WEISER FAMILIES IN AMERICA

Prepared for the three-hundredth anniversary of
the birth of
John Conrad Weiser (1696-1760)

Volume Two

under the general editorship of
Frederick S. Weiser
with
Paulette J. Weiser and Edward H. Wiser

New Oxford, Pennsylvania:
The John Conrad Weiser Family Association
1997

PENOBSCOT PRESS

The graphic on the dustjacket is a document dated 1475. The top portion of the document contains the first reference to members of the Weiser family of Kleinaspach in the thirty-second and thirty-third lines from the top: "Clausen Weißher Schultheißen zu Kleinaspach, Georg Weißher sein Brudern".
The first signature on the cloth spine is of Jacob Weysser (d. 1685), the last member of the Weiser family to live and die in Germany. The second signature on the cloth spine is of Johann Conrad Weiser Sr. (d. 1746), the first member of the Weiser family to live in America.
The graphic on the last page of Volume 2 is a reproduction of the wax seal of Conrad Weiser, Jr. (1796-1760).

Copyright © 1997 John Conrad Weiser Family Association
International Standard Book Number 0-89725-298-5
Library of Congress Catalog Card Number 97-65544

First Printing June 1997

This book is available from:
John Conrad Weiser Family Association
55 Kohler School Road
New Oxford, Pennsylvania 17350

Manufactured in the United States of America
Printed on 60# acid-free paper

CF41A24	Margaret Kehl m James B. Hermanek. Timberlake SD.
CF41A25	Charles Kehl m . WWI.
CF41A3	Joseph Gramley Kehl m Kate Nail. Jewel IA.
CF41A31	DeVere Kehl. WWI.
CF41A32	Marguerite Kehl
CF41A4	Andrew Jasper Kehl (b 22 Aug 1860, Webster City IA) m Annie K. Ley
CF41A41	David J. Kehl m Eva Lyon. Marble Rock IA.
CF41A411	Donald J. Kehl
CF41A412	Gerald Charles Kehl
CF41A413	Ley Miller Kehl
CF41A42	Maggie G. Kehl m Robert White. Vulcan Alta CAN.
CF41A421	Jean Marian White
CF41A422	Joyce Roberta White
CF41A423	Jewel Audrey White
CF41A43	Olive A. Kehl m Clarence Stone. Webster City IA
CF41A431	Leona Stone
CF41A432	Vernon Stone
CF41A44	Charles L. Kehl m Vera Hitsman. WWI.
CF41A45	Bertha Kehl. Webster City IA.
CF41B	Thomas Jefferson Kehl (1836-9 Jul 1923) m 1) Anna Keller (d 9 Jun 1862); m 2) Mary Kiplinger (1831-1923)
CF41B1	Clara Kehl m William Henry Kehl
CF41B11	Irene Kehl m Carl Paulson
CF41B111	Robert Paulson
CF41B112	Marion Paulson
CF41B113	Jack Paulson
CF41B2	William Kehl
CF41B3	Katie Kehl m George L. Brown. Beloit WI.
CF41B31	Maude Brown m Harry Hoover

CF41B311   Catherine Hoover

CF41B32   Margaret Brown m Clark Gilman

CF41B4   George Kehl

CF41B5   Charles H. Kehl. Lena IL.

CF41B6   Margaret A. Kehl. Lena IL.

CF41C   Frank Kehl (1843-1892) m Abbie Mowery (1837-1913). Bur Earlville IA.

CF41C1   Henry Kehl (1860-1885) m

CF41C11   Frank Kehl

CF41C2   Jennie Kehl m Frank Miller

CF41C21   Lizzie Miller m   Walt

CF41C211   Forest Walt

CF41C212   Donald Walt

CF41C213   Frances Walt

CF41C214   Edna Walt

CF41C215   Moras Walt

CF41C3   Mary Kehl m Dick Mattingly

CF41C31   Hope Mattingly m   Denkman

CF41C311   Anna Denkman

CF41C312   Hope Denkman

CF41C313   Elmer Denkman

CF41C314   Raymond Denkman

CF41C315   Mary Louise Denkman

CF41C4   Nora Kehl m   Long

CF41C5   Leah Kehl (15 Nov 1867-13 Sep 1930) m 25 Feb 1892, Horace Waldo (18 Jul 1863-25
Mar 1939)

CF41C51   Myrtle Waldo (24 Mar 1894-24 Feb 1957) m 11 Jun 1919, Bruce Derry

CF41C511   Virginia Derry m 19 Oct 1947, John Smith

CF41C52   Geneva Waldo (B 13 Jul 1895) m 22 Aug 1917, Herman Ackman (b 29 Apr 1891)

CF41C521   Carl Ackman (b 18 Aug 1918) m Bessie Wessel

CF41C522   Keith Ackman (b 4 Jun 1921) m Marilyn Karr

CF41C523   Bruce Ackman (b 1 Dec 1925) m Roberta Boles

CF41C524   Donald Ackman (b 6 Apr 1928) m Joann Louense

CF41C525   Hubert Ackman (b 15 Sep 1930) m Geneva West

CF41C53   Harry Waldo (30 Apr 1898-22 Nov 1920)

CF41C54   Fred A. Waldo (b 14 Mar 1902) m 5 Aug 1924, Mildred Fowler (b 29 Aug 1907)

CF41C541   Renne Waldo (b 13 Jun 1926) m 15 Jul 1945, Clyde Grapes

CF41C542   Robert Waldo (b 23 Aug 1928) m Jacqueline

CF41C6   Ella Kehl m   Robinson. Waterloo IA.

CF41C61   Earl Robinson. Strawberry Point IA.

CF41C62   John Robinson m

CF41C621   Litta Robinson

CF41C63   Mae Robinson m Jack Muntz

CF41C631   Robert Muntz

CF42   Catharine Kehl (daughter of John Jacob and Anna Catharine (Weiser) Kehl)(13 Apr 1784, Berks Co PA-11 Jan 1863, near Sunbury PA) married Thomas Snyder (6 Dec 1781-13 Apr 1828, near Sunbury PA), son of Casper Snyder (1745-1821) and Elizabeth Ferst (or Ferster) Snyder (1754-1823), pioneer settlers of Northumberland Co PA. Thomas Snyder was a corporal in Capt. Jacob Kimmel's Company (Lt. Col. Weirich), Pennsylvania Militia, 24 Sep-15 Dec 1814. His widow applied for a land warrant in 1855 for this service. They are buried in the old Sunbury cemetery.

Children of Thomas and Catharine (Kehl) Snyder:

CF421   Jacob Snyder

CF422   Casper Snyder

CF423   Elizabeth Snyder, 13 Jun 1806.

CF424   Catharine Snyder, 13 Apr 1809.

CF425   Sarah Snyder, 11 Aug 1811

CF426   Susan Snyder (d.y.)

CF427   Simon Snyder, 9 Mar 1814.

CF428   Maria Snyder, 5 Mar 1816

CF429   Thomas Kehl Snyder, 3 Dec 1822.

CF421   Jacob Snyder m Catharine Long.

CF4211   Elizabeth Snyder (26 Oct 1834-28 May 1862) m John C. Lytle. Bur Mile Run (Malick's)
U.B. Cemetery.

CF4212   Thomas Snyder m Martha Lytle.

CF422   Casper Snyder (13 Jun 1806, near Sunbury PA-5 Mar 1888, Corsica, Clarion Co. PA) m
Mary (Mollie) Houghton (12 Oct 1809, near Sunbury PA-14 Jan 1875, Corsica PA), daughter of Richard
Houghton (1772-1831) and Mary Snook (1774-1831).

CF4221   Catherine Snyder (9 Nov 1832-25 Nov 1887, Duke Centre PA) m J.P. Stephens. Bur near
Newmansville PA.

CF42211   Anna Stephens m Samuel Blair

CF42212   Burt Stephens

CF42213   Rulofson Stephens (d in Civil War)

CF42214   Lodema Stephens m Thomas Blair

CF42215   Amanda Stephens

CF42216   Margaret Stephens

CF42217   Vesta Stephens

CF42218   Carrie Stephens (10 Apr 1872, Clarion Co PA-12 Mar 1935, Petrolia PA) m William Harps
(15 Apr 1861, Clarion Co PA-15 Nov 1897, Marienville PA).

CF422181   Mabel Gertrude Harps (4 Feb 1894, Marienville PA-7 Jan 1943, Kane PA) m Claude D.
Jackson (26 Nov 1892, Rixford PA-12 Sep 1961, Warren PA).

CF4221811   Willis C. Jackson (b 30 May 1913, Kane PA) m Iris Carolyn Fridy (24 Feb 1914-29 Oct
1958, Pittsburgh PA).

CF42218111   Alan L. Jackson (b 29 Apr 1947, Pittsburgh PA)

CF42218112   Sue Anne Jackson (b 9 May 1952, Pittsburgh PA)

CF42219   Chloe Stephens m   Moriarit

CF4222   Simon Snyder (b 9 Sep 1834) m Mary Clark. Lived near Pine Grove, Clarion Co PA.

CF42221   Kate Snyder m   Blair

CF42222   James Snyder

CF42223   Clara Snyder m Edward Wilson

CF422231   Cora Wilson m William Russell

CF422232   Fred Wilson m Tressa Songer

CF422233   Allen Wilson

CF422234   Marie Wilson m James MacKay

CF422235	Ray Wilson
CF422236	Clarence Wilson
CF422237	Howard Wilson
CF422238	Paul Wilson
CF422239	Wade Wilson. Cleveland OH.
CF42223A	Thomas Wilson m Dorothy Rowland
CF42223B	Morris Wilson
CF42223C	Ella Wilson m Shippen. Cleveland OH.
CF42223C1	Joan Shippen
CF42223C2	Donald Shippen
CF42224	Ira Snyder m Remsel
CF42225	Cora Snyder
CF42226	Margaret Snyder
CF42227	Clarence Snyder m Clinger
CF42228	Francis Snyder
CF42229	Ollie Snyder m George Slike. Sigel PA.
CF4222A	Lucy Snyder m Slick
CF4222B	Charles F. Snyder
CF4223	Sarah Snyder (21 Aug 1836-6 Oct 1836)

CF4224   Elizabeth Snyder (22 Sep 1837-1925) m John E. Carroll (d 1916). Lived and died at Corsica PA. Bur Mt. Pleasant Baptist Cemetery.

CF42241	John E. Carroll
CF42242	Stella May Carroll (b 11 Nov 1863) m Isaac H. Smith
CF422421	Stanley R. Smith
CF422422	Wiley C. Smith
CF422423	Bessie June Smith m Walter Schwab
CF422424	Lulu M. Smith m Pierce Geist
CF422425	Florence Irene Smith m Albert Weaver
CF422426	Ethel Alberta Smith m John Burns

CF422427   Eva Adeline Smith (d 1933) m Braden Wood

CF4225   Richard B. Snyder (22 Sep 1837-1928) m Margaret C. Carroll (1838-1927). Lived at
Corsica PA

CF42251   Minnie Snyder (1861-1945) m William Anthony

CF422511   Robert Anthony

CF422512   William Anthony

CF422513   Pearl Anthony

CF422514   Elizabeth Anthony

CF422515   Ruth Anthony

CF422516   Claire Anthony

CF422517   George Anthony

CF423   Elizabeth Snyder (13 Jun 1806-17 Aug 1875) m 1) Thomas Smith (War of 1812); m 2)
Ada Renn (1781-1853). Bur old Sunbury Cemetery, Sunbury PA.

CF4231   Lewis Smith m   Long

CF4232   William Smith m   Willett

CF4233   Simon Snyder Renn (1829-1883) m Catherine Hane Willett

CF42331   Adaline Renn m C.L. Seibert

CF42332   Emma L. Renn

CF42333   Rachel Renn m John I. Reeser

CF42334   Lulu Jane Renn (1 Oct 1866-12 Mar 1883)

CF42335   Alfred Willett Renn. Philadelphia PA.

CF42336   Stella Renn m C.A. Lindeman. Lewisburg PA.

CF42337   Harry M. Renn (d age 7)

CF42338   Walter C. Renn. Philadelphia PA.

CF4234   Abraham Renn (22 Oct 1831-26 Oct 1892, Shamokin Tp PA) m 1) Martha Lytle (23 Feb
1843-7 Mar 1873); m 2) Sarah S.   . Martha bur Miles Run PA. He, Co. B, 172nd P.V.I.

CF42341   Thaddeus R. Renn (1860-28 May 1920) m Maggie M.

CF423411   Maude E. Renn (d 12 Sep 1922) m Arthur I. Derk. No chn. Treverton PA.

CF423412   Bertha B. Renn m   Welker, div.

CF423413   Claude A. Renn

CF42342   Thomas Jefferson Renn (28 Sep 1861, Lower Augusta PA-20 Sep 1941) m 1) 24 Jun 1882, Viola Mae Yeager (3 Jun 1864-2 Jul 1900); m 2) 22 Apr 1905, Charlotte Snyder. Bur Rush Tp PA.

CF423421   Thomas Jefferson Renn, Jr. (19 Jan 1884, Lower Augusta Tp PA-1901)

CF423422   Evelyn Roselia Renn (b 19 Dec 1885, Catawissa PA) m 29 May 1903, Elmira NY, Charles E. Yost (7 Apr 1886-29 Jan 1952). Shamokin PA.

CF4234221   Lillian Mae Yost (b 25 Jun 1904, Shamokin PA) m 24 Oct 1924, Hugo Winter (Northumberland PA-3 Dec 1937); m 2) David Barber

CF42342211   Evelyn Louise Winter (b 9 Aug 1925) m 1942, Robert Mull

CF423422111   Robert Mull, Jr. (b 21 Aug 1943)

CF423422112   Earnest Mull (b 19 Feb 19)

CF423422113   Lillian Mull (b 30 Nov 1955)

CF42342212   Ruth Winter (30 Jul 1926) m 2 Sep 1944, Fred E. Strouse

CF423422121   Thomas Delroy Strouse (b 1 Jun 1945) m 8 Jun 1963, Glenda Joyce Good (b 6 Jan 1946). Dairy & grain farmer.

CF4234221211   Thomas Delroy Strouse, Jr. (b 6 Dec 1963) m 4 Dec 1993, Cheryl Marie Wagner. Dairy & grain farmer.

CF4234221212   Thonda Richelle Strouse (b 6 Feb 1970) m 10 Mar 1990, Thomas Swank, div.

CF42342212121   Tomisha Rayelle Swank (b 28 Sep 1990)

CF42342212122   Trinity Richelle Swank (b 14 Sep 1992)

CF4234221213   Amanda Marie Strouse (b 9 Jul 1980)

CF4234222   Robert Lee Yost (b 20 Oct 1906, Shamokin PA) m 29 Jun 1935, Kathryn Negherton

CF42342221   Patricia Ann Yost (b 26 Apr 1936) m 30 Aug 1958, Bernard Essip

CF42342222   Catherine Marie Yost (b 30 Jun 1938) m Jun 1955, Thomas Henninger

CF423422221   Michael Henninger (b 30 Oct 1956)

CF423422222   Thomas Henninger (b 16 May 1958)

CF4234223   Earl Edward Yost (b 12 May 1909, Shamokin PA) m. 9 Sep 1929, Irene Troutman. Shippensberg PA.

CF42342231   Earl Edward Yost, Jr. (b 5 Jul 1933) m Shippensberg PA, Jane   . No chn.

CF42342232   Jeanette Ann Yost (b 29 Aug 1938) m Galen Asper

CF423422321   Roxanne Asper (b 22 Dec 1955)

CF423422322   Wade Asper (b 1958)

CF42342233   Mary Catherine Yost (b 20 Apr 1948)

CF4234224   Charles Henry Yost (b 30 Dec 1911, Shamokin PA) m 18 May 1940, Ruth Arter

CF42342241   Debora Ann Yost (b 28 Jan 1952)

CF42342242   Lillian Evelyn Yost (b 30 Nov 1955)

CF42342243   Charles Henry Yost, Jr. (b 17 Jan 1959)

CF4234225   Helen B. Yost (28 Aug 1914, Shamokin PA) m 22 Aug 1952, George E. Kline. No chn.
Northumberland PA.

CF4234226   Harriet S. Yost (b 15 Apr 1917, Shamokin PA) m Walter Cambell. No chn.

CF4234227   George Daniel Yost (b 15 Nov 1919, Shamokin PA) m 21 Jun 1947, Bettie Kalcich.
Sunbury PA.

CF42342271   Rita Elizabeth Yost (b 30 Aug 1948)

CF42342272   Elaine Susanne Yost (b 19 Nov 1949)

CF42342273   Frances Elizabeth Yost (b 20 Oct 1951)

CF42342274   George Daniel Yost, Jr. (b 17 Mar 1954)

CF42342275   Vincent Peter Yost (b 22 Mar 1959)

CF4234228   Sarah Elizabeth Yost (b 10 Mar 1922, Shamokin PA) m 10 Aug 1940, Walter Knopp.
Shamokin PA.

CF42342281   Walter George Knopp (b 15 Jun 1944)

CF42342282   David Charles Knopp (b 4 May 1951)

CF42342283   Timothy Renn Knopp (b 5 Feb 1953)

CF4234229   John Calvin Yost (b 5 Aug 1924, Shamokin PA) m 30 Mar 1946, Jean L. Bower

CF42342291   Ronald C. Yost (b 19 Dec 1949)

CF42342292   Judith Lorraine Yost (b 26 May 1953)

CF423422A   Thomas Hugo Yost (b 2 Oct 1925, Shamokin PA) m 29 Jun 1946, Mildred Stalkoski

CF423422A1   Donna Jean Yost (b 26 Jul 1948)

CF423422A2   Joan Louis Yost (b 27 Jul 1949)

CF423422B   Albert G. Yost (b 14 May 1927, Shamokin PA) m 6 Jun 1950, Anna Hall. No chn.
Montoursville PA

CF423422C   Jane Lois Yost (b 13 May 1929, Shamokin PA) m 27 Sep 1952, Charles Bruce

CF423422C1   Charles Bruce, Jr. (b 26 Jul 1953)

CF423422C2   Barbara Lorraine Bruce (b 10 Sep 1954)

CF423422C3   Richard Lee Bruce (b 18 Feb 1956)

CF423422D   Jean Louise Yost (13 May 1929, Shamokin PA-24 Oct 1943)

CF423423   Gertrude Ellen Renn (b 19 Dec 1885, Catawissa PA) m 20 Apr 1905, Everett Gray.
Shamokin PA.

CF4234231   Miles W. Gray (b 16 Jun 1906) m Kathryn Lewis

CF42342311   Margaret Gray m John Avilino

CF4234232   Harold E. Gray (b 21 Aug 1908) m Margaret Charles

CF42342321   Connie Gray (b 26 Dec 1939)

CF42342322   Glenn Gray (b 25 Apr 1941)

CF4234233   Blanche I. Gray (b 27 Aug 1910-25 Apr 1925)

CF4234234   Forrest E. Gray (10 Mar 1913-22 Mar 1920)

CF4234235   Walter C. Gray (b 20 Jun 1914) m Mary Conrad. Selinsgrove PA.

CF42342351   Kenneth Gray

CF423424   George Keefer Renn (17 Mar 1888-2 Dec 1946) m 1) Ida Riegle; m 2) 21 Feb 1930, Mae
Meckowiak

CF4234241   Esther L. Renn (b 26 Sep 1909) m 23 Jun 1928, William J. Lauer. Shamokin PA.

CF42342411   William E. Lauer (b 23 May 1929) m 8 May 1948, Janet Hunter

CF423424111   Ronald L. Lauer (b 10 Aug 1949)

CF42342412   Kenneth L. Lauer (b 5 Aug 1931) m 11 Feb 1953, Newfoundland CAN, Constance
Bartlett. Shamokin PA.

CF423424121   Cynthia Louise Lauer (b 22 Jan 1954)

CF42342413   Robert G. Lauer (b 14 Aug 1934) m 23 Aug 1958, Elizabeth Kleman. Shamokin PA.

CF423424131   Robert M. Lauer (b 4 Aug 1959)

CF423424132   Ronald F. Lauer (b 4 Aug 1959)

CF42342414   Gene A. Lauer (b 30 Jun 1937) m 1 Nov 1958, Entbaugh, Germany, Karen Thumm.
Shamokin PA.

CF42342415   Arthur E. Lauer (b 20 Oct 1942)

CF42342416   Donald R. Lauer (b 1 Feb 1945)

CF4234242   Anna M. Renn m Eugene Crocker. Miami FL.

CF42342421   Karen Jean Crocker (b 23 May 1955)

CF4234243   Margaret Renn m Paul Clark

CF4234244   Phyllis K. Renn (b 21 Nov 1932) m 11 Feb 1956, James H. Kline. New Cumberland PA.

CF42342441   Rose Marie Kline (b 3 Jan 1958)

CF4234245   Rose Marke Renn (b 24 Dec 1934) m 6 Aug 1955, John Chervanick. Shamokin PA.

CF42342451   Susan Chervanick (b 4 Sep 1958)

CF423425   Mary Elizabeth Renn (18 Apr 1890, Lower Augusta Tp, Northumberland Co PA-19 Aug 1959, Shamokin PA) m 14 Nov 1908, Shamokin PA, Harry B. Wheary (5 Jun 1887, Shamokin PA-22 Feb 1957, Philadelphia PA).

CF4234251   Edward VanLeer Wheary (6 Oct 1916, Shamokin PA-9 Sep 1917, Shamokin PA). Bur Trevorton PA.

CF4234252   Catherine Wheary (b 28 Apr 1918, Shamokin PA) m 30 Aug 1941, Shamokin PA, Raymond E. Marr (b 15 Mar 1917, Shamokin PA). Factory foreman, Rochester NY.

CF42342521   Russell Glenn Marr (b 1 Mar 1950, Rochester NY) m 18 Jul 1981, Rochester NY, Karen Christenson (b 11 Sep 1953).

CF423425211   Amy Christine Marr (5 Jul 1985, Rochester NY)

CF423425212   Ryan Christopher Marr (1 Aug 1987, Rochester NY)

CF42342522   Richard Allen Marr (b 1 Mar 1950, Rochester NY) m 20 Jun 1981, Rochester NY, Brenda Maier (b 9 May 1951, Rochester NY).

CF423425221   Suzanne Marie Marr (b 16 Aug 1984, Rochester NY)

CF423425222   Kristin Michelle Marr (b 8 Aug 1989, Rochester NY)

*CF4234253   Dorothy Ellen Wheary (b 1 Oct 1920, Shamokin PA) m 1 Oct 1940, Shamokin PA, Daniel Worhacz (b 14 Apr 1918, Shamokin PA). Mechanic, New Port Richey FL.

*CF42342531   Sandra Lee Worhacz (b 6 Jan 1942, Shamokin PA) m 25 Nov 1959, Rochester NY, John Charles Wihlen (b 24 Aug 1939, Rochester NY). Res Rochester NY.

CF423425311   Brenda Ann Wihlen (b 19 Mar 1961, Rochester NY) m 27 Aug 1994, Timothy Driscoll (b 11 Oct 1953, Rochester NY). Teacher, Rochester NY.

CF4234253111   Patrick Timothy Driscoll (b 13 Mar 1996, Rochester NY)

CF423425312   John Daniel Seth Wihlen (b 30 Jul 1963, Rochester NY) m 20 Sep 1986, Rochester NY, Traci A. Boardman (b 29 Feb 1964, Rochester NY). Res Rochester NY.

CF4234253121   John Matthew Seth Wihlen (31 Jul 1987, Rochester NY)

CF4234253122   Deanne Chelsie Wihlen (23 Mar 1991, Rochester NY)

CF423425313   Edward Vanleer Wihlen (b 24 Jan 1972, Rochester NY) m 28 Aug 1993, Rochester NY, Jaclyn N. Bestram (b 26 Dec 1969).

CF4234253131   Jaclyn Casandra Wihlen (b 25 Nov 1995)

CF42342532   Linda Mae Worhacz (b 9 Oct 1943, Shamokin PA) m 22 Aug 1964, Livonia NY, Thomas Martin Riley (b 31 Jan 1941, Rochester NY). Res Lakeville NY.

CF423425321   Karen Ann Riley (b 10 Aug 1965, Rochester NY) m 29 Jun 1991, Geneseo NY, Michael A. Smith (b 29 Nov 1965). Theol Sch, Livonia NY.

CF423425322   Kathleen Ann Riley (b 9 Oct 1967 Rochester NY) m 15 Jul 1989, Houghton NY, Timothy S. Trezise (b 23 Sep 1965). AB, Houghton Col; math teacher, Houghton NY.

CF423425323   Kristine Ann Riley (15 Dec 1970, Rochester NY-16 Nov 1977, Rochester NY). Bur Geneseo NY.

Mark Andrew Riley (b 9 Sep 1979, Rochester NY)(adopted)

CF42342533   Daniel Lynn Worhacz (b 19 Oct 1947, Shamokin PA) m 24 May 1969, Webster NY, Judith A. Scudlark (b 13 May 1947, Webster NY). Res Holcomb NY.

CF423425331   Sarah Elizabeth Worhacz (b 15 Jul 1979, Rochester NY)

CF423425332   Seth Daniel Worhacz (b 11 Jun 1982, Rochester NY)

CF4234254   Mable Mae Wheary (b 25 Apr 1924, Shamokin PA) m 28 Jun 1947, Shmamokin PA, William Joseph Spatzer (b 31 May 1920, Shamokin PA)

CF42342541   Shelby Mae Spatzer (b 8 Feb 1952, Danville PA) m 10 Apr 1971, Rochester NY, Thomas de Jong (b 8 May 1951, Rochester NY).

CF423425411   Kimberly Ann de Jong (b 16 Feb 1974, Rochester NY)

CF423425412   Jason de Jong (b 2 Sep 1977, Rochester NY)

CF42342542   Randy Spatzer (b 24 Sep 1954, Rochester NY) m 30 Apr 1977, Duryea PA, Kathy Welsh (b 12 Sep 1955, Pittston PA). AB, Bloomsburg (PA) U; printing company, Duryea PA.

CF423425421   Holly Spatzer (b 27 Sep 1980, Scranton PA)

CF423425422   Megan Spatzer (b 18 Aug 1984, Scranton PA)

CF42342543   Debra Jean Spatzer (b 11 Apr 1956, Rochester NY) m 6 May 1978, Rochester NY, Michael Cairns (22 Apr 1942, Rochester NY-30 Jun 1995). He, cremated. Researcher, Eastman Kodak; res Hilton NY.

CF42342544   William J. Spatzer (b 19 Dec 1959, Rochester NY) m 28 Dec 1985, Buffalo NY, Susanne Sifel (b 16 Aug 1961, Buffalo NY). MA, Fredonia (NY) Col; teacher, Kenmore NY.

CF423425441   Lauren Spatzer (3 May 1990, Buffalo NY)

CF423425442   Alexander William Spatzer (b 4 Jun 1993 Buffalo NY)

CF42342545   Roxanne Spatzer (26 Apr 1961, Rochester NY). Insurance mgr, Syracuse NY.

CF423426   Emerson Monroe Renn (b 6 Aug 1892, Rush Tp PA) m Ida Lott. Selinsgrove PA. No chn.

CF423427   Clinton Smith Renn (7 Jan 1895-Jul 1895)

CF423428   David Blair Renn (b 27 Apr 1896) m Mabel Chesney

CF4234281   Allen Renn

CF4234282   Florence Renn m Nicholas Sheblesky. Shamokin PA.

CF42342821   David Renn Shebelsky

CF4234283   Jean Renn m Charles Ray

CF4234284   Carl Renn (1935-1956)

CF423429   Viola Mae Renn (2 Jun 1898-1900)

CF42342A   Alma S. Renn (b 31 Oct 1906). Unm.

CF42342B   Beulah G. Renn (b 9 Sep 1908) m 1929, Jack L. Levin

CF42342B1   Jack Douglas Levin (b 17 Jul 193) m Janet Neer

CF42342B11   Douglas Levin (b Jan 1957)

CF42342B2   David Thomas Levin (b 7 Feb 193) m Barbara Diver

CF42342B21   Mary Beth Levin (b Feb 1957)

CF42342B3   Michael Levin (b 31 Jul 193). Unm.

CF42342B4   Carol Alma Levin (b 8 Apr 1945)

CF42342C   John Renn (1910-1928)

CF42342D   Martha Ann Renn (b 22 Jul 1913) m 1) 15 Jan 1932, James R. Greenwood (d 5 Jan 1945);
m 2) 14 Feb 1949, Joseph Wodzak. Elysburg PA.

CF42342D1   James R. Greenwood, Jr. (b 23 Mar 1933) m 20 Sep 1959, Dolores Karpiak

CF42342D2   Betty L. Greenwood (b 1 Feb 1937) m 2 Aug 1958, Russell Welsh

CF42342D3   Alma JoAnn Greenwood (b 3 Jun 1938) m 23 Mar 1957, William Parry

CF42342D31   William Thomas Parry (b 11 May 1958)

CF42342D32   Randy Lee Parry (b 8 Sep 1959)

CF42342D4   Gloria Jean Greenwood (b 15 Oct 1940)

CF42342D5   Nancy Lee Greenwood (b 6 Mar 1943)

CF42342D6   Thomas William Wodzak (b 28 Jul 1950)

CF42342D7   Mary Jane Wodzak (b 5 Jul 1952)

CF42342D8   Donna Marie Wodzak (b 28 Aug 1953)

CF42342D9   Cynthia Joy Wodzak (b 14 Nov 1956)

CF42342E	Ralph Jacob Renn (b 19 Jun 1917) m 16 Mar 1935, Alda Unger. Shamokin PA.
CF42342E1	Mary Lee Renn (b 3 May 1942)
CF42342E2	Ralph Jacob Renn, Jr. (b 19 Feb 1945)
CF42342E3	Foster Unger Renn (b 8 Jul 1950)
CF42342E4	Daniel Jefferson Renn (b 23 Feb 1954)
CF42343	Mary Jane Renn (1864-Aug 1928) m. Joseph Kramer (1857-1918). Bur Sunbury PA.
CF423431	Esther Kramer (11 Nov 1894-7 Dec 1928) m 2 Feb 1917, William E. Splain (b 8 Sep 1894). Sunbury PA.
CF4234311	Erd Splain (b 22 Feb 1918) m Ida . USA in Germany, WWII.
CF42343111	Neil Splain
CF4234312	Joe Daniel Splain (27 Dec 1919-29 Jan 1935)
CF4234313	Vivian Splain (b 5 Nov 1921) m William Scott. Dornsife PA.
CF42343131	Stephen Scott (b 1950)
CF42343132	Robert Scott (b 1956)
CF42343133	Terry Scott (b 1958)
CF4234314	Neil Splain (18 Sep 1925-26 Apr 1946). Bur Leghorn, Italy. USA Eng Corps (killed).
CF4234315	Ned Kramer Splain (28 Feb 1928-24 Jul 1930)
CF423432	Edward Kramer (1898-1955) m
CF42344	Elizabeth A. Renn (15 Feb 1866-25 Apr 1940) m Frank S. Seasholtz (4 Nov 1867-4 Mar 1937)
CF423441	Franklin Bruce Seasholtz (1893-10 Aug 1950) m Ethel Yordy
CF4234411	Fred E. Seasholtz (b 16 Aug 1916)
CF4234412	Jack Y. Seasholtz (7 Feb 1918-1924)
CF423442	Della Seasholtz m Paul Snyder. Sunbury PA.
CF4234421	Mildred Snyder m Charles Krouse
CF42344211	Sherry Krouse
CF4234422	Virginia Snyder m Miles Showers. Alexandria VA.
CF42344221	Sonny Showers (b 1938)
CF42344222	Bonny Showers (b 1940)

CF4234423   Mary Snyder m Kenneth Ruch. Northumberland PA.

CF423443   Frederick Albert Seasholtz (d 15 Apr 1925). USA.

CF423444   Joseph Seaxholtz (1895-1914). Bur Sunbury PA.

CF423445   Robert Seasholtz (d.y.). Bur Sunbury PA.

CF423446   Corleen Seasholtz (d.y.). Bur Sunbury PA.

CF423447   Roberta Seasholtz (d.y.). Bur Sunbury PA.

CF42345   Truman J. Renn (b 1868). No record.

CF42346   Mark Blair Renn (5 Aug 1870-19 Sep 1906) m 1) 23 Aug 1891, Katie E. Tharp; m 2) 9 May 1900, Olive Margaret Mutchler (13 Oct 1870-14 Nov 1924)

CF423461   Calvin Blair Renn (12 Jun 1901, Sunbury PA-14 Apr 1956) m 21 Dec 1921, Helen Dailey (b 1905) Bur Sunbury PA. Miller.

CF4234611   Theo Irene Renn (b 21 Jul 1922) m 8 Dec 1945, John Harold Smith

CF42346111   Scott Smith (b 7 Dec 1947)

CF42346112   Connie Jean Smith (b 27 Aug 1950)

CF4234612   Daniel Blair Renn (b 14 Jul 1924) m 22 Apr 1950, Dorothy Stetler

CF42346121   Lonna Renn (b 9 Jun 1946)

CF42346122   Paul Renn (b 19 Jul 1949)

CF42346123   Albert Renn (b 19 Aug 1952)

CF42346124   Debbie Renn (b 19 Mar 1957)

CF4234613   Viola Mae Renn (b 10 Sep 1926) m 3 Aug 1946, John Lenig. Hummels Wharf PA.

CF42346131   Lucille Lenig (b 12 Mar 1947)

CF42346132   Marilyn Lenig (b 31 Oct 1948)

CF42346133   William Lenig (b 25 Mar 1950)

CF42346134   Kenneth Lenig (b 3 Aug 1951)

CF42346135   Stephen Lenig (b 3 Aug 1951)

CF42346136   Janet Lenig (b 27 Feb 1957)

CF4234614   Samuel Lewis Renn (b 6 Jun 1929) m 11 Feb 1950, Alice Ferster. Sunbury PA.

CF42346141   Carol Ann Renn (b 18 Aug 1952)

CF42346142   Cheryl Renn (Oct 1955-Dec 1956)

CF42346143   Douglas Samuel Renn (b Aug 1957)

CF4234615   Constance Eileen Renn (b 25 Sep 1930) m 5 Sep 1948, Charles Fegley. Sunbury PA.

CF42346151   Alan Daniel Fegley (b 1 Jun 1952)

CF42346152   Wendy Lee Fegley (b 29 Apr 1954)

CF4234616   Donald Keith Renn (b 21 Sep 1930) m 24 Jun 1950, Nancy Hetrick. Sunbury PA.

CF42346161   Richard Keith Renn (b 7 Apr 1951)

CF42346162   Ann Louise Renn (b 12 Aug 1953)

CF4234617   Calvin Markly Renn (b 31 Aug 1932) m 19 Jun 1951, Pearl Osman

CF42346171   Teresa Susanne Renn (b 23 Mar 1953)

CF42346172   Blaine Markly Renn (b 17 Mar 1956)

CF4234618   Helen Joann Renn (b 1 Nov 1939).

CF4234619   Susan Joyce Renn (b 2 Mar 1942)

CF423461A   Teresa Diane Renn (b 2 Jan 1946)

CF423462   Alwilda Esther Renn (b 2 Jan 1907) m Jun 1939, Harold Miller. Alexandria VA.

CF4234621   Suzanne Benay Miller (b 9 Oct 1939)

CF4235   Sarah Ellen Renn (b 1834) m Abraham Lytle (29 Nov 1833-4 Jan 1900). Bur Old Sunbury
Cem.

CF42351   Martin Luther Lytle (1865-1918) m Elizabeth A. Garman (1862 - 1936)

CF423511   Gilbert Ambrose Lytle (b 1892) m 1918, Sula Newman (1900-1958)

CF4235111   Luther Lytle (b 9 Nov 1919) m Faye Smith. Middleburg PA.

CF42351111   Willard Kenneth Lytle (b 6 Dec 1938)

CF42351112   Leon Dennis Lytle (b 23 Jul 1945)

CF42351113   Larry Elwwod Lytle (b 7 Jan 1947)

CF423512   Elizabeth F. Lytle (24 Mar 1897-29 Nov 1918)

CF42352   George B. Lytle (3 Mar 1865-25 Mar 1896). Bur Sunbury PA.

CF42353   Minnie T. Lytle (21 Dec 1866-17 Apr 1871)

CF42354   Franklin Pierce Lytle (21 Jun 1868-15 Feb 1889)

CF42355   Frances E. Lytle (12 Jun 1870-18 Apr 1899)

CF42356   Sarah A. Lytle (19 Apr 1872-11 Apr 1873)

CF4236   Hattie Renn (b 1840) m Eli Gaugler. Monroe Tp, Snyder Co PA. No chn.

CF424   Catharine Snyder (13 Apr 1809-19 Sep 1893) m 20 Dec 1829, John Cooper (19 Aug 1807-3 Sep 1879). Bur Sunbury PA. Farmer, Upper Augusta Tp, Northumberland Co PA.

CF4241   Hiram Peter Cooper (25 Sep 1830-18 Jun 1899, Goshen IN) m 6 Apr 1855, Margaret Simpson (24 May 1838, Millersburg IN-20 Jan 1931, Goshen IN)

CF42411   John L. Cooper (9 Sep 1856-25 Mar 1910) m 4 Jun 1883, Mary Neufer (23 Sep 1856-14 Mar 1924). City engineer, Goshen IN.

CF424111   Vera Cooper m August Beyer. Orrville OH.

CF4241111   Mary Beyer

CF4241112   Betty Beyer

CF424112   Marian Cooper m Dr. Lyman Gould. Ft. Wayne IN.

CF4241121   Muriel Gould

CF4241122   John Gould

CF42412   Luther J. Cooper (31 Jul 1858-20 Aug 1940) m 3 Jan 1891, Maude B. Vallance (b 19 Jun 1871). Ligonier IN.

CF424121   Mildred Cooper (b 30 Nov 1897) m 2 Jun 1918, Arthur Judson Dillon (b 31 Jul 1891, Culver IN)

CF4241211   Arthur Judson Dillon (b 26 Sep 1920)

CF4241212   Barbara Dillon (b 15 Feb 1925)

CF42413   Mary T. Cooper (8 Feb 1860-21   1925) m 12 May 1882, Franklin Pierce Conrad (b 1855). Goshen IN.

CF42414   Horatio Semour Cooper (11 May 1862-8 Apr 1946) m 5 Apr 1898, Florentine Getz. United Brethren clergyman, Michigan.

CF424141   Paul Cooper (b 16 Feb 1899)

CF424142   Bertram Cooper (b 2 Dec 1901)

CF424143   Churchill Cooper (b 30 Jan 1907)

CF42415   Carrie M. Cooper (31 Oct 1864-15 Mar 1948) m 3 Dec 1890, James T. McLean (d 14 Nov 1936). Presbyterian clergyman, Gulfport FL.

CF42416   Florence Cooper (28 Dec 1866-5 May 1926) m 18 Feb 1889, Topeka, LaGrange Co IN, Samuel S. Neufer

CF424161   Luther Earl Neufer (b 17 Jan 1891) m 3 Aug 1922, Lula Plank

CF424162   Joan R. Neufer

CF424163   John E. Neufer

CF424164   Harriet Neufer

CF42417   Homer H. Cooper (b 22 Dec 1868) m 31 May 1900, Mary Baily (b 3 Apr 1881). Supt of schools, Knightstown IN

CF424171   Lowell B. Cooper (b 19 Mar 1904) m 2 May 1948, Thelma McConnaughey (b 4 Jun 1921)

CF4241711   Mary Jule Cooper (b 29 Jun 1950)

CF4241712   Lowell David Cooper (b 1 Mar 1954)

CF424172   Miriam Winifred Cooper

CF42418   Effie Cooper (31 Aug 1870-18 Mar 1935). Presbyterian church missionary to China, 11 yrs. Goshen IN

CF4242   Jermiah Cooper (18 May 1832-15 Jan 1888) m 1) Jemima Seaholz (10 Dec 1837-25 Dec 1872); m 2) Mrs. Martha (Riland) Keller. Bur Sunbury PA. Farmer.

CF42421   Thomas Newton Cooper (13 Jan 1858-1931) m 1) Mary Ella Krouse (22 Jan 1859-6 Jul 1888); m 2) Jenetta Christina Baker. Sunbury PA.

CF42422   Thadeus S. Cooper m 1) Rachel Slough; m 2) Candes Myers. Winfield PA.

CF424221   Elsie Cooper m John Wilson

CF4242211   Elizabeth Wilson

CF4242212   John Cooper Wilson

CF4242213   Rachel Cooper

CF4242214   Ruth Cooper

CF424222   Mabel Cooper (30 Sep 1890, Sunbury PA-5 Nov 1977, Sunbury PA) m James Calvin Dodge (28 Dec 1885, Northumberland PA-23 Jun 1965, Northumberland PA)

CF4242221   James Cooper Dodge, Jr. (3 Jul 1917, Northumberland PA-9Dec 1986, Northumberland PA) m Lois June Walker (b 10 Sep 1025, Northumberland PA). Florist.

CF42422211   James Howard Dodge (b 9 Jun 1951, Sunbury PA) m Nancy Louise Betzko (b 10 Feb 1951). Florist.

CF424222111   Stephanie Ann Dodge (b 30 Dec 1977, Danville PA)

CF424222112   James Christopher Dodge (b 16 Jun 1979, Danville PA)

CF424222113   Michael Dodge (b 9 Mar 1984)

CF424222114   Steven Todd Dodge (b 18 Dec 1985)

CF42422212   John Thomas Dodge (b 11 Jun 1954, Sunbury PA) m Diane Marotto

CF424222121   Nicole Adrian Dodge (b 14 Aug 1982)

CF424222122   Aubrie Sue Dodge (b 5 Jul 1989)

CF42422213   Edward Fayne Dodge (b 17 Sep 1961, Sunbury PA) m Terri Teck (b 2 Apr 1962)

CF424222131   Shawn Dodge (b 26 Mar 1979, Sunbury PA)

CF424222132   Matthew Dodge (b 25 Aug 1984, Sunbury PA)

CF424222133   Gregory Dodge (b 4 Aug 1986, Sunbury PA)

CF4242222   Shirley Dodge (b 21 Sep 1921, Northumberland PA) m 23 May 1943, Northumberland PA, Robert Glenwood "Zip" Crouser (b 24 Dec 1917, Northumberland PA)

CF42422221   James Firm Crouser (b 25 May 1948, Sunbury PA) m Susan Specht

CF424222211   Robert James Crouser (b 15 Jun 1981, Danville PA)

CF424222212   Hilary Ann Crouser (b 15 Jun 1981, Danville PA)

CF4242223   Dickson Dodoge m Mildred Curwin

CF42422231   Robert Dodge

CF42422232   Daniel Dodge

CF4242224   Gloria Dodge m Robert Henninger

CF42422241   Robert Henninger

CF42422242   Ursala Henninger

CF424223   Elmira Cooper m Donald Bloom

CF4242231   June Louise Bloom

CF4242232   Eleanor Bloom

CF424224   Edward Cooper

CF424225   Robert Cooper

CF424226   Paul Cooper

CF424227   David Cooper m   Kitchen

CF42423   Anna Laura Cooper m Grant App

CF424231   Ruth App m Edward Hutchinson

CF424232   Helen App m Russell Kemp

CF42424   William Bewvin Cooper m Elsie

CF424241   William Cooper

CF42425   Mary Alice Cooper (4 Aug 1861 - 10 Jan 1869)

CF42426   Harris Cooper (4 May 1865 - 20 Jul 1866)

CF42427   Edward Bertram Cooper (1870-13 Mar 1932) m Annie Brand (1874-6 Mar 1939). Bur Sunbury PA. MD; lst Lt, Med Corps, 90th Reg Inf, WWI.

CF424271   Harold David Cooper

CF424272   Edward Brand Cooper, Jr. (1909-Feb 1962, Atherton CA) m

CF4242721   James Cooper (b 1943)

CF4242722   Judith Cooper (b 1944)

CF4242723   Janice Cooper (b 1953)

CF4243   Isaac Newton Cooper (29 Jul 1834-4 Mar 1914) m 26 Jan 1860, Mary Snyder (3 Jan 1842-9 Dec 1899)

CF42431   Calvin Crake Cooper (12 Nov 1860-11 Jan 1916) m Mary Arnold (4 Dec 1860-29 Jun 1924). Bur Sunbury PA. Railroad engineer.

CF424311   Ella M. Cooper (9 Apr 1883-25 Mar 1903)

CF424312   Albert Clayton Cooper (12 Aug 1884-5 Nov 1960) m Jun 1912, Anna V. Shingora (10 Oct 1890-1952)

CF4243121   Albert Clayton Cooper, Jr. (b 7 Feb 1913) m Betty Clark. Evangelical United Brethren clergyman, Clearfield Co PA.

CF42431211   Garry Cooper

CF42431212   David Cooper

CF42431213   Marie Cooper

CF42431214   Daniel Cooper

CF42431215   Richard Cooper

CF42431216   Lewis Cooper

CF4243122   Paul Edward Cooper (b 17 Jul 1914) m Patricia Stanley. Portland ME.

CF42431221   Paul Edward Cooper, Jr.

CF42431222   Preston Cooper

CF42431223   John Cooper

CF4243123   Marie Catharine Cooper (b 6 Feb 1920) m 1942, James E. Fisher. Sunbury PA.

CF42431231   Sherry Ann Vannette Fisher (b 6 May 1946)

CF42431232   James R. Fisher (b 18 Oct 1953)

CF42431233   Paul Edward Fisher (b 26 Jul 1957)

CF4243124   James David Cooper (b 10 Jan 1923) m. Elizabeth Renninger. Northumberland PA.

CF42431241   Elizabeth Pearl Cooper (b 1943)

CF4243125   Raymond Henry Cooper (b 31 Aug 1925) m Naomi Miller. Mansfield PA.

CF42431251   Connie Lou Cooper (b 17 Oct 1953)

CF42431252   Cyndie Lee Cooper (b 25 Dec 1956)

CF42431253   Cathy Louise Cooper (b 27 Dec 1957)

CF424313   Henry Isaac Cooper (b 24 Dec 1892) m Harriet B. Lyons (b 1897). Sunbury PA.

CF4243131   Calvin L. Cooper (7 May 1914-23 Nov 1958). Unm. S/Sgt. Ord. Supp., WWII.

CF4243132   Robert James Cooper (b 1 Oct 1915) m Margaret Hoover.

CF42431321   Harriet Ann Cooper (b 3 Mar 1947)

CF42431322   Robert James Cooper (b 9 Sep 1952)

CF4243133   Jesse Cooper (b 2 Mar 1918) m Freda Kline

CF42431331   Susan Eileen Cooper (b 30 Dec 1942)

CF42431332   Karen Cooper (b 21 Apr 1947)

CF42431333   Jess Cooper, Jr. (b 22 Apr 1948)

CF42431334   James Cooper (b 1 May 1949)

CF424314   Margaret A. Cooper (1894-1947) m George R. Young (1891-1926)

CF4243141   Ray Young

CF4243142   William C. Young (1918-1942). S/Sgt. Signl Corps, WWII; killed in Pacific.

CF4243143   Robert D. Young (1919-1942). 2nd lt, 105th Inf Divn, WWII; killed at Saipan.

CF4243144   Albert Young

CF4243145   Mary Jane Young

CF424315   Maude J. Cooper (20 Aug 1896-23 Apr 1897)

CF42432   Lloyd Elmer Cooper (6 Jul 1862-6 Mar 1924) m Elizabeth May Dailey

CF424321   Bertha Cooper (d.y.)

CF424322   Herbert H. Cooper (5 Oct 1893-23 May 1948)

CF424323   Charles E. Cooper (15 Mar 1899-11 Nov 1961) m Lorraine Wetzel.

CF4243231   Agnes L. Cooper (b 1921) m   Niland. 5 chn.

CF42433   David Melanchthon Cooper (16 Sep 1865-11 Jan 1868)

CF42434   John Howard Cooper (30 Dec 1866-4 Mar 1937) m Gertrude Weitzel (20 Nov 1870-28 Jun 1957). Railroad conductor.

CF424341   Grace Cooper (1888-1902)

CF424342   Emma Cooper m Thomas Johnson

CF4243421   Howard Johnson (b 18 Jun 1922) m Joyce Witmer

CF42434211   Michael Johnson (b 15 Feb 1946)

CF42434212   Christopher Johnson (b 28 Jun 1951)

CF424343   William Cooper (b 1896) m Emma Bartholomew.

CF424344   Hattie Cooper (11 Oct 1898-28 Jul 1958) m Benjamin Lauer.

CF4243441   Emma Lauer (b 15 Sep 1915) m Clarence Schreiber.

CF4243442   John Lauer (b 5 Jun 1917) m Edna

CF424345   Ruth Cooper (b 1901) m Earl Brotemarkel

CF424346   Helen Cooper (b 1904) m 1) Ralph Bloom; m 2) Walter Tepper

CF4243461   Elaine Bloom (b Sep 1924) m William Powell

CF42434611   William Powell, Jr. (b 1943)

CF42434612   Elaine Powell (b 1951)

CF4243462   Robert Bloom (b Apr 1926) m

CF42435   Jacob Harvey Cooper (b 25 Apr 1870) m 1) Ellen Freed; m 2)   . Railroad engineer.

CF424351   Bruce Cooper

CF42436   Katie May Cooper (29 Mar 1871-10 Nov 1919) m Samuel Monroe Fenton (5 Sep 1870-17 Dec 1920). Railroad engineer.

CF424361   Harvey Jacob Fenton (1 Dec 1892-22 May 1942) m Mamie Newman. Dauphin PA.

CF4243611   Martha Fenton m Samuel Mumma

CF4243612   James Fenton (d Aug 1934)

CF4243613   Samuel Fenton

CF4243614   Earl Fenton

CF4243615   Louise Fenton m Kenneth Dunlap

CF4243616   Tressa Lucille Fenton

CF4243617   Joan Fenton m Michael Summers

CF424362   Mary Edna Fenton (20 Sep 1894-11 Jun 1954) m Joseph Oyster. Sunbury PA.

CF4243621   Helen Oyster m Francis Wiegand. Northumberland PA.

CF4243622   Gwendolyn Oyster m Jack Eister. Baltimore MD.

CF4243623   Shirley Oyster

CF4243624   Margaret Oyster (d.y.)

CF424363   Viola May Fenton (b 3 May 1896) m George Heivner.

CF4243631   Mervin Heivner

CF4243632   Thelma Heivner m Harold Reichart

CF4243633   Kathryn Heivner (d.y.)

CF4243634   Betty Heivner m Edward Lentz

CF4243635   Jean Heivner

CF424364   Anna Gertrude Fenton (28 May 1898-1946) m Robert Fletcher (d). Northumberland PA.

CF4243641   Samuel Fletcher. Northumberland PA.

CF4243642   Robert Fletcher. State College PA.

CF424365   William Isaac Fenton (b 6 May 1900). Unm.

CF424366   Samuel Hoffman Fenton (b 11 Jun 1902). Unm. Winfield PA.

CF424367   Elsie Catherine Fenton (25 Sep 1903-22 May 1958) m Alvin Bardell. Newark NJ.

CF4243671   Alvin Bardell, Jr.

CF424368   Kehres Franklin Fenton (26 Dec 1906-1950, Sunbury PA). Unm.

CF424369   Lena Elizabeth Fenton (b 10 Jan 1909, Northumberland PA) m Clarence E. Bollinger

CF4243691   Clarence E. Bollinger, Jr. (b 15 Oct 1931)

CF4243692   Doris Bollinger m. Lee Bettleyon (b 18 Apr 1934)

CF42436921   Lee Ann Bettleyon (b 13 Oct 1954)

CF42436922   David Bryne Bettleyon (b 28 Jan 1957)

CF4243693   Anna Elizabeth Bollinger m Luther Culp (b 22 May 1940). Sunbury PA.

CF42436931   Luther B. Culp, Jr. (b 3 Oct 1957)

CF42436932   LuAnn Culp (b 13 Dec 1958)

CF42436A   Bertha Lucille Fenton (b 27 Jun 1911). Unm.

CF42436B   Jessie O. Fenton (18 Apr 1914-17 Jan 1917)

CF42437   Daniel Caris Cooper (b 4 Mar 1876) m 1) Cora Adams; m 2)   ; m 3)

CF424371   Howard Cooper

CF424372   Elda Cooper

CF424373   Ruth Cooper

CF424374   Robert Cooper

CF42438   George Peter Cooper (b 1 Feb 1878). Unm. Carpenter.

CF42439   Mary Elda Cooper (21 Feb 1881-1923) m C.P. Wolverton. Bur Snydertown PA.

CF424391   Dorothy Wolverton

CF4244   Thomas Gabriel Cooper (15 Nov 1836, Upper Augusta Tp PA-22 Feb 1879, Sunbury PA) m 6 Apr 1859, Mary Elizabeth Rorhbach (4 Mar 1837, Sunbury PA-7 Feb 1923, Sunbury PA). Bur Sunbury PA.

CF42441   Charles Edward Cooper (17 Dec 1859-4 Nov 1926) m Miriam Linder. No chn. Railroad supt, Pottsville and Pittsburgh PA.

CF42442   George Palmer Cooper (6 Feb 1862-3 Mar 1871)

CF42443   Mary Catharine Cooper (25 Sep 1865-16 May 1942, Sunbury PA) m. 4 Nov 1883, Walton Francis Rhoads (22 Sep 1860, Hecla, Schuylkill Co PA-24 Nov 1927, Sunbury PA). Bur Sunbury PA. Cashier, First National Bank, Sunbury PA.

CF424431 Banker.   Florence Edna Rhoads (1884-4 Dec 1951, Sunbury PA) m Bruce G. Frick (d 1931).

CF4244311   Bruce G. Frick, Jr. (b 18 Dec 1911). Unm. Insurance agent, Sunbury PA.

CF4244312   Mary Edna Frick (b 24 Jul 1914) m James P. Ruch (b 15 Mar 1913)

CF42443121   James Allen Ruch (b 30 Jan 1947)

CF42443122   Patricia Ann Ruch (b 19 Nov 1948)

CF42443123   Mary Frick Ruch (b 7 Oct 1951)

CF4244313 Banker.   Thomas Rhoads Frick (b 2 Mar 1916) m 12 Apr 1936, Jenniebell Stumpff (b 2 Apr 1917).

CF42443131   Thomas Rhoads Frick, Jr. (b 6 Dec 1936) m 28 Sep 1958, Suzanne Grugan.

CF42443132   Terrance Craig Frick (b 28 May 1940) m 1 Oct 1961, Judith L. Merrill

CF4244314   Jean Catherine Frick (b Sep 1918) m Jun 1940, John H. Snyder

CF42443141   John P. Snyder (b 5 Dec 1942)

CF42443142   Joel David Snyder (b 1944)

CF42443143   Jeffrey Snyder (b 12 Apr 1947)

CF4244315   Martha Frick (b Aug 1920)

CF42443151   Charles Dewey (b 14 Jul 1948)

CF42443152   Linda Dewey (b 17 Aug 1952)

CF424432   Bertha Irene Rhoads m George H. Bucher. Pres, Westinghouse Elec & Mfg Co., Pittsburgh
PA.

CF4244321   Martha Elizabeth Bucher

CF4244322   Ruth Bucher

CF4244323   Alma Bucher

CF4244324   Irene Bucher

CF4244325   George David Bucher

CF424433   Alma Catherine Rhoads (1891-27 Mar 1906)

CF424434   Thomas William Rhoads (5 May 1893-26 May 1921, Sunbury PA). Unm. Sgt Maj, WWI.
George Washington U; clerk, First National Bank, Sunbury PA.

CF424435   Mary Cooper Rhoads (b 1901) m Stanley L. Whetstone. PhD; NJ.

CF4244351   Stanley L. Whetstone

CF4244352   Janice Whetstone

CF4244353   Mary Whetstone

CF424436   Walton Francis Rhoads, Jr. (1904-1919, Sunbury PA).

CF424437   Martha Elizabeth Rhoads (b 1911) m Resford R. Beal. Mansfield OH.

CF4244371   Linda Beal

CF4244372   Douglas Beal

CF4244373   Alison Beal

CF42444   Harriet Elizabeth Cooper (28 Jul 1868, Sunbury PA-14 Jul 1899, Sunbury PA) m 8 Oct
1889, Ira Thorne Clement Dissinger (7 Feb 1867, Sunbury PA-2 Jan 1912, Sunbury PA). Bur Sunbury PA.
Mbr of first graduating class of Sunbury High School, 1883. Prothonotary of Northumberland Co, 1907.

CF424441   David C. Dissinger (2 Sep 1890, Sunbury PA-17 Nov 1897, Sunbury PA). Bur Sunbury
PA.

CF424442   Charles Edward Dissinger (7 Sep 1894, Sunbury PA-23 Nov 1986) m. 20 Nov 1919, Helen
Ambrose Ellenberger (20 Sep 1895, Tampa FL-27 Sep 1995). Bur Sunbury PA. Brig Gen, USA.

CF4244421   Helen Elizabeth Dissinger (16 Jun 1921, Ft. Sam Houston TX-13 Apr 1985) m 1) 22 Mar
1947, Carl Frederick Holden, Jr. (b 23 Jan 1922, Bangor ME); m 2) Hubert W. Coleman. Bur Aron Park FL.
Holden, Lt, USN.

CF42444211   Carl Frederick Holden III (b 20 Apr 1948, Bethesda MD). Lt Col, USA.

CF42444212   Patricia Holden (b 19 May 1950, Philadelphia PA) m 2) 31 May 1986, James Gose

CF4244422   Mary Patricia Dissinger (b 15 Oct 1922, Ft. Sam Houston TX) m 21 May 1949, Capt. Robert Busill Tully (b 12 Nov 1923, Ft. Sam Houston TX)

CF42444221   Robert Bussill Tully, Jr. (b 15 Jul 1950, Ft. Campbell KY) m Patricia Galeher (b 13 Apr 1951)

CF42444222   Charles Dissinger Tulley (b 25 May 1952, Ft. Benning GA) m Constance Ash

CF42444223   Michael Merit Tulley (b 31 Jan 1955, Ft. Benning GA) m Maureen Blake

CF42444224   Elizabeth Rust Tulley (b 5 Aug 1957, Augsburg, Germany) m Andrew Simoff

CF424443   Ira Thorne Clement Dissinger, Jr. (24 Jun 1897, Sunbury PA-22 Feb 1937, Sunbury PA). Unm. Bur Sunbury PA.

CF424444   Mary Elizabeth Dissinger (28 Feb 1899, Sunbury PA-3 Jun 1985) m 18 Jun 1927, Harold E. Flack (30 Dec 1899, Plymouth PA-19 Jul 1984). State senator; Wilkes Barre PA.

*CF4244441   Charles Dissinger Flack (20 Jan 1928, Wilkes-Barre PA-17 Jul 1979) m 18 Sep 1948, Joan Powell (b 24 Jun 1931, Wilkes-Barre PA)

CF42444411   Janet Elizabeth Flack (b 11 Jul 1949, Wilkes-Barre PA)

CF42444412   Charles Dissinger Flack, Jr. (b 21 Nov 1954, Wilkes-Barre PA) m Katlin Stine (b 17 Mar 1954). Exec.

CF424444121   Charles Dissinger Flack III (b 16 Aug 1983)

CF424444122   Jamie Ann Flack (b 26 Sep 1986)

CF424444123   Alex Eckman Flack (b 26 Sep 1986)

CF42444413   Harold Eben Flack (b 21 Nov 1958, Wilkes-Barre PA)

CF4245   Harriet Sevilla Cooper (8 Oct 1838-24 Dec 1926) m J. Edward Muench (d 1900). Major, Civil War.

CF4246   John Landis Cooper (19 Dec 1840-14 Jun 1915) m 20 Sep 1866, Emma Amelia Hummel (28 Jul 1845-17 May 1926). Civil War.

CF42461   Nora Elsie Cooper (b 9 Oct 1867) m 9 Oct 1891, Robert S. Bannen. DD, Lutheran clergyman.

CF424611   Paul Cooper Bannen (6 Jun 1893-13 Dec 1933) m Janett Myers

CF42462   Arthur Eugene Cooper (b 23 Jun 1872) m 15 Nov 1894, Carrie Elizabeth Ulsh (b 16 Sep 1869). Lutheran clergyman.

CF424621   Florence Anita Cooper (b 14 Dec 1895) m William Boyd Tobias

CF4246211   Richard Boyd Tobias (b 3 Sep 1917)

CF4246212　　　　Lois Jean Tobias (b 8 May 1921)

CF4246213　　　　June Anita Tobias (b 18 Mar 1924)

CF424622　　　　Robert Ulsh Cooper (b 4 Jun 1898) m Kathryn Alvin. MD.

CF424623　　　　John Andrew Cooper (b 20 Nov 1904). PhD.

CF424624　　　　Kathryn Lois Cooper (b 5 Aug 1907)

CF4247　　　　Simon Cooper (1 Jul 1842-2 Jun 1850)

CF4248　　　　David William Cooper (3 Aug 1844-27 Dec 1916) m 1) 15 Feb 1872, Hannah Fasold (1845-23 Feb 1884); m 2) 28 Mar 1888, Emma Lesher

CF42481　　　　George Cooper (1873-1890)

CF42482　　　　Catherine Pearl Cooper (1889-1904)

CF4249　　　　Mary Catherine Cooper (4 Oct 1846-31 Oct 1927) m Dec 1879, Amos K. Zimmerman. Lutheran clergyman, Watsontown and Rebersburg PA.

CF42491　　　　Martha Catherine Zimmerman (b 25 Dec 1880) m Henry Dies. Lutheran clergyman, Hornell and Utica NY

CF424911　　　　Catherine Dies (b Jul　　) m Ralph Austin (b Jul　　). No chn.

CF424912　　　　Dorothea H.O. Dies. No chn.

CF42492　　　　Harriet May Zimmerman (b 14 Sep 1882). Unm. Teacher, Selinsgrove PA.

CF42493　　　　Stella C. Zimmerman (b 25 Mar 1884). Graduate nurse.

CF424931　　　　Christie Zimmerman. Lutheran missionary, Gunter S. India

CF424A　　　　Joseph Melanchthon Cooper (1 Feb 1849-1913) m Isabel Bardner. MD; Reading PA.

CF424A1　　　　Charles David Cooper (1882, Gratz PA-1954) m 1906, Cottie Gutilla Albright. BS, Bucknell U; PhD, Cornell Un; dir of athletics, Millersville S Col.

CF424A2　　　　George W. Cooper

CF424A3　　　　Claire Cooper (b 1884) m Sadie Moyer

CF424A4　　　　Robert Q. Cooper

CF424A5　　　　Edna E. Cooper (d 1919) m J.B. Hauk

CF424A51　　　　Joseph Hauk

CF424A52　　　　Robert Hauk

CF424A6　　　　Harriet Cooper m Frank Patchin

CF424A61　　　　Joseph Patchin

CF424A7   Helen C. Cooper m R.J. Washburn

CF424A8   Ethel U. Cooper. Unm. Teacher, Kansas City MO.

CF424A9   Thomas Baker Cooper (d.y.)

CF424B   Luther Snyder Cooper (3 May 1851-24 Jan 1937) m Lucy Alice Keefer (See CF1626)

CF425   Sarah Snyder (11 Aug 1811-29 Sep 1835). Unm.

CF426   Susan Snyder (ca 1813-d.y.)

CF427   Simon Snyder (9 Mar 1814-10 Oct 1854) m Mary Kreamer (26 Nov 1813-15 Dec 1894).
Bur Sunbury PA.

CF4271   Mary Catharine Snyder (d 12 May 1875) m Henry Clay Malick, Sr.

CF42711   Florene Malick (28 Sep 1858-8 Jun 1927) m John A. Krohn (1854-1895)

CF427111   Hattie Krohn (1884-1951) m George L. Hepler (1897-1956)

CF42712   Sarah Elizabeth Malick (22 Sep 1867-28 Mar 1928) m Benjamin Franklin Krohn (18 Jun
1865-28 Mar 1928)

CF427121   John Krohn m Hattie Jones

CF4271211   John Benjamin Krohn

CF4271212   Elizabeth Krohn

CF427122   Dora Mary Krohn (30 Jun 1889-18 Jan 1926)

CF42713   Henry Clay Malick m Mary Snyder

CF427131   Henry Clay Malick

CF427132   Hazel Malick m Harold Howard

CF42714   Harriet Malick m Herbrt B. Shaffer. Sunbury PA.

CF427141   Clayton Shaffer (b 1890) m 1) Edna Bitner; m 2) Ella Cummings

CF427142   Verna Shaffer (b Dec 1892). Unm.

CF427143   Florine Shaffer m 1) Henry Stevenson; m 2) James Naulty

CF4271431   Helen Stevenson

CF427144   Scott H. Shaffer (b 1898)

CF427145   Hilda Shaffer m 1) Walter Libby; m 2) William Neitz

CF4271451   Russell Libby

CF427146   Mary Shaffer m 1)   Wetzel; m 2) Harry Bennett. No chn.

CF4272   Albert Snyder (6 Dec 1845-13 Sep 1854). Bur Old Sunbury Cemetery.

CF4273   Sarah Elizabeth Snyder (1842-1921) m 6 Nov 1877, Martz Coovert

CF42731   Mollie Coovert m Harry March (d 12 Sep 1921, Jersey City NJ)

CF427311   George March m Mary Masterson

CF4273111   Mary March m John Tammon

CF427312   Coovert March m

CF4273121   Harry Elwood March

CF4273122   Clara Anna March

CF427313   Ida Laura March m Fred Lang

CF4273131   Ida Laura Lang

CF42732   Ida Coovert m George Rhoderick. Bayonne NJ

CF427321   Harold Rhoderick

CF427322   Ann Rhoderick

CF427323   Grace Rhoderick m William Kay

CF4273231   Rhoderick Kay

CF42733   William Coovert (d 16 Dec 1899). Unm.

CF4274   Lydia Snyder (11 Oct 1847-28 Feb 1928) m 24 Jul 1870, Jacob Bell (14 Nov 1845-22 Jul
1884)

CF42741   Charles Shafer Bell (27 Nov 1873-8 Apr 1929) m 1) 24 Sep 1891, Mary Alice Kempton;
m 2) Olive May Stahlnecker

CF427411   Jean Mae Bell (29 Sep 1892-18 May 1962) m 30 Jun 1916, Grant Barrett Gossler (3 Apr
1895-3 May 1971). Bur Sunbury PA. Res Renovo PA.

CF4274111   Helen Elinor Gossler (b 15 Sep 1925, Sunbury PA) m 3 May 1947, Renovo PA, John Paul
Martin, Jr. (b 10 Apr 1926, Hinton VA). She, RN; he, food processor serviceman. Res Sarasota FL.

CF42741111   Dawn Louise Martin (6 Mar 1948, Harrisonburg VA) m 1) 8 Aug 1970, Dayton VA,
Robert Timmons (b 12 Apr 1950, Fort Bragg NC) div; m 2) 15 Aug 1983, Harrisonburg VA, Melvin James
Shank (b 3 Aug 1945, Newport News VA). She, BSN, VA Commonwealth U, 1071; nurse, VA Hosp. He,
barber. Res Charlottesville VA.

CF427411111   Michele Lynn Timmons (24 Mar 1971, Richmond VA) m 15 Aug 1989, Charlottesville
VA, Charles Swingler (b 23 Aug 1966, Charlottesville VA). She, office worker; he, policeman. Res
Ruckersville VA.

CF4274111111   Ashley Dawn Swingler (30 Oct 1990, Charlottesvilla VA)

CF427411112   Lisa Diane Timmons (4 Jul 1973, Richmond VA) m 14 Jan 1994, Charlottesville VA,

Burke Zimmerman (b 26 Oct 1969, Charlottesville VA). She, homemaker; he, merchandising.

CF4274111121   Zachary Burke Zimmerman (b 7 Jul 1995, Charlottesville VA)

CF42741112   Diane Lee Martin (6 Mar 1948, Harrisonburg VA) m 1) 12 Sep 1970, Pearson GA, Jimmy Cole Vickers, Jr. (b 20 Jan 1948, Douglas GA), div; m 2) 25 Jun 1983, Bridgewater VA, Mark John Huffman (b 14 Jun 1948, Harrisonburg VA). She, homemaker; he, highway dept supervisor. Res Mt. Crawford VA.

CF427411121   Daphne Ann Vickers (b 6 Jun 1976, Jacksonville FL)

CF427411122   Jimmy Cole Vickers (b 1 Aug 1980, Harrisonburg VA)

CF427411123   Megan L. Huffman (b 24 May 1984, Harrisonburg VA)

CF427411124   Dane Mark Huffman (b 4 Sep 1985, Harrisonburg VA)

CF42741113   John Grant Martin (b 29 Jul 1949, Harrisonburg VA) m 9 Aug 1970, Dayton VA, Rebecca Jane Farley (b 15 Sep 1950, Harrisonburg VA). He, dairy, poultry farmer. She, BS, Madison (VA) Col, 1973, farm business mgr; kindergarten teacher, Dayton VA.

CF427411131   John Grant Martin, Jr. (b 17 Aug 1971, Harrisonburg VA). VA Tech U, 1973; food processing firm serviceman, Dayton VA.

CF427411132   Jason Daniel Martin (b 17 Sep 1984, Harrisonburg VA)

CF427411133   Craig Robert Martin (b 21 Jan 1986, Harrisonburg VA)

CF42741114   Glenn Douglas Martin (b 27 May 1952, Harrisonburg VA) m 9 Dec 1972, Dayton VA, Deborah Sue Evans (b 22 Oct 1951, Harrisonburg VA). He, trucker; she, nurse, Bridgewater VA.

CF427411141   Douglas Donald Martin (b 14 Apr 1974, Harrisonburg VA), Dairy specialties firm, Bridgewater VA.

CF427411142   Keith Scott Martin (b 2 Sep 1976, Harrisonburg VA)

CF427412   Helen E. Bell (b 10 Mar 1894) m 15 Jun 1913, Samuel Guy Dreese (17 Nov 1893-10 Dec 1969). Bur Stonington PA. Res Sunbury PA.

CF4274121   Samuel Guy Dreese (17 Oct 1919-8 Jan 1970). Unm. Bur Stonington PA.

CF427413   Charles Graham Bell (9 May 1898-1975) m 2 Apr 1917, Mildred Daisy Snyder (18 Jan 1898-15 Oct 1992). Bur Northumberland PA.

CF427414   Mabel Irene Bell (18 Mar 1900 - 2 Mar 1902)

CF427415   Glenwyn V. Bell m Curtis Umplebee

CF4274151   Curtis Umplebee

CF4274152   Carol Umplebee m   Yoke

CF427416   Dorothy Verla Bell (12 Sep 1909-13 Mar 1986) m 24 Jul 1931, David Norman Linderman (19 Aug 1906-4 Jul 1978). Auto salesman, Stroudsburg PA.

*CF4274161   Patricia Ann Linderman (b 20 Feb 1933) m 1) 7 Mar 1954, John William Osborn, div 1965; m 2) 2 Feb 1968, Clemens Peter Gesek. Civil employee, USA.

CF42741611   Diane Elizabeth Osborn (b 31 Mar 1955)

CF42741612   Gretchen Louise Osborn (b 22 Sep 1957)

CF42741613   John William Osborn (b 14 Nov 1959)

CF4274162   Dawn E. Linderman (b 8 Mar 1936) m 10 Apr 1959, Lester Slutter (b 7 Apr 1934)

CF42741621   Sandra Jo Slutter (b 14 Jun 1960) m 2 Jun 1989, Doyle Walter Young III

CF42741622   Steven David Slutter (b 20 Jul 1961)

CF42741623   Scott Slutter (b 6 Apr 1966)

CF4274163   Diane O. Linderman (8 Mar 1936-1 Jul 1936)

CF4274164   Linda Jo Linderman (b 18 Jul 1943) m 1) 22 Aug 1961, Dory Richard Wismer (b 13 Apr 1943), div 1964; m 2) 21 Aug 1965,   Rau, div 1971; m 3) 27 Sep 1974, Lawrence Bailey

CF42741641   Laurie Jo Wismer (b 22 Apr 1962) m 1) 9 May 1982, Mark Bonneau, div; m 2) 18 Jun 1985, John Lee McCormick, div 1991.

CF427416411   Jaimee Bonneau (b 28 Sep 1982)

CF427416412   Kristee Lee McCormick (b 1 Feb 1985)

CF427416413   Cody McCormick (b 14 Jul 1986)

CF42741642   David Richard Wismer (b 17 Aug 1963) m 4 Jul 1984, Marianne Carr

CF427416421   David Robert Carr (b 30 Jun 1990)

CF42741643   John George Rau (b 21 Mar 1966)

CF42741644   Jeffrey Darren Rau (b 1 Feb 1968)

*CF4274165   Susan Linderman (b 23 Aug 1947) m 1) 22 Oct 1968, William Alder Martin (b 29 Sep 1944), div 1980; m 2) 19 May 1985, Daniel Ralph Paul (b 17 May 1939)

CF42741651   Christopher Alden Martin (b 30 May 1969)

CF42741652   Cory William Martin (b 29 Jan 1975)

CF427417   Marlyn E. Bell (b ca 1911-1990)

CF427418   Myron L. Bell (d 28 May 1914)

CF427419   E. Maxine Bell (n 11 Jun 1917) m 24 Dec 1934, Arthur Ernest Grove (b 1 Jan 1913)

CF4274191   Ronald Norman Grove (b 30 Nov 1938)

CF4274192   David Michael Grove (b 4 Dec 1941)

CF4274193   Nancy Sue Grove (b 16 Feb 1945)

CF4274194   Sandra Jean Grove (b 14 Aug 1948)

CF4274195   Arthur Ernest Grove (b 21 May 1953)

CF42742   Mayde Bell (d 16 Apr 1877)

CF42743   Harry Bell (25 May 1878-1978) m 14 Apr 1917, Mattie Elmeda Garey (b 25 Jun 1879)

CF42744   Helen Bell (b 18 Aug 1881)

CF42745   Ethel Bell (3 Jul 1882-25 Sep 1959) m 25 Dec 1904, William R. Donmoyer

CF427451   Henry Charles Donmoyer (d.y.)

CF427452   Winter Eugene Donmoyer m Hazel Brownewell. No chn.

CF427453   Mable Donmoyer m Benjamin Hall

CF427454   Harry R. Donmoyer (b 12 May 1913) m 4 Feb 1937, Elizabeth Hickman (b 20 Jan 1917)

CF4274541   Harry R. Donmoyer, Jr. (b 27 May 1938)

CF4274542   Sue Ann Donmoyer (b 12 Sep 1939) m 15 Feb 1958, Robert G. Erdman (b 16 Jun 1935)

CF42745421   Dean Allen Erdman (b 28 Aug 1959)

CF4274543   Marie Donmoyer (23 Aug 1940-8 May 1941)

CF4274544   Carol Maria Donmoyer (b 28 Aug 1941)

CF4274545   Mary Louise Donmoyer (b 23 Aug 1942)

CF4274546   Ethel Elizabeth Donmoyer (b 29 Dec 1944)

CF4274547   David Fredrick Donmoyer (b 6 Nov 1946)

CF4274548   Christy Eugene Donmoyer (b 27 Jan 1953)

CF4275   Sarah Jane Snyder (Jul 1858-2 Aug 1858)

CF428   Maria Snyder (5 Mar 1816-8 May 1817)

CF429   Thomas Kehl Snyder (3 Dec 1822-8 Mar 1889) m 10 Jan 1850, Julia Ann Wolverton (22 Apr 1830-19 Dec 1897). Bur Sunbury PA.

CF4291   Ira W. Snyer (30 Sep 1850-10 Dec 1889) m Sarah Moyer (26 Jul 1854-22 Mar 1916). He bur Winfield PA; she, Montandon PA.

CF42911   Mary Snyder (13 Apr 1875-2 Feb 1931) m Elwood Fasold (24 Aug 1874-6 Apr 1959)

CF429111   Amy Fasold

CF429112   Raymond Fasold (b 11 Dec 1900) m Lottie Dietz. Northumberland PA.

CF4291121   Doris Fasold m Robert H. McDowell. Sunbury PA.

CF42911211   Michael McDowell (b 1949)

CF4291122   Willard R. Fasold m Joan Shaffer. Sunbury PA.

CF42911221   Craig Fasold (b 1955)

CF42911222   Janelle Fasold (b 1956)

CF429113   Thelma Sarah Fasold (b 13 May 1903) m 25 Oct 1926, Earl Rhone (b 16 Aug 1901).
Sunbury PA.

CF4291131   Earl Rhone, Jr. (b Apr 1928) m Elizabeth Reitz. Monroe LA.

CF42911311   Deborah Lynn Rhone (b 11 Nov 1954)

CF4291132   Marylou Rhone (b 25 Jul 1932) m Charles Williams. Sunbury PA.

CF42911321   Stephen Elwood Williams (b 2 Nov 1957)

CF4291133   William Elwood Rhone (b 11 Aug 1941)

CF429114   Theron Reuben Fasold (25 Oct 1906, Sunbury PA-31 Mar 1982, Danville PA) m 5 Jul
1928, Hazel Amber Wands (7 Mar 1904, Milton PA-16 Oct 1989, Danville PA). Electrical contractor,
Northumberland PA.

CF4291141   Donald Robert Fasold (b 3 Jun 1929, Sunbury PA) m 27 Sep 1852, Sunbury PA, Joan
Swope (b 15 Jun 1929, Lancaster PA)

CF42911411   Theron George Fasold (b Aug 1953, Sunbury PA) m Michelle Rogers, div.

CF42911411111   Amie Nichole Fasold (b 20 Feb 1982, Sunbury PA)

CF42911412   Timothy Robert Fasold (b 9 Dec 1955, Sunbury PA) m Debra Croak (b 25 Sep 1957)

CF429114121   Diane Elizabeth Fasold (24 Apr 1980, Danville PA)

CF429114122   Dawn Amber Fasold (b 15 Aug 1982, Danville PA)

CF429114123   Terra Renee Fasold (b 7 Jun 1993, Danville PA)

CF42911413   Terry Ray Fasold (b 1 Dec 1961, Sunbury PA-18 Mar 1986, Franklin PA)

CF4291142   Jack Elwood Fasold (b 12 Jun 1931) m 13 Apr 1952, Northumberland PA, Fay Slear (b
24 Aug 1932, near Selinsgrove PA)

CF42911421   Jeffrey Lee Fasold (b 19 Dec 1955, Sunbury PA) m 31 Jul 1976, Dorothy Hanetta Steese
(b 15 Dec 1954, Sunbury PA)

CF429114211   Lisa Jane Fasold (b 5 Apr 1979, Sunbury PA)

CF429114212   Jason Lee Fasold (b 24 May 1981, Sunbury PA)

CF429114213   Justin Lynn Fasold (b 26 Jun 1984, Sunbury PA)

*CF42911422   Darlene Kay Fasold (b 24 Jun 1960, Sunbury PA) m 30 Jun 1979, Northumberland PA,
William Engle (b 22 Sep 1956, Sunbury PA)

CF429114221   Scott Eric Engle (b 3 Mar 1983, Lewisburg PA)

CF429114222   Matthew Ryan Engle (b 14 Feb 1988, Lewisburg PA)

CF4291143   Beverly Jane Fasold (b 20 Jan 1933) m 28 Aug 1954, Northumberland PA, Leon Joseph Lenker (28 Aug 1928-1 May 1993). She, RN.

CF42911431   Kim Alan Lenker (b 18 Jan 1955, Sunbury PA) m 26 Mar 1980, Faith Rogers, div.

Jacob Kehres (b 17 Apr 1978, Sunbury PA)(Adopted by Kim A. Lenker)

CF429114311   Kevin David Lenker (b 17 Sep 1980, Sunbury PA)

CF429114312   Nicholas Isaiah Lenker (b 19 Jun 1982, Lewisburg PA)

CF429114313   Aaron Joseph Lenker (b 28 Apr 1984, Lewisburg PA)

CF429114314   Elizabeth Naomi Lenker (b 1 Nov 1985, Lewisburg PA)

CF42911432   Kevin Dean Lenker (23 Oct 1957-20 Oct 1967)

CF42911433   Linda Lou Lenker (b 7 Apr 1967, Sunbury PA) m 8 Oct 1988, Mark Gregory Graybill (b 1 Jan 1967, Sunbury PA)

CF429114331   Amanda Noel Graybill (b 2 Nov 1990, Lewisburg PA)

CF429114332   Cody James Graybill (b 16 Apr 1993, Lewisburg PA)

CF429115   Forrest Elwood Fasold (b 9 Feb 1910) m Olive Karns. Sunbury PA.

CF4291151   David Fasold m

CF4291152   Barbara Fasold m

CF4291153   Forrest Elwood Fasold, Jr.

CF4291154   Carole Fasold

CF4291155   John Fasold

CF429116   Paul Snyder Fasold (b 6 Apr 1918) m Alice Engle. Electrical contractor, Northumberland PA.

CF4291161   James Paul Fasold

CF4291162   Robin Fasold

CF42912   Harry T. Snyder (b 1880) m Emma Macker. Penn RR, Chester PA.

CF429121   Pearl Snyder

CF429122   Harry Snyder, Jr.

CF42913   William W. Snyder (6 Apr 1882-17 Apr 1901)

CF42914   Frank Snyder (b 1885) m   . No chn. Bur Arlington National Cemetery; WWI.

CF42915   Lula Snyder (19 Apr 1889-15 Nov 1950) m Harry Moyer (b 31 Dec 1888). York PA.

CF429151   Brooke Snyder Moyer (b 25 Jul 1908) m Grace Byers. Northumberland PA.

CF4291511   Lois Moyer (b 27 Jan 1930) m Jerry Moore. Erie PA.

CF42915111   Kathleen Moore (b 1 Nov 1948)

CF42915112   Keith Moore (b 29 Apr 1952)

CF42915113   Kerry David Moore (b 24 Sep 1957)

CF42915114   Tamme Lou Moore (b 1 May 1959)

CF42915115   Danne Layne Moore (b 7 Jul 1964)

CF4291512   Jacqueline Moyer m Richard Smith. No chn. Northumberland PA.

CF4291513   Paul Moyer (b 19 Sep 1935) m Sandra M.   . USA, Germany.

CF42915131   Lisa Dee Moyer (b 24 Nov 1961)

CF42915132   Terry Lee Moyer (b 12 Sep 1964)

CF429152   Vera Snyder Moyer (b 9 Sep 1910) m 1) Gurney Kissinger; m 2) Richard Ballou. York
PA.

CF4291521   Audrey Jean Kissinger (b 2 Feb 1929) m Howard Rohrbaugh. York PA.

CF42915211   Deborah Ann Rohrbaugh (b 15 Jan 1949)

CF42915212   Robin Elaine Rohrbaugh (b 22 Jun 1954)

CF429153   Ruth Snyder Moyer (b 20 Jun 1916) m Howard W. Eura Jenkins (b 16 Jul 1910). Sunbury
PA.

CF4291531   William Douglas Jenkins (15 Apr 1935-24 Dec 1956). USMC.

CF4291532   Philip Howard Jenkins (b 25 Nov 1945)

CF4292   Sarah Snyder (Jul 1858-2 Aug 1858)

CF4293   Charles Nevin Snyder (1859-Nov 1918). Unm.

CF4294   Annie Elizabeth Snyder (16 Nov 1863-Aug 1935) m 10 Oct 1888, William Ayresman
Shipman (11 Sep 1861-11 May 1921). Bur Sunbury PA. Undertaker and furniture dealer, Sunbury PA. See
Biography, Floyd, *Northumberland County Biography*, 1911, p. 194.

CF42941   Myrtle Elizabeth Shipman (b Apr 1891). Unm. Sunbury PA.

CF42942   Russell Conwell Shipman (18 Aug 1892-1967) m 7 Jun 1917, Nelle Stevens (b Sep 1891).
Bur Shamokin Dam PA. BS, Bucknell U, 1915. Funeral director and electrical engineer.

CF429421   William Stevens Shipman (7 Apr 1918-17 Nov 1974) m Sara Rohrbach. Bur Shamokin
Dam PA. Insurance agent, Sunbury PA.

CF4294211   William Stevens Shipman, Jr. (b 8 Mar 1948, Danville PA) m 20 Apr 1985, Latimore Tp,
Adams Co PA, Linda Louetta Leer (b 13 Jan 1954, Gettyburg PA). He, BA, Susquehanna (PA) U, 1969;

MDiv, Lutheran Sch of Theol, Chicago, 1973; STM, Lutheran Theol Sem, Gettysburg PA, 1989. Lutheran pastor, 1973- ; Lightstreet-Canby, Elliottsburg, Brickville and Lemoyne PA.

CF42942111   Eric Stephen Shipman (b 7 Jun 1986, Harrisburg PA)

CF42942112   Norah Marie Shipman (b 30 Apr 1988, Harrisburg PA)

CF429422   Margaret Shipman (1920-1920)

CF429423   Nancyann Shipman (b 6 Feb 1923, Sunbury PA) m 15 Feb 1944, William Cole (4 Jun 1921, Elrama PA-14 Nov 1979, Danville PA). Bur Shamokin Dam PA. He, WWII, USAAC. BS, U Pittsburgh, 1944; pharmacist, Sunbury PA.

CF4294231   William Russell Cole, Jr. (b 24 Oct 1947, Danville PA) m 1) 13 Jun 1965, Northumberland PA, Linda Louise Bird (b 3 Oct 1948), div 1975; m 2) 5 Sep 1981, Doreen Loeffler (b 8 Nov 1955, Glen Ridge NY), div 1989. Jail guard.

CF42942311   Wendy Sue Cole (b 1 Nov 1965, Sunbury PA) m 16 May 1992, Chad Matthew Rice (b 2 Jul 1965)

CF429423111   Cale David Rice (b 14 Oct 1994, Danville PA)

CF42942312   William Russell Cole II (b 22 Nov 1969, Harrisburg PA)

CF42942313   Kymberley Ann Cole (b 7 Sep 1984, Lewisburg PA)

CF4294232   Robert King Cole (b 26 Feb 1950, Danville PA) m 18 Jun 1977, Christie Seiple (b 23 Feb 1952, Danville PA). He, BS, U Pittsburgh, 1973, pharmacist; she, BS, U Pittsburgh.

CF42942321   Jason Robert Cole (b 9 Oct 1978, Danville PA)

CF42942322   Zachary William Cole (b 3 Oct 1980, Danville PA)

CF4294233   Michael Stevens Cole (b 12 Mar 1953) m 27 Jun 1979, Kay Renn (b 19 Mar 1957). He, pharmacy; she, beautician.

CF42942331   Michael Vincent Cole (b 22 Oct 1982, Sunbury PA)

CF42942332   Daniel Blair Cole (b 25 Feb 1986, Sunbury PA)

CF42942333   Chelsea Jo Cole (b 25 Feb 1986, Sunbury PA)

CF42943   Harley Nevin Shipman (24 Aug 1894-30 Aug 1951) m 12 Jun 1920, Ruth Killian Mettler (2 Apr 1899-27 Jun 1960). WWI. BS, civil engineering, Bucknell (PA) U, 1917; funeral director.

CF429431   Martha Elizabeth Shipman (b 31 Jul 1923) m Minor Stein, Jr. Grad, Miss Gibbs School.

CF4294311   Harley Nevin Stein (b 1945)

John George Brungart (1788-1877)   CF43 Salome Kehl Brungart (1787-1863)

CF4294312   Robert Stein (b 1955)

CF42944   William Ayersman Shipman, Jr. (b 13 Jul 1897) m Marjorie Hanna. No chn. Insurance, Sunbury PA.

CF42945   Helen Snyder Shipman (b 19 Oct 1907) m 29 May 1930, Robert Elias Diehl (b 7 Mar 1908). She, grad. Natl Park Sem, Washington DC, 1927. He, BS, PSU, 1929; public accountant.

CF429451   Julie Ann Diehl (6 Aug 1932-9 Aug 1932)

CF429452   Barbara Jean Diehl (b 24 Jan 1934). BS, Dickinson Col, 1953; teacher, Toms River NJ.

CF429453   Robert Elias Diehl, Jr. (b 23 Jun 1935) m 1) Nancy Hawk; m 2) Wendy L. Walborn. BA, Gettysburg Col, 1957; Dickinson Sch of Law, 1960; LLM, NYU Sch of Law, 1964.

CF4294531   Robert Elias Diehl III (3 Jan 1959, Carlisle PA) m Billie Jo Moist

CF42945311   Shannon A. Diehl (b 2 Sep 1982)

CF4294532   Michael Irvin Diehl (b 21 Apr 1962, Sunbury PA) m Melissa Updegraff

CF42945321   Jacob Robert Diehl (b 18 Oct 1995)

CF4294533   Chelsie Gabrielle Diehl (b 26 Jun 1992, Danville PA)

CF429454   William Shipman Diehl (b 13 May 1937) m 1959, Margaret Beers. BA, Gettysburg Col, 1959.

CF429455   Bonnie Sue Diehl (b 10 Jun 1944)

CF429456   John Michael Diehl (b 27 Feb 1950)

CF43   Salome Kehl (daughter of John Jacob and Catharine (Weiser) Kehl)(14 Jan 1787, near Sunbury PA-8 Dec 1863, Brush Valley, Centre Co, PA) m 9 Apr 1811, John George Brungart (20 Jul 1788, Manheim Tp, York Co, PA-21 Dec 1877, Brush Valley PA). Bur Rebersburg PA. Farmer in Centre Co PA; also proprietor of tannery. He developed a plow which became famous in local annals, known as the Brungart plow.

CF431   Catharine Brungart (20 Jan 1812-30 May 1857, Miles Tp, Centre Co PA) m 29 Nov 1829, Jacob W. Erhard (19 Jun 1804-19 Sep 1857)

CF4311   William Erhard (b 30 Nov 1830) m 1) Mary Bickel; m 2) Hannah Jamison

CF43111   Agnes Erhard (10 Dec 1854-10 Aug 1931) m William Coldren. Bur Pleasant Gap PA.

CF431111   John I. Coldren (b Selinsgrove PA) m 23 Feb 1905, Mayme Poethes. Bur Georges Valley Cem, Centre Co PA.

CF4311111   George W. Coldren. Unm.

CF4311112   Agnes Coldren m 31 Jan 1924, Merlo Feehrer

CF43111121   Janette Feehrer (b 13 Sep 1925)

CF43111122   Jean Feehrer (b 1 May 1931)

CF43111123   Joan Feehrer (b 1 May 1931)

CF43111124   Medora Susanna Feehrer (b 15 May 1937)

CF4311113   Inadora Coldren m 17 Dec 1938, Harry L. Richardson.

CF4311114   Irvin J. Coldren m 31 Aug 1939, Lillian Rosenolt

CF43111141   Irvin J. Coldren

CF4311115   Elizabeth Coldren

CF431112   Marion Coldren (b 29 Mar 1882, Georges Valley PA) m William H. Bilger. Bur Georges Valley Cemetery.

CF4311121   Herbert H. Bigler. Pittsburgh PA.

CF431113   James E. Coldren (Pleasant Gap PA-1921) m Mabel Karstetter

CF4311131   James Russell Coldren (1908-27 Feb 1931). Unm.

CF431114   Harry W. Coldren. Unm. Bur Pleasant Gap PA.

CF431115   Roy O. Coldren m Rhoda Swartz

CF4311151   William O. Coldren

CF43112   Emma Caroline Erhard m Nathanile Zettle

CF431121   Clarence Zettle m Fay McClintock

CF4311211   Helen Zettle

CF431122   John Erhard Zettle m Ethel Mare

CF431123   Mary P. Zettle. Unm.

CF431124   Helen Lula Zettle

CF43113   Anna Catharine Erhard (d 1 Feb 1931) m Fred Drake (d 3 Jan 1930)

CF43114   Charles Laundes Erhard (2 Jan 1860-30 Nov 1864)

CF43115   Mary M. Erhard (25 Mar 1862-3 Dec 1864)

CF43116   John Clyner Erhard (b 12 Jul 1866) m Emma Eisenberg (d 1917)

CF43117   Jacob Newton Erhard

CF43118   George W. Erhard m Kate Raymond

CF431181   Paul W. Erhard m Mary Malone

CF4311811   Paul William Erhard (b 10 Aug 1926)

CF4311812   Esther C. Erhard (b 9 Jul 1928)

CF431182   Robert H. Erhard

CF431183   John N. Erhard

CF431184   Harry Erhard

CF431185   Ruth Erhard

CF4312   Caroline Erhard (18 Mar 1832-28 Jul 1857)

CF4313   Aaron B. Erhard (b 27 Dec 1833) m Mary Miller

CF43131   Robert Lewis Erhard (4 Sep 1878-3 Sep 1926) m 1) Mary Morgan; m 2) 14 Apr 1922,
Sara Christ. Methodist clergyman.

CF431311   Elinor C. Erhard (9 Mar 1911) m F.E. Gromo

CF431312   Kate Roberta Erhard (d 19 Nov 1935) m T.F. Swope. Pastor.

CF431313   Janette R. Erhard m H.L. Gromo

CF431314   Harriet Gertrude Erhard m Fred Perkins

CF431315   John M. Erhard m Pearl Shope

CF4313151   Robert W. Erhard

CF4313152   Mildred Erhard

CF431316   Charles Clark Erhard m Margaret Crawford

CF4313161	Charles Clark Erhard, Jr.
CF4313162	Jane Erhard m George W. Rittenhouse
CF431317	Louise C. Erhard m E.H. Miller. Methodist clergyman.
CF4313171	Betty Louise Miller
CF4313172	Elinor Mae Miller
CF431318	Mary J. Erhard (d 18 Apr 1918)
CF43132	John Erhard
CF43133	William H. Erhard (b 1897) m Laura Hackenburg
CF431331	William Erhard
CF431332	Gertrude Erhard
CF431333	Ray Erhard
CF43134	Alice Gertrude Erhard m William Nycum
CF43135	John Calvin Erhard m Lula Fessler
CF431351	Raymond Erhard
CF431352	Calvin Erhard
CF43136	Ursinus Erhard m Kate Lellard
CF431361	Zacharias Erhard
CF431362	Dorothy Erhard
CF43137	Jacob Wilkinson Erhard m Gertrude Wagner
CF431371	Herbert Erhard
CF43138	Harry Miller Erhard m Nellie Rosa Kirby
CF431381	Paul Eugene Erhard m Florence Babcock
CF4313811	Harry Erhard
CF4313812	Charlotte Erhard
CF431382	Ferrille Harry Erhard m Florence Woody
CF431383	Naomi Erhard m Leo Cook
CF4313831	Veronica Cook
CF4313832	Leo Cook

CF4313833   William Cook

CF431384   Lucille Dorothy Erhard m   Long

CF431385   Carita Erhard

CF4314   Thomas George Erhard (15 Jan 1835, Miles Tp PA-7 Sep 1914, Perth KS) m Sarah
Guisewite (26 Jan 1836, Haines Tp-23 Jun 1901, Perth KS). Bur Perth KS.

CF43141   Allen C. Erhard (b 19 May 1858) m Anna Wert (16 Jun 1863-26 Sep 1919)

CF431411   Guy Erhard (b 14 Mar 1882) m Susie Gump (b 30 Mar 1886)

CF4314111   Eveline Erhard (b 22 Dec 1907) m Erwin Templeton (b 14 Aug 1902)

CF4314112   Nora Erhard (b 11 Oct 1910)

CF4314113   Lloyd Erhard (b 15 Dec 1914)

CF4314114   William Erhard (11 Jun 1904-11 Feb 1906)

CF431412   Harry Erhard (b 10 Jul 1885) m Della Iddings (b 3 Mar 1888)

CF4314121   Homer Erhard (b 2 Aug 1908)

CF4314122   Mona Erhard (b 12 Oct 1910)

CF4314123   Letha Erhard (b 25 Jul 1912)

CF4314124   Carl Erhard (b 26 Jun 1914)

CF4314125   Dorothy Erhard (b 19 Feb 1916)

CF4314126   Dean Erhard (b 14 Jul 1918)

CF4314127   Frances Erhard (b 6 Jul 1919)

CF4314128   Denice Erhard (b 3 Dec 1920)

CF4314129   Phyllis Erhard (b 13 Mar 1924)

CF431412A   Wanda Lee Erhard (b 23 Jul 1926)

CF431413   Irene Erhard (16 May 1887-23 Feb 1888)

CF431414   Maude Erhard (b 20 Dec 1889) m Henry Buchannon (b 5 Apr 1895)

CF4314141   Beulah Buchannon (b 20 Jul 1908)

CF431415   Vernie Erhard (b 5 Nov 1895) m Rolla Slothour

CF4314151   Arimetta Slothour (b 1912)

CF4314152   Deloris Slothour (b 1914)

CF431416   Mary B. Erhard (b 6 Jan 1897) m Charles Rerrick (b 6 Mar 1892)

CF431417	Myrtle Erhard (b 25 Dec 1899) m Ray Berringer (b 18 May 1901)
CF43142	George N. Erhard m Lizzie Musser
CF431421	Bertha E. Erhard m Ira Parker
CF4314211	Lola Parker m Clyde Hopper
CF43142111	Clyde Hopper, Jr.
CF43142112	Alberdine Hopper
CF4314212	Luelle Parker
CF4314213	Luther Parker
CF4314214	Buck Parker
CF4314215	Elizabeth Parker
CF4314216	Nellie Parker
CF431422	Delphia Erhard m James Parker
CF4314221	Ralph Parker
CF4314222	John Parker
CF4314223	George Parker
CF4314224	Orville Parker
CF4314225	Mona Parker
CF4314226	Lois Parker
CF4314227	Harold Parker
CF4314228	Blanche Parker
CF431423	Fannie Erhard m E.E. Fox
CF4314231	Floyd Fox
CF4314232	Roy Fox
CF4314233	Evelyn Fox
CF4314234	Ruth Fox
CF4314235	Earl Fox
CF4314236	Cleo Fox
CF4314237	Frances Fox

CF4314238   Dale Fox

CF431424   Thomas N. Erhard m Minnie McLain

CF4314241   Catharine Erhard

CF4314242   Lucille Erhard

CF4314243   Florence Erhard

CF4314244   Alberdine Erhard

CF4314245   Mary Edith Erhard

CF431425   Sadied R. Erhard m Cobus Zimmerman

CF431426   Ethel E. Erhard

CF431427   Ruth Erhard

CF43143   Samuel E. Erhard (b 16 Jun 1863) m Lula Jacobson

CF431431   Clymer Jacobson Erhard m Beatrice Hardin

CF431432   Clarence E. Erhard m Faye Carter

CF431433   Margery Erhard m Andrew Taxis

CF4314331   Edith Taxis

CF431434   Frederick Erhard

CF431435   Millard Erhard

CF431436   Ivy Erhard

CF431437   Edward Erhard

CF43144   Jacob C. Erhard (8 May 1866-1914). Unm.

CF43145   Alice Olivia Erhard (d 8 Jul 1857). Unm.

CF4315   Michael Jeremiah Erhard (26 Feb 1837-14 Dec 1847)

CF4316   Rebecca Erhard (27 Apr 1839-7 Dec 1893) m William McKibben (23 Aug 1840-26 Sep
1908)

CF43161   Catherine McKibben (1865-1941) m Charles Bowes (1861-1955)

CF431611   Thomas McKibben Bowes (b 1912) m 30 Aug 1932, Hazel Rovena Helsleg. Howard PA.

CF4316111   Ruth Arlene Bowes (b 1934) m 8 Oct 1955, Marvin Weaver.

CF43161111   Lori Marie Weaver (b 18 Sep 1956)

CF4316112   Thomas C. Bowes (b 1941)

CF43162   David Allison McKibben (1865-1951) m 1) Clara M. Bicket (1877 - 1911); m 2) Mary R. Bridges Wolf (1874-1923); m 3) Lorilla Hayes (b 22 Apr 1877)

CF43163   Mary Viola McKibben (13 Sep 1869-30 Nov 1889). Bur Howard PA.

CF43164   Harmon Huton McKibben (2 Oct 1871-16 Jul 1956) m 23 Jul 1895, Lucetta Allison (14 Jun 1874-6 Mar 1945)

CF431641   Mary Rebecca McKibben (b 17 Nov 1896) m 24 Dec 1921, Clyde A. Johnson (b 2 Nov 1892)

CF4316411   Clyde A. Johnson, Jr. (b 27 Oct 1931)

CF431642   Joseph Allison McKibben (b 20 Apr 1899) m 20 Dec 1919, Ethel Waite

CF4316421   Kenneth George Huston McKibben (b 15 Feb 1921) m Kathryn Cohick (b 3 Aug 1923)

CF43164211   Bonna Kay McKibben (b 4 Oct 1942)

CF43164212   Patricia Ann McKibben (b 23 Oct 1945)

CF43164213   Sandra Lee McKibben (b 26 Nov 1946)

CF43164214   Kenneth LeRoy McKibben (b 7 Nov 1947)

CF4316422   Romayne Ruth McKibben (b 9 Apr 1922) m William Brunner

CF4316423   Maetta J. McKibben (b 28 Mar 1926) m Robert Hoover

CF431643   Jessie Catherine McKibben (b 9 May 1901)

CF431644   William Brady McKibben (1 Apr 1903-23 Sep 1924) Bur Howard PA.

CF431645   Ruth McKibben (2 Oct 1907-7 Apr 1922). Bur Howard PA.

CF431646   Isabella McKibben (10 Apr 1909, Howard PA-10 Sep 1909).

CF431647   Lucetta McKibben (b 17 Jul 1914)

CF4317   Amos B. Erhard (b 12 Jan 1842) m Tillie Woodling. Grad, Susquehanna U and theol sch; Lutheran clergyman.

CF43171   Emma Pauline Erhard (b 31 May 1867) m J. Frank Schrader

CF431711   Ethel C. Schrader

CF43172   Mary C. Erhard

CF43173   Vernie Armetta Erhard

CF4318   Cyrus Erhard (24 Aug 1844-10 Sep 1900) m Catharine Brungart (b 1846)

CF43181   Rose Elizabeth Erhard (1868-1922) m William W. Hackman (1857-1938). Bur Rebersburg PA.

CF431811   Ruth Catherine Hackman (17 Apr 1877-7 Nov 1918) m Thomas Adams

CF4318111   Malden Adams

CF4318112   Trilby Adams (2 Aug 1910-7 Jan 1911)

CF431812   Walter Erhard Hackman (1890, Rebersburg PA-12 Oct 1965) m Pearl Royer. Bur Rebersburg PA.

CF4318121   Harold Hackman

CF431813   Lula Mae Hackman (24 Apr 1892, Rebersburg PA-30 Oct 1958, Millheim PA) m 25 Dec 1917, Rebersburg PA, William Norman Duck (23 Oct 1888, Mallheim PA-Sep 1978, Lancaster PA). Teacher, farmer, Millheim PA.

CF4318131   William Norman Duck, Jr. (b 9 Feb 1920, Millheim PA) m 10 Jun 1944, Camden NJ, Dorothy Jane Hampton (b 27 Dec 1920, Gibbstown NJ)

CF42181311   Elizabeth Helen Duck (b 7 Mar 1947, Philadelphia PA). Unm. Beautician, Lancaster PA.

CF43181312   William Norman Duck III (b 6 Jun 1953, Philadelphia PA) m Jun 1989, Amy Crapper (b 6 Jun 1953). Organ Builder, Lancaster PA.

CF431813121   William Norman Duck IV (b 4 Jun 1991, Lancaster PA)

CF4318132   John Jacob Duck (8 Oct 1922, Millheim PA-21 Feb 1991, Akron OH) m 5 Jun 1948, Akron OH, Lilian Ruth Babak (b 10 Feb 1924, Akron OH). Carpenter, Akron OH.

CF43181321   John Jacob Duck, Jr. (b 28 Jan 1951, Bellefonte PA) m 2 Feb 1973, Pat Johnson. BS, MS, PhD. Environmental control, Export PA.

CF431813211   Michael John Duck (b 23 May 1976)

CF431813212   Susan Duck (b 17 Aug 1981)

CF431813213   Matthew Duck (b 13 Jun 1983)

CF43181322   Jamie Norman Duck (b 18 Aug 1954, Akron OH). Unm. U Akron, horalogist, Cuyahoga Falls OH.

CF43181323   Jeanine Lynn Duck (b 9 Dec 1964, Akron OH) m 19 Sep 1987, Oakhurst NJ, Glenn Charles Dietz (b 24 May 1964, Neptune NJ). BS, OSU, 1987; homemaker, Oakhurst NH.

CF431813231   Kevin Jacob Dietz (b 30 Oct 1993)

CF431813232   Christine Leanne Dietz (b 6 Oct 1995)

CF4318133   Mary Elizabeth Duck (b 30 Jul 1926, Bellefonte PA) m 1) 23 Jul 1949, Northumberland PA, Henry Harter Haddon, Jr. (b 27 Nov 1924, Northumberland PA); m 2) 13 Apr 1985, Biglerville PA, Richard Seymour (d 2 Jul 1991).

CF43181331   Mary Beth Haddon (b 27 Jun 1950, Philadelphia PA). Unm. Managerial, Tampa FL.

CF43181332   Diane Victoria Haddon (b 1 Dec 1951, Philadelphia PA) m Bernard Balleweg. MS; social worker, Missoula MT.

CF43181333   Harry Harter Haddon III (17 May 1955, Chambersburg PA) m 19 Sep 1993, Sharon Sachs. Computer programer, Lancaster PA.

CF43181334   David Anthony Haddon (b 14 Sep 1957, Chambersburg PA) m 22 Aug 1981, Kathy Fitzgerald. Auto body work, Lancaster PA.

CF431813341   Mara Faith Haddon (b 11 Jul 1985)

CF431813342   Julia Ann Haddon (b 11 Jun 1988)

CF431813343   Caleb Haddon (b 28 Sep 1993)

CF431814   Paul Raymond Hackman (b 6 Jun 1894, Rebersburg PA) m 30 Sep 1915, Verna Reish (21 Apr 1897, Zion PA-2 Apr 1966). Bur Rebersburg PA.

CF4318141   Gladys Viola Hackman (b 26 Mar 1916, Rebersburg PA) m 8 Apr 1939, Merle Edwin Gephart (b 20 Jan 1918, Rebersburg PA)

CF43181411   Donna Mae Gephart (b 19 Nov 1939, Bellefonte PA) m 27 Nov 1963, R. Edward Weber (b 22 Mar 1940, Rebersburg PA). Secretary, Rebersburg PA.

CF431814111   Kevin Edward Weber (b 13 Feb 1965, Rebersburg PA). Unm. PSU. Construction work, Rebersburg PA.

CF431814112   Michele Dawn Weber (b 18 Jul 1966, Rebersburg PA) m 19 May 1993, Rebersburg PA, Larry Breon, Jr. Accountant, Fort Steward GA.

CF43181412   Martha Ann Gephart (b 28 Jul 1941, Lock Haven PA) m 14 Feb 1964, Max Dinges (b 29 Nov 1944, Coburn PA). Engineer, Coburn PA.

CF431814121   Tanya Lee Dinges (b 22 Jul 1964, Bellefonte PA)

CF431814122   Troy Scott Dinges (n 15 Jan 1967, Bellefonte PA)

CF43181413   Rosemary Gephart (n 28 Oct 1945, Lock Haven PA) m 23 May 1964, Robert Lewis Kerstetter (b 2 Sep 1942). She, beautician; he, truck driver, Beech Creek PA.

CF431814131   Robin Lynn Kerstetter (b 21 Nov 1964, Bellefonte PA) m Danny Caparelle. Laboratory tech, Bellefonte PA.

CF4318141311   Tony Marie Caparelle (b 26 Sep 1987)

CF4318141312   Josie Caparelle (b 3 Feb 1991)

CF431814132   Lorinda Lou Kerstetter (b 5 May 1970, Bellefonte PA) m 15 Aug 1992, Donald Peters. She, beautician; he, deputy sheriff, Milesburg PA.

CF4318141321   Colby Robert Peters (b 13 Jan 1994)

CF431814133   Jennifer Jo Kerststter (b 8 Sep 1972, Bellefonte PA). Res Beech Creek PA.

CF4318142   Cleora Geraldine Hackman (28 Jun 1922, Rebersburg PA-29 Mar 1965, Rebersburg PA) m 11 Oct 1941, Rebersburg PA, Calvin Stieger Breon (26 Jan 1923, Spring Mills PA-18 Apr 1994). Bur Rebersburg PA.

CF43181421   Patricia Ann Breon (b 30 Apr 1942, Bellefonte PA) m 17 Jun 1962, Rebersburg PA, Clarence Gene Haugh (b 11 Oct 1936, Spring Mills PA). She, BS, 1964, MS, 1969, Purdue U; teacher, real estate agent. He, BS, PSU, 1958, MS, U IL, 1959, PhD, Purdue U, 1964; engineer, prof VPI, Blacksburg VA.

CF431814211   Amy Elizabeth Haugh (b 15 Dec 1967, Lafayette IN) m 17 Jun 1995, Blacksburg VA, Lawrence Donald Dodds (b 31 Mar 1967, Ogdensburg NY). She, BS, VPI, 1990; MEd, U NC, 1995. He, AB, Hamilton Col, 1989. Stafford PA.

CF431814212   Jennifer Lea Haugh (b 8 Sep 1969, Lafayette IN) m 17 Apr 1993. Blacksburg VA, Michael Joseph Ulsh (b 20 Jan 1969, Harrisburg PA). BS, VPI, 1992; interior designer, architectural firm. He, BS, VPI, 1992; MS, U CO, 1996.

CF431814213   Mitchell Breon Haugh (b 8 Oct 1973, Lafayette IN)

CF431815   Mary Elizabeth Hackman (7 Nov 1896, Rebersburg PA-1 Aug 1899, Rebersburg PA). Bur Rebersburg PA.

CF431816   William Henry Hackman (b 24 Sep 1902, Rebersburg PA)

CF431817   Miriam Hackman (b 10 Aug 1907, Rebersburg PA). Unm.

CF431818   Esther L. Hackman (7 Mar 1918-10 Oct 1918)

CF43182   Delphia Ardella Erhard (8 Nov 1870, Rebersburg PA-10 Feb 1943, Ann Arbor MI) m 28 Mar 1893, John David Wynn (17 Feb 1869, Perry MO-17 Feb 1941, Lawrence KS). Bur Lawrence KS.

CF431821   Edith Arnetta Wynn (b 10 Sep 1895, Perth KS) m 24 Jun 1921, William Arthur Daugherty (28 Jan 1894, Carterville MO-26 Jul 1953, Tulsa OK)

CF4318211   Mary Katherine Daughterty (b 27 Aug 1922, Tulsa OK) m 26 Apr 1942, Russell E. Bryant (b 3 Dec 1917, Excelsior Springs MO)

CF43182111   Edith Ann Bryant (b 18 Jul 1943, Tulsa OK)

CF43182112   James Edward Bryant (b 30 Jul 1944, Seattle WA)

CF43182113   Charles Arthur Bryant (b 2 Dec 1946, Seattle WA)

CF43182114   Russell E. Bryant, Jr. (b 12 Apr 1956, Buffalo NY)

CF4318212   Elizabeth Rey Daugherty (b 12 Apr 1925) m 7 Oct 1948, Joseph A. Stivers (b 25 Dec 1923, Tulsa OK)

CF43182121   David Arthur Stivers (b 30 Nov 1950, Houston TX)

CF4318213   Virginia Lee Daugherty (b 23 Jan 1929, Tulsa OK) m 7 Oct 1950, Robert E. Buck (b 3 Aug 1927, Wichita KS).

CF43182131   David Daugherty Buck (b 8 Apr 1953, Wichita KS)

CF43182132   Katheryn Elizabeth Buck (b 28 Oct 1957, Wichita KS)

CF431822   Luella Mayflower Wynn (23 Mar 1899, Perth KS-22 Apr 1964, Santa Fe NM) m 10 Jul 1923, Herbert Augustus Olsen (b 12 Apr 1899, Lawrence KS)

CF4318221   Dale Gorden Olsen (b 20 Jan 1928, Ann Arbor MI) m 21 Jun 1958, Natalie Evelyn Filion (b 22 Aug 1928, Brattleboro VT)

CF43182211   Janet Lynn Olsen (b 21 Jun 1959, Oakland CA)

CF43182212 Jennifer Ann Olsen (b 24 Aug 1961, Hayward CA)

CF431823 Warren Hershel Wynn (b 22 Oct 1900, Perth KS) m 5 Aug 1931, Myrl Waters (10 Nov 1910, Pawnee OK-23 May 1953)

CF4318231 Warren Robert Wynn (b 27 Aug 1939, Shawnee OK) m 24 May 1959, Virginia Louise Carter

CF4318232 Albert Lee Wynn (b 6 Jan 1941, Tulsa OK)

CF431824 Glen Erhardt Wynn (b 11 Dec 1902, Tulsa OK) m 28 Jan 1931, Marjorie Scott (b 17 Jan 1905, Marietta OH)

CF4318241 Glen Erhardt Wynn (b 20 Nov 1933) m 1 Sep 1956, Eddie Mae Gregory (b 17 Dec 1935, Tulsa OK)

CF4318242 John David Wynn (b 31 Aug 1937, Tulsa OK) m 27 Jun 1959, Bonnie Jean Johnstone (b 15 Jun 1939, Grove City PA)

CF431825 Ruel Emanuel Wynn (20 Jun 1905, Tulsa OK-20 Jun 1906, Tulsa OK)

CF431826 John Delphian Wynn (b 19 Oct 1908, Tulsa OK) m 6 Aug 1934, Ruth Shambrger (b 14 Nov 1911, White House MD)

CF4318261 Janet Kay Wynn (b 9 Jun 1941, Vincennes IN)

CF4318262 David Everett Wynn (b 6 Dec 1945)

CF431827 Albert Fletcher Wynn (b 18 Sep 1912, Tulsa OK) m 11 Jul 1936, Portia Arlene Drennen (b 24 Nov 1912, Benton AR)

CF4318271 Josephine Ann Wynn (b 24 Oct 1944, Alexandra LA)

CF4318272 Michael Lee Wynn (b 14 Oct 1950, Little Rock AR)

CF4318273 Delphia Sue Wynn (b 23 Jun 1953, Calgary, Alberta)

CF43183 Sarah Catherine Erhard (b 1872) m Edwin S. Bierly.

CF431831 Meyer Bierly (21 Jul 1900-21 Apr 1919)

CF43184 Clyde Walter Erhard (21 Aug 1877, Rebersburg PA-21 Oct 1952) m 20 May 1907, Laura Mae Heidle. Bur Murfreesboro TN. Methodist clergyman.

CF431841 Elaine Ballast Erhard (b 9 Sep 1908, Ballast Island OH)

CF431842 Adeline Catherine Erhard (b 13 Aug 1911, Bangor MI) m 1) 16 Mar 1929, Miller; m 2) 31 Dec 1953, Edward Dolphus Green

CF431843 Clyde Walter Erhard, Jr. (b 4 Jul 1921, Bardwell KY) m 1) 24 Dec 1943, Emily Julia Yarborough; m 2) 5 Sep 1952, Carolyn Dozier

CF4318431 Julia Joyce Erhard (b 5 Feb 1945, Anderson SC)

CF4318432 Michael Clyde Erhard (b 9 Apr 1955, Decatur GA)

CF4318433   Britton Dozier Erhard (b 3 Mar 1958, Clinton SC)

CF43185   Lula Erhard (d 2 Feb 1935) m Harry Sweet

CF4319   Ellen Erhard (23 Sep 1847-5 Nov 1897) m Harvey H. Miller (27 Jun 1847-19 Jun 1915)

CF43191   Wallace Miller m 1) Mary Denton; m 2) Anna Virginia Geise

CF431911   Genevieve Miller m Charles Friel

CF431A   Mary Malinda Erhard (24 Jun 1850-15 Oct 1891) m 1869, Samuel G. Gutelius (6 Nov 1834-30 Jul 1895). Bur Millheim PA. Civil War. Dentist, Millheim PA.

CF431A1   Fredrick Erhard Gutelius (4 Oct 1870, Aaronsburg PA-11 May 1930, Millheim PA) m 22 Apr 1896, Bessie Stover (d Millheim PA). Bur Millheim PA. Dentist.

CF431A11   Mary Louise Gutelius (b 10 Jan 1897) m 9 Oct 1924, Sylvester Gutelius

CF431A12   Violet May Gutelius (b 20 May 1902) m 8 Jul 1928, Fred Cecil Dawe

CF431A121   Kitty Lou Dawe

CF431A122   Fred Cecil Dawe, Jr. (b 27 Dec 1933)

CF431A13   Catherine Gutelius (b 30 May 1908) m. 30 Mar 1935, Horace H. Martin

CF431A14   Louise Gutelius (b 8 Aug 1912)

CF431A2   Lydia Ella Gutelius (b 12 Oct 1872) m Thomas Oscar Morris

CF431A21   Harold G. Morris m 5 Jun 1922, Helene Shook. Dentist

CF431A211   John Robert Morris

CF431A212   Thomas Clinton Morris

CF431A22   Frederick Morris m 5 Jan 1934, Mary Roberta Boyd

CF431A23   Margaret Morris m 8 Oct 1927, Kenneth Bucher

CF431A231   Polly Ann Bucher (b 19 Dec 1928)

CF431A232   James Kenneth Bucher (b 16 Oct 1934)

CF431A3   Daniel Brungart Gutelius (b 24 Jan 1887) m 17 Jan 1910, Louise Weil

CF431A31   Harold Gutelius

CF431B   Franklin Pierce Erhard (b 27 Feb 1853) m Ella Heiter

CF431B1   Lizzie M. Erhard (b 22 Sep 1875) m C.D. Loudenslager.

CF431B11   Donald Franklin Loudenslager m 27 Oct 1924, Faye Smith

CF431B111   Robert Donald Loudenslager (b 3 Apr 1925)

CF431B112   Kenneth B. Loudenslager (b 3 Feb 1927)

CF431B113   Bettie Eunice Loudenslager (b 26 Aug 1928)

CF431B114   James Loudenslager (b 26 Dec 1932)

CF431B2   Clark D. Erhard (25 Jun 1876-24 Mar 1933) m Eva Elizabeth Gutelius

CF431B21   Harold Gutelius Erhard m Lucille Phelps

CF431B211   Harold Erhard

CF431B22   Fred Erhard

CF431B3   George Randall Erhard (25 Apr 1879-14 Jun 1936) m Rose Wilson Hursh

CF431B4   Frank Heiter Erhard (b 6 Jun 1881) m Victoria Warsing

CF431B5   Amy Augusta Erhard (b 30 Oct 1883) m William Emmet Kneiple

CF431B51   Amanda Geneva Kneiple m Herbert Corbett

CF431B511   Patricia Fay Corbett

CF431B52   Dorothy Louise Kneiple m L. Guy Frank

CF431B53   Frances Ellen Kneiple

CF431B54   George Erhard Kneiple

CF431B55   William Emmet Kneiple, Jr.

CF431C   Eliza Jane Erhard (14 Jan 1857-19 Apr 1857)

CF432   Jacob Brungart (9 Jan 1814, Miles Tp PA-20 Sep 1893, Rebersburg PA) m 28 May 1838, Sarah Corman (1 Sep 1819-7 Nov 1907). Bur Rebersburg PA.

CF4321   Thomas Brungart (22 Aug 1839-d.y.)

CF4322   Franklin Brungart (17 Jan 1841-8 Apr 1890). Unm.

CF4323   Sydney Brungart (5 Aug 1842-8 Apr 1922) m 1) Sylvester Gramley (8 Oct 1839, Miles Tp PA-17 Jul 1868); m 2) John Hoy

CF43231   Ira Gramley (14 Aug 1860, Miles Tp PA-14 Dec 1935, Millheim PA) m Susan Stover (26 Feb 1862-12 Dec 1933, Aaronsburg PA). Bur Wolf's Chapel.

CF432311   Joseph S. Gramley (29 Aug 1880, Haines Tp PA-16 Aug 1948, Battle Creek MI) m Lizzie Bower

CF432312   Sydney May Gramley (17 May 1883, Miles Tp PA-1 Feb 1944) m Miles Arney

CF4323121   Mary Arney m Harold Brumstead

CF43231211   Susanne Brumstead

CF4323122   Helen Arney m William Buck

CF43231221   William Buck, Jr.

CF43231222   Gary Buck

CF4323123   George Arney (d.y.)

CF4323124   Ruth Arney

CF432313   Orvis Stover Gramley (28 Feb 1894, Haines Tp PA-Dec 1967, Millheim PA) m 28 Aug 1915, Carrie Emerick (b 23 Sep 1893, Gregg Tp PA)

CF4323131   Homer Gramley (b 16 Apr 1916, Millheim PA) m Esther Crabb (b 11 Sep 1922, Millheim PA)

CF43231311   Janet Gramley (b 18 Jun 1944, Millheim PA) m Dean Crater

CF432313111   Mindy Sue Crater

CF432313112   Vicky Jo Crater

CF43231312   Alan Gramley (b 14 Dec 1948, Millheim PA) m Donna Arnold.

CF432313121   Jeffrey Alan Gramley (b 8 Aug 1974)

CF432313122   Susan L. Gramley (b 2 Feb 1979)

CF4323132   Edna Gramley (b 10 Aug 1918, Millheim PA) m William Weaver (b 16 May 1914)

CF43231321   Linda Weaver (b 30 Jul 1947)

CF43231322   Dennis Weaver (b 24 Jan 1952)

CF4323133   Harold Eugene Gramley (b 18 Aug 1932, Millheim PA) m 12 Mar 1954, Etta Bennett (b 22 Aug 1932)

CF43231331   Gary Gramley (b 9 Aug 1956, Bellefonte PA)

CF43231332   David Gramley (b 5 Sep 1957, Bellefonte PA)

CF432314   Jennie Gramley (b 22 Nov 1895, Haines Tp PA) m George F. Kolb (14 Feb 1882-15 Dec 1933, Aaronsburg PA)

CF43232   Alice Gramley (b 21 May 1864) m 1) Adam Auman; m 2) 19 Sep 1926, Jasper Gramley. Bur Rebersburg PA.

CF432321   Mary Auman (6 Sep 1884, Miles Tp PA-2 Jan 1947) m 1904, Allen S. Winkelblech (b 9 Dec 1882, Haines Tp PA)

CF4323211   Marion Winkelblech (b 8 Aug 1906, Rebersburg PA) m 1) 2 Jan 1928, Roy Jacob Homan (22 Dec 1904-8 Oct 1951); m 2) John M. Long

CF43232111   Carl Eugene Homan (b 11 May 1929, Aaronsburg PA) m Louise Morgan

CF432321111   Susan Homan (b 12 Apr 1955, Aaronsburg PA)

CF432321112   Michael Homan (b 23 Aug 1957)

CF43232112   Alice Homas (b 25 Jun 1930, Aaronsburg PA) m Richard Wance (b 7 Aug 1928, Aaronsburg PA). Trenton NJ

CF432321121   Brenda Wance (b 27 Aug 1955, Aaronsburg PA)

CF43232113   Bruce Homan (b 18 Sep 1931, Aaronsburg PA) m Evelyn P. Zim (b 10 Oct 1928, Aaronsburg PA). Cecil WI.

CF432321131   Mark Homan (b 15 Apr 1957)

CF43232114   Leonard A. Homan (b 15 Feb 1934, Aaronsburg PA) m Marcy Adams. Kingston NJ.

CF432321141   Minnie L. Homan (b 20 Jun 1954)

CF432321142   Wandy Homan (b 29 May 1955)

CF43232115   Donald Homan (b 1 May 1935, Aaronsburg PA) m Mollie Zigne. Plainsboro NJ.

CF432321151   Donna Homan

CF432321152   Debra Homan

CF432321153   Joseph Homan

CF43232116   Dean Homan (b 5 Oct 1937, Aaronsburg PA) m Patricia Parr (b 14 Oct 1936). Plainsboro NJ.

CF432321161   Robert Homan (b 21 Nov 1957)

CF432321162   Douglas Homan (b 11 Jul 1959)

CF43232117   Shirley Homan (b 9 Jan 1939, Aaronsburg PA). Chanute AFB IL.

CF43232118   Wayne Homan (b 20 Nov 1941, Aaronsburg PA)

CF43232119   Larry Homan (b 4 Aug 1942, Aaronsburg PA)

CF4323211A   Nancy Homan (b 3 Sep 1945)

CF4323212   Alice Winkelblech (6 Jun 1908, Rebersburg PA-20 Sep 1939) m 28 Jan 1932, Emanuel Mensch. Millmont PA.

CF43232121   Lynn Mensch (b 19 Feb 1937)

CF4323213   Ardrenna M. Winkelblech (b 15 Apr 1910, Rebersburg PA) m 4 Mar 1928, John M. Weaver (b 9 Apr 1908, Hublersburg PA)

CF43232131   Harry Allen Weaver (b 3 Jan 1929, Hublersburg PA) m 19 Aug 1950, Ruth Olive Styers

CF432321311   John Allen Weaver (b 22 May 1951, San Bernardino CA)

CF432321312   Marlin R. Weaver (b 22 May 1957, Bellefonte PA)

CF43232132   Marvin Eugene Weaver (b 6 Nov 1930, Rebersburg PA) m 3 Aug 1950, Vivian Jane Lamey

CF432321321   Eugene Forrest Weaver (b 1 Oct 1951, Lock Haven PA)

CF432321322   Marvin Junior Weaver (b 23 Nov 1952, Lock Haven PA)

CF432321323   Robert M. Weaver (b 6 Jan 1954, Lock Haven PA)

CF432321324   James E. Weaver (b 6 Dec 1955, Lock Haven PA)

CF43232133   Gerald Franklin Weaver (b 24 Dec 1932, Rebersburg PA) m 25 Sep 1955, Joyce Maureen
Weaver

CF432321331   Gregory William Weaver (b 24 Jan 1957, Bellefonte PA)

CF43232134   Mary Louise Weaver (16 Apr 1934, Rebersburg PA-20 Feb 1935, Rebersburg PA).

CF43232135   John William Weaver (b 29 Jan 1936, Rebersburg PA)

CF43232136   Yvonne Marie Weaver (b 15 Jan 1942, Rebersburg PA)

CF4323214   Harold Winkelblech (b 26 Apr 1912, Rebersburg PA) m Elsie Showers (b 18 Oct 1916,
Rebersburg PA)

CF43232141   Lois Winkelblech (b 9 Dec 1952, Rebersburg PA)

CF43232142   Cindy Winkelblech (b 4 Oct 1955, Rebersburg PA)

CF4323215   Mahlon Winkelblech (b 13 Jan 1914, Rebersburg PA) m Eleanor Wheaton. Brackney PA.

CF43232151   Mary Winkelblech (b 8 Jan 1940)

CF43232152   Mahlon Winkelblech, Jr. (b 27 Feb 1941, Rebersburg PA)

CF43232153   Merle Winkelblech (b 12 Jan 1946, Rebersburg PA)

CF4323216   Bertha Winkelblech (b 18 Aug 1916, Rebersburg PA) m Donald Willow. Mifflinburg PA.

CF43232161   Donald Willow, Jr. (b 30 May 1936, Mifflinburg PA)

CF43232162   Joan Willow (b 8 Jan 1941, Mifflinburg PA)

CF4323217   Lodi Winkelblech (b 12 Jan 1919, Rebersburg PA) m 2) Emanuel Mensch (see
CF4323212?). Millmont PA.

CF43232171   Mary Mensch (b 17 May 1946)

CF432322   Clarence Auman (b 20 Oct 1872) m. Gertrude Huddlestine. Montandon PA.

CF4323221   Richard Auman (b 7 Dec 1916). Montandon PA.

CF43233   Hester Gramley (7 Oct 1867, Miles Tp PA-16 Dec 1942, Howard PA) m William Loder
(d 30 May 1935). Bur Howard PA.

CF432331   Venda Raymond Loder (14 Sep 1887-1 Nov 1897)

CF432332   Victor Loder (28 May 1890-7 Jul 1890)

CF432333   Maurice Loder (12 Aug 1891-18 Mar 1909)

CF432334   Alice Elizabeth Loder (b 26 Apr 1896) m 1) George Quay; m 2) Jacob Frye. Howard PA.

CF4323341   Leona Frye

CF432335   Son Loder (b 24 Dec 1897)

CF432336   Ray Loder (10 Sep 1899-18 Nov 1899)

CF43234   Edward S. Hoy (b 1 May 1883) m Mary Vonada. Bur Hublersburg PA. No chn.

CF4324   Alice Brungart (4 Mar 1844-21 Mar 1926) m 25 Feb 1866, Jacob R. Sholl (1839-1890). Brush Valley PA.

CF43241   Emma Jane Sholl (25 May 1867-1936) m 19 Nov 1896, Rebersburg PA, Harry Hix Noll (6 Sep 1873, PA-1932). Bur Zion PA. Blacksmith shop, Walker Tp, Centre Co PA.

CF432411   William Jacob Noll (18 Jun 1897, Wolfe Store PA-31 Aug 1979, Delray FL) m Iva Belle Williamson. Bur Montoursville Cem, Lycoming Co PA. Die maker at Williamsport Tool & Die Co. He adopted Iva's two daughters from a previous marriage.

Back: CF432411 William Jacob Noll (1897-1979) and CF432412 Charles Edwin Noll (1899-1961)
Front: Harry Hix Noll (1873-1932) and CF43241 Emma Jane Sholl Noll (1867-1936)

CF432412   Charles Edwin Noll (13 Feb 1899, Sprucetown PA-23 Sep 1961, South Williamsport PA) m 16 Mar 1921, Elmira NY, Edna Victoria Krape (14 May 1894, Green Tp, Clinton Co PA-11 Dec 1983, Williamsport PA). Bur Zion PA. Machinist, Darling Valve Mfg Co., Williamsport PA.

CF4324121   Jacquelyn Emma Noll (b 7 Jun 1923, Williamsport PA) m 1) 20 Apr 1946, South Williamsport PA, Wilbur Conrad Heuser (5 Mar 1918, Marine IL-21 Oct 1989, Marine IL); m 2) 12 Apr 1992, Arthur Michel, div 1994. Teacher and artist in Marine IL; now res Pinellas Park FL. Heuser, postmaster, Marine IL.

CF43241211   Curtis Noll Heuser (b 30 Nov 1948, St. Louis MO) m 13 Jun 1976, Judith Ann Hetland (26 Aug 1951-10 Jun 1995, Lake Villa IL). Lake Villa IL.

CF432412111   Timothy Scott Heuser (b 17 Feb 1979, Chicago IL)

CF432412112   Daniel Curtis Heuser (b 29 Sep 1980, Chicago IL)

CF432412113   Brian Michael Heuser (b 29 Nov 1981, Chicago IL)

CF432412114   Thomas Gordon Heuser (b 12 Dec 1983, Chicago IL)

CF43241212   Alleen Deborah Heuser (11 Feb 1951, Springfield IL) m Larry Stuffle, div. Pittsburgh PA.

CF432412121   Christopher Michael Stuffle (b 21 Feb 1974, Springfield IL)

CF4324122   Bettie Jane Noll (7 Jun 1923, Williamsport PA) m 9 Jun 1945, Dayton OH, David Duncan (6 Jan 1909, Aetnaville KY-Sep 1980, Edwardsville IL); m 2) Earl Matter, div; m 3) 8 Apr 1988, Edwardsville IL, Victor Ramsey (b 2 Feb 1925). She, S IL U; teacher, Edwardsville IL.

CF43241221   Jane Ellen Duncan (b 10 Jun 1946, Chicago IL) m Jun 1965, Marine IL, Ronald Wohlgemuth, div; m 2) 25 Jun 1975, Edwardsville IL, Orville Bradshaw (b 10 Aug 1940, Edwardsville IL), div; m 3) May 1980, Edwardsville IL, Aaron Bradshaw (b 8 May 1936, Edwardsville IL).

CF432412211   Penny Ellen Wohlgemuth (17 Oct 1966, Galesburg IL-11 Oct 1991, Belleville IL) m Michael Pierson. Bur Glen Carbon IL. No chn. She, health service, Alton IL.

CF432412212   Andrea Sue Wohlgemuth (8 Sep 1968, Galesburg IL). Food service, Cincinnati OH.

CF432412213   Bettie Jane Wohlgemuth (b 18 Sep 1970, Highland IL) m 2 Mar 1992, Edwardsville IL, Jeffery D. Mifflin (b 28 Nov 1969, Alton IL).

CF4324122131   Jordon Denton Mifflin (b 12 Jan 1992, Alton IL)

CF4324122132   Magen Mifflin (3 Sep 1993, Alton IL)

CF432412214   David Orville Bradshaw (b 3 Mar 1976, Alton IL)

CF43241222   Robert Mallis Duncan (b 23 Jul 1949, Batesville AR) m 19 Dec 1969, Litchfield IL, Kathy Jean Pierce (b 16 Jul 1949, Chicago IL). He, BS, E Il U, 1976; car salesman. She, BS, 1972, MS, 1975, E IL U; investment banker, Findlay IL.

CF432412221   Rebecca Ann Duncan (b 3 Dec 1971, Portsmouth VA), Investment banker, Findlay IL.

CF432412222   Corrie Jean Duncan (b 27 Apr 1978, Urbana IL)

CF432412223   Andrew David Duncan (b 17 Nov 1981, Urbana IL)

CF4324123   Charles Irvin Noll (b 15 Feb 1925, Phelps NY) m 29 Dec 1962, Williamsport PA, Jane Marjorie Kunkle (3 Jan 1938, Williamsport PA). USN, Aug 1942-Feb 1946 on board ship and Naval Air Sta, Pascal WA. Steamship pilot first class, Republic Steel, Cleveland OH, 1952-64; Penn Liquor Control Board. Montoursville PA. She, trust officer.

*CF43241231   Charlene Marie Noll (23 Sep 1963, Williamsport PA) m 1) 26 May 1984, Williamsport PA, Kenneth A. Hoover, div 1980; m 2) 2 Mar 1996, Harrisburg PA, Larry Bruce Strohecker (b 19 Jan 1968, Harrisbutg PA). No chn. AD, Harrisburg Area Comm Col; exec secretary, Harrisburg PA; res Camp Hill PA.

CF43241232   Rebecca Louise Noll (b 14 Dec 1965, Williamsport PA) m 1 Oct 1989, New Cumberland PA, Joseph Fitzgerald Kelly (b 13 May 1964, New Cumberland PA). Assoc paralegal degree, Harrisburg Comm Col; New Cumberland PA.

CF432412321   Brittany Ann Kelly (b 31 Oct 1990, Harrisburg PA)

CF432412322   Shannon Noll Kelly (b 30 Aug 1993, Harrisburg PA)

CF43242   Anna Mazy Sholl (1 Oct 1868-17 Aug 1869)

CF43243   John Thomas Sholl (b 17 Nov 1869)

CF43244   Elizabeth Clara Sholl (30 Sep 1871-24 Dec 1913) m Jonas Malachi Stover. Farmer.

CF432441   Sallie Phoebe Stover (d Jun 1969)

CF432442   Minnie Althea Stover (1901-1909). Bur Zion PA.

CF432443   Belle Marie Stover (d 7 Jul 1938)

CF432444   Goldie Lucretia Stover (b 1913, Walker Tp, Centre Co PA) m Jun 1935, Tusseyville PA, William Edward McCormick. He, BS, PSU; chemist, Akron OH.

CF4324441   John Franklin McCormick (May 1936-1980, CA) m 1958, IN, Patricia Ann Aechard. Purdue U, 1960; civil engineer.

CF43244411   Russell William McCormick (b 17 Jul 1961) m 1984, Bloomington IN, Lisa Kay Branson

CF432444111   Zachary Tyler McCormick (b 11 Dec 1990, Indianapolis IN)

CF432444112   Trevor Ryan McCormick (b 22 Apr 1991, Indianapolis IN)

CF43244412   Daniel Martin McCormick (b 12 Apr 1964) m 1 Jun 1990, Susanne Frechette. No chn.

Marjorie Lynn McCormick (b 14 May 1965, Hollywood CA)(Adopted by John F. McCormick)

CF4324442   Kirk William McCormick (b 4 Mar 1943, W. Reading PA) m Oct 1973, Akron OH, Marilyn Kay Sehiltz. Draftsman. No chn.

CF432445   Newton Stover. Bur near Millheim PA.

CF432446   Charles Stover. Bur near Millheim PA.

CF432447   Stover

CF43245   Verna Sally Sholl (2 Jul 1873-1927) m Charles H. Bierly. Harrisburg PA. Farmer.

CF432451   Daunn Bierly

CF43246   Minnie Kate Sholl (17 May 1877, Rebersburg PA-3 Apr 1963) m 12 Jun 1902, Centre Hall PA, Clarence Emanuel Noll (25 Oct 1881, Pleasant Gap PA-28 Apr 1940). Bur North Vesailles PA. Dairyman, Pitcairn PA.

CF432461   Paul Leroy Noll (b 25 Oct 1924, Pitcairn PA) m 8 Oct 1928, Cumberland MD, Mildred Blythstone (b 21 Jun 1910). Dairyman, Trofford PA.

CF4324611   Dorothy Jean Noll (b 6 Mar 1930) m Bruce P. Marstellar. Greensburg PA.

CF43246111   Bruce P. Marstellar

CF432461111   Kimberly Marstellar

CF432461112   Katey Marstellar

CF43246112   Kevin Marstellar

CF4324612   James Clarence Noll (15 Apr 1933) m Gail Martz. Harrison City PA.

CF43246121   David Scott Noll

CF43246122   Jeffrey M. Noll

CF43246123   Matthew P. Noll

CF4324613   Kenneth Leroy Noll (1 Mar 1938) m Sylvia Cooley. Mesa AZ.

CF43246131   Sylvia Noll

CF43246132   Ross Noll

CF43246133   Wynn Noll m

CF432461331   Bailey Noll

CF4324614   Charles Edwin Noll m Dorothy Maynor. No chn. Trafford PA.

CF4324615   Nomi Eilien Noll m Richard Bowers, div

CF43246151   Rhonda Bowers

CF43246152   Lynn Bowers m Tommy Shakoske

CF432461521   Ronny Shakiske

CF43246153   Robert Bowers

CF43246154   Debra Bowers

CF43247   Elinora Sholl (21 Feb 1879-1932, Lewsiburg PA) m Howard Ziegler. Bur Millheim PA.
Farmer, Spring Mills PA.

CF43248   William Jacob Sholl (24 Aug 1883 -18 Sep 1961) m Anna Rhoads. New Columbia PA.

CF432481   John William Sholl (b 1921) Milton PA.

CF43249   Daughter Sholl (31 Dec 1880-4 Jan 1881)

CF4325   Newton Brungart (1 Sep 1845, Miles Tp, Centre Co PA-8 Mar 1926, Mifflinburg PA) m
23 Jun 1867, Lucy Ann Shaffer (4 Apr 1849, Spring Tp, Centre Co PA-30 Sep 1925, Mifflinburg PA). Bur
Mifflinburg PA. Farmer.

CF43251   Samuel Irwin Brungart (21 Jan 1869, Miles Tp, Centre Co PA-22 Sep 1885, Rebersburg
PA). Bur Rebersburg PA.

CF43252   Edwin Monroe Brungart (31 Oct 1871, Rebersburg PA-15 Mar 1960, Sunbury PA) m 5
Jun 1901, Winifred Wolfe (b Rebersburg PA). Grad, Susquehanna U, 1900; prof of education, Susquehanna
U, 1904-41.

CF432521   Sarah Christine Brungart (19 Oct 1905, Selinsgrove PA-4 Nov 1957, Selinsgrove PA) m
15 Jun 1931, Frederick C. Stevens (b 23 Nov 1902, Bezil ME). Registrar, Susquehanna U.

CF432522   Lois Brungart (b 21 Dec 1910, Selinsgrove PA) m 10 Jun 1938, Bruce B. Bendigo (b 21
Oct 1909, Tower City PA). Grad, Susquehanna U.

CF43253   Herbert Isaiah Brungart (1 Apr 1873, Miles Tp PA-4 Mar 1956, Columbus OH) m 27 Nov
1901, Viola Walter (1 Aug 1878, Scottdale PA-9 Mar 1956, Columbus OH). Grad, Susquehanna U, 1900;
teacher, sales manager.

CF432531 Herbert Isaiah Brungart, Jr. (b 11 Apr 1914, Columbus OH) m 21 Jul 1936, Edna Moore. OSU; drug salesman.

CF4325311 Madeliene Lee Brungart (b 8 Jul 1937, Columbus OH)

CF432532 John Walter Brungart (b 8 Jan 1916, Columbus OH) m 27 Jun 1937, Doris Cooper (b 2 Jul 1916, Thornville OH). OSU; druggist, Coshocton OH.

CF4325321 Sara Ann Brungart (b 10 Nov 1942, Lima OH)

CF4325322 John Cooper Brungart (b 30 Apr 1945, Lima OH)

CF43254 Jacob Wallace Brungart (14 Nov 1877, Miles Tp PA-27 Apr 1960, York PA) m 23 Dec 1902, Bertha V. Dice (b 15 Dec 1882, Glen Rock PA). Bur York PA. Sign painter and craftsman, Glen Rock PA. Some of the models of Penn rural life in the 19th century made by J. Wallace Brungart are exhibited at the Hershey Museum, Hershey PA.

CF432541 Leila Elizabeth Brungart (b 10 Dec 1903, Glen Rock PA) m Milligan.

CF432542 Franklin Dice Brungart (b 23 Jul 1907, Glen Rock PA) m 14 Jul 1934, Elsie L. Sullivan (b 13 Feb 1910, Hagerstown MD). Bookkeeper, Hagerstown MD.

CF4325421 David Lee Brungart (b 9 Apr 1939, Hagerstown MD)

CF4325422 Evelyn Elaine Brungart (b 12 Apr 1947, Hagerstown MD)

CF43255 John Victor Brungart (b 24 Feb 1882, Rebersburg PA) m 29 Jun 1904, Lida B. Yearick (8 Aug 1879, Hubersburg PA-Aug 1966, Rebersburg PA). Teacher, farmer, insurance agent.

CF432551 Harold Newton Brungart (11 Jan 1906, Smulltown PA-7 Nov 1975) m 16 Mar 1930, Sarah Jane Zerby (24 Mar 1900, Aaronsburg PA-25 Sep 1992, State College PA). PSU, Col of Dairying; breeder, Smulltown PA.

CF432552 Randal Eugene Brungart (b 24 Jan 1908, Rebersburg PA) m 12 Oct 1935, Mary Lipscomb (b 31 Mar 1913, Low Moor VA). PSU; chemical engineer, Covington VA.

CF4325521 Nancy Williams Brungart (b 12 Jan 1938, Covington VA)

CF4325522 Jane Louise Brungart (b 19 May 1941, Covington VA)

CF4325523 Randal Victor Brungart (b 11 Aug 1942, Covington VA)

CF432553 Malcolm Victor Brungart (b 5 Aug 1918, Rebersburg PA)

CF43256 Harry Roy Brungart (11 Apr 1891, Rebersburg PA-25 Feb 1957) m 28 Dec 1912, Irene Rishel (27 Oct 1884, Farmers Mills PA-27 Jan 1957). Salesman, Pittsburgh PA.

CF432561 Newton Rishel Brungart (b 24 Dec 1914, Wilkinsburg PA) m 12 Mar 1944, Margaret Nelson DeBardeleben (b 12 May 1922, Birmingham AL). Syracuse U; hydraulic joist, conveyers and cranes firm.

CF4325611 Newton Rishel Brungart, Jr. (b 28 Apr 1945, Memphis TN)

CF4325612 Charles Debardeleben Brungart (b 12 May 1947, New York City NY)

CF4325613 Nelsen DeBardeleben Brungart (b 21 Jul 1949, Birmingham AL)

CF4326   Henry C. Brungart (5 Sep 1847-22 Oct 1901) m Margaret Leitzell (17 Jun 1848-15 May 1904)

CF43261   Lawrence Brungart

CF43262   Carrie Mae Brungart m Albert Wood

CF432621   Margaret Wood m William Patterson

CF4326211   Mary Elizabeth Patterson m 13 Feb 1943, Charles J. Messner

CF432622   Charles Brungart Wood m Beulah Ridenour

CF4326221   Charles Richard Wood (b 14 Aug 1926)

CF4327   Cyrus Brungart (20 Nov 1851-8 Jun 1929) m Dolly Emerick (1 Dec 1862-30 Mar 1935)

CF43271   Sallie Brungart m John S. Getchell

CF432711   Wendel B. Getchell

CF432712   Ralph Getchell

CF43272   Anna Brungart (d 16 Jul 1883)

CF43273   Cora Brungart m   Keefer

CF432731   Agnes Keefer

CF432732   Thomas B. Keefer

CF4328   Miranda Brungart (18 Aug 1854, Miles Tp PA-11 Apr 1934) m. 9 Mar 1875, James Adam Wert (28 Nov 1854, Haines Tp PA-19 Mar 1941). Farmer.

CF43281   Sarah Jane Wert (16 Oct 1875, Boalsburg PA-30 Apr 1931, Boalsburg PA) m. 24 Oct 1894, David C. Bohn (17 May 1868, Boalsburg PA-13 Mar 1959, Bellefonte PA). Farmer.

CF432811   George James Bohn (2 Jun 1895, Tusseyville PA-17 Aug 1977) m 1) 24 Dec 1917, Ruth Yarnell (27 Feb 1894, State College PA-31 Aug 1971); m 2) 22 May 1972, Roxey Johnson (b 6 Nov 1914). WWI. General store merchant; county commissioner; school director.

CF432812   John Edward Bohn (28 Feb 1897, Tusseyville PA-24 Sep 1967) m 30 Oct 1920, Estella Elizabeth Musser (b 8 Jan 1897 Aaronsburg PA)

CF4328121   Musser James Bohn (b 1 May 1921, Centre Hall PA) m 18 Nov 1950, Betty Nadine Turner (b 8 Aug 1922, Topeka KS).

CF43281211   Gary James Bohn (b 5 Aug 1951, Washington DC)

CF4328122   Larry Edward Bohn (b 19 Dec 1952, Washington DC) m 24 Apr 1979, Angelia Marie Dicampli (b 22 Jul 1953).

CF432813   Carl Henry Bohn (9 Jul 1878, Colyer PA-25 Mar 1971) m 18 Aug 1927, Helen Edna Neese (b 15 Mar 1897, Pine Grove Mills PA). Accountant.

CF4328131   Carl Henry Bohn (b 29 Jan 1934, Akron OH) m 10 Aug 1958, Sarah Alice Spradlin (b 29 Sep 1935, Millstone KY). Teacher.

CF43281311   Robert John Bohn (b 6 Sep 1959)

CF43281312   Sara Lynne Bohn (b 4 Oct 1963)

CF4328132   John David Bohn (b 6 Jun 1935, Akron OH) m 8 May 1964, Faith Felicia Alyward (b 6 Sep 1941).

CF43281321   Maria Anne Bohn (b 6 Feb 1965)

CF43281322   John Andrew Bohn (b 22 Nov 1966)

CF43281323   Rebecca Rachel Bohn (b 19 Oct 1973)

CF432814   Miranda Ruth Bohn (May 1901, Potters Mills PA-16 Feb 1993) m 3 Jun 1924, Frank Edgar MacIntire (8 Oct 1898, Philadelphia PA)

CF4328141   Grace Keyser MacIntire (b 26 Feb 1925, Binghamton NY) m 14 Aug 1946, Warren Lewis Gardner (b 10 Oct 1924, Marathon NY).

CF43281411   Clarence George Gardner (b 12 Mar 1947, Kansas City MO) m Rebecca Rhodes

CF432814111   Jonathan Gardner

CF432814112   Virginia Gardner

CF432814113   David Gardner

CF43281412   Warren Lewis Gardner II (b 29 Sep 1948, Montrose PA) m Sarah Sisbarro

CF432814121   Matthew Gardner

CF43281413   Reginald Jay Gardner (b 17 Aug 1951, Binghamton NY) m Jeanene Knight

CF432814131   Heather Gardner

CF43281414   William James Gardner (b 23 Sep 1957, Binghamton NY) m Lori Offringa

CF432814141   Jennifer Gardner

CF43281415   Wilson Keyser Gardner (b 23 Sep 1957, Binghamton NY) m Victoria Phillips

CF432814151   Vanessa Gardner

CF432814152   Scott Gardner

CF432814153   Emily Gardner

CF43281416   Paul Gardner (23 Jun 1959, at _____)

CF4328142   Sarah Miranda MacIntire (b 27 Jul 1926, Binghamton NY) m 14 Aug 1951, Stephen Kostona (b 22 Sep 1919, Bronx NY).

CF43281421   Patricia Lee Kostona (b 2 Oct 1952, Brooklyn NY) m Scott Woodbury

CF432814211   Jennifer Kostona (Woodbury?) (b 23 Dec 1980)

CF43281422   Charles Kostona (b 11 Apr 1954)

CF43281423   Michael Kostona (b 19 Apr 1955)

CF432814231   Jennifer Kostona (b 23 Dec 1980)

CF43281424   Merry Lynn Kostona (b 1 Apr 1958)

CF43281425   Daniel Kostona

CF43281426   Candie Kostona

CF4328143   Susan Anna MacIntire (b 22 Sep 1927, Binghamton NY) m 20 Jan 1952, Frank Paul Kalesinskas (16 May 1927)

CF43281431   Mark Francis Kalesinskas (b 2 Dec 1952, Binghamton NY) m Cheryl Webster

CF43281432   Carl Kalesinskas (b 18 Jan 1955)

CF43281433   Kipen Kalesinskas (b 22 Jul 1956) m Leslie Schurman

CF4328144   Frances Alverta MacIntire (b 2 May 1929, Binghamton NY) m 13 Nov 1952, Joseph W. Wrana (b 30 Oct 1923)

CF43281441   Jay Wrana (b Jan 1955)

CF43281442   Ross Wrana (b Sep 1956)

CF4328145   Frank Edgar MacIntire III (b 20 Apr 1932, Bellefonte PA) m Judith Aleen Brull (b 17 Aug 1937)

CF43281451   Frank Edgar MacIntire IV (17 Nov 1957, Courtland NY)

CF43281452   Scott MacIntire (30 Jun 1959)

CF43281453   Aleen MacIntire (17 Jul 1969)

CF4328146   Wilson Filmore MacIntire (24 Feb 1935, Binghamton NY)

CF43281461   Greg MacIntire

CF43281462   Bruce MacIntire (b 24 Mar 1968)

CF43281463   Jennifer MacIntier (b 10 Jul 1970)

CF4328147   Mary Louise MacIntire (b 30 May 1937, Montrose PA)

CF432815   Russell William Bohn (28 Apr 1904, Potters Mills PA-19 Jan 1983) m 26 Dec 1932, Margaret Elizabeth Smith (b 13 Mar 1906, Centre Hall PA).

CF432816   Faye Elizabeth Bohn (30 Oct 1905, Potters Mills PA-30 Jan 1983) m 1 Sep 1928, Paul Wesner Huprick (b 16 Feb 1905, Baltic OH). District supt, Armor and Co., Lexington MA.

CF4328161   Paul Richard Huprick (b 12 Nov 1933, Akron OH) m 16 Jun 1956, Nancy Orne Eustes (b 28 Oct 1933, Waterville ME).

CF43281611   Kathryn Orne Huprick (b 20 Dec 1956, Smithtown NY) m 25 Jul 1981, Christopher Allen Krietsch (27 Jan 1951)

CF432817   James David Bohn (b 9 Jun 1908, Boalsburg PA) m 20 Aug 1938, Anna Mary Moyer (b 12 Aug 1909, Mifflinburg PA). Salesman.

CF4328171   James David Bohn II (b 12 Sep 1941, Englewood NJ) m 8 Jul 1967 Carol Jane Bronner (b 17 Jun 1943). He, DDS; dentist, Mifflinburg PA.

CF43281711   James David Bohn III (b 3 May 1970)

CF43281712   Jason Duehn Bohn (b 24 Apr 1973)

CF4328172   Jeffrey Charles Bohn (b 30 Apr 1948, Englewood NJ) m 29 Oct 1977, Gay Michelle Fields (b 11 Dec 1946).

CF432818   Sarah May Bohn (b 4 Nov 1909, Boalsburg PA) m 6 Feb 1932, William Hoy Neff (2 Dec 1905, Potters Mills PA-4 Aug 1982)

CF4328181   Virginia May Neff (b 28 Jul 1936, Boalsburg PA) m 2 Sep 1961, H. Thomas Swank (b 4 Mar 1935).

CF43281811   Thomas Brent Swank (b 8 Jan 1963)

CF43281812   Julia Louise Swank (b 27 May 1965, Boalsburg PA)

CF4328182   Marjorie Louise Neff (b 13 Oct 1941, Boalsburg PA) m 18 Sep 1965, Eugene Bennett (b 13 Feb 1937)

CF43281821   Pamela Elaine Bennett (b 22 Jul 1968)

CF43281822   Brian Eugene Bennett (23 Mar 1972, at _____)

CF432819   Frederick Bohn (15 Oct 1911, Boalsburg PA-13 Jan 1981) m 22 Apr 1933, Anna Mary Williams (b 15 Aug 1911, Rock Springs PA). Farmer.

CF4328191   Shirley Anne Bohn (b 19 Feb 1934, Rebersburg PA) m 14 Nov 1954, James Ronald Russell (b 18 Oct 1933).

CF43281911   James Kraig Russell (20 Aug 1956, Doylestown PA)

CF43281912   Holly Joy Russell (12 Dec 1959, at _____)

CF4328192   Frederick James Bohn II (b 12 Feb 1936, Rebersburg PA) m 15 Oct 1960, Lois Marion Smith (b 21 Jul 1941).

CF43281921   Susan Jo Bohn (b 3 Jul 1964)

CF43281922   Scott Erie Bohn (b 4 Jul 1964)

CF4328193   Barbara Jean Bohn (b 18 Oct 1937, Rebersburg PA) m 11 Oct 1959, Tilbert Clark Bryner (b 15 Feb 1938).

CF43281931   Tilbert Clark Bryner (b 26 Aug 1960) m 10 Oct 1981, Leslie Jo Keister (b 28 Jul 1967)

CF43281932   Randy Clark Bryner (b 13 May 1964)

CF43281933   David Clark Bryner (b 2 Jan 1966)

CF4328194   Ray William Bohn (b 20 Feb 1943, Pompton Plains NY) m 24 Aug 1974, Sandra Lee Taylor (b 27 May 1945).

CF43281A   Charles Wert Bohn (b 25 Jul 1913, Boalsburg PA) m 21 Jun 1941, State College PA, Geraldine Meckley (b 6 Nov 1916, Fountain PA). US Postal Service, State College PA.

*CF43281A1   Donna Jean Bohn (b 19 Jun 1946, Bellefonte PA) m 20 Jun 1964, Deep Creek MD, Gerald Frances Moody, Jr. (b 14 Nov 1943, Fairchance PA). Banking, Irwin PA.

*CF43281A11   Michelle Ann Moody (b 25 Nov 1966, Clearfield PA) m 20 Oct 1990, Norristown PA, Steven Gregory Wrick (b 4 Apr 1965, Norristown PA). BA, Lock Haven U, 1987; exec asst. He, BS, Lock Haven U, 1986; programmer, analyst, Ambler PA, 1990- .

CF43281A12   Kelly Susanne Moody (b 15 Feb 1970, Waynesburg PA). Unm. BA, NYU, 1992; MA, NY Inst Fine ARts, 1994; Admin asst, Bard Graduate Center, New York NY.

CF43281A13   Dawn Heather Moody (b 1 Jul 1971, Waynesburg PA) m 7 May 1994, Portsmouth VA, Robert Eugene Hess (b 2 Sep 1969, Portsmouth VA). X-ray tech, Portsmouth VA.

CF43282   John Brungart Wert (22 Jul 1877-27 Aug 1977) m 25 Dec 1902, Gertrude Rossman (10 Apr 1882-23 May 1971).

CF432821   Mary Rebecca Wert (31 Dec 1903, Tusseyville PA-26 Jan 1963) m 23 Apr 1927, George Charles Trevorrow (b 3 Aug 1901)

CF4328211   Nancy Jane Trevorrow (b 24 Oct 1928) m 25 Nov 1959, Joseph Carbonara (30 Jan 1932-19 Aug 1973). Teacher.

CF4328212   Joseph Wert Trevorrow (b 26 Nov 1930) m 1) 13 Dec 1951, Kathleen Ann O'Mahoney (b 13 Nov 1934), div; m 2) 28 Nov 1958, Elaine Lee Barger (27 Jun 1935), div; m 3) 6 Jan 1981, Anne Cavender (b 26 Sep 1941).

CF43282121   Michael Joseph Trevorrow (b 4 May 1952)

CF43282122   Steven John Trevorrow (b 30 Dec 1953)

CF43282123   Kimberlee Ann Trevorrow (b 13 Nov 1963)

CF4328213   George Charles Trevorrow (b 27 Apr 1932) m 8 Aug 1959, Helen Marie Kamenos (b 10 Mar 1934).

*CF43282131   Thomas Charles Trevorrow (b 15 Sep 1967). MD, ophthalmologist, Indiana PA.

CF43282124   Nancy Catherine Trevorrow (b 29 Dec 1935)

CF432822   Michael Rossman Wert (3 Jan 1906, Tusseyville PA-3 Mar 1996, Worcester PA) m 2 Mar 1929, Bertha Sarah Buzzard (b 17 Jan 1905). Bur Worcester PA. Consulting actuary, Philadelphia PA.

CF4328221   Gail Abbie Wert (b 14 May 1940) m 10 Aug 1963, Robert Leroy Williams (b 15 Nov 1939)

CF43282211   Scott Rossman Williams (b 27 Nov 1965)

CF43282212   Wendy Gail Williams (b 21 Sep 1968)

CF432823   James Kenneth Wert (21 Mar 1908, Tusseyville PA-17 Apr 1943) m 30 May 1936, Eleanor M. Culbertson (15 Oct 1901-31 May 1985)

CF4328231   Mary Ann Wert (b 21 Dec 1937, Loysville PA) m 3 Aug 1958, Don Evans Frazier (b 2 Mar 1935)

CF43282311   Jacqueline Ann Frazier (b 10 Oct 1964)

CF43282312   Kenneth Wert Frazier (b 29 Mar 1967)

CF4328232   Ruth Naomi Wert (9 Nov 1939, Tusseyville PA-23 Jul 1945, Centre Hall PA).

CF432824   Martha Ruth Wert (b 7 May 1910, Tusseyville PA) m 21 Jul 1931, Ralph Henry Dale (b 6 Jan 1901)

CF4328241   John Luther Dale (b 2 Jul 1938, Bellefonte PA) m 1) 4 Jun 1960, June Talpey (b 5 Jun 1940), div; m 2) 26 Jul 1977, Martha Willis Anderson (b 28 Jul 1940)

CF43282411   John Luther Dale, Jr. (b 30 Dec 1960)

CF43282412   Jeffrey Brian Dale (b 13 Feb 1963)

CF432825   John Brungart Wert, Jr. (b 22 Dec 1912, Tusseyville PA) m 7 May 1932, Myla Catherine Spyker (b 30 Oct 1913)

CF4328251   Joanne Barbara Wert (b 1 Nov 1932) m 9 Apr 1954, Philip Henry Blazer (b 10 Jul 1931)

CF43282511   John Edward Blazer (b 11 Aug 1954, Bellefonte PA)

CF43282512   James Lynn Blazer (b 5 Sep 1955, Bellefonte PA) m 15 Jun 1974, Penny Rae Price (b 21 Nov 1955)

CF43282513   Philip Henry Blazer (b 23 May 1958, Bellefonte PA) m 23 May 1978, Constance Sue Bunting Cole (b 23 Sep 1954)

CF432825131   Adam Philip Blazer (2 Feb 1980-3 Feb 1980)

CF43282514   Robert Wert Blazer (b 24 Jan 1964)

CF432826   Anna Elizabeth Wert (b 5 Dec 1916, Tusseyville PA) m 24 Mar 1940, James M. Law (b 1 Oct 1916).

CF4328261   James Michael Law (b 28 Jul 1943) m 14 Apr 1964, Rose Ellen Bowes (b 7 Jan 1944)

CF43282611   James Michael Law, Jr. (b 15 Apr 1965)

CF43282612   Julie Anne Law (b 21 Jun 1967)

CF4328262   Robert John Law (b 23 Nov 1947) m 18 Aug 1967, Lucinda Mae Shope (b 11 May 1947)

CF43282621   Michael Andrew Law (b 30 Apr 1970)

CF43282622   Trevor Allen Law (b 15 Apr 1974)

CF43283   Claude Edward Wert (12 Aug 1883, Boalsburg PA-5 Jul 1963) m 18 Oct 1905, Lillian Pearl Frank (21 Jul 1888, Madisonburg PA-16 Feb 1978)

CF432831   Kathryn Miranda Wert (4 May 1906, Tusseyville PA-9 Jan 1996, State College PA) m 3 Dec 1935, Lynn Breon (b 8 Jul 1913, Centre Hall PA). Secretary, PSU, Centre Hall PA.

CF4328311   Lynn Donald Breon (16 Jun 1937, Bellefonte PA). Unm. Centre Hall PA.

CF4328312   James Ronald Breon (b 16 Jun 1937, Bellefonte PA) m 24 Sep 1961, Viola Jane Grenoble (b 22 Sep 1943). Apalachin NY.

CF43283121   Kent Michael Breon (b 21 Jan 1975, NJ)

CF43283122   Julie Marie Breon (b 30 Oct 1976, NJ)

CF432832   Philip Frank Wert (12 Jan 1911-12 May 1911, Tusseyville PA).

CF432833   Martin Luther Wert (b 25 Nov 1912, Tusseyville PA) m 11 Nov 1935, Mary Irene Corman (b 9 May 1907, Smulltown PA). Niles MI.

CF4328331   Patricia Ann Wert (b 19 Jun 1939, Rebersburg PA) m 16 Jun 1957, Gerald Earl Travernier (b 17 Jun 1937)

CF43283311   Cary Andrew Tavernier (b 15 May 1958, Norfolk VA) m 10 Oct 1981, Mary Reed (b 27 Apr 1951).

CF43283312   Bruce Alan Tavernier (b 5 Mar 1964, IN) m 5 Jun 1982, Cynthia Alice Bradley (b 4 Nov 1963)

CF432833121   Kimberly Ann Tavernier (b 17 Oct 1982, MI)

CF43283313   Alicia Rae Tavernier (b 27 Dec 1968) m 31 Aug 1991, Timothy Jujawski (b 20 Dec 1965)

CF432834   Jacob Cyrus Wert (b 15 Feb 1915, Tusseyville PA) m 17 May 1936, Lyndall Whitehead (b 5 May 1915, MA). Bellefonte PA.

CF4328341   Robert Lindsey Wert (b 29 May 1937, Bellefonte PA) m 5 Dec 1958, Molly Ellen Ishler (b 15 Feb 1940, Bellefonte PA)

CF43283411   Gerald Robert Wert (b 3 Mar 1960, Bellefonte PA) m 10 Jul 1993, Debra Annette Dotson (b 30 Jun 1965, VA).

CF432834111   Gerald Robert Wert II (b 6 Sep 1994)

CF43283412   Susan Rae Wert (b 3 Jun 1963, Bellefonte PA) m 14 May 1983, Donald Frederick Kline (b 14 Jan 1962).

CF432834121   Ashley Rae Kline (b 1 Dec 1983, Bellefonte PA)

CF432834122   Brittany Dawn Kline (b 9 Oct 1985, Bellefonte PA)

CF43283413   Heidi Jane Wert (b 13 May 1964, Bellefonte PA). Unm.

CF43283414   Michael William Wert (b 25 Mar 1966, Bellefonte PA). Unm.

CF4328342   Joanne Marie Wert (b 12 Apr 1940, Boalsburg PA) m 1) 22 May 1959, Howard Wesley Blare (b 6 Dec 1937); m 2) 6 Jun 1973, Fred Harrison Bailey (b 14 Apr 1946). No chn.

CF4328343   James Cyrus Wert (30 Jan 1945, Axeman PA) m 24 Aug 1968, Alice King (b 1 May 1950).

CF43283431   Jason Christopher Wert (b 13 Jan 1971, Bellefonte PA)

CF43283432   Justin Dale Wert (b 30 Dec 1973, Bellefonte PA)

CF432835   Margaret Lucille Wert (b 2 Jul 1917, Tusseyville PA) m 1) 30 Apr 1939, Harry Trauger (b 19 Jan 1919-1 Jun 1990), div; m 2) 10 Jun 1978, Charles E. Watkins (10 Apr 1917-6 Jun 1979)

CF4328351   Harry Martin Trauger (b 29 Nov 1939, Philadelphia PA) m 3 Apr 1960, Connie Lee Stover (b 10 Feb 1944)

CF43283511   Scott Allen Trauger (b 18 Sep 1960, Bellefonte PA) m 13 Dec 1981, Joy Lynn Confer (b 15 Mar 1961)

CF432835111   Jennifer Lynn Trauger (b 19 Jan 1984, State College PA)

CF432835112   Jeime Lee Trauger (b 27 Mar 1987, State College PA)

CF43283512   Robb Martin Trauger (b 1 Apr 1965, Bellefonte PA) m 27 Nov 1985, Roxanna Garcia (b 11 Apr 1960, TX)

CF432835121   Zachary Sebastian Trauger (b 25 Jan 1994, Philadelphia PA)

CF43283513   Todd Michael Trauger (b 24 Jun 1971, State College PA)

CF4328352   Barbara Ann Trauger (b 13 Aug 1942, Philadelphia PA) m 1) Myron Kinsey (b 10 Dec 1937), div; m 2) 24 Nov 1968, Gerald Lee Toschner (b 29 Jun 1933).

CF43283521   Joanne Marie Kinsey (b 1 Jul 1963, CA)(adopted by G. Toschner) m 2 Oct 1982, Alan Joseph Lachapell (b 25 Dec 1957)

CF432835211   Scott Allen Lachapell (b 3 Feb 1984, WI)

CF432835212   Becky Marie Lachapell (b 10 Jun 1986, WI)

CF43283522   Darlene Ann Kinsey (b 29 Jan 1965, CA)(Adopted by G. Toschner)

CF432835221   Sean Michael Kinsey

CF4328353   Howard Albert Trauger (b 1 Sep 1946, Bellefonte PA) m 27 May 1978, Shirley Ann Ambrose (b 9 Feb 1948)

CF43283531   William Victor Trauger

CF432836   Dean Edward Wert (b 3 Feb 1922, Tusseyville PA) m 12 Jun 1949, Dorothy Mae Boozer (b 30 Dec 1930)

CF4328361   Dean Edward Wert (18 Apr 1950, Bellefonte PA) m 2 Sep 1981, Wilma Catherine Griffin (b 20 Aug 1952, Kerr PA).

CF43283611   William Claude Wert (b 30 Jan 1982, Lancaster PA)

CF43284   David Sparr Wert (b 14 May 1890, Boalsburg PA) m 24 Feb 1912, Eva Elizabeth Fleisher (3 Nov 1890, Colyer PA-8 Jan 1959, Harrisburg PA)

CF432841   Beatrice Madaline Wert (b 16 Dec 1913) m 1) 15 Jul 1934, Philip A. Vonada (7 Oct 1908-23 Oct 1972); m 2) 15 May 1976, Robert D. Haslop (b 30 Dec 1918)

CF4328411   Douglas Sparr Vonada (b 27 Apr 1935, Bellefonte PA) m 20 Aug 1960, Deloris Jane Quimbly (b 27 Mar 1937)

CF43284111   Debra Susan Vonada (b 23 Jan 1965)

CF43284112   Deanne Jean Vonada (b 3 May 1967)

CF432842   Donald Stanford Wert (3 Nov 1916-15 May 1942, Carthage Tunis Africa). WWII; USAAC.

CF4329   George Luther Brungart (27 Oct 1856-15 Nov 1873)

CF432A   Jacob Clayton Brungart (17 Nov 1857-9 Aug 1947) m 1) Margaret Rute (1 Feb 1862-26 Dec 1888); m 2) Sarah Crouse

CF432A1   Sarah Brungart m William Brungart

CF432A11   Mildred Brungart m 26 Jan 1927, Owen Ernest Kiser

CF432A111   Donald Owen Kiser (b 12 Jan 1929)

CF432A112   Barbara Sue Kiser (b 23 Jul 1931)

CF432A113   Joan Kiser (b 3 Dec 1932)

CF432A114   Nancy Kiser (b 3 Dec 1932)

CF432A12   Etta Mae Brungart m Roy Pass

CF432A13   Sarah Brungart m 11 Mar 1929, A. Harley Stanger

CF432A2   Matilda Brungart (13 Aug 1882-2 Dec 1882)

CF432A3   John R. Brungart (4 Jun 1886-28 Jul 1930) m Dorothie Crandal

CF432A4   Child Brungart (12 Dec 1880-12 Dec 1880)

CF432B   Jermiah Brungart (9 Mar 1860-31 Jan 1935) m 28 Oct 1878, Tena Lamey

CF432B1   Sadie Brungart (27 Mar 1879-2 Feb 1923) m Forest Emerick

CF432B11   John Emerick (b 30 Dec 1897) m 27 Jun 1941, Margaret McClennahan

CF432B12   Marion Emerick (b 12 Dec 1901) m Paul Brenner

CF432B121   Paul C. Brenner

CF432B122   Polly Ann Brenner

CF432B123   Joseph Brenner (b 5 Apr 1939)

CF432B13   Dorothy Emerick (b 24 May 1905)

CF432B14   Sarah Emerick (b 25 Jun 1907) m 24 Jun 1933, Edward Arnold Kolar

CF432B141   Ronald Kolar

CF432B2   Anna M. Brungart (b 21 Jun 1886) m Charles E. Miller (24 Apr 1885-15 Jul 1951)

CF432B21   Howard Miller m 28 Nov 1936, Mae Reid

CF432B3   Brungart (d 19 Apr 1881)

CF432C   Ira Brungart (25 Jul 1861, Brush Valley PA-13 May 1930, Rebersburg PA) m Ella M.
Snook (d 6 Sep 1948)

CF432C1   Bertha Catherine Brungart (25 Nov 1892-15 Mar 1897)

CF432C2   Clarence Clebe Brungart (13 Nov 1884-16 Jul 1925) m Lula Mowery. Bur Logantown PA.

CF432C21   Kermit Harry Brungart

CF432C22   Thelma Marion Brungart m 17 Jul 1927, Paul H. Cummings (b 24 Sep 1907)

CF432C221   Dean Brungart Cummings (b 18 May 1930)

CF432C23   Geraldine Brungart (b 20 Apr 1915, Loganton PA) m 17 Jun 1938, Albin Edgar Jacobson
(b 26 Jul 1915, Lanse PA)

CF432C231   Patricia Ann Jacobson (b 15 Mar 1952, Williamsport PA)

CF432C24   Harold Brungart (b 8 Jul 1917, Rebersburg PA) m Florence Bechtol (b 6 Jan 1917,
Woodward PA)

CF432C241   Clarence Brungart (b 1950)

CF432C242   Peggy Jean Brungart (b 23 Mar 1952)

CF432C25   Harry Brungart m

CF432C251   Harry Joseph Brungart (21 Sep 1945)

CF432C252   Paul Clarence Brungart (b 17 Feb 1947)

CF432C26   William Brungart

CF432C3   Estella Brungart (b 6 Mar 1887, Wolfs Store PA) m 8 Aug 1910, William C. Witmer (b
25 Feb 1887, Lemont PA)

CF432C31   Leonard Witmer (b 30 May 1911, Lemont PA) m 25 Dec 1935, Emma Lydia Hoffman
(b 24 Apr 1910, Montgomery PA)

CF432C311   Lynn R. D. Witmer (b 7 Aug 1938, Bellefonte PA)

CF432C312   Martha Doris Witmer (b 28 Aug 1939, Bellefonte PA)

CF432C32   Dick Aubry Witmer (b 6 Mar 1927, Bellefonte PA) m Hilda Weisheit.

CF432C321   Keith D. Witmer (b 14 Nov 1955)

CF432C322   Kevin Alan Witmer (b 12 Apr 1959, Dewart PA)

CF432C4   Edgar Samuel Brungart (b 27 May 1890, Rebersburg PA) m Estella Witmer

CF432C5   Raymond Jacob Brungart (b 12 Aug 1892, Rebersburg PA) m Irene Anderson (b 11 Aug 1892, Rush Co IN). Takoma Park MD.

CF432C51   Robert Raymond Brungart (B 2 Nov 1925, Detroit MI) m Elizabeth Johnson (b 26 Sep 1925, Washington DC). Second secretary, NATO embassy, Paris France.

CF432C511   William Raymond Brungart (b 20 Jun 1953, Frankfort, Germany)

CF432C512   Ralph Walter Brungart (b 25 Nov 1954, West Berlin Germany)

CF432C513   Karen Louise Brungart (b 5 Apr 1956, Berkeley CA)

CF432C52   Marjorie Jean Brungart (b 31 May 1929, Detroit MI) m Jun 1951, James N. Chomko (b 12 Jul 1928, Olyphant PA). U MD; capt, USA.

CF432C521   Lisa Karen Chomko (b 22 Jun 1953, Ft. Jackson MO)

CF432C522   Linda Cynthia Chomko (b 3 Jan 1955, Ft. Bragg NC)

CF432C523   Eric Nicholas Chomko (b 24 Jul 1958, Monterey CA)

CF432C6
Jun 1898)   Wilbur Reuben Brungart (b 29 Jun 1895, Rebersburg PA) m Velma E. Hosterman (b 3

CF432C61   Pauline Susan Brungart (10 Oct 1921, Rebersburg PA) m Nevin Wehr.

CF432C62   Phyllis Ella Brungart (9 May 1925, Rebersburg PA) m Russell Rossman

CF432C621   Russell Rossman, Jr. (2 Feb 1953)

CF432C622   Ronald James Rossman (5 Mar 1959, San Francisco CA)

CF432C63   Wilbur Reuben Brungart, Jr. (7 Aug 1930, Rebersburg PA) m Wanda Griest

CF432C7
Rebersburg PA.   Walter Snook Brungart (18 Oct 1899, Rebersburg PA-2 Mar 1899, Rebersburg PA). Bur

CF432C8   Charles Henry Brungart (7 Sep 1901, Rebersburg PA-7 Nov 1904, Rebersburg PA).

CF433   Johannes Brungart (son of George and Salome (Kehl) Brungart)(9 Mar 1817-10 Jan 1828)

CF434   Susanna Brungart (daughter of George and Salome (Kehl) Brungart)(10 Mar 1819-22 Mar 1862) m Jeremiah Haines (23 May 1818-14 Apr 1893)

CF4341   Emma J. Haines (6 Sep 1846-7 Dec 1924) m Thomas E. Royer (1840-1912)

CF43411   Susan Royer (4 Oct 1870-1939) m John Long

CF43412   Harry H. Royer (b 6 Oct 1874) m Lula Stover (b 5 Dec 1874)

CF4342   George B. Haines (6 Aug 1849-1924) m 1870, Emma J. Berkert (10 Aug 1852-1918)

CF43421
1869-17 Nov 1916)   William Burkert Haines (29 May 1869-24 Apr 1930) m 1890, Lydia Ocker (21 Jun

CF434211   Harry Haines (b 1891) m 1) Elizabeth Murphy; m 2) Mary Smith

CF4342111   Charles Haines

CF4342112   George Haines

CF4342113   Harry Haines, Jr.

CF43422   Charles M. Haines (1870-1914)

CF43423   Elizabeth Haines m Orvis Walker

CF43424   Claude Haines (15 Jan 1878-10 Apr 1933) m Alma Gramley (b 8 Mar 1883)

CF434241   Kenneth Gramley Haines (b 20 May 1906)

CF435   George Brungart (son of George and Salome (Kehl) Brungart)(4 Feb 1821-20 Mar 1898) m 10 May 1847, Anna Maria Wohlfert (25 Aug 1829-20 Nov 1897)

CF4351   Mary Jane Brungart (29 Aug 1847-1920) m 25 Dec 1865, William M. Waite (22 Aug 1843-28 Oct 1906). Bur Rebersburg PA.

CF43511   George Adam Waite (1866-28 Sep 1924) m Mary Kreamer

CF435111   Jay Waite

CF43512   Samuel A. Waite (b 13 May 1868, Rebersburg PA) m Jane Wohlfert

CF435121   Boyd Waite m Helen Davis

CF435122   Mary Lucretia Waite (b 21 Oct 1894) m Charles Gilbert

CF4351221   Earl Gilbert

CF4351222   Gladys Gilbert

CF4351223   Arthur Gilbert

CF4351224   Dorothy Gilbert

CF435123   Charles Albert Waite (b 7 Feb 1897) m Mary Geisel

CF435124   Lula Annie Waite (b 27 Feb 1899) m William Frederick

CF4351241   Pauline Frederick

CF4351242   William Charles Frederick

CF4351243   Dorothy Frederick

CF43513   Thomas N. Waite m 1) Mayme Stratoon; m 2) Kate Haas

CF435131   Verna Waite

CD435132   LeRoy Waite m Irene Como

CF4351321   Leroy Waite

CF4351322   Virginia Waite

CF435133   Clarence Waite (b 3 May 1912)

CF43514   Mazie M. Waite (8 Feb 1872, Rebersburg PA-25 Feb 1894). Bur Rebersburg PA.

CF43515   Anna Rose Waite (9 Jul 1874-8 Jun 1925) m Huston Shreckengast

CF435151   Charles Huston Shreckengast

CF43516   William H. Waite

CF43517   Clyde M. Waite (11 Mar 1882-12 Dec 1941) m Elsie Stover (b 17 Apr 1886, Penn Tp,
Centre Co PA)

CF435171   Mildred Waite (b 14 Jul 1903) m Orvis Orndorf

CF4351711   Bernice Orndorf (b 27 May 1927) m Eugene Warntz

CF4351712   Harold Orndorf (b 24 Aug 1928)

CF435172   Esther Waite (b 24 Nov 1920) m Kenneth Swartz

CF4351721   David Swartz (b 24 Aug 1943)

CF4351722   Richard Swartz (b 17 Apr 1947)

CF4351723   Paul Swartz (b 24 Jul 1948)

CF4351724   James Swartz (b 10 Jan 1956)

CF4351725   Susan Swartz (b 12 Feb 1958)

CF43518   Dolly J. Waite (13 Jun 1886-1918). Bur Rebersburg PA.

CF4352   Lewis Brungart (9 Oct 1848-31 Oct 1916) m 23 Jan 1870, Maria Wise (28 Arp 1848-14
May 1895). Farmer.

CF43521   Paul Brungart (2 Feb 1881-12 Feb 1881)

CF43522   Vera Catherine Brungart (b 26 Aug 1882). Attorney, Washington DC.

CF4353   Amanda Brungart (15 May 1850-11 Nov 1927) m David Yoder (14 Oct 1842-8 Jul 1897).
51st Penn Vol Regt, Civil War.

CF43531   Lizzie Yoder m Calvin Royer (d 1 Apr 1935)

CF435311   Hoyt Royer m Gertrude Ziegler

CF4353111   Gershon Toyer m 17 Jun 1936, Catharine C. Albright

CF435312   Glenn H. Royer m Elizabeth Archey

CF4353121   Archey Royer

CF4353122   Dean Royer

CF4353123   Charles Calvin Royer

CF43532   Catharine Yoder (b 13 Dec 1871) m William Tyson

CF435321   Harry Benjamin Tyson (b 18 Dec 1892) m Ada Campbell

CF435322   Sidney Brown Tyson (b 22 Aug 1895) m Lillian Letch

CF4353221   William Henry Tyson

CF4353222   James Tyson

CF435323   Annie Tyson m 2 Apr 1928, Blair Tate

CF4353231   Annie Kathry Tate

CF435324   Paul Tyson (13 Jul 1900-10 Oct 1910)

CF435325   Raymond L. Tyson (b 20 May 1902)

CF43533   Emma Yoder (b 22 Sep 1897) m Samuel Wilson Seyler

CF435331   Paul H. Seyler (d 1951) m Esther Reigel

CF4353311   Miriam Henrietta Seyler

CF435332   Myrtle Leonore Seyler (d 13 Nov 1991) m Carroll Eugene Hursh

CF4353321   Frances Hursh

*CF4353322   Barbara Hursh m Leo Karcher

CF43533221   Richard Karcher

CF43533222   Anne Karcher

CF43533223   Mary Jane Karcher

CF43533224   Thomas Karcher

CF4354   Susan Brungart (25 Mar 1852-21 Oct 1855)

CF4355   William L. Brungart (2 Dec 1853-25 Nov 1928) m 6 Jun 1875, Ellen Rowe (15 Oct 1854-27 Dec 1922)

CF43551   George W. Brungart (b 21 Nov 1875) m 1) 15 Mar 1930, Clara Ann Confer (1875-17 Nov 1913); m 2) Mrs. Emma Myers Brungart (see CF43553)

CF435511   Lester Larue Brungart (b 1 Sep 1907)

CF435512   Violet Brungart (b 3 Sep 1910)

CF43552   Mary Ellen Brungart (b 10 Oct 1877) m 25 Sep 1917, Chester Albright Stoltz (b 11 Jul 1890)

CF43553   John Rowe Brungart (17 Jul 1883-13 Dec 1916) m 27 Jun 1909, Emma Meyers (b 11 Jul 1890) (see CF43551)

CF435531   William Charles Brungart (b 12 Jul 1910)

CF435532   John Stanley Brungart (b 31 Jan 1912)

CF4356   Catharine Brungart (1 Mar 1855-16 Jan 1871). Unm.

CF4357   Sophia Brungart (19 Aug 1856-21 May 1934) m 1) Pierce Zellers; m 2) Harvey Laubach

CF43571   Lula May Zeller (b 1 Jun 1889) m Robert Sitler

CF435711   Mabel Sitler (b 23 Dec 1903) m Hollis Beach

CF4357111   Patricia Ann Beach (b 10 Sep 1931)

CF435712   Harvey Howis Sitler (b 3 Nov 1910) m Ella Livermore

CF4357121   William Sitler (b Jun 1931)

CF4357122   Glenn Sitler (b 3 Sep 1933)

CF435713   Lydia Eleanor Sitler (b 16 Mar 1913)

CF435714   Evelyn Pearl Sitler (22 Aug 1915-30 Aug 1933). Unm.

CF43572   Edna Maria Laubach (b 4 Jul 1899) m 24 Sep 1919, Alfred Mantel, Jr.

CF435721   Gertrude Eleanor Mantel (b 15 Dec 1921)

CF435722   Nevin Wentworth Mantel (b 16 Aug 1923)

CF435723   Ralph Del Roy Mantel (b 14 Sep 1925)

CF435724   Paul Joseph Mantel (b 18 Aug 1927)

CF435725   Isabel Lydia Mantel (b 9 Dec 1929)

CF435726   Alfred Boyd Mantel (b 4 Jan 1932)

CF435727   Marjorie Helen Mantel (b 11 Sep 1933)

CF435728   Richard B. Mantel (b 29 Mar 1936)

CF43573   Lydia May Laubach (b 29 Sep 1896) m 9 May 1917, Charles Fenstermaker

CF435731   Edna Ruth Fenstermaker (b 8 Mar 1918) m 30 Aug 1935, Harold W. Lamey

CF4357311   Charles Dale Lamey (b 11 Nov 1935)

CF4357312   Virginia Ann Lamey (b 12 Nov 1936)

CF435732   Lois Marguerite Fenstermaker

CF435733   Martha Elizabeth Fenstermaker (b 28 Feb 1922)

CF435734   Evelyn Grace Fenstermaker (b 15 Nov 1923)

CF435735   Doris Jane Fenstermaker (b 27 Jan 1932)

CF4358   Adam Noah Brungart (b 21 Nov 1857) m 22 Nov 1882, Mary Crouse (b 12 Apr 1857)

CF43581   Nora May Brungart (b 14 Mar 1884) m 18 Mar 1911, Allen Guisewhite

CF435811   Delphia Elizabeth Guisewhite (b 9 Sep 1911) m 7 Apr 1934, Miller L. Stamm

CF453812   Irene Catherine Guisewhite (b 7 Apr 1914) m 4 Jan 1934, John Wesley Long

CF435813   Glenn Sidney Guisewhite (b 5 Oct 1922) m

CF435814   Edward Clarence Guisewhite (22 Jan 1927-27 Jan 1927)

CF43582   Harry Cleve Brungart (b 16 May 1885, Rebersburg PA) m 1) 18 Nov 1908, Linnie Weaver (29 Jan 1881-31 May 1913); m 2) Laura Weaver

CF435821   Harry Weaver Brungart

CF43583   Beulah Elizabeth Brungart (12 Aug 1886, Rebersburg PA-6 Sep 1959) m 3 Oct 1914, Lee Luther Wolfe (b 5 Apr 1892)

CF435831   Mary Lorena Brungart (b 1 Jun 1908) m 29 Apr 1931, Vilas Wise (b 4 Jul 1897)

CF435832   Rosaline Wolfe (b 15 Mar 1914) m Russell G. Jackson

CF4358321   Edwin Jackson

CF435833   Virginia Wolfe (3 Jul 1916-21 Feb 1955) m John Wilcox (b 30 Jul 1914)

CF4358331   John Wilcox (b 2 Apr 1938)

CF4358332   Wanda Wilcox (b 22 May 1940) m Harlan Bowersox (b 21 Jul 1938)

CF435834   Donald Wolfe (b ca 1918, Rebersburg PA) m Mildred Dowdy (b 14 Aug 1918, Loganton PA)

CF4358341   Robert Wolfe (b 30 May 1939, Rebersburg PA)

CF4358342   Richard Wolfe (b 17 Nov 1941, Rebersburg PA)

CF4358343   Carol Wolfe (b 21 Oct 1947, Rebersburg PA)

CF4358344   Doreen Wolfe (b 5 Oct 1955, Rebersburg PA)

CF435835   Marion Wolfe (b 28 Oct 1919) m Paul Dinges

CF4358351   Regina Elizabeth Dinges (b 13 May 1939, Aaronsburg PA)

CF4358352   Larry Paul Dinges (b 15 Jul 1943, Aaronsburg PA)

CF4358353   Lynn Lee Dinges (b 19 Apr 1945, Aaronsburg PA)

CF435836   Leotta Wolfe (7 Jun 1922-2 Mar 1923)

CF43584   Delphia Lorena Brungart (26 Jan 1888-11 Nov 1922) m Paul Walkey

CF435841   Robert Edward Walkey (adopted by uncle George B. Brungart)

CF435842   Evelyn Walkey (b 3 Dec 1920) m Arthur Thomas

CF43585   George Bloomer Brungart (b 21 Sep 1889) m Alvira Smith

CF43586   Robert Crouse Brungart (21 Jan 1891-5 Dec 1897)

CF43587   Norman W. Brungart (17 Dec 1895-15 Dec 1930) m 5 Nov 1921, Alverta Bierly (13 Aug 1899, Tusseyville PA-May 1973, Nyack NY). Bur Rebersburg PA.

CF435871   Madaline Viola Brungart (b 25 Dec 1922)

CF435872   Evelyn Mildred Brungart (b 8 Aug 1924) m   Schultz

CF435873   Eugene Richard Brungart (b 8 Jan 1928)

CF43588   John Rufus Brungart (b 20 Mar 1897) m Ruth Royer (b 20 Feb 1903)

CF435881   Helen May Brungart (b 14 Jun 1922) m Dean R. Matter (b 25 Aug 1918, Smullton PA)

CF43589   Rufus Brungart (5 Sep 1900-5 Oct 1900)

CF4359   Alfred Brungart (18 Aug 1860, Livonia PA-7 Apr 1937, Mifflinburg PA) m 17 Oct 1880, Meda O. Mader (18 Nov 1860, Mifflinburg PA-15 Jun 1927, Mifflinburg PA).

CF43591   Mary Mabel Brungart (Apr 1881-2 Feb 1909, Madisonburg PA) m. Samuel C. Yearick (b 1882). Bur near Centre Hall PA.

CF435911   Anona Yearick (b 3 Mar 1900, Mifflinburg PA) m 20 Aug 1918, Orien Reish

CF4359111   Donald Reish (b 9 Apr 1919) m 7 Jun 1941, Olive Dennis (b 22 Dec 1919)

CF43591111   Bruce Reish (b 4 Mar 1946)

CF43591112   Laurence Reish (b 7 May 1950)

CF4359112   Glenn Reish (b 30 May 1921) m 9 Sep 1942, Doris Doll

CF43591121   Glenn Reish, Jr. (b 25 Aug 1942)

CF43591122   Brian Reish (b 20 Jan 1947)

CF4359113   Leonard Samuel Reish (b 17 Mar 1925) m 16 Jan 1943, Alice Hennet (b 17 Aug 1925)

CF43591131   Sharon Reish (b 21 Nov 1946)

CF43591132   Brenda Reish (b 22 Oct 1948)

CF43591133   Dwayne Reish (b 13 Jan 1951)

CF4359114   Hazel Viola Reish (b 18 Jul 1926) m Elwood Fenner

CF4359115   Talitha Reish (b 20 Dec 1927) m 18 May 1945, Theodore Bush

CF43591151   Scott Bush

CF4359116   Gene Reish (b 6 Jun 1933) m 26 May 1956, Beatrice Smith

CF43591161   Craig Reish (b 8 May 1957)

CF4359117   Joan Reish (b 9 Oct 1938) m Robert Bentzoni

CF4359118   Gary Reish (b 2 Aug 1943)

CF435912   Vesta Yearick m Lester Miller

CF4359121   Paul Miller

CF4359122   Jeanne Miller

CF435913   Ruth Yearick (b 17 Oct 1904, Madisonburg PA) m 22 Jan 1927, Paul Fetterolf (b 19 Mar 1906, Penns Creek PA)

CF4359131   Deloris Fetterolf (b 4 Jul 1927, Madisonburg PA) m Marvin Bair

CF43591311   Marvin Bair, Jr.

CF43591312   Dennis Eugene Bair

CF43591313   Samuel Eudell Bair

CF43591314   Darla Mae Bair

CF43591315   David Bair (b 13 Mar 1959)

CF4359132   Isabella Fetterolf (b 14 May 1930, Madisonburg PA) m William Coppenhaver

CF43591321   Michael William Coppenhaver

CF4359133   Leon Paul Fetterolf (b 27 Mar 1933, Madisonburg PA) m 1 Oct 1957, Elinor Stover

CF4359134   Gerald Samuel Fetterolf

CF435914   Wilbur Yearick m 11 Jun 1927, Victoria Fetterolf (b 14 Apr 1908, Troxelville PA)

CF4359141   Marlin Richard Yearick (1 Oct 1927- 19 Oct 1927)

CF4359142   Nelson Yearick (b 26 Mar 1929) m 7 Mar 1952, Iris Ripka

CF43591421   Luzetta Yearick (b 23 Jul 1956)

CF43591422   Keith Douglas Yearick (b 1 Aug 1958)

CF4359143   Leotta Yearick (b 11 Nov 1932) m 3 Feb 1951, Carl Long, Jr.

CF43591431   Beverly Diane Long (b 23 Jun 1951)

CF43591432   Kevin Douglas Long (b 4 Aug 1954)

CF43591433   Curtis Wayne Long (b 3 Aug 1955)

CF43591434   Carla Mae Long (b 3 Apr 1957)

CF4359144   Mary Kathleen Yearick (b 24 Sep 1934) m 23 Oct 1953, Leon Steiger

CF43591441   Kathy Lee Steiger (b 23 Jun 1954)

CF4359145   Edward Wayne Yearick (b 22 Oct 1936)

CF4359146   Elaine Yearick (b 12 May 1941) m. Richard Shivery

CF43591461   Tina Jean Shivery (b 2 Apr 1958)

CF4359147   Philip Samuel Yearick (b 19 Nov 1949)

CF435915   May Elizabeth Yearick (b 16 Jan 1909) m 10 Sep 1927, Paul Franklin Stover

CF4359151   Paul Calvin Stover (b 4 Dec 1927)

CF4359152   Ruth Stover

CF4359153   Robert Eugene Stover (b 27 Jun 1932)

CF4359154   Ronald Stover

CF43592   Vesta Viola Brungart (5 Feb 1883, Wolfs Store PA-10 Jul 1929, Mifflinburg PA) m 1)
25 Jun 1903, John Kleckner (d. 5 Nov 1919); m 2) Irvin Moyer (b 22 Nov 1878)

CF435921   Kathleen Winifred Kleckner (b 22 Jan 1904) m 1 May 1924, Joseph Laher

CF4359211   Joseph Kleckner Laher (b 24 Oct 1925) m 6 Apr 1946, Catherine Wolfe

CF43592111   Joe K. Laher (b 24 Feb 1948)

CF43592112   David Bruce Laher (b 31 Aug 1950)

CF43592113   Diane Kathleen Laher (b 14 Jan 1954)

CF435922   John Kleckner, Jr. (2 Dec 1918-2 Dec 1918)

CF43593   Paul A. Brungart (3 Jan 1884-1964) m 18 Mar 1914, Verda Moyer (20 Feb 1885-1963)

CF43594   Harry Milton Brungart (16 Jan 1885-18 Apr 1945) m 1) 21 Feb 1907, Annie Fisher
(1885-Mar 1912); m 2) 19 Sep 1912, Mary Herman

CF435941   Dorothy Mae Brungard (b 29 Jan 1912, Snyder Co PA) m 19 May 1934, Hagerstown MD,
George Nolan Royer, Jr.(13 Nov 1916, Mifflinburg PA-5 Apr 1973, Mifflinburg PA)

CF4359411   Joanne Marie Royer (b 25 Oct 1936) m Donald E. Sleet

CF43594111   Gregory Sleet

CF43594112   David Sleet

CF43594113   Brian Sleet

CF4359412   Donna Mae Royer (b 19 Oct 1938, Lewisburg PA) m Paul Robert Zirkel

CF43594121   Paul Eric Zirkel

CF43594122   Charles Robert Zirkel

CF43594123   Chad Detrick Zirkel

CF4359413   Harry George Royer (b 25 Sep 1940, Lewisburg PA). Unm. Clergyman.

CF43595   William Henry Brungard (28 May 1886, Centre Co PA-13 Jan 1956, Mifflinburg PA) m 12 Dec 1906, Mifflinburg PA, Dora Catherine Bingaman (22 Mar 1885, Union Co PA-29 Jul 1974, Lewisburg PA). Bur Mifflinburg PA. He, Mifflinburg Body Works; she, clothing factory, Mifflinburg PA.

CF435951   Clair Bingaman Brungard (18 Oct 1907, Union Co PA-Dansville NY) m 8 Jun 1933, Washington DC, Josephine Corine Strickler (17 Jun 1914, Union Co PA-1994). Commonwealth employee; res Mifflinburg PA.

CF4359511   Joseph Dean Brungard (b 12 Nov 1935, Mifflinburg PA) m 1) Catherine Benner, div; m 2) 9 Nov 1963, Canaseraga NY, Amanda Ellis (b 3 Nov 1941, Albany NY), div; m 3)   . He, AB, Lycoming (PA) Col; MA, U VI.

CF43595111   Scott Brungard (d.y.)

CF43595112   Joseph Dean Brungard, Jr. (b 4 Nov 1964, Hornell NY)

CF43595113   Megan Denae Brungard (b 28 Jul 1971, Albemarle VA)

CF4359512   Michael Clair Brungard (b 11 Jun 1945, Lewisburg PA) m Irma Hoffman (b 30 Jun 1947)

CF43595121   Evert Clair Brungard (b 27 Jun 1973, Rochester NY)

CF43595122   Erik Edwin Brungard (b 20 May 1977, Rochester NY)

CF435952   Oren Bingaman Brungard (4 Jun 1910, Mifflinburg PA-14 Feb 1985, Wilkes-Barre PA) m 24 Nov 1930, Baltimore MD, Violet Katherine Miller (see CF511141)(29 Jun 1902, Upper Augusta Tp, Northumberland Co PA-24 Feb 1995, Hummels Wharf PA).

*CF4359521   William Addison Brungard (b 11 Dec 1930, Sunbury PA) m 28 Dec 1948, Point Tp, Northumberland Co PA, Betty Jane Bird (b 30 Jun 1929, Williamsport PA). He, jet engine parts factory. She, AD, Susquehanna U, 1985; teacher, genealogist.

CF43595211   Steven Roger Brungard (b 6 Oct 1949, Phoenixville PA) m 18 Jun 1971, Danville PA, Connie Elizabeth Reibsome, div; m 2) 4 Mar 1978, Snyder Co PA, Desiree Jean Scholl Kline, div. He, BS, PSU; taxi and delivery service, Enola PA.

CF435952111   Anthony Everett Brungard (b 21 Jan 1972, Danville PA)(adopted by Bickhart)

CF435952112   Darii Karenina Brungard (b 20 Apr 1978, Lewisburg PA)

CF43595212   Karen Ruth Brungard (b 2 Nov 1951, Sunbury PA) m 24 May 1980, Northumberland PA, Norbert F. Toussaint, Jr. (b 20 May 1949). She, BS, Mansfield S Col; MD, U PA; fellowship, Mayo Clinic; internal medicine physician. He, BS, Notre Dame U; MD, St. Louis U; fellowship, Mayo Clinic; ophthamalogist. Res Madison WI.

CF435952121   Brian William Toussaint (b 4 Mar 1983, Madison WI)

CF43595213   Nevin Randall Brungard (b 21 Mar 1955, Sunbury PA) m 1976,Northumberland PA, Tracey Wojchehoski, div; m 2) 20 Jun 1981, Point Tp, Northumberland Co PA, Pamela Sue Botticher (b 28 Sep 1962). Bowling lanes proprietor, Sunbury PA; res Northumberland PA.

CF435952131   Nichole Erin Brungard (b 9 Feb 1977, Lewisburg PA) m 10 Jun 1995, Sunbury PA, Garry Max Romig, Jr.

CF435952132   Jamie Sue Brungard (b 4 Dec 1984, Lewisburg PA)

CF4359522   Oren Bingaman Brungart, Jr. (b 28 Apr 1933, Sunbury PA) m 18 Oct 1958, West Reading PA, Marie Boulanger (b 19 Oct 1936, Yugoslavia). Res Wyomissing Hills PA.

CF43595221   Thomas Michael Brungart (b 26 Nov 1959, West Reading PA) m 15 Aug 1992, College Park MD, Bridget Urbany. BS, Bloomsburg S Col, 1983.

CF435952211   Brooke Lee Brungart (b 13 Jun 1993, MD)

CF43595222   Julie Marie Brungart (b 29 Aug 1962, West Reading PA) m 1) 27 Oct 1984, Reading PA, Anthony Miller, div; m 2) 9 Oct 1993, Newburg MD, Colin Edward Rooney

CF435952221   Colin Edward Rooney, Jr. (b 6 Aug 1995, White Plains MD)

CF43595223   Amy Lynn Brungart (b 27 Mar 1970, West Reading PA) m 31 Oct 1992, Sinking Springs PA, Christopher Dean Ott

CF4359523   Jacqueline Suzanne Brungart (1 Jan 1936, Sunbury PA-22 Jun 1967, Danville PA) m Apr 1955, Sunbury PA, Max Lewis Leitzel, Jr. (b 11 Jan 1934, Hummels Wharf PA). Crane operator near Selinsgrove PA.

CF43595231   Susan Beth Leitzel (b 6 Mar 1955, Sunbury PA) m 24 Aug 1979, Robert Lauver. Medical supply business, CP02. Res Selinsgrove PA. No chn.

CF43595232   Cathy Jo Leitzel (b 30 Jun 1959, Sunbury PA) m 17 Aug 1985, Selinsgrove PA, Benjamin Joe Keiser. She, Lock Haven S Col; teacher and coach, Selinsgrove PA.

CF435952321   Ryan Benjamin Keiser (b 24 Jun 1991, Lewisburg PA)

CF435952322   Justin Max Keiser (b 11 Jan 1993, Sunbury PA)

CF43595233   Janette Louise Leitzel (b 20 May 1963, Sunbury PA) m Michael Scott Krebs (b 11 Oct 1962, Lewisburg PA). She, dental asst; he, USA; contraction. Res Bloomsburg PA.

CF435952331   Nathaniel Charles Krebs (b 9 Jul 1992, Bloomsburg PA)

CF4359524   Sonja Roxanna Brungart (b 19 Nov 1937, Sunbury PA) m 24 Sep 1960, Hummels Wharf PA, James Hassinger (b 9 Feb 1938), div 1974. She, beautician, then secretary, Milton PA

CF43595241   Craig Allen Brungard (10 Oct 1957, Mechanicsburg PA) (Adopted by great uncle Lloyd L. Brungard, CF435954) m 26 Apr 1980, Mechanicsburg PA, Debra Ann Steele (b 2 Nov 1957, Allentown PA), div. IBM employee, Mechanicsburg PA.

CF435952411   Angela Marie Brungard (b 19 Mar 1983, Carlisle PA)

CF43595242   Lisa Jean Hassinger (b 31 Aug 1963, Danville PA). Unm. LPN, Danville PA.

CF43595243   Eric James Hassinger (b 19 Jul 1970, Danville PA). Unm.

CF4359525   Vera Catherine Brungart (17 Aug 1941, Sunbury PA-24 Jan 1959, Sunbury PA). Bur Sunbury PA.

CF435953   Samuel Brungard (15 Nov 1913, Mifflinburg PA) m 1) 11 Mar 1938, Gene Meckley (b 1912-1963); m 2) 25 Jul 1964, Baltimore MD, Katie Holiday Barnes (b 19 Dec 1930, Norfolk VA)

CF4359531   Yvonne Marie Brungard (b 23 Jul 1966, Baltimore MD)

CF435954   Lloyd Klose Brungard (6 May 1915, Mifflinburg PA-26 Sep 1989, Mechanicsburg PA) m Frances Elizabeth Smith (29 Jun 1916, Mifflinburg PA-21 Jan 1991, Mechanicsburg PA). Bur Mechanicsburg PA. (Adopted Craig Brungard, CF43595241)

CF43596   Velira May Brungart (b 6 Oct 1888) m 19 May 1907, Norman Duck (3 Jun 1883, Millheim PA-23 Nov 1958, Beaver Springs PA). Bur Mifflinburg PA.

CF435961   Beatrice Eleanor Duck (b 1 Aug 1911, Centre Mills PA) m 2 Jul 1943, Donald Goodwin

CF4359611   Donald Bruce Goodwin (b 28 Oct 1944)

CF4359612   David Cary Goodwin (b 23 Sep 1946)

CF435962   Winifred Anabel Duck (26 Jul 1917-29 Jun 1918)

CF435963   Hazel Vila Duck (b 24 Oct 1920) m 11 Nov 1943, Paules J. Gibson

CF4359631   Jeanne Marie Gibson (b 27 Aug 1946)

CF4359632   Pamela Ann Gibson (b 31 Jul 1951)

CF43597   Rama Blanche Brungart (1 Nov 1892-1 Jan 1893)

CF43598 Blakely   Jodia Onita Brungart (b 2 Feb 1895) m 1) Charles Aaron Miller; m 2) 19 Jul 1925, George

CF435981   Donald Miller (b 17 Dec 1912) m Mirian Corman

CF4359811   Richard Neil Miller (b 6 Jul 1932)

CF4359812   Kathleen Miller

CF4359813   Barry Miller

CF435A   Emma Brungart (d 5 Nov 1933) m Levi Frazier

CF435A1   Clyde Frazier (d 18 Dec 1926) m Caroline Walker

CF435A2   Matilda Frazier m James Bridgens

CF435A21   Edward Bridgens m Grace Killinger

CF435A211   Mildred Bridgens

CF435A212   Edward Bridgens

CF435A213   Shirley Marian Bridgens (b 15 Dec 1926)

CF435A214   Bridgens (b 18 Aug 1931)

CF435A22   Frazier Bridgens m Sarah Frye

CF435A221   Bettie Louise Bridgens

CF435A222   Clara Lauvan Bridgens (b 6 Oct 1927)

CF435A23   Trenna Bridgens m Bruce Bowman

CF435A231   Maxine Hope Bowman

CF435A24   Harry Bridgens

CF435A25   Cora Bridgens

CF435A26   Sidney Bridgens

CF435A3   William Frazier m Effie J. Stuzman

CF435A4   Cora Frazier m Irvin Harry. Mill Hall PA.

CF435A41   Donald Harry

CF435A5   Sidney Frazier m Bertha I. Brown. Mill Hall PA.

CF435A51   Clyde W. Frazier (b 20 Jun 1930)

CF435B   Alice Brungart (b 25 May 1866) m Calvin J. Crouse (10 Jun 1860-17 Dec 1927). Bur
Rebersburg PA.

CF436   Daniel Brungart (son of George and Salome (Kehl) Brungart)(4 Jul 1823-8 Jul 1897) m
17 May 1846, Phoebe Ann Royer (19 Feb 1825-16 Oct 1920)

CF4361   Elmira Elizabeth Brungart (6 Feb 1847-28 Dec 1850)

CF4362   Jasper Royer Brungart (17 Jun 1851-14 Dec 1936) m 3 Oct 1876, Mary Elizabeth Long
(28 Jun 1850-12 May 1914)

CF437   Sarah Brungart (daughter of George and Salome (Kehl) Brungart)(22 Apr 1825, Brush
Valley, Centre Co PA-1 Sep 1866) m 28 Feb 1843, Samuel Frank (25 Apr 1821-9 Jan 1906). Assoc judge,
Centre Co PA.

CF4371   Pauline Frank (22 Mar 1868-29 Sep 1923) m Reuben D. Bierly (3 Feb 1844-8 Jul 1912)

CF43711   Salome (Sallie) Jane Bierly (27 Sep 1869-29 Sep 1916) m Thomas Aaron Auman (30 Dec
1871, Bald Eagle Valley PA-26 Aug 1940). Bur. Rebersburg PA. He, teacher, barber, carpenter.

CF437111   Miriam Eulalia Auman (6 Apr 1893, Rebersburg PA-23 Mar 1986, Rebersburg PA) m 14
Aug 1914, Rebersburg PA, Harry Franklin Confer (30 Jun 1890, Haines Tp, Centre Co PA-26 Nov 1973,
Rebersburg PA). Auto sales and garage.

CF4371111   Bernard Auman Confer (27 Aug 1914, Rebersburg PA-17 Sep 1988) m 11 Oct 1947, New
York City NY, Hallie Rose Baker (b 14 Apr 1921, Youngwood PA). He, Lutheran World Relief; she, secretary.

CF43711111   David Franklin Confer (b 17 Jul 1948, New York City NY) m. 30 Apr 1977, Wayne NJ,
Patricia Anne Hutson (b 23 Oct 1957). He, Lutheran clergyman; she, nurse.

Joseph Samuel Confer (b 7 Dec 1972)(Adopted)

CF437111111   Alexis Nicole Confer (b 17 Jul 1982)

CF437111112   Nickolas Hutson Confer (b 3 Oct 1987)

CF43711112   Ruth Anne Confer (b 26 Sep 1949, Teaneck NJ). Unm.

CF43711113   Joyce Elaine Confer (b 6 Aug 1951, Teaneck NJ) m 26 May 1979, New York City NY, Samuel Joseph Liberto, Jr. (b 29 Aug 1952). Both, teachers.

CF437111131   Samuel Joseph Liberto III (b 5 Aug 1980)

CF437111132   Hallie Rose Liberto (b 24 Mar 1982)

CF437111133   Spencer Bernard Liberto (b 19 Jun 1993)

CF43711114   Miriam Lynn Confer (b 21 Sep 1957, Teaneck NJ). Unm. Dietician.

CF4371112   Doyle Berten Confer (b 12 Jan 1916, Rebersburg PA) m 18 Feb 1943, Amarillo TX, Isabel Elinor Musser (b 12 Mar 1921, Spring Mills PA). He, mechanic; she, banking.

CF43711121   Sharilou Confer (b 30 Nov 1946, Bellefonte PA) m 5 Feb 1972, Millheim PA, David Lawrence Grim (b 11 May 1947, New Cumberland PA). Both, teachers. No chn.

CF43711122   Dana Joel Confer (b 2 Feb 1956, Bellefonte PA) m 31 Aug 1991, Rebersburg PA, Tanya Dinges (b 22 Jul 1964, State College PA). He, landscaping; she, physical therapist.

CF437111221   Cole Jarrett Confer (b 1 May 1995, State College PA)

CF4371113   Helen Charlotte Confer (b 17 Oct 1917, Rebersburg PA) m 9 Sep 1949, Millheim PA, Kenneth LeRoy Royer (30 Apr 1918, Bellefonte PA-20 Dec 1994). Bur Madisonburg PA. She, beautician; he, USA Air Corps, US Natl Guard.

CF43711131   Deborah Miriam Royer (b 19 Oct 1950, Bellefonte PA) m 27 Sep 1975, Madisonburg PA, Ronald Allen Strouse (b 3 Jan 1949, Bellefonte PA). She, secretary; he, electronics.

CF437111311   Andrew Bryan Strouse (b 11 May 1981, State College PA)

CF437111312   Amber Helen Strouse (b 28 Sep 1984, State College PA)

CF437111313   Alidia Jane Strouse (b 22 Jul 1992, State College PA)

CF43711132   LeRoy Allen Burns Royer (b 7 May 1952, Bellefonte PA) m 6 Jan 1979, Palmyra PA, Sharon Louise Boyer, div. Corporate financier.

CF437111321   Jessica Nicole Royer (b 26 Nov 1982, Lebanon PA)

CF437111322   Nathan Allen Royer (b 6 May 1986, Lebanon PA)

CF43711133   Hope Pearle Royer (b 1 Jun 1955, Bellefonte PA) m 12 Nov 1977, Madisonburg PA, William Thomas Miller (b 28 Oct 1954). She, sales; he, electrician.

CF437111331   Joshua William Miller (b 28 Apr 1980, State College PA)

CF437111332   Jeb Kenneth Miller (4 Aug 1981, State College PA)

CF437111333   Cody Haynes Miller (20 Feb 1990, State College PA)

CF4371114   Laird Harold Confer (20 Mar 1923, Madisonburg PA - 27 Apr 1923, at _____). Bur. _____

CF437112   Russell Frank Auman (21 Apr 1899, Rebersburg PA-27 Apr 1972) m 1) Lillian B. Rennick (21 Feb 1898, Butler PA-24 Apr 1948); m 2) Helen Rennick. He, Lutheran clergyman.

CF4371121   Naomi Pauline Auman (26 Jul 1928, Yeagertown PA) m John Hutko. Medical lab technician.

CF43711211   Jane Elizabeth Hutko (b 12 Feb 1961, Akron OH)

CF43711212   John Russell Hutko (b 12 Jan 1966, Akron OH)

CF4371122   Adah Jane Auman (18 Jun 1931, Yeagertown PA-d) m 18 Feb 1951, Wesley W. Walker

CF43711221   Wesley Walker, Jr. (b 19 Feb 1957)

CF43711222   Russell Walker (b 18 Apr 1958)

CF43711223   Jim Walker (b 4 Jul 1959)

CF437113   Harold Bierly Auman (20 Aug 1902, Rebersburg PA-1988) m 1) 28 Dec 1919, Scarsdale NY, Martha Irene Foote (6 May 1905-23 Mar 1949, Millheim PA); m 2) 5 Sep 1953, Lyma Jandrew (d 1987). Bur Millheim PA. He, teacher and railway express. No chn.

CF43712   Willis F. Bierly (31 Aug 1873-5 Dec 1958) m Lottie Weber (13 Mar 1880-19 Apr 1964). Bur Rebersburg PA.

CF437121   Robert W. Bierly (11 Dec 1896, Rebersburg PA-24 Aug 1965) m 30 Jan 1919, Madaline Cabel (b 3 Jan 1903, Millheim PA). Res Rebersburg PA.

CF4371211   Clarence Willis Bierly (b 9 Aug 1919, Rebersburg PA) m Lois Jeannette Neff (b 9 Jul 1920, Howard PA). Rebersburg PA.

CF43712111   Simone Adette Bierly (b 26 Sep 1938, Rebersburg PA) m Emory Florey

CF437121111   Emory Florey, Jr.

CF43712112   Karen Melanie Bierly (b 26 Feb 1942, Rebersburg PA) m Allen Drew Hammer (b 20 Sep 1941, Millheim PA)(see CS1513332)

CF43712113   Clarissa Willow Bierly (b 30 Jan 1945, Rebersburg PA) m Emery Floray

CF437121131   Jody Bierly

CF43712114   Candace Mariette Bierly (b 19 Apr 1946, Rebersburg PA) m Edward Hanson

CF437121141   Bruce Johnson

CF43712115   Jonathan Michael Bierly (b 16 Jun 1947, Rebersburg PA) m Bonnie Weaver

CF437121151   Anne Bierly

CF43712116   Timothy Richard Bierly (b 13 Aug 1948, Rebersburg PA) m Sandra Walker

CF437121161   Duane Bierly

CF437121162   Denise Bierly

CF43712117   Peter Kipling Bierly (b 6 Dec 1949, Rebersburg PA) m Loretta Stitzer

CF437121171   Anthony Bierly

CF43712118   Mark Stephen Bierly (b 4 Jul 1951, Rebersburg PA) m 27 Jan 1973, Lonnie Harter

CF437121181   Tiffany Dawn Bierly (b 2 Jan 1974)

CF43712119   David Derek Bierly (b 27 Jul 1952, Rebersburg PA)

CF4371211A   Jon Russell Bierly (b 8 Apr 1955, Rebersburg PA)

CF4371212   Margaret Ruth Bierly (b 6 Jun 1921, Rebersburg PA) m Franklin Beaver (b 20 Apr 1918). Lemont PA.

CF43712121   Thomas E. Beaver (b 30 Jun 1940)

CF43712122   Barbara Ann Beaver (b 13 Dec 1945)

CF4371213   Donald Eugene Bierly (b 1 Mar 1923) m. Maudella Rockey (b 27 Aug 1920, Bellefonte PA). Rebersburg PA.

CF43712131   Barry Lynn Bierly (b 26 Apr 1947, Bellefonte PA)

CF43712132   Susan Kay Bierly (b 28 Sep 1953, Bellefonte PA) m 16 Jul 1972, Jack De Sousa

CF43712133   Donald Eugene Bierly, Jr. (b 19 Jun 1957, Bellefonte PA)

CF4371214   Anabel May Bierly (30 May 1925-16 Jan 1926). Bur Rebersburg PA.

CF4371215   Catherine Irene Bierly (b 18 Mar 1927, Rebersburg PA) m Philip Meyer (b 27 Nov 1923, Millheim PA). Rebersburg PA.

CF43712151   Philip Duane Meyer (b 24 Jan 1947, Bellefonte PA)

CF4371216   Hazel Bierly (b 3 Apr 1929, Rebersburg PA) m Robert Zerby (b 24 Apr 1928). Spring Mills PA.

CF43712161   Linda Zerby (b 2 Aug 1948, Bellefonte PA)

CF43712162   Robert Zerby (b 5 Nov 1958, Bellefonte PA)

CF4371217   Robert Bierly, Jr. (b 14 Jul 1931, Rebersburg PA) m Nancy Eichman (b 13 Oct 1935, Middleburg PA). Rebersburg PA.

CF43712171   Robert Mark Bierly (b 8 Aug 1958, Rebersburg PA)

CF4371218   Harold Bierly (b 12 Jan 1934, Rebersburg PA) m Iris DeGarmo (b 28 Apr 1935, Rebersburg PA). Rebersburg PA.

CF43712181   James Devon Bierly (b 14 Nov 1954, Rebersburg PA)

CF43712182   Steven Kirk Bierly (b 25 Mar 1957, Rebersburg PA)

CF43712183   Tina Louise Bierly (b 15 Aug 1959, Rebersburg PA)

CF4371219   Susan Bierly (b 8 Sep 1935, Rebersburg PA) m Glenn Benner (b 30 Sep 1929, Madisonburg PA). Rebersburg PA.

CF43712191   Sharon Lynette Benner (b 20 Feb 1955, Rebersburg PA)

CF43712192   Glenn William Benner (b 7 Feb 1957, Rebersburg PA)

CF437121A   Donna Bierly (b 7 Sep 1937, Rebersburg PA) m Harold Bowersox (b 25 Jun 1938, Smullton PA). Spring Mills PA.

CF437121B   Sandra Bierly (b 23 Jul 1939, Rebersburg PA) m Patrick McGovern (b 4 Jan 1940). Rebersburg PA.

CF437121B1   Tracey McGovern (b 9 Jul 1960, Bellefonte PA) m 21 Jun 1981, Rebersburg PA, Kevin Rimmey (b 13 Aug 1960, NJ). RN, Altoona Hospital Sch of Nursing. Washington Courthouse OH.

CF437121B11   Jason Daniel Rimmey (b 16 Sep 1984, Baltimore MD)

CF437121B12   Jennifer Diane Rimmey (b 22 Aug 1988, State College PA)

CF437121B13   Andrew Patrick Rimmey (b 21 Dec 1990, State College PA)

CF437121B2   Stephanie McGovern (b 20 Apr 1964, Bellefonte PA) m 11 Jul 1986, Rebersburg PA, Jonathan Taylor (b 8 Jun 1964, Bellefonte PA). AD, PSU. Millheim PA.

CF437121B21   Madeline Lee Taylor (b 12 Apr 1990, State College PA)

CF437121B22   Elena Kathryn Taylor (b 5 Feb 1993, State College PA)

CF437121B3   Patricia McGovern (b 30 Oct 1965, Bellefonte PA) m 27 Oct 1990, Rebersburg PA, Thomas McKenna (b 1 Nov 1964, Kane PA). Wylie TX.

CF437121B31   James Michael McKenna (28 May 1993, Garland TX)

CF437121C   Samuel Bierly (b 8 Dec 1942, Rebersburg PA)

CF437121D   Nancy Bierly (b 12 Jan 1944, Rebersburg PA) m Charles Foust (b 24 Sep 1941, Centre Hall PA). Centre Hall PA.

CF437121D   Timothy Scott Foust (b 15 Sep 1959, Bellefonte PA)

CF437121E   Janie Bierly (b 9 Jan 1948, Rebersburg PA)

CF437122   Norman R. Bierly (4 Dec 1899, Rebersburg PA-11 Jul 1963) m Marie Leister (b 27 Sep 1903, Rebersburg PA). Millheim PA.

CF4371221   Evelyn Irene Bierly (b 16 Oct 1921, Rebersburg PA) m Henry Kurtz Weiser (b 4 Jul 1917, Altoona PA). Major, USAF Reserves, Rockville MD.

CF43712211   Gregory Kurtz Weiser (b 17 May 1949, Fayetteville NC)

CF4371222   Lucille Lorraine Bierly (b 27 Nov 1925, Millheim PA) m Carl Bohn (b 29 Jul 1922, Millheim PA). Enola PA.

CF43712221   Steven Carl Bohn (b 11 Feb 1958, Enola PA)

CF4371223   Dean Jacob Bierly (15 Aug 1928, Rebersburg PA-18 Aug 1928, Rebersburg PA). Bur Rebersburg PA.

CF437123   Hilda Pauline Bierly (b 23 Sep 1903) m John Ocker (b 20 Apr 1901)

CF4371231   Jeanne Catherine Ocker (b 19 Sep 1921)

CF4371232   Julia Marie Ocker (b 3 Oct 1926)

CF437124   Palmer C. Bierly (3 Jul 1906, Rebersburg PA-20 Apr 1992, Bellefonte PA) m 1) Neta Smull; m 2) 19 Jul 1942, Kathleen R. Burd. Bur Rebersburg PA. He, US Postmaster, Rebersburg PA; office equipment store, automobile dealer, auto auction, bus line.

CF4371241   William Charles Bierly (18 Sep 1929, Rebersburg PA-25 Feb 1948). Bur Rebersburg PA. Unm.

CF4371242   David Bierly (10 Jul 1934, Rebersburg PA-10 Jul 1934, Rebersburg PA).

CF4371243   Darryl Wayne Bierly (b 5 Apr 1939, Rebersburg PA)

CF4371244   Roger A. Bierly (b Jun 1943, Rebersburg PA). Register of wills, Centre Co PA.

CF4371245   Correen Rebecca Bierly (b 22 Jun 1945, Rebersburg PA)

CF4371246   Palmer Keith Bierly, Jr. (b 22 Mar 1949). Commissioner, Centre Co PA.

CF43713   Charles C. Bierly (3 Jul 1875-12 May 1934) m 28 Jan 1897, Ada Weber (b 24 Apr 1877)

CF437131   Doretha Bierly (17 May 1907 - 15 Sep 1934). Unmarr?

CF43714   Melvin Clyde Bierly (7 May 1878, Rebersburg PA-10 Jun 1882, Rebersburg PA). Bur Rebersburg PA.

CF43715   Curtis Melancthon Bierly (22 Apr 1880, Smullton PA-26 Sep 1964, Hershey PA) m 1907, Mayme Wolfe (24 Mar 1893, Smullton PA-7 Sep 1958, Rebersburg PA).

CF437151   Stanley Curtis Bierly (4 Oct 1908, Dent's Run, Elk Co PA-5 May 1992, Centre Hall PA) m 13 Jun 1936, Phyllis W. Wagner (b 26 Nov 1913, Spring Mills PA). AB, PSU; plumbing firm, Millheim PA.

CF4371511   Stanley Curtis Bierly (b 6 Dec 1941, Millheim PA) m

CF43715111   Alexander Patrick Bierly m 5 Sep 1992, State College PA, Candace Anne Shaffer

CF43715112   Stanley Curtis Bierly III

CF4371512   Herbert Eugene Bierly (b 21 Apr 1945, Millheim PA)

CF437152   Paul W. Bierly (15 Dec 1911, Dent's Run, Elk Co PA-10 Nov 1991, State College PA) m 2 Jan 1943, Evalyn Gingrich (b 7 Jul 1920, Altoona PA). State College PA.

CF4371521   Douglas P. Bierly (b 9 Mar 1945)

CF4371522   Jeffrey D. Bierly (b 12 Feb 1950)

CF4371523   Richard A. Bierly (b 21 Aug 1955)

CF437153   Eugene Bierly. Manasquan NJ.

CF437154   Woodrow W. Bierly (b 8 Dec 1917, Rebersburg PA) m Phillis Deal (b 26 Oct 1925, Williamsport PA)

CF4371541   Harold W. Bierly (b 2 Dec 1954)

CF4371542   Cynthia D. Bierly (b 6 Dec 1956, State College PA)

CF437155   Edith I. Bierly (b 8 Dec 1917, Rebersburg PA) m May 1940, Charles Franklin Kreamer (b 7 Apr 1915, Penn Tp, Centre Co PA)

CF4371551   Mary Ann Kreamer (27 Nov 1940, Rebersburg PA) m 1) Sep 1961, James E.L. Van Kirk (1940-1971); m 2) May 1976, Paul Snyder. Newmanstown PA.

CF43715511   David J. Van Kirk (b 15 Dec 1962)

CF4371552   Jeff Franklin Kreamer (b 13 Nov 1943, Harrisburg PA) m 14 May 1978, Mt. Aetna PA,
Rhonda Fisher

CF4371553   Jane Adelle Kreamer (b 5 May 1948, Harrisburg PA) m 6 Sep 1969, Jonestown PA,
Charles Bomberger (1940-1991).

CF43715531   Andrew Charles Bomberger (b 30 Jul 1977, Annville PA)

CF43715532   Matthew James Bomberger (b 15 Jan 1979, Annville PA)

CF43715533   Aaron Nathanael Bomberger (b 26 Feb 1981, Annville PA)

CF4371554   Barbara Ellen Kreamer (b 30 Oct 1953, Harrisburg PA)

CF437156   Ruth Bierly (b 14 Nov 1921, Rebersburg PA) m 22 Dec 1940, S. John Gray (b 24 Jun 1916, Reedsville PA). Bellefonte PA.

CF4371561   Susan Jane Gray (b 28 Jun 1942, Bellefonte PA)

CF4371562   Samuel Eugene Gray (b 23 Feb 1945, Bellefonte PA)

CF4371563   Rachel Mae Gray (b 11 May 1946, Bellefonte PA)

CF4371564   Clara Marie Gray (b 8 Dec 1948, Bellefonte PA)

CF4371565   Charles Oscar Gray (b 17 Jul 1953, Bellefonte PA)

CF4371566   John Curtis Gray (b 7 Jul 1955, Bellefonte PA)

CF4371567   Edna Mary Gray (b 22 Sep 1958, Bellefonte PA)

CF437157   Bruce Allen Bierly (27 Sep 1925-8 Jun 1927). Bur Rebersburg PA.

CF43716   Samuel A. Bierly (12 May 1883, Rebersburg PA-19 Jan 1958) m. Lydia Pearl Shaffer (20
Jul 1890-1950)

CF437161   Joanna Bierly (1908-1909)

CF437162   Elizabeth Bierly (17 Jan 1912, Rebersburg PA-2 Sep 1992, State College PA) m 6 Sep 1933, Eugene Lee (15 Mar 1908, Linden Hall PA-21 Mar 1989)

CF4371621   Donald Eugene Lee (b 4 Apr 1935, Bellefonte PA)

CF4371622   David B. Lee (b 15 Jun 1937, Bellefonte PA)

CF4371623   Richard James Lee (b 25 Nov 1939, Bellefonte PA)

CF437163   Madaline Ruth Bierly (1915-1915)

CF437164   Ruth Madaline Bierly (1915-1915)

CF437165   Loris Louise Bierly (b 10 Apr 1925, Rebersburg PA) m Robert Korman (b 19 Apr 1923, Rebersburg PA)

CF43717   Ray Spurgeon Bierly (3 Feb 1893, Rebersburg PA-5 Apr 1919). Bur Rebersburg PA.

CF4372   James Polk Frank (4 Feb 1849, Rebersburg PA-3 Oct 1905, New Castle PA) m Margaret Spangler (18 Jun 1848, Laurelton PA-1 Jan 1926, Rebersburg PA). Bur Rebersburg PA. Farmer.

CF43721   Samuel S. Frank (14 Dec 1871, Centre Co PA-22 Jul 1913, Rebersburg PA) m 6 Dec 1891, Gertrude Kreamer (29 Jul 1872, Rebersburg PA-27 Dec 1948, Loganton PA). Bur Centre Co PA. Railroad clerk.

CF437211   Clarence Kreamer Frank (28 Mar 1892, Rebersburg PA-22 Jul 1916, Harrisburg PA) m 20 Mar 1914, Grace Ida Bailets (6 Oct 1892, Maytown PA-1 May 1960, Franklintown PA). Bur Rebersburg PA. Draftsman, Bell Telephone.

CF4372111   James Samuel Frank (b 30 Mar 1916, Maytown PA) m 5 Feb 1941, Loganton PA, Helen June Shilling (b 26 May 1922, Clintondale PA). He, rural mail carrier, she, nurse, both retired, Loganton PA.

CF43721111   Joan Elaine Frank (b 20 Sep 1941, Loganton PA) m 27 Oct 1962, Jerry Pershing Lamey (b 10 Apr 1942, Lock Haven PA). She, librarian, Mt. Juliet TN.

CF437211111   Brian Scott Lamey (b 13 Jan 1964, Lock Haven PA) m 13 Jan 1987, Lebanon TN, Teresa Youngblood (b 3 Oct 1966). He, police officer, Mt. Juliet TN.

CF4372111111   Jarrad Van Lamey (b 23 Oct 1990, Lebanon TN)

CF437211112   Chad Eric Lamey (b 16 May 1972, Lock Haven PA). Mt. Juliet TN.

*CF43721112   James David Frank (b 10 Mar 1954, Lock Haven PA) m 30 Apr 1977, Lock Haven PA, Nancy Lee Thomas (b 22 Jun 1955, Carlisle PA). Both BS, Lock Haven S Col; both, teachers; Harrisburg PA. He, member of The John Conrad Weiser Family Assn board of directors.

*CF437211121   Allison Elizabeth Frank (b 24 Jan 1985, Harrisburg PA)

CF437211122   Ashley Alyssa Frank (b 27 Feb 1988, Harrisburg PA)

CF43722   Charles Orvis Frank (17 Apr 1880, Rebersburg PA-19 Sep 1942, Rebersburg PA) m 23 Aug 1905, Rebecca Covert (27 Aug 1881, Selinsgrove PA-9 Oct 1962). Grad, Susquehanna U; Gettysburg Sem; Lutheran clergyman.

CF437221   Elizabeth Covert Frank (26 May 1906, Bloomsburg PA-22 Sep 1961, Wilkinsburg PA) m Alton B. Smeltzer (b 15 Oct 1906, Vandergrift PA). She, teacher.

CF4372211   Elizabeth Jean Smeltzer (b 18 Apr 1939, Pittsburgh PA) m 16 Jul 1960, Donald F. Stoneburner. PhD, Carnegie Inst of Tech, 1960.

*CF437222   Mary Catherine Frank (b 23 Jul 1908, Bloomsburg PA) m 25 Dec 1930, John Dyer Fernwalt (20 Apr 1908-12 Oct 1976). She, RN, Lankenau Hospital, Philadelphia PA; he, mgr, farmers' cooperative.

CF4372221   John Dyer Fernwalt, Jr. (b 28 Jul 1932, Mt. Holly NJ) m 8 Aug 1953, Mildred Clark. Dairy farmer, Medford NJ.

CF43722211   Jeffrey Dale Fernwalt, Jr. (15 Apr 1955-23 Sep 1991)

CF43722212   Brian Douglas Fernwalt (b 24 Jun 1956) m 24 Apr 1983, Marcia Bonwell

CF437222121   Tanya Jo Fernwalt (b 23 Jan 1985)

CF43722213   John David Fernwalt (b 10 Sep 1957) m 11 Sep 1982, Bonnie Brown, div

CF437222131   Bergen Fernwalt (b 19 Mar 1983)

CF43722214   Scott Clark Fernwalt (b 30 Jan 1963) m 11 Jun 1983, Sharon Crew

CF437222141   Shane Fernwalt (b 6 Jun 1991)

CF437222142   Lacey Fernwalt (b 9 Jan 1996)

*CF4372222   Joan Elizabeth Fernwalt (b 6 Apr 1935, Mt. Holly NJ) m 30 Jun 1956, Gordon Newell Lockhart. He, MD.

CF43722221   Elaine Louise Lockhart (b 10 Aug 1957, Camp Lejeune NC) m 19 Aug 1975, Scott Molnar. Mt. Holly NJ.

CF43722222   Nancy Elizabeth Lockhart (b 24 Apr 1960) m 2 Sep 1990, Christopher Ben

CF437222221   Leah Elizabeth Ben (b 14 Mar 1992, Mt. Holly NJ)

CF437222222   Grace Catherine Ben (b 14 May 1995, Mt. Holly NJ)

CF43722223   Charles Newell Lockhart (b 5 Nov 1964, Mt. Holly NJ)

*CF4372223   Bonnie Frank Fernwalt (b 2 Apr 1945, Mt. Holly NJ) m 10 Dec 1966, Mt. Holly NJ, Allan Julian Hill. Dairy farmer, Kennedyville MD.

CF43722231   David Allan Hill (b 11 Oct 1968, Chestertown MD) m 7 Nov 1992, Elizabeth Mary Shaw (b 22 Sep 1967)

CF43722232   Dianne Marie Hill (b 31 Oct 1969, Chestertown MD) m 2 Jun 1990, Steven Rolph Townshend (b 20 May 1969)

CF437222321   Jesse Allan Townshend (b 20 Apr 1995, Towson MD)

CF437223   James Newton Frank (b 4 Jun 1910, Huntington PA) m 1) 24 Jul 1935, Jean Vaughan (d May 1951); m 2) Oct 1953, Edith Yeager. Chaplain, WWII. Thiel (PA) Col; Lutheran Theol Sem, Philadelphia PA; Lutheran clergyman, New Brighton PA.

CF437224   Charles E. Frank (b 1 May 1914, Philipsburg PA) m 5 Apr 1939, Betty Jane Sipher. PSU; PhD, OSU; Cincinnati OH.

CF4372241   Diane Frank (b 9 Mar 1943, Wilmington DE)

CF4372242   Galen Frank (b 21 Jul 1947, Wilmington DE) m 24 May 1975, Cincinnati OH, Freddie Hurt. Teacher.

CF43722421   Nicholas Hurt (b 22 Nov 1983, Jackson WY)

CF43722422   Ashley Hurt (b 29 Jun 1987, Cincinnati OH)

CF4372243   Robin Frank (26 May 1955, Cincinnati OH) m 27 Sep 1980, Cincinnati OH, John Rupp. Geologist.

CF43722431   Jonathan Rupp (b 23 Mar 1982, Midland TX)

CF43722432   Stephen Rupp (b 18 Jul 1985, Bloomington IN)

CF4373   George S. Frank (22 Oct 1859-13 Apr 1940) m Malissa Miller (d 30 Oct 1939). MD, Jefferson Med Col, 1883; physician, Millheim PA.

CF4374   Luther B. Frank m Mary C. Wolfe

CF438   Margaret Brungart (15 Mar 1827-25 Apr 1849, Miles Tp PA) m 30 Nov 1848, John Hosterman (26 Dec 1826-28 Sep 1909)

CF437224 Charles Edward Frank

CF44   John Peter Kehl (son of John Jacob and Anna Catharine (Weiser) Kehl)(22 Dec 1789, near Sunbury PA-9 Dec 1873, Sugar Valley, Clinton Co PA) m Sarah Haun (9 Nov 1794-11 Apr 1872)

CF441   Catherine Kehl

CF442   Sallie Kehl

CF443   John C. Kehl (1834-22 Sep 1898) m Catherine Bailey

CF444   Jacob Kehl m Elizabeth Fehr

CF4441   William Aaron Kehl m Emma Coleman

CF44411   Arthur Kehl m Grace Becke

CF4442   Maggie Kehl m Cyrus Howe. Lena IL.

CF44421   Julia Howe m Harry Quinters

CF444211   Robert Quinters

CF444212   Marion Quinters

CF44422   Clayton Howe m Lizzie Fox

CF444221   Isabella Howe

CF44423   Irene Howe m   Rabie

CF444231   Ira Rabie

CF44424   Clarence Howe m

CF44425   Chester Howe m Louise Mart. Winslow IL.

CF4443   Jasper Kehl m Mary Alice Stover-Meyers-Emery

CF445   George Kehl (1 May 1821-2 Feb 1904) m Sarah Herring (17 Oct 1829-1 Mar 1914)

CF4451   Jeremiah Kehl (1862-21 May 1869)

CF4452   Emma Kehl m John Warntz (1844-19 Sep 1927)

CF44521   Maude Myrtle Warntz (b 1882, Sunbury PA)

CF44522   Iva Gay Warntz (b 3 Sep 1892) m Harry Specht. Sunbury PA.

CF44523   Raymond Joy Warntz (b 16 Jun 1897)

CF44524   Harry Walter Warntz (b 23 Oct 1899)

CF446   Peter Kehl (15 Feb 1828-5 Jun 1898) m Ellen Beck (9 Jun 1842-31 Oct 1908)

CF4461   Mary Jane Kehl (20 Jul 1861-21 Jun 1904) m Charles Conrad

CF44611   Howard Leslie Conrad m Annie Heimadinger

CF446111   George Conrad

CF446112   Glenn Conrad

CF44612   Grant Conrad

CF44613   Earl Conrad

CF44614   Morris Conrad

CF4462   Henry H. Kehl (b 3 Mar 1863) m 5 Feb 1885, Stephenson Co IL, Sophia Hoeffer (4 Dec 1863-8 May 1932). Grundy Centre IA.

CF44621   Earl J. Kehl (1887-1902)

CF44622   Edna A. Kehl (1887-1919) m H.M. Trego

CF446221   Sadie Trego m Ray Palmer

CF4462211   Virginia Louise Palmer

CF446222   Dorothy Trego

CF44623   Lester A. Kehl m Alma Popp. Cedar Falls IA.

CF446231   Kenneth Kehl

CF446232   Howard Kehl

CF44624   Hazel A. Kehl m Arthur Gravenstine. Grundy Centre IA.

CF446241   Donald Gravenstine

CF446242   Lois Jeanne Gravenstine

CF44625   Charles Kehl (1902-1902)

CF4463   Rufus H. Kehl m Lou Lower. Nora IL.

CF44631   Iva Kehl m Harry Dreibilbis. Warren IL.

CF446311   Kenneth Dreibilbis

CF446312   Kathryn Dreibilbis

CF446313   Carole Mae Dreibilbis

CF446314   Robert Dreibilbis

CF44632   Jessie Kehl m Osborne Shaffer. Lenark IL.

CF446321   Ralph Shaffer

CF446322   Harry Shaffer

CF446323   Lester Shaffer

CF446324   Earl Shaffer

CF446325   Grace Shaffer

CF446326   Margaret Shaffer

CF44633   Miles Kehl m   . Elizabeth IL.

CF446331   Miles Kehl, Jr.

CF44634   Ruth Kehl m Roy Murry. Freeport IL.

CF44635   Russell Kehl

CF44636   Dorothy Kehl

CF44637   Helen Kehl

CF4464   Agnes Kehl m Charles Lower. Polo IL.

CF44641   Luther Lower m   . Brookville IL

CF446411   Maxine Lower

CF446412   Darlene Lower

CF44642   Gladys Lower m John Moser. Polo IL.

CF446421   Paul Moser

CF446422   Hazel Moser

CF4465   John Kehl m Anna Koertner. St. Cloud MN.

CF44651   Clayton Kehl m

CF446511   Clayton Kehl, Jr.

CF446512   Constance Kehl

CF446513   Beverley Kehl

CF44652   Agnes Kehl m M. Bean

CF446521   Clarence Bean

CF446522   Floyd Bean

CF446523   Robert Bean

CF44653   Evelyn Kehl m John Enger. Oakes ND.

CF446531   Norma Enger

CF446532   Jack Enger

CF4466   William Kehl m 1)   ; m 2)   . Chicago IL.

CF4467   Ada Kehl m 1) Pierce Betz; m 2) Thomas O. Musser. Maywood IL.

CF44671   Carmi Betz

CF44672   Denver Betz

CF44673   Emogene Musser m Ray C. Quandt

CF446731   Raymond C. Quandt, Jr.

CF447   Amelia Kehl m John Smull

CF4471   Sarah Smull m Charles Sullivan

CF44711   Jennie Sullivan m Frank Smith

CF44712   Myron Sullivan m Rose Thompson

CF447121   Philip Sullivan

CF4472   Miron P. Smull m 1) Ella Lusk; m 2) Tillie Sullivan. McConnell IL.

CF44721	Thomas Smull m Mabel Wells
CF447211	Homer Wells
CF44722	Mildred Smull m Rowe
CF4473 Larrow	Newton Smull m 1) Sadie Shippy; m 2)
CF4474	John G. Smull (1855-27 Dec 1858)
CF448 m Louise Strohecker (b 25 Jul 1839)	Samuel Kehl (8 Apr 1833-30 Apr 1898)
CF4481 m Catherine Rowe (13 Sep 1860-7 Dec 1912)	Daniel Kehl (3 Aug 1860-14 Jan 1913)
CF44811 Kleckner	Maude Kehl (b 7 Dec 1882) m John
CF448111	Ruth N. Kleckner (b 18 Aug 1900)
CF448112	Raymond Kleckner (b 20 Aug 1903)
CF44812 W.W. Bryant	Laura Mae Kehl (b 28 Sep 1881) m Dr.

Lawrence Stover (1833-1904) and
CF44A Susan Kehl (1835-1915)

CF44813	Anna Louise Kehl (b 13 Feb 1884)
CF44814	Mayme Ellen Kehl (b 28 Nov 1886) m George Douty
CF448141	Roy Lee Douty
CF448142	Harold Allen Douty
CF448143	Lena Gwendolyn Douty
CF448144	Helen Irene Douty
CF448145	Bernice Eliene Douty
CF449	Elizabeth Kehl m John Greninger
CF44A	Susan Kehl (8 Jul 1835-23 Feb 1915) m Lawrence Stover (1 Mar 1833-21 Mar 1904)
CF44A1 Livonia PA.	Adam Kehl Stover (1863-1945) m 24 Sep 1885, Jesse Freemont DeLong (1861-1948).
CF44A11 Livonia PA. Loganton PA.	Leslie Myron Stover (12 Aug 1886-1960) m 24 Jul 1908, Martha Snook (1886-1964). Bur
CF44A111	Julia Jesse Stover (6 Jan 1910-1976) m Charles De Haas (1893-1968). Teacher.
CF44A1111 Conflict. Machinist.	Charles De Haas (b 1935) m 1) Donna Yanarella, div; m 2) Mildred Leathers. Korean

CF44A11111   Patrick De Haas

CF44A11112   Rochelle De Haas

CF44A1112   Richard De Haas (b 1942) m Mary Louise McKissick (b 1942)

CF44A11121   Keith Allen De Haas (b 1961). Lab technician.

CF44A11122   William Charles De Haas (b 1968). Car salesman.

CF44A12   Herbert Elisha Stover (15 Jan 1888, Livonia PA-Feb 1963, Lock Haven PA) m 9 Jun 191 , Bellefonte PA, Elva Kathryn Tyler (1892, Lock Haven PA-1955, Williamsport PA). Bur Dunnstown PA. Teacher, author.

CF44A121   Anna Jane Stover (b 1918, Austin PA) m 9 Apr 193 , Towson MD, Edward Thomas McFate (1916, Ridley Park PA-1971, Chicago IL). Teacher.

CF44A1211   Kathryn Virginia McFate (b 1940, Ridley Park PA) m 7 Sep 1957, Mill Hall PA, Raymond L. Harmon (b 16 Feb 193 , White Pine PA), div 1990. Residential aide, Tylersville PA.

CF44A12111   Wendy Jo Harmon (b 1958, Williamsport PA) m 5 Jul 1980, Jeffrey Breon (b 1958, Williamsport PA). Homemaker, Tylersville PA.

CF44A121111   Jordon Parse Breon (b 1982, State College PA)

CF44A121112   Gary Breon (b 1983, State College PA)

CF44A121113   Ryan Breon (b 1984, State College PA)

CF44A12112   Molly Lee Harmon (_____ 1960, Williamsport PA) m 1) 1978, Tylersville PA, Michael Embick (b 1958, Tylersville PA), div; m 2) Donley Gum

CF44A121121   Lauren Kay Embick (1979, Jersey Shore PA-1984, Williamsport PA). Bur Sugar Valley PA.

CF44A121122   Anthony Gun (b 1993, Morgantown WV)

CF44A12113   Patrick Daniel Harmon (b 13 Nov 1962, Gary IN) m 14 Feb 1988, Tylersville PA, Vicky Mark (b 4 Oct 1968, Williamsport PA). Penn DOT employee. Res Tylersville PA.

CF44A121131   Danielle Harmon (b 1988, Williamsport PA)

CF44A121132   Sarah Ann Harmon (b 1990, Williamsport PA)

CF44A1212   Barbara Ann McFate (b 1945, Buffalo NY) m 1) 1966, Gary IN, James Demetrakis (b Chios Greece), div; m 2) 1973, Richmond VA, Larry Evans, div. Paralegal, union representative, AL.

CF44A12121   James Demetrakis (b 1971, Gary IN) m 1995, NC, Christy Sellers (b 1970, Winston Salem NC), U NC, business mgr, FL.

CF44A122   Elva Marjorie Stover (b 1921, Lock Haven PA) m 1961, Edward D. Murray (b 1907, Catawissa PA). Bloomsburg (PA) U; U MI; teacher, psychologist. Podiatrist.

CF44A123   Herbert Lewis Stover (1923, Lock Haven PA-1923, Lock Haven PA). Bur Dunnstown PA.

CF44A124   Donald Wayne Stover (1924, Lock Haven PA-1942, Sunbury PA). Bur Dunnstown PA.

CF44A2   Monasses Stover m 24 Nov 1900, Maggie E. Wohlfert. Livonia PA

CF44A21   Nelson Arthur Stover (b 25 Jan 1902)

CF44A22   Dora Olive Stover (b 24 Apr 1903) m 24 Mar 1928, Randal E. Bowersox

CF44A23   Cecille Estella Stover (b 1 Dec 1904)

CF44A24   Loretta Stover (b 25 May 1908)

CF44A3   Mary Alice Stover (1869-1926) m 1) William D. Meyers; m 2) Henry H. Emery; m 3)
Jasper Kehl

CF44B   Barbara Kehl

CF46   Margaret Ann Kehl (daughter of John Jacob and Anna Catharine (Weiser) Kehl)(26 Jan
1800-16 Jan 1892, Stephenson Co IL) m 6 May 1820, Henry Kiplinger (9 Dec 1799-1 Jan 1879)

CF461   Jacob Kiplinger m

CF4611   Henry Kiplinger m

CF46111   Mildred C. Kiplinger

CF4612   Charles Kiplinger

CF4613   Cora Ida Kiplinger m   Boden

CF46131   Fanny Margaret Boden

CF46132   Patrick Boden

CF462   Michael Kehl Kiplinger m 1) Hannah Rebecca McDonnel; m 2) May Gishwiller

CF4621   Thomas Kiplinger m Emmie McGullah

CF46211   Lula Kiplinger

CF4622   Charles Kiplinger m Agnes Giles

CF46221   Lloyd Kiplinger

CF4623   Irving Kiplinger m Mable Stahl

CF46231   Carl Kiplinger m

CF462311   Donald Kiplinger

CF4624   Edward Kiplinger m Ruth Howard

CF46241   Ward Kiplinger m Georgie Hotchkiss

CF462411   Ward Kiplinger

CF462412   George Edward Kiplinger

CF462413   Howard Kiplinger

CF462414   Franklin Ervin Kiplinger

CF462415   John Kiplinger

CF462416   Albert Kiplinger

CF46242   Edith Kiplinger m   Pulphry. Ten chn.

CF4625   Oliver Kiplinger m Florence Oliver

CF46251   Gladys Kiplinger m

CF4626   Mary Kiplinger m 1) George Rudy; m 2) Adolph Schirmacker

CF46261   Mabel Rudy m   Miner

CF46262   Mertie Rudy m   Wines

CF4627   Lucy Jane Kiplinger m James Miller

CF4628   Fannie Kiplinger m Joseph Sallee

CF46281   George Sallee

CF46282   Florence Sallee

CF463   Sally Kiplinger m Anthony Bolinger

CF4631   Michael Bolinger m   Rickey

CF46311   Lawrence Bolinger

CF46312   Stella Bolinger m Samuel Birk

CF463121   Paul Birk

CF4632   Jacob Bolinger m

CF46321   Howard Bolinger

CF4633   Fannie Bolinger m   Knepper

CF46331   Albert Knepper m

CF463311   Grace Knepper

CF463312   Gerald Knepper

CF463313   Paul Knepper

CF463314   Jean Knepper

CF463315   Beryl Knepper

CF46332	Harvey Knepper m
CF463321	Frances Knepper
CF463322	Maro Knepper
CF463323	Evelyn Knepper
CF46324	Kean Knepper
CF46325	Othel Knepper
CF4634	Mary Bolinger m Henry Wetters
CF46341	William Wetters m Lizzie Bechtold
CF463411	Ethel Wetters
CF463412	Louise Wetters
CF463413	Vada Wetters m Albert Layman
CF46342	Edward Wetters m Grace
CF463421	Donald Wetters
CF463422	Gertrude Wetters
CF46343	Esty Wetters m William Torpy
CF463431	Milon Torpy
CF463432	Lelia Torpy
CF464	Mary Kiplinger m Thomas Kehl
CF4641	Charles H. Kehl
CF4642	Margaret Kehl
CF465	Margaret Kiplinger m John Lapp
CF4651	Charles Lapp m Florence Fote
CF46511	Irene Lapp
CF46512	Mabel Lapp
CF46513	Vernon Lapp
CF46514	Norman Lapp
CF4652	John Lapp m Ethel Shippy
CF4653	Alfred Lapp m Annie Schwoob

CF4654   Thomas Lapp m Tillie Shelhase

CF46541   Wilbur Lapp

CF46542   Raymond Lapp

CF4655   Meda Lapp m Nerrel Baysinger

CF46551   Maude Baysinger m Charles Hudson

CF465511   Donald Hudson

CF465512   Ruth Hudson

CF465513   Darrel Hudson

CF46552   Ralph Baysinger m   Hudson

CF465521   Richard Baysinger

CF465522   Hazel Baysinger

CF465523   Evelyn Baysinger

CF46553   Royal Baysinger

CF46554   Alice Baysinger m Delmer Aurand

CF465541   Robert Aurand

CF465542   Lois Aurand

CF465543   Katherine Aurand

CF465544   Doloris Aurand

CF46555   Corra Baysinger

CF46556   Vera Baysinger

CF46557   Ruth Baysinger

CF46558   Mattie Baysinger

CF46559   Ethel Baysinger

CF4655A   Clarence Baysinger

CF4655B   Lloyd Baysinger

CF4656   Lura Lapp m Peter Schwoob

CF46561   Mary Schwoob m   Brunner

CF465611   Jackie Brunner

CF46562	Joseph Schwoob
CF46563	John Schwoob
CF46564	Florence Schwoob
CF46565	Irene Schwoob m Mizner
CF46566	Bernice Schwoob
CF46567	Ida Schwoob
CF46568	Clarence Schwoob
CF466	Lydia Kiplinger m Charles Hayes. California
CF4661	Lillian Hayes m 1) Dr. Larue; m 2) Robert Graham
CF46611	Hazel Larue m
CF46612	Margaret Graham (blind)
CF4662	Mamie Hayes m Wesley Fry
CF4663	Frank Hayes
CF4664	Arthur Hayes
CF4665	Hubert Hayes
CF467	Catherine Kiplinger m Charles Ferrell
CF4671	Mary Ferrell m Eli Meyers
CF46711	Annie Meyers
CF46712	Charles Meyers
CF4672	Lydia Ferrell m Andrew Kehl
CF4673	Ella Ferrell m Robert Sherman
CF468	Barbara Kiplinger
CF469	Fannie Kiplinger (1844-1927) m Alfred Daws. Guthrie Centre IA.
CF4691	Nettie Daws m 1) Jones; m 2) Farmer
CF46911	Fredia Jones
CF46912	Anna Jones
CF4692	Addie Daws m Slater
CF46921	James Slater

CF46922	Skyler Slater
CF46923	Fannie Slater
CF4693	Rolie Daws m
CF46931	Lester Daws
CF46932	Freda Daws
CF4694	Charles Daws m
CF46941	Harley Daws
CF46942	Haring Daws
CF46943	Helen Daws
CF4695	Skyle Daws
CF4696	Lily Daws
CF4697	Alice Daws
CF4698	Frank Daws
CF4699	Sidney Daws
CF469A	Hubert Daws

CF5. Peter Weiser ([1762]-1829)

Peter Weiser, son of Frederick and Anna Amelia (Zeller) Weiser, was born 7 Feb [1762], near Womelsdorf, PA. There is some question as to the year of his birth, for if his tombstone is read literally, his birth was in 1760, but the birth of his sister Catharine is dated 1760, and since it is known that she was elder than he, it is assumed that he was born in 1762. There is no record of his baptism or confirmation to ascertain these matters. His wife's name was Elizabeth, and it is believed that their marriage is that dated 16 Aug 1787, and that her maiden name was Minchausin, which is probably the feminine of Minchaus.[65]

Peter Weiser was eleven years old when his father died, but Frederick willed him the share of his father's lands recently divided, a tract of about 300 acres in what is now Northumberland Co and an island of 50 acres opposite in the Susquehanna River.[66] This land was to be part of what Conrad Weiser received from his service to the colony on a blanket warrant for 4000 acres in any part of lands recently purchased from the Indians. It was warranted 21 Jan 1755 and surveyed 9 Jun 1755. No one realized, surprisingly not even Conrad himself, that this land lay north of the line of the 1749 Indian purchase in land the colony did not acquire until 1768. Conrad's claim to it was inauthentic, therefore, but the heirs deeded it to Frederick, Frederick willed it to Peter, and Peter settled on it in due time. Obviously aware of the weakness of Weiser's claim Arthur Auchmuty applied 24 May 1769 for the Northern portion of this tract as well as other land nearby, which he warranted 1 Aug 1810 and patented the same day. The Auchmuty or Moodys were sued for ejection by Peter, who also attempted to sell the upper portion of his tract to James Silverwood in 1791. The matter finally reached the state supreme court which ruled against Weiser and in favor of Moody in 1796, after Peter tried forceably to eject Moody.[67] The portion of the land which Peter managed to retain was apparently

---

[65]See records of Christ Lutheran Church, Stouchsburg.

[66]Northumberland Co deeds I-107, P-79.

[67]See Decisions of Pennsylvania Supreme Court.

patented by his son George after his death. As a result of all of his problems, he died a relatively poor man. George Weiser, Peter's son, then tried to claim that a covenant to guarantee title was implied in the deed of partition by suing David Weiser and John Bossler, administrator of Conrad Weiser. This, too, went before the state supreme court in Jun 1836, which ruled against George's claim.

Peter Weiser died 9 Mar 1829. His wife, who was born 15 Jul 1763, died 17 Aug 1829. They are buried at Fishers Ferry, overlooking the River.[68]

Children of Peter and Elizabeth (Minchaus) Weiser:[69]

CF51   Catharine Weiser (b 2 Jan 1788).

CF52   Samuel Weiser (b 28 Jan 1791) 1790 on some lists.

CF53   George Weiser (b 29 Dec 1792).

CF54   Margaret Weiser (13 Apr 1795-13 Nov 1809) bur Fishers Ferry.

CF55   Jacob Weiser (11 Aug 1797-11 Nov 1822) bur Fishers Ferry.

CF56   Peter Weiser (b 24 Feb 1800).

CF57   John Weiser (b 19 Oct 1802).

CF58   Sarah Weiser (25 Apr 1803-9 Aug 1807).

CF51   Catharine Weiser (daughter of Peter and Elizabeth (Minchaus) Weiser) (2 Jan 1788, Fishers Ferry PA-3 Dec 1874, Fishers Ferry PA) m John Hart (10 Jun 1790-9 Aug 1858, Fishers Ferry PA). Both bur Fishers Ferry. A complete list of their children has not been discovered.[70]

CF511   Elizabeth Hart (12 Sep 1818, Fishers Ferry PA-18 Dec 1860, Fishers Ferry PA) m 10 Mar 1842, George Seiler (16 Dec 1812-25 Mar 1901). Bur Fishers Ferry PA.

CF5111   Catherine E Seiler (21 Oct 1843-24 Dec 1925) m 1868, John N Snyder (5 Mar 1838-Jul 1913, Sunbury PA) Bur Lantz Church. Co C, 136th Reg PVI, re-enlisted in Co H, 5th PA Cav, GA, Sunbury PA.

CF51111   Hubert Eugene Snyder (18 Jun 1868-23 Mar 1931) m 3 Aug 1908, Edna Stamm (31 May 1880-24 Jun 1950) Farmer and dairyman. See Floyd, *Genealogical and Biographical Annals of Northumberland County*, p 837.

CF511111   John William Snyder (b 30 Sep 1909, Sunbury PA) m Helen Fegley.

CF5111111   John William Snyder (b 1 Jun 1929) m Marian Krankoskie.

CF51111111   James Robert Snyder (b 2 Feb 1954).

CF51111112   William Russell Snyder (b 2 Sep 1958.)

CF5111112   Gladys Snyder (b 7 Feb 1931) m Harry Trego.

---

[68]Tombstones in Fishers Ferry Cemetery.

[69]George Weiser Family Bible, owned by Weiser Family Association.

[70]Data contributed (1960) by Charles F Snyder. Family Bible and marriage certificate owned by The Rev. Lloyd H Seiler. Additional data (1996) from The Rev. Lloyd H Seiler, Ruth S Summers.

CF51111121   Nancy Trego (b 1951).

CF51111122   Harry Trego Jr (b 1953).

CF51111123   Thomas Trego (b 1954).

CF51111124   Richard Trego (b 1965).

CF5111113   Robert Snyder (b 26 Feb 1933).

CF5111114   Martha Snyder (b 3 Oct 1936) m Russell Stroup.

CF51111141   Brenda Lee Stroup (b 31 Dec 1956).

CF51111142   Stephen Stroup (b 1958).

CF5111115   Larry Snyder (b 7 Oct 1941) m Virginia Anderson.

CF51111151   Larry Snyder (b 22 May 1959).

CF5111116   Carl Snyder (b 18 Apr 1944).

CF5111117   David Snyder (b 3 Apr 1949).

CF511112   Ruth O Snyder (b 4 Feb 1911) m 29 Dec 1945, Fred A Moyer (b 7 May 1913).

CF511113   Myrtle May Snyder (b 16 Feb 1913) m Albert Pittiglio.

CF5111131   Lindo Pittiglio (b 1943).

CF5111132   Theodore Pittiglio (b 1944).

CF511114   Catharine Grace Snyder (24 Oct 1916-15 Dec 1918).

CF511115   Henry Clay Snyder (b 24 Oct 1918) m Jan 1943, Romayne Fenstermacher.

CF5111151   Gretchen Louise Snyder (b 5 Mar 1959).

CF511116   Mary Gladys Snyder (15 Apr 1921-28 Feb 1924).

CF511117   Sarah Marguerite Snyder (b 15 Nov 1923) m Ralph Nerino.

CF5111171   Ralph Anthony Nerino (b 1942).

CF5111172   Ruth Ann Nerino (b Aug 1943).

CF5111173   Barbara Jean Nerino (b Aug 1944).

CF5111174   Michael Nerino (b Feb 1957).

CF51112   George Adren Snyder (24 Apr 1872-Jul 1932, Sunbury PA) unm.

CF51113   Claude Howard Snyder (5 Jun 1874-Jun 1930, Sunbury PA) unm.

CF51114   Eva Elizabeth Snyder (18 Jan 1877-17 Jul 1913) m 31 Aug 1899, Addison C Miller (28 Oct 1872, Paxinos PA-10 Nov 1936, Sunbury PA).

CF511141   Violet Kathryn Miller (29 Jun 1902, Sunbury PA-24 Feb 1995, Hummels Wharf PA) m 1) 13 Jul 1919, Alvin Luther Yeager (d 24 Dec 1973) div; m 2) 24 Nov 1929, Oren B Brungard (CF4359521 q.v. for her fourth-eighth children) (4 Jun 1910, Mifflinburg PA-14 Feb 1985, Wilkes-Barre PA).

CF5111411   John Franklin Yeager (b 13 Feb 1923) m Bessie Adelaide McLawhon (b 14 Feb 1919).

CF51114111   Michael Joseph Yeager (b 23 Jun 1948) m 1) Dixie Lee Parker, div 1980; m 2) Lisa Marie Kahler.

CF511141111   Angela Kay Yeager (b 26 Jun 1974, Sunbury PA).

CF511141112   Valerie Ann Yeager (b 14 Sep 1977, Sunbury PA).

CF511141113   John Michael Yeager (b 14 Oct 1988).

CF51114112   Lorraine Yeager (b 24 Feb 1955, Philadelphia PA) m 1) Samuel Wolfe, div; m 2) 25 Sep 1976, Hummels Wharf PA, Ralph Leon Blett Jr.

CF511141121   Gina Collette Wolfe (b 23 Apr 1973, Sunburg PA) m 2 Sep 1995, Steven Michael Keen (b 10 Jan 1972).

CF5111411211   Kayla Berlin Keen (b 2 Sep 1993).

CF511141122   Kyle RJ Blett (b 29 Mar 1978, Sunbury PA).

CF51114113   Valerie Yeager (24 Feb 1955, Philadelphia PA-Jun 1955, Philadelphia PA) Bur Sunbury PA.

CF5111412   Madelon June Yeager (b 2 May 1925, Sunbury PA) m 9 Jun 1945, Sunbury PA, Richard L Lindner (15 Dec 1923, Sunbury PA-24 May 1983, Allentown PA) Bur Allentown PA.

CF51114121   Carol Lee Lindner (b 29 Oct 1947, Reading PA) m 1) Leonard Hauser, div; m 2) 2 Sep 1972, Allentown PA, Roger Baldwin.

CF511141211   Stephanie Lynn Hauser (b 29 Nov 1965), adopted by Roger Baldwin, m 2 Jun 1990, Michael Paul Weiss.

CF511141212   Hope Vanessa Baldwin (b 18 May 1975, Allentown PA).

CF511141213   Eric Baldwin (b 14 May 1980, Baldwin PA).

CF51114122   Stephen Allender Lindner (b 7 Oct 1951, Reading PA) m 5 Nov 1988 Denise A Miller, div.

CF51114123   Terrence Lee Lindner (b 8 Oct 1953, Reading PA) m 1) Terri Sweitzer, div; m 2) Melyne Sherie Keyser.

CF511141231   Melanie Lee Lindner (b 9 Sep 1978, Allentown PA).

CF511141232   Lee Allender Lindner (b 21 Jun 1982, Allentown PA).

CF51114124   Ann Louise Lindner (b 5 Oct 1957, Reading PA) m Patrick Crosland.

CF511141241   Sean Michael Crosland (b 21 Aug 1979, Allentown, PA).

CF5111413   Shirley Arlette Yeager (b 25 Nov 1926, Sunbury PA) m 28 Feb 1948, Sunbury PA, Carl Homer Goodling (23 Nov 1922, Stonington PA-13 Apr 1987, Sunbury PA).

CF51114131   Jeffrey Lee Goodling (b 10 Dec 1950, Sunbury PA) m 1) 22 May 1971, Allentown PA, Diane M Persing (b 2 Oct 1950, Philadelphia PA) div 1985; m 2) 2 Nov 1985, Allentown PA, Donna Marie Kish (b 23 Jan 1957, Allentown PA).

CF511141311   Megan Elizabeth Goodling (b 16 Dec 1978, Allentown PA).

CF511141312   Matthew Lee Goodling (b 9 May 1991, Allentown PA).

CF51114132   Scott Lee Goodling (b 28 Jan 1955, Sunbury PA) m 1) 6 Sep 1980, Northumberland PA, Tammy Kay Kreider (b 18 Sep 1958, Sunbury PA) div 1983; m 2) 10 Oct 1987, Allentown PA, Sheryl Lynn Trzesniowski (b 16 Jul 1959, Meadville PA) He, BA, Muhlenberg Col, 1977; MSW, U PA, 1979.

CF511141321   Alexander Carl Goodling (b 29 Sep 1988, Allentown PA).

CF511141322   Zachary John Goodling (b 17 Mar 1992, Phoenixville PA).

CF51115   Keturah May Snyder (30 Mar 1881, Rockefeller Tp, Northumberland Co PA-15 Dec 1959, Sunbury PA) m 1) 23 Mar 1912, John D Bucher (5 Jun 1874-27 Jan 1932); m 2) 3 Jan 1957, Arthur Llewellyn (d 26 Aug 1947) Bur Sunbury PA. Llewellyn, Presbyterian minister.

CF51116   Jennie E Snyder (23 Apr 1883-7 Nov 1954, Sunbury PA) m Horace B Neff (1 Apr 1885-14 Aug 1953, Sunbury PA).

CF511161   John H Neff (1914-14 Jul 1926).

CF511162   Francis H Neff (b 1917) m Bessie Riland.

CF5111621   Doris J Neff (b 1941) m 29 Oct 1961, Todd W Broscious.

CF5111622   George Neff (b 1945).

CF5112   Mary Amanda Seiler (17 Mar 1848-12 Dec 1927, Sunbury PA) m Newton W Snyder (6 Sep 1846-2 Nov 1914, Sunbury PA) No chn.

CF5113   John Airsman Seiler (legally changed to Airsman John Seiler) (14 May 1852-12 Jan 1937) m Rosetta J Snyder (5 Aug 1857-11 Mar 1933) Bur Fishers Ferry PA. Farmer.

CF51131   George Henderson Seiler (28 Dec 1888, Fishers Ferry PA-16 May 1957, Sunbury PA) m 4 Apr 1911, Fisherville PA, Anna Yeager (17 Apr 1889, Halifax PA-14 Apr 1977, Millersburg PA) Bur Stonington PA. He, AB, Susquehanna U PA, 1909, BD, Lutheran Theological Seminary, Gettysburg PA, 1924. Lutheran pastor Shanksville PA; Jefferson, Lineboro, MD.

CF511311   Ruth Josephine Seiler (b 10 Nov 1914, Point Tp, Northumberland Co PA) m 20 Jun 1937, Jefferson MD, Eric Christian Summers (5 Mar 1907, Frederick County MD-3 Apr 1982, Cape Coral FL) She, AB, Hood Col, 1935; MA, WI U, 1936. Teacher.

CF5113111   Faith Ann Summers (b 18 Sep 1938, Hagerstown MD) m 5 Jun 1960, Fairmont WV, Frederick Arthur Foltz (b 7 Apr 1937, Sunbury PA) She, AB, WV U, 1960; he, AB, Gettysburg Col, 1959; BD, Yale Divinity School, 1962, DD, Gettysburg (PA) Col, 1996. She, teacher; he, Lutheran pastor, Espy and Gettysburg PA.

CF51131111   Franz Allen Foltz (b 22 Mar 1963, Bloomsburg PA) AB, 1985; MA, 1988, PSU; Ph D, Rensselaer Polytechnic Institute, 1996. Environmentalist.

CF51131112   Freda Ann Foltz (b 19 Jun 1965, Bloomsburg PA) m 11 Jul 1987, Gettysburg PA, Michael Joseph Martine (b 11 Apr 1960, Islip NY) She, BA, Bryn Mawr Col, 1987; Ph D, Cornell U, 1996. He, BA,

PSU, 1982; M Div., Lutheran Theological Seminary, Gettysburg,1986. She, English professor; he, director, Camp Beisler, New Jersey Synod, ELCA; ordained 14 Jan 1996; Lutheran pastor, Mt Joy PA.

CF511311121   Kayla Marie Martine (b 14 Sep 1992, Port Murray NJ).

CF511311122   Eric Arthur Marine (b 16 Apr 1996, Mt Joy PA).

CF51131113   Frances Ann Foltz (b 1 Mar 1968, Gettysburg PA) m 2 Jan 1993, Gettysburg PA, David Allen Sonnenberg (b 3 Mar 1969, Pittsburgh PA) She, AB, Muhlenberg Col, PA, 1990; JD, Cornell U, 1993; he, AB, Muhlenberg Col, 1991; M Div., Lutheran Theological Seminary, Gettysburg, 1996. She, attorney.

CF511311131   Rachel Foltz Sonnenberg (b 12 Dec 1995, Gettysburg PA).

CF5113112   Mark Lee Summers (b 17 Aug 1940, Hagerstown MD) m 11 Apr 1968, Wuppertal, Langerfeld, Anne Monica Knoerle (b 7 Sep 1942, Wuppertal, Langerfeld Germany) He, AB, PA U, 1962. CPA controller. Munich Germany.

CF51131121   Robert Christian Summers (b 25 Mar 1969, Munich Germany) m 17 Aug 1994 at Munich Germany, Gudrun Gerilinde Spiegel (b 30 Jan 1969, Munich Germany) She, MD, U Munich, 1996.

CF511311211   Anna Marlene Summers (b 15 Jan 1995, Munich Germany).

CF5113113   Jeanne Clare Summers (b 27 Nov 1943, Hagerstown MD) m 18 Jun 1968, Greensboro PA, Charles Thomas Myers (b 12 Dec 1942, Mt Vernon IL) She, AB, WV U, 1965; he, AB, Shimmer Col, 1964; MA, IL U, 1965. He, computer specialist; she, credit counsellor.

CF51131131   Carolyn Jeanne Myers (b 30 May 1969, Laurel MD) AB, Dickinson Col, 1991; anthropologist.

CF51131132   Christina Leigh Myers (b 8 Aug 1972, Columbia MD) AB, BS, WV U, 1994. Computer specialist.

CF51131133   Cynthia Anne Myers (b 14 May 1976, Columbia MD) AB, WV U, 1998.

CF51131134   Eric Charles Myers (b 4 Jun 1979, Columbia MD).

CF511312   Roland Yeager Seiler (8 Dec 1917, Point Tp, Northumberland Co PA-14 Feb 1983, Selinsgrove PA) m 20 Jan 1943, Tonapah NV, Mary Edith Mainhart (b 26 Oct 1921, New Market MD) Bur Stonington PA. WWII: US Air Corps Pilot. Mobile home, modular dealer, Selinsgrove PA.

CF5113121   Linda Rebecca Seiler (b 8 Jun 1947, Danville PA) m 12 Sep 1967, Selinsgrove PA, Charles Ronald Stuck (b 16 Jul 1944, Sunbury PA) She, beauty salon owner, operator; he, used car dealer, Selinsgrove PA.

CF51131211   Lori Ann Stuck (b 26 May 1971, Danville PA) m 3 Apr 1993, Shamokin Dam PA, Charles Richard Lehman III (b 25 Jul 1973, Sunburg PA) She, fitness cntr operator; he, forklift operator, Kreamer PA.

CF511312111   Jared Kristopher Lehman (b 20 Aug 1993, Danville PA).

CF51131212   Ronda Lynn Stuck (b 25 Aug 1979, Danville PA).

CF5113122   Sue Ann Seiler (b 12 May 1952, Danville PA) m 4 Aug 1984, Thomas Alan Beachell (b 4 Jan 1952, Sunbury PA) She, financial counselor, Geisinger Medical Center, Danville PA; he, Conrail car inspector, Enola PA.

CF511313   Lloyd Henderson Seiler (b 5 Feb 1919, Point Tp, Northumberland Co PA) m 22 Nov 1945 at Hartsville SC, Flora Harrell Lee (b 24 Feb 1917, Lydia SC) WWII: 1939 Capt 112th Infantry Regt, 28th Division, commanding Co. I in Normandy and 3rd Bn in northern France. AB, Gettysburg Col, PA; BD, Lutheran Theological Seminary, Gettysburg PA, 1947; STM, same, 1977. Lutheran pastor Haralson, Oglethorpe, Rossville GA; Starkville MS; Silver Run MD; Fairfield, Boalsburg PA. Res. Hartsville SC.

CF113131   Lloyd Henderson Seiler (b 9 Dec 1951, Oglethorpe GA) Art collector, Hartsville SC.

CF5113132   Wilhelmina Lee Seiler (b 24 Oct 1957, Starkville MS) m 18 Aug 1978, Hartsville SC, William Walton Luther Jr (b 5 Dec 1950, Florence SC) He, merchant, Hartsville SC.

CF51131321   William Walton Luther III (b 12 Jul 1995, Florence SC).

CF5114   Keturah Angelina Snyder (11 Jul 1858-1918) m 1898, Robert F Little.

CF51141   George Fleming Little (b 9 Dec 1903, McAlevy's Fort, Huntington Co PA) m 1) Elizabeth Dodson McKeague (b 7 Jan 1904, Jersey Shore PA) div; m 2) Vincenza Delores Aiello (b 11 Jan 1917).

CF511411   George Fay Little (b 14 Oct 1925, Sunbury PA) m Stella Florence Zielinki (b18 Apr 1930, Cleveland OH).

CF5114111   George Fay Little Jr (b 15 Apr 1954).

CF5114112   Nancy Pauline Little (b 29 Aug 1956).

CF511412   Jean Elizabeth Little (b 10 Dec 1930) m David Joseph Hric (b 28 Jun 1930, Cleveland OH).

CF5114121   Kathleen Elizabeth Hric (b 24 Oct 1956).

CF52   Samuel Weiser (son of Peter and Elizabeth (Minchaus) Weiser) (28 Jan 1791, Fishers Ferry, Northumberland Co PA-7 Apr 1868, Greencastle, Bloom Tp, Fairfield Co OH) m ca 1813, Augustaville, Augusta Tp, Northumberland Co PA, Margaret Hart (28 Apr 1792, Berks Co PA-21 Apr 1878, Greencastle OH) Bur Greencastle OH. They were communicants of Zion Lutheran Church, Augustaville PA. They moved to Greencastle in 1818, and he was a blacksmith there for over 40 years. Postmaster, township treasurer, Justice of the Peace for 35 years. Member and officer of the Presbyterian Church there for 50 years. His initial purchase in Greencastle is dated 16 Apr 1827.

Children of Samuel and Margaret (Hart) Weiser:

CF521   Peter Weiser (b 23 Jan 1814, Northumberland Co PA) No further record.

CF522   Elizabeth (b 10 Sep 1815).

CF523   Catharine Weiser (9 Sep 1817-apparently dy) She was baptized at Augustaville.

CF524   John Weiser (b 6 Nov 1819, Bloom Tp, Fairfield Co OH) He is listed as a carpenter, aged 32, on the 1850 census for Bloom Tp, but there is no further record of him.

CF525   Sarah Weiser (b 6 Dec 1821).

CF526   Matilda Weiser (b 17 Feb 1824).

CF527   Samuel Weiser (b 22 Dec 1825).

CF528   Andrew Jackson Weiser (b 10 Feb 1828).

CF529   George Washington Weiser (b 17 Dec 1829).

CF52A   Mary M Weiser (b 27 Apr 1831).

CF52B   Lavina Weiser (b 18 Aug 1833).

CF52C   Harriet Weiser (b 24 Nov 1836).

CF52D   Levi Weiser (b 14 Apr 1839, Bloom Tp, Fairfield Co OH, aged 10 on 1850 census; no further record)[71]

CF522   Elizabeth Weiser (10 Sep 1815, Augustaville PA-23 Sep 1856, near Greencastle OH) m 2 Sep 1834, Jacob Grubbe Courtright (23 Sep 1808, near Greencastle OH-14 Jun 1864, Greencastle OH) Bur Greencastle OH. Farmer, stock dealer.[72]

Children of Jacob and Elizabeth (Weiser) Courtright:

CF5221   Infant daughter (Nov 1835-May 1836) Bur Greencastle OH.

CF5222   John Ezra Courtright (b 16 Aug 1827).

CF5223   Samuel Marion Courtright (10 May 1840-8 Jun 1849).

CF5224   Thomas Hamer Courtright (b 27 Jan 1842).

CF5225   Infant son (16 Aug 1844-23 Aug 1844).

CF5226   Infant daughter (27 Jul 1845-30 Jul 1845).

CF5227   Margaret Irene Courtright (b 10 May 1846).

CF5228   Infant son (b 1 Sep 1848) stillborn.

CF5229   George Bigelow Courtright (b 15 Apr 1850).

CF522A   Jacob Felix Courtright (b 12 Jul 1852).

CF522B   Mary Elizabeth Courtright (b 17 Sep 1854).

CF5222   John Ezra Courtright (16 Aug 1837, near Greencastle OH-16 Nov 1896, Springfield OH) m 5 Oct 1858, Lorinda Williamson (28 Jun 1834-29 Jul 1910, Grover Hill OH) Bur Lithopolis OH. Owner of hardware, Rockford OH.

CF52221   Theodore Eugene Courtright (16 Mar 1860, near Greencastle OH-25 Mar 1914, Columbus OH) m 18 Jun 1885, Circleville OH, Minnie Frances Bunker (28 Aug 1859, near Mechanicsburg OH-26 Jun 1928, Columbus OH) Bur Columbus OH. Physician.

CF522211   Ivan Stanley Courtright (b 5 Nov 1886, Basil OH) m 2 Dec 1926, Columbus OH, Alma Z Watts (b 30 Sep 1895, Columbus OH) PA RR clerk.

CF5222111   Alden Stanley Courtright (27 Nov 1927, Columbus OH-18 Sep 1938, Philadelphia PA) Bur Drexel Hill PA.

---

[71]Data about Samuel Weiser and his children contributed by Dorothy W Seale and Lillian McNeill.
[72]Data compiled (1960) by George W. Weiser, with additions (1996) by Sarejo Green.

CF5222112   Dean Watts Courtright (b 9 Sep 1931, Columbus OH) m 6 Feb 1955, Sunbury PA, Patricia J Keithan (b 11 Feb 1932, Sunbury PA) Sales representative of Dell Publishing Co of NY in Philadelphia area.

CF52221121   Diane Sue Courtright (b 24 Dec 1956, Chester PA).

CF52221122   Donna Lynn Courtright (b 17 Apr 1959, Chester PA).

CF52222   Amanda Almina Courtright (7 Jan 1862, near Greencastle OH-2 Jul 1915, Rockford OH) m Lithopolis OH, Luther Leroy Shultz (2 Feb 1859-31 May 1918, Rockford OH) Bur Rockford OH. Painter.

CF522221   Besse Albertina Shultz (b 9 Apr 1884, Lithopolis OH) m 19 Apr 1905, Rockford OH, Carl Cornelius Smith (10 Apr 1880, Rockford OH-26 Feb 1953, Rockford OH) Bur Rockford OH. Banker and farmer.

CF5222211   Max Smith (b 15 Mar 1906, Rockford OH) m 6 Mar 1937, Wellston WVA, Mary Elizabeth Walling (b 21 Oct 1915, Cleveland OH) Farmer.

CF5222212   Neil Smith (b 21 Dec 1907, Rockford OH) m 29 Jan 1928, Toledo OH, Bertha Elizabeth Lilly (b 17 Sep 1909, Crooksville OH) Realtor.

CF52222121   Jack David Smith (b 30 Aug 1929, Drayton Plains MI) m 15 Mar 1958, Oklahoma City, OK, Rita Watson. USAF, Sgt.

CF522221211   Diane Kay Smith (b 7 Feb 1959, Oklahoma City OK).

CF52222122   Karen Sylvia Smith (b 25 Sep 1934, Rockford OH) m 22 May 1959, Phoenix AZ, Charles Watkins.

CF5222213   Josephine Smith (b 16 Jun 1911, Rockford OH) m 23 Mar 1931, Newport KY, George Edward Raudabaugh (b 2 Nov 1907, St Mary's OH) Foreman, Goodyear Tire & Rubber Co, St Mary's OH.

CF52222131   George Edward Raudabaugh II (b 3 Nov 1934, St Mary's OH) m 9 Jun 1956, St Mary's OH, Jeanette Marie Wendall (b 28 Mar 1935, Coldwater OH) Industrial Manager, Goodyear Aircraft, Akron OH.

CF522221311   George Edward Raudabaugh III (b 6 Mar 1958, Akron OH).

CF52222132   Carl Joseph Raudabaugh (b 29 Oct 1938, St Mary's OH) Checker, Goodyear Tire and Rubber Co, St Mary's OH.

CF5222214   Nadine Smith (b 16 Jun 1911, Rockford OH) m 27 Jul 1931, Celina OH, Wilbert Ralph Bruns (b 19 Jan 1902, Wendelin OH) Operator of Northmoor Motel, Celina OH.

CF52222141   Donald Joseph Bruns (15 Jan 1933, Celina OH-16 Jan 1933) Bur Celina OH.

CF52222142   Richard Leon Bruns (b 24 Feb 1934, Celina OH) Manager of Northmoor Marina, Celina OH.

CF52222143   Dennis Michael Bruns (b 11 Apr 1936, Celina OH) USA, Fort Lewis WA.

CF52222144   Linda Louise Bruns (b 24 Nov 1938, Celina OH) m 31 Jan 1959, Celina OH, Richard A Whyte (b 8 Aug 1938).

CF5222215   Marjorie Nan Smith (b 12 Jul 1914, Rockford OH) m 4 Dec 1936, Decatur IN, Ashley Benoit Beams (b 27 Nov 1909, Washington Tp, Mercer Co OH) Builder and machine operator.

CF52222151 Nancy Anne Beams (b 26 Sep 1937, Celina OH) m 23 Dec 1956, Celina OH, Robert Eugene Jamieson (b 8 Aug 1937) Truck driver.

CF52222152 Roberta June Beams (b 3 Jun 1941, Celina OH).

CF52222153 Donald Blair Beams (b 10 Dec 1947, Rockford OH).

CF5222216 Carlotta Cornelia Smith (b 8 Aug 1916, Rockford OH) m 1 Jun 1941, Rockford OH, David Guy Gilbert (b 16 Nov 1908, Phoenix AZ) Rancher.

CF52222161 Nada Jo Gilbert (b 15 Aug 1942, Casa Grande AZ).

CF52222162 Miriam Sue Gilbert (b 26 May 1944, Casa Grande AZ).

CF52222163 Carol Margaret Gilbert (b 30 Apr 1949, Case Grande AZ).

CF5222217 Jack Daniel Smith (b 5 Dec 1919, Rockford OH) m 25 Feb 1945, San Raphael CA, Myrtle Elizabeth Wilson (b 14 Feb 1919, Square Butte MT) Salesman.

CF52222171 Mark Daniel Smith (b 8 Mar 1951, Pittsburgh PA).

CF5222218 Blair Shultz Smith (b 18 Jun 1922, Rockford OH) m 26 Oct 1942, Cleveland OH, Laura Jane Giffin (b 1 Jul 1922, Mt Vernon OH).

CF52222181 Lana Jean Smith (b 15 Jul 1943, Mt Vernon OH).

CF52222182 Carl Cornelius Smith (b 20 Jan 1946, Mt Vernon OH).

CF52222183 Elizabeth Ann Smith (b 22 Dec 1948, Mt Vernon OH).

CF52222184 Steven Dennis Smith (b 13 Apr 1951, Mt Vernon OH)

CF52222185 Byron Douglas Smith (b 5 Feb 1955, Mt Vernon OH)

CF5222219 Gloria Sue Smith (b 23 Jan 1926, Rockford OH) m 19 Apr 1947, Weatherford TX, Robert Thomas Kelley Jr (b 21 Dec 1923, Aledo TX) Reg Mtr, Youngstown Kitchen.

CF52222191 Nannette Kelley (b 21 Jun 1951, Phoenix AZ).

CF52222192 Cynthia Dianne Kelley (b 20 Aug 1953, Tucson AZ).

CF522222 Hazel Irene Shultz (b 6 Jul 1887, Rockford OH) m 16 Feb 1910, Rockford OH, John William Lloyd (b 12 Aug 1885, Rockford OH) Ford dealer.

CF5222221 Eleanor Lloyd (22 Apr 1914, Rockford OH-18 Jun 1932, Rockford OH) Bur Rockford OH.

CF5222222 James Richard Lloyd (b 20 Sep 1918, Rockford OH) m 20 Dec 1940, Rockford OH, Mary Margaret Crone (b 4 Oct 1917, Payne OH) Ford dealer and oil distributor.

CF52222221 Jonell Kay Lloyd (b 7 Sep 1942, Celina OH).

CF52222222 Kevin Richard Lloyd (b 7 Nov 1952, Lima OH).

CF5222223 Robert Leroy Lloyd (b 18 Feb 1922, Rockford OH) m 3 Sep 1946, Lexington KY, Betty Ruth Shindeldecker (b 4 Dec 1925, Rockford OH) Ford dealer and oil distributor.

CF52222231   Barry Robert Lloyd (b 28 Sep 1947, Van Wert OH).

CF52222232   Barbara Anne Lloyd (b 13 Jul 1954, Celina OH).

CF522223   Anna Catherine Shultz (14 Jan 1891, Rockford OH-27 Aug 1947, Rockford OH) m 18 Jan 1917, Ann Arbor MI, Russell Leroy Straubinger (3 Dec 1888, Willshire OH-2 Dec 1943, Rockford OH) Bur Rockford OH. Salesman.

CF5222231   Marilyn Straubinger (b 10 Nov 1923, Van Wert OH) m 4 Jan 1947, Fort Wayne IN, Hobart Walter Steward (b 11 Jul 1922, Fort Wayne IN) Mechanic.

CF52222311   Dennis Michael Steward (b 22 Jul 1947).

CF52222312   Benjie Allen Steward (b 8 Jul 1951).

CF5222232   Donald Leroy Straubinger (b 24 Aug 1926, Rockford OH) m 16 Jun 1949, Celina OH, Jo Ann Ruth Herman (b 10 Apr 1928, Burkettsville OH) Aircraft instructor.

CF52222321   Eric Joseph Straubinger (b 19 Apr 1950, Van Wert OH).

CF52222322   Lynn Anne Straubinger (b 3 Aug 1953, Van Wert OH).

CF52222323   Brent Joseph Straubinger (b 8 Dec 1855, Chillicothe OH).

CF52222324   Jane Ann Straubinger (b 22 Oct 1958, Chillicothe OH).

CF522224   Helen Courtright Shultz (b 23 Dec 1897, Rockford OH) m 6 May 1921, Ann Arbor MI, Lynn Clark Winans (b 30 Apr 1897, Waldron MI) Architect.

CF5222241   John Robert Winans (b 15 Apr 1923, Toledo OH) m 12 Mar 1949, San Diego CA, Helen Louise Robson (b 23 May 1925, Marion OH) Insurance.

CF52222411   John Preston Winans (b 15 May 1951, Hawthorne CA).

CF52222412   Donald Clausen Winans (b 18 Nov 1954, San Diego CA).

CF52222413   William Robert Winans (b 10 Apr 1956, San Diego CA).

CF5222242   Jo Lynn Elizabeth Winans (b 7 Sep 1926, Toledo OH) m 7 Nov 1948, San Diego CA, Harry John Twohig (b 6 Jul 1922, Chicago IL) CPA.

CF52222421   Kevin John Twohig (b 18 Aug, 1949, Phoenix AZ).

CF52222422   Lynne Ann Twohig (b 22 Oct 1951, Phoenix AZ).

CF52222423   Joseph Anthony Twohig (b 5 Jun 1956, Phoenix AZ).

CF52222424   Michael Gerard Twohig (b 1 Nov 1959, Phoenix AZ).

CF52223   Martha Irene Courtright (4 Jul 1864, near Greencastle OH-25 Dec 1939, Paulding OH) m Reuben Gipe (d Paulding OH) Operator of dept store and hotel, Grover Hill OH. Bur Lithopolis OH.

CF52224   Hiram Vinton Courtright (b 19 Dec 1866, near Greencastle OH) m Ida E Beer (ca 1868-ca 1942, Chicago IL) Bur Chicago IL.

CF52225   George Seymour Courtright (6 Jun 1869, near Greencastle OH-1943, New Lexington OH) m Urbana OH, Helen Bridget Graham (Urbana, OH-1947, Zanesville OH) Bur New Lexington OH. Dentist, New Lexington OH.

CF522251   Geraldine Mary Louise Courtright (New Lexington OH) m New Lexington OH, Charles Michael Bennett. He, banker, Crooksville OH. She, dentist, New Lexington OH.

CF522252   Cleyta Coletta Courtright (New Lexington OH) m New Lexington OH, James Euman. He, reamer plant worker, New Lexington OH. She, teacher, Junction City OH.

CF522253   Catherine Helena Courtright (New Lexington OH) unm AB, OH U, Athens OH, 1931. Sales, Columbus OH.

CF522254   John Graham Courtright (b 19 Feb 1908, New Lexington OH) m 18 Jan 1930, Columbus OH, Ellen Lucille Reiss (b 25 Oct 1909, Bakersville OH) Insurance.

CF5222541   Patricia Ellen Courtright (b 24 Aug 1931, Youngstown OH) m 25 Jul 1953, Arlington VA, Cary Brown Hutchinson (b 10 May 1930, Ft Leavenworth KS) West Point Grad, 1953, USA.

CF52225411   Steven Cary Hutchinson (b 4 Aug 1954, Washington DC).

CF52225412   Susan Ellen Hutchinson (b 27 Apr 1956, Maiwnheim Germany).

CF5222542   John Rodney Courtright (b 3 Jun 1939, Washington DC).

CF5222543   Kathleen Graham Courtright (b 13 Oct 1944, Washington DC-25 Jan 1945, Washington DC) Bur Arlington VA.

CF52226   Albert Maywood Courtright (20 Nov 1871, near Greencastle OH-12 Apr 1950, Peoria IL) m 26 Jul 1896, Paulding OH, Grace Dell Bashore (b 14 Nov 1877, Paulding OH) Bur Peoria IL. Grain dealer, Peoria Board of Trade, Peoria IL.

CF522261   Albert Maywood Courtright II (b 17 Jan 1898, Paulding OH) m 1 Sep 1927, Muskegon Heights MI, Yvette Cote (b 14 Feb 1900, Trois Pistoles, Quebec Canada) She, first lady mayor of Muskegon Heights MI. He, degree in electrical engineering, MI U; Master in Mus., Columbia. Teacher, Muskegon Heights MI.

CF5222611   Yolande Irene Courtright (b 13 Jun 1928, Muskegon Heights MI) unm MA, MI U. Librarian, CA U, Berkeley.

CF5222612   Alan Maywood Courtright (b 8 May 1930, Muskegon Heights MI) unm AB, UT U; AM, AK U. Fish & Wild Life Service, Nome AK.

CF522262   Raymond Douglas Courtright (b 21 Aug 1899, Paulding OH) m 2 Oct 1921, Fort Wayne IN, Leeta Lavalla Dixon (b 4 May 1900, Knox IN) President, Bowser International Inc, NY, NY-Export Division of Bowser Inc, Fort Wayne IN.

CF5222621   Grace Elizabeth Courtright (b 17 Mar 1926, London England) m 11 Nov 1948, White Plains NY, Frank Warren Lynn (b 30 Apr 1922, Wilmington, DeKalb Co IN) Welder.

CF52226211   Sandra Kay Lynn (b 12 Feb 1951, Toledo OH).

CF52226212   Deborah Ann Lynn (b 11 Jul 1954, Toledo OH).

CF5222622   Constance Marie Courtright (b 21 Jun 1930, Fort Wayne IN) m 7 Jan 1956, White Plains NY, Richard Gray Willard (b 22 Jan 1914, Binghamton NY) Radio announcer and producer, WOR, Newark NY.

CF52226221   Connie Lou Willard (b 21 Dec 1957, White Plains NY).

CF5222623   Robert Carl Courtright (b 28 Sep 1934, Fort Wayne IN) m 2 Aug 1958, Mooresville NC, Deborah Hunt Sink (b 3 Apr 1936, Mooresville NC) BS, Biology, OR S Col, Corvallis OR.

CF522263   Evalyn Ruth Courtright (b 15 Sep 1901, Paulding OH) m 19 Jun 1926, Peoria IL, Henry Whitney Warner (b 27 Dec 1901, Buffalo NY) He, engineer and owner of Columbus Testing Laboratory, Columbus OH. She, AB, Bradley U, Peoria IL. Teacher.

CF5222631   Priscilla Dell Warner (b 3 Mar 1929, Osborn OH) m 10 Jun 1951, Columbus OH, James Marshall Berry (b 4 Dec 1924, Burnsville WVA) He, dentist, Akron OH. She, degree in home economics.

CF52226311   Cynthia Dell Berry (b 31 Jan 1956, Akron OH).

CF52226312   James Whitney Berry (b 25 Aug 1958, Akron OH).

CF5222632   David Brooks Warner (b 30 Apr 1934, Columbus OH) m 10 Aug 1957, Dayton OH, Joyce Shannon (b 15 Sep 1937, Dayton OH) Degree in chemical engineering. USAF, 1st Lt; meteorologist, Madrid Spain.

CF52226321   Jeffrey Shannon Warner (b 4 May 1959, Madrid Spain).

CF522264   Brooks Hiram Courtright (b 8 Oct 1903, Paulding OH) m 4 Aug 1929, Bloomington IL, Eleanor Amourette Cherry (b 9 Jan 1909, Cowden IL) MA in physics and education. Teacher and county superintendent of schools, Watseka IL.

CF5222641   John Brooks Courtright (b 16 Jun 1931, Cissna Park IL) m 12 Feb 1956, Chicago IL, Marie Raymond (b 30 Nov 1933) Physician, USAF Medical Service, Craig Air Force Base, Selma AL.

CF52226411   Steven Brooks Courtright (b 1 Sep 1958, Washington DC).

CF5222642   Joanne Eleanor Courtright (b 29 Aug 1932, Cissna Park IL) m 13 May 1953, Sheldon IL) He, teacher. She, degree in home economics, Eastern IL S Col. Teacher.

CF5222643   Terry Robert Courtright (b 16 Mar 1946, Sheldon IL).

CF522265   John Earl Courtright (9 Feb 1906, Paulding OH-21 Dec 1946, Michigan City IN) m 13 May 1939, Chicago IL, Jane Wilcox (Holland MI-21 Dec 1946, Michigan City IN) Bur Peoria IL. Commercial artist.

CF5222651   Jan Courtright (22 Nov 1941, Chicago IL-21 Dec 1946, Michigan City IN) Bur Peoria IL.

CF5222652   Cathy Courtright (24 Dec 1942, Chicago IL-21 Dec 1946, Michigan City IN) Bur Peoria IL.

CF522266   Florence Irene Courtright (b 4 Nov 1907, Paulding OH) unm AB, Bradley U; MA, Columbia U. Link trainer instructor during war. Teacher, Peoria IL.

CF522267   Claris Bill Courtright (b 1 Dec 1910, Paulding OH) m 12 Jul 1941, Washington DC, Violet Blanche Boisvert (b 4 Feb 1907, Woonsocket RI) AB, Bradley U. Budget officer, Information Center Service, US Government, Washington DC.

CF5224   Thomas Hamer Courtright (27 Jan 1842, Greencastle OH-23 Dec 1916, Greencastle OH) m 1 Sep 1864, Greencastle OH, Minerva Fellers (2 Apr 1845, near Carroll OH-20 May 1927, Greencastle OH) Bur Lithopolis OH. Farmer and storekeeper.

CF52241 Myrta Elfleda Courtright (3 Oct 1865, Greencastle OH-10 Feb 1943, Greencastle OH) unm Bur Lithopolis OH.

CF52242 Drusilla Florence Courtright (10 Mar 1867, Greencastle OH-24 Aug 1903, Greencastle OH) m 4 May 1892, Greencastle OH, Alvah Victor Weiser (3 May 1860, Greencastle OH-12 Jun 1943, Canal Winchester OH) Bur Lithopolis OH. Carpenter.

CF522421 Cecil Courtright Weiser (21 Dec 1899, Greencastle OH-18 Mar 1906, Greencastle OH) Bur Lithopolis OH.

CF52243 Ernest Woods Courtright (8 Aug 1869, Greencastle OH-27 Mar 1871, Greencastle OH).

CF52244 Clara Bertha Courtright (19 Jun 1871, Greencastle OH-21 Feb 1873, Greencastle OH).

CF52245 Thurman Thomas Courtright (16 Oct 1873, near Greencastle OH-16 Mar 1954, Lancaster OH) m 17 Oct 1906, Greencastle OH, Hazel Kirk Richards (b 23 Jul 1884, Lancaster OH) Bur Lancaster OH. Admitted to bar, 1900; elected prosecuting attorney, 1908; appointed postmaster by Woodrow Wilson, 1918, served 6 years; attorney and prosecuting attorney of Fairfield County.

CF522451 Thurman Thomas Courtright Jr (b 24 Aug 1911, Lancaster OH) m 25 May 1938, Lancaster OH, Elizabeth Vernon Theis (3 Mar 1915, Newark OH-1 Aug 1986, Lancaster OH) Bur Lancaster OH. Attorney.

CF5224511 Ann Courtright (b 3 Oct 1939, Lancaster OH) m 1) 18 Mar 1962, Lancaster OH, Steven Ream (b 14 Dec 1940, Columbus OH) div; m 2) Thomas Rodney Swearingen (b 24 Mar 1938, St Joseph MO) BS. Writer, editor, Columbus OH.

CF52245111 Douglas Allan Ream (b 23 Jun 1966, Columbus OH).

CF52245112 Daniel Thomas Ream (b 11 May 1970, Columbus OH).

CF5224512 Lynn Courtright (b 16 May 1943, Lancaster OH) m 5 Mar 1962, Lancaster PA, Thomas Hall (b 10 Feb 1936, Lancaster PA) Engineer, Lancaster PA.

CF52245121 Kristen Lynn Hall (b 11 Apr 1968, Lancaster OH) m Michael Hill.

CF52245122 Erin Lynn Hall (b 18 Jun 1971, Lancaster OH).

CF52245123 Matthew Hall (b 28 Jun 1974, Lancaster OH).

CF52246 Eura Maude Courtright (6 Feb 1877, Greencastle OH-17 Aug 1957, Canal Winchester OH) m 2 Dec 1896, Greencastle OH, John Clinton Hummell (26 Sep 1876, near Greencastle OH-20 Oct 1953, Canal Winchester OH) Bur Lithopolis OH. Farmer.

CF522461 Byron Courtright Hummell (26 Jun 1897, Greencastle OH-11 Dec 1953, Lancaster OH) m 25 Dec 1919, Carroll OH, Effie Elizabeth Courtright (b 8 Apr 1895, Lancaster OH) Bur Lancaster OH. General Manager, Lumber co, Lancaster OH.

CF5224611 Marilyn Louise Hummell (b 24 Sep 1924, Lancaster OH) m 31 May 1953, Lancaster OH, Richard Newton Matheny (b 31 May 1920, Lancaster OH) Architect.

CF52246111 Thomas Richard Matheny (b 30 Apr 1955, Columbus OH).

CF52246112 Mark Hummell Matheny (b 16 Jan 1958, Columbus OH).

CF522462 Ivan Maywood Hummell (b 24 Feb 1900, Greencastle OH) m 10 Jul 1926, Columbus OH,

Anna Mildred Black (b 23 Nov 1902, Walnut Tp, Pickaway Co OH) She, teacher, Canal Winchester OH. He, elementary principal, Obetz-Hamilton Tp.

CF5224621   Gene Maywood Hummell (b 12 Nov 1926, Greencastle OH) m 17 Jun 1950, Columbus OH, Reba Jeannine Lane (b 28 May 1930) Engineer, Martin Missile, Orlando FL.

CF52246211   Gregory Lane Hummell (b 21 Apr 1953, Columbus OH).

CF52246212   Gene Michael Hummell (b 13 Mar 1956, Columbus OH).

CF5224622   Richard Lee Hummell (b 7 Jan 1930, Greencastle OH) m 22 May 1954, Obetz OH, Bernita Nance.

CF52246221   Robbin Lynn Hummell (b 2 May 1956, Columbus OH).

CF5224623   Lois Jane Hummell (b 31 Jul 1932, Greencastle OH-1 Nov 1932, Greencastle OH) Bur Lithopolis OH.

CF522463   Marguerite Fern Hummell (b 2 Jul 1905, Greencastle OH) m 4 Sep 1926, Canal Winchester OH, Lewis Wendell Hanners (b 20 Aug 1906, Madison Tp, Franklin Co OH) Deputy County Auditor, Franklin Co OH.

CF5224631   John Lewis Hanners (b 22 Jan 1929, near Canal Winchester OH) m 27 Mar 1951, Columbus OH, Barbara Ann Newell (b 20 Aug 1928, Marion OH) Inspector, Jeffrey Mfg Co, Columbus OH.

CF52246311   John Steven Hanners (b 11 Aug 1953, Columbus OH).

CF52246312   Mark Newell Hanners (b 12 Apr 1958, Columbus OH).

CF5224632   Roger William Hanners (b 4 Mar 1931, near Canal Winchester OH) m 21 Mar 1951, Canal Winchester OH, Ruth Eileen Black (b 5 Jun 1926, West Union OH) Salesman, Harley-Davis Sporting Goods Co, Columbus OH. Former baseball pitcher, NY Yankee farm system, 1949-1954; now scout for Pittsburgh Baseball Club.

CF52246321   William Chris Hanners (b 25 Nov 1951, Columbus OH).

CF52246322   Charles Cary Hanners (b 8 Sep 1953, Columbus OH).

CF52247   Harlow Brice Courtright (9 Sep 1880, Bloom Tp, Fairfield Co OH-22 Dec 1947, Columbus OH) m 20 Nov 1907, near Greencastle OH, Sarah Anise Phelps (22 Oct 1883, Greenfield Tp, Fairfield Co OH-27 Oct 1978, Columbus OH) Bur Lithopolis OH. She, saleslady, Lazarus, Columbus OH. He, bookkeeper and salesman, Columbus OH.

CF522471   Shirley Alma Courtright (b 1 Sep 1912, Columbus OH) unm Librarian, St. Library, Columbus OH.

CF522472   Josephine Virginia Courtright (21 Aug 1915, Columbus OH-18 Jun 1994, Columbus OH) m 24 Sep 1938, Columbus OH, Arthur George Green (b 14 Dec 1911, Columbus OH) Bur Lithopolis OH. President, CEO, and Chairman, Columbus and Southern Ohio Electric Co, Columbus OH.

CF5224721   George Frederick Green (b 13 Jun 1947, Columbus OH) m 15 Aug 1970, Coreopolis PA, Janellen Newman (b 27 Oct 1946, Pittsburgh PA) He, AB, Princeton U, MA, Carnegie Mellon U. She, BA, Seton Hall Col; MA, Duquesne U. He, management, Kodak, Rochester NY.

CF52247211   Amy Catherine Green (b 22 Apr 1984, London England).

*CF5224722 Sarajo Courtright Green (b 30 Jun 1952, Columbus OH) div. BS, OSU; MSN TX U, San Antonio. Teacher, Columbus, OH. RN. Nurse Educator, Capital U, Columbus OH.

CF52248 Ruth Olive Courtright (25 May 1883, Greencastle OH-2 Jun 1955, Columbus OH) m 17 Oct 1906, Greencastle OH, Edward Beaty Roller (1 Aug 1878, near Greencastle OH-15 Jun 1968, Columbus OH) Bur Lithopolis OH. Physician, Lithopolis OH.

CF52249 Fannie Ester Courtright (25 Oct 1885, Greencastle OH-31 May 1969, Sabina OH) m 15 Sep 1909, Greencastle OH, John Courtright Phelps (6 Mar 1881, Lawrenceburg TN-7 Mar 1970, Sabina OH) He bur Lithopolis OH. Electrical engineer.

CF522491 Ruth Jocelyn Phelps (b 26 Oct 1916, St Paris OH) m 30 Jun 1939, Sabina OH, Paul Edgar Fitzwater (b 1 Jan 1914, West Manchester OH) She, BA, Wilmington (OH) Col; he, BA, Miami (OH) U. Both music teachers, Sidney OH, Public Schools.

CF5224911 Jane Ellen Fitzwater (b 21 Jul 1943, Columbus OH) m 31 Jul 1965, Sidney OH, Gerald Paul Parke (b 26 Aug 1943, Sidney OH) She, BA, Miami (OH) U; he, BA, OSU. She, teacher; he, management, Houston TX.

CF52249111 Andrew Parke (b 17 Apr 1969, Livonia MI) m 20 Nov 1993, Wallis TX, Donna Marie Banes (b 3 Dec 1969, Wallis TX) Both BA, TX A&M. He, USN.

CF52249112 Brian Parke (b 17 Oct 1970, Livonia MI) unm BA, SW TX U, San Marcos. Stockbroker, Houston TX.

CF52249113 Elizabeth Parke (b 7 Jun 1981, Humble TX).

CF5224912 Julie Anne Fitzwater (b 25 Sep 1944, Columbus OH) m 17 Jun 1967, Sidney OH, Eberhard George Preuninger (b 14 Feb 1942, Germany) She, BA, Miami (OH) U; he, BA, U Cincinnati. She, office admin; he, hospital admin, Ashville NC.

CF52249121 Todd Preuninger (b 10 Feb 1970, New Richmond OH) unm Researcher.

CF52249122 Lissa Preuninger (b 21 Sep 1971, New Richmond OH).

CF5224913 Jean Elizabeth Fitzwater (b 13 Oct 1947, Sidney OH) m 15 Nov 1973, London OH, Harold Dean Bussell (b 6 Jun 1934, Pineville KY) She, BA, OH Wesleyan U; MSW, OSU; he, BA, Shorter (GA) Col; MSSW, U Louisville. She, exec dir Reading Recovery Council of NA; he, businessman, Columbus OH.

*CF52249131 Jennifer Lynne Bussell (b 24 Apr 1975, Columbus OH).

CF5224914 John Phelps Fitzwater (b 10 Jun 1951, Sidney OH) unm Nurse.

CF522492 Frances Elizabeth Phelps (6 Jul 1921, Sabina OH-5 Mar 1991, Bozman MD) m 26 Nov 1944, New York NY, John Howard Newcomer (b 15 May 1916, Smithsburg MD) Airline pilot.

CF5224921 Barbara Newcomer (b 4 Mar 1949, Norfolk VA) m 24 Dec 1976, Florham Park NJ, Roger Pope (b 13 Feb 1945, Marietta OH) Teachers, Marietta OH.

CF5224922 Joanne Newcomer (b 3 Aug 1952, Summit NJ) m 12 Oct 1974, Florham Park NJ, Blaine Brown (b 19 Feb 1952, Doylestown PA).

CF52249221 Carrie Ann Brown (b 4 May 1984, Doylestown PA).

CF52249222 Amanda Beth Brown (b 31 May 1986, Philadelphia PA).

CF5227   Margaret Irene Courtright (10 May 1846, Greencastle OH-23 May 1882, Greencastle OH) m 19 Jan 1865, John Ray Fellers (27 Aug 1841-23 Sep 1880, Greencastle OH) Bur Lithopolis OH. Farmer.

CF52271   Mary Alice Fellers (27 Jun 1865, Greencastle OH-7 Mar 1946, Greencastle OH) m 11 Mar 1883, Greencastle OH, William Robert Cofman (16 Feb 1859, near Carroll OH-1 Jun 1945, Greencastle OH) Bur Canal Wincester OH. Farmer.

CF522711   Chalmer Curtis Cofman (19 Apr 1884, near Greencastle OH-27 Oct 1944, Canal Winchestr OH) m 1 Nov 1911, near Groveport OH, Edith Ardell Zwayer (b 28 Nov 1885, near Groveport OH) Bur Canal Winchester OH. Farmer and school bus driver.

CF5227111   William Ervin Cofman (b 29 May 1923, Columbus OH) unm Maintenance manager, Nationwide Insurance Co, Lynchburg VA.

CF522712   Glenn Courtright Cofman (12 Mar 1891, near Greencastle OH-11 Jul 1937, Columbus OH) m 14 May 1925, Lithopolis OH, Ruby Belle Miskell (b 15 Nov 1894, Murray City OH) Bur Canal Winchester OH. Supt, City Asphalt Plant, Columbus OH.

CF5227121   Mary Judith Cofman (25 Jul 1930, Canal Winchester OH-11 Dec 1931, Canal Winchester OH) Bur Canal Winchester OH.

CF522713   Ray Cofman (b 31 Jan 1896, Greencastle OH) m 27 Nov 1923, Lithopolis OH, Ada Rebecca Wagner (b 14 Mar 1901, Greencastle Tp, Fairfield Co OH) Retired farmer.

CF5229   George Bigelow Courtright (15 Apr 1850, Greencastle OH-24 Jul 1914, Greencastle OH) m 18 May 1869, Canal Winchester OH, Clara Eve Fellers (13 Feb 1850, near Carroll OH-24 Aug 1938, Greencastle OH) Bur Greencastle OH. Farmer.

CF52291   Nellie A Courtright (2 Sep 1870, Greencastle OH-10 Nov 1870, Greencastle OH) Bur Greencastle OH.

CF52292   Minnie Elnora Courtright (26 Jun 1873, Greencastle OH-20 Aug 1947, Bloom Tp, Fairfield Co OH) m 30 Apr 1898, Thomas Roller (13 Apr 1868, Canal Winchester OH-4 Feb 1951, Bloom Tp, Fairfield Co OH) Bur Lithopolis OH. Country Commissioner, farmer, painter, Greencastle OH.

CF522921   Helen Courtright Roller (30 Jul 1899, Greencastle OH-25 Jul 1951, Columbus OH) m Oct 1922, Dayton OH, Ellsworth McCain (30 Jan 1894, Portsmouth OH-15 Nov 1953, Dayton OH) Bur Lithopolis OH. Employee, Columbus (Army) General Depot.

CF5229211   Dorothy Elnora McCain (b 6 May 1923, Amanda Tp, Fairfield Co OH) m 16 Aug 1943, Dayton OH, Jerrald Walter Swift (b 24 Aug 1920, Akron OH) Aircraft mechanic, Wright-Patterson Air Force Base, Dayton OH.

CF5229212   Boyd Ellsworth McCain (b 10 May 1927, Amanda Tp, Fairfield Co OH) m 9 Sep 1951, near Ashville OH, Norma Scarbarry (b 7 Dec 1928, near Ashville OH) Foreman, Sucher's Packing Co, Dayton OH.

CF52292121   Pamela Sue McCain (b 9 Aug 1953, Dayton OH).

CF52292122   Bruce David McCain (b 21 Oct 1954, Dayton OH).

CF5229213   Paul Edward McCain (b 24 Apr 1929, Amanda Tp, Fairfield Co OH) m 7 Feb 1954, Coronado CA, Joann Flynn (b 28 Sep 1932, Oradell NJ) Radio man, USN.

CF52292131   Paula Maureen McCain (b 27 Nov 1954, St Albans NY).

CF52292132   James Robert McCain (b 25 Jun 1956, Sagamihara Japan).

CF52292133   John Stephen McCain (b 11 Jan 1958, Kahuku HI).

CF522922   Wayne Leroy Roller (7 Jan 1902, Bloom Tp, Fairfield Co OH-3 Jun 1956, Royalton OH) m 8 Jan 1927, Greenup KY, Georgia Jeretha Grove (b 24 Nov 1897, Pleasant Tp, Fairfield Co OH) Bur Amanda Tp, Fairfield Co OH. Supt of Highways, Fairfield Co OH.

CF5229221   Mildred Marie Roller (b 23 Oct 1927, Bloom Tp, Fairfield Co OH) m 27 Jun 1959, Cleveland OH, Thomas Scott Mitchell (b 26 Jun 1918, Cleveland OH) International representative for Communication Workers of America.

CF5229222   May Alice Roller (b 30 Aug 1929, Amanda Tp, Fairfield Co OH) m 3 Oct 1855, Columbus OH, Lawrence Valentine Dolan Jr (b 23 Jun 1928, Brooklyn NY) Manager, Sherwin-Williams store, Columbus OH.

CF52292221   Laura Ann Dolan (b 11 Oct 1956, Columbus OH).

CF52292222   Joseph Wayne Dolan (b 7 Jan 1959, Columbus OH).

CF52293   Edith Fellers Courtright (15 Oct 1878, Bloom Tp, Fairfield Co OH-26 Aug 1970) m 7 Dec 1904, Bloom Tp, Fairfield Co OH, Earl Wilson (11 Nov 1876, Madison Tp, Franklin Co OH-3 Mar 1961, Groveport OH) Both bur Lithopolis OH. Retired farmer.

CF522931   Alice Courtright Wilson (b 15 Nov 1905, Madison Tp, Franklin Co OH) m 7 Oct 1936, Gahanna OH, Lee Daniel Poth (b 25 Jul 1906, Gahanna OH) Shop worker, PA RR, Columbus OH.

CF5229311   Marilyn Lee Poth (b 8 Nov 1943, Columbus OH) m 23 Jun 1968, Columbus OH, Eugene Francis Cloninger (b 28 Dec 1941) div. She, BA, Kent State U(OH), 1965.

Amy Lynn Cloninger (b 30 Jul 1974) Adopted by Eugene and Marilyn Lee Poth Cloninger.

CF522932   Clara Loretta Wilson (2 Jun 1907, Madison Tp, Franklin Co OH-Nov 1980) m 1 Jun 1932, Madison Tp, Franklin Co OH, John Ralston Leidy (b 12 Nov 1909, near Brice OH) Bur Canal Winchester OH. Farmer.

CF5229321   Barbara Alice Leidy (b 25 Jul 1935, Madison Tp, Franklin Co OH) m 25 Jul 1954, Madison Tp, Franklin Co OH, Robert Dale Cullison (b 17 Sep 1933, Madison Tp, Franklin Co OH) Employee, Highway Dept.

CF52293211   Mark Robert Cullison (b 27 Oct 1959, Logan OH) United Parcels employee.

CF52293212   Denise Leidy Cullison (b 5 Sep 1962, Logan OH) m John L Linton (b 25 Jul 1963, Logan OH) He, USAF

CF5229322   Edith Emma Leidy (b 16 Jan 1938, Madison Tp, Franklin Co OH) m 23 Mar 1958, Madison Tp, Franklin Co OH, Rodney Kent Wildermuth (b 10 Feb 1937, Madison Tp, Franklin Co OH) Farmer.

CF52293221   Annetta Kay Wildermuth (b 2 Feb 1960, Columbus OH) m 25 Jun 1988, Robert Seman. She, BA, U Dayton; teacher. He, social worker, Columbus OH.

CF52293222   Jerry Kent Wildermuth (b 25 Jun 1961, Columbus OH) m Lina M Peffer (b 25 Sep 1960, Maysville KY) He, BA, Wilmington Col, 1984; she, BA, Wilmington Col, 1982.

CF522932221   Scott Christopher Wildermuth (b 22 Feb 1988, Columbus OH).

CF522932222   Jodi Marie Wildermuth (b 8 Feb 1990, Columbus OH).

CF522932223   Christi Lauren Wildermuth (b 29 Oct 1992, Columbus OH).

CF52293223   Susan Lynn Wildermuth (b 25 Nov 1968, Columbus OH).

CF522933   Edith Eloise Wilson (b 18 Aug 1908, Madison Tp, Franklin Co OH) m 23 Jun 1931, Groveport OH, Robert Hempy Rohr (b 12 Jan 1909, Bellefontaine OH) Carpenter.

CF5229331   Lois Janet Rohr (b 30 May 1932, Madison Tp, Franklin Co OH).

CF522934   George Andrew Wilson (29 Aug 1910, Madison Tp, Franklin Co OH-4 Feb 1989) m 1) 22 Jan 1931, Greenup KY, Vada Belle Abbott (28 May 1911, Groveport OH-4 Dec 1934, Columbus OH) Bur Groveport OH; m 2) 2 Dec 1944, Madison Tp, Franklin Co OH, Edna Faye Fridley (b 26 Dec 1917, Madison Tp, Franklin Co OH) Bur Lithopolis OH. Mechanic and farmer.

CF522935   Mary Elnora Wilson (b 20 Aug 1913, Madison Tp, Franklin Co OH) m 27 Sep 1937, Madison Tp, Franklin Co OH, Robert Louis Stevenson (b 30 Jul 1912, Canal Winchester OH) Lab technician, Columbus and Souther Ohio Electric Co, Columbus OH.

CF5229351   William Earl Stevenson (b 13 Feb 1942, Columbus OH) m 1) 12 May 1962, Rosie Marie Frans, div; m 2) 10 Oct 1992, Grovesport OH, Margaret Graves (b 4 Feb 1971) Powers company, Columbus OH.

CF52293511   Mary Elizabeth Stevenson (b 16 Jun 1963, Columbus OH) BA, OSU, 1986. Teacher, Columbus OH.

CF52293512   William Todd Stevenson (b 22 Jul 1965, Columbus OH) m Janel Shumaker (b 4 Feb 1971, Lancaster OH) AB, Columbus (OH) State. Power company employees.

CF522935121   Alisha Ann Stevenson (b 29 Jan 1991, Lancaster OH).

CF522935122   Brent Michael Stevenson (b 21 Feb 1994, Lancaster OH).

CF522935123   Carey Marie Stevenson (b 20 Jun 1996, Lancaster OH).

CF5229352   Thomas Wilson Stevenson (b 15 Jun 1945, Columbus OH) m 20 Nov 1971, Virginia Mae Manker (b 25 Jun 1945, Erie PA) AB, OSU, 1968; MA, 1975. USA, Vietnam; school administrator. She, AB, OSU, 1967. Sales.

CF522936   Earle Eugene Wilson (b 27 Oct 1918, Madison Tp, Franklin Co OH) unm Farmer.

CF522937   Martha Elizabeth Wilson (b 22 Feb 1921, Madison Tp, Franklin Co OH) m 25 Dec 1945, Groveport OH, Donald Cullen Fisher (b 19 Jan 1918, Carroll OH) Glass worker, Anchor Hocking Glass Co, Canal Winchester OH.

CF5229371   Carol Ann Fisher (b 27 Nov 1950, Columbus OH) m 7 Apr 1973, Chelan WA, David Keathley. She, AB, OSU, 1973.

CF5229372   Donna Jean Fisher (b 29 Apr 1954, Columbus OH) m 24 Nov 1973, Robert J Henson, div.

CF5229373   Mary Louise Fisher (b 6 Jul 1961) m Michael Anson (b 19 Feb 1961) USAF.

CF52293731   Meghan Marie Anson (b 10 Feb 1993, Melbourne FL).

CF52294   Blanche C Courtright (7 Nov 1883, Bloom Tp, Fairfield Co OH-19 Sep 1898, Greencastle OH) Bur Greencastle OH.

CF52295   Jacob G Courtright (27 Jun 1889, Bloom Tp, Fairfield Co OH-4 Feb 1891, Greencastle OH) Bur Greencastle OH.

CF522A   Jacob Felix Courtright (12 Jul 1852, Greencastle OH-1911) m Mary Viola Whitzel (1855-1889) Bur Greencastle OH.

CF522A1   Harley M Courtright (27 Aug 1874, Greencastle OH-31 Aug 1874, Greencastle OH) Bur Greencastle OH.

CF522A2   Nell Courtright. Bur Lithopolis OH. unm.

CF522A3   Edna Courtright (1887-1930) m Emil Bailey. Bur Lithopolis OH. Carpenter.

CF522B   Mary Elizabeth Courtright (17 Sep 1854, Greencastle OH-9 Nov 1885, Canal Winchester OH) m John Albert Whitzel (3 Aug 1850, New Lexington OH-16 Aug 1922, Columbus OH) Bur Canal Winchester OH. Storekeeper, Greencastle OH; Clerk, Lazarus Dept Store, Columbus OH.

CF522B1   Dora Agnes Whitzel (27 Oct 1872, Greencastle OH-15 Aug 1890, Columbus OH) Bur Canal Winchester OH. unm.

CF522B2   Lou Edith Whitzel (8 Jan 1874, Greencastle OH-17 Nov 1947, Columbus OH) Bur Canal Winchester OH. unm.

CF522B3   Grace Courtright Whitzel (15 Oct 1875, Greencastle OH-18 Feb 1945, Columbus OH) Bur Canal Winchester OH. unm.

CF522B4   Maggie Whitzel (30 Mar 1878, Greencastle OH-19 Apr 1878, Greencastle OH) Bur Canal Winchester OH.

CF522B5   Bertha A Whitzel (27 May 1879, Bloom Tp, Fairfield Co OH-27 Aug 1881, Bloom Tp, Fairfield Co OH) Bur Canal Winchester OH.

CF522B6   Mary Effie Whitzel (9 Mar 1884, Bloom Tp, Fairfield Co OH-18 Aug 1948, Columbus OH) m 7 Sep 1929, Columbus OH, Earl R Erkine (d Akron OH) She bur Canal Winchester OH; he bur Akron OH. Owner, rug cleaning store, Akron OH.

CF525   Sarah Weiser (b 6 Dec 1821, Bloom Tp, Fairfield Co) m 1) Rockey; m 2) 23 Aug 1858, Henry Ward Bicher. Cobbler.

CF5251   Pierce Rockey (d near Ashville OH) m Nancy Solt. Cobbler.

CF5252   Kate Rockey m Rufus Hedrick. Farmer. No chn.

CF5253   Eliza C Bicher (b ca 1854) m John Durant. Laborer.

CF5254   Lorenzo D Bicher (ca 1860-near Greencastle OH) m. Bur Salem U.B. Church Cemetery, Fairfield Co OH.

CF52541   Thurman Bicher m.

CF52542   Ethel Bicher m John Talbot.

CF526   Matilda Weiser (17 Feb 1824-8 Apr 1855) m 22 Jun 1853, John Beaty (15 Feb 1824-24 Mar 1856) Bur Greencastle OH.

CF5261   Emily Olivia Beaty (13 Apr 1854, Greencastle OH-12 Mar 1912, Bloom Tp, Fairfield Co OH) m 8 Feb 1877, Jacob Lamb Alspach (25 Aug 1853, Greenfield Tp, Fairfield Co OH-Nov 1932, Lancaster OH) Bur Lancaster OH. Farmer.

CF52611   Henry Albert Alspach (8 Dec 1877, Bloom Tp, Fairfield Co OH-30 Apr 1931, Lancaster OH) m 7 Mar 1900, Royalton OH, Della May Bookman (25 May 1879, Bloom Tp, Fairfield Co OH-11 May 1956, Lancaster OH) Bur Lancaster OH. City treasurer; Mayor of Lancaster OH, and real estate broker.

CF526111   Edna Lee Alspach (b 24 Spetember 1900, Bloom Tp, Fairfield Co OH) m 24 Dec 1923, Lancaster OH, Charles Lenlie Pierce (14 Sep 1895, Clear Creek Tp, Fairfield Co OH-21 Oct 1944, Lancaster OH) Bur Lancaster OH. He, US mail carrier.

CF526112   Dora Hester Alspach (b 8 Jun 1902, Bloom Tp, Fairfield Co OH) m 17 Jun 1922, Greenup KY, Clay Grove (15 Sep 1901, Walnut Tp, Fairfield Co OH-2 Dec 1963) Bur Lancaster OH. Supervisor, Borden Co, Elgin IL.

CF5261121   William Albert Grove (b 21 Feb 1933, Lancaster OH) m 28 Apr 1956, Aurora IL, Sue Pearson (b 27 Apr 1935, Aurora IL) Asst Administrator, Grant Hospital, Chicago IL.

CF52611211   Penny Sue Grove (b 22 Dec 1956, Aurora IL).

CF52611212   William Clay Grove (b 27 Jul 1958, Aurora IL).

CF526113   Olive Pauline Alspach (b 21 Oct 1909, Lancaster OH) m 24 Jun 1934, Lancaster OH, Harry Tripelette Kerr Jr (b 3 Dec 1905, Fort Worth TX) Office executor, Pitney Bowes, Stamford CT.

CF5261131   Betty Lee Kerr (b 23 Feb 1938, Kansas City MO) Apprentice designer.

CF52612   Lester Beaty Alspach (25 Sep 1879, Greenfield Tp, Fairfield Co OH-25 Aug 1955, Cleveland OH) m 1) 10 Apr 1902, Lancaster OH, Myrtie J Markwood (1 Dec 1880, Greenfield Tp, Fairfield Co OH-2 Oct 1906, Lancaster OH) Bur Lancaster OH; m 2) Jennie Rowles (1883-1948, Cleveland OH) Bur Lancaster OH. Carpenter and mechanic.

CF526121   Helen Mae Alspach (b 11 Apr 1904, Lancaster OH) m 4 Jun 1924, Columbus OH, Carl George Ruh (b 26 Aug 1901, Columbus OH) Pressman.

CF526122   Clarence Alspach (b 21 Aug 1906, Lancaster OH) m 13 May 1931, Greenup KY, Bertha Estella Unks (b 8 May 1912, Lancaster OH) Projectionist, Lyric Theater, Lancaster OH.

CF526123   Mildred Alspach (b 19 Nov 1916, OH) m James Mathias.

CF5261231   Marshall Mathias.

CF5261232   Clark Mathias.

CF5261233   Holly Mathias.

CF5261234   Marcine Mathias.

CF52613   Oscar Dale Alspach (b 26 Aug 1882, Bloom Tp, Fairfield Co OH) m 30 May 1908, Columbus OH, Edythe Gail Carnes (19 Oct 1886, Carroll OH-19 Dec 1957, Lancaster OH) Bur Carroll OH. Farmer.

CF526131   Dorothy Evelyn Alspach (b 9 Apr 1909, Bloom Tp, Fairfield Co OH) m Columbus OH, Fred J Wilson. She, Master's Degree in Ed., NY U, 1937, He, teacher; civilian employee in foreign embassies; US Dept of Agriculture, Columbus OH.

CF526132   Denver Carnes Alspach (b 9 May 1912, Bloom Tp, Fairfield Co OH) m 6 Nov 1937, Carrollton KY, Mary Catherine Kuhlman (b 22 Feb 1915, Carrollton, KY) Area supervisor, Carnation Milk Co.

CF5261321   John Dale Alspach (b 22 Dec 1943, Mt Sterling KY).

CF5261322   Elizabeth Anne Alspach (b 21 Aug 1945, Murfreesboro TN).

CF525133   Robert Corwin Alspach (b 30 Nov 1916, Bloom Tp, Fairfield Co OH) m 1) 24 Dec 1938, Lancaster OH, Dorothy Elizabeth Baker (b 11 Mar 1916, Lancaster OH); m 2) 29 May 1947, Springfield OH, La Donna Hendricks (b 25 Dec 1916, Champaign Co OH) Sales manager, Armour & Co, Memphis TN.

CF5261331   Robert Keith Alspach (b 1 Sep 1943, Lancaster OH).

CF5261332   Stephen Lynn Alspach (b 18 Jul 1948, Springfield OH).

CF527   Samuel Weiser (22 Dec 1825, Greencastle OH-22 Apr 1908, Greencastle OH) m 4 Jul 1852, Fairfield Co OH, Eve Ann Carris (10 Oct 1829, Baden Germany-2 Jul 1909, Greencastle OH) He was a plasterer in Greencastle and was a charter member of the IOOF lodge chapter there begun in 1871. They were members of the Greencastle Presbyterian Church, where they are buried.[73]

CF5271   George Renaldo Weiser (10 Jan 1853, Greencastle OH-18 Mar 1936, Lithopolis OH) m 17 Nov 1886, Olive Weeks Shultz (1864-1946) Bur Lithopolis OH. Hardware merchant and funeral director, Lithopolis OH. President, Trustees of Memorial Library, Lithopolis OH.

CF52711   Blanche Marie Weiser (b 11 Dec 1891, Lithopolis OH) m 1) 15 Aug 1917, I Elmer Jones (d 7 Apr 1949) MD; m 2) 31 May 1950, Percy Q Williams. She, VA Col, 1913; Westminster Col, 1915. Music teacher.

CF527111   Virginia Louise Jones (b 5 Dec 1918, Lancaster OH) m 20 Sep 1941, John Henry Mohn. USAF, Lt Col.

CF5271111   John Randolph Mohn (b 27 Aug 1943, Stockton CA).

CF5271112   Thomas Michael Mohn (b 15 Aug 1945, Toledo OH).

CF5271113   Suzanne Louise Mohn (b 28 May 1948, Washington DC).

CF52712   Olive Felonise Weiser (b 20 Sep 1900, Lithopolis OH) m 14 Jan 1928, Charles William Chappelear. She, Miami U; teacher. He, Asst Mgr, London and Lancashire Insurance Co, Hartford CT.

CF527121   David Conrad Chappelear (b 2 Mar 1931, Dayton OH) m 10 Jun 1967, Brenda Miller. Yale U, Princeton U graduate studies.

*CF5271211   Christopher William Chappelear (b 28 Aug 1968, Springfield MA) BA, Yale U, 1991. Financial analyst, Health Insurance Plan of Greater New York, NY.

CF5271212   Thomas Daniel Chappelear (b 17 Aug 1971, Springfield MA) BA, Yale U, 1993.

CF527122   Daniel Norman Chappelear (b 1 Mar 1935, Dayton OH) m 5 Jun 1976, Palo Alto CA, Kathern Ann Bradshaw. MI U. He, Naval architect.

CF5272   Charles F Weiser (25 Dec 1854, Greencastle OH-1 Nov 1951, Columbus OH) m 3 Oct 1880, Nancy Jane Swank (5 Jun 1856, Bloom Tp, near Greencastle OH-9 Feb 1944, Greencastle OH) Bur Lithopolis OH. Farmer.

---

[73]Samuel Weiser data submitted by Christopher Chappelear, Dorothy W Seale, Donald C Weiser, Richard C Weiser, Martin W Weiser, Donald L Schaffner, Robert C Weiser, Richard R Weiser.

CF527 SAMUEL WEISER AND FAMILY

Back row: CF5277 Clara Evaline Weiser Brenner (1868-1935); CF527 John Edgar Weiser (1866-1934); CF527 Samuel Weiser (1825-1908); CF5275 Mary M. Weiser (1863-1955); CF5272 Charles F. Weiser (1854-1951); CF5274 Almeda Emma Weiser Schaffner (1859-1918). Front row: CF5279 Thomas Hamer Weiser (1873-1952); CF5271 George Renoldo Weiser (1853-1936); Eve Carris Weiser (1829-1909); CF5273 Calvin Wallace Weiser (1857-1944); CF5278 Jesse Woods Weiser (1871-1938)

CF52721   Recie Hazel Weiser (3 May 1889, Greencastle OH-27 May 1894, Greencastle OH).

CF52722   Lula Weiser (14 Feb 1891, Greencastle OH-25 Apr 1894, Greencastle OH).

CF52723   Lester George Weiser (18 Dec 1892, Greencastle OH-25 Jul 1893, Greencastle OH).

CF52724   Gladys Opal Weiser (24 Dec 1896, Greencastle OH-7 Feb 1977) m 24 Feb 1920, Greencastle OH, Bryan Whittier Rager (15 Dec 1896, Groveport OH-19 Jan 1987) Farmer.

CF527241   Eileen Elnora Rager (b 6 Jan 1921, near Groveport OH) m 15 Dec 1941, Greenup KY, William Woodrow Weber (b 18 May 1918, Brice OH) Plumber.

CF5272411   Linda Lou Weber (b 18 Sep 1942, Canal Winchester OH) m Ken Rutherford.

CF52724111   Kim Rutherford (b 28 Dec 1960).

CF527241111   Scott Bobo (b 14 Jan 1984).

CF527241112   Brittany Dolbow (b 13 Mar 1990).

CF52724112   Stacy Rutherford (b 20 Mar 1962).

CF527241121   Courtney Hollingshead (b 1 Jul 1985).

CF527241122   Codi Hollingshead (b 20 Jul 1990).

CF527241123   Shelly Sears (b 6 Jul 1991).

CF5272412   Sharon Sue Weber (b 6 Oct 1943, Canal Winchester OH).

CF527242   Margaret Jean Rager (b 13 Feb 1922, near Groveport OH) m 1) 26 Sep 1943, Columbus OH, Melvin Willard Dobbs (23 Dec 1915, Sloan's Valley KY-10 Aug 1975); m 2) 9 Oct 1976, Glen H Fankhouser (b 2 Sep 1921) Dobbs: Attorney, Columbus OH.

CF5272421   James Bryan Dobbs (b 19 Jun 1945, Columbus OH) m 15 Jun 1968, Debra Young. Attorney.

CF52724211   James Bryan Dobbs (b 19 Jan 1970).

CF52724212   John Brennan Dobbs (b 15 Sep 1973).

CF52724213   Jenny Baker Dobbs (b 30 Mar 1975).

CF5272422   Donna Jane Dobbs (b 17 Aug 1948, Columbus OH) m 1) Sep 1967, Jan Crawford, div; m 2) Apr 1987, William Bricker.

CF52724221   Lori Crawford (b 21 Jun 1970).

CF52724222   Josh Crawford (b 27 Apr 1973).

CF527243   Mary Jane Rager (b 28 Oct 1925, Amanda Tp, Fairfield Co OH) m 22 Jun 1946, Columbus OH, Frank Wallace Kyle (b 9 Mar 1922, Lancaster IN) Logistic Manager, Air Force Ground Support Equipment and Test Equipment.

CF5272431   Rebecca Lee Kyle (b 26 Jul 1951, Dayton OH) m David Wendt.

Hazel Eleanor McKean Weiser (1893-1952)

CF52731 Harry Boyer Weiser, PhD (1887-1950)

CF5272432 Susan Denise Kyle (b 3 Feb 1956, Dayton OH) m Randy Marksburg.

CF527244 Bobby Lee Rager (23 Oct 1932, Amanda Tp, Fairfield Co OH-11 May 1993) m 30 Nov 1952, Canal Winchester OH, Margaret Loene Haynes (b 16 Aug 1934, Canal Winchester OH) Farmer.

CF5272441 Robin Loene Rager (b 1 Oct 1955, Columbus OH) m 27 Jun 1989, Columbus OH, Michael Thomas Hummel. Farmer.

CF5272442 Karen Sue Rager (b 12 Dec 1956, Columbus OH) m 12 Jul 1985, Douglas Steven Mutchler.

CF52724421 Robbie Douglas Mutchler (b 24 Oct 1986).

CF52724422 Katelyn Michelle Mutchler (b 15 Sep 1989).

CF5272443 Michael Lynn Rager (b 28 Jun 1963, Columbus OH) m 7 Jan 1989, Sherri Chapman. Farmer, fertilizer dealer.

CF52724431 Kirsten Reba Rager (b 19 Aug 1989).

CF52724432 Ryan Michael Rager (b 4 Oct 1991).

CF5273 Calvin Wallace Weiser (13 Aug 1857, Greencastle OH-2 Dec 1944, Columbus OH) m 29

Sep 1886, near Jefferson, Bloom Tp OH, Mary Boyer (24 Nov 1863, Greencastle OH-1 Nov 1939, Greencastle OH) Bur Lithopolis OH. Merchant, Greencastle OH.

CF52731 Harry Boyer Weiser (5 Sep 1887, Greencastle OH-27 Sep 1950, Houston TX) m 18 Sep 1915, Columbus OH, Hazel Eleanor McKean (3 Jun 1893, Akron OH-24 Sep 1981, Dallas TX) Bur Houston TX. He, BA 1911, MA 1912, OSU; Ph D, Cornell, 1914. Dean, Professor of Chemistry, dept chairman, Rice U, Houston TX, 1915-1950. Author, seven colloid chemistry text books, over 150 journal publications. Captain, Chemical Warfare Service, USA, WWI; confidential National Defense Research investigator, WWII. Many honors came to him. A Weiser scholarship in his memory exists at Rice U. She, BS, OSU, 1915.

*CF527311 Dorothy Boyer Weiser (b 2 Oct 1916, Houston TX) m 15 Jun 1940, Houston TX, William Wesley Seale Jr (b 7 Feb 1914, San Antonio TX) She, BA, Rice U, 1937. Secretary and teacher; author *Mat(t)hias Milestones* (1984) He, BS, Rice U, 1939, USNR, WWII. Oil company supervisor, Port Arthur TX. Arvada CO.

*CF5273111 William Boyer Seale (b 4 Feb 1946, Houston TX) m 19 Nov 1994, Peaceful Valley CO, Ann France Dederer (b 16 Jul 1957, Summit NJ) He, BA, CO Col, 1968; MD, Columbia U, 1972. Radiologist, Boulder CO. She, BA, Bucknell U, 1979; MA George Washington U, 1982.

*CF5273112 Mark Wesley Seale (b 17 Nov 1948, Port Arthur TX) m 9 Jul 1983, Estes Park CO, Linda Kay Dorn (b 28 Feb 1954, Flint MI) He, BS, CO U, 1972. Petroleum landman. She, BA, DU, 1976; MA, UNC, Greeley, 1983. Teacher. Res Monument CO.

CF52731121 Hilary Dorn Seale (b 4 Jun 1986, Amarillo TX).

CF52731122 Scott William Seale (b 4 Oct 1988, Amarillo TX).

*CF527312 Marjorie McKean Weiser (b 24 Sep 1922, Houston TX) m 12 Jul 1945, Houston TX, Horace Trabue Witherspoon Jr (7 Aug 1918, Galveston TX-21 Feb 1990, Irving TX) Bur Dallas TX. She, BFA, CO U, 1944. He, WWII: USAF; airline captain, Irving TX.

CF5273121 John Trabue Witherspoon (b 27 Apr 1946, Houston TX) m 1) 24 Jan 1970, Dallas TX, Judith Diane Shearin, div 1977; m 2) 1 Dec 1979, Newport Beach CA, Jeffre' Lynne Pierce (b 17 May 1953, Riverside CA) div 1987; m 3) 14 Jul 1989, St Paul MN, Carol Ann Cohoes Rivet (b 12 Sep 1950, St Paul MN) He, BA, OK U, 1968; Rivet: BA, MN U, 1973. He, sales manager, Woodbury MN.

CF52731211 Jaime Allyson Witherspoon (b 24 Feb 1983, St Paul MN).

CF52731212 Amanda Jo Witherspoon (b 17 Sep 1984, St Paul MN).

CF5273122 Harriet Ann Witherspoon (b 22 Nov 1949, Dallas TX) m 1970, Texarkana TX, Gregory Scott Myers (b 2 Mar 1948, Binghamton NY) div 1980. She, flight attendant, legal secretary, office manager, Irving TX.

CF52731221 Shannon Ann Myers (b 26 Dec 1970, Texarkana TX) m 21 May 1994, Southlake TX, John Charles McCrary (b 10 Oct 1968, El Paso TX) div 1996. BS, Tarleton (TX) S U, 1993.

CF52731222 Rebecca Jenn Myers (b 7 Feb 1976, Dallas TX).

CF5273123 Jean Boyer Witherspoon (b 4 Feb 1952, Great Falls MT) m 1) 3 Jan 1974, Irving TX, Don Stephen Jackson, div 1982; m 2) 30 Jun 1984, Irving TX, Larry Dean Flynn (b 10 Aug 1956, Nowata OK) She, flight attendant, realtor, Southlake TX. Jackson: BA, TX U, 1978; JD, St Mary's U (San Antonio) 1981. Flynn: attorney. Res Southlake TX.

CF52731231 Tyler Trabue Flynn (b 6 May 1985, Dallas TX).

CF52732 Ardrie Brighton Weiser
(1890-1961)

Hazel Kathleen Codner Weiser
(1890-1959)

CF52731232   Sarah Boyer Flynn (b 25 Aug 1987, Dallas TX).

CF52732   Ardrie Brighton Weiser (21 Mar 1890, Greencastle OH-13 Jun 1961, Canal Winchester OH) m 19 Jun 1919, Canal Winchester OH, Hazel Kathleen Codner (30 Jul 1890, Radnor OH-18 Jan 1959, Columbus OH) He, BA, OSU, MA, Columbia U. Supt of Schools, Canal Winchester OH. She, Otterbern (OH) Col, teacher.

*CF527321   Donald Codner Weiser (b 15 Jun 1923, Columbus OH) m 15 Sep 1946, Canal Winchester OH, Minnie Maxine Kerns (b 8 Apr 1924, Lake Worth FL) WWII: USAF. Banker, Columbus OH.

*CF5273211   Kristine Kay Weiser (b 18 Jul 1949, Columbus OH) m 5 Sep 1970, Canal Winchester OH, Anthony Roman Jr (b 11 Feb 1947, Lares Puerto Rico) She, BA, Capital (OH) U, 1995, banker; he, BA, OSU, 1971, construction firm president.

CF52732111   Alex Anthony Roman (b 31 Jul 1977, Columbus OH).

CF52732112   Erik Kristofer Roman (b 24 May 1979, Columbus OH).

CF52732 Ardrie B and Hazel Codne- Weiser Family, 1986

*CF5273212   Kile Kerns Weiser (b 5 May 1952, Columbus OH) m 21 Jun 1975, Canal Winchester OH, Anna Louise Schumick (b 25 Feb 1953, Columbus OH) div 1992. He, banker; she, hospital therapist, Canal Winchester OH.

CF52732121   Zachery Kerns Weiser (b 29 Jul 1976, Columbus OH).

CF52732122   Erin Johnine Weiser (b 11 Mar 1978, Columbus OH).

CF52732123   Allison Brighton Weiser (b 20 May 1982, Columbus OH).

*CF5273213   Kevin Codner Weiser (b 22 May 1955, Columbus OH) m 6 Apr 1974, Pauline J Hanna (b 6 Oct 1953, Columbus OH) President, Weiser Inc, Canal Winchester OH.

                  Stephanie Dawn Hanna Weiser (b 6 May 1973, Canal Winchester OH) adopted by Kevin Weiser.

CF52732131   Deidre Ann Weiser (b 31 Jul 1976, Canal Winchester OH).

CF52732132   Deena Lynn Weiser (b 31 Jul 1976, Canal Winchester OH).

*CF527322   Richard Conrad Weiser (b 26 Oct 1924, Columbus OH) m 18 Jun 1949, Betty Jo Woltz (b 3 Aug 1926, Bucyrus OH) He, BS, OSU, 1949. Architectural engineer. She, BS, OU, 1948. Teacher, Canal Winchester OH.

*CF5273221   Todd Conrad Weiser (b 19 Jun 1955, Columbus OH) m 31 Oct 1981, Groveport OH, Colleene Lou Fagan (b 9 Oct 1956, Columbus OH) He, President, TC Weiser Construction Co, Canal Winchester OH.

                  Rex Richard Weiser (b 26 Jul 1994, Columbus OH).

CF527323   Anne Codner Weiser (8 Jun 1927, Columbus OH-10 Feb 1953, Colorado Springs CO) m 21 Apr 1951, Canal Winchester OH, Richard Tatum (5 Nov 1924, Trinidad CO-10 Feb 1953, Colorado Springs CO) Bur Colorado Springs CO. He, US Naval Academy; USN. She, BS, OSU, medical technologist.

*CF527324   William Calvin Weiser (b 30 Jul 1931, Columbus OH) m 21 Dec 1956, Canal Winchester OH, Palma Marcella Martin (b 27 Mar 1935, St Paul MN-17 May 1992, Canal Winchester OH) Bur Canal Winchester OH. He, BSME, OSU; design engineer. She, BS, OSU, 1956; art teacher.

*CF5273241   Martin William Weiser (b 10 Jan 1959, Columbus OH) m 28 Jul 1985, Sacramento CA, Patricia Burt (b 29 Feb 1960, Salt Lake City UT) He, BS, OSU, 1981; MS, 1985; Ph D, 1987, UCA, Berkeley. Professor of mechanical engineering, U NM. She, BA, UCA, Berkeley, 1982.

CF52732411   Matthew William Weiser (b 17 Oct 1989, Albuquerque NM).

CF52732412   John Christopher Weiser (b 5 Dec 1992, Albuquerque NM).

*CF5273242   Mark Codner Weiser (b 11 May 1961, Columbus OH) m 21 May 1988, Cleveland Heights OH, Mary Catherine Moody (b 17 Jun 1963, Cleveland Heights OH) He, BA, OSU, 1986; photo lab technician. She, BS, 1986, MS, 1987, OSU; Ph D, OSU, 1992. Research fellow.

CF52733   Mary Helen Weiser (20 Jun 1897-5 Dec 1898, Bloom Tp, Fairfield Co OH) Bur Lithopolis OH.

CF5274   Almeda Emma Weiser (11 Nov 1859, near Greencastle OH-27 Aug 1918, Greencastle OH) m 13 May 1891, John Schaffner (20 Apr 1842, Basil Switzerland-25 Mar 1927, Basil OH) Bur Basil (Baltimore) OH. Farmer and butcher.

CF52741 Calvin Leroy Schaffner (20 Nov 1891, Basil OH-8 Apr 1972) m 12 Mar 1928, Basil OH, Mellie Bennettie Snider (Keller) (17 Jan 1883, Basil OH-5 Aug 1965) Bur Basil OH. Manager, general store, Basil OH.

CF52742 Samuel Stanley Schaffner (29 May 1893, Basil OH-30 Mar 1970, Columbus OH) m 29 May 1922, Newark OH, Pauline Edith Stalter (13 Mar 1904, Etna Tp, Licking Co OH-22 Jun 1982) Bur Reynoldsburg OH. Restaurant and carry-out business, Baltimore OH.

CF527421 Samuel Stanley Schaffner Jr (b 14 Dec 1923, Basil OH) m 21 Jun 1947, Ocean Grove NJ, Carole Jean Flay (5 Jan 1927, Bayonne NJ-21 Nov 1978, Baltimore OH) Bur Basil OH. WWII: USA Air Corps,. Jeweler.

CF5274211 Larey Dean Schaffner (b 3 Feb 1948, Lancaster OH) m 26 May 1973, Lockport NY, Nancy Jean Yeager (b 21 Feb 1952, Tucson AZ) She, teacher; he, engineer.

CF52742111 Adam Lyle Schaffner (b 24 Oct 1877, Columbus OH).

CF52742112 Aaron Jason Schaffner (b 24 Oct 1977, Columbus OH).

CF52742113 Matthew Kerel Schaffner (b 21 Sep 1980, Columbus OH).

CF52742114 Ethen Anton Schaffner (b 31 May 1985, Lancaster OH).

CF5274212 Nancee Lee Schaffner (b 26 Jun 1950, Lancaster OH) unm MD.

CF5274213 JoDell Jean Schaffner (b 3 Jun 1954, Columbus OH) m 9 Oct 1976, Buckeye Lake OH, Thomas Charles Siefert (22 Oct 1953, Columbus OH) He, sales; she, court reporter.

CF5274214 Scott Stanley Schaffner (b 20 Mar 1958, Baltimore OH) m 28 Sep 1985, Columbus OH, Linda Reed (b 13 Aug 1958, Columbus OH) He, engineer.

CF527422 Bruce Patrick Schaffner (b 17 Mar 1929, Basil OH) m 30 Jan 1954, Liberty IN, Roberta Irene Rostofer (b 8 Mar 1933, Violet Tp, Fairfield Co OH) Korean Conflict: USA. Timekeeper, North American Aviation, Columbus OH.

CF5274221 Sheree Sue Schaffner (b 14 Jan 1957, Columbus OH) Accountant.

CF5274222 Bruce Patrick Schaffner II (b 6 Nov 1959, Columbus OH) m 10 Jul 1993, Jackson OH, Lori Diane Mercer (b 22 Sep 1962, Jackson OH) She, nurse; he, pharmacist.

CF527423 John Albert Schaffner (b 24 Dec 1937, Basil OH) m 6 Jul 1962, Columbus OH, Luray Schirtinger. Artists.

CF5274231 Shawn Michael Schaffner (b 12 Aug 1964, Columbus OH) m 29 Aug 1987, St Louis MO, Andrea Leigh Maechling (b 3 Aug 1964, St Louis MO) She, production manager; he, sales.

CF5274232 John Michael Schaffner (b 7 Mar 1969, Columbus OH) Scientist.

CF52743 Mary Ruth Schaffner (b 3 Apr 1895, Basil OH) m 21 Jun 1921, Lancaster OH, Charles Ernest Nisley (b 26 Aug 1891, Hebron OH) Restaurant and carry-out business, Baltimore OH.

CF527431 Donna Jean Nisley (b 28 Mar 1922, Basil OH) m 9 Jul 1950, Basil OH, Homer Herbert Schoffner (b 2 Mar 1925, Basil OH) Electrical inspector in quality control, North American Aviation, Columbus OH.

CF5274311 Mitchell Patrick Schoffner (b 17 Apr 1953, Lancaster OH) m 14 Dec 1974, Etna OH,

Peggy Sue Heimberger (b 30 Jan 1954, Pataskola OH) Both BS, OH U, Athens. She, teacher; he, insurance industry.

CF52743111   Megan Nicole Schoffner (b 25 Apr 1984, Columbus OH).

Frederick Kyle Schoffner (b 6 Jun 1990) adopted 6 Apr 1995, Columbus OH.

CF5274312   Cecelia Beth Schoffner (b 16 May 1957, Lancaster OH) m 14 Jul 1978, Gahanna OH, Robert D Smeck.

CF527432   Richard Ernest Nisley (b 10 Mar 1926, Basil OH) m 22 Feb 1948, Canal Winchester OH, Lorna Lou Calvin (b 6 Aug 1928, Wilkesville OH) Chief electrician, Poston Plant of Columbus and Southern Ohio Electric Co, Athens OH.

CF5274321   Cheryl Legene Nisley (b 9 Jan 1949, Columbus OH).

CF5274322   Andrew Richard Nisley (b 17 Aug 1950, Athens OH).

CF5274323   Zella Lou Nisley (b 1 Apr 1952, Athens OH).

CF5274324   Matthew Scott Nisley (b 8 Oct 1954, Athens OH).

CF52744   Russell John Schaffner (18 Jul 1897, Basil OH-5 Nov 1983, Grove City OH) m 29 Dec 1926, Toledo OH, Ruth Viola Lilly (24 Nov 1904, Hemlock OH-28 Mar 1995, Columbus OH) Storekeeper, OSU, Columbus OH.

CF527441   Doris Marie Schaffner (b 25 Aug 1929, Etna OH) m 25 Oct 1952, Columbus OH, Ronald Louis Johnson (b 4 Nov 1928, South Connelsville PA) OSU, Columbus OH. Lab supervisor. Producers of ZMO healing oil, Grove City OH.

CF5274411   Keith Ronald Johnson (b 17 Aug 1953, Columbus OH) m 20 Mar 1981, Ft Wayne IN, Cheryl Ann Johnston (18 Oct 1955, Ft Wayne IN) Director-manager, West Ohio Conf., United Methodist Church, Circuit Rider, Galena OH.

CF52744111   Bernadine Elizabeth Johnson (b 3 Jul 1982, Columbus OH).

CF52744112   R Johnston Wayne Johnson (b 9 Oct 1984, Westerville OH).

CF52744113   Skye Marie Johnson (b 4 Apr 1993, Westerville OH).

CF5274412   Karla Marie Johnson (b 13 Jun 1957, Columbus OH) m 13 Aug 1977, Westerville OH, Kenneth Lynn Beamer (b 19 Oct 1949, Dennis OH) RR conductor, Hilliard OH.

CF52744121   Kathryn Michelle Beamer (b 9 Jul 1981, Columbus OH).

CF52744122   Kimberly Louise Beamer (b 2 Jul 1983, Columbus OH).

CF52744123   Kevin Mac Kenzie Beamer (b 12 Dec 1985, Westerville OH).

CF52744124   Kendra Gail Beamer (b 3 Sep 1988, Columbus OH).

CF5274413   Kyna Lynn Johnson (b 15 May 1958, Columbus OH) m 23 Sep 1978, Westerville OH, Andrew Edward Shindle (b 7 May 1959, Columbus OH) Graphic Arts, Hilliard OH.

CF52744131   Denver Andrew Shindle (b 26 Jun 1981, Columbus OH).

CF52744132   Holly Lynn Shindle (b 15 Dec 1983, Columbus OH).

CF527442   Donald Leroy Schaffner (b 22 Dec 1933, Etna OH) m 22 Aug 1958, Columbus OH, Marie Ellen Walp (b 28 Mar 1936, Springfield OH) Inventory clerk, OSU, Columbus OH. Producer of ZMO healing oil, Grove City OH.

CF5274421   Philip Leroy Schaffner (b 27 Oct 1960, Columbus OH) Landscape architect, Columbus OH.

CF5274422   Timothy Scott Schaffner (b 10 Aug 1962, Columbus OH) m 18 May 1985, Grafton OH, Karen Ann Hobar (b 28 Mar 1962, Elyria OH) Building inspector, Reynoldsburg OH.

CF5274423   Ruth Ellen Schaffner (b 10 Jun 1966, Columbus OH) m 7 Jan 1989, Michael Dwayne Meade (b 2 Dec 1965, Columbus OH) Carpenter, Columbus OH.

CF52744231   Misty Michelle Meade (b 8 Oct 1985, Columbus OH).

CF52744232   Megan Christine Meade (b 9 May 1989, Columbus OH).

CF52744233   Jessica Ellen Meade (b 21 Jul 1991, Columbus OH).

CF527443   Donna Lee Schaffner (b 22 Dec 1933, Etna OH) m 10 Sep 1955, Columbus OH, Robert Howard Miller (b 2 Dec 1932, Columbus OH) US Postal Service, Grove City OH.

CF5274431   Karen Ann Miller (b 27 Apr 1957, Columbus OH) m 20 Jun 1981, David Treece Simpson (b 6 Jul 1954, Findlay OH) Restaurant manager, Columbus OH.

CF52744311   Diana Christine Simpson (b 10 Jun 1985, Columbus OH).

CF52744312   Bethany Loren Simpson (b 26 Oct 1986, Columbus OH).

CF5274432   Gary Dean Miller (b 9 May 1960, Columbus OH) m 10 Nov 1984, Columbus OH, Lisa Christine Board (b 28 Jun 1963, Steubenville OH) US Postal Service, Columbus OH.

CF52744321   Renee Christine Miller (b 6 Sep 1987, Westerville OH).

CF52744322   Danielle Nicole Miller (b 26 Feb 1989, Westerville OH).

CF5274433   Carol Lynn Miller (b 2 Jan 1962, Columbus OH) Fitness director, Canton OH.

CF52745   Zella Mae Schaffner (2 Apr 1901, Basil OH-2 Oct 1992) m 25 Jun 1925, Basil OH, Harold Raymond Macklin (5 Jun 1897, Basil OH-19 May 1958, Baltimore OH) Bur Baltimore OH. Paper mill mechanic, Baltimore, OH.

CF527451   Sharma Joan Macklin (6 Apr 1928, Basil OH-14 Sep 1984, Basil OH) m 20 Apr 1949, Basil OH, Ralph Clinton Seever (b 26 Sep 1929, Basil OH) Laborer.

CF5274511   JaLinda Eloise Seever (b 18 Oct 1949, Lancaster OH) m 25 Jun 1972, Baltimore OH, James Haughn (b 9 Feb 1948, Columbus OH) Accounting and process manager.

CF52745111   Kyle Matthew Haughn (b 16 Dec 1984, Lancaster OH).

CF5274512   Jeffrey Ralph Seever (b 21 Nov 1953, Lancaster OH) Accounting.

CF5275   Mary M Weiser (1 Apr 1863, Greencastle OH-1955, Columbus OH) unm Bur Lithopolis OH.

CF5276   John Edgar Weiser (3 Feb 1866, Greencastle OH-14 Apr 1934, Walnut Tp, Pickaway Co OH) m 30 Mar 1892, Lillie Bell Noggle (16 Apr 1868-6 Apr 1946) Bur near Asheville OH. School teacher; merchant, Walnut Corners, Pickaway Co; clerk of township trustees and of board of education.

CF52761   Rayman Stanley Weiser (1 Jan 1893, Pickaway Co OH-30 Aug 1975) m 28 Jun 1919, Nelle Hoffhines (4 Oct 1893, Pickaway Co OH-9 Mar 1981) Teacher, Toledo OH.

CF527611   Robert Hoffhines Weiser (26 Jun 1921, Toledo OH-15 Apr 1982, Westwood MA) m 16 Nov 1944, Charlotte Flynn (b 21 Dec 1922, Fitchburg MA) Sales manager engineer, heating and cooling.

*CF5276111   Robert Charles Weiser (b 14 Feb 1946, Fitchburg MA) m 27 Dec 1969, Marsha Monahon (b 30 Jul 1948, Newton MA) Utility executive; social worker, Brewer ME.

CF52761111   Heidi Lynn Weiser (b 25 Sep 1971, Landstuhl, Germany) CPA, Boston MA.

CF52761112   Scott Travis Weiser (b 18 Feb 1976, Rutland VT).

CF5276112   Susan Marie Weiser (b 28 Mar 1948, Fitchburg MA-24 Aug 1974, New York NY) m 15 Feb 1969, Robert McKnight.

CF52761121   Kevin McKnight (b 4 Oct 1971, NJ) CO.

CF52761122   Kerrie Anne McKnight (b 29 Oct 1973, New York NY) New York NY.

CF5276113   Betty Jo Weiser (b 19 Jan 1952, Pawtucket RI) m 1) 1 Jul 1979, Ronald Gallaher; m 2) 20 Jun 1992, Joseph Caouette. Recreational director, Westwood MA.

CF52761131   Kylee Gallaher (b 28 Sep 1981, Redwood City CA) Westwood MA.

CF52761132   Devin Gallaher (b 24 Mar 1983, Redwood City CA) Westwood MA.

CF5276114   Thomas Rayman Weiser (b 14 Nov 1954, Pawtucket RI) unm Laborer, Westwood MA.

*CF5276115   Peter Anthony Weiser (b 26 Jun 1956, Attleboro MA) unm Software project manager, Oakland CA.

CF527612   Doris Weiser (b 5 Oct 1922, Toledo OH) m 20 Jan 1944, George M Lynn. San Diego CA.

CF5276121   Catherine Ann Lynn (b 19 Apr 1948, Akron OH) m 22 Nov 1972, Donald Glover. Teacher, San Diego CA.

CF52761211   Jeffrey Thomas Glover (b 16 May 1976, Los Gatos CA).

CF52761212   Kristin Lynn Glover (b 24 Nov 1978, Poway CA).

CF5276122   Barbara Sue Lynn (b 8 Apr 1950, Normal OK) m 4 Aug 1972, Ronald Sexton (b Eagle Point OR).

CF52761221   Robert Carrol Sexton (b 14 Feb 1979, Sacramento CA).

CF52761222   Andrew James Sexton (b 9 Feb 1983, Sacramento CA).

CF5276123   Thomas Michael Lynn (b 8 Jun 1954, Palo Alto CA) m 7 Jul 1984, Kathy Sims (b El Dorado Hills CA).

CF52761231   Michael Clayton Lynn (b 25 Jan 1987, San Diego CA).

CF52761232   Jonathon Thomas Lynn (b 14 Nov 1990, Sacramento CA).

CF52762   Harold Samuel Weiser (30 Nov 1897, Walnut Tp, Pickaway Co OH-2 Mar 1960, Beloit WI) m 21 Oct 1925, Geraldine Hope Roush (4 Aug 1898, Columbus OH-25 Apr 1984, Beloit WI) Bur Beloit WI. Owner, Bud Weiser Motors, Beloit WI.

CF527621   Nancy Lida Weiser (27 Oct 1927, Chicago IL-23 Aug 1974, Concord MA) Beloit Col, 1950.

*CF527622   John Roush Weiser (b 21 Nov 1928, Chicago IL) m 18 Feb 1961, Rockton IL, Mary Ellen Shappstrom (b 3 Jan 1937, Moline IL) USAF. WI U, Beloit Col. Owner, Bud Weiser Motors, Beloit WI.

CF5276221   James Scott Weiser (b 5 Sep 1961, Rockford IL) m 31 Dec 1989, Jamaica, Kathleen Anne Johnson McNabb (b 31 Mar 1964, Beloit WI) Used car mgr, Budweiser Motors, Inc.

CF52762211   Cole Jordan Weiser (b 27 Sep 1990, Beloit WI).

CF52762212   Maci Kaitlin Weiser (b 29 Jun 1993, Beloit WI).

CF5276222   Susan Lynn Weiser (b 27 Apr 1963, Rockford IL) m 14 Jul 1984, Robert David Penn (b 27 Aug 1962, Cedar Rapids IA) Both, Cornell Col, IA; investment broker.

CF52762221   Lauren Ashley Penn (b 17 Jan 1987, Cedar Rapids IA).

CF52762222   Robert David Penn (b 2 Aug 1989, Cedar Rapids IA).

CF52762223   Jonathan David Penn (b 9 Mar 1992, Cedar Rapids IA).

CF5276223   Paul Richard Weiser (b 19 Nov 1965, Rockford IL) WI U. Computer programmer, Madison WI.

CF5276224   Katherine Ann Weiser (b 28 Mar 1967, Rockford IL).

CF52762241   Nicole Hope Weiser (b 19 May 1992, Beloit WI).

CF52763   Frances Loraine Weiser (26 Jul 1900, Walnut Tp, Pickaway Co OH-Jan 1981) m 17 Feb 1951, Samuel Ridge (b 20 Mar 1895, Chagrin Falls OH) Teacher, Canton OH. No chn.

CF52764   Orville Berneal Weiser (14 Oct 1903, Walnut Tp, Pickaway Co OH-3 Jan 1970) m 1 Jan 1938, Evelyn Fisher (b 15 Dec 1905, New Philadelphia OH) City tax solicitor, Canton OH.

CF5277   Clara Evaline Weiser (29 Jun 1868, Greencastle OH-26 May 1935, Canal Winchester OH) m 15 May 1895, Henry Newton Brenner (16 Mar 1871, near Canal Winchester OH-23 Mar 1961, Canal Winchester OH) Bur Canal Winchester OH. Farmer.

CF52771   Mary Edith Brenner (6 Apr 1898, Canal Winchester OH-23 Dec 1987, Canal Winchester OH) unm Secretary.

CF52772   Evelyn May Brenner (b 12 Dec 1902, Canal Winchester OH) unm Owner, Groveport Hardware.

CF52773   Ivan Graeff Brenner (19 Jan 1906, Canal Winchester OH-25 Jan 1995, Newark OH) m 2 Jun 1942, Newark OH, Carrie Hoskinson (b 5 Mar 1905, Newark OH) Owner, Ivan G Brenner Mfg Co, Newark OH.

CF52774   Noel Arden Brenner (2 Jan 1911, Canal Winchester OH-26 Mar 1996) m 21 Dec 1940,

Violet Tp, Fairfield Co OH, Lucille Bickel (b 24 Mar 1915, Hocking Co OH) Bur Carroll OH. Farmer.

CF527741   Richard Lee Brenner (b 17 Feb 1946, Columbus OH) m 30 Jan 1985, Columbus OH, Patricia Horne (b 12 Dec 1955).

CF5277411   Jason Richard Brenner (b 14 May 1988, Canal Winchester OH).

CF5277412   Justin Lee Brenner (b 1 Oct 1990, Canal Winchester OH).

CF527742   Marilyn Lucille Brenner (b 23 Nov 1947, Columbus OH) m 28 Jul 1973, Joseph Lo Schiavo (b 4 Sep 1947) OSU. Teacher, Columbus OH.

CF5277421   Andrew Joseph Lo Schiavo (b 24 May 1978, Columbus OH).

CF5278   Jesse Woods Weiser (11 Feb 1871, Greencastle OH-16 Apr 1938, near Canal Winchester OH) unm Bur Lithopolis OH. Farmer.

CF5279   Thomas Hamer Weiser (4 Nov 1873, Greencastle OH-8 Mar 1952, Columbus OH) m 4 Apr 1904, Columbus OH, Nelle Florence Black (20 Jan 1874, Groveport OH-5 Feb 1954, Columbus OH) Bur Lithopolis OH. President, Coulson Glass Co, Columbus OH.

CF52791   Clyde Alden Weiser (b 11 Feb 1905, Columbus OH) m 12 Oct 1927, Columbus OH, Edith Mae Ashbrooke (b 22 Jan 1906, Columbus OH) President, Coulson Glass Co, Columbus OH. No chn.

CF52792   Robert Thomas Weiser (b 1 May 1910, Columbus OH) m 16 May 1936, Columbus OH, Jean Elizabeth Ervin (14 Sep 1910, Middleport OH-28 Aug 1992, Sarasota FL); m 2) 9 Apr 1994, Sarasota FL, Kathryn Soderstrom (b 20 Jul 1918, DeSoto IL) Personnel director, Rochester Products Division of General Motors Corp, Rochester NY; later Buick Division, Flint MI.

CF527921   Thomas Ervin Weiser (b 2 Nov 1941, Columbus OH) unm USA, 1964-68. Rochester Products Division, GMC.

*CF527922   Richard Robert Weiser (b 2 Apr 1946, Lynwood CA) m 25 Jun 1983, Portland MI, Annette Kay Gensterblum (b 29 Jul 1950, Lansing MI) Vietnam Conflict: USA, 1968-69. BA, OH Wesleyan U, 1968; JD MI U, 1972. Attorney, Lansing MI.

CF5279221   Kathryn Elizabeth Weiser (b 3 Apr 1986, Lansing MI).

CF5279222   Laura Jean Weiser (b 25 Apr 1989, Lansing MI).

CF52793   Thomas Edwin Weiser (15 Aug 1915, Columbus OH-1972) m 4 Sep 1943, Camp Pickett VA, Trella Louise Duffey (b 25 Aug 1918, Toledo OH) Vice President, Coulson Glass Co, Columbus OH.

CF527931   Elaine Weiser (b 2 Aug 1948, Columbus OH) m John Backey.

CF527932   Philip Alden Weiser (b 28 Jan 1951, Columbus OH) m Janice   . DDS. Dentist, Columbus OH.

CF528   Andrew Jackson Weiser (10 Feb 1828-14 Jun 1921, Canal Winchester OH) m 17 Jan 1860, Fairfield Co OH, Margaret Effie Green (6 Jan 1839-30 Jan 1908, Greencastle OH) Bur Lithopolis OH. Bricklayer.

CF5281   Alvah Victor Weiser (3 May 1860, Greencastle OH-12 Jun 1943, Canal Winchester OH) m 1) 4 May 1892, Greencastle OH, Drusilla Florence Courtright (10 Mar 1867, Greencastle OH-24 Aug 1903, Greencastle OH); m 2) 1904, Lithopolis OH, Tillie Warner (Hartman) (4 May 1867, Mifflintown PA-11 Oct 1936, Canal Winchester OH) Bur Lithopolis OH. Carpenter.

CF52811 Cecil Courtright Weiser (21 Dec 1899, Greencastle OH-18 Mar 1906, Greencastle OH) Bur Lithopolis OH.

CF52812 Margaret Irene Weiser (b 9 Jan 1906, Greencastle OH) unm Church organist.

CF529 George Washington Weiser (17 Dec 1829, Greencastle OH-29 May 1905, Columbus OH) m 15 Jan 1856, Fairfield Co OH, Mary Jane Homrighous (5 Oct 1836-29 Aug 1905) Bur Lithopolis OH.

CF5291 William Lee Weiser (5 Apr 1858, Dyersville IA-1940) m Belle Staley. Bur Lithopolis OH. Grocer.

CF5292 Ervin Miner Weiser (22 Aug 1861, Greencastle OH-24 Oct 1928, Los Angeles CA) Bur Glendale CA. unm Toolmaker.

CF5293 Samuel Elmer Weiser (14 Aug 1862, Greencastle OH-1942, Tampa FL) m Minnie Faust. Bur Tampa FL.

CF52931 Ivan Weiser (b Cardington OH) m. Musician, violonist.

CF52932 William Weiser (b Cardington OH) m. Barber.

CF529321 Jay Weiser (b Tampa FL) Musician.

CF529 George Washington Weiser
(1829-1905)

CF5294 Emma Caroline Weiser (20 Sep 1864, Greencastle OH-24 Janaury 1940, Los Angeles CA) m 20 Jun 1906, Columbus OH, Henry L Blair (1856, Morrow Co OH-13 Oct 1928, Los Angesles CA) Bur Glendale CA. Teacher and secretary. No chn.

CF5295 Angeline Weiser (5 Jun 1867, Greencastle OH-6 Jun 1867, Greencastle OH) Bur Greencastle OH.

CF5296 Lillian Elnorah Weiser (25 Apr 1868, Greencastle OH-10 Jun 1932, Los Angeles CA) m 18 Aug 1905, Cleveland OH, William Gordon Hamilton (London England-Los Angeles CA) Her ashes scattered; he bur Los Angeles CA. No chn.

CF5297 Clara Margaret Weiser (9 May 1872, Lithopolis OH-3 May 1926, Los Angeles CA) m 8 Jun 1910, Columbus OH, Sherman Lewis Porter (29 Jan 1868, Knox Co OH-22 Jan 1946, Los Angeles, CA) Bur Inglewood CA. Secretary.

*CF52971 Lillian Mary Porter (27 Apr 1912, Columbus OH-13 Jul 1996) m 1) 17 Oct 1930, Los Angeles CA, George Philip Bennett (b 7 Sep 1908, Mt Gilead OH) div 1934; m 2) 28 Jun 1935, Long Beach CA, Thomas J McNeill (b 29 Jan 1904, Oklahoma Territory) Warrant officer; civil service.

CF529711 Philip Alan Bennett (13 Aug 1931, Los Angeles CA-15 Apr 1992, San Diego CA) Bur at sea. BA, MA, San Diego S U. Teacher, speech therapist.

CF529712 Patricia Lynne McNeill (b 28 Oct 1951, San Diego CA) m 2 Jun 1973, San Diego CA, Dennis L Weikel (b 7 Apr 1950, San Diego CA).

CF5297121 Larissa Ann Weikel (b 24 Jun 1976, La Mesa CA).

CF5297122 Travis Scott Weikel (b 27 Dec 1978, Ada OK).

CF5298   Jessie Lorinda Weiser (27 Jul 1874, Lithopolis OH-25 May 1875, Lithopolis OH) Bur
Lithopolis OH.

CF5299   Hattie Druscilla Weiser (27 Jul 1874, Lithopolis OH-5 Aug 1875, Lithopolis OH).

CF52A   Mary M Weiser (27 Apr 1831-28 Aug 1907) m 26 Oct 1854, Reese H Bunn (26 Sep 1827-
9 Oct 1897, Greencastle OH) Bur Lithopolis OH. Livestock dealer; owner, tavern-hotel, Greencastle OH.

CF52A1   George W Bunn (20 Feb 1856, Greencastle OH-27 Mar 1866, Greencastle OH) Bur
Greencastle OH.

CF52A2   Ida M Bunn (1857-1945) m William A Solt (1848-1906) Bur Lithopolis OH.

CF52A21   Birdy Bunn Solt (9 Feb 1877-9 Feb 1877, Bloom Tp, Fairfield Co OH).

CF52A22   Fred Solt.

CF52A3   Fanny D Bunn (17 Apr 1859, Greencastle OH-5 Feb 1862, Greencastle OH) Bur
Greencastle OH.

CF52A4   Mary E Bunn (19 Nov 1861, Greencastle OH-5 Feb 1862, Greencastle OH) Bur
Greencastle OH.

CF52A5   Samuel Bunn m. School teacher, Greencastle OH.

CF52A6   Chester Bunn m. Window dresser in dept store.

CF52A61   Daughter (d 1913, Columbus OH).

CF52A7   Charles Bunn. Sheepherder, ID.

CF52A8   Herbert Bunn. Physician.

CF52A9   Maude Bunn (b 27 May 1877, Greencastle OH) m Hoskins.

CF52B   Lavina Weiser (18 Aug 1833, Bloom Tp, Fairfield Co OH-22 Dec 1905, Bloom Tp,
Fairfield Co OH) m 25 Mar 1852, Paul Alspaugh (25 Feb 1833, Bloom Tp, Fairfield Co OH-7 Aug 1896,
Bloom Tp, Fairfield Co OH) Bur Bloom Tp, Fairfield Co OH. Farmer.[74]

CF52B1   Henry Edward Alspaugh (29 Apr 1854, Bloom Tp, Fairfield Co OH-18 Oct 1912, Canal
Winchester OH) m 29 Aug 1876, Lithopolis OH, Sarah Samantha Courtright (26 Sep 1855, Fairfield Co OH-11
Jan 1901, Lithopolis OH) Bur Lithopolis OH. Farmer.

CF52B11   Gertrude Alspaugh (11 Jun 1877, Bloom Tp, Fairfield Co OH-10 Dec 1950, Canal
Winchester OH) unm Bur Lithopolis OH. Housekeeper.

CF52B12   Paul John Alspaugh (24 Dec 1878, Bloom Tp, Fairfield Co OH-Mar 1942, New
Philadelphia OH) m Jun 1919, Martha McCoy (d New Philadelphia OH) Bur New Philadelphia OH. Physician.
No chn.

CF52B13   Maude Lavina Alspaugh (ca 1881, Bloom Tp, Fairfield Co OH-11 Sep 1957, Columbus
OH) unm Bur Lithopolis OH. Clerk, Lazarus Dept Store, Columbus OH.

---

[74]Data compiled by George W Weiser. 1996 supplement by The Rev. Daniel A Kiger.

CF52B14   Infant daughter (15 Aug 1884-15 Aug 1884, Bloom Tp, Fairfield Co OH) Bur near Hooker OH.

CF52B2   Margaret Elizabeth Alspaugh (11 Nov 1856, Bloom Tp, west of Rock Mill OH-3 Sep 1940, Lancaster OH) m 8 Mar 1883, Bloom Tp, Fairfield Co OH, Silas S Mathias (16 Mar 1861, Hocking Co near Rockbridge OH-16 Mar 1949, Cuyahoga Falls OH) Bur Carroll OH. Farmer.

CF52B21   Bertha Alice Mathias (b 11 Jun 1889, Greenfield Tp, near Carroll OH) m 8 Mar 1911, Roy Lamb (2 Mar 1886, Bloom Tp, Fairfield Co OH-10 Nov 1974, Greenfield Tp, Fairfield Co OH) Farmer.

CF52B211   Neil Woodrow Lamb (1 Oct 1912, Bloom Tp, Fairfield Co OH-29 Apr 1952, Silver Spring MD) m 20 Jul 1935, Columbus OH, Alberta Mae Wolfe (b 30 Jun 1912, Fairfield OH) Bur Arlington VA. WWII: USA. Veteran's Administration, US Government. She, nurse.

CF52B2111   Neil Woodrow Lamb Jr (b 6 Aug 1937, Columbus OH) m 20 Jun 1964, Baltimore MD, Patricia Anne Farley (b 17 Feb 1941, Atlanta GA) USN; U Maryland; dentist.

CF52B21111   Tracy Lynn Lamb (b 26 Nov 1965, Portsmouth VA).

CF52B21112   Eric Neil Lamb Jr (b 21 Feb 1968, Frederick MD).

CF52B2112   Alan Roy Lamb (b 10 Mar 1940, Salt Lake City UT) m Murray Houston (b 29 Jul 1942) Air traffic control, Memphis TN.

CF52B21121   Michelle Kathleen Lamb (b 26 Sep 1964).

CF52B2113   Joan Ellen Lamb (b 31 Oct 1942, Canal Winchester OH) m 7 Dec 1963, Bethesda MD, Eugene Arnow (nee Arnowitz) (b 12 Apr 1935, Brooklyn NY) She, transcriber.

CF52B21131   Aaron Eugene Arnow (b 14 Aug 1964, Washington DC).

CF52B21132   Nathan Alan Arnow (b 28 Jul 1966, Silver Spring MD).

CF52B2114   John Marc Lamb (b 7 Aug 1950, Columbus OH) m Louise Cecilia Grady (b 7 Sep 1949, Riverdale MD).

CF52B212   Margaret Leota Lamb (b 22 Mar 1917, Bloom Tp, Fairfield Co OH) m 14 Aug 1944, near Carroll OH, Charles Albert Evers (b 3 Dec 1910, Cleveland OH) Electrical engineer, Warren OH. She, home economics teacher.

CF52B2121   Judith Adele Evers (b 2 Nov 1944, Lakewood OH) m 26 Jun 1965, Robert Wilson Flinn (b 3 Aug 1940, Kenton OH) Mechanical engineer. She, artist.

CF52B21211   David Eric Flinn (b 16 Sep 1969, Cleveland OH).

CF52B2122   Brian Lee Evers (b 8 Sep 1946, Lakewood OH) m 10 Jul 1968, Cleveland OH, Annette Kay Veits (b 20 Jan 1946, Warren OH) He, computer programmer; she, teacher.

CF52B2123   Bruce Albert Evers (b 8 Sep 1946, Lakewood OH) m 16 Dec 1972, Youngstown OH, Georgeann A Garritano (b 19 Nov 1948, Youngstown OH) He, laboratory sales; she, teacher.

CF52B22   Roy Silas Mathias (b 19 Sep 1891, Greenfield Tp, near Carroll OH) m 1 Aug 1919, Akron OH, Sadie Marie Semler (b 24 Feb 1896, Greensburg OH) Experimental engineer, BF Goodrich Rubber Co, Akron OH.

CF52B221   Evelyn Marie Mathias (b 1 May 1920, Akron OH) m 20 Sep 1944, Cuyahoga Falls OH,

Dudley A Colloran (b 30 Jun 1914, Los Angeles CA) Insurance salesman.

CF52B2211 Richard Roy Colloran (b 21 Mar 1947, Pleasantville NJ).

CF52B2212 Virginia Marie Colloran (b 21 Oct 1949, Oakland CA).

CF52B2213 Dorothy Louise Colloran (b 15 Mar 1953, Oakland CA).

CF52B222 Audrey Elene Mathias (b 15 Dec 1930, Akron OH) m 11 Dec 1948, Cuyahoga Falls OH, Robert Joseph Lucien (b 5 Dec 1925, Akron, OH) div; m 2) 1 Aug 1965, John Wise Logue, div; m 3) 15 Feb 1974, James Floto. Lucien: buyer for O'Neil Co.

CF52B2221 Daryl Eugene Lucien (b 23 Jun 1949, Akron OH).

CF52B3 Levi Renaldo Alspaugh (8 Apr 1859, Bloom Tp, Fairfield Co OH-9 Feb 1921, Lancaster OH) m Lancaster OH, Anna E Smith (22 Sep 1859, near Lancaster OH-21 Feb 1930, Lancaster OH) Bur Lancaster OH. PA RR section worker.

CF52B31 Caroline Elizabeth Alspaugh (13 Sep 1882-8 Feb 1884) Bur Bloom Tp, Fairfield Co OH.

CF52B32 Herbert Paul Alspaugh (4 Nov 1884-7 Oct 1886) Bur Bloom Tp, Fairfield Co OH.

CF52B33 Gertrude Ethel Alspaugh (16 Mar 1890, Fairfield Co OH-1 Jan 1925, near Lancaster OH) m Henry Cook. Bur near Lancaster OH. Retired glass worker.

CF52B331 Ann Louise Cook (29 Aug 1913, Lancaster OH-8 Dec 1937, Lancaster OH) m 28 Aug 1937, Lancaster OH, Clark Pierce. Bur near Lancaster OH. No chn.

CF52B332 Charles Edward Cook (b 5 Oct 1915) m 1 Oct 1938, near Baltimore OH, Dorothy Paugh. No chn.

CF52B34 Ruth Lavina Alspaugh (29 Sep 1893, Lancaster OH-19 Feb 1956, Lancaster, OH) m 24 Nov 1919, near Lancaster OH, Paul Holmes Rife (b 16 Dec 1894, Lancaster OH) Bur Lancaster OH. Custodian.

CF52B341 Mary Jane Rife (b 9 Dec 1920, Lancaster OH) m 19 Nov 1942, Lancaster OH, Paul Frederick Kitchen (b 3 Feb 1918, Lancaster OH) Fireman, PA RR. No chn.

CF52B342 Donald Eugene Rife (b 24 Feb 1923, Lancaster OH) m 5 Jun 1943, Josephine Margaret Straits. Salesman.

CF52B3421 Donald Eugene Rife Jr (b 23 Aug 1946, Lancaster OH).

CF52B3422 Nancy Rife (b 10 Feb 1949, Lancaster OH).

CF52B35 Mable Evaline Alspaugh (8 Nov 1900-16 Dec 1900).

CF52B4 Mary Alice Alspaugh (5 Jan 1863, Bloom Tp, Fairfield Co OH-25 Sep 1942, Columbus OH) m 16 Feb 1888, Bloom Tp, Fairfield Co OH, Jonathan Monroe Glick (3 Nov 1865, Bloom Tp, Fairfield Co OH-17 Aug 1927, Bloom Tp, Fairfield Co OH) Bur Lithopolis OH. Farmer and livestock dealer.

CF52B41 Coral Agnes Ruth Glick (b 25 Dec 1891, Bloom Tp, Fairfield Co OH) m 18 Nov 1915, Lithopolis OH, Frank Scott Busby (b 19 Apr 1890, Pleasant Tp, Fairfield Co OH) Farmer.

CF52B411 Alice Louise Busby (b 31 Oct 1916, Bloom Tp, Fairfield Co OH) m 18 Jun 1942, Bellevue KY, Delatus Earl Brown (b 4 Oct 1916, Columbus OH) Ophthalmologist. No chn.

CF52B412   Jonathan Glick Busby (b 30 Jan 1923, Bloom Tp, Fairfield Co OH) m 2 Sep 1944, Columbus OH, Mary Ellen Bachman (b 2 Jan 1924) Obstetrician, Columbus OH.

CF52B4121   Susanna Bachman Busby (b 26 Mar 1949, Columbus OH).

CF52B42   Magdalene Glick (b 19 Nov 1895, Bloom Tp, Fairfield Co OH) m 31 Mar 1918, Lithopolis OH, George Powell Boyer (17 Jan 1896, Canal Winchester OH-7 Mar 1949, Fremont OH) Bur Canal Winchester OH. District Sales Mgr, Purina Co, Northern Ohio.

CF52B421   Jack Monroe Boyer (b 11 Jun 1923, Dallas TX) m 1953, Sandusky OH, Lillian A Lee (b 1921, WVA) Mgr, Gray Drug Stores, Southwestern Ohio. Pharmacist.

CF52B4211   Candace Magdalene Boyer (b 10 Dec 1953, Columbus OH).

CF52B4212   Jack Monroe Boyer Jr (b 7 Oct 1956, Columbus OH).

CF52B4213   Jill Maureen Boyer (b 20 Apr 1958, Columbus OH).

CF52B422   George Powell Boyer Jr (b 15 Oct 1925, Dallas, TX) m 11 Mar 1956, New York NY, Sandra Davidson Scott (b 16 Nov 1931, Glen Falls NY) Architectural designer.

CF52B4221   Amy Scott Boyer (b May 1959, New York NY).

CF52B423   Mary Ann Boyer (b 4 Mar 1930, Bowling Green OH) m 12 Jun 1952, Fremont OH, Thomas G Baker (b 1927, Geneva OH) Artist Painter, Smithsonian.

CF52B4231   Deborah Glen Baker (24 Jul 1953, Washington DC-3 Jul 1959, Washington DC) Bur Arlington VA.

CF52B5   Samuel Solomon Alspaugh (18 Jun 1864, Bloom Tp, Fairfield Co OH-2 Jul 1940, Columbus OH) m 10 Dec 1890, Greencastle OH, Alma Viola Stuckey (28 Jun 1869, Greencastle OH-1 Nov 1950, Greenfield Tp, Fairfield Co OH) Bur Amanda Tp, Fairfield Co OH. Farmer.

CF52B51   Leota May Alspaugh (b 16 Oct 1892, Bloom Tp, Fairfield Co OH) m 30 Jun 1925, Columbus OH, Galy George Geer (1884, Vinton Co OH-11 Feb 1954, Columbus OH) Bur Lithopolis OH. Miller and carpenter.

CF52B511   Infant son (6 Jun 1926, Lancaster OH-28 Jun 1926, Lancaster OH) Bur Amanda Tp, Fairfield Co OH.

CF52B52   Ray Paul Alspaugh (b 1 Dec 1894, Bloom Tp, Fairfield Co OH) m 1932, Columbus OH, Helen Steele. Guard, Columbus Army Depot.

CF52B521   Gerald Lee Alspaugh (b Columbus OH) m 9 Aug 1959, Bourbonnais IL, Bethel Griffin.

CF52B522   Gloria Rae Alspaugh (b Columbus OH).

CF52B523   Carroll Alspaugh (b Hillards OH).

CF52B53   Otto Edward Alspaugh (29 Dec 1896, Bloom Tp, Fairfield Co OH-15 Sep 1903, Bloom Tp, Fairfield Co OH) Bur Amanda Tp, Fairfield Co OH.

CF52B54   Dorothy Marie Alspaugh (11 May 1900, Bloom Tp, Fairfield Co OH-18 Nov 1900, Bloom Tp, Fairfield Co OH) Bur Amanda Tp, Fairfield Co OH.

CF52B55   Effie Avinia Alspaugh (25 Sep 1902, Bloom Tp, Fairfield Co OH-15 Aug 1915) Bur Amanda Tp, Fairfield Co OH.

CF52B56   Kenneth Russell Alspaugh (b 12 May 1905, Bloom Tp, Fairfield Co OH) m 14 Nov 1929, Lancaster OH, Ruth Ann Royal (b 14 Nov 1905, Quincy KY) Glass worker, Coulson Glass Co, Columbus OH.

CF52B561   Kenneth Eugene Alspaugh (b 25 Nov 1930, Columbus OH) m 9 Jun 1957, Marion OH, Helen B Bauer (b 29 Aug 1933) Aircraft mechanic.

CF52B5611   Anne Louise Alspaugh (b 16 Mar 1959, Marion OH).

CF52B562   Geneva Ann Alspaugh (b 6 Apr 1932, Columbus OH) m 12 Sep 1952, Madison Tp, Franklin Co OH, Paul Nixon Morehart (b 16 Apr 1931, near Canal Winchester OH) Air Force pilot, Harlingen TX.

CF52B5621   Teri Ann Morehart (b 16 Sep 1956, Harlingen TX).

CF52B5622   Lisa Ann Morehart (b 4 Oct 1958, Harlingen TX).

CF52B563   Alice Jane Alspaugh (b 3 Jun 1937, Columbus OH) m 28 May 1955, Libert IN, John Laverne Ripley (b 27 May 1932, Columbus OH) Electric lineman, Columbus and Southern Ohio Electric Co, Columbus OH.

CF52B5631   Marilyn Jane Ripley (b 7 May 1956, Columbus OH).

CF52B5632   Carolyn Jean Ripley (b 16 Apr 1957, Columbus OH).

CF52B57   Viola Etta Alspaugh (b 17 Apr 1909, Greenfield Tp, Fairfield Co OH) m 28 Oct 1929, Lancaster OH, Walter Frederick Wagner (b 16 Aug 1909, near Lancaster OH) Greenskeeper, Lancaster Country Club.

CF52B571   Charles Robert Wagner (b 14 Dec 1930, near Lancaster OH) m 20 Sep 1952, Lancaster OH, Janet Belle Wilson (b 10 Jun 1930, Lancaster OH) Field representative, Alten Machine Co, Lancaster OH.

CF52B5711   Charlesia Ann Wagner (b 11 Aug 1957, Lancaster OH).

CF52B5712   Elizabeth Ann Wagner (12 Sep 1959, Lancaster OH-14 Sep 1959, Lancaster OH) Bur Sugar Grover OH.

CF52B572   Anna Marie Wagner (b Jul 1932, Lancaster OH) m 5 Jan 1952, Lancaster OH, William Farrow (b 10 May 1929, near Lancaster OH) Machine operator, Kaiser Aluminum Co, Newark OH.

CF52B5721   Janie Farrow (b 29 Oct 1953, Lancaster OH).

CF52B5722   William Farrow Jr (b 1 Dec 1957, Lancaster OH).

CF52B573   Ada Mae Wagner (b 5 Dec 1936, Lancaster OH) unm Saleslady, Hickle Co, Lancaster OH.

CF52B6   Luch Malinda Alspaugh (16 Jul 1868-28 Jun 1870) Bur Bloom Tp, Fairfield Co OH.

CF52B7   Cora Ann Alspaugh (30 Sep 1870, Bloom Tp, Fairfield Co OH-15 Oct 1913, Lancaster OH) m 7 Oct 1891, Bloom Tp, Fairfield Co OH, Charles Franklin Bell (6 Jan 1868, near Cedar Hill OH-7 Jan 1933, near Rock Mill OH) Bur Amanda Tp, Fairfield Co OH.

CF52B71   Esther Agnes Bell (b 7 Sep 1897, near Cedar Hill OH) m 18 Oct 1919, Lancaster OH, Harold Oscar Lamb (b 12 Nov 1894, near Carroll OH) Farmer.

CF52B711   Mary Kathryn Lamb (b 20 Oct 1920, near Carroll OH) m 19 Apr 1956, Portland IN, Joseph Daniel Kramer (b 1 Jul 1898, near Plain City OH) Contractor, NuBric Co, Lancaster OH.

CF52B712   Pauline Loretta Lamb (b 10 Sep 1923, near Carroll OH) m 19 Nov 1943, Santa Barbara CA, Donald Eugene Delp (b 20 Nov 1926, Lancaster OH) Air Conditioning and Heating Co, Columbus OH.

CF52B7121   Donald Eugene Delp Jr (b 25 Sep 1958, Columbus OH).

CF52B72   Irma Mildred Bell (b 14 Jan 1902, Walnut Tp, Pickaway Co OH) m Mar 1919, Greenup KY, Asher Gundy Lamb (b 16 Nov 1889, Greenfield Tp, Fairfield Co OH) Farmer.

CF52B721   Hugh Lamb (b 24 Oct 1919, Fairfield Co OH) m 23 Oct 1943, Knoxville TN, Dixie Sarah Gant (b 31 May 1918, Nashville TN) Veterinarian, Athens TN.

CF52B7211   Robert Hugh Lamb (b 13 Dec 1944, Knoxville TN).

CF52B7212   James David Lamb (b 16 Aug 1947, Athens TN).

CF52B7213   William Asher Lamb (b 31 Dec 1950, Athens TN).

CF52B722   Helen Ruth Lamb (b 19 Apr 1923, Amanda Tp, Fairfield Co OH) m 26 Jul 1941, Point Pleasant WVA, Charles Page McCray (b 16 May 1922, Madison Tp, Pickaway Co OH) Farmer.

CF52B7221   Charles Jeffrey McCray (b 31 Jan 1943, Circleville OH).

CF52B7222   Judith Ann McCray (b 27 Jul 1945, Circleville OH).

CF52B7223   Michael David McCray (b 1 Apr 1948, Columbus OH).

CF52B7224   Ruth Michelle McCray (b 18 Sep 1949, Columbus OH).

CF52B8   Irvin Ellsworth Alspaugh (1 Jan 1872, Bloom Tp, Fairfield Co OH-2 Feb 1959, Columbus OH) m 29 Nov 1899, Franklin Co OH, Etta Haas (23 Sep 1873, Amanda Tp, Fairfield Co OH-23 Aug 1948, Columbus OH) Bur Amanda Tp, Fairfield Co OH. Graduate, OH Northern U. Farmer and banker.

CF52B81   Ralph Benjamin Alspaugh (b 24 Oct 1902, Clear Creek Tp, Fairfield Co OH) m 26 Nov 1928, Chicago IL, Lillian Mae Haas (b 8 Aug 1907, Chicago, IL) She, BA, Chicago U; MA, OSU; professional lecturer and officer of American Association of U Women. He, BA, MA, OSU; professor, Long Beach Col, Long Beach CA. No chn.

CF52B82   Harold Paul Alspaugh (b 16 Janaury 1907, Clear Creek Tp, Fairfield Co OH) m 8 Aug 1936, Amanda OH, Vina Belle McFarland (b 17 Dec 1902, Clear Creek Tp, Fairfield Co OH) She, BS, MS, OSU. He, BA, MA, Ph D, OSU; in charge of Marketing in Standard Rates and Data, Evanston IL.

CF52B821   Donn Paul Alspaugh (b 16 Nov 1937, Columbus OH) m 1 Jun 1957, Wabash IN, Kathleen Kenton Duffey (b 28 Sep 1838, Wabash IN) BA, U of IL; trainee of Northern Trust Co, Chicago IL.

CF52B8211   Ann Elizabeth Alspaugh (b 6 Apr 1958, Champaign IL).

CF52B83   Donald Judson Alspaugh (b 11 Nov 1908, Amanda Tp, Fairfield Co OH) m 15 Aug 1936, Columbus OH, Ada Elizabeth Eisele (b 29 Dec 1912, Columbus OH) She, BA, OSU. He, BS, MD, OSU; physician and obstetrician; Health Commissioner and School Physician, Bexley OH; Member of American Col of Obstetrics and Gynecology.

CF52B831   Judith Kay Alspaugh (b 9 Oct 1941, Columbus OH) Sweet Briar Col, Sweet Briar VA.

CF52B832   Donald Judson Alspaugh II (b 3 Sep 1944, Columbus OH).

CF52B833   Jonathan Paul Alspaugh (b 9 Oct 1949, Columbus OH).

CF52B9   Mertie I Alspaugh (10 Oct 1875-5 Feb 1876) Bur Bloom Tp, Fairfield Co OH.

CF52BA   Emma Ethel Alspaugh (11 May 1877, Bloom Tp, Fairfield Co OH-10 Oct 1965, Lancaster OH) m 13 Dec 1903, Canal Winchester OH, George Orval Kiger (1 Sep 1876, Amanda Tp, Fairfield Co OH-25 Feb 1953, Columbus OH) Bur Amanda Tp, Fairfield Co OH. School teacher and farmer.

CF52BA1   Emily Lucille Kiger (b 11 Apr 1905, Bloom Tp, Fairfield Co OH) m 4 Dec 1928, Greenup KY, Clarence E Shriner (b 21 Janaury 1901, Fairfield Co OH) Farmer; glass worker, Hocking Glass Factory. No chn.

CF52BA2   Eugene Orville Kiger (b 16 Feb 1907, Bloom Tp, Fairfield Co OH) m 11 Feb 1939, Lancaster OH, Dorothy Porter (b 2 Nov 1915, Glouster OH) Maintenance worker, Lancaster Glass Co.

CF52BA21   Carl Rhoderick Kiger (b 19 Aug 1940, Lancaster OH).

CF52BA22   Sally Ann Kiger (b 2 Jan 1947, Lancaster OH).

CF52BA23   Stephen Eugene Kiger (b 2 Nov 1951, Lancaster OH).

CF52BA3   Frances Lavina Kiger (b 13 Oct 1909, Bloom Tp, Fairfield Co OH) m 19 Sep 1953, Carroll OH, David Stephen Pearce (b 2 Jan 1907, Fairfield Co OH) Landlord. No chn.

CF52BA4   Paul William Kiger (b 29 Sep 1911, Bloom Tp, Fairfield Co OH) m 1 Oct 1932, Greenup KY, Martha Helen Speaks (9 Jun 1914, Lancaster OH-4 Mar 1996, Marion OH) Dairy salesman for the Borden Co, Lancaster OH.

CF52BA41   Thomas William Kiger (b 26 Jun 1933, Lancaster OH) m 1) 14 Aug 1954, Cleveland, Elizabeth Anne Manning (b 10 Mar 1932, Sao Paulo Brazil); m 2) 16 Sep 1978, Cincinnati OH, Kay C Battell. Cost accountant, Cincinnati, OH.

CF52BA411   Russell Thomas Kiger (b 29 May 1957, Tachikawa Air Force Base, Japan).

CF52BA412   Paul William Kiger II (3 Aug 1960, Cincinnati OH-2 Nov 1994, Gainesville FL) unm.

CF52BA413   Jonathan Manning Kiger (b 7 Apr 1963, Cincinnati OH).

CF52BA42   Carol Ann Kiger (b 11 Dec 1934, Lancaster OH) m 2 Jul 1960, Berkley CA, Leland Cullen Allen (b 3 Dec 1926, Cincinnati OH) She, Colby Col, San Francisco S Col, U PA; professor, Rutgers U. He, Ph D, Massachusetts Institute of Technology; professor, Princeton U.

CF52BA421   Abigail Louise Allen (b 16 Mar 1963, Princeton NJ) Attorney.

CF52BA422   Ethan Cullen Allen (b 18 Oct 1967, Princeton NJ).

CF52BA423   Emily Helen Allen (b 2 Nov 1969, Princeton NJ).

CF52BA43   June Ellen Kiger (b 26 Jun 1938, Lancaster OH) m 26 Jun 1960, Larry Gail Baughman (b 4 Jun 1940, Lancaster OH) She, OH Wesleyan U, Delaware OH. Teacher. Professor, Baldwin-Wallace Col.

CF52BA44   Daniel Alspaugh Kiger (b 22 Apr 1947, Lancaster OH) m 30 Jun 1973, Columbus OH, Judy Anne Boyd (b 20 May 1948, Columbus OH) United Methodist clergyman, 1974.

CF52BA441   Daniel Boyd Kiger (b 18 Oct 1974, Columbus OH) AB, Princeton U; MD, Harvard U.

CF52BA442   Matthew Benjamin Kiger (b 9 Oct 1976, Columbus OII).

CF52BA5
Frederick Philip Kiger (b 12 Mar 1914, Bloom Tp, Fairfield Co OH) m 30 Apr 1938, Lancaster OH, Anna Cecelia Snyder (b 21 Nov 1913, Lancaster OH) Employee, Hocking Glass Factory, Lancaster OH.

CF52BA51 David Charles Kiger (b 20 Feb 1939, Lancaster OH) Col, Dayton, OH.

CF52BA52 Philip Frederick Kiger (b 13 Sep 1940, Lancaster OH) USA.

CF52BA53 Emma Lou Kiger (b 21 Nov 1942, Lancaster OH).

CF52BA54 Stanley Leo Kiger (b 26 May 1945, Lancaster OH).

CF52C Harriet Weiser Belote Alspach (1836-1895)

CF52BA55 Timothy Edward Kiger (14 Jun 1950, Lancaster OH-9 Nov 1958, Columbus OH) Bur Lancaster OH.

CF52C Harriet Weiser (24 Nov 1836, Greencastle OH 23 Oct 1895, Bloom Tp, Fairfield Co OH) m 1) 5 Oct 1858, George W Belote (20 Nov 1828-28 Dec 1862, Greencastle OH) Bur Greencastle OH; m 2) 25 Aug 1874, Charles Alspach (15 Oct 1833, Bloom Tp, Fairfield Co OH 24 Feb 1919, Bloom Tp, Fairfield Co OH) Bur Bloom Tp, Fairfield Co OH. Belote: Teacher; Alspach: Farmer.[75]

CF52C1 Flora Minnesota (Minnie) Belote (21 Jun 1859, Greencastle OH-24 May 1922, Bloom Tp, Fairfield Co OH) m 30 Apr 1882, Amanda OH, Edward Monroe Heister (1 Mar 1858, Bloom Tp, Fairfield Co OH-9 Mar 1937, Bloom Tp, Fairfield Co OH) Bur Lithopolis OH. Farmer.

CF52C11 Bertha Olive Heister (b 6 Sep 1886, Bloom Tp, Fairfield Co OH) m 1) 25 Dec 1909, Bloom Tp, Fairfield Co OH, Charles Foster Hummell (26 Feb 1881, near Greencastle OH-27 Apr 1929, Hooker's Station, Hooker OH) Bur Lithopolis OH; m 2) 17 Apr 1933, Wellston OH, Clyde Bert DeLapp (d 25 Jun 1944, Lancaster OH) Bur Lithopolis OH. Hummell: Grocer, Royalton OH; DeLapp: Stock dealer.

CF52C111 Juanita Bernadine Hummell (b 9 Nov 1911, Amanda Tp, Fairfield Co OH) m 8 Dec 1922, New York NY, James Waldron Dunn. Retired Army Major.

CF52C1111 James Waldron Dunn Jr (b 27 Dec 1942, New York NY).

CF52C1112 Robert Kimberly Dunn (b 18 Aug 1951, Alexandria VA).

CF52C1113 Timothy Kyle Dunn (b 10 Sep 1953, Westfield MA).

---

[75]Data provided by George W. Weiser, Thelma Brown and Alberta Cordier.

CF52C112   Flora Maxine Hummell (b 3 Dec 1913, Bloom Tp, Fairfield Co OH) m 29 Jul 1934, Amanda OH, Floyd Brigner. Owner, grocery store, Darbyville OH.

CF52C1121   Phyllis Jean Brigner (b 8 Dec 1934, Muhlenburg Tp, Pickaway Co OH) Stenographer.

CF52C1122   Jerry Eugene Brigner (b 31 Jan 1942, Circleville OH) Salesman and farmer.

CF52C113   Willis Heister Hummell (b 13 May 1916, Royalton OH) m 14 Feb 1935, KY, Mildred Leist. Rural mail carrier.

CF52C1131   Charles Kermit Hummell (b 20 Sep 1935, Circleville OH) m 23 Nov 1955, Royalton OH, Barbara Lee Schaeffer. USA, Germany.

CF52C114   Betty Jane Hummell (30 Dec 1922, Royalton OH-5 Oct 1946, Logan OH) m Jun 1939, KY, Lawrence Klinebriel. Bur Lithopolis OH.

CF52C1141   David Leonard Klinebriel (b 11 Jul 1941, Lancaster OH).

CF52C1142   Ronald Doyle Klinebriel (b 12 Aug 1944, Lancaster OH).

CF52C115   Doyle Edward Hummell (b 11 Jul 1928, Royalton OH) m 25 Jun 1949, Millersport OH, Norma Jean Binns (b 17 Jan 1930, Pancoastburg OH) Bookkeeper.

CF52C1151   Peggy Lee Hummell (b 18 Jan 1950, Columbus OH).

CF52C1152   Deborah Kay Hummell (b 22 Apr 1951, Columbus OH).

CF52C1153   Connie Sue Hummell (b 10 Aug 1954, Columbus OH).

CF52C1154   Bonnie Lou Hummell (b 10 Aug 1954, Columbus OH).

CF52C1155   Kent Edward Hummell (b 26 Nov 1958, Columbus OH).

CF52C12   Forrest Raymond Heister (b 18 May 1892, Bloom Tp, Fairfield Co OH) m 7 Apr 1928, Canton OH, Dora Belle Cline (Freeland) (20 Nov 1895, near Athens OH-8 Jun 1950, Lancaster OH) Farmer. Bur Lithopolis OH.

CF52C121   Raymond Edward Heister (b 13 Jan 1929, Bloom Tp, Fairfield Co OH) Ohio National Guard, Capt, Lancaster OH; farmer.

CF52C122   Jeannette Eloise Heister (b 30 Aug 1930, Bloom Tp, Fairfield Co OH) m 6 Apr 1952, Lockbourne Air Force Base, south of Columbus OH, George Stiffler. USAF.

CF52C1221   George Stiffler Jr (b 30 Sep 1953, Lancaster OH).

CF52C1222   Dora Lynn Stiffler (b 6 Apr 1956, Lancaster OH).

CF52C13   Viola Josephine Heister (b 6 Apr 1896, Bloom Tp, Fairfield Co OH) unm Teacher.

CF52C2   Carrie Margaret Belote (3 Sep 1863, Greencastle OH-2 Apr 1934, Lancaster OH) m 9 Oct 1902, Royalton OH, Ervin Elmer Kiger (27 Feb 1863, Royalton OH-1 Apr 1944, Lancaster OH) Bur Lancaster OH. Farmer

CF52C21   Infant son (b 1904) stillborn.

CF52C22   Arleta Fern Kiger (b 31 Jul 1906, Hooker OH) m 15 Jan 1938, Lancaster OH, William

Karl Hoffman (b 29 Mar 1902, Pleasantville OH) Government employee. No chn.

CF52C3   Elvie Melvina Alspach (7 Aug 1875, Bloom Tp, Fairfield Co OH-8 Mar 1954, Bloom Tp, Fairfield Co OH) m 1 Jan 1907, Royalton OH, Charles Henry Kiger (18 Nov 1875, Amanda Tp, Fairfield Co OH-5 Jul 1963, Millersport OH) Bur Amanda Tp, Fairfield Co OH. Farmer.

CF52C31   Lily Lee Alspach (30 Dec 1896, Bloom Tp, Fairfield Co OH-29 Mar 1987, Pottstown PA) m 22 Apr 1916, Lancaster OH, Joseph George Brown Jr (28 Aug 1893, Marion IN-6 Apr 1965, Philadelphia PA) Bur Camden NJ. Glassworker.

CF52C311   Baby girl Brown (b 20 Mar 1917) Bur Lancaster OH.

CF52C312   Robert Brown (5 Aug 1918, Lancaster OH-2 Oct 1926, Columbus OH) Bur Lancaster OH.

*CF52C313   Thelma Mae Brown (b 3 May 1920, Lancaster OH) WWII.

*CF52C314   Carolyn Jean Brown (b 2 Jul 1928, Lancaster OH) m 17 Jun 1961, Miami FL, Omer Clayton Williamson Jr (b 28 Aug 1928, Commerce GA)

CF52C3141   Terry Jean Williamson (b 19 Sep 1966, Coral Gables FL) m 22 Jun 1991, Baltimore MD, Steven William Monteith (b 28 Oct 1960, Buffalo NY) She, BA, FL International U, 1987; MBA, U MD, 1989; he, BA, Columbia U, 1982; MBA, U MD, 1989. She, account executive; he, US Postal Service.

CF52C3142   Amy Lynn Williamson (b 21 May 1970, Coral Gables FL) m 17 Feb 1996, Miami FL, Matthew David Marks (b 26 Jan 1969, Miami FL) BS, U of Miami, 1994. Consultant. He, Florida National Guard, 1987-91.

*CF52C315   Coralee Brown (b 2 Dec 1930, Bloom Tp, Fairfield Co OH) m 6 Aug 1955, Moorestown NJ, John Alexander Dailey III (6 Sep 1926, Emory GA-18 Jul 1990, San Mateo CA) div 1973. Bur San Francisco CA.

CF52C3151   Baby girl Dailey (b 21 Oct 1961).

*CF52C3152   John Alexander Dailey IV (b 2 Apr 1963, Inglewood CA) unm Warehouse foreman.

CF52C316   Claralee Brown (2 Dec 1930, Bloom Tp, Fairfield Co OH-9 Jul 1965, Philadelphia PA) m 29 Nov 1952, PHiladelphia PA, Elmer Robert Goebel (b 6 Nov 1928, Philadelphia PA) Bur Philadelphia PA. He, sales.

CF52C3161   Robert Gary Goebel (6 Jul 1956, Philadelphia PA-23 Jan 1961, Woodbury NJ) Bur Philadelphia PA.

*CF52C3162   Susan Claire Goebel (b 15 Mar 1958, Philadelphia PA) m 18 Oct 1980, Lafayette Hill PA, David Gary Gutekunst (b 17 Mar 1957, Phildelphia PA) He, USN; submarine service.

CF52C31621   Lindsay Allison Gutekunst (b 16 Jan 1983, Groton CT).

CF52C31622   Matthew Robert Gutekunst (b 15 Feb 1986, Groton CT).

*CF52C3163   Karen Lee Goebel (b 14 May 1960, Philadelphia PA) m 13 Jun 1987, Lafayette Hill PA, Philip C Goodwin (b 2 Feb 1959, Rockville CT) div 1995. She, office manager; he, BS, Bowdoin Col, ME, sales.

CF52C31631   Hannah Lee Goodwin (b 26 Jul 1987, Pittsfield MA).

CF52C31632   Alec Brown Goodwin (b 17 Sep 1989, Hartford CT).

*CF52C3164   Peter David Goebel (b 21 May 1961, Philadelphia PA) m 1) Oct 1982, Panama City Panama, Julie Pitrowski (b Decatur IL) div 1984; m 2) 6 Jun 1987, Devon PA, Lori Anne Valentino (b 17 Apr 1961, New York NY) He, USA; computer field service; she, BA, PA S U, 1984.

*CF52C31641   Daniel Robert Goebel (b 17 Apr 1983, Ft Hood TX).

CF52C31642   Zachary Ryan Goebel (b 11 Nov 1990, West Chester PA).

CF52C31643   Taylor Morgan Goebel (b 1 Mar 1994, West Chester PA).

*CF52C3165   Ellen Jeanne Goebel (b 31 May 1963, Philadelphia PA) m 30 Jun 1990, Philadelphia PA, Matthew A Stewart (b 24 Jun 1965, Philadelphia PA) She, BS, Temple U, 1991; education coordinator, Providence RI. He, BA, U PA, 1991; staff assistant, *The New Yorker*.

*CF52C32   Alberta Fern Kiger (b 5 Sep 1908, Bloom Tp, Fairfield Co OH) m 16 Jun 1928, Elkhart IN, Lester Joseph Cordier (8 Sep 1907, South Bend IN-7 Mar 1982, Tucson AZ) Bur Tucson AZ. She, clerical work.

*CF52C321   Charles Ira Cordier (b 30 Nov 1933, Oceola IN) m 4 Apr 1953, Florence AZ, Thelma Joy Rowley (b 30 Apr 1935, Tucson AZ) He, civil service.

CF52C3211   Joy Lynne Cordier (b 15 Feb 1954, Tucson AZ) m 2 Aug 1974, Tucson AZ, Raymond Lee Green (b 28 Aug 1954, Tucson AZ) She, developmental specialist.

CF52C32111   Samantha Brea Green (b 26 Jan 1978, Tucson AZ).

CF52C32112   Marnie Paige Green (b 10 Jun 1987, Tucson AZ).

*CF52C3212   Charles Kevin Cordier (b 21 Jan 1956, Tucson AZ) m 3 Jun 1978, Lesley Joan Brookbank (b 28 Oct 1956, Songea, Tanzania Africa) He, sales.

CF52C32121   Anastasia Dru Cordier (b 13 Feb 1982, Tucson AZ).

CF52C32122   Andrea Lee Cordier (b 25 Aug 1983, Tucson AZ).

CF52C32123   Kendall Jean Cordier (b 22 Nov 1985, Tucson AZ.)

CF52C32124   Breanne Fern Cordier (b 12 Nov 1987, Tucson AZ).

CF52C3213   Scott Rowley Cordier (b 24 Jan 1961, Tucson AZ) m 28 May 1983, Tucson AZ, Rebecca Lynn Wagelie (b 23 Jun 1961, Chicago IL) Human service youthworks.

CF52C32131   Kye Gan Cordier (b 17 Feb 1986, Tucson AZ).

CF52C32132   Charles Austin Cordier (b 19 Jan 1991, Tucson AZ).

CF52C3214   Linda Joal Cordier (b 17 Nov 1962, Tucson AZ) m 20 Feb 1986, Tucson AZ, Donald Frank Di Guardi (b 1 Sep 1964, Reading PA) She, BFA, U AZ; graphic artist.

CF52C32141   Brand Donald Di Guardi (b 18 Oct 1986, Tucson AZ).

CF52C3215   Dennis Allen Cordier (b 5 Sep 1967, Tucson AZ) m 2 Jul 1995, San Diego CA, Shauna Renee Mullins (b 30 Nov 1968, San Bernardino CA. He, zookeeper.

*CF52C322   Larry Neil Cordier (b 3 Aug 1936, Osccola IN) m 23 Aug 1958, Tucson AZ, Mary Ellen Van Kirk (b 22 Jun 1937, Paterson NJ) BS, U AZ; financial manager.

*CF52C3221   Kerry Lynn Cordier (b 11 Jul 1959, Tucson AZ) m 23 Oct 1982, Scottsdale AZ, Clifford Lamar Merrill (b 1 Mar 1958, Mesa AZ) div 1990. She, emergency room nurse. She has resumed her maiden name.

CF52C32211   Kylene Marie Merrill (b 20 Sep 1987, Phoenix AZ) Her name has been legally changed to Cordier.

CF52C3222   Kellie Dianne Cordier (b 24 Jul 1960, Tucson AZ) m 1) 24 Apr 1982, Scottsdale AZ, William Edward O'Connor (b 18 May 1955, New York NY) div 1987; m 2) 14 Oct 1989, Paradise Valley AZ, John Philip French Jr (b 24 Nov 1959, Topeka KS).

CF52C32221   Ashley Diane O'Connor (b 1 Jan 1983, Scottsdale AZ).

CF52C32222   Malori June O'Connor (b 5 Oct 1984, Scottsdale AZ).

CF52C32223   Cassidy Alexandra French (b 16 Oct 1990, Scottsdale AZ).

CF52C32224   Rylee Rebekah French (b 23 Apr 1992, Scottsdale AZ).

CF52C3223   Laurie Ellen Cordier (b 23 May 1962, Tucson AZ) m 10 Nov 1990, Scottsdale AZ, Robert Charles Coffman III (b 8 Oct 1964, Teaneck NJ) Administrative positions.

CF52C32231   McKenna Renae Coffman (b 1 Jun 1992, Orange CA).

CF52C32232   Austin Alexander Cordier (b 11 Jul 1994, Scottsdale AZ).

CF52C3224   Michele Therese Cordier (b 11 May 1965, Tucson AZ) m 19 Mar 1988, Phoenix AZ, Anthony Thomas Capone (b 19 Jan 1961, Freeport IL) div 1995.

CF52C32241   Dominic Joseph Capone (b 2 Jun 1988, Phoenix AZ).

CF52C32242   Lysandra Noelle Capone (b 1 Feb 1993, Glendale AZ).

*CF52C3225   Michael Andrew Cordier (b 10 Feb 1967, Tucson AZ) m 4 Aug 1990, Phoenix AZ, Gina Maria Plescia (b 26 May 1967, Paterson NJ) BA, U AZ, 1989; JD, U San Diego, 1992. Attorney.

CF52C32251   Lauren Elizabeth Cordier (b 12 Jun 1993, Tucson AZ).

*CF52C323   Frank Eugene Cordier (b 7 Jul 1943, Mishawaka IN) m 1) 18 Dec 1965, Tucson AZ, Cheryl Lynn Baker Grimes (b 16 Oct 1943, Warren OH) div 1981; m 2) 22 Jan 1982, Marana AZ, Pamela Jeanne DeGreen Bryans (b 29 Nov 1948, Tucson AZ)

*CF52C3231   Sean Eugene Cordier (b 4 Oct 1966, Boulder City NV) m 12 Aug 1989, Eager AZ, Stacy Elaine Mensching (b 28 Jul 1966, Glendale AZ) Hydrogeologist.

CF52C3232   Jon Lester Cordier (19 Aug 1968, Boulder City NV-20 Aug 1968, Boulder City NV) Bur Tucson AZ.

CF52C3233   Jody Lynn Cordier (b 20 Feb 1970, Santa Barbara CA) m 17 Sep 1988, Las Vegas NV, Joseph Donald La Blanc (b 4 Apr 1958, Duluth NM)

CF52C32331   Joseph Sterling La Blanc (b 17 Jul 1990, Las Vegas NV).

CF52C32332   Alyssa Bryanne La Blanc (b 26 May 1992, Las Vegas NV).

CF52C3234   Joseph Keith Everett Cordier (b 3 May 1974, Tucson AZ).

CF52C3235   Nicole Kristene Cordier (b 1 Jan 1976, Tucson AZ).

CF52C33   Ernest Ellsworth Kiger (b 13 Oct 1911, near Canal Winchester OH) m 24 Oct 1935, Floyd VA, Esther Akers (b 1 Mar 1912, Floyd VA) div 1950. Laborer, Columbus OH.

CF52C331   Mildred Jane Kiger (b 13 Dec 1936, near Lancaster OH) m 1) 13 Oct 1956, Maple Grove NJ, John Raymond Rems, div; m 2) Edward Olsen.

CF52C3311   Carl Edward Olsen (b 3 Feb 1970, Oxnard CA).

CF52C332   Lloyd Ellsworth Kiger (b 3 Jul 1938, Rockbridge OH) m 27 Mar 1959, Gates NC, Mary Elizabeth Casper (b 14 Oct 1937, Gatesville NC) Maintenance mechanic.

CF52C3321   Randolph Ellsworth Kiger (b 24 Oct 1960, Suffolk VA) m 24 Oct 1978, Elizabeth City NC, Barbara Jean Stephenson (b Suffolk VA) Mechanic.

CF52C33211   Thomas Ellsworth Kiger (b 17 Mar 1982, Jacksonville NC).

CF52C33212   Stephen Allen Kiger (b 27 Mar 1982, Jacksonville NC).

CF52C33213   Pamela Jean Kiger (b 4 Dec 1985, Jacksonville NC).

CF52C3322   Philip Eugene Kiger (b 21 Oct 1965, Suffolk VA) unm Store manager.

CF52C3323   Allen Wayne Kiger (b 17 Mar 1971, Suffolk VA) Plumber.

CF52C333   Russell Lee Kiger (b 2 Feb 1940, Greenfield OH) m 3 Sep 1967, New Lexington OH, Charlene La Raye Starner (b 19 Feb 1948, New Lexington OH).

CF52C3331   Karlene Rose Kiger (b 24 Nov 1969, Lancaster OH) m 14 Feb 1993, Lancaster OH, Shawn Stewart Brown (b 19 Feb 1973, Columbus OH) Cashier.

CF52C3332   Marvin Russell Kiger (b 16 Aug 1974, Lancaster OH).

CF52C3333   Alex Ray Kiger (b 6 Feb 1977, Lancaster OH).

CF52C334   Lincoln Ernest Kiger (b 9 Aug 1942, Violet Tp, Fairfield OH) m 1 Jan 1961, Lancaster OH, Helen Kaye Cook (b 6 Dec 1941, Lancaster OH) BS, OSU. Manufacturing engineer.

CF52C3341   Scott Anthony Kiger (b 28 Jul 1961, Lancaster OH) unm Bookkeeper.

CF52C3342   Cheryl Arlene Kiger (b 18 Mar 1966, Lancaster OH) unm.

CF52C335   David Eugene Kiger (b 16 Oct 1944, Lancaster OH) unm.

CF52C336   Randy Alan Kiger (b 18 Nov 1946, Lancaster OH) adopted by Harry and Martha Miller, assumed surname Miller, m 27 Mar 1967, Toledo OH, Joyce Ann Griffith (b 11 Feb 1939, Marion OH) BS, BA. Sales.

CF52C34   Paul Russell Kiger (29 Aug 1912, Lancaster OH-23 Jul 1987, Lancaster OH) m 18 Nov 1933, Lancaster OH, Julia Stewart (18 Nov 1916, Mt Sterling OH-6 May 1976, Lancaster OH) Bur Lancaster OH. Glass tester, Lancaster OH.

CF52C341   Paul Robert Kiger (b 4 Jun 1935, Lancaster OH) m 4 Apr 1964, Columbus OH, Anna Jayne Steiner (b 29 Dec 1942, Columbus OH) Machinist.

CF52C3411   Craig Robert Kiger (b 9 Oct 1969, Columbus OH).

CF52C3412   Brad Alan Kiger (b 14 Oct 1974, Lancaster OH).

CF52C342   James Arthur Kiger (b 14 Sep 1938, Lancaster OH) m 1) 7 Jul 1956, Richmond IN, Brenda Mae Wilson (b 18 Jan 1939, Lancaster OH) div; m 2) 1965, Lancaster OH, Jean Young, div 1968; m 3) 18 Oct 1969, Satellite Beach FL, Malcenia Jane Martin (b 4 Jul 1934, Owensboro KY).

CF52C3421   James Alan Kiger (b 1 Feb 1957, Lancaster OH) m 1980, Lancaster OH, Vicki Carroll (1956, Bremen OH) div 1991.

CF52C34211   Jon Jacob Kiger (b 21 Jan 1980, Lancaster OH).

CF52C34212   Linsi Nicole Kiger (b 22 Dec 1981, Lancaster OH).

CF52C3422   Vicki Lynn Kiger (b 29 Sep 1958, Lancaster OH).

CF52C34221   Jimi Jo Kiger (b 30 Sep 1977, Lancaster OH).

CF52C34222   Dean Dwight Kiger (b 3 Jun 1979, Lancaster OH).

CF52C34223   Jason Kiger (b 4 Aug 1983, Lancaster OH).

CF52C3423   Karen Mae Kiger (b 6 Jul 1960, Lancaster OH) m 1) 18 Nov 1983, Lancaster OH, David Davis; m 2) Myles Gordon (b 15 Sep 1964, Lancaster OH).

CF52C34231   David Michael Gordon (b 2 Nov 1979, Redmond OR).

CF52C34232   Sharon Mae Gordon (b 30 Mar 1981, Redmond OR).

CF52C34233   Annette Gordon (b 30 Mar 1981, Redmond OR).

CF52C343   Donald Lee Kiger (b 25 Nov 1939, Lancaster OH) m 1) 20 Dec 1965, Lancaster OH, Frances M Nimon, div 1972; m 2) Grovesport OH, Dixie L Reinhart (b 8 Feb 1948, Fairfield OH).

CF52C3431   Donnie L Kiger.

CF52C3432   Andrew T Kiger.

CF52C344   Larry Russell Kiger (b 12 Janaury 1944, Lancaster OH) m 1) 17 Aug 1963, Pamela Marlene Poland Thimmes (b 13 Apr 1943) div 1972; m 2) 10 Nov 1972, Lancaster OH, Judy Combs Kitchen (b 6 Aug 1943, Lancaster OH) Mechanic.

CF52C3441   Kimberly Rai Kiger (b 19 Mar 1964, Lancaster OH).

CF52C3442   Kerry Lynn Kiger (b 24 Apr 1967, Dayton OH).

CF52C345   Kenneth Richard Kiger (b 7 Jul 1947, Lancaster OH) m 6 Apr 1968, Lancaster OH, Nita Rae Huddle (b 30 Jul 1948, Lancaster OH) Managerial.

CF52C3451   Scott Richard Kiger (b 4 Nov 1971, Lancaster OH) BA, ITT, Dayton OH. Ornamental iron works firm.

CF52C3452   Michele Christine Kiger (b 1 Dec 1972, Lancaster OH) AB, Pittsburgh Art Institute.

CF52C346   Ruth Ann Kiger (b 19 Jan 1950, Lancaster OH) m 10 Jul 1971, Lancaster OH, Daniel Lee Keller (b 23 Nov 1949, Lancaster OH) Interior decorator.

CF52C3461   Christine Alison Keller (b 6 Jun 1979, Columbus OH).

CF52C3462   Corey Lynn Keller (b 9 Jun 1982, Columbus OH).

CF53   George Weiser (son of Peter and Elizabeth (Minchaus) Weiser) (29 Dec 1792, Fishers Ferry-15 May 1877, Sunbury PA) m 1 Jan 1821, Barbara Oswald (31 Dec 1798-3 Oct 1872, Sunbury PA). Bur Sunbury PA. He was a private in Captain Snyder's Co, War of 1812, and organized the Andrew Jackson Riflemen. He was captain and later colonel of the 45th regiment of PA militia. He was a contractor, railroad builder, dam and locks builder in civilian life. From 1829-1834, he was treasurer of Northumberland Co; and from 1851-1856, an associate judge.[76]

Children of George and Barbara (Oswald) Weiser:

CF531   Angelina Weiser (b 19 Jul 1821).

CF532   Mary Weiser (b 17 Jan 1823).

CF533   George Washington Weiser (b 22 Feb 1825).

CF534   John B Weiser (b 17 Jan 1827).

CF535   Sarah Elizabeth Weiser (17 Oct 1828, Sunbury PA-6 Jun 1837, Sunbury PA).

CF536   Samuel Young Weiser (b 19 Jan 1831).

CF537   Peter Oswald Weiser (b 10 Aug 1833).

CF538   Jacob Weiser (b 18 Mar 1836).

CF539   Catharine Louisa Weiser (b 15 Jul 1838).

CF53A   Margaret Weiser (20 Mar 1841, Sunbury PA-14 Jul 1843).

CF53B   William Henry Weiser (13 Mar 1844-15 Mar 1844).

CF531   Angelina Weiser (19 Jul 1821, Sunbury PA-6 Aug 1898, Wamejo KN) m 12 Nov 1850, John E Smick (5 Jun 1821-7 Apr 1871, Sunbury PA) Bur Sunbury PA.

CF5311   Eliza W Smick (Jun 1851-3 Aug 1851) Bur Sunbury PA.

CF5312   Austin Weiser Smick (25 Dec 1858-25 Mar 1873) Bur Sunbury PA.

CF5313   Oscar Smick (1858-1924) m Mary   (1858-1924).

CF52131   Stewart Smick (1887-1910) Bur Sunbury PA.

CF532   Mary Weiser (17 Jan 1823, Sunbury PA-18 Mar 1850, Sunbury PA) m 15 May 1845, Samuel Snyder (18 Jun 1824-6 Feb 1865, Sunbury PA) Bur Sunbury PA.

CF5321   George W Snyder.

---

[76]See George Weiser Family Bible owned by Weiser Family Association; data contributed (1960) by Charles F Snyder, George W Weiser, Harry B Weiser, Mrs. F.H. Lohafer, Mrs. W.I. Mudd Jr., Mrs. Frederick Melville, William M Hoffman, Mrs. Granville Hooper; 1996 by the above and Merrill F Long Jr., George P Weiser, Camelita J Hinds, Henrietta Bebber Loy, Paul E Slattery, Connie D Smith, Norma Johnson, Luther Bathurst.

CF533   George Washington Weiser (22 Feb 1825, Sunbury PA-5 Aug 1903) m 28 Dec 1854, Priscilla Morris Patton (29 Jan 1834-6 May 1918).

CF5331   George Patton Weiser (10 Nov 1855-11 Apr 1865).

CF5332   Alice Patton Weiser (14 Nov 1858-1946).

CF5333   Thomas Patton Weiser (22 Feb 1861, Steubenville OH-14 Dec 1951, Albuquerque NM) m Laura Maire Seltzer (27 Sep 1871, Hamburg PA-7 Jun 1948, Long Beach CA) Bur Albuquerque NM.

CF53331   George Washington Weiser (b 27 Nov 1891) m 1) 4 Aug 1913, Anna Bernice Phillips (d 28 Feb 1949); m 2) 10 Feb 1950, Adelina Phillips.

*CF533311   George Phillips Weiser (b 30 Dec 1915) m 24 Jul 1943, Nathalie Ohlson (b 17 Apr 1921) div 1943.

CF5333111   Richard George Weiser (b 3 May 1944, Miami FL) m Sandra Grimm (b 14 May 1940, Hingham MA) div.

CF53331111   Kimberly Weiser (b 26 Apr 1964) unm.

CF53331112   Erik Weiser (b 28 Jun 1966) unm.

CF53331113   Deirdre Weiser (b 21 Aug 1970) unm.

CF5333112   Robert Victor Weiser (b 29 Aug 1946, Fresno CA) unm.

CF533312   Russell Eugene Weiser (b 15 Aug 1918, Albuquerque NM-15 May 1973) m 1) 20 Jul 1939, Marlyn Miller (b 8 May 1920, Fresno CA) div; m 2) 3 Jun 1956, Phyllis Parker (b 12 Aug 1923, Fresno CA).

CF5333121   Kenneth Eugene Weiser (b 20 Apr 1940, Fresno CA).

CF53332   Ruth Amelia Weiser (30 Oct 1893, Paola KS-29 Oct 1972, Albuquerque NM) m 17 Jun 1919, Albuquerque NM, Frank Leslie Hinds (8 Mar 1888, Paola KS-15 Apr 1956, Albuquerque NM) Bur Albuquerque NM.

CF533321   Frank Leslie Hinds Jr (b 7 Mar 1920, Albuquerque NM) m 16 Dec 1949, Albuquerque NM, E Gladys Madole (b 23 May 1930, Edgewood, NM) USN, 1937-1940; WWII: USN, 1942-1945. Fireman: Albuquerque NM, 1941-42, Kirkland AF Base 1945-72. Security officer: BCMC Hospital, Albuquerque NM, 1972-82.

*CF533322   Thomas Edward Hinds (b 30 Nov 1922, Albuquerque NM) m 13 Jul 1957, Fort Collins CO, Carmelita June Senander (b 17 Apr 1933, Burlingame KS) WWII: USN, 1943-46. BS, 1958, MS, 1963, CO U. Research plant pathologist, US Forest Service, Fort Collins CO 1950-84.

CF5333221   Carl Edward Hinds (b 26 Oct 1959, Fort Collins CO) m 26 Jan 1991, Lafayette CA, Alexis Anne Barrios (b 29 Jul 1964, Oakland CA) BS, AZ S U, 1988. Nuclear engineer, Vallejo CA 1989-90; San Jose CA 1990-present.

CF53332211   Ryan Alexander Hinds (b 28 Feb 1993, Walnut Creek CA).

CF53332212   Julia Rose Hinds (b 12 Sep 1995, Walnut Creek CA).

CF5333222   Kevin Lake Hinds (b 25 Apr 1962, Fort Collins CO) m 1 Jul 1989, Fort Collins CO, Stacy Lynda Story (b 26 Jul 1963, Pasadena CA) BS, CO S U, 1985. Geotechnical engineer, Cheyenne WY 1985-

1990; Fort Collins CO 1990; Westminister CO 1990-1996; Boulder CO 1996-present.

CF53332221   Kyle William Hinds (b 23 Nov 1990, Fort Collins CO).

CF53332222   Mitchell Thomas Hinds (b 3 Jun 1994, Westminister CO).

CF5333223   Keith Michel Hinds (b 31 May 1964, Fort Collins CO) Construction management engineer, Denver CO 1991-present.

CF533323   Margaret Alice Hinds (b 26 Feb 1926, Albuquerque NM) m 16 Jan 1953, Albuquerque NM, Herbert L Duniven (b 30 Nov 1926, Amarillo TX) Mountain Bell, Albuquerque NM 1949-54; Citicorp Diners Club, Denver CO 1975-88.

CF5333231   Edward Lee Duniven (b 15 Jan 1954, El Paso TX) Self employed, San Francisco CA.

CF5333232   Victoria Leigh Duniven (b 5 Jan 1957, Denver CO) m 1) 16 Jun 1955, Denver CO, Rick Morud, div 1988; m 2) 1 Nov 1991, Woodland Park CO, Michael J Reynolds (b 13 Sep 1948, England) Paramedic, Woodland Park, CO.

CF53332321   Jason Michael Morud (b 25 May 1984, Denver CO).

CF53332322   Ashleigh Morud (b 5 Mar 1986, Denver CO).

CF5333233   Rebecca Lynn Duniven (b 28 May 1962, Scottsdale AZ) m Jun 1987, Denver CO, Douglas Crisp, div 1992.

CF53332331   Courtney Marie Crisp (b 11 Sep 1989, Denver CO).

CF533324   Robert Leonard Hinds (b 29 Aug 1927, Albuquerque NM) m 14 Sep 1950, Pueblo CO, Marie Estella Porreea (b 28 Apr 1925, Pueblo CO) div 1979. USA, 1945-46. X-ray technician, Albuquerque NM 1949-51; Industrial engineer technician, Pueblo CO 1951-74, Carmichael CA 1974-85.

CF5333241   Robert Leonard Hinds Jr (b 21 Oct 1951, Pueblo CO) m 1) 28 Nov 1973, Kiama, NSW, Australia, Lue Ann Allen, div 1980; m 2) 6 Aug 1988, Kiama, NSW, Australia, Vickie McFarland (b 16 Jun 1955, Sydney Australia) Secondary Industrial Arts instructor, Kiama Australia 1974-90. Secondary Computer instructor, Kiama Australia 1990-present.

CF53332411   Sandi Ann Hinds (b 12 Jan 1973, Kiama Australia).

CF53332412   Mary Lou Hinds (b 3 Nov 1974, Kiama Australia).

CF53332413   Robert Steve Hinds (b 1 Jul 1991, Kiama Australia).

CF53332414   Jessica Hinds (b 12 Sep 1994, Kiama Australia).

CF53333   Henrietta Morris Weiser (5 Aug 1895, Paola FL-29 Sep 1982, Albuquerque NM) m 20 Sep 1916, Albuquerque NM, Chester Francis Bebber (20 Sep 1894, Chicago IL-25 Mar 1968, Albuquerque NM) Bur Albuquerque NM. She, teacher.

*CF533331   Henrietta Marie Bebber (b 21 Oct 1917, Albuquerque NM) m 3 Dec 1942, Albuquerque NM, Arthur Edson Loy (b 2 May 1914, Tontogany OH) She, AB, 1939, MA, 1960, U NM. Teacher, social studies coordinator, Albuquerque schools.

CF5333311   Laura Louise Loy (b 30 Aug 1945, El Paso TX) m 3 Feb 1968, Albuquerque NM, Daniel Herbert Dennison Jr (b 19 Sep 1945, Minneapolis MN) BS, U NM, 1968; MS Emerson (MA) Col, 1971; Ed S, U Miami, 1978. Speech pathologist, St Petersburg FL.

CF53333111 Fletcher Loy Dennison (b 12 Jan 1980, St Petersburg FL).

CF5333312 David Edson Loy (b 11 Jan 1950, Albuquerque NM) m 4 Jun 1977, Las Vegas NV, Laura Christine Morgan (b 18 May 1950, North Hampton MA) BS, U NM, 1973; MLS U CA, Berkeley, 1976. Computer programmer, Palo Alto CA.

CF53333121 Benjamin Allen Loy (b 8 Aug 1980, Oakland CA).

CF53333122 Rebecca Nicole Loy (b 2 Aug 1982, Oakland CA).

CF533332 Ruth Elizabeth Bebber (b 29 Jan 1921, Albuquerque NM) BA, U NM, 1942, MS, USCA, 1948; Ph D, USCA, 1956. Teacher, Albuquerque; professor, Hollywood CA and S OR S Col, Ashland OR 1954-86.

CF533333 Chester Francis Bebber Jr (b 10 Apr 1927, Albuquerque NM) m 3 Sep 1949, Glendo WY, Doelores Helen Weimer (b 11 Jan 1929, Glendo WY) WWII: USAC. AB, U MT, 1957. Geologist, US and overseas.

CF5333331 Sharon Ann Bebber (b 5 Jan 1951, Albuquerque NM) m 1) 20 Sep 1969, Denver CO, M William Bejarmo (d 1980) div 1970; m 2) 13 Oct 1974, Richard Raymond Rowan (b 3 Jan 1946, Rochester NY) BA, Met S Col, 1989, MA, U N CO, 1993. Elementary teacher, Adams Co.

CF53333311 Eric James Bejarmo (b 8 Mar 1970, Denver CO) adopted by Richard R Rowan.

CF53333312 Cory Patrick Rowan (b 8 Oct 1975, Denver CO).

CF53333313 Leah Michelle Rowan (b 25 Mar 1977, Denver CO).

CF53333314 Todd Garrett Rowan (b 25 Aug 1979, Denver CO).

CF5333332 Kurt Conrad Bebber (b 4 Jul 1955) m 8 Oct 1974, Denver CO, Edie Ann Ester (b 11 Aug 1955) div 1991. BA, Ft Louis (CO) Col.

CF53333321 Brett Matthew Bebber (b 17 Oct 1979, Denver CO).

CF53333322 Jordan Michelle Bebber (b 2 Apr 1987, Denver CO).

CF5333333 Duane Thomas Bebber (b 22 Sep 1956, Denver CO) Automobile mechanic, Denver CO.

CF5333334 Gary Owen Bebber (b 30 Dec 1958, Denver CO) m 21 Aug 1982, Denver CO, Karen Elizabeth Heim (b 19 Aug 1959) BA, U N CO, 1981. Accountant, Denver CO.

CF53333341 William Ryan Bebber (b 11 Jan 1983).

CF53333342 James Andrew Bebber (b 4 Nov 1986).

CF533334 Marilyn Theresa Bebber (b 2 May 1936, Albuquerque NM) m 8 Jun 1957, C Dwayne Sheppard (b 4 Nov 1934, Albuquerque NM-18 Apr 1992, Albuquerque NM).

CF5333341 Theresa Lynn Sheppard (b 26 Sep 1958, Albuquerque NM).

CF5333342 Mary Kathleen Sheppard (b 30 Nov 1959, Albuquerque NM) m 9 Apr 1987, Albuquerque NM, W Brent Cummings (b 14 Dec 1959, Waco TX) BA, U NM, 1981, MA, U TX, 1987. Special Ed, Albuquerque NM 1981-84, Austin TX 1987-94.

CF53333421 Lindsay Janiece Cummings (b 22 Sep 1994).

CF5333343   Dwayne Francis Sheppard (b 12 Dec 1960, Albuquerque NM) m 28 Dec 1983, Jacqueline Susan Jones (b 9 May 1960, Reno NV) BS, U NM, 1982. Mechanical engineer.

CF5333344   Lori Jean Sheppard (b 29 Jun 1962, Albuquerque NM).

CF5333345   Barbara Elaine Sheppard (b 28 Sep 1963, Albuquerque NM) m 14 Jun 1985, Christopher John McCulloch (b 24 Jun 1962, Pueblo CO) BS, U NM, 1985. Marketing, Albuqeurque NM.

CF53333451   Ryan Christopher McCulloch (b 26 Dec 1990, Albuquerque NM).

CF53333452   Tyler Sheppard McCulloch (b 8 Apr 1993, Albuquerque NM).

CF5333346   Elizabeth Marie Sheppard (b 28 Sep 1966, Albuquerque NM) BA, U NM, 1988. Aquatic recreation.

CF5333347   Thomas Ferrel Sheppard (b 23 May 1968, Albuquerque NM) m 12 Jun 1993, Rosemary Helen Zimsen (b 20 Dec 1969, Bremerton WA) BA, NM S U, 1991. Media information director.

CF53333471   Bailey Susanne Sheppard (b 24 Feb 1959, Denver CO).

CF533335   William Thomas Bebber (b 20 Aug 1938, Albuquerque NM) m 5 Aug 1967, Reno NV, Jacqueline Kay Wood (b 2 Sep 1944, St Louis MO) BS, S OR Col, 1963. OR Nat gd, 1957-67. Construction worker.

CF5333351   Charles Clary Bebber (b 7 Jan 1974, Chico CA).

CF5333352   Kirsta Ann Bebber (b 20 Jan 1977, Chico CA).

CF5334   Anna Barbara Weiser (1 Apr 1867-1948).

CF534   John B Weiser (17 Jan 1827, Sunbury PA-1902, Shamokin PA) m Elizabeth Musselman (d Shamokin PA) Bur Sunbury PA. Lime and hay business, Sunbury PA, until he became blind; moved to Shamokin PA, with son George.

CF5341   Elmira A Weiser (Mar 1854, Sunbury PA-4 Sep 1856, Sunbury PA) Bur Sunbury PA.

CF5342   George Weiser (15 Aug 1854, Sunbury PA-17 Oct 1917, Shamokin PA) m Anna Cook (d 24 Feb 1896, Shamokin PA) Bur Shamokin PA.

CF53421   Charles Weiser (dy).

CF53422   George Weiser (dy).

CF53423   Albert Weiser (dy).

CF53424   Helen Weiser (b 22 Jun 1885, Shamokin PA) m 25 Oct 1905, Shamokin PA, Harry Kramer (b 2 Jan 1886, Shamokin PA).

CF534241   Dorothy Kramer (b 17 Aug 1910, Shamokin PA) m 23 Jun 1934, Shamokin PA, Robert Rhoades.

CF5342411   Nancy Rhoades (b 24 Nov 1941, Shamokin PA).

CF5342412   Robert Rhoades (b 14 Oct 1945, Shamokin PA).

CF534242   Louise Kramer (b 15 Nov 1918, Shamokin PA) m 27 Dec 1939, Shamokin PA, Albert Weller (b 22 Nov 1914).

CF5342421
Joan Weller (b 29 Sep 1943, Shamokin PA).

CF5342422
Ronald Weller (b 15 Nov 1946, Shamokin PA).

CF53425
Bertha Weiser (b 5 Jan 1887, Shamokin PA) m 28 Jun 1916, Louis Krouse.

CF534251
Elizabeth Krouse (b 16 Apr 1917, Allentown PA) m 2 Aug 1940, Syracuse NY, Robert Fiske.

CF5342511
Roberta Fiske (b 23 Apr 1947, Bethlehem PA).

Left to right: CF536 Samuel Young Weiser (1831-1919); CF537 Peter Oswald Weiser (1833-1933); CF538 Jacob Weiser (1836-1916)

CF53426
Harry Budson Weiser (8 Jan 1891, Shamokin PA-31 Jul 1961) m 5 Nov 1927, Shamokin PA, Helene Dreher (b 25 May 1895, Shamokin PA) Professional ball player, 19 years; part with Philadelphia Phillies.

CF5343   Dora Weiser (b Sunbury PA) m   Summers. Bur Washington DC.

CF5344   Catherine E Weiser (21 Feb 1859-3 Mar 1859, Sunbury PA).

CF5345   William E Weiser (1860, Sunbury PA-4 Jan 1885, Sunbury PA) unm Bur Sunbury PA.

CF5346   Charles B Weiser (23 Jul 1862, Sunbury PA-15 Sep 1882, Sunbury PA) unm Bur Sunbury PA.

CF5347   Ida Jane Weiser (4 Sep 1853-23 Dec 1932) m Emanuel Diebler (22 Dec 1853-17 Jan 1921).

CF53471   Mabel Elizabeth Diebler (b 25 Dec 1891) m Guy Stanford Tucker (9 Dec 1880-6 Mar 1957).

CF53472   Blanche Diebler (b 4 Apr 1893).

CF536   Samuel Young Weiser (19 Jan 1831, Sunbury PA-1919, Washington IL) m 1) Virginia (ca 1839, IL-ca 1865, Washington IL) m 2) 10 Jun 1869, Maria H Roberts (7 Dec 1842-3 Aug 1909, Washington IL) Bur Washington IL. Cobbler, Washington IL.

CF5361   George Weiser (b ca 1857, IL).

CF5362   Andrew C Weiser (b Nov 1861, Washington IL) m Fannie M   (b Feb 1862, IL) They lived in Washington IL, then in Plymouth NE, and later in Walton KS.

CF53621   Hearley Weiser (b Sep 1886, Plymouth NE).

CF53622   Ethel Weiser (b Jul 1887, Plymouth NE).

CF53623   Nannie B Weiser (b Sep 1890, Plymouth NE).

CF53624   Alvin F Weiser (b Jun 1891, Plymouth NE).

CF53625   Edith LB Weiser (b Jun 1892, Plymouth NE).

CF53626   Viola M Weiser (b Jan 1896, Plymouth NE).

CF53627   Blanch P Weiser (b Jan 1899, Plymouth NE).

CF53628   Fannie Mae Weiser (b ca 1901, Plymouth NE).

CF53629   Mattie Lucille Weiser (b ca 1903, Plymouth NE).

CF5362A   Orville M Weiser (b ca 1907).

CF5363   Samuel W Weiser (b Jul 1862, Washington IL) m 1) Josie Anna (b May 1868, IL) Lived in Washington IL, later Nemaha and Beatrice NE.

CF5364   Mary Weiser (Jun 1880-1956) m John H Weichmann (1883-1929) Bur Washington IL.

CF537   Peter Oswald Weiser (10 Aug 1833, Sunbury PA-22 Jan 1933, Shelby NE) m 28 Dec 1871, Evelyn Metts. Civil War: 2 Iowa Volunteer Cavalry, Co. K, Private. Bur Shelby NE.

CF5371   George Edmond Weiser (29 Sep 1872, Shelby NE-Nov 1955) m 10 Oct 1899, Belle McGimpsey. Bur Shelby NE. Farmer, garage owner, Shelby NE.

CF53711   George Andrew Weiser (30 Mar 1903-19 May 1962) m 30 Mar 1931, Kathryn Ernst, Omaha NE.

CF537111   Judith Marie Weiser (b 4 Dec 1932, Omaha NE) BS, U Omaha, 1958; teacher, Ohaha NE.

CF53712   Carl Weiser (b 26 Sep 1905, Shelby NE) m Ina Davis. No chn.

CF53713   Dorothy Ellen Weiser (12 Mar 1901, Shelby NE-15 Mar 1944, Omaha NE) m 27 Jun 1927, James Jensen. Bur Shelby NE.

CF537131   James Marvin Jensen (b 15 Jan 1931, Lincoln NE) m 14 Sep 1954, Mary Ann Griener. Korean conflict: USMC, Corp, purple heart; industrial engineer.

CF5371311   Debra Ann Jensen (b 14 Sep 1955, Omaha NE).

CF5371312   Kathryn Sue Jensen (b 1 Apr 1958, Omaha NE).

CF53714   Oscar Oswald Weiser (b 12 Feb 1912, Shelby NE) m 4 Jul 1934, Mildred Treadway. WWII; restaurant owner.

CF537141   Marjorie Weiser (b 8 Sep 1935, Omaha NE) m 19 Dec 1954, Paul Rosenberry.

CF5371411   Michael Paul Rosenberry (b 27 Sep 1955).

CF5371412   Julie Ann Rosenberry (b 16 Jul 1957).

CF537142   Gary Weiser (b 25 Jan 1938, Yakima WA).

CF5372   Minnie May Weiser (b 14 Sep 1875, Shelby NE) m 22 Feb 1897, Shelby NE, Charles W Bockoven.

CF53721   Peter Weiser Bockoven (b 6 Feb 1899, Seward NE) m Vera Foster. Sales manager, Sioux Fall SD.

CF537211   Milton Bockoven (b 22 May 1922, Lincoln NE) m. USA, Capt.

CF5372111   Dagan Bockoven (b 13 May 1946, WY).

CF5372112   Lorraine Bockoven (b 14 May 1953, Chicago IL).

CF537212   Minnie May Bockoven (b 27 Jun 1925, Lincoln NE) m Feb 1945, Ernest Peterson.

CF5372121   Kenneth Peterson (b 20 Dec 1945, Lincoln NE).

CF5372122   Carla Rae Peterson (b 13 Dec 1947, Lincoln NE).

CF5372123   Stenison Peterson (b 7 Jun 1951, Albuquerque NM).

CF53722   Ralph Edward Bockoven (b 16 Jul 1909, Shelby NE) m 21 Apr 1935, Elizabeth Sharp. Printer, Lincoln NE.

CF537221   Joyce Bockoven (b 26 Feb 1937, Lincoln NE) m Apr 1955, Richard Bittinger.

CF5372211   Douglas Bittinger (b Feb 1956, Amarillo TX).

CF5372212   Laura Bittinger (b Aug 1957, Amarillo TX).

CF5372213   David Lee Bittinger (b 16 Aug 1958, Wichita Falls TX).

CF537222   Leanne Bockoven (b 14 Nov 1942, Lincoln NE).

CF537223   Pamela Bockoven (b 9 Jul 1946, Lincoln NE).

CF5373   Kathryn Mary Weiser (29 May 1880, Shelby NE-14 Nov 1956, Lincoln NE) m 12 Aug 1903, Clyde F. Babcock. Bur Shelby NE.

CF53731   Evelyn Marie Babcock (b 23 Jun 1916, Shelby NE) m 9 Apr 1943, York, NE) m 12 Aug 1903, Clyde E Babcock. Bur Shelby NE.

CF537311   Glen Irwin Ulrich (b 3 Jul 1944, Shelby NE).

CF538   Jacob Weiser (18 Mar 1836, Sunbury PA-5 Mar 1916, Sunbury PA) m 24 Jun 1858, Martha A Potts (13 Jun 1838, Lancaster PA-May 1915, Sunbury PA) Bur Sunbury PA. Civil War: Co F, 11th Regiment, PVI; band of the 45th PA Regt; Co G, 185th PVI. Carpenter, PA RR, Sunbury PA.

CF5381   Catharine I Weiser (17 Jan 1860, Sunbury PA-28 Oct 1861, Sunbury PA) Bur Sunbury PA.

CF5382   Mary Alice Weiser (27 Sep 1861, Sunbury PA-2 May 1935) m 2 Oct 1879, Milton PA, George Feiser Wise (28 Apr 1855, Milton PA-2 May 1935) Tailor, Sunbury PA.

CF53821   William Jacob Wise (18 Sep 1880, Sunbury PA-29 Nov 1929, Sunbury PA) m 26 Sep

1906, Ada L Heffner. Tailor, Sunbury PA.

CF538211   Charles Janton Wise (11 Dec 1907, Sunbury PA-31 Aug 1958, Sunbury PA) m 31 Mar 1934, Oswego NY, Ida May Mitchell. Steward, Sunbury PA.

CF5382111   Robert Vincent Wise (b 2 Oct 1934, Sunbury PA).

CF5382112   Ada Lee Wise (b 6 Oct 1936, Sunbury PA) m 5 Feb 1956, Arden Neil Newman.

CF53821121   Arden Charles Newman (b 6 Sep 1956, Sunbury PA).

CF53821122   Scott Allen Newman (b 23 Nov 1957, Sunbury PA).

CF53821123   Lori Lee Newman (b 25 Nov 1959, Sunbury PA).

CF53821124   Lisa Mae Newman (b 10 May 1961, Sunbury PA).

CF5382113   Edward David Wise (b 1 Apr 1938) m 17 Jun 1961, Sunbury PA, Beverly Bingaman.

CF53821131   Edward Charles Wise (b Sunbury PA).

CF538212   William Vincent Wise (b 26 Jul 1910, Sunbury PA) m 20 Oct 1939, Lewisburg PA, Bessie Fegley. Postal clerk, Sunbury PA.

CF5382121   Charles Wise.

CF53822   Sara Lily Wise (3 Nov 1883, Sunbury PA-30 Jan 1949, Sunbury PA) m 15 Aug 1911, Frank Baylor Crites (20 Aug 1882, Catawissa PA-17 Mar 1959) Bur Sunbury PA.

CF538221   Madelyn Wise Crites (1 Apr 1912, Sunbury PA-5 Mar 1943, Harrisburg PA) m James Reuben Moyer (b 25 May 1913, Sunbury PA-27 Aug 1978) Railroad employee.

CF5382211   James Robert Moyer (b 2 May 1932, Sunbury PA) m Sabina Klara Josephine Hans (b 20 Jun 1928).

CF53822111   Victor Herbert Moyer (18 Apr 1952-22 Mar 1996) m Sharon Lori Campbell (b 18 Feb 1954).

CF538221111   Kyle Campbell Moyer (b 9 Sep 1978).

CF538221112   Trevor Campbell Moyer (b 18 Feb 1980).

CF53822112   Steven Michael Moyer (b 28 Mar 1953) m Eileen Joan Wujcik (b 28 Apr 1953).

CF53822113   Patricia Ann Moyer (b 27 May 1954).

CF53822114   Gary Richard Moyer (b 14 Jun 1957).

CF53822115   Kathy Susan Moyer (b 30 May 1966) m 1) Walter Anthony Williams (b 9 Nov 1966); m 2) Wayne Bruce Diedrich (b 22 Nov 1964).

CF538221151   Alexa Renee Williams (b 27 Nov 1991).

CF5382212   Donald Carl Moyer (b 24 Jul 1934, Sunbury PA).

CF5382213   Frank Hurley Moyer (b 25 Aug 1938, Sunbury PA).

CF538222   Frank Harold Crites (5 Dec 1913, Sunbury PA-5 Aug 1960) m 3 Sep 1935, Elkton MD, Almeda Inez Snyder (b 23 Jul 1914, Sunbury PA) Machinist, Sunbury PA.

CF5382221   Sharon Eileen Crites (b 15 Oct 1943, Sunbury PA).

CF5382222   Dolores Diane Crites (b 15 Jun 1952, Sunbury PA).

CF538223   Myrtle Jane Crites (b 24 Jul 1927, Sunbury PA) m 25 Mar 1946, Alexandria VA, Harold Melvin Wynn (b 25 Apr 1920, Sunbury PA) Employee, US Dept of Justice, Fed Bureau of Prisons, Sunbury PA.

CF5382231   Gail Elizabeth Wynn (b 24 Sep 1947, Sunbury PA).

CF5382232   Melvin Keith Wynn (b 28 Dec 1948, Sunbury PA).

CF5382233   Barbara Ann Wynn (b 15 Sep 1950, Washington DC).

CF5382234   Frances Louise Wynn (b 2 Feb 1952, Washington DC).

CF5382235   Jo Ann Wynn (b 2 Feb 1952, Washington DC).

CF53823   Rachel Leah Wise (20 Nov 1889, Sunbury PA-31 Dec 1961) m 24 Jul 1916, Sunbury PA, Oliver Samuel DeLancey (d 17 Oct 1950, Ottawa IL).

CF538231   Merton Miles DeLancey (b 25 Mar 1918, Washburn WI) m 6 Dec 1941, Virginia Claire Skerry (b 4 Apr 1918, Louviers CO) BS, U WI, 1941; Engineer, Charlestown WVA.

CF538232   Oliver Samuel DeLancey Jr (b 24 Feb 1922, Tacoma WA) m 24 Aug 1946, La Salle IL, Mary Anna Wacker (b 20 Nov 1922, Peru IL) WWII: USA, Air Corps, 1942-46. B Arch, U MI, 1950. Architect, Ann Arbor, Detroit MI.

CF5382321   Jane Ann DeLancey (b 7 Oct 1949, Ann Arbor MI) BFA, U MI, 1979. Graphic designer, Ann Arbor MI.

CF5382322   John Oliver DeLancey (b 7 Sep 1951, Ann Arbor MI) m 31 May 1980, Grosse Pointe Shores MI, Barbara Lee Lange (b 27 Nov 1953, Detroit MI) BA, Oberlin Col, 1973; MD, U MI, 1977. Physician, Detroit, Ann Arbor MI.

CF53823221   John Oliver Lang DeLancey (b 17 Apr 1982, Ann Arbor MI)

                Claire Elizabeth Lang DeLancey (b 3 Mar 1990, Ann Arbor MI) adopted by John Oliver and Barbara DeLancey.

CF53823222   Lang Carl DeLancey (b 17 Dec 1994, Ann Arbor MI)

CF5382323   Julie Anne DeLancey (b 4 Apr 1965, Ann Arbor MI) BA, U MI, 1987. Faculty, NE MO U, Kirksville MO.

CF53824   Ida Leah Wise (20 Nov, Sunbury PA-21 Feb 1932, Harrisburg PA) m 15 Jul 1920, Sunbury PA, Merrill Franklin Long (21 Apr 1890, Sunbury PA-20 Nov 1969, New Cumberland PA) Bur Sunbury PA. Bank secretary, Harrisburg PA.

*CF538241   Rachel Louise Long (b 15 Mar 1923, Harrisburg PA) m 3 Feb 1944, New Cumberland PA, William Irving Mudd Jr (b 11 Dec 1920, Harrisburg PA) Both, AB, Dickinson (PA) Col, 1950. Draftsman, Pittsburgh PA.

*CF5382411   William Irving Mudd III (20 Sep 1946, Mechanicsburg PA-1 May 1993, Pittsburgh PA) Bur Camp Hill PA. unm USN. AB Wesleyan U, 1968; LLB, American U, 1981. Attorney, accounting firm, Washington DC.

*CF5382412   Christopher Stephen Mudd (b 6 Jul 1951, Mechanicsburg PA) m 28 Jul 1984, Barbara Ann Foscato (b 6 Dec 1948, Holden MA) div 1990. AB, Design sales compensation, Worcester MA.

CF53824121   Stephen Morgan Mudd (b 28 May 1988, Worcester MA).

*CF5382413   Rebecca Louise Mudd (b 25 Jun 1954, West Reading PA) m 17 Apr 1982 William James Lewis (b 22 Dec 1951, Pittsburgh PA) She, B. Mus, Wittenberg (OH) U, 1976; M. Mus., Northwestern U, 1979. He, B. Mus., W VA U, 1973; M. Mus., LA S U, 1974. Programmer analyst, Pittsburgh PA.

CF53824131   Eric Grant Lewis (b 28 Sep 1984, Pittsburgh PA).

CF53824132   Jennifer Louise Lewis (b 25 Feb 1987, Pittsburgh PA).

*CF538242   Merrill Franklin Long Jr (b 6 May 1926, Harrisburg PA) m 4 Jun 1949, New Cumberland PA, Mary Catherine Lutz (b 29 Jun 1930, Red Lion PA) Navy computer systems designer.

*CF5382421   Jerry Paul Long (b 1 Jun 1951, Harrisburg PA) m 1) Cheryl Lynn Drackley (2 Apr 1953, Brookline MA-17 Dec 1987, Camp Hill PA); m 2) 2 Dec 1989, Judith Ann Rawa (b 7 Jan 1947, Brookville PA) BS, Lehigh U; MBA, U Pittsburgh, 1981. Director of Worldwide Logistics, Calgon Co, Pittsburgh PA.

          Matthew Gilbert Long (b 20 Jul 1983, Pittsburgh PA). Adopted.

          Jeffrey William Long (b 16 Mar 1985, Pittsburgh PA). Adopted.

*CF5382422   Elizabeth Dee Long (b 27 Apr 1953, Harrisburg PA) m 22 Jan 1993, Boonesville VA, David Lynn McDonald (b 26 May 1956, Belleville IL) BS, IUP U. US Govt service, Staunton VA.

CF5382423   Richard Franklin Long (b 21 Jul 1955, Harrisburg PA) m 15 Jun 1985, New Cumberland PA, Debra Frances Deller (b 9 Jul 1953, Dallastown PA) BS, PSU. Senior systems analyist, AMP, Inc, Harrisburg PA.

CF5382424   David Edward Long (b 29 Dec 1956, Harrisburg PA) m 2 Nov 1988, Telford PA, Pamela Dawn (nee Royer) O'Brien (b 12 May 1953, Lansdale PA) Insurance auditor, Hatfield PA.

          Timothy Bruce Long (b 12 Dec 1974, Hatfield PA). Adopted.

          Joshua Lee Long (11 Mar 1981, Hatfield, PA). Adopted

CF5382425   Marilee Kay Long (b 19 Aug 1958, Harrisburg PA) m 31 Dec 1986, George Marshall Houtz Jr (b 7 Aug 1949, Middletown PA).

CF53824251   Michele Mary Houtz (b 26 Jun 1978, Harrisburg PA).

CF53824252   Suzette Lee Houtz (b 24 Jan 1982, Harrisburg PA).

CF53824253   Jacqueline Kay Houtz (b 25 May 1983, Harrisburg PA).

CF53824254   Juliette Georgette Houtz (b 5 Mar 1987, Harrisburg PA).

CF53824255   Mary Agnes Houtz (b 11 Apr 1992, Hershey PA).

CF5382426   Jack Merrill Long (b 21 Oct 1964, Harrisburg PA) m 8 Oct 1994, Pocono Manor PA, Lori

Ann Crosby (b 16 Nov 1969, Bellwood PA) Computer specialist.

CF53825　　　　Myrtle Steckman Wise (2 Jan 1892, Sunbury PA-9 Jun 1963, Sunbury PA) m 6 Oct 1950, Earl Houser (19 Aug 1893, Sunbury PA-25 Oct 1957, Sunbury PA) Bur Sunbury PA.

CF5383　　　　Flora Emma Weiser (27 Jul 1863, Sunbury PA-6 Aug 1940, Williamsport PA) m 15 Sep 1885, Elmer Grieb Ritter (27 Jul 1863, Nipponee Valley PA-9 Jun 1936, Williamsport PA) Bur Williamsport PA. Machinist.

CF53831　　　　Nellie May Ritter (b 1887) m Steven Anthony Slattery. Bur Williamsport PA. Machinist.

CF538311　　　　Catherine Louise Slattery (1906-21 Feb 1919, Williamsport PA).

CF538312　　　　Eugene Anthony Slattery (11 Mar 1908, Williamsport PA-7 Sep 1988, Jeffersonville IN) m Grace Pauline Rider (22 Jul 1910, Eagles Mere PA-13 Aug 1993, Hughesville PA). Environmental, air pollution control, Louisville KY. Res. Jeffersonville IN.

CF5383121　　　　Louise Catherine Slattery (b 4 Feb 1931, Sonestown PA) m 15 Jul 1950, Muncy PA, Harold F Adams (b 26 Nov 1925, Muncy PA). Store cashier, Montoursville PA.

CF53831211　　　　David Steven Adams (b 4 Jan 1952, Williamsport PA) m 1) 26 Apr 1980, Robin McNet, div; m 2) 1992, Stewart FL, Terry Savory (b 28 Jul 1955) He, electrician; she, bridal attire shop.

CF53831211l　　　　Ashley Marie Adams (b 25 Oct 1987).

CF53831212　　　　Lynda Susan Adams (b 21 Mar 1954, Williamsport PA) m 22 Jul 1978, Montoursville PA, Daniel Wright (b 29 Jun 1952, Roanoke VA) He, teacher, wrestling coach; she, secretary, Montoursville PA.

CF538312121　　　　Brian Adam Wright (b 16 Mar 1982, Williamsport PA).

CF538312122　　　　Gregory Daniel Wright (b 4 Sep 1984, Williamsport PA).

CF53831213　　　　Richard Eugene Adams (b 11 Aug 1955, Williamsport PA) m 3 Oct 1981, Kitty Haussock, div. Musician, Montoursville PA.

*CF5383122　　　　Paul Eugene Slattery (b 9 May 1938, Sonestown PA) m 18 Jan 1958, Jeffersonville KY, Shirley Jean Nelson (b 25 May 1940, Louisville KY) He, KY and IN National Guard; firefighter: she, nurse's assistant, New Albany IN.

*CF53831221　　　　Paul Eugene Slattery Jr (b 26 Sep 1958, New Albany IN) m 12 Sep 1986, New Albany IN, Robin Bright. Welder, Clarksville IN.

CF538312211　　　　Stephanie Renee Slattery (b 28 Dec 1986, New Albany IN).

CF538312212　　　　Daniel Anthony Slattery (b 30 Apr 1991, New Albany IN).

*CF53831222　　　　Terry Renee Slattery (b 26 Oct 1959, New Albany IN) m 25 Oct 1987, Clarksville IN, Kenny Robinson (b 1 Mar 1961, Jeffersonville IN) Environmental control, New Albany IN.

CF538312221　　　　Ashley Nicole Robinson (b 26 Jan 1990, Louisville KY).

CF5383123　　　　Diane Mae Slattery (b 19 Mar 1948, Muncy PA) m Muncy PA, Ron Hilner, div 1986.

CF53831231　　　　Michelle Renee Slattery (b 26 Jun 1967, Muncy PA) m 25 May 1991, Hughesville PA, Carl Parker (b 14 Jun 1966, Muncy PA) Federal penitentiary guard, Muncy PA; she, retail store manager. No chn.

CF53832   Margaret Anne Ritter (11 Dec 1887-1 Mar 1972) m 1) William Wycoff; m 2) Charles Dimm.

CF53833   Marie Viola Ritter (d 27 Mar 1971, Nauvoo PA) m William David Dawson (d 27 Apr 1967, Orange NJ). Bur Williamsport PA.

CF538331   Marie Iola Dawson (14 Mar 1912, Elmire NY-23 Jan 1978, Willaimsport PA) unm.

CF538332   Donald William Dawson (29 May 1914, Auburn NY-29 Aug 1914). Bur Williamsport PA.

CF538333   Conrad Weiser (Connie) Dawson (b 19 Aug 1921, Clinton MA) m 28 Apr 1943, Williamsport PA, William Knoop Smith (15 Sep 1921, Williamsport PA-6 Oct 1992, Williamsport PA).

CF5383331   William Daniel Smith (b 10 Jun 1946, Williamsport PA) m 15 Jun 1968, Denver CO, Lorraine Bernice Roberts (b 31 Jan 1951, Denver PA).

CF53833311   William Robert Smith (b 19 Aug 1972, Williamsport PA) Band director, USAF Academy, Colorado Springs CO.

CF53833312   Michael Daniel Smith (b 23 Dec 1975, Denver CO).

CF5383332   Debra Larie Smith (b 27 Apr 1949, Williamsport PA) m 23 Nov 1968, Williamsport PA, Henry Edward Bashnick (b 31 Aug 1947, Williamsport PA).

CF53833321   Brian Patrick Bashnick (b 17 Mar 1969, Little Rock AR) The mother of his child is Susan Marie Wagner (b 7 Jan 1967, Williamsport PA).

CF538333211   Tanner Patrick Bashnick (b 14 Dec 1995, Williamsport PA).

CF53833322   Keith Edward Bashnick (b 11 Mar 1974, Williamsport PA) The mother of his child is Linda Marie Coleman (b 9 Nov 1972).

CF538333221   Megan Trease Coleman (b 15 Jun 1994, Williamsport PA).

CF53833323   Heath William Bashnick (b 11 Mar 1974).

CF5383333   Robert Charles Smith (b 22 May 1951, Williamsport PA) m 26 Jun 1971, Pamela Susan Younkin (b 29 Jun 1953, Williamsport PA).

CF53833331   Tatum Rachelle Smith (b 24 Jan 1976, Williamsport PA).

CF53833332   Ady Elizabeth Smith (b 25 Aug 1980, Williamsport PA).

CF538334   William David Dawson (b 30 Jan 1924, Sterling MA) m 31 Jan 1948, Williamsport PA, Phyllis Ethel Kaufman (b 24 Dec 1926, Williamsport PA).

CF5383341   William David Dawson (b 3 Mar 1949, Williamsport PA) m 13 Oct 1984, Pittsburg PA, Joan Ellen Birsic (b 27 Apr 1956, Pittsburgh PA).

CF53833411   Jennifer Ann Dawson (b 8 Oct 1989, Pittsburgh PA).

CF53833412   Karen Margaret Dawson (b 3 Aug 1992, Pittsburgh PA).

CF5383342   Sanford Kent Dawson (b 10 Jan 1952, Williamsport PA) m 1 Aug 1981, Taichung Taiwan, Debra Chupang, aka Chung Tai Hai (b 12 Mar 1956, Taiwan).

CF53833421   Kelly Ann Dawson (b 8 Dec 1982, Pittsburgh PA).

CF53833422   Kevin William Dawson (b 29 Mar 1991, Hong Kong).

CF53834   Raymond Augustus Ritter (b 17 Dec 1890, Sunbury PA) m 7 May 1913, New York NY, Lillian Mae Jester (b 5 Jan 1893, New York NY) Machinist, South Williamsport PA.

CF538341   Dorothy Flora Ritter (b 15 Mar 1917, New York NY) m 28 Oct 1939, Clifton Charles Robbins (2 Nov 1912, Newberry PA-17 May 1987, Williamsport PA).

CF5383411   Jan Clifton Robbins (b 19 May 1943, Williamsport PA) m 19 Aug 1967, Nancy Lee Brown.

CF538412   Margaret Ruth Ritter (29 Jun 1919, Williamsport PA-21 Apr 1994, Springfield VA) m 18 Jul 1943, Howard Kenneth Emert (b 22 Mar 1918, Williamsport PA).

CF5383421   Gary Howard Emert (b 3 May 1947).

CF5383422   Linda Ann Emert (b 30 Jan 1949) m 12 Jul 1969, Fairfax VA, Roy Lester Kearns (b 3 May 1947).

CF53834221   Leslie Ann Kearns (b 28 Feb 1971).

CF53834222   Roy Lester Kearns (b 1 Feb 1974).

CF5383423   Karen Louise Emert (b 1 Jan 1953).

CF5383424   Ronald Scott Emert (b 17 Nov 1956) m Julie Durkin (b 6 Mar 1967).

     Scott Francis Durkin (b 28 Dec 1984, Fairfax VA) Adopted by Ronald Scott Durkin.

CF53834241   Sara Ann Emert (b 13 Dec 1991, Woodbridge VA).

CF53835   Conrad Weiser Ritter (22 Nov 1898, Williamsport PA-7 Jun 1912, Williamsport PA).

CF53836   Barbara Thelma Ritter (7 Oct 1902, Auburn, NY-28 Sep 1985, Seminole FL) m 1) 9 Nov 1920, Elmira NY, Robert Edward Rook (3 Sep 1901-30 Jan 1972, Rochester NY) div 1935; m 2) 7 Jan 1936, Frederick Rudolph Melville (6 Apr 1877, CA-5 Mar 1954, Wilkes-Barre PA) div 1944; m 3) Nov 1944, Williamsport PA, Charles Leander Hubler (b 16 Nov 1914, PA) div 1956. Melville, Spanish-American War.

CF538361   Norma Lorraine Rook (b 24 Feb 1922, Williamsport PA) m 1) 12 Apr 1941, Williamsport PA, William Bard Carn Jr (12 Apr 1918, Williamsport PA-13 Mar 1988, Williamsport, PA) div 1946; m 2) Apr 1946, Chester L Eyler (b 14 Apr 1922, Williamsport, PA, div 1948; m 3) 4 Jan 1950, Lock Haven PA, Robert Milton Johnson (b 29 Sep 1927, Bellefonte PA).

CF5383611   William Bard Carn III (b 10 Apr 1943, Williamsport PA) m 23 Nov 1963, Largo FL, Joyce Ann Miller (b 3 Aug 1942) Meat cutter.

CF53836111   Theresa Lorraine Carn (b 12 Feb 1965, St Petersburg FL) m 21 Sep 1985, Brooksville FL, Michael Thomas Gregory (b 17 May 1965, Brooksville FL).

CF538361111   Ashleigh Nicole Gregory (b 13 Oct 1987).

CF53836112   Sophia Lorraine Carn (b 26 Oct 1967, St Petersburg FL) m 20 aug 1988, Brooksville FL, Charles Andrew Nix (b 26 Jan 1967, Brooksville FL).

CF538361121   Brittany Ann Nix (b 10 Apr 1991, Brooksville FL).

CF538361122   Charles Andrew Nix (b 16 Jan 1988, Brooksville FL).

CF53836113   William Bard Carn IV (b 10 Sep 1969, St Petersburg FL) m 12 Jan 1990, Brooksville FL, Dorothy Ann Woodcock (b 31 Aug 1964, Niagara Falls, NY) div 1992.

CF538361131   April Dawne Carn (b 10 Apr 1991, Springfield IL).

CF538361132   William Bard Carn V (b 10 Mar 1993, New Port Richey FL).

CF53836114   Robert Milton Johnson Carn (b 6 Apr 1971, Largo FL) m 4 Jan 1989, Brooksville FL, Christine Louise Mullins (b 27 Nov 1971, Brooksville FL).

CF538361141   Brandon Robert Michael Carn (b 12 Dec 1989).

CF538361142   Christopher Carn (b 3 Mar 1992).

CF53836115   Bryan Bradley Carn (b 11 Aug 1972, Largo FL) unm.

CF53836116   Dawne Lynna Carn (b 17 Sep 1973, St Petersburg FL) unm. The father of her child is
Alexander Chew.

CF538361161   Austin Alexander Chew (b 8 Apr 1992).

CF538362   Lamonte Frederick Melville (b 20 Jan 1937, Williamsport PA) m 24 Sep 1955, Williamsport PA, Lois Arlene Wanamaker (b 7 Jul 1938, Williamsport PA) div 1979; m 2) 25 Jul 1982, St Petersburg FL, Kathleen Francis Hunter (b 10 Oct 1942, Detroit MI)

CF5383621   Mickie Lynn Melville (b 9 Mar 1960, Williamsport PA) m 22 Feb 1986, St Petersburg FL, William Harold Schilling (b 11 Nov 1955).

CF53836211   Jennifer Nicole Schilling (b 6 Dec 1987, Pinellas Park FL).

CF5383622   Jodi Lee Melville (b 4 Dec 1964, St Petersburg FL) m 1)   ; m 2) 14 Sep 1985, Lake Seminole Park FL, George De Bellis; m 3) 23 Nov 1994, St Petersburg FL, Mark Lewis.

CF53836221   Dustin George De Bellis (b 26 Jan 1985).

CF53836222   Eric Michael De Bellis (b 8 Oct 1988).

CF5383623   Teri Rae Melville (b 28 Feb 1967, St Petersburg FL) m 1) 28 Feb 1987, St Petersburg FL, James Malti; m 2) 12 Jun 1995, Charles Willis.

CF5384   Ida Jane Weiser (13 Sep 1866, Sunbury PA-11 Sep 1951, Upper Darby PA) m 13 Sep 1890, Sunbury PA, Charles A Malick (24 Feb 1864, Sunbury PA-11 Feb 1914, Sunbury PA) Bur Sunbury PA.

CF53841   Helen Marie Malick (27 Oct 1891, Sunbury PA-6 May 1973, Sunbury PA) m 8 Oct 1914, Sunbury PA, William Luther Hoffman (15 May 1892-9 Sep 1967, State College PA) Bur Sunbury PA.

CF538411   Elizabeth Shaner Hoffman (28 Aug 1915, Sunbury PA-2 Nov 1994, Pleasant Gap PA) m 1) Sunbury PA, James R Bathurst (5 Sep 1914, Sunbury PA-12 Sep 1964, State College PA) m 2) Tobias Plozner (b 11 Oct 1920, Bellefonte PA) Bur Pleasant Gap PA.

CF5384111   James R Bathurst Jr (b 31 Jan 1937, Sunbury PA) m 11 Jun 1977 Huntsville AL, Dana B Brewer (b 17 Jun 1945, Washington DC).

CF53841111   Curtis Jamison Bathurst (b 24 Jun 1979, Huntsville AL).

CF5384112   Judith Rue Bathurst (b 25 Nov 1938, Sunbury PA) m 22 Jan 1960, State College PA, Thomas Gilbert Mulraney (b 12 Apr 1938, Mt Pleasant PA).

CF53841121   Thomas Gilbert Mulraney Jr (b 28 Mar 1961, Bellefonte PA) m 13 Jun 1987, Southgate MI, Patricia Rose McGee (b 23 Feb 1961, Wyandotte MI).

CF538411211   Megan Rose Mulraney (b 7 Feb 1995, Wyandotte MI).

CF53841122   James Edward Mulraney (b 30 Jun 1965, Greensburg PA) m 22 Jun 1991, Trenton MI, Michele Diane Cole (b 15 Nov 1967, Dearborn MI).

CF5384113   Jeanne Rochelle Bathurst (b 5 Oct 1940, Sunbury PA) m 28 May 1966, Du Bois PA, Ronald Markle London (b 22 May 1943, Du Bois PA).

CF53841131   Kenneth Monroe London (b 1 Nov 1967, Du Bois PA) m 17 May 1991, Du Bois PA, Penny Jean Shenkle (b 17 Mar 1969, Du Bois PA).

CF53841132   Leonard Raine London (b 11 Nov 1968, Du Bois PA).

CF53841133   Ronald Wayne London (b 29 Oct 1971, Du Bois PA).

*CF5384114   Luther Earl Bathurst (b 14 Nov 1948, State College PA) m 10 Jul 1971, Du Bois PA, Phyllis Catharine Fink (b 29 Mar 1949, Du Bois PA).

CF53841141   Melinda Anne Bathurst (b 25 Aug 1978, Towson MD).

CF53841142   James Earl Bathurst (b 27 Jul 1981, Towson MD).

CF5384115   John Charles Bathurst (b 11 Aug 1951, Bellefonte PA) m 1) 24 Apr 1982, Bayshore NY, Beth Ann Strine (b 13 May 1955, Milton PA) div; m 2) 14 May 1993, Johnstown PA, Cynthia Marie Dyda (b 3 May 1966, Johnstown PA).

CF53841151   Nicholas John Bathurst (b 25 Jun 1987, State College PA).

*CF538412   William Malick Hoffman (b 16 Feb 1917, Sunbury PA) m 23 Mar 1940, Betty St Clair (b 7 Nov 1917, Harrisburg PA) AB, Bucknell U, 1938. WWII: USN, Lt JG. District manager, GMC.

*CF5384121   William St Clair Hoffman (b 2 Oct 1940, Philadelphia PA) m 10 Jun 1967, Monterey CA, Diane Baker (b 29 Apr 1939, Santa Monica CA) MA, George Washington U. USN, Cmd, Springfield VA.

CF53841211   Shannon St Clair Hoffman (b 26 Oct 1971, Bethesda MD) AB, N VA Comm Col, 1994. Receptionist, Springfield VA.

CF53841212   Cynthia Marie Hoffman (b 28 Feb 1975, Philadelphia PA).

*CF5384122   Rodger Hodge Hoffman (b 6 Jan 1942, Philadelphia PA) m 28 Apr 1963, Birmingham AL, Margaret Bethell (b 3 Dec 1939, Jasper AL) U AL; USA. Sales, Birmingham AL. She, AB, U Montevallo(AL); MS, U AB, 1991.

*CF53841221   Rodger David Hoffman (b 11 Oct 1963, Chinon France) m 27 Jun 1987, Kentwood MI, Sandra Berg (b 7 Jul 1964, Detroit MI) AB, U AL, 1985. Insurance auditor.

CF538412211   Warren David Hoffman (b 3 Jun 1989, Birmingham AL).

CF538412212   Mary Catherine Hoffman (b 10 Jul 1991, Birmingham AL).

CF538412213   Nolan Rodger Hoffman (b 22 Jun 1993, Birmingham AL).

CF53841222   Paul William Hoffman (8 Oct 1964, Birmingham, AL) AB, Jacksonville (AL) U. Social security admin., Birmingham AL.

CF53841223   Margaret Elizabeth Hoffman (22 Jun 1968, Jacksonville, FL) AB, U AL, 1992. Teacher, Leeds AL.

CF538412231   Elizabeth Megin Hoffman (b 20 Jan 1989, Birmingham AL).

CF53841224   Betty Hodge Hoffman (b 31 Mar 1974, Jacksonville FL).

*CF53841225   William Malick Hoffman III (b 19 Feb 1978, Jacksonville FL).

CF538413   Robert Andrew Hoffman (14 Oct 1919, Sunbury PA-18 Aug 1977, Danville PA) m Betty Burgard (28 Mar 1920, Sharon PA-18 Feb 1990, Manchester NM) USA, Capt.

CF5384131   Susan Hoffman (b 16 Jan 1947, Dover NJ) m 3 Aug 1968, Morristown NJ, Randall Lee Parker (b 6 Sep 1946, Syracuse NY).

CF53841311   Randall Todd Parker (b 30 Jul 1972).

CF53841312   Jonathan Andrew Parker (b 4 Oct 1974).

CF5384132   Linda Hoffman (b 29 Nov 1950, Dover NJ) m 11 Oct 1975, Northumberland PA, William Winter Whelan (b 28 Nov 1949, Chappaqua NY) She, secretary, Pleasanton CA.

CF53841321   Donald Victor Whelan (b 31 Aug 1977).

CF53841322   Robert William Whelan (b 11 May 1979).

CF53841323   Andrew Turner Whelan (b 2 Dec 1982).

CF5385   George Frank Weiser (13 Dec 1868, Sunbury PA-6 Nov 1936, Williamsport PA) m 1899, Mary Ellen Lower (21 Aug 1881, near Dalmatia PA-6 Nov 1932, Sunbury PA) Bur Sunbury PA Employee, silk mill.

CF53851   Florence Weiser (b 6 Jul 1902, Sunbury PA) m 8 Oct 1922, El Paso TX, Walton Kirpatrick.

CF538511   June Kirpatrick (b 8 Jul 1923, Sunbury PA) m 1) Oct 1946, Joe Vollene; m 2) 12 Aug 1858, Gale Harris.

CF5385111   Ellen Vollene (b 17 Nov 1947).

CF5385112   JoAnn Vollene (b 7 Dec 1952).

CF5385113   Debbie Vollene (b 10 Feb 1956).

CF538512   Mary Kirkpatrick (b 16 Oct 1924, Sunbury PA) m Mar 1944, George Young.

CF5385121   Robert C Young (b 22 Oct 1947).

CF5385122   William S Young (b 10 Apr 1949).

CF538513   Robert Kirkpatrick (b 24 Feb 1934, Scranton PA) m 14 Dec 1957, Shearley DeVore.

CF5385131   Elisa Kirkpatrick (b 15 Nov 1958).

CF53852   George Francis Weiser (b 2 Aug 1913, Sunbury PA) m 17 Aug 1937, Edythe J Wynn. Board mill refiner operator, Sunbury PA.

CF538521   Mary Frances Weiser (b 22 Oct 1944, Sunbury PA).

CF5386   Edward James Weiser (20 Dec 1871, Sunbury PA-24 Apr 1943, Sunbury PA) m 11 Dec 1892, Lewisburg PA, Miriam Olga Geiss (7 Oct 1875, Monroe Tp, Snyder Co PA-13 Jan 1929, Sunbury PA) Bur Sunbury PA.

CF53861   Harold Martin Weiser (11 Apr 1894, Sunbury PA-22 May 1948, Salinas CA) m 14 May 1921, Sunbury PA, Grace Hornberger.

CF539 Catherine Louise Weiser Musselman
(1838-1909)

CF538611   Robert Elwood Weiser (b 6 Sep 1922, Sunbury PA) m Nov 1943, Gladys Myers.

CF5386111   Diana Louise Weiser (b 11 Mar 1947, Salinas CA).

CF5386112   Martin Weiser (b 18 Aug 1855, Sunbury PA).

CF538612   Eunice Miriam Weiser (b 13 Jul 1923, Sunbury PA) m Marlin Smith.

CF5386121   Michael David Smith (b 11 Dec 1946, Sunbury PA).

CF538613   Edward James Weiser (b 10 Feb 1925, Sunbury PA) m May 1951, Mary Stevens. No chn.

CF538614   Philip Conrad Weiser (b 3 Jan 1927, Sunbury PA) m 1) 1948, Inez Fancher; m 2) 19 Jan 1952, Leolla Annette Phillips.

CF5386141   James Allen Weiser (b 2 Feb 1949, Salinas CA).

CF5386142   Linda Lou Weiser (b 24 Jun 1953, Sunbury PA).

CF5386143   Rebecca Ann Weiser (b 9 Jun 1955, Sunbury PA).

CF5386144   Tracey Jo Weiser (b 25 Jul 1956, Sunbury PA).

CF539   Catherine Louise Weiser (15 Jul 1838, Sunbury PA-28 Jul 1909) m 23 Dec 1857, William Henry Musselman (2 Mar 1834-27 Sep 1884) Bur Templeville MD.

CF5391   Catherine Elizabeth Musselman (6 Dec 1858-19 Dec 1858).

CF5392   Annie Virginia Musselman (13 Jan 1859-ca 1930) m 12 Sep 1880, John A Dunkelberger (b 17 Apr 1854).

CF53921   Harry A Dunkelberger m Lucy   . Train dispatcher, PA RR, Philadelphia PA.

CF53922   Maude Dunkelberger (d about 12 yrs of age, Shamokin PA).

CF5393   George Thomas Musselman (24 Feb 1863, Sunbury PA-16 Dec 1916, Cambridge MD) m 25 Feb 1891, Marydel MD, Mary Viola Powell (21 Apr 1872-30 Dec 1954) Bur Cambridge MD. Railway postal clerk, US Government.

CF53931   Elizabeth Louise Musselman (8 Feb 1892, Marydel MD-14 May 1930, Hagerstown MD) m 25 Nov 1915, Cambridge MD, Raymond L Mowbray (8 Jun 1880, Aireys MD-4 May 1983) He bur Frederick MD. She bur FL. Teacher; Methodist clergyman.

CF539311   James Emerson Mowbray (b 30 Oct 1916, West Grove PA).

CF539312   Jay Byron Mowbray (b 23 Dec 1917, Wilmington DE) m 19 Apr 1947, Munich Germany, Sheila Grantham. PhD, Tulane U, 1952; WWII: USA, Lt Col; instructor, Fort Benning GA.

CF5393121   Alison Joan Mowbray (b 23 Nov 1948, New Orleans LA) m 27 Jun 1990, Ojai CA, Robert Joseph Cummings (b 6 Jul 1948) She, BS, U CA, 1970; writer. He, BS, U CA, 1970; computer programmer.

*CF539313   George Hamilton Mowbray (b 24 Dec 1921, Taylorsville MD) m 28 Nov 1946, Forest Hill MD, Phyllis Louise Wagner (b 25 May 1922, Baltimore MD) He, BA, MA, Johns Hopkins U, 1950; PhD, Cambridge U, England, 1953. WWII: USAF, Sgt. He, research, experimental psychologist, winemaker, Westminster MD; she, librarian.

CF5393131   Paul Nicholas Hamilton Mowbray (b 23 Dec 1954, Washington DC) Stage technician, Atlantic City NJ.

CF5393132   Claire Mowbray (b 27 Jun 1958, Washington DC) m 26 Sep 1981, Westminster MD, Dominic Golding (b 20 Sep 1959, Tichfield England) She, BA, Washington Col, Chestertown MD, 1980. Editor, Worcester MA. He, BA, Oxford U, England, 1981; PhD, Clarke U, Worcester MA, 1988.

CF53931321   Heather Louise Golding (b 6 Jun 1991, Bethesda MD).

CF53931322   Emma Elizabeth Golding (b 15 Mar 1995, Worcester MA).

CF539314   John Edwin Mowbray (b 28 Nov 1923, Walkersville MD) m 6 Mar 1944, Overlea MD, Charlotte Doris Wilkerson (b 25 Sep 1922, Baltimore MD) WWII: USAF. Manufacturing executive, travel agency, Wilmington NC. She, bookkeeper.

CF5393141   Barry Nelson Mowbray (b 8 Sep 1947, Baltimore MD) m 1) 30 Jun 1973, Judith Dahlin, div 1986; m 2) 8 Nov 1989, Mary Lawson Groseclose. BA, Duke U, 1969; USN Reserve; Travel agency, Wilmington NC.

CF53931411   David York Mowbray (b 22 Apr 1976, Wilmington NC).

CF53931412   Brian Jay Mowbray (b 27 Jul 1978, Wilmington NC).

CF5393142   Kenneth Brian Mowbray (b 14 Nov 1952, Wilmington NC) m 25 Feb 1977, Wilmington NC, Margaret Ann Cogdill (b 16 Jun 1953) div 1991. BA, U NC, Chapel Hill, 1973. Travel agency, Wilmington NC.

CF53931421   Adam Nolan Mowbray (b 26 Jun 1981, Wilmington NC).

CF53931422   Margaret Elaine Mowbray (b 8 May 1985, Wilmington NC).

CF53931423   Anna Paige (b 19 Mar 1987, Wilmington NC).

CF539315   Ruth Louise Mowbray (b 30 May 1929, Hagerstown MD) m 4 Oct 1947, Forest Hill MD, Robert Delevett Pyle (b 16 Dec 1924, Forest Hill MD) He, woodworker; she, secretary.

CF5393151   Jeffrey Musselman Pyle (b 10 Apr 1949, Havre de Grace MD) m 13 Oct 1979, Ft Monroe VA, Mary Christine Cornetta, div 1989. BA, U MD, 1972; MA, Morgan S U, 1977. Urban planning; mortgage banker.

CF5393152   Jennifer Jane Pyle (b 7 Mar 1953, Havre de Grace MD) BFA, U WA, 1976. Graphic screen printer.

CF5393153   Jeanne Laurie Pyle (b 4 Apr 1954, Havre de Grace MD) m 27 Mar 1976, Bothell WA, Donald C Martin, div 1980. BA, U WA, 1976.

CF53932   William Powell Musselman (b 16 Nov 1894, Marydel MD) m 27 Nov 1917, Philadelphia PA, Bessie May MacIntosh. Owner and manager, Aetna Felt Co, New York NY.

CF539321   Ellen Virginia Musselman (b 13 May 1919, Philadelphia PA) m 15 Apr 1944, Carl Theodore Kepler.

CF5393211   Pamela Kepler (b 1947) m 10 Jun 1967, Troy R Frodge.

CF53932111   Didi Frodge (b 11 May 1968).

CF53932112   Pamela Frodge (b 1970).

CF5393212   Carl Theodore Kepler (b 14 Jun 1948).

CF5393213   Penelope Kepler (b 17 Jan 1955).

CF539322   Lysbeth Anne Musselman (b 17 May 1920, Philadelphia PA) m 1946, Clark Outcault (d Nov 1960).

CF5393221   Susan Mary Outcault (b 1947).

CF5393222   Lysbeth Ann Outcault (b Aug 1950).

CF5393223   Timothy Outcault (b Oct 1954).

CF539333   Andrew Roe Musselman (1896-1896) Bur Marydel MD.

CF53934   Anna Beatrice Musselman (9 Mar 1897, Marydel MD-4 May 1979, Cambridge MD) m 15 Jun 1921, Cambridge MD, Granville Hooper. She, teacher; he, owner, coal and fuel oil business, Cambridge MD.

CF539341   Anne Hooper (b 21 Apr 1924, Cambridge MD) m 1) 29 Oct 1941, Richmond VA, Robert Elwood Andersen, div; m 2) 25 Oct 1982, James Sanders (b 12 Jun 1927, Hartsville SC).

CF5393411   Robert Elwood Andersen Jr (b 15 May 1942, Baltimore MD) m 1) 19 Sep 1965, Esther Gale Herrin, div; m 2) 8 Dec 1990, Nancy Harriss.

CF53934111   Noel Elise Andersen (b 15 Aug 1968).

CF53934112   Robert Christian Andersen (b 6 Aug 1973).

CF5393412   Timothy Hanks Andersen (b 20 Apr 1944, Cambridge MD) m Janice Marie Vequist.

CF5393413   Patrick Alan Andersen (b 18 May 1947, Hagerstown MD) m 1) 5 Jun 1971, Debra Ann Hughes, div; m 2) 16 Apr 1978, Lynette Little Floyd.

CF5393414   John Granville Andersen (b 27 Jun 1948, Hagerstown MD) m 28 Apr 1984, Roxanne Baker.

CF5393415   Linda Joanne Andersen (b 28 Jul 1961, Tampa FL) m 23 Oct 1991, Allen Brissenden.

CF5393416   Jane Elizabeth Andersen (b 26 Feb 1963, Atlanta GA).

CF539342   Jane Hooper (b 23 Jan 1927, Cambridge MD) m 21 Jan 1947, Hagerstown MD, Robert Thomas Keating.

CF5393421   Claire Marie Keating (b 30 Nov 1947, Carlisle PA) m 15 Jun 1968, John David Bloomfield.

CF53934211   Randall Hooper Bloomfield (b 10 Mar 1969).

CF53934212   Melynda Gayle Bloomfield (b 15 Jul 1970).

CF5393422   Kathy Anne Keating (b 2 May 1949, Carlisle PA) m 3 Jul 1970, Paul W Deminck.

CF5393423   Michael Robert Keating (b 30 Jun 1950, Elmira NY).

CF5393424   Kerry Thomas Keating (b 10 Sep 1951, Elmira NY).

CF5393425   Bernard Andrew Keating (b 21 Nov 1953, Elmira NY) m Marlene   .

CF53934251   Benjamin Michael Keating (b 12 Oct 1975).

CF53934252   Sean Robert Keating (b 1 Apr 1977).

CF5393426   Stephen Christoper Keating (b 12 Oct 1954, Canandaigua NY) m 16 Sep 1977, Cathy .

CF5393427   Theresa Keating (b 14 Aug 1957, Canandaigua NY).

CF5393428   Ellen Keating (b 28 Aug 1959, Canandaigua NY).

CF5393429   Maria Keating (b 12 Dec 1960, Canandaigua NY).

CF53935   George Thomas Musselman Jr (14 Jul 1899, Chestertown MD-14 Jun 1947, Wilmington NC) m 1 Oct 1924, Wilmington NC, Emma Donnelly Yopp. Bur Wilmington NC.

CF539351   Emma Donnelly Yopp Musselman (b 4 Jun 1928, Wilmington NC) m 11 Jun 1952, Wilmington NC, Clarence Chappell Council.

CF5394   Maude Estelle Musselman (24 Dec 1867-Oct 1947, Wilmington DE) m Samuel H Pippin (1862-1941) Bur Templeville MD.

CF53941   Claude Musselman Pippin (1890-1937).

CF53942   Robert Percy Pippin (1901-1935).

CF5395   William Henry Musselman III (6 May 1870-10 Mar 1871).

CF5396   Katie Leonore Musselman (19 Mar 1872-ca 1938) m 24 Nov 1897, Altoona PA, Irving G Braucher. Bur Altoona PA. No chn.

CF5397   Jennie Weiser Musselman (16 Apr 1874-16 Nov 1874).

CF56   Peter Weiser (son of Peter and Elizabeth (Minchaus) Weiser) was born 24 Feb 1800, Augusta Tp, Northumberland Co PA and died 27 May 1879, Marshall IL. He married Mary Elizabeth Winn (Potomac IL). He was confirmed in 1821 at Zion Lutheran Church, Augustaville PA. By 1830 he and his brothers Samuel and John had moved to Bloom Tp, Fairfield Co OH. By 1850 he was a farmer in Urbana Tp, Champaign Co OH. About 1858 he moved to Marshall Tp, Clark Co IL, where he farmed the rest of his life. He is buried there. His widow lived with her son George after his death and is buried at Potomac IL.[77] His tombstone gives his birthdate as 22 Feb.

CF561   Sarah Jane Weiser (b 1822).

CF562   Barbara Ellen Weiser (b 1830).

CF563   Elizabeth Jane Weiser (b ca 1831).

CF564   Samuel W Weiser (b 20 Mar 1831).

CF565   Absalom Weiser (b 1833).

CF566   John Decatur Weiser (b Jul 1841).

CF567   George M Weiser (b 8 Sep 1844).

CF568   Charles Jefferson Weiser (b 30 Jan 1848).

CF561   Sarah Jane Weiser (1822, PA-1881) m 12 Oct 1843, Fairfield Co OH, William Henry Kearns (d 30 Aug 1862, near Richmond VA) Civil War: Private, Co G, 16 IN Vol.

CF5611   Elizabeth Jane Kearns (b 1844, OH) m Drew Williams.

CF5612   James Fellen Kearns (dy).

CF5613   Seraphine Kearns (20 Jul 1848, Mt Finley OH-8 Oct 1936, Niagara Co NY) m 31 Jul 1867, Putnam Co IN, Robert Nelson (18 Jun 1841, Bedford Co PA-23 Feb 1911, Niagara Co NY).

CF56131   Ida May Nelson (24 Mar 1868, IN-dy).

CF56132   Odie Dell Nelson (b 28 Jan 1870, IN).

CF56133   Hiram Walter Nelson (b 12 Jun 1971, IN).

CF56134   Sarah Adena Nelson (b 30 Jan 1973, IN).

CF56135   Mary Bell Nelson (18 May 1874-dy).

CF56136   Eliza Jane Nelson (19 Oct 1875-dy).

---

[77]Data on Peter Weiser provided by Noreen Armerding, Betty L. Turner, Velma Remlinger of Clark Co (IL) Genealogical Society, Don Doran and Bill Wiser.

CF56137   Edward David Nelson (11 Feb 1878, Jefferson IN-17 Jun 1954, Waitsburgh WA) m 14 Jun 1905, Waitsburgh WA, Osa Ellen Angell (28 Jul 1885, Dayton WA-4 Dec 1972, Walla Walla WA) Both chiropractors.

CF561371   Robert Edward Nelson (24 Mar 1906, Waitsburgh WA-13 Jan 1990, Arlington MA) m 26 Aug 1938, Spokane WA, Margaret Hoffman (b 26 Aug 1916, Spokane WA) Bur Concord MA. BS, U WA, 1932; MD, U OR, 1937.

CF5613711   Trina Margaret Nelson (b 2 Jul 1940, Spokane WA) m 31 Oct 1964, David Murphy (b 21 Apr 1939, Arlington MA).

CF56137111   Kenneth William Murphy (b 9 May 1967, Arlington MA).

CF56137112   Richard David Murphy (b 21 Mar 1969, Arlington MA) m 2 Aug 1992, Oahu HI, Natalie Plourde (b 27 Jul 1962).

CF561371121   Margaret Murphy (b 1 Mar 1993, Naval Air Station, St Mary's Co, MD).

CF5613712   Kristine Louise Nelson (b 2 Jul 1942, Spokane WA-11 Mar 1977, Concord MA) m 16 Jun 1963, Belmont MA, Edwin Rodney Sage (b 4 Aug 1937).

CF56137121   Robert Charles Sage (b 31 Oct 1968, Concord MA).

CF56137122   Peter Sage (b 12 Apr 1966, Beaver Park WI).

CF561372   Raleigh P Nelson (10 Oct 1908, Waitsburgh WA-20 Nov 1958, Los Angeles CA) m 26 Feb 1930, NY, Margaret Bowman (b 9 Dec 1914, Dundee Scotland) BS, U WA, 1932. CPA, Los Angeles CA.

CF5613721   Noreen Rennie Nelson (b 16 Jun 1947, Los Angeles CA) m 14 Jun 1969, Las Vegas NV, J Peter Armerding (b 20 Dec 1942, Boston MA) BA, CA S U, 1968. Elementary teaching credential, 1969.

CF56137211   Gretchen Elizabeth Armerding (b 9 Dec 1976, Culver City CA).

CF56137212   James William Armerding (b 23 Nov 1980, Culver City CA).

CF561373   Vera Sally Nelson (b 4 Apr 1910) m 1) 14 Jun 1936, Albert Schwank; m 2) 23 Oct 1972, Leroy Kelly.

CF5613731   Gary Schwank (b 18 Mar 1937, WA).

CF5613732   Sherri Schwank (b 16 Aug 1940, WA) m Darrell Stamper.

CF56137321   Michael Stamper (b 23 May 1959, WA).

CF56137322   Larry Stamper (b 18 Oct 1961, WA).

CF561374   Verda Nelson (4 Sep 1925, WA-25 May 1952) unm.

CF56138   Susan Ruth Nelson (19 Oct 1879, IN-1965, NY) m Guy Gerald Muir (1875-1931).

CF561381   Rose Muir (b 17 Nov 1899, NY) m Lewis Wheeler.

CF561382   Blanch Muir (1903, NY-19 Oct 1920, NY).

CF561383   Marian Muir (b 16 Aug 1911, NY) m Peter Mudge.

CF5613831   William Mudge.

CF5613832   James M Mudge.

CF561384   Anne Muir (b and d 1914, NY).

CF561385   Elmira Muir (b and d 1914, NY).

CF561386   Lewis Muir m Helen   .

CF5613861   Barbara Muir.

CF561387   Eva Muir.

CF56139   Jessie Garfield Nelson (b 9 Jun 1881, IN).

CF5613A   Harvey Lane Nelson (b 4 Jun 1883, IN).

CF5613B   Eva Ruby Nelson (22 Dec 1886, IN-23 Apr1984, Waitsburgh WA) m 22 Jul 1906, Charles
Neace (b 1887).

CF5613B1   Charles Neace (b 1910, WA).

CF5613B2   Winnifred Neace (b 1915, WA) m Joseph Mc Cown.

CF5613C   Wilbur S Nelson (b 1889, IN).

CF5613D   Grover Cleveland Nelson (b 9 Mar 1893, IN) m Mable   .

CF5613D1   Theresa Nelson (b 1918, NY).

CF5614   Mary Catherine Kearns (1 Mar 1850-dy).

CF5615   William Marchel Kearns (b 5 Jun 1853).

CF5616   Barbara Ellen Kearns (b 9 Nov 1854) m 9 Nov 1875, Clay Co IN, John Morton.

CF56161   Margaret Morton (b 1877, IN).

CF5617   Martha Belle Kearns (b 24 Jan 1857) m Orville E Gibson (b Jul 1850, Clay Co IN)
Painter.

CF56171   Sarah Pearl Gibson (b 1876, IL).

CF56172   Maggie Gibson (1878, IL-dy).

CF56173   Charles A Gibson (b 22 Feb 1880, Marshall Tp, Clark Co IL) m Laina E   (b 1883, IL)
In 1920, Moultice Co IL.

CF561731   Mary E Gibson (b 1904, IL).

CF56174   girl Gibson (b 3 Mar 1882, Marshall Tp, Clark Co IL).

CF56175   Byrd Gibson (b Oct 1886, IL) m Wilmina   (b ca 1887, IL) In 1920, Douglas Co IL.

CF561751   Avery Gibson (b 1910, IL).

CF561752   Anna B Gibson (b 1915, IL).

CF561753   Martha B Gibson (b 1917, IL).

CF56176   Shelby Gibson (b Apr 1891, IL) m Vera   (b 1890, IL).

CF561761   Wilmont Gibson (b 1910, IL).

CF56177   Ruby Gibson (b 1891, IL).

CF5618   George Washington Kearns (b 30 Nov 1858, Clark Co IN).

CF5619   John Edward Kearns (b 20 Jun 1860, IN).

CF562   Barbara Ellen Weiser (ca 1831-1 Apr 1878, Clark Co IL) m 10 Nov 1854, Clark Co IL,
John W Barlow (ca 30 Aug 1830-1 Apr 1878) He, MD.

CF5621   Belle Barlow (b 1855, IL) m 21 Nov 1876, Clark Co IL, Richard T Houghton.

CF5622   Typy Barlow (b ca 1857, IL).

CF5623   Charles W Barlow (b Dec 1857, IL).

CF5624   Byrd Barlow (b ca 1879, IL).

CF563   Elizabeth Weiser (b ca 1832) m 9 Jan 1846, Fairfield Co OH, Joseph Jameson (b ca 1822)
Wagonmaker, Marysville IL.

CF5631   Charles A Jameson (b Mar 1847, OH) m Amelia   (b May 1852, IL).

CF56311   Margaret Jameson (b 1870).

CF56312   Lulu Jameson (b 1872).

CF56313   Robert Jameson (b Aug 1872).

CF5632   David Merrill Jameson (b 18 Apr 1848, OH) m 1872, Mary E   .

CF56321   Fred Jameson (b 18 Mar 1873).

CF56322   Jessie Jameson (b Oct 1881).

CF56323   William Jameson (b Jun 1889).

CF5633   James E Jameson (b Mar 1849, OH) m Anna   (b Mar 1857).

CF56331   Earl B Jameson (b Jul 1883, IL).

CF56332   Clarence S Jameson (b Sep 1886, IL).

CF5634   George E Jameson (b Mar 1866, IL) m F E L (b Jul 1875).

CF56341   Gladys E Jameson (b Jan 1897, IL).

CF56342   Glenn V Jameson (b Apr 1899, IL).

CF564   Samuel W Weiser (20 Mar 1830, PA-18 Mar 1916, Cleone IL) m 6 Sep 1863, Clark Co IL, Francis M Donaldson (30 Jul 1842-14 Oct 1918, Cleone IL) Bur Cleone IL.

CF5641   Carrie Weiser (13 Jun 1864-17 Sep 1865, Clark Co IL).

CF5642   Greenough Luther Wiser (21 May 1866, Clark Co IL-1 Aug 1940, Clark Co IL) m 14 Nov 1891, Marshall IL, Jessie Best (15 Mar 1874, Parker Tp, Clark Co IL-13 Sep 1937) Bur Cleone IL.

CF56421   Clem Wiser (21 Apr 1892, Parker Tp, Clark Co IL-1965, Miami FL) m 19 Dec 1915, Martinsville IL, Cecile Inez Winters (b 30 Nov 1898, Martinsville IL) div 1945. Postmaster, Martinsville IL. Ford garage.

CF564 Samuel W. Weiser
(1830-1916) and his wife,
Francis M. Donaldson Weiser
(1842-1918)

CF564211   Evelynne Maurine Wiser (b 9 Dec 1916, Martinsville IL) m 1) 18 Aug 1934, Marshall IL, Harrold Overpeck (b 20 Apr 1900, Darlington IN) div 1935; m 2) 1 Sep 1940, Henderson KY, Harris Loring Hitt, div 1941; m 3) 2 Sep 1942, St Charles MO, Ralph Arden Medsker (b 1 Mar 1912, West Union IL) div 1946; m 4) 8 Dec 1946, Scottsburg IN, George William Deahl (11 Aug 1911, Martinsville IL--26 Apr 1952, Paris IL); m 5) 4 Oct 1952, Effingham IL, John Nathan Stephenson (24 Mar 1921, KY-1 Dec 1954, Miami FL); m 6) 16 Aug 1956, Key West FL, John Henry Burke (b 5 Mar 1912, Exeter NH).

CF5642111   Bruce Allen Burke (b 22 Jul 1957, Hialeah FL).

CF564212   Lois Elaine Wiser (b 8 May 1918, Martinsville IL) m 25 Nov 1936, Brazil IN, Herbert Alver Barber (b 31 Dec 1915) div 1942; m 2) 1 Feb 1946, William Harold Logue (b 17 Mar 1915, Martinsville IL).

CF5642121   Alice Elveira Barber (b 11 Jan 1938, Terre Haute IN) m 18 Jan 1958, Casey IL, Marion Eugene Davidson (b 4 Jul 1925, Casey IL).

CF56422   Ala Wiser (24 May 1894, Parker Tp, Clark Co IL-1972) m 16 Feb 1916, Charles Luther Hammond (7 Mar 1890, Dolson Tp, Clark Co IL-1970) Bur Cleone IL.

CF564221   Evan Ronald Hammond (b 10 Jan 1917, Clark Co IL) m 1 Mar 1940, Martinsville IL, Henrietta Jean Weldon (b 6 Feb 1920, Pierce Co IN).

CF5642211   David Weldon Hammond (b 1 Jul 1941, Marinsville IL).

CF5642212   Susan Elizabeth Hammond (b 25 Jan 1945, Martinsville IL).

CF5642213   Jefry Alan Hammond (b 8 Jan 1950, Lima OH).

CF564222   Haven Wiser Hammond (23 Feb 1923, Clark Co IL-1 Dec 1995) m 24 Nov 1948, Gwendolyn Louise Hardway (b 23 Oct 1928, Masonville KY) Bur Martinsville IL.

CF5642221   Debra Lee Hammond (b 16 Oct 1949, Terre Haute IN).

CF5642222   Lora Ann Hammond (b 20 Sep 1952, Terre Haute IN).

CF5642223   Jill Ellen Hammond (b 18 Feb 1956, Terre Haute IN).

CF564223   Dallas Eugene Hammond (b 19 Jan 1926, Clark Co IL) m 9 Sep 1950, Martinsville IL, Doris Brenner (b 28 Oct 1931, Martinsville IL) div 1951; m 2) Waldraut Grueneberg (b 28 Jan 1931, New York NY).

CF5642231   Robert Dallas Hammond (b 10 Oct 1956, Evanston IL).

CF5642232   Roy William Hammond (b ca 1965-15 Feb 1985, Scottsdale AZ).

CF56423   Orion Wiser (8 Dec 1896, Parker Tp, Clark Co IL-Jun 1959, Paris IL) m 1 Mar 1923, Marshall IL, Dorothy Idella Berger (24 May 1904, Martinsville IL-12 Mar 1982, Urbana IL).

CF564231   Mary June Wiser (27 Mar 1924, Martinsville IL-2 Nov 1945, Martinsville IL) m Rex Eugene Stephens (b 2 Nov 1919, Martinsville IL) div.

CF56424   Best Wiser (21 Dec 1907-24 Dec 1907, Clark Co IL) Bur Cleone IL.

CF5643   Charles R Weiser (8 Jun 1867-16 Aug 1868, Clark Co IL).

CF5644   Sallie Weiser (31 Aug 1869-6 Feb 1876, Clark Co IL).

CF565   Absalom Weiser (1833, PA-1892) m 14 Aug 1873, Marshall IL, Elizabeth Willoughby (8 Sep 1852, near Cincinnati OH-22 Nov 1931, Anna IL) Bur Marshall IL.

CF5651   Charles Frederick Weiser (27 Oct 1874, Marshall IL-10 Feb 1960, near Charleston IL) m 8 Oct 1904, Marshall IL, Mary Pearl Anderson (6 Jul 1884, near Marshall IL-8 Feb 1944, near Charleston IL) Bur Cleone IL.

CF56511   Forrest Weiser (b 16 May 1905, near Kansas IL) unm. Farmer, near Greenup IL.

CF56512   Dorsey Eugene Weiser (b 7 Oct 1906, near Kansas IL) m 13 Apr 1927, Marshall IL, Thelma Lorine Combs (b 23 Nov 1907, Brocton IL) No chn.

CF56513   Emma Jane Weiser (b 5 Aug 1908, Cleone IL) m 16 Oct 1926, Charleston IL, Francis Edward Eaton (b 26 May 1908, Ashmore IL) Oil co foreman, Springfield IL.

CF565131   Mary Elizabeth Eaton (b 27 Dec 1927, Charleston IL) unm.

CF565132   Francis Dwain Eaton (b 22 Jan 1930, Springfield IL) m 23 Nov 1951, Springfield IL, Betty Lucille Tuckerman (b 18 Dec 1931, Springfield IL).

CF5651321   Michael Dwain Eaton (b 23 Aug 1952, Springfield IL).

CF5651322   Mark Kevin Eaton (b 31 Dec 1957, Springfield IL).

CF565133   Joan Ruth Eaton (b 3 Aug 1932, Springfield IL) m 6 Sep 1951, Springfield IL, Donald Allen Poland (b 2 Mar 1933, South Charleston IL).

CF5651331   Vicki Lynn Poland (b 9 Aug 1953, Springfield IL).

CF5651332   Douglas Allen Poland (b 23 Jul 1954, Springfield IL).

CF5651333   David Alden Poland (b 23 Jul 1954, Springfield IL).

CF5651334   Kathy Jo Poland (b 13 Dec 1957, Springfield IL).

CF56514   Lola Ethel Weiser (b 16 Aug 1912, Cleone IL) m 18 Jun 1937, Toledo IL, Francis Thomas Carpenter (b 19 May 1911).

CF565141   Barbara Jean Carpenter (b 30 Aug 1934, Charleston IL) m 12 Oct 1951, Roy Lester Mc Cammon. Farmer, Dryden WA.

CF5651411   David Wayne Mc Cammon (b 19 Aug 1953, Paris IL).

CF5651412   Douglas Eugene Mc Cammon (b 3 Dec 1954, WA).

CF5651413   Audry Lynn Mc Cammon (b 5 Mar 1955, WA).

CF565142   Thomas Leroy Carpenter (b 29 Jul 1938, Charleston IL).

CF565143   Carolyn Ann Carpenter (b 24 Dec 1940, Charleston IL) m 20 Oct 1959, Charleston IL, Donald Gene Gordon (b 26 Jul 1935, Decatur IL) Construction worker, Charleston IL.

CF56515   Catherine Weiser (2 Nov 1915, Cleone IL-Jan 1916, Cleone IL) Bur Cleone IL.

CF56516   Ala Maybell Weiser (b 25 Apr 1917, near Martinsville IL) m 5 Aug 1939, Maysville KY, Ernest Francis Gladman, div 1944. m 2) 19 Nov 1951, Charleston IL, Eugene Leland Murphy (b 14 Feb 1919, Valeria KY).

CF565161   Sandra Lee Gladman (b 28 Feb 1940, Springfield IL) m 24 Apr 1958, Gary Lee Ryan (b 13 May 1936, Jonesville IL) Grocer, Charleton IL.

CF56517   Mary Pearl Weiser (b 6 Jul 1919, near Martinsville IL) m 30 Sep 1939, Charleston IL, Harry Ivan Rienbolt (b 14 Jul 1915, Casey IL) Printer, Danville IL. Res. Charleston IL.

CF565171   Darrell Ivan Rienbolt (b 18 Jan 1942, Charleston IL).

CF565172   Jimmy Lynn Rienbolt (b 28 Feb 1955, Charleston IL).

CF5652   Le Roy Weiser (31 May 1877, Marshall IL-20 Jun 1908, Terre Haute IN) unm. Bur Marshall IL.

CF5653   Emma Selecta Weiser (26 Jun 1880, Marshall IL-27 Dec 1932, Paris IL) m 29 Mar 1899, Clark Co IL, Howery Delvin Bullard (29 Jan 1877, Livingston Co IL-1 Jun 1955, Bartow FL) Bur Marshall IL.

CF56531   Edith Myrle Bullard (2 Sep 1899, Marshall IL-15 Dec 1918, Martinsville IL) unm. Bur Marshall IL.

CF56532   Ethel Lucile Bullard (b 2 Apr 1902, Marshall IL) m 16 May 1936, Marion IN, David Carl Berk (b 5 Oct 1901) No chn.

CF56533   John Delvin Floyd Bullard (b 8 Sep 1906, Marshall IL) m 15 Sep 1930, Marshall IL, Thelma Lois Blankenbecker (b 13 Apr 1910, Orange Tp, Clark Co IL).

CF565331   Patricia Bess Bullard (b 25 Mar 1936, Martinsville IL).

CF56534   Leroy Taft Bullard (b 19 Oct 1908, Marshall IL) m 1) Alice Naomi Mayfield, div; m 2) Louise   .

CF565341   Barbara Dian Bullard (b 5 Aug 1934, Robinson IL) m 1 Mar 1953, Waycross GA, Arthur James Mitchell (b 23 Nov 1919, Atlanta GA) Insurnace adjuster, Ferguson MO.

CF5653411   Jeffrey Thomas Mitchell (b 23 Apr 1954, Lakeland FL).

CF5653412   Gregory Arthur Mitchell (b 21 Jul 1956, St Louis MO).

CF5653413   Nancy Joan Mitchell (b 12 Nov 1958, St Louis MO).

CF56535   Mary Belle Bullard (b 23 Aug 1911, Marshall IL) m 13 Jan 1932, Robert Lee Moore (b 15 Feb 1912).

CF565351   Phyllis Nan Moore (b 17 Jan 1934, Martinsville IL) m 28 Jun 1953, Martinsville IL, Doyle Albert Jewell (b 31 Aug 1928, Farmersburg IN).

CF5653511   Drew Alan Jewell (b 8 Jun 1956, Sullivan IN).

CF5653512   Valerie Lee Jewell (b 16 Jun 1959, Sullivan IN).

CF56536   Harry Allen Bullard (23 Aug 1911, Marshall IL-23 Nov 1911, Clark Co IL) Bur Marshall IL.

CF566   John Decatur Weiser (Jul 1841-1910) m Lortainna F Berry Carter (1858-13 Feb 1917, Potomac IL) Wagonmaker, Marysville IL. Apparently no chn.

CF567   George M Weiser (8 Sep 1844, Greencastle OH-12 Dec 1924, Potomac IL) m 9 Jul 1866, Marshall IL, Nancy C Offord (17 Aug 1847, Huntington WV-15 Dec 1906, Potomac IL) Bur Potomac IL. Farmer, Marysville IL.

CF5671   Mary Weiser (1867, Marshall IL-1917) m Frank P Golliday (1864-1930) Bur Potomac IL.

CF56711   Floyd Golliday m Lois Bussey.

CF56712   Blanche Golliday m Alfred Talbott.

CF56713   Ida Golliday m Harry Merritt.

CF5672   Lucy Weiser (13 Jun 1868, Clark Co IL-28 Nov 1949) m 1892, Hugh Duncan (2 Mar 1854, State Line IN) Bur Bismarck IL.

CF56721   Cora Ellen Duncan (b 4 Aug 1889, Potomac IL) m 15 Aug 1909, Roy L Bryan.

CF56722   Nancy Sidney Duncan (b 9 Jun 1893, Alvin IL) m 23 May 1920, Francis D Mc Cormick.

CF56723   James Asa Duncan (b 24 Jun 1895, Alvin IL) m Sep 1921, Edith Pearl Clem.

CF56724   George Weiser Duncan (b 2 Mar 1897, Alvin IL) m Feb 1917, Grances Degan.

CF56725   Mary Emaline Duncan (b 14 Dec 1900, Alvin IL) unm.

CF56726   Hugh Albert Duncan (5 Jul 1903, Alvin IL-Jun 1904).

CF5673   Harry Weiser (9 Nov 1870, Marshall IL-30 Nov 1870, Marshall IL) Bur Marshall IL.

CF5674   Johnnie Weiser (18 Dec 1873, Marshall IL-28 Jan 1877, Marshall IL). Bur Marshall IL.

CF5675   Clara Weiser (6 Jun 1875, Marshall IL-3 Sep 1924) m 1893, Frank Hall (8 Mar 1869-19 Sep 1945).

CF56751   Ruth Vivian Hall (b 17 Sep 1894, Potomac IL) m Morris Jones.

CF56752   George Weiser Hall (b 12 Dec 1895, Rantoul IL) m Oakie Cressey.

CF56753   Mary Elizabeth Hall (b 29 Jun 1899, Potamac IL) m Ben Clemmons.

CF56754   Rachel Drusilla Hall (1902-1904).

CF56755   Marion Elisha Hall (b 14 Jun 1904, Potamac IL) m Emma Adams.

CF56756   Frield Offord Hall (b 7 Nov 1906, Potamac IL) m Thelma Wrench.

CF56757   Gwendolyn Alice Hall (b 10 Apr 1910, Potamac IL) m Samuel Adams.

CF56758   Isis Voss Hall (ca 1915-ca 1917).

CF56759   Frances Adeline Hall (b 25 Nov 1915, Potamac IL) m Russell Myler.

CF5675A   Helen Agatha Hall (7 Mar 1918-1918).

CF5675B   Clara Eunice Hall (b 29 Jan 1920, Potomac IL) m Earl Myler.

CF5676   Charles Decatur Weiser (13 Jun 1879, Marshall IL-31 Dec 1960, Danville IL) m 1) 10 Apr 1879, Cora Tarpening (Jan 1882, Mc Clean IL-28 Aug 1948, Potomac IL); m 2) 19 Dec 1951, Zora Griffin. Bur Potomac IL.

CF56761   infant Weiser (b 1909).

CF56762   Mildred June Weiser (30 Jun 1910, Potomac IL-Jun 1976, Potomac IL) m Harry Earnest Doran (30 Nov 1900, Rankin IL-26 Jun 1965, Potomac IL) Bur Potomac IL.

CF567621   Don Eugene Doran (b 10 May 1934, Paxton IL) m 6 Mar 1955, Margaret Ruth Howell (b 1 Aug 1936, Colison IL) No chn. Machine shop, Potomac IL.

CF56763   Elizabeth Weiser (b and d 1921, Potomac IL).

CF5677   Elizabeth S Weiser (b 14 Nov 1881, Marshall IL) m Frank L Rice (1875, Piper City IL-1950, Piper City IL) Bur Piper City IL.

CF56771   Wilma Margaret Rice (b 2 Mar 1913, Potomac IL) m Dean K Finch.

CF56772   Lloyd Eugene Rice (b 11 Nov 1918, Potomac IL) m Dorothy Wiese.

CF56773   Pauline Elizabeth Rice (b 24 Jul 1922, Potomac IL) m William Meuhler.

CF568   Charles Jefferson (Jeffet) Weiser (30 Jan 1848-8 Feb 1936, Marshall IL) m 18 May 1879, Marshall IL, Martha Ann Baird (30 Jul 1857, Marshall IL-28 Mar 1914, Marshall IL) Bur Marshall IL.

CF5681   Susie Edith Weiser (6 Apr 1880, Marshall IL-1967) m 1) 29 Jan 1902, Marshall IL, John Wesley Mundy (1 Feb 1878, York IL-1966) div; m 2) 24 Feb 1931, Hiram Hilbert (no chn).

CF56811   Harold Jay Mundy (6 Jul 1903, York IL-16 Oct 1948, Virdon IL) m 1) Luella Taylor, div; m 2) 30 Nov 1931, Lincoln IL, Lois Laudermilk (b 13 Mar 1903, Virdon IL) No chn. Bur Virdon IL.

CF56812   Dema Alice Mundy (b 20 Jul 1910, York Tp, Clark Co IL) m 1) Harry Williams, div 1953; m 2) H Higginbotham.

CF568121   Billy Leo Williams (b 22 Mar 1932, West Union IL) m 1) 26 Oct 1950, Louise Jackson (b 10 Jun 1932, Olney IL); m 2) 11 Mar 1955, Phyllis Finbiner. No chn.

CF568122   Jack Morris Williams (b 12 May 1934) m 6 Apr 1958, West Union IL, Dea Katherine Hammond (b 13 Apr 1939, Paris IL).

CF5682   Wilton Raymond Wiser (9 Oct 1881, Marshall IL-3 Dec 1937, Terre Haute IN) m 28 May 1910, Marshall IL, Ethel Clair Clough (b 6 Aug 1888, Darwin Tp, Clark Co IL).

CF56821   Wilma Wiser (b 20 Dec 1908, Darwin IL) m Boyd Burns, Wayne OH.

CF568211   Barbara Burns m   Tyson.

CF568212   Mary Jo Burns.

CF568213   Paul Burns.

CF56822   Robert Dean Wiser (6 Feb 1911, Marshall IL-2 Nov 1958, Marshall IL) m 24 Jun 1935, Marshall IL, Dale Martin (10 Aug 1915, West Union IL-4 Dec 1986, Bonita Springs FL) Bur Marshall IL. Truck driver.

CF568221   Bill Eugene Wiser (b 13 Jan 1939, Terre Haute IN) m 1) 2 Feb 1963, Cheryl Friedrich (b 21 Feb 1944, Milwaukee WI) div 1988; m 2) 29 Jan 1989, KY, Connie Zeigler (b 31 Mar 1944, Terre Haute IN) Machine shop, Casey IL.

CF5682211   Teri Jo Wiser (b 14 Apr 1966, Terre Haute IN) m 7 Dec 1986, Everett Brandt. No chn. Martinsville, IL.

CF5682212   Tammy Lee Wiser (b 23 Jun 1969, Terre Haute IN) m Copace Tyler.

CF56822121   Copace Tyler Jr (b 2 Dec 1993, Springfield IL).

CF5682213   Lisa Kay Wiser (b 8 Aug 1970, Terre Haute IN) m Michael Alb.

CF56822131   Caley Alb (b 3 Mar 1995, Bloomington IL).

CF5682214   Margaret Wiser (b 8 Feb 1974, Terre Haute IN).

CF56823   Harley Duane Wiser (b 25 Aug 1919, Marshall IL) m 1) 24 Sep 1939, St Louis MO, Emma Faye Miller (b 11 Dec 1913) div 1947; m 2) 6 Sep 1947, Terre Haute IN, Mildred Hershfield (b 1 Apr 1922, Terre Haute IN) No chn. Bur Marshall IL. Civilian employee, Albuquerque AF Base, NM.

CF5683   Anna Mae Wiser (3 Dec 1885, Marshall IL-31 Dec 1958, Terre Haute IN) m 1) 21 Apr 1906, Marshall IL, Charles LaVern Thompson (b 27 Mar 1885, Wabash Tp, Clark Co IL) div 1912; m 2) 4 Mar 1914, Terre Haute IN, Edgar Grant Nay (30 Dec 1868, Dolson Prairie, Clark Co IL-23 Sep 1943, Marshall IL) Bur Marshall IL.

CF56831   Gerald Raymond Thompson (b 11 Sep 1908, Marshall IL) m 7 Jul 1934, Margaret Walute. Gadsden, AL.

CF568311   Jeffrey Lee Thompson (b 8 Oct 1945, Milwaukee WI).

CF5684   Clara Belle Wiser (1 May 1887, Marshall IL-31 Dec 1957, Milwaukee WI) m 1) 24 Jun 1908, Thomas Seiburn Riley Jr (8 Dec 1887, Marshall IL-8 Nov 1918, Marshall IL); m 2) Silas Mc Clellan Davis (18 Mar 1884, Clinton IN-23 May 1959, Milwaukee WI) Bur Marshall IL. Davis, Foundry worker.

CF56841   Charles Eugene Riley (b 30 May 1909, Marshall IL) m 4 Sep 1933, Marshall IL, Mary V Kutz (b 21 Aug 1914, Milwaukee WI) Receiving clerk, Milwaukee WI.

CF568411   Robert Ronald Riley (b 1 Mar 1937, Milwaukee WI) m 15 Mar 1958, Milwaukee WI, Gladys Ella Hildebrandt (b 18 Oct 1939, Town Herman WI) Auto dealer, Milwaukee WI.

CF5684111   Erin Lynn Riley (b 28 Jul 1958, Milwaukee WI).

CF5684112   Wynne Jill Riley (b 20 Jan 1960, Milwaukee WI).

CF568412   Miles Owen Riley (b 27 Dec 1938, Milwaukee WI).

CF568413   Timothy Patrick Riley (b 4 Feb 1957, Milwaukee WI).

CF56842   William Myles Riley (b 18 Jun 1911, Marshall IL) m 6 Jul 1932, Milwaukee WI, Zora Javorina (b 9 May 1912, Milwaukee WI) Woodworker, Milwaukee WI.

CF568421   Thomas Myles Riley III (b 2 Jun 1936, Milwaukee WI) m 14 Jun 1958, Karen Nancy Matthias (b 30 Jul 1938, Milwaukee WI) Tool and die maker, Milwaukee WI.

CF568422   Sharon Lynne Riley (b 16 Feb 1940, Milwaukee WI).

CF56843   Martha Baird Riley (b 27 Jul 1913, Milwaukee WI) m 1) 11 Mar 1933, Raymond Henry Braatz (20 May 1905, Oshkosh WI-28 Oct 1951, Milwaukee WI) div 1946; m 2) 5 Aug 1950, John Henry Costa (b 20 Oct 1914, Milwaukee WI) Riley, truck driver; Costa, construction worker, Milwaukee WI.

CF568431   Evelyn Rae Braatz (b 26 Feb 1936, Milwaukee WI) m 11 Aug 1956, Milwaukee WI, Jack Lee Farris (b 26 Dec 1932, Marshall IL) Service technician, Milwaukee WI.

CF5684311   Julie Ann Farris (b 19 Aug 1957, Milwaukee WI).

CF5684312   Michael Craig Farris (b 23 Aug 1959, Milwaukee WI).

CF5685   Lucia Weiser (1889, Marshall IL-1894, Marshall IL) Bur Marshall IL.

CF5686   Denton Jay Weiser (1891, Marshall IL-1892, Marshall IL) Bur Marshall IL.

CF57   John Weiser was born 19 October 1802 at Fishers Ferry, Northumberland Co PA. He was confirmed at Zion Lutheran Church, Augustaville, in 1821. His first children were born in PA, but about 1837 he moved to Bloom Tp, Fairfield Co OH with his brother Peter and not far from his brother Samuel. He remained there about a decade and went to Florence Tp, then to Wapello, Louise Co, IA. He is in the 1860 census there but not in the 1870. His wife Lydia Shipman was 35 in 1850 and a native of NJ, but she died about 1849. He was a farmer. He died in 1869.[78] They had nine children.

CF571   Andrew J Weiser (b ca 1832, PA).

CF572   Mary A Weiser (b ca 1834, PA).

CF573   Susan Weiser (b ca 1836, PA).

CF574   Elizabeth Weiser (b ca 1838, OH).

CF575   John D Weiser (b ca 1844, OH) m Elizabeth   (b ca 1841, VA).

---

[78]Data on John Weiser submitted by Noreen Armerding and Mrs. Edith Perry of Adair Co (IA) Genealogical Society.

CF5751   Lidia Weiser (b ca 1867, IA).

CF5752   Samantha Weiser (b ca 1869, IA).

CF576   Thomas H Benton Weiser (22 Dec 1846, near Morningsun IA-23 Feb 1919, near Fontanelle IA) m 15 Feb 1877, Wapello IA, Sarah Josephine Newell (22 Apr 1853, Wapello IA-7 Oct 1939, near Fontanelle IA) Farmer, Prussia Tp, Adair Co IA in 1879. Bur Fontanelle IA.

CF5761   Daisy May Weiser (12 Mar 1878, near Wapello IA-24 Mar 1924, Clarinda IA) unm.

CF5762   Thomas Weiser (1 Apr 1879, IA-24 Aug 1880).

CF5763   Myrtle Weiser (Jul 1882, PA-1942) unm.

CF5764   Roscoe W Weiser (2 Jan 1886, near Fontanelle IA-7 Mar 1959, Phoenix AZ).

CF5765   Samuel H Weiser (b 11 Feb 1888, near Fontanelle IA) m Gladys M   (Grants Pass OR)
WWI.

CF5766   Sprague N Weiser (b 26 Nov 1894, near Fontanelle IA) m. WWI.

CF577   Zachariah Weiser (b Oct 1854, IA) m Harriet R   (b Aug 1858, IA).

CF5771   Thomas R Weiser (b Feb 1894, IA).

CF6.   Hannah Weiser (1764-   )

Hannah Weiser (daughter of Frederick and Anna Amelia (Zeller) Weiser) was probably born about 1764, near Womelsdorf, although no definite record of her birth or confirmation has come to light to authenticate this. According to the records of Christ Lutheran Church, Stouchsburg, she married George Kehl, 3 Nov 1782. Likely he is the John George Kehl, son of Michael Kehl, born 18 Oct 1760. He served in the Seventh Company under Capt. Jacob Kremer in the US Revolution. They moved to Green Township, Franklin Co PA, where George and his son Jacob purchased ten acres from Hugh Ferguson on 15 Apr 1815. Hannah predeceased her husband before he wrote a will in 1838, which was probated 30 Sep 1845 after his death. He does not name his wife, but says he has ten children or their heirs, although only eight are named.[79]

Children of John George and Hannah (Weiser) Kehl:

CF61   Maria Catharine Kehl, 17 Dec 1783

CF62   John Jacob Kehl, 22 Oct 1785

CF63   Anne Marie Kehl, 9 Aug 1787

CF64   John Peter Kehl, 7 May 1789

CF65   Henry Kehl, ca 1791

CF66   George Kehl, 20 Feb 1792

CF67   Sarah "Sally" Kehl, 17 Dec 1793

CF68   Eva Elizabeth Kehl, 5 Aug 1795

---

[79]Records of Christ Lutheran Church, Stouchsburg PA. 1996 data provided by Martha Kahle Neal.

CF69   Elizabeth Kehl, 26 Jun 1801

CF6A   Jonathan Kehl, 7 May 1805

CF61   Maria Catharina Kehl (b 17 Dec 1783, near Stouchsburg PA). Probably unm. She is identified as her father's housekeeper in his will and special provision is made for her.

CF62   John Jacob Kehl (22 Oct 1785, Stouchsburg PA-11 Feb 1865) m 1) 25 Jun 1809, Reading PA, Catherine Spatz; m 2) 9 Dec 1847, Chambersburg PA, Sophia Salzberger, nee Jaerck. He purchased land in Green Tp, Franklin Co PA, with his father and added to his holdings in 1813 and 1817. The censuses of 1830 and 1840 list perhaps six sons and four daughters and suggests that his first wife was dead by 1840, but data on only one daughter is presently available. Bur Fayetteville PA.

CF621   Catherine Kahl (11 Sep 1815, PA-23 Nov 1873, Tipton IA) m 9 Aug 1837, John Moreland (6 Oct 1817-11 Dec 1905, Tipton IA). Bur Tipton IA.

CF6211   William Moreland (11 Sep 1838-5 Nov 1897)

CF6212   David Moreland (9 Oct 1839-22 Jun 1865)

CF6213   Elizabeth Moreland (27 Dec 1841-27 Jan 1864) m Mahlon Nerman

CF6214   Ann Amandy Moreland (b 6 Feb 1845)

CF6215   George Washington Moreland (17 May 1854, Tipton IA-? Jun 1919, Cedar Rapids IA) m 18 Nov 1854, Tipton IA, Sarah Almira Bagley, div ca 1905. He bur Tipton IA.

CF62151   Jonathan Carlton Moreland (14 Apr 1880, Tipton IA-25 Feb 1970) m 9 Aug 1908, Sonora CA, Ella Steinmetz

CF63   Anna Maria Kehl (8 Sep 1878, near Stouchsburg PA-10 Jan 1840, Stark Co OH) m 30 Mar 1807, Stouchsburg PA, James Beaty (2 May 1782, Ireland-19 Jul 18--, Massillon OH). They moved to Ohio in 1817. He was killed enroute to a camp meeting when he was thrown from his buggy. She was known as Polly.

CF631   George Beaty (8 Dec 1809, Berks Co PA-1900, Brady Tp, Williams Co OH) m 15 Mar 1838, Mary Jane Weiser

CF632   John Beaty (b 1810) m Mary Ann Albinger

CF633   Infant Beaty (b 1811)

CF634   James Beaty (b 1813)

CF635   Infant Beaty (b 1815)

CF636   Henry Beaty (b 16 Dec 1816, Franklin Co PA) m 1) Agnes Tinkler; m 2) 15 Mar 1853,
Jame Roberts

CF637   Hannah Beaty (1818-1865) m Henry Zerbe

CF638   Sarah Ann Beaty (1819-1897) m Moses Shoemaker

CF639   Jonathan Beaty (1821-1900) m 15 Apr 1858, Caroline Shoup

CF63A   Mary Beaty (31 Oct 1824, Stark Co OH-Jul 1901, Franklin Tp, Fulton Co OH) m 16 Mar 1846, Williams Co OH, Joseph McLaughlin

CF64   John Peter Kahl (7 May 1789, near Stouchsburg PA-2 Dec 1862) m Christina   . Bur
Jeromesville PA.

CF65   Henry Kahle (ca 1791-7 Nov 1870, Medina Co OH) m Susan Rank

CF66   George Kahl (20 Feb 1792, near Stouchsburg PA-ca 1863, Green Tp, Franklin Co PA)
m Mary Dechart

CF661   Levi Kahl (b ca 1815)

CF662   Jonathan Kahl (ca 1816-26 Apr 1901)

CF663   Elizabeth Kahl (b ca 1817). Probably unm.

CF664   Amalia Kahl (b ca 1819)

CF665   George Davis Kahl (b ca 1820)

CF666   Elenor Kahl (b ca 1822)

CF667   Mary Kahl (b ca 1825)

CF668   David Kahl (b ca 1827)

CF669   John Dechart Kahl (11 Dec 1829-15 Jan 1912, Finleyville PA). Moved to Washington Co
PA ca 1849. Farmer.

CF6691   John B. Kahl (b 1855) m 1882, Jeannetta (Janet) Clark (21 May 1858-Mar 1939)

CF66911   Maurice C. Kahl m Mertie Farson

CF6692   Anna M. Kahl (b ca 1858) m Ed Cochran

CF6693   George McClellan Kahl (18 Sep 1861, Nottingham Tp, Washington Co PA-13 Aug 1932,
Finleyville PA) m 5 Aug 1883, Clara Lucina Nicholson (13 Apr 1859, Union Tp, Washington Co PA-14 Aug
1936, Finleyville PA)

CF66931   Maude Ermina Kahl (1 Nov 1884-18 Jun 1967) m 3 Oct 1903, Pittsburgh PA, William
Jonas Fawcet

CF66932   William Dechart Kahl (4 Sep 1887, Ginger Hill, Washington Co PA-12 Dec 1959) m Clara
Parkinson (4 Nov 1888-15 Jun 1948)

CF669321   William Dechart Kahl, Jr. (23 Sep 1914, Monongahela PA-9 Jul 1983, Monogahela PA)
m 29 May 1942, Dorothy Ruth Broadhead (b 3 Oct 1922). He, BS, Carnegie Mellon U; mechanical engineer.

CF6693211   Emilie Marie Kahl (b 28 Oct 1943) m Edmund O'Kefe. Ba, PSU; flight attendant.

CF6693212   David William Kahl (b 19 Feb 1947) m Judith Huber. BS, PSU; civil engineer.

CF6693213   Harold James Kahl (b 10 Jul 1948) m Judith Huber. BA, PSU; electrical engineer.

CF6693214   Edgar T. Kahl (b 28 Jan 1950) m Cynthia Leaver. BA, PSU; telecommunications.

CF6693215   Raymond George Kahl (b 7 Apr 1951) m Victoria Pucel. Electrician.

CF6693216   Clara Lucile Kahl (b 5 Nov 1953) m John DeBiase. Nurses aide.

CF6693217   Ann Elizabeth Kahl (b 11 Jun 1954) m Duane Kell. BS, California (PA) U; data entry clerk.

CF6693218   Jane Ellen Kahl (b 3 Aug 1958) m William Olson. BS, Carnegie Mellon U; metallurgical engineer.

CF669322   James Richard Kahl (b 5 Dec 1915, Monongahela PA) m 28 Jun 1940, Lucretia Catherine Beazell (b 22 Jan 1919, Carroll Tp, Washington Co PA)

CF6693221   Lucretia Kathryn Kahl (b 30 Apr 1941). Legal secretary, Washington DC.

CF6693222   James Earl Kahl (b 31 Jul 1946) m 18 Jun 1971, Mary Kay Knudson. Mathematics teacher.

CF6693223   Thomas Earl Kahl (b 26 Jan 1948) m 17 Dec 1994, Grace Elizabeth Hill. Mathematics teacher.

CF669323   George DeWitt Kahl (23 May 1924-8 Jun 1984) m Doris Louise Stewart (31 Dec 1930-28 Aug 1985)

CF6693231   Donna Kahl (b 13 Oct 1949) m Jun 1975, Fred Geer

CF6693232   Dorene Kahl (b 21 May 1955) m Donald Zancanella

CF6693233   Margaret Elizabeth Kahl (b 8 Mar 1964)

CF66933   Mary Lucina Kahl (1 Dec 1890-13 Feb 1921) m 24 Jun 1911, Geroge Ernest Watson

CF66934   Ernest McClellan Kahl (15 Mar 1893, Finleyville PA-30 Sep 1971) m 22 Dec 1919, McKeesport PA, Della Corinne Troutman (30 Sep 1896, Gastonville PA-24 Dec 1979) Bur Mingo PA. BA, U Pittsburgh; teacher.

CF669341   Sydney Georgeanne Kahle (b 23 Nov 1923) m Paul Bloom

CF669342   Donald Foster Kahle (4 Dec 1926, Union Tp, Washington Co PA-1 Jul 1976, Wassenaar Holland) m 3 Oct 1947, Winchester Va, Martha Ann Ashcraft (b 24 Feb 1930, Monongahela PA). He, U Pittsburgh; petroleum engineer; pres, Con-Am Oil Co. She, computer consultant. She m 2) William G. Neal.

CF6693421   Robert Wayne Kahle (b 31 Jul 1948, Pittsburgh PA) m 24 Nov 1973, Coshocton OH, Claire Larsen. He, AB, Muskingum (OH) Col; geologist.

CF6693422   Gary Michael Kahle (b 3 May 1951, Pittsburhg PA) m 26 Jun 1986, Bridgeville PA, Teresa Marie Catherine Schoenig. Mail handler.

CF6693423   Sheri Kathleen Kahle (b 23 Aug 1964, Houston TX) m 29 Jun 1991, Baldwin PA, William John Taylor. She, AB, Carnegie Mellon U; psychologist.

CF66935   Sarah Mildred Kahl (7 Feb 1896-26 Aug 1957) m 1 Aug 1917, Robert A. Openshaw

CF66936   Grace Estella Kahl (8 May 1902-27 Apr 1996) m 14 Apr 1920, Robert Wilson Thomas. Bur Finleyville PA.

CF6694   Josephine Kahl (b ca 1864) m   McKubber

CF6695   Elizabeth Kahl

CF6696   Catherine M. "Kate" Kahl (May 1869-1900) m 12 Jul 1888, Albert "Bert" Withrow. Bur Ginger Hill, Washington Co PA.

CF6697   Jane Kahl m A.W. Lusk. Dunningville, Washington Co PA.

CF66A   Hannah Kahl

CF67   Sarah "Sally" Kahl (b 17 Dec 1793, near Stouchsburg PA) m Robert Beaty

CF68   Eva Elizabeth Kahl (5 Aug 1795, near Stouchsburg PA-probably d.y.)

CF69   Elizabeth Kahl (b 26 Jun 1801, near Stouchsburg PA) m Peter Spence

CF6A   Jonathan Kahl (b 7 May 1805, near Stouchsburg PA)

CF8.   Salome Weiser (1769-   )

Salome Weiser, daughter of Frederick and Anna Amelia (Zeller) Weiser, was born about 1769, judging from her confirmation at age fifteen in 1784 at Christ Lutheran Church, Stouchsburg. She married John Peter Kehl of Tulpehocken Township on 21 Dec 1790, according to the Schwarzwald Church records. He was a blacksmith in Bethel Township, Berks County, in the late 1790s. Some records cite her given name as Sarah, an English equivalent of Salome. On the 1810 census for Miles Tp, Centre Co, John "Cale" was a resident. His will there was dated 17 May 1812 and probated 31 August 1812. He names no wife but children Frederick, Jacob, Catharine and Eve.[80]

Children of John Peter and Salome (Weiser) Kehl:

CF81   Catharine Kehl, 11 Feb 1792

CF82   Maria Kehl, 1793 or 1794

CF83   Frederick Peter Kehl, 17 May 1795

CF84   Jacob Weiser Kehl, 13 Mar 1799

CF85   Eve Kehl

CF83   Frederick Peter Kehl (son of John and Salome (Weiser) Kehl) was born March 17, 1795, and baptized 3 May 1795, at St. Daniel's Lutheran Church, Robesonia PA. The middle name Peter is not given in his baptismal record. Frederick and Sarah Bechtel served as sponsors. According to an old tradition, in 1824, he migrated to Shippenville PA, and in May 1836, removed to Eldred Township, Jefferson County, at a place since called Kahletown. He was a nonacademic veterinarian. He married on 27 Aug 1816 at Warriors Mark Tp, Huntingdon Co PA, to Elizabeth Hyskell (daughter of George and Eve (Grey) Hyskill)(3 May 1797-21 May 1884). He died 24 Nov 1878. They are buried at Kahletown Methodist Church. They had thirteen children, ten boys (of whom two died young) and three girls.[81]

Children of Frederick and Elizabeth (Hyskell) Kehl:

CF81   Anlesey Kahle, 12 Oct 1817

CF832   John D. Kahle, 16 Feb 1819

CF833   Jacob R. Kahle, 4 Jan 1821

---

[80]Ibid. See also Northumberland County deeds, K-408, May 29, 1799, appointing John Kehl as attorney for Anna Amelia Weiser. See St. Daniel's Lutheran Church records. Centre County Wills.

[81]Data contributed in 1960 by Mrs Vincent Race, except as otherwise indicated, and in 1996 by Esther Kahle Best. The original marriage certificate and partial listing of the Frederick P. Kahle children is owned by Martha Kahle Rodeheaver. Anna Crumrine sent data and pictures.

CF83 Frederick Peter Kehl
(1795-1878)

Elizabeth Hyskell Kehl
(1797-1884), wife of
Frederick Kehl

CF834   Frederick Peter Kahle, 19 Aug 1823

CF835   George Lowry Kahle, 12 Oct 1824

CF836   Washington Whistler Kahle, 11 Feb 1826

CF837   Hensen G. Kahle, 30 Mar 1827

CF838   Perry J. Kahle, 11 May 1829

CF839   David R. Kahle, 6 Mar 1832

CF83A   Heiskell Kahle, 1834

CF831   Anlesey Kahle, 12 Oct 1817-d.y.

CF832   John D. Kahl (16 Feb 1817-19 Oct 1891) m Chrisin   (b England). Bur. Kahletown PA.
On the 1850 and 1860 census was a resident of Eldred Tp, Jefferson Co PA.

CF8321   Elizabeth Kahl (b 1857)

CF8322   John Kahl (b 1858)

CF8323   Beaumont Kahl (b 1860)

**CF833 Jacob R. Kahle (1821-1882)
and Family**
Seated, left to right: CF8337 Rosanna F.
Kehl DeForest (1859-1937); CF833 Jacob R.
Kahle; Sarah Carter Kahle (1825-1877);
CF8335 Jacob Hall Kahle (1855-1924);
CF8336 Almeda Jane Kahle (1856-1949).
Standing, left to right: CF833A Grace Sarah
Kahle McCoy (1864-1889); CF8333 James
W. Kahle (b 1850); CF8332 Amanda Allison
Kahle McGill Bassin (b 1849); CF8339 David
Abrem Kahle (1862-1937)

CF833   Jacob R. Kahle (4 Jan 1821, Huntingdon Co PA-8 Apr 1882, Brookville PA) m 1) Sarah Ann Carter (1825, Franklin PA-30 Sep 1877, Caseville PA); m 2) Anna H. Chivers (1848, England-11 Sep 1970, Pittstown PA). Bur Brookville PA. Methodist clergyman, Youngstown PA, 1873-74, Phillipsburg PA, 1875-76, Cassville PA, 1876-77, Brookville PA, 1879-81, Stahlstown PA, 1881-82.

CF8331   Frederick Peter Kahle (11 Sep 1846-2 Oct 1862). Bur Kahletown PA.

CF8332   Amanda Allison Kahle (b 1849) m 1) John McGill; m 2) Calvin Bassin

CF83321   Sadie McGill

CF83322   Harry Bassim (d 1953) m Minnie

CF833221   Thelma Corelli Bassim (b 10 Feb 1900) m Mark W. Beham (28 Jul 1895-30 Jun 1966)

CF8333   James W. Kahle (b 1850) m Lizzie Simpon (b 1852)

CF83331   James M. Kahle (b 1878)

CF83332   Bess Kahle

CF83333   Marie Kahle m Charles Phillips

CF833331   Charles Phillips

CF833332   Mary Jane Phillips m   Goodrich

CF833333   Roland S. Phillips (27 Oct 1923, Oil City PA-27 Aug 1981, Oil City PA) m 23 Aug 1958, Freda Brooks

CF833334   Kenneth Phillips

CF833335   Palmer J. Phillips

CF833336   David Phillips

CF83334   Nell Kahle

CF8334   Frances C. Kahle (9 Mar 1853-12 Feb 1854). Bur Kahletown PA.

CF8335   Jacob Hall Kahle (25 Jan 1855, Jefferson Co PA-10 Dec 1924, Bradford PA) m 1883, Sarah Alice Payne (22 Oct 1885, Jefferson Co PA-22 Apr 1928, Bradford PA). Bur Bradford PA. Oil producer.

CF83351   Sarah Edna Kahle (6 Jun 1885-5 Jun 1942, McKean Co PA) m 30 Dec 1905, Clarence Edward Bolles (11 Feb 1882-8 Apr 1970, McKean Co PA). Bur Lafayette PA.

CF833511   Pearl Maxine Bolles (b 14 Sep 1908, Bradford PA) m Richard Willis Robinson (b 18 Jan 1905, Beaver Falls PA). Massillon OH.

CF8335111 Mary Jane Robinson (b 21 May 1932, Massillon OH) m Nov 1952, Massillon OH, Dallas Earnest Baird (31 Jan 1932-1988, FL). Waynesburg OH.

CF83351111 Deborah Kay Baird (b 16 Jan 1954, Massillon OH) m 1 Nov 1975, Donald Edward Esber (b 4 Feb 1955, Canton OH)

CF83351112 Lisa Ann Baird (b 25 Feb 1956, Denver CO)

CF83351113 Susan Louise Baird (b 21 Dec 1957, Massillon OH) m 21 Jul 1979, Craig Joseph Tovissi (b 16 Aug 1959)

CF833511131 Tristan Tovissi (b Aug 1986)

CF83351114 Robin Collette Baird (b 11 Jun 1959, Massillon OH) m John R. Aston (b 22 Dec 1956, Parma Heights OH)

CF83351115 Dallas Earnest Baird (b 1 Jan 1964, Massillon OH) m Susan Miller

CF833511151 Sarah Marie Miller (b 30 Nov 1986)

CF8335112 Richard Edward Robinson (19 Jun 1937, Massillon OH-19 Nov 1954, Massillon OH). Bur Massillon OH.

CF833512 Alda Marie Bolles (12 Sep 1910, Duke Center PA-4 May 1995, Mesa AZ) m Henry W. Harvey (8 Aug 19 -1 Aug 1976, Mesa AZ)

CF8335121 Barbara Marie Harvey (b 21 Nov 1930) m Raymond Williams (10 Jun 1929-29 Jul 1976, Holbrook AZ)

CF83351211 Gayle Marie Williams (b 11 May 1953)

CF83351212 Gary Stanton Williams (4 Mar 1956-4 Mar 1956)

CF83351213 Teresa Louise Williams (b 4 Jul 1957)

CF83351214 Raymond Gary Williams (b 26 Nov 1960)

CF83351215 Jon Stanton Williams (b 21 Jan 1966)

CF83352 Katherine D. Kahle (3 Oct 1886-7 Oct 1939, Bradford PA) m George F. Ballou. Bur Bradford PA.

CF83353 Frederick William Kahle (4 Nov 1890, Rew PA-12 Apr 1964, Olean NY) m. 10 May 1917, Olean NY, Florence Olive Everitt (13 Aug 1899, Duke Center PA-11 Jan 1974, Olean NY). Bur Lafayette PA. Oil producer, Duke Center PA, 1917-74.

CF833531 Margaret Isabel Kahle (b 27 Nov 1917, Duke Center PA) m 6 Aug 1949, Ceres NY, Robert Carnes (b 23 Apr 1924, Allegany NY). St Marys PA.

CF8335311 Robert Dee Carnes (b 6 Nov 1952, Olean NY) m 1) 8 Sep 1984, Mary Margaret Schrift (b 21 Dec 1955); m 2) 26 Aug 1995, Patty Weis. St. Marys PA.

CF833532 Earl Frederick Kahle (3 Nov 1919, Duke Center PA-18 Apr 1993, Cheetowoga NY) m 25 Jun 1947, Eldred PA, Charlotte LaComte (b 23 Aug 1919). WWII, USAAC.

CF8335321 Kathleen Ann Kahle (b 7 May 1948, Olean NY) m 1) 13 May 1967, Ronald Michael Farr (b 27 Mar 1945), div; m 2) 14 Feb 1977, George Thomas Sawyer (b 17 Jan 1953, Condersport PA). Clarence Center NY.

CF83353211   Jeffrey Scott Farr (b 12 Dec 1967, Olean NY) m 1) Kathy Nettles, div; m 2) Sep 1994, Diana Cerezo

CF833532111   Morgan Nochole Farr (b 23 Aug 1992)

CF83353212   Timothy Robert Farr (b 30 Nov 1969) m 1) Dec 1988, Melanie Saylor, div; m 2) Claire Sue Hoisington

CF833532121   Samantha Renee Farr (b 14 Jul 1989, Orlando FL)

CF833532122   Stormy Ann Farr (b 23 Aug 1993)

CF83353213   George Thomas Sawyer (b 25 Aug 1978, Olean NY)

CF8335322   Sue Ann Kahle (b 8 Oct 1950, Olean NY) m 1) 4 Dec 1971, Frank Anthony Zdrojowy (b 7 Apr 1950), div; m 2) Loren Crawford (b 17 May 1942), div; m 3) Dennis Desso

CF83353221   Matthew Alexander Zdrojowy (b 27 Jan 1973)

CF83353222   Jared Joseph Zdrojowy (b 22 Sep 1974)

CF8335323   Stephen Earl Kahle (b 16 Jan 1953, Olean NY) m 22 Jun 1974, Cindy Mazza (b 10 Feb 1953, Olean NY). Res Olean NY.

CF83353231   Jessica Jane Kahle (b 25 Nov 1974, Olean NY)

CF833532311   Gregory Joseph Kahle (b 13 Dec 1993, Olean NY)

CF83353232   Juliet Elizabeth Kahle (b 13 Jan 1979, Olean NY)

CF8335324   Judith Lynn Kahle (b 26 Oct 1957, Olean NY) m 23 May 1987, Gary Lee Wetherby (b 4 Feb 1955). Ischua NY.

CF833533   Thomas Jacob Kahle (b 31 Dec 1920, Duke Center PA) m 19 Sep 1941, Frances Higley (b 3 Mar 1923). WWII, USA. Eldred PA.

CF8335331   Larry James Kahle (b 22 Jun 1942, Olean NY) m 1) 26 Dec 1960, Kathleen Patricia Scollard (b 10 Nov 1941), div; m 2) 13 May 1995, Penny Lee Claycomb

CF83353311   Laura Dee Kahle (b 5 Apr 1963) m 1) P.J. Neff, div; m 2) 16 Oct 1993, Bryan Jeffery Williams (b 20 Nov 1967)

CF833533111   Zachary Todd Neff (b 23 Sep 1984)

CF833533112   Aaron Creed Williams (b 24 Jul 1994)

CF83353312   Cris Patrick Kahle (b 25 Nov 1964) m 1) 6 Aug 1983, Kimberly Joy Martin, div; m 2) 1 Dec 1990, Christine Marie Thompson (b 12 Nov 19)

CF833533121   Casey Marie Kahle (b 15 Jul 1985)

CF833533122   James Patrick Kahle (b 27 Jan 1986)

CF833533123   Rachael Elizabeth Kahle (b 31 May 1991)

CF8335332   Janet Elaine Kahle (b 11 Feb 1945, Olean NY) m 1 Aug 1964, Basil John Holly (b 11 Nov 1943). Duke Center PA.

CF83353321   Gary Christopher Holly (b 17 Jul 1964)

CF8335333   Thomas Jay Kahle (b 25 Mar 1949) m 1) 10 Jul 1970, Cathy De Petrio (b 21 Dec 1946), div; m 2) 14 May 1983, Olean NY, Laurie Ann Wright

CF83353331   Lisa Nicole Kahle (b 3 Apr 1972, Olean NY)

CF83353332   Martin Thomas Kahle (b 12 Jul 1975, Olean NY)

CF833534   Everitt William Kahle (b 6 Jul 1923, Bradford PA) m 1) 25 Aug 1945, Francis Pugh, div; m 2) 3 Jan 1953, Pascagoula MS, Vera Louise Pruett (b 1 Sep 1927, Dawes AL). WWII, USMC. Res Youngstown FL.

CF8335341   William Eugene Kahle (14 May 1946-24 Apr 1965)

CF8335342   Bonnie Ann Kahle (b 28 Mar 1948) m   Campbell

CF8335343   Destiny Ann Kahle (23 Apr 1953, Mobile AL) m 27 Nov 1972, Panama City FL, William Joseph Arden (b 10 Dec 19   )

CF83353431   Tanya Lynette Arden (b 19 Aug 1976, Panama City FL)

CF83353432   Melissa Michelle Arden (b 10 Jun 1978, Panama City FL)

CF83353433   William Joseph Arden (b 23 Jun 1980, Georgetown SC)

CF8335344   Thomas Frederick Kahle (b 11 Jun 1954, Mobile AL) m 18 Nov 1978, Lynn Haven FL, Karla Glenda Seale (b 16 Jun 1958)

CF83353441   Krista Jade Kahle (b 31 Aug 1989, Panama City FL)

CF8335345   James Everitt Kahle (b 13 May 1962, Mobile AL) m 4 Sep 1982, Panama City FL, Cheryl Lynn Smith (b 5 Sep 1965), div

CF83353451   Travis Taylor Kahle (b 14 Sep 1983, Panama City FL)

CF83353452   Megan Lynne Kahle (b 29 Jan 1985)

CF8335346   Philip Lee Kahle (b 3 Feb 1966, Mobile AL) m 31 Jun 1986, Angela Lynn Childree (b 25 Aug 1969)

CF83353461   Philip Harlan Kahle (b 24 Sep 1986, Panama City FL)

CF83353462   Sarah Lynn Kahle (b 18 Nov 1989, Panama City FL)

CF83353463   Jimmy Lee Kahle (b 16 Sep 1992, Panama City FL)

CF833535   Philip Eugene Kahle (b 1 Aug 1926, Bradford PA) m 7 Oct 1950, Dulcie Stroup (b 14 Sep 1927). WWII, USN. Duke Center PA.

CF8335351   Amarylis Lynn Kahle (b 4 Jul 1953) m 31 Apr 1974, Duke Center PA, Roland G. Hollowell (b 2 Jun 1951)

CF83353511   Philip Richard Hollowell (b 29 Oct 1978, Olean NY)

CF83353512   Melissa Lynn Hollowell (b 4 Dec 1981, Olean NY)

CF83353513   Arthur Daniel Hollowell (b 4 Sep 1983, Olean NY)

CF833536   Eleanor May Kahle (b 19 Mar 1928, Bradford PA) m 3 Apr 1948, Duke Center PA, Frederick Russell Schwab (16 Dec 1927, Bradford PA-21 Apr 1986, Duke Center PA)

CF8335361   Sharon Lynn Schwab (b 18 Jun 1952, Williamsport PA). BS, Houghton Col, 1975; MSDiv, United Theol Sem. Methodist minister.

CF8335362   Tina Marie Schwab (b 11 Sep 1955, Olean NY) m 23 Nov 1975, Duke Center PA, Dennis Duane Crandell (b 28 Aug 1955). Rixford PA.

CF83353621   Nickole Autumn Crandell (b 3 Oct 1983, Olean NY)

CF8335363   Anita Louise Schwab (17 Jan 1966, Olean NY) m 22 Mar 1986, Duke Center PA, William Joseph Prescott (b 5 Dec 1965). Duke Center PA.

CF83353631   Brigitte Joleen Prescott (b 1 Mar 1990, Olean NY)

CF83353632   Rebecca Noelle Prescott (b 24 Nov 1992, Olean NY)

*CF833537   Esther Arlene Kahle (b 29 Dec 1930, Bradford PA) m 7 Jun 1953, Duke Center PA, Charles Eugene Best (b 3 Mar 1932, Ceres Tp, McKean Co PA). Church secretary, 1975-90, Coldspring TX.

CF8335371   Michael Alan Best (b 10 Feb 1956, Rome NY) m 11 Nov 1978, Cypress TX, Donna Renee Enlow (b 2 Nov 1960), div. Auto parts store mgr, Houston TX.

CF83353711   Michelle Ann Best (b 27 Apr 1980, Houston TX)

CF8335372   Cynthia Lee Best (b 8 Mar 1957, Greenville PA)

CF833538   Ronald Lee Kahle (b 30 Mar 1936, Bradford PA) m 13 Dec 1958, Duke Center PA, Marilyn Ann Fuss (b 14 Nov 1936). Duke Center PA.

                    David Robert Kahle (b 7 Mar 1964, Olean NY)(Adopted)

                    Leanne Marie Kahle (b 26 Nov 1965, Olean NY)(Adopted)

CF8335381   Rona Lynn Kahle (b 4 Jun 1977, Olean NY)

CF833539   James Clinton Kahle (b 14 Nov 1937, Bradford PA) m 1) 3 Mar 1962, Adele CA, Mae Roby, div; m 2) 19 Sep 1970, Rochester NY, Barbara Welker (b 19 Apr 1940)

CF8335391   April Lee Kahle (b 17 Dec 1962) m 1)   Rizzo, div; m 2) William Lee Tenny

CF83353911   Anthony William Rizzo (b 30 Dec 1977)

CF83353912   Angelina Maria Rizzo (b 3 May 1979)

CF83353913   William Lee Tenny (b 21 Dec 1987)

CF8335392   June Renee Kahle (b 5 Dec 1964). Unm.

CF8335393   Coral Ann Kahle (b 4 Jan 1966) m 30 Aug 1985, Mark Pratt (b 1 May 1965)

CF83353931   Scott Christopher Kahle (b 29 Jun 1983)

CF83353932   Melissa Elaine Kahle (b 29 Jan 1987)

CF83353933   Melinda Elaine Kahle (b 20 Apr 1989)

           Kim Welker Kahle (b 12 Aug 1963)(Adopted)

CF83354   Grace Alice Kahle (14 Jul 1892-10 Nov 1989, Gerry NY) m 1) 1 Sep 1909, Fred L. Berry (Feb 1882, ME-1918); m 2) , Henry Yale (d 22 Apr 1953)

CF833541   Andrew Jackson Berry (b 10 Jun 1910, Duke Center PA) m 1) Jessie Cummings (10 May 1911-Jun 1942); m 2) Bernice Heinz (b 21 Nov 1917, WI)

CF8335411   Sandra Lee Berry (b 25 Dec 1934)

CF8335412   Oliver Hazard Berry (b 4 May 1942, Niagara Falls NY) m Shirley Pratt (b 13 Feb 1944, Springville NY)

CF83354121   Ross Allen Berry (b 24 Jun 1967

CF83354122   Brian Berry (b 2 Apr 1969)

CF8335413   Andrew Jackson Berry (b 13 Feb 1947, Niagara Falls NY)

CF8335414   Clifford Alvin Berry (b 13 Apr 1949, Niagara Falls NY) m Margaret Donovan (b 8 Sep 1950, Amesbury MA)

CF83354141   Craig Andrew Berry (b 25 Mar 1971)

CF83354142   Kimberly Jean Berry (b 25 Nov 1974)

CF8335415   Lorrie Ann Berry (b 31 May 1954, Elma NY)

CF8335416   Linda Lee Berry (b 30 Mar 1962, Elma NY)

CF833542   Frederick Levi Berry (29 May 1911-20 Mar 1988) m Sarah Holmes

CF8335421   Judith Ellen Berry (b 11 Mar 1936) m Carl Jennejahn

CF83354211   Laura Diane Jennejahn (b 22 Sep 1965)

CF83354212   Barry Carl Jennejahn (b 20 Dec 1967)

CF83354213   Matthew Frederick Jennejahn (b 26 Apr 1972)

CF8335422   Daniel Holmes Berry (b 28 Dec 1939) m 1963, Naomi Campbell (b 10 Oct 1938). Methodist minister.

CF83354221   James Daniel Berry (b 29 May 1964)

CF83354222   Gregory Fred Berry (b 18 Nov 1967)

CF83354223   Sharon Lorraine Berry (b 9 Aug 1974)

CF8335423   Priscilla Lynn Berry (b 2 May 1945) m 1967 Tom Smiley (b 23 Feb 1945)

CF83354231   Amy Beth Smiley (b 27 Mar 1972)

CF83354232   Mark Thomas Smiley (b 29 Dec 1973)

CF83354233   Sara Cathleen Smiley (b 1975, England)

CF833543   Doris Imogene Berry (14 May 1912-12 Dec 1980) m Ralph Melton (d Nov 1972)

CF8335431   Barry Leroy Melton (b 17 May 1942) m Doreen   (b Oct 1943)

CF83354311   Renee Melton (b 19 Mar 1963)

CF83354312   Randy Melton (b 19 May 1967)

CF83354313   Michelle Melton (b 1 Jan 1970)

CF83354314   Gregory Melton (b 2 Apr 1971)

CF833544   Reba May Berry (14 Dec 1913, Bradford PA-7 Dec 1991, Gerry NY)

CF833545   Sarah Alice Berry (b 18 Dec 1914) m Homer Thompson (b 6 Jun 1914)

CF8335451   Bonnie Kay Thompson (5 Jun 1935-5 Jun 1935)

CF8335452   Robert Steven Thompson (b 21 May 1946) m Olivia B. Howell (b 2 Apr 1947)

CF83354521   Meghan Rebecca Thompson (b 18 Nov 1978, Omaha NE)

CF83354522   Andrew Howell Thompson (b 9 Jul 1982, Omaha NE)

CF833546   Daniel Easton Berry 9b 20 Jun 1918, Bradford PA) m 22 Aug 1949, North Chili NY,
Bethany Jane Smith (b 13 Jul 1917, Urbana PA)

CF8335461   Grant Easton Berry (b 22 Sep 1950, Mason City IA) m Diane Wilson (b 4 Oct 1955)

CF83354611   Rebeckah Berry (b 26 Mar 1978)

CF8335462   David Kahle Berry (b 18 Oct 1951, Rochester NY) m 1) Lois Stafford (b 22 Sep 1950,
Cuba NY), div; m 2) Ann Bailey (b 15 Apr 1959, Parkersburg PA)

CF83354621   Jennifer Ann Berry (b 17 Nov 1972)

CF83354622   Shawn Daniel Berry (b 20 Sep 1974)

CF8335463   Susan Gay Berry (b 21 Jul 1957, Pittsburgh PA)

CF8335464   Elizabeth Jane Berry (b 3 Jul 1959, Pittsburgh PA) m Reggie Ames (b 16 Nov 1956)

CF833547   Richard Kahle Yale

CF83355   Arthur Daniel Kahle (10 Apr 1894, Rew PA-19 Jan 1960) m Aug 1922, Ruth Emma
Minnich (Jul 1898-1976). Bur Lafayette PA. Oil producer.

CF833551   Jane Olive Kahle (10 Apr 1923-5 Apr 1970) m Bob Richards

CF8335511   Dana Lee Richards m James Edgar Di Blasi

CF833552   Arthur Donald Kahle (b 5 Nov 1924, Duke Center PA) m 31 Aug 1951, Port Allegany NY, Ann Bouden (b 31 Dec 1926)

CF8335521   Daniel Arthur Kahle (11 Mar 1953, Alliance OH-Jul 1992) m 2 May 1981, Grove City PA, Gail Ann Kaiser (b 21 Oct 1954, Grove City PA)

CF83355211   Andrew Daniel Kahle (b 18 Dec 1985, Franklin PA)

CF83355212   Patrick Eugene Kahle (b 30 Dec 1987, Franklin PA)

CF8335522   Jeffrey Stephen Kahle (b 13 Sep 1954, Alliance OH) m 25 Oct 1986, Seneca Tp, Venango Co PA, Doris J. Boyd (b 1 Oct 1961, Oil City PA)

CF8335523   Timothy Michael Kahle (b 1 Mar 1956, Oil City PA) m 25 May 1985, Oil City PA, Pamela A. Work (b 28 Aug 1957, Oil City PA)

CF83355231   Emily Ann Kahle (b 17 Jun 1987, Franklin PA)

CF83355232   Joshua Work Kahle (b 10 Aug 1988, Oil City PA)

CF8335524   Susan Jane Kahle (b 10 Dec 1958, Oil City PA)

CF8335525   Jonathan Andrew Kahle (b 9 Sep 1960, Oil City PA)

CF8335526   Robert Matthew Kahle (b 2 Dec 1962, Oil City PA)

CF833553   Richard Minnich Kahle (b 18 Jul 1930) m Eileen Piper (b 22 Sep 1930, Lamartine PA)

CF8335531   Rick Stephan Kahle (b 18 Aug 1951) m Barbara Ann   (b 27 Jul 1952)

CF83355311   Megan Nicole Kahle (b 31 Jan 1976)

CF83355312   Erica Hiliary Kahle (b 22 Aug 1978)

CF8335532   Joseph Dean Kahle (b 21 Apr 1953) m Laurie Rosenswie (b 8 Mar 1953)

CF83355321   Derek Joseph Kahle (b 15 May 1978)

CF83355322   Justin Daniel Kahle (b 14 Mar 1980)

CF83355323   Sarah Elizabeth Kahle (b 10 Jun 1987)

CF83356   Paul Easton Kahle (10 Nov 1896-31 Jul 1976) m 1) Pearl Starr (1898-1945); m 2) Marie Teresa Kopp (b 1901). Bur Lafayette PA. Oil producer.

CF833561   Stanley Jay Kahle (5 Apr 1919-22 Jul 1955, Duke Center PA) m 1) Joan Shuman (b 25 Dec 1919), div; m 2) Barbara App (b 26 Oct 1926). Bur Duke Center PA.

CF8335611   Jay Paul Kahle (b 12 May 1940) m 1) Frances Ann Klimek, div; m 2) Jacqueline Clark. Attorney, Smethport PA.

     Sara Elizabeth Kahle(Adopted)

CF8335612   William Franklin Kahle (9 Mar 1943-11 May 1966)

CF8335613   Paul Stanley Kahle (b 28 Jan 1950)

CF8335614   Molly Ann Kahle (b 18 Aug 1952)

CF8335615   Mark Allan Kahle (b 18 Aug 1952)

CF8336   Almeda Jane Kahle (5 Aug 1856, Jefferson Co PA-16 Jun 1949) m 5 May 1880, Brookville PA, Sylvester Newton Martin (4 Jan 1855, Dayton PA-Jun 1937). Bur Lewis Co WA.

CF83361   Roy Martin (15 Jun 1881-6 Sep 1947) m Mary Calhoun

CF83362   Lela Pearl Martin (8 May 1884-1957) m 1) Frank M. Davis; m 2) Charles Thompkins

CF833621   Howard Davis (1903-1953) m June Day

CF833622   Claude Davis (1905-1983) m Jesse Grove

CF833623   Katherine A. Davis (1907-1973) m Eugene Carter

CF833624   Blanche Davis (1909-1954) m Thomas Swisher

CF833625   John L. Davis (1911-1989) m Adda

CF833626   Clair Davis (b 1913)

CF833627   Arelo Davis (b 1915) m Jack Bergdorf

CF833628   Pearl Davis (1917-1985) m Harvey Kaser

CF833629   Garnett Davis (1919-1985) m Kenneth Eckman

CF83362A   Frank M. Davis (1920-1970) m Ellen

CF83362B   Doyle Davis (1929-d.y.)

CF83363   Robert Wesley Martin (3 Nov 1885-23 Jun 1968) m 1) Elva Daisy Cook (1887-1933); m 2) Edith L. Hanley (16 Mar 1908-15 Jul 1986)

CF833631   Opal Arola Martin (9 Oct 1910-6 Sep 1979) m Johnny Raymond Spears (b 17 Jan 1910)

CF8336311   Martin Lyle Spears (b 30 Oct 1934) m Phyllis Jean Bates (b 22 Dec 1936)

CF83363111   Gordon Eugene Spears (b 22 Feb 1956) m 1) Kim Arlene Christensen (16 Aug 1957-2 Mar 1982); m 2) Betty Harvey

CF833631111   Josiah Spears (b 29 Oct 1981)

CF833631112   Katlyn Spears (b 29 Jul 1988)

CF83363112   Jeffary Spears (b 25 Apr 1959) m Karen Thompson

CF833631121   Clinton Allen Spears (b 28 Oct 1989)

CF83363113   Mark Spears (b 17 Dec 1969)

CF8336312   John Raymond Spears (b 16 Jan 1937) m Patricia Lindsey (b 1 Dec 1938)

CF83363121   Dana Marie Spears (b 5 May 1964) m Carl Frank Miller

CF83363122   Shawn Spears (b 3 Apr 1965) m Linda Anderson (b 23 Jul 1964)

CF8336313   Mary Ann Spears (b 18 Jul 1945) m Larry Wilson (b 13 May 1943)

CF83363131   Jennifer Wilson (b 22 Feb 1972)

CF83363132   Craig Wilson (b 22 Apt 1975)

CF8336314   Patricia Louise Spears (b 13 Jul 1947)

CF833632   Manford Adrian Martin (26 Mar 1912-16 Jun 1968) m Mildred Cecil Green (b 29 Dec 1912)

CF8336321   Noel Allen Martin (b 24 Aug 1933) m Mary Louise Donaldson (b 10 May 1936)

CF83363211   Noel Paul Martin (b 25 Mar 1956) m Gail Saunders

CF833632111   Kelli Ann Martin (b 1 Jan 1983)

CF833632112   Noel Daniel Martin (d at two months)

CF833632113   Amanda Jeanne Martin (b 13 Feb 1988)

CF83363212   John Manford Martin (b 15 Aug 1957) m Lisa Switzer

CF833632121   Rachael Martin (b 25 Nov 1986)

CF83363213   Stacey Jane Martin (b 11 Mar 1964) m Steven Denny (b 12 Jul 1965)

CF83363214   Robert James Martin (b 14 Jun 1966) m Cheryl Ramsey (b 4 Jan 1967)

CF8336322   James Manford Martin (b 24 Jul 1939) m Roberta Shultz (b 24 Sep 1949)

CF8336323   Beverly Sue Martin (b 14 Feb 1946) m Craig Tresidder (b 20 Dec 1943)

CF8336324   Kent Gordon Martin (b 11 Jul 1951) m Marcella Aslin (b 6 Sep 1949)

CF83363241   Amanda Marie Martin (b 27 May 1971)

CF83363242   Paul Adrian Martin (b 4 Jul 1972)

CF83363243   Jacob Martin (b 25 Mar 1976)

CF83363244   Rebecca Martin (b 6 Jun 1978)

CF83363245   Glen Martin (b 9 Jul 1980)

CF83363246   Stuart Martin (b 25 Nov 1983)

CF83363247   Molly Martin (b 17 Jul 1984)

CF83363248   Jennifer Martin (b 7 Feb 1986)

CF83363249   James Martin (b 29 Jul 1987)

CF8336324A   Sarah Martin (b 29 Mar 1989)

CF8336324B   Elizabeth Marian Martin (b 9 Apr 1991)

CF833633   Kenneth Sylvester Martin (13 Sep 1913-26 Mar 1960) m Pauline Shultz (b 19 Dec 1910)

CF833634   Gwendolyn Sadie Martin (b 26 Apr 1915) m Floyd Epperson (b 24 Jul 1908)

CF8336341   Thomas Floyd Epperson (9 Jan 1943-1 Apr 1971)

CF8336342   Claude Shelby Epperson (b 3 Jun 1947) m 1) Jolie Sasseville; m 2) Melanie

CF83363421   Elise Gwen Epperson

CF83363422   Derrick Epperson (b 17 Mar 1987)

CF8336343   Dean Shelden Epperson (b 3 Jun 1947) m Karen Gertrude Carola Seibel (b 3 Jul 1950)

CF83363431   Sherry Epperson (b 14 Nov 1970)

CF83363432   Mikko Epperson (b 7 Feb 1974)

CF833635   Jack Martin (Jun 1918-d at three weeks)

CF833636   Virginia Almeda Martin (b 12 Sep 1920) m Weikko Arvid Korhonen (b 13 Dec 1920)

CF8336361   Michael Arvid Korhonen (b 21 Nov 1942) m Evelyn Garman (b 30 Aug 1939)

CF83363611   Kimberly Ann Korhonen (b 16 Dec 1962)

CF83363612   Michael Arvis Korhonen (b 28 Feb 1965)

CF8336362   Allen Keith Korhonen (b 27 Mar 1945) m Laddene Ingram (b 25 Feb 1947)

CF83363621   Krista Korhonen (b 31 May 1970)

CF83363622   Kara Gwen Korhonen (b 12 Jun 1972)

CF83363623   Pierce Korhonen (b 3 Oct 1978)

CF8336363   Elva Sue Korhonen (b 13 Dec 1949) m Lee Porter (b 30 Jun 1948)

CF83363631   Kevin Porter (b 11 Nov 1970)

CF83363632   Christopher Porter (b 15 Mar 1974)

CF83363633   Corey Porter (b 12 Sep 1977)

CF8336364   Kenneth Paul Korhonen (b 25 Apr 1961) m Shannon Greene (b 29 Jul 1968)

CF833637   Robert Wesley Martin, Jr. (b 10 Aug 1922) m Margaret Meyer (b 26 Jul 1920)

CF8336371   Robert Wesley Martin III (b 10 Aug 1948)

CF8336372   Terry Lee Martin (b 9 Dec 1949) m Judy Jean Hempel (b 27 Sep 1952)

CF83363721   Tanner Lee Martin (b 29 Nov 1989)

CF833638   Thomas Haney Martin (b 15 Mar 1945) m Diane Erickson (b 15 Jul 1946)

CF8336381   Marcy Martin

CF8336382   Brad Martin

CF83364   Harry Earl Martin (25 Aug 1888-18 Nov 1964) m Mattie O. Shaffer (Dec 1889-1973)

CF833641   Violet Keith Martin (23 Nov 1917-9 Jan 1986) m Lawrence E. Williams

CF8336411   Danny Lee Williams (b 10 Jan 1944) m Karen Rapp (b 24 Jul 1947)

CF83364111   Kimberly Dawn Williams (b 26 Feb 1973)

CF83364112   Chrystal Lynn Williams (b 13 Apr 1977)

CF83364113   Robert Edward Williams (b 3 Oct 1982)

CF8336412   Charles Dean Williams (b 4 Jun 1947) m Molly

CF8336413   Patrick James Williams (b 10 Aug 1959) m Barbara Louise Wright

CF83364131   Benjamin Charles Williams (b 3 Oct 1983)

CF83364132   Jacqueline Elizabeth Williams (b 25 Sep 1986)

CF833642   Harry Earl Martin, Jr. (b 27 Sep 1919) m Marilyn Butterfield

CF8336421   Steven Wayne Martin (b 2 Mar 1949) m Nancy Evans (b 13 Apr 1954)

CF83364211   Sean Martin (b 20 Aug 1986)

CF8336422   Lori Ellen Martin (b 5 Sep 1960)

CF833643   James Newton Martin (b 15 Sep 1920) m Faye Edith Ross (b 8 Sep 1922)

CF8336431   Linda Lee Martin m Bill Zeisener

CF83364311   Martin Zeisener

CF83364312   Ross Zeisener

CF83364313   Adrian Zeisener

CF83364314   Joanna Zeisener

CF83364315   Michael Zeisener

CF83364316   Bobby Zeisener

CF8336432   Kenneth James Martin (b 25 Aug 1949) m Doris Ann Griggs

CF83364321   James Edward Martin (b 6 Jul 1971) m 1) Georgia Kaye Brown (b 8 Dec 1964); m 2)
Kimberly

CF833643211   Anthony George (Brown) Martin (b 30 Jul 1986)

CF833643212   Angela Christine Martin (b Jul 1991)

CF833643213   Kimberly Martin

CF8336433   Alisa Faye Martin (b 9 Jan 1960) m 1) Bill Snodderly; m 2) David Score

CF83364331   Thomas James Snodderly (b 1980)

CF83364332   Teri Lynn Snodderly (b 1982)

CF833644   Raymond Dean Martin (b 22 Jul 1922) m Mildred Ann Brodland (b 5 May 1923)

CF8336441   Larry Dean Martin (b 6 Jul 1948) m Christine Leigh Olsen (b 2 Nov 1954)

CF83364411   Andrew Dean Martin (b 6 Jun 1982)

CF83364412   Rachael Leigh Martin (b 20 Jun 1984)

CF8336442   Richard George Martin (b 30 Apr 1950) m Susan Lynn Rosinbum (b 12 Aug 1949)

CF83364421   Justin Re Martin (b 20 Oct 1976)

CF83364422   Scott Mathew Martin (b 31 Jan 1983)

CF83365   Sadie Grace Martin (12 Oct 1890-Sep 1961) m Fred Tate (1888-1928)

CF833651   Sarah Almeda Tate (b 5 Nov 1913) m Paul Bigler (b 1904)

CF8336511   Nancy Ann Bigler (b 8 Sep 1945) m James Kersey

CF833652   May Irene Tate (May 1918-May 1918)

CF833653   June Grace Tate (b 4 Jun 1921) m Julian Wilkins

CF83366   Claude Alonza Martin (20 Sep 1891-30 Oct 1953) m Elsie Hattie Klander (d 16 Jul 1986)

CF833661   Leroy Newton Martin (27 Oct 1917-4 Jun 1923)

CF833662   Manuel Walter Martin (15 Mar 1919-8 Jun 1959) m Rose Ann Newman

CF8336621   Lorraine Ann Martin (b 24 Sep 1947) m Ronald William Walters (b May 1942)

CF83366211   Michael Andrew Walters

CF833663   Douglas Dee Martin (17 Sep 1920-7 May 1969) m Rosalie

CF83367   James Clarence Martin (2 Nov 1896-7 Mar 1985) m 1) Ethel Colvin; m 2) Eva Mae Williams (b 28 Aug 1895); m 3) Ruby Schoonover

CF833671   Glen Martin m Ruth Cunningham

CF8336711   Terry Martin (b 4 Jun 1957) m Gary Arnold

CF83367111   Corey James Arnold

CF83367112   Christopher Lee Arnold

CF8336712   James Martin (b 22 Jul 1960) m Judy Schultz

CF833672   Rose Ann Almeda Martin m 1) Donald Deck; m 2) Leland Gardner; m 3) Henry Cecil
Robinson

CF8336721   Almeda Rose Gardner (b 27 Aug 1952) m Manford James Davis, Jr. (b 14 Jan 1946)(see
CF8336821)

CF83367211   Davis (b 1988)

CF8336722   James Lee Gardner (b 21 Jan 1955) m Irene

CF83367221   Jamie Ann Gardner

CF83367222   Aaron Lee Gardner

CF83367223   Anita Marie Gardner

CF8336723   David Thomas Gardner (b 17 Apr 1958) m Dixie Lee Cutter (b 26 Apr 1961)

CF83367231   Stephanie Dawn Gardner (b 9 Sep 1977)

CF83367232   Kalista Lee Gardner (b 24 Oct 1979)

CF8336724   Angela Mae Robinson (b 18 Apr 1961) m John Hammond

CF8336725   Henry Cecil Robinson III (b 20 Sep 1964) m Dawna Caminzind

CF833673   Fred Allen Martin (b 11 Feb 1939) m Maureen Alice Keller (b 2 Mar 1941)

CF8336731   Susan Pauline Martin (b 13 Jul 1962) m Kenneth William Bergman

CF83367311   Corothy-Ann Maureen Bergman (b 29 May 1982)

CF83367312   Rebekah Sue Bergman (b 27 Jul 1984)

CF8336732   Lynn Michelle Martin (b 1 May 1964) m Donald Foster

CF8336733   Pamela May Martin (b 25 May 1966)

CF83368   Ruth M. Martin (21 Sep 1898-7 Jan 1991) m 1) Walter Y. Davis (27 May 1889-13 Feb
1963); m 2) Harry Handschin

CF833681   Almeda Jane Davis (b 16 May 1922) m 1) Owen Eldon Carmine; m 2) Allwin Brockway

CF8336811   David Walter Carmine (b 11 Sep 1953)

CF83368111   Takota Carmine

CF83368112   Carmine (b Jan 1990)

CF8336812   Lisa Marie Carmine (b 4 Dec 1957) m 1)   ; m 2) Ron

CF83368121   Kelsey   (b 1983)

CF83368122   Trey   (b 1987)

CF833682   Manford James Davis (18 Apr 1927-16 Apr 1982) m Pauline Rich (b 6 Nov 1926)

CF8336821   Manford James Davis, Jr. (b 14 Jan 1946) m 1) Linda Faye Glenn (b 7 May 1947); m 2)
Almeda Rose Gardner (b 27 Aug 1952)(see CF8336721)

CF83368211   Dawn Davis (b 15 Jun 1968)

CF83368212   Monroe York Davis (b 1 Jul 1977)

CF83368213   Sarah Davis (b 27 Oct 1979)

CF8336822   Esther Marie Davis (b 16 Jan 1947) m 1) Doug Kelley (b 2 May 1949); m 2) Fernando
Aguirre

CF83368221   Ronald Shane Kelley (b 5 Feb 1968) m Trina Thompson

CF83368222   Sean Wesley Kelley (b 9 Mar 1971)

CF83368223   Sharlee Pauline Kelley (b 9 Mar 1981)

CF83368224   Shadd Manford Kelley (b 6 May 1982)

CF8336823   Linda Sue Davis (b 24 Jun 1948) m William Walter Arnold (b 5 Jun 1948)

CF83368231   Heath York Arnold (b 29 Jan 1972)

CF83368232   Aaron Mathiew Arnold (b 22 Dec 1974)

CF83368233   Corey Noel Arnold (b 27 Aur 1976)

CF83368234   Brock Adams Arnold (b 12 Sep 1978)

CF8336824   Mark Wesley Davis (b 23 Apr 1958) m Delores Dianne Cornwell (b 14 Jun 1959)

CF83368241   Wesley Robert Davis (b 28 Oct 1981)

CF83368242   Lacey Jean Davis (b 23 Mar 1984)

CF8336825   Rock Even Davis (b 14 Jul 1961) m Gloria Deneen Maher (b 8 Aug 1964)

CF83368251   Jessica Davis

CF8336826   Kerry Owen Davis (b 1 Feb 1964)

CF833683   Lois Esther Davis (b 6 Jan 1930) m Buster Brown Green (b 9 Jan 1932)

CF8336831   Nancy Kaye Green (b 13 Oct 1955) m Paul Bonner Jackson (b 25 Feb 1952)

CF83368311   Emily Helen Jackson (b 3 Aug 1981)

CF83368312   Anne Elizabeth Jackson (b 9 Jul 1983)

CF83368313   Paul Edward Jackson (b 11 Feb 1986)

CF9336832   Douglas Alan Green 9b 13 Sep 1956) m Natasha Katarski (b 25 Feb 1957)

CF8336833   Diane Ruth Green (b 7 Apr 1962)

CF8337   Rosanna F. Kahle (1859-Jun 1937) m William Andrew DeForest (27 Sep 1854, Franklin Co PA-6 May 1921, Huntingdon Co PA). Bur Cassville PA.

CF83371   James E. DeForest

CF83372   William L. DeForest (b 1878)

CF833721   Richard DeForest

CF8338   Sarah Elizabeth Kahle (20 Mar 1861-26 Feb 1863)

CF8339   David Abrem Kahle (12 Jan 1862, Cassville PA-28 Sep 1937, McKean Co PA) m Hanna Marian Payne (6 Jan 1865-20 May 1936). Bur Clarion PA.

CF83391   William Roy Kahle (b Sep 1886-17 Jun 1888)

CF83392   Alda Mae Kahle (6 Sep 1889-11 Feb 1969) m Don Groft (3 Feb 1894-3 Jan 1970). No chn.

CF83393   Albert Wesley Kahle (22 Apr 1895-Aug 1973, Greenville PA) m 4 Sep 1920, Ada Mae Patchell (28 Nov 1897, Karthaus PA-23 Mar 1989, Tucson AZ). Bur Clarion PA.

CF833931   Dorothy Marie Kahle (b 28 Sep 1923, Butler PA) m 1) 1 Sep 1943, William Joseph McCann, Jr. (b 24 Oct 1922), div; m 2) 8 Oct 1994, James Crawford

CF8339311   Gayle Marie McCann (b 22 Jun 1947, Sharon PA) m 28 May 1966, André Pillott Tillman, Jr. (b 2 Feb 1946, Miami FL)

     Charlsie Tillman (b 2 Oct 1979, FL)

CF83393111   André Pillott Tillman III (b 2 Feb 1981, St. Louis MO)

CF83393112   Sarah Wellons Tillman (b 21 Mar 1984, Athens GA)

CF8339312   David Allen McCann (b 1 Jan 1948, Sharon PA) m 14 Jul 1968, Linda Gayle Black (b 16 Jul 1949, Athens GA)

CF83393121   Anthony McCann (b 5 Sep 1972, Ft. Worth TX)

CF83393122   Joy Marie McCann (b 27 Jun 1975, Tishamingo OK)

CF83393123   Marcus Kahle McCann (b 26 Jun 1981, Tulsa OK)

CF8339313   Gary Edward McCann (b 19 Oct 1953, Sharon PA) m 1) 1973, Susan Fortson, Athens GA, div 1978; m 2) 27 Jun 1980, Renata Dudley (b 21 Oct 1954, Athens GA)

CF83393131   Jennifer Leigh McCann (b May 1974)

CF833932   Patsy Ruth Kahle (b 22 Oct 1925) m 10 Dec 1943, Clarence Lee VanCleef, Jr. (9 Jan 1925-16 Dec 1989, Oxnard CA), div.

CF8339321   Alan Lee VanCleef (b 17 Dec 1946, Sharon PA) m 1 Jan 1971, Margaret Mitchell (b 9 Jul 1949, Barbourville KY)

CF83393211   Brandi Cossan VanCleef (b 22 Aug 1971, Petersburg VA)

CF83393212   Alan Lee VanCleef, Jr. (b 19 Oct 1973, Louisville KY)

CF83393213   Christopher George VanCleef (b 21 Jan 1975, Louisville KY)

CF8339322   Deborah VanCleef (b 30 Mar 1948, Sommerville NJ) m 6 Apr 1974, Gary Jones (b 12
Dec 1946, NC)

CF83393221   Symantha Jones 9b 21 Dec 1974, Wallhalla NC)

CF8339323   David VanCleef (b 6 Sep 1955, Los Angeles CA) m 11 Apr 1984, Teresa

CF833933   David B. Kahle (b 14 Oct 1931) m 9 Mar 1956, Connie Lou Winner (b 16 May 1937)

CF833A   Grace Sarah Kale (25 Aug 1864-23 Aug 1889) m 4 Jul 1881, Jefferson Co PA, Dallas
McCoy (3 Jan 1858-12 Jun 1936). Bur Kahletown PA.

CF833A1   Gertrude McCoy (22 Jun 1882-May 1938, Oil City PA) m William Shottenberg (6 May
1881, Marienville PA-28 Dec 1962, Brookville PA). Bur Kahletown PA.

CF833A11   Nellie Pearl Shottenberg (b 6 Apr 1908, Oil City PA) m 18 Jun 1929, Oil City PA, James
Monkern (10 Jun 1904, Oil City PA-14 Dec 1979, Oil City PA)

CF833A111   Arnold James Monkern (b 12 Mar 1941, Oil City PA) m 1962, Judy McCandless
(1941-Sep 1974, Columbia Station OH)

CF833A1111   Kimberly Ann Monkern (b 19 Jun 1965, Cleveland OH)

CF833A1112   Jaqueline Sue Monkern (b 9 Mar 1967, Cleveland OH)

CF833A1113   Lisa Marie Monkern (b 11 Mar 1970, Cleveland OH)

CF833A12   Dorothy G. Shottenberg (21 Jan 1910-11 Apr 1993) m Edgar Perry (b 27 Aug 1911)

CF833A121   Ronald Perry

CF833A122   Robert Perry

CF833A2   Pearl Hannah McCoy (18 Sep 1885-18 Sep 1962) m 1) Joseph Clark Girt (6 Jun 1885-19
Jan 1928); m 2) Frank Stanyard

CF833A3   Lee McCoy

CF833B   Justine D. Kahle (b 1879) m Burt Davis

CF834   Frederick Peter Kahle (19 Aug 1823, Shippenville PA-3 May 1914, Lima OH) m 22 Nov
1849, Kahletown PA, Isabel McCutcheon (18 May 1831-6 Dec 1916, Lima OH). Bur Franklin PA. Oil
business.[82]

CF8341   Benton Tilden Kahle (15 Jan 1851-1928) m Elizabeth Rumabugh

CF83411   Edna Kahle (b ca 1880) m Walter Brown

---

[82]Data on the Frederick P. Kahle family contributed in 1960 by Mrs. Aleen K. Froehlich.

CF83412   Claude A. Kahle (b ca 1882). Unm.

CF8342   Manuel Wilson Kahle (2 Apr 1852-16 Oct 1886) m 20 Jan 1877, Martha Jane Sharp (10 Mar 1856-28 Oct 1895)

CF83421   Wilkie Beatricke Kahle (b 15 Jun 1885) m Orrin Philip Gifford, Jr. (b 14 May 1885)

CF834211   Martha Jane Gifford (b 13 Oct 1913) m Charles E. Meinhardt (b 1 Sep 1911)

CF8342111   Charles Anne Meinhardt (b 27 Jun 1944)

CF8342112   Susan Meinhardt (b 2 Nov 1945)

CF834212   Florence Beatrice Gifford (b 28 Dec 1915) m Victor Garibaldi (b 28 Jun 1908)

CF8343   Hanna Emily Kahle (17 Jul 1853-15 Jan 1862)

CF8344   Clarence W. Kahle (24 Feb 1855-11 Apr 1941) m Lucy Grace Barber (24 Aug 1862-27 Dec 1940)

CF834 Frederick Peter Kahle (1823-1914); CF83471 Aleen Wilma Kahle Mowen Froehlich (b 1890); CF83472 Helen Louise Kahle Wicke (b 1892); Isabel McCutcheon Kahle (1831-1916)

CF83441   Charles Kahle (b 28 Oct 1882) m Bess   . No chn.

CF83442   Frances Kahle (b 14 Dec 1899) m 23 Apr 1925, Ralph Homeward Espach (5 Aug 1900-6 Aug 1956)

CF834421   Marian Kahle Espach (b 23 Feb 1928) m Frank S. Cordiner

CF8344211   Deborah Anne Cordiner (b 15 Jan 1953)

CF8344212   Michael Peter Cordiner (b 7 May 1954)

CF834422   Ralph Homeward Espach, Jr. (b 10 May 1932). Unm.

CF8345   Albert Wesley Kahle (30 Sep 1856, Jefferson Co PA-12 Feb 1955, Houston TX) m 28 Oct 1891, Clara Metheany Lynch (20 Jul 1866, Lima OH-15 Jun 1958). Bur Lima OH. MD, Col of Physicians and Surgeons, Baltimore MD, 1883; physician, Lima OH, 1886-1930.

CF83451   Richard Benton Kahle (5 Nov 1892, Lima OH-25 Jun 1969) m Helen Ruth Dodd (28 Jan 1897, Zanesville OH-20 Jan 1976, Houston TX)

CF834511   Martha Ruth Kahle (b 21 Sep 1917, Halifax NS CAN) m 27 Jun 1939, Old Greenwich CR, Joseph Newton Rodeheaver, Jr. (5 Oct 1911, Brookings SD-4 Apr 1971, Orinda CA).

CF8345111   James Richard Rodeheaver (b 29 Jul 1941, Boston MA) m Oct 1967, Lynn M. Hardie (b 3 Mar 1945, CA)

CF8345112   Thomas Newton Rodeheaver (b 5 May 1945, Houston TX) m 21 Apr 1973, Nancy Joan Huff (b 1 May 1945)

CF8345113   Myra Ruth Rodeheaver (b 12 Sep 1946, Newton Center MA) m 18 Dec 1971, Thomas S. Bamberger (b 6 Apr 1938)

CF8345114   Barbara Ann Rodeheaver (b 26 Jun 1952, Boston MA) m 1 Jul 1979, Ronald Warren Fong (b 7 Mar 1950)

CF834512   Richard Benton Kahle, Jr. (29 Apr 1920, E. Orange NJ-23 Mar 1987, Kingsville TX) m 1) Ann Williams; m 2) Lareva.

CF8345121   Judy Kahle

CF834513   Myra May Kahle (b 1 May 1924, Shreveport LA) m Oct 1944, James Frederick Horsey, Jr.

CF8345131   Carol Ruth Horsey (b 25 Nov 1945) m 1)   Van Russell; m 2) Ralph Katz

CF8345132   James Frederick Horsey III (b 14 Aug 1947)

CF8345133   Katherine Dale Horsey (b 11 Mar 1953) m Roger Lankford

CF83452   Raymond Frederick Kahle (20 Oct 1895, Lima OH-1 Jan 1919, Colorado Springs CO). Unm.

CF83453   Warren Francis Kahle (6 Oct 1898, Lima OH-Houston TX) m Katherine Greer. Physician.

CF834531   Warren Greer Kahle (b 28 Dec 1943)

CF834532   Roger Neal Kahle (b 10 Jul 1945)

CF8346   Sarah Elizabeth Kahle (25 Mar 1858-27 Mar 1858)

CF8347   Raymond David Kahle (4 Mar 1860, Kahletown PA-16 Jun 1933, Lima OH) m 24 Mar 1887, Nellie Adelle Strickland (6 Apr 1862, Red House NY-10 Aug 1940, Lakeside OH). MD, Med Crpt of UCNY; physician, Lima OH.

CF83471   Aleen Wilma Kahle (b 6 Dec 1890) m 1) Hugh Lester Mowen (18 Apr 1891); m 2) Frederick William Froelich (b 30 Nov 1867)

CF834711   Kenneth A. Mowen (b 2 Jul 1914) m 3 Jul 1939, Anna Gauch (b 16 Aug 1910)

CF8347111   Ann Mowen (b 6 Mar 1943)

CF8347112   Kay Mowen (b 29 Oct 1945)

CF83472   Helen Louise Kahle (b 4 Oct 1892) m 31 Oct 1919, Elbert A. Wickes (b 30 Nov 1884)

CF834721   Thomas Kahle Wickes (b 9 Nov 1921) m. 13 Jun 1942, Mary Ellen Miller (b 16 Jun 1920)

CF8347211   Bradford Thomas Wickes (b 1 Dec 1951)

CF8347212   Lauren Ann Wickes (b 5 Feb 1953)

CF8347213   Susan Lee Wickes (b 30 Jul 1955)

CF834722   Philip McCutcheon Wickes (b 21 Jan 1924). Unm.

CF83473   Katherine Isabel Kahle (b 16 Apr 1899) m 3 Sep 1924, Oliver Lockwood Williams (b 21 Jan 1899)

CF834731   David Lockwood Williams (b 3 Jan 1928) m 28 Jul 1951, Virginia Talley (b 30 Jul 1928)

CF8347311   Katherine Virginia Williams (b 7 Jul 1954)

CF8347312   Amy Elizabeth Williams (b 6 May 1957)

CF83474   Raymond Strickland Kahle (b 15 Apr 1903) m Iola Warren

CF834741   Raymond David Kahle II (b 22 Oct 1930) m 29 Aug 1953, Patricia Raymond (b 19 Jan 1932)

CF8347411   Patricia Lynn Kahle (b 7 Aug 1954)

CF8347412   Janet Rae Kahle (b 22 Jun 1957)

CF834742   Warren Kahle (b 21 Sep 1932). Unm.

CF8348   Frederick Leander Kahle (18 Apr 1862, Jefferson Co PA-Mar 1921) m May 1888 Mary Galbreath (d 1930). Attorney, 1886- .

CF83481   Anna Kahle (b 18 Sep 1891). Unm.

CF83482   Clarence Courtney Kahle (18 Mar 1894-2 Oct 1918, France). Distinguished Service Cross, French Legion of Honor. WWI, USA.

CF8349   Alice Arminta Kahle (25 Dec 1863-Easter 1916) m Don Carlos Elsworth Henderson (b 13 Feb 1862)

CF83491   Dudley Kahle Henderson (7 Jan 1893-1957) m Irene

CF834911   Jeanne Henderson m Howard Palmer

CF834912   Patricia Henderson m Leonard Wagner

CF834913   Shirley Henderson m Ronald Paolucci

CF83492   Marjorie Isabel Henderson m 1) 30 Oct 1917, Clarence E. Carnes; m 2) 26 Oct 1932, Phillip R. Markey. No chn.

CF834A   William Andrew Kahle (21 Jul 1865, Kahletown PA-7 Mar 1899). Unm. Bur Franklin PA. Surgeon, Sp-Am War.

CF834B   Charles Edgar Kahle (12 Feb 1867-15 Sep 1943, Oklahoma City OK) m Elizabeth Blanch Hayes (d Aug 1942)

CF834B1   Charles Edgar Kahle, Jr. (b 23 Feb 1902)

CF834B2   Keith Kahle (b 25 Sep 1909)

CF834C   Francis Urbin Kahle (10 Feb 1871, Plummer PA-8 Mar 1947) m 27 Sep 1892, Mary Louise Lewis (b 27 May 1860)

CF834C1   Julian L. Kahle (b 16 Jul 1895) m Katherine Lascalles (b 4 Sep 1903)

CF834C11   Nancy Kahle (b 18 Apr 1926)

CF834C12   Joan Kahle (b 4 Nov 1928)

CF834C13   Jay Kahle (b 29 Jan 1934)

CF834C2   Isabelle L. Kahle (b 5 Jul 1897) m 7 Jan 1928, George Frederick Betts Johnson (b 10 Jul 1898)

CF834C21   Georgia Johnson (b 17 Feb 1929) m Montgomery G. Pooly (b 21 Jul 1916)

CF834C22   Wolcott Howe Johnson (b 19 May 1930)

CF834C3   Elizabeth L. Kahle (b 27 Sep 1900). Unm.

CF834C   Philip Ainsworth Kahle (b 3 Jul 1874, Plummer PA) m 5 May 1897, Augusta Rosamond McKibben (b 11 Jun 1874). Attorney.

CF834D1   Roween Minerva Kahle (b 15 Oct 1898) m 1) 30 Jun 1920, William Lester Allgire, div; m 2) 4 Sep 1928, DeGrasse Fox Smith (b 26 Oct 1888)

CF834D11   Caroline Jane Allgire (b 16 Jul 1921) m Everett Taylor Eyman (b 10 Nov 1914)(Adopted by DeGrasse Smith)

CF834D2   Dorothy Dean Kahle (b 4 Jun 1903) m 15 Jun 1927, Paul Bartlett McDaniel (b 22 Feb 1903)

CF834D21   Charles Ainsworth McDaniel (b 30 Aug 1930) m 25 Sep 1954, Margaret Diane Childerhose (b 8 Apr 1936)

CF834D211   Shawn Ainslee McDaniel (b 1 Jan 1958)

CF834D3   Philip Ainsworth Kahle, Jr. (16 Jul 1905-5 Apr 1971, Sarasota FL) m 1 Sep 1930, Ethel Mae Robson (b 7 Jul 1906)

CF834D31   Barbara Ann Kahle (b 6 Mar 1932)

CF834D32   Elizabeth McKibben Kahle (b 29 Sep 1935) m 29 Dec 1962, Martin Charles Mondor (b 24 May 1931)

CF834E   Harry Vinton Kahle (10 Jun 1876, Plummer PA-29 Sep 1941, Oklahoma City OK) m 1 Apr 1900, Kate Gertrude Byrne (30 Apr 1883, Toronto Ont CAN-19 Dec 1919, Oklahoma City OK). Attorney.

CF834E1   Gertrude Amelia Kahle (3 Mar 1901, Lima OH-1978, Breencastle IN) m 19 Oct 1923, Calvin Russell Davis (19 Jul 1897-19 Jun 1955, St. Louis MO)

CF834E11   Calvin Russell Davis, Jr. (b 25 Jul 1925) m 24 Jun 1950, Milwaukee WI, Carol Gertrude Fuller (b 24 Aug 1931)

CF834E111   Calvin Russell Davis III (b 19 Aug 1951) m 1) 3 May 1975, Kerry Krummell; m 2) 23 DEc 1994, Cathy

CF834E1111   Kelly Faye Davis (b 22 Apr 1978)

CF834E1112   Casey Anne Davis (b 29 Mar 1980)

CF834E112   Linda Susan Davis (b 22 Oct 1952) m 1) 21 Jan 1974, Craig Sallendar; m 2) 9 Jun 1984, Norman Reiling (b 17 Jan 1958)

CF834E1121   Linnaea Sallendar (b 24 Jun 1974) m Jason Rextraw

CF834E11211   Ashlee Elizabeth Rextraw (b 13 Feb 1996)

CF834E1122   Eric Andrew Sallendar (b 13 Aug 1977)

CF834E1123   Russell Reiling (b 21 Mar 1985)

CF834E1124   Kahlyn Davis Reiling (b 27 Mar 1987)

CF834E113   Mary Anne Davis (b 21 Apr 1958) m 5 Jul 1985, Dan Franck (b 5 May 1947)

CF934E1131   Gabriel Merrill Davis Franck (b 1 Apr 1995)

CF834E12   John Vinton Davis (b 10 Nov 1926, Cleveland OH) m 4 Sep 1954, Webster Groves MO, June Schumacher (b 1 Jun 1933, St. Louis MO)

CF834E121   Cynthia Marie Davis (b 27 Mar 1963)

CF834E122   Richard Kahlc Davis (b 10 Mar 1972)

CF834E2   Loren Frederick Kahle (b 31 Dec 1903) m 10 Feb 1927, Helen Herr (b 31 Aug 1902)

CF834E21   Loren Frederick Kahle, Jr. (b 28 Feb 1930) m 20 Jun 1953, Elizabeth Ann Knebel (b 28 Feb 1928)

CF834E211   Randolph Stuart Kahle (b 31 May 1955) m 1) Pamela Fish; m 2) 2 Jan 1993, Lyle Confrey (b 28 Jun 1950)

CF834E2111   Nissa Confrey Kahle (b 9 Dec 1986)

CF834E2112   Nowell Confrey Kahle (b 28 Mar 1989)

CF834E212   Charles Frederick Kahle (b 30 Dec 1957) m 13 May 1989, Ruth Jessica Rogovoy (b 14 Feb 1963)

CF834E2121   Emma Carolyn Kahle (b 8 Jul 1992)

CF834E2122   Bernard Moses Kahle (b 27 Dec 1993)

CF834E213   James Allan Kahle (b 25 Nov 1960) m 24 Sep 1988, Mary Madeline Closman (b 6 Aug 1962)

CF834E2131   Charles Nicholas Kahle 9b 26 Sep 1991)

CF834E2132   Heidi Marie Kahle (b 7 Apr 1993)

CF834E2133   Kenneth Philip Kahle (b 25 Jul 1995)

CF834E22   Robert Vinton Kahle (b 10 Dec 1932) m 1) 25 Jun 1955, Margaret M. Lurton (b 15 Dec 1932); m 2) 2 Apr 1983, Annabella Shcafer (b 9 Aug 1942)

CF834E221   Allison Lurton Kahle (b 5 Apr 1959)

CF834E222   Brewster Lurton Kahle (b 21 Oct 1960) m 12 Sep 1992, Mary Katherin Auston

CF834E2221   Carlon Reed Auston Kahle (b 16 Aug 1994)

CF834E23   Richard Allan Kahle (b 2 Jul 1939, Caripito, Venezuela) m 1) 4 Mar 1964, Shreveport LA, Mary Easterwood (b 5 Jul 1941, Shreveport LA) ; m 2) 26 Nov 1981, Sherman TX, Carole Jane Smith (b 24 Jun 1939)

CF834E231   Kimberly Ann Kahle (b 7 Jun 1969, Bonton MA) m 3 Aug 1985, Rendon TX, Donald Wayne Lasater (b 21 Sep 1965, Grande Prairie TX)

CF834E2311   Donald Wayne Lasater III (b 28 Feb 1992, Burlington TX)

CF834E2312   George Brandon Lasater (b 16 Feb 1994, Ft. Worth TX)

CF834E2313   Lauren Madison Kahle Lasater (b 15 Sep 1995, Ft. Worth TX)

CF834E232   Steven Christopher Kahle (b 28 Jan 1969, Burlington TX)

CF834E233   Christopher Allen Kahle (b 18 Dec 1972, Norwalk CT)

CF835   George Loury Kahle (12 Oct 1824, Eldred Tp, Jefferson Co PA-24 Oct 1917, Fairview OK) m 4 Jan 1850, Mary Ann Terwilliger (22 Apr 1832, NY-2 Dec 1901, Fairview OK). Bur Fairview OK. In 1850, resident of Eldred Tp, Jefferson Co PA, with brother Frederick P. Kahle.

CF8351   Priscilla Jane Kahle (b 1851, Eldred Tp, Jefferson Co PA) m James Thompson Travis (22 Dec 1848-Sep 1933)

CF8352   Mary Ellen Kahle (18 Aug 1853, Eldred Tp, Jefferson Co PA-2 Mar 1945) m Frank
Wetzel

CF8353   Phoebe Ann Kahle (19 Sep 1854, Eldred Tp, Jefferson Co PA-13 Apr 1944) m 1872,
George A. Cook

CF8354   William Perry Kahle (18 Aug 1857, Eldred Tp, Jefferson Co PA-25 Aug 1925)

CF8355   George H. Kahle (10 Aug 1859, Eldred Tp, Jefferson Co PA)

CF8356   Lovenia Princetia Kahle (b 29 Feb 1861)

CF8357   Lorenzo Bert Kahle (26 Oct 1863-23 Apr 1918, Jackson CA) m Mary Victoria Noreiga (b 23 Dec 1873). Bur Campo Seco CA.

CF83571   Gertrude Katherine Kahle (b 14 Jun 1899, Valley Springs CA) m Charles C. Cullers

CF83572   Blanche Kahle (b 18 Jul 1900, Valley Springs CA) m 7 Sep 1921, Raymond Campbell
Miller

CF83573   George William Kahle m Florence Tyler

CF83574   Lora Bessie Kahle (b 24 Apr 1903, Valley Springs CA-24 Apr 1904, Valley Springs CA)

CF8358   Sylvanus Bascom Kahle (b 30 Jan 1865)

CF8359   Charles Edgar Kahle (14 May 1867-28 Oct 1957) m 25 Dec 1901, Agnes Wheeler

CF835A   Estella Uphema Kahle (1 Feb 1874, Independence KS-21 Feb 1967, Spearman TX) m 13 Aug 1892, Hardy Duncan Phebus (6 Jul 1872, Covington IN-22 Jul 1950, Perryton TX). Bur Perryton TX.

CF835A1   Leroy Phebus (13 Jun 1893, Duck Creek KS-30 Jun 1973) m Aug 1915, Myrtle Mills

CF835A2   Mabel Ellen Phebus (23 Feb 1895, Neodesha TX-13 Aug 1972, Perryton TX) m 20 Jun 1929, James Lynch Dodson (b 12 Jun 1887, Oenaville TX)

CF836 Washington Whistler Kahle (1826-1921)

CF835A21   James Lynch Dodson, Jr. (b 3 Oct 1931, Perryton TX) m 11 Aug 1970, Marcia Linda Clyburn

CF835A3   Grace May Phebus (b 27 Dec 1897, Neodesha KS) m 1 Jan 1916, George Lamb Thompson

CF835A4   Lula Mildred Phebus (b 10 Feb 1902, Fairview OK) m 19 May 1921, Melvin Herbert Flock

CF835A5   Joy Phebus (27 Nov 1904, Fairview OK-17 Feb 1905)

CF835A6   George Milton Phebus (b 14 Jul 1906, Fairview OK) m 25 Oct 1925, Maggie Painter

CF835A7   Everett Samuel Phebus (b 15 Mar 1908, Fairview OK) m 1928, Lucy Ellen Taft

CF835B   Bessie Mae Kahle (31 Mar 1879, Independence KS-16 Nov 1952) m 9 Feb 1897, Charley St. John

CF836   Washington Whistler Kahle (11 Feb 1826, Shippenville PA-22 Dec 1921) m 28 Mar 1850, Elizabeth Arthurs (28 May 1831-9 Feb 1906). Bur Kahletown PA.[83]

CF8361   Cemantha Kahle (2 May 1851-22 Dec 1919) m 26 Jul 1870, John Truby (8 Oct 1847-27 Jun 1913). Bur Eldred Tp, Jefferson Co PA. Farmer.

CF83611   Della Maude Truby (24 Dec 1870-24 May 1949) m 5 Oct 1892, William Mert Grant (29 Sep 1872-22 Oct 1950). Bur Kahletown PA.

CF836111   Hazel May Grant (b 15 Feb 1894) m 28 May 1913, John Ralph Baker (22 Aug 1888-12 Dec 1957). Bur Kahletown PA.

CF836112   John Dale Grant (b 2 Aug 1896) m 22 Mar 1920, Madge Frost (1894-1960)

CF8361121   Margarette Grant m John Ewers

CF83611211   Patricia Ewers

---

[83]Data supplied by Miss Phalla I. Gruver and Mrs. Vincent Race in 1960 and Esther Kahle Best and Elizabeth G. Weitzel in 1996.

CF83611212   Karen Ewers

CF8361122   James Grant (b 24 Dec 1920)

CF8361123   Ralph Grant m Joan Baughman

CF83611231   Dale Jay Grant

CF83611232   David Lee Grant

CF83611233   Ralph Wayne Grant

CF8361124   Louise Grant

CF836113   Wayne Cliffton Grant (b 18 Feb 1904) m 27 Nov 1929, Edith Heppinger

CF83612   Ida May Truby (10 Jan 1873-10 Apr 1949) m 1 Sep 1891, J.W. Daniels (2 Sep 1866-8 Oct 1957). She bur Eldred Tp, Jefferson Co PA. Farmer.

CF836121   Glenn Daniels (5 Sep 1892-23 Dec 1892). Bur Barnett Tp, Jefferson Co PA.

CF836122   Twila Maude Daniels (b 23 Mar 1894) m 16 Jul 1920, Leo Stanley Boyles (b 30 Mar 1891). She, teacher.

CF8361221   James Michael Boyles (16 Apr 1921-1 Dec 1949)

CF836123   Clair McKinley Daniels (b 21 Sep 1899) m 17 Jun 1944, Viola Croyle (b 24 Oct 1911)

CF836124   Cadmus Paul Daniels (30 Apr 1902-5 Nov 1907). Bur Barnett Tp, Jefferson Co PA.

CF83613   Bertha Larue Truby (10 Jan 1873-3 Sep 1925) m 10 Sep 1895, John N. Grove (28 Jul 1870-11 Jan 1956). He bur Eldred Tp, Jefferson Co PA.

CF836131   George Parker Grove (16 Nov 1896-7 Nov 1958) m 15 Jul 1918, Lottie Belle Hagan

CF8361311   Eleanor Grove (b 10 Feb 1919) m 27 Apr 1938, Elmer E. Beach

CF83613111   Sandra Pearl Beach (b 15 Aug 1939) m 30 Aug 1958, Stephen Frank Fento

CF83613112   Thomas George Beach (b 6 Jul 1942)

CF83613113   Charlotte Diane Beach (b 29 Jul 1947)

CF83613114   Linda Kay Beach (3 Sep 1951)

CF83613115   Daniel Alan Beach (22 Sep 1955)

CF83613116   Lori Jo Beach (25 Jul 1959)

CF836132   Verna Belle Grove (b 31 Mar 1899)

CF836133   Olive Blanche Grove (12 Dec 1900-16 Jan 1904). Bur Eldred Tp, Jefferson Co PA.

CF836134   Mathew Stanley Grove (b 20 Sep 1903) m 17 Jun 1934, June Rohrbach (b 18 Jun 1914)

CF8361341   Anna Louise Grove (b 15 Jul 1935) m 8 Aug 1959, Richard G. Johnson (b 30 Nov 1934)

CF8361342   Stanley Mathew Grove (b 6 Feb 1937) m 28 Nov 1959, Marcia Frances Matthews (b 29 Aug 1938)

CF83614   Laura Verna Truby (b 1 Jul 1882) m 28 Apr 1903, Charles Albert Wolfe (b 23 Aug 1874)

CF836141   Daughter Wolfe (9 Sep 1906-9 Sep 1906)

CF836142   George Harold Wolfe (b 27 Mar 1908) m 30 Sep 1931, Kathryn Louise Grace (b 2 Nov 1909)

CF8361421   Daughter Wolfe (1 Jun 1932-1 Jun 1932)

CF8361422   Dorothy Louise Wolfe (b 5 Aug 1934) m 13 Mar 1954, Herbert Lee Chatley (b 21 Jan 1935)

CF83614221   Diane Joy Chatley (b 2 Jun 1953)

CF83614222   Mark Allen Chatley (b 31 Dec 1957)

CF836143   Delbert Kaye Wolfe (b 23 Mar 1910) m 9 Apr 1938, Mary Ellen Daniels (b 2 Sep 1919)

CF8361431   Marilyn Kay Wolfe (b 11 Dec 1945)

CF8361432   Linda Lee Wolfe (b 4 Jul 1950)

CF836144   Vesta Larue Wolfe (b 8 Jan 1919) m 23 Oct 1937, Kenneth Arthur McKinley (b 17 Jul 1915)

CF8361441   Kenneth Robert McKinley (b 7 Jun 1938) m. 12 Nov 1957, Janet E. Shields (b 16 Dec 1937)

CF83614411   Victoria Ann McKinley (b 3 Aug 1958)

CF8361442   Mary Elizabeth McKinley (b 25 Jul 1940) m 6 Jun 1956, James Samuel Hamilton (b 18 Oct 1937)

CF83614421   Kathleen Sue Hamilton (b 2 Jan 1959)

CF8361443   Delbert Charles McKinley (b 17 Apr 1943)

CF8361444   Donna Larue McKinley (b 15 Jun 1946)

CF8361445   Ramona Bonita McKinley (b 23 Feb 1957)

CF83615   George Oscar Truby (4 May 1885-1963) m 8 Mar 1911, Alla Mae Hagerty (1891-1974). Bur Eldred Tp Jefferson Co PA.

CF836151   Esther Truby (b 31 Jul 1911) m 26 Jul 1954, Marc J. De Barti

CF836152   John Truby (b 30 Sep 1912) m 9 Jun 1936, Iva Aldine Moore

CF8361521   Esther Marie Truby (b 13 Nov 1938)

CF8361522   Catherine Ann Truby (b 3 Jun 1940)

CF8361523   John Frederick Truby (b 14 Sep 1943)

CF836153　　　　Lola Truby (8 Sep 1914-6 Oct 1914). Bur Eldred Tp, Jefferson Co PA.

CF836154　　　　Ralph Truby (b 2 May 1916) m 1943, Josephine Specuzza

CF8361541　　　James Frank Truby (b 19 Mar 1944)

CF8361542　　　Lana Lee Truby (b 21 Jan 1947)

CF836155　　　　Clair Truby (20 Aug 1921-8 Jun 1944). WWII.

CF836156　　　　Phalla Louise Truby (20 Oct 1925-27 Jul 1926). Bur Eldred Tp, Jefferson Co PA.

CF8362　　　　　Lucinda Kahle (12 Jul 1853-21 Jun 1927) m 22 Dec 1870, Frank Forsythe (1840-1916)

CF836272　　　　Gertrude Asel

CF836273　　　　Wayne Asel

CF836274　　　　Eva Asel

CF836275　　　　Elizabeth Asel

CF836276　　　　Twila Asel

CF836277　　　　Ray Asel

CF836278　　　　Elsie Asel

CF83621　　　　Viola Lou Forsythe (1871-1950) m W.R. McCracken

CF836211　　　　Burton Leroy McCracken (1894-1913) m Mary Margaret Tillotson (1896-1976). Bur
Reynoldsville PA.

CF8362111　　　Chauncey Leroy McCracken m Ruby Matilda Krob

CF83621111　　Chauncey Leroy McCracken, Jr.

CF83621112　　Rita Louise McCracken

CF83621113　　Kenneth Lee McCracken

CF83621114　　William James McCracken

CF83621115　　Mary Anne McCracken

CF836212　　　　Walter Ray McCracken

CF836213　　　　Charles Ellsworth McCracken m Gertrude McFadden

CF8362131　　　Ruth Evelyn McCracken m James Foley

CF83621311　　David Daniel Foley

CF83621312　　James Foley

CF8362132　　　Daniel William McCracken m Marion Cribbs

CF83621321   Lynn Joy McCracken

CF83621322   Dale Ellsworth McCracken

CF83621323   Dean Michael McCracken

CF83621324   Brady Lee McCracken

CF836214   J. Franklin McCracken (1900-1901)

CF83622   Bert Forsythe (1875-1955) m Eva Thompson (1881-1916). Bur Brookville PA.

CF836221   Howard Forsythe

CF836222   Clifford Forsythe

CF836223   George Forsythe

CF83623   Edna Forsythe (1871-1921) m James C. Stahlman (1869-1947) Bur Jefferson Co PA.

CF83624   Fannie Elizabeth Forsythe (1 Jun 1877-1960) m Archie Stahlman (20 Nov 1871-1951). Bur Jefferson Co PA.

CF83625   Ellsworth Forsythe m Ethel Jones

CF836251   Leone Forsythe

CF83626   Kate Forsythe m Clifton Siaro

CF836261   Clifton Siaro

CF836262   Robert Siaro

CF83627   Myrtle G. Forsythe (1885-1948) m James C. Asel (1883-1948). Bur Eldred Tp, Jefferson Co PA.

CF836271   Claude Asel

CF83628   Wesley Forsythe

CF83629   Lillian Forsythe m George Horton

CF836291   Donald Horton

CF836292   Dorothy Horton

CF8362A   Milton K. Forsythe (1894-1895)

CF8363   Sarah E. Kahle (20 Mar 1855-26 Feb 1863). Bur Kahletown PA.

CF8364   Violet Jane Kahle (25 Apr 1857-12 Jul 1933) m 3 Oct 1879, John Milton Gruver (17 Nov 1853-20 Oct 1936)

CF83641   Ethel Sydney Gruver (b 11 Apr 1881) m 14 Dec 1906, William Hunter (11 Apr 1879-9 Oct 1952). Oil contractor.

CF83642   Lauren Clark Gruver (b 26 Mar 1883) m 23 Jun 1909, Edna Husler

CF836421   Jane Husler Gruver (b 29 Jun 1929) m 29 Mar 1952, Shelly Marks (b 24 Jan 1924)

CF8364211   Candice Marks (b 8 Nov 1953)

CF83643   Harold Gruver (1886-12 Mar 1892)

CF83644   Phalla Imogen Gruver (b 25 Feb 1889)

CF83645   William Milton Gruver (1890-25 Mar 1892)

CF83646   Winifred Gruver (1895-14 Oct 1896)

CF8365   Oceana Grace Kahle (10 Sep 1859-2 Mar 1909) m 3 Oct 1880, Thomas Allen Ewing
(1858-1936). Bur Richardsville PA.

CF83651   Clyde Ellis Ewing (6 Aug 1881-4 Aug 1959, Tenstrike MN) m Sena Thompson

CF836511   Warren Ewing (1908-1949)

CF836512   Dale Ewing (b 1910)

CF836513   Clyde Ewing, Jr. (b 1915) m

CF8365131   Diane Ewing

CF836514   Stanley Ewing (b 1917)

CF836515   Russell Ewing (b 1919)

CF836516   Arnold Ewing (b 1921)

CF83652   Mabel Ewing (1883-1895)

CF83653   William Calvin Ewing (1885-1908)

CF83654   Lulu Caroline Ewing (15 Jan 1887-1958) m William D. Cartwright (b 10 Jun 1862)

CF836541   Joseph Ewing Cartwright (b 16 Dec 1908)

CF836542   William Ewing Cartwright (b 31 Aug 1913) m

CF8365421   Joel Cartwright

CF836543   Jean Eleanor Cartwright (b Dec 1924)

CF83655   Margaret Ewing (b 20 Jan 1889) m O.W. Morrison (b 23 Dec 1881)

CF836551   Dorothy Fae Morrison (b 1 Jun 1910) m Thomas McNally

CF8365511   Richard Thomas McNally m

CF8355512   Shirley Ann McNally m

CF8365513   Deborah Lynn McNally

CF836552   Thomas Mac Morrison (b 3 Jan 1914) m Dot Mae Atkinson

CF8365521   Wayne Edward Morrison

CF8365522   Joyce Faye Morrison

CF836553   Willa Marie Morrison (b 18 Nov 1918) m Francis Hanmore

CF836554   Grace Louise Morrison (b 4 Apr 1921) m Robert Wayne Hartzell

CF8365541   Richard Wayne Hartzell

CF8365542   John Robert Hartzell

CF83656   Franklin Eugene Ewing (b 15 Mar 1891) m 10 Apr 1911, Anna Mary Zuber (b 27 Jul 1891)

CF836561   Grayce Louelle Ewing (b 17 Jan 1912) m 1 Apr 1933, Edwin Wilson Henderson (b 19 Aug 1905)

CF836562   Gene Marie Ewing (b 21 Feb 1918) m Willard Woodrow Beach (b 30 May 1915)

CF8365621   Georgia Ann Beach (b 22 Jun 1944)

CF836563   George Thomas Ewing (b 8 Nov 1920) m 7 Jun 1948, Erie Elizabeth Smith (b 17 Nov 1922)

CF83657   Annie Elizabeth Ewing (b 1893) m 28 Mar 1923, Edwin Aggers

CF836571   Margaret Louise Aggers (b 1926) m 1947, Thomas Robinson

CF8365711   John Robinson (b 1947)

CF8365712   Thomas Robinson (b 1951)

CF8365713   Janet Robinson (b 1957)

CF836572   Donald Edwin Aggers (b 1928)

CF836573   Dale Robert Aggers (b 1930) m 1951, Avanella Sweeney

CF8365731   Robert Aggers (b 1954)

CF8365732   Debra Lynn Aggers (b 1957)

CF83658   Jennie Violet Ewing (b 22 Apr 1895) m 15 Oct 1917, Carl J. Hartmann (d 24 Jan 1919). She, RN, Passavant Hospital, Pittsburgh PA; he, tinner, roofer and bookkeeper.

CF836581   Charles Jacob Hartman (8 Sep 1918-4 Jan 1958) m Oct 1937, Jane Smith

CF8365811   Katherine Lee Hartman (b 29 Feb 1940)

CF8366   Elmer E. Ellsworth Kahle (3 Feb 1862, Sigel PA-20 Aug 1942) m 24 Dec 1889, Brookville PA, Amanda Wolf (b 1868, Armstrong Co PA)

CF83661   Lionel Wayne Kahle (21 Nov 18901-15 Mar 1892)

CF83662   Oren Edmund Kahle (28 Jan 1893-20 Oct 1918). WWI.

CF83663   Mary Elizabeth Kahle (26 Apr 1895-20 Dec 1942) m Jun 1916, Wayne Smith

CF836631   Mary Elizabeth Smith (b 6 Dec 1921) m John H. Bastic

CF83664   Arthur Pearl Kahle (1 Mar 1897-13 Sep 1902)

CF83665   Melvina Lucinda Kahle (b 2 Aug 1904) m Howard P. Potts

CF836651   Patrick Howard Potts (b 13 Nov 1931)

CF836652   Kay Lee Potts (b 4 Feb 1934)

CF83666   Edith Elaine Kahle (b 17 Mar 1915) m 13 May 1935, Egil M. Jensen

CF836661   Patricia Elaine Jensen (b 29 Feb 1940)

CF836662   Linda Ann Jensen (b 1 Feb 1943)

CF8367   Maggie Narcissa Kahle (28 Mar 1864-31 Jul 1865). Bur Kahletown PA.

CF8368   Lillian Catherine Kahle (14 Sep 1866-2 Dec 1908) m 14 Nov 1892, Francis James Rusk
(8 Feb 1865-12 Dec 1943)

CF83681   Irene Beatrice Rusk (b 30 Aug 1893) m 1) 14 Sep 1911, Paul James Smith, div; m 2) 18
Jun 1938, John E. Mitchell

CF836811   Kathryn Margaret Smith (b 6 Jan 1913) m 1) 4 Jun 1930, William H. Codrick (d WWII);
m 2) 16 Oct 1948, Louis S. Brochetti

CF8368111   Joanne Irene Codrick (b 26 Dec 1933) m. 26 Aug 1949, Gilbert Olds

CF83681111   Sharon Kathryn Olds (b 31 Mar 1957)

CF8368112   Louis S. Brochetti, Jr. (b 26 Jan 1949, Ft. Lauderdale FL)

CF836812   Madge Lucille Smith (b 29 May 1917) m 1) 9 Nov 1933, Armand H. Kirouac (d 21 Apr
1955); m 2) 21 Jun 1955, Earl Schultz. Both men, USN.

CF83682   Ethel Marie Rusk (b 5 Apr 1895) m Fred Lutz (b 12 Feb 1892)

CF836821   Harold Francis Lutz (b 26 Apr 1918) m Helen Hamilton (b 1 Jun 1920)

CF8368211   Harold Francis Lutz (b 11 Sep 1945)

CF836822   Betty Jean Lutz (b 1 Jun 1922) m 1941, Gene Dobson (b 1920)

CF8368221   Wayne Dobson (b 1943)

CF8368222   Donna Dobson (b 1948)

CF8368223   Timmy Dobson (b 1950)

CF836823   Peggy Louise Lutz (b 1 Feb 1929) m 17 Jan 1957, Norman Jansik (b 25 Dec 1929)

CF83683   Lillian Kathleen Rusk (b 1 Mar 1897, Heidelberg PA) m 11 May 1939, Rupert Alvin Jenkins (b 15 Aug 1897, McDonald PA)

CF836831   Gordon James Jenkins (b 19 Dec 1919, McDonald PA) m 6 Oct 1942, Marjory Barns Shelton (b 19 Oct 1923, Madison NC)

CF8368311   Ronald Gordon Jenkins (b 2 Jul 1943, Greensboro NC)

CF8368312   Jamie Alton Jenkins (b 17 Feb 1945, Reidsville NC)

CF8368313   Adonna Faye Jenkins (b 17 Oct 1945, Greensboro NC)

CF8368314   Sandra Kaye Jenkins (b 21 Oct 1952, Greensboro NC)

CF83684   Helen Lucille Rusk (b 22 Aug 1898, Heidelberg PA) m 31 Oct 1922, Marshall Craig

CF836841   Virginia Marie Craig (b 23 Oct 1918, McDonald PA) m Anthony John Mentz (b 10 Aug 1918, Oakdale PA)

CF8368411   David Anthony Mentz (b 4 Nov 1946, Oakdale PA)

CF8368412   Nancy Marie Mentz (b 9 May 1952, Oakdale PA)

CF836842   Thomas Marshall Craig (b 29 Nov 1923, McDonald PA) m Betty May Robinson (b 28 Apr 1925)

CF8368421   Marsha Ellen Craig (b 5 Sep 1950, McDonald PA)

CF8368422   Shannon Dale Craig (b 3 Dec 1954, McDonald PA)

CF836843   Mary Lou Craig (b 2 Jan 1924, McDonald PA) m   Garret

CF8368431   Thomas Marshall Garret (b 27 Mar 1949, McDonald PA)

CF8368432   Charlotte Helen Garret (b 3 Dec 1955, McDonald PA)

CF8368433   Charles Garret (b 13 Jan 1957, McDonald PA)

CF836844   Jack DeForest Craig (26 Dec 1926-15 Oct 1951)

CF8368441   John DeForest Craig (b 16 Dec 1948, Oakdale PA)

CF8369   George Calvin Reeser Kahle (22 Sep 1868-9 Feb 1930) m 7 May 1895, Nancy Wolford (11 Nov 1873-14 May 1970)

CF83691   Son Kahle (22 Feb 1896-22 Feb 1896)

CF83692   Phalla Blossom Kahle (21 Feb 1897-29 Oct 1913)

CF83693   Madge Evelyn Kahle (b 4 Mar 1899) m 1) 5 Aug 1919, Guy W. Hetrick; m 2) 20 Dec 1958, James Patrick Winslow

CF836931   Marilyn Kay Hetrick (b 1 Sep 1927) m 20 May 1948, Lee G. Detar, Jr.

CF8369311   Pamela Kay Detar (b 26 Jun 1955)

CF8369312   Jill Nancy Detar (b 11 Jul 1958)

CF83694   Azia Lenore Kahle (19 Nov 1901-16 Feb 1954) m 1 Jun 1927, Walter K. Heeter.

CF83695   Keith Karolyn Kahle (b 21 Mar 1906) m 20 Mar 1931, James Gleason Wheeler

CF836951   Nola Keith Wheeler (b 26 Mar 1932, Pittsburgh PA) m 15 Jul 1950, Theodore McKim

CF8369511   Kenneth Michael McKim (b 2 Mar 1953)

CF8369512   Dana Lyn McKim (b 17 Jul 1955)

CF8369513   Victoria Keith McKim (b 19 Aug 1957)

CF83696   Erle Wolfod Kahle (b 13 Jul 1913) m 17 Oct 1937, Ensie Jane Chesnut

CF836961   Dennis Erle Kahle (b 30 May 1944)

CF836962   James Walter Kahle (b 10 Feb 1948)

CF836A   Washington Klemer Kahle (28 Jun 1871-4 May 1955) m 1897, Lizzie Heft

CF836A1   Edger Milton Kahle (25 Oct 1898-25 Oct 1898)

CF836A2   Claude Winston Kahle (5 Sep 1900-29 Mar 1919)

CF836A3   Wendell Malcolm Kahle m 15 Sep 1937, Ethel Offerlee (b 28 Sep 1904)

CF836A31   Joan Eloise Kahle (b 13 Nov 1938) m 2 Nov 1957, Donald Scott Himes (b 10 Oct 1937)

CF836A311   Michael Scott Himes (b 17 Mar 1959)

CF836A32   James Sherman Kahle (b 1 Oct 1946)

CF836A4   Leila Fay Kahle (b 20 Apr 1904) m 15 Sep 1923, James Lucas (b 12 Jul 1901)

CF836A41   Margaret Jane Lucas (b 21 Jun 1924) m 16 Mar 1942, Charles F. Stillings (b 24 Jul 1921)

CF836A411   Dorothy Jane Stillings (b 20 Oct 1942)

CF836A412   Charles Robert Stillings (b 28 Mar 1944)

CF836A42   Jennette Irene Lucas (b 29 Jan 1928) m 20 Apr 1946, Jack E. Dailey (b 24 Feb 1925)

CF836A421   James Theron Dailey (b 13 Nov 1946)

CF836A422   Jane Elaine Dailey (b 4 Dec 1954)

CF836A43   Mary Ann Lucas (b 30 Apr 1933) m 13 Oct 1956, Richard Frederick Gustafson (b 13 Jun
1933)

CF836A5   Belva Lee Kahle (b 26 Oct 1905) m 1) Joseph W. Wood; m 2) Jul 1933, Glenn Howard
Patch (b 7 Aug 1905)

CF836A51   Helen Lee Wood (b 31 Mar 1925) m Cecil Howles (7 Feb 1921)

CF836A511   David Lewis Howles (b 21 Oct 1946)

CF836A512   Douglas Lee Howles (b 2 May 1949)

CF836A513   Diana Lynn Howles (b 9 Jun 1951)

CF836B   Arthur Lauren Kahle (13 Oct 1874-5 Nov 1942) m 1) 11 Sep 1901, Mura Pearsall (see CF83624); m 2) 1 May 1906, Elsie May Aharrah (19 May 1884-29 Sep 1976. Bur Eldred Tp, Jefferson Co PA.

CF836B1   Howard Jay Kahle (b 5 Feb 1907) m 21 Nov 1932, Winifred Geer (b 7 Jan 1912)

CF836B11   Elsie Emma Kahle (b 8 Mar 1934) m 1) 11 May 1950, George Mark Delgrasso; m 2) 14 Oct 1955, Norman Samuel Smith

CF836B111   George Mark DelGrasso (b 1 Aug 1950)

CF836B112   Donald Robert Smith (b 16 Apr 1956)

CF836B12   Donald Howard Kahle (b 17 Nov 1935) m Donna Breland

CF836B13   Laurence Arthur Kahle (b 14 Mar 1938) m Apr 1958, Claudette Weisse

CF836B14   Ruth Marie Kahle (b 4 Sep 1939) m 11 Aug 1957, Donald Wayne Scott

CF836B141   Donna Marie Scott (b 14 Feb 1958)

CF836B2   Paul Frederick Kahle (27 Jan 1911-12 Oct 1976, Guam) m 1) 4 Jul 1930, Alice Edgerton (b 25 Oct 1915); m 2) 25 Nov 1953, Guadalupe Lizama

CF836B21   Carolyn Alice Kahle (b 31 Jan 1932) m 28 Jun 1953, Ott Howard Davis (b 22 May 1931)

CF836B211   Richard Ott Davis (b 28 Jun 1960)

CF836B3   Wayne Kahle (24 Jul 1910-25 Mar 1930). Bur Eldred Tp, Jefferson Co PA.

CF836B4   Lauren Chester Kahle (11 Aug 1916, Sigel PA-5 Mar 1958, Huntington WV) m 10 May 1942, Beulah Ferguson

CF836B41   Lauren Edwin Kahle (b 3 Jun 1943)

CF836B42   Kathcrine Jeanette Kahle (b 28 Dec 1953)

CF836C   Winifred Arda Kahle (31 Aug 1876-24 Jan 1939) m 12 Nov 1895, Charles Albert Goble (22 Feb 1875-15 Nov 1939)

*CF836C1   Muriel Mae Goble (9 Feb 1896-1995, Greenville PA) m 23 Feb 1918, Floyd Raymond Harbison (3 May 1893-8 Apr 1954). Westinghouse Service

CF836C11   Hobert Goble Harbison (16 Feb 1919-29 Mar 1927)

CF836C12   Phyllis Maxine Harbison (b 29 Oct 1920) m 13 May 1944, James Gunther Martin (b 6 Jan 1920). Commercial artist.

CF836C121   Randy Floyd Martin (b 29 May 1945)

CF836C122   James Harbison Martin (b 25 Nov 1947)

CF836C123   Dan Bradley Martin (b 21 Jun 1951)

CF836C124   Lori Kay Martin (b 21 Jul 1957)

CF836C13   Winnie Aleene Harbison (b 14 Aug 1923) m 29 Jan 1948, William Norman Adams (b 15 Aug 1923). Hardware salesman.

CF836C131   Larry Dean Adams (b 18 Dec 1950)

CF836C132   William Dale Adams (b 7 Nov 1955)

CF836C133   Sidney Gay Adams (b 25 Sep 1958)

CF836C14   Martha Graham Harbison (b 14 Nov 1924) m 8 Dec 1944, Paul Brown (b 7 Oct 1921). Westinghouse mgr in sales.

CF836C141   Geoffery Gordon Brown (b 20 May 1945)

CF836C15   Gordon Charl Harbison (14 Aug 1928-19 Sep 1956) m 23 Feb 1952, Frances Mary Monahan (b 27 Dec 1927)

CF836C151   Gordon Floyd Harbison (b 4 Sep 1952)

CF836C2   Winifred Priscilla Goble (b 6 Sep 1897) m 4 Sep 1919, Elisha William Ripple (13 Mar 1896-Feb 1926). Laborer, gas and oil field.

CF836C21   Elisha Ripple, Jr. (13 Jun 1920-Feb 1926)

CF836C22   Elizabeth Arda Ripple (b 3 Mar 1922) m 10 Jul 1943, James Allen Cannon (b 9 Oct 1922)

CF836C23   Albert LeRoy Ripple (b 7 Oct 1925) m 31 Mar 1949, Margaret Ellen Dunmire (b 10 Jul 1926). Laborer, gas and oil field.

CF836C231   William Glenn Ripple (b 24 Jun 1951)

CF836C232   Albert LeRoy Ripple (b 10 Jul 1954)

CF836C233   Charlie Edward Ripple (b 3 Apr 1956)

CF836C24   Ruth Cleone Ripple (b 12 May 1927) m 2 Jan 1947, Bud McGregor (b 28 Jul 1925)

CF836C241   Rickey Allen McGregor (b 17 Sep 1947)

CF836C242   Vickey Ellen McGregor (b 2 Sep 1953)

CF836C25
Plumber.   Donald Goble Ripple (b 28 Jan 1929) m 5 Mar 1949, Ruth Sheafnocker (b 9 Aug 1928).

CF836C251   Ronald Dee Ripple (b 19 Dec 1949)

CF836C252   Debra Ann Ripple (b 19 Jun 1951)

CF836C253   Kelly Jane Ripple (b 7 Jan 1957)

CF836C3   Floyd Charles Goble (b 20 Nov 1899) m Feb 1924, Hazel Shobert (b 13 Jan 1903). Gas
driller.

CF836C31   Muriel Elaine Goble (b 23 May 1925) m 30 Jul 1948, Charles Clinton Pratt (b 24 Aug
1922)

CF836C311   Melanie Diane Pratt (b 24 Feb 1949)

CF836C312   Jeffrey Clinton Pratt (b 14 Apr 1951) m 16 Aug 1975, Kathi Reid

CF836C313   Steven Charles Pratt (b 27 Jul 1954)

*CF836C4   Elizabeth Sylvia Goble (b 6 Jan 1907) m 1) 29 Jan 1927, Max Weldon Frost (19 Feb
1907-10 Mar 1958); m 2) Rudolph Weitzel (d 4 Jul 1982). She and Weitzel, podiatrist.

CF836C41   Billie Mae Frost (b 14 Oct 1928) m Sep 1950, Ernest Squitter (b 12 Apr 1923). Salesman,
tire co.

CF836C411   Mark Douglas Squitter (b 10 May 1951)

CF836C412   Shawn Rennee Squitter (b 12 Jun 1952)

CF836C413   Judd Eric Squitter (b 28 Jan 1955)

CF836C42   Weldon Goble Frost (b 28 Jan 1931). Geologist.

CF836C5   Nellie Violet Goble (b 31 Oct 1910) m 23 Oct 1938, Vincent Race (b 29 Aug 1902).
Contractor.

CF836C51   Rosalind Ann Race (b 23 Jul 1943)

CF836C6   Joe Kahle Goble (b 24 Nov 1912) m Hattie Curran. Driller, gas wells.

CF836C61   Joan Goble (b 26 Dec 1933) m 27 Apr 1953, Harold Tetrick (b 4 Feb 1929). USMC.

CF836C611   Terry Tetrick (b 26 Feb 1954)

CF836C612   Kelly Kay Tetrick (b 3 Aug 1955)

CF836C62   Betty Kay Goble (b 25 Sep 1935)

CF837   Hensen G. Kahle (30 Mar 1827-d.y.)

CF838   Perry J. Kahle (11 May 1829-25 Jun 1907) m Ellen B. Thompson (21 Sep 1834, Clearfield
City PA-16 Aug 1902). Bur Kahletown PA.

CF8381   John Wesley Kahle (8 Jun 1854-29 Jun 1925) m Margaret E. Martin (1852-1925)

CF83811   Alvin N. Kahle (26 Sep 1879-27 Apr 1903). Bur Kahletown PA.

CF83812   Leota Ellen Kahle (5 Jan 1882, Sigel PA-26 Apr 1943, Sheffield PA) m Thomas Harrson
Jefferson (11 Feb 1879, Lake City PA-4 Sep 1953, Sheffield PA. Bur Sheffield PA.

CF838121   Freda Jefferson

CF838122   Minnie Jefferson

CF838 Perry J. Kahle (1829-1907)

CF838123   Edith Jefferson

CF838124   Claire Jefferson

CF838125   Howard Jefferson (d)

CF838126   Tom Jefferson (d)

CF838127   Pearl Almeda Jefferson (30 Dec 1912, Loleta PA-6 Jun 1972, Warren PA) m 15 Jun 1933, Frewsbury NY, Charles Frederick Edwards (26 Dec 1907, Emporium PA-14 Feb 1971, Warren PA). Bur Warren PA.

CF8381271   Carol Louise Edwards (b 2 Jul 1939, Sheffield PA) m 25 Jul 1959, Theodore Leroy Snyder (b 6 Oct 1937)

CF838128   Shorty Jefferson

CF83813   W. Wade Kahle (1884-1943) m Emma McCall (1897-1952). Bur Kahletown PA.

CF838131   Lois Kahle m   Gross

CF838132   Margaret Kahle m Ken Alt

CF838133   Elmerdeen Kahle m Bob Glosser

CF838134   Neil Kahle

CF83814   Frank P. Kahle (2 Jun 1890, Eldred Tp, Jefferson Co PA-4 Feb 1896, Eldred Tp, Jefferson Co PA). Bur Kahletown PA.

CF83815   Nettie Kahle m Dwight Orcutt

CF838151   Everett Orcutt

CF838152   Lee Orcutt

CF838153   Donald Orcutt

CF838154   Emery Orcutt

CF838155   Margaret Orcutt

CF83816   Don Kahle m Aleine Hulings

CF838161   Ruth Kahle

CF838162   Pauline Kahle

CF838163   John Vernon Kahle

CF838164   Maxine Kahle

CF838165   Don Kahle, Jr.

CF8382   Narcissa Florence Kahle (9 Jul 1856-30 Nov 1937) Winfield Pearsole. Clergyman.

CF83821   Winnie Pearsole (d) m Ralph Jack

CF83822   Harley Pearsole m Carrie

CF838221   Clarence Pearsole

CF838222   Emma Pearsole

CF838223   John Pearsole

CF838224   Harold Pearsole

CF838225   Mary Pearsole

CF83823   Effie Pearsole m Walter Riggs

CF838231   Annabelle Riggs m   Vandermont

CF8382311 Patricia Vandermont

CF83824   A. Myra Pearsole m. Arthur Kahle (see CF836B)

CF8383   Mary Ellen Kahle (7 Apr 1858-1924) m 1887, Charles H. Shawkey (b 1858, Venango Co
PA)

CF83831   Minnie A. Shawkey m Harry Matson

CF83832   H. Dallas Shawkey m Pauline

CF838321   John Shawkey

CF838322   Adam Shawkey

CF838323   Mary Shawkey

CF838324   Rita Shawkey

CF83833   Merle Shawkey m Nora McQuiston

CF838331   Clinton Shawkey

CF83834   Blanche Shawkey m William Garmany

CF83835   Edna Shawkey

CF83836   Zula Shawkey m Lewis Shoffer

CF8384   Catharine Elizabeth Kahle (1859-d.y.)

CF8385   Emma Jane Kahle (30 Dec 1860-d.y.)

CF8386   Wilbur Perry Kahle (21 Apr 1861-Oct 1933) m Myrtle Carroll. He bur Kahletown PA;
she bur Pittsburgh PA.

CF83861 Lillian Clare Kahle (14 Apr 1884, Sigel PA-26 Jun 1984, New Bethlehem PA) m 3 Sep 1901, Robert W. English (6 Oct 1880, Sigel PA-10 Nov 1976, New Bethlehem PA). Bur New Bethlehem PA.

CF838611 Claud B. English

CF838612 Loyall Pitts English (d 1958)

CF838613 Helen English m Paul Shaffer

CF838614 Ruth English m Philip Keirn

CF83862 George Carroll Kahle (b 10 Dec 1888) m Coral Noble (d 10 Apr 1963, Ahsville NY)

CF838621 Clarence Glade Kahle (b 14 Sep 1907) m Carla Lucille Johnston

CF8386211 Mary Sue Kahle (b 13 Nov 1944)

CF838622 Banks LeRoy Kahle (b 31 Mar 1909) m 1) ; m 2) Louise Goddard

CF8386221 Sheila Justine Kahle (b 17 Apr 1940)

CF8386222 Brian Banks Kahle (b 18 Apr 1945)

CF8386223 Ronald Eugene Kahle (b 26 Sep 1950)

CF8386224 Onalee Kahle (b 18 Apr 1955)

CF838623 Richard William Kahle (b 17 Jun 1914) m Maryon Hegstedt

CF8386231 Richard Noble Kahle (b 20 Sep 1934) m Shirly Timblin

CF83862311 Vicki Jean Kahle (b 9 Oct 1954)

CF83862312 Michael Jo Kahle (b 13 Aug 1956)

CF83862313 Julliann Kahle (12 Jun 1958)

CF83863 Dale W. Kahle (b 1891) m Olive Hidey. WWI. No chn.

CF83864 Noble Watson Kahle (24 Nov 1892-1916) m Edna Cannan. He bur Kahletown PA.

CF838641 Everett Kahle

CF838642 Harry Kahle

CF838643 Ruth Kahle

CF83865 Frederick Clarence Kahle (b 1892) m Pearl Lerch

CF838651 Arthur Kahle

CF838652 Kenneth Kahle

CF83866 Lyla Kahle (24 Aug 1898-1971) m 1) Hiram Newton; m 2) William Ogilvie; m 3) H. Johnson

CF838661   Beatrice Newton m Burdett Clarence Julian

CF8386611   Bruce Clarence Julian (b 4 Mar 1944, Jamestown NY)

CF8386612   Linda Carroll Julian (b 1 May 1945, Abilene TX)

CF8386613   Beth Elaine Julian (b 11 Dec 1949, Jamestown NY)

CF83867   Twila Belle Kahle (b 1 Sep 1900) m Albin Anderson

CF838671   Larue Anderson

CF838672   Marylin Anderson

CF838673   Harrison Anderson

CF83868   Harrison Kahle (1909-1910)

CF8387   Franklin Edgar Kahle (20 Aug 1864, Sigel PA-1944) m 17 Dec 1887, Brookville PA,
Elizabeth Stover (1862, Venango Co PA-1953). Bur Kahletown PA.

CF83871   Florence Kahle m E. Reep

CF838711   Marie Kahle

CF838712   Mildred Kahle

CF838713   Floyd Kahle

CF83872   Beulah Kahle m H. Castner

CF838721   Esther Castner

CF838722   Dorothy Castner

CF838723   Thelma Castner

CF83873   Mervin E. Kahle (1892-1916). Bur Kahletown PA.

CF83874   Otis Kahle (d)

CF83875   Rena Kahle (13 Aug 1897, Hallton PA-17 Jan 1981, Warren PA) m R. Barber. She bur
Kahletown PA.

CF838751   Lorraine Barber m Richard McHenry

CF838752   Eleanor Barber

CF83876   Mary M. Kahle m E. Bowen

CF838761   Dallas Bowen

CF838762   Everett Bowen

CF838763   David Bowen

CF838764   Earl Bowen

CF838765   William Bowen

CF838766   Arthur Bowen

CF838767   Harry Bowen

CF83877   Alma Kahle (b 1901)

CF83878   James Kahle (1904-1904). Bur Kahletown PA.

CF83879   Norman Kahle (1905-1961). Bur Kahletown PA.

CF8387A   North Erie Kahle (3 Apr 1909-25 Sep 1985)

CF8388   James Warren Kahle (24 Mar 1866-1950) m Arminta Cook (1863-1909). Bur Kahletown
PA.

CF83881   Vinnie Kahle m George Thomas

CF83882   Blanch Kahle m Arden McKindree

CF838821   Lee McKindree

CF838822   Delbert McKindree

CF838823   Teddy McKindree

CF83883   Cora Kahle (23 Aug 1892, Redcliff PA-20 Jun 1965, Marienville PA) m 3 Jul 1916,
Tionesta PA, John Chesterfield Kifer (4 Dec 1886, Guilfoyle PA-12 Sep 1985). Bur Marienville PA.

CF838831   Edith Rose Kifer (b 17 Apr 1917, Butler PA) m 10 Feb 1940, Charles Cunningham (27
Jun 1911-7 Mar 1977). Bur Oakdale CA. WWII; worked on Hanford plutonium project, Richland WA.
Construction and grocer, Oakdale CA.

CF8388311   James Hayes Cunningham (b 31 Jan 1947) m 1973 Sandra (Gunther) Smith (b 25 Jun
1946)

                  Pat Smith (b 3 Mar 1966)

                  Tiffany Smith (b 7 Mar 1970)

                  Larry Smith (b 12 Dec 1971)

CF83883111   Derrick Allen Cunningham (b 27 Aug 1975)

CF8388312   Donna Charleen Cunningham (b 15 Oct 1949) m 26 Nov 1977, Robert Cameron (b 1 Jun
1946), div 1989

CF8388313   Maxine Lynn Cunningham (b 22 Nov 1951) m 10 Jan 1973, Richard Jewell (b 14 Aug
1951). Vietnam Conflict; USA.

CF83883131   Toni Leann Jewell (b 30 Jul 1969) m Marc Joseph

CF838831311   Raymon Anthony Joseph (b 27 Jul 1986)

CF838831312   Devin Richard Joseph (b 17 Sep 1990)

CF838831313   Lindsay Joseph (b 1995)

CF83883132   Ryan Owen Jewell (b 24 Jul 1974) m Prisalla   . USA, 82nd Airborne.

CF838831321   Ty Owen Jewell (b 2 Apr 1995)

CF83883133   Scott Harley Jewell (b 25 Jul 1980)

CF8388314   Florina Lou Ann Cunningham (b 18 Jan 1955) m 16 Jun 1973, Gerald Walter Taylor (b 12 Feb 1955). USAF.

CF83883141   Christine Lou Ann Taylor (b 9 Jan 1974) m Jinno Magno

CF83883142   Jinno Antonia Magno (b 1989, Iceland)

CF83883143   Joseph Cristiano Magno (b 30 Oct 1994)

CF838832   Raymond Chesterfield Kifer (b 23 Sep 1919, Tionesta PA) m 26 Jun 1946, Butler PA, Lilly Jane Hindman (b 24 Jul 9123). WWII, USA medics corps. Insurance salesman, Butler PA.

CF8388321   David Chesterfield Kifer (6 Sep 1947, Butler PA). Viet Nam Conflict, USA.

CF8388322   Thomas Ira Kifer (b 18 Feb 1951, Butler PA)

CF8388323   Esther Ellen Kifer (b 2 Apr 1954, Butler PA) m 27 Sep 1975, Barry Lane Street (b 26 Nov 1953)

CF83883231   Benjamin Wayne Street (b 13 Sep 1977)

CF83883232   Rachel Jane Street (b 10 Aug 1983)

CF83883233   Jonathan Raymond Street (b 6 May 1985)

CF838833   Kenneth Wesner Kifer (b 27 Dec 1920, Kane PA) m 30 Jun 1947, Rosalie Ann Secino (b 10 Dec 1922, Fitchburg MA). WWII, USN. Production engineer, Fitchburg MA.

CF8388331   Kenneth Daniel Kifer (b 24 Apr 1951, Fitchburg MA) m 22 Jul 1972, Deborah June Hines (b 25 Sep 1952)

CF83883311   Jennifer Leigh Kifer (b 2 Mar 1973, Concord MA)

CF83883312   Adam Kenneth Kifer (b 29 Oct 1977, Concord MA)

CF83883313   Stephanie Corinne Kifer (b 4 Jan 1980, Concord MA)

CF8388332   John Chesterfield Kifer (b 7 Jul 1953, Fitchburg MA) m 1) 30 May 1976, Joyce Hachey (b 19 Mar 1956), div 1979; m 2) 3 Oct 1981, Darlene Minnis Duval (b 1 Jun 1953)

                Randy Duval (b 26 Dec 1970, Fitchburg MA)

                Jason Duval (b 12 Mar 1973, Fitchburg MA)

                Neisha Duval (b 16 Mar 1979, Fitchburg MA)(assumed Kifer surname)

CF83883321   Tracy Ann Kifer (b 4 Jun 1982, Greenville SC)

CF3838333   Robert Steven Kifer (b 2 Jan 1962, Fitchburg MA) m 27 Jun 1987, Leslye Karen DeVeau (b 14 May 1965, Havervhill MA)

CF838834   Floyd Richard Kifer (b 20 Jan 1923, Kane PA) m 8 Sep 1941, KY, Virginia Lee Moser (b 15 Jul 1923, WV). WWII, USN. Steelworker, Sharon PA.

CF8388341   Bonnie Lee Kifer (b 22 Jun 1942, Butler PA) m Rev. George Jones (b 25 Sep 1940)

CF83883411   Dawn Elizabeth Jones (b 19 Feb 1960) m 22 Aug 1981, Michael McMicken (b 13 Apr 1960)

CF838834111   Benjamin McMicken

CF838834112   Jonathan McMicken (b Jan 1988)

CF838834113   Christopher Layne McMicken (b 8 Nov 1989)

CF83883412   Douglas Todd Jones (b 2 Jun 1961) m 16 Jul 1983, Julie Lynn Wilton (b 25 Oct 1960)

CF838834121   Douglas Todd Jones, Jr. (b 3 Jan 1984)

CF838834122   Jessica Lee Jones (b 6 Apr 1985)

CF83883413   Timothy Brett Jones (b 23 Jul 1963) m 28 Jul 1984, Anna Elizabeth Savelle (b 11 Feb 1965)

CF838834131   Sarah Elizabeth Jones (b 8 Dec 1992)

CF83883414   Christopher Ladd Jones (b 4 Jun 1965)

CF83883415   Peter Matthew Jones (b 19 Arp 1969, Cuba NY)

CF83883416   Jennifer Lee Jones (b 17 Apr 1971) m 1)   Wix, div; m 2) 20 Mar 1993, Michael David Schiltz, div; m 3) 1995,

CF838835   Lois Adelia Kifer (b 19 Sep 1927, Kane PA) m 6 Jun 1964, Butler PA, Charles Aharrah, Jr. (b 1930, Sigel PA)

CF8389   George Haskill Kahle (25 Dec 1867-15 Jul 1891) m Elizabeth Confer (1868-1891). Bur
Kahletown PA.

CF83891   Harry Kahle

CF838911   Glen Kahle

CF838912   Grace Kahle

CF838913   Helen Kahle

CF838A   David Ernest Kahle (14 Jan 1870-1950) m Mary Elizabeth Fox (1870-1943). Bur
Kahletown PA.

CF838A1   Edward Kahle m Elizabeth Tarbox

CF838A11	Eleanor Kahle
CF838A12	Audrey Kahle
CF838A13	Marilyn Kahle
CF838A14	Elaine Kahle
CF838A15	Phyllis Kahle
CF838A2	Albert Kahle m Madge Raught
CF838A3	Merle F. Kahle (1900-1966) m Clair Anthony (b 1900)(see CF838C2). Bur Kahletown PA.
CF838A31	Mildred Kahle m Donald Bobbet
CF838A311	Jimmie Bobbet
CF838A32	Ray Kahle
CF838A33	Mervin Kahle
CF838A34	Hazel Kahle
CF838A35	Dorothy Kahle
CF838A4	Lou Kahle m Alice Zipfel
CF838A41	Michael Kahle
CF838A42	Barbara Kahle
CF838A5	William Kahle
CF838A6	Wesley Kahle
CF838A7	Floyd Kahle m Mary Snyder
CF838A71	Richard Kahle
CF838B Kahletown PA.	Sarah Alice Kahle (6 Dec 1871-1946) m 14 Mar 1888, Harry Confer (1866-1944). Bur Kahletown PA.
CF838B1	Ernest Confer
CF838B2	Shelby Confer
CF838B3	Ima Confer (1894-1972) m Clyde Payne (1889-1967). Bur Kahletown PA.
CF838B31	Marie Payne
CF838B32	Robert Payne
CF838B33	Lyle Payne
CF838B34	Rex Payne

CF838B35   Lulu Belle Payne

CF838B36   Georgiana Payne

CF838B37   Pauline Payne

CF838B38   Audrey Payne

CF838B39   Kenneth Payne (d 20 Dec 1944). WWII.

CF838B4   Lulu Confer m Whisner Kierman

CF838B41   Freeman Keirman

CF838C   Frederick Plummer Kahle (20 Nov 1873-Mar 1938) m 20 Feb 1900, Ruby Edna Van Tassell (1 Sep 1884-28 May 1961). Bur Kahletown PA.

CF838C1   Mildred Irene Maze Kahle (born out of wedlock to Frederick Plummer Kahle and Sara Maze (1898-1971) m Allen Woodward (1888-1962)

CF838C11   William Reynolds Woodward (1918-1992). Unm.

CF838C12   Stanley Ellsworth Woodward (1921-1957). Unm.

CF838C13   Allan Woodward (b 1922) m Arloween Steward

CF838C14   Lewanda Eileen Woodward (b 1924) m Frank Crawford

CF838C15   Echo Virginia Wave Woodward (1928-1977) m Lewis Michael Kovach (b 1925)

CF838C151   Lewis Michael Kovach (b 1949). Unm.

CF838C152   Anna Maria Kovach (b 1951) m Michael Tod Crumrine (b 1947)

CF838C1521   Laura Echo Elizabeth Crumrine (b 8 Oct 1990)

CF838C153   Stephen Allen Kovach (b 1957). Unm.

CF838C16   Gerald Laverne Woodward (b 1932) m Georgia Asel

CF838C17   Son Woodward (b 1933)

CF838C2   Lester Vernon Kahle (3 Mar 1901, Sigel PA-26 Feb 1981, Kane PA) m 24 Dec 1921, Esther Johnson. Bur Kane PA.

CF838C21   Louise Kahle m Harold Asp

CF838C22   Ruby Kahle m Richard Dillon

CF838C23   Patty Kahle m James Bostaph

CF838C24   Peggy Kahle m Wayne Phillips

CF838C25   Evelyn Kahle

CF838C3   Esther Emma Kahle (b 23 Sep 1902-15 Nov 1903). Bur Kahletown PA.

CF838C4   James Doyle Kahle (5 Nov 1904-5 Mar 1905). Bur Kahletown PA.

CF838C5   Daughter Kahle (25 May 1906-29 May 1906). Bur Kahletown PA.

CF838C6   Ivan F. Kahle (d 26 Jun 1908). Bur Kahletown PA.

CF838C7   Iva F. Kahle (d 26 Jun 1908). Bur Kahletown PA.

CF838C8   Raymond Kahle m 3 Dec 1938, Estella E. Clyde (30 Sep 1914, Halltown PA-12 Oct 1981,
Marienville PA)

CF838C81   Doris Kahle m Robert Zierden

CF838C82   Carol Kahle m Douglas Lambert

CF838C83   Donna Kahle m Edward Hedke

CF838C84   Grace Kahle m William Post

CF838C85   Jean Kahle m Jerry Cast

CF838C86   Deborah Kahle m James Morgan

CF838C9   Bertha Evelyn Kahle (b 1918)

CF838CA   Russell Leroy Kahle (b 1920) m Marie Walley

CF838CB   Grace Aletha Kahle (9 Mar 1921, Marienville PA 13 Aug 1982, Wilcox PA) m 1942,
Joseph Zimmerman (d 1970). She bur Holy Cross Cem, Rasselas PA.

CF838CB1   Richard Zimmerman

CF838CB2   Judy Zimmerman m Robert Wurm

CF838CC   Dorothy Ruby Kahle (1911-1932) m Clair Anthony (see CF838A3)

CF838CD   Sherman Dallas Kahle (1917-1980) m Betty Jean Edwards

CF838CE   Richard Jean Kahle (1923-1946). Unm.

CF838CF   Robert Dean Kahle (1923-1927)

CF838CG   Hazel Geraldine Kahle

CF838D   Eva Lottie Kahle (b 9 Aug 1875)

CF838E   Louise Candess Kahle (b 10 Feb 1878) m Alexander Irwin

CF838E1   Fred Irwin

CF838E2   Orpha Irwin m Fred Hinnesy

CF838E3   Florence Irwin

CF838E4   Claude Irwin

CF838E5   Howard Irwin

CF838E6   Lulu Irwin

CF838E7   Dessie Irwin (d) m Clifford Decker

CF838E8   Alma Irwin m   Grunden

CF838E9   Wilma Irwin m   Van Cook

CF838EA   Sherman Irwin

CF839   David R. Kahle (6 Mar 1832, Clarion Co PA-18 Jul 1904, Sigel PA) m Catherine Elizabeth
Thompson (13 Mar 1840-25 Nov 1927). Bur Kahletown PA.

CF8391   Ella Verna Kahle (1874-1935) m Edward R. Alford (1872-1960). Bur Kahletown PA.

CF83921   Roland Alford

CF8392   Nettie Maple Kahle (b 1874) m George W. Procious

CF8393   Lulu Maude Kahle (b 1878) m Mark McClelland

CF83A   Almeda Kahle (b 1832)

CF83B   Heiskell Kahle (b 1834)

CF83C   Margaret Kahle m John Kahle

CF83D   Grace Kahle

CF83E   Edna Kahle (d.y.)

CF83F   Claude Kahle (d.y.)

CF84   Jacob Weiser Kehl

CF84   Jacob Weiser Kehl was born 10 Mar 1799 in Heidelberg Tp, Berks Co, and baptized
shortly thereafter with Jacob and Maria Lechner as sponsors. On 10 Dec 1818 he moved to Huntingdon Co
PA in Warriors Mark Tp. In 1826 he moved to Shippenville, Venango Co, where he lived the remainder of
his life, and died 1 Dec 1875. He married 10 Dec 1818 to Sarah Jane Hyskell (21 Feb 1799-13 Feb 1871).
They are buried at Shippenville PA. The name Weiser does not occur in his baptismal record. He was an
associate judge of Clarion Co PA, 1857.

Children of Jacob Weiser and Sarah Jane (Hyskell) Kehl:

CF841   George Hyskell Kahle, 20 Sep 1819

CF842   John Wesley Kahle, 28 Dec 1821

CF843   Mary Ann Kahle, 29 Apr 1825

CF844   Nancy Jane Kahle, 13 Apr 1828

CF845   Wilder Mark Kahle, 28 Jan 1831

Sarah Jane Hyskell (1799-1871) and
CF84 Jacob Weiser Kehl (1799-1875)

CF841 George Hyskell Kahle
(1819-1898)

CF846   Jacob Weiser Kahle, 21 Sep 1832

CF847   Nathaniel Lang Kahle, 18 Jun 1836

CF848   Sarah Catherine Kahle, 11 Feb 1839

CF849   Harriet B. Kahle, 1842

CF84A   Thomas Muhlenberg Kahle, 8 Mar 1843

CF841   George Hyskell Kahle (20 Sep 1819, Warriors Mark Tp, Huntingdon Co PA-13 Apr 1898, Shippenville PA) m 1840, Matilda Shiffer (27 Jan 1823, Union Co PA-10 Jan 1906, Shippenville PA). Bur Strattonville PA. Farmer, collier, teamster, oil business.[84]

CF8411   Sarah Jane Kahle (1841, Shippenville PA-31 Mar 1897) m Jonas Botzer (1848-1916). Bur
Venus PA.

CF84111   William W. Botzer (1873-1931). Bur Venus PA.

CF8412   Levi Wesley Kahle (20 Jul 1842, Shippenville PA-21 Jan 1939, Pine City PA) m Chloe C. Wood (18 Nov 1847-12 May 1899). Bur Pine City PA. Blacksmith, oil business, farmer.

CF84121   Nellie Beryl Kahle (27 Jan 1874-12 May 1899). Unm.

CF84122   Ivan Dana Kahle (8 Aug 1875, Pine City PA-1 Jan 1951, Knox PA) m 11 Dec 1897, Margie R. Boyer. Clarion S Normal Sch; MD, Col of Physicians & Surgeons, Baltimore MD, 1905; physician, Wick WV and Knox PA. Served three terms, PA House, 1926; PA Senate, 1934.

CF841221   Kathleen Kahle (b 29 Jul 1898) m Leland Sheffer

CF8412211   Leah Ruth Sheffer

CF8412212   Naomi Sheffer

CF8412213   Shirley Sheffer

CF841222   Standish Calvert Kahle (b 15 Apr 1903) m Helen Burguin

CF8412221   Rosamond Kahle

CF84123   Levi Norval Kahle (13 Mar 1877-28 Nov 1962) m Aylia Underwood. Physician, Richwood
WV.

CF841231   Wesley Melvin Kahle

CF841232   Marie Kahle

CF841233   Levi Norval Kahle

CF84124   Marie Rosalia Kahle (11 May 1878-17 Dec 1968). Unm.

CF84125   Glenalvan Wood Kahle (8 Feb 1880-1 Aug 1952) m Maude Moore. Oil business,
Lawrenceville IL.

---

[84]Data on Jacob W. Kehl and family submitted by Marlene Carrier, Laura McQuaid and Helen Kahle Kolbe.

CF84126   Harold Hurlburt Kahle (21 Nov 1881-1 Jun 1954) m Lillie Amsler. Physician, Leeper PA.

CF841261   Emily Kahle

CF841262   Mildred Kahle

CF841263   Wesley Kahle

CF841264   Geraldine Kahle

CF84127   Gail Warren Kahle (23 May 1883-12 Mar 1980). Physician, Hadley PA.

CF84128   Alexander Edward Kahle (4 Jun 1885-16 Jan 1951) m Myrtle Kribbs. Merchant, Pine City PA.

CF841281   Infant Kahle

CF841282   Alvin Kahle

CF841283   Wayne Kahle

CF84129   Infant boy Kahle

CF8412A   Infant boy Kahle

CF8413   James Polk Kahle (1 Sep 1844-12 Jun 1929) m Olive Springer (15 Jun 1850-27 Sep 1880). He bur Strattonville PA.

CF84131   Lottie L. Kahle (27 Oct 1870-24 May 1934) m 27 Apr 1898, Lemuel Gilmore Stover (15 Aug 1857-7 Jun 1931)

CF84132   James Homer Kahle (30 Apr 1872-1955) m 1899, Sarah Agnes Dearolph (Jun 1871-18 Jul 1946). Bur Monroe PA.

CF84133   Mary Matilda Kahle (7 Aug 1873-6 Feb 1913) m Artemus F. Huldings (18 Jul 1872-1938). Bur Union City PA.

CF84134   Charles Newton Kahle (7 Aug 1873-27 May 1964) m 5 Oct 1898, Nancy Ida McElrany (2 Oct 1875-22 May 1964). Bur Strattonville PA.

CF8414   Matilda Victoria Kahle (4 May 1846-20 Jul 1846)

CF8415   George Washington Kahl (15 Jul 1847-14 Jul 1896) m Margaret Baker (1854-29 Jan 1930). Bur Shippenville PA.

CF84151   Daisy Pearl Kahl (4 Mar 1875-26 Jul 1894). Bur Shippenville PA.

CF84152   Clyde Kahl

CF84153   Myrtle Kahl

CF84154   Fred Kahl

CF8416   Jacob Weiser Kahle (10 Mar 1849, Shippenville PA-27 Aug 1933, Shippenville PA) m Rosella Reed (8 Apr 1853-29 Aug 1890, Shippenville PA). Bur Milo PA.

Alice Leona Stover (1882-1963) and CF84161 Franklin Howard Kahle (1877-1973) on their wedding day, 3 Jun 1902.

CF84161   Franklin Howard Kahle (16 Feb 1877, Knox PA-13 Oct 1973, Clarion PA) m 3 Jun 1902, Alice Leona Stover (11 Nov 1882, 24 Mar 1963, Shippenville PA). Bur Elmox PA. He, farmer, businessman. She, first female professional photographer in PA.

CF841611   Aliene Rosella Kahle (15 Dec 1902, Elmo, Clarion Co PA-3 Jul 1989, Kittanning PA) m 2 Jan 1922, Guy Edgar Toy (25 Dec 1900, Wnetlings Corners near Knox PA-30 Jun 1970). Bur Knox PA.

CF8416111   Benjamin Wayne Toy (b 23 Sep 1923) m 3 Jul 1944, Janet Lewis Titsler. WWII, USN, Sea Bees. Le Canto FL.

CF84161111   Dennis Wayne Toy (b 1 Nov 1946) m Doneci Dickey

CF841611111   Sean M. Toy

CF841611112   Nicole Louise Toy

CF84161112   Deborah Lynn Toy (b 29 Oct 1949) m 1) Douglas Smith, div; m 2) John Somers

CF841611121   Troy S. Smith

CF841611122   Holly Lynn Smith

CF841611123   John Somers

CF841611124   Curtis J. Somers

CF841611125   Katelin Dee Somers

CF8416112   Martha Jean Toy (b 29 Oct 1925, Knox PA) m 14 Dec 1945, Los Angeles CA, William James Katterhenry (26 Sep 1908, Evansville IN-14 Dec 1985, Kittanning PA). She, Penn DOT; he, barber.

CF84161121   Matilda Louise Katterhenry (b 18 Nov 1946, Los Angeles CA) m 1) 3 Feb 1964, Butler PA, Albert Edmund Morvik (b 27 Aug 1942, Kittanning PA), div; m 2) 2 Feb 1991, Samuel Saloum (b 16 Oct 1941, Kittanning PA). Ford City PA.

CF841611211   Albert Edmun Morvik III (b 20 May 1964, Kittanning PA) m Desiree Mendez. Sales

CF8416112111   Alexandria Lee Morvik (b 5 Apr 1996, Atlanta GA)

CF841611212   William James Morvik (b 10 Jun 1968, Kittanning PA). Unm.

CF8416112121   James Andrew Morvik (b 24 May 1991, Kittanning PA)

CF8416113   Guy Edgar Toy, Jr. (b 30 Jul 1933) m 12 Oct 1957, Shirley Morita McIntire (b 13 Apr 1937). USMC.

CF84161131   Guy Edgar Toy III (b 9 Aug 1962) m 1) 7 May 1983, Michelle Renee Schaeffer, div 1994; m 2) 18 Mar 1995, Joni Lynn Meyers (b 21 Jan 1964)

CF841611311   Cody Adam Toy (b 28 Apr 1988)

CF841611312   Dylan Jacob Toy (b 26 Feb 1991)

CF84161132   Harold McIntire Toy (b 5 Mar 1965) m 19 May 1990, Pamela Joy Troutman (b 23 Jan 1967)

CF841611321   Clayton Harold Toy (b 21 Nov 1993)

CF841612   Cecil Phipps Kahle (11 Dec 1906, Knox PA-2 Mar 1994, Holiday FL) m 1) 9 Sep 1933, Oil City PA, Kathryn Virginia Hughes (29 Dec 1911, Oil City PA-2 Dec 1970, Oil City PA); m 2) 2 Jun 1972, Salina PA, Dorothy Fink McVeigh (b 15 Feb 1909, Oil City PA). Bur Oil City PA. Railroad worker; grape farmer.

CF8416121   Marlene Virginia Kahle (b 30 Dec 1934, Oil City PA) m 21 Nov 1953, Oil City PA, Gary Dane Carrier (b 10 Jun 1934, Kane PA). She, political activist, creator of political memorabilia; mbr, PA Mental Health Brd, 1994- ; past pres PA Counsel of Republican Women. He, truck driver.

CF84161211   Deborah Ann Carrier (b 26 Oct 1954, Oil City PA) m 9 Oct 1976, Mercer PA, Robert Edwin Johnson. She, BA, Thiel Col, 1976; insurance office; he, exec, sanitation co.

CF841612111   Robert Michael Johnson (b 12 Apr 1978, Jeanette PA)

CF841612112   Dana Victor Johnson (b 1 Oct 1980, Greensburg PA)

CF841612113   Benjamin Hughes Johnson (b 6 Sep 1985, Greensburg PA)

CF84161212   Dennis Gary Carrier (b 19 Jun 1957, Oil City PA). Unm. Chef.

CF84161213   Laura Lynn Carrier (b 4 Apr 1961, Grove City PA) m 18 Oct 1986, Steelton PA, Jeffrey Edward McQuaid (b 22 Apr 1956, Harrisburg PA). She, AB, Indiana U of PA; paralegal, children's advocate. He, auditor, Penn Treasury Dept.

CF841612131   Shane Joseph McQuaid (b 28 Oct 1987, Harrisburg PA)

CF841612132   Kayla Marlene McQuaid (b 21 Feb 1992, Harrisburg PA)

CF8416122   Edward Hughes Kahle (b 26 Jul 1942, Oil City PA) m 1) 8 Jan 1965, Linda Mlochowski (b 30 Jun 1944, Buffalo NY), div; m 2) 11 Jul 1970, Mayville NY, Susan VanVolkenburg (b 8 Jun 1952, Mayville NY), div; m 3) 1 Oct 1982, Lucy Appleby Engstrom (b 10 Aug 1938, Waterford PA). USN. Truck dispatcher.

CF84161221   Cynthia Lynn Kahle (b 12 Sep 1965, Westfield NY)

CF84161222   Jeffrey Joseph Kahle (b 28 Feb 1967, Westfield NY)

CF84161221   Kelly Ann Kahle (b 27 Jun 1972, Westfield NY) m Kevin Jackson. She, insurance sales; he, military.

CF84161221   Bryant Matthew Jackson (b 19 Jun 1991, Staunton VA)

CF84161222   Eric Hughes Kahle (b 16 May 1976, Westfield NY)

CF8416123   Kathryn Ann Kahle (b 27 Sep 1951, Oil City PA) m 23 Aug 1971, Ripley NY, Larry Lee McCauley (b 9 Nov 1949, Oil City PA). He, GE engineer.

CF84161231   Christopher Michael McCauley (b 25 Aug 1974, Erie PA). BS, RN.

CF84161232   Mark Edward McCauley (b 11 Apr 1977, Erie PA)

CF84161233   Kenneth Robert McCauley (b 1 Jun 1980, Erie PA)

CF841613   Harriet Aida Kahle (b 8 May 1909, Shippenville PA) m 1) Donaducci, div; m 2) John Perish

CF8416131   Ingles Jane Donaducci (b 17 Jul 1933)(Adopted by John Perish) m 28 Jun 1958, John L. Wertz (b 8 Dec 1930)

CF84161311   Eric Wertz (b 26 Nov 1960)

CF84161312   Lisa Wertz (b 6 Sep 1963)

CF84161313   Mark Wertz (b 18 Oct 1964)

CF8416132   Shirley Ann Donaducci (b 2 Nov 1931)(Adopted by John Perish) m 4 Sep 1956, Clarence E. Roberts (b 26 Nov 1926)

CF84161321   Kenneth Kahle Roberts (b 29 Jun 1951) m Mary Pat Keeler (b 21 Aug 1959)

CF841613211   Jessica Roberts (b 20 Jul 1987)

CF841613212   Alexandra Roberts (b 23 Nov 1989)

CF841613213   Erica Roberts (b 24 Feb 1993)

CF84161322   David Paul Roberts (b 19 Oct 1952) m Karen Russell

CF841613221   David Roberts (b Apr 1983)

CF84161323   Sharon Lynn Roberts (b 14 Jul 1954) m John Joseph Clow III (b 16 Sep 1952)

CF841613231   John Joseph Clow IV (b 3 Sep 1975)

CF841613232   Jason Perish Clow (b 9 Sep 1976)

CF841613233   Justin Ryan Clow (b 25 Oct 1980)

CF841613234   Joshua Wayson Clow (b 13 Jan 1983)

CF84161324   Robbin Roberts (3 Sep 1955-12 Jan 1992) m James Glandon

CF841613241   Nicholas Glandon (b 29 Feb 1988)

CF84161325   Robert Roberts (b 4 Mar 1959). Unm.

CF84161326   Alice Mae Roberts (b 31 Aug 1961). Unm.

CF841613261   Luke Roberts (b 7 Apr 1993)

CF84161327   Sally Jane Roberts (b 25 Oct 1962) m Barry Russell

CF841613271   Barry Russell

CF841613272   Zachary Russell (b Feb 1993)

CF841614   Franklin Howard Kahle (8 Dec 1912, Elmo PA-22 Oct 1939, Clarion Co PA) m 6 Dec 1929, Ripley NY, Margaret Lucille McGregor (30 Sep 1909, Kittanning PA-11 Dec 1995, Sligo PA). Bur Clarion Co PA. He, proprietor, Kahle Coal Co, truck driver; she, clerk, merchant, state hospital supervisor.

CF8416141   Beverly Deane Kahle (b 17 Aug 1930, Texarkana AR) m 26 Aug 1956, John Zessis. He, teacher; she, shoe store, photography.

CF84161411   Jane Lynn Zessis (b 24 Sep 1963, Kittanning PA) m 16 May 1992, New Bethlehem PA, William Girard Lyons (b 10 Nov 1963, Pittsburgh PA). BA, MS, Duquesne U; He, BS, U Pittsburgh. Bankers.

CF8416142   Diane B. Kahle (b 5 Apr 1938) m 16 Jan 1960, New Bethlehem PA, John Joseph Panciera (b 6 Jan 1925). She, secretary; he, factory work.

CF84161421   Joel K. Panciera (b 9 Jan 1961, Brookville PA) m Susan Elizabeth Lensink (b 19 Mar 1960, Bozeman MT). He, BA, Oberlin (OH) Col; MA, Westminster Choir Col; teacher and conductor, Lindsborg KS. She, BA, St. Olaf Col; teacher, Bethany Col, Lindsborg KS.

CF841614211   Lyke Andrew Panciera (b 18 Jul 1994, Norman OK)

CF84161422   Mark David Panciera (b 3 Dec 1961, Brookville PA) m 21 May 1994, Houtzdale PA, Cheryl L. Tubo. Conservationists, Conneaut Lake PA.

CF841615   Kenneth Keating Kahle (b 21 Oct 1914, Elmo PA-d) m 30 Sep 1939, Dorothy Evelyn Propheter (b 1 Apr 1916). Farmer.

CF8416151   Dean Kahle

CF8416152   Diane Kahle

*CF841616   Donald Edgar Kahle (b 8 Apr 1917, Shippenville PA) m 1) Pauline Sempreviva (11 Jun 1917-8 Mar 1986); m 2) Dorothy Evelyn Propheter (widow of Kenneth Kahle (CF841515). Kahle Coal Co.

CF8416161   Donna Marie Kahle (b 22 Nov 1944, Clarion Co PA) m 29 Jan 1969, Richard De Novellis (b 28 Sep 1943), div. She, MA, EdD.

CF84161611   Kimberly Kahle De Novellis (b 14 Sep 1979)

CF8416162   Donald Edgar Kahle (b 26 Aug 1946, Clarion CoPA) m Pamela Mattern (b 2 Oct 1955). He, BS; coal company. She, RN.

CF84161621   Brian Jacob Kahle (b 23 Mar 1978)

CF84161622   Lindsay LeAnn Kahle (b 27 Nov 1987)

CF84161623   Nicholas Ryan Kahle (b 22 May 1991)

CF8416163   Carol Elzine Kahle (b 16 Dec 1948, Clarion Co PA) m 31 Aug 1974, David Williams (b 5 Nov 1952). She, BS, MA. He, MD.

CF84161631   Kathryn Kahle Williams (b 26 Aug 1978)

CF84161632   Mark Alexander Williams (b 28 Jan 1981)

CF84161633   Laura Diane Williams (b 26 Jan 1984)

CF8416164   Alice Loreta Kahle (b 9 Oct 1950, Clarion Co PA) m 17 Aug 1974, John Sampson (b 3 Jun 1952)

CF84161641   Paula Dawn Sampson (b 9 Jun 1967). JD.

CF84161642 Laurie Jayne Sampson (b 1 Jul 1980)

CF84161643 Donald Alec Sampson (b 1 Mar 1982)

CF8416165 Jayne Leigh Kahle (b 20 Oct 1952, Clarion Co PA) m 21 Apr 1973, Michael Scott Lloyd

CF84161651 Michael William Lloyd (b 12 Dec 1973)

CF84161652 Aaron Kahle Lloyd (b 6 May 1975)

CF84161653 Jessica Anne Lloyd (b 31 Oct 1977)

CF84161654 Nathan David Lloyd (b 6 Apr 1980)

CF84161655 Grace Susanna Lloyd (b 24 Apr 1983)

CF84161656 Rachel Elizabeth Lloyd (b 4 Jul 1986)

CF8416166 Charles Hugo Kahle (b 14 Jun 1954, Clarion Co PA) m 22 Jun 1974, Dena Spittler (b 10 Feb 1955). Coal company.

CF8416167 Franklin Howard Kahle III (b 22 Nov 1957, Clarion Co PA) m 15 Oct 1994, Sherry Russel (b 3 May 1961). Coal company.

CF84161671 Sarah Marie Kahle (b 21 Feb 1996)

CF841617 Walter Wadell Kahle (6 Apr 1921, Elmo PA-11 Jan 1993) m Phyllis Do Barr (b 23 Apr 1929, Kinzoo PA). No chn.

CF841618 Buddy Dean Kahle (6 Dec 1922, Elmo PA-17 Apr 1925, Shippenville PA)

CF84162 John Royal Kahle (22 Jan 1879, Shippenville PA-17 Apr 1952). Unm. WWI.

CF84163 (1877-1950) George William Kahle (30 Nov 1880, Shippenville PA-2 Feb 1958) m Sara Adelaide Irwin

CF841631 Clara Mae Kahle (b 4 May 1906) m Harold Leroy Loveless (b 1908)

CF8416311 Charles William Loveless (b 30 Aug 1933) m Jean Rembold

CF84163111 Cynthia Jean Loveless (b 28 Sep 1954)

CF84163112 Richard Brant Loveless (b 8 Mar 1956)

CF84163113 Bradford Scott Loveless (b 28 Nov 1958)

CF84163114 Charles William Loveless, Jr. (b 28 Arp 1960)

CF8416312 Richard Leroy Loveless (b 23 Jan 1935) m Wilma Smith

CF84163121 Lesa Leigh Loveless (b 26 Dec 1958)

CF84163122 Lynne Marcel Loveless (b 8 Feb 1960)

CF84163123 Chris Edward Loveless (b 21 Dec 1962)

CF8416313   Nancy Ann Loveless (b 17 Dec 1938) m Ronald D. Sell (b 12 Apr 193)

CF84163131   Kimberly Sue Sell (b 8 Feb 1961)

CF841632   Jane Elizabeth Kahle (b 7 Dec 1909) m William Edward Cameron (b 1910)

CF8416321   Jane Elizabeth Cameron (b 26 Aug 1937)

CF8416322   Sally Kay Cameron (b 5 Jan 1944)

CF841633   Sara Adeline Kahle (b 24 Dec 1911) m Lloyd Merritt Bracken

CF8416331   John Lloyd Bracken (b 7 Dec 1938)

CF841634   George William Kahle, Jr. (b 1 Oct 1914) m Beatrice Lauffer (b 31 Oct 1918)

CF8416341   Susan Adelaide Kahle (b 10 Sep 1950)

CF8416342   Philip Alan Kahle (b 25 Feb 1952)

CF841635   James Weiser Kahle (b 3 Jun 1917) m Loretta Mae Wilson

CF8416351   Virginia Ann Kahle (b 8 Sep 1941)

CF8416352   Alice Loretta Kahle (b 22 May 1947)

CF841636   Robert Leslie Kahle (b 31 Jan 1921) m Grayce Arlene Lang (b 31 Jan 1921)

CF8416361   Grayce Arlene Lang (b 31 Jan 1921)

CF8416362   Suellen Leslie Kahle (b 3 Mar 1954)

CF841637   Jack Wade Kahle (b 23 Sep 1923) m Lola Mae Detrie (b 1928)

CF8416371   Jack Curtis Kahle (b 15 Nov 1954)

CF8416372   Gretchen Lee Kahle (b 4 Aug 1957)

CF8416373   Kelly Lucretia Kahle (b 1963)

CF84164   Mary Kahle (1 Nov 1881-2 Nov 1882)

CF84165   Edna Gertrude Kahle (b 10 Oct 1882) m 1900, Charles Leslie Cook

CF841651   Clair Wilson Cook (b 1900)

CF841652   Hazel Blanche Cook m   Kerr

CF8416521   Margaret Jane Kerr m Kenneth Himrod

CF84165211   Glenn Allen Himrod

CF84165212   June Ann Himrod

CF84165213   Chris Edward Himrod

CF841653   Juniata Jewel Cook m William Engel

CF84166   Elizabeth Grace Kahle (b 31 Jan 1886, Shippenville PA) m 30 Nov 1912, Benjamin Harrison Bickel (b 25 Sep 1889)

CF841661   Dorothy Pauline Bickel (b 29 Jun 191) m 19 Feb 1921, Arden Mapes (b 26 Mar 19??)

CF8416611   Lois Louise Mapes (b 31 Aug 1922) m Trevan Woolbright (b 25 Jan 1922)

CF84166111   Larry Lelan Woolbright (b 21 Sep 1941) m 14 Oct 1961, Hazel Marie Moore (b 20 Sep 1943)

CF841661111   Child Woolbright

CF841661112   Trevan Woolbright, Jr. (b 23 Jun 1950)

CF841661113   Gary Lee Woolbright (b 18 Aug 1952)

CF841661114   Roxanne Woolbright (b 9 Aug 1953)

CF841661115   Gregory Woolbright (b 23 Nov 1956)

CF8416612   Mary Elizabeth Mapes (b 7 Apr 1924) m Nicolas Chancey (b 21 Oct 1908)

CF84166121   Myrna Lee Chancey (b 29 Apr 1941) m John B. Fretina (b 14 Dec 1941)

CF841661211   Myrna Renee Fretina (b 7 Feb 1959)

CF841661212   John Fretina Ib 6 Jan 1961)

CF84166122   Nicolas Chancey (b 25 Oct 1952)

CF84166123   Susan Mary Chancey (b 17 Jul 1956)

CF84166124   Lisa Jo Chancey (b 4 Feb 1957)

CF84166125   Donna Alfreda Chancey (4 Feb 1962-21 Apr 1962)

CF8416613   Vivian Lorraine Mapes (b 21 Mar 1926) m Max Snoberger (b 31 May 1930)

CF84166131   Max Snoberger (16 Feb 1954-6 Jun 1954)

CF84166132   Maxine Lorraine Snoberger (b 25 Sep 1956)

CF84166133   Mary Katherine Snoberger (b 8 Jul 1958)

CF84166134   James Allen Snoberger (b 16 Jul 1959)

CF84166135   Donald Steven Snoberger (b 4 Jul 1960)

CF8416614   Joan Jane Mapes (b 16 Jun 1929) m 13 Apr 1957, Lewis Wilbur Hallman (b 28 Sep 1924)

CF84166141   George Lewis Hallman (b 4 Mar 1960)

CF8416615   Phyllis Jenn Mapes (b 21 May 1931) m Max Chrisman (b 18 Jan 19)

CF84166151   Jack Leroy Chrisman (b 16 Mar 1951)

CF84166152   Karen Chrisman (b 9 Nov 1955)

CF8416616   Arden Clifford Mapes (b 23 Jan 1934) m Dora Ruth Ace (b 12 Feb 1939)

CF84166161   Scott Mapes (b 13 Jun 1960)

CF84166162   Laura Pauline Mapes (b 4 Apr 1062)

CF8416617   Nancy Rosella Mapes (b 24 Mar 1936) m Nov 1965, Robert Boyer

CF8416618   Emma Lou Mapes (b 8 Sep 1940)

CF8416619   Sandra Lee Mapes (b 26 Oct 1944)

CF841662   Eleonor Leona Bicket (b 7 Nov 1913) m 25 Jun 1930, Lawrence Luther Kahle (b 5 Jan
1901)

CF8416621   Emma Leona Kahle (b 8 May 1931) m Donald Land

CF84166211   Diana Susan Land (b 12 Nov 1953)

CF84166212   Ronald Lee Land (b 1956)

CF84166213   Alan James Land (b 3 Oct 1957)

CF84166214   Everett Wilson Land (b 1960)

CF8416622   Lawrence Harrison Kahle (b 7 Feb 1934) m Dolores Patten

CF84166221   Everett Lawrence Kahle (b 2 Jun 1953)

CF84166222   Wayne Allen Kahle (b 8 May 1955)

CF8416623   Charles Edward Kahle (b 20 Sep 1936) m Laura Chrispin

CF84166231   John Charles Kahle (b 19 Jan 1956)

CF84166232   Cindy Sue Kahle (b 4 Jul 1958)

CF84166233   David Lee Kahle (b 24 Mar 1961)

CF8416624   Donald Dean Kahle (b 5 Nov 1939) m 19 Nov 1960, Rose Marie Zacherl (b 26 May 1941)

CF84166241   Christine Kahle (b 1961)

CF8416625   Ruth Anne Kahle (b 20 Dec 1941) m 1961, Dallas Earl Deemer (b 10 Feb 1941)

CF84166251   Robert Lee Deemer (b Mar 1962)

CF8416626   Doris Mae Kahle (b 25 Jun 1943)

CF841663   Everett Leroy Bicket (b 9 Dec 1916) m 2 Sep 1939, Cora Mae Dunkerly (b 28 Nov 1921)

CF8416631   Dixie Lee Bicket (b 26 Nov 1940)

CF8416632   Beverly Jean Bickel (b 13 Jul 1944)

CF841664   Elizabeth Bicket (b 13 Dec 19)

CF84167   Grover Cleveland Kahle (9 Sep 1887-25 Dec 1942). Unm. WWI, USA, cook for General Pershing.

CF84168   Rosella Kahle (17 Aug 1890, Shippenville PA-29 Dec 1965, Clarion Co PA). Unm. Teacher; author *The Reed Genealogy.*

CF8417   Maria Kahle (b 4 Feb 1852) m John McDowell. Smithboro IL.

CF84171   Harvey McDowell

CF84172   Alfred McDowell m Mamey Robinson

CF84173   May McDowell m   Glenn

CF84174   Howard McDowell

CF84175   Pearl McDowell m   Glenn

CF8418   Laura Ann Kahle (4 Feb 1854-6 Apr 1858)

CF8419   Nathaniel Wilbur "Billy" Kahle (6 May 1857-21 Aug 1933) m Emma Ebinger. Bur Strattonville PA.

CF84191   Verna Kahle m William Lintz

CF84192   David Edward Kahle (9 May 1886-21 Jun 1968). Bur Sturbrick PA.

CF84193   Max Kahle m Mae Stover. Cleveland OH.

CF84194   Lawrence Lloyd Kahle m Eleanor Bickel. Clarion PA.

CF84195   Esther E. Kahle (d 28 Feb 1970) m Wayne Slater

CF84196   Ross Wayne Kahle (10 Feb 1896-7 Mar 1980) m 1913, Florence P. Cyphert (1896-1964). Bur Venus PA.

CF841A   Mary Elizabeth Kahle (1 Nov 1859-6 Sep 1889) m James H. Fleming (1863-1944). Bur Strattonville PA.

CF841A1   Ralph Newton Fleming (17 Aug 1889-17 Sep 1889)

CF841B   Alice Arabella Kahle (11 Jan 1862-16 Sep 1929) m Francis Albert Showers (16 Mar 1865-16 Jul 1931). Bur Strattonville PA. Farmer near Williamsburg PA.

CF841B1   Margaret Showers (31 Mar 1889-30 Nov 1952) m John Snider

CF841B2   Mary Irene Showers (19 Dec 1891-17 Jan 1967). Un. Bur Strattonville PA.

CF841B3   Gerald Bird Showers (8 Mar 1894-24 Nov 1978) m Anna Shawley

CF841B4   Elva Showers (b 23 Sep 1896) m 1) James O Collett (6 Mar 1898-25 Jul 1952, New Rehoboth PA); m 2)   Frazier, div

CF842 John Wesley Kahle (1821-1895)

CF841B5   Samuel Albert Showers (17 May 1899-1976) m Evelyn Carson (b 8 Aug 1906). Bur Strattonville PA.

CF841B6   Bessie J. Showers (b 17 Oct 1900) m John H. Moore (19 Jul 1878-14 Feb 1938). Bur Strattonville PA.

CF841B7   Evelyn Showers (b 5 Mar 1903) m Edward Magee

CF841B8   Sara Pearl Showers (8 May 1905-22 Aug 1974) m 5 Dec 1929, Willis Magness (26 Apr 1905-31 Mar 1964). Bur Strattonville PA. WWII, USN. No chn.

CF841C   Edward Kahle (May 1866-28 May 1944) m Belle Martha Neil (2 Oct 1869-25 Apr 1927). Bur Strattonville PA.

CF841C1   Dora Pearl Kahle (28 May 1890-11 Dec 1979) m 14 Jan 1914, Floyd L. Spangler. Bur Strattonville PA. Res Strattonville PA.

CF841C2   Stanley W. Kahle (3 Nov 1891-28 May 1954) m Nina Reed (b 30 May 1897)

CF841C3   Ruby Philistia Kahle (30 Mar 1893-Aug 1968) m Bert E. Standley (b 1900)

CF841C4   Gusta Matilda Kahle (11 Dec 1895-19 Dec 1980). Bur Strattonville PA. Unm. Culpepper VA.

CF841C5   Rena Belle Kahle (b 8 Oct 1897) m W. Preston Hunt

CF841C6   Roy Edward Kahle (19 Nov 1900-30 Nov 1966). Bur Strattonville PA. WWII, USA.

CF841C7   Ernest Neil Kahle (8 Nov 1902-28 Jun 1969) m Orpha Blauser (b 25 Aug 1903)

CF841C8   Thomas Neade Kahle (8 Feb 1907-4 Mar 1977) m 1) Kathryn Lewis; m 2) 4 Apr 1946, Evelyn P. Davison (31 Dec 1916-6 Oct 1981). Bur Strattonville PA.

CF841C9   Kathryn E. Kahle (b 1 Jul 1909). Culpepper VA.

CF841CA   Bruce Kahle (29 Jan 1916-Jul 1966) m Wilma Stone (d 16 May 1955)

CF841D   Loretta May Kahle (28 Jan 1868-1 Apr 1868)

CF842   John Wesley Kahle (28 Dec 1821, Warriors Mark Tp, Huntingdon Co PA-21 Feb 1895) m 1845, Ann Cheers (15 Jul 1823-24May 1898). Bur Venus PA. Penn Assembly, 1878.

CF8421   Dorsey Kahle (1845-1930) m Rosanna B. (1845-1917). Oil operator, inventor.

CF84211   Eugene Corma Kahle (1870-1954) m Mary G. Cetar (1878-1958)

CF84212   Maude M. Kahle (1874-1957)

CF84213   Harry P. Kahle (1880-1926) m Olive M. Detar (1885-1967)

CF8422   Lucinda Jane Kahle (b 1848) m   Gayetty

CF8423   Allis Rosanna Kahle (1850) m Benjamin Springer

CF8424   Mary Kahle (1852-1937) m Allison J. Sigworth (1853-1937)

CF8425   James Crum Kahle (14 May 1855-27 Jul 1936) m Hattie L. Hahn (7 Jan 1868-1914). Oil City PA.

CF8426   J. W. Kahle (b 1858)

CF8427   Letitia Kahle (b 1861) m   Clewell. Cleveland OH.

CF8428   Ap Kahle (b 1866)

CF843   Mary Ann Kahle (b 29 Apr 1825, Warriors Mark Tp, Huntingdon Co PA)

CF844   Nancy Jane Kahle (b 13 Apr 1828, Elk Tp, Venango Co PA)

CF845   Wilder Mark Kahle (b 28 Jan 1831)

CF846 Jacob Weiser Kahle
(1832-1924)

CF846   Jacob Weiser Kahl (21 Sep 1832-17 Aug 1924, Shippenville PA) m 19 Apr 1866, Maria Byers (30 Jun 1842-27 Feb 1934). Bur Perry Chapel graveyard. Civil War, Co D, 57th Regt Pa Vols. Farmer near Shippenville PA.

CF8461   Albert L. Kahle (5 Jul 1867-28 Nov 1918)

CF84611   Kathryn Pearl Kahle

CF84612   Ida Virginia Kahle

CF8462   Sarah Quintilla Kahle (16 Nov 1868-27 Mar 1871). Bur Pine City PA.

CF8463   Mary Blanche Kahle (11 Dec 1870-1959) m Harvey R. Mong (1869-1946). Bur Pine City PA.

CF84631   Scott Kahle Mong (1894-1970) m Helen H.   (b 1900). Bur Pine City PA.

CF84632   Vera Myrtle Mong (1898-1948) m Frank McBride. Bur Pine City PA.

CF846321   Frank McBride

CF846322   Jean McBride

CF8464   Lillian Estella Kahl (30 Aug 1877-11 Mar 1886). Bur Pine City PA.

CF8465   Maria Pearl Kahl (b 26 Jun 1880) m William Lynn McClintic. SD.

CF84651   Harold Kahle McClintic (28 May 1909-28 May 1995) m 23 Sep 1937, Irene Louise Hedlind

CF847 Nathaniel Lang Kahle
(1836-1885)

CF856511　　　　Marie Louise McClintic (b 31 Dec 1938) m 1) Norman Knispel; m 2) Lawrence Schnaidt. Res Groton SD.

CF8465111　　　　Kelly Knispel

CF8465112　　　　Mathew Knispel

CF8465113　　　　Christi Knispel

CF8465114　　　　Eric Knispel

*CF846512　　　　Gerda Irene McClintic (b 6 Jul 1940) m 16 Jun 1962, James Arthur Phoenix. Res Los Alamos NM.

CF8465121　　　　Howard Kahle Phoenix (b 30 Oct 1965)

CF8465122　　　　Elizabeth Phoenix (b 12 Mar 1967) m 27 Nov 1992, Charles Kennock Martin

CF846513　　　　William Kahle McClintic (b 25 May 1943) m, div. Res Watertown SD.

CF8465131　　　　Michelle McClintic

CF846514　　　　Carol Lynn McClintic (b 19 Jan 1945) m 1) James Bernhardt; m 2) David Lawrance. Res Forest Falls CA.

CF8465141　　　　Chad Bernhardt

CF8465142　　　　Lisa Lawrance

CF846515　　　　Susan Pearl McClintic (b 22 Jul 1947) m Robert Mabee. Res Sioux Falls SD.

CF8465151　　　　Linda Mabee

CF8465152　　　　Laura Mabee

CF84652　　　　Gerda McClintic m 1) Harvey Crow; m 2) Leonard M. Mason. Gusby MD.

CF846521　　　　Harvey Crow, Jr. Attorney, Rapid City SD.

CF846522　　　　Maria Crow

CF8466　　　　Elma Kahl (11 Oct 1882-23 Mar 1886). Bur Pine City PA.

CF847　　　　Nathaniel Lang Kahl (28 Jun 1836, Pine City PA-25 Mar 1885, Pine City PA) m 25 Dec 1866, Ketura Phipps (14 May 1844, Elmo PA-8 Sep 1928, Oil City PA). Bur Pine City PA. Civil War, Co F, 83rd Penn Vol Inf; later 121st Penn Vol Inf. Farmer, Pine City PA.

CF8471　　　　Ida LuAdda Kahle (9 Apr 1869, Pine City PA-17 Oct 1923, Oil City PA). Unm. Bur Pine City PA.

CF8472　　　　John Lemoyne Kahle (7 Dec 1871, Pine City PA-29 Apr 1962, Bradford PA) m 1) 25 Dec 1894, Clara Alwilda Swab (11 Apr 1872, Pine City PA-28 Apr 1913, Aiken PA); m 2) 20 May 1922, Little Valley NY, Lillian Louise Myers (29 Sep 1893, Johnsonburg PA-28 Jan 1964, Rochester NY). Clara bur Pine City PA; he and Lillian bur Lafayette PA. Oil driller, OK and PA.

CF84721   Clifford LeRoy Kahle (17 May 1896, Pine City PA-5 Feb 1965, Oil City PA) m 1) 10 Jun 1919, Jenny Camp (10 Jun 1896, Oil City PA-2 Aug 1936, near Oil City PA); m 2) 28 Aug 1937, Mary Kerr (5 Sep 1906, Oil City PA-4 Jan 1980, Orlando FL). Bur. Oil City PA. Co. D, 16th Reg, NGP, 1916-19, WWI. CPA, Oil City PA.

CF847211   Robert LeRoy Kahle (b 8 Mar 1921, Oil City PA) m 1) 12 May 1941, Erie PA, Julia Rose Jack, div; m 2) Mar 1949, Gooding ID, Mary Fertig (b 1921); m 3) St. George UT, Barbara Jean Norfleet (13 Jan 1938-May 1983). WWII, USN. Radio, tv, St. George UT.

CF8472111   Gennilee Kahle (b 10 Feb 1942, Erie PA) m 31 Aug 1962, Las Vegas NV, Douglas Claude Abbott (b 9 Apr 1941, Las Vegas NV). St George UT.

CF84721111   Scott LeRoy Abbott (b 12 May 1962, Las Vegas NV) m Karen Conley. Richfield UT.

CF847211111   Torrey Abbott (b 31 May 1979, Richfield UT)

CF847211112   Kacy Scott Abbott (b 16 Dec 1982, St. George UT)

CF84721112   Jeffrey Claude Abbott (b 13 Jul 1963, Las Vegas NV) m Debbie Diltz (b 9 May 1964)

CF847211121   Krystal Anne Abbott (b 12 Mar 1986)

CF847211122   Chelsea Jean Abbott (b 10 Feb 1990)

CF84721113   Rebecca Sue Abbott (b 11 Nov 1964, Las Vegas NV) m Bryan Smethurst

CF847211131   Bryan Douglas Smethurst (b 2 May 1983, St. George UT)

CF847211132   Ashlee Dawn Smethurst (b 25 Mar 1987, St. George UT)

CF847211133   Wendell Jaco Smethurst (b 11 Nov 1992, St. George UT)

CF84721114 Kimberly Kay Abbott (b 4 Jun 1968, Las Vegas NV) m 11 Mar 1986, Washington UT, David Layne Sullivan (b 4 Apr 1967, St. George UT), div 1994. St. George UT.

CF847211141   David Lamar Sullivan (b 10 Mar 1986, St. George UT)

CF847211142   Kelsie Marie Sullivan (b 10 Apr 1990, St. George UT)

                Christopher Michael Abbott (b 22 Sep 1971, Las Vegas NV)(Adopted)

CF84721115   Matthew Elias Abbott (b 4 May 1976, St. George UT)

CF84721116   Gena Rose Abbott (b 28 Jun 1977, St. George UT)

CF84721117   Nicole Marjorie Abbott (b 17 May 1979, St. George UT)

CF84721118   Emilie Anne Abbott (b 4 Jun 1986, St. George UT)

CF8472112   Clifford LeRoy Kahle II (b 23 Feb 1943, Niagara Falls NY) m 1) 20 Apr 1963, Linda Lewis, div; m 2) 2 Aug 1974, Myrtle Ruth Lee (b 15 Jan 1948, Nachez MS), div; m 3) Cindy   (b 19 Aug 1949). Las Vegas NV.

CF84721121   Clifford LeRoy Kahle III (b 25 Aug 1965). MD; obstetrician-gynecologist, Las Vegas NV.

CF84721122   Aaron Kahle (b 11 Sep 1967)

CF84721123   Amber Kahle (b 11 Aug 1970)

CF84721124   April Kahle

CF8472113   Frederick Kahle

CF8472114   Robert LeRoy Kahle, Jr. (b 15 Dec 1964, Holbrook AZ) m May 1993, St. George UT, Bobbie Sue Neilson

CF847212   James Edward Kahle (b 7 Oct 1928, Oil City PA) m 8 May 1957, Palmer AL, Anne Bettine Lewis Cain (b 30 Mar 1934, Auburn WA). He, BS, U of AK; MA, UCLA; geologist, St of CA. She, BS, MS, U of AK; PhD, UCLA; geophysicist, NASA. Topanga Canyon CA.

                    Richard Daryl Cain (b 10 Apr 1955)(Adopted by James Kahle). BS, UCLA. Unm.

CF8472121   Sheree Lynn Kahle (b 22 Sep 1956, Nome AK) m 22 Sep 1992, Edward Rex Luttrell. She, BS, E OR U; MS, CA S, Humboldt; wildlife management.

CF84721211   Kolle Kistrell Riggs (b 17 Mar 1981, OR)

CF84721212   Katie Ann Luttrell (b 9 Mar 1994)

CF8472122   Vickie Irene Kahle (b 3 Apr 1958, Nome AK) m 1 Oct 1980, Michael Alan Kowalski, div

CF84721221   Ian Kowalski (b 26 Oct 1982)

CF8472123   Jeffrey Peter Kahle (b 11 May 1959, Nome AK)

CF847213   Kay Wildamarie Kahle (b 1 Apr 1942, Oil City PA) m 30 Jul 1966, Oil City PA, David Thomas Winger (b 20 Nov 1941, Oil City PA). She, BA, Westminster (PA) Col; MEd, U Ctrl FL; principal. He, BSEd, Clarion (PA) S U; MEd, U Miami, Coral Gables; coordinator of testing, Seminole Co, FL.

CF8472131   Kristin Kay Winger (b 11 Dec 1971, Orlando FL). Unm.

CF8472132   Matthew David "Jake" Winger (b 20 Apr 1975, Winter Park FL). Unm.

CF84722   Harmon Phipps Kahle (31 Dec 1897, Pine City PA-6 Feb 1979, Bradford PA) m 1) 1930, Oil City PA, Margaret Lucille Balsiger (4 Aug 1910, Karn City PA-20 Jul 1988, Bradford PA), div 1932; m 2) 25 Feb 1939, Bradford PA, Marion Johnson (15 Feb 1912, Bradford PA-31 Aug 1982, Bradford PA). He and Marion bur McKean PA; Margaret bur Bradford PA.

CF847221   Peggy Joan Kahle (b 11 May 1931, Bradford PA) m 1) 7 Apr 1951, Bradford PA, John Hartman Nicholson (7 Feb 1925, Pittsburgh PA-6 Mar 1956, Pittsburgh PA); m 2) Jan 1970, Bradford PA, Thomas Maxwell Neilly (b 25 Jun 1930), div 1972. She, surveyors office, banker, Bradford PA. Nicholson, USA.

CF8472211   Michael Charles Nicholson (b 17 Jun 1972, Punxsatawny PA). Unm. BS, Hampton-Sydney Col; MS, U FL, Tampa; teacher, Tampa FL.

CF8472212   Lynn Nicholson (b 5 Jul 1955, Punxsatawny PA) m 17 May 19 , Cooperstown NY, Robert Donald Lundgren (b 12 Apr 1947). Editor, Phienix AZ.

CF84722121   Gayle Lundgren (b 18 Jun 1984, Phoenix AZ)

CF847222   John Lemoyne Kahle II (b 12 Nov 1940, Bradford PA) m 1962, Bradford PA, Marilyn Breese (b 1942). Journeyman electrician.

CF8472221   Douglas Kahle (b 16 Nov 1962)

CF8472222   Dianne Kahle (b 17 Sep 1963)

CF8472223   Richard Kahle (b 1 Jun 1964)

CF847223   Gordon Johnson Kahle (b 31 May 1942, Bradford PA) m 1) 1964, Smethport PA, Sandra Lorshbaugh, div; m 2) 1976, Paulette Grolemund (b 25 Mar 1950). Chemist, Olean NY.

CF8472231   Brett Kahle (b 21 Sep 1968)

CF8472232   Kimberly Kahle (b 4 Aug 1977, Bradford PA)

CF8472233   Kristan Kahle (b 21 Jul 1980, Bradford PA)

CF84723   Velma Elverda Kahle (28 Oct 1897, Pine City PA-16 Apr 1979, Indiana PA) m 12 Sep 1942, Bradford PA, Harold W. Neptune, div 1946. She, gas firm, Oil City and Port Allegany PA. No chn.

CF84724   Georgina Terrilla Kahle (17 Jun 1904, Pine City PA-21 Mar 1993, Eustis FL) m 16 Jul 1926, Little Valley NY, James Charles Balsiger (26 Dec 1905, Karns City PA-1 Jan 1990, Eustis FL). She, nurse-receptionist, Oil City PA. He, oil co., gasoline station, grocery store, gunsmith. Bur Lafayette PA.

CF847241   Barbara Jeanne Balsiger (b 30 Jan 1927, Bradford PA). Unm. BSEd, Indiana (PA) U, 1951; MA, U IA, 1955; Fulbright Scholar; PhD, U Pittsburgh, 1970; prof of art history, Indiana (PA) U, 1966-89.

CF84725   John Nathaniel Kahle (28 Apr 1913, Aiken PA-28 Apr 1913, Aiken PA).

CF84726   John Kahle (1923-1923).

CF84727   Kenneth Eugene Kahle (27 Jul 1924, Bradford PA-23 Apr 1981, Elyria OH) m 1946, Warren PA, Mary Louise Moyer (b 2 Jun 1925, Kane PA). Bur Lafayette PA. WWII, USA; Korean Conflict, USAF. Air traffic controller, FAA.

CF847271   Kenneth Eugene Kahle, Jr. (b 13 Feb 1947, Kane PA) m 1967, Flint MI, Linda Dee Ray (b 1 Dec 1948, Elyria OH). BS, AZ St Un, 1974; USAF, 1970-90; major on retirement; F-15 pilot and instructor. Res Elyria OH.

CF8472711   Kenneth Eugene Kahle III (b 13 Jan 1968, Columbus OH). Unm. Phoenix AZ

CF847272   Stacey Lee Kahle (b 17 Apr 1958, Mt. Lebanon PA) m 22 Jun 1979, Elyria OH, Debra Lynn Pennington (b 4 Jun 1960, Selma AL). USN, 1977-79. Air traffic controller, FAA. Berthoud CO.

CF8472721   Christopher Lee Kahle (24 Mar 1989, Longmont CO-24 Mar 1989, Longmont CO).

     Samantha Jo Kahle (b 22 Sep 1989, Seoul, Korea)(Adopted)

CF8472722   Nicole Maree Kahle (b 7 Mar 1991, Longmont CO)

CF8472723   Michelle Lee Kahle (b 10 Nov 1993, Longmont CO)

CF847273   Amber Louise Kahle (b 14 Oct 1960, Mt. Lebanon PA) Ciba-Geigy, Lorain OH.

CF847274   Pamela Lynn Kahle (b 6 Oct 1961, Mt. Lebanon PA). Police dept, Phoeniz AZ.

*CF84728   Helen Marie Kahle (b 18 Oct 1927, Bradford PA) m 24 Jun 1949, Rew PA, John Lyon Kolbe (b 16 Dec 1926, Bradford PA). She, BA, Houghton (NY) Col, 1956; MS, library/information science,

Catholic U, 1972; population information specialist, technical advisor to the office of the President (USA), 1980-82, UN international consultant. He, BS, Carnegie Inst Tech, 1951; MBA, Loyola (MD) Col, 1978; chemical engineer, PA, SD, MD.

CF847281   Karen Deborah Kolbe (b 10 Dec 1952, Olean NY) m 18 Oct 1976, Columbia MD, Charles Gene Edwards (11 Aug 1935, Lonestar TX-9 Jan 1996, Woodbine MD). Bur Arlington VA. She, America Online, senior buyer. He, electronics technician, Johns Hopkins U Applied Physics Lab, Laurel MD. No chn.

CF847282   John Lyon Kolbe (5 Apr 1954, Olean NY). Unm. BS, U ID, 1979 and 1982; Peace Corps; int. forestry consultant, Harrison ID.

CF847283   Kevin Warner Kolbe (b 7 Jul 1956, Olean NY) m 16 Aug 1980, Silver Spring MD, Beth Ann Russell (b 9 Aug 1957, Canton OH). He, newspaper circulation sales mgr, WV and MD; accountant, Columbia MD. She, day care teacher, Howard Co. MD.

CF8472831   Amanda Lee Kolbe (b 18 Jun 1983, Martinsburg WV)

CF8472832   Andrew Ian Kolbe (b 21 Mar 1987, Martinsburg WV)

CF847284   Jeffrey Kahle Kolbe (b 11 Nov 1957, Olean NY) m 9 Mar 1991, The Dalles OR, Ronna Dee Johanson (b 19 Jul 1954, Killeen TX). BA, U ID, 1982; JD, Willamette U, 1986; deputy dist attorney, Wasco Co and Clackamas Co OR; Arizona Bar. No chn.

CF84729   Marilyn Kahle (26 Jul 1934, Smethport PA-8 Sep 1976, Churchville NY) m 9 Oct 1953, Rew PA, Marlin Ross Smith (b 17 Apr 1934, Juniata PA). RN, Bradford Hospital, Bradford PA, 1955; nursing director, Churchville NY. He, BS, St. Bonaventura U, Allegany NY, 1957; teacher, Olean, Rochester NY. Bur Lafayette PA.

CF847291   Marcia Lynn Smith (b 2 Oct 1956, Olean NY) m 7 Aug 1976, North Chili NY, Shaun Michael O'Brien (b 28 Feb 1954, Rochester NY). She, AB, Rochester Inst Tech, 1984; MBA, U Rochestr, 1989; banker and financial consultant.

CF847292   Melinda Smith (4 Apr 1958, Olean NY-4 Apr 1958, Olean NY). Bur Lafayette PA.

CF847293   Michaelyn Smith (21 Nov 1959, Olean NY) m 1) 7 Jun 1980, North Chili NY, David Mack, div 1988; m 2) 12 Oct 1991, North Chili NY, Carey Parker (b 2 Jun 1955, Antiqua WI). She, RN, St. Elizabeth's Hospital, Utica NY. Res Dover PA.

CF8472931 name, Feb 1994)   Marlee Mack (b 13 Mar 1981, Woodbridge VA)(Adopted by Carey Parker and assumed

CF8472932 name Feb 1994)   Annette Marie Mack (b 15 Dec 1982, Torrance CA)(Adopted by Carey Parker and assumed

CF8472933 Feb 1994)   Jesse Mack (b 28 Dec 1986, Rochester NY)(Adopted by Carey Parker and assumed name

CF8472934   Lauren Ruth Parker (b 27 Jul 1993, Schenectady NY)

CF847294   Marlin Thomas Smith (b 22 Nov 1961, Brockport NY)

CF847295 Baltimreo MD.   Melanie Leigh Smith (b 21 Aug 1963, Brockport NY). Building maintenance technician,

CF8473 Teacher.   Elverda Christina Kahl (13 Dec 1874, Pine City PA-10 Jan 1957, Port Allegany PA). Unm.

CF8474 Harmon Nathaniel Kahle (14 Feb 1881, Pine City PA-24 May 1882, Fertig PA). Bur Pine City PA.

CF848 Sarah Catherine Kahle (11 Feb 1839-1925) m 5 Dec 1867, Alex W. Phipps (1837-1914)

CF849 Harriet B. Kahle (1842-1861). Unm. Bur Shippenville PA.

CF84A Thomas Muhlenberg Kahle (8 Mar 1843, Elk Tp, Clarion Co PA-23 Sep 1922) m 4 Sep 1865, Harriet Henlen (23 Jan 1846-1 Sep 1934). Bur Shippenville PA. Veterinarian.

CF84A1 Neoskelita Pearl Kahle (25 Jul 1869-17 Feb 1955) m Harrison Lewis Mahle (26 Nov 1867-12 Sep 1928). Bur Shippenville PA.

CF84A11 Bernice Eleanor Mahle (23 Oct 1909-18 Mar 1987) m 19 Jul 1941, Fred Sheldon Goble (13 Dec 1898, Arthurs PA-22 Jan 1980). Bur Shippenville PA.

CF84A111 Thomas Albert Goble (b 10 Jul 1949) m 14 Jun 1969, Tamalyu Kay Fye (b 2 Aug 1949)

CF84A1111 Jessica Kathleen Goble (b 8 Dec 1969)

CF84A2 Lillian Kahle (21 Apr 1883-1965) m 20 Oct 1910, John Clark Walker (21 Nov 1882-1944). Bur Shippenville PA.

CF84A Thomas Muhlenberg Kahle (1843-1922)

CHAPTER FOUR D

CR Peter Weiser (1730-ca 1785)

Peter Weiser, son of Conrad and Anna Eva (Feg) Weiser, was born February 27, 1730, at Tulpehocken Township, Berks County, Pa. He married Catharine, whose married name is unknown, and evidently resided in Reading until the mid-1770s, when he took up residence in Penns Township, Northumberland County, on the tract that was divided between the Weiser heirs there. On 2 November 1772, Henry Muhlenberg Junior gave Peter a list of his four surviving children with their birthdates, in the English language, no doubt in anticipation of their move to the land in what is now Snyder County. Peter returned to Berks County about 1779 and sold his share of one of the tracts in Northumberland. The remainder was sold by the sheriff of Northumberland County in 1785.[85]

The deeds he executed in Berks County identify him as a saddler, but he likely farmed when he was in Northumberland County. On his return to Berks, he seems to have resided in Womelsdorf. No definite record of his death exists. However, no document over his name is found after 1785 and his wife is identified as a widow in 1787. Of her last days and of their burial, nothing is known. There are no estate records for him in Berks or Northumberland Counties.

Children of Peter and Catharine (   ) Weiser:

CR1   Eva Elizabeth Weiser (29 Jan 1753, Reading PA-Apr 1831, Reading PA) m.1768, Edward McCabe. No ch. No further record.

CR2   John Philip Weiser (21 Sep 1755).

CR3   Solomon Weiser (27 May 1761, Reading PA-dy before 1772).

CR4   Henry Solomon Weiser (14 May 1763,Reading PA).

CR5   John Melchior Weiser (7 Feb 1767, Reading PA-9 Nov 1768, Reading PA)

CR6   Mary Catharine Weiser (8 Oct 1769).[86]

CR2. John Philip Weiser (1755-   )

John Philip Weiser, son of Peter and Catharine (   ) Weiser, was born 21 Sep 1755 and confirmed in 1770. His wife's name is not recorded, but several children are all listed on the records of Christ Lutheran Church, as baptized 7 Jun 1787. This is all the record there is of Philip, except that he seems to be the Philip listed in the 1790 and 1800 census for Heidelberg Township.

Children of John Philip and (   ) Weiser:

CR21   Benjamin Weiser (b 18 May 1778).

CR22   Peter Weiser (b 3 Oct 1781).

CR23   John Jacob Weiser (b Mar 1783).

---

[85]Conrad Weiser to Peter Weiser, 12 Dec 1752, lot 34 in Reading, of which Peter and Catharine sold half in Feb 1754 and the other half 9 Jul 1774 (A-1-323, B-3-166). On 31 Jul 1770, they sold lot 38 in Reading which they had purchased in 1753 (9-247). cf. Northumberland County deeds D-182, C-338. The original paper given by Pastor Muhlenberg to Peter Weiser is in the JCWFA Collection.

[86]Records of Trinity Lutheran Church, Reading PA.

CR24   Marie Margaret Weiser (b 18 Jun 1786).[87]

CR21   Benjamin Weiser (b 18 May 1778, probably in or near Womelsdorf PA). He may be the father and grandfather of the following Weisers:[88]

CR211   Benjamin Weiser (b ca 1800) m. Elen   (b ca 1801). According to the 1850 census, the last four of the following children were still in the home:

CR2111   Emanuel Weiser (b ca 1827) m Maria   . (He is in the 1870 census).

CR2112   Catharine Weiser (b ca 1833) m ca 1852, Daniel Weber.

CR2113   Sarah Weiser (b ca 1839).

CR2114   Jacob Weiser (b ca 1840).

CR2115   Benjamin Weiser (b ca 1844).

CR212   Jacob Weiser m Jane Rolley.

CR2121   John Weiser (b ca 1830) m Martha   .

CR2122   Isaac Weiser.

CR21221   Mary Weiser (b ca 1865).

CR21222   George W Weiser (b ca 1868).

CR21223   Lewis Weiser (b ca 1870).

CR21224   William J Weiser (b ca 1876).

CR2123   Ellen Weiser.

CR2124   Jacob Franklin Weiser (b 29 Jan 1838, Bunell Tp, Armstrong PA) m 11 Jul 1860, Mary Ellen Meckling (3 Dec 1834-31 Sep 1899, Kittanning PA). Civil War. Carpenter, oilman, railroader.

CR212411   William H Weiser (16 Nov 1861).

CR212412   Jacob M Weiser (29 Feb 1864).

CR212413   Hannah Jane Weiser (19 May 1866).

CR212414   Rebecca Ellen Weiser (31 Jan 1868-24 Aug 1876).

---

[87]Records of Christ Lutheran Church. Baptisms for Catharine Weiser, 16 Dec 1791, daughter of Philip and Barbara Weiser, sponsor at baptism, 1 Jan 1792, Catharine Wohlfarth; and for Catharine Elizabeth Weiser, 1 Mar 1795, to Philip and Mary Weiser; sponsor at baptism on 6 Apr 1795, Catharine Elizabeth Weiser - may be for this man. There seems to be no other likely Philip Weisers in the community at the time. The tax registers of Heidelberg Township record Philip Weiser as paying minimal tax from at least 1780 until 1803, sometimes as a resident of "Middletown" (Womelsdorf), sometimes in the township, and in 1803 as Philip "Sr" of Middletown. This distinguished him from CP31 Philip Weiser (1776-1827), who married in 1800. It should be noted that 1) not all years' lists have survived; 2) there is a gap from 1810 to 1830; and 3) Philip is listed in 1788 in Middletown, but not at all in 1789, 1791, and 1792. He is listed in 1793 and 1795 in Middletown. His absence from the list may reflect poverty rather than physical absence from the area.

[88]Data on this family comes from census records without proof of relationship to CR21 Benjamin Weiser.

CR212415   John Franklin Weiser (24 Jul 1870-21 Oct 1882).

CR212416   Mary Martha Weiser (24 Feb 1872-25 Oct 1874).

CR212417   Anna Bell Weiser (21 Aug 1874).

CR212418   Samuel James Weiser (11 Mar 1876).

CR212419   Myran A Weiser (6 Oct 1878

CR21241A   Loisa Bell Weiser (25 Jan 1884).

CR22   Peter Weiser (b 3 Oct 1781).(It is possible that he is the Peter Weiser named as a member of the Lewis and Clark expedition, from whom the Weiser River and city of Weiser, Idaho, are named-especially because he would be about the right age for the position.)

CR23   John Jacob Weiser (20 or 22 Mar 1783, Probably Heidelberg TP, Berks Co PA-1837, Monroe Tp, Clarion Co PA) m Mary Myers (16 Sep 1781-29 Oct 1854, Monroe Tp, Clarion Co PA). He moved by 1810 to Union Township, Mifflin Co PA; to Monroe Tp Armstrong Co (now in Clarion Co) PA in 1827. Bur. Churchville, Clarion Co PA.[89]

CR231   Philip Weiser (4 Dec 1805-26 Sep 1822). No chn.

CR232   Samuel Weiser (20 Oct 1807-29 Mar 1818).

CR233   Elizabeth Weiser (31 Jul 1809, Union Tp, Mifflin Co PA-12 Sep 1857, Clarion Co PA) m 23 Sep 1830, Clarion Co PA, Michael Harringer (19 Jun 1806-8 Sep 1892, Clarion Co PA). Bur Clarion Co PA.

CR2331   Jacob Harringer (27 Sep 1831, Monroe Tp, Clarion Co PA-21 Apr 1833, Monroe Tp, Clarion Co PA).

CR2332   John Harringer (24 Jan 1832 [sic], Monroe Tp, Clarion Co PA). Farmer, near Kalamazoo MI.

CR2333   Mary Harringer (24 Dec 1834, Monroe Tp, Clarion Co PA) m Jacob Hetrich. Farmer near Kalamazoo MI.

CR2334   Henry Harringer (17 Jan 1837, Monroe Tp, Clarion Co PA) m 26 Dec 1865, Monroe Tp, Clarion Co PA, Sarah Myers (13 Apr 1845, Piney Tp, Clarion Co PA). Civil War: Co H, 155th PA Vol Inf, 1862-1865.

CR23341   Jennie M Harringer (30 Oct 1866, Monroe Tp, Clarion Co PA) m James Campbell. Farmer, Piney Tp, Clarion Co PA.

CR233411   Vera Campbell (25 Aug 1885).

CR233412   Lillie May Campbell (15 Sept 1896).

CR23342   P Emery Harringer (14 Aug 1868, Monroe Tp, Clarion Co PA).

CR23343   Bertin C Harringer (24 Jun 1871, Monroe Tp, Clarion Co PA).

---

[89]Data on the descendants of John Jacob Weiser was submitted by Margaret R. Vandeuren, Clara Seigworth Oiesen, Pat Rhoads, Doris Raybould, Frances Walter, Margaret Weiser, Jack Coder, and Milton Udell Wiser.

CR23344   J Earl Harringer (19 Sep 1876, Monroe Tp, Clarion Co PA).

CR23345   James Mc C B Harringer (21 Sep 1887, Monroe Tp, Clarion Co PA).

CR 2335   Phillip Harringer (25 Mar 1893, Monroe Tp, Clarion Co PA). Wagonmaker, Du Bois PA.

CR2336   Washington Harringer (17 Apr 1841, Monroe Tp, Clarion Co PA-1863). Civil War: 83rd
PA Vol Inf.

CR2337   Daniel Harringer (13 Dec 1844, Monroe Tp, Clarion Co PA). Blacksmith, Greenville PA.

CR2338   James L Harringer (9 Jan 1847, Monroe Tp, Clarion Co PA). Farmer, near White Cloud
MI.

CR2339   Alexander Harringer (29 Mar 1850, Monroe Tp, Clarion Co PA).

CR234   Mary Jane "Polly" Weiser (b 29 Aug 1811, Union Tp, Mifflin Co PA).

CR235   Catherine Weiser (b 4 Sep 1813, Union Tp, Mifflin Co PA).

CR236   Sarah Weiser (b 26 Sep 1815, Union Tp, Union Co PA).

CR237   Magdalena (aka Martha) Weiser (5 Dec 1817, Union Tp, Mifflin Co PA-15 May 1906,
Newcomerstown OH) m Henry R Coder (b 1810-6 Dec 1884, Newcomerstown OH). Bur Newcomerstown OH.
In adulthood she used Martha, the name assumed to be translation of Magdalena.

CR2371   Clara A Coder (ca 1845-20 Nov 1895).

CR2372   Mary B Coder (b ca 1846).

CR2373   William S Coder (1848-23 Dec 1931, Akron OH) m 24 Dec 1931 McConnel. Bur
Newcomerstown, OH.

CR2374   Jacob J Coder (1849-Newcomerstown, OH). Unm. Bur Newcomerstown OH.

CR2375   Martha J Coder (d 1921) m 3 Feb 1884, Emanuel Mumma.

CR2376   Susan Coder (b Sligo, Clarion Co PA) m 20 Apr 1879, Wm T Willoxen.

CR2377   Fannie Francis Coder (22 Feb 1857, Shippenville PA-8 Jan 1912, Westerville OH). Unm.
Bur Newcomerstown OH.

CR2378   Henry Milton Coder (8 Mar 1859, Coshocton OH-Jan 1917, Hampton IL) m. 11 Dec 1884,
Rock Island IL, Elma Jane Donahoo (13 Apr 1865, Zuma, Rock Island Co IL-18 Jun 1944, Hampton IL). Bur
Hampton IL.

CR23781   Stella Mary Coder (28 Apr 1884, Zuma IL-1964) m Lewis Taylor.

CR23782   Susan Coder (b 12 Nov 1886, Oxford Tp OH).

CR23783   Nettie May Coder (18 Nov 1887, Newcomerstown OH-10 Jun 1979, Hampton IL) m
Alfred F Hofstetter.

CR237831   Harold Hofstetter.

CR23784   Elsie Lela Coder (24 Jul 1889, Newcomerstown OH-22 Dec 1979, Moline IL) m. 22 Aug

1924, Charles Toptien (d 1959). Owner, Moline Consumers Co, Moline IL.

CR23785   John Robert Coder (31 Mar 1891, Columbus OH-1959,Hampton IL). Merchant, Hampton IL.

CR23786   Wilbur Milton Coder (24 Mar 1895, Newcomerstown OH-1948).

CR23787   Bernice Elizabeth Coder (11 Sep 1897, Newcomerstown OH--21 Oct 1992, Hampton IL) m 1) Harry Rylander; m 2) Fred Vance.

CR237871   Robert Rylander.

CR237872   Elma Jane Vance.

CR23788   Leonard Cecil Coder (28 Sep 1900, Joslin IL-1956, Hampton IL).

CR23789   Harold William Coder (11 Jan 1905, Joslin IL-12 Jan 1988, Hampton IL) m 12 Apr 1925, Hampton IL, Gertrude Marie Duncan (23 Feb 1904, Blandensville IL). Postal clerk, Hampton IL.

CR237891   Betty Marie Coder (14 Feb 1926, Hampton IL) m 1 Mar 1947, East Moline IL, Herman Eggericks (b 29 June 1924, Barrington IL). Realtor, Hampton IL.

CR2378911   Steven Eggerichs.

CR2378912   Terry Lee Eggerichs.

CR2378913   Allan L Eggerichs.

CR237892   Harold William Coder Jr (5 May 1927, Hampton IL) m 1960, Jackie Conklin. Lawyer, Judge, Great Falls MT

CR2378921   Craig William Coder (15 Nov 1963, Missoula MT).

CR2378922   Chandra Elizabeth Coder (21 Jan 1966, Great Falls MT).

CR2378923   Kurt M Coder (16 Nov 1968, Great Falls MT).

CR2378924   Kyle M Coder (27 Jan 1972, Great Falls MT).

CR237893   Clifford Lee Coder (24 Jan 1929, Hampton IL) m 1) Jeannette Harker; m 2) Helen Wheeler.

CR2378931   Sue Ellen Coder (29 Dec 1957).

CR2378932   Dustin John Coder (2 Jun 1960).

CR2378933   Sarah Louise Coder (7 Aug 1962).

*CR237894   Jack Coder (b 8 Jul 1930, Moline IL) m 26 Dec 1954, Hampton IL, Beverly Ann McNeal (9 May 1930, Moline IL). AB, Augustana College, 1952; MA, U of IA, 1960; high school counselor, Hampton IL.

CR2378941   Christopher McNeal Coder (27 Oct 1955, Moline IL) m Flagstaff AZ, Marcelle Zumlauf. BA, Augustana (IL) Col; MA, U AZ. Dept of Interior, Flagstaff, AZ.

CR23789411   Hannah Coder.

CR23789412   Claire Coder.

CR2371942   Tad William Coder (b 25 Sep 1959) m Sheri Bentley. J AB, Augustana (IL) College. Recreational director, Hampton IL.

CR23719421   Katie L Coder.

CR23719422   Jack B Coder.

CR23719423   Merry E Coder.

CR2371943   Elizabeth Ellen Coder (8 Jan 1962, Moline IL) m 18 Aug 1994, Rock Island IL, Dan Kosminsky (20 Sep 1955, New Jersey). She, AB, Augustana (IL) College; MA, U IL. Director of Career Center, Augustana College, Rock Island IL.

CR23719431   Rebecca Anne Kosminsky (18 Jul 1995, Moline IL).

CR2378A   Clifford Donahoo Coder (11 Aug 1908, Hampton IL-27 Dec 1965, Hampton IL) m Helen Moran. Painter, Wichita KS.

CR2378B   Ray Franklin Coder (12 Aug 1910, East Moline IL-1977, Hampton IL) m Pauline Marson. Deere Company foreman, Hampton IL.

CR2378B1   David Coder.

CR2379   Emma Coder (7 Jan 1863-1946) m 25 Dec 1885, Charles Langhead.

CR237A   Bernice Coder m GW Burris.

CR237B   Sadie G Coder.

CR238   Jacob Jackson Weiser (5 Dec 1817, Union Tp, Mifflin Co. PA-24 Oct 1886, Tylersburg, Farmington Tp, Clarion Co PA) m 1840, Mary Ann Kuhn (10 Jan 1819-2 Mar 1902). Bur Lickungville PA. Teamster on the 1850 census in Monroe Tp, Clarion Co; farmer after 1854 in Farmington Tp, Clarion Co PA.

CR2381   John Kuhn Weiser (9 Oct 1841, Reidsburg, Clarion Co PA-23 Dec 1911, Farmington Tp, Clarion Co PA) m 1867, Mary Ann Imhoof (3 Feb 1843, Lucinda Furnace, Clarion Co PA-26 Jul 1918, Farmington Tp, Clarion Co PA). Bur. Tylersburg PA. Farmer, Tylersburg, PA.

CR23811   William H Weiser (12 Jun 1868, Farmington Tp, Clarion Co PA-17 Jan 1944) m 7 Aug 1900, Sarah E Smathers (26 Feb 1863-4 Mar 1961).Bur. Tylersburg PA. General storekeeper, Tylersburg PA.

CR238111   Hazel Weiser.

CR238112   Harry Weiser.

CR238113   Clarence Weiser.

CR23812   Webster W Weiser (b ca 1870, Farmington Tp, Clarion Co PA). Married and had a family. Moved away and lost.

CR23813   Sarah Etta Weiser (19 Mar 1872, Farmington Tp, Clarion Co PA-16 Mar 1945, Beaver Tp, Clarion Co PA) m 24 Sep 1889, Tylersburg PA, Jacob Frederick Seigworth (2 Apr 1863, Farmington Tp, Clarion Co PA-29 Dec 1946, near Knox PA). Bur near Fryburg, Clarion Co PA. Farmer, blacksmith.

CR238131   George Mahle Seigworth (7 Jul 1890, Lickingville, Clarion Co PA-16 Apr 1966, Clarion

PA) m 24 Mar 1915, Franklin PA, Lena May Prichard (11 Jun 1887, Dempsytown, Venango Co PA-20 Aug 1976, Clarion Co PA). Bur. Asbury PA. Teacher, farmer, miner, Polk PA; county commissioner, Clarion Co PA.

*CR2381311   Howard Prichard Seigworth (3 Sep 1916, Polk PA) m 1) 20 Dec 1940, Strattanville PA, Dorothy Ruth Reighard (30 Jan 1916, Fisher PA-8 Jan 1989, Clarion Co PA); m. 2) 28 Jul 1989, Strattanville PA, Shirley Leadbetter Armagost (2 Aug 1929, Strattanville PA). Trucker, school bus firm; Dorothy, BS, Clarion SU; teacher.

CR23813111   Kathleen Mae Seigworth (11 Jul 1941, Brookville PA-7 Oct 1943, Strattanville PA). Bur Clarion Tp, Clarion Co PA).

*CR23813112   Noreen Ruth Seigworth (b 21 Oct 1942, Brookville PA) m 2 Sep 1961, Clarion PA, Raymond Albert Ganoe (b 3 May 1941, Clarion PA). She, B.S., M.Ed Clarion SU, 1969, teacher; he, BS, Clarion State U., 1965, teacher, tire store proprietor, Cocoa FL; Harcourt Brace Publishers, Orlando FL.

CR238131121   Marcia Rayleen Ganoe (3 Mar 1967, Brookville PA) BA, US Military Academy, 1984; MS, Boston U; mechanical engineer, Cocoa FL; marketing.

CR238131122   Cheri Ann Ganoe (24 Apr 1963, Brookville PA) m 2 May 1987, Merritt Island FL, Allen Ridgdill Zeman (b 6 Nov 1963, Gainesville FL).She, BS, MS, FL SU; he, PhD. Special assistant, secretary of the Navy, Washington DC; Res Alexandria VA.

CR2381311221   Brittany Ann Zeman (4 May 1988, Tallahassee FL).

CR2381311222   Benjamin Allen Zeman (20 Jan 1990, Arlington VA).

CR2381311223   Aaron Keith Zeman (28 Aug 1992, San Diego CA).

CR2381311224   Alese Kristine Zeman (28 Aug 1992, San Diego CA).

CR238131123   Steven Ray Ganoe (2 Apr 1969, Brookville PA). Unm. Ship captain, Ft Lauderdale FL. Owner-Maritime Exporter; G & G Marine, Ft Lauderdale FL.

CR23813113   Ralph Dan Seigworth (b 25 Aug 1944, Brookville PA) m 14 Dec 1968, Pittsburgh PA, Joan Eileen Thompson (b 10 Apr 1943, Pittsburgh PA). AB, Lycoming C; MS, Edinboro U PA; teacher, principal. She, BS, Clarion State U, teacher.

CR238131131   Michael Scott Seigworth (b 5 Jan 1971, Brookville PA). MS, Clarion U PA. Computer Specialist.

CR238131132   Kristin Ann Seigworth (b 14 Jul 1973, Brookville PA). BA Grove City C, MA, BGSU.

CR2381312   Glenn Wilson Seigworth (25 May 1919, Polk PA). World War II service. Trucker, bus driver.

*CR2381313   Twila Alene Seigworth (b 4 May 1923, Strattanville PA) m 31 Dec 1945, Franklin PA, Joseph Desko, Jr (b 7 Aug 1922, Ambridge PA). R.N., Western PA Hospital, Pittsburgh; he, World War II, sheet metal mechanic, electrician.

CR23813131   Alene Lynn Desko (b 24 Apr 1947, Franklin PA) m 19 Aug 1967, Franklin PA, John Donald Cooper (b 19 Feb 1947, Terre Haute IN) div 1984. She, A.B., Point Park C, Pittsburgh PA, communications; relious broadcasting marketing director, LaVerne CA.

CR238131311   Nicole Leigh Cooper (b 15 Aug 1974, Washington PA) m 25 Oct 1991, Little Rock AR, Kristopher Robert Michol (b 13 Nov 1972, Woodbury NJ). Secretary, La Verne CA.

CR2381313111   Jessica Caitlyn Michol (b 18 Aug 1993, Vernon Parish, Los Angeles CA).

CR238131312   Erik John Cooper (b 5 Feb 1976, Washington PA).

CR23813132   Luanne Kay Desko (b 30 Aug 1949, Franklin PA) m 8 Jun 1968, Franklin PA, Dennis Lynn Jones (b 31 Oct 1947, Franklin PA), div 1995. Real estate broker, Ft Myers FL.

CR238131321   Jill Ellen Jones (b 29 Jul 1969, Franklin PA). Unm. BS, U FL. Special Ed teacher, Ft Myers FL.

CR238131322   Jason Todd Jones (b 20 Sep 1974, Franklin PA). Unm.

CR238132   Harvey Truman Seigworth (7 Jun 1892, Lickingville PA-4 Apr 1961, near Knox PA) m 24 Jul 1912, Clarion PA, Letha Iona Sanner (27 Sep 1892, Fisher PA-5 Feb 1973, Clarion PA). Bur Fryburg PA. Farmer, logger.

CR2381321   Edna Maxine Seigworth (b 20 Jun 1912, Lickingville PA) m 1 Oct 1935, near Shigo PA, Cyrus Emberson Wolfgong (b 7 May 1912, Mayport PA). Farmer, miner, custom construction work.

CR23813211   James Edward Wolfgong (b 10 Jul 1936, Hawthorn PA) m 2 Jan 1960, Franklin PA, Barbara Sharp (b 19 Feb 1936, Franklin PA). Factory worker, Franklin PA.

CR238132111   James Edward Wolfgong Jr (b 12 Dec 1960, Franklin PA) m 20 Oct 1979, Franklin PA, Karen Elizabeth Minnick (b 4 Jul 1961, Franklin PA). US Navy.

CR2381321111   Deanna Sue Wolfgong (11 Oct 1984, Spain).

CR2381321112   Amber Rena Wolfgong (b 13 Dec 1987, Jacksonville FL).

CR238132112   Michael Scott Wolfgong (b 26 Apr 1964, Franklin PA) m 21 Jul 1990, Franklin PA, Heather Marie Stahlman (b 8 Sep 1966).

CR238132113   Joyce Darlene Wolfgong (b 11 Jul 1968, Franklin PA) m 3 Dec 1988, Franklin PA, William James McGinnis (b 17 Aug 1965). Office worker, Franklin PA.

CR2381321131   Alyssa Jade McGinnis (26 Jun 1989, Franklin PA).

CR2381321132   Mackenzie Alayna McGinnis (24 Jan 1992, Franklin PA).

CR238132114   Shawn Robert Wolfgong (6 Mar 1972, Franklin PA). US Navy, Norfolk VA.

CR23813212   Allen Harold Wolfgong (b 16 Jul 1937, Shannondale PA) m 31 Jul 1963, Franklin PA, Mary Louise Hines (b 8 Sep 1941). US Army, tank driver, Franklin PA.

CR238132121   Allen Harold Wolfgong Jr (b 12 Oct 1964, Franklin PA) m 26 Nov 1983, Franklin PA, Dawn Lea Barickman (b 4 Jun 1964, Butler PA). US Army. Automobile worker, trucker, Franklin PA.

CR2381321211   Justin Scott Wolfgong (b 16 Jul 1986, Franklin PA).

CR2381321212   Jessica Rozanna Wolfgong (b 18 Jan 1988, KY).

CR238132122   Edward John Wolfgong (b 3 Jul 1972, Franklin PA).

CR238132123   Susan Marie Wolfgong (b 30 Dec 1976, Franklin PA).

CR23813213   Letha Mae Wolfgong (b 6 Mr 1939, Shannondale PA) m 25 Mar 1960, Smicksburg PA,

Daniel Vernon McGarry (b 22 Apr 1937, Venango PA). She, automobile dealer salesperson; he, electrical co.

CR238132131   David Lant McGarry (b 30 Aug 1963, Oil City PA) m 17 Aug 1985, Oil City PA, Monique Ann Smith (b 12 Apr 1962, Oil City PA). Pilot.

CR2381321311   Christopher Ryan McGarry (b 9 Feb 1990, Daytona FL).

CR238132132   Patricia Ann McGarry (b 28 Jul 1965, Oil City PA) m 13 Jun 1987, Oil City PA, Eric Charles Elliot (b 12 Nov 1965, Oil City PA). Trust secretary, Seneca PA. He Welder.

CR2381321321   Courtney Alyson Elliot (b 18 Jun 1992, PA).

CR23813214   Thomas Lee Wolfgong (b 1 Apr 1940, Shannondale PA). Unm. Graphics firm, Chambersburg PA and Smyrna DE. US Army.

CR23813215   Cyrus Dean Wolfgong (b 4 Jun 1941, Shannondale PA) m 11 Oct 1968, Emlenton PA, Francine White Smith (b 10 Apr 1943, Clinton PA). U.S. Air Force. Oil firm employee.

CR23813216   Donald Wayne Wolfgong (b 21 May 1942, Shannondale PA) m 1) 17 Jun 1966, Sheryl Bean, div; m 2) 3 Jan 1970, Christine Rankin (b Greenville PA). US Army, Vietnam. Maintenance firm.

CR238132161   Dawn Marie Wolfgong (b 17 Aug 1967, Oil City PA) m 1) 28 Oct 1988, Greenville PA, Edward Duane Thompson III (b Sharon PA), div; m 2) 14 Feb 1992, Greenville PA, Roert Williams (b Greenville PA).

CR2381321611   Cherish Amber Thompson (b 11 Oct 1989, Sharon PA).

CR2381321612   Tyler Steven Williams (b 15 Aug 1992, Greenville PA).

CR238132162   Tammy Darlene Wolfgong (b 1 Feb 1973, Greenville PA) m 10 Jun 1994, Greenville PA, Robert Eckard (b Sharon PA).

CR238132163   Edward Wayne Wolfgong (b 12 Oct 1975, Greenville PA).

CR23813217   Larry Frank Wolfgong (b 25 Aug 1945, Shannondale PA) m 28 Jul 1973, Oil City PA, Mary Ann Skiba (b 6 Aug 1947, Oil City PA). US Army; shoe salesman.

CR238132171   Matthew Thomas Wolfgong (b 22 Apr 1976, Franklin PA).

CR238132172   Christopher Ryan Wolfgong (b 8 Apr 1979, Franklin PA).

CR23813218   Timothy Ronald Wolfgong (b 10 Sep 1955, Oil City PA) m 5 May 1979, Oil City PA, Jeanette Dawn Benton (b 12 Mar 1957, Oil City PA). He, telephone co, Oil City PA; she, sales clerk.

CR238132181   Lindsey Benet Wolfgong (8 Feb 1983, Franklin PA).

CR238132182   Wesley William Wolfgong (3 Apr 1990, Franklin PA).

CR2381322   Arthur Jacob Seigworth (b 20 Aug 1913, near Strattanville PA) m 14 Jun 1932, Charlene Esther Wilson (20 May 1914-23 Oct 1983). Farmer, laborer, Pampas TX and Knox PA.

CR23813221   Iona Maxine Seigworth (1935, TX-d at two weeks, TX). Bur Pampas TX.

CR23813222   Shyrlee Idella Seigworth (b 28 Sep 1937, Knox PA) m 11 Sep 1954, Knox PA, Raymond Edgar Smith (b 5 Nov 1937).

CR238132221   Arthur Lynn Smith (b 27 Mar 1956) m 14 Sep 1991, Knox PA, Wendy Nelson Jamtor.

CR238132222   Deborah Ann Smith (3 Oct 1957-Dec 1958).

CR238132223   Paul Leroy Smith (25 Aug 1960-24 Jan 1990). Bur Providence PA.

CR23813223   Jack Vernon Seigworth (18 Jul 1939-6 Jan 1987) m 24 Jul 1961, Knox PA, Barbara Jean
Clark. Laborer.

CR238132231   Jackie Iona Seigworth (b 28 Jun 1962) m 7 Jun 1986, William Joseph Dilley. Law
enforcement, Knox PA.

CR2381322311   Anthony Michael Dilley (20 Jul 1989, Clarion PA).

CR2381322312   Caleb Alexander Dilley (b 27 Jan 1992, Clarion PA).

CR238132232   Cindy Jo Seigworth (b 11 Jun 1963).

CR2381322321   Brandon James Seigworth (b 10 Jun 1989, Clarion PA).

CR2381322322   Amanda Lynn Seigworth (b 3 Dec 1992, Clarion PA).

CR238132233   Peggy Lea Seigworth (b 11 Apr 1967).

CR23813224   Harvey Arthur Seigworth (7 Oct 1941, Knox PA-16 Apr 1988, Clarion PA) m. 14 Oct
1967, Clarion PA, Calie E. Slagle (b 24 Apr 1948). Bur Washington Tp, Clarion PA. Trucker, Fisher PA.

CR238132241   Rebecca Lynn Seigworth (b 7 Oct 1968, Clarion PA) m 10 Aug 1990, Sigel PA, Michael
Reed (b 1 Nov 1964, Clarion PA). BS, Clarion U; accounting, Clarington PA.

CR2381322411   Todd Michael Reed (31 Oct 1994, Brookville PA).

CR238132242   Daniel Francis Seigworth (b 29 Dec 1970, Carion PA).

CR2381322421   Deanna Grace Seigworth (1 Feb 1994, Du Bois PA).

CR2381322422   Jacob Daniel Seigworth (1 Feb 1994, Du Bois PA).

CR238132243   Susan Marie Seigworth (b 24 Oct 1974, Clarion PA).

CR23813225   Norman Paul Seigworth (b 24 Dec 1943) m 25 Aug 1967, Barbara Kay Knight.

CR238132251   John Arthur Seigworth (b 2 Mar 1968).

CR238132252   Michele Ann Seigworth (b 7 Jul 1969).

CR23813226   Phyllis Marie Seigworth (b 31 Jul 1948) m 18 Apr 1973, Edward Geisel, div. 1994. Store
clerk, Du Bois PA.

CR238132261   Melissa Lea Geisel (b 26 Jun 1968) m Bill Reynolds.

CR2381322611   Justin Reynolds (b 18 Sep 1987, Tacoma WA).

CR2381322612   Amber Lynn Reynolds (b 26 Feb 1989, Tacoma WA).

CR2381322613   Heather Reynolds (b 17 Jul 1992, Tacoma WA).

CR238132262   Arthur Neil Geisel (b 9 May 1970). US Army.

CR238132263   Joel Edward Geisel (b 14 Aug 1976).

CR238133   Clemens Lloyd Seigworth (22 Feb 1894, Lickingville PA-29 Feb 1952, Clarion PA) m 17 Dec 1927, Clearfield PA, Besse Irene Shaffer (b 3 Mar 1900, Knox Tp, Jefferson Co PA). Bur. Strattanville PA. Driller, Strattanville PA. US Army, WWI.

*CR2381331   Harold Lloyd Seigworth (b 2 May 1927, Strattanville PA) m 1) 14 Aug 1949, Sacramento CA, Thelma Ivers (1 Apr 1924, Bisbee AZ), div 10 Mar 1969; m 2) 20 Dec 1969, Riverside CA, Margaret Elizabeth Prewitt (b 16 Aug 1950, Riverside CA), div 8 Nov 1988; m 3) 16 Jun 1990, Barstow CA, Mary Lou Gleasman White Humphries (b 14 May 1934, Rome NY). BS, MS, U of CA; teacher, Riverside CA; farm supply business, Fallon NV.

CR23813311   Mark Lloyd Seigworth (b 21 Dec 1956, Riverside CA) m 24 Jun 1978, San Rafael CA, Deborah Lee McNear (b 16 Jun 1956, San Rafael CA). BS, CA St Polytechnic U; landscape designer, contractor, Auburn CA; ABE teacher CA.

CR238133111   Corey Adam Seigworth (b 1 Oct 1979, Sacramento CA).

CR238133112   Shari Dawn Seigworth (b 9 Jun 1982, Racklin CA).

CR23813312   Scott David Seigworth (b 12 Jun 1972, Riverside CA) m 26 Jun 1993, Fallon NV, Emily Theresa Lowe (b 1 Feb 1971, Reno NV). Inspector, draftsman, Twin Falls ID.

CR23813313   Matthew George Seigworth (b 25 Nov 1980, Reno NV).

*CR2381332   Margaret Patricia Seigworth (b 24 Dec 1928, Strattanville PA) m 1) 25 Jun 1947, Strattanville PA, Thomas Dale Moore (b 31 Jan 1926, Brookville PA), div Dec 1969; m 2) 17 Jan 1970, Hazen, Jefferson Co PA, Eugene Lorraine Rhoads (b 19 Nov 1926, Lamertine PA) div May 1977. BS, 1970, M.Ed., Clarion (PA) S Col; teacher, Brookville PA.

CR23813321   Robin Diane Moore (b 21 Aug 1949, Brookville PA) m 24 Jan 1970, Clarion PA, James David Fagley (b 31 Aug 1946, Paint Tp, Clarion Co. PA) div 1992. District manager, Clarion Co Conservation District. Legislative assistant, Clarion PA.

*CR238133211   Kelly Lynn Fagley (b 16 Oct 1970, Clarion PA). Unm. B.S., civil engineering, PSU, 1993. Engineer, Fairfax VA.

CR238133212   Kimberly Joyce Fagley (b 26 Feb 1974, Rochester PA). Unm.

CR23813322   Kevin Wayne Moore (b 16 Feb 1951, Brookville PA) m 7 Aug 1971, Clarion PA, Patricia Jean Magrini (b 17 Apr 1951, Brookville PA). Corporate sales manager, Loveland OH.

CR238133221   Lori Ann Moore (b 10 Oct 1974, York PA). BS, PSU, 1996.

CR238133222   Paul Thomas Moore (b 12 Sep 1977, Erie PA).

CR238133223   Jeffrey Augustine Moore (b 6 Dec 1978, Milford MA).

CR23813323   Julia Moore (b 2 Sep 1959, Clarion PA) m 26 Jul 1986, Brookville PA, Paul Edward Ferraro (b 29 Apr 1950, Brookville PA). BS, IN U., PA, 1981; MEd 1988; teacher, Du Bois PA.

CR238133231   Alex Paul Ferraro (b 16 Oct 1989, Du Bois PA).

CR238133232   Emily Marie Ferraro (b 17 Aug 1993, Brookville PA).

CR2381333 William Albert Seigworth (b 31 Aug 1930, Clarion PA) m 1) 6 Oct 1947, Clarion PA, Betty Lee Walters (b 3 Jan 1930, Clarion PA) div; m 2) Maureen Ekard Wiser (b 10 Jul 1949, Norfolk VA). Beverage distributor, Seneca PA.

CR23813331 Delores Yvonne Seigworth (b 7 Mar 1948, Brookville PA) m 22 Aug 1970, Seneca PA, Thomas Alan Wenner (b 24 Jun 1948, Brookville PA). BS, Clarion (PA) S Col, 1970.

CR238133311 Michael Jason Wenner (b 4 Nov 1974, Oil City PA).

CR238133312 Matthew Eric Wenner (b 9 Oct 1978, Clarion PA).

CR23813332 William Leslie Seigworth (b 26 Sep 1950, Brookville PA) m 24·Apr 1976, Erie PA, Debra Jean Wier (b 10 Jan 1950, Erie PA). Beverage distributor, sales representative, Seneca PA.

CR238133321 Bryan Michael Seigworth (b 19 Oct 1977, Franklin PA).

CR238133322 Jeffrey Paul Seigworth (5 Oct 1979, Franklin PA).

CR238133323 Kevin Patrick Seigworth (5 Dec 1983, Franklin PA).

CR238133324 Corey William Seigworth (17 Feb 1985, Franklin PA).

CR23813333 Denise Renee Seigworth (b 17 Aug 1953, Brookville PA) m 1) 28 Feb 1976, Oil City PA, William E Allaman (b 13 Mar 1953, Oil City PA) div. 23 Mar 1984; m. 2) 27 May 1994, Richard Alan Falvo (b 10 Aug 1955, Sharon PA). BS, accountant, Erie PA C.

CR23813334 David Russell Seigworth (b 7 Jan 1958, Clarion PA) m 4 Oct 1980, Oil City PA, Margaret Sue Stone (b 23 Mar 1957, Oil City PA). Trucker, Seneca PA.

CR238133341 Russell David Seigworth (b 31 Mar 1981, Franklin PA).

CR238133342 Ryan Andrew Seigworth (b 4 May 1983, Franklin PA).

CR23813335 Bruce Leigh Seigworth (b 2 Dec 1966, Clarion PA) m 15 Apr 1989, Seneca PA, Jeanne Elizabeth Whitling (b 1 Mar 1967, Oil City PA). Sales, Seneca PA.

CR2381334 Ronald Colburn Seigworth (b 9 Apr 1932, Strattanville PA) m 7 Mar 1959, Clarion PA, Donna I Smith (b 23 Apr 1939, Clarion PA). US Army. Glass and plastics maker, carpenter.

CR23813341 Jodi Lynn Seigworth (b 14 Sep 1959, Clarion PA) m 25 Oct 1986, Marienville PA, Lewis Gary Kamin (b 5 Oct 1945, Brooklyn NY). Teacher, State Col PA.

CR23813342 Ronald Gregory Seigworth (b 18 Nov 1960, Clarion PA). Carpet installer, Alexandria VA.

CR23813343 Lori Lee Seigworth (b 22 Feb 1964, Clarion PA) m 28 Jun 1991, Manassas VA, John Joseph Maceda (b 8 Mar 1949, Nantucket MA). CIA, McLean VA.

CR238133431 Alexander Joseph Maceda (b 3 Feb 1992, Manassas VA).

CR2381335 Richard Frederick Seigworth (b 30 Oct 1934, Strattanville PA) m 1) 27 Aug 1951, Patricia Ruth George, div. 1961; m 2) 19 Sep 1964, Seneca PA, Brenda J. Daugherty (b 23 Aug 1941, Seneca PA). Petroleum equipment sales and service, Pittsburgh PA.

CR23813351 Steven Richard Seigworth (b 2 Mar 1952, Brookville PA) m 16 Sep 1972, Terri L Reed, div. Welder, Clarion PA.

CR238133511   Scott Alan Seigworth (b 18 Apr 1973, Brookville PA).

CR238133512   Corrie Jan Seigworth (b 29 Jun 1978, Clarion PA).

CR23813352   Christina Lynn Seigworth (20 Jul 1953, Oil City PA) m 16 Sep 1994, Las Vegas NV, Glenn Evans.

*CR23813353   Tracy Diane Seigworth (b 22 Nov 1966, Butler PA) m 19 Aug 1989, Mc Kees Rocks PA, Edward Jerome Kosis III (b 21 Jan 1959, Sewickley PA). Accountant, Clinton PA.

CR2381336   Marilyn Louella Seigworth (b 2 Nov 1938, Strattanville PA) m 22 Dec 1954, Monroe Twp., Clarion Co PA, Christian Amos Fox (b 30 Aug 1936, Monroe Tp, Clarion Co PA). Office clerk, Sligo PA.

CR23813361   Karen Suzanne Fox (b 22 Jul 1955, Clarion PA) m 24 Sep 1977, New Bethleham PA, Glenn Alan Eschborn (b 24 Mar 1952, Lakewood OH). Claims adjustor, Dublin CA.

CR238133611   Jill Briana Eschborn (b 28 Jun 1980, Batavia NY).

CR238133612   Valerie Lynn Eschborn (b 10 May 1982, Batavia NY).

CR238133613   Heather Dawn Eschborn (b 3 Sep 1984, Walnut Creek CA).

CR23813362   Cinthia Lynn Fox (b 1 Apr 1957, Clarion PA) m 10 Mar 1979, Clarion PA, Jonathan Harvey Stants (b 15 Aug 1953, West Monterey PA). She, BS, U of Pittsburgh, 1978; dental hygienist, Strattanville PA.

CR238133621   Keaton Jon Stants (b 9 Aug 1979, Clarion PA).

CR238133622   Calla Christine Stants (b 28 May 1982, Clarion PA).

CR23813363   Eric Chris Fox (b 21 Mar 1958, Clarion PA) m 25 Aug 1979, Distant PA, Cindy Lou Doverspike (b 23 Mar 1961, Brookville PA), div 3 Jan 1992. Sales, Sligo PA.

CR238133631   Natalie Ann Fox (b 27 Dec 1981, Franklin PA).

CR238133632   Erin Leah Fox (b 1 Jun 1984, Franklin PA).

CR238133633   Cami Linn Fox (b 18 Mar 1986, Franklin PA).

CR23813364   Sandra Ann Fox (b 30 Nov 1959, Clarion PA) m 4 Feb 1984, Oil City PA, David Mark Emig (b 14 Sep 1958, New Castle PA). BS, Clarion St C, 1980; cost accounting manager, New Castle PA.

CR238133641   Andrew James Emig (b 18 Mar 1987, New Castle PA).

CR238133642   Paul Thomas Emig (b 13 Mar 1988, New Castle PA).

CR2381337   Linda Lee Seigworth (b 2 Nov 1938, Grove City PA) m 27 Nov 1954, Strattanville PA, Fredrick Wayne Heasley (b 2 Jan 1933, Clarion PA). She, housing authority project manager, Strattanville PA. He, U.S. Army.

CR23813371   Cameron Wayne Heasley (b 17 Jun 1955, Brookville PA) m 25 Oct 1975, Wooster OH, Deborah Kathleen Raber (b 1 Nov 1956, Morgantown WV). Factory supervisor, Atlanta GA.

CR238133711   Jason Wayne Heasley (8 Mar 1977, Clarion PA).

CR238133712   Jessican Kathleen Heasley (27 Jul 1979, Clarion PA).

CR238133713   Jennifer Lee Heasley (24 Oct 1980, Franklin PA 12 Feb 1984, Du Bois PA). Bur Strattanville PA.

CR23813372   Brian Merve Heasley (b 29 May 1957, Brookville PA) m 24 Sep 1988, Strattanville PA, Laura Lynn Dolby (b 19 Sep 1962, Brookville PA). Factory worker, Strattanville PA.

CR23813373   Deanna Lynn Heasley (27 Aug 1966, Brookville PA) BS, BA, Clarion U of PA; J.D., Duquesne U; attorney, Erie PA.

CR2381338   Thomas Lowell Seigworth (b 2 Feb 1940, Strattanville PA) m 20 Sep 1957, Clarion PA, Ella May Winters (b 8 May 1939). Wholesale building supplies, mining, lumber, farmer, USDA Soil Conservation Service.

*CR23813381   Allan Thomas Seigworth (b 8 Aug 1958) m 31 Jul 1982, Susan Lynn Rhines (b 16 Jun 1962). Farmer,Brookville PA.

CR238133811   Rebecca Lynne Seigworth (b 29 Aug 1986).

CR238133812   Megan Sue Seigworth (b 29 Nov 1990).

CR23813382   Carol Ann Seigworth (b 21 Sep 1959) m 31 Aug 1984, Alvin Glenn Emery Jr (b 18 Dec 1952). Clerk, Brookville PA.

CR23813383   Gary Lee Seigworth (b 13 Dec 1962) m 20 Oct 1983, Robin Elaine Hoffman (b 27 Oct 1964). Mechanic, Brookville PA.

CR238133831   Adam Lee Seigworth (b 28 Feb 1988).

CR238133832   Justin Todd Seigworth (b 26 Nov 1991).

CR238134   Solomon Curtis Seigworth (27 Jan 1896, near Strattanville PA-22 Feb 1976, Orlando FL) m 1) 26 Jun 1918, Corsica PA, Ruth Lillian Shingledecker (8 Aug 1898, Pinecreek Tp, Jefferson Co PA-25 Jul 1967, Brookville PA); m 2) 9 May 1970, Du Bois PA, Daisy Susanna Johnston (23 Jul 1899, Fisher PA-7 Dec 1990). US Army, WWI. Blacksmith, miner, lumber mill, building inspector, organ installer, car salesman, Clarion PA. Bur Strattanville PA.

CR2381341   Margaret Lucille Seigworth (b 18 Apr 1920, near Strattanville PA) m 10 Dec 1943, Du Bois PA, Ralph Leroy Spangler (17 Apr 1916, Venus PA-22 Jun 1971). She, BS, Clarion (PA) S Col; teacher, payroll clerk, jury commissioner's clerk.

CR23813411   Jerry Lee Spangler (b 25 Sep 1946, Grove City PA) m 6 Jul 1968, Rixford PA, Mary Lou Whiteman (b 22 Oct 1943). BS, Clarion S C; insurance agent, Brookville PA.

CR238134111   Judy Lynn Spangler (b 28 Sep 1970, Oil City PA).

CR238134112   Jamie Lynn Spangler (b 5 Oct 1973, Oil City PA).

CR23813412   Gary Ralph Spangler (b 10 Apr 1949, Grove City PA) m 1) 24 Nov 1973, Tallahassee FL, Joetta Long, div; m 2) 4 Apr 1981, Tallahassee FL, Margaret Ann McCann. He, B.A., PSU; MA, PhD, FL S U; contractor, Tallahassee FL.

CR238134121   Nathan Campbell Spangler (b 13 Aug 1986, Tallahassee FL).

CR23813413   Jeffrey Alan Spangler (28 Jun 1957, Clarion Co PA-21 May 1982, Pittsburgh PA). Bur Strattanville PA.

*CR2381342   Doris Ruth Seigworth (25 Oct 1921, near Strattanville PA) m 1) 12 Jun 1944, near Strattanville PA, Robert Amos Mortland (18 Jun 1921, Clarion PA-19 Nov 1951, Mohave Desert CA); m 2) 22 Apr 1962, Rockville MD, Merrill Ernest Raybould (b 5 Jan 1912, Phillipsburg PA). She, BS, Clarion (PA)S Col, 1942; teacher, Montgomery Co MD. Mortland, BS, US Military Academy, West Point; MA, Princeton; WWII; test pilot, USAF. Raybould, proofreader, editor, US Government Printing Office; staff assis, House Armed Services Committtee, ret.

CR23813421   Erica Lynn Mortland (b 11 May 1945, Oil City PA). Insurance claims adjustor, Rockville MD.

CR23813422   Robert Amos Mortland Jr (b 20 Sep 1946, Grove City PA) m 1) 3 Feb 1968, Kensington MD, Ana-Maria Ward (b 25 Jan 1949, Panama Canal Zone) div; m 2) 29 Jun 1973, Rockville MD, Carol Elaine Jansen (b 4 May 1947, Washington DC). US Air Force; garage owner, Du Bois PA.

CR238134221   Sara Dianna Mortland (b 16 Aug 1969, Okinawa). Legally adopted by Dr. Stuart Ross, her mother's second husband. Children by 1) Michail Sapienza (d 7 Aug 1990); 2) Wayne Wood Jr.

CR2381342211   Anthony Bradford Christopher Ross-Sapienza (b 15 Dec 1988, Silver Spring MD.

CR2381342212   Jesse Wayne Ross Wood (b 7 Feb 1994, Freehold NJ).

CR23813423   Dan Seigworth Mortland (b 20 Sep 1950, Ft Dix NJ) m 19 Feb 1972, Cane PA, Cheryl Eileen Stark (b 6 Mar 1950, Kane PA). BS, Clarion (PA)S Col; Regional sales manager, Jamison PA.

CR238134231   Robert Carl Mortland (b 16 Jan 1976, Warren PA).

CR238134232   Karen Eileen Mortland (b 11 Oct 1977, Manchester NH).

CR23813424   Ruth Ada Raybould (b 16 Mar 1965, Washington DC) m 5 Aug 1989,Silver Spring MD, David Paul Carmi (b 13 Nov 1963, Beirut, Lebanon) BA, Towson U MD. Homemaker, Elkridge MD.

CR238134241   Paul David Carmi (b 10 May 1993, Columbia MD).

CR238134242   Matthew Merrill Carmi (b 26 Aug, Columbia MD).

CR2381343   Donald Curtis Seigworth (b 7 Jun 1925, near Strattanville PA) m 3 Mar 1946, Paradise Valley PA, Verda Mae Deily (b 22 Nov 1926, New Bethlehem PA). USAF; miner, trucker, driller, motel, manufacture electric signs; Shippenville PA.

CR23813431   Carol Diane Seigworth (b 27 Jan 1948, Grove City PA). Director of admissions, rehab center, Delray Beach FL.

CR23813432   Gregory Curtis Seigworth (b 25 Jun 1953, Brookville PA) m 22 Jun 1987, Brookville PA, Elisabeth Anne Bullers (b 29 Nov 1960, Brookville PA) Construction estimator, environmental remediation, Farmington CT.

CR238134321   Alicia Kay Seigworth (b 6 Dec 1991, Farmington CT).

CR238134322   Shirey Mae Seigworth (b 3 Jan 1995, Farmington CT).

CR23813433   Robert Scott Seigworth (b 9 Apr 1959, Brookville PA) m 30 May 1981, Fruitland Park FL, Suzanne Le Francois (b 17 Aug 1961, Weymouth MA). Electrical technician, Bartow PA.

CR238134331   Robyne Elizabeth Seigworth (b 25 May 1983, Gainesville FL).

CR238134332   Sara Lynn Seigworth (b 25 May 1983, Gainesville FL).

CR238134333   Robert William Seigworth (b 8 Jan 1986, Eustis FL).

CR238134334   James Curtis Seigworth (b 19 Apr 1988, Eustis FL).

CR238134335   Laura Marguerite Seigworth (b 20 Nov 1991, Eustis FL).

CR238134336   Anne Elyse Seigworth (b 28 Apr 1994, Lakeland FL).

CR2381344   Raymond Leonard Seigworth (b 28 Feb 1930, Strattanville PA) m 2 May 1954, Peggy Jean Graybill (b 31 Jan 1934, Fisher PA). USAF; engineer, Orlando FL.

CR23813441   Cinthia Kay Seigworth (b 14 Dec 1954, Niagara Falls NY) m 30 Dec 1972, Orlando FL, Jeffrey Herbert Rinne (b Pittsburgh PA).

CR238134411   Brian Jeffrey Rinne (b 14 Jan 1979, Ocala FL).

CR23813442   Melinda Jean Seigworth (b 9 Mar 1958, Niagara Falls NY) m 19 Mar 1977, Orlando FL, Carl Thomas Rinne (b Pittsburgh PA). She, secretary, Deltona FL; he, nurseryman, landscape gardener, Enterprise FL.

CR238134421   Thomas Curtis Rinne (13 May 1981, Deltona FL).

CR238134422   Kelly Megan Rinne (18 Mar 1987, Deltona FL).

CR238134423   Mallory Jean Rinne (30 Dec 1989, Deltona FL).

CR23813443   Tina Marie Seigworth (22 Aug 1963, Orlando FL) m 26 Apr 1986, Orlando FL, Brian Rodney Frew (b Jefferson City MO). Clerk, Atsugi, Japan.

CR23813444   Raymond Leonard Seigworth, Jr. (b 3 Aug 1970, Orlando FL) m 10 Sep 1994, Orlando FL, Carol E Hofma (b Tallahassee FL). BS; sales, Orlando FL.

CR238135   Lewis Lee Seigworth (8 Jul 1898, Strattanville PA-10 Aug 1978, Clarion PA) m 19 Apr 1921, Clarion PA, Corothea Helen Reid (8 Nov 1901, Clarion PA-27 Sep 1980, Clarion PA). Bur Strattanville PA. Farmer, driller, construction worker, Knox and Strattanville PA, Baltimore MD.

CR2381351   Eleanor Mary Seigworth (23 Jul 1922, Strattanville PA-9 Feb 1923, Clarion PA). Bur Strattanville PA.

CR2381352   Velma Leona Seigworth (29 Dec 1924, Jackson Tp, Venango Co PA-12 Jan 1927, Clarion PA). Bur Strattanville PA.

CR2381353   Juanita Alma Seigworth (b 27 Jun 1929, Strattanville PA) m 17 Jan 1948, Clarion PA, Harold E McKinney (b 12 Feb 1928, Rimersburg PA).

CR23813531   Sandra Diane McKinney (b 16 Dec 1948, Brookville PA) m 23 Aug 1969, Wesleyville PA, Robert Edwin Ludwig (b 26 Feb 1949, Erie PA). M Ed; teacher, Brookville PA.

CR238135311   Scott William Ludwig (b 29 Dec 1971, Erie PA). BS.

CR238135312   Heather Ludwig (b 4 May 1974, Erie PA). BS.

CR23813532   Kathleen Ann McKinney (b 30 Apr 1952, Brookville PA) m 13 Aug 1977, Wesleyville PA, Arthur James Hoffman III (b 4 Jul 1952, Erie PA). Electronics engineer, Williamsport PA.

CR238135321   Jason Lee Hoffman (b 1 Mar 1980, Roanoke VA).

CR238135322   Christopher James Hoffman (b 24 May 1982, Roanoke VA).

CR23813533   Marsha Lynne McKinney (b 28 Oct 1961, Erie PA) m 5 May 1979, Wesleyville PA, Robert Lynn Wilder (b 16 May 1956, Erie PA). State highway dept, Erie PA.

CR238135331   Amanda Lynn Wilder (b 20 Aug 1979, Erie PA).

CR238135332   James Robert Wilder (b 15 Feb 1982, Erie PA).

CR238135333   Holly Kristine Wilder (b 20 Jan 1988, Erie PA).

CR2381354   Edward Lee Seigworth (b 17 Oct 1935, Clarion PA) m 30 Aug 1950, Milwaukee WI, Marjorie Selma Moeller (b 26 Mar 1929, Milwaukee WI). USAF; M Ed, administration, U of WI, Milwaukee; teachers, Milwaukee WI.

CR23813541   Susan Melinda Seigworth (31 May 1962, Milwaukee WI) m 4 Jun 1983, Cedarburg WI, Marc David Simpson (11 Feb 1962, Marshall MN). AB, St Olaf C, 1984; MA Hunter Col, 1986. Dance therapist, Mpls MN.

CR23813542   John Edward Seigworth (b 9 Jul 1964, Milwaukee WI) m 20 Jun 1992, Minneapolis MN, Louise Jacobwith (b 31 Oct 1968, Minneapolis MN). BS, U of WI, restaurant manager, Mpls MN.

CR2381355   Phyllis Marie Seigworth (b 13 Aug 1937, Clarion PA) m 18 May 1957, Clarion PA, Charles Joseph Aaron (b 30 Mar 1934, Clarion PA). She, drugstore employee. He, USMC; postal worker, Clarion PA.

CR23813551   David Charles Aaron (b 4 Feb 1959, Clarion PA) m 29 Sep 1984, Clarion PA, Theresa Ann Godfrey (b 25 Feb 1956, Hollidaysburg PA). BS, Clarion (PA) U; factory worker, Shippenville PA.

CR238135511   Matthew David Aaron (7 May 1987, Clarion PA).

CF238135512   Benjamin James Aaron (12 Aug 1991, Clarion PA.)

CR23813552   Steven Edward Aaron (26 May 1961, Clarion PA) m 2 Feb 1980, Clarion PA, Jane Elizabeth Rapp (26 Jan 1962, Marble PA). Trucker, Shippenville PA.

CR238135521   Margaret Jane Aaron (20 Nov 1982, Clarion PA).

CR238135522   Alex Andrew Aaron (19 Oct 1989, Clarion PA-19 Oct 1989, Clarion PA). Bur PA.

CR238136   Donnie Day Seigworth (3 Aug 1900, Strattanville PA-23 Sep 1900, Strattanville PA). Bur near Fryburg PA.

CR238137   Arnold Banks Seigworth (1 Aug 1901, Clarion Tp, Clarion Co. PA-6 Oct 1968, Brookville PA) m 9 Oct 1933, Bradford PA, Mary Gladys Best (27 Sep 1906, Perry Tp, Clarion Co PA-3 Jul 1989, Clarion PA). Bur Strattanville PA. Driller, farmer, trucker, merchant, Knox Strattanville PA.

CR2381371   Donna Gae Seigworth (b 31 Jul 1934, Knox PA) m 26 Nov 1960, Clarion Tp, Clarion Co PA, Howard Dale Reitz (b 21 Jul 1933, Heathville PA). He, clergyman in various PA towns.

CR23813711   Tammy Denise Reitz (b 19 Nov 1961, Meadville PA) m 23 Oct 1982, Bradford PA, Patrick Michael Holleran (b 25 Oct 1957, Bradford PA). She, physician's secretary, Bradford PA.

CR238137111   Tricia Ann Holleran (11 Apr 1983, Bradford PA).

CR238137112   Joseph Michael Holleran (b 21 Jul 1984, Bradford PA).

CR238137113   Joshua Patrick Holleran (b 11 Mar 1987, Bradford PA).

CR2381372   Arnold Vaughn Seigworth (b 17 Jun 1935, Beaver Tp, Clarion Co PA) m 20 Oct 1956, Alliquippa PA, Margret Delores Barlett (b 18 Nov 1938, Leatherwood PA). No chn. Instructor, Glenwillard PA.

CR2381373   Darwin Jay Seigworth (b 13 Sep 1937, Beaver Tp, Clarion Co PA) m 29 Dec 1990, Strattanville PA, Virginia Louella Orris (b 27 May 1926). Lumbermill employee, Knox PA.

CR2381374   Sarah Rachel Seigworth (b 13 Oct 1942, Beaver Tp, Clarion Co PA). Secretary, Clarion PA.

CR238138   Arley Thelma Seigworth (16 Sep 1904, Strattanville PA-19 Jun 1984, Beaver Tp, Clarion Co PA) m 8 May 1924, Mayville NY, Clarion Heeter Stover (5 Mar 1899, Turniphole, Licking Tp, Clarion Co PA-24 Nov 1952, Beaver Tp, Clarion Co PA). Bur near Knox PA. Railroader, hauling, Strattanville and Knox PA.

CR2381381   Blaine Eugene Stover (b 12 Aug 1925, Beaver Tp, Clarion Co PA) m 29 Dec 1950, Clarion PA, Amy Rose Kelleher. USAF; BS, Clarion S C, 1948; MS, PSU; teacher.

CR23813811   Blaine Eugene Stover Jr (b 25 Jul 1951, State College PA) m 1) 25 Aug 1973, Tallahassee FL, Dorothy Estella Brown, div; m 2) 11 Nov 1993, Marty   . Scuba instructor.

CR2381382   James Richard Stover (16 Aug 1927, Beaver Tp, Clarion Co PA-10 Aug 1976, Oil City PA) m 1) 2 Jul 1948, Middletown PA, Connie Reynolds (b 19 Sep 1930, Harrisburg PA), div 1951; m 2) 6 Sep 1954, Beaver Tp, Clarion Co. PA, Virginia Corbett. Bur Beaver Tp, Clarion Co PA. US Army; electrical technician.

*CR23813821   Dennis Lee Stover (26 Oct 1948, Harrisburg PA) m 8 Sep 1973, Harrisburg PA, Louise Hicks (b 28 Dec 1950, Harrisburg PA). Realtor, Middletown PA.

CR238138211   Elizabeth Leigh Stover (b 13 Jan 1978, Harrisburg PA).

CR238138212   Phillip Alan Stover (b 27 Apr 1981, Harrisburg PA).

CR2381383   Dwight Nelson Stover (b 12 Jun 1933, Knox PA) m 5 Jun 1953, Emlenton PA, Carole Marlene Shick (b 17 Jun 1933, Emlenton PA). Sawmill, real estate, drilling, Knox PA.

CR23813831   Laura Lee Stover (b 9 Jun 1954, Oil City PA) m 29 May 1976, Knox PA, Charles James Rogan (b 2 Dec 1952, New Castle PA). She, BS, Clarion S C; nurse, Christiana PA. He, BS, Clarion S C; teacher, Quarryville PA.

CR238138311   Jennifer Lee Rogan (b 21 May 1977, Oil City PA).

CR238138312   Julie Renee Rogan (b 23 Nov 1979, Wilmington DE).

CR238138313   Emily Sue Rogan (b 11 Feb 1982, Wilmington DE).

CR23813832   Daniel Frederick Stover (b 16 Jul 1955, Oil City PA) m 20 Apr 1985, Long Beach Island NJ, Johannah Carol Anglin (b 17 Mar 1956, England). BS, PSU; engineer, Anchorage AK.

CR238138321   Hannah Clarion Stover (5 Mar 1986, Cody WY).

CR238138322   Archibald Daniel Stover (28 Jan 1994, Aberdeen Scotland).

CR23813833   Paul Andrew Stover (b 25 Jul 1958, Oil City PA) m 15 Oct 1983, Coatesville PA, Nancy

Suzanne Jones (b 17 Nov 1959, West Chester PA). AB, Clarion (PA) S Col; teacher, Fullerton CA.

CR238138331   Andrew Christian Stover (6 Sep 1988, Fullerton CA).

CR238138332   Abigail Grace Stover (4 Feb 1992, Fullerton CA).

CR23813834   Curtis Dwight Stover (27 Feb 1960, Oil City PA) m 18 May 1991, Knox PA, Brenda R Thompson (6 May 1967, Tucson AZ). Natural gas and oil technician, Knox PA.

CR238138341   Adrienne Nicole Stover (b 4 Sep 1991, Clarion PA).

CR238138342   Matthew Curtis Stover (b 22 Nov 1993, Du Bois PA).

CR23813835   Michael Joseph Stover (b 11 Jun 1964, Oil City PA) m 17 Sep 1988, Gryburg PA, Julie Ann O'Neill (b 7 Nov 1964, Oil City PA). PSU; petroleum and natural gas engineer, Houston TX.

CR2381384   Cornelius GW Stover (16 Jan 1935, Beaver Tp, Clarion Co PA) m 6 Aug 1954, Beaver Tp, Clarion Co. PA, Pauline Ruth Monrean (27 Jan 1934, Beaver Tp, Clarion Co PA) Merchant, Knox PA.

CR23813841   Elizabeth Karen Stover (b 17 May 1956, Oil City PA) m 6 Jun 1975, Beaver Tp, Clarion Co PA, Ronald Eugene Allaman (b 24 Oct 1947, Brookville PA). BS, Clarion S Col; teacher, Knox PA.

CR238138411   Angela Joyc Allaman (b 24 Sep 1977, Oil City PA).

CR238138412   Justin Todd Allaman (b 26 Jun 1980, Sayre PA).

CR23813842   Kerry Allen Stover (b 13 Jun 1958, Oil City PA) m 30 Jun 1979, Brookville PA, Beverly J Brosius (b 25 Dec 1959, Oil City PA). Auto technician, Knox PA.

CR238138421   Remington Allen GW Stover (b 25 Jan 1984, Clarion PA).

CR238138422   Felicia Joy Stover (b 5 Oct 1993, Franklin PA).

*CR2381385   Elizabeth Jane Stover (b 3 Apr 1940, Beaver Tp, Clarion Co PA) m 9 Jun 1962, Beaver Tp, Clarion Co PA, James Thomas Hach (b 3 Apr 1941, Oil City PA). She, BS, PSU, 1962; BS, Rochester Inst Tech, 1981; dietitian, Webster NY. He, BS, Clarion S Col, 1964; MA, PSU, 1968; research laboratory.

CR23813851   Charles Thomas Hach (b 12 Apr 1968, Bellefonte PA). Ph.D., Alfred U, NY. Ceramic engineer, Alexandria VA.

CR23813852   Matthew James Hach (b 9 Aug 1969, Rochester NY). MA, Oswego U, NY. Chemist, Xerox Corp, Webster NY.

CR23813853   Susan Jane Hach (b 2 Nov 1970, Rochester NY). MA, Alfred U NY; school counselor, Norwich NY.

CR2381386   Dale Francis Stover (b 17 Feb 1946, Beaver Tp, Clarion Co. PA) m 29 Jun 1968, Salem Tp, Clarion Co. PA, Patricia Elaine Say (b 27 Nov 1946, Oil City PA). AB, Clarion S Col, 1968; manager of chemical procurement, Chagrin Falls OH.

CR23813861   Heather Elizabeth Stover (b 27 Nov 1974, Cleveland OH).

CR23813862   Heidi Suzanne Stover (b 27 Nov 1974, Cleveland OH).

*CR238139   Mary Rosanna Seigworth (21 Aug 1906, Strattanville PA-3 Mar 1995, Oil City PA) m 5 Jun 1929, Shippenville PA, Ralph Leonard Klingler (13 Feb 1900, Mariasville, Venango Co PA-28 Jun 1974, Oil City PA). Bur Emlenton PA. She, teacher; he, driller.

*CR2381391   Norma Jean Klingler (b 15 Oct 1930, Franklin PA) m 16 Oct 1954, Emlenton PA, Jack Clifford Sanford (b 3 Mar 1921, Franklin PA). She, secretary. Franklin PA.

CR23813911   Nancy Ellen Sanford (b 17 Dec 1956, Franklin PA) m 28 Nov 1981, Windsor CT, Glenn Theodore Stafford (b 7 Apr 1956, Springfield OH), div 1994. She, BS, 1979,Baldwin Wallace Berea OH; MS,VA Tech, Blacksburg VA, 1995.

CR238139111   Meredith Anne Stafford (1 Apr 1985, Richmond VA).

CR23813912   Susan Elaine Sanford (28 Aug 1959, Franklin PA) m 28 May 1983, Oil City PA, Mike David Painter (13 Oct 1956, Brookville PA), div 1994. She, BS, Clarion U, 1995. She teacher, Franklin PA.

CR238139121   Stephanie Susanne Painter (b 24 Oct 1985, Franklin PA).

CR238139122   Erin Michelle Painter (b 8 Dec 1988, Franklin PA).

CR2381392   Betty Jean Klingler (b 10 Mar 1932, Emlenton PA) m 26 Jul 1952, Oil City PA, Donald Keith Bowser (b 15 Oct 1931, Butler PA).

CR23813921   Andrew Keith Bowser (b 23 Jul 1959, Butler PA) m 2 Jul 1983, Wellsboro PA, Paula Kay Hazelett (b 30 Jun 1959). He, BS, PSU, 1982; architectural engineer, Bedford TX. She, AB, PSU; accountant.

*CR2381393   Richard Harrison Klingler (b 4 Aug 1937, Emlenton PA) m. 26 Aug 1961, Emlenton PA, Kay Ruth Weiser (b 30 Sep 1940, Oil City PA). He, BS, PSU, 1959, MS, Carnegie Mellon, 1961; Retire Exec, chemical co, Baton Rouge LA.

CR23813931   David Allen Klingler (b 13 Jul 1963, Summit NJ) m 20 Jul 1991, Sulphur Springs TX, Michelle Moore (b 3 Feb 1965, Sulphur Springs TX). AB, MA, PSU; JD, U of TX; attorney, Plano TX.

CR23813932   Marianne Klingler (13 Dec 1966, Summit NJ) m 2 Sep 1995, Baton Rouge LA, John Robert Schnell (b 23 Oct 1969, Decatur IL). BA, PSU. She, Paralegal, Birmingham LA.

CR23813933   Jennifer Gaye Klingler (b 21 Feb 1972, Summit NJ). BS, PSU, 1994. International marketing, Phoenix AZ.

CR2381394   Robert Meredith Klingler (2 Jan 1941, Emlenton PA-11 Jun 1951, Emlenton PA). Bur Emlenton PA.

*CR23813A   Clara Adda Seigworth (17 Oct 1908, Strattanville PA-27 Nov 1995, Oil City PA) m 30 Jul 1932, Franklin PA, Raymond Frederick Oiesen (2 Dec 1893, Oil City PA-27 Nov 1969, Oil City PA). Bur Cranberry PA. She, secretary; he, piano and pipe organ repair and tuner, Franklin and Oil City PA.

*CR23813A1   Sarah Lavina Oiesen (b 19 Mar 1934, Oil City PA) m 21 Jul 1956, Oil City PA, James Leonard Williams (b 26 Oct 1934, St. Louis MO).BS Music, Brown U; Wheaton Col adm, Wheaton IL.

CR23813A11   Kimberly Joy Williams (stillborn, 16 Apr 1958,St Louis MO). Bur St Louis MO.

CR23813A12   David Oiesen Williams (b 27 Oct 1960, Alton IL) m 16 Aug 1980, Wheaton IL, Lois Lee Herndon (b 16 Mar 1959, Summit NJ). Real estate, Wheaton IL.

CR23813A121   David Garrett Williams (b 28 Aug 1982, Wheaton IL).

CR23813A122   Melissa Lee Williams (b 29 Sep 1985, Wheaton IL).

CR23813A123   Rachel Ann Williams (b 11 Oct 1989, Wheaton IL).

CR23813A124   Daniel James Williams (b 12 Aug 1993, Wheaton IL).

*CR23813A13   Beth Erica Williams (b 13 Sep 1961, Alton IL) m 31 Jul 1982, Wheaton IL, Kevin Jay Wierenga (b 3 May 1960, Grand Rapids MI). BA, North Central Col; corporation manager, Grand Rapids MI.

CR23813A131   Natalie Claire Wierenga (b 11 Apr 1988, Grand Rapids MI).

CR23813A132   Lauren Avery Wierenga (b 27 Mar 1991, Grand Rapids MI).

CR23813A2   Charles Raymond Oiesen (b 21 Jun 1938, Oil City PA) m 1) 21 Aug 1965, Oil City PA, Judith Kay Miller (b 22 Jun 1942, Allison Park PA), div; m 2) 17 Aug 1991, North East PA, Carol L Maas (9 Dec 1940, North East PA). BS CAU; organ builder, Stuart's Draft VA.

*CR23813A21   Eric Andrew Oiesen (b 9 Nov 1966, Oil City PA) m 2 Jan 1993, Colonial Heights VA, Cory Ann Browder (b 30 Mar 1968, Colonial Heights VA). MA, VA Poly Inst; electrical engineer, Sunnyvale CA.

CR23813A22   Todd Charles Oiesen (b 9 Jan 1970, Erie PA).

CR23813A23   Peter Raymond Oiesen (b 19 Nov 1972, Waynesboro VA) m 25 Jun 1994, Charleston SC, Angela Dawn Bowick (b 8 Oct 1973, Charleston SC). US Navy, Norwalk CT.

CR23813B   Burdett Weiser Seigworth (12 Dec 1910, Strattanville PA-17 Sep 1965, Franklin PA) m 10 Apr 1943, East Brady PA, Rose Lucille Spudic (b 20 Mar 1923, Rimersburg PA). Bur near Knox PA. Farmer, Knox PA.

CR23813B1   Karen Diane Seigworth (4 Jun 1944, near Knox PA) m 11 Jan 1969, Emlenton PA, Ray Louis Minor (2 Nov 1946, Fowler CA). She, hospital employee; he, Commonwealth of PA employee.

CR23813B11   Michele Lee Minor (b 7 Oct 1972, Washington DC).

CR23813B12   Jason Burdett Minor (b 28 Oct 1977, Norwood MA).

CR23813B2   Robert Burdett Seigworth (b 16 Jun 1946, near Knox PA) m 8 Oct 1977, North Charleston SC, Mary Louise Coudle (b 27 Nov 1953, St. Johns, Newfoundland). US Navy; engineer, Atlanta GA.

CR23813B21   Nicole Alice Seigworth (8 Oct 1980, Hawaii-11 Aug 1984, Charleston SC). Bur Goose Creek SC).

CR23813B22   Hannah Elizabeth Seigworth (b 9 Jan 1990, Mt Pleasant SC).

CR23813B23   Sarah Rose Seigworth (b 28 May 1993, Peach Tree City GA).

CR23813B3   Janice Elaine Seigworth (b 25 Feb 1948, near Knox PA) m 1) 18 Nov 1967, Emlenton PA, Harry Michael Jessen (b 6 Jul 1946, Bloomington IN), div 1977; m 2) 31 Jul 1984, Augusta GA, James David Mousseau (b 31 Jul 1951, Renton WA). BS, Burnaw Col GA; US Army, Ft Gordon GA.

CR23813B31   Angela Christine Jessen (b 11 Nov 1968, Chitose Japan) m 2 May 1992, Augusta GA, John Matthew Crews (b 3 Aug 1969, Augusta GA). Program specialist, Grovetown GA.

CR23813B32   Denise Carmon Jessen (b 18 May 1972, Kimbrough Army Hospital, MD). Director, gymnastics center, Harlen GA.

*CR23813B4   Clifton Francis Seigworth (b 9 Dec 1956, near Knox PA) m 9 Jan 1993, Sumter SC, Shanna Marie Sircy (b 31 Dec 1969, Ft Bragg NC). USAF, Lakenheath, England.

CR23813C   Jacob Frederick Seigworth (b 8 May 1919, Strattanville PA) m 19 Sep 1937, Knox PA, Irma Iona Beck (b 8 Sep 1918, Knox PA). Farmer, gun dealer, school bus contractor,storekeeper, local government officeholder near Knox PA.

CR23813C1   Kenneth Robert Seigworth (b 24 Feb 1938, near Knox PA) m 12 Mar 1960, Knox PA, Malvene Adelle Creese (b 23 Mar 1939, Harmorville PA). Merchant, Knox PA.

CR23813C11   Gregory James Seigworth (b 18 Sep 1961, Clarion PA) m 13 Apr 1985, Turkey City PA, Jacqueline Elizabeth Benn (b 22 Oct 1961, Grove City PA). MA, Clarion S Col PA, PhD, U of IL; professor, Millersville U, Millersville PA.

CR23813C111   Kendall Roseanne Seigworth (b 25 Apr 1993, Champaign IL).

CR23813C12   Alan Frederick Seigworth (b Aug 1963, Clarion PA) m 13 May 1989, Knox PA, Heather Lynnette Wetcel (b Dec 1968, San Diego CA). Merchant, Knox PA.

CR23813C121   Timothy Steven Seigworth (b 29 Apr 1991, Franklin PA).

CR23813C122   Lynn James Lon Seigworth (b 21 Sep 1993, Franklin PA).

CR23813C13   Kenneth Lon Seigworth (b 12 Dec 1966, Clarion PA) m 17 Mar 1990, Dutch Hill PA, Cynthia Faye Callander (b 4 Feb 1968, Brookville PA). Merchant, Emlenton PA.

CR23813C131   Alyssn Cheyenne Seigworth (b Sep 1990, Franklin PA).

CR23813C132   Jeffery Robert Seigworth (b Sep 1993, Franklin PA).

CR23813C2   Judith Ann Seigworth (b Nov 1944, Knox PA) m 23 Feb 1962, Knox PA, David Paul Weber (11 Apr 1942, Franklin PA). She, personnel manager, Franklin, PA. He, policeman.

CR23813C21   Janet Suzette Weber (b Sep 1962, Ft Lee VA) m 25 Aug 1984, Franklin PA, Michale Paul Anderson (b Mar 1962, Franklin PA). She, AB, PSU, 1984; he, PSU; trade specialist, Erie PA.

CR23813C211   Morgan Renae Anderson (b 14 Mar 1991, Franklin PA).

CR23813C212   Johanna Lea Anderson (b 24 Aug 1992, Erie PA).

CR23813C22   Tracy Ann Weber (b 11 Sep 1966, Clarion PA). Lab tech, St Petersburg FL.

CR23813C23   Jill Marie Weber (b 1 Jun 1975, Pittsburgh PA).

CR23813C3   Russell Alan Seigworth (b 9 Jun 1946, Beaver Tp Clarion Co. PA) m 15 Dec 1971, Patricia Ann Pappal (b 16 Jul 1947, Indiana PA). Accountant, Latrobe PA.

CR23813C31   Kelly Lynn Seigworth (b 31 Oct 1971, Clarion PA) m 12 Feb 1994, Indiana PA, John Alan David (b 3 Dec 1971, Merced CA). BS, IN U, PA; accountant, Greensburg PA.

CR23813C32   Kristine Ann Seigworth (b 15 Apr 1974, Oil City PA).

CR23813C33   Kimberly Rae Seigworth (b 19 Jun 1976, Indiana PA).

CR23813C34   Mark Russell Seigworth (b 23 Jun 1979, Indiana PA).

CR23814   John Franklin Curtis Weiser (30 Aug 1873, Farmington Tp, Clarion Co PA-25 Jan 1962, Strattanville PA) m 17 Apr 1901, Tionesta PA, Ada Lavina Miller (17 Mar 1874, Tylersburg PA-6 May 1945, Strattanville PA). Bur Strattanville PA. General store, Strattanville, 1905-55.

CR238141   Milburn Arthur Weiser (8 Apr 1902, Tylersburg PA-6 Dec 1981, Los Angeles CA) m 1926, Clarion PA, Edith Johnson (b 10 Oct 1906) div;. No chn. Bur Los Angeles CA. Mechanic.

CR2381411   John Curtis Weiser (b 24 Feb 1927, strattanville PA) m 16 Mar 1952, Du Bois PA, Elvera Hyberg (b 15 Jun 1925, Kane PA). he, supervisor, Brockway Glass co. She, employee, same.

CR2381412   Charles Eugene Weiser (b 28 Aug 1929, strattanville PA) m 23 Nov 1947, Bonnie Elizabeth Moore (b 28 Jun 1918, Allen Mills PA). He, art and design, brockway Glass Works.

CR23814121   Robert Charles Weiser (b 7 May 1949, Brockway PA). auditor, Ft Lauderdale FL.

CR238142   Alberta Belle Weiser (21 Feb 1904, Tylersburg PA-8 Feb 1969, Erie PA) m 1 Mar 1923, Ripley NY, John Hornbaugh (15 Mar 1893-26 May 1964, Erie PA). Bur Strattanville PA. He, coal industry.

CR2381421   Karl Burton Horbaugh (b 28 Feb 1924, Strattanville PA) m 21 Oct 1950, New Britain CT, M Rosalie Bednarik.

CR23814211   Karla Hornbaugh.

CR23814212   Donna Hornbaugh.

*CR238143   Margaret Althea Weiser (b2 Dec 1906, Strattanville PA) m 15 Oct 1931, Clarion PA, Rene Gustave Vandeuren (15 Nov 1900, Jumet Belgium-30 Oct 1973, Erie PA). Bur Strattanville PA. He, tool and die maker.

*CR2381431   Jeannine Marie Vandeuren (b 10 May 1932, Clarion PA) m 23 Nov 1974, Ridgewood NJ, Harry Rimassa, div BA, PSU, 1954; teacher, Wykoff NJ.

CR2381432   Frances Yvonne Vandeuren (b 11 Mar 1934, Clarion PA) m 10 Aug 1957, Lakewood OH, Ralph Edward Hiskey (b 1 Aug 1934, Lakewood OH). She, BS, PSU, 1956, home economics; he, B.S., U of Rochester, 1956; vice president, U.S. West, Seattle WA.

CR23814321   Susan Elizabeth Hiskey (b 24 Jul 1958, Lakewood OH) m 16 Aug 1986, Ridgewood NJ, Mark Richard Bauer (b 10 Oct 1957, Cincinnati OH). She, BA, Miami U, 1980, medical technologist. He, BS, Denison U, 1980; MS, MI SU, 1983; Ph.D., MSU, 1986; research scientist, Battelle Memorial Institute Columbus OH.

CR238143211   Erin Marie Bauer (b 10 Apr 1988, Delaware OH).

CR238143212   Anne Katherine Bauer (b 17 Oct 1989, Delaware OH).

CR23814322   David Brian Hiskey (b 21 Feb 1960, Lakewood OH) m 2 Jul 1983, Ridgewood NJ, Lois Margaret Freimuth (b 10 Aug 1960, Hackensack NJ). He, BS, Arizona SU, 1982; construction project manager. She, BA, Fairleigh Dickinson Un., 1982, teacher.

CR238143221   Robert Andrew Hiskey (b 7 May 1986, Ridgewood NJ).

CR238143222   Elizabeth Anne Hiskey (b 29 Nov 1988, Ridgewood NJ).

CR238143223   Sarah Katherine Hiskey (b 28 Aug 1992, Ridgewood NJ).

*CR23814323   Karen Elaine Hiskey (b 1 Sep 1965, Canfield OH) BA, MI SU, 1987; sales administration, Seattle WA.

CR238144   Kathryn Pauline Weiser (3 Aug 1909, Strattanville PA-30 Apr 1975, Meadville PA) m 6 Dec 1934, Meadville PA, James Wesley Hickernell (10 Jul 1900, Meadville PA-17 Feb 1966, Meadville PA). Bur Strattanville PA. She, RN, Meadville City Hospital; he, railroad engineer.

CR2381441   Kathryn Kay Hickernell (b 12 Nov 1935, Meadville PA) m 1959, Willis Williams.

CR23814411   Pamela Kay Williams (b 25 Jul 1960, Meadville PA).

CR2381442   Susan Jane Hickernell (b 25 Nov 1936, Meadville PA)m 21 Jun 1958, William A McWilliams, div. She, RN, Meadville City Hospital.

CR23814421   John Charles McWilliams (b 8 Feb 1959, Meadville PA) m 1) 8 Jun 1979, Meadville PA, Susan Marie Bulger, div; m 2) 14 Sep 1991, Carolyn Walton (b 25 Mar 1949).

CR238144211   Brandon John McWilliams (b 15 Jul 1979[?], Meadville PA).

CR238144212   Jessica Marie McWilliams (b 28 Feb 1980, Honolulu HI).

CR23814422   Steven James McWilliams (b 6 Nov 1960, Meadville PA) m 15 Jan 1980, New Richmond PA, Pamela McElhaney, div.

CR238144221   Summer McWilliams (b 23 Jul 1980, Meadville PA).

CR23814423   Bruce Allen McWilliams (b 6 Nov 1961, Meadville PA). Computer tech.

CR23814424   Douglas Eugene McWilliams (b 23 Dec 1966, Meadville PA). Delivery service.

CR23814425   Darrell Duane McWilliams (b 22 Jun 1971, Meadville PA). Produce specialist.

CR23815   James Elmer Weiser (30 May 1875, Tylersburg PA-1 Dec 1946, Strattanville PA) m 23 Apr 1902, Fanny Alice Keefer Hiles (17 Jul 1873, Armstrong PA-6 Sep 1910, Strattanville PA). Bur Strattanville PA. Farmer.

CR238151   Blanda Mae Weiser (20 Mar 1903, Strattanville PA-22 Mar 1987, Pittsburgh PA) m 1) 9 Sep 1921, Limestone PA, Floyd Edison Lewis (25 Feb 1895, Reidsburg PA-9 Jan 1959, Strattanville PA); m 2) 6 Nov 1966, Strattanville PA, Howard O Wilson (1896, Strattanville PA-7 May 1976, Sarasota FL). Blanda and Floyd bur Strattanville PA; Howard bur. Clarion PA. Floyd, lumberer and miner.

CR2381511   Frances Rose Lewis (b 28 Nov 1922, Pittsburg PA) m 20 Apr 1946, Miola PA, Donald Walter (b 4 Dec 1921, Fisher PA). Corporate vice president, Strattanville PA.

CR23815111   H Donald Walter Jr. (b 2 Nov 1946, Brookville PA) m 2 Sep 1967, Fisher PA, Sarah Clinger (b 31 Dec 1948, Brookville PA). He, Clarion & Syracuse U, math & physics teacher, Gowanda NY. She, Bradford Nursing School.

CR238151111   Veronica Dawn Walter (b 9 Oct 1970, Jamestown NY) m 3 Jun 1990, Gowanda NY, Tom Lawson (b 4 Dec 1968, Gowanda NY). She, Fredonia U, computer science, 1993. He, Fredonia U criminology, 1992. Res Marlton NJ.

CR238151112   Wendy Renee Walter (b 4 Dec 1973, Jamestown NY).

CR23815112   Ronald Paul Walter (b 2 Sep 1948, Brookville PA) m 24 Jun 1972, Clarion PA, Carole Lane (b 16 Jan 1952, Elmira NY). He, Slippery Rock U; phys ed teacher, Sigel PA. She, Clarion U, elementary education.

CR238151121   Barbra Frances Walter (b 29 May 1976, Du Bois PA).

CR238151122   Caron Paulann Walter (b 11 Apr 1982, Du Bois PA).

CR2381512   Paul Wade Lewis (7 Feb 1924, Pittsburgh PA-9 Aug 1964, Pittsburgh PA) m 10 May

1947, Strattanville PA, Leona Blachier (31 May 1926, Strattanville PA). Bur Strattanville PA. Mechanic.

CR23815121   Robert Paul Lewis (b 2 May 1948, Brookville PA) m 2 Aug 1972, Strattanville PA, Margaret Beers (b 17 Nov 1951, Brookville PA). He, Pittsburgh Electronics Inst; electronic tech, Newark OH.

CR238151211   Maris Leigh Lewis (b 28 Aug 1977, Newark OH).

CR238151212   Corey Robert Lewis (b 29 Aug 1980, Newark OH).

CR23815122   Carol Ann Lewis (b 22 Apr 1951, Brookville PA) m 1) 26 Jun 1971, Foxburg PA, David Best (10 Jul 1950, Butler PA-13 Jan 1973, Oil City PA); m 2) 31 Mar 1990, Strattanville PA, Terry Slagle (b 11 Jun 1947, Brookville PA). Best bur Perryville Cemetery. She, Slippery Rock U; data processing manager, cost accountant, Leeper PA. Best, PA S Slagle, PA S; bookkeeper.

CR23815123   Susan Marie Lewis (b 28 Oct 1959, Brookville PA) m 11 Aug 1984, Strattanville PA, David Buzard (b 15 Jan 1958, Strattanville PA).He, factory worker; reside Corisca PA.

CR238151231   Kari Lynn Buzard (b 13 Mar 1986, Clarion PA).

CR238151232   Katelin Nicole Buzard (b 26 Jul 1989, Clarion PA).

CR2381513   Mabel Mae Lewis (b 26 Sep 1925, Strattanville PA) m 28 May 1960, Big Run PA, Eli Blachier (b 9 Jan 1920, Suttersville PA). He, plumber. Res Strattanville PA.

CR23815131   James Eli Blachier (b 18 Dec 1960, Brookville PA) m 28 May 1988, Strattanville PA, Mary Reed (b 6 Nov 1965, Strattanville PA). Res Strattanville PA.

CR238151311   Joshua Eli Blachier (b 1 Jul 1989, Brookville PA).

CR238151312   Robert James Blachier (b 18 Dec 1991, Brookville PA).

CR23815132   John Allen Blachier (b 25 1962, Brookville PA) m 25 Jun 1962, Clarion PA, Jean Huefner (b 28 Oct 1963, Brookville PA). Grad from automotive school. Res Clarion PA.

CR238151321   Nathan Tyler Blachier (b 8 Jul 1990, Franklin PA).

CR238152   Truman Wade Weiser (b 2 Feb 1906, Strattanville PA-18 Mar 1986, Clarion PA) m 21 Jun 1941, Margaret Elder (b 7 Dec 1905, Strattanville PA). No chn.. Bur Clarion PA. Carpenter, Clarion Co. PA. Res Clarion PA.

CR238153   Twila Ruth Weiser (11 Jul 1908, Strattanville PA-23 May 1988, Meadville PA) m Meadville PA, Norman Appenrodt (21 Oct 1911, Pittsburgh PA-12 Apr 1980, Meadville PA). No chn. Bur Meadville PA. He, timekeeper.

CR238154   Sarah Alice Weiser (b 5 Sep 1910, Strattanville PA) m 30 Sep 1939, Summerville PA, Paul Fowler (21 Sep 1913, Rimersburg PA-13 Jun 1967, Natrona Heights PA). No chn. Bur Lower Burrell PA. He, millwright. She, res Apollo PA.

CR23816   Isabel Weiser.

CR23817   Jacob Clyde Weiser (23 Dec 1878, Farmington Tp, Clarion Co PA-13 Mar 1944, Warren PA) m Blanche Girts (9 Jun 1878, Tylersburg PA-1957, Sheffield PA). Bur Tylersburg PA. General store, Sheffield PA.

CR238171   Lawrence Keith Weiser (b 17 May 1903, Tylersburg PA) m 1) 1923, Jamestown NY, Violet Slack (d 1926); m 2) 30 Apr 1935, Jamestown NY, Ethel Weiser (b 11 Oct 1909, Sugargrove PA).

CR2381711   Lawrence Keith Weiser Jr (b 26 Nov 1924, Jamestown NY) m 18 Sep 1948, Bemus Point NY, Phyllis L Carlson. Supervisor, Stromberg Carlson Digital Systems Center, Sanford FL.

CR23817111   Lawrence Keith Weiser III (b 22 Apr 1950, Jamestown NY) m 15 Aug 1970, Largo FL, Elaine Hamilton.

CR238171111   Amy Lynette Weiser (b 16 Jan 1973, Tampa FL).

CR238171112   Jennifer Nicole Weiser (b 17 Aug 1975, Tampa FL).

CR2381712   Craig Arthur Weiser (b 25 Sep 1962, Tampa FL). USAF, 1980.

CR238172   Marion Josephine Weiser (25 Jan 1906, Kellettville PA-2 Feb 1978, sheffield PA) m Gilbert Carl Lundquist (d 1976).

CR2381721   Jean Lundquist m Raymond Lord.

CR238173   Ariel Weiser (b 17 Apr 1911, Kellettville PA).

CR238174   Burdette C Weiser (29 Mar 1918, Kellettville PA-2 Oct 1969, Warren PA)m 4 Aug 1939, Russell PA, Delma Tome (b 19 Jun 1918) 4 ch; 7grch. Bur Sheffield PA.

CR23818   Ida Weiser m Ira King.

CR238181   Ruby King.

CR238182   Milo King.

CR238183   William King.

CR238184   Wesley King.

CR238185   Clem King. Unm.

CR238186   Ruth King.

CR238187   Mabel King.

CR23819   Albert Wade Weiser (19 Jun 1884,Farmington Tp, Clarion Co PA-21 Aug 1939, Farmington Tp, Clarion Co PA) m Iva Zerbe. Coal miner, Tylersburg PA.

CR238191   Albert Wade Weiser Jr.

CR238192   Leonard Weiser. Unm.

CR238193   Paul Weiser.

CR2381931   Son Weiser.

CR2381932   Daughter Weiser.

CR238194   Raymond Milburn Weiser (b 8 Mar 1922, Leeper PA) m 11 Nov 1946, Oil City PA, Anna Marie Workman (b 14 May 1927, Oil City PA). He, laborer; she, secretary, Oil City PA.

CR2381941   Raymond Paul Weiser (b 19 Mar 1947, Oil City PA) m 19 Nov 1975, Erie PA, Francis Morgan (b 15 Aug 1952, Erie PA). No chn. USA, 1968-72. Both GE factory, Erie PA.

CR2381942   Jennifer Leigh Weiser (b 25 Jan 1949, Oil City PA) m 1) 1966, Jacksonville NC, Fred Swires; div 1970; 2) 10 Aug 1974, Oil City PA, Joseph Curran (b 29 May 1938, Oil City PA). She, LPN. He factory Worker.

CR23819421   Debora Ann Swires (b 6 Nov 1968, Jacksonville NC). Unm.; adopted by Joseph Curran.

CR238194211   Danielle Curran (b 19 Mar 1986).

CR238194212   Joshua Perry (19 Jun 1987-1 Dec 1987).

CR238194213   Millissa Ann Grinnell (b 8 Oct 1990).

CR238194214   Devin Robert Curran (b 4 Jan 1993).

CR23819422   Jason Aaron Curran (b 28 Aug 1976, Oil City PA).

CR23819423   Megan Suzanne Curran (b Apr 1980, Oil City PA).

*CR2381943   Thomas Earl Weiser (b 15 Apr 1952, Oil City PA) m 17 Feb 1973, Oil City PA, Margaret Julia Martin (b 7 Oct 1952, Oil City PA). PSU, 1978, City employee, 1972, Oil City PA.

CR23819431   Thomas Earl Weiser Jr (b 31 Aug 1974, Oil City PA). PSU, 1991.

CR23819432   Margaret Suzann Weiser (b 2 Mar 1977, Oil City PA).

CR23819433   Christopher Conrad Weiser (b 8 Dec 1980, Oil City PA).

CR23819434   Sandra Pamela Patricia Weiser (b 22 Sep 1990, Oil City PA).

CR2381944   William Joseph Weiser (b 9 Oct 1952, Oil City PA) m 8 Apr 1978, Franklin PA, Sally Jo Knezevich (b 16 May 1952, Pittsburgh PA). UPS driver, Oil City PA.

CR23819441   Daniel William Weiser (b 24 Oct 1982).

CR2381945   Mary Martha Weiser (b 1 Jan 1956, Oil City PA) m 30 Jun 1979, Oil City PA, Ronald Martyna (b 19 Feb 1954, Oil City PA). He, US Postal Service, Charlotte NC.

CR23819451   Jamie Marie Martyna (b 3 Mar 1981).

CR23819452   Kristy Leigh Martyna (b 1 Jun 1982).

CR2381946   James Albert Weiser (b 1 Apr 1958, Oil City PA) m 16 May 1981, Franklin PA, Nancy Jo Romanchek (b 25 Apr 1958, franklin PA). PSU, PA DOT, Franklin PA.

CR23819461   Stephenie Jo Weiser (b 23 Sep 1983).

CR23819462   Tiffeny Marie Weiser (b 13 Jul 1986).

CR2381947   Susan Joanna Weiser (b 15 Oct 1963, Oil City, PA) m 9 Oct 1987, Oil City PA, Christopher Steward (b 15 Oct 1963, Oil City PA). No chn.. He U Pitt; engineer; she, U Pitt, A Band MA, physician's office, Franklin PA.

CR2382   George B Weiser (1843, Farmington Tp, Clarion Co-19 Jun 1864, near Petersburg VA). Unm. Killed, Civil War. Bur City Point National Cemetery.

CR2383   Joseph A Weiser (20 Jul 1845-13 Dec 1912) m Helen   . Farmer, 1870, Loborer, Farminton Tp, Clarion Co PA, 1880.

CR23831   George B Weiser (b 16 Aug 1869).

CR23832   Isabel Weiser.

CR238321   Weiser m RC Ely.

CR238323   Arley J Weiser (b ca 1871, Farmington Tp, Clarion Co PA) m Sydney Lynch.

CR2383231   Helen Weiser m GC McCandless.

CR2383232   Joseph Weiser.

CR2383233   Helen Weiser.

CR2383234   Bud Weiser.

CR238324   Winfried N Weiser (b ca 1873, Farmington Tp, Clarion Co PA).

CR238325   Albert S Weiser (b ca 1877, Farmington Tp, Clarion Co PA).

CR238326   Calista M Weiser (b ca 1879, Farmington Tp, Clarion Co PA).

CR2384   Mary Jenny Weiser (b 1848, Monroe Tp, Clarion Co PA).

CR2385   Washington Scott Weiser (b 1850, Monroe Tp, Clarion Co PA).

CR2386   Margaret Weiser (b 1852, Clarion Co PA) m Samuel Reyner.

CR2387   Rose Ann Weiser (b 1854, Clarion Co PA) m Reed.

CR2388   Lucinda Carrie Weiser (b 1857, Clarion Co PA) m Henry Lockwood.

CR2389   William H Weiser (b 1860, Farmington Tp, Clarion Co PA).

CR239   Susannah Weiser (b 12 Jun 1820, Union Tp Mifflin Co PA) m Jacob Myers (2 Mar 1820, Union co PA-6 Apr 1886). No chn.. She was a domestic in Monroe Tp, Clarion Co PA on the 1860 Census. She was his second wife; he, weaver.

CR23A   John Washington Weiser (9 Dec 1822, Union Tp, Mifflin Co PA-2 Oct 1900, Reidsburg PA) m 1845, Jane Henry (Jan 1824, Clarion Co PA-27 May 1912, Reidsburg PA). Bur Reidsburg, Clarion Co PA. He changed the spelling of the surname to Wiser. Farmer and carpenter, Reidsburg and Carroll Co PA.

CR23A1   Robert H Wiser (5 Oct 1846,Monroe Tp, Clarion Co PA-1 Oct 1906, Curtisville PA) m 18 Sep 1871, Limestone PA, Sara Eleanor King (20 Sep 1849, Limestone Tp, Clarion Co PA-14 Mar 1926, Los Angeles CA). He, bur Clarion Co PA; she, bur Los Angeles. Teacher, carpenter, postmaster, justice of the peace, Curllsville PA, 1892.

CR23A11   Kate (Census:Occelia E) Wiser (b 21 Nov 1872, Monroe Tp, Clarion Co PA-21 Apr 1955, Los Angeles CA) m 1899, PA, Scott Benson Conrad (d 1916, Forrest City AR). He bur Forrest City AR; she, Los Angeles CA.

CR23A111   Rober Benson Conrad (Forrest City AR-Forrest City AR).

CR23A112   Estelle Conrad (Forrest City AR-Forrest City AR).

CR23A113   Eleanor Mary Conrad (b 7 Mar 1913, Forrest City AR) m 9 May 1936, Los Angeles CA,

Harry Gassetty (b 30 Sep 1905, Golden MO). Machinist, San Gabriel CA.

CR23A1131   Wayne Conrad Cassetty (b 21 Jul 1940, Los Angeles CA) m 22 Mar 1963, Las Vegas NE, Glenda Henson (b 28 Feb 1944, Sanger CA). He, Redlands U, CA; US Dept of Justice, Cary IL.

CR23A11311   Michael Frederick Cassetty (b 18 May 1964, Pasadena CA).

CR23A11312   David Robert Cassetty (b 19 Sep 1966, Pasadena CA).

CR23A1132   Donald Elery Cassetty (b 18 Feb 1942, Los Angeles CA) m 18 Jun 1965, Alhambra CA, Carol Ann Keele (b 23 Dec 1944, Los Angeles CA). AB Redlands U; MA, U OR, Teacher, Eugene OR.

CR23A11321   Julia Ann Cassetty (b 24 Nov 1969, San Gabriel CA).

CR23A11322   Jennifer Lynn Cassetty (b 31 Mar 1973, Eugene OR).

CR23A12   Audley Marie Wiser (b Oct 1874, Clarion Co PA) m 1) Bessie Wakefield (b Apr 1881, PA) div; m 2) Mrs Lottie Bender Lived Jackson Tp, Butler Co PA.

CR23A121   Chester Wiser (b Jun 1899, Butler Co PA).

CR23A122   Ralph Wiser (b Butler Co PA).

CR23A123   Gladys Wiser (b Butler Co PA).

CR23A13   Verda V Wiser (17 Jan 1877, Monroe Tp, Clarion Co PA-26 Dec 1941, Huntington Park CA) m John W McMillan (b 1877). No chn. Lived Butler Co PA, 1909; Los Angeles CA; San Antonion CA.

CR23A14   Floyd K George Wiser (27 Mar 1879, Monroe Tp, Clarion Co PA-11 Aug 1949, Harmony PA) m 1899, Harmony PA, Carrie Enslon (30 Mar 1877, Harmony PA-6 Feb 1960, Harmony PA). Bur Harmony PA. Driller.

CR23A141   Delmont Clem Wiser (16 Sep 1899, Jackson Tp, Butler Co PA-Feb 1969, Harmony PA) m Carrie Isabell Kristophel (b 23 Dec 1901). Bur Harmony PA. Oil driller, Harmony PA

CR23A1411   Robert Edward Wiser (16 Aug 1924, Harmony PA-16 Nov 1944, England). Bur Arlington VA. WWII.

CR23A1412   Thomas Floyd Wiser (b 14 May 1928, Harmony PA) m 29 Dec 1951, Beaver Falls PA, Nancy Fern Shimer (b 25 Aug 1930). Car painter, PA.

CR23A14121   Robert Edward Wiser (b 21 Oct 1952, New Brighton PA m 1) Elaine Fletcher, div; m 2) 1 Jun 1991, Brighton ME, Marita Gorham. Carpenter.

CR23A141211   Jeremy Benjamin Wiser (b 28 May 1975, Ellwood City PA).

CR23A141212   Rosemary Isabelle Wiser (b 30 Mar 1992, N Conway NH).

CR23A141213   Margurite Adele Wiser (b 7 Feb 1994, N Conway NH).

CR23A14122   Cathy Lynn Wiser (b 11 Nov 1954, New Brighton PA) m 15 Jul 1975, Fombell PA, Timothy David Beige (b 23 Jul 1953, Ellwood City PA). He, Geneva Col, Beaver Falls PA. Computer Programmer, Goddard Space Flight Center; res Laurel MD.

CR23A141221   Benjamin Garrett Beige (b 11 Feb 1980, Ellwood City PA).

CR23A141222   Jonathan David Beige (b 26 Dec 1981, Ellwood City PA).

CR23A141223   Anna Marie Beige (b 18 Jun 1990, Boston MA).

CR23A141224   Caleb Edward Beige (b 15 Aug 1994, Peterboro NH).

CR23A14123   Thomas Michael Wiser (b 2 Nov 1956, Ellwood City PA) m Fallston PA, Sandra Ann Bowser. US Army. Welder, Fombell PA.

CR23A141231   Derek Michael Wiser (b 7 Oct 1980, Ellwood City PA).

CR23A141232   Nikki Ann Wiser (b 7 May 1986, Tacoma WA).

CR23A14124   Emily Belle Wiser (b 9 Oct 1964, Ellwood City PA) m 17 Mar 1983, Lynchburg VA, Michael Edward Kelosky (b 15 Sep 1960, Ellwood City PA). Steam fitter.

CR23A141241   Christopher David Kelosky (b 7 Jan 1985, Manchester NH).

CR23A141242   Zachary Andrew Kelosky (b 4 May 1986, Ellwood City PA).

CR23A141243   Carrie Elizabeth Kelosky (b 4 Apr 1988, Ellwood City PA).

CR23A141244   Travis Michael Kelosky (b 26 Mar 1989, Butler PA).

CR23A14145   Chance Edward Kelosky (b 26 Mar 1989, Butler PA).

CR23A142   Dorothy Belle Wiser (b 3 Jun 1902, Harmony PA). Telephone co, Zelienople PA; res Harmony PA.

CR23A143   Helen Alice Wiser (b 5 Feb 1904, Harmony PA) m 5 Jun 1935, Manheim PA, Ralph Benjamin McQuiston (20 Dec 1903, Butler PA-22 Feb 1975, Harmony PA). Bur Harmony PA. Druggist, Harmony PA; she, teacher.

CR23A2   Albert Jacob Wiser (4 Oct 1849, Curllsville, Monroe Tp, Clarion Co PA-21 Oct 1912, Westville PA) m 14 Nov 1872, Clarion Co PA, Elizabeth Jane Klingensmith (19 Dec 1848, Clarion PA-23 Mar 1935, Clarion Co PA. Carpenter, undertaker, Westville PA. Bur Washington Tp, Jefferson Co PA.

CR23A21   Harry Vanlear Wiser (23 Aug 1872, Sligo PA-21 Jan 1922, Detroit MI) m 23 Nov 1897, Clarion PA, Sarah Kerry (b Nov 1878). He bur Indiana PA. Automobile factory, Detroit MI.

CR23A211   Ellis H Wiser (b 25 May 1898, Bradford PA) m Rose Kingsley. No chn.

CR23A212   Everal A Wiser (b 27 Jul 1900). Unm.

CR23A22   H Clark Wiser (5 Apr 1875, Sligo PA-26 Jul 1877, Sligo PA). Bur Sligo PA.

CR23A23   Cora Belle Wiser (22 May 1877, Sligo PA-1956, Clarion PA) m 24 Mar 1900, Westville PA, John Harry Orr (15 Oct 1870, Clarion Co PA-13 Nov 1934, Clarion PA). He, then she, postmaster, Clarion PA.

CR23A231   Eleanor Alice Orr (10 May 1901, Clarion PA-21 Feb 1954, Clarion PA) m Frederick Muller, div. No chn.. She Clarion U; teacher. He, exec, Brockway Glass Co.

CR23A232   Irene Leona Orr (7 Feb 1902, Clarion Pa-25 Apr 1913, Clarion PA). Bur Clarion PA.

CR23A24   John Edward Wiser (19 Sep 1878, Sligo PA-24 Jan 1955, Du Bois PA) m 3 May 1905,

Du Bois PA, Ruth Almira Calhoun (2 Feb 1883, Beechwoods PA-1 May 1957, Du Bois PA). Bur Beechwoods PA. Miner, merchant, Falls Creek PA.

CR23A241   Mildred Evelyn Wiser (26 Jul 1906, Coal Glen PA-30 Aug 1980, Du Bois PA) m 1) William Peterson, div; m 2) William E Tufts (b 1 Oct 1901);. No chn. She, bur Beechwoods PA. She RN.

CR23A242   Chester Albert Wiser (31 May 1908, Westville PA-5 May 1978, Falls Creek PA) m 9 Feb 1935, Little Valley NY, Leona Priscilla McLaughlin (18 Sep 1915, Coal Glen PA). Bur Jefferson Co PA. Trucker, later welder, Ridgway, callensburg, Spangler and Falls Creek PA.

CR23A2421   Barbara Laree Wiser (b 4 Sep 1935, Ridgway PA) m 16 Apr 1955, Hastings PA, Robert Melvin Routch (b 22 Oct 1931, Clearfield PA). Quality control, Ford Motor Co; Hastings PA.

CR23A24211   Bryan Robert Routch (b 18 Jul 1957, Berea OH) m 16 Jul 1983, Strongville OH, Valerie Lynn Millhoane (b 14 Feb 1958, Berea OH). Jet mechanic, delta Airlines, Lawrenceburg IN).

CR23A242111   Heidi Lynne Routch (b 30 Jun 1986, Atlanta GA).

CR23A242112   Cory Evan Wiser Routch (b 23 Sep 1988, Concinnati OH).

CR23A24212   Douglas Drew Routch (b 29 Jul 1960, Berea OH) m 25 Sep 1982, Strongville OH, Gayle Ann Oldenburg (b 26 Jan 1964), div 1988. Meatcutter, Curwensville PA.

CR23A242121   Allen Douglas Routch (b 25 Dec 1983, Du Bois PA).

CR23A24213   Gregory Allen Routch (b 9 Oct 1964, Berea OH). Unm. Carpenter, Stafford VA.

CR23A24222   Gwendolyn Jean Wiser (b 21 Aug 1941, Spangler PA) m 10 Jun 1962, Gary Brosch (b 12 Jun 1941) div. He USA;she res Woodbridge VA.

CR23A24221   Tracey Lynne Brosch (b 26 Feb 1964, Berea OH) m 1) 10 Mar 1984, VA, Mark McCluney (b 28 May 1961) div; m 2) 14 May 1989, John Billings (b 10 Jun 1963, Washington DC). Res Spotsylvania VA.

CR23A242211   Meagan Lynn McCluney (b 15 Mar 1985, Woodbridge VA).

CR23A242212   Rebekah Chelsea Billings (b 27 Sep 1989, Fairfax VA).

CR23A242213   Christopher Kyle Billings (b 3 aug 1990, Fairfax VA).

CR23A24222   Shelley Ann Brosch (b 19 Jun 1969, Medina OH) m 7 May 1994, Springfield VA, Kenneth Brian Herzer (b 4 Nov 1966, Fairfax VA). Computer, tele-comm tech, Warrenton VA.

CR23A243   William Russel Wiser (27 Jun 1910, Westville PA-24 May 1990, Richardville PA) m 1) 12 Jun 1937, Brockway PA, Margaret Caroline Perrine (22 Oct 1912, Hazen PA-9 Dec 1982, Sebring FL); m 2) 20 Jun 1987, Richardsville PA, Julia Marin Lindemuth Long (29 Oct 1915, Belgiumtown PA). Bur Beechwoods PA. Highway Inspector, Comm PA.

CR23A2431   Margaret Jane Wiser (b 4 Apr 1938, Du Bois PA) m 6 Aug 1955, Du Bois PA, Jack Stradofsky (b 18 Aug 1936, Du Bois PA).

CR23A24311   Deborah Lynn Stradofsky (b 13 Oct 1955, Du Bois PA) m 1 Oct 1982, Treasure Lake PA, Michael Collins (b 12 May 1950, Du Bois PA). No chn. Res Treasure Lake PA.

CR23A24312   Cynthia Leigh Stradofsky (b 24 Sep 1962, Du Bois PA).

CR23A243121   Jackie K Stradofsky (b 4 Sep 1982, Du Bois PA).

CR23A244   Margaret Irene Wiser (b 20 Sep 1913, Westville PA) m 30 Jun 1937, Homesteadh PA, George Robert Degenkalb (3 Oct 1906, Hays PA-16 Mar 1981, McKeesport PA). Bur McKeesport PA. He, floor refinisher; she, RN, Munhall PA.

CR23A2441   Ruth Irene Degenkolb (b 31 Dec 1942, Pittsburgh PA) m div. Organist, choir director, Munhall PA.

CR23A245   Cecil Marie Wiser (b 26 Mar 1917, Rockdale PA) m 23 Apr 1936, Camp Hill PA, Maurice Edgar Berty (b 12 Dec 1912, Falls Creek PA). Floor covering firm, Falls Creek PA.

CR23A2451   Robert Maurice Berty (b 30 Oct 1936, Du Bois PA) m 25 Jun 1960, Camp Hill PA, Jeannette Louise Butler (b 1 Jul 1938, Roaring Spring PA. Insurance, realty firm, Robinson IL.

CR23A24511   Donna Lynn Berty (b 16 Oct 1963, Springfield IL) m 3 Aug 1984, Robinson IL, Robin Allen Wetherell (b 22 Jun 1957, Champaign IL). He, dental surgeon, Vienna IL U, DDS, Louisville IL.

CR23A245111   Kristen Ann Wetherell (b 17 Feb 1989, Vienna IL).

CR23A24512   Scott Robert Berty (19 Nov 1965, Robinson IL) m. 1 Sep 1989, Robinson IL, Nancy Marie Buczko (24 Oct 1968, Detroit MI). CPA, Mt Carmel IL.

CR23A245121   Alexander Scott Berty (b 30 Dec 1991, Robinson IL).

CR23A245122   Nicholas William Berty (b 12 Oct 1955, Mt Carmel IL).

CR23A2452   Donna Marie Berty (b 29 Dec 1940, Du Bois PA) m 10 Aug 1963, Falls Creek PA, Richard A Daugherty (b 29 Apr 1941, Falls Creek PA). No chn. She, Clarion UPA, MA, Saginaw (MI) U; he, Indiana UPA. She, teacher; he, managing engineer, Ford Motor Co, Utica MI.

CR23A24521   Julie Ann Daugherty (b 29 Jun 1966, Utica MI). Unm. BA, MA, MSU, psychologist.

CR23A24522   Robert Douglas Daugherty (b 28 Aug 1968, Utica) m 11 May 1996, Miami FL, Michelle Klutz (b 23 May 1969, New York NY). AB, MA, U MI. Manager, fitness center; plans and engineers fitness centers.

CR23A24523   Steven Craig Daugherty (b 17 Dec 1971, Utica MI). Unm. MSU. Exterior lighting designer, Ford Motor Co, Utica MI.

CR23A246   Edwin Charles Wiser (3 Mar 1920, Jefferson Co PA-30 Apr 1935, Beechwoods PA). Bur Beechwoods PA.

CR23A25   Frank Lenville Wiser (12 Feb 1882, Sligo PA-10 Feb 1919, Buffalo NY) m 8 Jun 1909, Westville PA, Rena Deluth Fiddler (5 May 1888, Coal Glen PA-12 Sep 1982, Kenmore NY). Bur Beechwood PA. He, painter, carpenter, undertaker, builder, Buffalo NY; she, factory forelady.

CR23A251   LeOttis Aldine Wiser (16 May 1910, Westville PA-7 Nov 1993, Kenmore NY) m 29 Nov 1933, Buffalo NY, Ralph Emerson Hill (16 Jul 1907, Scottsdale MI-24 Feb 1991, Kenmore NY). No chn.. US Army. Interior decorator, Kenmore NY.

CR23A252   Milton Udell Wiser (b 9 Sep 1911, Westville PA) m 20 Aug 1934, Buffalo NY, Katherine Louise Wiswell (b 6 Apr 1911, Albany NY). No chn. Corporate financial officer. Res Lakeland FL.

CR23A26   Anna Clara Wiser (4 Jun 1884, Sligo PA-31 Dec 1957, Du Bois PA) m 1) 28 Nov 1900, Westville PA, Allen McKay, div; m 2) 13 Jul 1913, Samuel Garfield Patton (13 Oct 1881-26 Feb 1954, Du

Bois PA). Bur Beechwoods PA.

CR23A261   Bessie McKay (b 5 May 1902) m Jack Buckholz.

CR23A2611   Lee Jack Buckholz (b 17 May 1921).

CR23A26111

CR23A26112

CR23A26113

CR23A26114

CR23A2612   Betty E Buckholz m Joseph Lang.

CR23A26121

CR23A2613   William Buckholz m Manlyn Ritter. No chn.

CR23A262   Gilbert James Patton (b 26 Jun 1914, Westville PA) m 27 Jun 1942, Philadelphia PA, Eileen Jane Bennett (b 17 Jun 1918, Du Bois PA). Superintendent of Measurement Regulations, southern MI, gas company. Res Coldwater MI.

CR23A2621   Sidney Jane Patton (b 9 May 1947, Du Bois PA) m 30 Sep 1972, Union City MI, Duane Harold Paradine (b 27 May 1947, Coldwater MI).

CR23A26211   James Kenyon Paradine (b 17 Jan 1980, Kalamazoo MI).

CR23A26212   Corey Lynn Paradine (b 8 Mar 1981, Kalamazoo MI).

CR23A2622   Cheryl Ann Patton (b 7 Jul 1948, Du Bois PA) m 12 Jun 1969, Coldwater MI, Michael Duane Easterday (b 20 Sep 1948, Coldwater MI). Product line manager, Frankfurt IN.

CR23A26221   Leslie Ann Easterday (b 3 Nov 1970, Coldwater MI). Unm. Administrative asst, Lafayette IN.

CR23A26222   Patrick Michael Easterday (b 5 Feb 1974, Coldwater MI).

CR23A26223   Christopher Matthew Easterday (b 10 Jul 1978, Coldwater MI).

CR23A263   Thomas Irvin Patton (b 4 Mar 1916, Du Bois PA) m 25 Oct 1945, Du Bois PA, Adelia Cashmere Lepionka (4 Mar 1919, Du Bois PA-22 Oct 1975, Du Bois PA). Bur Du Bois PA. Rockwell International, Du Bois, PA.

CR23A2631   Robert Thomas Patton (b 12 Dec 1946, Du Bois PA) m 14 Aug 1971, Du Bois PA, Sheila Ann Boyle (b 6 Jun 1947, Du Bois PA). No chn. He plant manager, Du Bois PA; she, purchasing.

CR23A2632   Thomas Lee Patton (b 22 Sep 1949, Du Bois PA) m 1) div; m 2) 14 Jul 1979, Christine Levendusky (b 25 Sep 1957, Du Bois PA).

CR23A26321   Christopher John Patton (b 18 Sep 1970, Du Bois PA). Unm.

CR23A26322   Britt Michelle Patton (b 22 Nov 1972, Du Bois PA). Unm.

CR23A26323   Jeremy August Patton (b 3 Oct 1980, Cicero IL).

CR23A26324   Evan Reed Patton (b Cicero IL).

CR23A26325   Amanda Lee Patton (b 26 Dec 1986, Cicero IL).

CR23A2633   Marcia Kaye Patton (b 11 Nov 1951, Du Bois PA-1 Apr 1994, Du Bois PA) m John Michael Vitarelli.

CR23A26331   Shawn Patton (b 7 Jan 1973). USN.

CR23A26332   John Michael Vitarelli (b 7 Dec 1989).

CR23A26333   Kimberly Lynn Vitarelli (b 6 Mar 1993).

CR23A264   Eleanor Oleta Patton (b 8 Apr 1919, Du Bois PA) m 28 Dec 1937, Du Bois PA, Quentin Calvin Snyder (b 11 Jun 1914, Bennezette PA). Meteorologist, Du Bois, PA.

CR23A2641   Gilbert Lee Snyder (b 4 May 1938, Du Bois PA) m Lola Ann Ellis (b Aug 1946, KS. Electrical Engineer, Wheaton MD.

CR23A26411   Brian Kirk Snyder (b 18 Nov 1968, Bethesday MD) m 20 Dec 1991, Baltimore MD, Elizabeth Bell. AAB, PSU; MD, San Diego Medical School, physician, San Diego, CA.

CR23A26412   Sean Lee Snyder (b 20 May 1971, Bethesda MD). Unm. AB, U IN.

CR23A2642   William March Snyder (b 10 Feb 1940, Du Bois PA) m 15 Jul 1966, Ogden UT, Sharen Sue White (23 May 1946, Ogden UT). USAF, Ogden UT.

CR23A26421   Bradley John Snyder (b 27 Feb 1965, Ogden UT) m 21 Aug 1982, Eden UT, Louise Keyes (b 1963, Ogden UT).

CR23A264211   Amanda Louise Snyder (b 21 Feb 1983, Ogden UT).

CR23A264212   Tonya Leigh Snyder (b 22 Jul 1984, Ogden UT).

CR23A26422   William March Snyder (b 20 Dec 1966, Ogden UT). Unm.

CR23A26423   Jason Ernest Snyder (b 27 Apr 1970, Ogden UT). Unm. U UT, Marriott Motels,CA.

CR23A265   Claire Elaine Patton (30 Dec 1921, Du Bois PA-13 Dec 1968, Youngstown OH) m 30 Jan 1945, Luthersburg PA, Joseph Alvin Miller (19 Aug 1913, Du Bois PA-27 Sep 1988, Youngstown OH). Bur Austintown OH.

CR23A2651   Joelene Ann Miller (10 Nov 1945, Youngstown OH-11 Jul 1965, Youngstown OH). Bur Austintown OH.

CR23A2652   Jaye Patricia Miller (b 26 Nov 1948, Youngstown OH) m 1) 29 Dec 1966, Youngstown OH, Ronald Barb (b 18 Dec 1947, Youngstown OH), div 1 Nov 1973, m 2) 2 May 1986, Youngstown OH, John Louis Christoff (b 17 May 1957, Youngstown OH). General Motors Co. Res New Middletown OH.

CR23A26521   Joelene Ann Barb (b 11 Aug 1967, Youngstown OH) m 12 Sep 1986, Youngstown OH, Charles A Navy (b 10 Sep 1964, Youngstown OH). Health Spa owner, Ft Myers FL.

CR23A265211   Chelsea Joel Navy (b 6 Aug 1992, Ft Myers FL).

CR23A265212   Vincente Antonio Navy (b 27 Jun 1995, Ft Myers Fl).

CR23A26522   Sharlene Ann Barb (b 17 Oct 1970, Youngstown OH) m 24 Oct 1995, Youngstown OH, Merris Steven Hearvall (b 6 Mar 1968, Akron OH). She, Youngstown SU, USA National Guard, geologist; he, window replacement service.

CR23A2653   Deborah Lee Miller (b 18 Dec 1951, Youngstown OH) m 29 Sep 1979, Youngstown OH, John Stephen Michael Markota (b 15 Oct 1945, Youngstown OH), div May 1987.

CR23A26531   Aubrey Claire Markota (b 17 Jun 1981, Youngstown OH).

CR23A27   Irvin Wiser (6 Jun 1886, Sligo PA-11 Nov 1886, Sligo PA).

CR23A28   Auley Zathoe Wiser (24 Jan 1888, Clarion Co PA-26 May 1966, Union Lake MI) m 7 Jun 1911, Westville PA, Harry C Fraser (17 Dec 1887, PA-20 Mar 1971, Union Lake MI). Bur Union Lake MI. Automobile dealer. Res Union Lake MI.

CR23A281   Burnell Fraser (2 Apr 1912) m 1) div; m 2) Marion Roberts.

CR23A2811   Nancy Lee Fraser.

CR23A2812   Joanne Roberts Fraser.

CR23A282   Elizabeth Mae Fraser m Earl Potts.

CR23A2821   Earl Potts Jr.

CR23A2822   Pamela Potts.

CR23A2823   Timmy Potts.

CR23A2824   Randolph Potts.

CR23A3   Thomas Carson Wiser (Oct 1853, Monroe Tp, Clarion Co PA-1932, Falls Creek PA) m 1879, Sadie C (b 1860-1923, Falls Creek PA). Bur Washington Tp, Jefferson Co PA. Laborer and carpenter.

CR23A31   Lena P Wiser (Jan 1883-PA). Bur PA.

CR23A32   Irvin Clyde Wiser (Dec 1884, Clarion Co PA-30 May 1932, 1932, Falls Creek PA) m Tillie May Morse (24 Apr 1886, Keene NH-1974). Bur Washington Tp, Jefferson Co PA.

CR23A321   Gerald Clyde Wiser (23 Apr 1912, Falls Creek PA-13 Nov 1993, Du Bois PA) m 22 Oct 1932, Falls Creek PA, Mabel Evelyn Reddinger (b 23 May 1912, Brookville PA). He, bricklayer, Du Bois PA.

CR23A3211   Gerald Allen Wiser (19 Jun 1933, Falls Creek PA-10 May 1991, Pittsburgh CA) m 24 Dec 1958, San Diego, CA, Geraldine E Penn (b 16 Dec 1935). USA. Purchasing agent, Pittsburt CA. Bur Beechwoods PA.

CR23A32111   Linnea Wiser (b 26 Oct 1960, Antioch CA). Unm.

CR23A32112   Cyrene Wiser (b 25 Mar 1964, Antioch CA) m 8 Nov 1990, Alamo CA, Douglas Hatcher (b 12 Apr 1956, San Rafael CA). He, retail management. Res Totawa NJ.

CR23A3212   Marla Ann Wiser (b 8 Jul 1939, Falls Creek PA) m 1 Jun 1963, Ridgway PA, John Richard Newman (b 11 Sep 1931, Du Bois PA). He, Catholic U, Washington DC; teacher. Res Du Bois PA.

CR23A32121   Anthony John Newman (b 20 Feb 1964, St Marys PA). Indiana PA U. National Guard.

CR23A32122   Barbara Ann Newman (b 6 May 1967, St Marys PA).

CR23A32123   John Mark Newman (b 27 Sep 1968, St Marys PA) m 10 Jul 1993, Ridgway PA, Cindy Salvamosce (b 4 Oct 1970, St Marys PA). Lumber brooker, Wilcox PA.

CR23A32124   Michael Gerald Newman (b 19 May, 1970, St Marys PA). PSU. Health care researcher, Washington DC.

CR23A3213   Beth ArleneWiser (b22 Aug 1944, Falls Creek PA) m 21 May 1965, Falls Creek PA, Thomas Robert Crawford (b 9 Sep 1942, Du Bois PA). Both, Clarion U PA. He, teacher, Falls Creek PA.

CR23A32131   Lucas Mark Crawford (b 9 Mar 1970, Du Bois PA) m 12 Feb 1994, Sykesville PA, Cathy Kennis (b 13 Mar 1972, Du Bois PA). Solid Waste Specialist, PA DOT. Res Montoursville PA.

CR23A32132   Tori Elizabeth Crawford (b 10 Nov 1974, Du Bois PA).

CR23A3214   Kenneth Alvin Wiser (b20 Jul 1946, Du Bois PA). Unm. AB, Mansfield PA U; teacher, Falls Creek PA.

CR23A322   Helen Wiser M Woodridge. Res (1991) Orlandon FL.

CR23A4   Clara Jane Wiser (13 Apr 1856, Monroe Tp, Clarion Co PA-Detroit MI) m 18 Sep 1879, Clarion Co PA, Thomas Irvin Klingensmith (11 Dec 1854, Clarion Co PA-1937, Detroit MI). Bur Detroit MI. Carpenter, Clarion Co and Westville PA; 1919, automotive worker, Detroit MI.

CR23A41   Arthur Earl Klingensmith (23 Jul 1880, Clarion Co PA-15 Aug 1880, Clarion Co PA).

CR23A42   Myrtle Mae Klingensmith (11 Oct 1881, Clarion Co PA-29 Nov 1881, Clarion Co PA).

CR23A43   Willis Wiser Klingensmith (11 Jul 1883, Clarion Co PA-14 Aug 1883, Clarion Co PA).

CR23A44   Clair Albert Klingensmith (11 Jul 1884, Clarion Co PA-Detroit MI) m 24 Jun 1914, Jefferson Co PA, Martha Elizabeth Calhoun (b Beechwoods PA-Detroit MI). Bur Detroit MI. Miner, Westville PA, 1919-automotive worker, Detroit MI.

CR23A441   Dale Klingensmith m Betty   .

CR23A4411   Robert Klingensmith.

CR23A4412   Judith Klingensmith.

CR23A442   Faye Klingensmith.

CR23A45   Cora Blanch Klingensmith (11 Oct 1887, Clarion Co PA-20 Jan 1968, Detroit MI). Unm. Bur Detroit MI.

CR23A46   Preston Glenn Klingensmith (3 Jan 1891, Clarion Co PA-Detroit MI) m 15 May 1916, Jefferson Co PA, Mae Elizabeth McDowell (10 Feb 1890, Jefferson Co PA-Detroit MI). Teacher, Westville PA; automotive worker, Detroit MI.

CR23A461   Albert Willis Klingensmith (b 20 Nov 1921) m Doris   .

CR23A4611   Ruth Klingensmith (b 1947, Detroit MI).

CR23A4612   William Klingensmith.

CR23A4613   James Klingensmith.

CR23A47   Harry Hall Klingensmith (19 Apr 1893, Westville PA-Detroit MI) m Ethel   .

CR23A48   Hazel Fern Klingensmith (30 Jul 1895, Westville PA-d infancy).

CR23A5   Andrew Leroy Wiser (or John A in 1850/1870 census)(Jul 1859, Monroe Tp, clarion Co PA-1939) m 1880, Margaret Ullman (b Mar 1865). Laborer, carpenter, Brinkerton, Porter Tp, Clarion Co PA.

CR23A51   John H Wiser (1882, Clarion Co PA-1913, Clarion PA). Unm. Garm laborer; miner.

CR23A52   Blanch Clara Wiser (4 Sep 1884, Sligo PA-Jun 1915, Emlenton PA) m 8 apr 1903, Sligo, Malvern Allen Eddinger (b 9 Jan 1881, Turkey city PA-6 May 1966, Franklin PA). Bur Emlenton PA. (This surname has various spellings.)

CR23A521   Mary Margaret Eddinger (3 Feb 1904-11 Jul 1995) m 1 Jun 1929, William David Anderson.

CR23A522   Leslie Allen Eddinger (19 Feb 1906-19 May 1989) m 1 Dec 1928, Pearl Genevieve Plant.

CR23A5221   Barbara Eddinger m Richard Carr.

CR23A523   Cecile Luella Eddinger (b 23 Oct 1907) m 26 Jul 1934, Floyd Eugene Campbell.

CR23A524   Lilian Mae Eddinger (31 Aug 1909-8 Nov 1994) m 19 Sep 1944, Charles Anthony Mere.

CR23A525   John Delbert Eddinger (28 Apr 1913-1958).

CR23A526   Charles Andrew Eddinger (11 Apr 1910, Emlenton PA-11 Nov 1968, Oil City PA) m Aug 1939, Ruth Margaret Ferguson (b 20 Mar 1915, Emlenton PA). Bur Emlenton PA. Teacher, coach.

CR23A5261   Richard Allen Eddinger (b 23 Jun 1936, Emlenton PA) m 4 May 1957, Knox PA, Margaret Ann Beisel (b 13 Nov 1937, Beaver Tp, Beaver Co PA). BD, Wesley Seminary. Clergyman, Du Bois PA.

CR23A52611   Cynthia Lee Eddinger (b 23 Feb 1958, Oil City PA) m 14 Jun 1980, Valier PA, Ronald Paul Hoover. Res Indiana PA.

CR23A526111   Vanessa Lyn Hoover (b 3 May 1981, Indiana PA).

CR23A526112   Melissa Sue Hoover (b 23 Sep 1984, Indiana PA).

CR23A52612   Brenda Ann Eddinger (b 1 Jun 1959, Oil City PA) m 21 Jun 1987, Valier PA, William Harry Means. Res Punxsutawney PA.

CR23A526121   Erica Lynn Means (b 15 Mar 1989, Indiana PA).

CR23A526122   Sarah Ruth Means (b 29 Oct 1991, Indiana PA).

CR23A52613   David Allen Eddinger (b 30 Dec 1963, Butler PA). Unm.
Res Erie PA.

CR23A52614   Dena Marie Eddinger (b 1 Mar 1965, Butler PA) m 28 May 1988, Sligo PA, Kevin Scott Johnston. Res Sligo PA.

CR23A526141   Brandon Scott Johnston (b 27 Aug 1989, Clarion PA).

CR23A526142   Kelsey Nicole Johnston (b 8 Dec 1992, Clarion PA).

CR23A526143   Tiffany Brianne Johnston (b 3 Mar 1995, Clarion PA).

CR23A5262   Carolyn Jane Eddinger (18 Feb 1935, Emlenton PA-19 Feb 1991). Bur Lamertine PA.

CR23A5263   Charles Robert Eddinger (b 21 Feb 1939, Emlenton PA). Unm. BA, MA, PhD, U of HI. College Professor, Honolulu, HI.

CR23A527   Ruth Lucille Eddinger (b 7 May 1905, Emlenton PA) m Robert Jeremiah Grimm (b 2 Nov 1904, Emlenton PA). Res Emlenton PA.

CR23A5271   Roberta Lucille Grimm (b-d 16 aug 1946, Franklin PA).

CR23A5272   Robert Allen Grimm (b 14 Nov 1950, Grove City PA) m 10 Jun 1968, Emlenton PA, Melanie Ann Dreibelbis (b 19 Jun 1950, Lansdown PA. Commercial artics, Boardman OH.

CR23A52721   Lynn Errin Grimm (b 9 Sep 1968, Oil City PA) m 7 May 1994, Akron OH, Jay Johnson. He, painter and decorator. Res Cleveland Heights OH.

CR23A52722   Leslie Ann Grimm (b 11 Sep 1969, Pittsburgh PA). Picture framer and sometimes caterer. Res Cleveland Heights OH.

CR23A53   Albert Wiser (Nov 1889, Clarion Co PA-1965, Clarion Co Pa). Unm.

CR23A54   Jennie Wiser (27 Nov 1891, Sligo PA-25 apr 1972, Sewickley PA) m 6 Jul 1911, Sligo PA, David Fletcher Rupert (11 Sep 1889, Easton PA-18 May 1972, Sewickley PA). Bur Sewickley PA. Painting contractor.

CR23A541   Cecile Leone Rupert (7 Nov 1913, Sewickley PA-1 Jan 1987, Pittsburgh PA) m 24 Dec 1932, Pittsburgh PA, Joseph Kenneth Coukart (17 Jun 1907, Pittsburgh PA-1956, Monaca PA).

CR23A5411   Patricia Coukart (b 27 Jun 1939, Sewickley PA)m 1)   Butler,div; m 2) 5 Oct 1976, Sewickley PA, Claude Charles Frelke (8 Nov 1938, Pittsburgh PA-23 Jun 1995, Corapolis PA. He limo driver.

CR23A54111   Kenneth Allen Butler (b 1 Nov 1965, Rochester PA). USAF, Tampa FL.

CR23A54112   Keith David Butler (b 1 Nov 1965, Rochester PA). USA, Panama.

CR23A54113   Kirk Michael Butler (b 1 Jun 1967, Rochester PA). Sales representative, Chicago IL.

CR23A542   David Ardell Rupert (b 7 Apr 1916, Sewickley PA) m 27 Sep 1936, Corapolis PA, Shirley Mason Fye, (b 24 Sep 1918, Ambridge PA). Steel worker, Coraopolis PA.

CR23A5421   Shirley Jean Rupert (b 10 Oct 1937, McDonald PA) m   Cavin. Res Baltimore MD.

CR23A5422   Mary Lou Rupert (b 31 May 1941, Sewickley PA) m 6 Jul 1962, Groveton PA, Anthony Joseph Masciola (6 Jul 1938, McKees Rocks PA). Police officer, Coraopolis PA.

CR23A54221   David Leroy Linn Masciola (b 24 Sep 1961, Sewickley PA). Roofer and electrician, NC.

CR23A54222   Denise Marie Masciola (b 15 Mar 1963, Sewickley PA) m 1) Paul Homer Tischhauser, div; m 2) 14 Nov 1992, Jacksonville FL, Dan Cooper (b 3 Mar 1952, OH). She, chief Petty Officer in the USN. He, welder and truck driver, Jacksonville FL.

CR23A542221   Paul Anthony Tischhauser (b 18 Aug 1983, Orlando FL).

CR23A542222   Tarah Nicole Tischhauser (b 9 Mar 1988, Puerto Rico).

CR23A55   Lillie Wiser (6 Mar 1894, Sligo PA-23 Nov 1894, Sligo PA). Bur Churchville PA.

CR23A56   Tillie Wiser (b 6 Mar 1894, Sligo PA) m Robert Hull.

CR23A57   Nell Wiser (b Sligo PA) m Floyd Rodgers.

CR23A58   William Homer Wiser (Oct 1896, Sligo PA-1981, Sligo PA) m 1 May 1918, Sligo PA, Martha Johanna Hackbarth (16 Aug 1900, Karns City PA-24 Jan 1974, Sligo PA). Bur Sligo PA. Miner, Sligo PA.

CR23A581   Merle Edwin Wiser (b 24 Dec 1919, Sligo PA) m 27 Jun 1962, Clarion PA, Norma Loraine Sanesi (b 27 Aug 1930, McWilliam PA). AB, Clarion PA U; JD, Dickenson Law School. Attorney, Judge, Clarion PA.

CR23A5811   Mark Erik Wiser (b 31 Jul 1963, Brookville PA). U Pitt. Union employee, Sacramento CA.

CR23A582   Jack Leroy Wiser (b 4 Dec 1921, Sligo PA) m 14 Jun 1944, Wellsboro VA, Virginia Lucille Shoup (7 Apr 1924, Lawsonham PA-12 Dec 1986, Sligo PA)

CR23A5821   Ann Marie Wiser (b 9 Jan 1946, Sligo PA) m 6 Nov 1965, Jack Claude Laughlin (b 5 May 1945, Rimersburg PA). Trucking business, Sligo PA.

CR23A58211   Robert J Laughlin (b 6 Mar 1967, Brookville PA). Trucking business, Sligo PA.

CR23A582111   MacKenzie Rose Divins (b 20 Jan 1994, Clarion PA)

CR23A58212   Amy J Laughlin (b 4 Apr 1970, Brookville PA) m 13 Oct 1990, Sligo PA. Brent Robert Shirey. She Medical Assistant; he, electrical engineer.

CR23A582121   Kelsey Blaire Shirey (b 15 Oct 1993, Arlington VA).

CR23A5822   Marcia Lee Wiser (b 11 Jun 1948, Sligo PA) m 3 Jul 1970, Harrisville PA, Delmar Arthur Wiley (b 29 May 1948, Ellwood City PA). Both Slippery Rock U PA. He, school teacher.

CR23A58221   Brent Arthur Wiley (b 15 Aug 1975, New Brighton PA).

CR23A583   Richard Eugene Wiser (b 22 Feb 1924, Sligo PA) m 31 Mar 1944, Rimersburg, Clarion Co, Jean Louise Seybert (28 Dec 1923, Rimersburg PA-9 Nov 1994, Sligo PA). Glass worker. Res Sligo PA.

CR23A5831   Richard Eugene Wiser Jr (b 11 Sep 1944, Maplegrove PA) m 29 May 1944, Rimersburg PA, Vivian Lucille Eddy (b 7 Jan 1947, Madison Tp, Clarion Co PA). He, Legal Secretary. Res Elyria OH.

CR23A58311   Dawn Christen Wiser (b 11 Nov 1965, Oberlin OH). Unm. AB, Muskingum Col, New Concord OH. MA, PhD, Colorado SU. Chaemist, Seabrook TX.

CR23A58312   Susan Beth Wiser (b 20 May 1971, Oberlin OH) m 12 Aug 1995, Elyria OH, Dean John Schneider (b 7 Jun 1970, Elyria OH). She, marketing; he, customer service rep.

CR23A5832   Ronald Paul Wiser (b 19 Feb 1946, Maplegrove PA).

CR23A5833   Gloria Jean Wiser (b 22 Nov 1947, Sligo PA) m 18 Feb 1966, Sligo PA, Arthur John Deitz (b 15 Febb 1947, Bradford PA). Glass installation company, specializing in heavy equipment glass replacement. Res Sligo PA.

CR23A58331   Terri Jean Deitz (b 25 Jul 1966, Brookville PA). Unm. Employed at Clarion Col, PA.

CR23A58332   Daniel Ray Deitz (b 15 Mar 1968, Butler PA) m 11 Jun 1994, Golden Co, PA, Kathleen Diana McCoy (b 27 Sep 1959). He, mechanic, Continental Airlines, Burlington VT.

CR23A58333   Jeffrey Allen Deitz (b 11 May 1972, Brookville PA) m 2 Jul 1994, Clarion PA, Charlotte Susan Bish (b 18 Dec 1974, Clarion PA). Clarion U of PA. He, WV Glass Co.

CR23A583331   Shawn Jeffrey Deitz (b 2 Jun 1994).

CR23A5834   Pauline Jean Wiser (b 21 Nov 1950, Sligo PA) m 29 May 1968, Sligo PA, Larry Ray Keefer (b 14 Apr 1949, Brookville, PA). Carpenter. Res Sligo PA.

CR23A58341   Scott Allen Keefer (b 20 May 1971, Sligo PA). PSU. Res Sligo PA.

CR23A58342   Shannon Noel Keefer (b 24 May 1977, Sligo PA). Lock Haven U, PA. Res Sligo PA.

CR23A584   Robert Clarence Wiser (1928, Sligo PA-1939, Sligo PA).

CR23A585   Carl ("Curt") David Wiser (1932, Sligo PA-1980, Titusville PA) m 1) 25 Aug 1949, Emlenton, Ella Irene McCall (b 15 Aug 1932, Piney Tp, Clarion Co PA) div; m 2) 1960, Patricia Larson (d 1978, Titusville PA). Meat cutter.

CR23A5851   William Merle Wiser (b 25 Jan 1950, Butler PA). Adopted by Virgil Wiant Conner m 4 Aug 1978, Santa Ana CA, Nancy Lynn Delameter (b 11 Aug 1954, Trenton NJ). He, Slippery Rock U, PA; Biola U, La Mirada CA. She, Criss Business Col, Anaheim CA. He concrete finsher.

CR23A58511   Heather Lynn Conner (b 2 Feb 1980, Orange CA).

CR23A58512   Brian Aaron Conner (b 21 Oct 1982, Santa Ana CA).

CR23A58513   Ashley Lynn Conner (b 3 Jul 1991, Orange CA).

CR23A5852   Robert Carl Wiser (b 20 Feb 1951, Brookville, PA). Adopted by Virgil Wiant Conner.

CR23A5853   Carla Wiser. (Mother was Dolores Leadbetter).

CR23A586   Kenneth Ray Wiser (b 23 Jul 1936, Sligo PA) m 24 Oct 1991, Sandra Lavay Darby (b 4 Aug 1945, Los Angeles CA). No chn.

CR23A587   Anna Kaye Wiser (b 23 Dec 1938, Sligo PA) m 27 Aug 1954, Parker PA, Richard Dean Heeter (b 19 Dec 1936, Callensburg PA. He, railroader. Res Callensburg PA.

CR23A5871   Debra Kaye Heeter (b 23 Jan 1955, Brookville PA) m 30 Aug 1974, Callensburg PA, Larry Edward Goheen (b 14 Mar 1954, Brookville PA). Manufacturer, Clarion PA.

CR23A58711   Marta Jenna Goheen (b 5 Mar 1973, Brookville PA).

CR23A58712   Garrett Edward Goheen (b 6 Oct 1975, Brookville PA).

CR23A58713   Deena Kaye Goheen (b 4 Mar 1978, Clarion PA).

CR23A5872   Shelley Jean Heeter (b 26 Dec 1956, Brookville PA) m 1) Joseph Leroy Hilliard (b 22 Oct 1955, Kittanning PA) div 1992; m 2) 24 Jul 1993, Shippenville PA, Benjamin Edward Kahle (b 5 Oct 1966, Brookville PA). Factory worker, Shippenville PA.

CR23A58721   Billie Jo Hilliard (b 19 Nov 1975, Franklin PA).

CR23A58722   Jennifer Leigh Hilliard (b 14 May 1983, Pittsburgh PA).

CR23A58723   Kyle Richard Joseph Hilliard (17 Jun 1988, Franklin PA).

CR23A5873   Merle Edwin Heeter (b 12 Jun 1960, Brookville PA) m 28 Mar 1981, Knox PA, Sharon Kaye Eisenhuth (b 10 Jun 1960, Oil City PA). He, employee tractor factory, Knox PA. Res Knox PA.

CR23A58731   Amanda Kaye Heeter (b 23 Feb 1983, Clarion PA).

CR23A58732   Alysha Kaye Heeter (b 17 Jan 1988, Clarion PA).

CR23A58733   Amber Kelly Heeter (b 28 Sep 1989, Clarion PA).

CR23A5874   Kimberley Raye Heeter (b 21 Aug 1962, Brookville PA) m 13 Jun 1980, Callensburt PA, Charles Raymond Renninger (b 24 Aug 1958, Clarion PA). He, employed tractor factory, Callensburg PA. Res Callensburg PA.

CR23A58741   Kenneth Raymond Renninger (b 14 Dec 1979, Clarion PA).

CR23A58742   Brandi Ann Renninger (b 9 Mar 1982, Clarion PA).

CR23A58743   Julie Richelle Renninger (b 28 Dec 1983, Clarion PA).

CR23A588   William Terry Wiser (b 2 Mar 1943, Sligo PA) m 4 Oct 1968, Sandra Lee Philipps (b 3 Jun 1936, New Bethleham PA). Laborer. Res Sligo PA.

CR23A5881   Chad Edward Wiser (b 6 Apr 1971, Brookville PA). Delivery service. Res Sligo PA.

CR23A5882   Todd Andrew Wiser (b 17 Oct 1972, Brookville PA).

CR23A5883   Ryan Steven Wiser (b 16 Apr 1976, Brookville PA).

CR23A59   Mary Viola ("Nell") Wiser (19 Jul 1899, Sligo PA-8 Apr 1958, Sligo PA) m ca 1917, Seth Alvin Simpson (17 May 1897, Hamler PA-3 Sep 1955, Reynoldsville, Jefferson Co PA. Bur Sligo PA. Miner, Sligo PA.

CR23A591   Ruth Leone Simpson (26 Oct 1918, Sligo PA-15 Dec 1994) m   Rummel.

CR23A592   Betty Mae Simpson (b 29 Sep 1920, Sligo PA) m 12 Oct 1948, Winchester VA, John Roland Bishop (b 19 Jun 1921, Karns City, Butler Co PA).

CR23A593   William Andrew Simpson (1922, Sligo PA-16 May 1977, Pittsburgh PA). Bur Sligo PA.

CR23A594   Jennie Evelyn Simpson (b 17 Mar 1924, Sligo PA) m Francis Clair Haun.

CR23A595   Kenneth Dean Simpson (b 15 Mar 1926, Sligo PA) m 1) 15 May 1953, Knox PA, Doris Ilene Dunkle (b 13 Oct 1932, Mars, Butler Co PA); m 2) 20 Jun 1992, Sligo PA, Bernice Louise Switzer (b 22 Dec 1927, Rimersburg PA). Res Sligo PA.

CR23A5951   Susan Ann Lanteline (d 5 May 1994, Sligo PA).

CR23A5952   Patricia Louise Simpson (d 13 Oct 1995, Sligo PA) m   Elder.

CR23A5A   Elbert Wiser.

CR23A5B   Mary Wiser (b Jul 1899).

CR23A6   Wilson Wiser (b ca 1860, Monroe Tp, Clarion Co PA).

CR23A7   William Wiser (b 1862, Monroe Tp, Clarion Co PA).

CR4. Henry Solomon Weiser

Henry Solomon Weiser, son of Peter and Catharine Weiser, was born in Reading on 14 May 1763. He married Marie Wenger, according to their son's obituary. Although he must have been very young, he is the private listed in the Pennsylvania Archives in the American Revolution.[90] His name appears on the Heidelberg Township census for 1800 and 1810, but after that there is no record of him. He died September 2, 1829, in Bern Township, Berks County, Pennsylvania. Marie died in January 1824.

Children of Solomon and Marie (Wenger) Weiser:

CR41   Peter Weiser, 17 Jan 1784.

CR42   Maria Catharine Weiser, b 30 Mar 1787

CR43   Henry Solomon Weiser (4 Mar 1789-dy)

CR44   Francisca Weiser, 30 Jun 1790

CR45   Solomon Weiser, 4 Mar 1793.[91]

CR41   Peter Weiser (son of Solomon and Marie (Wenger) Weiser) (17 Jan 1784, Womelsdorf PA-4 Sep 1868, near Womelsdorf PA) m 20Apr 1824, Maria Elizabeth Krunkelman. Bur Christ Lutheran Church. Peter was a shoemaker in Heidelberg Township until 1811, when he appointed Solomon Weiser, very likely his father, as his power-of-attorney. He then moved to Montgomery Township, Franklin Co, where relatives lived for some time, returning to Berks Co prior to 1820. Solomon sold a tract of land in Heidelberg Township which Peter had owned in June 1811, and another tract of thirty acres was sold the same year by the sheriff of the county. In 1820, when he was back in Heidelberg Township, he sold all of his property, obligations and assets to Philip Weiser and Solomon Weiser (perhaps a cousin and his father; there is no definite way of proving the relationship) for $1.00. Family tradition states that it was believed he would never marry, and accordingly the son of his brother Solomon was named for him, traditionally in order to inherit whatever he had. However, in 1824 he did marry and left five children when he died at an advanced age in 1854 in Marion Township.

Children of Peter and Mary Elizabeth (Krunkelman) Weiser:

CR411   Catherine Weiser, 15 Jun 1824.

CR412   Maria Elizabeth Weiser, 8 Sep 1825.

CR413   Salome Weiser, 13 Dec 1831.

CR414   Margaret Rebecca Weiser, 17 Mar 1833.

---

[90]PA 5-2-893; 7-4-30, 48; Cf Pension Application for Solomon Wiser, R11740.

[91]Records of Christ Lutheran Church; see death notice of Peter Weiser quoted by Mrs. Ida Krick to Frederick Weiser, 21 Sep 1957. See CP3 for Wenger family.

CR415   George E. Weiser, 10 Aug 1838.[92]

CR411   Catherine Weiser (15 Jun 1824-5 Jun 1897, Miamisburg OH) m 17 Sep 1849, William Peter Hoffert. Bur Miamisburg OH.[93]

CR4111   Daniel Peter Hoffert (28 May 1849, Stouchsburg PA-31 Mar 1931, Miamisburg OH) m 21 Apr 1880, West Carrollton OH, Mary Catherine (Hippert) Burns (26 Apr 1859, Stouchsburg PA-5 Apr 1913, Franklin OH). Bur Miamisburg OH. Farmer, Montgomery and Butler Cos OH.

CR41111   Franklin Jacob Hoffert (29 Jan 1881, near Miamisburg-1 Jun 1954) m Lulu Howell (b Nanchester OH. He, bur Newport KY; she, Maysville KY. Steel worker, Cincinnati OH.

CR41112   Grace Lucilla Hoffert (b 2 Sep 1890, near Miamisburg OH) m 30 Mar 1907, near Poasttown OH, Charles Eugene Witters (17 Feb 1888, Bachman OH-20 Dec 1953, Middletown OH). Bur Poasttown OH. Carpenter and machinist, Middletown OH.

CR411121   Harry Edward Witters (25 May 1908, Middletown OH-28 Jun 1947, Middletown OH) m 16 Jun 1934, Middletown OH, Lucile May Williamson (b 25 Sep 1914) Bur Poasttown OH. Factory worker.

CR4111211   Donald Lee Witters (30 Apr 1935, Middletown OH-25 Nov 1937, Middletown OH). Bur Poasttown OH.

CR4111212   Charles Elsworth Witters (b 28 Aug 1938, Middletown OH) Lineman, Middletown OH.

CR4111213   Carolyn May Witters (b 9 Apr 1940, Middletown OH). Ohio St Sch for the Deaf, Columbus OH.

CR411122   Luella May Witters (b 18 Mar 1910, Poasttown OH) m 26 Oct 1929, Middletown OH, Dennis Ebert Smith (b 16 Nov 1901, Clarksburg WV). Millwright supt, Middletown OH.

CR4111221   Patricia Ann Smith (b 23 Jul 1930, Middletown OH) m 22 Oct 1949, Middletown OH, Joseph Kovac. He, truck driver, Middletown OH; she, private secretary.

CR41112211   David Eugene Kovac (28 Jul 1951-19 Jun 1952, Middletown OH). Bur Middletown OH.

CR4111222   Eileen Grace Smith (b 24 Feb 1938, Middletown OH). Vocalist, Covington KY.

CR4111223   Linda Marrol Smith (b 9 Jun 1939, Middletown OH) m 28 Jan 1956, Middletown OH, Marvin Peter Blankenship, Jr. (10 Nov 1933, Middletown OH). Steel worker, Middletown OH.

CR41112231   Mitchell Lee Blankenship (b 4 Oct 1956, Middletown OH)

CR412   Maria Elizabeth "Polly" Weiser (8 Sep 1825-16 Feb 1889) m 23 Nov 1850, Jonathan Witman (15 Jan 1829-16 Jun 1881). They are buried at Stouchsburg PA. They had a family, but descendants have not been located.

---

[92]Records of Christ Lutheran Church; Berks County deeds, 31-308. Miscellaneous records, 5-312; tradition quoted by Mrs. Harry Wright.

[93]Data contributed by W.A. Rabold.

CR413 Sarah Weiser Rabold (1831-1915), on the left

CR413   Sarah (Salome) Weiser (baptized at Schaefferstown as Salome on 8 Apr 1832)(13 Dec 1831, Berks Co PA-24 Mar 1915, near Dayton OH) m 4 May 1850, Berks Co PA, John Rabold (29 Dec 1825-10 Feb 1904, near Miamisburg OH). Bur Ellerton Cemetery, Jefferson Tp, Montgomery Co OH. Farmer, Berks Co PA and Montgomery Co OH.[94]

CR4131   Franklin Jacob Rabold (20 Apr 1852, Newsmanstown Lebanon Co PA-18 Dec 1916, Miamisburg OH) m 1) 4 Jul 1882, Miamisburg OH, Lydia Ann Fox (23 Sep 1863, near Miamisburg OH-3 Sep 1885, Miamisburg OH); m 2) 28 Nov 1889, Miamisburg OH, Clara Lavina Gebhart (29 Feb 1871, Miamisburg OH-13 Nov 1948, Miamisburg OH). Bur Miamisburg OH. Farmer, Montgomery Co OH.

CR41311   John Alexander Rabold (b 26 Dec 1882, near Miamisburg OH) m 29 Jun 1905, Miamisburg OH, Roena Geneva Sellers (10 Nov 1886, Clarksville OH-16 Feb 1959, Dayton OH). Bur Miamisburg OH. Farmer, Montgomery Co OH.

CR413111   Raymond Franklin Rabold (b 2 Nov 1905, near Ellerton OH) m 1) 28 Jun 1927, Newport KY, Elizabeth Jane Booher (b 25 Jul 1908, Dayton OH); m 2) 26 Dec 1941, St. Charles MO, Anna Agnes Berish (b 20 Aug 1908, Heilwood PA). Farmer, Clarksville OH.

CR4131111   Betty Jane Rabold (12 Sep 1927, near Liberty OH-14 Dec 1946, Dayton OH). Bur Dayton OH.

CR4131112   Raymond Kenneth Rabold Jr. (b 15 Aug 1930, near Liberty OH) m 4 Jun 1953, Conway SC, Mary Faye Turner (b 5 Oct 1931, Hanover Co NC). Laborer, Dayton OH.

CR41311121   Susan Jill Rabold (b 29 Jan 1958, Wilmington, Clinton Co OH)

CR413112   Glenna Frances Rabold (19 Oct 1907, near Liberty OH-11 Jun 1942) m 15 Jan 1929, Liberty OH, Russell Elmer Wolf (b 24 Oct 1907, near Liberty OH). Bur Dayton OH. Purchasing agent, Lebanon OH.

CR4131121   Marla Joy Wolf (b 22 Feb 1930, near Liberty OH) m 6 Aug 1948, Liberty OH, Glen Hoffman Weaver (6 Aug 1921, New Paris PA). Purchasing agent, Dayton OH.

CR41311211   Robin Sue Weaver (b 23 Nov 1951, Dayton OH)

CR41311212   Ginger Ramona Weaver (b 4 Jul 1955, Dayton OH)

CR41311213   Kevin Scott Weaver (b 27 Apr 1958, Dayton OH)

CR4131122   Carolyn Jean Wolf (b 7 Apr 1934, near Liberty OH) m 25 May 1957, Liberty OH, James Henry Lang (b 18 Jan 1935, Dayton OH). Sales engineer, Dayton OH.

CR41311221   Gregory Alan Lang (b 4 Feb 1959, Dayton OH)

CR4131123   Richard Russell Wolf (b 19 Apr 1938, near Liberty OH) m 23 Dec 1958, Brookville OH, Donna Jean Cunningham (b 26 May 1938, Walton KY). He, Co-op, U of Cincinnati; mechanical engineer, Dayton OH. She, school teacher, Brookville OH.

CR413113   Mable Vida Rabold (b 27 Nov 1909, near Liberty OH) m 17 Aug 1929, Germantown OH, Lester Obadiah Schenck (b 23 Mar 1910, Ellerton OH). Owner, furniture store, Ellerton OH.

CR4131131   Wanda Lee Schenck (b 13 Mar 1930, Ellerton OH) m 15 Jan 1955, Liberty OH, Joseph Henry Sute (6 Sep 1929, Laura OH). Electric and gas serviceman, Dayton OH.

---

[94]Data contributed by W.A. Rabold, and updated in 1996 by Donald A. Smith.

CR41311311   Judy Lynn Sute (b 16 Jan 1956, Dayton OH)

CR41311312   Jerel Michael Sute (b 8 May 1957, Dayton OH)

CF4131132   Larry Nelson Schenck (b 12 May 1938, Ellerton OH). Furniture salesman, Ellerton OH.

CR413114   Russell Marion Rabold (4 Oct 1911, near Liberty OH) m 1) 10 Oct 1931, Dayton OH, Catherine Lucille Fisher (b 12 Sep 1909, Ludlow Falls OH); m 2) 10 Jul 1943, Dayton OH, Phyllis Lucille DeLora (b 30 Sep 1917, Dayton OH). X-ray salesman, Dayton OH.

CR4131141   Clarabelle Rabold (b 24 Jun 1933, Liberty OH) m 22 Nov 1957, Ellerton OH, Charles F. Linebaugh (b 4 May 1930, Ellerton OH). Motor rewinder, Dayton OH.

CR4131142   Nancy Ellen Rabold (b 7 Jan 1947, Dayton OH)

CR4131143   Julie Ann Rabold (b 19 Sep 1953, Dayton OH)

CR41312   Cordie May Rabold (b 1 Jan 1885, near Miamisburg OH) m 5 Feb 1903, Miamisburg OH, John Henry Urschel (11 May 1876, Miamisburg OH-16 Jan 1938, Miamisburg OH). Bur Miamisburg OH. Millwright, Miamisburg.

CF413121   Esther Elizabeth Urschel (28 Jan 1904, Miamisburg OH-d.y.). Bur Miamisburg OH.

CR413122   Helen Irene Urschel (3 Apr 1905, Miamisburg OH-15 Jan 1952) m 17 Jun 1922, Miamisburg OH, Edgar Joseph Pickle (b 5 Oct 1898, Germantown OH). Bur Miamisburg OH. Core maker, Dayton OH.

CR4131221   Marvin Joseph Pickle (b 17 Jun 1923, Miamisburg OH) m 26 Apr 1946, Miamisburg OH, Nellie Frances Scarborough (b 21 Dec 1925, Germantown OH). Tool checker, Dayton OH.

CR41312211   Pamela Ann Pickle (b 18 Sep 1947, Miamisburg OH)

CR41312212   Creig Marvin Pickle (b 4 May 1950, Miamisburg OH)

CR41312213   Robert Edgar Pickle (b 28 Apr 1953, Miamisburg OH)

CR4131222   Alma Louise Pickle (b 3 Sep 1926, Miamisburg OII) m 2 Jun 1945, Miamisburg OH, Robert Lee Miller (15 Aug 1921, Farmersville OH). Crating laborer, Dayton OH.

CR41312221   Ronald Lee Miller (b 27 Aug 1946, Miamisburg OH)

CR41312222   Janice Irene Miller (b 21 Feb 1952, Miamisburg OH)

CR4131223   Delbert John Pickle (b 18 Dec 1927, Miamisburg OH) m 23 May 1952, Dayton OH, Glenna Jeanette Chester (b 31 Jan 1933, Franklin OH). AB, General Motors Inst of Tech, Flint MI; industrial engineer, Dayton OH.

CR41312231   Virginia Ann Pickle (b 30 Jan 1954, Miamisburg OH)

CR41312232   Michael John Pickle (b 18 Jul 1955, Vandalia OH)

CR41312233   Steven Douglas Pickle (b 16 Nov 1957, Vandalia OH)

CR4131224   Janet Maxine Pickle (b 15 Dec 1931, Miamisburg OH) m 1) 11 Jul 1949, Salmouth KY, Ralph Edward Powell (15 Jan 1927, Salmouth KY-22 Jul 1951, Miamisburg OH); m 2) 14 Jun 1952, Miamisburg OH, William Gerald Sauter (2 Jun 1930, Franklin OH). Farmer, near Franklin OH.

CR41312241 Sandra Kay Powell (b 31 Mar 1950, Miamisburg OH)

CR413123 Edgar Wilson Urschel (b 10 Feb 1908, Miamisburg OH) m 24 Nov 1927, Miamisburg OH, Vera Corine Reiling (b 8 Aug 1910, Miamisburg OH). Shoe cobbler, Lakeview OH.

CR4131231 Phyllis Ann Urschel (b 16 Dec 1928, Miamisburg OH) m 23 Sep 1945, Miamisburg OH, Beryl Harrison Howard (b 1 Mar 1928, Camden OH). Assembler, Dayton OH.

CR41312311 Connie Sue Howard (b 9 Apr 1946, Miamisburg OH)

CR41312312 Vicky Lynn Howard (b 20 Nov 1947, Miamisburg OH)

CR41312313 Michael Alan Howard (b 13 Apr 1952, Miamisburg OH)

CR41312314 Patricia Ann Howard (b 15 Apr 1954, Carlisle OH)

CR41312315 Thomas Lee Howard (b 8 Apr 1958, Farmersville OH)

CR4131232 Charles Irvin Urschel (19 Jul 1932, Miamisburg OH) m 7 Mar 1951, Germantown OH, Anna May Kuhn (8 Feb 1933, Dayton OH). Deliveryman, Dayton OH.

CR41312321 Debra Ann Urschel (b 18 Feb 1954, Fayetteville NC)

CR41312322 Stephen Charles Urschel (b 8 Oct 1955, Miamisburg OH)

CR41312323 Susan Dianne Urschel (b 21 Dec 1957, Miamisburg OH)

CR4131233 Shirley Ann Urschel (b 29 Mar 1935, Miamisburg OH). Punch press operator, Dayton OH.

CR413124 Clarence Elwood Urschel (b 11 Sep 1910, Miamisburg OH) m 1) 22 Feb 1936, Miamisburg OH, Ellen Irene Ewing (b 4 Apr 1916, near Centerville OH); m 2) 1 Feb 1947, Miamisburg OH, Marcella May Payne (b 12 Apr 1919, Miamisburg OH). Millwright, Dayton OH.

CR4131241 Larry Alan Urschel (28 Aug 1947, Miamisburg OH-3 Jul 1949, Miamisburg OH). Bur Miamisburg OH.

CR4131242 Brenda Jean Urschel (b 28 Apr 1953, Miamisburg OH)

CR413125 Ruby Christine Urschel (26 May 1914, Miamisburg OH-26 Dec 1936, Miamisburg OH) m 30 May 1936, Miamisburg OH, Charles Byron Snyder (b 30 Jul 1910, Dayton OH). Laborer, Miamisburg OH. No chn.

CR413126 Ethel Louise Urschel (b 26 Oct 1917, Miamisburg OH) m 18 Aug 1946, Miamisburg OH, Theodore Roosevelt DeHart (b 10 May 1918, Dayton OH). Time clerk, Dayton OH.

CR413127 Harry Wilbur Urschel (b 16 Aug 1920, Miamisburg OH) m 21 Mar 1941, Miamisburg OH, Emma Jeane Jones (b 14 Mar 1920, Menfee Co KY). Office clerk, Dayton OH.

CR4131271 Harry Wilbur Urschel, Jr. (b 10 Dec 1943, Miamisburg OH)

CR4131272 Richard Eugene Urschel (b 3 Feb 1952, Miamisburg OH)

CR4131273 John Thomas Urschel (b 3 Feb 1952, Miamisburg OH)

CR4131274 Kathryn Louise Urschel (b 4 Jun 1956, Miamisburg OH)

CR41313 Jennie Frances Rabold (8 May 1890, near Miamisburg OH-17 Apr 1956, Centerville OH) m 20 Jan 1909, Miamisburg OH, Clarence Mahan (10 Aug 1887, Centerville OH-1 Jul 1939, Centerville OH). Bur Centerville OH. Telephone lineman.

CR413131 Ethel Viola Mahan (b 12 Aug 1909, Miamisburg OH) m 22 Nov 1927, Newport KY, Raymond Otis Cook (b 27 Feb 1906, Warren Co OH). Truck driver and road maintenance, Miamisburg OH.

CR4131311 Phyllis Marian Cook (b 17 Oct 1928, Centerville OH) m 27 Jun 1946 Middletown OH, Richard Wallace Diver (b 18 May 1923, Butler Co OH). Farmer, near Germantown OH.

CR41313111 Carol Ann Diver (b 30 Jun 1947, Butler Co OH)

CR41313112 Connie Ann Diver (b 15 Oct 1950, Montgomery Co OH)

CR41313113 Scheri Diana Diver (b 4 Sep 1952, Montgomery Co OH)

CR41313114 Jennie Frances Diver (b 30 Aug 1955, Montgomery Co OH)

CR4131312 Kenneth Lee Cook (b 20 Aug 1930, Miamisburg OH) m 2 Jul 1949, Miamisburg OH, Geneva Pauline Wagner (b 16 Mar 1931, Miamisburg OH). Truck driver, Miamisburg OH.

CR41313121 Karen Rae Cook (b 30 Jun 1950, near Miamisburg OH)

CR41313122 Becky Jo Cook (b 11 Apr 1952, near Miamisburg OH)

CR4131313 Ellen Jane Cook (b 17 Oct 1933, near Miamisburg OH) m 13 Jun 1953, Miamisburg OH, Richard Beals (b 21 Mar 1930). BS, OSU; chemical engineer, Shell Chemicals Co., Houston TX.

CR41313131 Richard Nathan Beals (b 11 Sep 1954, Norfolk VA)

CR41313132 James Allen Beals (b 5 Aug 1956, Houston TX)

CR41313133 Susan Kay Beals (b 31 Aug 1957, Houston TX)

CR41313134 Steven Ray Beals (b 22 Oct 1958, Houston TX)

CR413132 John Luther Mahan (b 24 Sep 1910, Centerville OH) m 26 Mar 1938, Richmond IN, Minnie Elizabeth (Weidle) Baker (b 28 Apr 1916, Miamisburg OH). Farmer, Montgomery Co OH.

CR4131321 Roger Lee Mahan (b 28 Mar 1936, near Miamisburg OH)

CR4131322 Wilbur Gene Mahan (b 1 Dec 1938, near Centerville OH)

CR4131323 Joyce Ann Mahan (b 25 Jan 1940, near Miamisburg OH)

CR4131324 John Luther Mahan, Jr. (b 27 Jan 1941, near Miamisburg OH)

CR4131325 James Edgar Mahan (b Jul 1943, near West Middletown OH)

CR4131326 Robert Donald Mahan (b 1 Apr 1945, near Miamisburg OH)

CR413133 Drucilla Pauline Mahan (b 24 Jan 1914, near Centerville OH) m 1) 12 Dec 1936, Richmond IN, Lawrence Edward Alsop (15 Nov 1914, Cincinnati OH-24 Dec 1952, Centerville OH); m 2) 29 Dec 1956, Miamisburg OH, William Bradford Davis (b 12 Sep 1912, near Walton KY). Alsop bur Centerville OH; insurance salesman, Dayton OH. Davis, truck driver, Dayton OH.

CR4131331   Lynda Rae Alsop (b 20 Jul 1943, Centerville OH)

CR4131332   Edward Kent Alsop (b 21 Sep 1946, Dayton OH)

CR413134   Clarence Everett Mahan (b 8 Jul 1919, near Centerville OH) m 1) 29 Jul 1938, Richmond IN, Elsie Hazel Crouch (b 30 Jul 1918, Bloomer OH); m 2) 4 Dec 1953, Dayton OH, Florence Viola (Kennel) Weikert (b 24 Sep 1913, Dayton OH). Salesman, Dayton OH.

CR4131341   Clarence Everett Mahan (b 1 Jan 1939, Covington OH)

CR4131342   Betty Frances Mahan (b 21 Nov 1941, Covington OH)

CR41314   Charles Amos Rabold (b 28 May 1891, near Miamisburg OH) m 23 Jan 1913, Miamisburg OH, Mable Luetta Frazee (b 23 Jul 1893, Miamisburg OH). Farmer, Montgomery Co OH.

CR413141   Esker Glenwood Rabold (b 16 Oct 1914, near Miamisburg OH) m 16 Oct 1949, Centerville OH, Reba Louise Miller (20 Aug 1916, near Centerville OH-14 Jan 1957, near Centerville OH). Bur Centerville OH. Factory worker, Dayton OH.

CR413142   Norman Robert Rabold (b 23 Apr 1916, near Miamisburg OH). Farmer, Montgomery Co OH.

CR413143   Pauline Marcella Rabold (b 22 Jul 1918, near Miamisburg OH) m 25 Jan 1936, Dayton OH, Francis Melvin Silver (b 21 Apr 1915, Dayton OH). Salesman, tool designer, Dayton OH.

CR413144   Don Elvin Rabold (b 18 Apr 1924, near Miamisburg OH) m 17 Sep 1946, Covington KY, Barbara Alberta Whitaker (24 Jan 1926, Miamisburg OH). Mill operator, Dayton OH.

CR4131441   Charles Steven Rabold (b 29 Mar 1955, near Miamisburg OH)

CR413145   Dale Melvin Rabold (b 18 Apr 1924, near Miamisburg OH) m 31 Oct 1947, Centerville OH, Iva May Bowersox (19 Dec 1929, Dayton OH). Machine operator, Dayton OH.

CR4131451   Kathy Jo Rabold (b 21 Jun 1953, Dayton OH)

CR413146   Charles Everat Rabold (b 25 Dec 1929, near Miamisburg OH). Farmer, Montgomery Co OH.

CR41315   Lillian Rabold (b 6 Feb 1896, near Miamisburg OH) m 19 Sep 1922, Muncie IN, Arnold Melbourn Martin (14 Sep 1894, Blackford Co IN-12 Jul 1956, Miamisburg OH). Machine tool builder, Dayton OH.

CR41316   Gladys Irene Rabold (b 17 Feb 1899, near Miamisburg OH) m 18 Jan 1930, Cincinnati OH, Julius Victor Sprague (b 29 Apr 1895, Goshen OH). Printer, Bellefontaine OH.

CR413161   Bonnie Lee Rabold (b 7 May 1918, Miamisburg OH) m 13 Feb 1937, Centerville IN, William Elmer Prather (b 21 Jan 1915, Brown IL). U of Dayton; president, plants and facilities, Lau Blower Co., Dayton OH.

CR4131611   Carol Lee Prather (b 13 Oct 1937, Miamisburg OH) m 30 Jun 1956, Miamisburg OH, Roy Edward Kidwell (b 25 Nov 1934, Miamisburg OH). USAF; paint and body worker, Miamisburg OH.

CR41316111   John William Kidwell (b 24 Apr 1957, Cocoa FL)

CR4131612   Bonnie Sezanne Prather (b 13 Dec 1940, Miamisburg OH)

CR4131613   Billye Kay Prather (b 20 May 1944, Miamisburg OH)

CR41317   Robert Henry Rabold (b 30 Sep 1902, near Miamisburg OH) m 31 Dec 1925, Dayton OH, Betty Bronner (b 29 Aug 1904, Somerset KY). Owner, drapery shop, Gallup NM.

CR4132   Wellington Peter Rabold (15 Dec 1853, Berks Co PA-30 Aug 1910, Dayton OH) m 3 Feb 1876, Miamisburg OH, Mary Agnes Reedy (6 Dec 1859, Miamisburg OH-12 Mar 1933, Miamisburg OH)

CR41321   Infant Rabold (stillborn, Dec 1876)

CR41322   Howard Wilson Rabold (10 Dec 1877, Miamisburg OH-26 Sep 1950, Miamisburg OH) m 1 Dec 1896, Dayton OH, Pauline Eleanor Wannamaker (22 Jun 1877, Ottowa OH-29 Sep 1956, Dayton OH). Bur Miamisburg OH. Cigar maker, Dayton and Lima OH.

CR413221   Earl Jerome Rabold (19 May 1897, Dayton OH-24 May 1953, Dayton OH). Bur Miamisburg OH. Factory foreman, Dayton OH.

CR413222   Raymond Alexander Rabold (b 24 Nov 1898, Dayton OH-3 Oct 1954, Dayton OH) m 1) 4 Mar 1917, Lima OH, Orpha Lenora Hayes (b 22 May 1897, Lima OH), div; m 2) 17 Nov 1945, Dayton OH, Annes (Mason) Smith (b 27 Jun 1902, Princeton IN). Bur Hill Grove Cemetery, Miamisburg OH. Bar tender, Dayton OH.

CR4132221   Robert Raymond Rabold (16 Jul 1918, Lima OH-7 Apr 1919, Dayton OH). Bur Dayton OH.

CR413223   Albert Vincent Rabold (5 Jun 1902, Miamisburg OH-20 Dec 1902, Miamisburg OH). Bur Miamisburg OH.

CR413224   Dorothy Pauline Rabold (18 Jan 1904, Dayton OH-17 Jan 1993, Dayton OH) m 24 Apr 1920, Dayton OH, Andrew Sanders (25 Jul 1901, Austria-Hungary-30 Mar 1960, Dayton OH). She, bur Miamisburg OH; he, bur Dayton OH. Bar tender, Dayton OH. No chn.

CR413225   Alice Marie Rabold (b 28 Jul 1905, Dayton OH) m 5 Jul 1958, Dayton OH, William Bonadio (21 Nov 1894, Nicastro Italy-3 Jun 1969, Dayton OH). Bur Dayton OH. Tax collector, Dayton OH. No chn.

CR413226   Virginia May Rabold (19 Mar 1912, Miamisburg OH-12 Aug 1973, Dayton OH) m 14 Jul 1934, Richmond IN, Elmer Fredrick Cosby (12 Feb 1908, Dayton OH-28 Sep 1973, Dayton OH). Bur Dayton OH.

CR4132261   Sandra Lee Cosby (b 31 May 1942, Dayton OH) m 28 Jul 1973, Chicago IL, James Leight (b 26 Jan 1946, Chicago IL), div 1986. Sales asst, trade show coordinator; res Chicago IL.

CR41323   Lulu Viola Rabold (3 Dec 1879, Miamisburg OH-16 Feb 1951, Dayton OH) m 1) 4 Apr 1900, Dayton OH, Charles James Klump (4 Apr 1876, Dayton OH-10 Aug 1944, Dayton OH), div; m 2) 4 Apr 1912, Miamisburg OH, Jerome Mauer (b 1891, Nashville TN), div. Klump bur Dayton OH; Lulu bur Miamisburg OH. Baker, Chicago IL.

CR413231   Russell Albert Klump (20 Feb 1901, Dayton OH-2 Aug 1968, Dayton OH) m 9 Sep 1945, Dayton OH, Ruth Elizabeth (Paxton) Dear (22 Mar 1904, Bellefontaine OH-d Dayton OH). Bur Miamisburg OH. Postal clerk, Dayton OH. No chn.

CR413232   Hazel Irene Klump (b 3 Jul 1904, Miamisburg OH-3 Feb 1907, Miamisburg OH). Bur Miamisburg OH.

CR413233   Donald Jerome Mauer (31 Jul 1913, Miamisburg OH-28 Sep 1990, Dayton OH) m 13 Jun

1936, Covington KY, Mary Nell Hyman (b 30 May 1918, Palmyra NC). Bur Miamisburg OH. Factory worker, Dayton OH.

CR41324   Charles Vincent Rabold (23 Jul 1883, Miamisburg OH-30 Nov 1887, Miamisburg OH). Bur Miamisburg OH.

CR41325   Elsie May Rabold (23 Oct 1887, Miamisburg OH-10 May 1966, Miamisburg OH) m 30 Apr 1908, Miamisburg OH, Arthur Ray Sharritts (8 Nov 1885, Miamisburg OH-13 Dec 1963, Miamisburg OH). Bur Miamisburg OH. Factory worker, Dayton OH.

CR413251   Mary Lenora Sharritts (22 Nov 1908, Miamisburg OH-15 May 1994, Miamisburg OH) m 27 Jan 1927, Miamisburg OH, Alfred Charles Hetzel (1 Dec 1902, Miamisburg OH-6 Nov 1976, Dayton OH). Bur Miamisburg OH. Inspector, Dayton OH.

CR4132511   Phyllis Ann Hetzel (b 22 Sep 1927, Miamisburg OH) m 5 May 1951, Miamisburg OH, Quillard Abney (b 5 Nov 1925, Berea KY). She, banker; he, WWII, USA; steam engineer, Miamisburg OH.

CR41352111   Mary Ann Abney (b 25 Oct 1951, Miamisburg OH) m 1 Sep 1973, Miamisburg OH, James Ronald Alspaugh (b 30 Dec 1950, Dayton OH). She, statistical specialist. He, USA, 1970-72; ABA, Sinclair (OH) Col, 1982; self-employed.

CR413251111   Douglas Reginold Alspaugh (b 1 Feb 1977, Dayton OH)

CR413251112   Jessica Elizabeth Alspaugh (b 21 Jul 1982, Cincinnati OH)

CR41325112   Lee Ann Abney (b 28 Feb 1955, Miamisburg OH) m 24 Jun 1978, Miamisburg OH, Michael Lee Kurtz (b 22 Oct 1952, Cincinnati OH). Both factory workers. No chn.

CR4132512   Marilyn Joyce Hetzel (b 5 Dec 1929, Miamisburg OH) m 27 Jan 1949, Miamisburg OH, Charles Walter Gilbert (b 1 Jun 1922, Miamisburg OH). She, retired banker; he, WWII, USA; factory worker, Miamisburg OH

CR41325121   Sue Ann Gilbert (b 26 Mar 1951, Miamisburg OH) m 22 Aug 1970, Miamisburg OH, Michael S. Pierce (b 19 Aug 1948, Dayton OH). She, utility company service representative; he, self-employed.

CR413251211   Eric Stuart Pierce (b 19 Dec 1975, Dayton OH). Roofer.

CR413251212   Stephanie Sue Pierce (b 24 Apr 1980, Dayton OH)

CR41325122   Pamela Jo Gilbert (b 5 Nov 1953, Miamisburg OH) m 1) 23 Oct 1971, Miamisburg OH, Marc Frazer (b 25 Sep 1953, Dayton OH), div 1982; m 2) 18 Jun 1993, Union KY, Randy Presley (b 7 Apr 1962, Dayton OH), div 1995.

CR413251221   Michelle Ann Frazer (b 18 May 1972, Dayton OH). Student, Wright S (OH) U.

CR413251222   Marc Andrew Frazer (b 14 Apr 1975, Dayton OH). USMC.

CR4132513   Lola Jean Hetzel (b 5 Mar 1940, Miamisburg OH) m 2 May 1964, Miamisburg OH, Jay Emmons (b 11 Dec 1942, Dayton OH). She, insurance; he, self-employed in insurance.

CR41325131   Jennifer Jo Emmons (b 2 Jan 1968, Dayton OH) m 24 Jun 1995, Cincinnati OH, Gregory Benedict Karpinsky (b 3 Dec 1964, Peninsula OH). She, BS, Miami (OH) U; sales management, Cincinnati OH. He, BS, BA, U Akron; football coach, U Cincinnati.

CR41325132   Jeffrey Emmons (b 16 Jun 1971, Dayton OH). BS, Miami (OH) U; computer sales, Phoenix AZ.

CR413252   Norman Edward Sharritts (8 Feb 1910, Miamisburg OH-10 Apr 1910, Miamisburg OH). Bur Miamisburg OH.

CR41326   Homer Roy Rabold (4 Apr 1892, Miamisburg OH-12 Jul 1937, Miamisburg OH) m 1) 26 Mar 1917, Lima OH, Bernadine Wehrkamp (7 Jul 1899, Carthegena OH-18 Nov 1922); m 2) 28 May 1925, Covington KY, Ruth Inez Parker (b 22 Dec 1907, Lima OH). Homer bur Miamisburg OH; Bernadine bur Lima OH.

CR413261   James Frederick Rabold (18 Feb 1917, Lima OH-d NM) m 5 Aug 1942, Wichita Falls TX, Thelma Estelle Swain (b 20 Aug 1912, Mundy TX). Bur NM. WWII, USA; security inspector, Albuquerque NM.

CR4132611   Roberta Lynn Rabold (b 17 Aug 1946, Albuquerque NM)

CR4132612   James Gregory Rabold (b 18 Jun 1948, Albuquerque NM)

CR4132613   Kathryn Anne Rabold (b 18 Jun 1952, Albuquerque NM)

CR413262   Robert Kenneth Rabold (14 Aug 1918, Lima OH-d MI) m 17 Oct 1944, Monroe MI, Vivian Vondale Smith (b 22 Oct 1920, Lima OH). Bur MI. He, factory worker; she, Affiliated Theaters, Detroit MI. No chn.

CR4133   Mary Rebecca Rabold (4 May 1857, Berks Co PA-7 Jul 1939, near Ellerton OH) m 17 Dec 1874, Ellerton OH, Samuel Schell (28 Dec 1854, near Ellerton OH-7 Aug 1922, near Ellerton OH). Bur Ellerton OH. Farmer, near Ellerton OH.

CR41331   Harry Wilson Schell (16 Oct 1876, near Ellerton OH-7 Jan 1930, Ellerton OH) m 4 Feb 1897, Ellerton OH, Florence Estella Getter (17 Aug 1877, near Ellerton OH-15 Sep 1951, Ellerton OH). Bur Ellerton OH. Farmer, near Ellerton OH.

CR413311   Beatrice Pauline Schell (24 Jan 1901, near Ellerton OH-17 Dec 1941, Ellerton OH) m 15 May 1923, Ellerton OH, Robert Ellis Forrest (30 Aug 1901, near Liberty OH-26 Apr 1971, Ellerton OH). Bur Ellerton OH. Supervisor, supply dept, Dayton OH. He, Miami Valley Milk Producer.

CR4133111   Lois Elaine Forrest (b 2 Nov 1925, near Ellerton OH) m 6 Apr 1946, Ellerton OH, Richard Elwood Schenck (b 31 Dec 1924, near Liberty OH). Appraiser, Dayton OH. He, WWII, USA.

CR41331111   Sue Anne Schenck (b 2 Oct 1948, Ellerton OH) m 1 Mar 1969, Pittsburg OH, Lyle Thomas Storlie (b 30 Apr 1948, Minneapolis MN), div 1994.

CR413311111   Amanda Elizabeth Storlie (b 25 May 1972, Saginaw MI) m 30 Sep 1995, Lake Placid FL, Jesse Gallegos, Jr. (b 16 Sep 1972, Clewiston FL)

CR413311112   Holly Kathryn Storlie (b 13 Jun 1975, Saginaw MI)

CR413311113   Sarah Anne Storlie (b 18 Dec 1977, Traverse City MI)

CR41331112   Robert Schenck (b 28 Dec 1951, Centerville OH) m 1) 22 Dec 1972, Mitchell SD, Teresa Anne Pederson (b 15 Jun 1952, Brown Co SD), div 1980; m 2) 3 Jul 1992, Mitchell SD, Cristine Stewart Martin (b 18 Nov 1958, Chanute KS). He, AB, Augustana (SD) Col, 1976.

CR413311121   Benjamin Forest Schenck (b 30 Jan 1976, Sioux Falls SD)

CR413311122   Joshua Paul Schenck (b 2 Jan 1978, Sioux Falls SD)

CR4133112   Jean Marcella Forrest (b 14 May 1930, Ellerton OH) m 1) 15 Oct 1949, Ellerton OH,

Albert George Lucas (31 Aug 1927, Flint MI-10 Nov 1958, near Dayton OH); m 2) 8 Jun 1962, Tokyo Japan, William E. Roberts (b 2 Dec 1929, Flemingsburg KY). Lucas bur Ellerton OH. Delivery supervisor, Dayton OH. Roberts, USAF; US Postal Service. She, grocery employee.

CR41331121   Jane Ann Lucas (b 25 Jun 1950, Ellerton OH) m 2 Aug 1969, Ellerton OH, David Leslie Guinn (b 22 Nov 1947, Dayton OH). She, firefighter, paramedic; he, General Motors, fire chief.

CR413311211   Christine Renee Guinn (b 2 Jun 1970, Dayton OH). US Postal Service.

CR413311212   Leslie Ann Guinn (b 28 Jan 1975, Dayton OH). Secretary.

CR41331122   Patti Lynn Lucas (b 30 Mar 1956, Centerville OH) m 18 Jun 1977, Paul Marquis Stoll (b 1 Dec 1954, Dayton OH). She, banker; he, landscape design. No chn.

CR41331123   Elizabeth Ellen Roberts (b 13 Dec 1966, Limestone ME) m 15 Jul 1989, Troy Eugene Holtrey (b 5 Jan 1965, Dayton OH). Both, Lee (TN) Col; teachers.

CR413311231   Cassidy Elizabeth Holtrey (b 4 Feb 1995, Dayton OH)

CR4133113   Richard Ellis Forrest (b 30 May 1935, Ellerton OH) m 5 Mar 1955, Ellerton OH, Carol Ann Fleischman (b 18 Jun 1935, near Ellerton OH)(see CR4134241). BS, General Motors Inst of Tech, Flint MI, 1958; mechanical engineer, Dayton OH. She, secretary, bookkeeper.

CR41331131   David Ellis Forrest (b 27 Jul 1956, Ellerton OH) m 2 Sep 1989, Conton OH, Lauri Cost (b 3 Mar 1960, Syracuse NY). He, executive hcf, Syracuse NY. She, office mgr.

CR413311311   Elizabeth Amanda Forrest (b 8 Sep 1992, Syracuse NY)

CR41331132   Douglas Eugene Forrest (b 26 Sep 1958, Dayton OH) m 8 Feb 1985, Lebanon OH, Cheri Dawn Leyes (b 27 Nov 1959, Harveysburg OH). BS, U Cincinnati, 1981; telecommunications mgt, Dayton OH.

                Charles Adam Leyes (b 7 Aug 1982, Harveysburg OH) (Adopted by Douglas Eugene Forrest)

CR413311321   Douglas Daniel Forrest (b 18 Aug 1985, Lebanon OH)

CR41331133   Donald Eric Forrest (b 24 Feb 1963, Huber Heights OH) m 25 Jun 19 , Lima OH, Linda Marie Griffo (b 27 Dec 1967), div. BS, Franklin (OH) U, 1987; sales representative, Columbus OH.

CR413312   Mable Irene Schell (10 Aug 1904, near Ellerton OH-30 Aug 1977, Dayton OH) m 1 Jul 1927, Ellerton OH, Myron Francis Eberly (b near Ellerton OH-29 Nov 1987, Dayton OH). Bur Ellerton OH. Accountant, Dayton OH.

CR4133121   Nancy Marlene Eberly (b 10 Nov 1934, Ellerton OH) m 12 Nov 1955, Ellerton OH, Richard Allan Horvath (b 28 Jul 1937, Dayton OH). Draftsman, Dayton.

CR41331211   Keith Allan Horvath (b 26 Oct 1956, Dayton OH). MD; pediatrician.

CR41332   Elmer Clarence Schell (3 Dec 1881, near Ellerton OH-7 Jul 1953, Ellerton OH) m 8 Apr 1903, Ellerton OH, Bessie Olive Getter (21 Oct 1881, near Ellerton OH-1 Apr 1958, Ellerton OH). Bur Ellerton OH. Farmer; stock clerk, Dayton OH.

CR413321   Walter Emerson Schell (b 5 Aug 1905, near Ellerton OH) m 23 Jun 1928, New Philadelphia OH, Christine Becker (b 11 May 1907, near Dayton OH). Carpenter, Miamisburg OH.

CR4133211   Barbara Ann Schell (b 23 Nov 1946, near Dayton OH)

CR413322   Mary Louise Schell (b 12 Mar 1909, near Ellerton) m 30 Jul 1934, Ellerton OH, Herbert Arthur Schmidt (b 16 Jun 1910, Ansonia OH). Accountant, Dayton OH.

CR4133221   Carolyn Sue Schmidt (b 2 Mar 1939, Greenville OH)

CR413323   Paul Luther Schell (b 15 Dec 1919, near Ellerton OH) m 27 Jun 1942, Lewisburg OH, Mary Etta Routzahn (b 25 Apr 1923, Germantown OH). Pilot, American Airlines, Grapevine TX.

CR4133231   Thomas Warren Schell (b 31 Oct 1945, Dayton OH)

CR41333   Vernie Herbert Schell (13 Sep 1885, near Ellerton OH-27 Mar 1943, Ellerton OH) m 1) Daisy Alverta Belleman (21 Mar 1887, near Dayton OH-29 Nov 1924, Ellerton OH); m 2) 29 Oct 1927, New Philadelphia OH, Vinnie Rebecca Wenner (b 23 Oct 1886, near Dayton OH). Bur Ellerton OH. Farmer and truck driver, Ellerton OH.

CR413331   Marguerite Lucille Schell (b 3 Jul 1909, near Ellerton OH) m 28 Nov 1929, near Farmersville OH, Paul Everet Holp (6 Feb 1910, near Farmersville OH-3 Feb 1959, New Lebanon OH). Bur near Farmersville OH. County engineer, New Lebanon OH.

CR4133311   Anita Joan Holp (b 29 May 1930, near Farmersville OH) m 11 Jun 1950, near Farmersville OH, Frederick William Bellew (15 Aug 1927, Detroit MI). Radar technician, Dayton OH.

CR41333111   Patricia Jo Bellew (b 16 Jul 1952, Vandalia OH)

CR41333112   Mark William Bellew (b 19 Jul 1954, Vandalia OH)

CR41333113   Daniel Paul Bellew (b 23 Jun 1958, Vandalia OH)

CR4133312   Roland Emerson Holp (b 9 Jun 1932, near Farmersville OH) m 7 Jun 1952, near Farmersville OH, Abygail Smithers (b 30 May 1935, Dayton OH). Wholesale drug salesman, sw OH, Fairfield OH.

CR41333121   Jon Joel Holp (b 19 Aug 1953, Dayton OH)

CR41333122   Timothy Michael Holp (b 21 Dec 1956, near Farmersville OH)

CR4133313   Sheralyn Kay Holp (b 19 Aug 1944, New Lebanon OH)

CR4133314   Jennifer Sue Holp (b 17 Apr 1947, New Lebanon OH)

CR413332   Herbert Elwood Schell (b 13 Jan 1912, near Ellerton OH) m 1) 6 Feb 1937, Dayton OH, Mildred A. Swope (b 16 Mar 1913, Dayton OH); m 2) 25 Oct 1952, Hamburg NY, Louvell Maxine Nutter (b 13 Mar 1920, Dodd Co WV). Automation equipment maker, Angola NY.

CR4133321   Thomas Herbert Schell (b 1 Jul 1939, Dayton OH). USAF, Charleston SC.

CR4133322   Michael James Schell (b 11 Nov 1953, Lackawanna NY)

CR4133323   Patrick Herbert Schell (b 1 Feb 1956, Lackawanna NY)

CR4133324   Richard Warren Schell (b 2 Jul 1957, Lackawanna NY)

CR4134   John Irvin Rabold (30 Jun 1859, Berks Co PA-26 Jul 1892, near Miamisburg OH) m 17 Aug 1882, Miamisburg OH, Elizabeth Catherine Fox (11 Oct 1860, near Miamisburg OH-5 Feb 1940, Liberty

OH). Bur Miamisburg OH. Farmer, near Miamisburg OH.

CR41341   Walter Alvin Rabold (13 Jan 1883, near Miamisburg OH-4 Jan 1970, Dayton OH) m 21 Aug 1902, near Liberty OH, Maude Elvira Forrest (19 Jan 1884, near Liberty OH-27 Nov 1981, Dayton OH). Bur Ellerton OH. AB, Schauck's Col Prep; Refrigeration Inst School teacher; publisher; architect; professional engineer. Editor and publisher, "School Visitor," 1906-10; editor and publisher, "Christian Advocate," 1908-10; author, "Short Cuts in Concrete Design with Marked Slide Rule," 1909. Dayton OH.

CR413411   Forrest Alvin Rabold (9 Jan 1903, near Liberty OH-20 Dec 1962, Dayton OH) m 1) 14 Aug 1923, Canton OH, Vera Stonebrook (b 8 Aug 1903, Canton OH; m 2) 8 May 1936, Richmond IN, Bernice Neely (b Sep 1915, Elida OH); m 3) 8 Feb 1942, Richmond IN, Juanita Opal Dumus (b 8 Aug 1906, Gettysburg OH); m 4) 11 Nov 1950, Indianapolis IN, Isla Marie (Pattison) Wallaver (b 25 Jul 1902, Appleton WI); m 5) 13 Nov 1951, Dayton OH, Santa Mary Bottigaglia (b 2 Nov 1902, Italy). Tool maker, Dayton OH.

CR413412   Margaret Elizabeth Rabold (b 24 Oct 1906, Johnsville OH) m 19 Jun 1924, Canton OH, Joseph Addison Van Horn (11 Oct 1904, Youngstown OH-11 Aug 1976, Canton OH). Bur Canton OH. Trade ruler and book binder, Canton OH.

CR4134121   Delores Elizabeth Van Horn (b 25 Nov 1924, Canton OH) m 21 Jun 1947, Canton OH, Paul Richard Holl (b 9 Mar 1921, Canton OH). Carpenter, Canton OH.

CR41341211   Susan Dianne Holl (b 30 Jun 1948, Canton OH) m 1) 1968, Vancouver BC, Paul Yermaatt (b 1948, Netherlands), div 1970; m 2) 1975, Vancouver BC, James Hulse (b 8 Jun 1945, England). She, social worker; he, nurse. No chn.

CR41341212   Kim Richard Holl (b 29 Mar 1952, Canton OH) m 1975, Norfolk VA, Debbie Hoy (b 19 Sep 1952, Austria). He, musician, USN Band, Vero Beach VA.

        Sean Holl (b 3 Nov 1973, Memphis TN)(Adopted by Kim R. Holl). USN.

        Scott Holl (24 Apr 1977, Memphis TN)(Adopted by Kim R. Holl).

CR4134122   Robert Joseph Van Horn (b 29 Oct 1926, Canton OH) m 19 Nov 1948, Canton OH, Jean Marie Myers (b 31 Jul 1930, Canton OH). Binderyman, Marblehead OH. Social Security representative.

CR41341221   Gail Marie Van Horn (b 25 Aug 1950, Canton OH) m 1) 9 Sep 1972, Cleveland OH, Dennis Lynn Golko (b Cleveland OH), div 1987; m 2) 1990, Columbus OH, Michael Whitcomb (b 6 Nov 1940, Cincinnati OH). She, homemaker; he, physician.

CR413412211   Lynne Marie Van Horn Golko (b 21 Aug 1977, Columbus OH)

CR41341222   Denise Kay Van Horn (b 22 Oct 1952, Canton OH) m 26 Feb 1977, Nashville TN, Harry Thomas Haigler (b 7 Jul 1952, Charlotte NC). He, MD; pathologist, Irvine CA.

CR413412221   Evan Michael Haigler (b 27 May 1982, Costa Mesa CA)

CR413412222   Neil Haigler (b 26 Apr 1991, Irvine CA)

*CR413413   Dorothy Luella Rabold (b 11 Oct 1909, Franklin OH-13 Dec 1991, Dayton OH). Unm. Bur Brookville OH. Sales clerk, Dayton OH.

*CR413414   Catherine Rosella Rabold (b 10 May 1915, Dayton OH) m 1) 22 Jun 1933, Richmond IN, Archie Ford Smith (8 Jan 1910, Dayton OH-13 Feb 1973, Dayton OH); m 2) 22 Nov 1982, Findlay OH, Donald E. Woodward (13 Feb 1913, Findlay OH-15 Sep 1993, Columbus OH). Smith, bur Brookville OH; Woodward bur Washington Tp, Hancock Co OH. She, bookkeeper, res Findlay OH. Smith, outside mill supply salesman, Dayton OH; Woodward, barber.

*CR4134141   Donald Archie Smith (b 23 Feb 1934, Liberty OH) m 18 May 1955, Nashua NH, Joan Sandra Speedie (b 9 Jan 1936, Newton MA). AB, Harvard U, 1956; OSU; aerospace engineer, Columbus OH; financial vice president in aerospace and church, IN; deputy genl secr, health benefits, United Methodist Church, Evanston IL. She, tax assistant.

CR41341411   Douglas Alan Smith (b 28 May 1956, Columbus OH) m 23 Jun 1976, Stuttgart, Germany, Evelyn Weide (b 16 May 1958, Stuttgart, Germany). He, USA, 1974-94; restaurant manager, St. Joseph IL

CR413414111   Stefanie Flora Smith (b 25 Jul 1980, Berlin, Germany)

CR41341412   Keith Cameron Smith (b 25 Sep 1957, Columbus OH) m 7 Aug 1982, Frankfort IN, Lisa McIntosh (b 20 Dec 1960, Frankfort IN). He, BS, Purdue U, 1981; aerospace engineer, Indianapolis IN.

CR413414121   Andrew Eric Smith (b 9 Jun 1985, St. Louis MO)

CR413414122   Alexander James Smith (b 27 Aug 1986, Cincinnati OH)

CR413414123   Caitlin Joan Opal Smith (b 15 Apr 1988, Cincinnati OH)

CR41341413   Dierdre Lynne Smith (b 17 Dec 1959, Columbus OH) m 1) 15 Apr 1978, Columbus OH, Kevin David Shonk (b 22 Jul 1957, Columbus OH), div 1994; m 2) 29 Aug 1994, Lebanon OH, Stuart Platt Delaney (b 20 Dec 1960, Cincinnati OH). She, BS, Franklin U, 1978; corporate vice president finance; he, carpenter, Grove City OH.

CR41341414   Neal Ramsey Smith (b 10 Oct 1962, Dayton OH) m 16 Jul 1988, Vandalia OH, Katherine St. Marie (b 27 Jan 1969, Dayton OH). He, sales; she, executive secretary, Dayton OH.

Donald William Smith (b 28 Jan 1985, Dayton OH) (Adopted)

CR413414141   Alexander Ramsey Smith (b 7 Apr 1990, Dayton OH)

CR4134142   Marcia Ann Smith (b 18 Jul 1936, Findlay OH) m 28 Jul 1956, Dayton OH, James Edward Shields (b 2 Oct 1931, Riverside CA). Sales engineer, Dayton OH.

CR41341421   Stan Michael Shields (b 14 Sep 1957, Dayton OH). Unm. Real estate, Eaton OH.

CR41341422   Jon Alan Shields (b 6 May 1971, Dayton OH). Unm. BS, OSU, 1995. Sales representative, Orlando FL.

CR41341423   Beth Ann Shields (b 11 Apr 1972, Dayton OH) m 29 Aug 1995, Liverpool, England, Michael Peter Falder (b 24 Mar 1973, Penketh, England). OSU, U Hamburg, Germany. Computer systems analyst, Nottingham, England.

CR41342   Hallie Vester Rabold (17 Nov 1884, near Miamisburg OH-14 Nov 1970, Dayton OH) m 25 Dec 1907, Ellerton OH, Eva Maude Loy (11 Oct 1889, near Miamisburg OH-30 May 1942, Ellerton OH). Bur Ellerton OH. Farmer, New Lebanon, Montgomery Co OH.

CR413421   Ormal Loy Rabold (19 Aug 1908, near Liberty OH-24 Sep 1966, near Liberty OH) m 15 Apr 1933, Richmond IN, Gladys Irene Brelsford (6 Mar 1912, near Lewisburg, Preble Co OH-4 Oct 1990, Dayton OH). Bur West Alexandria OH. Farmer, Dayton OH.

CR4134211   Roger Roy Rabold (25 Feb 1939, near Liberty OH-16 Jul 1992, Lexington KY) m 29 Aug 1959, West Carrollton OH, Barbara Ann Carr (b 15 Apr 1939, Dayton OH). Bur West Carrollton OH. USN. Barber and truck driver, West Carrollton OH.

CR41342111   Matthew Theodore Rabold (b 27 Sep 1960, Dayton OH). Truck driver, Dayton OH.

CR41342112   Marie Rabold (b 25 Apr 1963, Dayton OH). Home associate, Dayton OH.

CR4134212   Kathleen Ann Rabold (b 21 Jul 1945, near Liberty OH) m 8 Jul 1972, Liberty OH, Phillip Eugene Coffman (b 25 Aug 1947, Dayton OH). BS, U Dayton; school librarian. He, factory worker and farmer, Farmersville OH.

CR41342121   Eric Richard Coffman (b 9 May 1973, Dayton OH)

CR41342122   Kevin Michael Coffman (b 29 Aug 1977, Dayton OH)

CR4134213   Karl Russell Rabold (b 26 Apr 1948, near Liberty OH) m 25 Oct 1975, Farmersville OH, Betty Ann Emrick (b 13 Sep 1956, Middletown OH). He, BS, Miami (OH) U. Photographer and assembly technician. She, bus driver. Res Liberty OH.

CR41342131   Adrian Marie Rabold (b 6 Oct 1980, Dayton OH)

CR41342132   Allison Melisse Rabold (b 13 Jun 1982, Dayton OH)

CR41342133   Aaron Marcus Rabold (b 24 May 1984, Dayton OH)

CR41342134   Adam Mitchell Rabold (b 31 May 1986, Dayton OH)

CR413422   Myrtle Estella Rabold (12 Jun 1910, Drexel OH-17 Nov 1981, Dayton OH) m 23 Aug 1930, Ellerton OH, Lawrence Heiney Caylor (3 Aug 1909, near Dayton OH-6 Dec 1978, Dayton OH). Bur Ellerton OH. Chief of Police, Dayton OH.

CR4134221   Lois Ann Caylor (b 18 Oct 1932, Dayton OH). Unm. Office worker, Dayton OH.

CR4134222   Arlene Louise Caylor (b 9 Dec 1934, Dayton OH-28 Jul 1964, Dayton OH) m 1) 1 Jun 1952, Dayton OH, John David Lundberg (b 25 May 1934, Dayton OH), div; m 2) 3 Mar 1956, Dayton OH, Thomas Potter Lees (b 22 Mar 1932, near Dayton OH). Lundberg, high school teacher, Mansfield OH. Lees, USAF; BS, OSU.

CR41342221   James Lawrence Lundberg (b 15 Mar 1953, Dayton OH) (Adopted by Thomas P. Lees)

CR41342222   Gary Roscoe Lees (b 2 Dec 1956, Rantoul IL) m 22 Aug 1981, Molly Conroy

CR413422221   John William Lees (b 12 Jul 1988)

CR413422222   Thomas Conner Lees (b 26 Dec 1991)

CR41342223   Thomas Gregory Lees (b 3 Apr 1958, Youngstown OH) m 20 Jul 1985, Peggy Holliday

CR413422231   L'Erin Jordan Lees (b 19 Aug 1980)

CR413422232   Megan Brittany Lees (b 10 Feb 1987)

CR413422233   Kristin Nicole Lees (b 15 Nov 1988)

CR41342224   Daniel Steven Lees (b 17 Jun 1961) m 1) 16 Aug 1986, Maryanne (Amendt) Carter; m 2) 23 Nov 1994, Lori (Garman) Kurtz

CR413422241   Gregory Michael Lees (b 4 Mar 1988)

CR4134223   Lowell Howard Caylor (b 17 Jun 1941, Dayton OH) m 1) 15 Aug 1960, Lavonne Childress; m 2) 21 Jul 1969, Audrey Lanzisera; m 3) 12 Jun 1981, Becky Lou Copley (b 12 Aug 1948)

CR41342231   Lisa Dawn Kendell Caylor (b 20 Feb 1961) m 16 Nov 1991, Seth McLaughlin

CR413422311   Madison Margaret McLaughlin (b 22 Jul 1993)

CR41342232   Lori Ann Kendell Caylor (b 21 Oct 1964) m 13 Jul 1991, John Jervis

CR413422321   Trenton Alexander Jervis (b 20 Sep 1993)

CR413422322   Logan Troy Jervis (b 30 Nov 1994)

CR41342233   Stacey Lee Caylor (b 15 Dec 1969)

CR413423   Irene Louise Rabold (b 25 Sep 1912, near Dayton OH) m 7 Oct 1933, Richmond IN, Robert William Shyrigh (11 Jan 1912, Urbana OH-17 Jun 1993, Dayton OH). Job setter, Dayton OH.

CR4134231   John Mitchell Shyrigh (b 9 Feb 1935, Dayton OH) m 16 Sep 1954, Eldorado OH, Barbara Garber (b 13 Apr 1934, near Eaton, Preble Co OH). USN; drill press operator, Dayton OH.

CR41342311   Luann Marie Shyrigh (b 9 Sep 1957, Dayton OH) m 1) 14 Feb 1976, Montgomery Co OH, Gary Armbruster (Apr 1957-26 Jan 1983, Daytn OH; m 2) 22 Oct 1983, Montgomery Co OH, Kenneth Miller (b 23 Jun 1957, Dayton OH). She, RN, New Lebanon OH.

CR413423111   Heidi Armbruster (b 5 Aug 1976, Dayton OH)(Adopted by Kenneth Miller)

CR413423112   Marcus Armbruster (b 26 Mar 1980, Dayton OH)(Adopted by Kenneth Miller)

CR413423113   Ryan Miller (b 12 Oct 1984, Dayton OH)

CR413423114   Nicholas Miller (b 21 Dec 1989, Dayton OH)

CR41342312   Jan Arthur Shyrigh (b 17 Aug 1958, Dayton OH) m 1) 27 Dec 1979, Norfolk VA, Shelby Spicrey, div; m 2) 2 Nov 1989, Montgomery Co OH, Lyn Hupp. He, automotive repairman, Miamisburg OH.

CR41342313   Jeffrey Shyrigh (b 7 Mar 1961, Montgomery Co OH) m 12 May 1984, Jennifer Clauve (b 12 Dec 1962) Welder, Germantown OH.

CR41342314   Lynne Shyrigh (b 25 Mar 1962, Montgomery Co OH) m 30 Jun 1986, Montgomery Co OH, Denis Bussard (b 3 Feb 1961). Res Germantown OH.

CR413423141   Kelly Bussard (b 14 Oct 1987, Dayton OH)

CR413423142   Danielle Bussard (b 26 Oct 1994, Dayton OH)

CR4134232   Nancy Lee Shyrigh (b 26 Aug 1936, Dayton OH) m 26 Feb 1955, Johnsville OH, Gene Dafler (b 6 Feb 1932, Dayton OH). BS, General Motors Inst of Tech, Flint MI; mechanical engineer, Dayton OH.

CR41342321   Denise Lyn Dafler (b 22 May 1956, Dayton OH) m 1) 6 Feb 1981, Montgomery Co OH, Charles Nem, div; m 2) 15 Dec 1990, Dayton OH, Donald Jadwin II. Seamstress, Dayton OH.

CR413423211   Donald Jadwin III (b 20 Dec 1990, Dayton OH)

CR41342322   Betsy Ann Dafler (b 28 Aug 1957, Dayton OH) m 24 Dec 1979, Montgomery Co OH, John Harsh. RN, Englewood OH.

CR413423221   Katherine Harsh (b 19 Nov 1993, Dayton OH)

CR413423222   Christopher Harsh (b 23 Dec 1994, Dayton OH)

CR41342323   Gary Lee Dafler (b 27 Oct 1958, Dayton OH) m 14 Aug 1982, Montgomery Co OH, Juanita Smith (b 13 Feb 1962). Musical instrument repairman, Brookville OH.

CR413423231   Marie Dafler (b 16 Oct 1986, Dayton OH)

CR413423232   Andrew Dafler (b 25 Dec 1988, Dayton OH)

CR413423233   Jay Dafler (b 1 Jun 1991, Dayton OH)

CR41342324   Gregg Dafler (28 Jul 1960, Montgomery Co OH-4 Jun 1974, Dayton OH). Bur New Lebanon OH.

CR41342325   Gail Dafler (b 21 Nov 1966, Montgomery Co OH). Social worker, Dayton OH.

CR4134233   Kenneth Neil Shyrigh (b 3 Oct 1941, Johnsville OH) m 1) 9 Oct 1960, Montgomery Co OH, Donna Ault, div; m 2) 18 Oct 1985, Sharon Bonnecutter, div; m 3) 20 Jul 1991, Marlene Cunningham. Construction, West Alexandria VA.

CR413424   Evelyn May Rabold (b 18 Jan 1917, near Ellerton OH) m 22 Jan 1935, Richmond IN, George Esterly Fleischman (1 Sep 1916, Indianapolis IN). Pressman, Dayton OH.

CR4134241   Carol Ann Fleischman (b 18 Jun 1935, Dayton OH) m 5 Mar 1955, Ellerton OH, Richard Ellis Forrest (b 30 May 1935, Ellerton OH)(see CR4133113). He, BS, General Motors Inst of Tech, Flint MI; mechanical engineer, Springboro OH. She, secretary, bookkeeper.

CR41342411   David Ellis Forrest (b 27 Jul 1956, Ellerton OH) m 2 Sep 1989, Laurie Cost (b 3 Mar 1960, Syracuse NY). He, executive chef; she, office manager, Syracuse NY.

CR413424111   Elizabeth Amanda Forrest (b 8 Sep 1992, Syracuse NY)

CR41342412   Douglas Eugene Forrest (b 26 Sep 1958, Dayton OH) m 9 Feb 1985, Lebanon OH, Cheri Dawn Leyes (b 27 Nov 1960, Clarksville OH). Factory manager, Dayton OH.

Charles Adam Leyes (b 7 Aug 1982, Waynesville OH) (Adopted by Douglas Forrest)

CR413424121   Douglas Daniel Forrest (b 18 Aug 1985, Lebanon OH)

CR41342413   Donald Eric Forrest (b 24 Feb 1963, Dayton OH) m 25 Jun Lima OH, Linda Marie Griffo (b 27 Dec 1967), div, sales representative, Westerville OH.

CR4134242   Della Marie Fleischman (b 14 Apr 1937, Dayton OH) m 10 Nov 1956, Ellerton OH, Joseph Binkley Carr (b 23 Apr 1936, Zoar, Clermont Co, OH). Plant manager, Ossian IN.

CR41342421   Michael Alan Carr (b 18 Apr 1958, Dayton OH) m 27 Jun 1981, Bluffton OH, Cynthia Kay Longenberger (b 2 Oct 1951, Decatur IN). He, BS, Manchester (IN) Col; CPA. She, elementary teacher. Bloomington IL.

CR413424211   Ryan Michael Carr (b 11 Nov 1983, Peoria IL)

CR413424212   Matthew Allen Carr (b 24 Apr 1985, Peoria IL)

CR41342422   Steven Joseph Carr (b 12 Jan 1960, Dayton OH) m 11 May 1985, Bluffton IN, Lori Ann Deam (b 10 Mar 1961, Bluffton IN) He, BS, Manchester (IN) Col; sales representative. She, child care. Bluffton IN.

CR413424221   Allison Nichole Carr (b 18 Nov 1991, Kendallville IN)

CR413424222   Aaron Charles Carr (b 4 Jun 1993, South Bend IN)

CR41342423   James Scott Carr (b 9 Oct 1963, Siloam Springs AR) m 3 Apr 1993, Fort Wayne IN, Sarah Marie Kilfoil (b 13 Mar 1968, Fort Wayne IN). He, BS, Wabash (IN) Col; bank loan officer. She, high school teacher. Indianpolis IN.

CR41342424   Susan Marie Carr (b 10 Aug 1968, Bluffton IN) m 25 Nov 1989, Ossian IN, Neil Everett Stoppenhagen (b 29 May 1968). She, travel agent. He, tool and die maker and farmer. Fort Wayne IN.

CR413424241   Ethan Everett Stoppenhagen (b 14 Sep 1995, Fort Wayne IN)

CR413424242   Graham Neil Stoppenhagen (b 14 Sep 1995, Fort Wayne IN)

CR41342425   Sharon Leigh Carr (b 10 Aug 1968, Bluffton IN). BS, IN U; mercantile manager, Destin FL.

CR4134243   Donna Jean Fleischman (b 20 Jun 1939, Dayton OH) m 21 Feb 1959, Ellerton OH, George Bruce Phillabaum (30 Jun 1936, Germantown OH). She, day care asst; he, home builder, Germantown OH.

CR41342431   Mark Bruce Phillabaum (b 23 Oct 1959, Germantown OH) m 8 Jun 1979, Germantown OH, Susan Ann Shirley. He, fireman; she, computer arts. Germantown OH.

CR413424311   Candice Leigh Phillabaum (b 29 Jul 1981, Germantown OH)

CR413424312   Ashley Lauren Phillabaum (b 8 Sep 1984, Germantown OH)

CR41342432   Kelly Jean Phillabaum (b 22 Mar 1962, Germantown OH) m 30 Jan 1982, Germantown OH, Michael Eugene Shell (b Farmersville OH). She, Germantown Press; he, precision systems, Germantown OH.

CR413424321   Melynda Kelly Shell (b 25 Jul 1982, Germantown OH)

CR413425   Edith Luella Rabold (b 7 Oct 1914, near Ellerton OH) m 4 Feb 1933, Richmond IN, Ray Denver Werts (12 Sep 1911, near West Alexandria OH-31 Dec 1975, Dayton OH). Bur Dayton OH. Factory foreman, Dayton OH.

CR4134251   Barbara Jean Werts (b 20 May 1933, Dayton OH) m 18 Oct 1952, Dayton OH, Donald Paul Moyer (b 3 Aug 1932, Dayton OH). Stationary engineer, Dayton OH

CR41342511   Douglas Paul Moyer (b 26 Apr 1954, Dayton OH) m 15 Jun   1974, Bellbrook OH, Judy (b 4 Oct 1954, Middletown OH). BS, Purdue U; process automation engineer. Auburn KY.

CR413425111   Jennifer Moyer (b 26 May 1976, Hammond IN)

CR413425112   Christine Moyer (b 26 May 1976, Hammond IN)

CR413425113   Lisa Moyer (b 26 Jul 1981, Hammond IN)

CR413425114   Nicholas Moyer (b Nov 1994, Bowling Green KY)

CR41342512   Deborah Lynn Moyer (b 1 May 1957, Dayton OH) m 1) 4 May 1977, Lima OH, Paul Kunkleman, div 1982; m 2) 13 Feb 1993, Timothy Reid (b 11 Mar 1955, St. Paul MN). She, LPN and RN; nurse. He, U MN and Augsburg (MN) Col; truck driver. Belleville MI.

CR413425121   Sylvia Kunkleman (b 13 Oct 1979, Lima OH)

CR4134252   Ronald Ray Werts (b 18 Feb 1936, Dayton OH) m 9 Jul 1955, Dayton OH, Betty Lou Zambrum (b 23 Aug 1932, Brookville OH). USN, Norfolk VA.

CR41342521   Ronald Ray Werts, Jr. (b 1 Jul 1957, Dayton OH) m 3 Mar 1976, Covington KY, Christine , div 1978. Machine shop, Moraine OH.

CR413425211   Ronald Ray Werts (b 2 Dec 1976, Dayton OH)

CR413425212   Robert W. Werts (b 24 Jan 1978, Dayton OH)

CR4134253   Jane Ellen Werts (b 5 May 1940, Dayton OH) m 6 May 1957, Dayton OH, Donald Dale Curtis (b 23 Dec 1938, NJ), div 1958; m 2) 20 Jun 1959, Ralph E. Brown (b 15 Aug 1931, Shelby OH). Curtis, actor, New York City. Res Brooksville FL.

CR41342531   Brenda Kay Curtis (b 26 May 1958, Dayton OH) m 29 May 1976, Tiffin OH, Jeffery Cook (30 Dec 1955, Tiffin OH-3 Mar 1989, Bucyrus OH). Bur Bucyrus OH. RN, nurse, Bucyrus OH.

CR413425311   Heather Cook (b 24 Oct 1976, Tiffin OH)

CR413425312   Deric Cook (b 30 Jun 1979, Bucyrus OH)

CR413425313   Ashley Cook (b 6 Jun 1985, Bucyrus OH)

CR41342532   Ray Brown (b 23 Aug 1960, Dayton OH) m Jun 1981, FL, Sharina   (b 9 Nov 1959, FL). Construction, FL.

CR413425321   Ray Brown, Jr. (b 26 Nov 1982, FL)

CR413425322   Jordan Brown (b 10 Nov 1985, FL)

CR413425323   Rebecca Brown (b 7 May 1987, FL)

CR413425324   Jerod Brown (b 1 Jul 1993, FL)

CR41342533   Larry Brown (b 14 Feb 1963, Dayton OH). Construction, Tiffin OH.

CR41342534   Regan Brown (b 3 Sep 1966, Tiffin OH) m 10 Aug 1985, Rhonda   (b 28 Dec 1966, Shelby OH). Pizza chain manager, Prestonburgh KY.

CR413425341   Samantha Brown (b 26 Jul 1986)

CR413425342   Jennifer Brown (b 5 Nov 1987)

CR413425343   Ashley Brown (b 20 Jun 1991)

CR41342535   Ryan Brown (b 17 Jul 1970, Tiffin OH) m 31 Dec 1988, Rhoda   (b 1 Jan 1971, Willard OH). He, mechanic; she, nursing home asst, Masontown WV.

CR413425351   Nathan Brown (b 16 Oct 1989, FL)

CR413426   Hazel Marie Rabold (b 17 Aug 1917, near Ellerton OH) m 29 Jun 1940, Ellerton OH, Herbert Lee Peck (4 Dec 1918, near Germantown OH-1 Sep 1992, Kettering OH). Machine adjustor, Germantown OH.

CR4134261   Beverly Ann Peck (b 15 Mar 1947, Dayton OH) m 1967, Germantown OH, David Strader (b 1 Aug 1945, Dayton OH). Landscaper, farmer, Miamisburg OH.

CR4134262   Marvin Kent Peck (b 26 Oct 1956, Dayton OH). Construction worker, Dayton OH.

CR413427   Thelma Lucile Rabold (b 19 Oct 1921, near Ellerton OH) m 20 Jul 1939, Newport KY, George Richard Yost (27 Aug 1919, near Gratis, Preble Co OH). Farmer, Preble Co OH.

CR4134271   Harold Eugene Yost (b 4 Dec 1939, Dayton OH) m 1) 8 Aug 1960, Karen Ancha Bok, div; m 2) 19 Aug 1968, Dayton OH, Barbara Robinson (d 23 Aug 1983, Dayton OH); m 3) 28 Jan 1972, Lufkin TX, Diana Frost (b 23 Mar 1949, Dayton OH). USAF. BS, Stephen Austin (TX) S U; industrial engineer, Lufkin TX.

CR41342711   Allen Richard Yost (b 26 Dec 1973, Lufkin TX) m 21 Jun 1995, Guam, Candy Truesdale (b 1973, Ogden UT). USA, Guam.

CR4134272   Clara Louise Yost (b 8 Jun 1941, Dayton OH) m 1) 13 Jun 1964, Farmersville OH, Robert Trissel (b 5 Nov 1943, Dayton OH), div; m 2) 18 Mar 1970, Dayton OH, Ronald Calhoun (b 25 Jul 1945, WV), div; m 3) 12 Nov 1988, New Carlisle OH, Roger Belton (b 9 Feb 1949, Springfield OH). She, trust clerk; he, cab driver, Dayton OH.

CR41342721   Edward Trissel (b 1 Jun 1965, Dayton OH) m 5 Oct 1990, Mary Page (b 30 Apr 1968, Mount Gilead OH). Newspaper mailer, Dayton OH.

CR413427211   Christopher Trissel (b 22 Jan 1988, Dayton OH)

CR413427212   Jason Trissel (b 8 Nov 1989, Dayton OH)

CR41342722   Denise Calhoun (b 26 May 1974, Dayton OH). Newspaper mailer, Dayton OH.

CR41342723   Christopher Calhoun (b 5 Nov 1975, Dayton OH). Construction worker, Dayton OH.

CR4134273   Frances Winifred Yost (b 9 Aug 1942, Dayton OH) m 1) 10 Feb 1962, Farmersville OH, David Cobb, div; m 2) Dayton OH, James Londergam (b 13 Aug 1939, London OH). Factory worker, Dayton OH.

CR41342731   Robert Allen Cobb (b 20 Jan 1964, Dayton OH). BS, Butler U; computer operator, New Lebanon OH.

CR41342732   George Michael Cobb (b 26 May 1967, Dayton OH) m 28 Apr 1990, Dayton OH, Melissa Bliss (b 22 May 1966, Dayton OH). Aircraft mechanic, Jamestown OH.

CR4134274   Doris Elaine Yost (b 18 Oct 1945, Dayton OH) m 20 Feb 1965, Farmersville OH, Kyle A. Fuller, Jr. (b 12 Jun 1943, Columbus OH). Antique dealer, realtor, Columbus OH.

CR4134275   Norma Jean Yost (b 16 Feb 1948, Dayton OH) m 1) 26 Feb 1965, Fairhaven OH, Robert Crothers, div; m 2) 1979, Troy OH, Walter Torres (El Paso TX-1993, Dayton OH). Factory worker, Eaton OH.

CR41342751   Rhonda Ann Crothers (b 18 Aug 1965, Richmond IN) m 12 Oct 1983, Byesville OH, Timothy David Zigler (b 25 Oct 1958, Warren OH). Electrician, Grove City OH.

CR413427511   David Timothy Zigler (b 27 Aug 1984, Warren OH)

CR413427512   Rebekah Leah Zigler (b 7 Mar 1988, Columbus OH)

CR41342752   Rebecca Sue Crothers (b 21 Oct 1968, Dayton OH). BS, OSU; claim processor, Columbus OH.

CR41342753   James Richard Crothers (b 15 Jan 1971, Dayton OH) m 14 Aug 1995, TN, Stacey June Bailey (b 30 Dec 1970, Dayton OH). He, mason; she, asst bank manager, West Alexandria OH.

CR413428   Ruth Arlene Rabold (b 13 Feb 1927, near Liberty OH) m 14 Jun 1947, Liberty OH, Roy Wilbur Strader (b 1 Sep 1925, Dayton OH). She, employee of Jefferson Tp Brd of Education; he, firefighter, Wright-Patterson AFB, Dayton OH.

CR4134281   Sandra Sue Strader (b 25 Jul 1948, near Liberty OH) m 21 Apr 1967, Liberty OH, Drew Alan Wardlaw (b 9 Oct 1945). She, care center activity director; he, electrician.

CR41342811   Tarla Sue Wardlaw (b 17 Jul 1971, Dayton OH)

CR41342812   Alana Dawn Wardlaw (b 16 Apr 1974, Dayton OH)

CR41342813   Wardlaw (b 28 Apr 1977, Greenville OH)

CR4134282   Marcia Eloise Strader (b 27 Feb 1951, near Liberty OH) m 1) 21 Sep 1968, Liberty OH, David Lee Smith (b 14 Mar 1950, Dayton OH), div 1985; m 2) 12 Mar 1988, Farmersville OH, Thomas Robert Franks (b 29 Nov 1955, Dayton OH). She, retail manager; he, communications technician, Aurora CO.

CR41342821   Brian Anthony Smith (b 3 Apr 1969, Dayton OH) m 9 Sep 1995, Carey OH, Julie Marie Miller (b 24 Mar 1971, Findlay OH). He, BS; industrial sales representative. She, BBA; auditor. Owings Mills MD.

CR41342822   Dwight Scott Smith (b 30 Nov 1969, Dayton OH) m 4 May 1991, Farmersville OH, Josie Marie Patch (b 15 Nov 1967, Cincinnati OH). Plumber, Brookville OH.

CR413428221   Kathryn Elizabeth Smith (b 1 Feb 1994, Dayton OH)

CR4134283   Cheryl Kay Strader (b 4 Jun 1954, near Liberty OH) m 6 Oct 1979, Liberty OH, Timothy Alan Zink (b 23 Dec 1953, Dayton OH). She, sales; he, laboratory technician. Kettering OH.

CR41342831   Zachary Zane Zink (b 6 Mar 1984, Kettering OH)

CR41342832   Travis Daniel Zink (b 27 Nov 1986, Kettering OH)

CR4134284   Lynn Arlene Strader (b 3 Nov 1955, near Liberty OH) m 28 Dec 1974, Rocky River OH, James John Walker (b 6 Oct 1955, Cleveland OH). She, U Toledo; CPA, computer programmer; He, BS, Wright S (OH) U; software company officer, Blythewood SC.

CR41342841   Alexander Scott Walker (b 3 Jan 1984, Lexington SC)

CR41342842   Jennifer Leslie Walker (b 17 Mar 1988, Lexington SC)

CR4134285   Jerry Dwayne Strader (b 3 Jan 1963, Dayton OH). USA. Truck driver, West Carollton OH.

CR41343   Bessie Luella Rabold (b 11 Feb 1887, near Miamisburg OH-11 Feb 1987, Medway OH) m 7 Mar 1915, Ellerton OH, John Wesley Izor (23 Jul 1884, near Germantown OH-21 Apr 1979, Medway OH). Bur New Lebanon OH. Gas and oil station tender, Dayton OH.

CR413431   Catherine Louise Izor (b 24 Mar 1916, near Liberty OH) m 1) 16 Dec 1938, New Castle IN, Leonard Garland Moats (b 29 Aug 1914, near Liberty OH), div 1945; m 2) 6 Apr 1947, Medway OH, Robert Maxon Welter (b 3 Oct 1920, New Carlisle OH). Moats, factory worker, Dayton OH. Welter, farmer, near New Carlisle OH.

CR4134311   Myrna Rae Moats (b 3 Nov 1941, Liberty OH)(Adopted by Robert M. Welter) m 1962,

KY, James Payne, div 1964. Self-employed, New Carlisle OH.

CR41343111   Mary K. Payne (b 22 Apr 1963, Dayton OH) m 22 May 1994, Dayton OH, Mark Kuse (b 1 Nov 1958, MO). She, secretary; he, construction. Reseda CA.

CR413431111   Quintin Allen Kuse (b 19 Mar 1995, Reseda CA)

CR4134312   Gloria Jean Welter (b 7 Oct 1948, New Carlisle OH) m 25 Sep 1983, Centerville OH, William Robb Turner. She, Wright-Patterson AFB; he, self-employed. Medway OH.

CR41343121   Lauren Robb Turner (b 13 Feb 1988, Dayton OH)

CR413432   Ralph Emerson Izor (20 Aug 1918, near Liberty OH-5 Nov 1918, Dayton OH). Bur near Farmersville OH.

CR413433   Loren Edison Izor (b 18 Jun 1920, near Liberty OH) m 21 Mar 1942, Miamisburg OH, Martha Jane Korn (b 13 Dec 1922, Miamisburg OH), div 1984. Gas and oil station leasee, Dayton OH.

CR4134331   Kim Eugene Izor (b 31 Jan 1957, Miamisburg OH) m 1984, Cincinnati OH, Peggy Sugino. U Cincinnati; mechanical engineer, Miamisburg OH.

CR41343311   Alexis S. Izor (b 8 May 1989, Cincinnati OH)

CR41344   Forrest Irvin Rabold (10 Aug 1892, near Miamisburg OH-23 May 1978, Dayton OH) m 1) 10 Jan 1910, Ellerton OH, Minnie Catherine Wilson (24 May 1891, near Liberty OH-9 Jun 1982, Dayton OH), div 1939; m 2) 5 Oct 1954, Dayton OH, Thelma Ruth Stewart (b 29 May 1914, Dayton OH). Bur Ellerton OH. Owner, Dayton Letterhead Co., Dayton OH.

CR413441   Mildred Arlene Rabold (3 Jun 1910, Dayton OH-17 Feb 1974, Dayton OH) m 27 Oct 1934, Ellerton OH, Albert Lewis Boehringer (24 Dec 1907, Dayton OH-22 Oct 1987, Dayton OH). Bur Dayton OH. Clerk, Dayton OH. No chn.

CR4135   Kate Elizabeth Rabold (3 Jan 1861, Berks Co PA-12 Feb 1945, Beavertown OH) m 5 Sep 1879, Miamisburg OH, Lewis Michael Gebhart (15 Mar 1858, near Miamisburg OH-14 Mar 1941, Beavertown OH). Bur Miamisburg OH. Farmer, Montgomery Co OH.

CR41351   Emma Idella Gebhart (20 Jul 1880, near Miamisburg OH- 14 Dec 1952, Dayton OH) m 24 Apr 1900, Dayton OH, Edwin Johnson Weaver (14 Nov 1877, Arcanum OH-8 Nov 1936, Dayton OH). Bur Dayton OH. Construction supt, Dayton OH.

CR413511   Bernice Lucile Weaver (b 5 Apr 1901, Dayton OH) m 10 Sep 1920, Dayton OH, Charles Edgar Leonard (b 1 Sep 1900, Dayton OH). Building contractor, Waynesville OH.

CR4135111   Don Edmund Leonard (b 10 Nov 1926, Dayton OH) m 4 Sep 1952, New York NY, Eunice Patricia Quidley (b 5 Jun 1932, Baltimore MD). Tool and die maker, Dayton OH.

CR41351111   Donna Patricia Leonard (b 19 Sep 1953, Dayton OH)

CR41351112   Roy Edmund Leonard (b 7 Dec 1954, Dayton OH)

CR41351113   Debra Lee Leonard (b 23 Oct 1957, Dayton OH)

CR41352   Anna Elizabeth Gebhart (b 1 Apr 1884, near Miamisburg OH) m 25 Dec 1901, Miamisburg OH, Ira Franklin Weaver (5 Aug 1879, Arcanum OH-19 Aug 1942, Dayton OH). Bur Dayton OH. Construction foreman, Wright-Patterson Military Field, Dayton OH.

CR413521 Grace Catherine Weaver (b 22 Mar 1902, Dayton OH) m 5 Sep 1936, Dayton OH, Curtis Daniel Rhoades (b 17 Mar 1900, Miamisburg OH). Administrative asst, Wright-Patterson AFB, Fairborn OH.

CR413522 Margaret Viola Weaver (31 Aug 1905, Dayton OH-19 Oct 1909, Dayton OH). Bur Dayton OH.

CR413523 Ira Franklin Weaver, Jr. (b 4 Jul 1910, Dayton OH) m 4 Sep 1931, Cincinnati OH, Elsie May Wamsley (b 15 May 1911, Eaton IN). Office worker, Dayton OH.

CR4135231 Wayne Conrad Weaver (b 28 Jul 1933, Dayton OH) m 1) 4 Feb 1954, Richmond IN, Helen Mitman (b 29 Jan 1935, Albuquerque NM), div; m 2) 14 Mar 1955, Bernadeni Margaret Jernee (b 16 Jan 1932, WY). Plant manager, Dayton OH.

CR41352311 Wayne Conrad Weaver, Jr. (b 24 Nov 1954)

CR4135232 Roger Lee Weaver (b 3 Sep 1934, Dayton OH) m 8 Feb 1959, Englewood OH, Phyllis Jeanne Thomas (b 5 Nov 1937, Dayton OH). Salesman, Dayton OH.

CR41353 William Ernest Gebhart (b 20 Jan 1886, near Miamisburg OH) m 6 Sep 1905, Miamisburg OH, Olie Catherine Cook (b 19 Apr 1888, near Miamisburg OH). Farmer, Montgomery and Preble Cos OH.

CR413531 Dorothy Lucile Gebhart (b 16 Oct 1906, near Centerville OH) m 1) 6 Apr 1926, Dayton OH, William Lewis Bayham (b 3 Mar 1900, Dayton OH); m 2) 22 Sep 1940, Union OH, Ira Lee Richard; m 3) 16 Oct 1958, Richmond IN, Ralph Baker Marker (b 29 May 1904, near Eaton, Preble Co OH). Grinder, Dayton OH.

CR4135311 Betty Virginia Bayham (b 9 Sep 1926, Dayton OH) m 18 Jul 1947, Dayton OH, Robert James Johnson (b 2 Apr 1926, Dayton OH). Group leader, Dayton OH.

CR413532 Orville Abertus Gebhart (21 Apr 1909, near Dayton OH-12 Aug 1945) m 11 May 1932, Eaton OH, Mary Elizabeth Siepel (b 26 Aug 1916, Fremont OH). Bur Miamisburg OH. Job setter, Dayton OH.

CR4135321 Robert Allen Gebhart (b 23 Oct 1932, Dayton OH) m 30 May 1956, Eaton OH, Betty Joyce Hignite (b 8 Mar 1937, Richmond IN). Store clerk, Richmond IN

CR41353211 Linda Sue Gebhart (b 27 Apr 1957, Richmond IN)

CR41353212 Judy Ann Gebhart (b 29 Dec 1958, Richmond IN)

CR4135322 Beverly Jean Gebhart (b 15 Oct 1935, Dayton OH) m 1 Aug 1955, Richmond IN, Don Eugene Rike (b 29 Mar 1931, Dayton OH). Trucker, Eaton and vicinity, Eaton OH.

CR413533 Lewis William Gebhart (b 12 Dec 1910, near Centerville OH) m 12 Dec 1938, Dayton OH, Edith Alma McGrew (b 4 May 1904, Fairborn OH). Drillpress operator, Dayton OH.

CR413534 Hazel Lavone Gebhart (b 9 May 1913, near Dayton OH) m 28 Jan 1938, Louisville KY, Clifford Hanna Howard (26 Nov 1896, Moorehead KY-27 Jan 1955, Dayton OH). Bur Dayton OH. He, tool maker; she, mail clerk, Dayton OH.

CR4135341 Gerald William Howard (b 9 Apr 1939, Evansville IN)

CR413535 Lloyd Dale Gebhart (b 10 Nov 1915, near Dayton OH) m 12 Jun 1935, Richmond IN, Twila Franklin (b 7 Jun 1919, Spencer SD). Assembler, Dayton OH.

CR4135351 Dale Leroy Gebhart (b 11 May 1936, Dayton OH) m 17 Jun 1955, West Carrollton OH, Patricia Shumard (b 2 Jan 1940, Dayton OH). Grocery clerk, West Carrollton OH.

CR41353511   Dale Leroy Gebhart, Jr. (b 15 Mar 1955, Dayton OH)

CR41353512   Mary Twila Gebhart (b 2 Feb 1958, Hollywood FL)

CR413536   Verna Viola Gebhart (b 19 Dec 1916, Dayton OH) m 29 Jul 1934, Dayton OH, Paul William Robertson (b 20 Aug 1915, Dayton OH). Tool checker, Mesa AZ.

CR4135361   Ted Eugene Robertson (b 30 Sep 1940, Dayton OH)

CR413537   Wanda Ellen Gebhart (15 Nov 1919, Dayton OH-29 Feb 1920, Dayton OH). Bur Miamisburg OH.

CR413538   Warren Elden Gebhart (b 15 Nov 1919, Dayton OH) m 28 Nov 1950, Dayton OH, Anna May Wells (b 17 Feb 1928, Middletown OH). Automobile mechanic, Dayton OH.

CR4135381   Warren Elden Gebhart (b 9 Jan 1953, Dayton OH)

CR413539   Richard Eugene Gebhart (b 7 Oct 1924, Dayton OH) m 8 Dec 1945, Dayton OH, Betty May Hixon (b 27 Feb 1925). Mechanic, Dayton OH.

CR4135391   Barry Lynn Gebhart (b 10 Mar 1947, Dayton OH)

CR4135392   Larry Dean Gebhart (b 24 Feb 1950, Dayton OH)

CR4135393   Garry Lamar Gebhart (b 19 Jan 1951, Dayton OH)

CR41353A   Donald Leroy Gebhart (b 12 Jun 1926, Dayton OH) m 28 Nov 1947, Mary Jane (Lutz) Baker (b 7 Dec 1921, Miamisburg OH). Appliance repairman, Xenia OH.

CR41353A1   Gloria Dianne Gebhart (b 10 Dec 1949, Dayton OH)

CR41354   Lottie Pearl Gebhart (b 20 Jul 1889, near Miamisburg OH) m 14 Oct 1908, Centerville OH, Clyde Clifton Long (b 25 Aug 1883, Miamisburg OH). Farmer and committeeman, Dept of Agriculture, near Centerville, Montgomery Co OH.

CR413541   Mildred Louise Long (b 21 Feb 1910, West Carrollton OH) m 16 Jun 1934, Dayton OH, George Larone Bunnell (b 7 Apr 1908, Waynesville OH). Supt, Wilmington Schools, Wilmington OH.

CR4135411   Larry Lerone Bunnell (b 15 Oct 1936, Dayton OH). OD, Kirksville (MO) Col of Osteopathic Med; osteopath.

CR4135412   Karen Louise Bunnell (b 20 Nov 1942, Dayton OH)

CR413542   Kermit Elden Long (b 28 Jun 1911, West Carollton OH) m 12 Jun 1937, Centerville OH, Margorie Jane Pasco (b 3 Apr 1914, Dayton OH). Insurance agent, Dayton OH.

CR4135421   Michael Elden Long (b 28 Feb 1940, Dayton OH). USN.

CR4135422   Dianne Raye Long (b 25 Apr 1945, Dayton OH)

CR4135423   Kermit Dennis Long (b 4 Jan 1949, Dayton OH)

CR413543   Roland Eugene Long (b 18 Nov 1912, West Carrollton OH) m 19 Feb 1936, Dayton OH, Marie Elizabeth Mockabee (b 20 Nov 1912, Dayton OH). Farmer, near Miamisburg OH.

CR4135431   Ronald Gene Long (b 27 Oct 1938, Dayton OH). OSU.

CR4135432   Jane Kay Long (b 29 Mar 1941, Dayton OH)

CR4135433   James Douglas Long (b 5 Aug 1947, Miamisburg OH)

CR4135434   Roger Allan Long (b 11 Dec 1950, Miamisburg OH)

CR413544   Hilda Drusilla Long (b 30 Dec 1914, West Carrollton OH) m 19 Oct 1940, near Centerville OH, Kenneth Leroy Stewart (b 16 Jul 1912, Alpha OH). General mgr, Alpha Seed and Grain Co., Alpha OH

CR4135441   Kathleen Ann Stewart (b 22 Jul 1946, Alpha OH)

CR4135442   David Kenneth Stewart (b 15 Jun 1949, Alpha OH)

CR41355   Etta Viola Gebhart (21 Feb 1892, near Centerville OH-15 Feb 1981, Kettering OH) m 30 Apr 1913, Dayton OH, Fred Daughters (24 Mar 1888, Warren Co OH-7 Sep 1959, Dayton OH). Bur Waynesville OH. Cement contractor, Dayton OH.

CR413551   Thelma Pauline Daughters (20 Sep 1914, Centerville OH-27 Dec 1978, Kettering OH) m 14 Apr 1930, Waynesville OH, Joseph Charles Fritz (12 Nov 1910, Indianapolis IN-7 Oct 1971, Kettering OH). Bur Kettering OH. He, silversmith; she, buyer for department store, Dayton OH.

CR4135511   Joseph Charles Fritz II (28 Apr 1931, Dayton OH-1 Oct 1983, Mesa AZ) m 1) 19 Nov 1952, Liberty IN, Elaine Rae Dellar (b 19 Jul 1932, Dayton OH), div; m 2) May 1965, Dayton OH, Connie Wright. Bur Mesa AZ. Policeman, Dayton OH.

CR41355111   Steven Ray Fritz (b 25 Aug 1953, Dayton OH). Unm.

CR41355112   Joseph Charles Fritz III (b 29 Dec 1954, Dayton OH). Unm.

CR41355113   Kimberly Sue Fritz (b 14 Aug 1957, Dayton OH). Unm.

CR4135512   Carol Elaine Fritz (b 21 Apr 1932, Dayton OH) m 22 Feb 1954, Dayton OH, Ronald Lewis De Pasquale (b 13 Apr 1934, Cleveland OH). BS, U of Dayton, 1961; quality control, Beavercreek OH.

CR41355121   Lawrence Paul De Pasquale (b 27 Mar 1955, Dayton OH) m 1) 1976, Kettering OH, Kathlene Grier (b 1956, Dayton OH), div; m 2) 19 Mar 1986, Dayton OH, Patricia Chandler (b 12 Jun 1959, Cincinnati OH).

CR413551211   Paul Lawrence De Pasquale (b 26 Dec 1982, Dayton OH)

CR413551212   Joseph Antonio De Pasquale (b 29 Apr 1988, Dayton OH)

CR413551213   Lawrence Paul De Pasquale, Jr. (b 22 Jan 1992, Dayton OH)

CR41355122   Daniel Lewis De Pasquale (b 4 Nov 1957, Dayton OH) m 13 Feb 1985, Dayton OH, Deborah Sue Thiele (b 21 Mar 1956, Dayton OH)

CR413551221   Aaron Michael De Pasquale (b 25 Feb 1986, Dayton OH)

CR413551222   Nicholas Paul De Pasquale (b 29 Mar 1989, Dayton OH)

CR41355123   Christopher Joseph De Pasquale (b 27 Jun 1960, Dayton OH). Unm. Chef, Fairborn OH.

CR413552   Lowell Gebhart Daughters (12 Nov 1916, Dayton OH-13 Apr 1980, Kettering OH). Unm. Bur Centerville OH. Accountant, Chicago IL.

*CR413553   Lorraine Winifred Daughters (b 22 Nov 1918, Dayton OH) m 7 Oct 1941, Dayton OH, Walter Frederick Hartmeier, Jr. (b 11 Feb 1919, Dayton OH). She, secretary, Kettering OH. He, factory worker, Dayton OH.

*CR4135531   Kathlyn Jill Hartmeier (b 22 Aug 1948, Dayton OH) m 29 May 1971, Dayton OH, Ronald A. Morgan (b 3 Jul 1941, Youngstown OH). She, secretary, Fairfield OH. He, president, Ramcrete Pumping Co.

*CR41355311   Ronald Lewis Morgan (b 16 Aug 1976, Dayton OH)

*CR41355312   Todd Landon Morgan (b 25 Jul 1978, Dayton OH)

CR413554   Garnet Louise Daughters (b 1 Nov 1920, Centerville OH) m 1) 8 Jan 1941, Dayton OH, Royal Emerson Sawyer (b 30 May 1919, Dayton OH), div; m 2) 20 Mar 1956, Dayton OH, Irvin Michael Kuhn (b 10 Jul 1927, Wapakoneta OH). Sawyer, tool designer, Dayton OH; Kuhn, office worker, Dayton OH.

CR4135541   Thomas Lee Sawyer (b 28 Sep 1941, Dayton OH)

CR4135542   Connie Lynne Sawyer (b 30 Aug 1944, Dayton OH)

CR4135543   Dennis Robert Kuhn (b 24 Mar 1957, Dayton OH)

CR413555   Alice Virginia Daughters (b 30 Oct 1922, Dayton OH) m 30 Oct 1941, Dayton OH, John Philip Jonas (14 Apr 1920, Dayton OH-2 Sep 1987, Dayton OH), div. Bur Miasmisburg OH. She res Kettering OH. He, machinist, Dayton OH.

CR4135551   Gary Philip Jonas (b 4 Feb 1943, Dayton OH) m 1963, Indianapolis IN, Barbara L. Branham (b 27 Apr 1945, Dayton OH). Draftsman.

CR41355511   Kellie Elaine Jonas (b 27 May 1965, Dayton OH) m 4 Jan 1987, Robert Allen Praydis (b 23 Nov 1963, Baltimore MD). USN.

CR4135552   Gail Elaine Jonas (b 4 Jun 1946, Dayton OH) m 1) 5 Jun 1965, Dayton OH, Paul Joseph Wabler, Jr. (b 21 Nov 1944, Dayton OH), div; m 2) 16 Nov 1978, Robert Bruce Kiehne (b 19 Dec 1954, Oak Park IL). Building contractor.

CR41355521   Jeffrey Philip Wabler (b 12 Nov 1966, Dayton OH) m 7 Jun 1986, Dayton OH, Cheryl Joleen Barse (20 Sep 1968, Wilmington OH).

CR413555211   Danielle Nicole Wabler (b 1 Apr 1987, Fayetteville NC)

CR413555212   Paul Joseph Wabler III (b 30 Nov 1988, Troy OH)

CR413556   Wynne Lamar Daughters (b 20 Dec 1927, Dayton OH) m 29 Jul 1952, Valdosta GA, Lois Marie Baldy (b 11 Oct 1929, Fitzgerald GA). BS, GA Tech; aeronautical engineer, Marietta GA. USAF. She, real estate broker, Roswell GA.

CR4135561   Gary William Daughters (b 1 Nov 1959, Atlanta GA). Unm. BA; television news journalist, CNN, Atlanta GA.

CR4135562   Scott Douglas Daughters (b 16 Dec 1962, Atlanta GA). Unm. Landscaping supervisor, Atlanta GA.

CR4136   Sallie Rabold (6 Jan 1863, Berks Co. PA-30 Mar 1935, Miamisburg OH) m 12 Oct 1882, Miamisburg OH, Charles Aquilla Maxwell (1 Jul 1858, near Bellbrook, Warren Co. OH-19 Apr 1932, Miamisburg OH). Bur Centerville OH. Farmer, Montgomery Co OH.

CR41361 Daisy May Maxwell (4 Dec 1883, near Centerville OH-18 Feb 1944) m 27 Oct 1910, Ellerton OH, Charles Evan Shade (b 8 Feb 1881, near Ellerton OH). Bur Ellerton OH. Farmer, Montgomery Co OH.

CR413611 Luther William Shade (b 12 Feb 1904, near Miamisburg OH) m 13 Oct 1934, Covington KY, Zella May Tillison (b 27 May 1914, Bristol TN). Technical engineer, Dayton OH.

CR4136111 Charles William Shade (b 4 Feb 1936, Miamisburg OH) m 29 May 1958, Miamisburg OH, Patricia Heckathorn (b 30 Dec 1937, Miamisburg OH). Photographer, Dayton OH.

CR41361111 Neal Martin Shade (b 20 Nov 1958, Miamisburg OH)

CR4136112 Nancy Lee Shade (b 20 Aug 1937, Miamisburg OH) m 8 Dec 1956, Liberty IN, Eugene Leroy Hull (b 19 Jan 1929). Factory worker.

CR41361121 Robert Eugene Hull (b 28 Mar 1957, Miamisburg OH)

CR41361122 Johnny Joe Hull (b 19 Mar 1958, Miamisburg OH)

CR4136113 Michael Lewis Shade (b 27 Jul 1948, Miamisburg OH)

CR4136114 Susan Ann Shade (b 27 Jul 1948, Miamisburg OH)

CR4136115 Jeffrey Paul Shade (b 29 Mar 1956, Miamisburg OH)

CR413612 Herbert Emerson Shade (b 6 Jun 1905, near Miamisburg OH) m 14 Oct 1939, Miamisburg OH, Lillian Lovell Hill (b 27 Apr 1907, Harrison KY). Owner, boat and auto trim shop, Miamisburg OH.

CR413613 Russell Nelson Shade (b 19 Aug 1908, near Miamisburg OH) m 23 Jul 1930, Newport KY, Willie Gertrude Tillison (b 25 Oct 1911, Bristol TN). Manufacture of boats, Miamisburg OH.

CR4136131 Judith Ellen Shade (b 9 Apr 1938, Miamisburg OH) m 16 Mar 1951, Richmond IN, Chester Alexander (b 26 Oct 1935, Loveland OH). Steel worker, Middletown OH.

CR41361311 Karen Sue Alexander (b 11 Aug 1957, Middletown OH)

CR4136132 Carol Jean Shade (b 20 Mar 1940, Miamisburg OH) m 14 Sep 1958, Miamisburg OH, William Lewis McNabb (b 20 Nov 1936, West Carrollton OH). Factory worker, West Carrollton OH.

CR41361321 Richard Lewis McNabb (b 27 Mar 1958, West Carrollton OH)

CR4136133 Richard Nelson Shade (b 23 Oct 1946, Miamisburg OH)

CR4136134 David Allen Shade (b 24 Apr 1948, Miamisburg OH)

CR41362 Carry Luella Maxwell (b 23 Jun 1886, near Centerville OH) m 22 Aug 1912, Miamisburg OH, Otto Christian Betz (15 Jan 1881, Miamisburg OH-25 Feb 1957, Miamisburg OH). Shoe repairman, Miamisburg OH.

CR413621 Vera Viola Betz (b 28 Jan 1914, Miamisburg OH) m 5 Apr 1944, Miamisburg OH, John McDaniel (19 Feb 1907, Dayton OH-26 Aug 1946, Dayton OH). Bur Dayton OH. Factory worker, Franklin OH.

CR413622 James Robert Betz (b 19 Apr 1919, Miamisburg OH) m 1) 16 Dec 1945, Miamisburg OH, Naomi Marie Cadle (b 8 Feb 1924, Hamilton OH); m 2) 16 May 1953, Miamisburg OH, Margie Jean Myers (b 24 Nov 1930, Miamisburg OH). Carpenter, Miamisburg OH.

CR41362221   Cynthia Darlene Betz (b 8 Oct 1946, Hamilton OH)

CR4136222   Cheryl Kay Betz (b 3 Sep 1948, Hamilton OH)

CR4136223   Judy Marie Betz (b 28 Oct 1955, Miamisburg OH)

CR41363   Bessie Viola Maxwell (b 20 Aug 1888, near Centerville OH) m 26 Oct 1905, Ellerton OH, George Alfred Schell (b 1 Mar 1886, near Ellerton OH). Farmer, Montgomery Co OH.

CR413631   Carol Maxwell Schell (b 30 Dec 1906, near Ellerton OH) m 1 Jun 1935, Dayton OH, Betty Elizabeth Braun (b 25 Nov 1912, Dayton OH). Mechanical engineer, Dayton OH.

CR4136311   Betty Jo Schell (b 7 Feb 1939, Dayton OH) m 26 Nov 1958, Ellerton OH, Theodore John Colbert (b 16 Mar 1937, Marion OH). Meter reader, Dayton OH

CR4136312   Molly Beth Schell (b 3 Oct 1949, Centerville OH)

CR413632   Lawrence G. Schell (13 Nov 1908, near Ellerton OH-11 Mar 1921). Bur Ellerton OH.

CR413633   Mary Adeline Schell (b 7 Dec 1911, near Ellerton OH) m 23 Aug 1934, New Lebanon OH, James Edward Wolf (b 13 Sep 1911, near Liberty OH). Farmer, near New Lebanon, Montgomery Co OH.

CR4136331   Larry Lee Wolf (b 2 Jan 1937, near New Lebanon OH) m 30 Nov 1957, Connersville IN. Farm Bureau employee, Germantown OH.

CR4136332   Gloria Jean Wolf (b 4 Jan 1941, near New Lebanon OH)

CR413634   Emerson Dewitt Schell (b 15 Oct 1917, near Ellerton OH) m 1) 22 Jun 1940, near Liberty OH, Esther McNay (5 Jan 1918, Liberty OH-7 Oct 1947, near Liberty OH); m 2) 30 Jul 1949, Drexel OH, Edna Christian (b 6 Jul 1921, Dayton OH). Bur Ellerton OH. Plaster precision moulder, Cincinnati OH.

CR4136341   Jerry Lynn Schell (b 27 Jul 1944, Montgomery Co OH)

CR413635   Donald Edwin Schell (b 22 Aug 1921, near Ellerton OH) m 28 Jun 1941, Dayton OH, Henrietta Hilda Busse (b 30 Apr 1922, Dayton OH). Dairyman, West Alexandria OH.

CR4136351   David John Schell (b 6 Mar 1943, near Liberty OH)

CR4136352   Douglas Eugene Schell (b 18 Jun 1946, near Liberty OH)

CR4136353   Joellen Schell (b 22 Aug 1948, near Liberty OH)

CR41364   Harry Wilson Maxwell (b 17 Nov 1890, near Miamisburg OH) m 27 Dec 1909, Ellerton OH, Ruth Naomi Patten (b 21 Oct 1891, Ellerton OH). Farmer, Montgomery and Butler Cos, West Middletown OH.

CR413641   Doris Mable Maxwell (23 May 1910, Ellerton OH-25 Jun 1958, near Minneapolis MN) m 1 Jan 1928, Ralph Lee Henning (b 28 Mar 1908, Miamisburg OH). Bur near Minneapolis MN. Assemblyman, Minneapolis MN.

CR4136411   Richard Lee Henning (b 22 May 1928, Miamisburg OH)

CR4136412   Barbara Jean Henning (b 16 May 1931, Miamisburg OH) m Thomas Campbell. Salesman, Newport Beach CA.

CR41364121   Gary Lee Campbell (b 25 Feb 1949, Minneapolis MN)

CR4136413   Beverly Ann Henning (b 1 Oct 1935, Miamisburg OH)

CR4136414   Charlotte Kay Henning (b 22 Apr 1941, Miamisburg OH)

CR4136415   Peggy Jo Henning (b 29 Dec 1944, Dayton OH)

CR4136416   Cynthia Lou Henning (b 12 Apr 1951, Minneapolis MN)

CR4136417   Todd William Henning (b 21 Aug 1954, Minneapolis MN)

CR413642   Robert Byron Maxwell (b 11 Jan 1912, Centerville OH) m 25 Mar 1939, Ellerton OH, Violet Elizabeth Baker (b 21 Apr 1915, Drexel OH). Office worker, Dayton OH.

CR4136421   Daniel Eugene Maxwell (b 28 Jan 1945, Dayton OH)

CR413643   Charles Woodrow Maxwell (b 19 Mar 1913, Ellerton OH) m 1) 24 Nov 1936, Miamisburg OH, Norma Elizabeth Buchanan (24 Jun 1915, Miamisburg OH-28 May 1940); m 2) 31 Jan 1941, Lewisburg OH, Helen McKee (b 6 Mar 1918, near West Manchester, Darke Co OH). Parts manager, West Chester OH.

CR4136431   Ramon Lee Maxwell (b 15 Nov 1937, Miamisburg OH)

CR4136432   David Charles Maxwell (b 29 Aug 1939, Miamisburg OH)

CR413644   Esther Ruby Maxwell (b 3 Feb 1915, Ellerton OH) m 1) 5 Dec 1936, Ellerton OH, Donald Virgil Wrights (b 17 Nov 1915), div; m 2) 8 Sep 1952, Chester Allen Powers (b 1 Jan 1894). Assembler, Xenia OH.

CR413645   Mark Alsworth Maxwell (b 5 Dec 1917, Miamisburg OH) m 2 Mar 1946, Germantown OH, Treva G. Miller (b 1 Jan 1922, Germantown OH). Factory worker, Hamilton OH.

CR4136451   Anthony Walter Maxwell (b 16 Dec 1947, Middletown OH)

CR413646   Lowell Edison Maxwell (b 4 Jun 1922, Franklin OH) m 24 Jun 1941, Lewisburg OH, Nina Marie Mattis (b 20 Dec 1921, Lewisburg OH). Shipping and receiving clerk, Dayton OH.

CR4136461   Michael Lowell Maxwell (b 26 Jan 1945, Dayton OH)

CR4136462   Thomas Wilson Maxwell (b 20 Dec 1947, Dayton OH)

CR413647   Phyllis Irene Maxwell (b 11 Nov 1924, Miamisburg OH) m 24 Nov 1942, Germantown OH, Kenneth Miller (b 1 Jul 1923, Germantown OH). Press operator, Middletown OH.

CR4136471   Robert Gene Miller (b 9 Nov 1943, Germantown OH)

CR4136472   Linda Lou Miller (b 26 Jun 1946, Germantown OH)

CR4136473   Terry Lee Miller (b 3 Oct 1947, Germantown OH)

CR4136474   Marilyn Ann Miller (b 8 Aug 1951, Germantown OH)

CR413648   Lucille Jean Maxwell (b 1 Feb 1927, Miamisburg OH) m 15 Feb 1944, Middletown OH, Scharold Dean Eckhardt (b 24 Jun 1920, Middletown OH). Guard, Middletown OH.

CR4136481   Larry Douglas Eckhardt (b 19 Dec 1944, Middletown OH)

CR4136482   James Alfred Eckhardt (b 17 Sep 1946, Middletown OH)

CR4136483   Virginia Lee Eckhardt (b 8 Sep 1948, Middletown OH)

CR4136484   Steven Scharold Eckhardt (b 7 Mar 1957, Middletown OH)

CR41365   Ernest Victor Maxwell (25 Dec 1892, near Centerville OH-14 Jul 1932, Dayton OH) m 1) 28 Sep 1911, Ellerton OH, Glena Viola Smith (b 2 Apr 1892, near Ellerton OH); m 2) 11 Feb 1912, Dayton OH, Carrie May Highfield (b 22 May 1891, Centerville OH). Bur Centerville OH.

CR413651   Clarence Thurman Maxwell (17 Feb 1912, near Ellerton OH-4 Jun 1931, Ellerton OH). Bur Ellerton OH.

CR413652   Earl Victor Maxwell (b 11 Oct 1914, near Germantown OH) m 24 Jun 1944, Dayton OH, Vivian Madge Fenner (b 26 Sep 1915, Little York OH). Salesman, Dayton OH.

CR413653   Harold Glen Maxwell (b 19 Apr 1918, Miamisburg OH) m 30 Jun 1945, Waterbury CT, Clare Jean Bartlett (b 11 Mar 1923, Springfield MA). Partnership owner, A.F. Leis, Inc., Dayton OH.

CR4136531   Douglas Bartlett Maxwell (b 5 Nov 1946, Dayton OH)

CR4136532   Debra Leigh Maxwell (b 6 Feb 1950, Dayton OH)

CR413654   Estele Lee Maxwell (b 4 Sep 1919, near Germantown OH) m 15 May 1943, Los Angeles CA, Margery Estelle Hathaway (b 28 Mar 1921, Dayton OH). Owner, Dayton Window Co, Dayton OH.

CR4136541   Larry Lee Maxwell (b 27 Aug 1944, Dayton OH)

CR413655   Margery Allen Maxwell (b 19 Apr 1925, Dayton OH) m 9 Jun 1946, Dayton OH, Wilmer Yewis Moyer (b 3 May 1922, Mt. Cory OH). Electronic engineer, Dayton OH.

CR41366   Florence Marie Maxwell (b 24 Jul 1895, near Centerville OH) m 4 Nov 1914, Miamisburg OH, Noble Alexander Graham (30 Jan 1889, Jackboro TN-20 Mar 1943, Miamisburg OH). Bur Centerville OH. Factory foreman, Miamisburg OH.

CR413661   Peggy Lou Graham (b 9 Dec 1919, Dayton OH) m 25 Oct 1941, Miamisburg OH, William Henry Schneider (b 26 Sep 1915, Hamilton OH). Fireman, Miamisburg OH.

CR4136611   William Fredrick Schneider (b 28 Apr 1943, Miamisburg OH).

CR4136612   Thomas Maxwell Schneider (b 8 Aug 1948, Miamisburg OH)

CR4136613   Cinda Louise Schneider (b 4 Dec 1952, Miamisburg OH)

CR4136614   Constance Marie Schneider (b 24 Jan 1958, Miamisburg OH)

CR4137   William Rabold (12 Feb 1864, Berks Co PA-29 Oct 1931, Dayton OH) m 26 Jan 1895, West Carrollton OH, Elizabeth Catherine Fox. Bur Ellerton OH. Farmer, 1892-1909; grocery store owner.

CR4138   Emma Rabold (23 Feb 1866, Berks Co PA-18 Oct 1879, near Ellerton OH). Bur Ellerton OH.

CR4139   Harry Wilson Rabold (14 Jun 1869, Berks Co PA-5 Feb 1945, Dayton OH) m 18 Feb 1892, Miamisburg OH, Emma Gaiser (28 Apr 1868, Miamisburg OH-18 Apr 1948, Dayton OH). Bur Miamisburg OH. Carriage painter, Miamisburg OH.

CR41391   Ernest Edward Rabold (29 Mar 1893, Miamisburg OH-16 Nov 1958, Dayton OH) m 12 Oct 1910, Miamisburg OH, Ruby May Baker (b 7 Feb 1892, Miamisburg OH). Bur Miamisburg OH. Laundry foreman, Dayton OH.

CR413911   Donald Wilson Rabold (b 19 May 1911, Miamisburg OH) m 20 Sep 1933, Richmond IN, Helen Bernice Fitzpatrick (b 2 Jan 1916, Covington KY). Homemaker, MacAllen TX.

CR4139111   Donald Carlton Rabold (b 3 Mar 1935, Dayton OH) m 15 May 1954, Liberty IN, Janet May Woodbury (b 10 Sep 1937, Dayton OH). Salesman, southern part of OH, KY and IN, Dayton OH.

CR41391111   William Edward Rabold (b 23 Dec 1954, Dayton OH)

CR41391112   Jeffrey Lynn Rabold (b 31 May 1956, Dayton OH)

CR41391113   Sherryl Lyn Rabold (b 27 Jan 1958, Dayton OH)

CR4139112   Robert Eugene Rabold (b 11 Apr 1940, Dayton OH)

CR4139113   John Ernest Rabold (b 28 Jun 1943, Dayton OH)

CR4139114   Susan Elaine Rabold (b 9 May 1945, Dayton OH)

CR4139115   Rebecca Jane Rabold (b 26 Apr 1953, Dayton OH)

CR413912   Dorothy Jane Rabold (17 Oct 1914, Dayton OH-6 Dec 1914, Dayton OH). Bur Miamisburg OH.

CR413913   James Melvin Rabold (b 11 Dec 1915, Dayton OH) m 1) 28 Mar 1937, Dayton OH, Catherine Tyleman Furnas (b 4 Oct 1917, West Milton OH); m 2) 24 Oct 1944, Newport KY, Elizabeth Patricia Hall (b 14 Feb 1920, Dayton OH). Interior decorator, Dayton OH.

CR4139131   Scotte Lynne Rabold (b 2 Sep 1945, Dayton OH)

CR413914   Richard Carlton Rabold (b 6 Dec 1917, Dayton OH) m 15 Dec 1943, Nashville TN, Mary Helen Cooksey (b 23 May 1925, Bowling Green KY). Time study engineer, Dayton OH.

CR4139141   Keith Allen Rabold (b 23 Mar 1946, Dayton OH)

CR4139142   Thomas Edward Rabold (b 6 Jan 1951, Dayton OH)

CR4139143   Christopher Lance Rabold (b 21 Aug 1955, Dayton OH)

CR413915   Betty Jane Rabold (b 17 Aug 1925, Dayton OH) m 21 Apr 1943, Dayton OH, Curtis Cummins Atkinson (b 13 Apr 1922, Vincennes IN). Iron worker, Dayton OH.

CR4139151   Richard Curtis Atkinson (b 20 Dec 1943, Dayton OH)

CR4139152   Carlton Arden Atkinson (b 23 Nov 1945, Dayton OH)

CR4139153   Patricia Ann Atkinson (b 20 Dec 1950, Dayton OH)

CR4139154   Michael David Atkinson (b 24 Dec 1953, Dayton OH)

CR41392   Edith May Rabold (28 May 1895, Miamisburg OH-4 May 1918, Miamisburg OH) m 6 Mar 1915, Miamisburg OH, Byron Dawson (b 11 Oct 1893, Dayton OH). Bur Miamisburg OH.

CR413921   Harold William Dawson (b 26 Feb 1916, Dayton OH) m 18 Apr 1939, Carlton KY, Gladys Harriet King (b 31 Dec 1910, Chicago IL). Factory foreman, Brookville OH.

CR4139211   James William Dawson (b 30 Nov 1940, Dayton OH). Operator of farm ditcher,

CR414 MARGARET REBECCA WEISER SOUDERS AND FAMILY
Seated, left to right: CR4147 John Robert Souders (1872-1938); CR4141 Sallie Souders Wagner; CR414 Margaret Rebecca Weiser Souders (1833-1918); Thomas Tobias Souders (1837-1917). Standing, left to right: CR4144 Emma Helen Souders Stiely (1866-1941); CR4146 Margaret Elizabeth Souders Bechtel (1870-1935); CR4142 Mary Ann Souders (1862-1946)

Montgomery, Miami and Preble Cos, Clayton OH.

CR4139212   Thomas King Dawson (b 5 Jun 1943, Dayton OH)

CR4139213   Catherine Marie Dawson (b 15 May 1950, Dayton OH)

CR4139214   Bruce Harold Dawson (b 26 Jul 1954, Dayton OH)

CR413922   Robert Nelson Dawson (b 15 Jul 1918, Dayton OH) m 28 Apr 1938, Dayton OH, Edna May Miller (b 14 Jun 1920, Dayton OH). Furniture jobber, Miami FL.

CR4139221   Robert Nelson Dawson, Jr. (b 28 Apr 1940, Dayton OH)

CR41393   Mable Alberta Rabold (26 Mar 1898, Miamisburg OH-10 Oct 1949, Dayton OH) m 28 Dec 1923, Dayton OH, Carlton MacChesney (b 1 Jun 1900, Middletown OH). Bur Miamisburg OH. Salesman, Dayton OH.

CR41394   Lawrence Wilbur Rabold (b 7 Nov 1902, Miamisburg OH) m 1) 18 Jun 1923, Dayton OH, Betty Schumann; m 2) 12 Sep 1944, Norfolk VA, Russiea Banks (b 1 Dec 1905, Greenville TX). Owner, "Therm-O-Glare of Florida," Miami FL.

CR414   Margaret Rebecca Weiser (17 Mar 1833, Womelsdorf PA-1918, Womelsdorf PA) m PA, Thomas Tobias Souders (1837, PA-1917, PA). Bur Womelsdorf PA.[95]

CR4141   Sarah Souders m   Wagner

CR41411   Minnie Wagner m   Kelley

CR414111   Clifford Kelley

CR41412   Ella Wagner m Lou Ingram

CR41413   William Wagner

CR4142   Mary Ann Souders (1862, Womelsdorf PA-1946, Womelsdorf PA). Unm. Housekeeper, Womelsdorf and Sinking Spring PA.

CR4143   Kate Viola Souders (2 Sep 1865, Womelsdorf PA-Jun 1935, m Apr 1887, John Charles
Oberly

---

[95]Data contributed in 1996 by Ruth Deibert, Mary Weiser Evans, Marilyn Poore, and Allison P. Koch.

CR41431 Esther May Oberly (b 19 Feb 1888) m 1) 1908, Frank Bertram Brandreth; m 2) 1918, Walter Bayard Statton

CR414311 Frank Bertram Brandreth (b 12 Sep 1909, Royersford PA)

CR414312 Walter Bayard Statton, Jr. (b 1 Jun 1920)

CR41432 Edith Gertrude Oberly (20 Jun 1889). Unm.

CR4144 Emma Helen Souders (18 Dec 1866, Stouchsburg PA-5 Dec 1941, Reading PA) m 28 Jan 1899, Reading PA, Charles Stiely (22 Feb 1866, Wernersville PA-19 Jul 1937, Reading PA). Bur Womelsdorf PA.

CR41441 Paul Robert Weiser Moyer (7 Jan 1888, Womelsdorf PA-9 Oct 1967, Womelsdorf PA) m Joann

CR414411 Catherine Irene Moyer (b 16 Jun 1906, Reading PA) m Charles I. Folk (1 Nov 1901, Reading PA-7 Sep 1970). Dyer.

*CR4144111 Ruth Grace Folk (b 10 May 1938, Reading PA) m 1) 10 May 1958, Russell Richard Manwiller (b 13 Jan 1938), div 1981; m 2) 14 Feb 1982, William John Deibert

CR41441111 Lori-lynn Manwiller (b 24 Sep 1960) m 29 Mar 1980, Robert Lee McWilliams

CR414411111 Ryan Lawton McWilliams (b 4 Oct 1981)

CR414411112 Michaell Timothy McWilliams (b 8 Feb 1985)

CR41441112 Michael Bradley Manwiller (b 20 Jul 1965) m 25 Jun 1988, Letitia Shomo

CR414411121 Sarah Ashley Manwiller (b 27 Mar 1989)

CR414411122 Tyler Curtis Manwiller (b 4 Feb 1991)

CR41441113 Bradley Michael Manwiller (b 20 Jul 1965) m 19 Apr 1986, Lynn Elizabeth Buchanan (b 6 Aug 1964)

CR414411131 Valcrie Lynn Manwiller (b 21 Jun 1990)

CR414412 Beatrice Amelia Moyer (b 13 Oct 1907, Reading PA) m 8 Nov 1924, Howard Samuel Peifer (b 27 Jun 1904, Reading PA). Utility man, Metropolitan Electric Co., Reading PA.

*CR4144121 Pauline Beatrice Peifer (b 11 Apr 1925, Reading PA) m 8 May 1943, Stanley Bertolette Hepler (b 5 Feb 1922, Reading PA). Knitter, Berkshire Knitting Mills, Wyomissing PA.

CR41441211 Jacqueline Lee Hepler (b 5 Aug 1944, PA) m 9 Sep 1967, Michael Craig Aten (b 11 May 1944)

CR414412111 Michael Craig Aten (b 29 Oct 1968)

CR414412112 Scott Keith Aten (b 17 Jul 1971)

CR41441212 Stanley Bertolette Hepler, Jr. (b 23 Oct 1958). Unm.

CR4144122 Howard John Peifer (b 5 Sep 1926, Reading PA) m 9 Jul 1947, Reading PA, Betty DeDamio (b 27 Mar 1934, Reading PA)

CR41441221   Howard Samuel Peifer (b 12 Feb 1948, Reading PA) m 25 Jun 1978, Charlotte

CR414412211   Troy Anthony Peifer (b 12 Nov 1980, Reading PA)

*CR414413   Mary Evelyn Weiser Moyer (b 9 Oct 1909, Hyde Park PA) m Robert Dudly Evans

CR4144131   Beverly June Wise (b 29 Sep 1934-29 Jun 1956) m   Ranck

CR41442   Margaret Florence Stiely (8 Apr 1901, Reading PA-8 Jul 1987, Reading PA) m 20 Mar 1926, Reading PA, Samuel Manning Longenecker (b 9 Sep 1906, Reading PA). Cremated. Homemaker and clerk, Reading and West Lawn PA.

CR414421   Patricia Aline Longenecker (b 14 Jun 1928, Reading PA) m 10 May 1952, Reading PA, Robert Steven Rentschler (b 21 Mar 1927, Reading PA). Secretary and homemaker, West Lawn and Reading PA.

CR4144211   Kim Robin Rentschler (b 12 May 1953, West Reading PA) m 11 May 1974, Reading PA, Harold Tommy Leibensperger (b 12 Nov 1952, Reading PA). Administrative asst, West Lawn and Mohrsville PA.

CR41442111   Cory Hannah Leibensperger (b 27 Apr 1979, West Reading PA)

CR41442112   Abbey Michelle Leibensperger (b 22 Feb 1981, West Reading PA)

CR41442113   Ahri Noel Leibensperger (b 11 Jul 1989, West Reading PA)

CR41442114   Kesh Alex Leibensperger (b 27 Dec 1990, West Reading PA)

CR4144212   Keath Steven Rentschler (b 31 Mar 1954, Reading PA) m 30 Sep 1982, Elkton MD, Felicia Ann Valle (b 26 Sep 1956, West Reading PA). Warehouse manager, Reading and Bethel PA.

CR41442121   Zubulon Robert Rentschler (b 1 May 1985, West Reading PA)

CR41442122   Luke Daniel Rentschler (b 14 Sep 1986, West Reading PA)

CR41442123   Jason Steven Rentschler (b 21 Apr 1990, West Reading PA)

CR4144213   Kristie Lynn Rentschler (b 26 Apr 1963, West Reading PA) m 21 May 1990, Key West FL, Eugene Michael Hudzik (b 30 Jul 1962, Reading PA). Sales clerk, Reading PA.

CR41442131   Cody Eugene Hudzik (b 23 Jan 1993, Reading PA)

CR41442132   Zoe Aline Hudzik (b 15 Jun 1995, Reading PA)

*CR414422   Marilyn Ann Longenecker (b 20 Jun 1932, Reading PA) m 11 Jun 1955, Reading PA, Franklin Emmett Poore III (1 Apr 1933, West Reading PA-21 Jul 1987, Wyomissing Hills PA). BS, Kutztown (PA) U, 1954; librarian, Wyomissing Hills PA.

CR4144221   Jocelyn Elaine Poore (b 29 Sep 1956, Pensacola FL) m 9 Jul 1983, Wyomissing PA, John Leroy Moyer, Jr. (b 17 Sep 1956, West Reading PA). BS, Indiana U of PA, 1978; preschool teacher, Wyomissing Hills and Wernersville PA.

CR41442211   Drew Franklin Moyer (b 12 Jul 1989, West Reading PA)

CR41442212   Kyle John Moyer (b 30 Sep 1991, West Reading PA)

CR4144222   Bradley Scott Poore (b 7 Oct 1958, Edenton NC) m 19 Dec 1981, West Reading PA, Beth Ann Parks (b 10 Jan 1958, West Reading PA). BA, Elizabethtown (PA) Col, 1980; financial consultant, Wyomissing Hills PA.

CR41442221   Jenna Marie Poore (b 2 Feb 1988, West Reading PA)

CR41442222   Erin Lynn Poore (b 4 Sep 1990, West Reading PA)

CR4144223   Roderick Alan Poore (b 13 Apr 1964, West Reading PA) m 19 Aug 1989, Philadelphia PA, Mary Ann Williams (b 30 Sep 1961, Philadelphia PA). BS, PSU, 1986; MADiv, Westminster Theol Sem, 1990; youth pastor, Wyomissing Hills and Philadelphia PA.

CR41442231   Gabrielle Alexis Poore (b 19 Apr 1991, Philadelphia PA)

CR41442232   Talitha Amaris Poore (b 30 Mar 1993, Philadelphia PA)

CR41442233   Karis Adina Poore (b 24 Feb 1995, Philadelphia PA)

CR41442234   Jesse Amos Poore (b 24 Feb 1995, Philadelphia PA)

*CR4144224   Allison Leigh Poore (b 15 Mar 1971, West Reading PA) m 5 Nov 1995, Wyomissing PA, William George Koch, Jr. (b 26 Nov 1966, West Reading PA). BS, Elizabethtown (PA) Col, 1993; public accountant, Wyomissing Hills PA.

CR414423   Lee Carl Longenecker (b 6 May 1934, Reading PA) m 11 Nov 1961, Reading PA, Julia Suzanne Myersburg Ritter (b 19 May 1928, Rio Grande NJ). Electrician, Reading PA.

CR4144231   Beth Anne Longenecker (b 14 Oct 1964, West Reading PA) m 6 Feb 1988, West Lawn PA, Shane Lee Turner (b 8 Jan 1963, Pomona CA). Homemaker, Sinking Spring PA.

CR41442311   Troy Nathan Turner (b 11 Oct 1991, West Reading PA)

CR41442312   Shelby Lee Turner (b 3 Jun 1993, West Reading PA)

CR414424   Douglas Allan Longenecker (b 29 Sep 1945, Reading PA) m 12 Dec 1970, Wernersville PA, Helen Antoinette Boulanger (b 11 Dec 1934, West Reading PA). BS, 1971, MLS, 1974, Kutztown (PA) U; librarian, Reading PA. No chn.

CR41443   Elsie May Stiely (14 Dec 1902, Reading PA-14 Jan 1994, Reading PA) m 24 Feb 1945, Reading PA, Ephraim Hartman (6 Jun 1892, Reading PA-9 Aug 1972, Reading PA). Bur Reading PA. Hosiery mill worker. No chn.

CR41444   Helen Mary Stiely (27 Apr 1905, Reading PA-20 Dec 1977, PA) m Willard Leroy Farrell (3 Jul 1906, Reading PA-22 Dec 1980, PA). Pattern maker, Reading PA.

CR414441   Willard Charles Farrell (b 23 Oct 1927, Reading PA) m 31 Aug 1946, Alverta Sara Wolfe (b 16 Nov 1928, Pine Grove PA). Reading School District, retired, Reading PA.

CR4144411   Michael David Farrell (b 24 Apr 1947, Reading PA) m. Painter and school bus driver, Reading PA.

CR41444111   Matthew Michael Farrell (b 6 Dec 1966, Reading PA) m 10 Sep 1988, Amy Marie Gaul (b 11 Oct 1967, Reading PA). Carpenter.

CR41444112   Megan Kathleen Farrell (b 21 Sep ca 1972, Reading PA).

CR4144412   Jeffrey Willard Farrell (b 25 Jan 1954, Reading PA) m 10 May 1973, Susan Carol Showers (b 19 Mar 1954). He, building contractor; she, secretary.

CR41444121   Justin Jeffrey Farrell (b 20 Aug 1976, Reading PA)

CR41444122   Sara Jean Farrell (b 27 Jul 1985, Reading PA)

CR414442   Elaine Louise Farrell (b 28 Oct 1929, Reading PA) m 20 Nov 1948, George Massy Stewart (b 2 Sep 1924, Reading PA). Telephone co.; consignment store owner, Reading PA.

CR4144421   Stephanie Layne Stewart (b 30 Jun 1951, Reading PA) m 22 Jul 1972, Larry Arnold Bundens (b 9 Apr 1950, Reading PA). He, steel factory; she, consignment store manager, Reading PA.

CR41444211   Michael Thomas Bundens (b 8 Sep 1972, Reading PA)

CR41444212   Megan Elizabeth Bundens (b 19 Mar 1976, Reading PA)

CR4144422   Suzanne Libeth Stewart (b 23 Aug 1952, Reading PA) m 12 May 1978, John Joseph Murray (b 4 Aug 1956, Reading PA). She, RN; he, chemical engineer.

CR4144423   Mark Farrell Stewart (b 30 Jul 1954, Reading PA) m 6 Apr 1991, Kay Louise Homuth (b 24 Sep 1953, Minneapolis MN). He, laser service manager; she, secretary.

CR4144424   Martha Jane Stewart (b 23 Jul 1958, Reading PA) m 15 Jun 1979, Daniel Lee Davidheiser (b 7 Nov 1954, Reading PA). She, consignment shop sales; he, tree trimmer.

CR41444241   Melissa Lynne Davidheiser (b 17 Dec 1979, Reading PA)

CR4144425   Amy Helen Stewart (b 26 Feb 1961, Reading PA) m 29 Feb 1992, Darron Reed Yeager (b 14 Jul 1963, Reading PA). She, consignment shop sales; he, brick mason, Reading PA. No chn.

*CR4144426   Elizabeth Jo Stewart (b 1 Mar 1967, Reading PA).

CR4145   Lilly Jane Souders (b 13 Apr 1868, PA-24 May 1883, Womelsdorf PA). Bur Womelsdorf PA.

CR4146   Margaret Elizabeth Souders (b 8 Feb 1870, Womelsdorf PA-5 Jan 1935, Reading PA) m 24 Dec 1891, Womelsdorf PA, Walter Lincoln Bechtel. Cigar maker.

CR41461   Christine Rebecca Bechtel (b 6 Feb 1896, Womelsdorf PA) m 3 Oct 1925, Mark M. Lindenmuth (b 11 Dec 1898, Sutter Tp, Berks Co PA). Clerk, bookkeeper, Reading PA. No chn.

CR4147   John Robert Souders (15 Oct 1872, Marion Tp, Berks Co PA-3 Sep 1938, Philadelphia PA) m 4 Nov 1899, Reading PA, Viola Hartman (b Reading PA). Bur Sinking Spring PA. Clerk, transportation dept, Reading Terminal, Philadelphia PA.

CR41471   Ruth Souders. Unm.

CR415   George E. Weiser (10 Aug 1838, Lebanon Co PA-16 Jul 1927, Dayton OH) m Bernville PA, Mary Ann Grime (29 Nov 1846, Bernville PA-6 Dec 1916, Dayton OH). Bur Dayton OH. Civil War, Co. E, 14th Regt, PVI.[96]

CR4151   Charles Herbert Weiser (24 Nov 1864, Bernville PA-22 Mar 1870, Bernville PA). Bur Bernville PA.

---

[96]Supplemental data (1996) submitted by Ada Weiser Florek.

CR4152   Wilson Grant Weiser (28 Sep 1866, Bernville PA-14 May 1868, Bernville PA). Bur Bernville PA.

CR4153   William Harry Weiser (24 Aug 1868, Bernville PA-29 Apr 1945, Cleveland OH) m 19 Dec 1893, Florence B. Finch (10 Apr 1873, Liberty IN-11 Aug 1941, Lynn IN). Bur Spartanburg IN. Teacher and woodturner.

CR41531   Marion F. Weiser (27 Jul 1894, Connersville IN-10 Oct 1959, Richmond IN) m 1) Jan 1914, Eva Mason; m 2) 18 Mar 1927, Pearl Hood. WWI; woodworker and piano tuner.

CR415311   William Wesley Weiser (b 18 Dec 1914, Centerville IN) m 25 Dec 1934, Helen Madge (b 18 May 1914, Richmond IN).

CR4153111   Patty Ann Weiser (b 8 Aug 1939, Richmond IN) m May 1957, Dale Wallace

CR41531111   Cynthia Lynn Wallace (b 26 Oct 1959)

CR4153112   Bonnie Sue Weiser (b 14 Oct 1945, Richmond IN)

CR415312   Mary Ellen Weiser (b 2 May 1917, Centerville IN) m 17 Oct 1936, Wallace Moore (b 1914)

CR4153121   Robert Moore (b 4 May 1938, Richmond IN) m 6 Aug 1956, IN, Louan Tanner (b 14 Apr 1941, Centerville IN)

CR41531211   Jeffrey Scott Moore (b 29 Oct 1958, Panama City FL)

CR4153122   Ronine Moore (b 11 Jan 1942, Richmond IN)

CR4153123   Sandra Moore (b 12 Nov 1946, Richmond IN)

CR41532   Mary Esther Weiser (b 19 Oct 1897, Centerville IN) m 24 Dec 1921, William Herbert Napiere (3 Jun 1887, Liberty IN-31 Aug 1961). WWI; telegraphist, Lynn IN.

CR415321   Stanley Leon Napiere (b 10 Oct 1922, Liberty IN) m 1) 29 Mar 1945, Esther Lee Patterson; m 2) 13 Jun 1958, Jeraldine Menger

CR4153211   Diana Lee Napiere (b 16 Jul 1946)

CR4153212   Timothy William Napiere (b 11 Apr 1954)

CR41533   Raymond Everett Weiser (b 15 Jun 1906, Connersville IN) m 15 Nov 1939, Josephine Jetters. Woodworker.

CR415331   Charles Earl Weiser (b 9 Jun 1942, Lynn IN)

CR415332   Billy Jo Weiser (b 30 Apr 1948, Lynn IN)

CR4154   Katie Weiser (10 Jul 1870, Bernville PA-28 Mar 1948, Dayton OH) m 1910, John Coblentz. Bur Dayton OH. No chn.

CR4155   Anna Dora Weiser (24 Oct 1872, Miamisburg OH-4 Feb 1957, New Madison OH) m 25 Dec 1889, OH, McCoy Miller (d 20 Jan 1944). Bur Dayton OH. Engineer, Longfellow School, Dayton OH.

CR4156   Harvey George Weiser (11 Dec 1874, Chambersburg OH-27 May 1927) m 2 Aug 1902, OH, Ella M. Winters (20 Sep 1882, near Brownsville IN-6 Sep 1958). Bur Brownsville IN.

CR41561   Maybelle E. Weiser (b 22 Sep 1904, Brownsville IN) m 19 Oct 1922, Ivan W. Clevenger
(b 21 Jun 1898)

CR415611   Doris Clevenger (b 30 Sep 1924, Brownsville IN). Unm. Although blind, a telephone
dictation stenographer, Indianapolis IN.

CR415612   Inez Clevenger (b 20 Jun 1927, Brownsville IN) m 1) Feb 1947, John Ankrom; m 2) 1953,
Dewey Swinney

CR4156121   Dale Edward Ankrom (b 3 Sep 1949)

CR4156122   Timothy Lee Swinney (b 28 Jan 1956)

CR415613   Gilbert Clevenger (b 2 Feb 1935, Brownsville IN) m 12 Sep 1954, Alice Cargal (b 5 Sep
1936)

CR4156131   Denyce Lin Clevenger (b 14 Jan 1956)

CR4156132   Douglas Lee Clevenger (b 7 Feb 1958)

CR41562   Roy W. Weiser (b 2 Sep 1907, Brownsville IN) m 1925, Elizabeth Jane Elliott (b 1 Feb
1908)

CR415621   Robert Eugene Weiser (b 7 Mar 1926) m Marian

CR4156211   James E. Weiser (b 11 Dec 1946)

CR4156212   Jeanette Weiser (b 4 Jul 1951)

CR415622   Mona Louise Weiser (b 13 Aug 1928) m Jan 1947, Marion Scotten (b Apr 1927)

CR4156221   Ella Jean Scotten (b 14 Sep 1947)

CR4156222   Carol Susan Scotten (b 5 Jun 1953)

CR415623   Donald Edward Weiser (b 14 Oct 1930) m Jun 1957, Nancy Park

CR4156231   Dale Alan Weiser (b 7 Sep 1958)

CR415624   Billy Gene Weiser (b 26 Aug 1934) m Nov 1955, Deanna

CR4156241   Jerry Dean Weiser (b 10 Jun 1956)

CR4156242   Mark Allen Weiser (b 7 Nov 1957)

CR4156243   Danny Lee Weiser (b 6 Aug 1958)

CR415625   Mary Kathryn Weiser (b 7 Oct 1939) m Feb 1956, Richard Beck

CR4156251   Michael Dean Beck (b 23 Sep 1956)

CR4156252   Kathryn Ann Beck (b 15 Oct 1957)

CR4157   Franklin Milton Weiser (6 May 1877, Miamisburg OH-20 Dec 1949, Panama City FL)
m 1) 18 Sep 1899, IN, Ada Mae Stelle (24 Aug 1877, Fayette Co IN-10 Jun 1920, Fayette Co IN); m 2) Lulu
Frances Stuart. Ada bur Connersville IN; he, bur Dayton OH.

*CR41571   Robert Vernon Weiser (21 May 1901, Connersville IN-10 Apr 1972, Bradenton FL) m 2 Jul 1927, Dayton OH, Dorothy Esther Shanor (21 Apr 1904, Dayton OH-27 Mar 1996, Dayton OH). Bur Dayton OH. Inspector; she, teacher.

*CR415711   Ada Lee Weiser (b 29 Aug 1931, Dayton OH) m 25 Jun 1955, Dayton OH, Francis Florek (b 8 Oct 1929, Toledo OH). Proofreader. Huber Heights OH.

CR4157111   Pamela Sue Florek (b 23 Jan 1956, Dayton OH) m 9 Oct 1982, Huber Heights OH, Marlin Marcum (b 2 Mar 1958, Dayton OH).

CR41571111   Stephen Edward Marcum (b 18 Jan 1985, Dayton OH)

CR41571112   Katie Elizabeth Marcum (b 16 Nov 1989, Dayton OH)

CR4157112   Sharon Ann Florek (b 15 Jan 1958, Dayton OH) m 12 Jun 1976, Dayton OH, Charley Timmy Hobbs (b 10 Jul 1959, Norton VA)

CR41571121   Jannifer Rae Hobbs (b 23 Dec 1976, Dayton OH)

CR41571122   Julie Marie Hobbs (b 29 Jun 1980, Dayton OH)

CR41571123   Jonathan Allen Hobbs (b 29 Jun 1983, Dayton OH)

CR4157113   Robert Michael Florek (b 9 Nov 1960, Dayton OH) m 1) 14 Feb 1981, Dayton OH, Carol Ann Pesch (b 31 Dec 1960), div 1982, m 2) 14 Feb 1985, Lori Vernier Burnash (b MI), div 1983; m 3) 20 May 1988, Troy OH, Tami Elizabeth Moore (b 1 Jul 1967, Bangor ME)

CR41571131   Francis Clinton Florek (b 22 Jul 1981, Wright-Patterson AFB OH)

CR41571132   Megan Elizabeth Florek (b 10 Feb 1990, Dayton OH)

CR41571133   Allison Renee Florek (b 9 Dec 1993, Napoleon OH)

CR4157114   Laura Marya Florek (b 29 Sep 1965, Dayton OH) m 27 Aug 1988, Huber Heights OH, Timothy Francis Joliat (b 9 Apr 1963, Canton OH)

CR41571141   Philip Kent Joliat (b 12 Jan 1991, Wright-Patterson AFB OH)

CR41571142   Jared Adam Joliat (b 26 Jan 1994, Dayton OH)

CR4151143   Carter Louis Joliat (b 26 Jun 1996, Dayton OH)

*CR415712   David Robert Weiser (b 30 Mar 1933, Dayton OH) m 8 Mar 1958, Richmond VA, Elizabeth Anne Nunn (b 12 Sep 1939, Richmond VA)

CR4157121   David Lee Weiser (b 9 Dec 1958, Richmond VA) m 19 Jan 1985

CR41571211   Matthew Bennett Weiser (b 26 May 1991, Richmond VA)

CR4157122   Raymond Vernon Weiser (b 5 Jul 1961, Richmond VA) m 2 Jul 1983, Highland Springs VA, Sharon Elizabeth Cole (b 21 Sep 1963, Richmond VA)

CR41571221   Jacquline Ray Weiser (b 21 Dec 1984, Richmond VA)

CR41571222   Nicholas Vernon Weiser (b 19 Mar 1987, Richmond VA)

CR41571223   Victoria Elizabeth Weiser (b 21 May 1991, Richmond VA)

CR4157123   Elizabeth Anne Weiser (b 29 Sep 1962, Richmond VA) m 8 Sep 1990, Highland Springs VA, Joseph Edward Broocks (b 13 Feb 1962, Richmond VA)

CR41571231   Joseph Robert Broocks (b 31 May 1995, Richmond VA)

CR41572   Ruth Viola Weiser (b 6 Jul 1906, Dayton OH) m William Stewart

CR415721   Ada Mae Stewart (b 1 Dec 1931, Eaton OH)

CR415722   Sara Nancy Stewart (b Eaton OH)

CR41573   Rachel Vera Weiser (b 13 Mar 1910, Connersville IN)

CR41574   Gladys Weiser

CR4158   Edward Weiser (b 11 Oct 1879, Miami Tp, Montgomery Co OH)

CR4159   Margaret Viola Weiser (7 Jul 1881, Miamisburg OH-13 Apr 1945, Dayton OH) m 29 Nov 1900, John Wesley Cottingham (b 9 Jan 1870). Bur Dayton OH.

CR41591   John Virgil Cottingham (b 29 Sep 1901, Dayton OH)

CR41592   Frances Aline Cottingham (b 1 Dec 1902, Dayton OH) m 30 Sep 1933, Kenneth Early Risner (d 18 Jan 1955, Dayton OH). Building and loan assn, Dayton OH.

CR415921   Douglas Stuart Risner (b 21 Oct 1938, Dayton OH). Miami (OH) U; music.

CR415922   Jeffrey Kenneth Risner (b 26 Nov 1940, Dayton OH). Heidelberg (OH) Col; music.

CR41593   Mary Vesta Cottingham (Sep 1908-dy)

CR415A   Lillie May Weiser (15 Aug 1883, Montgomery Co OH-1 May 1897, Montgomery Co OH).
Bur Dayton OH.

CR415B   Robert Milton Weiser (b 1886) m Nellie St. John

CR415B1   Lillian Weiser m Monroe Parker

CR415B11   Robert Parker

CR415B12   Mary Ann Parker

CR415B13   Stephen Parker

CR415B2   Naomi Weiser m Charles Naugle

CR415B21   Thomas Naugle

CR415B22   Charles Naugle

CR415B221   Naugle

CR415B222   Naugle

CR415B223   Naugle

CR415B3   Mary Weiser m Dan Poliquin

CR415B4   Betty Weiser m 1)   ; m 2) Rolla Bimley

CR415B41   Douglas

CR415B5   Arthur Nelson Weiser m Lucille

CR415B51   Arthur Nelson Weiser, Jr. m

CR415B52   Shirley Weiser m

CR415B6   Florence Weiser (1911-1913, Dayton OH)

CR42   Maria Catharine Weiser (b 30 Mar 1787) m Oct 1810, John Reigart

CR43   Henry Solomon Weiser (4 Mar 1789-d.y.)

CR44   Francisca Weiser (daughter of Solomon and Marie (Wenger) Weiser) was born 30 Jun 1790, and married in May 1816 to Michael Frederick. It is believed that she was the mother of Elizabeth Weiser, born June 21, 1811, a ward of Solomon Weiser (Francisca's brother) in later years. Of any family to Frederick, there is no record. She was dead by 1854.[97]

CR441   Elizabeth Weiser (21 Jun 1811 PA-4 Feb 1889, Womelsdorf PA) m 14 Apr 1834, Joseph Weiss (6 Mar 1815-12 Mar 1891, Womelsdorf PA). Bur Womelsdorf PA.

CR4411   Sarah Weiss (9 Oct 1834, Womelsdorf PA-10 Oct 1875, Womelsdorf PA) m Henry
Hoffman

CR44111   J.H. Hoffman (3 Sep 1853-7 Feb 1911) m Fannie W. Clouse (1 Dec 1853-31 Oct 1897)

CR441111   Sarah L. Hoffman (1 Oct 1876-19 Feb 1879)

CR4412   Mary Weiss (b 12 Sep 1836)

CR4413   Levi Weiss (13 Oct 1838-19 Apr 1913) m Mary   (21 May 1841-14 Jun 1898). Capt., Co. B, 93rd Penn Vol Inf, Civil War.

CR44131   William S. Weiss (9 Apr 1866-29 Oct 1872).

CR44132   Harry S. Weiss (1867-1927)

CR44133   John L. Weiss (1870-1933) m Florence M.   (b 1876)

CR44134   Charles G. Weiss (b 1872-1927) m Maggie M. (b 1873)

CR441341   Harry W. Weiss (1894-1897)

CR44135   Fred L. Weiss (1874-1930)

CR44136   Joseph F. Weiss (b 1877) m Lena V.

---

[97]Mrs. Ida Krick to Frederick Weiser, 21 Sep 1957; tonbstones, Womelsdorf PA.

CR44137   Eddie G. Weiss (25 Mar 1883-6 Nov 1887)

CR4414   Joseph Weiss (b 17 Oct 1840)

CR4415   Frank Weiss

CR4416   William H. Weiss (31 Jul 1849-23 Jul 1917). Civil War.

CR4417   Elmira W. Weiss (7 Mar 1856-7 Mar 1925) m Jacob P. Matthews

CR44171   Fred H. Matthews (22 Aug 1876-27 Jul 1911)

CR45   Solomon Weiser (son of Solomon and Marie (Wenger) Weiser) was born 4 Mar 1793, at Womelsdorf PA and died there 11 Jan 1866. He married in September 1818 to Maria Susan Zerbe (27 Sep 1797, Womelsdorf PA-17 Mar 1857, Womelsdorf PA). They are buried at Womelsdorf PA. Solomon, at least in his later years, was keeper of the tollgate east of Womelsdorf, and his daughter Elvina Arnold made her home with him. She tended the gate during his illness, when he was confined to a chair.[98]

CR451   Matilda Weiser (1 Jan 1819, Womelsdorf PA-12 Aug 1824, Womelsdorf PA). Bur Womelsdorf PA.

CR452   Elvina Weiser (4 Feb 1820, Womelsdorf PA-18 Sep 1893, Reading PA) m 17 Oct 1840, PA, George Arnold (b PA-1862, Battle of Seven Pines VA). She, bur Womelsdorf PA; his body never located. Pvt, Co. G, 93rd PVI; brickmaker, Womelsdorf PA.

CR4521   Mary Ann Elizabeth Arnold (17 Dec 1840, Womelsdorf PA-6 Aug 1902, Reading PA) m 1) PA,   Warren; m 2) Damon D. Schultz (1840-1925). Bur Womelsdorf PA.

CR45211   Ella Susan Martha Shearer (22 Feb 1860, Womelsdorf PA-Sep 1912, Reading PA). Unm. Bur Womelsdorf PA.

CR45212   Mamie Warren (1874-1927) m 1)   Brown; m 2)   Briner

CR452121   Raymond Brown (dy)

CR4522   Rebecca Arnold (4 May 1842, Womelsdorf PA-dy)

CR4523   John Peter Arnold (12 Oct 1843, Womelsdorf PA-17 Apr 1904, St. Joseph MO) m Apr 1865, Frances Chellew (14 Jun 1848, England-24 Dec 1913, St. Joseph MO). Bur St. Joseph MO. Civil War, Co. B, 90th PVI.

CR45231   Ida Arnold (23 Feb 1866, Womelsdorf PA-28 Aug 1911, St. Joseph MO) m Charles Stiers

CR45232   William Henry Arnold (b 2 Apr 1868, Womelsdorf PA) m Bertha Smallwood

CR452321   Herbert Aubrey Arnold

CR45233   George Benjamin Arnold (1869, Hamilton MO-May 1928, St. Joseph MO) m 30 Aug 1927, MO, Frances Straubie. No chn.

CR45234   John Franklin Arnold (26 Jun 1878, Hamilton MO-19 Aug 1936) m 20 Oct 1897, Effie Kueker (b 22 Dec 1878, Boon Co IN)

---

[98]Data submitted by Mrs. Ida Krick, Mrs. John I. Arnold, Harry F. Arnold, Roscoe H. Arnold, Russell M. Arnold, Mrs. Cosmus Kleinfelter, and Mrs. Harry Wright. Supplemental data (1996) sent by Mary K. Putman and Ruth K. Norton.

CR452341   Harry Franklin Arnold (b 10 Oct 1899, St. Joseph MO) m 4 Jun 1921, St. Joseph MO,
Margaret Lemser

CR4523411   Dorothy Arnold (b 29 Jun 1922) m 2 Jan 1940, Val C. Fandel

CR45234111   Diane Fandel (b 8 Oct 1942)

CR45234112   Richard Fandel (b 17 Feb 1946)

CR45234113   Valarie Fandel (b 28 Oct 1949)

CR45234114   Vincent Fandel (b 6 May 1951)

CR4523412   Robert E. Arnold (b 4 Sep 1924, St. Joseph MO) m 10 Jan 1947, Lois Bickmore

CR45234121   Christina Arnold (b 14 Dec 1947)

CR45234122   Annette Arnold (b 10 Jun 1949)

CR45234123   Glenn Arnold (b 23 Jul 1951)

CR45234124   Phillipp Arnold (b 31 Dec 1952)

CR452342   George Albert Arnold (b 10 Jun 1902, St. Joseph MO) m 10 Sep 1935, Savana MO, Ola
Limbie

CR452343   Frances Virginia Arnold (b 22 Aug 1904, St. Joseph MO). Unm.

CR45235   Clarence Felix Arnold (b ca 1880) m

CR452351   Clarice Arnold

CR452352   Clarence Arnold

CR4524   Alice Rebecca Arnold (28 Jul ca 1845-46, Womelsdorf PA-dy)

CR4525   Matilda Rebecca Arnold (Aug ca 1847-48, Womelsdorf PA-1913, Harrisburg PA) m
William Weir. Bur Womelsdorf PA.

CR45251   Alma F. Kern (Sep 1865-1946) m Victor John Larsen (1859, Denmark-1926). Bur
Womelsdorf PA.

CR45252   Ida E. Weir (1880-1945) m 1) Charles L. Wingard (16 Aug 1873-14 Dec 1919); m 2)
Saylor. Bur Womelsdorf PA.

CR452521   Charles Clifford Wingard (5 Sep 1899-19 Oct 1930). BurWomelsdorf PA. Unm.

CR45253   Mamie Weir. Unm.

CR45254   Harry Weir

CR4526   George W. Arnold (7 Feb 1849, Womelsdorf PA-12 Aug 1925, Lebanon PA) m Emma
Clara Light (6 Mar 1847-7 Feb 1916). Bur Lebanon PA. Ironworker.

CR45261   William L. Arnold (8 Jul 1869, Lebanon PA-21 Jul 1950, Lebanon PA) m Sally Rebecca
Zeller (Aug 1871-1932). Ironworker, Lebanon PA.

CR452611   Roscoe H. Arnold (b 29 Feb 1892, Lebanon PA) m 26 Dec 1912, Ella Louise Maus (b 13 Mar 1893). Wholesale confectioner, Reading PA.

CR452612   Ida May Arnold (b 25 Jun 1893, Lebanon PA) m George Anne (b 23 Oct 1868)

CR452613   William L. Arnold, Jr. (30 Mar 1896, Lebanon PA-1945) m 1) Mildred   ; m 2)   ; m 3)

CR4526131   Frederick Arnold

CR4526132   William L. Arnold

CR452614   Naomi Arnold (b 6 Apr 1898, Lebanon PA) m 8 Jan 1919, Jay P. Clymer. Mechanical engineer,

CR4526141   Gwen N. Clymer (b 2 Feb 1920, Lebanon PA) m Arthur M. Niemi

CR45261411   Jeffrey Eric Niemi (b 7 Aug 1951)

CR45261412   Natalie Gwen Niemi (b 20 Nov 1955)

CR4526142   Jay P. Clymer, Jr. (b 31 Jul 1923, Fleetwood PA) m Jeanette Arnold (b 21 Nov 1925). Mechanical engineer.

CR45261421   Jay P. Clymer, III (b 23 Jun 1951)

CR45261422   Julia Clymer (b 22 Sep 1953)

CR4526143   Sallie Alice Clymer (28 Apr 1926-25 Jan 1927, Reading PA).

CR4526144   Louise Patricia Clymer (b 10 Oct 1927, Reading PA)

CR4526145   Mary Elizabeth Clymer (b 28 Jul 1929, Reading PA) m John D. Ayers (b 5 Dec 1930). Electrical engineer.

CR45261451   Philip J. Ayers (b 25 Dec 1953)

CR45261452   John D. Ayers (b 13 Sep 1955)

CR45261453   Deborah Sue Ayers (b 31 Dec 1957)

CR45262   Miles Grant Arnold (23 Oct 1871, Lebanon PA-1 Dec 1954, Avon Lake OH) m 9 Jul 1892, Fannie Dohner. Bur Avon OH. Steelworker.

CR452621   Paul Henry Arnold (b 24 Jul 1900, Lebanon PA) m 1 Jun 1924, Edythe Detwiler. Printer, Washington DC.

CR4526211   Russell Burnell Arnold (b 18 Oct 1926) m 3 Dec 1946, Betty Hucker. Physician and surgeon, Washington DC.

CR45262111   Donna Marie Arnold (b 1 Dec 1949)

CR45262112   Linda Joanne Arnold (b 28 Apr 1952)

CR45262113   Pamela Jean Arnold (b 19 Dec 1954)

CR45262114   Rhonda Kay Arnold (b 16 Dec 1955)

CR452622   Russell Miles Arnold (b 31 Jan 1903, Lebanon PA) m 22 Jul 1924, Helen Dessain. AB, MD; physician and surgeon, Avon Lake OH.

CR4526221   Marianne Arnold (b 20 Jan 1934) m James Raymond Higgins

CR45262211   Nina Kathyleen Higgins (b 18 Sep 1955)

CR45262212   James Russell Higgins (b 7 Sep 1957)

CR4526222   Louis Dessain Arnold (b 21 Mar 1936)

CR4526223   Russell Grant Arnold (b 21 Mar 1936). AB.

CR452623   Esther Violet Arnold (b 5 Nov 1905, Lebanon PA) m 3 Jul 1928, Ed Kinter. Cleveland OH.

CR4526231   Doris Elaine Kinter (b 10 Feb 1931) m 19 Aug 1951, Frank Domiyan

CR45262311   Frank Domiyan (b 22 Sep 1952)

CR45263   Gertrude Arnold (b Lebanon PA) m 2 Jul 1895, Cosmus Kleinfelter

CR452631   Edith I. Kleinfelter m Charles Zearfoss

CR452632   May E. Kleinfelter m Jacob Zearfoss

CR452633   George H. Kleinfelter m Mable Klein

CR452634   Sterling Kleinfelter m Lillie Miller

CR452635   Raymond A. Kleinfelter m Erma Grimes

CR452636   Miles Kleinfelter m Martha Bean

CR452637   Harry Kleinfelter (d 23 May 1929). Unm.

CR452638   Hilda Kleinfelter m Leroy Werner

CR45264   Barbara Arnold (b 23 Apr 1885) m William Billman (b 1 Mar 1882)

CR45265   Earl Arnold. Unm.

CR4527   William Franklin Arnold (26 Sep 1850, Womelsdorf PA-25 Nov 1935, St. Joseph MO) m 24 May 1877, St. Joseph MO, Felixitus Volk (21 Jun 1856, Bavaria-20 Oct 1925, St. Joseph MO)

CR4528   Ida Relma Arnold (9 Apr 1858, Womelsdorf PA-20 Oct 1938, Reading PA) m 1882, Camden NJ, Robert F. Kredell (7 Nov 1858, Reading PA-20 Jun 1909, Reading PA). Bur Reading PA.

CR45281   Harry Damon Kredell (11 Nov 1882, Reading PA-1 Jan 1970, Womelsdorf PA) m 18 Jun 1906, Reading PA, Jenny Musser (Aug 1882, Lancaster PA-20 Jun 1958, Reading PA). Bur Womelsdorf PA. No chn.

CR45282   Ida Relma Kredell (26 Dec 1887, Reading PA-29 Oct 1978, Sinking Spring PA) m 22 Oct 1908, Reading PA, Irvin Luther Krick (17 Feb 1888, Sinking Spring PA-11 Dec 1940, Reading PA). Salesman.

*CR452821   Mary Elizabeth Krick (b 29 Nov 1910, Reading PA) m 22 Nov 1939, Reading PA, Carl Eugene Putman (b 2 Feb 1911, Rockford OH). BS, Albright (PA) Col.

*CR4528211   Carol Jean Putman (b 11 Dec 1942, Reading PA) m 1) 23 Sep 1961, Chicago IL, Edwin Arthur Ullrich (b 1 Aug 1940, Chicago IL), div; m 2)4 May 1974, Wilmette IL, Samuel A. Williams (b 16 Jan 1899, Chicago IL). She, MBA, Northwestern U, 1980.

CR45282111   Katharen M. Ullrich (b 15 Apr 1962, Chicago IL) m 29 Apr 1989, Chicago IL, Brian M. Beringer (9 Mar 1964, Elkhorn WI). He, AB, Elgin (IL) Community Col, 1985.

CR452821111   Nicole Elizabeth Beringer (b 2 Nov 1990, Woodstock IL)

CR452821112   Samantha Lynn Beringer (b 15 Jul 1952, McHenry IL)

CR452822   Ruth Frances Krick (b 10 Sep 1912, Reading PA) m 20 Jul 1940, Reading PA, Frederic William Norton (b 17 Sep 1915, Reading PA). BA, Albright (PA) Col.

*CR4528221   Frederic Weiser Norton (b 8 Jul 1942, Ft. George Meade MD) m Madelyn Benham. BS, CA S U.

CR45282211   Leana Kristine Norton (b 28 Aug 1967, Mason City IA) m 18 May 1990, Benjamin Franklin Griffin III (b 2 Sep 1964, Sacramento CA)

CR452822111   Benjamin Franklin Griffin IV (b 31 Oct 1990, Sacramento CA)

CR452822112   Katherine Nicole Griffin (b 18 Apr 1992, Sacramento CA)

CR45282212   Frederic Weiser Norton, Jr. (15 Jun 1970, Sacramento CA) m 14 Jul 1994, Shannon Kay Whitehead (b 23 May 1968)

CR45282213   Leon Peter Norton (14 May 1973, Grand Forks ND). Unm.

*CR4528222   Ann Elizabeth Norton (b 31 Jan 1944, Reading PA) m 6 Aug 1960, Charles Leverne Fye (12 Jul 1934, Lancaster PA-1991), div

CR45282221   Lora Louise Fye (b 23 Dec 1960) m Sep 1980, Dennis Fisher

CR452822211   Jessica Ann Fisher (b 2 Nov 1988, Lancaster PA)

CR45282222   Angela Dee Fye (b 2 Aug 1964, Livermore CA)

CR45283   Robert Blee Kredell (b 13 Feb 1890, Cleveland OH) m 15 May 1914, Reading PA, Stella Wilhelmina Heffelfinger (17 Jun 1892, Reading PA-25 Jan 1960, Clifton NJ).

CR452831   Donald Harley Kredell (b 19 Feb 1916, Hornell NY) m Aug 1942, Clifton NJ, Matilda Seidel (b 19 Jul 1918, Clifton NJ).

CR4528311   Linda Elaine Kredell (b 3 Jul 1943, Clifton NJ)

CR4528312   Susan Estelle Kredell (b 21 May 1946, Clifton NJ)

CR452832   Carol Ruth Kredell (b 20 Oct 1924, Patterson NJ). BS, Pratt Inst; MA, U of WI. Home economist, PSU, York PA.

CR45284   Conrad Weiser Kredell (b 4 Apr 1896, Reading PA) m Ester Middendorf

CR453   Peter Emanuel Weiser (12 Jun 1822, Womelsdorf PA-19 Dec 1890, Philadelphia PA) m 16 Mar 1854, Sarah D. Shearer (daughter of Samuel and Susan Shearer)(30 Dec 1828, Robesonia PA-28 Dec 1915, Philadelphia PA). Bur Philadelphia PA.

CR4531   Susan Ella Weiser (b 24 Nov 1854, Heidelberg Tp, Berks Co PA) m 10 Jan 1884, Frank Hendley

CR45311   Eleanor Hendley

CR45312   Clara Hendley (d 1977)

CR45313   Francisca Dorothea Hendley m Charles David Williams

CR4532   Henry Shearer Weiser (8 Aug 1858, Philadelphia PA-16 Nov 1952, Philadelphia PA) m 29 Nov 1898, Anna Idabel Sailer (b 19 Apr 1872, Philadelphia PA). Merchant tailor, Philadelphia PA.

CR45321   Frances Sailer Weiser (b 1 Sep 1900, Philadelphia PA) m 11 Sep 1930, Philadelphia PA, Harry Wright (b 27 Jan 1896, Philadelphia PA).

CR4533   Jennie Florence Weiser (20 Jan 1867, Philadelphia PA-18 Apr 1943, Philadelphia PA).

CR6   Mary Catharine Weiser (1769 - 1852)

Mary Catharine Weiser, daughter of Peter and Catharine (   ) Weiser, was born in Reading, 8 Oct 1769, and died in Lebanon, Pennsylvania, 21 Jun 1852. She married Robert McConell. At the time of her death, this notice appeared in the *Berks and Schuylkill Journal* (3 Jul 1852):

Died-On the 21st of June, in Lebanon,Catharine McConnel, widow of Robert McConnel, aged 82 years. The deceased was the daughter of the late Peter Weiser, and the only surviving granddaughter of Conrad Weiser. She was born in Reading on Oct. 8, 1769.[99]

Children of Robert and Mary Catharine (Weiser) McConnell:

CR61   Frederick Augustus McConnell

CR62   Rebecca McConnell, 30 Mar 1790

CR63   Louisa McConnell, 6 Sep 1792

CR64   Maria McConnell, 17 Feb 1797

CR65   Evan McConnell, ca 24 Mar 1799

CR66   Morris McConnell, 1802

CR67   Peter Muhlenberg Weiser McConnell, 31 Jan 1805

CR68   Esther McConnell, 2 Jul 1807

CR69   James McConnell, 22 Jul 1809

CR6A   Catherine Amelia McConnell, 12 Sep 1810[12]

---

[99]See records of Trinity Lutheran Church, Reading PA.

CR6B   Oliver Robert Reily McConnell, 27 Feb 1814[100]

CR61   Frederick Augustus McConnell (son of Robert and Mary Catherine (Weiser) McConnell) m 5 Feb 1812, Elizabeth Schaeffer

CR611   John Schaeffer McConnell (b 29 Nov 1817)

CR612   McConnell m Pine Grove PA, Francis Robinson

CR62   Rebecca McConnell (daughter of Robert and Mary Catherine (Weiser) McConnell)(b 30 Mar 1790)

CR63   Louisa McConnell (daughter of Robert and Mary Catherine (Weiser) McConnell)(b 6 Sep 1792)

CR64   Maria McConnell (daughter of Robert and Mary Catherine (Weiser) McConnell)(b 17 Feb 1797)

CR65   Evan McConnell (son of Robert and Mary Catherine (Weiser) McConnell)(ca 24 Mar 1799-4 Oct 1834). Died aged 35 years, 6 months, 10 days.

CR66   Morris McConnell (son of Robert and Catharine (Weiser) McConnell)(17 Jul 1802, Womelsdorf PA-4 Jul 1876, Washington DC) m 1830, Sarah Christ (9 Dec 1806-Jul 1887, Washington DC). Bur Washington DC.[101]

CR661   Esther Margaret McConnell (21 Jul 1831, Stouchsburg PA- 2 Dec 1896, Washington DC) m 8 Jun 1854, Washington DC, Hubert Schutter (11 Feb 1826, Bonn, Germany-16 Jul 1904, Washington DC). Artist.

CR6611   Mary Ellen Schutter (20 Apr 1855, Washington DC-1 Oct 1936, South Pasadena CA) m 1) 2 Jun 1874, Washington DC, Charles Cary Ewer (9 Jan 1839, Barnstable MA-13 Feb 1879, Washington DC); m 2) 16 Oct 1890, Washington DC, Frank Evan Johnson (1856, VA-26 Mar 1935, Los Angeles CA). Bur Los Angeles. Treasury Dept agent.

CR66111   Maidee Schutter Ewer (25 May 1875, Washington DC-6 Feb 1946, Washington DC). Unm. Bur Washington DC. Educator.

CR66112   Pauline Ryder Ewer (24 Feb 1877, Washington DC-3 Nov 1957, Los Angeles CA) m 12 Sep 1900, Washington DC, Edward Sumner Glavis (30 Jun 1878, Newark NJ-3 Jan 1939, Washington DC). Bur Arlington VA. Government official, Washington DC.

CR661121   Pauline Ewer Glavis (1 Jun 1901, Washington DC-2 Apr 1972, San Diego CA). Unm. Secretary, Los Angeles CA.

CR661122   Edward Sumner Glavis, Jr. (7 Oct 1903, Washington DC-4 Nov 1977, Cottage Grove OR) m 7 Feb 1924, South Pasadena CA, Frances Mary Mason (9 Nov 1903, Des Moines IA-6 Dec 1954, Cottage Grove OR).

CR6611221   Edward Sumner Glavis, III (b 2 Jan 1925, Glendale CA) m 22 Jul 1950, Hobart IN, Judith Otto. Hospital administrator.

CR66112211   Edward Glavis (b 19 Oct 1952) m

---

[100]See records of Christ Lutheran Church, Stouchsburg; Zion Lutheran Church, Womelsdorf PA.
[101]Data provided by Miss Pauline E. Glavis and L.S. Bailey.

CR661122111   Brandon Glavis

CR661122112   Jennifer Glavis

CR66112212   Susan Glavis (b 3 Dec 1954) m   Portwood

CR661122121   Kim Portwood

CR661122122   Mandy Portwood

CR66112213   Cheryl Glavis (b 22 Aug 1959)

CR6611222   Mary Mason Glavis (b 10 Jun 1933, Oakland CA). Unm. BS, Natl Col of Educn, 1955. Teacher, Cottage Grove OR.

CR661123   Margaret Glavis (5 Nov 1906, Washington DC-11 Oct 1993, Longwood FL) m 1) 20 Mar 1929, S Pasadena CA, Charles C. Yates; m 2) 19 May 1943, Honolulu HI, Elbert Armstrong. She, nurse.

CR661124   Maidee Virginia Glavis (18 Jun 1911, New Baltimore VA-1991) m 1) 19 Aug 1931, Los Angeles CA, James McMillan; m 2) John Edward Ellis

CR6611241   Barbara Ann McMillan (b 14 Feb 1936, Los Angeles CA) m

CR66112411   Laura Ann   (b 15 Feb 1965)

CR66112412   Bradley   (b 28 Oct 1968)

CR66112413   Brian   (b 28 Oct 1968)

CR661125   Frank Johnson Glavis (b 13 Oct 1913, New Baltimore VA) m 7 Sep 1940, Cheltenham PA, Doris Ashworth

CR6611251   Wendy Glavis (b 8 Nov 1943, Elkins Park PA). Unm. Educator. Res England.

CR6612   Jessie Hubertine Schutter (16 Feb 1865, Washington DC-6 Aug 1911, Washington DC) m 27 Nov 1889, William R. Bailey. Civil engineer, Washington DC. Bur Arlington VA.

CR66121   Lionel Schutter Bailey (18 May 1892, Washington DC-13 Dec 1965, San Marino CA) m 27 Dec 1929, San Diego CA, Helga Sjaastad. Civil engineer, San Marino CA.

CR661211   William Lionel Bailey (b 23 Apr 1931, Pasadena CA) m 24 Mar 1961, Anne Vine

CR6612111   Brent William Bailey (b 5 Apr 1964)

CR6612112   Eric Lionel Bailey (b 21 Mar 1966)

CR6612113   Stuart Vine Bailey (b 21 Dec 1967)

CR661212   Bergetta Hubertine Bailey (b 23 Apr 1931, Pasadena CA) m 20 Jul 1957, John Lyman Bunce

CR6612121   John Lyman Bunce (b 27 Aug 1958)

CR6612122   Katharine Anne Bunce (b 18 Sep 1960, Atlantic IA)

CR6612123   William Bailey Bunce (b 18 May 1967, Atlantic IA)

CR66122   William Robert Bailey (23 Aug 1894, Washington DC-14 Feb 1941, Rocky Mount NC) m 12 Sep 1936, Richmond VA, Edna Elizabeth Powell. Bur Richmond VA. Postal clerk.

CR6613   Clara Schutter (6 Apr 1862, Washington DC-16 Mar 1937) m 22 Feb 1883,   Murphy

CR662   Ellen McConnell (b 1837). Unm.

CR663   Sarah Elizabeth McConnell (17 Jun 1842, Washington DC-8 Feb 1928, Washington DC) m 10 Sep 1872, Washington DC, Charles Warren Hills (30 Jul 1840, Mayfield OH-11 Jan 1908, Washington DC). Bur Washington DC. Civil War, 71st OVI; civil servant.[102]

CR6631   Grace Muhlenberg Hills (22 Mar 1874, Cleveland OH-1 Feb 1948, Chicago IL) m 16 Sep 1917, Washington DC, Henry C. Morris (b Chicago IL-29 Jul 1948, ME). Bur Washington DC. Diplomatic service.

CR6632   Ralph Warren Hills (7 Jun 1875, Cleveland OH-21 May 1940, Cumberland MD) m 1901, Washington DC, Mary Edna Gorman (1 Mar 1876, Howard Co MD-4 Jul 1944, Baltimore MD). Bur Washington DC. Historian.

CR66321   Ralph Gorman Hills (b 19 Jan 1902, Washington DC) m 11 Aug 1928, Missoula MT, Mary Joe Dixon (b 7 Aug 1906, Missoula MT). MD, Johns Hopkins Med School, 1929; asst prof, internal medicine, Johns Hopkins U; trustee, Princeton U; councilor, medical and chirugical faculty of MD.

CR663211   Joseph Dixon Hills (b 30 Nov 1932, Baltimore MD)

CR663212   Ralph Warren Hills (b 7 Jun 1939, Baltimore MD)

CR66322   Mary Gorman Hills (b 27 Jan 1905, Washington DC) m 1 Nov 1934, Washington DC, Stuart H. Gillmore (b 17 Jan 1896)

CR663221   Mary Gorman Burns Gillmore (b 8 Dec 1937)

CR663222   James Clarkson Gillmore (b 11 Mar 1940)

CR66323   Elizabeth Warren Hills (b 18 Jul 1910, Washington DC) m 20 Jun 1928, Washington DC, William Journey Roome III (b 4 Dec 1905, Plainfield NJ)

CR663231   William Journey Roome IV (b 16 Jun 1929)

CR663232   Rodney Hills Roome (b 28 Jun 1932)

CR66324   Arthur Gorman Hills (b 5 Aug 1915, Washington DC). Unm. MD, Johns Hopkins, 1942; assoc prof of medicine, Miami (FL) U.

CR664   Mary Susan McConnell (2 Apr 1847, Washington DC-1 Apr 1918, Olney MD) m 26 Sep 1866, Washington DC, Henry Clay Sherman (26 Sep 1842-29 Sep 1896, Olney MD). Bur Sandy Spring MD. He, attended Rittenhouse Academy, Washington DC, and completed a musical education under private instructors; served as organist in Washington churches, including St. Aloysius Roman Catholic, All Souls' Unitarian, and St. Thomas Episcopal Churches.[103]

CR6641   Charles Albert Sherman (6 Sep 1867, Washington DC-Aug 1906, Chevy Chase MD). Bur Washington DC.

---

[102]Data provided by Ralph G. Hills.
[103]Data provided by Mrs. J.W. Jones.

CR6642   Margaret Elgar Sherman (12 Jun 1871, Washington DC-28 Aug 1966) m 20 Apr 1898, Washington DC, Josiah Waters Jones (2 Apr 1870, Olney MD-6 Sep 1946, Olney MD). Bur Sandy Spring MD.

CR66421   Margaret Sherman Jones (b 4 Jul 1899, Washington DC) m 3 Apr 1929, Olney MD, William Howard Gilpin (b 2 Apr 1899, Sandy Spring MD). She, AB, Goucher (MD) Col. He, George School, PA; insurance agent, Olney MD.

CR664211   Josiah Jones Gilpin (b 4 Mar 1930, Olney MD) m 13 Dec 1950, Olney MD, Joanne Lois Grey (b 10 Sep 1927). He, George School; forestry. She, RN, Olney MD.

CR6642111   William Edward Gilpin (b 19 Oct 1954, Olney MD)

CR6642112   Steven Brooke Gilpin (b 29 Jun 1957, Olney MD)

CR664212   Margaret Elgar Gilpin (b 23 Nov 1940, Olney MD)

CR66422   Ruth Sherman Jones (b 16 Oct 1905, Washington DC) m 24 Jun 1936, Olney MD, James Arthur Richards (b 17 Sep 1913, Patrick Co VA). She, Peabody Inst, Baltimore. He, STD, DD; Methodist minister, Elizabeth NJ.

CR664221   Ruth Lackey Richards (b 1 Mar 1938, Baltimore MD)

CR664222   James Arthur Richards II (b 21 Jun 1939, Baltimore MD)

CR66423   Mary Elizabeth Sherman Jones (b 12 Mar 1910, Washington DC) m 13 Jun 1936, Olney MD, Charles Gibson Grey (b 20 May 1908, Washington DC). She, RN, Garfield Memorial Hosp, Washington DC. He, deputy director, Dept of Agric, Washington DC; Howard Co MD.

CR664231   Peter Gibson Grey (b 8 Apr 1937, Washington DC)

CR664232   Elizabeth Gibson Grey (b 9 Jul 1939, Washington DC)

CR664233   Margaret Elgar Grey (b 30 Jun 1941, Lincoln NE)

CR664234   Robert Waters Grey (b 12 Oct 1943, Olney MD)

CR66424   Elgar Sherman Jones (b 4 Aug 1911, Washington DC) m 22 Aug 1936, Olney MD, Robert Campbell Gilmore (b 16 Jun 1910, VA). Insurance agent, Bethesda MD. She, AB, U of MD, Peabody Convervatory.

CR664241   Anne Elgar Gilmore (b 17 Mar 1949, Bethesda MD)

CR6643   Mary Lois Sherman (5 Jan 1875, Washington DC-29 Dec 1948, Chevy Chase MD) m 12 May 1897, Washington DC, Samuel Scoville Paschal (1875, Washington DC-1917, Chevy Chase MD). She, bur Sandy Spring MD; he, bur Georgetown, Washington DC.

CR66431   Barbara Paschal (1900-1900). Bur at sea, Pacific Ocean.

CR66432   Guy Sherman Paschal (b 14 Aug 1901, Washington DC) m 1) 12 Oct 1926, NY, Dorothy Iselin; m 2) Melanie

CR664321   Barbara Paschal (b 1927)

CR664322   Samuel Paschal (b 1930)

CR664323   Guy Paschal (b 1933)

CR66433   Mary Lois Paschal (b 7 Nov 1904, Washington DC) m 13 May 1936, Donald Davis. Chevy Chase MD.

CR665   Peter Muhlenberg Weiser McConnell (b ca 1849-50, Washington DC-d Lititz PA). Unm.

CR67   Peter Muhlenberg Weiser McConnell (son of Robert and Catherine (Weiser) McConnell)(b 31 Jan 1805, Womelsdorf PA) m Sarah Miller

CR671   Barbara Anne McConnell (28 Sep 1827, Womelsdorf PA-Jan 1828, Womelsdorf PA). Bur Womelsdorf PA.

CR68   Esther McConnell (daughter of Robert and Catherine (Weiser) McConnell)(b 2 Jul 1807, Womelsdorf PA) m 5 Jun 1830, Lebanon PA, Daniel Miller

CR69   James McConnell (son of Robert and Catherine (Weiser) McConnell)(b 22 Jul 1809)

CR6A   Catherine Amelia McConnell (daughter of Robert and Catherine (Weiser) McConnell)(b 12 Sep 1810)

CR6B   Oliver Robert Reily McConnell (son of Robert and Catherine (Weiser) McConnell)(27 Feb 1814-7 Jun 1893) m 1 Mar 1836, Lebanon PA, Rebecca Noecker (d 9 May 1890)

CR6B4   Cecilia McConnell (d 1 Sep 1889) m John W. Allwein

CR6B41   Emma Louise Allwein m 26 Apr 1887, William H. Morrette

CR6B411   Leigh Morrette

CR6B412   Alonza Boyer Morrette

CHAPTER FOUR E

[CA] Margaret Weiser (1734-1777)

Margaret Weiser, daughter of Conrad and Anna Eva (Feg) Weiser, was born on 28 January 1734, near Womelsdorf, Pennsylvania. She married first, November 1754, the Reverend John Diedrich Matthias Heintzelmann (1726, Salzwedel, Germany-9 Feb 1756, Philadelphia PA). He was buried in St. Michael's Church in Philadelphia. Heintzelman was ordained a Lutheran pastor on 11 Jul 1751, at Wernigerode in the Harz Mountains; he arrived in Philadelphia 1 Dec 1751. Following his death, she married Anthony Fricker (ca 1731 in Europe-27 Nov 1796, Reading PA). Fricker was a Roman Catholic and Margaret apparently joined his church, which accounts for both the special provision in Conrad Weiser's will concerning her children and the legal action Henry Melchior Muhlenberg took to gain custody of her son by her first marriage. Anthony Fricker was an innkeeper and shopkeeper in Reading. Margaret died early in 1777, for under date of 2 Feb 1777, Henry Melchoir Muhlenberg records the fact that news of her death, due to an accidental fall down a flight of stairs, was received. Her funeral is not recorded in the Lutheran or Roman Catholic church registers.

Following Margaret's death, Fricker married Maria Eva Becker, the widow of John Zweger. They had several children, only one of whom, ironically, is named in his will. Children of his first wife are: Anthony (eldest son), Peter, Thomas, Catharine, George (also called Henry), John and Margaret. It is highly likely, therefore, that the daughter Mary, who married John Frantz (whose descendants are partially reported in *The Weiser Family*, 1960) is from the second marriage, as were Mary Eva (1780-1844), married 24 Jun 1804 to John Miller; William (1783-ca 1831); and Magdalen (b 1785). On 14 Aug 1790, three children of Anthony Fricker over age 14 selected him as their guardian. They were John, Thomas, and Stephen. The occasion for this is not clear, but it may have to do with money they received from their grandfather Weiser's estate. Stephen is not mentioned in his father's will, and it is unclear which woman was his mother. There is no birth record for him.[104] Fricker died in 1807. It seems likely that a good percentage of Fricker's descendants by Margaret Weiser did become Lutherans.

Child of Rev. J.D.M. and Margaret (Weiser) Heintzelmann:

CA1   Henrich Israel Heintzelmann (10 Feb 1756, Philadelphia PA-12 Sep 1774, Ebenezer GA). He was born the day after his father's death. Henry Keppele, a prominent member of the Lutheran Church in Philadelphia, was appointed his guardian in 1762, by which time his mother had married Anthony Fricker. In 1773 Israel was sent to Georgia to work for John Adam Treutlen, where he fell from a horse and died the next day.[105]

Children of Anthony and Margaret (Weiser) Fricker:

CA2   Anthony Fricker

CA3   Margaret Fricker

CA4   Peter Fricker

CA5   Henry George Fricker

CA6   Catharine Fricker

CA7   Mary Catharine Fricker

---

[104]Charles H. Glatfelter, *Pastors and People* (Breinigsville PA, 1980), 55-56; the registers of the Goschenhoppen (Bally PA) Roman Catholic Church. See also Peggy Joyner, *Ancestors and Descendants of Joseph Shomo (Shammo)* (Baltimore 1983), 363-72.

[105]Tappert and Doberstein, *op. cit.,* I, 509-10.

CA8   John Frederick Fricker

CA9   Thomas Fricker

CAA   Stephen Fricker[106]

CA2   Anthony Fricker (ca 1760, Reading PA-1821, Womelsdorf PA) m 27 Nov 1799, near Stouchsburg PA, Anna Maria Kerrstahler. He served in the American Revolution. Hatmaker, later gunsmith and metalsmith, in Womelsdorf PA. In 1821 George Brownewell, his brother-in-law and his estate's administrator, petitioned the orphans court for permission to sell Anthony's property in Womelsdorf to pay his debts.[106]

CA21   Maria Margaretha Fricker (13 Mar 1800, probably at or near Womelsdorf-before 1821 without heirs)

CA22   John Fricker (b 12 Feb 1802, Womelsdorf PA). No further record.

CA23   William Fricker (16 Sep 1806, Womelsdorf PA-29 Aug 1871, Reading PA) m 22 Jul 1832, Reading PA, Elizabeth Gravel (ca 7 Jun 1810-18 Oct 1875, Reading PA). Bur Reading PA.

CA 231   Maria Fricker (b 14 Jan 1833, Reading PA)

CA232   John Franklin Fricker (b 31 Mar 1834, Reading PA)

CA233   Anna Maria Fricker (b 28 Jun 1836, Reading PA)

CA234   Mary Jane Fricker (21 Oct 1838, Reading PA)

CA235   Henrick Fricker (23 Aug 1841, Reading PA)

CA236   Ellen Rebecca Fricker (25 Dec 1843, Reading PA)

CA24   Henriette Fricker (28 Feb 1808, Womelsdorf PA). No further record.

CA3   Margaret Fricker (b ca 1762, Reading PA). She received 25 pounds in her father's will, probably the unpaid share of her inheritance from Conrad Weiser.

CA4   Peter Fricker (b ca 1764, Reading PA-1828). He received one shilling in his father's will, which probably means some of his share from Conrad Weiser had already been given him. But his father mentions that he owes him money from his grandfather which, minus what Peter owed his father, was to be paid him. Revolutionary War service.

CA5   Henry George Fricker (b Jan 1766) m Barbara Siegfried. He received 25 pounds in his father's will, which indicates that the sum George owes to his father is to be deducted from his share of his grandfather Conrad Weiser's bequest. Private, Von Heer's dragoons.

CA51   George Fricker (b 29 Feb 1796, Reading PA)

CA6   Catherine Elizabeth Fricker (19 Nov 1767, Reading PA-probably d.y.)

CA7   Mary Catharine Fricker (b 15 Aug 1769, Reading PA) m 20 Dec 1789, Jacob Merckel.

---

[106]Tappert and Doberstein, III, 314; of Gary T. Hawbaker, *Ledger of Anthony Fricker*, Gunsmith, Womelsdorf, Heidelberg Township, Berks County, Pennsylvania, 1814-1821 (Hershey PA, 1985). Records of Altalaha Lutheran Church, Rehersburg PA; Zion Lutheran Church, Womelsdorf PA; Trinity Lutheran Church, Reading PA.

As Catharine she received one shilling in her father's will.

CA71   Francisca Merckel (b 3 Oct 1790, Reading PA)

CA72   Lydia Merckel (b 27 Nov 1791, Reading PA)

CA73   Anna Margaretha Merckel (b 11 Jan 1793, Reading PA)

CA8   John Frederick Fricker (29 Apr 1771, Reading PA-1808). Known as John, he received 80 pounds in his father's will. He was "an artificer in Capt. James Sterret's company of artillery, USA" in his estate papers.

CA9   Thomas Fricker (b 21 Dec 1773, Reading PA). He received one shilling in his father's will.

CAA   Stephen Fricker (d 1816, Reading PA)

CHAPTER FOUR F

[CS] Samuel Weiser (1735-1796)

Samuel Weiser (son of Conrad and Anna Eva (Feg) Weiser) was born on the Weiser farm near Womelsdorf on 23 Apr 1735. He was baptized by his brother-in-law Henry Melchior Muhlenberg. Samuel married 28 May 1760, Judith Levan, at St. Michael's Lutheran Church in Philadelphia.[107]

Samuel was the most intimately associated of all Conrad Weiser's sons with his father's relations with the Indians. "Sammy" appears in his father's correspondence as messenger and companion. In 1751, Sammy went to live with the same Mohawks who had taught Conrad his knowledge of their language, and he was official successor as Indian interpreter for the government.[108]

Sammy also saw service in the French and Indian War. He served as a "Captain-Lieutenant" in the independent PA company, first battalion, from 3 Jul 1755 and was stationed at Ft. Henry. He was located at Ft. Ligonier under Colonel Bouquet until he wrote his father in April 1759 of his desire to resign. His resignation became official on 15 May 1759.[109]

Following his services in various battles and his marriage, he lived in Reading. In 1770 Muhlenberg reported that he had baptized sick children of Samuel in Reading.[110] Sometime in the 1770s he moved to the tract he inherited in the division of his father's lands in 1773. It lay in Mahonoy Tp, Northumberland Co about equally divided along the east side of the Susquehanna River on each side of the Mahonoy Creek where it enters the Susquehanna. He lived there until his death, probably in July 1796.

Samuel wrote his will 24 Nov 1794. It was probated 28 Jul 1796. An inventory of his possessions was made 14 Aug 1796. His will provided for his wife Judith including the use of a tenant house. The property was to be divided between the children (the Mahonoy Creek forming the boundary of the halves). Neither was married in 1794. Should they die without issue, Samuel provided that Benjamin's part should go to his godson Samuel, son of Peter, his nephew nearby, who had to pay twenty pounds to the Lower Lutheran Congregation of Mahonoy Township (probably St. Peter's, Red Cross) nearby for the poor. If Maria Margaret died without issue, her property went to his other godson Samuel Feather of Reading, son of Peter, who had to pay his brother Jacob (see below) fifty pounds and ten pounds each to the Church Wardens of the Lutheran and Reformed congregations of Sanbury for the poor. Although Samuel and Judith probably had children who died in infancy or childhood, both Benjamin and Margaret lived and presently married. The inventory of Samuel's possessions shows him to be a typical Pennsylvania German farmer.[111]

Samuel's will provided that if either child sold his farm, the other had the first right to buy it. Thus when Benjamin sold his part to William Witman of Reading in 1800, Margaret Weiser and her husband Jacob Feather joined in the deed.[112]

Jacob and Margaret Feather sold their portion on 30 Apr 1807 to Peter Wentle or Wertle of Mahonoy Township, including a small island and a 118 A tract of woodland which had been warranted to Samuel and patented to Maria Margaret in 1807. Her mother Judith gave power-of-attorney 20 Feb 1806 to Jacob Feather to collect any debts due Samuel's estate and act as his substitute executor, a document recorded 22 Aug 1810.[113] [114] Judith likely died in this period of time. She may be buried at St. Peter's Church with Samuel,

---

[107]Judith Levan was a daughter of Isaac Levan (1700-1783) and Mary Margaret   , he, a son of Daniel Levan and Maria Beau, who came to America in 1715. Anna Maria Levan who married Samuel's son Benjamin was a daughter of Abraham and Esther Levan. Abraham was a son of Isaac Levan (d 1800) and Mary Anna Ellmaker, daughter of Leonard Ellmaker of Lancaster County.

[108] Wallace, *op. cit.*, 323 ff; Richards, *op. cit.*, 83.

[109]*Ibid.*, 560-561; PA 2-1-62, 108, 713, 714.

[110]*Journals of Henry Melchior Muhlenberg.* II, 466.

[111]Northumberland County wills, I-174. Xerox copies of the will and inventory, JCWFA.

[112]Northumberland County deeds L-630.

[113]Northumberland County deeds A-103, Q-112.

but no evidence confirms that or her death date.

Children of Samuel and Judith (Levan) Weiser:

CS1   Benjamin Weiser (b 1766).

CS2   Maria Margaret Weiser.

CS12   Benjamin Weiser m Eleanora (or Judith Redinger). Of his death and final whereabouts, nothing is known. No chn survived.

CS121   Samuel Weiser (26 Dec 1824-10 Sep 1827) Bur Aaronsburg PA, Wolf's Chapel.[115]

CS13   Esther Weiser (daughter of Benjamin and Maria (Levan) Weiser) (30 Jun 1803-24 Nov 1850) m 31 Apr 1822, Henry Winkleman (16 Oct 1793-11 Apr 1863) She bur Snydertown PA; he bur St. Paul's Church near Aaronsburg PA. Farmer, Nittany PA.[116]

CS131   Mary Ann Winkleman (16 Mar 1824-4 Feb 1850) m David Snyder.

CS1311   Amanda Jane Snyder (7 Oct 1845-6 Feb 1855).

CS1312   Hetty Catharine Snyder m Miller.

CS1313   James Snyder. Orangeville IL.

CS132   Margaretha Winkleman (23 Feb 1827-29 May 1833).

CS133   Samuel Weiser Winkleman (24 Apr 1829-5 Jun 1833).

CS134   Benjamin Schneck Winkleman (22 Jul 1834, Nittany PA-22 Dec 1894, Nittany PA) m 16 Aug 1855, Amanda L Wise (1 Feb 1834-17 Feb 1889, Nittany PA) Bur Snydertown PA. Farmer.

CS1341   James Buchanan Winkleman (13 Nov 1856, Nittany PA-14 Mar 1890) m Sarah Catharine Neese. Bur Snydertown PA.

CS13411   Merrill Winkleman (dy).

CS13412   Minnie Mae Winkleman (b 5 Jun 1887, Knox Tp, Clearfield Co PA) m 25 Jun, Joseph Weaver (2 Oct 1882-1955) Bur Hublersburg PA. Guard, steel mill, Bellefonte PA.

CS134121   Kathryn Madeline Weaver (1 Sep 1905-2 Aug 1921) Bur Hublersburg PA.

CS134122   James Russell Weaver (1 Jul 1909-1970, Bellefonte PA) m 1944, Mary Ellen Gheen. Steel mill furnace operator, Harrisburg PA.

CS1341221   Rosemary Weaver (b 9 Nov 1945).

---

[114]Richards, op. cit., p. 84. Records of Trinity Lutheran Church, Reading; tombstones, Wolf's Chapel Cemetery near Aaronsburg, PA. See papers in the estate files of Henry and Rebecca (Weiser) Hess for children of Benjamin and Anna Maria (Levan) Weiser, Centre County records, Bellefonte, PA. Estate No. 1919.

[115]See Richards, op. cit., p. 84, which cites Benjamin's wife as Judith Redinger. The baptismal record of CS121 Samuel gives his mother's name as Eleanora.

[116]Data provided by Mrs. C. W. Casner; see also will of Henry Winkleman, C-45 and Benjamin S. Winkleman, E-93, Centre County records. Updated (1996) by Bonnie Futey.

CS1341222   Marsha Ann Weaver (b 11 Nov 1946).

CS1341223   James J Weaver (b 5 Jul 1948).

CS1341224   Linda Weaver (b 28 Sep 1950).

CS1341225   Ronald Weaver (b 3 Oct 1952).

CS13413   Benjamin Winkleman m Mabel   . Mechanic, Downingtown PA.

CS134131   Benjamin J Winkleman m Margaret.

CS1341311   Carol Winkleman (b 11 Sep 1954).

CS1342   John Henry Winkleman (16 Nov 1857-6 Mar 1873).

CS1343   Derbin Iona Winkleman (6 Sep 1859-5 Mar 1861).

CS1344   Horace Wise Winkleman (4 Apr 1861, Nittany PA-10 Sep 1931, Altoona, Juniata PA) m
14 Feb 1885, Lock Haven PA, Mary Mauck (4 Jul 1862-17 Apr 1893, Nittany PA) Bur Cedar Hill, Clinton
Co PA.

CS13441   Roy Mauck Winkleman (b 15 Oct 1886, Nittany PA) m 27 Dec 1906, Carrie Belle
Letterman (b 5 Aug 1887).

CS134411   Harry Leroy Winkleman (b 16 Jul 1907) m Dorothy Wadsworth.

CS1344111   Pearl Winkleman (dy)

CS1344112   Bernice Winkleman (b 1931).

CS134412   Boyd James Winkleman (b 28 Nov 1908) m Clevella Wadsworth. Supt, water lines, Lock
Haven PA.

CS1344121   Boyd James Winkleman Jr (dy).

CS1344122   Betty Winkleman (b 1931).

CS134413   Forest Kermit Winkleman (b 23 Nov 1910) m 1) Helen Nicols; m 2).

CS1344131   John Winkleman.

CS134414   Leonard Guy Winkleman (b 23 Aug 1912) m 1) Margaret McGill; m 2) Thelma Mackey.

CS134415   Donald Bertram Winkleman (b 28 Sep 1914) m Geraldine Young.

CS1344151   William Winkleman m.

CS1344152   Genevieve Winkleman.

CS134416   Clair Franklin Winkleman (b 28 Apr 1923) m Malissa Moore.

CS1344161   Bonny Winkleman (b 1945).

CS1344162   Greggy Winkleman (b 1956).

CS134417 Genevieve Winkleman (28 Jul 1926-15 Apr 1931, Lock Haven PA) Bur Avis PA.

CS134418 Richard Jay Winkleman (b 27 Oct 1928) m Alice Vangorder.

CS1344181 Sharon Winkleman.

CS1344182 Vicky Winkleman.

CS1344183 Richard Winkleman.

CS1344184 Larry Winkleman.

CS13442 Veva Pearl Winkleman (25 Dec 1888, Nittany PA-9 Jul 1977, Altoona PA) m Aug 1907, Howard F Brickley (12 Nov 1883-20 Apr 1958, Cottonwood AZ) Bur Howard PA. Engineer, Penna RR.

CS134421 Chester Arthur Brickley (25 Mar 1908-26 Dec 1976, Coupon PA) m 24 Sep 1928, E Kathryn Harkinson. WWII: Quartermaster Corps, awarded medal for heroism. Engineer, Penna RR. Bur Howard PA.

CS134422 Helen Pearl Brickley (1 Oct 1909, Altoona PA-12 Dec 1994, Mechanicsburg PA) m 8 Jun 1940, Altoona PA, Walter McAlarney (12 Sep 1912, Altoona PA-12 Sep 1952, Altoona PA) WWII, Korean Conflict. He, Machinist, PA RR; She, BS, Shippensburg (PA) U, MS, PSU. Teacher, Altoona PA.

CS1344221 Annetta Lou McAlarney (b 1 Apr 1949, Altoona PA) m 30 Sep 1967, Altoona PA, Hershel E Simington Jr (b 5 Sep 1945) Res. Mechanicsburg PA.

CS13442211 Kimberly Robin Simington (b 25 Jun 1973).

CS13442212 Kerensa Carlee Simington (b 30 Dec 1976, Camp Hill PA).

CS13442213 Kassandra Lynette Simington (b 24 May 1979).

CS1344222 Monique Kay McAlarney (b 9 Mar 1952, Altoona PA) m 18 Jul 1970, Craig J Marasco, div; m 2) 27 Mar 1982, AA King, div.

CS13442221 Desiree M Marasco (b 18 Sep 1975).

CS13443 Mirian Winkleman (b 3 Mar 1890) unm.

CS13444 Esta Minerva Winkleman (21 Apr 1891, Nittany PA-15 May 1981, Altoona PA) m 17 Nov 1909, Lock Haven PA, Charles Wesley Casner (2 Sep 1983, Ryde PA-13 Dec 1962, Altoona PA) Bur Altoona PA. Freight conductor, Penna RR.

CS134441 John Wesley Casner (25 Aug 1910, Altoona, Juniata PA-17 Dec 1987, Altoona PA) m Ruth Alma Baker (14 Nov 1911-20 Oct 1986, Altoona PA) Bur Altoona PA. WWII. Dept head, Sears Roebuck and Co, Altoona PA.

CS134442 Charles Horace Casner (13 Dec 1912, Altoona, Juniata PA-24 Jan 1967, Oteen NC) m June Metzer (b 6 Jun 1921) Bur Altoona PA. Store manager, Jacksonville FL.

CS1344421 Edward Casner (b 29 Jul 1938, Altoona PA) m 27 Apr 1957, Jeanne Mary Heide (b 13 Apr 1938) Owns paint store, Washington DC.

CS13444211 Christine Elisa Casner (b 15 Dec 1958, Jacksonville FL) m 14 Oct 1978, Brian J Skidds.

CS134442111 Jason Skidds (b 2 Jul 1979).

CS13444212   John Edward Casner (b 10 Mar 1960) m Kelly Brooks.

CS13444213   Celeste Casner (b 27 Dec 1965) unm.

CS134443   Kathryn Mae Casner (19 Jul 1916, Altoona, Juniata PA-26 Apr 1976, Baltimore MD) m 25 Jul 1942, Altoona PA, Al Cohen (b 19 Mar 1910, Altoona PA) Bur Altoona PA. Storekeeper, Altoona PA. No chn.

CS134444   Dorothy Louise Casner (5 Dec 1918, Altoona, Juniata PA-12 Oct 1944, Altoona, Juniata PA) m Sep 1935, Altoona PA, Albert Chase (25 Nov 1922, Altoona PA-9 Dec 1960, Tucson AZ) Bur Altoona PA. Railroader.

CS1344441   Joan Esta Chase (b 25 Aug 1936, Juniata PA) m 22 Sep 1953, Altoona PA, Mitchell Karalis (b 16 Aug 1930, Brooklyn NY) Silkscreen Artist, Glendale CA.

CS13444411   John Michael Karalis (b 20 May 1962, Burbank CA) m 11 Jan 1992, Burbank CA, Paulina Fulster (b 22 Jun 1967, Manilla PI) Construction, Burbank CA.

CS134444111   John Nathaniel Karalis (b 1 Feb 1995, Glendale CA).

CS13444412   Nicholas Peter Karalis (b 8 Jul 1963, Burbank CA) Res. La Crescenta CA.

CS13444413   Robert Mitchell Karalis (b 10 Jun 1964, Burbank CA) m 19 Aug 1989, La Canda CA, Danielle Lefeu. Aircraft servicing manager, San Diego CA.

CS13444414   Kristy Lee Karalis (b 27 Feb 1967, Burbank CA) Res. Hollywood CA.

CS134444141   Adrian Marie Karalis (b 18 Sep 1993, Los Angeles CA).

CS13444415   Julie Anne Karalis (b 15 Jun 1969, Burbank CA) BA, U San Diego. Santa Monica CA.

CS1344442   Kay Lenora Chase (15 Aug 1943, Altoona PA-20 Jun 1984, Altoona PA) adopted by Eugene and Betty (Casner) Brunell; m 21 Dec 1968, Hollidaysburg PA, Franklin Metz. Bur Altoona PA.

CS13444421   Jeffrey Scott Brunell (b 23 Apr 1963, Altoona PA) m 4 Dec 1982, Altoona PA, Paula Riley (b 24 Jul 1962, Philadelphia PA) MBA, National U, 1991.

CS134444211   Audrey Kay Brunell (b 16 Jan 1991, Santa Ana CA).

CS134444212   Trevor Scott Brunell (b 8 Dec 1993, Altoona PA).

CS134445   Cecil Cloyd Casner (9 Dec 1920, Altoona, Juniata PA-29 Jan 1923, Altoona PA) Bur Altoona PA.

CS134446   Betty Marie Casner (b 17 May 1924, Altoona PA.) m 11 Jan 1941, Winchester VA, Eugene A Brunell (b 6 Apr 1918, Altoona PA) Electrician, Penna RR.

CS1344461   Ronald Eugene Brunell (31 Dec 1943, Altoona PA-7 Feb 1944, Altoona PA) Bur Altoona PA.

*CS1344462   Bonnie Jeanne Brunell (b 20 Nov 1951, Altoona, PA) m 27 Apr 1974, Hollidaysburg PA, John Steven Futey (b 23 Nov 1949, Altoona PA) She, Insurance agent secretary; He, Electrical engineer, Ligonier PA. No chn.

CS134447   Jeanne Renetta Casner (20 Nov 1928, Altoona, Juniata PA-23 Jul 1969, Altoona PA) m 29 Sep 1953, Winchester VA, Edward Stiffler (b 28 Apr 1927, Altoona PA) Truck driver, Hollidaysburg PA.

CS1344471   Donald Eugene Stiffler (b 9 Jan 1953, Altoona PA) adopted by Edward and Jeanne Stiffler; m 15 Jul 1972, Hollidaysburg PA, Mitzie Stiver (b 5 Dec 1958, Roaring Springs PA) Truckdriver.

CS13444711   Amie Jeanne Stiffler (b 3 Jan 1973, Roaring Springs PA).

CS13444712   Donald Ashley Stiffler (b 16 Aug 1977, Altoona PA).

CS13444713   Jennie Marie Stiffler (b 11 Oct 1981, Altoona PA).

CS1344472   Deborah Stiffler (b 5 Mar 1958, Philadelphia PA) adopted by Edward and Jeanne Stiffler; m 25 Jun 1977, Altoona PA, Rhett Shoemaker (b 14 Nov 1955, Bedford PA).

CS13444721   Travis James Shoemaker (b 31 Jan 1984, Bedford PA).

CS13444722   Amanda Jo Shoemaker (b 6 Jan 1988, Bedford PA).

CS1345   Irvin Holloway Winkleman (2 Oct 1862, Nittany PA-12 Sep 1906, Flemington PA.) m Rose A Weaver (14 Oct 1862, Centre Hall PA-16 Apr 1944, Altoona PA) He bur Snydertown PA; she bur Altoona PA. Carpenter.

CS13451   Ethel Elena Winkleman (b 25 Mar 1890, Nittany PA) m 22 Nov 1951, Clyde Willow (b 23 Apr 1890, Lock Haven PA) Engineer, NYC RR. No chn.

CS13452   Lulu Bell Winkleman (b 23 Sep 1891, Nittany PA) m 19 Dec 1911, George Miller (b 28 Aug 1888, Lock Haven PA) Telegraph operator.

CS134521   Ethel Miller (b 28 Aug 1913, Flemington PA) m 18 Aug 1933, William Wescott (15 Oct 1911, Clearfield PA-8 Jan 1952) NYC employee.

CS1345211   Sally Wescott (b 8 Mar 1933, Clearfield PA).

CS1345212   Joyce Wescott (b 7 Jan 1936, Clearfield PA).

CS134522   Dorothy Miller m Bumbarger (b Clearfield PA).

CS1345221   Carol Bumbarger (b 9 May 1936, Clearfield PA) m 29 Aug 1957, Samuel Carns (b 1936, Clearfield PA).

CS1345222   John Oral Bumbarger (b 28 Jan 1952, Clearfield PA).

CS13453   Derbin Iona Winkleman (1 Apr 1893, Nittany PA-16 Jan 1895, Lamar PA) Bur Snydertown PA.

CS13454   Violet Mayburn Winkleman (29 Mar 1896, Nittany PA-2 Sep 1915, Flemington PA) unm Bur Snydertown PA.

CS13455   Paul Matthew Winkleman (28 Jan 1899, Nittany PA-30 Jan 1900, Nittany PA) Bur Snydertown PA.

CS13456   Naomi Grace Winkleman (b 28 Jan 1899, Nittany PA) m 4 May 1927, Oscar Calvert (24 Apr 1899, Altoona PA-16 Oct 1956) Bur Altoona PA.

CS13457   Sylvia Marcella Winkleman (19 Jun 1903, Nittany PA-23 Jan 1995, Fullerton CA) m 11 Jul 1924, Louise Saleme (1904, Altoona PA-Altoona PA) Salesman.

CS134571   Gloria June Saleme (9 May 1925, Altoona PA-26 Jun 1995, Fullerton CA) m 25 Sep 1948,

Altoona PA, John D Cuzzolina (b Altoona PA).

CS1345711   Nan Cuzzolina (b 15 May 1950) m Gerald L Cruce. Res. Yorba Linda CA.

CS1345712   John Cuzzolina (b 12 Sep 1952) unm Res. Riverside CA.

CS1345713   Jan Cuzzolina (b 4 Jan 1958) unm Res. Fullerton CA.

CS1346   Minnie Mayburn Winkleman (5 Jul 1864, Nittany PA-23 Oct 1939, Audubon PA) m 26 Jun 1906, Henry Adolphenus Clark (7 May 1873, Burchardsville PA-23 Dec 1939) Bur Bristol PA. Engineer, Penna RR.

CS1347   Mittie Ora Winkleman (12 Jul 1866, Nittany PA-16 Feb 1920, Nittany PA) Bur Snydertown PA.

CS1348   Urah Boyd Winkleman (12 Feb 1868, Nittany PA-21 Feb 1895) m Hattie Agnes Ferree (d 28 May 1943).

CS13481   Herbert Ollan Winkleman (b 6 Jun 1890) m 25 Feb 1914, Verna Margaret Waite Tressler (b 6 Jan 1895) Machinist, Lock Haven PA.

CS134811   Guy Tressler Winkleman (b 17 Aug 1915) m 30 Jun 1931, Gertrude McGonigal (b 16 Dec 1915) Salesman.

CS1348111   Shirley Ann Winkleman (b 29 Oct 1932) m 19 Jan 1950, Harold Roy Barrett (b 30 Oct 1931).

CS13481111   Cindy Ann Barrett (b 24 Aug 1953).

CS13481112   Robin Kay Barrett (b 15 Mar 1955).

CS13481113   Candy Sue Barrett (b 29 Aug 1956).

CS13481114   Harold Roy Barrett (b 4 Jul 1959).

CS1348112   Guy Herbert Winkleman (b 8 Jan 1934) m.

CS13481121   Kenneth Guy Winkleman (b 12 Nov 1956).

CS1348113   Larry Lyn Winkleman (b 25 Oct 1937).

CS1348114   Garry Lee Winkleman (b 17 Sep 1941).

CS1348115   Barbara Kay Winkleman (b 6 Aug 1944).

CS134812   Mary Cathrine Winkleman (b 22 Jul 1918) m 4 Nov 1938, Richard Lee Powers (b 22 Jan 1920).

CS1348121   Carla Ann Powers (b 5 Oct 1939).

CS1348122   Jerry Lee Powers (b 15 Oct 1940) m 28 Aug 1959, Rita Gale Wheeler.

CS134813   Robert Allan Winkleman (b 19 Jul 1922) m 25 Apr 1941, Tessie Marie Confer.

CS1348131   Leslie Marie Winkleman (b 29 Nov 1942).

CS1348132   Robert Gaylord Winkleman (b 8 Dec 1943).

CS134814   Richard Herbert Winkleman (b 19 Jul 1922) m 1) 25 Jul 1941, June Lehman; m 2) 18 Mar 1952, Helen Brooks.

CS1348141   Audrey June Winkleman (b 16 Mar 1942) m 30 Nov 1956, Richard Satteson.

CS13481411   Cindy Jo Satteson (b 23 Jul 1957).

CS13481412   Vicki Ann Satteson (b 18 Nov 1958).

CS1349   Arthur Percival Winkleman (4 Jul 1870-21 Aug 1870) Bur Snydertown PA.

CS134A   Ellwood Bellmont Winkleman (12 May 1872, Nittany PA-26 May 1951) m 1) 3 Dec 1904, Gertrude Albertina Ertley (2 Dec 1878, Nittany PA-14 Apr 1909); m 2) 30 Oct 1911, Mary Hopple (27 Mar 1878, Loganton PA-3 Mar 1955) Ertley bur Jacksonville PA.

CS134A1   Jeannette Fay Winkleman (b 11 May 1905) m Clyde Robert Schleh (b 7 Jun 1902) Clerk, Naugatuck CT.

CS134A2   Anna Louise Winkleman (b 8 Mar 1907, Altoona PA) m 1923, Homer Yearick (d 14 Mar 1954) Bur Jacksonville PA. Railroader.

CS134A21   Mary Ellen Yearick (b 24 Dec 1924, Newbury PA) m Howard Coon (b Painted Post NY).

CS134A211   Barbara Coon (b 1947).

CS134A212   Joyce Ellen Coon (b 1952).

CS134A22   Betty Yearick (b 24 Dec 1926) m John Klingler (b Rochester NY).

CS134A221   Jack Klingler (b 1944).

CS134A222   Scott Klingler (b 1952).

CS134A23   Allen Yearick (b 28 Aug 1929) m Mary Ellen Gruver. Warehouse manager, Shamokin Dam PA.

CS134A231   Sally Ann Yearick (b 1953).

CS134A232   Pat Yearick (b 1956).

CS134A3   Loy Winkleman (b 28 Nov 1911) m Doris Snyder.

CS134A31   Connie Winkleman (b 1944).

CS134A4   Margaret Winkleman (b 21 Oct 1913) m James Murphy. Fireman, Naugatuck CT.

CS134A41   James Murphy (b 1937).

CS134A42   Mary Ann Murphy (b 1941).

CS134A5   Gertrude Winkleman (b 12 Nov 1915) m Bruce Robbins.

CS134A51   Bruce Robbins.

CS134A52   Mary Louise Robbins.

CS134B   Mary Belle Winkleman (11 Aug 1874, Nittany PA-6 May 1904) m Daniel Newton Dorman (12 Oct 1872, Hublersburg PA-7 Oct 1949) She bur Snydertown PA; he bur Jacksonville PA.

CS134B1   Minnie Marie Dorman (b 2 Mar 1895, Nittany PA) m 24 Aug 1912, Jerry Milo Randall (b 17 Jun 1893) Machinist, Penna RR.

CS134B11   Sara Josephine Randall (b 6 Jan 1914, Jersey Shore PA) m 1) 6 Feb 1938, Wharton Fosselman; m 2) 19 Oct 1952, Holland; m 3) 15 Sep 1964, Gleason Lewis (d 1963).

CS134B111   Randall Josiah Fosselman (30 Mar 1939-19 Apr 1966) m 30 May 1964, Helen McCarthy.

CS134B1111   Brenda Lee Fosselman (b 7 Oct 1965).

CS134B1112   Randall J Fosselman Jr (b 12 Nov 1966).

CS134B12   Geraldine Julia Randall (b 1 Mar 1919, Altoona, Juniata PA) m 30 Dec 1942, Eugene Howard Bay (b 22 Nov 1918) Janitorial supply co owner, Washington DC.

CS134B121   Josephine Marie Bay (b 3 May 1945) m John E Ridgeway.

CS134B1211   Geraldine Lynn Ridgeway (b 24 Feb 1964).

CS134B1212   John E Ridgeway Jr (b 13 May 1967).

CS134B122   Eugene Howard Bay Jr (b 17 Sep 1948) USMC.

CS134B13   Richard Paul Randall (6 Apr 1924, Altoona PA-19 Apr 1966, Claysville PA) m 17 Nov 1945, Margaret Godfrey. Janitorial supply co owner, Washington DC.

CS134B131   Margaret Hope Randall (b 29 Nov 1946).

CS134B132   Richard Paul Randall (b 27 Aug 1948).

CS134B133   Mack Wayne Randall (b 20 Nov 1954).

CS15   Samuel Weiser (son of Benjamin and Anna Maria (Levan) Weiser) (2 Jun 1808, Miles Tp, Centre Co PA-20 Nov 1886, Millheim PA) Bur Millheim PA. Blacksmith.[117]

Children of Samuel and Elizabeth (Snavely) Weiser:

CS151   Henry Hess Weiser (b 18 May 1831).

CS152   Susan Weiser.

     Aaron Weiser (dy) twin; not named in will.

     Sarah Weiser (dy) twin; not named in will.

CS153   William R Weiser (6 Oct 1836-11 Feb 1915, Millheim PA) m Julia Ann Hess (May 1832-1903, Millheim PA).

---

[117]Data provided by David D. Weiser, Miss Bertha Harter, Frank I. Grove, Ronald E. Weiser, Edward L. Weiser. Updated (1996) by Charlotte Weiser and Robert Harter.

CS154   Samuel J Weiser (17 Nov 1837, Millheim PA-30 Nov 1898, Mifflinburg PA).

CS155   Charles Weiser (1844-1921) m Mary Louise Otto (1848-1946) Bur Burbank OH, 148 PA Vol Inf Co A. No chn.

CS156   Elizabeth Weiser.

CS157   Benjamin Weiser (b 12 Jul 1849).

CS151   Henry Hess Weiser (son of Samuel and Elizabeth (Snavely) Weiser (18 May 1831, Millheim PA-26 Dec 1895, Millheim PA) m 9 Jun 1853, Catherine Long (14 Apr 1833-26 Feb 1921, Millheim PA) Bur Millheim PA.

CS1511   Samuel Weiser (28 Oct 1853, Millheim PA-22 Jan 1912, Millheim PA) m 14 Nov 1875, Clara June Cantner (1858-1932, Millheim PA) Bur Millheim PA.

CS15111   Ward Weiser (5 Jun 1876, Millheim PA-2 May 1927, Millheim PA) unm Bur Millheim PA.

CS15112   Bertha Weiser (1882, Millheim PA-1954) m Charles Breon (1889-1957) Bur Millheim PA.

CS151121   Emerson Weiser Breon (5 May 1908-11 Apr 1910, Millheim PA).

CS151122   Dean Breon (b 27 Nov 1921, Millheim PA) m Audrey Crust (b 4 Sep 1931).

CS1511221   Nancy Breon (b 14 Apr 1947).

CS1511222   Charles Breon (b 26 May 1949).

CS1511223   Gary Breon (b 5 Jul 1951).

CS1511224   Janet Breon (b 1 Dec 1956).

CS1511225   Deborah Breon (b 28 May 1958).

CS15113   Emerson Edgar Weiser (9 Dec 1889, Millheim PA-4 May 1938) m 1) Jennie K Decker (12 May 1886-30 Jan 1913, Millheim PA); m 2) Stella May Border. Auto dealer, State College and Bellefonte PA.

CS151131   Emerson E Weiser Jr (26 Nov 1916-24 Oct 1921, Millheim PA)

CS151132   Marcia Lucille Weiser (b 1918, Huntington PA) m 27 Sep, Eugene Shultz.

CS1511321   James Andrew Shultz (b 10 Jan 1950, Bellefonte PA).

CS1511322   David Eugene Shultz (b 3 Nov 1953, Bellefonte PA).

CS1511323   Robert William Shultz (b 2 Jul 1955, Greenwood IN).

CS151133   Richard Paul Weiser (b Mar 1920, Huntington PA) m Dorothy Sunday.

CS1511331   Judith Ann Weiser (b Jan1943, Philadelphia PA) m Damian Neuberges.

CS1511332   Cinthia Louise Weiser (b 16 Feb 1945, Philadelphia PA).

CS1511333   Sandra June Weiser (b 16 Feb 1945, Philadelphia PA).

CS1511334   Richard Carl Weiser (23 Jul 1947, Bellefonte PA-Dec 1966, Memphis TN).

CS151134   Eugene Robert Weiser (b 27 Aug 1921, Huntington PA) m Mary Gingher (b Bellefonte PA).

CS1511341   Sheri Lynn Weiser (b 30 Mar 1952, Bellefonte PA).

CS1511342   Robin Cathleen Weiser (b 14 Jun 1958, Johnstown PA).

CS1512   Solomon Long Weiser (6 Nov 1855, Millheim PA-21 Nov 1935, Marion OH) m 24 Sep 1889, Mary K Shirley (26 Sep 1859, Mt Gilead OH-29 Mar 1927, Marion OH) Bur Marion OH. Sheet metal worker, Marion OH.

CS15121   Emerson Frederick Weiser (23 Dec 1886, Marion OH-19 Mar 1950, Marion OH) m 2 Jul 1916, Marion OH, Nellie Ethel Morgan (20 Sep 1896, Marion OH-9 Mar 1957, Marion OH) Bur Brush Ridge OH. Auto radiator and garage shop, Marion OH.

CS151211   Mary Claire Weiser (27 May 1917, Marion OH-28 Aug 1983) m Covington KY, WW Wanamaker (b 11 Sep 1916, Bucyrus OH).

CS1512111   Danny Wanamaker (22 Oct 1944, Marion OH-1966, Vietnam) USA.

CS1512112   Gary Wanamaker (b 15 May 1952, Marion OH) m Mary Ann   .

CS15121121   Danny Wanamaker.

CS1512113   Debby Wanamaker (b 18 May 1954, Marion OH).

CS151212   Ronald Emerson Weiser (21 May 1919, Marion OH-31 Aug 1985) m 5 Oct 1940, Russell KY, Elizabeth I. Loren (b 12 Jul 1919, Morrow Co OH) Auto radiator shop and garage, Marion OH.

CS1512121   Larry Lee Weiser (b 20 May 1941, Galion OH) m 25 Nov 1961, Ella Pemberton (b 17 Aug 1944).

CS15121211   David Allen Weiser (b 18 Jul 1962, Columbus OH) m Tina Reese, div.

CS151212111   Timmy Lee Weiser (b 22 Oct 1984, Tucson AZ).

CS151212112   Tara Nadine Weiser (b 4 Jan 1986, Tucson AZ).

CS151212113   Nickolas David Weiser (b 14 Oct 1994, Tucson AZ).

CS15121212   Donald Emerson Weiser (b 7 Jul 1963, Columbus OH) m Christina Spanyard, div.

CS151212121   Courtney Elizabeth Weiser (b 23 Jun 1982, Tucson AZ).

CS1512122   Judy A Weiser (b 3 Dec 1943, Marion OH) m 1) 20 Jul 1963, Marion OH, James W Potter, div 1974; m 2) 6 Aug 1982, Merle G Smith (b 8 Aug 1928, Cardington OH).

CS15121221   Douglas U Potter (b 26 Oct 1964, Marion OH) m 1) Jun 1986, Kimberly Hupp, div 1994; m 2) 3 Sep 1995, Marion OH, Robin R Adkins.

CS151212211   Tara R Potter (b 6 Mar 1986, Marion OH).

CS151212212   Douglas J Potter (b 30 Aug 1989, Marion OH).

CS151212213   Joseph U Potter (b 1 Mar 1995).

CS15121222   Vance W Potter (b 8 Mar 1967, Marion OH) m 1) 31 Dec 1986, Oklahoma City OK. Jennifer A Tucker, div; m 2) 5 Nov 1994, Marion OH, Korene S Ballard.

CS151212221   Zackery I Potter (b 14 Mar 1989, Okinawa, Japan).

CS151212222   Andrew U Potter (b 22 May 1991, Lubbook TX).

CS1512123   Pamela J Weiser (b 3 Nov 1949, Marion OH) unm.

CS15121231   Timothy M Weiser (b 25 Nov 1971, Marion OH).

CS1512124   Ronnie Ray Weiser (b 4 May 1954, Marion OH) unm.

CS151213   Edward Leroy Weiser (b 29 Jan 1926, Marion OH) m 12 Apr 1952, Marion OH, Dorothy Gail Stephenson (b 14 Jun 1919, Marion OH) Machinist, Marion OH.

CS1512131   Stephanie Rachelle Weiser (b 19 Aug 1953, Marion OH) m 13 Aug 1977, Stuart H Carter, div 1980. She B Mus., OH Wesleyan U, 1975; M Mus., IN U, 1977.

CS15121311   Seth E Carter (b 25 Jun 1980).

CS151214   Betty Ann Weiser (b 19 Mar 1930, Marion OH) m 4 Jun 1950, Marion OH, Carlton Cook (b 15 May 1928, Marion OH).

CS1512141   Robert S Cook (b 26 Jun 1952, Marion OH) m Debra Campbell (b 10 Nov 1952, Marion OH).

CS15121411   Tiffanie L Cook (b 7 Mar 1979).

CS15121412   Kyle R Cook (b 3 Oct 1982).

CS1512142   Bradley C Cook (b 1 Jul 1953, Marion OH) m 1) Mary C Richards (b 26 May 1955) div 1992; m 2) 30 Oct 1994, Michelle Cahela.

CS15121421   Jon B Cook (b 13 Nov 1975, Marion OH).

CS15121422   Amy Cook (b 5 Mar 1977).

CS15121423   Amber Cook (b 12 Apr 1979).

CS15121424   Jamie Cook (b 22 Aug 1981).

CS1512143   Jeffrey T Cook (b 5 Apr 1957, Marion OH) m Jay Steiner, div 1984; m 2) 1984, Jeanine A Robson (b 18 Feb 1967).

CS15121431   Carl B Cook (b 28 Dec 1985, Aiken SC).

CS15121432   Joseph M Cook (b 8 Jun 1988, Spartanburg SC).

CS15121433   Brian J Cook (b 14 Mar 1990, Spartanburg SC).

CS1513   Franklin Fleming Weiser (17 Feb 1860, Millheim PA-19 Jul 1946, Millheim PA) m Sarah Jane Summers (19 Feb 1862-5 Sep 1946, Millheim PA) Bur Millheim PA.

CS15131 Henry Kurtz Weiser (Nov 1883-30 Jun1960, Altoona PA) m Emma C Wicker (1883-27 Jan 1973, Torrance CA) Bur Altoona PA.

CS151311 Clair D Weiser (b 29 Mar 1903) m 1) Lorene Martin, div; m 2) Anna K Yokum. Bur CA.

CS1513111 Richard D Weiser (b 1 Aug 1922, PA) m 1) Dorothy Meyer, div; m 2) Maurine Graces.

CS15131111 Carol Ann Weiser (b 16 Feb1944) m   Gonzales.

CS151311111 James Gonzales (b 15 May 1968).

CS151311112 Robert Gonzales (b 19 Jul 1969).

CS151311113 Summer Gonzales (b 7 Jul 1976).

CS15131112 Joyce Weiser (b 10 Jan 1947) m Ed Disney.

CS151311121 Samantha Disney (b 11 Sep 1973).

CS151311122 Holly Disney (b 5 Nov 1977).

CS15131113 Richard M Weiser (b 21 Nov 1949) m Jenny Forbes.

CS151311131 Jennifer Weiser (b 3 Feb 1979).

CS15131114 Doralene Weiser (b 1955) m.

CS151311141 Lavon (b 11 Feb 1977).

CS1513112 Vivian L Weiser (b 26 Feb 1925, PA) m Jack E Donahue (b PA) div.

CS15131121 Steven Donahue (b 22 Mar 1944) m Carmen Woods.

CS151311211 Karen Donahue (b 19 Oct 1968).

CS151311212 Susan Donahue (b 13 Dec 1970).

CS151311213 Jeffrey Donahue (b 18 Mar 1977).

CS15131122 Nancy Donahue (b 27 Apr 1949) m.

CS151311221 Kristine   (b 26 Jan 1968).

CS151311222 Kari   (b 4 Mar 1970).

CS15131123 Terri Donahue (b 6 Sep 1950) m Fields.

CS151311231 Jennifer Fields (b 22 Aug 1979).

CS151311232 Ryan Fields (b 25 Jan 1981).

CS15132 Grace Beryl Weiser (22 Aug 1888, Aaronsburg PA-4 Jun 1984, Altoona PA) m 8 Oct 1907, Harry B Chevalier (7 Sep 1888, Sinking Valley PA-26 Aug 1957, Altoona PA) Bur Blair Co PA.

CS151321 Kathryn E Chevalier (1 Mar 1909, Altoona PA-8 Dec 1972, Altoona PA) unm Bur Blair Co PA.

CS151322   Harry Elwood Chevalier (b 21 Jan 1912, Altoona PA) m 19 Aug 1929, Violet LaRue Bollinger (11 Mar 1910, Cumberland MD-30 Oct 1983, Altoona PA) Bur Blair Co PA.

CS1513221   Charles Elwood Chevalier (b 31 Dec 1930, Altoona PA) m 20 Jun 1958, Ruth Emily Kurpjuweit (b 4 Jan 1927, Charleroi PA) BS, MS, PSU.

CS1513222   Donna Jean Chevalier (b 17 Jul 1932, Altoona PA) m 14 Feb 1953, Clarence Gene Ingram (b 13 Jul 1926, Altoona PA).

CS15132221   Steven Gene Ingram (b 23 Sep 1953, Altoona PA) m 19 Jun 1980, Debra Franks (b 8 May 1954) He, U Akron.

CS151322211   Kristoffer Steven Ingram (b 10 Jan 1981).

CS1513223   Harry Richard Chevalier (b 28 Jan 1940, Altoona PA) m 28 Dec 1962, Sharon Sullivan (b 26 Aug 1938).

CS15132231   Michelle Renee Chevalier (b 18 Sep 1964).

CS1513224   Gary E Chevalier (b 2 Nov 1954, Altoona PA).

CS151323   Mildred Grace Chevalier (b 8 Jun 1914, Altoona PA) m 1 May 1940, David Wesley Kuhn (b 7 Oct 1916, Holidaysburg PA).

CS1513231   Linda Lee Kuhn (b 22 Aug 1942, Towson MD) m 23 Aug 1963, George Washington Tilghman (b 13 Nov 1938, Crisfield MD) BA, Towson S U.

CS15132311   George Christopher Tilghman (b 27 Feb 1968, Towson MD).

CS15132312   Laura Elizabeth Tilghman (b 18 Jul 1970, Towson MD) m Aug 1993, Michael Hielmot Daugstrop (b 21 Aug 1970, Avon Lake OH) BS, OSU.

CS15132312   Erin Marie Tilghman (b 25 Feb 1977, Seaford DE).

CS151324   Clair DeWitt Chevalier (7 Jan 1919, Altoona PA-1 Mar 1995, Wilmington DE) m Marjorie Ellen Williams (b 23 Jul 1923) WWII: USA. BS, Shippensburg (PA) U; MS, PSU. Bur Minquadale DE.

CS1513241   Carol Ann Chevalier (b 3 Apr 1952, Baltimore MD) m Christopher Pilsbury (b 2 Jan 1952, Wolverhampton England) She, BS, MS, U DE.

CS15132411   Sarah Beth Pilsbury (b 28 Sep 1977, Wilmington DE).

CS1513242   Alan Clair Chevalier (13 Feb 1955-22 Feb 1955, Wilmington DE) Bur Wilmington DE.

CS1513243   Barry Clair Chevalier (b 4 Jul 1956, Wilmington DE) m Donna Bear (b 28 Nov 1955, DE).

CS15132431   Suzanne Kay Chevalier (b 22 Dec 1981, Wilmington DE).

CS15132432   Barry Clair Chevalier (b 20 Sep 1986, Wilmington DE).

CS1513244   Mark David Chevalier (b 10 Apr 1960, Wilmington DE).

CS151325   David Chevalier (b 25 Jun 1922, Altoona PA) m 17 Apr 1943, Lois Weaver (b 2 Jul 1924, Sayton PA) WWII: USA.

CS1513251   Leah Debra Chevalier (b 31 May 1944, Altoona PA) m Harry Hatterman.

CS15132511   David Ernest Hatterman (b 19 Jul 1976).

CS15133   David DeWitt Weiser (14 Sep 1895, Aaronsburg PA-29 Oct 1989, Bellefonte PA) m 23 May 1914, Milheim PA, Helen E Kreamer (11 Apr 1895, Millheim PA-26 May 1990, Milheim PA) Room assignment officer in Dept of Housing at PSU. Bur Millheim PA.

CS151331   David Franklin Weiser (b 18 Aug 1915, Millheim PA) m 1937, Mildred J Wingard (b 5 Nov 1917, Coburn PA) Federal government employee, Midwest City OK.

CS1513311   Harry DeWitt Weiser (b 3 Dec 1937, Milheim PA) m 14 Dec 1958, El Paso TX, Simona Martinez (b 28 Jan 1939, El Paso TX) Federal government employee, Midwest City OK. OSA.

CS15133111   Harry DeWitt Weiser Jr (b 14 Aug 1959, El Paso TX) m 26 Jun 1982, Karen Smith (b 17 Mar 1940, Jackson MS) Federal government employee, Midwest City OK. USAF.

CS15133112   David Franklin Weiser (b 26 Mar 1961, El Paso TX) m 27 Dec 1980, Midwest City OK, Karen Michelle Allnutt (b 31 Jul 1961, Merced CA).

CS15133 David DeWitt Weiser
(1895-1989)

CS151331121   Sarah Michelle Weiser (b 13 Mar 1982, Midwest City OK).

CS151331122   Joshua Joseph Weiser (b 19 Dec 1983, Midwest City OK).

CS15133113   Donald Alan Weiser (b 18 Apr 1962, El Paso TX) m 30 Aug 1982, Midwest City OK, Glenda Lee Reames (b 4 Oct 1961, Midwest City OK) Federal government employee, Midwest City OK.

                Michael Louis Weiser (b 17 Feb 1980, Okla City OK) adopted by Donald Alan Weiser.

CS151331131   Brandon Conrad Weiser (b 10 May 1983, Midwest City OK).

CS151331132   Amanda Marie Weiser (b 16 Aug 1985, Midwest City OK).

CS1513312   Elysbeth Ann Weiser (b 11 Sep 1942, Harrisburg PA) m James Angeloff (b 21 Aug 1939, Steelton PA).

CS15133121   Beth Ann Angeloff (b 24 Mar 1960, Harrisburg PA) m William David Soisson (b 2 Sep 1957, Sewickley PA) div.

CS151331211   Caroine Soisson.

CS1513313   Helen Mabelle Weiser (b 17 May 1952, Bellefonte PA) m 12 Nov 1970, Thomas Trent (b 18 Aug 1950, Oklahoma City OK).

CS15133131   Lori Elaine Trent (b 23 May 1972, Oklahoma City OK).

CS15133132   Eric Tommy Trent (b 3 Aug 1974, Oklahoma City OK) USAF.

CS15133133   Amy Alyse Trent (b 24 Oct 1975, Oklahoma City OK) m May 1993, Howard Wilson (b

20 Nov 1971, Pensacola FL) USAF.

CS151331331   Heidi Simone Wilson (b 2 Dec 1993, Ft Leonard Wood MO).

CS151331332   Katherine Alyse Wilson (b Sep 1995, Landstubl, Germany).

CS151332   Henry Kurtz Weiser (b 4 Jul. 1917, Altoona PA) m Evelyn Bierly (b 16 Oct 1921, Rebersburg PA) WWII: USA. Major in USAF Reserves.

CS1513321   Gregory Kurtz Weiser (b 17 May 1949, Fayetteville NC).

CS151333   Evelyn Elizabeth Weiser (b 10 Dec 1918, Altoona PA) m 5 Sep 1935, Cumberland MD, Alvin Hammer (b 3 Jun 1917, Cumberland MD) div.

CS1513331   Phyllis Evelyn Hammer (b 11 Oct 1936, Bellefonte PA) m Raymond Warfel (b 25 Jun 1934, Lancaster PA).

CS15133311   David Scott Warfel (b 22 Jun 1958, Lancaster PA) BS, Millersville (PA) U.

CS15133312   Lori Beth Warfel (b 25 Jun 1961, Lancaster PA) BA, M Ed, Millersville (PA) U.

CS15133313   Rae Ann Warfel (b 7 Sep 1965, Lancaster PA).

CS151333131   Luke Julian Gomez (b 3 Dec 1990, Lancaster PA).

CS151333132   Blake Adam Gomez.

CS1513332   Allan Drew Hammer (b 20 Sep 1941, Millheim PA) m 14 Dec 1963, Karen Melanie Bierly (b 26 Feb 1942, Rebersburg PA).

CS15133321   Kelly Lynn Hammer (b 14 Dec 1964, Pittsburgh PA).

CS15133322   Kimberly Lee Hammer (b 27 Dec 1971, Pittsburgh PA).

CS15133323   Kristy Louise Hammer (b 8 Dec 1974, Pittsburgh PA).

CS151334   Frances Jane Weiser (13 Feb 1920, Altoona PA-8 Mar 1995, Columbia PA) m 11 Apr 1946, Robert J Cassidy (9 Jun 1922, Philadelphia PA-22 Apr 1984, Lancaster PA) Bur Millheim PA. WWII: USA.

CS1513341   David Joseph Robert Cassidy (b 9 Dec 1947, Bellefonte PA) m 6 Oct 1973, Pittsburgh PA, Katherine Ann Allen (b 7 May 1950, Pittsburgh PA) USA, Vietnam.

CS15133411   Matthew Allen Cassidy (b 10 Aug 1977, Lancaster PA).

CS15133412   Colleen Suzanne Cassidy (b 9 Aug 1980, Lancaster PA).

CS15133413   Alana Katherine Cassidy (b 28 Oct 1984, Lancaster PA).

CS1513342   Robert John Cassidy (b 16 Feb 1950, Kyoto, Japan) m 11 Oct 1975, Darlene Eidemiller (b 19 Sep 1954, Lancaster PA) USA, Vietnam.

CS15133421   Michael Tyler Cassidy (b 9 Oct 1978, Lancaster PA).

CS15133422   Kate Elizabeth Cassidy (b 19 Oct 1983, Lancaster PA).

*CS151335 Charlotte Mae Weiser (b 30 Jun 1922, Bigler PA) unm BS, U of Miami, MA, Columbia U, WWII: Waves, Lt Navy Nurse Corps, RN.

CS151336 Donald DeWitt Weiser (b 13 Sep 1924, Altoona PA) m Bremerhaven, Germany, Marian Wagner (b 15 Jul 1934, Bremerhaven, Germany) div. USA.

CS1513361 Barbara Kaye Weiser (b 25 Jun 1953, Bremerhaven, Germany) m Alvin L Roegge (b 8 Jul 1953, Monterey CA).

CS15133611 Ryan Alexandra Roegge (b 1 Oct 1984, Denison TX).

CS1513362 Susanna Helen Weiser (b 5 Dec 1954, Bellefonte PA).

CS1513363 Karen Elsie Weiser (b 29 May 1958, Fort Knox KY) m Ralph Vaughn.

CS15133631 Ralph Eric Vaughn (b 28 Apr 1987, Thousand Oaks CA).

CS15133632 Lindsay Renee Vaughn (b 29 Jun 1990, Thousand Oaks CA).

CS151337 Helen Virginia Weiser (b 18 May 1926, Altoona PA) m 6 Jan 1946, Donald R Boob (b 13 Feb 1926, Coburn PA).

CS1513371 Donna Marie Boob (b 15 May 1947, Bellefonte PA) m 1) 26 Oct 1968, Aaronsburg PA, Gary Price (b 26 May 1943) div; m 2) 10 Oct 1987, James Ditlow (b 9 Mar 1954, Harrisburg PA) She, BS, St Francis Col; RN, Polyclinic, Hosp.

CS15133711 Shane Adam Price (b 1 Dec 1971, Harrisburg PA) USN.

CS15133712 Erin Lynn Price (b 26 Sep 1973, Harrisburg PA).

CS1513372 Dana Ray Boob (b 29 May 1948, Bellefonte PA) m 12 Aug 1972, Joy Helen Leslie (b 11 Mar 1951, Philadelphia PA) He, BS, PSU. USA.

CS15133721 Christopher Jason Boob (b 17 Feb 1973, Harrisburg PA).

CS15133722 Craig Michael Boob (b 12 Jun 1976, Harrisburg PA).

CS1513373 Douglas Lee Boob (b 16 Dec 1951, Bellefonte PA) m 20 May 1972, Connie Lee Henry (b 19 Apr 1951, Lewiston PA) He, BS, PSU. USMC.

CS15133731 Nathan Lee Boob (b 11 Dec 1975, State College PA).

CS15133732 Neil Tyler Boob (b 6 Jan 1980, Renton WA).

CS151338 Dorothy Jean Weiser (b 6 Feb 1928, Altoon PA) m 12 Nov 1947, Stuart Bowersox (b 4 Feb 1929, Smullton PA).

CS1513381 Leslie Dianne Bowersox (b 4 Jan 1949, Bellefonte PA) m James Lester Homan (b 23 Feb 1948).

CS15133811 Jaime Dyann Homan (b 18 Jul 1968) m 8 Jun 1991, Millheim PA, Scott Edward Swartz.

CS151338111 Matthew James Swartz (b State College PA).

CS151338112 Maverick Brook Swartz (b 23 Feb 1995, State College PA).

CS15133812   Julia Denise Homan (8 Nov 1971, State College PA-27 Mar 1993, Aaronsburg PA) m 6 Oct 1990, Millheim PA, Ryan P Eckenroth (1 Dec 1971, Bellefonte PA-27 Mar 1993, Potter Tp, Centre Co PA) Bur Aaronsburg PA.

CS151338121   Shane Elizabeth Eckenroth.

CS151338122   Dakota Ryanne Eckenroth (b Tyrone PA).

CS1513382   Rodney Steven Bowersox (b 6 Feb 1952, Bellefonte PA) m 1) Sharlyn Mae Vonada, div; m 2) Carol Walter.

CS15133821   Mark David Bowersox (b 21 May 1972, Bellefonte PA).

CS151339   Katherine Louise Weiser (11 Jan 1930, Altoona PA-2 Jan 1936, Altoona PA) Bur Altoona PA.

CS15133A   Ruth Ann Weiser (15 Feb 1932, Altoona PA-14 Mar 1984, Rochester NY) m 19 Jun 1953, Glenn Richard Haugh (b 28 Feb 1929, Gregg Tp, Centre Co PA) RN. Bur Milheim PA.

CS15133A1   Elizabeth Ann Haugh (b 11 Apr 1955, Jersey Shore PA) m 6 Aug 1983, Williamson NY, Ted Allen Kerschner (b 30 May 1959, Syracuse NY).

CS15133A11   Gregory Allen Kerschner (b 12 May 1985, Newark NY).

CS15133A12   Kara Elizabeth Kerschner (b 27 Jan 1987, Newark NY).

CS15133A2   Mary Jane Haugh (b 31 May 1956, Lock Haven PA) m 4 Aug 1979, Williamson NY, Rolf David Paschke (b 1 Nov 1954, Sodus NY) She, AB, Rochester Institute of Technology.

CS15133A21   Eric David Paschke (b 20 May 1987, Rochester NY).

CS15133A22   Leah Elizabeth Paschke (b 21 Dec 1989, Rochester NY).

CS15133A3   Suzanne Marie Haugh (b 26 Aug 1958, Lock Haven PA) m 17 Jul 1982, Williamson NY, John William Krahe (b 27 Mar 1951, Oak Park IL) BA, U NY(Fredonia).

CS15133A31   Catherine Rose Krahe (b 28 Apr 1984, LaCeiba Honduras).

CS15133A32   John Michael Krahe (b 18 Dec 1985, Harvard IL).

CS15133A33   Laura Ruthann Krahe (b 25 Sept 1988, Marian IL).

CS15133A4   Glenda Ruth Haugh (b 13 Apr 1961, Sodus NY) m 7 Nov 1987, Syracuse NY, Luis Jazier Suarez (b 16 Nov 1957, San Juan Puerto Rico) She, RN.

CS15133A41   Cecilia Jane Suarez (b 29 Aug 1990, Syracuse NY).

CS15133A42   Luis Suarez (b Nov 1995, Cincinnati OH).

CS15134   Katherine Amelia Weiser (14 Aug 1898, Aaronsburg PA-8 Sep 1966, State College PA) m 24 May 1921, Paul W Myers (29 Oct 1896, Boalsburg PA-18 Mar 1950, Aspinwall PA) Bur Millheim PA.

CS151341   Paul DeWitt Myers (b 29 May 1922, Millheim PA-13 Aug 1969, Pittsburgh PA) m 23 Jul 1942, Evelyn Eisenhaur (b 29 Feb 1924, Millheim PA) Bur Millheim PA. WWII: USA.

CS1513411   Dennis Allen Myers (b 9 Jun 1943, Millheim PA) m 1) Aleta Glasgow, div; m 2) Kim Henninger.

CS15134111   Valeria Christine Myers (b 6 Mar 1966, Bellefonte PA).

CS15134112   Scott Fitzgerald Myers (b 21 Mar 1967, Bellefonte PA) m M Mong, div.

CS151341121   Nicholas Fitzgerald Myers.

CS15134113   Bradley Myers (b 10 Apr 1968, Bellefonte PA).

CS15134114   Denise Myers (b 28 Feb 1970, Bellefonte PA).

CS15134115   Dennis Allen Myers (b 21 Nov 1981, NC).

CS15134116   Shawn Myers (b 25 Oct 1982, State College PA).

CS15134117   Brittany Myers (b 30 Nov 1987, State College PA).

CS1513412   Maureen Ann Myers (b 23 Jan 1950, Lock Haven PA) m 1) 1969, Robert Catherman (b 18 Nov 1950) div; m 2) 8 Jun 1975, Dennis Roberts (b 9 Sep 1951, Snow Shoe PA).

CS15134121   Nicole Maureen Catherman (b 4 Aug 1969, Bellefonte PA) m Todd Urbanik (b 12 Dec 1959, Bellefonte PA).

CS151341211   Jon-Paul Richner (b 14 Dec 1986, State College PA).

CS151341212   Amber Lynn Barner (b 26 Jan 1992, State College PA).

CS151341213   Ethan Urbanik (b 29 Sep 1994, State College PA).

CS15134122   Colleen Ann Catherman (b 13 Oct 1970, Bellefonte PA) m Douglas Flipse (b 28 Oct 1959) div.

CS151341221   Franklin Robert Flipse (b 11 Sep 1990, State College PA).

CS1513413   Timothy Paul Myers (b 29 Jul 1954, Lock Haven PA).

CS1513414   Martin Charles Myers (b 13 Aug 1956, Lock Haven PA) m Vivian Shawver.

CS15134141   Paul Myers (b 25 Mar 1974).

CS15134142   Kristopher Myers (b 9 May 1976, State College PA).

CS15134143   Carrie Marie Myers (b 21 Nov 1981, State College PA).

CS1514   Edwin Morris Weiser (18 Jan 1862, Millheim PA-15 Mar 1873, Millheim PA) Bur Millheim PA.

CS1515   Sarah Minerva Weiser (27 Aug 1865, Millheim PA-Larned KS) m Millheim PA, Alfred J Grove (4 Mar 1861, Center Hall PA-2 Jul 1909, Larned KS) Bur Larned KS. Miller.

CS15151   Harry Fern Grove (13 Feb 1885, Millheim PA-2 Feb 1952, Larned KS) m 21 Dec 1911, Nettie Elizabeth Sloon (b 2 Feb 1890, Gorham KS) Bur Larned KS. Mail carrier.

CS151511   Roberta Maxine Grove (21 Jul 1912, Larned KS-Mar 1937, Larned KS) m Apr 1935, Henry Garringer (b OK) Bur Larned KS. No chn.

CS151512   Harriet Fern Grove (b 24 Jul 1917, Larned KS) m 27 Jan 1941, Ned McKinley Brown (b

3 Oct 1917, Larned KS) Manager, Doerr Co.

CS1515121   Michael Grove Brown (b 12 Sep 1941, Larned KS).

CS1515122   Robert Ned Brown (b 30 Dec 1947, Larned KS).

CS1515123   Debra Gar. Brown (b 14 Nov 1952, Larned KS).

CS15152   Jay Weiser Grove (24 Jul 1887, Larned KS-21 Dec 1944, Larned KS) m Jun 1912, Minnie A Brown (b 5 May 1892, Bucklin KS) Farmer.

CS151521   Giles Gordon Grove (b 31 Aug 1914, Larned KS) m Bernie Franklin (b 17 Nov 1911, Pawnee Co KS) Mortician.

CS1515211   Gale Allan Grove (b 12 Jul 1952, Sdgwick Co KS).

CS151522   Harry Kenneth Grove (b 24 Jun 1916, Bucklin KS) m Merle Hendershot (b 24 Jan 1914) TV announcer.

CS1515221   Rebecca Ann Grove (b 6 Oct 1944, Oceanside CA).

CS151523   Jay Weiser Grove Jr (b 18 Aug 1918, Larned KS) m Josephine Allred (b 16 Jan 1928) Salesman.

CS1515231   John Jay Grove (b 3 Nov 1951, Great Bend KS).

CS1515232   Carolyn Sue Grove (b 29 Sep 1953, Great Bend KS).

CS15153   Frank Irvin Grove (b 18 Nov 1890, Larned KS) m 31 Mar 1929, Ellen Mae LaRue (b 21 Apr 1902, Phillipsburg KS) Plant engineer, Johnson Pontiac Co, Colorado Springs CO.

CS151531   Kenneth W Grove (18 Jan 1930, Elkhart KS-22 Feb 1957, Colorado Springs CO) Bur Colorado Springs CO.

CS151532   Keith LaRue Grove (b 18 Jan 1930, Elkhart KS) m June Marie Hartwell (Swan Lake Canada) USAF, S/Sgt.

CS1515321   Grant Keith Grove (b 23 Jul 1954, Altus OK).

CS1515322   Debra Diane Grove (b 21 Aug 1956, Swan Lake Canada).

CS1515323   Glenn Kenneth Grove (b 14 May 1958, Las Vegas NV).

CS15154   Ruth Cathern Grove (28 Dec 1897, Larned KS-22 Jul 1944, Colorado Springs CO) m 1912, Charles Meeker (1887, Russel KS-12 Dec 1925, Colorado Springs CO) She bur Colorado Springs CO; he bur Larned KS. Farmer.

CS151541   Maxine Mae Meeker (b 25 Jan 1915, Larned KS) m Frank D Reed Jr (b 2 Feb 1916, Forder CO) Mechanic. No chn.

CS151542   Vergene Meeker (b 2 May 1920, Larned KS) m Duane L Christiansen. USAF, Officer.

CS1515421   Sandra Lee Christiansen (b 12 Dec 1943, Los Angeles CA).

CS15155   James M Grove (24 May 1900, Larned KS-16 Apr 1935, Hutchinson KS) m 1925, Marie Purcell (4 Feb 1894, LaCross KS-8 Mar 1943, Larned KS) Bur Larned KS. Shoe store manager.

CS151551   Gwendolyn Joan Grove (b 9 Jul 1926, Cripple Creek CO).

CS151552   James Robert Grove (b 1 May 1931, Hutchinson KS) m Beverly Ann Jones (b 9 Sep 1932, Kansas City MO).

CS1515521   Hollis Kay Grove (b 27 Mar 1957, Houston TX).

CS1515522   Jay Robert Grove (b 14 Jan 1959, Houston TX).

CS1516   Harriet Teresta Weiser (28 Aug 1870, Millheim PA-Mar 1961, Bridgewater SD) m 6 Dec 1888, Robert Elery Harter (11 Sep 1868, Millheim PA-2 Jun 1965, Bridgewater SD) Bur Bridgewater SD. Lumberman, Millheim PA to 1901; farmer and street commissioner, Bridgewater SD.

CS15161   Harry Harter (15 Mar 1889, Millheim PA-3 Apr 1900, Millheim PA) Bur Millheim PA.

CS15162   Frank Gurn Harter (b 3 May 1891, Millheim PA-30 May 1990) m 28 Feb 1933, Helen Kressman (b 20 Jun 1898, Bridgewater SD) Farmer, Bridgewater SD. Honored in 1987 as South Dakota's oldest farmer.

CS15163 Ralph Weiser Harter
(1893-1989)

CS151621   Roger Harter (b 17 Feb 1935, Bridgewater SD) m 13 Jul 1956, Virgene Ecker (b 16 Apr 1937, Lake Benton MN) Carpenter and teacher, Kalispell MT.

CS1516211   Cindey Jane Harter (b 26 Sep 1957, Lead SD) m 27 Jun 1977, Kalispell MT, Allen Greenwood Bardwell. He, county employee; she, news agency, Kalispell MT.

CS1516212   Terri Harter (b 2 Jan 1960).

CS15162121   Orion   (b Jul 1988).

CS1516213   David Harter (b 14 Feb 1961) USA. Draftsman, Kalispell MT.

CS1516214   Susan Gay Harter (b 29 Nov 1962, Lead SD) m Gary Giberson (b 5 Jul 1961) He, USA; she, USA, civilian secretary.

CS1516215   Donald Allen Harter (b 22 Jun 1964, Lead SD) USAF, Tacoma WA.

CS151622   Noel Harter (b 28 Oct 1936, Bridgewater SD).

CS15163   Ralph Weiser Harter (19 Sep 1893, Millheim PA-1 Nov 1989, Sioux Falls SD) m 28 Jun 1930, Hudson Falls NY, Mary Kellogg Monty (28 Apr 1898, Hudson Falls NY-21 Oct 1991, Sioux Falls SD) Bur Bridgewater SD. BS, U SD (Vermillion). WWI: USA, Food chemist, Nabisco, New York NY; farmer, Bridgewater SD.

*CS151631   Robert Preston Harter (b 12 Apr 1932, Orange NJ) m 30 Dec 1955, Emma Leonora Myer (7 Jul 1936, Ashton SD) BS, SD S Col. USAF, Korean conflict. Realty specialist, Federal Highway Adm. 1963, Fairfax VA. She, BS Cornell U; teacher, school secretary.

CS1516311   Kathleen Mary Harter (b 24 Aug 1956, Brookings SD) unm Telephone co. employee, physical therapist.

CS1516312   Carol Marie Harter (b 18 Dec 1959, Sioux Falls SD) m 5 Sep 1981, Marc Creigh Joseph (b 9 Feb 1948) div. He, marketing; she, BS, George Mason U. Finance officer, Fairfax VA.

CS15163121   Marc Nathan Joseph (b 21 Feb 1983, Falls Church VA).

CS151632   Mary Lou Harter (b 19 Jul 1934, Orange SD) m 1) 19 Sep 1953, Joseph Anthony Romano (b 14 Mar 1932, Brockton MA) div; m 2) 5 Nov 1982, Earl Baxter Patterson (b 7 May 1948) Romano: USAF, security firm, Brockton MA; Patterson: cabinetmaker, auto sales, Sioux Falls SD and Waynesboro VA. She, secretary, Sioux Falls SD and Waynesboro VA.

CS1516321   Joseph Anthony Romano Jr (b 8 Dec 1954, Brockton MA) USAF.

CS1516322   Katherine Gina Marie Romano (b 1 Mar 1960, Germany).

CS15164   Leora Katherine Harter (15 Dec 1895, Millheim PA-5 Sep 1983, Sioux Falls SD) m 22 Dec 1928, Mitchell SD, Charles A Harvison (9 Jan 1894, White Lake SD-8 May 1941, White Lake SD) He, rural mail carrier, dance band. She, teacher. Bur White Lake SD.

*CS151641   Marilyn Jeanette Harvison (b 6 Jul 1930, Mitchell SD) m 21 Jul 1950, Bridgewater SD, Keith E Eide (b 6 Oct 1928, Yankton SD) div 1982. He, music teacher; She, B Mus., Lewis and Clark Col, 1968; M Mus., Lewis and Clark Col, 1970; M Adm., Portland S U, 1978. Music teacher, elementary principal.

CS1516411   Gail Montelle Eide (b 3 Apr 1952, Yankton SD) m 1) 19 Jul 1973, Larry Street, div; m 2) Estes Kiger, div; m 3) 18 Jun 1988, San Jose CA, William McGraw Vanderhoof (b 29 Oct 1955, Columbus OH) She, AB, Lewis and Clark Col, 1973; he, BS, San Jose S, 1978.

CS15164111   William Talbot McGraw Vanderhoof (b 29 Aug 1989, San Jose CA).

CS15164112   Harry James Eugene Vanderhoof (b 10 Apr 1992).

CS1516412   Judd Keith Eide (b 20 Jun 1954, Yankton SD) m 25 Dec 1985, Agana Guam, Rose Techur (b 4 Sep 1960, Palau Micronesia) He, helicopter pilot; she, teacher.

CS15164121   Bradlee Eide (b 1 Jan 1987, Agana Guam).

CS15164122   Harlee William Eide (b 8 Dec 1992, Agana Guam).

CS1516413   Keith Charles Eide (b 24 Jun 1958, Juneau AK) m 23 May 1992, San Francisco CA, Kari Feibelman (b 1 Oct 1967) He, BA, U OR, 1978.

CS15164131   Parker Alexander Eide (b 6 Mar 1994, Alameda CA).

CS1516414   Kevin Gregg Eide (b 24 Jun 1958, Juneau AK) m 28 Jun 1986, Sausalita CA, Catherine Garcia (b 13 Jan 1959) He, BA, U OR, 1977. She, RN, 1977.

CS15164141   Stephan Tyler Eide (b 6 May 1989, NC).

CS15164142   Alyssa Marianna Eide (b 17 Jul 1992, CA).

CS151642   Byron George Harvison (b 31 May 1933, Mitchell SD) m 23 Dec 1954, Flandreau SD, Wilma Duncan (b 20 Oct 1935, Flandreau SD) USN pilot; corporate jet pilot, Nashville TN.

CS1516421   Steven Charles Harvison (b 11 May 1959, Pensacola FL) m 12 Sep 1987, Huntsville AL, Linda Lee (b 2 Feb 1962, Huntsville AL).

CS15164211   Stephanie Lee Harvison (b 8 Apr 1990, Huntsville AL).

CS1516422 Kristen Diane Harvison (b 25 Apr 1966, China Lake CA) m 4 May 1991, Naperville GA, Michael Dean Hinson (b 1 May 1961, Cordele GA).

CS15164221 Jennifer Diane Hinson (b 13 Jul 1995, Atlanta GA).

CS151643 Jerome Charles Harvison (b 9 May 1935, Mitchell SD) m 1) 19 Aug 1960, Anacortes WA, Karen Albers, div; m 2) 6 Jun 1970, Watertown SD, Marcile Herding (b 6 Jun 1970, Watertown SD) div; m 3) Shirley Clark. He, highway maintenance.

CS1516431 Susan Katherine Harvison (b 19 Dec 1962, Flandreau SD) m 1 Oct 1982, Joseph M Heavican (b 23 Apr 1962, Schuyler NE).

CS15164311 Matthew Joseph Heavican (b 4 Mar 1983, Schuyler NE).

CS15164312 Melinda Sue Heavican (b 17 Sep 1987, Schuyler NE).

CS15164313 Mitchell Zachary Heavican (b 8 Oct 1994, Schuyler NE).

CS1516432 Leesa Maurine Harvison (b 7 Nov 1963, Flandreau SD) m 12 May 1984, Schuyler NE, Timothy Richtig (b 19 Feb 1959, Schuyler NE).

CS15164321 Kristina Lee Richtig (b 10 Sep 1985, Schuyler NE).

CS15164322 Aaron Timothy Richtig (b 5 Mar 1988).

CS15164323 Brittany Michelle Richtig (b 20 Feb 1991).

CS1516433 Daniel Charles Harvison (b 30 Apr 1964, Flandreau SD) m 16 Jul 1995, San Diego CA, Corinne Rachelle.

CS15165 Bertha Harter (b 21 May 1901, Millheim PA) unm Telephone co, silent movie pianist, Bridgewater and Chamberlain SD.

CS15166 Margaret Elizabeth Harter (b 30 Apr 1912, Bridgewater SD) m 31 Dec 1932, William Lowell Hancock (b 24 Mar 1909, Oklahoma City OK) Engineer.

CS1517 Anna Elizabeth Weiser (b 24 Sep 1872, Millheim PA-14 Aug 1873, Millheim PA) Bur Millheim PA.

CS152 Susan Weiser (b 1834) m Peter Rearick (Altoona PA-22 Jan 1904, Altoona PA).

CS1521 Daughter m Charles Ross. No chn.

CS153

CS1531 Sarah Weiser (b ca 1859).

CS154 Samuel Weiser (17 May 1837-30 Nov 1898) m Sarah Henrietta Thompson (b 1843, Mifflinburg PA).

CS1541 Thompson Weiser (b Jul 1870).

CS156 Elizabeth Weiser (daughter of Samuel and Elizabeth (Snavely) Weiser) (ca 1847, Millheim PA-Millheim PA) m Henry B Brown. Bur Millheim PA.

CS1561 Edward Brown (1877-1948, Pleasant Gap PA) m Margaret Keller (1870-1947, Pleasant

Gap PA) Bur Pleasant Gap PA.

CS15611   Helen Brown (b 1909) m.

CS15612   Ruth Brown (b 2 Apr 1911) m 25 Aug 1927, Harrison Shawley.

CS156121   Calvin Edward Shawley (b 5 Apr 1928, Lewiston PA) m Constance Weir (b 30 Sep 1927).

CS1561211   Jeanne Louise Shawley (b 21 Jan 1949).

CS1561212   Daniel Edward Shawley (b 12 Dec 1950).

CS1561213   Virginia Lee Shawley (b 11 Feb 1952).

CS1561214   Michael Calvin Shawley (b 19 Oct 1955).

CS157   Benjamin Franklin Weiser (12 Jul 1849, Millheim PA-4 Aug 1891, Millheim PA) m 1) Sophia Jane (5 May 1849-26 Oct 1874, Millheim PA); m 2) Ellen Smith (16 Feb 1849-7 Sep 1915, Millheim PA) Bur Millheim PA.

CS1571   William Franklin Weiser (Apr 1872, Millheim PA-1946) m Priscilla Howell (1879-1959) Bur Millheim PA.

CS15711   Irene May Weiser.(b ca 1906).

CS1572   Anna Mary Weiser (1874-1941) m 1892, James Calvin Keen (22 Sep 1872, Millheim PA-31 Mar 1959, Altoona PA) Bur Altoona PA.

CS15721   William Weiser Keen (14 Apr 1893, Millheim PA-18 Dec 1966, Altoona PA) m 26 Sep 1912, Bertha Throssell (11 Jul 1893-7 Feb 1986, Altoona PA) Bur Altoona PA.

CS157211   William Andrew Keen (b 29 Sep 1913, Altoona PA) m 2 Oct 1944, Jane Burns (b 30 Mar 1922, Altoona PA) WWII: USA.

CS1572111   William Andrew Keen (b 14 Oct 1946, Altoona PA) m Barbara Coble.

CS15721111   Matthew Keen (b 4 Jul 1974).

CS15721112   Christopher Keen (b 1977).

CS15721113   Jeffrey Keen (b 1981).

CS157212   James Calvin Keen (23 Feb 1917, Altoona PA-5 Mar 1956, Altoona PA) m Lois Baker.
Bur Altoona PA.

CS157213   John Keen (b 2 Jul 1919, Altoona PA) m Mary Rose Irwin (d 9 Aug 1991, Altoona PA)
Bur Altoona PA.

CS157214   Elizabeth Keen (b 14 Jun 1921, Altoona PA) m Glenn E Lloyd (d 7 Dec 1974) div.

CS1572141   Samuel G Lloyd (b 25 Mar 1950, Altoona PA) unm.

CS1572142   Lee Ann Lloyd (b 27 Mar 1955, Altoona PA) m 8 Jul 1978, Larry Merlo (b Charleroi PA)
She, BS, U Pittsburgh.

CS15721421   Kristen Victoria Merlo (b 12 Aug 1994, RI).

CS15722   Edna Rose Keen (b 16 Feb 1895, Millheim PA) m Frank Hesser Louder (1884-1953).

CS157221   James Robert Louder (b 4 Dec 1920, Chicago IL) m 25 Nov 1945, Laguna Beach CA, Margaret Rose Power (b 17 Jun 1925).

CS1572211   Laurie Rose Louder (b 23 Jan 1955, Santa Monica CA) m 15 Jan 1988, Lake Tahoe CA, C Michael Bilbruck (b 30 Nov 1946).

CS15722111   Alexandra Rose Bilbruck (b 23 May 1990, Anaheim Mills CA).

CS1572212   Frederick Keen Louder (b 12 Nov 1956, Santa Monica CA) m 12 Sep 1987, Canyon CA, Vickie Marie Sudick (b 12 Aug 1961).

CS15722121   Christopher James Louder (b 10 Jul 1989, Los Angeles CA).

CS15722122   Jared Scott Louder (b 16 May 1994, Los Angeles CA).

CS157222   Donald Raymond Louder (b 18 Mar 1924, Chicago IL) m 1953, Pasadena CA, Betty Jean Githen (b 3 May 1930).

CS1572221   Steven Wayne Louder (12 Jan 1953-27 May 1984).

CS1572222   Ronald Allen Louder (b 14 Apr 1954, Santa Monica CA) m 1) Cindy   , div; m 2) Beth Merry; m 3) Robin .

CS15722221   Ryan Elizabeth Louder (b 25 Apr 1981).

CS15722222   Kevin Broc Louder (b 16 Jul 1986).

CS1572223   Donna Jean Louder (Jul 1956-4 Dec 1960).

CS1572224   James Raymond Louder (b 8 May 1958, Santa Monica CA) m 22 Jun 1985, Valencia CA, Debra Gay Rostadt.

CS15722241   April Lynn Louder (b 4 Apr 1986, Valencia CA).

CS15722242   Steven James Louder (b 31 Dec 1993, Sulmar CA).

CS15723   Ralph John Keen (26 May 1902, Millheim PA-1984) m Mary Harter (b 18 Oct 1908, Bellefonte PA).

CS157231   David Calvin Keen (b 21 Jun 1933, Altoona PA) m Patricia White (b 12 Oct 1934).

CS1572311   David A Keen (b 7 Feb 1959, Altoona PA).

CS1572312   Paul Fay Keen (b 18 Apr 1961, Jacksonville FL).

CS1572313   Donna Christine Keen (b 12 Dec 1963, Altoona PA).

CS157232   Dorothy Margaret Keen (b 29 Jun 1929, Altoona PA) m 1) Melvin Waters (b 22 May 1928); m 2)   Settle.

CS1572321   Richard Waters (b 22 Apr 1951, Altoona PA).

CS15724   Helen Harriet Keen (1904-1976) m 1922, Walter J Smith (d 3 May 1986).

CS157241   Dorothy Smith m Thomas Novak.

CS157242   Robert T Smith m 1) Maggie   ; m 2) Margaret   .

CS157243   Walter Smith m Pilar   .

CS157244   Patrick Smith m Mary   .

CS15725   Marguerite Kees Keen (b 17 Jul 1906) m James Willis Gibboney (14 Apr 1904-16 May
1985).

CS157251   Richard A Gibboney (b 6 Feb 1927) m Roberta Henderson. He Ph D; professor, U OK.

CS1572511   Diane Gibboney (b 19 Jul 1954) m Thomas Carr.

CS1572512   Richard Gibboney II (b 30 Jun 1957).

CS157252   Phyllis Elaine Gibboney (b 25 Jan 1930) m 1) Richard Goetz; m 2) William Hultman (14
Sep 1921-1994).

CS1572521   Elaine Goetz (b 18 Mar 1951) m Daniel Walters.

CS15725211 Daniel J Walters (b 30 Dec 1976).

CS15725212 David Walters (b 3 Apr 1978).

CS15725213 Justine Walters (b 30 Jan 1980).

CS1572522   Eve Ann Goetz (b 30 Jun 1955) m Paul Ruscio.

CS15725221 Kathryn M Ruscio (b 21 Aug 1978).

CS15725222 Michelle M Ruscio (b 8 Jan 1981).

CS1572523   Ruth Ellen Goetz (b 29 Aug 1957).

CS157253   Jean Louise Gibboney (b 7 Apr 1972) m James Weiksner Jr (b 15 Sep 1924).

CS1572531   Jeffries Weiksner (b 28 Feb 1958).

CS1572532   Lynn Weiksner m David Paul Odenwalt.

CS15725321 David Paul Odenwalt Jr (b 3 Aug 1982).

CS15725322 Amanda Odenwalt (b 10 Aug 1987).

CS15725323 Matthew Odenwalt (b 17 Sep 1989).

CS1572533   James F Weiksner III (b 13 Nov 1971).

CS15726   Eugene Keen (1909-1911) Bur Altoona PA.

CS1573   Charles Wesley Weiser (29 Jul 1877, Millheim PA-16 May 1941) m 26 Nov 1912, Clara
Helena TenHaeff. AB, 1901; AM, 1906, Gettysburg Col, Gettysburg Seminary, 1906. Lutheran pastor, 1908-
1911; postal and railway employee.

CS1574   John Weiser (b 1880, Millheim PA) m Martha (b 1887).

CS1575   Edwin Weiser (Millheim PA-Thompsontown PA) m Caroline Schwartz (d 4 Feb 1973) He bur Thompsontown PA; she bur Millheim PA.

CS1576   Minerva Weiser (20 May 1880-5 Jan 1957) m Elmer J Miller (30 Nov 1887, Glasco PA-21 Nov 1959) Bur Altoona PA.

CS15761   Victor Charles Miller m Pleasanton CA.

CS15762   Dorothy Miller (b 5 Aug 1910, Altoona PA) m Lester L Calderwood (b 16 Feb 1907, Altoona PA).

CS157621   Phyllis Calderwood (b 10 Mar 1935, Altoona PA) m Donald F Tarner (b 24 Dec 1932, Altoona PA).

CS1576211   Donald Scott Tarner (b 16 Nov 1957, Altoona PA).

CS157622   Kathleen Marie Calderwood (b 23 May 1944, Altoona PA).

CS15763   Robert Miller m Wheaton IL.

CS15764   Marjorie E Miller (b 17 Dec 1925, Altoona PA) m Ernest Weierick (b 11 May 1923, Altoona PA).

CS157641   Rebecca A Weierick (b 9 Apr 1946, Altoona PA).

CS157642   Dianne F Weierick (b 1 Nov 1947, Altoona PA).

CS157643   Robert B Weierick (b 9 Oct 1949, Altoona PA).

CS16   Maria Magdalena Weiser (daughter of Benjamin and Anna Maria (Levan) Weiser (14 Dec 1810, Miles Tp, Centre Co PA-14 Mar 1860) Their tombstones have evidently been removed from the local cemeteries. They had one surviving child.[118]

CS161   James Clay Smith (26 Feb 1853-6 Oct 1933) m Sarah Lydia Mauck (24 Dec 1859-22 Oct 1932) Bur Millheim PA.

CS1611   Robert Smith (25 Feb 1877-21 Jun 1954) m Bertha Miller (b 13 Apr 1878) Bur Pine Halls PA.

CS16112   Irene Smith (b 24 Jan 1902, Millheim PA) m State College PA, David Harry Ruhl (b 26 Jun 1899).

CS161121   David Harry Ruhl Jr (b 11 Jan 1920) m Bernice Straussner.

CS161122   Robert E Ruhl (b 26 Sep 1921) m State College PA, Arla Hackenberg.

CS1611221   Valli Denise Ruhl.

CS161123   Donald Gene Ruhl (b 22 Oct 1925) m Mary Homan.

CS16113   James Harry Smith (b 14 Feb 1905) m State College PA, Ruth Bechers (b 15 Jan 1911).

---

[118]Data provided by David D. Weiser and James Daniel Bower, Jr.

CS161131   Nancy Lee Smith (b 27 Aug 1939).

CS16114   Robert Paul Smith (b 29 Jan 1908) m Jeanne Saussman.

CS16115   Russell S Smith (b 20 Jan 1910) m Virginia Beatty.

CS16116   William Marshall Smith (30 Aug 1917-10 Aug 1932).

CS16117   Sarah Marjorie Smith (8 Jun 1921-18 Mar 1922).

CS1612   Harry Smith m NJ, Elizabeth Weiland.

CS16121   Kenneth Smith.

CS1613   Paul Smith m Philadelphia PA, Grace Auman.

CS16131   Grace Smith.

CS16132   Emeline Smith (b TX).

CS16133   Andrew Smith (b CA).

CS16134   Louise Smith (b FL).

CS16135   Richard Smith (b Philadelphia PA).

CS16136   Elaine Smith (b Tuckerton NJ).

CS1614   Esta Smith (29 Mar 1880, Millheim PA-1 Mar 1965, Beach Haven NJ) m 25 Feb 1903, Martin Riley Bower (d Washington DC).

CS16141   James Daniel Bower (16 Apr 1905-29 Apr 1974, Somers Point NJ) m 28 Oct 1935, Rochester NY, Edna Rose Hegele (29 May 1913, Cherry Flats PA-21 Aug 1966, Tuckerton NJ) Bur Tuckerton NJ.

*CS161411   James Daniel Bower Jr m 1) 2 Jun 1962, Janet Ann Rubright, div; m 2) 7 Oct 1976, Elsie Heinricks.

CS1614111   Lauri Ann Bower.

CS1614112   James Bower.

CS161412   Brenda Bower m Joseph Carrington III.

CS1614121   Donna Michel Carrington.

CS16142   Martin Bower.

CS16143   Sarah Bower m Alexandria VA or Washington DC, Donald Black.

CS1615   Minerva Smith m Bridgeton NJ, Vilas Chapman.

CS16151   James Chapman.

CS1616   Rose Smith m Charles Mallory. Bur Rebersburg PA.

CS16161   Sarah Mallory m Nevada Beach GA, George Pierce.

CS16162   Genevieve Mallory m Scranton PA, Donald Stearns.

CS1617   Thomas Smith.

CS17   Catharine Weiser (daughter of Benjamin and Anna Maria (Levan) Weiser) (13 Feb 1814-11 Nov 1848, near Aaronsburg PA) m Daniel Warntz (20 Jun 1818-9 Apr 1880, near Aaronsburg PA) Bur Wolf's Chapel, cemetery near Aaronsburg PA.[119]

CS171   Sarah A Warntz unm No record.

CS172   Rebecca Warntz m Albuquerque NM, Jeremiah Oliver.

CS1721   John Oliver (b Albuquerque NM).

CS1722   Regina Oliver m Albuquerque NM, McCoy.

CS1723   Elmer Oliver (12 Mar 1863-2 Dec 1863) Bur Wolf's Chapel, cemetery near Aaronsburg PA.

CS18   Sarah Weiser (daughter of Benjamin and Anna Maria (Levan) Weiser) (17 Jun 1816, Lycoming Co PA-9 Mar 1904, Bellefonte PA) m John Wagner (9 Nov 1806, Augusta Tp, Northumberland Co PA-4 Feb 1900, Bellefonte PA) Bur Bellefonte PA.[120]

Children of John and Sarah (Weiser) Wagner:

CS181   Emaline Wagner (b 18 Mar 1839).

CS182   Susanna Wagner.

CS183   Henry Franklin Wagner (11 Apr 1845, Harris Tp, Centre Co PA-28 Feb 1892, Miles City MT).

CS184   John Calhoun Wagner.

CS181   Emaline Wagner (18 Mar 1839, Gregg Tp, Centre Co PA-2 Feb 1925, Bellefonte PA) m 24 Dec 1861, Michael Hess (5 Aug 1835, Pine Grove Mills PA-26 Aug 1906, Bellefonte PA).

CS1811   Newton Edgar Hess (b 23 Nov 1862, Pine Grove Mills PA) m 10 Mar 1889, Margaret McWilliams (20 Dec 1861, Fairbrook PA-22 Dec 1923, Pine Hall PA) Bur Pine Hall PA.

CS18111   Samuel McWilliams Hess (3 May 1889, Shingletown PA-19 Jun 1976) m 31 May 1914, Minnie Portzline (b 3 Apr 1892, Hoffer, Snyder Co PA).

CS181111   Newton Ernest Hess (b 31 Jan 1916, Ferguson Tp, Centre Co PA) m Charlene Tiehl.

CS1811111   Samuel Tiehl Hess (b 7 Nov 1955, Allentown PA).

CS181112   Sarah Hess (b 26 Oct 1917, Ferguson Tp PA).

---

[119]Data provided by David D. Weiser.

[120]Data provided by David D. Weiser and Mrs. Albert W. Gilmer, who owns the Wagner family Bible and other documents. Updates in (1990) by Richard A Bradbury, Charles C. Wagner, Eric H. Wagner, Lisa Carey, and Krista Miller Hain.

CS181113   Phyllis Hess (b 27 Jul 1922, Bellefonte PA) m 18 Apr 1946, George McWilliams.

CS1811131   Luke McWilliams (b 25 Jul 1948, Bellefonte PA).

CS1811132   Thomas McWilliams (b 13 Apr 1950, Bellefonte PA).

CS1811133   Phyllis McWilliams (b 16 Oct 1951, Bellefonte PA).

CS1811134   Gale McWilliams (b 1 Sep 1957, Bellefonte PA).

CS181114   David Hess (b 31 Dec 1924).

CS18112   John Michael Hess (2 Aug 1899, Ferguson Tp, Centre Co PA-30 May,1963) m 2 Nov 1921, Sarah Catherine McKinney (b 28 Oct 1901, Potters Mills PA).

CS181121   John E Hess (b 6 Jun 1927, Bellefonte PA) m 30 Jun 1954, Patricia Mark (b 5 Jun 1936).

CS1811211   Mark Allen Hess (b 17 Aug 1956, Bellefonte PA).

CS1812   Wilford Hess (6 Dec 1864-dy).

CS1813   Ernest Wagner Hess (12 Nov 1866, State College PA-1 Jan 1943, Boalsburg PA) m 21 Mar 1893, Blanche Felty (b 11 Jul 1872) Farmer.

CS18131   Edgar E Hess (b 3 Aug 1899, State College PA) m 6 Jun 1923, State College PA, Mary K Thompson (b 4 Aug 1904).

CS181311   Ernest William Hess (b 26 Aug 1924) m 13 Nov 1944, Stella Kepler (b Barboursville NJ).

CS1813111   Michael Aaron Hess (b Apr 1950).

CS1813112   Mary Ann Hess (b Sep 1952).

CS181312   Edna Marie Hess (b 26 Oct 1926) m 31 Oct 1949, Benjamin Whitacre (b Pleasant Gap PA).

CS1813121   Lewis Jay Whitacre (b 9 Feb 1951).

CS181313   Charles Ira Hess (b 1 May 1931) m 22 Oct 1956, Catherine Baney.

CS1813131   Kathy Jo Hess (b 15 Mar 1958).

CS181314   Virginia Ann Hess (b 11 Jul 1932) m 25 Nov 1954, Paul Luke Brobst (b Dayton OH).

CS1813141   Carol Ann Brobst (b 26 Nov 1956).

CS181315   Elizabeth Jane Hess (b 22 May 1940, State College PA).

CS18132   Emeline Wagner Hess (b 2 Apr 1902, Shingletown PA) m Paul Coxey (b 15 Jul 1901, Boalsburg PA) Salesman.

CS181321   Paul E Coxey Jr (b 27 Jan 1931, Indiana PA) m 30 Aug 1958, Donna Faye Fowkes (b 8 Nov 1937, Dembo PA).

CS181322   Sally Ann Coxey (b 23 Jul 1934, Greenburg PA) m 18 Dec 1954, Harry F Moyer (b 4 Mar 1935, Greenburg PA).

CS1813221 Fred Paul Moyer.

CS1813222 Boyd Allen Moyer.

CS1813223 June Ann Moyer.

CS18133 Robert Calvin Hess (b 9 Jun 1904, State College PA) m Fern Bennett (b 23 Oct 1903, Altoona PA).

CS181331 Joan Caroline Hess (19 Aug 1934-10 Aug 1949).

CS18134 Anna Mary Hess (b 11 Feb 1907, State College PA) m 30 Jun 1938, Fred Bruce Lonberger (b 16 Jul 1908) No chn.

CS18135 Virginia Hess (b 21 Mar 1913, State College PA) m 19 Oct 1938, David E Ailman. Ph D.

CS181351 Emiline Beth Ailman.

CS181352 David E Ailman.

CS1814 Nina Winona Hess (30 Oct 1868, Shingletown PA-26 Nov 1944, State College PA) m 25 Dec 1896, Shingletown PA, D Hall Bottorf (5 Mar 1868, Lemont PA-19 Jul 1933, Boalsburg PA).

CS18141 Sarah Margaret Bottorf (b 20 Jun 1897, Lemont PA) m 20 Jun 1921, Lemont PA, Harold Kersteter (26 Mar 1896, Pleasant Gap PA-State College PA)

CS181411 Ammon Kersteter (b 21 Mar 1924) m 14 Sep 1946, Lois Harpster (b 27 Mar 1927, Pine Grove Mills PA).

CS1814111 Cathy J Kersteter (b 13 Feb 1948, Bellefonte PA).

CS1814112 Michael A Kersteter (b 26 Nov 1951, Bellefonte PA).

CS1814113 Steven H Kersteter (b 10 Sep 1954, Bellefonte PA).

CS181412 Winona Ellen Kersteter (b 13 Oct 1934, Philipsburg PA) m 9 Sep 1956, Daniel Kent Fellows (b 17 Mar 1933).

CS18142 Mary Bottorf (4 Oct 1901, Lemont PA-31 Aug 1964) m 10 Jul 1923, Bellefonte PA, Guy Stearns (b 20 Jun 1899, Garden Grove IA).

CS181421 Dan W Stearns (b 20 Oct 1927, Lemont PA) m 5 Jun 1948, Bellefonte PA, Anna Hassinger (b 15 Sep 1927, Oak Hall PA).

CS1814211 Dianne Marie Stearns (b 19 Sep 1950, Bellefonte PA).

CS1814212 Dan T Stearns (b 1 Oct 1951, Bellefonte PA).

CS18143 Charles Irwin Bottorf (b 9 Jan 1911, Lemont PA) m 5 Sep 1936, Rhoda Swaim.

CS18144 Fred Bottorf (d Sep 1926) m Mary Miller. No chn.

CS18145 Frances Bottorf m Barnegatt NJ, William Engelsen.

CS181451 John Engelsen.

CS182 Susanna Wagner (1842-1919) and husband Adam Yeager Wagner (1843-1926)

CS18146   Mildred Bottorf m State College PA, William Driebelbis.

CS1815   Sarah Weiser Hess (27 Apr 1871, Shingletown PA-29 Dec 1950, Bellfonte PA) m 17 Oct 1900, Harvey Pierce Schaeffer (3 Mar 1868-23 Aug 1941, Bellefonte PA) Bur Bellefonte PA.

CS18151   Larue Hess Schaeffer (b 3 May 1909, Bellefonte PA) m 31 Aug 1937, Bellefonte PA, Albert W Gilmer (b 14 Mar 1910, Philadelphia PA).

CS181511   Susan Sarah Gilmer (19 May 1940, Abington PA-30 Jul 1982, Epping NH) m 30 Jun 1962, Chestnut Hill, Philadelphia PA, Richard Arthur Bradbury (b 2 Oct 1937, Charlotte NC).

CS1815111   Bruce Chapman Bradbury (b 27 Dec 1969, Concord NH) unm BA, U NH, 1995.

CS1815112   James Arthur Bradbury (b 16 Aug 1972, Champaign IL) unm BS, CO Col, 1995.

CS181512   William Schaeffer Gilmer (b 11 Nov 1945, Germantown PA) m 17 Sep 1985, Holderness NH, Mary Kienzle (b 7 Oct 1958, Daylestown PA).

CS1815121   Sarah Susan Gilmer (b 11 Jul 1986, Concord NH).

CS1816   Samuel Moser Hess (2 Oct 1876-9 Apr 1884).

CS1817   John Wagner Hess (b 26 Sep 1878).

CS182   Susanna Wagner (27 Jan 1842, Harris Tp, PA-7 Nov 1919, Bellefonte PA) m 25 Dec 1866, Adam Yeager Wagner (7 Mar 1843, Lebanon Co PA-2 May 1926, Bellefonte PA) Bur Bellefonte PA.

CS1821   Sabrina Sarah Wagner (27 Jul 1867, Rock Mills PA-27 Dec 1950, Lemont PA) m 21 Mar 1894, Boalsburg PA, Daniel Fye Houser (25 Dec 1867, Houserville PA-29 May 1944, Bellefonte PA) Bur Bellefonte PA.

CS18211   Paul Wagner Houser (b 5 Dec 1898, Rock Forge PA) m 21 Feb 1924, Lemont PA, Sarah Lenker (b 3 Jul 1901, Lemont PA).

CS182111   James Daniel Houser (b 19 Oct 1938, Bellefonte PA).

CS1822   John Wagner (7 Dec 1869-27 Dec 1869) Bur Centre Co PA.

CS1823   Curtis Yeager Wagner (12 Jan 1871, Rock Forge PA-2 Mar 1963, Bellefonte PA) m 9 Sep 1898, Pine Glenn PA, Margaret Beates (12 Dec 1868, Pine Glenn PA-3 Dec 1958, Bellefonte PA) Bur Bellefonte PA.

CS18231   Joseph Beates Wagner (11 Jul 1898, Bellefonte PA-1 Jun 1957, Philadelphia PA) m 21 Aug 1938, Bellefonte PA, Eleanor Schenk (26 Oct 1914, Bellefonte PA-1995, Bellefonte PA) Bur Bellefonte PA.

CS182311   Sarah Ellen Wagner (b 18 Jul 1947, Bellefonte PA) m Michael Alterio.

CS1823111   Kelly Alterio.

CS1823112   Michael Alterio.

CS182312   Susanna Wagner (b 1 Mar 1952, Bellefonte PA) m Lawrence Greenfield, div.

CS18232   Mildred Sarah Wagner (19 Aug 1901, Bellefonte PA-12 Sep 1971, Chattanooga TN) m 1) 25 Jun 1924, Bellefonte PA, Elliot Lyon Morris (Macon GA-3 Sep 1932, Searcy AR); m 2) 19 Oct 1934, New York NY, Delmas Kitchen.

CS182321   Barbara Morris (b 23 Apr 1925, Macon GA) Res. Franklin NC.

CS182322   Elliot Morris Jr (4 Aug 1926, Macon GA-23 May 1945, Phillippines) WWII: USA, Phillippines.

CS18233   Charles Harmon Wagner (16 Feb 1903, Bellefonte PA-2 Jun 1980, Mingoville PA) m 1) 21 Aug 1924, Snow Shoe PA, Fay Etta Kisling (2 Sep 1905, Snow Shoe PA-19 Aug 1978, Bellfonte PA) Mingoville PA, div; m 2) 1 Jun 1955, Newark NJ, Pauline Carner (12 Jan 1910, Walker Tp, PA-10 Jun 1990, State College PA).

CS182331   Nancy Jane Kisling Wagner (23 Aug 1925, Bellefonte PA-27 Mar 1977, Bellefonte PA) m 22 May 1944, Jonesboro AR, Robert Edgar Francis (27 Sep 1923-10 Dec 1985, Pocateelo ID) Bur Zion PA.

CS1823311   William Delbert Francis (b 9 Sep 1945, Bellefonte PA) unm Reporter.

CS1823312   Nancy Cheryl Francis (b 6 Jan 1949, Bellefonte PA) m 1) 10 Feb 1968, Bellefonte PA, Richard Chester Croyle (b 8 Feb 1943, Hollidaysburg PA) div; m 2) 21 Aug 1982, York PA, Lawrence Stultz (b 31 Dec 1945, Altoona PA) Communications.

CS18233121   James Ross Croyle (b 18 Nov 1968, Bellefonte PA) Manager.

CS18233122   Michael Bradley Croyle (b 1 Dec 1972, Bellefonte PA) m 23 Jan 1993, Fayetteville NC,

Pamela Ann Bradley (b 18 Sep 1975, Fayetteville NC) USA.

CS182331221   Jacob Lee Alan Croyle (b 15 Jul 1995, Fayetteville NC).

*CS1823313   Elizabeth Ann Francis (b 23 Dec 1959, Bellefonte PA) m 23 Jun 1984, Bellefonte PA, Michael Joseph Carey (b 18 Jun 1954, Boise ID) USN, Cdr.

CS18233131   Joanne Elizabeth Carey (b 30 Mar 1989, Portsmouth VA).

CS182332   Margaret Ann Wagner (b 17 Jan 1927, Bellefonte PA) m 1) 2 Dec 1944, Bellefonte PA, Thomas Davis (b 1927, Corry PA) div; m 2) 31 May 1952, Bellefonte PA, Donald Levan Seiler (b 21 Nov 1925, Harrisburg PA) York PA.

CS1823321   Thomas Niles Davis Seiler (b 14 Mar 1945, Bellefonte PA) m 17 Apr 1971, State College PA, Pamela Irvin, div. Manager, Seiler Facilities services, PSU.

CS1823322   Curtis Wagner Davis Seiler (b 23 Apr 1946, Bellefonte PA) m 24 Dec 1966, Mechanicsburg PA, Marjorie Burlison (b 19 Aug 1948, Mechanicsburg PA) USA, Lt Col; banker, Chattanooga TN.

CS18233221   James Curtis Seiler (b 11 Oct 1968, Fort Jackson SC) m 18 Jan 1991, Chattanooga TN, Susan Elizabeth Johnson (b 24 Jul 1966, Signal Mountain TN).

CS18233222   Kate Seiler (b 6 Sep 1970, Fort Knox KY) m 23 Jul 1994, Chattanooga TN, Michael P Foster.

CS1823323   Clarise Ann Seiler (b 25 Dec 1952) m 11 Sep 1971, Mechanicsburg PA, Michael Garrett (b 13 Jul 1952, Harrisburg PA).

CS18233231   Christopher Michael Garrett (b 18 Jan 1972, Mechanicsburg PA) m 22 Dec 1994, Schuylkill Haven PA, Lucinda L Phillips. USAF.

CS182332311   Dylon Mitchell Garrett (b 15 Aug 1995, Honolulu HI).

CS18233232   Maggi Anne Garrett (b 25 Nov 1974, Mechanicsburg PA).

CS18233233   Geoffrey Craig Garrett (b 25 May 1980, Harrisburg PA).

CS182333   Charles Curtis Wagner (b 8 Feb 1930, Bellefonte PA) m 22 Aug 1953, Mingoville PA, Elizabeth Anne Walker (b 13 Apr 1930, Bellefonte PA) Mongoville PA. USA, 1948-52. (Forestry) PSU, 1958; BS (Zoology) PSU, 1960; MS (Zoology) PSU, 1962. She, BA, Bucknell U, 1952. Fisheries biologist, PSU.

*CS1823331   Ivan Walker Wagner (b 29 Jan 1955, Bellefonte PA) m 18 Dec 1976, Benner Tp, Centre Co PA, Cindy Jean Milton (b 24 Apr 1954, Bellefonte PA) He, BS, PSU, 1977; MBA Vanderbilt U, 1986. Director of human resources, Truckstops of America.

CS18233311   Zachary John Wagner (b 18 Sep 1980, Merrillville IN).

CS18233312   Sean Adam Wagner (b 9 Jul 1986, Westlake OH).

*CS1823332   Eric Hicklen Wagner (b 25 Jan 1959, Bellefonte PA) m 13 Aug 1983, Bellefonte PA, Susan Lyn Sheckler (b 4 Mar 1963, Bellefonte PA) USAF. Advanced engineering aide, Mingoville PA.

CS18233321   Amanda Elizabeth Wagner (b 3 May 1987, State College PA).

CS18233322   Rebecca Lynn Wagner (b 25 May 1989, State College PA).

CS18233323   John Kurtis Wagner (b 20 Dec 1990, State College PA).

CS182334   William George Wagner (b 25 Jul 1935, Bellefonte PA) m 15 Jun 1957, Lockport NY, Barbara Lee McCarthy (b 5 Feb 1937).

CS1823341   Molly Lee Wagner (b 5 Jul 1959, Buffalo NY) m Eric Heller.

CS18233411   Erica Lee Heller-Wagner (b 10 Feb 1988, Buffalo NY).

CS18233412   Rachel Colleen Heller-Wagner (b 10 Aug 1990, Australia).

CS18233413   Gideon Jack Heller-Wagner (b 20 Mar 1992, Australia).

CS1823342   Carrie Margaret Wagner (b 9 Dec 1962, Buffalo NY) m 6 Aug 1983, Buffalo NY, Michael Wopperer, div.

CS18233421   Michael Jay Wopperer (b 23 Aug 1984, Buffalo NY).

CS18233422   Cheri Lisa Wopperer (b 7 May 1986, Buffalo NY).

CS18233423   Evan William Wopperer (b 29 Jul 1988, Buffalo NY).

CS182335   Susan Faye Wagner (b 14 Jul 1936, Bellefonte PA) m 15 Oct 1955, Bellefonte PA, Michael Edward Riglin (b 30 Aug 1934 Bellefonte PA) div; m 2) Edwin Dull, div. Bellefonte PA.

CS1823351   Margaret Anne Wagner Riglin (b 26 Apr 1956, Bellefonte PA) m 6 Sep 1975, John Osborne.

CS18233511   Rynne Megan Osborne (b 4 Aug 1977, Nasawatix VA).

CS18233512   Nicole Marie Vasco (b 7 Mar 1983, Harrisburg PA).

CS1823352   George Michael Riglin (b 26 Jun 1958, Bellefonte PA).

CS1823353   Nancy Jane Dull (b 9 Aug 1963, Bellefonte PA) m 14 Sep 1991, State College PA, Michael John Thorn, div.

CS1823354   Daniel Howard Dull (b 12 Apr 1965, Central City PA).

*CS18234   Anna Elizabeth Wagner (b 26 Oct 1905, Bellefonte PA) m 28 Aug 1930, Gettysburg PA, Mahlon Keister Robb (15 Jul 1906, Bellefonte PA-1994, Bellefonte PA).

*CS182341   Elizabeth Anne Robb (b 27 Jun 1931, Plainfield NJ) m 6 Sep 1952, Bellefonte PA, Marlin Ardell Miller (b 20 Aug 1930, Geistown PA) He, dentist, Chambersburg PA.

*CS1823411   Kathi Anne Miller (b 5 Jul 1953, Sault St Marie MI) m 12 Apr 1975, Chambersburg PA, Walter Calvin Bietsch III (b 17 Oct 1951, Chambersburg PA) She, Master of Education, Shippensburg (PA) U, 1974. Employment educator. He, US Army School of Engineering and Logistics, 1987. Employment Dept of Defense.

CS18234111   Timothy Miller Bietsch (b 29 Jul 1979, Chambersburg PA).

CS18234112   Matthew William Bietsch (b 12 Dec 1982, Chambersburg PA).

CS18234113   Philip Michael Bietsch (b 28 May 1985, Chambersburg PA).

*CS1823412   Michael Kevin Miller (b 2 Sep 1955, Philadelphia PA) m 31 Dec 1977, Chambersburg PA, Karen Lynn Lehman (b 27 Feb 1957, Chambersburg PA) He, Union Theological Seminary VA, 1995. She BS Medical Technology, Shippensburg (PA) U, 1979. Medical Technologist.

CS18234121   Jessica Lynn Miller (b 6 Aug 1982, Chambersburg PA).

CS18234122   Curtis Michael Miller (b 7 Dec 1984, Chambersburg PA).

*CS1823413   Richard Robb Miller (b 5 Sep 1957, Chambersburg PA) m 18 Jun 1983, Chambersburg PA, Sonya Kay Reese (b 13 Mar 1960, Chambersburg PA) He, Master of Safety Science, Indiana (PA) U, 1989. Industrial Hygenist. She, BA, Education in Special Education, Slippery Rock (PA) S Col, 1982; homemaker.

CS18234131   Joshua Robb Miller (b 3 Oct 1986, Harrisburg PA).

CS18234132   Benjamin Richard Miller (b 26 Nov 1988, Harrisburg PA).

CS18234133   Laura Anne Miller (b 30 Oct 1991, Harrisburg PA).

*CS1823414   Krista Suzanne Miller (b 21 Jul 1962, Chambersburg PA) m 2 Jun 1984, Chambersburg PA, Alan Paul Hain Jr (b 4 Aug 1962, Harrisburg PA) She, BA, Education in Library Science, Millersville (PA) U, 1984; homemaker. He, BS, Engineering Science, PSU, 1984. High School Math and Science teacher.

CS18234141   Stephen Alan Hain (b 16 Jan 1988, Rome NY).

CS18234142   Aaron Michael Hain (b 3 Oct 1990, Concord MA).

*CS1823415   Susan Gramling Weiser Miller (b 30 Oct 1964, Chambersburg PA) m 27 Nov 1993, Chambersburg PA, Michael Allen Stahl (b 20 Aug 1965, Waynesboro PA) She, BA, Education in Special Education, Slippery Rock (PA) U, 1986. Lincoln Intermediate Unit # 12 Secondary Special Education. He, Brake operator, Grove World Wide.

CS18235   George Adam Wagner (24 Sep 1912, Bellefonte PA-2 May 1975, Bellefonte PA) unm USAF. Bur Bellefonte PA.

CS1824   Harry Adam Wagner (30 Oct 1873, Rock Forge PA-1 Mar 1942, Boalsburg PA) m 25 Dec 1895, Minnie A Peters (b 11 Jul 1876, Pine Grove Mills PA) Bur Boalsburg PA.

CS18241   Ernest A Wagner (b 20 Jan 1897, near Bellefonte PA) m 17 Oct 1916, Marie Haupt. Railroad yard master, Cleveland OH.

CS182411   Harold E Wagner (b 25 Jun 1916, Bellefonte PA).

CS1824111   Robert Wagner (b 1950).

CS182412   Donald A Wagner (b 23 Sep 1920, Bellefonte PA).

CS18242   Frederick E Wagner (b 24 Dec 1899, Roopsburg PA) m 2 Nov 1928, Margery W Wright (b 17 Jun 1907, Atlanta GA).

CS182421   Dudley W Wagner (b 22 Feb 1930, South Pasadena CA).

CS182422   Grethen Susanna Wagner (b 23 Dec 1940, South Pasadena CA).

CS18243   Harold E Wagner (b 27 Jun 1902, Oak Hall Station PA) m. Hotel desk clerk, Allentown PA.

CS182431   Donna Wagner (b 22 Dec 1943).

CS182432   Harold Edward Wagner (b 18 Jun 1947).

CS18244   Nellie E Wagner (b 11 Apr 1904) m William E Sheldon. Personnel representative, Jersey Central Power and Light Co, Ashbury Park NJ.

CS18245   John A Wagner (18 Aug 1907, Oak Hall Station PA-Jun 1972, Bethlehem PA) m Carrie Walker. Steelworker, Bethlehem PA.

CS18246   Mary Susanna Wagner (b 3 Oct 1914, Oak Hall Station PA) m George A Northridge. Coast Sales Division Manager, Jersey Central Power and Light Co.

CS182461   Nancy Sue Northridge (b 15 Jul 1946, Neptune NJ).

CS1825   Emma Caroline Wagner (28 Jun 1876, Rock Forge PA-1965) m 27 Mar 1901, Bellefonte PA, George H Hazel (6 Aug 1872, Madisonburg PA-8 Jan 1962, Bellefonte PA) Bur Bellefonte PA.

CS18251   Thelma Susanne Hazel (12 Nov 1902, Bellefonte PA-10 Dec 1982, Bellefonte PA) m 16 Jun 1925, Bellefonte PA, William H Kline (b 8 Jul 1903, Bellefonte PA) Bur State College PA.

CS182511   Beverly Jane Kline (b 31 May 1926, Bellefonte PA) m 29 Nov 1951, Bellefonte PA, Francis E Cressley (b 19 Sep 1920, Kersey PA).

CS18252   Frances Helen Hazel (b 15 Sep 1913, Bellefonte PA) m 8 Jun 1936, York PA, Earl O Heverly (b 2 Nov 1913, Pittsburgh PA) Kenmore NY.

CS182521   James George Heverly (b 18 Feb 1948, Bellefonte PA).

CS1826   Nellie Nora Wagner (8 Dec 1878, Rock Forge PA-31 Aug 1883, Rock Forge PA) Bur State College PA.

CS1827   Bertha Wagner (24 Feb 1881, Rock Forge PA-15 Jun 1954, Bellefonte PA) m 29 Mar 1905, Bellefonte PA, Maurice Brachbill Runkle (2 Mar 1879-1966) Bur Bellefonte PA.

CS18271   Dorothy Wagner Runkle (b 12 Jun 1913, Lancaster PA) m 20 Jun 1933, Bellefonte PA, John Martin Montgomery (b 30 Aug 1908).

CS182711   Richard Martin Montgomery (b 26 Sep 1936) m 7 Apr 1957, Bellefonte PA, Ida Marie Derardis (b 13 Jul 1935).

CS1827111   Karen Lynn Montgomery (b 17 Nov 1957, Bellefonte PA).

CS182712   Dennis Michael Montgomery (b 10 Apr 1944) m Susan Wilkinson, div. Bellefonte PA.

CS182713   Thomas John Montgomery (b 21 May 1945).

CS184   John Calhoun Wagner m 1) Otilda Pickard; m 2).

CS1841   Mildred Estella Wagner (24 Aug 1877, Osage, Mitchell Co IA-12 Apr 1902, Bellefonte PA).

CS1842   Luella Wagner (b Freeport IL) m Howard Brutaker. No chn.

CS1843   John Pickard Wagner (Mar 1880, IA-Altoona PA) m 11 Mar 1903, Gertrude Meyers. No chn.

CS2   Maria Margaretha Weiser was probably born in Reading in the 1760s or early 1770s. About 1795 she married Jacob Feather, son of Peter and Maria Feather (sometimes Fedder) of Reading (he was born 1725 and died in 1801), members of the Reformed Church in Reading. Peter and Margaret lived on the farm her father left them, the part south of the Mahonoy Creek until 1807 when they sold it. They moved to New Berlin, across the river in what is now Union County, where Jacob bought a lot 29 Jun 1807 which he sold in 1808. He was living there in 1810. In 1810 he sold a claim due him which may suggest that he was leaving the area.[121] They probably had children, but nothing further has come to light.

----

[121]See Northumberland Co deeds X-452, O-304. Northumberland Co court records 179 Aug 1810. 31.

CHAPTER FOUR G

[CB] Benjamin Weiser (1744-   )

Benjamin Weiser was the youngest son of Conrad and Anna Eva (Feg) Weiser. He was born on the Weiser farm in Heidelberg Tp, Berks Co PA, on 12 Aug 1744.

He was a boy of 15 when his father died. He continued to live with his mother, although he also spent time in "Shamokin," the designation for the area around Sunbury. For instance, Henry Melchior Muhlenberg had to write him there in 1780 admonishing him and his brother Samuel (nine years his elder, but the next oldest sibling in the family who survived) to take better care of their mother. When she died 11 Jun 1781, Benjamin wrote to the Muhlenbergs to inform them, so that he must have been in Womelsdorf at the time.

When Frederick Muhlenberg conducted services on the Isle of Que in 1771, he reported that he visited Benjamin Weiser and "took a look at the larger portion of the Weiser land," as yet undivided. Benjamin was likely his guide; he was about six years older than Frederick.

When the acreage the senior Conrad received from the colony for his services was divided in 1773, Benjamin received 236 acres on the Isle of Que near Selinsgrove. He apparently lived there in a log cabin that stood into this century. The original of his bond to guarantee Jacob Fisher (who purchased the Muhlenbergs' share, the southernmost of the Isle of Que) a road of access, dated 27 Nov 1773, is in the collection of the Weiser Family Association.

Benjamin Weiser was a captain in the German Continental Regiment during the revolution from 8 July 1776, but was cashiered, apparently for misconduct, 31 Oct 1776 at Montressor's Island. Later he was a captain in the Northumberland County militia, 30 Jan 1777, at Philadelphia. He was a justice of the peace in 1772 and 1778.

Benjamin could not retain his land inheritance. He took out a mortgage 27 Dec 1774 using the land as collateral. The mortgage was satisfied on 17 Feb 1777, but on the same date he took out a new, larger mortgage for which no satisfaction is on file. There are a number of suits filed against him from 1775 through 1787. Most involved money he owed and various horses were levied upon and probably sold to satisfy the debt. Ultimately the entire tract was sold at sheriff's sale on 1 Mar 1787 to Adam Fisher, since Benjamin had no more goods to levy on. The writ does name certain pieces of personal property which are crossed off and replaced by "a tract of land where he lives" or perhaps "lived" - the original document is stained. Three suits from the year before also involve a George Troutner who seems to have been served the papers. The last suit, field Feb 1787, was by Ann Emilia Weiser and Daniel Levan, executors of Benjamin's brother Frederick. However the sheriff's return is endorsed "Nihil," meaning that Benjamin was gone and there was nothing left to attach. In 1791 the Weiser plaintiffs moved to set aside the sheriff's sale as the rest of the purchase price was not paid. Since there is no further reference, Fisher must have completed payments.

When Conrad Weiser's heirs sold the "Spring Tract" in Snyder County, Benjamin and wife Catherine sold his interest, too, to Christopher Gettig, Esq., on 5 Nov 1779. The witnesses to Benjamin's and Catherine's signatures 21 Dec 1784 were two separate sets of persons, suggesting that they had not appeared together. This is the only reference found to Benjamin's wife; either she died presently or they separated. They apparently had no children.

C.Z. Weiser cites a letter Benjamin wrote Simon Snyder on 2 Apr 1788 about recovering his father's possessions in New York. The last reference to any member of the Weiser family in the journals of Henry Melchior Muhlenberg is about Benjamin, dated 6 Aug 1787, two months before Muhlenberg's death:

Visit from my wife's brother, Benjamin Weiser, who is journeying to New York. He had a midday meal with me and took along my letter for the Rev. Dr. Kunze. He desired my signature and that of my wife for a document by means of which he hopes to find some additional land which the former government of New York promised to his father, Conrad Weiser, for his services among the Indians.

He will probably make his efforts in vain. It is like the dog in the fable who snapped at the shadow, etc. and lost the substance.

In a memo written 14 Dec 1840, Catharine Weiser McConnell, the last of Conrad Weiser's grandchildren, listed Conrad's children's names and wrote "has children" next to each except Benjamin. Later she added, "as from (sic) Benj. Weiser he left Pennsylvania this fifty years ago. I do not know if he has children or not. I have not heard of him since he left."[122]

---

[122]See Northumberland County deeds A-117, B-106, B-109, D-283. *Journals of Henry Melchior Muhlenberg*, III, 750. C.Z. Weiser, *The Life of (John) Conrad Weiser, the German Pioneer, Patriot, and Patron of Two Races* (Reading PA, 1876), 109-110. Ralph H. Schwalm combed Northumberland County court and deed records in order to provide more details about Benjamin's life.

CHAPTER FIVE

[MD] Anna Magdalena Weiser DeLong
and her descendants

Anna Magdalena Weiser, daughter of John Conrad and Anna Magdalena (Uebele) Weiser, was born about 1690-92, perhaps at Grossaspach or perhaps at some site associated with her father's military career. She emigrated with her father in 1709-10. She married 29 Sep 1712 at Kingston, New York, to Jan (or John) De Lang (also DeLong, Langen, or Langet). The marriage took place at a Dutch Reformed church and is recored in the register of the Poughkeepsie congregation, whose transcription cites her name as "Kyser." However, examination of the original showed that it is "Wyser." Jan DeLong moved from Ulster county (where he was born at Rochester) between 1713 and 1720 to Dutchess county. They may have moved to Grune County where a Jan and Magdalena were sponsors in 1763. He is taxed in Dutchess County, Rombout-Poughkeepsie, 1718-38, but the absence of his name thereafter is not clear evidence that he had left. He was overseer of the King's Highway, 2 April 1723. There are other scattered references to him and to her, but there is no clear record of their deaths that has been so far discovered. There is undisputed record of the birth and baptism of five children and five more are assumed to be their children on the basis of a study of all DeLongs along the Hudson completed some years ago by John D. Baldwin of Cleveland, Ohio. The fact that their children appear in Dutch Reformed and German Lutheran records suggests that her heritage played a role in their family life.

MD1   Arie DeLong (bp 1 Jan 1713, Kingston) m May 1737, Margareta Vlegelar

MD2   Gertrude DeLong (probably a Gertrude born ca 1714-15, Kingston) m 2 Feb 1733 to Isaac Wieler

MD21   Elizabeth Wieler (bp 11 Nov 1733)

MD3   Frans DeLong (probably a Franz born ca 1716-17) m by 1742, Catherina Dymant; perhaps m 2) Hannah Carley. He may be the Frans DeLong who shows up in the 1750s in Monroe Co PA.

MD31   John DeLong (bp 19 Sep 1742, Fishkill NY) m Rachel   . US Revolutionary War

MD32   Maria DeLong (bp 9 Jan 1744, St. Matthew's Lutheran Chruch, New York NY)

MD33   Benjamin DeLong (out of wedlock by Hannah Carley) (bp 1 Dec 1763, Smithfield PA)

MD34   Sarah DeLong (out of wedlock by Hannah Carley) (bp 1 Dec 1763, Smithfield PA)

MD35   Arie DeLong (After marriage to Hannah Carley) (bp 1 Dec 1763, Smithfield PA). US Revolutionary War.

MD4   Christina Magdalena DeLong (8 Apr 1718; bp 21 Jun 1718, St. Matthew's Lutheran Church, New York NY). A Leena DeLong m 31 May 1738 at Fishkill NY to Thoms Ceerber of Staten Island. The best evidence for this marriage being hers is that she was living at Poquajeck=Poughquag, a hamlet in the Beekman precinct, while her father worked nearby.

MD5   Jacobas DeLong (bp 12 Oct 1720, Poughkeepsie NY) probably m 1) Catherine   ; m 2) Elizabeth

MD6   Rachel DeLong (b Mar; baptized Nov 1722, St. Matthew's Lutheran Chruch, New York NY) probably m 9 Jan 1740, Fishkill, William Tanner (d 1786, Beekman NY)

MD61   Anna Magdalena Tanner (b 6 May 1742, Pacquesien NY)

MD62   William Tanner

MD63   Reuben Tanner

MD64   Samuel Tanner (1761-1823)

MD65   James Tanner

MD66   Hannah Tanner m   Thompson

MD67   Martha Tanner m   Thomas

MD68   Margaret Tanner m   Radel

MD69   Maribe Tanner m   Thompson

MD6A   Rachel Tanner m   McIntosh

MD7   Conrad DeLong (b ca 1723-24) m 18 Sep 1743, Catherine Freeling. Probably named for his grandfather.

MD71   Hendrick DeLong (14 oct 1765, Dutchess Co NY-Prince Edward, Ont, CAN) m Margaret Gosline/Joslin (ca Apr 1769-Little Nine Partners RI).

MD711   Hendrick/Henry DeLong (29 Nov 1803-1873, Prince Edward, Ontario Canada) m Mary Wanamaker (1799/1800-17 Jun 1836 or 1844, Ont CAN)

MD7111   Thurston DeLong (18 Feb 1835, Prince Edward, Ont CAN-28 Feb 1915, Staples MN) m 15 Feb 1857, Sauk Rapids MN, Sarah Cronk (6 Jul 1840, Prince Edward, Ontario Canada-16 Jan 1889, Benton MN)

MD71111   George DeLong (29 Dec 1865-14 Dec 1921, Benton MN) m 13 Nov 1890, Benton MN, Nellie M. Raber (16 Nov 1873, Jakesville MN-22 Mar 1960, Monticello MN)

MD711111   William Edward DeLong (13 Sep 1891, Benton Co MN-21 Dec 1960, St. Cloud MN) m 22 Mar 1916, Anna Mae Miller (16 Jul 1886, Stockton KS-6 Feb 1976, Grove Heights MN)

MD7111111   Gustie Isabel DeLong (b 22 or 30 Jun 1917, Morrill MN) m 4 Mar 1937, St. Paul MN, Richard Russell Edwards (17 Jun 1916, Des Moines IA-30 Aug 1974, St. Paul MN).

MD71111111   Herbert William Edwards (b 28 Jul 1943, St. Paul MN) m 2 June 1962, Janet Kay Engel (b 3 Dec 1946, St. Paul MN)

MD8   Maria DeLong (bp 1 or 11 Jun 1725, Poughkeepsie NY) Probably the mother of:

MD81   Martinus (out of wedlock to Martinus Osterle) (b 15 Feb 1743)

MD9   Catherine DeLong (27 Apr 1727; bp at St. Matthew's Lutheran Church, New York NY). Perhaps the Catherine who m Quirenius Light.

MDA   Johannes DeLong, (bp 16 Sep 1730, St. Matthew's Lutheran Church, New York NY)

CHAPTER SIX

[GF] George Frederick Weiser (ca 1697-1764)
and his descendants

Georg Frederick Weiser[123] was born about 1697[124] and emigrated with his father and family to New York in 1710. Faced with a large number of children to his deceased first wife, the senior Conrad (Georg Frederick's father) arranged for him to be apprenticed to Samuel Smith of Smithtown on Long Island. He thereby lost all contact with his father's family. He rapidly assimilated into Anglo-American life, became known as George, and settled at Winnecommack, now Commack, at the junction of Huntington, Smithtown and Islip in Suffolk Co NY.

George married first to a daughter, given name unknown, of Timothy Scudder, who presently died. He married second, 31 Dec 1729, Rebecca Udall, daughter of Joseph Udall of Huntington. George wrote his will 14 Mar 1763 and was dead when it was probated 7 Jun 1764. George Weiser became a member of the Anglican (later Episcopalian) Church and was a member of St. John's parish in Huntington. His widow apparently later married Timothy Scudder, father of Rebecca Weiser Scudder's husband Timothy. His known children are listed below.

Children of George Frederick Weiser:

GF1   Prudence Weiser, Oct 1723

GF2   Rebecca Weiser

GF3   George Weiser, bp 31 Dec 1752

GF1   Prudence Weiser (Oct 1723-5 Sep 1803, Dicks Mills, Huntington NY) m 23 Nov 1742, Huntington NY, Daniel Blachly (Blatchley) (ca 1721-25 Oct 1781). Bur Elwood, Huntington NY. She was baptized 11 Sep 1764 as an adult at First Church, Huntington, along with the first eleven of her children.

GF11   Sarah Blachly (ca 1746-27 Apr 1815, Winnecommack NY) m 1) 17 May 1764, Smithtown NY, Samuel Smith (d shortly thereafter); m 2) 3 Feb 1774, Moses Wickes. Bur Wickes Cemetery.

GF111   Elthanan Wickes

GF112   Joshua Wickes (3 Jun 1780-7 May 1846, Bay Shore NY) m 18 Jul 1802, Experience Haff
(see GF191)

GF113   Miriam Wickes m   Totten

GF114   Sarah Wickes. No chn.

GF115   Elizabeth Wickes. No chn.

GF12   Mary Blachly m 13 Feb 1767, James Hubbs. Descendants on Long Island.

GF13   Benjamin Blachly (d 29 Jul 1823, Winnecommack NY) m 23 Mar 1774, Smithtown NY, Sarah Wheeler. Bur Commack NY. Ensign, US Revolution, fled to Norwalk CT.

---

[123]See Herbert F. Smith, "The Connections of Prudence Weiser," *National Genealogical Society Quarterly*, XXV (1937), pp 36-44. Cf. will of George Weiser, Suffolk Co NY, 1764, and will of Rebecca Scudder, same, 1796. The Weiser Family Association has no contact with descendants of this family.

[124]The baptism of Georg Friedrich Weiser is not in the Grossaspach church register.

GF131   Carl Blachly

GF132   Susanna Blachly m 12 Nov 1815, Lewis Wickes

GF133   Experience Blachly m Daniel Haff (see GF194)

GF134   Mary Blachly m 8 Nov 1817, Joel Harned

GF135   Samuel Blachly m 10 Mar 1803, Freelove Carll, a widow.

GF136   Ebenezer Blachly m Nancy

GF137   Benjamin Blachly (d 22 Dec 1816, Commack NY)

GF138   Daniel Blachly, bp 1784

GF14   Daniel Blachly. Enlisted 7 Apr 1776 in Capt. Nathaniel Platt's (2nd) Company. Listed as sick and absent on Capt. Joshua Roger's Company and probably died unm shortly thereafter.

GF15   Ebenezer Blachly (d 1808) m 6 Jan 1782, Smithtown NY, Sarah Jarvis

GF151   Hannah Blachly m   Sandies

GF152   Jane Blachly

GF153   Prudence Blachly m   Saxton

GF154   Jemima Blachly m   Brown

GF155   Mary Blachly

GF156   Elizabeth Blachly m Jacob Pearsall

GF157   Sarah Blachly m Edward Bunce

GF158   Isaac Blachly

GF159   Henry Blachly (17 Jan 1802, Commack NY-17 May 1880) m 1822, Letty (Smith) Lewis. Descendants in NY.

GF15A   Israel Blachly. Unm.

GF16   Hannah Blachly (d 30 Jul 1784) m Alexander Rogers. Family not known.

GF17   Phoebe Blachly (probably dy)

GF18   Jemima Blachly m 12 Aug 1781, Huntington NY, Hubbard Ketcham. Had chn.

GF19   Freelove Blachly (b ca 1758-ca 9-12 Apr 1826) m James Haff. Bur Long Swamp, Huntington NY.

GF191   Experience Haff m Joshua Wickes (see GF112)

GF192   Polly Haff m 18 Jul 1802, Huntington NY, John Soper

GF193   Hannah Haff m 2 Jan 1806, Smithtown NY, Selah Wickes

GF194   Daniel Haff m Experience Blachly (see GF133)

GF195   Harriet Haff. In NY in 1818.

GF196   James Haff m Sarah   . Patchogue NY. Had chn.

GF1A   Rhoda Ann Blachly m Zachariah Rogers

GF1B   Jane Blachly m 16 Dec 1784, Charles Peters

GF1C   Moses Blachly m 5 Jan 1796, Huntington NY, Sarah Bryan

GF1D   Experience Blachly. Unm in 1781.

GF1E   Frances Blachly m John Wood

GF2   Rebecca Weiser (d 1796, Smithtown NY) m 19 Feb 1758, Huntingdon NY, Timothy
Scudder

GF21   Timothy Scudder

GF22   Sarah Scudder m Isaac Haff

GF23   Hannah Scudder m Thomas Higbie

GF24   Jerusha Scudder m Peter Ruland

GF25   Jemima Scudder m   Hudson

GF26   Rebecca Scudder

GF27   Elizabeth Scudder m   Weekes

GF28   Joel Scudder

GF3   George Weiser (bp 31 Dec 1752, Hampstead NY-ca 1779) m 2 Nov 1774, Hampstead NY,
Sarah Allen. She m 2) 27 Feb 1780, Smithtown NY, Thomas Robertson.

GF31   George Weiser m 5 Feb 1799, Smithtown NY, Marinda Bunce. With him the surname
apparently died out in this family.

GF32   Margaret Weiser

GF33   Rebecca Weiser (bp 25 Jan 1775, Huntington NY) m 5 Mar 1791, Lemuel Jarvis.

CHAPTER SEVEN

[RF] Christopher Frederick Weiser (1699-1768)
and his descendants

Christopher Frederick Weiser (son of John Conrad and Anna Magdalena (Uebele) Weiser) was born 24 Feb 1699 at Gross Aspach, in Wurttemberg, and emigrated to America with his father in 1710. In 1721 he married Elizabeth   (25 Dec 1702, 56564 Neuwied, Germany-29 Jul 1760, Heidelberg Tp, Berks Co PA). He was located in New Jersey at least by 1732, but in 1745 he was granted, as a gift, a farm in Tulpehocken Township by Caspar Wistar, a friend of Philadelphia. In 1746 Christopher joined the Moravian congregation in Heidelberg Township, Berks County, of which church he remained a member until his death. On 29 Jul 1762, he married Maria Catharine Roeder, widow of Johannes Knauss, born 24 Mar 1720 in 67112 Mutterstadt, Germany. In 1764 Christopher deeded his property to Jacob Weiser, his son, as he had moved to Emmaus, Pennsylvania, in 1762. He was a storekeeper at Emmaus and his second wife served as community midwife there for many years. Christopher died at Emmaus 16 Jun 1768, and is buried there.[125]

Children of Christopher Frederick and Elizabeth Weiser:

RF1   John Conrad Weiser (b 19 Sep 1725).

RF2   Margaret Weiser (28 Sep 1728-ca 1750).

RF3   Elizabeth Weiser (b 19 Apr 1730).

RF4   Maria Catharine Weiser (b 1732).

RF5   Christoph Weiser (18 Nov 1733-34, probably NJ-1754, Tulpehocken) unm Bu at Reed's
Church.

RF6   Jacob Weiser (b 22 Sep 1736).

RF7   Anna Weiser (b 5 Apr 1738) No further record.

RF8   Benjamin Weiser (b 8 Mar 1740).

RF9   Jabez Weiser (b 4 Aug 1742) No further record.

RFA   Georg Friedrich Weiser (b 22 May 1746) No further record.

---

[125]See records of the Moravian congregations at Tulpehocken and Emmaus.

CHAPTER SEVEN A

RF1 John Conrad Weiser (1725-1775)

John Conrad Weiser (son of Christopher Frederick and Elizabeth Weiser) was born 29 Sep 1725, and died in Sep 1775. He married 1) 29 Jan 1749, Maria Margaret Battorf (daughter of Martin and Maria Margaret Battorf) (10 Oct 1729-22 Dec 1772); m 2) 3 Feb 1774, Elizabeth Preiss. He was a farmer in Tulpehocken. His widow was appointed the guardian of her daughter Mary in Dec 1775. About the same time a petition was presented to the Orphans Court of Berks Co stating that he had died and left ten children: Martin, Catharine (wife of John Saltzgerber), Mary (wife of Henry Spycker), Christopher, John, Samuel, Eve, Elizabeth, Christina, and Mary. He was known as Johannes Weiser, perhaps to distinguish him from his uncle John Conrad, the Indian diplomat. He was an active member of Christ Lutheran Church and frequently an officer of the congregation and its delegate to Synod.[126]

Children of John Conrad and Maria Margaret (Battorf) Weiser:

RF11   Catharine Elizabeth Weiser (b 23 Jan 1759).

RF12   Martin Weiser (b 15 Oct 1751).

RF13   John Weiser (31 Mar 1754-dy).

RF14   Anna Maria Weiser (b 1 Apr 1754).

RF15   Christopher Weiser (b 9 Apr 1756).

RF16   Anna Eva Weiser (15 Sep 1758-dy).

RF17   Anna Eva Weiser (b 12 Feb 1761) No further record.

RF18   John Weiser (b 15 Dec 1762).

RF19   Samuel Weiser (b 16 May 1765).

RF1A   Elizabeth Weiser (b 6 Sep 1767).

RF1B   Christina Elizabeth Weiser (b 8 Jan 1770) No further record.

Children of John Conrad and Elizabeth (Preiss) Weiser:

RF1C   Mary Weiser (b Feb 1775) No further record.

RF11   Catharine Elizabeth Weiser (23 Jan 1750, Tulpehocken Tp, Berks Co PA-before 1783, probably Tulpehocken Tp, Berks Co PA) m 18 Jun 1771, Johannes Salzgeber (ca 15 Sep 1747-1 Apr 1829, probably Tulpehocken Tp. He married 2) as a widower, 25 Mar 1783, Maria Margreth Eisenmenger, single. Several children are recorded at Christ Lutheran Church to Johannes and Margreth, but none to him and Catharine Elizabeth.[127]

RF12   Martin Weiser (15 Oct 1751, Tulpehocken Tp, Berks Co PA-3 Nov 1822, York PA) m Maria Catharina (1754-20 Jul 1822, York PA) Martin's first two children were baptized at Christ Lutheran

---

[126]See records of Berks Co Orphans Court, 1773; registers of Christ Lutheran Church, Stouchsburg.

[127]See registers of Christ Lutheran Church, Stouchsburg PA.

Church, Stouchsburg. In 1780 he was taxed in Heidelberg Tp, Lancaster Co (now in Lebanon). He moved to York about 1783.[128]

RF121   John Henry Weiser (24 Feb 1775, probably Heidelberg Tp, Berks Co PA-York PA) m Florentine Klinefelter, widowed Roessler, (30 Jan 1770-6 Mar 1843, York PA) Henry is a resident of York on the 1800, possibly on the 1810 census for Dover Tp, York Co, and apparently not on the 1820 census at all. He is named as a living child in his father's will, by which he was given lifetime residence in part of a house and lot on Water Street, in York, providing he keep it in order and pay taxes on it. But upon his death, or if he did not comply with the terms, the property was to be sold and the proceeds divided among his children. This Martin Weiser's executors did. Since Henry subsequently died his share of Martin's estate went to his children who are named in the transaction. Probably buried at one of the cemeteries of Christ Lutheran Church, York.

RF1211   Maria Catharina Weiser (b 17 May 1796, York PA) m William Dobbin (Tobins).

RF12111   Anna Maria Dobbin (b 17 Oct 1825, York PA).

RF12112   Wilheim Henry Dobbin (b 2 Sep 1828, York PA).

RF12113   Samuel Dobbin (b 17 Feb 1831, York PA).

RF12114   Catharine Dobbin (b 21 Jan 1833, York PA).

RF1212   Samuel Weiser (7 Dec 1798, York PA-21 Jul 1867) m 22 Nov 1821, Cassandra Heckert (b York PA).

RF12121   Mary Weiser (b 24 Sep 1822, York PA) m 13 Oct 1844, Henry Deitch.

RF12122   Sarah Weiser (b 3 Nov 1824, York PA).

RF12123   Susan Weiser (b 9 Aug 1826, York PA) m 9 Mar 1854, John William Bowen.

RF12124   Elizabeth Weiser (b 17 Jun 1828, York PA)

RF12125   Lewis Weiser (b 27 Sep 1829, York PA).

RF12126   Levi Weiser (b 15 Dec 1830, York PA).

RF12127   Ellen Weiser (1 Jan 1832, York PA-8 Oct 1860) unm.

RF12128   Anna Weiser (12 Dec 1836-10 Jun 1864) unm.

RF12129   Albert Weiser (b 1839).

RF1212A   Emmaline Weiser (b 1842).

RF1213   Daniel Weiser (bp 11 Jun 1800, York PA-1836) m 1) Veronica   ; m 2) Maria   .

RF12131   Charles Weiser (12 May 1822-20 Sep 1899) m 1)   ; m 2) Mary Daron.

RF121311   m Frank Mann.

---

[128]Data on the descendants of Martin Weiser compiled from the registers of Christ Lutheran Church, York, PA; data at Historical Society of York County, PA; and material submitted by Isabel Scott Anderson, Elizabeth Anne Gluckert, Henry B. Leader, Gov. George M. Leader, William J. Weiser and Maria Weiser.

RF121312   Charles D Weiser (12 May 1859, Springettsburg Tp, York Co PA-31 Jan 1931) m 23 Nov 1865, Hallam Tp, York Co PA, Jane Agnes Fisher. Bur near Hallam PA.

RF1213121   Oliver David Weiser (b 6 Sep 1891, Hallam Tp, York Co PA) m 27 Nov 1919, Helen Joahan Luther (b 16 Dec 1895, Reading PA).

RF12131211   Betty Jane Weiser (b 11 Aug 1921, Philadelphia PA).

RF121313   Reuben Weiser.

RF121314   Agnes Weiser.

RF12132   Henry Weiser (15 Jan 1825, York PA-24 Aug 1887, Chaceford Tp, York Co PA) m Sarah A (nee Schmitt) Snodgrass (3 Sep 1828-11 Sep 1906) Bur Chanceford Tp, York Co PA, as are most of his children.

RF121321   Cassandra Ellen Weiser (27 May 1851-10 Mar 1910) m Henry Smeltzer. Bur Chanceford.

RF1213211   Bertha Smeltzer.

RF1213212   Charles Smeltzer.

RF1213213   Minnie Smeltzer.

RF1213214   James Smeltzer.

RF1213215   Ellen Smeltzer.

RF1213216   Harry Smeltzer.

RF1213217   Sallie Smeltzer.

RF1213218   Joe Smeltzer.

RF1213219   Ben Smeltzer.

RF121321A   Oliver Smeltzer.

RF121322   Mary Catherine Weiser (12 Nov 1852-22 Jan 1932) m Hiram Crone. Wrightsville PA.

RF1213221   Carrie Crone.

RF121323   Joseph Henry Weiser (6 Dec 1853-9 Sep 1855).

RF121324   Benjamin Franklin Weiser (27 Apr 1855-21 Jul 1855).

RF121325   Josephine Correanna Weiser (21 Sep 1856-8 Jun 1924) m George Sangrey.

RF1213251   Joseph Sangrey.

RF1213252   Lottie Sangrey m Ephie Snyder.

RF1213253   Carrie Sangrey m James Arnold.

RF1213254   Jennie Sangrey m Will Arnold.

RF1213255   Mary Sangrey.

RF121326   Elmira Jane Weiser (18 Jan 1858-9 May 1912) m   Tome.

RF1213261   Charles Tome.

RF1213262   Harry Tome.

RF1213263   Janie Tome.

RF121327   Daniel Wesley Weiser (17 Jan 1859-22 Jul 1859).

RF121328   Hannah Ann Weiser (10 Apr 1860-8 May 1860).

RF121329   Sarah Ann Weiser (2 Jul 1861-22 May 1870).

RF12132A   Henrietta Snodgrass Weiser (16 Oct 1862-14 Mar 1949) m Isaac Sample.

RF12132A1   Edith Sample m Clayton Snyder.

RF12132A11   Harold Snyder.

RF12132A2   Mary Sample m Enoch Smeltzer.

RF12132A21   Sterling Smeltzer.

RF12132B   Isabella Snodgrass Weiser (20 Dec 1863-23 May 1954) m James W Scott (15 Jul 1860-18 Feb 1936).

RF12132B1   Blanche Scott (1895-1922).

RF12132B2   Henry Oscar Scott (20 Apr 1899, Peach Bottom Tp, York Co PA-20 Feb 1989, York PA) m 19 Apr 1923, York PA, Cora Kraft Jones (14 Jan 1898, Spring Garden, York Co PA-9 Jun 1980, York PA) Bur York PA.

RF12132B21   Isabel Anne Scott (b 29 Jun 1925, York PA) m 26 Nov 1947, John Wallace Anderson (b 8 Apr 1924, Red Wing MN) He, Lutheran, then Orthodox pastor, missionary, seminary professor.

RF12132B211   Christina Anderson (b 19 Dec 1950) m 18 Apr 1970, Antoine Soueidi (b 28 Jul 1938).

RF12132B2111   Mark Soueidi (b 4 Apr 1972).

RF12132B2112   Elie Soueidi (b 3 Jun 1976).

RF12132B2113   Joseph Soueidi (b 4 Apr 1981).

RF12132B212   Eric Scott Anderson (b 17 Apr 1952) m 16 Sep 1972, Kathleen Brantner (b 22 Jan 1951).

RF12132B2121   Erica Anderson (b 20 Apr 1973).

RF12132B2122   Michael Anderson (b 1 Jan 1977).

RF12132B2123   Joshua Anderson (b 15 May 1980).

RF12132B213   John Mark Anderson (9 Sep 1953-27 Feb 1954).

RF12132B214   Per Seth Anderson (b 6 Dec 1954) m 5 Jun 1976, Renee Rosiek (b 12 Dec 1955).

RF12132B2141   Michelle Anderson (b 29 Aug 1978).

RF12132B2142   Christian Anderson (b 13 Aug 1981).

RF12132B2143   Stacy Anderson (b 21 Jun 1984).

RF12132B215   Sara Anderson (b 23 Sep 1956) m 11 Sep 1976, Galen Johnson (b 4 Feb 1955).

RF12132B2151   Benjamin Johnson (b 4 Mar 1978).

RF12132B2152   Forrest Johnson (b 26 Jan 1980).

RF12132B2153   Caleb Johnson (b 4 Jan 1982).

RF12132B216   Julia Anderson (12 Apr 1960-13 Apr 1960).

RF12132B217   Elizabeth Anderson (b 22 Jan 1966) m 18 Jul 1987, David Brewer (b 13 Jan 1960).

RF12132B2171   Julianna Brewer (b 15 Aug 1991).

RF12132B2172   Elysia Brewer (b 5 Apr 1994).

RF12132B218   Andrew Jesse Anderson (b 22 Jan 1966) m 12 May 1996, Karen Yared (b 10 Oct 1965).

RF12132C   Alexandria Snodgrass Weiser (20 Mar 1865-20 Aug 1965).

RF12132D   Ida Agnes Weiser (19 Aug 1866-23 Nov 1930) m Thomas Grove. Dallastown PA.

RF12132D1   Harry Grove (d 1917).

RF12132E   Hannah Elizabeth Weiser (11 Nov 1867-22 Jul 1968).

RF12132F   Willie Charles Weiser (31 Mar 1869-10 Aug 1902) m Maria B Kohler (b 1870) Bur
Chanceford Tp, York Co PA.

RF12132F1   Infant (b 19 Nov 1890).

RF12132G   John Edward Weiser (10 Apr 1871-10 Oct 1913) m Annie C Rikeard (2 Aug 1868-16 Oct
1944) Bur Chanceford Tp, York Co PA.

RF12132G1   Ethel E Weiser (b 31 Jan 1895) m Ernest O Moore (10 Dec 1894-26 Apr 1946) Bur
Chanceford Tp, York Co PA.

RF12132G11   Wilbur W Moore (b 16 Apr 1916) m Erma C Howard (b 15 Mar 1918).

RF12132G12   Shirley Maxine Moore (b 9 May 1939).

RF12132G2   Wilbur R Weiser (b 6 Feb 1903) m Reba M Craley (b 25 Sep 1911).

RF12132G21   Maxine Weiser (b 15 Oct 1931) m Edgar Leland Shade (b 6 Jun 1931).

RF12132G211   Dennis Lee Shade (b 9 Aug 1956).

RF12132G22   John Ernest Weiser (b 19 Sep 1932) m Fayne Elsesser (b 26 Apr 1933).

RF1214 Jonathan Weiser (b 16 Sep 1801, York PA) unm No chn.

RF1215 Maria Weiser (b 18 Oct 1802, York PA) unm No chn.

RF1216 Elizabeth Weiser (b 21 Jun 1805, York PA) m George Schiffner.

RF12161 Henry Schiffner (b ca 1840).

RF1217 Sarah Weiser m John Bonawitz.

RF1218 Anna Weiser (d 21 Aug 1845, Mt Joy PA) m John Lingafelter.

RF12181 Cassandra Lingafelter (b 9 May 1825, York PA).

RF12182 daughter (b 7 Feb 1840).

RF1219 Elizabeth Weiser (d 24 Jan 1842) m Joseph Neiman.

RF12191 Cassandra W Neiman (b 7 Jun 1826, York PA).

RF12192 Jacob Neiman (b 20 Mar 1829, York PA).

RF12193 Joseph Neiman (b 8 Mar 1831, York PA).

RF121A Cassandra Weiser (25 Feb 1812, York PA-17 Nov 1877, West Fairview PA) m 1 May 1838, Columbia PA, Thomas McClune (3 Mar 1814, Nantmeal PA-27 Jan 1882, York PA) Bur West Fairview PA.

RF121A1 Eliza Ann McClune (13 Feb 1837, Woodstock PA-18 Feb 1903) m John Minsker (1833-1908).

RF121A11 Thomas Minsker (1858-1859).

RF121A12 John Minsker (1865-1866).

RF121A13 Harry Minsker (1868-1869).

RF121A14 Anna Minsker (1871-1951) m Stallsmith. No chn.

RF121A15 Theodore Minsker (1880-1930) m Trumbore (b 1879).

RF121A151 John Minsker (b 1908) m Rosen.

RF121A152 Robert Minsker (b 1911) m Warner.

RF121A153 Isabella Minsker (b 1912) m Grant.

RF121A2 Florinda Susan McClune (19 Feb 1840, Rockbridge Co VA-27 Feb 1902, West Fairview PA) m 6 Mar 1862, West Fairview PA, Theodore McKendrie Moltz (19 Aug 1832, East Pennsboro Tp Cumberland Co PA-3 Apr 1906, West Fairview PA) Bur Enola PA. Grocer, postermaster, photographer, West Fairview PA.

RF121A21 George Thomas Moltz (b 8 Dec 1862, West Fairview PA-28 Jun 1936, Harrisburg PA) m 12 Jul 1896, Susan Marcella Wagner (11 Apr 1874, Harrisburg PA-17 Jun 1948, Harrisburg PA) Teacher, West Fairview PA.

RF121A211   Frank Kenneth Moltz (20 Aug 1908, West Fairview PA-4 May 1975, Kauai, HI) m Sarah ; div. No chn. Naval employee, Kauai HI. Cremated.

RF121A212   John Minsker Moltz (2 May 1897, West Fairview PA-17 Nov 1984, Harrisburg PA) m 26 Jun 1926, Lancaster PA, Elizabeth Louise Kinzer (20 Oct 1903, New Holland PA-25 Mar 1985, Harrisburg PA) He, WWI: USA; AB, U PA; PA Dept of Highways engineer; cement representative, 1935-1962. She, RN.

RF121A2121   Nancy Louise Moltz (b 10 May 1927, Harrisburg PA) m 25 Jun 1949, Harrisburg PA, Donald F Hilbush (b 13 Jan 1926, Harrisburg PA) BS, PSU.

RF121A21211   Kathryn Louise Hilbush (b 25 Jul 1950, Harrisburg PA) m 5 Jun 1975, Baltimore MD, David McGlaughlin (b 29 Oct 1950, Gettysburg PA).

RF121A212111   Matthew David McGlaughlin (b 21 Jan 1982, Philadelphia PA).

RF121A21212   Victoria Patricia Hilbush (b 4 Apr 1958, New Brunswick NJ) m 19 Sep 1982, Bon Aire MD, Walter Hundley Chandler (b 12 Feb 1957, Onancock VA) He, carpenter; she, secretary, receptionist.

RF121A212121   Amanda Elizabeth Chandler (b 25 Apr 1985, Richmond VA).

RF121A212122   Seth Hundley Chandler (b 23 Sep 1988, Richmond VA).

RF121A2122   Patricia Jean Moltz (b 3 Aug 1929, Harrisburg PA) m 20 Oct 1951, Harrisburg PA, Robert Hugh Snyder (b 26 Jul 1929, Altoona PA) She, secretary; he, inventory control clerk.

RF121A21221   Kristy Lee Snyder (b 31 Aug 1952, Geneva NY) m 21 Apr 1985, Harrisburg PA, Eric Paul Kessler (b 18 Nov 1955, Harrisburg PA) She, BA, Kutztown (PA) S U; MA, PSU. He, BA, Elizabethtown Col. Real estate, construction.

RF121A212211   Elizabeth Ann Kessler (b 17 Feb 1986, Harrisburg PA).

RF121A212212   Stephen Michael Kessler (b 18 Feb 1990, Harrisburg PA).

RF121A21222   Robert Hugh Snyder Jr (b 27 May 1955, Harrisburg PA) m 17 Sep 1977, Harrisburg PA, Dianne Klawitter (b 12 Jun 1954, Harrisburg PA).

RF121A212221   Nicole Marie Snyder (b 3 Mar 1980, Harrisburg PA).

RF121A212222   Jamie Lee Snyder (b 30 Apr 1985, Harrisburg PA).

RF121A2123   John Minsker Moltz Jr (b 17 Sep 1937, Harrisburg PA) m 10 Sep 1960, Harrisburg PA, Donna Rae Brownewell (b 6 Nov 1938, Harrisburg PA) USA, Lt Col. BA Gettysburg (PA) Col; BA, Baylor U; MA, Tarleton (TX) S U.

RF121A21231   Timothy John Moltz (b 21 Dec 1961, Munich Germany) m 28 Jun 1985, Hearne TX, Suzanne Hopkins (b 18 Nov 1961, Hearne TX) He, BS, Texas A&M.

RF121A212311   Anthony Kyle Moltz (b 19 Oct 1990, Bryan TX).

RF121A212312   Travis Daniel Moltz (b 12 Jul 1993, Austin TX).

RF121A21232   Michael William Moltz (b 13 Jun 1972, Ft Hood TX) AB, Tarleton (TX) S U.

RF121A213   George Wagner Moltz (5 Jul 1898, West Fairview PA-15 Feb 1975, Harrisburg PA) unm.

RF121A214   Martha Helen Moltz (4 Apr 1900, West Fairview PA-Dec 1989, Harrisburg PA) m Jack

WEISER FAMILIES IN AMERICA

L Froelich. No chn.

RF121A215   Susan Florinda Moltz (18 Jun 1903, West Fairview PA-17 Aug 1967, Southern Pines NC) m Hugh Lee Cobb (1 Nov 1891, Raleigh NC-Apr 1969, Southern Pines NC) No chn.

RF121A22   Gouverneur Warren Moltz (6 Feb 1864, West Fairview PA-13 May 1932, Harrisburg PA) m 6 May 1891, Steelton PA, Bessie Hiney (23 Apr 1866, Middletown PA-15 Jun1959, Harrisburg PA) Bur Enola PA.

RF121A221   Theodore Hiney Moltz (18 Jul 1892, West Fairview PA-Sep 1964, West Chester PA) m 26 Jun 1918, Downingtown PA, Mary Gertrude Boldridge (15 Dec 1890, near Downingtown PA-26 Apr 1977, Holland PA) Bur Downingtown PA

RF121A2211   Jeane Chase Moltz (b 5 Jun 1919) m 21 Mar 1942, Downingtown PA, Robert Bicking (b 8 Jan 1918, Pittsburgh PA) Auto sales.

RF121A22111   Mary Carol Bicking (b 11 Jan 1950, West Chester PA) m 30 Dec 1976, PA, Bradley Taylor.

RF121A22112   Joseph North Bicking (b 10 Oct 1944, VA) m 16 Jul 1966, PA, Wadell Bromley.

RF121A221121   Christopher North Bicking (b 17 May 1971, West Chester PA).

RF121A221122   Kimberly Ann Reilly Bicking (b 1 Aug 1973, West Chester PA).

RF121A2212   Mary Ellen Moltz (29 Sep 1925, West Chester PA-11 Jun 1991, Downingtown PA) m 19 Aug 1950, Downingtown PA, Earl Butler Wilkins (2 Dec 1908, Bucks Co PA-13 Sep 1970, Paoli PA) WWII: USA. He, AB, PSU, 1930; M Ed, U PA, 1934. Teacher, principal, Church Farm School, Exton PA, 1931-1970.

RF121A22121   Frances Madeline Wilkins (b 25 Jan 1956, PA) m 20 Aug 1977, Exton PA, Timothy Hayes Rooney, div; m 2) 10 Nov 1981, Marc Goldberg.

RF121A221211   Zoe Ellen Goldberg (b 18 Jul 1993, Philadelphia PA).

RF121A221212   Lily Ann Goldberg (b 9 Apr 1995, Philadelphia PA).

RF121A22122   Earl Boldridge Wilkins (b 10 May, 1958, West Chester PA) m 13 Jun 1981, Malvern PA, Karen Mary Borlase.

RF121A221221   Matthew Wilkins (b 21 Aug 1982).

RF121A221222   Jeffry Wilkins (b 12 Jun 1984).

RF121A221223   Keith Tyler Wilkins (b 10 Mar 1987).

RF121A2213   Theodore Hiney Moltz (b 21 Sep 1926, West Chester PA) m 27 Nov 1954, West Chester PA, Anita Knox (b 7 May 1928, West Chester PA) She, BS, West Chester (PA) U. He, farm machinery sales.

RF121A22131   Tobin Warren Moltz (b 2 Sep 1956, Canton OH) m 22 Jun 1985, West Chester PA, Cindy Petrondi Pratt.

RF121A221311   Khristine Moltz (b 10 Mar 1988).

RF121A221312   Katherine Moltz (b 10 Mar 1988).

RF121A22132   Marianne Moltz (b 18 Nov 1958, Canton OH) m 22 Aug 1982, West Chester PA, Randy

Sands (b 10 May 1958, PA).

RF121A221321   Lauren Sands (b 13 Nov 1986).

RF121A221322   Yardley Sands (b 6 Oct 1989).

RF121A222   Catharine Ghere Moltz (7 Jun 1895, Harrisburg PA-24 May 1967, Richland WA) m 1) 7 Jun 1916, Harrisburg PA, Melchinger John Lewis (22 Jun 1882, York PA-19 Mar 1919, Wilmington DE) Bur York PA; m 2) 5 Apr 1924, Harrisburg PA, Homer Carlton Yingst (13 Jul 1893, Hummelstown PA-16 Jul 1961, Richland WA) Bur Kennwich WA. She, musician, banker; Yingst, attorney, CPA.

RF121A2221   Melchinger Theodore Lewis (9 Jul 1917, Washburn WI-6 May 1992) m 17 May 1941, Oakmont PA, Helen Dorothy Kauffman (15 Apr 1918, Philadelphia PA-16 Feb 1992, Richland WA) Bur Kennwich WA.

RF121A22211   Melchinger Theodore Lewis Jr (b 19 Jul 1943, Joliet IL) m 29 Jun 1974, Twin Falls ID, Marilyn Arnold (b 11 Mar 1947, Spokane WA) BS, U ID. Nuclear engineer, Idaho Falls ID.

RF121A222111   Roman Brian Lewis (b 11 Nov 1976, Idaho Falls ID).

RF121A222112   Ivan Thomas Lewis (b 16 Sep 1978, Idaho Falls ID).

RF121A222113   Ryan Edward Lewis (b 29 Jul 1981, Idaho Falls ID).

RF121A22212   Kurt Bryan Lewis (b 7 Dec 1952, Richland WA) m 25 Nov 1972, Cheney WA, Cynthia Lynn Polster (b 18 Apr 1954, Richland WA) BA, E WA U, 1974. Teacher; nuclear engineer, Richland WA. She, RN.

RF121A222121   Jennifer Renee Lewis (b 3 Aug 1975, Werribee, Australia) RN.

RF121A222122   Kimberly Michele Lewis (b 23 Mar 1979, Richland WA).

*RF121A2222   Elizabeth Anne Lewis (b 20 Jun 1919, Harrisburg PA) m 1 Jan 1941, Oakmont PA, Francis Albert Gluckert (b 23 Nov 1917, Pittsburgh PA) She, BS, West Chester (PA) U; he, BS, PSU. Chemist.

RF121A22221   Jeanne Catharine Gluckert (b 21 May 1942, Louisville KY) m 28 Aug 1965, West Chester PA, James Clarence Wilson (b 26 Mar 1938, West Chester PA).

RF121A222211   Jennifer Lynn Wilson (5 Sep 1968, West Chester PA-16 Apr 1993) m 14 Feb 1993, Mark Sweezy (16 Feb 1959-16 May 1993) She, BS, Kutztown (PA) U. He, USN.

RF121A222212   Judith Ann Wilson (b 20 Sep 1973, West Chester PA).

RF121A22222   Suzanne Louise Gluckert (b 7 Jun 1944, Oak Ridge TN) m 24 Jun 1967, Wilmington DE, Mark Barton Weber (b 17 Jun 1944, Wilmington DE) She, BS, U MD; Retailer. He, BS, U DE; Developer.

RF121A222221   Christa Dawn Weber (b 11 Mar 1969, Charleston WV) m 24 Aug 1991, Dana Karl Stibolt (b 17 Oct 1967, MD) She U VA, 1991; he, computer service.

RF121A2222211   Weber Hans Stibolt (b 8 Mar 1994).

RF121A2222212   Oliva Ann Stibolt (b 18 May 1996, Annapolis MD)

RF121A222222   Julia Catharine Weber (b 27 Nov 1971, Washington DC) BS, U MD, 1993. unm Dance teacher.

RF121A22223   John Carlton Gluckert (b 25 Aug 1946, West Chester PA) m 30 Aug 1969, Washington DC, Mary Margaret Frick (b 25 Jun 1949, Alexandria VA) USGC. Yacht broker.

RF121A222231   Marianne Beech Gluckert (b 10 May 1970, Baltimore MD) m 16 Sep 1995, Scott Campbell Smith (b 1 Mar 1963, Washington DC) She, BA, BS, Emory Henry (VA) U; paralegal. He, auto sales.

RF121A222232   Mialisa Lewis Gluckert (b 25 Jul 1973, Key West FL) BS, Coastal Carolina U, 1995. Veterinary hospital.

RF121A22224   Diane Louise Gluckert (b 20 Jan 1950, West Chester PA) m 27 Nov 1971, Wilmington DE, Gary Lee Mahan (b 14 May 1940, Wilmington DE) She, law office; he, architect.

RF121A222241   Anna Melinda Mahan (b 4 Sep 1974, Jacksonville FL) BS, FSU, 1996.

RF121A222242   Sean Patrick Mahan (b 25 Mar 1976, Jacksonville FL).

RF121A222243   Amanda Beth Mahan (b 29 Nov 1978, Jacksonville FL).

RF121A3   Weiser Criley McClune (30 May 1849, West Fairview PA-9 Jun 1863, West Fairview PA) Bur Enola PA.

RF122   John Weiser (25 Jan 1778, Heidelberg Tp, Berks Co PA-14 Nov 1847, York PA) m Catharine   (1776-11 Mar 1852, York PA) Bur York PA. Farmer, York Tp. His will names his sons, but not his daughters.

RF1221   Eva Weiser (8 Feb 1801, York Tp, York Co PA-24 Mar 1885, York Tp, York Co PA) m 7 May 1819, Georg Lieder (Leader) (2 Oct 1794, Lower Chanceford Tp, York Co PA-27 Dec 1878, York Tp, York Co PA) Bur Paradise, Springfield Tp, York Co PA. Teacher and farmer, York Tp, York Co PA.

RF12211   Catharine Leader (b 12 Mar 1820).

RF12212   Charles Weiser Leader (b 25 May 1821).

RF12213   Susan Leader (b 22 Apr 1823).

RF12214   Priscilla Leader (9 Jun 1825-1898).

RF12215   Sarah M Leader (19 Mar 1827-30 Apr 1904) m John Stouch.

RF12216   George W Leader (19 Feb 1829-8 Nov 1910) m 3 Jul 1851, Fannie Newcomer (1829, Mountville PA-9 May 1908, York PA).

RF12217   Henry Leader (27 Dec 1830, York Tp, York Co PA-5 Feb 1916, Codorus Tp, York Co PA) m 8 Jan 1854, Leah E Wambaugh (12 Sep 1830, Springfield Tp, York Co PA- 12 Sep 1898, Codorus Tp, York Co PA) Bur Springfield Tp, York Co PA. Farmer and miller, York Co PA.

RF122171   Phebe Alice Leader (9 Sep 1855-2 Apr 1881, Springfield Tp, York Co PA) m Henry Dise.

RF122172   George Michael Leader (26 Jan 1858, York Tp, York Co PA-1937, Jacobus PA) m 1) 20 Nov 1881, Susan Myers; m 2) Mabel   (d 5 Jun 1962, York PA) Farmer, manufacturer, York Co PA.

RF1221721   Guy Alvin Leader (21 Oct 1887, Hametown Tp, York Co PA-15 Oct 1978, York PA) m Beulah Boyer (d 7 Nov 1965, York PA) Bur Jacobus PA. Teacher, poultryman. President, PA Poultry Assoc. PA State Senate, 1944-1948.

RF12217211   George Michael Leader (b 17 Jan 1918, near York PA) m 1939, Mary Jane Strickler.

WWII: USN, 1942-1946, Lt. BS, U PA, 1939. LLD, Temple U; LHD, Gettysburg (PA) Col; LLD, Elizabethtown (PA) Col; LLD Lincoln U; LLD, La Salle Col. PA State Senate, 1950-1954. Governor of PA, 1955-1959. Founder, Leader Nursing and Rehabilitation. Country Meadows, 1982-. Currently (1996) engaged in creative eductional opportunities for persons in Harrisburg PA inner city. Recipient 1995 of the 89th gold medal for distinguished achievement of the PA Society.

RF122172111   Michael Leader (b 1946).

RF122172112   Frederick Nolton Leader (b 1950).

RF122172113   Jane Ellen Leader (b 1954).

RF12217212   Henry B Leader m 8 Jun 1945, Doris Morrell (b 1923) He, AB, Swarthmore Col, 1942; LLB, Yale, 1947. USA. Attorney, York PA.

RF12217213   Paul H Leader (d 7 Dec 1991, York PA) m Mary Mc Dowell.

RF122172131   Nancy L Leader m   Snyder. Farmer, realtor, York PA.

RF122172132   Joanne L Leader m   Williams.

RF122172133   Linda L Leader m   Welles.

RF122172134   Jane L Leader m   Wells.

RF12217214   Guy Alvin Leader Jr.

RF12217215   Mary Leader m Raymond S Hovis.

RF12217216   Ruth Lois Leader m Harold B Collins.

RF12217217   Margaret Jean Leader m S Forry Eisenhart.

RF122173   Priscilla Leader m Joe L Trout.

RF122174   Leah Leader.

RF12218   Jesse Leader (12 Nov 1832-27 Dec 1914) Miller and farmer, Conewag Tp, York Co PA

RF12219   Elizabeth Leader (5 Dec 1834-15 Nov 1922) m 1) Jacob Stiles (1839-1920); m 2) William Glatfelter.

RF1221A   Lydia Leader (2 Nov 1836-26 Dec 1915) m David Willet.

RF1221B   Leah E Leader unm.

RF1221C   Eliza Ann Leader (b 1837) unm.

RF1221D   Anna Maria Leader (6 Aug 1841-19 May 1924) m William H Hartman.

RF1222   Helena Weiser (b 9 Apr 1803, York Tp, York Co PA) m 1825, York PA, John Lieder.

RF12221   Catharine Lieder (b 8 Sep 1826, York PA).

RF12222   Jacob Lieder (b 25 Aug 1828, York PA).

RF12223   John Frederick Lieder (b 30 Jan 1830, York PA).

RF12224   Joseph Lieder (b 3 Nov 1831, York PA).

RF12225   Marian Lieder (b 27 Sep 1834, York PA).

RF12226   Rebecca Ann Lieder (b 7 May 1837, York PA).

RF12227   Isaac Lieder (b 28 Dec 1838).

RF12228   Levi Lieder (b 18 Aug 1841).

RF1223   John Adam Weiser (aka John K Weiser) (12 Jul 1807, York Tp, York Co PA-14 Jun 1873, York PA) m 1) Elizabeth Crosby (6 May 1808-20 Apr 1863, York PA) m 2) 18 Dec 1864, Johanna Elizabeth Rieker (7 Jul 1806-11 Jan 1875) Hatter, merchant, York PA.

RF12231   Benjamin C Weiser (12 Mar 1829-4 Mar 1895, York PA) m 17 Apr 1851, York PA, Sarah Eisenhauer (4 Oct 1821-22 May 1897, York PA) Carpenter.

RF122311   Edward Weiser (b 27 Jun 1852).

RF122312   Benjamin Louis Weiser (b 5 Sep 1853).

RF122313   Samuel Harrison Weiser (2 Nov 1854-1913) m 3 Feb 1880, Anna M Myers (14 Jan 1850-21 Mar 1917, York PA).

RF1223131   Ida M Weiser (b May 1881).

RF1223132   Aaron Franklin Weiser (28 Nov 1884, York PA-18 Sep 1905, York PA) unm.

RF122314   Celinda Weiser (b ca 1856).

RF12232   John C Weiser (25 Jun 1830, York PA-11 Dec 1901, York PA) m 20 Mar 1853, Leah Jane Myers (13 Jun 1831-25 Sep 1896, York PA).

RF122321   William Henry Weiser (3 Dec 1853, York PA-1930, York PA) m 5 Mar 1876, Sarah Ann Landis (16 Oct 1859-4 Nov 1925, York PA).

RF1223211   Arthur E Weiser (8 Nov 1878, York PA-9 Jan 1969) m Lucinda Keller (6 Oct 1882-24 May 1954) Bur Jacobus PA.

RF12232111   William B Weiser (1906-1908).

RF12232112   Edward E Weiser (1909-1911).

RF12232113   Clarence Weiser (1921-1921).

RF1223212   Lillie Belle Flora Weiser (b 31 Oct 1880, York PA) m Eli Trout.

RF1223213   Francis James Weiser (13 Mar 1883, York PA-Jun 1942) m Carrie Weitkamp (b 1 Nov 1881).

RF12232131   Dorothy Weiser (b ca 1909).

RF12232132   Violet Weiser (b ca 1913).

RF1223214   Fannie M Weiser (20 Mar 1885, York PA-1 Apr 1885, York PA).

RF1223215   Estella May Weiser (4 Aug 1886, York PA-3 Mar 1964, Silver Spring MD) Bur Jacobus
PA. unm.

RF1223216   Clarence C Weiser (8 Feb 1889, York PA-15 Jun 1914) unm.

RF1223217   Cora Ellen Weiser (31 Aug 1891, York PA-13 Oct 1963) unm.

RF1223218   Jennie Weiser (4 May 1892, York PA-22 May 1892, York PA) Bur York PA.

RF1223219   Melvin Albert Weiser (3 May 1895, York PA-3 Jan 1900, York PA).

RF122321A   Mary Irene (Mazie) Weiser (b 1 Feb 1897, York PA) unm.

RF122321B   Ervin W Weiser (b 9 Feb 1901, York PA) m Mildred Ulshaffer (b 30 Aug 1902).

RF122322   Charles Franklin Weiser (5 Sep 1855, York PA-15 Oct 1887, York PA) m 26 Jan 1879,
Leah Leveknight. Blacksmith.

RF122323   Emma C E Weiser (17 Jul 1857-16 Aug 1932) unm Bur York PA.

RF122324   Emanuel John Weiser (17 Jan 1861, York PA-24 Apr 1918, York PA) m 3 Aug 1893,
Thirza M King (1868-Nov 1898).

RF1223241   Martha Weiser (b and d Sep 1894).

RF1223242   unnamed child.

RF1223243   John Henry Weiser (Nov 1897-Aug 1898).

RF122325   Carrie E Weiser (b 1871) m 1) 21 Oct 1898, Nelson Shepp; m 2) William Smith.

RF12233   Alexander Weiser (16 Jun 1834, York PA-19 Jan 1918, York PA) m Sarah J (3 Nov
1835-24 Sep 1899) Bur York PA. Businessman, York PA.

RF122331   Willis F Weiser (27 Feb 1857-5 Dec 1932).

RF122332   Samuel R Weiser.

RF122333   Edward Weiser m Mary S   .

RF122334   Laura Weiser m Ruhl   .

RF12234   Charles C Weiser (b 21 Apr 1836, York PA-1 Feb 1906, Codorus Tp, York Co PA) m
Celinda   . Civil War. Baker, York PA

RF12235   Emanuel C Weiser (26 Mar 1840-1865) unm Civil War.

RF12236   Granville Weiser (14 Nov 1845-18 Oct 1929) m 24 Mar 1870, Elizabeth Givens (16 Sep
1838-8 Sep 1921, Lancaster PA) Bur York PA. Baker, York PA.

RF122361   Minna May Weiser (25 Aug 1870-23 Aug 1953) m 1) 18 Oct 1893, Forest E Weller, div;
m 2) Joseph S Miller.

RF122362   Mary J Weiser m   Hodge.

RF12237		Mary Ann Weiser (9 Aug 1847-11 Oct 1920) m Adam Seeger. Bur York PA. Brillharts Station, York Co PA.

RF122371		James Irven Seeger (b 3 Jan 1890).

RF122372		Winfield S Seeger.

RF122373		Harry Seeger.

RF122374		G Ivan Seeger.

RF122375		Clara C Seeger m		Amsbaugh.

RF1224		Jacob K Weiser (5 May 1810, York PA-22 Mar 1876, York PA) m 12 Jun 1836, York PA, Sarah Reisinger.

RF12241		Sarah Weiser (b ca 1838).

RF12242		Catharine Weiser (b ca 1840).

RF12243		Eliza A Weiser (b Feb 1842).

RF12244		Mary Weiser (b Feb 1842).

RF12245		Samuel R Weiser (Sep 1844-22 Apr 1935, near Dover PA) m 14 Jul 1867, Mary Spangler (Sep 1847-1914) York, 1870-1880; Civil War 1891-; Norwood PA, 1900; York, 1910. Bur York PA. Railroad car builder, carpenter.

RF122451		Allen Blair Weiser (10 Apr 1868-13 Sep 1890).

RF122452		Sadie Weiser (b Sep 1869) m		Hartzell.

RF122453		Clement Samuel Weiser (b 4 Dec 1873) m Anna Hartzel (b Feb 1881).

RF1224531		Mary E Weiser (b ca 1901).

RF1224532		Clement R Weiser (b ca 1902).

RF1224533		George A Weiser (b ca 1904).

RF1224534		Anna E Weiser (b ca 1910).

RF122454		Mary Hattie Eliza Weiser (b 7 Mar 1883) m John W Crist.

RF12246		Jacob C Weiser (b Jul 1856) m Sarah		(b ca 1869) No chn.

RF12247		Matilda Ellen Weiser (b ca 1858).

RF1225		John George Weiser (dy).

RF1226		Daniel K Weiser (11 Sep 1816, York PA-4 Mar 1892, York PA) m 14 Nov 1852, York PA, Susanna Spangler (2 Nov 1815, York PA-19 May 1888, York PA) Bur York PA.

RF12261		William John Weiser (12 Sep 1853, York PA-10 Apr 1926, York PA) m Ella Everhart (17 Dec 1852-18 Sep 1943) Bur York PA.

RF122611   Oscar Weiser (b Oct 1886, York PA) m Nettie   .

RF1226111   Lawrence Weiser.

RF1226112   Helen Weiser.

RF122612   Ira Daniel Weiser (10 Mar 1886-14 Apr 1956) m 10 Aug 1918, Edna C Brillinger (b 1 Mar 1891) Bur York PA. He, gas company, county agricultural society; she, teacher.

RF1226121   Mary Ellen Weiser (16 Oct 1921, York PA-25 Aug 1994) Bur York PA. unm West Chester (PA) U, 1943. Teacher, Haverford PA.

*RF1226122   William Jacob Weiser (b 23 Feb 1925, York PA) m 24 Jul 1948, Mary Louise Sieber (b 25 Apr 1924, York PA) He, PSU, 1945; Metallurgist supervisor, Bethlehem Steel. She, Gettysburg Col, 1946. Res Hellertown PA.

RF12261221   Michael Lynn Weiser (b 29 Oct 1949, Lancaster PA) m 17 Dec 1988, Linda Susan Hunsberger (b 20 May 1949, Philadelphia PA) AB, Kutztown (PA) U, 1972; she, AB, Philadelphia Community Col, 1989. Media PA.

                Gina Ciarlente (b 22 Jan 1976) Adopted by Michael Lynn Weiser.

RF12261222   Thomas Christopher Weiser (b 19 Apr 1951, Fountain Hill PA) m 8 Aug 1980, Jeanne Marie Strisofsky (b 16 May 1952, Northampton PA) He, AB, PSU, 1973; she, Lehigh Community Col. Emmaus PA.

RF122612221   Carrie Lynn Weiser (b 16 Mar 1983, Allentown PA).

RF12261223   Margaret Ann Weiser (b 1 Oct 1953, Fountain Hill PA) m 10 Nov 1985, Leonard Mark Laxer (b 7 Dec 1959, Franklin Square NY) AB, Kutztown (PA) U, 1975; he, S U NY, Buffalo, 1981. Res Wantagh NY.

RF122612231   Brian Andrew Laxer (b 7 Oct 1986, Bethpage NY).

RF122612232   Allison Beth Laxer (b 12 Jan 1988, Bethpage NY).

RF12261224   John Timothy Weiser (b 8 Feb 1958, Fountain Hill PA) m 22 Oct 1995, Ann Marie Valuch (b 31 Oct 1958, Lancaster PA) He, Lehigh Community Col, 1982; she, AB, PSU, 1980, MBA, Shippenburg (PA) U, 1982.

                Michael Gilbert (b 23 Jun 1988, Lancaster PA).

RF122612241   Rebecca Ann Weiser (b 9 Mar 1996, Lancaster PA).

RF12261225   Heidi Ann Weiser (b 16 Dec 1967, Fountain Hill PA) m 2 Jun 1990, Christopher James Wrobel (b 27 Jun 1965, Allentown PA).

RF122612251   Audrey June Wrobel (b 25 Jun 1996, Philadelphia PA).

RF123   Benjamin Weiser (10 Feb 1780, Heidelberg Tp, Lancaster Co PA-9 Sep 1854, York PA) m 13 Sep 1801, Catharine Baumgardner (19 Oct 1785-24 Jan 1855, York PA) Bur York PA. Hatter, York PA.

RF1231   Daniel B Weiser (8 Jul 1803, York PA-10 Jun 1866, York PA) m Feb 1824, York PA, Margaret Matilda Pentz (29 Jan 1803-24 Jul 1875, York PA).

RF12311   Mary Louisa Weiser (23 Apr 1825, York PA-27 Apr 1829, York PA) Bur York PA.

RF12312   Henry Kanlock Weiser (3 May 1828, York PA-31 Mar 1875, York PA) m 22 Sep 1853, York PA, Matilda Jane Ziegler (17 Dec 1831-3 Jan 1869) MD. Physician, York PA.

RF123121   John Ziegler Weiser (4 Nov 1854, York PA-9 Oct 1928, York PA) m 1) Ida J   (16 Mar 1858-17 Feb 1897); m 2) 4 May 1899, Milvina J Clemens.

RF123122   Henry K Weiser (9 Feb 1856-6 Dec 1909).

RF123123   Barbara M Weiser (4 Aug 1857-22 Aug 1857).

RF123124   Jacob D Weiser (1863-1863).

RF12313   Catharina Dorothea Weiser (b 16 Apr 1831, York PA) m 12 Jun 1851, Jacob D Scholl.

RF12314   Johanna Elizabeth Weiser (22 May 1834, York PA-1 Mar 1839, York PA) Bur York PA.

RF12315   Margaret Matilda Weiser (6 Jun 1837, York PA-9 Mar 1893) m 15 May 1856, Edmund C Bender (22 Aug 1831-29 Aug 1883).

RF123151   Sarah M Bender (20 Jun 1858-9 May 1929).

RF123152   Helen V Bender (12 Sep 1865-17 Aug 1929).

RF12316   Sarah Magdalena Weiser (b 26 Aug 1841, York PA) m Emanuel Herman. Towson MD.

RF12317   Miriam Zipporah Weiser (b 30 Jul 1845, York PA) m 25 Feb 1869, Edward Gilberthorpe Stuck.

RF1232   Elizabeth Weiser (b 19 Jan 1806, York PA) m 25 Aug 1825, York PA, Henry Nes (20 May 1802, York PA-10 Sep 1850, York PA) MD. Physician, York PA. Member of Congress.

RF12321   Charles M Nes (26 Jun 1827, York PA-11 Jun 1896) m 1846, Caroline King.

RF123211   Henry Nes (b 1854, York PA) MD. Physician, York PA. Bank officer, president.

RF123212   Charles M Nes.

RF123213   E Gulick Nes.

RF123214   Elizabeth Nes m Eli Forney.

RF12322   Arabella Nes m EA King.

RF12323   Frederick Nes. US Coast Guard Survey.

RF12324   Margaret Nes m GW Doty.

RF12325   Henrietta (Ada) Elizabeth Nes m BF Spangler, MD.

RF1233   George Weiser (d 5 Dec 1858).

RF1234   Benjamin Henry Weiser (11 Feb 1823, York PA-28 Jan 1883, York PA) m 2 Apr 1844, York PA, Catharine Stine (1828-26 Oct 1907, York PA).

RF12341   George Benjamin Weiser (18 Feb 1845, York PA-18 Jul 1875, York PA) Bur York PA. unm MD.

RF12342   Edwin Reinke Weiser (27 Jan 1848, York PA-23 May 1870, York PA) Bur York PA. unm.

RF124   Maria Eva Weiser (b 2 Jul 1782, probably Heidelberg Tp, Lancaster Co PA) Not mentioned in her father's will.

RF125   Maria Catharina Weiser (b 1784, York PA) m Johannes Jost (Yost).

RF1251   Henry Yost (b 13 Mar 1803).

RF1252   John Yost (b 7 Mar 1805).

RF1253   Henrietta Yost (b 20 Apr 1807).

RF1254   Theresa Yost (b 15 Jun 1809).

RF1255   Lousiana Yost (b 9 Nov 1811).

RF1256   Jacob Yost (b 18 Jan 1814).

RF1257   Lydia Yost (b 14 Mar 1817).

RF1258   Catharine Yost (b 27 Nov 1819).

RF126   Lydia Weiser (b ca 1786, York Tp, York Co PA) m Oct 1818, York PA, Jacob Miller.

RF1261   Alexander Miller (b 12 May 1821, York PA).

RF127   Martin Jonathan Weiser (25 Aug 1789, York PA-22 Oct 1829, York PA) m 1812, York PA, Catharine Haller (29 May 1792-13 Feb 1882, York PA) Bur York PA.

RF1271   Susan Weiser (b 21 Jul 1813).

RF1272

RF1273   Maria Anna Weiser (b 12 Mar 1817).

RF1274   Caroline Weiser (b 1 Jun 1819).

RF1275   Catharine Weiser (11 May 1821-1897) m Charles Pfabler (1819-1893).

RF12751   Emma C Pfabler (1844-1897) m Charles Augustus Eisenhart (1845-1901).

RF127511   William S Eisenhart (1874-1941) m Lucy A Forry.

RF1275111   William S Eisenhart (b 1913) m Hazel Laity.

RF12751111   William Schmucker Eisenhart (b 1946).

RF127512   Luther Pfabler Eisenhart (b 1876) m 1) Anna D Mitchell; m 2) Catharine R Schmidt.

RF127513   Jacob C Eisenhart (1878-1946) m Rose Butt. Wall paper manufacturer, Hanover PA.

RF127514   Harry W Eisenhart (1880-1947) m Lillian Cleary. Mechanical engineer.

RF127515   M Herbert Eisenhart m Elsa M Bausch. President, Bausch and Lomb.

RF1276   Emilia (Emma) Weiser (b 20 May 1823) m 28 Sep 1852, Jacob F Martin.

RF1277   Martin Haller Weiser (23 Oct 1825, York PA-6 Jun 1887, York PA) m 1) 13 May 1851, Caroline Jane Peiffer (1826-15 Mar 1864, York PA); m 2) 29 May 1866, York PA, Mary E Tyler (1830-1913) Bur York PA.

RF12771   Edwin Christopher Weiser (b 10 Apr 1852, York PA) m Lucy   (b May 1865, MA).

RF127711   Richard M Weiser (b Apr 1893).

RF127712   Catherine Weiser (b May 1896).

RF127713   Helen Weiser (b Apr 1899).

RF12772   William Peiffer Weiser (b 5 Aug 1854, York PA) m Sallie F Logan (Oct 1859, PA-1900 or 1920, Camden NJ).

RF12773   Caroline Weiser (1 Jan 1857, York PA-30 Apr 1861, York PA) Bur York PA.

RF12774   Robert Haller Weiser (6 Sep 1860, York PA-5 May 1861, York PA) Bur York PA

RF12775   Horace Martin Weiser (22 Jan 1863, York PA-13 Aug 1863, York PA) Bur York PA

RF12776   Margaret Haller Weiser (12 Jul 1867, York PA-29 Aug 1901, York PA) Bur York PA

RF12777   Walter Rupert Weiser (b 13 Jan 1870, York PA).

RF12778   Martin Luther Weiser (b 5 Mar 1876, York PA).

RF1278   William M Hoffmeyer Weiser (20 Jan 1828, York PA-28 Mar 1861, York PA) m 29 May 1856, Sarah Elizabeth   (b 1834).

RF12781   Ida Kate Weiser (b 7 Mar 1857).

RF12782   Martin Edward Weiser (b 11 Aug 1859).

RF12783   Charles William Weiser (1 Aug 1859-26 Mar 1860).

RF12784   William Jacob Weiser (b 10 Sep 1861).

RF14   Anna Maria Weiser (1 Apr 1754, Tulpehocken Tp, Berks Co PA-11 Oct 1829, Lewisburg PA) m 29 Oct 1774, John Henry Spyker (29 Aug 1753-1 Jul 1817, Lewisburg PA) Bur Lewisburg PA. US Rev: 6th Battalion, Berks Co Militia, 1777, Lt Col. In 1795 he began to build the first brick house in Sunburg PA, which is still standing. Member, PA legislature, 1784-1790.[129]

RF141   John Peter Spyker (9 Aug 1775, Tulpehocken Tp, Berks Co PA-15 Mar 1832, Sciota OH) m 17 Jun 1800, Sophia Dreisbach (8 Apr 1780-5 Nov 1860, Packaway Co OH) Bur Tarlton OH.

RF1411   Peter Spyker.

RF1412   Anna Spyker (b 10 Jan 1806).

RF1413   Catharine Spyker (b 5 Feb 1807).

---

[129]Data on the descendants of Anna Maria Weiser Spyker provided by L.E. Tomlinson, James A. Dunlap, Beverly Jean Eckert.

RF1414   Mary Magdalene Spyker (b 28 May 1808).

RF142   Lidia Spyker (30 Jun 1777, Tulpehocken Tp, Berks Co PA-12 Jun 1811, on a journey to Sciota OH) m 24 May 1801, Martin Dreisbach (22 Mar 1876-25 Sep 1850, Ross Co OH).

RF1421   Jacob Dresbach (20 Aug 1805, Union Co PA-16 Oct 1849, Pickaway Co OH) m 18 Aug 1835, Pickaway Co OH, Elizabeth Harvey (22 Dec 1811-16 May 1879, Hallsville OH).

RF14211   Gedaliah Dresbach (5 Oct 1847, Hallsville OH-7 Dec 1910, Pickaway OH) m 22 Oct 1879, Paris IL, Helen Rosalta Dresbach (22 Nov 1861, Edger Co IL-18 Apr 1948, Hallsville OH).

RF142111   Judd Harvey Dresbach (1 Jan 1896, Hallsville OH-20 Sep 1967, Ashville OH) m 18 Jun 1928, Avis Grace Bee (b 28 Mar 1897, Doddridge Co VA).

RF1421111   Sue Dresbach (b 26 Feb 1929, Ross Co OH) m 29 Nov 1959, Myron F Gearhart (b 9 Aug 1923, Ross Co OH).

RF143   Catharina Spyker (11 Jun 1779, Tulpehocken Tp, Berks Co PA-3 Nov 1815, Ross Co OH) m 9 Aug 1803, John Dreisbach (3 Sep 1778-17 Jul 1843, Ross Co OH).

RF1431   Gabriel Dresbach (6 Jun 1805, PA-1871) m 8 Dec 1826, Ross Co OH, Maria A Pyles.

RF1432   Mary Magdalena Dresbach (b 13 Sep 1807, PA) m 20 Jul 1826, Ross Co OH, Christopher Ross.

RF1433   Amelia Dresbach (b 2 Aug 1808, PA).

RF1434   George Y Dresbach (b 2 Aug 1808, PA).

RF1435   John S Dresbach (13 Oct 1810-8 Sep 1884) m 20 Mar 1834, Pickaway Co OH, Polly Vincent.

RF1436   Anna Dresbach (22 Apr 1813-16 Aug 1884) m 30 Jul 1831, Pickaway Co OH, William Mc Grady.

RF1437   Catharine Dresbach (2 Jul 1815, Ross Co OH-18 Aug 1889, Allen Co KS) m 11 Sep 1834, Pickaway Co OH, Elijah Moore (b 11 Dec 1811) Bur Iola KS.

RF14371   John S Moore (1 Jun 1835, Ross Co OH-15 Apr 1919, Joplin MO) m 25 Aug 1861, Monticello IL, Leah Reed Dorris (8 May 1838, Chillicothe OH-24 Jun 1905, Joplin MO) Bur Joplin MO. Civil War: USA, IL Vol Co E 107, 1862-1865, 2 Corp

RF143711   Mary Alice Moore (b 9 Feb 1863, Piatt Co IL) m ca 1893.

RF143712   George Marley Moore (2 Feb 1867, Piatt Co IL-12 Mar 1949, Salmon ID) m 15 Mar 1891, Webb City MO, Gertie Myers (9 Nov 1868, IA-30 Apr 1908, Boulder CO) He bur Salmon ID; she bur Boulder CO.

RF1437121   Lulu May Moore (3 May 1892, Joplin MO-28 Nov 1969, San Bernardino CA) m 3 Aug 1911, Denver CO, Lee Glenn Tomlinson (15 Nov 1893, Boone Co MO-20 Jun 1960, Los Angeles CA) Bur Inglewood CA.

RF14371211   June Evelyn Tomlinson (b 9 May 1912, Denver CO) m 13 May 1939, Los Angeles CA, Franklyn Taylor Lindawood (b 15 Nov 1917, Brownwood TX).

RF143712111   Leona May Lindawood (b 4 Apr 1941, Los Angeles CA) m 1) Dave Cochran, div; m 2)

Ray Cadman, div; m 3) 11 Apr 1981, James Rodney Taylor.

RF1437121111   Cynthia Anne Cochran (b 15 Sep 1965).

RF1437121112   John Michael Cadman (b 2 Jul 1968).

RF143712112   Frances Louise Lindawood (b 3 Nov 1943, Los Angeles CA).

RF1437121121   Shawn Taylor Lindawood (b 27 Aug 1984).

RF143712113   Gail Inez Lindawood (b 4 May 1947, Austin TX) m 1) Steve Cushing, div; m 2) Chuck Steibers, div.

RF1437121131   Brooks Caren Cushing (b 3 Dec 1966).

RF1437121132   Michelle Lynn Cushing (b 28 Mar 1968).

*RF14371212   Lloyd Everett Tomlinson (b 1 Mar 1915, Salt Lake City UT) m 5 Sep 1936, Glendale CA, Inez Napier (b 30 Jun 1913, Leslie AR).

RF143712121   Marilyn June Tomlinson (b 10 Sep 1937, Inglewood CA) m 25 Mar 1961, Los Angeles CA, Dalton Erwin Canty Jr (b 7 Jul 1934, Crowley LA).

RF1437121211   Alan Lloyd Cantey (b 27 Feb 1964, Redlands CA).

RF1437121212   David Dalton Cantey (b 3 Dec 1965, Redlands CA).

RF143712122   Anna Lee Tomlinson (b 9 Nov 1940, Los Angeles CA) m 18 Aug 1962, Toronto Canada, Stepan Maziar (b 1 Jan 1926, Lvov Russia).

RF143712121221   Martha Inez Maziar (b 30 Sep 1963, Toronto, Ontario Canada) m 10 Jun 1982, San Jose CA, Gregory Hibbard (b 29 Mar 1961).

RF14371212211   Amanda Marie Hibbard (b 22 Mar 1983, Boulder CO).

RF14371212212   Nathaniel William Hibbard (b 23 Oct 1985, Boulder CO).

RF1437121222   Mark Gregory Maziar (b 3 Nov 1964, Toronto, Ontario, Canada).

RF1437121223   Lucia Diane Maziar (b 12 Jun 1966, Toronto, Ontario, Canada).

RF143712123   Diane Ethel Tomlinson (b 12 Mar 1945, Los Angeles CA) m 19 Jan 1968, W Los Angeles CA, Byron Jay Allen Jr (b 12 Dec 1935, Los Angeles CA).

RF1437122   John A Moore (4 Oct 1897, Boise ID-20 Jan 1899, Boise ID).

RF1437123   Reva Moore (13 Mar 1900, Parchute Co ID-7 Feb 1982, Boise ID) m 20 Jun 1921, Clyde Robert Gillespie Sr (b 13 Jun 1900, Clyde KS) Bur Boise ID

RF14371231   Gertrude L Gillespie (b 12 Aug 1922, Hailey ID) m 1) Russel Chrest (b Aug 1921, Iron Mountain MI) div; m 2) Dale Skinner.

RF143712311   Constance Lynn Chrest (b 24 Oct 1948, Marquette MI) m 24 Jan 1969, Princeton NJ, Donald Carl Branton (b 22 Oct 1946, Charlotte NC).

RF1437123111   Anna Lynn Branton (b 2 Jul 1975, Pocatello ID).

RF1437123112   Sarah Karleen Branton (b 4 May 1978, Goleta GA).

RF143712312   George Durian Chrest (b 27 May 1951, Marquette MI) m Sandra Clyne (b 19 Aug 1951, Nampa ID).

RF14371232   Doris Gillespie (b 31 Dec 1923, Stanley ID) m 1946, Philip Goodell (b 3 Apr 1920, Salmon ID).

RF143712321   Reva Anne Goodell (b 19 Nov 1952, Salmon ID) m 20 Aug 1977, Salmon ID, Richard Meadows (b 9 Jan 1950).

RF1437123211   Alexander Dickinson Meadows (b 9 Oct 1984, Seattle WA).

RF143712322   Philip Ransom Goodell II (b 26 Sep 1954, Salmon ID) m Mar 1979, St Maries ID, Nancy

RF1437123221   Carmen Marie Goodell (b 31 Jul 1980, Salmon ID).

RF1437123222   Amanda Rea Goodell (b 9 Jun 1984, Salmon ID).

RF14371233   Gerald Clyde Gillespie (3 Aug 1926, Hailey ID-31 Dec 1929, Boise ID).

RF14371234   Clyde Raymond Gillespie (b 5 Jul 1929, Hailey ID) m 1959, Tuana Corbet (b 17 Oct 1935, Salmon ID).

RF143712341   Clyde Gale Gillespie (b 8 Dec 1958, Salmon ID) m 21 Aug 1981, Cokeville WY, Lynda Sue Bannion (b 13 Feb 1962).

RF1437123411   Trenton James Gillespie (b 18 Sep 1982, Salt Lake City UT).

RF143712342   Kathryn Ann Gillespie (b 15 Jan 1961, Soda Springs ID) m 13 May 1983, Daryl Shane Rasmussen (b 13 Mar 1959).

RF1437123421   Ryan Shane Rasmussen (b 11 Jan 1985, Salt Lake City UT).

RF143712343   Karen Tuana Gillespie (b 29 Oct 1968, Evanston WY).

RF1437124   Alta Moore (b 14 Aug 1901, Parachute CO) m 1) 1927, Howard Johnson (b Nov 1894, Ogden UT) div; m 2) Orie Eckert.

*RF14371241   Beverly Jean Johnson Eckert (b 8 Aug 1928, Logan UT) m 23 Jan 1952, Sam Meln (b 16 Dec 1921, IL).

RF143712411   Mark Meln (b 30 Nov 1952, Seattle WA).

RF143712412   Paula Lee Meln (b 17 Aug 1955, Seattle WA).

RF14371242   Marley Howard Johnson Eckert (b 26 May 1932, Ogden UT) m Lenora Mc Gibbon (b 28 Mar 1931, Seattle WA).

RF143712421   Stephen Marley Eckert (b 20 Oct 1955, Seattle WA) m Nell Kimberly Endress (b 4 May 1958).

RF1437124211   Brook Marley Eckert (b 13 Oct 1978).

RF143712422   Paul Edward Eckert (b 30 Mar 1957, Seattle WA).

RF143712423 Billie Scott Eckert (b 26 May 1961, Seattle WA).

RF143712424 Theresa Rose Eckert (b 7 Sep 1963, Seattle WA).

RF143713 James Austin Moore (19 Jun 1869, Piatt Co IL-23 Aug 1949, Joplin MO) m Margaret Luinda Hullen (27 Oct 1873-26 Apr 1958) Bur Joplin MO.

RF1437131 Guy Earl Moore (19 Feb 1895-8 May 1955) m Joplin MO, Thelma Gibson (28 Aug 1898-26 Jan 1975) Bur Hood River OR.

RF14371311 Marguerita Moore (b 4 Mar 1916) m 7 Sep 1937, Richard Calvin (7 Oct 1913-May 1968).

RF143713111 Carolyn Calvin (b 21 Dec 1937) m 1) Arby Willard (b Jul 1935); m 2) Frank Bush (b 5 Oct 1936).

RF1437131111 Ronald Ray Willard (b 5 Sep 1956).

RF1437131112 Ronda Willard (b 8 Jan 1958).

RF1437131113 Roxanna Willard (b 13 Oct 1958).

RF1437131114 Richard Bush (b 17 Aug 1966).

RF143713112 Marilyn Calvin (b 17 Aug 1940) m Tony Casa Calvo, div.

RF1437131121 Tonya Kay Calvo (b Oct 1967).

RF14371312 Peggy Moore (b 2 Dec 1922, Picher OK) m 7 May 1941, Joplin MO, Bill Wetherell (b 22 Dec 1919, Halton WA).

RF143713121 William Thomas Wetherell (b 18 May 1944, Hood River OR) m 17 Apr 1970, Portland OR, Lynn K Rossiter (b 6 Nov 1942).

RF1437131211 Melissa Anne Wetherell (b 31 Dec 1971).

RF1437131212 William Michael Wetherell (b 30 Dec 1974).

RF1437131213 Rebecca Susan Wetherell (b 30 Sep 1979).

RF143713122 Sandra Lee Wetherell (b 21 May 1947) m 6 Nov 1966, Portland OR, Raymond J Hofmann (b Feb 1942).

RF1437131221 Karen Lee Hofmann (b 29 Dec 1969).

RF1437131222 Eric James Hofmann (b 11 Jul 1972).

RF143713123 Linda Karen Wetherell (b 28 Apr 1954).

RF14371313 Jo Ann Moore (b 12 Nov 1932, Joplin MO) m Howard Keeling (b 9 Feb 1932).

RF143713131 Sherry Keeling.

RF143713132 Terry Keeling.

RF143713133 Tommy Keeling (b 16 Nov 1961).

RF14371314   Gary Moore (b 21 May 1935, Joplin MO).

RF14371315   James Austin Moore (b 17 Feb 1943) m 10 Nov 1961, Imogene Marie Schalbert (b 20 Mar 1943).

RF143713151   Angela Marie Moore (b 20 Oct 1965).

RF143713152   Justin Lee Moore (b 23 Nov 1973).

RF1437132   Ray Arlie Moore (b 26 Mar 1897, Joplin MO).

RF1437133   Roy Johny Lucus Moore (b 28 Feb 1899, Joplin MO) m 1) Iva Baughtery; m 2) Haddie Davis (19 Aug 1903-3 Dec 1967).

RF14371331   Sybil Moore m Calvin Calberly.

RF143713311   Bob Calberly.

RF143713312   Cora Sue Calberly.

RF1437133121   Becky   .

RF143713313   Roy Lee Calberly.

RF14371332   Clyde Austin Moore (b 20 Mar 1929, Rankin TX) m 11 Dec 1956, Germany, Ilsa Blank
(b 21 Sept 1932).

RF143713321   Barbara Anne Moore (b 22 Sep 1957, Pampa TX) m 12 Jun 1976, David Fruit (b 18 Dec
1952, Borger TX).

RF143713322   James Scott Moore (b 19 Aug 1958) m Aug 1982, Cindy   .

RF143713323   John Austin Moore (b 26 Jun 1961) m 15 Dec 1978, Suzanna Paulsell.

RF1437133231   Amy Suzanna Moore (b 27 Jun 1979, Borger TX).

RF1437133232   John Austin Moore (b 16 Nov 1983, Borger TX).

RF14371333   Bobby Lee Moore (b 18 Nov 1931, Rankin TX) m 14 Jan 1955, Pampa TX Josephine
Ethel Parks (b 28 Oct 1935).

RF143713331   Kimela Kay Moore (b 25 Mar 1957, Pampa TX) m 1) 4 Aug 1974, Michael Harrell, div;
m 2) 16 Sept 1979, Bob Belasco (b 28 Jan 1951).

RF1437133311   Jason Michael Harrell (b 14 Aug 1976, Germany).

RF1437133312   Misty Dawn Harrell (b 31 Jul 1977, Ft Worth TX).

RF1437133313   Brandi Michelle Belasco (b 27 Mar 1980).

RF1437133314   Ashley Renee Belasco (b 24 Nov 1982).

RF143713332   Camela Fay Moore (b 23 Oct 1958) m 14 Feb 1981, Ronald Ray Creecy (b 27 May 1959).

RF1437133321   Ronald Scott Creecy (b 26 Oct 1983).

RF143713333   Donna Jo Moore (b 13 May 1962) m 25 Nov 1978, Raymond C Miles (b 11 May 1957).

RF1437133331   Jeremy Wayne Miles (b 2 Nov 1981, Hurst TX).

RF1437133332   Jodie Carman Miles (b 3 Nov 1984, Hurst TX).

RF14371334   Glenda Joy Moore (b 28 Dec 1936, Childress TX) m 30 Dec 1955, George E Cannedy (b 8 Nov 1934, Sawyer OK).

RF143713341   Melinda Carol Cannedy (b 10 Oct 1956, Dallas TX) m 24 Sep 1983, Clinton Bob Crumbie (b 3 May 1955).

RF143713342   Michael E Cannedy (b 16 Aug 1960, Grand Prairie TX).

RF143713343   Sheila Ann Cannedy (b 3 May 1964, Grand Prairie TX).

RF14371335   Shirlee Louise Moore (b 29 Jun 1940, Childress TX) m 13 Feb 1956, William Dale Gruver (b 10 Apr 1938).

RF143713351   Jeffrey Kurtis Gruver (b 26 Nov 1966, Euless TX).

RF143713352   Timothy Dale Gruver (b 4 Oct 1970, San Angelo TX).

RF1437134   Anna Leah Moore (3 Sep 1905-20 Feb 1907, Boulder CO).

RF1437135   Glenn Edwin Moore (11 Aug 1908, Joplin MO-20 Mar 1976) m 27 Sept 1936, Ruby Henderson, (9 Dec 1909-6 Aug 1980).

RF143714   Rene Moore (7 Jun 1871, Jasper MO-ca 1953, Pasadena CA) m Elmer Wyman (d 21 Dec 1946, Pasadena CA).

RF1437141   Paul Wyman.

RF143715   CG Moore (ca 1876, Jasper CO-ca 1882, Joplin MO).

RF143716   Warren H Moore (14 Jul 1879, Joplin MO-18 Oct 1965, Joplin MO) m Forest Lylian Davis (California MO-29 Mar 1957, Joplin MO) Bur Joplin MO.

RF1437161   Goldie Moore (b 20 Apr 1902, Joplin MO) m 1); m 2) 6 Jan 1933, Frederick Beardsley (21 Jul 1885, Derbyshire, England-10 Mar 1966, Joplin MO).

RF1437162   Robert L Moore (b 9 Oct 1905, Joplin MO) m Gerta   .

RF1437163   Mildred Moore (b 1910, MO).

RF14372   Eliza Jane Moore (b 8 May 1838, Ross Co OH) m 20 Mar 1858, Frank Schoch.

RF143721   Daniel E Schoch (lived near Ft Wayne, IN).

RF143722   Mary Catherine Schoch (lived near Ft Wayne IN).

RF143723   Sarah Ellen Schoch (d ca 1943) (lived near Ft Wayne IN) m George Gay (d ca 1900).

RF1437231   Frank Gay (b KS).

RF1437232   Ralph Gay (b KS).

RF1437233   Fred Gay (b KS).

RF1437234   Hubert Gay (b KS).

RF143724   Clara G Schoch (lived near Ft Wayne IN).

RF143725   Sophia M Schoch (lived near Ft Wayne IN) m William Yarges.

RF1437251   Estiline Yarges (b IN).

RF1437252   Estella Yarges (b IN).

RF143726   Georg L Schoch (lived near Ft Wayne IN).

RF143727   Henry D Schoch (lived near Ft Wayne IN).

RF143728   William F Schoch (lived near Ft Wayne IN).

RF14373   George W Moore (b 19 Aug 1840, Pickaway Co OH) m 1) 18 Feb 1869, Nashville TN, Annie Tucker (d 11 Aug 1872, Iola KS); m 2) 9 Jan 1873, Annie Owens. Civil War: USA, Co E, 107 IL Vol, 1862-1865.

RF143731   Charles E Moore (ca 1870, Nashville TN-TN) m Mamie Sullivan (b IA).

RF143732   Lottie E Moore (Nashville TN-Iola KS).

RF143733   George Frank Moore (ca 1874, Nashville TN-ca 1925) m.

RF1437331   Earle Moore.

RF1437332   Francis Moore.

RF143734   Compton Moore (1876, Nashville TN-Feb 1903, Denver CO).

RF14374   Jacob D Moore (b 22 Nov 1842, Ross Co OH) m 25 Aug 1868, Izelia Watson (b ca 1846) Civil War: USA, Co E, 107 IL Vol, 1862-1865.

RF143741   Effie C Moore (ca 1869, IL-near Bronson KS) m 1) Tom Matthews; m 2) William Gatt.

RF143742   Mary H Moore (ca Jan 1870, IL-Moran KS) m Richard Rumbel (d Moran KS).

RF1437421   Freddie Rumbel.

RF143743   Cora Bell Moore.

RF143744   Maud M Moore (ca 1873, Allen Co KS-near Moran KS) m Marian Anderson.

RF143745   Bertha D Moore (ca 1875, Allen Co KS-1938, Walnut KS) m AE Hewitt (d 1933, Walnut KS).

RF1437451   Forest Hewitt (b Walnut KS).

RF143746   Howard D Moore (b ca 1877, Allen Co KS) m Gertie Smith.

RF1437461   Bernice Moore.

RF1437462   Opal Moore.

RF1437463   Cecil Moore.

RF1437464   Arthur Moore.

RF1437465   Ray Moore.

RF143747   Arthur J Moore (b ca 1879, Allen Co KS) m Sadie   .

RF1437471   Chester Arthur Moore.

RF1437472   Marcia Moore.

RF143748   Abbie Moore (Allen Co KS-1945) m Vic Sloan.

RF1437481   Marie Sloan (b near Moran, KS).

RF1437482   Charlotte Sloan (b near Moran KS).

RF1437483   Mande Sloan (b near Moran KS).

RF1437484   Elgin Sloan (b near Moran KS).

RF143749   Ray Moore.

RF14374A   Hazel Moore (b Allen Co KS) m Ray Proctor.

RF14374A1   JD Proctor.

RF14374A2   Maxine Proctor

RF14375   Mary Ellen Moore (b 2 Feb 1845, Ross Co OH) m 6 Aug 1866, James Warren Stinson (b 10 Jun 1844, Carrel IN) Civil War: USA, Co E, 107 IL Vol, 1862-1865.

RF143751   Warren Edwin Stinson (1866-1872).

RF143752   Charles Alexander Stinson (b 29 Jan 1869) m 18 Aug 1892, Sophia Arnold.

RF1437521   Ester Stinson (b 1 Aug 1894) m Fred J McKinna (d Nov 1943).

RF14375211   Dean McKinna.

RF14375212   Frederick McKinna.

RF1437522   Harold Stinson (b 13 Mar 1896) m Vera Fultz.

RF14375221   Robert Stinson.

RF14375222   Mary Ann Stinson.

RF14375223   Susie Stinson.

RF143753   Rene R Stinson (23 Feb 1871-Oct 1874).

RF143754   Lillian C Stinson (b 23 May 1873) m Edward S Davis (d 4 Jul 1933).

RF1437541   Everett Davis (b 19 Sept 1897) m Enia Mae McCabe.

RF14375411   Florence Davis m Jimmie Cosh.

RF14375412   Velma Davis m Floyd Walton Jr.

RF1437542   Wallace Davis (b 3 Jun 1900) m Dale Striegel.

RF14375421   Arthur Striegel (b 29 Jun 1923) m Ida Louise Trisler.

RF14375422   Eleanor Striegel (b 15 Aug 1925).

RF14375423   Wayne Striegel (b 22 Aug 1931).

RF1437543   Kenneth Davis (b 14 Feb 1903) m Catherine Corey.

RF1437544   Clayton Davis (b 18 Nov 1905) m Martha Du Mars.

RF14375441   Marion Davis (b 22 Oct 1940).

RF14375442   John Edward Davis (b 11 Mar 1942).

RF14375443   Sarah Davis.

RF14376 OH).   Lafayette W Moore (b 26 Apr 1847, Ross Co OH) m 3 Sep 1871, Nancy Cox (b ca 1850,

RF143761   Clarence Moore (b ca 1869, Piatt Co IL).

RF143762   Estella Moore (b ca 1873, Piatt Co IL).

RF143763   Alonzo (Lonnie) Moore (b ca 1875, Piatt Co IL).

RF143764   Orella (Lauretta) Moore (b ca 1878, Piatt Co IL).

RF143765   Hephzibah (Hepsia) Moore (b 1880, Piatt Co IL).

RF143766   Hattie Moore.

RF143767   Katie Moore.

RF143768   Ella Moore.

RF143769   William Moore.

RF14377   Henry D Moore (b 24 Mar 1850, Ross Co OH) m 4 Nov 1874, Sarah Emma Weir.

RF143771   Mary Ellen Moore (b ca 1876).

RF143772   Sophia J Moore (b ca 1878) m Ray Goodrich.

RF1437721   Vera Goodrich.

RF1437722   Goodrich (boy).

RF143773   Walter Moore (b ca 1880).

RF143774   Ada Moore m Freemont Myers.

RF1437741   Harold Myers.

RF1437742   ALCA Myers.

RF143775   Leila Moore.

RF14378   Sophia C Moore (26 Sep 1853, Ross Co OH-Feb 1946) m 10 May 1875, Allen Co KS, Grafton D Whitaker Sr (b OH).

RF143781   Nettie Whitaker (10 May 1876, Carlyle KS-20 Feb 1843) m Fin Phillips.

RF1437811   Tina Phillips m WV Stevens.

RF14378111   Lloyd Stevens.

RF143782   May Whitaker (b 8 Jul 1878, Carlyle KS) m Will Douglas.

RF1437821   Mabel Jean Douglas.

RF143783   Mabel Whitaker (b Carlyle KS-dy).

RF143784   Edwin C Whitaker (b 4 Mar 1885, Carlyle KS) m Dell Ewing.

RF1437841   Dorothy Whitaker m Russell Hovey.

RF143785   Grafton D Whitaker Jr (b 18 Mar 1887, Carlyle KS) m Alta Croft.

RF1437851   Gene Whitaker m Cecil   .

RF14378511   Barbara Jean Whitaker m Rex Hobbs.

RF14378512   Roger Whitaker.

RF1437852   Mary Whitaker m Harold Zook.

RF14378521   Dean Zook.

RF14378522   Judy Zook.

RF1437853   Nellie Whitaker m Butler Thomas.

RF14378531   Philip Mark Thomas.

RF14378532   Karen Sue Thomas.

RF1437854   Sophia Whitaker m Kelton Maxfield.

RF1437855   Margaret Whitaker (dy).

RF1437856   Velma Whitaker m Paul Nicholson.

RF14378561   Larry Nicholson.

RF1437857   John Whitaker m Betty Somers.

RF14378571   Treva Whitaker.

RF14378572   Trella Whitaker.

RF14378573   John Clark Whitaker.

RF14378574   Mary Beth Whitaker.

RF1437858   Edwin Whitaker m Doris Brennanman.

RF14378581   Ronald Duvall Whitaker.

RF1437859   Warren Whitaker m Kay Ellis.

RF14379   Gabriel D Moore (b 7 Dec 1859, Piatt Co IL) m 8 Dec 1882, Sarah Alice Huston.

RF143791   Lottie C Moore (25 Sep 1883-20 Nov 1921) m Alva Skelton.

RF1437911   Gerald Skelton.

RF1437912   Clifford Skelton.

RF143792   Lester D Moore (8 Jan 1885-Feb 1944).

RF143793   June Moore (b 4 Jun 1897) m Branch Perry.

RF1437931   Kenneth Perry.

RF1437932   Edwin Perry.

RF1437933   David Perry.

RF1437934   John Perry.

RF144   Daniel Spyker (10 Feb 1781, Tulpehocken Tp PA-25 Jun 1855, Aaronsburg PA) m 13 Oct 1805, Magdalena Rausch (26 Aug 1784-27 Apr 1865, Aaronsburg PA) Bur Aaronsburg PA.

RF1441   Samuel Spyker (8 Aug 1806-20 Sep 1854) m Susan Wise (1806-1892).

RF14411   Rosetta Spyker (1830-1881) m   Tippery. Bur Alexandria PA.

RF14412   Daniel Spyker.

RF14413   George W Spyker.

RF14414   Alfred W Spyker (1840, Alexandria PA-1907) m Caroline Piper (1844, Alexandria PA-1935).

RF144141   Harry W Spyker (1863-1906) m Hattie Hamer.

RF1441411   Helen Spyker m Austin Thorton.

RF144142   William Peter Spyker (1865-1907) m M Salome Piper.

RF1441421   Mae Spyker m Gustave Graffius.

RF14414211   Helen Graffius m   Huhn.

RF14414212   Elizabeth Graffius m   Yocum.

RF14414213   Gustave Graffius.

RF14414214   Robert Graffius.

RF14414215   Salome Graffius m Alexandria PA,   Davis.

RF14414216   Henry Graffius.

RF1441422   Chester Alton Spyker (1889-1960) m Mary Donelson.

RF14414221   Myra Catherine Spyker (b 1913) m JP Wert Jr.

RF14414222   William Donnelson Spyker (b 1915).

RF14414223   John Alfred Spyker (b 1916).

RF14414224   Fred Bowers Spyker (b 1918).

RF14414225   Mary Alice Spyker (b 1918).

RF14414226   Sarah Jane Spyker (1922-1977) m Charles S Hosterman.

RF14414227   Martha Caroline Spyker (b 1925) m   Wagner.

RF14414228   Ruth Louise Spyker (b 1929) m   Barger.

RF144143   Samuel Ira Spyker (10 Oct 1876, Alexandria PA-1936).

RF144144   Ralph Spyker (1863-1943).

RF144145   Charles Abraham Spyker (25 Apr 1875-1936, Alexandria PA) m Oct 1898, Alexandria PA, Bertha Margaret Piper (25 Jan 1878-17 Dec 1955) Bur Alexandria PA.

RF1441451   Harold Leslie Spyker (13 Apr 1899-14 Oct 1965, Hares Valley PA) m 18 Aug 1919, Mabel Edith Aggar (b 24 Dec 1899, Hares Valley PA).

RF14414511   Sarah Margaret Spyker (b 12 Feb 1921, Alexandria PA) m 16 Mar 1940, Clearwater FL, Homer Norton Davis (11 Jan 1918, Atlanta GA-23 Jun 1969, Tampa FL) Bur Clearwater FL.

RF144145111   Joann Davis (b 9 Sept 1947, Clearwater FL) m 25 Oct 1969, Rome Italy, James Gordon Davis Sr (b 5 Aug 1947).

RF1441451111   Joanna Gay Davis (b 22 Mar 1971).

RF1441451112   James Gordon Davis Jr (b 28 Dec 1973).

RF1441451112   James Michael Davis (b 30 Mar 1951, Clearwater FL) m 1) 1 May 1971, Linda Maureen Zolinsky, div 1980; m 2) Cynthia Ann Campbell (b 25 Feb 1956).

RF1441451121   Sarah Melina Davis (b 14 Nov 1976).

RF1441451122   Benjamin Aaron Davis (b 25 May 1979).

RF14414512   Mary Louise Spyker (b 3 Jul 1923, Alexandria PA) m 1 Jun 1947, Clearwater FL, John Wesley Welsh (b 6 Feb 1920, Berea KY).

RF144145121   John Wesley Welsh III (25 Oct 1948, Clearwater FL-10 Jun 1970).

RF144145122   Mark Gilbert Welsh Sr (b 27 Dec 1950, Clearwater FL) m 12 Jun 1976, Kathleen Ann Casper (b 24 Jun 1952, Troy NY).

RF1441451221   Mark Gilbert Welsh Jr (b 21 Sept 1979).

RF1441451222   Kristine Anne Welsh (b 26 Jan 1981).

RF1441452   Eleanor Grace Spyker (b 26 Feb 1901, Alexandria PA) m 5 Sep 1928, Williamsport PA, Roland Sylvester Mickey (28 Dec 1902-29 Nov 1964) Bur Alexandria PA.

RF14414521   Marilyn Joanne Mickey (b 26 Sep 1930, Alexandria PA) m 11 Aug 1950, Robert Harold Giffin (b 28 Jun 1929).

RF144145211   Thomas Mickey Giffin (b 10 Feb 1954, Bellefonte PA) m 27 Nov 1976, Cindy Vickers (b 10 Oct 1954).

RF1441452111   Joel Samuel Giffin (b 13 Apr 1980).

RF1441452112   Aaron Thomas Giffin (b 12 Feb 1983).

RF144145212   Roger Leland Giffin (b 30 Jan 1956, Clearfield PA).

RF144145213   Paula Ann Giffin (b 29 Aug 1960, Clearfield PA).

RF14414522   Linda Louise Mickey (b 4 Sep 1939, Alexandria PA) m 21 Sep 1963, Huntingdon PA, Richard William Scialabba (b 10 Nov 1939, Huntingdon PA).

RF144145221   Joseph Mickey Scialabba (b 7 Nov 1964, Huntingdon PA).

RF144145222   Susan Michelle Scialabba (b 28 Aug 1968, Huntingdon PA).

RF144145223   Ann Michelle Scialabba (b 25 Mar 1970, Huntingdon PA).

RF1441453   Charles Norman Spyker (11 Mar 1903-14 Dec 1954) m Aug 1924, Ida Chilcoat (b 1906).

RF14414531   Betty Jane Spyker (b 8 Jan 1925) m   Norris.

RF144145311   Jeffrey Lynn Norris (b 13 Jun 1953).

RF14414532   William Norman Spyker (b 9 Sep 1927) m Jun 1948, Mary Jane Lenpel.

RF144145321   Berth L Spyker (b 1951).

RF144145322   William Piper Spyker (b 1955).

RF1441454   Walter Albert Spyker (10 Jan 1908-5 Mar 1962) m Arlene Wertman (b 1910) Bur Alexandria PA.

RF1441455   Miriam Isobel Spyker (b 3 Feb 1910) m 18 Jan 1930, Vinton L Moore (1 Sep 1905, Four Oaks NC).

RF1441456   Margaret Winifred Spyker (b 1 Sep 1913) m 1934, Clyde Rishel (10 Aug 1912-3 Aug 1978) Bur Alexandria PA.

RF14414561   John Charles Rishel (b 4 Aug 1944, PA) m 4 Nov 1972, Susan Brady Johnson (b 28 Feb 1940, NC).

RF144145611   Windy Sue Rishel (b 21 May 1973).

RF1441457   Richard Piper Spyker (23 Feb 1915-27 Dec 1944, Battle of the Bulge, France) m Jul 1940, Winchester VA, Madeline Yarnell (b 3 Jan 1921).

RF14414571   Charles Richard Spyker (b 2 Aug 1942, Huntingdon PA) m 1) Jun 1964, Conway SC, Renae K Howard (b Hampstead NC); m 2) 17 Oct 1970, Newport PA, Phyllis Lorraine Shull.

RF144145711   Jeffrey Kye Spyker (b 19 Mar 1965, Jacksonville NC).

RF144146   George Newton Spyker (d 14 Jun 1910, Huntingdon PA) m Ella B Stouffer.

RF1441461   Robert Newton Spyker (b 3 Jun 1909, Huntingdon PA) m 20 Aug 1938, Rebeca Pavin (b 18 Feb 1914, Reading PA).

RF14414611   Susanne Carylon Spyker (b 3 Jul 1940, West Chester PA) m Jan 1958, Lynn Barry Daniels.

RF14414612   John Parvin Spyker (b 14 Apr 1942, Reading PA) m 11 Jul 1964, Gertrude Elmira Ely.

RF14414613   Eleanor Jane Spyker (b 16 Aug 1947, Reading PA) m 19 Feb 1965, Charles Hilman.

RF1441462   Mary Elizabeth Spyker (b 10 Jan 1906, Huntingdon PA) m Apr 1936, Valley Forge PA, Preston Rebok (22 Dec 1897-14 Jul 1951, Philadelphia PA) Bur Germantown, Philadelphia PA.

RF14414621   Edward Newton Rebok (b 5 Jan 1938, Germantown, Philadelphia PA).

RF144147   Susan B Spyker (2 Nov 1879-26 Jul 1968) m Harry Stouffer.

RF14415   Francis N Spyker.

RF14416   Margaret A Spyker.

RF1442   William Spyker (23 Sep 1808-11 Oct 1846) m Lydia Poorman. Bur Aaronsburg PA.

RF14421   Mary Jane Spyker (b 13 Jan 1832) m Charles Durner.

RF14422   Susanna (or Rosanna) Spyker (5 Dec 1840-9 Feb 1870) Bur Aaronsburg PA.

RF14423   Sarah Matilda Spyker.

RF1443   Maria Spyker (17 Feb 1811, Aaronsburg PA-26 Apr 1888) m 28 Feb 1832, Henry Gast (13 Sep 1806-2 Nov 1897).

RF14431   Margaret Magdalina Gast (2 Mar 1834-2 Dec 1871) unm.

RF14432   John Daniel Spyker (24 Nov 1835-2 Dec 1903) m 7 Jan 1868, Elizabeth Piper.

RF144321   Harry A Gast (9 Apr 1869-1934) m Jan 1896, Anna Rothermel (1876-1940).

RF1443211   Elizabeth Gast.

RF144322   Margaret Gast (b 3 Oct 1870) m Robert E Snodgrass.

RF144323   Mayme Gast (b 26 Nov 1873) m 7 Nov 1901, Guy Roush.

RF144324   Katharine Gast (b 21 Jun 1875) m 1 Jun 1899, Newton A Kurtz.

RF1443241   Spyker Kurtz (d 5 Dec 1963).

RF1443242   Luther Daniel Kurtz (4 Oct 1907-27 Aug 1965) m 29 Nov 1934, Florence Anderson. Supervisor, Greensburg, PA.

RF14432421   Luther Daniel Kurtz III (b 15 Nov 1940) m 16 Jun 1965, Eileen Todd.

RF14433   George Calvin Gast (26 Oct 1837-18 Feb 1840).

RF14434   Oliver Henry Gast (31 Jan 1839-18 Feb 1839).

RF14435   John Reynolds Gast (7 Mar 1840-19 Nov 1921) m 1) Mary Bechtel (18 Oct 1847-23 Oct 1902); m 2) Blanche Reighard.

RF14436   Catharine Ann Gast (b 4 Jun 1842) m 8 Oct 1867, John Montelius.

RF144361   Charles Harry Montelius (28 Aug 1868-7 May 1869).

RF144362   Joseph K Montelius (b 17 Feb 1870) m 30 Nov 1898, Helen Stadler.

RF1443621   Harry Montelius (b 8 Sep 1899).

RF1443622   Catharine Montelius (b 8 Aug 1901).

RF1443623   Alfred Montelius (b 1 Feb 1903).

RF1443624   Ruth Montelius (b 29 Aug 1905).

RF144363   Margaret G Montelius (b 20 Mar 1871).

RF144364   George Montelius (b 30 Nov 1872) m 26 Jun 1900, Anna Stadler.

RF1443641   Charles Henry Montelius (b 23 Jun 1901).

RF1443642   Dorothy Helen Montelius (b 28 Mar 1907).

RF144365   John Montelius (b 10 Nov 1874) m 20 Jun 1899, Emilie McKinney.

RF144366   Mary Rebecca Montelius (b 17 Mar 1879) Piper City IL.

RF14437   Emma Gast (22 Apr 1846-8 Nov 1877).

RF1444   George Spyker (ca 1814-Jan 1888) m Leah Shank.

RF14441   Rosetta Spyker (b ca 1837).

RF14442   Mary Spyker (b ca 1842).

RF14443   Charles Spyker (b ca 1844).

RF1445   Henry Spyker (14 Feb 1816, Aaronsburg PA-7 Apr 1885) m 1) 17 Feb 1842, Elizabeth Kramer; m 2) 25 Oct 1881, Emma Peters.

RF14451   Mary Spyker (b ca 1847).

RF14452   Mazy Spyker (b ca 1849).

RF14453   Irene Spyker.

RF1446   Magdalena Margaret Spyker (1819, Aaronsburg PA-3 Feb 1846, Lebanon PA) m Solomon Meyer (21 Sep 1818-19 Jul 1872, Boalsburg PA) Bur Boalsburg PA.

RF14461   Alfred Meyer.

RF14462   Mary Elizabeth Meyer (20 Nov 1843, Centre Hall PA-29 Sep 1944, Mifflinburg PA) m Thomas Oliver Bogenrief (1 May 1844, Mifflinburg PA-30 Oct 1925, Mifflinburg PA) Bur Mifflinburg PA.

RF144621   Harriet Meyer Bogenrief (30 Jan 1875, Mifflinburg PA-18 Aug 1960, Elizabethtown PA) m John Calvin Prettyleaf (11 Aug 1880, Lewistown PA-30 Mar 1943, Lewistown PA) Bur Lewistown PA.

RF1446211   Jeanne Prettyleaf (b 18 Nov 1908, Lewistown PA-26 May 1989) m 8 Jun 1933, Lewistown PA, Charles Lester Lack (b 9 May 1907, Harrisburg PA) Lutheran pastor, Harrisburg PA, 1932-1940; USAF, 1940-1960, Chaplain, Lt Col; Teacher, 1960-.

RF14462111   Linda Sue Lack (b 4 Nov 1938, Harrisburg PA).

RF14462112   Brian Michael Stoever Lack (b 15 Jul 1942, Harrisburg PA) m 6 Jan 1964, Montpelier VT, Nan Marie Lomasney (b 3 Aug 1944, Schenectady NY).

RF144621121   Cynthia Marie Lack (b 30 Dec 1964, Barre VT).

RF1447   Jonathan Spyker (1 Sep 1823-17 Feb 1867).

RF145   Johann Henrich Spyker (27 Sep 1782, Tulpehocken Tp, Berks Co PA-30 Jan 1855, Shawnee OH) m 20 Aug 1810, Circleville OH, Elisabetha Todd (3 May 1795, VA-31 Oct 1878, Shawnee OH) Bur Allen Co OH. War of 1812.

RF1451   Samuel Spyker (13 Nov 1810, Circleville OH-23 Mar 1897, Shawnee OH) m 1) 13 Dec 1835, Sarah Weaver (13 Jan 1814, KY-30 Oct 1850, Shawnee OH); m 2) 13 Aug 1851, Margaret Lousch (12 Aug 1833, OH-21 Feb 1903, Allen Co OH).

RF14511   Martin Spyker (15 Oct 1834, Shawnee OH-8 Feb 1912, Shawnee OH) m 1 Aug 1864, Duchouquet, Auglaize Co OH, Ladema Cutler (4 Dec 1841, VA-21 Apr 1936, Shawnee OH).

RF145111   Thomas Corbett Spyker (27 May 1865, Duchouquet OH-19 Jan 1948, Columbus OH) m 28 Aug 1886, Goshen OH, Flora Estelle Haggard (26 Dec 1869, Goshen OH-27 Oct 1929, Goshen OH).

RF1451111   Harry Asbury Spyker (12 Dec 1888, Goshen OH-2 Dec 1970, Ottawa OH) m 14 May 1910, Kempton OH, Laura Belle Herrington (2 Sep 1885, German OH-Oct 1984).

RF14511111   Mitchell Alden Spyker (11 May 1911, Wayne Tp, Auglaize Co OH-12 Sep 1986) m 26 Apr 1941, Cincinnati OH, Catherine Smith (b 12 Oct 1913, Farrell PA) WWII: USA, 1942-1945. Physician.

RF145111111   Stephanie Joan Spyker (b 26 Aug 1946, Columbus OH).

RF145111112   Gregory Alden Spyker (b 2 Sept 1947, Columbus OH).

RF145111113   Melanie Caye Spyker (b 9 Jun 1949, Waltham MA).

RF14512   Lewis Spyker (b 1837).

RF14513   Allen Spyker (b ca 1839).

RF14514   Elizabeth Spyker (b 1841).

RF14515   Mary Spyker (b 1843).

RF14516   Henry Spyker (b 1845).

RF14517   Jacob Spyker (b 1848).

RF14518   Susan Spyker (b 1850).

RF14519   Jonathan Spyker (b 1852).

RF1451A   Sarah Spyker (b 1854).

RF1451B   Samuel Spyker (b 1856).

RF1451C   Peter Spyker (b 1858).

RF1451D   Effie Spyker (b 1859).

RF1451E   Theodore Spyker (b 1861).

RF1451F   Charles Spyker (b 1863).

RF1451G   Joel Spyker (29 Mar 1864, Shawnee Tp, Allen Co OH-17 Nov 1950, Allen Co OH) m
1887, Mary Belle Driscoll (9 Feb 1863, Williams City OH-29 Jan 1950, Allen Co OH).

RF1451G1   Lawrence K Spyker (14 May 1888, Allen Co OH-28 Sep 1976) m 19 Jun 1912, Helen
Vortkamp (10 Jan 1891, Cincinnati OH-12 Oct 1976).

RF1451G11   Lawrence Spyker (b 2 May 1913) m Alice Rousculp.

RF1451G111   Daniel Spyker (b 15 Nov 1942) m 22 Dec 1977, Mary Saiomiveber (b 23 Apr 1949).

RF1451G1111   Meghan R Spyker (b 19 Jan 1979).

RF1451G1112   Abigail L Spyker (b 20 Nov 1980).

RF1451G112   Stephen L Spyker.

RF1451G113   Jack A Spyker (21 Jul 1949-Jan 1974).

RF1451G12   Richard D Spyker (b 6 Feb 1916) m 1953, Dorothy Aska (b 18 Jul 1917).

RF1451G121   Jonathan L Spyker (b 15 May 1954).

RF1451G122   David E Spyker (b 15 May 1955).

RF1451G1221   Dawn N Spyker (b 21 Jan 1979).

RF1451G123   Nancy Jane Spyker (b 2 Sep 1957) m 26 Jul 1980, David A Fine (b 7 Nov 1954).

RF1451G13   David A Spyker (b 22 Oct 1917) m 9 Apr 1942, Margene Whitney.

RF1451G14   Joel B Spyker (b 31 Jan 1919) m 30 Sep 1961, Eulice Murphy (b 7 Dec 1928).

RF1451G15   Helen Jean Spyker (b 25 Sep 1954, Lima OH).

RF1451G2   Gertrude Spyker (b 1890).

RF1451G3   Florence Spyker (b 1892).

RF1451G4   Dale Spyker (1895-1900).

RF1451G5   Irma Spyker (b 1898).

RF1451G6   Eleanor Spyker (b 1899).

RF1451H   George Spyker.

RF1451I   Nettie Spyker (b 1868).

RF1451J   Addie Spyker (b 1871).

RF1452   Mary Spyker.

RF1453   Julia Ann Spyker.

RF1454   Luther Spyker (18 Dec 1818, Pickaway Co OH-14 Mar 1888, Auglaize Co OH) m 22 Apr 1846, Allen Co OH, Mary Ann Petit (b 1829).

RF14541   Levi Spyker (17 Nov 1847-3 Jan 1901, Allen Co OH) m 15 Sep 1869, Sarah Anna Butler (4 Mar 1841-22 Aug 1899, Allen Co OH).

RF145411   Sarah Spyker (b 23 Nov 1872, Auglaize Co OH).

RF145412   George Allen Spyker (28 Dec 1875, Auglaize Co OH-28 Jul 1940, Crawford Co IL) m 25 Dec 1898, Auglaize Co OH, Sarah Melissa Sellers (28 Oct 1877, Auglaize Co OH-26 Feb 1960, Crawford Co IL).

RF1454121   Blanche Cecil Spyker (9 Oct 1899-7 Sep 1939, Crawford Co IL) m John Gaddis.

RF14541211   Ruth Alma Gaddis m Leroy Catt.

RF14541212   Frank Arthur Gaddis.

RF14541213   Clyde Albert Gaddis.

RF14541214   Mary Alice Gaddis m Bill McClure.

RF14541215   Lois Ann Gaddis m John White.

RF14541216   Thelma Gaddis.

RF1454122   Roland Vern Spyker (b 3 Jan 1902) m Edith Meyers.

RF14541221   Vera Spyker.

RF14541222   Warren Spyker.

RF1454123   Hazel Elsie Spyker (12 Jul 1904-26 Nov 1960, Olney IL).

RF14541231   Charles Spyker.

RF14541232   Albert Spyker.

RF1454124   Edna Belva Spyker (b 22 Jan 1907) m William Henry Vernia.

RF14541241   Francis Vernia m 31 Jan 1948, Orlin Stephens.

RF145412411   Darrell Eugene Stephens (b 15 Jun 1948, Crawford Co IL) m 1) Feb 1967, Phyllis Matheny; m 2) Dec 1973, Shirley Nave; m 3) Dec 1993, Sue Tracy.

RF1454124111   Beth Ann Stephens (b 18 Sep 1967) m Chris Kirk.

RF1454124112   Darrell Eugene Stephens II (b 28 Mar 1969).

RF1454124113   Dennis Jo Stephens (b 15 Jun 1971) m Brandy   .

RF1454124114   Daniel Lee Stephens (b 6 Jun 1972).

RF1454124115   Kevin Eugene Stephens (b 10 Jul 1975).

RF145412412   Diana Kae Stephens (b 15 Jan 1951) m Doyle Graham.

RF1454124121   Douglas Ray Graham (b 20 Mar 1975).

RF145412413   Anita Rowene Stephens (b 25 Jan 1955) m Philip Otey, div.

RF1454124131   Jrissa Marie Otey (b 4 Feb 1975).

RF1454124132   Cindy Mae Otey (b 14 Nov 1976).

RF145412414   Terri Louise Stephens (b 11 Nov 1957) m John Beacher.

RF145412415   Vicky Sue Stephens (b 26 May 1959).

RF1454124151   Linda Marie (b 10 Oct 1976).

RF1454124152   Liza May (b 28 Mar 1979).

RF145412416   Brian Douglas Stephens (b 10 Feb 1963) m 14 Oct 1989, Karen Sue Bowman.

RF145412417   Kelly Jo Stephens (b 29 Apr 1965).

RF14541242   Betty Lou Vernia m Jim Jones.

RF14541243   Mary Vernia.

RF14541244   Dorthy Vernia.

RF1454125   Frances Clarence Spyker (b 28 Aug 1909).

RF1454126   Nellie Catherine Spyker (14 Aug 1912, Spencerville OH-21 Sep 1971, Hutsonville IL) m 24 Sep 1930, Lyman Leroy Lowe.

RF1454127   Ellen Elizabeth Spyker (b 28 May 1915, Crawford Co IL) m 24 Jun 1938, Owensboro KY, George Dunlap (19 Dec 1915, Crawford Co IL-5 Dec 1985, Crawford Co IL).

RF14541271   Mary Ann Spyker (b 4 Nov 1935, Crawford Co IL) m 1) Doyle Quincy Patton; m 2) 10 Nov 1960, Ronald William Cox (b 28 May 1927) Interstate trucker.

RF145412711   David Allen Patton (b 29 Mar 1953, Crawford Co IL).

RF14541272   George Ray Dunlap (b 26 Jun 1939, Crawford Co IL) m 1 Jul 1972, Lake Co IN, Jacqueline Sue Mathews (b 9 Nov 1947) He, Boilermaker; she, RN.

RF145412721   Jeremy Scott Dunlap (b 21 Feb 1980, Cook Co IL).

RF145412722   Jonathon Ray Dunlap (b 15 Feb 1984, Cook Co IL).

RF145412723   Janna Kaye Dunlap (b 1 Aug 1985, Cook Co IL).

RF14541273   Doris Sue Dunlap (b 1 Jun 1941, Crawford Co IL) m 1) Gene Bryant; m 2) Ronald Casmir LaBada (b 18 Jul 1936) She, refinery operator.

RF145412731   Kimberly Ann Dunlap (b 9 Oct 1963).

RF145412732   Julie Dawn Dunlap (b 24 Jan 1965).

RF145412733   Mary Ellen Bryant (b 7 Jun 1967).

RF145412734   Daniel Scott LaBada (b 23 Aug 1978).

RF14541274   Sarah Belle Dunlap (b 11 Jun 1943, Crawford Co IL) m 22 Dec 1962, Crawford Co IL, Robert Lee Shidler (b 14 Nov 1941) She, foreman; he, construction worker.

RF145412741   Linda Darlene Shidler (b 1 Jul 1963, Crawford Co IL) m 23 May 1987, Crawford Co IL, Glenn Patrick Lattz (b 19 Oct 1965, Crawford Co IL).

RF1454127411   Cameron Ross Shidler-Lattz (b 21 Mar 1989, St Louis MO).

RF1454127412   Brook Nicole Shidler-Lattz (b 11 Jul 1990, Urbana IL).

RF145412742   Jame Ann Shidler (b 24 Nov 1964, Crawford Co IL) m 20 Dec 1985, Crawford Co IL, Brian Kenneth McCall (b 3 Mar 1963, McCall IL) She, principal; he, petro engineer, Traverse City MI.

RF145412743   Christy Jo Shidler (b 4 Oct 1974, Crawford Co IL) m 26 Nov 1994, Crawford Co IL, Nathan Gunter Arnstowski (b 18 Apr 1974, Stratford, Ontario Canada).

RF14541275   John Wesley Dunlap (b 6 Jun 1945, Crawford Co IL) m 14 Nov 1964, Crawford Co IL, Judith Ann Maxey (b 13 Nov 1946) Construction worker.

RF145412751   Katherine Louise Dunlap (b 26 Jan 1966).

RF145412752   Leonard Ray Dunlap (b 12 May 1968).

RF14541276   Nancy Ellen Dunlap (25 Jun 1947, Crawford Co IL-13 Aug 1952, Crawford Co IL).

*RF14541277   James Albert Dunlap (b 4 Jan 1950, Crawford Co IL) m 26 May 1973, Jasper Co IL, Sandra Belle Woodard (b 30 Nov 1955, Richland Co IL) Ceramic caster, Baptist pastor.

RF145412771   James Albert Dunlap Jr (b 16 Apr 1974, Richland Co IL).

RF145412772   Robert Eugene Dunlap (b 8 Dec 1975, Richland Co IL).

RF145412773   Eric Daniel Dunlap (b 20 May 1978, Richland Co IL).

RF145412774   Shane Christopher Dunlap (b 20 Jan 1982, Richland Co IL).

RF145412775   Adam Joseph Dunlap (b 20 Dec 1986, Richland Co IL).

RF145412776   Sara Elisabeth Dunlap (b 16 Sep 1989, Richland Co IL).

RF14541278   Charles Francis Dunlap (b 8 Dec 1952, Crawford Co IL) m 22 Sep 1984, Carol Jean Hess (b 28 Dec 1952, Gary IN) He, Children's entertainment.

RF145412781   Evan Andrew Dunlap (b 29 Aug 1986, Tulsa OK).

RF14541279   Naomi Ruth Dunlap (b 15 Jan 1955, Crawford Co IL) m 1) 20 Apr 1974, Hammond IN, Godofredo DeJesus (b 19 Nov 1954, Puerto Rico) div 1984; m 2) 19 May 1984, Bossier City LA, Peter William Smith (b 12 Jul 1954, Spain) div 1991; m 3) 11 Apr 1993, Haughton LA, Brian Keith Leatherwood (b 15 Nov 1966, Dennison TX) He, USA, Lt.

RF145412791   Kevin Anthony DeJesus (b 11 Sep 1975, Hammond IN).

RF145412792   Elisabeth Ashley Smith (b 30 Nov 1985, Bossier City LA).

RF1454127A   Janice Joan Dunlap (b 16 Oct 1959, Crawford Co IL) m 24 Dec 1977, Hammond IN, Terry Gene Shelton (b 12 Dec 1959).

RF1454127A1   Amy Marie Shelton (b 19 Oct 1980).

RF1454127A2   Beth Ann Shelton (b 28 Feb 1983).

RF1454128   Jennie Marie Spyker (b 3 Nov 1918, Crawford Co IL) m 24 Jun 1936, Crawford Co IL, Thomas Eugene Dunlap (b 15 Nov 1915, Crawford Co IL).

RF14541281   Paul Gene Dunlap (b 6 Oct 1936, Crawford Co IL) m Shirley Kay Wells (b 12 Nov 1941).

RF145412811   Debbie Jean Dunlap (b 2 Jun 1959).

RF145412812   Patty Jo Dunlap (b 6 Apr 1962).

RF145412813   Thomas Andrew Dunlap (b 7 Jan 1964).

RF14541282   Jerry David Dunlap (b 29 Nov 1938, Crawford Co IL) m 23 Dec 1959, Crawford Co IL, Doris June Allison.

RF145412821   Vickie Dunlap (b 7 Aug 1960).

RF145412822   Kelly Jo Dunlap (b 23 Apr 1967).

RF145412823   David Lee Dunlap (b 2 Oct 1970).

RF14541283   Harry Allen Dunlap (b 7 Apr 1941, Crawford Co IL).

RF14541284   Franklin Dunlap (b 23 Aug 1943, Crawford Co IL) m Donna Kaye Biggs (b 7 Dec 1947).

RF145412841   Ralph Eugene Dunlap (b 23 Feb 1965).

RF145412842   Sherry Ann Dunlap (b 24 May 1969).

RF145412843   Susan Kay Dunlap (b 22 Sep 1970).

RF145412844   Frankie Dunlap (b 20 Feb 1977).

RF14541285   Sally Ann Dunlap (b 16 Nov 1946, Crawford Co IL).

RF14541286   James Leroy Dunlap (b 31 Aug 1948, Crawford Co IL) m 26 Feb 1979, Crystal Darlene Hires (b 9 Jan 1956, Charleston IL).

RF145412861   Billy Joe Dunlap (b 15 Feb 1979).

RF14541287   Larry Joe Dunlap (b 21 Sep 1950, Crawford Co IL) m 30 Oct 1971, Betty Jean Brush (b 25 Aug 1951, Indianapolis IN).

RF145412871   Brian Lee Dunlap (b 27 Jul 1978, Lawrenceville IL).

RF145412872   Malisa Ann Dunlap (b 11 Jan 1982, Robinson IL).

RF14541288   Harold Dean Dunlap (b 22 Aug 1952, Crawford Co IL) m 10 Apr 1975, Crawford Co IL, Hellen Lvonne Atteberry (b 30 Nov 1957).

RF145412881   Christina Marie Dunlap (b 31 Jun 1975).

RF14541289   Gary Lee Dunlap (b 6 Jun 1954, Crawford Co IL) m 30 Dec 1977, Cherl Lynn Koen (b 2 Aug 1953, Flora IL) No chn.

RF1454128A   Roger Wayne Dunlap (b 10 Dec 1956, Crawford Co IL) m 18 Feb 1979, Robinson IL, Donna Carol Mendenhall (b 9 Feb 1959, Sullivan IL).

RF1454128A1   Jedidiah David Dunlap (b 28 Oct 1980).

RF1454128B   Ricky Lynn Dunlap (b 26 Nov 1958, Crawford Co IL).

RF1454128C   Sharon Kay Dunlap (b 11 Jan 1962, Crawford Co IL).

RF145413   William Spyker (b ca 1880).

RF145414   Rosetta Spyker (b Nov 1881) m Youlyes Thomas Granger.

RF145415   Mary Spyker m John Ramsey.

RF14542   Eliza Jane Spyker (b 1850) m 1878, William Hesner.

RF14543   Elizabeth Spyker (1856-6 Aug 1916) m 1876, James A Wilson.

RF14544   Warren Spyker (1858-18 Sep 1859).

RF14545   William Spyker (b 1862).

RF1455   Henry Spyker.

RF1456   Eliza Spyker (31 Jan 1828, Salt Creek Tp, Pickaway Co OH-22 Jun 1897) m 1) 15 May 1848, Allen Co OH, John Longshore; m 2) John Van Atta.

RF1457   Levi Spyker m 1846, Mary Osman. Died in Libby Prison.

RF1458   Rachel Spyker.

RF146   Jonathan Spyker (12 Mar 1785, Tulpehocken Tp, Berks Co PA-29 Dec 1862) m 9 Jul 1815, Elisabetha Hosterman (5 Nov 1789-4 Dec 1868).

RF1461   Catharina Spyker (b 5 Apr 1816) m 12 Oct 1847, Levi Starner.

RF1462   Israel Spyker (8 May 1817-26 Mar 1818).

RF1463   Maria Spyker (1 Feb 1819-24 May 1893).

RF1464   Amanda Spyker (27 Jan 1821-11 Jan 1877) m 15 Apr 1823, George Schnure.

RF1465   Elizabeth Spyker (27 Jan 1823-21 Oct 1823).

RF1466   Franklin Spyker (5 Oct 1824-8 Jan 1899) m 1 Oct 1851, Agnes Selin Davis (21 Feb 1824-13 Jun 1875).

RF14661   Jonathan Schnure Spyker (26 Aug 1852-31 Dec 1885).

RF14662   James K Davis Spyker (4 Dec 1854-15 Aug 1855).

RF14663   Agnes Selin Davis Spyker (12 Jul 1856-12 Apr 185.7)

RF14664   Franklin Davis Spyker (1 Feb 1858-3 Jul 1917) m 12 Apr 1900, Margery E S Cornelius.

RF14665   George Sylvester Spyker (1 Oct 1860-14 Nov 1863).

RF14666   Mary Catharine Spyker (Dec 1862-Dec 1862).

RF14667   Henry S Eyer Spyker (4 Oct 1865-30 Jul 1931, Williamsport PA) m 3 Sep 1889, Mary Miller Fairchild (20 Jul 1865-14 Feb 1944, Williamsport PA).

RF146671   Maria Agnes Spyker (b 7 Jan 1891, Lewisburg PA).

RF146672   Baker Fairchild Spyker (12 Apr 1895, Lewisburg PA-13 Oct 1918, in action, WWI) unm Bur Romaque-sous-Montfineon, France.

RF146673   Elizabeth Fairchild Spyker (b 7 Jan 1897, Lewisburg PA) m 30 Dec 1931, Lewisburg PA, Archibald Alexander Owen (11 Aug 1891-3 Nov 1970).

RF1466731   Archibald Alexander Owen (b 4 Oct 1932, Nashville TN) m Glenda Allen .Brown.

RF14667311   Archibald Alexander Owen (b 25 Nov 1959).

RF14667312   Carter Brown Owen (b 8 Aug 1961).

RF14667313   Henry Spyker Owen (b 3 Oct 1966).

RF1466732   Henry Eyer Spyker Owen (b 6 Mar 1934, Locust Grove GA) m 12 Apr 1958 Polly Ann Keller.

RF14667321   Susan Spyker Owen (b14 Dec 1959).

RF14667322   Timothy Keller Owen (b 4 Jan 1961).

RF14667323   Molly Carrington Owen (b 20 Mar 1964).

RF14667324   Douglas R Owen (b 12 Mar 1970).

RF1467   Ledy Ann Spyker (29 May 1827-30 Mar 1830).

RF147   Maria Margaretha Spyker (5 Jul 1786, Tulpehocken Tp, Berks Co PA-18 Mar 1863) m 8 Jan 1807, Alexander Graham (17 Jul 1783, Magherafelt Ireland-1839, Lewisburg PA).

RF1471   Thompson W Graham (1806-22 Jul 1859).

RF1472   Margaret Graham (1808-1 Jun 1870) m 17 Feb 1829, Joseph Flavel Grier. Physician.

RF14721   John A Grier, Civil War: USN.

RF147211   Margaret Graham Grier (b Chicago IL).

RF1473   Henry Graham (1809-28 Aug 1868).

RF1474   Caroline Graham (b ca 1810) m Robert G Hayes (ca 1795-2 May 1854).

RF1475   Henrietta Graham (1812-9 May 1872) m John W Elliott (1817-20 Jan 1857).

RF1476   Mary Graham (24 Sep 1814-21 Nov 1890) m PB Marr (1808-27 Jan 1874).

RF14761   Addison Graham Marr (b 24 Jan 1844).

RF147611   William Price Marr (1 Jun 1872-9 Dec 1957, Racine WI) m Helen Augusta Stocking (7 Jul 1871-Jun 1933).

RF1476111   Helen Winifred Marr (b 23 Jul 1904, RacineWI) m 30 Jun 1928, Racine WI, Bernard Parker Mullen (b 25 Nov 1892, Sturgeon Bay WI) Surgeon, Seattle WA.

RF14761111   Marr Parker Mullen (b 13 Jul 1929, Seattle WA) m 12 Sep 1959, Nancy Jay Heathe (b 11 Jan 1936, Spokane WA).

RF147611111   Kathi Lynn Mullen (b 5 Jun 1960, Seattle WA).

RF147611112   Richard Marr Mullen (b 11 Sep 1961, Spokane WA).

RF14761112   Bernard James Mullen (b 29 Oct 1936, Seattle WA) m 29 May 1964, Cumberland MD, Rebecca Haines.

RF147611121   Elizabeth Anne Mullen (b 25 Aug 1967, Okinawa).

RF147611122   William Gregory Mullen (b 17 Apr 1969, Rochester MN).

RF1476112   Katharine Julia Marr (b 31 Jan 1907, Racine WI) m 29 Aug 1929, Paul Bernard
Buckwalter.

RF14761121   Shirley Ann Buckwalter (b 23 Jul 1930, Evanston IL) m 18 Oct 1952, Dreer Purvin
Langhauser.

RF147611211   Andrew Marr Langhauser (b 4 Jan 1956, New Haven CT).

RF147611212   Amy Katharine Langhauser (b 19 Aug 1958, Hartford CT).

RF147611213   Derek Peter Langhauser (b 20 Feb 1962, Hartford CT).

RF1476113   Jeannette Marr (b 25 Sep 1910, Racine WI) m 1 Sep 1934, Racine WI, Hunter Corbett
(b 14 Aug 1910, Peking China).

RF1477   Thomas Graham (1822-20 Aug 1864).

RF1478   George W Graham.

RF1479   Rosetta Graham (1823-4 Aug 1872) m J Grier Boggs.

RF147A   Lucinda Graham m 1) Thomas Van Valzah Jr (d 23 May 1842) Physician; m 2) Charles
Elder.

RF147B   Alice Graham.

RF148   Eva Elizabetha Spyker (31 Oct 1788, Tulpehocken Tp, Berks Co PA-16 Mar 1790).

RF15   Christopher Weiser (9 Apr 1756, Tulpehocken Tp, Berks Co PA-30 Mar 1818, near
Lewisburg PA) m Barbara   . Bur Lewisburg PA. 5th PA Btln, Peter Decker's Co, Sgt. He was taxed in
Heidelberg Tp, now in Lebanon Co in 1780.[130]

RF151   Eva Elizabeth Weiser (22 Jan 1779-1818) m John Henry Pontius (22 Dec 1773-1812).

RF1511   Henry Pontius (1801-1859) m Sarah Hammer (1812-1868).

RF15111   Andrew Jackson Pontius (1838-1885) m Sarah Trucken Miller (1848-1928).

RF151111   Pierce Benjamin Pontius (1878-1954) m Lenora Leek (1880-1976).

*RF1511111   Andrew Leek Pontius.

RF1511112   Chester Warren Pontius.

RF1511113   Harold Jackson Pontius.

RF152   Christopher Weiser (25 Oct 1780, Tulpehocken Tp, Berks Co PA-25 Oct 1813, near
Lewisburg PA) unm.

RF153   Maria Margaret Weiser (b Feb 1782) Evidently died before Christopher, her brother, as
she was not mentioned in his will.

---

[130]Information from Bell's *History of Northumberland County*, 454; data from Miss Bell Schuh, Eileen Johnson, Wayne W. Weiser;
Linn's *Annals of Buffalo Valley*, 442. Additional data provided in 1996 by Andrew L. Pontius, Elizabeth Sills Mortenson, Dr. John
C. Weiser, and George T. Weiser.

RF154　　　　　George Weiser (25 Jan 1785, Tulpehocken Tp, Berks Co PA-2 Jul 1857, Sunbury PA) m 1 Jun 1809, Elizabeth Bucher (6 Jan 1787-17 Jan 1871, Sunbury PA) Bur Sunbury PA. Tanner; associate judge of Northumberland Co, 1834-1842; County treasurer, 1825-1827,1844-1845.

RF1541　　　　　Henry Weiser (20 May 1810, Sunbury PA-22 Jun 1811, Sunbury PA) Bur Sunburg PA.

RF1542　　　　　John B Weiser (4 Nov 1811, Sunbury PA-7 Oct 1832, Sunbury PA) Bur Sunburg PA. unm.

RF1543　　　　　Amelia Catharine Weiser (26 Sep 1813, Sunbury PA-5 Jun 1915, Sunbury PA) m 1831, Richard Adams Fisher (26 Oct 1805, Heidelberg Tp, Berks Co PA-27 Jan 1857, Sunbury PA) Bur Sunbury PA. Reformed pastor, Sunbury, PA 1827-1854.

RF15431　　　　Albert W Fisher (b 1832, Sunbury PA) m Elizabeth Wise. Physician, Toledo, OH.

RF154311　　　Charles E Fisher (12 Sep 1867, Toledo OH-26 Feb 1929, Toledo OH) m Apr 1912, Elizabeth M Herb.

RF154312　　　William H Fisher (25 Feb 1870, Toledo OH-1936, Toledo OH) Physician, Toledo, OH.

RF154313　　　Albert Fisher.

RF154314　　　Nevin Fisher.

RF154315　　　Dolly Fisher.

RF154316　　　Lillian A Fisher

RF154317　　　Catharine Fisher.

RF154318　　　Frank Fisher.

RF15432　　　　Nevin Fisher (1834, Sunbury PA-1848, Sunbury PA).

RF15433　　　　Amelia Susan Fisher (b 22 Dec 1836, Sunbury PA) m Edward Masser Bucher. No chn.

RF15434　　　　Louisa Fisher (1838, Sunbury PA-1910, Sunbury PA) Bur Sunbury PA. unm.

RF15435　　　　Elizabeth Fisher (1841, Sunbury PA-1861, Sunbury PA) Bur Sunbury PA. unm.

RF15436　　　　Charles Fisher (b 1843, Sunbury PA) unm.

RF15437　　　　Richard Adams Fisher Jr (1845, Sunbury PA-Sunbury PA) Bur Sunbury PA. unm Constable, Sunbury PA.

RF15438　　　　George Zwingli Fisher (b 1847, Sunbury PA) Lima OH.

RF15439　　　　Florence L Fisher (1849, Sunbury PA-8 Sep 1880, Sunbury PA) m 5 Jul 1870, Cornelius A Reimensnyder. Attorney, Sunbury PA.

RF154391　　　Charles Cornelius Reimensnyder (1871, Sunbury PA-13 Jul 1873, Sunbury PA).

RF154392　　　Daisy Reimensnyder (1875, Sunbury PA-21 Sep 1956) m Ira Teitsworth. Dentist.

RF1543921　　Alfred Teitsworth. Dentist.

RF154393   Junius T Reimensnyder (9 Aug 1879, Sunbury PA-10 Sep 1879, Sunbury PA).

RF1543A   Millard Fillmore Fisher (b 1851, Sunbury PA) m Louisa D   (14 Aug 1856-3 May 1897).

RF1543B   John Calvin Fisher (6 Feb 1854, Sunbury PA-27 Sep 1857, Sunbury PA) Bur Sunbury PA.

RF1544   Harriet Weiser (Oct 1814, Sunbury PA-21 Apr 1816, Sunbury PA) Bur Sunbury PA.

RF1545   Elizabeth Mary Weiser (16 May 1818, Sunbury PA-10 Jan 1892, Sunbury PA) m 10 Apr 1851, John Conrad Weiser Bassler. See CP173.

RF1546   George Bucher Weiser (9 Feb 1819-7 Oct 1887, Millersburg PA) m 24 Feb 1857, Susan Ressler (10 Jan 1829-1 Mar 1911) Bur Millersburg PA. MD, Jefferson Medical Col 1842. Physician, PA, Millersburg, Spring Mills, Dalmatia, Selinsgrove.

RF15461   Charles Leon Weiser (7 May 1862, Sunbury PA-10 Oct 1931, St Paul MN) m May 1910, St Paul MN, Henrietta Zeiser (31 May1880, Red Lake Falls MN-1 Apr 1952, White Bearlake MN) Bur St Paul MN. Salesman.

*RF154611   Ruth Pauline Weiser (b 31 Aug 1912, St Paul MN) m 8 May 1943, Milen TN, Oren Peter Sills (31 Jul 1912, Minneapolis MN-28 Jan 1977, Bemidjin MN) Bur Fort Snelling MN.

RF1546111   Elizabeth Ann Sills (b 13 Apr 1948, St Paul MN) m 18 Jul 1970, Pine City MN, Gerald Mortenson (b 18 Feb 1946) div 1975. Federal worker.

RF15461111   Erik Allan Mortenson (b 31 Jan 1972).

RF15462   George Rollin Weiser (13 Feb 1864, Sunbury PA-19 Feb 1887, Millersburg PA) Bur Millersburg PA. unm. Journalist.

RF15463   Frank Ressler Weiser (10 Nov 1865, Sunbury PA-22 May 1925, Windom MN) m 1 Mar 1894, Jeanette A Schock (27 Jul 1865-29 Jun 1950) Bur Windom MN. Physician, Windom MN.

RF154631   George Conrad Weiser (26 Jun 1897, Windom MN-19 Mar 1980, Alexandria VA) m 1) 11 May 1921, Wells MN, Lola Irene Anderson (11 Jan 1897, Wells MN-6 Feb 1954, Bethesda MD); m 2) 30 Dec 1957, Little Rock AR, Margaret Martin Paepper (17 Jul 1906, Montgomery AL-25 Oct 1995, Alexandria VA) Bur Alexandria VA. DDS, U MN, 1920; Seabury Western Seminary, 1931. Episcopal priest, MN, MI, VA, AR. She, RN.

RF1546311   John Conrad Weiser (b 7 Jan 1922, St Paul MN) m 11 Jun 1947, Ft Madison IA, Lenora May Brewster (b 3 Jun 1927, Wyaconda MO) WWII: USMC, 1942-45. BA, 1948, MA, 1949, U IA; PhD, Western Reserve U, 1961. Professor, Kent, 1949-1982. Radio broadcaster.

RF15463111   John David Weiser (b 3 Sep 1948, Iowa City IA) m 1973, Rebecca Smith, div 1976. USMC, 1968-72; 1974-77. BS. Electronics sales and security, Sacramento CA.

RF15463112   Michael Alan Weiser (b 16 Nov 1950, Ravenna OH) unm BA, Sacramento S U, 1989; JD, U N CA School of Law, 1995. Attorney, New Concord CA.

RF15463113   James Richard Weiser (b 1 Jan 1957, Ravenna OH) m 15 Dec 1982, Lisa Antognoli (b 16 Mar 1957, Akron OH) He, BA, 1979, BS, 1982, Kent State (OH) U. Teacher, Wooster OH. She, BA, 1979, MLS, 1991, Kent State U. Librarian.

RF154631131   Noelle Weiser (b May 1994, China).

RF1546312   Marilyn Jeanette Weiser (b 27 Aug 1923, St Paul MN) m 17 Oct 1947, Ft Madison IA,

James A Peck (b 20 Sep 1925) She, RN.

RF15463121   Thomas Richard Peck (b 28 Jul 1949).

RF15463122   Margaret Katherine Peck (b 20 May 1953).

RF1546313   Frank Robert Weiser (b 25 May 1928, St Paul MN) m 24 Sep 1949, Arlington VA, Ruth Ann Ramsdell (b 13 Jul 1926).

RF1546313l   Conrad Arthur Weiser (b 2 Oct 1954).

RF1546314   George Thomas Weiser (b 17 Sep 1931, St Paul MN) m 24 Apr 1954, Arlington VA, Joyce Ann Proctor (b 9 Jul 1934, Washington DC) Fingerprint technician. She, word processor and actress.

RF15463141   William Edward Weiser (b 17 Aug 1958, Washington DC) m 6 Jun 1981, Washington DC, Sarah Dabney Peyton (b 25 Mar 1959, Washington DC) BS, Col of William and Mary, 1979; PhD, Purdue U, 1986. Analytical chemist. She, sociologist.

RF154631411   Caroline Peyton Weiser (b 24 Feb 1989, Durham NC).

RF154631412   Catherine Stuart Weiser (b 14 Nov 1991, Durham NC).

RF15463142   Laurie Jean Weiser (b 14 Nov 1961, Bethesda MD) m 27 Dec 1986, Arlington VA, Luis A Logrono (b 1 May 1959, Santo Domingo, Dominican Republic) BS, James Madison U, 1984. Teacher. He, physician.

RF154631421   Alexander Jose Logrono (b 6 Mar 1990, Milwaukee WI).

RF154631422   Caitlin Anne Logrono (b 15 Oct 1991, Milwaukee WI).

RF154632   Helen Schock Weiser (b 16 Dec 1901, Windom MN) Bur Windom MN. unm Teacher, Hurley WI, International Falls MN.

RF15464   William Henderson Weiser (8 Feb 1867, Millersburg PA-17 Aug 1953) m 28 Sep 1893, Cora Herrold (30 Mar 1873-9 Aug 1950) Bur Millersburg PA. Painter and decorator.

RF15465   Spencer Bucher Weiser (17 May 1873, Millersburg PA-21 Dec 1923) m Jane Isabella Hutton (5 Jun 1874-16 Dec 1945) Bur Bellingham WA. Pharmacist, Bellingham WA.

RF154651   John Hutton Weiser (b 2 Aug 1903, St James MN) m 23 Jun 1930, Ellen Shirley Nelson (b 15 May 1905) Advertiser.

RF1546511   John Hutton Weiser (b 20 Jul 1934, CA) unm.

RF154652   Spencer Kenneth Weiser (b 24 Sep 1906, St James MN) m 8 Oct 1935, Florence Mildred Randolph (b 18 Mar 1910).

RF1546521   Spencer Randolph Weiser (b 22 Jun 1941).

RF1546522   Christy Lynn Weiser (b 13 Jan 1945).

RF1547   Louisa Weiser (b 10 Jan 1821) m 3 Jun 1852, Charles J Bruner (17 Nov 1820, Sunburg PA-15 Mar 1885) Civil War: Co F, 11th PA Vol; Co D 3rd Reg PA Militia, capt. Collector, internal revenue, 1869-1883.

RF15471   Mary Gray Bruner m 28 Mar 1888, Clarence G Voris (29 Jan 1851, Danville PA-2 Jul

1909, Philadelphia PA) Attorney, Milton PA.

RF154711   Clarence A Voris.

RF154712   Charles William Voris.

RF15472   Elizabeth Bruner.

RF15473   Louisa Bruner.

RF15474   Charles Bruner.

RF15475   William W Bruner (d 7 Dec 1901, Sunburg PA) unm.

RF15476   Franklin Bruner.

RF1548   Francis Franklin Weiser (18 Aug 1824, Sunburg PA-5 Oct 1827, Sunburg PA).

RF1549   Charles Peter Shindel Weiser (7 Aug 1827, Sunburg PA-23 May 1862, Sunburg PA) m
Sarah C Brosius (b 7 Sep 1827) MD, Jefferson Medical Col, 1850.

RF15491   Elizabeth Weiser unm.

RF15492   George Broscius (Bucher) Weiser (7 Sep 1857, Dalmatia PA-23 Mar 1948) m 2 Oct 1890,
Selinsgrove PA, Sarah Catharina Schoch (13 Oct 1861, Selinsgrove PA-24 Feb 1948, New Ulm MN) Bur New
Ulm MN.

RF154921   Katharine Georgia Weiser (b 2 Jan 1900, New Ulm MN) m 10 Jun 1925, New Ulm MN,
Clifford Thoren Ekelund. She, BA, Sweetbriar Col, 1923; librarian. He, UMN Medical Col.

RF1549211   Sarah Ann Ekelund (b 8 May 1926, Hibbing MN) m 19 Jul 1947, Newton Skillman. She,
BA, MSU, 1947; He, U MI, 1948. Engineer.

RF15492111   Christopher Thoren Skillman (b 10 Jun 1949, Pontiac MI).

RF15492112   Amy Elizabeth Skillman (b 21 Nov 1952) BA, St Lawrence U, Canton, NY, 1975; MA,
UCLA, 1979. Folklorist.

RF15492113   Newton Skillman III (b 25 Jan 1953).

RF15492114   Stephen Walker Skillman (b 8 Jan 1957).

RF15492115   Timothy George Skillman (b 20 Aug 1958).

RF1549212   Mary Sue Ekelund (b 10 Dec 1928) Mary Washington Col ; UVA, 1951. Secretary.

RF1549213   Georgia Katharine Ekelund (b 7 Sep 1932, Pontiac MI) m 16 Jun 1952, Brewster Holmes
Smith.

RF15492131   David Clifford Smith (b 20 Mar 1954).

RF15492132   Michael Shaw Smith (b 1957).

RF15492133   Gregory George Smith (b Sep 1958).

RF154(10)   Margaret Malinda Weiser (b 4 Aug 1829, Sunburg PA).

RF155 David Weiser (d 1824, Penns Tp, Union Co PA) m Barbara . Left 3 children, one was born after his death.

RF1551 Mary Weiser m 17 Mar 1833, David Druckemiller.

RF1552 Harriet Weiser m 6 Sep 1836, Daniel Durst.

RF156 Daniel Weiser (24 Nov 1792, near Lewisburg PA-8 Oct 1816, near Lewisburg PA) Bur near Lewisburg PA. unm.

RF18 John Weiser was born 15 Dec 1762 in western Berks Co PA and baptized at Christ Church 1 Jan 1763 with Simon Koppenhoffer and his wife Maria Elizabeth Batdorf serving as sponsors. When his father died in 1775, guardians were appointed in December for his young children including John. There is a document in the Weiser Family Association collection in which Christopher Weiser (1756-1817) mortgages a 68 acre tract in Buffalo Tp, Northumberland Co (now Union) to secure a series of bonds totally 450 pounds Christopher owed John Weiser of Frederick, Frederick Co MD and Philip "Phuneta" (Von Neida) of Buffalo Tp on 6 May 1790. (Also recorded in Northumberland Co deeds D-468). A power of attorney executed by John Weiser of Louden Co VA on 19 Sep 1791 is recorded in Northumberland Co deeds G-533. It is a fair assumption that the John involved in this transaction was the brother of Christopher and if that is so, it is the last unequivocal reference to that John so far found.

RF19 Samuel Weiser (16 May 1765, Tulpehocken Tp, Berks Co PA-15 Jan 1838, York PA) m Eva Catharine Pfluger (or Pflieger) (29 Sep 1769-5 Jan 1856, York PA) Bur York PA Samuel was the first of the family to move to York County. He was married there and is on the 1790 Census as a resident of the borough of York. He began as a hatter which he continued until 1822; in 1808 he also opened a dry goods store. The often-printed pictures of Conrad Weiser and his wife are in fact drawings made by Jacob Maentel in the York area in the 1820s or 1830s; they are probably of this couple.[131]

RF191 Samuel Weiser (3 May 1788, York PA-20 Jul 1856, York PA) m 1) May 1813, York PA, Susan Gaertner (1794-22 Apr 1826, York PA); m 2) 15 Nov 1827, York PA, Anna Marin Ilgenfritz (18 May 1808, York PA-23 Jan 1876, York PA) Bur York PA. Hatmaker in York; bought a farm south of York in 1840.

RF1911 Augustus Gardner Weiser (5 Dec 1813, York PA-18 Dec 1879, York PA) m 27 Oct 1839, Sarah Ann Gotwalt (20 Dec 1819, York PA-3 Jun 1895, York PA) Bur York PA. Farmer south of York PA.

RF19111 George Samuel Weiser (10 Mar 1840, near York PA-25 Aug 1853, near York PA) Bur York PA.

RF19112 Marcellus Gotwalt Weiser (b 23 Mar 1842, near York PA) m 1) 30 Nov 1862, Martha Ellen Rively (d 9 Nov 1863); m 2) Isabella .

RF191121 Annie Sue Weiser (b 27 Feb 1868).

RF191122 Curtis Augustus Weiser (b 9 Oct 1869).

RF19113 Augustus Weiser (5 Jun 1844, near York PA-1917) m 5 Jul 1865, Catharine C Hoke (1840-1923).

RF191131 Sarah Ellen Weiser (5 Jan 1866-15 Sep 1891) unm.

RF191132 Annie Kate Weiser (b 20 Jan 1868).

---

[131]Data compiled from the registers of Christ Lutheran Church, York; US census records: data at the Historical Society of York PA, and from Harry N. Weiser Jr., Lucille Winstead, Oliver C. Weiser, Mary Jane Mann, and Helen M Rehberg.

RF191133   James Percy Weiser (b 25 Dec 1869).

RF191134   Delilah Cecilia Weiser (b 2 Feb 1874).

RF191135   Lottie Florence Weiser (b 6 Apr 1879).

RF19114   John Elias Weiser (b 5 Apr 1846, near York PA) unm.

RF19115   Henrietta Christianna Weiser (b 13 May 1848) m 29 Aug 1866, Samuel Ilgenfritz.

RF19116   Samuel Gardner Weiser (b 1 Aug 1851, near York PA) Had a family.

RF19117   Martha Susan Weiser (b 20 Oct 1853, near York PA).

RF19118   Anna Kate Weiser (b 31 Jan 1856, near York PA).

RF19119   Emma Catherine Weiser (20 Sep 1858, near York PA-14 Dec 1938, York PA) m 24 Sep 1876, John Rockey (1852-7 Mar 1897) Clerk, freight depot, York PA.

RF191191   Gertrude M Rockey (3 Apr 1877, York PA-22 Oct 1936) m Herman S Ralph (31 Oct 1879, Brooklyn NY-31 Dec 1955) Salesman.

RF1911911   Williamine Whitall Ralph (22 Mar 1904, Philadelphia PA-21 Dec 1970, Philadelphia PA) m 18 Mar 1926, Harry Ifill Lauer (b 26 Aug 1901, Philadelphia PA) Wesleyan U. Banker, Philadelphia PA.

RF19119111   Harry Ifill Lauer Jr (b 16 Mar 1927, Philadelphia PA) m 13 May 1952, Audrey Ann Breitinger (b 9 May 1930, York PA) BS, Yale U; MA, U PA; BD, Epis. Theol. School, Cambridge MA.

RF191191111   Jane Bladen Lauer (b 24 Sep 1953).

RF191191112   Harry Ifill Lauer III (b 24 Jul 1957).

RF191191113   Audrey Ann Lauer (b 27 Jul 1958).

RF1911912   Julian F Ralph (1 Mar 1908, Philadelphia PA-1908) m 15 Oct 1938, Helen Rudolph. Salesman.

RF19119121   Suzanne Ralph (b 25 May 1942) m 8 Jun 1963, Richard Gross.

RF19119122   John Rockey Ralph (b 26 Jun 1948) m.

RF191192   Ida J Rockey (b Jan 1881, York PA) m George W Allison. Bur York PA.

RF1911921   George W Allison (1906, York PA-Jan 1959) Bur York PA.

RF191193   Edna C Rockey (1885, York PA-Sep 1957) m 1938, William H Ottemiller (1871, York PA-1946) Bur York PA. She, teacher; he, businessman, York PA.

RF1911A   Ida Jane Weiser (b 4 Aug 1859, near York PA) Living 1900.

RF1912   Alexander Samuel Weiser (9 Jun 1815, York PA-14 Aug 1867, York PA) Bur York PA. unm.

RF1913   Henrietta Weiser (b 4 Jan 1818, York PA)

RF1914   Louisa Weiser (7 Nov 1820, York PA-25 Oct 1877, York PA) m 23 Jan 1842, John

Ensminger (10 Oct 1814-9 Jan 1889, York PA) Bur York PA.

RF19141   Louise Ensminger (3 Aug 1844-10 May 1860, Conewago Tp, York Co PA.

RF19142   Ellen Ensminger (17 Jan 1847, York PA-22 Oct 1922, York PA) Bur York PA. unm.

RF19143   Florence Ensminger (16 Sep 1851, York PA-16 Aug 1929, York PA) Bur York PA. unm.

RF19144   Emma Ensminger (b 9 Sep 1855, York PA).

RF1915   Catharine Weiser (b 8 Nov 1821, York PA).

RF1916   Eliza Anna Weiser (b 28 Jan 1824, York PA).

RF1917   Maria Johanna Weiser (b 28 Jan 1824, York PA).

RF1918   Margaret Eva Weiser (b 29 Aug 1825, York PA) m 12 May 1846, Berlin, Somerset Co PA, Josiah Poorbaugh.

RF19181   Lizzie R Poorbaugh (b 1854) m Cyrus Dort (b 15 May 1833) Clergyman.

RF19182   Ann Poorbaugh m Ziegler.

RF191821   Weiser Ziegler.

RF19183   Henry N Poorbaugh.

RF191831   Katherine Poorbaugh m Charles K Edwards, MD.

RF1919   Magdalena Weiser (b 14 Jun 1828).

RF191A   Anna Maria Weiser (24 Sep 1829, York PA-1 Jul 1913, York PA) m 17 May 1858, York PA, David Ziegler (8 Nov 1827, Gettysburg PA-17 Oct 1899, York PA. Bur York PA.

RF191A1   Lucy H Ziegler.

RF191A2   R William Ziegler. Druggist, York PA.

RF191A3   Edgar David Ziegler (b 29 Aug 1868, York PA) m 10 Jan 1910, York PA, Annie J Fauth, widow of Charles G Shenberger.

RF191A31   Edgar D Ziegler (17 Aug 1911, York PA-3 Jan 1995, York PA) m Dorothy M Doll. Lutheran pastor.

RF191A311   David W Ziegler.

RF191A312   Elizabeth Ziegler m   Ebel.

RF191A4   Albert L Ziegler. Druggist, York PA.

RF191A5   C Walter Ziegler. Manufacturer, York PA.

RF191A6   Samuel Weiser Ziegler. Teacher, York PA.

RF191B   Maria Jane Weiser (b 17 Jul 1831, York PA).

RF191C   Albertus Weiser (6 Jul 1833, York PA-1894, Preston MN) m 1) 1860, Olive M Rogers; m 2) 1875, Preston MN, Ida Mae Norman (Feb 1860-2 Mar 1945, Los Angeles CA) He bur Preston MN; she bur Glendale CA. Pharmacist, Preston MN.

RF191C1   Enos Halleck Weiser (1862-1936) unm. Hotel proprietor, Waterloo IA.

RF191C2   Roger Albert Weiser (1867-1930) m 1872, WI, Mary W   . Hotel proprietor, Des Moines IA.

RF191C21   Victor A Weiser (b 11 Aug 1895).

RF191C211   Victor A Weiser Jr.

RF191C22   Madge Amelia Weiser (b 1899, WI) m 1) Charles Wilson (b 1896, IA); m 2) Charles J Kennedy.

RF191C221   Weiser White Wilson (May 1919, IA-Germany) unm WWII: USA.

RF191C3   Olive Alma Weiser (Sep 1863-1943) unm.

RF191C4   Samuel Lincoln Weiser (b 18 Mar 1879, Preston MN) m 23 Nov 1921, St Paul MN, Signe Marie Foss. He, U MI, 1901. Attorney, St Paul MN. She, RN, St Paul MN. No chn.

RF191C5   Maud Ann Weiser (20 Dec 1880-5 Nov 1884, Preston MN) Bur Preston MN.

RF191C6   Albert Norman Weiser (7 May 1884, Preston MN-30 Jul 1912).

RF191C7   Beulah Helen Weiser (b Nov 1886, Preston MN) m 1) Edwin J Kampschroer; m 2) Fricker. Sunland CA.

RF191C71   Robert Kampschroer (b Sunland CA) m.

RF191C711   James Kampschroer.

RF191C712   Joanne Kampschoer.

RF191C72   Jack Weiser Kampschoer. MGM Studios, Hollywood CA.

RF191C721   Christine Kampschoer.

RF191C722   Jacqueline Kampschoer.

RF191C8   Emelius Ilgenfritz Weiser (16 Apr 1835, Spring Garden Tp, York Co PA-28 Oct 1902) m 2 Feb 1854, near Decorah IA, Maria Louise Van Hoff (b 18 Nov 1843, Mechanicsburg IA) Pharmacist, Decorah IA, having moved there in 1856.

RF191C81   Infant (b 1 Apr 1865, stillborn).

RF191C82   Emilius James Weiser (3 Jan 1867, Decorah IA-8 Feb 1937) m 17 May 1893, Decorah IA, Grace E Marsh (23 Apr 1869, Decorah IA-8 Jul 1929) Bur Fargo ND. BA, Northwestern U, 1888. Banker, Fargo ND.

RF191C821   Charlotte Marsh Weiser (27 Jun 1900, Ortonville MN-23 Aug 1940) Bur Fargo ND.

RF191C822   Gretchen Von Hoff Weiser (b 2 Jan 1903, Ortonville MN) m 4 Jan 1930, Fargo ND, Robert Hoole Fayfield (b 9 May 1900, Buffalo NY).

RF191C8221   Marsha Weiser Fayfield (b 5 Jun 1932, Minneapolis MN) m 4 Sep 1954, David W Walsh (b 22 Jan 1930, Escanaba MI) Gladstone MI.

RF191C82211   Kathleen Jo Walsh (b 5 Feb 1956, Escanaba MI).

RF191C82212   Mark David Walsh (b 25 Nov 1957, Escanaba MI).

RF191C8222   Robert Weiser Fayfield (b 29 May 1940, Minneapolis MN).

RF191C83   William Walter Weiser (24 Aug 1870, Decorah IA-13 Jul 1872, Decorah IA) Bur Decorah IA.

RF191C84   Samuel Von Hoff Weiser (19 Sep 1872, Decorah IA-17 Sep 1942, Decorah IA) m 17 Jun 1896, Edna May Tierny. Bur Decorah IA.

RF191C85   Harry Martin Weiser (22 Sep 1884, Decorah IA-27 Apr 1938, Decorah IA) m 31 Oct 1907, Decorah IA, Grace Jane Shea.

RF191D   Mary Magdalena Weiser (15 Oct 1836, York PA-dy).

RF191E   Emma Weiser (16 Apr 1838, York PA-29 Sep 1881, York PA) m 18 Jul 1865, Martin Bender (21 Mar 1832-5 Jan 1908).

RF191E1   Willie Bender (dy).

RF191E2   Helen Bertha Weiser Bender (b 19 Jul 1874, York PA).

RF191F   Samuel Weiser (13 Sep 1841, York PA-12 Feb 1843, York PA) Bur York PA.

RF191G   Helen Weiser (6 Apr 1843, York PA-26 Nov 1933, York PA) unm.

RF191H   Camilla Adda Weiser (10 Oct 1844, York PA-dy).

RF191I   Florence Weiser (24 Mar 1846, York PA-11 May 1871, York PA) Bur York PA. unm.

RF191J   Martha Susan Weiser (16 Jun 1848, York PA-dy).

RF192   John Jacob Weiser (26 Jul 1792, York PA-7 Jun 1874, York PA) m 1)   ; m 2) Sarah Kraber (d 23 May 1833, York PA); m 3) 9 Nov 1837, Ann Lanius (8 Jun 1798-15 Nov 1874, York PA) Bur York PA. Partner with brother Charles in dry goods business to 1818; thereafter partner with brother Daniel in lumber business.

RF1921   Amanda Christina Weiser (4 Mar 1822, York PA-7 Dec 1854, York PA) Bur York PA. unm.

RF1922   Franklin Samuel Weiser (25 Sep 1825, York PA-20 Oct 1887, York PA) m 25 Mar 1852, York PA, Barbara Sophia Stable (20 Oct 1827, York PA-22 Jan 1886, York PA) Bur York PA. Box factory owner, York PA.

RF19221   John Robert Weiser (5 Mar 1853, York PA-5 May 1857, York PA) Bur York PA.

RF19222   Sarah Ann Weiser (19 Jan 1855, York PA-19 Nov 1863, York PA) Bur York PA.

RF19223   Jacob Stable Weiser (14 Jun 1858, York PA-9 Aug 1863, York PA) Bur York PA.

RF19224   Harry Kraber Weiser (13 Oct 1860, York PA-20 Apr 1943, York PA) m 23 Apr 1885, York PA, Ella Sheaffer (30 Dec 1861, York PA-22 Sep 1933, York PA) Bur York PA. Purchasing agent, York PA.

RF192241   Franklin Sheafer Weiser (b 30 Mar 1886, York PA) m Martha   . Middlebury CT. No chn.

RF192242   Harry Norman Weiser (18 Feb 1890, York PA-5 Nov 1967, York PA) m 5 Jun 1920, Columbus OH, Emily Church Benham (19 Jul 1886, Columbus OH-21 Nov 1959, York PA) Bur York PA. Sales manager, York PA.

RF1922421   Harry Norman Weiser Jr (b 6 Apr 1921, Columbus OH) m 1) 7 Apr 1945, Brisbane Australia, Gwendolyn Dorothea Bergman, div 1957; m 2) 7 June 1958, York PA, Phyllis Amanda Hueter (b 10 Mar 1926, Front Royal VA) USAF. Chemist, York PA.

RF19224211   Darryl Bergman Weiser (b 9 May 1959, York PA).

RF19224212   Stacy June Weiser (b 15 Jun 1957, York PA).

RF1922422   Sara Church Weiser (b 24 Dec 1924, Columbus OH) m 26 Jun 1944, York PA, Palmer E Dice (19 May 1924, York PA-6 Jan 1987, York PA) Bur York PA.

RF19224221   Marcia Lou Dice (b 16 Mar 1946, York PA).

RF19224222   Jeffery Kenneth Dice (b 3 Jul 1948, York PA).

RF192243   Janella Sheafer Weiser (18 Sep 1897, York PA-20 Apr 1928, York PA). Bur York PA. Unm. Secretary, York PA.

RF19225   William Franklin Weiser (2 Oct 1865, York PA-21 Mar 1915, York PA) m Jun 1889, York PA, Nettie Virginia Smyser (12 Jun 1866, York PA-1 Apr 1938,York PA) Bur York PA. Lumber business; banker, York PA.

RF192251   Martin Smyser Weiser (10 May 1891, York PA-7 Oct 1918, Ft McHenry MD) Mexican border incident, 1st Cavalry; later, USA, Quartermasters Corps, 1st Lt. unm.

RF192252   Jacob Spangler Weiser (1892-1892, York PA).

RF192253   William Donald Weiser (1894-1895, York PA).

RF192254   Mary Julia Weiser (b 26 Dec 1895, York PA) m 18 Nov 1926, York PA, Edwin Augustus Barnitz. Bur York PA. Postmaster, York PA.

RF19226   Eugene Francis Weiser (16 May 1874, York PA-28 Aug 1948, York PA) m 17 Jun 1903, Lulu Kindig. Bur York PA. Insurance business, York PA.

RF1923   Maria Johanna (Mary Jane) Weiser (2 Sep 1827, York PA-14 Apr 1910, York PA) m 1) 19 Feb 1850, Jacob Smyser; m 2) Nathaniel Weigle (12 Apr 1823, York PA-28 Apr 1825, York PA) Bur York PA. No chn.

RF1924   Marcellus Albertus Weiser (29 Feb 1830, York PA-11 Sep 1831, York PA) Bur York PA.

RF1925   Sarah Ann Weiser (18 Jul 1831, York PA-21 Apr 1854, York PA) Bur York PA.

RF1926   Marcellus Graber Weiser (17 May 1833, York PA-dy).

RF1927   Ellen Lanius Weiser (21 Dec 1838, York PA-17 Jul 1839, York PA).

RF1928   James Lanius Weiser (8 Dec 1840, York PA-26 Jul 1841, York PA).

RF193   Catharine Weiser (16 Mar 1795, York PA-19 Aug 1885, Easton PA) m 7 Jan 1816, York PA, John Augustus Probst (1792, Saxony-Easton PA) Bur Easton PA. He emigrated 1811; ordained Lutheran pastor 1813; Centreville PA, 1813-. Recorder of deeds, Northampton Co PA, 1836.

RF1931   Franklin Probst. unm. MD.

RF1932   Emilius Probst (ca 1816-1905) unm.

RF1933   Cecilia E Probst (d 1887) m Jacob B Illick.

RF19331   Mary C Illick. unm. Easton PA.

RF194   John Carl (Charles) Weiser (29 Dec 1796, York PA-17 Jul 1867, York PA) m 26 Mar 1822, Anna Maria Spangler (1 Apr 1800-5 Jan 1873, York PA) Bur York PA. In 1856 he established a private bank in York PA. Dry goods merchant, York PA. Owner of the "Weiser Building" on the southeast corner of Continental Square, York PA.

RF1941   Johanna Anna Weiser (15 Feb 1823, York PA-9 Jul 1824, York PA) Bur York PA.

RF1942   John Augustus Weiser (31 Jul 1824, York PA-21 Mar 1889, York PA) m 1) 13 Feb 1851, Georgianna Eichelberger (10 Dec 1828-22 Jun 1855, York PA); m 2) 14 Dec 1858, Mary Jane Upp (26 Sep 1839-7 Mar 1914, York PA) Bur York PA. Banker; President, York and Gettysburg Turnpike Co.

RF19421   Harry Percival Weiser (10 Mar 1852, York PA-4 Jul 1923, York PA) m 8 May 1877, York PA, Irene Amanda Stauffer (12 Feb 1856, York PA-16 Sep 1926, York PA) Bur York PA. Yale U. Merchant and banker, York PA.

RF194211   Marie Eichelberger Weiser (3 Jul 1879, York PA-13 Nov 1961, Fairfield CT) m 28 Oct 1909, York PA, William Smith Heiges (8 Aug 1869-16 Sep 1926, York PA)

RF1942111   Lucille Weiser Heiges (b 18 Jun 1914, York PA) m 29 Dec 1934, Richmond VA, Victor Lee Winstead (29 Sep 1905, Roxboro NC-6 Aug 1987, Boston MA) Bur Roxboro MA.

*RF19421111   Elizabeth Weiser Winstead (b 6 Dec 1939, York PA) m 5 Aug 1967, York PA, Donald Michael Flynn (b 11 Jan 1939, Philadelphia PA) She, BA, High Point (NC) Col, 1962. He, PhD.

RF194211111   Elizabeth Florence Flynn (b 5 Dec 1968, Abington PA) BS, Elizabethtown (PA) Col, 1990.

RF194211112   Michael Winstead Flynn (b 3 Sep 1971, Abington PA).

*RF19421112   Victor Lee Winstead Jr (b 29 Mar 1943, York PA) unm.

*RF1942112   Marie Irene Heiges (b 14 Nov 1915, York PA) m 29 Jun 1940, York PA, William Fleming Major (b 21 Jan 1912, Richmond VA) Fairfield CT, 1953-1977; York PA, 1977-.

RF19421121   William Fleming Major Jr (b 3 Sep 1945, York PA) m 1) 15 Jun 1968, Fairfield CT, Diana Louise Kirsten (b 7 Dec 1947, Fairfield CT) div 1981; m 2) 23 Jan 1982, Weston CT, Marjorie McAlpin Bolgard Dail (b 25 Aug 1938 New York NY) BS, Bucknell U, 1967. Engineer, Fairfield CT.

RF194211211   William F Major III (b 30 Apr 1975, Bridgeport CT).

RF19422   Bertha Weiser (14 Jul 1860, York PA-22 May 1940, York PA) m 15 Apr 1886, York PA,

Robert Doudel Croll (19 Jan 1857-20 Dec 1926, York PA) Bur York PA. Realtor, York PA.

RF194221   John Shelby Croll (1 May 1887, York PA-1 May 1887, York PA) Bur York PA.

RF194222   Horace Doudel Croll (b 26 Nov 1888, York PA) m 10 Nov 1927, York PA, Kathryn Zeigler (b 4 Nov 1904, Rossville PA) Bur York PA. Realtor, York PA. No chn.

RF194223   Anna Weiser Croll (24 Jul 1891, York PA-3 Feb 1941, York PA) m 4 Jul 1918, York PA, William Heinly Schellhammer (19 Oct 1892, York PA-21 Mar 1952, York PA) Bur York PA. MD. Physician, York PA.

RF19423   George Upp Weiser (28 Oct 1862, York PA-6 Dec 1945, York PA) m 1) 18 Apr 1901, Sarah Catharine Eyster (31 Oct 1869, York PA-28 Mar 1910, York PA); m 2) Mabel S   .

RF194231   Charles S Weiser (26 Jan 1902, York PA-10 Aug 1985, York PA) m 2 Dec 1950, Roberta J Yost (d 13 Jul 1989, York PA) Bur York PA. Eyster, Weiser Co; banker, York PA. No chn.

RF194232   Sarah Catharine Eyster Weiser (29 Feb 1904, York PA-15 Nov 1954, York PA) m 30 Apr 1938, York PA, Henry B Martin.

RF1942321   Mary Weiser Martin (b 3 Mar 1939, York PA).

RF19424   Patterson Sterrett Weiser (30 Apr 1864, York PA-19 Jun 1928, York PA) m 2 Jan 1890, York PA, Hattie A Stubbins (b Dec 1864) Bur York PA.

RF194241   John A Weiser (18 Sep 1890, York PA-2 May 1962) m 9 Jan 1915, Helen Frances Robinson (b 1896, MA).

RF1942411   Virginia Helen Weiser (b 13 Nov 1915) m Charles T Redfern. Oklahoma.

RF194242   Katharine Fahs Weiser (2 Jul 1893, York PA-21 May 1908, York PA) Bur York PA.

RF19425   Mary Louisa Weiser (b 29 Aug 1865) m Norman Alexander Patterson. Oxford PA.

RF194251   Elizabeth Patterson m C Walter Dawson.

RF19426   Anna Spangler Weiser (8 Dec 1867, York PA-28 Feb 1935, York PA) m 11 Nov 1897, York PA, Franklin Gillespie (24 Mar 1866, Principio MD-23 Aug 1905, Oxford PA) Bur York PA. Physician.

RF194261   Elizabeth Armstrong Gillespie (22 Aug 1898, Oxford PA-22 Aug 1898, Oxford PA).

RF194262   Charles Weiser Gillespie (b 7 Oct 1899, Oxford PA) Physical therapist, York PA.

RF1943   Erastus Hay Weiser (28 Jan 1826, York PA-11 Jul 1872, York PA) m 12 Octo 1852, York PA, Annie Franklin (30 Sep 1830-16 Apr 1871, York PA) Bur York PA.

RF19431   William Franklin Weiser (28 Aug 1858, York PA-1 Apr 1906, York PA) Bur York PA. unm.

RF19432   Charles Weiser (b 16 Apr 1871, York PA).

RF1944   Horace Spangler Weiser (22 Oct 1827, York PA-19 Jul 1875, Decorah IA) m 14 Jul 1859, Louise M Amy (21 Apr 1837, Salsbury VT-8 Nov 1898, Decorah IA) Bur Decorah IA. Yale Col, one of the founders of the college fraternity, Alpha Sigma Phi, 6 Dec 1845; moved to Decorah, 1855. Banker, Decorah IA.

RF19441   Amy Spangler Weiser (5 Jul 1861, Decorah IA-14 Jun 1940) m 21 Feb 1881, Decorah IA, Edwin Carlisle (8 Apr 1860, Montreal-Mar 1932, Santa Monica CA) Insurance.

RF194411   Horace Carlisle (Chicago IL-Las Vegas NM) unm.

RF194412   Charles Carlisle (b Chicago IL) m 23 Aug 1923, Salt Lake City UT, Lorva A Garrett (b Salt Lake City UT) Insurance, San Jose CA.

RF194413   Louise Carlisle (b 20 Nov 1891, Chicago IL) unm. Secretary at a girls school, Los Angeles CA.

RF19442   Anna J Weiser (b Dec 1869) m Robert Jones.

RF194421   Robert Jones.

RF194422   Lawrence Weiser Jones (b 12 Nov 1905) m 3 Sep 1927, Janet Young Henson.

RF1944221   Lawrence Weiser Jones (b 2 Feb 1932) m 15 Feb 1957, Edith Joneu Mitchell (b 23 Nov 1933).

RF19442211   Lawrence Weiser Jones (b 23 Jul 1957).

RF19442212   Susan Grace Jones (b 23 Jul 1957).

RF1944222   Robert Graham Milburn Jones (b 6 Jul 1937) m 20 Jun 1959, Ruth Agnes Freel (b 21 Jan 1939).

RF19443   Charles John Weiser (1864, Decorah IA-1944, Los Angeles CA) m Abbie Bullis (12 Aug 1873, Decorah IA-12 Feb 1955, Los Angeles CA) Bur Los Angeles CA. Banker, Decorah IA.

RF194431   Horace Spangler Weiser II (22 Mar 1898, Decorah IA-31 Jul 1963, Los Angeles CA) m 19 Feb 1929, Cresco IA, Mary Inman (b 2 Mar 1912, Davenport IA). Realtor, Los Angeles CA.

RF1944311   Abbie Gail Weiser (b 30 Dec 1929, Decorah IA) m 25 Nov 1957, Malibu CA, Jack Vogel (b 2 Oct 1922, Passaic NJ) He, editor, Ran Corp; she, secretary, painter, Los Angeles CA.

RF19443123   Mary Carroll Weiser (b 24 May 1931, Decorah IA) m 14 Nov 1957, Rio de Janeiro, Brazil, Carlos E V DeMello. Oil refining, Rio de Janeiro; president, International Land and Development Co, Los Angeles CA.

RF19443121   Michael Vieira DeMello (b 3 Jun 1959).

RF1944313   Charles John Weiser III (b 7 Feb 1933, Long Beach CA).

RF1944314   Jane Louise Weiser (b 10 May 1934, Long Beach CA) Secretary, Los Angeles CA.

RF194432   Charles John Weiser Jr (b 31 Dec 1901) m 12 Jan 1924, Dorothy Reeves (b 8 Jan 1906, Trenton NJ).

RF1944321   Sarah Weiser (b 24 Dec 1924) m David T Blake (b 23 Aug 1921, Princeton NJ).

RF19443211   Catherine Blake (b 17 Sep 1948, Trenton NJ).

RF1943212   Teresa Grier Blake (b 18 Jun 1954, Princeton NJ).

RF194433   Hubert Holway Weiser (b 14 Feb 1908, Decorah IA) m 28 Oct 1955, Eagle Rock CA,

Miriam Morningstar (b 11 Apr 1923, Middletown OH) Banker, Los Angeles CA. No chn.

RF1945   Josephine Mary Weiser (29 May 1829, York PA-13 Jul 1889, York PA) m 14 Apr 1853, York PA, Edward H Pentz (21 Jan 1826-30 Nov 1973, York PA. Bur York PA. MD. Physician, York PA.

RF19451   Edward H Pentz (16 Nov 1877, York PA-20 Dec 1883, York PA).

RF19452   Bransby Pentz.

RF1946   Theodosia Eliza Weiser (11 Dec 1830, York PA-30 Dec 1889, York PA) Bur York PA.
unm.

RF1947   Arabella Catharine Weiser (17 Aug 1832, York PA-13 Dec 1868, York PA) Bur York PA.

RF1948   Amelia Weiser (b 4 Sep 1834, York PA) m 25 Oct 1872, Meredith S Green.

RF1949   Adelaide Ann Weiser (27 Jul 1836, York PA-23 Feb 1897, York PA) m 10 Jan 1861, York PA, Jeremiah Carl (21 Jul 1829, York PA-23 Nov 1909, York PA) Bur York PA. Banker, York PA.

RF19491   Charles Weiser Carl (22 Mar 1864, York PA-27 Feb 1882, York PA) Bur York PA.

RF19492   Bella Weiser Carl (b 29 Aug 1873, York PA) m 5 Nov 1896, William A Keyworth.

RF194A   Charles Smyser Weiser (13 Mar 1838, York PA-1909, York PA) m Isadora Brown (1842-1915) Bur York PA. Banker, York PA.

RF194A1   Charles Weiser (24 Mar 1867, York PA-31 Aug 1867, York PA) Bur York PA.

RF194B   George Weiser (31 Oct 1839, York PA-25 Nov 1844, York PA) Bur York PA.

RF194C   Camilla Jane Weiser (26 Dec 1841, York PA-25 Nov 1844, York PA) Bur York PA.

RF194D   Infant (16 Feb 1844, York PA-21 Feb 1844, York PA) Bur York PA.

RF194E   Edwin Fahnestock Weiser (29 Apr 1845, York PA-11 Jul 1846, York PA) Bur York PA.

RF195   Mary Weiser (16 May 1799, York PA-21 Jul 1827, Lancaster PA) m 11 Apr 1826, Daniel Heitshu. Bur Lancaster PA.

RF196   Daniel Weiser (22 Feb 1901, York PA-29 Nov 1848, York PA) m 9 Mar 1824, Catherine Jameson.

RF1961   Gates Jameson Weiser (b 2 Jul 1824, York PA) m Elmira Brown (b 1825).

RF19611   Gates B Weiser. m Minnie M Blummer (b 1852).

RF196111   Isadore E Weiser.

RF19612   James Weiser.

RF19613   Millard Fillmore Weiser (1856-15 Apr 1861, York PA).

RF1962   Emily Weiser (b 3 Mar 1826).

RF1963   David A Weiser (9 Dec 1827, York PA-1890, York PA) m 15 Jan 1852, Emma F Meyers (Mar 1831-1913).

RF19631   James B Weiser (Aug 1858-1913) m Grace E   (b Nov 1875).

RF196311   Corita Weiser (b 1902).

RF19632   Lucy Ann Weiser (b 1862).

RF1964   Amelia Weiser (b 2 Dec 1829, York PA).

RF1965   Thomas Weiser (d 26 Feb 1833).

RF1966   Oliver Thomas Weiser (24 May 1836, York PA-1889, York PA) m York PA, Maria L Hibner (1839, York PA-1898, York PA) Bur York PA. Grocer, York PA.

RF19661   Emily Weiser (1858, York PA-1924, York PA) m John Heaps (d Delta PA) Bur York PA. MD. Physician, York PA. No chn.

RF19662   Grace Weiser (1860, York PA-Oct 1926, Bradley Beach NJ) m York PA, James Davis (Jersey City NJ-Bradley Beach NJ) Bur Jersey City NJ. Judge. No chn.

RF19663   Elmer E Ellsworth Weiser (4 Mar 1860, York PA-1868, York PA) Bur York PA.

RF19664   Oliver Weiser (22 Aug 1862, York PA-24 Feb 1904, Delta PA) m 8 May 1884, York PA, Rowena B List (27 Mar 1867, York PA-Jan 1950, York PA) He bur York PA; she bur Philadelphia PA. US Postal Service.

RF196641   Arthur Clinton Weiser (19 Jun 1888, Birmingham AL-Apr 1951, Philadelphia PA) Bur Philadelphia PA. unm.

RF196642   Oliver Clinton Weiser (27 Jul 1890, Birmingham AL-3 Sep 1964, Ocean City NJ) m Hannah Morgan Armons. Bur Oakford PA. No chn. Restaurant owner.

RF196643   Grace Weiser (19 Mar 1893, Delta PA-Oct 1931, Hamburg PA).

RF1966431   Rowena Houck.

RF196644   Emily Weiser (15 Dec 1896, Delta PA-14 Nov 1957).

RF196645   Matthew Stanley Quay Weiser (b 27 Jul 1898, Delta PA) m 1) Lucille Taylor; m 2) Helen Anthony; m 3) Mignon   .

RF1966451   Quay Taylor Weiser.

RF1966452   Barbara Weiser (b 2 Feb 1946, Burlingame CA).

RF196646   Dorothy Weiser (b 21 Jan 1900, Delta PA) m 19 Mar 1927, Cheltenham PA, Harold Butterworth.

RF1966461   Roy Stanley Butterworth (b 27 Jul 1929, Woodbury NJ) m 11 Feb 1956, Westville NJ, Kathryn Nolan.

RF1967   Thomas Davis Weiser (b 26 Aug 1838, York PA) m 1 Jun 1859, Philadelphia PA, Annie M Parker (b 1841, Tuckerton NJ).

RF1968   Jane Weiser (b 8 Mar 1841, York PA).

RF1969   Catharine Margaret Weiser (22 Jun 1843, York PA-10 Sep 1845, York PA) Bur York PA.

RF197   Margaret Weiser (24 Nov 1802, York PA-14 Aug 1859, Friends Cove PA) m 5 Sep 1826, York PA, Charles Frederick Hoffmeier (24 Sep 1803, Hellertown PA-19 Apr 1877, Lancaster PA) Clergyman of the German Reformed Church, ordained 19 Nov 1843. Served at Newville, Bendersville, and Gettysburg, Minersville, Womelsdorf Palmyra, Somerset, Friend's Cove, McConnellsburg, Rebersburg New Berlin, Liverpool, Troutville, all in PA. She bur Friend's Cove; he bur Lancaster PA.

RF1971   Mary Hoffmeier. m Thornton Benford.

RF19711   Margaret Benford.

RF19712   Angie Benford.

RF19713   Arthur Benford.

RF19714   Edgar Benford.

RF1972   Emmie Hoffmeier m 5 Sep 1860, Elias D Shoemaker.

RF19721   Charlotte Shoemaker (d Dec 1950) m William H Gilchrist.

RF197 Margaret Weiser Hofmeier (1802-1859) and RF1978 Josephine Margaret Hofmeier (1849-1874)

RF197211   Edgar Gilchrist (1 Oct 1885, Bedford PA-1 Oct 1885, Bedford PA).

RF197212   Pauline Gilchrist (27 Sep 1886, Philadelphia PA-Nov 1976) m 1) Henry Beck Reagle (1886-1976); m 2) 16 May 1931, Lansdowne, Henry Barel Strock (1868-Bedford PA) Reagle, clergyman; Strock, physician. Bur Bedford PA.

RF197213   Marguerite Gilchrist (8 Sep 1888, Philadelphia PA-196?, Philadelphia PA) m 2 Nov 1914, Sharon Hill PA, Edwin B Callow.

RF197214   Miriam Gilchrist (11 May 1890, Philadelphia PA-1975, Philadelphia PA) unm.

RF197215   Helen Gilchrist (27 Apr 1892, Philadelphia PA-Feb 1969) m 3 Jun 1922, Philadelphia PA, James Anderson Mann (5 Mar 1895-24 Nov 1966) Bur Drexel Hill PA.

*RF1972151   Mary Jane Mann (b 26 Jun 1923, Philadelphia PA) unm. Bell Atlantic.

RF1972152   Helen Elizabeth Mann (b 10 May 1925, Philadelphia PA) m 10 Oct 1953, Lansdowne PA, George Bernard Rehberg (b 22 May 1929, Brooklyn NY) He, fire chief.

*RF19721521   George James Rehberg (b 15 Apr 1955, Middletown CT) m 12 Jul 1975, Westbrook CT, Beverly Welch (b 22 May 1956, Middletown CT) div 1982. Carpenter.

*RF197215211   Jason Allan Rehberg (b 16 Sep 1980, New Haven CT).

*RF19721522   Virginia Jane Rehberg (b 13 Nov 1957, Middletown CT) m 13 Oct 1990, Brookline MA, Joseph Salami (b 19 Apr 1955, Boston MA) No chn. AB, U CT. Career counselor.

*RF19721523   John Tyler Rehberg (b 15 Jun 1959, Middletown CT) m 20 Sep 1986, Seybrook CT, Linda Jean Porter (b 5 Mar 1962, New Haven CT) Emergency radio dispatcher.

*RF197215231   Jordan Tyler Rehberg (b 10 Nov 1991, Middletown CT).

*RF197215232   Emma Elizabeth Rehberg (b 14 Dec 1994, Middletown CT).

*RF197215233   Edward Garrit Rehberg

*RF197215234   David Weiser Rehberg

RF1972153   Virginia Anderson Mann (4 Dec 1926, Philadelphia PA-19 Jan 1987, Chadds Ford PA) unm. Bur Drexel Hill PA. U PA. Bookkeeper.

RF19722   Mary Shoemaker (d 19 Aug 1946, Lansdowne PA) m William H Sexton. Bur Philadelphia PA.

RF19723   Emmie Shoemaker (d 22 Dec 1948) m Karl Collings.

RF19724   John Nevin Shoemaker m Amye Victoria Sides (d 15 Dec 1956, Tujunga CA).

RF197241   Kathryn Shoemaker (d 9 Jun 1986, CA) m William H von Brockhagen. Bur CA.

RF1972414   Charlotte Gilchrist Mann (29 Dec 1932, Philadelphia PA-29 Dec 1932, Philadelphia PA) Bur Drexel Hill PA.

RF1973   Henry W Hoffmeier.

RF1974   Angeline Hoffmeier (23 Aug 1824, Lancaster PA-19 Mar 1906, Lancaster PA) unm. Bur Lancaster PA.

RF1975   Thomas Franklin Hoffmeier (30 Oct 1837, Lancaster PA-1 Nov 1902) m. German Reformed clergyman.

RF19751   Anna Gertrude Hoffmeier m N A Sharretts.

RF19752   Frank Newcomer Hoffmeier m Nellie I Cordell.

RF19753   Mary Catherine Hoffmeier.

RF19754   Henry Asen Hoffmeier.

RF19755   Emily Leman Hoffmeier.

RF19756   Helen Weiser Hoffmeier.

RF1976   John Hoffmeier.

RF1977   Emelius Hoffmeier m Luch Defibaugh.

RF19771   Cora Hoffmeier. No chn.

RF19772   Nellie Hoffmeier.

RF19773   Charles Hoffmeier.

RF19774   Edgar Hoffmeier m Hester Levan.

RF197741   Catherine Hoffmeier.

RF197742   Levan Hoffmeier.

RF19775   Arthur Hoffmeier.

RF19776   Angie Hoffmeier.

RF19777   Homer Hoffmeier.

RF19778   Josephine Margaret Hoffmeier (14 Jan 1849, Minersville PA-12 Sep1874, Troutville PA)
unm. Bur Friend's Cove PA.

RF198   John Weiser (28 Dec 1805, York PA-7 Jun 1813, York PA) Bur York PA.

RF199   Elizabeth Weiser (b 8 Jun 1807, York PA) m 24 Dec 1829, Samuel Ilgenfritz (d Oct
1835).

RF1991   Ilgenfritz.

RF19911   Blanch T Ilgenfritz m Theodore Warner.

RF19912   M Marcella Ilgenfritz m L B Benton.

RF19A   Cassandra Weiser (5 May 1811, York PA-19 Nov 1861, York PA) m 16 May 1836, York
PA, Emanuel K Zeigler.

RF1A   Elizabeth Weiser (b 6 Sep 1767, Tulephocken Tp, Berks Co PA) m 1 Nov 1789,
Tulpehocken Tp, Berks Co PA, Henry Wiegand.

RF3   Elizabeth Weiser (b 19 Apr 1730, although some records state 19 Apr 1730-?) m Johann
Philip Breitenbach (8 Oct 1725, Germany-26 Oct 1790, probably Tulpehocken Tp, Berks Co PA) Probably bur
Stouchsburg PA.[132]

RF31   Christoph Breitenbach (30 Sep 1754-18 Nov 1818) m 29 Feb 1780, Elizabeth
Koppenhoffer (b 16 Mar 1758).

RF311   Christine Elizabeth Breitenbach (b 14 Feb 1781).

RF32   Maria Breitenbach (b ca 1754) m 11 Jun 1778, Christian Fischer (3 Dec 1751-20 Sep
1831) Probably bur Stouchsburg PA.

RF321   Christian Fischer (b 5 Apr 1779) m 7 May 1807, Catharine Zimmermann (ca 5 Aug 1782-
25 Nov 1838).

RF322   Johannes Fischer (b 1781).

RF323   Anna Elizabeth Fischer (b 21 Feb 1784).

RF324   Catharine Fischer (b 5 Feb 1789) m 2 Feb 1808, Johannes Feg.

RF325   Jacob Fischer (b 16 Dec 1792).

RF326   Johannes Fischer (4 Mar 1795-11 Mar 1840).

---

[132]Data on the Breitenbach-Breidenbaugh family compiled by the Rev. David C. Burnite and from the registers of Christ Lutheran
Church, Stouchsburg PA.

RF3421 The Rev. Edward
Breidenbaugh (1821-1906)

RF34213 Edward Swoyer
Breidenbaugh (1849-1926)

RF33   Elizabeth Breitenbach (b ca 1759, she was confirmed at age 13 years, 5 months on Pentecost 1773) m 25 Sep 1783, John Kuster (b 15 Apr 1762).

RF331   Johannes Kuster (b Aug 1784).

RF332   Isaac Kuster (b 11 Jan 1788).

RF333   Marie Elizabeth Kuster (b 7 Oct 1789).

RF334   Philip Frederick Kuster (b 29 Aug 1792).

RF335   Johnathan Kuster (b 27 Jun 1799).

RF34   Philip Breitenbach (14 Apr 1764, Tulpehocken Tp, Berks Co PA-15 Oct 1826) m 3 Feb 1789, Catharine Walborn (9-10 Oct 1759-3 Jul 1823).

RF341   John Philip Breitenbach (11 Dec 1789-Dec 1826).

RF342   Frederick Breitenbach (13 Dec 1792, Stouchburg PA-20 Apr 1823) m 7 Jan 1821, Anna Maria Ulrich.

RF3421   Edward Breitenbach/Breidenbaugh (17 Dec 1821, Myerstown PA-12 Jul 1906, Gettysburg PA) m 16 Mar 1847, Catherine Elizabeth Swoyer (1825 Newville PA-29 Dec 1911, Gettysburg PA) Bur Gettysburg PA. He, AB, Gettysburg (PA) Col, 1842. Ordained a Lutheran pastor, 1846; served Newville, Pine Grove, Greencastle, Gettysburg PA.

RF34211   Mary Julia Ida Breidenbaugh (b 16 Dec 1851, Pine Grove PA) m 6 Oct 1880, Jacob Yertzy (24 May 1847, Myersdale PA-13 Jun 1927).

RF34212   Annie L Breidenbaugh (Greencastle PA-11 Apr 1934, Johnstown PA) m 20 May 1880, William Alfred Shipman (9 Sep 1852, Springfield NJ-16 Apr 1934, Johnstown PA).

RF342121   Minot Martineau Shipman.

RF34213   Edward Swoyer Breidenbaugh (14 Jan 1849 Newville PA-5 Sep 1926, Gettysburg PA) m 20 Nov 1873, Philadelphia PA, Mary Ida Kitzmiller (31 Aug 1847, Pine Grove PA-1 Oct 1931, Gettysburg PA) Bur Gettysburg PA. He, AB, Gettysburg (PA) Col, 1868; Lutheran Theological Seminary, Gettysburg; ScD, Gettysburg Col, 1887. Professor, Gettysburg Col, 1874-1924. Author of chemistry studies. Breidenbaugh Hall at Gettysburg Col is named for him.

RF342131   Edna Kitzmiller Breidenbaugh (1 Aug 1875, Gettysburg PA-28 Feb 1963, Gettysburg PA) m 15 Oct 1895, Gettysburg PA, George Barlow Zane II (b 1864) div 1903. Bur Gettysburg PA.

RF3421311   Ida Dorothy Zane (2 May 1897, Palmyra NJ-9 Feb 1959, Gettysburg PA) m 1) 26 Dec 1917, John Benjamin Duckstead (31 Aug 1890, Fertile MN-6 Sep 1918, France); m 2) 15 Jun 1920, Kenderton Smith Lynch (14 Dec 1868, Philadelphia PA-9 Mar 1937, Gettysburg PA) Bur Gettysburg PA.

RF34213111   Eric Edward Duckstad (23 Jun 1918, Gettysburg PA-20 Dec 1982, Palo Alto CA) m 1) 5 Jun 1943, Donna M Roach (b 11 Feb 1924) div 1953; m 2) 17 Sep 1954, Joyce E Campau (b 26 Aug 1928, East Grand Rapids MI).

RF342131111   Eric Edward Duckstad II (b 8 Mar 1944, Louisville KY).

RF342131112   Neils Christian Duckstad (b 17 Mar 1948, Palo Alto CA).

RF342131113   Tracy Duckstad (b 25 Jun 1957, Palo Alto CA).

RF34213112   Kenderton Smith Lynch II (b 29 Mar 1921, Gettysburg PA) m 3 Mar 1944, Berkeley CA, Frances Katherine Saxton (b 26 May 1921).

RF342131121   Kimberly Ann Lynch (b 13 Apr 1950, San Francisco CA) m 1) 14 Feb 1973, Charles Richard Abraham (b 20 Nov 1944), div 1976; m 2) 3 Dec 1978, Walter Craig Kolb (b 2 May 1947).

RF3421311211   Kelley Starr Abraham (b 21 Feb 1974, Walnut Creek CA).

RF3421311212   Courtney Dayton Kolb (b 18 May 1981, Berkeley CA).

RF342131122   Kenderton Smith Lynch III (b 18 Oct 1951, San Francisco CA) m 7 Feb 1986, Stephanie Lynn Krafchak.

RF342131123   Michal Lauren Lynch (b 19 Dec 1953, San Francisco CA) m 1) 5 Nov 1979, James Robert Menzies II, div 1982; m 2) 1 May 1991, Patrick Brendan Rogers.

RF3421311231   Quinn Dylan Rogers (b 6 Mar 1992).

RF34213113   Ann (Nancy) Masters Lynch (b 4 Jan 1923, Gettysburg PA) m 1) 2 Jan 1946, Al Hansen (b 23 Mar 1914) div 1959; m 2) 14 May 1962, Laurence Montgomery Peet (b 24 Jun 1921), div 1974.

RF342131131   Sue Ann Hansen (b 7 May 1950, San Mateo CA) m 1) 25 Sep 1976, William Law; m 2) 8 Aug 1992, Marnix Zettler.

RF3421311311   Gavin Law (b 8 Nov 1978).

RF342131132   Eric Masters Peet (b 27 Jan 1963, San Mateo CA).

RF342131133 Kirsten Katrine Peet (b 27 Jun 1967).

RF342132 Ida May Breidenbaugh (30 Mar 1882, Gettysburg PA-17 Apr 1939, Pittsburgh PA) m 5 Oct 1904, Gettysburg PA, David Clark Burnite IV (24 Apr 1875, Harrisburg PA-28 Nov 1952, Zelienople PA) Bur Harrisburg PA. He, AB, Gettysburg (PA) Col, 1901; BD, Lutheran Theological Seminary, Gettysburg, 1904; ordained a Lutheran pastor, 1904. Served Ghent NY; York PA; Galion OH; Danville PA; Cambridge OH; Warren OH; Sharpsburg PA.

RF3421321 Edward Breidenbaugh Burnite (3 Jun 1906, York PA-13 Sep 1907, York PA) Bur Gettysburg PA.

RF3421322 Mary Ida Burnite (19 May 1916, Galion OH-29 Dec 1992, Langhorne PA).

*RF3421323 David Clark Burnite V (b 30 Sep 1919, Danville PA) m 1) 2 Jun 1943, Sharpsburg PA, Florence Haller Frey (19 May 1918, York PA-10 Sep 1975, Gettysburg PA); m 2) 11 Aug 1976, Ruth Elizabeth Stark Coleman (b 16 Dec 1917, York PA) He, AB, Wittenberg (OH) U, 1940; BD, Lutheran Theological Seminary, Gettysburg PA, 1943; ordained a Lutheran pastor, 1943. Served at Turtle Creek PA; York PA; Montoursville PA; USN chaplaincy; Reading PA; Clarks Summit PA.

RF34213231 David Clark Burnite VI (b 31 Aug 1944, McKeesport PA) m 1) 10 Mar 1977, Kathryn Louisa Bedsworth (b 14 Aug 1948, Miami FL) div 1977; m 2) 9 Jun 1979, Katherine Marie Pauli Egan (15 Oct 1949, Detroit MI-13 Jun 1990 Miami FL).

RF342132311 Keron Patrick Burnite (b 13 Sep 1969).

RF342132312 Patricia Marie Burnite (b 11 Jan 1971).

RF34213232 Martha Jeanne Burnite (b 7 Dec 1946, York PA) m 1) 12 Jul 1969, Wyomissing PA, Randolph Wilson Roberts (b 8 Oct 1946) div; m 2) 3 Jul 1987, Randallstown MD, Walter James Alston II (b 3 Jun 1944).

RF342132321 Gwendolyn Suzanne Roberts (b 2 Sep 1975, Baltimore MD).

RF342132322 Ryan Weylin Roberts (b 8 Mar 1979, Baltimore MD).

RF3421324 Elizabeth Edna Burnite (b 21 Jan 1923, Cambridge OH) m 26 Dec 1955, Frank Richard Segina (b 18 May 1930, Milani Yugoslavia).

RF34213241 Karen Ellen Segina (b 22 Feb 1957, Pittsburgh PA).

RF34213242 Lissa Kathleen Segina (b 22 Aug 1958, Pittsburgh PA) m 11 Apr 1987, Pittsburgh PA, Frank S Holland II.

RF342132421 Dylan Stewart Holland (b 12 Jan 1994).

RF34213243 Julie Ann Segina (b 15 Apr 1966, Pittsburgh PA) m 19 Sep 1992, Pittsburgh PA, Charles Phillip Meyette.

RF35 Johannes Breitenbach (16 Jan 1767-26 Oct 1818, Lebanon PA) m 6 Oct 1798, Lebanon PA, Hannah Ort. Justice, Lebanon PA.

RF351 John Henry Breitenbach (11 Jan 1798-2 Jun 1805).

RF352 Jeremias Ort Breitenbach (2 Nov 1799-24 Apr 1800).

RF353 Henrietta Breitenbach (b 19 Nov 1801).

RF354					Joseph Breitenbach (b 22 Feb 1804).

RF355					Catarine Breitenbach (25 Aug 1807-Mar 1811).

RF356					Francis Augustus Breitenbach (b 17 Dec 1811).

RF357					Alfred Breitenbach (b 1 Oct 1815).

RF4					Maria Catharine Weiser (29 Jan 1733-1789) m ca 1754, Conrad Rahm (1734-1782) He was a farmer near Philadelphia, later near Harrisburg PA. US Rev: Capt Weiser's Co, German Continentals, Corp.[133]

RF41					John Michael Rahm (7 Mar 1753-20 Apr 1795) m Mrs. Mary Sophia Toot Ross (14 Jun 1761, York PA-27 Dec 1815, Elizabethtown PA) US Rev: Innkeeper, Hummelstown PA.

RF411					Catharina Rahm (22 Dec 1779-21 Apr 1849) m John Earnest (24 Mar 1773-20 Nov 1840) Bur Hummelstown PA. Tollkeeper, Hummelstown PA.

RF4111					David Earnest (1 Jul 1798-7 Sep 1854, Hummelstown PA) m 1) Christina Hummel (16 May 1797, Hummelstown PA-18 Sep 1834, Hummelstown PA); m 2) Mary (b 1822) Farmer, Hummelstown PA. Bur Hummelstown PA.

RF41111					Valentine Hummel Earnest Sr (21 May 1819, near Hummelstown PA-12 Aug 1878, Miami Co OH) m 8 Dec 1842, Miami Co OH, Susanna Minnich (18 Dec 1818, Dauphin Co PA-5 Aug 1882, Pleasant Hill OH) Farmer.

RF411111					David Wendel Earnest (b 6 Apr 1943) m 9 Jan 1868, Darhe Co OH, Mary Yount.

RF411112					Mary Jane Earnest (b 15 Feb 1845) m 24 Mar 1861, Darhe Co OH, Joseph Trump.

RF411113					Eleanor Earnest (b 11 Nov 1847) m 5 Feb 1868, Darhe Co OH.

RF411114					Valentine Hummel Earnest Jr (15 Feb 1849, Miami Co OH-10 Jan 1928, North Loup NE) m 16 Nov 1873, Pleasant Hill OH, Elizabeth Clara Harp (12 Aug 1855, Darhe Co OH-22 Nov 1922, North Loup NE) Farmer.

RF4111141					Mary Belle Earnest (25 Dec 1874, Darhe Co OH-13 Nov 1963, North Loup NE) m 2 Oct 1901, North Loup NE, Walter Cummins (21 Apr 1979, Buffalo NY-8 Mar 1954, North Loup NE).

RF4111411					Fanny Dorothy Cummins (b 18 Jun 1902, North Loup NE) m 29 Sep 1936, Taylor NE, Lloyd Francis Johnson (b 23 Dec 1910, Tomaro NE).

RF4111412					Austin Cummins (25 Mar 1904, North Loup NE-3 Sep 1979, Julesburg CO) m 1) 2 Oct 1926, Big Springs NE, Buena Comer (31 Aug 1905-9 May 1939, Big Springs NE); m 2) 12 Feb 1948, Laveda Albers (b 11 Nov 1920, Blue Hill NE) Farmer.

RF411114121					Dorothy Ilene Cummins (b 13 Jan 1926) m 1 Jul 1944, Pueblo CO, Francis Mullin (b 16 Nov 1923).

RF4111141211					Julia Ellen Mullin (b 28 Feb 1946, Schenectady NY) m 22 Jun 1968, Brooklyn NY, William Winfield Swan (b 15 Dec 1944, Huntington WV).

RF41111412111					Amanda Morgan Swan (b 21 May 1981 Newburg NY).

---

[133]Data on the Rahm descendants submitted by Robert E. Strock, Jean J. Holder, and Gloria H. Kinback.

RF4111141212   Patricia Ann Mullin (b 18 Sep 1952) m 14 Feb 1970, Brooklyn NY, Thomas Andrew Kochie (b 6 Jun 1948, Easton PA).

RF41111412121   Chanda Larisse Kochie (b 25 Mar 1971, Rochester NY).

RF41111412122   Brian Christopher Kochie (b 1 Mar 1974, Syracuse NY).

RF4111141213   Maureen Elizabeth Mullin (b 3 Jan 1955).

RF411114122   Alice Ruth Cummins (b 28 Aug 1927, Ord NE) m 23 Nov 1948, Imperial NE, Frank Clements (b 29 Oct 1928, Imperial NE).

RF4111141221   Linda Kay Clements (b 12 Dec 1951, Imperial NE) m 23 Nov 1972, Imperial NE, David Michael Cummings (b 5 Apr 1951, Sedan KS).

RF41111412211   Justin Michael Cummings (b 28 Jul 1978, Lincoln NE).

RF41111412212   Joshua Luke Cummings (b 18 Mar 1981 New Orleans LA).

RF4111141222   Scott Leo Clements (b 18 Feb 1955, Imperial NE).

RF4111141223   Diane Clements (b 20 Apr 1962, Imperial NE).

RF411114123   Janice Marie Cummins (b 13 Sep 1943, Lewellen NE) m 5 Oct 1962, Denver CO, Jackson Le Roy Wiggins (b 10 Jun 1937, Galveston TX).

RF4111141231   Austin Le Roy Wiggins (b 13 Nov 1963, Denver CO).

RF4111141232   Shawn Eric Wiggins (b 20 Jun 1965, Denver CO).

RF4111141233   Jennifer Marie Wiggins (b 9 Jul 1966, Denver CO).

RF4111141234   Michelle Kay Wiggins (b 9 Nov 1968, Denver CO).

RF411114124   Carrie Kay Cummins (b 13 Apr 1948, Lewellen KS) m 16 Feb 1967, Julesburg CO, Gary Wayne Johnson (b 9 Nov 1946, St Joseph MO).

RF4111141241   Dale Aaron Johnson (b 15 Jun 1967, Julesburg CO).

RF4111141242   Dean Allen Johnson (b 15 Jun 1967, Julesburg CO).

RF4111141243   Mark Anthony Johnson (b 11 Jun 1971, Ogallala NE).

RF411114125   Lois Ann Cummins (4 Mar 1953, Lewellen NE-18 Nov 1973, Beatrice NE).

RF41111413   Florence Cummins (b 19 May 1905, Valley Co NE) m 1) 7 Aug 1923, Valley Co NE, Wayne Elmer King (11 Nov 1899, Valley Co NE-4 Jun 1976, Ord NE); m 2) 23 Jan 1979, Burwell NE, Elmer Vergin (d 27 Jan 1982, Ord NE).

RF411114131   Mary Elizabeth Anne King (b 2 Jul 1927, Valley Co NE) m 1) 22 May 1949, Ord NE, Lyle Dean Manchester (b 7 May 1928, North Loup NE); m 2) 29 Mar 1981, Sierra Vista AZ, Ray Hooper (b Newton MA).

RF4111141311   Michael Gene Manchester (b 18 Apr 1950, Ord NE) m 7 Jul 1969, Aurora CO, Rebecca Louise Freiss Arbauthnot (b 3 Jul 1952, Omaha NE).

RF41111413111   Jon Patrick Manchester (b 16 Jan 1970, Norfolk NE).

RF41111413112   Eric Paul Manchester (b 21 Jun 1977, Wurzburg Germany).

RF411114132   Joyce Rosalie King (b 14 Nov 1928, Valley Co NE) m 2 Jan 1952, Ord NE, Calvert Burton Bresley (b 14 Oct 1909, Valley Co NE).

RF4111141321   Leon Calvert Bresley (b 3 Nov 1952, Ord NE) m 2 Jan 1972, St Paul NE, Donna Preskocil (b 7 Apr 1956, Ord NE).

RF41111413211   Dustin Zane Bresley (b 27 May 1973, St Paul NE).

RF41111413212   Crystal Dawn Bresley (b 29 Sep 1975, St Paul NE).

RF41111413213   Bill Jo Bresley (b 11 Jul 1979, St Paul NE).

RF4111141322   Rebecca Dawn Bresby (b 6 Nov 1953, Ord NE) m 25 Apr 1973, North Loup NE, Vincent C Hanson (b 22 Jul 1954, Williston ND).

RF41111413221   Tanya Christine Hanson (b 21 Dec 1974, Wurzburg Germany).

RF41111413222   Joshua Craig Hanson (b 28 Jun 1978, Junction City KA).

RF4111141323   Tanya Elaine Bresley (b 2 Jul 1956, Ord NE) m 11 Sep 1972, North Loup NE, Randy Adamek (b 10 Feb 1955, Ord NE).

RF41111413231   Heather Wayne Adamek (b 28 Mar 1973, Ord NE).

RF41111413232   Ryan Allan Adamek (b 25 Nov 1977, Ord NE).

RF411114133   Raymond Wayne King (b 28 Jan 1930, Valley Co NE).

RF41111414   Hazel Ruth Cummins (18 Feb 1907, Valley Co NE-14 Jun 1982, Lincoln NE) m 1) 28 Jun 1928, Burwell NE, Albert Haught (17 Nov 1902 New York NY-25 Aug 1946, North Loup NE); m 2) 16 May 1952, Grand Isle NE, Reggie McLain (9 Dec 1895, Ord NE-31 Dec 1974, Mesa AZ).

RF411114141   Walter Richard Haught (b 28 Mar 1928, Valley Co NE) m 2 Apr 1954, Wichita Falls TX Patsy Merlyn Knox (b 17 May 1934, Oklahoma City OK).

                              Terry Wayne Haught (b 3 Aug 1953) Adopted.

RF4111141411   Richard Charles Haught (b 9 Mar 1955, Wicheta Falls TX) m 1 Dec 1973, Logan UT,
Julie Nickelson.

RF41111414111   Michael Brandon Haught (b 6 Feb 1975, Mt Home UT).

RF41111414112   Matthew Adam Haught (b 19 Jun 1978, Boise ID).

RF4111141412   Nikki Sue Haught (b 25 Sep 1967, Goldsboro NC).

RF411114142   Donald Albert Haught (3 Feb 1931, Valley Co NE-19 Apr 1971, Grand Island NE) m 20 Jun 1958, Fremont NE, Shirley Yanke (b 19 Apr 1925, Richland NE).

RF4111141421   Sheri Haught (b 3 Feb 1963 Idaho Falls ID).

RF411114143   Kathleen Haught (b 6 Nov 1933, Valley Co NE) m 15 Feb 1951, North Loup NE, Charles

Davis (b 28 Nov 1938, Ord NE).

RF4111141431   Cathy Joe Davis (b 2 Oct 1951, Grand Island NE) m 7 Dec 1968, Pinehurst ID, Danny Hill (b 13 Dec 1950, Kellogg ID).

RF41111414311   Kelly Sue Hill (b 2 Mar 1969).

RF41111414312   Josie Marie Hill (b 28 Dec 1972).

RF4111141432   Thomas Davis (b 29 Nov 1952, Grand Island NE).

RF4111141433   Amy Ruth Davis (b 22 Sep 1961 Idaho Falls ID).

RF4111141434   Albert Davis (b 2 Jun 1965 Idaho Falls ID).

RF4111141435   Joseph Robert Davis (b 6 Sep 1970, Pinehurst ID).

RF411114144   Dennis Haught (b 8 Feb 1944, Valley Co NE) m 1) 26 Sep 1963, San Rafael CA, Yvonne Pester (b 24 Feb 1946, Arcadia NE); m 2) 24 Jun 1978, Lake Tahoe NV, Ellen Lee Kennedy (b 29 Oct 1948).

RF4111141441   Heidi Lou Haught (b 3 Feb 1966, San Pablo CA).

RF41111415   Helen Elizabeth Cummins (b 30 Aug 1906, Valley CO NE) m 28 Mar 1928, Marysville KS, William Valentine Earnest (14 Feb 1895, Valley Co NE-12 Jan 1984, Ord NE).

RF411114151   Daryl William Earnest (b 6 Nov 1928, North Loup NE) m 1) 12 Jun 1955, North Loup NE, Joan Burrows; m 2) 1959, Ord NE, Doris Marie Studnicka (b 18 Aug 1938, Farwell NE).

RF4111141511   Sheryl Rose Earnest (b 13 Nov 1959, Spalding NE) m 9 Mar 1979, Amherst NE, Craig Harmoney (b 13 Nov 1959, Kearney NE).

RF41111415111   Joshua Craig Harmoney (b 25 Sep 1979, Kearney NE).

RF41111415112   Jason Michael Harmoney (b 18 Jun 1981, Lexington NE).

RF4111141512   Michael William Earnest (b 20 Mar 1961, Spalding NE) m 27 Aug 1983, Riverdale NE, Teresa Henncy (b 18 Mar 1965, Fairmont NE).

RF4111141513   Patricia Rae Earnest (b 4 Dec 1962, Valley NE) m 20 Aug 1982, Kearney NE, Martin Moore (b 3 May 1962, Overton NE).

RF41111415131   Sarah Michelle Moore (b 27 Jan 1983, Kearney NE).

RF4111141514   Terri Lynn Earnest (b 25 Jan 1965, Valley NE) m 29 Mar 1985, Minden NE, Richard Thomas Petersen (b 20 Jan 1965, Fremont NE).

RF411114152   Dorothy Jean Earnest (b 8 Dec 1929, North Loup NE) m 7 Oct 1951, North Loup NE, Vernon Merriman (b 18 Feb 1930, Lincoln NE).

RF4111141521   Douglas Dale Merriman (b 6 Sep 1956, Lincoln NE) m 29 Sep 1979, Lincoln NE, Margaret Adams.

RF4111141522   Debra Lynn Merriman (b 19 May 1959, Lincoln NE).

RF4111141523   Dianne Lee Merriman (b 4 Sep 1966, Lincoln NE).

RF411114153   Mary Joan Earnest (b 12 Dec 1932, North Loup NE) m 17 Feb 1952, North Loup NE, Ernst Eugene Bahm (b 13 Sep 1924, Colon NE).

RF4111141531   Allen Ernst Bahm (b 4 Feb 1954, Memphis NE) m 2 Feb 1975, Memphis NE, Debra Push (b 1 Jul 1956, Omaha NE).

RF41111415311   Jennifer Ann Bahm (b 12 Aug 1975, Wahoo NE).

RF4111141532   Steven Craig Bahm (17 Sep 1956, Memphis NE-14 Jul 1972, Memphis NE).

RF4111141533   Gregory Eugene Bahm (b 25 Mar 1961, Memphis NE).

RF4111141534   Laura Helen Bahm (b 12 Dec 1970, Memphis NE).

RF411114154   Dale Dean Earnest (b 17 Mar 1936, North Loup NE) m   1959, Everett WA, Donna Welborn.

RF4111141541   Carol Jean Earnest (b 28 Nov 1960, Everett WA).

RF4111141542   Randal Dean Earnest (b 11 May 1962, Everett WA).

RF4111141543   Julie Ann Earnest (b 28 Mar 1965, Everett WA) m Jun 1982, Marysville WA, Kevin Maude.

RF41111415431   Shala Marie Maude (b 19 Apr 1983, Minot ND).

RF4111141544   Karin Earnest (b 20 Nov 1966).

RF41111416   Anthony Earnest Cummins (b 12 Aug 1911, Valley Co NE) m 2 Nov 1934, Ord NE, Doris Flynn (28 Jan 1917, Ord NE-18 Jun 1984, Mesa AZ).

RF411114161   Geraldine Fay Cummins (3 Nov 1935, Davis Creed NE-5 Oct 1944, Ord NE).

RF411114162   Phyllis Jean Cummins (b 23 Apr 1937, Valley Co NE) m 1) 4 Apr 1964, Alan Knobel (b 17 May 1931); m 2) 16 Jul 1982, Brooklyn SD, William Dohrmann (b 21 Oct 1934, Pine Island MN).

RF4111141621   Richard Alan Knobel (b 17 Oct 1964, Zumbrota MN).

RF4111141622   Kimberly Anne Knobel (24 Feb 1967, Zumbrota MN-19 Jun 1974, West Concord MN).

RF411114163   Virginia Lee Cummins (b 25 Jul 1938, Valley Co NE) m 1 Dec 1956, Madrid IA, George Thorngate (b 16 Feb 1938, North Loup NE).

RF4111141631   David Allen Thorngate (b 25 Mar 1959, Lincoln NE).

RF4111141632   Rodney Ray Thorngate (b 8 Jun 1961, Lincoln NE).

RF4111141633   Bradley Dale Thorngate (b 28 Aug 1964, Lincoln NE).

RF4111141634   Scott Allison Thorngate (b 14 Sep 1968, Lincoln NE).

RF411114164   Robert Le Roy Cummins (b 6 Sep 1939, Valley Co NE).

RF41111417   Clinton Paul Cummins (b 26 Dec 1912, Arcadia NE) m 1) 19 Jul 1936, Francie Osborn (b 7 Jul 1920, Mayetta KS); m 2) 24 Dec 1949, Port Angeles WA, Pauline Virginia Palmer (b 27 Oct 1910, Nellie NC).

RF411114171   Thelma June Cummins (b 15 Jun 1937, North Loup NE) m 21 Jul 1956, Port Orchard WA, Ronald E Brown.

RF4111141711   David Mike Brown (b 23 Feb 1957, Duarte CA).

RF4111141712   Dwayne Edward Brown (b 30 Jan 1959, Duarte CA).

RF4111141713   Deanna June Brown (b 31 Oct 1963, Duarte CA).

RF41111418   Comfort William Cummins (b 13 Oct 1914, Arcadia NE) m 3 Aug 1941, Burwell NE, Doris Mae Tolen (b 9 Oct 1927, Taylor NE).

RF411114181   Ronald Eugene Cummins (b 19 Jun 1942, North Loup NE) m 26 Jun 1969, Florence AZ, Marie Juanita Valenzuela (b 17 Jul 1933, Phoenix AZ).

RF4111141811   Sabrina Ranee Cummins (b 13 Apr 1970, Mesa AZ).

RF4111141812   Rhonda Mae Cummins (b 6 Aug 1971, Phoenix AZ).

RF411114182   Gary Dean Cummins (b 14 Jun 1943, North Loup NE) m 14 Jul 1969, Las Vegas NV, Zylphia Honeycutt (b 4 Jul 1949, Riverton WY).

RF4111141821   Brian Eric Cummins (b 29 Jan 1969, Tempe AZ).

RF4111141822   Brett William Cummins (b 20 Apr 1971, Tempe AZ).

RF411114183   Carol Ann Cummins (b 4 May 1945, North Loup NE) m 1) 28 Jul 1962, Fremont NE, Ross Belmore Cottrell (b 28 Jan 1941, Fremont NE), m 2) 12 Apr 1980, Fremont NE, Wayne Stark.

RF4111141831   Tracy Lynn Cottrell (b 8 Feb 1963, Fremont NE) m 28 Apr 1984, William Campbell.

RF41111418311   Kelly Ann Campbell (b 15 Oct 1983, Fremont NE).

RF4111141832   Terry Lee Cottrell (b 2 Jun 1964, Fremont NE) m 16 Jul 1983, Shenandoah IA, Cindy Poe.

RF4111141833   Robbie Dean Cottrell (b 15 Jun 1968, Fremont NE).

RF4111142   Milton David Earnest (1 Jul 1876, Gettysburg OH-17 Nov 1959, La Mesa CA) m 1 Dec 1900, North Loup NE, Vio (Beulah) Bell Knapp (3 Dec 1881, Vinton IA-17 Jan 1973, El Cajon CA) Banker.

RF41111421   Leland Clinton Earnest (7 May 1906, North Loup NE-5 Mar 1976, El Cajon CA) m 13 Apr 1928, Grand Island NE, Florentine Felecia Osantowski (29 Jul 1908, Elba NE-9 Apr 1975, El Cajon CA).

RF411114211   Russell David Earnest (b 20 Mar 1938, San Diego CA) m 13 Jun 1964, Gresham OR, Corinne Faye Pattie (b 6 Sep 1942, Amarillo TX) Wildlife biologist.

RF4111142111   Patricia Corinne Earnest (b 8 Aug 1966, Denver CO).

RF4111142112   Russell David Earnest (b 2 Dec 1968, San Rafael CA).

RF411114212   Ronald Lee Earnest (b 9 Jul 1939, National City CA) m 24 Jun 1964, LaMesa CA, Diana Gerrard (b 20 May 1938, Owens South, Ontario CA).

RF4111142121   Robert Larry Earnest (b 26 Jun 1946, La Mesa CA).

RF41111422   Lyle Milton Earnest (b 13 Nov 1922, North Loup NE) m 1) 20 Dec 1947, Chula Vista

CA, Ruby Corinne Wright (21 Aug 1921, San Diego CA-7 Apr 1966, San Diego CA); m 2) 12 May 1967, Las Vegas NV, Jean Marilyn (nee Parkinson) Stewart (b 27 Jul 1928, Lincoln NE) Banker.

RF411114221   Jeri Lee Earnest (b 19 Jun 1950, San Diego CA) m 1) 19 Sep 1970, San Diego CA, Joseph Warren Cabral (b 19 Feb 1950, San Diego CA); m 2) 1975, Dale Jones (b 5 Dec 1952, ID).

RF4111142211   Rebecca Marie Jones (b 2 Mar 1976, Oceanside CA).

RF4111142212   Christopher Michael Eugene Jones (b 27 Sep 1978, Memphis TN).

RF411114222   Janice Corine Earnest (b 14 Jun 1954, San Diego CA) m 26 Jun 1976, La Mesa CA, Richard Watkins (b 17 Nov 1950, IL).

RF4111143   Charles Omer Earnest (15 Jan 1878, Gettysburg OH-17 Sep 1968, Alpine CA) m 28 Aug 1899, Ord NE, Lucy Elizabeth Clark (30 May 1879, Carlyle IL-28 Dec 1958, San Diego CA) Banker.

RF41111431   Mildred Marie Earnest (b 15 Aug 1900, North Loup NE) m 1) 22 Dec 1927, San Diego CA, Clifton Donald Rock (27 May 1900, Onward IN-21 Dec 1954, San Diego CA); m 2) 7 Jun 1962, Seattle WA, Stuart Whitehouse (22 Mar 1902, Walla Walla WA-7 Feb 1964, Honolulu HI); m 3) 28 Sep 1979, Honolulu HI, Harry Lardin. She, teacher.

RF41111432   Nellie Earnest (b 23 Jun 1902, North Loup NE) m 25 Jun 1927, San Diego CA, Lon Elliot Wheeler (30 May 1905, Lincoln NE-6 Nov 1966, El Cajon CA) She, teacher.

RF411114321   Richard Lon Wheeler (5 Aug 1932, San Diego CA-13 Mar 1977, Springfield OR) m 1) 26 Jun 1952, Springfield OR, Deanne Holling (b 24 Nov 1933); m 2) 9 Dec 1956, Reno NV, Gloria Phibbs (b 26 Feb 1933, Dexter OR).

RF4111143211   Kimberly Ann Wheeler (b 17 Nov 1953, Eugene OR) m 1) 23 Mar 1974, San Jose CA, Gary Geser; m 2) 8 Jun 1980, Elmira OR, Tom Zavola.

RF41111432111   Kayla Dee Geser (b 19 Sep 1975, San Jose CA).

RF41111432112   Travis Edward Zavola (b 29 Dec 1980, Elmira OR).

RF4111143212   Shelby Wheeler (b 17 Jun 1957, Springfield OR) m 1) 24 Dec 1972, Leaburg OR, Douglas Baldwin (b 26 Mar 1955); m 2) 25 Aug 1979, Springfield OR, Russell Hoover.

RF41111432121   Lonnie Kirk Baldwin (b 7 Mar 1973, Springfield OR).

RF4111143213   Richard Lance Wheeler (11 Nov 1958, Springfield OR-30 May 1968, Leaburg OR).

RF4111143214   Kari Lynette Wheeler (b 25 Nov 1959, Springfield OR) m 1 Mar 1980, Springfield OR, Larry Alberts.

RF41111432141   Melissa Lea Alberts (b 25 Jan 1981, Springfield OR).

RF411114322   Frank Earnest Wheeler (b 28 Jun 1934, San Diego CA) m 4 Feb 1956, Reno NV, Luella Daughenbaugh (b 9 Jun 1936, Springfield OR).

RF4111143221   Susan Kay Wheeler (b 6 Jan 1957, Eugene OR).

RF4111143222   Mary Ellen Wheeler (b 27 Jan 1959, Eugene OR) m 10 Jun 1978, McKenzie Bridge OR, Charles H Haring (b 28 Feb 1958).

RF41111432221   Nicholas Charles Haring (b 28 Sep 1979, Springfield OH).

RF4111143223   Douglas Lon Wheeler (b 3 Jan 1960, Eugene OR).

RF41111433   Lester Elvin Earnest (b 24 Apr 1905, North Loup NE) m 22 Nov 1928, Yuma AZ, Sue Wolfer (b 19 Sep1907, Grand Fords ND) Administrator.

RF411114331   Lester Donald Earnest Jr (b 17 Dec 1930, San Diego CA) m 13 Apr 1955, Wencote PA, Joan Patton (b 5 Jan 1927, Camden NJ).

RF4111143311   Mark Patton Earnest (b 29 Oct 1955, Phoenixville PA).

RF4111143312   Jo Ann Earnest (b 7 Jan 1957, Philadelphia PA).

RF4111143313   Ian Kenneth Earnest (b 29 Jan 1959, Arlington MA).

RF411114332   Patricia Sue Earnest (b 28 Apr 1933, San Diego CA) m 1) 24 Jun 1967, San Diego CA, Hugh P Boyle (b 8 Jun 1933, Hartford CT); m 2) 1 Jan 1980, Herbert Bernstein (b 18 Jul 1932, Brooklyn NY).

RF4111143321   Kristin Elizabeth Boyle (b 2 Sep 1969, San Diego CA).

RF4111143322   Jennifer Lee Boyle (b 12 Oct 1971, San Diego CA).

RF4111143323   John Christopher Boyle (b 21 Aug 1973, San Diego CA).

RF4111144   Lola Irene Earnest (b 14 May 1908, North Loup NE) m 29 Jan 1931, Yuma AZ, Rollo Tinkham Pearson (3 Jul 1903, Baraboo WI-4 May 1945, San Diego CA) Secretary.

RF41111441   Charles Rollo Pearson (b 23 Feb 1933, San Diego CA) m 11 Feb 1951, Yuma AZ, Lillian Ann Wilcox (b 26 Jul 1934, Chicago IL).

RF411114411   Edward James Pearson (b 21 Dec 1952, San Diego CA).

RF411114412   Michael Dean Pearson (b 5 Dec 1954, San Diego CA) m 12 Oct 1974, Alpine CA, Carol Savoie (b 12 Dec 1956, San Diego CA).

RF4111144121   Jeffrey Charles Pearson (b 25 Feb 1975, San Diego CA).

RF4111144122   Corrine Jeanette Pearson (b 12 Jan 1977, San Diego CA).

RF411114413   Eric Charles Pearson (b 27 Jul 1958, San Diego CA) m 17 Nov 1979, La Mesa CA, Lonie Hamel (b 2 May 1961, San Diego CA).

RF4111144131   Janine Lee Pearson (b 17 Jan 1979, San Diego CA).

RF4111144132   Eric Charles Pearson Jr (b 26 May 1981, San Diego CA).

RF411114414   Cathleen Marie Pearson (b 5 Mar 1961, San Diego CA).

RF41111442   Beverly Eunice Pearson (b 18 Feb 1936, San Diego CA) m 1) 7 Jun 1954, San Diego CA, Frederick Marten Leonhardt (21 Mar 1935, St Louis MO-27 Dec 1974, Huntington Beach CA); m 2) 30 Oct 1982, John Kercheval.

RF411114421   Patricia Kaye Leonhardt (b 13 Nov 1954, San Diego CA) m 13 May 1977, Westminster CA, John Andrew Munsterman (b 12 Aug 1954).

RF411114422   Peter Marten Leonhardt (b 5 Jun 1957, San Diego CA) m 1 Jul 1978, Huntington Beach CA, Elizabeth Pinkston (b 21 Mar 1958).

RF411114423   Penelope Ann Leonhardt (b 20 May 1961, San Diego CA).

RF411114424   Pamela Lucy Leonhardt (b 28 Sep 1966, San Diego CA).

RF4111145   Blanche Olive Earnest (6 Jul 1880, Gettysburg OH-16 Feb 1956, Ord NE) m 4 Jan 1899, North Loup NE, Asa Clark Leonard (11 Dec 1867, Middleville MI-23 Oct 1934, Ord NE).

RF41111451   Vere Perry Leonard (27 Sep 1899, Ord NE-7 Sep 1949, North Loup NE) m 15 Mar 1922, North Loup NE Nellie Pearl Eberhart (8 Oct 1897, Avoca IA-5 Sep 1981, Lincoln NE) Farmer, laborer.

RF411114511   Arnold George Leonard (b 4 Feb 1924, North Loup NE) m 12 Jul 1945, Loup City NE, Catherine Odel John (b 10 Aug 1922, Loup City NE) Insurance executive.

RF4111145111   Constance Marie Leonard (b 19 Dec 1950, Superior NE) m 12 Jun 1973, West Point NY, Donald Edward Brown (b 1 Nov 1951, Panama Canal Zone).

RF41111451111   Annemarie Marguerite Brown (b 29 Jun 1979, Ft Huchuca AZ).

RF41111451112   Julie Christine Brown (b 27 Aug 1981, Hinesville GA).

RF4111145112   Catherine Anne Leonard (b 9 Mar 1952, Superior NE) m 29 May 1976, Roeland Park KS, Donald F Bayer (b 13 Feb 1949, Dickinson ND).

RF41111451121   Catherine Odel Bayer (b 2 Dec 1978, Kansas City MO).

RF4111145113   Christine Priscilla Leonard (b 21 Jun 1961, St Louis MO) m 8 Sep 1984, Ann Arbor MI, Kevin Earl Raquepaw (b 6 Oct 1959, Saginaw MI).

RF411114512   Carol Ruby Leonard (6 Aug 1928, North Loup NE-28 Oct 1942, North Loup NE).

RF411114513   Lester Gordon Leonard (b 19 Apr 1931, North Loup NE) m 1) 6 Aug 1952, Las Vegas NV, Corinne Pinto (b 1 Nov 1932, Richmond CA); m 2) 29 Jun 1979, Rough and Ready CA, Theresa Olszyk (b 23 May 1940, Wilkes-Barre PA).

RF4111145131   Deborah Ann Leonard (b 18 Apr 1953, Anchorage AK) m 11 Apr 1978, Modesto CA, David Butler (b 18 Mar 1956, Modesto CA).

RF41111451311   Candy Butler (6 Feb 1979-7 Mar 1979).

RF41111451312   Crystal Butler (6 Feb 1979-31 Aug 1979).

RF41111451313   Vanessa Dawn Butler (b 21 Jul 1980, Vacaville CA).

RF4111145132   Michele Leonard (b 23 Mar 1957, San Pablo CA).

RF4111145133   Cheryl Lynn Leonard (b 1 Apr 1958, San Pablo CA).

RF4111145134   Michael Allen Leonard (b 12 Jan 1961, Pinole CA).

RF41111452   Myrnie Ruby Leonard (25 Dec 1902, Ord NE-17 Mar 1926, Ord NE) m 27 Mar 1923, Ord NE, Walter John Foth (23 Aug 1898, Ord NE-26 Dec 1971, Ansley NE).

RF411114521   Lyle Leon Foth (b 2 Mar 1926, Ord NE) m 19 Feb 1950, Grand Island NE, Ruth Elma Meier (b 7 Mar 1931, Grand Island NE).

RF4111145211   Kay Jolene Foth (b 1 Jan 1951, Ord NE) m 8 Jan 1972, Ord NE, Terrance Scott Hines (b 17 Nov 1950, Omaha NE).

RF4111145212   Christine Ruth Foth (b 10 Jan 1952, Ord NE) m 7 Aug 1977, Ord NE, Bruce Reinboth (b 29 May 1950, Deshler NE).

RF41111452121   Shannon Kay Reinboth (b 22 Mar 1979, North Platte NE).

RF41111452122   Brett Allen Reinboth (b 28 Aug 1981, North Platte NE).

RF41111452123   Katie Marie Reinboth (b 14 Nov 1983, North Platte NE).

RF4111145213   Gretchen Sue Foth (b 15 Oct 1953, Ord NE).

RF4111145214   Eileen Marie Foth (b 22 Jun 1957, Ord NE) m 15 Jun 1979, Ord NE, David Ray Kuhule (b 7 Aug 1956, Cedar Rapids IA).

RF4111145215   Kimberly Ann Foth (b 26 Nov 1952, Ord NE).

RF41111453   Asa Leslie Leonard (13 Jul 1906, Ord NE-16 Jan 1981, Mesa AZ) m 8 Jun 1929, Ord NE, Carol Bessie Flynn (b 4 Nov 1908, Valley Co NE) Farmer, implement dealer.

RF411114531   Donald Eugene Leonard (b 17 Mar 1933, Ord NE) m 8 Jun 1954, Lincoln NE, Joan Follmer (b 3 Jun 1931, Lincoln NE) Lawyer.

RF4111145311   William Follmer Leonard (b 18 Aug 1957, Lincoln NE).

RF4111145312   John Allen Leonard (b 4 Feb 1960, Lincoln NE) m 4 Sep 1982, Kansas City MO, Gaye Lynn Peterson (b 30 Oct 1959, Kansas City MO).

RF4111145313   James Donald Leonard (b 4 Jul 1965, Lincoln NE).

RF41111454   Olive Pearl Leonard (16 May 1914, Ord NE-12 Dec 1969, Ord NE) m 8 Apr 1937, Burwell NE, Glenn Walter Bremer (b 21 May 1912, Scotia NE).

RF411114541   Sharon Kay Bremer (b 28 Feb 1941, North Loup NE) m 7 Jun 1964, North Loup NE, Ira Joe Condley (b 3 Dec 1937, Wabbaseka AR) Teacher.

RF4111145411   Stacy Joelle Condley (b 22 Oct 1970, Fresno CA).

RF4111145412   Lisa Danielle Condley (b 25 Apr 1973, Fresno CA).

RF411114542   Richard Glenn Bremer (b 30 Jan 1944, Scotia NE) PhD.

RF41111455   Evelyn Violet Leonard (b 7 Dec 1916, Ord NE) m 18 Feb 1934, Ord NE, Melvin Frederick Koelling (b 28 Jan 1913, North Loup NE) Clergyman.

RF411114551   Dennis Duane Koelling (b 5 Mar 1939, Ord NE) m 25 Jul 1969, Sioux Falls SD, Lynne Marie Larson (b 4 Jun 1943, Muscatine IA).

RF4111145511   Bryce David Koelling (b 27 May 1972, Spencer IA).

RF4111145512   Suzanne Marie Koelling (b 31 Jan 1975, Sioux Falls SD).

RF411114552   Charlene Lucienne Koelling (b 24 Mar 1942, North Loup NE) m 3 Mar 1967, Honolulu HI, Walter Kenichi Takahashi (b 7 Feb 1941, Eva HI).

RF4111145521   Tess Leina Takahashi (b 29 Dec 1968, Honolulu HI).

RF4111145522   Trevor Kekoa Takahashi (b 29 Jul 1971, Honolulu HI).

RF4111145523   Amy Leiland Takahashi (b 23 May 1973, Honolulu HI).

RF4111145524   Sara Keolani Takahashi (b 31 Jul 1974, Honolulu HI).

RF411114553   Gary Eugene Koelling (b 24 Feb 1947, Aurora IL) m 1) 29 May 1971, Estherville IA, Sheila Mary Harrold (12 Mar 1952, Ft Dodge IA-2 Sep 1982, Spirit Lake IA); m 2) 29 Jul 1983, Estherville IA, Cathy Jean (nee Rogness) Feiler (b 26 Aug 1952, Clarion IA) Teacher.

RF4111145531   Kristine Kathleen Koelling (b 21 Feb 1978, Spirit Lake IA).

RF4111145532   Kimber Lee Koelling (b 29 Feb 1980, Spirit Lake IA).

RF411114554   Rodney Allen Koelling (b 14 Mar 1949, Aurora IL) m 22 Aug 1987, Austin TX, Victoria Stephanie Rieck Harrison.

RF4111146   Hazel Ruth Earnest (1 Aug 1898, Valley Co NE-8 Mar 1903, Valley Co NE).

RF411115   Margaret Ann Hannah Earnest (b 4 Nov 1851) m 10 Nov 1890, Darke Co OH, John Smith.

RF411116   Rosanna Barbara Earnest (25 Feb 1854-11 Feb 1856).

RF411117   Susan Elizabeth Earnest (b 6 Mar 1856) m 10 Mar 1872, Darke Co OH, Warren Davis.

RF411118   Jacob Frederick Earnest (25 Aug 1860, Darke Co OH-18 Feb 1945, North Loup NE) m 16 Mar 1887, Darke Co OH, Henrietta Couding (2 Feb 1867 OH-Apr 1930, North Loup NE).

RF4111181   Ethel Edna Earnest (b 5 May 1888, Darke Co OH) m 1)   Hemkin; m 2) Ralph Craft; m 3) Dwaine Clark.

RF41111811   Lawrence Hemkin (11 Jan 1908, North Loup NE-Jun 1944, CA).

RF41111812   Ina Lou Craft (b 13 Oct 1912, North Loup NE).

RF4111182   Murel Joy Earnest (b 1 Jul 1893, Valley Co NE) m 4 Jan 1913, North Loup NE, Lon Newcomb.

RF41111821   Dorys Etta Newcomb (b 28 Dec 1914, North Loup NE) m Loren Redman.

RF41111822   Twyla Jean Newcomb (b 21 May 1917, North Loup NE) m Phillip Grider.

RF41111823   Bernard Newcomb (b 14 Dec 1922, North Loup NE).

RF4111183   William Valentine Earnest (14 Feb 1895, Valley Co NE-12 Jan 1984, Ord NE) m 28 Mar 1928, Marysville KA, Helen Elizabeth Cummins (b 30 Aug 1909, Valley Co NE) See RF31111415.

RF4111184   Guy David Earnest (28 Jul 1903, Valley Co NE-15 Nov 1972, Rapid City SD) m 15 Oct 1931, Central City NE, Lucille Callaway (b 7 May 1911, Ravenna NE).

RF41111841   Howard Rollin Earnest (b 24 Jan 1934, Scotia NE) m 21 Dec 1959, St Paul NE, Beth Reasland.

RF411118411   Mitchael Dean Earnest (b 20 Aug 1960, Grand Island NE).

RF411118412   Michelle Ann Earnest (b 18 Aug 1961, Grand Island NE) m 9 Jun 1984, Cairo NE, Cornell Pollock.

RF411118413   Jeffrey Howard Earnest (b 16 Mar 1963, Grand Island NE).

RF411118414   Douglas Guy Earnest (b 28 Aug 1972, Grand Island NE).

RF41111842   Velma Arlene Earnest (b 26 Nov 1935, North Loup NE) m 1) 28 Aug 1955, Ravenna NE, Harold Wallace; m 2) 31 Mar 1962, Omaha NE, Le Roy Foreman (b 19 Aug 1936).

RF411118421   Karen Kay Wallace (b 31 Mar 1956, Omaha NE; adopted by Le Roy Foreman) m 26 Jun 1976, Omaha NE, Ron Duane Johnson.

RF4111184211   Ryan David Johnson (b 5 Mar 1981, Omaha NE).

RF4111184212   Eric Daniel Johnson (b 30 Oct 1982, Omaha NE).

RF411118422   Hal Eugene Wallace (b 12 Nov 1957, San Gabriel CA) m 24 Apr 1982, Omaha NE, Mary Nekola.

RF4111184221   Andrew James Foreman (b 6 Feb 1983, Omaha NE).

RF41111843   Thelma Darlene Earnest (b 26 Nov 1935, North Loup NE) m 4 Aug 1957, Ravenna NE, Leland Kirkland.

RF411118431   Russell Lee Kirkland (b 12 Apr 1958, West Point NE) m 25 Sep 1982, Stanton NE, Ruth Pinkston.

RF41111844   Melvin Russell Earnest (b 7 Jul 1937, North Loup NE) m 27 Jun 1965, Grand Island NE, Rita Devone Bilslend.

RF411118441   Joy Lynn Earnest (b 22 Jul 1966, Grand Island NE, stillborn).

RF411118442   Brian Dwight Earnest (b 7 Nov 1968, Grand Island NE).

RF411118443   Bradley Duane Earnest (b 21 Mar 1970, Grand Island NE).

RF411118444   Brenda Jo Earnest (b 1 Apr 1977, Grand Island NE).

RF41112   Eleonora Earnest (4 Jan 1822-9 Apr 1831).

RF41113   John Quincy Adams Earnest (b 9 Sep 1827).

RF41114   Ann R Earnest (ca 1829-9 Apr 1831).

RF41115   Michael S Earnest (7 Jun 1833-20 Jul 1833).

RF41116   Elmira Earnest (b 1846).

RF41117   Juliana Earnest (b 1849).

RF4112   Anna Earnest m Jacob Maze.

RF4113   Sophia Earnest (1803-5 Jan 1846) m 24 Jan 1826, Jacob Earnest Jr.

RF4114   Rachel Earnest (8 Feb 1805, Hummelstown PA-20 Aug 1878, Wayne Tp OH) m Isaac Johnson (23 Jul 1803-24 Feb 1869, Wooster OH).

RF41141   Pleasant Ann Johnson (25 Nov 1829, Wayne Co PA-4 Jul 1893, Wooster Tp OH) m 1) 3 Jun 1854, Wayne Co OH, Philip Troutman (1 Jan 1824, Berkeley Co VA-16 Feb 1880, Wooster Tp, Wayne Co OH) Farmer, Wooster Tp, Wayne Co OH.

RF411411   Ada Troutman (11 Dec 1855-Wooster Tp, Wayne Co OH-24 Dec 1945, Wooster OH) m 1 Jan 1880, Clinton Tp, Wayne Co OH, Daniel Webster Strock (b 28 Jun 1852, Wooster Tp, Wayne Co OH) Farmer near Wooster OH.

RF4114111   Frank Troutman Strock (28 Aug 1881, Wooster Tp, Wayne Co OH-1 Apr 1978, Auburn IN) m 20 Mar 1905, Hudson IN, Ada Grieve Ketchum (b 3 Oct 1884, Hudson IN) Grain elevator owner, onion farmer; bank president. Bur near Hudson IN.

RF41141111   Paul Wayne Strock (10 Oct 1911, Hudson IN-27 Jul 1985, Ft Wayne IN) m 12 Oct 1940, Kendallville IN, Helen Mary Bruner (b 26 Sep 1911, Kendallville IN) He, BA, Miami (OH) U, 1933. Grain elevator, Hudson IN).

RF411411111   Stephen Frank Strock (b 9 Oct 1947, Angola IN) m 22 Sep 1973, Karen Spike (b 18 Oct 1942, Chelsea MI).

RF4114111111   Michelle Lynn Strock (b 23 Feb 1975, Ann Arbor MI).

RF4114111112   Jeremy Frank Strock (b 2 Oct 1976, Ann Arbor MI).

RF41141112   Carl Ashton Strock (b 24 Aug 1918, Hudson IN) m 1) 10 Oct 1945, Grace Newnam Iddings (b 16 Nov 1916, Kendallville IN); m 2) 12 Oct 1985 PA, Doris Gertrude Hodges. AB, DePauw (IN) U, 1941. Hardware, men's wear merchant, Angola IN. No chn.

RF4114112   Jay Philip Strock (3 Oct 1883, Millbrook IN-22 Feb 1974, Dalton OH) m 1) 23 Nov 1904, Vera M Filger (b 26 Sep 1885, Plain Tp, Wayne Co OH); m 2) 1923, IN, Viola Wildman Smith (b 24 Feb 1879, Wolcottville IN).

RF41141121   Gertrude Ellen Strock (b 23 Oct 1911, Wooster OH) m 28 Dec 1935, Robert Allen Cook (b 22 Jun 1911, Holmes Co OH) She, teacher.

RF411411211   Mary Frances Cook (b 26 Jan 1937, Wooster OH) m 23 Aug 1959, Wooster OH, Jonathan B Howes (b 12 Apr 1937, Knoxville TN) She, AB, Wittenberg (OH) U; MA, U NC. He, AB, Wittenberg (OH) U; MA, U NC; MA, Harvard U. She, travel consultant; he, professor, U NC; director, Center of Urban and Regional Studies, U NC; Mayor, Chapel Hill NC, 1988-1991.

RF4114112111   Anne B Howes (b 5 Jul 1960, Chapel Hill NC) m 25 Nov 1989, David Anderson. She, AB, Col of Wooster OH; MA, U NC. Swimming coach, Col of William and Mary (VA).

RF41141121111   Margaret Hannah Anderson (b 26 Feb 1991, Williamsburg VA).

RF4114112112   Mary Elizabeth Howes (b 26 Jan 1963, Washington DC) m 2 May 1992, Charles Bean. She, BA, Wellesley (MA) Col; MA, Harvard U. Federal reserve employee, New York NY.

RF4114112113   Robert Cook Howes (b 1 May 1965, Falls Church VA) m 30 Jun 1990, Patricia Olovo. BA, Denison (OH) U. Legislative assistant to member of Congress, Elizabeth Patterson.

RF411411212   Donald Lawrence Cook (b 14 May 1940, Wooster OH) m 22 Jun 1968, Denver CO, Rose Naglack (b 29 Oct 1943) He, BA, Wittenberg (OH) U; MA, JD, U Denver. Vietnamese conflict: USAF, Capt. Attorney, Denver CO. She, AB, U CT; MA, U Denver. Sociologist, Cherry Creek Co school system, Denver.

RF41141122   Mary Frances Strock (b 17 Apr 1913, Wooster OH) m 5 Feb 1908 OH, Eugene Kendig (b 5 Feb 1908, Nanhin OH) AB, Ashland U, 1934; Lake Erie Col for Women, 1963. Teacher OH and Ft Myers FL.

RF411411221   Edward Strock Kendig (b 27 Jun 1946, Painesville OH) m 16 Apr 1983, Becky Peters.

RF4114112211   Katy Kendig (b 21 Feb 1985, CO).

RF411411222   Robert Dean Kendig (b 18 Jan 1950, Painesville OH) m 20 May 1978, Jane Alice Belcher.

RF4114113   Earl Wayne Strock (3 Oct 1886, Wooster Tp, Wayne Co OH-9 Jul 1962, Wooster OH) m 1) 25 Nov 1909, Millersburg OH, Blanche McDonald Adams (b 28 Jul 1886, Millersburg OH); m 2) 26 May 1920, Columbus OH, Mona Pauline Thomas (b 29 Dec 1891, Union Co OH).

RF41141131   James Robert Strock (11 Apr 1911, Wooster OH-6 Sep 1980, Wooster OH) m 21 May 1928 New Cumberland VA, Norabelle Parkinson (b 20 Mar 1909, Millersburg OH) Bur Wooster OH.

RF411411311   Robert Earl Strock (b 11 Oct 1934, Wooster OH) m 16 Jun 1957, Wooster OH, Esther Jane Miller (b 3 Apr 1938, Westfield Tp, Medina Co OH) USAF, 1956-1960. Radio engineer, Laramie WY; research technologist, Garland TX; communications technician, Wooster OH. Genealogist.

RF4114113111   Thomas Wayne Strock (b 28 Mar 1960, Laramie WY) m 21 Jun 1908, Kidron OH, Elaine Sue Huntsberger (b 25 Dec 1959, Orrville OH) He, BSME, RPI; MSME, U MO, 1989. Engineer, St Louis MO, 1982-1991; project engineer, research and development, Alliance OH.

RF41141131111   Melanie Lynette Strock (b 8 Apr 1984, St. Louis MO).

RF41141131112   Katherine Liane Strock (b 12 Jan 1986, St. Louis MO).

RF41141131113   Robert William Strock (b 13 Jun 1988, St. Louis MO).

RF4114113112   Carol Ann Strock (b 20 Mar 1961, Laramie WY) m 2 Jun 1984, Massillon OH, Rickie Eugene Archer (b 22 May 1962, Orrville OH) Systems analyst, Akron OH.

RF41141131121   Erica Ann Archer (b 6 Apr 1900, Akron OH).

RF41141131122   Maria Elizabeth Archer (b 12 Jun 1992, Akron OH).

RF4114113113   John Robert Strock (b 4 Jul 1964, Garland TX) m 30 Mar 1985, Kidron OH, Angela Dawn Steiner (b 24 May 1966, Orrville OH) AB, Ashland (OH) Col, 1986. Television production.

RF41141131131   Trevor Alan Strock (b 19 Aug 1985, Orrville OH).

RF41141131132   Adrian Marie Strock (b 3 Dec 1988, Orrville OH).

RF411411312   William James Strock (b 12 Aug 1937, Wooster OH) m 1) 10 Feb 1962, MD, Carole Jane Housely (b 18 Aug 1945); m 2) 30 Aug 1975, Springfield MA, Maureen Hondros Wilson (b 10 Apr 1948, Springfield MA).

RF4114113121   Cynthia Renee Strock (b 18 Dec 1962, Hartford CT) m 16 Jun 1990, Frankfort ME, Kenneth Robert Thompson (b 9 Sep 1944, ME) She, banker, Bangor ME.

RF41141131211   Spencer Thompson (10 Dec 1990, Bangor ME-11 Dec 1990, Bangor ME).

RF41141131212   Miranda Carole Thompson (b 1 Jun 1992, Bangor ME).

RF4114113122   Tracy Leigh Strock (b 21 Apr 1965, Hartford CT) AB, Centre (KY) Col, 1987. Banker.

RF4114113123   Charles James Strock (b 19 Aug 1978, Manchester KY).

RF411411313   Daniel Parkinson Strock (12 Oct 1940, Wooster OH-5 Dec 1995, Canton OH) unm. Banker, Wooster OH.

RF41141132   James Thomas Strock (26 Dec 1922, Wooster OH-26 Sep 1982, Normandy Park, Medina Co OH) m 5 Jun 1943, Marilyn Eleanor Neilson (b 23 Jul 1921, Bellevue PA) WWII: USAC, South Pacific. Businessman, Wooster OH. She, WWII: USMC. Bur Wooster OH.

RF411411321   Diane Marilyn Strock (b 17 Jan 1947, Wooster OH) m 16 Aug 1969, Wooster OH, Ronald Dale Vanden Dorpel (b 21 Apr 1947) AB, OSU, 1969; Creighton Law. Attorney, Chicago IL. No chn.

RF411411322   James Neilson Strock (b 18 Jul 1949, Wooster OH) m 2 Aug 1975, Chula Vista CA, Claudia Jean Smyth. No chn.

RF411411323   Frederick Thomas Strock (b 31 Jul 1952, Wooster OH) m 11 Oct 1980, Ft Sill OK, Judy Elaine Jarecke (b 7 Jul 1959) OSU; USMC.

RF4114113231   Adam James Strock (b 3 Nov 1981, Ft Belvoir VA).

RF4114113232   Andrew Robert Strock (b 20 Jun 1983, Camp Pendleton CA).

RF4114113233   Amy Marilyn Strock (b 31 Mar 1985, Camp Pendleton CA).

RF411411324   John Allan Strock (b 22 Feb 1956, Wooster OH) m 21 Aug 1981, Wooster OH, Joan Elizabeth (nee Schmid) Galford (b 7 Feb 1956, Wooster OH) Field foreman, Wooster OH.

RF41141133   Sarah Mae Strock (18 Apr 1927, Wooster OH-15 Mar 1988, Akron OH) m 19 Dec 1948, Sherman Sheridan Dalbey (b 1923, Mansfield OH) Bur Wooster OH. No natural chn.

RF4114114   Mary Pleasent Strock (5 May 1889-10 Aug 1921, Robertsdale AL) m 18 Nov 1917, Bucyrus OH, Carl A Gearhart.

RF41141141   John Daniel Gearhart (b 8 Oct 1917, Wooster OH) m 11 May 1943, Mary Evelyn Wright (b 28 Mar 1921, Lexington AL) IRS, 1941-1972.

RF411411411   Betty Louise Gearhart (b 29 Aug 1945, Florence AL) m 1) 11 Jun 1966, Robert Keith Wetzel; m 2) 24 Dec 1976, Herbert Bateman Williams (b 10 Sep 1943, Fayetteville NC).

RF4114114111   Herbert Bateman Williams Jr (b 30 May 1978, Alexandria VA).

RF4114114112   Dawn Michelle Williams (b 15 Jun 1981, Pensacola FL).

RF411411412   Jane Louise Gearhart (b 17 Jul 1921) m 22 Jun 1941, Harold Pete Jones.

RF4114114121   Infant son (b and d 16 Feb 1946, Mobile AL) Bur Bay Minette AL.

RF4114114122   Carl Jackson Jones (b 19 Feb 1950, Bay Minette AL) m 27 Sep 1975, Monica Lou Meyers (b 9 Oct 1950).

RF41141141221   Carl Jackson Jones II (b 10 Mar 1980, Mobile AL).

RF41141141222   Lee Byrne Jones (b 12 Mar 1985, Mobile AL).

RF4114114123   Harold Byrne Jones (2 Mar 1955, Bay Minette AL-5 Nov 1975, Bay Minette AL) Bur Bay Minette AL.

RF4114115   Frances Baumgardner Strock (26 Oct 1891, Wooster OH-10 Nov 1983, Long Beach CA) m 15 Oct 1913, CA, Andrew Gladstone Wilson (b 10 Oct 1892, Wayne Co OH).

RF41141151   John Strock Wilson (b 30 Jul 1914, Long Beach CA) m 6 Oct 1940, CA, Helen Gregg (b 10 Jul 1921).

RF41141152   Andrew Gladstone Wilson Jr (b 23 May 1916, Long Beach CA) m 4 Jun 1938, Vera Mercer (b 13 Jan 1917).

RF411441521   Robert Andrew Wilson (b 24 Jan 1940, CA) m 9 Jun 1962, Sandra Thomas.

RF4114115211   Chris Wilson (b 25 Jun 1964, CA).

RF4114115212   Shara Wilson (b 16 Nov 1967, CA).

RF411441522   Donald Michael Wilson (17 Mar 1943, CA-3 May 1943, CA).

RF411441523   Nancy Lee Wilson (b 17 Oct 1944, CA) m Jan 1962, Joseph Johnson.

RF4114115231   Joseph Johnson II (b 25 Nov 1962).

RF4114115232   Jennifer Johnson (b 14 Jul 1966).

RF411441524   Sharon Lyn Wilson (b 13 Nov 1947, CA) m Dec 1970, Greg Redding.

RF41141153   Florena Elizabeth Wilson (6 Dec 1918, Long Beach CA-22 Dec 1919, Long Beach CA).

RF41141154   Gordon Charles Wilson (b 11 Jul 1921, Long Beach CA) m 1) 22 Jul 1950, Adriana Bayz (b 27 Sep 1927); m 2) 8 May 1964, Barbara Williams (b 11 Oct 1932).

RF411441541   Margaret Elizabeth Wilson (b 15 May 1951, CA) m 15 Aug 1987, CA, Andrew Deloje.

RF4114115411   Adam Deloge (b 20 May 1988, CA).

RF4114115412   Daniel Deloje (b 28 Sep 1991, CA).

RF411441542   Diana Leigh Wilson (b 1 Oct 1953, CA).

RF411441543   Andrew Gladstone Wilson (b 5 Jan 1967, CA).

RF41141155   Donald Wallace Wilson (b 3 Nov 1923, Long Beach CA) m 28 Jan 1949, Lois Jean Johnson (b 1 Mar 1928, Inglewood CA).

RF411441551   Buckner Strock Wilson (b 6 Mar 1950, Long Beach CA).

RF411441552   Kimberly Ann Wilson (b 1 Feb 1993, Long Beach CA) m 7 May 1983, Stephen Rose.

RF4114115521   Scott Wilson Rose (b 10 Aug 1985, Tampa FL).

RF4114115522   Michael Wilson Rose (b 23 May 1988, Tampa FL).

RF411441553   Susan Diane Wilson (b 29 Jan 1955, Long Beach CA) m 1975, Rafael Lopez.

RF4114115531   Tanya Brooke Lopez (b 4 Jan 1976, Austin TX).

RF4114115532   Zachariah Caine Lopez (b 20 Jun 1978, Georgetown TX).

RF41141156   Frances Ann Wilson (b 22 Oct 1926, Long Beach CA).

RF4114116   Florence Eakin Strock (10 May 1894, Wooster Tp, Wayne Co OH-13 Oct 1985, Silver Springs MD) m 21 Apr 1920, Reginald Hylton Larkins (b 9 Jan 1887, Hazelton PA).

RF41141161   Infant (b and d Sep 1927, Wooster OH) Bur Wooster OH.

RF41141162   Richard Hylton Larkins (b 4 Nov 1923, Wooster OH) m 17 Sep 1949, Nancy Ellen Vititoe (b 22 Sep 1922, Evansville IN).

RF411411621   Victoria Ann Larkins (b 29 Apr 1951, Jacksonville FL) m David Allen.

RF411411622   Nancy Richelle Larkins (b 24 Jun 1952, Jacksonville FL) m Richard Reed.

RF411411623   Sarah Elizabeth Larkins (b 8 Mar 1955, Jacksonville FL).

RF411412   Jessie Troutman (13 Mar 1858, Wooster Tp Wayne Co OH-6 Feb 1943, Wayne Co OH) m 1) 16 Aug 1882, Wayne Co OH, Richard Parker Redick (b 10 Jan 1840); m 2) 18 Jun 1889, Wayne Co OH, Charles Ports (b 4 Nov 1843, Wayne Co OH) Bur Wooster OH. Redick, clergyman.

RF4114121   Richard Ralph Redick (7 May 1884, Wooster OH-18 Mar 1919, Wayne Co OH) Bur Wooster OH.

RF4114122   Mildred Ports (b 21 Jun 1895, Wayne Co OH) m Apr 1921, Fred Leroy Ohler.

RF41141221   Lois May Ohler (b 7 Sep 1923 m Charles Sofield.

RF41141222   Dorothy Ohler (b 16 Oct 1926) m 20 Jul 1947, Richland Co OH, Thomas Yontz (b 6 Nov 1926).

RF411412221   Steven Jay Yontz (b 8 Dec 1951).

RF411412222   Jeffrey Dee Yontz (b 13 Sep 1954).

RF411412223   Barry Scott Yontz (24 Aug 1956-26 Aug 1956).

RF411413   Otto Troutman (11 Jun 1860, Wooster Tp Wayne Co OH-22 Apr 1939, Ripley TP Holmes Co OH) m 23 Sep 1890, Jeromesville OH, Effie Van Niman (b 1866 OH).

RF4114131   Fred V Troutman (b 9 Jan 1893, Shreve OH).

RF4114132   Edward Troutman (23 Apr 1896, Shreve OH-11 Sep 1943, Wooster OH) m 28 Oct 1931, Phyllis Higgins. AB, LLB, Harvard U. Attorney, Wooster OH. WWI: USN. No chn.

RF411414   Mary Troutman (9 Aug 1862, Wooster Tp Wayne Co OH-12 Feb 1932, Wooster OH) m 16 Feb 1893, Wooster OH, Silas Troxel (b 25 Mar 1858) No chn.

RF411415   John J Troutman (15 Oct 1864, Wooster Tp Wayne Co OH-16 Dec 1938, Springfield OH) unm. Bur Wooster OH.

RF411416   Morse Troutman (8 Jul 1867, Wooster Tp Wayne Co OH-5 May 1947, Wayne Co OH) m 16 Feb 1892, Wayne Co OH Ida M Keister (b 19 May 1869, Wayne Co OH).

RF4114161   Philip Keister Troutman (28 Nov 1892, Clinton Tp Wayne Co OH-20 Jun 1982, Ashland OH) m 1) Bess R Matthews (b 1892); m 2) Apr 1926, Clora Baughman (b 1895) No chn. WWI: USA; OSU, 1916. Engineer.

RF4114162   Karl Andrew Troutman (b 2 Feb 1903, Clinton Tp Wayne Co OH) m 28 Jun 1933, Wayne Co OH, Mary Doratha Stuckey (b 19 Jul 1907, near Butler OH).

RF41141621   William Morse Troutman (b 9 Nov 1934, Wooster OH) m 4 Dec 1955, Wooster OH, Doris Arleen Geitgey (b 9 Aug 1937, Franklin Tp Wayne Co OH).

RF411416211   Jeffrey Karl Troutman (b 27 Oct 1956, Wooster OH) m 1) 27 Aug 1978, Plain Tp Wayne Co OH, Brenda Franks; m 2) 1 Jul 1988, Orrville OH, Christie Peterinelli (b 16 Jun 1963, Greensburg PA).

RF4114162111   Harmony Dawn Troutman (b 31 May 1979, Wooster OH).

RF4114162112   Chantalle Dee Ann Troutman (b 10 Sep 1988, Wooster OH).

RF4114162113   Rachelle Le Ann Troutman (b 18 Nov 1990, Wooster OH).

RF411416212   Alan Wayne Troutman (b 4 Jun 1960, Wooster OH) m 28 Mar 1980, Wayne Co OH, Marla Franks.

RF4114162121   Melissa Ann Troutman (b 7 Mar 1981).

RF411416213   Lori Maree Troutman (b 4 Mar 1964, Wooster OH) m 25 May 1986, Johnstown OH, Richard Dean Hinderer (b 6 Nov 1964).

RF41141622   Kenneth Roger Troutman (b 18 Jun 1939, Millersburg OH) m 19 Jul 1968, Perrysville OH, Louise Ackerman (b 26 Apr 1939, Ashland OH).

RF411416221   Charles Louann Troutman (b 31 Aug 1972, Mansfield OH).

RF411416222   Philip Parke Troutman (b 6 Sep 1973, Mansfield OH).

RF41141623   Philip Arlen Troutman (b 25 Aug 1941, Wooster OH) m 1) 9 Jul 1966, Deerfield OH, Lynn Hoskins (b 20 Apr 1943, Portage Co OH); m 2) 26 Apr 1980, Las Vegas NV, Judi Holland Bare (b 8 Aug 1947).

RF411416231   Bryan Ray Troutman (b 14 Apr 1970, Fontana CA).

RF411416232   Mark Allen Troutman (b 29 Aug 1971, Fontana CA).

RF41141624   Robert Karl Troutman (b 7 Jul 1944, Wooster OH) m 18 Jun 1967, Millersburg OH, Rosemary Bigler (b 15 Oct 1946, Millersburg OH).

RF411416241   Andrew Christian Troutman (b 27 Jan 1973, Wooster OH).

RF411416242   Sara Jean Troutman (b 10 Sep 1977, Wooster OH).

RF411416243   Amanda Grace Troutman (b 20 Sep 1983, Wooster OH).

RF41141625   Linda Grace Troutman (b 28 Mar 1947, Wayne Co OH).

RF411417   Parke Troutman (28 Jun 1870, Clinton Tp Wayne Co OH-1 Jan 1957, Wayne Co OH) m 14 Sep 1898, Wayne Co OH, Cora Orilla Shaffer (b 17 Sep 1876) Bur Wooster OH.

RF4114171   Clark R Troutman (b 6 Oct 1901) m 1) Sep 1919, Wayne Co OH, Etha Sarah Shelby; m 2) ca 1973, Margaret Crawford.

RF41141711   Clyde M Troutman (b 13 Feb 1923, Wayne CO OH) m 1) 8 Jun 1942, Greenup KY, Betty Irene Finn (b 9 Mar 1924, Overton OH); m 2) 13 May 1950, Phyllis Pfouts (b 9 Oct 1929, Wooster OH); m 3) 13 Sep 1988, Wayne Co OH, Betty Dawson (b 28 Aug 1923).

RF411417111   James Rodger Troutman (b 18 Jan 1943, Wooster OH) m 1) 1966, Marylin B Miller (b 1 Mar 1947); m 2) 26 Oct 1979, Wooster OH, Dianna Jeannene Ferris Riley (b 7 Jun 1949).

RF4114171111   Nancy Ann Troutman (b 18 Jul 1967, Wooster OH) m 18 Oct 1986, Wooster OH, James Craft.

RF4114171112   Linda Lou Troutman (b 28 Jun 1969, Wooster OH) m 18 Sep 1993, West Salem OH, Robert Earl Shover.

RF411417112   Paul Allen Troutman (b 4 Aug 1944, Lodi OH, adopted by Charles Stevens, who married his mother) m 18 Sep 1962, Wooster OH, Sharon Ann Weiker (b 28 Sep 1943, Wooster OH).

RF4114171121   Jadea Marie Stevens (b 27 Sep 1964).

RF4114171122   Steve Shane Stevens (b 12 Apr 1970, Wooster OH).

RF411417113   Shelly Marie Troutman (b 9 Jul 1955, Wooster OH) m 12 Dec 1975, Wooster OH, Jeffrey Blake Lehman (b 12 Aug 1953).

RF4114171131   Joshua Blake Lehman (b 1 Oct 1977, Orrville OH).

RF41141712   Leta Mae Troutman (b 18 Jan 1926, Wayne Co OH) m 1) 25 Jan 1943, Clarence A McKinley; m 2) 21 Dec 1952, George Zook; m 3) 18 Aug 1974, Clark Wood Jr; m 4) 30 May 1980, John Dellafare.

RF411417121   Milo M McKinley (b 10 Jan 1944).

RF4114171211   Melisa Marie McKinley (b 14 Dec 1966).

RF411417122   Terry Lee McKinley (b 28 May 1947).

RF4114171221   Gary Lee McKinley (b 2 Sep 1966).

RF411417123   Mary Jean McKinley (b 14 Sep 1949, Wooster OH) m ca 1969 Newark OH, Bobby Ross.

RF4114171231   Raymano Clark McKinley (b 15 Sep 1964, Wooster OH).

RF411417124   Virginia Maire Zook (b 20 Sep 1951, Alexandria VA) m Dan Ramsier.

RF4114171241   Kevin Lee Ramsier (b 21 Dec 1971).

RF411417125   Donna Arlene Zook (b 5 May 1957, Fairfield OH) m John A Napier.

RF4114171251   Shadrack William Napier (b 5 Mar 1976, Medina OH).

RF4114171252   Amanda Arlene Napier (b 20 Feb 1979, Medina OH).

RF4114172   Emil J L Troutman (10 May 1903, Wayne Co OH-22 Jan 1908, Wayne CO OH) Bur Wooster OH.

RF4114173   Mary M Troutman (15 Sep 1906, Shreve OH-28 Feb 1980, Wooster OH) m Stanford Clell Barton (b 1901).

RF41141731   Marion Barton m Frances Troutman.

RF411417311   Sherrie Barton.

RF411417312   Randy Barton.

RF411417313   Terry Barton

RF41141732   Hershel Barton m Ross   .

RF411417321   Robert Barton.

RF411417322   Cheryl Barton.

RF411417323   Mark Barton.

RF411417324   Christopher Barton.

RF411417325   Debbie Barton.

RF411417326   Mike Barton.

RF41141733   Janet E Barton m Larry R Wile.

RF411417331   Ty Wile.

RF41141734   Helen Barton m 1) Don Lacy; m 2) Richard Uhler.

RF411417341   Lisa Uhler.

RF411417342   Mitchel Uhler.

RF41141735   Geraldine Barton (b 30 Aug 1945) m 28 Aug 1966, Wooster OH, Robert Edward Schmid (b 1 Feb 1945).

RF411417351   Stacy Renee Schmid (b 3 Jun 1968, Corpus Christi TX) m 27 Mar 1993, Wooster OH, Patrick Allen Swyers.

RF411417352   Kevin Michael Schmid (b 20 Sep 1970, Wooster OH).

RF411417353   Jody Marie Schmid (b 30 Aug 1975, Wooster OH).

RF41142   John Johnson (1831 PA-1889).

RF41143   Andaline Johnson (11 Nov 1833, Dauphin Co PA-11 Sep 1912, Wooster Tp, Wayne Co OH) m 7 Feb 1854, Wooster OH, William N Smith (b 9 Apr 1830, Franklin Tp, Wayne Co OH).

RF411431   Hiram W Smith (22 Mar 1855, Wooster Wayne Co OH-8 Feb 1879, Wooster OH) m 14 Nov 1872, Jane Donalson. Bur Wooster OH.

RF4114311   Edna Smith (ca 1875-16 Jun 1962, Wooster OH) m William R Curry. Bur Wooster OH.

RF41143111   James Rowland Curry (b 29 Dec 1903).

RF41143112   Richard R Curry (b 29 Jan 1908, Wooster OH).

RF411432   Isaac Johnson Smith (1857, Wooster Tp, Wayne Co OH-18 Jun 1918, Wayne Tp, Wayne Co OH) m 4 Dec 1881, Wayne Co OH, Eunice Milbourn.

RF4114321   Harvey Smith.

RF4114322   Laura Smith.

RF4114323   Luella Smith.

RF4114324   Isaac Johnson Smith Jr.

RF4114325   Glenna E Smith (1888-9 Nov 1918, Wayne Co OH) m Walter O. Elliott. Bur Wooster OH.

RF4114326   William Newton Smith (27 Nov 1893, Wayne Tp, Wayne Co OH-17 Jun 1963, Wooster OH) m 3 Apr 1930, Ruth E Uhl (3 Dec 1900, Holmes Co OH) Bur Wooster OH. WWI: USAF. Garage owner, highway employee.

RF41143261   Miriam Ruth Smith (b 4 Oct 1933, Wooster OH) m 28 Aug 1955, Larry Edward Kettlelake (b 13 Oct 1933, Springfield OH) He, AB, 1955; MDiv, 1958, Wittenberg (OH) U; DDiv, Hamma Divinity Sch, 1974. Ordained 1958. Pastor, West Alexandria, Minton Bay Village, Greenville OH. Director, counselling center, 1974-78.

RF411432611   Cheryl Kettlelake (b 9 Nov 1956) m 18 Aug 1979, Robert Basel. She, secondary teacher; he, clinical psychologist.

RF4114326111   Christopher Robert Basel (b 21 Jun 1986).

RF4114326112   Nicholas Stephen Basel (b 13 Apr 1988).

RF411432612   David Kettlelake (b 20 Jul 1959) m 20 Apr 1985, Lisa Martin.

RF4114326121   Nicole Linn Kettlelake (b 12 Jul 1986).

RF4114326122   Aaron William Kettlelake (b 8 Aug 1988).

RF411432613   Daniel Kettlelake (b 5 Oct 1963) m Julia Parker

RF4114326131   Joshua Parker Kettlelake (b 19 May 1987).

RF4114327   Ira Milbourne Smith (1895-21 Jul 1978) Bur Wooster OH.

RF41144   Isaac Johnson Jr (10 Jan 1836, Wayne Tp, Wayne Co OH-18 Apr 1900, Mansfield OH) m 25 Nov 1858, Wooster OH, Catharine McClure (b 12 Feb 1837) Bur Wooster OH. Studied law, admitted to Wayne Co Bar 1868; probate judge, 1881. Attorney, Wooster OH.

RF411441   Ella Lenore Johnson (12 Oct 1862, Wooster OH-3 Aug 1933, Belefontaine OH) m 24 Jun 1885, Wooster OH, John Edwin West (b 8 Feb 1858, Bellefontain OH).

RF4114411   Johnson Edwin West (31 Mar 1886, Bellefontain OH-6 May 1945, Troy OH) m 14 June 1916, Laura Anderson (b 20 Sep 1885) No natural chn.

RF4114412   Clara Elizabeth West (13 Aug 1887, Bellefontain OH-28 Jan 1972) m 11 Sep 1912, George J Rogers (b 17 Mar 1876).

RF41144121   Elizabeth Rogers (b 15 Jul 1913) m 29 Jan 1939, Gerald Shrader (b 21 Aug 1913).

RF411441211   Joanna Shrader (b 31 Jul 1944) m 20 Aug 1966, William Panning (b 22 Sep 1944).

RF4114412111   Stephan Eric Panning (b 22 May 1970).

RF4114412112   Matthew West Panning (b 7 May 1974).

RF4114412113   Jennifer Panning (b 25 Jun 1976).

RF411441212   Frances Shrader (b 8 Feb 1946).

RF411441213   Lee Theodore Shrader (b 16 Nov 1955) m 24 Jun 1978, Elaine Welbourne (b 29 Sep 1956).

RF4114412131   Sarah Elissa Shrader (b 22 Mar 1980).

RF4114412132   Ryan West Shrader (b 16 Mar 1982).

RF41144122   John West Rogers (b 22 Dec 1914) m 3 Oct 1942, Nancy Morris (b 21 May 1914).

RF411441221   John West Rogers Jr (b 17 Oct 1944) m 20 Dec 1969, Amelia Valentina (b 2 Sep 1939).

RF4114412211   Christopher Carlo Rogers (b 11 Apr 1972).

RF4114412212   Benjamin West Rogers (b 23 Jan 1977).

RF411441222   Rebecca Mary Rogers (b 22 Dec 1946) m 14 Jun 1975, James Swager (b 23 Sep 1943).

RF4114412221   Richard Henry Swager (b 5 Aug 1981).

RF41144123   James Patterson Rogers (6 Nov 1916-19 May 1944) m 13 Sep 1943, Elizabeth Patterson
(b 13 Jan 1921).

RF411441231   James Patterson Rogers III (b 15 Jul 1944) m 29 Apr 1973, Linda Hardy (b 17 Feb 1949).

RF4114412311   Adam Hampton Rogers (b 18 Aug 1979).

RF41144124   Eleanor Rogers (b 12 Dec 1920) m 10 Oct 1942, Warren DeBolt (b 19 Sep 1920).

RF411441241
No natural chn.   John Robert DeBolt (b 11 Feb 1944) m 15 May 1968, Patricia Simon (b 10 May 1946)

RF411441242   Bruce Rogers DeBolt (b 7 Dec 1947) m 6 Oct 1973, April Stencer.

RF4114412421   Nicola DeBolt (b 11 Oct 1976).

RF4114412422   Alex DeBolt (b 10 Apr 1983).

RF411441243
He, dentist.   Anne Elizabeth DeBolt (b 1 Sep 1950) m 11 Aug 1973, E Dean Blair (b 12 Oct 1947)

RF4114412431   Gregory Davis Blair (b 22 Jan 1983).

RF411441244   Margaret West DeBolt (b 4 Jul 1954) m 16 May 1981, David Esch (b 7 Mar 1954).

RF4114412441   Joanna Jackson Esch (b 7 Jan 1986).

RF41144125   Joanna Rogers (b 7 Dec 1923) m 25 Oct 1958, Harold Retzler (b 19 Nov 1922).

RF411441251   Nancy Louise Retzler (b 1 Jul 1949) m 8 Oct 1971, Miken Ondercin (b 4 Mar 1949).

RF4114412511   Christopher Ondercin (b 17 Oct 1975).

RF4114412512   Heather Ondercin (b 9 Apr 1979).

RF411441252   Eleanor Rogers Retzler (b 6 Oct 1959) m 18 Oct 1986, Martin Ryan.

RF411441253   Mary Joanna Retzler (b 10 May 1961).

RF4114413   Samuel Earnest West (20 Jul 1889, Bellefontain OH-26 Jun 1952) m 9 Jul 914, Mabel Clevenger (b 22 Feb 1891).

RF41144131   Samuel Earnest West (b 6 Dec 1915) m 22 Jun 1940, Mary Aileen Cies (b 28 Aug 1915)
Clergyman.

RF411441311   Samuel Earnest West (1 Jan 1942-28 Mar 1960).

RF411441312   Michael Herbert West (b 28 Jan 1944) m 7 Jul 1979, Elaine Branham.

RF411441313   Carolynn Jane West (b 22 Aug 1947) m 18 May 1973, C Richard Mullen (b 1935).

RF4114413131   Heidi Lynn Hess (b 12 Mar 1970).

RF411441314   James Newell West (b 10 May 1951) m 8 Sep 1974, Nancy West.

RF4114413141   James Johnson West (b 14 Feb 1976).

RF411441315   Sarah Catherine West (b 8 Nov 1957) m 11 Sep 1983, Robert Mcinnis Schneider (b 4 Jan 1955).

RF41144132   Jane West (b 4 Mar 1918) m 1 May 1943, Jack W Gardner (b 20 Aug 1912).

RF411441321   Mary Elizabeth Gardner (b 18 Feb 1945) m 5 May 1969, Michael Taylor (b 28 Jul 1943).

RF4114413211   Tracie Ann Taylor (b 4 Jul 1973).

RF4114413212   Deborah Jane Taylor (b 27 Apr 1983).

RF411441322   Patricia Ann Gardner (b 18 Feb 1948) m 3 Apr 1972, Bruce Malone (b 18 May 1945).

RF4114413221   Scott Andrew Malone (b 10 May 1974).

RF4114413222   Michael Sean Malone (b 19 Aug 1977).

RF411441323   Charles Gardner (b 13 Jul 1950) m 11 Jul 1980, Josephine Santore (b 19 May 1956).

RF41144133   Johnson Edwin West (b 31 Oct 1921) m 2 Jun 1947, June Cale (b 8 May 1927)
Clergyman.

RF411441331   Marcia West (b 29 Nov 1952).

RF411441332   Mark Johnson West (b 26 Apr 1954) m 25 Nov 1982, Caroline Gurber (b 18 Jan 1955).

RF411441333   Deborah Cale West (b 8 Jan 1956) m 15 Dec 1979, Richard Hanson (b 14 Aug 1946).

RF4114414   Katharine West (25 May 1893, Bellefontain OH-4 Dec 1979, Salem OR) m 14 Oct 1919, Malcolm Pratt (b 5 Aug 1892).

RF41144141   John Lester Pratt (27 Oct 1920-22 Jan 1943).

RF41144142   Sarah Pratt (b 14 Jul 1922) m 9 Jun 1945, Edwin Snider (b 30 Jun 1920).

RF411441421   Malcolm Snider (b 5 Apr 1947) m 1) Kathleen M Melhuse (b 20 Jan 1949); m 2). Physician.

RF4114414211   Matthew Snider (b 28 Sep 1967).

RF411441422   Thomas Nathan Snider (b 13 Dec 1949) m 20 Mar 1976, Jolene Cooley (b 30 Nov 1949).

RF4114414221   Keeley Snider (b 23 Mar 1979).

RF4114414222   Devin Delane Snider (b Jul 1984).

RF411441423   Kathrine Louise Snider (b 12 Apr 1951) m 28 Jun 1974, William Hagarty (b 16 Apr 1941).

RF4114413231   Finn Edwin Hagarty (b 2 Feb 1977).

RF4114414232   Simon Paul Hagarty (b 25 Sep 1981).

RF411441424   John Eric Snider (b 11 Sep 1952) m 12 Sep 1981, Traci Lee Horn (b 4 Nov 1960).

RF4114414241   Frankie Lee Snider (b 27 Sep 1982).

RF4114414242   Kati Snider (b Jul 1984).

RF4114414243   Emili Snider (b Sep 1987).

RF411441425   Kristina Lynn Snider (b 11 Jan 1954) m 9 Aug 1974, Tom Belknap (b 10 Feb 1947).

RF4114414251   Kaya Sarah Belknap (b 29 Aug 1985).

RF4114414252   Belknap (b 1988).

RF411441426   Jefferson Snider (b 9 Jun 1956) m 6 Aug 1988, Mary Alice Snider.

RF41144143   Mary Katharine Pratt (b 9 Nov 1924) m 1 Oct 1952, Jorma Salovaara (b 7 Oct 1916).

RF411441431   Lauri Mikael Salovaara (b 8 Feb 1954) m 30 Oct 1982, Beth Stewart (b 20 Nov 1956).

RF4114414311   Salovaara (b 1988).

RF411441432   Kaarina Salovaara (b 18 Apr 1955).

RF411441433   Jonn Alexis Salovaara (b 6 Jul 1956) m May 1984, Bobbye Middendorf.

RF411441434   Katharine Pratt Salovaara (b 3 Aug 1958) m 30 Apr 1988, Joseph Martin Brower (b 26 Oct 1959).

RF411441435   Kristian Robert Salovaara (b 19 Nov 1960) m 27 Aug 1988, Carol Alice Matthews (b 11 Apr 1960).

RF411441436   Erik Jorma Salovaara (b 14 Jun 1967).

RF41144144   Jane Pratt (b 22 Jan 1928) m 31 May 1953, Eric Parker (b 19 Jun 1928) USA, Lt Col.

RF411441441   Amy Jane Parker (b 9 Jan 1956).

RF411441442   William Bratton Parker (b 20 Sep 1959) m 20 Sep 1986, Cynthia Christine Smith (b 24 Oct 1961).

RF411441443   Katharine Parker (b 9 Oct 1961).

RF411441444   Marit Brunhilda Parker (b 14 Oct 1963) m 21 May 1988, Ruben Dirado (b 19 Jan 1963).

RF411441445   Sarah Parker (2 Oct 1966-4 Apr 1970).

RF4114415   Margaret Jeannette West (5 Oct 1896, Bellefontain OH-19 Apr 1974, Sidney OH) m 2 Dec 1922, William Frank Milligan (b 4 Oct 1896).

RF41144151   William West Milligan (b 24 Dec 1923, Bellefontain OH) m 23 Jun 1956, Logan Co OH, Suzane Crimm (b 10 Jun 1931).

RF411441511   Edith Crimm Milligan (b 22 Oct 1958) m 1 Sep 1984, Paul Alan Delphia (b 2 Jun 1958).

RF411441512   Martha Sae Milligan (b 4 Aug 1960).

RF411441513   Clara Ruth Milligan (b 27 Sep 1968).

RF41144152   Samuel Johnson Milligan (31 Aug 1925, Bellefontain OH-23 Aug 1987, Sidney OH) m 13 Aug 1949, Marilyn Liechty (b 17 Feb 1927).

RF411441521   Margaret Ann Milligan (b 25 Dec 1950).

RF411441522   John David Milligan (b 27 Jun 1954) m Apr 1987, Linda Oxley.

RF411441523   Jeffrey Samuel Milligan (b 3 Aug 1958) m 30 Jun 1984, Julie Dunlap (b 10 Aug 1957).

RF4114415231   Paul Samuel Milligan (b 3 Feb 1988).

RF411441524   Paula Jean Milligan (b 2 May 1960) m 9 Aug 1986, David Kiel.

RF41144153   Patrick Henry Milligan (b 9 Jun 1928) m 22 Dec 1951, Carol Benson (b 8 Mar 1930).

RF411441531   Mary Elizabeth Milligan (b 10 Sep 1955) m 11 Sep 1979, Charles Sheaffer (b 25 Sep 1953).

RF4114415311   Caitlin Margaret Milligan Sheaffer (b 3 Mar 1985).

RF4114415312   Hannah Clare Milligan Sheaffer (b 8 Sep 1988).

RF411442   Florence G Johnson (ca 1866, Wooster OH-15 Feb 1924) Bur Wooster OH.

RF411443   Catherine J Johnson (31 Aug 1868, Wooster OH-15 Nov 1924, Wooster OH) m Ned Harris. Bur Wooster OH. Physician.

RF411444   Rachel E Johnson (b 2 Mar 1874, Wooster Tp, Wayne Co OH).

RF411445   Elizabeth Earnest Johnson (2 Feb 1875 Wooster OH-28 Nov 1945, Chillicothe OH) m 11 Jul 1906, Wooster OH, Edwin Slasser Wertz (b 7 Aug 1875, Dalton OH). Bur Wooster OH. Attorney.

RF4114451   William Henry Harrison Wertz II (25 Mar 1910, Wooster OH-11 Jul 1988, Wooster OH) m 11 Mar 1938, Wooster OH, Bonnie Jean Foster (b 24 Jun 1917) AB, Washington and Lee (VA) U, 1933; LLB, George Washington (DC) U, 1936. Attorney. Common pleas judge, Wayne Co OH. WWII: USMC.

RF41144511 F Robinson Jr.   Mardie Foster Wertz (b 12 Feb 1939, Wooster OH) m Aug 1960, Wooster OH, Beauford

RF411445111   Beauford Robinson m Kelley Ford.

RF411445112   John William Robinson.

RF411445113   Amanda Jean Robinson.

RF41144512   Edwin Slusser Wertz (b 12 Jan 1942, Wooster OH) m 27 Sep 1970, Margaret Riley.

RF411445121   William Henry Harrison Wertz III.

RF41144513   Bonnie Jean Wertz (b 21 Aug 1943, Wooster OH).

RF4114452 Clark Evans Jr.   Catharine Virginia Wertz (27 Mar 1910, Wooster OH-1987, Chillicothe OH) m Charles

RF41144521   William E Evans (b 15 Dec 1934, Akron OH) m Roberta Nancy. He, physician.

RF411445211   Catharine Evans.

RF411445212   William Evans m Jill .

RF4114452121   Katie Lee Evans.

RF411445213   Carol Evans.

RF41144522   Robert Clark Evans (b 22 Jul 1936, Chillicothe OH) m Patricia Steitler.

RF411445221   John Evans.

RF411445222   Jennifer Evans.

RF411445223   Julia Evans.

RF4114453 M Stellhorn.   Caroline S Wertz (13 Aug 1912, Wooster OH-May 1988, Santa Anna CA) m Frederick

RF41144531   Michael Stellhorn (b 10 May 1936) m Honarie .

RF411445311   Elisa Stellhorn.

RF41144532   Susan Stellhorn.

RF41144533   Frederick Stellhorn (b 1 Jun 1943) m Diane Dobkowitz. He, physician.

RF411445331   Robert Stellhorn.

RF411445332   Jim Stellhorn.

RF41144534   Patrick Stellhorn (b 9 Jan 1951).

RF41144535   Cisca Stellhorn (b 9 Jan 1951).

RF4114454   Elizabeth Earnest Johnson Wertz (b 27 Mar 1915, Wooster OH) m 23 Jul 1932 Newcastle PA, Robert Gardner Schultz (b 15 Jan 1915).

RF41144541   Robert G Schultz Jr (b 29 Dec 1934, Wooster OH) m Carol A Weirath.

RF411445411   Alison M Schultz m Todd Broadbridge.

RF4114454111   Edwin Broadbridge.

RF411445412   Robert F Schultz m Robin   .

RF4114454121   Erica Schultz.

RF4114454122   James Schultz.

RF4114454123   Lesley Schultz.

RF4114454124   Andrew H Schultz.

RF4114454125   Jason R Schultz.

RF41144542   Andrew J Schultz (b 13 Aug 1937, Wooster OH) m Melinda Kolb.

RF411445421   Melissa Schultz.

RF411445422   Margaret Schultz.

RF41144543   James H Schultz (b 22 Mar 1943, Wooster OH) m Nancy K Stevens.

RF411445431   Adam Johnson Schultz.

RF41145   Rachel Earnest Johnson (15 May 1838, Wayne Tp, Wayne Co OH-19 Aug 1903, Columbus OH) m 24 Nov 1859, Wooster OH, John Clark Barton (28 Dec 1837, Creston OH-29 Jun 1924, NY) div. Bur Wooster OH.

RF411451   Pleasant Johnson Barton (18 Jun 1864, Wooster OH-12 Feb 1924, Grandview Heights OH) m 31 Dec 1899, Wooster OH, Frank Morgan Higgs (26 Aug 1862, Wheeling WV-5 Dec 1937, Grandview Heights OH) He, furniture store; she, secretary, court reporter clerk, teacher.

RF4114511   Pleasant Alleyne Higgs (7 Aug 1904, Columbus OH-31 May 1987, Columbus OH) m 18 Sep 1926, Grandview Heights OH, Ira Stanton Jones (15 Jul 1897, Centerville OH-13 Nov 1969, Grandview Heights OH) She, BS, OSU, dietician. He, principal, coach, teacher. He, WWI.

RF41145111   Joyce Alleyne Jones (b 5 Feb 1928, Grandview Heights OH) m 14 Nov 1951, Alfred P Alibrando.

RF411451111   Julie Anne Alibrando (b 1953) unm.

RF411451112   Karen Joyce Alibrando (b 1957) m William Brekke.

*RF41145112   Jean Anne Jones (b 16 Jan 1930, Columbus OH) m 6 Aug 1955, Columbus OH, Robert William Holder (b 17 Jan 1931, Waterloo IA) She, BS, OSU; MA, U ID; teacher. He, BS, MS, U ID. Korean Conflict: USN. Stockbroker.

RF411451121   Infant girl (b 2 Aug 1956, stillborn).

RF411451122   Michael Robert Holder (b 9 Jul 1959, Moscow ID) unm.

RF411451123   Suzanne Holder (15 Jul 1962, Spokane WA-16 Jul 1962, Spokane WA).

RF411451124   William Stanton Holder (b 30 Dec 1963, Spokane WA) m Nancy Elizabeth Johnson (b 1967).

RF411451125   Ann Barton Holder (b 19 Nov 1965, Spokane WA) m 26 Aug 1990, Bellevue WA, David Allan Strand (b 28 Jul 1966) She, BS, U WA; MTh, Fuller Sem. He, BS, U WA; MDiv, Fuller Sem. Youth Minister, Boulder CO.

RF4114511251   Zachary Strand (b 10 Nov 1992, Glendale CA).

RF4114511252   Charlie Winter Strand (b 16 Nov 1995, Louisville CO).

RF41145113   Stanton I Jones (b 7 Sep 1934, Grandview Heights OH) m 1) 11 Jun 1960, Joanne Evelyn Nichols (b 1935); m 2) 28 Dec 1988, Meigs Co OH, Lynne Elizabeth Shepard Bader (b 28 Dec 1938 Newark OH).

RF411451131   Stanton I Jones Jr (b 1961) m Laura Dee Blake (b 1961).

RF4114511311   Jordan Blake Jones (b 1992).

RF411451132   Sue Ellyn Jones (b 1964) unm.

RF4114512   Frank Lott Higgs (1908-1945) m Diann Menzies (d 1975).

RF41146   Catherine Johnson (18 May 1841, Wayne Tp, Wayne Co OH-28 Jan 1846, Wayne Tp, Wayne Co OH) Bur Wooster OH.

RF41147   Ellen C Johnson (b 10 Oct 1843, Wayne Tp, Wayne Co OH) m 5 May 1964, Wooster OH, Isaac Grimes.

RF411471   Edna Grimes.

RF411472   Hazel Grimes.

RF41148   Theodore Johnson (24 Sep 1845, Wayne Tp, Wayne Co OH-10 Nov 1885, El Cajon CA) Bur Wooster OH.

RF41149   Martha Johnson (4 Dec 1859, Wayne Tp, Wayne Co OH-10 Apr 1964, Wayne Tp, Wayne Co OH) Bur Wooster OH.

RF4115   Michael Earnest (29 Apr 1806-20 Jul 1833).

RF4116   William Earnest (4 Sep 1809, Hummelstown PA-6 Jun 1873, Jonestown PA) m Leah Desh (4 Mar 1821, Fredericksburg PA-Feb 1902).

RF41161   Child (dy).

RF41162   John P Earnest (b Pine Grove PA) Spanish American War: 4th Reg, PA Vol, Lt Col.

RF41163   Catherine Earnest m Jonathan Schnader, Harrisburg PA.

RF41164   Napoleon Earnest (b 13 Mar 1850, Fredericksburg PA) m 4 Jul 1872, Hummelstown PA, Mary A Hoffer (b 9 Jun 1846, near Elizabethtown PA).

RF411641   William H Earnest (b 3 Jul 1875, Jonestown PA) m Estelle Penney. Lafayette Col. Educator, Honesdale PA; attorney, Harrisburg PA.

RF4116411   Ernest Penney Earnest (b 17 Sep 1901).

RF4116412   Joel Gates Earnest (b 10 Apr 1904).

RF41165   Elias Earnest, Hummelstown PA.

RF41166   David M Earnest, Jonestown PA.

RF4117   Catherine Earnest (b 23 Oct 1811) m John Zerfoss.

RF4118   Sarah Earnest (b 31 Dec 1813).

RF4119   John Earnest (b 13 dec 1815).

RF411A   Priscilla Earnest (b 11 May 1818).

RF411B   Joseph Hummel Earnest (b 14 Mar 1821).

RF411C   Rebecca Earnest (21 Aug 1822-16 Oct 1823).

RF412   Melchior Rahm (11 Dec 1781-1 Jan 1847) m 21 May 1805, Sarah Kapp (10 Nov 1787-7 Jan 1849).

RF4121   Sophia Catharina Rahm (24 Mar 1806-8 Jan 1870).

RF4122   Michael Rahm (3 Dec 1807-25 Dec 1881) m Mrs. Bartell.

RF41221   William Duffield Rahm.

RF41222   George Rahm.

RF41223   Elizabeth Rahm m   Howard.

RF41224   Rebecca Rahm m   Colendence.

RF41225   Margaret Rahm m   Johnson.

RF412126   Sophia Rahm m   Fraser.

RF4123   Martin A Rahm (27 Oct 1809 PA-15 Sep 1889, CA) m 30 Mar 1836, Gettysburg PA, Catherine Benedict (1818 PA-ca 1903).

RF41231   Francis Marion Rahm (3 Feb 1839 PA-1912, CA) m Helen A Gaddis (1846, Waukegan MI-Dec 1924, Oakland CA).

RF412311   Marion Rahm (1867-1921).

RF412312   Francis Rahm (1868-1949).

RF412313   Elmer Rahm (1870-1927) m Ella Welch.

RF412314   Roscoe Rahm (1872-1931) m 1898 Nella Kaerth.

RF4123141   Edith Rahm (b Aug 1898) m 1932, Enoch W Crozer.

RF4123142   June Rahm (b Sep 1916).

RF412315   Helen Rahm (b 1876) m 1900, Edwin R Thompson.

RF4123151   Norman Rahm Thompson (1906-1912).

RF4123152   Peter Rahm Thompson (b 1916) m 1941 Jane Inkster.

RF41231521   Peter Rutledge Thompson (b 29 Apr 1944).

RF41231522   Sarah Ann Thompson (b 18 Oct 1946).

RF41231523   Mark Frederick Thompson (b 28 April 1950).

RF41231524   Edwin John Thompson (b 23 Jan 1953).

RF41231525   Helen Elizabeth Thompson (b 24 Dec 1953).

RF412316   Ethel Rahm (b 1883) m 1929 Jacob E Peregrine.

RF41232   Melchior Rahm.

RF41233   Frank Rahm.

RF41234   Sarah Rahm.

RF41235   Edward Rahm.

RF4124   David Rahm (7 Dec 1811-May 1882) m Hannah Pugh Davis.

RF41241   John Melchior Rahm (25 Sep 1839-Jun 1915) m Anne Amelia Ennes.

RF412411   Mildred Louis Rahm m Edward Luther Smith.

RF4124111   David Rahm Smith, WWI: USA.

RF41241111   David Rahm Smith Jr.

RF41241112   James Edward Rahm Smith.

RF4124112   Eleanor Scott Smith m Webster   .

RF4124113   Elizabeth Learned Smith (dy).

RF412412   Susan Rahm.

RF412413   Sarah Rahm.

RF412414   Ross Rahm.

RF4125   Sarah Rahm (19 Jan 1814-30 Mar 1901).

RF4126   Elizabeth Rahm (1 Sep 1816-14 Jul 1895) m John Jones.

RF41261   Henry Jones.

RF41262   Rhoda Jones.

RF41263   Barbara M Jones.

RF41264   Sophia Jones.

RF41265   Louisa Jones.

RF41266   Ida Jones.

RF4127   Edward Cronch Rahm (23 Oct 1818, Middletown PA-3 Jul 1885, Oakland CA) m 1) 2 Apr 1857, Fairfield IA, Louisa Maria Moeller (23 Mar 1836, Somerset OH-24 Jan 1875); m 2) 1890, Mary Acres Miller, Somerset OH. In 1862 moved to California, settling in 1868 in Benicia. Bur Benicia CA.

RF41271   Edith Catherine Rahm (14 Dec 1857, Fairfield IA-9 Sep 1879).

RF41272   Mary Elizabeth Rahm (15 Feb 1859, Fairfield IA-30 Sep 1860).

RF41273   Jessie Amanda Rahm (16 Nov 1861, Fairfield IA-25 Jul 1932, Alameda CA) m Ludwig Erdman.

RF412731   Fred Martin Erdman (b 26 Apr 1890) m Emma Wolf.

RF4127311   William Erdman.

RF4127312   Edith Erdman m Collins Bradley.

RF41274   Louisa Rahm (23 Mar 1866, Carson City NV-1 Apr 1922, Oakland CA) m Charles C Davidson.

RF412741   Ray Davidson (24 Jun 1893-Dec 1894).

RF41275   Martha Frederica Rahm (b 11 Apr 1869, Benicia CA) m William H Morrison.

RF412751   Mabel Emily Morrison (b 26 Jun 1892).

RF412752   Florence Long Morrison (b 16 Jun 1895) m Richard K Ham.

RF4127521   Robert Ham.

RF4127522   Kimball Ham.

RF4127523   Donald Morrison Ham.

RF412753   Martha Helena Morrison (b 17 Jul 1911) m Kenneth M Churchill.

RF41276   Mabel Rahm (20 Dec 1870, Benicia CA-27 May 1919, Berkeley CA) m Nelson Hoyt
Chamberlain.

RF412761   William Edward Chamberlain (b 6 Aug 1892) m Genevieve Owen.

RF4127611   Owen Chamberlain.

RF4127612   Elizabeth Ann Chamberlain.

RF412762   Pauline Chamberlain (b 22 Feb 1894) m Allen Morrow.

RF4127621   Marian Morrow.

RF4127622   Allen Morrow Jr.

RF412763   Leon Chamberlain m Irene Yeatman.

RF4127631   Eleanor Chamberlain.

RF4127632   William Chamberlain.

RF412764   Marian Chamberlain (b 14 Jan 1900) m Bayard Brewster.

RF4127641   Alta Brewster.

RF41277   Edna Margarita Rahm (b 21 Sep 1892, Benicia CA) m Horace Patterson.

RF4128   Mary Rahm (8 Oct 1820-6 Feb 1877).

RF4129   Harriet Rahm (7 Feb 1823-28 Sep 1892) m Calvin Weinbruener.

RF41291   Louis Weinbruener m Harriet Young.

RF41292   Melchior Weinbruener.

RF41293   Edward Weinbruener.

RF412A   Margaret Rahm (15 Mar 1825-18 Feb 1871) m Charles Rahm.

RF412A1   Francis M Rahm.

RF412A2   Edward Rahm.

RF412A3   Sarah Virginia Rahm m   Fortune.

RF412A4   Charles Rahm m   Johnson.

RF412A41   Charles Rahm Jr.

RF412A5   Louisa Rahm m   Enfield.

RF412A51   Paul Enfield.

RF412B   John Andrew Rahm (3 Feb 1827-9 Mar 1906) m Jemima Fisher.

RF412B1   Mary Alice Rahm, Wooster OH.

RF412B2   Edward Fisher Rahm. Civil War: Co C-139 Reg. ONG.

RF412C   Eleanor J Rahm (14 Oct 1829-17 Mar 1890) m Isaac Herring.

RF412C1   Nina Herring (dy).

RF413   Rahm (d 1845).

RF414   David Rahm (b1783).

RF415   Rebecca Rahm (1786-1792).

RF42   John Jacob Rahm (b 17 June 1757) m Barbara Byers.

RF43   Margaretha Rahm (b 20 Apr 1759) m   Byers.

RF44   Melchior Muhlenberg Rahm (13 Feb 1762, near Middletown PA-31 Oct 1820, Harrisburg PA) m Mary King (d 6 Oct 1822, Harrisburg PA) US Rev: Lancaster Co Militia, 6th Btm, 2nd Lt. PA State Senate. Tavernkeeper, Harrisburg PA.

RF441   Jacob Rahm (d 20 Oct 1834) m 9 Oct 1810, Rebecca Harris.

RF4411   George Rahm (31 Aug 1812-17 Aug 1813, Harrisburg PA).

RF442   Rebecca Rahm (1789-2 Jan 1831).

RF443   John Rahm (b 14 Jul 1793) m 22 Mar 1827, Golconda IL, Juliette C Field (17 Dec 1810-26 Apr 1872). Changed spelling to Raum.

RF4431   Mary Eliza Raum (12 Feb 1828-26 Oct 1830).

RF4432   Green Berry Raum (3 Dec 1829-18 Dec 1909) m 15 Oct 1851, Maria Field (13 Apr 1832-1915) Civil War Commissioner, Record and Pension Div, US War Dept, 1892.

RF44321   Jessie Raum (1 Oct 1852-9 Oct 1857).

RF44322   Effie Raum (b 7 Oct 1854) m 16 Oct 1876, Winfield S S Walters (d 17 Sep 1889) Clerk, US Treasury Dept.

RF443221   David Raum Walters (b 1 Oct 1877).

RF443222   Henry McCoy Walters (b 21 Jun 1880).

RF44323   Daniel Field Raum (b 10 Feb 1857) m Jan 1888, Rae Copley. Attorney, Peoria IL.

RF44324   Maude Raum (b 17 Mar 1859) m 14 Feb 1885, Frank Z Maguire.

RF443241   Frank Raum Maguire (b 29 Nov 1885).

RF44325   John Raum (b 17 Jul 1861).

RF44326   Green Berry Raum Jr (b 10 May 1864) m 2 Jan 1890, Annie I Rogers. Attorney, New York NY. Civil servant.

RF443261   Berry Rogers Raum.

RF44327   Maria Raum (b 8 Apr 1867) m 23 Oct 1889, Frank J Moses. USMC, Capt.

RF44328   Mabel H Raum (b 5 Sep 1868) m 16 May 1889, James Reed Little.

RF443282   Joseph Reed Little (b 13 Oct 1891).

RF44329   Fanny Raum (b 7 Feb 1871) unm.

RF4432A   Dick Raum (18 Nov 1874-25 Mar 1875).

RF4433   William Henry Clay Raum (23 Dec 1831-25 Apr 1833).

RF4434   John Melchior Raum (b 1 Dec 1833) m 29 Sep 1868, Mary Caroline Sloan. Civil War: 120 IL Vol, Major.

RF4435   William Wallace Raum (28 Aug 1836-2 Aug 1861).

RF4436   Mary Eliza Raum (13 Sep 1838-29 Aug 1839).

RF4437   Ada Raum (b and d 25 Nov 1841).

RF4438   Stella Smith Raum (25 Nov 1856-2 Jun 1857).

RF444   Magdalina Rahm.

RF445   Catharine Rahm (ca 1797-25 Aug 1822).

RF446   Martin Rahm m Anna Maria Rahm Anshutz (1788-1878).

RF4461   Anna Maria Rahm (1813-1894) m   Johnston.

RF44611   Sarah Jane Johnston (1841) m   Miller.

RF446111   Maria Louisa Miller, Blairsville PA.

RF447   George Rahm (14 Apr 1799, Harrisburg PA-13 Sep 1808, Harrisburg PA).

RF448   Samuel Rahm (b 13 Apr 1801, Harrisburg PA) m 29 Dec 1818, Harrisburg PA, Elizabeth Hain.

RF449   Henry Rahm (b 3 April 1803, Harrisburg PA).

RF44A   William King Rahm (b 1 Apr 1805, Harrisburg PA).

RF44B   Mary Ann Rahm (1809, Harrisburg PA-11 Jun 1849, Harrisburg PA) m 4 Jul 1826, Harrisburg PA, Christopher Cuel Hynicka (27 Feb 1799, Princeton NJ-18 Nov 1853, Harrisburg PA) Bur Harrisburg PA. Shoemaker.

RF44B1   Catharine Ann Hynicka (8 Feb 1827, Harrisburg PA-25 Oct 1847, Harrisburg PA) Bur Harrisburg PA.

RF44B2   Luther Reilly Hynicka (30 Dec 1828, Harrisburg PA-8 Aug 1872, Lebanon PA) m 1) 15 Jun 1858, Lebanon PA, Mary Elizabeth Moyer (10 Mar 1834-8 Jan 1864, Myerstown PA); m 2) 8 Jan 1866, Lebanon PA, Caroline Moyer (her sister; d 27 Apr 1909, Lebanon PA) Bur Lebanon PA. Hydraulic engineer.

RF44B21   Rudolph Kelker Hynicka (6 Jul 1859, Myerstown PA-22 Feb 1927, St Petersburg FL) m

1) 1884, Laura Elizabeth Campbell (d 17 Apr 1908, Cincinnati OH); m 2) 1918, Dorothy Dresselhouse. Bur Lebanon PA. Newspaper reporter.

RF44B211   Caroline Elizabeth Hynicka (4 Mar 1895, Cincinnati OH-31 Oct 1955, Lebanon PA) m 1) 19 Jul 1918, Lebanon PA, David Carl Fox, div; m 2) Paul Shenk Leslie (1903-2 Mar 1944, Lebanon PA) Bur Lebanon PA.

RF44B2111   Joan Hynicka Fox (21 Mar 1919, Lebanon PA-1 Feb 1952, Lebanon PA) m Charles Delmar Euston (d 1978) She bur Lebanon PA.

RF44B21111   Barbara Graham Euston (b 9 Jun 1939, Lebanon PA) m 1) 1958, Richard D Amy, div; m 2) 9 May 1964, Richard Charles Knight (b 19 Jul 1935, Reading PA) Res Baton Rouge LA.

RF44B211111   Tawn Elizabeth Amy (b 25 Nov 1959, Norristown PA; adopted by Richard Charles Knight).

RF44B211112   Richard Charles Knight Jr (b 4 Aug 1965, Reading PA).

RF44B211113   Charles William Knight (b 1 July 1967, Reading PA).

RF44B22   Alice Adalaide Hynicka (18 Dec 1860, Myerstown PA-15 Aug 1862, Myerstown PA) Bur Lebanon PA.

RF44B23   Lemuel Klein Hynicka (21 Jun 1862, Myerstown PA-31 Mar 1931, Lebanon PA) Bur Lebanon PA. Civil engineer. unm.

RF44B24   Robert Griffith Hynicka (5 Oct 1866, Lebanon PA-18 Aug 1938, Lebanon PA) Bur Lebanon PA. unm. Horse breeder, Lebanon PA.

RF44B25   Luther Reilly Hynicka Jr (4 Jan 1869, Lebanon PA-4 Sep 1870, Lebanon PA) Bur Lebanon PA).

RF44B26   Elizabeth Gobin Hynicka (19 Dec 1871, Lebanon PA-23 Jun 1949, Lebanon PA) m 18 Oct 1892, Lebanon PA, Grant L Miller (1869-1930) Bur Lebanon PA. She, RN.

RF44B3   Adelaide Hynicka (29 Sep 1831, Harrisburg PA-8 Jul 1916, Harrisburg PA) m 18 Oct 1860, Richard Fox (8 Nov 1813, Hummelstown PA-30 Jun 1874, Hummelstown PA) He bur Hummelstown PA; she bur Harrisburg PA) Businessman, banker, Hummelstown PA.

RF44B31   Anna Patton Fox (4 Nov 1861-28 Dec 1942, Harrisburg PA) m 5 Sep 1888, Edgar Van Sant Einstein (1859-24 Jul 1924, Philadelphia PA) Bur Harrisburg PA. Merchant, Harrisburg PA.

RF44B311   Richard Fox Einstein (6 May 1889-8 Feb 1952, Harrisburg PA) m 30 Jun 1943, Mildred Martha Kulp (1889-29 Jul 1964, Harrisburg PA) Bur Harrisburg PA. Insurance broker.

RF44B32   May Fox (1863-1930, Santa Ana CA) Bur Hummelstown PA. Artist.

RF44B33   Richard V Fox m 7 Nov 1916, Marie Burns. Commonwealth employee, Harrisburg PA.

RF44B34   Elizabeth Fox (3 Apr 1866-23 Oct 1940, Philadelphia PA) m 11 Apr 1894, William James Walton (23 Oct 1858-6 Dec 1946, Philadelphia PA) Bur Philadelphia PA.

RF44B341   Robert Allen Walton (15 Dec 1896-27 Feb 1978) m 1) 12 May 1934, Dorothy Edwards; m 2) 23 Nov 1957, Elise Luck Penrock.

RF44B4   George Hynicka (3 Oct 1832, Harrisburg PA-13 Nov 1913, Hampton VA) m Harrisburg

PA, Catherine C Vollmar. He bur Hampton VA. Civil War: PA 127th Inf. Building contractor.

RF44B41   Frederick H Hynicka (b Harrisburg PA-10 Jul 1858, Harrisburg PA) Bur Harrisburg PA.

RF44B42   Theodore K Hynicka (b 1859, Harrisburg PA) m Sarah . Res New York NY. Policeman.

RF44B43   Charles Frederick Hynicka (21 Aug 1861, Harrisburg PA-30 Jul 1935, Johnstown PA) m 19 May 1898, Apollo PA, Anna Christina Martin (23 Sep 1878, Johnstown PA-13 Dec 1952, Washington DC) Bur Johnstown PA. Steelworker.

RF44B431   Adelaide Esther Hynicka (6 Jul 1900, Johnstown PA-13 Dec 1943, Johnstown PA) m 24 Dec 1923, Emmett Darlington Reed (Jan 1902, Derry PA-12 Aug 1971, Johnstown PA) Fireman and machinist, Johnstown PA. Bur Johnstown PA.

RF44B4311   Emmett Darlington Reed Jr (1925-1925, Johnstown PA) Bur Johnstown PA.

RF44B4312   Alyce Ann Reed (b 17 Jul 1931, Johnstown PA) m 1) 29 Aug 1949, Cumberland MD, Howard Eugene Hershberger (b 24 Dec 1926, Johnstown PA) div 1970; m 2) 20 Nov 1970, Johnstown PA, Robert Cornell Kinsey (b 2 Sep 1924, Pittsburgh PA) div 1995. Res Somerset PA.

RF44B43121   Carol Ann Hershberger (b 10 Mar 1951, Johnstown PA) m 26 July 1969, Johnstown PA, Joseph John Vitko Jr (Mar 1949-25 Apr 1991, Ebensburg PA) Bur Ebensburg PA. Res Ebensburg PA.

RF44B431211   Joseph John Vitko III (b 2 Feb 1970, Summerville NJ) Pitcher, NY Mets, 1989-1995.

RF44B431212   Lori Ann Vitko (b 16 May 1973, Columbus OH).

RF44B431213   Ashley Rebecca Vitko (b 29 April 1986, Johnstown PA).

RF44B43122   Gloria Jean Hershberger (25 Sep 1952, Johnstown PA-3 Oct 1985, Johnstown PA) m 11 August 1973, Johnstown PA, Daniel John Barkley. She bur Johnstown PA.

RF44B431221   Jennifer Lynn Barkley (b 7 Sep 1972, Johnstown PA) m 30 Sep 1988, Kevin Cox. Res Imler PA.

RF44B4312211   Elizabeth Ann Cox (b 30 May 1990, Windber PA).

RF44B431222   Daniel John Barkley Jr (b 2 Oct 1973, Johnstown PA).

RF44B431223   Lisa Marie Barkley (b 27 Feb 1981, Johnstown PA).

RF44B43123   Cindy Lee Hershberger (b 11 Aug 1954, Johnstown PA) m 19 Sep 1972, William James Warhul Jr, div. Res Somerset PA.

RF44B431231   Michelle Lynn Warhul (b 29 Jan 1973, Johnstown PA) m 26 Aug 1994, Cumberland MD, Michael Harbaugh.

RF44B4312311   Shuree Leneah Harbaugh (b 5 Feb 1993, Somerset PA).

RF44B4312312   Abby Nicole Harbaugh (b 29 Aug 1995, Somerset PA).

RF44B431232   William James Warhul III (b 3 Dec 1973, Johnstown PA).

RF44B431233   Darlene Suzanne Warhul (b 24 May 1983, Somerset PA).

RF44B431234   Christine Suzanne Warhul (b 24 May 1983, Somerset PA).

RF44B43124   Susan Joy Hershberger (b 20 Dec 1955, Johnstown PA) m 1) 11 Jul 1971, Robert Edward Lester, div, 1986: m 2) 14 Jul 1995, Somerset PA, Rodger Andrew Tomko.

RF44B431241   Robert Edward Lester Jr (b 8 Nov 1971, Johnstown PA).

RF44B431242   Keri Ann Lester (b 4 Sep 1975, Johnstown PA).

RF44B4312421   Samantha Kay Lowry (b 4 Aug 1993, Somerset PA).

RF44B432   Charles Frederick Hynicka Jr (10 Sep 1902, Johnstown PA-13 Jan 1983, Ebensburg PA) m 20 Mar 1926, Johnstown PA, Anna Viola Yunga (18 May 1903, Walsall PA-16 Jan 1983, Johnstown PA) WWII: USN. Bur Johnstown PA. Policeman, Johnstown PA.

RF44B4321   Nancy Carol Hynicka (b 2 June 1944, Johnstown PA) m 8 Oct 1966, Windber PA, Richard George Wargo (b 2 Jan 1938, Windber PA) Sales. Res Johnstown PA.

RF44B433   Eugene William Hynicka (26 Nov 1905, Johnstown PA-13 Mar 1969, Johnstown PA) m 28 Nov 1929, Johnstown PA, Anna Popovich (b 19 Sep 1907, Johnstown PA) Bur Johnstown PA. Fireman, 1925-1968, steelworker, Johnstown PA. She res Johnstown PA.

RF44B4331   Eujean Louise Hynicka (b 2 Sep 1930, Johnstown PA) m 23 Jun 1951, Windber PA, Leslie L Faust, div 1972. She RN. Res Cleveland OH.

RF44B43311   Dawn Leslie Faust (24 Feb 1953, Windber PA-15 Dec 1971, Streetsboro OH) Bur Twinsburg OH.

RF44B43312   Leslie Leroy Faust (b 11 Apr 1955, Windber PA) m 1) 15 Mar 1980, Boulder CO, Amy Patricia Ruggles (b 1 Feb 1957, Ravenna OH) div 1986; m 2) 15 Apr 1989, GA, Sherry Phillips (b 29 May 1955, Bedford OH). He, carpenter, Big Pine Key, FL.

RF44B433121   Tyler Patrick Faust (b 21 Oct 1983, Ravenna OH) Kent OH.

RF44B4332   Donna Claire Hynicka (b 4 Nov 1931, Johnstown PA) m 14 Feb 1954, Johnstown PA, Melvin Oliver Allison (b 16 Oct 1931, Johnstown PA) She, RN. He, BS, U (PA) Pittsburgh, 1955. Chemical engineer, Akron OH.

RF44B43321   Marjorie Sue Allison (b 16 Nov 1957, Akron OH) BS, St Johns Col, Annapolis MD, 1980. Res. Denver CO.

RF44B43322   Ann Adair Allison (b 9 Jan 1960, Niagara Falls NY) m 6 June 1981, Akron OH, Mark Phillip Stoehr (b 8 June 1957, Terre Haute IN) She, BS, U Houston, 1982; he, BS, Purdue U, 1980. CPA, The Woodlands TX.

RF44B433221   Matthew Blake Stoehr (b 1 Jul 1992, Houston TX).

RF44B433222   Brett Thomas Stoehr (b 7 Apr 1994, Houston TX).

RF44B43323   Amy Lynn Allison (b 4 Oct 1966, Akron OH) BS, TX A&M, 1989; MBA, U TX, Austin, 1996. Houston TX.

*RF44B4333   Gloria Marie Hynicka (b 7 Apr 1933, Johnstown PA) m 21 Jan 1955, Winchester VA, Harold Thomas Kinback (b 21 Jan 1934, Johnstown PA) He, USAF, 1954-58. BS, U (PA) Pittsburgh, 1962; MS, Stanford (CA) U, 1970. Civil engineer. Springfield VA.

RF44B43331   Debora Ann Kinback (b 19 Mar 1957, Anchorage AK) m 1) Jun 1977, Annandale VA, Paul Langley, div 1982; m 2) 27 June 1986, Middleburg VA, John Edward Holmes (b 2 Nov 1953, Queens

NY) BS Rensselaer Polytechnic I, 1975; JD, George Washington U, 1978. Patent lawyer, Washington DC. Res Woodbridge VA.

RF44B433311   John Christopher Holmes (b 31 Mar 1991, Fairfax VA).

RF44B43332   Harold Thomas Kinback Jr (b 23 Feb 1960, Johnstown PA) m 4 Jan 1980, Fairfax VA, Havyn Patrice Hendricks (b 17 June 1961, Ft Benning GA) BS, George Mason (VA) U, 1984. College loan officer. Res Springfield VA.

RF44B433321   Andrew Thomas Kinback (b 12 Aug 1980, Falls Church VA).

RF44B433322   Kyle David Kinback (b 15 Jul 1986, Falls Church VA).

RF44B433323   Brett Alexander Kinback (b 9 Nov 1991, Falls Church VA).

RF44B43333   Mary Christine Kinback (b 29 Sep 1962, Pittsburgh PA) m 16 Jul 1984, Alexandria VA, Jeffrey Lamont Calloway (b 1 Jun 1962, Tecumseh MI) She, sales; he, construction contractor. Springfield VA.

RF44B433331   Jeffrey Lamont Calloway Jr (b 20 Sep 1989, Fallbrook CA).

RF44B433332   Samantha Marie Calloway (b 22 Sep 1991, Jackson CA).

RF44B43334   Karen Jean Kinback (b 19 Jun 1964, Pittsburgh PA) m 2 Aug 1986, Burke VA, John Gregory Barker (b 6 May 1964, Coronado CA) He, construction contractor. Stephens City VA.

RF44B433341   Ryan Gregory Barker (b 1 Jul 1993, Fairfax VA).

*RF44B4334   Rebecca Ann Hynicka (b 3 Nov 1946, Johnstown PA) BS, Indiana (PA) U, 1968. Teacher; Girl Scout executive; RR Donnelley and Sons, Lancaster PA.

RF44B44   George Washington Hynicka (22 Feb 1864, Harrisburg PA-21 Aug 1944 New Cumberland PA) m Myrtle M Rudy (May 1867, WI-26 June 1943, New Cumberland PA) Bur Harrisburg PA. Steelworker, Harrisburg PA.

RF44B45   Harry R Hynicka (16 April 1866, Harrisburg PA-26 Sep 1933, Schwenksville PA) m 1) 27 Dec 1885, Katharine Hubley (b Sep 1868) div 1909; m 2) 7 Sep 1910, Harrisburg PA, Katie M Kober (5 Jun 1885-9 Mar 1951) Bur Harleysville PA.

RF44B451   Ray S Hynicka (b Harrisburg PA) m 25 Aug 1906, Ardella M Aumiller. Res Paxtang PA.

RF44B4511   Kathryn Hynicka (2 Jun 1907-26 Nov 1981, Narberth PA) m Leroy Sohland (d 27 Sep 1987) Bur Ardmore PA.

RF44B45111   Anne Elizabeth Sohland (b 19 Apr 1939, Philadelphia PA) m 23 Jun 1962, Ardmore PA, Elton Phillips Richards (b 24 Jul 1932, Philadelphia PA) She, teacher; he, AB, Dickinson Col, 1954; BD, Lutheran Theol Sem, Philadelphia, 1959; ThM, Princeton Theo Sem, 1966. Ordained Lutheran pastor, 1959. Pastor, Ardmore, Levittown, Reading PA; West DesMoines IA.

RF44B451111   Elton Russell Richards (b 14 Dec 1964, Bristol PA).

RF44B451112   David Roy Richards (b 24 Oct 1966, Bristol PA).

RF44B452   Ella Hynicka (b Harrisburg PA) m Charles Brenisholtz. Res Harrisburg PA.

RF44B4521   Charles Brenisholtz Jr (d aged 16).

RF44B4522   Ken Brenisholtz m Doris Stauffer, div.

RF44B453   Thomas Harry Hynicka (20 Mar 1892, Harrisburg PA-20 Nov 1952, Lancaster PA) m 25 Nov 1914, Harrisburg PA, Nellie Hilda Gast (9 Jan 1893, Lancaster PA-5 Oct 1981, Mountville PA) Bur Lancaster PA.

RF44B4531   Dorothy E Hynicka m Andrew D Hartman.

RF44B4532   Margaret Catherine Hynicka (b 12 Jul 1917, Lancaster PA) m 1) 1938, Albert Gerwer, div 1961; m 2) 1963, Donald S Rutt (d 4 Apr 1988) Res Lewisburg PA.

RF44B45321   Shirley Anne Gerwer (b 10 Jun 1939, Lancaster PA) m 1960, Edward Frailey. Res Lancaster PA.

RF44B453211   Traci Frailey (b 4 Sep 1968, Lancaster PA).

RF44B45322   Richard A Gerwer (b 10 Nov 1943, Lancaster PA) m 1964, Elaine Messner. Res Lititz PA.

RF44B453221   Michelle L Gerwer (b 13 Sep 1965, Lancaster PA) m 1) Robin Capwell, div; m 2) Scott Trompeter.

RF44B4532211   Amber Sue Capwell (b 9 May 1987, Lancaster PA) Adopted by Scott Trompeter.

RF44B453222   Christopher Gerwer (1971, Lancaster PA-1983).

RF44B45323   Margaret L Gerwer (b 1 Apr 1945, Lancaster PA) m 1967, Michael Powl. Res Macungie PA.

RF44B453231   Michael Powl Jr (b 9 Feb 1971, Lancaster PA).

RF44B453232   Jeffrey Powl (b 6 Nov 1973, Lancaster PA).

RF44B4533   Ruth Grace Hynicka (b 25 Apr 1921, Lancaster PA) m 5 Mar 1941, Ross Kendig Bare (b 21 Sep 1910, Lancaster PA) Res Lancaster PA.

RF44B45331   Judith Anne Bare (b 21 June 1942, Lancaster PA) m 2 Apr 1966, J Vincent Becker. He, salesman, Lancaster PA. She, RN.

RF44B453311   Tracey Lynn Becker (b 10 Mar 1968, Lititz PA).

RF44B453312   Stephanie Lee Becker (b 10 May 1970, Lititz PA).

RF44B453313   Deron Vincent Becker (b 10 May 1975, Bedford PA).

RF44B45332   Ross Kendig Bare Jr (b 24 Jul 1943, Lancaster PA) m 1) 20 Apr 1963, Anita Louise Hallman, div; m 2) 20 Oct 1990, Susan Wenger Ludwig.

RF44B453321   Fredrick Paul Bare (b 28 Sep 1963, Lancaster PA).

RF44B453322   Charles Anthony Bare (b 5 May 1967, Lancaster PA).

RF44B45333   Sandra Kay Bare (b 12 Feb 1952, Lancaster PA) m 6 May 1972, Carl Lowell Smoker. Res Lancaster PA.

RF44B453331   Michael Shann Smoker (b 9 Apr 1974, Lancaster PA).

RF44B453332   Kim Elayne Smoker (b 12 Sep 1976, Lancaster PA).

RF44B4534   Walter Thomas Hynicka.

RF44B4535   Richard Harry Hynicka (b 13 May 1925, Lancaster PA) m 3 Jul 1948, Mary Anne Dickey (b 2 Mar 1925, Berlin PA) TV manufacturing, Lancaster PA. Res Mountville PA.

RF44B45351   Robert Richard Hynicka (b 16 Aug 1950, Lancaster PA) m 7 Jul 1973, Kathleen Szemborski.

RF44B453511   Dallas Troy Hynicka (b 5 July 1975, Lancaster PA).

RF44B453512   Elizabeth Ann Hynicka (b 15 July 1976, Lancaster PA).

RF44B453513   Adrianne Yvonne Hynicka (b 15 Mar 1978, Lancaster PA).

RF44B45352   Robin Michael Hynicka (b 4 Sep 1953, Lancaster PA) Missionary pastor, Cookman United Methodist Church, Philadelphia PA.

RF44B45353   Stephen Franklin Hynicka (b 31 Mar 1956, Lancaster PA) m 6 Sep 1980, Kathleen Cooke. Factory superintendent, Lancaster PA.

RF44B453531   Lauren Marie Hynicka (b 4 Sep 1983, Lancaster PA).

RF44B453532   Justin David Hynicka (b 27 June 1985, Lancaster PA).

RF44B4536   Betty J Hynicka m John Overly. Lancaster PA.

RF44B46   Christian F Hynicka (ca 1869, Harrisburg PA-12 Jul 1871, Harrisburg PA) Bur Harrisburg PA.

RF44B47   Edward Orth Hynicka (1871, Harrisburg PA-22 Apr 1930, Harrisburg PA) m 31 Oct 1911, Philadelphia PA, Louisa A Huber, div 1917. Bur Harrisburg PA. Landscaper, state capitol, Harrisburg PA.

RF44B5   Rebecca Hynicka (30 Sep 1834, Harrisburg PA-22 May 1918, Harrisburg PA) m Richard Hogan Jr (17 Aug 1823-27 Jan 1891, Harrisburg PA) Bur Harrisburg PA. He, merchant; she, teacher, Harrisburg PA.

RF44B51   Adelaide Hogan (30 Dec 1866, Harrisburg PA-20 Apr 1869, Harrisburg PA) Bur Harrisburg PA.

RF44B52   Mary Hynicka Hogan (2 Mar 1870, Harrisburg PA-12 Sep 1937, Harrisburg PA) Bur Harrisburg PA. Supt of Art, Harrisburg Schools, Harrisburg PA.

RF44B6   Mary Magdalena Hynicka (6 Feb 1837, Harrisburg PA-22 Jun 1837, Harrisburg PA) Bur Harrisburg PA.

RF44B7   John Melchior Hynicka (3 Oct 1838, Harrisburg PA-5 Feb 1903, Kansas City MO) Bur MO. Civil War: 1st PA Inf, 127th PA Inf. unm.

RF44B8   Mary Ann Hynicka (17 Dec 1840, Harrisburg PA-29 Jun 1912, Harrisburg PA) Bur Harrisburg PA. unm.

RF44B9   Christopher Cuel Hyricka Jr (7 Dec 1842, Harrisburg PA-21 Mar 1864, Richmond VA) Bur Richmond VA. Civil War: 76 PA Inf. POW 11, Jul 1863. unm.

RF44B10   Edward Orth Hynicka (20 Sep 1845, Harrisburg PA-19 Oct 1857, Harrisburg PA) Bur Harrisburg PA.

RF44B11   Fanny Elizabeth Hynicka (20 May 1849, Harrisburg PA-11 Jul 1869, Harrisburg PA) Bur Harrisburg PA.

RF44C   Elizabeth Rahm (1816, Harrisburg PA-9 Jul 1873, Bellefonte PA).

RF45   John Rahm (b 22 Aug 1765).

RF46   Catharine Rahm (20 Jul 1769-9 Mar 1810) m Andrew Albright Jr (28 Feb 1770, Bethlehem PA-24 Nov 1822, Sunburg PA).

RF47   Rebecca Rahm (22 Nov 1773, near Hummelstown PA-31 Dec 1843, Harrisburg PA) m 1794, Christian Henry Orth (24 Mar 1773, Lebanon Tp, Lebanon Co PA-1816) She bur Harrisburg PA. He, ironmaster; sheriff of Dauphin Co 1797-1801; state senator 1801-1804; flour inspector, port of Philadelphia, 1809; merchant, Philadelphia and Baltimore. After his death she operated a boarding house, Harrisburg PA.

RF471   Catharine Elizabeth Orth (b 1 Jan 1795) m 1) John Whitehill; m 2) William Piper.

RF472   Rebecca Orth (1796-15 Oct 1854, Harrrisburg PA) m Luther Reily (7 Dec 1794, Myerstown PA-20 Feb 1854, Harrisburg PA) Bur Harrisburg PA. War of 1812: Pvt, Capt Richard M Crain's Co, assistant surgeon. Physician, Harrisburg PA. Member, 25th Congress; manager Harrisburg Cemetery, 1843-1849.

RF4721   R Elizabeth Reily (1824-2 Aug 1882, Harrisburg PA) Bur Harrisburg PA. unm.

RF4722   Emily Reily m George W Porter.

RF4723   John A Reily (1826-1901) m Catherine Olewine (1827-1909) Bur Harrisburg PA.

RF47231   Martha L Reily (1853-1855) Bur Harrisburg PA.

RF47232   William P Reily (1858-1933) Bur Harrisburg PA.

RF47233   George E Reily (1862-13 Feb 1934, Washington DC) m Esther Minnich (d 1959) Bur Harrisburg PA.

RF472331   William H Reily (1895-1895) Bur Harrisburg PA.

RF47234   John F Reily (b and d 1865).

RF47234   George Wolf Reily (30 Nov 1834, Harrisburg PA-8 Feb 1892, Harrisburg PA) m Elizabeth Hannah Kerr (1841-28 Sep 1922) Bur Harrisburg PA.   Yale Col, 1854; MD, U PA, 1859. Physician, Harrisburg PA, to 1870; banker and corporation director, Harrisburg PA.

RF47241   Elizabeth Hummel Reily (13 Oct 1867-5 Sep 1849) m 2 Oct 1889, Edward Bailey (19 Oct 1861-17 Oct 1938) Bur Harrisburg PA. Nail manufacturer; later, banker, Harrisburg PA.

RF472411   Elizabeth Scott Bailey.

RF472412   Martha Bailey.

RF472413   George Reily Bailey (16 Mar 1899-8 Jan 1981) Bur Harrisburg PA. Banker, Harrisburg PA.

RF47242   George Wolf Reily Jr (21 Nov 1870, Harrisburg PA-5 Jun 1954, Philadelphia PA) m 29 Apr 1903, Louisa Hoxall Harrison (1878-21 Mar 1915, Philadelphia PA) Bur Harrisburg PA. Yale U, 1912; banker to 1897; National Bank Examiner, 1897-1902; banker, 1902-.

RF472421   George Wolf Reily II (b 27 Dec 1905).

RF47243   Mary Emily Reily (1875-1942) Bur Harrisburg PA.

RF47244   Caroline Reily.

RF4725   Caroline M Reily (1836-2 Apr 1897) Bur Harrisburg PA.

RF473   Adam Henry Orth (22 Apr 1799-15 Oct 1833, Coxestown PA) m 3 May 1832, Elizabeth Cox (1813-13 Jan 1836) Bur Harrisburg PA. Attorney, Harrisburg PA; district attorney, Dauphin Co PA. Transcribing clerk PA House of Representatives.

RF4731   Adam Orth (dy) Bur Harrisburg PA.

RF474   Henry Orth (1803-1821).

RF475   William Orth (1806-1824) Bur Harrisburg PA.

RF476   Caroline Orth (1812-10 Jan 1848) m 17 Apr 1828, Otto Witman. Bur Harrisburg PA.

RF4761   Henry Orth Witman.

RF4762   Luther Reily Witman.

RF4763   Edward Lawrence Witman.

RF4764   Rebecca Catherine Witman m Robert H Moffitt, DDS.

RF477   Edward Lawrence Orth (4 Jan 1814, baltimore MD-15 Apr 1861, Harrisburg PA) m Martha Cummins Kerr (1818-20 Jun 1907, Harrisburg PA) Bur Harrisburg PA. MD, Jefferson Medical Col, 1834. Physician, Harrisburg PA.

RF4771   Mary W Orth (d 23 Aug 1911, Harrisburg PA) m Jacob F Seiler (d 14 Apr 1907, Harrisburg PA) Bur Harrisburg PA. Supt, Harrisburg Academy; mgr, Harrisburg Cemetery, 1879-1907.

RF47711   Martha Orth Seiler (1867-1873) Bur Harrisburg PA.

RF47712   Sue Seiler (1869-1949) Bur Harrisburg PA.

RF4772   Henry L Orth (17 Aug 1842, Harrisburg PA-18 May 1920, Harrisburg PA) m 30 June 1868, Elizabeth Bridgeman Dixon. Bur Harrisburg PA. Civil War: USA medical cadet. Yale Col, 1859. MD, U PA, 1866. Physician, Harrisburg PA; 1891, supt and physician, Harrisburg State Hospital.

RF47721   Edward Lawrence Orth (Aug 1872-Nov 1931) Bur Harrisburg PA.

RF47722   Roberta Elizabeth Orth (d 3 May 1954) Bur Harrisburg PA.

RF47723   Anna Shipley Orth (d 25 Aug 1950) Bur Harrisburg PA.

RF4773   James Wilson Orth (1845-1924) m Bertha E Ross. Bur Harrisburg PA.

RF4774   Rebecca Reily Orth (1848-9 Apr 1918, Pittsburgh PA) Bur Harrisburg PA.

RF478   Martin Rahm (b 4 Oct 1776).

RF6. Jacob Weiser (1736-1808)

Jacob Weiser was born 22 Sep 1736 New Jersey (as stated on his tombstone) and died 1 Jan 1808, Tulpehocken Tp, Berks Co PA. He married Anna Elizabeth Kurr (5 Jun 1740-1 Oct 1805), Tulpehocken Tp, Berks Co PA). They are buried at Christ Church. US Revolution, Corporal in Captain Michael Schaffer's Co, 1st Btn, Berks Co Militia, and other records. In 1764 he purchased his father's farm, which he sold in 1806 to his son John. In 1790 he purchased the Col Conrad Weiser farm which he sold in 1795 to his son John, who sold part of it, disposing of the balance in 1822.   On the father's tract, in Tulpehocken Tp, he erected a large stone house in 1783 which bore this date mark:

"Gott gesegnet dieses Haus
Und were da ein oder aus gehet
17 Jacob Weiser and Elizabeth Weiser 83"
(God bless this house and whoever goes in and out of it)[134]

Children of Jacob and Anna Elizabeth (Kurr) Weiser:

RF61   Anna Elizabeth Weiser (b 23 Dec 1763).

RF61 Anna Elizabeth Weiser
Etschberger (1763-1827)

RF62   John Weiser (b 23 Jan 1766).

RF63   John Jacob Weiser (5 Sep 1774, Tulpehocken Tp PA-30 Jun 1793, Tulpehocken Tp) Bur Christ Church. unm.

RF64   Anna Maria Weiser (b 17 May 1778, Tulpehocken Tp PA) m 2 Apr 1799, George Illig.

RF61   Anna Elizabeth Weiser (23 Dec 1763, Tulpehocken Tp, Berks Co PA-10 Jun 1837, Tulpehocken Tp, Berks Co PA) m 1785, John Peter Etschberger (26 Apr 1760, Jackson Tp, Lebanon Co PA-30 Oct 1823) Bur Stouchsburg PA.

RF611   Elizabeth Etschberger (13 Mar 1786-12 Jun 1863) m 22 Mar 1825, Jacob Stewart (29 Dec 1784-2 Jan 1854) Bur Myerstown PA.

RF6111   Lemuel Stewart.

RF6112   Clementine Stewart.

RF612   John Etschberger (27 Sep 1787-dy).

RF613   Marin Etschberger (17 Aug 1790-14 Dec 1862) m John Tice (10 Aug 1785-17 Jun 1845) Bur Lebanon PA (8 children).

RF614   John Peter Etschberger (4 Nov 1794-15 Nov 1885) m 8 Apr 1821, Elizabeth Walborn (4 Feb 1802-29 Mar 1858) Bur Stouchsburg PA. War of 1812: 5th Btn, 1st Brg PA Inf, Capt Jerimiah Rees's Co, Sgt.

---

[134]See records of Christ Lutheran Church, Stouchsburg. Data furnished (1960) by Mrs. Thomas Jenkins, Mrs. Vaneta Cobaugh, Mrs. Emma Gohl, Mrs. Carrie Haupt, James A Seibert, and Linda Gunder.

RF6141   Franklin Etschberger (24 Nov 1822-8 May 1906) m 15 Feb 1845, Elizabeth Snyder (d 31 May 1906).

RF61411   Ezra Etschberger (b 20 Sep 1845).

RF61412   William Etschberger (b 22 Feb 1847).

RF61413   Amanda Etschberger (b 22 Aug 1849) m William Deck.

RF61414   Emma Etschberger (b 17 Oct 1850) m Henry Sutsing.

RF6142   Priscilla Etschberger (16 Sep 1823-8 Feb 1902) m 24 Oct 1847, Jacob Miller (10 May 1824-17 Feb 1895).

RF61421   Levi Miller (b 20 Sep 1848) m 8 May 1869, Maria Walborn.

RF61422   Emanuel Miller (b 18 Jan 1853).

RF61423   Catherine Miller (b 24 May 1856).

RF61424   Rebecca Miller (b 10 Mar 1859).

RF61425   William Miller (b 17 Aug 1864) m 26 Jun 1886, Kate Ney.

RF6143   Levi Etschberger (b 6 May 1826) m 9 Jun 1844, Sarah Conrad (19 Dec 1821-17 Aug 1899, Louisville OH) Bur Louisville OH. She moved to OH in 1855.

RF61431   Melissa Etschberger (31 Jan 1846, Stouchburg PA-15 Jul 1926, East Cleveland OH) m 26 Dec 1871, Cleveland OH, Benjamin Franklin Matthias (23 Jul 1840, Louisville OH-12 Sep 1913, Alliance OH) Bur Louisville OH. He, Civil War: 86th OH Vol, Co 8; 26th OH Ind Battery, 1862-1865. Res Louisville, Alliance, Augusta OH, and Kiowa KS. Farmer and grain merchant near Minerva OH.

RF614311   Lulu Gertrude Matthias (28 Sep 1872, Louisville OH-24 Sep 1931, Lakewood OH) m 19 Jun 1895, Alliance OH, Lewellyn Orrin Eldredge (13 Mar 1867, Edinburgh OH-9 Jul 1949) Bur Rocky River OH. He, Methodist clergyman.

RF6143111   Franklin Eugene Eldredge (7 Jun 1897, East Palestine OH-5 Oct 1961, Los Angeles CA) m. Bur Rocky River OH. No chn. Entertainer, Hollywood CA.

RF6143112   Mary Elizabeth Eldredge (b 17 May 1900, Peninsula OH) m 1) 21 Aug 1923, Xenophon Kaylor Critchfield (6 Oct 1900-17 Jan 1957); m 2) Larry Weiderman; m 3) 15 Sep 1951, LaVerne Traphagen (d 27 Mar 1960); m 4) 28 Nov 1968, Canton OH, Samuel Losos Davis (b 23 Aug 1903, Girardsville PA).

RF61431121   Xenophon Kaylor Critchfield Jr (b 14 Jul 1924, Canton OH) m 31 Dec 1946, Pauline Bowers (b 19 Nov 1925, Ellet OH) Insurance salesman, Wooster OH.

RF614311211   David Milton Critchfield (b 12 Jul 1948, Canton OH) m 8 Jul 1972, Butler PA, Leslie Foster (b 10 Jan 1950, Butler PA) Insurance, Wadsworth OH.

RF6143112111   Kiersti Critchfield (b 3 Oct 1977, Gaylord MI).

RF6143112112   Thomas Eldredge Critchfield (b 10 Oct 1952, Warren OH) Music teacher, U Pittsburgh.

RF6143112113   Vickie Lynn Critchfield (b 22 Jan 1955, Wooster OH) Insurance underwriter, Canton OH.

RF6143113   Helen Marguerite Eldredge (b 11 Aug 1901, Rootstown OH) m 28 Sep 1929, Vermillon

OH, Ray Collins Siggens (10 Dec 1898, Sandusky OH-1 May 1968, Park Ridge IL) She, teacher; he, USN; Oberlin Col, 1923; teacher, book publisher. Bur Rocky River OH.

RF61431131   Richard (Skip) Eldredge Siggens (b 1 Apr 1935, Evanston IL) USA, 1954-56. Aircraft technician, Park Ridge IL.

RF61431132   James Alfred Siggens (b 24 Sep 1936, Evanston IL) m 1965, Linda Lee Merryfield (b 4 Feb 1945, Seattle WA) Public relations, Bothell WA.

RF614311321   Eric Scott Siggens (b 26 Jun 1966, St Paul MN).

RF614311322   Laura Marie Siggens (b 5 Mar 1969, St Paul MN).

RF6143114   Alice Gail Eldredge (b 31 Aug 1911, St Clairsville OH) m 21 Dec 1933, Lakewood OH, Edgar Powell Baird (b 18 Jun 1911, Pittsburgh PA).

RF61431141   Barbara Anne Baird (b 18 Mar 1935, Cleveland OH) m 26 Aug 1956, Oakhurst NJ, Harold James Schaaff (b 15 Sep 1933, Jersey City NJ).

RF614311411   Susan Marie Schaaff (b 31 Dec 1958, Ft Benning GA).

RF614311412   Harold James Schaaff Jr (b 10 Jun 1960, Cape Cod MA).

RF614311413   Robert Paul Schaaff (b 18 Sep 1965, Long Branch NJ).

RF61431142   Harold Powell Baird (b 28 Mar 1937, Cleveland OH) m 6 Jun 1965, Asbury Park NJ, Elizabeth Ann Sammons (b 3 Jun 1943 Newark NJ).

RF614311421   Diane Elizabeth Baird (b 17 Oct 1968, Neptune NJ).

RF61431143   Dorothy Jeanne Baird (b 15 Aug 1940, Cleveland OH) m 3 Mar 1969, Ft Lauderdale FL, Robert James Renner (b 2 Nov 1923, Hoboken NJ).

RF614312   Emma E Matthias (5 Apr 1875, Louisville OH-1878, Louisville OH) Bur Louisville OH.

RF614313   Fred Matthias (1 Jan 1877, Louisville OH-18 Sep 1877, Louisville OH) Bur Louisville OH.

RF614314   Kathryn M Matthias (7 Jan 1878, Louisville OH-30 Mar 1923, Akron OH) m 15 Mar 1898, Alliance OH, Lester Schory. Bur Louisville OH.

RF6143141   Wilda Schory (15 Sep 1908, Akron OH-7 Dec 1964, Cleveland OH) m 18 Jul 1945, Paul O'Connell. Bur Cleveland OH.

RF6143142   James Schory (b 7 Aug 1911, Akron OH) USAF.

RF6143143   Eleanor Muriel Schory (b 28 Nov 1912, Akron OH) unm.

RF614315   Julia Etchberger Matthias (7 Jan 1878, Louisville OH-22 May 1955, Hartsdale NY) m 25 Mar 1907, Jersey City NJ, Arthur H Harrison (13 May 1885, Williamsport PA-Feb 1948, Hartsdale NY) Bur Hartsdale NY. She, teacher. He, stock broker, investment banker, Hartsdale NY.

RF6143151   Catherine Crain Harrison (b 15 Dec 1907, New York NY) m 1) 19 Jun 1928, George Frederic Church II (b 1 Sep 1906, St Louis MO) div 1941; m 2) 29 Jun 1950, Hartsdale NY, Stanley J Sittenfield (b 3 Aug 1915, New York NY) WWII: USA, Sittenfield, Capt. Church, salesman.

RF61431511   George (Rick) Frederic Church II (b 11 Aug 1930, Highland Park IL) m Mary Milano (b 8 Jun 1930, White Plains NY) div. USN.

RF614315111   Julie Ellen Church (b 24 May 1956, Guantanamo Cuba) Secretary, Hartford CT.

RF614315112   Carol Elizabeth Church (b 15 May 1959, Montreal Canada).

RF61431512   Rodney Harrison Church (b 12 Feb 1933, Highland Park IL) m 2) 4 May 1979, New Hebrides, Margaret Poole Comerford (b 29 Jan 1973, CA) USA; BA, U MO; teacher, pool designer, realtor, Cupertino CA.

RF61431513   Linda Church (b 15 Jul 1956, Highland Park IL) m 11 Jul 1956, Norfolk VA, Glenn Thomas Allison (b 26 Jun 1931) div; m 2) Alan Mostow (b 6 June 1942) Medical secretary, St Louis MO.

RF614315131   Gregory Thomas Allison (b 14 Apr 1958, Kansas City MO).

RF614315132   Susan Diane Allison (b 28 May 1962, Kansas City MO) m 20 Mar 1981, St Louis MO, Robert Morton Lydon (d 14 Feb 1983).

RF6143151321   Melissa Sue Lydon (b 22 Sep 1981, St Louis MO).

RF614315133   Keith Christopher Allison (b 15 Sep 1968, St Louis MO).

RF614316   Henry Gilbert Matthias (25 Jun 1880, Louisville OH-7 Oct 1935, East Cleveland OH) Bur Louisville OH. unm.

RF614317   Charles Franklin Matthias (16 Jul 1882, Louisville OH-16 Nov 1947, Cleveland OH) Bur Louisville OH. unm. MA, Columbia U. Teacher, Cleveland OH.

RF614318   Wilda Grace Matthias (25 Nov 1885, Louisville OH-3 Aug 1977, Cleveland OH) m 14 Jun 1924, Johnstown PA, Vincent Roy Peterson (15 Jan 1890-9 Dec 1972) Bur Cleveland OH. He, MA, 1934; PhD, 1941, Western Reserve U. Both teachers.

RF6143181   David Walborn Peterson (b 3 Mar 1927, Cleveland OH) m 14 Jun 1952, Cleveland OH, Donna Jean Terrill (b 7 Aug 1928) He, USN; AB, Mt Union (OH) Col, 1950. She, BS, Mt Union (OH) Col, 1952. He, industrial sales; she, nurse, Jericho NY.

RF61431811   Gary Matthias Peterson (b 25 Jan 1956, Evansville IN) BA, SUNY, 1980.

RF61431812   Wesley Conrad Peterson (b 2 Mar 1958, Evansville IN) BSA, SUNY.

RF61431813   Sandra Darlene Peterson (b 30 Dec 1959, Mineola NY).

RF614319   Adah Viola Matthias (6 Apr 1889, Louisville OH-6 Apr 1982, Scottsdale AZ) m 29 Mar 1911, Canton OH, Oakley Ross Iden (28 June 1886, Oneida OH-15 May 1964, Scottsdale AZ) Bur Phoenix AZ. She, milinary designer; he, railroad agent.

*RF6143191   Virginia Iden (b 22 Mar 1912, Alliance OH) m 24 Oct 1942, Phoenix AZ, Duard Louis Ferguson (b 19 Jul 1909, Dayton OH) No chn. He, advertising photographer, yacht broker; she, advertising photographer.

RF61432   William Jonathan Etschberger (14 Aug 1847-ca 1920) m Margaret Matthias (1842-17 Jul 1890) Bur Louisville OH. No chn.

RF61433   Jacob Milton Etschberger (b 26 Feb 1849) Bur Louisville OH. unm.

RF61434   Emma Catherine Etschberger (2 Oct 1850-1870s) Bur Louisville OH.

RF6144   Angeline Elizabeth Etschberger (24 Dec 1828-25 Jul 1898) Bur Stouchsburg PA. unm.

RF6145   Rebecca Catherine Etschberger (16 Jan 1832-29 Jan 1901) m 2 Jan 1869, William Fegley (d 14 Apr 1878) Bur Stouchburg PA.

RF61451   William Fegley (b 14 Nov 1869).

RF6146   Emma Clarissa Etschberger (24 Nov 1841-31 Jul 1842) Bur near Myerstown PA.

RF615   Catherine Etschberger (9 Jun 1798-14 Feb 1863) m John Brown (16 Mar 1804-28 Feb 1862) Bur Chambersburg PA.

RF6151   Amanda Brown m   Rodgers.

RF616   John Jacob Etschberger (b 19 Apr 1801) Bur near Clear Spring MD. unm.

RF617   George Philip Etschberger (19 Mar 1807-28 Mar 1877, Falling Water VA) m 10 Jan 1839 (9 Dec 1808-20 Feb 1878) Bur Chambersburg PA. (6 children) Moved to Chambersburg 1837.

RF617 George Philip
Etschberger (1807-1877)

RF62   John Weiser (23 Jan 1766, Tulpehocken Tp, Berks Co PA-7 Nov 1825, Tulpehocken Tp, Berks Co PA) m 22 Feb 1789, Elizabeth Anspach (7 Feb 1769-14 Mar 1841, Tulpehocken Tp, Berks Co PA) They are buried at Christ Church. He was a farmer, owning both the Conrad Weiser homestead and the Christopher Frederick Weiser property, purchased from his father in 1806. John sold this to his son-in-law, Thomas Rehrer, who sold it to another son-in-law, Peter Brown, from whom it passed, 1839, out of the family.

RF621   Peter Weiser (25 May 1789, Tulpehocken Tp, Berks Co PA-18 May 1843, Juniata Co PA) m 1); m 2) 16 Apr 1830, Sarah Moore (21 Sep 1808-6 Feb 1847).[135]

RF6211   Jonathan Weiser (15 Nov 1818-6 Mar 1880, Susquehanna Tp, Snyder Co PA) m 1851, Mary Gilfillan (1 Jan 1827-18 Apr 1889, Susquehanna Tp PA) Miller, Susquehanna Tp PA. Erected mill 1858, storekeeper and postmaster, 1849-1866, Mahontango PA.

RF62111   Alice Weiser (1853, Mahontango Tp PA-1918) m John G App (1851-1923) She bur near McKees Half Falls, Snyder Co PA.

RF621111   Carleton Smith App (1886-1925) unm.

RF621112   Gilfillan App.

RF621113   Charles App.

RF62112   Jay Gilfillan Weiser (1855, Mahontango Tp PA-1935) unm. Bur Chapman Tp PA. UPA. Attorney, Middleburg PA.

RF62113   Mary Laura Weiser (8 Mar 1859, Mahontango Tp PA-16 Jun 1936) m 24 Nov 1898, Alton B McLinn. Bur Harrisburg PA. No chn.

RF62114   Charles Brandt Weiser (8 Jun 1861, Mahontango Tp PA-17 Oct 1905, Mahontango Tp PA) Bur near McKees Half Falls, Snyder Co PA.

---

[135]Data furnished by Mrs. Thomas Jenkins, Mrs. Vaneta Cobaugh, Mrs. Emma Gohl and James A. Dibert.

RF62115 Jennie Ida Weiser (11 Oct 1863, Mahontango Tp PA-15 Feb 1879, Mahontango Tp PA) Bur near McKees Half Falls, Snyder Co PA.

RF62116 Johnathan Lewis Weiser (10 Mar 1857, Mahontango Tp PA-26 May 1904, Mahontango Tp PA) m 5 Oct 1881, Elizabeth Eve Holman (24 May 1859, near Millerstown PA-30 Jul 1915, Mahontango Tp PA) Bur near McKees Half Falls, Snyder Co PA.

RF621161 John Holman Weiser (6 Aug 1882, Mahontango Tp PA-20 May 1949, Mifflintown PA) m 6 May 1925, Topeka KS, Margaret S Gilfillan. Bur Mahontango Tp PA.

RF621162 Mary Gilfillan Weiser (20 Jun 1889, Mahontango Tp PA-26 Jun 1975, Ardmore PA) m 5 Apr 1921, Thomas Jenkins (b 30 Aug 1881, Bethlehem PA) USA, Lt Col; Civil engineer. She, AB, Bucknell U

RF6211621 Holman Weiser Jenkins (b 19 Jan 1922, Bethlehem PA) m Apr 1955, Barbara Robinson. She, AM, PhD, UPA. Teacher.

RF62116211 Caroline Elizabeth Jenkins (b 9 Jan 1958, Philadelphia PA) m 14 Aug 1981, Paul Wesley Kreamer.

RF621162111 Heidi Elizabeth Kreamer (b 18 Nov 1983).

RF621162112 Jonathan Paul Kreamer (b 8 Aug 1985).

RF621162113 Mary Robin Kreamer (b 1 Apr 1987).

RF621162114 Catherine Faith Kreamer (b 8 Nov 1989).

RF62116212 Holman Weiser Jenkins (b 1 Apr 1959, Philadelphia PA).

RF62116213 Thomas Ellsworth Jenkins (b 17 Apr 1962, Philadelphia PA).

RF6211622 Ruth Elizabeth Jenkins (b 15 Apr 1925, Bethlehem PA) AB, Radcliffe (MA) Col.

RF621163 Ruth Elizabeth Weiser (6 Jan 1893, Mahontango Tp PA-26 May 1919, Mifflintown PA) Bur near McKees Half Falls PA.

RF6212 Josiah Weiser (2 Feb 1821-25 Aug 1849, Chapman Tp PA) m 1849, Mary Fryer. Bur Juniata Co PA.

RF6213 Jacob Weiser (3 Mar 1823-10 Oct 1887, Chapman Tp PA) m 14 Mar 1848, Margaret Niemond (14 Sep 1827-25 Feb 1903, Chapman Tp PA) Bur Juniata Co PA. Storekeeper; erected Weiser's Folly, 1873, south of Mahontango Creek.

RF62131 Melinda Weiser (30 Dec 1848-3 Oct 1919) m Edward G Shaeffer (14 Jul 1846-25 Aug 1931) Bur McKees Half Falls PA.

RF621311 E Clay Sheaffer.

RF6213111 Lillian Mae Sheaffer m Stanley C Barner Sr.

RF62131111 Leroy E Barner m Helen Victoria Trimble.

RF62132 Amanda Weiser (11 Dec 1851, Mahontango PA-12 Dec 1878) Bur Mahontango PA.

RF62133 James Weiser (10 Mar 1854-21 Aug 1920) Bur Mahontango PA. unm.

RF62134   Catherine Weiser (7 Mar 1856-21 Aug 1920) Bur Mahontango PA. unm.

RF62135   Jacob Weiser (10 May 1860-29 Jun 1933) Bur Mahontango PA. unm.

RF62136   Elinor Weiser (1863-1864).

RF62137   William Weiser (28 Jul 1864-14 Aug 1864) Bur Mahontango PA.

RF62138   Susan Weiser m Ed Long.

RF62139   Frank Weiser, unm.

RF6214   Isaac Weiser (4 Oct 1825-14 Feb 1883, Chapman Tp PA) m 8 Dec 1848, Catherine Houseworth (10 Jun 1831-22 Jun 1881) Bur Mahontango PA. Miller.

RF62141   Elizabeth Weiser (8 Mar 1849-7 Dec 1919, Chester PA) m Mar 1866, Thomas Newman (Aug 1839-23 Mar 1916) Bur Chapman PA. Farmer, Hoffers PA.

RF621411   John Newman (b Oct 1866) m Eva Leech. Bur Herndon PA.

RF6214111   Earl Newman.

RF62141111   Doris Newman m Howard Wetzel. Herndon PA.

RF62141112   Ivan Newman. Herndon PA.

RF62141113   Lila May Newman.

RF62141114   Thomas Newman.

RF62141115   Robert Newman.

RF62141116   Larry Newman. Herndon PA.

RF621412   Catherine Newman (b 26 Aug 1870, Hoffers PA) m 26 Dec 1889, Edward Straub (12 May 1864, Hoffers PA-28 Nov 1949, Herndon PA) Bur Herndon PA. Owner and editor, Herndon *Star*.

RF6214121   Mamie Ruth Straub (b 27 Oct 1892, Centerville, Snyder Co PA) m 10 Mar 1914, Clarence M Malick, MD (3 Sep 1886, Greenbrier, Northumberland Co PA-13 Sep 1955, Danville PA) Bur Herndon PA.

RF62141211   Lillian Kathryn Malick (b 20 Feb 1916, Herndon PA) m 5 Jun 1937 Nevin W Knerr (26 Mar 1912, Pillow PA-29 Feb 1968, Harrisburg PA) Bur Herndon PA.

RF621412111   Joan Yvonne Knerr (b 30 Dec 1939, Danville PA) m 16 Jun 1962, Harrisburg PA, Charles W Wentling II (b 1 Apr 1934, Harrisburg PA).

RF6214121111   Kim Louise Wentling (b 17 Mar 1964, Harrisburg PA) m 10 Sep 1988, Laurel MD, Christian Walter VandenAssem (b 3 Jan 1963, Paterson NJ).

RF62141211111   Chelsea Elizabeth VandenAssem (b 4 Jan 1990, Washington DC).

RF6214121112   Michael Charles Wentling (b 6 Oct 1967, Washington DC) m 21 Nov 1992, Nicole M Hughes (b 10 Dec 1970).

RF621412112   Don Malick Knerr (b 4 Feb 1943, Harrisburg PA) m 10 Sep 1966, Harrisburg PA, Fern Koehler (b 10 Mar 1947).

RF6214121121 Don Malick Knerr Jr (b 20 Sep 1968) m 12 Jun 1993, Ellen Stoop.

RF6214121122 Lauren Kay Knerr (b 24 Apr 1970).

RF6214121123 Steven Winfield Knerr (b 25 Oct 1975).

RF621413 Annie Newman (31 Dec 1876, Hoffers PA-2 Jun 1930, Chester PA) m George Wilson.
Bur Chapman PA.

RF62142 Jonathan H Weiser (24 Sep 1851-25 Sep 1925) m Fietta Schlegal (3 Sep 1846-20 Dec 1917).

RF621421 Ira Weiser (11 oct 1875-1 Oct 1908).

RF621422 Thomas Edward Weiser (13 Oct 1880-14 Dec 1881).

RF621423 Annie Catherine Weiser (15 Nov 1885-22 Dec 1958) m Issac Dewitt Kline (10 Feb 1884-14 Feb 1944).

RF6214231 Ruth Irma Kline (5 Jun 1904-15 Dec 1946) m Chester Keller.

RF62142311 Chester Keller Jr. Williamsport PA.

RF62142312 Donald Keller. Freeburg PA.

RF62142313 Ned G Keller. Camp Hill PA.

RF6214232 Mary Elizabeth Kline (b 5 Jun 1907) m Melvin Broome.

RF62142321 Melvin Paul Broome m 7 Jun 1949, Annie Sue Kline.

RF621423211 Gail Elaine Broome (b 18 Jan 1954).

RF6214233 Paul Cyrus Kline (b 16 Sep 1909) m 14 Oct 1933, Florence Irene Keithan.

RF62142331 Charlotte Ann Kline (b 15 Nov 1936) m James C Foulke.

RF62142332 Richard Paul Kline (b May 1940).

RF62142333 Lois Kay Kline (b 21 Nov 1945).

RF6214234 Francis Odea Kline (b 31 Dec 1911) m Thomas Goodley. Chester PA.

RF62142341 Donald Goodley.

RF6214235 Ida Nadine Kline (b 28 Nov 1914) m Beldon Neidig.

RF62142351 Joan Neidig m James Mertz, Sunbury PA.

RF62142352 David Neidig (b 1941) Sunbury PA.

RF62143 Daniel Weiser (15 Jan 1859-1 Feb 1906) m 9 Nov 1889, Mary Shirk. Bur Manontango PA.

RF621431 Stella Weiser m Dressler.

RF62144   Emma Weiser (6 Nov 1860-25 Sep 1910, Independence PA) m Wellington Herold (12 Jan 1847-14 Jan 1924, Independence PA) Bur Chapman PA.

RF621441   Milton Herold (3 Dec 1888-Dec 1918, Herndon PA).

RF6214411   Catherine Herold (b 18 Mar 1910, Sunbury PA) m Dell Schoomaker. Williamsport PA.

RF6214412   Irene Herold (b 14 Dec 1910, Sunbury PA) m Herman Stettler.

RF6214413   George C Herold (b 22 Oct 1913) Sunbury PA.

RF6214414   Paul Herold (b 15 Nov 1915) m Bell Enders.

RF6214415   Ruth Herold (b Jan 1917, Herndon PA) m James Duff. Sunbury PA.

RF6214416   Betty Herold (b May 1919, Lewisburg PA) m Fred Fisher.

RF62144161   Fred Fisher.

RF62144162   Betty Fisher.

RF621442   Eva May Herold (b 22 Jun 1893) m George Paige in 1912. Bur Chapman PA.

RF621443   Annie Herold (b 14 Nov 1894, Chapman PA) m 1916, Paul Lenig (26 Jan 1895, Paxinos PA-10 Nov 1951, Sunbury PA) Bur Grubbs Church, near McKees Half Falls PA.

RF6214431   Robert Lenig (b 14 Feb 1917, Chapman PA) m Beatrice Aucker, Selinsgrove PA.

RF62144311   Duane Lenig (b 1 May 1946).

RF62144312   Janice Lenig (b 28 Jun 1951).

RF6214432   Lawrence Lenig (b 5 Nov 1918, Chapman PA) m Jun 1947, Ann Barnett.

RF62144321   Larry Lenig (b 20 Sep 1948, Dallas TX).

RF62144322   Richard Lenig (b 24 Mar 1954, Dallas TX).

RF621444   Nelson Herold (16 Aug 1896, Chapman PA-1950, Sunbury PA) m Barbara Lenig.

RF6214441   Maurice Herold (b 12 Jul 1915) m Mary Ellen Bryan.

RF62144411   Michael Herold (b 1950).

RF62144412   Marcia Herold (b 1944).

RF62145   Jacob Weiser (b 1862) m Sarah Harold (1856-1920) Independence PA.

RF62146   Catherine Weiser (1865-1909) m George W Attinger (1862-1944) Bur Chapman, Snyder Co PA.

RF621461   William Attinger, unm. Bur Shamokin Road PA.

RF621462   Charles Attinger m. Sunbury PA.

RF6214621   Lithia Attinger.

RF6214622   Elaine Attinger.

RF6214623   Betty Attinger.

RF6214624   Horace Attinger.

RF6214625   Paul Attinger.

RF6214626   William Attinger.

RF6214627   Charles Attinger.

RF621463   Roy Attinger (b 1897) m Hope Marie Herr (b Sep 1898) RD, Herndon PA.

RF6214631   Helen Attinger (d) Bur Herndon PA.

RF6214632   Reginald Attinger (b Mar 1917) m Elma Lebo, RD, Sunbury PA.

RF62146321   Lonnie Attinger (b 1940).

RF62146322   Wayne Attinger.

RF62146323   Terry Attinger.

RF62146324   Dale Attinger (b 1953).

RF6214633   Mary Attinger (b Nov 1920) m Charles Daniels, RD, Herndon PA.

RF62146331   Betty Daniels (b 1938).

RF62146332   Evely Daniels (b 1940).

RF62146333   Stanford Daniels (1944-1944) Bur Red Cross PA.

RF6214634 PA.   Ernest Attinger (b Jul 1921) m Sep 1945, Rene Deibler (b 20 Mar 1928) New Cumberland PA.

RF62146341   Joyce Attinger (b 19 May 1946, Herndon PA).

RF62146342   Janet Attinger (b 26 Jun 1947, Herndon PA).

RF62146343   Judy Attinger (b 31 Oct 1951, Mechanicsburg PA).

RF6214635   Mark Attinger (b Mar 1923) m York PA.

RF62146351   Marlin Attinger (b 1944).

RF6214636   Edith Attinger (dy).

RF6214637   Evelyn Attinger (b 1925) m Allen Snyder. Richfield PA.

RF62146371   Raymond Snyder (b 1942).

RF62146372   Barbara Snyder (b 1944).

RF62146373   Carol Snyder (b 1945).

RF62146374   Grace Snyder (b 1947).

RF62146375   Allen Ernest Snyder (b 1954).

RF6214638   Grace Attinger (b 1927) m Earl Erdman, RD, Herndon PA.

RF62146381   Bryant Erdman (b 1954).

RF62146382   Kim Erdman (b 1956).

RF6214639   Effie Attinger (b Nov 1929) m Raymond Lahr. Richfield PA.

RF62146391   Fay Lahr (b 1947).

RF62146392   Ronald Lahr (b 1948).

RF62146393   Donna Lahr (b 1949).

RF62146394   Lester Lahr (b 1950).

RF62146395   Jean Lahr (b 1951).

RF62146396   Thomas Lahr (1952-1953) Bur Red Cross PA.

RF62146397   Raymond Lahr Jr (b 1953).

RF62146398   Mark Lahr (b Dec 1959).

RF621463A   Bertha Attinger (b 1934) m Sev Laskowski. Harrisburg PA.

RF621463A1   Kevin Laskowski (b 1951).

RF621463A2   Rickey Laskowski (b 1952).

RF621463A3   Tania Laskowski (b 1959).

RF621463B   Jean Attinger (b 1936) m William Buffington, RD, Millersburg PA.

RF621463B1   Karen Buffington (b 1954).

RF621463B2   Randy Buffington (1955-1955).

RF621463B3   Kathy Buffington (b 1956).

RF621463B4   Steve Buffington (b 1958).

RF621463B55   Shirley Buffington (b Nov 1959).

RF621463C   Carlos Attinger (b Apr 1938) m Nancy Benner, York PA.

RF621463C1   Keith Attinger (b 1957).

RF621463C2   Jeffrey Attinger (b 1958).

RF621463D   Barry Attinger (b 1941) unm. RD, Herndon PA.

RF621464 Ralph Attinger (b 6 Nov 1899, Herndon) m Katie Goodman (31 May 1907-6 Aug 1945) Bur Dalmatia PA. Linglestown PA.

RF6214641 Lillian Attinger (b 18 Dec 1924) m Ernest Nye. RD, Linglestown PA.

RF62146411 Lucille Nye (b 17 Jun 1942).

RF62146412 Nancy Nye (b 3 Sep 1946).

RF62146413 Susan Nye (b 19 Jun 1949).

RF62146414 Ernest Ray Nye (b 25 Feb 1957).

RF6214642 Robert Attinger (b 20 Aug 1927, Red Cross PA) m Betty Eutzy (b 3 Apr 1928) RD, Linglestown PA.

RF62146421 Sandra Lee Attinger (b 12 Jan 1946).

RF62146422 Dorothy Mae Attinger (b 11 Jul 1949).

RF62146423 Robert Attinger Jr (b 11 Jul 1949).

RF6214643 George Attinger (6 Mar 1931-1954, Huntingdon PA) m Donna Burdge. Bur Hurlock PA.

RF62146431 George Ernest Attinger Jr (b 1951).

RF62146432 Stephen Attinger (b 1952).

RF62147 Henry Weiser (d MI).

RF621471 Daughter.

RF62148 Benton Weiser (b Apr 1854, PA) m Niles MI, Lydia (b Aug 1856, PA).

RF62149 Sally Weiser m Joseph Lipp.

RF6215 John Weiser (27 Nov 1827-between 1850 and 1860) unm.

RF6216 William Wesley Weiser (6 Mar 1831-8 Jan 1836).

RF6217 Martin Moor Weiser (b 7 Apr 1833) Lost.

RF6218 Uriah Peter Weiser (11 Apr 1835-6 Apr 1911, Sunbury PA) m 12 Jul 1855, Mary Kratzer (d 22 Dec 1878, Herndon PA) Bur Mahontango PA. Hotel owner.

RF62181 Sarah Jane Weiser (5 Oct 1855, Snyder Co PA-23 Dec 1943, Sunbury PA) m Washington C Reichenbach (6 Nov 1848-13 Oct 1903, Northumberland PA) Civil War: USA, 208th Reg, Co Ca. Bur Northumberland PA.

RF621811 Arthur William Milton Dunn (b 21 May 1875) Glendale CA.

RF621812 Thomas Wesley Reichenbach (10 Apr 1879-11 Jan 1909, Northumberland PA) m Jennie Irene Kreps (b 16 Apr 1885 Parde PA) Spanish-American War: 10th Inf, Co Ca. Bur Northumberland PA.

RF6218121 Martha May Reichenbach (b 28 Jan 1904, Northumberland PA) m 24 Dec 1930, Newberry PA, Arthur Ervin Bingaman (b 14 Feb 1908, Lewisburg PA) Northumberland PA.

RF62181211   Ronald Irvin Bingaman (b 24 Jul 1934, Northumberland PA) m 1954, Sunbury PA, Rose Marie Schultz (b 2 Feb 1937).

RF62181212   Wesley Howard Bingaman (b 26 Jan 1957, Sunbury PA).

RF62181213   John Arthur Bingaman (b 23 Jul 1959, Sunbury PA).

RF621813   William Banks Reichenbach (23 Apr 1882-16 Dec 1907) Bur Northumberland PA. unm.

RF621814   Howard Morris Reichenbach (11 Mar 1885-16 Sep 1941, Tower City PA) m 24 Oct 1909, Algie Kniss. Bur Tower City PA.

RF6218141   Francis Reichenbach (b 1 Jul 1911) m Millersburg PA.

RF621815   Margie May Reichenbach (24 Feb 1887-25 Jan 1909) Bur Northumberland PA. unm.

RF621816   Elizabeth Reichenbach (4 Apr 1889-8 Mar 1906) Bur Northumberland PA. unm.

RF621817   George Weiser Reichenbach (7 Aug 1891-28 Jul 1926, Coatesville PA) m. WWI: 68th T Cavalry. Bur Northumberland PA.

RF62182   John Weiser (8 Nov 1857, Mahontango PA-10 Mar 1863).

RF62183   William Wesley Weiser (21 Nov 1860, Mahontango PA-3 Mar 1935, Groton CT) m 30 Dec 1890, Sarah Jennie Bixler (d 16 Jan 1932) Bur New London CT.

RF621831   James Russell Weiser (30 Sep 1893-3 Sep 1960, St Petersburg FL) m 1) 16 Jun 1921, Eshcol PA, Florence Randall (12 Apr 1899-6 Jul 1932); m 2) 29 Jul 1933, Phyllis McCann (28 Sep 1906-2 Jan 1969, St Petersburg FL).

RF6218311   Doris Ellen Weiser (21 Feb 1926-16 Jan 1927).

RF6218312   Earl Randall Weiser (b 17 Jun 1928) m Geraldine Blanchard.

RF621832   Margaret Helen Weiser (b 14 Oct 1894, NY) m Howard Mcafee. St Petersburg FL.

RF621833   Laurence Arthur Weiser (d Dec 1898, NY).

RF621834   Katherine Elizabeth Weiser (4 Jan 1899, NY-18 Feb 1969, Tampa FL) m   Turner. St Petersburg FL.

RF621835   Clarence William (Charles) Weiser (b 7 Oct 1903, ME) St Petersburg FL.

RF621836   Mary Eleanor Weiser (b 2 Oct 1907, ME) m   Romanella. St Petersburg FL.

RF62184   Mary Priscilla Weiser (22 Apr 1862, Mahontango PA-23 Oct 1916, Philadelphia PA) m 1) Robert Ross Zerbe (d 1888) m 2) Carlisle PA, William Mcatee (d) She bur Philadelphia PA; Zerbe bur Harrisburg PA.

RF621841   Robert Ross Zerbe (Mcatee) (24 May 1886, Harrisburg PA-4 Feb 1967) m 22 Aug 1916, Cornwell's Heights PA, Anna Veronica McFadden (b 9 Dec 1892) Philadelphia PA.

RF6218411   Donald Robert Mcatee (b 22 Dec 1925, Philadelphia PA) m 20 Jul 1946, Jacksonville Naval Air Station Chapel FL, Constance Marie Maguire.

RF62184111   Suzanne Marie Mcatee (b 13 Jul 1947, Philadelphia PA).

RF62184112   Patricia Mcatee (b 28 Nov 1948, Philadelphia PA).

RF62185   Samuel Sylvester Weiser (5 Nov 1864, Mahontango PA-9 Oct 1918, Harrisburg PA) m 15 May 1887, Ella C Cannon (d 31 Oct 1921, Lemoyne PA) Bur Harrisburg PA.

RF621851   Mary C Weiser (b 2 Nov 1890, Harrisburg PA) m Earl Stone (d 1934) RD, Etters PA.

RF621852   Warren M Weiser (25 Apr 1889, Harrisburg PA-May 1950, Elizabethtown PA) m. Bur Highspire PA.

RF62186   Emma Margaret Weiser (b 15 Feb 1868, Mahontango PA) m 21 Jan 1884, Philadelphia PA, George Agustus Gohl (5 Aug 1865, Harrisburg PA-27 Jul 1922, Fishing Creek Valley PA) Owner and operator of bakery, Harrisburg PA. Bur Harrisburg PA.

RF621861   Norman Sylvester Gohl (12 Aug 1886, Harrisburg PA-21 Feb 1888, Harrisburg PA) Bur Harrisburg PA.

RF621862   George Agustus Gohl Jr (6 Dec 1888, Harrisburg PA-15 Nov 1950, Lebanon PA) unm. Bur Harrisburg PA.

RF621863   Frederick Weiser Gohl (21 May 1891, Harrisburg PA-28 Aug 1959, Harrisburg PA) m 26 Jan 1913, Oil City PA, Vina Blanche Forshey (15 Jun 1890, Blair Co PA-1 Nov 1957, Harrisburg PA) Bur Harrisburg PA.

RF6218631   Emma Vaneta Gohl (b 6 Jul 1914, Williamsburg PA) m 28 Jul 1934, Westminster MD, John J Cobaugh (b 21 Jan 1913, Chambersburg PA) She, interior decorator; co-owner Windsor House, Harrisburg PA. He, WWII, USN, Chief Electrician's Mate S U6, USNR Third Fleet, electrical contractor, Harrisburg PA.

RF62186311   Nancy Rae Cobaugh (b 29 Jul 1935, Harrisburg PA) m 28 May 1955, Harrisburg PA, James W Middaugh (b 17 Aug 1929, Harrisburg PA) 12th Inf Reg Med Co 4th Div, 1951-53. Salesman.

RF621863111   Kim Doreen Middaugh (b 12 Jul 1959, Harrisburg PA).

RF6218632   Frederick Weiser Gohl Jr (b 7 Jul 1915, Harrisburg PA) unm WWII: USA, Inspector, Phoenix Iron and Steel Co, Harrisburg PA.

RF6218633   Earl Forrest Gohl (b 24 Sep 1917, Fishing Creek Valley PA) m 15 Nov 1945, Harrisburg PA, Mary Elizabeth Baker (b 2 Sep 1923, Harrisburg PA) He, co-owner Windsor House, interior decorator, Harrisburg PA.

RF62186331   Mary Kathryn Gohl (b 6 Dec 1947, Memphis TN).

RF62186332   Earl Forrest Gohl II (b 15 Apr 1950, Harrisburg PA).

RF6218634   Harold Dewain Gohl (b 23 Oct 1919, Fishing Creek Valley PA) unm WWII; Electrician of inter-communication systems, Harrisburg PA.

RF6218635   Betty Virginia Gohl (b 26 Oct 1922, Harrisburg PA) m 27 Jun 1942, Harrisburg PA, Roger Henry Williams (b 12 Jun 1914, Carlisle PA) USA; Employee, United Telephone Co, Harrisburg PA.

RF62186351   Kurt Ralph Williams (b 12 Sep 1951, Harrisburg PA).

RF62186352   Craig Frederick Williams (b 2 Oct 1953, Harrisburg PA).

RF6218636   Barbara Ann Gohl (b 18 Oct 1928, Harrisburg PA) m 15 May 1954, New Cumberland PA, Clifford Paul Lowe (b 24 Jun 1929, Highspire PA) 452nd Div Batt B 7th Army. Harrisburg PA.

RF62186361   Jeffrey Hale Lowe (b 23 Jun 1955, Harrisburg PA).

RF62187   Waldo Wittenmyer Weiser (2 Apr 1872, Chapman PA-Oct 1952, York PA) unm Bur York Co PA.

RF62188   Minnie Metilda Weiser (31 Sep 1870, Mahontango PA-9 Apr 1871, Mahontango PA) Bur Mahontango PA.

RF62189   David M Weiser (1 Aug 1875, Mahontango PA-1 Apr 1932, Harrisburg PA) m 19 Aug 1895, Harrisburg PA, Sarah A Henderson (6 Oct 1876, Green Park PA-3 Jun 1953, Harrisburg PA) Bur Harrisburg PA.

RF621891   Miriam Frances Weiser (b 17 Sep 1899, Harrisburg PA) m 31 Dec 1923, Philadelphia PA, Lester H Butler (b 17 May 1892, Harrisburg PA) Camp Hill PA.

RF621892   Esther Gladys Weiser (9 Apr 1903, Harrisburg PA-18 Apr 1952, Lemoyne PA) m 1919, John A Schaeffer. Bur New Cumberland PA.

RF6218921   John David Schaeffer (14 Feb 1920, Lemoyne PA-17 June 1944, India) Transport Command, China-Burma Area; Crew Chief 1st Transport Grp 13th Squadron. Bur New Cumberland PA.

RF621893   Iverna Weiser (b 23 Oct 1911, Eddington PA) unm.

RF6219   Catherine Jane Weiser (18 Apr 1837-23 Oct 1909, Seven Points PA) m Peter M Reitz (8 Oct 1819-13 Feb 1897) Bur Wolf's Cross Roads Lutheran Church.

RF62191   Urias P Reitz (30 Sep 1856, Seven Points PA-17 Jan 1943) m Clara Farnsworth (1857-1927, Sunbury PA) Bur Irish Valley PA.

RF621911   Annie Reitz (16 Aug 1885, Seven Points PA-8 Jan 1959, Seven Points PA) m Christopher Fasold (30 Jan 1880-1 Feb 1958, Seven Points PA) Bur Stoneyton PA.

RF621912   Bessie Reitz (Mar 1887, Seven Points PA-Oct 1952, Clearwater FL) m Roy Dunkleberger. Bur Clearwater FL.

RF6219121   Mable Dunkleberger (b 3 Jul 1920, Sunbury PA) m Robert Wallace. Sarasota FL.

RF621913   Pearl Reitz (b 1891, Seven Points PA) m Nathaniel Kerstetter. Lewisburg PA.

RF6219131   Ellis K Kerstetter.

RF6219132   Leroy Kerstetter.

RF6219133   Doris Kerstetter.

RF621914   Charles A Reitz (1893, Seven Point PA-Jan 1960, MI) Bur MI.

RF6219141   Catherine Reitz.

RF6219142   Robert Reitz.

RF6219143   Madaline Reitz.

RF6219144   Doris Reitz m Richard Cochenour. Romulus MI.

RF6219145   Kenneth Reitz.

RF6219146   Jerry Reitz.

RF621915   Ellis Gordon Reitz (b 12 Nov 1895, Seven Points PA) m Maude Delp (b 30 Jan 1898).

RF6219151   Clair Arthur Reitz (b 29 Jan 1920, Sunbury PA) m 1940, Martha Raker (b 6 Jan 1921)
Sunbury PA.

RF62191511   Nancy Reitz (b 8 Feb 1941, Sunbury PA).

RF62191512   Judy Reitz (b 5 Nov 1942, Sunbury PA).

RF62191513   Ronald Reitz (b 5 Apr 1949, Sunbury PA).

RF62191514   Eric Reitz (b 11 Sep 1954, Sunbury PA).

RF6219152   Goldie Arlene Reitz (b 18 Mar 1923, Sunbury PA) m Frank Ritchie.

RF62191521   Iova Ritchie (b 5 Jun 1940, Sunbury PA).

RF62191522   Jerry Ritchie (b 14 Jan 1942, Sunbury PA).

RF62191523   James Ritchie (b 21 May 1944, Sunbury PA).

RF62191524   Carson Ritchie (b 3 Jul 1948, Sunbury PA).

RF6219153   Betty May Reitz (12 Nov 1925, Sunbury PA-12 Nov 1925, Sunbury PA) Bur
Northumberland Co PA.

RF62192   David C Reitz (23 Apr 1859-26 Jul 1936, Sioux City IA) Hotel business.

RF62193   Jonathan Edward Reitz (25 May 1861-5 Jun 1917) m Sara Jane   (1863-1932).

RF62194   Daniel N Reitz (21 Nov 1864-3 Aug 1937) m Clara A   (6 Sep 1865-17 Aug 1915).

RF62195   Anna Rebecca Reitz (6 May 1869-7 Oct 1947, Seven Points PA) m Fraser Wolf.

RF62196   Katie Jane Reitz (18 Jul 1872-29 Aug 1938) m Herbert Miller.

RF62197   Laura Weiser Reitz (11 Mar 1878-12 Aug 1938) m Bert Williams.

RF621A   David R Weiser (1 Dec 1839-31 Jan 1893) m Rebecca Krotzer (26 Aug 1847-24 Jul 1897)
Bur McKees Half Falls PA.

RF621A1   Minnie Catherine Weiser (25 Aug 1864-4 May 1926, Millersburg PA) m Levi A Dressler
(1 Oct 1863-28 Aug 1920, Millersburg PA) Farmer and shoemaker. Bur Millersburg PA.

RF621A11   Jennie Dressler (16 Apr 1883, McKees Half Falls, Chapman Tp, Snyder Co PA-June 1933)
m Albert Christian. Bur Millersburg PA.

RF621A111   Jay C Christian (b 4 Mar 1903, Millersburg PA) m 24 Nov 1924, Hegins PA, Bessie
Klinger (b 10 Jun 1902, Elizabethville PA) Millersburg PA.

RF621A112   Lester C Christian m Clara Michael.

RF621A1121   Betty Christian m   Sloan.

RF621A113   Lloyd Franklin Christian m Ruth Neidigh.

RF621A1131   William Christian.

RF621A114   Clair E Christian (b 29 Jul 1910) m Mary Kapp.

RF621A115   Florence Christian (b 17 Jul 1911) m James Heffner.

RF621A1151   Wallace G Heffner.

RF621A116   Alma Christian m Robert Worth.

RF621A117   Graydon W Christian m Ruth Rothermel Grocer. Sunbury PA.

RF621A1171   Helen M Christian m Fred Baston.

RF621A12   Norman Dressler (1885-5 Mar 1890) Bur McKees Half Falls PA.

RF621A13   Arthur Dressler (8 Jun 1887-24 Aug 1934, Millersburg PA) m Myrl Snyder (b 3 Jan 1891, Upper Paxton Tp PA) Bur Millersburg PA.

RF621A131   Ruth Dressler (21 Jun 1908, Millersburg PA-26 Oct 1948, Brooklyn NY) m Karl Beyer. Bur Millersburg PA.

RF621A1311   Ann Elizabeth Beyer (b 14 Jul 1947).

RF621A14   Clair Eugene Dressler (b 11 Jan 1891, Chapman Tp, Snyder Co PA) m 1) Kathryn Brown (17 Nov 1893, Herndon PA-7 Aug 1937, Millersburg PA); m 2) 9 Oct 1943, Millersburg PA, L Mabel Straub (b 3 Nov 1900, Berrysburg PA) Brown bur Millersburg PA.

RF621A141   Marlin J Dressler (b Mar 1912, Millersburg PA) m 1) 1930, Lykens PA, Mary Pearl Nichilo (d 13 June 1954, Jacksonville FL); m 2) Gertrude Sykes. Nichilo bur Jacksonville FL. Jacksonville FL.

RF621A1411   Dolores Dressler (b 1931, Millersburg PA) m GA, John P Thompson. Jacksonville FL.

RF621A14111   Rebecca Marlene Thompson (b Jacksonville FL).

RF621A14112   John Thompson (b Jacksonville FL).

RF621A1412   James R Dressler (b 1933, Millersburg PA) m 1954, Florence Lasco. Attorney, Cocoa FL.

RF621A14121   Donna Dressler (b 1955, FL).

RF621A14122   Theresa Dressler (b 1957, FL).

RF621A14123   James Dressler (b 6 Jan 1960, FL).

RF621A1413   Patricia Dressler (b 1937, Millersburg PA) m Robert E Hill. Jacksonville FL.

RF621A142   Robert E Dressler (b 29 Jul 1914, Millersburg PA) m Spring Glen PA, Lillian Klinger. Halifax PA.

RF621A1421   Robert E Dressler Jr (b Mar 1948).

RF621A143   Gladys M Dressler (b 12 Jan 1922, Millersburg PA) m 23 Dec 1949, Millersburg PA, Bruce S Wells. Insurance agent, Camp Hill PA.

RF621A1431   Barbara Wells (b 6 Aug 1951, Indianapolis IN).

RF621A1432   Linda Ann Wells (b 25 Dec 1953, Harrisburg PA).

RF621A15   Marcia Louise Dressler (b 22 Jul 1893, Chapman Tp, Snyder Co PA) m 12 Feb 1910, Millersburg PA, Lloyd Lehman (17 Oct 1889-19 Jun 1956, Millersburg PA) Bur Millersburg PA.

RF621A151   Evelyn Lehman (b 24 Aug 1911, Millersburg PA) m June 1939, Millersburg PA, William Dunker. New York NY.

RF621A1511   William Weiser Dunker (b 16 Jan 1943, New York NY).

RF621A1512   Susan Eleanor Dunker (b 21 Jun 1947, New York NY).

RF621A152   Ralph Lehman (b 14 Sep 1913, Millersburg PA) m 16 Dec 1939, Millersburg PA, Eleanor Wilson. Shoe salesman, Millersburg PA.

RF621A1521   Todd Wilson Lehman (b 30 Apr 1941, Harrisburg PA).

RF621A1522   John Vincent Lehman (b 22 Jan 1944, Harrisburg PA).

RF621A1523   Marcia Louise Lehman (b 18 Jul 1947, Harrisburg PA).

RF621A153   Eleanor Lehman (b 4 Apr 1917, Millersburg PA) m 12 Feb 1935, Mercersburg PA, Charles Sheetz (b 9 Oct 1910) Auditor, Millersburg PA.

RF621A1531   Charles Lehman Sheetz (b 5 Jul 1937, Harrisburg PA) Shippensburg (PA) Col. Teacher.

RF621A1532   Jonathan Weiser Sheetz (b 13 Jan 1948, Harrisburg PA).

RF621A1533   Christina Rose Sheetz (b 19 Dec 1949, Harrisburg PA).

RF621A1534   Gretchen Abigal Sheetz (b 3 Feb 1959, Harrisburg PA).

RF621A16   Weiser Lewis Dressler (1886, Snyder Col PA-1900) Bur McKees Half Falls PA.

RF621A17   John McKinley Dressler (9 May 1897, Snyder Co PA-25 Jun 1967, Williamsburg PA) m 28 Jun 1919, Millersburg PA, Bertha Mae Shoop (19 Sep 1897, Enders PA-20 Dec 1981, Millersburg PA) Bur Millersburg PA.

*RF621A171   John Henry Dressler (b 21 Apr 1920, Millersburg PA) m 28 Apr 1943, Hampton VA, Helen Constance Hale (b 4 Mar 1921, Hampton VA) He, BS, Lebanon Valley Col, 1941; MBA, Syracuse U, 1963. US Civil Service, Ft Monroe VA, 1941-73; Commissioner of Revenue, Poquoson VA, 1977-85.

RF621A1711   Anne Hale Dressler (b 25 Jun 1944, Hampton VA) Accountant, Alexandria VA.

RF621A1712   Margaret Lee Dressler (b 27 Apr 1949, Hampton VA) AB, Appalachian U, 1970. Teacher, Tabb VA.

RF621A172   Gloria M Dressler (b 21 May 1931, Millersburg PA) Music teacher, Philadelphia PA.

RF621A18   Allen Dressler (1900-dy, Millersburg PA).

RF621A19   Ester M Dressler (9 Jan 1900-19 Jun 1957, Millersburg PA) m Richard R Miller.

RF621A191   Miller m Thomas Long.

RF621A192   Richard H Miller.

RF621A193   Donald E Miller.

RF621A194   Jack L Miller.

RF621A1A   Violet Gertrude Dressler (14 Sep 1902, Millersburg PA-1 Jun 1969, Harrisburg PA) m 5 Apr 1919, Millersburg PA, Cataldo Muggio.

RF621A1A1   Joseph Levi Muggio (31 Oct 1919, Millersburg PA-25 Apr 1994, Millersburg PA) m 19 Nov 1937, Hagerstown MD, Pauline Elizabeth Troutman (b 19 May 1921, Upper Paxton Tp, Dauphin Co PA).

RF621A1A11   Joseph Henry Muggio (b 18 Apr 1938, Harrisburg PA) m 17 Jun 1961, Darby Anne Daniels (b 21 Apr 1938, Harrisburg PA).

RF621A1A12   Bonia Marie Muggio (b 22 Oct 1939) m 1) William Mace; m 2) Robert Barber.

RF621A1A121   Bari Muggio.

RF621A1A122   Cynthia Mace.

RF621A1A123   David Mace.

RF621A1A13   Michael Jon Muggio (b 27 Feb 1947) m Nancy   .

RF621A1A14   Anthony Gene Muggio (b 25 Jun 1955) m Barbara Wertz.

RF621A1A141   Tony C Muggio (b 1 Nov 1979).

RF621A1A2   Kathryn Madaline Muggio (b 25 Aug 1921, Millersburg PA) m 1) Nov 1943, Millersburg PA, Harold Heinbaugh (d 20 Aug 1944); m 2) 2 Nov 1946, Millersburg PA, Elwood (Nip) Rothermal (13 Aug 1920-14 Jun 1983) WWII: Heinbaugh, Pilot.

RF621A1A21   Harold Herbert (Bud) Heinbaugh Jr (b 24 Apr 1944) m 1) 22 Feb 1964, Palmyra PA, Claudia Boris, div; m 2) Patricia Manning (b 4 Nov 1940).

RF621A1A211   Kathryn Heinbaugh (b 27 Jan 1967).

RF621A1A212   Erik Heinbaugh (b 16 Jul 1968).

RF621A1A213   Heather Heinbaugh (b 29 Jun 1970).

RF621A1A22   Donald Rothermal (b 2 Jun 1947, Harrisburg PA) m Sandra Viccaro (b 12 Mar 1944, Harrisburg PA).

RF621A1A221   Tammy Rothermal (b 29 Sep 1968, Harrisburg PA).

RF621A1A222   Lisa Diann Rothermal (b 27 Feb 1973, Harrisburg PA).

RF621A1A23   Linda Rothermal (b 6 Feb 1951, Harrisburg PA).

RF621A1A231   Ryan McKinley (b 17 Jun 1974, Pittsburgh PA).

RF621A1A232   Kyle McKinley (b 1 Mar 1977, Lancaster PA).

RF621A1A3   Sabelle Muggio (b 4 Oct 1923, Millersburg PA) m 26 Apr 1941, Millersburg PA, Joseph Sherman Baker (12 Apr 1922, Millersburg PA-26 Apr 1987, Millersburg PA).

RF621A1A31   William L Baker (b 27 Jan 1942, Harrisburg PA) m Linda Hanna.

RF621A1A311   Michael Baker (b 23 Feb 1965).

RF621A1A312   Susan Baker (b 7 Jul 1967).

RF621A1A313   Jessica Baker (b 24 Mar 1970).

RF621A1A32   Joette D Baker (b 3 Jul 1944, Harrisburg PA) m 1) Ray Weaver; m 2) Leon Wells.

RF621A1A321   Wendy S Weaver (b 15 Sep 1962) m Jordan Sander.

RF621A1A322   Gary R Weaver (b 17 Aug 1965).

RF621A1A323   Steven D Weaver (b 18 Aug 1967).

RF621A1A324   Jodi A Weaver (b 17 Mar 1970).

RF621A1A33   Judy E Baker (b 26 Apr 1946, Harrisburg PA) m 25 Dec 1964, Larry Snyder.

RF621A1A331   Douglas Snyder (b 28 Jan 1965).

RF621A1A332   Tara Snyder.

RF621A1A34   Stephanie D Baker (b 24 Aug 1958, Harrisburg PA) m   Wentzel.

RF621A1A341   Ryan M Wentzel (b 9 Aug 1980).

RF621A1A4   Lois Marie Muggio (b 11 Nov 1925, Millersburg PA) m 26 Nov 1946, Millersburg PA, Frederick Carl Beuchle (6 Jan 1924, West Bend IA-27 Dec 1990, Lebanon PA).

RF621A1A41   Carolyn Marie Beuchle (b 23 Feb 1952, Panama Canal Zone) m 20 Jun 1970, Palmyra PA, James Andrew Dibert (b 25 Oct 1942, Altoona PA).

RF621A1A411   Kristin Marie Dibert (b 28 Jul 1972, Philadelphia PA) m 22 Jun 1991, Lebanon PA, Timothy Garvey.

RF621A1A42   Rebecca Ann Beuchle (b 19 May 1956, Harrisburg PA) m 1) 17 Apr 1976, Lebanon PA, Robert Kling, div; m 2) 22 Dec 1979, Lebanon PA, Joseph Francis Arnold, div.

RF621A1A421   Gretchen Amelia Arnold (b 7 Feb 1981, Hershey PA).

RF621A1A5   Janet Marcia Muggio (b 4 Sep 1927, Dauphin PA) m 9 Mar 1946, Leroy Walter Chubb (b 14 Jun 1918, Millersburg PA).

RF621A1A51   Beverly Elaine Chubb (b 2 Oct 1946, Harrisburg PA) m 19 Dec 1962,   Dreker (11 Nov 1943-1995).

RF621A1A511   Mark Dreker.

RF621A1A52   Todd Douglas Chubb (b 29 Aug 1964, Harrisburg PA) m 26 May 1990, Christine Marie Reichard (b 2 Jun 1965).

RF621A1A6   Thomas James Muggio (b 27 Aug 1930, Baltimore MD) m 1) 25 Jul 1953, Millersburg PA, Joyce Witmer, div; m 2) 3 Dec 1977, Millersburg PA, Gloria D Spidel Whitmire Blose.

RF621A1A61   Angela M Muggio (b 5 Nov 1961, Harrisburg PA) m Keith Leitzel.

RF621A1A611   Jessica Leitzel.

RF621A1A7   Ralph Eugene Muggio (b 15 Jan 1933, Millersburg PA) m 10 Aug 1957, Millersburg PA, Peggy C Witmer(b 3 Jan 1941, Harrisburg PA) div.

RF621A1A71   Tommye Jean Muggio (b 11 Jan 1958, Harrisburg PA) m Fred M Margerum (b 6 Nov 1953).

RF621A1A8   Florence Fairlee Muggio (b 26 Jan 1936, Millersburg PA) m 5 Mar 1955, Hagerstown PA, Donald L Underkoffler (b 3 Sep 1931, Lykens PA).

RF621A1A81   Donna Lee Underkoffler (b 24 Oct 1955, Harrisburg PA) m 1) Craig Sheesley (b 21 Jul 1950) div; m 2) Robert Minck (b 21 Dec 1947, York PA).

RF621A1A811   Michell L Sheesley (b 23 Aug 1974, Harrisburg PA).

RF621A1A812   Erik B Minck (b 30 Jun 1980, Hershey PA).

RF621A1A82   Shari Lyn Underkoffler (b 13 Sep 1962, Harrisburg PA) m Robert G Darling.

RF621A1A821   Natalie Lea Darling (b 15 May 1989).

RF621A1A9   Larry William Muggio (b 16 Feb 1939, Millersburg PA) m 29 Jun 1957, Mary Marie Boyer (b 7 May 1939).

RF621A1A91   Stacie Marie Muggio (b 17 Jun 1960, Pottsville PA) m 1) John Lucas; m 2) Terry Bordner.

RF621A1A911   Johnny William Lucas.

RF621A1A912   Cory David Lucas.

RF621A1A92   Larry William Muggio Jr (b 22 May 1965, Pottsville PA) m 1) 18 Jun 1987, Williamstown PA, Judy Massari, div; m 2) 31 Mar 1990, Jodi Underkoffler.

RF621A1AA   Harold Lamar (Mugs) Muggio (b 9 Jul 1940, Millersburg PA) m 16 Nov 1962, Charlotte Miller, div.

RF621A1AA1   Pamela Muggio (b 1 Jun 1963) m Joel Filius (b 15 Apr 1963).

RF621A1AA11   Lauren Filius (b 3 Dec 1987).

RF621A1AA12   Jessica Filius (b 23 May 1989).

RF621A1AA2   Kristine Muggio (b 24 Mar 1972).

RF621A1B   Kathryn M Dressler (21 Dec 1904, Millersburg PA-5 Nov 1952, Millersburg PA) m 1922, Millersburg PA, Earl Fralick. Bur Millersburg PA.

RF621A1B1   Ruth M Fralick (16 Feb 1923, Millersburg PA-22 Mar 1945, Millersburg PA) unm Bur Millersburg PA.

RF621A1C   Levi Dressler (dy) Bur Millersburg PA.

RF621A2   Cochran A Weiser (28 Sep 1867-18 Oct 1870) Bur McKees Half Falls PA.

RF621A3   Sarah Adda Weiser (2 Oct 1870-16 March 1884) Bur McKees Half Falls PA.

RF622   Maria Weiser m 28 Jul 1810, near Myerstown PA, Daniel Seltzer (1 Mar 1788, Stouchburg PA-23 Aug 1823, Amity Tp, Berks Co PA. Innkeeper, Amity Tp, Berks Co PA.

RF6221   Edward Weiser Seltzer (b 14 Jan 1812, Womelsdorf PA) m 21 Feb 1845, St Louis MO, Hannah Maria Williams (b 1828, NJ) Farmer, Coltlerville, Dardenne Tp, St Charles Co MO.

RF62211   Sarah M Seltzer m 23 May 1894, Denver CO, Ross Davis.

RF62212   William Henry Seltzer (9 Dec 1849, St Louis MO-5 Nov 1916, Long Beach CA) m 19 Apr 1880, Denver CO, Sarah Dickinson Laughlin (24 Dec 1830, Zane OH-10 Feb 1916, Los Angeles CA) Broom manufacturer, Denver CO.

RF622121   Herbert Eugene Seltzer (4 Apr 1881, Denver CO-16 Jan 1936, Los Angeles CA) m 26 Apr 1903, Denver CO, Matilda Loretta Hezel.

RF622122   William Henry Seltzer Jr (1884, Denver CO-ca 1956, Los Angeles CA).

RF622123   Maria Seltzer (ca 1890, Denver CO-Stockton CA).

RF622124   John Pool Seltzer (ca 1890, Denver CO-Saugus CA).

RF622125   Raymond Seltzer (ca 1894, Denver CO-ca 1964, Burbank CA).

RF62213   Frances M Seltzer (ca 1856, MO) m ca 1878, KS,   Stephans.

RF62214   Edward J Seltzer (b Dec 1857, MO) m 31 Oct 1894, Helen Peterson.

RF62215   Hubert Lee Seltzer (6 Nov 1863, St Charles MO-31 Dec 1868, Leavenworth KS) Bur Leavenworth KS.

RF6222   Catharine Priscilla Seltzer (29 Oct 1814, near Stouchsburg PA-14 Apr 1901, Spearfish SD) m 1 Mar 1840, Jeremiah Diefenbach (27 Apr 1815-15 Jun 1902, Spearfish SD).

RF62221   Edward Deffebach (9 Oct 1849, Manche, St Louis Co MO-2 Jul 1983, Los Angeles CA) m 4 Feb 1867, Franklin Co MO, Nancy Crow (21 Jul 1850, Franklin Co MO-20 Nov 1930, Los Angeles CA).

RF622211   Jesse Ross Deffebach (25 Nov 1887, Pierre SD-12 Jun 1978, Placentia CA) m 25 Aug 1910, Marie Agnes Myers (14 Mar 1887, Springfield MO-6 Jul 1988, Los Angeles CA).

RF6222111   Richard E Deffebach (b 4 Aug 1912, Los Angeles CA) m 31 Dec 1941, Mildred E Connell (b 6 Nov 1916, Burke SD).

RF6223   Jonathan Seltzer (26 Mar 1817-1817) Bur Womelsdorf PA.

RF6224   William Seltzer.

RF623   Catharine Weiser (b 3 Jan 1793, Tulpehocken Tp, Berks Co PA) m 1 Jan 1816, Leonard Kreutzer.

RF624   Jonathan Weiser (b 24 Nov 1794, Tulpehocken Tp, Berks Co PA) living as of 1825.

RF625   Salome Weiser (3 Jan 1797, Tulpehocken Tp, Berks Co PA-30 Oct 1842).

RF6251   Erastus Godfrey Rehrer.

RF6252   Clarissa Rehrer m George Dock.

RF62521   Lillian Dock m 1)   Finley; 2)   Hastings.

RF625211   Clara Dock Finley.

RF6253   Clementine Margaret Rehrer, Harrisburg PA.

RF626   Thomas Weiser (He was living in1825, but his share of his father's estate was to be invested and the interest paid to him annually by the executor or his guardian or guardians).

RF627   Jacob Weiser (31 Dec 1803, Tulpehocken Tp, Berks Co PA-17 Apr 1865) m 10 Apr 1825, Maria Magdalena Eicholtz (Highhold, Henchhold) (1 Dec 1800-1 Apr 1874, Herndon PA) Carpenter, Herndon PA. Bur Red Cross PA.

RF6271   Rebecca Weiser m Jul 1848, George Diehl.

RF6272   Reuben Weiser (26 Sep 1828-1 Mar 1878) m Esther Malick (1 Jan 1830-20 Aug 1907) Bur Red Cross PA.

RF62721   Ellen Lavinia Weiser (d 9 Jan 1919, Shamokin PA) m Samuel Shoppell.

RF62722   Emma Caroline Weiser (1860-1941) m 15 Jan 1880, John Wirt (1854-1925).

RF627221   Jennie Wirt m Fred Drumheller.

RF627222   Earl Wirt.

RF6272221   Ethel Wirt.

RF6272222   Emma Jane Wirt.

RF627223   Beulah R Wirt.

RF62723   Mary Cordelia Weiser (d 1895) m Harvey Heintzelman.

RF62724   Sarah Alice Weiser (15 Apr 1855-12 Jun 1936) m 1 Mar 1874, Elias Gonser (25 Jan 1849-26 Aug 1927).[136]

RF627241   Emma Jane Gonser (Feb 1875-Mar 1875).

RF627242   Catharine May Gonser (7 Jun 1876-14 Nov 1944) m 1898, George B Kerstetter (d 2 Apr 1938) General store keeper.

RF6272421   Leon V Kerstetter m 1) 1924, Eliza Henninger (d 1924); m 2) Jun 1929, Elanore Newberry. Painter.

RF62724211   Emma Kerstetter (b 14 Dec 1924) m 20 Sep 1947, Nelson Weikel.

RF627242111   Todd Weikel (b 14 Aug 1950).

RF62724212   Louise Kerstetter (b 27 Dec 1929) m Richard Davidson.

---

[136]Data provided by Mrs. Carrie Haupt, Gowen City, PA.

RF6272422   Edith M Kerstetter m 1924, Frank Cotterall. Plumber.

RF62724221   Francis Cotterall (b 20 Apr 1925).

RF62724222   George Cotterall (b Nov 1928).

RF62724223   Catherine Cotterall (b Jun 1930) m Joseph McBride.

RF6272423   Margarette Kerstetter.

RF627243   Carrie Ellen Gonser (17 Mar 1878-9 Dec 1963, Danville PA) m 1900, Albert W Haupt (d 2 Nov 1955) General store merchant, Gowen City PA.

RF6272431   Russell G Haupt (9 Jan 1902-25 Mar 1942) m 17 Nov 1925, Grace E Long.

RF62724311   Richard L Haupt (25 Aug 1929-5 Jun 1949).

RF627244   Annie Clarissa Gonser (17 Apr 1880-25 Apr 1952) m 1896, Sylvester S Henninger (d 2 Jan 1957) Coal miner.

RF6272441   Leroy Henninger (1 Apr 1897-Oct 1897).

RF6272442   Lloyd Henninger (b 1 Apr 1897) m Jun 1918, Edna Henninger. Coal miner and grocer.

RF62724421   Shirley Henninger (1925-1943).

RF62724422   Nona Henninger (1928-1946).

RF6272443   Alice Henninger (5 Feb 1899-10 Oct 1937) m 1) 1917, Charles Kerstetter (d 1919); m 2) 1930, John Boback.

RF6272444   Edna Henninger (1901-1925).

RF6272445   Elwood Henninger.

RF6272446   Clyde Henninger (7 May 1904-Jan 1929).

RF6272447   Lorraine Henninger (b 24 May 1914) m Jun 1950, Ben Snick.

RF62724471   Rene   (b 1939).

RF627245   Son (b 1882, stillborn).

RF627246   Grace Violet Gonser (25 Aug 1886-1 Jan 1918) m 3 Aug 1917, John Bird.

RF6273   John Weiser.

RF6274   Caroline Weiser (b 5 Feb 1832) m 3 Dec 1853, Henry Kline, Schuylkill Co PA.

RF6275   Elizabeth Regina Weiser m Moses Leitzell, Schuylkill Haven PA.

RF62751   Elizabeth Leitzell.

RF62752   Mary Ellen Leitzell (b 1858) m Andrew K Whalen.

RF627521   Ellen Elizabeth Whalen (b 1886).

RF627522   Howard Arthur Whalen (b 1888).

RF627523   Earl Leitzell Whalen (b 1897).

RF62753   Anna Leitzell m Samuel Cummings.

RF62754   Frances Maria Leitzell (14 Apr 1860-1928) m John William Stroh (15 Nov 1859-July 1923).

RF627541   Frank Clifford Stroh (b 8 Feb 1884) m Grace Viola Seiler (4 Apr 1888-10 Apr 1953) Accountant, Sunbury PA.

RF6275411   Ruth Seiler Stroh (1920-1920).

RF6275412   William Richard Stroh (b 5 May 1923).

RF627542   Raymond Weiser Stroh (b 22 Nov 1889) m Elizabeth J Kerchner.

RF62755   Sarah Leitzell m William Stitzer.

RF6276   Emanuel Weiser, Emrichsville, Jefferson Co PA, had 4 daughters.

RF62761   Lizzie Weiser.

RF62762   Olley Weiser m Fletcher Haines.

RF6277   Levi Weiser.

RF6278   Lavina Jane Weiser (1836-Jun 1915, Sunbury PA) unm.

RF6279   Clementine Weiser m   Wentzel. Herndon PA.

RF627A   Sarah Ann Weiser (1841-Mar 1914, Sunbury PA) unm.

RF627B   Jeremiah George Weiser (20 Nov 1844-1 Apr 1865).

RF627C   Jonathan Weiser.

RF628   Rebecca Weiser m 18 Apr 1824, Womelsdorf PA, Peter Brown (b 26 Oct 1800).

RF6281   Edward Brown (b 2 Sep 1825, near Stouchsburg PA).

RF6282   Bateisa Brown (b 11 May 1827, near Stouchsburg PA).

RF6283   Calina (Carolina) Brown (b 27 Nov 1828, near Stouchsburg PA).

RF6284   Melanchthon Martin Brown (14 Jul 1832-13 Nov 1832).

RF629   John Weiser.

RF62A   Elizabeth Weiser (1807-1891, Mendota IL) m John Jacob Reed (12 Oct 1799-1870, Mendota IL) Settled in Dayton OH, 1840, later moved to Mendota, where they are buried.

RF62A1   Elmire S Reed (1830-1887) unm Bur Mendota IL.

RF62A2   Amanda E Reed (b 27 Oct 1832) m Henry Miller. Paris IL.

RF62A21   Chester W Miller (b 1867).

RF62A3   Emma M Reed (1834-1909) unm Bur Mendota IL.

RF62A4   Miranda E Reed (1836-1857) unm Bur Mendota IL.

RF62A5   Amelia Reed m Ambrose Best.

RF62A6   Jacob Reed, unm.

RF62A7   Richard Reed m. No chn.

RF62A8   John Reed m Phoebe Munson.

RF62A81   Fannie Reed m James H Eckels.

RF62A811   Phoebe Eckels m John A Stevenson. Chicago IL.

RF62A82   Winnifred Reed m Kennesaw Mt Landis (20 Nov 1866, Millville OH-25 Nov 1954, Chicago IL) US Judge. Commissioner of baseball.

RF62A821   Reed Landis.

RF62A822   Susanne Landis m   Phillips.

RF62A9   George W Reed (1844-1907) unm Bur Mendota IL.

RF62AA   Mary Reed (1846-1883) m Henry Thayer. Bur Mendota IL.

RF62AA1   Millie Thayer.

RF62AB   Edward A Reed (b 8 Sep 1852, Dayton OH) m Letitia A Porter.

RF62AB1   Elizabeth A Reed (b 17 Apr 1882) m Raymond H Officer.

RF62AB11   Elizabeth Reed Officer (b 24 Oct 1920) m George D Kilgo. Buffalo NY.

RF62AB111   Martin D Kilgo (b 1 Nov 1943).

RF62AB112   Sharon E Kilgo (b 16 Apr 1947).

RF62AB2   Chester P Reed (b 1 Oct 1884).

RF62B   Caroline Weiser m 14 Dec 1835, Jacob Eckert.

RF62C   Lavinia Weiser (31 Jan 1813-1872) m 21 Aug 1833, John Stamm Good.

RF62C1   John Stamm Weiser Good (1834-1864) m Lavinia Schmeck.

RF62C11   Mary Lavinia Good (b 1860).

RF62C2   Oscar R Good (1836-1871) unm.

RF62C3   Joseph N Good (1838-1890) unm.

RF62C4   Mary Cecilia Good (b 1840) m Abraham R Royer. Philadelphia PA.

RF62C41	Daisy Lavinia Royer (b 1875) m Walter S March.
RF62C5	Emma Merinda Good (11 Oct 1843-25 Jan 1902) m 21 Sep 1865, James Miller Landis.
RF62C51	Bertha May Landis (b 1869) m Howard W Curry. Hartford CT.
RF62C511	Harriette Emma Curry (b 1895).
RF62C512	Jean Landis Curry (b 1897).
RF62C52	Herbert Davis Landis (1870-1871).
RF62C53	Charles Alfred Landis (1872-1878).
RF62C54	Edward Horace Landis (b 1876).
RF62C55	Arthur Spencer Landis (1879-1880).
RF62C56	Osbourn Landis (b 1880).
RF62C6	Amanda Lavinia Good (b 1847).
RF62C7	William Good (dy) unm.
RF64	Anna Maria Weiser (b 17 May 1778, Tulpehocken Tp, Berks Co PA) m George Illig.
RF641	Margaret Illig (b 16 Apr 1801).
RF642	Samuel Illig (b 20 Sep 1802).
RF643	Jacob Illig (b 13 Jun 1804).

RF8. Benjamin Weiser (1740-1782)

Benjamin Weiser, son of Christopher Frederick and Elizabeth   Weiser, was born 8 May 1740 and died 24 Nov 1782 at Womelsdorf PA. He married 7 Feb 1772 at Douglassville PA, Esther Levan (24 Nov 1752-29 Jul 1798, Womelsdorf PA), daughter of Daniel and Susanna (Siegfried) Levan. Following his death, Esther married 11 Jul 1784 John Bleiny. Benjamin Weiser was a merchant at Womelsdorf and a member of the Pennsylvania legislature in 1782.[137]

Children of Benjamin and Esther (Levan) Weiser:

RF81	Daniel Weiser.
RF82	Elizabeth Weiser (b 30 Jun 1776).
RF83	Benjamin Weiser (b 10 Nov 1778).
RF84	John Weiser.
RF81	Daniel Weiser (bap 15 Jan 1776) m Feb 1797, Elizabeth Copeland (d 1825, Hickory MD),

---

[137]See will of Benjamin Weiser, Berks Co. 2-55. Data supplied (1960) by Mrs. C Wadsworth Schwartz and Mrs. Vera Naiden Johns, supplemented in 1996 by Betty L Ramsay, The Most Rev. William Clifford Newman, The Rev. Eugene K Culhane, SJ and Dorothy W Seale.

RF813 Martha Weiser Ryder
(1802-1885)

daughter of Issac Copeland. She bur Churchville MD. He is on the 1800 census in Womelsdorf, the 1810 census in Schaefferstown, but not on the 1820 census when his widow Elizabeth appears with a son and a daughter between 16 and 26.

RF811 Eleanore Weiser (22 Aug 1798-1873) unm.

RF812 Elizabeth Weiser (10 Mar 1800-dy).

RF813 Martha Weiser (15 Mar 1802, near Womelsdorf PA-7 Mar 1885, Pylesville MD) m 15 Apr 1819, George Ryder (4 Mar 1787, Emmitsburg MD-16 Feb 1865, Hickory MD) Bur Hickory MD. Proprietor of "The Hickory Hotel," Hickory MD. (There are family records which cite her birthdate variously as 29 or 31 Jan 1802).

RF8131 Lavinia Ryder (2 Feb 1821-14 Feb 1898) m James Quinlan (25 Feb 1840-9 Nov 1887).

RF81311 Thomas Albert Quinlan (b 12 Dec 1840).

RF81312 James Quinlan Jr (b 1 Feb 1842).

RF81313 Martha Elizabeth Quinlan (23 Feb 1845-12 Jul 1904) m 1) 6 May 1865, Baltimore MD, Thomas Glenn (1 Apr 1817-5 Jan 1872); m 2) Benjamin F Darbie (d 7 Feb 1923).

RF813131 Emily Helen Glenn (20 Jul 1866 29 Dec 1940) m George P Speidel (8 Aug 1896-19 Jun 1937).

RF8131311 Glenn Paul Speidel (13 Aug 1897 27 Sep 1963) m Elinore Lee Newall (b 20 Oct 1918) MD.

RF81313111 Paul Lionel Speidel (b 27 Sep 1940) m 27 Feb 1965, Denise Maitzen (b 1 Aug 1941).

RF813131111 Paul Lionel Speidel (b 16 Nov 1965).

RF8131312 Elizabeth Helen Speidel (14 Jul 1899-Jan 1954) m 28 Jun 1927, Thomas Gerald Stapleton (22 Mar 1898-Jul 1959).

RF81313121 Patricia Ann Stapleton (b 23 Jul 1928) m 11 Jun 1949, Louis Leo Funk (b 21 Mar 1923).

RF813131211 James Louis Funk (b 3 Oct 1951).

RF813131212 Ann Elizabeth Funk (b 22 Nov 1953).

RF813131213 Thomas Michael Funk (b 13 Aug 1956).

RF813131214 Terrence Patrick Funk (b 15 Jan 1958).

RF81313122 Thomas George Stapleton (b 2 Dec 1930).

RF81313123 James Gene Stapleton (b 15 Feb 1934).

RF8131313 Mary Naomi Speidel (b 26 Jul 1902) m 16 Feb 1926, Arthur Fitzgerald (b 21 Nov 1897).

RF81313131   Mary Joan Fitzgerald (b 2 Oct 1928).

RF81313132   Thomas Butler Fitzgerald (b 1 Jan 1930) m 29 Jun 1957, Marjorie Coupe (b 20 Nov 1935).

RF813131321   Thomas Coupe Fitzgerald (b 23 Nov 1958).

RF813131322   Mary Patricia Fitzgerald (b 28 May 1965).

RF81313133   Nancy Glenn Fitzgerald (b 30 May 1931) m 8 Sep 1952, Raymond Debacker (b 10 Sep 1930).

RF813131331   Mary Joan Debacker (b 9 Jul 1953).

RF813131332   Nancy Debacker (b 25 Aug 1955).

RF813131333   Amy Debacker (b 28 Sep 1957).

RF813131334   John B Debacker (b 8 Feb 1960).

RF81313134   Arthur Fred Fitzgerald (b 5 Mar 1939) m 4 Sep 1965, Ruth Holzfaster (b 28 Jan 1942).

RF81313135   Suzanne Hanorah Fitzgerald (b 18 Sep 1940).

RF8131314   Thomas Speidel (10 Feb 1908-30 Nov 1957) m 27 Dec 1934, Edna Warweg (b 14 Jun 1908) DDS.

RF81313141   Thomas Michael Speidel (b 17 Apr 1936).

RF81313142   John Joseph Speidel (b 17 Sep 1937).

RF81313143   Ann Elizabeth Speidel (b 4 Dec 1939) m 4 Sep 1961, John Maxwell Ferren (b 21 Jul 1937).

RF813131431   Andrew John Ferren (b 15 Oct 1964).

RF813132   Benjamin Darbie.

RF81314   Lewis Edward Quinlan (b 18 Dec 1846).

RF81315   Laura Theresa Quinlan (b 15 Oct 1848) m James Stansbury.

RF81316   Anna Quinlan (b 23 Apr 1854) m   Poulson.

RF81317   Sarah Louisa Quinlan (b 26 Dec 1857).

RF81318   Joseph Quinlan (6 Sep 1863-Apr 1918) m 27 Apr 1889, Margaret Loretta Dorman. Dentist.

RF813181   Albert Edward Quinlan (28 May 1891, Brooklyn NY-Nov 1911, Liberty NY).

RF813182   Edna Marie Quinlan (b 14 Oct 1893, Brooklyn NY) m 1) 28 Jul 1923, Anthony Brown; m 2) William F Cunningham.

RF8131821   Marguerite Brown (b 12 Sep 1926, Brooklyn NY) m 31 Mar 1951, Frank J Herron.

RF81318211   Francis Joseph Herron (b 19 Jul 1953).

RF81318212   Jane Marie Herron (b 14 Jan 1955).

RF813183   Joseph Augustine Quinlan (b 5 Feb 1895) m 30 Apr 1928, Katherine Louise McGurk.

RF8131831   Joseph Augustine Quinlan (b 9 May 1931, Columbus OH) m 10 Jan 1959, Redempta Burr
Larkin.

RF813184   Victor Raymond Quinlan (b 9 Sep 1897) m 15 Sep 1956, Tersa Mulvihill. Insurance
broker.

RF8132   Alexander B Ryder (b 7 Oct 1821) m Sara McDevitt.

RF81321   Helen Ryder.

RF81322   Thiel Ryder.

RF8133   Edward Ryder (29 May 1823-4 Apr 1869) m Anna Elder (d 1849).

RF81331   George Ryder.

RF81332   Thomas Ryder.

RF8134   Thomas Ryder (b 14 Dec 1827) m Emily Helen Lawrence. He, DDS.

RF81341   Jenny Ryder m Alexander Fisk.

RF81342   Grace Ryder m Harry Anderson.

RF81343   Dottie Ryder.

RF8135   Anie Ryder (b 30 Apr 1829).

RF8136   May Ryder (b 29 Dec 1829) m John O'Donnell.

RF81361   Theresa O'Donnell (b 1 Dec 1850).

RF81362   Rosalia O'Donnell.

RF81363   Mary Suzanne O'Donnell (b 13 Oct 1855).

RF8137   Martha Caroline Ryder (7 Sep 1832-3 Mar 1917) m Benjamin Minnick (1829-5 Aug 1900)
Bur Hickory MD.

RF81371   Corine Mary Minnick (15 Oct 1857-3 Feb 1929) m Fred Nelson Ramsay (28 Oct 1863,
Delta PA-28 Nov 1954) div. Bur Slate Ridge MD. Telephone company.

RF813711   Marie Viola Ramsay (15 Oct 1891-1 Nov 1987) m Ralph David Gemmill.

RF8137111   Rita Lietta Gemmill (b 27 May 1912) m 1) John McElwain; m 2) Spurgeon Lehman.

RF81371111   Merle McElwain (b 9 Jun 1938) m Jeanne Rempel.

RF813711111   Vicky McElwain (b 27 May 1959).

RF81371112   Muriel McElwain (b 4 Jun 1943) m 1) Robert Neally; 2) Donald Smith.

RF813711121   Shawn Neally (b 10 Dec 1964).

RF813711122   Ryan Smith (b 26 Jul 1971).

RF8137112   Clyde Joseph Gemmill (b 14 Jul 1914) m Leah Gillian.

RF81371121   Ralph Gemmill m Debra Welch.

RF813711211   Ralph Edward Gemmill (b 1974).

RF813711212   David Gemmill m Marianne McVeigh.

RF8137112121   James Joseph Gemmill (b 20 Jun 1983).

RF813712   Cletus Benjamin Ramsay (19 Sep 1893-14 Jan 1955) m 2 Nov 1917, Sylvia Anita
Pomranning Duncan (20 Aug 1896-25 Dec 1933) He bur York PA; she bur New Park PA.

RF8137121   Duncan Cletus Ramsay (29 May 1918-7 Aug 1984) m 16 Apr 1949, Mary Louise Seitz
(b 5 Aug 1928) Bur York PA.

RF81371211   Debra Cheryl Ramsay (b 31 Aug 1956) m 25 Jan 1991, Todd K McWilliams. No chn.

RF8137122   Laura Corine Ramsay (6 Sep 1921-15 Jun 1988) m 19 Dec 1946, Elick Zak. Bur York
PA. No chn.

RF8137123   Arthur Hilton Ramsay (8 Mar 1923-25 May 1934) Bur New Park PA.

RF813713   Fred Hilton Ramsay (b 10 May 1896) m 20 May 1916, Florence McFadden.

RF8137131   Hazel Louise Ramsay (19 Nov 1916-14 Jul 1966) m James Westerman. Bur Delta PA.

RF8137132   Charles Frederick Ramsay (2 Feb 1920-16 Sep 1977) m 1937, Maxine Greer. Bur Slate
Ridge MD.

RF81371321   Charles Ramsay (b 15 Jun 1939) m 21 Jan 1959, Ann Bowman.

RF813713211   Mark Ramsay (b 17 Aug 1959).

RF81371322   William Ramsay (b 30 Aug 1945) m Nettie   .

RF8137133   Gloria Florence Ramsay (19 May 1922-4 May 1982) m Ramsay Montgomery. Bur Slate
Ridge MD.

RF81371331   Ronnie Montgomery (30 Mar 1939-28 Mar 1965) m Charlotte Rocky.

RF813713311   Ronald Michael Montgomery (b Nov 1957).

RF813713312   Randal Lee Montgomery (b Dec 1959).

RF8137134   Eunice Merle Ramsay (7 Nov 1924-14 Jul 1976) m 8 Oct 1955, William Kilgore. Bur
Slate Ridge MD.

RF81371341   Connie Sue Ramsay (b 27 Jan 1961).

RF81371342   Betty Lynn Ramsay (b 22 Nov 1966).

RF8137135   Corine Mary Ramsay (b 24 Mar 1929) m 24 Feb 1956, Harold Wiley.

RF81371351   Harold Todd Wiley (b 31 Oct 1959).

RF813714   Joseph Edward Ramsay (9 May 1898-13 May 1967) m 1916, Olive Boyle.

RF8137141   Ramsay (d 11 Nov 1922).

RF8137142   Donald Ramsay (dy).

RF8137143   Lois Virginia Ramsay (b 27 Sep 1921) m 1) Joseph Lewis (d); m 2) Calvan Davidson.

RF81371431   Ronnie Lewis.

RF81371432   Karen Lewis.

RF8137144   Thelma Corine Ramsay (b 23 Aug 1923) m Charles Faville.

RF81371441   Charles Faville.

RF81371442   Douglas Faville.

RF81371443   Gary Faville.

RF8137145   Robert Adare Ramsay (b Jun 1926) m Dorothy Freddrick.

RF81371451   Robert Adare Ramsay Jr.

RF8137146   Jo Ann Marie Ramsay (b 1932).

RF81371461   Carol Ramsay.

RF813715   Cora Cecilia Ramsay (b 18 Jun 1903) m 26 Sep 1936, William E Taylor (d 14 Sep 1940); m 2) 8 Apr 1944, John M Cogan (d 10 Mar 1954) No chn.

RF81372   Florence Mae Minnick (12 Dec 1867-25 Jan 1942) Bur Pylesville MD, unm.

RF81373   Laura Teresa Minnick (2 Mar 1869-9 May 1916) m William Basil Newman (d 20 Apr 1950, Baltimore MD) Bur Baltimore MD.

RF813731   Clinton Joseph Newman (1895-3 Nov 1958, FL) m Jocelyn Burke. USN. No chn.

RF813732   Martha Evelyn Newman (1896-27 Mar 1963, Baltimore MD) m Edward Eickorn. She, RN; he, sales. No chn.

RF813733   William Clifford Newman (6 Jan 1897, Trenton NJ-17 Sep, Baltimore MD) m 20 Jul 1918, Elliott City MD, Mable Catherine Evans (12 Sep 1897, Baltimore MD-20 Oct 1986, Baltimore MD) He, sales; she, homemaker.

RF8137331   Maryalma Cecilia Newman (b 8 Feb 1919, Baltimore MD) Sister Mary Pierrre Newman, School Sisters of Notre Dame, 1940-. BA, Col of Notre Dame, 1953; MA, Villanova U, 1961.

RF8137332   Catherine Patricia Newman (b 17 Mar 1920, Baltimore MD) m 7 Feb 1948, Baltimore MD, Joseph Ross Franck (17 Mar 1910, Baltimore MD-18 Jan 1993, Baltimore MD) Bur Baltimore MD. She, homemaker; he, trade association supervisor.

RF81373321   Mary Patricia Franck (b 10 Aug 1948, Baltimore MD) m 25 Sep 1970, Stephen Stewart Olin (b 15 Jan 1942, Indianapolis IN) He, PhD, Purdue U; she BS, U MD; PA, George Washington U. He, cancer research; she, physician's associate.

RF813733211   Jennifer Rain Olin (b 29 Jul 1971).

RF813733212   Peter Jason Olin (b 3 Oct 1975).

RF81373322   Catherine Anne Franck (b 17 Sep 1949, Baltimore MD) unm Bank teller.

RF81373323   June Francis Franck (b 29 Nov 1950, Baltimore MD) m 1 May 1970, Baltimore MD, Guy Girard Dowell (b 17 Jun 1950, Baltimore MD) She, homemaker; he, manufacturer's rep.

RF813733231   Jimmy Francis Dowell (b 8 Oct 1970).

RF813733232   Jamie Michelle Dowell (b 22 Jun 1979).

RF81373324   Bernadette Eileen Franck (b 26 Jan 1952, Baltimore MD) m 30 Oct 1971, Baltimore MD, Dominick Anthony Battaglia Jr (b 6 Sep 1951, Baltimore MD) She, pre-school teacher; he, police lieutenant.

RF813733241   Michael Joshua Battaglia (b 13 Nov 1972).

RF813733242   Matthew Ryan Battaglia (b 25 Sep 1975).

RF81373325   Theresa Suzanne Franck (b 28 Jul 1953, Baltimore MD) unm Nurses aide, Baltimore MD.

RF81373326   Jane Evelyn Franck (b 20 Jan 1957, Baltimore MD) m 25 Apr 1981, Baltimore MD, Edward Gerald Giblin (b 12 Oct 1942, Bridgeport CT) She, BA, Towson (MD) S U, 1979; homemaker.

RF813733261   Bethany Jane Giblin (b 30 Mar 1983).

RF813733262   Evelyn Grace Giblin (b 31 Jul 1986).

RF81373327   Joseph Ross Franck Jr (b 19 Jun 1960, Baltimore MD) m 12 Oct 1985, Baltimore MD, Deborah Nocar (b 7 Jan 1965, Baltimore MD).

RF813733271   Timothy Andrew Franck (b 2 Feb 1986).

RF813733272   Ryan Michael Franck (b 2 Aug 1989).

RF8137333   Rita May Newman (13 May 1923, Baltimore MD-9 Oct 1979, Baltimore MD) Bur Glen Arm MD. School Sisters of Notre Dame, 1943-1979. AB, Col of Notre Dame; MA Villanova U.

RF8137334   June Marie Newman (b 1 Jun 1921) m 17 Jan 1948, Baltimore MD, Henry J Ruth (28 Apr 1922, Baltimore MD-9 Jan 1985, Elliott City MD) Bur Baltimore MD. She, homemaker; he, government employee.

RF81373341   Harry Joseph Ruth (7 Feb 1952-5 Feb 1961).

RF81373342   Dolora Anne Ruth (b 11 Aug 1955, Baltimore MD) m 7 Nov 1992, Albert Gregory Stoffa (b 1 Mar 1957, Baltimore MD) He, BS, MS; she BS, BSN. He, IBM.

RF813733421   Gregory Joseph Stoffa (b 14 Mar 1994).

RF81373343   William Newman Ruth (b 14 Sep 1962, Baltimore MD) unm BS, Towson (MD) S U, 1985. CPA, Baltimore MD.

RF8137335   Doris Elizabeth Newman (b 27 Nov 1925, Baltimore MD) m 12 Oct 1946, Baltimore MD, Michael Joseph Piasecki (b 2 Jan 1921, Baltimore MD) She, Telephone Co, homemaker; he, accountant.

RF81373351   Mary Regina Piasecki (b 16 Jun 1947, Baltimore MD) m 26 May 1973, Leroy John Duckett (b 3 Dec 1945, Philadelphia PA) BS, Towson (MD) S U, 1973; MA, George Washington U, 1979. Social security administration, 1965-83; health care financing admin, 1983-.

RF813733511   Sean Michael Duckett (b 11 Feb 1980).

RF813733512   Scott Matthew Lee Duckett (b 6 Jun 1983).

RF81373352   Mary Joan Piasecki (b 16 Jun 1947, Baltimore MD) unm BA, Notre Dame (MD), 1972. School Sisters of Notre Dame, 1965-1972. Program analyst, Social Security admin, 1973-.

RF81373353   Michael Joseph Piasecki III (b 5 Mar 1949) m 1) 8 Aug 1970, Baltimore MD, Katherine Moershell (b 6 Aug 1949) div; m 2) 18 Nov 1983, Shannon Mary Maloney Huth (b 15 Feb 1947) USAF. Electronic technician, 1973-85; boat sales, Kent Island, MD, 1985-.

RF813733531   Michael Vernon Piasecki (b 8 Aug 1977).

RF813733532   Robert George Piasecki (b 8 Jan 1979).

RF81373354   Timothy Mark Piasecki (b 3 Jul 1953, Baltimore MD) m 15 Apr 1981, Newtown PA, Kathleen Brady Sweeney (b 15 Feb 1951, Philadelphia PA) Motor mechanic, maintenance supervisor, plant manager, Gallatin NJ.

RF813733541   Matthew Curtis Piasecki (b 31 Aug 1982).

RF81373355   Susan Marie Piasecki (b 14 Jul 1954, Baltimore MD) m 13 Oct 1973, Avalon NJ, William Thomas Colavito (b 30 Nov 1951, Philadelphia PA).

RF813733551   Justin Andrew Colavito (b 29 Apr 1979).

RF813733552   Lisa Anne Colavito (b 28 Sep 1983).

RF81373356   Thomas William Piasecki (b 13 Jul 1956, Baltimore MD) m 20 Nov 1982, Morrisville PA, Wendy Jane Safka (b 4 Mar 1956, Bristol PA) Electronic technician, Springhouse PA.

RF813733561   Jason Thomas Piasecki (b 1 Aug 1987).

RF813733562   Meredith Piasecki (b 28 Mar 1991).

RF81373357   Elizabeth Ann Piasecki (b 21 Dec 1957, Baltimore MD) m 1) 23 Aug 1980, Thomas Richard Brown (13 Sep 1939, Philadelphia PA-15 Jun 1985, Longhorne PA); m 2) 19 Mar 1987, John Arthur Day (b 2 Sep 1941, Philadelphia PA) No chn. Accountant, Steamboat Springs CO.

RF81373358   Gerard David Piasecki (b 26 May 1961, Baltimore MD) m 1) 14 Jun 1980, Levittown PA, Mary Arleth (b 17 Nov 1961, Trenton NJ) div 1995; m 2) 20 Oct 1995, Levittown PA, Cathleen (nee McNeill) Imhof (b 12 Jul 1959, Holyoaks MA) Policeman.

RF813733581   Gerard David Piasecki Jr (b 14 Mar 1980).

RF813733582   Daniel Robert Piasecki (b 11 Feb 1985).

RF81373359   Christopher Francis Piasecki (b 15 Nov 1966, Baltimore MD) m 22 Jul 1994, Honolulu HI, Nancy Jean Jerdon Womack (b 23 Sep 1954, Philadelphia PA) Sales, Delran NJ.

RF8137336   Martha Evelyn Newman (b 13 Dec 1926, Baltimore MD) m 15 Jun 1957, Baltimore MD, Robert Thomas Brown (b 28 May 1930, Stockton CA) She, RN; he, MD, UC, San Francisco, 1958. Family practice, Stockton CA.

RF81373361   Kathleen Anne Brown (b 7 Apr 1958) unm.

RF81373362   Anne Marie Brown (b 19 Mar 1969) unm.

RF8137337   William Clifford Newman Jr (b 16 Aug 1928, Baltimore MD) BA, St Mary's Seminary and U, Baltimore MD, 1950; STL, Catholic U of America, 1954; M Ed, Loyola (Baltimore MD) Col, 1965, DD. Ordained Roman Catholic priest, 1954. Served parishes in Baltimore, high school principal; Superintendent of Catholic schools, Baltimore, 1967-76; Rector of Cathedral of Mary Our Queen, Baltimore, 1981-84; Auxillary bishop of Baltimore, 1984-. Ordained bishop, 2 Jul 1984.

RF8137338   Bernadette Theresa Newman (14 Oct 1933, Baltimore MD-29 Mar 1996, Baltimore MD) m 18 May 1957, Baltimore MD, Howard William Uhl (b 1 Jul 1929, Baltimore MD) He, BS, U MD, 1951. Plant supervisor. She, homemaker.

RF81373381   Carole Anne Uhl (b 7 May 1958, Baltimore MD) m 7 Nov 1995, Baltimore MD, Mark Edward Chouinard. She, secretary; he, electrician.

RF81373382   Jennifer Anne Uhl (b 7 Apr 1959, Baltimore MD) m 6 Sep 1986, Kenneth Jean Bergman (b 8 Jul 1947) She, BS, 1981; MS, Loyald (MD) Col, 1982. Speech therapist. He, purchasing.

RF813733821   Kenneth James Bergman (b 1 Dec 1987).

RF813733822   Aimee Grace Bergman (b 25 Sep 1990).

RF813733823   Andrew Howard Bergman (b 28 Sep 1993).

RF81373383   Gregory Howard Uhl (b 13 May 1960, Baltimore MD) m 31 Jul 1993, Chicago IL, Carol Lynn Callanan (b 17 Dec 1961, Chicago IL) He, BS, James Madison (VA) U, 1982; MBA, U Baltimore, 1992; she, BS, U MI, 1983. Both computer programming.

RF813733831   Sylvia Nicholette Uhl (b 11 Feb 1989).

RF813733832   Isabelle Bernadette Uhl (b 13 Nov 1994).

RF81373384   Peter Joseph Uhl (b 6 Sep 1963) BS, James Madison (VA) U, 1985. Computer programming, Washington DC.

RF8138   Ellen Frances Ryder (23 Dec 1839-9 Dec 1873) m 3 Jan 1861, Michael Ignatius Wheeler. Farmer, Harford Co MD.

RF81381   George Edward Wheeler.

RF81382   Albert Ignatius Wheeler m Gussie Whitford.

RF81383   Michael Oswald Wheeler m.

RF81384   Helen Wheeler m Archer Price.

RF813841   Nettie Price.

RF813842   Emily Price.

RF813843   Sylvan Price.

RF81385   Clara Wheeler.

RF81386   Loretta Wheeler m Charles McGuigan.

RF813861   Stella McGuigan m   Mason.

RF813862   Irene McGuigan m   Hall.

RF813863   Howard McGuigan.

RF813864   Walbert McGuigan.

RF813865   Lillian McGuigan.

RF81387   Elizabeth Wheeler m Richard Miller.

RF81388   Emily May Wheeler.

RF81389   Martha Frances Wheeler m Edward Caulk.

RF813891   Elizabeth Caulk.

RF813892   Howard Caulk.

RF813893   Ed Caulk.

RF8138A   Marian Wheeler m 1) Walter Hurt, div.; m 2) Walter Allan.

RF813A   Henry Ryder (Jun 1843-19 Mar 1889) m Margurete Zalm.

RF813A1   Martha Ryder

RF813A2   George Ryder

RF814   Edward Copeland Weiser (15 Feb 1804-ca 1818).

RF815   Lydia Weiser (b 7 Jan 1806) m John Smith.

RF816   Maria Weiser, unm.

RF817   Thomas Boyd Weiser (22 Mar 1810, Schaefferstown PA-Oct 1882, Brooklyn NY) m 22 Feb 1846, Ann Teresa Farrell (12 Jun 1824, Ireland-19 Nov 1894) Tailor.

RF8171   Mary Weiser (20 Oct 1847-19 Mar 1850).

RF8172   Thomas Weiser (15 May 1849-1 Nov 1850).

RF8173   James Francis Weiser (9 Jul 1851-14 Aug 1852).

RF8174   Elizabeth Teresa Weiser (12 Jul 1853-7 Sep 1924) m 12 Aug 1874, Brooklyn NY, Patrick John Kenedy (4 Sep 1843-4 Jan 1906) Bur St Andrews on the Hudson, Poughkeepsie NY. Catholic Book publisher.

RF81741   John Kenedy (20 Jun 1875-Dec 1875) Bur Queens NY.

RF81742   Loretto (Lauretta) Anne Kenedy (17 Dec 1876-24 Feb 1951) m 2 Aug 1911, New York NY, Robert Culhane (1874-1939) Bur Poughkeepsie NY.

RF817421   Robert Patrick Culhane (21 May 1912, Flushing NY-29 Aug 1922) Bur Poughkeepsie NY.

RF817422   Eugene Kenedy Culhane (b 11 Oct 1913, Flushing NY) Ordained Jesuit priest, 31 Jul 1945; PhD, Fordham U, 1956. Managing Editor, *America.*

RF817423   Elizabeth Marie Culhane (24 Aug 1918, Flushing NY-23 Aug 1971, Gardena CA) m 6 Apr 1946, Woodstock MD,   Janowicz. Bur Los Angeles CA. AB, Col of St Vincent, Bronx NY, 1940.

RF8174231   Carol Ann Janowicz (b 7 Feb 1947, Inglewood CA) m 12 Dec 1968, Gardena CA, David Michael Trowbridge (b 1945) div 1979. MA, UC Santa Barbara, 1972. Personnel specialist.

RF8174232   Thomas Eugene Janowicz (b 5 Nov 1948, Inglewood CA) m 27 Sep 1975, Gardena CA, Susan Jo Edson (b 1953) div 1980.

RF81742321   Jamaica Elizabeth Janowicz (b 4 June 1976, Torrance CA).

RF8174233   Linell Marie Janowicz (b 29 Apr 1950, Los Angeles CA) m 4 Sep 1976, Danville WA, Charles Lloyd Miller (b 1941) BS, UCA Santa Clara, 1972. Accountant, realtor.

RF81742331   Nathaniel Joseph Miller (b 10 Sep 1977, Grand Forks, British Columbia Canada).

RF81742332   Benjamin Charles Miller (b 10 Apr 1979, Grand Forks, British Columbia Canada).

RF8174234   Mark Peter Janowicz (b 2 Oct 1952, Los Angeles CA) m 4 Jul 1984, Hualien, Republic of China, Lee-wun Judith Hong (b 1960) BA, San Francisco S U, 1977; MA, WA S U, 1990. EFL instructor, marble importer.

RF81742341   Edward Eugene Janowicz (b 29 Sep 1986, Hualien, Republic of China).

RF81742342   Patrick Joseph Kenedy Janowicz (b 18 May 1989, Manila Phillipines).

RF8174235   Jane Marian Janowicz (b 3 Dec 1954, Los Angeles CA) m 24 Aug 1981, Torrance CA, John Michael Van Sky (b 1949) div 1984; m 2) 14 Oct 1985, San Diego CA, Jan Bruce Metzger (b 1959) She, RN, hospital administrator.

RF81742351   Elizabeth Ashley Metzger (b 26 Jun 1989, Albany NY).

RF81742352   Alexander Bryant Metzger (b 14 Aug 1991, Albany NY).

RF81743   Arthur Patrick Kenedy (30 Apr 1878, New York NY-3 Feb 1951, New York, Manhattan NY) m 1 Oct 1912, Anna Mercedes Reid (1883-1918) Bur Poughkeepsie NY. Catholic book publisher.

RF817431   Mary (Moira) Elizabeth Kenedy (21 Jul 1913, Edgemere NY-27 Apr 1987, Bay Shore NY) m 17 Sep 1940, New York, Manhattan NY, John Lawrence Belford II (1911-1982) Bur Bay Shore NY.

RF8174311   John Lawrence Belford III (b 15 Aug 1941, New York, Manhattan NY) m 5 Aug 1967, Bay Shore NY, Mary Susan Parker (b 1942) BS, Holy Cross, 1963; LLB, Columbia U, 1968. Attorney.

RF81743111   John Lawrence Belford IV (b 24 Apr 1968, Rockville Centre NY).

RF81743112   Timothy Charles Belford (b 23 Jan 1971, Rockville Centre NY).

RF81743113   Brian Arthur Belford (b 30 Sep 1973, Rockville Centre NY).

RF81743114   Mary Elizabeth Belford (b 20 Oct 1979, West Islip NY).

RF8174312   Paul Arthur Belford (b 5 May 1943, Bay Shore NY) m 3 Jun 1972, Washington DC, Michaele Anne Connors (b 1948) BS, Boston Col; MA Fordham U, 1967. Executive search consultant.

RF81743121   Peter Thomas Belford (b 11 Jun 1974, Saigon Vietnam).

RF81743122   David John Belford (b 9 Sep 1977, Washington DC).

RF81743123   Claire Connors Belford (b 31 Mar 1981, Washington DC).

RF8174313   Michael Kenedy Belford (b 27 Apr 1947, Bay Shore NY) m 21 Jul 1979, Bay Shore NY, Donamarie Jones (b 1952) BS, Boston Col; JD, Fordham U, 1972. Attorney.

RF81743131   Reid Michael Belford (b 22 Nov 1981, West Islip NY).

RF81743132   Elizabeth Jane Belford (b 22 Dec 1983, West Islip NY).

RF81743133   Luke Conor Belford (b 11 Feb 1989, West Islip NY).

RF8174314   Andrew James Belford (b 5 Jul 1949, Bay Shore NY) AB, Holy Cross, 1971.

RF8174315   Anne Reid Belford (b 1 Apr 1951, Bay Shore NY) m 8 Jun 1974, Bay Shore NY, Terrence Paul Lambert (b 1947).

RF81743151   Emily Anne Lambert (b 13 Aug 1977, West Islip NY).

RF81743152   John Gallagher Lambert (b 4 Jan 1979, West Islip NY).

RF81743153   Nora Kenedy Lambert (b 20 Nov 1980, West Islip NY).

RF81743154   Mary (Molly) Belford Lambert (b 13 Nov 1982, West Islip NY).

RF817432   Arthur Reid Kenedy (b 9 Aug 1914, Edgemere NY) m 11 May 1937, New York, Manhattan NY, Mary Alice McGuirk (1913-27 Mar 1994) AB, Georgetown U, 1936. Catholic book publisher.

RF8174321   Arthur Reid Kenedy Jr (b 21 Aug 1938, Bay Shore NY) m 2 Sep 1961, Winnetka IL, Sheilah Ann Wilson (b 1940) AB, Holy Cross, 1959. Publisher.

RF81743211   Susan Alene Kenedy (b 20 Sep 1962, Manhattan NY) m 27 Sep 1986, Holliston MA, Steven Albert Hood (b 1960) BS, IA S U, 1984. TV Reporter, anchorperson.

RF817432111   Eliot Kenedy Hood (b 6 Jun 1989, Frederick MD).

RF817432112   Elizabeth Maria Hood (b 12 Aug 1990, Frederick MD).

RF81743212   Kathleen Anne Kenedy (b 2 Sep 1964, New York, Manhattan NY) m 1 Aug 1987, Omaha NE, John Peter Hayden (b 1962) BS, IA S U, 1985. Commercial artist.

RF81743213   William Wilson Kenedy (b 27 May 1968, Bronxville NY) m 28 Dec 1990, Omaha NE, Linda Anne Splittberger (b 1968) BS, St John (MN) U. Accountant.

RF81743214   Megan Mariah Kenedy (b 20 Jan 1972, Omaha NE).

RF8174322   Anne Loretta (Annie Laurie) Kenedy (b 17 Nov 1941, Bay Shore NY) m 16 Oct 1966, Bay Shore NY, James Michael MacEvitt III (b 1936).

RF81743221   Amanda Michaelene MacEvitt (b 11 Oct 1968, Ft Sill OK).

RF81743222   Christopher Hatch MacEvitt (b 22 Oct 1972, Honolulu HI).

RF8174323   Gael Elizabeth Kenedy (b 16 Feb 1944, Bay Shore NY) m 14 Oct 1972, New York, Manhattan NY, John Winand Greene (b 1941).

RF81743231   Caroline Reid Greene (b 24 Apr 1973, Baltimore MD).

RF81743232   John Winand Greene Jr (b 9 Mar 1976, Baltimore MD).

RF81743233   Marie (Molly) McGuirk Greene (b 13 May 1980, Baltimore MD).

RF8174324   Mark William Kenedy (b 2 May 1945, Bay Shore NY) m 6 Aug 1971, Bay Shore NY, Joan Marie Accettella (b 1946) President, sand and gravel business.

RF81743241   Jed Foster Kenedy (b 6 May 1975, West Islip NY).

RF81743242   Jamie Alizabeth Kenedy (b 26 Feb 1980, West Islip NY).

RF81743243   Kristen Elizabeth Kenedy (b 12 Jan 1988, West Islip NY).

RF8174325   David Gerard Kenedy (b 14 Jun 1946, Bay Shore NY) m 7 Mar 1971, Euclid OH, Mary Ann Gornick (b 1947) BS, Col of Steubenville. Comptroller.

RF81743251   David Bradley (Brad) Kenedy (b 8 Feb 1974, West Islip NY).

RF81743252   Julie Ann Kenedy (b 17 Dec 1977, West Islip NY).

RF8174326   Daniel Joseph Kenedy (28 Jun 1949, Bay Shore NY-16 Sep 1975) Bur Bay Shore NY.

RF817433   Eugene Thomas (Hap) Kenedy (21 Apr 1918, New York, Manhattan NY-5 Mar 1980) m 1) 17 Jun 1940, Bellport NY, Joan McAvoy (1919-1952); m 2) 4 Aug 1965, West Babylon NY, Marguerite Bloomingdale (1906-1986) Bur Calverton NY.

RF8174331   Sheila Marie Kenedy (15 Aug 1941, Port Jefferson NY-20 Aug 1980, Tampa FL) m Howard William Kinderman (b 1941).

RF81743311   William Walter Kinderman (b 17 Mar 1961, Bay Shore NY) m 19 Jun 1993, Davis CA, Kim Susanna Haag (b 1966) BA, UC Davis, 1990.

RF817433111   Mary Anastasia Kinderman (b 18 Apr 1994, Stockton CA).

RF8174332   Eugene Timon Kenedy (b 8 Aug 1946, Port Jefferson NY) m 1 Jul 1982, New York, Manhattan NY, Olga Josephine Silva (b 1948).

RF81743321   David Patrick Kenedy (b 13 Jan 1984, Washington DC).

RF81743322   Katherine Elizabeth Kenedy (b 9 Sep 1985, Washington DC).

RF81743323   Christopher Brian Kenedy (b 1 Apr 1989, Fairfax VA).

RF81743324   Kelly Ann Kenedy (b 4 Dec 1990, Fairfax VA).

RF81744   Eugene Thomas Kenedy (10 Feb 1880, Brooklyn NY-19 Oct 1964) Bur Poughkeepsie NY. Ordained Society of Jesus, 28 Jun 1914, Woodstock MD. WWI: Chaplain.

RF81745 Louis Kenedy (13 Oct 1882, Brooklyn NY-16 Nov 1956, New Rochelle NY) m 19 Apr 1909, New York, Manhattan NY, Gabrielle Marie Barzaghi (1885-1966) Bur Valhalla NY. Catholic book publisher.

RF817451 Louis Arthur Kenedy (17 Jul 1910, Stamford CT-25 Jul 1991, Bridgewater Nova Scotia Canada) m 28 Jul 1936, Bridgetown Barbados, Patricia Greenridge (b 1915) Bur Lunenburg Nova Scotia Canada. Sea captain.

RF8174511 Brian Patrick Kenedy (b 3 May 1937, Bridgetown Barbados) m 5 Jun 1959, Nassau Bahamas, Barbara Ann Sameth (b 1936) Executive.

RF81745111 Brian Patrick Kenedy Jr (b 18 Oct 1960, Jersey City NJ) m 25 Apr 1992, Woodside CA, Linda Ann Gallagher (b 1962).

RF817451111 Shannon Ruth Kenedy (b 25 Sep 1992, San Francisco CA).

RF81745112 Shaun Michael Kenedy (28 Feb 1964, Nice France-10 Oct 1982, Twenty Nine Palms CA) Bur Belle Haven VA. USMC.

RF81745113 Jennifer Ann Kenedy (b 10 Jan 1969, Fairfax VA).

RF8174512 Patricia Anne Kenedy (b 26 Aug 1943, Bridgewater Nova Scotia Canada) m 3 Dec 1973, Bridgetown Barbados, G William Bolling III (b 1928).

RF8174513 Gabrielle Barzaghi Kenedy (b 11 Aug 1947, Bridgewater Nova Scotia Canada) m 28 Oct 1966, Nassau Bahamas, Richard Herbert Lightbourn (b 1945).

RF81745131 Tiffany Ann Lightbourn (b 5 May 1967, London England) BA, Boston U.

RF81745132 Sabrina Nicole Lightbourn (b 20 Sep 1972, Nassau Bahamas).

RF8174514 Rosemary Susan Kenedy (b 16 Jul 1954, Bridgewater Nova Scotia Canada) m 27 Jun 1980, Nassau Bahama, Marcus Homen Mitchell (b 1957) Resort owner.

RF81745141 Justin Patrick Mitchell (13 Sep 1980-14 Sep 1980, Nassau Bahamas).

RF81745142 Melissa Anne Mitchell (b 13 Apr 1982, Ft Lauderdale FL).

RF81745143 David Patrick Mitchell (b 17 Jun 1983, Nassau Bahamas).

RF81745144 Amanda Rose Mitchell (b 22 Feb 1985, Nassau Bahamas).

RF81745145 Lauren Alexandra Mitchell (b 20 Oct 1986, Nassau Bahamas).

RF817452 Rosemary Gabrielle Kenedy (5 Oct 1914, Stamford CT-29 Sep 1972, New York, Manhattan NY) Bur Valhalla NY. Biology researcher.

RF817453 Patricia Joan Kenedy (14 Nov 1916, Stamford CT-28 Mar 1929, New York, Manhattan NY) Bur Valhalla NY.

RF817454 John Leopold Kenedy (2 Mar 1918, Stamford CT-21 Apr 1985, Sanibel FL) m 1) 7 Jan 1961, Hull England, Angela Downs (b 1928) div 1965; m 2) 30 Dec 1973, Spring Lake NJ, Lorraine Swan Walker (b 1918) Catholic book publisher.

RF8174541 John Justin Kenedy (23 Mar 1963, Hull England-28 Oct 1963, Red Bank NJ) Bur Valhalla NY.

RF817455   Thomas Boyd Kenedy (b 5 Nov 1919, Stamford CT) m 18 Oct 1945, Pelham NY, Rita Filomena Cuzzi (b 1921) Catholic book publisher. Received *Pro Ecclesia et Pontifice* award from Bishop Loverde, Ogdensburg NY, 1995.

RF8174551   Patricia Joan Kenedy (b 16 Oct 1946, Mt Vernon NY) m 22 Jul 1972, Saranac Lake NY, Joseph Patrick Crowley (b 1946).

RF81745511   Peter Thomas Crowley (b 14 Jan 1975, Chapel Hill NC).

RF81745512   Timothy Daniel Crowley (b 6 Oct 1977, Chapel Hill NC).

RF81745513   John William Crowley (b 14 Oct 1981, Montgomery AL).

RF81745514   Rita Mary Crowley (b 26 May 1984, Montgomery AL).

RF81745515   Mark Joseph Crowley (b 10 Nov 1985, Montgomery AL).

RF8174552   Elizabeth (Betsy) Ann Kenedy (b 5 Oct 1948, Mt Vernon NY) m 1 May 1982, New York, Manhattan NY, Karl Swanson (b 1950) div 1991.

RF81745521   Jeffrey Kenedy Swanson (b 23 Jan 1985, Boston MA).

RF8174553   Paul John Kenedy (b 7 Dec 1952, Mt Vernon NY).

RF8174554   Carmela Therese Kenedy (b 4 Aug 1956, Mt Vernon NY) m 6 Sep 1986, Boston MA, Timothy Joseph Martell (b 1957).

RF81746   Elizabeth (Lillian) Mary Kenedy (14 Apr 1884, Brooklyn NY-6 Jan 1927) m 19 Apr 1917, New York, Manhattan NY, Charles M O'Keefe (1885-1928) Bur Poughkeepsie NY.

RF81747   Clara Kenedy (29 Aug 1885-1 Sep 1885, Great Neck NY).

RF81748   Marie Agnes Kenedy (13 May 1891, New York, Manhattan NY-30 Aug 1985) m 2 Sep 1914, Stamford CT, Charles Wadsworth Schwartz (1891-1957) Bur Valhalla NY. Her name was legally changed to Wadsworth after his death.

RF817481   Thomas Wadsworth Schwartz (b 1 Feb 1918, Brookline MA) m 28 Jan 1955, Bronxville NY, Georgine Ernestine LaMontagne (b 1920) BS, NYU, 1942.

RF8174811   Nancy Marie Schwartz (b 24 Mar 1957, Wilmington, DE) m 19 Jan 1990, Greenwich CT, Brian David Tracy (b 1956).

RF817482   Kenneth Schwartz (b 9 Mar 1921, White Plains NY) m 16 Aug 1958, Brewster NY, Virginia Wells (b 1923) BS, Yale U, 1947.

RF8174821   Philip Wadsworth Schwartz (b 18 Jul 1959, New York, Manhattan NY) BS, N#A2#U, 1983. Aviation engineer.

RF8174822   Charles Crosby Schwartz (b 2 Mar 1961, New York, Manhattan NY) m 10 Oct 1987, Louisville KY, Elizabeth Hunt (b 1963) BS, U CO; MBA, U Louisville, 1989. Financial consultant.

RF81749   Isabel Mercedes Kenedy (4 Jan 1895, New York, Manhattan NY-12 Sep 1983, New Rochelle NY) m 5 Jul 1924, White Plains NY, Charles E Egan Jr (1890-1967) Bur Poughkeepsie NY.

RF817491   Charles E Egan III (b 19 Nov 1925, Stamford CT) m 25 Feb 1949, New York NY, Ethel Anderson (1926-1990).

RF8174911   Cheryl Ann Egan (b 31 Mar 1951, New York, Manhattan NY) m 10 Aug 1974, Schenectady NY, Steven Mead Schrade (b 1948) AB, Russell Sage Col; MST, Union Col, 1990. Teacher.

RF81749111   Kelly Ann Schrade (b 17 May 1977, Niskayuna NY).

RF81749112   Amy Lynn Schrade (b 22 Oct 1980, Niskayuna NY).

RF81749113   Kyle Egan Schrade (b 22 Feb 1983, Niskayuna NY).

RF8174912   Charles Anderson Egan (b 16 Apr 1953, Elmont NY) m 10 Sep 1977, Washingtonville NY, Barbara Christine Thumann (b 1952) Food sales manager.

RF81749121   Sara Christine Egan (b 29 Sep 1979, Kingston NY).

RF81749122   Heather Lynn Egan (b 18 Nov 1981, Poughkeepsie NY).

RF81749123   Patrick Charles Egan (b 13 Oct 1983, Poughkeepsie NY).

RF8174913   Jerome John Egan (19 Jul 1957, Roslyn NY-1 May 1993, New Paltz NY) m 18 Mar 1978, Hialeah FL, Aileen Ann Mertes (b 1958) Bur Kingston NY.

RF81749131   Alissa Yvonne Egan (b 2 Dec 1980, Hollywood FL).

RF81749132   Jeremy John Egan (b 21 Jul 1983, Kingston NY).

RF8174914   Jean Karen Egan (b 21 Jun 1958, Roslyn NY) m 20 Mar 1982, Poughkeepsie NY, Stephen John Smith (b 1958) BA, Vassar Col, 1980.

RF81749141   Christopher Charles Smith (b 6 Jul 1987, Suffern NY).

RF81749142   Kaitlyn Marie Smith (b 21 Feb 1990, Suffern NY)

RF8174915   Meg Ann Egan (b 28 Jan 1965, Great Neck NY) m 1 Jul 1989, West Point NY, David Seth Dworkin (b 1965) BS, Union Col, 1987.

RF81749151   Jacob Charles Dworkin (b 27 Mar 1993, Newton MA).

RF817492   Isabel Irene (Betty) Egan (b 27 Mar 1927, Stamford CT) Concert, opera singer; classical pianist.

RF8175   Charles Weiser (8 Apr 1856, New York NY-1964) m Emma

RF81751   Emma Weiser m   Keith.

RF8176   Henry Weiser (11 Dec 1857, New York NY-19 Dec 1860).

RF8177   Louis Weiser (b 7 Nov 1860, Brooklyn NY) Real estate broker.

RF82   Elizabeth Weiser (30 Jun 1776-16 Nov 1848) m 21 Mar 1796, John George Ruck (Rick) (8 Nov 1755-14 Jun 1821) Farmer, Bern Tp.

RF821   Charles Rick (22 Dec 1804-28 May 1878) m Ellen Louise Ruth (13 Jun 1813-31 Aug 1880) Reading PA.

RF8211   Cyrus Rick (2 Sep 1837, Bern Tp PA-1895, Reading PA) m 1868, Emma R Madeira (Muhlenberg Tp PA) Banker, hardware manufacturer.

RF82111   Infant (dy).

RF82112   Ella Rick m Samuel Spang.

RF821121   Emily R Spang.

RF821122   Mary Spang.

RF82113   Anna E Rick, unm.

RF82114   Mary E Rick, unm.

RF82115   Charles Rick.

RF8212   John Rick (d 1900) m Emma C Ammon. Hardware manufacturer. Civil War: Co C, 42nd
Regt, PVI.

RF82121   George Ammon Rick (b 23 Oct 1877, Reading PA) m 12 Nov 1903, Margaret Hunter.
Financier; President, Council, Reading PA. Pvt, Co A, 4th Regt, PVI.

RF821211   John Hunter Rick (b 31 Aug 1904).

RF821212   Margaret Marion Rick (b 8 Nov 1906).

RF82122   John Rick.

RF82123   Paul Ammon Rick (b 22 May 1882, Reading PA) m Pearl Bingaman. Hosiery
manufacturer.

RF821231   Charlotte Augusta Rick (b 31 Mar 1902).

RF8213   Ellen Louise Rick (1846-1903) m William Augustus Arnold (1836-1906) Banker.

RF82131   William Augustus Arnold Jr (b 5 Feb 1873, Reading PA) m 23 May 1901, Katharine L
Bowers (b 5 Aug 1876, Hamburg PA) Hatter, Reading PA.

RF82132   Ellen Rick Arnold.

RF82133   Franklin Dundore Arnold (b 24 May 1881, Reading PA) BS, U PA, 1902, LLB, 1905; U
Munich. American Diplomatic Service, 1909-.

RF82134   Mary Dundore Arnold m Edward Vose Babcock (see *Who's Who in America*).

RF82135   John Arnold.

RF82136   Anna Arnold.

RF8214   James Rick (b 28 Jun 1844).

RF82141   James Rick.

RF82142   Harrison Rick.

RF82143   Albert Rick.

RF82144   Edward Rick (d 19 Oct 1918, age 32) m Caroline August Schlechter.

RF821441   Edward Rick.

RF821442   Richard Rick.

RF821443   Daughter.

RF8215   Charles Rick (15 Nov 1840-27 Nov 1909) m Emma Augusta Pauli (d 16 Mar 1921) Civil War: Co E, 128th Regt. Hardware manufacturer.

RF82151   Mary Rick m Frederick Hunter Muhlenberg.

RF82152   Rick m John M Frame (6 Aug 1875, Reading PA-3 Feb 1925) Attorney.

RF82153   Rick m Herbert A Green.

RF82154   Rick m Harry Weile.

RF82155   Rick m Lindsay McCandlish.

RF82156   Arthur Rick (b 22 Dec 1878, Reading PA) m 9 Mar 1900, Alice M Spang. Coal dealer, Reading PA.

RF821561   Arthur Rick Jr (b 16 Aug 1911).

RF821562   Sarah Annie Rick (b 9 May 1914).

RF8216   Mary Rick m Franklin Dundore, Philadelphia PA.

RF82161   Charles Dundore.

RF82162   Frank Dundore.

RF82163   Ella Dundore.

RF83   Benjamin Weiser (10 Nov 1778-1808, Womelsdorf PA) m 15 Dec 1802, Lebanon PA, Catharine Hyde; m 2)   Smith.

RF831   Siegfried Weiser (b 29 Dec 1803, Womelsdorf PA) m Sarah   (b ca 1810) Five children died in youth. In 1850, he, a tailor, and Sarah were residents of Middle Ward, Philadelphia; in 1870 they were in Des Moines IA.

RF832   Esther Weiser (b 29 Jan 1805) unm.

RF833   Elizabeth Weiser, unm.

RF834   Levan Weiser, unm.

RF835   Reuben Benjamin Weiser (20 Jan 1807, Womelsdorf PA-8 Dec 1885, Georgetown CO) m 10 Sep 1833, Sarah Bossart (31 Oct 1814, Ft McCord, near Chamersburg PA-12 May 1898) Bur Georgetown CO. Reuben Weiser graduated from Lutheran Theological Seminary, Gettysburg PA, and was ordained in 1834. He served pastorates in Pennyslvania, Maryland, West Virginia, Illinois, and Iowa. Moved to Georgetown CO in 1872, entered mining interest. DD, Gettysburg Col, 1876. Author of *Luther by a Lutheran* and other works.

RF8351   Floritine Cordelia Margaret Weiser (b 28 May 1835, Martinsburg WV) m James R Lackey (b 22 Feb 1829, Bloomsburg PA) Railroad brakeman and conductor.

RF83511   Charles Weiser Lackey m Linnie Gardner.

RF835111   Charles W Lackey (dy).

RF835112   Madeline Clare Lackey (dy).

RF83512   Sarah Larue Lackey (dy).

RF83513   Mary Gertrude Lackey m Harry Wire, Grinnell IA.

RF8352   Elizabeth Larue Weiser (24 Mar 1837, St Thomas PA-18 Mar 1923, near Ft Morgan CO) m 9 May 1871, Minersville PA, Alexander Cree (18 Mar 1840, Newport OH-22 Apr 1919, near Ft Morgan CO) Bur Ft Morgan CO. Civil War. Mining newspaper proprietor.

RF83521   Jennie Weiser Cree (4 Apr 1872, Minersville PA-21 Nov 1958, Boulder CO) m 9 Mar 1904, Leroy Sherman Allnatt (3 Aug 1856, Villanova NY-21 Jun 1952, Boulder CO) Bur Boulder CO. Miner near Eldora CO. No chn.

RF83522   Elbert Chappee Cree (1 Dec 1874, Georgetown CO-28 Aug 1876, Georgetown CO) Bur Georgetown CO.

RF8353   Sarah Madeline Weiser (28 Sep 1838, Woodsboro MD-13 Dec 1904, Woodward IA) m 7 Jun 1860, James Owen Sanks, MD (17 Nov 1825, Imsville, Frederick Co MD-Jan 1891, Woodward IA) Bur Woodward IA. Practiced medicine, Woodward IA. Had ten children, only one survived.

RF83531   Carrie Winifred Sanks (13 May 1863, Xenia IA-28 Jun 1928) m 24 Oct 1884, Henry Richard Naiden (9 Apr 1859, Edgerton WI-8 Sep 1925) Bur Woodward IA. Druggist, Woodward IA.

RF835311   Viva Gertrude Naiden (30 Nov 1885, Woodward IA-Jan 1974) m 4 Aug 1859, Woodward IA, Floyd Jones (6 Jun 1886, Independence IA-1965) She, U IA, 1910; he, 1911.

RF835312   Fred Sanks Naiden (15 Jun 1887, Woodward IA-25 May 1939, Marshalltown IA) m 18 Jun 1913, Chariton IA, Sara Maude Abernathy (1 Feb 1887, Republic Co KS-17 Aug 1974, Iowa City IA) IA S U, 1909; civil engineer.

RF8353121   James Richard Naiden (b 2 Feb 1915, Adel IA) m 4 Jul 1942, San Antonio, TX, Norma Frances Robinson (b 26 Aug 1916, St Louis MO) PhD, Columbia U; Latin teacher, Lakeside School, Seattle WA. Part-time instructor, U Seattle.

RF83531211   James Richard Naiden (b 24 Sep 1943, San Antonio TX) Poet, editor, radio announcer, Minneapolis MN.

RF83531212   Mary Madeleine Naiden (b 13 Nov 1944, San Antonio TX) m 1965, Nigeria, John Gibson (b 1942, OK) He, engineer; she, realtor, Seattle WA.

RF835312121   Sean Paul Gibson (b 16 Jan 1968).

RF835312122   Janie Elisa Gibson (b 29 Sep 1973).

RF83531213   Norman John Naiden (b 26 Jun 1946 , New Brunswick NJ) m 1) Vintonne A Maiden, MD, div; m 2) Sep 1978, Yolanda Rivera (b 1955, Puerto Rico) He, physician; she computer programmer, Yakima WA.

RF835312131   Jason Naiden (b May 1971).

RF83531214   Norma Frances Naiden (b 5 Oct 1947 , New Brunswick NJ) m 1974, Reno NV, Greg

Newell (b 1946, Aberdeen WA) She, pharmacist, Ferndale WA.

RF835312141   Misty Dawn Newell (b 1 Aug 1974).

RF835312142   Daniel Douglas Newell (b Jan 1977).

RF83531215   Dorothy Ann Naiden (b 4 Aug 1949, Seattle WA) m 14 Jun 1970, Seattle WA, Glenn Nelson (b 3 Dec 1948, Seattle WA) He, attorney, Seattle WA.

RF8355312151   Erick Paul Nelson (b 24 Oct 1978, Seattle WA).

RF83531216   Sarah Maude Naiden (b 2 May 1951, Seattle WA) m 1) 1970, David Bast, div; m 2) 1978, Seattle WA, Lance Newell. She, nurse, Ferndale WA.

RF835312161   Sabrina Bast (b 13 Oct 1971).

RF83531217   Emelia Elizabeth Naiden (b 6 Mar 1953, Seattle WA) m 1969, Seattle WA, Bruce Allen Nevers (b 25 Nov 1950, Spokane WA) He, park worker; she, waitress, Kirkland WA.

RF835312171   Jennifer Ida Nevers (b 4 Jan 1970).

RF835312172   Vanessa Nevers (b 10 Jul 1974).

RF83531218   Catherine Ida Naiden (b 23 Feb 1956, Seattle WA) m 1977, Seattle WA, Wolfgang Lill (b Germany) He, machinist; she waitress, Seattle WA.

RF83531219   Theresa Louise Naiden (b 27 Sep 1957, Seattle WA).

RF8353122   Neil David Naiden (b 4 Jan 1918, Adel OA) m 1) 13 Jul 1944, Helena, MT, Eulaine Halners (b 28 Nov 1920, Monarch MT) div 1973; m 2) Eva Lavonne Haupert (b 18 Oct 1917, Perry IA) He, JD, U IA; she, MD, George Washington Medical School, DC. He, attorney; Halners, physician.

RF83531221   Fred Sanks Naiden (b 12 Mar 1953, Washington DC) Amherst Col, 1976. TV writer, New York NY.

RF83531222   Noel Marie Naiden (b 7 Jan 1955, Tarrytown NY).

RF835313   James Henry Naiden (24 Jul 1889, Woodward IA-16 Mar 1931, Sandwich IL) m 3 Oct 1917, Richmond IN, Helen McMinn (b 31 Jan 1899, Richmond IN) IA S U, 1912.

RF8353131   Dorothy Ann Naiden (b 10 Jul 1918, Indianapolis IN) m 13 Jun 1942, William Donohue Ellis (b 23 Sep 1918, Riverton NJ) BA, Wesleyan, 1941. She, school librarian, Rocky River OH.

RF83531311   William Naiden Ellis (b 1 Jan 1952, Lakewood OH) m 29 Jun 1974, Manchester England, Sue Elizabeth McCreery (b 8 May 1952, Manchester England) Purchasing agent, Huron OH.

RF835313111   William McCreery Ellis (b 8 Aug 1978, Huron OH).

RF83531312   Sarah Elizabeth Ellis (b 22 Jun 1955, Lakewood OH) AB, Wittengberg (OH) U, 1977. Teacher.

RF835314   Carrie Winifred Naiden (15 Apr 1891, Woodward IA-17 Aug 1968, Perry IA) m 21 Aug 1912, near Woodward OH, Clifford C Noland (b 21 Aug 1892, near Woodward IA-21 Dec 1950, Ft Dodge IA) div 1940. Bur Woodward IA.

RF8353141   Georgia Jean Noland (27 Jun 1915, Woodward IA-27 Jul 1921, Woodward IA).

RF8353142   Earl Lorraine Noland (5 Sep 1917, Woodward IA-13 May 1929, Sioux City IA).

RF8353143   Dean Carroll Noland (26 Jul 1919, Woodward IA-18 Aug 1963, Waterloo IA) m 1) 21 Aug 1943, Johanna Wilaminia Vandenberg (1919, Detroit MI-Jan 1944); m 2) 21 Jul 1947, Frances Ellen Lonergan (b 14 Jan 1921, Reinbeck IA) She, secretary, Waterloo IA.

RF83531431   Michael Allen Noland (b 12 May 1949, Waterloo IA) m 13 Aug 1977, Denver CO, Cyndi Geist (b 2 Nov 1953, Waterloo IA) He, machinist, Denver CO.

RF83531432   Ann Marie Noland (b 23 Aug 1951, Waterloo IA) m 25 Nov 1972, Jerry Mensch (b 14 Feb 1952, Plymouth IA) He, silversmith, jeweler; she, nursing instructor, Mason City IA.

RF835314321   Joel Mensch (b 25 Feb 1977, Mason City IA).

RF83531433   Kim Louise Noland (b 10 Mar 1953, Waterloo IA) m 18 Sep 1976, Waterloo IA, Daniel P Nissen (b 30 Jan 1952, Waterloo IA) He, realtor; she, factory worker, Waterloo IA.

RF83531434   Christopher Dean Noland (b 20 Jul 1954, Waterloo IA) m 17 Jul 1976, Waterloo IA, Mary Ann Kaumanns (b 23 Aug 1953) He, distributor; she, secretary, Waterloo IA.

RF83531435   Mary Kay Noland (b 4 Apr 1961).

RF8353144   Allen Kay Noland (b 22 Jul 1925, La Mars IA) m 1) 13 Sep 1952, Colorado Springs CO, Gerda Irmgard Erica Schultz (b 30 Nov 1928, Berlin, G D) div 1964; m 2) 26 Aug 1967, Colorado Springs CO, Roberta Gayle Ringer (b 13 Sep 1942, Quintes KS) He, WWII: USA, Major; office equipment services; she, teacher, Colorado Springs CO.

RF83531441   Barry Allen Noland (b 7 Jan 1954, near Ft Carson CO) Electrician assembler, Colorado Springs CO.

RF83531442   Sharon Kay Noland (b 28 Dec 1954, San Francisco CA) m 9 Aug 1972, Colorado Springs CO, Marrin Eugene Olson (b 27 Aug 1953, Austin MN) He, sales; she, restaurant hostess, Grand Junction CO.

RF835315   Mary Madeleine Naiden (24 Dec 1892, Woodward IA-11 Dec 1908, Woodward IA) Bur Woodward IA.

RF835316   Earl Larue Naiden (2 May 1894, Woodward IA-20 Sep 1944, Bend OR) m 1) 20 Dec 1919, Mary Seman (b 3 Dec 1895, Uniontown PA); m 2) Katharine Capel (d Dec 1939); m 3) 4 Jul 1943, Satchie Sholars Cooper (b 24 Jun 1906, Monroe LA) WWI and II: Flyer, West Point, 1915. No chn.

RF835317   Elma Jean Naiden (28 Jul 1896, Woodward IA-8 Dec 1969, Long Beach CA) m 1) 13 Sep 1915, Emory Perry Wells (19 Feb 1885, Madrid IA-22 Oct 1954, OR); m 2) 27 Oct 1934, William L Coburn (b 17 Jul 1906, Lane SD).

RF8353171   Carra Elizabeth Wells (14 Feb 1918, Omaha NE-14 Jun 1973, Long Beach CA) m 18 Jan 1939, Des Moines IA, Charles Albert Lounsbury (b 7 Jan 1918, Corwith IA) Bur Westminster CA. Grocer, Long Beach CA. No chn.

RF8353172   Henry Robert Wells (28 Feb 1920, Des Moines IA-10 Mar 1968, Long Beach CA) m 1 Aug 1942, Princeton MO, Mildred Maxine Manuel (b 16 Dec 1919, Vinton IA) Invester.

RF83531721   Thomas Robert Wells (b 4 Oct 1943, Ft Benning GA) m 6 Jun 1964, Las Vegas NV, Linda Lee Anderton (b 3 Apr 1945, Long Beach CA) He, municipal waterworks; she, sales, Oroville CA.

RF835317211   Lorina Lee Wells (b 26 Sep 1965, Long Beach CA).

RF835317212   Nicholas Robert Wells (b 15 Apr 1968, Long Beach CA).

RF8353173   Willa Jeanne Coburn (b 10 Jul 1937, Des Moines IA) m 28 Jun 1957, Bellflower CA, George Edward Traucht (b 12 Aug 1933, Jenera OH).

RF83531731   Timothy Edward Traucht (19 Apr 1958-26 Apr 1958).

RF83531732   Katrina Jeanne Traucht (b 13 Jul 1963).

RF835318   Vera Naiden (18 Jun 1899, Woodward IA-12 May 1972) m 3 Feb 1922, Daryl D Johns (b 31 Aug 1898, Colfax IA) She, Drake U, 1931; he, Drake U; attorney.

RF8354   Virginia Catharine Weiser (24 Aug 1842, Chambersburg PA-25 Sep 1921, Denver CO) m 10 Jul 1877, Joseph A Love (11 Jul 1829, Coshocton Co OH-3 Jan 1908, Georgetown CO) Bur Denver CO. No chn.

RF8355   Reuben Bossart Weiser (26 Sep 1846, Selinsgrove PA-30 Jan 1922, Denver CO) m 1869, Sarah C Stenbury (27 Sep 1848, Manchester MD-17 Apr 1931, Denver CO) Bur Denver CO. DDS, Baltimore Dental Col, 1968. State Senator; President State Board of Dental Examiners, State Dental Association.

RF83551   Mary May (Mamie) Weiser (4 May 1871, Manchester MD-29 May 1921, Denver CO.

RF83552   Flora Virginia Weiser (1873, Georgetown CO-24 Feb 1879, Georgetown CO) Bur Georgetown CO.

RF83553   William Straussburg Weiser (Apr 1878, Georgetown CO-26 Aug 1878, Georgetown CO) Bur Georgetown CO.

THE FAMILY OF JOHN WEISER (1817-1881)

J   John Weiser, born 6 Aug 1818, to John Weiser and Barbara Witman, although his tombstone says born 1817. He was confirmed at the age of 16 in 1833 at Rehrersburg PA. Barbara Witman, widow of Christopher Witman, was also the mother of Esther Weiser, confirmed 1831, at age 16, at Rehrersburg. She married Elijah Lantz of Miami Tp, Montgomery Co OH, on 15 Dec 1832, at Christ Lutheran Church. (See Berks Co, Misc. Book F-443.) John Weiser died 22 Dec 1881. He married, 19 Nov 1842, Magdalena Himmelberger (27 Mar 1815-21 Mar 1878). Bur Host Church[138]

J1   Rebecca Maria Elizabeth Weiser (7 Jun 1844-10 Mar 1901) m Henry S. Keener (25 Feb 1849-22 Aug 1905). She bur Host Church; he bur Strausstown PA. No chn.

J2   Adam Weiser (1 Oct 1845-1 Mar 1919) m Catherine Ann Mast (5 Jul 1852, Penn Tp, Berks Co PA-28 Apr 1932, Strausstown PA). Bur Host Church.

J21   John Weiser (25 Nov 1876, Strausstown PA-1949, Reading PA) m 25 Nov 1911, Anna Baum (b 21 May 1891, Bethel PA)

J211   Samuel Adam Weiser (5 Sep 1911, near Bethel PA-27 Sep 1944, Baltimore MD) m 28 Jan 1933, Nellie Blanche Dishong (b 24 Apr 1914, Everett PA). Bur Bethel PA.

J2111   Samuel John Weiser (b 5 Aug 1939, Everett PA) m 16 Mar 1959, Sandra Lee Asbury

J2112   Ruth Ellen Weiser (b 8 Jan 1941, Everett PA) m 28 Dec 1957, John Marshall (b 24 Jun 1925, Cazenovia NY). USN.

J21121   John Duley Marshall (b 16 Jan 1959, Fort Dix NJ)

J2113   John Melvin Weiser (b 25 Apr 1942, Everett PA)

J2114   Floyd William Weiser (b 17 Sep 1943, Baltimore MD)

J212   Annie Emma Weiser (b 19 Apr 1913, near Bethel PA) m 21 Jan 1934, Floyd Durant (b 8 Apr 1907, Manceona NY)

C2121   Virginia Mary Durant (b 5 Mar 1935, Vernon Center NY) m 29 Jun 1957, Keith Strong (b 24 Jan 1926, Knoxbara NY)

J21211   Diana Catherine Durant (b 24 Sep 1952)(Adopted by Keith Strong)

J2122   Priscilla Ann Durant (b 17 Jul 1939, Oneida NY)

J2123   Isabell Catherine Durant (b 16 Jun 1944, Oneida NY)

J2124   Lindia Elizabeth Durant (b 21 May 1948, Oneida NY)

---

[138]John Weiser was baptized 9 Dec 1821, Christ Lutheran Church, Stouchsburg PA, the son of John Weiser and Barbara Witman. The record cites his birthdate as 6 Aug 1818. His sponsors were Peter Zerbe and his wife Elizabeth. The identification of the John Weiser who was his and Esther's father is a problem. Since all the records of this family point to the area of Rehrersburg, the most likely candidate is RF62 John Weiser (1766-1825), who lived in Tulpehocken Tp nearby. The record of the children implies illegitimacy, but provides no further information about him. There were other John Weisers in Berks County at the time and this identification must be considered extremely tentative. Data provided by Schuyler Brossman, Dr. Ed Wiser, Carrie Hoffert, Arthur Witman, Elmer Weiser, Nellie D. Weiser and Annie E. Durant.

J22   Jane Weiser (19 Nov 1878, Strausstown PA-1952, Strausstown PA). She had the following son with Harry Bordner:

J221   Herbert Calvin Bordner (b 15 Feb 1914, Strausstown PA) m Marion Nagel

J2211   Joan M. Bordner (b 4 Feb 1944)

J2212   Janice A. Bordner (b 17 Aug 1945)

J2213   Curtis C. Bordner (b 22 Feb 1947)

J2214   Kathleen A. Bordner (b 11 Oct 1948)

J2215   Pearl E. Bordner (b 16 Aug 1950)

J2216   Brian G. Bordner (b 8 Aug 1952)

J2217   Shirley A. Bordner (b 12 Jun 1955)

J2218   Susan L. Bordner (b 3 Jan 1958)

J23   Kate Weiser (1 Mar 1881, North Heidelberg Tp, Berks Co PA-12 Aug 1955) m 27 Jun 1903, William Hoffert. Womelsdorf PA.

J231   Carrie Hoffert (b 16 May 1903) m Carl Foust

J2311   Yvonne R. Foust (b 17 Jul 1924) m Ray C. Dinkel

J23111   Pamela Y. Dinkel (b 26 Sep 1948)

J23112   Todd R. Dinkel (b 15 Aug 1956)

J23113   Tara K. Dinkel (b 23 Jun 1957)

J24   Adam Weiser (9 Jun 1883-7 Apr 1962, Reading PA). Unm.

J25   Emily (Emma) Weiser (1885-1886)

J3   John Weiser (17 Nov 1847, Strausstown PA-27 Sep 1873, Reading PA) m 2 Jul 1870, Reading PA, Emma Elizabeth Hoefer (Hafer) (b 1854)

J31   Deborah Lavinia Weiser

J4   Deville Weiser (12 Mar 1849, Strausstown PA-13 Feb 1850). Bur Stouchsburg PA.

J5   Isaac Daniel Weiser (10 Jan 1852-2 Nov 1923, Strausstown PA) m Elizabeth Heister (d 10 Jul 1917, Reading PA). He bur Rehrersburg PA; she bur Reading PA.

J51   Ella M. Weiser (1874, Struasstown PA-1941) m 17 Feb 1900, Reading PA, William Henry Himmelberger

J52   Charles W. Weiser (15 Dec 1876, Strausstown PA-21 Jun 1952, Reading PA)

J53   Elizabeth (Lizzie) K. Weiser (Dec 1878, Tulpehocken Tp, Berks Co PA-1946) m 8 Jul 1913, Reading PA, Willis (Wallace) C. Witman

J531   Arthur Willis Witman (b 4 Nov 1920, Reading PA) m Mary E. (b 8 Sep 1924). USPO
employee.

J54   Sally Weiser m   Hartman

J55   Paul Weiser (4 Mar 1884, Strausstown PA-4 Feb 1954, Reading PA). Unm. Bur Reading
PA.

J56   Harry Weiser (19 Oct 1885, Strausstown PA-28 Jul 1941, Reading PA). Unm. Bur Reading
PA.

J57   John Elmer Paul Weiser (8 Aug 1897, Strausstown PA-4 Nov 1976) m Emma S. Banks
(20 Feb 1895-23 Dec 1975). Bur Reading PA. Metal sheetworker, Reading PA.

J6   Willoughby (William) James Weiser (17 Dec 1854-14 Apr 1941) m 31 Jul 1880, Diana
Himmelberger

J61   Elnora Weiser (1881-1956) m 4 Oct 1902, Jacob Bright

J7   Catherine Weiser (26 Mar 1856-1 Mar 1881). Bur Host Church.

W   William Weiser (6 Apr 1843-14 Apr 1921) m 4 Jun 1864, Anna Maria Schrack (19 Oct
1844-4 Jan 1901). Bur Rehrersburg PA.[139]

W1   Javan Semore Weiser (24 Nov 1864-25 Nov 1875). Bur Rehrersburg PA.

W2   Clara Jane Weiser (7 Feb 1866-10 Dec 1912). Unm. Bur Rehrersburg PA.

W3   Lizzie Catharine Weiser (1 Dec 1867-14 Nov 1875). Bur Rehrersburg PA.

W4   Milton Samuel Weiser (30 May 1869-10 Feb 1950, Utica NY) m Ella Virginia Powell (3
Jan 1869-11 Dec 1934). Bur Philadelphia PA.

W5   Amanda Ebeiem Weiser (24 Jun 1870-10 Jul 1871). Bur Rehrersburg PA.

W6   Mary Agnes Weiser (12 Jul 1873-23 Sep 1889). Bur Rehrersburg PA.

W7   William Franklin Weiser (21 Nov 1874, Tulpehocken Tp, Berks Co PA-25 Jan 1920) m
18 Dec 1897, Strausstown PA, Annie Lengel (1872-8 Jan 1939). Bur Philadelphia PA.

W71   Beulah May Weiser (8 May 1898-30 Dec 1975). Bur Philadelphia PA.

W72   Marie Rebecca Weiser (2 Aug 1899-Feb 1982). Bur Philadelphia PA.

W73   Earl Lengel Weier (5 Apr 1901-22 Aug 1978) m Helen Lenn (b 21 Mar 1904). Bur
Philadelphia PA.

W731   Earl William Weiser (b 5 May 1931, Philadelphia PA)

---

[139]William Weiser was baptized 10 Sep 1843 at Christ Lutheran Church, Stouchsburg, and is called a son of John Weiser and
Rebecca Rollman. It is a fairly safe assumption that his father was the J - John Weiser (1817-1881) above and that he was conceived
about August 1842 prior to his father's marriage to Magdalena Himmelberger in November 1842. Descendants own the family Bible
of Rebecca Rollman's family. She was born 4 Nov 1815 and died 23 Jan 1876. She never married. She is buried at Rehrersburg on her
son's plot. Data provided by Schuyler Brossman, Dr. Ed Wiser, the Rev. Paul W. Weiser and William F. Weiser, Sr.

W732   Richard Lenn Weiser (b 21 Aug 1932, Philadelphia PA) m 29 Jul 1967, Jeraldine Rose
(b 3 Jun 1939)

W7321   Robert Brian Weiser (b 5 Jun 1969, Philadelphia PA) m 28 Feb 1995, Patricia Epting (b
1 Aug 1969)

W7322   Christian Eric Weiser (b 30 Jun 1971, Philadelphia PA)

W74   Conrad William Weiser (17 Jul 1902, Philadelphia PA-5 Aug 1979, Anniston AL) m Katie
Estella Cousey (10 Apr 1907-10 Nov 1955). Bur Anniston AL.

W741   Conrad William Weiser, Jr. (20 Jul 1926, Anniston AL-31 Jan 1978, Virginia Beach VA)
m 8 Apr 1950, Betty Williams (b 9 Jan 1932)

W7411   Conrad William Weiser III (b 16 Aug 1951, Virginia Beach VA) m Jul 1970, Diane
Reynolds (b 26 Oct 1952)

W74111   Conrad William Weiser IV (b 20 Apr 1972, Virginia Beach VA)

W74112   Luann Elizabeth Weiser (b 21 Nov 1974, Virginia Beach VA)

W7412   Janis Weiser (b 16 Jul 1953, Virginia Beach VA) m 1) Robert Teets, div; m 2) Paul Tesner

W74121   Michele Elizabeth Teets (b 13 Dec 1973, Virginia Beach VA)

W74122   Cheryle Lynn Teets (b 13 Dec 1973, Virginia Beach VA)

W7413   Susan Weiser (b 17 Sep 1957, Virginia Beach VA) m David Hyers (b 25 Jul 1958)

W74131   Daniel Collins Hyers (b 14 Jun 1982, Virginia Beach VA)

W742   William Franklin Weiser (b 21 Apr 1943, Philadelphia PA) m 3 Feb 1962, Anniston AL,
Kathy Ward (b 21 Jul 1946, Anniston AL). Petroleum equipment co executive, Anniston AL.

W7421   Denise Renee Weiser (b 4 Jan 1968, Anniston AL) m Alan Sisco (b 25 Dec 1960)

W74211   Love Marie Sisco (b 18 Feb 1994)

W7422   William Franklin Weiser, Jr. (b 15 Jul 1970, Anniston AL) m Linda Christopher

W74221   Whitney Weiser (b 5 Nov 1991, Anniston AL)

W75   Paul Michael Weiser (4 Feb 1904-9 Sep 1953) m 13 Jan 1929, Ethel Irene Wineland (b
14 Jun 1907). Bur Philadelphia PA.

W751   Paul Wineland Weiser (b 17 Oct 1929, Allentown PA) m 30 May 1954, Joan Elaine
Poulon (b 10 May 1930). Clergyman, Allentown PA.

*W7511   Mark Kevin Weiser (b 22 Feb 1956) m 8 May 1982, Becky Budd (b 16 Feb 1961). USA,
O'Fallon IL.

W75111   Seth Michael Weiser (b 13 Oct 1983)

W75112   Phillip Conrad Weiser (b 9 Jun 1988)

W75113   Daniel Aaron Weiser (b 9 Jan 1988)

W75114   Mark David Weiser (b 1 Aug 1989)

W7512   Scott Keith Weiser (b 28 Aug 1957)

W7513   Paul Konrad Weiser (b 22 Sep 1958) m 1) Jean Frank (b 28 Apr 1959); m 2) Debbie
Braswell (b 7 Mar 1959)

W75131   Joshua Aaron Weiser (b 23 Feb 1982)

W75132   Jillian Andrea Weiser (b 4 Jul 1987)

W7514   Paula Michelle Weiser (b 9 Jan 1960) m Wayne Chopin (b 13 Jun 1959)

W75141   Kyle Aaron Chopin (b 14 Oct 1982)

W75142   Keith Wayne Chopin (b 14 Jan 1988)

W76   Anna Violet Weiser (3 Mar 1907-24 Mar 1960) m William C. Johnston (28 Jun 1905-4
Sep 1965). Bur Philadelphia PA.

W761   Jean Maryann Johnston (b 7 Dec 1932) m Herbert Cole, Jr

W7611   Herbert W. Cole (b 29 Apr 1955) m Marian V. Vasquez

W76111   Lisa Marie Cole (b 1 Dec 1982)

W76112   Laura Jean Cole (b 8 May 1990)

W76113   Kathryn A. Cole (b 2 Jun 1992)

W7612   Susan L. Cole (b 18 Mar 1958) m Randal Bowers (b 7 Jun 1957)

W76121   David Cole Bowers (b 15 Oct 1986)

W76122   Christine Lee Bowers (b 16 Sep 1989)

W7613   Patricia Ann Cole (b 2 Nov 1959) m Michael E. Bittner (b 27 Feb 1957)

W76131   Daniel E. Bittner (b 20 Apr 1988)

W76132   Allison Ann Bittner (b 28 Sep 1989)

W77   Emma Estelle Weiser (c 1909-5 Dec 1925). Bur Philadelphia PA.

W8   Anna Deborah Weiser (14 Nov 1877-11 Dec 1938). Unm.

W9   Cora Alice Weiser (b 12 Jun 1884)

CHAPTER EIGHT

[BP] Anna Barbara Weiser Pickert
and her descendants[140]

Anna Barbara Weiser, daughter of John Conrad and Anna Magdalena (Uebele) Weiser was born 17 Oct 1700 in Grossaspach. She emigrated with her father and family to New York. About 1722 she married Nicholas Pickert, who was baptized 23 Feb 1701 in the Dutch Reformed Church at Schenectady NY, the son of Bartholomew and "Eechje Clazz" (Eva Klaas) Pickert. Nicholas probably grew up at "Verrebergh" (far hill), the Pickert farm six miles west of Albany. The Pickerts seem to have lived at Schoharie for a while, inherited land from his father in Stone Arabia, which they sold, and were residents near Canawadagy in 1750 when her brother Conrad visited them. Nicholas was named executor of an estate in 1778, but there is no records of the death or burial of either of them. While there is no records that states in so many words that Nicholas Pickert's wife was Anna Barbara Weiser, Conrad Weiser's statement that John Pickert was his sister's son clarifies her identity.

Children of Nicholas and Anna Barbara (Weiser) Pickert:

BP1   Johannes (John) Pickert

BP2   William Pickert

BP3   Bartholomew Pickert, 14 Feb 1726

BP4   Conrad Pickert, 5 Mar 1727

BP5   Leah Pickert

BP6   Jacobus (Jacob, James) Pickert

BP7   Rachel Pickert, 29 Oct 1733

BP1   Johannes (John) Pickert (d 4 May 1783 of wounds at the battle of Oriskany). Bur Stone Arabia. He married about 1750 to Anna Rosina Countryman. That his uncle Conrad's desire for him to serve as an interpreter, since by 1750 he had already learned the Mohawk tongue "tolerably well," was successful is borne out by a deed executed 30 Apr 1752 by which some Indians conveyed title to 950 acres of land (subsequently acquired by John's father-in-law Conrad Countryman) on which occasion John was sworn to serve as an interpreter. He was a member of the Tryon Co NY committee of safety and later quartermaster of Col. Samuel Campbell's Canajoharie Regiment, subse commanded by Col. Samuel Clyde, of the Tryon Co NY militia. He was a trustee of Christ Evangelical Lutheran Church ("Geisenberg Church") near Hallsville NY, which acquired its property in 1767.

BP11   John Pickert, Jr. m Maria Elizabeth

BP111   Anna Margeret Pickert (b 25 Jan 1775)

---

[140]Information about the Pickert family has been compiled from Marilyn Fox Anderson and Anna Carpenter Waite, Pickard and Allied Families (1979); George Christian Schempp The Schempp Family History (Baltimore, 1989); and correspondence with Donna R. Fleming, Clarence Mott Pickard, Irma Newberry Repas and Elaine Liepschultz. Since there is a recent history of the Pickard family, we have listed descendants to the great-great-grandchildren of Barbara Pickard except in cases in which descendants have provided us material not in Pickard and Allied Families. Marilyn Fox Anderson and Irma V. Newberry Pass are descendants of this family and are life members of the Weiser Family Association.

BP112   Wilhelm Pickert (perhaps)(b 22 Jul 1797)

BP12   Jacob Pickert

BP13   Henry Pickert

BP14   Nicholas Pickert (bp 6 Nov 1775, Stone Arabia NY) m Margaret Stenzel. Bur Hallsville
NY.

BP141   John Heinrick Pickert (ca 31 Jul 1776-6 Dec 1778)

BP142   Isaac Pickert m Anna Countryman

BP143   George N. Pickert (7 Aug 1778, Stone Arabis NY-1831, Minden NY) m Catherine
Bettinger (18 Aug 1778-12 Apr 1868). Bur Ft. Plain NY.

BP15   Anna Pickert (b 11 May 1754, Stone Arabie NY)

BP16   Maria Margaret Pickert (b 11 Mar 1756, Stone Arabia NY)

BP17   Isaac Pickert (7 Oct 1762, Montgomery Co NY-26 Apr 1843, Schroeppel NY) m 5 Feb
1793, Palatine NY, Magdalena Countryman (23 Mar 1771, Montgomery Co NY-23 Apr 1754, Schroeppel NY).
Bur Clay NY. He was a drummer from 7 Oct 1778, aged 16 years, under Capt. Jacob Diefendorf, Capt.
McKean and Col. Samuel Clyde. His widow Magdalena received a pension based on his service.

BP171   Christina Pickert (b 28 Apr 1794) m Edward Febrick

BP172   Johannes Pickert (1 Jan 1796-ca 1847) m 25 Jan 1818, Ft. Plain NY, Barbara Bauder

BP173   Anna Pickert (b 24 Mar 1798)

BP174   Isaac Pickert (7 May 1804, Montgomery Co NY-25 Jan 1862, Schroeppel NY) m 7 Jun
1829, Anna Sanders (5 Jun 1810, Montgomery Co NY-27 Mar 1899, Schroeppel NY), Bur Schroeppel NY.
Farmer.

BP1741   Soloman Pickard (b 29 May 1831)

BP1742   Lany Anna Pickard (b 7 Oct 1833)

BP1743   Delia Biancy Pickart

BP1744   Catherine Maria Pickart (b ca 1838)

BP1745   Almira Pickard

BP1746   Isaac Alonzo Pickert (14 Jul 1843-7 Dec 1918, Clay NY) m 30 Jun 1871, Oswego NY,
Barbara Cushman (22 Sep 1852, Germany-21 Jun 1914, Clay NY). Bur Phoenix NY. Farmer.

BP17461   Anna Christina Pickard

BP17462   Clarisa Amelia Pickard

BP17463   Estella Augusta Pickard

BP17464   William Alonzo Pickard (17 Apr 1876, Onondaga Co NY-23 Nov 1941, Dewitt NY) m
27 Nov 1897, Josie Snook (Jun 1876, Hastings NY-8 Mar 1939, Dewitt NY). Bur Collamer NY. Farmer.

BP174641   Robert Arnold Pickard

BP174642   Howard Pickard

BP174643   Ward Pickard

BP174644   Donald Pickard

BP174645   William Pickard

BP174646   Edwin Pickard

BP174647   Raymond Pickard (25 Dec 1909, Syracuse NY-24 Jun 1985, Ormond Beach FL) m 11 May 1929, Liverpool NY, Edna May Haberer (b 20 Mar 1911, Liverpool NY). Bur N. Syracuse NY. Farmer, home builder.

BP1746471   Lawrence Allen Pickard (b 19 Mar 1930, Syracuse NY) m 1) Kathryn Pryor (b 2 Jul 1929); m 2) 14 Feb 1981, Sherrill NY, Patricia Harris Moureau (b 14 Apr 1927, Beverly MA). BS, Syracuse U; electrical engineer.

BP17464711   James Raymond Pickard (b 12 Mar 1953, Syracuse NY) m Nov 1980, Syracuse NY, Kathleen Lazarro. BS, LeMoyne (NY) Col; contractor.

BP17464712   Karen Lynn Pickard (b 19 Jul 1957, Syracuse NY) m May 1985, Syracuse NY, William Lipke

BP17464713   Elizabeth Mary Pickard (b 4 Aug 1963, Syracuse NY) m 1) Sep 1986, Thomas Brimfield; m 2) 11 Apr 1992, Denver CO, Michal Hamner

BP1746472   Donna Rae Pickard (b 17 May 1941, Syracuse NY) m 1) 9 Dec 1960, Pensacola FL, Wann Edward Gays (b 11 Sep 1939, New York NY); m 2) 21 Nov 1981, Alexandria VA, Norwood Wall Fleming (b 23 Nov 1932, Camden NJ)

BP17464721   Machael Allen Gays (b 9 Jan 1962, Pensacola FL) m 3 Dec 1988, Falls Church VA, Susan Lynn Kuehn (b 9 Sep 1964). BBA, George Mason U; stock broker.

BP174647211   Brianna Lynn Gays

BP17464722   Thomas Henry Gays II (b 7 Jan 1963, Bremerhaven, Germany) m 4 Jun 1988, Richmond VA, Virginia Holmes Cary (b 19 Mar 1961, Richmond VA). BA, VA Commonwealth U; LLB, George Mason U; attorney.

BP174647221   Alyssa Cary Gays

BP174647222   Marchall Harrison Gays

BP17464723   Jon Daniel Gays (b 12 Nov 1968, Alexandria VA). Security.

BP174648   Ethel Pickard

BP174649   Ray Allen Pickard

BP17464A   Helen Pickard

BP17465   Wardwell Augustus Pickard

BP17466   Gertrude Almira Pickard

BP17468   Edith Julia Pickard

BP17469   Elmer Florentine Pickard

BP1747   Ezra Pickard (b ca 1845)

BP1748   Jacob Henry Pickard (b 8 May 1809)

BP1749   William Menzo Pickart

BP174A   George Sylvanus Pickard

BP174B   Charles Ely Pickard

BP175   Magdalena Pickert (b 18 Jun 1806)

BP176   Jacob Pickert (b 8 May 1809)

BP177   Maria Pickert (b 14 Apr 1810)

BP178   Daniel Pickert (b 16 Nov 1811)

BP179   Elizabeth Pickert (b 13 Jun 1813)

BP2   William Pickert m Elizabeth   . Butlers Rangers. Settled in Canada.

BP21   James Pickert. Private, Butlers Rangers.

BP22   Benjamin Pickert (d Aug 1757, Paris, Ont CAN). Drummer, Butlers Rangers.

BP23   Margaret Pickert m Jacob Deterick. Butlers Rangers.

BP24   Elizabeth Pickert m William Osterhaut. Private, Butlers Rangers. Settled in Niagara district,
Ontario, later in Scarborough Ont CAN.

BP241   Eliza Osterhaut (b 1807) m 1826, St. Catherine Ont CAN, John Smith

BP3   Bartholomew Pickert (14 Feb 1726, probably Canajoharie NY-17 Jan 1807) m Maria
Catherine   . Bur Manheim NY. In 1765 he purchased a farm at Manheim NY. He served in the militia in
1763 and 1769; as a private in Capt. John Cayser's Company at the battle of Oriskany in 1777; and was
captured by the British and Indians in 1780 and taken to Canada, where he was released 1 May 1783. He
continued farming and gave land for "Old Yellow Church," a Lutheran congregation at Manheim NY.

BP31   Conrad Pickert (dy)

BP32   Christian Pickert (26 Jul 1768-9 Jul 1836) m 1) 18 Oct 1795, Ann Windecker (d 14 Mar
1800); m 2) 7 May 1800, Margaret Keyser (10 Oct 1779-7 May 1844)

BP321   Catharina Pickert (b 26 Aug 1796)

BP322   Joseph Pickert (b 4 Apr 1798) m 1) 4 Jan 1835, Elizabeth Felter; m 2)

BP323   Ann Pickert (b 7 Feb 1800) m 6 Jan 1824, Gilbert Merrels

BP324   Gertrude Pickert (b 27 Jul 1802) m 7 Jan 1827, Robert Alexander

BP325   Mary Pickert (9 Dec 1804-9 Jul 1826)

BP326   William Pickert (b 2 Jul 1807)

BP327   Moses Pickert (b 4 Jul 1810)

BP328   Rebecca (Margaret) Pickert (b 7 Nov 1814) m 3 Oct 1836, Isaac Davis

BP329   Elizabeth Pickert (b 21 Feb 1824)

BP33   Bartholomew Pickert (10 May 1771-18 Mar 1813, Manheim NY) m 1) 3 May 1796, Dorothy Bishop (d 26 Jun 1802); m 2) 21 Nov 1802, Catherine

BP34   Frederick Pickert (1772-15 Mar 1857, Manheim NY) m 21 Dec 1799, Catherine Windecker (d 2 Jun 1866). Bur Manheim NY.

BP341   Daniel Pickert (b 14 Apr 1811)

BP342   Samuel Pickert (27 Dec 1812-6 Dec 1860) m Sally   (d 11 May 1857). Bur Manheim NY.

BP343   Ephraim Pickert (b 13 Aug 1815)

BP35   John Pickert (1777-15 Mar 1857) m Nancy (d 21 Sep 1862). Bur Manheim NY.

BP351   Lucina Pickert (b 12 Feb 1830)

BP352   Lelander Pickert (b 24 Sep 1831)

BP36   Dina Pickert m William Kissner

BP37   Eche Pickert m Elijah Goodell

BP38   Maria Pickert m Gerret Van Slyke

BP39   Peter Pickert (7 Aug 1784-28 Dec 1849, South Hammond NY) m Jemima Briggs. Bur South Hammond NY.

BP391   Elias Pickert (20 Jul 1814-1854) m Clarissa

BP392   Peter Pickert

BP393   Jane Pickert (b 1819) m Benjamin Franklin

BP394   Joseph Pickert (1822-1909) m 1844, Samantha Franklin

BP395   Charles Pickert (10 Dec 1826, near Middleville NY-14 Feb 1882, Redwood NY) m 8 Jan 1861, Louise De Garmo (1 Jan 1842, near Gansevoort NY-3 Aug 1898, Balston Spa NY). Steamboat operator on the Hudson River between Albany and New York City. Later resided Northumberland and Albany NY; finally farmer near Hammond NY.

BP3951   Jennie A. Pickert (23 Dec 1861, Northumberland NY-13 Nov 1950) m 23 Dec 1882, Canastola NY, William F. George (3 Feb 1861, Philadelphia PA-20 Sep 1938). Bur Ithaca NY.

BP39511   Leeta May George (10 Nov 1883-26 Aug 1970) m Charles Houghton

BP39512   Perle H. George (21 Oct 1884-15 Nov 1930) m Marie Rassmussen

BP39513   Jennie N. George (b 2 Sep 1887) m 28 Sep 1910, Ward Manchester

BP39514   Beatrice Cencei George (5 Nov 1889, Ithaca NY-25 Feb 1980, Ithaca NY) m 3 Jan 1912, Ithaca NY, George Christian Schempp II (14 May 1889, Tacoma WA-20 Jan 1919). He bur Tacoma WA; she Ithaca NY. BS, Cornell U; prof, U GA, Athens GA.

BP395141   Lucy Anne Schempp (b 24 Oct 1913, Albany GA) m 5 Jul 1941, Ernest H. Jacoby

BP3951411 Cook   Lucerne A. Jacoby (b 2 Jan 1947) m 1) 1964, James Morr; m 2) 26 Aug 1973, Thomas

BP39514111   Scott Morr (b 4 Jun 1965)(Adopted by Thomas Cook)

BP39514112   Brian Cook (b 19 Dec 1975)

BP39514113   Elizabeth Cook (b 24 Oct 1977)

BP3951412   Jeanneane H. Jacoby (b 3 Nov 1949) m 20 Dec 1969, Bruce Pelon

BP39514121   Holly Pelon (b 25 Jan 1975)

BP3951413   Ernest C. Jacoby (b 17 Sep 1951) m 14 Nov 1970, Joy Hughes

BP39514131   Jill Jacoby (b 23 Oct 1972)

BP3951414   Stephen A. Jacoby (b 22 Jun 1953) m 26 Jan 1983, Susan Brandes

BP39514141   Kip Jacoby (b 2 Sep 1983)

BP395142   Beatrice Cencei Schempp (b 10 Jun 1915, Albany GA) m 23 Dec 1937, Robert Reddick

BP3951421   Donald Reddick (b 16 Jul 1939) m 21 Jan 1967, Joyce Hellum

BP39514211   Eve E. Reddick (b 15 Apr 1968)

BP39514212   Ian Reddick (b 7 Oct 1973)

*BP395143   George Christian Schempp III (b 26 Sep 1916, Batavia NY) m 1) 30 May 1938, Kathryn Irene Marinso (b 23 May 1918, Ithaca NY), div 1946; m 2) 30 Oct 1946, Mary Elizabeth Finch (b 12 Jan 1912, Buffalo NY). Insurance executive, Ithaca NY; she, RN.

BP3951431   Charlotte Ann Schempp (b 8 Dec 1938, Ithaca NY) m 15 May 1959, William Homer Day (b 29 Sep 1934, Wilmington DE). BS, U DE; PhD, Cornell U, 1965; research entymologist, USDA, Newark DE.

BP39514311   Robert Steven Day (b 3 Jan 1960, Ithaca NY) m 31 Aug 1986, Joann Rosenberg (b 10 Oct 1962, Newark DE). He, research lab; she, computer specialist. Res Newark DE.

BP395143111   Melissa Christine Day (b 3 Oct 1987, Newark DE)

BP395143112   Steven James Day (b 20 Apr 1989, Newark DE)

BP3951432   George Christian Schempp III (b 19 Apr 1941, Ithaca NY) m 1) 4 Sep 1965, Elizabeth A. Isabell, div 1984; m 2) 15 Jul 1985, Carol Haber. Miami FL.

BP39514321   Natalie Elizabeth Schempp (b 15 Mar 1966, Syracuse NY). Real estate mgr, Pembroke Pines FL.

BP39514322   Leslie A. Schempp (b 14 Nov 1968, Syracuse NY). Lab technician, Davie FL.

BP39514323   Jeffrey Adam Schempp (b 20 Aug 1986, Miami FL)

BP3951433   William A. Schempp (b 11 Jun 1948)

BP395144   John Adams Schempp (b 15 Mar 1918, Camilla GA) m 6 Oct 1942, Isabel G. Poyer

BP3951441   Nancy L. Schempp (b 7 Apr 1944)

BP3951442   Beatrice A. Schempp (b 1 Feb 1946) m Robert Crocetta

BP39514421   Lisa Crocetta (b 3 Jun 1967)

BP39514422   Robert Crocetta (b 27 Aug 1969)

BP3951443   Mary J. Schempp (b 17 Sep 1949) m Lawrence Boyka

BP39514431   Michael Boyka (b 24 Mar 1977)

BP3951444   Susan M. Schempp (b 13 Nov 1951) m 13 Apt 1975, Robert McCue

BP39514441   Laura McCue (b 10 Jan 1978)

BP39514442   Erin McCue (b 31 Oct 1980)

BP39514443   Heather McCue (b 31 Oct 1980)

BP3951445   John Adams Schempp, Jr. (b 4 Apr 1957) m 26 Jul 1980, Bethany Fellman

BP39514451   Jennifer Schempp (b 25 Aug 1982)

BP39514452   Sarah Schempp (b 3 Jun 1986)

BP39515   Louisa George (b 7 Oct 1794(m Jun 1820, Lawrence Butler

BP3952   Louis Pickert m Fannie Makepeace

BP3953   Edith Pickert

BP3954   Morgan Pickert (28 Dec 1872-18 Mar 1957) m 18 Jan 1897, Ada Genung

BP3955   Guilbert Pickert (d 11 Dec 1898) m Josephine Sherwood

BP4   Conrad Pickard (5 Mar 1727, Palatine NY-5 Aug 1827, Owasco NY) m 30 Jun 1751, Anna May Margartha Walrath (Walrod). Probably bu in a cemetery which he established on his farm near Owasco NY.

BP41   Nicholas N. Pickard (3 May 1752, Montgomery Co NY-19 Mar 1825) m Jun 1781, Mary Linn (11 Aug 1763-19 Aug 1831). Bur Elbridge Tp, Onondaga Co NY. US Revolution, 1st Tryon Co. Had land in Camillus NY. He is called Doctor, but had no academic training; he has been styled by a descendant a "herb and root doctor who learned his pharmacology from the Indians."

BP411   Margaret Pickard (8 Mar 1782-19 Nov 1819) m 1 Jan 1799, Amos Robinson

BP412   Nicholas N. Pickard (16 Mar 1784-6 Dec 1869, Marion NY) m 1 Jan 1808, Jane Armstrong (bu 9 Dec 1856, Camillus NY)

BP413   Joseph Nicholas Pickard (25 Jun 1786, Onondaga Co NY-6 Jul 1847, Stephenson IL) m 1 Jun 1809, Julia Ann Coleman (b 19 Nov 1788)

BP4131   Julia Ann Pickard (10 Jan 1810, Cayuga Co NY-1 Oct 1882) m 15 Jun 1829, Peter Van Sickle (28 Feb 1806-19 May 1898)

BP4132   Jane Ann Pickard (3 May 1811, Cayuga Co NY-17 Sep 1835) m   Benson

BP4133   Nicholas Coleman Pickard (b 25 May 1813, Cayuga Co NY) m Hannah   . Lena IL.

BP4134   Squire Orthno (Orthonel) Pickard (b 16 Dec 1815, Cayuga Co NY) m 26 Feb 1837, Huron Co OH, Sarah Ann Way (d 4 Jul 1871). Moved to Stephenson Co IL, McLean Co IL, Iowa Co IA. She bur Marengo IA.

BP41341   Harriet Lois Pickard (b ca 1840) m   Leigh

BP413411   Jesse R. Leigh

BP413412   Clarence W. Leigh

BP413413   Jennie Leigh

BP413414   Harriet Lois Leigh

BP413415   Ivy Leigh

BP41342   Mary Jane Pickard (b ca 1842) m   Merritt

BP41343   Ola (Minnieola) Pickard m Bert Hastings

BP41344   Alta (Amelia) Pickard (b ca 1850) m Phillip Hahn

BP413441   Frank Willard Hahn

BP413442   Minnie Hahn m   Maxwell

BP413443   Jennie Hahn m   McLaughlin

BP413444   Vernon Hahn

BP413445   Fred Hahn

BP41345   Fred W. Pickard m

BP413451   Hazel Pickard m   Miller

BP413452   Edith Pickard m   Carlson

BP413453   Iva Pickard

BP413454   Alma Pickard

BP413455   Clifford Pickard

BP413456   Lois Pickard

BP413457   Helen Pickard

BP413458   Max Pickard

BP41346   Luther Henry Pickard (b ca 1844) m

BP413461   Adelbert D. Pickard

BP413462   Lulu Mae Pickard

BP413463   Edith Belle Pickard m   Booth

BP413464   Daisy Pickard m   Barkley

BP413465   Myrtle Pickard m   Mayer

BP413466   Veta Pickard

BP413467   Leigh Pickard

BP41347   Edwin Coleman Pickard (b ca 1847)

BP413471   Maude Pickard

BP413472   Leroy Pickard

BP413473   Ethel Pickard m   Kelley

BP41348   Bertrem Leander Pickard

BP413481   Ora Pickard

BP413482   Harry Pickard

BP413483   Clyde Pickard

BP41349   Charles Willard Pickard (10 Feb 1855, Stephenson Co IL-28 Apr 1932, Indianola IA) m 24 Oct 1888, Newton IA, Martha Ann Long (19 Jan 1856, Jasper Co IA-15 Feb 1950). Bur Indianola IA. Rancher, Chase Co KS, later farm real estate.

BP413491   Clarence Luther Pickard (28 May 1890, near Cedar Point, Chase Co KS-22 Dec 1982, Des Moines IA) m 7 Sep 1922, Des Moines IA, Sarah Mildred Mott (9 Mar 1895, Tipton IA-4 Dec 1987, Columbia MO). WWI, USN. MS, IA S U; teacher, county agent, farmer. In his 70s he and his wife joined the Peace Corps and served in India. She teacher and homemaker.

BP4134911   Clarence Mott Pickard (b 24 Oct 1923, Ames IA) m 9 Oct 1954, Florence Estelle (Erica) Carlan (b 20 Aug 1924, Everett MA). He, AB, Simpson Col; MD, Johns Hopkins U; teaching and consulting internist, Columbia MO. Active in patriotic societies, SAR, Huguenot Society, Sons and Daughters of the

Pilgrims, Founders and Patriots of the Jamestowne Society. She, medical illustrator, artist, master silversmith. Res Columbia MO.

BP41349111   Carlan Brent Pickard (b 18 Mar 1956, Kansas City MO)

BP41349112   Emmett Blair Pickard (b 4 Sep 1957, Columbia MO)

BP41349113   Reid Haskell Pickard (b 18 Mar 1958, Columbia MO)

BP41349114   Lydia Windsor Pickard (b 24 Oct 1959, Columbia MO). USNR.

BP4134912   David Charles Pickard (b 6 Mar 1925, Ames IA) m 22 Aug 1948, Edith McGehee (b 15 Dec 1923-1 Dec 1991). USN Air Corps. Pilot, Miami Springs FL.

BP41349121   Glen Charles Pickard (b 14 Aug 1950, Miami FL) m 23 May 1993, Vivian Ghatan. Engineer, Ringwood NJ.

BP41349122   Wayne Arthur Pickard (b 5 Mar 1952, Miami FL) m 26 May 1990, Lela Ruth Lilly, div 1994. MD; anesthesiologist, Tampa FL.

BP41349123   Kenneth Cameron Pickard (b 16 Jun 1954, Miami FL). Miami Springs FL.

BP41349124   Martin David Pickard (b 18 Jun 1958, Miami FL) m 11 Jan 1993, Kathryn Bohlmann. USN. Pilot.

          Marily Susan Pickard (b 28 Dec 1961, Miami FL)(Adopted by David and Edith Pickard) m 28 Dec 1988, Donald Meecham Dawson, Jr. Miami Springs FL.

BP413492   Wayne A. Pickard (named Way at birth, he assumed name Wayne and initial A.)(14 Nov 1891, near Cedar Point, Chase Co KS-22 Nov 1972, Phoenix AZ) m 12 Aug 1929, Lora Himstreet (14 May 1904-1 Feb 1985, Farmington NM). Bur Safford AZ. USA.

BP4134921   Paul Wayne Pickard (b 29 Jul 1931) m Wilma Jean Shreffler

BP41349211   Paula Jean Pickard (b 23 Sep 1956) m Mar 1988, Clifford Digby. Elizabeth CO.

BP41349212   William Wayne Pickard (b 9 Sep 1957) m Trudy Alexander. Aztec NM.

BP413492121   Tyrell Pickard (b 1982)

BP413492122   Cody Pickard (b 1984)

BP41349213   Creston Turner Pickard (b 23 Nov 1959) m April Whitehorn, div. Res Kirtland NM.

BP413492131   Dawn Marie Pickard (b Jun 1979)

BP413492132   Brandi Cheyenne Pickard (b 1989)

BP4134922   Frederick Charles Pickard (b 14 Jan 1934) m 1) Dora Thomas Kern; m 2) Arlene

BP41349221   Cynthia Ann Pickard (b 14 Apr 1963) m 4 Jun 1983, Michael Jacobson

BP413492211   April Lorraine Jacobson (b 7 Nov 1981)

BP41349222   James Frederick Pickard (b 1 Apr 1965)

BP41349223   Dionne Rebecca Pickard (b 2 Feb 1981)

BP413493   Fannie Pauline Pickard (b 2 Feb 1894, near Cedar Point, Chase Co KS) m 18 Feb 1922, Mora MN, Manley Earl Sweazy (20 Jul 1898, near Salem MO-22 Jun 1980, Tacoma WA). USN. Grad, IA U, Harvard U; hunter, wild life photographer; CLU, AK and Seattle WA.

BP4134931   Martha Ann Sweazy (b 8 Oct 1922, Cambridge MA) m 29 Jul 1950, Seattle WA, George Edward Gaby (b 22 Sep 1921). Social workers, Springfield MA.

BP41349311   David Paul Gaby (b 6 May 1955, Springfield MA) m 8 Jun 1985, Springfield MA, Bonita Faye Dillard. City planner, Springfield MA.

BP413493111   Alison Opal Jean Gaby (b 5 Nov 1985)

BP413493112   Lauren Elizabeth Gaby (b 29 Aug 1989)

BP413493113   Margaret Gaby (b 2 Nov 1990)

BP413493114   Lydia Faye Gaby (b 5 Mar 1992)

BP41349312   Margaret Elizabeth Gaby (b 13 May 1957, Springfield MA) m 1)   ; m 2) 12 Jul 1980, Darryl Kinney

BP413493121   Alexander Kinney (b 12 Aug 1982)

BP413493122   Daniel James Gaby Kinney (b 6 Apr 1985)

BP413493123   Mariel Christine Kinney (b 26 Jul 1988)

BP41349313   Paula Katherine Gaby (b 31 Oct 1960, Springfield MA)

BP4134932   Pauline Pickard Sweazy (b 20 Sep 1925, Seattle WA) m 12 Sep 1946, Seattle WA, Vance William Reeves (b 28 Sep 1924). Chemical engineer, teacher, Tacoma WA.

BP41349321   Katherine Claire Reeves (b 14 Mar 1948, Seattle WA)

BP41349322   Michael Stuart Reeves (b 26 Mar 1951, Seattle WA)

BP41349323   Martha Anne Reeves (b 31 Jul 1956, Tacoma WA) m 30 Jun 1984, Gregory Warren Wong (b 10 Aug 1957, Springfield MA)

BP4134933   Patricia G. Sweazy (b 5 Mar 1927, Seattle WA) m 26 Nov 1948, Seattle WA, Russell Paul Nelson (b 30 Aug 1924, Eau Claire WI), div 1991. She, management consulting, counseling.

BP41349331   Gregory Nelson (30 Jan 1951-31 Jan 1951, Pomona CA)

BP41349332   Geoffrey Nelson (30 Jan 1951-31 Jan 1951, Pomona CA)

BP41349333   Cynthia Gay Nelson (b 15 Feb 1952, Pomona CA) m Thomas Osborn. Olympia WA.

BP41349334   Andrea Marie Nelson (b 5 Mar 1954, Seattle WA) m John Bowen. West Seattle WA.

BP41349335   Barry Craig Nelson (b 15 Mar 1956, Seattle WA)

BP413494   Williard Charles Pickard (b 30 Jan 1896) m 21 Nov 1921, Irene Shenken (b 21 Nov 1902). Real estate appraiser, Cedar Rapids IA.

BP4134941   Charles Coleman Pickard (b ca 1940). Cedar Rapids IA.

BP414   Jonas Pickard (6 May 1788-27 Dec 1812)

BP415   Henry Pickard (18 Oct 1790, Cayuga Co NY-1855) m 1 Sep 1810, Cayuga Co NY, Jane
Coleman

BP416   Phoebe Pickard (26 Jan 1793-29 Aug 1876) m 1) 7 Feb 1811, John Rose; m 2) Jun 1821,
Daniel Perkins

BP417   Rachel Pickard (25 Sep 1795, Ovid NY-20 Oct 1826) m 6 Mar 1823, John Hawkins

BP418   Smith Wix Pickard (25 Sep 1795, Ovid NY-18 Oct 1874, Richland Co MI) m 1) 1816,
Affa Skeels, div 1853; m 2) Mrs. James. War of 1812. Moved to Camillus NY in 1831, to MI in 1838; then
to Lena IL.

BP419   Polly Pickard (b 19 Aug 1797) m 14 Feb 1819, Joseph Remington

BP41A   Andrew B. Pickard (b 21 Mar 1800) m 6 Jan 1827, Maria Lamb. Methodist pastor.

BP41B   Daniel Lynn Pickard (15 Jun 1802-12 Sep 1878, Rochester NY) m 25 Feb 1845, Phebine
H. Brown (b Jul 1825, Steuben Co NY)

BP41C   Susan L. Pickard (18 Aug 1804-1888) m 5 Jun 1827, Abner Mallory

BP42   Catherine Pickard (b 24 Apr 1754)

BP43   John Pickard (b ca 1756, Springfield NY) m 1772, Counegunda (Kinyet) Bratt (1756-5
Feb 1841, West Sparta NY). US Revolution. He spelled surname Pickertt.

BP431   Margaret Pickertt (b 1773) m Samuel Hill

BP432   John Pickertt, Jr. (b ca 1774)

BP433   Conrad Pickertt (b 25 Sep 1777, Cherry Valley NY) m Mary B. Van Alstine (b 9 Feb
1777, Cherry Valley NY)

BP44   George Pickert

BP45   Adolphus Pickert (ca 1761, Springfield, Otsego Co NY-23 Jul 1846, Orleans, Jefferson
Co NY) m Catherine Spaulding (ca 1771-1840, Jefferson Co NY). US Revolution.

BP451   Jonas Pickert (ca 1788-3 Oct 1878, Alton IL) m Roxy Conant

BP452   Meriam (Mary) Pickert (b ca 1789) m Jacob Turner

BP453   Jonathan N. Pickard (ca 1792-30 Sep 1868, Locke MI) m Mary Countryman (1801,
Canada-13 Apr 1892)

BP46   Mary Pickert (ca 1769, Springfield NY-1859) m ca 1789, Peabody Cook

BP461   Catherine Cook (b ca 1791)

BP462   Clariss Cook (ca 1793-dy)

BP463   Margaret Cook (ca 1795-dy)

BP464   Lucy Cook (b ca 1797) m Hiram Wiltse

BP465   Anna Margaret Cook (b ca 1799)

BP466   Susan Cook (b ca 1801)

BP467   Phebe Cook (b ca 1803)

BP468   Mary Cook (b ca 1805)

BP469   Elizabeth Cook (b ca 1806)

BP46A   Clarissa Cook (b ca 1807)

BP46B   Nelson Cook (b ca 1809)

BP47   William Pickert (b 6 Jul 1772) m Mary   . No chn.

BP48   Abraham Pickert (ca 1776-ca 1860) m Elinda Richardson (ca 1786-16 Oct 1868)

BP481   James H. Pickard (ca 1823, Springfield NY-16 Jan 1891, Kalamazoo MI) m 1) Anna
(d 19 Jan 1865); m 2) Marilla T.   (ca 1828-20 Aug 1876)

BP482   Fannie Mary Pickard (d 1896) m 22 Mar 1837, James M. White (d 9 Jan 1894)

BP5   Leah Pickert

BP6   Jacobus (James) Pickard (b ca 1730) m ca 1757, Gertrude Hartman

BP61   Anna Margrita Pickert (Bikkert) (b ca 1758) m 11 Apr 1784, German Flatts, Herkimer Co
NY, George Van Slyke (ca 1762-14 Sep 1832). US Revolution. Niagara Co NY.

BP611   Margaret Van Slyke (b ca 1785) m John Schyler

BP612   Garrett Van Slyke (b 11 Aug 1789) m Elizabeth Pickard (b 18 Dec 1795) (see BP684)

BP613   Eva Van Slyke (b ca 1794, Canajoharie NY) m John Christmas

BP614   Rachael Van Slyke m Jacob Kaharsh

BP615   John Van Slyke (b ca 1805) m Emily Zimmerman (b ca 1814)

BP616   George Van Slyke (b ca 1806)

BP617   Elizabeth Van Slyke m   Squires

BP62   Johannes (John) Pickert (28 May 1760, Little Falls NY-30 Aug 1827, Ellery NY) m 6 Jan
1784, Margaret Marie Garlock

BP621   Maria Margareta Pickard (22 Dec 1784/5, German Flats NY-24 Dec 1825, Ellery NY) m
15 Nov 1801, John Vanderwarker (b 22 Jan 1781, Montgomery Co NY)

BP622   Gertrude Charity Pickard (3 Oct 1785, German Flats NY-21 Nov 1867, Ellery NY) m ca
1804, Lawrence Story (30 Apr 1781-23 Jul 1860)

BP623   Adam I. Pickard (b 3 Oct 1786) m Polly (Mary) Richmond (9 Nov 1799, Madison Co

NY-6 Feb 1873). Bur Red Bird NY.

BP624   Catherine Pickard (2 Aug 1789-15 Jul 1845, Ellery NY) m James Pickard (see BP671)

BP625   Peter Pickard (17 Jan 1790, St. Johnsville NY-28 Sep 1872, Busti NY) m four times

BP626   James Pickard (ca 1793-16 May 1848)

BP627   John Pickard, Jr. (ca 1794-ca 1835)

BP628   Nancy Pickard (29 Apr 1798-5 Nov 1852, Ellery NY) m 30 Jan 1848, William H. Ludden

BP629   Sylvanus Pickard (8 Dec 1800-23 Jan 1880, Ogden IA) m Betsy Becker (d 17 Nov 1878)

BP62A   Henry Pickard (9 Jul 1803, Monroe Co NY-29 Dec 1882, Basti NY) m 1) Maria Vanderwark (28 Feb 1808-8 Jun 1860); m 2) Eunice A. Beck (d 17 Jan 1891)

BP62B   Albert Pickard (ca 1807-14 Jun 1852, Decatur Co IN)

BP62C   Abraham Pickard (21 Apr 1810, Sullivan NY-25 Apr 1896, Ellery NY) m 26 Jun 1831, Sally Ann Waite (d 28 Mar 1896)

BP63   Lea Pickard (b 1762) m 6 Jan 1784, German Flats NY, Andreas Balsley (Palsley)

BP631   Maria Balsley (b 1789)

BP632   Margretha Balsley (b 1792)

BP633   Nicholas Balsley (b 1793)

BP64   Isabel Pickard (b ca 1762)

BP65   Anna (Nancy) Pickard (b ca 1763) m 11 Apr 1784, German Flats NY, Martin Van Slyke

BP651   John B. Van Slyke (b ca 1805) m Mary Ann

BP652   James Van Slyke m Margaret Christmas

BP653   Nicholas Van Slyke

BP654   Dorothea Van Slyke m Sam Kittinger

BP655   Margaret Van Slyke m   Ostrander

BP656   Charity Van Slyke m John Keller

BP66   Catherine Pickard (b ca 1765) m 27 Dec 1785, Johannes Balsley

BP661   Pieter Balsley (b 1786)

BP662   Magdalena Balsley (b 1792)

BP67   Joseph Pickard (ca 1767-30 Jul 1823) m 27 Dec 1785, Magdalena Forth

BP671   Jacobus Pickard (12 May 1786-21 Sep 1859) m 1) ca 1808, Catherine Pickard (2 Aug 1789-15 Jul 1845); m 2) Mary Richmond (d 6 Feb 1873)(see BP624)

BP672   Andreas Pickard (b 1788) m Laura

BP673   Benjamin Pickard (b 1791)

BP674   Catherine Pickard (b 1792)

BP675   Rudolph Pickard (1793-1852) m Katherine Kelly (d 1858)

BP676   Joseph Pickard, Jr.

BP68   Nicholas Pickard (b ca 1769) m 29 Jan 1792, Barbara Stamm

BP681   Peter Pickard (b 26 Aug 1794, Palatine NY)

BP682   Adam N. Pickard (1793-5 Nov 1868, Centreville MI) m 3 Mar 1816, Sullivan NY, Nancy
Ale (d 6 Aug 1881, Leland MI)

BP683   Bartel Pickard m Mary Jan Becker (d 8 Jan 1828)

BP684   Elizabeth Pickard (b 18 Dec 1795) m Garret Van Slyke (see BP612)

BP69   Hartman Pickard (ca 1770-5 Nov 1823, Pendleton NY) m 21 Sep 1794, Dorothy (Dolly)
Stamm (5 Nov 1775-25 Mar 1839, Pendleton NY)

BP691   Ann Eva Pickard (1795-2 Dec 187) m Conrad Rickard (d 16 Feb 1859)

BP692   Lawrence A. Pickard (23 Apr 1797, Sullivan NY-15 Feb 1861, Pendleton NY) m Lucy
Woolover (7 Jul 1808-13 Nov 1879)

BP693   Mary (Polly) Pickard m 1) John Busch; m 2) John McCallister

BP694   Elizabeth Pickard m 1) Paul Kelly; m 2) John Golden

BP695   John Pickard (ca 1798-Feb 1851)

BP696   Gertrude Charity Pickard

BP697   Launna A. Pickard (1811-1818)

BP6A   Maria Pickard (b ca 1770) m 25 Oct 1791, Johann Dietrich Petri

BP6A1   Maria Petri (b 1791)

BP6B   Jacob Pickard (b ca 1772) m Kate

BP6C   Barbara Pickard (b ca 1772)

BP6D   Heindrick (Henry) Pickard (b ca 1773) m Anna Eva

BP6D1   Margaretha Pickard (b 20 May 1792)

BP6D2   Edwin Pickard (ca 1805-2 Dec 1851) m Rachael Schuyler

BP6D3   Richard Pickard (2 May 1815, Sullivan NY-25 Dec 1859, Ellery NY) m Mary Pickard (28
Nov 1819-9 Apr 1885)

BP6D4   Henry Pickard (ca 1818-1882) m Diana Becker

BP6D5   Polly Pickard

BP6D6   Susan Pickard

BP6D7   Catherine Pickard m Elijah Rappleyea

BP6E   Conrad Pickard (b ca 1774) m three times

BP6E1   Maria Pickard (b 25 Dec 1791, Herkimer Co NY)

BP6E2   Jonas Pickard (b Aug 1793, Herkimer Co NY)

BP6E3   Margaret Pickard (ca 1803-ca 1875, MI)

BP6E4   William Pickard (ca 1806-17 Jun 1885, Alamo MI) m 1)   ; m 2) Mrs. Susannah Wiles

BP6E5   Matilda Pickard (13 Dec 1808, Sullivan NY-29 Nov 1885, Ellery NY) m John Maybee

BP6E6   Conrad Pickard

BP6E7   Michael Pickard m ? Zelpha Martin

BP6F   Rachael Pickard (b ca 1776) m Jacob Lower

BP7   Rachel Pickard (b 29 Oct 1733) m   Countryman

BP71   Maria Countryman (b 1771) m Conrad Shimmel

BP711   Conrad Shimmel (b 1794) m Margaret Fickes

BP7111   Mary Ann Shimmel (b 27 May 1823, Jefferson Co NY) m Martin Shindler (2 Feb 1820, NY-30 Aug 1867, Alexandria Bay NY)

BP71111   Edgar Seymour Shindler (19 Jun 1868, Alexandria Bay NY-8 Sep 1957, Hammond NY) m 20 Oct 1886, Alexandria Bay NY, Janet Brown (7 Aug 1866, Fowler NY-30 Jan 1948, Hammond NY). Bur Hammond NY.

BP711111   Mattie Belle Shindler (10 Aug 1895, Pamelia NY-23 Sep 1983, Plattsburgh NY) m 19 Nov 1914, Hammond NY, Vernon Clay Newberry (22 Jan 1893, Ganonoque Ont CAN-19 Jun 1961, Hammond NY). Bur Alexandria Bay NY.

BP7111111   Irma Virginia Newberry (b 12 Jul 1929, Ogdensburg NY) m 26 Dec 1949, Syracuse NY, Gus Repas (b 8 Nov 1914, Plattsburgh NY)

BP71111111   Constance Repas

BP71111112   Maria Repas m   Arnold

CHAPTER NINE

[JW] Jacob Weiser (ca 1712-   )

Jacob Weiser, one of two sons of Hans Conrad Weiser by his second marriage to Anna Margaretha Muller, was probably born about 1712 in New York. Although we are not certain how long his mother lived or where she died, it seems probable that the entire family followed the senior Conrad in his movements.

After his return from England in 1721, Conrad was at first in Minisink, Orange Co NY (1726), then Bucks Co PA (1730), and, it would seem, in New Jersey in the early 1730s. At least his son Christopher Frederick was involved in a land transaction in Middlesex County in 1732. His daughter Anna Margaretha died unmarried in Rocky Hill, Somerset Co NJ, in late 1748. On that occasion, Jacob Wiser of Middlesex County, called her brother, was appointed her administrator, 13 Oct 1748. He and one John Deare of Perth Amboy took a bond for 400 pounds in her estate on that date. The record of it cites him as of New Brunswick and calls him a cordwainer (shoemaker).

Jacob's wife was named Sarah. The records of the New Brunswick First Reformed Church, published in the New Jersey Historical Society Proceedings, XI (1926), p. 412, cite the baptism of their son Jacob on 4 Aug 1745.[141] Jacob, Sr., seems to have had other children as well: a son Frederick, who was also a shoemaker, who had a daughter Susannah baptized at Christ Episcopal Church, New Brunswick, 24 Jul 1774, and who was buried unmarried on 4 May 1856 at the same church; perhaps a son Henry who married 11 Jul 1768 at Richmond, to Catherine Wynants; perhaps some daughters. Since there appears to be no estate record for Jacob, we are not certain about his family.

There is a marriage at Christ Church, New Brunswick, for a Jacob Weiser and Elizabeth Turner, 7 Mar 1783, who might be a grandchild of the senior Jacob.

Jacob Weiser was a witness to the will of Johannes Volkertse Van Noordstrand of Somerset Co NJ written 5 Jul 1753, probated 5 Apr 1756. He was also witness 9 Mar 1768 to the will of John Downey of New Brunswick. A William Oak or Oake was also a witness to each will.

Relationships between Jacob Weiser and the family of his half-brother Conrad seem to have been cordial. When Henry Melchior Muhlenberg was involved in the affairs of Lutheran congregations in New Jersey, he reported 14 Sep 1759 that "my wife's uncle, Mr. Jacob Weiser, and his wife came from Braunschweig (Brunswick) to pay us a visit." On 19 Nov 1759 Muhlenberg and his wife "drove fourteen miles further to Braunsweig to visit a relative Mr. Jacob Weiser and his family." In April 1760 he gave two pounds, fourteen shillings and six pence to be delivered to Jacob Weiser in Brunswick for a pair of boots and a pair of shoes.[142]

Perhaps more study of records from New York and New Jersey would uncover more about Jacob and his family. Whether he had descendants at all and whether he has any by the surname Weiser in any spelling is uncertain at this point.

---

[141]There is a gravemarker in St. Paul's churchyard in New York City for Jacob Weiser who died in 1785, aged 40. He was witness as a cordwainer on 4 Jun 1777 to the will of Anne Avory, late of New York City, but then of New Brunswick. An estate record for Jacob exists in New York City, letters to his wife Rebecca, granted 16 Aug 1785.

[142]Journals of Henry Melchior Muhlenberg I, pp. 414, 421, 428.

CHAPTER TEN

[RK]   Rebecca (Weiser) Klein (b ca 1713)[143]

Rebecca Weiser was born about 1713 and married about 1732 to Johann Friedrich Klein. Little is known about them, except that there are a number of children listed as born to them in various church records in the Hudson Valley, and that they sponsored various children born there.

Children of Johann Friedrich and Rebecca (Weiser) Klein:

RK1   Anna Catharine Klein, 8 Apr 1733, Kingston NY

RK2   Anna Margaretha Klein, 16 Feb 1735, Kingston NY

RK3   Jacob Klein, 16 Feb 1737, Tarbush NY

RK4   Johann Frederick Klein, 1 Mar 1739, Ancram NY

RK5   Rebecca Klein, 22 Apr 1741, Ancram NY

RK6   Johann Adam Klein, 5 Dec 1743, Ancram NY

RK7   Maria Klein, 2 Mar 1746, Ancram NY

RK8   Eva Klein, 24 Feb 1750, Ancram NY

---

[143]Data provided by Henry Z Jones, Jr.

CHAPTER ELEVEN

[JF] Johann Friedrich Weiser (1714-1769)
and his descendants[144]

Johann Friederich, or John Frederick, or simply Frederick (son of Johann Conrad and Anna Margaretha (Mueller) Weiser) Weiser was born 14 Nov 1714, in Schoharie NY. He is specifically called the third and youngest child of his parents in his "Personalia," the biographical sketch of him in the Hebron, Lebanon Co PA, Moravian records. He married 18 Apr 1738 at "Gochkameko" (Ancram) as noted in the records of the Lutheran congregation at Loonenburg NY to Anna Catharina Humrich (26 Feb 1718, Maxsain, Germany-8 Dec 1793, Annville PA). In the spring of 1744, he moved his family to the "Swatara Hohl" in Lebanon Co PA. He became a Moravian in 1749 after having attended their worship for most of his married life. He suffered during Indian raids in 1756, losing a son in an attack. In 1763 he moved into Lebanon where he lived until shortly before his death 2 Sep 1769. He was buried in the Moravian cemetery at Hebron, today in the eastern part of Lebanon PA. His widow married 12 Dec 1780 to Peter Hetrick from whom she was separated.

JF1   Maria Catharina Weiser (12 Jan 1739-dy)

JF2   Johann Friederich Weiser (21 May 1740, NY-26 Jun 1756, near Lebanon PA). He was scalped by the Indians and is buried at Bethel Moravian Church Cemetery in Swatara Tp, Lebanon PA.

JF3   Johann Jacob Weiser (b 3 Oct 1742, Rheinbeck NY). There is no clear proof that he settled anywhere, but it seems likely that he was married to a Catharine by whom he had a daughter baptized in Lebanon in 1769. There are deed records in Cumberland Co PA, by which Jacob Weiser, a merchant of Carlisle, and his wife Catharine sold property they had purchased in 1791. Another deed, 8 Jun 1795, records a purchase in West Pennsborough Township and yet another 2 Aug 1795 in Rye Township. There is also a transfer to Jacob Weiser in Dickinson Township 23 Nov 1795. Letters of administration were issued 2 Jan 1802 to John Crover of Carlisle in the estate of Jacob Weiser of Carlisle. Since there is no record specifically naming children (except the baptism of a daughter), we are at a loss to be certain if he had any at all. On the basis of proximity and nomenclature, admittedly circumstantial rather than factual evidence, we are suggesting that he had several children who may be responsible for various Weiser families we find in Cumberland and adjacent counties whom we have not placed elsewhere. There is a marriage record dated 1 Sep 1766 for Jacob Weiser and Jane Mitchelltree, the marriage performed by John Conrad Bucher at Carlisle, the same Reformed clergyman who baptized the child in 1769. It is possible the Jacob under discussion here was married twice, lived in Carlisle, then in Lebanon, and then in Carlisle again. However, none of this is absolutely clear from the records, nor is the data below to be assigned to this Jacob without question.

JF31   Jacob Weiser m Mary Myers. He acquired land in Rye Tp, now Perry Co PA, by land grant in 1794 and by purchase in 1795. He is on the 1800 census for Rye Tp, but not in 1810 nor in 1820. Mary, presumably his wife, is listed in 1830 and 1840. There is no estate record or any record of birth or death for him, nor a tombstone. Nor are there any baptismal records for his children, whose names are derived chiefly from the will of his son Jacob who died without issue.

JF311   Frederick Weiser (ca 1788, Cumberland Co PA-1855, Perry Tp, Franklin Co OH) m 1) Elizabeth ; m 2) Rachel   (b 1803). He appears to have moved to Plymouth Tp, Richland Co OH, by 1830, then into Franklin Tp, Perry Co, by 1840. His first wife was confirmed at Enola in 1827. This family is incomplete.

---

[144]The memorial notice of John Frederick Weiser is printed in German in H.M.M. Richards, "The Weiser Family" in Pennsylvania German Society, XXXII (1924), pp. 112-115. See also the records of the Moravian congregations at Bethel and Hebron, Lebanon Co PA, in the Moravian Archives, Bethlehem PA. The data about Catharine Humrich is in Annette K. Burgert and Henry Z Jones, Jr. *Westerwald to America* (Camden ME, 1989), III. See Dauphin Co deed records and tax lists, records of Tabor Reformed Church and Salem Lutheran Church, Lebanon; and extensive correspondence with Edna B. Eichler, Hilda M. Smith, Harry Lenig and Ralph B. Rainey (all JCWFA) has provided data and raised questions.

JF3111   Benjamin Weiser (b 18 Mar 1825, bp Enola PA)

JF3112   Jacob Weiser (b 21 Jan 1827, bp Enola PA)

JF3113   Flewell Weiser (b ca 1837, OH)

JF312   Mary Weiser (1792-1850, Rye Tp, Perry Co PA) m Thomas Barnett

JF3121   Frederick Barnett

JF3122   Sarah Barnett m   Shively

JF3123   Mathilda Barnett m   McClintock

JF3124   Mary Ann Barnett (20 Mar 1820-8 Aug 1900) m 11 Dec 1838, James Moore (13 Sep 1813-24 Jun 1874)

JF31241   Linus Moore

JF31242   William Barnett Moore

JF3125   Ester Barnett m   Fouler

JF3126   John Barnett

JF3127   William P. Barnett

JF313   Jacob Weiser (Jan 1794-12 Feb 1861) m   Jones. No chn. His will does not list a wife or children, but it does list nieces and nephews.

JF314   Jane Weiser m 1) William Wills (d 1838); m 2)   Putman

JF315   John Weiser m 20 Feb 1823, Mary Dentler

JF32   Catharine Elizabeth Weiser (b 17 Aug 1769, bp Lebanon PA)

JF33   Sarah Weiser (ca 1771-13 Apr 1830, Rye Tp, Perry Co PA) m 1) ca 1786, William Ogle (1749, New Castle Co DE-6 May 1806, Rye Tp, Perry Co PA); m 2) John Fry (d 1824).

JF331   John Ogle (10 Jan 1787-27 Mar 1824, Perry Co PA) m 28 Jun 1808, Martha Beatty (10 Feb 1788-26 Mar 1849, Rye Tp, Perry Co PA).

JF3311   Sarah Ogle (28 Feb 1810, Rye Tp, Perry Co PA-9 May 1868, Duncannon PA) m ca 1825, William Murphey.

JF3312   Martha Ogle (10 Dec 1811, Rye Tp, Perry Co PA-24 Mar 1874, Wheatfield Tp, Clinton Co IL) m ca 1828, Adam Yingst.

JF3313   William Ogle (21 Feb 1814, Rye Tp, Perry Co PA-8 Aug 1872, Wheatfield Tp, Clinton Co IL) m 12 Jan 1837, Perry Co PA, Susannah Collier

JF3314   Elizabeth Ogle (15 Jan 1817, Rye Tp, Perry Co PA-13 May 1855, Perry Co PA) m William Keel

JF3315   Lyman J. Ogle (25 May 1819, Rye Tp, Perry Co PA-15 Jan 1856, Duncannon PA) m ca 1843, Mary Ann Ogle

JF3316   Susannah Maria Ogle (17 Dec 1821, Rye Tp, Perry Co PA- 19 Oct 1862, Perry Co PA) m ca 1842, Nathaniel Collier.

JF3317   Elyann Ogle (19 Jan 1824, Rye Tp, Perry Co PA-11 Nov 1865, Clinton Co IL) m 1) ca 1842, Matthew W. Fisher; m 2) John Wade, Sr.

JF332   David Ogle (16 Sep 1788-before 1806)

JF333   William Ogle (9 Mar 1790-20 Mar 1829, Rye Tp, Perry Co PA) m Mary Steel

JF334   Jacob Ogle (9 Oct 1791-28 Jun 1867, Vigo Co IN) m 8 Jun 1813, Rye Tp, Perry Co PA, Sarah Beatty

JF335   James Ogle (11 Aug 1793, Rye Tp, Perry Co PA-3 Feb 1855, Perry Co PA) m 16 Oct 1816, Rachel Willis

JF336   Thomas Ogle (27 Jan 1796, Rye Tp, Perry Co PA-3 Jan 1816, Rye Tp, Perry Co PA). Unm.

JF337   Margret Ogle (30 Apr 1798, Rye Tp, Perry Co PA-before 1806)

JF338   Charlette Ogle (21 Apr 1800, Rye Tp, Perry Co PA-before 1806)

JF339   Edward Ogle (27 Aug 1803, Rye Tp, Perry Co PA-before 1806)

JF4   Elisabeth Weiser (15 Jan 1745, Lebanon Co PA-dy)

JF5   Johann Conrad Weiser (15 Mar 1747, Lebanon Co PA-dy)

JF6   Rebecca Weiser (5 or 16 Apr 1748, Lebanon Co PA-22 Jan 1815, Lebanon PA) m 3 Jul 1774, Johann Adam German (13 Dec 1750, Tulpehocken-3 Jul 1823, Lebanon PA). They had nine children of whom four sons and one daughter survived them.

JF61   Elizabeth German (5 Oct 1772-3 Apr 1829) m Philip Trump

JF62   Maria Otillia German (14 May 1775-29 Jan 1798). Unm.

JF7   Philippus Weiser (b 21 Aug 1750, near Lebanon PA) m Sabina   . He purchased property in Lebanon as a turner on 2 Apr 1779, which he sold 18 Nov 1783 to John Gloninger. He was taxed on this house and lot in 1782. That is the last clear reference we have to Philip. He does not seem to be on the 1790 census for Pennsylvania or any thereafter.

JF8   Johannes Weiser (7 Dec 1752-8 Dec 1760)

JF9   Conrad Weiser (1 Aug 1755-1757)

CHAPTER TWELVE

[HG] Hans Georg Weisser (1665-1740)
Schultheiss of Kleinaspach[145]

Hans Georg Weisser, the son of Jacob and Anna (Trefz?) Weisser, was born in Grossaspach on 1 Apr 1665 (or 10 Apr 1662) and died in Kleinaspach on 12 Apr 1740. He married 19 May 1685 in Kleinaspach to Anna Rosina Mueller (4 Nov 1663, Kleinaspach-16 Nov 1737, Kleinaspach). Hans Georg became a citizen of Kleinaspach on 4 Jun 1685. He was a baker, the proprietor of the Loewe Inn, a farmer, tax collector and appraiser there. His wife was the daughter of an old citizen of Kleinaspach, Michael Mueller (d 1685), also a baker, proprietor of the Loewe, and Buergermeister (then treasurer) of the town. The document settling the affairs of Georg Weisser's younger brother refers to him, Schultheiss of Kleinaspach, clearly as one of the siblings. Hans Georg was Schultheiss from 1689 to 1722/25 during the difficult period of the French invasion. Though it suffered in the invasion, Kleinaspach was not as battered as its larger parent neighbor from which Hans Georg had come. Its church records, which had been taken to Backnang "for safety," were burned there. In 1690 enemy troops extorted 20 gulden from Kleinaspach by taking Schultheiss Weisser to prison.

HG1   Anna Catharine Weisser (b 20 Feb 1687, Kleinaspach) m 27 Jan 1711, Kleinaspach, Johann Jacob Haiden, widower. He was a farmer and barrelmaker, Grossbottwar.

HG2   Hans Georg Weisser (1688, Kleinaspach-12 Mar 1700, Kleinaspach.

HG3   Anna Rosina Weisser (16 Dec 1690, Kleinaspach-10 Mar 1779, Kleinaspach) m Abraham Dorn, a son of Georg Dorn of Kleinaspach. Abraham was a farmer and Schultheiss, 1722-48.

HG4   Maria Elisabetha Weisser (b 22 May 1692, Kleinaspach) m 13 Apr 1717, Kleinaspach, Johann Melchior Bazinger (b at Neu-Lautern bei Loewenstein, a son of Georg Bazinger, glass producer at Neu Lautern). Johann Melchior was a baker in Kleinaspach.

HG5   Konrad Hans Weisser or Hans Konrad Weisser (b 12 May 1695, Kleinaspach) m 23 Jan Kleinaspach Anna Catharina Mehlin, daughter of Georg Mehlin of Allmersbach. Nothing is known of any children this couple might have had.

HG6   Angelika Weisser (13 Jun 1697, Kleinaspach-29 Feb 1744, Kleinaspach) m 15 Jul 1721, Kleinaspach, Johann Simon Dosselburger. Pattern weaver, Kleinaspach.

HG7   Matthaeus Weisser (12 Nov 1698, Kleinaspach-12 Nov 1698, Kleinaspach).

HG8   Matthaeus Weisser (20 Oct 1703, Kleinaspach-9 Jun 1775, Kleinaspach) m 19 Jun 1731, Kleinaspach, Anna Catharina Dorn, daughter of Veit and Barbara (Sayler) Dorn. Baker, farmer, proprietor of the Lowe, member of the town council and court; Burgermeister, Kleinaspach.

HG81   Conrad Johann Weisser (7 Sep 1732, Kleinaspach-7 Sep 1732, Kleinaspach).

HG82   Matthaeus Weisser (29 Jul 1734, Kleinaspach-29 Jul 1734, Kleinaspach).

HG83   Rosine Catharina Weisser (3 Jan 1736, Kleinaspach-Aug 1824, Gronau)

HG84   Johann Georg Weisser (23 Sep 1737, Kleinaspach-26 Mar 1809, Kleinaspach) m 1) 17 Jun 1766, Kleinaspach, Maria Magdalena Kirchner (d 26 Jul 1772, Kleinaspach); m 2) 9 Feb 1773, Kleinaspach, Barbara Haussner

---

[145]Data in this chapter provided by Francis C. Martin, Wolfgang Weisser, and from Rudolf Weisser, *Die Geschlechter der Weisser von Klein-Aspach*, 1475-1959 (Stuttgart-Degenbach, 1959).

HG85   Johann Abraham Weisser (19 Jul 1739, Kleinaspach-1809) m 13 Nov 1764, Backnang, Catharina Schneider (1748, Backnang-27 Jun 1819, Stuttgart). Baker, Kleinaspach, perhaps also Backnang and Stuttgart. No data about descendants.

HG86   Margarete Maria Weisser (b 27 May 1741, Kleinaspach)

HG87   Matthaus Weisser (27 Mar 1743, Kleinaspach-17 Dec 1829, Gronau) m 1) 26 Sep 1769, Gronau, Barbara Kirchner (20 Oct 1750, Gronau-7 May 1772, Gronau); m 2) 16 Feb 1773, Gronau, Regina Barbara Bezelberger (b 27 Dec 1753, Gronau)

HG871   Unnamed child Weisser (30 Apr 1772, Gronau-30 Apr 1772, Gronau)

HG872   Johann Jakob Weisser (10 Sep 1774, Gronau-29 Aug 1776, Gronau)

HG873   Christian Gottfried Weisser (2 Feb 1776, Gronau-14 May 1842, Gronau) m 2 May 1797, Gronau, Maria Rosine Bauer (26 Nov 1776, Gronau-22 Jun 1840, Gronau). Farmer, member of the town council, Gronau.

HG8731   Son Weisser (2 Nov 1798, Gronau-2 Nov 1798, Gronau)

HG8732   Christine Barbara Weisser (17 Oct 1799, Gronau-3 Jun 1867)

HG8733   Johann Georg Weisser (31 Jul 1802, Gronau-4 Jan 1803, Gronau)

HG8734   Johanna Christiane Weisser (30 Nov 1803, Gronau-19 Mar 1804, Gronau)

HG8735   Johanna Christine Weisser (11 May 1805, Gronau-9 Mar 1869, Gornau) m 11 Nov 1823, Gronau, Johann Georg Schlipp.

HG8736   Friederike Weisser (b 8 Jan 1808, Gronau) m 21 Sep 1829, Ludwigsburg, Jakob Friedrich Moll. Baker, Ludwigsburg.

HG8737   Johann Jakob Weisser (12 Feb 1811, Gronau-21 Jul 1885, Gornau) m 25 Jul 1837, Gronau, Rosine Katharine Bertsch (4 Jul 1802, Gronau-28 Jan 1872, Gronau), widow of Johann Ludwig Kunz (27 Jun 1797, Gornau-22 Aug 1834, Gronau). Baker and farmer, Gronau. Emigrated twice to the USA.

HG87371   Johann Gottlieb Weisser (17 Nov 1838, Gronau-3 Jul 1913, Gronau) m 9 Feb 1864, Gornau, Friederike Karoline Schaefer (1 May 1842, Billensbach-22 Feb 1913, Gronau). Farmer, Gronau.

HG873711   Christine Friederike Weisser (15 Jun 1866, Gronau-2 Feb 1869, Gronau)

HG873712   Johann Jakob Weisser (b 15 Jun 1866, Gronau) m 10 May 1894, Gronau, Karoline Rosine Beck (21 Jan 1871, Gronau-27 Sep 1916, Gronau). Farmer, Gronau.

HG8737121   Karl Wilhelm Weisser (b 23 Apr 1892, Gronau) m 1 Jul 1920, Hof und Limbach/Grossbottwar, Wilhelmine Feil (b 26 Oct 1897, Hof und Limbach).

HG87371211   Berta Weisser (b 10 Dec 1921, Gronau) m 23 Aug 1947, Gronau, Ernst Schick. Farmer, Gronau

HG87371212   Richard Weisser (19 Jan 1924, Gronau-26 Mar 1944, Italy). Killed in action.

HG87371213   Karl Weisser (6 May 1925, Gronau-7 Jul 1944, Kiriyewa). Killed in action.

HG87371214   Erna Hermine Weisser (b 18 Nov 1928, Gronau)

HG87371215   Ilse Weisser (b 13 Aug 1930, Gronau)

HG87371215   Waltraud Weisser (b 9 Apr 1939, Marbach/Neckar)

HG8737122   Emma Weisser (b 1 Oct 1894, Gronau) m 6 May 1920, Gronau, Karl Schassberger. Farmer, Horkheim bei Heilbronn.

HG8737123   Eugen Weisser (b 16 Aug 1896, Gronau) m 4 Mar 1920, Horkheim, Berta Zwirn (b 23 Jul 1897, Horkheim). Master mechanic, Gronau.

HG87371231   Gotthold Eugen Weisser (b 6 Dec 1921, Gronau)

HG87371232   Ruth Ester Weisser (b 20 Dec 1923, Gronau)

HG8737124   Mathilde Karoline Weisser (b 16 Apr 1904, Gronau)

HG8737125   Hermann Wilhelm Weisser (b 16 Jan 1908, Gronau)

HG873713   Karoline Gottliebe Weisser (29 Jun 1870, Gronau-22 Dec 1873, Gronau)

HG873714   Wilhelmine Rosine Weisser (b 4 Jul 1873, Gronau) m 13 Jul 1905, Gronau, Johann Christian Bauer

HG873715   Pauline Weisser (b 22 Dec 1912, Gronau) m 13 Jul 1905, Gronau, August Friedrich Baeuerle

HG87372   Christine Friederike Weisser (b 24 Feb 1840, Gronau)

HG87373   Christine Luise Weisser (b 8 Nov 1841, Gronau)

HG87374   Johann Gottfried Weisser (5 Nov 1843, Gronau-3 Feb 1844, Gronau)

HG87375   Johann Gottfried Weisser (11 Dec 1847, Gronau-21 Dec 1847, Gronau)

HG8738   Georg Gottlieb Weisser (21 Apr 1815, Gronau) m 6 Jun 1843, Beilstein, Anna Christiane Haerdtner (b 23 Nov 1823, Beilstein). Farmer, Beilstein.

HG87381   Christine Marie Weisser (b 28 Mar 1844, Beilstein)

HG87382   Christine Magdalene Weisser (b 23 May 1845, Beilstein)

HG87383   Carl Gottlob Weisser (b 7 Sep 1846, Beilstein)

HG87384   Rosine Catharine Weisser (b 26 May 1848, Beilstein)

HG87385   Caroline Weisser (b 13 Mar 1850, Beilstein)

HG87386   Gottlieb Weisser (n 26 Mar 1851, Beilstein)

HG87387   Wilhelm Weisser (b 19 Jun 1852, Beilstein)

HG87388   Christiane Weisser (b 22 Feb 1854, Beilstein)

HG87389   Wilhelmine Weisser (22 Nov 1855, Beilstein-28 Sep 1856, Beilstein)

HG8738A   Wilhelmine Weisser (b 4 Feb 1857, Beilstein)

HG8738B   Gottlob Weisser (b 24 Jan 1859, Beilstein)

HG8738C   Friedrich Heinrich Weisser (11 Sep 1860, Beilstein-19 Nov 1861, Beilstein)

HG8738D   Friederike Luise Weisser (b 6 Dec 1863, Beilstein)

HG8738E   Luise Weisser (b 10 Jan 1865, Beilstein)

HG8738F   Anna Pauline Weisser (b 6 Oct 1866, Dillstein)

HG8738G   August Weisser (b 18 Jan 1870, Dillstein)

HG8739   Rosine Karoline Weisser (11 Aug 1815, Gronau-25 Nov 1854)

HG874   Johann Matthaus Weisser (b 20 Jan 1784, Gronau) m 18 Nov 1808, Oberstenfeld, Eva Christine Retter. Farmer, Oberstenfeld, Beilstein.

HG88   Elisabeth Weisser (27 Mar 1746, Kleinaspach-27 Mar 1746, Kleinaspach)

HG89   Elisabeth Weisser (b 26 Jan 1748, Kleinaspach) m 1770, Kleinaspach, Johann Kaufmann. Butcher, Gronau.

HG8A   Georg Ludwig Weisser (18 Jul 1750, Kleinaspach-7 Jul 1820, Kleinaspach) m 19 Apr 1774, Anna Maria Haeusser (7 Sep 1755, Kleinaspach-27 Mar 1829, Kleinaspach). Farmer; proprietor of the Loewe; member of the town council and court, 1776; Schultheiss of Kleinaspach, 1787-1820.

HG8A1   Unnamed Weisser (3 Apr 1775-4 Apr 1775, Kleinaspach)

HG8A2   Georg Ludwig Weisser (9 Feb 1777, Kleinaspach-24 Oct 1777, Kleinaspach)

HG8A3   Barbara Weisser (2 Jan 1778, Kleinaspach-24 Oct 1779, Kleinaspach)

HG8A4   Johann Georg Weisser (31 Dec 1780, Kleinaspach-22 Dec 1827, Kleinaspach) m 12 Nov 1801, Kleinaspach, Maria Catharina Wolf (5 Aug 1780, Kleinaspach-16 Mar 1829, Kleinaspach. Farmer, Kleinaspach.

HG8A41   Rosine Barbara Weisser (23 Jul 1802, Kleinaspach-5 May 1883, Kleinaspach)

HG8A411   Friederich Weisser (b 8 May 1830, Kleinaspach). Father N. Seitz.

HG8A42   Georg Martin Weisser (26 May 1804, Kleinaspach-27 Apr 1811, Kleinaspach)

HG8A43   Johann Jakob Weisser (b 23 Sep 1806, Kleinaspach). In Kleinbottwar, 1834.

HG8A44   Maria Dorothea Weisser (b 22 Nov 1808, Kleinaspach)

HG8A45
Kleinbottwar   Georg Martin Weisser (8 Sep 1811, Kleinaspach-2 Jul 1851, Kleinaspach) m 1834,

HG8A46   Georg Ludwig Weisser (12 May 1814, Kleinaspach-8 Jul 1867, Stuttgart) m 24 Jul 1842, Stuttgart, Christine Bausch (15 Apr 1812, Lustnau bei Tuebingen-8 Feb 1879, Stuttgart). Carpenter, piano builder, piano construction firm of Maedler, Schoenleber & Co, Stuttgart.

HG8A461   Wilhelm Georg Ludwig Weisser (1 Dec 1842, Stuttgart-10 Mar 1919, Stuttgart-Degerloch) m 1) 21 Sep 1868, Reudern bei Nuertingen, Margarete Barbara Loser (29 Oct 1843, Stuttgart-23 Aug 1881, Stuttgart); m 2) 3 Nov 1883, Stuttgart, Maria Lautenschlager, widowed Weiss (28 Oct 1845, Stuttgart-1 Jan 1930, Stuttgart-Degerloch). Banker, insurance firm.

HG8A4611 Wilhelmine Marie Luise Weisser (b 24 Jan 1866, Stuttgart) m 18 Apr 1896, Stuttgart, Julius August Wagenmann (12 Jul 1869, Stuttgart-30 Jan 1936, Uhlbach). Mechanical designer.

HG8A46111 Julius Adolf Otto Wilhelm Wagenmann (13 Apr 1897, Canstatt-13 Jul 1897)

HG8A46112 Adolf Wilhelm Arthur Wagenmann (25 Jul 1898, Canstatt-4 Apr 1986, Stuttgart-Uhlbach) m 1) 28 Jul 1923, Luise Bader; m 2) Maria Sophie Koch (25 Nov 1910, Weil im Schoenbach); m 3) Emma Koch. Mechanical engineer.

HG8A461121 Lotte Gudrun Wagenmann (b 22 Jan 1943, Stuttgart) m Osarenkhoe

HG8A461122 Ellen Maria Wagenmann (b 3 May 1944, Stuttgart) m Brodersen

HG8A461123 Christa Wilhelmine Wera Wagenmann (b 12 May 1946, Stettin i. R.) m   Reicke

HG8A461124 Irma Eva Martha Wagenmann (b 27 Dec 1947, Stettin i. R.) m   Wagner

HG8A461125 Otto Wagenmann (b 24 May 1950, Winterbach)

HG8A46113 Irma Maria Martha Therese Wagenmann (2 Jul 1899, Canstatt-13 Apr 1987, Basel) m 28 May 1921, Erwin Hund (b 31 Mar 1896, Sulzbach a.d. Murr). Banker.

HG8A461131 Walter Erwin Adolf Hund (21 May 1925, Stuttgart-1 Mar 1933, Basel)

HG8A461132 Ewald Hund (b 2 Jul 1934, Basel) m Rosmarie Hatter

HG8A4611321 Monica Hund

HG8A4611322 Daniela Hund

HG8A461133 Dietmar Hund (b 13 Mar 1941, Basel)

HG8A46114 Kurt Gustav Wagenmann (31 May 1902, Canstatt-27 Jun 1988). m 1) 4 Jun 1926, Uhlbach, Maria Friesch (b 12 Dec 1899, Giengea/Brenz); m 2) 25 Jun 1936, Bad Canstatt,   (18 Jan 1907, Crailsheim)

HG8A461141 Edgar Otto Kurt Wagenmann (b 8 Nov 1926, Hedelfingen) m Gisela

HG8A461142 Marlis Wagenmann (b 10 Jul 1937, Esslingen/Neckar) m 1) 15 Feb 1958, Esslingen, Rolf Pingel (3 Aug 1931, Altona, Hamburg); m 2) Wolfgang Friedrich; m 3)

HG8A4611421 Kay-Thomas

HG8A4611422 Malte

HG8A4611423 Elke Friedrich

HG8A461143 Rainer Wagenmann (b 14 Oct 1939, Esslingen), cohabitation with Elke Lindenhahn

HG8A4611431 Caren Wagenmann

HG8A46115 Otto Josef Ludwig Wagenmann (10 Sep 1904, Canstatt-10 May 1986, Lorch) m 1) 10 Apr 1931, Wangen, Dora Gonser (b 10 Aug 1902, Dietersweiler); m 2) Hildegard Schilling. Dentist

HG8A461151 Joachim Wagenmann (b 18 Sep 1931, Stuttgart)

HG8A461152		Eckard Wagenmann (b 26 Sep 1934, Stuttgart)

HG8A461153		Daughter Wagenmann (13 Jul 1943, Stuttgart-13 Jul 1943, Stuttgart)

HG8A46116		Hermann Friedrich Wagenmann (20 May 1907, Canstatt-11 Jun 1911, Uhlbach)

HG8A4612		Martha Christine Dorothea Weisser (26 Jun 1867, Stuttgart-18 Jan 1951, Cologne). Roman Catholic nun, Cloister of the Good Shepherd, Cologne-Junkersdorf.

HG8A4613		Ludwig Wilhelm Christian Weisser (17 Apr 1869, Stuttgart-23 Feb 1919, Stuttgart) m 23 Aug 1897, Schweinfurt, Helene Karoline Hartmann (24 Oct 1868, Schweinfurt-23 Sep 1919, Stuttgart). Banker, teacher of merchandising, Stuttgart.

HG8A46131		Ludwig Weisser (23 Mar 1898, Stuttgart-23 Mar 1898, Stuttgart)

HG8A46132		Rudolf Ludwig Weisser (b 5 Jun 1900, Stuttgart) m 22 May 1926, Mathilde Stockburger (b 17 Nov 1895, Hellershof bei Gaildorf). Teacher, school administrator.

HG8A461321		Marieluise Helene Weisser (b 5 Aug 1927, Stuttgart) m 3 Apr 1954, Schenningen/Neckar, Karl Werner Schwab (b 2 Jan 1927, Breitenfeld). Violin case maker.

HG8A461322		Ingeborg Elisabeth Weisser (b 31 Mar 1931, Ludwigsburg) m 21 Sep 1957, Schwenningen/Neckar, Juergen Rupp (b 2 Jun 1929, Saulgan). Engineer. Two chn.

HG8A4614		Gustav Adolf Weisser (22 Aug 1870, Stuttgart-17 Jan 1915, Buffalo NY) m 7 Nov 1895, Canstatt, Emilie Friederika Schneider (30 Jan 1866, Canstatt-5 Dec 1908, Buffalo NY). Emigrated to USA Jun 1907. Cabinetmaker.

HG8A46141		Hans Weisser (30 Apr 1893, Canstatt-17 Jul 1893, Canstatt)

HG8A46142		Margaret Weisser (30 Apr 1893, Canstatt-21 Jul 1893, Canstatt)

HG8A46143		Willi Gustav Weisser (2 Nov 1894, Canstatt-15 Jul 1981, Wellsville NY) m 1) Elise (Elsie) Johanna Goerke (8 Apr 1896, Buffalo NY-18 Oct 1918, Buffalo NY); m 2) Cezelie (Celia) Schwier (b 6 Apr 1902, Buffalo NY); m 3) Millie . Carpenter, Rushford NY.

HG8A461431		Walter Wilhelm Weisser (b 3 Oct 1916, Buffalo NY) m 15 Jul 1939, Buffalo NY, Lorraine Thiele (b 14 Jul 1918, Buffalo NY). No chn. Gunsmith.

HG8A46144		Albert Emil Weisser (28 Apr 1896, Canstatt-22 Nov 1965, Williamsville NY) m 11 Jun 1932, Cinderella Marie Deazley (7 Sep 1896, Williamsville NY-28 Jun 1972, Williamsville NY). Bur Williamsville NY. Factory foreman.

HG8A461441		David Conrad Weisser (b 3 Mar 1933, Buffalo NY) m 3 Aug 1957, Marie Helen Bane (b 23 Oct 1934, Chicago IL). Mechanical engineer; she, teacher, realtor.

HG8A4614411		Beth Ann Weisser (b 2 Jul 1958, Buffalo NY). Nurse.

HG8A4614412		Timothy John Weisser (b 6 Sep 1961, Buffalo NY) m 5 Nov 1988, Rochester NY, Julie Nemeth (b 21 Nov 1960, Rochester NY).

HG8A46144121		John Weisser (b 30 Nov 1990, Amsterdam NY)

HG8A4614413		Thomas A. Weisser (b 29 May 1964, Buffalo NY) m 30 Jul 1994, Lisa Lanni (b 12 Feb 1964, Albany NY). He, construction manager; she, architect.

HG8A4614414   Susan Mary Weisser (b 13 Aug 1968, Silver Spring MD) m 22 Apr 1995, Fayetteville NC, Paul Schmitt. USA

HG8A46145   Ludwig Wilhelm Weisser (14 May 1897, Canstatt-4 May 1915, Buffalo NY)

HG8A46146   Martha Maria Weisser (3 Jun 1898, Canstatt-17 Mar 1916, Long Island NY)

HG8A46147   Maria Weisser (12 Jan 1900, Canstatt-25 Nov 1901, Stuttgart)

HG8A46148   Rudolf (Rudolph) Weisser (4 Mar 1902, Stuttgart-18 Jan 1987, Buffalo NY) m 1) Muriel Rettke (1 Oct 1909, Buffalo NY-1932); m 2) 3 Feb 1943, Ruth M Graham (b 25 Jan 1911, Buffalo NY). He, carpenter; she, office manager, caterer.

HG8A461481   Robert Rudolf Weisser (16 Oct 1929, Buffalo NY-6 Nov 1929, Buffalo NY)

HG8A461482   Arlene Weisser 6 Nov 1930, Buffalo NY-16 Mar 1931, Buffalo NY)

Laura Marie Weisser (7 Feb 1936, Buffalo NY-11 Oct 1980, Williamsville NY) m 18 Aug 1962, Williamsville NY, Kenneth W. Golding.

HG8A461483   Albert E. Weisser (b 5 May 1944, Buffalo NY) m 18 May 1968, Williamsville NY, Linda Mae Knab (b 16 Apr 1948, Buffalo NY). He, building inspector; she, secretary.

HG8A4614831   Julie Lynn Weisser (b 28 Sep 1975, Buffalo NY)

HG8A4614832   Kathryn Lynn Weisser (b 23 Aug 1984, Buffalo NY)

HG8A461484   Maryann M. Weisser (b 28 Jan 1946, Buffalo NY) m 1) James Robinson III; m 2) 30 Apr 1982, Williamsville NY, Anthony Orlando, Jr. (b 4 May 1955, Buffalo NY)

HG8A4614841   James Robinson IV (b 1 Sep 1968, Buffalo NY)

HG8A4614842   Lauri Marie Orlando (b 17 Sep 1982, Williamsville NY)

HG8A4614843   Melissa Suzanne Orlando (b 29 Aug 1983, Williamsville NY)

HG8A461485   Arlene Joan Weisser (b 11 Dec 1947, Buffalo NY) m 6 Sep 1969, Williamsville NY, Robert C. Bossert, Jr. (b 28 Jul 1947, Buffalo NY). She, BS, Rosary Hill Col, 1969; MS, Buffalo S Col, 1972; teacher. He, BS, Boston U, 1969; insurance.

HG8A4614851   Sara Elizabeth Bossert (b 18 Oct 1975, Buffalo NY)

HG8A4614852   Andrew Jason Bossert (b 4 Aug 1979, Buffalo NY)

HG8A4614853   Kristen Marie Bossert (b 17 Aug 1983, Buffalo NY)

HG8A46149   Marie Weisser (b 12 Jul 1904, Botnang near Stuttgart) m 15 Nov 1943, Earl R. Lutz (9 Sep 1899, Buffalo NY-30 Aug 1987, Williamsville NY). Bur Williamsville NY. No chn. Chiropractor; later railroader.

HG8A4614A   Emilie Weisser (27 Sep 1908, Buffalo NY-2 Oct 1908, Buffalo NY)

HG8A4615   Albert Christian Weisser (9 Feb 1872, Stuttgart-13 Feb 1944, Bowmansville NY) m 8 Apr 1901, Bowmansville NY, Katharine Selma Gessert (3 Jul 1868, Buffalo NY-11 Sep 1943, Bowmansville NY). Bur Bowmansville NY. Emigrated Aug 1890. Machinist.

HG8A46151   Katharine Louise Weisser (7 Oct 1903, Buffalo NY-15 Apr 1993, Bowmansville NY) m 27 Jun 1925, Buffalo NY, Francis Martin (14 Jul 1903, Saugerties NY-30 Jan 1996, Bowmansville NY). He, engineer.

*HG8A461511   Francis Carl "Bud" Martin (b 31 May 1927, Buffalo NY) m 11 Jun 1955, Bowmansville NY, Judith Diane Suckow (b 14 Apr 1934, Buffalo NY). He, BEP, 1951, MEP, 1953, Cornell U; electrical engineer. She, BS, U Buffalo, 1955; MS, SUNY, Buffalo, 1989; teacher.

HG8A4615111   Emily Clare Martin (b 30 Aug 1958, Buffalo NY) m 8 Aug 1987, Mounds View MN, Carl Josef Beckmann (b 31 May 1960, Minneapolis MN). She, BEE, Cornell U, 1980; MEE, U IL, 1984; electrical engineer. He, BS, Brown U, 1984, MS, 1989, PhD, 1993, U IL; electrical engineer.

HG8A46151111   Conrad Martin Beckmann (b 15 Nov 1992, Champaign IL)

HG8A4615112   Sally Helen Martin (b 29 Mar 1960, Buffalo NY) m 22 Jun 1991, Lancaster NY, Evan Hirsch (b 14 Nov 1961), div 1995. No chn. She, BMus, IN U, 1983; violinist.

HG8A4615113   Jenny Diane Martin (b 30 Jun 1962, Buffalo NY). BS, Alfred (NY) U, 1984; RN; nurse.

HG8A46151 Katharine Louise
Weisser Martin (1903-1993)

HG8A4615114   Carrie Lynn Martin (b 12 May 1964, Buffalo NY). BUSt, U ME, 1989.

HG8A461512   Albert Edward Martin (b 12 Aug 1928, Elmira NY) m 23 Dec 1950, Bowmansville NY, Shirley Margaret Warner (b 4 Apr 1928, Schenectady NY). He, BEE, Union (NY) Col, 1950; mechanical engineer. She, BA, Albany S Col, 1950; MS, Canisius (NY) Col, 1954; teacher.

HG8A4615121   Kathleen Noel Martin (b 21 Dec 1952, Buffalo NY) m 14 Aug 1982, Beacon NY, William Charles Hueston (b 8 Apr 1953, New York NY). She, BA, Hartwick (NY) Col, 1974; MS, S CT S Col, 1979; BS, New Paltz (NY) Col, 1991; bookkeeper. He, AB, Hartwick (NY) Col, 1975; MS, Union (NY) Col, 1978; computer systems.

HG8A46151211   Cara Martin Hueston (b 31 Oct 1985, Poughkeepsie NY)

HG8A46151212   Alana Martin Huewton (b 27 Oct 1989, Poughkeepsie NY)

HG8A4615122   Donna Lynn Martin (b 6 Apr 1955, Buffalo NY) m 29 May 1982, New Orleans LA, Robert Young (b 16 Mar 1953). She, BA, Hartwick (NY) Col, 1977; JD, Loyala of New Orleans, 1983; lawyer. He, BS, Tulane U; computer systems.

HG8A46151221   Natalie Kathryn Young (b 11 Sep 1995, Seattle WA)

HG8A4616   Hedwig Luise Weisser (24 Oct 1873, Stuttgart-2 Oct 1931, New York NY) m 7 Mar 1910, New York NY, Paul Kosubek (19 Oct 1868, Oberglogau, Upper Silesia-27 Mar 1932, New York NY). She, janitress; he, cook, janitor.

HG8A46161   Hedwig Kosubek (22 Sep 1911, New York NY-22 Sep 1911, New York NY)

HG8A4617   Rudolf Weisser (6 Nov 1878, Stuttgart-26 Dec 1970, Stuttgart) m 20 Jul 1920, Stuttgart,

HG8A46151111 Conrad Martin Beckmann (b 1992).
Der juengste Conrad. Photographed November 1994, Grossaspach.

Helene Wanner (27 Mar 1892, Stuttgart-7 Dec 1974, Stuttgart). Insurance agent; local historian, genealogist. Author, Die Geschlechter der Weisser aus Klein-Aspach, 1475-1959) (Stuttgart-Degerloch, 1959). No chn.

HG8A462 Marie Luise Catharine Christiane Weisser (20 Nov 1844, Stuttgart-d after 1912) m 22 Nov 1884, Stuttgart, Johann Bausch. Immigrated to USA, 1889. Tailor. Two daus.

HG8A463 Marie Emilie Weisser (24 Jun 1846, Stuttgart-25 Feb 1929, Stuttgart) m 26 Jun 1870, Stuttgart, Ludwig Kraus (12 May 1843, Mindelheim-17 Jan 1916, Stuttgart). Piano maker.

HG8A4631 Marie Christine Luise Kraus (16 Apr 1871-4 Feb 1931, Stuttgart)

HG8A4632 Anna Luise Kraus (20 Feb 1874-7 Mar 1916, Stuttgart)

HG8A4633 Julie Klara Kraus (b 19 Mar 1878). Secretary.

HG8A464 Christian Johannes Weisser (23 May 1850, Stuttgart-18 Feb 1931, Stuttgart) m 28 Sep 1907, Stuttgart, Katharine Schwarz (21 Dec 1858, Feuerbach-30 Dec 1914, Stuttgart). No chn. Piano maker.

HG8A47 Johann Georg Weisser (20 Dec 1816, Kleinaspach-1850). Moved to Stuttgart.

HG8A48 Johann Christian Weisser (26 Sep 1819, Kleinaspach-16 May 1890, declared dead)

HG8A49 Konrad Weisser (21 Dec 1822, Kleinaspach-9 Apr 1843, Kleinaspach)

HG8A5 Georg Ludwig Weisser (7 Dec 1783, Kleinaspach-24 Feb 1786, Kleinaspach)

HG8A6 Matthaeus Weisser (26 Apr 1786, Kleinaspach-3 Mar 1859, Kleinaspach) m 6 Mar 1810, Kleinaspach, Sibylla Friederika Essich

HG8A7 Georg Ludwig Weisser (27 May 1788, Kleinaspach-5 Mar 1815)

HG8A8 Martin Georg Weisser (9 Mar 1791-died in Russian campaign, missing in action, Napoleonic Wars)

HG8A9 Anna Maria Weisser (28 Jan 1794, Kleinaspach-6 Mar 1853)

HG8AA Christoph Weisser (1 Nov 1795, Kleinaspach-15 Apr 1796, Kleinaspach)

HG8AB   Georg Martin Weisser (b 2 Nov 1797, Kleinaspach). Moved to Winzerhausen.

HG8AC   Konrad Weisser (20 Jan 1802, Kleinaspach-13 Oct 1821)

HG8B   George Ludwig Weisser (12 Feb 1709, Kleinaspach-1769, Kleinaspach). No further
information.

CHAPTER THIRTEEN

[HC] Hans Conrad Weisser (1642-1720)
Stadtschreiber of Backnang[146]

Johann or Hans Conrad Weisser, son of Jacob Weisser I (ca 1595/ 1600-1668) was born 8 Feb 1642 in Grossaspach and died 13 Feb 1720 in Backnang. He was trained as a professional writer in Stuttgart, Heidenheim, and served as town clerk for Backnang, together with service as the town notary, from 1675 to 1720. He was also administrator of the sheriff's office (Vogtsamtsverweser). He married 15 Aug 1676 in Backnang to Anna Catherina Linde (7 Dec 1655, Oberbruden near Backnang-25 Jan 1733, Backnang). She was a daughter of Johann Jacob Linde, pastor in Sulzbach/Murr and Plieningen.

HC1   Maria Barbara Weisser (9 Nov 1677, Backnang-1706, Backnang) m 22 Nov 1698, Backnang, Andreas Baihinger (1676, Backnang-1713, Backnang). He was cloth cutter and fancy dyer in Backnang. He m 2) 1707, Backnang, Marie Barbara Natter.

HC2   Maria Catharine Weisser (3 Feb 1680, Backnang-1743, Backnang) m 1703, Backnang, Johann Michael Denzel (1673, Backnang-1742, Backnang). He was a merchant, Backnang; he m 1) 1695, Anna Sybilla Weihenmaier (1672-1702).

HC3   Frederick Jacob Weisser (14 Jan 1682, Backnang-ca 1716, Kornwestheim) m Anna Catharine N, who m 2) 7 Sep 1717, Muehlhausen/ Nackar, Johann Gustav Lamberti; goldsmith from Zweibruecken, Pfalz.

HC31   Catharine Margaretha Weisser (d 21 Feb 1699), born out of wedlock to Anna Murr, widowed Zwinckh (1666-1699)

HC4   Euphresina Dorothea Weisser (b 12 Feb 1684)

HC5   Friedrich Gottlieb Weisser (b 20 Jul 1685, Backnang) m ca 1710, Anna Barbara   . Town clerk substitute, Backnang, 1711-19.

HC51   Johann Gottfried Weisser (b 24 Oct 1711, Backnang)

HC52   Gottlieb Adam Weisser (17 Dec 1719-30 Dec 1719, Backnang)

HC6   Friedrich Carl Weisser (b 9 May 1687, Backnang)

HC7   Regine Dorothea Weisser (b 14 Feb 1689, Backnang) m 13 Sep 1733, Allmersbach, T.J.N. Weermann, a sergeant under "Obrist Leutnant Nostiz Companie"

HC71   Ludwig Bernhard Weisser (b 17 Dec 1724), out of wedlock

HC8   Helene Rosine Weisser (b 23 Feb 1691, Backnang)

HC9   Christian Friedrich Weisser (b 9 Apr 1693, Backnang)

HCA   Maria Elisabetha Weisser (1 Jul 1695, Backnang-1766, Backnang) m 1) 17 Jun 1721, Backnang, Andreas Gunter Rebitz (1690, Sachsen-Hildburghausen-1734, Backnang); m 2) 1753, Backnang, M. Heerman. Rebitz, apprentice board maker, Backnang; four children; Heermann, buttonmaker, Backnang.

---

[146]Contributed by Dr. Wolfgang Weisser

HCB   Christoph Friedrich Weisser (13 Dec 1697, Backnang-16 Jul 1763, Backnang) m 1) 6 Jan 1723, Backnang, Catharina Juliane Pfalzgraf (26 Dec 1791, Stuttgart-9 Mar 1737, Backnang), had four children; m 2) 9 Sep 1738, Aldingen/Nackar, Marie Luise Drommer, widowed Leussler (1717, Calw-21 Feb 1747, Backnang), she had been m 1) Viktor Leussler, administrator in Goeppingen, one child died young; m 3) 26 Sep 1747, Sophie Juliane Georgii (3 Jun 1710, Hornberg-10 Sep 1782, Backnang), one child. Trained as a scribe, Backnang; substitute, Murrhard, 1715; town clerk, Backnang, 1725-63.

HCB1   Philippine Elisabeth Friederike Weisser (28 Jun 1724, Backnang-21 Jan 1765, Stuttgart) m 26 Oct 1758, Allmersbach, Georg Jakob Finckh (1724, Freudenthal-1803, Stuttgart). Court servant, Stuttgart. He, m 2) 1766, Christiane Karoline Heller (1745-1802). Eight children.

HCB2   Helene Veronika Juliane Weisser (28 Jun 1724, Backnang-1801, Unterensingen) m 1) 9 Apr 1750, Backnang, Christian Ludwig Bazing (ca 12 Mar 1725-ca 12 May 1756); m 2) 17 Jan 1764, Allmersbach, Friedrich Sigmund Gess (b Ebingen-6 Aug 1766, Backnang). Bazing, second lieutenant and adjutant with a Prussian infantry regiment; Gess, town clerk, Backnang, 1764-66. No chn. The second marriage was arranged by the city council of Backnang.

HCB3   Johann Philipp Christoph Weisser (15 Feb 1726-29 Oct 1726, Backnang)

HCB4   Adolf Friedrich Weisser (1 Jan 1731, Backnang-1 May 1766, Backnang) m 2 Oct 1764, Marie Agnes Mueller (25 Jun 1742, Backnang-22 Apr 1817, Sulz/Neckar). No chn. She m 2) 9 Oct 1770, Sulz/Neckar, Johann Georg Bauder (1733-1814), pastor, dean, Sulz/Neckar, 1793-1814.

HCB5   Catharine Louisa Friederike Weisser (13 Sep 1743-11 Mar 1744)

HCB6   Johann Friedrich Christoph von Weisser (10 Dec 1752, Backnang-9 Apr 1833, Stuttgart) m 3 May 1783, Stuttgart, Regine Christine Bernhard (3 Nov 1758, Stuttgart-14 Mar 1821, Stuttgart). He was trained as a clerk at Backnang and Maulbronn, substitute at Kirchheim/Teck. Professor at the Hohe Carlsschule, Stuttgart, 1781-93; later councillor for church and expedition affairs, Stuttgart. Privy councillor, royal councillor, 1811. He was personally ennobled in 1806.

HCB61   Christiane Luise Weisser (21 May 1785, Stuttgart-15 Oct 1850, Reuthingen) m 4 Jun 1807, Stuttgart, Johan Christoph Reuchlin (22 Sep 1775, Mettinzimmern-27 Jan 1838, Heidenheim). Pastor , Markgroningen; dean, Heidenheim, 1820 ff

HCB62   August Friedrich Weisser (7 Aug 1788, Stuttgart-4 Jul 1835, Stuttgart) m 23 Nov 1816, Tuebingen, Wilhelmine Luise Uhland (2 Mar 1789, Tuebingen-21 Jun 1866, Stuttgart). He studied law at Tuebingen University; secretary and assessor, royal Wuerttemberg state ministry, Stuttgart; royal upper tribunal councillor, Wuerttemberg, Stuttgart.

HCB621   Luise Marie Weisser (9 Feb 1818, Stuttgart-7 Mar 1892, Stuttgart. Unm.

HCB622   Gotthold August Friedrich Weisser (29 Apr 1819, Stuttgart-10 May 1848, Stuttgart). Unm.

HCB623   Sophie Wilhelmine Weisser (14 Oct 1821, Stuttgart-4 Dec 1888, Tuebingen) m 23 Aug 1858, Tuebingen, Heinrich Adalbert von Keller (5 Jul 1812, Pleidelsheim-13 Mar 1883, Tuebingen). He, PhD; professor, German literature, Tuebingen University, 1841 ff. He m 1) 24 Aug 1837, Charlotte Scholl (1812-1856).

HCB624   Wilhelm Gotthold August Weisser (4 Oct 1826, Stuttgart-29 Apr 1863, Stuttgart). MD, Tuebingen University; practiced medicine, Stuttgart. Unm.

HCB63   Sophie Wilhelmine Weisser (10 May 1792, Stuttgart-26 Apr 1836, Stuttgart) m 16 Nov 1815, Stuttgart, Johann Friedrich Gottlob Rueff (16 Nov 1787, Berg bei Stuttgart-19 Nov 1819, Ellwangen). Royal Wuerttemberg accountant councillor; royal Wuerttemberg financial councillor, Ellwangen, 1819. Three chn.

HCB64   Karl Friedrich von Weisser (25 Sep 1796, Stuttgart-7 Jul 1873, Stuttgart) m 1) 28 May 1826, Stuttgart, Wilhelmine Waechter (10 Feb 1805, Waiblingen-27 May 1838, Stuttgart), three chn; m 2) 2 Mar 1840, Stuttgart, Charlotte Hartmann (6 Jan 1808, Stuttgart-20 Feb 1871, Stuttgart). No chn. Studied clerking, administration, Tuebingen. Royal Wuerttemberg ministerial secretary, Stuttgart, 1823; councillor to the chancellory; councillor to the administration, 1837, chancellory director of the privy council, 1847 ff. Personally ennobled, 1862.

HCB641   Karl Friedrich Weisser (13 Jul 1827, Stuttgart-9 Jul 1843, Stuttgart)

HCB642   Sophie Weisser (12 Feb 1831, Stuttgart-20 Oct 1878, Stuttgart). Unm.

HCB643   Paul Albert von Weisser (25 Dec 1832, Stuttgart-6 Mar 1917, Stuttgart) m 16 Apr 1861, Stuttgart, Karoline Luise Emilie Hoffmann (3 Mar 1836, Stuttgart-30 Jul 1924, Stuttgart). Studied law at Tubingen; judge, auditor, Marbach/Neckar; court councillor, Heilbronn, Stuttgart and Ravensburg. President of the royal Wuerttemberg senate, 1898 ff. Personally ennobled.

HCB6431   Wilhelm August Weisser (7 Sep 1864, Marbach/Neckar-21 Jan 1941, Stuttgart) m 3 Aug 1897, Ulm, Antonie Sofie Fernando Entress (22 May 1871, Stuttgart-30 Sep 1937, Ulm). Studied philosophy at Tuebingen and Geneva, PhD. Teacher and school administrator, Real gymnasium, Ulm, 1895; professor, Ulm, 1925 ff. Landscape painter; chairman of the Ulm branch of the German-Austrian Alpenverein.

HCB64311   Otto Weisser (9 Jun 1898, Ulm-4 May 1917, Arras, Flanders). Volunteer, Wuerttemberg Infantry Regiment 124. Unm.

HCB64312   Dietrich Weisser (9 Jun 1898, Ulm-26 Apr 1945, Berlin) 6 Oct 1924, Stuttgart-Feuerbach, Margarete Hartman (b 11 Sep 1902, Stuttgart). Dr. rer. pol. Tuebingen, 1922. Chief of personnel, Robert Bosch AG, Stuttgart. Oberleutnant, WWII, killed in action.

HCB643121   Erika Weisser (b 14 Sep 1926, Stuttgart-Feuerbach) m 1959, Stuttgart, Hartmut Zoller (b 1927). She, nurse; he, physician, Waiblingen. Two daughters.

HCB643122   Hans Dietrich Weisser (b 19 Jan 1929, Stuttgart) m 1959, Saulgau, Hedwig Lore Bauer (b 1935, Bad Waldsee). MD, Tuebingen U. Internist, Waiblingen.

HCB6431221   Bettine Weisser (b 1960, Waiblingen). Nurse.

HCB64312211   Wendelin Hans Weisser (b 31 Jan 1990, Tubingen)

HCB6431222   Carola Weisser (b 13 Oct 1961, Waiblingen) m 1991, Hans Christian Johnsen. He, pastor, Oberhauser.

HCB6431223   Mirjam Weisser (b 1965, Waiblingen). Midwife.

HCB6431224   Eva Weisser (b 1967, Waiglingen). Chemical technology assistant, Stuttgart.

HCB64313   Kurt Weisser (17 Jul 1899, Ulm/Donau-2 May 1929, Ulm) m 2 Aug 1923, Tuebingen, Gertrud Haendle (7 Feb 1901, Tuebingen). Studied Tuebingen; teacher, lieutenant.

HCB643131   Margarete Weisser (b 26 Feb 1926, Ulm) m Tuebingen, Hans Schulze. She, MD; physician, Wedel Holstein; he, same. Two chn.

HCB64314   Fritz Weisser (26 Apr 1901, Ulm-8 Jun 1940, Vailly, Aisne, France) m 12 Jun 1934, Stettin, Sigrid Becker (29 Jul 1911, Stettin-1994, Braunschweig). No chn. Dr. of agriculture, 1928, after studies at Stuttgart and Berlin. Teacher of agric, Griefenhagen, Oder, 1928 ff. Lieutenant, Pioneer Battalion, 1940; killed in action.

HCB64315   Gertrud Weisser (14 Nov 1904, Ulm-1 Dec 1987, Stuttgart) m 7 May 1932, Munich, Rolf Glauner (29 Jan 1905, Ludwigsburg-19 Jan 1976, Gerlingen). She, medical technology asst; he, MD; professor, directing physician, St. Mary's Hospital, Stuttgart, specialist in x-ray. Four chn.

HCB64316   Hans Bernhard Weisser (7 Jul 1908, Ulm-14 Dec 1977, Guettingen-Radolfzell) m 5 Jun 1934, Mirow, Mechlenburg, Luise Frieda Holz (31 Aug 1908, Pfirth, Ferrette, Alsace France-8 Apr 1986, Guttingen). Studied medicine at Tuebingen, Munich and Vienna. MD, Tuebingen U, 1934. Assisting physician, Heilbronn, 1934-37; practice, Tailfingen, 1937-68; Guettingen, 1968-77.

HCB643161   Bernhard Weisser (b 30 Sep 1935, Heilbronn) m 1962, Tailfingen, Helga Hermann (b 20 Jun 1940, Thuringia). Machine construction engineer, Reuthingen; she, physical therapist.

HCB6431611   Silke Weisser (b 26 Jan 1966, Reuthingen) m 1983, Reuthingen, Adolg Heiler (b 1941, Siggenhausen). Farmer, Siggenhausen. Two daughters.

HCB643162   Klaus Weisser (b 18 Jan 1937, Heilbronn) m 1966, Tuebingen, Ursula Braun (b 21 Jun 1943, Ruebingen). Firm director, Herbertingen.

HCB6431621   Brigitte Weisser (b 29 Feb 1968 Tuebingen-Buhl) m 4 Oct 1995, Silver Spring MD, USA, Stephan Hirsch. Mathematician, Stuttgart.

HCB6431622   Eva Weisser (b 15 Jun 1970, Tuebingen-Buehl)

*HCB643163   Wolfgang Weisser (b 27 Mar 1938, Tailfingen) m 23 Aug 1963, Tailfingen, Ingrid Gisela Grosse (14 Aug 1942, Dresden). Dr. med vet, Munich, 1962. Academic asst, U Stuttgart-Hohenheim, 1963-67; industry, Konstanz, 1967-68; institutional veterinarian, Stuttgart, 1969 ff; veterinary director.

*HCB6431631   Frank Weisser (b 17 Dec 1966, Stuttgart)

*HCB6431632   Nina Susanne Weisser (b 14 Feb 1970, Stuttgart)

HCB6431633   Jana Melanie Weisser (b 14 Jun 1977, Stuttgart)

HCB6431634   Julia Stephanie Weisser (b 3 Feb 1981, Stuttgart)

HCB643164   Lies Weisser (b 14 May 1939, Tailfingen) m 1962, Tailfingen, Ernst Schumacher (b 2 Jan 1931, Radolfzell). She, kindergarten teacher; he, typesetter.

HCB6431641   Hans Peter Schumacher

HCB6431642   Dieter Schumacher

HCB643165   Gudrun Weisser (b 1 Jan 1946, Tailfingen) m 7 Nov 1969, Freiburg, Dieter Kopf (b 1945, Ebingen). She, pediatric nurse; he, teacher, Salem.

HCB6431651   Michel Kopf

HCB6431652   Oliver Kopf

HCB643166   Konrad Weisser (b 9 Nov 1947, Tailfingen) m 1) 1970, Freiburg, Sigrid Wohnhas (1950, Ebingen-1975, Basel); m 2) 1977, Loerrach Sonja Albang (b 11 Jul 1950, Lorrach). Teacher, Loerrach; she, interpreter correspondent.

HCB6431661   Anna Katrin Weisser (b 25 Jul 1970, Frieburg)

HCB6431662   Carolin Weisser (b 7 May 1974, Haltingen)

HCB6431663   Florian Weisser (b 28 Mar 1978, Haltingen)

HCB6432   Anna Weisser (22 Feb 1866, Heilbronn-1947) m 14 Sep 1891, Ravensburg, Karl-Friedrich Mack (29 Aug 1857, Ludwigsburg-27 Jan 1934, Ludwigsburg). He, Dr. rer. nat.; Dipl-Ing; professor, physics and meteorology, Stuttgart-Hohenheim. Three chn.

HCB6433   Sophie Charlotte Weisser (11 Oct 1867, Heilbronn-15 Jan 1953, Friedrichshafen/Manzell) m 25 Apr 1892, Ravensburg, Gustav Uhland (26 Oct 1859, Ludwigsburg-14 Dec 1944, Schloss Horn, Kreis Biberach). Director of state court, Ravensburg, Stuttgart.

HCB6434   Karl Friedrich Weisser (18 Jul 1872, Stuttgart-1958, Leipzig) m 25 Jul 1905, Leipzig, Dagmar Lorch (28 May 1882, Riga, Latvia-1958, Leipzig). Book dealer, Leipzig; Insel-Verlag, Leipzig.

HCB64341   Erich Weisser (b 17 May 1906, Leipzig-Stuttgart) m 31 Aug 1936, Weidensahl, Helene Erika Schuster (b 1 Jun 1909, Weidensahl)

HCB643411   Eckart Weisser (b 20 Jan 1938, Istanbul, Turkey) m Bielefeld, Irmgard Linneweber (b 1937, Bielefeld). He, MD, Erlangen U; physician, Stuttgart, Gerlingen; organist.

HCB6434111   Ulrike Weisser (b 1967) m 28 Sep 1991, Gerlingen, Michael Germann (b 1967, Stuttgart)

HCB6434112   Alexander Weisser (b 1968). Organist.

HCB6434113   Markus Weisser (b 1971, Gerlingen)

HCB643412   Alfila Weisser (b 28 Apr 1940, Krefeld) m 1971, Augsburg, Edith Gingele (b Augsburg). Dipl-Ing; ship's motor engineer, Augsburg.

HCB6434121   Christoph Weisser (b 1972, Augsburg)

HCB6434122   Anne Kathrin Weisser (b 1974, Augsburg)

HCB643413   Konrad Weisser (b 22 May 1942, Krefeld) m Monica Sandross (b 5 Dec 1943). Printer and paper specialist, Stuttgart.

HCB6434131   Pamela Weisser (b 9 Nov 1971)

HCB64342   Ingeborg Weisser (11 Dec 1908, Leipzig-1988, Leonberg) Unm. Directress, student residence, social pedagogical women's seminar, Leipzig. Res after 1971, Ditzingen bei Stuttgart.

HCC   Euphrosine Rosina Weisser (27 Sep 1699, Backnang-Kleinbottwar) m 22 Jan 1732, Kleinbottwar, Johann Georg Felger. Shoemaker master, Kleinbottwar; member of the town council.

CHAPTER FOURTEEN

[DW]   David Weiser (ca 1719-1786)
of the Oley Valley, Berks County, Pennsylvania and his descendants

The first member of this family to arrive in Pennsylvania was Peter Weiser. No information has been found on when he arrived, but in his will dated 24 November 1738, he was identified as Peter Weiser of Oley. His will was probated on 18 January 1738/1739, so he must have died in December 1738 or January 1739. The inventory taken after his death showed him to have been a hatter.

Peter's will referred to his parents, Henry and Sybylla of the Bishopric of Worms, his sister Anne Marie and his brother David. News of his death must have been sent to Germany promptly, because on 3 September 1739 David Weiser arrived at Philadelphia on the Loyal Judith. David seems to have gone immediately to Oley, where he made arrangements with George Adam Weidner to marry his daughter Catharine, who had been recently widowed. David and Catharine settled in Oley, where they farmed and raised eight children.

In 1772, David made agreements with his two eldest sons, Christian and David Jr., by which he turned over his land to his sons, in exchange for which they agreed to take care of David and Catharine as well as making payments to the other six children. David died in 1786, and Catharine in 1787.

It may be noted that no records of David or his family have been found in the Lutheran and Reformed churches that were extant in the area around Oley at the time. The only dates that are available for the births of the children are on the gravestones, which because of the private cemeteries in the Oley Valley are in much better condition than might be expected given their age. Six of the children remained in Oley and all their gravestones have been found. For Sibilla and Jonathan, neither dates of birth or death are known.

It may also be noted that, particularly as compared with the other Weiser families, this family did very little migrating. It was not until the 1820s that one of the descendants left the area of Berks County, and it was not until almost 1850 that Samuel Weiser's family moved out of Pennsylvania, to Minnesota. There are still many of the descendants in Oley and Maxatawny townships. This has made the task of tracing the family much easier.[147]

DW   David Weiser (ca 1719, Germany-1786, Oley, Berks PA) m 1740 Catharine Weidner (ca 1715-22 Mar 1787, Oley, Berks PA). Farmer, Oley, Berks PA.

DW1   Christian Weiser (5 Mar 1741, PA-22 Jan 1807, Oley, Berks PA) m ca 1775, Magdalena Lobach (20 Nov 1760, Rockland, Berks PA-15 Apr 1812, Oley, Berks PA). Farmer, Oley, Berks PA.

DW11   John Weiser (ca 1775, PA-ca 1840) m 28 May 1806, Oley, Berks PA Elisabetha Lobach (d after 1827). Farmer, Oley, Berks PA.

DW12   Magdalena Weiser (20 Oct 1784, PA-8 Jun 1863) m 22 Feb 1807, Oley, Berks PA Daniel Levan (16 May 1782-31 Dec 1848). Farmer, Oley, Berks PA.

DW121   Son Levan (Nov 1807-28 Nov 1807).

DW122   Catharine Levan (29 Oct 1809-12 Mar 1833) m 15 Nov 1831, Daniel Y. Deturk (3 Dec 1808, PA-25 Dec 1881). Farmer, Oley, Berks PA.

DW123   Willi W. Levan (19 Oct 1814, PA-5 Jan 1885) m 11 Nov 1834, Daniel Y. Deturk (3 Dec 1808, PA-25 Dec 1881). Farmer, Oley, Berks PA.

---

[147]The list of descendants in this chapter has been limited to those with the surname Weiser (or Wiser), their spouses, and their children. The information in this chapter has come from the variety of sources. Edward Wiser has taken primary responsibility for assembling the material, which has come from a variety of sources. Particular appreciation is expressed to Bernice Sell of Kutztown for material in the Maxatawny area, to Charles W. Weiser of Douglassville for material from Oley, and to Charles A. Weiser of Schuylkill Haven for material from Schuylkill County.

DW13   Esther Weiser (4 May 1788, PA-20 Jul 1852) m John Youse.

DW131   Levi Youse (24 Sep 1819-6 May 1898) m 3 Apr 1842, Amelia (Emma) L. Haas (2 Apr 1822-5 Oct 1887). Tailor, Oley, Berks PA.

DW14   Daniel L. Weiser (ca 1790, PA-Aug 1814) m 27 Jan 1811, Reading PA, Hannah Mertz (15 May 1792, Rockland, Berks PA-12 Jan 1863). Farmer, Rockland, Berks PA.

DW141   Charles Weiser (16 Dec 1812, Oley, Berks PA-15 Feb 1893) m 26 Jan 1845, Catharine Diener (9 Jun 1815, PA-10 Mar 1888). Farmer, Rockland, Berks PA.

DW1411   Benjamin D. Weiser (Jun 1846, PA-1913) m 12 Jan 1873, Reading PA, Catharine S. Wertman (b Jul 1853, PA). Farmer, Rockland, Berks PA and Milton, Northumberland PA.

DW14111   Sylvania R. Weiser (b Dec 1885, PA).

DW1412   Susanna Weiser (28 Nov 1847, Rockland, Berks PA-26 Jul 1935). Unm. Rockland and District, Berks PA.

DW1413   Charles D. Weiser (11 Oct 1849, PA-8 Jun 1921). Unm. Rockland, Berks PA.

DW1414   Hannah Weiser (18 Apr 1851, PA-6 Feb 1918) m 5 Mar 1881, Charles Garman (10 Apr 1852-6 Apr 1924). Farmer, Rockland, Berks PA.

DW1415   Catharina (Kate) Anna Weiser (20 Apr 1852-13 May 1930, Rockland, Berks PA). Unm. Rockland and Maxatawny, Berks PA;

DW1416   Joel D. Weiser (8 Oct 1853, PA-25 Jun 1887, Lyons, Berks PA) m 4 Nov 1877, Alice Abbie Moyer (7 Nov 1857, PA-6 May 1911). Farmer, Rockland and Maxatawny, Berks PA.

DW14161   Lizzie Mae Weiser (7 May 1878, Maxatawny, Berks PA-26 Dec 1959, Lititz, PA) m 28 Nov 1903, Philadelphia, PA, John Albert Steierwald (1870, Lynn, Lehigh PA-1931). Farmer, Lyons, Berks PA.

DW14162   Charles William Weiser (b 4 Nov 1879, PA). Maxatawny, Berks PA and Grand Junction, CO.

DW14163   Laura May Weiser (b 3 Jul 1881, PA) m 27 Sep 1902, Lyons, Berks PA, Solan L. Parkes (1875, Maxatawny, Berks PA-1938). Farmer, Lyons, Berks PA.

DW14164   Abbie Catharine Weiser (14 May 1883, PA-Dec 1971). Unm. Maxatawny,   Berks PA and Bethlehem PA.

DW14165   Charlotte A. Weiser (28 Nov 1884, Lyons, Berks PA-1964) m 26 Mar 1910, Lyons, Berks PA, Linus Hammes (1886, Lyons, Berks PA-1976). Maxatawny, Berks PA.

DW1417   Sarah Anna Weiser (21 Jan 1858, PA-5 Feb 1940). Unm. Rockland, Berks PA.

DW15   Daughter Weiser (21 Jul 1797, PA-24 May 1798).

DW2   Sibilla Weiser (b ca 1743, PA) m Jacob Hoch (16 Dec 1738, Oley, Berks PA-29 Jan 1814). Farmer, Maidencreek, Berks PA.

DW21   David Hoch (30 Dec 1765-16 Aug 1834) m Elizabeth Schwoyer (26 Sep 1772-8 Dec 1830). Farmer, Maxatawny, Berks PA.

DW22   Esther Hoch m 11 Feb 1783 Conrad Preis. Ruscombmanor, Berks PA and Union PA.

DW3   Rosina Weiser (1 Feb 1746, PA-14 May 1798) m Nicholas Heist (d 26 Mar 1813. No ch. Drover, Oley, Berks PA.

DW4   David Weiser (9 Feb 1748, PA-17 Nov 1820, Oley, Berks, PA) m Maria DeTurk (16 Jul 1748, Oley, Berks, PA-3 Mar 1819). Carpenter, Oley, Berks PA.

DW41   Deborah Weiser (10 Mar 1774, PA-23 Jan 1837). Unm. Ruscombmanor, Berks PA.

DW42   Abraham Weiser (16 Aug 1775, PA-6 May 1835) m 1 Apr 1798, Sarah Schueck (2 Mar 1780-10 Dec 1843). Oley, Berks PA and Reading PA.

DW421   Mary ("Polly") Weiser (12 Jun 1800, PA-14 Feb 1860) m 25 Dec 1830, Solomon G. Rothermel (16 Jan 1799, Maidencreek, Berks PA-30 Jan 1860). Farmer, Maidencreek, Berks PA.

DW4211   Mary Rothermel (13 Mar 1832, PA-22 Aug 1918) m 1) 18 Jan 1857, Jacob Rausch (21 Jun 1833, PA-10 Mar 1860); m 2) Adam Hains (5 Mar 1834, Richmond, Berks PA-5 Feb 1902, Fleetwood PA). Maidencreek, Berks PA and Hamburg PA.

DW4212   Sophia Rothermel (13 Mar 1836, PA-1 Feb 1896) m 14 Sep 1855, PA, Owen K. Wesner (9 May 1834, PA-16 Jun 1907), Farmer, Maidencreek, Berks PA.

DW4213   Sarah Martha Rothermel (28 Nov 1844, PA-4 Jun 1882) m William Henry Boyer (10 Apr 1844-20 Jan 1917). Maidencreek, Berks PA.

DW422   Gideon Weiser (15 Jun 1802, PA-9 Jun 1849, Reading PA) m 11 Dec 1842, Margaretha Sigman (2 Mar 1821-18 May 1905). Reading PA.

DW4221   Sarah Margaret Weiser (19 Sep 1843, PA-30 Apr 1870) m 25 Apr 1867, Christopher (Cornelius) G. Gerhart. Reading PA.

DW4222   Abraham Sigman Weiser (17 Dec 1845, PA-Apr 1883). Reading PA.

DW423   Jesse Weiser (9 Sep 1806, PA-18 May 1863, Maidencreek, Berks PA) m 17 Jul 1826, Oley, Berks PA, Juliana Reiff (1805-27 Jan 1862).   Oley, Ruscombmanor and Ontelaunee, Berks PA.

DW4231   Esther Weiser (b ca 1 May 1826, PA).

DW4232   Mary Ann Weiser (b ca 1829, PA). Ontelaunee, Berks PA.

DW4233   Catharine Weiser (b Mar 1834, PA) m 31 May 1856, Moses Wolf (ca 1826, PA-2 Apr 1898). Maidencreek, Berks PA.

DW4234   William R. Weiser (6 Jan 1833, Berks PA-15 Oct 1872) m 24 Mar 1867, Rebecca Hinkle (Nov 1843, Berks PA-1935). Ontelaunee, Berks PA.

DW42341   William Franklin Weiser (15 Sep 1867, Berks PA-1869).

DW42342   Sally Ann Weiser (27 Sep 1869, Berks PA-1873).

DW42343   Clara Susan Weiser (27 Aug 1871, Berks PA-1886).

DW42344   Carrie C. Weiser (b Nov 1875, Berks PA) m 30 Jun 1921, Reading PA, Samuel A. Walters (b ca 1871, NY). Reading PA.

DW4235   Matilda Weiser (b 24 Jan 1835, PA).

DW4236   Isaac Weiser (b 17 Aug 1837, PA). Ontelaunee, Berks PA.

DW424   Sarah Weiser (7 Nov 1809, PA-24 Oct 1812, Oley, Berks PA).

DW425   Moses Weiser (11 Jan 1811, PA-1874) m ca 2 Mar 1833, Catharine Schenk (ca 1813, Hamburg, PA-1880). Carpenter, Hamburg PA and Minersville PA.

DW4251   John A. Weiser (29 Aug 1832, PA-8 Aug 1850, Minersville PA).

DW4252   Edward S. Weiser (13 Oct 1833, PA-8 Oct 1910) m Sarah E.   (12 May 1835, PA-29 Dec 1913). Minersville and Pottsville PA.

DW42521   George E. Weiser (23 Mar 1863, PA-14 Mar 1905). Unm. Pottsville PA.

DW42522   Edward A. H. Weiser (1 Oct 1868, Pottsville, PA-27 Feb 1946, Pottsville, PA) m 26 Oct 1899, Schuylkill PA, Mary L. Yaissle (b 13 Jan 1869, Pottsville, PA). No ch. Pottsville PA.

DW42523   Isabella Weiser (b Mar 1870, PA).

DW4253   Frederick Alexander Weiser (20 Jun 1836, Pottsville PA-28 Jan 1909, Schuylkill Haven PA) m Keziah A. DeLong (Jun 1839, PA-29 Jul 1917, Schuylkill Haven PA). Schuylkill Haven PA.

DW42531   Annie S. Weiser (15 Aug 1859, Schuylkill Haven PA-19 Jun 1894) m 17 Sep 1889, Schuylkill PA, Daniel M. Keller (b 28 Aug 1851, Berks PA). Schuylkill Haven PA.

DW42532   Olivia Evateny Weiser (12 Jul 1862, Schuylkill Haven PA-12 May 1942) m 8 Sep 1887, Schuylkill PA, Harrison J. Sterner (5 Aug 1862, Schuylkill Haven PA-1 Jan 1936). Schuylkill Haven PA.

DW425321   Frederick A. Sterner (9 Jul 1890, Schuylkill Haven PA-6 Nov 1966, Reading PA) m 1) 21 Jun 1914, Reading PA, Mary E. Kendig (23 Oct 1889, Lancaster PA-1 Sep 1945, Reading PA); m 2) Florence M.   (26 Aug 1903-26 Apr 1988, Reading PA). Reformed minister, Reading PA.

DW42533   Julius Theodore Weiser (Apr 1864, Schuylkill Haven PA-1942) m 26 Jul 1883, Berks PA, Kate E. Merkel (Mar 1860, Cressona PA-1942). Schuylkill Haven PA.

DW425331   Ada G. Weiser (b 7 Jan 1883, Cressona PA) m 12 Oct 1900, Schuylkill, PA, William R. Fetter (b 21 Mar 1879, Schuylkill Haven PA). Cressona and Schuylkill Haven PA.

DW4253311   Lauretta I. Fetter (b ca 1904, PA) m John Reiley. Schuylkill Haven PA.

DW4253312   Travis Fetter (b ca 1912, PA). Schuylkill Haven PA.

DW425332   Charles Franklin Weiser (1 Sep 1883, PA-1966) m 1) 1912, Lancaster, PA, Maude Mae Fetter (1883, PA-14 Mar 1921); m 2) 30 Jan 1926, Schuylkill Haven PA, Edith A. Adams; div 1932; m 3) 1934, Minnie Reichert (24 Feb 1892-3 Apr 1984). Schuylkill Haven PA.

DW4253321   Esther Madine Weiser (b 6 Feb 1913, PA) m 1) 1932, Ruppert Shollenberger; div 1934; m 2) 1942, Walter Pietrowicz (28 Jan 1919-26 Dec 1994, Reading PA). Reading PA.

DW42533211   Russell E. Shollenberger (b 5 Sep 1932) m ca 1951, Phyllis Bailey (b 22 Dec 1933).
Reading PA.

DW42533212   Nancy Jane Shollenberger (b 22 Sep 1934) m Theodore Mierzejewski (18 Feb 1929-30 Aug 1994).

DW4253322 Charles Alfred Weiser (b 15 Mar 1916, PA) m 1) Jun 1952, Elaine Yunker; div Oct 1953; m 2) 29 May 1957, Grace Amanda Otterbein (5 Feb 1911, Schuylkill Haven PA-15 May 1992). Schuylkill Haven PA.

DW42533221 Lawrence Y. Weiser (b 28 Jan 1954).

DW425333 Mamie O. Weiser (23 Oct 1884, Schuylkill Haven PA-1918) m 17 Oct 1903, Schuylkill PA, Newton Mull (b 18 Mar 1886, Maquoketa, IA). Cressona and Port Carbon PA.

DW4253331 Charles H. Mull (b 20 Apr 1905, Cressona PA) m Florence Mae Truscott (1 Mar 1905-15 Jan 1964).

DW4253332 Ruth I. Mull (b ca 1907, Cressona PA) m Leslie Hoffman. Philadelphia, PA.

DW4253333 Earl E. Mull (ca 1910, PA-dy).

DW4253334 George Mull (b ca 1914, PA). Reading PA.

DW425334 Violet Weiser (10 Mar 1887, PA-13 May 1963, Pottsville PA) m 1) Jacob W. Kramer (1 Nov 1884-27 Dec 1909); m 2) Daniel Kocher (1867-1943).

DW4253341 Lester Kramer (6 Jan 1906-6 Jan 1906).

DW4253342 LeRoy Kramer (20 May 1907-1982) m Grace Minnick. Tremont PA.

DW4253343 Mildred Kramer (b 21 Sep 1908) m Harvey Haas. Berks PA.

DW4253344 Dorothy Kramer (1909-19 Apr 1980) m Elmer Woodward. Reading PA.

DW4253345 Jennie Marie Kocher (b 30 May 1911) m 1) Ted Boyer; m 2) Luther Wolff (b 14 Jan 1910).

DW4253346 Eugene Victor Kocher (19 Dec 1912-1978). Pottstown PA.

DW4253347 Samuel Julius Kocher (29 Nov 1913-1986) m Esther Knopf.

DW4253348 Ina Naomi Kocher (Feb 1915-1991) m Marlin Lehman.

DW4253349 Kathryn Aletha Kocher (23 Sep 1918-1987) m Raymond Focht. Reading PA.

DW425334A Daniel Milton Kocher (27 Mar 1919-1983) m Ethel Morgan.

DW425334B Charles Kocher (b 28 Mar 1921) m Grace Moyer (b 26 Jun 1921).

DW425334C William Franklin Kocher (30 Mar 1923-1993) m May Zerbe.

DW425335 Harry A. Weiser (Jun 1888, Schuylkill Haven PA-1953) m 1) Clara Schappell (b ca 1888); div 1920; m 2) 14 Jun 1921, Schuylkill Haven PA, Ruth E. Henne (1894, South Manheim, Schuylkill PA-1974). Schuylkill Haven PA.

DW4253351 Earl Julius Weiser (b 25 Oct 1921) m 1) Emily Thomas; div; m 2) Julia Renchock (b 20 Nov 1918).

DW42533511 Ronald Weiser (b 9 Jul 1941) m Jacqueline Fisher (b 23 Apr 1944). Schuylkill Haven PA.

DW425335111 John David Weiser (b 14 Apr 1966) m Janet Smith (b 29 Jan 1967).

DW425335112   William K. Weiser (b 10 Jun 1969).

DW42533512   Robert Weiser (b 18 Mar 1948) m 1) Jacqueline Yerges; div; m 2) 9 May 1972, Stephanie Ann Hoffman. Lykens, Dauphin PA.

DW425335121   Robert Joe Weiser (b 31 Aug 1973).

DW425335122   Kayla Ann Weiser.

DW425335123   Dallas Weiser.

DW425335124   Marie Weiser.

DW425335125   James Weiser.

DW42533513   Judy Weiser (b 2 May 1950) m Dell Blank. Columbia MO.

DW4253352   June Irene Weiser (b 22 Jun 1925) m Milfred F. Klahr (7 Oct 1924-18 Aug 1994). Schuylkill Haven PA.

DW42533521   Pamela Klahr (b 8 Mar 1950). Lancaster, PA.

DW42533522   James Klahr (b 6 Apr 1957) m Maureen McKay. Wyomissing, Berks PA.

DW42533523   Sherri Klahr (b 1 Mar 1958) m Tony Sacco (b 1 Feb 1957).

DW425336   Edward George Weiser (Oct 1890, PA-ca 1945) m Mary J. McGugart (ca 1888, PA-Apr 1965). Schuylkill Haven PA.

DW4253361   Annie Evelyn Weiser (16 Jan 1908, PA-May 1983) m Stanley Aungst. Schuylkill Haven PA.

DW4253362   Leonard E. Weiser (6 May 1910, PA-May 1983) Schuylkill Haven PA.

DW4253363   Edward J. Weiser (b 15 Aug 1912, PA) m Doris Hawk (20 Oct 1918). Schuylkill Haven PA.

DW4253364   Kenneth F. Weiser (b 23 May 1921). Schuylkill Haven PA.

DW4253365   LaVern A. Weiser (b 2 Feb 1925) m Catherine Foose (b 12 Jun 1930).

DW42533651   Dennis Charles Weiser (b 21 Nov 1952). NM.

DW42533652   Genevieve M. Weiser (b 12 Jan 1954) m Jeffrey Fisher (b 10 Jun 1943). Schuylkill Haven PA.

DW42533653   Francine L. Weiser (b 31 Oct 1955) m Michael Dipe. Elizabethtown, Dauphin, PA.

DW425336531   Michael Dipe (b 17 Sep 1976).

DW425336532   Bryan Dipe (b 23 Jun 1978).

DW425336533   Sarah Dipe (b 12 May 1991).

DW42533654   Bryan L. Weiser (b 27 Sep 1957) m Mary Salakus (b 30 Dec 1958). Cumbola, Schuylkill,

PA.

DW425336541   Holly C. Weiser (b 12 Mar 1985).

DW425336542   Keith R. Weiser (b 12 Jul 1989).

DW425336543   Brett LaVern Weiser (b 28 Apr 1991).

DW42533655   Germaine M. Weiser (b 26 Jun 1961) m George Eichert.

DW425336551   Christine Weiser (b 12 Oct 1977).

DW42533656   Kevin G. Weiser (b 6 Feb 1964) m Julia Czeprusz (b 17 Oct 1967, NC).

DW425336561   Christian G. Weiser (b 25 Jan 1992).

DW425336562   Brandon M. Weiser (b 12 Oct 1994).

DW425337   Frederick E. Weiser (b Sep 1895, Schuylkill Haven PA) m 14 Apr 1922, Auburn PA, Anna L. Koch (b ca 1893, West Brunswick, Schuylkill PA). West Brunswick, Schuylkill PA.

DW4253371   Alberta A. Weiser (b 16 Mar 1923). Unm. Orwigsburg PA.

DW4253372   Alvin Earl Weiser (b 12 Feb 1926) m 1) Herta J. Bohrmann (b Germany); div; m 2) Evelyn R. Minchoff.

DW42533721   Evelyn R. Weiser m Robert Johns.

DW42533722   David J. Weiser (b 27 Mar 1955) m Cynthia   . Orwigsburg PA.

DW425337221   Christopher Weiser (b 3 Jan 1994).

DW425338   Isabella Weiser (Dec 1898, PA-1903).

DW42534   Alexander Benjamin Weiser (11 Jun 1866, Schuylkill Haven PA-15 Sep 1928, Schuylkill Haven PA) m 1) 23 Dec 1889, Schuylkill PA, Elizabeth S. Bohrman (Feb 1871, Schuylkill PA-1904); m 2) Ella J.   (b ca 1868, PA). Schuylkill Haven PA.

DW425341   Bessie C. Weiser (Apr 1891, PA-1981) m Alexander A. Ruff (1889-1972). Schuylkill Haven PA.

DW4253411   Edgar Ruff (19 Feb 1916-12 Dec 1995) m Leone Schlear (b 9 Jul 1928).

DW4253412   George Ruff m Esther Peterson. Orwigsburg PA.

DW4253413   Robert Ruff.

DW4253414   Bryan Ruff.

DW4253415   James Ruff.

DW425342   Bright Weiser (1893-1899).

DW425343   Esther H. Weiser (Oct 1896, PA-1965) m 1) 27 Feb 1915, Frackville PA, John Holsberger (b ca 1890, Harrisburg PA); m 2)   Simpson. Schuylkill Haven PA.

DW42535   Catharine Violet Weiser (28 Aug 1873, PA-4 Apr 1888).

DW42536   Edward Douglas Weiser (Jan 1878, PA-Apr 1953, Schuylkill Haven PA).   Schuylkill Haven PA.

DW4254   Charles Carroll Weiser (31 Dec 1838, PA-2 Jan 1851, Minersville PA).

DW4255   George W. Weiser (b 11 Apr 1841, PA) m Ida M.   (Apr 1852, PA-Aug 1947). Schuylkill PA and Philadelphia PA.

DW42551   Elwood Weiser (b Mar 1871, PA) m Louisa   (b Nov 1878, PA). Philadelphia PA.

DW425511   George H. Weiser (b Jul 1896, PA) m Gertrude C. Kirk (b ca 1894, PA). Philadelphia PA.

DW4255111   George H. Weiser (b ca May 1920, PA).

DW425512   Catherine Weiser (b Mar 1899, PA).

DW425513   Elwood Weiser (b ca 1901, PA).

DW425514   Roy Weiser (b ca 1904, PA).

DW425515   John Weiser (b ca 1906, PA).

DW425516   Lewis Weiser (b ca 1914, PA).

DW425517   Dorothy A. Weiser (b ca 1916, PA).

DW42552   Roy C. Weiser (b Jan 1873, PA). Philadelphia PA.

DW42553   Lee Weiser (b Apr 1877, PA). Philadelphia PA.

DW42554   Alice M. Weiser (b May 1881, PA). Philadelphia PA.

DW42555   Flossie Weiser (b Aug 1884, PA). Philadelphia PA.

DW42556   Mamie Weiser (b Aug 1887, PA). Philadelphia PA.

DW42557   Martha Weiser (b Mar 1889, PA). Philadelphia PA.

DW4256   James M. Weiser (30 Nov 1842, PA-7 Aug 1916, Minersville PA) m Ellen G. (Jan 1842, PA-before 1910). Minersville PA.

DW42561   Kate E. Weiser (Jan 1866, Minersville PA-Feb 1925) m 15 Dec 1890, Schuylkill PA, Frank Oerther (9 Jan 1855, Minersville PA-Feb 1915). Minersville PA.

DW425611   Abbie Oerther (b Nov 1882, PA).

DW425612   Robert Oerther (b Jun 1884, PA).

DW425613   Nellie Oerther (b Jan 1892, PA).

DW42562   Nellie Mae Weiser (Nov 1867, Minersville PA-Nov 1949) m 29 Jun 1889, Schuylkill PA, William A. Ernst (11 Dec 1866, Llewellyn, Schuylkill PA-Mar 1934). Minersville PA.

DW425621   Isabella M. Ernst (Oct 1892, PA-Feb 1975). Unm.

DW42563   Charles M. Weiser (Sep 1869, PA-before 1915). Minersville PA.

DW42564   James F. Weiser (Oct 1877, PA-Dec 1914). Minersville PA.

DW4257   Walter Weiser (b 26 Nov 1844, PA).

DW4258   Theodore Weiser (b 26 Nov 1846, Pottsville PA).

DW4259   Isabella Catherine Weiser (b 27 May 1849, PA) m Washington Littledales.

DW425A   Franklin P. Weiser (b 7 Aug 1852, PA) m 14 Dec 1882, Martha Landefeld (Nov 1859, PA-30 Apr 1936, Ashland PA). Ashland PA.

DW425A1   Maude Florence Weiser (b Jan 1884, PA) m Louis A. Fleck. Ashland PA.

DW425A11   Doris Weiser Fleck.

DW426   Rachel Weiser (5 Mar 1814, PA-Jan 1852). Reading PA.

DW427   Levi S. Weiser (ca 1820, PA-before 1850) m 13 Jan 1842, Matilda Henritze (6 Dec 1819, PA-Aug 1900). Reading PA.

DW4271   Henry Henritzy Weiser (11 Jan 1843, Berks PA-31 Dec 1883) m 24 Dec 1865, Sarah Hoag (28 Oct 1842, Berks PA-22 Mar 1920). Reading PA.

DW42711   Emily Margaret L. Weiser (b 31 Oct 1866, PA) m 16 Jan 1886, Reading PA, Samuel Hollenbach (b ca 1864).

DW42712   Ida May Weiser (b 18 Apr 1868, Berks PA) m 22 Jun 1889, Reading PA, Daniel Rissmiller (b Feb 1865, Muhlenberg, Berks PA). Reading PA.

DW427121   William B. Rissmiller (b Mar 1895, Reading PA) m on 25 Jun 1915, Reading PA, Blanch M. Bear (b ca 1895, Reading PA).

DW427122   Howard Rissmiller (b Aug 1899, PA).

DW42713   William Benjamin Weiser (13 Nov 1869, PA-1 Feb 1958) m 28 Jun 1900, Reading PA, Anna A. Stahler (Dec 1875-Jan 1942). Reading PA.

DW42714   Mary Matilda Weiser (25 Jul 1871, PA-1893) m 30 Mar 1889, Reading PA, Henry Jacob Wilker (b 13 Nov 1867). Reading PA.

DW427141   Mabel L. A. Wilker (b Sep 1889, Reading PA) m 29 Jun 1911, Reading PA, Ralph E. Johns (b ca 1890, Denver, Lancaster PA). Reading PA.

DW42715   Lydia Henrietta Weiser (17 Mar 1873, PA-6 Feb 1875).

DW42716   Cora Laura Weiser (b 13 Dec 1874, Alsace, Berks PA) m 18 Jun 1896, Reading PA, Isador Wise (b ca 1861, Reading PA). Reading PA.

DW42717   Harry (Henry) C. Weiser (Oct 1876, Pike, Berks PA-23 Feb 1945, Reading PA) m 30 Sep 1896, Reading PA, Claudia V. Hains (29 Oct 1873, Port Clinton PA-2 Apr 1918). Reading PA.

DW427171   Helen May Weiser (12 Apr 1897, PA-11 Sep 1968). Unm. Reading PA.

DW42718   Edwin Hoag Weiser (15 Feb 1878, Berks PA-Jan 1952) m 12 Jul 1924, Reading PA, Mary A. Breidenbach (b ca 1877). Reading PA.

DW42719   Clara Florence Weiser (25 Dec 1880, PA-Jul 1883).

DW4271A   Sarah Irene Weiser (12 Sep 1882, PA-Oct 1883).

DW43   Esther D. Weiser (22 Oct 1777, PA-22 Jul 1848). Unm. Ruscombmanor,   Berks PA.

DW44   Anna Weiser (26 Dec 1779, PA-11 Feb 1842) m 29 Nov 1803, Exeter, Berks PA, George Heaffer (14 Jul 1779-23 May 1839).

DW441   David Hafer (2 Sep 1804-18 Sep 1806).

DW442   Solomon Hafer (12 Nov 1805-26 Sep 1806).

DW443   Henry Hafer (11 Nov 1806, PA-14 Oct 1850) m 13 May 1828, Reading PA, Rebecca Hinnershitz (14 May 1808, PA-7 Feb 1860). Reading PA.

DW444   Benjamin W. Hafer (22 Oct 1807, PA-28 Sep 1893) m 19 Jan 1828, Reading PA, Mary Ann O. Nein (5 Nov 1807, Oley, PA-11 Jan 1893). Oley, Berks PA.

DW445   Daniel Hafer (b 22 Oct 1807).

DW446   John Hafer.

DW447   Isaac W. Hafer (7 Sep 1810, PA-21 Mar 1889) m 1) Esther   (14 Jul 1810, PA-1 Apr 1857); m 2) Sarah   (3 Jul 1812, PA-25 May 1888). Ruscombmanor, Berks PA.

DW448   Maria Anna Hafer (27 Jan 1814, PA-21 Sep 1863) m Peter Hauck (24 Apr 1810, PA-11 Jun 1868). Oley, Berks PA.

DW449   George Francis Hafer (13 Nov 1815, PA-17 Apr 1889) m 1) 30 Apr 1837, Reading PA, Esther B. Moyer (28 Sep 1814-18 Nov 1853); m 2) 26 May 1857, Mary Faust (18 Nov 1822, PA-29 Oct 1890). Ruscombmanor, Berks PA.

DW44A   Sarah Hafer (14 Feb 1818, PA-11 Jan 1900) m 10 Nov 1839, Samuel Marburger (29 Oct 1816, PA-8 Sep 1889). Exeter, Berks PA.

DW44B   Samuel Hafer (30 Sep 1819, PA-2 Dec 1897) m 5 Dec 1840, Elizabeth Reider (1 Aug 1816, PA-20 Dec 1899). Ruscombmanor, Berks PA.

DW45   Jacob Weiser (28 Mar 1781, PA-30 Apr 1849) m 9 Sep 1810, Oley, Berks PA, Catharine Levan (24 Dec 1785, PA-21 Nov 1863). Oley, Berks PA.

DW451   Daniel L. Weiser (21 Apr 1811, PA-25 Jul 1890) m 24 Jul 1860, Reading PA, Anna Elizabeth Reider (16 Dec 1840, PA-29 Aug 1919). Oley, Berks PA.

DW4511   Catherine R. Weiser (1861, PA-abt 1885) m Ammon B. Stitzer (2 Oct 1861, PA-5 Mar 1916). Oley, Berks PA.

DW45111   Ammon W. Stitzer (1884, Oley, Berks PA-1944) m 18 Feb 1911, Reading PA, Lillie M. Bloch (b ca 1891, Reading PA).

DW4512   Jacob Gideon Weiser (17 Jul 1862, PA-5 Oct 1863).

DW4513   Amelia Rebecca Weiser (b 31 Aug 1864, PA) m 21 Mar 1891, Oley, Berks PA, Harry (Henry) W. Kieffer (b ca 1868, PA) (DW8129). Reading PA.

DW45131   Ella Kieffer (b 3 Aug 1891).

DW45132   Valley (Valie) W. Kieffer (b Jan 1897) m   Degler.

DW4514   Mahlon R. Weiser (10 Aug 1866, PA-19 May 1943) m Katie S.   (1883-1973). No ch. Oley, Berks PA.

DW4515   Lydia R. Weiser (b 10 Jul 1868, Berks PA) m 1 Dec 1888, Friedensburg, Berks PA, George H. Schwartz (b Jan 1867). West Reading PA.

DW45151   Harrison M. Schwartz (b Feb 1889, Berks PA) m on 10 Jun 1916, Reading PA, Rosa E. Seidel (b ca 1893, Milwaukee, WI).

DW45152   Raymond Schwartz (b Jan 1891, PA).

DW45153   Ellen R. Schwartz (b May 1892, Berks PA) m 25 Nov 1915, Pinegrove, Schuylkill PA, Richard J. Egolf (b ca 1881, Fleetwood, Berks PA).

DW45154   Joseph D. Schwartz (b Aug 1897).

DW45155   Esther May Schwartz (b 27 Aug 1902).

DW45156   Pearl Schwartz.

DW4516   Anna R. Weiser (22 Oct 1869, Berks PA-24 Feb 1892) m 31 Jan 1891, Oley, Berks PA, Ammon T. Link (21 Aug 1869, Berks PA-9 Dec 1891). Oley, Berks PA.

DW45161   Warren W. Link (b 24 Jul 1891, Berks PA) m 20 Feb 1914, Reading PA, Mabel E. Troxell (b ca 1892, Lehigh, PA).

DW4517   Abigail R. Weiser (b 16 Jul 1871, PA) m 2 Apr 1892, Friedensburg, Berks PA, Samuel Z. Lykens (b 21 Nov 1865). Robeson, Berks PA.

DW45171   Bertha M. Lykens (b 8 Dec 1892, PA) m Preston McGowan.

DW45172   Ruth Viola R. Lykens (b 10 Apr 1896, PA).

DW45173   Samuel W. Lykens (b 20 Dec 1898, PA) m Florence Degler. Birdsboro PA.

DW45174   Helen E. Lykens (b 2 Feb 1901) m Thomas Kochel. Birdsboro PA.

DW45175   Florence C. Lykens (b 15 Aug 1903) m Vernon L. Rhoads (b 10 May 1901). Reading PA.

DW45176   J. Vernon Lykens (b 12 Aug 1905).

DW45177   Arthur S. Lykens (b 18 Apr 1907) m Francis Schnable.

DW45178   Mary Clementine Lykens (b 6 Aug 1910) m   Clauser.

DW45179   Esther L. Lykens (b 25 Aug 1911) m   Knabb.

DW4517A   Margaret L. Lykens (b 7 Sep 1914) m   Kerper.

DW4517B   Harold L. Lykens (b 15 Jul 1916).

DW4518   Daniel R. Weiser (15 Jan 1873, Oley, Berks PA-7 May 1962) m 17 Jul 1897, Athol, Berks PA, Kate B. Heist (May 1877, Oley, Berks PA-1952). Oley, Pike and Fleetwood, Berks PA.

DW45181   Paul Jeremiah H. Weiser (27 Aug 1897, Oley, Berks PA-1931) m 17 Jul 1920, Reading PA, Maude B. Yoder (ca 1903, Berks PA-1978). Oley, Fleetwood and Pike, Berks PA.

DW451811   Sadie Weiser m Henry Kulakowsky.

DW4518111   Janet Kulakowsky. Yardville, NJ.

DW4518112   Son Kulakowsky.

DW451812   Daniel Y. Weiser (b 6 Mar 1923, Rockland, Berks PA) m Marguerite Clauser (b 15 Sep 1926, Reading PA). Pike, Berks PA.

DW4518121   Scott Weiser m Lori Duggan.

DW45181211   Adam Weiser.

DW45181212   Daniel Weiser.

DW45181213   Katlyn Weiser.

DW451813   Paul Weiser m Mary Ellen   . Tucson AZ.

DW4518131   Marcus Weiser.

DW45182   Maude H. Weiser (11 Jan 1899, Berks PA-1989) m 17 Jan 1920, Reading PA, Clarence S. Yoder (5 Dec 1887, Berks PA-28 Jul 1965). Oley, Berks PA.

DW451821   Marie W. Yoder (b 1 Apr 1920) m Paul C. Strunk (19 Dec 1916-17 May 1994).

DW451822   Marion W. Yoder (b 18 Oct 1923) m Mary L. Wittman (23 Aug 1924-10 Dec 1974). Oley, Berks PA.

DW451823   Marvin W. Yoder (b 12 Jan 1931). Pottstown PA.

DW45183   Meda H. Weiser (13 Feb 1900, PA-24 Mar 1988) m 23 Dec 1922, Reading PA, Frank R. Wesner (1 Feb 1887-17 Nov 1967). No ch.

DW45184   Leon H. Weiser (b 28 Sep 1902, PA) m Mabel M. Behm (5 Nov 1906-24 Jun 1994). Pike, Berks PA.

DW451841   Leon Weiser.

DW451842   Pearl Weiser m   Frederick.

DW451843   Meda Weiser m   Stauffer.

DW451844   Miriam Weiser m   Carl.

DW451845   Edith I. Weiser (b 3 Jan 1931) m Edward W. Conrad (b 16 Aug 1926).

DW45185   Lena H. Weiser (b 19 Mar 1906, PA).

DW4519   Sallie R. Weiser (1874, PA-1951) m 24 Aug 1895, Friedensburg, Berks PA, Thaddeus K. Endy (1872, PA-1955). Reading PA.

DW45191   Harold Endy.

DW45192   Esther Endy m   Strausser.

DW45193   Edna Endy m   Aufferman.

DW45194   Solis W. Endy (1889-1989) m Pearl B.

DW45195   John W. Endy (b ca 1906).

DW45196   Harold W. Endy (b ca 1911).

DW451A   Maria R. Weiser (b Oct 1879, Oley, Berks PA) m 24 Nov 1903,   Schuylkill PA, John Claude Bolich (b 24 Aug 1874, Rauschs, Schuylkill PA). Auburn PA.

DW451A1   Joseph Weiser Bolich (13 Aug 1904-19 Jan 1905).

DW451A2   Sarah Elizabeth Bolich (b 21 Jan 1906, PA) m   Kundt.

DW451A3   Amy Kathryn Bolich (b 21 Jan 1908, PA) m   Orlando.

DW451A4   Mahlon Daniel Bolich (b 27 Mar 1910, PA).

DW451A5   Esther Mary Bolich (b 25 Sep 1911, PA).

DW451A6   Edna Orpah Bolich (b 8 Jun 1918, PA).

DW452   Abigail Weiser (28 Oct 1817, PA-9 Feb 1894) m 1843, Oley, Berks PA, Benjamin Keim (3 Aug 1817, Berks PA-18 Apr 1896). Pike, Berks PA.

DW4521   Isaac Weiser Keim (30 Mar 1845, Oley, Berks PA-17 Apr 1894) m 25 Dec 1878, Berks PA, Mary Ellen K. Marquette (13 Apr 1860, Oley, Berks PA-4 Jun 1907). Reading PA.

DW4522   Clara Catharine Keim (28 Feb 1849, PA-13 Feb 1932) m Nathaniel S. Merkel (22 Aug 1847, PA-23 Apr 1906).

DW4523   Benjamin Keim (b ca 1852, PA).

DW453   Maria Weiser (15 Aug 1828, PA-7 Sep 1910) m 28 Jan 1851, August Schenke (18 Jul 1828, Saxony-13 Aug 1895). Philadelphia PA.

DW4531   John Albert Schenke (16 May 1855, PA-5 Mar 1924). Philadelphia, PA.

DW4532   Charlotte Wilhelmina Schenke (b 22 Apr 1857, Philadelphia, PA) m Andrew Datz (b 24 Aug 1856, Germany). Philadelphia, PA and Merchantville, NJ.

DW4533   William A. Schenke (b ca May 1860, PA).

DW4534   Anna Schenke (5 Aug 1865-Nov 1927).

DW4535   Louisa C. Schenke (b 15 May 1869, Philadelphia, PA) m John M. Kelley (23 Sep 1867, PA-16 Jan 1927). Philadelphia, PA.

DW46   Samuel D. Weiser (5 Nov 1783, PA-17 May 1854, St. Paul, MN) m 22 Jan 1815, Reading PA, Mary ("Polly") Schroeder (1795-1879, Valley City ND). Berks PA and Shakopee MN.

DW461   Esther Weiser (29 May 1816, PA-24 Oct 1835).

DW462   William F. Weiser (27 Mar 1830, PA-11 Jun 1919, Everett, WA) m 1) on 9 Aug 1857, Scott MN, Mary Elizabeth Allen (d Sep 1865, Shakopee MN); m 2) 1868, Catherine Love McCallum (Jan 1847, Canada-17 Feb 1901). Shakopee MN; Barnes ND; Spokane WA.

DW4621   Flora Weiser (b ca 1857, MN).

DW4622   Cora Ann Weiser (b 9 May 1859, MN).

DW4623   John F. Weiser (b ca 1863, MN).

DW4624   William Walter Weiser (b 16 Jun 1868, MN) m Jessie Isadore   (b Nov 1877, OR). Spokane WA.

DW46241   Winona Weiser (b Jun 1896, OR).

DW46242   Howard Weiser (b Mar 1899, WA).

DW4625   Mary E. Weiser (b Feb 1870, MN).

DW4626   Ernest J. Weiser (b 17 Jan 1872, Scott MN) m Ruth   (b ca 1882, OR). Spokane WA.

DW4627   Vinnie E. Weiser (b 30 Mar 1873, MN).

DW4628   Jennie H. Weiser (b 25 Jun 1875, MN).

DW4629   Elwyn Roy Weiser (b 13 Nov 1877, MN).

DW462A   Joel Howard Weiser (b 7 Mar 1880, Barnes ND).

DW462B   Gertrude Weiser (b 23 Dec 1882, ND).

DW462C   Edna C. Weiser (b 21 Jun 1884, ND).

DW462D   Lois Adelaide Weiser (b 25 Feb 1888, ND).

DW463   Josiah S. Weiser (17 Aug 1832, PA-24 Jul 1863, Big Mound, ND) m Eliza   (b ca 1840, Canada). Shakopee MN. Shot and killed by Indians.

DW4631   Adda Weiser (b ca Jan 1860, MN).

DW464   Joel Schroeder Weiser (31 Aug 1834, PA-17 Jan 1925, Detroit, MN) m 10 May 1854, Oley, Berks PA, Louisa Cleaver (11 Oct 1835-8 Aug 1909). Amity, Berks PA; Shakopee MN; Valley City ND; Detroit Lakes MN.

DW4641   Mary Weiser (ca 1856, Shakopee MN-dy).

DW4642   James Weiser (ca 1858, Shakopee MN-dy).

DW4643   Rosa Ellen Weiser (b 30 Jan 1860, Shakopee MN) m Christ E. Schilling (b ca 1853, MO). Hermiston OR.

DW4644   Sarah Emma Weiser (b 11 Nov 1862, Shakopee MN) m 1) John McPherson (b ca 1859, England); m 2) George Phillips; m 3) William F. Kernkamp. Detroit MI.

DW4645   Hattie Clara Weiser (5 Oct 1863, Shakopee MN-25 Mar 1902, Pomona CA) m 5 Oct 1886, Valley City ND, Charles Edward Heidel. Shakopee MN. Valley City ND.

DW46451   Charles Sumner Heidel.

DW46452   Albert Weiser Heidel.

DW46453   Ewart Leslie Heidel.

DW4646   William C. Weiser (11 Apr 1866, Shakopee MN-25 May 1888).

DW4647   Joel Albert Weiser (23 Jan 1868, Shakopee MN-dy).

DW4648   Edith Weiser (ca 1870, Shakopee MN-dy).

DW4649   Lydia Annetta Weiser (b 7 Oct 1871, Shakopee MN) m Linwood Foster. Billings MT.

DW464A   Ida Mabel Weiser (b 23 Apr 1874, Shakopee MN) m John W. Sifton. Hood River OR.

DW464B   John Wesly Weiser (27 Jan 1876, Shakopee MN-1923, Valley City ND) He m 1904, Valley City ND, Margaret O'Brian (3 Dec 1876, Ireland-Mar 1965, Helena MT). Valley City ND.

DW464B1   John T. Weiser.

DW464B2   William J. Weiser.

DW464B3   Mary Weiser m   Winslow.

DW464B4   Lillian Weiser m Howard F. Wilkins.

DW464B5   Margaret Weiser.

DW464C   Lillian Annie Weiser (b 12 Apr 1878, Valley City ND) m James W. Neilson.

DW465   Annette Weiser (b 1839, PA).

DW47   David D. Weiser (7 Dec 1790, PA-22 Oct 1848) m 23 Oct 1814, Oley, Berks PA, Sarah Hoch (b ca 1794, PA). Reading PA.

DW471   Harriet Weiser (23 Feb 1816, PA-20 Jun 1844).

DW472   Helena Weiser (b 4 Feb 1818, PA).

DW473   Maria Weiser (b 4 Feb 1818, PA).

DW474   Amos High Weiser (27 Jul 1826, PA-29 Sep 1860, Pottsville PA) m 1) 9 Jul 1847, Reading PA, Rebecca Shaeffer (19 Feb 1826-4 Mar 1851); m 2) 2 Feb 1852, Reading PA, Elizabeth Anna Oberholtzer (b ca 1830, PA). Reading and Pottsville PA.

DW4741   John Edward Weiser (13 Apr 1849, PA-24 Jul 1850).

DW4742   John Weiser (ca 1851, PA-Apr 1857).

DW4743   Curdina{?} Weiser (b ca 1854, PA).

DW4744   Sarah Weiser (b ca 1856, PA).

DW4745   Mary E. Weiser (b ca 1857, PA).

DW4746   Annie A. Weiser (b ca 1859, PA).

DW475   Hiram High Weiser (b 24 Aug 1831, PA) m Mary A.   (b ca 1837, Wales). Suffield CT.

DW4751   Eugene Weiser (b ca 1854, CT).

DW4752   Charles Weiser (b ca 1857, CT).

DW476   Isabella Weiser (b 23 Feb 1833, PA) m 9 Feb 1852, Lebanon PA, Simon Noll (b ca 1818, PA). Minister, Spring Creek, Dauphin PA; Annville, Lebanon PA.

DW4761   Lawrence J. Noll (b ca 1859, PA).

DW4762   John H. Noll (b ca 1863, PA).

DW4763   Sarah Noll (b ca 1865, PA).

DW4764   Minnie V. Noll (b ca 1874, PA).

DW477   Sarah Jane Weiser (22 Feb 1836, PA-13 Apr 1854).

DW5   Susanna Weiser (12 Mar 1750, PA-21 Feb 1824) m Abraham Hoch (5 Sep 1745, Oley, Berks PA-4 Mar 1826). Farmer, Oley, Berks PA.

DW51   Abraham Hoch (5 Sep 1771-1 Dec 1838) m 23 Mar 1794, Exeter, Berks PA, Susanna Schneider (29 May 1772-14 Dec 1836). Farmer, Oley, Berks PA.

DW52   Susanna Hoch (30 Apr 1774, PA-19 Sep 1863) m 6 May 1794, Oley, Berks PA, Abraham Herbein (25 Jan 1768, Oley, Berks PA-14 Feb 1826). Farmer, Oley, Berks PA.

DW53   Esther Hoch (15 Apr 1789, Oley, Berks PA-25 Sep 1852) m 24 Nov 1811, Berks PA, Jacob Levan (16 May 1782, PA-29 Jun 1853). Farmer, Oley, Berks PA.

DW6   Jonathan Weiser (b ca 1752, PA) m? Eva Elisabeth Weiss. Oley, Berks PA.

DW61   Jonathan Weiser (b 27 Apr 1782, PA) m ca 1806, Magdaline Diener (9 Oct 1787-ca 1851).
Earl, Oley PA.[148]

DW611   Catharine Weiser (b 6 Dec 1808, PA).

DW612   Jes. Maria D. Weiser (b 13 Oct 1811, PA) m 2 Jun 1833, New Hanover, Montgomery PA,

---

[148]The baptism of Jonathan Weiser, son of Jonathan Weiser and Eva Weiss, is recorded in the church book of Salem Reformed Church in Oley. There can be no doubt that the father was (DW6). The fact that he left Oley in haste is also documented. However, his departure makes it more difficult to keep continuity in the life of his son. That the Jonathan who appeared first in 1798 at Hill Church and married Magdaline Diener was the same person who was born in 1782 cannot be documented. The conclusion that he was the same person is based on the facts that he was the right age to attend communion in 1798, that the mother Eva Weiss and her mother Eva Catherine were at the same communion, and that there were no other Weisers in the membership of Hill Church or any nearby church at the time.

Adam Dreher (18 Mar 1808-6 Nov 1861).

DW613 David D. Weiser (21 Aug 1813, PA-24 Dec 1874, Earl, Berks PA) m 26 Mar 1837, New Hanover, Montgomery PA, Catharine Ann B. Schoenly (1813-23 Mar 1895, Earl, Berks PA). Earl, Berks PA.

DW6131 Lydia S. Weiser (b ca 1840, PA) m 10 Aug 1861, Amity, Berks PA, George K. Sassaman (31 Jan 1836, PA-7 Aug 1904). Colebrookdale, Berks PA.

DW61311 Elmira Sassaman (b ca 1865, PA).

DW61312 Irvin Sassaman (b ca 1867, PA).

DW61313 Annie Sassaman (b ca Aug 1869, PA).

DW61314 Charles Sassaman (b ca 1876, PA).

DW6132 Jonathan S. Weiser (ca 1841, PA-1925).

DW6133 Catharine Ann Weiser (10 Apr 1845, PA-27 Feb 1885) m Daniel T. Botts (b ca 1845, PA). Frederick, Montgomery PA.

DW61331 Benjamin Daniel Botts (b 2 Apr 1875).

DW61332 Franklin Botts (b ca Sep 1879, PA).

DW6134 David S. Weiser (5 Oct 1847, PA-5 Feb 1924) m ca 1873, Mary Ann A. Bowman (13 Nov 1854, PA-6 Aug 1915). Earl, Berks PA.

DW61341 William Harrison B. Weiser (27 Jun 1874, Earl, Berks PA-1950) m 11 Mar 1905, Pennsburg, Montgomery PA, Harriet Ann Fretz (1879, PA-May 1965). Earl, Berks PA.

DW613411 Son Weiser (18 Apr 1906, PA-23 Apr 1906).

DW613412 Leon F. Weiser (1907, Earl, Berks PA-18 Dec 1983, Reading PA).

DW613413 Mary Edna Weiser (b 6 Jan 1910, PA) m Harold George Roberts (6 Aug 1908-6 Jul 1995). Douglassville, Berks PA.

DW6134131 Doris Bernice Roberts (b 18 Jan 1931, Pottstown PA).

DW613414 Harvey L. Weiser (ca 1914, Weavertown, Berks PA-9 Jun 1995) m 1939, Kathryn M. Hagenbuch. Pottstown and Boyertown PA.

DW6134141 Conrad W. Weiser (b 18 Nov 1939, Pottstown PA) m 29 Dec 1962, Norristown PA, Carol A. Lanz (b 7 May 1941, Norristown PA). Springtown, Bucks PA.

DW6134142 Harvey L. Weiser II. Gilbertsville, Montgomery PA.

DW61342 Charles B. Weiser (4 Jun 1875, PA-19 Jul 1880).

DW61343 Henry Augustus B. Weiser (9 Oct 1877, PA-15 Sep 1878).

DW61344 Catharine B. Weiser (1880, PA-1880).

DW6135 Jacob S. Weiser (14 Jul 1850, Earl, Berks PA-7 Nov 1912) m 10 Jul 1875, Reading PA, Sarah B. Snyder (17 Apr 1849, Reading PA-22 Jan 1936). Earl, Berks PA.

DW61351   Charles Elmer S. Weiser (Nov 1875, Earl, Berks PA-1960) m 9 Dec 1899, Reading PA, Sallie H. Haring (1 Dec 1878, Earl, Berks PA-16 Mar 1951, Earlville, Berks PA). Earl, Berks PA.

DW613511   Florence H. Weiser (23 Aug 1901, Earl, Berks PA-1979) m 18 Nov 1922, Reading PA, William A. Messner (1900, Lehigh, PA-1985).

DW613512   Mary Ellen Weiser (3 Mar 1905, PA-1 Jan 1906).

DW61352   John Weiser (4 Jan 1877, PA-15 Jun 1877, Earl, Berks PA).

DW61353   James Weiser (5 Jul 1878, PA-4 Jan 1887).

DW61354   Catharine Weiser (b 5 Oct 1880, PA).

DW61355   Mary S. Weiser (b ca 1881, PA) m 17 Dec 1904, Boyertown, Berks PA, Morris S. Stauffer (b ca 1879, Hereford, Berks PA).

DW61356   Ammon Franklin Weiser (27 Feb 1883, PA-23 Dec 1886).

DW61357   Sarah Rebecca Weiser (b 1 Sep 1884, PA) m 4 Feb 1911, Pottstown PA, Howard E. Acker (b ca 1889).

DW61358   Emma Elizabeth S. Weiser (b 9 Jan 1887, Earl, Berks PA) m 14 Dec 1912, Reading PA, Frank P. Stapleton (b ca 1883, Oley, Berks PA).

DW61359   Samuel S. Weiser (b Nov 1888, Earlville, Berks PA) m 6 May 1916, Oley, Berks PA, Mabel C. Schollenberger (b ca 1898, Earlville, Berks PA). Earl, Berks PA.

DW613591   Charles LeRoy Weiser (5 Aug 1916, PA-5 Jul 1971) m Laura Landis (b 10 Jun 1918).

DW6135911   Martin Weiser.

DW613592   Harold Weiser.

DW6135A   Daniel S. Weiser (22 Mar 1891, Earl, Berks PA-5 Dec 1952) m 14 Sep 1912, Boyertown, Berks PA, Bertha Mae Schaeffer (10 Sep 1895, Douglass, Berks PA-10 Sep 1949. Douglass, Berks PA.

DW6135A1   Eva Helena Weiser (b 23 Feb 1913, PA).

DW6135B   Minnie S. Weiser (b 15 Apr 1894, Earl, Berks PA).

DW6136   Hannah Weiser (24 Apr 1853, PA-9 Oct 1882) m? 1) Jesse Pannabecker; m 2) ca 1873, Alfred Leffel (9 Apr 1850, PA-21 Apr 1889). Earl, Berks PA.

DW61361   Mary Amanda Pannabecker (25 Oct 1871-26 Jan 1885).

DW61362   Mary Leffel (b ca 1873, PA).

DW61363   David Weiser Leffel (b 25 Jan 1875, Earl, Berks PA) m 4 Apr 1896, Pottstown PA, Hannah E. Yocum (b ca 1875, Douglass, Berks PA). Douglass, Berks PA.

DW61364   John William Leffel (b 19 Oct 1876, PA).

DW61365   Franklin Pierce Leffel (17 Jan 1878, PA-ca 1882).

DW61366   Sarah Catharine Leffel (b 23 Apr 1879, PA).

DW61367   Alfred Leffel (b 16 Oct 1880) m 19 Oct 1907, Pottstown PA, Ada L. Miller (b ca 1879). Pottstown PA.

DW61368   Mamie Lucinda Leffel (19 Apr 1882-ca May 1882).

DW6137   Darius (Grant) S. Weiser (14 Sep 1856, PA-23 Jan 1924). Unm. Earl, Berks PA.

DW614   Lewis D. Weiser (b 14 Feb 1817, PA) m 10 May 1840, Catharine Herb (30 Nov 1820, PA-12 Nov 1875). Pike and Washington, Berks PA.

DW6141   William H. Weiser (11 Sep 1840, PA-15 Apr 1895) m 3 May 1862, Catherine Weller (3 Jan 1843, PA-27 Jan 1914). Boyertown PA.

DW61411   Isabella W. Weiser (4 Jun 1863, PA-1943). Unm. Boyertown PA.

DW61412   Alfred Weller Weiser (25 Nov 1865, PA-3 Oct 1934) m 28 Feb 1889, Pottstown PA, Sarah Yost Henricks (2 Aug 1869, Slippery Rock, Lawrence PA-18 Mar 1960, Harrisburg PA). Musician and Chiropractor, Pottstown PA.

DW614121   William Henricks Wiser (28 Jan 1890, Pottstown PA-21 Feb 1961, Markleysburg PA) m 21 Dec 1916, Allahabad, UP, India, Charlotte Melina Viall (31 Aug 1892, Chicago, IL-19 Dec 1981, Raleigh, NC). Missionaries in North India.

DW6141211   Arthur Dana Wiser (b 22 Jul 1920, Naini Tal, UP, India) m 27 Dec 1941, Gowanda, NY, Mary Leona Raecher (b 31 Aug 1918). Members of Macedonia Community, Clarkesville GA and Hutterian Brethren, Ulster Park NY.

*DW61412111   Alan Wiser (b 13 Sep 1945, Clarkesville GA) m 24 May 969, Horsham PA, Susan Lydia Horel (b 6 Mar 1945, Philadelphia PA). Physician, Plymouth Meeting PA.

DW614121111   Jeffrey Alan Wiser (b 10 Apr 1973, Philadelphia PA).

DW614121112   Scott William Wiser (b 29 Apr 1976, Philadelphia PA).

DW614121113   Melissa Charlotte Wiser (b 23 Jan 1982, Philadelphia PA).

DW61412112   Rae Wiser (b 15 Feb 1948, Clarkesville GA) m 21 Aug 1971, Springville, Erie, NY, David Roland Whitehead (b 3 Jul 1945, Cambridge MD). Teachers, Ballston Spa NY.

DW614121121   Kirsten Mary Whitehead (b 11 Jul 1973, Saratoga Springs NY).

DW614121122   Rebecca Anne Whitehead (b 19 Feb 1975, Saratoga Springs NY).

DW614121123   Rachel Elizabeth Whitehead (b 28 Feb 1977, Saratoga Springs NY).

DW614121124   Jonathan David Whitehead (b 26 Jul 1987, Albany NY).

DW61412113   Stephen Wiser (b 31 Jan 1951, Clarkesville GA) m 22 Oct 1978, Rifton NY, Martha Ann Moody (b 14 Sep 1953, Greensboro NC). Members, Hutterian Brethren.

DW614121131   Conrad Douglas Wiser (b 18 Aug 1979, Poughkeepsie NY).

DW614121132   Elizabeth Ann Wiser (b 13 Feb 1981, Poughkeepsie NY).

DW614121133   Dorien Mary Wiser (b 17 Mar 1982, England).

DW61412114   Dana Wiser (b 29 Jun 1954, Demarest GA) m 16 Jun 1985, Rifton NY, Maureen Warren (b 31 Dec 1960, Poughkeepsie NY). Members, Hutterian Brethren, Rifton NY.

DW614121141   Trevor William Wiser (b 15 Apr 1986, Kingston NY).

DW614121142   Arthur Darrell Wiser (b 5 Sep 1987, Kingston NY).

DW614121143   Leona Jean Wiser (25 Oct 1988, Albany NY-13 Nov 1988, Albany NY).

DW614121144   Adrian Jack Wiser (b 10 Oct 1990, Rifton NY).

DW614121145   Lara Joy Wiser (b 15 Jul 1993, Rifton NY).

DW614121146   Ralph Samson Wiser (b 4 Jun 1995, Rifton NY).

DW614121147   Wesley Dana Wiser (b 10 Nov 1996, Rifton NY).

DW61412115   William Wiser (b 1 Oct 1957, Staunton VA) m 23 Feb 1986, Rifton NY, Grace Anna Domer (b 28 Oct 1957, Poughkeepsie NY). Members, Hutterian Brethren, Rifton NY.

DW614121151   Jesse Leonhard Wiser (b 14 Dec 1986, Kingston NY).

DW614121152   Earl Jacob Wiser (b 24 Jul 1988, Kingston NY).

DW614121153   Emmett Joseph Wiser (b 17 Dec 1989, Kingston NY).

DW614121154   Anna Louisa Wiser (b 4 Jun 1992, Winnipeg, MB, Canada).

DW614121155   Kayla Joy Wiser (b 30 Nov 1994, Kingston NY).

DW61412116   Helen (Gloria) Wiser (b 19 Jun 1959, Poughkeepsie NY) m 26 Apr 1987, Rifton NY, Martin Sheppherd Huleatt (b 13 Dec 1964, Poughkeepsie NY). Members, Hutterian Brethren, Ulster Park NY.

DW614121161   Chad Huleatt (b 18 Feb 1988, Uniontown PA).

DW614121162   Jay Warren Huleatt (b 9 Oct 1990, Uniontown PA).

DW614121163   Debra Talitha Huleatt (b 5 Jun 1991, Rifton NY).

DW614121164   Veery Maureen Huleatt (b 16 Apr 1993, Rifton NY).

DW6141212   Alfred Roswell Wiser (b 19 May 1924, Naini Tal, UP, India) m 1) 11 Jun 1949, Chicago IL, Lucille Reed (b 1925, Chicago IL); div 1958; m 2) 25 Oct 1958, Jefferson IA, Edna Pauline Price (b 16 Aug 1923, Jefferson IA). He, high school music teacher, Evanston IL, Jefferson and Ames IA. She, secretary, Ames, IA.

        Pamela Kay Wiser (b 25 Feb 1947, Iowa City IA; parents   Bertram and Edna Pauline Price, adopted by (DW6141212) Alfred Roswell Wiser) m 16 Aug 1969, Ames IA, Theodore Wier Millen (b 19 Oct 1945, Allahabad, UP, India). She, teacher. He, sales representative. Ames IA.

        Michael Kent Wiser (b 25 Feb 1949, La Crosse WI; parents   Bertram and Edna Pauline Price, adopted by (DW6141212) Alfred Roswell Wiser) m 25 Nov 1973, Ludington MI, Linda Lee Palmquist (b 17 Dec 1947, Ludington MI). He, Lutheran minister. She, nurse. Spokane, WA.

        Donald Reuben Wiser (b 22 Oct 1950, Jefferson, IA; parents   Bertram and Edna Pauline Price, adopted by (DW6141212) Alfred Roswell Wiser) m 8 Feb 1975, Ames IA, Ruthanne Clarke (b 2 Jul

1950, Des Moines IA). Teachers, Keokuk and Marshalltown IA.

DW61412121   Timothy Todd Wiser (b 15 Jul 1961, Jefferson IA) m 24 Jul 1982, Ames, IA, Kimberly Ann Blackmer (b 2 Jul 1962, Ames IA). He, real estate. She, business school. Ankeny IA.

DW614121211   Austin Thomas Wiser (b 1 Jul 1990, Tulsa OK).

DW614121212   Ashley Ann Wiser (b 6 Apr 1992, Des Moines IA).

DW61412122   Tad William Wiser (b 28 Jan 1963, Jefferson IA) m 20 Sep 1991, Maui, HI, Leona Leigh Jones (b 11 Jun 1963, Denver CO). Soft drink sales. Denver, CO.

DW6141213   Edward Hempstead Wiser (b 21 Jan 1931, Fatehgarh, UP, India) m 21 Dec 1957, Shelby OH, Betty Anne Hutchinson (b 12 May 1931, Shelby OH). He, university professor. She, gerontologist. Raleigh NC.

DW61412131   Carla Blanche Wiser (b 21 Nov 1961, Raleigh NC) m 2 May 1992, Raleigh NC, Lincoln Lounsbury (b 14 Jul 1958, Peterborough NH). Air traffic controllers, San Francisco and Washington National airports.

DW614121311   Laura Charlotte Lounsbury (b 16 Nov 1994, Hayward CA).

DW61412132   Conrad John Wiser (b 17 Jun 1963, Raleigh NC) m 27 Dec 1992, Winters CA, Lisa Louise Nixon (21 Jan 1966, Webster City IA). Officer, US Army.

Dustin Charles Brandon Nixon Wiser (b 24 Nov 1985, Fairfield CA; mother Lisa Louise Nixon, adopted by (DW61412132) Conrad John Wiser).

DW614121321   Ashley Louise Tahoe Wiser (b 28 Sep 1993, Ft. Riley KS).

DW614122   Dorothy Lenore Weiser (14 Jan 1892, Pottstown PA 3 Apr 1970) m 1 Jun 1926, William C. Kilpatrick (16 Feb 1889-11 Nov 1971). Episcopal minister.

DW6141221   James David Kilpatrick (b 1 Apr 1927) m 5 Aug 1950, Herminie Lacour (b 5 Jun 1929).

DW6141222   Kathleen Dorothy Kilpatrick (b 29 May 1934) m 23 Aug 1958, Andrew Beaton Jr. (b 12 Sep 1932).

DW614123   Mary Henricks Weiser (16 Aug 1893, Pottstown PA-25 Oct 1967, Pottstown PA) m 16 Aug 1923, Pottstown PA, Arthur Henderson Essick (21 Jul 1895, Coventryville PA-19 Nov 1986, Piqua OH). Pottstown PA.

DW6141231   Dorothy Faith Essick (b 4 Aug 1924, Pottstown PA) m 9 Jun 1946, Harrisburg PA, Wilbur Warren Shoemaker (b 1 Dec 1923, Stark, OH). Minister, Church of the Brethren, Bremen IN, Osceola and Springfield MO, West Manchester OH, Oaks PA and Piqua OH.

DW6141232   Forrest Weiser Essick (13 Nov 1926-30 May 1984) m 4 Jun 1949, Ruth Ehst Kolb (b 28 Nov 1926). Pottstown PA.

DW6141233   Ruth Virginia Essick (b 25 Mar 1930, Pottstown PA) m 3 Sep 1948, Ray Buckwalter (b 8 Feb 1929, Pottstown PA). North Lawrence OH.

DW614124   Daniel Weiser (29 Feb 1896, Pottstown PA-17 Apr 1896, Pottstown PA).

DW614125   Florence Weiser (16 Oct 1900, Pottstown PA-18 Oct 1900).

DW614126   Richard Wagner Weiser (14 May 1902, Pottstown PA-13 Aug 1981, Steubenville OH) m 1) 20 Apr 1927, Lynette Ellen Baldwin (6 Aug 1904, Pottstown PA-2 Oct 1978, Jewett OH); m 2) 7 Jan 1979, Mabel Lenora Brown (b 21 Aug 1904, Dillonvale OH). Family physician, Philadelphia PA, Kenmore NY, Cincinnati and Jewett OH.

DW6141261   Jacquelyn Lucille Weiser (b 22 Nov 1930, Philadelphia PA) m 13 Mar 1954, Jewett OH, Thomas Herbert Cunningham (b 20 Oct 1929, New Rumley, Harrison, OH). She, nurse. He, Christian radio program writer. Pittsville WI.

DW61412611   Kim Lynette Cunningham (b 11 Jul 1956, Cincinnati OH) m 14 Jun 1980, Pittsville WI, Michael Lee Knuth (b 21 Dec 1954, Sheboygan Falls WI).

DW61412612   Kathy Ann Cunningham (b 22 Feb 1958, Cambridge OH) m 23 Apr 1983, Timothy Donald Wunsch. She, occupational therapist.

DW61412613   Thomas Richard Cunningham (b 4 Aug 1959, Cambridge OH).

DW6141262   Marilyn Baldwin Weiser (b 29 May 1933) m 7 Apr 1954, Robert Dale Morgan (b 15 Sep 1931); div 1990. Zanesville OH.

DW61412621   Robert Daryl Morgan (b 15 Aug 1956) m 8 Aug 1986, Lisa Brooke (b 18 Sep 1963).

DW61412622   Richard Joseph Morgan (b 25 Mar 1959) m 1 Aug 1981, Lori Jane Reser (b 19 Feb 1960); div 1993.

DW61412623   Brian Dean Morgan (b 5 Aug 1960) m 11 Aug 1979, Judith Ann Downing (b 2 Feb 1961).

DW61412624   Brad Lee Morgan (b 9 Apr 1963) m 27 Oct 1990, Catherine Thomas (b 19 Mar 1962).

DW6141263   Gwendolyn Ruth Weiser (b 21 Dec 1939, Cincinnati OH) m 25 Sep 1965, Robert Leonard Stewart (b 19 Oct 1936, Jewett OH). Dairy farmer, Jewett OH.

DW61412631   Sandra Lee Stewart (b 23 Jan 1968, Dover OH) m 9 Sep 1990, Alan McKinney Thompson (b 11 May 1964, Dennison OH). Farmer, Jewett OH.

DW61412632   Steven Foster Stewart (b 6 Nov 1970, Dover OH) m 17 Apr 1993, Melissa Ann Baker (b 23 Aug 1971, Dover OH).

DW6141264   Lyndalyn Kaye Weiser (b 23 Jun 1941, Columbia SC) m 16 Feb 1963, Jewett OH, Geoffrey Llewellynn Jenkins (21 Jan 1943, Springfield IL). She, teacher. He, loan broker. Huntingdon Beach CA.

DW61412641   Deron Russell Jenkins (b 20 Dec 1967, Middletown OH). Cabinet maker.

DW61412642   Mark Edward Jenkins (b 21 Jun 1969, Middletown OH).

DW6141265   Richard Lynn Weiser (b 19 Jul 1942, Columbia SC) m 18 Mar 1967, Shreve OH, Janet Kay Merryman (9 Jun 1944, Steubenville OH). Laboratory manager, Cleveland OH.

DW61412651   Richard Kaye Weiser (b 10 Sep 1969, Dover OH). Engineer, Cleveland OH.

DW61412652   Dale Lynn Weiser (b 13 Jan 1970, Berea OH).

DW61412653   David Lee Weiser (b 4 Feb 1974, Parma OH).

DW614127   Ruth Madeline Weiser (b 1 Jul 1906, Pottstown PA) m 1 Sep 1927, Pottstown PA, John

Milhime Smith (b 15 Aug 1904, Catasauqua PA). She, music teacher. He, music superintendent. Valley Stream NY.

DW6141271   Sara Mae Smith (b 14 May 1931, Bronx NY) m 27 Jun 1953, Valley Stream NY, John ("Jack") Andrew MacNab (19 Jun 1931, Hartford CT). Engineer. Satellite Beach FL.

DW6141272   Mary Anne Smith (b 14 May 1931, Bronx NY) m 26 Jun 1954, Valley Stream NY, William Henry Munch (26 Aug 1930, Philadelphia PA-13 Dec 1995, Melbourne FL). Physical education teacher. Valley Stream NY.

DW61413   Helena Weiser (7 Feb 1868, PA-17 May 1952) m 7 Nov 1885, Boyertown PA, Walter S. Funk (8 Jun 1865, PA-26 Mar 1955). Boyertown PA.

DW614131   Sheldon Weiser Funk (7 May 1888, PA-1971) m Dorothy Eidell (16 Oct 1895-1975). Boyertown PA.

DW614132   Hildagard W. Funk (7 Sep 1890, Boyertown PA-27 Apr 1980) m 1) 21 Jun 1911, Boyertown PA, William E. Ott (19 Dec 1888, Bucks, PA-23 Jun 1912); m 2) 20 Nov 1920, Norristown PA, Clarence E. Benner (22 Oct 1885, Richlandtown, Bucks, PA-17 May 1963). Boyertown PA.

DW614133   Kathleen Funk (b 11 Sep 1896) m James R. Bower (b 21 Jul 1893). Oley PA.

DW61414   Emma M. Weiser (b 9 Sep 1869, PA) m 30 Mar 1889, Pottstown PA, William H. Moser (7 Jun 1867, District, Berks PA-3 May 1924). Pottstowm PA.

DW614141   Harry W. Moser (b 4 Jul 1890, PA) m Louise C. Vogan.

DW614142   Raymond W. Moser (15 Jul 1892-10 Dec 1913).

DW614143   William W. Moser Jr. (b 20 Oct 1898, PA) m Lucille Bleasdale (b 5 Sep 1900).

DW614144   Isabel Moser (15 Feb 1904-21 Aug 1904).

DW614145   Florence Moser (b 6 May 1906).

DW61415   Wilson W. Weiser (16 Nov 1870, Boyertown PA-22 Sep 1952, West Reading PA) m 27 Jun 1895, Reading PA, Sallie Alice Geiger (23 Jul 1871, Reading PA-21 Apr 1949). Reading and Boyertown PA.

DW614151   Catharine May Weiser (4 May 1896, Reading PA-13 Oct 1949) m 28 Dec 1922, Boyertown PA, Allen R. Hartzell (12 Dec 1894, Bucks, PA-25 Jun 1950). Boyertown PA.

DW6141511   Ralph Hartzell (26 Apr 1925-1925).

DW6141512   Elsie Janet Hartzell (b 8 Dec 1930) m 5 Sep 1953, Vinton Bowering (16 Feb 1928-3 Aug 1979). Universalist ministers.

DW614152   Grant Weiser (18 Nov 1897, Reading PA-13 Aug 1975, New York NY) m Elizabeth Hevener (17 Apr 1897-ca Aug 1975).

DW6141521   Ellen Weiser (b 26 Jul 1920) m Eugene Daggy. Tenafly NJ.

DW61415211   Ora Ellen Daggy (b 13 Feb 1951, Natick MA) m Richard Steinberger.

DW61415212   Neil Daggy (b 6 Nov 1955, Englewood NJ).

DW614153   Earl Herbert Weiser (22 Oct 1899, Reading PA-3 Sep 1991, San Antonio, TX) m Elizabeth Emery (27 Aug 1899-12 Sep 1981, San Antonio, TX).

DW614154   Alice G. Weiser (21 Feb 1902, Reading PA-1908).

DW614155   Elsie Mary Weiser (23 Feb 1905, Reading PA-5 Dec 1972, Lansdale, PA) m 1937, David E. Cowell (b 1903). Lansdale, PA.

DW6141551   David E. Cowell Jr. (1940, West Reading PA-28 Sep 1962).

DW614156   Paul Conrad Weiser (6 Aug 1907, Reading PA-16 May 1960, Boyertown PA) m Jean M. Meyrick (ca 1895, Shenandoah PA-8 Jul 1992).

DW6141561   Conrad Weiser.

DW6141562   Alice Jean Weiser (11 Jul 1938, PA-20 Jul 1938).

DW614157   Miriam G. Weiser (29 Aug 1909, Boyertown PA-31 Jan 1924).

DW614158   Daniel G. Weiser (19 Oct 1911, Boyertown PA-16 Feb 1973, Boyertown PA) m 2 Apr 1938, Boyertown PA, Jennie S. Kolb (24 Feb 1912-12 Jun 1977, West Reading PA).

DW6141581   Mary Alice Weiser (b 4 Oct 1938, Coatesville PA) m 5 Jun 1960, Boyertown PA, James J. Peck (b 26 Nov 1938).

DW61415811   Sherrie Lee Peck (b 15 Nov 1960, Pottstown PA).

DW61415812   Shellie Lynn Peck (b 24 Dec 1963, Lebanon PA).

DW6141582   Daniel W. Weiser (b 17 May 1942) m 22 Feb 1964, Boyertown PA, Joanna A. Schultz (b 20 Aug 1943).

DW61415821   Deborah Ann Weiser (b 29 Jan 1967).

DW61415822   Julie Ann Weiser (b 10 Jan 1973).

DW6141583   Charles W. Weiser (b 20 Sep 1947, Pottstown PA) m 9 May 1970, Mt. Penn, Berks PA, Anne L. Gehret (b 17 Apr 1939, Plainfield NJ).

DW61415831   David W. Weiser (b 16 Mar 1972, West Reading PA).

DW61415832   Steven C. Weiser (b 29 Nov 1979, West Reading PA).

DW61416   Mary W. Weiser (1 Apr 1873, Boyertown PA-1 Feb 1939) m 1) 7 Jan 1892, Boyertown PA, Charles U. Sands (3 Jan 1873-15 Jun 1904); m 2) 27 Jul 1909, Boyertown PA, Harry B. Mest (6 Sep 1874, Schultzville PA-12 Jan 1968). Boyertown PA.

DW614161   Pearl Sands (b 28 Apr 1892, Boyertown PA) m 15 Jan 1910, Boyertown PA, Robert S. Kern (b ca 1890, Maxatawny, Berks PA).

DW614162   Helen Eileen Mest (b 23 Dec 1909).

DW61417   Katie W. Weiser (4 Jun 1874, Boyertown PA-1940) m 22 Mar 1903, Boyertown PA, Albert B. Leidy (b 27 Dec 1880, Gilbertsville, Montgomery PA). Boyertown PA.

DW614171   Ruth Alberta Leidy (11 May 1910, Philadelphia, PA-13 Dec 1993, Topton, Berks PA) m

D. Richard Jafolla (d 6 Jan 1989).

DW61418 Olivia W. Weiser (2 Nov 1877, PA-13 Jan 1908, Boyertown PA) m 12 Aug 1901, Boyertown PA, George A. N. Romig (b ca 1879, Douglass, Berks PA). Olivia and Sallie died in the Boyertown opera house fire.

DW614181 Sallie Romig (7 Mar 1905-12 Jan 1908, Boyertown PA).

DW6142 Abraham Weiser (15 Sep 1843, PA-11 Nov 1857).

DW6143 Daniel H. Weiser (7 Feb 1852, PA-8 Mar 1926) m Elmira (Ellen) R. Giles (9 Jan 1853, PA-5 May 1922). Pottstown and Reading PA.

DW61431 Lewis G. Weiser (20 Nov 1869, Glendale, Montgomery PA-1944) m 23 Jan 1892, District, Berks PA, Emma L. Schmeck (1868, Longswamp, Berks PA-1920). Topton and Reading PA.

DW614311 Estella H. E. Weiser (13 Sep 1893, Longswamp, Berks PA-1918) m 12 Oct 1911, Reading PA, Elmer Edward Smith (b ca 1888, Lehigh, PA).

DW6143111 Hattie Bertha Smith (b 18 Nov 1911).

DW6143112 Elmer Edward Smith (b 26 Sep 1917). Philadelphia PA.

DW6143113 Dorothy Jennie Smith (b 13 Sep 1918, Lower Heidelberg, Berks PA). Philadelphia PA.

DW614312 Sarah May Weiser (b Mar 1897, Hemmingsville, Berks PA) m 17 Jun 1914, Topton, Berks PA, James Patrick Dillon (b ca 1892, Reading PA).

DW6143121 Arlene Dillon (b 30 Sep 1914).

DW6143122 James Arthur Dillon (b 17 Jun 1916).

DW614313 Catherine May Weiser (b 18 May 1898, Topton, Berks PA) m 1) Walter Miller; m 2) 19 Feb 1921, Reading PA, James E. Wartzenluft (6 Sep 1882, Berks PA-29 Feb 1976).

DW6143131 Lewis Walter Miller (b 27 Oct 1916).

DW61432 Wilson G. Weiser (b 26 Feb 1873, Earl, Berks PA) m 7 Nov 1891, Pottstown PA, Ida R. Heims (b Nov 1873, PA). Pottstown PA.

DW614321 Leroy W. Weiser (b Jun 1896, Pottstown PA) m 11 Oct 1917, Norristown PA, Alice Wampole (b ca 1893, Sumneytown, Montgomery PA).

DW614322 Thomas Edwin Weiser (b ca 1906, PA).

DW614323 George A. Weiser (b ca 1907, PA).

DW614324 John T. Weiser (b ca 1910, PA).

DW61433 William Henry G. Weiser (b 25 Feb 1875, PA).

DW61434 John G. Weiser (b Jan 1879, PA) m 16 Apr 1898, Pottstown PA, Ida M. Richards (b Mar 1879, PA). Pottstown PA.

DW614341 Mary E. Weiser (b Jul 1899, PA) m Garber. Pottstown PA.

DW6143411   Robert L. Garber (b ca Sep 1919, PA).

DW614342   Ralph Jacob Weiser (b ca 1901, Pottstown PA) m 9 Sep 1922, Reading PA, Thelma S. Kochel (b ca 1906, North Coventry, Chester, PA).

DW614343   Elmira Weiser (b ca 1904, PA).

DW614344   Jeanette Evelyn Weiser (b ca 1914, PA) m 1934, Charles Warren Smith.

DW61435   Mary G. Weiser (b Apr 1885, PA) m 1) 22 May 1902, Pottstown PA, Howard Baker (b 10 Nov 1881); m 2) Howard Miller.

DW614351   William H. Baker (b ca 1904).

DW61436   Charles Giles Weiser (27 Mar 1892, PA-2 Oct 1918) m 17 May 1911, Pottstown PA, Leona Mary Boyer (14 Mar 1886-1 Apr 1946). Pottstown PA.

DW614361   Fernley G. Weiser (8 Dec 1911, PA-21 Jan 1945). Pottstown PA.

DW614362   Mary A. Weiser (1913-1984) m 1946, Horace C. Shellenberger (1907-1972). Pottstown PA.

DW6144   Emma H. Weiser (14 Aug 1860, PA-13 Jul 1895) m ca 1881, William H. Miller. Pottstown PA.

DW61441   Anne Miller (b 24 Feb 1881).

DW61442   Mary Miller (b 5 Feb 1885).

DW61443   Emma Miller (b 18 Jun 1891).

DW615   Lea D. Weiser (b 5 Mar 1821, PA). Colebrookdale, Berks PA.

DW616   William D. Weiser (13 Aug 1822, PA-22 Feb 1902) m Sarah Ann Gehris (21 Oct 1821, PA-18 Mar 1899). Colebrookdale, Berks PA.

DW6161   Caroline G. Weiser (27 Mar 1845, PA-30 Mar 1913) m 11 May 1872, Boyertown PA, John N. Polster (17 Dec 1845, PA-6 May 1901).   Sumneytown, Montgomery PA.

DW61611   Agnes W. Polster (b ca 1873, Colebrookdale, Berks PA) m 23 Apr 1892, Boyertown PA, Ephraim G. Erb (b ca 1871, Washington, Berks PA). New Berlinville, PA.

DW61612   Lillie W. Polster (b Oct 1875, PA) m 23 May 1896, Montgomery PA, Clinton Kemmerer (b Oct 1877, PA). Marlboro, Montgomery PA. Sellersville PA.

DW61613   Sallie W. Polster (b Nov 1875, PA) m 1 Jun 1895, Green Lane PA, Corson B. Weber (b Aug 1876, PA). Quakertown PA.

DW61614   John W. Polster (b ca 1877, PA) m 20 Mar 1902, Sumneytown, Montgomery PA, Maggie F. Sowers (15 Oct 1880-5 Jan 1917). Frederick and Oaks, Montgomery PA.

DW61615   Edwin W. Polster (b ca 1881) m 1 Apr 1903, Sumneytown, Montgomery PA, Carrie M. Kieffer (b ca 1881).

DW61616   Warren W. Polster (b ca 1885, PA) m 21 Feb 1906, Sumneytown, Montgomery PA, Lizzie B. Emert (b ca 1887, PA). Emaus, Lehigh PA.

DW6162   Jonathan G. Weiser (16 Sep 1847, PA-16 Jul 1916) m 21 Feb 1874, Reading PA, Rose Ann Moser (30 Mar 1853-21 Oct 1925). Lebanon PA.

DW61621   Eva Victoria Weiser (15 Jul 1874, PA-29 Oct 1874).

DW61622   Sara Annette Weiser (12 Oct 1875, PA-13 Apr 1880).

DW61623   Clarence Monroe Weiser (26 Aug 1877, PA-29 Feb 1940, Allentown PA) m ca 1903, Sarah E. Biecher (12 Nov 1878-4 Jun 1973). Lebanon and Reading PA.

DW616231   J. Allen Weiser (1904, PA-1985) m Helen M. Neider (b 1906).

DW616232   Harold M. Weiser (b ca 1908, PA).

DW61624   Delphina Estella Weiser (b 5 Jun 1879, PA) m John H. Rakcr.

DW6163   Sarah G. Weiser (Jan 1854, PA-1922) m ca 1882, Henry H. Kolb (Mar 1859-1923). Colebrookdale, Berks PA.

DW617   Juliana D. Weiser (b ca 1826) m Isaac Moyer.

DW618   Benjamin Weiser (ca 1831, PA-1 Feb 1883). Cumru, Berks PA.

DW7   Anna Weiser (11 Apr 1755, PA-20 Jun 1829) m 4 Apr 1782, Abraham DeTurk (3 Mar 1752-19 Apr 1829). Farmer, Oley, Berks PA.

DW71   Abraham DeTurk (13 Apr 1785, PA-8 Oct 1865) m 17 Jul 1808, Oley, Berks PA, Esther Levan (24 Dec 1785-25 Sep 1847). Farmer, Oley, Berks PA.

DW72   Isaac DeTurk (2 Nov 1789, PA-3 May 1865) m Maria Weiser (DW83) (20 Jan 1786, PA-21 Jan 1846). Maxatawny, Berks PA. (For children, see DW83).

DW73   Catharine DeTurk (21 Mar 1792-24 Jan 1822) m 11 Mar 1821, Oley, Berks PA, Peter Deysher (21 Feb 1802-1 Jul 1892). Washington, Berks PA.

DW74   Hannah DeTurk m 16 Jul 1821, Reading PA, Josiah (Joshua) Hoch.

DW8   Daniel Weiser (1756, PA-29 Dec 1821, Maxatawny, Berks PA) m 31 Oct 1780, Esther Hoch Pott (27 Sep 1758-3 Nov 1834, Maxatawny, Berks PA). Farmer, Oley, Maxatawny and Longswamp, Berks PA.

DW81   William Weiser (24 Sep 1782, PA-12 Apr 1861) m? 1) Hannah Stoudt (27 Mar 1804-14 May 1879); m 2) Esther Bieber (9 Feb 1812, PA-23 Apr 1873). Maxatawny and Kutztown, Berks PA.

DW811   William S. Weiser (28 Apr 1825, Rockland, Berks PA-24 Jun 1900, Maxatawny, Berks PA) m 7 Feb 1847, Sarah Ann Fenstermacher (19 Nov 1821, PA-27 Jun 1906). Farmer, Rockland and Maxatawny, Berks PA.

DW8111   Leanda Weiser (19 May 1847, PA-7 Oct 1908) m 29 Aug 1867, Longswamp, Berks PA, Francis J. Schwoyer (11 Mar 1843, PA-4 Sep 1913). Rockland, Berks PA.

DW81111   Eliza Ellen Nora Schwoyer (20 Jul 1867, Maxatawny, Berks PA-20 Mar 1915) m 11 Jan 1886, Dryville, Berks PA, Peter Samuel Oswald (9 Aug 1860, Dryville, Berks PA-25 Dec 1914). Rockland, Berks PA.

DW81112   William A. Schwoyer (20 Aug 1870, PA-24 Apr 1947) m 9 Jul 1892, Bowers, Berks PA,

Annie L. Drey (23 Jul 1874-31 Aug 1960). Rockland, Berks PA.

DW81113   Eugene E. C. Schwoyer (1874, Rockland, Berks, PA-1957) m 23 Dec 1905, Dryville, Berks PA, Andora H. Herbein (1875, Rockland, Berks PA-1962). Rockland, Berks PA.

DW81114   Endora H. Schwoyer (1876, PA-1932) m Frank W. Danner (1871-1940). Rockland, Berks PA.

DW81115   Cyraneus J. Schwoyer (Dec 1879, PA-1948). Rockland, Berks PA.

DW81116   Astor I. Schwoyer (Feb 1882, Rockland, Berks PA-1945) m 30 Jul 1903, Kutztown, Berks PA, Hattie E. Fegely (1884, Rockland, Berks PA-1968). Rockland, Berks PA.

DW81117   S. Neida Schwoyer (Sep 1884, Rockland, Berks PA-10 Feb 1960, Reading PA). Unm.

DW8112   Alfred George Weiser (24 Jul 1849, Maxatawny, Berks PA-7 Jan 1897, Bowers, Berks PA) m ca 1873, Amanda Hilbert (3 Aug 1851, PA-27 Dec 1941). Farmer, Rockland, Berks PA.

DW81121   George Edward (Edwin) Weiser (7 Feb 1874, Bowers, Maxatawny, Berks PA-1943) m 2 Dec 1899, Kutztown PA, Emma (Emmalina) L. Miller (Mar 1883, Rockland, Berks PA-1947). Maxatawny, Berks PA.

DW811211   Raymond Alfred Weiser (22 Mar 1900, Rockland, Berks PA-Dec 1979, PA) m 3 Apr 1926, Kutztown PA, Hilda Hassler (1901, Lyons, Berks PA-1982). Maxatawny, Berks PA.

DW8112111   Robert A. Weiser (b 6 Aug 1926, PA) m 12 Jan 1952, Fleetwood, Berks PA, Loretta M. Brintzenhoff.

DW8112112   Budd Weiser m Catherine Berstler.

DW8112113   Buster Weiser.

DW8112114   Raymond Weiser (b 20 Mar 1931, PA).

DW81122   Elizabeth Victoria Weiser (24 Apr 1880, Bowers, Berks PA-6 Apr 1972, Almshouse, Berks PA). Unm. Maxatawny, Berks PA.

DW8113   David Albert Weiser (12 Mar 1852, PA-12 Mar 1873). Unm.

DW8114   Benjamin Cyrenius Weiser (12 Feb 1854, Rockland, Berks PA-7 Jan 1892, Villa Grove, CO) m Ellen J. Fegley (b ca 1855). Rockland, Berks PA. Villa Grove, CO.

DW81141   George Weiser (30 Oct 1878, Rockland, Berks PA-23 Jan 1885).

DW8115   Hannah Rebecca Weiser (22 Jun 1857, Rockland, Berks PA-5 Jun 1911) m 28 Apr 1878, Reuben L. Smith (3 Oct 1859, PA-30 Jan 1944). Maxatawny and Topton, Berks PA.

DW81151   Harry (Henry) E. Smith (b Oct 1879, PA).

DW81152   Harvey Irvin Smith (19 Nov 1881, Maxatawny, Berks PA).

DW81153   Helen L. R. Smith (b Aug 1891, PA).

DW8116   Oliver W. Weiser (26 Jul 1858, Berks PA-25 Oct 1933) m 8 Jan 1921, Bowers, Berks PA, Katie D. Rothermel (1900, Berks PA-1984). Maxatawny, Berks PA.

DW81161   Gladys Weiser (b ca 1920, PA) m Abraham Benner.

DW81162   William Oliver Weiser (b ca 1921, PA) m 1) 6 Mar 1943, Topton, Berks PA, Mary J. Hoppes (b ca 1917); m 2) Edna Hilbert (b ca 1921). Topton, Berks PA.

DW811621   William Oliver Weiser Jr. (b 1 Jun 1943, Topton, Berks PA).

DW8117   Allen Weiser (28 Jan 1861, PA-13 Dec 1863).

DW8118   Alvin Weiser (12 Apr 1863, Bowers, Berks PA-5 Apr 1932) m 16 Mar 1889, Maxatawny, Berks PA, Mary Evella Kutz (16 Mar 1866, Lyons, Berks PA-21 Apr 1947). Farmer, Maxatawny, Berks PA.

DW81181   Edgar David Weiser (5 Jul 1889, PA-7 Sep 1929) m Minnie Yenser (28 Sep 1890-10 Oct 1975). Maxatawny, Berks PA. Washington, DC.

DW811811   Mary J. Weiser (b ca Jan 1920, PA) m   Dolan.

DW811812   Edgar David Weiser (b 7 Sep 1928, PA) m Shirley Ann Goldberg. Leesport, Berks PA. Norfolk, VA.

DW8118121   Cheryl Joyce Weiser (1 May 1960, Phoenixville, Berks PA.

DW8118122   Michael D. Weiser m Lisa Marie Maxwell.

DW81182   Minnie Edna Weiser (b 8 Jan 1893, Bowers, Berks PA) m 17 Jun 1914, Kutztown PA, Walter B. Grim (4 Nov 1883, Bowers, Berks PA-17 Mar 1967). Maxatawny, Berks PA.

DW811821   Vera E. Grim (b 9 Jun 1914, Bowers, Berks PA).

DW811822   Kermit Moses Grim (b 16 Jun 1916, Rutherford, PA).

DW811823   Annie Louise Grim (b 13 Jul 1923).

DW811824   Marion Elizabeth Grim (b 4 Oct 1925).

DW81183   George William Weiser (8 Dec 1895, Maxatawny, Berks PA-11 May 1923) m 17 Jul 1918, Kutztown PA, Sadie E. Schearer (9 Sep 1896, Berks PA-30 Dec 1980). Maxatawny, Berks PA.

DW811831   Alma E. Weiser (b ca Aug 1918, PA) m Peter Dolan.

DW811832   Leon Charles Weiser (b 13 Apr 1922, PA) m Hilda   .

DW81184   Paul Alvin Weiser (31 Aug 1897, Bowers, Berks PA-Jun 1958) m 30 May 1925, Port Clinton PA, Hannah Mae Kauffman (b 1906, Hamburg, Berks PA). Maxatawny, Berks PA.

DW811841   Infant Weiser (19 Dec 1925, PA-19 Dec 1925).

DW811842   Paul Alvin Weiser (b 27 Jan 1936, Shillington, Berks PA).

DW81185   Mary Evella Weiser (16 Oct 1899, Maxatawny, Berks PA-26 Mar 1924). Unm. Maxatawny, Berks PA.

DW81186   Annie Elizabeth Weiser (12 Feb 1904, Maxatawny, Berks PA-Jun 1975). Unm. Maxatawny, Berks PA.

DW81187   Lillian Carolyn Weiser (21 Jul 1907, PA-17 Mar 1991) m Ed Earl O. Barto (26 Feb

1905-11 Mar 1974).

DW811871   Sam. Al. Barto (b 14 Jan 1932) m Eileen J. Rust. West Lawn PA.

DW811872   Peter L. Barto (b 16 Feb 1934) m 22 Feb 1958, Kutztown PA, Nancy F. Herber (b ca 1939). Laureldale, Berks PA.

DW81188   Forrest Conrad Weiser (b 18 Feb 1910, PA) m Mary Sheridan.

DW81189   Mark Wilson Weiser (b 26 Apr 1913, PA).

DW8119   Ellen Sarah Ann Weiser (19 Mar 1865, PA-17 Jul 1866).

DW811A   Amanda Priscilla Weiser (9 Sep 1867, Maxatawny, Berks PA-30 May 1932) m 7 Oct 1893, Maxatawny, Berks PA, John D. Grim (22 Dec 1867, Rockland, Berks PA-12 Jan 1939). Maxatawny, Berks PA.

DW811A1   William Edgar Grim (10 Feb 1895, Maxatawny, Berks PA-16 Oct 1968) m Minnie A. Lichtenwalner (25 Oct 1899-13 Mar 1975).

DW811A2   Sallie M. Grim (16 Jun 1896, Berks PA-7 Jan 1977) m 30 Sep 1920, Bowers, Berks PA, Raymond P. DeLong (25 Dec 1893, Berks PA-30 Oct 1873).

DW811A3   George A. Grim (b Jan 1900, Berks PA) m 14 Jul 1921, Kutztown PA, Lulu M. Zwoyer (b ca 1903, Berks PA).

DW812   Rachel B. Weiser (20 Nov 1830, Maxatawny, Berks PA-30 Nov 1906, Spangsville, Berks PA) m 30 May 1852, Oley, Berks PA, George S. Kieffer (2 Dec 1829, Oley, Berks PA-30 Jun 1905, Spangsville, Berks PA). Oley, Berks PA.

DW8121   Mary Alice Kieffer (14 Jun 1853, Maxatawny, Berks PA-18 Apr 1906, Spangsville, Oley, Berks PA) m   Sittler.

DW8122   Oliver Abraham Kieffer (7 Sep 1855, PA-25 Oct 1862).

DW8123   William Effinger Kieffer (22 Mar 1858, PA-4 Dec 1862).

DW8124   Charles Kieffer (10 Jan 1860, PA-28 Oct 1862).

DW8125   Ellen W. Kieffer (21 Oct 1861, Oley, Berks PA-28 Mar 1892) m 11 Jun 1881, Berks PA, Bower Daniel B. Griesemer (25 Jan 1857, Oley, Berks PA-8 May 1941, Griesemersville, Berks PA). Oley, Berks PA.

DW8126   Deborah Kieffer (7 Jul 1863-25 Oct 1868).

DW8127   George Ellworth W. Kieffer (5 Aug 1864, PA-3 Feb 1894) m Mary F. Mest (26 Dec 1863, Boyertown, Berks PA-12 Jul 1936). Oley, Berks PA.

DW8128   Caleb Kieffer (25 Oct 1866-2 Nov 1868).

DW8129   Harry (Henry) W. Kieffer (b ca 1868, PA) m 21 Mar 1891, Oley, Berks PA, Amelia Rebecca Weiser (b 31 Aug 1864, PA) (DW4513). Reading PA. See DW4513 for children.

DW812A   Irvin Lessly Kieffer (26 Nov 1870, Berks PA-1965) m 8 Apr 1893, Lillie E. Grim (Nov 1870, Berks PA-1955). Exeter, Berks PA.

DW812B   Thomas Elwood W. Kieffer (8 Sep 1872, Oley, Berks PA-1936) m 29 Jun 1895, Reading PA, Elizabeth F. Clauser (1875, Oley, Berks PA-1932).

DW812C   Catharine W. Kieffer (30 Jul 1874, PA-14 May 1956, Reading PA) m 2 Dec 1895, Oley, Berks PA, James M. Philips.

DW812D   Valeria Maud Kieffer (10 Aug 1876, PA-21 Nov 1942). Unm.

DW813   Leah Weiser (28 Jan 1833, PA-13 Feb 1836, Maxatawny, Berks PA).

DW814   Mary A. Weiser (28 Mar 1835, PA-30 Jul 1883) m 9 Oct 1859, George W. H. Long (12 Apr 1834-6 Aug 1862). Kutztown PA.

DW8141   Valleria Long (9 Dec 1859-1922) m Stanley S. Schwoyer (1858-1907). Maxatawny, Berks PA.

DW8142   Margrette Amelia Long (b 26 Jan 1861).

DW8143   George Washington Long (19 Aug 1862-10 Apr 1893).

DW815   Judith B. Weiser (25 Jan 1838, PA-9 Jun 1866) m 5 Jul 1858, Reading PA, William C. Kutz (b Oct 1834, PA). Reading PA.

DW8151   Hiester W. Kutz (b 19 Apr 1860, PA).

DW8152   Lincoln W. Kutz (20 Nov 1864-23 Jun 1866).

DW8153   Evella Kutz (ca 1866).

DW816   Susanna Weiser (24 Jun 1841, PA-28 Mar 1892) m 4 Jul 1857, Kutztown PA, Charles B. Bast (6 Mar 1825, PA-6 Mar 1878). Kutztown PA.

DW8161   Harvey C. Bast (b ca 1855).

DW8162   Percival Bast (22 Oct 1858, PA-28 Sep 1884).

DW8163   Mary Bast (19 May 1859, PA-10 Dec 1863).

DW8164   Belle Bast (b ca 1861, PA).

DW8165   Charles W. Bast (b ca 1863, PA).

DW8166   Ralph Bast (4 Feb 1865-10 Feb 1870).

DW8167   Lillie Susan Bast (30 Dec 1866, PA-14 Sep 1936, Cleveland, OH) m   Boyer.

DW8168   Archibald Walter Bast (22 Oct 1868-30 Mar 1870).

DW8169   Leslie Irvin Bast (22 Nov 1870, Kutztown PA-29 Mar 1903) m 17 Apr 1897, Kutztown PA, Lydia A. Wentzel (b ca 1877, Maxatawny, Berks PA). Queens, NY.

DW816A   Harper Lester Bast (10 Oct 1872, PA-12 Jan 1901).

DW816B   Roger S. Bast (1875, Kutztown PA-1937) m Jane ("Jennie") Sarah Eisenhard (13 May 1878, Lehigh, PA-25 Sep 1932). Kutztown PA.

DW816C   Mary Bast (23 May 1877-26 Oct 1878).

DW816D   Richard S. Bast (b ca 1877, PA).

DW817   Daniel Weiser (30 Mar 1845, PA-1 Jun 1845).

DW818   Bryan (George) Weiser (18 Mar 1850, PA-3 Aug 1854, Maxatawny, Berks PA).

DW819   Isadora Weiser (11 Oct 1853, PA-14 Nov 1860, Kutztown PA).

DW82   David P. Weiser (3 Aug 1784, PA-12 Feb 1828) m 19 Jan 1812, Esther L. Butz (30 Dec 1783-2 Aug 1848). Maxatawny, Berks PA.

DW821   Elijah (Elias) Weiser (14 Sep 1812, Maxatawny, Berks PA-29 Jun 1889, Maxatawny, Berks PA) m 28 Apr 1849, Reading PA, Esther Bieber (1 Sep 1822, PA-14 Jul 1882). Maxatawny, Berks PA.

DW8211   Emma Catharine Weiser (1 Jun 1850, Bowers, Berks PA-18 Jul 1933) m 27 Jul 1871, Longswamp, Berks PA, Moses K. Grim (8 May 1845, Bowers, Berks PA-25 Dec 1926). Maxatawny, Berks PA.

DW82111   Daniel U. Grim (5 Dec 1872, PA-27 Aug 1897).

DW82112   Jacob W. Grim (8 Mar 1876, Maxatawny, Berks PA-31 Jul 1964) m 11 Jun 1904, Reading PA, May C. Frey (20 Mar 1880, Kutztown PA-26 Sep 1956). Maxatawny, Berks PA.

DW82113   Louisa E. Grim (b Jun 1878, Maxatawny, Berks PA) m 12 May 1903, Bowers, Berks PA, Harry G. Kutz (b ca 1881, Reading PA).

DW82114   William G. Grim (b Apr 1881, PA).

DW82115   Walter B. Grim (4 Nov 1883, Bowers, Berks PA-17 Mar 1967) m 17 Jun 1914, Kutztown PA, Minnie Edna Weiser (DW81182) (b 8 Jan 1893, Bowers, Berks PA). Maxatawny, Berks PA. (For children, see DW81182).

DW82116   Ida May Grim (8 Mar 1886, Maxatawny, Berks PA-21 Jul 1975). Unm.

DW82117   Julius H. Grim (Jul 1888, PA-1962) m Mayme F. Wylie Kline (1883-1947).

DW82118   John E. Grim (Apr 1890, PA-1979) m Elda M.   (1893-1963).

DW8212   Louisa Allen Weiser (4 Dec 1851, PA-8 Nov 1907). Maxatawny and Rockland, Berks PA.

DW82121   Fred Weiser (b Apr 1886, PA).

DW82122   Richard Weiser (b Nov 1888, PA).

DW8213   Ezra Weiser (b 10 May 1854, PA).

DW8214   Andora Elizabeth Weiser (6 Feb 1857, PA-1 Nov 1947) m 10 Aug 1876, Bowers, Berks PA, Peter Charles Hamsher (6 Jun 1852-Jan 1948). Maxatawny, Berks PA.

DW82141   Jacob E. Hamsher (b May 1877, PA). Maxatawny, Berks PA. Florida.

DW82142   Kathryn Marie Hamsher (1883, PA-6 Feb 1976, Kenilworth, Chester, PA) m Charles Herbert Christman (27 May 1883-11 May 1968). Boyertown PA.

DW82143 Joseph Ezra Hamsher (8 Nov 1888, Bowers, Berks PA-1972) m 10 Jan 1911, Kutztown PA, Elda W. Fritsch (1885, Fleetwood, Berks PA-15 Nov 1980, Allentown, PA).

DW82144 Carrie A. Hamsher (30 Nov 1890, Maxatawny, Berks PA-20 Sep 1981, Hamburg PA) m 19 Nov 1910, Topton PA, Charles S. Fisher (22 Nov 1891, Topton PA-23 Nov 1982, Hamburg PA). Topton, Berks PA.

DW82145 Lydia L. Hamsher (b 1893, Bowers, Berks PA) m 26 Jul 1913, Bowers, Berks PA, LeRoy ("Roy") W. Danner (1895, Bowers, Berks PA-1967). Kutztown PA.

DW82146 Sallie S. Hamsher (b Jan 1894, Bowers, Berks PA) m 25 Jan 1913, Topton, Berks PA, John D. Carl (b ca 1894, Bowers, Berks PA). Harrisburg, PA.

DW82147 Alton P. Hamsher (30 May 1899-20 Jul 1899).

DW82148 Myrtle Esther Hamsher (20 Dec 1900, PA-24 May 1991, Kutztown PA) m Luther Daniel Zwoyer (b 8 Sep 1900, Berks PA). Maxatawny, Berks PA.

DW8215 Jorosa Hetty Ann Weiser (25 Oct 1858, Maxatawny, Berks PA-8 Nov 1888, Maxatawny, Berks PA) m 7 Dec 1878, Peter W. Kieffer (Oct 1858-1939). Maxatawny, Berks PA.

DW82151 Daniel E. Kieffer (16 Nov 1879, PA-28 Mar 1897).

DW82152 Peter Jacob Kieffer (24 Apr 1881-16 Sep 1881)

DW82153 Sallie Esther Kieffer (11 Apr 1882-20 Sep 1882).

DW82154 Hettie L. Kieffer (6 Sep 1883, Maxatawny, Berks PA-19 Jan 1930) m 12 Nov 1904, Topton PA, William H. Mertz (9 Feb 1884, Maxatawny, Berks PA-12 Jan 1962).

DW82155 Eva Victoria Kieffer (30 Dec 1885, Maxatawny, Berks PA-21 May 1917) m 15 Feb 1913, Kutztown PA, Frank H. Fegley (1876, Maxatawny, Berks PA-1962).

DW82156 Irvin Charles Kieffer (b 12 Aug 1887).

DW8216 Daniel (David) B. Weiser (25 Dec 1860, Maxatawny, Berks PA-12 Jul 1903, Columbus, OH) m Ida C. Batz (b ca 1865, PA).

DW82161 Annie Katie Elizabeth Weiser (b 26 Oct 1882, Berks PA).

DW8217 Mary A. S. Weiser (2 Jul 1864, Maxatawny, Berks PA-2 Mar 1890, Longswamp, Berks PA) m 27 Aug 1886, Jonathan B. DeLong (14 Jun 1861, PA-13 May 1926). Rockland, Berks PA.

DW822 Levi Weiser (14 Sep 1812, PA-6 Feb 1824).

DW823 William P. Weiser (11 Jul 1814, PA-21 Apr 1848) m 26 Mar 1837, Elizabeth Bieber (15 Jan 1814, PA-4 Jan 1869). Rockland, Berks PA.

DW8231 Daniel B. Weiser (13 Sep 1839, PA-24 Jan 1863, Maxatawny, Berks PA). Died in Civil War.

DW8232 David B. Weiser (19 Aug 1841, PA-17 Aug 1867).

DW8233 Sarah Weiser (b 15 Aug 1843, PA) m 10 Sep 1864, Allen Poh.

DW8234   William B. Weiser (b 16 Oct 1846, PA).

DW824   Esther Weiser (9 Oct 1819, PA-7 Mar 1863) m 22 Apr 1843, Daniel Wickey (22 Jan 1817, PA-17 Jul 1890). Kutztown PA.

DW825   David Weiser (11 Jun 1822, Maxatawny, Berks PA-25 Jan 1899, Topton, Berks PA) m 17 Dec 1854, Longswamp, Berks PA, Catharine Fisher (b Aug 1836, PA). Longswamp and Topton, Berks PA.

DW8251   Sarah Amanda Weiser (26 Aug 1855, PA-24 Mar 1924, Maxatawny, Berks PA) m 17 Nov 1877, John Shalter Schwoyer (16 Jan 1850, PA-1 Dec 1930). Maxatawny, Berks PA.

DW82511   Nora Minnie C. Schwoyer (13 Jan 1879, PA-1 Mar 1956). Unm.

DW82512   Stanley David Schwoyer (1 Sep 1882-8 Sep 1882).

DW82513   Florence Emma Schwoyer (b 31 Oct 1891, PA) m Edwin O. Bachman.

DW82514   John LeRoy Schwoyer (11 Aug 1895, PA-13 Jul 1963) m 10 Apr 1920, Kutztown PA, Mabel M. Shade (b 2 Apr 1901).

DW8252   Alvin Zacheus Weiser (22 Mar 1859, Topton PA-14 Mar 1927, Bowers, Berks PA) m 8 Sep 1883, Elizabeth E. A. Hanning (Aug 1864, Topton, Berks PA-1934). Longswamp, Berks PA.

DW82521   Herbert D. Weiser (b Dec 1883, PA).

DW82522   Walter A. Weiser (4 Dec 1888, Topton, Berks PA-4 Jun 1947) m 4 Jul 1914, Hamburg PA, Annie E. Folk (b ca 1895, Virginsville, Berks PA. Longswamp, Berks PA.

DW82523   Raymond W. C. Weiser (12 Oct 1890, PA-Sep 1967, PA) m Annie J. (b ca 1895, PA). Longswamp, Berks PA.

DW8253   Carl David Weiser (22 Jan 1864, PA-26 Feb 1864).

DW8254   Ellen C. H. Weiser (22 Feb 1869, Longswamp, Berks PA-23 Sep 1927) m 20 Jan 1894, Kutztown PA, Clarence W. Levan (b 3 Apr 1872, Kutztown PA). Topton PA.

DW82541   Kate Matilda Guldin Levan (21 Jan 1894, Topton, Berks PA-11 Aug 1894).

DW82542   Arline E. Levan (b Jan 1897, PA).

DW8255   Anna N. L. Weiser (17 Mar 1875, PA-15 Dec 1876).

DW83   Maria Weiser (20 Jan 1786, PA-21 Jan 1846) m Isaac DeTurk (DW72) (2 Nov 1789, PA-3 May 1865). Maxatawny, Berks PA.

DW831   Elijah (Elias) DeTurk (21 Nov 1809, PA-19 Jan 1876) m Julianna Levan (2 Oct 1808, PA-28 Sep 1898). Maxatawny, Berks PA.

DW84   Susanna Weiser (21 Jun 1788, PA-24 Jul 1842) m John Peter Ziegler (3 May 1783-12 Dec 1834).

DW841   David Ziegler (b 20 Apr 1811).

DW842   Eleanora Ziegler (9 Oct 1813, Maxatawny, Berks PA-12 Jan 1835) m Reuben Grim (17 Mar 1815, PA-19 Dec 1896). Rockland, Berks PA.

DW843   Edwin Ziegler (1 Apr 1815-ca Aug 1845) m Hannah   (b ca 1818, PA). Rockland and Maxatawny, Berks PA.

DW844   Weiser Ziegler (28 Feb 1819, Longswamp, Berks PA-29 Jan 1883). Sunbury and Reading PA.

DW845   William Ziegler (7 Jun 1820, PA-1868) m Henrietta   (b ca 1819, PA). Reading PA.

DW846   Julianna Ziegler (22 May 1821, Maxatawny, Berks PA-3 Oct 1895, Rockland, Berks PA) m 10 Oct 1852, Joshua DeLong (13 Aug 1829, PA-9 Nov 1898). Rockland, Berks PA.

DW847   James Ziegler (b 15 Feb 1824).

DW848   Susanna (Maria) Ziegler (b 26 Dec 1825) m David Bortz (13 Oct 1825-8 Jul 1853, Rockland, Berks PA). Lower Macungie, Lehigh PA.

DW849   Harrison{?} Ziegler (b 24 Mar 1828).

DW84A   Elijah{?} Ziegler (b 1 Mar 1830).

DW84B   C...{?} Ziegler (b 21 Jul 1833).

CHAPTER FIFTEEN

[AW] Adam Weiser (Wysor) (d 1804)
of Virginia and his descendants

Adam Weiser arrived in Philadelphia in 1751 on board the ship Neptune, and qualified on 23 September 1751. He spent a number of years in southeastern Pennsylvania, although it is not clear whether he was settled in any one place. It is stated that he was married to Elizabeth Beck, daughter of George Beck, in the records of St. Paul's (Blue) Lutheran Church in Upper Saucon Township, but the date was not recorded. Baptismal records for their two eldest children have not been found. The third and fourth children were baptized in 1759 and 1761 in St. Paul's, and the next three children were baptized between 1763 and 1768 in Dryland Union Church in Lower Nazareth Township, now in Northampton County.

Before 1771, when the next child was born, the family had moved to Frederick County, Virginia, where they remained until 1785 when they moved to a part of Montgomery County, Virginia that is now part of Pulaski County. The farm on which they settled was near the present town of Dublin.

It is not clear why the spelling of the family name was changed, but by 1797 court records referred to Adam Wysor. There is a story in the family that the wife of one of the sons, being of English ancestry, recommended the change. It is interesting to note, however, that Adam's son George Adam used a spelling Wiser which he carried into Russell County, Virginia and eventually to Laurel County, Kentucky. The descendants in Russell County later adopted the Wysor spelling, but those in Kentucky and their descendants who moved into Kansas and Missouri kept the Wiser spelling.[149]

AW   Adam Weiser (d 1804, near Dublin VA) m 6 Jul 1755, Elizabeth Beck. Lehigh PA; Frederick and Montgomery VA.[150]

AW1   Henry Wysor (15 Apr 1755, PA-12 Jan 1844, Pulaski VA) m 21 Apr 1777, Frederick VA, Barbara Ann Ripseed (14 Feb 1758-10 May 1837, Montgomery VA). Farmer, Montgomery VA.

AW11   George W. Wysor (14 Aug 1779, Frederick VA-May 1803).

AW12   Mary Wysor (22 Jul 1781, Montgomery VA-17 Oct 1856, Tazewell VA) m 21 May 1799, Montgomery VA, Peter Buise Dills (4 Aug 1779, NC-27 Jan 1853).

AW13   Elizabeth ("Betsy") Wysor (b 27 Dec 1783) m 28 Mar 1807, Montgomery VA, Ambrose Grayson (6 Nov 1785, Montgomery VA-13 Jul 1846, Wythe VA).

AW131   Randolph Grayson (23 Jan 1808, Wythe VA-29 Dec 1880, Bland VA) m 25 Apr 1837, Wythe VA, Cynthia Grayson.

AW132   Gordon Grayson (13 Jan 1810, Wythe VA-30 Dec 1811, Wythe VA).

AW133   Henry Grayson (1812, Wythe VA-1852).

---

[149]Most of the information on the early family in Pulaski County has been obtained from Jackson Darst and his book The Darsts of Virginia, Williamsburg, VA, 1972, and from Mark Steinke of St. Bernard, OH. Information for the more recent period in that area has been provided be Robert G. Wysor of Pulaski, VA. Information on the Russell and Tazewell County families has been collected by Robert B. Wysor of Clinton, TN. Some of the information on the family that moved to Laurel County, Kentucky has been provided by Judy Bayless of Bellingham, WA. Other material has been collected by Edward Wiser, who has assembled all the information and edited it in its present form.

[150]Jackson Darst, who has collected a large amount of information on the family, thinks that Adam Weiser and Elizabeth Beck were married on 6 July 1755. He thinks also that Adam's eldest son Henry was born on 15 April 1754, and that his mother must therefore have been someone else who was Adam's first wife. Documentation of both the marriage date and Henry's birth is not strong, and it may not justify the extra complication.

AW134   James W. Grayson (1818, Wythe VA-23 Mar 1864, Wythe VA) m 26 Jun 1850, Emily Steel.

AW135   Mary Grayson (b 1820, Wythe VA) m 27 Oct 1846, Wythe VA, John Grayson.

AW14   Henry Wysor Jr. (7 Aug 1786, Montgomery VA-20 Jul 1859, Pulaski VA) m 31 May 1811, Montgomery VA, Cynthia Charlton (3 Nov 1787-14 Jan 1866, Pulaski VA). Farmer, Montgomery and Pulaski VA.

AW141   Elvira Ann Wysor (11 Jul 1812, Montgomery VA-22 Jan 1869, Pulaski VA) m 6 Apr 1835, Montgomery VA, John Chandler Darst (11 Jun 1811, Rockbridge VA-28 Dec 1885, Princeton WV).

AW1411   Cynthia Elizabeth Ann Darst (6 Jan 1836, Montgomery VA-29 Aug 1861, Pulaski VA) m 15 Apr 1857, Pulaski VA, David Sidney Matthias Painter (12 Nov 1830, Wytheville VA-6 Jan 1899, Blacksburg VA).

AW1412   James Henry Darst (25 Jan 1838, Montgomery VA-25 Dec 1906, Dublin VA) m 17 Oct 1859, Dublin VA, Margaret Wesley Trolinger (28 Sep 1840, Dublin VA-29 Dec 1928, Dublin VA).

AW1413   John Benjamin Darst (17 Jul 1840, Pulaski VA-27 Feb 1897, Pulaski VA) m 10 Feb 1864, Pulaski VA, Mary Euphemia Yost (20 Dec 1841, Dublin VA-5 Feb 1930, Pulaski VA).

AW1414   Nancy Mary ("Nannie") Darst (7 Mar 1843, Pulaski VA-9 Jun 1904, Princeton WV) m 13 Aug 1867, Pulaski VA, Robert Andrew Glendy (9 Jun 1833, Augusta VA-29 Jun 1910, Princeton WV).

AW1415   Infant Darst (22 Oct 1845, Pulaski VA-22 Oct 1845).

AW1416   Aline ("Lena") Grigsby Darst (15 Aug 1847, Pulaski VA-5 Oct 1873, Natchez MS) m 15 Dec 1864, Pulaski VA, Charles Winthrop Babbitt (13 Jul 1834, Natchez MS-2 Aug 1903, Natchez MS).

AW142   Benjamin Franklin Wysor (24 Nov 1813, VA-26 May 1864, Pulaski VA) m 1 Nov 1847, Pulaski VA, Harriet Jane Jordan (29 Sep 1823, VA-1 Jun 1890). Lawyer, Pulaski VA.

AW1421   Hugh S. Legare Wysor (30 May 1847, VA-15 Apr 1938) m Alice M. Eads (22 Aug 1850, VA-19 Nov 1930). Pulaski VA.

AW14211   Frank Wysor (12 Dec 1871, Newbern VA-28 Feb 1900, Cebu, Philippines).

AW14212   Ethel Wysor (b Apr 1874, VA).

AW14213   Shirley Wysor (14 Feb 1876-26 Jun 1876).

AW14214   Wilkie Collins Wysor (30 Sep 1879, VA-24 Aug 1882).

AW14215   Jean Wysor (b May 1882, VA).

AW14216   Elizabeth A. Wysor (13 Dec 1884, VA-31 Mar 1968) m 26 Jun 1914, Pulaski VA, Frank Joseph Klingberg (25 Feb 1883-4 Jun 1968).

AW14217   Dorothy Wysor (May 1889, VA-1969) m Paul Jordan Smith (19 Apr 1885-17 Jun 1971).

AW14218   Jeffrey Wysor (b Dec 1892, VA).

AW1422   William Wirt Wysor (24 Sep 1848, VA-14 Apr 1897) m 23 Sep 1880, Lee AL). Vice-Consul, Cadiz, Spain.

AW1423   Michael Jordan Wysor (24 Oct 1850, Newbern VA-14 Feb 1936, Princeton WV) m 23 Sep 1880, Lee AL, Willie Edna Boynton (b Feb 1860, GA). Methodist minister, western Virginia and eastern Tennessee.

AW14231   Eula Wall Wysor (b Aug 1881, VA) m   McNutt.

AW14232   Boynton Wysor (4 Oct 1883-13 Dec 1883).

AW14233   Marion Boynton Wysor (b ca 1885).

AW14234   Michael Lamar Wysor (b Dec 1888, VA).

AW1424   Cynthia Elizabeth Wysor (27 Apr 1853, Pulaski VA-3 Jul 1853).

AW1425   James Henry Wysor (17 Sep 1855, Pulaski VA-May 1863).

AW1426   Joseph Cloyd Wysor (17 Sep 1855, Pulaski VA-5 Sep 1919) m 2 Oct 1879, Pulaski VA, Jennie May Gardner (4 Sep 1858, VA-18 Apr 1928). Lawyer, Pulaski VA.

AW14261   Emma May Wysor (16 Aug 1880, VA-11 Apr 1963) m 17 Nov 1904, Pulaski VA, Robert Finley Dunlap (b ca 1872).

AW142611   Emma Dunlap.

AW142612   May Dunlap.

AW14262   John Franklin Wysor (26 Aug 1881, VA-8 Oct 1954).

AW14263   Joseph Lawrence Wysor (1 Oct 1883, VA-27 Dec 1948).

AW14264   Harriet Isabella Wysor (13 Mar 1886, VA-10 May 1964) m 2 Jun 1908, Pulaski VA, Robert C. Graham (b ca 1884).

AW14265   Elizabeth Jordan Wysor (19 Feb 1888-2 Sep 1892).

AW14266   Mary Anderson Wysor (7 Aug 1890-11 Aug 1892).

AW14267   Mary Elizabeth Wysor (22 Jul 1892, VA-1 Apr 1979) m 9 Nov 1916, Pulaski VA, Robert Hall Smith III (10 Mar 1888, Baltimore MD-18 Jun 1960).

AW142671   Robert Hall Smith IV (b 5 Aug 1917) m 14 Mar 1950, Catherine A. Muhlenberg (b 18 Mar 1917).

AW142672   Joseph Wysor Smith (b 24 Feb 1919) m 6 Feb 1943, Frances Leigh Ellett (b 21 Jun 1919).

AW142673   Mary Gardner Smith (b 26 Sep 1920) m 8 Nov 1941, Carter Lane Burgess (b 31 Dec 1916).

AW142674   Margaret Donnell Smith (b 9 Nov 1922) m 7 Feb 1948, David Comfort Watkins (b 21 Apr 1917).

AW142675   Jane Stuart Smith (b 29 Sep 1926).

AW14268   William Henry Wysor (15 Jun 1894, VA-9 Apr 1946) m 7 Nov 1917, Pulaski VA, M. Pierce Lyon (31 Oct 1894-5 Feb 1961).

AW142681   William Henry Wysor Jr. (18 Nov 1923-26 Jul 1979) m 5 Jul 1947, Pulaski VA, Jane Divers (b 22 May 1926). Pulaski VA.

AW1426811   Jane Wysor (b 30 Dec 1948) m 7 Jul 1971, Switzerland, Ray Walker (b 7 Mar 1951).

AW14268111   Evan Walker (b 3 Mar 1972).

AW14268112   Megan Walker (b 25 Mar 1975).

AW1426812   William Henry Wysor III (b 28 Mar 1951) m 12 Nov 1976, Susan Wohlford (b 21 Feb 1957).

AW14268121   Josh Wysor (b 3 Jun 1981).

AW14268122   Sean Wysor (b 13 Jul 1983).

AW1426813   Ann Wysor (b 26 May 1954) m 25 May 1974, England, Max Harris (b 26 Mar 1949).

AW14268131   Joel Harris (b 24 Apr 1978).

AW14268132   Matthew Harris (b 10 Aug 1981).

AW1426814   Robert G. Wysor (b 27 Aug 1963).

AW14269   Annie Wysor (8 May 1897-18 Jun 1897).

AW1426A   Nannie Lucile Wysor (8 May 1897-15 Aug 1897).

AW1427   Nancy Carter Wysor (30 Jul 1858-15 Dec 1929) m 22 Jun 1880, Pulaski VA, George Washington Muirhead.

AW1428   Morehead Jordan Wysor.

AW1429   Belle Wysor (28 Aug 1861, Pulaski VA-10 Oct 1861, Newbern VA).

AW142A   Betty Wysor (28 Aug 1861, Pulaski VA-28 Apr 1862, Newbern VA).

AW143   George Washington Wysor (26 Jul 1817, Montgomery VA-1 Oct 1883) m 19 Dec 1843, Margaret Ann Miller (17 Dec 1825, VA-18 Aug 1907). Farmer, Pulaski VA.

AW1431   James Miller Wysor (17 Aug 1845, VA-27 Nov 1929) m Laura A. Ware (28 Sep 1857, IA-10 Jan 1937). Pulaski VA.

AW14311   Hannah Miller Wysor (b Nov 1879, MN).

AW14312   James Miller Wysor Jr. (9 Jul 1882, MN-26 Aug 1901).

AW14313   Mary Ware Wysor (21 Aug 1894, VA-4 Jan 1939) m 28 Aug 1920, Pulaski VA, Kaakon G. Koltukian (b ca 1893).

AW14314   Raymond Ware Wysor (b Feb 1899, VA).

AW1432   Henry Charlton Wysor (21 Oct 1847, VA-7 Aug 1927) m Mary Elizabeth Shipp (24 Oct 1846, Charlotte NC-21 Aug 1922). Pulaski VA.

AW14321   Mary Shipp Wysor (4 May 1876, VA-Apr 1925).

AW14322   William Washington Wysor (Mar 1878, VA-1935) m Mamie F.   (b ca 1889, VA). Railroad superintendent, Baltimore MD.

AW143221   Dorothy H. Wysor (b ca 1912, PA).

AW143222   William J. Wysor (8 Jul 1913, PA-Apr 1985, Bucks PA).

AW143223   Louise F. Wysor (b ca 1915, PA).

AW143224   Mary D. Wysor (b ca Jun 1917, MD).

AW143225   Ida S. Wysor (b ca Oct 1918, MD).

AW14323   Henry Wysor Jr. (20 Apr 1880, VA-Jan 1967, Easton PA) m 28 Aug 1906, Pulaski VA, Mary Belle Ernest (b ca 1881). Chemist, Lafayette College, Easton PA.

AW143231   Elizabeth Wysor (b 14 May 1908). Wagnerian opera singer, Europe, and professor, Northwestern University, Evanston IL.

AW143232   Ginnie Wysor m Douglas Purdy.

AW14324   Cora Reid Wysor (b Jul 1881, VA) m 2 Mar 1907, Pulaski VA, Henry W. Marsh (b ca 1884).

AW14325   Rufus Johnston Wysor (8 Dec 1885, VA-11 Jun 1967, Brunswick GA) m Mary E.   (b ca 1896, CO). President, Republic Steel Corporation.

AW143251   Jeanne M. Wysor (b ca Jan 1918, PA).

AW143252   Carolyn Wysor (b ca Aug 1919, PA).

AW14326   Davidson Charlton Wysor (21 Nov 1888, VA-May 1982, Bergen NJ). Geologist, General Chemical Co.

AW1433   George Washington Wysor Jr. (26 Dec 1849, VA-1930) m 21 Feb 1877, Smyth VA, Mary Martha Price Templeton (Apr 1849, VA-1924). Pulaski VA and Lubbock TX.

AW14331   James Miller Wysor (b Apr 1878, VA) m Ida May   (b ca 1873, OH).

AW14332   George Edward Wysor (b Apr 1880, VA) m Anna   (b ca 1881, OH).

AW143321   Stanley Wysor (b ca 1907, OH).

AW143322   Ruth Wysor (b ca 1911, OH).

AW14333   Fannie Naff Wysor (b Jan 1882, VA) m   Torrance.

AW14334   Ruth Wysor (b Aug 1883, VA) m   Atkinson.

AW14335   Frederick Johnston Wysor (20 Jul 1885, WV-Jan 1972, Tampa FL) m Ethel   (b ca 1886, AL).

AW14336   John Lewis Wysor.

AW1434   Emma Clay Wysor (4 Feb 1852, VA-1923) m 6 Aug 1872, Pulaski VA, George William Walker (b ca 1844).

AW14341   John Ernest Walker m Emily Brown.

AW143411   Marjory Wysor Walker m William E. Depuy.

AW1435   John Chandler D. Wysor (12 May 1854, Pulaski VA-23 Feb 1919) m 27 Aug 1884, Alice Eugenia Pugh (18 Jul 1859, VA-3 Jan 1947). Surgeon-in-charge, Chesapeake and Ohio Railroad hospital, Clifton Forge VA.

AW14351   Julia Bentley Wysor (b Jul 1887, VA) m   West.

AW14352   Frank Laird Wysor (10 Oct 1888, VA-Jul 1985, Clifton Forge VA) m Jennie   (b ca 1896, VA). Physician.

AW1436   Margaret Ann Wysor (10 Aug 1856, Pulaski VA-10 Oct 1947).

AW1437   Ellen Webster Wysor (2 Oct 1858, Pulaski VA-4 Nov 1919).

AW1438   Elizabeth F. Wysor (5 Nov 1860, Entry Branch, Pulaski VA-May 1864, Pulaski VA).

AW1439   Robert Edward Wysor (21 Dec 1862, Pulaski VA-6 Sep 1936) m 1) Marguerite Simpson (29 Sep 1863-12 Feb 1900); m 2) Lelia Dickinson (8 Nov 1873, VA-24 May 1939). Pulaski VA.

AW14391   Robert Edward Wysor Jr. (b ca 1892, VA.

AW14392   John Donald Wysor (27 Aug 1893, VA-Feb 1977, Dublin VA) m 2 Sep 1918, Pulaski VA, Cecil Moomaw (b ca 1893, VA).

AW14393   Julia Margaret Wysor (b ca 1895) m 3 Sep 1919, Pulaski VA, John A. Blakemon (b ca 1895).

AW143A   Lucy Jackson Wysor (20 Jan 1865, Pulaski VA-26 Oct 1890).

AW143B   Mittie Lawrence Wysor (10 Jul 1867, Pulaski VA-5 Mar 1953).

AW143C   Nettie M. Wysor (9 May 1869, Pulaski VA-11 Jul 1966).

AW144   Nancy B. Wysor (1819, VA-16 Nov 1860, Dublin VA) m 19 Feb 1839, Montgomery VA, George W. Baskerville (d 1849).

AW1441   Cynthia M. Baskerville (b ca 1840, Pulaski VA).

AW1442   Martha ("Mattie") Baskerville (ca 1842-Jun 1854, Pulaski VA).

AW1443   Henry Baskerville.

AW1444   John B. Baskerville (b ca 1847, Pulaski VA).

AW1445   George Spencer Baskerville (b ca 1849, Pulaski VA).

AW145   James Lawrence Wysor (1824, Montgomery VA-1826).

AW146   Cynthia Mary Wysor (20 Nov 1827, VA-13 Feb 1894) m 14 Dec 1853, Pulaski VA, Isaac Newton Naff (6 Oct 1817-12 Mar 1900).

AW1461   Fannie N. Naff (b ca 1855, Pulaski VA) m Charles W. Johnson.

AW1462   Harry Wysor Naff (b ca 1857, Pulaski VA).

AW1463   Mary Eunice Naff (b ca 1859, Pulaski VA).

AW1464   George J. Naff.

AW1465   Edith E. Naff.

AW1466   F. J. Naff.

AW15   John Wysor (11 Feb 1788, VA-Jul 1793).

AW16   Catharine Wysor (b 9 Oct 1790, VA) m 1) 11 Oct 1811, Montgomery VA, James Reyburn; m 2) Robert Blackwell (b ca 1783, TN).

AW161   James M. Reyburn (b 1816, Montgomery VA).

AW162   Mary Elizabeth Reyburn (7 Sep 1818, Montgomery VA-17 Mar 1890, Lytle TX) m 14 Dec 1837, Hot Springs AR, John B. House (14 Sep 1815, NC-27 Sep 1888, Lytle TX).

AW163   William Henry Blackwell (b ca 1825, MO).

AW164   Barbara Ellen Blackwell (b ca 1827, MO).

AW165   Jesse Blackwell (b ca 1835, MO).

AW17   Jacob Wysor (22 Sep 1793, VA-Oct 1819, Montgomery VA) m 5 Jan 1819, Montgomery VA, Margaret Miller (b ca 1798).

AW171   Jacob Henry Wysor (b Dec 1819, VA) m Sarah Richardson (b ca 1827, VA). Merchant and miller, Muncie IN.

AW1711   Virginia Wysor (b ca 1856, IN).

AW1712   Harry R. Wysor (b Apr 1858, IN) m Jennie R.   (b Jun 1858, IA).

AW17121   Sarah Wysor (b May 1885, IN).

AW17122   Mary Wysor (b Jul 1887, IN).

AW1713   Martha Wysor (b ca Dec 1859, IN.

AW1714   William Wysor (b ca 1862, IN).

AW18   William Wysor (16 Jun 1797, VA-ca 1830, Farmington MO) m Polly Miller.

AW19   James Wysor (18 Jun 1801, VA-1 Apr 1868).

AW2   Elizabeth Wysor (ca 1756, PA-ca 1812, Pulaski VA) m ca 1776, Christopher Trinkle (ca 1752, Winchester VA-16 Aug 1829, Washington IN).

AW21   Henry Trinkle (ca 1776, Winchester VA-5 Aug 1832, Washington IN) m Catherine Hornbarger (ca 1776-20 Oct 1857, Washington IN).

AW22   Elizabeth Trinkle (b 30 Mar 1777, Winchester VA) m 1804, Sampson Patton (d abt 1814).

AW23   Margaret Trinkle m 12 Mar 1806, Montgomery VA, Adam Stobaugh.

AW24   Stephen Trinkle (ca 1782, Winchester VA-6 Mar 1859, Pulaski VA) m 10 Feb 1810m Montgomery VA, Sarah Ann Trollinger (1 Mar 1794-25 Mar 1887, Pulaski VA).

AW25   Frederick Trinkle m Sally Hickman.

AW26   Jacob Trinkle (ca 1792, Montgomery VA-ca Mar 1831) m Margaret ("Peggy") Hickman (20 Jan 1791, Montgomery VA-20 Aug 1966).

AW27   Adam Trinkle m 31 Jul 1817, Washington IN, Hannah Rutherford.

AW28   John Trinkle m 1) Mary Gordon (d bef 1821); m 2) 20 Dec 1821, Washington IN, Sarah Patton (d bef 1830); m 3) 21 Jan 1830, Charlotte Broadwaters.

AW29   Catherine Trinkle (1794, Montgomery VA-1 Jul 1878, Washington IN) m 1) James Anderson Burress (d ca 1814); m 2) John Christopher Clark; m 3) Paul Kester (11 Apr 1781, PA-31 Oct 1855, Washington IN).

AW2A   Mary Trinkle (b ca 1797) m 20 Aug 1817, Washington IN, Jacob Colclazure (b ca 1795, KY).

AW3   Catharine ("Caty") Wysor (b 20 Jun 1759, Lehigh PA) m 26 Feb 1792, Montgomery VA, George Peck.

AW31   Henry Peck (b ca 1801, Montgomery VA) m Elizabeth   (b ca 1804).

AW4   Christina Wysor (1 Mar 1761, Lehigh PA-28 Jul 1846, Pulaski VA) m 24 Mar 1779, Frederick VA, Jacob Anderson (b 5 Jul 1758, Frederick VA).

AW41   George Anderson (b ca 1780, Winchester VA) m 2 Mar 1802 Mary Burton.

AW42   Elizabeth Anderson (ca 1783, Winchester VA-14 Jul 1867, Auglaize OH) m 27 Mar 1804, Botetourt VA, George G. Woolwine (ca 1782, Frederick VA-ca 1862, Madison KY).

AW43   Catherine Anderson (b 8 Aug 1785, Winchester VA) m 30 Jul 1804, Montgomery VA, Jacob Sherman (ca 1781-15 May 1862, Pulaski VA).

AW44   Margaret ("Peggy") Anderson (b 8 Aug 1785, Winchester VA) m 1) 6 Jun 1803, Montgomery VA, John King; m 2) 25 Nov 1838, Pope IL, Alexander Gray (5 Oct 1777-9 May 1849, Pope IL).

AW45   Mary Anderson (ca 1787-ca 1850, Pope IL) m 14 Feb 1808, Montgomery VA, Abraham Shufflebarger (ca 1788-ca 1868, Pope IL).

AW46   Eve Anderson (b ca 1790) m 22 Mar 1808, Montgomery VA, Jacob Songer (b ca 1784, VA).

AW47   Susannah Anderson m 1) John Thompson; m 2)   Hughes.

AW48   John Anderson m 15 Feb 1813, Montgomery VA, Catherine Kiplinger.

AW49   Jacob Anderson (20 Jul 1796, Montgomery VA-30 Mar 1874, Pope IL) m Drucilla (ca May 1795, MD-Sep 1868, Pope IL).

AW4A   Melinda Anderson.

AW4B   William Anderson (b 22 Jun 1805, Montgomery VA) m 1) 29 Jan 1829, Montgomery VA, Hetty Carper (Mar 1808, Montgomery VA-15 Jun 1859, Pulaski VA); m 2) 12 Oct 1869, Juliet Brooks.

AW4C   Nancy Anderson (b ca 1806, VA) m 6 Mar 1821, Montgomery VA, William Shepherd (b ca 1799, VA).

AW5   George Adam Wiser (7 Jun 1763, Northampton PA-1842, Laurel KY) m 28 Mar 1786, Frederick VA, Mary Luckleiter (b ca 1765). Montgomery and Russell VA, Claiborne TN and Laurel KY.

AW51   Adam Wiser (ca 1795, Montgomery VA-28 Jun 1887, Russell VA) m Russell VA, Mary (b ca 1797, Russell VA). Russell VA.

AW511   Catharine Wysor (b ca 1819, Russell VA) m   Jackson.

AW5111   Mary Jane Jackson (b ca 1843, VA).

AW5112   Margaret E. Jackson (b ca 1847, VA).

AW5113   Charles Jackson (b ca 1864, VA).

AW5114   Catharine Jackson (b ca 1865, VA).

AW512   James Wysor (21 Apr 1822, VA-22 Jun 1900) m Mary H. Steele (4 Feb 1824, VA-18 Jul 1907). Tazewell VA.

AW5121   George Whitten Wysor (21 Mar 1846, VA-5 Sep 1860).

AW5122   John William Wysor (1 Mar 1848, Tazewell VA-8 Sep 1926) m 1) 30 Nov 1867, Russell VA, Melissa A. Taylor (ca 1844, Russell VA-15 Aug 1891, Russell VA); m 2) 10 Sep 1894, Russell VA, Sally Price (25 Jan 1872, Russell VA-10 Apr 1956).

AW51221   James Harvey Wysor (May 1867, VA-Oct 1952) m Almeda E. Hayter (19 Jun 1876, VA-21 Nov 1963, Abingdon VA).

AW51222   John C. Wysor (b Jun 1874, Russell VA) m 8 Jan 1895, Russell VA, Mollie Calvert (b Aug 1870, Tazewell VA). Hughes OK.

AW512221   Son Wysor (23 Aug 1896-24 Aug 1896).

AW512222   Joseph Wysor (b Dec 1898, VA).

AW512223   Bert Wysor (22 Apr 1901, VA-Apr 1970, Holdenville OK).

AW512224   Gussie Wysor (b ca 1904, TX) m   McHenry.

AW512225   Johnnie Wysor (b ca 1908, OK) m   Poteet.

AW51223   Henry Franklin Wysor (Oct 1876, Russell VA-Oct 1956) m 20 Jul 1898, Russell VA, Flora Gertrude Perkins (May 1875, Russell VA-ca 1962).

AW512231   William Clarence Wysor (13 Apr 1906-May 1965) m Stella Sneed.

AW5122311   Betty Buras Wysor.

AW5122312   Marian Frances Wysor (b 1931) m Clyde William Roth.

AW51223121   Liza Susanne Roth.

AW51224   Walter Kelly Wysor (3 Jun 1898, Elk Garden VA-3 Jan 1983, Roanoke VA) m 11 Jul 1928, Maybeury WV, Mima Arlene Smith (3 Jan 1899, Reading PA-2 Mar 1990).

AW512241   Jean Harriet Wysor (b 29 Mar 1930, Pageton WV) m 24 Mar 1949, John Comer Washburn.

AW5122411   John Wysor Washburn (b 20 Apr 1951) m 1) Robin Shockley; m 2) Susanne Porterfield.

AW51224111   Dallas James Washburn (b 21 Dec 1977).

AW51224112   Dustin John Washburn (3 Jan 1984, Roanoke VA-3 Jun 1993, Roanoke VA).

AW5122412   Anne Carol Washburn (b 3 Aug 1953, Roanoke VA) m 1) Roger Surber; m 2) Robert Shults.

AW51224121   Kristen Elizabeth Surber (b ca 1972, Roanoke VA).

AW51224122   Kelly Anne Surber (b ca 1978, Roanoke VA).

AW51225   Charles Mathias Wysor (26 Aug 1903, Russell VA-3 Jun 1960, Russell VA) m 30 Mar 1930, Russell VA, Lucille Munsey (16 Apr 1910, Russell VA-1 May 1972, Russell VA).

AW512251   Mildred Sue Wysor (b 27 Jan 1933, Lebanon VA) m 6 Oct 1956, Quantico VA, Robert Allen Haydock (b 21 Dec 1930, IL).

AW5122511   Jennifer Lynn Haydock (b 2 Aug 1957, Ottumwa IA) m   McMillan.

AW512252   Edith Ann Wysor (22 Jun 1937, Lebanon VA-19 Feb 1996, Fairfax VA) m 8 Jun 1963, Bobby Gene Hadaway (b 18 Jun 1937).

AW5122521   Charles Edward Hadaway (b 12 May 1965, Ft. Benning GA).

AW5122522   Robert Wysor Hadaway (b 26 May 1968, Alexandria VA).

AW51226   Joseph Earnest Wysor (14 Mar 1906, VA-4 Apr 1986, Bluefield WV) m 18 Jun 1938, Tazewell VA, Mary Inez ("Pat") Patterson (8 Nov 1913-12 Jun 1958).

AW51227   Elizabeth C. Wysor (b 20 Jul 1911, VA) m 16 Apr 1936, Kyle Taylor (25 Dec 1905-1 Nov 1975, Johnson City TN).

AW512271   Joyce Taylor (b 9 Feb 1937) m 2 Feb 1980, Cliff Bagot.

AW512272   Larry Joe Taylor (b 13 Mar 1939) m 16 Jun 1962, Nellie Barnett.

AW5122721   Larry Joe Taylor Jr. (b 28 Mar 1965) m Jennifer   .

AW51227211   Logan Blake Taylor (b 8 May 1994).

AW5122722   Jill Ann Taylor (b 14 Jan 1967).

AW512273   Jerry Lee Taylor (b 16 Mar 1943) m 3 Sep 1966, Reta June Good.

AW5122731   Jennifer Leigh Taylor (b 11 Sep 1969) m Mark Smith.

AW5122732   Jeanna Renea Taylor (b 3 Nov 1973) m Thomas Campbell.

AW512274   Julia ("Judy") Taylor (b 6 Feb 1951) m 1 Jun 1971, Gary Wayne Onks.

AW5122741   Ivy Elizabeth Onks (b 11 Mar 1974).

AW5122742   Daniel Wayne Onks (b 23 Dec 1975).

AW5123   Henry Franklin Wysor (b ca Oct 1849, VA).

AW5124   Robert Meshack Wysor (3 Feb 1852-8 Sep 1853, Tazewell VA).

AW5125   Eliza C. Wysor (3 Feb 1854, Tazewell VA-15 Mar 1936) m 7 Mar 1872, Tazewell VA, William H. Jackson (8 Jun 1839, Russell VA-18 Nov 1922).

AW51251   James M. Jackson (b ca 1872).

AW5126   Ralph Wysor (6 Jun 1856, Maiden Spring Fork, Tazewell VA-13 Sep 1943, Belfast VA) m 1) 13 Aug 1879, Russell VA, Josephine B. Honaker (1860, Russell VA-10 Oct 1888); m 2) 12 Nov 1890, Anna Nuckols (13 Jun 1873, Buchanan VA-21 Jan 1958). Russell VA.

AW51261   Myrtle Alice Wysor (10 Sep 1880, Russell VA-3 Aug 1967) m 28 Nov 1901, Russell VA, William H. Miller (b ca 1880, Russell VA). Casper WY.

AW512611   Cosby Ellen Miller (b 18 May 1906, New Garden, Russell VA).

AW51262   Dora Wysor (b 27 Sep 1883, Russell VA) m 20 Feb 1902, Tazewell VA, Henry E. Shamblin (b ca 1883, Russell VA).

AW512621   Earl H. Shamblin.

AW512622   Mabel Shamblin.

AW51263   William Whitten Wysor (7 Mar 1888, Russell VA-2 Dec 1952) m 22 Dec 1913, Wardell, Tazewell VA, Mabel Clara Stinson (30 Aug 1896, Russell VA-29 Dec 1951).

AW512631   Alta Octavia Wysor (12 Jun 1915, VA-1 Oct 1991) m 13 Apr 1936, Boyden Sawyer (b 21 Jun 1913).

AW512632   Mary Josephine Wysor (b 19 Mar 1919, VA) m 1944, Irvin Bastyr.

AW512633   Billy Ralph Wysor (b 22 Sep 1921, Richlands VA) m 5 Jul 1946, Bristol VA, Lula Roberta Lester (b 13 Jul 1922, Wardell, Tazewell VA). Richlands VA.

AW5126331   Billy Keith Wysor (b 4 Nov 1962, Richlands VA).

AW512634   George Oney Wysor (b 8 Sep 1924) m Carrol Ory.

AW5126341   Esther Irene Wysor.

AW512635   Earl Kenneth Wysor (b 3 Feb 1930, Richlands VA) m 30 May 1953, Tazewell VA, Norma Joan Reedy (b 28 May 1934, Jewell Ridge VA). Mayor, Richlands VA.

AW5126351   Sandra Lyn Wysor (b 12 Apr 1955) m 29 Jun 1974, Joseph Randall Tatum (b Nov 1950).

AW51263511   Chad Michael Tatum (b 4 Jul 1979, Abingdon VA).

AW51263512   Benjamin Mathus Tatum (b 27 Jul 1981, Abingdon VA).

AW51263513   Clarissa Eva Tatum (b 8 Jan 1983, Abingdon VA).

AW5126352   Clara Ann Wysor (b 25 Aug 1958, Richlands VA) m 16 Dec 1978, Harold Lee Dye II (b 7 Aug 1955, Richlands VA).

AW51263521   Nathan Wysor Dye (b 15 Aug 1995).

AW51264   Edward Lyle Wysor (8 Apr 1893, VA-16 Feb 1962) m 17 Nov 1914, Maude Ellen Call (ca 1895, VA-27 Mar 1983).

AW512641   Madge Kathleen Wysor (20 Aug 1918, VA-30 Apr 1990) m William Riley Keesee (b 11 Jul 1915).

AW512642   Harry Dillard Wysor (3 Oct 1920-12 May 1983) m 23 Mar 1941, Marjorie Buckles (b 22 Jun 1923). Orlando FL.

AW5126421   Carolyn Wysor (15 Dec 1941-17 Dec 1993) m Fred Hageman.

AW51264211   Amy Lynne Hageman (b 11 Nov 1964, Orlando FL) m 22 Oct 1988, Brian L. Kelly (b 8 Jun 1964).

AW51264212   Frederick Todd Hageman (b 30 Mar 1970, Orlando FL) m 12 Oct 1988, Shelly Teddy.

AW512642121   Eric Hageman (b ca 1989).

AW512642122   Julie Hageman (b ca 1991).

AW51265   Charles Naff Wysor (12 Apr 1895, Elk Garden, Russell VA-16 Jan 1979, Lebanon VA) m 10 Jun 1922, Russell VA, Martha Elizabeth Martin (7 Oct 1901, Russell VA-29 Sep 1986, Wytheville VA). Honaker VA.

AW512651   Betty Lou Wysor (b 21 Jan 1925, WV) m 12 Mar 1944, Northfork WV, Ray C. Walls (7 Feb 1917, WV-25 Nov 1986, Wytheville VA).

AW5126511   Teena Rae Walls (b 10 Aug 1949, Radford VA) m Garrett Austin ("Autie") Cochran (b 26 May 1953).

AW51265111   Christina Elizabeth Cochran (b 8 Aug 1968).

AW51265112   Anthony Ryan Cochran (b 16 Sep 1977).

AW51265113   Tamara Leigh Cochran (b 11 May 1979).

AW5126512   Charles Thomas Walls (13 Apr 1952, Radford VA-13 Jan 1956, Wytheville VA).

AW5126513   Debra Lynn Walls (b 30 May 1957, Radford VA) m Terry Wolford.

AW51265131   Michael Wolford (b 30 Aug 1983, Wytheville VA).

AW51265132   Lauren Wolford (b 19 Mar 1992, Wytheville VA).

AW5126514   Catherine Elizabeth Walls (b 27 Aug 1958, Radford VA) m Robert Howe.

AW51265141   Liam Walls Howe (b ca 1985).

AW51265142   Charles Thomas Howe (b ca 1988).

AW512652   Billy Burke Wysor (ca 1926, War WV-ca 1927).

AW512653   Robert Burns Wysor (b 13 Mar 1928, War WV) m 24 Aug 1950, Bassett VA, Esther Lee Ingram (b 24 Aug 1929, Bassett VA).

AW5126531   Karen Lee Wysor (b 1 Sep 1952, Wilmington DE) m 23 Apr 1994, Knoxville TN, Ward Allen Reeves (b 6 Sep 1961).

AW5126532   Robert Wesley Wysor (b 25 Sep 1955, Wilmington DE) m 10 Jun 1989, Lenoir City TN, Karen Sue Mahan (b 13 Aug 1964).

AW51265321   Sarah Katherine Wysor (b 10 Nov 1996, Knoxville TN).

AW5126533   John Conrad Wysor (b 10 Nov 1961, Birmingham AL) m 7 Aug 1993, Knoxville TN, Regina Gwen Lawson (b 7 Feb 1964).

AW51265331   Austin Conrad Wysor (b 15 Sep 1995, Knoxville TN).

AW512654   Joan Wysor (6 Nov 1930, Russell VA-21 Apr 1992, Kingsport TN) m 19 Feb 1950, Russell VA, Jack Donald Howard (14 Jul 1926, Russell VA-3 Jun 1989, Russell VA).

AW5126541   Vickie Ruth Howard (b 24 Dec 1950, Richlands VA) m 22 Oct 1994, Rosedale VA, Charles Langdon Scott (b 6 Apr 1951).

AW5126542   Mary Lynn Howard (b 10 Apr 1952, Richlands VA) m 31 May 1975, Bluefield WV, Michael Malamisura (b 3 Jan 1953).

AW51265421   Chris Malamisura (b 10 Aug 1979).

AW51265422   Andrea Malamisura (b 1 Jun 1983).

AW5126543   Donna Jo Howard (b 5 Aug 1953, Richlands VA) m 3 Sep 1977, Bob Burgess (b 29 Jan 1937).

AW51265431   Robert Burgess (b 21 Mar 1982).

AW51265432   Cody Burgess (b 23 Dec 1989).

AW5126544   Martha Jane Howard (b 16 Nov 1954, Richlands VA) m 20 Jul 1974, Richard Randal Waddell (b 16 Sep 1954).

AW51265441   Seth Waddell (b 22 Jun 1980).

AW51265442   Rebecca Waddell (b 29 Aug 1984).

AW5126545   Jack Donald Howard (b 20 Nov 1956, Richlands VA) m ca Mar 1976, Ginger Browning (b ca 3 Jul 1958).

AW51265451   Jill Howard (b 17 May 1987).

AW51265452   Ethan Howard (b 9 Apr 1989).

AW5126546   Charles R. Howard (b 9 Aug 1958, Bluefield WV).

AW512655   Charles Naff Wysor Jr. (b 20 Oct 1932, Honaker VA) m 20 Oct 1971, Katie Jo Owens
(b 26 Aug 1949).

AW5126551   Charles Douglas Wysor (b 7 Jul 1974).

AW5126552   Tracy Jo Wysor (b 3 May 1976).

AW512656   Patty Jean Wysor (b 22 Sep 1934, Honaker VA) m 20 Sep 1952, William Burl Wyatt (b
30 May 1934).

AW5126561   William David Wyatt (b 19 Jul 1954, Richlands VA) m 19 Oct 1978, Bristol TN, Karen
Sue Cole (b 15 Apr 1958, Richlands VA).

AW51265611   Kara Alexandria Wyatt (b 14 Jul 1990).

AW5126562   Elizabeth Wyatt (b 16 Jun 1956).

AW5126563   Charles Richard Wyatt (b 16 Jan 1958) m 1) 8 May 1982, Janet Louise Dooley; m 2) m
30 Jun 1991, Rebecca Carol Faucette.

Farrah Wyatt (b 20 May 1987).

AW512657   James Larry Wysor (13 Sep 1942, Honaker VA) m 1) 11 Sep 1959, Mary Lynn Van Dyke
(b 20 Sep 1942); 2) 6 Apr 1995, Honaker VA, Carolyn Keene (b 14 Aug 1948, Lebanon VA).

AW5126571   Robert Chet Wysor m Gayetta   .

AW51265711   Sara Elizabeth Mae Wysor (b 12 Sep 1991).

AW5126572   Cindy Wysor (b 21 Jan 1966) m Randy Newberry.

AW51265721   Kandis Newberry (b 7 Jan 1987).

AW51265722   Joshua Newberry (b 5 May 1889).

AW51266   Vernon Clyde Wysor (20 Mar 1897, Elk Garden, Russell VA-15 Sep 1984, Bluefield WV)
m 3 Dec 1924, Beulah Mae Jackson (8 Dec 1903, Honaker VA-29 Mar 1990, Bluefield WV).

AW512661   Donald Jack Wysor (b 30 Dec 1925) m 7 Aug 1945, Peggy Jane ("Pete") Lambert.

AW5126611   Donald Gary Wysor (b ca 1946) m Janet Gail   (11 Apr 1940-7 Jun 1989, Bluefield
VA).

AW5126612   Margaret Alta Wysor.

AW5126613   Judy Marie Wysor.

AW512662   Clyde Edward ("Lank") Wysor (b 8 Apr 1927, Honaker VA) m 13 Sep 1952, Tazewell
VA, Virginia Ida Richardson (b 3 Apr 1926, Bluefield WV).

AW512663   Joe Ralph Wysor (b 22 Mar 1929) m 1) Alice   ; m 2) Phyllis   .

AW5126631   Donna Marie Wysor.

AW5126632   Davy Joe Wysor.

AW5126633   Nikki Ann Wysor.

AW5126634   Jackie Edward Wysor.

AW5126635   John Paul Wysor.

AW51267   Paul S. Wysor (10 Feb 1907, Elk Garden, Russell VA-20 Feb 1981, Bluefield WV) m 27 Dec 1934, Tazewell VA, Anna Gladys Harris (15 Jun 1911-5 Jul 1986, Mercer WV).

AW5127   Rose Anna E. ("Betty") Wysor (b 8 Jun 1858, Indian Creek, Tazewell VA) m 21 Feb 1878, Tazewell VA, Napoleon B. Honaker (b Dec 1858, VA).

AW51271   Rose Honaker (b Dec 1880, VA) m   Howard.

AW51272   Ella Honaker (b 21 Feb 1884, Russell VA) m Charles Abrams Fuller.

AW51273   James Honaker (b Jan 1888, VA).

AW51274   Molly Honaker (b Dec 1890, VA) m   Butt.

AW5128   Samuel Thomas Wysor (5 May 1860, VA-12 Jan 1942, Tazewell VA).

AW5129   Serena Cordelia Wysor (6 Feb 1862, VA-17 Aug 1950, Tazewell VA).

AW512A   Charles Beverly Wysor (4 Feb 1864, VA-6 Jun 1947, Tazewell VA) m 28 Apr 1909, Nellie Audrey Gaussoin (23 Aug 1886, VA-4 Jun 1951).

AW512A1   Mary Emma Wysor (9 Feb 1912, VA-30 Mar 1995) m Orr Ferrell.

AW512A2   James Robert Wysor (b ca 1913, Wardell, Tazewell VA) m 22 Dec 1951, Narrows VA, Hazel Matilda Hilt (b ca 1911, Tannersville VA).

AW512A3   George Henry Wysor (b ca 1927) m Lorraine Dales.

AW512A31   Debra Wysor m   Lambert.

AW512A32   Charles Henry Wysor.

AW513   Mary Wysor (5 Aug 1825, Russell VA-22 Oct 1859, Russell VA) m 1843 James Harvey Fuller (b 27 May 1822, Honaker VA).

AW5131   Lucinda C. Fuller (b 12 May 1844, Russell VA) m Spencer Tunnell Ball (b 10 Mar 1845, Russell VA).

AW5132   Julia Ann Fuller (b ca 1846, Russell VA).

AW5133   Ira Reynolds Fuller (b ca 1849, Russell VA) m Phoebe C. Thompson (b ca 1856, Russell VA).

AW514   William L. Wysor (ca 1826, Russell VA-ca 1858) m Catharine   (b ca 1836, VA).

AW5141   Maria A. Wysor (20 Jul 1855, Russell VA-29 Aug 1887, Russell VA) m 8 Apr 1873, Russell VA, Charles H. Boyd (b ca 1852, Russell VA).

AW51411   William S. Boyd (b ca 1874, VA).

AW51412   Sarah K. Boyd (b ca 1877, VA).

AW5142   Beverly Wysor (31 Jan 1856, Russell VA-31 Jan 1856, Russell VA.

AW515   John G. Wysor (16 May 1830, Russell VA-15 Jul 1904) m 1) 3 Nov 1854, Lebanon VA,
Mary Jane Lee (6 Jul 1839, Russell VA-25 Jun 1877); m 2) m 4 Nov 1879, Russell VA, Elizabeth Stinson (16
Sep 1846, Russell VA-3 Nov 1916). Russell VA.

AW5151   Beverly J. Wysor (Jan 1856, VA-ca Jan 1913, Russell VA) m Laura A. Clark (b Apr 1859,
VA).

AW51511   Myrtle M. Wysor (b ca 1876, VA) m   Davis.

AW51512   Adolphus A. Wysor (May 1880, VA-8 Aug 1945, Richlands VA) m 1) 11 Aug 1903,
Narcie B. Brown (b ca 1884, VA); m 2) Nell Davis (b ca 1912).

AW515121   Laura Clark Wysor (b ca 1905, VA) m   Repass.

AW5152   Albert C. Wysor (ca Dec 1858-6 Jun 1859, Russell VA).

AW5153   Sylvester A. Wysor (3 Apr 1859, New Garden, Russell VA-6 Jun 1860, New Garden,
Russell VA).

AW5154   Cordelia Wysor (30 Aug 1859, New Garden, Russell VA-10 Apr 1861, New Garden,
Russell VA).

AW5155   John William Wysor (May 1862, Russell VA-Dec 1944) m 26 Dec 1895, Russell VA,
Laura A. Smith (May 1876, Russell VA-Jun 1959).

AW51551   Elsie Wysor (1904, VA-1994) m Guy Overstreet.

AW51552   Carrie Wysor (1906, VA-1990) m Paul Gillespie.

AW515521   Jean Gillespie.

AW515522   Bill Gillespie.

AW51553   Henry Stuart Wysor (4 Jul 1910, Honaker VA-3 Nov 1981, Bristol VA) m Lakie Hughes
(b 1916).

AW515531   Daniel C. Wysor (b Oct 1938) m Faye Bays.

AW5155311   Stephanie Page Wysor (b ca 1967).

AW5155312   Kevin Matthew Wysor (b ca 1972).

AW5156   Maggie Wysor (b ca 1881, Russell VA) m 12 Sep 1899, Russell VA, A. D. Shoemaker
(b ca 1863, Russell VA).

AW5157   Carrie Wysor (b Mar 1884, Russell VA) m 18 Dec 1903, Russell VA, W. J. Weinman (b
ca 1872, Campbell VA).

AW5158   Charles Henry Wysor (26 Nov 1886, VA-4 Jan 1903).

AW516   Serena Wysor (b ca 1835, Russell VA) m 9 Jul 1853, Russell VA, Charles Johnson (b ca
1829, Russell VA).

AW52 Henry Wiser (b ca 1796, Montgomery VA) m 1) Ruth ; m 2) 20 Aug 1852, Laurel KY, Louisa Catching (b ca 1811, KY). Russell VA, Claiborne TN and Laurel KY.[151]

AW521 Mary Wiser (ca 1818, Russell VA) m 2 Jan 1838, Harlan KY, William T. Coldiron.

AW522 Daughter Wiser (ca 1819, Russell VA).

AW523 John G. Wiser (ca 1824, Russell VA-ca 1853) m Mary (ca 1824, KY). Laurel KY.

AW5231 Charles Wiser (ca 1845, KY).

AW5232 John H. Wiser (b Aug 1850, KY) m 17 May 1876, Owen KY, Mary Frances Smoot (b Feb 1856, KY).

AW52321 Lizzie M. Wiser (b Apr 1878, Owen KY).

AW52322 Bessie Wiser (b Aug 1881, KY).

AW52323 James D. Wiser (4 Jun 1888, KY-21 Oct 1968, Owenton KY) m Susan (b ca 1893, KY).

AW523231 Leona Wiser (b ca 1912, KY).

AW523232 Gayle Wiser (7 Sep 1914, Owen KY-31 Oct 1986, Owen KY).

AW52324 Joseph D. Wiser (Apr 1891, KY-6 Nov 1958, Owen KY).

AW52325 Charles Wiser (b Nov 1895, KY).

AW5233 William Wiser (b ca 1852, KY).

AW524 Lewis Christopher Wiser (b 8 May 1825, Claiborne TN) m 13 Dec 1853, Laurel KY, Mary Ann Points (b 10 Dec 1828, TN). Laurel and Pulaski, KY and Mitchell KS.

AW5241 Sarah Jane Wiser (b 24 Sep 1854, Laurel KY) m 23 Sep 1875, Somerset KY, Walter Estel Ingram (b 30 May 1854, Pulaski KY.

AW5242 Martha M. Wiser (b 2 Mar 1857, Laurel KY).

AW5243 John Wiser (28 Dec 1858, Laurel KY-9 Jul 1900, Beloit KS) m Maggie E. Thompson (12 Feb 1867-28 Oct 1898). Mitchell KS.

AW52431 Lulu Wiser (b ca 1894, KS).

AW52432 Lillian Wiser (22 Oct 1895, KS-Jan 1976, Mitchell KS).

AW5244 Mary C. Wiser (b 4 Sep 1861, Laurel KY).

AW5245 James H. Wiser (b May 1865, KY). Clinton MO.

AW5246 William C. Wiser (b ca 1867, KY).

[151]No documentation has been found to prove that Henry was a son of George Adam, and some lists of the family do not include his name. However, he travelled with George from Russell County to Claiborne County and was still with George when he died in Laurel County, Kentucky. This behavior seems adequate proof that he was a son.

AW5247   Robert L. Wiser (b Sep 1870, KY) m Flora   (b ca 1882, MO). Clinton MO.

AW52471   Lulu Wiser (b ca 1904, MO).

AW52472   Lela Wiser (b ca 1907, MO).

AW52473   Pearl Wiser (b ca 1909, MO.

AW52474   Edna Wiser (b ca 1911, MO).

AW52475   Ray Wiser (b ca 1913, MO).

AW52476   John Wiser (b ca 1915, MO).

AW52477   Myrtle Wiser (b ca Jan 1920, MO).

AW525   Son Wiser (b ca 1827, Claiborne TN).

AW526   James Wiser (b ca 1829, Claiborne TN) m 13 Jan 1853, Laurel KY, Mary Ann Williams
(b Mar 1834, KY). Laurel and Pulaski KY.

AW5261   Lewis Christman Wiser (23 Apr 1854, Laurel KY-19 Apr 1933, Covington KY) m 26 Nov
1874, Pulaski KY, Sarah C. McBee (b Mar 1852). Pulaski KY.

AW52611   Ophelia Wiser (b 11 Sep 1875, AR).

AW52612   William Wiser (b 1 May 1878, Pulaski KY).

AW52613   Everett Wiser (b ca 1880, KY) m Dora S. Price (b ca 1889, KY). Pulaski KY.

AW526131   Raymond D. Wiser (b ca 1908, KY).

AW526132   Pretzel L. Wiser (b ca 1910, KY).

AW526133   Hubert Opal Wiser (b 8 Jan 1911, Pulaski KY).

AW526134   Leonie E. Wiser (b 24 Sep 1912, Pulaski KY).

AW526135   Louis Edith Wiser (b 9 Dec 1913, Pulaski KY).

AW526136   Earl Wiser (27 Feb 1915, Pulaski KY-Jul 1987, Dayton OH).

AW526137   Terrell Wiser (b 28 Feb 1915, Pulaski KY).

AW526138   Paris V. Wiser (4 Mar 1916, Pulaski KY-Jun 1980, Dayton OH).

AW526139   Adolphus Wiser (15 Aug 1918, Pulaski KY-28 Nov 1919, Pulaski KY).

AW52613A   Vernon Wiser (22 Jun 1920, Pulaski KY-8 May 1993, Montgomery OH).

AW52614   Dora Wiser (b Nov 1888, KY).

AW52615   Molly Wiser (b Oct 1890, KY).

AW52616   Charles Wiser (27 Jun 1891, KY-May 1968, Covington KY).

AW52617   Cora Wiser (b Feb 1895, KY).

AW52618   Ben Wiser (5 Feb 1896, Pulaski KY-21 Aug 1913, Kenton KY).

AW5262   David Wiser (b 3 Oct 1856, Laurel KY).

AW5263   Henry Wiser (b 19 Dec 1858, Laurel KY) m 13 Jan 1876, Pulaski KY, Rebecca McBee (b Sep 1854).   Pulaski KY and McLean IL.

AW52631   Nora Wiser (3 Feb 1878, Pulaski KY).

AW52632   Otis Wiser (Mar 1880, KY-ca 1912) m Orlina P.   (b ca 1880, KY).   McLean IL.

AW526321   Beulah I. Wiser (b ca 1905, IL).

AW526322   Vola Wiser (b ca 1907, IL).

AW526323   Clarence Wiser (b ca 1910, IL).

AW526324   Clarissa Wiser (b ca 1910, IL).

AW52633   Louis T. Wiser (b Jun 1882, KY) m Ophelia   (b ca 1883, KY).   McLean IL.

AW526331   Hubert Joplin Wiser (24 Sep 1902, KY-Jul 1974, Bloomington IL).

AW526332   Myrtle R. Wiser (b ca 1905, IL).

AW526333   Charles T. Wiser (29 Aug 1906, IL-Oct 1983, Bloomington IL).

AW526334   Lela Mabel Wiser (b ca 1909, IL).

AW526335   Oliver Wiser (b ca 1911, KY).

AW52634   Lillie Wiser (b Feb 1885, KY).

AW52635   James T. Wiser (b Feb 1887, KY) m Martha Agnes   (b ca 1893, IL).   Peoria IL.

AW52636   Willie Wiser (b Jul 1889, KY).

AW52637   Lula D. Wiser (b Sep 1893, KY).

AW52638   Ora Wiser (b Sep 1896, KY).

AW5264   Martha J. Wiser (b ca 1864, KY) m 10 Mar 1881, Pulaski KY, Josiah Hays.

AW5265   Charles C. Wiser (b ca 1867, KY).

AW5266   Nancy M. Wiser (b ca 1869, KY).

AW5267   Virgie Wiser (b ca 1874, KY).

AW5268   John D. Wiser (b ca 1878, KY).

AW527   William G. Wiser (ca 1832, TN-5 Dec 1862, Laurel KY) m 25 Dec 1855, Laurel KY, Elizabeth Lewis (31 Mar 1840, Laurel KY-31 Jan 1933, Stony Point, Clinton MO).   Laurel KY.

AW5271   Henry Clay Wiser (Oct 1856, KY-1925, MO) m 23 Oct 1879, Clinton MO, Willie May Brown (b 1 Feb 1855, MO). Clinton MO.

AW52711   William C. Wiser (b Dec 1880, MO).

AW52712   Jesse A. Wiser (b Apr 1882, MO).

AW52713   Mannie E. Wiser (b Feb 1887, MO).

AW52714   Charles Wiser (b Jul 1888, MO) m Zona   (b ca 1891, MO).

AW5272   Lucinda Catherine Wiser (17 Sep 1858, Laurel KY-1938, MO) m ca 1878, MO, John Henry Brown (Dec 1854, MO-1933, MO).

AW5273   Milton Green Wiser (1 Jan 1862, Laurel KY-11 Jun 1941, Clinton MO) m 20 Nov 1884, Clinton MO, Ida Davis Brown (7 Dec 1861, Clinton MO-10 May 1956, Amarillo TX). Clinton MO.

AW52731   Agnes Olivia Wiser (b 8 May 1886, Clinton MO) m 22 Dec 1909, Clinton MO, Henry P. Smith.

AW52732   Milton Eldon Wiser (30 Nov 1891, Clinton MO-27 May 1965, Lubbock TX) m 21 Dec 1910, Clinton MO, Frances Pearl Wheatley (12 Aug 1893, Bath KY-26 Apr 1969, Lubbock TX). Clinton MO and Lubbock TX.

AW527321   Milton Harold Wiser (26 Aug 1912, Clinton MO-21 Sep 1993, Sun City CA) m 29 Jul 1945, St. Joseph MO, Catherine Harriet Schanafelt.

AW527322   Evelyn May Wiser (b 15 May 1917, Clinton MO) m 1 Aug 1942, St. Joseph MO, Robert E. Hudspeth.

AW527323   Robert Maxey Wiser (b 11 Nov 1919, Clinton MO) m 31 May 1941, St. Joseph MO, Mary Lee Allison (b 2 Feb 1922, Buchanan MO).

AW5273231   Judy Kay Wiser (b 6 Mar 1944, St. Joseph MO) m 19 Jun 1965, Lubbock TX, Guy Walter Bayless (b 2 Dec 1941, Harrison TX).

AW5273232   Merle Jean Wiser (b 15 May 1946, St. Joseph MO) m Leslie Ray White.

AW528   Elizabeth Wiser (b ca 1836, TN).

AW529   Martha Ann Wiser (7 Jul 1853-24 Jul 1853).

AW53   James Wiser.

AW54   George Wiser.

AW55   Mary Wiser.

AW56   Elizabeth Wiser (ca 1804, VA-2 Jun 1877, Laurel KY).

AW6   John Jacob Wiser (b 11 Sep 1765, Northampton PA) m 16 Jun 1794, Montgomery VA, Eve Helm (b ca 1776, Winchester VA).

AW7   Maria Margaret ("Peggy") Wysor (12 Jan 1768, Northampton PA-ca 1835, Tazewell VA) m 24 Dec 1787, Montgomery VA, James Cecil (ca 1765, MD-17 Oct 1801, Tazewell VA).

AW71   Susannah Cecil m Samuel Gibson.

AW72   Thomas Cecil (ca 1789-8 Jan 1873, Floyd KY) m 11 Aug 1811, Tazewell VA, Jane ("Jennie") Stratton (b ca 1790, VA).

AW73   Samuel Cecil (18 Sep 1791, VA-21 Feb 1871, Cedar Bluff VA) m 1) 18 Dec 1817, Tazewell VA, Rebecca Smith (13 Feb 1795-20 Mar 1839); m 2) 30 Sep 1841, Tazewell VA, Nancy Corell (b ca 1808).

AW74   Zachariah Cecil (ca Jun 1794, VA-27 Mar 1882, Green, Fayette OH) m 1) 1823, Tazewell VA, Abigail Quinn (d ca 1842, Fayette OH); m 2) 26 Dec 1843, Fayette OH, Mary Johnson (b ca 1813, VA).

AW75   Rebecca Cecil m 25 Dec 1832, Tazewell VA, John McGuire.

AW76   Henry W. Cecil (b ca 1797, VA) m 2 Aug 1821, Tazewell VA, Rebecca Claypool (ca 1800-1863).

AW77   John Cecil m 18 Aug 1835, Tazewell VA, Nancy Harmon.

AW78   Margaret ("Peggy") Cecil (d 1887, Lee VA) m 7 Jun 1832, Tazewell VA, John Pruett.

AW79   James Cecil.

AW7A   Elizabeth Cecil (ca 1800-ca 1842) m 1823, Tazewell VA, Isaac Dailey (27 Dec 1786, Montgomery VA-12 Mar 1861).

AW7B   Witten Cecil (ca 1801-ca 1871) m 1) 13 Aug 1846, Tazewell VA, Angeline Peery (b ca 1822); m 2) 30 Jun 1868, Tazewell VA, Elizabeth M.

AW7C   Mitchell Cecil (11 Jan 1803-4 Apr 1887, Dryden VA) m 11 Jul 1833, Lee VA, Mary S. Pennington (11 Nov 1817, Lee VA-6 Feb 1901, Dryden VA).

AW7D   Madison ("Matt") Cecil (21 Feb 1809-2 Feb 1893) m Mary A. Taylor (b ca 1816, VA).

AW8   Mary Wysor (ca Dec 1771, Winchester VA-27 Mar 1861, Pulaski VA) m 3 Sep 1791, Montgomery VA, Elias Shufflebarger (12 Feb 1762, York PA-ca 1826, Montgomery VA).

AW81   John Shufflebarger (11 Jul 1794-1862, Johnson TN) m 4 Nov 1817, Montgomery VA, Mary White.

AW82   Jacob Shufflebarger (ca 1796-19 Mar 1862, Pulaski VA) m 27 Mar 1825, Phoebe Katherine Trollinger (b ca 1807).

AW83   Simon Shufflebarger (9 Dec 1798, Montgomery VA-11 Feb 1835, Pope IL) m 9 Mar 1820, Clark IN, Hannah Beanard (b ca 1792, Montgomery VA).

AW84   Elias Shufflebarger (b ca 1801) m 9 Dec 1824, Montgomery VA, Nancy Carper (b ca 1804).

AW85   David Shufflebarger (b ca 1803) m 26 Jan 1826, Montgomery VA, Mary Carper (ca 1805-1 May 1862, Montgomery VA).

AW86   Charles Shufflebarger (b ca 1805) m 24 Mar 1828, Montgomery VA, Mary Carper (b ca 1808).

AW87   Isaac Shufflebarger (ca Feb 1808-9 Jun 1879, Madison, Fayette OH) m 1) 12 Jun 1828,

Montgomery VA, Mary Elizabeth Surface; m 2) 23 Oct 1839, Pulaski VA, Mary Deck (15 Nov 1818, VA-3 Oct 1895, Madison, Fayette OH).

AW88   Hiram Shufflebarger (b ca 1811) m 1) 3 Dec 1832, Montgomery VA, Hannah Yearout (b ca 1813); m 2) 16 Mar 1858, Washington MO, Lucinda McMurty.

AW89   Adam Shufflebarger (b ca 1813) m 28 Jun 1844, Montgomery VA, Mary Jane Hawley (b ca 1818).

AW9   Eve Wysor (ca 1776, Frederick VA-24 Jan 1853, Pulaski VA) m 5 Jan 1796, Montgomery VA, Jacob Peck (ca 1770, VA-ca Jan 1854, Pulaski VA).

AW91   Mary Peck m   Brookman.

AW92   Fadela Peck m   Burton

AW93   Nancy Peck m 12 Dec 1835, Montgomery VA, Benjamin Burton.

AW94   Elizabeth Peck m 19 Mar 1822, Montgomery VA, Augustine Martin.

AW95   Rebecca Peck m 3 Oct 1822, Montgomery VA, John Brookman.

AW96   William Peck (b ca 1805, VA) m 5 Sep 1835, Montgomery VA, Susan Cooksey (b ca 1816).

AW97   Christopher Peck.

AW98   Catherine Peck m Robert H. Weeks.

AW99   Louisa Peck (b ca 1818) m 10 Jan 1840, Pulaski VA, Thomas Robinson(?) (b ca 1819).

CHAPTER SIXTEEN

[SC] Christian Weiser (ca 1750-1804)
of Cumberland County PA[152]

The earliest concrete reference found to Christian and Susanna Weiser is a baptismal certificate for their son Jacob, born 13 Oct 1781, in "Berlin" Township, Cumberland County. We have only a translation of it and not a copy of the original. Most likely someone not fully familiar with German script read Berlin for "Lurgan" (since a German script L looks like a capital B.) In fact, the family dwelt in Southampton Township later on and it adjoins Lurgan. Both of these are near Shippensburg, and it is in the records of the Lutheran church there that we find the next contemporary references to Christian. He and his wife Susanna Kunckel (whose maiden name is cited at the baptism of a child) were parents, sponsors and communicants until 12 May 1804. Jacob was a deacon of the Lutheran congregation in the 1780s.

Letters of administration in his estate were granted 4 Dec 1804 to Susannah, his widow. He is called Christopher in the documents pertaining to his estate, a not uncommon error English clerks made. The German nickname for Christopher is Stophel, but for Christian it is Christ, pronounced to rhyme with grist. On 30 Nov 1807, Philip Laufman (who is called an administrator in 1807, but not in 1804) and Henry Cress and Susannah, his wife, formerly Weiser, appeared to report a balance in the estate of 399 pounds, five shillings, a sizeable estate. On 17 May 1808 guardians were appointed for the children above 14, but not yet 18: for Susannah and Samuel, their brother Jacob; for Sally Philip Laufman. Although the children are called orphans Susannah Kress is listed as communing until 30 May 1819.

Efforts to determine the parentage of Christian Weiser have proved frustrating. A birthdate of about 1750 seems necessary, especially if Susannah's last child was Samuel, born 1794, which posits a possible birthdate of about 1751 for her. We do not have a complete list of their children. Kunckels were to be found in the 1790 census in Philadelphia, York, Northumberland, Lancaster and Lynn Tp, Northampton (now Lehigh) Counties. While the given names Christian and Samuel, Jacob and John, sound like the family of David Weiser of Oley, there is no way Christian could be part of them. There is nowhere in the family of Conrad Weiser or his brothers to assign him either. There is no immigration record for him. The children of Christian and Susannah (Kunckel) Weiser of whom there is record were:

SC1   John Weiser, ca 1775, a communicant in 1801.

SC2   Maria Weiser, ca 1777, married Peter Drechsler/Trexler.

SC3   Elizabeth Weiser, a communicant in 1801. No further record.

SC4   Jacob Weiser, 13 Oct 1781, a communicant in 1801.

SC5   Anna Catharine Weiser, 5 May 1787, bp at the Shippensburg Lutheran Church, 27 Sep 1787, Michael and Elisabeth Kraus Drechsler sponsors. No further record.

SC6   Salome, Sally or Sarah Weiser, ca 1790, m ca 1810 Jonas Grubb (b 4 Nov 1787).

SC7   Susannah Weiser, ca 1792, m   Keef or Kreaf.

SC8   Samuel Weiser, bp 19 Mar 1794, Shippensburg Lutheran Church.

SC1   Johannes Weiser, born ca 1775, died 8 Nov 1858, Dublin Tp, Huntingdon Co PA, where he is buried in the Methodist cemetery called Possumtown Cemetery near Shade Gap. His tombstone there

---

[152]Data provided, 1959-1996, by Rev Tracy Wiser, Lola Lovell, William Albright, Clifford Wiser, D.T. Talmadge, Mary Ann Likes, Gertrude Wiser Butcher; records of Memorial Lutheran Church, Shippensburg; US census; Cumberland Co (PA) estate records; Huntingdon Co deeds and estate records.

gives his date of death and says, "Aged about 83 years." While no existing record calls him a son of Christian Weiser, he communed with them in the Lutheran congregation at Shippensburg in 1801 (and his brother Jacob). He was certainly married to Barbara who was confirmed and communed at Shippensburg in 1819 and served as a sponsor in 1821. John does not seem to be on any census until 1850. He purchased a 75 acre farm in Dublin Tp from his brother Samuel in 1836 (Huntingdon Co deeds, D-2-439) out of which he and Barbara sold a 44 perch lot to the trustees of the Methodist Episcopal Church of Shade Gap for a burial ground in 1852 (Huntingdon Co deeds, O-8-447). Barbara is also buried there. She died 6 Mar 1866, "Aged about 71 years," which gives a birthdate of about 1794. Her will (Huntingdon Co Will book 6, p 171) was written 5 March. She calls herself Barbara A; certainly Anna was her middle name, given to her godchild in 1821. She divided her estate, half to her son John, a quarter each to her daughter Susannah Hegie and son Samuel Wiser and directed payments to $20 each to grandchildren Barbara [sic] and Daniel Webster Wiser. Both their Lutheranism and the spelling Weiser disappeared as the family moved to Huntingdon County about 1830.

SC11   Susanna Weiser (b 10 Nov 1817) m   Hegie

SC12   Catharine Anna Weiser (28 Jul 1822-dy)

SC13   Johannes Weiser (18 Apr 1826-after 1870). Unm. Lived at home, then as a farmworker with Henry Shearer who was his mother's executor.

SC14   Jacob Weiser (b 21 Oct 1828). He was a resident of the Huntingdon Co Poor House in 1860 and called insane. Predeceased his mother.

SC15   Samuel A. Weiser (29 Jan 1831, Franklin Co PA-Apr 1895, Tell Tp, Huntingdon Co PA) m Hannah C. Runk (b 1833). Lived in Dublin Tp, later Tell Tp, Huntingdon Co. They owned a 2 1/2 acre tract in the former, which they sold to George Fulton 6 Apr 1868 (Huntingdon Co deeds 3-2-454) and purchased a 128 acre, 85 perch farm at public sale 25 Apr 1889 in Tell Tp (Huntingdon Co deeds B-4-362), which fell to his wife (Orphans Court docket R-250, 258) upon his death. He also worked in a sawmill.

SC151   John A. Wiser (b 1856) m Sarah J. Jones

SC1511   Willis H. Wiser, Sr. (4 Dec 1884-8 Sep 1954) m Frances Shoop (25 Dec 1885-19 Jul 1970)

SC15111   Pauline Wiser (b 13 Feb 1907)

SC15112   Jennie Wiser (b 13 Feb 1907) m   Cyphers

SC15113   Willis Wiser, Jr. (b 25 Oct 1912)

SC15114   Gladys Wiser (b 9 Jun 1915) m   Snyder

SC15115   Gerald Wiser (b 2 May 1918)

SC15116   Paul Wiser (b 19 Mar 1919)

SC15117   Calvin Wiser (b 10 Nov 1925)

SC1512   Blanche Wiser m Blaine Welch

SC152   Mary J. Wiser (b 1858) m   Tarxler

SC1521   Melissa Tarxler m   Cowan

SC153   Barbara Wiser (b 1861) m Alexander Mort

SC1531   Harvey Wiser (b to   Mills and Barbara Wiser) m Beulah Cisney (c 5 Dec 1884-11 May 1967)

SC15311   Hilda M. Wiser (b 2 Jul 1902) m 1)   Gardner; m 2)
Rorer

SC153111   Hope Gardner (b 8 Oct 1924) m   Gourley

SC153112   Paul Gardner (b 21 Oct 1927)

SC15312   Florence Wiser (b 4 Dec 1904) m   McCartney

SC153121   Fred McCartney (b 4 Feb 1930)

SC15313   Thelma Wiser (b 24 Jan 1914) m   Shearer

SC153131   Ronald Shearer (b 15 Jun 1933)

SC153132   Sandra Shearer (b 10 Oct 1939) m   Bossert

SC15314   Donald H. Wiser (12 Apr 1918-1977)

SC153141   Ray Wiser (b 30 Dec 1945)

SC153142   Kay Wiser (b 30 Dec 1945) m   Clugston

SC154   Charlotte R. "Emma" Wiser (b 1863)

SC155   Melissa Wiser (b ca 1865)

SC156   Daniel G. Wiser (b 1867). Unm. Farmer, lived with his brother William F. Wiser.

SC157   James M. Weiser (1868-ca 1890)

SC158   Samuel B. Wiser (b 1872)

SC1581   Bruce Wiser

SC1582   Clarence Wiser

SC159   Martha Ellen "Ella" Wiser (b 1874) m 1) Frank Yocum; m 2) Albert Holland

SC15A   William Franklin Wiser (6 Nov 1875, Shade Gap PA-2 Aug 1949, East Waterford PA) m 26 Jan 1897, Mary Catherine Clemens (3 Jul 1882, Wayne Tp, Mifflin Co PA-6 Feb 1947). Bur Knossville PA. Farmer and sawmill laborer.

SC15A1   Lambert M. Wiser (13 Jul 1897-2 Dec 1955) m Mary E. Planch (21 May 1899-29 May 1965)

SC15A11   Albert Wiser

SC15A12   Weasley Wiser

SC15A13   Helen Wiser

SC15A14   Edna Wiser

SC15A2   Bertha L. Wiser (6 Mar 1901-9 Mar 1901)

SC15A3   Carl A. Wiser (4 Apr 1903-12 Jun 1987) m 1) Ola Clugston, div; m 2) Ommie   (5 Jun 1900-6 Jun 1987). Farmer, Bloserville PA.

SC15A31   Carl Wiser, Jr.

SC15A32   Mary Wiser m   Moore

SC15A4   John A. Wiser (26 May 1905-6 Jun 1981) m Lois Gibbons. Farmer, school bus driver.

SC15A41   Wayne Wiser

SC15A42   Ward Wiser

SC15A43   John Wiser

SC15A5   Ellen Beatrice Wiser (8 Aug 1907-10 Jan 1908)

SC15A6   William Theodore Wiser (24 Mar 1910, near Knossville PA-13 May 1966, Lurgan PA) m 11 Jun 1929, Dorsey MD, Helen Marjorie Smith (2 Apr 1911, Horse Valley PA). Bur Mongul PA. Farmer, Todd Tp, Huntingdon Co and Lurgan Tp, Franklin Co PA.

SC15A61   William Cecil Wiser (b 15 Mar 1930) m 24 Dec 1949, Beulah Anna Zook (b 15 Dec 1930, Franklin Co PA)

SC15A611   Kenneth Lynn Wiser (b 29 Nov 1949, Chambersburg PA) m 13 Apr 1968, Mongul PA, Barbara Jean Johnson (b 30 May 1947, Orrstown PA)

SC15A6111   Ronald Lynn Wiser (b 16 Jul 1969, Chambersburg PA)

SC15A6112   Daniel Kenneth Wiser (b 21 Apr 1971, Chambersburg PA)

SC15A612   Dennis Eugene Wiser (b 1 Apr 1952, Chambersburg PA) m 16 Jul 1972, Chambersburg PA, Teena Kay Sterner (b 12 Jul 1953, Hanover PA). Vietnam; USMC, 1970-74.

SC15A6121   Lisa Marie Wiser (b 16 Sep 1972, Chambersburg PA)

SC15A6122   Sheila Anna Wiser (b 13 Mar 1976, Chambersburg PA)

SC15A613   Bonnie Jean Wiser (b 9 Oct 1959, Chambersburg PA) m 15 Oct 1978, Chambersburg PA, Timothy Mellott (b 14 Aug 1957)

SC15A6131   Michelle Lynn Mellott (b 5 Feb 1980)

SC15A6132   Tamara Jean Mellott (b 20 Jan 1982)

SC15A614   Donna Rae Wiser (b 9 Feb 1962, Chambersburg PA) m 26 Jun 1982, Dana Gettel (b 4 Jun 1963, Chambersburg PA)

SC15A6141   Adam Wade Gettel (b 4 Feb 1986, Carlisle PA)

SC15A6142   Taina Rene Gettel (b 3 Jun 1988, Carlisle PA)

SC15A6143   Austin William Gettel (b 6 Feb 1992, Carlisle PA)

SC15A62   Theodore Sylvester Wiser (b 23 Sep 1932, Todd Tp, Huntingdon Co PA) m 1) 21 Mar 1951, Hagerstown MD, Lena Jane Beidel (b 29 Jun 1933, Willow Hill PA), div 1967; m 2) 4 Jun 1977, Mabel Luella Rhoades (b 4 Jun 1930). USA, 1953-55.

SC15A621   Theodore Ray Wiser (b 20 Nov 1955, Chambersburg PA) m 12 Jan 1974, Shippensburg PA, Ruth Marie Goodhart (b 19 Nov 1954)

SC15A6211   Gayle Elaine Wiser (b 14 Jan 1976) m 14 Aug 1993, Mainsville PA, Casey Wayne Mowers (b 6 Feb 1970)

SC15A62111   Garrett Dalton Mowers (b 20 Feb 1994, Chambersburg PA)

SC15A6212   Jessica Lynn Wiser (b 24 May 1979)

SC15A6213   Kristin Nadine Wiser (b 20 Nov 1987)

SC15A622   Tracy Lee Wiser (b 3 Jul 1959, Chambersburg PA) m 1 Dec 1989, Thurmont MD, Patricia Lee Culler (b 30 May 1959, Frederick MD). BA, Hood (MD) Col, 1996. Licensed minister, Church of the Brethren; ministry to the deaf, Frederick MD.

SC15A6221   Wesley Aaron Wiser (b 13 May 1992, Frederick MD)

SC15A6222   Matthew Noah Wiser (6 Nov 1995, Frederick MD)

SC15A623   Terry Lynn Wiser (b 2 Oct 1963, Chambersburg PA) m 1) 21 Jul 1984, Debra Diane Cramer (b 15 Apr 1964), div; m 2) 13 Jan 1987, Shippensburg PA, Shirley Jean Parson (b 2 Mar 1960)

SC15A6231   Nathan William Wiser (b 4 Jan 1988)

SC15A63   Janice Marlene Wiser (b 28 May 1939) m 4 Jun 1960, Harold Baer, Jr. (b 15 Sep 1938)

SC15A631   Randy Eugene Baer (b 15 Feb 1964) m 10 Dec 1981, Tammy Forrester

SC15A6311   Randi Lee Baer (b 4 Dec 1981)

SC15A6312   Amanda Sue Baer (b Dec 1986)

SC15A6313   Wesley Eugene Baer (b 7 Mar 1989)

SC15A632   Michael Todd Baer (16 Dec 1968-16 Dec 1968)

SC15A633   Tammy Marlene Baer (20 Jan 1970-20 Jan 1970)

SC15A634   Rita Renee Baer (b 5 Mar 1972)

SC15A64   Helen Louise Wiser (b 9 Aug 1943) m 11 Jul 1961, Hagertown MD, Larry Donald Rosenberger, Jr. (b 12 Feb 1942, Chambersburg PA)

SC15A641   Larry Donald Rosenberger, Jr. (b 18 Jan 1962, Chambersburg PA) m 1) 1 Jun 1980, Bobbie Jo Kriner (b 1 Jun 1961), div 1991; m 2) 23 Dec 1992, Gloria (Johnson) Coy (b 24 Jul 1947)

SC15A6411   Larry Donald Rosenberger III (b 15 Oct 1980, Chambersburg PA)

SC15A6412   Rebecca Marie Rosenberger (b 16 Feb 1984, Carlisle PA)

SC15A642   Rickey Lynn Rosenberger (b 6 May 1964, Chambersburg PA) m 1) 16 Apr 1983,

Orrstown PA, Pamela Sue Ocker (b 7 Feb 1967, Chambersburg PA), div 1980; m 2) 24 Mar 1984, Hagerstown MD, Doreen Baillor

SC15A6421   Rickey Lynn Rosenberger II (b 22 Nov 1983, Chambersburg PA)

SC15A643   Bradley Eric Rosenberger (b 12 Sep 1968, Chambersburg PA). Had child with Teresa Murphy Gunder (b 2 Apr 1967)

SC15A6431   Taylor Bradley Rosenberger (b 15 Jun 1988, Waynesboro PA)

SC15A644   Bryan Curtis Rosenberger (b 21 Apr 1971, Chambersburg PA)

SC15A7   Elmer LeRoy Wiser (3 May 1914-10 Feb 1960, Dry Run PA) m Julia Stewart

SC15A71   Iline Wiser

SC15A72   Sandy Wiser

SC15A73   Mark Wiser

SC15A74   Sue Wiser

SC15A8   Mary E. Wiser (30 Jul 1917-20 Sep 1918)

SC15A9   Darrell S. Wiser (16 Oct 1922-1 Aug 1986) m Beulah C. Cooper

SC15AA   Darrell Eddie Wiser

SC15AB   Randy F. Wiser

SC16   Christopher Columbus Wiser (ca 1835, Dublin Tp, Huntingdon Co PA-ca 1865) m Jane
   , who m 2)   Parsons. In 1850 he is a laborer, aged 16, in Taylor Tp, Fulton Co PA, with Sol, aged 31, and Hannah, aged 28, Scallman

SC161   Daniel Webster Wiser. Resident of Lutheran orphanage, Loysville PA.

SC162   Mary E. Wiser (d 5 Nov 1874). Resident of Lutheran orphanage, Loysville PA.

SC2   Maria Weiser, born ca 1777, married ca 1797, Peter Drechsler or Trexler. She was confirmed on 27 Aug 1797 as Maria Weiser, married to Drechsler. The only Drechsler who appears married to a Maria is a Peter. The following children are baptized at the Shippensburg Lutheran Church; there may have been more:

SC21   Susanna Drechsler (b 17 Jan 1798)

SC22   Johannes Drechsler (b 4 Jul 1804)

SC23   Samuel Drechsler (b 22 Apr 1807)

SC24   Sara Anna Drechsler (b 5 Jan 1810)

SC25   Maria Drechsler (b 7 Jun 1812)

SC26   Helena Drechsler (b 21 Dec 1815)

SC3   Elizabeth Weiser

SC4   Jacob Weiser was born 13 Oct 1781, in Lurgan Township, now in Franklin Co PA. He served as guardian for his siblings, was occasionally a baptismal sponsor and communicant at the Shippensburg Lutheran Church (in 1807 for his sister Maria Drechsler), but does not seem to appear there after 1808. By 1820, he had settled in Erie Co NY. In 1820 the census lists him at Amhurst, Niagara Co; in 1830 there is no Jacob in New York; in 1840 there is a Jacob at Amherst, Erie Co.

SC41   Henry Phillip Weiser (2 Feb 1820-26 Jun 1884) m Elizabeth Ely. Bur Skinnerville NY. Farmer, clergyman; Little Falls, Herkimer Co NY (1860); Lancaster Tp, Erie Co NY (1880). Had 16 children.

SC411   Melvina Weiser (b 1845)

SC412   Jacob Weiser (b 1847)

SC413   Henry Weiser (b 1849)

SC414   Samuel Weiser (b 1852)

SC4141   Ralph Wiser

SC415   Solomon Wiser (b 1853)

SC416   Eliza Weiser (b 1854)

SC417   Elizabeth Weiser (b 1856)

SC418   Henry Weiser (b 1858)

SC419   Mary Weiser (b 1859)

SC41A   Sarah Jane Weiser (21 Feb 1861, Little Falls NY-20 Aug 1944, Salamanca NY) m 6 Oct 1880, Bowmansville NY, Henry Smith Kissinger

SC41A1   Nora Kissinger

SC41A2   Willis Kissinger

SC41A3   Elizabeth Kissinger

SC41A4   Florence Kissinger

SC41A5   Henry Weiser Kissinger

SC41A6   Edith Mildred Kissinger m   Stoddard

SC41A7   DeWitt Talmadge Kissinger. Yorkshire NY.

SC42   Samuel Wiser (16 Aug 1821-16 May 1891) m Fanny   (b 1826). Bur Skinnerville NY. Purchased land near Lockport NY, 1857.

SC421   Margaret Wiser (b 28 Jan 1844)

SC422   Catherine A. Wiser (b 4 Jul 1847)

SC423   Ella Wiser (b 1851)

SC424   Jacob Peter Franklin Wiser (29 Oct 1852-1923) m Caroline   (b 1851, Germany)

SC4241   Oliver Wiser (b 1877)

SC4242   Lee Wiser (b 1880) m Flora V.

SC42421   Lenola C. Wiser m Ralph C. Hanson

SC4243   Clifford F. Wiser (b 1885)

SC425   Josephine E. Weiser (b 16 Jan 1855)

SC426   George Weiser (b 1859)

SC427   Mary E. Weiser (b 6 Jul 1861)

SC428   Henrietta E. Weiser (b 4 Nov 1862)

SC429   George W. Weiser (b 2 Sep 1869)

SC43   Solomon Weiser (b 1823) m Martha   (b 1830)

SC431   Elizabeth Wiser (b 1849)

SC6   Salome Weiser (b ca 1790) m ca 1810, Jonas Grubb (b 4 Nov 1787). Lived in Crawford Co PA. Moved to Quincy IL, 12 Jul 1839. Eleven children, all born in Pennsylvania, 1811-37. She was confirmed at the Shippensburg Lutheran Church as Salome in 1810, but when her guardian was appointed in 1808, her name is given as Sally, sometimes also as Sarah.

SC7   Susannah Weiser (ca 1792)

SC8   Samuel Weiser/Wiser (b 19 Mar 1794, Southampton Tp, Cumberland Co PA) m ca 1817, Elizabeth   (Aug 1800-24 Dec 1874). He is on the 1820 census for Southampton Tp, Cumberland Co, with one male between 16 and 26, one female under 10, and one female, 16-26. In 1830 he is on the census for Dublin Tp, Huntingdon Co PA, with one male over 25, one male between three and four, two females over 25, two females between five and ten, one female between ten and 15, and one female between three and four. He is on the 1840 census in Franklin Tp, Summit Co OH. It seems probable that he died in the 1840s. By 1850 his son Samuel and widow Elizabeth were in Stark Co OH; they may have gone there as early as 1838 when the daughter Susanna was married there. Elizabeth married a second time on 2 Oct 1851 to Abram Stevens. She is buried in Union Cemetery, Stark Co OH.

SC81   Susanna Weiser (23 Jan 1818, bp at Shippensburg Lutheran Church-30 Jan 1879) m 13 Feb 1838, Stark Co OH, Michael Trexler (11 Feb 1800-25 Mar 1876). Bur Pioneer Cemetery near Alvordton, Williams Co OH. She had a number of children. They moved to northwestern Ohio.

SC82   Mary Jane Weiser (b 23 Oct 1819, baptized at Shippensburg Lutheran Church)

SC83   John Weiser (b 29 Nov 1821, baptized at Shippensburg Lutheran Church)

SC84   Elizabeth Weiser (b 24 Jun 1823, baptized at Shippensburg Lutheran Church)

SC85   Ellen Weiser (1825-6 Feb 1893) m 22 Jan 1846, Stark Co OH, George Johnson (1825-1870). Bur Monterey IN. They moved to Fulton Co IN, near Culver, where they had a farm. The names of their children are not necessarily in order of birth.

SC851   William Johnson (d in his teens)

SC852   Melissa Johnson (d in her teens)

SC853   Elizabeth Johnson m William Duff. No chn.

SC854   Mary Johnson m Dan Carr. Ten chn.

SC855   Nancy Johnson m Jasper Davis. Five chn.

SC856   Finley Johnson m Mary Young. Three chn.

SC857   Emma M. Johnson m George Davis

SC8571   Harley Almon Davis m Evelyn Peckhart

SC8572   Eva M. Davis (25 Mar 1887-31 Dec 1975) m 29 May 1912, Joseph D. Heiser

SC8573   Carrie Ethel Davis m Leroy C. Huff

SC8574   George L. Davis m Anita M. Heres

SC8575   Harry Elmer Davis

SC8576   Floyd Eugene Davis m Ruth Schnabel

SC858   Simon Johnson m Mary Widman. Eight chn.

SC859   Almon Johnson m Mary Shriver. One son.

SC85A   Ida Johnson (1870-1925) m Birt Young. Eight chn.

SC85B   Clara Belle Johnson m Ralph Decker. Eight chn.

SC86   Samuel Findley Wiser (Jun 1829-8 Aug 1898, Columbus OH) m 29 Jan 1850, Canal Fulton OH, Nancy McCullom (23 Jan 1828, Muskingum Co OH-14 Jul 1924, Marion IN). Bur Marion IN. In 1850 he was a boatman; later he was a railroad engineer.

SC861   Ellen Maria Wiser (9 Sep 1850-13 Aug 1851). Bur near Canal Fulton OH.

SC862   Clara Belle Wieser (1853, Canal Fulton OH-26 Dec 1928, Marion IN) m 1) Joseph Wiggins; m 2) Gideon Turner

SC8621   Louise Wiggins m Frank Saylor

SC8622   Nelle Wiggins (16 Feb 1879-5 May 1958) m 2 Mar 1903, Charles Clair Brackett

SC8623   Josephine Wiggins (b 3 Oct 1887, Columbus OH) m 1) 9 Dec 1909, James Long Reed; m 2) Frederick Louis Hunzicker

SC8624   Harry G. Wiggins m Florence Arnold

SC8625   Ruth Turner

SC863   Adelia Wiser (27 Dec 1854, Canal Fulton OH-18 Jun 1943, Lafayette IN) m 1927, Christian Mellinger. Marion IN.

SC864   Katherine Wiser (1858, Canal Fulton OH-24 Nov 1919, Marion IN) m Henry Beshore

SC865   Winifred Wiser (18 Feb 1862, Stark Co OH-21 Jul 1945, Canal Winchester OH) m

Lafayette Stevenson

SC866   Alva Ellis Wiser (22 Nov 1864, Union Station OH-7 Jul 1953, South Bend IN) m 18 Jun 1894, Marion IN, Mary Caroline Doremiss (24 Feb 1874, Russiaville IN-3 Aug 1937, South Bend IN)

SC8661   Guy Brown Wiser (10 Feb 1895, Marion IN-30 Mar 1983, Fallbrook CA) m 12 Sep 1922, Mishawaka IN, Grace Irene Clark (9 Nov 1900, Elkhart IN-1 May 1970, Los Angeles CA). BArch, Cornell U; faculty, OSU, Scripps Col; artist.

SC86611   Nancy Charlotte Wiser (29 Jan 1929, Columbus OH-1 Dec 1992) m 1 Apr 1951, A.C.
Clower

SC866111   Craig Clower (b 12 Jul 1953, San Francisco CA)

*SC86612   Clark Austin Wiser (b 6 Jul 1938, Los Angeles CA) m 5 Jul 1971, Durham NC, Ellen King. Presbyterian pastor.

SC866121   Rebekah Campbell Wiser (b 10 Apr 1973)

*SC8662   Miriam Gertrude Wiser (b 13 May 1898, Jonesboro IN) m 1) 31 Dec 1929, Ray Walter Nelson (b 4 Nov 1896, South Bend IN); m 2) 5 May 1939, William A. Butcher (1880-1954)

SC86621   Ray Walter Nelson (18 Sep 1928, South Bend IN-25 Oct 1985, Playa del Rey CA)(name changed to Walter W. Butcher) m 21 Dec 1963, N. Hollywood CA, Colleen Sidle (d 17 Feb 1990)

SC8663   Harriet Lucille Wiser (7 Aug 1904, South Bend IN-4 Aug 1961, Whittier CA) m 1) Edward Grimm; m 2) 26 Oct 1935, Harry Joseph Hess (14 Aug 1903, Canton OH-24 Feb 1971, Whittier CA)

SC86631   Alan Joseph Hess (b 26 May 1928, Pico CA) m 1) 15 Jun 1962, Tuscon CA, Virginia Ann Alex; m 2) 21 Jan 1977, Barbara Palmer

SC866311   David Joseph Hess (b 26 Oct 1967, Whittier CA)

SC866312   Donald Alan Hess (b 7 Sep 1969, Whittier CA)

SC867   Samuel Olis Wiser (18 Nov 1866, OH-20 Sep 1870, Marion IN)

SC868   Gertrude Wiser (19 Mar 1870, Marion IN-19 Jul 1968, Los Angeles CA) m 1889, Arthur
Evans. Doctor.

SC87   John Wiser

SC88   William Wiser (9 May 1827, PA-30 Sep 1886) m Margaret Wilson (14 Feb 1837-30 Apr
1882)

SC881   John C. Weiser (b Sep 1862) m Cora A.   (b Jun 1866). In 1900, in Norton Tp, Summit
Co OH.

SC8811   Eva M. Wiser (b Feb 1893)

SC8812   Raymond A. Wiser (b Feb 1895)

SC882   Ann M. Wiser (b 1864)

SC883   Emma Wiser (b 1866)

SC89   Simon Wiser (15 Jul 1841, Canal Fulton OH-7 May 1904, Canal Fulton OH). Unm.
Railroader.

CHAPTER SEVENTEEN

[CJ] John Weiser (ca 1760-1841)
of Cumberland and Clearfield Counties PA

One of the most difficult problems in Weiser genealogy is clarifying the ancestry of John Wiser who appears in Clearfield Co PA on the census from 1810 to 1840. Once he is there, his biography is easily traced: he is on the 1806 assessment for the first time. When his wife Mary died in Boggs Tp on 26 Dec 1847, aged 81 years (yielding a birth year of about 1766), a notice in the Clearfield Democratic Banner, 1 Jan 1848, reported that they had come to the county in 1804. The assessments list his estate as 100 acres (for which no deed to him exists) until 1837 when it was assessed to John Weiser, Jr., who purchased it 13 Jun 1837 -- 112 acres -- from William and Sarah Samson (Clearfield Co deeds L-589). Obviously, as frequently happened, John Sr. paid taxes on land he was considered responsible for by the tax collector, either because he was in the process of buying it or because he was renting it with the obligation to pay the taxes. He continued to be assessed with one cow through 1841. In 1842, he is listed as deceased; he died in 1841 or 1842 therefore. There is no tombstone for him or his wife at the Stoneville Cemetery where many of their descendants are buried in Boggs Tp, Clearfield Co, and no reference to him in the deed records nor in the estate records of Clearfield County.

Descendants have believed that his wife's name was Elizabeth but can find no documentation for it. The obituary cited above clearly states that it was Mary. It seems highly probable, therefore, that he is the Johannes Weiser who with wife Maria had three children baptized at the Lutheran church in Shippensburg, Cumberland County: Maria (b Mar 1798), Susanna (b Aug 1799) and Johannes (b 23 Mar 1801). These birth dates mesh somewhat with the known children of John and Mary Weiser of Clearfield Co, for few of whom precise birth dates seem to have been found. Regrettably, no contemporary documentation of genealogical data for this family has come to light. Since the Shippensburg record has no later children, a departure about 1804 is possible. The fact that there are no earlier children may be because the Lutheran records are spotty in the late 1780s and early 1790s. It may also mean that John had come into the area from elsewhere shortly before 1798. The 1800 census does not clarify the matter. He and Anna Maria sponsored Elizabeth, the daughter of Bernhart and Maria Elizabeth Kleber at Shippensburg, born 10 Dec 1798.

Who was John Weiser or Wiser who died in Clearfield County about 1842? There is a temptation to tie him to RF6 John, son of John Conrad, but the discovery of records locating that John in Maryland and Virginia at the time this John has children born in Pennsylvania rules that out. Among the assumed descendants of John Frederick Weiser (see Chapter Eleven) there is no probability of a John, born about 1760-65. The remaining possibility is that John of western Cumberland Co and Boggs Tp, Clearfield Co, was a brother of Christian Weiser of Shippensburg. If we had clear evidence about their father, we might even learn of another brother or more who could be ancestors of other Weisers in central Pennsylvania (see Chapter 21). The existence of these people without clear evidence of their lineage is a source of considerable frustration.[153]

CJ1   Elizabeth Weiser (24 Jan 1789-17 Sep 1852, Bigler Tp, Clearfield Co PA) m Benjamin S. Smeal (Schmehl)(2 Aug 1783, Maxatawny Tp, Berks Co PA-23 Jul 1867, Bradford Tp, Clearfield Co PA). Bur Bigler PA.

CJ11   Abraham Smeal m Ellen Bradley. IN.

CJ12   George Smeal (ca 1810-1 Apr 1859, Pike Tp, Clearfield Co PA) m Elizabeth Bailey

CJ121   Maria Smeal (1848, Pike Tp, Clearfield Co PA-1902) m Jeremiah Dressler

CJ122   Samuel Alfred Smeal (1850, Pike Tp, Clearfield Co PA-1927) m Julia Salisday

CJ123   Sarah Elizabeth Smeal (1852, Pike Twp, Clearfield Co PA-1917) m William Pinchios

---

[153]Data on John Weiser family compiled primarily by Leona Nelson with additional assistance from Edward Wiser, Chris Watson and Phyllis Hatcher.

CJ124   Mary Melinda Smeal (1853, Pike Tp, Clearfield Co PA-1921) m 1) Isaac Pentz; m 2)
William Reesinger

CJ125   Henry Barnet Smeal (1856-1879)

CJ126   George W. Smeal (1856, Pike Tp, Clearfield Co PA-28 Oct 1922, Pike Tp, Clearfield Co
PA) m Alda Courtney

CJ13   Jacob Smeal (ca 1811-10 Jul 1896, Wallaceton PA) m JoAnna Conaway

CJ14   John Smeal (b ca 1812) m ca 1832, Elizabeth Conaway

CJ141   Nancy Jane Smeal (b Dec 1832) m ca 1851 George Kephart

CJ142   Elizabeth Smeal (b 1834)

CJ143   Mathew Smeal (b 1836)

CJ144   John Smeal (b 1840)

CJ145   George Smeal (b 1842)

CJ146   Henry Smeal (b 1844)

CJ15   Sarah Ann Smeal (19 Jul 1813-19 May 1826). Bur Bigler PA.

CJ16   Daniel Smeal (8 Sep 1815-24 Feb 1902) m 16 Feb 1837, Elizabeth Logan

CJ17   Elizabeth Smeal (19 Nov 1817-21 Oct 1908, Wallaceton PA) m 13 Apr 1837, James H.
Turner

CJ18   Mary A. Smeal (2 Oct 1820-12 Jul 1848) m Absolom Pearce, Jr.

CJ19   Infant Smeal (b 1822)

CJ1A   Benjamin Smeal (1824-1877) m Elizabeth Barger (1823-1879)

CJ1B   Samuel Smeal (3 Jan 1826-11 Aug 1910) m Ellen Flegal

CJ1B1   Isiah Smeal (1853-1934) m 1) Elmira Shimel; m 2) Mary Stives

CJ1B2   Matilda Smeal (1854-1940) m William Shoemaker

CJ1B3   Hezekiah Smeal (1857-1923) m 1893, Tillie Oster Henry

CJ1B4   Josiah Smeal (1859-1922)

CJ1B5   Nellie Smeal (1862-1922) m George Smith

CJ1B6   Lila Smeal (1863-d.y.)

CJ1B7   Jennie Smeal (1865-1944) m Otis Williams

CJ1B8   Grant Smeal (1866-1941) m Matilda Kramer

CJ1B9   Samuel Smeal (1868-1944) m Alice Peters

CJ1BA   Harry Smeal (1870-1950) m Ann McTavish

CJ1BB   Eva Lilly Smeal (1872-1955) m William Ward

CJ1BC   Cora Smeal (1875-1965) m Howard Williams

CJ1BD   Rosy Smeal (1878-d.y.)

CJ1C   Sarah Ann Smeal (20 Nov 1827-23 Jan 1895) m Samuel Flegal

CJ1C1   Joanne Flegal (1848-1916) m J.M. McKelvey

CJ1C2   Lucetta Flegal (1850-1920) m Israel Ghue

CJ1C3   Jerome Flegal (b 1855) m Maggie Kellock

CJ1B4   Aaron Flegal (b 1858) m Maggie Phillips

CJ1C5   Mahlon Flegal (1860-1934) m 1) Lizzie Wymer; m 2) Elizabeth Miller

CJ1C6   Irene Flegal (b 1860) m Daniel Smith

CJ1C7   Elvina Flegal (b 1865) m W.B. McGuire

CJ1D   Henry M. Smeal (22 Dec 1829-30 Mar 1904) m Sarah J. Cowder

CJ2   Catharine Weiser (ca 1792-6 Mar 1876, Stoneville, Boggs Tp, Clearfield Co PA) m
Andrew Kephart (Gephart)(ca 1788, probably Macungie Tp, Northampton Co PA-1868, Freeport IL)

CJ21   John Asbury Kephart (7 Oct 1812, Clearfield Co PA-28 Jan 1891, Clearfield Co PA) m
Martha Jane Haney (16 Jul 1819 5 Dec 1904). Bur Stoneville, Boggs Tp, Clearfield Co PA.

CJ211   Mary J. Kephart (b 1839)

CJ212   Rachel Ellen Kephart (1841-ca 1870) m Andrew L. Kephart (ca 1834-6 Mar 1915, Decatur
Tp, Clearfield Co PA)

CJ2121   Martha Kephart m George Zimmerman

CJ2122   Elmira Kephart m William J. Motherbough

CJ2123   Annie Kephart (1864-1878)

CJ2124   Viola Catherine Kephart (22 Jul 1865, Osceola Mills PA-24 Mar 1952, Philadelphia PA)
m 29 Jul 1884, William K. Turner (CJ3257)

CJ2125   Catherine Kephart

CJ2126   Benny Kephart (d.y.)

CJ213   Margaret E. Kephart (7 Jun 1842-12 Sep 1891) m Jesse Wisor (1831-1906)(RF1655)

CJ214   Catherine E. Kephart (1845-1935) m 1866, Edward S. Turner (22 Dec 1836, Boggs Tp,
Clearfield Co PA-22 May 1918). Bur Bigler PA.

CJ2141   Mary Ann Turner m Calvin Parks

CJ215   John Kephart (b 1847) m Mina Ogden

CJ2151   A.J. Kephart (b 1887)

CJ2152   Lodie May Kephart (b 1889)

CJ2153   Louella Kephart (b 1891) m George Peters

CJ2154   Lyda May Kephart (1900-1971) m 1) James Good; m 2) John Coudriet

CJ216   Jacob Kephart (b 1849) m Matilda Hochenberry

CJ2161   Jacob Kephart (b 1879)

CJ2162   Amelia Kephart (b 1880) m Stacy Hampton

CJ2163   Winfield Kephart (b 1882) m 1) Cora Ogden; m 2) Edith Antes

CJ2164   Paul Kephart (b 1883) m Nettie Good

CJ2165   Cleveland Kephart (b 1885) m Bertha Hampton

CJ2166   Cordie Kephart (b 1886) m William Hallman

CJ2167   Edith Kephart (b 1888) m Benjamin Hallman

CJ2168   Charlott Kephart (b 1890)

CJ2169   Jacob Kephart (b 1891)

CJ216A   Clark Kephart (b 1893)

CJ216B   Myrtle Kephart (b 1895)

CJ217   Amelia Kephart (b 1851)

CJ218   Elizabeth Kephart (b 1853)

CJ219   Christina Kephart (b 1855) m William Ashley

CJ2191   William Ashley (b 1876)

CJ21A   Benjamin Kephart (b 1857)

CJ21B   Mary "Molly" Kephart (b 1860) m Thomas Parks (b 1855)(CJ532)

CJ22   Mary Kephart (15 Jan 1815, Clearfield Co PA-26 Mar 1895) m 1) Alexander Stone (19
May 1801, England-8 Nov 1856, Clearfield PA); m 2)   . Bur Stoneville, Boggs Tp, Clearfield Co PA.
Stone, innkeeper, lumberman, founder of Stoneville PA.

CJ221   Elizabeth Stone (7 May 1834-9 Jun 1904) m Daniel H. Dugan (b 13 Nov 1826, NY)

CJ222   Thurdy J. Stone (1836-d.y.)

CJ223   Jane Stone m 2 Feb 1854, John Blair

CJ224   Mary Ann Stone (18 Jan 1843-29 Jun 1863) m 15 May 1860, Patrick Gallaher

CJ225   John Stone (21 Aug 1845-1922) m 1) 2 Feb 1862, Josephine Lumadur (d Nov 1875); m 2) 1879, Emma Odell. Farmer.

CJ2251   Alexander Stone

CJ2252   William Stone

CJ2253   Franklin J. Stone

CJ2254   Earl Stone

CJ2255   Harry Stone

CJ2256   Sybil Stone

CJ2257   Ara Stone

CJ2258   John Stone

CJ226   Sharlotte Stone (1848-d.y.)

CJ23   Catherine Kephart (1 Mar 1816, Clearfield PA-26 Jan 1901, Beresford SD) m Oct 1834, Clearfield PA, Samuel Milliken

CJ231   Mary Jane Milliken (5 Jul 1835, Centre Co PA-16 Nov 1906, Dundy Co NE) m 1) 9 Aug 1853, Stephenson Co IL, Samuel Neil; m 2) 19 Oct 1858, Jacob Ochs

CJ232   Margaret Ellen Milliken (19 Oct 1836, Centre Co PA-1899, Black Hawk Co IA) m 3 Nov 1856, Stephenson Co IL, John DeGraff

CJ233   Rebecca H. Milliken (10 Nov 1838, Centre Co PA-30 Mar 1925, Black Hawk Co IA) m 1) 4 Mar 1858, Stephenson Co IL, Thomas Hood (d Apr 1862); m 2) 24 Dec 1868, Henry Bucher

CJ234   Sarah E. Milliken (19 Jun 1841, Centre Co PA-29 Dec 1906, Buchanan Co IA) m 7 Sep 1858, Stephenson Co IL, George Northrup

CJ235   Amelia Ann Milliken (19 Mar 1843, Centre Co PA-3 Mar 1919, Lisbon ND) m 1) 22 Oct 1863, Black Hawk Co IA, Sal Stoner; m 2) 27 Jan 1898, Levi Lamberton; m 3) 1908, E.B. Martin

CJ236   John Thomas Milliken (5 Jul 1845, Centre Co PA-13 Oct 1914, Stratton NE) m 24 Mar 1867, Black Hawk Co IA, Ann Merwin (27 Oct 1847, Wesleyville IL-2 Aug 1929, Stratton NE)

CJ2361   Dick Merwin Milliken (2 Feb 1872, Black Hawk Co IA-10 Oct 1930, Topeka KS) m 30 Apr 1895, Forsyth Co MO, Eugenie Allen (7 May 1874, Pella IA-30 Jan 1953, Frankfort KS)

CJ23611   Merwin Monroe Milliken (13 Aug 1902, Morrowville KS-5 May 1987, Wichita KS) m 6 Jun 1929, Waterville KS, Lorena Belle Seaton (14 Feb 1895, Barnes KS-6 May 1975, Norman OK)

CJ236111   Anne Seaton Milliken (28 Aug 1930, Hannibal MO) m 14 Jun 1953, David Edward Herrick (30 Jul 1925, Kansas City KS)

CJ237   Alice Catherine Milliken (3 Aug 1849, Stephenson Co IL-5 May 1927, Fayette Co IA) m 15 Jul 1870, Waterloo IA, David Schrack

CJ238   James Oscar Milliken (23 Mar 1854, Freeport IL-2 Feb 1911, Pleasant Tp SD). Unm.

CJ239   William Henry Milliken (11 Sep 1855, Freeport IL-15 Jul 1925, Beresford SD) m 23 Nov 1884, Lincoln Co SD, Dora Hummerly

CJ23A   Armenica Janette Milliken (28 Aug 1857, Stephenson Co IL-2 Jun 1927, Lincoln Co SD) m 1 Jan 1874, Black Hawk Co IA, Job Pierce

CJ23B   Samuel David Milliken (1 Dec 1859, Freeport IL-17 May 1939, Beresford SD) m 28 Oct 1895, Lincoln Co SD, Rosa Becker

CJ23C   Luella May Milliken (10 Feb 1861, Stephenson Co IL-21 Jan 1917, Beresford SD) m 13 Jun 1886, SD, Oscar Pierce

CJ23D   Charles Leslie Milliken (6 May 1866, Waterloo IA-2 Apr 1941, Beresford SD) m 22 Oct 1891, Lincoln Co SD, Louise Vogeli

CJ24   Tamer Kephart (b ca 1817) m Michael Walker

CJ25   Rachel Kephart (2 Mar 1822, Clearfield Co PA-1906, DuBois PA) m 1840, John Logan

CJ251   Hannah Logan (b 1844) m Reuben Miller

CJ252   Jane Logan (b 1845) m Isaac Goss

CJ253   Margaret Logan (b 1848)

CJ254   Mary Ann Logan (b 1850) m Joshua Kephart

CJ255   Joseph Logan (b 1853)

CJ256   Minnie Logan (b 1863) m 23 Dec 1884, Phillip Cordelius

CJ257   Ida Logan (b 1867)

CJ26   Isaac Kephart (15 Nov 1824, Clearfield Co PA-19 May 1883, Stephenson Co IL) m 28 Sep 1862, Green Co WI, Elizabeth Koehler (11 Oct 1830-1 Apr 1897, Stephenson CO IL)

CJ261   Caroline Kephart (b ca 1863, Stephenson Co IL) m William Kegel

CJ262   Mabel Kephart (b ca 1878, Stephenson Co IL) m Earl Howe

CJ27   Nancy Jane Kephart (b ca 1827) m 1845, Alexander Hess (ca 1823-3 Feb 1873, Cherokee Co KS)

CJ271   George Auster Hess (b 6 Feb 1847, Clearfield Co PA) m Lucy

CJ272   Francis Boyington Hess (8 Jun 1849, Clearfield Co PA-Jul 1851)

CJ273   Andrew Ewelace Hess (b 25 May 1851, Clearfield Co PA) m 20 Mar 1874, Ida A. Whitney

CJ274   Dayton Richard Hess (8 Mar 1855, Stephenson Co IL-18 Feb 1861)

CJ275   Josephine Florence Hess (6 Feb 1856, Stephenson Co IL-12 Jun 1932, Seattle WA) m 28 Aug 1873, Robert Perry Wright (28 Oct 1851, Lawrenceville IL-15 Nov 1937, Seattle WA)

CJ2751   Lillian May Wright (5 May 1875, Eagle NE-13 Jan 1899) m 16 Sep 1891, Benjamin
Franklin McIntyre

CJ2752   Frederick A. Wright (b 3 Apr 1878, Eagle NE) m 18 May 1909, Bessie Richard

CJ2753   Mamie R. Wright (2 Jan 1880, Palmyrae NE-23 Jan 1955) m 2 Jul 1901, Will A. Robison

CJ2754   Eva Ann Wright (1 Jan 1882, Lincoln NE-4 Mar 1964) m 19 Jul 1903, Howard Otis
Darnell

CJ2755   Mable Pearl Wright (8 Apr 1885, Ord NE-18 Dec 1971) m 23 Feb 1909, William Tilden
Burns

CJ2756   Ethel Amanda Wright (b 28 Jun 1887, Ft. Hartsuff NE) m 1) 3 Jun 1904, George B. Flick;
m 2) Herbert Smith

CJ2757   Lucy Jane Wright (23 Mar 1889, Ord NE-28 Apr 1972, Riverside CA) m 18 Apr 1908,
Arthur Bennett

CJ758   Hazel Charmenia (Charmain) Wright (2 Apr 1893, Bean Creek NE-7 Feb 1980) m 1) 24
Dec 1915, Albert R. McLean; m 2) 19 Jul 1940, Frank V. Erickson

CJ2759   Ruby F. Wright (7 Jan 1895, Garfield Co NE-29 Dec 1942) m 9 Jun 1918, Dewey E.
Gilman

CJ275A   Myrtle I. Wright (2 Mar 1897, Garfield Co NE-8 Nov 1990) m   Olliphant, div

CJ275B   William R. Wright (1 May 1899, Chelan Co WA-26 Feb 1958) m 1) 9 Sep 1918, Mabelle
Emery, div; m 2) Dorothy

CJ28   Jacob Kephart (ca 1829-ca 1905) m Sarah Ann Kephart

CJ281   William L. Kephart (b 1851) m Deborah Medershett (Hendershot)

CJ282   Phebe Kephart (b 1853) m Harvey Walker

CJ283   Lavine Kephart (b 1854)

CJ284   Hiram Kephart (b 1855) m Charlotte Kephart

CJ285   Mary Ann Kephart (b 1856) m Jacob Walker

CJ286   Samuel Kephart (1857-1928) m Margaret Graham

CJ287   John C. Kephart (b 1860) m Margaret Knyper

CJ288   Daniel Columbus Kephart (6 Apr 1864-20 Oct 1944) m 1888, Ellen Frances Ritchey

CJ289   Jacob Kephart (b 1866) m Phoebe Myers

CJ28A   Andrew Kephart (b 1868) m 1889, Rachael Alexander

CJ28B   Barbara Kephart (b 1870) m 1892, Richard Mathews

CJ28C   Alfred Kephart (1873-ca 1906) m 14 Jun 1894, Madera, Clearfield Co PA, Elveretta
Maines (31 Oct 1875-7 Apr 1954)

CJ28C1 Jonathan Clair Kephart (27 Jul 1896, Bigler Tp, Clearfield Co PA-1 Aug 1952, Philipsburg PA) m 6 Feb 1918, Martha Selina Granville (28 Dec 1894, Bigler Tp, Clearfield Co PA-10 Nov 1963, Philipsburg PA)

CJ28C11 Harold Kephart (stillborn, 2 Sep 1920, Bigler Tp, Clearfield Co PA)

CJ28C12 Betty Rosalie Kephart (24 Dec 1921, Bigler Tp, Clearfield Co PA) m 11 Oct 1937, William Arthur Raab

CJ28C13 Rella Maxine Kephart (7 Dec 1924, Bigler Tp, Clearfield Co PA) m   Henrich

CJ28C14 Shirley LaRue Kephart (19 Nov 1926, Bigler Tp, Clearfield Co PA) m 28 Aug 1948, Philipsburg PA, Harold Eldon Mills

CJ28C15 Elwood Clair Kephart (4 Feb 1928, Bigler Tp, Clearfield Co PA-1975) m 24 Dec 1948, Philipsburg PA, Lucy Jane Adams

CJ28C16 Leonard Eugene Kephart (26 Oct 1930, Bigler Tp, Clearfield Co PA) m 28 Oct 1950, Philipsburg PA, Peggy Anne Blout

CJ28C2 Elva Kephart (dec 1899) m Alfred Foster

CJ28C3 Berton S. Kephart (5 Jan 1902-16 Jun 1984) m Mary Florence Swatsworth

CJ29 George Kephart (ca 1831-d IL) m 1) Nancy Jane Smeal (b Dec 1832); m 2) Mary (Grimsley) Clark

CJ291 Andrew E. Kephart (4 Aug 1851, Clearfield Co PA-3 Jul 1923, Waterloo IA) m 27 Aug 1855, LaPorte City IA-16 Jul 1929)

CJ2911 Jennifer Kephart (20 Aug 1875, Benton IA-31 Jul 1956) m 1893, Wilbert Clinton Wallingford (b 1873)

CJ29111 Pearl Celeta Wallingford (1893, West Liberty IA-25 Dec 1947, Washington Co IA) m 31 Jan 1912, Clinton Grant Morrisey (16 Sep 1891, Stacysville IA-22 Jun 1951, Waterloo IA)

CJ291111 Lawrence K. Morrissey (3 Apr 1913, Mitchell Co IA-27 Jan 1989, Waterloo IA) m 11 Sep 1942, Lorraine Doyle

CJ291112 Elna Esther Morrissey (1914-14 Dec 1991, Cedar Falls IA) m 13 Jan 1933, Laurtis E. Henriksen

CJ291113 Mildred Morrissey (3 Dec 1916, Mitchell Co IA-9 Jan 1917)

CJ291114 Delbert Morrissey (20 Aug 1918-1 Nov 1918)

CJ291115 Virgil Lee Morrissey (17 May 1925-Jul 1972, Las Vegas NV) m Heidi

CJ291116 Merle Dean Morrissey (2 Feb 1927-1 Apr 1980, Bellevue NE) m 5 Apr 1952, Alvira Riccardo Sausedo

CJ29112 Earl Wallingford (b 1895)

CJ29113 Violet Edna Wallingford (b 1896, Riceville IA) m 1 Jul 1916, Peter Robert Winker (b 1894, WI)

CJ29114   Otis Leroy Wallingford (8 Apr 1898, Riceville IA-Jan 1978, Yakima WA) m 16 May 1916, Bertha Pearl Henke (b 1897 WI)

CJ29115   George Wallingford (27 Jan 1902, Riceville IA-Jul 1982)

CJ29116   May Wallingford (1905, Riceville IA) m Frank Panek

CJ29117   Margaret Wallingford (5 Aug 1907, Riceville IA) m William Ernst

CJ2912   Rosetta Kephart (3 Feb 1877-Jun 1953) m 1897, Roy H. Barkolow (b 1 Feb 1877)

CJ29121   Glen Paul Barkolow (b 5 Dec 1900)

CJ29122   Mildred Alice Barkolow (b 4 Apr 1904)

CJ29123   Gladys Marie Barkolow (b 20 Oct 1906)

CJ29124   Eva Mae Barkolow (b 4 Sep 1908)

CJ29125   Leland Roy Barkolow (b 18 Oct 1916)

CJ2913   Pearl C. Kephart (3 Feb 1879-18 Feb 1946) m 18 Feb 1902, George Burkhurst

CJ2914   Nellie C. Kephart (3 Jun 1881-7 Sep 1956) m Jan 1900, Byrd Oscar Slogel

CJ2915   Edward Kephart (1883-29 Jan 1954) m Lulu Stucker

CJ2916   Ernest Kephart (7 Oct 1885-6 Nov 1943, Riceville IA) m 1906, Jennie Ochiltree

CJ2917   William Kephart (28 Dec 1888-17 Feb 1942) m 1) 11 Aug 1912, Ella Stormer (11 Aug 1894m Muscatine IA 11 Dec 1918, Pleasant Prairie IA); m 2) Sarah (Knox) Bradley

CJ29171   Victor Melvin Kephart (b 24 Apr 1913) m 12 Dec 1936, Ruth Erickson

CJ291711   Jerold Wayne Kephart (b 12 Jun 1939) m 15 Aug 1959, Anna Mae McKee

CJ2917111   Cindy Ann Kephart (b 24 Feb 1961)

CJ2918   Raymond Kephart (2 Sep 1890-15 Mar 1959) m Bess

CJ2919   Mable Kephart (5 Oct 1895-Apr 1983) m 22 Apr 1914, Rolland T. Graber

CJ291A   Della Kephart (14 Jul 1898-Mar 1972) m Aug 1921, J.E. Warner

CJ292 Germany)   John Kephart (1853, IL-15 Apr 1912) m 16 Oct 1877, Elizabeth Young (b Dec 1858,

CJ2921   Emma Kephart (b 1877) m 2 Mar 1893, Albert Chase

CJ2922   Cora Kephart (b 1879) m 4 Jun 1899, Roy Simmons

CJ2923   William Kephart (b Aug 1880)

CJ2924   Frank Kephart (b Mar 1885)

CJ2925   Adie Kephart (b Jul 1887)

CJ2926   Fred Kephart (b Jul 1894)

CJ2927   John E. Kephart (b May 1896)

CJ293   Douglas James Kephart (27 Nov 1860, Freeport IL-26 Dec 1939, Riceville IA) m 19 Jun 1878, Independence IA, Elizabeth Lane (1 Apr 1861, Black Hawk Co IA-7 May 1953, Mason City IA). Bur Riceville IA.

CJ2931   Floyd William Kephart (13 Jan 1895, Vinton IA-3 Apr 1967, Mankato MN) m 22 May 1918, Mitchell Co IA, Stella Louise Morris

CJ29311   Violet Lucille Kephart (7 Mar 1921, Morrow IA) m 27 Sep 1944, Joseph Michael Bauer

CJ2932   Rose Jane Kephart (18 Feb 1881-12 May 1972) m Oscar Barkhurst

CJ2933   Grace B. Kephart (b 8 Sep 1883) m Charles Norris

CJ2934   Albert J. Kephart (b 18 Apr 1886)

CJ2935   Minnie E. Kephart (9 Oct 1890-23 Jan 1975) m Frank Comstock

CJ294   Emaline Kephart (b 1862) m 24 Sep 1877, Anson Miller

CJ295   Pernina "Minnie" Kephart (1864, IL-1894, Adair IA) m 1) 4 Mar 1882, I.G. Joseph Langer; m 2) 4 Sep 1889, Buchanan Co IA, Christopher H. "Carl" Garver (Feb 1852, Lancaster Co PA-20 Jun 1928, Salem OR)

CJ2951   Leslie H. "Rex" Garver (b Nov 1890, Adair IA)

CJ2952   Lela B. Garver (Mar 1893, Adair IA-1968, Miami FL) m Howard

CJ2953   Olive Grace Manetta Garver (1 Sep 1894, Adair IA-12 Oct 1966, OK) m 1 May 1915, Villisca IA, Cecil Stanley Gill

CJ296   Charles Kephart (Apr 1865, IL-3 Aug 1902) m 1 Dec 1891, IA, Stella M. Long (b Dec 1875)

CJ2961   Gilbert Kephart (b. Oct 1893, IA)

CJ2962   Preston Kephart (b Sep 1895, IA)

CJ2963   Myrtle Kephart (b Jul 1897, IA)

CJ297   Caroline Kephart (b 1868, IL)

CJ298   George H. Kephart (b 1878)

CJ299   May Belle Kephart (b Feb 1880) m 1) 6 May 1895, James B. Dingsley; m 2) 24 Dec 1906, Walter Koenig

CJ29A   Minnie Kephart (b 27 Mar 1883)

CJ2A   Lavina Kephart (ca 1835-ca 1865/1870) m ca 1855, David J. Kephart (16 May 1835, Newcastle PA-3 Feb 1912, Sedro Wooley WA). Bur Sedro Wooley WA.

CJ2A1   Foster Alexander Kephart (29 Jan 1857, Clearfield Co PA-2 May 1930, Everett WA) 1884,

Clearfield Co PA, Addie Lorissa Kephart (16 Dec 1867, Clearfield Co PA-11 Jan 1956). Bur Everett WA.

CJ2A11   Infant Kephart (22 Oct 1885-22 Oct 1885)

CJ2A12   Susan Harriett Kephart (Dec 1887-30 Mar 1904, Gibbon NE)

CJ2A13   Evron N. Kephart (9 May 1889-1 Jul 1893)

CJ2A14   Cordelia Kephart (5 Jul 1891-5 Jul 1893)

CJ2A15   Percy O. Kephart (17 May 1894-May 1894)

CJ2A16   Burton C. Kephart (14 Apr 1896-21 Apr 1979, Chelan WA) m Leona Lane (b 26 Feb 1899)

CJ2A161   Kenneth Kephart (b 22 Apr 1916)(adopted by Norris) m 10 May 1943, Vella Meints

CJ2A162   Gilbert Kephart (b 11 Jan 1918)(adopted by Norris)

CJ2A17   Infant Kephart (18 Jun 1898-18 Jun 1898)

CJ2A18   Millard Filmore Kephart (18 May 1899, Clearfield Co PA-2 Sep 1958, Everett WA) m 24 Mar 1920, Monica Scott (b 24 Mar 1900, Denver CO). WWI; USA. Bus driver.

CJ2A181   Jean Kephart (b 25 May 1921, Everett WA) m 24 Mar 1941, Everett WA, Allen Moomey

CJ2A182   Audrey Kephart (b 20 Oct 1923, Everett WA) m 20 Feb 1943, Seattle WA, Ralph Dearing

CJ2A183   Joy Kephart (b 27 Apr 1934, Everett WA) m 3 Sep 1955, Tacoma WA, Gwinn Dunham

CJ2A19   Louella Kephart (26 Sep 1902, Grand Junction CO-12 Jul 1969, Arlington WA) m 25 Dec 1919, Snohomish WA, William Glandon (11 Nov 1899, Mt. Pleasant IA-28 Jul 1962, Arlington WA)

CJ2A191   Bertha Glandon (b 10 Nov 1922, Coos Bay OR) m 13 Mar 1948, Everett WA, Waid A. Myers

CJ2A192   Hazel Glandon (b 28 Oct 1924, Snohomish WA) m 1 Jan 1948, Merle Lee

CJ2A193   Irene Glandon (b 7 Aug 1930, Everett WA) m 10 Aug 1951, Arlington WA, George W. Rhods

CJ2A194   Velma Glandon (b 26 Apr 1932, Monroe WA) m Robert Krebs

CJ2A195   Wilma Glandon (b 26 Apr 1932, Monroe WA-11 Aug 1978)

CJ2A196   William Glandon (b 4 Jun 1939, Marysville WA) m 22 Jun 1961, Arlington WA

CJ2A197   Dale Glandon (b 22 Nov 1941, Everett WA)

CJ2A198   Joe Glandon (b 16 Apr 1943, Everett WA)

CJ2A1A   Alma Mae Kephart (28 Jan 1906-Jan 1906)

CJ2A1B   Rozella Kephart (30 Jun 1907, Grand Junction CO-7 Feb 1974, Everett WA) m Walter Jones

CJ2A1B1   Howard Jones

CJ2A1B2   Dewane Jones

CJ2A1C   Oskar "Howard" William Kephart (8 Jul 1910-1946) m Grace Cain

CJ2A1C1   George Foster Kephart (b 28 Oct 1927) m 30 Mar 1975, Shirley Shannon

CJ2A1C2   Harold Eugene Kephart (b 5 Apr 1930) m 15 Oct 1947, Zoe Mueller

CJ2A1C3   Doris Lorraine Kephart (b 26 Aug 1932) m 1 Dec 1950, Jack Chedgey

CJ2A1C4   Richard Barton Kephart (b 14 Dec 1934) m 6 Sep 1957, Joyce Steward

CJ2A1C5   Dorothy Mae Kephart (b 20 May 1936) m 15 Jan 1954, Marcus Anderberg

CJ2A2   Albert Kephart (b 1859, Clearfield Co PA). Lost.

CJ2A3   Alonzo Willard Kephart (10 Jun 1861, Clearfield Co PA-12 Nov 1944, Hayward CA) m
1) 1 Apr 1884, Monroe WI, Sarah Elizabeth Breon (20 Sep 1861, Shueyville WI-13 Jun 1929, Modesto CA);
m 2) Bernice Hammond (b 1900, Grand Junction CO)

CJ2A31   Mary Alta Kephart (18 Aug 1885, Winslow IL-11 Jan 1975, Klamath Falls WI) m 22 Jun
1910, Stockton CA, Jessa Cleveland Rightmier (25 Sep 1885, Merced CA-13 Feb 1955, Salem OR)

CJ2A311   William Rightmier (b 20 Aug 1913, Ray WA) m 28 Nov 1933, Audrey Robertson

CJ2A312   Virgil Alonzo Rightmier (b 21 Nov 1915, OR-5 Mar 1934, Modesto CA)

CJ2A313   Ray Allen Rightmier (b 30 Jan 1918, Orcutt CA) m 24 Jun 1944, Helen Crickton

CJ2A314   Marilyn Rightmier (b 10 Aug 1922, Turlock CA) m 18 Jun 1942, Paul Breithaupt

CJ2A32   Elmer Thomas Kephart (20 Aug 1887, Gibbon NE-6 Aug 1959, Modesto CA) m 20 Apr
1908, Stockton CA, Ida Ann Rightmier (5 Nov 1889, Julian CA-22 Jun 1982, Modesto CA)

CJ2A321   Clarence Kephart (b 20 Nov 1908, Modesto CA) m 3 Jul 1934, San Jose CA, Frances
Lorenzen (b 27 Jun 1911, San Juan Bautista CA)

CJ2A3211   Shirley Kephart (b 6 May 1938, Modesto CA) m 18 Dec 1960, Fred Bernadotti

CJ2A3212   Charlene Kephart (b 9 Oct 1940, Modesto CA) m 9 Mar 1963, James Hankal

CJ2A3213   Carol Kephart (b 26 Mar 1944, Modesto CA) m 31 Oct 1965, Larry Hager

CJ2A322   Lucille Viola Kephart (b 7 Jun 1918, Watsonville CA) m 18 Nov 1945, Modesto CA,
Albert Pester (20 May 12919, Oakland CA-4 Jul 1968, Sacramento CA)

CJ2A3221   Albert Edward Pester (11 Sep 1946, Sacramento CA) m 18 Sep 1965, Caroline Carfoll

CJ2A3222   Donald Elmer Pester (b 25 Feb 1948, Sacramento CA)

CJ2A3223   William Stanley Pester (b 8 Aug 1951, Sacramento CA)

CJ2A33   Oliver David Kephart (b 5 Nov 1889, Gibbon NE-16 Mar 1953, San Francisco CA) m 4

Jul 1909, Modesto CA, Helen Hammond (23 Jun 1881, Eagle Co NE-19 Oct 1969, IL)

CJ2A331 Ralph Kephart (b 19 Dec 1910, Modesto CA-12 Apr 1983, Erie ND) m 10 Jul 1937, Gladys Schroeder

CJ2A332 Francis Kephart (b 29 Mar 1912, Marshfield OR) m 1 Mar 1939, Ila Barbara Shanteau

CJ2A333 Marjorie Kephart (b 18 Nov 1915, Marshfield OR-10 May 1992, St. Jacob IL) m Raymond Bovinett

CJ2A34 Bertha Emma Kephart (b 1 Oct 1891, Tacoma WA-28 Mar 1985, San Jose CA) m 22 Feb 1913, Modesto CA, Lorenz Walter Ocken (9 Nov 1890, Cheyenne Wells CO-6 Apr 1983, San Jose CA)

CJ2A341 Merle Walter Ocken (b 6 Oct 1913, Dos Palos CA) m 2 Apr 1938, Josie Twedt

CJ2A342 Irene Eleanor Ocken (b 12 Sep 1915, Keyes CA) m 2 Jul 1935, Albert Johnson

CJ2A35 Ray Charles Kephart (12 Apr 1893, Tacoma WA 25 May 1969, Modesto CA) m 25 Nov 1920, San Jose CA, Genevieve Mae Fysh (19 Aug 1898, Lakeview OR-17 Apr 1993, Modesto CA). WWI; USAF; dairy farmer.

*CJ2A351 Leola Arlene Kephart (b 12 Sep 1923, Ft. Bragg CA) m 11 Aug 1946, San Jose CA, Eugene Alfred Nelson (23 Jan 1927, Clitherall MN)

CJ2A3511 Cheryl Lynn Nelson (b 2 May 1950, San Jose CA) m 2 Sep 1972, Modesto CA, Peter Lee Moore (b 5 Jul 1950, San Jose CA)

CJ62A35111 Jennifer Lynn Moore (b 16 Sep 1975, Modesto CA)

CJ2A35112 Jacinda Moore (b 16 Feb 1981, Modesto CA)

CJ2A3512 Janine Rae Nelson (b 19 Jun 1962, San Jose CA) m 24 Mar 1984, Modesto CA, Jerry Goubert (b 6 Apr 1961)

CJ2A35121 Julie Breon Goubert (b 13 Mar 1986, Modesto CA)

CJ2A35122 Justin Eugene Goubert (b 10 Apr 1988, Modesto CA)

CJ2A35123 Jillian Elisa Goubert (b 12 Jun 1990, Modesto CA)

CJ2A35124 Jordan Ernest Goubert (b 28 Sep 1994, Modesto CA)

CJ2A352 Richard Earl Kephart (b 2 May 1928, Modesto CA) m 20 Jul 1957, Kalamazoo MI, Mari Lugar (b 7 Apr 1935)

CJ2A3521 Susan Elaine Kephart (b 25 Jun 1958, Modesto CA) m 1) Jun 1977, Jim Arnold; m 2) 9 Oct 1982, Modesto CA, Kevin Conyers Finnerty (b 5 Apr 1957, Los Angeles CA)

CJ2A35211 Ryan Congers Finnerty (b 2 May 1987,Modesto CA)

CJ2A35212 Sara Brianne Finnerty (b 21 Apr 1990, Modesto CA)

CJ2A3522 Steven Kephart (b 11 Nov 1960, Modesto CA) m 28 Dec 1984, Reno NV, Kay Daly. No chn.

CJ2A3523 Tami Kephart (b 17 Jul 1963, Pascoe WA)

CJ2A3524   Alana Kephart (b 21 Mar 1965, Pascoe WA) m 2 Aug 1990, Las Vegas NV, Blaine Green

CJ2A35241   Cherise Megan Green (b 15 May 1991)

CJ2A35242   Miranda Arlene Green (b 17 Nov 1993, Modesto CA)

CJ2A35243   Serena Marie Green (b 2 Apr 1995)

CJ2A353   Delmar Charles Kephart (b 4 Sep 1934, Modesto CA) m 14 Feb 1972, Reno NV, Gladys
Nelson

CJ2A36   Vida May Kephart (12 Aug 1895, Gibbon NE-25 May 1969, San Jose CA) m 2 Sep 1915,
Forrest George Davis (20 May 1893, OR-30 Jul 1949, San Jose CA)

CJ2A361   Dean Presnell Davis (b 3 Sep 1927, San Diego CA) m 21 Jun 1958, Hillsborough CA,
Betty Ann Ahrens

CJ2A37   Milton Farrel Kephart (29 Mar 1897, Gibbon NE-3 Aug 1977, Salem OR) m 1) 12 Mar
1944, Clark Co WA, Alta Lois Martin (d 4 Jan 1990, Salem OR); m 2) Marian Taylor (1901-26 Nov 1991)

CJ2A38   Guy Franklin Kephart (18 Jul 1899, Gibbon NE-24 Nov 1971, Santa Rosa CA) m 5 Feb
1929, Reno NV, Dorothy Marie Johnson (24 Jul 1909, San Francisco CA). Chicken rancher.

CJ2A381   Delores Kephart (b 4 Apr 1930, Orland CA) m 16 Aug 1953, Joseph McGimley

CJ2A382   Rosalie Kephart (b 5 Feb 1934, Sacramento CA) m 23 Oct 1950, Anthony Morgan

CJ2A383   Neil Franklin Kephart (b 12 Dec 1938, Sacramento CA) m 19 Sep 1965, Kathleen Lampert

CJ2A384   Sharon Lee Kephart (b 17 May 1945, Auburn CA) m Jun 1968, Robert Wilson

CJ2A39   Viola Amy Kephart (20 Apr 1902, Grand Junction CO-29 Mar 1988, San Jose CA) m 16
Jun 1923, Orland CA, Orville John Colgan (11 Mar 1902, Salem OR-15 Sep 1954). Bur San Jose CA.

CJ2A391   Maxine Colgan (b 16 Nov 1925, Salem OR) m 1) Kenneth Jensen; m 2) Bill Kelly

CJ2A392   Jack Eugene Colgan (b 15 May 1930, Modesto CA) m 2 Sep 1956, Sonia Shafto

CJ2A3A   Helen Lucille Kephart (12 Apr 1905, Modesto CA-18 Nov 1987, San Jose CA) m 1) 23
Jun 1924, William Hartford Kirkpatrick; m 2) 19 Oct 1941, Wynia Garrett (12 Aug 1910, Yakima WA-22 Dec
1980, San Jose CA)

CJ2A3A1   Jeanne Eileen Kirkpatrick (b 17 Dec 1926) m 9 Jun 1946, Dale Dikkers

CJ2A3A2   Janice Margie Kirkpatrick (b 30 Jan 1929) m 18 Aug 1951, Richard Jacobs

CJ2A3A3   Gary Wayne Wynia (b 6 Jun 1943) m Ann Jobe

CJ2A3B   Woodrow Franklin Kephart (b 13 Jan 1931, Hayward CA) m 1) Dorothy Eldridge (d
1956); m 2) 4 Jun 1957, Reno NV, Kathleen Y. James

CJ2A3B1   Girl adopted by Eldridge family

CJ2A3B2   Girl adopted by Eldridge family

CJ2A3B3   Karin Lexine Kephart (b 25 Nov 1958, Seattle WA) m 16 Nov 1982, Reno NV, Dennis Allen Barth

CJ2A3B4   Franklin Scott Kephart (b 23 Sep 1960, Seattle WA)

CJ2A3B5   Stacey Leigh Kephart (b 16 Feb 1962, Seattle WA) m 31 Dec 1983, San Diego CA, Michael Patrick Shannon

CJ2A3C   Violet Kephart (b 17 May 1935, Hayward CA) m 5 Aug 1956, San Jose CA, Norman Eighmy (b 5 Mar 1921, Springbrook WI)

CJ2A3C1   Norman Eighmy (b 16 Oct 1957, Modesto CA) m 16 May 1981, Kellie Morgan

CJ2A3C2   Linda Eighmy (b 18 Mar 1959, Modesto CA) m 6 May 1978, Modesto CA, Dennis Anderson

CJ2A3C3   Annette Eighmy (b 3 Mar 1965, Modesto CA)

CJ2A4   Cordelia Kephart (3 Apr 1862, Clearfield PA-20 Dec 1893, Boggs Tp, Clearfield Co PA) m 29 Jun 1880, Clearfield PA, George Latimer Barger (19 Jan 1857-1942)

CJ2A41   Harvey William Barger (4 Jun 1881-14 Dec 1893)

CJ2A42   Ada Barger (12 Apr 1884-7 Oct 1904) m 13 Oct 1902, Franklin Shedrick Kephart (28 Sep 1873-23 Sep 1961)

CJ2A421   Sidna Kephart (b Sep 1904) m Fred Eckley

CJ2A43   Charles Barger m 1) 1909, Margaret Anderson (d 8 Dec 1919); m 2) 1921, Marie Fisher

CJ2A44   Guy Barger (1 Aug 1890-30 Jan 1930) m 2 Jun 1903, Sarah Keller

CJ2A45   David Foster Barger (2 Jul 1891-4 Jan 1894)

CJ2A46   George Barger (b 5 Apr 1893)

CJ2B   Pernina Kephart (b ca 1839) m Amasa Wilkes

CJ2B1   Susanna Wilkes (b 1859)

CJ2B2   John Wilkes (b 1861)

CJ2B3   Mary Wilkes (b 1863)

CJ2B4   William Wilkes (b 1865)

CJ2B5   Amasa Wilkes (b 1868)

CJ2B6   Clara Wilkes (b 1871)

CJ2B7   Sudie Wilkes (b 1873)

CJ2B8   Etta Wilkes (b 1877)

CJ2C   Susannah Kephart (b ca 1841) m John Coder (1827-1918)

CJ2C1   Amasa Coder (b 1860)

CJ2C2   William A. Coder (b 1861)

CJ2C3   Mary Catherine Coder (1864-1951) m Martin Hoover Bloom

CJ2C4   Julia Coder (1868-1881)

CJ2C5   Jane Coder (b 1872)

CJ2C6   Sudie Coder (b 1877) m Bert Smith

CJ2C7   Effie Coder (b 1880)

CJ2C8   Myrtle Coder (b 1883)

CJ2C9   Bessie Coder (b 1885) m Pete Johnson

CJ3   Susanna Weiser (1796-12 Jul 1852, Bigler PA) m 1819, Samuel Henry Turner (ca 1770 Centre Co PA-1833, Mahoning Tp, Mercer Co PA). Bur Bigler PA. Miller, Boggs Tp and Bradford Tp, Clearfield Co PA.

CJ31   Adeline Turner (1 Jan 1820, Philipsburg PA-7 Dec 1887, Clearfield PA) m John Phillips (16 Jan 1811-4 Apr 1863, Clearfield PA)

CJ311   Susanna Phillips (29 Dec 1839-29 Nov 1892) m Samuel Snyder Kephart

CJ312   Shaderick Phillips (22 Feb 1840-20 Aug 1863). Unm.

CJ313   Meshuk Phillips (22 Feb 1842-18 Nov 1862). Unm.

CJ314   Obednigo Phillips (7 Dec 1844-25 Nov 1878)

CJ315   Sarah Catharine Phillips (19 Mar 1847-12 Jul 1894)

CJ316   Eliza Jane Phillips (29 Apr 1849-31 Oct 1891)

CJ317   Emma Marie Phillips (14 Mar 1851-11 Feb 1906)

CJ318   Mary Phillips (11 Oct 1855-12 Jun 1870)

CJ319   Levi Phillips (28 Dec 1857-23 May 1917)

CJ32   John Worth Turner (23 Mar 1822, Philipsburg PA-23 Aug 1893, Graham Tp, Clearfield Co PA) m 3 Jul 1842, Martha Dixon (1824-1875)

CJ321   E.B. Turner

CJ322   Margaret Turner m Martin Taylor

CJ323   Elias Kay Turner (12 Feb 1852, Graham Tp, Clearfield Co PA-24 Sep 1938, Graham Tp, Clearfield Co PA) m 24 Aug 1876, Jane Graham (30 Apr 1854, Bradford Tp, Clearfield Co PA-20 Apr 1930)

CJ3231   J. W. Turner

CJ3232   Effie Turner m Frederick Fuge

CJ3233   Carrie Viola Turner (23 Nov 1881, Graham Tp, Clearfield Co PA-9 Oct 1983, Clearfield PA) m 28 Jul 1898, Alfred Clark Hummel (15 May 1880, Graham Tp, Clearfield Co PA-31 Dec 1957, Graham Tp, Clearfield Co PA)

CJ32331   Ethel Verda Hummel (30 Oct 1900, Graham Tp, Clearfield Co PA-26 Oct 1975, Decatur Tp, Clearfield Co PA) m 24 Dec 1917, Bruce Dare Bock (12 Jan 1898, Boggs Tp, Clearfield Co PA-5 Nov 1975, Altoona PA)

CJ323311   Melvin Bock (19 Sep 1920, Wallaceton PA). Unm.

CJ3234   Ella Turner m Orvis Hubler

CJ3235   Gwen Turner

CJ3236   Anna Turner (1893-1970) m John Hubler (1888-1959)

CJ32361   Jean Hubler (b 15 Jun 1915) m Clarence Carr

CJ3237   Mabel Turner

CJ3238   William Turner

CJ3239   Ernest Turner

CJ323A   Lynn Turner

CJ323B   Wendell Turner

CJ324   Ann Elizabeth Turner (28 Mar 1825, Bradford Tp, Clearfield Co PA-6 Jan 1915, Clearfield Co PA) m Daniel Phillips

CJ325   David Joshua Turner (13 Mar 1828, Bradford Tp, Clearfield Co PA-1889, Wallaceton PA) m 1) Catherine Martha Cowfer (ca 1830-ca 1863); m 2) Mrs. Mary Bressler

CJ3251   Nancy Turner (b 30 Jan 1848) m 29 Apr 1880, John Hoffman

CJ3252   Samuel E. Turner (22 Dec 1850-12 Feb 1915, Woodward Tp, Clearfield Co PA) m Ann Margareet Kephart (b 29 Jan 1853). Bur Woodward Tp, Clearfield Co PA.

CJ32521   Clara M. Turner (10 Aug 1871-25 Jan 1894)

CJ32522   Nora Belle Turner (b 1878) m 1898, Richard Lloyd

CJ32523   William John Turner (17 Jun 1883-18 Mar 1963, Coalport PA) m 29 Sep 1904, Annie Bennett

CJ32524   Annie Crissie Turner (13 Nov 1886-23 Jul 1892, Punxatawney PA) m Thomas Trombull

CJ32525   Cleveland G. Turner (8 Feb 1889-15 Aug 1897)

CJ32526   Ruth Iva Turner (b 1892) m 1916, NJ, Amos Groom

CJ32527   Carrie Mae Turner (b 1896) m 1916, Guy Muthersbaugh

CJ3253   James Turner (1852-1911, Jefferson Co PA) m 1) Mary   ; m 2) Alice Knuppenberg

CJ3254   Matilda Elizabeth Turner (23 Jun 1853, Clearfield PA-10 Jun 1892, Dillwyn KS) m 25 Mar 1868, Clearfield Co PA, Henry Speaker Kephart (3 Aug 1846, Pittsburgh PA-9 Apr 1916, Dillwyn KS). Bur Dillwyn

CJ32541   Mary Ann Kephart (24 Jan 1870, Cedar Rapids IA-5 Jun 1956) m 25 Dec 1889, John Long

CJ32542   William David Kephart (20 Dec 1871-d.y.). Bur Dillwyn KS.

CJ32543   Rachel Susan Kephart (16 Apr 1874, Scandia KS-14 Feb 1945) m 7 Aug 1895, Thomas
Ed Baker

CJ32544   Joseph Albert Kephart (5 Jun 1876, Scandia KS-14 Apr 1928) m 1905, Amanda Elizabeth
Dimmitt

CJ32545   Nancy May Kephart (14 Sep 1878, Scandia KS-25 Mar 1952) m 10 Aug 1895, William
Williams

CJ32546   Florence Katherine Kephart (12 Oct 1880, Scandia KS-16 Apr 1930) m William Lamb

CJ32547   George Washington Kephart (16 Jun 1883, Scandia KS-21 Nov 1940) m 3 Mar 1903,
Maude Clouse

CJ32548   Henry Hunter Kephart (14 Jul 1889, Dillwyn KS-19 Dec 1941) m Delilah Jane Rowe

CJ2255   David Turner (1856-1887) m 8 May 1876, Lucinda Knuppenberg

CJ3256   John Turner (17 Apr 1860-17 Jan 1937, Falls Creek, Jefferson Co PA) m Emma Catherine
Kephart

CJ3257   William K. Turner (2 Aug 1862-30 Aug 1929, Philadelphia PA) m 29 Jul 1884, Houtsdale PA, Viola Catherine Kephart (22 Jul 1865, Osceola Mills PA-24 Mar 1952, Philadelphia PA). Bur Grampian PA

CJ32571   Ai Turner (9 Aug 1883, Clearfield Co PA-Dec 1957, Noewport OR) m 26 Feb 1902, Lumber City PA, Vida Tereasa Mahaffey (21 Feb 1885, Clearfield Co PA-ca 1947, Toledo OR). Bur Newport OR.

CJ325711   Viola Edith Turner (b 13 Feb 1904, PeEll OR) m 1) Albert Hazelton; m 2) Kenneth
Gossett

CJ325712   Raymond Turner (Apr 1906-1935, Newport OR)

CJ325713   Silvia Turner (16 Dec PeEll OR) m 21 Oct 1928, Portland OR, George Schmidt/Smith

CJ325714   Chester Turner (12 Feb 1909, Corvallis OR-31 Jan 1964, Newport OR) m 1) Mona Moss Martin; m 2) Millicent Broadwell; m 3) Doris   ; m 4) Esther

CJ325715   Eva May Turner (10 Oct 1910, Corvallis OR-8 Nov 1970, North Bend OR) m Robert Mitts

CJ325716   Esther Bernice Turner (13 Mar 1914, Corvallis OR016 Nov 1933) m Samuel Henry

CJ325717   Williard Turner (b 8 Apr 1915, Corvallis OR) m 15 Apr 1936, Toledo OR, Lavine Mary
Beers

CJ325718   Milton Lloyd Turner (b Oct 1924, Toledo OR) m Marchita

CJ32572   Martha Turner (b Jan 1885)

CJ32573   Thomas Turner (22 Nov 1886, Clearfield Co PA-28 Dec 1951) m 9 Nov 1912, Evie
Bonsall

CJ32574   William K. Turner, Jr. (11 Aug 1888, Sanborn PA-13 Jul 1944, Grampian PA) m 1915,
Nadine Rowles

CJ32575   David J. Turner (26 Mar 1892, Sanborn PA-Jun 1957, Whitewash PA) m 16 Apr 1913,
Martha Elizabeth Shimp

CJ32576   Andrew Turner (b 8 Apr 1894, Clearfield PA) m Celia

CJ32577   Cora L. Turner (b 12 Jul 1896, Clearfield PA) m Bert Philips

CJ32578   Viola May Turner (b Sep 1899, Clearfield PA) m Richard Michelson

CJ32579   Albert Turner m Lillian

CJ3257A   James E. Turner (14 Jan 1901, Curwinsville PA-3 Dec 1979, Warren OH) m 13 Oct 1919,
Vada Stevens

CJ3257B   Agnes Turner m   Duganitz

CJ4   Sarah Weiser (24 Jun 1796-9 Jul 1869) m Henry Shimmel (10 Apr 1792-13 Dec 1870).
Bur Bigler PA.

CJ41   Maria Shimmel (2 Aug 1819-13 Dec 1870) m 20 Aug 1868, Jacob Darger

CJ42   Catharine Shimmel (22 Aug 1821-1880) m 1836, Abraham Hummel

CJ421   Lydia Hummel (1840-1909) m David Smeal

CJ422   Henry Hummel (1841-1892) m Hannah Lowe

CJ423   George W. Hummel (1847-1923) m Mary A. Baker

CJ424   Matilda Hummel (1848-1928) m Thomas Fuge

CJ425   James A. Hummel (b 1850) m 1) Priscilla Emiegh; m 2) Jane Walker

CJ426   Mary Ann Hummel (1852-1932) m 1) Frank Conklin; m 2) Robert Sykes

CJ4261   Minnie Conklin

CJ427   John F. Hummel (1857-1946) m Charlotte Smeal

CJ428   Catherine Hummel (1859-1934) m Isaac Smeal

CJ429   Anna J. Hummel (1862-1944) m James Beatie

CJ43   Sarah Shimmel (3 Jan 1825-1882) m 20 Feb 1848, James Dickson (1825-1875).
Blacksmith.

CJ431   Joel Dickson (1848-1915) m Martha Lines

CJ432   Mary Dorcas Dickson (1850-1912)

CJ433   William Dickson (1851-1912) m Ellen Graham

CJ434   Emily Dickson (b 1854) m 1) Lindsey Wisor; m 2) Berton Merritt

CJ435   Anna Martha Dickson (1855-1920) m Jeremiah Graffius

CJ436   Jerome Dickson (b 1856) m June Dimeling

CJ437   John Dickson (1858-1914) m Cynthia Miller

CJ438   Sarah Dickson (1859-1932) m Joseph Peters

CJ439   Nancy Dickson (1861-1939) m Amos Graham

CJ43A   Susan Dickson (1862-1874)

CJ43B   Martha Dickson (1865-1906) m Lewis Lamadue

CJ43C   Minnie Dickson (1866-1945) m John Thompson

CJ44   George W. Shimmel (30 Apr 1827-10 Mar 1897) m 1) 1 Aug 1852, Mary Jane Bush, div;
m 2) 1874, Fannie Peters. Farmer and lumberman.

CJ441   Sarah E. Shimmel (b 1853) m Thomas Kyler

CJ442   Henry M. Shimmel (b 20 Sep 1854) m Clara Botts (1862-1937)

CJ4421   Nile Shimmel (1882-1962) m May Williams

CJ44211   Albert Shimmel

CJ44212   Robert Shimmel

CJ44213   Gerald Shimmel

CJ44214   Melvin Shimmel

CJ44215   Nile Shimmel m Phyllis Stone

CJ4422   Mae Shimmel (1884-1950) m John Rothrock (1887-1955)

CJ44221   Cledes Rothrock (b 1910)

CJ44222   Zola Rothrock (b 1912) m 1) Paul Wisor; m 2) Edward Graffins; m 3) Ernest Mitchell

CJ44223   Wesley Rothrock (b 1915) m Jane Shimmel

CJ44224   Marvin Rothrock (b 1918) m Florence Middleton

CJ44225   Marcine Rothrock (b 1923) m   Short

CJ44226   Elwood Rothrock (1929-1968) m Anna Droll

CJ4423   Roxanna Shimmel (b 1889) m Joseph Fleck

CJ44231	Raymond Fleck m Alberta Bodle
CJ44232	Donald Fleck
CJ44233	Weldon Fleck
CJ44234	Duane Fleck
CJ44235	Esther Fleck
CJ44236	Charles Fleck m Smeal
CJ4424	Rosa Nellie Shimmel (1891-1913)
CJ4425	Thomas Shimmel (1895-1945) m Margaret Emeigh
CJ44251	Norman Shimmel (1915-1978) m Bernice Cowder
CJ442511	Thomas Shimmel
CJ442512	Glenn Shimmel
CJ44252	Nellie Shimmel (b 1918) m Chester Graham
CJ44253	Marion Shimmel (1926-1983) m Samuel Dixon
CJ4426	Hannah Shimmel (1897-1986) m Willard Goss
CJ44261	Louise Goss m Byers
CJ44262	Dorothy Goss m William Jordan
CJ44263	Eldon Goss m Barbara Good
CJ44264	Cleo Goss m Harry Fleck
CJ44265	Erla Goss m Robert Jordan
CJ4427	Morris Shimmel (1900-1964) m Iola May Knepp
CJ44271	Helen Shimmel m Hipps
CJ44272	Phyllis Shimmel
CJ44273	Gail Shimmel m Kenneth Shimmel
CJ44274	Diane Shimmel
CJ44275	Irene Shimmel m Conaway
CJ44276	Morris Shimmel
CJ44277	Darwin Shimmel
CJ44278	Raymond Shimmel

CJ44279   Donald Shimmel

CJ4427A   Elda Shimmel

CJ4427B   Lois Shimmel

CJ4427C   William Shimmel

CJ4428   Cecil Shimmel (1903-1976) m Imelda Milligan

CJ44281   Nesta Shimmel m Wallace Kephart

CJ443   Laura A. Shimmel (b 1856) m Ed Lamadue

CJ45   Nancy Shimmel (22 Aug 1828-12 Jul 1904). Unm. Bur Bigler PA.

CJ46   Matilda Shimmel (12 Oct 1832-19 Feb 1906). Unm. Bur Bigler PA.

CJ47   Mary Ann Shimmel (6 Jun 1836-3 Feb 1913) m William D. Moyer

CJ48   Henry Ellis Shimmel (28 Feb 1838-3 Feb 1913) m Margaret Elizabeth Hummel (1843-1924). Bur Bigler PA. Farmer, Boggs Tp, Clearfield Co PA.

CJ481   John Henry Shimmel (b 1868) m Ada Wople. Bur near Wallaceton PA.

CJ4811   Ralph Shimmel m Zana Hummel

CJ4812   Vivian Shimmel

CJ4813   Ethel Shimmel m 1) Lloyd Hummel; m 2) Ezekial Buck

CJ4814   Kenneth Shimmel

CJ482   George McClellan Shimmel (1874-1944) m Tillie Smeal

CJ4821   Mary Shimmel

CJ4822   Hazel Shimmel m Earl Clark

CJ4823   Jack Shimmel

CJ4824   George Shimmel

CJ4825   Edith Shimmel m   Fernandez

CJ4826   Dorothy Shimmel m   Cambria

CJ4827   Pauline Shimmel

CJ4828   Miles Shimmel

CJ4829   Paul Shimmel (1919-1980)

CJ482A   James Shimmel

CJ482B   Irene Shimmel

CJ5   John Wiser (1800-1848) m Elizabeth Derrick (ca 1805-1865)

CJ51   Catherine Wiser (1824-1887) m John Rowles

CJ511   Jane Rowles (b 1846)

CJ512   John Rowles (b 1848)

CJ513   Elizabeth Rowles (b 1851)

CJ514   Sarah Rowles (b 1853)

CJ515   Susanna Rowles (b 1855)

CJ516   Ann Rowles (b 1857)

CJ517   Adeline Rowles (b 1861)

CJ518   Tina Rowles (b 1864)

CJ519   Andrew Rowles (b 1869)

CJ52   George Wiser (14 Jun 1825-18 Feb 1887) m Mary Derrick (7 Jul 1830-7 Dec 1907). Bur
near Woodland PA.

CJ521   Enoch Wisor (Nov 1849-1912) m 29 Aug 1871, Clearfield PA, Jane Louder (1850-1913)

CJ5211   George W. Wisor (1872-1951) m Adeline Ruth Lamadue (b 1875)

CJ52111   Bertha Wiser (b Jan 1896)

CJ52112   Alta B. Wiser (b Apr 1898)

CJ52113   Olive Wiser (b ca 1904)

CJ52114   Josephine Wiser (b ca 1909)

CJ52115   Dorcas Wiser (b ca 1913)

CJ5212   Frederick R. Wisor (1875-1950) m S. Melissa Druggs (1882-1954)

CJ52121   Nancy Wisor (b ca 1901)

CJ52122   Lloyd Alfred Wisor (1903-1932)

CJ52123   Bessie Wisor (b ca 1907)

CJ52124   Irene Wisor (1909-1985) m Buford I. Smith (1908-1991)

CJ52125   Homer L. Wisor (1912-1986) m 31 Dec 1976, Adoree J.
(b 1937)

CJ52126   Clive E. Wisor (b 5 Oct 1914) m Catherine   (4 Nov 1917-17 Feb 1992)

CJ521261   Reuben E. Wisor Ib 30 Nov 1946)

CJ52127   Merrill E. Wisor (1917-1971) m Bernice L.   (1922-1996)

CJ52128   Nellie Mae Wisor (1922-1936)

CJ5213   Maude Wisor (Feb 1880-1960)) m Blair Adams

CJ5214   Allen M. Wisor (26 Feb 1882-28 Aug 1942) m 1) Retta A. Hitchings (b ca 1887); m 2)
Alfaretta Mitchell (4 Jan 1887-6 Aug 1955)

CJ5215   John "Jake" Wisor (1885-1918) m ca 1906, Sarah Shovestall

CJ52151   Miles Wiser (b ca 1906)

CJ52152   Pearl Wiser (b ca 1907)

CJ52153   Elsie Wiser (b ca 1908)

CJ5216   Blanche Wisor (Dec 1886-1938) m David E. Lansberry

CJ52161   Earl Lansberry (b ca 1903)

CJ52162   Raymond Lansberry (b ca 1905)

CJ52163   Clare Lansberry (b ca 1907)

CJ52164   Alice Lansberry (b ca 1909)

CJ22   Nancy Elizabeth Wiser (1852-1941) m 1) William Wisor; m 2) 5 Mar 1877, George
Louder

CJ23   Manning Wiser (b Apr 1853)

CJ524   John E. Wiser (12 Aug 1856-9 Feb 1873)

CJ25   Morris Wisor (May 1859-1931) m Martha E. Woodel (Mar 1868-1930)

CJ5251   Bertha Wisor (b 1887) m Harry Baney

CJ5252   Miles Wisor (1890-1979)

CJ5253   George Wisor (b 29 Dec 1892)

CJ5254   Guy R. Wisor (29 Dec 1892-12 Nov 1918)

CJ5255   Gladys Wisor (b ca 1904)

CJ26   Emma J. Wiser (18 Feb 1862-16 Jun 1875)

CJ27   Ella Wiser (b 1865) m Isaac Black

CJ28   Mary Ann Wiser (b 1868) m Alfred Hull

CJ29   George J. Wiser (4 Feb 1871-28 Mar 1871)

CJ52A   Miles Wiser (6 Jul 1872, Bradford Tp, Clearfield Co PA-1945) m Alvina Freeman (b Jul
1876)

CJ52A1   Enlo Wisor (Apr 1899-1978) m Inez Caldwell

CJ52A2   Ella Wisor (b 1900)

CJ52A3   Clifford Wisor (b 1902) m Iva Mae Irvin

CJ52A4   Eva Wisor (b 1903) m 1) Earl Weaver; m 2) James Smith

CJ52A5   Harry Wisor (b 1904)

CJ52A6   Erma Fay Wisor (b 1906) m Ira Weber

CJ52A7   Merrill Wisor (b 1907) m Gladys Aughenbaugh

CJ52A8   Miles Jefferson Wisor (b ca 1909)

CJ52A9   Ruth Wisor (1910-1910)

CJ52AA   Charles Lewis Wisor (b 1911) m 1) Ruth Hurley; m 2) Helen Wilson

CJ52AB   Erie Belle Wisor (b 1913) m Curtis Aughbaugh

CJ52AC   James Arthur Wisor (b 1915)

CJ52AD   Edith Wisor (b 1920) m Willard Caldwell

CJ52B   Margaret Wiser (28 Apr 1875-5 May 1875)

CJ52C   Sarah Wiser (b 1878) m Harry Green

CJ53   Nancy Jane Wiser (17 Aug 1826-1 Mar 1925) m 28 Mar 1850, Thomas Parks (1827, Huntlngdon Co PA-3 Dec 1896). Bur Bigler PA.

CJ531   James Parks (b 1853)

CJ532   Thomas Parks (b 1855) m Mary Kephart (b 1860)(CJ21B)

CJ5321   William Parks (b 1876) m Adda Peters

CJ5322   Cora Parks (b 1878) m William R. Stevens

CJ5323   Ray Edward Parks (25 Jun 1880, Woodland PA-22 May 1964) m Olive Parks

CJ5324   Lula Parks (b 1882) m 1) John Briggs; m 2) Robert Spence

CJ5325   Preston Parks (b 1889)

CJ5326   Duella Parks (1892-1898)

CJ5327   Charles Parks (1894-1894)

CJ5328   Dorothy Parks (b 1899) m Clyde Curry

CJ5329   Millie Parks (1905-1984) m Alton McKee

CJ533   Sarah Parks (1857-26 Nov 1892) m 1) Louder; m 2) Joseph Hull

CJ534   Jacob R. Parks (1859-1923) m Minnie Ruffner (1866-1933)

CJ5341   Arthur Parks (b 1882) m Anna Graham

CJ5342   Ella Parks (b 1883)

CJ5343   Theresa Parks (1885-1927)

CJ5344   Benjamin Parks (1887-1962) m Flora Wisor (1888-1970)

CJ5345   Annie Parks (b 1895) m Roy Goss

CJ5346   Sadie Parks (b 1896)

CJ5347   Clark Parks (b 1898) m Edith Waple

CJ535   John Calvin Parks (b 1860) m Mary Ann Turner

CJ5351   Warren A. "Piney" Parks (3 Jun 1900-24 Oct 1982) m 1) Alice Mooney; m 2) Maude
Peterson

CJ5352   Maynard Parks

CJ5353   Erma Parks m   Wintergill

CJ5354   Zona Parks m   Sheesley

CJ5355   Goldie K. Parks (30 Apr 1895-4 Jun 1969) m 29 Dec 1906, Willis Eckley. Bur Bradford
PA.

CJ5356   Gertrude Parks (17 Mar 1883-30 Jun 1970) m James Lumadue. Bur Bigler PA.

CJ5357   Violet Parks m Ellis Mainer (1891-1986)

CJ5358   Arnold F. Parks (8 Mar 1902-24 May 1978) m Mary Stevens. Bur Bradford PA.

CJ5359   Vivian Parks (11 Sep 1906-31 Dec 1979) m Murray F. Barrett. Bur Bradford PA.

CJ536   Elizabeth Parks (b 1862) m John B. Davis

CJ537   George Parks (1865-1876)

CJ54   Mary Wiser (b 1828) m William Rowles

CJ55   Jesse Wisor (1831-11 Jun 1906) m Margaret E. Kephart (1844-1903)

CJ551   Abraham Wisor (17 Jun 1858-3 Dec 1899) m 30 Jun 1878, Sarah Alice Shimmel (13 Sep
1861-1 Aug 1927)

CJ5511   Burton Wisor (Apr 1880-1941) m Ruth Fullerton (b 1883)

CJ55111   Sallie Wisor (b ca 1900)

CJ55112   Earl Wisor (b ca 1903)

CJ55113   Gordon Wisor (b ca 1904)

CJ55114   Grace Wisor (b ca 1906)

CJ55115   Willard W. Wisor (b ca 1915)

CJ55116   Lester W Wisor (b ca 1917)

CJ55117   George E. Wisor (b ca 1919)

CJ5512   Nora E. Wisor (1882-1960) m Curtis Phillips

CJ5513   Harry Wisor (23 May 1883-11 Jul 1883)

CJ5514   Maggie Wisor (1884-1924) m Edward Haney

CJ5515   Ernest Wisor (b Apr 1887) m Gertrude Hendricks (b ca 1882)

CJ5516   Lewis W. Wisor (Mar 1891-May 1963) m Katie A. Root (1893-1965)

CJ55161   Paul W. Wisor (1910-1910)

CJ55162   Kenneth Wisor (b 1911)

CJ55163   Clarence Roy Wisor (1913-1970)

CJ55164   George Wisor (b 1916)

CJ55165   Sylvia K. Wisor (1918-1923)

CJ55166   Lois Wisor (b ca 1920)

CJ55167   Hestor Wisor (1925-1925)

CJ55168   Lestor Wisor (1925-1925)

CJ5517   Clarence Wisor (Jun 1894-1978) m 1) Pearl   ; m 2) Lavina Litz; m 3) Mary J. Coudriet

CJ5518   Roy Wisor (25 Jun 1895-18 Jun 1968) m 1) Bessie Rowles; m 2) Bessie Dunlap

CJ5519   Lloyd Wisor (b Dec 1897) m Zella Coudriet

CJ55191   Edward Wisor (b 1917)

CJ55192   Elva Wisor (b 1918)

CJ552   Ann Jane Wisor (1860-1891) m 15 Mar 1877, Harry Graham

CJ5521   Ella Nora Graham (1878-1951) m Newton Dixon

CJ5522   Anna Graham (b 1880) m Arthur Parks

CJ5523   Harvey Graham (1882-1953) m Beryl Williams

CJ5524   Molly Graham (b 1883) m 1) William Banner; m 2) Crieghton Blo

CJ5525   Emma Graham (b 1884) m 1) Steward Peters; m 2) Charles Sheck

CJ5526   Cora Graham (b 1886) m Joseph Palmer

CJ5527   William Graham (1890-1986) m Mabel Turner

CJ553   Alfred Wisor (Jul 1862-1915) m Mary E. Druggs (1867-1959)

CJ5531   Jesse Henry Wisor (3 Jul 1883-Aug 1962) m Lottie Shovestall (b 1886)

CJ55311   Raymond A. Wisor (1904-1977) m 1) Clara C. Leppert (1906-1942); m 2) Edna Graham

CJ553111   Infant Wisor (1939-1939)

CJ55312   Joseph A. Wisor (1905-1936) m Lenora Parks

CJ55313   Grace Wisor (b 1908) m Kenneth Knepp

CJ55314   Clare W. Wisor (1910-1976) m Hazel B.   (1906-1975)

CJ55315   Verna Wisor (1913-1913)

CJ5532   Charles A. Wisor (Apr 1885-1954) m Gertrude J. Wisor (Dec 1890-1965)(CJ582)

CJ55321   Roy Wisor (1904-1977) m Edna Graham (1915-1972)

CJ553211   Jean Wisor m Ed Hatcher

CJ5532111   Phyllis Jean Hatcher

CJ5533   Foster H. Wisor (Mar 1887-1960) m Lula Greene (1889-1956)

CJ55331   Harold Wisor

CJ55332   Edna Wisor

CJ55333   Emma Wisor

CJ5534   May Belle Wisor (May 1889-1915) m Benjamin Knepp

CJ5535   Lelia Wisor (Jun 1892-1910) m William George Mullen

CJ5536   Cora Jane Wisor (Apr 1894-1963) m Earl Peters

CJ5537   Dorse Wisor (1897-1973) m Anne Shovestall (1900-1983)

CJ55371   Elizabeth Wisor (b ca 1919)

CJ55372   Ethel Wisor

CJ55373   Bernice Wisor

CJ55374   Arnold Wisor (1920-1978)

CJ55375   Shirley Wisor

CJ55376   Herman J. Wisor (1924-1928)

CJ5538   Verna Wisor (1900-1901)

CJ5539   Chloe Wisor (b 1902) m William Coulter

CJ553A   Bessie Wisor (b 1905) m 1) Vernon Smeal; m 2) Francis Rodgers

CJ553B   Beryl Wisor (b 1908) m Henry Rogers

CJ56   John Wiser (b 1833) m   Shomo

CJ57   Sarah Wiser (26 Oct 1835-10 Jun 1919) m Joel Wolstencroft

CJ571   James Wolstencroft (b 1862)

CJ572   Joel Wolstencroft (b 1865) m Rella Louder

CJ573   Nancy Wolstencroft (b 1868) m William Wis

CJ574   John Wolstencroft (b 1875) m Mamie Holt

CJ575   Thomas Wolstencroft (b 1877) m Alma Shuga

CJ576   George Wolstencroft (b 1880)

CJ58   Abraham W. Wisor (b 1838) m Anne Mease (1837-1914)

CJ581   Alice Wisor (1861-1948) m 1) William Haines; m 2) Harry Goss

CJ582   Flora Wisor (b 1863)

CJ583   Albert Louis Wisor (18 Feb 1867, Boggs Tp, Clearfield Co PA-1945, Salem PA) m 10 Jul 1887, Mary A. Kephart (d 1930). Farmer and miner

CJ5831   Flora A. Wisor (1888-1970) m Benjamin Parks (1887-1962)(CJ5344)

CJ5832   Gertrude J. Wisor (15 Dec 1890, Boggs Tp, Clearfield Co PA-11 Jan 1965, Clearfield PA) m Charles Wisor (1885-1954)(CJ5532). Bur Bradford PA.

CJ58321   Allen L. Wisor (1907-1975) m Esther A. Green (1907-1988)

CJ58322   Earl E. Wisor (27 Mar 1909-25 May 1965) m Bessie Wisor

CJ583221   Ronald D. Wisor (8 Jul 1931-11 Jul 1955)

CJ583222   Eleanor Wisor (1833-1933)

CJ583223   Vonnie Wisor (1937-1937)

CJ583224   Gerald Wisor (1943-1943)

CJ583225   Son Wisor (1943-1943)

CJ58323   Leonard Wisor (14 Feb 1912-21 Jul 1989) m Madeline Aveni

CJ58324   Henry C. Wisor

CJ58325   Mary E. Wisor (1916-1993) m Paul S. Rauch (1916-1982)

CJ58326   Lenora Wisor (b 1918) m Merrill Lumadue

CJ58327   Raymond Wisor

CJ58328   Paul Wisor

CJ58328   Dorothy Wisor m Frederick Knepp

CJ5833   Lettie M. Wiser (31 Dec 1892, Boggs Tp, Clearfield Co PA-29 Oct 1957, Warren PA) m
Earl Williams. Bur Morrisdale PA.

CJ58331   LeRoy Williams

CJ58332   Ottis Williams

CJ58333   Albert Williams

CJ58334   Harry Wiliams

CJ58335   Mabel Williams m   Holt

CJ58336   Eleanor Williams m   Lansberry

CJ58337   Irene Williams m Arthur Smeal

CJ58338   Donna Williams m Robert Dinant

CJ5834   Harry Irvin Wisor (1895-23 Jun 1966, Niles OH) m Verna Graffius (b 1898). USA; WWI.
Steelworker, Niles OH.

CJ58341   Francis Wisor

CJ58342   Clair Wisor

CJ58343   Alice Jeanine Wisor m Irvin Cribbs

CJ58344   Maurice Wisor (1927-1927)

CJ58345   James Wisor

CJ5835   Verna Wisor (20 Nov 1896, Boggs Tp, Clearfield Co PA-22 Jul 1988, Clearfield PA) m
Lloyd Guthrie. No chn. Cook.

CJ5836   Abraham B. Wisor (13 Aug 1899, Bradford Tp, Clearfield Co PA-5 Jun 1983, Clearfield
PA) m Mabel L. Robinson (1901-1980). Bur Bigler PA.

CJ58361   Catherine Wiser (b 1919) m James Lombardo

CJ58362   Elmer A. Wiser

CJ58363   Abram Wiser

CJ58364   Thomas Wiser

CJ58365   Burton Wiser

CJ58366   Barton Wiser

CJ5837   Grace Wisor (12 Mar 1901, Boggs Tp, Clearfield Co PA-25 Sep 1991, Salem PA) m
Ralph Bodle (d 6 Apr 1982)

CJ58371   Albert W. Bodle

CJ58372   Alberta Bodle m Paul Fleck

CJ58373   LaVaughn Bodle m James Glosser

CJ58374   Pauline Bodle m   Dixon

CJ58375   Ronald Bodle

CJ58376   Norma Bodle m Arthur Kerfoot

CJ58377   Norman R. Bodle

CJ5838   William Burton Wisor (b 1904) m 1) Dorcas   ; m 2) Josephine Wisor; m 3) Virginia
Conaway

CJ5839   Mary Martha Wisor (1907-1980) m Calvin Woods

CJ583A   Edith Wisor (b 1910) m Roy Johnson

CJ583B   Milfred A. Wisor (1914-1914)

CJ583C   Ethel Wisor (b 1916) m Bernard Shaw

CJ584   Mary Lettie Wisor (1869-1914) m Harry Goss

CJ585   James Wisor (Nov 1871-1951) m Grace Yaeger (b May 1875)

CJ5851   Bertha Wisor (b Feb 1894)

CJ5852   Bessie Wisor (b Feb 1900)

CJ5853   Maude Wisor (1901-1986) m Sheridan Wisor (Feb 1891-1971)

CJ58531   Chester Wisor

CJ58532   Walter Wisor

CJ58533   Eda Jean Wisor m Rex Monague

CJ5854   James Ashley Wisor (1908-1987) m Verna M. Stonebraker (b 1911)

CJ5855   Anna Wisor m Kenneth Straw

CJ586   David Wisor (1875-1947) m Gertrude Wisor (Aug 1883-1966)(CJ7224)

CJ5861   Jeanette Wisor (12 Jan 1900-14 Nov 1918) m Girard Butler

CJ5862   Lena Wisor (1903-1975) m Clark Williams

CJ5863   Donald Wisor (29 Aug 1905-23 Apr 1906)

CJ5864   Roy Wisor (1907-1979) m Miriam Foster

CJ5865   Cloyd Wisor (10 Jul 1909-14 Jul 1909)

CJ5866   Geneva Wisor (1912-1982) m Wayne Maines

CJ5867   Lucretian Wisor (b 1915)

CJ5868   Thelma Wisor (b 1918) m   Foster

CJ5869   Edna Wisor (b 1920) m 1) Maynard Foster; m 2) Ren Dixon

CJ586A   Floyd Wisor (1922-1982)

CJ587   Frony Jane Wisor (May 1878-1954) m Jonathan Falconer

CJ588   Hannah Wisor (Nov 1881-21 Apr 1966) m G. Burton Davis

CJ5881   Willis Davis (b ca 1904)

CJ59   Angeline Wiser (1843-1920) m Shedrick Butler

CJ591   Harry Butler (b 1869) m Emma Beish

CJ5A   David R. Porter Wiser (1846-13 Jun 1887) m 1) Jane Jordan (d before 1877); m 2) Cynthia
Miller

CJ5A1   John E. Wisor (1868-1921) m Blanche R. Lansberry (1872-1959)

CJ5A11   Thomas Wisor (14 Nov 1890-30 Oct 1960) m M. Margaret Fleming (10 Mar 1897-19 Jun
1981)

CJ5A111   Earl Wisor (b 1917)

CJ5A112   Elnora Wisor (b 1919)

CJ5A12   Oscar Wilson Wisor (1892-1892)

CJ5A13   Edward L. Wisor (Jan 1895-1969) m Lucy Palmer

CJ5A131   Robert Wisor (b 1916)

CJ5A14   Carl W. Wisor (25 Mar 1900-1961) m Ora E.   (1901-1984)

CJ5A15   Esther Leona Wisor (b 1908) m Leon Schenk

CJ5A2   Phoebe Wisor (b 1878) m Frank Waple

CJ5A3   Sarah Elizabeth Wisor (1879-1897) m Robert Clark

CJ5A4   Irene Wisor (1883-1903)

CJ5A5 Godal	Nancy E. Wisor (1885-1937) m 1) William Joseph Wisor (1877-1920)(CJ7221); m 2) John
CJ5A51	Viola Wisor (b ca 1906)
CJ5A6	David R. Wisor (1886-1943) m Pearl Lansberry
CJ5A61	Ruth Wisor (b ca 1905)
CJ5A62	Edna Wisor (b ca 1907)
CJ5A63	Lois Wisor (b ca 1908) m Nicholls
CJ5A64	Lena Wisor (b 1910)
CJ5A65	Paul Wisor (b ca 1914)
CJ5A66	Marshall Wisor (1915-1989) m Ruth Keith
CJ5A67	Ethel Wisor (b 1918) m Hoover
CJ5A68	Harold Wisor (1920-1952)
CJ5A69	Pauline Wisor m Ball
CJ5A6A	Brooks Wisor
CJ5A6B	David Wisor, Jr. (8 Feb 1926-19 Feb 1926)
CJ6	Nancy Wiser (b 1801) m Phillip Bennehoof/Benehof (aka Bennekorf)
CJ61	Mary Bennehoof (b 1827) m Levi Louder
CJ62	John Bennehoof (b 1830)
CJ63	Sarah Bennehoof (b 1832) m Thomas Mease
CJ64	Susanna Bennehoof (1834-1917) m Hamilton Geoffius
CJ65	Henry Bennehoof (b 1839) m 1) Martha Borges; m 2) Catherine Geoffius
CJ66	Ellen Bennehoof (b 1841) m Isaac Beish
CJ67	Levi Bennehoof (b 1842)
CJ68	Lavina Bennehoof (b 1846) m Wesley Graham
CJ7 Bur Bigler PA.	Jonathan Wiser (12 Mar 1803-27 Apr 1877) m Sarah Beers (24 Sep 1809-1 Dec 1890).
CJ71	Elizabeth Weiser (b 1829)
CJ72 PA). Bur Kyler PA.	Jonathan Weiser (1830-1909) m Catherine Hess (c 5 Mar 1833-23 Apr 1896, Woodland
CJ721	William Ellis Wisor (1852-1874) m Elizabeth Wisor

CJ7211   Rhoda Wisor (1873-1965) m 1) James Polkingham; m 2) Isaac Sayers

CJ722   John Henry Wisor (Mar 1854-1929) m Martha S. Hummel (1859-1921)

CJ7221   William Joseph Wisor (1877-1920) m 1) Nancy Wolstencraft (2 Jul 1868-10 Sep 1909); m 2) Nancy E. Wisor (1885-1937) (CJ5A5)

CJ72211   Viola Wisor

CJ7222   Nora Wisor (1879-1879)

CJ7223   Blanche Wisor (1881-1966) m James Pearce

CJ7224   Gertrude Wisor (1883-1966) m David Wisor (1875-1947) (CJ586), q.v.

CJ7225   Katie Wisor (Mar 1885-1976) m Ephraim Davis

CJ72251   James Davis (b ca 1906)

CJ72252   John Davis (b ca 1908)

CJ72253   Catharine Davis (b ca 1910)

CJ7226   Orvis Wisor (14 Jan 1888-18 Apr 1966) m Anna Goss (8 Aug 1892-13 Jul 1973)

CJ72261   Howard Wisor (1908-1974) m Mildred Michaels (1909-1991)

CJ72262   Clyde Wisor (1909-1986) m Dorothy Lowder (1916-1989)

CJ72263   Ethel M. Wisor (28 Jul 1912-27 Apr 1936)

CJ72264   Arthur Wisor (b ca 1915)

CJ72265   Wilford B. Wisor (17 Apr 1921-24 Apr 1921)

CJ72266   Maynard E. Wisor (2 Dec 1921-4 May 1930)

CJ72267   Betty L. Wisor (17 Apr 1923-4 Jun 1930)

CJ7227   Susan Wisor (b 1890) m Thomas Smeal

CJ7228   Sam Wisor (b Feb 1890)

CJ7229   Sherman Wisor (1891-1968) m Pearl Ritchie (1893-1981)

CJ72291   Evelyn Wisor (1911-1985) m Marlin Parks

CJ72292   Clarence J. Wisor (28 Apr 1913-26 Jan 1988) m Bessie Hunt (b 29 May 1919)

CJ722921   Arnold Wisor

CJ722922   Melvin Wisor

CJ722923   Arthur Wisor

CJ722924   Barbara Wisor

CJ722925   Gail Wisor

CJ72293   Ralph W. Wisor (1917-1991) m 1) Olive B.   (1923-1949); m 2) Beryl E. Hall

CJ722931   Gerald Duane Wisor (8 Sep 1948-30 Mar 1949)

CJ72294   Franklin Wisor (1919-1941)

CJ72295   Russell Wisor (1921-1938)

CJ72296   Esther Wisor m Wilbur Dixon

CJ72297   Minabelle Wisor m Harold Woods

CJ72298   Gerald Wisor

CJ72299   Sherman Wisor

CJ7229A   Hye Ray Wisor

CJ7229B   Rhoda Wisor m Arthur Smith

CJ7229C   Katherine Wisor m Oliver Millinder

CJ722A   Sheridan Wisor (Feb 1891-1971) m Maude M Wisor (1901-1986)

CJ722A1   Chester Wisor

CJ722A2   Walter Wisor

CJ722A3   Eda Jean Wisor m Rex Monague

CJ723   Jacob Wiser (b 1856) m Sophia Rowles (1861-1910)

CJ7231   Mable Wisor (b 1878) m Lorenzo Woodle

CJ7232   Della Wisor (b ca 1881) m Warren Aughenbaugh

CJ7233   Dom Wisor

CJ7234   Effie Wisor (b May 1886) m W.F. Steeler

CJ7235   Wilbert Wisor (b May 1891) m Edna Hamilton

CJ72351   Margaret Wisor (b ca 1912)

CJ72352   Orel Wisor (b ca 1914)

CJ72353   Wilbert Wisor (b ca 1918)

CJ72354   Kenneth Wisor (b ca 1919)

CJ7236   Edna Wisor (b Jul 1893)

CJ7237   Willis Wisor (b Jun 1895) m Goldie Pennington

CJ7238   Gordon Wisor (b 1900) m Dorcas Rauch

CJ7239   Theodore Wisor (b 1903)

CJ724   Jonathan Wisor (1858-1859)

CJ725   Sarah A. Wisor (1860-1886) m 9 Nov 1882, Jacob Hummel

CJ726   Harvey Wisor (1862-1873)

CJ73   Henry Wiser (21 Apr 1832-20 May 1902) m Mary Ann Odell (20 Apr 1838-30 Mar 1907).
Civil War.

CJ731   Ella Wisor (1861-1944) m 20 Apr 1882, David E. Flegal

CJ732   Ida Wisor (1863-12 May 1947) m 12 Jun 1881, Clearfield PA, George Shugarts (17 Oct
1862, Knox Tp, Clearfield Co PA-23 Sep 1958). Bur Stoneville, Clearfield Co PA.

CJ7321   Frank Shugarts (22 Dec 1881-12 May 1968) m Laura Penvose

CJ7322   Foster Shugarts (d 1918) m Sep 1906, Bessie Bell Peters (23 Nov 1888-12 Jun 1970)

CJ73221   Wava Annabell Shugarts (5 Feb 1907-Feb 1992) m Harry Rexford (29 Sep 1898-12 Feb
1968)

CJ732211   Dorothy Rexford (b 26 Aug 1925) m Harold Buckets (19 Feb 1922-Jun 1992)

CJ7322111   Robert Buckets (b 29 Aug 1950) m 1) Oct 1977, Vicki Volovich; m 2) Roxanne   . No
chn.

CJ7322112   Thomas Buckels (b 28 Jul 1952) m May 1977, Deborah Fitch

CJ73221121   Matthew Buckels

CJ73221122   Justin Buckels

CJ7322113   James Buckels (b 6 Sep 1954). Unm.

CJ73221131   Tess Buckels

CJ7322114   Barbara Joyce Buckels (b 6 Sep 1966) m Kerry Kotyk

CJ732212   Joyce Rexford (b 20 Jun 1928) m David Kipp (d May 1992)

CJ7322121   George Kipp. Unm.

CJ7322122   David Kipp (d)

CJ7322123   Harry Burton Kipp m Sue

CJ73221231   Tyler Kipp

CJ7322124   Sam Kipp (twin). Unm.

CJ7322125   Sandy Kipp (twin). Unm.

CJ732213   Barbara Rexford (b 9 Apr 1933) m James Adams

CJ7322131   James Adams m Linda

CJ73221311   Steven Adams

CJ73221312   David Adams

CJ7322132   Tim Adams m Debbie

CJ73221321   Nicole Adams

CJ7322133   Cecelia Adams. Unm.

CJ73221331   Amber

CJ7322134   Theresa Adams. Unm.

CJ73221341   Jamie

CJ7322135   Mary Adams. Unm.

CJ732214   George Burton Rexford (b 15 May 1937) m Tillie

CJ7322141   Heidi Rexford. Unm.

CJ73221411   Christina

CJ7322142   Jeffrey Rexford. Unm.

CJ7322143   Tammy Rexford m Daniel Claycomb

CJ73221431   Nicole Claycomb

CJ73221432   Claycomb

CJ73222   Earl Dayton Shugarts (b 24 May 1908) m 30 Jun 1937, Zoe Rae Frankhouser (b 21 Dec
1916)

CJ732221   Ralph Roland Shugarts (b 26 Feb 1938) m Linda Stamen

CJ7322211   Tara Lee Shugarts

CJ7322212   Keith Stamen Shugarts

CJ732222   Earl Dayton Shugarts, Jr. (b 25 Apr 1939) m Janet Dinardi

CJ7322221   John Michale Shugarts (b 15 Feb 1961) m Tracy Prough

CJ732223   Barry Lee Shugarts (b 1 Dec 1940) m Stephanie Bersinger

CJ7322231   Bryon Lee Shugarts (b 24 Nov 1966)

CJ7322232   Toni Rae Shugarts (b 3 Apr 1969)

CJ73223   George Benjamin Shugarts (199-May 1957). Unm. No chn.

CJ73224   Merlin A. Shugarts (6 May 1913-30 Oct 1977) m 20 Dec 1939, Esther Banks

CJ732241   Gary Elwood Shugarts m Ramona Dinardi

CJ7322411   David Martin Shugarts m Marie

CJ73224111   Bradley Shugarts

CJ732242   Joyce Marie Shugarts m S. Duane Thomas

CJ7322421   Dennis Thomas m

CJ73224211   Georgina Thomas

CJ73224212   Denise Thomas

CJ73224213   Lucas Thomas

CJ7322422   Danny Thomas m   . Two chn.

CJ7322423   Penney Thomas m   . Two chn.

CJ7322424   Toni Thomas m   . Three chn.

CJ732243   Shelva Jean Shugarts m W. Dale Smith

CJ7322431   Cindy Smith m   Valdevio

CJ73224311   Nicholas Valdevio

CJ73224312   Natalie Valdevio

CJ73224313   Lauren Valdevio

CJ7322432   Gary Dale Smith m Chris

CJ73224321   Brittany Smith

CJ73224322   Merlin Jacob Dale Smith

CJ7322433   Jodi M. Smith m Mark Booher

CJ73224331   Morgan Booher

CJ73324332   Logan Booher

CJ732244   Georgia Lee Shugarts (b 14 Oct 1941) m 18 Jan 1960, Eugene Moore

CJ7322441   Brenda Moore m Richard Swanson

CJ73224411   Joshua Swanson

CJ73224412   Kent Swanson

CJ73224413   Michael Swanson

CJ7322442	Daniel William Moore. Unm.
CJ73224421	Jamie Moore
CJ7322443	Patty Moore m Greg
CJ73224431	Matthew
CJ73224432	Eric
CJ73224433	Keith
CJ7322444	Kevin Moore. Unm.
CJ73224441	Devin Moore
CJ732245	Carolann Shugarts m 1) Darwin Harshbarger; m 2) William Weyandt
CJ7322451	Terri Rae Harshbarger. Unm.
CJ73225 Nov 1992)	Betty Ruth Shugarts (11 Jun 1915-7 Apr 1995) m Edward Earl Nelson (15 May 915-21
CJ732251	Wava Joan Nelson (3 Oct 1937-26 Feb 1993) m Harper R. Smith
CJ7322511	Tammy Jo Smith (b 10 Feb 1959) m 20 Dec 1980, Eugene W. Park (b 28 Oct 1952)
CJ73225111	Michelle Lee Park
CJ73225112	David Thomas Park
CJ73225113	Eric James Park
CJ7322512	Debra Lynn Smith (b 6 May 1962) m 8 Oct 1988, Kenneth Losh
CJ73225121	Ashley Rochelle Losh (b 17 Jan 1990)
CJ73225122	Erin Elizabeth N. Losh (b 1 Sep 1993)
CJ7322513	David Gerald Smith m 28 May 1992, Andrea Prough
CJ73225131	Alyssa Smith (b 17 Sep 1993)
CJ73225132	Katy Sue Smith (b Oct 1994)
CJ732252	Bonnie Rita Nelson (b 8 Nov 1942) m 30 May 1964, Harold E. Benson (b 4 Jan 1942)
CJ7322521	Christy DeLynn Benson (b 13 May 1965). Unm.
CJ7322522	Ryan Scott Benson (b 27 Mar 1968). Unm.
CJ73225221	Alexis Betty Ruth Benson (b 26 May 1995)
CJ7322523	Patty Jean Nelson (b 1 May 1952) m Michael Kent McElwee
CJ73225231	Shelley Jean McElwee

CJ73225232   Andrew McElwee

CJ7323   Alma Shugarts (29 Apr 1883-7 Oct 1941) m Thomas Wilsoncroft

CJ7324   Date Vern Shugarts (18 Feb 1887-14 Jan 1931) m Katheryn Hinds

CJ7325   Tressie Dee Shugarts (26 Nov 1889-3 May 1917) m Adam H. Good

CJ7326   Frederick George Shugarts (29 Jun 1894, Boggs Tp, Clearfield Co PA-21 Mar 1968, Clearfield PA) m Naomi Bell Wilsoncroft (10 Aug 1898-30 Jul 1971). USPS, Clearfield PA.

CJ73261   Kenneth Barkley Shugarts (31 Aug 1915-29 Jan 1976) m Eleanor. One daughter.

CJ73262   John Pershing Shugarts (25 Aug 1918-9 Jan 1957) m Anna

CJ73263   Ethel Elizabeth Shugarts (b 11 Sep 1920) m 5 Dec 1941, Chester Railing (20 Jan 1909-d)

CJ732631   Kim Railing (b 19 Dec 1957)

CJ73264   Mable Luella Shugarts (27 May 1922-ca 1990) m Steven Kruczek

CJ732641   Marian Kruczek

CJ732642   Steven Kruczek

CJ73265   William Fredrick Shugarts (10 Jun 1925-d) m Gussie. Chn

CJ73266   Robert Harold Shugarts (b 2 Apr 1928) m Lois

CJ732661   Barbara Ann Shugarts (b 17 Mar 1955) m 10 Jun 1978, Joe Porter

CJ732662   Martin Robert Shugarts (b 17 Sep 1956)

CJ732663   Robert Harold Shugarts, Jr. (b 23 Dec 1957)

CJ73267   Dessie Mae Shugarts (25 Nov 1930-ca 1981) m Richard Conrad

CJ732671   Debra J. Conrad (b 19 Feb 1953) m James R. Prendergast

CJ7326711   Jennifer Brooke Prendergast (b 16 Aug 1977)

CJ732672   Richard D. Conrad (b 25 Oct 1955)

CJ732673   Penny L. Conrad (b 17 Oct 1959)

CJ73268   Franklin Delano Shugarts (b 16 Nov 1932) m Ann. Chn.

CJ73269   Winifred Joyce Shugarts (b 13 May 1941) m Carl Undercofler. One son, one daughter.

CJ7326A   Janet Darlene Shugarts (b 11 Mar 1942). Unm.

CJ7327   Blake B. Shugarts (7 Feb 1897-26 Mar 1951) m 19 Jan 1922, Lulu Wilsoncroft

CJ7328   Anna Shugarts (28 Jun 1898, Boggs Tp, Clearfield Co PA-9 Mar 1975, Clearfield PA) m 23 Dec 1918, Cumberland MD, Clyde Knepp (23 Feb 1898, Renovo PA-19 May 1971, Clearfield PA). Bur Hyde City PA.

CJ73281   Eva Knepp (b 28 Aug 1919, Curwensville PA) m Lev Kirby

CJ73282   A Harvey Knepp (b 2 Dec 1920, Curwensville PA) m 4 Sep 1945, Oahu HI, Mary Robinson (25 Sep 1921, Cambridge MA). He, USA, WWII, Korean Conflict; US Natl Guard Reserve. BS, Harvard Col, 1949; MS, Bucknell (PA) U, 1951; teacher, principal, 1951-81, Dover NH. Pres, New England Assoc of Secondary School Principals, 1975-76.

CJ732821   Christine Knepp (b 18 Nov 1949, Sunbury PA) m 1) Stanley Ellis (1981, Anchorage AK); m 2) 1983, Michale Sitbon

CJ732822   Patricia Knepp (b 1 Aug 1951, Stoneham MA) m Monte Oglesby. BS, U NH, 1977.

CJ732823   Robert Clyde Knepp (b 18 Jun 1953, Stoneham MA) m 1980, Scotch Plains NJ, Maureen O'Donnell. BS, Alderson-Broaddus Col; teacher, Nashua NH.

CJ7328231   Patrick Dennis Knepp (b 15 Jan 1989, Manchester NH)

CJ7328232   Janice Lynn Knepp (b 15 Apr 1992, Manchester NH)

CJ73283   R. Russel Knepp (4 Sep 1928, Curwensville PA-26 Oct 1978) m Beverly Dickenson

CJ73284   Fay Knepp (26 Jun 1932, Curwensville PA-Sep 1990) m Harvey Goiher

CJ73285   Jay Knepp (b 26 Jun 1932, Curwensville PA) m Joyce Bloom

CJ73286   Curley Brinton Knepp (b 26 Dec 1933, Pike Tp, Clearfield Co PA) m 1) 27 Jun 1962, Dallas TX, Kathleen Carlos (b 22 Mar 1933, Elstow, Sask, Canada), div 1994; m 2) 28 Feb 1994, Seoul, South Korea, Mak Ye Kang (b 15 Jan 1964, Kangjin-Kun, Korea). USA, Korean & Vietnam Conflicts. BS, NH Col, 1979; civil servant.

CJ732861   Michele Catherine Knepp (b 14 Mar 1963, White Sands Missile Range NM)

CJ732862   Linda Antonio Knepp (b 8 Aug 1964, White Sands Missile Range NM)

CJ732863   Eva Marie Knepp (b 26 Feb 1970, Fort Monmouth NJ)

CJ73287   Ronald Knepp (3 Oct 1935-1955)

CJ73288   Phyllis Knepp (b 3 Oct 1939, Curwensville PA) m 17 Jul 1959, New Millport PA, Kenneth Bauman (24 Jan 1932, Clearfield PA-25 Oct 1995, Faunce PA). She, nursing asst.

CJ732881   Kathy Bauman (b 27 Jun 1960, Clearfield PA) m 18 Oct 1980, Sanborn PA, Marlin Freeman (b 21 Dec 1958)

CJ7328811   Derek Freeman (b 15 Jun 1982, State College PA)

CJ7328812   Katie Freeman (b 4 Jun 1986, State College PA)

CJ732882   Kelly Bauman (b 8 Mar 1962, Clearfield PA) m 1) 29 Oct 1983, Clearfield PA, Scott Mullin (b 10 Sep 1962), div 1991; m 2) 10 Jul 1993, Clearfield PA, Duane Luzier (b 26 May 1963)

CJ7328821   Miranda Mullin (b 8 May 1989, Clearfield PA)

CJ7328822   Mitchell Mullin (b 26 Jun 1990, Clearfield PA)

CJ732883   Kenneth Bauman III (b 25 Aug 1963, Clearfield PA) m 13 Sep 1986, near Houtzdale PA,

Melissa Weatherholtz (b 8 Oct 1966). Auto body work.

CJ7328831   Amber Bauman (b 2 Mar 1988, Clearfield PA)

CJ7328832   Nickolos Bauman (b 23 Aug 1990)

CJ732884   Kara Bauman (b 7 Dec 1965, Clearfield PA) m 28 Sep 1985, Jeff Finney (b 4 Oct 1964). Beautician, Middletown PA.

CJ7328841   Bryan Finney (b 25 Oct 1993, Harrisburg PA)

CJ7329   Helen Shugarts (13 Mar 1901, Boggs Tp, Clearfield Co PA-3 Oct 1966) m Andrew
McGaughey

CJ73291   Kathryn "Kay" Eloise McGaughey (b ca Oct 1918) m 1)   (d) ; m 2)   Favro (d)

CJ732911   Michael Andrew Favro (b 19 Aug 1943) m

CJ7329111   Michelle Favro

CJ7329112   Mark Favro

CJ732912   Sheila Dee Favro (b 28 Sep 1952) m   Moore

CJ73292   Russell McGaughey (b ca 1920-d)

CJ73293   Emory Blake McGaughey (b 10 Feb 1922) m Vivian

CJ73294   Edmund McGaughey (d 1926)

CJ73295   Barbara McGaughey (b 21 Mar 1936) m 1)   Lines (d); m 2) George Smeal

CJ732951   Maxine Dee Lines (b 28 Nov 1954) m   . One chd.

CJ732952   Russell J. Smeal (b 11 Jan 1957

CJ732953   Sandra K. Smeal (b 29 Nov 1958)

CJ732954   Clayton C. Smeal (b 12 Apr 1961)

CJ732955   Rock S. Smeal (b 24 Jan 1963)

CJ732956   Dustin L. Smeal (b 14 Aug 1964)

CJ733   Agnes Wisor (b 1866) m Frank B. Eberts

CJ734   Catherine Wisor (1866-1946)

CJ735   Cordelia Wisor (1872-1947) m 1) P.H. Flegal; m 2) Loy Gilman

CJ736   Frederick B. Wisor (1874-1948) m May A. Gallaher (1881-1952)

CJ7361   Clifford Wisor (b ca 1904)

CJ7362   Paul C. Wisor (1909-1943) m Zola B.   (1912-1994)

CJ7363	Angeline Wisor (b ca Jun 1919)
CJ74	Susanna Wiser (b 1834) m 1852, George C. Greene
CJ741	Salina Greene (b 1857)
CJ742	John Greene (b 1858)
CJ743	Michael Greene (b 1860)
CJ744	Rosannah Greene (b 1862)
CJ745	James Greene (b 1864)
CJ746	Veronica Greene (b 1865)
CJ747	Claudius Greene (b 1867)
CJ748	Celestine Greene (b 1869)
CJ749	Sarah Greene (b 1872)
CJ74A	Mary Greene (b 1874)
CJ75	Jared (Jeremiah) Wiser (b 1836) m Salina
CJ751	John Wisor (b 1866)
CJ752	Lettic Mae Wisor (b 1867)
CJ753	Laura Belle Wisor (b 1869)
CJ754	Adda Wisor (b 1872)
CJ755	Willis Wisor (b 1874)
CJ756	Myrtle Wisor (b 1878)
CJ757	Chester Wisor (b 1886)
CJ76	Hannah Wisor (1838-1910) m William Batts
CJ761	Henry Batts (1859-1887)
CJ762	Clara Batts (1862-1937) m Henry Shimmel
CJ763	Hiram Batts (b 1865)
CJ764	Hallie Batts (1869-1952) m John Croder
CJ765	Ella Batts (b 1872) m George Stine
CJ766	Eurman Batts (b 1879) m Barnard Leigey
CJ77	Sarah Wisor (1839-8 Dec 1889) m Lindsey Stone

CJ78   Mary Wiser (b 1842) m Joseph Yothers

CJ79   Emanuel Wiser (28 Apr 1843-18 Dec 1868)

CJ7A   Israel Wiser (1845-1923) m Carrie Gallaher (1850-1928)

CJ7B   Alexander Wiser (b 1846) m Annie E.

CJ7B1   Alexander Wiser (b ca 1875)

CJ7B2   Nancy T. Wiser (b ca 1878)

CJ7C   Lindsey Wiser (19 Sep 1848-29 Dec 1883) m Emily Dixon

CJ7C1   Fanny A. Wiser (b ca 1871)

CJ7D   Lewis Wiser (b 1850) m Katie Root

CJ7E   Marjorie Wiser (b 1852) m Henry Young

CJ7F   Sophia Wiser (1853-1916) m 1873, Tyrone PA, William Varner

CHAPTER EIGHTEEN

[GW]   George Wieser (d ca Aug 1809)
of Berks and Lehigh Counties, Pennsylvania and his descendants

There is a family that seems to have originated in Berks County, Pennsylvania in the late 1700s that spelled its name Wieser or Wisser, although on occasion local officials mistakenly spelled their name Weiser. Sometimes in the early records the name was spelled Wiesner, and this may have been the correct spelling for the first immigrants. In later generations most of the family had moved into Lehigh County, where the spelling Wieser was continued, although family members in Berks County now generally use the spelling Wisser. It has all become so confused that, as an example, some known descendants of Abraham Wieser are using the spelling Wisser while others are using the spelling Weiser.

The first person using this spelling who arrived in the area seems to have been Caspar, for whom early spellings of his last name include Wisser, Wiser, Weiser, and Wieser. Caspar arrived in Philadelphia on 16 September 1751 on the Edinburgh. He is next found as a sponsor for a baptism at Hill Church in Berks County on 8 June 1755, when he was listed as a single man. At another baptism at Hill Church on 30 March 1760, he was again a sponsor with his wife Maria Dorothea. By 1765, he was located in Rockland Township, Berks County, where he was listed in the tax rolls of 1765 through 1771. On 15 April 1770, he and his wife Barbara were listed as parents of a daughter named Dorothea. Nothing further about this family has been found.

The man who started the family to be documented in this chapter is George Wieser, who appeared first in the tax lists for Maxatawny Township of Berks County in 1762. He may have been somehow related to Caspar, or he may have been the Johan Georg Weisser who arrived in Philadelphia on 16 October 1751 on the Duke of Wirtenberg. He remained in Maxatawny through 1770 when he moved to Greenwich Township, where he remained until his death in 1809. There are a number of records in the New Bethel Zion Lutheran Church at Grimville that mention him and his wife Maria Barbara during that period. He wrote his will on 17 March 1808, mentioning his wife Maria Barbara, his sons Jacob and John and a deceased daughter Maria Reimer, wife of Matthias. The will was probated on 14 August 1809.[154]

GW   George Wieser (d ca Aug 1809, Greenwich, Berks, PA) m Maria Barbara.

GW1   Maria Wieser m Matthias Reimer.

GW11   Hans Jacob Reimer (4 Apr 1776).

GW2   Jacob Wieser (d ca 1819) m ca 1779, Greenwich, Berks PA, Catharina (14 Dec 1750-16 Dec 1839).

GW21   John George Wieser (6 Feb 1783, Greenwich, Berks PA-19 Jul 1856, Hamilton OH) m 1) Sarah   ; m 2) Elizabeth   (15 Jan 1783-4 Oct 1858, Hamilton OH).

GW211   Maria Anna Wieser (10 Oct 1802-17 May 1829).

GW212   Catherina Wieser (b 1804).

GW213   Samuel Wieser (18 Oct 1806, Reading PA-19 Nov 1874) m Catharine Roseboon (6 Jun 1806, OH-5 Sep 1888).

---

[154]The information in this chapter was collected by Edward Wiser, who also prepared it in the present format. Family background information for Greenwich and Maxatawny Townships was provided by Bernice Sell of Kutztown. Specific information was provided by Anna Schroeder of Hamburg for the Wissers of Berks County, by Evelyn Stefan of Chicago for the family of John George Wieser of Ohio, and by Ann Wieser of Gustine CA for the family of Daniel Wieser in Nebraska and California. Many others including Conrad Walton Weiser of Durham NC and Robert A. Wieser of Hamilton MT provided information on their own families.

GW2131   William Wieser (b Apr 1837, OH).

GW2132   Nathaniel Wieser (Aug 1838, OH-31 Oct 1909) m Belinda Hoel (Jan 1842, OH-28 Oct 1929, Hamilton OH).   Hamilton OH.

GW21321   William H. Wieser (b Nov 1868, OH) m Lottie   (b Feb 1874, OH).

GW21322   Alice Wieser (b ca 1871, OH) m Malott.

GW213221   Clarence W. Malott (b ca 1896, OH).

GW213222   Eva Malott (b ca 1902, OH).

GW21323   Bertha Wieser (b Sep 1874, OH).

GW21324   Edward Wieser (1 Dec 1877, OH-17 Apr 1937) m Ethel G.   (b ca 1883).

GW213241   Ethel G. Wieser (b ca 1902, OH).

GW213242   Ruth M. Wieser (b ca 1904, OH).

GW213243   Thomas Edward Wieser (b ca 1906, OH).

GW213244   Dorothy Wieser (b ca 1912, OH).

GW213245   Robert Wieser (b ca 1915, OH).

GW21325   Clara Wieser (b Jul 1884, OH) m   Tuley.

GW213251   Nathan H. Tuley (b ca 1905, OH).

GW213252   James Tuley (b ca 1907, OH).

GW214   Harriet (Hattie) Wieser (b 1808) m   Sell.

GW215   Nathan Wieser.

GW216   Ann Wieser m 1)   Davis; m 2)   Kohlfrat.

GW2161   Jane Davis.

GW217   Isaac Wieser (28 Feb 1814, Reading PA-13 May 1891) m 10 Jul 1841, St. Louis MO, Rosina Kistner (8 Sep 1808, Goettingen, Germany-Dec 1879).

GW2171   Edward Wieser (15 Apr 1842-29 Jul 1842).

GW2172   Elizabeth Wieser (b 21 Aug 1843, OH) m C. W. Schoenfeld (b ca 1833, Hanover, Germany).

GW21721   Frederick Schoenfeld (b ca 1870, OH).

Isaac Wieser (1814-1891)

GW21722   Rosa Schoenfeld (b ca 1873, OH).

GW21723   Ida Schoenfeld (b ca 1878, OH).

GW2173   Matilda Wieser (2 Mar 1846-1873).

GW2174   Caroline Wieser (21 May 1848, OH-May 1934) m Oscar E. Thiel (1846, Posen, Germany-1905).

GW21741   Ida Thiel (b 2 Dec 1866).

GW21742   Olga Thiel (b 6 Nov 1874) m Edward Loll.

GW21743   Walter E. Thiel (b 13 Dec 1876, Cincinnati OH) m Elizabeth Williams (b 22 May 1876, Chicago, IL).

GW217431   Evelyn Thiel (b 28 Mar 1904, Chicago, IL) m George W. Stefan (25 Feb 1905-20 Oct 1987).

GW2174311   Margo Evelyn Stefan (b 10 Mar 1939, Chicago, IL).

GW217432   Edwin Jacob Oscar Thiel (5 Jan 1906, Chicago, IL-31 Dec 1981) m Margerite Seabloom (b 11 Jul 1905, Sweden).

GW21744   Norma Thiel (b 8 Jan 1879).

GW21745   Howard Thiel (b 18 Jul 1880).

GW21746   Oscar Thiel (b 26 Aug 1882).

GW21747   Irwin Thiel (b 12 Aug 1883).

GW21748   Meta Thiel (b 16 Sep 1884).

GW21749   Elisa Thiel (b 1 Dec 1885).

GW2174A   Alma Thiel (10 Dec 1887-1 Apr 1962).

GW2174B   Irene Thiel (b 19 Nov 1890) m Arthur Amundsen.

GW2175   Lillian Wieser (b 10 Aug 1850) m 18 Mar 1885, Hamilton OH, Dominic Emminger.

GW2176   Ida Wieser (2 Dec 1852-1858).

GW218   Elizabeth Wieser (b 22 Aug 1816, Reading PA).

GW22   Catharina Wieser (4 Nov 1785, Greenwich, Berks, PA).

GW23   Samuel Wieser (16 Sep 1788, PA-15 Apr 1873) m 7 Nov 1819, Elizabeth Wertz (16 Jun 1796-12 Sep 1866).

GW231   Carolina Wieser (b 29 Oct 1822).

GW232   Daniel Wieser (19 Aug 1824-28 Aug 1894) m 30 Jan 1847, Judith Lichty (10 Sep 1825-27 Apr 1895, Greenwich, Berks, PA).

GW2321   Oliver T. Wieser (5 Jun 1847-5 Apr 1871).

GW2322   Wilson Wisser (4 Dec 1849, PA-2 Jul 1921, Weisenberg, Lehigh PA) m 19 May 1877, Grimsville, Berks PA, Christianna Hanna Brunner (27 Aug 1849-27 Nov 1925).

GW23221   Oliver Lewis Wisser (17 Dec 1877, Greenwich, Berks PA-22 May 1879).

GW23222   Anna Kate Malara Wisser (b 27 Apr 1879, Greenwich, Berks PA) m 14 Jun 1913, Fred G. Smith.

GW232221   Edna Wisser Smith (b 4 Aug 1915, Weisenburg, Lehigh PA).

GW232222   George Fred Smith (b 20 Aug 1919, Lynn, Lehigh PA).

GW232223   Florence Annie Smith (b 17 Apr 1921, Lynn, Lehigh PA).

GW232224   Paul Wilson Smith (b 18 Nov 1922, Lynn, Lehigh PA).

GW23223   George Freddie Wisser (7 Jul 1880, Greenwich, Berks PA-Aug 1964, PA) m 12 Nov 1910, Grimsville, Berks PA, Ida C. Bittner (1890, Jordan, Lehigh PA-1967).

GW232231   Viola Ida Wisser (14 Mar 1913, Weisenberg, Lehigh PA-Dec 1967, PA).

GW23224   Edward Wilson Wisser (b 12 Aug 1881, PA).

GW23225   Addie Viola Wisser (26 Apr 1894-1986) m 6 Nov 1914, New Tripoli, Lehigh PA, George C. Derr (1890-1974).

GW232251   Beatrice Addie Derr (9 May 1917, Lehigh PA-1919).

GW232252   Lester George Derr (4 Apr 1919, Upper Macungie, Lehigh PA-1920).

GW232253   Cleon Carl Derr (b 10 Nov 1920, Upper Macungie, Lehigh PA) m Lillian M. L.   (b 16 Oct 1921).

GW2323   Mary Ann Wieser (13 Dec 1851-11 Sep 1882) m Martin A. L. Grim (20 Jan 1850-9 Dec 1923).

GW23231   Alice J. R. Grim (1 Dec 1871-2 Jan 1873).

GW23232   Oliver Daniel Grim (26 Mar 1877-24 Jun 1929) m 29 Nov 1902, Minerva Victoria Siegfried (26 Sep 1882-25 Sep 1925).

GW232321   Homer Harold Grim (b 25 Apr 1907, Greenwich, Berks PA).

GW232322   Ruth Edith Grim (b 4 May 1911, Albany, Berks PA).

GW232323   Edna Miriam Grim (b 24 Nov 1913, Greenwich, Berks PA).

GW232324   Russel Ralph Grim (b 29 Jan 1917, Lynn, Lehigh PA).

GW23233   Lenius Abraham Grim (b 24 Dec 1878).

GW23234   Chester Eugene Grim (3 Nov 1880-1958).

GW2324   Sarah Elizabeth Wieser (3 Feb 1854, PA-19 May 1876) m 4 Jul 1875, Grimsville, Berks

PA, Lenius Reinhart (b 23 Sep 1853).

GW23241   Infant Reinhart (May 1876-19 May 1876).

GW2325   Morris Wieser (31 Oct 1856, Greenwich, Berks PA-30 Jul 1929, Berks PA).

GW2326   Carolina Margaret Wieser (19 Dec 1858-6 Mar 1860).

GW2327   Diana Wieser (b 3 Feb 1861, PA).

GW2328   Daniel Adam Wisser (22 Jul 1863, Greenwich, Berks PA-22 Sep 1934) m 26 Mar 1883, Greenwich, Berks PA, Emma Mary Old (10 Jan 1858-5 Mar 1929, Seiberlingville,PA).

GW23281   Gertrude Estella Mary Wisser (b 9 Jun 1883, Greenwich, Berks PA) m 6 Dec 1902, Ebenezer, Lehigh PA, Albert C. Dengler (b ca 1882).

GW232811   Franklin Elias Dengler (b 1 Feb 1905).

GW232812   Clara Ida Dengler (b 24 Oct 1906).

GW232813   Charles Albert Dengler (b 31 Oct 1907).

GW232814   Addie May Dengler (b 27 Oct 1908).

GW232815   Andrew Aaron Dengler (b 9 Feb 1910).

GW232816   Menno Paul Dengler (16 Jun 1912-10 Jan 1959) m Mildred M.   (8 Aug 1920-26 Oct 1983).

GW232817   James Milton Dengler (b 19 Apr 1917).

GW232818   William Moses Dengler (b 24 Mar 1919).

GW232819   Estella Gertie Dengler (b 29 May 1920).

GW23281A   Paul Thomas Dengler (b 12 Jul 1923).

GW23281B   Mabel Martha Dengler (b 4 Sep 1925).

GW23281C   Albert Moses Dengler (b 12 Jan 1927).

GW23282   Daisy May Jane Wisser (8 Jun 1884, Greenwich, Berks PA-11 Sep 1919) m 2 Jun 1906, Grimsville, Berks PA, Bartolette Owen Schlenker (17 Apr 1877, Greenwich, Berks PA-28 Aug 1941).

GW232821   Edith Susannah Schlenker (b 15 Sep 1906, Greenwich, Berks PA).

GW232822   Lester Harlan Schlenker (21 Mar 1918, Greenwich, Berks PA-1981).

GW23283   Charles Ambrose Wisser (7 Aug 1886, Grimsville, Berks PA-26 Sep 1963, Berks PA) m 23 Jan 1909, Stony Run, Berks PA, Mary Eva Roth (24 Jan 1887, PA-17 Apr 1935).

GW232831   Elda Pauline Wisser (19 Mar 1911, Greenwich, Berks PA-1992) m 24 Nov 1938, Kutztown PA, Walter L. Herber (1904-1986).

GW232832   Irvin Charles Wisser (5 Feb 1916, Greenwich, Berks PA-23 May 1977).

GW232833   Arline Elizabeth Wisser (22 Mar 1919, Maxatawny, Berks PA-2 Sep 1919).

GW232834   Anna Mary Wisser (b 10 Aug 1920, Maxatawny, Berks PA) m Warren Charles Wesner.

GW2328341   Richard Warren Wesner (b 31 Dec 1942, Kutztown PA).

GW232835   Irma Catharine Wisser (b 30 Aug 1923, Maxatawny, Berks PA) m William Franklin Bond.

GW2328351   Eileen Elda Bond (b 28 Feb 1943).

GW2328352   William Franklin Bond Jr. (b 10 Jan 1945).

GW23284   Andrew Walton(?) Wisser (4 Nov 1888, Greenwich, Berks PA-20 Jun 1959) m 3 Oct 1908, Grimsville, Berks PA, Mary A. Gehringer (26 Apr 1892, Weisenberg, Lehigh PA-17 May 1962).

GW232841   Marvin John David Wisser (10 Apr 1909, Weisenberg, Lehigh PA-4 Sep 1986) m Marguerite Kuhns.

GW2328411   Mellis Marvin Wisser (21 Sep 1928, Kutztown PA-14 Jul 1957) m Joyce A.   (b 8 Dec 1927).

GW232842   Stewart Andrew Wisser (9 May 1924, Weisenberg, Lehigh PA-Nov 1970).

GW2329   Louis Wieser (14 Oct 1870-24 Sep 1872).

GW233   Samuel Wisser (13 May 1827, Greenwich, Berks PA-17 Apr 1907) m Julia Ann Rhoads (17 Jun 1833-8 Jun 1922).

GW2331   Ann Eliza Wisser (13 Apr 1851, PA-25 Jun 1866).

GW2332   Stephen Sylvester Wisser (13 Jan 1853, Ephrata, Lancaster PA-17 Oct 1916, Reading PA) m 26 Aug 1876, Harriet M. Reinhold (20 Mar 1855, PA-22 Jun 1934).

GW23321   Daisy May Wisser (26 May 1877, Denver, Lancaster PA-15 Jan 1958) m 9 Jun 1903, Walter L. Heckman (5 Nov 1877, Reading PA-20 Jun 1964).

GW233211   Cleora I. Heckman (b ca 1905).

GW233212   Thorma M. Heckman (b ca 1906).

GW23322   Bertha Blanche Wisser (20 Dec 1878, Shoeneck, Lancaster PA-17 Feb 1939) m Nelson Boltz (29 Jun 1881, Upper Tulpehocken, Berks PA-14 Nov 1936).

GW23323   L. Olive Wisser (11 Apr 1885-25 Dec 1885).

GW23324   LeRoy Lester Wisser (30 Dec 1887-27 Jan 1896, West Reading, PA).

GW23325   Charles F. Wisser (30 Oct 1889, West Reading, Berks PA-9 May 1970) m Mary Trommatter(?) (13 Jun 1893, Pottsville PA-6 Aug 1958).

GW23326   Stephen S. Wisser Jr. (25 May 1891, PA-15 Apr 1978) m 3 Jun 1914, Hattie Bosch (2 Oct 1887-20 Oct 1965).

GW233261   Stephen S. Wisser III (b 6 Sep 1915) m 30 Jun 1940, Janet Scheifley (b 1 May 1918).

GW2332611   Stephen Wisser IV (b 1 Nov 1944) m ca 1965, Jane Mayer.

GW23326111   Laurie Wisser (b 16 Jun 1965).

GW233262   Ferd H. Wisser (b 10 Jan 1924) m 3 Jun 1945, Birdina Mickle (b 7 Feb 1921).

GW2332621   Louise Wisser (b 3 Jun 1953) m 15 Jun 1974, Brian Frawley (b 14 Feb 1954).

GW234   Harriet (Henrietta) Wieser (17 Nov 1828, Greenwich, Berks PA-17 Nov 1900) m 4 Apr 1852, Michael Bailey (15 Jul 1823, PA-4 May 1900).

GW2341   Daniel Bailey (6 Jun 1852, PA-6 Sep 1926) m Maria   .

GW23411   Ida B. Bailey (5 Feb 1875-18 Dec 1877).

GW23412   Hetty Jenette Bailey (b 24 Mar 1877).

GW23413   Katie Bailey (18 May 1880-14 Aug 1880).

GW2342   H. Alfred Bailey (b ca 1854, PA) m 1) Emma Elisabeth Benigkoff (7 May 1856-7 Oct 1877); m 2) Ellamanda M. Gehringer.

GW23421   Charles William Bailey (17 Sep 1877-15 Dec 1877).

GW23422   Mantana Bailey (b 21 Jun 1882).

GW23423   Lewis Bailey (22 Oct 1884-26 Jan 1893).

GW23424   Katie Elizabeth Bailey (b 29 Dec 1887).

GW2343   Charles Bailey (b ca 1856, PA).

GW2344   Benjamin Bailey (b ca 1858, PA).

GW2345   Samuel Bailey (25 Dec 1861, Greenwich, Berks PA-13 May 1941) m 4 Mar 1882, Lizzie A. Snyder (3 Oct 1861, PA-4 Jan 1921).

GW23451   Edwin Martin Bailey (2 Jun 1884, PA-27 Jan 1904).

GW23452   Franklin M. Bailey (6 Dec 1886, PA-12 Jan 1887).

GW23453   Cora Missouria Bailey (b 13 Apr 1887).

GW23454   Emma Henriette Bailey (6 May 1888-20 Mar 1926) m Charles James Grim (22 Aug 1888-8 May 1954).

GW23455   Ellen L. Bailey (28 Nov 1891, PA-18 Mar 1966) m Robert E. Muse (28 Feb 1890-4 Jul 1970).

GW234551   Paul R. Muse (11 Jul 1912-6 Oct 1978).

GW23456   Ida Clara Bailey (5 Aug 1893, PA-19 Jul 1913) m 11 Jan 1913, Alvin S. Hoffman.

GW234561   George S. Hoffman (19 Jul 1913-17 Aug 1913).

GW2346   Jonathan Bailey (5 Jun 1864, PA-28 May 1936) m Mary A. Miller.

GW23461   Daniel Oswin Bailey (b 31 May 1886).

GW23462   Oliver J. Michael Bailey (1 Apr 1888-26 Aug 1889).

GW23463   Solomon Edgar Bailey (b 5 Apr 1898, Albany, Berks PA).

GW2347   M. Elizabeth Bailey (b ca 1867, PA).

GW2348   Emma Bailey (b ca 1869, PA).

GW235   Elizabeth Ann Wieser (3 May 1833, Greenwich, Berks PA-1 May 1896, Maxatawny, Berks
PA) m 5 Jun 1856, Benjamin Kemp (27 Apr 1837-21 May 1902).

GW2351   Sarah E. Kemp (22 Mar 1858-8 Mar 1925) m Daniel J. Metzger.

GW2352   Amelia Kemp (2 Feb 1860-24 Jun 1926) m Penrose Herring.

GW24   Jacob Wieser (b ca 1795) m Esther   (13 Feb 1791-18 Mar 1835, Maxatawny, Berks
PA).

GW241   Rudolph Wieser (31 Jan 1814, Maxatawny, Berks PA-21 May 1893, Berks PA) m Rachel
Kline (b ca 1816, PA).

GW2411   John Wieser (6 May 1842, Richmond, Berks PA-4 Jun 1916, Berks PA) m Selias Daniel.

GW24111   Adam Monroe Wieser (b 30 Mar 1863).

GW2412   Esther Wieser (b ca 1844, PA) m 14 Feb 1867, Reading PA, Charles Eckspellen (b ca
1845, PA).

GW24121   Daughter Eckspellen (2 Jul 1868-12 Jul 1868).

GW2413   Elias Wieser (4 Mar 1847-2 Dec 1886, Berks PA) m 26 Aug 1871, Weisenberg, Lehigh
PA, Hala Werley.

GW2414   Deborah K. Wieser (15 Mar 1849, PA-20 Mar 1904) m 8 Jul 1871, Daniel F. Moyer (2
Nov 1847-24 Oct 1895).

GW2415   Gabriel Wieser (18 Mar 1852-8 May 1916, Berks PA.

GW2416   Lucy Ann Wieser (6 Aug 1855-29 Sep 1886) m 11 Feb 1882, Reading PA, Jerome Cunius
(b ca 1856, Reading PA).

GW24161   Mary Ellen Cunius (b 25 Mar 1883).

GW242   Harrison Wisser (b 30 Jan 1818, Greenwich, Berks PA) m 13 Feb 1842, Maria Bast.

GW2421   Judith Wisser (b ca 1846) m 13 Apr 1867, Alexander Schwanger.

GW24211   William Henry Harrison Schwanger (13 Nov 1867-5 Jan 1870).

GW2422   Mary Elizabeth Wisser (8 May 1848-24 Dec 1848).

GW2423   Susanna Wisser (b ca 1852).

GW2424   Harrison H. Wisser (b Mar 1855, PA) m Rose   (b Dec 1865, PA). Henry OH and
Alcona MI.

GW24241   Winnie Wisser (b Aug 1889, OH).

GW24242   Frederick J. Wisser (b Nov 1891, OH) m ca 1910,

GW242421   Elva A. Wisser (b ca 1911, MI).

GW242422   Freda G. Wisser (b ca 1913, MI).

GW242423   Arthur J. Wisser (b ca 1914, MI).

GW242424   Clifford E. Wisser (b ca Nov 1915, MI).

GW242425   Mary E. Wisser (b ca Jul 1918, MI).

GW24243   Charles F. Wisser (b Apr 1892, OH) m Ruth   (b ca 1898, MI).

GW242431   Josephine Wisser (b ca Sep 1915, MI).

GW242432   Oren Wisser (b ca Jan 1918, MI).

GW24244   Helen (Ella) M. Wisser (b Aug 1896, OH).

GW24245   Golda Wisser (b May 1897, OH).

GW24246   George Harry Wisser (b Dec 1899, OH).

GW24247   Mabel F. Wisser (b ca 1902, OH).

GW24248   Julia M. Wisser (b ca 1904, OH).

GW24249   Matilda V. Wisser (b ca 1905, OH).

GW2424A   Lawrence E. Wisser (b ca 1907, OH).

GW2424B   Bruce E. Wisser (b ca 1910, OH).

GW2424C   Dora A. Wisser (b ca Oct 1915, MI).

GW243   Elizabeth Wieser (13 Nov 1819-10 Mar 1843) m William Reber.

GW244   Matilda Wieser (b 4 Jul 1821).

GW245   William Wieser (b 11 Apr 1824, Greenwich, Berks PA).

GW246   Carl Wieser (b 14 Dec 1825).

GW247   Esther Wieser (b 14 Oct 1828).

GW3   John Wieser (Nov 1758, Maxatawny, Berks PA-ca Feb 1810, Greenwich, Berks PA) m Elisabeth Kohler (19 Jul 1764-22 Mar 1844, South Whitehall, Lehigh, PA).[155]

---

[155]The county history states that one Daniel Wisser came to Lehigh County from Greenwich Township in Berks County and lists five children: Jonas, Daniel, Elizabeth, Jacob and a daughter married to Mr. Aldendorfer. The son Daniel is said to have been born in 1803. The problem is that there is no record of a Daniel in Greenwich Township, although there was a Daniel Weiser from the Oley Valley family in the adjacent Maxatawny Township. It is assumed here that the history must have been referring to John (GW3), son

GW31   John Wieser (b ca 1786) m Magdalena   .[156]

GW311   Benjamin Wieser (19 Jan 1812-1 Apr 1892) m 14 Sep 1834, Christina Rausch (25 Aug 1811-5 Nov 1890).

GW3111   Catharina Wieser (5 Feb 1835-12 Oct 1838).

GW3112   Mary Ann Wieser (16 Jan 1838-20 Jun 1862, Maxatawny, Berks PA) m 1 Dec 1861, Benjamin Fritz.

GW31121   Alice Fritz (b 1862).

GW3113   Henry R. Wieser (ca 1842, Maxatawny, Berks PA-22 Sep 1897, Earl, Berks PA) m 1) 26 May 1883, Reading PA, Rebecca R. West (ca 1856, Centre, Berks PA-Apr 1887); m 2) 16 Oct 1894, Boyertown PA, Elizabeth Mary Gunsenhouser (b Sep 1874, Phoenixville, Chester PA).

GW31131   William Milton Wieser (b 14 Dec 1886, Blandon, Berks PA).

GW31132   Chester Wieser (14 Oct 1896, Goosetown, Berks PA-28 Dec 1896, Earl, Berks PA).

GW31133   William Henry Wieser (b 16 Nov 1897, Earl, Berks PA).

GW3114   Daniel Wieser (10 Jun 1841, PA-15 Jun 1921, North Loup, Valley NE) m 1) 23 Nov 1862, Mary Louisa Frey (24 Aug 1841, PA-10 Mar 1908); m 2) Martha   (b ca 1853, IN).

GW31141   Ida Wieser (b ca 1863, PA).

GW31142   Clara Wieser (b ca 1865, PA).

GW31143   Benjamin Jacob Wieser (2 Oct 1867, PA-19 Nov 1940) m 1) ca 1889, Margaret Eisenhauer (28 Dec 1865, IL-16 Sep 1914, Spalding NE); m 2) 23 Mar 1915, Fullerton NE, Martha M. Settles (b ca 1872, MO); m 3) 15 Oct 1939, Central City NE, Sarah Marie Glines (10 May 1885-Apr 1975).

GW311431   Joseph Benjamin Wieser (28 Aug 1891, Fullerton NE-8 May 1942, Kit Carson, CO) m 1) 2 Sep 1915, Greeley NE, Margaret Alwisha Kinny (18 Nov 1898, York NE-15 Mar 1919, Keystone NE); m 8 Nov 1923, McCook NE, Mary Estelle Buchanan (20 Nov 1897, Kanorado, KS-21 Feb 1976).

GW3114311   Chester Aaron Wieser (b 24 Dec 1915, Greeley NE) m 12 Nov 1936, Bushnell NE, Ruth Alvina Hartman (b 8 Jan 1918, Idalia, CO).

GW31143111   Joyce Elaine Wieser (b 14 Nov 1940, St. Francis, KS).

GW31143112   Connie Ilene Wieser (10 Apr 1948, Idalia, CO-10 Apr 1948).

GW31143113   Chester Aaron Wieser Jr. (b 18 May 1950, Idalia, CO) m 25 Aug 1973, Judy McCoy.

---

of George, and that the children named were John's children.

[156]There is a problem for the family of John (GW31). The births of four children can be documented from church records between 1825 and 1837. However, the 1820 Census for his household shows two boys and three girls less than 10 years old, and the 1830 Census lists two boys under 5, one boy 5-10, one boy 10-15, one young man 15-20, two girls 5-10, two girls 10-15 and one young woman 15-20. There was a son born between 1810 and 1815 and a son born between 1815 and 1820 who are not otherwise documented, as well as more younger children. This is important because there are two men who lived in the area who used the name Wieser but whose parentage has not been otherwise documented, Benjamin who was born in 1812 and Abraham who was born in 1818. No conflicting evidence having been found, they are therefore added to John's family.

GW311431131   Lori Ann Wieser (b 13 Mar 1977).

GW311431132   Dennis Aaron Wieser (b 27 Jan 1979).

GW31143114   Roger Eugene Wieser (b 20 Dec 1951, Idalia, CO) m 4 Apr 1983, Trudi Dale Strangway (b 19 Apr 1957).

GW311431141   Katie Marie Wieser (b 25 Feb 1986).

GW31143115   Dean Alan Wieser (b 8 Nov 1954, Idalia, CO) m 23 Jun 1974, Susan Alice Riedesel (b 6 Sep 1955).

GW311431151   Grant Alan Wieser (b 22 Mar 1976).

GW311431152   Joan Alice Wieser (b 9 Dec 1979).

GW311431153   Pamela Sue Wieser (b 2 Mar 1981).

GW311431154   Michael Dean Wieser (b 3 Jan 1992).

GW3114312   Willard Joseph Wieser (6 Jun 1918, Keystone NE-12 Feb 1980, Riverton, WY) m 28 Feb 1939, Esther Maxine Funk (b 7 Feb 1922).

GW31143121   Beverly Ann Wieser (b 23 Mar 1940).

GW31143122   Wilma Jane Wieser (b 3 Jun 1941).

GW31143123   Shirley Maxine Wieser (b 10 Apr 1943).

GW31143124   Donna Carol Wieser (b 10 Jan 1946).

GW31143125   Joyce Marie Wieser (2 Feb 1948-15 Nov 1964).

GW31143126   William Joseph Wieser (b 6 May 1950).

GW31143127   Betty Lou Wieser (b 23 May 1953).

GW3114313   Clarice June Wieser (b 18 Jun 1924) m 4 Jun 1942, Howard Armknecht (4 Jan 1922-15 Sep 1994).

GW31143131   Elaine Armknecht (b 3 Mar 1943) m 1) Jerry Soto; m 2) Richard Montgomery.

GW31143132   Marcia Gay Armknecht (b 11 Aug 1946) m 1) Ron Franzen; m 2) Ray Alverado.

GW31143133   Debra May Armknecht (b 1 May 1948) m Richard Allen.

GW31143134   William Joseph Armknecht (b 11 Aug 1949) m 1) Karen   ; m 2) Bamcy Mershon.

GW31143135   Cindy Ray Armknecht (b 17 Jul 1951) m Don Vorque.

GW31143136   Connie Fay Armknecht (b 21 Jul 1952) m Dave Johnson.

GW3114314   Benjamin Christopher Wieser (2 Oct 1926-21 Mar 1994) m 1) ca 1945, Lois Nelson; m 2) 3 Nov 1952, Myrtice Wilson (b 3 Nov 1934).

GW31143141   Donald Wieser.

GW31143142   Dennis Wieser.

GW31143143   Kathy B. Wieser (26 Sep 1956-29 Dec 1969).

GW31143144   Gary B. Wieser (b 20 Jun 1967).

GW3114315   Wayne Dean ("Jack") Wieser (b 14 Dec 1928) m 1) 30 Jan 1950, Barbara Hensley (b 9 Sep 1928); m 2) 1 Jan 1975, Geline Stearns (b 11 Mar 1939).

GW31143151   Norma Jean Wieser (b 5 Aug 1950) m   Russell.

GW311431511   Matthew Russell.

GW311431512   Sarah Russell.

GW311431513   Andrew Russell.

GW31143152   Nancy Ellen Wieser (b 4 Oct 1951) m   Ruge.

GW311431521   Tanner Ruge.

GW311431522   Caron Ruge.

GW31143153   Christine Dee Wieser (b 29 Jan 1954) m   Perry.

GW311431531   Regan Perry.

GW3114316   Ray Daniel Wieser (21 Dec 1931-25 Feb 1994) m 1) 14 Dec 1952, Dorothy Borst (b 14 Dec 1933); m 2) 12 Jun 1970, Patricia Wood (b 19 Mar 1936).

GW31143161   Dennis Ray Wieser (b 1 Jan 1954).

GW311431611   Blake Wieser.

GW31143162   Donald Leroy Wieser (b 7 Dec 1954).

GW31143163   Douglas Eugene Wieser (b 7 Nov 1955).

GW31143164   Doyle Allen Wieser (b 26 Jul 1957).

GW311431641   Dylon Wieser.

GW311431642   Daniel Wieser.

GW3114317   Dale Clifton Wieser (b 28 Jul 1934) m 20 Dec 1952, Betty Jeannine McCurry (b 19 Dec 1935).

GW31143171   Deborah Ellen Wieser (b 12 Mar 1954).

GW31143172   Aaron Dale Wieser (b 28 Oct 1956).

GW31143173   Ray Dean Wieser (b 17 Dec 1958).

GW3114318   Lois Ilene Wieser (b 18 Jun 1938) m 13 Oct 1962, Dean Sutherland (b 20 Apr 1932).

GW31143181   Aaron Dean Sutherland (b 27 Jan 1965).

GW31143182   Karen Eileen Sutherland (b 13 Nov 1967).

GW31143183   Kyle Eugene Sutherland (b 31 Dec 1970).

GW3114319   Larry Elton Wieser (8 Dec 1941-7 Apr 1960) m 13 Dec 1959, Shirley Bradshaw (b 9 Aug 1943).

GW31143191   Marty Roy Wieser (b 5 May 1960).

GW311432   Elsie Marinda Wieser (28 Apr 1893, Fullerton NE-25 Jul 1978, Fresno CA) m 11 Nov 1914, Spalding NE, Peter Henning ("Henry") Lund (14 Apr 1890-21 Oct 1949, Sun Valley CA).

GW3114321   Alice Josephine Lund (b 1 Apr 1916) m 11 Nov 1939, Ralph Bishop ("Jerry") Rubeck (b 10 Dec 1915).

GW31143211   Melvin Douglas Rubeck (b 17 Jun 1940, St. Paul NE).

GW31143212   Glenda Lee Rubeck (b 27 Oct 1945, Glendale CA).

GW3114322   Hazel Irene Lund (1 Oct 1924-12 May 1996, Chico, Butte CA) m Robert Baumann.

GW31143221   Gail Ann Baumann (b 4 Mar 1946, Sun Valley CA) m Harry Kennedy.

GW3114323   Jessie Bernice Lund (b 17 Sep 1928) m 26 Feb 1949, Milton Eugene Hench (b 24 Feb 1928).

GW31143231   Bryan Eugene Hench (7 Oct 1951, San Fernando CA-7 May 1971).

GW31143232   Karen Lynn Hench (b 11 Oct 1955, San Fernando CA).

GW31143233   Alan Melvin Hench (b 2 Feb 1958, San Fernando CA).

GW3114324   Margaret Elna Lund (b 11 Dec 1932) m 28 Apr 1951, Gerald Elwood Enochs (b 14 Dec 1932).

GW31143241   David Elwood Enochs (b 4 Aug 1955, San Fernando CA).

GW31143242   Dennis Elwood Enochs (b 10 Sep 1957, San Fernando CA).

GW311433   Daniel Peter Wieser (16 Nov 1894, Fullerton NE-17 Dec 1971, St. Paul NE) m 7 Dec 1916, Greeley NE, Susan Delina Crumrine (18 Aug 1897, NE-15 Nov 1993, Grand Island NE).

GW3114331   Francis Daniel Wieser (19 Feb 1923, Greeley NE-17 Jul 1987, FL) m 1) 17 Feb 1945, Columbus OH, Margaret Josephine Brown; m 2) Genevieve   .

GW31143311   Francis Daniel Wieser (b 2 Sep 1946, FL).

GW31143312   Gary Steven Wieser (b 19 Mar 1948, FL).

GW3114332   Harold Benjamin Wieser (29 Jul 1924, Greeley NE-1994, St. Paul NE) m Anna Belle Berney (b 24 Apr 1926, Spalding NE).

GW31143321   Sheryl Lynne Wieser (b 16 Oct 1948) m 8 Feb 1969, Barry A. Huston (b ca 1947).

GW311433211   Amy Elizabeth Huston (b 20 Oct 1971).

GW311433212   Sarah Katherine Huston (b 29 Dec 1973).

GW311433213   Meghan Ann Huston (b 21 Jan 1981).

GW31143322   Terry Alfred Wieser (b 22 Mar 1952) m 18 Dec 1976, Diane Winkler.

GW311433221   Cara Adria Wieser (b 12 Dec 1978).

GW311433222   Adam Benjamin Wieser (b 9 Apr 1983).

GW311433223   Ingrid Marielle Wieser (b 6 Jun 1985).

GW31143323   William Benjamin Wieser (b 29 Jun 1955) m 25 Jun 1983, Jeannette Munyon (b 30 Oct 1956).

GW311433231   Sharyln Brooke Wieser (b 25 Jul 1985).

GW311433232   Dylan Benjamin Wieser (b 28 Mar 1989).

GW3114333   Danny Eugene Wieser (b 27 Jan 1932) m 1) 25 Mar 1951, Charlene F. Wetzel (b ca 1935, North Loup NE); m 2) Marian Tuenge; m 3) 7 Apr 1972, Ruth Jane Sherlock (b 1 Jan 1932).

GW31143331   Lavonne Kay Wieser (b 14 Jun 1953).

GW311434   Guy Milton Wieser (4 Apr 1896, Fullerton NE-4 Sep 1963, Stockton CA) m 2 Jun 1919, Spalding NE, Johanna Louise Heinz (28 Mar 1899, Ewing NE-13 Dec 1995, Sacramento CA).

GW3114341   Donald Edwin Wieser (22 Nov 1921, Spalding NE-29 May 1996, Sacramento CA) m 29 Jun 1946, Canton OH, Betty Bittner (b 4 Dec 1919, Meyersdale PA).

GW31143411   Edward Charles Wieser (b 7 May 1947) m 13 Jun 1992, Lynne Shannon (b 30 Mar 1960).

GW311434111   Evan Robert Wieser (b 9 Jan 1994).

GW311434112   Sean Edwin Wieser (b 16 May 1996).

GW31143412 ("Dean") Banks.   Dorothy Louise ("Dottie Lou") Wieser (b 5 Jul 1948) m 13 Jul 1968, Sherman Wayne

GW311434121   Justin Eliot Banks (26 Nov 1976-18 May 1988).

GW311434122   Benjamin Jacob Banks (b 12 Jun 1979).

GW31143413   Guy Franklin Wieser (13 Aug 1949-15 Aug 1949).

GW31143414   Douglas Jacob Wieser (b 25 Dec 1951) m Donna Sudderth (b 15 Nov 1966).

GW31143415   Marcy Ann Wieser (b 10 Feb 1953) m 13 Jul 1981, Michael O'Day (b 26 Mar 1953).

GW311434151   Casey Ann O'Day (b 25 Jul 1989).

GW31143416   Donald Edwin ("Dewey") Wieser (9 Sep 1963-3 Jan 1966).

GW3114342   Bernadine Louise ("Bunny") Wieser (b 4 Jan 1924, Spalding, Greeley NE) m 4 Jan 1944, Sacramento CA, Raymond John Thielen (b 15 Feb 1924, Chicago IL).

GW31143421   Raymond John Thielen Jr. (b 29 Oct 1943, Sacramento CA) m 5 Jun 1969, Sacramento CA, Dorothy Moe.

GW311434211   Raymond John Thielen III (b 1969, Sacramento CA).

GW311434212   Andrew Carl Thielen (b 29 Apr 1971, Sacramento CA) m 12 Aug 1995, Sacramento CA, Leslie Ann Shaw.

GW3114342121   Nicholas Andrew Thielen (b 29 Jan 1995).

GW3114342122   Joseph Edgar Thielen (b 15 Mar 1996).

GW31143422   Diana Thielen (b 29 Nov 1946, Fort Sill OK) m 1) 15 Jul 1967, Sacramento CA, William Von Phul; m 2) 31 Dec 1974, Carson City NV, Richard Lowe.

GW311434221   Tracy Thielen Von Phul (b 19 Feb 1969, Ft. Lewis WA).

GW311434222   Patricia Diane Von Phul (b 19 Oct 1972, Sacramento CA).

GW31143423   Donald Thomas Thielen (b 22 Jun 1949, Fort Meade MD) m 1) 22 Aug 1971, Kathy McCoy; m 2) Karen Crumbley; m 3) Debbie   .

GW311434231   Jennifer Michele Thielen.

GW311434232   Donald Thomas Thielen Jr.

GW311434233   Daniel Thielen.

GW31143424   Mary Jo Thielen (b 31 May 1953) m Douglas Farrell.

GW311434241   Kevin Farrell.

GW311434242   Jacob Farrell.

GW31143425   Mark William Thielen (1 Sep 1961, Fort Sill OK-12 Dec 1961).

GW3114343   Delores Eileen ("Dodie") Wieser (b 28 Nov 1925, Spalding NE) m 4 Feb 1946, Sacramento CA, Francis Anderson ("Bubby") Williams (21 Jul 1924-1992).

GW31143431   Robert Adrian Williams (b 21 Mar 1947) m Laurie   .

GW311434311   Robert Agustus Williams (b 7 Apr 1979).

GW31143432   Patricia Ann Williams (b 15 Apr 1951).

GW311434321   Jessica   .

GW31143433   Johanna ("Jodie") Williams (b 7 Oct 1954) m Chris Deaton.

GW311434331   Brianna Deaton (b 1982).

GW311434332   Elana Deaton.

GW31143434   Evelyn Williams (b 4 Feb 1957) m   Norstrom.

GW311434341   Adrian Norstrom (b 25 Dec 1976).

GW31143435   Francis Anderson ("Andy") Williams II (b 25 Nov 1961) m Angela Zito.

GW311434351   Johanna Anna Williams (b ca 1988).

GW311434352   Francis Anderson ("Trey") Williams III (b ca 1992).

GW311434353   Nicolas James Williams (b 4 Dec 1995).

GW31143436   Barbara Elizabeth Williams (b 20 Apr 1964) m Brian Kahrs.

GW311434361   Brian Andrew Kahrs (b 7 May 1990).

GW311434362   Brandon Norstrom Kahrs (b 15 Apr 1996).

GW3114344   Thomas Charles Wieser (b 27 May 1927, Greeley NE) m 1) 1952, Stateline NV, Laura Lee Weir; m 2) 1955, Placerville CA, Leota Madge Cox; m 3) 8 Sep 1961, Gustine CA, Ann Elizabeth Bunker (b 17 Apr 1937, Newman CA).

GW31143441   Russell ("Rusty") Wieser (b ca 1953).

GW31143442   Christine Marie Wieser (b 13 Apr 1962, Gustine CA) m 18 Nov 1989, Concord CA, Michael Stephan Punty (b 27 Apr 1963).

GW311434421   Scott David Punty (b 2 Jul 1981, Oakland CA).

GW311434422   Zachary Stephan Punty (b 12 Oct 1991, Oakland CA).

GW311434423   Christopher Michael Punty (b 20 Dec 1993, Oakland CA).

GW31143443   Elizabeth Ann Wieser (b 13 Apr 1962, Gustine CA) m 1) 8 Dec 1980, Gustine CA, Jefferson Charles Galatro; m 2) 29 Sep 1990, Carson City NV, Matthew Dunn (b 7 Jun 1965).

GW311434431   Sarah Elizabeth Dunn (b 24 Jun 1981, Los Banos CA).

GW311434432   John Carl Dunn (b 17 Jan 1983, Modesto CA.

GW31143444   Katherine Mary Wieser (b 14 Mar 1964, Gustine CA) m 13 Jun 1987, Long Beach CA, James Anthony De Bois (b 19 Jul 1961, Long Beach CA).

GW311434441   Tricia Lee De Bois (b 1 Dec 1987, Long Beach CA).

GW311434442   Felicia Ann De Bois (b 15 Sep 1989, Long Beach CA).

GW31143445   Karl William Wieser (b 17 Jul 1965, Gustine CA) m 30 Jun 1996, Sacramento CA, Louise Chase Shaw (b 5 Jul 1968, San Diego CA).

GW31143446   Susan Patricia Wieser (b 8 Sep 1967, Gustine CA) m 9 Oct 1987, San Francisco CA, Raphael Pazo (b 26 Apr 1960, Puerto Rico).

GW311434461   Thomas Raphael Pazo (b 23 Apr 1988, San Francisco CA).

GW311434462   Daniel Yitzhack Pazo (b 26 Nov 1989, Tracy CA).

GW311434463   Anthony Andrew Pazo (b 22 Dec 1991, Sacramento CA).

GW311434464   Juliann Margaret Pazo (b 29 Oct 1993, San Mateo CA).

GW3114345   Mary Adeline Wieser (b 25 Jul 1929, Wallace NE) m 1 Feb 1951, Salem OR, Lewis Leon Gray (b 15 Oct 1928, Corvallis OR).

GW3114346   Shirley Lorraine Wieser (b 15 Nov 1931, Ericson NE) m 8 Aug 1953, Sacramento CA, Buford Leroy ("Jim") Wright (b 9 Nov 1928, Madera CA).

GW31143461   Karen Lea Wright (b 14 Jan 1958, Sacramento CA) m 1) Aug 1978, Charles Taylor; m 2) 24 Nov 1990, Sacramento CA, John Patrick Keller.

GW311434611   Brianne Marie Taylor (b 6 Apr 1981, Sacramento CA).

GW31143462   Matthew Carl Wright (b 22 Nov 1959, Sacramento CA) m 16 Nov 1991, Jody Steffan (b 11 Aug 1965).

GW311434621   Amanda Glynn Wright (b 30 Mar 1988, Sacramento CA).

GW311434622   Joshua Matthew Wright (b 3 Apr 1992, Sacramento CA).

GW31143463   Stevan James Wright (b 24 Jul 1962, Sacramento CA).

GW31143464   Julie Lorraine Wright (b 1 Jan 1964, Sacramento CA) m 12 May 1990, Sacramento CA, Stacy Collins.

GW311434641   Kyle Sean Collins (b 21 Mar 1991, Sacramento CA).

GW311434642   Austin Alan Collins (b 25 Mar 1993, Sacramento CA).

GW3114347   Joan Margaret Wieser (b 2 Dec 1933, Spalding NE) m 8 Jan 1955, Sacramento CA, Charles Hugh McGee (b 19 Mar 1934, Sacramento CA).

GW31143471   Cathleen Marie McGee (b 9 Dec 1955, Oakland CA) m May 1976, Stateline NV, James Young.

GW31143472   Dennis Michael McGee (b 24 Apr 1957, Sacramento CA) m 16 May 1987, Willows CA, Patricia Ann Sykes.

GW31143473   Timothy Patrick McGee (b 5 Aug 1959, Sacramento CA) m 2 Jun 1984, Sacramento CA, Jill Katherine Ahrendt.

GW311434731   Laura Ashley McGee (b 2 Sep 1986, Sacramento CA).

GW311434732   Tara Leanne McGee (b 8 Mar 1989, Sacramento CA).

GW31143474   Hugh Frances McGee (b 18 Oct 1961, Sacramento CA) m 1) Apr 1985, Sacramento CA, Pamela Hayes; m 2) 17 Sep 1995, Sacramento CA, Tina Marie Stahley.

GW3114348   Bertha Jean ("Bertie") Wieser (b 17 Sep 1936, Spalding NE) m 1 Oct 1955, Sacramento CA, Earle Leroy Travis (b 16 May 1932, Cheriton VA).

GW31143481   Michael Earle Travis (b 12 Oct 1959, Sacramento CA) m 7 Jul 1984, Eureka CA, Kathleen Eleanor Hiscox (b 8 Jan 1962).

GW311434811   Brandon Michael Travis (b 3 Jun 1986).

GW311434812   Brittany Jean Travis (b 31 Dec 1990).

GW31143482   Teresa Lynn ("Terry") Travis (b 21 May 1961, Sacramento CA) m 14 Jun 1980, Sacramento CA, Daniel Theodore Mandella (b 12 Feb 1960).

GW311434821   Bryan Adam Mandella (b 8 Jun 1985, Sacramento CA).

GW311434822   Danielle Nicole Mandella (b 9 Oct 1986, Sacramento CA).

GW31143483   Ronald Eugene Travis (b 14 Aug 1963, Wichita Falls TX).

GW311434831   Sarah April Travis (b 25 Sep 1986).

GW311434832   Erica Marie Travis (b 29 Mar 1988).

GW31143484   Anne Marie Travis (b 24 Nov 1967, Clovis NM) m 7 Aug 1993, Carmichael CA, Kevin Richardson McCutcheon (b 17 Dec 1959).

GW311434841   Nathaniel Gregory McCutcheon (b 20 Oct 1995).

GW31143485   Gregory Alan Travis (b 6 May 1968, Wichita Falls TX) m 1 Oct 1993, Carmichael CA, Leanne Kay Hartsgrove (b 26 Nov 1962).

GW311434851   Jordan Jedediah Travis (b 13 Jul 1994, Sacramento CA).

GW311434852   Rachael Kimberlee Travis (b 8 Aug 1996, Sacramento CA).

GW3114349   Roberta Jeannine Wieser (b 11 Nov 1938, Spalding NE) m 20 Aug 1961, Sacramento CA, Edward Carl Brady.

GW31143491   Jack Carl Brady (b 29 Jul 1962, Sacramento CA) m Sep 1992, Christine Raczkowski.

GW31143492   Jeanine Brady (29 Aug 1967, Sacramento CA-29 Aug 1967).

GW31143493   Jeanine Marie Brady (b 17 Apr 1969, Sacramento CA) m Rene Villa.

GW31143494   Michelle Jennifer ("Shellie") Brady (b 23 Aug 1977, Sacramento CA).

GW311434A   Bernard Joseph ("Butch") Wieser (b 18 Mar 1941, Spalding NE) m 24 Mar 1969, Antoinette Bernice McLoughlin (b 7 Mar 1951).

GW311434A1   Erika Jean Wieser (b 15 Sep 1969, Sacramento CA) m 13 Aug 1994, Sacramento CA, Michael Paul Goyette (b 13 Nov 1968).

GW311434A11   Julia Nicole Goyette (b 5 Jul 1995, Wichita KS).

GW311434A2   Tanya Marie Wieser (b 9 Nov 1972, Sacramento CA) m 20 Jan 1996, Fair Oaks CA, Ward Houston Roberts (b Apr 1969).

GW311434B   Michael Jerome Wieser (b 24 Mar 1944, Sacramento CA) m 1) Kathy Brown; m 2) Mary Ann Quay.

GW31144   George Milton Wieser (Aug 1871, PA-12 Dec 1910, Denver, Adams NE) m ca 1890, Ida Giersdorf (b Aug 1875, NE).

GW311441   Mabel Mary Wieser (7 Sep 1891, Nance NE-8 Jul 1970) m 25 Feb 1912, Albion NE, Marshall Lee Oakley.

GW3114411   Fred M. Oakley (b ca 1913).

GW3114412   Mildred Oakley (b ca 1914).

GW3114413   Lloyd R. Oakley (b ca Jun 1917).

GW3114414   Edna M. Oakley (b ca Oct 1918).

GW311442   Emma Wieser (b Sep 1893, NE) m   Brown.

GW3114421   Robert Brown.

GW311443   Dora Wieser (b Sep 1895, NE).

GW311444   Lottie Wieser (b Nov 1896, NE) m 1) Joe Sallach; m 2) Leslie Danbaum.

GW3114441   Son Sallach.

GW311445   Lloyd Milton Wieser (Jan 1900, Belgrade NE-ca 1981) m 21 Dec 1918, Fullerton NE, Elizabeth ("Bessie") Elliot (b 1900, Cushing NE).

GW3114451   Velda E. Weiser (b ca 1922) m 12 Sep 1942, St. Paul NE, Marvin L. Christensen (b ca 1919).

GW3114452   Lloyd Weiser Jr..

GW3114453   Wayne Weiser.

GW3114454   Melvin Weiser.

GW3114455   Shirley Weiser m Irving Goerhing.

GW311446   Jessie Wieser (b 1902) m Pearson.

GW311447   Halverson H. Wieser (15 May 1903, Belgrade NE-21 May 1985, Albion NE) m 10 Dec 1939, Brandish NE, Ruth B. Fusselman (29 Aug 1907-Jul 1994).

GW3114471   Halver William Wieser (b 18 Jun 1942) m 9 Aug 1969, Spalding NE, Eileen M. Reuter (b 7 Aug 1949, Spalding NE).

GW31145   Alice Sidney Wieser (8 Dec 1874, PA-4 Aug 1930, Kearney NE) m 22 Sep 1908, NE, Cyrus N. Baker (b 1848, IA).

GW31146   Lizzie C. Wieser (b Sep 1881, Nance NE) m 25 Dec 1902, NE, Charles Erickson (b 1870, Sweden).

GW311461   Harley Erickson (1904-1907).

GW311462   Dannie C. Erickson (b ca 1908, NE).

GW311463   Nellie A. Erickson (b ca 1910, NE).

GW31147   Harvey Wieser (b Apr 1885, NE).

GW3115   Amelia Wieser (b ca 1844).

GW3116   Sarah Ann Wieser (12 Sep 1845, Mertztown, Berks PA-26 Aug 1920, Topton PA) m 2 Feb 1872, Franklin Fritsch.

GW31161   Katie Christina Alice Fritsch (22 Apr 1872, Longswamp, Berks PA-18 Sep 1878).

GW31162   Jonas Fritsch (21 Feb 1874, District, Berks PA-30 Sep 1878, District, Berks PA).

GW31163   Alfred Fritsch (13 Nov 1877, District, Berks PA-17 Nov 1878, District, Berks PA).

GW31164   Sarah Fritsch (b 7 Aug 1879, District, Berks PA).

GW31165   Jennie Fritsch (b 17 May 1881, District, Berks PA).

GW31166   Martha W. Fritsch (17 Nov 1882, District, Berks PA-4 May 1952) m Jacob M. Gehris (8 Feb 1883-21 Apr 1976).

GW31167   Elda W. Fritsch (1885, Fleetwood PA-15 Nov 1980, Allentown PA) m 10 Jan 1911, Kutztown PA, Joseph Ezra Hamsher (8 Nov 1888, Bowers, Berks PA-1972).

GW311671   Daughter Hamsher (26 Feb 1912-12 Mar 1919).

GW311672   Joseph Fritch Hamsher (b 15 Mar 1914) m 4 Jun 1940, Zionsville, Lehigh PA, Mildred Reppert (b 27 Nov 1910, Maxatawny, Berks PA).

GW3116721   Ronald Hamsher m Georgine Lucas.

GW31167211   Brett Hamsher.

GW31167212   Douglas Hamsher.

GW31167213   Elizabeth Hamsher.

GW3116722   Neil Hamsher m Cassandra Miller.

GW31167221   Christopher John Hamsher.

GW311673   Paul Fritch Hamsher (7 Jul 1915-28 Feb 1916).

GW311674   Sarah E. Hamsher (b 30 Oct 1919, Bowers, Berks PA) m 15 Mar 1941, Kingstree, SC, Charles D. Kuhns (b 15 Feb 1918).

GW3116741   Carol Joy Kuhns (b 11 Jan 1942) m 31 Dec 1966, Raymond Teske.

GW31167411   David Gregory Teske (b 23 Aug 1967).

GW31167412   Patrick Charles Teske (b 25 May 1973).

GW311675   Anna Fritch Hamsher (b 16 Nov 1925) m Jack DeHaven.

GW3116751   Cynthia DeHaven m James Boscov.

GW3116752   Suzanne L. DeHaven m Michael A. Fox.

GW3117   Catharine Wieser (b ca 1849) m 1) 31 Jan 1874, Eli F. Frederick; m 2) 27 Feb 1886, Reading PA, Harrison W. Preston (b ca 1864).

GW3118   Benjamin Franklin Wieser (8 Jul 1853, Maxatawny, Berks PA-2 Oct 1853, Maxatawny, Berks PA).

GW312   Abraham Wieser (1818, Albany, Berks PA-16 Aug 1901, Berks PA) m 1) Lucinda Leiby (11 Sep 1824-24 Dec 1866, Windsor, Berks PA); m 2) 18 Jul 1869, Hamburg PA, Ruhama Estella Lord.

GW3121   Mary Ann A. Wieser (10 Dec 1846, PA-16 Feb 1920) m Samuel Behler (25 Oct 1849, PA-8 Dec 1911).

GW31211   Charles Behler (b ca 1866, PA).

GW3122   John Harrison Wieser (b ca 1849, PA).

GW3123   William Wilson Wieser (b 27 Jan 1853, Berks PA) m 30 Dec 1903, Schuylkill PA, Annie J. Barr (b 8 Jul 1864, Jefferson PA).

GW3124   Sarah A. Wieser (27 Apr 1856, PA-11 Sep 1914) m 7 Jun 1874, Albert B. Miller (14 Feb 1856-15 Mar 1939).

GW31241   Cora Miller (12 Feb 1880-Jul 1911) m Henry B. Hollenbach (23 Dec 1876-5 Jul 1955).

GW31242   Elvesta Miller (23 Oct 1881-22 May 1941) m 1) A. Wilson Wentzel (26 Nov 1875-31 Oct 1918); m 2) George Foorman.

GW312421   Edna C. Wentzel (4 Jul 1898-13 Mar 1933).

GW31243   Oscar Frank Miller (13 Sep 1885-5 Jun 1941, Jacobs, Lehigh PA).

GW31244   Annie Wilma Miller (17 Aug 1886-1950) m John Wink (1890-1968).

GW31245   Harvey G. Miller (b 1895) m Sallie A. Bailey.

GW3125   Anna Maria Matilda Wieser (b 9 Jul 1858, PA).

GW3126   Benjamin Franklin Wisser (29 Jan 1862, Windsor, Berks PA-6 Oct 1931, Lenhartsville PA) m 12 Jun 1886, Bernville(?) PA, Ellen Susanna Bauscher (26 Jan 1868, Greenwich, Berks PA-3 Dec 1940, Lenhartsville PA).

GW31261   Herbert Franklin Wisser (30 Mar 1888, Lenhartsville PA-25 May 1954) m 20 May 1916, Kutztown PA, Helen M. Moll (10 May 1898-31 Oct 1990, Hamburg PA).

GW312611   Joseph Thomas Wisser (19 Oct 1916, Maxatawny, Berks PA-25 Apr 1980, Hamburg PA) m 8 Feb 1941, Lenhartsville PA, Earlene Luella Binner (b 30 Oct 1922, Strausstown PA).

GW3126111   Barry Neil Wisser (b 17 May 1941) m 1) Virginia Harriet Adam; m 2) 11 Dec 1993, Gloria Jean Berger (b 20 Jul 1956).

GW31261111   Kimberly Sue Wisser (b 26 Apr 1968).

GW3126112   Steven Joseph Wisser (b 17 Aug 1943) m 2 Sep 1962, Hamburg PA, Sandra Kay Uberti (b 6 Jun 1944).

GW31261121   Steven Todd Wisser (b 8 Sep 1963, Reading PA) m 24 Nov 1985, Hamburg PA, Barbara Ann Miller (b 20 May 1960).

GW312611211   Emily Anne Wisser (b 7 Nov 1986).

GW312611212   Jacob Benjamin Wisser (b 8 Jan 1988).

GW31261122   Stephanie Luann Wisser (b 23 Sep 1964, Reading PA) m 24 Feb 1990, Barry Lee Riegel
(b 2 Jan 1955).

GW312611221   Jennifer Kay Wisser (b 13 Dec 1982, Reading PA).

GW312611222   Justin Matthew Riegel (b 20 Jan 1990).

GW31261123   Samuel Scott Wisser (b 25 Jan 1966, West Reading PA) m 1) Kristin Leigh Wentzel; m
2) 21 May 1994, Hamburg PA, Shannon Sue Gerner (b 26 Feb 1972).

GW312611231   Samuel Nicholas Wisser (b 25 Dec 1989).

GW312611232   Derick Joseph Wisser (b 19 Oct 1994).

GW31261124   Susan Marie Wisser (b 19 May 1971, Reading PA) m 3 Dec 1988, Hamburg PA, Randy
Alan Specht (b 26 Dec 1962).

GW312611241   Kasondra Lynn Specht (b 10 Jul 1989).

GW312611242   Jasmine Marie Specht (b 6 Aug 1991).

GW3126113   Evelene(?) Wisser (1952-1952).

GW312612   Ella May Wisser (b 9 Mar 1918) m 1) 9 Nov 1940, Lenhartsville PA, Thomas H. Reed;
m 2) 24 Dec 1949, Edenberg PA, Carl Edwin Strittmatter (b 1 May 1921).

GW3126121   Carla Rae Strittmatter (b 6 Mar 1954).

GW312613   Lillian Alice Wisser (7 Dec 1919-29 Jan 1990) m 17 Jun 1941, Lenhartsville PA, Sterling
Ivan Rudolph Smith (b 7 Feb 1918).

GW3126131   Donald Lee Smith (b 18 Dec 1941).

GW3126132   Dennis Lynn Smith (17 Jul 1945, West Reading PA-19 Feb 1968, Norristown PA).

GW3126133   David Lloyd Smith (b 5 Mar 1947).

GW312614   Donald Wesley Wisser (b 22 Jan 1921) m 21 Mar 1959, Trexlertown PA, Ethel Cecelia
Gorr (b 15 Jul 1929).

GW3126141   Karen Kay Wisser (b 9 Apr 1959).

GW3126142   Mark Alan Wisser (b 26 Jun 1960).

GW312615   John Allen Wisser (b 25 Apr 1923, Greenwich, Berks PA) m 31 Jul 1964, Schnecksville
PA, Verna Louisa Weiss (b 28 Dec 1927).

GW3126151   John Allen Wisser Jr. (b 28 Sep 1964, Allentown PA) m 3 Aug 1991, Wayne PA, Elaine
Marie Lawless (b 25 Sep 1964).

GW31261511   Jacob John Wisser (b 8 Mar 1994).

GW312616   Harold Lloyd Wisser (b 4 Aug 1925) m 22 Jul 1950, Edenberg PA, Fern Viola Binner (b
26 Feb 1932).

GW3126161   Linda Mae Wisser (b 9 Oct 1950) m 30 Jun 1973, Fleetwood PA, Ronald John Mohap (b 10 Aug 1949).

GW3126162   Scott Alan Wisser (13 Jan 1954-17 Dec 1992).

GW3126163   Jane Louise Wisser (b 7 Jul 1965).

GW312617   Russell Matthew Wisser (b 28 Aug 1926) m 24 Dec 1953, Lenhartsville PA, Delores Lois Burkert (b 26 Jun 1934, Reading PA).

GW3126171   Gretta Renee Wisser (b 25 Sep 1955, Reading PA) m 22 Dec 1973, Leon John Seyler (b 31 Oct 1945).

GW31261711   Justin Matthew Seyler (b 25 May 1980).

GW31261712   Brandon Vernon Seyler (b 2 May 1982).

GW31261713   Jordan Zachary Seyler (b 13 Mar 1990).

GW3126172   Denise Lynn Wisser (b 7 Dec 1956).

GW3126173   Jennifer Kay Wisser (b 5 Jun 1958).

GW3126174   Andrea Lee Wisser (b 30 Sep 1966, Reading PA) m 29 Jun 1991, Andrew Paul Pellegrino (b 10 Apr 1964).

GW312618   Herbert Charles Wisser (b 15 Feb 1928) m 25 Jul 1953, Edenberg PA, Jean Marie Moyer (b 28 Jul 1934).

GW3126181   Keith Allen Wisser (b 13 Jan 1954) m 31 Dec 1988, Windsor Castle, Berks PA, Kathleen Marie Zabrinski (b 1 Aug 1954).

GW3126182   Kathleen Jean Wisser (b 12 Sep 1955) m Nov 1973, Vernon Drake Geisinger (b 31 Aug 1955, Kutztown PA).

GW31261821   Andrew Drake Geisinger (b 23 Apr 1974).

GW3126183   Mary Helen Wisser (b 29 Apr 1959) m 4 Nov 1978, Lenhartsville PA, William Edward Lillington (b 23 Sep 1958).

GW31261831   Christa Helen Lillington (b 28 Dec 1974).

GW31261832   Jon Edward Lillington (b 25 Sep 1976).

GW31261833   Darren Edward Lillington (b 17 Mar 1978).

GW31261834   Joseph Charles Lillington (b 15 Oct 1990).

GW31261835   Joshua William Lillington (b 26 May 1994).

GW3126184   Faith Ann Wisser (b 24 Mar 1961) m 11 Jan 1982, Lenhartsville PA, Dennis Allen Miller (b 30 Nov 1958).

GW31261841   Daniel Adam Miller (b 17 May 1982).

GW31261842   Lindsey Ann Miller (b 27 Feb 1986).

GW31261843   Michael Allen Miller (b 23 Oct 1990).

GW312619   Murrill Ralph Wisser (b 3 Aug 1931, Greenwich, Berks PA) m 20 Jun 1964, Lenhartsville PA, Mary Alice Hill (b 12 Dec 1928).

GW31261A   Robert Lee Wisser (5 Dec 1932-26 Dec 1932).

GW31261B   Helen Loraine Wisser (b 28 Sep 1933) m 2 Oct 1954, Windsor Castle, Berks PA, Elmer Sylvester Sonon (b 27 Dec 1930, Maidencreek, Berks PA).

GW31261B1   Jeffrey Lynn Sonon (b 13 Dec 1954).

GW31261B2   Gregory Lee Sonon (b 21 Nov 1955).

GW31261B3   Craig Alan Sonon (b 24 Feb 1964).

GW31261B4   Philip Alan Sonon (b 29 Sep 1971).

GW31261C   Son Wisser (13 Mar 1935-13 Mar 1935).

GW31261D   Son Wisser (26 Dec 1935-26 Dec 1935).

GW31261E   Carl Robert Wisser (b 22 Dec 1936, Lenhartsville PA) m 17 Jun 1961, Lenhartsville PA, Shirley Anne Schumaker (b 26 Nov 1942, Allentown PA).

GW31261E1   Robin Renee Wisser (b 7 Mar 1962, Allentown PA).

GW31261E2   Anita Anne Wisser (b 13 May 1964, Reading PA) m 18 Mar 1989, Kutztown PA, John Francis Muzopappa (b 14 Jan 1964).

GW31261E3   Colin Scott Wisser (b 19 Sep 1970, Reading PA) m 8 Apr 1995, Reading PA, Lori Anne Schlottman (b 30 May 1973).

GW31261F   Barbara Ann Wisser (b 11 Sep 1938) m Franklin Stump.

GW31262   Scott Llewellyn Wisser (15 Feb 1890, Bernville PA-12 May 1956) m 14 May 1910, Grimsville, Berks PA, Emma Louisa Kistler (6 Jun 1890, Greenwich, Berks PA-19 Mar 1939).

GW312621   Daughter Wisser (4 Mar 1911-11 Mar 1911, Albany, Berks PA).

GW312622   Alvin Paul Wisser (1 Sep 1912, Albany, Berks PA-19 Mar 1970) m 30 Mar 1935, Grimsville, Berks PA, Elsie Mae Sechler (8 May 1912-4 Dec 1982).

GW3126221   Grace Marie Wisser (b 29 Sep 1935, Lynn, Lehigh PA) m 7 Aug 1954, Irvin Luther Ketner (b 31 May 1934).

GW31262211   David Lee Ketner (b 9 Jan 1955).

GW31262212   Linda Lou Ketner (b 29 Mar 1958).

GW31262213   Julianne Lynne Ketner (b 29 Dec 1963).

GW3126222   Nevin Alvin Wisser (29 Jan 1942-16 Apr 1942).

GW3126223   Carl Rau Wisser (b 12 Mar 1943).

GW312623   Milton Stanley Wisser (18 Jun 1914, Albany, Berks PA-15 Sep 1979).

GW312624   Gertrude Emma Wisser (28 Jun 1916, Albany, Berks PA-1995) m Edgar Harvey Berger (23 Mar 1909, Greenwich, Berks PA-25 Dec 1979).

GW3126241   Son Berger (18 Apr 1954-18 Apr 1954).

GW312625   Mildred Florence Wisser (b 2 Mar 1918, Albany, Berks PA) m 23 Mar 1940, Kutztown PA, Lawrence U. Wertman.

GW3126251   Lawrence Uriah Wertman (b 21 Aug 1940, Lynn, Lehigh PA).

GW3126252   Joanne Mildred Wertman (b 31 Oct 1944).

GW3126253   Diane Marie Wertman (b 5 Mar 1955).

GW312626   Herman Lester Wisser (b 21 Sep 1919, Albany, Berks PA).

GW312627   Elda May Wisser (b 26 Mar 1921, Albany, Berks PA) m Robert Edwin Brobst (20 Apr 1919, Kirbyville, Berks PA-4 Mar 1991).

GW3126271   Dale Robert Brobst (b 12 Aug 1942).

GW3126272   Barry Lee Brobst (b 12 Jan 1949).

GW3126273   Jeffrey Lynn Brobst (b 20 Aug 1956).

GW3126274   Gary Gene Brobst (b 6 Jun 1958).

GW312628   Clayton Scott Wisser (28 Apr 1922, Albany, Berks PA-5 Jan 1945).

GW312629   Norman Ralph Wisser (b 3 Oct 1923, Albany, Berks PA) m 21 Sep 1946, Hamburg PA, Helen Catharine Derr (b 4 May 1928).

GW3126291   Sharon Marie Wisser (b 29 Sep 1952, Allentown PA) m 4 Mar 1972, Lenhartsville PA, Dean Francis Weidman.

GW31262911   Scott Christopher Weidman (b 27 Aug 1973).

GW31262912   Erica Lynn Weidman (b 13 Jun 1977).

GW3126292   Brenda Kay Wisser (b 1 May 1962, Reading PA) m 15 Jun 1985, Hamburg PA, David Paul Loeb (b 13 Jun 1961).

GW31262921   Brandon David Loeb (b 22 Jul 1986).

GW31262922   Tyler Allen Loeb (b 27 Jan 1988).

GW31262923   Courtney Nicole Loeb (b 16 Apr 1990).

GW31263   Anna Lucinda Wisser (27 Jun 1891, Lenhartsville PA-13 May 1946) m 27 Aug 1910, Stony Run, Berks PA, Herbert L. Stump (18 Sep 1890, Greenwich, Berks PA-2 May 1955).

GW312631   Elsie Grace Stump (b 5 Jan 1911, Greenwich, Berks PA).

GW312632   Kermit Leroy Stump (25 Feb 1914, Albany, Berks PA-22 Jul 1919).

GW312633   Herbert Walter Stump (b 1 Sep 1916, Wessnersville, Berks PA).

GW312634   Melvin Ralph Stump (20 Dec 1918, Kempton, Berks PA-22 Jul 1978) m Eva M.   (b 27 Mar 1919).

GW312635   Kenneth Herman Stump (b 29 Nov 1921, Kempton, Berks PA) m Mae E.   (b 1924).

GW312636   Roma Evelyn Stump (b 5 Sep 1924, Greenwich, Berks PA).

GW312637   Shirley Ann Stump (b 14 Sep 1928, Greenwich, Berks PA).

GW31264   Ada Mary Wisser (18 Sep 1893, Greenwich, Berks PA-4 Jan 1961) m 25 Dec 1911, Stony Run, Berks PA, Edwin Newton Kunkel (19 Apr 1893, Albany, Berks PA-1 Apr 1956).

GW312641   Mildred Hilda Kunkel (3 Jun 1912, Greenwich, Berks PA-1 Aug 1983, Kutztown PA) m Samuel A.   (1909-1966).

GW312642   Alegra Pauline Kunkel (22 Oct 1913, Lenhartsville PA-7 Feb 1982).

GW312643   Marie Naomi Kunkel (29 Mar 1915, Greenwich, Berks PA-9 Jan 1990).

GW312644   Lee Edison Kunkel (b 16 Mar 1917, Greenwich, Berks PA).

GW312645   Son Kunkel (b 16 Jul 1918).

GW312646   Norman Ralph Kunkel (13 Oct 1920, Greenwich, Berks PA-2 Apr 1991) m Dorothy R. Kline (b 26 Sep 1916).

GW312647   Kathryn Elizabeth Kunkel (b 28 Mar 1922, Greenwich, Berks PA).

GW312648   Nello Arlington Kunkel (b 3 Jul 1925, Greenwich, Berks PA).

GW312649   Josephine Mary Kunkel (b 22 Feb 1928, Greenwich, Berks PA).

GW31264A   Son Kunkel (b 27 Jul 1933).

GW31264B   Lynn Carson Kunkel (b 22 Feb 1936, Maxatawny, Berks PA).

GW31265   Martha Ellen Wisser (7 Dec 1895, Greenwich, Berks PA-14 Jun 1989) m 18 Oct 1919, Kutztown PA, Francis David Kunkel (28 Aug 1898, Berks PA-14 Feb 1951).

GW312651   Violet Evelyn Kunkel (b 28 Dec 1920, Albany, Berks PA) m Luther I. Bieber (b 1917).

GW312652   Carl Arlan Kunkel (b 19 Sep 1923, Albany, Berks PA).

GW312653   Jean Martha Kunkel (b 21 Jan 1929, Albany, Berks PA).

GW31266   Minnie Alvenia Wisser (22 May 1898, Greenwich, Berks PA-3 Oct 1987) m 20 Oct 1917, Reading PA, Thomas Harrel Bailey (19 Dec 1896, Douglassville, Berks PA-18 May 1958).

GW312661   Marian Ellen Bailey (b 18 May 1918).

GW312662   Harlan Thomas Bailey (b 24 Apr 1920).

GW312663   Vernon Franklin Bailey (b 16 Apr 1924).

GW312664   Gene Mary Bailey (5 Jul 1925-22 Sep 1925).

GW312665   Elaine Kathleen Bailey (b 16 May 1936).

GW31267   Irwin Anson Wisser (13 Nov 1900, Greenwich, Berks PA-3 Jun 1972) m 29 Mar 1922, Carrie Esther Merkel (24 Jul 1905-27 Sep 1978).

GW312671   Rachel May Wisser (b 7 Sep 1922, PA) m 4 Jun 1938, Richmond, Berks PA, Warren James David Miller (17 Aug 1917-17 Apr 1983).

GW3126711   Richard Lee Miller (b 10 Dec 1938, PA) m 1) 23 Feb 1957, Richmond, Berks PA, Donna Joan Price (b 6 Oct 1939); m 2) Donna Jean Kerschner; m 3) Dawn Miller.

GW31267111   Scott Richard Miller (b 8 Aug 1957, Reading PA).

GW31267112   Tracey Noreen Miller (b 16 Jul 1961, PA).

GW31267113   Kristen Lee Miller (b 20 Nov 1865).

GW31267114   Richard Lee Miller Jr. (b 4 Sep 1970).

GW3126712   Robert Allen Miller (b 25 Jul 1953, PA) m 17 Sep 1986, Elizabeth Ann Hails (b 21 Mar 1961).

GW312672   Dorothy Marie Wisser (b 15 Jun 1926, PA) m 12 Dec 1942, Richmond, Berks PA, Dewey Paul Spohn (6 May 1924-23 Jul 1963).

GW3126721   Sandra Lee Spohn (b 9 Aug 1943, PA).

GW3126722   Ronald Barry Spohn (b 4 May 1945, PA).

GW3126723   Debra Susan Spohn (b 15 Apr 1956).

GW3126724   Cheri Lyn Spohn (b 5 May 1966).

GW312673   William Paul Wisser (b 18 Sep 1929, PA) m 20 Apr 1948, Reading PA, Anna Theresa Neagle (b 7 Feb 1927).

GW3126731   William Paul Wisser Jr. (b 20 Apr 1952, PA) m 13 Oct 1990, Whitfield PA, Lori Louise Walton (b 9 Sep 1960).

GW31267311   Emily Louise Wisser (b 10 Aug 1992).

GW31267312   Sarah Anne Wisser (b 2 Apr 1995).

GW312674   Norman Carl Wisser (b 1 Jun 1936) m 1) Tina Yenser; m 2) Beverly   .

GW3126741   Lois(?) Wisser (b Oct 1960).

GW3126742   Heidi Ann Wisser (b 10 Mar 1966).

GW312675   Nelson Lee Wisser (b 4 May 1939, PA) m 2 Jul 1960, Fleetwood PA, Sally Ann Freeman (b ca 1935, PA).

GW3126751   Darryl Lynn Wisser (b 3 Dec 1958).

GW3126752   Lisa Diane Wisser (b 31 Dec 1960).

GW3126753   Sheryl Lee Wisser (b Feb 1966).

GW31268   Luella May Wisser (14 May 1903, Greenwich, Berks PA-26 Jul 1982) m 1) 1 Jan 1920, Kutztown PA, Paul Willoughby Seidel (24 Sep 1900, Berks PA-18 Aug 1929); m 2) 20 Dec 1930, Kutztown PA, Leroy Elmer Hess (18 Jun 1907-15 Feb 1989).

GW312681   Wayne Allen Seidel (6 Jul 1920, PA-12 Nov 1931).

GW312682   Florence May Seidel (b 8 May 1922, PA).

GW312683   Son Seidel (10 Dec 1924-10 Dec 1924).

GW312684   Margaret Ellen Seidel (b 12 Sep 1926, PA).

GW312685   Darwin Leroy Hess (21 Apr 1931-7 Apr 1986).

GW312686   Lucille Elinore Hess (b 26 May 1937).

GW312687   Dale Richard Hess (b 16 Aug 1941, Tilden, Berks PA).

GW31269   Gertrude Irene Wisser (26 Jan 1905, Greenwich, Berks PA-28 May 1971) m 10 Apr 1925, Grimsville, Berks PA, Floyd Walter Gehringer (4 May 1904, Albany, Berks PA-4 Oct 1988).

GW312691   Son Gehringer (27 May 1926-27 May 1926).

GW312692   Robert Lee Gehringer (b 15 Jul 1931).

GW3126A   Florence Evelyn Wisser (24 Apr 1907, PA-7 Jan 1988, Kutztown PA) m 20 Mar 1926, New Tripoli, Lehigh PA, Miles Leroy Schroeder (29 Mar 1904-9 Jan 1990).

GW3126A1   Warren Miles Schroeder (b 24 Sep 1926).

GW3126A2   Randall Wisser Schroeder (b 8 Feb 1929).

GW3126A3   Carl Stanley Schroeder (b 8 Aug 1932) m 21 Nov 1953, Anna Violet Adam (b 24 Apr 1932, Windsor, Berks PA).

GW3126A31   Monte Carl Schroeder (b 17 May 1954).

GW3126A32   Kirk Daryl Schroeder (b 11 May 1955).

GW3126A33   Karen Beth Schroeder (b 27 Jul 1957).

GW3126A34   Todd Denton Schroeder (b 8 Nov 1958).

GW3126A35   Chris Mitchell Schroeder (b 29 Dec 1968).

GW3126A4   Miriam Ruth Schroeder (b 5 Sep 1934) m Dale Miller.

GW3126A5   Denton Jacob Schroeder (b 8 Nov 1936).

GW3126A6   Sandra Faye Schroeder (b 26 Jul 1943) m Ernst Platfoot.

GW3126B   Herma Frances Wisser (29 Apr 1909, Greenwich, Berks PA-10 Jul 1982) m 23 Mar 1929,

Kutztown PA, George Edgar Meitzler (24 Jun 1902-1 Jan 1967).

GW3126B1   Eleanor June Meitzler (10 Jun 1929-25 Jun 1929, Kutztown PA).

GW3126B2   Jack Richard Meitzler (b 20 Aug 1930, Klinesville, Berks PA) m Dolores Heffner.

GW3126B21   Gary Richard Meitzler (b 5 Jun 1954).

GW3126B22   Carol Lynn Meitzler (b 13 Jan 1956).

GW3126B23   Kim Lee Meitzler (b 3 Aug 1960).

GW3126B24   Randy Brian Meitzler (b 16 Mar 1968).

GW3126B3   Joanne Marie Meitzler (b 9 Jan 1937) m Donald Sweda.

GW3127   Charles Henry Weiser (15 Jun 1865, PA-3 Apr 1906, WV) m 1) 7 Apr 1882, Hamburg PA, Catharine Meave(?); m 2) 1 Nov 1892, Bluefield WV, Cora Matilda Schwank (Jan 1871 19 Mar 1903, Norton VA); m 3) 8 Jun 1904, Mt. Pleasant NC, Sarah Jane Moriah Fisher (1 Aug 1866, Rowan NC-21 Aug 1943, Salisbury NC).

GW31271   Fred William Wisser (b 12 Apr 1884).

GW31272   Mary Jane Wisser (25 Mar 1885-4 Sep 1887).

GW31273   Daughter Weiser (28 Oct 1893-1893, Bluefield WV).

GW31274   Carl Elbert Weiser (3 Nov 1894, WV-Jun 1976, Oyster Bay, NY) m Ora   (10 Apr 1894-Oct 1975, Oyster Bay, NY).

GW312741   Leota Weiser (ca 1915-ca 1976) m Jack Hansen (d ca 1975).

GW31275   Pearl Hannah Weiser (13 Oct 1896, WV-ca 1983, Plainview, TX) m Malcolm Pursiful.

GW312751   Vernon Pursiful (ca 1927-ca 1945) m Lillie   .

GW3127511   Verna Pearl Pursiful.

GW3127512   Judy Pursiful.

GW31276   Edna Mae Weiser (30 Nov 1897, Bluefield WV-5 May 1985, Bluefield WV) m 7 Sep 1919, George Richard Linkenhoker (16 Apr 1890, Hinton WV-5 Dec 1947).

GW312761   George Richard Linkenhoker Jr. (16 Jul 1920, Bluefield WV-28 Apr 1994) m Jun 1950, Essie Smith.

GW312762   Albert Lee Linkenhoker (2 Apr 1922, Bluefield WV-Nov 1984, Miami FL) m 7 Dec 1945, Monica Lois James.

GW3127621   Albert Lee Linkenhoker Jr. (b 6 Sep 1954, Williamson WV).

GW312763   Elsie Marie Linkenhoker (24 Dec 1923, Bluefield WV-10 Apr 1977, Roanoke VA) m 5 Feb 1944, Charles Mitchell Frangowlakis (b 9 Sep 1920).

GW3127631   Linda Sue Frangowlakis (b 7 Sep 1945, Quantico VA) m 1) Walter Krueber; m 2) George T. Mahoney.

GW3127632   George Ray Frangowlakis (b 15 Jul 1948, Williamson WV) m Mary Bryant.

GW31276321   John Kevin Frangowlakis (b 3 Jul 1972).

GW3127633   Edna Gaynell Frangowlakis (b 21 Nov 1955, Williamson WV) m 1) May 1976, Lester Darnell Osborne.

GW31276331   Scott Darnell Osborne (b 11 Jul 1975, Roanoke VA).

GW31276332   Ollie Gaynell Osborne (b 3 Oct 1976, Roanoke VA).

GW3127634   Elsie Marie Frangowlakis (b 21 Nov 1955, Williamson WV).

GW3127635   Charles Mitchell Frangowlakis Jr. (b 15 Jul 1962, Williamson WV) m Jean   .

GW31276351   Charles Mitchell ("Chad") Frangowlakis III (b 7 Feb 1983).

GW31276352   Elizabeth Marie Frangowlakis (b 18 Jan 1993, Roanoke VA).

GW312764   Dorothy May Linkenhoker (b 14 Oct 1924, Williamson WV) m 7 Feb 1953, Davis Theotie Maxey (b 25 Jul 1925, Franklin VA).

GW3127641   Karen Virginia Maxey (b 24 Jul 1953, Roanoke VA) m 1) Harold David Vaught; m 2) Jerry Lyn Wright.

GW3127642   Dreama Beth Maxey (b 23 Sep 1953, Roanoke VA).

GW3127643   Loren Ogden Maxey (b 29 Dec 1956, Roanoke VA) m 7 Jan 1988, Elizabeth Ann Key (b 11 Apr 1960).

GW31276431   James Davis Maxey (b 2 Sep 1988, Roanoke VA).

GW31276432   Garret Allen Maxey (b 24 Jun 1993, Roanoke VA).

GW312765   Betty Louise Linkenhoker (9 Oct 1933, Williamson WV-30 May 1978) m 7 Sep 1954, Peter Gasper Leginus.

GW3127651   Belinda Ann Leginus (b 10 Apr 1959) m 1) Ralph Buckner Wade; m 2) Bruce Gerristein; m 3) Neal Golden.

GW3127652   Kenneth Michael Leginus (b 2 Oct 1965, Roanoke VA) m 1 Jun 1991, Stewartsville VA, Jeannette Haskins.

GW31276521   Taylor Lauren Leginus (b May 1993, Roanoke VA).

GW31277   William Walton Weiser (6 Jul 1899, WV-2 Dec 1913).

GW31278   Anna Nira Weiser (29 Jun 1901, Bluefield WV-ca 1988, Tampa FL) m Winfrey ("Slim") Standefer (1 Oct 1901, MI-Dec 1971, Tampa FL).

GW31279   Daughter Weiser (19 Mar 1903, Bluefield WV-21 Mar 1903, Bluefield WV).

GW3127A   Charles Henry Weiser (5 Sep 1906, Mt. Pleasant NC-7 Aug 1985, Salisbury NC) m 19 Dec 1937, Mt. Ulla NC, Byrd Misenheimer (b 20 Feb 1915, Rowan, NC).

GW3127A1   Conrad Walton Weiser (b 22 May 1939, Salisbury NC) m 8 Apr 1978, Raleigh NC, Susan

Louise Coon (b 29 Jun 1952, New York NY).

GW3127A11   Sarah Emily Jane Weiser (b 27 Feb 1982, Raleigh NC).

GW3127A12   Philip Konrad Richard Weiser (b 7 Oct 1987, Durham NC.

GW3128   Catharine Wieser (b ca 1878, PA).

GW313   Daniel Wieser (b 10 Dec 1825, Greenwich, Berks, PA).

GW314   Carolina Wieser (b 27 Oct 1827, Greenwich, Berks, PA).

GW315   Judith Wieser (7 Oct 1829, Greenwich, Berks PA-27 Apr 1895, Greenwich, Berks PA).

GW316   William Wieser (26 Jan 1837, Kutztown PA-27 Feb 1904, Berks PA).

GW32   Maria Elizabeth Wieser (b ca 1788) m 29 Jan 1811, George Michael Zettelmoyer.

GW321   Salome Zettelmoyer (b 1812).

GW33   Maria Margaret Wieser (b ca 1790) m George Zieger.

GW34   Susanna Wieser (4 May 1792-15 May 1862) m John Jacob Laury.

GW341   Susanna Anna Laury (b 5 Jan 1825).

GW35   Catherine Wieser (b ca 1794).

GW36   Jacob Wisser (25 Feb 1796, Grimsville, Berks PA-3 Mar 1886, Fullerton, Lehigh PA) m 28 Oct 1824, Anna Maria Davidheiser (3 Sep 1806-28 Oct 1887).

GW361   Josua Wisser (b 1 May 1825, Greenwich, Berks PA).

GW362   Julianna Wisser (b 29 Oct 1826, Greenwich, Berks PA).

GW363   Solomon Wisser (15 Aug 1828, Greenwich, Berks PA-24 May 1912, South Whitehall, Lehigh PA) m 23 Jul 1854, Caroline Fenstermacher (17 Nov 1830, Lowhill, Lehigh PA-4 Dec 1893).

GW364   Jesse Wisser (Apr 1830, Upper Macungie, Lehigh PA-2 Mar 1911, South Whitehall, Lehigh PA) m 4 Jun 1854, Malinda Muthhard (12 May 1833, Weisenberg, Lehigh PA-19 Nov 1904).

GW3641   Alvin T. Wisser (Jun 1855, PA-1931) m 8 Sep 1877, Emma E. Butterweck (b Oct 1858, PA).

GW36411   Luther P. Wisser (30 Nov 1877, PA-Aug 1962, PA) m 19 Mar 1898, Ft. Washington PA, Anna Eliza Moore (b Sep 1874, PA).

GW364111   Leroy Wisser (b ca 1906, PA).

GW364112   Norton Wisser (b ca 1910, PA).

GW36412   Irwin R. Wisser (26 Feb 1880, Allentown PA-4 Oct 1954) m 1) Gertrude   (29 May 1879-22 Jun 1956); m 2) Mabel   (b ca 1881, PA).

GW364121   Franklin A. Wisser (b ca 1914, PA).

GW364122   Kenneth I. Wisser (b ca May 1915, PA).

GW36413   Mabel K. Wisser (b ca 1892, PA).

GW3642   Rosa Wisser (b ca 1859, PA) m 13 Jul 1878, George A. Beisel (28 Feb 1856-6 Sep 1886).

GW3643   Amanda Wisser (b ca 1860, PA).

GW3644   Ida Wisser (b ca 1863, PA).

GW3645   Alice M. Wisser (b ca 1865, PA) m 12 Sep 1886, Weisenberg, Lehigh PA, William F.
Klein.

GW3646   Annie Wisser (b ca 1871, PA).

GW365   Abraham Wisser (1832, PA-8 Sep 1905, Whitehall, Lehigh PA) m Sarah Ann Hartman(?)
(1833, PA-14 Feb 1898, Whitehall, Lehigh PA).

GW3651   Phaon P. Wisser (b ca 1859, PA).

GW3652   Louisa L. Wisser (b ca 1860, PA) m William Hartman.

GW366   Deborah Wisser (b 12 Feb 1834) m 23 Aug 1853, Western Salisbury, Lehigh PA,
Benjamin Seiders.

GW367   Maria Catharina Wisser (b 20 Apr 1836).

GW368   Amandus Wisser (b 5 Oct 1836, Greenwich, Berks PA).

GW369   Emma (Emmetria) Wisser m 19 Feb 1856, Lewis Acker.

GW36A   Sarah Wisser (b ca 1839) m Peter Hoy (b ca 1839).

GW36A1   William Hoy (b ca 1866).

GW36A2   Benjamin Hoy (b ca 1869).

GW36B   Hezekiah (Ezekiel) J. Wisser (30 Jan 1841, Crackersport, Lehigh PA-25 Oct 1921) m 1)
Sarah Tevilia Knerr (14 Oct 1844-1 May 1874); m 2) ca 1880, Elisabeth Deisher (b May 1863, PA).

GW36B1   Emma E. Wisser (1868-1959) m Charles A. Frey (1868-1920).

GW36B2   Anna Wisser (b ca 1871, PA) m 20 May 1893, Maxatawny, Berks PA, Alfred W. Leiby
(b ca 1873).

GW36B3   Irvin J. Wisser (b Apr 1881, PA) m ca 1904, Eline (Elma) Epler (b ca 1883, PA).

GW36B31   Eva E. Wisser (b ca 1906, PA).

GW36B32   Helen M. Wisser (b ca 1907, PA).

GW36B33   Paul J. Wisser (b ca 1909, PA).

GW36B4   Allen (Alvin) N. Wisser (14 Dec 1882, Fullerton PA-21 Jul 1951) m 1907, Esther E.
Kercher (16 Sep 1887, PA-19 Mar 1960).

GW36B41   Arline E. Wisser (b ca 1910, PA).

GW36B42   Mabel E. Wisser (b ca 1911, PA).

GW36B43   Myrtle May Wisser (22 Jun 1913, PA-3 Sep 1924).

GW36B44   Ellen E. Wisser (b ca 1916, PA).

GW36B45   Allen N. Wisser Jr. (25 Jun 1920-26 Mar 1978).

GW36B5   Estella Wisser (b Sep 1885, Maxatawny, Berks PA) m 10 Aug 1907, Hancock, Berks PA, Herbert W. Pauley (b ca 1886, Longswamp, Berks PA).

GW36B6   Ida May Wisser (b 2 Feb 1888).

GW36B7   Edwin E. Wisser (8 Jun 1889, PA-5 Jun 1973) m Pearl N.   (21 Mar 1894, PA-5 Sep 1965).

GW36B71   Dorothy E. Wisser (b ca 1913, PA).

GW36B72   Edna E. Wisser (b ca 1914, PA).

GW36B73   William W. Wisser (b ca 1916, PA).

GW36B8   Beulah M. Wisser (b Dec 1890, Upper Macungie, Lehigh PA) m 9 Jan 1909, Topton PA, Howard C. Drey (b ca 1886, Maxatawny, Berks PA).

GW36B9   William E. Wisser (b Oct 1892, PA).

GW36BA   Herbert Alvin Wisser (b Nov 1894, PA).

GW36C   Emanuel Wisser (7 May 1843-22 Sep 1923, Guthsville, Lehigh PA) m 1) ca 1865, Mary Ann (Margaret) Krause (Jun 1842-17 Nov 1911); m 2) Lillie   (b ca 1874).

GW36C1   Mantana Wisser (b Jan 1864) m 20 Dec 1890, Lewis Stephen.

GW36C11   Eva Florence Stephen (b 25 Jan 1892).

GW36C12   Edgar Lewis Daniel Stephen (b 5 Mar 1897).

GW36C2   Anna M. M. Wisser (ca 1865-1951) m 1) Harvey Stauffer; m 2) 5 Dec 1891, Orwin (Orville) E. Kuhns (1868-1940).

GW36C21   Ralph Washington Stauffer (b 16 Apr 1889).

GW36C22   Clarence Daniel Stauffer (b 17 Oct 1890).

GW36C23   Howard Jesse Kuhns (b 22 Dec 1892).

GW36C24   Messrin(?) Elias Kuhns (b 26 Mar 1895).

GW36C25   Oscar Phaon Kuhns (b 24 Mar 1899).

GW36C26   Milton Irvin Kuhns (b 24 Nov 1903).

GW36C3   Ellen R. Wisser (b Nov 1869) m 24 May 1890, Milton J. Buchman.

GW36C31   Stella Mary Buchman (b 2 Aug 1891).

GW36C32   Oliver Henry Buchman (b 4 Sep 1897).

GW36C33   Clyde Emmanuel Buchman (b 14 Aug 1901).

GW36C4   Oliver F. Wisser (2 Mar 1872, South Whitehall, Lehigh PA-19 Aug 1957, Allentown PA) m 23 Aug 1890, Jordan, Lehigh PA, Amanda A. Hammel (Jun 1872-10 May 1941, Allentown PA).

GW36C41   Edwin James Wisser (25 Nov 1890, PA-19 Mar 1964, PA) m 1) Leleh M.   (b ca 1884); m 2) 20 Mar 1926, Allentown PA, Katie Priscilla Strauss (d 15 Mar 1936, Allentown PA).

GW36C411   Mabel S. Wisser (b ca 1915).

GW36C412   Emanuel L. Wisser (b ca Feb 1918).

GW36C413   Charles Benjamin Wisser (b 5 May 1930, Allentown PA).

GW36C414   Joyce Mae Wisser (b 25 Feb 1932, Crackersport, Lehigh PA).

GW36C415   Norman Robert Wisser (b 10 Dec 1933, Allentown PA).

GW36C416   Frederick Paul Wisser (26 Jul 1937, Crackersport, Lehigh PA-Jan 1982, PA).

GW36C42   Sevilla L. Wisser (b Jul 1894) m   Seidel.

GW36C43   Mary Ann Kate Wisser (4 Sep 1895-23 Aug 1940) m 2 Oct 1915, Hamburg PA, Floyd
Milton Merkel.

GW36C431   Helen Beulah Merkel (b 16 Jan 1917) m Earl Sunday.

GW36C432   Ellwood Solon Merkel (b 30 Apr 1919).

GW36C433   Eldon Floyd Merkel (b 30 Apr 1919).

GW36C434   Norman Oliver Merkel (b 15 May 1920).

GW36C435   Earl Thomas Merkel (b 4 Dec 1921) m Edna R. Schollenberger.

GW36C436   Betty Virginia Merkel (b 26 Apr 1932).

GW36C44   Robert Emanuel Wisser (13 Apr 1897-20 Feb 1989) m ca 1919, Annie   (b ca 1899).

GW36C441   Dorothy Wisser (b ca Jan 1920).

GW36C45   James J. Wisser (1901, Allentown PA-8 Jun 1981) m 1) Bertha T. (b ca 1897); m 2)
Noxen, Luzerne PA, Elsie Kocher.

GW36C451   Ralph Wisser.

GW36C452   Robert Wisser.

GW36C453   Dale E. Wisser.

GW36C454   Evelyn Wisser m 3 Jun 1942, Kutztown PA, Curtis F. Schlenker (28 May 1920-25 Jun
1980).

GW36C4541   Curtis Ronald Schlenker (b 27 Aug 1942, Greenwich, Berks PA).

GW36C455   Katherine Wisser m   Ruppert.

GW36C46   George W. Wisser (b ca 1906).

GW36C47   Beulah M. Wisser (b ca 1909) m   Weidner.

GW36C5   Oscar E. Wisser (25 Dec 1876, South Whitehall, Lehigh PA-7 May 1935, Walberts, Lehigh PA) m 24 May 1902, Maria S. Hunsicker (ca 1880, Guth's Station, Lehigh PA-25 Dec 1935, South Whitehall, Lehigh PA).

GW36C51   Sadie Maria Wisser (b 1 Jun 1903).

GW36C52   Herbert Lewis Emanuel Wisser (19 Sep 1904-2 Jun 1956, Allentown PA).

GW36C53   Morris Eugene Wisser (27 Aug 1907, PA-Jun 1986, PA).

GW36C54   Elmer Oscar Wisser (24 Sep 1909, PA-9 Feb 1988, PA).

GW36C55   Pauline S. Wisser (b ca 1913).

GW36C6   Jennie Wisser m Edwin Reichard.

GW36D   William Wisser (b ca 1846) m Angelina   (b ca 1848).

GW36E   Lewis Wisser (Jan 1849, PA-1934) m ca 1877, Anna Maria Paterson (b Aug 1852, PA).

GW36E1   Lizzie Wisser (b ca 1877, PA).

GW37   Jonathan Wieser (18 Oct 1797, Berks PA-13 Apr 1884, Allentown PA) m 8 Apr 1827, Egypt, Lehigh PA, Hannah Henninger (22 Apr 1809, Whitehall, Lehigh PA-7 Feb 1849).

GW371   Jonathan H. Wieser (12 Nov 1827-24 Sep 1902, Hanover, Lehigh PA) m 6 Nov 1853, Caroline Eisenhardt (Jan 1835, Upper Macungie, Lehigh PA-17 Oct 1916, Allentown PA).

GW3711   Morgan Wieser (b ca 1853).

GW3712   Isabella Jane Wieser (b 31 Dec 1855).

GW3713   Jonathan D. Wieser (Oct 1857, PA-19 Nov 1934, Allentown PA) m ca 1878, Mary Alice Donnecker (b Sep 1857, PA).

GW37131   Jacob J. Wieser (b Apr 1880, PA).

GW37132   Edwin H. Wieser (b Mar 1882, PA) m ca 1904, Sadie I.   (b ca 1887, PA).

GW371321   Josephine C. Wieser (b ca 1905, PA).

GW371322   Catharine M. Wieser (b ca 1907, PA).

GW371323   Dorothy P. Wieser (b ca 1911, PA).

GW37133   Robert G. C. Wieser (12 Aug 1884-4 Oct 1887).

GW37134   Elizabeth Isabella Wieser (b 19 Jul 1886).

GW37135   Harry U. Wieser (b May 1888, PA) m 6 Feb 1911, Rittersville, Lehigh PA, Ella A. Fritz.

GW37136   Minnie E. Wieser (b Dec 1890, PA) m Harvey E. Roth.

GW371361   Hester Ella Roth (b 27 Mar 1913, Allentown PA).

GW37137   Gertrude M. Wieser (b May 1893, PA).

GW37138   Hannah C. Wieser (b 19 Dec 1894, PA) m John Yosko.

GW371381   Bernard James Yosko (b 20 Apr 1913, East Allentown, Lehigh PA).

GW37139   Florence A. Wieser (b Mar 1897, PA).

GW3713A   Anna May Wieser (b Jun 1898, PA) m 20 Nov 1909, Rittersville, Lehigh PA, Arthur J.
Fisher (b ca 1890, PA).

GW3713A1   Catharine Gertie Fisher (b 3 Nov 1910, East Allentown, Lehigh PA).

GW3713A2   Dorothea Elizabeth Fisher (b 3 Feb 1913, Rittersville, Lehigh PA).

GW3713A3   Alton Fisher (b ca Oct 1918, PA).

GW3713B   George P. Wieser (b Feb 1900, PA).

GW3714   William Wieser (b Nov 1859, PA) m Sarah A.   (b Jan 1852, PA).

GW37141   Paul H. Wieser (b Sep 1890, PA) m Stella   (b ca 1895, PA).

GW371411   Dorothy P. Wieser (b ca May 1915).

GW3715   Laura Elizabeth Wieser (b ca 1863, PA-1886, East Allentown, Lehigh PA) m Preston A.
Biegley.

GW37151   Lucy Laura Biegley (1886-1887).

GW3716   Stephen F. Wieser (24 Dec 1865-12 Apr 1895, Hanover, Lehigh PA) m 1) 31 Oct 1886,
Ida Hattie Gehris (16 Dec 1868-17 May 1891); m 2) ca 1892, Katie Gehris.

GW37161   Carrie Catharine Wieser (b 9 Jan 1889).

GW37162   Lottie May Wieser (15 Apr 1891-2 Aug 1891).

GW37163   Grover (George) Stephen Wieser (23 Mar 1893-9 Oct 1895).

GW37164   Elsie Priscilla Wieser (b 20 Sep 1895).

GW3717   Ellie Wieser (b ca 1868, PA).

GW3718   Thomas B. Wieser (b Mar 1870) m ca 1890, Matilda R. Hohl (b Oct 1870, PA).

GW37181   Irwin Thomas Wieser (b 9 Mar 1889) m 10 Jun 1909, Rittersville, Lehigh PA, Florence
M. Deily (b ca 1891).

GW371811   Clarence Irvin Wieser (b 13 Dec 1909, PA).

GW37182   Bertha Agnes Wieser (b 26 Aug 1890).

GW37183   Annie May Wieser (b 5 May 1892).

GW37184   Gertrude Rebecca Wieser (b 7 Jul 1893).

GW37185   Eugene Howard Wieser (b 9 Jul 1898, Rittersville, Lehigh PA) m Elsie I. Ritter (b ca 1901, PA).

GW371851   Arthur E. Wieser (b ca 1918, PA).

GW37186   Arthur E. Wieser (18 Oct 1900, PA-May 1984).

GW37187   Mabel Irene Wieser (b 4 Jun 1907, East Allentown PA).

GW37188   Martin Luther Wieser (2 Aug 1909, East Allentown PA-7 Jun 1941) m 2 Aug 1930, Macungie, Lehigh PA, Bertha Althea Rathburn (7 Feb 1914, Allentown PA-21 May 1945, Allentown PA).

GW371881   James Martin Wieser (b 11 May 1931).

GW371882   Donald Lee Wieser (b 21 Jun 1932).

GW371883   Robert Arthur Wieser (b 1 Oct 1933) m Phyllis Christine Whitney (b 14 Apr 1931).

GW3718831   Robert A. Wieser (b 18 Aug 1958) m Kimberly Ryan.

GW37188311   Megan Michelle Wieser (b 24 Jan 1990).

GW37188312   Matthew Ryan Wieser (b 10 Jun 1993).

GW3718832   Victoria Lynn Wieser (b 15 Jun 1961) m 4 Oct 1986, William Andrew Simmel.

GW37188321   Madeline Francine Simmel (b 15 Apr 1992).

GW37188322   Blake Andrew Simmel (b 27 Oct 1995).

GW371884   Shirley Althea Wieser (b ca 1935).

GW371885   Ronald Dale Wieser (b 26 Jul 1939).

GW371886   Martin Leon Wieser (b 1 Jul 1941).

GW3719   Maggie Cora Wieser (b 4 Sep 1873) m William Brong.

GW37191   Warren Daniel Brong (b 2 Oct 1905, East Allentown, Lehigh PA).

GW371A   Milton Cyrus Wieser (b 30 Mar 1875).

GW371B   Matilda Agnes Wieser (b 17 Feb 1877) m ca 1897, Edward Beck (b ca 1872).

GW371C   Charles Wieser (b Mar 1879, PA).

GW371D   George Winfield Wieser (22 Sep 1881-1 Sep 1883).

GW371E   Martin Luther Wieser (b 11 Jul 1884, PA).

GW372   Adeline Wieser (b 13 Feb 1829) m William Ritter.

GW373   Stephen Wieser (b 12 Aug 1830).

GW374   Abigail Wieser (b 22 Nov 1832, PA).

GW375   Susanna Wieser (b 3 Sep 1835).

GW376   Mariann Wieser (b 12 Jul 1839, PA) m Edward Eisenhard.

GW377   Henry William Wieser (3 Dec 1842, South Whitehall, Lehigh PA-11 Oct 1922, Allentown PA) m 3 Jun 1869, Louisa S. Lentz (b Jul 1847, PA).

GW3771   Edwin W. Wieser (b 4 Dec 1870, PA).

GW378   Gideon Wieser (7 Feb 1845, PA-7 Sep 1913, Bedford, Taylor IA) m 11 Apr 1871, Louisville KY, Elizabeth Hersch (b May 1848, KY).

GW3781   Albert J. Wieser (b ca 1872, KY).

GW3782   Katie Wieser (b ca 1873, KY).

GW3783   Lillie Wieser (b ca 1874, KY).

GW3784   William Wieser (b Oct 1876, IA).

GW3785   Laura Wieser (b 1879, IA).

GW3786   Effie E. Wieser (b May 1883, IA).

GW3787   Victor G. Wieser (b May 1885, IA) m Glenna   (b ca 1891, MO).

GW37871   Frederick H. Wieser (b ca 1912, MO).

GW37872   Charles W. Wieser (b ca 1914, MO).

GW37873   John E. Wieser (b ca Feb 1916, MO).

GW37874   Hubert B. Wieser (b ca Oct 1918, IA).

GW3788   Mamie M. Wieser (b Jun 1887, IA).

GW3789   Lottie A. Wieser (b Jan 1890, IA).

GW378A   Charles E. Wieser (b Jan 1894, IA) m Ruth S.   (b ca 1897, IA).

GW378A1   Catherine Wieser (b ca Sep 1916, IA).

GW378A2   Mary N. Wieser (b ca Apr 1919, IA).

GW379   Thomas Lewis Wieser (28 Oct 1847, North Whitehall, Lehigh PA-2 May 1924, Allentown PA) m Emma S. Beidelman (b Oct 1849).

GW3791   Charles Wieser (b Nov 1872, PA) m Ada   (b Nov 1873).

GW37911   Lillie M. Wieser (b Mar 1895).

GW37912   Jennie M. Wieser (b Dec 1896).

GW37913   Esther E. Wieser (b Dec 1898).

GW37914   Winfield Wieser (13 Mar 1902-Oct 1973, Lehigh PA).

GW37915   Miles Wieser (15 Jun 1907, PA-Jun 1985, Lehigh PA).

GW37916   Forrest Wieser (25 Apr 1911, PA-Mar 1982, Allentown PA).

GW3792   Samuel Jonathan Wieser (b Mar 1879, PA) m Mamie A. Hagenbuch (b ca 1880, PA).

GW37921   Isabella C. Wieser (b ca 1907, PA).

GW38   Sarah (Salome) Wieser (11 Nov 1799-12 Aug 1875, Greenwich, Berks PA) m Jacob Altenderfer (1 Nov 1799-21 Jul 1874, Greenwich, Berks PA).

GW381   Jacob Jonas Altenderfer (b 31 Jul 1826, Greenwich, Berks PA) m Catharine Dietrich (b 15 Dec 1821, Berks PA).

GW382   Maria Altenderfer (14 May 1829, Berks PA-29 Mar 1907, Kutztown PA) m Charles Edwin Kutz (b 21 Apr 1831, Kutztown PA).

GW383   Sarah Altenderfer (b 1 Aug 1834, Greenwich, Berks PA) m John B. Niefert (b 4 Sep 1829, Berks PA).

GW384   Catharine Altenderfer (b 20 Feb 1839, Greenwich, Berks PA) m Jacob Kunkel (b 3 Jan 1836, Berks PA).

GW385   John Altenderfer (b ca 1844, Berks PA) m Catharine Trexler (b 24 Dec 1843, Berks PA).

GW39   Rebecca Wieser (b ca 1801) m Jonathan Reinhard.

GW3A   Daniel Wisser (21 Dec 1803, Berks PA-13 Feb 1895, South Whitehall, Lehigh PA) m 6 May 1827, Lydia Miller (28 Dec 1807, South Whitehall, Lehigh PA-6 Jan 1865).

GW3A1   Jesse Wisser (b ca 1827) m Susanna   (b ca 1830).

GW3A11   Jacob Wisser (b 20 Jun 1851).

GW3A12   Mary J. Wisser (b ca 1856) m 23 Oct 1875, Allentown PA, Tilghman Seip (b ca 1854).

GW3A121   William Seip (b ca 1876).

GW3A122   Lizzie J. Seip (b ca 1879).

GW3A2   David Wisser (9 Jan 1830, Allentown PA-23 Mar 1902, Whitehall, Lehigh PA) m 1) 6 May 1855, Lydia Eliza Roth (17 Mar 1832-29 Jan 1858); m 2) Susanna Wright (2 Nov 1838-19 Mar 1898).

GW3A21   Franklin P. Wisser (b Aug 1856) m Bertha E.   (b Mar 1861).

GW3A211   Samuel D. Wisser (b Sep 1884) m Pearl Frances Dankel (b ca 1887).

GW3A2111   Francis Loraine Wisser (b 17 Sep 1909).

GW3A2112   Cynthia L. Wisser (b ca 1913).

GW3A2113   Franklin H. Wisser (b ca Aug 1919).

GW3A212   Sallie Wisser (b Apr 1887).

GW3A213   Annie E. Wisser (b Sep 1894).

GW3A22   Ida E. Wisser (b ca 1862) m Daniel I. Schreiber.

GW3A221   Alfred D. Schreiber (22 Feb 1890-6 Dec 1918).

GW3A23   Mary Wisser (b Jan 1870).

GW3A24   Annie Wisser (b Dec 1878) m ca 1899, Charles Heffelfinger (b Mar 1878).

GW3A241   Clara Heffelfinger (b Sep 1899).

GW3A3   Elizabeth Wisser (b ca 1832) m 9 Oct 1856, William Wenner.

GW3A4   Mary Wisser (1 Jul 1834-9 Nov 1854, Egypt, Lehigh PA).

GW3A5   Paul Wisser (b ca 1838).

GW3A6   Daniel Wisser (15 Nov 1839, Allentown PA-13 Feb 1895, South Whitehall, Lehigh PA) m 23 Nov 1867, Rosa S. Faust (b Nov 1848, Upper Macungie, Lehigh PA).

GW3A61   Mary L. Wisser (b ca 1869) m 24 Sep 1887, Allentown PA, John M. Haas.

GW3A611   Irene J. Haas (b Feb 1893).

GW3A62   Jane ("Jennie") R. Wisser (b May 1875).

GW3A7   Mary Ann Wisser (19 Jul 1842-21 Dec 1854).

GW3A8   Samuel Wisser (1844-1869).

GW3A9   Lydia Wisser (b ca 1847).

GW3AA   Ellenmina Wisser (30 Apr 1851-29 Apr 1854, Egypt, Lehigh PA).

GW3AB   Matilda Wisser (29 Mar 1854, Allentown PA-28 Dec 1854, Egypt, Lehigh PA).

GW3B   Lydia Wieser (28 Mar 1807-6 Jul 1881) m John C. Sichting (7 Oct 1796-15 Feb 1881).

CHAPTER NINETEEN

[BW]   Benjamin Wiser (b ca 1744)
of Haverhill, New Hampshire and his descendants

No information has been found concerning the ancestry of Benjamin Wiser.[157] He was probably born between 1740 and 1750. The first record of him that has been found is for his service during the Revolutionary War. He was in Captain Luther Richardson's Company raised for the defense of the Frontier on and adjacent to the Connecticut River. Pay commenced 6 April 1778, and he served for eleven months and twenty-five days. Luther Richardson owned a tavern in the Town of Haverhill, Grafton County, New Hampshire, and the company was presumably raised from that area.

Benjamin was definitely a resident of the Town of Haverhill before 1784, when he was warned out of town by the authorities, probably because of poverty. Evidently the warning was not effective, because he was still living in Haverhill at the time the Census was taken in 1790. However, by 1800 he and most of his family had moved to Cazenovia Township, Madison County, NY to a place now called New Woodstock. The 1812 tax assessment is the last record that has been found for Benjamin.

In the 1820 Census, four of his sons were heads of household in Truxton Township, Cortland County, NY. Some of their descendants remain in that area. However, one of the grandsons joined the Mormon migration to Utah, and his descendants constitute the majority of the family today.

His son Benjamin remained in New England, and was listed in several towns in New Hampshire and Vermont through 1850. Many of his descendants are still in New England.[158]

BW   Benjamin Wiser (ca 1744-after 1812, Cazenovia NY) m Kezia (b ca 1748). US Rev, NH Vols. Farmer, Haverhill NH; Cazenovia NY.

BW1   Allice Wiser (b ca 1770).

BW2   Alithea Wiser (b ca 1772) m 2 Sep 1788, Haverhill NH, Luther Morse. Haverhill NH; Cazenovia NY.

BW3   Benjamin Wiser (1774, Bath, Grafton NH-after 1850, Corinth, Orange VT) m 1) Sally Turner (ca 1772, NH-1818, Bath, Grafton NH); m 2) 12 Oct 1822, Bath, Grafton NH, Sarah Orn (1784, Alfred ME-14 Dec 1860, Corinth, Orange VT). Farmer, Haverhill NH; Corinth VT.

BW31   Benjamin Wiser (1804, NH-1864, Haverhill NH). NH.

BW32   Mary ("Polly") Wiser (b ca 1806, Haverhill NH) m 10 Jan 1825, Haverhill NH, Brigham Woods. Bath NH.

BW33   Levi Wiser (b ca 1808, Haverhill NH-after 1830). Littleton NH.

BW34   Nathan Wiser (1810, Haverhill NH-1 Jan 1870, Northfield NH) m Sarah Nichols (b 1830, Concord NH). Joiner, Concord NH.

BW341   Joseph Wiser (b 1844, NH).

---

[157]There may be a relationship to the family of Benjamin and Sarah Wiser of Worcester, Massachusetts, who are listed in the International Genealogical Index. In particular, the birth of their son Benjamin is listed on 7 Feb 1753.

[158]The list of descendants in this chapter has been limited to those with the surname Wiser and their spouses, simply because the total number of descendants is far too large for a single chapter of this book. The information is taken from an unpublished compilation submitted by Ron G. Wiser, of Roswell, New Mexico, which contains a much more complete list of descendants. See also "Wiser Family - Genealogy and History", compiled by Thelma King Woodland. Providence, Utah. 1981.

BW342   Melissa Ann Wiser (b 1846, NH).

BW343   Sarah Armina Wiser (20 Dec 1849, Concord NH-16 Jun 1923, Concord NH) m 9 Feb 1867, Hooksett NH, Peter Momble (Apr 1852, Canada-5 Sep 1928, Boscawen, Merrimack NH). Concord NH.

BW344   Nathan Benjamin Wiser (1852, Concord NH-1 Jun 1925, Concord NH). Concord NH.

BW345   George H. Wiser (b ca 1862, Laconia NH) m 7 Mar 1888, Loudon, Merrimack NH, Sarah Stevens (b 1866, Belmont NH). Concord NH.

BW35   Lucinda Wiser (1811, NH-26 Jul 1887, Boscawen, Merrimack NH).

BW36   John R. Wiser (5 Jun 1812, Haverhill NH-31 Dec 1877, Laconia NH) m 15 Feb 1835, Bridgewater, Grafton NH, Betsey Spiller (1 May 1816, Bethel ME-15 Mar 1895, Raymond NH). Peg manufacturer, Laconia NH.

BW361   Sarah T. Wiser (20 Aug 1836, NH-5 Mar 1870) m 20 Aug 1859, Bridgewater, Grafton NH, Patrick Henry Rowen (3 Mar 1840, Ireland-5 Apr 1903, Laconia NH). Laconia NH.

BW362   Clarice J. Wiser (7 Aug 1841-Fall 1849).

BW363   Nathan S. Wiser (7 Jun 1845, Alexandria, Grafton NH-10 Oct 1885, Laconia NH) m 1) 4 May 1867, Bridgewater, Grafton NH, Sarah E. Blodgett (b VT); m 2) 17 Jun 1879, Laconia NH, Harriet M. Bedell (10 Dec 1858, Springvale ME-16 Feb 1933, Sanbornton, Belknap NH).

BW3631   John Henry Wiser (30 Jul 1869, Springfield VT-27 Nov 1887, Laconia NH).

BW364   Betsy H. Wiser (8 May 1848, NH-29 Oct 1875) m 11 Jun 1871, Bridgewater, Grafton NH, Wallace F. Baker.

BW365   Eliza J. Wiser (2 Mar 1850, Bridgewater, Grafton NH-23 Feb 1899, Raymond NH) m 30 Apr 1888, Raymond NH, Chase Ebenezer Osgood (b 9 Jun 1839, Raymond NH).

BW366   Charles H. Wiser (4 Dec 1859, Laconia NH-16 Mar 1878, Laconia NH).

BW37   Thomas Jefferson Wiser (1813, Haverhill NH-after 1847). Lisbon NH.

BW38   Solomon Wiser (ca 1815, Haverhill NH-before 1847) m 23 Aug 1840, Bridgewater, Grafton NH, Judith C. Spiller (15 Jul 1819, Gilead, Oxford ME-22 Jan 1864, Laconia NH).

BW381   Norman Wiser (15 Jan 1841, Bridgewater, Grafton NH-29 Aug 1909, Bridgewater, Grafton NH) m 14 Jun 1863, Bridgewater, Grafton NH, Mary Jane Heath (31 Jul 1841, Bridgewater, Grafton NH -23 Jun 1927, Ashland NH).

BW3811   Orrin W. Wiser (23 Dec 1866, Bridgewater, Grafton NH-23 Jan 1899, Bridgewater, Grafton NH).

BW3812   Orra S. Wiser (23 Dec 1866, Bridgewater, Grafton NH-22 Dec 1885, Bridgewater, Grafton NH).

BW3813   Elmer P. Wiser (30 May 1869, Bridgewater, Grafton NH-18 Jun 1957, Bridgewater, Grafton NH) m 1) 30 May 1889, Bridgewater, Grafton NH, Evelyn Belle Mitchell (18 Apr 1870, Bridgewater, Grafton NH-24 Aug 1905, Bridgewater, Grafton NH); m 2) 1908 M. Alice Veasey (12 May 1884, NH-25 Nov 1955, Plymouth NH).

BW38131   Maud ("Ina") M. Wiser (21 Jun 1890, Bridgewater, Grafton NH-31 Jan 1954, Bridgewater,

Grafton NH) m Everett E. Atwood (1884, NH-1955, Bridgewater, Grafton NH).

BW38132	E. Byron ("Bud") Wiser (28 Jun 1911, Bridgewater, Grafton NH-16 Nov 1977, Ashland NH).

BW38133	A. Georgianna Wiser (31 May 1914, Bridgewater, Grafton NH-Jul 1974, Edgewood MD) m Erbett Comette (18 Dec 1912-14 Apr 1966).

BW38134	Herman Kenneth Wiser (b 13 Jan 1916, Bridgewater, Grafton NH) m Madeline Whiting.

BW381341	Richard Wiser m Nancy .

BW3813411	Michael Wiser.

BW381342	Dianne Wiser m Venoit.

BW38135	A. Bernice Wiser (b 8 May 1918, Bridgewater, Grafton NH) m Philip Eastman (b ca 1920, NH).

BW38136	Ernest Wiser (15 Nov 1921, Bridgewater, Grafton NH-13 Jan 1944). WWII: USA, Pvt.

BW3814	Clara Belle Wiser (12 Apr 1873, Bridgewater, Grafton NH-22 Jan 1962, West Thornton, Grafton NH) m 1) 4 Aug 1887, Holderness NH, Norman B. Tobine (22 Nov 1864, Springfield, Sullivan NH-13 Jan 1923, Canterbury, Merrimack NH); m 2) Chester Evans; m 3) 28 Apr 1922, Henry Lauriston Gault (1869, NH-1959)

BW39	Marian W. Wiser (b 1816, VT) m 1) 8 Sep 1844, Corinth, Orange VT, James C. Bedee; m 2) 6 Jul 1850, Concord NH, William P. Hook

BW3A	Charles S. Halley Wiser (23 Nov 1818, Corinth, Orange VT-29 Jul 1880, Meredith NH) m Maria Hartford (1843, Cambridge MA-19 Aug 1893, Weirs, Belknap NH).

BW3B	Sarah J. Wiser (27 Aug 1827, Washington, Orange VT-1 Jan 1892, Corinth, Orange VT) m 1844, Orford, Grafton NH, Aaron B. Ford (6 Feb 1821, VT-10 Mar 1894, Corinth, Orange VT).

BW3C	Daniel Wiser (24 Apr 1830, Corinth, Orange VT-20 Apr 1909, Sanbornton, Belknap NH) m 12 Mar 1870, Hill, Merrimack NH, Ellen M. Growe (14 Nov 1833, Gaysville, Windsor VT-3 Jul 1914, Sanbornton, Belknap NH).

BW4	Josiah Wiser (b ca 1776, Haverhill NH) m Philena . No chn. Cortland NY; Harrison IN.

BW5	Kezia Wiser (b ca 1781, Haverhill NH).

BW6	Abigail Wiser (ca 1783, Haverhill NH-after 1821). Cazenovia NY.

BW7	Samuel Wiser (1784, Haverhill NH-1834, Truxton, Cortland NY) m ca 1820, Truxton, Cortland NY, Elizabeth Babcock (ca 1790, Pittsfield MA-1839, Jo Daviess IL). Elizabeth also married Theodore Wiser (BW9). War of 1812. Farmer, Truxton, Cortland NY.

BW71	Amanda Wiser (1821, Truxton, Cortland NY-13 May 1886, Cascade IA) m 1) 20 Feb 1840, Jo Daviess IL, Marshall Cottle (b 1806, MO); m 2) Patrick McManus (1808, Cork, Ireland-26 Oct 1885, Cascade IA). Jo Daviess IL; Cascade IA.

BW72	Temperance M. Wiser (8 Jul 1821, Truxton, Cortland NY-13 Jan 1881, Bennezette, Butler IA) m 2 Jan 1842, Jo Daviess IL, William J. Adams (22 Feb 1812, MA-30 Mar 1888, Bennezette, Butler IA).

Farmer, Clayton IA; Butler IA.

BW73   Ezra Wiser (b ca 1824, Truxton, Cortland NY).

BW74   John McCormick Wiser (22 Jun 1826, Truxton, Cortland NY-25 Jul 1897, Lewiston UT)
m 1) 22 Feb 1849, Jackson IA, Sarah Ann Silsbee (1831, Berkshire, Tioga NY-27 Dec 1849, Jackson IA); m
2) 1851, Big Cottonwood, Salt Lake UT, Martha McKinney Frost (7 Oct 1825, Knoxville TN-26 Aug 1902,
Lewiston UT); m 3) 21 Oct 1896, Logan UT, Elizabeth Baker (26 Mar 1824, London, England-16 Mar 1907,
Lewiston UT). Farmer, Jackson IA; Alpine UT.

BW741   Child Wiser (Dec 1849, Jackson IA-Dec 1849, Jackson IA).

BW742   Sarah Ann Wiser (26 Feb 1852, Alpine, Utah UT-1 Mar 1853, Alpine, Utah UT).

BW743   Amanda Jane Wiser (13 Jun 1854, Draper UT-1 Jul 1899, Lodi, Fremont ID) m 10 Aug
1873, Lewiston UT, Heber Chase Smith (23 Oct 1846, Pottawattamie IA-3 Oct 1921, Marysville ID). Heber:
railroader.

BW744   Mary Olive Wiser (11 Feb 1856, Alpine, Utah UT-12 Mar 1906, Salt Lake City UT) m
21 Mar 1875, Lewiston UT, Hyrum R. Cunningham (12 Jan 1855, Salt Lake City UT-11 Jul 1945, Manti UT).
Hyrum: farmer.

BW745   John Harvey Wiser (9 Apr 1858, Alpine, Utah UT-6 Feb 1950, Lewiston UT) m 4 Jan
1883, Salt Lake City UT, Eustacia Rawlins Cunningham (30 Apr 1862, Salt Lake City UT-9 Oct 1947,
Lewiston UT). Farmer.

BW7451   John Andrew Wiser (22 Oct 1884, Lewiston UT-31 Jul 1968, Brigham City UT) m 1) 17
Jun 1908, Logan UT, Luella Budge (2 Mar 1886, Paris ID-9 Mar 1952, Logan UT); m 2) Evelyn Hansen.
Farmer.

BW74511   Ruth Nora Wiser (8 Dec 1909, Lewiston UT-1 Feb 1988, Salem OR) m 26 Jul 1933,
Logan UT, Floyd Manuel Packer (b 12 Jun 1908, Franklin ID).

BW74512   Andrew Scott Wiser (b 7 Apr 1913, Logan UT) m 3 Oct 1935, Salt Lake City UT, Zelpha
May Nelson (b 8 Oct 1916, Franklin ID).

BW745121   Carol Wiser (26 Mar 1938, Logan UT-7 Nov 1951)

BW745122   Norma Wiser (17 Oct 1939, Logan UT-1 Nov 1939)

BW745123   Joyce Wiser (b 17 Jun 1941, Logan UT) m 2 Sep 1966, Oakland CA, Garreth Lee Bogar
(b 17 Dec 1937, Mason City, Okanogan WA).

BW745124   Dean Scott Wiser (b 18 Sep 1943, Logan UT) m 20 Feb 1965, Idaho Falls ID, Barbara
Ann Taylor (b 30 Jan 1944, Rexburg, ID.

BW7451241   Shane Scott Wiser (b 4 Apr 1968, Blackfoot ID).

BW7451242   Shawna Ann Wiser (b 16 Aug 1970, Blackfoot ID).

BW745125   Reed Andrew Wiser (b 30 Jun 1946, Logan UT) m 10 Aug 1973, Ogden UT, Marilyn
Wren (b 3 May 1945, Blackfoot ID).

BW7451251   Teresa Wiser (b 2 Oct 1975, Blackfoot ID).

BW7451252   Tammy Wiser (b 20 Dec 1977, Blackfoot ID).

BW745126   Lynn Guy Wiser (b 10 Nov 1949, Logan UT) m 10 Dec 1971, Idaho Falls ID, Linda Lee Stott (b 25 Jan 1952, Blackfoot ID).

BW7451261   Raelyn Wiser (b 19 Aug 1976, Idaho Falls ID).

BW74513   Grant Budge Wiser (b 4 May 1927, Logan UT) m 9 May 1952, Salt Lake City UT, Fae Reeves (b 17 Jan 1927, Cedar City UT).

BW745131   Brenda Wiser (b 2 Mar 1953, Salt Lake City UT).

BW745132   Susan Wiser (b 26 Feb 1955, Salt Lake City UT) m 26 Aug 1976, Salt Lake UT, David Allen Williams.

BW745133   Steven Grant Wiser (b 11 Sep 1956, Salt Lake City UT) m 2 Jun 1978, Salt Lake UT, Becky Cutler.

BW745134   Julie Wiser (b 13 May 1959, Salt Lake City UT).

BW7452   William Harvey Wiser (26 Feb 1887, Lewiston UT-29 Nov 1977, Salt Lake City UT) m 12 Mar 1913, Logan UT, Emma Jones Haslam (21 Jul 1887, Wellsville UT-1 Feb 1979, Salt Lake City UT).

BW74521   George Haslam Wiser (20 Jun 1914, Lewiston UT-20 Jun 1914, Lewiston UT).

BW74522   William Don Wiser (9 Sep 1916, Fairview, Franklin ID-May 1982, Hurricane UT) m 25 Nov 1936, Gretta Rawlings (b 11 Oct 1914, Fairview, Franklin ID).

BW745221   Irwin Don Wiser (b 15 Feb 1938, Salt Lake City UT).

BW745222   Marcia Wiser (b 8 Jul 1940, Salt Lake City UT) m 9 Jun 1961, Utah UT Brent Evans Boyack (10 Jun 1940, Provo UT).

BW745223   William Lee Wiser (b 5 Feb 1944, Salt Lake City UT) m 23 Nov 1968, Salt Lake UT, Joann S. Longson.

BW745224   Van Rawlings Wiser (b 10 Oct 1945, Salt Lake City UT) m 1) Ann; m 2) Sharon Pugmire.

BW7452241   Michelle Wiser.

BW7452242   Darrell Wiser.

BW7452243   Travis Wiser.

BW7452244   Danielle Wiser.

BW74523   Myrl Haslam Wiser (12 Jul 1918, Fairview, Franklin ID-6 Feb 1922).

BW74524   Eva Wiser (22 Jul 1920, Fairview, Franklin ID-14 May 1995, Albuquerque NM) m Paul Nelson Davis (29 May 1918, Preston ID-Feb 1984, Hurricane UT).

BW74525   Wendell Haslam Wiser (b 16 Dec 1922, Fairview, Franklin ID) m 1) 13 Jun 1947, Salt Lake City UT, Yvonne Helen Wendrich (2 Dec 1928, Salt Lake City UT-16 Mar 1968, Bountiful UT); m 2) 12 Aug 1969, Salt Lake City UT, Barbara Carr (b 20 Apr 1940, Salt Lake City UT).

BW745251   Jerald Wendrich Wiser (b 7 Jan 1956, Cedar City UT) m 13 Aug 1981, Salt Lake UT, Susan Jeanine Johnson (b 12 Oct 1957, Colorado Springs CO).

BW7452511   Benjamin Jerald Wiser (b 4 Aug 1982, Salt Lake City UT).

BW7452512   Lance Michael Wiser (2 Aug 1984, Salt Lake City UT-2 Aug 1984).

BW7452513   Austin Lance Wiser (b 5 Sep 1985, Salt Lake City UT).

BW7452514   Timothy Grant Wiser (b 8 Jul 1987, Salt Lake City UT).

BW7452515   Zachary William Wiser (b 25 Sep 1989, Salt Lake City UT).

BW745252   David Wendrich Wiser (b 17 Jul 1957, Seattle WA) m 23 May 1985, Price UT Senna Marie Parker.

BW745253   Gregory Wendrich Wiser (b 13 Feb 1960, Auckland, New Zealand) m 1) 24 Aug 1984, Davis UT, Debbi Lynn Conrad; m 2) 11 Jun 1987, Davis UT, Lisa Morley (b 4 Jul 1969, Rantoul IL).

BW7452531   Ashley Yvonne Wiser (b 7 Jan 1988, Ogden UT).

BW7452532   Jake Gregory Wiser (b 14 Aug 1989, Ogden UT).

BW745254   Diane Wiser (b 30 Apr 1962, TeAroha, Thames, New Zealand).

BW745255   Sharon Wiser (b 21 Sep 1973, Salt Lake City UT).

BW74526   Helen Wiser (1 Dec 1924, Fairview, Franklin ID-19 Nov 1994, Salt Lake City UT) m 3 Apr 1950, Salt Lake City UT, Clyde Compton Child (b 7 Mar 1918, Ogden UT).

BW74527   Verl Haslam Wiser (15 Nov 1926, Fairview, Franklin ID-before 1995) m 16 May 1946, Logan UT, Colleen Hurst (b 13 May 1926, Logan UT); div.

BW745271   Steven H. Wiser (b 4 Dec 1959, Provo UT).

BW74528   Van Haslam Wiser (16 Oct 1931, Fairview, Franklin ID-1 Feb 1933).

BW7453   Clarence Cunningham Wiser (8 Oct 1888, Lewiston UT-15 Jun 1956, Salt Lake City UT) m 19 Nov 1913, Logan UT, Eurilla Emeline Kent (12 Aug 1888, Lewiston UT-9 Jan 1968, Ogden UT).

BW74531   Paul Kent Wiser (b 9 Oct 1924, Logan UT) m 28 Jun 1946, Logan UT, Lois Clawson (b 12 Dec 1926, Hyrum UT).

BW745311   Kent Clawson Wiser (b 12 Jul 1947, Logan UT) m 13 Sep 1972, Los Angeles CA, Susan Richards (b 14 Apr 1950, Salt Lake City UT).

BW7453111   Allison Wiser (b 23 Jun 1975, La Mesa CA).

BW745312   Marianne Wiser (b 9 Aug 1950, Logan UT) m 1 Jun 1973, Manti UT, Vaughn O. Judi (b 15 Jun 1948, Price UT).

BW745313   Gayla Wiser (b 28 Jul 1952, Logan UT) m 3 Sep 1971, Salt Lake UT, John David Petersen.

BW745314   Pauline Wiser (b 18 Apr 1954, Logan UT) m 21 Aug 1975, Logan UT, Donald Lee Dodge (b 4 Mar 1953, Las Vegas NV).

BW745315   Neil Paul Wiser (b 9 Nov 1958, Silverton OR) m 23 Apr 1982, Utah UT, Amy Michelle Westfall.

BW74532   Horace Wiser (28 Sep 1926, Lewiston UT-28 Sep 1926).

BW74533   Harvey Wiser (28 Sep 1926, Lewiston UT-28 Sep 1926).

BW74534   Margaret Wiser (b 2 Jun 1930, Lewiston UT) m 19 Mar 1947, Preston ID, William Jasper Turner (b 18 Feb 1925, Lewiston UT).

BW7454   Myron Cunningham Wiser (29 May 1891, Lewiston UT-30 Jul 1963, Lewiston UT) m 21 Apr 1915, Logan UT, Zelma Smith (13 May 1894, Lewiston UT-May 1986, Lewiston UT). Farmer.

BW74541   Edna Wiser (4 Mar 1916, Lewiston UT-30 Sep 1917).

BW74542   Philip Smith Wiser (b 4 Mar 1920, Logan UT) m 5 May 1944, Logan UT, Marian Naomi Sudekum (b 8 Nov 1923, Nashville TN).

BW745421   Janell Wiser (21 Aug 1946, Logan UT-May 1986, Salt Lake City UT) m 26 Jan 1967, Idaho Falls ID, Wayne L. Gardner (b 22 Jul 1944, Idaho Falls ID).

BW745422   John Philip Wiser (b 11 May 1948, Preston ID) m 25 Sep 1971, St. George UT, Martha McFarlane (b 30 Apr 1952, Provo UT).

BW7454221   Tawnee K. Wiser (b 30 Mar 1973, Anchorage AK).

BW745423   Joseph Dallan Wiser (b 16 Dec 1950, Blackfoot ID) m 16 Dec 1972, St. George UT, Gaye Lynne Gubler (b 14 May 1953, St. George UT).

BW7454231   Jacinta Wiser (b 15 Oct 1973, St. George UT).

BW7454232   Jeremiah Joseph Wiser (b 3 Sep 1974, St. George UT).

BW7454233   Tyson Horatio Wiser (b 29 Mar 1977, St. George UT).

BW745424   Alison Wiser (18 Jan 1953-17 Dec 1989, Henderson NV).

BW745425   Melanie Wiser (b 30 Apr 1956, Idaho Falls ID) m 6 Oct 1973, Hurricane UT, Karl Kent Wilson (b 7 Sep 1953, St. George UT).

BW745426   Kellee Jene Wiser (b 12 Jan 1959, Rexburg ID) m 21 Jul 1978, St. George UT, Ronald James Smith (b 16 Apr 1957, Provo UT).

BW745427   Gary Myron Wiser (b 12 Apr 1961, Rexburg ID).

BW745428   Jerry Lyman Wiser (b 12 Apr 1961, Rexburg ID).

BW745429   Charles DeWayne Wiser (29 Sep 1963, Rexburg ID-Nov 1985)

BW74543   Lyman Smith Wiser (b 5 Oct 1921, Logan UT) m 21 Nov 1944, Logan UT, Ramona Palmer (b 27 Mar 1925, Samaria, Oneida ID).

BW745431   Kevin Lyman Wiser (b 16 Jun 1961).

BW745432   Hal Wiser.

BW74544   Wallace Winston Wiser (b 2 Aug 1923, Lewiston UT) m 27 Nov 1945, Salt Lake City UT, Beatrice Faye Harmer (b 23 May 1925, Woods Cross UT).

BW745441   Thomas Lynn Wiser (b 27 Aug 1947, Logan UT) m 9 Jul 1971, Logan UT, Gail Neal (b 6 Sep 1950, Tremonton UT).

BW7454411   Kyla Wiser (b 3 Jun 1977, Twin Falls ID).

BW745442   Cheryl Lee Wiser (b 9 Oct 1948, Preston ID) m 6 May 1967, Terry W. Smith.

BW745443   Bradley H. Wiser (b 16 May 1956, Preston ID) m 30 May 1980, Logan UT, Patti Bowcutt.

BW74545   Theron Telford Wiser (b 27 Nov 1926, Lewiston UT) m 1) 11 Sep 1952, Logan UT, Fern Hansen (28 Jul 1932, Redmond, Sevier UT-17 Jan 1974, Salt Lake City UT); m 2) 26 Jun 1985, Salt Lake UT, Katherine Hunt.

BW745451   Mark Theron Wiser (b 26 Jan 1954, Salt Lake City UT) m 9 Jun 1973, Salt Lake UT, Carol Crandall.

BW745452   Lucinda Wiser (b 4 Jun 1958, Salt Lake City UT).

BW745453   Timothy L. Wiser (b 20 Jul 1960, Salt Lake City UT).

BW74546   Lawrence Clare Wiser (b 7 Oct 1929, Lewiston UT) m 9 Dec 1948, Logan UT, Billie Lou Gilbert (b 14 Jan 1929, Fairview, Franklin ID). Farmer.

BW745461   Marilee Wiser (b 1 May 1951, Logan UT) m Kelly Spackman (b 7 Jan 1951).

BW745462   Lu Ann Wiser (b 14 Feb 1953, Ogden UT) m 9 Jun 1972 Todd Jensen.

BW745463   Larry Gilbert Wiser (b 7 Dec 1954, Preston ID) m 4 Jun 1977, Patricia Ann Barber.

BW7454631   Landon Larry Wiser (b 9 Aug 1978, Logan UT).

BW745464   Daniel Ralph Wiser (b 18 Apr 1956, Rexburg ID) m 15 Apr 1976, Logan UT, Cyndi Lee Earl (b 18 Nov 1956, Logan UT).

BW7454641   Ondulyn Wiser (b 10 Jul 1978, Logan UT).

BW7454642   Jeanette Wiser (b 28 Nov 1979).

BW745465   Nanette Wiser (b 25 Jan 1960, Preston ID) m 15 Mar 1980, Logan UT, Tom Nutthall.

BW74547   Lois Wiser (b 2 Jun 1931, Lewiston UT) m 28 Sep 1951, Logan UT, Robert Melroy Ballard (b 9 Jun 1925, Benson, Cache UT).

BW7455   Leda Pearl Wiser (1 Apr 1893, Lewiston UT-23 Feb 1920, Lewiston UT) m 20 Jun 1917, Logan UT, Earl Delore Olson (14 Jan 1894, Millville, Cache UT-29 Aug 1973, Salt Lake City UT).

BW7456   Leora Wiser (28 Feb 1896, Lewiston UT-1 Sep 1978, Lewiston UT) m 19 Jun 1918, Logan UT, La Vere King (8 Aug 1897, Logan UT-Jan 1989, Lewiston UT).

BW7457   Hyrum Leon Wiser (19 Oct 1898, Lewiston UT-3 Jan 1899)

BW7458   Cliff Wiser (21 Aug 1900, Lewiston UT-Feb 1986, Logan UT) m 18 Dec 1924, Logan UT, Leona Lowe (b 26 Dec 1901, Franklin ID). Farmer.

BW74581   Emery Lowe Wiser (b 27 Oct 1925, Franklin ID) m 16 May 1945, Logan UT, Aliene Thain (b 14 Mar 1925, Logan UT). Farmer, manufacturer.

BW745811 Thayne Bradley Wiser (b 16 Jan 1947, Logan UT) m 19 Mar 1971, Logan UT, Kay Louise Wing (b 12 Aug 1951, Twin Falls ID).

BW7458111 Bradley Thayne Wiser (b 19 Feb 1972, Logan UT).

BW7458112 Clayne Jason Wiser (b 27 Jul 1973, Twin Falls ID).

BW7458113 Talon Scott Wiser (b 11 Jul 1975, Twin Falls ID).

BW7458114 Kurtis Elwood Wiser (b 21 Jul 1977, Logan UT).

BW745812 Shauna Wiser (b 10 Mar 1949, Logan UT) m 29 May 1969, Logan UT, Garold William Busch (b 23 Sep 1946, Sacramento CA).

BW745813 Machel Wiser (b 17 Aug 1953, Logan UT) m 27 Dec 1975, Logan UT, Louis Ted Stimpson (b 8 Sep 1951, Burley ID).

BW745814 DeLaine Wiser (b 2 Nov 1959, Wenatchee WA) m 27 Jul 1984, Utah UT, Gary Jay Shenton.

BW74582 Carma Wiser (b 23 Apr 1929, Lewiston UT) m 26 Nov 1952, Logan UT, Joseph Milton Hawkes (b 8 Dec 1931, Pocatello ID).

BW74583 John Merle Wiser (b 2 Jan 1937, Logan UT) m 11 Dec 1959, Logan UT, Marlene Jones (b 6 Sep 1937, Logan UT).

BW745831 LaDawn Wiser (b 2 Feb 1961, Preston ID).

BW745832 Brian John Wiser (b 30 Apr 1963, Preston ID).

BW745833 Annette Wiser (b 10 Apr 1968, Chicago IL)

BW745834 Steven Cliff Wiser (b 25 Oct 1970, Chicago IL)

BW7459 Orville Wiser (b 1 Dec 1905, Lewiston UT) m 24 Dec 1930, Logan UT, Norma Rebecca Gyllenskog (6 Aug 1903, Logan UT-27 May 1980, Logan UT). Farmer.

BW746 Nancy Alvira Wiser (8 Apr 1860, Alpine, Utah UT-24 Mar 1865).

BW747 Samuel Frost Wiser (23 Oct 1862, Richmond UT-3 Jun 1947, Lewiston UT) m 23 Oct 1884, Logan UT, Rebecca Ann Telford (16 Jan 1862, Brigham City, Box Elder UT-7 Jan 1954, Lewiston UT). Farmer.

BW7471 Effie Lenore Wiser (22 Feb 1886, Lewiston UT-14 Aug 1974, Logan UT).

BW7472 Samuel Glenn Wiser (25 Dec 1887, Lewiston UT-28 Jul 1959, Ogden UT) m 1) 12 Mar 1913, Logan UT, Verna Gertrude Van Orden (25 Dec 1887, Lewiston UT-28 Jul 1959, Ogden UT); m 2) Emerett Millar (b 29 Aug 1900, American Fork UT). Farmer, bus driver.

BW74721 Glenn Van Orden Wiser (17 Aug 1915, Lewiston UT-18 Aug 1915).

BW74722 Shirley Wiser (b 30 Jun 1916, Lewiston UT) m 27 Jan 1934, Lewiston UT, Edgar Orchard (8 Nov 1908, Lewiston UT-25 Jan 1942, Sacramento CA).

BW74723 Paul Van Orden Wiser (20 Sep 1918, Lewiston UT-3 Oct 1918).

BW74724   Louise Wiser (b 16 Oct 1921, Lewiston UT) m 23 Mar 1942, Salt Lake City UT, Alvin Theodore Kiholm (b 30 Sep 1919, Shelley ID).

BW74725   Robert Van Orden Wiser (23 Dec 1924, Lewiston UT-23 Dec 1924).

BW74726   Roland Glenn Wiser (3 Dec 1931, Lewiston UT-6 Feb 1932).

BW74727   Cara Lou Wiser (b 8 Dec 1932, Logan UT) m 7 Mar 1957, Salt Lake City UT, Clarence Lee Vance (b 19 Mar 1930, Fairview UT).

BW74728   Wendell Mark Wiser (b 11 Mar 1934, Lewiston UT) m 16 Apr 1954, Logan UT, Priscilla Price (b 18 Aug 1934, Pleasantview, Oneida ID).

BW747281   Wendelene Wiser (b 27 Apr 1957, Shirley MA) m 14 Jun 1983, Salt Lake City UT, Kevin Darrell Watts.

BW747282   Susan Rae Wiser (b 28 Oct 1958, Nurnberg, Germany) m 1) 27 May 1977, Daniel Alfred Delgado; m 2) 26 Aug 1985, Salt Lake UT, Robert J. Eaton.

BW747283   Lucilla Wiser (b 29 Nov 1960, Salt Lake City UT) m 15 Oct 1979, Salt Lake UT, David Clifford Bevan.

BW747284   Patricia Ann Wiser (b 18 Aug 1967, Pocatello ID) m 15 May 1991, Salt Lake City UT, Steven Ray Williams.

BW747285   John Wendell Wiser (b 26 Jun 1971, Kettering OH).

BW747286   William Mark Wiser (b 31 Mar 1976, Albuquerque NM).

BW74729   Farrell Dean Wiser (b 3 Dec 1935, Lewiston UT) m 16 May 1958, Na Dene Kent (b 6 May 1940, Lewiston UT).

BW747291   Luana Wiser (b 22 Mar 1959, Preston ID) m 2 Feb 1979, Davis UT, Mark Edwin Erickson.

BW747292   Sharon Wiser (b 16 Jun 1960, Brigham City UT).

BW747293   Darla Wiser (b 23 Sep 1961, Brigham City UT).

BW747294   Douglas Kent Wiser (b 7 Oct 1964, Brigham City UT) m 14 Mar 1989, Davis UT, Sky Lyn Matthew.

BW747295   Darren Glen Wiser (b 30 Mar 1967, Brigham City UT).

BW747296   Ryan Seth Wiser (b 24 Jun 1971, Brigham City UT).

BW747297   Clifton Ross Wiser (b 21 Oct 1975, Bountiful UT).

BW7472A   Maxine Wiser (b 9 Oct 1938, Richmond UT) m 18 May 1962, Salt Lake City UT, Charles Russell Cummings Jr. (29 Dec 1935, Fort Wayne IN-30 Nov 1989, Kirtland NM).

BW7472B   Cordell Wiser (b 19 Nov 1941, Richmond UT) m 30 Jul 1965, Los Angeles CA, Ruth Elaine Richards (b 5 Sep 1945, Inglewood CA).

BW7472B1   Robert Glenn Wiser (b 12 Dec 1967, Inglewood CA).

BW7472B2   Aaron Jeffrey Wiser (b 14 May 1970, Inglewood CA).

BW7472B3   Michael David Wiser (b 12 Jul 1975, Inglewood CA).

BW7473   Nilus Wiser (19 Jul 1890, Lewiston UT-18 Dec 1968, Salt Lake City UT) m 1 Oct 1919, Logan UT, Alma Sharp Packer (4 Oct 1892, Franklin ID-30 Aug 1973, Salt Lake City UT). Alma: WWI, USA.

BW7474   Venus Wiser (16 Sep 1892, Lewiston UT-1 Jun 1970, Helsinki, Finland) m 17 Sep 1913, Logan UT, George Allen Lufkin (25 Jul 1888, Salt Lake City UT-24 Nov 1956, Idaho Falls ID). George: farmer.

BW7475   Lorin Frost Wiser (23 Oct 1894, Lewiston UT-18 Sep 1930, Logan UT) m 29 Nov 1922, Logan UT, Eliza Lewis King (21 May 1895, Logan UT-22 May 1958, Lewiston UT). Lorin: farmer. Eliza: teacher.

BW74751   Phyllis Wiser (b 15 May 1924, North Logan UT) m 9 Mar 1945, Logan UT, Earl Raymond Anderson (b 2 Apr 1919, Logan UT).

BW74752   Lorin Kenneth Wiser (b 28 Dec 1925, North Logan UT) m 8 Sep 1952, Logan UT, Mary Arlene Hansen (b 8 Sep 1929, Logan UT). Teacher.

BW747521   Marianne Wiser (b 8 Sep 1953) m 16 Dec 1978, Ogden UT, W. Kent Parker.

BW747522   Randall Kenneth Wiser (b 3 Jun 1955, Ogden UT) m 21 Jun 1977, Ogden UT, Becky Ann Brown.

BW747523   Janice Wiser (b 4 Dec 1956) m 31 Mar 1978, Ogden UT, Kevin W. Toyn.

BW747524   Kraig Lorin Wiser (b 21 Oct 1959).

DW74753   Milton King Wiser (21 Aug 1927, North Logan UT-2 Sep 1952, Logan UT) m 9 Aug 1946, Logan UT, Muriel Lucile Johnson (b 22 Jan 1929, North Logan UT). Farmer.

BW747531   Lorin Milton Wiser (b 23 Jan 1949, Logan UT) m 12 Aug 1972, Alice Analee Carlin.

BW7475311   Joshua Lorin Wiser (b 8 Jul 1976, Gridley CA).

BW74754   Rey Lamar Wiser (b 12 Feb 1929, Lewiston UT) m 19 Jun 1959, Manti UT, Koa Jean Ogden (b 22 Aug 1936, Richfield UT). Teacher.

BW747541   Diane Wiser (b 16 Oct 1960, Preston ID).

BW747542   Gary LeMar Wiser (b 12 Dec 1962, Preston ID).

BW747543   Jean Wiser (b 14 Jun 1964, Preston ID).

BW747544   Ruth Wiser (b 3 Sep 1965, Preston ID).

BW747545   Linda Wiser (b 23 Oct 1967, Logan UT).

BW747546   Debbie Wiser (b 30 Jan 1970, Logan UT).

BW747547   David Rey Wiser (b 22 Nov 1975).

BW74755   Lewis Frost Wiser (b 30 Oct 1930, Lewiston UT) m 25 Mar 1960, Logan UT, Louise

Bright (b 27 May 1937, Lewiston UT). Farmer.

BW747551　　　　Sheldon Lewis Wiser (b 14 Oct 1961, Logan UT) m Judy.

BW747552　　　　Kristine Wiser (b 16 Mar 1963, Preston ID).

BW747553　　　　Darrell Lorin Wiser (b 11 Oct 1964, Preston ID).

BW747554　　　　Douglas Wesley Wiser (b 6 Sep 1966, Logan UT).

BW747555　　　　Sherwin Andrew Wiser (b 2 Oct 1968, Logan UT).

BW747556　　　　Kathleen Wiser (b 18 Jan 1970, Logan UT).

BW747557　　　　Anthony William Wiser (b 4 Aug 1971, Logan UT).

BW747558　　　　Aaron Frost Wiser (b 9 Dec 1972, Logan UT).

BW747559　　　　Jarred Samuel Wiser (b 20 Jan 1976, Preston ID).

BW74755A　　　　Jonathan Hazen Wiser (b 13 Mar 1978, Preston ID).

BW74755B　　　　Daniel King Wiser (b 9 Mar 1981).

BW7476　　　　Wayne Telford Wiser (26 Dec 1896, Lewiston UT-29 Sep 1972, Lewiston UT) m 30 Nov 1921, Logan UT, Eva Almira England (19 Mar 1899, Logan UT-3 Dec 1973, Logan UT). Farmer, railroader.

BW74761　　　　Barbara Wiser (b 5 Jun 1923, Logan UT) m 6 Oct 1942, Logan UT, Rex Gibson Plowman (31 Oct 1923, Smithfield UT-29 Dec 1994, Logan UT). Rex: bank president & CEO.

BW74762　　　　Gayle Wiser (9 Apr 1928, Lewiston UT-28 Sep 1994, TX) m 5 Nov 1946, Idaho Falls ID, Jack Eldon Leavitt (b 9 Aug 1926, Cornish UT).

BW74763　　　　Marilyn Wiser (b 28 Apr 1931, Lewiston UT) m 1) 2 Aug 1949, Logan UT, Layle Odis Talbot (24 Jun 1931, Logan UT-13 Oct 1971, Twin Falls ID); m 2) 22 Jun 1974, Wesley Harrop Poole.

BW74764　　　　Janet Wiser (b 10 Nov 1933, Lewiston UT) m 22 Sep 1952, Logan UT, Milton Delbert Petersen (b 27 Aug 1933, Logan UT).

BW74765　　　　Dahl Wayne Wiser (b 23 Apr 1936, Lewiston UT) m 27 Feb 1959, Logan UT, Karen Buhler (b 29 Apr 1938, Sandy UT).

BW747651　　　　Kevin Dal Wiser (b 4 May 1964, Ogden UT).

BW747652　　　　Kim Wiser (b 29 May 1967, Ogden UT).

BW7477　　　　Erwin Douglas Wiser (29 Apr 1902, Lewiston UT-28 Nov 1985, Preston ID) m 1) 21 Jun 1922, Logan UT, Wanda Thompson (6 Feb 1901, Richmond UT-25 Mar 1974, Ephrata WA); m 2) 14 Oct 1978, Moab UT, Rosanna Sullivan (19 Apr 1911, Leeds UT-29 Aug 1990, Preston ID). Farmer.

BW74771　　　　Erwin Dee Wiser (b 28 Jan 1923, Lewiston UT) m 11 Aug 1948, Logan UT, Lorna Shumway (b 13 Jul 1930, Franklin ID). Farmer.

BW747711　　　　David Earl Wiser (b 1 Oct 1957, Moses Lake WA) m 13 Sep 1978, Salt Lake City UT, Malinda Pearce (b 14 Nov 1959, Salt Lake City UT); m 2) 2 Feb 1984, Pasco WA, Gayle Breen (b 2 Aug 1957); m 3) 1 Apr 1994, KY, Ronnie Dee Willis (b 10 May 1972). Medical technologist.

BW7477111   Whitney Wiser (b 13 Feb 1980, Wenatchee WA).

BW7477112   Preston Charles Wiser (b 22 Feb 1988, San Antonio TX).

BW7477113   Carly Dee Wiser (b 26 Nov 1991, San Antonio TX).

BW747712   Joleen Wiser (b 17 Apr 1961, Spokane WA) m 19 Sep 1980, Salt Lake City UT, Thomas Wade Comstock (b 19 Feb 1958, Ephrata WA).

BW747713   Perry Douglas Wiser (b 13 Dec 1963, Spokane WA) m 22 Jul 1988, Boise ID, Evelyn Leavitt Carter (b 22 Sep 1967, Caldwell ID).

BW7477131   David Leavitt Wiser (b 18 Nov 1987, Provo UT).

BW7477132   Rachel Kathryn Wiser (b 1 Aug 1990, Wenatchee WA).

BW7477133   Perris Evelyn Wiser (b 17 Dec 1991, Spokane WA).

BW747714   DeAnn Wiser (b 24 Nov 1966, Davenport WA) m 7 May 1990, Ephrata WA, Mark Francis Lefebvre (b 31 Mar 1962).

BW74772   Genevieve Wiser (b 11 Aug 1924, Lewiston UT) m 30 Nov 1942, Mare Island CA, George Telford Denning (19 Oct 1920, Iona ID-18 Aug 1994, Payson UT).

BW74773   Sylmar Thompson Wiser (b 28 Apr 1926, Lewiston UT) m 10 Sep 1948, Salt Lake City UT, Karma Page (30 Jan 1928, Logan UT-9 Aug 1995, Ogden UT). Air force base worker.

BW747731   Jeffrey Blake Wiser (b 26 Jul 1961, Salt Lake City UT) m 2 Aug 1984, Ogden UT, Lesa Joan Higley (b 13 Oct 1965, Ogden UT). Mechanic.

BW7477311   Maddison Paige Wiser (b 13 Oct 1994, Ogden UT).

BW747732   Janet Wiser (b 26 Jul 1963, Ogden UT).

BW74774   James Gordon Wiser (b 10 Dec 1927, Lewiston UT) m 17 Feb 1955, Logan UT, Eva Lou Blair (b 30 Sep 1935, Lewiston UT). Engineer.

*BW747741   Ron Gordon Wiser (b 14 Sep 1956, Glendale CA) m 6 Jun 1986, Mesa AZ, Cynthia Marie Shupe (b 7 Oct 1961, Ft. Leonard Wood, Pulaski MO). Ron: CPA, bank president & CEO. Cynthia, CPA.

BW7477411   Joshua Thompson Wiser (b 4 Apr 1987, Albuquerque NM).

BW7477412   Logan Patrick Wiser (b 20 Feb 1990, Albuquerque NM).

BW7477413   Andrew William Wiser (b 24 May 1993, Albuquerque NM).

BW747742   Bob Harold Wiser (b 13 Mar 1959, San Jose CA) m 19 Dec 1980, Logan UT, Beverly Thalman (b 22 Jan 1960, Logan UT). CPA, finance director.

BW7477421   Trina Wiser (b 10 Dec 1981, Logan UT).

BW7477422   Robert James Wiser (b 21 Apr 1983, Logan UT).

BW7477423   LaTisha Wiser (b 18 Jan 1986, Salt Lake City UT).

BW7477424   David DeLoy Wiser (b 5 Jan 1988, Salt Lake City UT).

BW747743   Shelly Wiser (b 6 Dec 1962, Bellevue WA). Accountant.

BW74775   Denzel Nolan Wiser (b 25 May 1930, Lewiston UT) m 8 Sep 1955, Salt Lake City UT, Beverly Ann Morgan (b 10 Aug 1934, Burley ID). Engineer.

BW747751   Deborah Ann Wiser (b 25 Aug 1956, Seattle WA) m 20 Aug 1977, Oakland CA, Donald Howard Fry. Computer programmer.

BW747752   Jay Douglas Wiser (b 27 Dec 1957, San Jose CA) m 18 Mar 1981, Ogden UT, Deborah Lee Jensen. Air traffic controller.

BW7477521   Jason Nolan Wiser (b 13 Jan 1982, Ogden UT).

BW7477522   Kenneth James Wiser (b 20 Jun 1986, Tacoma WA).

BW7477523   Rebecca Ann Wiser (b 5 Jun 1989, Carbondale IL).

BW7477524   Paul Wiser (b 30 Nov 1992, Huron SD).

BW7477525   Jennifer Lee Wiser (b 20 Jun 1994, Huron SD).

BW747753   Steven Bruce Wiser (b 27 Nov 1959, San Jose CA) m 1) 28 Dec 1982, Bellevue WA, Laurie Lynn Gilbert; m 2) 30 Jul 1994, Seattle WA, Barbara Larsen.

BW7477531   Lindsay Rebecca Wiser (b 18 Aug 1986, Bellevue WA).

BW7477532   Kelsey Lauren Wiser (b 14 Jun 1989, Bellevue WA).

BW747754   David Bryan Wiser (b 29 Jun 1962, San Jose CA) m 3 Jan 1984, Bellevue WA, Sandra Kay Merrell.

BW7477541   Krysti ReAnn Wiser (b 22 Oct 1985, Provo UT).

BW7477542   Ashley Marie Wiser (b 3 Aug 1987, Seattle WA).

BW7477543   Joshua David Wiser (b 3 Nov 1989, Bellevue WA).

BW747755   Michael Dennis Wiser (b 22 Jul 1964, San Jose CA) m 1 Aug 1987 Los Angeles CA, Anyolina Olivas.

BW7477551   Jessica Christine Wiser (b 6 Jan 1989, Bellevue WA).

BW7477552   Clarissa Janeen Wiser (b 19 Jun 1991, Oxnard CA).

BW747756   Paul Jeffrey Wiser (1 Jun 1967, San Jose CA-1 Jun 1967).

BW74776   Anita Wiser (b 9 May 1931, Lewiston UT) m 13 Jul 1949, Logan UT, Cleve Al Raymond (b 6 Apr 1929, Smithfield UT).

BW74777   Robert Clayne Wiser (18 Sep 1933, Lewiston UT-5 Feb 1935, Lewiston UT).

BW74778   Gwen Wiser (b 10 May 1940, Lewiston UT). Computer analyst.

BW74779   Burdette Wiser (b 2 Feb 1944, Lewiston UT).

BW7478   Horace Verne Wiser (28 Apr 1904, Lewiston UT-9 Jul 1964, Bountiful UT) m 23 Nov

1927, Logan UT, Nellie Telford (27 Jan 1904, Richmond UT-ca 1994). Veterinarian.

BW74781   Rhea Kathleen Wiser (b 8 Sep 1928, Logan UT) m 1) 31 Jul 1946, Salt Lake City UT, Claude Edwin Purles (b 14 Aug 1927, Salt Lake City UT); m 2) 1 Apr 1987, Salt Lake UT, Jerry Lynne Cruise.

BW74782   Horace Clare Wiser (b 26 Jan 1933, Lewiston UT) m 19 Jun 1953, Sharon Heslop (b 25 Jun 1933, Ogden UT). College professor.

BW747821   Cherie Wiser (b 25 Dec 1955, Roswell NM).

BW747822   Steven J. Wiser (b 7 Aug 1957, Big Spring TX).

BW747823   Jolene Wiser (b 7 Jan 1962, Pullman WA).

BW747824   Shawn Douglas Wiser (b 9 Dec 1965, Pullman WA).

BW74783   Richard Verne Wiser (b 23 May 1940, Salt Lake City UT) m 20 Dec 1963, Salt Lake City UT, Helma Edelburg Schindler (b 5 Mar 1944, Falkenov, Germany).

BW747831   Brian Wiser (b 29 Apr 1969, Bountiful UT).

BW7479   Marjorie Wiser (b 1 Sep 1910, Lewiston UT) m 22 Mar 1928, Logan UT, Lowell Christian Titensor (b 17 Sep 1910, Cove, Cache UT). Farm equipment company owner.

BW748   Child Wiser (ca 1864, Richmond UT); stillborn.

BW749   George Harmon Wiser (11 Oct 1867, Richmond UT-17 Feb 1941, Lewiston UT) m 14 Dec 1892, Logan UT, Alice Asenath Glover (13 Oct 1871, Farmington UT-29 Apr 1951, Fairview ID).

BW7491   Ada Wiser (25 Oct 1894, Lewiston UT-29 Mar 1958, Franklin ID) m 1) 25 Feb 1914, Logan UT, Walter Smith (9 Apr 1893, Fairview ID-31 Jan 1930, Preston ID); m 2) Harry Siddoway Gamble (17 Aug 1894-26 Jun 1966, Logan UT).

BW7492   NaVella Wiser (11 Oct 1898, Lewiston UT-27 Feb 1981, Ogden UT) m 30 Jan 1919, Manti UT, Oscar Richard Rawlings (24 Dec 1897, Fairview ID-11 Nov 1974, Fairview ID).

BW7493   La Moin Harmon Wiser (8 Nov 1902, Lewiston UT-7 Aug 1977, Logan UT) m 10 Feb 1932, Logan UT, Sara Gunnell Poppleton (23 Dec 1909, Wellsville UT-20 Oct 1988)

BW74931   Gerald Lamoin Wiser (b 29 Jul 1933, Lewiston UT) m 1) 15 Jan 1960, Pasadena CA, Joan Ada Grant (8 Jul 1933, Wilkes-Barre PA-16 Jun 1991); div; m 2) Jane.

          Victoria Joan Wiser (b 9 Aug 1968, Los Angeles CA).

BW74932   Dean Clell Wiser (4 Feb 1935, Lewiston UT-11 Mar 1936).

BW74933   Marie Wiser (b 28 Jun 1938, Lewiston UT) m 14 Sep 1956, Tracy Homer Daines (b 21 Dec 1936, Smithfield UT); div.

BW74934   Judy Wiser (b 28 Apr 1942, Lewiston UT) m Teddy Brooks.

BW74935   Joyce Wiser (b 26 Nov 1946, Logan UT) m Alan Don Watterson (b 11 Aug 1947).

BW74936   John Steve Wiser (b 6 Feb 1955, Logan UT) m Teresa Ann Fullmer.

BW749361   Nicole Wiser (29 Feb 1980, Logan UT-21 Jul 1980).

BW7494   Chloey Wiser (1 Oct 1904, Lewiston UT-Apr 1986, Ogden UT) m 1) 5 Jul 1922, Logan UT, Harold Floyd Creger (b 9 Sep 1897, Shelley ID); m 2) George Esterholdt (2 Jul 1884, Dingle, Bear Lake ID-22 May 1952, Montpelier ID); m 3) 24 Sep 1953, Soda Springs ID, Alfred Moroni Dayton (b 26 Nov 1893, Dingle, Bear Lake ID).

BW7495   Devon Glover Wiser (14 Oct 1906, Lewiston UT-16 Apr 1989, Logan UT) m 25 Nov 1931, Logan UT, May Elizabeth Nielsen (b 2 Apr 1907, Hyrum UT).

BW74951   Bryce Devon Wiser (b 18 Jul 1932, Hyrum UT).

BW74952   Clayne Harmon Wiser (25 Jul 1934, Lewiston UT-Oct 1986, Logan UT) m 27 Jun 1958, Logan UT, Dixie Lee Balling (b 15 May 1940, Logan UT). Plumbing company owner.

BW749521   Boyd Clayne Wiser (b 13 Jul 1964, Ogden UT).

BW749522   Shauna Lee Wiser (b 6 Jul 1966, Logan UT) m Eric Abram Zollinger.

BW749523   Kathy Wiser (b 6 Mar 1968, Logan UT) m Kraig Packer.

BW749524   Kim Cheree Wiser (b 6 Nov 1969, Logan UT) m Darin Lloyd Hinton.

BW749525   Jerry Devon Wiser (b 7 Apr 1971, Logan UT) m Brandi Lee Atkinson.

BW749526   Martin Harold Wiser (b 5 Sep 1976, North Logan UT).

BW749527   Michael Joseph Wiser (b 13 Jun 1980, North Logan UT).

BW74953   Eugene Gail Wiser (19 Nov 1936, Lewiston UT-8 Jan 1937).

BW74954   Joan May Wiser (b 24 Apr 1938, Hyrum UT) m 31 Dec 1966, Layton UT, James Green Weaver (b 27 Nov 1917, Layton UT).

BW74955   Brant Marvin Wiser (b 21 Jan 1941, Hyrum UT) m 1) Carolyn Ruth Rose; m 2) Sandra Snyder Yager; m 3) Caryol Timms (b 26 Oct 1939).

BW749551   Marci Caryol Wiser (b 24 May 1974).

BW74956   Mayvon Wiser (b 19 Aug 1944, Logan UT) m 1) 9 Jun 1967, Salt Lake City UT, Barry Jellette Brown (b 16 Feb 1945, Ogden UT); m 2) 7 Jul 1969, Edward Fallows; m 3) 23 Nov 1974, Saratoga WY, Ronald Ralph Platt.

BW74957   DeMont Clell Wiser (b 22 Jun 1950, Logan UT) m 6 Mar 1972, Logan UT, Karen Alexander (b 18 Mar 1947).

BW749571   Karmon Wiser (b 6 Dec 1972, Pocatello ID).

BW749572   Bryce DeMont Wiser (b 28 Apr 1975, Pocatello ID).

BW749573   Clark Devon Wiser (b 28 Sep 1977, Payson UT).

BW749574   DeAnn Wiser (b 13 May 1980, Gunnison UT).

BW7496   Carl William Wiser (3 Sep 1908, Lewiston UT-26 Jan 1959, Fresno CA) m 1) 6 Aug 1930, Logan UT, Zona Blair (23 Feb 1909, Lewiston UT-27 Nov 1940, Lewiston UT); m 2) Alta Van Orden (b 17 Mar 1913, Lewiston UT).

BW74961   Carol Wiser (b 11 Jul 1931, Lewiston UT) m Dallan Bingham Spackman (b 12 Dec 1930, Smithfield UT).

BW74962   Faye Wiser (1 Jul 1936, Logan UT-Feb 1987, Logan UT) m 8 Apr 1955, Fairview, Franklin ID, Edwin Malcolm Hyde (b 20 Nov 1935, Logan UT).

BW74963   Richard Carl Wiser (27 Nov 1940, Lewiston UT-15 Oct 1993, Fairview, Franklin ID).

BW7497   Harold John Wiser (b 4 Apr 1912, Lewiston UT) m 8 Feb 1933, Logan UT, Pearl Biggs Hampton (b 13 May 1914, Franklin ID).

BW74971   Darrell H. Wiser (b 27 Jan 1934, Franklin ID) m 22 May 1953, Ogden UT, Marian Thornley (b 2 Aug 1935, Ogden UT).

BW749711   Karie Wiser (b 9 Jan 1957, Las Vegas NV) m Wallace Kent Eggleston.

BW749712   Kathy Wiser (b 22 Mar 1961, Ogden UT).

BW74972   Glade H. Wiser (b 28 Aug 1943, Logan UT) m 1) 24 Mar 1962, Ogden UT, Karol Kay Smith (b 14 Mar 1943, Ogden UT); m 2) 18 Nov 1967, Kathryn Ence (b 26 May 1945, Richfield UT).

BW749721   Krystal Wiser (b 17 Sep 1963, Ogden UT) m Kevin L. Johnson.

BW749722   Karen Wiser (b 13 Jan 1965, Ogden UT).

BW749723   Mikel Jon Wiser (b 13 Jul 1969, Ogden UT).

BW749724   Jason Andrew Wiser (b 8 Mar 1971, Ogden UT).

BW749725   Jennifer Anne Wiser (b 21 Feb 1975, Ogden UT).

BW749726   David Harold Wiser (b 29 Sep 1976, Ogden UT).

BW74A   Alla Arminda Wiser (24 Feb 1870, Richmond UT-27 Jul 1952, Ogden UT) m 28 Jan 1891, Logan UT, William Dorris Hendricks (23 Sep 1870, Richmond UT-12 Jul 1938, Rupert ID).

BW75   Samuel S. Wiser (b ca 1829, Truxton NY)

BW76   Matilda Ann Wiser (1832, Truxton NY-1861, Dubuque IA) m 9 Sep 1847, Jo Daviess IL, James Gregory (1826, Ireland-after 1865).

BW77   William Henry Wiser (b ca 1834, Truxton NY)

BW8   James Wiser (b 1785, Haverhill NH) m 1) Anna Kingsley (1796, NY-after 1860, Boone, Harrison IN); m 2) Amanda (1800, MA-16 Mar 1885, Cortland NY). Farmer, Cortland NY.

BW81   Mary ("Polly") Wiser (1812, Cazenovia NY-after 1870) m 17 Aug 1831, Harrison IN, Fielding Steele.

BW82   Lucy Ann Wiser (1823, NY-after 1883) m 9 Jul 1840, Harrison IN, Joseph Claspill (1819, IN-10 Jul 1853). Harrison IN.

BW83   Cloa S. Wiser (b 1824, NY) m 1) 25 Apr 1840, Harrison IN, Thomas Thornberry; m 2) 19 Apr 1845, Harrison IN, Washington Canady, m 3) 17 Feb 1852, Harrison IN, James ("Jack") Bean.

Harrison IN.

BW84   Mariam Elis Wiser (d 28 Jul 1850, New Albany IN) m 26 Jul 1841, Harrison IN, George Washington Benton (28 Nov 1818, GA-12 Apr 1911, Evansville IN). Harrison IN.

BW85   Levi Wiser (10 Jan 1835, Truxton NY-8 Mar 1903, Virgil NY) m 15 Jul 1860, Chenango, Cortland NY, Lucy Amelia Pike (1845, NY-1 Sep 1892, South Cortland NY).

BW851   Frank L. Wiser (15 Jul 1861, Solon, Cortland NY-12 Feb 1917, Ithaca NY) m Agnes (b 1865, NY). Fireman, Ithaca NY.

BW852   Jessie Evlin Wiser (b 26 Apr 1870, NY) m 1) James A. Harris (6 Aug 1875, MI-26 Aug 1932, Ithaca NY); m 2) 31 Dec 1932, David William Shroff (b 13 Jan 1902, Lebanon PA).

BW853   Edwin Ernest Wiser (10 Oct 1876, Cortland NY-25 Jul 1940, Cortland NY) m 1) 22 Nov 1901, Carrie L. Hilsinger (16 Oct 1883, NY-11 Jun 1911); m 2) 7 Feb 1912, Lillian Eleanor Scott (b 1885, Port Crane, Broome NY). Railroader, Cortland NY.

BW8531   Herbert Grayson ("Bud") Wiser (12 Dec 1902, Texas Valley, Cortland NY-8 May 1985, Barker, Broome NY) m 11 Jun 1927, Chenango Forks, Broome NY, Bertha Benedict (20 Sep 1908, Barker, Broome NY-4 Oct 1969, Johnson City, Broome NY).

BW85311   Warren Herbert Wiser (b 27 Aug 1931, Binghamton NY) m 21 Sep 1963, Apalachin NY, Wanda Barton (b 30 Oct 1932).

BW853111   Marlene Louise Wiser (b 14 Jul 1963, Syracuse NY) m 24 Jul 1981, Kevin Donald Morgan (b 26 Jul 1959).

BW853112   Michael Christopher Wiser (b 19 Jul 1964, Johnson City NY) m 19 Jul 1991, Terrie Hertzog.

BW8531121   Sydney Marie Wiser (b 11 Apr 1992).

BW8531122   Aaron Todd Wiser (b 9 Dec 1993).

BW85312   Gerald Ethan Wiser (b 11 Oct 1932, Binghamton NY) m 1) Topeka KS, Edna Burgoyne; m 2) 20 Oct 1957, Thelma Louise Shaefer (b 5 Jan 1940, Spirit Lake IA).

BW853121   Elizabeth Grace Wiser (b 8 Jun 1954, Johnson City NY) m 23 Jul 1977, John Christenson (b 20 Apr 1954).

BW853122   Lori Jean Wiser (b 12 May 1962).

BW853123   Lisa Kay Wiser (b 20 Dec 1963).

BW853124   Jerry Lee Wiser (b 31 Dec 1965).

BW853125   Cathy Jo Wiser (b 24 Jul 1969) m 21 Aug 1993, Michael William Hamblen.

BW85313   Leo Clifton Wiser (b 7 Oct 1933, Barker, Broome NY) m 1) 25 Jul 1953, Chenango Bridge, Broome NY, Joyce Alice Bush (b 20 Nov 1936); m 2) 7 Dec 1974, Binghamton NY, Rebecca Johnson (b 20 Nov 1946).

BW853131   Leo Clifton Wiser (b 17 Aug 1954, Johnson City NY) m Greenville SC, Carol.

BW8531311   Toni Jean Wiser (b 16 Jan 1982).

BW8531312   Henry Wiser.

BW853132   Jeffrey Lyn Wiser (b 1 Oct 1954, Johnson City NY) m 1) Jan 1980, Dottie; m 2) ca 1980, Linda.

BW8531321   Matthew Noah Wiser (b 19 Jul 1976).

BW8531322   John Daniel Wiser (b 29 Jun 1983).

BW853133   Timothy James Wiser (b 16 Oct 1957, Johnson City NY) m 17 Jul 1981, Doris Bowers (b 24 Nov 1955).

BW8531331   Trisha Dee Wiser (b 23 Sep 1982).

BW8531332   Katie Lauren Wiser (b 18 May 1989).

BW853134   Debra Marlene Wiser (b 4 Dec 1958, Johnson City NY) m 3 Sep 1977, Jeffrey Trammell.

BW853135   Cynthia Louise Wiser (b 14 Jan 1961, Johnson City NY) m Dolby.

BW853136   Kevin Grayson Wiser (b 2 Mar 1963, Binghamton NY).

BW853137   Daniel Ervin Wiser (b 28 Jan 1977, Johnson City NY).

BW853138   Matthew David Wiser (b 26 Sep 1978, Johnson City NY).

BW85314   Richard LaVerne Wiser (b 15 Dec 1934, Barker, Broome NY) m 10 Nov 1956, Tunnel, Broome NY, Joanne Hurlburt (31 Oct 1938-21 Jun 1995, Binghamton NY).

BW853141   Linda Ann Wiser (b 27 Dec 1958, Johnson City NY) m 4 Nov 1989, Frederick Frasier Vlele (b 8 Mar 1955).

BW853142   Mark Richard Wiser (b 21 Jul 1960, Johnson City NY).

BW853143   Douglas LaVerne Wiser (b 20 Nov 1962, Johnson City NY) m 23 Apr 1988, Joann Kublo (b 17 May 1964).

BW8531431   Douglas Michael Wiser (b 13 Aug 1989, Binghamton NY).

BW853144   James Grayson Wiser (b 30 Mar 1967, Johnson City NY) m 14 Aug 1993, Barbara Byroads (b 18 Jan 1970).

BW8531441   Grayson John Wiser (b 3 Dec 1993, Cortland NY).

BW85315   Harold Everett Wiser (b 30 Sep 1936, Barker, Broome NY) m 15 Oct 1958, Whitney Point, Broome NY, Mary Lou Smith (b 5 Apr 1939).

BW853151   Julie Lynn Wiser (b 10 Feb 1960, Johnson City NY) m 20 Nov 1982, Charley Patterson.

BW853152   Jane Lynnette Wiser (b 25 Apr 1961, Johnson City NY) m 17 Jul 1982, Castle Creek, Broome NY, David Lewis (b 23 Jun 1959).

BW853153   Vicki Lee Wiser (b 1 Dec 1962, Johnson City NY) m 26 Jun 1982, Timothy E. Ross (b 19 Dec 1960).

BW853154   Carrie Adele Wiser (b 26 Apr 1973, Johnson City NY).

BW85316   Lois Marlene Wiser (b 1 Aug 1940, Barker, Broome NY) m 12 Jul 1989, Woodbine IA, Richard Russell Dilworth (b 24 Oct 1944, Flushing NY).

BW8532   Elwin Erford Wiser (13 May 1904, Cincinnatus, Cortland NY-26 Dec 1977, Fenton, Broome NY) m 22 Feb 1930, Brookvale, Broome NY, Anna Mary Elizabeth Amelia Shufeldt (b 28 Sep 1911, Cincinnatus, Cortland NY).

BW85321   Ernest Dewitt Wiser (b 6 Mar 1934, Binghamton NY) m 1) 1 Feb 1958, Ruth Marie Ayers; div; m 2) 12 Oct 1978, Wanda McCormick (b 4 Jun 1946).

BW853211   Diane Lynn Wiser (b 11 Nov 1958) m 29 May 1981, Scott Reiman (b 12 Aug 1956).

BW853212   Penny Marie Wiser (15 Oct 1962-13 Apr 1966).

BW853213   Pamela Jo Wiser (b 15 Oct 1962) m 1) 27 Feb 1982, Martin John Maples (b 28 Oct 1961); m 2) 8 Nov 1991, Benjamin O. Boyst.

BW85322   Paul Erford Wiser (b 14 Aug 1941, Binghamton NY) m 1) 19 Apr 1964, Martha Lee Steinbrecher; div; m 2) 10 Oct 1971, Elizabeth ("Becky") Ann Cahill; div; m 3) 15 Dec 1991, Juanita McCallister (b 11 Feb 1938).

BW853221   Paul Erford Wiser (b 22 Jan 1965).

BW853222   Stephanie Ann Wiser (b 7 Oct 1972) m 7 May 1991, Terrence Simmons.

BW85323   Jack Burt Wiser (b 2 Mar 1943, Binghamton NY) m 1) Pat Sodan; div; m 2) 3 Sep 1966, Faye Henry; div; m 3) 18 Aug 1979, Laureen Porter.

BW853231   Floyd Robert Wiser (3 Aug 1961-10 Apr 1984).

BW85324   Dale Lee Wiser (b 29 Aug 1944, Binghamton NY) m 24 Sep 1966, Elizabeth Myers.

BW853241   Lorraine Ann Wiser (b 31 Mar 1967) m 18 Jul 1992, Eugene H. Hulbert Jr.

BW853242   Thomas Dale Wiser (b 13 Apr 1968) m 2 Jul 1994, Kelly Ann Briggs.

BW853243   Daniel Lee Wiser (b 18 Jun 1970).

BW8533   Edwin Ernest Wiser (15 Jun 1906, Cortland NY-29 Sep 1967, Colesville, Broome NY) m 25 Dec 1928, Nettie C. Thurston (8 Dec 1911, Whitney Point, Broome NY-4 May 1977, Colesville, Broome NY).

BW85331   Robert Warren Wiser (12 Sep 1929, Binghamton NY-20 Jul 1976, Anaheim CA) m 4 Dec 1948, Dorothy Nabinger.

BW853311   Lynette LaVerne Wiser (b 27 May 1950, Binghamton NY) m 1) 3 Nov 1968, Randy Taylor; m 2) 24 May 1975, Mark W. Bales (b 18 Mar 1955).

BW853312   Gail Marie Wiser (b 5 Sep 1951, Binghamton NY) m 1) Dale Jude Kinder; m 2) Sep 1978, Richard Brown.

BW853313   Peggy Ann Wiser (b 24 Oct 1953, Binghamton NY) m 8 Dec 1973, Paul Prestridge; div.

BW85332   Donald Edwin Wiser (11 Feb 1931, Binghamton NY-18 Feb 1932, Binghamton NY).

BW85333   Dawn Marie Wiser (b 15 May 1933, Binghamton NY) m 23 Aug 1952, Raymond Joseph

Warner (b 17 Feb 1930, Binghamton NY).

BW854   Fannie J. Wiser (26 Mar 1882, NY-21 Aug 1969, Willard, Seneca NY); unm. Ithaca NY.

BW9   Theodore Wiser (ca 1787, Haverhill NH-ca 1840, Jo Daviess IL) m 1) Elisa Hunt (d before 1832); m 2) after 1832, Elizabeth ("Betsey") Babcock (ca 1790, Pittsfield MA-1839, Jo Daviess IL). She was previously married to his brother Samuel (BW7).

BW91   Prudence Wiser (10 Sep 1817, Elmira NY-18 Feb 1903, Lanesboro MN) m 4 Dec 1845, Jo Daviess IL, Earl S. Emmons (13 Feb 1817, PA-17 May 1896, Lanesboro MN). Farmer, Fillmore MN.

BW92   Samuel Henry Wiser (3 Feb 1819, Truxton, Cortland NY-21 Mar 1893, Joliet IL) m 18 Nov 1841, Canton OH, Elizabeth Joney (Sep 1825, Nova Scotia, Canada- after 1900, Will IL). Meat market, Wilmington and Joliet IL.

BW921   Theodore L. Wiser (ca Mar 1844, OH-3 Sep 1868, Wilmington IL).

BW922   Alonzo Wiser (31 Mar 1846, OH-17 Feb 1888, Chicago IL) m Elizabeth (b 1850, Germany). Harness maker, Wilmington IL.

BW9221   Carrie Wiser (b 1868, IL).

BW9222   Alice May Wiser (28 Jun 1871, Joliet IL- after 1947) m 1) ca 1887, George E. Hickey (1870, Chicago IL-18 Mar 1899, Chicago IL); m 2) Alexander B. Boyle (b 1870, IN). Boyle, Stonecutter, Chicago IL.

BW923   William H. Wiser (b Aug 1848, OH) m Ella (Aurelia) Rogers (b Aug 1859, MO).

BW9231   Pearl Wiser (b Dec 1882, IL).

BW9232   Gertrude Wiser (b Feb 1884, IL).

BW924   Florence Belle Wiser (15 Sep 1860, Florence, Will IL-11 Jan 1935, Joliet IL) m 6 Oct 1880, Joliet IL, Conrad Barringer (14 Oct 1854, NY-3 Jan 1926, Joliet IL). Painter, Joliet IL.

BW93   Albert Henry Wiser (b 1838, Truxton, Cortland NY).

BWA   Maisilva{?} Wiser (b ca 1789, Haverhill NH).

CHAPTER TWENTY

[PW]   Philip Wiser (d Oct 1798) and Michael Wiser (d ca 1804) of North Carolina and their descendants

The name of Philip Wiser appears in a list of 47 names of 'natives of Germany' who were naturalized in September 1763 by the Superior Court, District of Salisbury in North Carolina. The name was spelled Wiser in that list, and that spelling was kept by the family. No prior record of a Wiser in North Carolina has been found, and it is not known how, when or why Philip arrived in the Salisbury area.

Records for Mecklenburg County were incomplete prior to 1774, and this may explain the lack of any further records until 1779, when the name of Michael also appears. In 1779, both Philip and Michael applied for land grants in the same area, which in 1793 became part of Cabarrus County. In 1782, Philip petitioned for permission to build a mill on his land, but there is no record that the mill was completed. Both their names appear on a number of deeds and jury records through the years, and it is apparent that they were respected members of the community.

Philip wrote his will on 5 October 1798 and it was probated in the October session of the court in 1798, which indicates that he must have died almost immediately after writing the will. There is no mention of a wife in his will, but he listed four daughters: Susannah Hunter, Deborah Townsend, Elisabeth Wiser, and Ann Whitaker; and three sons: Philip, John and David. Executors were John Culpeper and David Wiser, and witnesses were Henry Townsend and William Hunter, who may have been his sons-in-law.

There are no records of the ages of the children, except for John who was born in 1768 according to family records. Philip was the first one married, before 1790, so it is likely that he was born before 1768. David was the last one married and remained at home after the others had left. It seems strange that he would be named executor if he were the youngest, but it is possible that Philip and John had already left home before their father died. It will be assumed therefore that they were listed in the will in order of age.[159]

PW   Philip Wiser (d Oct 1798). Cabarrus NC.

PW1   Philip Wiser (ca 1767, NC-ca 1813) m ca 1789, Mary   (b ca 1768).

PW2   John Wiser (14 Oct 1768, NC 6 Feb 1854) m 17 Jul 1797, Cabarrus NC, Margaret Cook (2 Jun 1772, NC-6 Sep 1826).

PW3   David Wiser (b ca 1766, NC) m 17 Mar 1803, Cabarrus NC Ruth Chamberlin.

PW4   Susannah Wiser m William(?) Hunter.

PW5   Deborah Wiser m Henry(?) Townsend.

PW6   Elizabeth ("Betsy") Wiser.

PW7   Ann Wiser m   Whitaker.

Michael Wiser

There is nothing in the records to identify the relationship of Michael to Philip, but given the proximity of their land holdings it seems likely that they were brothers.

---

[159]Although much additional information has been assembled, the list of members of this family has been limited to those with the surname Wiser and their spouses. This has meant excluding all the descendants of Philip's daughters, and all of Michael's family, as well as all of the other descendants of daughters of Wisers. Data on the families of Philip Wiser Sr. and Michael Wiser was assembled by Edward Wiser, to supplement information provided by members of the three families. Edward Wiser was also responsible for the editing of the entire chapter to its present form.

There are two records of marriages involving a Michael Wyser in New York. The first is to Rachel DeVou on 29 October 1761 at New York City and on 1 November 1761 at the Old Dutch Church, Tarrytown, NY. The second is to Elizabeth Murray on 1 October 1763 at New York City. There is a baptism recorded on 16 September 1764 by the Lutheran Church in New York of a daughter Catharine born to Michael Weiser and Elisabeth Leibacher, and a baptism recorded on 28 September 1766 at the same church of a daughter Elisabeth born to Michel and Elisabeth Wiser.

Michael wrote his will on 6 October 1801, but it was not probated until the January session of court in 1805. He mentioned his wife Elizabeth and three daughters: Polly (and her husband Mathias Beam), Catharina (and her husband Henry Furr) and Batsy (and her husband George Berringer). No sons are mentioned. Also mentioned are grandsons John Furr and Jacob Wiser, first born son of daughter Batsy (apparently born prior to her marriage). The executor was Henry Furr, son-in-law, and witnesses were George Guttman and George Feil. It is interesting to note that, whereas all of Philip's sons-in-law were of English descent, all of Michael's were of German descent.

The similarities between the names in the New York records and the will implies that these were all records of the same family. This would suggest that Philip and Michael may both have arrived in New York around 1760, that Philip moved soon after to North Carolina, and that Michael remained in New York until some time after 1766 before moving south. It may be noted that Henry Wiser (discussed in a separate chapter) appeared in Maryland from New York in 1769, suggesting that he was somehow related.

Except for Jacob Wiser, there were no descendants with the name Wiser, so none of Michael's descendants will be traced here. Unfortunately, there were a number of Jacob Wisers in the eastern states at that time, and it will be difficult to find out what happened to Michael's grandson Jacob. He may have even been adopted by his stepfather George Berringer.

MCW   Michael Wiser (d ca 1804, NC) m 1) 1 Nov 1761, Tarrytown NY, Rachel DeVou; m 2) 1 Oct 1763, NY, Elizabeth Murray. New York and Cabarrus NC.

MCW1   Mary ("Polly") Wiser m Oct 1801, Mathias Beam.

MCW2   Catharine Wiser (b ca Sep 1764, NY) m ca 1782 Henry Furr (1762-1851).

MCW3   Elisabeth ("Betsy") Wiser (b ca Sep 1766, NY) m George Berringer.

MCW31   Jacob Wiser (b before 1801).

Philip Wiser (Jr.)

Philip Wiser appeared with his wife in a household separate from his father in 1790. There were no children in the family, so it is likely that he had been married the previous year. No marriage bond for him has been found. Also, because his name cannot be distinguished from his father's in the records, it is not possible to tell when he appeared in jury records.

Philip seems to have left North Carolina either before or almost immediately after his father's death, because he was listed on the tax rolls in Washington County, Kentucky in 1799 with his brother John. Unlike his brother, however, he seems to have liked it there, because by 1800 he had purchased land on the Big South Branch of the Rolling Fork, in part of Lincoln County which became Casey County in 1807. He remained there until his death, and many of his descendants are still in the same area.[160]

PW1   Philip Wiser (ca 1767, NC-ca 1813) m ca 1789, Mary   (b ca 1768). Cabarrus NC and Lincoln KY.

PW11   David Wiser (b 1792, KY) m 1)   ; m 2) m 18 Jun 1820, Theresa Murphy; m 3) m 12 Apr 1821, Casey KY, Polly Young (ca 1800-ca 1848). Casey KY.

---

[160]Information on the family of Philip Wiser Jr. was assembled by John Thomas Wiser of Lebanon KY and Clara R. Wiser of Mooresville IN.

PW111   Philip Wiser (ca 1818, KY-ca 1864) m Margaret Cox (b ca 1817, KY).

PW1111   Sylvanus Wiser (b ca 1840, KY).

PW1112   Daniel Wiser (b 1843, Casey KY).

PW1113   Melissa E. Wiser (b ca 1845, KY) m 23 Aug 1866, Casey KY, Benjamin F. Wash.

PW1114   Uriah Wiser (b 1846, Casey KY).

PW1115   Sophrona Wiser (b ca 1850, KY).

PW1116   Amanda Wiser (b 1858, Casey KY).

PW112   Polly Wiser (b ca 1829, KY).

PW113   Nancy I. Wiser (b ca 1831, KY) m 19 Apr 1858, Casey KY, John B. Cooley (b ca 1840,
KY).

PW114   Elizabeth Wiser (b ca 1831, KY).

PW115   Patsy Wiser (b ca 1834, KY).

PW116   Amanda Wiser (b ca 1838, KY) m 8 Apr 1855, Winkfield Shreve (b ca 1833, KY).

PW117   Hector(?) Wiser (b ca 1838, KY).

PW118   Maranda Wiser (b ca 1841, KY).

PW12   Daniel Wiser (ca 1794-ca 1826) m Betheny ("Theany")   (b ca 1785, VA).

PW121   Daniel Wiser (b 1824, Casey KY) m 1) 16 Mar 1849, Casey KY, Nancy (Mary) Taylor
(b ca 1829, KY); m 2) 24 Jul 1856, Caroline Frost (b ca 1839).

PW1211   Sarah E. Wiser (b 1849, Casey KY) m 24 Feb 1867, Micajah C. Bronson.

PW1212   Nancy Wiser (b ca 1853, KY).

PW1213   Priar P. Wiser (b Jun 1857, KY) m Laura   (b Sep 1861, IL).

PW12131   Walter E. Wiser (b Nov 1884, IL) m Ella O.   (b ca 1885, IL).

PW121311   Eva B. Wiser (b ca 1905, IL).

PW121312   Doris M. Wiser (b ca 1910, IL).

PW121313   Charles P. Wiser (b ca 1913, IL).

PW121314   Byron D. Wiser (b ca Jul 1916, IL).

PW12132   Effie E. Wiser (b Aug 1887, IL).

PW1214   Matilda F. Wiser (b ca 1861, KY).

PW1215   Susan M. Wiser (b ca 1863, KY).

PW1216   Annie Wiser (b ca 1865, KY).

PW1217   Amanda Wiser (b ca 1867, KY).

PW1218   Laura Wiser (b ca 1869, KY).

PW1219   Ettie Wiser (b ca 1871, IL).

PW121A   Bertha Wiser (b ca 1874, IL).

PW121B   Hattie Wiser (b ca 1877, IL).

PW122   Philip Wiser (b ca 1826, KY) m Sarah J.   (b ca 1830, MO).

PW1221   David A. Wiser (b May 1851, MO) m Susan A.   (b Dec 1850, MO).

PW12211   Archie W. Wiser (b ca 1876, KS).

PW12212   Bertha A. Wiser (b Dec 1878, KS).

PW1222   Benjamin F. Wiser (b ca 1854, MO) m Sarah C.   (b ca 1877, KS).

PW12221   Philip G. Wiser (b ca 1912, KS).

PW1223   Nancy Wiser (b ca 1858, KS).

PW1224   William F. Wiser (b ca 1862, KS).

PW1225   Philip C. Wiser (b ca 1864, KS).

PW1226   Ida Hilda Wiser (b 24 Nov 1866, Lecompton, Douglas KS) m ca 1889, Charles Edward
Greaser.

PW1227   Nettie Wiser (b Aug 1869, KS).

PW123   Polly Wiser (b 1827, Casey KY).

PW13   Elizabeth Wiser (b ca 1800) m 20 Feb 1820, Casey KY, Elijah Cox.

PW14   John Wiser (b ca 1801, KY) m 12 Mar 1829, Casey KY, Polly Anderson (b ca 1810, KY).

PW141   Sarah A. Wiser (b ca 1832, KY) m 23 Sep 1860, Robert Russel (b ca 1828, KY).

PW142   Lucinda Wiser (b ca 1834, KY).

PW143   Minerva Wiser (b ca 1841, KY).

PW15   Nicholas Wiser (ca 1804-ca 1841) m 30 Mar 1831, Liberty KY, Polly Weatherford (b ca
1812, KY).

PW151   Franklin Wiser (b Feb 1832, KY) m 24 Aug 1852, Casey KY, Nancy Amanda Glazebrook
(b ca 1836, KY).

PW1511   Mary A. Wiser (b ca 1855, KY).

PW1512   Ellen B. Wiser (b ca 1857, KY).

PW1513   Laura Wiser (b ca 1858, KY).

PW1514   Susan B. Wiser (b ca 1862, KY).

PW1515   Mattie L. Wiser (b ca 1868, KY).

PW152   Amanda Wiser (b ca 1841, KY).

PW16   Joseph Wiser (ca 1805, KY-1 Feb 1855) m 25 Oct 1829, Elizabeth Peyton (b 1803, KY).

PW161   Madison Wiser (b ca 1832, KY).

PW162   Mary E. Wiser (b ca 1835, KY).

PW163   James J. Wiser (Aug 1840, KY-ca 1917, Casey KY) m 1 Nov 1860, Casey KY, Sophronia Peyton (Mar 1845, KY-Apr 1910, Casey KY).

PW1631   Mary Belle Wiser (17 Feb 1864, Casey KY-8 Apr 1929) m 20 Dec 1879, Casey KY, George W. Cox (b ca 1859, KY).

PW1632   Sarah Alice Wiser (Jan 1868, Casey KY-ca 1902) m 17 Sep 1882, Casey KY, Frank Sears.

PW1633   Lucinda Helen Wiser (20 Apr 1869, Casey KY-25 Sep 1918, Casey KY) m 9 Oct 1884, Casey KY, William Montgomery (b 1866).

PW1634   John Wiser (b Jan 1870, KY).

PW1635   James Madison Wiser (14 Sep 1873, KY-25 Jan 1929, Chilton, Casey KY) m 1) 30 Jun 1892, Casey KY, Nancy F. Peyton (Mar 1876, Casey KY-1901); m 2) 5 Mar 1911, Casey KY, Perry Amanda Cummins (10 Sep 1875, KY-22 Jan 1929, Chilton, Casey KY).

PW16351   Rosa Etta Wiser (24 Jun 1893, Casey KY-22 Jun 1976, Brodhead, Rockcastle KY) m 26 Mar 1911, Casey KY, Thomas Frank Cummins.

PW16352   William M. Wiser (b Sep 1896, Casey KY) m 12 May 1917, Chilton, Casey KY, Wavie Peck (b Jul 1898, Casey KY). Knoxville TN.

PW163521   Monroe Lewis Wiser (6 Feb 1918, Casey KY-Dec 1974, Knoxville TN).

PW163522   William Bradley Wiser.

PW163523   Ray Wiser.

PW163524   Ruby R. Wiser (17 Dec 1925, KY-21 Dec 1925, Danville KY).

PW16353   John Wallace Wiser (13 Oct 1899, Casey KY-30 Jan 1969, Marion KY) m Grace Lee Russell (25 Nov 1903, Casey KY-18 Nov 1980, Lebanon KY).

PW163531   William Thomas ("Pete") Wiser (4 Dec 1921, Casey KY-12 Aug 1972, Franklin IN) m 1) Alma Jean Wright (b 23 Jan 1931, Marion KY); m 2) Helen Dyer.

PW1635311   Faye Carol Wiser (b 3 Sep 1947, Lebanon KY) m 21 Aug 1965, Jackson TN, Willie Garland Cochran (b 17 Apr 1943, Liberty KY).

PW1635312   William Seidgel Wiser (b 18 Mar 1949, Marion KY) m 1) June Shepherd; m 2) 13 Apr 1979, Gatlinburg TN, Cathy Sharp (b 13 Apr 1959).

PW16353121   Rhonda June Wiser (b 5 Dec 1973, Lebanon KY) m Ricky Leigh.

PW16353122   William T. Wiser (b 4 Mar 1979, Lebanon KY).

PW16353123   Waylon S. Wiser (b 29 Nov 1981, Lebanon KY).

PW1635313   John Thomas Wiser (b 11 Nov 1950, Marion KY) m 1) 7 May 1969, Lebanon KY, Connie Sue Oldson (b 11 Apr 1951, Taylor KY); m 2) 25 Sep 1979, Bradfordsville KY, Donna F. Coffman (b 19 Apr 1955).

PW16353131   Carolyn Sue Wiser (b 30 Aug 1970, Lebanon KY) m 1 Oct 1988, Greensburg KY, Richard Wayne Shirley (b 28 Jan 1967, Green KY).

PW163531311   Jonathan William Wiser (b 10 Jun 1987, Campbellsville KY).

PW16353132   Rona Jean Wiser (b 1 Jul 1974, Danville KY) m James Roland Johnson.

PW16353133   Joni Lynn Wiser (b 28 Oct 1981, Danville KY).

PW1635314   Howard Shelton Wiser (b 13 Mar 1952, Marion KY) m 14 Sep 1979, Pamela Bagby (b 3 Jul 1959, Taylor KY).

PW16353141   Nicholas S. Wiser (b 11 Mar 1980, Marion KY).

PW1635315   Robert Ray Wiser (b 23 Oct 1953, Marion KY) m Kathy Jean Brown (b 22 Sep 1955, Taylor KY).

PW16353151   Jennifer Michelle Wiser (b 1 Sep 1973, Taylor KY).

PW16353152   Tammy Renee Wiser (15 Jun 1977, Taylor KY-27 Apr 1992).

PW1635316   Brenda Lee Wiser (b 29 May 1955, Marion KY) m 1) 10 Apr 1971, Christopher Whitehouse (b 7 May 1948, Marion KY); m 2) Steven Hafley.

PW1635317   Mary Linda Wiser (b 29 May 1955, Marion KY) m 1) 11 Jul 1972, Jerry E. Cooley (b 10 Jul 1953, Marion KY); m 2) 27 Sep 1984, James Otis Raley.

PW1635318   Debra Lynn Wiser (b 26 Feb 1957, Marion KY) m Garland Lane (b 24 Aug 1952, Casey KY).

PW1635319   Ronald ("Rocky") Keith Wiser (b 10 Jul 1958, Marion KY) m 4 Oct 1979, Marion KY, Pamela Mattingly.

PW16353191   Bradley Keith Wiser (b 3 Dec 1982, Campbellsville KY).

PW16353192   Stewart Paul Wiser (b 26 Jan 1987, Campbellsville KY).

PW163531A   Betsy Ann Wiser (b 14 Aug 1959, Marion KY) m 26 Aug 1980, Bradfordsville KY, Randall Wilson (b 8 Jun 1949, Boyle KY).

PW163531B   William Thomas ("Sam") Wiser.

PW163531C   Billie Wiser.

PW163531D   Debbie Wiser.

PW163531E   Marilyn Wiser.

PW163532   Wilbur Lee ("Tootsie") Wiser (3 Jul 1923, Casey KY-28 Jun 1943, Marion KY).

PW163533   James Wesley ("Matt") Wiser (13 May 1925, Casey KY-15 Jul 1980, Lebanon KY) m 31 Mar 1950, Marion KY, Mary George Stayton (b 16 Dec 1933, Marion KY).

PW1635331   John Thornton Wiser (b 28 Aug 1951, Marion KY) m 27 May 1969, Ethel Marie Cox.

PW16353311   Jimmy D. Wiser (b 21 Aug 1973, Marion KY).

PW16353312   Amy M. Wiser (b 2 Sep 1978, Marion KY).

PW1635332   James Allen Wiser (b 21 Feb 1954, Marion KY) m 1) Marsha Wilson; m 2) Karen Caldwell; m 3) 6 Feb 1980, Donna Sue Johnson.

PW1635333   George Clay Wiser (b 5 Apr 1955, Marion KY) m 22 Sep 1973, Donna Jean Cox.

PW16353331   Mary J. Wiser (b 15 Apr 1974, Marion KY).

PW1635334   Terry Wayne Wiser (b 24 Feb 1958, Marion KY).

PW1635335   David Lewis Wiser (b 7 Dec 1962, Marion KY) m   Stone.

PW1635336   Diane Renee Wiser (b 9 Jun 1964, Marion KY) m 12 Jun 1982, Gary Alan Ruley.

PW1635337   Donna Jean Wiser (b 8 Aug 1965, Marion KY) m 31 Jan 1984, Thomas Lawrence Bradshaw.

PW1635338   Rita Michelle Wiser (b 25 Oct 1966, Marion KY).

PW163534   Loretta Fay Wiser (b 4 Aug 1927, Casey KY) m Lewis Thomas Wright.

PW163535   Russell Clay Wiser (b 22 Nov 1929, Marion KY) m 1) Libby   ; m 2) Edith Ann Roution.

PW1635351   Connie Michelle Wiser (b 1 Jul 1957, Jefferson KY) m   Carver.

PW1635352   Dallas Lee ("Candy") Wiser (b 22 Sep 1959, Jefferson KY) m   Aschbacher.

PW1635353   Russell Clay ("Rusty") Wiser (7 Dec 1961, Jefferson KY-27 Jun 1995, Jeffersonville IN) m Debra Nellis.

PW16353531   Robyn L. Wiser (b 19 Aug 1982, Jefferson KY).

PW1635354   Lori Ann Wiser (b 21 Mar 1963, Jefferson KY) m   Byerly.

PW1635355   John Thomas Wiser (b 30 Nov 1972, Jefferson KY).

PW163536   Oscar Coleman Wiser (b 7 Nov 1931, Marion KY) m Edith Ann Howell.

PW1635361   Betty Ann Wiser (b 23 Jan 1955, Marion KY) m   Mattingly.

PW1635362   Ronald Coleman Wiser (13 Jul 1956, Marion KY-16 Dec 1956, Shelby TN).

PW1635363   Roger Dale Wiser (b 6 May 1959, Marion KY).

PW163537   Bessie Belle Wiser (b 9 Mar 1934, Casey KY) m Edward Clark.

PW163538   John Wallace Wiser Jr. (b 15 Aug 1936, Casey KY) m 1) Geraldine Slack; m 2) Judy Rogers (b 17 Mar 1941).

PW1635381   Bette Corine Wiser (b 24 May 1956, Marion KY).

PW1635382   John Richard Wiser (b 22 Oct 1957, Taylor KY).

PW1635383   Barbara Joyce Wiser (b 7 Jan 1959, Taylor KY) m   Abell.

PW1635384   Joseph Wiser (21 Feb 1960, Marion KY-21 Feb 1960, Marion KY).

PW1635385   Donald Wayne Wiser (b 19 Jun 1962, Shelby KY).

PW1635386   Gerry Lynn Wiser (b 28 Feb 1965, Jefferson KY).

PW1635387   Katherine D. Wiser (b 24 May 1966, Hardin KY).

PW1635388   Connie Wiser (b 16 Nov 1973).

PW1635389   Michael Todd Wiser (b 27 Oct 1976).

PW163539   Carl Ray Wiser (b 14 Sep 1938, Marion KY) m Mary Alice Vaught.

PW1635391   Carl Eddie Wiser (b 10 Jun 1962, Mercer KY).

PW1635392   Sandra Kay Wiser (b 31 May 1964, Boyle KY) m 4 Nov 1988, Derrick Allen Drury.

PW16353A   Corine Wiser (7 Apr 1940, Marion KY-31 Aug 1994) m Isaac Morgan Hudson.

PW16353B   Orlean Irvin Wiser (29 Dec 1942, Marion KY-3 Jan 1943).

PW16353C   Arnold B. Wiser (b 20 Mar 1944, Marion KY) m Barbara Ann Green.

PW16353C1   Bridget Ann Wiser (b 8 Jul 1967, Marion KY).

PW16353C2   Mark Arnold Wiser (b 23 May 1968, Marion KY).

PW16353C3   Kevin Ray Wiser (b 6 Aug 1973, Marion KY).

PW16353D   William Howard ("Harry") Wiser (b 28 Apr 1947, Marion KY) m 8 May 1967, Faye
Walden.

PW16353D1   Tracy Wiser.

PW16353D2   Billy Wiser.

PW16354   Thomas Coleman Wiser (17 Jan 1912, Chilton, Casey KY-2 May 1942, Ft. Benjamin
Harrison IN).

PW16355   Addie Clay Wiser (8 Oct 1913, Chilton, Casey KY-25 Sep 1981, Franklin IN) m 9 Jun
1961, Eva A. Yates.

PW16356   James Madison Wiser Jr. (4 May 1916, Chilton, Casey KY-12 Jul 1983, Liberty KY) m
1) 18 Sep 1934, Liberty, Casey KY, Gracie ("Hazel") Vanoy (17 Oct 1919, Casey KY-5 Jul 1993, Danville

KY); m 2) 28 Jan 1946, Danville KY, Dessie ("Christine") Whited (b 13 Sep 1926, Brush Creek, Casey KY).

PW163561   William Randall Wiser (b 24 Jun 1935, Casey KY) m 6 Apr 1957, Liberty KY, Clara Rae Lucas (b 17 Apr 1936, Yosemite, Casey KY).

PW1635611   William ("Kevin") Wiser (b 5 May 1958, Bexar TX) m 30 Sep 1989, Martinsville IN, Amy Jo Allen.

PW1635612   James ("Brian") Wiser (b 21 Jul 1959, Bexar TX) m 31 Mar 1984, Mooresville IN, Julie Ann Even.

PW163562   DeAnna Christine Wiser (b 14 Jan 1947, Danville KY) m 10 Jul 1965, Liberty KY, Aubrey Lee Wesley.

PW163563   DeAngelo Nathaniel Wiser (b 30 Dec 1952, Danville KY) m 1 Apr 1978, Lexington KY, Nancy Ann Moss.

PW16357   Son Wiser (25 Jul 1918, KY-25 Jul 1918, KY).

PW16358   Warren G. Harding ("Bud") Wiser (31 Oct 1920, Chilton, Casey KY-1 Sep 1983, Indianapolis IN) m 23 May 1954, Irvington, Marion IN, LaVonne Lorraine Robinson (b 23 May 1935, Marion IN).

PW163581   Sheryl Mae Wiser (b 11 Oct 1957, Indianapolis IN) m 5 Sep 1981, Mooresville IN, Paul Anthony Racic.

PW163582   Warren G. H. ("Buddy") Wiser Jr. (b 3 Mar 1960, Indianapolis IN).

PW163583   Gregory Charles Wiser (b 27 Feb 1961, Indianapolis IN).

PW163584   James Edward Wiser (b 9 Sep 1964, Indianapolis IN)

PW1636   Hardin Wiser (11 Jul 1874, Casey KY-27 Sep 1921, Casey KY) m 6 Oct 1892, Casey KY, Mary Richards (b Apr 1872, KY).

PW16361   Pearl L. Wiser (b May 1896, KY) m 2 Aug 1913, Casey KY, Christie Cox.

PW16362   Bertha E. Wiser (6 Oct 1899, KY-Jan 1975, Indianapolis IN) m 24 Feb 1918, Casey KY, Elmer Ross.

PW16363   Grace Wiser (b ca 1903, Casey KY) m 7 Nov 1920, Ellisburg, Casey KY, Ira C. Sears.

PW16364   Melvin E. Wiser (b ca 1906, Casey KY).

PW16365   Lillie Wiser (b ca 1909, Casey KY).

PW1637   Elijah Wiser (b 1878, Casey KY).

PW1638   Amanda E. Wiser (b Oct 1879, KY).

PW1639   Nancy Jane Wiser (2 Jun 1882, Casey KY-21 Aug 1970) m 23 Jul 1899, Casey KY, Arthur Reeves.

PW163A   Victoria Wiser (15 Mar 1887, Casey KY-13 Dec 1952) m 7 Apr 1909, Casey KY, Burrell Lewis Reeves (b ca 1892, KY).

PW17   Jacob C. Wiser (b ca 1807, KY).

PW171   Daniel(?) Wiser (b ca 1840, KY).

PW172   Charlotte F. Wiser (b ca 1843).

John Wiser

John Wiser appeared in jury records as early as 1795, and a bond was issued in Cabarrus County, NC on 17 July 1797 for his marriage to Margareth Cook. There is a record in the possession of his descendants which seems to have been written by a member of his immediate family which lists the birth dates of John, his wife and all of his children. Someone else has added death dates to the record.

John had been listed with his father in the 1790 Census, but he had left North Carolina before 1800, and is not found on a census record again until 1830, in Tennessee. Tax lists for Kentucky list him in Washington County in 1799 with his brother Philip, but he doesn't seem to have stayed there. He spent several years in Cumberland County with his brother David, where he is found in the 1805 tax list, the only one extant, and he was listed as owning land there as late as 1819, although by then he had almost certainly moved to Tennessee. He is found in a tax list in Bedford County, Tennessee as early as 1812, and finally settled on the headwaters of Noah's Fork of the Duck River in what became Coffee County where he died in 1854.[161]

PW2   John Wiser (14 Oct 1768, NC-6 Feb 1854) m 17 Jul 1797, Cabarrus NC, Margaret Cook (2 Jun 1772, NC-6 Sep 1826).

PW21   Daniel Wiser (4 Dec 1797, NC-5 Sep 1857, Coffee TN) m Cynthia   (ca 1806, TN-ca 1855).

PW211   William H. Wiser (26 Oct 1826, Coffee TN-Sep 1909, Coffee TN) m Dora   (b ca 1833, TN).

PW2111   Joseph H. Wiser (b May 1850, TN) m 25 Sep 1873, Coffee TN, Mary ("Mollie") F. Gibson (b Aug 1857, TN). Baylor TX and Howard AR.

PW21111   Delleener(?) Wiser (b ca 1878, TN).

PW21112   Katy Wiser (b ca 1879, TX).

PW21113   James W. Wiser (b Feb 1881, TX) m Mattie   (b ca 1886, AR).

PW211131   J. B. Wiser (b ca 1905, AR).

PW211132   Lela F. Wiser (b ca 1907, AR).

PW211133   Clinton B. Wiser (b ca 1910, AR).

PW211134   Cleo E. Wiser (b ca 1912, OK).

PW211135   Aline E. Wiser (b ca 1914, OK).

PW211136   Jessie E. Wiser (b ca 1916, OK).

PW211137   Hazel P. Wiser (b ca 1919, OK).

---

[161] Most of the information on the family of John Wiser was assembled by Gerald Wiser of Lebanon TN. Other contributors include Ovalee Wiser and Ruth Davenport of McMinnville TN, Ellen and Tammy Wiser of Pulaski TN, and Bonnie Coatney of Dallas TX.

PW21114   David(?) A. Wiser (b Jun 1887, TX).

PW21115   King Wiser (10 Feb 1894, TX-Mar 1977, McCurtain OK).

PW2112   Louisa Wiser (b 19 Apr 1852, TN).

PW2113   Thomas A. Wiser (b Apr 1854, TN) m 6 Sep 1875, Coffee TN, Angeline Gibson (b ca 1839, TN).

PW21131   Thomas Edgar Wiser (b Oct 1878, TN) m 1) Mary M.   (b Mar 1879, MS); m 2) Kittie May   (b ca 1879, GA).

PW211311   May Lorene Wiser (9 Feb 1908, TX-Jan 1983, Kaufman TX).

PW2114   Sarah Ann Wiser (b ca 1858, TN) m 9 Sep 1880, Coffee TN, A. R. Hammer.

PW2115   Melvin L. Wiser (b May 1865, TN) m 1) 25 Sep 1890, Nancy Rains; m 2) 3 Sep 1902, Josie Pilkington (1 Dec 1877, Rutherford TN-7 Jun 1937, Beech Grove, Coffee TN).

PW21151   Mary Lila Wiser (b Sep 1895).

PW21152   Keron Wiser (21 Apr 1905, TN-Sep 1972) m 7 Nov 1923, Beauford Banks.

PW21153   Eran Wiser (b ca 1907, TN).

PW21154   Mcfee L. Wiser (19 Apr 1908, TN-Dec 1971) m Lou

PW211541   Melvin McKenzie Wiser (14 Mar 1932, TN-25 Oct 1933, Coffee TN).

PW21155   Lois Wiser (b ca 1911, AR) m 22 Apr 1938, Raymond Hoover (b ca 1907).

PW21156   David Ledbetter Wiser (20 Feb 1914, TX-7 Sep 1977, Manchester TN).

PW2116   Mollie(?) Wiser (b ca 1869, TN).

PW2117   Alvin William Wiser (8 Jan 1872, Coffee TN-27 Feb 1940, Coffee TN) m 24 Dec 1895, Owa Runnels (b Aug 1868, OH).

PW21171   Cyril Wiser (22 Jan 1898, TN-1 Dec 1973, Wartrace TN) m 12 Feb 1922, Mary E. (b 29 Jun 1905).

PW211711   Sylvia Wiser (Jan 1923-Feb 1923).

PW211712   Dalton Wiser.

PW211713   Leighton Wiser.

PW211714   Katricia Wiser.

PW21172   Victor Wiser (18 Apr 1901, TN-Jan 1971, Manchester TN) m 22 Nov 1923, Ruth Cheney.

PW21173   Odessa Wiser (b ca 1906, TN).

PW21174   Ruby Wiser (b ca 1908, TN).

PW21175   Daughter Wiser (b 1 Mar 1911, Coffee TN).

PW21176   Emma Wiser (b ca 1912, TN).

PW21177   Geneva Wiser (b ca Oct 1915, TN).

PW2118   Ollie Wiser (4 Jun 1873, TN-23 Dec 1964) m 1 Jan 1896, John Thomas Arnold (26 Jul 1872, Coffee TN-14 Aug 1939, Coffee TN).

PW212   Jane Wiser (ca 1829, TN-1915).

PW213   Louisa C. Wiser (b ca 1831, TN) m 21 Sep 1865, Coffee TN, Jackson Crosslin (b ca 1832).

PW214   Newton Daniel Wiser (30 Apr 1834, Coffee TN-5 Sep 1903, Coffee TN) m 14 Aug 1873, Coffee TN, Margaret Darnell (25 Sep 1852, TN-7 Sep 1895).

PW2141   Margaret A. Wiser (1874, Coffee TN-1909) m Albert Teal (1869-1950).

PW2142   Mary ("Mollie") N. Wiser (11 Jun 1876, TN-28 Nov 1962) m 23 Apr 1893, Andrew Jack Harmon (26 Oct 1871-17 Oct 1933).

PW2143   Martha J. Wiser (b Apr 1878, TN).

PW2144   Clinton W. Wiser (b Mar 1879, TN) m 17 Dec 1899, Sara Ann Reynolds (b ca 1875, TN).

PW2145   Julia Wiser (b Feb 1882, TN).

PW2146   Josie Maud Wiser (25 Feb 1884, TN-28 Feb 1964) m 3 Feb 1902, William Powell Morton (14 Feb 1883-2 Nov 1953).

PW2147   Frank Wiser (15 Sep 1889, TN-Feb 1966, Forney, Kaufman TX).

PW2148   Grover Wiser (b Feb 1891, TN).

PW2149   Leone Wiser (b Feb 1894, TN).

PW215   John M. Wiser (15 Sep 1836, Coffee TN-12 Sep 1913, Coffee TN) m 11 Nov 1869, Coffee TN, Oregon T. Mankins (30 Sep 1847, Rutherford TN-23 Oct 1924).

PW2151   Walter Winthrope Wiser (14 Aug 1875, Coffee TN-23 Mar 1940, Bedford TN) m 1) 28 Dec 1897, Rettie Jett (b Dec 1881, TN); m 2) 12 Apr 1904, Tabitha Jane Messick (Oct 1887, Coffee TN-May 1972, Coffee TN).

PW21511   Jessie Ola Wiser (Jul 1899, TN-1968) m 17 Sep 1916, James Mack Jernigan (1894-1969).

PW21512   Nolan Wiser.

PW21513   Lula Catherine Wiser (26 Apr 1905, Coffee TN-4 Feb 1979, Bedford TN) m Charlie Jasper Floyd (28 Sep 1905, Coffee TN-2 Oct 1956, Bedford TN).

PW21514   Willie Jonah Wiser (15 Sep 1906, Coffee TN-2 Jan 1934, Bedford TN) m 1 May 1931, Jessie Ruth Messick (25 Dec 1909-13 Feb 1992).

PW215141   Elizabeth Wiser (b 2 Apr 1933) m 14 Nov 1959, Lewis Edward Wright (b 21 Feb 1940).

PW21515   Irene Amazon Wiser (23 Jan 1908, TN-9 Dec 1987) m 13 Dec 1936, Morgan Wyatt Butler

(14 Dec 1908-Feb 1969, Wartrace TN).

PW21516   Lorene Lavergne Wiser (23 Jan 1908, TN-23 Mar 1976, Wartrace TN) m 19 Dec 1930, Carl Ray Messick (26 Mar 1908-15 May 1990).

PW21517   Lathorne O. Wiser (b 1 Oct 1909, Coffee TN) m 24 Dec 1937, Callie Ruth Turner (b 4 Feb 1920, Shelbyville TN).

PW215171   La Ruth Wiser (b 19 Apr 1939) m 24 Sep 1955, Bobby Reynolds.

PW215172   Linda Carol Wiser (b 6 Nov 1948) m 18 Nov 1967, Stephen Lyle Taylor.

PW21518   Virgie Eugene Wiser (Feb 1911, Coffee TN-2 Nov 1995) m 20 Mar 1936, George Marvin Sullivan (21 Apr 1907-Oct 1977, Shelbyville TN).

PW21519   Carl T. Wiser (28 Jan 1913, TN-Dec 1986, Shelbyville TN) m 22 Dec 1934, Shelbyville TN, Ruth Womble (31 Jul 1912-4 Oct 1989).

PW215191   Hilda Jean Wiser (b 25 Aug 1941) m 23 Feb 1960 Roy London (b 13 Apr 1939).

PW2151A   Woodrow Wilson Wiser (11 Dec 1914, TN-Nov 1986, Pulaski TN).

PW2151B   Lelon Wiser (21 Nov 1917, TN-Oct 1981, Peoria IL) m Madge Riner (b 1926).

PW2151B1   Sandra Wiser.

PW2151B2   Patsy Wiser (17 Nov 1944-17 Oct 1988).

PW2151B3   Barbara Wiser (b 24 Nov 1947).

PW2151B4   Bobby Wiser (24 Nov 1947-5 Nov 1948)

PW2151C   Elon Wiser (21 Nov 1917, TN-1920).

PW2151D   Gertha Wiser (4 Jan 1919, TN-19 Oct 1969) m 2 Dec 1939, Bedford TN, Willie Fred Marr (29 Jun 1921-14 Nov 1992, Fayetteville TN).

PW2151E   Gerda Wiser (b 4 Jan 1919, TN) m Claude Edward Bingham (25 Aug 1917-May 1985, Granville, Jackson TN).

PW2151F   Wilbur Dean Wiser (b 24 Jan 1921) m 20 Aug 1943, Dorothy Pearl Riner (b 15 Jul 1927).

PW2151F1   Billy Rodney Wiser (b 31 Jan 1945) m Jessi Lynn Talley (b 25 Aug 1944).

PW2151F11   Mathew W. Wiser (b 28 Mar 1974).

PW2151F12   Laura Rachael Wiser (b 11 Mar 1977).

PW2151F13   John David Wiser (b 23 Nov 1979).

PW2151F14   Aaron Talley Wiser (b 26 Jan 1981).

PW2151F2   Cherry Lynn Wiser (b 28 Apr 1949) m 23 Jun 1974, Bill Bush (b 23 Jun 1949).

PW2151G   Josephine Wiser (b 24 Jan 1921) m Alfred Bingham.

PW2152   Sophia Josephine Wiser (10 Dec 1880, Coffee TN-29 Dec 1947) m 16 Mar 1899, Marion Glenn Wiser (PW21A3).

PW2153   Commodore Young Wiser (b Sep 1884, TN) m Reatha McKee (b ca 1893, MS).

PW21531   Avis Barilla Wiser (10 Sep 1910, TX-Sep 1992, Orange TX) m Sam Smith.

PW21532   Noland Douglas Wiser (4 Mar 1912, TX-15 Jan 1975, Kaufman TX) m 4 Jun 1933, Frances McKee (b 15 Nov 1913, MS).

PW215321   Joanna Wiser (b 1 Jul 1935, Kaufman TX) m 1) 1951, Milton Lanehart Land; m 2) Burk.

PW215322   Charles Douglas Wiser (b 20 Nov 1939) m Barbara Stone.

PW2153221   Christi Michelle Wiser (b 9 Nov 1970).

PW2153222   Ashley Nicole Wiser (b 11 May 1983).

PW21533   Forest Young Wiser (2 Jan 1917, TX-Feb 1968, Kaufman TX) m Dorothy   .

PW21534   Commodore McKee Wiser m Kathleen Trammel.

PW21535   Leotta Wiser.

PW2154   Forest Wiser (b Sep 1884, TN) m 12 Apr 1908, Adie Ferrell.

PW216   Joseph Wiser (b ca 1839, TN).

PW217   Rachel M. Wiser (1841, TN-1913) m 8 Jun 1865, Coffee TN, Romulus Burks.

PW218   Margaret Ann Wiser (b ca 1843, TN) m 7 Feb 1865, Coffee TN, Isham Duncan.

PW219   Isaac Wiser (b ca 1846, Coffee TN) m 1) 13 Feb 1873, Sarah Margaret Simpson (b ca 1852); m 2) 30 Jan 1876, Coffee TN, Elizabeth Ann C. Crocker (ca 1859, Coffee TN-ca 1887; m 3) 25 Sep 1888, Mary ("Mollie") Reynolds (b Mar 1861, TN).

PW2191   Sarah Jane ("Jennie") Wiser (25 Oct 1876, TN-14 Aug 1937) m 26 Sep 1897, Dixon L. Darnell (1 Jan 1874, Coffee TN-24 Jul 1937, Coffee TN).

PW2192   Robert E. Wiser (b Jun 1879, TN) m 23 Sep 1899, Minnie Spindle (b Feb 1883, TN).

PW21921   Luther Wiser (b ca 1901, TN) m Bertha Ann Grimes (16 Jan 1905, Dallas TX-16 Aug 1996, Dallas TX).

PW219211   L. Eugene Wiser m Wanda   .

PW2192111   Tanya Wiser m Alan Nelson.

PW21922   Eddie Wiser (b ca 1907, TN).

PW2193   Isaac Daniel Wiser (6 Mar 1881, Hoodoo, Coffee TN-13 Sep 1944, Tullahoma TN) m Emma Inus Morton (15 Nov 1888, TN-31 Oct 1973).

PW21931   Marcus Lee Wiser (2 Sep 1905, TN-19 Mar 1964, Gary IN) m 1) Marian Charlotte Puent (b 15 Aug 1910, La Crosse WI); m 2) 26 Dec 1939, Odell Arnold (b ca 1917).

PW219311   Harry Lee Wiser (b 22 Dec 1931) m 2 Sep 1968, Merrillville IN, Lola Henley (b 6 Dec 1931).

PW219312   Donna Clara Wiser (b 22 Oct 1933, Gary IN) m Henry John Denslaw (18 Dec 1930).

PW219313   Charlotte Ann Wiser (b 20 Dec 1936, Gary IN) m 4 Sep 1964, Gary IN, Lawrence Bernard Gresser (b 3 Jan 1940).

PW219314   Mark Douglas Wiser (28 Sep 1941, Gary IN-18 Aug 1969, Crown Point IN) m 3 Jun 1960, Merrillville IN, Sandra Kay Fricke (b 20 Sep 1944).

PW2193141   Cheryl Lynn Wiser (b 10 Oct 1961).

PW2193142   Shelly Ann Wiser (b 14 Aug 1964).

PW2193143   Randell Lee Wiser (b 10 Jun 1966).

PW21932   Jesse Daniel Wiser (b 13 Jul 1907, TN) m Alice Josephine Gold (21 Jan 1913, Lewisburg TN-Sep 1984, Murfreesboro, TN).

PW219321   Michael Dennis Wiser (b 16 Apr 1949) m Diane Farmer (b 1954).

PW2193211   Douglas Daniel Wiser (b 3 Aug 1975).

PW21933   Borthal C. Wiser (5 Jul 1909, Coffee TN-30 Oct 1962, Coffee TN) m Roxie Holter.

PW219331   Bruce H. Wiser (b 1939).

PW219332   Shirley Ann Wiser (b 1943) m   Toner.

PW21934   Frances Lois Wiser (b 20 Sep 1911, Hoodoo, Coffee TN) m 18 Oct 1937, Tony DeGeorge (b ca 1911).

PW21935   Wade Clifton Wiser (8 Jan 1914, Coffee TN-18 Mar 1985, Middletown OH) m Louise Rigney (b 1919). Coffee County TN school superintendent and teacher, Middletown OH.

PW219351   Judy Wiser m   Grandillo.

PW2194   Houston Wiser (b Jan 1883, TN).

PW2195   Austin Calvin Wiser (b Jan 1886, Hoodoo, Coffee TN) m 15 Nov 1909, TN, Mary Ellen ("Mollie") Uselton (b ca 1893, Hoodoo, Coffee TN).

PW21951   Eunice P. Wiser (b ca 1910, TN).

PW21952   William Dewey Wiser (b 15 Dec 1911, Noah, Coffee TN).

PW21953   Emma G. Wiser (b ca Jan 1916, TX).

PW2196   Beulah Wiser (b Dec 1889, TN) m 26 Aug 1906, Martin L. McCullough (24 Nov 1886-Nov 1987, Dallas TX).

PW2197   Eula Wiser (Sep 1899, TN-1968) m 4 Nov 1916, Howard Green.

PW21A   Francis Marion Wiser (28 Oct 1848, Coffee TN-26 Dec 1934, Coffee TN) m 30 May 1872, Coffee TN, Mary Magdalene Allison (15 Aug 1852, KY-13 Nov 1925).

PW21A1   James D. Wiser (3 Nov 1872, Coffee TN-18 Nov 1964, Bedford TN) m Jul 1890, Laura Ferrell (3 May 1873, Coffee TN-19 Apr 1961).

PW21A11   Ernest James Wiser (11 May 1891, Bedford TN-3 Mar 1966, Collin TX) m 5 Sep 1909, Mary ("Mollie") Lemons (21 Sep 1893, Bedford TN-Apr 1975, Collin TX).

PW21A111   Theodore James Wiser (3 Feb 1911, TN-22 Apr 1973).

PW21A112   Loise Wiser (8 Dec 1912, TN-14 Feb 1990, Collin TX).

PW21A113   Christina Wiser (b 1916, TN).

PW21A114   Elizabeth Wiser (b 17 May 1918, TN).

PW21A115   Ollie Mae Wiser (b 29 Apr 1920).

PW21A116   Daughter Wiser (26 Nov 1924, Coffee TN-26 Nov 1924, Coffee TN).

PW21A117   Clarence Wiser (30 Apr 1926-28 Jun 1992, Duncanville, Dallas TX).

PW21A12   Ethel Elmer Wiser (8 Dec 1892, TX-19 Feb 1961, Bedford TN) m 20 Apr 1913, Bedford TN, Sara Ann ("Sadie") Reynolds (7 Dec 1895, Coffee TN-30 Dec 1965, Bedford TN).

PW21A121   Mildred Louise Wiser (b 11 Mar 1914, TN) m 30 Mar 1935, Wartrace TN, Audry Lee Frazier (b 1913).

PW21A122   James Eldred ("Dr.") Wiser (b 31 Dec 1915, Bedford TN) m Louisa Marsean Houck (b 18 Dec 1911).

PW21A1221   Eldred Houck ("Dr.") Wiser (b 9 Mar 1943) m Rebekah Earle Griffitts (b 8 Jul 1941).

PW21A12211   Eldred Jonathan Wiser (b 13 Aug 1971).

PW21A12212   Elizabeth Brittian Wiser (b 6 Nov 1972).

PW21A12213   Sarah Houck Wiser (b 30 Jul 1975).

PW21A123   Ethel Eunice Wiser (b 26 Apr 1918, Bedford TN) m 10 Sep 1937, Manchester TN, J. C. Driver (b 9 Jul 1916, Bedford TN).

PW21A124   Verlon Elmer Wiser (b 15 Feb 1921) m 20 Dec 1941, Mary Nadine Hatchett (b 14 May 1924).

PW21A1241   Wanda Evelyn Wiser (b 13 Dec 1942) m 1) 15 Sep 1961, John Harold Sloop (3 Oct 1939-14 Apr 1985); m 2) 20 Jan 1978, Joe Nottingham (b 18 Jan 1939).

PW21A1242   Betty Jo Wiser (b 4 Apr 1945) m 1) 15 Jun 1965, Armand Alexander III; m 2) 28 Dec 1985, Don Kvernes (b 10 Oct 1956).

PW21A125   Cyrus Wymer Wiser (b 14 Jan 1923) m Laura Frances Gribble (b 9 Sep 1923).

PW21A1251   Linda Carolyn Wiser (b 14 Dec 1947) m George William Saddler (b 12 Mar 1946).

PW21A1252   Cyrus Wymer Wiser (b 5 Jan 1951) m Regina Delores Genesis (b 2 Aug 1960).

PW21A12521   Hannah Leigh Wiser (b 23 Apr 1992).

PW21A12522   Ellis Reid Wiser (b 21 Aug 1996).

PW21A1253   Gary Gribble Wiser (b 22 Feb 1952) m Vivian Gayle Pope (b 19 Jun 1952).

PW21A12531   Andrea Michelle Wiser (b 4 Mar 1972).

PW21A12532   Lauren Antone Wiser (b 12 Apr 1976).

PW21A12533   Gary Gribble Wiser Jr. (b 26 Mar 1981).

PW21A126   Winfred L. Wiser (b 14 Jun 1926).

PW21A13   Bertha Wiser (8 Oct 1894, TN-21 Oct 1970) m 15 Mar 1918, Bedford TN, S. H. Throneberry (4 Jan 1897-24 Jul 1968, Wartrace TN).

PW21A14   Owen Wiser (29 Feb 1896, TN-2 Sep 1972, Wartrace TN) m 24 Dec 1922, Wattie Mae Marris(?).

PW21A15   Newman Wiser (2 Apr 1898, TN-1 Dec 1963, TN) m 8 Jun 1919, Pearl Mankins (b ca 1904, TN).

PW21A151   James Thomas Wiser (b Dec 1920).

PW21A152   Cletus Wiser (b 30 Apr 1923) m Lorraine   .

PW21A153   Ruby Dean Wiser (b 23 Jul 1926).

PW21A154   Garnetta B. Wiser (b 19 Jul 1928).

PW21A155   Kenneth W. Wiser (b 9 Mar 1931) m 8 Aug 1953, Edwina Cates (b 27 Feb 1932, Detroit MI).

PW21A1551   David Kenneth Wiser (26 May 1954-13 May 1973, Shelbyville TN).

PW21A1552   Dan Edwin Wiser (b 24 Jan 1957, Shelbyville TN) m 8 Aug 1984, Sevierville TN, Kay Brinkley Smotherman.

PW21A1553   Dennis Mark Wiser (b 21 Mar 1958, Shelbyville TN) m 3 Nov 1979, Murfreesboro TN, Cecile Pinkston.

PW21A15531   Caroline Lindsey Wiser (b 3 Jan 1984).

PW21A15532   Matthew Kenneth Wiser (b 9 Feb 1990).

PW21A15533   Anna Marie Wiser (b 25 Jan 1992).

PW21A1554   Ted Keith Wiser (b 6 Oct 1959, Shelbyville TN) m 3 Jan 1987, Westmoreland TN, Alice Lynn Couch.

PW21A15541   Andrew Chase Wiser (b 12 May 1988).

PW21A15542   Nicholas Reed Wiser (b 2 Nov 1992).

PW21A16   Archie Wiser (b 9 Sep 1900, Coffee TN) m 23 Dec 1923, Bedford PA, Algie Cook (29 Jun 1895, Bedford TN-Jul 1985, Bedford TN).

PW21A161   Willard E. Wiser (b 13 Jun 1925, Fairfield TN) m 1) Mildred Mae Robinson (1 Jul 1927, Coffee TN-27 Mar 1995); m 2) Margaret Sons.

PW21A1611   Gerald E. Wiser (b 17 Feb 1948, Shelbyville TN) m 20 Jun 1969, Wartrace TN, Mary Virginia Owen (b 15 Aug 1949, Nashville TN).

PW21A16111   Letitia Lynn Wiser (b 4 Sep 1972) m Charles Eric Johnson.

PW21A16112   Christie Carmine Wiser (b 8 Feb 1978).

PW21A1612   Sylva Katherine Wiser (b 25 Nov 1951, Bedford TN) m James William Thompson (b 24 Feb 1949, Bedford TN).

PW21A1613   Larry Doyal Wiser (b 2 Oct 1956, Bedford TN) m Rebecca Marie Crowell (b 21 Mar 1961, Bedford TN).

PW21A16131   Brittany Nicole Wiser (b 4 Dec 1985).

PW21A16132   Brian Daniel Wiser (b 17 Oct 1989).

PW21A162   Windell Wiser (b 17 Jul 1929, Bedford TN) m 16 Feb 1952, Charlotte Brothers (b 3 Mar 1932).

PW21A1621   James Edward Wiser (b 27 Jun 1953, Laurel KY) m Denna Depew (b 9 Jun 1952).

PW21A16211   Martha Ann Wiser (b 22 Jun 1974) m Kevin Bowers (b 30 Apr 1969).

PW21A16212   Melissa Wiser (b 25 Jan 1976).

PW21A16213   James E. Wiser (b 19 Dec 1977).

PW21A1622   Martha G. Wiser (b 9 Aug 1954, Laurel KY) m Tim Hall (b 19 Sep 1955).

PW21A1623   John Wiser (b 23 Jun 1957, Athens AL) m Miriam Gateley (b 28 Nov 1961).

PW21A16231   Emily Wiser (b 4 Sep 1982).

PW21A1624   Paul Wiser (b 8 Feb 1959, Athens AL) m Kim McLeod (b 3 Aug 1964).

PW21A16241   Jason Wiser (b 2 Feb 1985).

PW21A16242   Josh Wiser (b 6 Jul 1986).

PW21A16243   Kaila Wiser (b 12 Jun 1993).

PW21A1625   Mary Wiser (b 6 Jul 1960, Athens AL) m Douglas Fields (b 13 Aug 1960).

PW21A1626   Julie Wiser (b 14 Nov 1961, Athens AL) m Dennis Craig (b 2 Aug 1958).

PW21A1627   Anna Wiser (b 18 Jan 1963, Athens AL) m Dennis Terry.

PW21A163   Marie Wiser (b 8 Jul 1931, Bedford TN) m 8 Mar 1952, Dewey Warren (b 17 Nov 1931).

PW21A164   James Franklin Wiser (b 15 Feb 1934, Bedford TN) m 15 Jun 1957, Jacqueline Elaine Will (b 1 Apr 1936).

PW21A1641 Paulette Elaine Wiser (b 29 Nov 1957) m 5 Mar 1976, Joseph Anthony Stuve (b 12 Jun 1956).

PW21A1642 Gordon Edward Wiser (b 5 Jan 1960).

PW21A1643 Linda Marie Wiser (b 22 Apr 1961) m 30 Jun 1984, Terrel Jay Faul (b 14 Nov 1949).

PW21A1644 Robin Lynne Wiser (b 1 Apr 1962) m 26 Sep 1992, Dawson William Kelly (b 21 Mar 1964).

PW21A165 Lorine Wiser (b 25 Mar 1935, Bedford TN) m 12 Sep 1954, Harold Clark (b 1 Apr 1934).

PW21A166 Mary Catherine Wiser (b 14 Oct 1942) m John A. Ankenbauer.

PW21A17 Verna Wiser (b 3 Mar 1903, TN) m Rumble(?).

PW21A18 Winston Wiser (23 Jan 1910, Bedford TN-1 Apr 1961, Shelbyville TN) m 26 Jul 1929, Bedford TN, Katherine Morris (1911-1991).

PW21A181 Robert Gordon Wiser (b 21 Apr 1934) m Mattie Ray Atnip (b 22 Aug 1930).

PW21A1811 Max Gordon Wiser (b 20 Jul 1956).

PW21A1812 Hal Milton Wiser (b 15 May 1958).

PW21A182 Eddie Wiser.

PW21A1821 Eddie Wiser.

PW21A183 Judy Wiser.

PW21A2 Mary F. Wiser (10 Aug 1874, TN-24 Sep 1956) m 9 Aug 1888, Charley H. Griffy (b 30 Oct 1860).

PW21A3 Marion Glenn Wiser (18 Oct 1875, Coffee TN-5 Jan 1958) m 16 Mar 1899, Sophia Josephine Wiser (PW2152).

PW21A31 Willie Josephine Wiser (2 Jan 1900, Noah, Coffee TN-5 Feb 1944, Barton Hill TN) m 30 Sep 1917, James Vivian Frazier (4 Feb 1895, Gnat Hill TN-17 Dec 1971, Barton Hill TN).

PW21A32 Cap Nolan Wiser (26 Jul 1902, TN-13 May 1969, Shelbyville TN) m 12 Oct 1923, Ruggie Trail (19 Mar 1908, Coffee TN-16 Jul 1940, Bedford TN).

PW21A321 Florence Lillian Wiser (b 13 May 1925, Coffee TN) m John Robert ("J. R.") Wiser (PW21A46).

PW21A322 Thelma Wiser m George Adcox.

PW21A323 Glen Wiser m Eleanor Genvo(?).

PW21A3231 Holly Wiser.

PW21A3232 Alan Wiser.

PW21A324 Johnnie Lindel Wiser m Lois Booker.

PW21A3241   Kay Wiser.

PW21A3242   Connie Wiser.

PW21A3243   Johnnie Wiser.

PW21A3244   James Wiser.

PW21A3245   Faye Wiser.

PW21A3246   Ann Wiser.

PW21A325   Huey Wiser (b 31 Aug 1936) m 27 Mar 1954, Joyce Howard (b 23 Jan 1939).

PW21A3251   Huey Wayne Wiser (8 Mar 1955, TN-Sep 1974) m Dana   .

PW21A32511   David Wiser (b 25 Jul 1974) m Carol Mooneyham.

PW21A325111   Shelby Wiser (b 12 Dec 1993).

PW21A325112   Brently Wiser (b 18 Jul 1996).

PW21A3252   Ruggie Wiser (b 27 May 1956) m   Parker.

PW21A3253   Teresa Wiser (b 10 Sep 1957) m   Cook.

PW21A3254   Peggy Wiser (b 23 Mar 1959) m   Hill.

PW21A3255   Melissa Wiser (b 19 Mar 1962) m   Williams.

PW21A326   Jimmie Wiser m Charlene Halleberg(?).

PW21A33   Raymond L. Wiser (14 Feb 1905, TN-Oct 1959) m Hazel Townsend(?).

PW21A331   Barbara Wiser.

PW21A332   Hazel Wiser.

PW21A333   Beverly Wiser.

PW21A334   Raymond Wiser.

PW21A34   Alene Wiser (b 1908, Coffee TN) m 1) 27 Jul 1928, Ardith E. Trail (29 Jul 1903, Coffee
TN-Jun 1963); m 2) George Wilson.

PW21A341   Ardith E. Trail (b Aug 1933, Coffee TN).

PW21A35   Daughter Wiser (b 27 Jun 1911, Coffee TN).

PW21A36   Bertie Lee Wiser (ca 1913, TN-4 Sep 1987) m 1) 30 Jun 1934, Manchester TN, James A.
Arnold (12 Dec 1892-19 Apr 1968, Wartrace TN); m 2) Calvin Lester Mullins.

PW21A37   Coleman Wiser (24 Apr 1915, TN-Nov 1975).

PW21A38   Marion Wiser (18 Jun 1918, TN-Feb 1983, Hopkins TX) m Mildred Adcox.

PW21A381   Judy Wiser.

PW21A382   Ronnie Wiser.

PW21A383   Dale Wiser.

PW21A384   Dennis Wiser.

PW21A385   Brenda Wiser.

PW21A39   Russell Cleveland Wiser (15 Nov 1921-1 Apr 1989, Shelbyville TN) m 1 Nov 1947, Shelbyville TN, Olive Vibbart (b ca 1908).

PW21A4   George Watson Wiser (5 Oct 1880, Coffee TN-19 Oct 1960) m 1) 13 Nov 1905, Sammie Ferrell (4 Dec 1886, TN-29 Oct 1912); m 2) 13 Apr 1913, Johnnie Lee Townsend (8 Mar 1897, Coffee TN-13 Jul 1944, Giles TN).

PW21A41   Virgie Wiser (24 Jul 1908-9 Jan 1990) m Cliff Lewis.

PW21A42   Elzie Lee Wiser (16 Apr 1910, Giles TN-14 Oct 1974, McMinnville TN) m 13 May 1928, Bessie Ferrell (13 May 1910, Coffee TN-26 Jan 1984).

PW21A421   Edward Allen Wiser.

PW21A422   Virgil Watson Wiser (b 1 Oct 1931, Coffee TN) m 25 Nov 1950, Davidson TN, Jo Dean Whaley (b 1 Sep 1935).

PW21A4221   David Carl Wiser (b 6 Dec 1951, Davidson TN) m 11 Jul 1969, Davidson TN, Patsy Piper (b 11 Jul 1951, Davidson TN).

PW21A42211   Kimberly Diane Wiser (b 22 Mar 1973, Davidson TN).

PW21A42212   Kelly Dawn Wiser (b 12 May 1976, Davidson TN) m Mike Gooch (b 21 Oct 1976).

PW21A4222   Stanley Bruce Wiser (b 5 Jan 1955, Davidson TN) m 18 Aug 1973, Davidson TN, Debra Sue Baker.

PW21A42221   Christi Alana Wiser (b 11 Feb 1978, Davidson TN).

PW21A42222   Stanley Benjamin Wiser (b 11 Mar 1980, Davidson TN).

PW21A4223   Randall Virgil Wiser (b 9 Sep 1964, Davidson TN) m 18 Jun 1988, Davidson TN, Carol Anne Dillingham.

PW21A42231   Jacob Randall Wiser (b 25 Jun 1990, Davidson TN).

PW21A42232   Hannah Catherine Wiser (b 4 May 1992, Davidson TN).

PW21A42233   Abigail Marie Wiser (b 26 Feb 1996, Davidson TN).

PW21A423   Judy Wiser m   Vaughn.

PW21A424   Naomia Wiser.

PW21A425   Valeria Wiser (31 May 1941, Giles TN-15 Apr 1943, Giles TN).

PW21A43   George Watson Wiser Jr. (b 25 Mar 1912, Giles TN) m 16 Jul 1935, Giles TN, Nellie Mae Sanders (b 20 Jan 1910, Giles TN).

PW21A431   Ila Mae Wiser (12 Jan 1937, Marshall TN-12 Jan 1937, Marshall TN).

PW21A432   Nellie Delois Wiser (b 18 Jun 1938, Giles TN) m 25 Dec 1958, James Dwain Glossup (b 6 Jan 1935, Giles TN).

PW21A433   Jerry Donald Wiser (2 Jul 1946, Jefferson KY-19 May 1948, Jefferson KY).

PW21A434   Geraldine Wiser (20 Jul 1948, Jefferson KY-20 Jul 1948, Jefferson KY).

PW21A44   Marvin David Wiser (1 Oct 1914, Coffee TN-8 Mar 1966, Giles TN) m 19 Dec 1936, Gladys Rebecca Warren (b 14 Feb 1920).

PW21A441   Mary Laverne Wiser (b 3 May 1938, Giles TN) m 20 Jun 1956, Giles TN, Robert Leroy Leonard (b ca 1931).

PW21A442   Joe Wiser (b 21 Aug 1941, Giles TN) m Kathy Harwell (b 28 Apr 1945).

PW21A4421   Hope Denise Wiser (b 21 Mar 1964, Lincoln TN).

PW21A4422   Marvin Eric Wiser (b 9 Dec 1966, Lincoln TN) m Bridget Bean.

PW21A44221   Marvin Lane Wiser (b 31 Mar 1985).

PW21A4423   Gregory Joe Wiser (b 28 May 1971, Lincoln TN).

PW21A443   Richard Wiser (b 24 Apr 1943, Giles TN) m 1) Martha Morton (b 22 Nov 1945, Lincoln TN); m 2) Lynn Martin.

PW21A4431   Mandy Gay Wiser (b 20 Oct 1966, Bedford TN) m 6 Aug 1988, Lincoln TN, Bob Edlin.

PW21A4432   Heather Wiser (b 9 May 1974, Bedford TN).

PW21A444   Carolyn Wiser (b 29 Feb 1944, Giles TN) m 28 Apr 1967, James Wesley Beverly (b 26 Oct 1945).

PW21A45   James William Wiser (26 Apr 1916, TN-10 Jan 1996) m 21 Sep 1935, Nola Ellen Sanders (b 18 Nov 1919, Giles TN).

PW21A451   James Herbert Wiser (b 14 Dec 1937, Pulaski TN) m 1) Genene Gaines (b 4 Mar 1939, Giles TN); m 2 Nancy Susan Cromwell (b 12 Sep 1946, Townsend TN).

PW21A4511   Jeffery Wiser (17 Oct 1965-17 Oct 1965).

PW21A4512   Leigh Ann Wiser (b 18 May 1967, Davidson TN).

PW21A46   John Robert ("J. R.") Wiser (14 Apr 1919, Coffee TN-Oct 1984, Giles TN) m Florence Lillian Wiser (PW21A321).

PW21A461   Linda Wiser (b 22 Jun 1945, Giles TN) m 27 Oct 1967, Kerry Duane Ezell (b 5 Jul 1947).

PW21A462   Mary Ruth Wiser (7 Feb 1947, Giles TN-7 Feb 1947, Giles TN).

PW21A463   John Robert Wiser Jr. (b 1 Feb 1948) m 20 Dec 1971, Renee Storey (b ca 1951).

PW21A464   Margaret Wiser (b 25 Mar 1950, Giles TN) m 1) 9 May 1966, Woodrow Robert Thompson Jr. (b ca 1945); m 2)   Thomas; m 3) Dalton Hall (b 6 Feb 1941, Giles TN).

PW21A465   Jannie Wiser (b 18 May 1953) m 20 Dec 1980, Dwayne D. Williams (b ca 1951).

PW21A466   Rickie Lee Wiser (b 29 Aug 1955, Marshall TN).

PW21A47   Thurman Chester Wiser.

PW21A471   Renee Wiser.

PW21A472   Son Wiser.

PW21A48   Cecil Watson Wiser (4 Jul 1924, Coffee TN-27 Mar 1987) m Christine Edwards (b 21 Mar 1926, TN).

PW21A481   Roger Dennon Wiser (b 9 Jan 1952) m 1) 12 Dec 1992, Anne Susan Bailey (b ca 1954); m 2) 19 Jun 1992, Reba Lynn Hamlett (b ca 1960).

PW21A4811   Nickole Wiser (b 10 Mar 1978).

PW21A4812   Leigh Bailey Wiser (b 13 Feb 1980, Giles TN).

PW21A482   James Donald ("Jack") Wiser (11 Jan 1957-27 May 1989) m 19 Dec 1981, Patricia Ann Gibson (b 12 May 1953).

PW21A4821   Sandy Wiser (b 20 Jun 1982).

PW21A4822   Laura Jane Wiser (b 20 Dec 1984).

PW21A49   Kattie Ruth Wiser m 1) Daley Tucker (b 16 Feb 1925); m 2) Cleo Baughman.

PW21A4A   Rubye Ellen Wiser (b 3 Jan 1929) m Marvin Eugene Moore (b 31 Aug 1924).

PW21A4B   Mamie Earline Wiser (b ca 1933) m 5 Oct 1957, John Earl Moore (b ca 1928).

PW21A4C   Clarence Samuel Wiser (b Aug 1935) m Joyce   (b 30 Aug 1942, Moline IL).

PW21A5   Osdenie Wiser (19 Apr 1883-19 Oct 1883).

PW21A6   Henry Boston ("Boss") Wiser (31 Mar 1885, TN-17 Jan 1966, Lewisburg TN) m Martha Elizabeth Townsend (28 Apr 1889, TN-1 Sep 1963).

PW21A61   Francis Lee Wiser (31 Jan 1911, TN-30 Apr 1996) m 8 Nov 1931, Lewisburg TN, Agnes Gertie Curlee (b ca 1913).

PW21A611   Calvin Henry Wiser.

PW21A612   Cora Wiser.

PW21A62   Charles Henry Wiser (14 Feb 1913, TN-11 Jul 1982, Lewisburg TN) m Virginia Louise Smith (b 20 Mar 1922).

PW21A621   Shirley Ann Wiser.

PW21A622   Alice Faye Wiser.

PW21A623   Martha Carolyn Wiser.

PW21A624   Dorothy Mae Wiser.

PW21A625   Bobby Lee Wiser.

PW21A626   Roger Dale Wiser.

PW21A627   Barry Neal Wiser.

PW21A63   Eugene Wiser (b 16 Jun 1916, Lewisburg TN) m 25 Dec 1937, Anna Ophelia Wells (b 28 Jul 1919, Petersburg TN).

PW21A631   Myra June Wiser (b 16 Sep 1940).

PW21A632   Thomas Edward Wiser (b 14 Mar 1943).

PW21A633   Linda Joyce Wiser (b 16 Jul 1946).

PW21A634   Roy Lee Wiser (b 28 Apr 1950).

PW21A64   Mary Alice Magdalene Wiser (16 Jan 1919, TN-18 Dec 1989) m Bernice Brown (12 Dec 1917-Jun 1978, Memphis TN).

PW21A65   Hazel Mai Wiser (b 3 Mar 1921) m Wilfred Wilkerson (3 Apr 1917-Jan 1975).

PW21A66   Clyde Boston Wiser (18 Feb 1923-9 Jul 1954) m 14 Oct 1939, Kathleen Richardson (29 Jan 1918-5 Mar 1987).

PW21A661   Barbara Jo Wiser (b 16 Dec 1940) m 1) Aug 1962, Mack Leonard Young (d ca 1968); m 2) Ron Preas.

PW21A6611   Eddie Wayne Young (b 26 Oct 1963).

PW21A6612   Carrie Maletha Young (b 6 Dec 1965).

PW21A662   Donna Sue Wiser (b 25 Nov 1943) m 1 Jul 1961, Jerry Tyrone Morrow.

PW21A663   Danny Clyde Wiser (b 7 Mar 1952) m 1) 18 Mar 1969, Patricia Ann Allison (b ca 1955); m 2) 1984, Teresa Jackson.

PW21A6631   David Clyde Wiser (b 27 Aug 1969) m 1 Jul 1994, Ginger Lee Hayes (b ca 1971).

PW21A6632   Stacey Ann Wiser (b 1 Oct 1971).

PW21A6633   Daniel Wiser (b 3 Sep 1985).

PW21A67   Clayborn G. Wiser (b 31 May 1927) m Sue King.

PW21A671   Chris Wiser.

PW21A672   Kimberly Wiser.

PW21A68   Marcus Edward Wiser (b 6 Jan 1931) m Geraldine Lassiter.

PW21A681   Ricky Wiser.

PW21A682 Tim Wiser.

PW21A683 Jeff Wiser.

PW21A7 Oscar Wiser (30 Aug 1887, TN-28 Jul 1975, Manchester TN) m 18 May 1907, Judy Florence Arnold (20 Aug 1887, Coffee TN-12 Sep 1967).

PW21A71 Grace Wiser (b ca 1907, TN) m 15 Apr 1924, Grover Green.

PW21A72 Ozell Wiser (b ca 1913, TN) m 19 Jun 1937, Marvin Trail (b ca 1911).

PW21A73 Buford Wiser (21 Mar 1923-30 Oct 1995, Summitville TN).

PW21A8 Lena Eva Wiser (26 Feb 1890, TN-4 May 1977, Shelbyville TN) m Thomas Dave Curlee (21 Nov 1883-13 May 1970, Shelbyville TN).

PW21A9 Horace Wiser (16 Apr 1893, TN-29 Dec 1978, Cornersville TN) m 1) 19 Dec 1912, Leona Erma Rohelier (25 Nov 1897, Grundy TN-10 Mar 1930, Bedford TN); m 2) 27 Oct 1932, Mattie Knowis, m 3) Bessie Colvette (b 8 Oct 1908).

PW21A91 Denver L. Wiser (b ca 1914, TN).

PW21A92 Mary E. Wiser (b 1917, TN) m Ernest Fisher.

PW21A93 Vera Wiser m P. T. Holloway.

PW21A94 Virginia Wiser m 1) Woodrow Richardson; m 2) Buddy Wagoner; m 3) Joe Scott.

PW21A95 Horace Wiser Jr. m 8 Jul 1939, Miriam B. Fox.

PW21A96 James Thomas Wiser m 1 Jul 1965, Sharon June Edwards.

PW21A97 Martha Faye Wiser m 15 Jul 1967, John Frederick Scarbrough III.

PW21A98 Peggy Wiser.

PW21A99 Brenda Kay Wiser m 31 Dec 1969, Daryll Keith Sweeney.

PW21B Cynthia Evelyn Wiser (1850, TN-1910, Coffee TN) m 16 Sep 1869, Lafayette ("Fate") Thomas (1851-1919).

PW22 Abigail Wiser (23 Jun 1800, KY-18 Oct 1874, Coffee TN).

PW23 John B. Wiser (3 Jan 1803, KY-17 Jun 1884, Coffee TN) m Matilda Sallie Rhoten(?) (b ca 1811, NC).

PW231 William Harrison Wiser (17 Jul 1839, Manchester TN-19 Sep 1908, Rutherford TN) m 21 Dec 1865, Coffee TN, Docia Tennessee Adams (18 Dec 1840, Readyville, Cannon TN-20 May 1921, Ferris, Ellis TX).

PW2311 Eliza R. Wiser (2 Nov 1866, TN-1 Jul 1906) m 15 Jul 1886, Coffee TN, Thomas Henry Keel (12 Oct 1857, TN-1 Aug 1920).

PW2312 Matilda Florence Wiser (19 Mar 1869, TN-18 Sep 1907) m 2 Jan 1889, John Washington Peay (14 Jul 1861-16 Apr 1924).

PW2313   Ollie B. Wiser (b ca 1872, TN) m Tom Jones.

PW2314   William Harry Wiser (11 Nov 1874, Readyville, Cannon TN-7 Feb 1962, Waxahachie TX) m 21 Jul 1904, Waxahachie TX, Alva Rilla Moore (1 Sep 1883, Fulton MS-10 Oct 1969, Waxahachie TX).

PW23141   Girtie Lee Wiser (5 Feb 1907, Ferris TX-17 May 1986, Lancaster TX) m 24 Jan 1926, Lancaster TX, Chester Harrison Rogers (27 Jan 1898, Booneville MS-24 May 1990, Lancaster TX).

PW23142   Docia Dorothy Wiser (28 Aug 1914, Ferris TX) m 16 May 1936, Waxahachie TX, Virgil A. McCarly (27 Sep 1909, Sweetwater TX-8 Jan 1980, San Diego CA).

PW23143   Mildred Lois Wiser (7 Jul 1917, Ferris TX-28 Aug 1994, Waxahachie TX) m 7 Sep 1935, Waxahachie TX, Elvis Davis Ellis.

PW23144   Virginia Jane Wiser (b 8 Apr 1922) m 29 Oct 1944, Yuma AZ, Frank Marcos Murillo.

PW2315   Sarah L. Wiser (b May 1878, TN) m William D. Barr (b ca 1854, TN).

PW2316   Calvin Claud Wiser (23 Jul 1882, TN-21 Jun 1950, Waxahachie TX) m 15 Nov 1917, Mattie Ethel Culver (12 Dec 1900, Groesbeck, Limestone TX-17 Sep 1978, Waxahachie TX).

PW23161   Delbert Ray Wiser (b 18 Apr 1919, Ferris TX).

PW23162   Bobbie Lorene Wiser.

PW23163   Margarite Louise Wiser (b 29 Nov 1921, Ferris TX).

PW23164   Rose Nell Wiser (b 21 Sep 1924, Ferris TX).

PW23165   Joy Fay Wiser (b 28 Nov 1925, Chillicothe TX).

PW23166   Frances Willie Wiser (b 22 Mar 1928, Ferris TX).

PW23167   Billy Eugene Wiser (b 5 Sep 1934, Ferris TX).

PW2317   Nancy Jane Wiser (28 Nov 1885-7 Sep 1899).

PW232   Margaret Wiser (b ca 1843, TN) m 28 Feb 1860, Coffee TN, J. K. Burks.

PW24   Margaret Wiser (6 May 1805, Cumberland KY-6 Apr 1883, Coffee TN) m Hamilton Lewis Duncan (10 Nov 1806-18 Mar 1869, Coffee TN).

PW25   Isaiah Wiser (15 Apr 1808, KY-15 Apr 1843, Coffee TN) m Nancy   (b ca 1807).

PW251   John D. Wiser (b Oct 1832, TN) m 1 Jun 1856, Coffee TN, Nancy Ann Elizabeth Redden (b ca 1839, TN).

PW2511   James William H. Wiser (b Apr 1860, TN) m Nancy A. Seagroves (b Jul 1870, TN.

PW25111   Lela M. Wiser (b Jul 1893, TN).

PW2512   Mary Ella Wiser (b ca 1867, TN).

PW2513   James Wilburn ("Webb") Wiser (b 10 Oct 1868, Coffee TN) m 13 Jun 1891, Coffee TN, Hettie Ann Alice Jernigan (b Dec 1872, TN).

PW25131   Walter Newman Wiser (b 2 May 1892, Coffee TN) m   Lonan (b ca 1895, TX).

PW251311   Woxie Wiser (b ca 1918, TX).

PW251312   Odessa Wiser (b ca Nov 1919, TX).

PW25132   Mary E. Wiser (b Oct 1893, TN).

PW25133   Oscar Ransome Wiser (21 Sep 1895, Coffee TN-Jan 1966, TX) m 29 Jul 1917, Plano,
Collin TX, Sallie Frances Taylor (b ca 1901, TN).

PW251331   Marion Quentin Wiser (b 18 Jun 1918, Grapevine, Tarrant TX).

PW251332   Juanita Wiser (b ca Nov 1919, TX).

PW25134   John Marion Wiser (b 16 Jan 1898, Grapevine, Tarrant TX).

PW25135   Porter Wilson Wiser (21 Sep 1899, Grapevine, Tarrant TX-Jun 1968, Tarrant TX).

PW25136   Iva M. Wiser (b ca 1903, TX).

PW25137   William Lawrence Wiser (11 Mar 1905, Grapevine, Tarrant TX-Nov 1974, Houston TX).

PW25138   Bessie Wiser (b ca 1908, TX).

PW25139   Alva Eunice Wiser (b ca Oct 1909, TX) m 4 Oct 1930, Grapevine, Tarrant TX, Eldy
Vernon Anderson.

PW2513A   James W. Hubert Wiser (b 25 Dec 1915, Grapevine, Tarrant TX).

PW2514   Margaret Wiser (b May 1870, TN).

PW2515   Nancy Wiser (b ca 1872, TN).

PW2516   Harvey Wiser (b Dec 1879, TN) m 1) 15 Mar 1900, Mabel Teal (b Oct 1884, TN); m 2)
Lillie   (b ca 1897, AR).

PW2517   Birdie E. Wiser (b 16 Jun 1881, Coffee TN).

PW2518   George W. Wiser (b Jan 1884, TN) m Annie M. Bush (b ca 1889, TN).

PW252   Thomas J. Wiser (b ca 1834, TN) m 7 Feb 1856, Martha Mary A. Stacy (b Jul 1835, TN).

PW2521   William H. Wiser (b ca 1856, TN) m Margaret Ivy (ca 1856, TN-ca 1897).

PW25211   Willie Wiser (b Feb 1882, MS).

PW25212   Isaac Wiser (b Feb 1886, MS).

PW25213   Della Wiser (b Feb 1889, MS).

PW25214   Ella Wiser (b Feb 1889, MS).

PW25215   Ona Wiser (b May 1891, MS).

PW25216   Etta Wiser (b Jun 1894, MS).

PW2522   John Henry Wiser (b ca 1858, TN) m 18 Dec 1880, Coffee TN, Virginia Baker.

PW2523   Francis E. Wiser (b Mar 1861, TN) m ca 1903, Gertrude E. Lane (b ca 1870, TN).

PW25231   Hattie Wiser (b ca 1905, TN).

PW25232   Mary E. Wiser (b ca 1908, TN).

PW25233   Jesse Elbert Wiser (8 May 1910, Gibson TN-31 May 1943, Madison TN) m Hattie James.

PW2524   Martha J. Wiser (b ca 1863, TN) m Parley M. Jacobs.

PW2525   Mary T. Wiser (b ca 1870, TN).

PW253   Margaret Ann Wiser (ca 1836, TN-Sep 1868).

PW254   David R. C. Wiser (12 Jan 1838, Coffee TN-9 Sep 1910, Havana AR) m 1) 21 Jun 1855,
Coffee TN, Lydia Jane St. John (1832, TN-4 Mar 1884); m 1 Nov 1885, Yell AR, Barbara Clara Morsback
(b Mar 1856, WI).

PW2541   Isaiah T. Wiser (b ca 1856, TN).

PW2542   Nancy A. Wiser (2 May 1858, Coffee TN-28 Apr 1898, Havana AR).

PW2543   John Robert Wiser (b Nov 1859, Coffee TN) m 24 Nov 1889, Danville AR, Bonnie
Bushart (b 21 Aug 1870, AR).

PW25431   Ora Wiser (b 21 Aug 1891, Havana AR) m 5 Sep 1912, Paris, Logan AR, Omar Benjamin
King (b 11 May 1890, Havana AR).

PW25432   William Bryan Wiser (25 Nov 1892, Havana AR-3 Jan 1898, Havana AR).

PW25433   Wealtha Wiser (27 Feb 1895, Havana AR-23 Feb 1988, Fayetteville TN) m 7 Jan 1914,
Eufala OK, James Edgar Valentine (9 Mar 1892-Jul 1980, Gentry, Benton AR).

PW25434   Oliver Lafayette Wiser (b 1 Jan 1899, Havana AR) m Jessie Armstrong.

PW25435   Robert E. Lee Wiser (19 Aug 1902, Havana AR-Mar 1970, Oklahoma City OK) m Amy
Parsons.

PW25436   Claudia Iris Wiser (b 6 Feb 1906, Havana AR) m Clarence Baker.

PW25437   Infant Wiser (3 Apr 1908, Havana AR-3 Apr 1908, Havana AR).

PW25438   Johnnie Mae Wiser (b 12 Jan 1910, Havana AR).

PW2544   William James Wiser (5 Oct 1861, TN-16 Jul 1945, Havana AR) m 26 Feb 1886, NcNairy
TN, Arie Ida Simpkins (29 Oct 1863, TN-17 Mar 1940, Havana AR).

PW25441   Grover Cleveland Wiser (Nov 1886, AR-1946).

PW25442   Zelma (Elmer) Wiser (b Apr 1888, AR) m ca 1909, Maggie   (b ca 1889).

PW254421   Margaret Wiser (b ca 1912, AR).

PW254422   James William Wiser (b ca 1914, AR).

PW25443   Porter H. Wiser (28 May 1890, AR-22 Mar 1973, Havana AR) m 19 Sep 1911, Ratha Omega Rogers (18 Aug 1893, AR-Mar 1977, Yell AR).

PW254431   William James Wiser (b 3 Jul 1913, AR) m 2 Aug 1936, Gussie Ellora Boss (b 19 Feb 1913).

PW2544311   Media Louisa Wiser (b 24 Jan 1941) m 16 Jun 1964, Stephen Mabry Snipes (b 5 Dec 1941).

PW2544312   Julian Porter Wiser (b 6 Jul 1943) m 1) Eugenia Lynn Perry; m 2) Dorothy   .

PW25443121   Brian Jeffrey Wiser (b 19 Dec 1973).

PW25443122   Julie Ann Wiser (b 16 Mar 1979).

PW25443123   Brandon Lee Wiser (b 5 Jun 1994).

PW25443124   Trevor Lee Wiser (b 5 Jun 1994).

PW254432   Porter Hulon ("Shug") Wiser (b 24 Apr 1915, AR) m 1) 16 Feb 1935, Geneva Pearl Robinson (20 Aug 1917-2 Jun 1995); m 2) 26 Apr 1996, Nell Baker.

PW2544321   James Clyde Wiser (b 19 Jun 1936, Havana AR) m Wanda Sue Manes (b 7 Jul 1938).

PW25443211   James Ricky Wiser (b 7 Aug 1959) m Sandra Kay Jones (b 10 Jan 1963).

PW254432111   James Ricky Wiser Jr. (b 10 Apr 1979).

PW254432112   Matthew Paul Wiser (b 22 Jun 1984).

PW25443212   Ronnie Lynn Wiser (b 13 May 1961) m 1) Karen Christine Bottom (b 12 Apr 1965); m 2) 3 Dec 1993, Nicole Lynn Holly.

PW254432121   Jonathan Keith Wiser (b 14 Jan 1986).

PW254432122   Kasey Irene Wiser (b 3 Apr 1987).

PW254432123   Jennifer Nicole Wiser (b 1 Sep 1990).

PW25443213   Tammy Sue Wiser (b 5 Jan 1963) m Daniel Lee Fincher.

PW25443214   Michael Shannon Wiser (b 10 Apr 1975).

PW2544322   William Lynn Wiser (b 17 Sep 1938) m Brenda Joyce Sims (b 4 Jan 1947).

PW25443221   William Lynn Wiser Jr. (b 10 Mar 1969).

PW25443222   Kevin Porter Wiser (b 14 Nov 1972).

PW25443223   Joseph Barry Wiser (b 1 Jul 1977).

PW254433   Robert Othorp Wiser (b 14 Apr 1917, AR) m Syble Eulalia Smith (b 12 Nov 1919).

PW2544331   Bobby Joe Wiser (b 30 Dec 1940) m Patricia Irene Wiley (b 7 Apr 1941).

PW25443311   Barbara Ann Wiser (b 17 Jun 1963) m Keith Allen Cotten (b 16 Aug 1963).

PW2544332   Johnny Lee Wiser (10 Dec 1943-5 Nov 1993) m Bonnie Jean Pollard (b 26 Oct 1946).

PW25443321   Debra Jean Wiser (b 23 Mar 1966) m Tracey Glen Stewart (b 26 Mar 1965).

PW25443322   Robert Lee Wiser (2 Feb 1967-15 Feb 1992) m Sherri Von Knoles.

PW25443323   Karen Sue Wiser (b 3 Aug 1968) m John Anderson.

PW25443324   Lisa Gay Wiser (b 9 Oct 1971) m 8 Sep 1990, Michael Lanina.

PW2544333   Caroline Omega Wiser (b 16 Jan 1949) m Charles Richard Melton (25 Aug 1942-6 Aug 1996).

PW254434   Mary Madlyn Wiser (15 Feb 1920-31 Mar 1923).

PW254435   Joseph Aaron Wiser (5 Jan 1922, AR-2 Nov 1978) m 16 Jan 1946, Ruth Patricia Yaeger (11 Aug 1924-25 Mar 1993).

PW2544351   Gary Lynn Wiser (b 22 Jul 1947) m Sylvia Jean Thompson (b 18 Sep 1949).

PW25443511   Robert Scott Wiser (b 24 Aug 1970) m Judith Ann Thomas (b 21 Mar 1969).

PW254435111   Andrew Scott Wiser (b 23 Jul 1992).

PW25443512   Tiffany Marie Wiser (b 18 Jul 1974) m 21 Apr 1996, Jeffrey Burle Kennedy.

PW2544352   Darline Faye Wiser (b 9 Jun 1950) m James William Blackwell (b 12 Apr 1944).

PW2544353   Darrell Wayne Wiser (b 29 Jun 1953) m 28 Aug 1981, Candie Lynn Janes (b 10 Dec 1956).

PW25443531   Athalie Marie Wiser (b 12 Jun 1982).

PW25443532   Mitchell Joseph Wiser (b 12 Jun 1985).

PW25443533   Samuel Isaiah Wiser (b 11 Jun 1988).

PW2544354   Dale Allen Wiser (b 30 Dec 1958) m Michelle Charlene Mongillo (b 22 Sep 1962).

PW25443541   Joseph Allen Wiser (b 7 Sep 1986).

PW25443542   Arielle Jane Wiser (b 15 Mar 1989).

PW2544355   Edward Ray Wiser (b 22 Dec 1961).

PW254436   Roger Lee Wiser (b 15 Feb 1924) m 15 Jun 1946, Mary Helen Mott (b 24 Jul 1927).

PW2544361   Jimmy Glenn Wiser (b 9 Oct 1947) m 17 Mar 1967, Marilyn Gail Harger (b 5 Nov 1947).

PW25443611   Tessa Lynn Wiser (b 13 Feb 1968) m 1) Eugene Potter; m 12 Dec 1990, James Brian Short.

PW25443612   Glenna Marie Wiser (b 25 Sep 1970).

PW25443613   Linda Gayle Wiser (b 14 Feb 1973) m 5 Oct 1991, Christopher Allen Hall.

PW2544362   Jacky Lynn Wiser.

PW2544363   Judy Lavon Wiser (b 24 Jun 1950) m 11 Aug 1972, James Edward Perry.

PW2544364   Janet Lee Wiser (b 9 Jan 1962) m 14 Sep 1979, Steven Edward Ridenour.

PW254437   Henry Lynn Wiser (b 12 Dec 1926) m 27 Apr 1947, Dortha Catlett.

PW2544371   Henry Lynn Wiser Jr. (b 2 Feb 1948) m 1) Pamela Sue Kroesen; m 2) Joyce Ann Bubbard Brown.

PW25443711   Kimberly Dianne Brown Wiser (b 5 Oct 1966) m Jadrian Marcus.

PW25443712   Tabitha Lynn Wiser (b 5 Apr 1974).

PW2544372   Ronald Stephen Wiser (b 12 Feb 1950) m Carolyn Jean Thompson.

PW25443721   Stacy Lynn Wiser (b 12 Jul 1968).

PW25443722   Julia Kay Wiser (b 19 Feb 1970) m John Nagy.

PW2544373   Steven Grant Wiser (b 2 Aug 1953) m Loretta Miller.

PW25443731   Stephen Maclain Wiser (b 5 Oct 1977).

PW25443732   Shasta Dawn Wiser (b 31 Jul 1980).

PW25443733   Latessa Ann Wiser (b 31 Mar 1983).

PW2544374   James Robert Wiser (b 26 Jan 1969) m 3 Dec 1988, Elizabeth McKenny.

PW25443741   Andrea Marie Wiser (b 7 Feb 1991).

PW254438   Ida Sue Wiser (b 30 Jul 1928) m Damon Dale Hall (14 Jun 1928-6 Nov 1995).

PW2544381   Michael Wayne Wiser (b 13 Mar 1952) m 11 Sep 1970, Polly Faye Moody.

PW25443811   Jeffrey Wayne Wiser (b 18 Feb 1973).

PW25443812   Michael Scott Wiser (b 30 Dec 1974).

PW254439   Betty Jean Wiser (b 5 Oct 1930) m 19 May 1956, Coy Eugene Reed.

PW25443A   Franklin Delano Wiser (b 13 Nov 1932, Havana AR) m 31 May 1958, Beatrice Faye Trost (b 27 Dec 1933, Green Forest AR).

PW25443A1   Cecilia Rae Wiser (b 10 Oct 1959).

PW25443A2   Grant Earl Wiser (b 9 Mar 1961).

PW25443B   Molly Maxine Wiser (b 27 Sep 1934) m 25 Sep 1953, Wesley Merle Fish (b 24 Aug 1929).

PW25444   Oswald Wiser (15 Nov 1896, AR-Mar 1974, Little Rock AR) m Barney Hall (13 Aug 1887-Feb 1976, Benton, Saline AR).

PW25445   Myrtle Wiser (23 Nov 1898, AR-Aug 1970, Little Rock AR) m Olice N. Martin (13 Dec 1898-20 Aug 1988, Hope, Hempstead AR).

PW25446   Roscoe Wiser (1902, AR-1902).

PW25447   Beauton C. Wiser (23 Jan 1904, AR-Apr 1976, Little Rock AR) m J. R. Wilson.

PW25448   Alma Wiser (b ca 1907, AR) m Clyde Lewis.

PW2545   Marion Jackson Wiser (2 Jan 1863, Coffee TN-6 Jun 1908, Havana AR) m 7 Nov 1888, Yell AR, Laura J. Walkup (b Sep 1869, AR).

PW25451   Willie Wiser (b Aug 1889, AR).

PW25452   Elzie E. Wiser (b Aug 1892, AR).

PW25453   Ethel Wiser (b Jan 1894, AR).

PW25454   Edna Wiser (b Apr 1898, AR).

PW25455   Marion Wiser (b Nov 1899, AR).

PW2546   David Robert Wiser (b Jan 1865, TN) m ca 1898, Laura McGar (b Jul 1874, AR).

PW25461   Boss(?) D. Wiser (b ca 1904, AR).

PW2547   Rosetta Jane Wiser (9 Jan 1867, Coffee TN-10 Jun 1951, Farmington AR) m Feb 1896, Steve Douglas Reed (15 Apr 1867, AR-Feb 1958, Farmington AR).

PW2548   Anna E. Wiser (b 27 Jul 1872, Coffee TN) m 1) 27 Dec 1894, Yell AR, J. H. Sexton; m 2) Doc Rowland.

PW2549   Frank Wiser (22 Feb 1877, Coffee TN-4 May 1934, Checotah OK) m 18 Sep 1900, Havana AR, Hattie Chapin (7 Aug 1879, AR-6 Mar 1915, Checotah OK).

PW25491   Harvey Wiser (19 Dec 1903, Havana AR-Sep 1983, San Bernardino CA) m Mattie Ellen Miller (b 27 Jun 1909, Meeker OK).

PW254911   Jerry Wiser.

PW254912   Frank Wiser.

PW25492   Infant Wiser (1 Mar 1905, Havana AR-23 Aug 1905, Havana AR).

PW25493   Orville Wiser (b 23 Aug 1906, Havana AR) m Wynona Miller.

PW254931   James Wiser.

PW25494   Edward Wiser (2 Nov 1908, Havana AR-17 Jan 1944, Tulsa OK) m Velma Alice Looney.

PW25495   Sibbel Wiser (19 Mar 1911, Havana AR-2 Aug 1924, Checotah OK).

PW25496   Eula Wiser (b 12 Feb 1913, Checotah OK) m Harold E. Elsey (16 Jan 1913-11 Oct 1989, Muskogee OK).

PW254A   Harvey A. Wiser (b ca 1879, AR) m 10 Nov 1909, Lillie Benefield (b ca 1894, AR).

PW254B   Esther Wiser (b Nov 1888, AR).

PW255   Isaiah Wiser (1840, Coffee TN-ca 1863).

PW256   William D. Wiser (1842, Coffee TN-ca 1863).

PW26   David Wiser (3 Feb 1811, TN-25 Sep 1867, Coffee TN) m Mary Elizabeth Duncan(?) (b ca 1818).

PW261   Margaret L. Wiser (b 20 Jan 1840, TN) m 30 Apr 1861, Coffee TN, Osburn Dye.

PW262   John William Wiser (25 Feb 1842, TN-Aug 1913, Coffee TN) m 1) 21 Feb 1866, Coffee TN, Lucina Nichols (ca 1845, TN-ca 1877); m 2) 26 Nov 1879, Coffee TN, Mary Elizabeth Adams (16 May 1864, Coffee TN-23 Apr 1916, Coffee TN).

PW2621   William Wiser (b Dec 1866, TN) m 11 Nov 1889, Emma Hayley (b Jul 1875, TN).

PW26211   James Robert Wiser (2 Jul 1894, Coffee TN-5 Feb 1980, Pulaski TN) m 1) 3 Sep 1916, Della May Lovett (b ca 1899, Giles TN); m 2) 6 Jan 1936, Flossie Garner (b 20 Mar 1902).

PW262111   James Allen Wiser (4 Jun 1917, Giles TN-4 Jun 1917, Giles TN).

PW262112   Raleigh Wiser (7 May 1918, TN-27 Sep 1944) m 21 Jan 1941, Mary Ellen Fralix (b ca 1912).

PW2621121   Jimmie Wiser (27 Nov 1942-27 Nov 1942).

PW2621122   Raleigh Glenn Wiser.

PW262113   Cordell Wiser (b 25 Sep 1920) m Mabel Chapman (30 May 1923-Nov 1992, Giles TN).

PW2621131   James Ronald Wiser (b ca 1948) m 1 Mar 1969, Cathy Jean Jones (b ca 1951).

PW26211311   Phillip Allen Wiser (b ca 1970) m 4 Sep 1992, Leslie Samantha McGill (b ca 1974).

PW2621132   Tammy Wiser.

PW262114   Alatha Wiser (b 6 Jan 1922) m John Whitehead.

PW262115   Kenneth Lewis Wiser (b 26 Jan 1926) m 14 Jan 1951, Marjorie Pearl Brewer (b ca 1930).

PW2621151   Carolyn Wiser.

PW2621152   Kenneth Wiser.

PW2621153   Dennis Wiser.

PW2621154   John Wiser.

PW262116   William Harold Wiser (12 May 1927-24 Mar 1976) m 20 May 1949, Martha Ruth Scott (b 16 Dec 1930).

PW2621161   Pamela Kay Wiser (b ca 1955) m 19 May 1973, Gary Winston Harwell (b ca 1952).

PW26212   Lora Bessie Wiser (b ca 1901, TN).

PW26213   Myrtle Wiser (b ca 1904, TN).

PW2622   Mary Wiser (b Dec 1869, TN).

PW2623   Martha Wiser (b ca 1875, TN).

PW2624   Thomas Alfred Wiser (7 Jan 1881, Coffee TN-6 Jun 1947) m 13 Dec 1903, Mary Wood Blanton (1 Oct 1887, Coffee TN-6 Dec 1945, Coffee TN).

PW26241   John Short Velaesco Wiser (16 Dec 1904, TN-20 Sep 1976, Manchester TN) m 12 Jun 1927, Minnie Leone Smith (b 23 Oct 1908).

PW262411   Bill Wiser (b 29 Sep 1928) m Betty Lafever.

PW2624111   Mitchell Ray Wiser m Jackie   .

PW2624112   William Robert Wiser.

PW262412   Horace Lee Wiser (b 3 Nov 1931) m 1) Ruth Kelly; m 2) Sonia   ; m 3) 12 Oct 1968, Tullahoma TN, Margaret Kay Kimbro (b ca 1947, TN); m 4) 19 Mar 1983, Coffee TN, Linda Ruth Haynes (b ca 1947, TN).

PW2624121   Valerie Wiser (b 29 Sep 1957) m Ken Hewlett.

PW2624122   Tammy Wiser (b 27 Aug 1962) m Stanton Mills.

PW262413   Stanley Wiser (b 1 May 1933) m Lena Grogan (b 20 Jul 1933).

PW2624131   Sherman Layne Wiser (b 1 Sep 1952, TN) m 7 Mar 1975, Brenda Faye Shelton (b 29 Apr 1953, TN).

PW26241311   Amanda Lane Wiser (b 29 Oct 1979).

PW26241312   James Aaron Wiser (b 30 Jul 1982).

PW2624132   Danny Earl Wiser (b 19 Jul 1954, TN) m 1) 2 Mar 1973, Coffee TN, Glinda Elaine Roberts (b ca 1955, TN); m 2) 4 Oct 1980, Coffee TN, Laura Leann Carey (b 12 Jun 1962, HI).

PW26241321   Whitney Wiser (b 28 Oct 1986).

PW26241322   Clay Wiser (b 27 Jul 1988).

PW2624133   Stanley Joe Wiser (b 5 May 1961) m Lisa O'Kelly.

PW26241331   Chantel Wiser (b 31 Aug 1983).

PW26241332   Samantha Wiser (b 27 Oct 1987).

PW262414   Nellie Wiser (b 26 Apr 1938) m Marlon Carter (b 1 Apr 1934).

PW262415   Mary Jane Wiser (b 2 Dec 1939, Coffee TN) m 8 Nov 1958, Manchester TN, Charles Allen Reed (b 5 Nov 1942, Coffee TN).

PW262416   Johnnie Kathleen Wiser (b 20 Jul 1944, TN) m 23 Mar 1963, Manchester TN, Arthur Wayne Stevens (b 22 Jun 1942, TN).

PW262417   Eddie Wayne Wiser (b 18 Feb 1946, TN) m 1) 28 Nov 1968, Tullahoma TN, Janice Elaine Bailey (b ca 1949, NC); m 2) 17 Dec 1971, Coffee TN, Melissa Joy Adams (b 16 May 1954, TN).

PW2624171   Angie Wiser (b 9 Jun 1973).

PW2624172   Heather Wiser (b 28 Oct 1976).

PW262418   Ronnie Wiser (b 4 May 1948, Coffee TN) m 30 Oct 1970, Deborah Perry (b 23 Apr 1953, Coffee TN).

PW262419   Son Wiser.

PW26242   Irene Elizabeth Wiser (9 Jan 1910, Coffee TN-10 Jan 1994) m 26 Dec 1926, William Marvin Crouch Jr. (b 17 Apr 1907).

PW26243   Alice Francis Wiser (7 Apr 1913, TN-27 Sep 1993) m 16 Dec 1939, William Fermon Davenport (4 Jul 1915-12 Feb 1989).

PW26244   James Robert ("J. R.") Wiser (4 Jul 1915, TN-11 Mar 1994) m 29 Mar 1941, Addie Riddle (b 13 Jan 1914).

PW262441   Theresa Wiser (b 6 Feb 1942) m Robbie Frame (b 21 Feb 1939).

PW262442   Mary Helen Wiser (b 24 Aug 1944) m Wendle Stokes (b 24 May 1939).

PW262443   Lucy Jane Wiser (b 31 Jul 1946, TN) m 3 Oct 1975, Coffee TN, Charles Roy Deal (b 21 Jan 1945, TN).

PW262444   Robert Andrew Wiser (b 6 Aug 1948, TN) m 5 Mar 1971, Coffee TN, Sheila Annette Woodward (b 15 Mar 1947, TN).

PW2624441   Greyson Wiser (b 26 Jan 1978).

PW2624442   Stephanie Andrea Wiser (b 19 May 1980).

PW2624443   Matthew Wiser (b 2 Oct 1986).

PW262445   Doris Fay Wiser (b 27 Oct 1952, TN) m 28 Dec 1973, Terry Michael Hines (b 30 Jan 1947, TN).

PW262446   Claude Edward Wiser (b 22 Nov 1954, TN) m 25 Aug 1979, Coffee TN, Debra May Rogers (b 7 Feb 1955, TN).

PW26245   David Cissrow Wiser (29 Jul 1918, TN-25 Jan 1991) m 24 Dec 1941, Maggie Ovalee Scott (b 7 Apr 1923).

PW262451   Carolyn Sue Wiser (b 20 Sep 1943) m 1) 10 Mar 1962, Paul W. Dotson; m 2) Nolen McGregor (b 18 May 1932).

PW262452   Jerry Martin Wiser (b 14 Mar 1945) m Alice Jewel Jones (b 25 Jun 1947).

PW2624521   Jill Ann Wiser (b 14 Oct 1966) m Stanley Phillips (b 16 Aug 1962).

PW2624522   Janet Lee Wiser (b 11 Oct 1969) m Ricky Phillips (b 23 Apr 1966).

PW262453   Carl Thomas Wiser (b 12 Sep 1946) m 16 Dec 1967, Brenda G. Adams (b 5 Feb 1947).

PW2624531   Carla Gail Wiser (b 30 Dec 1968) m Danny Catignanni.

PW2624532   Wendy Lynn Wiser (b 17 Mar 1972).

PW262454   Wanda Grace Wiser (b 17 Jul 1948) m 1) 28 May 1967, Jairon D. Spencer; m 2) Chester Sullivans (b 10 Jan 1942).

PW262455   Johnny William Wiser (19 Nov 1949-19 Nov 1949).

PW26246   Thomas Allen Wiser (29 Sep 1920-14 Jan 1989, Manchester TN) m Clara Throneberry (b 14 Feb 1929).

PW262461   Brenda Wiser (b 22 Nov 1949).

PW262462   Bianca Wiser (b 24 Jun 1954) m Druie Shelton (b 26 Aug 1952).

PW262463   Allen Lynn Wiser (b 19 Jun 1960, TN) m 1) 14 Dec 1977, Coffee TN, Pamela Joy Frazier (b ca 1959, IL); m 2) Kathy Simmons.

PW2624631   Tommy Wiser (b 10 Nov 1978).

PW2624632   Eric Wiser (b 2 Sep 1979).

PW2624633   Mindy Wiser (b 18 Jan 1982).

PW262464   Sheila Wiser (b 14 Apr 1965) m 1) Jeff Bush; m 2) Greg Sheets.

PW26247   Arlie Jean Wiser (4 Jan 1923-8 Jan 1985) m Howard Collins (b 13 Jun 1904).

PW26248   Anna Lou Wiser (6 Jul 1925-20 Oct 1981) m Ewell Zumbro (29 Mar 1911-14 Jun 1978).

PW26249   Wilbur Lee Arie Wiser (b 4 Jun 1929) m 25 Oct 1958, Francis J. Talley (b 31 Dec 1932).

PW262491   Jimmy Wiser (b 29 Jul 1964).

PW2625   Mary Wiser m William Banks.

PW2626   Josie Francis Wiser (1885, TN-1958) m 26 Dec 1905, A. L. Haley.

PW2627   Lucy E. Wiser (b 18 Jul 1890, TN) m James Stephens.

PW2628   James Harvey Wiser (21 Sep 1893, TN-29 Sep 1970, Manchester TN) m 1) 12 Dec 1915, Matty (Mollie) Fletcher (8 Dec 1891-17 Mar 1916); m 2) Dec 1916, Leota Morton (9 Sep 1896, TN-19 Jun 1954).

PW26281   Lorene Wiser (4 Mar 1916, TN-15 Aug 1990) m 9 Aug 1939, Horace McMahan (b ca 1919).

PW26282   Louis Hoyt Wiser (b 21 Sep 1918, TN) m 23 Mar 1940, Helen Ione Brown (b 19 Jun 1920).

PW262821   Patricia Lee Wiser (b 9 Jun 1941) m 14 Jun 1976, Gordon Eugene Lee (b ca 1933, TX).

PW262822   Louis Hoyt Wiser Jr. (b 1 Nov 1942, Coffee TN) m Barbara Gayle Robins (b 18 Oct 1944).

PW2628221   David Robins Wiser (b 5 Dec 1968, Coffee TN).

PW2628222   Derek Lee Wiser (b 1 Nov 1973, Humphries TN).

PW2629   Nancy Delilah Ann Wiser (b Jul 1897, TN) m 24 Mar 1918, Solomon Thomas Peek.

PW262A   David Wiser.

PW263   Thomas Daniel Wiser (20 Jul 1844, Coffee TN-Mar 1880) m 21 Nov 1867, Coffee TN, Rebecca Jane Thacker (11 Oct 1849, Coffee TN-10 Mar 1902).

PW2631   William Wiser (ca 1868, TN-4 Jul 1891, Coffee TN).

PW2632   Mary Lee (Mollie) Wiser (27 Oct 1870, TN-19 Jun 1953) m 16 Feb 1897, George Byrom (11 Mar 1858-9 Mar 1915).

PW2633   Jacob Thomas Hamilton Wiser (22 Oct 1872, Coffee TN-15 Aug 1939, Mt. View, Coffee TN) m 22 Feb 1903, Francis G. Blanton (30 Jan 1884, Coffee TN-18 Jul 1943, Coffee TN).

PW26331   William Alfred Wiser (9 Mar 1904, TN-7 Apr 1959) m 5 Sep 1925, Penny Irene Charles (12 Oct 1908-13 Sep 1986).

PW263311   Frances Elizabeth Wiser (9 Mar 1928-26 May 1996) m James Howard Huddleston (b 5 Jan 1913).

PW263312   Wilma Dean Wiser (b 26 Dec 1929) m 2 Jun 1949, John Louis Lassiter (b 16 Oct 1928).

PW263313   Herman Alfred Wiser (14 Nov 1931-Jun 1981, Nashville TN).

PW2633131   Rebecca Starr Wiser (b 17 Jan 1953) m James Albert Summer.

PW2633132   Freddie Ray Wiser (Nov 1954-Jan 1955).

PW263314   Jewel Mae Wiser (b 20 Nov 1933) m Charles Thomas Smartt (b 2 Jan 1929).

PW263315   Rebecca Louise Wiser (b 5 Jun 1939) m Robert Wright Peay (b 4 May 1929).

PW263316   John Clayton Wiser (b 4 Jan 1943) m Emily Marie Taylor (25 Nov 1942).

PW2633161   Jacqueline Kay Wiser (b 15 Jun 1962).

PW2633162   Deborah Diane Wiser (b 22 Sep 1963).

PW263317   Barbara Ann Wiser (b 17 Dec 1944) m 1)   Harrell; m 2) Jackie Allen Livesay.

PW263318   Leighton Clyde Wiser (b 2 Dec 1948) m Mildred ("Teedee") Hossler (b 26 Jan 1950).

PW2633181   Jenny Lynn Wiser.

PW2633182   Tommy Wiser.

PW2633183   Jimmy Wise.

PW26332   Mary Elizabeth Wiser (11 Feb 1906, TN-21 Apr 1985) m 29 Apr 1933, Franklin Pierce Ogle.

PW26333   Thelma Rebecca Wiser (21 Jun 1908, TN-4 Apr 1944) m 12 Nov 1932, Joe Edgar Aughinbaugh (2 Jul 1899-29 Apr 1960).

PW26334   Leonard Thomas Wiser (25 Mar 1910, TN-9 Nov 1984, Manchester TN) m Lillie Brandon (23 May 1903-5 Sep 1990).

PW26335   John Wilson Wiser (12 Jan 1913, Coffee TN-12 May 1986, McMinnville TN) m 3 May 1941, Mamie Magdalene Reynolds (b 3 Mar 1917, Warren TN).

PW263351   Jerry Wayne Wiser (26 Sep 1945, Warren TN-26 Sep 1945, Warren TN).

PW263352   Linda Janell Wiser (b 9 Jan 1951) m 7 Jun 1969, Larry Steven Sharpe (b 18 Feb 1949).

PW263353   Darrell Lynn Wiser (b 9 Oct 1957).

PW26336   Bernice Mae Wiser (b 19 Jul 1915, TN) m 31 Aug 1935, Charles Thomas Lafevor (27 Jun 1915-22 Dec 1983).

PW26337   Charles Edwin Wiser (26 Apr 1917, TN-14 Dec 1965) m Annie Bell Broadrick (b 13 Mar 1924).

PW263371   Kenneth Edwin Wiser (b 3 Jul 1946) m Carol   .

PW2633711   Phillip Wiser.

PW263372   Oral Dwight Wiser (b 16 Aug 1948) m Jan   .

PW263373   Dennis Wiser (b 21 Jan 1954) m Diane   .

PW26338   Alma Ruth Wiser (b 19 Jul 1921, TN) m 10 Jun 1939, Delter Ray Davenport (4 Sep 1908-21 Aug 1985).

PW2634   Nancy Virginia ("Birdie") Wiser (b ca 1875, TN) m 1 Jan 1901, James Riley Hodge.

PW2635   James Tilden Wiser (16 Sep 1876, Manchester TN-10 Apr 1964) m Lavada Bowden (21 Jan 1886, Manchester TN-4 Feb 1964).

PW26351   Fred C. Wiser (10 Sep 1907, TN-1 May 1995) m 1) 12 Feb 1928, Hazel D. Carroll (13 Apr 1908, Coffee TN-30 Dec 1967, McMinnville TN); m 2) 22 Jun 1968, Elizabeth W. Freeze (2 Feb 1902-Jun 1976).

PW263511   Joan Wiser.

PW263512   Helen Wiser.

PW263513   Fred C. Wiser Jr.

PW263514   Harold Wiser.

PW263515   Gary Wiser.

PW263516   Jerry Dow Wiser (1939-1939).

PW26352   Golden Bowden Wiser (b 20 Jun 1911, Manchester TN).

PW26353   J. T. Wiser (1912, TN-1964) m Polly A.   (b 1922).

PW26354   Thomas Baxter ("Jack") Wiser (26 Mar 1915, TN-17 Nov 1970) m 23 Dec 1934, Minnie P. Williams (1913-1996).

PW263541   Donald Wiser.

PW263542   Daughter Wiser m Billy Jarrell.

PW263543   Edward Austin Wiser (2 Aug 1939, Coffee TN-23 Jan 1963) m 20 Sep 1958, Manchester TN, Barbara Dean Farris (b ca 1939, Coffee TN).

PW263544   Paulette Wiser (b ca 1942, TN) m James Houston Thompson (b ca 1941, TN).

PW26355   John William Wiser (23 Nov 1918, Coffee TN-22 May 1972, Coffee TN) m 2 Jun 1940, Marselle Baltimore (15 Jan 1916-Feb 1989, Coffee TN).

PW263551   Daughter Wiser m Wayne Reynolds.

PW26356   Louise Mae Wiser (5 May 1922, TN-8 Nov 1922, Coffee TN).

PW26357   Mattie Jane Wiser (b ca 1925) m 24 Jul 1948, Alvis Owen West (b ca 1927).

PW26358   Howard A. Wiser (1 Sep 1926-4 Mar 1967).

PW264   David Poke Wiser (26 Mar 1847, TN-21 Sep 1925).

PW265   Mary Emeline Wiser (b 4 Jun 1850, TN) m   Lusk.

PW266   Louisa C. Wiser (b 4 Jun 1850, TN) m 29 Nov 1870, Coffee TN, George B. Duncan.

PW267   Nancy A. Wiser (b 10 Nov 1853, TN) m 2 Oct 1876, Coffee TN, John T. Roper (21 Jun 1852, Cherokee GA-6 Nov 1906, Hillsboro TN).

PW268   Eliza Wiser (b 31 Jan 1858, TN).

PW27   William Wiser (29 Jan 1815, TN-5 Aug 1868, Coffee TN) m 27 Nov 1843, Cannon TN, Violet Parker (ca 1823, TN-27 Apr 1897, Coffee TN).

PW271   Mary Ann Wiser (b ca 1845, TN).

PW272   Sarah Wiser (ca 1847, TN-Jan 1860, Coffee TN).

PW273   Newton Jasper Wiser (b Jan 1848, TN).

PW274   Caminza Jane Wiser (b 2 Mar 1850, TN) m 25 Aug 1870, Charles Calvin Trail (21 May 1848-29 Oct 1929).

PW275   Matilda C. Wiser (b ca 1853, TN) m 30 Dec 1885, Coffee TN, A. J. Crosslin (b ca 1845, Coffee TN).

PW276   Louise Wiser (b ca 1857, TN).

PW277   Tennessee E. Wiser (ca Aug 1859, TN-7 Aug 1949).

PW278   William H. Wiser (1860, TN-1926) m 25 Sep 1883, Anna S. Jacobs (1 Sep 1861, Coffee TN-26 Sep 1934, Coffee TN).

PW2781   Josie Lee Wiser (5 Jan 1885, TN-5 Feb 1958) m Alexander Marion Jacobs (1879-1968).

PW2782   Esther D. Wiser (23 May 1886, TN-1 Feb 1951) m James Riley Floyd (7 Jun 1882-6 Sep 1936, Coffee TN).

PW2783   Boss W. Wiser (15 May 1892, TN-26 Dec 1967) m Winnie Perry (29 May 1892, Bridgeport MI-4 May 1965).

PW27831   Boss Wiser Jr. (18 Apr 1921-13 Nov 1982, Beechgrove, Coffee TN).

PW27832   Evelyn Wiser (26 Jul 1925, Coffee TN-20 May 1939).

David Wiser

Except for his father's will, the first record of David Wiser is the bond issued in Cabarrus County on 17 March 1803 for his marriage to Ruth Chamberlin. Unlike his brothers, he seems to have remained in North Carolina for several years after his father's death, perhaps to settle the estate. By 1805, he was in Cumberland County, Kentucky with his brother John, but he seems to have stayed there longer than John did, still owning property there as late as 1824. He seems to have been in Bedford County, Tennessee for a short time before settling in 1824 in a part of White County that became Putnam County in 1842.

David does not seem to have prospered as much as his brothers, and he only had one son (none of his three daughters married); the result was that the family did not grow the way the others did. Eventually, the only descendants with the name Wiser left the area, and only a few descendants remain. Like the other families, money was not wasted on carved gravestones, and a cemetery that remains identified with the Wiser family has no readable stones.[162]

PW3   David Wiser (b ca 1766, NC) m 17 Mar 1803, Cabarrus NC Ruth Chamberlin. Cabarrus NC, Cumberland KY and White TN.

PW31   Susanna Wiser (b ca 1803, KY).

PW32   Rebecca Wiser (b ca 1806, KY).

PW33   David Wiser (ca 1807, KY-ca 1865, Putnam TN) m Eleanor Ladermon (b ca 1810, NC). White and Putnam TN.

PW331   Mary M. Wiser (b ca 1831, TN).

PW332   John L. Wiser (b ca 1834, TN).

PW333   W. C. Wiser (b ca 1836, TN).

PW334   Levina Wiser (b ca 1838, TN) m E. G. ("Gehaz") Reynolds.

PW335   Sarah F. Wiser (ca 1840, TN).

PW336   James Madison Wiser (23 Jan 1842, White TN-18 Jul 1923) m 1) Mary Elizabeth Rockwell (b Aug 1844, TN); m 2) Rebecca   (b ca 1850, TN). Putnam TN and Clay MO.

PW3361   Harvey D. Wiser (Feb 1866, TN-1952, Owosso MI) m ca 1884, Elizabeth   (b Mar 1865, TN). Putnam and Jackson TN and Owosso MI.

PW33611   Minnie L. Wiser (b Mar 1885, TN) m   Barnes.

---

[162]Information on the family of David Wiser was assembled by Michael Boniol of Crossville TN.

PW33612   Lillie D. Wiser (b Oct 1889, TN).

PW33613   Edwin C. Wiser (b Sep 1891, TN).

PW33614   Verna E. Wiser (b Jul 1893, TN).

PW33615   Jesse Allen Wiser (19 May 1898, TN-Sep 1972, Owosso MI) m 14 Dec 1916, Putnam TN,
Lydia Stewart.

PW33616   Robert Dennis Wiser (b Feb 1900, TN) m 13 Mar 1919, Putnam TN, Alma Ellis (b ca
1900, TN).

PW33617   Lola B. Wiser (b ca 1904, TN).

PW3362   Fredona Wiser (ca 1868, TN-1952) m Alexander Steelmon (1865-1953).

PW3363   Mary Wiser (b ca 1873, TN).

PW3364   Sarah Wiser (b ca 1879, TN).

PW3365   Thomas Franklin Wiser (13 Jun 1886, TN-Jan 1968, Malheur OR) m 1) 19 Jun 1910,
Putnam TN, Naomi Reynolds (b 3 Jan 1892, Putnam TN); m 2) Della   . Putnam TN and Fremont ID.

PW33651   Clara Lillian Wiser (b 9 May 1911, ID) m Ernest Rupert Kaneafter.

PW33652   Eugene Pierre Wiser (b 6 Sep 1912, ID) m Emily Steinman.

PW33653   Edward Jackson Wiser (b 7 May 1914, ID) m Idaho Falls ID, Elizabeth Jane Ostermiller
(b 20 Dec 1914, Newark NJ).

PW33654   Hazel Irene Wiser (b 5 Jul 1916, ID) m Warren Lewis Powell.

PW33655   James Lee Wiser (b 8 Apr 1918, Fremont ID).

PW33656   Helen Louise Wiser (b 18 Feb 1920, ID).

PW33657   Ruby Beverly Wiser (b 9 Sep 1922, ID).

PW33658   Ruth Bernice Wiser (b 5 Sep 1924, ID) m George Anthony Humble (10 Feb 1919-30 May
1996).

PW337   David Mitchell Wiser (ca 1844, TN-1883) m Mary E.   (b ca 1845, TN). Putnam TN.

PW3371   Henry D. Wiser (b ca 1866, TN).

PW3372   Fredona Wiser (b ca 1869, TN).

PW338   Eliza J. Wiser (b ca 1846, TN).

PW34   Narcissus ("Sissy") Wiser (b ca 1809, TN).

CHAPTER TWENTY-ONE

[HW]   Harmon Wiser (Harman Kreydenwys) (1769-1832)
of Albany County, New York and his descendants

Henderick Kreydenwys arrived in New York around 1759, married Rachel Campbell and settled near Ballston Spa in a part of Albany County which is now Saratoga County. He is supposed to have emigrated from Holland, and family notes indicate that his home was on the Rhine River.

Henderick served in the Revolution in the 12th Albany County Regiment under Colonel Jacobus Van Schoonhoven. It seems during that time that there were some problems with the spelling of the name, and the papers of the regiment list him as Henry Crydenwiser or Craydenwiser.

Henderick and Rachel are known to have had seven children, most of whom were baptized at the Dutch Reformed Church in Schenectady. Harmanus Kreydenwys was baptized on 5 April 1769. As the children grew up various spellings were used, but Harmanus eventually changed the name he used to Harmon Wiser. The other children retained names like Crydenwise.

Harmon and his first wife settled first in Milford in Otsego County, New York, where they were reported as Herman Wiser and family in the 1800 Census. He and his second wife were identified as H. Crydin and family in Middlefield, Otsego County in the 1810 Census, but in 1811 the family moved to Clarence Hollow in what was then Niagara County but is now Erie County. They were listed there in the 1820 Census as Harmon Crydenwise and family.

Finally, they moved in 1822 to Crawford County, Pennsylvania where the 1830 Census lists Harmon Wiser and family. Harmon died on 21 September 1832 and is buried in Linesville. Some of the family still live nearby in Ashtabula County, Ohio, but most of them moved farther away and are now scattered throughout the country. While there is a general belief that the Weiser and Wiser families in the United States are somehow related, this family by its origin is clearly not related to the others.[163]

HW   Harmon Wiser (13 Mar 1769, Albany NY-21 Sep 1832, Linesville PA) m 1) Eunice St. John; m 2) Mary Elizabeth Gallup (14 Mar 1783, Pownal VT-14 Aug 1855, Crawford PA). Otsego and Niagara NY. Crawford PA.

HW1   Abraham S. Wiser (1799, NY-30 Mar 1869, South Palmyra, Macoupin IL) m ca 1825, Crawford PA, Rachel Burwell (ca 1810, PA-6 Jul 1873, South Palmyra, Macoupin IL). Macoupin IL.

HW11   Hiram Wiser (b ca 1827, PA) m 16 Jan 1853, Pike IL, Della Gray (b ca 1834).
Sacramento CA.

HW111   Helen Jane Wiser (b ca 1854, IL) m 6 Apr 1873, Sacramento CA, Archibald Stewart.

HW112   Rachel A. Wiser (b ca 1856, IL).

HW113   Asenith P. Wiser (b ca 1858, IL).

HW114   Floy Wiser (15 Jul 1860, IL-15 Jul 1860, Macoupin IL).

HW115   Flora Wiser (b ca 1863).

HW116   Henry Wiser (b ca 1863).

---

[163]The list of descendants in this chapter has been limited to those with the surname Wiser and their spouses. Most of the information in this chapter was provided by Clem M. Wiser of Palo Alto, California. Additional material has been obtained from Laura S. Schnell of Milo, Maine, Brenda Jo Wiser of Ashtabula County, Ohio, Rosalie Hamilton of Fort Wayne, Indiana and Merald Wiser of Ashland, Ohio. Census data has been added by Edward Wiser, who also edited it into the present form.

HW12   Hannah Ann Wiser (ca 1832-ca 1868) m   Neighbert.

HW13   Harmon Walter Wiser (5 Nov 1836, PA-10 Mar 1906, Macoupin IL) m Deborah Jane
Strawmatt (27 Nov 1843, IL- 5 Dec 1922, Macoupin IL). Macoupin IL.

HW131   John Henry Wiser (1 Nov 1860, IL-20 Dec 1935) m 27 Apr 1885, Jewell KS, Emma
Privet (11 Aug 1866-11 Jun 1933).

HW1311   Henry Wiser (b Aug 1886, KS).

HW1312   Ora Wiser (b Jan 1890, KS).

HW1313   Hazel Wiser (b Jun 1892, KS).

HW1314   Rhoda Wiser (b Feb 1894, KS).

HW1315   Thomas Wiser (b Aug 1895, OK).

HW1316   Wilma Wiser (b Dec 1897, OK).

HW1317   Glenn Wiser (30 Jul 1902, OK-Jul 1966, Macoupin IL).

HW1318   Dale Wiser (18 Apr 1906, OK-Jul 1969, Carter MO).

HW1319   Velma Wiser (b ca 1909, OK).

HW131A   Eva Wiser (b ca 1913, IL).

HW132   Rhoda J. Wiser (10 Aug 1862, IL- 8 Jan 1936).

HW133   L. Ann Wiser (1865, IL-1887) m 4 Apr 1883, Palmyra IL, Eleazer T. Beatty.

HW134   Thomas H. Wiser (Dec 1867, IL-1943).

HW135   Hiram Wiser (b ca 1868, IL) m Melvina ("Vine") Lamar (b Jan 1876, IL). Custer OK and
Independence KS.

HW1351   Elva Wiser (b Mar 1894, IL).

HW1352   Oral Wiser (20 Jun 1895, IL-Apr 1970, Temple, Cotton OK).

HW136   Abraham St. John Wiser (1 Jul 1870, Palmyra IL-27 Feb 1946, Carlinville IL) m Esther
Jane Lyle (13 Jan 1872, TN-17 Jul 1957). Macoupin IL.

HW1361   Roena V. Wiser (8 Nov 1893, IL-16 Jun 1986) m 12 Sep 1912, Joseph D. Proctor.

HW1362   Mildred Irene Wiser (18 Mar 1895, IL-26 Apr 1930) m 24 Sep 1921, Owen Miller.

HW1363   Martha Eulah Wiser (17 Oct 1897, IL-8 Jun 1988) m 14 Jan 1928, Martin Diefenback.

HW1364   William Glenn Wiser (28 May 1899, IL-10 Apr 1956) m 15 Jan 1927, Arra Dell Dyer.

HW13641   Della Jane Wiser.

HW13642   Eulah Joyce Wiser.

HW13643   Edna Mae Wiser.

HW1365   Victor Lyle Wiser (6 May 1901, IL-18 Jan 1984, Granite City IL) m 29 Sep 1927, Ruth Hopper.

HW13651   Leonard Eugene Wiser.

HW13652   Ellen Wiser.

HW13653   Robert Wiser.

HW13654   Norma Wiser.

HW13655   Stanley Wiser.

HW13656   Herbert Wiser.

HW13657   Mary Wiser.

HW13658   Ruth Wiser.

HW13659   Ruby Wiser.

HW1365A   Raymond Wiser.

HW1365B   Martha Wiser.

HW1365C   William Wiser.

HW137   Melinda Wiser (3 Dec 1873, IL-18 Mar 1936) m Isaac Allen Hodges.

HW138   Laura Ellen Wiser (b 1875, IL) m 18 Apr 1894, Palmyra IL, George Robert Walker.

HW139   S. Arthur Austin Wiser (12 Mar 1879, IL-6 Jun 1933, Macoupin IL) m ca 1904, Stella J. Lloyd (1888, IL-1956. Macoupin IL.

HW1391   Lloyd Wiser (22 Jan 1905, IL-Dec 1962.

HW1392   Infant Wiser (16 Jul 1906, IL-16 Jul 1906, Macoupin IL).

HW1393   Velma Wiser (b ca 1908, IL).

HW1394   Faye Wiser (b ca 1911, IL).

HW1395   Pearl Wiser (1915, IL).

HW1396   Melvin Wiser (b 1919, IL).

HW13A   Walter Harmon Wiser (23 Nov 1883, IL-4 Dec 1950, Macoupin IL) m Sarah L. Norton (1885, IL-1961, Macoupin IL). Macoupin IL.

HW13A1   Anna S. Wiser (b ca 1907, IL).

HW13A2   Nellie J. Wiser (b ca 1908, IL).

HW13A3   Dorothy Wiser (b ca 1911, IL).

HW13A4   George Wiser (26 Jan 1913, IL-28 Jan 1993, Palmyra IL).

HW13A5   Ernest Wiser (29 Aug 1917, IL-11 Jun 1992, Waverly, Morgan IL).

HW14   Mary Rebecca Wiser (15 Apr 1839, Macoupin IL- 4 Sep 1907, Palmyra IL) m 9 Mar 1856, Prosper Miller Johnson (16 Dec 1838, Albany ME-24 Feb 1927, Macoupin IL).

HW15   Rhoda I. Wiser (ca 1842, Macoupin IL-1852, Macoupin IL).

HW16   Aseneth Arvilla Wiser (b 25 Jun 1844, Macoupin IL) m George W. Scouten (b ca 1842, IL).

HW17   Abraham J. Wiser (b Mar 1847, Macoupin IL) m ca 1867, Dorothy C.   (b Jan 1848, IL). Jewell KS and Custer OK.

HW171   Ida A. Wiser (b ca 1868, IL).

HW172   Lorena Wiser (b ca Feb 1870, IL).

HW173   Sylvester Wiser (b ca 1872, IL).

HW174   May Wiser (b ca 1875, IL).

HW175   Isaac William Wiser (b Dec 1876, IL).

HW176   Ira Lawrence Wiser (b Sep 1879, IL) m Myrtle   (b ca 1881, KS).

HW1761   Roland Wiser (b ca 1907, OK).

HW1762   Max Wiser (b ca 1912, OK).

HW1763   Devert Wiser (b ca Jan 1920, KS).

HW177   Artimus A. Wiser (27 Jan 1882, KS-Apr 1971, Riley KS) m Lucy I. Chaney (b ca 1884, KS). Cloud KS.

HW1771   Clarence A. Wiser (b ca 1910, OK).

HW178   Ada O. Wiser (b Sep 1884, KS).

HW179   Roy E. Wiser (b Mar 1887, KS).

HW18   Isaac B. Wiser (Jun 1850, Macoupin IL-1862, Macoupin IL).

HW19   Rachel Elizabeth Wiser (15 Jun 1852, Macoupin IL-4 Oct 1912) m 24 Nov 1870, Macoupin IL, William E. Vaughan (b 22 Mar 1849).

HW2   Rachel Wiser (b ca 1800, Otsego NY).

HW3   Harmon Wiser (b ca 1802, Otsego NY).

HW4   Henry Wiser (30 Jun 1806, Otsego NY-1887, Jennings, Crawford IN) m Lucretia Head (ca 1811, NY-1862, Jennings, Crawford IN). Crawford IN.

HW41   Benjamin Franklin Wiser (b Jun 1830, Crawford PA) m 1) Sarah M. Beedle (1833, NY-26 Jul 1862, Linesville PA); m 2) 1869, Linesville PA, Mary Jane Allen (b Apr 1841, Crawford PA). Crawford

PA and Decatur KS.

HW411 Sylvania Wiser (b ca 1853, Linesville PA) m 2 Mar 1876, George Hughes.

HW412 Frank Clayton Wiser (22 Jan 1870, Lineville PA- 3 Feb 1955, North Hollywood CA) m Bertha Easley (b Apr 1874, KS). Physician, Falls City NE.

HW4121 Nellie E. Wiser (b May 1896, NE).

HW4122 Joseph A. Wiser.

HW41221 Lavon Wiser.

HW42 Henry Wiser (b ca 1831, Crawford PA).

HW43 Mary Wiser (29 Feb 1832, Conneaut, Crawford PA-23 Nov 1915) m 23 Aug 1849, Crawford PA, Solomon Oats (ca 1826, PA-1893, Summit, Crawford PA).

HW44 Eunice Wiser (b ca 1833, PA).

HW45 Filetta Wiser (11 Oct 1835, Crawford PA- 8 Mar 1898) m 2 Jul 1852, Crawford PA, Amos L. Gilliland (1832, PA-1901).

HW46 Eliza Jane Wiser (b ca 1837, Crawford PA) m 25 Jan 1855, Crawford PA, Isaiah B. Henry (b ca 1833, PA).

HW47 Mary Anne Wiser (b ca 1840, Crawford PA) m 10 Mar 1859, Crawford PA, Elisha Henry Patrick (b ca 1836, IN).

HW48 Rachel Wiser (b ca 1842, Crawford PA) m 18 Apr 1861, Crawford IN, Henry Andrew Rothrock.

HW49 Elmira Wiser (b ca 1844, PA) m 20 Nov 1864, Crawford IN, Paul Strickland.

HW4A Levi Wiser (b Oct 1843, Crawford PA) m 1) Lynch; m 2) Sarah S. (b Aug 1839, OH). Crawford IN.

HW4A1 Levi Wiser (b ca 1879, IN).

HW4B Asa Wiser (b Sep 1849, Crawford PA) m 17 May 1874, Crawford IN, Margaret Melcome (b ca 1850, IN). Crawford IN.

HW4B1 Albert Wiser (b May 1875, IN).

HW4B2 Mary Wiser (b ca 1877, IN).

HW4B3 Anna Wiser (b ca 1879, IN).

HW4B4 Ettie Wiser (b Aug 1880, IN).

HW4B5 Lola Wiser (b Jan 1884, IN).

HW4B6 Sarah Wiser (b Feb 1888, IN).

HW4B7 Willoughby Wiser (b Feb 1890, IN).

HW4C   Solomon Wiser (b ca 1853, PA) m Sarah J.   (b Dec 1853, IN). Crawford IN.

HW4C1   Mona L. Wiser (b Jan 1881, IN) m   Duckman.

HW4C2   William Don Wiser (b Apr 1885, IN).

HW5   Hiram Gallup Wiser (1807, Otsego NY-1882, Bethel, Branch MI) m 15 Sep 1828, Clarence NY, Mary Bates (13 Nov 1810, Newsted, Erie NY-15 Jan 1897, Bethel, Branch MI). Branch MI.

HW51   Eunice Wiser (b 12 Jul 1832, Clarence NY) m 6 May 1858, Branch MI, Charles Segur.

HW52   Levi Sanford Wiser (24 Jul 1834, Clarence NY-24 Jul 1910, Branch MI) m 15 Apr 1857, Branch MI, Mary E. Barnes (1839, MI-1896). Branch MI.

HW521   Traverse L. Wiser (Apr 1859, Branch MI-25 Dec 1868, Bronson MI).

HW522   Hiram Lewis Wiser (b 19 Apr 1863, MI) m 6 Aug 1882, Branch MI, Edith A. Miner (b Jun 1866, MI). Branch MI.

HW5221   Bernard F. Wiser (b Jul 1884, MI) m Gertie   (b ca 1889, MI).

HW52211   Jessie Wiser (b ca 1907, MI).

HW52212   Ola Wiser (b ca 1908, MI).

HW52213   Urban Wiser (b ca 1911, MI).

HW52214   Eloise Wiser (b ca 1914, MI).

HW52215   Eva Wiser (b ca 1916, MI).

HW52216   Edith Wiser (b ca Feb 1919, MI).

HW5222   Leo Wiser (b Feb 1888, MI).

HW523   Violet A. Wiser (b ca 1865, MI).

HW524   Chauncy Lucius Wiser (Dec 1865, Branch MI-25 Dec 1878, Bethel MI).

HW525   Hugh G. Wiser (b Jan 1868, MI) m Eunice G.   (b May 1870, MI). Branch MI.

HW5251   Alva Gerald Wiser (23 Mar 1891, MI-May 1966, MI) m Lottie Wiser (14 Nov 1897, MI-Feb 1970, Branch MI). Branch MI.

HW52511   Lloyd Wiser (b ca Mar 1920, MI).

HW526   Ira Wiser (b Apr 1869, MI).

HW527   Eva Wiser (b ca 1874, MI).

HW528   Lottie Wiser (b ca 1877, MI).

HW53   Elizabeth Wiser (Sep 1835, Bethel, Branch MI-26 Oct 1879, Branch MI) m Isaac Rupright (Apr 1835, OH-6 Dec 1890, Branch MI).

HW54   Alonzo Hollister Wiser (Feb 1839, Bethel, Branch MI-1923, Branch MI) m 15 Jun 1862,

Branch MI, Lucina Minerva Larabee (b Oct 1842, MI). Branch MI.

HW541   Lennie A. Wiser (b Feb 1868, MI-1935) m Jennie   (b ca 1874).

HW542   David C. Wiser (b Oct 1874, MI) m Lenna C.   (b ca 1880, MI).

HW5421   Rex H. Wiser (2 Jun 1909, MI-May 1987, Branch MI).

HW5422   Carol Wiser (b ca 1912, MI).

HW55   Mary Anne Wiser (b 1841, Bethel, Branch MI) m 10 Mar 1860, Branch MI, Winard Van Gilder.

HW56   Amanda S. Wiser (b 1843, Bethel, Branch MI) m 8 Apr 1866, Branch MI, George W. Jules.

HW6   Asa Gallup Wiser (12 Mar 1809, Otsego NY-14 Jun 1845, Crawford PA) m 16 Jun 1830, Crawford PA, Anna Mary Bennett (ca 1809, Shenango, Crawford PA- 4 Mar 1882, Linesville PA). Crawford PA.

HW61   Fidelia Wiser (30 Mar 1831, Linesville PA-28 Mar 1910, Erie PA) m 15 Apr 1849, Crawford PA, Levi Dudley (27 Nov 1829, NY-2 Nov 1921).

HW62   Harmon Wiser (1832, Linesville PA-Mar 1837, Linesville PA).

HW63   Sarah Ann Wiser (22 May 1834, Crawford PA-20 Dec 1915) m 24 Nov 1852, Linesville PA, Isaac Litwiler (14 Aug 1833-Nov 1918).

HW64   Marie Antoinette Wiser (Jun 1836, Crawford PA-1877, Summit, Crawford PA) m Terrill.

HW65   Cathcrine Wiser (7 Sep 1838, Pine, Crawford PA-3 Oct 1901, Thetford MI) m 29 Jan 1857, Hiram Bishop (13 Feb 1833, Pine, Crawford PA-16 May 1928, Saginaw MI).

HW66   Ellen Wiser (b ca 1841, PA).

HW67   Harvey Wiser (b ca 1845, PA).

HW7   Eunice Wiser (b 2 Jun 1810, Otsego NY).

HW8   Elias B. Wiser (5 Dec 1812, Clarence Hollow, Erie NY-ca 1868, Linesville PA) m 1838, Crawford PA, Mary Elizabeth Slocum (b 2 Oct 1816, Monkton VT). Crawford PA.

HW81   Samuel E. Wiser (8 Jun 1839, Pine, Crawford PA-2 Mar 1907, Decatur IL) m ca 1860, Linesville PA, Laura Amanda Foote (b Aug 1840, PA). Crawford PA and Macon IL.

HW811   John M. Wiser (b Dec 1861, Linesville PA).

HW812   Lena E. Wiser (b ca 1863, PA).

HW813   William Wiser (b ca 1867, PA).

HW814   Laura Wiser.

HW815   Leroy Elliott Wiser (29 Oct 1881, Mattoon IL-12 Jul 1955, Los Angeles CA) m 26 Nov 1902, Decatur IL, Mary Ellen Schmink (20 May 1883, Decatur IL-12 Jul 1955, Los Angeles CA). Macon IL.

HW8151   Edith Mae Wiser (30 Nov 1904, Decatur IL- 9 Mar 1966) m 11 Nov 1922, Decatur IL, James Hubert Burgess.

HW8152   Samuel Leroy Wiser (26 Oct 1906, Decatur IL-13 Feb 1978) m ca 1943, Margaret   .

HW8153   Wynona Clarissa Wiser (b 6 Dec 1909, Oklahoma City OK) m 4 Nov 1928, Bloomington IL, Harold Winfred Kerny.

HW8154   Kenneth Barnett Wiser (13 Oct 1911, Decatur IL-8 May 1914, Decatur IL).

HW8155   Caroline Lanell Wiser (28 Oct 1913, Decatur IL-24 Mar 1975) m 20 Apr 1929, Cecile Higdon.

HW8156   Augusta Jewell Wiser (b 7 May 1917, Decatur IL) m 19 Dec 1936, Wilmer Gasaway.

HW8157   Elizabeth Rachel Wiser (b 24 May 1921, Decatur IL).

HW82   Harmon Levi Wiser (8 Jun 1839, Pine, Crawford PA-22 Apr 1927, Denmark, Ashtabula
OH) m 1) Mary   ; m 2) Mary Elizabeth Frey (11 Jun 1842-6 Sep 1865, Crawford PA). Crawford PA and
Ashtabula OH.

HW821   James M. Wiser (Mar 1860, Crawford PA-Sep 1865, Crawford PA).

HW822   Henry Eli Wiser (26 Jan 1862, Linesville PA-24 Nov 1924, Pierpont OH) m 4 Jul 1883, Nancy Ann Hart (15 Nov 1863, Crawford PA-9 May 1947). Crawford PA and Ashtabula OH.

HW8221   Florence Belle Wiser (26 Jan 1885, Erie PA-2 Mar 1953, Pierpont OH) m m 1) 28 Aug 1909, Ashtabula OH, George A. Harvey (1882-1941); 2) Jay Strock.

HW8222   Earl Monroe Wiser (1 May 1887, Erie PA-19 Mar 1965, Eagleville OH) m 31 Aug 1914, Jefferson OH, Mattie Belle Taylor (1890, WV-26 Jul 1963). Ashtabula OH.

HW82221   Garnet Idalene Wiser (b ca Jan 1916, OH).

HW82222   Dorothy Madeline Wiser (b ca Apr 1918, OH).

HW82223   Ruth Wiser.

HW8223   Mary Etta Wiser (17 Aug 1889, Erie PA-2 Sep 1890, PA).

HW8224   Alice Josephine Wiser (16 Jan 1891, Erie PA-16 Jun 1971, Butler PA) m 29 Jun 1910, Jefferson OH, Quinn O. Harvey (d 9 Mar 1952).

HW8225   Nelda Idalene Wiser (15 Sep 1893, Erie PA-27 Dec 1984) m 3 Apr 1915, Alva Augustus Thompson (9 Feb 1893-14 Apr 1978).

HW8226   Edna Irene Wiser (7 Mar 1896, Erie PA-20 Mar 1969) m 17 Nov 1915, Jefferson OH, Frank Harold Asp (1889-1973).

HW8227   Esther Elizabeth Wiser (21 May 1898, Meadville PA-18 Mar 1983, North East PA) m 10 Jan 1921, Jefferson OH, John Baptist Jacquel III (12 Mar 1898, Erie PA-18 Jan 1985, Erie PA).

HW8228   Vernon Victor Wiser (9 Jul 1900, Sharon PA-11 Feb 1976, Erie PA) m 22 Jun 1926, Erie PA, Gladys Metzler.

HW82281   Harold Victor Wiser (b 8 Jun 1927) m Norma   .

HW82282   Marion Irene Wiser (b 17 Jul 1930).

HW82283   Gordon Vernon Wiser (b 17 Jan 1935).

HW8229   Charles Henry Wiser (15 Apr 1903, Sharon PA-7 Jan 1974, Jefferson OH) m 17 May 1926, Ripley NY, Helen Cadwell Leonard (19 Feb 1909-Sep 1974, Jefferson OH). Ashtabula OH.

HW82291   Maynard Lee Wiser.

HW82292   Charles Henry Wiser.

HW82293   Bernice Marie Wiser.

HW82294   Mary Wiser.

HW822A   Anna Mae Wiser (14 May 1906, West Middlesex PA-5 Jan 1985, Meadville PA) m 26 Jun 1926, Richard Price (d 24 May 1972).

HW822B   Ralph Alvin Wiser (1 Apr 1909, Pierpont OH-Feb 1991) m 13 Jan 1932, Edna Hakalinen (b 1915). Ashtabula OH.

HW822B1   William Henry Wiser (b 1932) m Donna   .

HW822B11   Victoria Wiser.

HW822B12   William Wiser.

HW822B2   Raymond Eugene Wiser (b 1935) m Mary Jane Partch (b 1941). Ashtabula OH.

HW822B21   Deborah Lou Wiser (b 1959) m Alan Nelson.

HW822B22   Glenn Alvin Wiser (b 1960) m Pepha Salinas.

HW822B221   Raymond Scott Wiser.

HW822B222   Jason Lee Wiser.

HW822B223   Tonya Maureen Wiser.

HW822B224   Glenn Alvin Wiser Jr.

HW822B23   Cheryl Ann Wiser (b 1962) m George Gray.

HW822B24   Michael Lee Wiser (b 1966) m 1) Gail Roghbaugh; m 2) Bede Harold.

HW822B241   Nicole Wiser.

HW822B242   Michael Andrew Wiser.

HW822B243   Erica Wiser (b 11 Jan 1996).

HW822B25   Brenda Jo Wiser (b 1971).

HW822B3   Lila Marie Wiser (b 1937).

HW822B4   James Wiser (b 1941) m Barbara   .

HW822B41   Joseph Wiser (b ca 1967).

HW822B42   Eric Wiser (b ca 1969).

HW823   John Sherman Wiser (24 Jul 1865, Linesville PA-10 Feb 1933, Dorset, Ashtabula OH) m 1) 28 Nov 1889, Andover OH, Jennie Elvira Tobias (2 May 1869, Andover OH-17 Apr 1909, Ashtabula OH); m 2) 3 Apr 1918, Alice Furber (19 Nov 1879, OH-4 Feb 1950). Ashtabula OH.

HW8231   Harry S. Wiser (b Oct 1890, OH).

HW8232   Edith Wiser (3 Sep 1896, Ashtabula OH-31 Mar 1987, Auburn IN) m 9 Feb 1915, Ashtabula OH, Jesse Haiflich (13 Mar 1893, Uniondale IN-11 Jul 1976, Bluffton IN).

HW8233   Lewis J. Wiser (1901-1903).

HW8234   Carlton L. Wiser (18 Feb 1904, OH-1 Aug 1961).

HW8235   Lottie May Wiser (b 23 Apr 1924, Denmark, Ashtabula OH) m 17 Jul 1948, Jefferson OH, Lyle Marcy (b 18 Jan 1922).

HW8236   Merald S. Wiser (b 7 Dec 1920, Ashtabula OH) m 1947, Dorset, Ashtabula OH, Marie Allen (b 1920). Cleveland and Ashland OH.

HW82361   James A. Wiser (b 8 Oct 1948) m Patricia   . Ashland OH.

HW823611   Tricia Wiser (b Mar 1975).

HW823612   Heather Wiser (b 1976).

HW823613   Brandon Wiser (b 1 Oct 1981).

HW82362   Bruce D. Wiser (b 2 Jan 1951) m Carrie Paullin.

HW82363   John Wiser (b 5 Jun 1953). Winter Park FL.

HW82364   Dale N. Wiser (b 15 Feb 1954).

HW82365   Kathy Wiser (b 22 Feb 1957) m Steve Shull.

HW83   Marcus L. Wiser (8 Jun 1842, Linesville PA-21 Feb 1924, Louisville KY) m 27 Mar 1864, Owen, Clark IN, Nancy M. Bowyer (14 Feb 1846, Bowyers Landing, Clark IN-19 Jan 1936, Louisville KY). Clark IN and Louisville KY.

HW831   Marcus L. Wiser Jr. (7 Oct 1864, Linesville PA-12 Dec 1900, Louisville KY) m 5 Dec 1892, Mary Etta Adams (27 May 1872, KY-20 Jul 1954, Louisville KY). Louisville KY.

HW8311   Anna Leora Wiser (25 Jan 1894, Louisville KY-28 Sep 1971, Louisville KY) m 26 Nov 1913, Andrew E. Cook (25 Dec 1889, Rome KY-5 Dec 1958, Louisville KY).

HW8312   Marcus Clement ("C. M., Bud") Wiser (15 Oct 1896, Louisville KY-5 Mar 1960, Pikeville KY) m 1) Charlotte Mae Gibbs; m 2) 4 Jul 1923, Catlettsburg KY, Mary Nell Sword (b 28 Jul 1907, Pikeville KY). Pikeville KY.

HW83121   Clem M. Wiser Jr. (b 25 May 1924, Pikeville KY) m 8 Jun 1944, San Francisco CA, Olga Diaz-De-Leon (b 23 Jul 1923, Mazatlan, Sinaloa, Mexico). Palo Alto CA.

HW831211   John Mark Wiser (b 13 Jun 1947, San Francisco CA) m 1) 21 Jun 1969, Los Angeles CA, JoAnn Carol Hull (b 22 Mar 1945, Covina CA); m 2) 21 Mar 1994, Orcas Island WA, Harriet Meier (b 24 Feb 1939, Hamburg, Germany).

HW8312111   Ryan H. Wiser (b 13 Aug 1971, Portland OR) m 29 Dec 1995, Santa Clara CA, Maureen Calderon.

HW8312112   Morgan N. Wiser (b 18 Sep 1973, Portland OR).

HW831212   Yvette Marie Wiser (b 1 Aug 1949, San Francisco CA) m 28 Aug 1971, Harrisburg OH, William T. Custer (b 31 Jan 1951, Parkersburg WV).

HW831213   Clem M. Wiser III (b 1 May 1955, San Francisco CA) m 1979, Patricia Tumbaga.

HW831213l   Michael James Wiser (b 31 Jan 1980, Palo Alto CA).

HW831214   Mark Steven Wiser (b 22 Nov 1956, San Francisco CA).

HW83122   Marguerite Dale Wiser (b 24 Jan 1928, Pikeville KY) m 21 Mar 1947, Paintsville KY, John B. Polley (b 28 Jan 1926).

HW83123   June Audrey Wiser (b 18 Sep 1930, Pikeville KY) m 7 Oct 1949, Pikeville KY, Joseph Raymond Justice (b 12 Apr 1928, Louisa KY).

HW8313   Claudine A. Wiser (10 Feb 1900, Louisville KY-Mar 1988, Louisville KY) m 1) 3 Jul 1915, J. M. Eckert (d 17 Dec 1942); m 2) 17 Jul 1927, Harry Robert Dages.

HW832   George W. Wiser (3 Jun 1866, Linesville PA-17 Jul 1937, Birmingham AL) m Mary Elizabeth Paley (16 Dec 1871, IN-2 Jun 1957, Birmingham AL). Birmingham AL.

HW8321   Maggie Wiser (b ca 1893, KY).

HW8322   Nellie Wiser (b ca 1895, MS).

HW8323   Elizabeth Wiser (b ca 1897, KY).

HW8324   Edna Wiser (b ca 1907, MS).

HW833   William H. Wiser (31 May 1867, Charlestown IN-25 Dec 1943, Louisville KY) m 1) 11 Jun 1887, Clark IN, Margaret Elizabeth Clark (1868-4 Apr 1892); m 2) 14 Jun 1893, Clark IN, Margaret Isabell Rogers (b Dec 1872, IN-14 Jan 1952, Louisville KY). Louisville KY.

HW8331   Eva May Wiser (b 31 Oct 1887, KY) m Charles Reardon.

HW8332   Albert Hughes Wiser (15 Feb 1890, KY-9 Aug 1970, Louisville KY) m 1917, Louise Julia Walter (b ca 1894, KY). Louisville KY.

HW83321   Mildred L. Wiser (b 12 Aug 1918, Louisville KY).

HW83322   Albert Hughes Wiser Jr. (b 6 Dec 1922, Louisville KY) m 1942, Juanita Joyce Jameson.

HW833221   Karen Denise Wiser (b 16 May 1949, Louisville KY) m 1969, Stephen Earl Powers.

HW833222   Lisa Alison Wiser (b 21 Apr 1952, Louisville KY).

HW83323   Kenneth Walter Wiser (b 14 Sep 1924, Louisville KY) m 1947, Mary Ethelyn Bennet.

HW833231   Cynthia Louise Wiser (b 1949, New Albany IN) m 1970, John R. Riddle.

HW833232   Pamela Joyce Wiser (b 1953, New Albany IN).

HW8333   William H. Wiser Jr. (27 Mar 1892, Jefferson KY-28 Jan 1967, Louisville KY) m Edna Mae Lemasters (ca 1895, IN-15 Feb 1968, KY).

HW8334   Margaret Isabell Wiser (b Dec 1894, KY) m Tyler Arthur Busey.

HW834   Samuel E. Wiser (14 Dec 1868, Whitley IL-17 Mar 1955, Tamalpais CA) m 2 Sep 1891, Clark IN, Martha E. Johnson (Feb 1869, IN-12 Feb 1957, Tamalpais CA). Clark IN.

HW8341   Stella Mae Wiser (b 7 Apr 1892, Louisville KY) m 25 Jun 1924, San Mateo CA, Arthur F. Martin.

HW8342   Jesse Carl Wiser (4 Feb 1895, Marble Hill, Clark IN-Mar 1972, Tamalpais CA).

HW8343   Lillian Macel Wiser (b Jun 1897, Rabbitsburg KY) m 1)   Justice; m 2)   Marchisio.

HW8344   Grace Cleone Wiser (b 19 Jul 1899, Prather, Clark IN) m 1) Stanley Port; m 2)
Marchisio.

HW835   John F. Wiser (14 Feb 1871, Charlestown IN-1 Aug 1900) m 18 Nov 1897, Lillian Quenton (b Mar 1875, KY). Mercer KY.

HW8351   Mary G. Wiser (b Sep 1898, KY).

HW836   Lillian May Wiser (b 14 Oct 1875, Charlestown IN) m 1900, W. S. Van Arsdale.

HW837   Claudia A. Wiser (8 Jun 1878, Charlestown IN-19 Mar 1919) m James Connors.

HW838   Arthur G. Wiser (19 Apr 1881, Charlestown IN-18 Oct 1939, Louisville KY) m Verda (--).

HW839   Jesse E. Wiser (4 May 1885, Charlestown IN-Sep 1966, Louisville KY) m Amelia Joyce (b ca 1887, KY). Louisville KY.

HW8391   Harold K. Wiser (b ca 1908, KY).

HW8392   Edna May Wiser (b ca Jan 1916, KY).

HW83A   Infant Wiser.

HW83B   Infant Wiser.

HW84   Mary E. Wiser (b ca 1846, Linesville PA).

HW85   Amanda A. Wiser (b ca Nov 1849, Linesville PA).

HW86   William H. Wiser (6 Oct 1852, Linesville PA-26 Oct 1907, Meadville PA) m Ellen (b Jan 1858, NY). Crawford PA.

HW861   Agnes Wiser (1873, Meadville PA-Aug 1874, Meadville PA).

HW862   Mary Elizabeth Wiser (4 Jul 1875, Meadville PA-23 Sep 1964) m   Belden.

HW863   Malcolm William Wiser (13 Apr 1889, Meadville PA-1 Jan 1967, Meadville PA) m Opal (b ca 1895, PA).

HW864   Ellen Wiser (1890, Meadville PA-Jul 1892, Meadville PA).

HW865   Andrew Vincent Wiser (14 Apr 1892, PA-5 Dec 1969).

HW866   Lewis A. Wiser (19 Jul 1894, Meadville PA-ca 1940, Detroit MI) m Tillie   (b ca 1895, PA). Detroit MI.

HW8661   Lewis B. Wiser (b ca 1913, PA).

HW867   Mercedith L. Wiser (b 3 Jun 1896, Meadville PA) m 1)   Haughey; m 2)   Brutcher.

HW868   James Maxwell Wiser (1 Sep 1898, Meadville PA-15 Apr 1962, Meadville PA) m Cleo A. Smith.

HW869   Daughter Wiser (31 Jan 1902-31 Jan 1902).

HW9   Nathaniel G. Wiser (1 Mar 1814, Clarence Hollow, Erie NY-8 Jan 1877, Linesville PA) m Electa Tabor (24 Jan 1823, PA-24 Dec 1893, Cleveland OH). Crawford PA.

HW91   John H. Wiser (20 Jun 1843, Linesville PA-10 Feb 1864).

HW92   Roselle Virginia Wiser (3 Apr 1845, Linesville PA-31 Oct 1881) m 20 Nov 1879, Hiram OH, Arthur C. Pierson (b ca 1852, IA).

HW93   Clinton Brock Wiser (9 Nov 1846, Linesville PA-15 Nov 1926) m 1) Effie Killebrew (d ca 1878); m 2) Audrey Ella   (b May 1869, IL). Chicago IL.

HW931   Daisy E. Wiser (b Oct 1874, PA).

HW932   Blanche W. Wiser (b ca 1877, PA).

HW94   Son Wiser (9 Nov 1846, Linesville PA-1846).

HW95   Rogene Wiser (b 5 May 1848, Linesville PA) m 1)   Reno; m 2)   Anderson.

HW96   Frank W. Wiser (13 Apr 1850, Linesville PA) m Clara Hulmes.

HW97   Aaron Brown Wiser (12 Jun 1854, Linesville PA-30 May 1913) m Edna Belle Carpenter.

HW98   Alta May Wiser (12 Aug 1857, Linesville PA- 4 Dec 1888) m 8 Feb 1883, Arthur Chester Pierson.

HW99   Addie Belle Wiser (b 9 Apr 1860, Linesville PA) m Alex M. Kincaid.

HWA   Levias B. Wiser (1 Jul 1815, Clarence Hollow, Erie NY-24 Jul 1879, Evansburg PA) m Sarah Hill (ca 1830, Fairfield, Crawford PA-20 Aug 1899, Sandy Lake, Mercer PA). Crawford PA.

HWA1   Rosanna A. Wiser (b 28 Apr 1850, Crawford PA) m 17 Sep 1868, Uriah McKay.

HWA2   Rosaltha Wiser (20 Oct 1854, Crawford PA-20 Aug 1924, Meadville PA) m 1) Lewis M. Brown; m 2)   Rhodes.

HWA3   Frederick Wiser (b ca 1855, Crawford PA).

HWA4   John Wiser (b ca 1857, Crawford PA).

HWA5   Charles Wiser (b ca 1859, Crawford PA).

HWA6   Elvina Wiser (b ca 1862, Crawford PA).

HWA7   Almira Wiser (b ca 1862, Crawford PA) m 14 Dec 1882, Andrew Slater.

HWB   Alvah B. Wiser (17 Oct 1816, Clarence Hollow, Erie NY-22 Feb 1846, Crawford PA) m
Sarah Graham (2 Feb 1823, Linesville PA-5 Jun 1911, Meadville PA). Crawford PA.

HWB1   Mary Wiser (15 Nov 1837, Crawford PA-26 Jan 1849, Crawford PA).

HWB2   Alvah B. Wiser (b 1 Mar 1846, Crawford PA) m 21 Oct 1868, Pontiac MI, Catherine Anna
Lanning (b Feb 1851, MI). Saginaw MI and Hand SD.

HWB21   Alvah B. Wiser (b 22 Apr 1874, Saginaw MI) m 18 Mar 1903, Danforth, Hand SD, Grace
Lillie Fountain.

HWB211   Milo Alvin Wiser (8 Jan 1904, Danforth SD-Jan 1971, Gila AZ).

HWB212   Eva Faye Wiser (b 16 Feb 1906, Danforth SD).

HWB22   Verna Ruth Wiser (b 22 Apr 1898, Hand SD).

HWC   John Wiser (27 Jul 1818, Clarence Hollow, Erie NY-9 Mar 1893, Bethel MI) m 1) 1839,
Patty Ann Crocker; m 2) 19 Jan 1845, Branch MI, Rosina Fields (b ca 1827); m 3) 4 Jul 1869, Branch MI,
Louisa   (b ca 1833, NY). Branch MI.

HWC1   Edward Henry Wiser (b ca 1849, Branch MI).

HWC2   Mary L. Wiser (b 1852, Branch MI) m 20 Dec 1869, Branch MI, Munson P. Ioles.

HWC3   Alonzo Wiser (b 1854, Branch MI) m Elva   (b 1853, IN). Steuben IN.

HWC31   Mina M. Wiser (b ca 1878, IN).

HWD   Mary Anne Wiser (13 Apr 1821, Clarence Hollow, Erie NY-23 Dec 1900, Bowling Green
OH) m ca 1845, Stephen Deriar (b Jun 1827, NY).

CHAPTER TWENTY-TWO

Other Weiser/Wiser families in America

[BRW] Bartholomaus Weisser (1813-1889)
of "Dahlheim", Wurttemberg and Marietta, Pennsylvania

Bartholomaus Weisser's dates are found on a tombstone in Marietta, Lancaster Co PA: 16 Nov 1813-14 Dec 1889. He and his wife Catharine had a son Jacob whose marriage on 15 Jul 1863, recorded at Zion Lutheran Church in Marietta, was to Sarah Grass, born 18 Nov 1840, Warren Tp, Franklin Co PA.

Jacob's birthdate is given as 13 Apr 1840 at Dahlheim, Wuerttemberg, probably one of five places named Talheim listed in Wuerttemberg in the German postal directory. Jacob died 16 Dec 1900, the result of a railroad accident at Watts Station PA. The burial record at Zion Church and his tombstone give his birth year as 1839. Sarah died 30 Oct 1877, according to her tombstone at Marietta.

The 1870 census lists Barth Wiser, age 65, from "Wurtenburg" in East Donegal Tp, Lancaster Co, with Mary, age 19; Jacob and Sarah above; and Bartholomew, 30, born in "Wurtenburg," his wife Mary, 26, born in Switzerland, and children Frank, 7; Jacob, 6; George, 3; Minnie, 1; and Catharine Wiser, 18, also born in "Wurtenburg."

In 1880 they have these children as well as William, 9; Henry J., 7; Cornelia M., 5; and Rosa M., 2. On that census John, 66, a native of Wurtemberg, lives with Jacob in Marietta; John likely being Bartholomew. There are likely descendants of this family in Columbia PA, near Marietta.

BRW   Bartholomaus Weiser (16 Nov 1813, Wurttemberg-14 Dec 1889) m Catharine   .

BRW1   Bartholomew Weiser (b Jan 1836, Wurttemberg) m Mary E.   (b Apr 1844,
Switzerland).

BRW11   Frank B. Weiser (b ca 1862, PA) m Susan M. Young (b Oct 1872, PA).

BRW111   Frank P. Weiser (b Oct 1888, PA) m Anna Kimberly (b ca 1894, PA).

BRW1111   Frances Weiser (b ca 1913, PA).

BRW112   George M. Weiser (b Nov 1889, PA).

BRW113   Christina M. Weiser (b Feb 1891, PA).

BRW114   Clara Weiser (b Aug 1892, PA).

BRW115   Mary E. Weiser (b May 1894, PA).

BRW116   Ella R. Weiser (b Jan 1897, PA).

BRW117   Sarah Weiser (b Jan 1900, PA).

BRW118   Alice A. S. Weiser (b ca 1907, PA).

BRW119   Elizabeth A. Weiser (b ca 1910, PA).

BRW12   Jacob B. Weiser (b May 1864, PA) m Minnie   (b Feb 1877, PA).

BRW121   Catherine Weiser (b ca Sep 1915, PA).

BRW13   George M. Weiser (b Jul 1866, PA) m Flora B.   (Sep 1872, PA-ca 1919).

BRW131   George C. Weiser (b May 1898, PA).

BRW132   Paul L. Weiser (b ca 1902, PA).

BRW133   John H. Weiser (b ca 1904, PA).

BRW134   Sarah W. Weiser (b ca 1907, PA).

BRW135   Harold Weiser (b ca 1911, PA).

BRW136   Edward Weiser (b ca 1915, PA).

BRW137   Helen Weiser (b ca Jul 1917, PA).

BRW14   Mary (Minnie) E. Weiser (b ca 1868, PA).

BRW15   William P. Weiser (b Feb 1871, PA) m Mary C.   (b Dec 1871, PA).

BRW151   Catherine A. Weiser (b Dec 1899, PA).

BRW152   William B. Weiser (b ca 1902, PA).

BRW153   Edmund J. Weiser (b ca 1904, PA).

BRW154   Mary E. Weiser (b ca 1905, PA).

BRW155   Swidbert E. Weiser (b ca 1907, PA).

BRW156   Gertrude F. Weiser (b ca 1910, PA).

BRW16   Henry J. Weiser (b May 1873, PA) m Rose L.   (b ca 1882, PA).

BRW161   Henry J. Weiser (b ca 1910, PA).

BRW162   Joseph V. Weiser (b ca 1912, PA).

BRW163   Charles A. Weiser (b ca 1913, PA).

BRW164   Vincent Weiser (b ca 1915, PA).

BRW165   Barton Weiser (b ca Feb 1917, PA).

BRW166   Leo F. Weiser (b ca Mar 1919, PA).

BRW17   Cornelia (Amelia) M. Weiser (b Oct 1875, PA).

BRW18   Rosa M. Weiser (b Mar 1878, PA).

BRW19   Ellen (Ella) M. Weiser (b Oct 1880, PA).

BRW1A   Charles B. Weiser (b May 1882, PA).

BRW1B   Bart C. Weiser (b Jul 1887, PA) m Ethel M.   (b ca 1892, PA).

BRW1B1   Joseph Weiser (b ca 1913, PA).

BRW1B2   James Weiser (b ca 1914, PA).

BRW1B3   Gladys Weiser (b ca Mar 1916, PA).

BRW1B4   Dorothy Weiser (b ca Jan 1918, PA).

BRW1B5   Rosamund Weiser (b ca Mar 1920, PA).

BRW1C   Joseph V. Weiser (b Oct 1891, PA) m Mary Link (b ca 1899, PA).

BRW2   Jacob Weiser (13 Apr 1840, Talheim, Wurttemberg -16 Dec 1900, Watts Station PA) m
Sarah Grass (18 Nov 1840, Warren, Franklin PA-30 Oct 1877).

BRW21   Sarah Catharine Weiser (31 May 1864, Chichies, Lancaster Co PA-16 Jun 1910) m 24 Jan
1901, John M. Lamparter (30 Oct 1866, Marietta PA-13 Aug 1912).

BRW22   David Weiser (b or d 15 Mar 1870). Bur Marietta PA.

BRW23   Mary A. Weiser (b 3 Aug 1874, Chickees PA) m 22 Mar 1896, Charles W. Roth (b 26
Jan 1870, Marietta PA). Four children are recorded at Zion Church.

BRW3   Mary Weiser (b ca 1851, PA).

[BJW] Benjamin Weiser (b ca 1810)
of Cumberland County, Pennsylvania and Linn County, Iowa

Benjamin Weiser (b ca 1810) married Maria   . He was confirmed at the Lutheran Church at Enola,
Cumberland Co PA in 1827. By 1840 he was a resident of Johnson Co IA; in 1850 he was a carpenter in Linn
Co IA, in 1860 he was a farmer in Rock Island Co IL.

BJW   Benjamin Weiser (b ca 1810) m 1) ca 1829, Maria   (d ca 1848); m 2) ca 1851, Mary
Jane Moore (b ca 1821, OH).

BJW1   Sarah Rebecca Weiser (b 26 Jan 1831, near Enola PA) m 11 Mar 1849. Cedar Rapids IA,
Simeon Dewitt Loveless (b 3 Nov 1827, NY). Moved to Austin TX.

BJW11   Charles Henry Loveless (5 Dec 1849, Cedar Rapids IA-26 Sep 1850, IA).

BJW12   George Malcolm Loveless (5 Apr 1852, IA-1902, TX).

BJW13   Mary Tesianna Loveless (b 14 Aug 1855) m   Freeman.

BJW14   Jennie Rebecca Loveless (30 Nov 1858-30 Nov 1870).

BJW15   Sarah Elizabeth Loveless (3 May 1862-16 Feb 1926) m   Oatss.

BJW16   William Benjamin Loveless (3 Dec 1864-29 Oct 1946).

BJW17   Ellen Maria Loveless (5 Dec 1868-3 Dec 1878).

BJW2   Maria Magdalena Weiser (b 13 Jan 1833 near Enola PA).

BJW3   Malcolm Wiser (b ca 1841, IA) m Amelia   (b Apr 1846, IA). Moved to San Antonio
TX.

BJW31   James Wiser (b ca 1871, IL).

BJW32   Mildred Wiser (b ca 1873, IL).

BJW33   Ada J. Wiser (b Feb 1875, IL) m F. H. Cooper.

BJW4   Phoebe Jane Weiser (b ca 1846, IA).

BJW5   Sierra Nevada Weiser (b ca 1852, IA).

BJW6   Luella Weiser (b ca 1858, IL).

[CHW]   Christian Weiser (1821-1887)
of Lehigh County, Pennsylvania

Christian Weiser was born in Wurttemberg in 1821 and came to the United States about 1850. He settled in Salisbury Township of Lehigh County, near the town of Emaus.[164]

CHW   Christian Weiser (26 Sep 1821, Wurttemberg-19 Feb 1887, Salisbury, Lehigh PA) m 1858, Angelina Theresa Knauss (5 Oct 1837, Emaus PA-29 May 1877).

CHW1   S. Elmira Weiser (14 Feb 1859, Lehigh PA-11 Sep 1887) m Isaac O. Kramer (10 Dec 1853-30 Oct 1910).

CHW2   Charles A. Weiser (23 Jul 1861, Lehigh PA-10 Apr 1938) m 5 Dec 1882, Malinda B. Shaffer (4 Feb 1862, OH-15 Sep 1936).

CHW21   John Edwin Weiser (20 Jun 1883, Wayne OH-22 Apr 1946) m 18 Oct 1911, Loanda Octavia ("Queen") Day (6 Sep 1889, OH-30 Apr 1985).

CHW211   Ruth Elizabeth Weiser (15 Jul 1912, Cleveland OH-26 Jul 1947) m Robert Cruickshank.

CHW212   Dorothy Anne Weiser (b 14 Mar 1923, Wayne OH) m 1) 16 Jun 1943, Rodney Gene Stafford (7 Jan 1920-1 Mar 1978, Akron OH); m 2) 27 Sep 1983, Wooster OH, Robert F. Snyder.

CHW213   John Edwin Weiser (b 8 May 1928, Wayne OH) m 1) 3 Aug 1947, Nancy Tunison; m 2) 17 Feb 1967, Judy Karrer.

CHW2131   Linda Jean Weiser (b 20 Mar 1949, Wayne OH).

CHW2132   John Edwin Weiser (b 28 Jul 1950, Wayne OH).

CHW2133   Jaqueline Ruth Weiser (b 5 Nov 1951, Wayne OH).

CHW2134   Rebecca Sue Weiser (b 22 Dec 1953, Wayne OH).

CHW2135   Elizabeth Anne Weiser (b 23 Jan 1956, Wayne OH).

CHW2136   Barbara Lee Weiser (b 2 Jul 1958, Wayne OH).

CHW2137   Matthew William Weiser (b 13 Dec 1960, Wayne OH).

CHW22   Forest A. Weiser (20 Aug 1884, Wayne OH-22 Oct 1956) m Mary C. Gorman (b ca 1886, OH).

---

[164]The information on this family was assembled by J. Owen Weiser. It has been edited in the present form by Edward Wiser.

CHW221   Violet M. Weiser (b 18 Aug 1914, Cleveland OH).

CHW222   Vivian C. Weiser (b 24 Jan 1916, Cleveland OH) m Frank Cook.

CHW223   Forest Weiser Jr. (b 17 Nov 1920, Cleveland OH) m Marlene Allen.

CHW2231   Jacqueline May Weiser (b 12 Feb 1947) m Jim Walesch.

CHW2232   Kathleen Mae Weiser (b 2 Aug 1948).

CHW23   Clyde L. Weiser (4 May 1886, Wayne OH-22 Nov 1955) m 3 May 1909, Helen Agusta Moran (28 Jul 1885, Buffalo NY-5 Apr 1977).

CHW231   Helen Edna Weiser (b 22 Jul 1922, Orrville OH) m 1 Dec 1945, Anthony Yonto (b 16 Feb 1921).

CHW232   Charles Richard Weiser (26 Sep 1925, Orrville OH-1945).

CHW24   Bessie Weiser (b 15 Feb 1890, Wayne OH) m 22 Dec 1922, William A. Wagner (2 Sep 1894-24 Feb 1975).

CHW25   Glenn V. Weiser (2 Dec 1895, Wayne OH-23 Nov 1970) m 14 May 1923, Grace Ludwick (21 Jul 1891-10 May 1970).

CHW26   Perry W. Weiser (14 Mar 1901, Wayne OH 17 Sep 1971) m 1) Lucille Dow; m 2) 29 Dec 1958, Ethel Anderson Miller (b 2 Jan 1912).

CHW261   Norma Jean Weiser (b 5 Dec 1927) m 8 Mar 1952, David A. Muller (b 5 Oct 1920).

CHW3   Ellen M. Weiser (b 25 Feb 1864, Lehigh PA) m 1) George Weaver (d 11 Jan 1904); m 2) Edwin Bertch.

CHW4   Edwin Joseph Weiser (17 May 1866, Lehigh PA-30 Aug 1929) m 1) 25 Jul 1891, Salinda B. Cook (20 Sep 1862, Wayne OH-19 Apr 1921); m 2) Mae McFadden (d 4 Nov 1959).

CHW41   Forest E. Weiser (17 Feb 1892, Wayne OH-30 Sep 1918).

CHW42   Carl E. Weiser (b 21 Oct 1895, Wayne OH) m 20 Aug 1927, Effie Mae Weidman (2 Feb 1892, Wayne OH-22 Aug 1963).

CHW421   Opal Fae Weiser (b 28 Sep 1930, Wayne OH) m 21 Jul 1951, Noble Flener (b 17 Jan 1925).

CHW422   Pearl Mae Weiser (b 2 Dec 1931, Wayne OH) m 13 Dec 1949, Richard A. Young (b 30 Aug 1929).

CHW43   Pearl M. Weiser (8 Jan 1898, Wayne OH-27 Jul 1957, Portland OR) m Sep 1925, Vancouver WA, Thomas Gilpin (d 4 Nov 1969).

CHW44   John Owen Weiser (18 Oct 1900, Wayne OH-29 Nov 1978) m 17 Jul 1923, Flora D. Fittler (b 10 Apr 1905, Barberton OH).

CHW441   Margaret Weiser (b 10 Jun 1924, Portland OR) m 18 Sep 1943, William Leitch (b 6 Feb 1920, Youngstown OH).

CHW442   Forest E. Weiser (b 25 May 1926, Wayne OH) m 12 Jan 1947, Lillie Mackey (b 4 Jan

1927, Holmes OH).

CHW4421   Ronald Lee Weiser (b 7 Sep 1948, Wayne OH) m 30 Jul 1966, Lynn Patterson (b 13 Jun 1948, Wayne OH).

CHW44211   Lisa Jean Weiser (b 18 Feb 1967, Wayne OH).

CHW44212   Thomas Matthew Weiser (b 21 Oct 1970, Wayne OH).

CHW4422   Bonnie J. Weiser (b 5 Mar 1951) m Jay Richard Kinney (b 2 Nov 1955, Ashland OH).

CHW443   Richard E. Weiser (b 22 Jul 1927, Wayne OH) m 2 Jul 1950, Shirley Rae Costell (b 30 Jul 1928, Wooster OH).

CHW4431   Diana Rae Weiser (b 23 Jun 1951, Wooster OH) m 14 Apr 1973, Jack Schmidt.

CHW4432   Ralph E. Weiser (b 16 Dec 1952, Wooster OH) m 1976, Judy Begler (b 9 Feb 1957, Wooster OH).

CHW44321   Joshua Lee Weiser (b 18 Oct 1978, Wooster OH).

CHW4433   Vicki Lynn Weiser (b 22 Mar 1957, Wooster OH) m 10 Apr 1976, David Straits (b 31 Jan 1956, Millersburg OH).

CHW4434   Jeffery S. Weiser (b 9 May 1960, Wooster OH).

CHW4435   Douglas Arthur Weiser (b 21 Feb 1962, Wooster OH).

CHW4436   Bradley A. Weiser (b 14 Apr 1966, Wooster OH).

CHW444   William O. Weiser (b 21 May 1930, Wayne OH) m 8 Aug 1951, Evelyn Mattie Shaver (b 22 Feb 1932, Tyler TX).

CHW4441   Stephen O. Weiser (b 1 Sep 1952, Wayne OH).

CHW4442   David E. Weiser (b 3 Dec 1953, Tyler TX).

CHW4443   Sharon K. Weiser (b 17 Jul 1957, Wayne OH) m 7 Aug 1977, Paul Winther Gray.

CHW4444   Keith A. Weiser (b 22 Jun 1961, Wayne OH).

CHW445   Carolyn J. Weiser (b 8 Sep 1931, Wayne OH) m 15 Aug 1948, Donald D. Hughes (b 22 Mar 1930, Wayne OH).

CHW446   Earl C. Weiser (b 23 Dec 1932, Wayne OH) m 6 Sep 1956, Lela Hughes (b 26 May 1926, Wayne OH).

CHW447   Clifford D. Weiser (b 13 Sep 1934, Wayne OH) m 17 Apr 1956, Joyce Bobby Adamson (b 10 Sep 1936, Liberty, DeKalb KY).

CHW4471   Debora Kay Weiser (b 24 Mar 1957, Murfreesboro TN) m 10 Jun 1978, Louis Frank Gilliland (b 15 Dec 1954, Murfreesboro TN).

CHW4472   Kevin D. Weiser (b 26 Jun 1961, Moses Lake WA).

CHW4473   Kerry Dale Weiser (b 20 Feb 1975, Lebanon TN).

CHW448   Gary Lee Weiser (b 15 Feb 1939, Wayne OH) m 12 Dec 1964, Colette Lene Anthony (b 7 Feb 1944, Seattle WA).

CHW4481   Rebecca Lynn Weiser (b 23 Oct 1966, Wooster OH).

CHW4482   Vincent Lee Weiser (b 3 Jun 1969, Wooster OH).

CHW4483   Rachel Laura Weiser (b 17 Oct 1976, Wooster OH).

CHW449   Jeanette Alice Weiser (b 22 Mar 1942, Wayne OH) m 1) 3 Dec 1961, Ramon Zappone (b 31 Oct 1929, Wooster OH); m 2) 12 Dec 1966, Raymond Tennant (b 14 Apr 1935, PA).

CHW5   Emma E. Weiser (25 Nov 1868, Lehigh PA-30 Aug 1946) m Wilson M. Berry (d Sep 1954).

CHW6   William O. Weiser (12 May 1871, Lehigh PA-31 Oct 1947) m 6 Dec 1892, Alice R. Shaffer (Feb 1865, OH-26 Oct 1945).

CHW7   George J. Weiser (12 Aug 1873, Lehigh PA-13 May 1956) m Alice Elsie (Dec 1879, IA-24 Dec 1952).

CHW71   Nellie Alice Weiser (10 Mar 1900, Weatherby MO-25 Jan 1976) m 1) 12 May 1917, Mercer MO, Bazil Trail (b 20 Jul 1893); m 2) 10 Sep 1947, Henry Grone (d 25 Nov 1952).

CHW72   Louis Floyd Weiser (b 17 Apr 1901).

CHW73   Opal Irene Weiser (b 12 Jan 1915, Mount Ayr IA) m 16 Nov 1934, Bethany MO, Bert Lee Mitchell (b 5 Jan 1890, Red Cloud NE).

CHW8   Laura Theresa Weiser (22 Apr 1876-17 Aug 1941).

[CRW]   Cornelius Wiser (b ca 1777)
of New York

Cornelius Wiser was born about 1777 in New York according to census records. He appeared for the first time in Charlestown, Montgomery County, New York in the 1810 Census, when he already had a number of children. By 1820, he had moved to the eastern part of Monroe County, and remained in that area through 1850. His descendants had moved by 1860 to Michigan.

Nothing is known about the ancestry of Cornelius. He could have been a son of Nicholas, who was in Canajoharie in 1790, or of John, who was in Amsterdam in 1800. There is also a possibility, with an apparently Dutch given name, that like Harmon Wiser he might have changed his surname from a longer Dutch name.

CRW   Cornelius Wiser (b ca 1777, NY) m Hannah   (b ca 1776, NY).

CRW1   Hiram Wiser (b 22 Apr 1805, Webster, Monroe NY) m Marsha Goodnow (b ca 1814).

CRW11   Charles M. Wiser (b 16 Oct 1831, NY) m 1) ca 1852, Jane(?) H.   (b ca 1833, NY); m 2) Charlotte   (b ca 1845, Canada).

CRW111   Albert N. Wiser (b Apr 1852, NY) m Mary Van Gordon (b Aug 1850, MI).

CRW1111   Ida Wiser (b ca 1878, MI).

CRW1112   Ettie Wiser (b Jul 1880, MI).

CRW1113   Hiram Wiser (b Mar 1884, MI) m Edith   .

CRW1114   Charles D. Wiser (b Jan 1892, MI) m Alma E.   (b ca 1888, OH).

CRW11141   Charles Wiser (b ca Apr 1916, MI).

CRW11142   Robert Donald Wiser (b ca Apr 1918, MI).

CRW1115   Harold Wiser (b Apr 1894, MI).

CRW112   Eva(?) A. Wiser (b ca 1858, MI).

CRW12   Marcus Wiser (b 17 Jul 1834, NY).

CRW13   Newton P. Wiser (b 10 Dec 1836, NY).

CRW14   Milon W. Wiser (b 19 Nov 1839, NY) m Mary Elizabeth   (b Oct 1845, MI).

CRW141   Nora A. Wiser (b ca 1870, MI).

CRW15   Adeline E. Wiser (b 7 Jul 1841, NY).

CRW16   George A. Wiser (b 22 Mar 1845, NY).

CRW17   James Franklin Wiser (b 15 Jul 1846, NY) m ca 1871, Jessie E.   (b Jan 1848, England).

CRW171   Edwina M. Wiser (b 1 Sep 1871, MI).

CRW172   George H. Wiser (b Jul 1873, MI) m Tilla M.   (b ca 1873, MI).

CRW1721   Lela Wiser (b ca 1905, MI).

CRW173   Newton A. Wiser (26 Sep 1876, MI-Nov 1962, MI) m Rose H.   (b ca 1878, MI).

CRW1731   J. Frank Wiser (b ca 1903, MI).

CRW1732   Bessie E. Wiser (b ca Oct 1913, MI).

CRW174   Bessie P. Wiser (b Apr 1888, MI).

CRW18   John B. Wiser (b 30 Oct 1847, NY).

CRW2   Amanda Wiser (b ca 1815, NY).

[FSW]   Foster Weiser (1815-1852)
of Delaware County, Ohio

Foster Weiser (10 Oct 1815-22 Oct 1852) married Eleanor Coleman (21 Jan 1820-13 Jun 1894). They lived in or near Delaware OH, where there are descendants remaining.

In 1880 Philip Weiser reported to the census taker that he was born in Ohio, but both his parents were born in Pennsylvania. Foster Weiser is in Marlborough Tp, Delaware Co OH in 1840, but not on the 1850 census nor, apparently, is his family. The given name Foster does not occur with any known Weiser in Pennsylvania, so that placing him there is not possible at this time.

FSW   Foster Weiser (10 Oct 1815-22 Oct 1852) m 25 Mar 1840, Delaware OH, Eleanor Coleman (21 Jan 1820-13 Jun 1894).

FSW1   John Weiser (31 Mar 1840-3 Oct 1865). Civil War.

FSW2   Philip Weiser (30 Jun 1845, OH-29 Aug 1899) m 21 Apr 1866, Marion OH, Mary Jane Culp (24 Nov 1845, OH-Feb 1893).

FSW21   Sherman J. Weiser (b Aug 1866, OH) m Jennie R.   (b Mar 1867, OH).

FSW211   Herbert C. Weiser (b Oct 1892, OH).

FSW212   Lewis P. Weiser (b Sep 1894, OH).

FSW213   Gertrude Weiser (b ca 1901, OH).

FSW214   Lucy Weiser (b ca 1903, OH).

FSW215   Walter Weiser (b ca 1907, OH).

FSW22   John Weiser (b Feb 1871, OH) m Ada A. Hunt (b Mar 1876, OH).

FSW221   Ruth M. Weiser (b Dec 1895, OH).

FSW23   Eleanor Weiser (b 9 Nov 1873, Delaware OH).

FSW24   Foster S. Weiser (b Dec 1876, OH) m Ada B.   (b ca 1888, OH).

FSW241   Paul A. Weiser (b ca 1907, OH).

FSW242   Ray J. Weiser (b ca 1910, OH).

FSW243   Eva C. Weiser (b ca 1912, OH).

FSW244   Lawrence Weiser (b ca Aug 1916, OH).

FSW25   Nina Groll Weiser (b Dec 1878, OH).

FSW26   Mina Beebe Weiser (b Dec 1878, OH).

FSW27   Everett E. Weiser (b Apr 1880, Marlboro, Delaware OH) m Amelia   (b ca 1890, OH).

FSW271   Gerald C. Weiser (b ca 1909, OH).

FSW28   Hartley Weiser.

FSW29   Solomon Weiser (b Jan 1885, OH).

FSW2A   Eva Hoke Weiser (b Jun 1887, OH).

FSW2B   Grace Fivecoats Weiser (b Nov 1891, OH).

FSW2C   Agnes Weiser.

FSW2D   Mollie Weiser.

FSW3   Henry Weiser.

FSW4   Margaret Weiser m   Smith. Marion OH.

Henry Weiser (1806-1895)
of Hampden Township, Cumberland County, Pennsylvania

The 1860 census of Hampden Township, Cumberland Co PA, calls Henry Weiser, aged 41, a native of Switzerland and a farm laborer. His will, written 28 Mar 1885, was supplemented with a codicil on 3 Apr 1893 (Cumberland County Wills, U-356). These documents and an entry in the Miscellaneous Docket 15, page 563, of the Cumberland County records, clarify his relatives.

He bequeathed $300 for missionary work to St. John's Lutheran Church at Shiremanstown PA, $1000 to the same for general purposes, $500 to St. Mark's Lutheran Church in Mechanicsburg, and the remainder to his relatives, who are unnamed, and without precise instructions about his estate's division. The codicil provided $1000 and personal items to Solomon Beck and his wife for treating him kindly since his return from the "West several years ago."

The burial records of St. John's Church record the death of Henry Weiser on 21 Feb 1895, aged 88 years, two months and six days, of a broken arm and paralysis. This yields a birthdate of 15 Dec 1806. The confirmation of Henry Weiser on 23 May 1829 is also recorded.

John and Mary Weiser are communicants at the church for the first time on 29 May 1819 (as Johannes and Maria) and commune fairly regularly thereafter. Jacob and Susanna Weiser, single, were confirmed in 1825. John communed for the last time on 6 May 1827. Maria and Henry communed from 1829 until the last time in 1835. With them is Joseph Will and his wife Susanna, likely a daughter whose husband was baptized and confirmed the same day as Henry in 1829. The 1830 census lists a Hy (Henry) in East Pennsboro Tp.

Tombstones difficult to read in the Friedens Church cemetery (an older name of St. John's Church) are for Maria Weiser, died 18 Dec 1836, aged 63 or 68 years, six months, and eleven days (which yields a possible birthdate of 7 Jun 1773 or 1768), aand for Susanna Wiser, 25 Mar 1804-8 Jun 1836, aged 32 years, two months and thirteen days.

The legatees of Henry Weiser were John Will, Muscatine Co IA; Elizabeth Weaver, Kingman Co KS; Catharine Hoover, Macon Co IL; and the children of Mary Pool: W.A. Pool, Pottawattomie Co IA; Mrs. Lois Shane, Cook Co IL; J.H. Pool, Logan Co OK; Mrs. Libbie E. Birchard, St. Louis Co MO; and J.S. Pool, Stearns Co MN. Apparently, Henry remained unmarried or, if married, had no issue.

[HJW]   Henry J. Weiser (1806-1864)
of Princeton, Wisconsin

Henry J. Weiser was a native of Goettingen, Germany. Born in 1806, he was a tailor by trade. He was married and had several children, before coming to the United States in 1853. He and his family settled on a farm near Princeton, WI[165].

HJW   Henry J. Weiser (5 May 1806, Germany-7 Sep 1864, Princeton WI) m ca 1844, Hanover, Germany, Christine Elizabeth Henke (15 Jun 1821, Hanover, Germany-28 Dec 1898). Farmer, Princeton WI.

HJW1   Mary Weiser (13 May 1845, Germany-19 Mar 1877) m 27 Mar 1861, Hosea Quimby (6 Feb 1844, Racine WI-13 Aug 1907).

HJW2   Caroline Weiser (b 13 May 1845, Germany-19 May 1927, Mankato MN) m 16 Feb 1878, Hosea Quimby (6 Feb 1844, Racine WI-13 Aug 1907).

HJW3   Henry Carl Wiser (3 Jun 1847, Hanover, Germany-28 Aug 1931) m Julia Maria Stacy (23 Jul 1852, Russell MA-24 Mar 1917, Gridley CA).

---

[165]Information for this family has been obtained from a manuscript by Lillian E. Mathias of Tulare CA, compiled in 1969. Minor changes based on Census records have been added by Edward Wiser, who also edited to the present format.

HJW31   Malvern Leroy ("Vern") Wiser (15 Dec 1872, Princeton WI-9 Aug 1918, Sacramento CA) m ca 1897, Edith Ann Williams (b 1 Aug 1874, IA). Farmer, Gridley CA.

HJW311   Vern Leroy ("Roy") Wiser (5 Aug 1898, IA-May 1980, Gridley CA) m 1) Ruth Johnson; m 2) Florence Wilder Edwards (3 May 1894-Sep 1979, Gridley CA).

HJW3111   Gwen Wiser (b 9 Oct 1922).

HJW312   Ray Beyer Wiser (b 5 Oct 1900, IA) m 1) Elizabeth Haller; m 2) Julie   .

HJW3121   Harry Malvern Wiser (b 4 Jan 1925).

HJW3122   Ray Haller Wiser (b 9 Feb 1927).

HJW3123   Emerson Ernest Wiser (b 28 Jan 1929).

HJW3124   Betty Jean Wiser (b 19 Nov 1933).

HJW313   Henry David ("Harry") Wiser (b 20 Jan 1908, Gridley CA) m Aug 1930, Inez Louise Wilson (b 19 Aug 1911, Hennessy OK). President, Chaffey College.

HJW3131   Melba Harryette Wiser (b 6 Jul 1931, Oroville CA) m 17 Jun 1953, Palo Alto CA, Robert Bruce Mathias (b 17 Nov 1930, Tulare CA). Olympic decathlete, US Congress.

HJW3132   Nancy Ann Wiser (b 6 Nov 1935, San Mateo CA) m 14 Jun 1959, Mare Island CA, Edward Mitchell Kocher. US Navy, Pentagon.

HJW314   Glen Williams Wiser (30 Aug 1911, CA-Jan 1980, CA) m Adeline Eager.

HJW32   Mary Iona Wiser (8 Jun 1874, Princeton WI-16 Sep 1956).

HJW33   Almeda Wiser (23 Jun 1876, IA-1967) m 14 Feb 1901, Domenick Killaran.

HJW34   Ralph Stacy Wiser (4 Jun 1878, IA-25 Dec 1948) m 24 Mar 1906, Jeanette McEachram (b ca 1884, IL).

HJW341   Stacy B. Wiser (b ca 1908, IA).

HJW342   Irene L. Wiser (b ca 1909, IA).

HJW343   Edith J. Wiser (b ca 1910, IA).

HJW344   Ralph Wiser.

HJW345   Paul ("Pete") Wiser.

HJW35   Claude Henry Wiser (18 Apr 1884, IA-4 Jul 1965, Mifflinburg PA) m 23 Mar 1913, Mary Jane Ittings (b ca 1884, IA). Teacher, PA.

HJW351   Florence Wiser.

HJW352   Winston Wiser.

HJW353   Malvern Wiser.

HJW354   Mary Wiser.

HJW36   Lola Irene Wiser (14 Apr 1886, IA-12 Dec 1963, Sutter CA) m 1) Jessie A. Rice; m
Edward Thurston.

HJW37   Clyde Prentice Wiser (7 Apr 1888, IA-May 1964, CA) m 10 Jun 1922, Edith Henshaw
(9 Dec 1897-Jun 1977).

HJW371   Prentice Wiser (16 Jan 1925-Aug 1985).

HJW372   Richard Wiser.

HJW373   Carl Wiser.

HJW374   David Wiser.

HJW38   Gladys Wiser (b 28 Nov 1891, IA) m 19 Dec 1925, Wheeler Abernathy.

HJW4   Wilhelmina Weiser (17 Dec 1849, Hanover, Germany-3 Jan 1925) m 17 Mar 1874, Julius
Kopplin (13 Dec 1849, Prussia, Germany-6 Jun 1897).

HJW5   Louisa A. Weiser (14 Mar 1853, Hanover, Germany-1921, Princeton WI).

HJW6   Albert Henry Weiser (b 21 Aug 1855, Princeton WI) m 15 Jan 1881, Green Lake WI,
Mary Elizabeth Hopkins (b ca 1863, WI).

HJW61   Ethel Weiser m   Perry.

HJW7   Alvira Weiser (5 Jul 1857, WI-15 Jun 1864, WI).

HJW8   Evaline (Eva) J. Weiser (1859, WI-1927, Princeton WI).

HJW9   Daughter Weiser (16 May 1861-12 May 1866, WI).

[JRW]   Jeremiah Wiser (b ca 1769)
of Oneida County, New York

Jeremiah Wiser was baptized on the 6th of August 1769 in Dutchess County, New York. His father was identified as Johannes Wiser. The next record of him that has been found is in the 1810 Census in Trenton Township, Oneida County, New York. He remained there or in adjacent Deerfield Township through 1850.

No records of his family have been found, and the census records are unclear. In 1810, there were three J. Wisers listed in Oneida County, and it is not possible tell who they were. There were three boys and a girl in his household in 1820, but there were three young men, two older men, a young woman and an older woman in the household, indicating that there may have been more than one family in the household. The 1830 Census, in fact, lists a man and woman both between 50 and 60 years old (presumably Jeremiah and his wife), as well as a man between 80 and 90 years old, who could have been the father of one of them. In the 1840 Census, Jeremiah was listed as between 70 and 80 years old, inconsistent with the previous census, but suggesting that his age may have been close to the limit of 60 in 1830 and 70 in 1840. His wife was identified in the 60 to 70 year bracket, indicating that she must have been slightly younger than he. In the 1850 Census, Jeremiah no longer had his own household, but was living with his son Stephen.

A number of other Wiser families are also found in the census records for these two and other adjacent townships. It is likely that they are somehow related, but census records confirm only that Stephen Wiser was a son of Jeremiah. The families are listed separately below, with the hope that documentation can be found to define the relationships.

JRW   Jeremiah Wiser (b 1769, Dutchess NY). Farmer, Oneida NY.

JRW1   Stephen D. Wiser (b ca 1799, NY) m Lucretia   (b ca 1805). Farmer, Oneida NY.

JRW11   David Wiser (b ca 1829).

JRW12   Cornelia Wiser (b ca 1830) m 17 Oct 1850, South Trenton, Oneida NY, Alonzo Chapin.

JRW13   Maria Wiser (b ca 1833).

JRW14   Orrin Wiser (b ca 1837).

. . .

JRWA   Jonas(?) W. Wiser (b ca 1814, NY) m Lydia E.   (b ca 1815, NY). Farmer, Milwaukee
and Fond du Lac WI.

JRWA1   Jeremiah E. Wiser (b ca 1837, NY).

JRWA2   George Henry Wiser (b 1 Aug 1838, Oneida NY) m Mary J.   (b Nov 1842, Canada).
Carpenter, Corvallis OR and San Diego CA.

JRWA21   Etta Wiser (b ca 1868, WI).

JRWA22   James E. Wiser (b ca 1869, WI).

JRWA23   Frank Wiser (b ca 1872, WI).

JRWA24   Georgia M. Wiser (b Aug 1883, OR).

JRWA3   Charles H. Wiser (b ca 1848, WI).

JRWA4   Edwin Wiser (b ca 1855, WI).

. . .

JRWH   Hiram H. Wiser (b ca 1814, NY) m Mary J.   (b ca 1816, England). Railroader, Utica
and Rochester NY.

JRWH1   Mary E. Wiser (b ca 1843, NY).

JRWH2   Albert H. Wiser (b ca 1845, NY).

JRWH3   Charles Henry Wiser (b Jan 1851, NY) m ca 1876, Lena   (b ca 1857, IL). Chicago
IL.

JRWH31   Nellie M. Wiser (b Feb 1878, IL).

JRWH32   Louise J. Wiser (b Oct 1879, IL).

JRWH33   Fanny M. Wiser (b Aug 1881, IL).

JRWH34   George R. Wiser (b Dec 1884, IL).

JRWH4   Edward B. Wiser (b ca 1855).

. . .

JRWI   Isaac J. Wiser (b ca 1795, NY) m Mary   (b ca 1793, PA).

JRWI1   John Wiser (b ca 1825, NY).

JRWI2   Sarah E. Wiser (b ca 1836, NY).

. . .

JRWJ   Jeremiah Wiser (b ca 1806, NY) m Diana H.   (b ca 1804, NY).

JRWJ1   Harriet Wiser (b ca 1837, NY).

. . .

JRWM   Martin Wiser (b ca 1782, NY) m Sophia   (b ca 1811, NY).

JRWM1   Calvin(?) Wiser (b ca 1851, NY).

. . .

JRWR   Ira Wiser (b 15 Sep 1808, Deerfield, Oneida NY) m Rebecca Joslin (b ca 1810, NY).

. . .

JRWW   William H. Wiser (b ca 1809, NY) m Nancy   (b ca 1813, NY).

JRWW1   Nancy H. Wiser (b ca 1836, NY).

JRWW2   Sarah Cornelia Wiser (b ca 1838, NY).

JRWW3   Henry S. Wiser (b ca 1845, NY).

[JMW]   Jeremiah Wiser (b ca 1809)
of Cumberland County, New Jersey

Jeremiah Wiser appeared first in the 1850 Census for Cumberland County, New Jersey. There is a marriage recorded in the International Genealogical Index of Samuel Wiser and Hepzebah Ridgeway on 14 Jul 1807 at Cumberland, New Jersey, which makes them Jeremiah's probable parents. However, none of these names appear in the census records prior to 1850, and no other records of a Samuel Wiser in the area.

JMW   Jeremiah Wiser (b ca 1809, Cumberland NJ) m 29 Jul 1831, Cumberland NJ, Deborah
Errickson (b ca 1808, Cumberland NJ).

JMW1   Deborah Wiser (b ca 1837, PA) m 25 Aug 1856, Maurice River, Cumberland NJ, James
W. Fithian.

JMW2   George Wiser (b Oct 1839) m Mattie   (b Apr 1853, NJ).

JMW21   James Wiser (b Jan 1868, NJ).

JMW22   Maggie Wiser (b ca 1870, NJ) m Elmer Alsener(?).

JMW3   Sarah Wiser (b ca 1841).

JMW4   William Wiser (b Mar 1845, NJ) m Mary   (b Sep 1850, PA).

JMW41   Thomas M. Wiser (b Dec 1869, NJ) m Emma M. Reed(?) (Aug 1867, WV).

JMW411   Harry S. Wiser (b Nov 1893, IN).

JMW412   Charles Wiser (b ca 1907, IL).

JMW42   William Wiser (b Apr 1874, NJ).

JMW43   Clara Wiser (b Nov 1876, NJ).

JMW5   Susan Wiser (b ca 1847, NJ).

JMW6   Hepzibah M. Wiser (b 20 Jul 1850, Maurice River, Cumberland NJ) m 22 Apr 1873, Millville, Cumberland NJ, Joseph Shaw.

[JJW]   John Jacob Wiser (b ca 1796) of Louisville, Kentucky

John Jacob Wiser arrived in Kentucky sometime between 1800 and 1820, probably directly from Germany. After marrying Louisiana Arnold in 1821, he settled on a farm in Jefferson County, Kentucky, just outside Louisville and started farming.

JJW   John Jacob Wiser (b ca 1796, Germany) m 17 May 1821, Jefferson KY, Louisiana ("Lucy") Arnold (b ca 1806, KY). Farmer.

JJW1   Anthony Wiser (b Jul 1822, KY) m 20 Mar 1845, Jefferson KY, Margaret Snawder (b Jan 1824, KY). Farmer.

JJW11   Julia Ann Wiser (b Mar 1846, KY).

JJW12   John D. Wiser (Feb 1848, KY-31 Mar 1922, Jefferson KY) m Margaret   (b Jun 1854, KY).

JJW121   Anthony J. Wiser (Mar 1877, KY-27 Dec 1945, Jefferson KY) m Mattie B. Probst (12 May 1890, KY-15 Mar 1979, Jefferson KY).

JJW1211   Mildred Wiser (b 8 Mar 1914, Jefferson KY).

JJW1212   Authurie Wiser (b 17 Feb 1918, Jefferson KY).

JJW1213   Eugene A. Wiser (b 2 Mar 1919, Jefferson KY).

JJW1214   Richard L. Wiser (b 22 Apr 1923, Jefferson KY).

JJW122   Raymond Wiser (Jul 1879, KY-2 Apr 1966, Jefferson KY).

JJW123   Nora Wiser (b Aug 1881, KY).

JJW124   Alexander Wiser (10 Jan 1886, KY-27 May 1973, Jefferson KY) m May E.   (b ca 1895, KY).

JJW1241   Martin Wiser (4 Oct 1912, KY-7 Oct 1978, Louisville KY).

JJW1242   May D. Wiser (b ca 1916, KY).

JJW125   Agnes Wiser (b Nov 1887, KY).

JJW126   Augustus Wiser (Jan 1890, KY-12 Mar 1932, Jefferson KY).

JJW13   Eliza Wiser (b 1850, KY).

JJW14   Louisiana Wiser (b ca 1852, KY).

JJW15   Frederick Wiser (Aug 1857, KY-4 Jan 1911, Jefferson KY).

JJW16   Alexander Wiser (Oct 1859, KY-5 Feb 1931, Jefferson KY) m Caroline   (b Nov 1849,
KY).

JJW2   George Wiser (b ca 1824).

JJW3   David Wiser (b ca 1825, KY) m Margaret   (b ca 1831, Bavaria).

JJW31   Mahala (Amelia) Wiser (b ca 1848, KY).

JJW32   Thomas Wiser (b ca 1850, KY) m Annie M.   (b ca 1850, GA).

JJW321   Eugene Wiser (b ca 1875, KY).

JJW322   Eileen Wiser (b ca 1877, TN).

JJW33   John H. Wiser (Aug 1851, KY-11 Jun 1934, Jefferson KY).

JJW34   George Wiser (Nov 1855, KY-8 Mar 1942, Jefferson KY) m Mary J.   (b Oct 1857,
KY).

JJW341   Maggie Wiser (b ca 1879, KY).

JJW342   Mamie Wiser (b Oct 1880, KY).

JJW343   Lizzie Wiser (b Jan 1883, KY).

JJW344   John Edward Wiser (Jan 1885, KY-22 Oct 1961, Jefferson KY) m Ada G. Kelly (19 Oct
1888, KY-13 Dec 1982, Jefferson KY).

JJW3441   Mabel M. Wiser (b ca 1911, KY).

JJW345   Harry L. Wiser (9 Jan 1889, KY-30 Apr 1975, Jefferson KY).

JJW346   Cora E. Wiser (b Feb 1891, KY).

JJW347   Annie M. Wiser (b Aug 1893, KY).

JJW348   Frances E. Wiser (b Nov 1895, KY).

JJW349   George Wiser (b Feb 1900, KY).

JJW35   Barbara Wiser (b ca 1858, KY).

JJW36   Anthony Wiser (b ca 1859, KY).

JJW37   Mary Wiser (b Feb 1861, KY).

JJW38   Martha Wiser (b ca 1863, KY).

JJW39   Francis Wiser (Mar 1865, KY-8 Mar 1955, Jefferson KY).

JJW3A   Joseph Wiser (Apr 1867, KY-4 Nov 1922, Jefferson KY).

JJW3B   Lawrence Wiser (Feb 1870, KY-15 Mar 1957, Jefferson KY).

JJW3C   Anna Wiser (b ca 1870, KY).

JJW3D   Philip Wiser (Jan 1874, KY-11 Mar 1953, Jefferson KY).

JJW4   Hiram Wiser (b Aug 1826, KY) m Lena   (ca 1837, Prussia-7 Oct 1917, Jefferson KY).
Farmer.

JJW41   Henry T. Wiser (Oct 1854, KY-14 Feb 1940, Jefferson KY) m 1)   ; m 2) Katie   (Nov 1875, KY-27 Jun 1959, Jefferson KY).

JJW411   Frank Wiser (b Jul 1882, KY).

JJW412   Mattie Wiser (b Sep 1888, KY).

JJW413   Floyd Wiser (ca 1901, KY-12 Jan 1960, Jefferson KY).

JJW414   Irvin Wiser (ca 1903, KY-22 Jul 1961, Jefferson KY).

JJW42   William R. Wiser (Oct 1858, KY-10 Jan 1916, Jefferson KY) m Georgia A.   (Sep 1860, KY-6 Apr 1915, Jefferson KY).

JJW421   Samuel Wiser (Feb 1886, KY-27 Apr 1911, Jefferson KY).

JJW422   Emma A. Wiser (b Feb 1889, KY).

JJW43   Nicholas Wiser (Sep 1859, KY-30 Dec 1924, Jefferson KY) m Annie K.   (Apr 1869, KY-9 Sep 1926, Jefferson KY).

JJW431   Lillian F. Wiser (b Aug 1891, KY).

JJW432   Mary Theresa Wiser (b Aug 1895, KY).

JJW433   Mollie C. Wiser (b Aug 1897, KY).

JJW434   Frank B. Wiser (4 Jun 1900, KY-1 Jun 1979, Jefferson KY).

JJW435   Albert Wiser (b ca 1904, KY).

JJW44   Laura Wiser (b ca 1861, KY).

JJW45   John Wiser (b ca 1863, KY).

JJW46   Catharine Wiser (b ca 1865, KY).

JJW47   Mary Wiser (b ca 1867, KY).

JJW48   Anna Wiser (b ca 1869, KY).

JJW49   Philip E. Wiser (Sep 1873, KY-29 Dec 1912, Jefferson KY) m Josie M.   (b May 1881, KY).

JJW491   C. Jn. Wiser (b ca 1900, KY).

JJW4A   Wickey Wiser (b ca 1873, KY).

JJW4B   Maggie Wiser (b ca 1875, KY).

JJW4C   Victor Wiser (May 1878, KY-14 Oct 1946, Jefferson KY) m Mabel Gray (ca 1884, KY-20 Apr 1962, Jefferson KY).

JJW4C1   Virginia Agnes Wiser (b ca 1908, KY).

JJW4D   Charles Wiser (11 Jun 1882, KY-2 Sep 1968, Jefferson KY) m Mary   (b ca 1889, KY).

JJW4D1   Viola Wiser (b ca 1906, KY).

JJW4D2   Evelyn Wiser (b ca 1912, KY).

JJW5   Mahala Wiser (b ca 1832, KY).

JJW6   Elizabeth Wiser (b ca 1833, KY).

JJW7   Charles Wiser (ca 1836-27 Mar 1921, Jefferson KY) m 21 Apr 1860, Jefferson KY, Diana Elizabeth Ward (b 1840, KY).

JJW71   Frederick T. Wiser (Jun 1866, KY-8 Oct 1945, Jefferson KY) m Mary   (Jan 1871, KY-10 Dec 1941, Jefferson KY).

JJW711   Jesse James Wiser (10 Jan 1893, KY-21 Feb 1983, Jefferson KY) m Mattie Caple(?) (29 Aug 1895, KY-28 Jul 1981, Jefferson KY).

JJW7111   Evangeline F. Wiser (b 23 Feb 1919, Jefferson KY).

JJW7112   Estelle V. Wiser (b 17 Nov 1925, Jefferson KY).

JJW712   Edward A. Wiser (b ca 1901, KY).

JJW72   Ida Wiser (b ca 1869, KY).

JJW73   Elizabeth Wiser (b ca 1871, KY).

JJW74   America Wiser (b ca 1874, KY).

JJW75   Zacharias Wiser (Apr 1878, KY-14 Jul 1952, Jefferson KY) m ca 1901, Minnie   (ca 1882, KY-11 Aug 1960, Jefferson KY).

JJW751   Leonard Wiser (28 Jul 1901, KY-29 Sep 1976, Jefferson KY).

JJW76   Minnie Wiser (b Sep 1882, KY).

JJW77   Lawrence Wiser (May 1884, KY-1 Feb 1946, Jefferson KY) m Emma   (28 Dec 1883, KY-13 Jan 1982, Jefferson KY).

JJW771   Walter A. Wiser (b ca 1906, KY).

JJW8   Henry Wiser (Apr 1840, KY-1 Nov 1917, Jefferson KY) m Sophia   (Oct 1848, KY-5 Feb 1920, Jefferson KY).

JJW81   Emma M. Wiser (b ca 1869, KY).

JJW82   Abbie (Allie) L. Wiser (b Jul 1875, KY).

JJW83   Henry Clay Wiser (Feb 1878, KY-7 Feb 1943, Jefferson KY) m Nettie   (b ca 1883, KY).

JJW831   Horace C. Wiser (b ca 1903, KY).

JJW832   Walter C. Wiser (b ca 1908, KY).

JJW833   Jeanette Wiser (b 11 Feb 1913, Jefferson KY).

JJW84   Clara May Wiser (b 1880, KY).

JJW85   Clem Wiser (23 Feb 1883, KY-30 May 1974, Louisville KY) m Alice S. Gagel (ca 1890-30 Jun 1929, Jefferson KY).

JJW851   Clarence Wiser (21 Aug 1914, KY-2 Jul 1986, Jefferson KY).

JJW852   Edna Wiser (b 7 Feb 1916, Jefferson KY).

JJW853   Gladys Wiser (b 20 Aug 1917, Jefferson KY).

JJW854   Alfers C. Wiser (b 19 Jul 1920, Jefferson KY).

JJW855   Ray H. Wiser (b 23 Nov 1924, Jefferson KY).

JJW86   Frudie B. Wiser (b Jun 1885, KY).

JJW87   Clara Florence Wiser (b Nov 1887, KY).

JJW88   Flora Wiser (b Nov 1895, KY).

JJW9   Kitty Elizabeth Wiser (b ca 1847, KY).

Johann Jacob Weisser (1814-1892)
of Schopfloch, Wuerttemberg, and Lancaster, Pennsylvania[166]

Johann Jacob Weisser was born at 72296 Schopfloch in Wuerttemberg, near Freudenstadt, on 24 May 1814. He was the son of Christian Weisser (10 May 1789, Schopfloch-18 Nov 1854 at 72172 Hopfau), who married 3 Aug 1814, Barbara Eberhardt (d 16 Nov 1854).

Christian was a farmer and proprietor of the Sonne Inn. His father Georg Friedrich Weisser (8 Sep 1745-10 May 1827) married Elizabetha Helber (8 Nov 1754-3 Feb 1811), and was also proprietor of the Sonne and a judge in Schopfloch. Georg's parents were Joseph Weisser, innkeeper and judge in 72290 Wittendorf, and Elizabetha Gottlieben Nussborn.

Children of Christian and Barbara (Eberhardt) Weisser:

1. Johann Jacob Weisser.

2. Johann Weisser (b 22 Sep 1815) m 1848 and moved to Reunthausen(?).

---

[166]Data provided by Charles F. Weisser, Lancaster, and from the records of Zion Lutheran Church, Lancaster, and the registers of the Lutheran churches at Schopfloch and Oberiflingen.

3. Maria Christina Weisser (b 4 Apr 1817) m 1848 and moved to Rodt.

4. Christina Weisser (b 12 Oct 1819) m 28 Feb 1843, 72296 Oberiflingen.

5. Elisabetha Katharina Weisser (b 22 Dec 1823) m 1848 and moved to 72355 Schomberg.

6. Barbara Weisser (b 11 Sep 1825). The church register at Oberiflingen says she went to America. According to the family of Jacob, she married and lived in Philadelphia.

Johann Jacob was confirmed at Oberiflingen on 20 Apr 1828. The family had moved there in 1823. He probably emigrated about 1849. He was naturalized at Lancaster, application dated 1855, and final naturalization 1858. The records of Zion Lutheran Church in Lancaster record these children of Jacob Weiser and wife Agnes Sengler or Single (1824-1901):

1. Catharine Weisser (25 Aug 1850-1866).

2. Mary Weisser (1852, but not in the Zion records-1908), unmarried.

3. Johan Jacob Weisser (5 Jan 1854-1937). He had a son Charles F. Weiser, who lived in Lancaster.

4. Barbara Weisser (22 Nov 1857-1947).

5. Johann Weisser (b 15 Oct 1859). Bur Philadelphia PA.

6. Christine Weisser (b 17 Jul 1865). No further record.

7. Christian Weisser (b 10 Jun 1869). No further record.

It seems highly likely that this family descends from the large Black Forest Weisser family, which seems to have centered at 78126 Buchenberg.

[JNW]   John Wiser (d 1884)
of Port Matilda, Centre County, Pennsylvania

John Wiser, age 25, is reported as resident in a boarding house in Snyder Tp, Blair Co PA, on the 1850 census. In 1860, age 28, he and wife Margaret, age 26, and children William, 9, Joseph, 6, and Wilder, 2, are in Houston Tp, Centre Co, with Elizabeth Ardy, 54, a widow, born in Pennsylvania and perhaps the parent of one of them.

In 1880 he is a widower in Port Matilda, Worth Tp, Centre Co, age 61. He says he was born in Pennsylvania, and that both his parents were also. His household contains Wildres F., 21; Loney A.C., 18; Nora E, 15; Emma R.S., 12; and Annie May, 10.

His will, signed 7 May 1884, was probated 21 July; his date of death is given as 13 Jul 1884. He names children Williams James, Wilders Susan, Aplona Regina, Norah Ellen, Emma Arsila, and Anna May. Later estate documents indicated that Aplona married a Hardy, Norah Ellen a Marks, and perhaps Wilders Susan married a Stephens. There is an Ellis Poorman named who may be Emma Arsila.

William James Wiser (born 15 Nov 1851, according to the family) is listed in Centre County in 1910, age 58, with wife Rachel J., 51, and children George C., 25, with wife Ella, 20, and a child Clair T.; Myrtle I., 23; Thurman C., 21; Lena M., 19; Gordon H., 16; Pearl A., 14; and Belle E., 13. Apparently a William E., age 46 in 1920, is also a son. His wife was Susie S., 47, and they had William, 11; Gilbert, 10; and James, 5. In 1920 the senior William and wife have Clair T. Wiser, 11, in their home. Thurman C., 31 (born 6 Oct 1888, Port Matilda, according to the family), and wife Sarah E. Woodring (b 17 Aug 1891, Port Matilda PA), have Thurman Jr., 3, and Gerald, 9/12 of a year, in their home in Trafford Tp, Westmoreland Co. According to family information, his first wife was a Patton.

Descendants in Port Matilda suggest that John Wiser might have come from Bellwood, Antis Tp, Blair County. Since his age varies so greatly on the decennial census reports (1850: 25; 1860: 28; 1880: 61), it is difficult to be precise about a birthdate. No birthdate confounds determining his parentage.

JNW   John Wiser (d 13 Jul 1884) m Margaret   (b ca 1834, PA).

JNW1   William James Wiser (b 15 Nov 1851, PA) m Rachel J.   (b ca 1859, PA).

JNW11   George C. Wiser (b ca 1885, PA) m Ella   (b ca 1890, PA).

JNW111   Clair T. Wiser (b ca 1909, PA).

JNW12   Myrtle I. Wiser (b ca 1887, PA).

JNW13   Thurman C. Wiser (b 6 Oct 1888, Port Matilda PA) m Sarah E. Woodring (b 17 Aug 1891, Port Matilda PA).

JNW131   Thurman C. Wiser (b 13 May 1916, Trafford PA) m 30 Aug 1942, Port Matilda PA, Grace Rosalie (b 21 Dec 1919, Port Matilda PA).

JNW132   Gerald A. Wiser (17 Aug 1919, Trafford PA-1 Feb 1992, Altoona PA) m 16 Nov 1937, Jane E. Williams. He, USA, Lt. Col.,1942-46; PSU.

JNW1321   Barbara Wiser.

JNW1322   Larry R. Wiser.

JNW1323   Beatrice M. Wiser m   Filewich.

JNW1324   Steven R. Wiser.

JNW14   Lena M. Wiser (b ca 1891, PA).

JNW15   Gordon H. Wiser (b ca 1894, PA).

JNW16   Pearl A. Wiser (b ca 1896, PA).

JNW17   Bella E. Wiser (b ca 1897, PA).

JNW2   Joseph Wiser (b ca 1854, PA).

JNW3   Wilders Susan Wiser (b ca 1858, PA).

JNW4   Aplona (Loney) Regina A. C. Wiser (b ca 1862, PA) m   Hardy.

JNW5   Norah Ellen Wiser (b ca 1865, PA) m   Marks.

JNW6   Emma Arsila S. Wiser (b ca 1868, PA).

JNW7   Anna May Wiser (b ca 1870, PA).

[JTW]   Jonathan Weiser (1828-1912) of Bedford County, Pennsylvania

The earliest clear reference to Jonathan Weiser or Wiser, whose tombstone reports a birthdate of 31 Dec 1828, is a statement sworn before a justice of the peace in Bedford County in 1859. In it, he is said to be a resident of East Providence Tp, Bedford Co, and is attempting to gain exemption from military service due to a hernia. He was, however, a private in the Civil War, enrolling in Co. E, 49th PA Volunteers on 13 Aug

1863. He was discharged 20 Jun 1865 to his home at Wells Tannery, Fulton Co.

He does not seem to be anywhere on the 1850 or 1860 censuses, but in 1870, he is in Broad Tp, Bedford Co, as he is in 1880. In 1900 he is in Hopewell Tp, Bedford Co, and again in 1910. He reports his birthplace as Pennsylvania in each enumeration and in 1880 gives Pennsylvania as his parents' birthplace.

He married Matilda ("Tillie") Adams (Jun 1833-), and they had James W. (b ca 1854); Nancy S. (b ca 1857); Mary (b 1860); Amy R. (b 1862), who married John R. Letcher, Jr.; Ella (Jun 1867-1938), who married John Fox; and Harry Bartley (24 Jun 1870-6 Jan 1948), who married Mary Nash and left some descendants who spell the surname Wiser. They are buried at Hopewell, Bedford Co.

No clear candidate for Jonathan's father is evident unless they are members of the Christian Weiser family of Shippensburg not known to us. The fact that Jonathan does not seem to be on the 1850 census (when he might have been in or near his parental home) or the 1860 census seems to block potential clues.

JTW   Jonathan Wiser (b 31 Dec 1828, PA) m Matilda Adams (b Jan 1833, PA).

JTW1   Henry James Wiser (b Aug 1853, PA) m Lessie N.   (b Feb 1845, PA).

JTW11   James Nepper Wiser (b Jul 1877, PA).

JTW12   Zora Wiser (b Jan 1880, PA).

JTW13   Harry Wiser (b Mar 1885, PA).

JTW2   Nancy S. Wiser (b ca 1857, PA).

JTW3   Mary A. Wiser (b ca 1860, PA).

JTW4   Amy (Annie) Roselphia Wiser (b 21 Dec 1862, Hopewell, Bedford PA) m John R. Letcher.

JTW5   Ella E. Wiser (Jun 1867, PA-1938) m John Fox.

JTW6   Harrison Bartley Wiser (24 Jun 1870, PA-6 Jan 1948) m Mary Nash (b Sep 1875,
England).

JTW61   James Henry Wiser (b Jul 1897, PA) m Pearl L.   (b ca 1895, PA).

JTW611   Lois M. Wiser (b ca Jul 1916, PA).

JTW612   Cyril Wiser (b ca Jul 1919, PA).

JTW62   Cecil Adams Wiser (b Oct 1899, PA).

JTW63   Verrie(?) Wiser (b ca 1902, PA).

JTW64   Alberta (Alverta) Wiser (b ca 1905, PA).

JTW65   Edwin Wiser (b ca 1913, PA).

JTW66   Frances Wiser (b ca Sep 1915, PA).

JTW67   Justina Wiser (b ca Dec 1918, PA).

[LVW]   Levi Weiser (b ca 1821)
of Lebanon County, Pennsylvania

Levi Weiser, who appears on the 1850 census in Jackson Township, Lebanon Co, PA, reported his age as 26 and that he was born in Pennsylvania. His wife Sophia, also a Pennsylvanian, was 25, and they had two small children. In 1860 he was said to be 39, which facts give him a birthdate between 1821 and 1824. By 1870 Sophia is a widow. His parentage is unknown.

LVW   Levi Weiser (b ca 1821, PA) m Sophia   (b Feb 1822, PA).

LVW1   William Weiser (b ca 1846, PA).

LVW2   George Weiser (b ca 1849, PA).

LVW3   Mayberry Weiser (b Sep 1851, PA) m 1) Amelia   (b Dec 1849, PA); m 2) ca 1906, Kate.

LVW31   Mary Weiser (b ca 1871, PA) m   Moor.

LVW311   Charles Moor (b Nov 1890).

LVW32   Lizzie Weiser (b Aug 1872, PA).

LVW33   Willie Weiser (b ca 1876, PA).

LVW34   Kate Weiser (b Dec 1877, PA).

LVW4   Allen E. Weiser (b Nov 1852, Myerstown PA) m Caroline Sarah Geasy (29 Oct 1849, Myerstown PA-14 Jan 1934, Reading PA).

LVW41   Harry Rambler Weiser (Dec 1874, Myerstown PA-19 Feb 1958, Reading PA) m 23 Oct 1919, Reading PA Mary Elizabeth Clouser (17 Oct 1876, Lancaster IL-26 Nov 1937).

LVW42   George L. Weiser (b Nov 1876, PA) m 9 Apr 1912, Reading PA, Elizabeth A. Cassidy (b ca 1885, PA).

LVW421   George F. Weiser (b ca 1913, PA) m 9 Dec 1944, Mary E. O'Reilly.

LVW4211   George E. Weiser.

LVW4212   Gloria F. Weiser m   Gilmore.

LVW4213   Bernard J. Weiser.

LVW422   J. William Weiser (b ca 1915, PA).

LVW423   Robert F. Weiser (b ca 1916, PA).

LVW424   Gerald J. Weiser (ca 1918, PA-13 Jun 1995, Spring, Berks PA) m Jean M. Lochman.

LVW4241   Diane E. Weiser m Carl L. Leas.

LVW4242   Marcia A. Weiser m Walter R. Holbrook.

LVW4243   Barbara E. Weiser m Walter M. Leis.

LVW425   Virginia Weiser m Robert Hollenbach.

LVW426   Bernice Weiser m   Cate.

LVW43   Sarah M. Weiser (b Nov 1878, PA).

LVW44   Robert L. Weiser (Dec 1880, PA-15 Jun 1936) m Mame E. Felker (1879, PA-24 May 1964).

LVW441   William A. Weiser (b ca 1907, PA).

LVW442   Christina C. Weiser (1909, PA-1985) m Paul K. Reinert (1911-1967).

LVW443   Jennie V. Weiser (b ca 1919, PA) m Webster Conrad.

LVW45   Stella E. Weiser (b Feb 1886, PA) m   Herbein.

LVW451   Russell Herbein (b ca 1910).

LVW452   Edgar Herbein (b ca 1912).

LVW453   Ralph Herbein (b ca 1915).

LVW46   Ella Stella Weiser (Feb 1886, Myerstown PA-9 Nov 1964) m 7 Sep 1907, Reading PA, Morris M. Bohn (10 Dec 1878, Reading PA-27 Sep 1959, Reading PA).

LVW47   Minnie M. Weiser (b Nov 1889, Reading PA) m 28 Sep 1912, Reading PA, William M. Kauffman (b ca 1885, Berks PA).

LVW48   Florence M. Weiser (b Dec 1891, Reading PA) m 10 Jun 1916, Reading PA, Howard Zeller (b ca 1892, Bethlehem PA).

LVW49   James C. Weiser (b Feb 1895, Reading PA) m 28 Oct 1916, Reading PA, Lydia S. Brod (b ca 1890, Danville PA).

LVW5   Samuel Weiser (b 5 Feb 1855, PA).

LVW6   Elizabeth Weiser (b ca 1857, PA).

LVW7   Aaron Weiser (b ca 1859, PA).

LVW8   Robert A. Weiser (b 12 Feb 1861, PA) m ca 1883, Lillie L. Blecher (b Dec 1866, PA).

LVW81   Clinton Robert Weiser (3 Jul 1884, PA-Jul 1970, PA) m Sarah C. DeVanney (b ca 1886, PA).

LVW811   Clinton Robert Weiser Jr. (5 Aug 1907, PA-May 1980).

LVW812   Regina M. Weiser (b ca 1910, PA).

LVW813   Marie K. Weiser (b ca 1912, PA).

LVW82   May Weiser (30 May 1889-25 Apr 1897).

LVW83   William Glen Weiser (b 7 May 1893, PA).

LVW84   Ralph Russell Weiser (20 Nov 1898, PA-Jul 1975, PA) m Katherine M. Tshudy (1897-1950). Bur Palmyra PA.

LVW85   Harold Weiser (2 Jun 1903, PA-18 Apr 1956). Bur Palmyra PA.

LVW9   John Andrew Weiser (12 Aug 1864, Myerstown PA-4 May 1932) m 22 Dec 1883, Berks

PA, Bertha Lily Carver (2 Jan 1865, Frystown PA-29 Dec 1920, Gibbsboro NJ).

LVW91 George H. Weiser (Oct 1885, Lebanon PA-5 Jun 1967, PA) m 24 Dec 1912, Reading PA, Susan C. Leinbach (b ca 1879, Fleetwood PA).

LVW92 Earl E. Weiser (19 Aug 1887, Myerstown PA-29 Jun 1973) m 1) 26 Mar 1910, Reading PA, Stella Sarah Messner (Sep 1889, Pinegrove, Schuylkill PA-Jul 1941); m 2) Edna S. (19 Jul 1902-12 Aug 1970).

LVW93 Conrad Casper Weiser (19 Oct 1892, PA-Jan 1943) m Katie M. Hoch (b 6 Sep 1904).

LVW94 John Bryan Weiser (20 Apr 1897, Wernersville PA-12 Apr 1971) m 1) 23 Feb 1916, Reading PA, Miriam Palm (May 1899, Reading PA-Mar 1928); m 2) Lucy R. (Mar 1897-Nov 1975).

LVW941 Dorothy Ella Weiser (b 10 Jul 1916, PA).

LVW942 May M. Weiser (b ca 1919, PA).

LVW943 Janet Lillian M. Weiser (b 11 Jul 1923).

LVW95 Thomas Levi Weiser (5 Apr 1906-8 Jun 1908).

Louis Weiser
of Lancaster, Pennsylvania

The records of Zion Lutheran Church, Lancaster PA, register the marriage of Louis Weiser of Wuerttemberg to Maria Mold, 5 Apr 1856, and the birth of Maria Dorothea (b 21 Nov 1856), Jacob (b 17 Nov 1859), and Albrecht Ludwig (b 1862). There is a naturalization for Louis in Lancaster.

[MTW] Martin Weiser
of Allentown, Pennsylvania

Martin Weiser appeared in the 1800 Census at Easton, Pennsylvania, from where he moved to Allentown where he spent the rest of his life selling and repairing clocks. He appears to have been born in the 1770s, but his origin is unclear. According to the History of Lehigh County, he was a descendant of Conrad Weiser, and his name was common to Conrad's family. However, his presence so early in the country makes it impossible that he could have descended from Conrad, and it is more likely that he had come from Germany.

This family was an unusually important one, given its small size. Martin's son Nelson was a politician and newspaperman in Allentown, and his son was a newspaper editor.

MTW Martin Weiser m Mary Ann (b ca 1792, PA).

MTW1 Nelson Weiser (b 6 Aug 1823, PA) m 26 Apr 1851, Elemina R. (b Aug 1822, PA).

MTW11 Anna E. Weiser (b ca 1852, PA) m 8 Feb 1872, Thomas B. Leisenring.

MTW12 Mary C. Weiser (b ca 1854, PA).

MTW13 Sarah Weiser (b ca 1859, PA).

MTW14 Charles W. Weiser (b Apr 1863, PA) m Sarah A. (b ca 1882, PA).

MTW141 Charles K. Weiser (b ca 1905, PA).

MTW142 Helen C/R. Weiser (b ca 1908, PA).

MTW143   Nelson A. Weiser (b ca 1910, PA).

MTW144   George K. Weiser (b ca 1919, PA).

Mary Margaret Weiser Reed (1802-1884)
of Lycoming County, Pennsylvania

Mary Margaret Weiser is reported by descendants to have been born 3 Jan 1802 in "Bucks" County, probably actually Berks County. She married Jacob Reed (1802-1850) and eventually they settled at Okome, Lycoming Co.

There is a baptism for Harriet Reed, born to Jacob Reed and his wife Mary Weiser, on 18 May 1826 at Zion Church, Augustaville PA, Northumberland County. There are baptisms for two other children at Friedens Church in Lycoming County: Getura [Keturah], born 18 Apr 1835, baptized 24 May 1835, and Maria Margareth, born 28 Aug 1839, to Jacob Rieth and Marie, nee Weiser, baptized 19 Apr 1840 with Katharina Schreiner as sponsor. Family sources name further Matilda, Melinda, Julianna, Jackson, a boy who died at age eight, and Lydia Alice (7 Aug 1844-28 Apr 1931). Lydia married George Brion (12 Aug 1832-4 Mar 1900) in 1863 and had six children.

The marriage to a Reed surely suggests that she might have been part of the Tulpehocken Weisers. Descendants claim that her father's name was reported as John Weiser, but all of the couples in the Conrad or Christopher Frederick Weiser families who could have been having children around 1802 either have a child that year or were not yet married. The three men named John who might fit were CP33 John Weiser (1779-1824), who married Catharine Fengel; RF42 John Weiser (1766-1825); and RF16 John Weiser (b 1762). The first had a daughter born in 1802. The second left a will carefully naming all his children, but does not list a Mary or a Margaret. Of the third, nothing is known. Probably only the discovery of a privately-held document will clarify her parentage.

[MW]   Michael Wiser (1758-1845)
of Fauquier County, Virginia

There have been several reports of people named Wiser in Virginia during the early 1700s, but it has not been possible to trace them to any of the existing families. This family seems to have originated with a miller named Henry Weiser, who appeared in Frederick County, Maryland in 1769. He was said to be of 'New York Government', but no reference to his presence in New York has been found.[167]

On 20 April 1769 Henry entered into a contract with one Thomas Beall to lease a 150-acre tract of land which was located where Rock Creek Park in Washington, DC is now located. Under the contract, Henry could occupy the land and use the grist mill in exchange for seventy pounds rent annually. He was also required to plant five hundred apple trees. However, he seems to have been unable to meet the financial requirements because in September 1770 he sold many of his possessions to Thomas Beall for ninety pounds, and in 1771 he appeared on the tax rolls of Loudoun County, Virginia. He was still there in 1782, but was listed on the tax rolls of Fairfax County, Virginia in 1790. There is no indication of what he was doing during that time and no later records of his presence have been found, and it is not known where or when he died.

Michael Wiser enlisted in the 7th Maryland Regiment of the Continental Line in June 1778 for a term of three years. He fought at the Battle of Monmouth Courthouse in New Jersey, but was captured by the British at Camden, South Carolina and was held prisoner at Charleston, South Carolina for a year. After the war he appeared on the Loudon County tax rolls in 1782 and then moved to Fairfax County, where he was listed on the tax rolls from 1783 through 1806. From this pattern of movement it is inferred that he was the son of Henry, but there is no documentation of their relationship. Michael had moved to Fauquier County, Virginia by 1811, where he was listed on the tax rolls through 1823, but his son Thomas remained there and Michael is thought to have remained there until he died in 1845.

Michael lived long enough to file an application for a pension, from which most of the information about him has been obtained. He prepared the application in March 1823 while he was in Fauquier County. He stated that he was 64 years old in December 1822, that his wife Nelly was then 58 years old and that he was living with a son who was 34 years old. The pension file shows that he had sons Henry and Thomas who were

---

[167]For a possible link with the family of Michael and Philip Wiser of North Carolina, see that chapter.

grown men in 1814, that he was married before 1 January 1794, and that he died 26 April 1845.[168]

MW   Michael Wiser (1758-26 Apr 1845, Fauquier VA) m 10 Apr 1782, Fairfax VA, Nelly Beach (ca 1764-ca 1848, Fauquier VA).

MW1   Henry Wiser(b ca 1788, VA) m 30 Apr 1840, Monongalia VA, Mary Ann Keener.

MW11   George Wiser (b ca 1840, VA).

MW2   Thomas Wiser (b ca 1790, Fairfax VA-ca 1855, Fauquier VA) m 22 Mar 1825, Fauquier VA, Elizabeth Willingham (b ca 1794, VA).[169]

MW21   Henry Thomas Wiser (29 Apr 1826, Fauquier VA-4 Mar 1862, Enon MO) m 12 Jul 1847, Fauquier VA, Jane Ann Davis (28 Mar 1826, VA-4 Nov 1917).

MW211   Sarah Ellen Wiser (11 Sep 1848, VA-25 May 1936).

MW212   James Edward Wiser(9 Mar 1850, VA-5 Apr 1923) m 4 Aug 1872, Francis Caroline Enloe (23 Jun 1854, MO-6 Aug 1929).

MW2121   Benjamin Walter Wiser (5 Jul 1873, MO-26 Scp 1955) m Delia Matheis (1892-1935).

MW2122   E. S. Marelda Wiser (26 May 1875-12 Jan 1878).

MW2123   Marvella Elizabeth Wiser (21 Apr 1878, MO-12 Jan 1968) m 22 Aug 1900, Walter William Campbell (29 Mar 1877-25 Aug 1940).

MW2124   Henry Thomas Wiser II (28 Feb 1881, MO-8 Mar 1958) m 27 Nov 1901, Effie Jane Long (3 Dec 1880-17 Jul 1955).

MW21241   Alma Frances Wiser (b 28 Apr 1904, MO) m 21 Mar 1936 Jess Thornbrugh (3 Jul 1885-15 Dec 1968).

MW21242   Herbert Willard Wiser (22 Apr 1910, MO-6 Nov 1990) m 14 Oct 1933, Ruby Ann Scott (b 30 Sep 1915).

MW212421   Rita Joyce Wiser (b 10 May 1935).

MW212422   Carol Sue Wiser (b 1 Jun 1938) m 8 Mar 1969, James Lee Shikles (b 13 Jan 1938).

MW212423   Gary Kent Wiser (b 23 Aug 1943) m 22 Aug 1965, Saundra Sue Tising (b 14 Dec 1943).

MW2124231   Sarah Beth Wiser (b 1 Jul 1970).

MW2124232   Sheryl Lynn Wiser (b 16 Jan 1974).

---

[168]Most of the material in this chapter has been collected by Jeffrey C. Wiser of Suffolk, VA. Some material has been added by Edward Wiser, who edited the information into the present format.

[169]There was another Thomas Wiser who had a grist mill in Henrico County, Virginia. He purchased the property in 1820, and remained there until he died in 1835. His will identified his wife Ann as sole beneficiary. It has not been possible to determine why there were two men with the same name, about the same age, with the same trade, and in such close proximity. Because Michael was living with the Thomas in Fauquier County, it is most likely that he is Michael's son, which leaves the identity of the Thomas in Henrico County unknown.

MW212424   Sonya Ann Wiser (b 30 Apr 1945) m 16 Jun 1963, Robert Harold Baysinger (b 18 Oct 1943).

MW2125   Sallie Ann Wiser (4 Apr 1883, MO-21 Aug 1968) m 24 Feb 1901, John Fount Long (8 Apr 1876-23 May 1966).

MW213   Ann Elizabeth Wiser (11 Mar 1851, VA-16 Dec 1932) m 21 Sep 1873, Moniteau MO, Allen Shackels (15 Feb 1852-24 Jan 1902).

MW214   John Henry Wiser (26 Jan 1854, VA-30 Jul 1921) m 1) 17 Dec 1874, Moniteau MO, Nancy Jane Gray (1857, MO-10 Nov 1891); m 2) Mary Rebecca Son (18 Feb 1867, MO-25 Feb 1904); m 3) Margaret E.   (b ca 1859, MO).

MW2141   Isom S. Wiser (4 Oct 1875-17 Oct 1876).

MW2142   William Wesley Wiser (22 Jul 1877, MO-May 1965, MO) m 26 Feb 1901, Ida McBroom.

MW2143   Henry O. Wiser (1878-1879).

MW2144   Minnie L. Wiser (23 Apr 1881-11 Jun 1918) m 10 Aug 1899, Creed Hayes.

MW2145   Nellie M. Wiser (21 Feb 1883-24 Feb 1884).

MW2146   Chester A. Wiser (26 Feb 1885-9 Aug 1969, Bowie TX) m 28 Jan 1908, Ella Austin (ca 1888, MO).

MW21461   John Wiser (b ca 1910, MO).

MW2147   Lillie J. Wiser (18 Oct 1888, MO-18 Feb 1904).

MW2148   Nancy Ellen Wiser (10 Nov 1891, MO-Feb 1969) m 24 Mar 1909, Charles Roscoe Arney (27 Apr 1886-17 Jan 1956).

MW2149   Roy Stanley Wiser (10 May 1894, MO-27 Dec 1979) m Edith Lunceford.

MW21491   Emmett Wiser.

MW21492   Gertrude Wiser.

MW21493   Dwaine Wiser.

MW214A   Mary Alice Wiser (18 Feb 1896, MO-3 Sep 1922) m 17 Aug 1919, Christopher Enloe Campbell (15 Aug 1882-12 Dec 1956).

MW214B   Earnest Ray Wiser (15 Mar 1898, MO-14 Oct 1931) m 14 Aug 1919, Vedah Milburn (b 9 Jan 1899, MO).

MW214B1   Ruby Maxine Wiser (b 29 Jun 1920).

MW214B2   Helen Marie Wiser (b 14 Oct 1921).

MW214B3   Eula Mae Wiser (b 12 Jul 1927).

MW214C   John Earl Wiser (2 Jul 1900, MO-17 Sep 1937) m 19 Aug 1923, Olean MO, Sadie Larcenia Amos (b 10 Jul 1901).

MW214C1   Ruth Marie Wiser (b 14 Dec 1924) m 14 Jun 1959, Nathaniel Cole.

MW214C2   Dale Henry Wiser (b 24 Dec 1927) m 12 Jun 1949, Erma Wave Palmer.

MW214C21   Deborah Ann Wiser (b 19 Jan 1952).

MW214C22   Daniel Wayne Wiser (b 12 Nov 1953).

MW214C23   Floyd Paul Wiser (b 12 Jul 1958).

MW214C3   Robert Marvin Wiser (b 19 Feb 1934, Olean MO) m 17 Jun 1961, Baumholder, Germany, Barbara Charlene Creekmore (b 13 Feb 1937, Portsmouth VA).

MW214C31   Lynne Annette Wiser (b 16 May 1962) m Thomas Stockman.

MW214C32   Jeffrey Charles Wiser (b 8 Feb 1964, Charlottesville VA) m 21 May 1988, Ft. Monroe VA, Judith Ann Roberson (b 16 Sep 1961, Amarillo TX).

MW214C321   Garrett Michael Wiser (b 16 Jan 1991, Bethesda MD).

MW214C322   Logan Robert Wiser (b 15 Apr 1992, Bethesda MD).

MW214C33   James Earl Wiser (b 17 Jul 1970).

MW214C4   Bonnie Margaret Wiser (b 19 Feb 1934).

MW215   Marie Catherine Wiser (6 Oct 1855, VA-22 Feb 1895) m 19 Dec 1883, Moniteau MO, George Washington Uptergrove (Oct 1861-Sep 1904).

MW216   William Oscar Wiser (13 Sep 1857, VA-15 Jan 1948) m 1) 12 Oct 1879, Miller MO, Martha Kansas Long; m 2) 31 Jul 1884, Miller MO, Cordelia Maria Wyrick (b ca 1866, MO).

MW2161   Tensie West Wiser m 17 Nov 1898, Wesley Farris.

MW2162   Mertie Elizabeth Wiser (14 Jul 1885-17 Feb 1938) m 13 Sep 1903, Edwin Silver Bond (2 Aug 1884-15 Sep 1966).

MW2163   Charley Ira Wiser (4 Sep 1887-Nov 1969, MO) m 20 Dec 1908, Zona Lee West (3 Mar 1890-15 Mar 1947).

MW21631   Ethelyn C. J. Wiser (b 10 Dec 1909).

MW21632   Oscar Benjamin Wiser (22 Apr 1911-26 Nov 1956) m 5 Jun 1933, Eva Carrie Scott (17 Apr 1916-10 May 1980).

MW216321   Marvin Ellsworth Wiser (b 15 Apr 1934) m 12 Jun 1955, Arletta Jerene Blackburn (b 15 Mar 1937).

MW2163211   Pamela Denise Wiser (b 22 Dec 1956) m 22 Jun 1974, Michael Rackers (b 16 Aug 1955).

MW2163212   Justin Lloyd Wiser (b 25 Jul 1962).

MW216322   Gail Edward Wiser (b 19 Oct 1936) m 21 Jun 1958, Jo Ann Martin (b 23 May 1939).

MW2163221   Tammy Jo Wiser (b 8 Apr 1959) m 8 Apr 1977, Randy Jacobs (b 18 Jul 1958).

MW2163222   Bradley Allen Wiser (b 16 Nov 1961).

MW2163223   Scott Edward Wiser (b 26 May 1967).

MW216323   Delores June Wiser (b 2 Aug 1941) m 18 Jun 1960, James Clyde Plaster (b 7 Jul 1939).

MW216324   Stephen Leon Wiser (b 17 Aug 1947) m 26 Jan 1974, Susan Marlene Jackson (b 16 Feb 1950).

MW2163241   Benjamin Steven Wiser (b 24 Sep 1982).

MW21633   Lionel L. Wiser (23 May 1912-30 Aug 1960) m Ethel Brizendine (d 23 Nov 1977).

MW216331   Jerry Wiser (b 22 Feb 1936) m Martha Good.

MW2163311   Dean Wiser.

MW2163312   Sandra Wiser.

MW2163313   Paul Wiser Jr.

MW216332   Emma Lee Wiser (b 25 Nov 1937) m William Lee Lewis.

MW216333   Larry Duane Wiser (b 18 Jan 1940) m Sharon Lee Lewis.

MW216334   Patricia Lynn Wiser (b 7 Feb 1942) m 1) Howard Powell; m 2) Eldin Shueffield.

MW216335   Sherry Joann Wiser (b 11 Feb 1943) m Buck Schooler.

MW216336   Ray Allen Wiser (13 Oct 1945-Jul 1983).

MW2163361   Byron Wiser.

MW216337   Joyce Wiser (b 8 Dec 1947) m Harold Fred Sappington.

MW216338   Lionel Lester Wiser Jr. (b 9 Nov 1948) m Becky   .

MW2163381   Zachery Wiser.

MW216339   Debbie Wiser (b 26 Aug 1955) m David Bruce.

MW21633A   Rickey Don Wiser (b 27 Oct 1958).

MW21633A1   Rickey Wiser Jr.

MW21633B   Roy Dale Wiser (b 4 Jan 1959) m Peggy   .

MW21633B1   Roy Dale Wiser Jr.

MW21634   Delpha Lucille Wiser (b 8 Nov 1913) m 1) 28 Jul 1931, Edward Kelsey; m 2) 23 Jun 1934, Everett Brizendine.

MW21635   Helen Lorene Wiser (b 29 Mar 1916) m 3 Mar 1934, Alvin Brizendine.

MW21636   Charles Leland Wiser (27 Mar 1918-9 Feb 1972, Pettis MO) m 29 Jul 1939, Della McNeal (b 20 Jul 1915).

MW216361   Ronald Charles Wiser (b 6 Jun 1940).

MW216362   Kathryn Darlene Wiser (b 2 Feb 1944) m Freddie Dale Sisemore.

MW216363   William Dwain Wiser (b 8 Jul 1943) m Gloria Gonzales.

MW2163631   Cynthia Ann Wiser.

MW2163632   Kathy Sue Wiser.

MW216364   Billy Gene Wiser (b 7 Feb 1945) m 6 Nov 1966, Janice Fisher.

MW2163641   Peggy Ilene Wiser (b 28 May 1967).

MW2163642   Charles Travis James Wiser (10 Jul 1972-1 Jun 1981).

MW216365   Donnie Wray Wiser (b 15 May 1951) m 5 Mar 1971, Teressa Williams.

MW2163651   Michelle Ann Wiser (b 20 Jul 1972).

MW216366   Michael Dean Wiser (17 Jul 1952-3 Nov 1970).

MW216367   Judy Frances Wiser (20 Mar 1956-21 Mar 1956).

MW216368   Rickey Lee Wiser (b 23 May 1957) m Mona Lee Smith.

MW2163681   Eric Kristin Wiser (b 27 Nov 1978).

MW2163682   Brandi Lynn Wiser (b 26 Oct 1979).

MW21637   Raymond A. Wiser (Feb 1920-22 Aug 1921).

MW21638   Viola Marie Wiser (b 13 Sep 1921) m 29 Jul 1939, Harold Sousley.

MW21639   Johnny Ellsworth Wiser (19 Jul 1923-21 Feb 1978, Spokane WA) m 25 May 1945, Inez
McCoy.

MW216391   Wanda Marie Wiser (b 25 Mar 1946).

MW216392   Lina Wiser (b 19 Mar 1948).

MW216393   Jimmy Dale Wiser (b 17 Jan 1950).

MW2163A   Geneva Ruth Wiser (b 10 Sep 1925) m 12 Jun 1946, Louis H. Schmidt.

MW2163B   Wanda Lee Wiser (b 5 Jan 1930) m 24 Apr 1948, Dwight Akin.

MW2163C   Lonnie Ralph Wiser (b 8 Nov 1933) m Alice Faye Williams.

MW2163C1   Zona Fay Wiser (b 23 Dec 1954).

MW2163C2   Jerri Dawn Wiser (b 20 Dec 1956).

MW2164   Barney Wiser (Mar 1888-1920) m 17 Aug 1909, Safrona Mamey Enloe.

MW21641   Virgil Arvin Wiser (b 11 Jul 1914) m 23 Apr 1937, Dorothy Pauline Sosley (b 18 Mar
1919).

MW216411   Dale Wiser (b 5 Dec 1938) m Clara Jo Charlton.

MW2164111   Donald Wiser (b 29 Apr 1958).

MW2164112   David Wiser (b 7 Jun 1963).

MW216412   Lavonna Wiser m 1952, Leslie Ray Harris.

MW2165   Allie Wiser.

MW2166   Marie Wiser (b ca 1890, MO).

MW2167   Byron W. Wiser (b ca 1891, MO) m Fronie   (b ca 1890, MO).

MW21671   Virgil Wiser (b ca 1915, MO).

MW2168   Ruth Wiser (b ca 1894, MO).

MW2169   Annie Wiser (23 Nov 1895-14 Jan 1981) m 17 Jan 1915, William Zoll Smith (22 Sep
1882-1 Aug 1965).

MW216A   Lewis Ellsworth Wiser (10 Mar 1898-Sep 1962) m 20 Feb 1919, Anna Bell Slavens (28
Feb 1899-16 Feb 1989, Moniteau MO).

MW216A1   Helen M. Wiser (b 1 Jul 1920) m 29 Oct 1938, William Franklin Coleman (31 Jul
1909-1982).

MW216A2   Lewis Wiser Jr. (b 12 Aug 1926) m Hallie Stanch.

MW216A21   Lewis Ellsworth Wiser III m Beverley Valentine.

MW216A22   Steven Joseph Wiser (b 20 May 1955) m Kathy Kruger.

MW216A221   Christopher Wiser (b 1973).

MW216A222   Sissie Wiser (b 1974).

MW216A223   Cathy Jo Wiser (b 1976).

MW216A23   Rickey Don Wiser m Robin Kerr.

MW216A231   Karla Wiser.

MW216A24   Dennis Ray Wiser (b 2 Feb 1965).

MW216A3   LaFawn Wiser (b 20 Feb 1937) m 14 Feb 1953, John Lee Mock (b 16 Jan 1935).

MW217   Margaret Virginia Wiser (22 Jul 1859, VA-21 Sep 1896) m 22 Dec 1880, John William
Uptergrove (19 Sep 1860-1935).

MW218   George Washington Wiser (24 Apr 1861, MO-24 May 1925) m 20 Dec 1883, Moniteau
MO, Sarah Rutha Leslie (29 Oct 1864, MO-23 Nov 1928).

MW2181   Pearl Jane Wiser (20 Oct 1884, MO-9 Jun 1966) m 1 Mar 1908, Harry Webster Morrow
(1 Dec 1883, MO-25 Dec 1960).

MW2182   Joseph Henry Wiser (29 Mar 1890, MO-1965) m 6 Sep 1914, Bessie Myrtle Rea (21 Jan
1895, MO-1974).

MW21821   Geneva LaVerne Wiser (b 29 Apr 1916, MO) m Virgle Henry Funk (b 1914).

MW21822   Joseph Edward Wiser (26 Apr 1919, MO-11 Nov 1955) m Betty Ross Sayler.

MW218221   Dennis Edward Wiser (b 21 Oct 1939) m Janette Rosemarie Driver.

MW2182211   Richard James Wiser (b 1965).

MW2182212   David Edward Wiser (b 1969).

MW2182213   Allison Clarie Wiser (b 1970).

MW2183   Della Edward Wiser (30 Sep 1895, MO-23 Dec 1943) m Erva Starke.

MW21831   Della Margaret Wiser (b 26 Oct 1924) m Don Wilton Nelson.

MW2184   Delie Emma Wiser b (30 Sep 1895, MO) m James Clyde Campbell (b 21 Jan 1895).

MW2185   Leona Jeanette Wiser (b 25 Mar 1904, MO) m 5 May 1925, James Patterson (20 Mar
1902-3 Aug 1966).

MW22   Mary A. Wiser (b 29 Apr 1826, VA).

MW23   Charles Wiser (b ca 1829, VA) m 24 Mar 1851, Fauquier VA, Ricey G. Moore.

MW231   Adalade G. Wiser (b 16 Jun 1858) m Aug 1881, John Irvin Woodward.

MW232   Virginia A. Wiser (b 16 Jun 1858).

MW233   Anna E. Wiser.

MW24   John L. Wiser (b ca 1833, VA) m 20 Dec 1857, Fauquier VA, Frances Ann Alexander
(b ca 1836).

MW241   John Thomas Wiser (18 Jun 1858-11 Mar 1919) m 10 Jan 1884, Fauquier VA, Nancy A.
Allison (1868-22 Dec 1910).

MW2411   John Carrol Wiser.

MW2412   Irvin Milton Wiser.

MW2413   William Emmett Wiser (b 14 Apr 1890, Marshall VA) m Hilda Louise Russell (b ca 1897,
DC).

MW24131   Gilbert E. Wiser (b ca 1917, DC).

MW24132   Robert E. Wiser (b ca 1917, DC).

MW24133   Mary L. Wiser (b ca 1918, DC).

MW24134   Thomas Richard Wiser (b 1922, MD).

MW2414   Leona Maude Wiser.

MW2415   Clarence Ennis Wiser (24 Nov 1894, VA-Jun 1954, Fauquier VA) m Bettie   (b ca 1895, VA).

MW24151   Mollie N. Wiser (b ca Apr 1917, VA).

MW24152   Bessie T. Wiser (b Dec 1919, VA).

MW2416   James William Wiser.

MW2417   Jack Grimsley Wiser.

MW2418   Raymond Edward Wiser (25 Jun 1902, VA-Dec 1983, Fairfax VA).

MW2419   Henry Hunton Wiser.

MW241A   Elton M. Wiser (b ca 1908, VA).

MW241B   Joseph Willard Wiser (b ca 1909, VA).

MW241C   Charles Collins Wiser.

MW25   Jonah Wiser (b ca 1835, VA).

MW26   William J. Wiser (b ca 1837, VA).

[NCW]   Nicholas Wiser
of Canajoharie, Montgomery County, New York

Nicholas Wiser is found in the 1790 Census for Canajoharie, Montgomery County, New York. The record shows three young men under 16, and five females, possibly his wife and four daughters. There is no record for Nicholas in the 1800 Census, although there is a record for John Wiser at Amsterdam in Montgomery County.

According to Biographical Sketches of Richard Ellis, by E. R. Ellis, two Weiser sisters married two Ellis brothers. According to this book, Rachel and Mary Weiser were daughters of Nicholas Weiser and his wife Margaret Walrad, who were from the Mohawk valley in Montgomery County, NY but settled in Ellisburg, NY in the early 1800s. The book further states that Nicholas Weiser was a soldier in the Revolutionary war, famous as a scout, and a son of Conrad Weiser. No documentation has been found to support any of this statement, and Nicholas certainly could not have been a son of Conrad Weiser.

Rachel Weiser is reported to have married James Ellis (1792-1823) in about 1815, from which it is estimated that she was born around 1795. She is also said to have died in Ellisburg in 1858. Mary Weiser (1798-ca 1879) married Robert Ellis (1794-1863) in 1816, according to the book. No further references to the Weiser family are found in the book.

No records of the presence of any Weiser family have been found in Ellisburg until 1830, when Benjamin and Isaac Weser are listed in the census records for Ellisburg. Both Benjamin and Isaac are listed in the 1830 Census as being between 40-50 years old, with no sons, wives that are slightly younger, and one or two daughters. The ages given by the census put them in the right age range to be sons of Nicholas, and brothers of Rachel and Mary. No explanation has been found for why the Weser spelling was used, or why no records at Ellisburg have been found prior to 1830.

In 1840, Isaac Wezar was still at Ellisburg, and in 1850 Isaac Wesar, age 71, born in NY was still there with his wife Maria Ann, age 55, born VT, and no children. Benjamin had moved to Sandy Creek in adjacent Oswego County, where he was identified as Benjamin Wise(?) in 1840 and Benjamin Weser in 1850, age 63, born in NY, with a wife Lydia, age 53, born NY, and no children.

There are baptisms listed for several children of Nicholas and Margaret Wiser in the records of the Dutch Reformed Church at Stone Arabia in Montgomery County, New York. Combining all of these records gives us the following family:

NCW   Nicholas Weiser m Margaret Walrad.

NCW1   Elisabeth Wiser (baptized 18 Sep 1774, Stone Arabia NY).

NCW2   Isaac Weser (baptized 6 Mar 1779, Stone Arabia NY) m Miriam Sturdevant (b 13 Apr 1795, Rutland VT). Ellisburg NY and Sandy Creek, Oswego NY.

NCW3   Benjamin Weser (b ca 1787, NY) m Lydia   (b ca 1797, NY). Ellisburg NY and Sandy Creek, Oswego NY.

NCW4   Amalia Wiser (bapt 8 Jan 1792, Stone Arabia NY).

NCW5   Rachel Wiser (b ca 1796, Montgomery NY) m ca 1815, Ellisburg NY, James Ellis (12 Aug 1792-1823, Ellisburg NY).

NCW6   Mary Wiser (b ca 1798, NY) m 1816, Ellisburg NY, Robert Ellis (24 Mar 1794-1863).

[PTW] Peter Wisser (ca 1810-ca 1852)
of Lehigh County, Pennsylvania

Peter Wisser was an ore miner born in Prussia. He went first to Mexico to work in the silver mines. This work was interrupted by a revolution there and he returned first to Prussia, and then came to the United States in about 1848. He was killed in a cave-in in about 1852.

PTW   Peter Wisser (ca 1810, Prussia, Germany-ca 1852) m Mary Wickel (ca 1810, Germany-ca 1892).

PTW1   Pauline (Caroline) Wisser (b ca 1839) m Abraham Kuhns.

PTW2   Boniface ("Fassio") Wisser (b May 1840, Mexico) m Geneva ("Jennie") Latzer (b Oct 1841, Europe).

PTW21   Edward Wisser (b Dec 1864, PA) m ca 1896, Theresa (b Dec 1869, Germany).

PTW211   Joseph M. Wisser (b Mar 1896, PA).

PTW212   Mary J. Wisser (b May 1897, PA).

PTW213   Alfred W. Wisser (Aug 1898, PA-1983).

PTW214   Matilda A. Wisser (b ca 1901, PA).

PTW215   George C. Wisser (b ca 1902, PA).

PTW216   Bernhard Wisser (b ca 1906, PA).

PTW22   William H. Wisser (b 17 Nov 1866, Allentown PA) m Sep 1899, Sophia Miller (Aug 1871, PA-ca 1920).

PTW221   Andrew A. Wisser (b ca 1901, PA).

PTW222   Anna M. Wisser (b ca 1903, PA).

PTW223   Charles Wisser (b ca 1904, PA).

PTW224   Josephine H. Wisser (b ca 1906, PA).

PTW225   Emma J. Wisser (b ca 1908, PA).

PTW226   Elizabeth S. Wisser (b ca 1910, PA).

PTW227   Louise D. Wisser (b ca 1912, PA).

PTW228   Genline(?) Wisser (b ca 1914, PA).

PTW229   William Wisser (b ca 1916, PA).

PTW22A   Sophia Wisser (b ca Nov 1919, PA).

PTW23   Charles Wisser (b Jun 1870, PA).

PTW24   Joseph Wisser (b Sep 1875, PA).

PTW25   Leo Wisser (b Mar 1879, PA).

PTW26   Frank Wisser (b Oct 1881, PA).

PTW3   Elizabeth Wisser (b ca 1847) m William Sacks.

PTW4   Sarah Levina Wisser (b ca 1852, PA) m John Miller.

[RNW]   Ransome Wiser (1825-1862)
of New York and Indiana

   Ransome Wiser is found first in the 1850 Census in northern Indiana, where he and his family settled. The census records show that both he and his wife were born in New York around 1825, that the two eldest children were born there, and that the family moved to Indiana around 1848.

   Unconfirmed sources state that his wife and the two children were born in Macedon, Wayne County, New York, which was on the Erie Canal. The only Wiser families in that part of New York during that time period were the family of Cornelius Wiser, his son Hiram, and John Wiser, who were in the adjacent part of Monroe County. No documentation on the relationship between these families has been found.

RNW   Ransome Wiser (17 Oct 1825, NY-6 Jul 1862, Culver IN) m ca 1841, NY, Amanda Elvina Douglas (1 Oct 1825, NY-24 Sep 1890, Culver IN).

RNW1   Susan Wiser (29 Aug 1842, NY-31 May 1866, Culver IN) m 7 Aug 1864, Harrison Stotler.

RNW11   Susan Amanda Stotler (21 May 1864-23 Sep 1865).

RNW2   Martin Wesley Wiser (11 Apr 1845, NY-20 Sep 1918, Steuben IN) m Emaline   (b Nov 1851, IN).

RNW21   Martha Wiser (b Mar 1870, IN).

RNW22   Anna V. Wiser (b Jan 1877, IN) m Harry Vaughn (b Mar 1875, IN).

RNW23   Eva E. Wiser (b Dec 1880, IN).

RNW24   Ada R. Wiser (b Mar 1884, IN).

RNW3   Adelaide Wiser (19 Feb 1849, Marshall IN-28 Jan 1851, Culver IN).

RNW4   William J. Wiser (1 Nov 1852, Marshall IN-26 Dec 1852, Culver IN).

RNW5   Stephen Douglas Wiser (18 Jul 1854, Marshall IN-27 Nov 1937, Culver IN) m 27 Mar 1875, Isabelle Marie Alleman (b Apr 1853, IN).

RNW51   Amanda Wiser (b ca 1877, IN).

RNW52   Alda Wiser (b Apr 1882, MO).

RNW53   William M. Wiser (b Apr 1885, IN) m Lottie N.   (b ca 1891, IN).

RNW531   Naomi L. Wiser (b ca 1910, IN).

RNW532   Isabell M. Wiser (b ca 1912, IN).

RNW533   Florence E. Wiser (b ca 1914, IN).

RNW54   Myrtle Wiser (b Aug 1890, IN).

RNW6   Albert Eugene Wiser (Mar 1858, IN-1927, Rochester IN) m 27 Nov 1880, Emma Nellans (b May 1860, OH).

RNW61   Nellie Wiser (b Jun 1884, IN) m   Reiter.

RNW62   James Guy Wiser (30 Aug 1891, IN-Jul 1969, IN).

RNW7   Finley Clarence Wiser (b Aug 1860, IN) m 11 Apr 1878, Alvina Agina Nellans (b Oct 1857, OH).

[VLW]   Valentine Wiser (b ca 1780)
of Bucks County, Pennsylvania

The first census record of any Wiser in Bucks County, Pennsylvania is in 1840, when Jacob Wiser is listed in Warminster Township with a wife and two sons, aged between 5 and 10. There are births of five children listed in the International Genealogical Index, four of which are confirmed in the census records in 1850. The International Genealogical Index also indicates that Jacob's parents were Valentine Wiser and Elizabeth Jung, and that he was born on 18 Jan 1806 at Hilltown in Bucks County. No census record has been found for Valentine Wiser.

VLW   Valentine Wiser (b ca 1780) m Elizabeth Jung (b ca 1784).

VLW1   Jacob Wiser (b 18 Jan 1806, Hilltown, Bucks PA) m 25 Nov 1830, Abington, Montgomery PA, Elizabeth Marple (b 2 Jun 1808, Warminster, Bucks PA).

VLW11   Thomas M. Wiser (b 21 Aug 1831, Hilltown, Bucks PA) m Eliza   (b May 1831, PA).

VLW111   Eramanda Wiser (b ca 1855, PA).

VLW112   Elizabeth Wiser (b ca Sep 1859, PA).

VLW113   Owen Jacob Wiser (b Jun 1864, PA) m 1) Lydia   (b Nov 1873, PA); m 2) Mary E. Anderson (b ca 1865, PA).

VLW1131   Blanche Wiser (b Aug 1891, PA).

VLW1132   Owen J. Wiser (26 Feb 1897, PA-Mar 1969, Philadelphia PA) m Marguerite D.   (b ca 1900, PA).

VLW11321   Marguerite D. Wiser (b ca Apr 1920, PA).

VLW1133   Marie C. Wiser (b ca 1901, PA).

VLW12   Nathan Marple Wiser (b 30 Sep 1833, Hilltown, Bucks PA) m Wilhelmina Snyder (b 7 Oct 1834, Hilltown, Bucks PA).

VLW121   John P. Wiser (b 6 Sep 1857).

VLW122   Elizabeth H. Wiser (b 3 Jun 1859, PA).

VLW123   Charles Oscar Wiser (b 17 Jan 1861, PA) m 25 Dec 1884, Bucks PA, Hannah Harrison Larzeler (b Nov 1865, PA).

VLW1231   Benjamin L. Wiser (10 Mar 1886, PA-Apr 1981).

VLW1232   Nathan Marple Wiser (b 30 Dec 1888, Bucks PA) m Mabel F.   (b ca 1886, PA).

VLW12321   Nathan Wiser (13 Nov 1909, PA-Jun 1973, Doylestown PA).

VLW12322   Robert A. Wiser (b ca 1912, PA).

VLW1233   Ethel Wiser (b Apr 1895, PA).

VLW124   Alfred Wiser (b 7 Nov 1862).

VLW125   Emma Matilda Wiser (b 30 Nov 1864, Eureka, Montgomery PA) m Edwin Lewis Thompson (b 8 Dec 1853, Eureka, Montgomery PA).

VLW126   Walter Bernard Wiser (b 1 Oct 1867, PA).

VLW13   Edith Ann Wiser (b 21 Jul 1837, Hilltown, Bucks PA).

VLW14   Jacob P. Wiser (b 23 Jan 1839, PA).

VLW15   Martha Louisa Wiser (b 10 Jun 1847, Hilltown, Bucks PA).

[WW]   William Weiser (1780-1845)
of Cumberland County, Pennsylvania and Richland County, Ohio

William Weiser was born (as computed from his age on his tombstone) on 6 Aug 1780 and died 14 Apr 1845. He is buried, as is his wife, at St. Peter's Lutheran Church, Shelby OH.

He married Barbara Creutzer on 6 Jul 1807 at Zion Lutheran Church, Harrisburg PA. She died 7 Jul 1843, aged 59 years, eleven months, seven days, which yields a birthdate of about 30 Jul 1783. They moved to Richland Co OH about 1828. Their children were variously baptized in Harrisburg (1807, 1811, 1813), Carlisle (born 1814, 1816, 1819, and baptized on the same day), and Enola (born 1824, 1827, 1828 and baptized on the same day). One daughter either remained in PA or returned there. There is no clear evidence of his parentage, but there are other Weisers in Cumberland County with whom he may fit.

WW   William Weiser (6 Aug 1780, PA-14 Apr 1845) m 6 Jul 1807, Harrisburg PA, Barbara Creutzer (ca 30 Jul 1783-7 Jul 1843).

WW1 Jacob Weiser (28 Nov 1807, PA-1887) m 1) Mary Ann Hershiser (1815-1846); m 2) 11 Mar 1848, Margaret Ann (ca 1812, PA-ca 1851); m 3) 1 Dec 1853, Richland OH, Catharine Hart (b ca 1814, PA).

WW11 John William Weiser (1834, OH-1921) m 29 Dec 1857, Richland OH, Lucinda Kingsborough (1838, OH-1906).

WW111 Jennie Mary Weiser (b ca 1859, OH) m 1 Sep 1875, Richland OH, Daniel W. Douglass.

WW112 Emmett E. Weiser (b Sep 1860, OH) m Jeanette (b Dec 1864, OH).

WW1121 Vina Weiser (b Feb 1886, IN).

WW1122 John (Floyd) L. Weiser (b Feb 1890, IN).

WW1123 Charles P. Weiser (13 Oct 1891, IN-Aug 1968).

WW1124 George Weiser (b ca 1908, IN).

WW113 Alida A. Weiser (b ca 1864, OH).

WW114 Lulu N. Weiser (b ca 1868, OH) m Leonard Elston.

WW115 Harry Weiser (b ca 1871, OH) m Ree Humbert.

WW1151 Martha M. Weiser (b 17 Sep 1896, Shelby OH).

WW116 Annie Weiser (b ca 1873, OH).

WW117 Verta(?) Weiser (b 11 May 1877, Shelby OH).

WW118 Smith F. Weiser (b 28 Sep 1880, Shelby OH) m 17 Sep 1902, Richland OH, Helen Knabershue (b ca 1882, OH)

WW119 John K. Weiser (b 16 Mar 1884, Shelby OH) m 3 Jul 1905, Richland OH, Alberta W. Andrews.

WW12 Catherine E. Weiser (b ca 1837, OH) m 4 Oct 1866, Richland OH, John K. Cumberworth.

WW13 Amanda J. Weiser (b ca 1841, OH) m 18 Jun 1865, Richland OH, Le Grand St. John.

WW14 Cinderella Weiser (b ca 1843, OH) m 4 Jan 1866, Richland OH, George W. Burger.

WW15 David Weiser (b ca 1844, OH).

WW16 Harriet Weiser (b ca 1845, OH).

WW17 Samuel Weiser (b ca 1849, OH).

WW18 Josiah Weiser (b ca 1851, OH).

WW19 Charlotte Weiser (b ca 1855, OH) m 7 Oct 1880, Richland OH, James E. Lantz.

WW1A Emma J. Weiser (b ca 1857, OH) m 12 Apr 1881, Coggswell Perdew.

WW2 Eliza Weiser m Fesler.

WW3   Adam Weiser (24 Sep 1811, Dauphin PA-24 Mar 1896, Arcadia OH) m 30 Nov 1836, Richland OH, Susannah Bender (16 Jul 1819, PA-7 Jul 1889, Jackson, Seneca OH). Bur Shelby OH.

WW31   Sarah Jane Weiser (b 11 Nov 1837, OH) m 31 Dec 1857, Solomon Feighner.

WW32   Susan Weiser (b 16 Jul 1840, OH) m 31 Dec 1865, Richland OH, John St. John.

WW33   Barbara Weiser (14 May 1842, Richland OH-16 Oct 1928) m 12 Mar 1862, Richland OH, David Dick (28 May 1836, Richland OH-2 Apr 1921, Arcadia OH). Bur Arcadia OH. Res Washington, Hancock OH.

WW331   George W. Dick (1864-1943) m Jessie F.   (1869-1941). Bur Arcadia OH. Res Washington, Hancock OH.

WW3311   Virgil O. Dick (dy). Bur Arcadia OH.

WW3312   Arla L. Dick (dy). Bur Arcadia OH.

WW332   Daughter Dick m Alvin B. Davidson. Fostoria OH.

WW333   Charles F. Dick. Washington, Hancock OH.

WW334   Ada May Dick (ca 28 Feb 1872-14 Feb 1882, Hancock OH). Bur Arcadia OH.

WW335   Infant Dick.

WW336   John Adam Dick (6 Nov 1876, Washington, Hancock OH-29 Sep 1971, Washington, Hancock OH) m Naomi Wyant. Bur Arcadia OH. Farmer. Washington, Hancock OH.

WW34   John B. Weiser (b 14 Apr 1844, OH) m 12 Aug 1865, Richland OH, Amanda Daub (b ca 1845, PA).

WW341   Ida Weiser (b ca 1866, OH).

WW35   Harriet Weiser (b 1847, OH) m 1 Oct 1868, Jonas Feighner.

WW36   Infant son Weiser (b 1847, OH).

WW37   Infant daughter Weiser (b 30 Jan 1850, OH).

WW38   Jacob Bender Weiser (b 14 Dec 1850, OH) m 2 Dec 1875, Richland OH, Susan Briner (b Aug 1848, OH). Montpelier OH.

WW381   Jennie M. Weiser (b ca 1878, OH).

WW382   Adam Weiser (b Jan 1880, OH) m Maude   (b ca 1884, MI).

WW383   Verna Weiser (b May 1882, OH).

WW39   Adam H. Weiser (11 Jun 1852, OH-4 May 1938) m 1) 22 Oct 1874, Richland OH, Barbara E. Lybarger (18 Sep 1851-30 Apr 1910); m 2) 15 Oct 1914, Richland OH, Augusta Fromm (b ca 1868, OH). Bur Shelby OH.

WW391   Arch C. Weiser (b 17 Mar 1876, Cass, Richland OH) m 4 Oct 1899, Richland OH, Clida L. Earick (b ca 1876, OH).

WW3911   Roscoe M. Weiser (b ca 1902, OH).

WW392   Otto H. Weiser (b 16 Dec 1878, Cass, Richland OH) m 25 Feb 1905, Richland OH, Flossie A. Gates (b ca 1880, OH).

WW393   Lewis Weiser (b 16 Jan 1881, Cass, Richland OH).

WW3A   William Franklin Weiser (30 May 1855, OH-18 Oct 1942) m 21 Dec 1876, Hancock OH, Mary Catherine Sherman (22 May 1851, Washington, Hancock OH-20 May 1923, Washington, Hancock OH). Bur Fostoria OH.

WW3A1   Jessie Weiser (11 Dec 1878, Washington, Hancock OH) m 15 Feb 1900, Hancock OH, Clinton L. Ebersole (5 Aug 1879, Hancock OH). Orrville OH.

WW3A11   Franklin C. Ebersole (b 8 Dec 1900, Marion, Hancock OH).

WW3A12   James E. Ebersole (1902, Hancock OH-28 Nov 1915, Washington, Hancock OH). Bur Arcadia OH.

WW3A13   Blanche May Ebersole (18 Jan 1905, Washington, Hancock OH-8 Aug 1907, Washington, Hancock OH). Bur Arcadia OH. Died of gunshot wound.

WW3A14   Mary Adella Ebersole (b 12 Sep 1908, Arcadia OH).

WW3A15   William Lee Ebersole (b 25 Jan 1915, Washington, Hancock OH).

WW3A2   Blanche B. Weiser (16 Jan 1881, Washington, Hancock OH-5 Jul 1955, Fostoria OH) m 14 Mar 1901, Hancock OH, John W. Wyant (14 Mar 1878, Washington, Hancock OH-14 Jan 1967, Findlay OH). Farmer, Washington, Hancock OH. No known chn.

WW3A3   Carney S. Weiser (22 Jun 1889, Washington, Hancock OH-by 1929) m 1) 21 Sep 1911, Seneca OH, Mary Esther Woodruff (3 Nov 1892 or 1893, Deerfield MI-8 May 1917, Washington, Hancock OH); m 2) 3 Sep 1919, Seneca Co OH, Minnie M. Kissaberth (b 13 Aug 1889, Loudon, Seneca OH). Bur Fostoria OH. Teamster and farmer. Res Fostoria and Washington, Hancock OH.

WW3B   Alice Eliza Weiser (9 Aug 1857, OH-3 Dec 1920) m 30 Nov 1876, Richland OH, William
H. Sherman.

WW3C   Mary B. Weiser (b 30 Nov 1860, OH) m 15 Oct 1885, Richland OH, George K. Sutter.
Shelby OH.

WW4   Wilhelm Weiser (10 Mar 1813-dy).

WW5   Maria Weiser (b 7 Jan 1814, PA) m 28 Oct 1841, Richland OH, Peter Keller.

WW6   Juliana Weiser (b 24 Jul 1816, PA) m   Ebersole. Lived in PA.

WW7   Rosina Weiser (b 9 Feb 1819, PA) m 13 Feb 1844, David Boyd.

WW8   John Weiser (27 Jan 1824-16 Jul 1839). Bur Shelby OH.

WW9   Wilhelm Weiser (12 Aug 1827-29 Apr 1835). Bur Shelby OH.

MEMORIAL CONTRIBUTIONS

TO 1960 EDITION

The Rev. Dr. Edward Fry Bartholomew
  from his children

The Rev. Frederick Ludwig Bergstresser
  from his daughters

Gertrude Fister Bond

Henry G. Brehm
  from Mrs. Annie B. Erdman

Charles Henry Brocious
  from his sons

Mr. and Mrs. John George Brungart
  from Miss Vera Catherine Brungart

Elizabeth H. Deppen
  from her son, Joseph Deppen

The Henry Faoold Family
  from Mrs. J.J. Shuman

Lovina Weiser Fossinger
  from her granddaughter, Mrs. James Llewellyn

The Rev. Charles O. Frank
  from his children

Emma Weiser Gohl
  from her granddaughter, Vaneta Cobaugh

William Lutz Krigbaum
  from his children

Mrs. Richard Mason
  from her daugher, Mrs. James Llewellyn

Frederick W. Nicolls, Sr
  from his son, Frederick S. Nicolls, Jr

Sue M. Sherman
  from her daughter, Mrs. J.W. Jones

Arthur George Weiser
  from his family

Charles Luther Weiser
  from his family

Mr. and Mrs. Donald Koehler Weiser
  from their children

Eugene Francis Weiser
  from his children

Elmer Sherman Weiser
  from his children

Jacob Shaffer Weiser
  from his family

George Renaldo Weiser
  from his daughter, Mrs. C.W. Chappelear

Oliver Weiser
  from his son, Oliver Weiser

Mrs. Oliver Weiser
  from her son, Oliver Weiser

Paul William Weiser
  from his children

Peter Weiser
  from his family

Stephen Bertram Weiser,
  from his son, George Weiser

Samuel Weiser
  from his son, Donald K. Weiser

Samuel Henry Weiser
  from his family

William Weiser
  from his family

The Rev. William Walter Weiser
  from his wife and children

Frederick Witmer
  from his son, Frederick D. Witmer

Mr. and Mrs. John T. Woolridge
  from their children, Albert Woolridge and James L. Woolridge

CONTRIBUTIONS TO THE 1996 EDITION

In memory of Rose Marie Weiser Clevenger
by Rev. Raymond K. Clevenger

In memory of William M. Hiester
by Elizabeth F. Hiester

In memory of Matilda Klaiss
by Caroline Wagaman

In memory of Luella R. Kreider
by Martha K. Rudnicki

In memory of Leah R. Muliali
by Martha K. Rudnicki

In memory of Donald Koehler Weiser
by Harriette W. Russell
Dorothy W. Seale
Rev. Frederick S. Weiser

In memory of Helen Grace Weiser
by Martha Marybelle Anderson

In memory of Frederick Daniel Witmer
by Lynn Witmer Doss

Melva Appleton

Mrs. James Arbegast

Nancy Weiser Baue

Anne Bender

William A. Bender, MD

Elia Bubenik

Gertrude Wiser Butcher

Marlene Carrier

Alberta Cordier

+John Croll, Jr

Virginia Cochran Del Cour

James L. Dodson

Joyce Weiser Dorrell

Lynn Witmer Doss

John H. Dressler

Donald R. Eberhart

Samuel M. Eppley, MD

Judith Eshleman

Frederick E. Frey

Ardelle A. Graeff

Robert Harter

Wanda Weiser Hebel

Elizabeth F. Hiester

Carmelita J. Hinds

Robert William Hoffman

William M. Hoffman

Mr. and Mrs. Weiser Hughes

David L. Johnson

Thomas Krigbaum

Dean Leibold

Effie Alice Henrietta Loy

Francis Martin

Laura J. Martin

Valerie Martz

Frances Mason

Laura McQuaid

Vera M. Morford

Susie Morris

+William I. Mudd

John D.S. Muhlenberg

Leola K. Nelson

Gail Porter

Janet Raddon

Mary Jane Randall

Helen Mann Rehberg

Martha K. Rudnicki

Robin Frank Rupp

Nancy Strode Ryan

Thomas R. Scanlan

George C. Schempff

Winthrop deV. Schwab

Dorothy Weiser Seale

John E. Shettel

Robert E. Shirck

Harold F. Springer

Louise Zimmerman Stahl

James G. Stauffer, MD

Evelyn Wieser Stefan

Wayne Steward

Charlene Noll Strohecker

Deane A. Tack

Rene G. Vandeuren

Edward W. Wagaman

Mrs. Elvin Wagner

William M. Wagner, Jr

Charlotte Weiser

Conrad John Weiser

Donald C. Weiser

Frederick Sheely Weiser

Hazel Weiser

James Haldor Weiser

John Conrad Weiser

M. Everett Weiser

Paul Kenneth Weiser

Paulette J. Weiser

Pauline S. Weiser

Richard C. Weiser

Stanley Weiser

Stanley P. Weiser

Milton U. Wiser

Robert L. Woolridge

Michelle Wrick

The Weiser Family Association
55 Kohler School Road
New Oxford, PA 17350

Encourages persons who could
correct data in this book,
add to data in this book,
or have questions about possible
relationships to any Weiser
family to contact us.

EVERY NAME INDEX

The following Every Name Index compiled by Picton Press contains a total of 83,114 entries. Women are indexed whenever possible under both their maiden and married name(s). Maiden names are given in parentheses, thus Mary (Smith) Weiser. When the maiden name is unknown, it is given thus: Mary (--) Weiser. As always, readers are cautioned to check under all conceivable spellings.

[UNKNOWN]
--, 467, 960, 962, 987, 993, 1062, 1122, 1211, 1240, 1720
Barbara, 634
Barbara Ann (McMillan), 1357
Beatrice (Shotsberger), 983
Betty (Weiser), 1349
Bradley, 1357
Brian, 1357
Burk, 1798
Christina, 1715
Cornelius, 273
Cynthia Louise (Wiser), 1781
Darsey D, 614
daughter, 1417
Delores Gail (Ross), 202
Dolby, 1781
Donald, 983
Douglas, 1349
Eleanor Scott (Smith), 1505
Eric, 1717
Fern (Wetzel), 471
Greg, 1717
Heidi (Hottenstein), 63
Heinrich, 965
Hilda M (Wiser) Gardner, 1671
Howard, 1688
Jan, 1405
Janis Lee (Adams), 960
Jennifer Lee (Jones), 1240
Jessica Renee, 401
Joanne Eleanor (Courtright), 1122
John, 202
Jolyn, 648
Karen Allinson (Frost), 993
Kari, 1377
Kathryn, 1720
Kay-Thomas, 1599
Keith, 1717
Kelsey, 1211
Ken, 63
Kimberly Jo (Fahlbeck), 962
Kristine, 1377
Laura (Weiser), 1424
Laura Ann, 1357
Lavon, 1377
Leilani, 214
Lela B (Garver), 1688
Letha, 549
Lewis Jr, 576
Linda Marie, 1448
Lisa Marie (Carmine), 1211
Liza May, 1448
Lodi (Winkelblech), 1062
Loma, 549

Magdalena, 1405
Malte, 1599
Margaret Elizabeth (Gaby), 1581
Margaret Kathleen, 399
Mary (Kephart) Stone, 1682
Matthew, 214, 1717
Maxine Dee (Lines), 1720
Mildred Hilda (Kunkel), 1748
Orion, 1385
Orlia Rae, 399
Patty (Moore), 1717
Pearl (Steel), 965
Rachael Lynn, 273
Rebecca Dawn, 273
Ron, 1211
Ruhl, 1424
Ruth Irene (Degenkolb), 1298
Samuel A, 1748
Scott, 64
Sharon (Player), 214
Susie (Radabaugh), 987
Trey, 1212
Vera, 1184
Webster, 1505
Will, 471

AARON
Alex Andrew, 1283
Benjamin James, 1283
Charles Joseph, 1283
David Charles, 1283
Jane Elizabeth (Rapp), 1283
Margaret Jane, 1283
Matthew David, 1283
Phyllis Marie (Seigworth), 1283
Steven Edward, 1283
Theresa Ann (Godfrey), 1283

ABBOTT
Chelsea Jean, 1261
Christopher Michael, 1261
Debbie (Diltz), 1261
Douglas Claude, 1261
Emilie Anne, 1261
Frank Raymond, 579
Gena Rose, 1261
Gennilee (Kahle), 1261
Jeffrey Claude, 1261
Juanita, 801
Kacy Scott, 1261
Karen (Conley), 1261
Kimberly Kay, 1261
Krystal Anne, 1261
Matthew Elias, 1261
Nicole Marjorie, 1261
Pamela Marlene, 579
Rebecca Sue, 1261
Scott LeRoy, 1261
Shirley Maxine (Miller), 579
Torrey, 1261

Vada Belle, 1128
ABDELMALEK
Shahira, 746
ABE
Shiho, 178
ABELL
--, 1792
Barbara Joyce (Wiser), 1792
ABERNATHY
Doris Ann (Karr), 473
Gladys (Wiser), 1852
Jodi, 473
Sara Maude, 1562
Wheeler, 1852
ABNEY
Lee Ann, 1317
Mary Ann, 1317
Phyllis Ann (Hetzel), 1317
Quillard, 1317
ABRAHAM
Charles Richard, 1474
Kelley Starr, 1474
Kimberly Ann (Lynch), 1474
ABRAMS
Charlotte, 426
Kay, 367
ACCETTELLA
Joan Marie, 1556
ACE
Dora Ruth, 1256
ACHEY
Mary, 896
ACHILLES
Augusta, 309
ACHTERT
Alfred, xi, 940
Alfred Carl Robert, 131
Alfred Carl Robert III, 131
Alfred Carl Robert Jr, 131
Delores Marie (Hoppes), 131
Douglas Conrad, 132
Geraldine (Shollenberger), 131
Jacquelyn Marie, 132
Jennifer Kristin, 132
Johanna (Dallas), 132
Kenneth Fred, 132
Vinette Mary (Brown), 132
Walter Scott, 132
ACKER
Emma, 1754
Howard E, 1628
Jean, 426
Lewis, 1754
Sarah Rebecca (Weiser), 1628
ACKERMAN
Barbara Kay, 519
Bernadine Elizabeth (Brewer), 520

Bessie Elsie (Mason), 520
Brock, 519
Carrie Lynn, 520
Colleen Vivian (Woodard), 520
Darla (Schaad), 519
Dennis, 128
Dorothy Marie, 520
Edith, 597
Erna Aubra, 519
Ernest Franklin, 520
Jaqueline (Long), 519
Jessica Nicole, 519
Kathlynn Louise (Boutwell), 519
Kathryn Marie (Morehead), 519
Kelly Sue (Willoughby), 128
Leonard Wesley, 520
Leslie Newton, 520
Lester, 519
Louise, 1493
Lucas, 519
Mary Joanna, 520
Pamela Dianne, 520
Randall Lynn, 519
Richard Allan, 519
Robert Allan, 519
Rosa Estelle (Fisher), 519
Rosemary Kay, 520
Sara Louise, 519
Sondra Jean, 520
Stephanie Alane, 519
Steve Franklin, 520
Timothy Scott, 520
ACKERMANM
Louise, 1493
ACKERS
Elaine Louise, 616
Emmabelle (Baker), 616
Harold Paul, 616
Janet Nadine, 616
Linda Kay, 616
Max Murl, 616
ACKEY
George, 843
John, 843
Maggie (Auspach), 843
Margaret, 843
May, 843
ACKMAN
Bessie (Wessel), 1012
Bruce, 1013
Carl, 1012
Donald, 1013
Geneva (Waldo), 1012
Geneva (West), 1013
Herman, 1012
Hubert, 1013
Joann (Louense), 1013
Keith, 1013
Marilyn (Karr), 1013
Roberta (Boles), 1013

ADAIR
Adaline (Shettel), 876
Carol Ann (Hoaster), 876
Elsa, 479
George Benjamin, 876
Larry Robert, 876
son, 876
ADAM
Anna Violet, 1750
Virginia Harriet, 1743
ADAMEK
Heather Wayne, 1478
Randy, 1478
Ryan Allan, 1478
Tanya Elaine (Bresley), 1478
ADAMS
Ailean Elizabeth, 980
Alva Alphys, 960
Amber, 1715
Andrew Jay, 569
Ashley Marie, 1171
Barbara (Rexford), 1715
Bessie I, 682
Beulah Emeline, 743
Bill, 621
Blair, 1702
Blanche McDonald, 1489
Brenda G, 1819
Carol Ann, 814
Carolyn Kay (Herring), 569
Carolyn Marie, 573
Carrie (Kehl), 980
Cathie Ann (Goodling), 228
Cecelia, 1715
Cecil, 576
Chana Esther, 569
Clarence, 228
Clarence Tappen, 743
Cora, 1033
Dale Douglas, 960
Dana, 491
David, 1715
David Lee, 461
David Steven, 1171
Debbie (--), 1715
Dee Ann (Rowland), 191
Docia Tennessee, 1809
Dorothy Ann (Tingler), 461
Dorothy Rae, 461
Edith A, 1614
Egbert Watson, 742
Elizabeth (Eister), 742
Emma, 1189
Erin Lee (Hursen), 228
Ervin Ellis, 960
Gail Hayes, 121
Garfield, 980
Geraldine (Williams), 576
Gordon Kehl, 980

ADAMS (continued)
Gwendolyn Alice (Hall), 1189
Harold, 980
Harold Dean, 461
Harold Edward, 461
Harold F, 1171
Harriet Elizabeth, 743
Heide Jo (Blair), 451
Ida May, 743
James, 1715
Jamie, 1715
Janis Lee, 960
Jay Howard, 569
Jeanne, 980
Joanne, 231
Joe Dan, 191
Judy (Payne), 562
Kathryn Minnette (Hayes), 121
Katie Odera, 742
Keith Randall, 228
Kelly, 562
Kitty (Haussock), 1171
Kristin, 562
Larry Dean, 1232
Linda (--), 1715
Lois Genevieve (Ehrgott), 960
Lonnie, 562
Loraine Izetta, 442
Louisa (Eister), 743
Louise Catherine (Slattery), 1171
Lucy Jane, 1686
Lynda Susan, 1171
Mable (Hare), 743
Malden, 1054
Marcy, 1061
Margaret, 1479
Margaret (Helwick), 743
Martha, 813
Mary, 1715
Mary (Weiser), 934
Mary Elizabeth, 1817
Mary Etta, 1836
Mary Kathryn (Burkholder), 228
Matilda, 1862
Maude (Wisor), 1702
Melissa Joy, 1819
Melissa Susan, 258
Nicholas Scott, 451
Nicole, 1715
Novelda (Rhodes), 608
Richard Eugene, 1171
Roberta Faye (Ehrgott), 960
Robin (McNet), 1171
Robin Renee, 569
Romona Rae (Brown), 621
Ruth, 980
Ruth Catherine (Hackman), 1053
Ryan Keller, 228
Samuel, 1189
Samuel Eugene, 121
Scott, 451
Scott Thomas, 228
Sidney Gay, 1232
Steven, 1715
T L, 934
Temperance M (Wiser), 1765
Terry (Savory), 1171
Theresa, 1715
Thomas, 1053

Thomas Randall, 228
Tim, 1715
Trilby, 1054
Walter Franklin, 743
William, 608
William Dale, 1232
William Glenn, 980
William J, 1765
William Norman, 1232
William Terry, 608
Winnie Aleene (Harbison), 1232
ADAMSON
Joyce Bobby, 1846
ADCOX
George, 1803
Mildred, 1804
Thelma (Wiser), 1803
ADDINGTON
Dennis Keith, 530
Joy Michelle (Riggs), 530
ADELINE
Adeline, 468
Augustus John Lotge, 468
ADKINS
Joan, 122
Lewana Sue, 611
Robin R, 1375
ADNEY
Sharon Sue, 573
ADRIAN
Sue, 179
AECHARD
Patricia Ann, 1065
AESCHLIMAN
Beth Ann (Grieser), 632
Kalia Jo, 632
Karla Sue, 632
Kevin Lee, 632
Steve, 632
AGGAR
Mabel Edith, 1441
AGGERS
Annie Elizabeth (Ewing), 1227
Avanella (Sweeney), 1227
Dale Robert, 1227
Debra Lynn, 1227
Donald Edwin, 1227
Edwin, 1227
Margaret Louise, 1227
Robert, 1227
AGRIN
Glen, 117
Lynn Carol (Krigbaum), 117
AGUIRRE
Esther Marie (Davis), 1212
Fernando, 1212
AHARRAH
Charles Jr, 1240
Elsie May, 1231
Lois Adelia (Kifer), 1240
AHRENDT
Jill Katherine, 1739
AHRENS
Betty Ann, 1692
Ruth, 617
AIELLO
Gretchen Ann, 169
AIKEN
Elizabeth, 30

AIKENS
Kathleen Ann, 917
Margaret H (Spengler), 917
Mary Kathleen (Klaiss), 917
Paul Evans, 917
Paul Wayne, 917
Susan, 917
AILLS
Brenda Kay (Weiser), 453
Joseph George, 453
Marlin Lee, 453
Melanie Lee, 453
Valerie Jean, 453
AILMAN
David E, 1395
Emiline Beth, 1395
Virginia (Hess), 1395
AILTS
Amy Ann (Easton), 197
Derek Weston, 197
AIPPERSPACH
Amber Maria, 411
Eileen Sara (Saville), 410
Nicole Estelle, 410
Robert Ruben, 410
Troy Robert, 410
AITWELL
Edith Abbiegail (Lenker), 674
Russell, 674
AKENHEAD
Elizabeth Emma (Fausold), 728
W R, 728
AKERMAN
Adeline J, 518
Alta (Rise), 521
Andrew Jackson, 513
Arminta (Guagey), 513
Axel L, 517
Barbara J, 518
Bertha (Van Valkenbergh), 513
Carl Don, 514
Charles E, 518
Charles T, 518
Chester E, 518
Christian, 514
Clarissa Jane (Campbell), 521
Clifford E, 518
Don R, 517
Edna (Mae), 518
Edwin, 514
Elizabeth (May), 521
Elizabeth (Rocher), 517
Emma M, 521
Ethel Pauline, 518
Eugene, 521
Eva, 519
Eve, 513
Fanny Loretta (Holman), 521
Forest D, 518
Frederick E, 519
Genevieve Gertrude (Wentz), 514
George Homer, 513
Gladys (Hadley), 518
Gladys M, 518
Glenn C, 518
Hattie, 514
Hope, 514
Iva (Crannery), 518

James R, 518
Joan L, 518
John, 521
John J, 517
John J Jr, 517
John M, 517
Juntta, 521
Keziah, 518
La Dene, 517
Laura Margaret, 514
Letitia May, 514
Linda K, 514
Loran E, 521
Mae (Frederick), 514
Marcelle, 517
Margaret M, 519
Martha Juanite, 517
Mary (Workman), 517
Mary B, 518
Mary E, 518
Maxine, 513
Myra E, 513
Nellie (Lewis), 517
Nellie (Tabler), 513
Nellie M, 518
Newton, 521
Norman E, 518
Norton J, 521
Parthenia (Denny), 521
Phyliss C, 518
Robert J, 518
Samuel Baird, 513
Samuel D, 517
Sarah (Fisher), 521
Vernon W, 518
Violet H, 518
Walter E, 514
William, 518
William D, 513
William N, 521
Wilma L, 519
Winifred E (Farr), 518
AKERS
Chester Arthur, 520
Esther, 1158
Rosemary Kay (Ackerman), 520
AKIN
Dwight, 1871
Glenn Houston, 202
Patricia Sue (Sturm), 202
Wanda Lee (Wiser), 1871
AKINS
Alice (Van Halen), 111
Amanda (Deppen), 111
Andrew, 111
Andrew Robert, 420
Arabelle (Padrick), 111
Bertha, 111
Charles, 111
Charles S, 111
Christine (Brown), 420
Deborah Ann, 420
Della, 111
Dollie, 111
Donna Kae (Weiser), 420
Ivy (Lacy), 111
John, 111
John W, 111
John William Jr, 111
Leila L, 111
Margaret E, 111
Mary (Shaw), 111
Peter Eugene, 421
Robert Eugene, 420
Sarah Elizabeth, 420

Winnie Maud, 111
AL NAQEEB
Farris Hamed, 44
Hamed Mohamed Said, 44
Mary Elizabeth (Mason), 44
ALAND
Kurt, 279
ALB
Caley, 1190
Lisa Kay (Wiser), 1190
Michael, 1190
ALBANG
Loerrach Sonja, 1608
ALBAUGH
Hazel R, 613
ALBERS
Karen, 1387
Laveda, 1476
ALBERT
--, 472
Amos Melanction, 466
Anna, 463
Anne Catherine, 467
Archie L, 467
Barbara (Beckley), 472
Charles Henry, 467
Christina, 464
Claydie, 468
Daniel, 466
Don, 473
Elizabeth Jane (Shrider), 467
Emma Luceria, 467
Francis Marion, 467
George W, 466
Hannah (Reed), 466
Ida E, 467
Iva Isadore, 467
James, 468
Jefferson, 468
Jennie, 468
Kate (Macklin), 467
Lillie, 468
Lydia Ann (Binkley), 466
Mabel Fern (Baumgardner), 467
Margaret, 793
Mary Alice, 467
Mary Catherine (Mechling), 467
Mary Jane, 467
Matilda Ieadora, 471
Matilla, 467
Nancy (Griner), 466
Patricia (Karr), 473
Sarah Ellen, 467
Sarah Isabelle (Coe), 466
Simon Peter, 467
Stella, 468
Susan, 467
Thomas, 467
ALBERTS
Kari Lynette (Wheeler), 1482
Larry, 1482
Melissa Lea, 1482
ALBINGER
Mary Ann, 1193
ALBRECHT
Elisabeth Johanna Lulu Daisy (von Gevekot), 323
Helmut, 323
Karin, 323
Meike, 323

ALSPAUGH (continued)
Donn Paul, 1151
Dorothy Marie, 1149
Douglas Reginold, 1317
Effie Avinia, 1149
Emma Ethel, 1152
Etta (Haas), 1151
Geneva Ann, 1150
Gerald Lee, 1149
Gertrude, 1146
Gertrude Ethel, 1148
Gloria Rae, 1149
Harold Paul, 1151
Helen (Steele), 1149
Helen B (Bauer), 1150
Henry Edward, 1146
Herbert Paul, 1148
infant daughter, 1147
Irvin Ellsworth, 1151
James Ronald, 1317
Jessica Elizabeth, 1317
Jonathan Paul, 1151
Judith Kay, 1151
Kathleen Kenton
  (Duffey), 1151
Kenneth Eugene, 1150
Kenneth Russell, 1150
Lavina (Weiser), 1146
Leota May, 1149
Levi Renaldo, 1148
Lillian Mae (Haas), 1151
Mable Eveline, 1148
Margaret Elizabeth, 1147
Martha (McCoy), 1146
Mary Alice, 1148
Mary Ann (Abney), 1317
Maude Lavina, 1146
Mertie I, 1152
Otto Edward, 1149
Paul, 1146
Paul John, 1146
Ralph Benjamin, 1151
Ray Paul, 1149
Ruth Ann (Royal), 1150
Ruth Lavina, 1148
Samuel Solomon, 1149
Sarah Samantha
  (Courtright), 1146
Vina Belle (McFarland), 1151
Viola Etta, 1150
ALSTAETLER
Edith Ethel, 626
ALSTON
Martha Jeanne
  (Burnite) Roberts, 1475
Walter James II, 1475
ALT
Ken, 1234
Margaret (Kahle), 1234
ALTENDERFER
Catharine, 1761
Catharine (Dietrich), 1761
Catharine (Trexler), 1761
Jacob, 1761
Jacob Jonas, 1761
John, 1761
Maria, 1761
Sarah, 1761
ALTERIO
Kelly, 1397
Michael, 1397

Sarah Ellen (Wagner), 1397
ALTHOUSE
Claude, 249
Connie Lynn, 947
Elizabeth (Dillon), 947
Ida May (Loy), 249
Janice Clair, 947
Jeannett (Clemmer), 947
John Cosgrove, 947
John Joseph, 947
John Skyles, 946
Kathy Jeanne, 947
Kurt William, 947
Mary Jane, 947
Patricia Doris, 249
Sonia (Moyer), 947
Viola Dean, 947
Viola Dean (Cosgrove), 946
William C, 947
ALTLAND
Beth Ann, 687
ALTON
Alta Ellen, 799
Amelia Ann (Weiser), 798
Bessie Maude, 798
Celese, 801
Charles L, 801
Clinton Weiser, 798
Darrell, 801
Hugh Emerson, 801
Janice Louise, 799
Juanita (Abbott), 801
Madaline Elizabeth, 798
Mancel D, 798
Margaret, 801
Marie Elnor
  (Tombough), 801
Mary Lynn, 801
Miles, 799, 801
Myrtle Belle, 799
Phoebe Emma (Conn), 798
Robert Ellis, 801
Thelma Louise
  (Mondorf), 799
ALUMBAUGH
--, 103
Marjorie Eloise (Blair), 103
ALVERADO
Marcia Gay
  (Armknecht) Franzen, 1733
Ray, 1733
ALVIN
Kathryn, 1036
ALYWARD
Faith Felicia, 1069
AMAIL
Gisela, 610
AMARINE
Audrey Eulala, 446
Bertha Helen, 447
Louis, 446
Miriam Mabel
  (Rhoads), 446
AMBROGI
Emma Katherine, 313
Nicholas Sigifrido, 313
Robert Raymond, 312
Sarah Baldwin
  (Schwab), 312
AMBROSE
Bill, 146

Dorothy (Evans), 146
Karen, 146
Kenneth B, 146
Scott, 146
Shirley Ann, 1075
AMBROSINO
Austin J, 808
Georgene Shissler
  (Keefer), 808
Jarod Austin Keefer, 808
Michelle Lynn, 808
AMBROZA
Abraham John, 145
Antony Lee, 145
Barry Russell, 144
Deborah Loraine
  (Hughes), 144
AMENDT
Maryanne, 1323
AMERSON
Pauline, 213
AMES
Elizabeth Jane (Berry), 1204
Reggie, 1204
AMMON
Emma C, 1560
Jordan Lee, 144
Mark, 144
Tamara Renee
  (Fuelling), 144
AMON
Eleanor Ruth (Gasser), 83
George Washington III, 83
AMOS
Mary Starnes, 441
Sadie Larcenia, 1868
AMOSS
Alice Rebecca
  (Eikelberner), 276
Harold William, 276
Helen Elizabeth, 276
Walter R, 276
AMSBAUGH
--, 1425
Clara C (Seeger), 1425
AMSLER
Lillie, 1247
AMSPAUGH
Virginia, 839
AMSTUTZ
Michael David, 196
Selma, 612
AMUNDSEN
Arthur, 1725
Irene (Thiel), 1725
AMUNDSON
Cora Louise, 989
David, 989
Evan Jacob, 989
Janet (Bernard), 989
John, 989
Kathleen, 989
Kelly Ann (Gossard), 599
Nan (Finkelstein), 989
Robert, 599
AMY
Barbara Graham
  (Euston), 1510
Louise M, 1466
Richard D, 1510
Tawn Elizabeth, 1510
ANDERBERG
Dorothy Mae (Kephart), 1690

Marcus, 1690
ANDERSEN
Anne (Hooper), 1179
Debra Ann (Hughes), 1180
Esther Gale (Herrin), 1179
Jane Elizabeth, 1180
Janice Marie (Vequist), 1180
John Granville, 1180
Linda Joanne, 1180
Lynette Little (Floyd), 1180
Nancy (Harriss), 1179
Nole Elise, 1179
Patrick Alan, 1180
Robert Christian, 1179
Robert Elwood, 1179
Robert Elwood Jr, 1179
Roxanne (Baker), 1180
Timothy Hanks, 1180
ANDERSON
--, 992, 1839
-- (--), 777, 992
Albin, 1237
Alexander Dayton, 310
Alva Eunice (Wiser), 1811
Andrew Jesse, 1416
Ann Marie (Gardner), 438
Anne B (Howes), 1488
Betty, 871
Betty Joy (Brown), 459
Betty Louise
  (LeVasseur), 426
Beverly, 599
Caitrin Castine, 310
Carl Lawrence, 426
Carl Stephen, 398
Carl William, 426
Caroline Augusta
  (Muhlenberg), 285
Catherine, 1654
Catherine (Kiplinger), 1654
Celine (--), 992
Charles A Jr, 133
Cheryl Louise, 870
Christian, 1416
Christina, 1415
Christina (Wysor), 1654
Dana Ray, 601
David, 1488
David Robert, 134
David Scott, 399
David William, 310
DaVolla, 663
Debora Sue, 426
Della Marie (Burd), 162
Delwin Mauritz, 285
Dennis, 1693
Diane Maurine
  (Bennett), 398
Donald, 992
Donald Blain, 426
Drucilla (--), 1654
Earl Raymond, 1773
Eddie, 663
Eldy Vernon, 1811
Eleanore (Kline), 868
Elizabeth, 1416, 1654
Elizabeth Leonore, 810
Elvia, 870
Eric Scott, 1415

Erica, 1415
Ethel, 1558
Ethel Goldie (Yinger), 869
Eva, 390
Eve, 1654
Fay (Stoner), 869
Florence, 1444
Frances Anita
  (Cochran), 44
Frances Jean (Beam), 426
Francis Fencil, 869
George, 1654
Gertrude (--), 992
Glenn, 395
Glenn Alfred, 459
Grace (Ryder), 1547
H Emmett, 991
Hallie, 431
Harrison, 1237
Harry, 1547
Helen Grace (Weiser), 398
Hetty (Carper), 1655
Homer, 992
Irene, 1078
Isabel Anne (Scott), 1415
Isabel Scott, 1413
Jacob, 1654
JaNelle Roberta (Hall), 175
Janet E (Meeker), 395
Janet Suzette (Weber), 1288
Johanna Lea, 1288
John, 992, 1654, 1814
John Mark, 1415
John Wallace, 1415
Joshua, 1415
Joyce Arline, 162
Judy, 124
Julia, 1416
Julia Ann (Leffel), 439
Juliet (Brooks), 1655
K T, ix, 361, 777
Karen, 869
Karen (Yared), 1416
Karen Sue, 398
Karen Sue (Wiser), 1814
Kathleen (Brantner), 1415
Katrina Thurston
  (Schwab), 310
Kevin Vernon, 870
Knut Theodore, 809
Kristin Marie, 398
Larue, 1237
Laura, 1496
Laura Jane (Ditzler), 991
LeRoy, 162
Linda, 996, 1207
Linda (Eighmy), 1693
Linda Gail (Williams), 459
Linda Marie (Haney), 398
Lloyd Lee, 175
Lola Irene, 1456
Lu Ann, 124
Mae, 830
Margaret, 1654, 1693
Margaret Catharine, 810
Margaret Hannah, 1488

ANSPACH (continued)
William M, 598
William Ray, 839
William Theodore, 842
Wilmer, 838
Wilmer John, 838
ANSTED
Carolyn Jane, 483
ANTES
Edith, 1682
ANTHONY
Alice, 815
Anna Elizabeth, 814
Barbara Jane, 814
Brenda, 815
Carol Ann (Adams), 814
Caroline, 814
Clair, 1241, 1243
Claire, 1016
Colette Lene, 1847
Cora May, 814
David, 815
Dean Ralph, 579
Dean Scott, 579
Donna (Summerville), 815
Dorothy Ruby (Kahle), 1243
Elizabeth, 1016
George, 1016
Grace, 815
Harlene B (Miller), 579
Helen, 1469
James Clyde, 814
Jerome Martin, 579
Joseph Emmett, 814-815
Margie, 815
Michael, 815
Minnie (Snyder), 1016
Nancy, 815
Pearl, 1016
Robert, 1016
Ruth, 1016
Shirley Diane, 815
Violet, 815
Violet Jane (Womelsdorf), 814
William, 1016
ANTILL
Gary Edward, 448
Jane, 446
Jane Elizabeth (Sweeting), 448
Jaron Miles, 448
Jeremy Miles, 448
Kisha Jean (Gilbert), 448
Simon Peter, 448
ANTOGNOLI
Lisa, 1456
APELT
Julie, 318
APGAR
Ellen, 850
APLIN
Alfred Campbell, 439
Alice Faye, 439
Donald Graham II, 439
Donald Graham III, 439
Gordon Frederick, 439
Jean Catherine, 440
John Alfred, 439
John Benjamin, 439
Judith (Wright), 439
Michael Stewart, 439
Peter Campbell, 439

Susan Elvira, 439
Zola Elvira (Knecht), 439
APOSTOLAKOS
Mary, 86
APP
Alice (Weiser), 1522
Anna Laura (Cooper), 1028
Barbara, 1205
Carleton Smith, 1522
Charles, 1522
Daniel, 83
Gilfillan, 1522
Grant, 1028
Helen, 1028
Henry, 83
Herman, 83
John G, 1522
Lulu, 794
Ruth, 1028
Sarah (Bassler), 83
APPEL
Luella W, 176
APPENRODT
Norman, 1291
Twila Ruth (Weiser), 1291
APPLEBY
Ann May, 40
Anna, 33
Caroline Elizabeth (Willey), 40
Grace Ellen (Bradley), 40
Janet Lee, 40
Katherine Elizabeth (Carlton), 40
Laura Ida Belle, 41
Laurie Elizabeth, 40
Louie Lorena, 40
Minnie Marvin, 40
Myrtle Willey, 41
Samuel Roy, 40
Susan Grace, 40
William Allen, 40
APPLETON
Melva, 119, 1884
Melva Pauline (Tack), 130
Norman, 130
APT
Alda, 833
Elmer, 833
Elmer S, 833
Helen Grace (Womelsdorf), 833
Kenneth, 833
Oscar C, 833
ARBAUTHNOT
Louise Freiss, 1477
ARBEGAST
-- (--), 1884
Christopher James, 175
Collette B (Paul), 174
Elizabeth Ann, 174
Ella Nora (Woolridge), 174
Gloria (Kamps), 174
Jacke (Devona), 175
James, 1884
James Lee, 175
James Lee Jr, 175
Lee Milton, 175
Lee Milton Jr, 175
Linda K (Marion), 175
Lori (Coppinger), 175
Margaret Marie, 174
Nancy Joan, 175

Nina (Tiller), 175
Pamela, 174
Richard Jesse, 174
Richard Jesse Jr, 175
Toni Marie, 174
Virginia Louise, 174
William, 174
William J, 174
William John, 174
ARBOGAST
Angelina (Koppenheffer), 643
Beth, 917
Catharine Marie, 246
Don, 917
Dorthy Pauline (Lawver), 717
Emmaline, 652
Faye Evelyn, 717
Ida Elizabeth, 661
Israel, 643
Kathleen Ann (Aikens), 917
Mary Agnes, 643
Michael, 917
Randal Wayne, 717
Russell, 717
ARCHER
Cora (Cromley), 995
Erica Ann, 1489
Maria Elizabeth, 1489
Rickie Eugene, 1489
Vick, 995
ARCHEY
Elizabeth, 1080
ARCHIBALD
Amanda Marlane, 991
Kathryn, 141
Mark, 991
Marlane Judith (Wand), 991
Matthew Frederick Lawrence, 991
Timothy Mark, 991
ARDELL
Kristin Ann, 355
ARDEN
Anna Margaretta (Ward), 336
Destiny Ann (Kahle), 1201
Elizabeth Vaughn (Jones), 336
Helen, 336
John, 336
Melissa Michelle, 1201
Tanya Lynette, 1201
Thomas B, 336
Thomas Boyle, 336
William Joseph, 1201
AREHART
Ermal Maxine, 208
Everett Earl, 208
Grace Hazel (Weiser), 208
Lorine Elizabeth, 208
ARENDS
Britney Lucille, 543
Charles Stone, 543
Heather Lisa (Tews), 543
ARGOTSINGER
Amber Koren, 124
Apryl Lynne, 124
Bryce W, 124
Colleen Mae (Weiser), 124
Darcie Dane, 124
David Paul, 124

Dereck Paul, 124
Gabriel Isaac, 124
Kathy Jo (Marshall), 124
Margaret Ann (Kuhn), 124
Mathew James, 124
Michael Evan, 124
Rebecca Lynn, 124
Ruth Elaine, 124
Samuel David, 124
Steven Elwood, 124
ARIAIL
James Meryle, 69
Nancy Lee (Martin), 69
ARILLO
Marie, 911
ARINGTON
Reda Jo, 583
ARKIN
Millie, 842
ARLETH
Mary, 1551
ARMAGOST
Shirley Leadbetter, 1273
ARMBRUSTER
Gary, 1324
Heidi, 1324
Luann Marie (Shyrigh), 1324
Marcus, 1324
ARMERDING
Gretchen Elizabeth, 1182
J Peter, 1182
James William, 1182
Noreen, 1181, 1191
Noreen Rennie (Nelson), 1182
ARMITAGE
Frances Lee (Knecht), 431
Wilson, 431
ARMKNECHT
Bamcy (Mershon), 1733
Cindy Ray, 1733
Clarice June (Wieser), 1733
Connie Fay, 1733
Debra May, 1733
Elaine, 1733
Howard, 1733
Karen (--), 1733
Marcia Gay, 1733
William Joseph, 1733
ARMONS
Hannah Morgan, 1469
ARMSTRONG
Elbert, 1357
James, 401
James Nathan, 401
Jane, 1578
Jessie, 1812
Margaret (Glavis) Yates, 1357
Phyllis Nadine (Moore), 401
ARNETT
Michelle Ann, 198
ARNEY
Charles Roscoe, 1868
George, 1060
Helen, 1060
Mary, 1059
Miles, 1059
Nancy Ellen (Wiser), 1868

Ruth, 1060
Sydney May (Gramley), 1059
ARNOLD
--, 1586
-- (--), 1350-1352
Aaron Mathiew, 1212
Alice Rebecca, 1351
Angela Marie, 441
Angela Rose, 498
Anna, 1560
Annette, 1351
Arvilda Jane, 498
Ashley Nicole, 169
Barbara, 1353
Bertha (Smallwood), 1350
Bertie Lee (Wiser), 1804
Bessie Arvilda (Kern), 498
Betty (Hucker), 1352
Betty Maxine, 533
Brenda (Howe), 533
Brock Adams, 1212
Carrie (Sangrey), 1414
Christina, 1351
Christopher Lee, 1211
Clarence, 1351
Clarence Felix, 1351
Clarice, 1351
Corey James, 1210
Corey Noel, 1212
Daniel Christopher, 498
Debra Sue, 498
Della Nadene, 533
Donald Eugene, 671
Donna, 1060
Donna Marie, 1352
Dorothea, 251
Dorothy, 753, 1351
Earl, 1353
Edith, 617
Edythe (Detwiler), 1352
Effie (Kueker), 1350
Ella Louise (Maus), 1352
Ellen Louise (Rick), 1560
Ellen Rick, 1560
Elvina (Weiser), 1350
Emma Clara (Light), 1351
Emma J, 81
Esther Violet, 1353
Fannie (Dohner), 1352
Felixitus (Volk), 1353
Florence, 1677
Frances (Chellew), 1350
Frances (Straubie), 1350
Frances Virginia, 1351
Franklin Dundore, 1560
Frederick, 1352
Gary, 1210
George, 1350
George Albert, 1351
George Benjamin, 1350
George W, 1351
Gerald DeWayne, 533
Gertrude, 1353
Glenn, 1351
Gregory Lee, 498
Gretchen Amelia, 1537
Harold F, 1350

ATWOOD (continued)
Maude, 1764
Stephan A, 65
AUCHMUTY
Arthur, 357, 1110
AUCKER
Beatrice, 1526
AUFFERMAN
--, 1623
Edna (Endy), 1623
AUGENSTEIN
Bonnie Mae, 465
AUGHBAUGH
Curtis, 1703
Erie Belle (Wisor),
1703
AUGHENBAUGH
Della (Wisor), 1713
Gladys, 1703
Warren, 1713
AUGHINBAUGH
Jerry Wayne, 1822
Joe Edgar, 1822
John Wilson, 1822
Leonard Thomas, 1822
Lillie (Brandon), 1822
Mamie Magdalene
(Reynolds), 1822
Thelma Rebecca
(Wiser), 1822
AUGUSTINE
Scott Michael, 550
Sheila Jane (Kreisher),
550
AUKER
Mary, 599
AULERMAN
Garn, 555
Martha E (Johnson),
555
Sione, 555
AULT
Donna, 1325
AUMAN
Adah Jane, 1092
Adam, 1060
Alice (Gramley), 1060
Alton, 982
Clarence, 1062
Gertrude (Huddlestine),
1062
Grace, 1392
Harold Bierly, 1092
Helen (Rennick), 1092
Lillian B (Rennick),
1092
Lyma (Jandrew), 1092
Martha Irene (Foote),
1092
Mary, 1060
Minnie (Bierly), 982
Miriam Eulalia, 1090
Naomi Pauline, 1092
Pauline, 982
Richard, 1062
Russell Frank, 1092
Salome, 1090
Thomas Aaron, 1090
AUMILLER
Ardella M, 1513
AUNGST
Annie Evelyn (Weiser),
1616
Stanley, 1616
AURAND
Alice (Baysinger),
1108
Clarence, 1108
Corra, 1108

Delmer, 1108
Doloris, 1108
Ethel, 1108
Katherine, 1108
Lloyd, 1108
Lois, 1108
Mattie, 1108
Robert, 1108
Ruth, 1108
Vera, 1108
AUSTIN
Alice Anne, 152
Alma Ruby, 150
Alta Lucille, 151
Alyssa Lynne, 152
Amy Linette), 152
Andy Ray, 153
Barbara Jean, 153
Bernice Louise, 153
Betty June (Gordon),
150
Beverly Ann, 153
Bobbi Jean, 153
Bradley Scott, 152
Brian Scott, 152
Catherine (Dies), 1036
Christina Annette, 150
Cindy Lynne (Johnson),
152
Clarissa Helen (Stolz),
154
Cory Ray, 152
Dale Rick, 152
Daniel Lee, 152
Darrell Wayne, 154
Darren Mark, 154
Debra Marie, 153
Denine Marie
(Lehman), 152
Dollie Louise Ellen
(Noah), 152
Dollie Pearl, 153
Donald Ray, 152
Elaine Joyce (Hanson),
152
Ella, 1868
Ellsworth, 596, 599
Emily Anne, 152
Eric Ryan, 152
Evelyn (Moretti), 150
Frank, 948
George Ernest, 150
Goldie Mae, 150
Herbert Leroy, 150
Jamie Sue, 152
Jane Ellen, 150
Jerome Noah, 153
Kathi (Keller), 152
Kathryn Louise, 151
Kenneth Neal, 150
Laura Frances, 151
Linda Marie, 154
Lori Maurene (Moore),
152
Louise Grace (Landis),
151
Lovena Ellen (Vorhees),
596, 599
Margaret Ella, 151
Marjorie Nora, 150
Martha Elizabeth
(Spurgeon), 150
Martha Nelley
(Sowers), 152
Mary E, 596, 599
McKenzie Marie, 152
Melissa Dawn, 153
Michael Ray, 153
Myrtle (Crump), 948

Ralph, 1036
Ray, 948
Raymond Lee, 152
Richard, 948
Richard Cecil, 151
Rickey Dale, 152
Robert Stanley, 152
Robert Wendell, 152
Roberta Norma
(Billington), 152
Roy Ernest, 150
Ryan Nicholas, 152
Scott Daniel, 152
Shane William, 152
Sheryl Lee (Barkeleu),
152
Stephen Lowell, 152
Virginia Irene (Kline),
150
Wendell Eugene, 151
AUSTON
Mary Katherin, 1220
AUTEN
Italene, 545
AVANTS
Loretta Jane, 527
AVENI
Madeline, 1707
AVERY
Grace I, 492
AVILINO
John, 1019
Margaret (Gray), 1019
AVIS
Debra Anne
(Bernbrock), 636
Geoffrey, 636
AVITT
Lisa Christine, 424
AVORY
Anne, 1587
AX
Albert, 479
Viola (Payne), 479
AXON
Joyce Ellen, 933
AYERS
Anne, 299
Betty Jane, 100
Deborah Sue, 1352
Delores Marie, 737
John D, 1352
Mary Elizabeth
(Clymer), 1352
Philip J, 1352
Ruth Marie, 1781
AYRES
Elwood Bowers Jr, 835
Frances (Venderchen),
835
Gail, 835
BABAK
Lilian Ruth, 1054
BABBITT
Aline, 1648
Charles Winthrop,
1648
BABCOCK
Anita Louise (Knapp),
630
Clyde E, 1167
Dawn Marie, 630
Edward Vose, 1560
Elizabeth, 1765, 1782
Evelyn Marie, 1167
Evelyn Marie
(Babcock), 1167
Florence, 1049
Julene Gail, 630

Karen Elaine, 630
Kathryn Mary (Weiser),
1167
Kenneth, 630
Mary Dundore
(Arnold), 1560
BABER
Thelma June, 146
BABIONE
Alice Mae, 503
BABYNSKI
Mary, 661
BACH
Kathi Lou, 918
BACHMAN
Cody Jonathan, 249
Edwin O, 1644
Eric John, 249
Florence Emma
(Schwoyer), 1644
Joanne Onata, 916
Lillian, 72
Marci Jo (Mundell),
249
Romaine Elizabeth
(Brehm), 916
William, 916
BACHTAL
Betty, 716
BACKEY
Elaine (Weiser), 1144
John, 1144
BADDORF
Lois Marie, 653
BADER
Luise, 1599
Lynne Elizabeth
Shepard, 1503
BADERTSCHER
Beth Ellen, 612
Frank, 612
Patty (Long), 612
BADMAN
Angela Suzette, 745
Betty Elnora (Klinger),
745
Brett Josiah, 745
Clarence Edwin, 745
Heather Johnne, 745
Leon Reynold, 745
Margaret Ann, 745
Renold Lee, 745
Vonda Charlene
(Fishburn), 745
BAER
Amanda Sue, 1673
Donna, 1378
Harold Jr, 1673
Janice Marlene (Wiser),
1673
Mary Kimmel, 281
Michael Todd, 1673
Randi Lee, 1673
Randy Eugene, 1673
Rita Renee, 1673
Tammy (Forrester),
1673
Tammy Marlene, 1673
Wesley Eugene, 1673
BAEUERLE
August Friedrich, 1597
Pauline (Weisser),
1597
BAGBY
Pamela, 1790
BAGLEY
David Todd, 373
Floyd Eugene, 622
Joanne Elinor

(Edwards), 622
Linda Jean (Seaman),
373
Sarah Almira, 1193
Stefani Jean, 373
Steven David, 373
BAGOCIUS
Celia, 767
BAGOT
Cliff, 1656
Joyce (Taylor), 1656
BAHM
Allen Ernst, 1480
Debra (Push), 1480
Ernst Eugene, 1480
Gregory Eugene, 1480
Jennifer Ann, 1480
Laura Helen, 1480
Mary Joan (Earnest),
1480
Steven Craig, 1480
BAHNER
Irene Grace, 646
Margaret, 786
BAHR
Jacob, 914
Susanna (--), 914
BAICHTAL
Janis Lee (Adams), 960
Kerry, 960
BAIHINGER
Andreas, 1605
Maria Barbara
(Weisser), 1605
Marie Barbara (Natter),
1605
BAILETS
Grace Ida, 1097
BAILEY
--, 985
Alletta Nathalie, 337
Alletta Remsen (Lynch),
337
Ann, 1204
Ann Mary, 337
Anne (Vine), 1357
Anne Susan, 1807
Barbara Jeanette
(Ortez), 436
Benjamin, 1729
Bergetta Hubertine,
1357
Brent William, 1357
Caroline, 1517
Caroline M, 1517
Catherine, 1099
Charles, 982, 985,
1729
Charles William, 1729
Christine Amora, 469
Cora Missouria, 1729
Dale Henry, 436
Daniel, 1729
Daniel Oswin, 1729
David Winfield, 436
Dorothy Jean (Roberts),
436
Earnest, 597
Edna Elizabeth
(Powell), 1358
Edward, 1516
Edwin Martin, 1729
Elaine Kathleen, 1749
Eliza Meier (Lorillard),
337
Elizabeth, 1679
Elizabeth Hummel
(Reily), 1516
Elizabeth Scott, 1516

BALL (continued)
Marshall Edgar, 298
Mildred (Johnson), 978
Pauline (Wisor), 1711
Philena Selewella
   (Bower), 978
Ray, 978
Spencer Tunnell, 1661
Tracy Ann, 928
Walter Earl, 298
BALLAH
Norma Jean, 454
BALLARD
Korene S, 1376
Lois (Wiser), 1770
Robert Melroy, 1770
BALLENGER
Charles Paul, 607
Daniel Eugene, 607
Darrell DeWayne, 607
Dora (Robles), 607
Herbert Eugene, 607
Mary Elaine, 607
Mary Etta (Craig), 607
Paul, 607
Roger Lee, 607
Roger Paul, 607
William Charles, 607
Zelpha Margaret
   (Rhodes), 607
BALLENTINE
Mary Ellen, 815
Mildred Inez, 815
BALLEW
Frank K, 163
Frank Kaywood, 163
Joan Ellen, 163
Ronald Eugene, 163
Thelma Genevieve
   (Burd), 163
BALLEWEG
Bernard, 1054
Diane Victoria
   (Haddon), 1054
BALLING
Dixie Lee, 1778
BALLINGER
Anne Sheridan
   (Holmes), 65
Carl Richardson, 65
Elizabeth Ann
   (Massey), 65
John Montgomery, 65
Louise Renn, 65
Marlene Janet, 605
Maude, 575
Michael Cummings, 65
Nicholas Massey, 65
Scott Sheridan, 65
Tillie, 603
BALLOU
George F, 1199
Katherine D (Kahle),
   1199
Richard, 1044
Vera Snyder (Moyer),
   1044
BALSIGER
Barbara Jeanne, 1263
Gerogina Terrilla
   (Kahle), 1263
James Charles, 1263
Margaret Lucille, 1262
BALSLEY
Catherine (Pickard),
   1584
Johannes, 1584
Magdalena, 1584
Pieter, 1584

BALSLEY/ PALSLEY
Andreas, 1584
Lea (Pickard), 1584
Margretha, 1584
Maria, 1584
Nicholas, 1584
BALTIMORE
Marselle, 1823
BAMBERGER
Myra Ruth
   (Rodeheaver), 1216
Thomas S, 1216
BANE
Marie Helen, 1600
BANES
Donna Marie, 1125
BANEY
Bertha (Wisor), 1702
Catherine, 1394
Harry, 1702
BANKS
Beauford, 1795
Benjamin Jacob, 1736
Donna (Sudderth),
   1736
Dorothy Louise, 1736
Douglas Jacob, 1736
Emma S, 1568
Esther, 1716
Guy Franklin, 1736
Justin Eliot, 1736
Keron (Wiser), 1795
Martha Jane, 148
Mary (Wiser), 1820
Russiea, 1340
Sherman Wayne, 1736
William, 1820
BANNEN
Arthur Eugene, 1035
Carrie Elizabeth (Ulsh),
   1035
Nora Elsie (Cooper),
   1035
Paul Cooper, 1035
Robert S, 1035
BANNER
Molly (Graham), 1705
William, 1705
BANNION
Lynda Sue, 1432
BANTER
Abraham W, 548
Barbara Jane, 564
Benjamin J, 549
Berlie (Swagger), 563
Bessie, 548
Betty Louise, 564
Beverly (Jones), 562
Bonnie Jean, 561
Carrie (Murray), 563
Charamae, 563
Christena (Herring),
   548
Clarence, 548
Cora Bell, 561
Daniel, 564
Darlene, 562
Della (--), 561
Dellia May, 549
Delmar, 548
Demarus, 561
Diane, 562
Dica May, 548
Donald, 548
Dora, 548
Eddie Leroy, 563
Edna Mae, 564
Eileen (Ford), 561
Eliza, 525

Ellen, 564
Elsie Leota, 563
Eva Adaline, 548
Fern (Pugh), 563
Flossie, 548
Frederick Leo, 562
Freida (Highley), 561
Gene, 564
George, 548
Harlen, 561
Harley Jackson, 561
Harry, 564
Hattie May, 549
Hattie May (Banter),
   549
Helen (Canter), 561
Henery, 548
Howard, 561
Ileen, 564
infant son, 564
Jack, 564
James Leroy, 562
Janet (Harrold), 561
Jason A, 564
Jay, 548
Jay W, 564
Jennette, 548
Jerry W, 563
Jessie (Smith), 561
Jessie Ernest, 563
Joan, 565
Joe, 564
John Robert, 563
John W, 561
Joyce, 564
Katie, 564
Kurt, 561
Lena Lavon, 563
Leo Harley, 561
Lester J, 561
Letetia Mae, 563
Lillian Arrel, 562
Lillie Ann (Herring),
   561
Linda, 565
Linnie, 548
Lola (Welch), 564
Lorada Ilene, 562
Margaret Ann, 563
Maria, 564
Martha A, 549
Martha Louise, 562
Mary Ethel, 564
Mary Jane, 548
Michelle (Gregerson),
   564
Mike, 564
Milford Leon, 561
Millie (Boxell), 561
Ora, 549
Orpha (Lake), 561
Oscar Lee, 563
Patricia, 564
Perry, 549
Rex, 564
Rita Diane (Bell), 563
Robert, 563
Rosa D, 548
Rosetta, 548
Russell, 564
Ruth (Hunt), 564
Samuel, 564
Samuel F, 561
Sarah A (Leverich),
   548
Sarah Ella, 548
Sarah Jill, 564
Stephen, 561
Teresa (Cahue), 561

Terri (Clock), 563
Thomas A, 549
Timothy, 561
Tracy, 561
Tyson, 561
Vickie, 563
Violet (Richey), 564
Virginia (McCoy), 563
Walter J, 563
Wanda, 565
Wilma Gertrude, 563
Zada Elizabeth, 563
BARB
Jaye Patricia (Miller),
   1300
Joelene Ann, 1300
Ronald, 1300
Sharlene Ann, 1301
BARBE
Marian Lucille, 799
Myrtle Belle (Alton),
   799
Orrin Willis, 799
Rosa Louise, 799
BARBER
Alice Elveira, 1185
Angela Grace, 860
Bonia Marie (Muggio)
   Mace, 1536
Carolyn Marie, 860
Dale Stanley, 857
David, 1017
Eleanor, 1237
Herbert Alver, 1185
Joseph, 860
Laura Beth (Shettel),
   860
Lillian Mae (Yost),
   1017
Lois Elaine (Wiser),
   1185
Lorraine, 1237
Lucy Grace, 1215
Mary Beth (Stauffer),
   857
Patricia Ann, 1770
R, 1237
Rena (Kahle), 1237
Robert, 1536
Rose Ann, 583
Rose Marie, 921
BARBOSA
Michael, 938
Tammy Lou (Weiser)
   Klopp, 938
William Madosta, 938
BARBUSH
Clara L, 919
BARCLAY
Henry Anthony, 829
Leslie Boocock (de
   Caraegna), 829
Lyda Murray
   (Womelsdorf), 829
Rutgers, 829
Susan Lefevre, 829
BARDEBABAN
Waurena, 57
BARDELL
Alvin, 1032
Alvin Jr, 1032
Elsie Catherine
   (Fenton), 1032
BARDILL
Margaret, 727
BARDON
Donald J, 942
Douglas Donald, 942
Maxine Jean (Starner),

942
Neil James, 942
Rebecca Sue, 942
Robert Allen, 942
BARDWELL
Allen Greenwood,
   1385
Cindey Jane (Harter),
   1385
BARE
Anita Louise (Hallman),
   1514
Charles Anthony, 1514
Frederick Paul, 1514
Judi Holland, 1493
Judith Anne, 1514
Ross Kendig, 1514
Ross Kendig Jr, 1514
Ruth Grace (Hynicka),
   1514
Sandra Kay, 1514
Susan Wenger
   (Ludwig), 1514
BARGDILL
Sherrie Lynn, 453
BARGER
--, 1441
Ada, 1693
Barbara Jane (Anthony),
   814
Charles, 1693
Clair, 815
Cordelia (Kephart),
   1693
David Foster, 1693
Edward, 815
Edward Avon, 814
Elizabeth, 1680
Elmira, 824
George, 1693
George Latimer, 1693
Guy, 1693
Harvey William, 1693
Jacob, 1697
James, 815
Joseph, 815
Lori, 815
Margaret (Anderson),
   1693
Margie, 815
Maria (Shimmel), 1697
Marie (Fisher), 1693
Ruth Lousie (Spyker),
   1441
Sarah (Keller), 1693
Tracy, 815
BARICKMAN
Dawn lea, 1274
BARKELEU
Sheryl Lee, 152
BARKER
Bryan Lee, 614
Carol (Baker), 613
Frank, 435
John Gregory, 1513
Karen Jean (Kinback),
   1513
Kenneth, 613
Olive Neoma (Smith),
   435
Rhonda Lynn, 614
Ryan Gregory, 1513
BARKHURST
Oscar, 1688
Rose Jane (Kephart),
   1688
BARKLEY
--, 1579
Daisy (Pickard), 1579

BAUM
-- (Weisser), 6
Anna, 1566
Jacob, 6
BAUMAN
Amber, 1720
Ernest Lenard, 654
Jane Marie, 654
Kara, 1720
Kathy, 1719
Kelly, 1719
Kenneth, 1719
Kenneth III, 1719
Melissa (Weatherholtz), 1720
Nickolos, 1720
Phyllis (Knepp), 1719
Virginia Mabel (Heller), 654
BAUMANN
Gail Ann, 1735
Hazel Irene (Lund), 1735
Robert, 1735
BAUMER
Jim, 478
Marsha (Miller), 478
BAUMGARDNER
Catharine, 1426
Diana, 626
John, 387
Mabel Fern, 467
Martha Elizabeth (Moneysmith), 387
Nancy, 387
BAUSCH
Christine, 1598
Elsa M, 1428
Johann, 1603
Marie Luise Catharine Christiane (Weisser), 1603
BAUSCHER
Ellen Susanna, 1743
BAUSERMAN
Francis Pauline (Eltzroth), 534
George M, 534
BAUSHKE
Pamela Lynn, 817
BAUSUM
Felicia, 273
Janet (Trapp), 273
Jeff, 273
Ryan Dale, 273
Seth Joseph, 273
Zane Allen, 273
BAVIS
Helen Maud, 256
BAXTER
Charles Franklin, 802
Charlotte Ruth (Wilson), 801
Clovia Faye (Dean), 584
Cyntha Ann (Rashid), 802
Diane, 777
Gregory Neil, 584
James Patrick, 802
Janice Jo, 802
Jodi Lea (Norquist), 802
Kathy Jean (Krohmer), 802
Kayla Lynae, 802
Kelly Ellen, 801
Kelsey Lynn, 802
Kenneth Darrell, 801

Kenneth David, 801
Kenneth Walter, 802
Kip Wilson, 802
Kirk Darrell, 801
Kylie Jean, 802
Marissa Ann, 802
Mark Wayne, 584
Mary Ann (Borgman), 802
Mary Bernadette, 802
Michael David, 802
Neva, 663
Paul Anthony, 802
Paul Samuel, 584
Paulette Leigh, 584
Zelda Diane, 802
Zelda Maxine (Edison), 801
BAY
Eugene Howard, 1373
Geraldine Julia (Randall), 1373
Josephine Marie, 1373
BAYARD
Eliza Ann, 337
BAYER
--, 1
Catherine Anne (Leonard), 1484
Catherine Odel, 1484
Donald F, 1484
BAYHAM
Betty Virginia, 1331
Dorothy Lucile (Gebhart), 1331
William Lewis, 1331
BAYLER
Susanna, 929
BAYLESS
Daniel, 997
Guy Walter, 1666
Judy, 1647
Judy Kay (Wiser), 1666
Kari (Shirck), 997
BAYS
Faye, 1662
BAYSINGER
-- (Hudson), 1108
Alice, 1108
Evelyn, 1108
Hazel, 1108
Maude, 1108
Meda (Lapp), 1108
Nerrel, 1108
Ralph, 1108
Richard, 1108
Robert Harold, 1868
Royal, 1108
Sonya Ann (Wiser), 1868
BAYZ
Adriana, 1491
BAZE
David Stephens, 310
Lucy Titcomb (Schwab), 310
BAZING
Christian Ludwig, 1606
Helene Veronika Juliane (Weisser), 1606
BAZINGER
Georg, 1595
Johann Melchior, 1595
Maria Elisabetha (Weisser), 1595
BEACH
Charlotte Diane, 1222
Daniel Alan, 1222

Eleanor (Grove), 1222
Elmer E, 1222
Gene Marie (Ewing), 1227
Georgia Ann, 1227
Hollis, 1082
Linda Kay, 1222
Lori Jo, 1222
Mabel (Sitler), 1082
Michelle Darlene, 406
Nelly, 1867
Patricia Ann, 1082
Sandra Pearl, 1222
Thomas George, 1222
Willard Woodrow, 1227
BEACHELL
Sue Ann (Seiler), 1115
Thomas Alan, 1115
BEACHER
John, 1448
Terri Louise (Stephens), 1448
BEADLE
Cindy, 992
Cora Elizabeth, 726
Donald John, 725
Elsie (--), 726
Gertrude (Hepner), 725
John Elwood, 726
John Henry, 725
John Randolph, 726
Kenneth, 726
Madaline, 725
Madeline (Dershaw), 725
Malvin, 725
Mary Jane, 725
Rachel Ellen, 725
Rose (Flarski), 725
Wilfred, 726
William, 725
BEADLES
Helen Alicia, 801
BEAL
Alison, 1034
Douglas, 1034
Linda, 1034
Martha Elizabeth (Rhoads), 1034
Resford R, 1034
BEALE
Anna (Wagner), 906
Augustus, 330
Gertrude Withers (Tuttle), 330
Sarah (Mader), 906
Susanna (Brightbill), 906
William, 906
BEALL
Thomas, 1866
BEALS
Ellen Jane (Cook), 1314
James Allen, 1314
Manford, 789
Mildred (Crone), 789
Richard, 1314
Richard Nathan, 1314
Steven Ray, 1314
Susan Kay, 1314
BEAM
Frances Jean, 426
Mary, 1786
Mathias, 1786
BEAMER
Adam Gilcrest, 163
Carleton Alonzo, 812

Cathie Sue, 163
Evan Thomas, 163
Gail (Gleeson), 163
Karla Marie (Johnson), 1140
Kathryn Michelle, 1140
Kendra Gail, 1140
Kenneth Lynn, 1140
Kevin MacKenzie, 1140
Kimberly Louise, 1140
Lynn Elspeth (McIntyre), 811
Mildred Marie (Bordlemay), 163
Ray, 163
Thomas Ray, 163
BEAMS
Ashley Benoit, 1118
Donald Blair, 1119
Marjorie Nan (Smith), 1118
Nancy Anne, 1119
Roberta June, 1119
BEAN
Agnes (Kehl), 1102
Ann (McGrady), 371
Anna (Emrick), 769
Bridget, 1806
Charles, 1488
Clarence, 1102
Cloa S (Wiser) Thornberry Canady, 1779
Daniel, 769
Elaine Lynn, 371
Floyd, 1102
James, 1779
Jewel Alberdine (Griffis), 371
John E, 363
John Eugene, 371
John Lyn, 371
M, 1102
Martha, 1353
Mary Elizabeth (Howes), 1488
Robert, 1102
Sheryl, 1275
BEANARD
Anita Kay, 751
Darrin Paul, 751
David Allen, 750
Evelyn Faye (Whyde), 750
George Michael, 751
Glen Howard, 751
Hannah, 1667
Harold Albert, 750
Howard Allen, 750
Isabella Irene (Eister), 750
Janice Roberta, 750
Kathleen Faye, 750
Kay Marie (Kopchop), 751
Mary Roberta (Weaver), 750
Myrna Jane (Whittach), 751
Paul David, 751
Stephen Mark, 751
Ted Allen, 750
Ted Allen Jr, 750
Timothy Paul, 750
BEAR
Addie (Gedney), 960
Alice, 848
Blanch M, 1619

Charles A, 960
Clarence, 960
Cora, 848
Ethel, vi
Ethel L, 940
Ethel Lena, 960
Hazel (Stephens), 960
Herman, 960
Irma, 960
Jennie (Hill), 960
Lois Irene (Hill), 960
Wilbur Eugene, 960
BEARD
Alma (Walters), 853
Amy M, 924
Arthur Colt, 899
Bonnie, 853
Brian Bollman, 899
David, 853
Deborah M, 788
Elaine Anne, 651
Fred Stanley, 899
Judith Ann (Bollman), 899
Larry, 853
Pearl (Potteiger), 899
Richard Godshalk, 899
Wesley, 853
BEARDEN
Michael, 53
Michelle Elizabeth, 53
Miriam Camille (Maier), 53
BEARDSLEY
Frederick, 1435
Goldie (Moore), 1435
BEARY
Donald Paul, 816
Jennifer, 816
Jodi Lynn (Motter), 816
Jody Edward, 816
Karen Juanita, 816
Lula Melinda (Priester), 816
Theresa Ann, 816
Wanda Lynette, 816
Willard Eugene, 816
BEASLEY
Ina Marcella, 402
BEATES
Margaret, 1397
BEATIE
Anna J (Hummel), 1697
James, 1697
BEATON
Andrew Jr, 1631
Kathleen Dorothy (Kilpatrick), 1631
BEATTY
Eleazer T, 1828
L Ann, 1828
Martha, 1592
Mary, 729
Sarah, 1593
Virginia, 1392
Virginia Mae, 892
BEATY
Agnes (Tinkler), 1193
Anna Maria, 1193
Caroline (Shoup), 1193
Emily Olivia, 1130
George, 1193
Hannah, 1193
Henry, 1193
infant, 1193
Jame (Roberts), 1193
James, 1193

BEATY (continued)
John, 1129, 1193
Jonathan, 1193
Mary, 1193
Mary Ann (Albinger), 1193
Mary Jane (Weiser), 1193
Matilda (Weiser), 1129
Robert, 1196
Sarah, 1196
Sarah Ann, 1193
BEAU
Maria, 1365
BEAUCHAMP
William M, 19
BEAUDETTE
Janet Lee (Knecht), 431
Robert Joseph, 431
BEAVENS
Dessel Eugene, 527
BEAVER
Barbara Ann, 1093
Bertha, 147
Blanche, 147
Emma Rebecca (Weiser), 147
Franklin, 1093
Kathryn, 226
Louise, 147
Margaret Ruth (Bierly), 1093
Peter, 30
Samuel, 147
Thomas E, 1093
BEAVERSON
Ann (Cox), 633
Doloras Merlin, 632
Ellen Marie, 633
Jana Sue, 633
Juanita Fern, 632
Karen Jean, 633
Lelia Anna (Smith), 632
Lisa Ann, 633
Lowell, 632
Lowell Vernell, 633
Susan Jane, 633
BEAZELL
Lucretia Catherine, 1195
BEBBER
Brett Matthew, 1163
Charles Clary, 1164
Chester Francis, 1162
Chester Francis Jr, 1163
Delores Helen (Weimer), 1163
Duane Thomas, 1163
Edie Ann (Ester), 1163
Gary Owen, 1163
Henrietta Marie, 1162
Henrietta Morris (Weiser), 1162
Jacqueline Kay (Wood), 1164
James Andrew, 1163
Jordan Michelle, 1163
Karen Elizabeth (Heim), 1163
Kirsta Ann, 1164
Kurt Conrad, 1163
Marilyn Theresa, 1163
Ruth Elizabeth, 1163
Sharon Ann, 1163
William Ryan, 1163
William Thomas, 1164

BECHERS
Ruth, 1391
BECHLET
Mary, 190
BECHMANN
--, 327
Almuth, 327
Friedhelm, 327
Kathe (Schrader), 327
Klaus-Helmut, 327
Walter, 327
BECHT
Dora Hannah, 231
BECHTEL
Anna Mary (Eppley), 891
Christine Rebecca, 1344
Frederick, 1196
Jamie Yvonne, 924
Jay Oliver, 891
Joan, 126
Kenneth Eugene, 891
Margaret Elizabeth (Souders), 1340, 1344
Mary, 1444
Mary Alice, 832
Mildred, 144
Sarah (--), 1196
Walter Lincoln, 1344
BECHTOL
Brittany Lee Ann, 142
Dawn Elaine (Hughes), 142
Florence, 1077
Thomas Scott, 142
BECHTOLD
Lizzie, 1107
BECK
--, 1
-- (--), 1850
Abner, 914
Albert Leon, 437
Arabella, 982
Brian, 438
Cynthia Jane, 807
David Bruce, 438
Edward, 1759
Eileen Renee, 437
Eleanor Amelia, 830
Eleanor P (Huhn), 348
Elizabeth, 1647
Ellen, 1100
Eunice A, 1584
Fharal (Jean), 437
Franklin Eli, 438
Gabriele Luise, 322
George, 914, 1647
Hannah C, 914
Henry W, 348
Irma Iona, 1288
James Wesley, 436
Jennifer Annette, 437
John, 914
Jonathan David, 438
Karin Lynne (Sweeney), 436
Karoline Rosine, 1596
Kathryn Ann, 1346
Kendra (Getter), 438
Kilde (Kaufmann), 438
Kira Marie, 437
Larry John, 438
Lela Neoma, 572
Louise Marie (Mannone), 436
Marguerite Echo, 436
Maria (Spitler), 914
Martin, 914

Mary Edna, 756
Mary kathryn (Weiser), 1346
Matilda Agnes (Wieser), 1759
Michael Dean, 1346
Michelle, 437
Miriam Tilghe, 348
Nephi David, 437
Nephi Nolan, 436
Pamela Louise (Manseau), 436
Patty, 431
Peter, 914
Richard, 1346
Richard James, 437
Richard James III, 437
Robert Nolan, 436
Rochelle Marie, 437
Sarah, 914
Shirley Mae (Quast), 437
Solomon, 1850
Sophie Margaretta, 829
Stephanie Marie, 438
Teresa, 536
Tirzah Jay, 437
Veva Leola (Knecht), 436
Veva Leota, 437
William Martin, 436
William Martin III, 437
BECKE
Grace, 1099
BECKER
Alice Margaret (Fasold), 812
Anna Catharine, 88
Anna Christina, 22
Anna Louise, 777, 790
Anna Margaretha, 22
Beryl Jean (Hoffman), 751
Betsy, 1584
Carl, 812
child, 847
Christine, 1319
Darline Alice (Kistner), 868
Deron Vincent, 1514
Diana, 1586
Elizabeth (--), 22
Harvey M, 790
J Vincent, 1514
James Lee, 751
Joan S, 734
Jodi Lynn, 751
Judith Anne (Bare), 1514
Lillian, 847
Louise, 255
Maria Eva, 1361
Martin, 22
Mary, 511
Mary Jan, 1585
Maud O (Keefer), 790
Michael Robert, 255
Morris L, 847
Pamela Kay, 738
Rosa, 1684
Sadie Amelia (Anspach), 847
Scott David, 751
Shirley Anne, 218
Sigrid, 1607
Stephanie Lee, 1514
Terry Robert, 868
Thomas, 255
Tracey Lynn, 1514

Vera Arlene (Brehm), 255
William, 255
BECKLEY
Barbara, 472
Billie Dianne, 472
Delene R (Wetzel), 472
Delores, 471
Frank L, 472
Joyce, 472
Linda, 472
Ruth Ann, 472
Thomas, 471
William, 471
BECKMAN
Bruce Merlin, 150
Laura Christine, 150
Marjorie Nora (Austin), 150
BECKMANN
Carl Josef, 1602
Conrad Martin, 1602-1603
Emily Clare (Martin), 1602
BECKNER
Jeanine Grace (Osborne), 101
Joe, 101
Marcia Jo, 101
BEDDOW
Ginger, 477
BEDEE
James C, 1765
Marian W (Wiser), 1765
BEDELL
Harriet M, 1764
BEDFORD
Etta Sophia (Knabe), 879
George Elmer, 879
Victor DeWitt, 879
BEDLOW
Harriet Hall, 337
BEDNARIK
M Rosalie, 1289
BEDSWORTH
Kathryn Louisa, 1475
BEE
Avis Grace, 1430
BEEKER
Blanche Marie (Rafferty), 500
Harold Philip, 500
Mary Frances, 500
Ruth Ann, 500
BEEKMAN
Florence Edith (Wickham), 527
George, 527
Jo Lester, 527
Norman Lester, 527
Ruby Jo (Brown), 527
Vera Belle, 527
BEEKS
Marie, 53
Mary Charlotte (Bond), 40
R W, 40
BEEM
Geraldine Thelma, 761
BEER
Ida E, 1120
BEERS
--, 750
Lavine Mary, 1696
Margaret, 1046, 1291
Sandra Lee

(Eckenrode), 750
Sarah, 1711
Tamea Lynn, 750
BEESON
Hazel Hortense, 403
BEGANI
Elva Darlene (Buffington), 642
Michael, 642
BEGHON
Emilie Dorothea (Confer), 242
Jean Baptiste, 242
BEGLER
Judy, 1846
BEHAM
Mark W, 1198
Thelma Corelli (Bassim), 1198
BEHLER
Charles, 1743
Mary Ann A (Wieser), 1743
Samuel, 1743
BEHM
Mabel M, 1622
BEHRENS
Helen Emma (Moyer), 772
William Henry, 772
BEHRLE
Elizabeth May, 256
BEIDEL
Lena Jane, 1673
BEIDELMAN
Emma S, 1760
BEIDLEMAN
Estelle (Shettel), 875
George, 875
BEIGE
Anna Marie, 1296
Benjamin Garrett, 1295
Caleb Edward, 1296
Cathy Lynn (Wiser), 1295
Derek Michael, 1296
Jonathan David, 1296
Nikki Ann, 1296
Sandra Ann (Bowser), 1296
Thomas Michael, 1296
Timothy David, 1295
BEISEL
George A, 1754
Margaret Ann, 1303
Rosa (Wisser), 1754
BEISH
Ellen (Bennehoof), 1711
Emma, 1710
Isaac, 1711
BEISLEY
Carla Mae (Conklin), 428
Douglas Phillip, 428
Julie Lynn, 428
Perry, 428
BEISTLINE
Pearl E, 874
BEITENMAN
Edna Virginia, 245
Frederick, 245
Frederick Rugus, 245
Gertrude Rebecca, 245
Lulu Wolff, 245
Virginia (Wolff), 245
BEITZEL
Alma I, 222

BEJARMO
Eric James, 1163
Sharon Ann (Bebber), 1163
William, 1163
BELASCO
Ashley Renee, 1434
Bob, 1434
Brandi Michelle, 1434
Kimela Kay (Moore), 1434
BELCHER
Jane Alice, 1489
BELDEN
--, 1838
Mary Elizabeth (Wiser), 1838
BELEW
Christine Leanne, 996
Elizabeth Anne, 996
Karen Louise (Shirck), 996
William, 996
BELFORD
Andrew James, 1555
Anne Reid, 1555
Barbara Ann, 109
Brian Arthur, 1554
Charlotte (Eckley), 109
Claire Connors, 1555
David John, 1555
Delbert, 109
Delbert Jr, 109
Donamarie (Jones), 1555
Elizabeth Jane, 1555
Elizabeth M, 464
John Lawrence II, 1554
John Lawrence III, 1554
John Lawrence IV, 1554
Luke Conor, 1555
Marjorie C, 109
Mary, 1554
Mary Elizabeth, 1555
Mary Susan (Parker), 1554
Michael Kenedy, 1555
Michaele Anne (Connors), 1555
Paul Arthur, 1555
Peter Thomas, 1555
Raymond, 109
Reid Michael, 1555
Roy A, 109
Sidney E, 109
Timothy Charles, 1554
Vera Rose, 41
BELIN
Wendy Sue, 650
BELKNAP
--, 1499
Kaya Sarah, 1499
Kristina Lynn (Snider), 1499
Tom, 1499
BELL
--, 919
Anna, 729
Baynard Norman, 209
Betty Jean (Dillon), 550
Brenda Sue, 550
Charles Franklin, 1150
Charles Graham, 1039
Charles Shafer, 1038
Christine Marie, 746
Clara N (Riggs), 554

Clarissa May, 442
Cora Ann (Alspaugh), 1150
David, 944
Debra Jean, 550
Donna Colleen, 539
Dorothy, 367
Dorothy Verla, 1039
E Maxine, 1040
Elizabeth, 1300
Esther Agnes, 1150
Ethel, 1041
Glenwyn V, 1039
Harry, 1041
Helen, 1041
Helen E, 1039
Irma Mildred, 1151
Jack, 902
Jacob, 1038
Jane Shirley (Matz), 902
Jean Mae, 1038
Jeffery Paige, 209
John Jefferson, 554
Judy Marie (Snyder), 746
Katherine Irene, 848
Leigh Ann, 209
Lisa Ann, 848
Lydia (Snyder), 1038
Mabel Irene, 1039
Mark, 944
Marlyn E, 1040
Mary Alice (Kempton), 1038
Mary Cooper, 50
Mattie Elmeda (Garey), 1041
Mayde, 1041
Michael, 902
Mildred Daisy (Snyder), 1039
Myron L, 1040
Nathan Lee, 746
Nathan Lee Jr, 746
Nicole Diane, 209
Olive May (Stahlnecker), 1038
Pamela Anne, 550
Rita Diane, 563
Sheila Jean, 384
Shelly Diane (Hughes), 209
Sherrell, 550
Sherry Marie, 612
Suzanne (Dwyer), 209
Vicki Lynn (Weiser), 919
Wilma Jane (Keller), 944
BELLAMY
Ora, 116
BELLEMAN
Daisy Alverta, 1320
BELLESFIELD
Dorothy (Smeltzer), 816
Marlin John, 816
BELLEW
Anita Joan (Holp), 1320
Daniel Paul, 1320
Frederick William, 1320
Mark William, 1320
Patricia Jo, 1320
BELOTE
Carrie Margaret, 1154
Flora Minnnesota,

1153
George W, 1153
Harriet (Weiser), 1153
BELSON
Arthur Ernest, 916
Joanne Onata (Bachman), 916
BELTON
Clarra Louise (Yost) Trissel Calhoun, 1328
Roger, 1328
BEMIS-SCHAAP
--, 370
Lois (Steward), 370
BEN
Christopher, 1098
Grace Catherine, 1098
Leah Elizabeth, 1098
Nancy Elizabeth (Lockhart), 1098
BENANTI
Nanette E, 43
BENDER
Alan Marshall, 223
Allison Christine, 222
Alma I (Beitzel), 222
Anne, 1884
Anne Warfel, 222
Bessie V, 221
Beverly J (McNaul), 223
Bradley Frank, 222
Brian William, 223
Brook Elizabeth, 222
Bruce Robert, 223
Bryan Elliott, 223
Charles, 226
Charles Alfred, 222
Charles Alfred Jr, 222
Charles Conrad, 223
Charles Samuel, 221
Charles Samuel II, 222
Christine Lillian, 223
Clara D, 221
Craig Douglas, 223
Cynthia Lee, 223
Daisy Elizabeth (Ulrich), 73
David Alan, 223
Diane, 938
Dollie (Burkholder), 221, 226
Donna Irene (Eberman), 222
Edmund C, 1427
Eleanore, 221
Elizabeth Teall, 70
Emma (Weiser), 1463
Eric David, 223
Evelyn Marie (Shuler), 222
Frank Hoover, 222
George Eldon, 223
Grace Ann, 222
Grace Elizabeth, 222
Helen Bertha Weiser, 1463
Helen V, 1427
Jacklyn Abbie, 222
Jane Louise, 223
Janet (Rampone), 223
Jennifer (Rowe), 223
John Douglas, 223
Kathryn E (Warfel), 222
Kay Louise, 222
Laura Alice, 220
Linda Lou (Elliott), 223

Lottie (--), 1295
Margaret Matilda (Weiser), 1427
Marian, 156, 222
Marian (Burkholder), 221
Martin, 1463
Mary Alverda, 221
Mary M (Maxwell), 222
Mildred S (Shull), 221
Patricia (McNaul), 223
Paul Alan, 223
Rachel Suzanne, 223
Samuel Alfred, 222
Sandra D (Weiser), 165
Sarah Grace (Hoover), 221
Sarah M, 1427
Scan Galen, 223
Shane Mikel, 938
Sierra Elizabeth, 223
Susannah, 1880
Vic, 165
W A, 215
William, 73
William A, 1884
William Allison, 221-222
Willie, 1463
BENDIGO
Bruce B, 1066
Lois (Brungart), 1066
BENEDICT
Bertha, 1780
Catherine, 1504
BENEFIELD
Lillie, 1816
BENFER
Alma, 887
BENFORD
Angie, 1470
Arthur, 1470
Edgar, 1470
Margaret, 1470
Mary (Hottmeier), 1470
Thornton, 1470
BENHAM
Madelyn, 1354
Mary Ellen, 375
BENN
Carol Ann (Seibert), 255
Jacqueline Elizabeth, 1288
Maurice, 255
Tiffany L, 255
Troy M, 255
BENNEHOOF
Ellen, 1711
Lavina, 1711
Mary, 1711
Sarah, 1711
Susanna, 1711
BENNEHOOF/BENEHOF/ BENNEKORF
Catherine (Geoffius), 1711
Henry, 1711
John, 1711
Levi, 1711
Martha (Borges), 1711
Nancy (Wiser), 1711
Philip, 1711
BENNER
--, 273
Abraham, 1639

Catherine, 1087
Clarence E, 1633
Gladys (Weiser), 1639
Glenn, 1094
Glenn William, 1094
Hildagard W (Funk) Ott, 1633
Nancy, 1528
Sharon Lynette, 1094
Susan (Bierly), 1094
Vickie (Sanders), 273
BENNET
Mary Ethelyn, 1837
BENNETCH
Alice (Richards), 354
Alice Ellen (Brader), 354
Alice Richards, 353
Alice Van Leer, 353, 356
Bradley Muhlenberg, 354
Charles Thomas, 356
Charlotte Anges (Pennington), 355
Christopher Matthew, 354
Cordelia Anne, 356
Dawn (Schaeffer), 354
Elizabeth Fisher (Schwanger), 355
Helen Strickler, 354
Ira Leonard, 353-354
James Ira, 356
Janet Kathleen (Watson), 356
Jeremy Phillip, 356
Joanna Claire, 354
John Henry Richards, 353, 355
John Muhlenberg, 354, 356
Leonard M, 345
Leonard Muhlenberg, 353-354
Marilyn Janice (Phillips), 356
Mark Andrew, 354
Nathan John, 356
Sue (Kusman), 354
BENNETT
Anna Mary, 1833
Annie, 1695
Arthur, 1685
Brian Eugene, 1071
Charles Robert, 367
Clara E, 696
Diane Maurine, 398
Eileen Jane, 1299
Etta, 1060
Eugene, 1071
Fern, 1395
George Philip, 1145
Harry, 1037
Inez Eleanor (Krigbaum), 116
Kay (Abrams), 367
Keith Linn, 367
Lance Allan, 367
Lillian Mary (Porter), 1145
Lucy Jane (Wright), 1685
Marjorie June (Bauder), 367
Marjorie Louise (Neff), 1071
Mary (Shaffer), 1037
Pamela Elaine, 1071

BITTINGER (continued)
Joyce (Bockoven), 1167
Laura, 1167
Richard, 1167
BITTNER
Alison Cook, 188
Allison Ann, 1570
Betty, 1736
Daniel E, 1570
Frank, 188
Ida C, 1726
Leslie Hill, 188
Martha Anna, 353
Michael E, 1570
Patricia Ann (Cole), 1570
Shirley Rae (Snyder), 188
BIVOY
Barbara, 1006
BIXBY
Moses, 30
Peter, 30
BIXLER
Alverta Romaine (Mace), 645
Andrew Robert, 645
Bruce Leroy, 645
Christina, 463
Clark Albert, 644
Clayton Andrew, 644
Craig Alan, 644
Don Eugene, 645
Doris Jo Ann, 656
Doris Marie (Updegrave), 645
Faye, 981
Francis Bruce, 645
Garvin S, 922
George, 463
George Allen, 645
Helen Mae (Wiest), 644
Jennifer Lynn, 645
Jennifer Lynn Iachini (Jago), 645
Kathy Lynn (Blyler), 645
Lindsay Kay, 645
Michael Allen, 645
Palmer Forrest, 644
Pamela Janine, 644
Patricia Ellen (Weiser), 922
Polly Jadene, 644
Sarah Jennie, 1530
Sherry Ann, 645
Stacy Ann, 645
Stephanie Mae (Kline), 645
Steven Bruce, 645
Steven Bruce Jr, 645
BLACHIER
Eli, 1291
James Eli, 1291
Jean (Huefner), 1291
John Allen, 1291
Joshua Eli, 1291
Leona, 1291
Mabel Mae (Lewis), 1291
Mary (Reed), 1291
Nathan Tyler, 1291
Robert James, 1291
BLACHLY
Benjamin, 1407-1408
Carl, 1408
Daniel, 1408

Ebenezer, 1408
Elizabeth, 1408
Experience, 1408-1409
Frances, 1409
Freelove, 1408
Freelove (Carll), 1408
Hannah, 1408
Henry, 1408
Isaac, 1408
Israel, 1408
Jane, 1408-1409
Jemima, 1408
Letty (Smith), 1408
Mary, 1407-1408
Moses, 1409
Nancy (--), 1408
Phoebe, 1408
Prudence, 1408
Rhoda Ann, 1409
Samuel, 1408
Sarah, 1407-1408
Sarah (Bryan), 1409
Sarah (Jarvis), 1408
Sarah (Wheeler), 1407
Susanna, 1408
BLACHLY/BLATCHLEY
Daniel, 1407
Prudence (Weiser), 1407
BLACK
Aliene, 634
Anna Mildred, 1124
Coral (Smith), 634
Daniel Robert, 649
Donald, 1392
Elizabeth V, 62
Ella (Wiser), 1702
Hazel Evelyn (Wickham), 526
Isaac, 1702
Jessica Marie, 649
John T, 526
Josephine Francis, 771
Judith Ann, 606
Linda Gayle, 1213
Nelle Florence, 1144
Nicole Lynn, 649
Orlo, 634
Patricia Ann, 526
Ruth Eileen, 1124
Sarah (Bower), 1392
Tina Marie (Wiest), 649
BLACKBURN
Arletta Jerene, 1869
Deborah Diane (Young), 134
Jessica Jewel, 134
Kimberly Lynn, 134
Lee Ann, 119
Richard, 134
BLACKETTER
Betty Marie, 670
Charles W, 670
Charles W Jr, 670
James K, 670
Lillian Ethel (Fulkroad), 670
Michael J, 670
Sherry Ann, 670
BLACKMAN
Hermaine, 470
John, 469
Myrtle Eleanor (McGowin), 469
BLACKMER
Kimberly Ann, 1631

BLACKWELL
Barbara Ellen, 1653
Catharine (Wysor) Reyburn, 1653
Darline Faye (Wiser), 1814
James William, 1814
Jesse, 1653
Robert, 1653
William Henry, 1653
BLADE
Jantina, 273
Kim, 273
Phyllis Jean (Sanders), 273
Robert, 273
BLADES
Lisa Jo, 43
Peggy Jo (Perryman), 43
Robert Eugene, 43
BLAGUS
Barbara Jo, 636
Carol (Buckberry), 636
Christine Louise, 636
Doris (Dussezu), 636
Geraldine (Murray), 636
Gregory Stephen, 636
Jeffery Richard, 636
Jennifer L (Payette), 636
Marcia Anne, 636
Mary (Turby), 636
Pearl Helena (Fisher), 636
Richard Stephen, 636
Rita Anne (Mellott), 636
Ronald Earl, 636
Ronald Stephen, 636
Sharon Louise, 636
Stephen, 636
Tanya (Lyons), 636
BLAHUSCH
Barbara Jean (Yohe), 854
Charles, 854
Janice, 854
Mark, 854
BLAINE
Mabel G, 115
BLAIR
--, 1014
Alexis (--), 899
Anna (Stephens), 1014
Anne Elizabeth (DeBolt), 1497
Beulah Irene (Weiser), 805
Beverly Maudeline, 103
Brenda Kay (Weiser), 920
Charles Woodbury III, 899
Charles Woodbury Jr, 899
Chauncy G, 584
Chauncy Garland, 584
Claree (Hoover), 584
Debra Lynn, 103
Donald Gene, 584
E Dean, 1497
Elise, 103
Emma Caroline (Weiser), 1145
Eva Lou, 1775
Forrest Taavah, 899

George Williard, 584
Georgie Grace, 584
Gregory Davis, 1497
Harriet Lavene, 806
Harry E, 806
Heide Jo, 451
Henry L, 1145
Jane (Stone), 1682
Jane Elizabeth (Bollman), 899
Janet, 894
Jean (Schmitt), 584
Jo-Anne, 103
John, 1682
Jonathon Larue, 584
Karen B, 169
Kary, 899
Kate (Snyder), 1014
Kathy Jane, 899
Kenneth Merle, 920
Kenneth Merle Jr, 920
Lisa Leigh, 899
Lodema (Stephens), 1014
Lori Ann, 899
Margie, 423
Marjorie Eloise, 103
Mary Jane (Hocker), 584
Michael, 899
Mildred (Daulton-Stidham), 584
Paul, 103
Paul Franklin, 103
Phyllis Ellen, 103
Ramona, 584
Ruby Grace (Walden), 103
Samuel, 1014
Sandra Sue, 103
Sharron Louise, 584
Shirley Jean (Clevenger), 451
Steve Dale, 584
Theresa (--), 899
Thomas, 1014
Timothy, 899
Timothy Wayne, 584
William, 451
William Albert, 584
Williams T, 777
Winona, 584
Zona, 1778
BLAISDELL
Amanda Ann, 646
Bradley David, 646
Tammy Ann (Mace), 646
BLAKE
Catherine, 1467
David T, 1467
Laura Dee, 1503
Maureen, 1035
Sarah (Weiser), 1467
Teresa Grier, 1467
BLAKELEY
Belva Virginia, 130
BLAKELY
George, 1089
Jodia Onita (Brungart), 1089
BLAKEMON
John A, 1652
Julia Margaret (Wysor), 1652
BLAKESLEE
Helen Alice, 58
BLAMER
Dorothy Aileen

(Griffis), 371
James Eugene, 371
Lori Lyn, 371
Robert James, 371
BLANCHARD
Evaland, 973
Geraldine, 1530
BLAND
Emma (Veley), 34
George, 34
James Carl, 726
John, 726
John Forrest, 726
John Henry, 726
La Rue Myrtle, 726
Leslie Martha, 286
Liona Grace, 726
Rebecca (Hepner), 726
Richard William, 726
Robert James, 726
Ruth Elizabeth (Wilson), 726
BLANK
Dell, 1616
Ilsa, 1434
Judy (Weiser), 1616
BLANKEBECKER
Thelma Lois, 1187
BLANKENSHIP
Linda Marrol (Smith), 1309
Marvin Peter Jr, 1309
Mitchell Lee, 1309
BLANTON
--, 149
Charles, 529
Charles Jr, 529
Dollie Gladys (Spurgeon), 149
Francis G, 1821
Glendoris (Wickham), 529
Gregory Allen, 529
Mary Wood, 1818
BLARE
Howard Wesley, 1074
Joanne Marie (Wert), 1074
BLASE
Betty Jean Sheldon, 235
Carol Ann Sheldon, 235
Jean Marie (Gibbons), 235
Patricia Marie, 235
Raymond Michael, 235
Richard James, 235
BLATT
Susan Barbara, 310
BLAUSER
Orpha, 1258
BLAUSEY
Albert Frederick Ernst, 482
Emery Albert, 482
Gladys Myrtle (Seem), 482
Kristy Ann, 483
Marilyn Yvonne, 486
Marylene Mae, 483
Melissa Ann (Heilman), 483
Paul Allan, 483
Richard, 483
Sharon Joyce, 483
Viola Mae (Schott), 482

BLAZER
Adam Philip, 1073
Constance Sue Bunting
(Cole), 1073
James Lynn, 1073
Joanne Barbara (Wert),
1073
John Edward, 1073
Penny Rae (Price),
1073
Philip Henry, 1073
Robert Wert, 1073
Tamara, 196
BLEASDALE
Lucille, 1633
BLEAVINS
James N, 117
Jason James, 118
Lorraine Susan
(Krigbaum), 117
BLECHER
Lillie L, 1864
BLEINY
Esther (--) Weiser,
1544
John, 1544
BLESSLEY
Ann Elizabeth
(Fountain), 159
Anna Mary, 157, 159
Ellen Elizabeth, 159
James William, 159
John Weiser, 159
Lee James, 159
Levi, 157, 159
Levi Fountain, 159
Martha Ellen (Weiser),
159
Miriam Elizabeth
(Fetrow), 159
Samuel Henry, 159
BLETT
Kyle R J, 1113
Lorraine (Yeager),
1113
Ralph Leon Jr, 1113
BLEVINS
Bonnie, 263
Gary DeWayne, 590
Janie Marie (Hocker),
590
Sandra Kay, 590
Tommy, 590
BLICK
Alan Lee, 35
Pamel Kay (Sheehan),
35
BLINKER
Ruth Elizabeth (Sager),
979
William, 979
BLISS
Brian Michael, 193
Kelly Elizabeth, 193
Lawrence, 193
Mark Christopher, 193
Mary Ellen (Morris),
193
Melissa, 1328
Ruth Baldwin, 310
Tracey Lynn, 193
BLITZ
Elizabeth, 244
Judy Ellen, 996
BLO
Creighton, 1705
Molly (Graham)
Banner, 1705

BLOCH
Lillie M, 1620
BLOCKERT
Jean, 252
BLODGETT
Arzuba, 576
Sarah E, 1764
BLOIR
Adam Thomas, 632
Beryl Lynn, 631
Kimberly Rochelle
(Sands), 632
Muriel Avis (Harvey),
631
Robert, 631
Steven Charles, 632
Susan Theo, 631
Thomas Robert, 632
BLOOM
Donald, 1028
Elaine, 1031
Eleanor, 1028
Elmira (Cooper), 1028
Helen (Cooper), 1031
Joyce, 1719
June Louise, 1028
Martin Hoover, 1694
Mary Catherine
(Coder), 1694
Paul, 1195
Ralph, 1031
Robert, 1031
Sydney Georgeanne
(Kahle), 1195
BLOOMFIELD
Claire Marie (Keating),
1180
John David, 1180
Linda Sue (Shumaker),
611
Marcus Wayne, 611
Melynda Gayle, 1180
Randall Hooper, 1180
BLOSE
Gloria D Spidel
Whitmire, 1537
BLOSER
Elizabeth Ann, 889
BLOSS
Donald, 865
Joann (Shettel), 865
BLOSSER
Angela Renee, 265
BLOUT
Peggy Anne, 1686
BLOYD
Bingley, 128
Eva Ophelia, 127
Goldia La Veta, 128
Philip Hester, 127
Phoebe Elizabeth
(Weiser), 127
BLUBAUGH
Mary Joan, 378
BLUM
Lillian, 611
BLUMMER
Minnie M, 1468
BLUNK
Amber Dale, 402
David Allen, 402
Renée Denise (Weiser),
402
Sandy Dell, 402
BLUST
Anna Fay (Weiser),
919
Audrey, 918
Audrey Maureen, 919

Daniel Franklin, 919
Sheila Arlene, 919
BLYLER
Kathy Lynn, 645
BLYTHSTONE
Mildred, 1065
BOARD
Lisa Christine, 1141
Lucy, 821
BOARDMAN
Traci A, 1020
Trudy, 549
BOAS
Catharine
(Womelsdorf), 904
Jeremiah, 904
BOATMAN
Beverly B, 178
Kathleen, 267
BOBBET
Donald, 1241
Jimmie, 1241
Mildred (Kahle), 1241
BOBO
Scott, 1133
BOCK
Bruce Dare, 1695
Ethel Verda (Hummel),
1695
Melvin, 1695
Thresa, 594
BOCKOVEN
Charles W, 1167
Dagan, 1167
Elizabeth (Sharp), 1167
Joyce, 1167
Leanne, 1167
Lorraine, 1167
Milton, 1167
Minnie May, 1167
Minnie May (Weiser),
1167
Pamela, 1167
Peter Weiser, 1167
Ralph Edward, 1167
BODECKER
Elizabeth Ann
(Brouches), 596
Frank, 596
BODEN
--, 1105
Cora Ida (Kiplinger),
1105
Fanny Margaret, 1105
Patrick, 1105
BODKIN
Deanne Margaret, 580
BODLE
Albert W, 1709
Alberta, 1699, 1709
Grace (Wisor), 1709
LaVaughn, 1709
Norma, 1709
Norman R, 1709
Pauline, 1709
Ralph, 1709
Ronald, 1709
BOEHLING
Christopher Wayne,
959
Marilyn (Lee), 959
Rebecca Lee, 959
William Anthony, 959
William Anthony Jr,
959
BOEHRINGER
Albert Lewis, 1330
David John, 129
Louis John Jr, 128

Matthew David, 129
Mildred Arlene
(Rabold), 1330
Rebecca Elaine
(Hinton), 129
Sheralyn Evon, 128
Wanda Deloris (Tippin),
128
Wendy Lou, 128
Wetonia Anne, 129
BOEKENHAUER
Lillian W, 843
BOERGE
Rhonda, 630
BOETTGER
Barbara, 125
BOGAN
Linda, 492
BOGAR
-- (--), 777
Alice Lorraine
(Cooper), 791
Garreth Lee, 1766
Joyce (Wiser), 1766
Lori Jeanne, 791
Luke, 777
Luke Emanuel Jr, 791
Matthew Dean, 791
Stephen Victor, 791
BOGARDUS
-- (--), 304
Andrew Lanark, 325
Egbert, 304
Egbert Hal, 325
Eric Hall, 325
Gordon, 325
Hannah Hutchins, 325
Jean (Claeys), 325
Julia Blair (Hunt), 325
Karen Rene, 325
Lisa Margaret, 325
Margaret Haskell, 325
Margaret Henrietta
(Klüpfel), 325
Peter Livingston, 325
Sidney Tuttle, 325
Sidney Tuttle Jr, 325
Sully Reeves
(McCauley), 325
William Reeves, 325
BOGARDUS/STEGEMANN
Adalia Lisa, 325
BOGDANOVIC
Catharine Elizabeth
(Lenker), 675
David Darryl, 675
Evelyn Jo-Ann, 675
Joan Elizabeth, 675
Miles John, 675
Steve, 675
Steven Marlin, 675
BOGENRIEF
Harriet Meyer, 1445
Mary Elizabeth
(Meyer), 1445
Thomas Oliver, 1445
BOGGS
Barbara Marion
(Koegel), 959
Brian James, 959
Eric James, 959
J Grier, 1454
Michael Stewart, 959
Rosetta (Graham),
1454
BOHDE
Earl Shelby, 591
Eunice Louise, 591
Janice Ann, 591

Mary Ellen (Carter),
591
Nancy Ruth, 591
Paul Nathaniel, 591
Rachel Sue, 592
Ronald Earl, 592
BOHENKAMP
Louise, 804
BOHLEN
Barbara Fulton
Masland, 228
BOHLMANN
Kathryn, 1580
BOHN
Angleia Marie
(Dicampli), 1068
Anna Mary (Moyer),
1071
Anna Mary (Williams),
1071
Barbara Jean, 1071
Betty Nadine (Turner),
1068
Carl, 1094
Carl Henry, 1068
Carol Jane (Bronner),
1071
Charles Wert, 1072
David C, 1068
Donna Jean, 1072
Ella Stella (Weiser),
1864
Estella Elizabeth
(Musser), 1068
Faith Felicia (Alyward),
1069
Faye Elizabeth, 1070
Frederick, 1071
Frederick James II,
1071
Gary James, 1068
Gay Michelle (Fields),
1071
George James, 1068
George M, 961
Geraldine (Meckley),
1072
Helen Edna (Neese),
1068
James, 554
James David, 1071
James David II, 1071
James David III, 1071
Jason Duehn, 1071
Jeffrey Charles, 1071
John Andrew, 1069
John David, 1069
John Edward, 1068
Larry Edward, 1068
Lois Marion (Smith),
1071
Lucille Lorraine
(Bierly), 1094
Margaret Elizabeth
(Smith), 1070
Maria Anne, 1069
Miranda Ruth, 1069
Morris M, 1864
Musser James, 1068
Nova May (Riggs), 554
Ray William, 1072
Rebecca Rachel, 1069
Robert John, 1069
Roxey (Johnson), 1068
Russell William, 1070
Ruth (Yarnell), 1068
Sandra Lee (Taylor),
1072
Sara Lynne, 1069

BOHN (continued)
Sarah Alice (Spradlin), 1068
Sarah Jane (Wert), 1068
Sarah May, 1071
Scott Erie, 1071
Shirley Anne, 1071
Steven Carl, 1095
Susan Jo, 1071
BOHNER
Adan Ansver, 706
Barbara Ann, 706
Beatrice Helen (Goldman), 706
Bertha M, 706
Carrie Malinda (Phillips), 706
Henry Morris, 706
Jean Eleanor, 706
Lloyd Palmer, 706
Mary A, 707
Roger Adan, 706
Sandra Phillips, 706
Sarah Anne (Koppenhaver), 706
BOHR
Hulda Pauline, 457
BOHRMAN
Elizabeth S, 1617
BOHRMANN
Herta J, 1617
BOJANINI
Fabiola Maria, 496
BOK
Karen Ancha, 1328
BOLAN
Charla Annis, 861
Charles, 861
Esther Dorcas (Shettel), 861
BOLDAN
Mary L, 976
BOLDRIDGE
Mary Gertrude, 1419
BOLE
Allen L, 526, 551
Amy Suzette, 527
Anna (Mower), 600
Anna Louise, 527
Carroll Edwin, 527
Charles, 527
Charles Kent, 527
Donald Lavon, 527
Goldie E (Wickham), 526
Harley Lavon, 527
Josephine (Rhinehart), 527
Leroy Raymond, 526
Lesley Allen, 526
Mabel Delight, 527
Madonna Lynn (McIlwain), 526, 551
Norma Jean, 527
Opal (Rinker), 526
Randy, 527
Raymond Dewayne, 526
Roy, 526, 600
Sandy, 527
Shelly, 527
Sherrie, 527
Shirley (Oswalt), 527
Thera Kay, 526
BOLEN
Opal, 616
BOLES
Clara Jane (Herring),

556
Connie Sue, 975
Dorothy Ann (Kratz), 975
Kenny, 975
Lem, 556
Marsha Ann, 975
Roberta, 1013
BOLICH
Amy Kathryn, 1623
Edna Orpah, 1623
Esther Mary, 1623
John Claude, 1623
Joseph Weiser, 1623
Mahlon Daniel, 1623
Maria R (Weiser), 1623
Sarah Elizabeth, 1623
BOLIG
Betty Ulrich (Wagenseller), 77
Harold, 77
John Everett, 712
Katelin Elizabeth, 712
Kay, 77
Nancy, 77
Sherri Lynn (Hommel), 712
BOLINGER
-- (--), 1106
-- (Rickey), 1106
Anthony, 1106
Carolyn Fay, 218
Fannie, 1106
Howard, 1106
Jacob, 1106
Lawrence, 1106
Mary, 1107
Michael, 1106
Sally (Kiplinger), 1106
Stella, 1106
BOLLES
Alda Marie, 1199
Clarence Edward, 1198
Pearl Maxine, 1198
Sarah Edna (Kahle), 1198
BOLLING
G William III, 1557
Patricia Ann (Kenedy), 1557
BOLLINGER
Amy Elizabeth, 228
Anna Elizabeth, 1032
Barbara Fulton Masland (Bohlen), 228
Clarence E, 1032
Clarence E Jr, 1032
Doris, 1032
Lena Elizabeth (Fenton), 1032
Mary Kathryn (Burkholder), 228
Robert, 228
Robert David III, 228
Robert David Jr, 228
Susan E (Remaly), 228
Violet LaRue, 1378
BOLLMAN
Agnes Celesa (Womelsdorf), 896
Agnes Dorothy, 900
Agnes Louise, 898
Barbara Lou, 897
Daniel Walter, 901
Donald Potteiger, 899
Edna Mae (Bucher), 897
Elizabeth Louise, 900

Elwood, 901
Frederick Godshalk, 898
George, 896
George Charles, 897
George Womelsdorf, 897
Jacqueline (Ely), 901
Jane Elizabeth, 899
Joan Jane (Oppasser), 897
Judith Ann, 899
Juli Lois, 898
Ladora (Lorah), 898
Laura Louise (Weiler), 898
Linda Audrea (Lehman), 899
Lori Louise, 897
Margaret Louis, 897
Marti Lynn, 898
Mary Harriett, 900
Mary P, 899
Minnie, 896
Paul Womelsdorf, 898
Richard Potteiger, 899
Steffi Lou, 898
Vinie S (Godshalk), 897
Wendi Lee, 897
BOLMAN
Cheryl Lynn (Hite), 568
Patrick Jerome, 568
BOLTON
Charles, 797
Florence Rose (Myers), 640
Greg, 797
John Arthur, 640
John Robert, 640
Karen Kay, 797
Lon Eugene, 640
Mary Helen (Rhodes), 797
Maude Eva (Bietz), 640
Rita Jane, 640
Terry Lee, 640
BOLTZ
Bertha Blanche (Wisser), 1728
Nelson, 1728
BOMBERGER
Aaron Nathanael, 1096
Andrew Charles, 1096
Barbara Mary, 922
Charles, 1096
Hannah Josephine (Koppenhaver), 707
Harry Frederick, 707
Harry Rudy, 707
Jane Adelle (Kreamer), 1096
Matthew James, 1096
BOMGARDNER
Cletus, 774
Martha (Weiser), 774
BONADIO
Alice Marie (Rabold), 1316
William, 1316
BONAWITZ
Amy Margaret, 715
Betty Mae, 668
Ida, 713
John, 1417
Sarah (Weiser), 1417

BOND
Adelva Louisa (Williey), 40
Agnes Louise, 40
Benjamin Ray, 40
Betty Jean, 243
Carrie Corena, 40
Charles Holbert, 40
Edwin Silver, 1869
Eileen Elda, 1728
Eleanor Louise, 243
Gertrude Elizabeth (Fister), 243
Gertrude Fister, 1883
Irma Catharine (Wisser), 1728
John Lorenz, 243
Mary Charlotte, 40
Mertie Elizabeth (Wiser), 1869
Pamela Inez, 747
William Benjamin, 40
William Franklin, 1728
William Franklin Jr, 1728
William Henry, 40
BONDONESE
Marisa Anne, 792
BONE
Lana Sue, 958
BONINE
Anthony N, 290
Floyd, 290
George Earl, 290
Margaret Ella (Ege), 290
Marie (Dunn), 290
Mary Darlene, 290
Roy St Clair, 290
William Clark, 290
BONIOL
Michael, 1824
BONNEAU
Jaimee, 1040
Laurie Jo (Wismer), 1040
Mark, 1040
BONNECARRE
Bruce, 469
Bruce Wayne, 469
Joan Cecilia (Sherrill), 469
BONNECUTTER
Sharon, 1325
BONNER
--, 107
Dellona Renee (Sikes), 107
Elizabeth, 107
Matthew, 107
BONNIE
Barbara, 64
Elizabeth, 64
BONSALL
Evie, 1697
BONWELL
Marcia, 1098
BOOB
Christopher Jason, 1381
Connie Lee (Henry), 1381
Craig Michael, 1381
Dana Ray, 1381
Donald R, 1381
Donna Marie, 1381
Douglas Lee, 1381
Helen Virginia (Weiser), 1381

Joy Helen (Leslie), 1381
Nathan Lee, 1381
Neil Tyler, 1381
BOOHER
Carl, 551
Dora May (Riggs), 551
Elizabeth Jane, 1311
Jody M (Smith), 1716
Lena Ruth, 574
Logan, 1716
Mark, 1716
Morgan, 1716
BOOKER
Lois, 1803
BOOKMAN
Della May, 1130
BOOKS
Grace R, 643
BOOKWALTER
Pamela, 606
BOONE
Richard, 289
Sarah (Ege), 289
BOOTH
--, 1579
Edith Belle (Pickard), 1579
Lillian Flenamen, 706
BOOZER
Dorothy Mae, 1075
BORDER
Stella May, 1374
BORDLEMAY
Ella Margaret (Weiser), 163
Harold, 163
Mildred Marie, 163
BORDNER
Alice, 254
Bertha Anna (Bettilyon), 780
Brian G, 1567
Curtis C, 1567
Harry, 1567
Herbert Calvin, 1567
J Stanley, 780
Janice A, 1567
Joan M, 1567
Kathleen A, 1567
Kathryn, 780
Margaret (Nuvinger), 758
Margareta, 759
Marion (Nagel), 1567
Pearl E, 1567
Peter, 758-759
Shirley A, 1567
Stacie Marie (Muggio), 1538
Susan L, 1567
Susanna, 758-759
Terry, 1538
Walter G, 780
BORGES
Martha, 1711
BORGESON
Nancy, 232
BORGMAN
Mary Ann, 802
BORING
Dorna Odette, 907
Fred, 208
Nancy Ellen, 603
Ruby May (Weiser), 208
Shirley Ann, 208
BORIS
Bernard, 664

BORIS (continued)
Claudia, 1536
Judith K (Hutchenson), 664
Tammy L, 664
Travis, 664
Tricia R, 664
Troy A, 664
BORLASE
Karen Mary, 1419
BOROFF
Shirley Ann Elaine, 956
BORRELL
Alfred, 250
Anna Mae, 250
Arthur Perry, 250
Catharine Elizabeth, 247
Ida Katherine, 250
Ida Rosanna (Fasig), 247
Jennie (Kramer), 250
Mary Matilda, 249
Mary Violet, 250
Mildred, 901
Perry, 247
BORROR
Donald LeRoy, 107
Donna Alice, 107
Nancy Ellen, 107
Opal Pearl (Starwalt), 107
Sue Ann, 107
BORST
Dorothy, 1734
BORTZ
David, 1645
Susanna, 1645
BOSCH
Hattie, 1728
BOSCOV
Cynthia (DeHaven), 1742
James, 1742
BOSENEILER
Adolph Bernard, 234
Bessie Pearl (Manon), 234
Betty Louise, 235
Donald Eugene, 235
Edna W K (Schwitters), 235
Frank Detrick, 235
Helen Margaret, 235
Joanne Mae, 235
Judith Kay, 235
LeRoy Bernhard, 235
LeRoy Larry, 235
Mary Margaret (Scanlan), 235
Terry Lee, 235
BOSS
-- (Weisser), 12
Gussie Ellora, 1813
Hans Conrad, 12, 15
Maria Catharina (Weisser), 15
BOSSART
Sarah, 1561
BOSSERT
--, 1671
Andrew Jason, 1601
Arlene Joan (Weisser), 1601
Kristen Marie, 1601
Robert C Jr, 1601
Sandra (Shearer), 1671
Sara Elizabeth, 1601

BOSSLER
John, 1111
BOSTAPH
Patty (Kahle), 1242
BOTCHLETT
David James, 604
Dorothy (Long), 604
Jill (Weisenborn), 604
Robert, 604
BOTHA
May Evelyne, 169
BOTTICHER
Pamela Sue, 1087
BOTTIGAGLIA
Santa Mary, 1321
BOTTOM
Karen Christine, 1813
BOTTORF
Ann, 1000
Anna Margaret, 714
Ardel, 1000
Betty, 1000
Charles Irwin, 1395
D Hall, 1395
daughter, 1000
Donald, 1000
Frances, 1395
Fred, 1395
Judy, 1000
Lynette, 1000
Mary, 1395
Mary (Miller), 1395
Mary Catherine, 1000
Mary Jane (--), 1000
Mildred, 1396
Mildred (Kelver), 1000
Nancy, 1000
Nina Winona (Hess), 1395
Rhoda (Swaim), 1395
Sarah, 1000
Sarah Margaret, 1395
son, 1000
Thorald, 1000
BOTTORFF
Jane, 357
BOTTS
Benjamin Daniel, 1627
Catharine Ann (Weiser), 1627
Clara, 1698
Daniel T, 1627
Franklin, 1627
BOTZER
Jonas, 1246
Sarah Jane (Kahle), 1246
William W, 1246
BOUDEN
An, 1205
BOUGHAN
Beverly K (Hughes), 143
Charles Michael, 143
Clara Jane (Brouches), 596
William Elmer, 596
BOUIC
Betty, 382
George, 382
Mary Elizabeth (Leibold), 382
BOULANGER
Helen Antoinette, 1343
Marie, 1088
BOULWARE
Bonnie Jean (Banter), 561
Don, 561

Drew, 561
Kathy, 561
Phillip, 561
BOUMAN
Bastian Nicholas, 926
Jeffrey Paul, 926
Julia Faith (Weiser), 926
BOUQUET
Col --, 1365
BOURDO, 465
Amy (Mikolajczyk), 465
Bonnie Mae (Augenstein), 465
Diana T (Szymanski), 465
Donald Frank, 465
Eleanor M (Bowman), 465
Erma Mae (Schabel), 465
Evelyn (McClanhan), 465
Frank, 465
Glen, 465
Gregg Alan, 465
Jeffrey Paul, 465
Julie (Panning), 465
Julie Mae, 465
Lulu Aleta (Gee), 465
Margaret Jean, 465
Matthew Paul, 465
Patricia Ann, 465
Raymond Gilbert, 465
Richard Blair, 465
Scott, 465
Stanley Arthur, 465
Terry Arthur, 465
Tom, 465
Trina Ann, 465
BOURGOIN
Giselle, 937
BOURNE
Susan Kay, 536
BOUTWELL
Kathlynn Louise, 519
BOVINETT
Marjorie (Kephart), 1691
Raymond, 1691
BOW
Ina, 205
BOWAN
Nellie (Hoke), 264
Robert, 264
BOWANSKI
Jenny E, 162
BOWCUTT
Patti, 1770
BOWDEN
Lavada, 1822
BOWEN
Andrea Marie (Nelson), 1581
Arthur, 1238
Dallas, 1237
David, 1237
E, 1237
Earl, 1238
Everett, 1237
Fannie E, 349
Harry, 1238
John, 1581
John William, 1413
Mary M (Kahle), 1237
Susan (Weiser), 1413
Violet Evelyn, 868
William, 1238

BOWER
Addison, 259
Alice Lillian, 977
Alphaline Elnora, 978
Amanda Jane, 977
Arlene, 974
Benjamin Franklin, 962
Bernard Leon, 977
Brenda, 1392
Brumeld, 978
Caroline Busby (Rufuer), 977
Catherine (Kehl), 961
Charles, 682
Clara, 260
Clara Catherine, 978
Clara Jane, 971
Clarence Arnold, 977
Darline, 978
Donald George, 977
Dorothy, 978
Edna Rose (Hegele), 1392
Edward Duane, 978
Elizabeth Sweigart (Switer), 962
Elsie (Heinricks), 1392
Elsie (Nichols), 971
Emily, 259
Esta (Smith), 1392
Ethel (Cates), 971
Florence Agnes, 977
Franklin Washington, 971
George Melvin, 974
Gertrude Mayme (Holverson), 977
Glenn, 971
Harold Richard, 977
Harriet Elizabeth (Smith), 978
Harriet L (Rosenkranz), 978
Harriet Lenora, 974
Harvey Swellyn, 978
Hattie Esther (Schultz), 260
Hattie Louisa (Michael), 682
Henry, 259
Henry Jacob, 259
Ira Sylvester, 977
James, 1392
James Daniel, 1392
James Daniel Jr, 1391-1392
James R, 1633
Janet Ann (Rubright), 1392
Jean L, 1018
Jessie (Donahue), 977
Jessie Murl, 977
John Hall, 259
Juanita, 978
Kathleen (Funk), 1633
Laurell, 978
Lauri Ann, 1392
Leelon Earl, 977
Lester Shuman, 977
Lizzie, 1059
Lloyd, 975
Margaret, 977
Margaret (Cates), 974
Margaret Olawa, 977
Martha Halstead (Stewart), 962
Martin, 1392
Martin Riley, 1392
Mary, 260

Mary (Hull), 259
Mary Elizabeth, 975
Mary L (Boldan), 976
Mary Rosetta, 971
Mary Wood, 259
Mella Mae, 972
Michael, 961
Michael Hamilton, 971
Michael Harvey, 978
Millisent Mirabel, 977
Miriam Andrea, 977
Miriam M, 682
Nilah Gwenlen, 977
Nomi Eilien (Noll), 1066
Patricia Nadine, 977
Philena Selewella, 978
Rebecca (Mengel), 259
Rhonda, 1066
Richard, 1066
Richard Paul Lamer, 977
Rita Francis, 378
Robert, 259
Rose (Donahue), 978
Royal, 977
Sarah, 975, 1392
Sarah Catherine, 962
Susan, 259
Susan (Peterson), 975
Susan (Zimmerman), 259
Thirza, 978
Thirzah Lenthena (Firman), 977
Vera, 971
Verlord, 975
W Gibson, 259
Waneta, 978
William, 259
William George, 260
William McMilken, 977
William Porter, 975
William Riley, 976
Woodward Dwight, 977
BOWERING
Elsie Janet (Hartzell), 1633
Vinton, 1633
BOWERMAN
Christopher Allen, 634
Julie Kay, 634
Laura Lea (Miller), 634
Richard, 634
BOWERS
Ada, 251
Adelaide C (Lewars), 251
Aline (Thomas), 251
Althea (Miller), 252
Anna (Kralick), 252
Anna Mae, 686
Anna Ruth, 917
Annie (Krick), 253
Annie E, 253
Annie E (Neischwender), 251
Barbara A, 252
Benton W, 252
Bessie M, 252
Betty K (Luke), 251
Carol A, 253
Charles E, 251
Charles E Jr, 251
Charles J, 252
Charles Jackson, 251

BOWERS (continued)
Christine Lee, 1570
David Cole, 1570
Debbie L, 253
Debra, 1066
Dennis L, 252
Doris, 1781
Earlene E, 253
Edna Mable (Rhodes), 606
Edwin A, 252
Eliza (Kirkwood), 252
Emma I (Nunsicker), 252
Enda M (Funk), 253
Estella (Knox), 252
F M, 238
Franklin L, 253
Fred M II, 251
Fred M III, 251
Frederick M, 251
Gladys (Link), 251
Gladys V, 252
Helen (Kammerer), 252
Jacqualine, 142
Jane E, 252
Janette L, 252
Jean (Blockert), 252
John Henry, 251
John W, 252
John W Jr, 252
Joyce Marie, 606
Judith Ann (Black), 606
Julie Edge, 312
Karen L, 251
Karl Peter, 252
Kate W (Carl), 251
Katharine L, 253, 1560
Kathleen A, 252
Kay M, 252
Kevin, 1802
Leroy R, 253
Leroy W, 253
Lorainc, 253
Louise (MacIntyre), 252
Lynn, 1066
Marion Dale, 606
Martha Ann (Wiser), 1802
Mary A, 251
Mary E (Robers), 251
Myron Dale, 606
Naomi T (Evans), 251
Noreene, 786
Pamela (Bookwalter), 606
Patricia (Diehl), 252
Pauline, 1519
Ralph C, 252
Randal, 1570
Ray William, 606
Richard K, 252
Robert, 1066
Robert W, 251-252
Roberta Agnes, 606
Sarah E, 252
Shane William, 606
Susan L (Cole), 1570
Susan S, 251
Warren C, 252
Warren C Jr, 252
Wellington C, 251
William E, 252
BOWERSOCK
Eileen, 139

BOWERSOX
--, 478
Carol (Walter), 1382
Donna (Bierly), 1094
Dora Olive (Stover), 1105
Dorothy Jean (Weiser), 1381
Evelyn, 505
Harlan, 1083
Harold, 1094
Iva May, 1315
Jayne (Miller), 478
Leslie Dianne, 1381
Mark David, 1382
Randal E, 1105
Rodney Steven, 1382
Sharlyn Mae (Vonada), 1382
Stuart, 1381
Tracey, 751
Wanda (Wilcox), 1083
BOWES
Andrew Leo, 956
Catherine (McKibben), 1052
Charles, 1052
Daniel Alexander, 956
Hazel Rovena (Helsleg), 1052
Krysten Lynn (Ernsting), 956
Patricia, 420
Rose Ellen, 1073
Ruth Arlene, 1052
Thomas C, 1052
Thomas McKibben, 1052
BOWICK
Angela Dawn, 1287
BOWLBY
Elsie, 917
BOWMAN
Ada Beatrice (Croy), 849
Ann, 1548
Anna Katherine, 502
Bruce, 1090
Charles, 908
Cora, 1090
Eleanor M, 465
Harry, 1090
Jody (Nace), 908
John Henry, 482
Karen (Godfrey), 908
Karen Sue, 1448
Lois V, 105
Lydia Matilda, 503
Margaret, 1182
Mary Ann A, 1627
Mary Elizabeth, 482
Matilda, 482
Maxine Hope, 1090
Rebecca Louise (Mader), 908
Robert E, 908
Robert Franklin, 849
Scott Allen, 908
Sidney, 1090
Solomon B, 482
Travis Allen, 908
Trenna (Bridgens), 1090
BOWMER
Christie Lynn (Fox), 537
William Randall, 537
BOWSER
Andrew Keith, 1286

Anthony Charles, 687
Betty Jean (Klingler), 1286
Beverly Ann (Howard), 687
Charles Benjamin, 687
Donald Keith, 1286
Paula Kay (Hazelett), 1286
Sandra Ann, 1296
Susan, 848
Susan Louise, 687
Terry Lee, 687
BOWSHER
Aaron Randall, 581
Alice (Fess), 557
Alice C (Lawrence), 581
Amanda (Hocker), 580
Ardrey Rudolph, 581
Betty Ruth (Wilson), 581
Brandon DeWitt, 580
Bruce Walter, 581
Carol Jean, 582
Catherine Lynn, 582
David Edward, 582
Deanne Margaret (Bodkin), 580
Ester (Brown), 580
Ethelind Joy, 581
Garnet Rae (Straight), 582
Gwendolyn Agatha, 582
Isola Eileen, 581
Jacob E, 580
Jeffery Michael, 582
Joseph Edward, 580
Kay Rosalie, 580
Kenneth Paul, 582
Lester Eugene, 581
Lori Thelma, 580
Lovel Constance, 581
Marian Emlie (Jones), 580
Marian Ethel, 581
Michael Edward, 582
Robin Deanne, 580
Ruth Elizabeth (Gobel), 582
Ruth June, 580
Sheila Leslie, 581
Waldo Gern, 580
Wendell Paul Atlee, 582
Wendy Joyce, 582
Willard, 557
BOWYER
Nancy M, 1836
BOXELL
Millie, 561
Nova P, 550
BOYACK
Brent Evans, 1767
Marcia (Wiser), 1767
BOYD
Charles H, 1661
David, 1881
Dazel (Willey), 39
Doris J, 1205
Jeffrey Neil, 406
Judy Anne, 1152
Maria A (Wysor), 1661
Mark James, 406
Mary Roberta, 1058
Ola Tippie, 121
Ronald Eugene, 405
Rosina (Weiser), 1881

Sandra Charlotte (Weiser), 405
Sarah K, 1662
Shirley Louise, 224
Weldon, 39
William S, 1661
BOYER
--, 1641
Alice Mary, 911
Amy Scott, 1149
Anna Clara (Eppley), 895
Anne (Albright), 93
Augustus, 93
Barbara (Cole), 93
Bertha Irene, 895
Beulah, 1421
Candace Magdalene, 1149
Carolyn, 83
Catharine A, 81
Charles Wesley, 93
Charlotte K (Francis), 895
Cindy Rae, 651
Delia, 507
Edward, 895
Edward Walter, 895
Elsie (Mader), 906
Elsie M, 841
Elsie Naomi (Mader), 910
Emma (Keyser), 895
Francis, 895
Francis Allard, 895
G Raymond, 895
Gary Lee, 93
George Elmer, 895
George Powell, 1149
George Powell Jr, 1149
Geraldine, 895
Hannah M, 740
Harry Boyer, 1135
Hazel Eleanor (McKean), 1135
Helen, 741
Herbert Monroe, 910
Herbert Monroe Jr, 910
Jack Monroe, 1149
Jack Monroe Jr, 1149
Jacob Edward, 895
James Joseph, 911
Jean Frances, 895
Jeffrey, 895
Jennie Catharine, 759
Jennie Marie (Kocher), 1615
Jill Maureen, 1149
Karen Ann, 911
Leona Mary, 1636
Lillian A (Lee), 1149
Lillie Susan (Bast), 1641
Linda Jeanette (Lukens), 93
Mabel, 729
Mable May, 657
Magdalene (Glick), 1149
Margaret Jane (Grimes), 93
Margie R, 1246
Marie (Arillo), 911
Martha Jane (Norbeck), 910
Mary, 1134
Mary (Cadwalter), 895
Mary (Hiltwine), 895

Mary Ann, 1149
Mary Edith, 705
Mary Marie, 1538
Marylou (Tyson), 93
Myra, 865
Nancy Rosella (Mapes), 1256
Permillia Arabella, 895
Ray, 895
Richard Keith, 93
Robert, 1256
Sandra Davidson (Scott), 1149
Sarah, 598
Sarah A (Miller), 66
Sarah Martha (Rothermel), 1613
Sharon Louise, 1091
Ted, 1615
Theresa Arline, 841
Vera Elizabeth, 925
Walter E, 895
William Henry, 1613
BOYKA
Lawrence, 1577
Mary J (Schempp), 1577
Michael, 1577
BOYLE
Alexander B, 1782
Alice May (Wiser) Hickey, 1782
David Michael, 73
Eleanor (Snyder), 132
Hugh P, 1483
James, 132
Jennifer Lee, 1483
John Christopher, 1483
Kelli Anne, 73
Kristin Elizabeth, 1483
Linda (Hunt), 73
Olive, 1549
Patricia Sue (Earnest), 1483
Paula Mevrice, 936
Sheila Ann, 1299
BOYLES
Anna Mae, 818
Daniel Henry, 818
Della Grace, 818
Edith Emma, 818
Ellen Jane (Chapman), 818
Eva Ann (Kreible), 818
Grace Elizabeth (Dettra), 818
James Michael, 1222
John Henry, 818
Leo Stanley, 1222
Lilly Jane, 818
Louis Henry, 818
Martha Ann, 818
Mary Elizabeth, 818
Mary Ellen, 818
Minerva Esther, 820
Nora Jane, 818
Ruth Elizabeth, 819
Stella Mae (Ralston), 818
Twila Maude (Daniels), 1222
Viola May, 821
BOYNTON
Willie Edna, 1649
BOYSEN
Shirley, 177
BOYST
Benjamin O, 1781
Pamela Jo (Wiser),

BREITENBACH
(continued)
Elizabeth (Weiser)
(continued)
1472
Francis Augustus, 1476
Frederick, 1473
Hannah (Ort), 1475
Henrietta, 1475
Jeremias Ort, 1475
Johann Philip, 1472
Johannes, 1475
John Henry, 1475
John Philip, 1473
Joseph, 1476
Maria, 1472
Philip, 1473
**BREITENBACH/
BREIDENBAUGH**
Catherine Elizabeth
(Swoyer), 1473
Edward, 1473
BREITHAPUT
Marilyn (Rightmier),
1690
Paul, 1690
BREITINGER
Audrey Ann, 1460
BREITSPRECHER
Ann Marie (Popham),
966
Christine Lynne, 966
Glen Fred, 965
Janice (Potratz), 966
Janis Elleen (--), 966
Joyce, 965
Judith Ann, 966
Mildred (Otterbeck),
965
Richard, 966
Robert Allen, 966
Russell Glen, 966
BREKKE
Iaren Joyce (Alibrando),
1503
William, 1503
BRELAND
Donna, 1231
BRELSFORD
Gladys Irene, 1322
BREMER
Glenn Walter, 1485
Mary, 85
Olive Pearl (Leonard),
1485
Richard Glenn, 1485
Sharon Kay, 1485
BRENISHOLTZ
Charles, 1513
Charles Jr, 1513
Doris (Stauffer), 1514
Ella (Hynicka), 1513
Ken, 1514
BRENIZER
Myrtle Belle, 875
BRENNANMAN
Doris, 1440
BRENNEMAN
Pearle Ella, 873
BRENNER
Carrie (Hoskinson),
1143
Clara Evaline (Weiser),
1132, 1143
Doris, 1186
Evelyn May, 1143
Henry Newton, 1143
Ivan Graeff, 1143
Jason Richard, 1144

Joseph, 1076
Justin Lee, 1144
Lucille (Bickel), 1144
Marilyn Lucille, 1144
Marion (Emerick),
1076
Mary Edith, 1143
Noel Arden, 1143
Paul, 1076
Paul C, 1076
Polly Ann, 1076
Richard Lee, 1144
BRENNICK
Camille, 172
BRENOBLE
Ruth Elizabeth, 701
BRENSINGER
--, 250
Mary Elva (Lau), 250
Michael Alan, 250
Randy, 250
BRENT
Gwen, 270
BREON
Audrey (Crust), 1374
Bertha (Weiser), 1374
Calvin Stieger, 1055
Charles, 1374
Cleora Geraldine
(Hackman), 1055
Dean, 1374
Deborah, 1374
Emerson Weiser, 1374
Gary, 1104, 1374
James Ronald, 1074
Janet, 1374
Jeffrey, 1104
Jordon Parse, 1104
Julie Marie, 1074
Kathryn Miranda
(Wert), 1074
Kent Michael, 1074
Larry Jr, 1055
Lynn, 1074
Lynn Donald, 1074
Michele Dawn (Weber),
1055
Nancy, 1374
Patricia Ann, 1055
Ryan, 1104
Sarah Elizabeth, 1690
Viola Jane (Grenoble),
1074
Wendy Jo (Harmon),
1104
BRESBY
Rebecca Dawn, 1478
BRESLEY
Bill Jo, 1478
Calvert Burton, 1478
Crystal Dawn, 1478
Donna (Preskocil),
1478
Dustin Zane, 1478
Joyce Rosalie (King),
1478
Leon Calvert, 1478
Tanya Elaine, 1478
BRESSLER
Dorothy, 1003
Katherine Irene, 239
Verna, 980
BRETT
Mary Baldwin
(Schwab), 312
Philip M Jr, 312
BRETZ
Alice Louise, 640
Amy Ellen, 640

Catharine Lavina
(Cook), 639
Charles Bryan, 640
Charles Thomas, 640
Charles Wesley, 640
Clara Belle (Case), 640
Dorothy Helen, 640
Elizabeth Joanne
(Crumrine), 640
Ethel Frances (Pogue),
640
Eugene Lincoln, 640
Gerald Case, 640
John Ammon, 639
Lester Leroy, 640
Maude Eva, 640
Michael David, 640
Percival Cook, 640
BREVIG
John R, 213
Norla Louse (Weiser),
213
Shirley Isabel, 213
BREWER
--, 849
Anna Elizabeth (Croy),
849
Berdina, 103
Bernadine Elizabeth,
520
Dana B, 1174
David, 1416
Elizabeth (Anderson),
1416
Elysia, 1416
Herbert Wm, 546
Julianna, 1416
Kathy Gail, 469
Kelly C, 546
Laurli, 546
Lois Marie (Wagoner),
546
Marjorie Pearl, 1817
Robin Jay, 546
Tyler Eugene, 546
BREWSTER
Alta, 1507
Bayard, 1507
Lenora May, 1456
Marian (Chamberlain),
1507
BRIAN
Caitlin Patricia, 671
Dean William, 671
Latisha M (Barnitz),
671
BRICKER
Ada (Carr), 576
Bertha Elizabeth, 576
Carl Jesse, 576
Crystal Ann, 576
Donna Jane (Dobbs),
1133
Dora Belle, 576
Iva May, 576
Jennie (Herring), 575
Leroy, 576
Levi, 576
Louise, 575
Rebecca, 565
Sarah Elizabeth, 582
Simon Peter, 575
William, 1133
BRICKLEY
Chester Arthur, 1368
E Kathryn (Harkinson),
1368
Helen Pearl, 1368
Howard F, 1368

Veva Pearl
(Winkleman), 1368
BRIDAGUM
Paul William Jr, 682
Randall Kevin, 682
Robert Keith, 682
Willa Mae
(Koppenhaver), 682
BRIDGE
Penola, 593
BRIDGENS
--, 1089
Bettie Louise, 1090
Clara Lauvan, 1090
Edward, 1089
Frazier, 1089
Grace (Killinger), 1089
James, 1089
Matilda (Frazier), 1089
Mildred, 1089
Sarah (Frye), 1089
Shirley Marian, 1089
Trenna, 1090
BRIDGES
Rose Maye, 108
BRIDLE
Caroline Boyer (Miller),
86
Herbert, 86
BRIGANCE
Bonnie, 172
BRIGGS
Ann Leah, 595
Jemima, 1575
John, 1703
Kelly Ann, 1781
Lula (Parks), 1703
BRIGHT
Elnora (Weiser), 1568
Jacob, 1568
Louise, 1773
Robin, 1171
BRIGHTBILL
Jestina (Mader), 907
Susanna, 906
William, 907
BRIGNER
Flora Maxine
(Hummell), 1154
Floyd, 1154
Jerry Eugene, 1154
Phyllis Jean, 1154
BRILES
Beverly Jean, 567
BRILL
Rachel Lynne, 455
BRILLINGER
Edna C, 1426
BRIMFIELD
Elizabeth Mary
(Pickard), 1573
Thomas, 1573
BRINER
--, 1350
Mamie (Warren)
Brown, 1350
Susan, 1880
BRINEY
Margaret, 166
BRINK
Evelyn Ruth
(Callender), 668
Karl Luther, 668
Karl Luther Jr, 668
Kerry Lynn, 668
BRINKMAN
Christopher T, 952
Clare Kathleen, 952
Danielle, 952

Elizabeth A (Brammer),
951
Nicholas A, 952
Phillip Michael, 952
Sarah Elizabeth, 952
Thomas P, 952
BRINTON
Julia Nadine, 781
BRINTZENHOFF
Loretta M, 1638
BRION
George, 1866
Lydia Alice (Reed),
1866
BRISSENDEN
Allen, 1180
Linda Joanne
(Andersen), 1180
BRISTOW
Shirley Ethel, 592
BRITCHER
Anna Margaret, 698
BRIZENDINE
Alvin, 1870
Delpha Lucille (Wiser)
Kelsey, 1870
Ethel, 1870
Everett, 1870
Helen Lorene (Wiser),
1870
BROADBRIDGE
Alison m (Schultz),
1502
Edwin, 1502
Todd, 1502
BROADHEAD
Dorothy Ruth, 1194
Margaret, 270
BROADRICK
Annie Bell, 1822
BROADWATERS
Charlotte, 1654
BROADWELL
Millicent, 1696
BROBST
Barry Lee, 1747
Carol Ann, 1394
Dale Robert, 1747
Elda May (Wisser),
1747
Gary Gene, 1747
Jeffrey Lynn, 1747
Paul Luke, 1394
Robert Edwin, 1747
Virginia Ann (Hess),
1394
BROCHETTI
Kathryn Margaret
(Smith), 1228
Louis S, 1228
Louis S Jr, 1228
BROCIOUS
Charles Henry, 1883
BROCK
Pamela Sue, 258
BROCKWAY
Allwin, 1211
Almeda Jane (Davis),
1211
BROD
Hans Michael, 11
Lydia S, 1864
BRODLAND
Mildred Ann, 1210
BROEKERS
Bradley, 276
David L, 276
Melea (Douglass), 276

BROGAN
Delia D, 841
Nettie Idella, 620
BROKAW
Una Fay, 445
BROMLEY
--, 509
Katie Lenora (Binkley),
509
Wadell, 1419
BRONG
Maggie Cora (Wieser),
1759
Milton Cyrus, 1759
Warren Daniel, 1759
William, 1759
BRONNER
Betty, 1316
Carol Jane, 1071
BRONSON
Cheryl Ann, 439
Janet (Dawkins), 439
Micajah C, 1787
Patricia Ann (Knecht),
439
Robert Charles, 439
Robert Charles Jr, 439
Sarah E (Wiser), 1787
BROOCKS
Elizabeth Anne
(Weiser), 1348
Joseph Edward, 1348
Joseph Robert, 1348
BROODER
Barbara Leonare, 445
BROOKBANK
Lesley Joan, 1156
BROOKE
-- (--), 299, 338
Annie Louise (Clingan),
303
Charles, 303
Edward, 303
Elizabeth Muhlenberg,
303
George, 302-303
George III, 299, 338,
342
Lisa, 1632
Lucille Polk (Carter),
303
Mary (Andrews), 303
Mary Baldwin (Irwin),
302
Mary Baldwin Irwin,
303
Virginia (Muhlenberg),
303
Virginia Dunham
(Muhlenberg), 342
BROOKENS
Charles, 389
E Lloyd, 389
Eleanor, 389
James, 389
Loma Ilo (Tuller), 389
Marjorie, 389
BROOKING
Alice (--), 818
Anna Mae (Boyles),
818
Florian, 818
Mary, 818
May (--), 818
Mildred (Rudelick),
818
Patricia Ann, 818
Robert Boyles, 818
Roberta Ann, 818

Teresa Ann, 818
BROOKMAN
--, 1668
Frances I, 389
John, 1668
Mary (Peck), 1668
Rebecca (Peck), 1668
BROOKS
Dollie Lenora, 397
Freda, 1198
Grace Nesbit, 744
Helen, 1372
John Alan, 763
Judy (Wiser), 1777
Juliet, 1655
Kelly, 1369
Linda June, 417
Marian Josephine
(Heckert), 763
Martin Alan, 763
Miriam, 773
Pearl (Still), 867
Sheila Elizabeth, 763
Teddy, 1777
William, 867
BROOME
Annie Sue (Kline),
1525
Gail Elaine, 1525
Mary Elizabeth (Kline),
1525
Melvin, 1525
Melvin Paul, 1525
BROSCH
Barbara (Stock), 92
Gary, 1297
Gwendolyn Jean
(Wiser), 1297
Richard, 92
Riki Ann, 93
Shelley Ann, 1297
Tracey Lynne, 1297
BROSCIOUS
-- (--), 737
Alice (Zimmerman),
737
Anne (Weaver), 739
Anne Marie (Wallach),
738
Benjamin Michael, 737
Brieanna Marie, 737
Charles Andrew, 740
Charles Henry, 737
Charles McClenehen,
739
Charlotte Louise
(Haupt), 738
Charlotte S (Rudisill),
737
Christopher James, 739
D S, 737
Darlene Grace (Toland),
740
David, 737
David Charles, 737
David Sebastian, 737
Delores Marie (Ayers),
737
Doris J (Neff), 1114
Elaine Patricia, 737
Elizabeth, 737, 740
Elna (Monroe), 737
Elsie Mea (Kreider),
737
Esther Elizabeth
(Everett), 739
Evan Charles, 738
Francis A, 737
Francis Abraham, 737

Gail Elizabeth, 737
Gussie May, 740
Harriet Louisa, 738
Henry H, 737, 740
Henry Hiram, 739
Herby Edward, 740
Jae (Hoffbauer), 739
James Charles, 740
Janine Louise (Updyke),
738
Jason Lee, 739
Jeanne Scott
(McClenahen), 739
Jennifer Lynn, 740
Jeremy David, 738
Joan Wallis (Zink), 737
John Allen, 738
Jonathan Matthew, 738
Josephine (Meyer), 739
Katherine, 737
Katherine Elizabeth
(Carolus), 739
Katherine Keller
(Mullally), 738
Katie Malinda, 740
Lee Raymond, 739
Louise (Fegle), 737
Mabel Ellen (Steffen),
737
Margaret E (Hepner),
736-737
Marion Pauline, 737
Mary Ann (Hartline),
736
Mary Etta, 740
Matthew Allen, 738
Michael David, 737
Nancy Jeanne, 738
Pamela Kay (Becker),
738
Patrick Douglas, 739
Philip Burl, 738
Rachael Elizabeth, 738
Randall John, 738
Raymond Francis, 739
Russell K, 737
Russell Karl, 739
Samuel, 736-737
Sarah, 768, 773
Sarah Lynn, 739
Scott David, 738
Sharon (Darrow), 739
Steven Charles, 738
Susan Blymyer, 739
Todd W, 1114
William Webster, 737
BROSIOUS
Ben Kirby, 684
Diane Marie, 70
Frances Helena, 684
Franklin Henry, 684
George E, 684
Grace Elizabeth
(Dockey), 684
June Pauline (Reitz),
684
Margareth (--), 638
Samuel, 638
BROSIUS
Beverly J, 1285
Elizabeth, 358
Sarah C, 1458
BROSSMAN
Schuyler, 1566
BROT
Robbin, 380
BROTEMARKEL
Earl, 1031
Ruth (Cooper), 1031

BROTHERS
Charlotte, 1802
BROUCHES
Adam, 595
Adam E, 596
Barbara (Fisher), 595
Barbara Ellen, 596
Barbarry E, 596, 599
Clara Jane, 596
Daisy (Estes), 596
David Andrew, 596
Elizabeth, 556, 597
Elizabeth Ann, 596
Eva Dell, 596
Frank Ervin, 596
George, 595
George W, 596-597
Hannah, 597
Jacob H, 597
John E, 596, 599
Lena (Siebert), 596
Lovina, 595
Margaret, 596
Mary Catherine, 596,
599
Melissa A
(Ransbottom), 597
Mina (Fleming), 596
Nancy (Fisher), 596,
599
Samuel, 596
Samuel Elbert, 596
Sarah (Evick), 596
Zada (Candler), 596
BROUGH
John Thomas, 475
June Louise (Dorobek),
475
BROWDER
Cory Ann, 1287
BROWER
Jenny Alrich (Stiles),
288
Joseph Martin, 1499
Katharine Pratt
(Salovaara), 1499
Kelly Stiles, 288
Kristopher Derek, 288
Kyle Richard, 288
Peter Thomas, 288
BROWN
--, 136, 390, 835, 910,
1350, 1408, 1741
Ada Levina, 557
Agnes Dorothy
(Bollman), 900
Agnes Suzanne, 900
Alan Dale, 610
Albert Edward, 440
Alberta Mae, 565
Alberta Olive, 440
Alice (Copeland), 184
Alice Louise (Busby),
1148
Allison Dorothy, 900
Alma, 971
Alma Grace, 440
Alva, 610
Alvin Harrison, 621
Amanda, 1522
Amanda Beth, 1125
Amy Frances (Walker),
331
Andrew James, 200
Andrew Mark, 172
Ann Allen, 184
Ann Marie, 425
Ann Susan, 185
Anne Marie, 1552

Annemarie Marguerite,
1484
Annette Irene (Delp),
167
Annie H, 834
Anthony, 1546
Arin Daniell, 545
Ashley, 1327
Avis, 551
baby girl, 1155
Barry Jellette, 1778
Bateisa, 1542
Bearl Bertram, 556
Becky Ann, 1773
Benjamin William, 484
Bernice, 1808
Bertha I, 1090
Betty (Coston), 184
Betty Ann (Shaffer),
484
Betty Joy, 459
Blaine, 1125
Bonnie, 1098
Brenda, 607
Bruce Carl, 673
Caitlin Marie, 275
Calina, 1542
Carl, 624
Carol (Morgan), 610
Carolyn (Dorsch), 610
Carolyn Jean, 1155
Carrie Ann, 1125
Catherine (Etschberger),
1522
Charity April, 484
Charles, 565, 621
Cheryl Anne
(Gustafson), 484
Chester E, 440
Christine, 420
Christine (Miller), 200
Christine Ann
(Douglass), 275
Christopher, 184
Christopher Edward,
610
Christopher Michael,
451
Claralee, 1155
Clarice, 946
Claudia Ann, 57
Claudie, 557
Cleo Marie (Shuck),
610
Constance Marie
(Leonard), 1484
Coralee, 1155
David Alan, 610
David Andrew, 484
David Bollman, 900
David Coston, 184
David Mike, 1481
Deanna June, 1481
Deanna Sue, 226
Debra Gar, 1384
Deedra Kay, 200
Delatus Earl, 1148
Dennis Lynn, 545
Dixie Evelyn, 556
Donald, 167
Donald Edward, 1484
Donald Eugene, 557
Donna Marie, 440
Donna May, 557, 621
Dorothy (Dolbin), 853
Dorothy Estella, 1284
Douglas Bollman, 900
Douglas Edward, 200
Dudley, 673

BROWN (continued)
Dwayne Edward, 1481
Earnest, 557
Ed, 275
Edna (Kahle), 1214
Edna Marie (Quinlan), 1546
Edward, 226, 440, 1387, 1542
Edwin Lewis, 440
Eldon Edison, 557
Eleanor Louise (Graham), 200
Elise Swicegood, 310
Elizabeth (Weiser), 1387
Elizabeth Ann (Piasecki), 1551
Elizabeth Ellen (Fess), 556
Elizabeth Louise (Bollman), 900
Ella (Hoffman), 769
Ella Nora (Woolridge), 174
Elmira, 1468
Emily, 910, 1652
Emma (Wiser), 1741
Emma Martha, 621
Emmett Marguette, 900
Emmett Marquette, 900
Ester, 580
Ethe Ray (Snyder), 183
Ethel Pearl (Cummings), 556
Eugene Mac, 425
Everett Charles, 565
Fletcher Moore, 185
Florence Irene (Shuck), 611
Franklin, 331
Fred Elmer, 971
Gail Marie (Wiser) Kinder, 1781
Geoffery Gordon, 1232
George, 720
George A, 769
George L, 1011
George Washington, 556
Georgia Kaye, 1209
Glenda Allen, 1452
Gloria, 557
Gloria Jean, 621
Harold, 459
Harriet Fern (Grove), 1383
Harvey Ames, 245
Helen, 266, 1388
Helen Crissie, 814
Helen Ione, 1820
Helen Oakley (Evans), 332
Henrietta Mabel (Walker), 331
Henry B, 1387
Henry L, 621
Henry Moore, 331
Herbert Glen, 610
Ida Davis, 1666
Ira, 971
Irene (Shelton), 440
Irma, 124
Isadora, 1468
J Ross Snyder, 185
Jack David, 900
James Aaron, 200
James Mark, 484
Jane (--), 60

Jane Ellen (Werts), 1327
Janet, 1586
Janet Louise, 441
Jason Ward, 107
Jay Chester, 556
Jay Weiser, 1384
Jeffrey Mark, 441
Jemima (Blachly), 1408
Jennie Lenore, 971
Jennifer, 1327
Jere (Moore), 185
Jere Moore, 185
Jerod, 1327
Jess, 174
Jessie Fern, 440
Jim, 107
Joanne (Newcomer), 1125
John, 1522
John Eric, 484
John Franklin, 971
John Henry, 1666
Jonathan Lee, 484
Jordan, 1327
Jordan Lee, 484
Joseph George Jr, 1155
Josephine (O'Neal), 621
Joshua Michael, 484
Joyce Ann Bubbard, 1815
Julia Bernice (Ege), 292
Julie Christine, 1484
Karen Lee, 440
Karlene Rose (Kiger), 1158
Kathleen Anne, 1552
Kathryn, 1534
Kathryn Elinor, 621
Kathy, 1740
Kathy Jean, 1790
Katie (Kehl), 1011
Kayla Marie, 484
Kenneth, 265
Kittie DeBrutz, 184
Kristin (Keihl), 900
Lafay Frank, 183
Lafay Frank III, 184
Lafay Frank IV, 184
Lafay Frank Jr, 184
Larry, 1327
Laura, 598
Lawrence, 621
Lee Rust, 184
Lee Rust Jr, 184
Leona Edith (Roughton), 624
Leroy, 853
Lesa Ann (Troxel), 484
Leslie Rae (Weiser), 425
Lewis M, 1839
Lily Lee (Alspach), 1155
Linda Jean (Herring), 545
Lucinda Catherine (Wiser), 1666
Lynn (Meyers), 901
M Tucker, 900
Mabel Lenora, 1632
Madaline Hazel, 621
Mamie (Warren), 1350
Mandy Rochell, 545
Marcia Wirtz, 184
Marcy Ann, 900
Margaret, 1012

Margaret (Keller), 1387
Margaret (Slack), 390
Margaret Josephine, 1735
Margaret Wilson (Womelsdorf), 835
Marge (Conn), 265
Marguerite, 1546
Marlene Winifred (Koppenhaver), 673
Martha (--), 184
Martha Evelyn (Newman), 1552
Martha Graham (Harbison), 1232
Martha H, 523
Martin Ross, 440
Mary, 158
Mary Alice Magdaline (Wiser), 1808
Mary Ann (Prownell), 184
Mary Anna, 621
Mary Elizabeth, 900
Mary Elizabeth (Kees), 556
Mary Emmaline (Edwards), 621
Mary Lou (Clevenger), 451
Mary Rosetta, 971
Matthew Lee, 200
Maude, 1011
Mayvon (Wiser), 1778
Melanchthon Martin, 1542
Melissa Ann, 901
Michael, 451, 783
Michael Allen, 200
Michael Grove, 1384
Michael Scott, 200
Michele Lynn, 901
Michelle Louise, 184
Mina Elverda, 556
Minnie A, 1384
Minnie A (Brown), 1384
Minnie Olive (Knecht), 440
Nancy Lee, 1173
Nancy Marie (Wagner), 783
Narcic B, 1662
Nathan, 1327
Ned McKinley, 1383
Nettie Alice, 621
Nettie Grace (Mason), 459
Nicholas Scott, 610
Nicole Anjeanette, 440
Oliver Andrew, 484
Packer, 910
Patricia Ann, 459
Patricia Ann (Mastric), 900
Patty, 266
Paul, 265, 1232
Paul A, 611
Paul Douglas, 425
Peter, 1522, 1542
Peter Bollman, 901
Phebine H, 1582
Philip, 25
Philip Matthew, 610
Philip S, 332
Phyllis, 861
Phyllis Lee (Courtney), 484

Priscilla (Wilcox), 136
Rachel Mae, 200
Ralph E, 1327
Ray, 1327
Ray Jr, 1327
Ray Leon, 46
Raymond, 1350
Rebecca, 1327
Rebecca (Weiser), 1542
Regan, 1327
Reva Arline, 441
Revah Geraldine (Edwards), 621
Rhoda (--), 1327
Rhoda Anne, 556
Rhonda (--), 1327
Richard, 1781
Richard Arlan, 593
Richard Hale, 185
Rita Kay (Cloud), 593
Robert, 60, 1155, 1741
Robert Charles, 621
Robert Emmett III, 172
Robert Emmett Jr, 172
Robert Ned, 1384
Robert Thomas, 1552
Roberta Lee, 484
Roland William, 900
Romona Rae, 621
Ronald E, 1481
Ronald Harley, 200
Rosaltha (Wiser), 1839
Ross F, 440
Ross Snyder, 184
Ruby Jo, 527
Russel, 556
Ruth, 1388
Ruth Enona, 858
Ruth M (Hansen), 226
Ryan, 1327
Sadie Alvena, 685
Sally Jane (Flemming), 910
Samantha, 1327
Sandra Jo (Fisher), 900
Sarah May (Oaks), 245
Sharina (--), 1327
Shawn Stewart, 1158
Shirley Ann, 611
Sidney Earl, 292
Spencer Todd, 910
Stella (Roddewig), 440
Steven Eric, 610
Steven Michael, 200
Sue Ann (Borror), 107
Susan, 610
Susan Annette, 200
Susan Diane (Leadbetter), 172
Susan Marie, 184
Suzanne, 756
Teresa Kalman, 900
Teresa Kalman (Brown), 900
Terry (Kahl), 1007
Thelma, 1153
Thelma June (Cummins), 1481
Thelma Mae, 1155
Thomas, 853
Thomas Richard, 1551
Tiffany Suzanne, 900
Timothy Nathaniel, 484
Tommy Paul, 611
Trena Marie, 673
Tressa (Reinholt), 265
Verna (Hepner), 720
Verna Vember

(Herring), 565
Vickie (Lauz), 440
Vicky Lee (Spears), 200
Victoria Ann, 200
Vinette Mary, 132
Virginia Middleton, 185
Walter, 1214
Warren Dudley III, 673
Wendy (West), 185
William, 1007
William Douglas, 900
William Snyder, 185
William Snyder Jr, 185
Willie May, 1666
Wilma Genevieve (Willey), 46
Zoe Elizabeth, 900
BROWNE
Curtis Northrop, 300
Winifred Wheelwright (Chisholm), 300
BROWNEWELL
Donna Rae, 1418
George, 1362
Hazel, 1041
BROWNING
Gayniel Sue, 397
Ginger, 1659
BROWNLEE
Barbara, 444
Frances (Weiser), 444
J Loren, 444
June, 444
BROXSON
Lisa, 827
BROZOVICH
Dorothy, 975
Katherine, 974
BRUBAKER
Brian Matthew, 541
Camille (Brennick), 172
Connie, 868
David Wallace, 172
Deborah Lee (Mitchell), 540
Donna Rae, 172
Drew Scott, 172
E Irvin, 220
Elizabeth, 215
Emma Elizabeth (Stouffer), 220
Helen Ilene (Mitchell), 540
Jennifer Marie, 172
Keith, 540
Maude (Kline), 868
Merrel, 540
Mitchell Jay, 541
Nathan David, 172
Robert, 868
Shannon Kai, 540
Stacy Allyn, 172
Thelma Mae (Protzeller), 172
Thomas Daniel, 172
Thomas Franklin, 172
BRUCE
--, 591
-- (Bruce), 591
Barbara Lorraine, 1019
Cassius Otto, 968
Charles, 1018
Charles Jr, 1018
Charles Otto Jr, 968
Daniel Earl, 591
Danna Michelle, 591

BRUCE (continued)
David, 1870
Debbie (Wiser), 1870
Herman, 591
Jane Lois (Yost), 1018
Linda Ellen, 591
Madona May (Rickey), 591
Mary Parrish, 415
Nellie Lewella (Hammond), 968
Richard Lee, 1019
Vada (--), 968
BRULL
Judith Aleen, 1070
BRUMBACH
Donna Lee (Rush), 298
Finney Charles, 298
Lulu Bell Rex (Ball), 298
Madison Cranford, 298
Madison Earl, 298
Mari Willodene (Cranford), 298
Mary Jane (Harkins), 298
BRUMBACK
Sandra Sue, 206
BRUMFIELD
Alfred, 530
Dorothy Arlene (Alexander), 530
Patricia Ann, 530
Phillip Alfred, 530
BRUMMET
Frances Jeannie, 663
BRUMSTEAD
Harold, 1059
Mary (Arney), 1059
Susanne, 1059
BRUNDIGE
Helen, 114
BRUNELL
Audrey Kay, 1369
Betty (Casner), 1369
Betty Marie (Casner), 1369
Bonnie Jeanne, 1369
Eugene, 1369
Eugene A, 1369
Jeffrey Scott, 1369
Kay Lenora, 1369
Paula (Riley), 1369
Ronald Eugene, 1369
Trevor Scott, 1369
BRUNER
Akyssa Kem, 539
Charles, 1458
Charles J, 1457
Danny Lee, 539
Elizabeth, 1458
Franklin, 1458
Helen Mary, 1488
Kyle Alexander, 539
Louisa, 1458
Louisa (Weiser), 1457
Mary Gray, 1457
Tammy Rae (Herring), 539
Todd Allen, 539
William W, 1458
BRUNGARD
-- (--), 1087
Amanda (Ellis), 1087
Anglea Marie, 1088
Anthony Everett, 1087
Betty, xiii, 737, 961
Betty Jane (Bird), 1087
Catherine (Benner),

1087
Clair Bingaman, 1087
Connie Elizabeth (Reibsome), 1087
Craig, 1089
Craig Allen, 1088
Darii Karenina, 1087
Debra Ann (Steele), 1088
Desiree Jean Scholl (Kline), 1087
Dora Catherine (Bingaman), 1087
Dorothy Mae, 1086
Erik Edwin, 1087
Evert Clair, 1087
Frances Elizabeth (Smith), 1089
Gene (Meckley), 1089
Irma (Hoffman), 1087
Jamie Sue, 1088
Joseph Dean, 1087
Joseph Dean Jr, 1087
Josephine Corine (Strickler), 1087
Karen Ruth, 1087
Lloyd Klose, 1089
Lloyd L, 1088
Megan Denae, 1087
Michael Clair, 1087
Nevin Randall, 1087
Nichole Erin, 1088
Oren B, 1113
Oren Bingaman, 1087
Oren Bingaman Jr, 1088
Pamela Sue (Botticher), 1087
Samuel, 1089
Scott, 1087
Steven Roger, 1087
Tracey (Wojchehoski), 1087
Violet Katherine (Miller), 1087
Violet Kathryn (Miller), 1113
William Addison, 1087
William Henry, 1087
Yvonne Marie, 1089
BRUNGART
--, 1077
-- (--), 1883
Adam Noah, 1083
Alfred, 1084
Alice, 1063, 1090
Alverta (Bierly), 981, 1084
Alvira (Smith), 1084
Amanda, 1080
Amy Lynn, 1088
Anna, 1068
Anna M, 1077
Anna Maria (Wohlfert), 1079
Annie (Fisher), 1086
Bertha Catherine, 1077
Bertha V (Dice), 1067
Beulah Elizabeth, 980, 1083
Brooke Lee, 1088
Carrie Mae, 1068
Catharine, 1047, 1053, 1082
Charles Debardeleben, 1067
Charles Henry, 1078
Child, 1076
Clara Ann (Confer),

1081
Clarence, 1077
Clarence Clebe, 1077
Cora, 1068
Cyrus, 1068
Daniel, 1090
David Lee, 1067
Delphia Lorena, 1083
Dolly (Emerick), 1068
Doris (Cooper), 1067
Dorothie (Crandal), 1076
Edgar Samuel, 1077
Edna (Moore), 1067
Edwin Monroe, 1066
Elizabeth (Johnson), 1078
Ella M (Snook), 1077
Ellen (Rowe), 1081
Elmira Elizabeth, 1090
Elsie L (Sullivan), 1067
Emma, 1089
Emma (Meyers), 1081
Emma Myers, 1081
Emma Myers (Brungart), 1081
Estella, 1077
Estella (Witmer), 1077
Etta Mae, 1076
Eugene Richard, 982, 1084
Eva May (Snyder), 982
Evelyn Elaine, 1067
Evelyn Mildred, 981, 1084
Florence (Bechtol), 1077
Franklin, 1059
Franklin Dice, 1067
George, 1078-1079, 1090
George B, 1084
George Bloomer, 1084
George Luther, 1076
George W, 1081
Geraldine, 1077
Harold, 1077
Harold Newton, 1067
Harry, 1077
Harry Cleve, 1083
Harry Joseph, 1077
Harry Milton, 1086
Harry Roy, 1067
Harry Weaver, 1083
Helen May, 1084
Henry C, 1068
Herbert Isaiah, 1066
Herbert Isaiah Jr, 1067
Ira, 1077
Irene (Anderson), 1078
Irene (Rishel), 1067
J W, 961
Jacob, 1059
Jacob Clayton, 1076
Jacob Wallace, 1067
Jane Louise, 1067
Jasper R, 961
Jasper Royer, 1090
Jermiah, 1076
Jodia Onita, 1089
Johannes Brungart, 1078
John Cooper, 1067
John George, 1046-1047, 1883
John R, 1076
John Rowe, 1081
John Rufus, 1084

John Stanley, 1082
John Victor, 1067
John Walter, 1067
Joseph, 982
Julie Marie, 1088
Karen Louise, 1078
Kermit Harry, 1077
Laura (Weaver), 1083
Lawrence, 1068
Leila Elizabeth, 1067
Lester Larue, 1081
Lewis, 1080
Lida B (Yearick), 1067
Linnie (Weaver), 1083
Lois, 1066
Lucy Ann (Shaffer), 1066
Lula (Mowery), 1077
Madaline Viola, 981, 1084
Madelinee Lee, 1067
Malcolm Victor, 1067
Margaret, 1099
Margaret (Leitzell), 1068
Margaret (Rute), 1076
Margaret Nelson (DeBardeleben), 1067
Maria (Wise), 1080
Marie (Boulanger), 1088
Marjorie Jean, 1078
Mary (Crouse), 1083
Mary Elizabeth (Long), 1090
Mary Ellen, 1081
Mary Jane, 1079
Mary Lorena, 980, 1083
Mary Mabel, 1084
Matlida, 1076
Meda O (Mader), 1084
Meyer C, 982
Mildred, 1076
Milton, 982
Miranda, 1068
Nancy Williams, 1067
Nelsen Debardeleben, 1067
Nelson Lendon, 982
Newton, 1066
Newton Rishel, 1067
Newton Rishel Jr, 1067
Nora May, 1083
Norman E, 981
Norman W, 1084
Paul, 1080
Paul A, 1086
Paul Clarence, 1077
Pauline Susan, 1078
Peggy Jean, 1077
Phoebe Ann (Royer), 1090
Phyllis, 982
Phyllis Ella, 1078
Ralph Walter, 1078
Rama Blanche, 1089
Randal Victor, 1067
Raymond Jacob, 1078
Robert Crouse, 1084
Robert Raymond, 1078
Rufus, 1084
Ruth (Royer), 1084
Sadie, 1076
Sallie, 1068
Salome (Kehl), 961, 1047, 1078, 1090
Salome Kehl, 1046
Samuel Irwin, 1066

Sara Ann, 1067
Sarah, 1076, 1090
Sarah (Brungart), 1076
Sarah (Corman), 1059
Sarah (Crouse), 1076
Sarah Christine, 1066
Sarah E (Bierly), 982
Sarah Jane (Zerby), 1067
Sonja Roxanna, 1088
Sophia, 1082
Susan, 1081
Susanna, 1078
Sydney, 1059
Tena (Lamey), 1076
Thelma Marion, 1077
Thomas, 1059
Thomas Michael, 1088
Velira May, 1089
Velma E (Hosterman), 1078
Vera Catherine, 1080, 1088, 1883
Vera Catherine (Brungart), 1080
Verda (Moyer), 1086
Vesta Viola, 1086
Viloa (Walter), 1066
Violet, 1081
Walter, 982
Walter Snook, 1078
Wanda (Griest), 1078
Wilbur Reuben, 1078
Wilbur Reuben Jr, 1078
William, 1077
William Charles, 1082
William L, 1081
William Raymond, 1078
Winifred (Wolfe), 1066
BRUNING
Cindy Kay, 79
BRUNK
Eric Michael, 970
Gregory Alan, 970
Heather Joy, 970
Janice (Burzyski), 970
Laura Ann, 970
Lori Johnell (Hantz), 970
Margie Velma (Smith), 970
Norman Peter, 970
Norman Peter Jr, 970
Patricia Elaine, 970
Scott Toy, 970
Sharon Dawn (Wilkens), 970
Steven Michael, 970
Thomas Walter, 970
Timothy James, 970
BRUNNER
--, 1108
Christianna Hanna, 1726
Jackie, 1108
Mary (Schwoob), 1108
Romayne Ruth (McKibben), 1053
William, 1053
BRUNOW
Katharine Ann, 409
BRUNS
Dennis Michael, 1118
Donald Joseph, 1118
Linda Louise, 1118
Nadine (Smith), 1118
Richard Leon, 1118

BRUNS (continued)
Wilbert Ralph, 1118
BRUNZ
Rose, 274
BRUSH
Betty Jean, 1451
BRUTAKER
Howard, 1401
Luella (Wagner), 1401
BRUTCHER
--, 1839
Mercedith L (Wiser)
Haughey, 1839
BRYAN
Cora Ellen (Duncan),
1188
Corbett, 621
Eileen Belinda, 133
Elizabeth Strode
(Entrekin), 173
Geneva, 621
Golda (Oakley), 102
Joseph, 850
Mary Ellen, 1526
Rebecca Jane
(Womelsdorf), 850
Ronald, 173
Roy L, 1188
Sarah, 1409
W W, 102
BRYANS
Pamela Jeanne
DeGreen, 1157
BRYANT
Alice Lillard, 381
Charles Arthur, 1056
Doris Sue (Dunlap),
1449
Edith Ann, 1056
Gene, 1449
James Edward, 1056
Laura Mae (Kehl),
1103
Mary, 1752
Mary Katerine
(Daugherty), 1056
Russell E, 1056
Russell E Jr, 1056
W W, 1103
BRYCE
Barbara Jean (Muir),
214
Christine (--), 214
Drea, 215
Kayla, 214
Larry, 214
Leigh Ann (--), 215
Nick Jason, 215
Nicole, 215
Scott Allan, 214
BRYNE
Eleanor May (Nelson),
973
Patrick R, 973
BRYNER
Barbara Jean (Bohn),
1071
David Clark, 1072
Leslie Jo (Keister),
1071
Randy Clark, 1071
Tilbert Clark, 1071
BUBB
Hilda, x
BUBENIK
Ashley Marie, 382
Cary Fred, 382
Diane Marie
(Cartesegna), 382

Elia, 1884
Elia (Leibold), 382
Elia Leibold, 375
Gertrude Wiser, 1884
Justin James, 382
Miles Blair, 382
Miles C, 382
BUCH
Kristine A, 118
BUCHANAN
Lisa Ann, 988
Lynn Elizabeth, 1341
Mackenzie Ann, 988
Mary Estelle, 1732
Nancy Joan, 988
Norma Elizabeth, 1337
BUCHANEN
Pres, 238
BUCHANNON
Beulah, 1050
Henry, 1050
Maude (Erhard), 1050
BUCHER
Alma, 1034
Amelia Susan (Fisher),
1455
Arthur James, 761
Barbara Ann, 760
Bertha Irene (Rhoads),
1034
Beulah Marie (Hoke),
761
Carrie Wilhemina, 761
Clarence Eugene, 760
Clarence Eugene Jr,
760
Corinne Eileen, 761
Edna Mae, 897
Edward Masser, 1455
Elizabeth, 1455
Ernest John, 761
Frances Elizabeth
(Casey), 760
George David, 1034
George H, 1034
Gerald Ernest, 761
Gerald Richard, 761
Geraldine Thelma
(Beem), 761
Henry, 1683
Irene, 1034
Irene Mildred, 761
James Edridge, 490
James Kenneth, 1058
John Conrad, 1591
John D, 1114
John Jacob, 760
Joyce Pauline
(Heileman), 490
Kathryn Henrietta, 760
Katie Elizabeth
(Snyder), 760
Kenneth, 1058
Kenneth Eugene, 761
Keturah May (Snyder),
1114
Linda Ann, 761
Mae Elizabeth, 761
Margaret (Morris),
1058
Margaret Eleanor, 761
Mark Robert, 761
Martha Elizabeth, 1034
Paul Lee, 761
Polly Ann, 1058
Ray Allen, 761
Ray Allen Jr, 761
Rebecca H (Milliken)
Hood, 1683

Rodney Lee, 761
Ronald Darwin, 761
Ruth, 1034
Steven Lloyd, 761
Tresa Elaine, 761
BUCHMAN
Clyde Emmanuel, 1756
Ellen R (Wisser), 1755
Milton J, 1755
Oliver Henry, 1756
Stella Mary, 1756
BUCK
Betty, 798
Billy Miles, 798
Carroll Warren, 798
Charlotte, 798
Cynthia (Wilson), 799
Danny, 799
David Daugherty, 1056
Diana Lyn, 798
Dorothy Phyllis, 798
Edwin Carroll, 798
Ethel (Shimmel)
Hummel, 1770
Ezekial, 1770
Gary, 1060
Gaylene Rachelle, 799
Gloria (Krell), 798
Grace Bergstresser,
890
Helen (Arncy), 1060
Inda, 63, 63
Jane Rosalie
(Hottenstein), 63
Katheryn Elizabeth,
1056
Katie Ann, 918
Madaline Elizabeth
(Alton), 798
Mary Pauline, 798
Mildred (Simpson),
798
Phoebe Madaline, 798
Robert E, 1056
Roy L, 63
Theodore Davis, 799
Timothy Michael, 799
Virginia Lee
(Daugherty), 1056
William, 1060
William Jr, 1060
William Miles, 798
BUCKBERRY
Carol, 636
BUCKELS
Barbara Joyce, 1714
Deborah (Fitch), 1714
James, 1714
Justin, 1714
Matthew, 1714
Roxanne (--), 1714
Tess, 1714
Thomas, 1714
BUCKERT
Delores Lois, 1745
BUCKETS
Dorothy (Rexford),
1714
Harold, 1714
Robert, 1714
Vicki (Volovich), 1714
BUCKHOLZ
--, 1299
Bessie (McKay), 1299
Betty E, 1299
Jack, 1299
Lee Jack, 1299
Manlyn (Ritter), 1299
William, 1299

BUCKLES
Johnathan, 757
Jovanah, 757
Joy Diane (Furman),
757
Marjorie, 1658
BUCKLEY
Dayle Ann, 517
Elizabeth Malinda, 642
Gayle Ann, 517
Kathleen, 517
Lillian Beatrice, 694
Marcelle (Akerman),
517
Wilbert E, 517
BUCKMAN
Jean Evelyn (Byrd),
578
William, 578
BUCKNER
Barbara, 545
Linda, 107
BUCKWALTER
Katharine Julia (Marr),
1454
Paul Bernard, 1454
Ray, 1631
Ruth Virginia (Essick),
1631
Shirley Ann, 1454
BUCZKO
Nancy Marie, 1298
BUDD
Anna, 302
Anna Carolina (Irwin),
302
Becky, 1569
Elizabeth, 302
Elizabeth (Maylan),
302
Emily, 302
Eugenia, 302-303
Irwin, 302
J B, 302
John, 302
Morgan, 302
Rose, 302
Susan, 302
BUDGE
Luella, 1766
BUERIIL
L, 621
BUFFINGTON
Alfreda Naomi, 763
Angela Marie
(Rothermel), 651
Daniel Harold, 776
Donald Arthur, 642
Donald Austin, 642
Douglas Harold, 775
Elizabeth Malinda
(Buckley), 642
Elva Darlene, 642
James Allen, 651
Janet Louise, 642
Jared Allen, 651
Jean (Attinger), 1528
Jennie Caroline
(Messersmith), 642
John, 638
Joseph Arthur, 642
Joshua David, 651
Joyce Darlene, 642
Karen, 1528
Kathy, 1528
Kevin Roy, 776
Lou Ann (Seiler), 775
Marqueen (Latsha),
775

Mary, 766
Mary Ann (Foster),
642
Randy, 1528
Roy, 775
Shirley, 1528
Stephanie Jan, 776
Steve, 1528
William, 1528
BUGHER
Conor William, 354
Daniel Charles, 354
Daniel Charles Jr, 354
Randee Louise
(Morrow), 354
BUGLASS
Camilla Oakley
(McRory), 333
Robert D, 333
BUHEL
Ethel, 797
BUHLER
Karen, 1774
BUIS
Sandra Elaine, 536
BULGER
Susan Marie, 1290
BULKLEY
Arthur Hanks, 334
Catharine Frederica
(Oakley), 334
Catharine Frederica
Kunze, 334
Charles Henry, 334
Edwin Adolphus, 334
Edwin Muhlenberg,
334
Edwin Muhlenberg Jr,
334
Eliza Jaffray, 334
Harold Kidder, 334
Helen Muhlenberg, 334
Katharine Frederica,
334
Lucy Kidder, 334
Lucy W (Kidder), 334
Mary Virginia, 334
Theodore Meier, 334
BULLARD
Alice Naomi
(Mayfield), 1187
Barbara Dian, 1187
Doreen Isabelle
(Herring), 534
Edith Myrle, 1187
Emma Selecta (Weiser),
1187
Ethel Lucile, 1187
Harry Allen, 1188
Howery Delvin, 1187
John Delvin Floyd,
1187
Leroy Taft, 1187
Louise (--), 1187
Mary Belle, 1188
Patricia Bess, 1187
Thelma Lois
(Blankebecker), 1187
Virgil W, 534
BULLERS
Elisabeth Anne, 1281
BULLIS
Abbie, 1467
BUMBARGER
Carol, 1370
Dorothy (Miller), 1370
John Oral, 1370
BUMGARTNER
Donald, 450

BUMGARTNER
(continued)
Donna May, 391
Jeffry David, 450
Kathryn Elizabeth
(Rowland), 450
Robert Wayne, 450
Tena Sue, 450
BUNCE
Bergetta Hubertine
(Bailey), 1357
Edward, 1408
John Lyman, 1357
Katharine Anne, 1357
Marinda, 1409
Sarah (Blachly), 1408
William Bailey, 1357
BUNCH
Mildred, 534
BUNDENS
Larry Arnold, 1344
Megan Elizabeth, 1344
Michael Thomas, 1344
Stephanie Layne
(Stewart), 1344
BUNDY
Billy, 546
Jennifer Bundy, 178
BUNGE
Clarence Edward, 286
Frederica Harriet
(Muhlenberg), 286
BUNKER
Ann Elizabeth, 1738
Minnie Frences, 1117
BUNN
George W, 1146
Ida M, 1146
Mary M (Weiser),
1146
Maude, 1146
Reese H, 1146
BUNNELL
George Larone, 1332
Karen Louise, 1332
Larry Lerone, 1332
Mildred Louise (Long),
1332
BUNTING
Lisa Lee, 930
BURCH
Amy Jane, 667
Carroll Junior, 667
Donald Emerald, 36
Donna Lee (Atkinson),
36
Emma Elizabeth
(Burkholder), 220
Linda Lou, 667
Lula Maxine (Stanley),
667
Mildred Elizabeth, 220
Norman, 220
Ralph Emerald, 36
Ruby, 263
Ruth, 979
BURCHAM
Annette Lynn, 572
Charles Jr, 572
Gayle Lynn (Herring),
572
Jeremy Scott, 572
BURCHELL
Sybilla, 303
BURD
Charles Edgar, 162
Della Marie, 162
Dorothy K (Smith),
162

Elizabeth, 911
Jeremiah, 161-162
Kathleen R, 1095
Maude Emma (Weiser),
161
Thelma Genevieve, 163
BURDEN
Victoria Lynn, 144
BURDGE
Donna, 1529
BUREL
Autumn Monique, 475
Christine Marie (Butts),
475
James H, 475
BURGARD
Betty, 1176
BURGE
Anna (Doyle), 270
Charles, 270
Floyd, 270
BURGER
Cinderella (Weiser),
1879
George W, 1879
BURGESS
Bob, 1659
Carter Lane, 1649
Cathy (Fausnaught),
367
Cody, 1659
Colin, 367
Donna Jo (Howard),
1659
Edith Mae (Wiser),
1834
James Hubert, 1834
Mary Gardner (Smith),
1649
Nickolas, 367
Robert, 1659
BURGET
Ethel Mary, 793
BURGOYNE
Edna, 1780
BURGUIN
Helen, 1246
BURHAM
Belle, 112
Bennett, 112
Blanche, 112
Cardie (Taylor), 112
Clifford, 112
Florence (Seamans),
112
Franklin A, 112
Hattie (Sullivan), 112
Larane, 112
Marian, 112
Minnie, 112
Myrtle M, 112
Ret, 112
Ruby M, 112
Solomon, 112
Thelma, 112
Thomas, 112
BURHANS
Samuel Jr, 20
BURINGTON
Andrea Robin, 36
BURKE
Bruce Allen, 1185
Evelynne Maurine
(Wiser), 1185
Jocelyn, 1549
John Henry, 1185
Margaret, 722
BURKES
Lillian E, 515

BURKETT
Anne Hall, 175
Austin Hugh, 175
Blake, 901
Candace, 901
Carolyn (Rhoads), 901
Dale L, 499
Darrell, 901
Edward A, 499
Fremont Walter, 498
Grace Mary, 498
Myrtle E (Heileman),
498
Richard, 901
Ronald, 175
Sarah Cathryn, 512
Sonja Glee (Hall), 175
BURKEY
Barbara Glennys, 225
BURKHARDT
--, 993
Eva Maria (Schwab),
317
Hillena Katharina, 317
Max Michael, 317
Michael, 317
Sandy (Hunt), 993
Verena Sarah, 317
BURKHART
Floyd, 799
Marian Lucille (Barbe),
799
BURKHOLDER
-- (--), 215
Ann Louise, 229
Anna, 216, 236
Beth Ann, 229
Brenda Jill, 226
Catharine M (Weiser),
237
Clara, 226
Dollie, 221, 226
Dorothy Elizabeth, 220
Ella Gertrude, 220
Ella Katherine, 216,
218
Emma Belle, 216, 221
Emma Elizabeth, 220
Emma Jane, 230
Emma Katherine
(Bartel), 227
Francis William, 228
Fred Bartel, 230
Gail Nancy, 227
George, 215-216, 218,
220-221, 227, 231,
236-237
George Clyde, 228
George Luther, 216,
221, 223
Gertrude, 227
Gertrude (Meseke),
220
Gloria Glea (Fisher),
226
H B, 215
Harry Benton, 220
Harry McDowell, 220
Hattie E (McDowell),
220
Hazel Lorena, 227
Irene (Ashenfelter),
228
John D I, 215
John Diehl, 228
John Diehl II, 228
John Diehl III, 228
John Diehl IV, 228

John Henry, 216, 227
Judith Ann, 228
Judy (Collins), 228
Karen (Logan), 228
Kathryn (Beaver), 226
Laura (Egolf), 228
Laura Alice (Bender),
220
Lila (Fogelsonger), 230
Lulu Edith, 227
Margaret Alice, 230
Margaret Rebecca, 216,
231
Marian, 216, 221
Marion Elizabeth, 229
Martin L, 215
Martin Luther, 226
Mary, 216
Mary (Diehl), 227
Mary Alice (Mohler),
228
Mary Allen (Dodd),
229
Mary Ann (Miller),
223
Mary E, 216
Mary Kathryn, 228
Mary Maye, 226
Maude (Feltcher), 229
Minnie Ellen, 226
Naida Anne, 220
Nancy J (Sample), 229
Paul K, 215
Paul Kauffman, 229
Rebecca (Weiser),
215-216, 218,
220-221, 227, 231,
236-237
Richard Mark, 229
Richard Martin, 226
Richard Mohler, 229
Samuel Weiser, 216,
231
Sarah Rebecca, 223
Susanna (Royer), 223
Violet, 227
Virginia Bell (Hughes),
228
Wesley John, 228
William, 237
William Leslie, 221
William Reuben, 216,
220
BURKHURST
George, 1687
Pearl C (Kephart),
1687
BURKINS
Janet Louise, 873
BURKITT
Edith Muhlenberg
(Robeson), 333
John de P, 333
Virginia Robeson, 333
BURKS
J K, 1810
Margaret (Wiser), 1810
Rachel M (Wiser),
1798
Romulus, 1798
Sally, 119
BURLISON
Marjorie, 1398
BURNASH
Lori Vernier, 1347
BURNETT
Carol Virginia, 603
BURNHAM
Amanda Lee, 1004

Julie Rae (Smith), 1004
Oliver Wendell, 1004
BURNITE
David C, 1472
David Clark IV, 1475
David Clark V, 1475
David Clark VI, 1475
Edward Breidenbaugh,
1475
Elizabeth Edna, 1475
Florence Haller (Frey),
1475
Ida May
(Breidenbaugh), 1475
Katherine Marie Pauli
(Egan), 1475
Kathryn Louisa
(Bedsworth), 1475
Keron Patrick, 1475
Martha Jeanne, 1475
Mary Ida, 1475
Patricia Maria, 1475
Ruth Elizabeth Stark
(Coleman), 1475
BURNS
Barbara, 1190
Boyd, 1190
Brittany Marie, 938
Chelsie Ann-Lynn, 938
Dillon Lee, 938
Ethel Alberta (Smith),
1015
Evelyn, 730
James Arthur, 387
James William, 387
Jane, 1388
John, 1015
Judy, 312
Lulu, 512
Mable Pearl (Wright),
1685
Martha Marie (Welch),
387
Mary Catherine
(Hippert), 1309
Mary Jo, 1190
Pamela Jean, 656-657
Paul, 1190
Peggy Lee, 387
Sarah, 168
Wendy Lou (Weiser)
Showers, 938
William, 938
William Tilden, 1685
Wilma (Wiser), 1190
BURNSIDE
James Burnell Jr, 201
James Nicholas, 201
Jason Kyle, 201
Teresa Diane (Allison),
201
BURNW
Marie, 1510
BURRESS
Catherine (Trinkle),
1654
BURRIER
Cleta Coleen
(Dinwiddie), 442
Cynthia Ann, 442
Raymond Jr, 442
Stephen Lee, 442
BURRIS
Bernice (Coder), 1272
G W, 1272
BURROUGHS
Albert Short, 347
Emily (Richards), 347
Helen, 347

CALDERON
Maureen, 1837
CALDERWOOD
Dorothy (Miller), 1391
Kathleen Marie, 1391
Lester L, 1391
Phyllis, 1391
CALDWELL
Christine I, 172
Donald, 610
Edith (Wisor), 1703
H L, 1008
Helen, 443
Helen (Sheehe), 610
Inez, 1703
Karen, 1791
Stephen Dow, 610
Vera (Kehl), 1008
Willard, 1703
CALE
June, 1498
CALHOUN
Christine Mary, 832
Christopher, 1328
Clair, 1003
Clara Louise (Yost)
Trissel, 1328
Denise, 1328
Eleanor (Smyer), 832
Helen Margaretta
(Womelsdorf), 830
Jeffrey, 1004
Laura, 832
Laura Diane
(Whitehead), 832
Lucy Anna, 137
Martha Elizabeth, 1302
Mary, 1206
Mary (Farwell), 1003
Maureen B (McCabe),
832
Norma Rosamond, 832
Richard Brown, 832
Ronald, 1328
Ruth Almira, 1297
Son, 1004
William John, 830, 832
CALIMAN
Cora Louise (Eppley),
884-885
Eunice Louise, 884-885
Lorraine Cheryl, 884
Lorraine Louise, 886
Louise Lorraine,
884-885
Monte Cristo, 884-885
Reba Ursula (Eppley),
881, 885
CALL
Dorothea Bernice, 213
Maude Ellen, 1658
CALLAN
James Evan Jr, 967
James Evan Sr, 967
Kristin Lynn (Howes),
967
CALLANAN
Carol Lynn, 1552
CALLANDER
Cynthia Faye, 1288
CALLAWAY
Carol, 276
Lucille, 1486
CALLENDER
Evelyn Ruth, 668
Faye Corrine
(Fulkroad), 668
Janet JoAnne, 668
William Landis, 668

CALLIHAN
Adeele Huston (Sharpe),
796
Cathryn (Wright), 796
Charles H, 796
Emma C, 795
Evelyn (de Grasse),
796
Flora B (Mull), 795
Forrest I (Harnest),
796
Frank P, 796
George H, 795
Jacob, 795
James R, 796
John Tressler, 796
Kathryn, 777
Kathryn G, 796
Lillian M, 796
Linda Kay, 796
Linnaeus D, 796
Margaret (Perkins),
796
Mary Catherine
(Weiser), 795
Minnie L (Sibert), 796
Patricia, 796
Phyllis, 796
Robert Lin, 796
Tressler W, 796
William H, 796
CALLINAN
Andrew Joseph, 405
Jean Louise
(Etherington), 405
Jenna Louise, 405
Neal Andrew, 405
CALLOW
Edwin B, 1470
Marguerite (Gilchrist),
1470
CALLOWAY
Jeffrey Lamont, 1513
Jeffrey Lamont Jr,
1513
Mary Christine
(Kinback), 1513
Samantha Marie, 1513
CALVERT
Mollie, 1655
Naomi Grace
(Winkleman), 1370
Oscar, 1370
CALVIN, 1433
Carolyn, 1433
James, 1027
Lorna Lou, 1140
Mabel (Cooper), 1027
Marguerita (Moore),
1433
Marilyn, 1433
Richard, 1433
CALVO
Marilyn (Calvin), 1433
Tony Casa, 1433
Tonya Kay, 1433
CAMBELL
Barbara Gail, 706
Carolyn Booth
(Koppenhaver), 706
Harriet S (Yost), 1018
Paul David, 706
Paul Douglass, 706
Walter, 1018
CAMBLIN
--, 548
Lois, 548
Rosa D (Banter), 548

CAMBRIA
--, 1770
Dorothy (Shimmel),
1770
CAMDEN
Joyce, 486
Kay Lyn (Kern), 486
Louis, 486
CAMERON
Catharine Elizabeth,
299, 343
Debra Lynn (Karr),
478
Donna Charleen
(Cunningham), 1238
Jane Elizabeth, 1254
Jane Elizabeth (Kahle),
1254
John, 299
Mary Magdalena
(Shulze), 299
Michael Rhoads, 478
Nan, 824
Robert, 1238
Sally Kay, 1254
William Edward, 1254
CAMINZIND
Dawna, 1211
CAMMANN
Abby (Patterson), 336
Amy Evelyn, 335
Anna Catharine, 335
Anna Catharine
(Lorillard), 335
Anna Margaretta, 335
child, 336
Cortland, 336
Donald Muhlenberg,
336
Edward Crary, 335
Elizabeth Schuyler, 336
Ella Cornelia (Crary),
335
Frances N (Schenck),
335
Frederic Almy, 335
George Philip, 335
George Philip Jr, 335
Grace H (Churchill),
335
Hamilton Fairfax, 336
Helena van Kortland
(Clarkson), 335
Henry Lorillard, 335
Herbert Schuyler, 335
Hermann Henry, 335
Hermann Muhlenberg,
335
Isabella Apolline (Mali),
335
Isabelle Mali, 335
Jacob Lorillard, 335
Jean B (Gallatin), 335
Katherine, 336
Katherine van
Ransselaer (Fairfax),
335
Marcia deForest (Post),
335
Marguerite Marie
(Villa), 336
Maria Margaretta, 335
Mary Evelyn, 335
Mary Lyman (Cox),
336
Nicholas Bayard, 336
Philip Gallatin, 335
Robert Fairfax
Livingston, 336

Robert Fulton, 335
Schuyler Van
Rensselaer, 335
Sophie Edwards
(Spencer), 336
Stephen Van
Rensselaer, 336
Stephen Van
Rensselaer Jr, 336
William Bayard, 336
William Edgar, 335
CAMMONN
Frances Worthington,
336
CAMP
Jenny, 1261
CAMPAU
Joyce E, 1474
CAMPBELL
--, 1201
Ada, 1081
Amanda, 566
Barbara Ann, 735
Barbara Jean (Henning),
1336
Bertin C, 1269
Bonnie Ann (Kahle),
1201
Carly Louise, 636
Catherine Louise, 75
Cecile Luella
(Eddinger), 1303
Charles, 170, 267, 566
Christine Louise
(Blagus), 636
Christopher, 636
Christopher Enloe,
1868
Cindy (Poe), 1481
Clarissa Jane, 521
Cynthia Ann, 1441
Debra, 1376
Delie Emma (Wiser),
1873
Elfrieda (Kasper), 740
Eliza, 463
Elizabeth (Smith), 170
Emily (Dunn), 740
Emma (Dorward), 170
Esther Louise (Shipe),
740
Ethel Hewitt, 267
Floyd Eugene, 1303
Fred, 566
Gary Lee, 1336
Glenn Alton, 740
James, 1269
James Clyde, 1873
Jane (Wilcox), 170
Janet Sue, 170
Jeanna Renea (Taylor),
1657
Jennie M (Harringer),
1269
Judith, 170
Katharine, 170
Kathy Ann (Witmer),
703
Kelly Ann, 1481
Laura Elizabeth, 1510
Lillie May, 1269
Lori Lee, 703
Margaret, 170
Marvella Elizabeth
(Wiser), 1867
Mary Alice (Wiser),
1868
Mary Ann (Eberly),
170

Mary Kathryn
(Williams), 599
Merle, 599
Minnie S (Protzeller),
170
Nancy Stratton (Ulrich),
75
Naomi, 1203
P Emery, 1269
Rachel, 1827
Richard Charles, 170
Roger Allen, 703
Roy, 170
Samuel, 1571
Sarah, 170
Sharon Lori, 1168
Shirley Irene, 990
Sterl Glenn, 740
Sterl Wesley, 740
Susanna, 929
Terry Lee, 1481
Thomas, 1336, 1657
Tracy Lynn (Cottrell),
1481
Vera, 1269
Vickie Lin, 267
Virginia Anne, 128
Walter William, 1867
Wanda Sue (Herring),
566
William, 170, 740,
1481
William E, 75
CAMPBILL
Clyde, 137
Juanita Martha
(Peoples), 137
CANADY
Cloa S (Wiser)
Thornberry, 1779
Washington, 1779
CANCILA
Anthony, 779
Arlene Evelyn, 779
Elizabeth, 779
Grace Mildred
(Bettilyon), 779
CANDLER
Zada, 596
CANNAN
Edna, 1236
Gudrida, 805
CANNEDY
George E, 1435
Glenda Joy h(Moore),
1435
Melinda Carol, 1435
Michael E, 1435
Sheila Ann, 1435
CANNON
Elizabeth Arda (Ripple),
1232
Ella C, 1531
James Allen, 1232
CANTER
Helen, 561
CANTNER
Clara June, 1374
CANTRELL
Wilda, 42
CANTY
Alan Lloyd, 1431
Dalton Erwin Jr, 1431
David Dalton, 1431
Marilyn June
(Tomlinson), 1431
CAOUETTE
Betty Jo (Weiser), 1142
Joseph, 1142

CAPARELLE
Danny, 1055
Josie, 1055
Robin Lynn
(Kerstetter), 1055
Tony Marie, 1055
CAPEL
Katharine, 1564
CAPLE
Mattie, 1858
CAPONE
Anthony Thomas, 1157
Dominic Joseph, 1157
Lysandra Noelle, 1157
Michele Therese
(Cordier), 1157
CAPONI
Susanna, 287
CAPPLEMAN
Mary Lavon, 592
CAPPS
Doris (Spurgeon), 148
James R, 148
CAPWELL
Amber Sue, 1514
Michelle L (Gerwer),
1514
Robin, 1514
CARBAUGH
Anna Leona, 189
Annie Leona Self
(Tatham), 190
Charles, 190
Christian, 190
Elmer Herman, 190
Howard Elmer, 190
Mabel Eleanor
(Kennedy), 190
CARBONARA
Joseph, 1072
Nancy Jane
(Trevorrow), 1072
CARBONI
Lorraine, 812
CARDOVA
Susan, 191
CARDWELL
Donald William, 812
Lindsay Noel, 812
Lynn Elspeth
(McIntyre), 811
Lynn McIntyre, 777
CARE
Nancy Jean, 457
CAREY
Carolyn Arleene
(Schuh), 50
Dyann Cecile, 227
Elizabeth Ann (Francis),
1398
Joanne Elizabeth, 1398
Joyce, 538
Laura Leann, 1818
Lisa, 1393
Micheal Joseph, 1398
Richard, 50
Richard Donald, 50
CARFOLL
Caroline, 1690
CARGAL
Alice, 1346
CARIS
Dola, 620
CARISS
Claire (Witmer), 766
Evan Daniel, 766
Joseph Gregory, 766
Mariah Lynn, 766
Nathanile Conrad, 766

CARL
--, 1622
Adelaide Ann (Weiser),
1468
Bella Weiser, 1468
Charles Weiser, 1468
Jeremiah, 1468
John D, 1643
Kate W, 251
Miriam (Weiser), 1622
Sallie S (Hamsher),
1643
CARLAN
Florence Estelle, 1579
CARLEN
Connie Sue, 105
David E, 105
Greg Lee, 105
Mark Alan, 105
Miriam Letha (Titus),
105
CARLEY
Hannah, 1405
CARLIN
Alice Analee, 1773
CARLISLE
Amy Spangler (Weiser),
1467
Charles, 1467
Edwin, 1467
Horace, 1467
Lorva A (Garrett),
1467
Louise, 1467
CARLL
Freelove, 1408
CARLOS
Kathleen, 1719
CARLSON
--, 1578
Barbara Sue (Crocker),
749
Canel Vail, 722
David Alan, 749
Dorothy Jean (Frey),
749
Edith (Pickard), 1578
Florence, 610
John, 749
Jonathan David, 749
Kari Sue (Larson), 749
Kelli Ann, 749
Lisa Dawne, 1004
Lynda Ann, 749
Matthew Alan, 749
Nancy Jean, 749
Phyllis L, 1292
Samantha Jeanne, 749
Wayne Michael, 749
CARLTON
Katherine Elizabeth, 40
CARMEAN
Darla, 275
Darrell, 275
Gary Robert, 275
Karen Sue (Gibbons),
275
CARMI
David Paul, 1281
Matthew Merrill, 1281
Paul David, 1281
Ruth Ada (Raybould),
1281
CARMICHAEL
child, 880
Edgar, 880
Harry, 880
Harry J, 880
Nancy Alma (Eppley),

880
Pauline, 880
Ruth, 880
CARMIN
Harold, 598
Vivian Leola (Gossard),
598
CARMINE
--, 1211
Almeda Jane (Davis),
1211
David Walter, 1211
Lisa Marie, 1211
Owen Eldon, 1211
Takota, 1211
CARN
April Dawne, 1174
Brandon Robert
Michael, 1174
Bryan Bradley, 1174
Christine Loiuse
(Mullins), 1174
Christopher, 1174
Dawne Lynna, 1174
Dorothy Ann
(Woodcock), 1174
Joyce Ann (Miller),
1173
Norma Lorraine
(Rook), 1173
Robert Milton Johnson,
1174
Sophia Lorraine, 1173
Theresa Lorraine, 1173
William Bard III, 1173
William Bard IV, 1174
William Bard Jr, 1173
William Bard V, 1174
CARNATHAN
Bess, 824
CARNER
Pauline, 1397
CARNES
Clarence E, 1217
Dorothy (Riggs), 554
Edythe Gail, 1130
Elsie Ann (Riggs), 554
Guy, 554
Margaret Isabel (Kahle),
1199
Marjorie Isabel
(Henderson), 1217
Mary Margaret
(Schrift), 1199
Patty (Weis), 1199
Robert, 1199
Robert Dee, 1199
Vaughn, 554
CARNEY
Minnie, 276
CARNICOM
Amos, 509
Ann, 509
Carrie A (Stine), 509
Clara (Engler), 509
Gloria, 485
Hannah (Binkley), 508
Helen (Sidney), 508
Idella, 508
Irvin Peter, 508
James C, 508
Lydia, 508
Mary, 509
Minnie M (Harning),
508
Myrtle, 509
Peter, 508
Sarah E, 509
Theodore Perry, 509

William H, 509
CARNS
Carol (Bumbarger),
1370
Samuel, 1370
CAROLL
Daniel Arthur, 575
Donald Russell, 575
Sharri Ann (Herring),
575
CAROLUS
Katherine Elizabeth,
739
CARPENTER
Barbara Jean, 1187
Carolyn Ann, 1187
Charlotte Mease, 356
Cordelia Anne
(Bennetch), 356
Edna Belle, 1839
Ellenor Paulson, 426
Francis Thomas, 1187
Joan, 117
John Halsey, 356
Kenneth H, 356
Lola Ethel Weiser,
1187
Patricia Anne, 356
Thomas Leroy, 1187
CARPER
Hetty, 1655
Mary, 1667
Nancy, 1667
CARR
Aaron Charles, 1326
Ada, 576
Allison Nichole, 1326
Anna Lodicie (Herring),
594
Barbara (Eddinger),
1303
Barbara Ann, 1322
Barbarra, 1767
Clarence, 1695
Cynthia Kay
(Longenberger), 1325
Dan, 1677
David John, 812
David Robert, 1040
Della Marie
(Fleischman), 1325
Diane (Gibboney),
1390
Eileen, 58
Ernest Merrill, 594
Helen, 942
Ilda Ione, 594
James Scott, 1326
Jean (Hubler), 1695
John Alden, 812
John Lewis, 594
Joseph Brinkley, 1325
Karen, 812
Laura, 613
Lori Ann (Deam),
1325
Lorraine (Carboni),
812
Marianne, 1040
Mary (Johnson), 1677
Mary Alice, 777, 812
Mary Catherine, 135
Matthew Allen, 1325
Michael Alan, 1325
Richard, 1303
Ryan Michael, 1325
Sarah Marie (Kilfoil),
1326
Sharon Leigh, 1326

Steven Joseph, 1325
Susan marie, 1326
Thomas, 1390
CARR-POTTER
Brendan Nathaniel, 812
Calli Isabella, 812
Noah Alden, 812
CARRICO
Norma Jean, 394
CARRIER
Deborah Ann, 1250
Dennis Gary, 1250
Gary Dane, 1250
Laura Lynn, 1250
Marlene, 1246, 1884
Marlene Virginia
(Kahle), 1250
CARRINGTON
Brenda (Bower), 1392
Donna Michel, 1392
Joseph III, 1392
CARRIS
Eve Ann, 1131
CARROLL
Catharine Lucille
(Johnson), 391
Charles F, 391
Damon John, 215
Elizabeth (Snyder),
1015
Hazel D, 1822
Jason Martin, 215
John E, 1015
Lezli Kae (Weiser),
215
Margaret C, 1016
Myrtle, 1235
Nicole Rene, 215
Stella May, 1015
Vicki, 1159
CARSON
Evlyn, 1258
Rosetta, 313
CARSTEN
Gladys, 178
CARTER
Anne Page, 301
Birdie Irene (Hocker),
591
Cameron Michael, 552
Candace Lynn, 592
Charles Kenneth, 592
Charles Virgil, 591
Connie Marie, 592
Cristin Michelle, 552
Daniel Michael, 592
David Phillip, 592
Dollie Glayds
(Spurgeon), 149
Dorothy Nadine, 592
Effie I (Binkley), 507
Eugene, 1206
Evelyn Leavitt, 1775
Faye, 1052
Gary, 487
Grace, 536
James Phillip, 592
Jason Anthony, 937
Jeanne Marie, 408
Jennifer Joyce (Filbert),
937
Jill Arlene (Cline), 552
Joyce Marie (Hall),
592
Katherine A (Davis),
1206
Katherine Michele, 926
Keneth Leroy, 592
Kenneth Kevin, 592

CHAPMAN
Ellen Jane, 818
James, 1392
Kate, 328
Lillie Pauline, 665
Mabel, 1817
Minerva (Smith), 1392
Sherri, 1134
Vilas, 1392
CHAPPELEAR
Brenda (Miller), 1131
C (Weiser), 1883
Charles William, 1131
Christopher, 1131
Christopher William, 1131
Daniel Norman, 1131
David Conrad, 1131
Katheyn Ann (Bradshaw), 1131
Olive Felonise (Weiser), 1131
Thomas Daniel, 1131
CHAPPELL
Catherine Julia, 43
Chad Crawford, 43
Julia Margaret (Collinson), 43
Kim Elizabeth, 43
Lisa Cunningham (Moseley), 43
Wayne Crawford, 43
CHARLES
Alice Marie, 520
Aurelia Lillian (Salada), 693
James, 78
Margaret, 1019
Mary Ellen Weiser (Bergstresser), 78
Penny Irene, 1821
Ralph William, 693
CHARLTON
Clara Jo, 1872
Cynthia, 1648
CHARMENIA/ CHARMAIN
Hazel, 1685
CHARNOSKY
Diane Christine, 860
CHASE
Albert, 1369, 1687
Dorothy Louise (Casner), 1369
Emma (Kephart), 1687
Joan Esta, 1369
Kay Lenora, 1369
Marianna (McDonough), 202
Richard Brian, 202
CHATLEY
Diane Joy, 1223
Dorothy Louise (Wolfe), 1223
Herbert Lee, 1223
Mark Allen, 1223
CHEATEM
Kathryn Elinor (Brown), 621
Kenneth, 621
CHEDGEY
Doris Lorraine (Kephart), 1690
Jack, 1690
CHEDISTER
Beverly, 478
CHEEK
Clarence William, 76
Debra Lynn, 76

Dennis William, 76
Dorothy (Womelsdorf), 824
John, 824
Laura Priscilla (Rockey), 76
Philip Warren, 76
CHEERS
Ann, 1258
CHEESMAN
Alice (Morris), 337
Bates, 337
Francis Morris Stewart, 337
CHELETTE
Dorothy Lee (Sherrill), 470
Evandon Marx, 470
Sharon Ann, 470
CHELLEW
Frances, 1350
CHENEY
Christopher, 203
Daniel, 203
Eunice (Long), 619
Loree Lynn (Smith), 203
Owen, 619
Ruth, 1795
CHERINGTON
Melissa, 487
CHERNEY
Anna Marie (Muhlenberg), 343
Christopher, 343
Marvin, 343
Mary Gabrielle, 343
CHERVANICK
John, 1020
Rose Marke (Renn), 1020
Susan, 1020
CHESNEY
Katherine M, 768
Mabel, 1022
CHESNUT
Ensie Jane, 1230
CHESSER
Donald, 388
Hazel Ilo (Manter), 388
Leo Ernest, 388
Robert, 388
CHESTER
Glenna Jeanette, 1312
CHESTNUT
Judy Ann, 817
CHEVALIER
Alan Clair, 1378
Barry Clair, 1378
Carol Ann, 1378
Charles Elwood, 1378
Clair DeWitt, 1378
David, 1378
Donna (Baer), 1378
Donna Jean, 1378
Gary E, 1378
Grace Beryl (Weiser), 1377
Harry B, 1377
Harry Elwood, 1378
Harry Richard, 1378
Kathryn E, 1377
Leah Debra, 1379
Lois (Weaver), 1378
Marjorie Ellen (Williams), 1378
Mark David, 1378
Michelle Renee, 1378
Mildred Grace, 1378

Ruth Emily (Kurpjuweit), 1378
Sharon (Sullivan), 1378
Suzanne Kay, 1378
Violet LaRue (Bollinger), 1378
CHEW
Alexander, 1174
Austin Alexander, 1174
CHIGAN
John, 60
Sophia (--), 60
CHILCOAT
Ida, 1442
CHILD
Clyde Compton, 1768
Helen (Wiser), 1768
CHILDERHOSE
Margaret Diane, 1218
CHILDREE
Angela Lynn, 1201
CHILDRESS
Lavonne, 1323
CHILTON
Delores Dean (Jones), 34
Elizabeth Dee, 34
Jeffrey Harding, 34
William II, 34
CHINLUND
Faye Evelyn (Arbogast), 717
Robert, 717
CHISHOLM
Barbara Muhlenberg, 300
Benjamin Ogden, 300
Donald Muhlenberg, 300
Dorothy Rogers, 300
Edith (Lawrence), 300
Elizabeth (Rhoades), 300
Elizabeth Harsen, 300
George Edings, 300
Henry Lawrence, 300
Jessie Edings, 300
John Rogers, 300
Margaret Willing, 300
Mary Ann (Rogers), 300
Mary Frederick, 300
Nina Rhoades, 300
Priscilla Pixton, 301
Wiliam Edings, 300
William Augustus Muhlenberg, 300
William Edings, 300
Winifred Wheelwright, 300
CHITTUM
Joseph Allen, 929
Mark W, 929
Mary Louise (Snyder), 929
CHIVALETTE
Andre, 757
Frank, 757
Sharon Dawn (Furman), 757
Yvonne Marie, 757
CHIVERS
Anna H, 1198
CHMURA
Audrey Louise (Ferfien), 970
Debbie Lynn, 970
Frank, 970
Stephen Paul, 970

CHOE
Kilja, 752
CHOLEWINSKI
Angie (Ketnas), 481
Charlene Mae, 481
Connie Mae (Karr), 481
Herman Adam, 481
Leonard Adam, 481
CHOMKO
Eric Nicholas, 1078
James N, 1078
Linda Cynthia, 1078
Lisa Karen, 1078
Marjorie Jean (Brungart), 1078
CHONE
Jessie, 112
CHOPIN
Keith Wayne, 1570
Kyle Aaron, 1570
Paula Michelle (Weiser), 1570
Wayne, 1570
CHOUINARD
Carole Anne (Uhl), 1552
Mark Edward, 1552
CHOUMAN
Dawn Linette (Casper), 246
Taisseer Ali, 246
CHREST
Constance Lynn, 1431
George Durian, 1432
Gertrude L (Gillespie), 1431
Russel, 1431
Sandra (Clyne), 1432
CHRISMAN
Jack Leroy, 1256
Karen, 1256
Max, 1255
Phyllis Jean (Mapes), 1255
CHRISPIN
Laura, 1256
CHRIST
George Matthew III, 146
Loreen Lynne (Evans), 146
Sara, 1048
Sarah, 1356
CHRISTENSEN
Angela Caryn, 151
Chad James, 151
Duretta Darlene (Roderick), 151
Jane Maurine, 290
Jennifer (Packer), 151
Joel Ross, 151
Kim Arlene, 1206
Kyle Ray, 151
Laura Ann, 151
Marvin L, 1741
Ross Leon, 151
Velda E (Weiser), 1741
CHRISTENSON
Elizabeth Grace (Wiser), 1780
Jerry Lee, 1780
John, 1780
Karen, 1020
Lisa Kay, 1780
Lori Jean, 1780
CHRISTIAN
Albert, 1533
Alma, 1534

Bessie (Klinger), 1533
Betty, 1533
Christopher M, 194
Clair E, 1534
Clara Michael, 1533
Edna, 1336
Eric Danon, 194
Florence, 1534
Graydon W, 1534
Helen M, 1534
Jay C, 1533
Jennie (Dressler), 1533
Lester C, 1533
Linda (Snyder), 194
Lloyd Franklin, 1534
Mark Lewis, 194
Mary (Kapp), 1534
Philip Austin, 194
Robert, 194
Ruth (Neidigh), 1534
Ruth Rothermel (Grocer), 1534
William, 194
CHRISTIANSEN
Duane L, 1384
Sandra Lee, 1384
Vergene (Meeker), 1384
CHRISTIANSON
Barnard, 989
Marie M (Barnard), 989
CHRISTINIDIS
Fred, 831
Janice Gayle (Dottie), 831
Jon Philip, 831
Mark Peter, 831
CHRISTMAN
Charles Herbert, 1642
Kathryn Marie (Hamsher), 1642
CHRISTMAS
Eva (Van Slyke), 1583
John, 1583
Margaret, 1584
CHRISTOFF
Jaye Patricia (Miller) Barb, 1300
John Louis, 1300
CHRISTOPHER
Linda, 1569
Linda Magrisi, 246
CHUBB
Anna Maria (Simpson), 915
Beverly Elaine, 1537
Catharine (Weiser), 915
Charles Clayton, 673
Christine Marie (Reichard), 1537
Elizabeth May, 673
Grace Alvest (Koppenhaver), 673
Janet Marcia (Muggio), 1537
Joseph, 915
Leroy Walter, 1537
Marian Jean, 673
Todd Douglas, 1537
CHUDZINSKI
Billie Dianne (Beckley), 472
John Arthur, 472
CHUNG
Sue, 351
CHUPAK
Matthew Michael, 792

CHUPAK (continued)
Michael V, 792
Patricia Ellen (Snyder), 792
Peter Michael, 792
CHUPANG
Debra, 1172
CHURCH
Andrew, 540
Carol Elizabeth, 1521
Catherine Crain (Harrison), 1520
George, 1520
George Frederic II, 1520
Julie Ellen, 1521
Linda, 1521
Lydia Ellen (Mitchell), 540
Margaret Poole (Comerford), 1521
Mary (Milano), 1520
Philip Floyd, 151
Rodney Harrison, 1521
Stacy Lynn (Taylor), 151
CHURCHILL
Bethany Rebekkah, 991
Dale Roberta (Ditzler), 990
Gordon Ralph, 990
Grace H, 335
Joshua Nathanael, 990
June Elizabeth (Craig), 990
Kenneth M, 1506
Martha Helena (Morrison), 1506
Shirley Irene (Campbell), 990
Warren Rupert, 990
CIES
Mary Aileen, 1498
CILDERMAN
Andrew A, 756
Christopher Andrew, 756
Matthew Scott, 756
Sarah Elnora (Furman), 756
CIN
Janie, 180
CINICIONE
Anthony, 867
Anthony Jr, 867
Louis, 867
Mark, 867
Marriettia (Gisner), 867
CINTURA
Arnulf B, 56
Eliza Eugenia (Maier), 56
CISNEY
Beulah, 1671
CITZLER
Naomi Hannah, 989
CLAEYS
Jean, 325
CLAFIN
Amy Marie, 485
Bobbi Lee, 485
Janet Lee (Knipp), 485
William Roy, 485
CLAIR
Elizabeth (Llewellyn), 835
Joseph, 835
Mary Beth, 835

CLAMPITT
Bonnie Lou (Studebaker), 523
Carrie Lynn, 524
Charles Jay, 523
Dean Kay, 524
Jay Mack, 523
Jered Andrew, 524
Juanice (Yeargan), 524
Kathy (Griffin), 524
Linda Kay, 524
Lois Margaret, 524
Lola Mae (McClurg), 523
Lucille (Coffin), 523
Mary Marjorie, 524
Rebecca Ann, 523
William Frederick, 524
William M, 523
CLARK
-- (--), 157
Abbie (Ege), 292
Ada, 251
Alice Requa, 308
Amy Elizabeth, 855
Barbara (Marshall), 855
Barbara Jean, 1276
Bessie Belle (Wiser), 1792
Bessie M, 878
Betty, 1029
Byron E, 292
Carl H, 946
Catherine (Trinkle) Burress, 1654
Charles R, 292
David, 482, 757
Devin Elizabeth, 453
Donald Crose, 106
Dwaine, 1486
Earl, 1770
Edith M, 292
Edna (Wilson), 878
Edward, 1792
Elizabeth (Knotter), 102
Ella Christine (Shettel), 855
Elva L, 841
Ernest Alwyn, 848
Esther Evelyn (Starwalt), 106
Ethel Edna (Earnest) Hemkin Craft, 1486
Evelyn M, 878
Gaylord, 855
Golda (Oakley), 102
Grace Irene, 1678
Harold, 1803
Hazel (Shimmel), 1770
Helen, 432
Henry Adolphenus, 1371
Ingrid (Fetter), 106
Jacqueline, 1205
James, 855, 878
James Jr, 855
Jeannetta, 1194
Jeffrey, 102
Jesse James, 453
John, 157, 159
John Christopher, 1654
Josephine (Schlesinger), 159
Judy, 933
Julia, 810
Kathaleen Gayle, 855
Kathleen Alice (Kohl),

757
Larry Wayne, 489
Laura A, 1662
Linda Christine (Barrell), 482
Linda Louise (Brauer), 489
Lorine (Wiser), 1803
Lucy Elizabeth, 1482
Margaret (Renn), 1020
Margaret Elizabeth, 1837
Marilyn Esther, 106
Mark, 102
Marvin Donald, 106
CLARK
Mary, 1014
CLARK
Mary (Shettel), 878
May Scott (Rodman), 337
Mildred, 1098
Minnie Mayburn (Winkleman), 1371
Molly Jo, 855
Nancy Lee, 102
Paul, 1020
Pauline Ida, 645
Robert, 1710
Robert S, 878
Robert Wilson, 878
Ruth, 878
Ruth H, 292
Sarah Elizabeth (Wisor), 1710
Sharon (Lee), 855
Sheldon, 102
Sheldon O, 102
Shirley, 1387
Stephanie Suzanne (Degner), 489
Stephen Paul, 489
Thelma, 878
Thomas Carl, 489
Thomas Lee, 489
Valerie Jean (Aills), 453
Vera Vesta (Croy), 848
Wibur D, 292
William Bayard, 337
Zoe Kathryn (Hanover), 946
CLARKE
Edward, 836
Elizabeth B (Llewellyn), 836
Ruthanne, 1630
CLARKS
Evelyn, 199
CLARKSON
Helena van Kortland, 335
CLARKSTON
Daniel, 491
Karen (Moore), 491
CLASPILL
Joseph, 1779
Lucy Ann (Wiser), 1779
CLASSEN
Anna Lore, 316
Emilie Henriette, 316
Gretel, 316
Henriette Schwab Weitbrecht, 315
Walter, 316
CLAUSEN
Eric David, 229
Jacob, 229

Jacob Willis Jr, 229
Kathryn Elizabeth (Jacobs), 229
Linda Michele, 229
Louise Grace (Smith), 229
Marc Adam, 229
Nancy Elizabeth, 229
Sandra Lee Mary (Tredway), 229
Susan Elizabeth (McMeans), 229
Tara Nicole, 229
William Daniel, 229
CLAUSER
--, 1621
Elizabeth F, 1641
Marguerite, 1622
Mary Clementine (Lykens), 1621
CLAUVE
Jennifer, 1324
CLAVENGER
Mabel, 1498
CLAWSON
Lois, 1768
CLAY
Cindy (--), 401
Daniel Nathan, 401
Danielle Deanne, 401
David Ray, 401
Dawn (--), 401
Deanne Marie, 401
Dennis Franklin, 401
Dennis Franklin Jr, 401
Diane (Kremmere), 401
Donnetta (Imel), 401
Dwight John, 401
Karla, 401
Lucas David, 401
Marion Franklin, 401
Nancy (Ebright), 401
Phyllis Nadine (Moore), 401
Ryan Matthew, 401
Timothy Jay, 401
CLAYCOMB
--, 1715
Daniel, 1715
Nicole, 1715
Penny Lee, 1200
Tammy (Rexford), 1715
CLAYMILLER
Betty Joe (Day), 524
Lora Lisa, 524
Monte, 524
Paul, 524
CLAYPOOL
Rebecca, 1667
CLAYTON
Helen, 396
CLEARY
Caitlin Caroline DelCour, 45
Conor Patrick Cochran, 44
Dylan Alexander Boucher, 45
Julia Ann Sloane (DelCour), 44
Lillian, 1428
Paul Joseph, 44
CLEAVER
Louisa, 1624
CLEM
Edith Pearl, 1188

CLEMENS
--, 983
Albert, 983
Clare, 984
Fred, 984
Harold, 984
Harry, 984
Junior, 984
Kate (Radabaugh), 983
Leonard, 984
Margaret, 984
Mary, 269
Mary Catherine, 1671
Milvina J, 1427
Pearl, 984
Robert, 984
Twilight, 984
CLEMENT
Betty Evelyn, 544
CLEMENTS
Alice Ruth (Cummins), 1477
Diane, 1477
Eva Dell (Brouches), 596
Frank, 1477
Gus, 596
Linda Kay, 1477
Scott Leo, 1477
Wendy (Crosby), 473
Wes, 473
CLEMISON
Nina Pearl, 126
CLEMMER
Jeannett, 947
CLEMMONS
Ben, 1189
Mary Elizabeth (Hall), 1189
CLENDENNING
John, 939
CLEVELAND
Alice Mae, 369
Gladys Bailey, 368
Grace Annabelle, 370
Jeanette Margaret, 370
Judith, 369
Loretta (May), 369
Margaret Marie (Bauder), 368
Marjory M, 369
Nora B, 115
Regina Lee, 369
Richard, 369
Richard Hall, 368-369
Robert L, 369
Sarah Elizabeth Bailey, 369
Vera Jean, 369
Verna (Klingle), 369
CLEVENGER
Alice (Cargal), 1346
Amy Lyn, 451
Angela Nicole, 451
Beverly Jane (Spicer), 452
Brett James, 469
Bruce Eric, 452
Carol Rose Draper, 451
Danielle Marie (Miller), 452
Denyce Lin, 1346
Donna Louise, 452
Doris, 1346
Douglas Lee, 1346
Gilbert, 1346
Harry Arthur, 451
Harry Arthur III, 451

CLEVENGER
(continued)
Harry Arthur Jr, 451
Inez, 1346
Irene Rose, 452
Ivan W, 1346
John Duane, 469
John Edward, 452
Joseph Patrick, 469
June Elklen, 452
Karl Edward, 452
Kathryn Alberta, 452
Kimberly Ann, 452
Laura Jean, 452
Mar Layna Danielle,
452
Marjorie Ann, 452
Mary Lou, 451
Maybelle E (Weiser),
1346
Paula Jean (Fisher),
451
Raymond K, 1884
Raymond Kenneth, 451
Raymond R, 446
Robert Leroy, 451
Rosa Lee Draper
(Stewart), 451
Rose Marie (Weiser),
451, 1884
Ruth Ann Taylor
(Harris), 451
Ryan Lewis, 469
Shirley Jean, 451
Susan Annette (Hunt),
452
Susan Clare (Davis),
469
Wesley Raymond, 469
CLEWELL
--, 1259
Letitia (Kahle), 1259
CLEWS
--, 659
Peggy (Klinger), 659
CLIFT
Amy Marlene (Cozad),
149
Thomas Arthur, 149
CLIFTON
Alexa R, 664
CLINE
Almora, 116
Doris Anna (Stinson),
552
Elizabeth, 240
Ethel Pauline
(Akerman), 518
Everett, 126
George, 518
Jill Arlene, 552
John Douglas, 126
Jonne Elaine, 552
Judy Ann, 552
William Alexander,
552
Youra, 240
Zirelda Tamsel
(Weiser), 126
CLINGAN
Annie Louise, 303
CLINGER
--, 1015
Sarah, 1290
CLIPPINGER
Anna Elizabeth, 187
Beulah, 182
Beulah Crilly (Snyder),
187

C H, 156
Charles Hamsher, 187
CLOCK
Terri, 563
CLOGSTON
Edwin Clare, 148
June Ann (Spurgeon),
148
Mabel June (Spurgeon),
148
CLONINGER
Amy Lynn, 1127
Eugene Francis, 1127
Marilyn Lee (Poth),
1127
CLOORE
Helen C, 510
Mildred, 510
Mima Florence
(Umbaugh), 510
Robert, 510
Vivian, 510
**CLORA
(BAUGHMAN)**, 1493
CLOSMAN
Mary Madeline, 1219
CLOUD
Corey C, 563
Frank Wayland, 593
Letetia Mae (Banter),
563
Nora, 521
Paul Dale, 563
Rita Kay, 593
Thomas Jay, 593
Wetoka N (Hocker),
593
CLOUGH
Drusilla Joan, 286
Ethel Clair, 1190
CLOUSE
Fannie W, 1349
Maude, 1696
Penalope Kay Lennon,
536
CLOUSER
-- (--), 851
Caroline E, 813
Carolyn E, 851
Carolyn Ruth (Eppley),
886
Dora Elmina, 693
Marcella Jean, 886
Mary Elizabeth, 1863
Megan Louise, 886
Melinda Kay, 886
William H, 851
William Harold, 886
CLOW
Jason Perish, 1251
John Joseph III, 1251
John Joseph IV, 1251
Johsua Wayson, 1251
Justin Ryan, 1251
Sharon Lynn (Roberts),
1251
CLOWER
--, 504
A C, 1678
Craig, 1678
Mary (Smith), 504
Nancy Charlotte
(Wiser), 1678
CLUGSTON
--, 1671
Kay (Wiser), 1671
Ola, 1672
CLYBURN
Marcia Linda, 1221

CLYDE
Estella E, 1243
Samuel, 1571-1572
CLYMER
David, 205
Gwen N, 1352
Jap P Jr, 1352
Jay P, 1352
Jay P III, 1352
Jeanette (Arnold), 1352
Julia, 1352
Louise Patricia, 1352
Mary Elizabeth, 1352
Naomi (Arnold), 1352
Sallie Alice, 1352
Sherry Louise (Smith),
205
CLYNE
Sandra, 1432
CO
Geraldine (Huffman),
570
William, 570
COATES
Marcy Carol, 143
COATS
Charles, 556
Delia E, 556
Donna M, 556
Doris M, 556
Effie (Johnson), 556
Joan, 556
Joe, 556
COBAUGH
Emma Vaneta (Gohl),
1531
John J, 1531
Nancy Rae, 1531
Vaneta, 1883
Vaneta (--), 1518, 1522
COBB
David, 1328
Frances Winifred
(Yost), 1328
George Michael, 1328
Hugh Lee, 1419
Marilyn, 954
Melissa (Bliss), 1328
Robert Allen, 1328
Susan Florinda (Moltz),
1419
COBLE
Barbara, 1388
COBLENTZ
John, 1345
Katie (Weiser), 1345
COBURN
Willa Jeanne, 1565
William L, 1564
COCHENOUR
Doris (Reitz), 1532
Richard, 1532
COCHRAN
Alice Sophia, 504
Anna M (Kahl), 1194
Anthony Ryan, 1658
Blanche R, 530
Charles Thomas, 1658
Christine Elizabeth,
1658
Cynthia Anne, 1431
Dave, 1430
Ed, 1194
Faye Carol (Wiser),
1789
Frances Anita, 44
Garrett Austin, 1658
Gertrude M, 505
Howard J, 505

Hugh L, 44
Isaac W, 505
Leona May
(Lindawood), 1430
Marjorie, 505
Opal Myrtle (Willey),
44
Sarah Matilda (Stine),
505
Tamara Leigh, 1658
Teena Rae (Walls),
1658
Vernell L, 505
Virginia Ellen, 44
Willie Garland, 1789
COCKERELL
Jan Marie (Potter), 91
Todd, 91
COCKLIN
Beatrice Justine, 863
Bertha Margaret
(Metzger), 718
Daisy V (Shettel), 863
Henry M, 863
Henry M Jr, 863
Ivy Irene, 863
Louise, 863
Nellie (Johnston), 863
Percy David, 718
William H, 863
CODDINGTON
Lynn, 284
CODER
--, 509
-- (McConnel), 1270
Amasa, 1694
Bernice, 1272
Bernice Elizabeth,
1271
Bertrude Marie
(Duncan), 1271
Bessie, 1694
Bessie (Dinkley), 509
Betty Marie, 1271
Beverly Ann (McNeal),
1271
Chandra Elizabeth,
1271
Christopher McNeal,
1271
Claire, 1272
Clara A, 1270
Clifford Donahoo,
1272
Clifford Lee, 1271
Craig William, 1271
David, 1272
Dustin John, 1271
Effie, 1694
Elizabeth Ellen, 1272
Elma Jane (Donahoo),
1270
Elsie Lela, 1270
Emma, 1272
Fannie Francis, 1270
Hannah, 1271
Harold William, 1271
Harold William Jr,
1271
Helen (Moran), 1272
Helen (Wheeler), 1271
Henry Milton, 1270
Henry R, 1270
Jack, 1269, 1271
Jack B, 1272
Jackie (Conklin), 1271
Jacob J, 1270
Jane, 1694
Jeannette (Harker),

1271
John, 1693
Julia, 1694
Katie L, 1272
Kurt M, 1271
Kyle M, 1271
Leonard Cecil, 1271
Magdalena (Weiser),
1270
Marcell (Zumlauf),
1271
Martha (Weiser), 1270
Martha J, 1270
Mary B, 1270
Mary Catherine, 1694
Merry E, 1272
Myrtle, 1694
Nettie May, 1270
Pauline (Marson), 1272
Ray Franklin, 1272
Sadie G, 1272
Sarah Louise, 1271
Sheri (Bentley), 1272
Stella Mary, 1270
Sudie, 1694
Sue Ellen, 1271
Susan, 1270
Susannah (Kephart),
1693
Tad William, 1272
William A, 1694
William S, 1270
CODGILL
Margaret Ann, 1178
CODNER
Hazel, 1137
Hazel Kathleen, 1136
CODRICK
Joanne Irene, 1228
Kathryn Margaret
(Smith), 1228
William H, 1228
COE
Alverta Eunice, 482
James, 508
Rosetta (Rinkley), 508
Sarah Isabelle, 466
COFFIN
Barbarry E (Brouches),
596, 599
Lucille, 523
William E, 596, 599
COFFMAN
Donna F, 1790
Eric Richard, 1323
Kathleen Ann (Rabold),
1323
Kevin Michael, 1323
Laurie Ellen (Cordier),
1157
McKenna Renae, 1157
Phillip Eugene, 1323
Robert Charles III,
1157
COFMAN
Adda Rebecca
(Wagner), 1126
Chalmer Curtis, 1126
Edith Ardell (Zwayer),
1126
Glenn Courtright, 1126
Mary Alice (Fellers),
1126
Mary Judith, 1126
Ray, 1126
Ruby Belle (Miskell),
1126
William Ervin, 1126
William Robert, 1126

COGAN
Cora Cecilia (Ramsay)
    Taylor, 1549
John M, 1549
COGGINS
Charles Edward, 56
Virginia Lee (Maier),
    56
COHEN
Al, 1369
Kathryn Mae (Casner),
    1369
COHENHOUR
Mary Elizabeth, 839
COHICK
Kathryn, 1053
COIL
Bertha, 622
COLAVITO
Justin Andrew, 1551
Lisa Anne, 1551
Susan Marie (Piasecki),
    1551
William Thomas, 1551
COLBERT
Betty Jo (Schell), 1336
Theodore John, 1336
COLBURN
Claire Ruth, 90
COLBURN-COLLIER
Dylan Charles, 90
Ryan Matthew, 90
COLCLAZURE
Jacob, 1654
Mary (Tinkle), 1654
COLDIRON
Mary (Wiser), 1663
William T, 1663
COLDREN
Agnes, 1047
Agnes (Erhard), 1047
Elizabeth, 1047
George W, 1047
Harry W, 1047
Inadora, 1047
Irvin J, 1047
James E, 1047
James Russell, 1047
John I, 1047
Lillian (Rosenolt),
    1047
Mabel (Karstetter),
    1047
Marion, 1047
Mayme (Poethes), 1047
Rhoda (Swartz), 1047
Roy O, 1047
William, 1047
William O, 1047
COLDSNOW
Dana Dee, 203
Deborah Lynn, 203
James Wilbur, 203
Sharon Kay, 203
Wilma Jean (Ross),
    203
COLE
--, 32
Amanda Catherine, 711
Barbara, 93
Chelsea Jo, 1045
Chester R, 571
Christie (Seiple), 1045
Constance Sue Bunting,
    1073
Cummins Stouffer, 219
Daniel Blair, 1045
Daniel Jay, 571
Daniel Robert, 571

Debra Kay, 453
Doreen (Loeffler),
    1045
Doris Delight, 571
Edward Joseph, 711
Grace Alberta
    (Herring), 571
Herbert Jr, 1570
Herbert W, 1570
Hilda L, 389
Jane Ann, 572
Janet Sue (Gard), 571
Jason Robert, 1045
Jay C, 571
Jean Maryann
    (Johnston), 1570
Jeffery D, 572
Jessie Katherine, 219
Jo Dee (Conklin), 32
Jo Ellen, 571
John Dene, 571
Karen Sue, 1660
Kathryn A, 1570
Kay (Renn), 1045
Kymberley Ann, 1045
Laura Jean, 1570
Linda Louise (Bird),
    1045
Lisa Marie, 1570
Lona Sue (Hommel),
    711
Marian V (Vasquez),
    1570
Mary Lavisa (Stouffer),
    219
Michael Stevens, 1045
Michael Vincent, 1045
Michele Diane, 1175
Nancyann (Shipman),
    1045
Nathaniel, 1869
Pamela Kay (Watson),
    204
Patricia Ann, 1570
Rebecca Susan
    (Fulcher), 571
Robert King, 1045
Rodger D, 571
Rose, 822
Ruth Marie (Wiser),
    1869
Sarah Marie (Barnes),
    571
Sharon Elizabeth, 1347
Susan L, 1570
Taylor Lea, 711
Wendy Sue, 1045
William, 1045
William Cummins, 219
William Russell II,
    1045
William Russell Jr,
    1045
Willie Ray, 204
Zachary William, 1045
COLEMAN
Absalom, 427
Andrew Bryan, 712
Annie (--), 930
Cathy (Remphrey), 712
Charlotte Amelia
    (Weiser), 427
Daren Eugene, 712
Eleanor, 1848
Emma, 1099
Gale Edward, 712
Gladys May, 924
Grace Harriet
    (Koppenhaver), 682

Helen Elizabeth
    (Dissinger), 1034
Helen M (Wiser), 1872
Helen Marie, 224
Hubert W, 1034
Jane, 1582
Josephine, 428
Judith Ellen (White),
    516
Julia Ann, 1578
Katie Beth, 712
Kelly Wagner
    (Sunbury), 712
Laura Leigh, 55
Linda Marie, 1172
Linda Susan (Stovall),
    55
Maggie Bri, 712
Marian Clark, 55
Matthias Clinton, 682
Megan Trease, 1172
Mitchell Daren, 712
Nelson Douglas, 516
Nyle Edward, 712
Phyllis Lorraine
    (Hommel), 712
Robert Kenneth II, 55
Robert Willie, 55
Ruth Elizabeth Stark,
    1475
Ryan Eric, 712
Sarah, 283
Terri Jean (Wagner),
    712
William Franklin, 1872
William Stovall, 55
COLENDENCE
--, 1504
Rebecca (Rahm), 1504
COLFLESH
Dorothy Marie, 394
Emma Ellen, 394
COLGAN
Jack Eugene, 1692
Maxine, 1692
Orville John, 1692
Sonia (Shafto), 1692
Viola Amy (Kephart),
    1692
COLLETT
Elva (Showers), 1257
James O, 1257
COLLIER
Alice, 89
Alice Louise
    (Tschanen), 90
Aliza Marie, 90
Catherine Anne, 90
Charles Theodore, 90
Claire Ruth (Colburn),
    90
Darla, 669
Karlee Ann, 90
Kevin Charles, 90
Mabel, 148
Margaret Maria (Grall),
    90
Michael Alan, 90
Nancy, 369
Nathaniel, 1593
Susannah, 1592
Susannah Maria (Ogle),
    1593
COLLINGS
Carol Ann (Ross), 749
Emmie (Shoemaker),
    1471
Karl, 1471
Robert, 749

COLLINS
--, 813
Anna Eva (Weiser),
    813
Arlie Jean (Wiser),
    1820
Ashley Michelle, 637
Ashley Nicole, 501
Austin Alan, 1739
Beverly Darlene (Reed),
    135
Bonnie Rachelle, 637
Carolyn Lynn
    (Johnson), 637
Chad, 997
Cheryl Lynn (Weiker),
    501
Clara Iona (Hammond),
    969
Clara Victoria (Willey),
    49
Deborah Lynn
    (Stradofsky), 1297
Debra, 544
Dorothy, 943
E D, 637
Edith Danielle, 637
Elizabeth Ann, 90
Eva Womelsdorf
    (Weiser), 813
Harold B, 1422
Harry S, 49
Howard, 1820
James Peter, 90
Jerry Lavoy, 501
John Patrick, 135
Judy, 228
Julie Lorraine (Wright),
    1739
Kari (Shirck), 997
Kyle Sean, 1739
Lenora Winifred, 71
Lois, 595
Martha Frances
    (Tschanen), 90
Michael, 1297
Michael Scott, 637
Nancy Jane, 91
Ruth Lois (Leader),
    1422
Stacy, 1739
Walter Claude, 969
Whitney Lynne, 501
COLLINSON
Anna Josephine
    (Farmer), 43
Florence, 48
Joanna, 43
John Leonard, 43
Julia Margaret, 43
COLLORAN
Dorothy Louise, 1148
Dudley A, 1148
Evelyn Marie (Mathias),
    1147
Richard Roy, 1148
Virginia Marie, 1148
COLOMBO
Lorrain Jeanette
    (Menges), 915
Samuel, 915
COLON
Garlan Delite (Eberly),
    629
Lee, 629
Ziglia A, 162
COLVETTE
Bessie, 1809

COLVIN
Ethel, 1210
COLWELL
Cathryn Jane, 825
COLYER
Lawrence Albert, 700
Viola Jane (Renno),
    700
COMBES
Abbott Carson, 308
Alice Clark (Schwab),
    308
Andrea Wallbridge,
    308
COMBS
Deborah M (Herring),
    534
Gregory J, 534
Thelma Lorine, 1186
COMER
Andrew Isaac, 582
Buena, 1476
Gwendolyn Agatha
    (Bowsher), 582
Jackie, 476
Larry Andrew, 582
Lora Lee, 582
Nayna Ruth, 582
COMERFORD
Margaret Poole, 1521
COMETTE
A Georgianna (Wiser),
    1754
Erbett, 1754
COMMERER
Alma Leora, 854
COMO
Irene, 1079
COMPTON
Anne Merrill (Schwab),
    310
Elijah, 362
James Neville, 310
Sarah Jane (Powell),
    362
COMSTOCK
Frank, 1688
Helen Oakley (Evans),
    332
Jean Oakley, 332
Joleen (Wiser), 1775
Minnie E (Kephart),
    1688
Stephen, 332
Thomas Wade, 1775
William James, 332
CONANT
Roxy, 1582
CONAUT
Laura R (Yeager), 710
T O, 710
CONAWAY
--, 1699
Amanda Louise, 703
Darwin, 1699
Elizabeth, 1680
Irene (Shimmel), 1699
JoAnna, 1680
Joshua Robert, 703
Melissa Sue (Witmer),
    703
Raymond, 1699
Robert Howard, 703
Virginia, 1709
CONDIT
Mabel E, 331
CONDLEY
Ira Joe, 1485
Lisa Danielle, 1485

CONDLEY (continued)
Sharon Kay (Bremer), 1485
Stacy Joelle, 1485
CONDO
John, 1006
Kelli Jo, 1006
Michele Leigh, 1006
Terry (Fryer), 1006
CONFER
Abbie (Kahl), 1007
Adam Joseph, 1007
Alexis Nicole, 1091
Bernard Auman, 1090
Bessie (Fister), 242
Calvin Zwingli, 1007
Clara Ann, 1081
Clayton, 1007
Cole Jarrett, 1091
Dana Joel, 1091
David Franklin, 1090
Dorothy (Mango), 1005
Elizabeth, 1240
Emilie Dorothea, 242
Ernest, 1241
Faye Adelaide Mengel (Ritter), 242
Franklin Paul, 242
Hallie Rose (Baker), 1090
Harry, 1241
Harry Franklin, 1090
Helen Charlotte, 1091
Ima, 1241
Jacob, 1005
Joseph Samuel, 1090
Joy Lynn, 1075
Joyce Elaine, 1091
Laird Harold, 1092
Lulu, 1242
Marc Tate Hardy, 1005
Miriam Eulalia (Auman), 1090
Nickolas Hutson, 1091
Patricia Anne (Hutson), 1090
Rita Hanna (Hardy), 1005
Ruth Anne, 1091
Ruth Gladys, 242
Sarah Alice (Kahle), 1241
Sharilou, 1091
Shelby, 1241
Tanya (Dinges), 1091
Tessie Marie, 1371
Thomas, 1005
Thomas Blair Hardy, 1005
Thomas Fister, 242
Thomas Ritter, 242
Wellington Jacob, 242
William, 1007
CONFREY
Lyle, 1219
CONKLIN
Amy, 428
Barbara (Nelson), 428
Carla Mae, 428
Charles, 32
Clifford Harry, 428
Clytie (Morey), 428
Curtis Allen, 428
Darrel Edward, 428
Deborah (Williams), 428
Edwin Lavan, 428
Elsie Belle, 427

Esther Amelia (Merfert), 427
Floyd Arthur, 428
Frank, 1697
Frederick Luther, 428
Gerald Wayne, 428
Harry Edward, 428
Heidi, 428
Jackie, 1271
Jo Dee, 32
Joyce Ann, 32
Judith Mary Esther, 428
Karen (--), 428
Kenneth Leroy, 428
Leona (Busacker), 428
Mabel Geneva, 427
Marcia Laree, 428
Margaret L, 146
Margie (Harrington), 428
Mary Ann (Hummel), 1697
Minnie, 1697
Nancy Jay (Welser), 32
Robert Lee, 428
Royce Jay, 428
Sally Lynn (--), 428
Thelma (Signor), 428
Virgil Lavan, 427
Virginia (Gillette), 428
CONKLING
Florence, 276
Frank, 276
George, 276
Rebecca Weiser (Eikelberner), 276
Sylvester, 276
Theodore, 276
CONLEY
Ann (Keller), 506
Barbara Jane (Weber), 452
Clovis, 452
Clovis Blake, 452
Clovis Seth, 452
Connell B, 52
Donnell Lee, 52
Dustin Daniel Ross, 456
Helen Louise (Herring), 569
Jackie David, 569
Jacqueline Ann, 569
James, 506
Josephine Margaret Virginia (Schuh), 52
Karen, 1261
Kathryn Alberta (Clevenger), 452
Kathy Lynn, 452
Linda Marie (Rheinscheld), 456
Mary (Shettel), 874
Melvin, 874
Nick Edward Ross, 456
Pamela Sue, 569
Sara Jeanne, 52
Sherrie Lea, 452
Susan Marie, 874
Theda (Elbrador), 52
William Henry, 52
CONN
Carol Ann (Johnson), 149
Ella, 270
Frank Ralph, 149
Marge, 265

Phoebe Emma, 798
CONNELL
Mildred E, 1539
CONNELLY
Florence Rockwell, 332
CONNER
Ashley Lynn, 1306
Bertha Belle, 826
Brenda Kay (Gibbons), 276
Brian Aaron, 1306
Edith, 514
Heather Lynn, 1306
Nancy Lynn (Delameter), 1306
Patrick, 276
Roberrt Carl, 1306
Virgil Wiant, 1306
CONNOOLEY
Judy Nadine, 36
CONNOR
Alice (Anspach), 841
Charles, 841
Jacob Kenneth, 712
Kylie Renee, 712
Lillian, 841
Marion, 841
Penny Lou (Bickhart), 712
Ralph, 841
Robert, 841
Timothy John, 712
William J, 841
CONNORS
Claudia A (Wiser), 1838
James, 1838
Michaele Anne, 1555
CONRAD
-- (--), 777
Alice Pearl (Fahringer), 794
Ann (Koser), 795
Annette L, 354
Annie (Heimadinger), 1100
Audrey, 787
Barbara Lee, 795
Bonnie Louise, 891
Charles, 1100
Debbi Lynn, 1768
Debra J, 1718
Delilah, 887
Dessie Mae (Shugarts), 1718
Doris Helen (Eppley), 891
Dorothy Alice (Haas), 913
Earl, 1100
Edith I (Weiser), 1622
Edward James, 891
Edward W, 1622
Eleanor Mary, 1294
Elizabeth (Frey), 787
Estelle, 1294
Eva, 778
Franklin Pierce, 1026
Gail, 787
George, 1100
Glenn, 1100
Grant, 1100
Howard Leslie, 1100
Jacob, 777
James Hoover, 891
Jane Isabelle, 794
Jane Marie, 913
Jennie V (Weiser),

1864
Judith Ann, 913
Kate (Wiser), 1294
Keith, 787
Mary, 777, 1019
Mary Jane (Kehl), 1100
Mary Melissa (Savidge), 794
Mary T (Cooper), 1026
Michael Robert, 795
Morris, 1100
Occelia E (Wiser), 1294
Oliver Nelson, 794
Pamela, 409
Penny L, 1718
Rhysann J (Ledden), 787
Richard, 1718
Richard D, 1718
Robert, 787, 913
Robert Benson, 1294
Robert Earl, 913
Roger Alan, 913
Russell Kirby, 795
Russell Lee, 795
Russell S, 777
Russell Savidge, 794
Sandra, 787
Sarah, 1519
Scott Benson, 1294
Sharon Marie, 891
Thomas William, 913
Wayne Allen, 891
Webster, 1864
CONRATH
Jessie Marie, 686
CONROY
Molly, 1323
CONSIGLIO
Anne Crilly (Wall), 187
Robert Allan, 187
Robert Allan Jr, 187
CONSTABLE
Mickie Jo, 569
CONSTANTINE
Margery Baldwin (Schwab), 311
William, 311
CONTI
Irma Anita, 953
CONTRIS
Charles, 520
Mary Joanna (Ackerman), 520
CONVERSE
Clayton Wallace, 193
Darrell, 193
Judith (Wallace), 193
Justin Jacob, 193
COOK
--, 1804
Algie, 1801
Alvie, 788
Amber, 1376
Amy, 1376
Andrew E, 1836
Ann Louise, 1148
Anna, 1164
Anna Beulah (Reigle), 642
Anna Leora (Wiser), 1836
Anna Margaret, 1583
Arminta, 1238
Arnetta Grace, 840
Ashley, 1327

Barbara (Fossinger), 459
Barbara Kay (Ackerman), 519
Beatrice Elva, 640
Becky Jo, 1314
Betty Ann (Weiser), 1376
Betty Louise (Ungard), 642
Beverly, 232
Bradley C, 1376
Brenda Kay (Curtis), 1327
Brian, 1576
Brian J, 1376
Carl B, 1376
Carlie (Rowe), 667
Carlton, 1376
Carmen Jo, 385
Catharine Lavina, 639
Catherine, 1582
Ceylon A, 642
Charles, 442
Charles Edward, 1148
Charles Leslie, 1254
Charles William, 640
Christie Ann, 385
Clair Wilson, 1254
Clara Jane (Snyder), 641
Clariss, 1582
Clarissa, 1583
Daisey (Weaver), 641
David Arthur, 585
Debra (Campbell), 1376
Deric, 1327
Donald Lawrence, 1488
Dorothy (Paugh), 1148
Earl Palmer, 840
Earnest, 522
Edna Gertrude (Kahle), 1254
Edwin Eugene, 641
Eleanor, 641
Elizabeth, 1576, 1583
Ellen Jane, 1314
Elva Daisy, 1206
Ethel Estella, 779
Ethel Viola (Mahan), 1314
Eva Esther (Umholtz), 640
Faye Georgianna, 641
Frank, 1845
Galen John, 641
Geneva Pauline (Wagner), 1314
George, 641
George A, 1220
Gerald Clinton, 642
Gertrude Ellen (Strock), 1488
Gertrude Ethel (Alspaugh), 1148
Glenda Gene, 641
Glenn, 522
Glenn Eugene, 641
Hazel Blanche, 1254
Heather, 1327
Helen Kaye, 1158
Henry, 1148
Hulda Mae (Fry), 641
Jamie, 1376
Jannetta Jane (Riggs), 522
Jay (Steiner), 1376

COSGROVE (continued)
Viola (Coutts), 946
Viola Dean, 946
Willis J, 941
COSH
Florence (Davis), 1438
Jimmie, 1438
COST
Lauri, 1319
Laurie, 1325
COSTA
John Henry, 1191
Martha Baird (Riley), 1191
COSTANZO
Margaret Louise, 960
COSTELL
Shirley Rae, 1846
COSTELLO
Joy Lynn, 917
COSTON
Betty, 184
COTE
Yvette, 1121
COTNER
Docia Brady, 271
Eunice (Staley), 597
Thomas J, 597
COTTEN
Barbara Ann (Wiser), 1813
Keith Allen, 1813
COTTERALL
Catherine, 1541
Edith M (Kerstetter), 1541
Francis, 1541
Frank, 1541
George, 1541
COTTINGHAM
Frances Aline, 1348
John Virgil, 1348
John Wesley, 1348
Margaret Viola (Weiser), 1348
Mary Vesta, 1348
COTTLE
Amanda (Wiser), 1765
Marshall, 1765
COTTRELL
Carol Ann (Cummins), 1481
Robbie Dean, 1481
Ross Belmore, 1481
Tracy Lynn, 1481
COUCH
Alice Lynn, 1801
COUDING
Henrietta, 1486
COUDLE
Mary Louise, 1287
COUDRIET
John, 1682
Lyda May (Kephart), 1682
Mary J, 1705
Zella, 1705
COUKART
Cecile Leone (Rupert), 1304
Joseph Kenneth, 1304
Patricia, 1304
COULTER
Chloe (Wisor), 1707
David Eugene, 572
Kathryn Sue, 572
Laura Jean, 572
Melissa Marie, 572
Regina Sue (Herring),

572
William, 1707
COUNCIL
Clarence Chappell, 1180
Emma Donnelly Yopp (Musselman), 1180
COUNTRYMAN
--, 1586
Anna, 1572
Anna Rosina, 1571
Conrad, 1571
Maria, 1586
Mary, 1582
Rachel (Pickard), 1586
COUNTS
Clark, 822
Gloria (Womelsdorf), 822
Robert Clark, 822
Ronald Gene, 822
COUPE
Marjorie, 1546
COURSEN
Henrietta Meier (Oakley), 333
Henrietta Oakley, 333
Henry Dee, 333
William A, 333
William A Jr, 333
COURTNEY
Alda, 1680
Barbara Hiester (Mills), 282
Mark, 282
Phyllis Lee, 484
COURTRIGHT
Alan Maywood, 1121
Albert Maywood, 1121
Albert Maywood II, 1121
Alden Stanley, 1117
Alma Z (Watts), 1117
Amanda Almina, 1118
Ann, 1123
Blanche C, 1129
Brooks Hiram, 1122
Catherine Helena, 1121
Cathy, 1122
Clara Bertha, 1123
Clara Eve (Fellers), 1126
Claris Bill, 1122
Cleyta Coletta, 1121
Constance Marie, 1121
Dean Watts, 1118
Deborah Hunt (Sink), 1122
Diane Sue, 1118
Donna Lynn, 1118
Drusilla Florence, 1123, 1144
Edith Fellers, 1127
Edna, 1129
Effie Elizabeth, 1123
Eleanor Amourette, 1122
Elizabeth (Weiser), 1117
Elizabeth Vernon (Theis), 1123
Ellen Lucille (Reiss), 1121
Ernest Woods, 1123
Eura Maude, 1123
Evelyn Ruth, 1122
Fannie Ester, 1125
Florence Irene, 1122
George Bigelow, 1117,

1126
George Seymour, 1120
Grace Dell (Bashore), 1121
Grace Elizabeth, 1121
Harley M, 1129
Harlow Brice, 1124
Hazel Krik (Richards), 1123
Helen Bridget (Graham), 1121
Hiram Vinton, 1120
Ida E (Beer), 1120
infant daughter, 1117
infant son, 1117
Ivan Stanley, 1117
Jacob Felix, 1117, 1129
Jacob G, 1129
Jacob Grubbe, 1117
Jan, 1122
Jane (Wilcox), 1122
Joanne Eleanor, 1122
John Brooks, 1122
John Earl, 1122
John Ezra, 1117
John Graham, 1121
John Rodney, 1121
Josephine Virginia, 1124
Kathleen Graham, 1121
Leeta Lavalla (Dixon), 1121
Lorinda (Williamson), 1117
Lynn, 1123
Margaret Irene, 1117, 1126
Marie (Raymond), 1122
Martha Irene, 1120
Mary Elizabeth, 1117, 1129
Mary Viola (Whitzel), 1129
Minerva (Fellers), 1122
Minnie Elnora, 1126
Minnie Frences (Bunker), 1117
Myrta Elfleda, 1123
Nell, 1129
Nellie A, 1126
Patricia Ellen, 1121
Patricia J (Keithan), 1118
Raymond Douglas, 1121
Reva, 490
Robert Carl, 1122
Ruth Olive, 1125
Samuel Marion, 1117
Sarah Anise (Phelps), 1124
Sarah Samantha, 1146
Shirley Alma, 1124
Steven Brooks, 1122
Terry Robert, 1122
Theodore Eugene, 1117
Thomas Hamer, 1117, 1122
Thurman Thomas, 1123
Thurman Thomas Jr, 1123
Viola, 490
Violet Blanche (Biosvert), 1122

Yolande Irene, 1121
Yvette (Cote), 1121
COUSE
Alice (Brungart), 1090
Calvin J, 1090
COUSEY
Katie Estella, 1569
COUSINS
Ann Marie, 1001
Byrl Jr, 798
Fred, 1000
Mary Pauline (Buck), 798
Sarah (Bottorf), 1000
son, 1000
COUTNEY
Bonnie, 1794
COUTTS
Viola, 946
COVA
Joseph Eugene, 954
Louise Ilene (Ludwick), 954
Robert Steven, 954
COVER
Thelma, 47
COVERT
Rebecca, 1097
COWAN
--, 1670
Mary Emma, 813
Maud (Spohn), 833
Melissa (Tarxler), 1670
W S, 833
COWANS
Harriet May, 664
COWDER
Bernice, 1699
Sarah J, 1681
COWELL
Cindy Lee, 206
David E, 1634
David E Jr, 1634
Elsie Mary (Weiser), 1634
Kenneth Lee, 206
Linda Ann (Smith), 206
Michael Edward, 206
COWFER
Catherine Martha, 1695
COWLEY
Elizabeth Robin, 314
Gary David, 314
Irene Elizabeth (Schwab), 314
Katrina Anne, 314
COX
Ann, 633
Christie, 1793
Donna Jean, 1791
Elijah, 1788
Elizabeth, 1517
Elizabeth (Wiser), 1788
Elizabeth Ann, 1511
Emma Rebecca, 119-120, 134
Emma Rebecca Kromess, 119
Ethel Marie, 1791
George W, 1789
Harold Eugene, 239
Hazel, 302
Jennifer Lynn (Barkley), 1511
Katherin Ann (Herkness), 239
Katherine, 238

Kevin, 1511
Leota Madge, 1738
Margaret, 1787
Mary Ann (Spyker) Patton, 1449
Mary Belle (Wiser), 1789
Mary Lyman, 336
Nancy, 1438
Opal, 110
Pearl L (Wiser), 1793
Ronald William, 1449
Ruby, 110
Tami Lyn, 858
COXEY
Donna Faye (Fowkes), 1394
Emeline Wagner (Hess), 1394
Paul, 1394
Paul E Jr, 1394
Sally Ann, 1394
COY
Gloria (Johnson), 1673
COZAD
Amy Marlene, 149
Dorothy May (Spurgeon), 149
Elmer Bigelow, 149
Fred, 149
Fred Albert Jr, 149
COZARD
Dorothy May, 149
COZART
Hazel Verna, 365
CRABB
Esther, 1060
CRABTREE
Andrea Kay, 386
Jimmy Allen, 386
Judith Kay (Leibold), 386
CRAFT
Alma Sue, 53
Ethel Edna (Earnest) Hemkin, 1486
Ina Lou, 1486
James, 1494
Nancy Ann (Troutman), 1494
Ralph, 1486
CRAIG
Adelaide Susanna (Richards), 348
Betty May (Robinson), 1229
Dennis, 1802
Fanny, 513
Gregory, 537
Helen Lucille (Rusk), 1229
Jack DeForest, 1229
Jacques van der Beek, 348
John DeForest, 1229
Julie (Wiser), 1802
June Elizabeth, 990
Juntta (Akerman), 521
Kim Lane (Miller), 537
Lane Regan, 538
Lylan Lee Robert, 538
Marsha Ellen, 1229
Marshall, 1229
Mary Etta, 607
Mary Lou, 1229
Sarah, 595
Shannon Dale, 1229
Thomas Marshall, 1229
Virginia Marie, 1229

CRAIG (continued)
Walter William, 521
CRAIN
Charlotte, 218
Richard M, 1516
CRALEY
Reba M, 1416
CRALTY
Thelma, 49
CRAM
Alicia Kathleen, 211
Joshua Daniel, 211
Kathleen Ruth (Weiser), 211
Kevin Brett, 211
Megan Kristine, 211
Ryan Joseph, 211
Tyler Benjamin, 211
CRAMER
Cheri Lyn (Rodgers), 138
Debra Diane, 1673
Gary Lynn, 138
Gary Lynn II, 138
Sara Kaye, 138
Wesley Arden, 138
CRAMPTON
Gloria Jean (Brown), 621
Howard, 621
CRANDAL
Dorothie, 1076
CRANDALL
Carol, 1770
CRANDELL
Dennis Duane, 1202
Nickole Autumn, 1202
Tina Marie (Schwab), 1202
CRANE
Mary A, 148
CRANFORD
Mari Willodene, 298
CRANNERY
Iva, 518
CRAPPER
Amy, 1054
CRARY
Ella Cornelia, 335
CRATER
Carol, 1003
daughter, 1003
Dean, 1060
Dorothy (Bressler), 1003
George Leroy, 1003
James, 1003
Janet (Gramley), 1060
Margaret (Fiedler), 1003
Mindy Sue, 1060
Vicky Jo, 1060
CRAUN
Rebecca, 463
CRAVENS
Colleen, 493
Darlene, 493
Jerry, 493
Virginia Loraine, 493
CRAWFOLD
Mildred, 159
CRAWFORD
Ada Levina (Brown), 557
Anna Elizabeth (Smith), 121
Beth Arlene (Wiser), 1302
Catharine Elizabeth

(Weiser), 120
Cathy (Kennis), 1302
Charles Franklin, 121
Charlotte Hartman, 121
Diana, 424
Donna Jane (Dobbs), 1133
Dorothy Marie (Kahle), 1213
Frank, 1242
Fred, 781
Harry Arthur, 121
Hoyt Grady, 432
James, 1213
Jan, 1133
Jessie M (Parks), 121
John, 120
Josh, 1133
Lewanda Eileen (Woodward), 1242
Loren, 1200
Lori, 1133
Lucas Mark, 1302
Margaret, 1048, 1494
Mary, 835
Maynard, 121
Melvin John Boyd, 121
Minette Priscilla, 120
Minnie Mabel (Bettilyon), 781
Ola Tippie (Boyd), 121
Ruby Mildred (Hillman), 432
Samuel Weiser, 121
Sue Ann (Kahle), 1200
Thomas Robert, 1302
Thomas Slayton, 557
Tori Elizabeth, 1302
Warren Gibson, 432
CRAYDENWISER
[SEE
KREYDENWYS],
CREACY
Delia Lea, 528
CREE
Alexander, 1562
Betty Packard (Neild), 790
Elbert Chappee, 1562
Elizabeth Larue (Weiser), 1562
Jennie Weiser, 1562
John Franklin, 790
John Franklin Jr, 790
Mary Edna (Keefer), 790
Nancy Winsor, 790
Peter Noel, 790
William Franklin, 790
CREECY
Camela Fay (Moore), 1434
Ronald Ray, 1434
Ronald Scott, 1434
CREEKMORE
Barbara Charlene, 1869
CREESE
Malvene Adelle, 1288
CREIGHTON
Grace, 755
CREMEAN
David Neal, 593
Diane (Lora), 593
Earl Lavern, 593
Estella Pauline, 594
Gretchen Ruth (Guy), 593
Helen Loraine (Bushong), 593

James W, 593
Joseph Edward, 593
Lora Sue, 593
Marion Calvin, 593
Stephen Joseph, 593
Susan (Hocker), 593
Susan Jane, 593
William Earl, 594
CRESS
Anna Elizabeth, 472
Anne Augustus (Muhlenberg), 299
Henry, 1669
J P, 299
Susannah (Weiser), 1669
CRESSEY
Oakie, 1189
CRESSLEY
Beverly Jane (Kline), 1401
Francis E, 1401
CRESWELL
Wilma Leoda, 677
CREUTZER
Barbara, 1878
CREVELING
Marian Jean, 911
CREW
Sharon, 1098
CREWS
Angela Christine (Jessen), 1287
John Matthew, 1287
CRIBBS
Marion, 1224
CRICKTON
Helen, 1690
CRIDER
Cloyd, 945
Cloyd Jr, 945
Shirley (Ward), 945
Virginia, 945
CRILLY
Alice, 186
Daniel, 186
Edward, 186
Elizabeth (Snyder), 186
Florence, 187
Frank, 186
Fred, 186
Harriet (Snyder), 186
Helen, 187
CRIMM
Suzane, 1500
CRISP
Courtney Marie, 1162
Douglas, 1162
Rebecca Lynn (Duniven), 1162
CRISS
Patricia Lynn, 489
CRISSINGER
Aaron Paul, 687
Abigail Ann, 687
Joshua David, 687
Karen Ann (Sterrett), 686
Kenneth William, 686
Nathan William, 687
Rachel Ann, 687
CRISSWEL
Alice Jane, 145
CRIST
Ida M, 863
John W, 1425
Kathryn C, 265
Mary Hattie Eliza (Weiser), 1425

CRITCHFIELD
David Milton, 1519
Kiersti, 1519
Leslie (Foster), 1519
Mary Elizabeth (Eldredge), 1519
Pauline (Bowers), 1519
Thomas Eldredge, 1519
Vickie Lynn, 1519
Xenophon Kaylor, 1519
Xenophon Kaylor Jr, 1519
CRITES
Almeda Inez (Snyder), 1169
Barbara Jean, 860
Cecelia Ann, 860
Dana Lynn (Sanderson), 860
Diane Christine (Charnosky), 860
Dolores Diane, 1169
Frank Baylor, 1168
Frank Harold, 1169
Madelyn Wise, 1168
Myrtle Jane, 1169
Robert Eugene, 860
Robert Harry, 860
Sara Lily (Wise), 1168
Sharon Eileen, 1169
Viola Evelyn (Shettel), 859
Viola Shettle, 851
CROAK
Debra, 1042
CROCETTA
Beatrice A (Schempp), 1577
Lisa, 1577
Robert, 1577
CROCKER
Anna M (Renn), 1019
Barbara Sue, 749
Elizabeth Ann C, 1798
Eugene, 1019
Karen Jean, 1020
Patty Ann, 1840
CROCKETT
Euabelle, 531
CROCKMEN
Donna, 459
CRODER
Hallie (Batts), 1721
John, 1721
CROFT
Alta, 1439
Donna Jean, 530
Evelyn Lucile (Alexander), 530
George, 530
Lerry Lee, 530
Mary Ellen (Staner), 508
William Henry, 508
CROLL
-- (--), 759
Amy Michelle, 936
Anna Weiser, 1466
Barbara (Weiser), 1465
Betty Carolyn, 770
Betty Jane (Decker), 770
Carrie (Hoffman), 769
Christopher Lee, 936
Eleanor (Hardin), 918
Heath Wayne, 935
Horace Doudel, 1466

John, 759, 770
John Harold, 918
John Jr, 759, 770, 1884
John Peter, 918
John Shelby, 1466
Katharine, 918
Kathryn (Zeigler), 1466
Margaret Viola (Klaiss), 918
Mende Lou (Bingaman), 935
P C, ix, 813
Philip C, 19
Robert Doudel, 1466
Susan, 918
Wayne, 935
Wesley Scott, 936
CROMER
Ella, 186
CROMLEY
Cora, 995
Frances Rebecca (Kehl), 995
Lizzie, 995
Wesley, 995
CROMWELL
Nancy Susan, 1806
CRONE
Carrie, 1414
Hiram, 1414
Mary Catherine (Weiser), 1414
Mary Margaret, 1119
Mildred, 685, 789
CRONISE
Armand E, 370
Eva Marie (Steward), 370
CRONISTER
Betty, 868
Charles, 868
Charles Jr, 868
Gladys (Kline), 868
Robert, 868
CRONK
Sarah, 1406
CROOK
John, 14
John Jr, 13
CROOKS
Cheryl (Robinson), 141
Dennis, 141
Fred, 141
Grace Lucy (Evans), 141
Jolene, 141
Kacie, 141
Karl F, 141
Kathryn (Archibald), 141
Loverne (Delahunty), 141
Marilyn (Rose), 141
Richard, 141
Robert, 141
Roger, 141
Scott, 141
CROOKSHANK
Sue, 629
CROSBY
Chris (Buthmann), 473
Elizabeth, 1423
Lori Ann, 1170-1171
Nathan, 499
Robin, 473
Sharon (Heileman), 499

CROSBY (continued)
Sharon Kay (Karr), 473
Troy, 473
W R, 473
Wendy, 473
CROSLAND
Ann Louise (Lindner), 1113
Patrick, 1113
Sean Michael, 1113
CROSS
Bernadine Ann (Olson), 232
Brad Allen, 232
Donna Fay, 516
Gene, 232
Harold J, 516
Lester H, 516
Marcella M (Tennis), 516
Robert L, 516
CROSSEN
Ida, 73
CROSSLEY
Anna Mae, 680
Flora Mae (Koppenhaver), 680
Harriet Elizabeth, 680
John Matthias, 680
Marjorie Grace, 681
Rachel Alice, 680
CROSSLIN
A J, 1823
Jackson, 1796
Louisa C (Wiser), 1796
Matilda C (Wiser), 1823
CROTHERS
James Richard, 1329
Norma Jean (Yost), 1328
Rebecca Sue, 1328
Rhonda Ann, 1328
Robert, 1328
Stacey June (Bailey), 1329
CROTINGER
Edna, 515
CROUCH
Elsie Hazel, 1315
Heath Aaron, 539
Irene Elizabeth (Wiser), 1819
Jay, 811
Jill Dawn, 539
Joel Duane, 539
Lisa J, 272
Michael Duane, 539
Pamela Jeanne (Dismore), 811
Theresa Elaine (Fischer), 539
William Marvin Jr, 1819
CROUGH
Ronda Lyn (Bishop), 153
Timothy, 153
CROUIE
Felicia Liane, 649
Kenneth Paul, 649
Michael Paul, 649
Sherry Lee (Leeper), 649
CROUSE
Mary, 1083
Sarah, 1076

CROUSER
Hilary Ann, 1028
James Firm, 1028
Robert Glenwood, 1028
Robert James, 1028
Shirley (Dodge), 1028
Susan (Specht), 1028
CROUSHORN
Jan, 172
CROUTHARMEL
Carl Allen, 660
Darryl Lee, 660
Dennis Ray, 660
Karen Diane, 660
Larry Kurtis, 660
Melba Catharine (Klinger), 660
Raymond Curtis, 660
Terry Gene, 660
CROW
Andes Forrest, 796
Brittany Wade, 283
Douglas Laird, 283
Dwin Charles, 393
Emily Theresa, 283
Estella Catherine, 600
Gerda (McClintic), 1260
Harvey, 1260
Harvey Jr, 1260
Helen Chloe (Duffie), 796
infant daughter, 283
Jennifer Wallis, 283
Laura Bruce (Harden), 283
Lori Jean (Foster), 393
Maria, 1260
Nancy, 1539
Rufus M, 796
CROWE
Mildred Marian, 594
CROWELL
Rebecca Marie, 1802
CROWL
Elizabeth Jane, 856
Mildred Geraldine (Kochenour), 622
Walter Ivan, 622
CROWLEY
John William, 1558
Joseph Patrick, 1558
Mark Joseph, 1558
Patricia Joan (Kenedy), 1558
Peter Thomas, 1558
Rita Mary, 1558
Timothy Daniel, 1558
CROXTON
Rose Marie, 819
CROY
Ada Beatrice, 849
Adrienne Libby, 848
Alice (Bear), 848
Allen L, 848
Altha May, 848
Amanda Lehman (Aldrich), 848
Anna Elizabeth, 849
Caroline (Womelsdorf), 847
Catherine Maria, 848
Charles Theodore, 848
Christine Annette, 849
Clara, 849
Cora (Bear), 848
Daisy Rosella (Fryman), 848

Daniel Lee, 849
David, 847
Dorothy (Whitehead), 849
Elsie Elizabeth, 849
Emma, 849
Eva Edie (Ramsey), 848
Florence Viola, 848
Frederick Michael, 848
Gloria Kay, 849
Henry David, 848
Henry Dewey, 849
John Charles, 848
John E, 813, 828
John Edwin, 848
Judy Katherine, 849
Katherine Irene (Bell), 848
Linda Sue (Butts), 849
Lisa Ann (Bell), 848
Louise, 849
Mabel Louise Wurm (Lust), 848
Madeline Teresa, 848
Marianna Elizabeth (Freese), 848
Mary Ellen, 847
Mary Karolyn (Kazmaier), 848
Milton, 848
Milton Ambrose, 848
Noah William, 848
Rhoda, 849
Rosemary, 849
Susan (Bowser), 848
Sylvester Scott, 848
Theodore William, 848
Thomas Jefferson, 848
Vera Vesta, 848
CROYLE
Jacob Lee Alan, 1398
James Ross, 1397
Michael Bradley, 1397
Nancy Cheryl (Francis), 1397
Pamela Ann (Bradley), 1398
Richard Chester, 1397
Viola, 1222
CROZER
Edith (Rahm), 1505
Enoch W, 1505
Mary A Watson, 204
Willis H, 204
CROZIER
--, 976
Eugene, 826
Laura Ellen (Womelsdorf), 826
Mattie (Rubendell), 976
CRUICKSHANK
Robert, 1844
Ruth Elizabeth (Weiser), 1844
CRUISE
Jerry Lynne, 1777
Rhea Kathleen (Wiser) Purles, 1777
CRULL
Ruth Elizabeth, 68
CRUM
Earl, 932
Linda Diane (Wilde) Galeone Ulery, 932
Lois, 793
CRUMBIE
Clinton Bob, 1435
Melinda Carol

(Cannedy), 1435
CRUMBLEY
Karen, 1737
CRUMP
Edward, 948
Eva Mae, 948
Jessie (Weiser), 948
Myrtle, 948
Winifred D, 366
CRUMRINE
Anna, 1196
Anna Maria (Kovach), 1242
Elizabeth Joanne, 640
Laura Echo Elizabeth, 1242
Michael Tod, 1242
Susan Delina, 1735
CRUSE
Eva Adaline (Banter), 548
female, 548
George, 548
Lucinda Francis, 536
male, 548
Samuel, 548
CRUSEY
Esther, 889
Ira, 889
Marjorie (Renard), 889
CRUST
Audrey, 1374
CRYDENWISE [SEE ALSO WISER],
CULBERTON
Patricia, 613
CULBERTSON
Eleanor M, 1073
CULHANE
Edward, 853
Elizabeth Marie, 1554
Eugene K, 1544
Eugene Kenedy, 1554
Loretto, 1554
Marion (Walters), 853
Patricia, 853
Patrick, 853
Richard E, 857
Robert, 1554
Robert Patrick, 1554
Sharon Lynn (Stauffer), 857
CULLEN
Emily Schwab (Mix), 309
Frank, 309
CULLER
Patricia Lee, 1673
CULLERS
Charles C, 1220
Gertrude Katherine (Kahle), 1220
CULLISON
Barbara Alice (Leidy), 1127
Denise Leidy, 1127
Mark Robert, 1127
Robert Dale, 1127
Violette B, 920
CULP
Anna Elizabeth (Bollinger), 1032
Bert C, 807
Curtis, 63
Jackie, 63
Kelly, 63
LuAnn, 1032
Luther, 1032
Luther B Jr, 1032

Mary Jane, 1849
Peggy, 83
Sally (Hottenstein), 63
Sara Claudine (Fasold), 806
CULPEPER
John, 1785
CULVER
Mattie Ethel, 1810
CUMBERWORTH
Catherine E (Weiser), 1879
John K, 1879
CUMMINGHAM
Patricia, 31
CUMMINGS
Albert R, 65
Albert S, 65
Alison Joan (Mowbray), 1178
Anna (Leitzell), 1542
Charles Russell Jr, 1772
David Michael, 1477
Dean Brungart, 1077
Dwight Emrick, 769
Elizabeth Katherine, 65
Ella, 1037
Ethel Pearl, 556
Jennie, 699
Jessie, 1203
Joan, 32
John, 63
Joshua Lake, 1477
Justin Michael, 1477
Linda Kay (Clements), 1477
Lindsay Janiece, 1163
Louise (Richter), 65
Louise Geise (Emrick), 768
Marjorie (Hottenstein), 63
Mary Kathleen (Sheppard), 1163
Maxine (Wiser), 1772
Nellie May, 66
Oscar Larry, 769
Paul H, 1077
Robert Joseph, 1178
Samuel, 1542
Thelma Marion (Brungart), 1077
W Brent, 1163
William John, 65
CUMMINS
Alice Ruth, 1477
Anthony Earnest, 1480
Austin, 1476
Brett William, 1481
Brian Eric, 1481
Buena (Comer), 1476
Carol Ann, 1481
Carrie Kay, 1477
Chad, 195
Christine (Wallace), 195
Clinton Paul, 1480
Comfort William, 1481
Doris (Flynn), 1480
Doris Mae (Tolen), 1481
Dorothy Ilene, 1476
Fanny Dorothy, 1476
Florence, 1477
Francis (Osborn), 1480
Gary Dean, 1481
Geraldine Fay, 1480
Hazel Ruth, 1478

DANNER (continued)
Erin McKenzie, 884
Frank W, 1638
James, 884
LeRoy, 1643
Lydia L (Hamsher),
1643
Mariam Marie, 678
Mary, 864
Rodney James, 800
Sharon (Eppley), 884
Shawn Patrick, 884
Viola, 864
Wanda Ann (Simmons),
800
DANYSCH
Catherine Frances, 191
DARBIE
Benjamin, 1546
Benjamin F, 1545
Martha Elizabeth
(Quinlan), 1545
DARBY
Alice J, 389
Bertha Edith (Slack),
389
Charles Edwin, 389
Charles W, 389
Mary Lou, 390
Paul W, 390
Sandra Lavay, 1306
DARLING
Natalie Lea, 1538
Robert G, 1538
Shari Lyn
(Underkoffler), 1538
DARNELL
Dixon L, 1798
Eva Ann (Wright),
1685
Howard Otis, 1685
Sarah Jane, 1798
DARON
Mary, 1413
DARONE
Donna F (Anspach),
846
Robert, 846
DARR
Darlene (Barnheiser),
504
John, 504
DARRAH
Anna Fern, 718
Hazel Carrie (Frymire),
718
LeRoy, 718
Sarah Grace, 718
DARRINGER
Hazel, 479
DARROW
Cecil, 978
Sharon, 739
DARST
Aline, 1648
Cynthia Elizabeth Ann,
1648
Elvira Ann (Wysor),
1648
Grace E, 819
Harry Vern, 819
infant, 1648
James Henry, 1648
John Benjamin, 1648
John Chandler, 1648
Margaret Wesley
(Trolinger), 1648
Mary Euphemia (Yost),
1648

Molly Elizabeth
(Sprinkle), 819
Nancy Mary, 1648
DARY
Dianne, 993
DASH
Barbara, 507
DATZ
Andrew, 1623
Charlotte Wilhelmina
(Schenke), 1623
DAUB
Amanda, 1880
DAUBERMAN
Edgar, 655
Janet Lorene (Neiman),
655
DAUGHENBAUGH
Luella, 1482
DAUGHERTY
Brenda J, 1278
Donna Marie (Berty),
1298
Edith Arnetta (Wynn),
1056
Elizabeth Rey, 1056
Julie Ann, 1298
Linda Carol, 480
Mary, 533
Mary Katerine, 1056
Michelle, 413
Michelle (Klutz), 1298
Richard A, 1298
Robert Douglas, 1298
Steven Craig, 1298
Virginia Lee, 1056
William Arthur, 1056
DAUGHTERS
Alice Virginia, 1334
Etta Viola (Gebhart),
1333
Fred, 1333
Garnet Louise, 1334
Gary William, 1334
Lois marie (Baldy),
1334
Lorraine Winifred,
1334
Lowell Gebhart, 1333
Scott Douglas, 1334
Thelma Pauline, 1333
Wynne Lamar, 1334
DAUGHTERY
Barbara Jean (Karr),
473
Marcella, 473
Paul, 473
DAUGSTROP
Laura Elizabeth
(Tilghman), 1378
Michael Hielmot, 1378
DAULTON-STIDHAM
Mildred, 584
DAVENPORT
Alice Francis (Wiser),
1819
Alma Ruth (Wiser),
1822
Cletus D, 93
Cynthia Lynn, 93
Delter Ray, 1822
Diana Jean (Kahl),
1007
Jennifer Lee, 93
Jill Melison, 93
Margaret (Grimes), 91
Margaret Jane (Grimes),
93
Ruth, 1794

Theresa Marie, 93
Timothy Allen, 93
Wesley Charles, 93
Westbrook, 1007
William Fermon, 1819
DAVEY
George, 643
Gladys Faye
(Messersmith), 643
Janet Faye, 643
DAVID
John Alan, 1288
June (Day), 1206
Kelly Lynn (Seigworth),
1288
DAVIDHEISER
Anna Maria, 1753
Daniel Lee, 1344
Martha Jane (Stewart),
1344
Melissa Lynne, 1344
DAVIDSON
-- (Dick), 1880
Adam Lewars, 753
Alice Elveira (Barber),
1185
Alvin B, 1880
Bruce, 758
Calvan, 1549
Carol Ann, 943
Charles C, 1506
Darlene Emma (Kohl),
758
Grace Louise, 753
Lois Virginia (Ramsay)
Lewis, 1549
Louisa (Rahm), 1506
Louise (Kerstetter),
1540
Marion Eugene, 1185
Nanette Louise
(Wright), 753
Norma Rosamond
(Calhoun), 832
Ray, 1506
Richard, 1540
Robert A, 832
DAVIES
Elizabeth, 989
Jane Ann, 448
DAVIS
--, 207, 984, 1211,
1441, 1662, 1724
Adda (--), 1206
Agnes Selin, 1452
Alice Marie, 424
Almeda Jane, 1211
Almeda Rose (Gardner),
1211-1212
Alta Lois (Martin),
1692
Andrew, 600
Angela Lea, 574
Anita M (Heres), 1677
Ann (Wieser), 1724
Arelo, 1206
Arlie, 822
Arthur Clinton, 1469
Benjamin Aaron, 1441
Bertha Maye, 585
Beth Jean (Herring),
574
Betty, 375
Betty Ann (Ahrens),
1692
Beverly Fay (Hamilton),
973
Blanche, 1206
Brent Lee, 574

Burt, 1214
Calvin Russell, 1218
Calvin Russell III,
1218
Calvin Russell Jr, 1218
Carla Jean, 207
Carol Gertrude (Fuller),
1218
Carolyn Alice (Kahle),
1231
Carrie Ethel, 1677
Casandra, 428
Casey Anne, 1219
Catharine, 1712
Catherine (Corey),
1438
Cathy (--), 1218
Cathy Joe, 1479
Charles, 1478-1479
Charles A, 773
Chester, 984
Clair, 984, 1206
Clara Belle (Wiser),
1190
Claude, 1206
Clayton, 1438
Clyde Jay, 781
Cynthia Ann
(Campbell), 1441
Cynthia Marie, 1219
Dale (Striegel), 1438
Daniel Gene, 428
Daren, 427
David, 1159
Dawn, 692, 1212
Dean, 984
Dean Presnell, 1692
Delores Dianne
(Cornwell), 1212
Donald, 1360
Donald George, 973
Donna Lee, 671
Doris, 984
Dorothy, 558
Dorris Ann, 45
Doyle, 1206
Drew Stephen, 119
Drucilla Pauline
(Mahan) Alsop, 1314
Edith Louise, 342
Edmund James, 671
Edward S, 1437
Elizabeth (Parks), 1704
Ellen (--), 1206
Elmer E Ellsworth,
1469
Elsie Belle (Conklin),
427
Emma m (Johnson),
1677
Enia Mae (McCabe),
1438
Ephraim, 1712
Esther Marie, 1212
Ethan Burks, 119
Eva (Wiser), 1767
Eva M, 1677
Evelyn (Peckhart),
1677
Everett, 1438
Florence, 1438
Floyd Eugene, 1677
Forest Lylian, 1435
Forrest George, 1692
Frances Margaurite
(Romberger), 671
Frank M, 1206
Freida L, 600
G Burton, 1710

Garnett, 1206
Gary Lynn, 207
George, 1677
George L, 1677
Gertrude Amelia
(Kahle), 1218
Gloria (Womelsdorf),
822
Gloria Deneen (Maher),
1212
Gloria Jean (Heideman),
207
Grace, 1469
Grace (Weiser), 1469
Grayson Edward, 469
Haddie, 1434
Hannah (Wisor), 1710
Hannah Morgan
(Armons), 1469
Hannah Pugh, 1505
Harley Almon, 1677
Harry Elmer, 1677
Helen, 1079
Homer Norton, 1441
Howard, 1206
Ina, 1166
Irene Lillian (Alleman),
773
Isaac, 1575
J C, 850
James, 1469, 1712
James Allen, 671
James Gordon, 1441
James Gordon Jr, 1441
James Michael, 1441
Jane, 739, 1724
Jane Ann, 1867
Jasper, 1677
Jean (Ingwerson), 427
Jennifer Christine, 207
Jesse (Grove), 1206
Jessica, 1212
Jessica Josephine
(Jones), 469
Jessie, 765
Joann, 1441
Joann (Davis), 1441
Joanna Gay, 1441
John, 1712
John B, 1704
John Edward, 1438
John L, 1206
John Vinton, 1219
Juen (Schumacher),
1219
Justine D (Kahle), 1214
Karen Irma, 972
Karen Mae (Kiger),
1159
Katherine A, 1206
Kathleen (Haught),
1478
Kathleen Ann
(Krigbaum), 119
Kathleen Susan (Webb),
781
Katie (Wisor), 1712
Kelly Faye, 1218
Kenneth, 1438
Kerry (Krummell),
1218
Kerry Owen, 1212
Lacey Jean, 1212
Larry Alan, 972
Laura (Womelsdorf),
850
Laura C, 76
Laura Denise, 973
Lela Pearl (Martin),

DAVIS (continued)
Lela Pearl (Martin)
(continued)
1206
Lillian C (Stinson),
1437
Lillian Ruth (Herring),
537
Linda Faye (Glenn),
1212
Linda Maureen
(Zolinsky), 1441
Linda Sue, 1212
Linda Susan, 1219
Lois, 984
Lois (Camblin), 548
Lois Esther, 1212
Loreta (Dill), 427
Lucille, 984
Manford James, 1212
Manford James Jr,
1211-1212
Margaret Ann
(Wagner), 1398
Marian (Taylor), 1692
Marion, 890, 1438
Mark Wesley, 1212
Martha (Du Mars),
1438
Mary (Stahl), 600
Mary Anne, 1219
Mary Elizabeth
(Eldredge), 1519
Mary Lois (Paschal),
1360
Matthew Dale, 428
Michael Edmund, 671
Michael Eugene, 973
Milton Farrel, 1692
Monroe York, 1212
Myra Colleen Lundy,
477
Myrtle M (Wysor),
1662
Nancy (Johnson), 1677
Nell, 1662
Oliver, 1469
Oliver Clinton, 1469
Ott Howard, 1231
Patricia Lynn (Swart),
973
Paul Nelson, 1767
Pauline (Rich), 1212
Pearl, 1206
Pearl (Clemens), 984
Phil, 548
Priscilla Pixton
(Chisholm), 301
Raymond Eugene II,
469
Raymond Michael, 469
Rebecca, 1575
Richard Kahle, 1219
Richard N, 301
Richard Ott, 1231
Rick Allen, 574
Robert Edward, 972
Robert Elton, 972
Robert Eugene, 972
Rock Even, 1212
Ronald Elton, 973
Ross, 1539
Rowena B (List), 1469
Russell Stephen, 119
Ruth (Schnabel), 1677
Ruth Estella
(Alexander), 972
Ruth M (Martin), 1211
Rylla Faye (Lowery),

973
Salome (Graffius),
1441
Samuel Losos, 1519
Sarah, 1212, 1438
Sarah M (Seltzer),
1539
Sarah Margaret
(Spyker), 1441
Sarha Melina, 1441
Shawne Dawn, 973
Sials McClellan, 1190
Susan Clare, 469
Susan Elizabeth
(Earnest), 1486
Susanne, 428
Sydney Leigh, 119
Teri Noel, 781
Thomas, 1398
Thomas Allan, 973
Timothy Wade, 973
Tommy D, 207
Tonya Renee, 207
Tyler Michael, 469
Velma, 1438
Vernie, 600
Vida May (Kephart),
1692
Viola Elizabeth, 685
Violet Jeanene (Knapp),
972
Virgil Clare, 427
Virginia Ann, 469
Virginia Mae, 972
Wallace, 1438
Walter, 537
Walter Y, 1211
Warren, 1486
Warren Gene, 427
Wesley Robert, 1212
Wilfred Clare, 427
William Bradford,
1314
William Chester, 973
Willis, 1710
Wilma Ann (Sherrill),
469
DAVISON
Dorothea Richards, 350
Dorothea Young
(Richards), 350
Evelyn P, 1258
John Richards, 350
Joseph Homer, 350
Kenneth, 178
Lois Jean (Woolridge),
178
DAWALD
Benjamin Franklin, 511
Hannah Margaret, 511
Minnie Alberta, 511
Samuel, 511
Sarah Ann (Zartman),
511
Sarah Viola, 511
DAWE
Fred Cecil, 1058
Fred Cecil Jr, 1058
Kitty Lou, 1058
Violet May (Gutelius),
1058
DAWKINS
Janet, 439
DAWS
-- (--), 1110
Addie, 1109
Alfred, 1109
Alice, 1110
Charles, 1110

Fannie (Kiplinger),
1109
Frank, 1110
Freda, 1110
Haring, 1110
Harley, 1110
Helen, 1110
Hubert, 1110
Lester, 1110
Lily, 1110
Nettie, 1109
Rolie, 1110
Sidney, 1110
Skyle, 1110
DAWSON
Ann Whiteman, 287
Betty, 1494
Bruce Harold, 1340
Byron, 1339
C Walter, 1466
Catherine Marie, 1340
Debra (Chupang), 1172
Donald Meecham Jr,
1580
Donald William, 1172
Edith May (Rabold),
1339
Edna May (Miller),
1340
Elaine Patricia
(Broscious), 737
Elizabeth (Patterson),
1466
Ember Dawn, 737
Gladys Harriet (King),
1339
Harold William, 1339
James William, 1339
Jennifer Ann, 1172
Joan Ellen (Birsic),
1172
Karen Margaret, 1172
Kelly Ann, 1173
Kevin William, 1173
Marie Iola, 1172
Marie Viola (Ritter),
1172
Marily Susan (Pickard),
1580
Marilyn, 177
Phyllis Ethel
(Kaufman), 1172
Robert Nelson, 1340
Robert Nelson Jr, 1340
Santord Kent, 1172
Thomas King, 1340
Tom, 737
Tristan Eric, 737
William David, 1172
DAY
--, 473
-- (--), 136
Anna Gail (Ward), 147
Barbara Joan, 524
Betty Joe, 524
Carol (Milner), 524
Charlotte Ann
(Schempp), 1576
Elbert, 524
Elizabeth Ann
(Piasecki) Brown, 1551
Ella Mary, 302
Ellery, 981
George W, 136, 147
Gwendolyn Louise,
147
Jerry Joe, 524
Joann (Rosenberg),
1576

John Arthur, 1551
June, 1206
Kelly Mack, 524
Laura Ellen (Wolfe),
981
Loanda Octavia, 1844
Lois Margaret
(Clampitt), 524
Marilyn (Schneider),
524
Melissa Christine, 1576
Patricia (Karr), 473
Robert Steven, 1576
Steven James, 1576
William Homer, 1576
DAYTON
Alfred Moroni, 1778
Chloey (Wiser) Creger
Esterholdt, 1778
DE BARTI
Esther (Truby), 1223
Marc J, 1223
DE BELLIS
Dustin George, 1174
Eric Michael, 1174
George, 1174
Jodi Lee (Melville),
1174
DE BOIS
Felicia Ann, 1738
James Anthony, 1738
Katherine Mary
(Wieser), 1738
Tricia Lee, 1738
DE CARAEGNA
Leslie Boocock, 829
DE GARMO
Louise, 1575
DE GRASSE
Evelyn, 796
DE HAAN
Anke Hilde, 320
Anna-Lynn, 321
Brigitte Hilde (Seitz),
320
Christian Hinrich
Homfeld, 321
Christina (Falkenberg),
320
Christina (Ruhe), 320
Derk Heinrich
Johannes, 320
Derk Lothar Jan Coobs,
320
Doris (Ruhmann), 321
Eduard Jacobus, 320
Fokko Walter, 320
Folma Marianne
Albertine, 321
Gerd Otto Klaus, 320
Gesa Marike Folma,
321
Griet Marianne Hedwig,
320
Hildegard Clementine
(Willich), 320
Hildegard Marianne,
320
Immo Ernst Heinrich,
320
Jan Albert Homfeld,
321
Jürgen Werner, 320
Karin Maria (Fabricius),
320
Marlin Katharina, 320
Rielke Lisbeth Paula,
321
Wilm Derk, 320

DE HAAS
Charles, 1103
Donna (Yanarella),
1103
Julia Jesse (Stover),
1103
Keith Allen, 1104
Mary Louise
(McKissick), 1104
Mildred (Leathers),
1103
Patrick, 1104
Richard, 1104
Rochelle, 1104
William Charles, 1104
DE JONG
Jason, 1021
Kimberly Ann, 1021
Shelby Mae (Spatzer),
1021
Thomas, 1021
DE LA TORRE
Anna Isabel, 404
Benjamin Oscar, 404
Joel David, 404
DE LEON
David Michael, 74
Keith Manuel, 74
Lisa Ellen (Rudnicki),
74
DE NOVELLIS
Kimberly Kahle, 1252
Richard, 1252
DE PASQUALE
Aaron Michael, 1333
Carol Elaine (Fritz),
1333
Christopher Joseph,
1333
Danielk Lewis, 1333
Deborah Sue (Thiele),
1333
Joseph Antonio, 1333
Kathlene (Grier), 1333
Lawrence Paul, 1333
Lawrence Paul Jr, 1333
Nicholas, 1333
Patricia (Chandler),
1333
Paul Lawrence, 1333
Ronald Lewis, 1333
DE PETRIO
Cathy, 1201
DE SOUSA
Jack De, 1093
Susan Kay (Bierly),
1093
DEAHL
Evelynne Maurine
(Wiser), 1185
George William, 1185
DEAKIN
Ann Amelia (Bauder),
367
W Albert, 367
DEAL
Agnes Antoinette
(Robinson), 121
Charles Roy, 1819
Lucy Jane (Wiser),
1819
Phillis, 1096
Walter H, 121
DEAM
Lori Ann, 1325
DEAMER
Catherine, 69
DEAN
Clovia Faye, 584

DEAN (continued)
Faye Pauline (Hocker), 584
Helen Muhlenberg (Bulkley), 334
Henry Emerson, 334
J J, 134
Lonnie Avery, 584
Lonnie Avery Jr, 584
Mina Geneva (Young), 134
Patricia Mae (Turner), 584
Scott Avery, 584
Stanley Ray, 584
Steven Roy, 584
Stuart Alan, 585
DEAR
Alice Frances, 459
DEARDUFF
Anna Louise (Bole), 527
Melba Joan, 527
Willard, 527
DEARE
John, 15, 1587
DEARING
Audrey (Kephart), 1689
Ralph, 1689
DEAROLPH
Sarah Agnes, 1247
DEATON
Brianna, 1737
Chris, 1737
Connie Louise, 434
Elana, 1737
Johanna, 1737
Verna Dene (Smith), 434
Waymen Wallace, 434
DEAZLEY
Cinderella Marie, 1600
DEBACKER
Amy, 1546
John B, 1546
Mary Joan, 1546
Nancy, 1546
Nancy Glenn (Fitzgerald), 1546
Raymond, 1546
DEBAILLJE
Crystal Mae, 568
DEBARDELEBEN
Margaret Nelson, 1067
DEBBLE
Carol Jean (Meeker), 393
Charles Gordon, 393
Darrell Brent, 393
Delia Gaye, 393
Gary Lawrence Regan, 393
Gordon Blaire, 393
DEBIASE
Clara Lucile (Kahl), 1195
John, 1195
DEBOLT
Alex, 1497
Anne Elizabeth, 1497
April (Stencer), 1497
Bruce Rogers, 1497
Eleanor (Rogers), 1497
John Robert, 1497
Margaret West, 1497
Nicola, 1497
Patricia (Simon), 1497
Warren, 1497

DECHART
Mary, 1194
DECK
Amanda (Etschberger), 1519
Donald, 1211
Mary, 1668
Rose Ann Almeda (Martin), 1211
William, 1519
DECKER
Betty Jane, 770
Bruce R, 747
Clara Belle (Johnson), 1677
Clifford, 1244
Dessie (Irwin), 1244
Hans Zachary, 747
Jennie K, 1374
Kristoff Jan-Gabriel, 747
LaJuana Cheryl (Klinger), 747
Ralph, 1677
Sashana, 747
Sonja Noelle, 747
DECLOEDT
Eleanor June (Stanley), 666
Ferdinance Clarence, 666
Fred Robert, 666
Stanley Philip, 666
DEDAMIO
Betty, 1341
DEDERER
Ann France, 1135
DEEL
June Elklen (Clevenger), 452
Nathan Roy, 452
Timothy Allen, 452
DEEMER
Dallas Earl, 1256
John, 245
Robert Lee, 1256
Ruth Anne (Kahle), 1256
Sarah Rebecca (Fasig), 245
DEFAZIO
Louise Marie, 379
DEFFEBACH
Edward, 1539
Jesse Ross, 1539
Marie Agnes (Myers), 1539
Mildred E (Connell), 1539
Nancy (Crow), 1539
Richard E, 1539
DEFFINBAUGH
Judith Ann, 591
Madona May (Rickey), 591
Robert, 591
DEFIBAUGH
Luch, 1471
DEFOOR
Alice Louraine (Smith), 433
Dorothy Ann, 433
Janice Lavane, 433
Jeanie Lorraine, 433
Marshall, 433
Mary Louise, 433
Vera Lee, 433
DEFOREST
James E, 1213

Richard, 1213
Rosanna F (Kahle), 1213
Rosanna F Kehl, 1198
William Andrew, 1213
William L, 1213
DEFRAIN
Ida, 784
DEFREES
Harriet E, 330
DEGAN
Grances, 1188
DEGARMO
Iris, 1093
DEGENKALB
George Robert, 1298
Margaret Irene (Wiser), 1298
DEGENKOLB
Ruth Irene, 1298
DEGEORGE
Frances Lois (Wiser), 1799
Tony, 1799
DEGLER
--, 1621
Florence, 1621
Valley, 1621
DEGNER
Stephanie Suzanne, 489
DEGRAFF
John, 1683
Margaret Ellen (Milliken), 1683
DEGREEN
Linda R, 912
Mary Louise, 912
Mary M (West), 912
Merrill, 912
Merrill Jr, 912
Nancy M, 912
Shirley E, 912
DEHART
Ethel Louise (Urschel), 1313
Theodore Roosevelt, 1313
DEHAVEN
Anna Fritch (Hamsher), 1742
Cynthia, 1742
Jack, 1742
Lillian, 794
Suzanne L, 1742
DEIBERT
Ruth, 1340
DEIBLER
Elizabeth, 758-759, 774
Mary, 672
Rene, 1527
Shirley Mae, 923
Susie, 978
DEILEMAN
Ann Elizabeth (Wagner), 415
Michael, 415
DEILY
Florence M, 1758
Verda Mae, 1281
DEININGER
Ehrgott Jonathan, 341
Emma Muhlenberg, 341
Mary Elizabeth Hiester (Muhlenberg), 341
DEISHER
Elisabeth, 1754

DEITCH
Henry, 1413
Mary (Weiser), 1413
DEITZ
Arthur John, 1305
Charlotte Susan (Bish), 1306
Daniel Ray, 1306
Gloria Jean (Wiser), 1305
Jeffrey Allen, 1306
Kathleen Diana (McCoy), 1306
Shawn Jeffrey, 1306
Terri Jean, 1306
DEIVERT
Shirley, 748
DEJESUS
Godofredo, 1450
Kevin Anthony, 1450
Naomi Ruth (Dunlap), 1450
DEL COUR
Virginia Cochran, 1884
DEL SECCO
Claudia, 763
DELAHUNTY
Loverne, 141
DELAMETER
Nancy Lynn, 1306
DELANCEY
Barbara Lee (Lange), 1169
Claire Elizabeth Lang, 1169
DELANCEY
Ethel Pearl, 714
DELANCEY
Jane Ann, 1169
John Oliver, 1169
John Oliver Lang, 1169
Julie Anne, 1169
Lang Carl, 1169
Mary Anna (Wacker), 1169
Merton Miles, 1169
Oliver Samuel, 1169
Oliver Samuel Jr, 1169
Rachel Leah (Wise), 1169
Virginia Claire (Skerry), 1169
DELANEY
Janet Sterling, 291
DELANGE
Dale E, 667
Kathrine, 667
Sally Ann (Parent), 667
DELANO
Jennifer Lynn, 775
Karen Marie (Wasson), 775
Salvatore, 775
Stephanie Ann, 775
DELAPP
Bertha Olive (Heister), 1153
Clyde Bert, 1153
DELBAUGH
Adam, 742
Carol Lyn, 742
Chris Allen, 742
Cory, 742
Debbie (Parker), 742
Debra Ann, 741
Dorothy (Atkinson), 741
Douglas Greg, 742
Edwin A Jr, 742

Edwin A Sr, 741
Ella Mae, 742
Floyd F, 741
Hannah Boyer (Neidig), 742
Harry Leroy, 742
Helen (Boyer), 741
Kelly, 742
Linda Kay, 742
Mary C (Shipe), 742
Mertie Selow (Neidig), 741
Nicole (Schrenk), 742
Norma Eileen, 742
Paul Harry, 742
Robert Leroy, 742
Susan Lee, 742
William Fenmore, 741
William Scott, 742
DELBOSCO
Rosa Mitchel Martinez, 931
DELCAMP
Carol Ann, 250
George, 250
Mary Violet (Borrell), 250
DELCOUR
Howard John, 44
Julia Ann Sloane, 44
Virginia Ellen (Cochran), 44
DELGADO
Daniel Alfred, 1772
Susan Rae (Wiser), 1772
DELGRASSO
Elsie Emma (Kahle), 1231
George Mark, 1231
DELIUS
Helene August, 325
Käthe Henrietta Flora, 326
DELL
Raymond, 681
Sadie Elizabeth (Koppenhaver), 681
DELLAFARE
John, 1494
Leta Mae (Troutman) McKinley Zook, 1494
DELLAR
Elaine Rae, 1333
DELLER
Debra Frances, 1170
DELOJE
Adam, 1491
Andrew, 1491
Daniel, 1491
Margaret Elizabeth (Wilson), 1491
DELONG
Ana Magdalena (Weiser), 1405
Anna Mae (Miller), 1406
Anna Magdalena (Weiser), 15
Arie, 1405
Benjamin, 1405
Brenda Joyce (Miller), 623
Catherina (Dymant), 1405
Catherine, 1406
Catherine (--), 1405
Catherine (Freeling), 1406

DELONG (continued)
Christina Magdalena,
1405
Conrad, 1406
David Edward, 623
Deborah Lea, 623
Elizabeth (--), 1405
DELONG
Emitt, 598
Ethelind Joy (Bowsher),
581
Flo Ellen (Williams),
598
DELONG
Frans/ Franz, 1405
George, 1406
Gertrude, 1405
Gustie Isabel, 1406
Hannah (Carley), 1405
Hendrick, 1406
Hendrick/ Henry, 1406
DELONG
Herbert Sylvester, 581
DELONG
Jacobas, 1405
Jerry Joseph, 623
Jesse Freemont, 1103
Johannes, 1406
John, 15, 1405
Jonathan B, 1643
Joshua, 1645
Julianna (Ziegler),
1645
Kevin Joseph, 623
Keziah A, 1614
Leena, 1405
Margaret (Gosline/
Joslin), 1406
Margareta (Vlegelar),
1405
Maria, 1405-1406
Martinus, 1406
Mary (Wanamaker),
1406
Mary A S (Weiser),
1643
Mary Kay (Utterback),
623
Nellie M (Raber), 1406
Rachel, 1405
Rachel (--), 1405
Raymond P, 1640
Sallie M (Grim), 1640
Sarah, 1405
Sarah (Cronk), 1406
Thurston, 1406
William Edward, 1406
**DELONG/ DELANG/
LANGEN/ LANGET**
Jan/ John, 1405
DELOZIER
Brian John, 528
Davida June
(Wickham), 528
Jennifer Beth, 528
Jeremy Ross, 528
John Ross, 528
DELP
Andrew Curtis, 827
Annette Irene, 167
Arlene Annette
(Weiser), 166
Bryan Christopher, 166
Charles, 827
Dennis Glen, 167
Donald Eugene, 1151
Donald Eugene Jr,
1151
Donald Richard, 167

Elizabeth S, 827
Glenn William, 166
James, 827
Kelly Annette, 167
Korey Lynn, 167
Larry Eugene, 166
Lois (Snyder), 167
Lorna C (Womelsdorf),
827
Margaret, 166, 813
Mary (Womelsdorf),
827
Maude, 1533
Pauline Loretta (Lamb),
1151
Sean Joseph, 166
Sharyl Diane (Richard),
167
DELPHIA
Clara Ruth, 1500
Edith Crimm (Milligan),
1500
Martha Sae, 1500
Paul Alan, 1500
Samuel Johnson, 1500
DEMARCO
Donna Jean, 145
DEMASTERS
Beatrice Alberta
(Herring), 565
Dorance, 565
Jessie Leroy, 565
DEMELLO
Carlos E V, 1467
Mary Carroll (Welser),
1467
Michael Vieira, 1467
DEMETRAKIS
Barbara Ann (McFate),
1104
James, 1104
DEMETRIKIS
Christy (Sellers), 1104
DEMINCK
Kathy Anne (Keating),
1180
DEMME
Carl Rudolph, 84
DEMMY
Clayton, 256
Dorothy Mabel
(Brehm), 256
DEMOSS
Daisy, 262
Eliza Jane
(Eikelberner), 262
Eva L, 262
Florence Pearl, 262
Minnie, 262
Ollie, 262
William, 262
DENGLER
Addie May, 1727
Albert C, 1727
Albert Moses, 1727
Andrew Aaron, 1727
Charles Albert, 1727
Clara Ida, 1727
Estella Gertie, 1727
Franklin Elias, 1727
Gertrude Estella Mary
(Wisser), 1727
James Milton, 1727
Mabel Martha, 1727
Menno Paul, 1727
Mildred M (--), 1727
Paul Thomas, 1727
William Moses, 1727

DENIS
Donald Dee, 956
Geri Ann (McMillian),
956
Jane Lee
(Renkenberger), 956
Julie Ann, 956
Kenneth Douglas, 956
Martha Jane, 956
DENKMAN
--, 1012
Anna, 1012
Elmer, 1012
Hope, 1012
Hope (Mattingly), 1012
Mary Louise, 1012
Raymond, 1012
DENN
Thelma Evelyn, 133
DENNING
Genevieve (Wiser),
1775
George Telford, 1775
DENNIS
Bonnie Lou, 602
John, 602
John Edward, 602
Kaye Marlene, 264
Nancy Marie, 602
Olive, 1084
Ronald Theodore, 602
Rose Marie
(Schlenbaker), 602
Wilma Jean, 602
DENNISON
Daniel Herbert Jr,
1162
Fletcher Loy, 1163
Laura Louise (Loy),
1162
DENNY
Mary, 289
Parthenia, 521
Stacey Jane (Martin),
1207
Steven, 1207
DENOVELLIS
Donna Marie (Kahle),
1252
DENSAVAGE
Rose, 778
DENSLAW
Donna Clara (Wiser),
1799
Henry John, 1799
DENSMORE
Delbert M Jr, 621
Donna May (Brown),
621
DENSTEN
--, 237
Blanche (Weiser), 237
DENTLER
Mary, 1592
DENTON
Anne Watkins, 402
Mary, 1058
DENZEL
Anna Sybilla
(Weihenmaier), 1605
Johann Michael, 1605
Maria Catharine
(Weisser), 1605
DEPASQUALE
Joyce Ellen, 738
DEPEW
Denna, 1802
Pamela L, 144

DEPHILLLIPS
Donald Allen, 748
Donna (Kerstetter), 748
Erik Lee, 748
Heather Renee, 748
John F, 748
Jonathan Richards, 748
Judy (Smith), 748
Kristy Marie, 748
Mary Gladys (Ross),
748
Nicholas John, 748
Richard Lee, 748
Shawn Bradley, 748
Stephen Jay, 748
Susan Kay, 748
Tonya Lynn, 748
Vickie (Narehood), 748
DEPPEN
Allen Grover, 98
Amanda, 97, 111
Catharine, 97, 110
Charles G, 109
Clara Edna, 104
Darius, 97
David, 97
Dora Belle, 104
Dora Isabel, 106
E E, 97
Effie Fern, 98
Elizabeth (Downing),
111
Elizabeth (Reed), 109
Elizabeth Eva, 774
Elizabeth H ( ), 1883
Ellen Jones (Evans), 98
Elmira, 98
Ethel (Door), 98
Eva Elizabeth
(Hoffman), 773
Flora Ellen, 104
George Edwin, 106
Gertrude Jane, 774
Harriet M (Uphold),
111
Hiram, 97-98
Hollie Cartmill
(Prather), 98
Horace Clinton, 104
Jane A, 111
Jesza Maurine, 99
John, 97, 111
John Lucien, 104
John William, 104
Joseph, 773, 1883
Joseph Henry, 774
Lenna Belle, 98
Lona Mae, 98
Louisa May, 109
Lucien, 97, 109
Lucy Frances (Shupe),
98
M L, 97
Margaret Jane
(Stirewalt), 104
Martha F, 106
Mary, 97, 112
Mary Ada, 773
Mary Ellen, 99, 110
Mathilda A, 111
Michael, 97, 109-110
Olive, 98
Paul Emerson, 106
Rosanna (Williams),
109
Samuel Weiser, 97,
111
Sarah (Weiser), 97,
109-110

Sarah Catharine, 106
Sue C, 764
Sylvia (Dooling), 98
William Theodore, 98
Zoe Augusta, 105
DEPUY
Marjory Wysor
(Walker), 1652
William E, 1652
DERACLEO
Jennifer Lynn, 857
Joseph Frederick, 857
Linda Marie (Stauffer),
857
DERADIS
Ida Marie, 1401
DERBY
Trista, 356
DERIAR
Mary Anne (Wiser),
1840
Stephen, 1840
DERK
Arthur I, 1016
Maude E (Renn), 1016
DERKS
Dixie Ann, 800
Donna Lou, 800
Lawrence Lee, 800
Mary Lu Cena (Long),
800
William Ray, 800
DERR
-- (--), 238, 719
A L, 719
Addie Juliet, 244
Addie Viola (Wisser),
1726
Adelaide Louise
(Wolff), 243
Beatrice Addie, 1726
Benneville, 238, 243
Bertha, 243
Charles, 719, 726
Charles Albert, 726
Cleon Carl, 1726
Cora Elizabeth (Beadle),
726
Elmira Rebecca (Wolff),
243
Elmira Rebecca Wolff,
243
Frances Patricia, 244
Frances Riehl (Weaver),
244
Frank Romeo, 244
Franklin G, 238
Franklin Geary, 244
George C, 1726
Helen Catharine, 1747
Helen Louise, 244
Lester George, 1726
Lillian M L (--), 1726
Margaret Verdilla
(Witmer), 719
Mary Catherine, 66
Mary Elizabeth, 244
Mary Elizabeth (Geary),
243
Michael David, 757
Susanne, 922
Yvonne Marie
(Chivalette), 757
DERRICK
-- (--), 908
Adam Troy, 908
Dorna Odette (Boring),
907
Edna Mae, 907

DERRICK (continued)
Elizabeth, 1701
Harry Robert, 907
Harry Troutman, 907
Hary Robert Jr, 908
Jane Louise (Simonson), 907
Karen (Miller), 908
Mary, 1701
Minnie Ellen (Mader), 907
Peggy Ann, 908
Robert Harry, 908
Wendy (--), 908
DERRINGER
Brenda Sue, 606
Cheryl Ann, 606
Don Eugene, 606
Duane Edward, 606
Janet Merlene, 606
Janice Eileen (Cary), 606
Mary Agnes (Rhodes), 606
Merlin LeRoy, 606
DERRY
Bruce, 1012
Myrtle (Waldo), 1012
Virginia, 1012
DERSHAW
Madeline, 725
DERSHEM
Barbara Joan (Bingaman), 683
Benjamin Lee, 683
Donald Leroy, 683
Doris Louise, 683
Grace Pauline (Michael), 682
James Franklin, 683
John Albert, 683
Marie Cathern, 682
Mary Ellen, 683
Rachel Louise, 683
Robert Eugene, 683
Ruth Elizabeth, 683
Simon Peter III, 683
Simon Peter Jr, 683
Simon Peter Sr, 682
William Edward, 683
DERSTETTER
Jennifer Jo, 1055
DESETH
Sharon Kay, 413
DESH
Leah, 1503
DESIDER
Jean, 83
DESKO
Alene Lynn, 1273
Joseph Jr, 1273
Luann Kay, 1274
Twila Alene (Seigworth), 1273
DESPOT
--, 276
Barbara (Vitello), 276
DESSAIN
Helen, 1353
DESSEZ
Sally Chew, 85
DESSO
Dennis, 1200
Sue Ann (Kahle), 1200
DETAR
Jill Nancy, 1230
Lee G Jr, 1229
Marily Kay (Hetrick), 1229

Olive M, 1258
Pamela Kay, 1229
DETERICK
Jacob, 1574
Margaret (Pickert), 1574
DETERS
David Paul, 373
Jessica Rose, 373
Patricia Jean (Lombardi), 373
DETRIE
Lola Mae, 1254
DETTLEBACH
Benjamin, 111
Inez D, 112
Mathilda A (Deppen), 111
DETTRA
Grace Elizabeth, 818
DETURCK
Barbara Louise, 249
Frederick, 249
Joan Marie, 249
Patricia Doris (Althouse), 249
DETURK
Abraham, 1637
Anna (Weiser), 1637
Catharine, 1637
DETURK
Catharine (Levan), 1611
Daniel Y, 1611
DETURK
Elijah, 1644
Esther (Levan), 1637
Hannah, 1637
Isaac, 1637, 1644
Julianna (Levan), 1644
Maria, 1613
Maria (Weiser), 1637, 1644
DETURK
Willi W (Levan), 1611
DETWILER
Edythe, 1352
Frank, 155
Nettie Irene (Howald), 155
DEVANNEY
Sarah C, 1864
DEVASHER
Guy, 137
Juanita Martha (Peoples), 137
Kathleen, 137
DEVAULT
Helen Muriel, 605
Ruth Pauling, 607
DEVEAU
Leslye Karen, 1240
DEVILLIERS
Kathrina Hendrina, 309
DEVINE
Daniel, 955
Elizabeth (Weiser), 955
Fred, 955
James, 93
Myrtle (Simons), 93
Nettie, 955
DEVITO
Barbara J, 144
DEVLIN
Mary, 724
Paul, 901
Viola (Rhoads), 901
DEVONA
Jacke, 175

DEVORE
Shearley, 1177
DEVOU
Rachel, 1786
DEVRIES
Carol Sue (Knapp), 630
Michael Paul, 630
Rhonda (Boerge), 630
Robert, 630
DEW
Carol Ann, 640
Jon Alan, 640
Ralph S, 640
Rita Jane (Bolton), 640
DEWALD
Albert, 512
Charles, 512
Clara, 512
Clarence Leroy, 512
Irvin, 512
Levi, 512
Mary Ann (Zartman), 512
DEWALD
Mary R, 95
DEWALD
Samuel E, 512
DEWEESE
Mattie Elizabeth, 204
DEWEY
Charles, 1034
Linda, 1034
DEWSNAP
Dorothea, 71
DEYOUNG
Emma, 652
DEYSHER
Bertha, 96
Catharine (DeTurk), 1637
Clayton, 96
Ellsworth, 96
Harvey, 96
Nellie (--), 96
Peter, 1637
Stella (Smith), 96
Vera, 96
Wilson, 96
DI BLASI
Dana Lee (Richards), 1205
James Edgar, 1205
DI GUARDI
Brand Donald, 1156
Donald Frank, 1156
Linda Joal (Cordier), 1156
DIAZ
Cory Patrick, 186
Douglas, 186
Marcia Ann (McKinnie), 186
DIAZ-DE-LEON
Olga, 1836
DIBBLE
Alford B, 681
Bernard Alford, 681
Bernard Emory, 681
Bernice Evelyn, 681
Catherine Ann, 681
Deborah Ann, 681
Harriet Aletta (Weatherill), 681
Kathryn (Galbeath), 681
Morrison Allan, 681
Sandra Elaine, 681

DIBERT
Carolyn Marie (Beuchle), 1537
James A, 1522
James Andrew, 1537
Kristin Marie, 1537
DICAMPLI
Angleia Marie, 1068
DICE
Bertha V, 1067
Carol Bernice (Maxson), 127
James Renfrow, 127
Jeffery Kenneth, 1464
Marcia Lou, 1464
Palmer E, 1464
Sarah Church (Weiser), 1464
DICK
--, 1880
Ada May, 1880
Arla L, 1880
Barbara (Weiser), 1880
Charles F, 1880
David, 1880
George W, 1880
infant, 1880
Jessie F (--), 1880
John Adam, 1880
Naomi (Wyant), 1880
Virgil O, 1880
DICKENSON
Beverly, 1719
DICKERING
Dolly, 823
Thomas, 823
DICKERSON
Angela Jean, 551
Kathy Gale (Riggs), 551
Terry, 551
DICKESON
Lou (Umbaugh), 510
William, 510
DICKEY
Doneci, 1249
Earnest, 522
Mary Ann, 1515
Maryetta (Riggs), 522
Wayne Edward, 522
DICKINSON
Lelia, 1652
DICKSON
Anna Martha, 1698
Cynthia (Miller), 1698
Ellen (Graham), 1698
Emily, 1698
James, 1697
Jerome, 1698
Joel, 1697
John, 1698
June (Dimeling), 1698
Martha, 1698
Martha (Lines), 1697
Mary Dorcas, 1698
Minnie, 1698
Nancy, 1698
Sarah, 1698
Sarah (Shimmel), 1697
Susan, 1698
William, 1698
DIEBERT
Ruth Grace (Folk) Manwiller, 1341
William John, 1341
DIEBLER
Blanche, 1165
Emanuel, 1165
Ida Jane (Weiser),

1165
Mabel Elizabeth, 1165
DIEDRICH
Gertrude Louise, 806
Kathy Susan (Moyer), 1168
Wayne Bruce, 1168
DIEFENBACH
Adam, 26
Catharine Priscilla (Seltzer), 1539
Jeremiah, 1539
DIEFENBACK
Martha Eulah (Wiser), 1828
Martin, 1828
DIEFENDERFER
Merion, 83
DIEFENDORF
Jacob, 1572
DIEFFENBACH
Brittany McCall, 429
Bruce M, 429
Carol Ann, 429
Eleanor, 375
Eleanor Ann (Hastedt), 429
Mark Bruce, 429
Sara Jane (Matthews), 429
DIEHL
Barbara Jean, 1046
Billie Jo (Moist), 1046
Bonnie Sue, 1046
Chelsie Gabrielle, 1046
D Harvey, 220
Daisy, 173
Ella Gertrude (Burkholder), 220
Elsie, 979
Eve, 33
George, 1540
Helen Snyder (Shipman), 1046
Jacob Robert, 1046
John Michael, 1047
Julie Ann, 1046
Margaret (Beers), 1046
Marion Elizabeth, 220
Mary, 227
Melissa (Updegraff), 1046
Michael Irvin, 1046
Nancy (Hawk), 1046
Patricia, 252
Rebecca (Weiser), 1540
Robert E Jr, 961
Robert Elias, 1046
Robert Elias III, 1046
Robert Elias Jr, 1046
Shannon A, 1046
Wendy L (Walborn), 1046
William Shipman, 1046
DIEM
Jeremy, 64
Kathy (McConnell), 64
Rebecca, 64
Robert K, 64
DIEMER
Becky, 804
David N, 804
Julia Ann (Kirby), 804
Stacy, 804
DIENER
Catharine, 1612
Charles H, 424
Dakota Edmund, 424

DIENER (continued)
Dylan Charles, 424
Jeffrey Allen Michael, 424
Jenny (Wimmergarm), 424
Joan Lucille (Weiser), 424
Magdaline, 1626
Steven Karl, 424
DIES
Catherine, 1036
Dorothea H O, 1036
Henry, 1036
Martha Catherine (Zimmerman), 1036
DIETRICH
Alvin Howard, 676
Alvin Howard Jr, 676
Bertha M, 791
Catharine, 1761
Debby Kay, 676
Deborah Ann (Mitcheff), 492
Grace, 492
Jim, 492
Melinda E, 464
Neal, 492
Pearl Marie (Lenker), 676
Ryan, 492
Valarie, 492
DIETZ
Alice Marie (Schutt), 236
Christine Leanne, 1054
Cindy Lee, 236
Donald William, 236
Doris Ann, 236
Ella Easter (Manon), 236
Glenn Charles, 1054
Jeanine Lynn (Duck), 1054
John Henry, 236
John Junior, 236
Joyce Arlene, 236
Kevin Jacob, 1054
Letha Marie (Hammelman), 236
Lottie, 1041
Marjorie Estelle (Larkey), 236
Michael Stephen, 236
Pamela Jon, 236
Peggy Lee, 236
Robert Louis, 236
Robin Lon, 236
Sally Marie, 236
Terry Donald, 236
Timothy Peter, 236
DIGAN
Sherry, 754
DIGBY
Clifford, 1580
Paul Jean (Pickard), 1580
DIKKERS
Dale, 1692
Jeanne Eileen (Kirkpatrick), 1692
DILDINE
Mary Elizabeth, 34
Newton, 34
Stella C (Warren), 34
DILL
Loreta, 427
DILLARD
Bonita Faye, 1581

Bradley Richard, 46
Brittany Diane, 46
Gena Rae (Gunn), 46
George Richard, 46
La Una Marie (Morris), 46
Richard Morris, 46
Stephen Michael, 46
Susan Lee, 46
DILLER
Francine Lou, 612
Mable Catherine, 893
Mary Ann (Eppley), 893
Paul, 893
Robert Paul, 893
DILLEY
Anthony Michael, 1276
Caleb Alexander, 1276
Jackie Iona (Seigworth), 1276
William Joseph, 1276
DILLIE
Amanda, 524
DILLINGHAM
Carol Anne, 1805
DILLMAN
Alice (Lemon), 525
Sidney M, 525
DILLON
Arlene, 1635
Arthur Judson, 1026
Barbara, 1026
Betty Jean, 550
Elizabeth, 947
Ellen, 598
Frank, 598
Gloria Jane, 550
James Arthur, 1635
James Patrick, 1635
Joyce Ann, 550
Margaret Annabelle (Riggs), 550
Mary Elinor (Herring), 595
Mildred (Cooper), 1026
Patty, 550
Richard, 1242
Ruby (Kahle), 1242
Sarah May (Weiser), 1635
Verlin Eli, 550
William Boyd, 595
DILLS
Mary (Wysor), 1647
Peter Buise, 1647
DILTS
Orvillo, 271
DILTZ
Debbie, 1261
DILWORTH
Lois Marlene (Wiser), 1781
Richard Russell, 1781
DIMELING
June, 1698
DIMICK
Bill Martin, 590
Kathleen Ruth (Duncan), 590
DIMM
Charles, 1172
Margaret Anne (Ritter), 1172
DIMMITT
Amanda Elizabeth, 1696

DINANT
Donna (Williams), 1708
Robert, 1708
DINARDI
Janet, 1715
Ramona, 1716
DING
Bee Yun, 386
DINGES
Larry Paul, 1083
Lynn Lee, 1083
Marion (Wolfe), 1083
Martha Ann (Gephart), 1055
Max, 1055
Paul, 1083
Regina Elizabeth, 1083
Tanya, 1091
Tanya Lee, 1055
Troy Scott, 1055
DINGSLEY
James B, 1688
May Belle (Kephart), 1688
DINKEL
Pamela Y, 1567
Ray C, 1567
Tara K, 1567
Todd R, 1567
Yvonne R (Foust), 1567
DINWIDDIE
Anna Lucille (Knecht), 441
Clarence Edward, 441
Cleta Coleen, 442
Gary Lee, 442
Jeffrey Joel, 442
Madeline Diane (Loudon), 442
Teresa Rene, 442
DIPE
Bryan, 1616
Francine L (Weiser), 1616
Michael, 1616
Sarah, 1616
DIPPERY
James W, 96
Louisa P (Weiser), 96
DIRADO
Marit Brunhilda (Parker), 1500
Ruben, 1500
DISE
Henry, 1421
Phebe Alice (Leader), 1421
DISHMAN
Vela, 553
DISHONG
Nellie Blanche, 1566
DISMORE
Frank Paden, 811
Frank Steglich, 811
Fredrick Charles, 811
Miriam Rebecca (Fasold), 811
Paden F, 777
Paden Fasold, 811
Pamela Jeanne, 811
Ruth, 811
Ruth (Steglich), 811
DISNEY
Benjamin, 576
Ed, 1377
Holly, 1377
Iva May (Bricker), 576

Joyce (Weiser), 1377
Robert Eugene, 576
Samantha, 1377
Wayne Leroy, 576
DISSINGER
Charles Edward, 1034
David C, 1034
George, 843
Harriet Elizabeth (Cooper), 1034
Helen Ambrose (Ellenberger), 1034
Helen Elizabeth, 1034
Ira Thorne Clement, 1034
Ira Thorne Clement Jr, 1035
Maggie (Anspach), 843
Mary Elizabeth, 1035
Mary Patricia, 1035
Robert, 843
DISTAL
Catherine Pauline, 473
DITLOW
Donna Marie (Boob), 1381
James, 1381
DITMARS
Alma Grace, 216
Bessie Bell, 216
Charles Spencer, 216
Charlotte, 218
Dorothy Agnes, 216
Frank Orville, 218
Helen Louise, 218
James Sherman, 216
Leslie Corrington (Gibson), 218
Mallie Maude, 217
Mary Alice (Lawlor), 216
Mary E (Burkholder), 216
Mattie May (Woodward), 216
Oma Blanche, 218
Rose Neola, 217
Ruth, 218
DITTES
Arthur C, 95
Florence E (Knodt), 95
Laura (Smith), 95
Norman, 95
DITTRICH
Carolyn Gale (Brauer), 489
Greg Alan, 489
Michael Wayne, 489
Rebecca Lynn, 489
Wendy Marie, 489
DITTY
Joy Christine, 741
DITZLER
Alison Diane, 990
Carmen Louise, 989
Charlotte (Willoughby), 993
Clayton Nathaniel, 989
Clayton Norman, 989
Dale Roberta, 990
Doris Delma, 991
Elizabeth (Davies), 989
Elsie (Gilbert), 989
Esther, 993
Gertrude (Pearce), 989
Ida Delilah, 988
Jakob Wilhelm, 988
Kenneth Leleand, 989
Laura Jane, 991

Leland William, 993
Leleand Peter, 989
Lois Marguerite, 989
Luella Catherine, 992
Mamie (Landon), 989
Mattie Lavina, 992
Michael Colin, 990
Roland Gilbert, 989
Rosetta Christiana (Kehl), 988
Shannon (Peters), 990
Shirley Eileen, 990
DIVER
Carol Ann, 1314
Connie Ann, 1314
Jennie Frances, 1314
Phyllis Marian (Cook), 1314
Richard Wallace, 1314
Scheri Diana, 1314
DIVERS
Jane, 1650
DIVINS
MacKenzie Rose, 1305
DIX
Charles, 949
Della (Weiser), 949
DIXON
--, 1709
Charles, 126
Dorothy Helen (Weiser), 126
Edna (Wisor) Foster, 1710
Elizabeth Bridgeman, 1517
Ella Nora (Graham), 1705
Emily, 1722
Esther (Wisor), 1713
Leeta Lavalla, 1121
Marion (Shimmel), 1699
Martha, 1694
Mary Joe, 1358
Newton, 1705
Pauline (Bodle), 1709
Ren, 1710
Samuel, 1699
Wilbur, 1713
DOBBIN
Anna Maria, 1413
Catharine, 1413
Samuel, 1413
Wilheim Henry, 1413
DOBBIN/ TOBINS
Maria Catharina (Weiser), 1413
William, 1413
DOBBS
Donna Jane, 1133
James Bryan, 1133
Jenny Baker, 1133
John Brennan, 1133
Margaret Jean (Rager), 1133
Melvin Willard, 1133
Naoma Zola, 585
DOBERSTEIN
John W, 20, 87, 279, 357
DOBKOWITZ
Diane, 1501
DOBSON
Betty Jean (Lutz), 1228
Donna, 1228
Gene, 1228
Judith A, 923
Timmy, 1228

DOBSON (continued)
Wayne, 1228
DOCK
Clarissa (Rehrer), 1540
George, 1540
Lillian, 1540
DOCKEY
Benjamin F, 684
Carrie Maylinda
(Koppenhaver), 684
Grace Elizabeth, 684
Homer Allen, 684
Lottie, 759
Martha Irene, 684
Roger, 684
DODD
-- (--), 777
Betty Marie, 590
Harper, 777, 794
Helen Ruth, 1215
Irene Lulu (Fasold),
794
Jack Fasold, 794
Mary Allen, 229
Teressa Lucille, 794
Vivian Hensel, 794
DODDS
Amy Elizabeth (Haugh),
1056
Lawrence Donald,
1056
DODGE
Aubrie Sue, 1027
Daniel, 1028
Diane (Marotto), 1027
Dickson, 1028
Donald Lee, 1768
Edward Fayne, 1028
Ethel, 383
Gloria, 1028
Gregory, 1028
James Calvin, 1027
James Christopher,
1027
James Cooper Jr, 1027
James Howard, 1027
Jeanne, 618
John Thomas, 1027
Lois June (Walker),
1027
Mabel (Cooper), 1027
Matthew, 1028
Michael, 1027
Mildred (Curwin),
1028
Nancy Louise (Betzko),
1027
Nichole Adrian, 1027
Pauline (Wiser), 1768
Robert, 1028
Shawn, 1028
Shirley, 1028
Stephanie Ann, 1027
Steven Todd, 1027
Terri (Teck), 1028
DODRILL
Barbara (Brownlee),
444
Donald L, 444
Nona June, 444
Walter Fred, 444
DODSON
Diane Kay, 952
James L, 1884
James Lynch, 1221
James Lynch Jr, 1221
Mabel Ellen (Phebus),
1221
Marcia Linda

(Clyburn), 1221
DOERR
Edward J, 955
Linda Lee (Servass),
955
Scott Edward, 955
DOERSOAM
Ethel, 606
DOHERTY
Diane Lee Allen, 776
DOHNER
Fannie, 1352
DOHRMANN
Phyllis Jean (Cummins)
Knobel, 1480
William, 1480
DOLAN
--, 1639
Alma E (Weiser), 1639
Cheryl Joyce, 1639
Joseph Wayne, 1127
Laura Ann, 1127
Lisa Marie (Maxwell),
1639
Mary J (Weiser), 1639
Michael D, 1639
Peter, 1639
DOLBIN
Benjamin, 853
Benjamin Jr, 853
Carolyn, 853
Dorcas (Miller), 853
Dorothy, 853
Peggy, 853
DOLBOW
Brittany, 1133
DOLBY
Laura Lynn, 1280
DOLE
Dorothy, 963
DOLL
Doreen, 144
Doris, 1084
Dorothy M, 1461
Linda Lee, 886
DOMBROWSKI
Holdherta, 321
DOMEIER
Folma Marianne
Albertine (de Haan),
321
Heinz Helmut, 321
Jan Frederik, 321
DOMER
Grace Anna, 1630
DOMIYAN
Doris Elaine (Kinter),
1353
Frank, 1353
DONADUCCI
--, 1251
Harriet Aida (Kahle),
1251
Ingles Jane, 1251
Shirley Ann, 1251
DONAHOO
Elma Jane, 1270
DONAHUE
--, 113
Carmen (Woods), 1377
Cynthia Ann, 92
Daniel, 92
Edith Jane (Mueller),
59
Edna, 431
Ethel (Grimes), 92
Florence M (--), 92
Jack E, 1377
Jeffrey, 1377

Jessie, 977
John Burrows, 59
Joseph, 92
Joseph Charles, 92
Joseph E III, 92
Joseph Jr, 92
Karen, 1377
Nancy, 1377
Rose, 978
Steven, 1377
Susan, 1377
Terri, 1377
Terry, 92
Vivian L (Weiser),
1377
DONALDSON
Francis M, 1185
Mary Louise, 1207
DONALSON
Jane, 1495
DONATO
Pat, 491
DONAVIN
Ella (Weiser), 155
Kirkwood, 155
DONELSON
Mary, 1441
DONLEY
Deck, 620
Kathryn M (Steele),
620
Lloyd, 620
DONMOYER
Carol Maria, 1041
Christy Eugene, 1041
David Fredrick, 1041
Elizabeth (Hickman),
1041
Ethel (Bell), 1041
Ethel Elizabeth, 1041
Harry R, 1041
Harry R Jr, 1041
Hazel (Brownewell),
1041
Henry Charles, 1041
Mable, 1041
Marie, 1041
Mary Louise, 1041
Sue Ann, 1041
William R, 1041
Winter Eugene, 1041
DONNE
Alene Bernice, 831
Claire M (Maloney),
832
Clay Webster, 830,
832
Coralie Jayne, 831
Cynthia Johan, 831
Daniel Womelsdorf,
830
Douglas Jay, 830
Edyth Adele, 830
Eleanor Beck, 831
Eva Mae (Freed), 830
Grace, 830
Helen Jean, 831
Helen Margaretta
(Womelsdorf), 830
Janice Gayle, 831
Lois Ann, 830
Mae (Anderson), 830
Margaret (Stewart),
830
Marion Amanda
(Freed), 831
Oscar Charles, 830
Oscar Charles
Womelsdorf, 830

Philip Womelsdorf,
831
Rebecca Alwilda, 830
Sherry Diane (Haddix),
830
Susan Jean, 830
DONNECKER
Mary Alice, 1757
DONNELLY
Kathleen Margaret
(Sherrill), 470
Ronald, 470
Ronald Joseph, 470
DONOVAN
Margaret, 1203
DOOLEY
-- (--), 215
Dorothy Agnes
(Ditmars), 216
Frank C, 215
Frank Cleo, 216
Janet Louise, 1660
Mary Lou, 216
Sandra Sue, 217
DOOLING
Sylvia, 98
DOOR
Ethel, 98
DORAN
Don, 1181
Don Eugene, 1189
Harry Earnest, 1189
Margaret Ruth
(Howell), 1189
Mildred June (Weiser),
1189
DORAZIO
Sherri Renee, 79
DOREMISS
Mary Caroline, 1678
DORMAN
Daniel Newton, 1373
Margaret Loretta, 1546
Mary Belle
(Winkleman), 1373
Minnie Marie, 1373
DORMER
Ann, 1001
Arlene (Schreckangast),
1001
Edward, 1001
DORN
Abraham, 1595
Agnes (Schumacher), 8
Anna Catharina, 1595
Anna Rosina (Weisser),
1595
Barbara (Sayler), 1595
Elisabeth, 319
Georg, 8, 1595
Linda Kay, 1135
Margaret, 203
Veit, 1595
DOROBEK
Abbie Lynn, 476
Belva Ann, 474
Beth Ann (Held), 476
Cheryl Lynn (Salyers),
476
Cynthia (Foos), 476
Daniel Lee, 476
Debra Ann, 475
Debra Lynne (Zienta),
476
Donna Jean
(Hallingshead), 476
Donna June (Mesnard),
475
Gloria Ann (Pisarsky),

476
Jac Leon, 476
Jackie (Comer), 476
James Steven, 474
Jamie Michael, 475
Janice Irene, 475
Jared Michael, 476
Jay Bernard, 476
Jean Marie (Lang), 476
Jeanette Louise, 474
Jeffrey Casmir, 476
Jennifer Irene, 475
Jerome Anthony, 475
Jerrold Lamar, 476
Jerry Leroy, 476
John Edward, 475
John Thomas, 475
Jonathan David, 476
Joseph Henry, 476
Joseph Henry II, 476
Judith Ann, 474
Julie Ann, 476
June Louise, 475
Kathryn Irene (Karr),
474
Kathryn Virginia, 474
Kenneth James, 474
Kevin Allen, 476
Linda Louise
(Harbottle), 475
Michelle Lynn, 475
Nicole Lynn, 476
Patricia Ann (Moran),
474
Paul Christopher, 476
Rita Marie (Reinbolt),
474
Stacy Ann, 476
Stephanie Marie, 475
Sylvia Ann, 474
Taylor James, 475
Timie Jo, 475
Vernoica Sue, 476
Walter, 476
Walter John, 476
DORPEL
Diane Marilyn (Strock),
1490
Ronald Dale Vanden,
1490
DORRELL
Cara Nicole, 425
Cassie Ann, 425
Codi Leigh, 425
Dena (Lawley), 425
Joshua Randall, 425
Joyce Bernice (Weiser),
425
Joyce Weiser, 1884
Kristine (Johnson), 425
Mitchell Lee, 425
Randall Mark, 425
Ronald Dean, 425
Ronda Sue, 425
Wendolyn Kaye
(Foster), 425
Wesley Jay, 425
DORRIS
Leah Reed, 1430
DORSCH
Carolyn, 610
DORSEY
Earl Edward, 393
Mildred Elizabeth
(Meeker), 393
Nancy Earlene, 393
DORT
Cyrus, 1461
Lizzie E (Poorbaugh),

DORT (continued)
Lizzie E (Poorbaugh)
(continued)
1461
DORTON
Claude, 554
Melba Nile (Riggs),
554
DORWARD
Emma, 170
DOSH
Annie (Kaiser), 464
Ardis Rae (Bentley),
463
Cynthia (Newland),
463
Doreen, 464
Doris, 464
Elise (--), 463
Elizabeth M (Belford),
464
George, 464
Grace Jeanette, 464
Ivan Leonard, 464
John Leonard, 463
Judith (Felter), 463
Kristine Rae, 463
Leona, 464
Leonard, 463
Linda (Seymour), 463
Loretta Marie (Burt),
463
Mary Viola (Binkley),
464
Maude Erm (Epley),
463
Mervin Charles, 464
Mervin Karl, 463
Muril Elizabeth (Smith),
463
Paul Henry, 463
Ralph L, 463
Raymond, 463
Raymond Curtis, 463
Rebecca (Craun), 463
Richard Dale, 463
Richard Lee, 463
Ruth (Thurston), 464
Sarah Jeanette, 463
Viola May, 463
DOSS
Ellen Lynne, 766
John Frederick, 766
John Roger, 766
Lynn W, 759
Lynn Witmer, 1884
Lynne (Witmer), 766
Maureen Patricia
Collette (Murphy), 766
DOSSELBURGER
Angelika (Weisser),
1595
Johann Simon, 1595
DOTSON
Carolyn Sue (Wiser),
1819
Christine Elizabeth,
859
Etta, 601
Jane Maria (Smith),
859
Jerry Wayne, 859
Paul W, 1819
DOTTS
David, 683
Marie Cathern
(Dershem), 682
William, 682

DOTY
G W, 1427
Margaret (Nes), 1427
Mary Artie, 240
DOUBLIN
Chad Sherman, 543
Christy Noel (Mages),
543
Clyde Sherman, 543
Courtney Spencer, 543
Nina Christina
(Herring), 543
Shannon Renee, 543
DOUGHERTY
Eliza Eugenia (Maier),
56
George W, 56
George W Jr, 56
Herbert Keys, 873
Janet Hazel (Shettel),
873
Sandy Elizabeth, 873
Sherry, 873
Sophia, 1008
William Christopher,
873
DOUGLAS
Amanda Elvina, 1876
Christopher, 516
Mabel Jean, 1439
May (Whitaker), 1439
Will, 1439
DOUGLASS
Billy, 275
Carole (Voss), 275
Christine Ann, 275
Cynthia Sue, 69
Daniel W, 1879
Elaine, 275
Irene Hazel
(Eikelburner), 274
Jamie, 275
Jennie Mary (Weiser),
1879
Jessie Willey (Staley),
39
John Edgar, 274
Joyce Ellen, 275
Kelsey Renee, 275
Larry Eugene, 39
Marilee (Zecheil), 276
Mary Irene, 274
Melanie (Southwood),
275
Melea, 276
Paul, 39
Steven Jon, 275
Thomas John, 276
Tracey, 275
William Frank, 275
DOUTY
Bernice Eliene, 1103
George, 1103
Harold Allen, 1103
Helen Irene, 1103
Lena Gwendolyn, 1103
Mayme Ellen (Kehl),
1103
Roy Lee, 1103
DOVE
Dorothy, 247
DOVERSPIKE
Cindy Lou, 1279
DOW
Lucille, 1845
DOWART
Claire, 864
DOWD
Christina Elizabeth, 45

Kathleen Mary, 71
Kevin Vincent, 45
Phyllys Rhea (Garton),
45
Ryan Patrick, 45
DOWDELL
Anna May, 41
Laura Ida Belle
(Appleby), 41
Richard Samford, 41
William James, 41
DOWDY
Mildred, 1083
DOWELL
Guy Girard, 1550
Jamie Michelle, 1550
Jimmy Francis, 1550
June Francis (Franck),
1550
DOWING
Clarissa Jane, 506
Ellen, 506
Elvira, 506
James, 506
John, 506
Joshua, 506
Marietta Marguerite,
506
Rosella, 506
Sarah (Binkley), 506
William H, 506
DOWNARD
Bertha, 510
Frank, 510
Leo W, 510
Sarah (Fisher), 510
DOWNEY
John, 1587
DOWNHOUR
Margaret, 627
DOWNHOWER
Charles G, 514
Darlene Ann, 514
Dennis L, 514
Edith (Conner), 514
Francis H Jr, 515
Francis Howard, 515
James Allen, 515
Jane Ellen, 514
Jerry F, 514
John H, 514
John Henry, 514
Margaret Bernice, 514
Mary Ann (Ramsey),
514
Matilda (Fritz), 514
Mildred L, 514
Muriel (Martin), 515
Nina (Wibberly), 514
Perry L, 514
Ruth (Rousch), 514
Samuel L, 514
Sharon L, 515
Walter J, 514
DOWNING
Betty Jane, 816
Elizabeth, 111
Elizabeth Juanita
(Womelsdorf), 815
Henry Paul
Womelsdorf, 816
Judith Ann, 1632
Judith LaVann, 826
Patricia Louise (Pizer),
816
Robert Haze, 815
DOWNS
Angela, 1557
Daniel M, 72

Eric Thomas, 72
Karen J, 72
Kathleen Elizabeth
(Ulrich), 72
Linda K, 72
Merle T, 72
DOWNTON
Carolyn, 101
DOYLE
Anna, 270
John, 270
Judith Laurel (Seaman),
374
Lorraine, 1686
Mark Laverne, 374
May, 873
Rebecca Elizabeth
(Eikelberner), 270
Sarah J, 549
DRAEGER
Darin Lee, 494
Heather Renee
(Timmons), 494
DRAKE
Anna Catharine
(Erhard), 1048
Fred, 1048
Gladys (Ford), 457
Marion, 457
Nellie, 114
DRAPER
Allen, 551
Carol Rose Clevenger,
451
Kathy Gale (Riggs),
551
DRECHSLER
Elisabeth (Kraus), 1669
Michael, 1669
DRECHSLER/
TREXLER
Helena, 1674
Johannes, 1674
Maria, 1674
Marie (Weiser), 1674
Peter, 1674
Samuel, 1674
Sara Anna, 1674
Susanna, 1674
DRECHSLER/TREXLER
Maria (Weiser), 1669
Peter, 1669
DREESE
-- (--), 961
Guy, 961
Helen E (Bell), 1039
Samuel Guy, 1039
DREHER
Adam, 1627
Helene, 1165
Mes Maria D (Weiser),
1626
DREIBELBIS
Helen Irene, 709
Jacob Franklin, 709
Leah Elizabeth, 709
Mable Grace, 709
Mary Alice
(Koppenheffer), 709
Melanie Ann, 1304
Phoebe M, 68
DREIBILBIS
Carole Mae, 1101
Harry, 1101
Iva (Kehl), 1101
Kathryn, 1101
Kenneth, 1101
Robert, 1101

DREISBACH
Martin, 1430
DREISBACH/
DRESBACH
Amelia, 1430
Avis Grace (Bee), 1430
Catharina (Spyker),
1430
Elizabeth (Harvey),
1430
Gabriel, 1430
Gedaliah, 1430
George Y, 1430
Helen Rosalta
(Dresbach), 1430
Jacob, 1430
John, 1430
John S, 1430
Judd Harvey, 1430
Lidia (Spyker), 1430
Maria A (Pyles), 1430
Polly (Vincent), 1430
DREKER
--, 1537
Beverly Elaine (Chubb),
1537
Mark, 1537
DRENNEN
Portia Arlene, 1057
DRESBACH
Anna, 1430
Catharine, 1430
Helen Rosalta, 1430
Mary Magdalena, 1430
Sue, 1430
DRESLER
Levi A, 1533
Minnie Catherine
(Weiser), 1533
DRESSELHOUSE
Dorothy, 1510
DRESSLER
--, 1525
Allen, 1535
Anne Hale, 1535
Arthur, 1534
Bertha Mae (Shoop),
1535
Clair Eugene, 1534
Dolores, 1534
Donna, 1534
Ester M, 1535
Faye Evelyn, 728
Florence (Lasco), 1534
Gladys M, 1534
Gloria M, 1535
Helen Constance (Hale),
1535
James, 1534
James R, 1534
Jennie, 1533
Jeremiah, 1679
John H, 1884
John Henry, 1535
John McKinley, 1535
Kathryn (Brown), 1534
Kathryn M, 1538
L Mabel (Straub), 1534
Levi, 1538
Lillian (Klinger), 1534
Marcia Louise, 1535
Margaret Lee, 1535
Maria (Smeal), 1679
Marlin J, 1534
Mary Pearl (Nichilo),
1534
Myrl (Snyder), 1534
Norman, 1534
Patricia, 1534

DRESSLER (continued)
Robert E, 1534
Robert E Jr, 1534
Ruth, 1534
Stella (Weiser), 1525
Theresa, 1534
Violet Gertrude, 1536
Weiser Lewis, 1535
DREWRY
Gray, 171
Susan Mary
  (Protzeller), 171
DREY
Annie L, 1638
Beulah M (Wisser),
  1755
Howard C, 1755
DRIEBELBIS
Mildred (Bottorf), 1396
William, 1396
DRIESBACH
Sophia, 1429
DRIFTMYER
--, 472
Linda Kay (Caskey),
  472
DRIGGUS
--, 187
Catharine (Gearhart),
  187
DRILLING
Gina Louise, 415
DRISCOLL
Brenda Ann (Wihlen),
  1020
Mary Belle, 1446
Patrick Timothy, 1020
Timothy, 1020
DRIVER
Elsie, 618
Ethel Eunice (Wiser),
  1800
J C, 1800
Janette Rosemarie,
  1873
DROKE
Clifford S, 992
Ellen Annette (Irvine),
  992
Kimberlee, 992
Kristen, 992
Mark, 992
DROLL
Anna, 1698
DROMMER
Marie Luise, 1606
DROZ
Gordon, 411
Nancy Nadean
  (Weiser), 411
DRUCKEMILLER
David, 1459
Mary (Weiser), 1459
DRUGGS
Mary E, 1706
DRUGS
S Melissa, 1701
DRUM
Carlene (Patterson),
  705
David Lawrence, 705
Dewey Lee, 705
Dewey Lee Jr, 705
George Earl, 705
Lillian Noll
  (Koppenhaver), 705
Peggy Anne, 705
DRUMHELLER
Fred, 1540

Jennie (Wirt), 1540
DRUMM
Bret Ann, 590
Danna Sue (Hocker),
  590
Pauline M (Owens),
  590
Richard Wayne, 590
DRURY
Derrick Allen, 1792
Sandra Kay (Wiser),
  1792
DRYER
Sudney Elizabeth, 249
DU MARS
Martha, 1438
DUBELL
Ada May (Wolff), 245
Isaiah N, 245
Stanley Wolff, 245
DUBOIS
Barbara Sievaright, 301
Daniel Joe, 268
David, 268
Debra Kay, 268
Donald, 268
Elizabeth Harsen
  (Chisholm), 300
Emily Stuart
  (Meirsmith), 327
DUBOIS
Freddie Lee, 268
DUBOIS
Henry Ogden, 327
James Richard, 268
Joe, 268
Josephine, 268
Madonna (Reinholt),
  268
Marcia, 268
Mary Constance, 327
Paula, 268
Robert Ogden, 300
Robert Ogden Jr, 301
Ruth (Smith), 268
Vicki Lynn, 268
Wanda, 268
DUCHMAN
Anna Eliza, 343
DUCK
-- (--), 961
Amy (Crapper), 1054
Beatrice Eleanor, 1089
Dorothy Jane
  (Hampton), 1054
Elizabeth Helen, 1054
Hazel Vila, 1089
Jamie Norman, 1054
Jeanine Lynn, 1054
John Jacob, 1054
John Jacob Jr, 1054
Lilian Ruth (Babak),
  1054
Lula Mae (Hackman),
  1054
Mary Elizabeth, 1054
Matthew, 1054
Michael John, 1054
Norman, 961, 1089
Pat (Johnson), 1054
Susan, 1054
Velira May (Brungart),
  1089
William N, 961
William Norman, 1054
William Norman III,
  1054
William Norman IV,
  1054

William Norman Jr,
  1054
Winifred Anabel, 1089
DUCKETT
Leroy John, 1551
Mary Regina (Piasecki),
  1551
Scott Matthew Lee,
  1551
Sean Michael, 1551
DUCKMAN
--, 1832
Hiram Gallup, 1832
Mary (Bates), 1832
Mona L (Wiser), 1832
William Don, 1832
DUCKSTAD
Eric Edward II, 1474
Neils Christian, 1474
Tracy, 1474
DUCKSTEAD
Donna M (Roach),
  1474
Eric Edward, 1474
Ida Dorothy (Zane),
  1474
John Benjamin, 1474
Joyce E (Campau),
  1474
DUCKWELL
John Lewis, 548
Rosetta (Banter), 548
DUDLEY
Barbara Lee (Trigg),
  403
Daniel, 403
Fidelia (Wiser), 1833
Levi, 1833
Nancy, 542
Renata, 1213
DUERR
Dorothy, 889
DUFF
Douglas Erwin, 608
Elizabeth (Johnson),
  1677
Erwin Jr, 608
Evelyn Faye (Klingler),
  608
James, 1526
Ruth (Herold), 1526
William, 1677
DUFFEY
Audrey Erma (Gee),
  466
Kathleen Kenton, 1151
Lawrence, 466
Trella Louise, 1144
DUFFIE
Amy Jo, 798
Carron Sue, 797
Cathy Lou, 797
Charles Edward, 796
Clement, 797
Donna (Kissick), 797
Ethel (Buhel), 797
Helen Chloe, 796
Jacqueline, 797
Janice Elaine, 797
John K, 797
John Luther, 797
Joyce Ann, 797
Lenus Lee, 797
Leona (Allison), 797
Lloyd Keith, 797
Lloyd Keith Jr, 797
Loren Douglas, 797
Loren Edgar, 797
Loren Richard, 797

Marie (Ingersoll), 796
Mary Elizabeth, 796
Michall, 797
Sarah Elizabeth
  (Weiser), 796
Susie (Wilkie), 796
William Hamilton, 796
DUFFY
Elizabeth Ann, 197
DUFRENSE
Arlene Louise (Shettel),
  855
Ronald Marcel, 855
Wayne Dennis, 855
DUGAN
Catherine, 768
Daniel H, 1682
Elizabeth (Stone), 1682
DUGANITZ
--, 1697
Agnes (Turner), 1697
DUGGAN
Debbie, 207
Lori, 1622
DUGHMAN
Minerva Ann, 190
DUININK
-- (--), 215
John, 215, 227
Violet (Burkholder),
  227
DUKE
--, 540
Tina Marie (Mitchell),
  540
DULEMBA
Edward, 492
Sandra Grace
  (Mitcheff), 492
Shane, 492
Tiffany, 492
DULL
Daniel Howard, 1399
Edwin, 1399
Nancy Jane, 1399
Susan Faye (Wagner),
  1399
DUMBROFF
Laurie Sue, 484
DUMUS
Juanita Opal, 1321
DUNBAR
Gregory Lee, 448
Margaret Ruth
  (Sweeting), 448
Robert Earl, 448
Scott Allan, 448
DUNCAN
Andrew David, 1064
Anthony Randall, 590
Bertrude Marie, 1271
Bettie Jane (Noll), 1064
Brenda (Miller), 589
Carole Jean, 589
Cora Ellen, 1188
Corrie Jean, 1064
Dan, 487
Daniel Lee, 590
Darlene Ann (Kern),
  487
David, 1064
Don Stephen, 590
Don Theodore, 590
Edith Pearl (Clem),
  1188
Esther Dorcas (Shettel),
  861
Floyd, 102
Frenchen Renee, 590

George B, 1823
George Weiser, 1188
Grances (Degan), 1188
Hamilton Lewis, 1810
Heather Ann, 487
Hugh, 1188
Hugh Albert, 1188
Isham, 1798
James Asa, 1188
Jane Ellen, 1064
Jo Ann, 589
John Edward, 590
Kathleen Ruth, 590
Kathy Jean (Pierce),
  1064
Kenneth, 487
Larry Dean, 589
Linda Sue, 590
Liza Dawn, 589
Louisa C (Wiser), 1823
Lucy (Weiser), 1188
M Nancy Elaine
  (Oldham), 590
Margaret (Wiser), 1810
Margaret Ann (Wiser),
  1798
Mark Lewis, 589
Mary Elizabeth, 1817
Mary Emaline, 1188
Max Edward, 589
Maxine Imogene
  (Hocker), 589
Nancy Sidney, 1188
Patricia Eileen
  (Hocker), 590
Patricia Jeanne, 590
Rebecca Ann, 1064
Robert Mallis, 1064
Sharla Jeanne, 590
Shirley Ann, 102
Silas Shettel, 861
Stephen Robert, 590
Sylvia (Oakley), 102
Sylvia Anita
  Pomranning, 1548
Vicki Leah, 589
Wendell Duane, 102
William O, 861
Wilma, 1386
DUNDORE
Anna, 847
Catharine Elizabeth,
  914
Charles, 1561
Ella, 1561
Frank, 1561
Franklin, 1561
Mary (Rick), 1561
DUNHAM
Gwinn, 1689
Harriet, 189
James Jackson, 534
Joy (Kephart), 1689
Valeria Ann (Herring),
  534
DUNIVEN
Edward Lee, 1162
Herbert L, 1162
Margaret Alice (Hinds),
  1162
Rebecca Lynn, 1162
Victoria Leigh, 1162
DUNKELBERGER
Annie Virginia
  (Musselman), 1177
Harry A, 1178
John A, 1177
Lucy (--), 1178
Maude, 1178

EARNEST (continued)
Mary Belle, 1476
Mary Jane, 1476
Mary Joan, 1480
Melvin Russell, 1487
Michael, 1503
Michael S, 1487
Michael William, 1479
Michelle Ann, 1487
Mildred Marie, 1482
Milton David, 1481
Mitchael Dean, 1487
Murel Joy, 1486
Napoleon, 1504
Nellie, 1482
Patricia Corinne, 1481
Patricia Rae, 1479
Patricia Sue, 1483
Priscilla, 1504
Rachel, 1488
Randal Dean, 1480
Rebecca, 1504
Rita Devone (Bilslend), 1487
Robert Larry, 1481
Ronald Lee, 1481
Rosanna Barbara, 1486
Ruby Corinne (Wright), 1482
Russell David, 1481
Sarah, 1504
Sheryl Rose, 1479
Sophia, 1487
Sophia (Earnest), 1487
Susan Elizabeth, 1486
Susanna (Minnich), 1476
Teresa (Henney), 1479
Terri Lynn, 1479
Thelma Darlene, 1487
Valentine Hummel Jr, 1476
Valentine Hummel Sr, 1476
Velma Arlene, 1487
Vio, 1481
William, 1503
William H, 1504
William Valentine, 1479, 1486
EASLEY
Bertha, 1831
EAST
Gloria Janice, 595
Jean DeeLee, 595
Vivian Oletha (Herring), 595
Warren E, 595
EASTERDAY
Cheryl Ann (Patton), 1299
Christopher Matthew, 1299
Leslie Ann, 1299
Michael Duane, 1299
Patrick Michael, 1299
EASTERWOOD
Mary, 1220
EASTLAKE
Hazel May, 145
EASTMAN
A Bernice (Wiser), 1754
Philip, 1754
EASTON
Amy Ann, 197
Bertha K, 188
Carrie Jean, 198
Elizabeth Ann (Duffy),

197
Flo Ann (Sours), 197
J Scott, 197
John, 197
Michal Anna, 187
Sharon Middleton, 105
EATON
Betty Lucille (Tuckerman), 1186
Emma Jane (Weiser), 1186
Evelyn (Alexander), 530
Francis Dwain, 1186
Francis Edward, 1186
Glenn Edwin, 530
Joan Ruth, 1186
Mark Kevin, 1186
Mary Elizabeth, 1186
Michael Dwain, 1186
Robert, 530
Robert J, 1772
Susan Rae (Wiser) Delgado, 1772
EAVES
Margaret, 130
EBBERTS
--, 821
Anabelle (Kreible), 821
EBEL
--, 1461
Elizabeth (Ziegler), 1461
Mary Elizabeth, 86
EBERHARD
--, 1
EBERHARDT
Barbara, 1859
Diane Patricia, 243
Edward A, 243
Eleanor Louise (Bond), 243
Patricia Ann, 243
Richard Charles, 243
EBERHART
--, 370
Andrew Watson, 771
Benjamin Charles, 929
Bruce, 370
Daniel Richard, 771
David, 370
David Robert, 771
Donald R, 1884
Donald Ralph, 771
Donna Kay (Snyder), 929
Duane leroy, 929
Elizabeth Laura (Fasnacht), 771
Elizabeth Rachel, 771
Gretchen, 771
Harry James, 771
Helenmae, 233
Janette, 370
Jason Andrew, 929
Jeanette (Watson), 771
Linda Susan, 771
Lizbeth Lee, 771
Marie Doris (Fleer), 370
Michael, 370
Nellie Pearl, 1484
Robert James, 771
Ruth Eleanor (Moyer), 771
Stacey Lynn, 929
Suzanne Moyer, 771
EBERLY
Anna Calarah (Spacht),

642
Charlotte Rose, 628
Garlan Delite, 629
Janice Wandalee (Harvey), 628
Jerilyn Jane, 628
Joenita Ann, 629
Lawrence Berdean, 628
Lawrence Dean, 628
Mable Irene (Schell), 1319
Margaret (Tinney), 628
Mary Ann, 170
Myron Francis, 1319
Nancy Marlene, 1319
Ray Hastings, 642
Teresa Lynn, 628
Verlyn R, 628
EBERMAN
Donna Irene, 222
EBERSOLE
--, 1881
Blanche May, 1881
Clinton L, 1881
Franklin C, 1881
James E, 1881
Jessie (Weiser), 1881
Juliana (Weiser), 1881
Mary Adella, 1881
William Lee, 1881
EBERTS
Agnes (Wisor), 1720
Frank B, 1720
EBINGER
Agnes (Uebele), 17
Emma, 1257
Thomas, 17
EBLING
Duane, 286
Jessica Jordan, 286
Marcella Daneker (Wagner), 286
EBRIGHT
Nancy, 401
EBY
Alvin Edward, 670
Annie Katharine, 668
Arthur Alvin, 670
Dorothy Frances (Shuey), 670
Edward, 670
Gertrude (McCord), 670
Herbert J, 670
Minnie Esther, 670
Nancy Jane (Witmer), 670
Sharon Kay, 670
Susan Agnes (Koppenheffer), 667
William Edward, 667
ECCLES
Gladys, 532
Leo, 945
Mary (Cosgrove), 945
Patricia Ann, 945
ECHOLS
--, 789
Georgiana (Hoagland), 789
James W, 789
ECK
Daniel Joseph, 867
David Robert, 867
Douglas Arthur, 867
Earl O, 867
Earl O Jr, 867
Edna Sophia (Still), 867

Georgia (Hall), 867
Harry James, 868
Merry, 604
Nancy Lee, 867
ECKARD
Robert, 1275
Tammy Darlene (Wolfgong), 1275
ECKELS
Fannie (Reed), 1543
Helen, 874
James H, 1543
Phoebe, 1543
ECKENRODE
Clinton C, 750
Myrtle Elnora (Ross), 750
Nancy Ann, 750
Patricia Ann, 750
Sandra Lee, 750
ECKENROTH
Dakota Ryanne, 1382
Julia Denise (Homan), 1382
Ryan P, 1382
Shan Elizabeth, 1382
ECKER
Virgene, 1385
ECKERSELL
Onduyln, 210
ECKERT
Alta (Moore) Johnson, 1432
Anton Friedrich, 321
Beverly Jean, 1429
Beverlyn Jean Johnson, 1432
Billie Scott, 1433
Brook Marley, 1432
Caroline (Weiser), 1543
Claudine A (Wiser), 1837
J M, 1837
Jacob, 1543
Johann Heinrich, 321
Katherina Barbara Brigitte (Willich), 321
Lenora (McGibbon), 1432
Marley Howard Johnson, 1432
Matthias, 321
Nell Kimberly (Endress), 1432
Orie, 1432
Paul Edward, 1432
Peter, 89
Stephen Marley, 1432
Theresa Rose, 1433
Thomas, 321
ECKHARDT
James Alfred, 1337
Larry Douglas, 1337
Lucille Jean (Maxwell), 1337
Scharold Dean, 1337
Steven Scharold, 1338
Virginia Lee, 1338
ECKHART
Charles Allen, 493
Michael Aldon, 493
Tammy Lynn, 493
Traci (--), 493
ECKHERT
Betty Joyce (Heileman), 492
Merle Allen, 492

ECKLES
Emma Burkhart, 880
ECKLEY
Charles, 109
Charlotte, 109
Ellen May, 109
Fred, 1693
Goldie K (Parks), 1704
Louisa May (Deppen), 109
Sidna (Kephart), 1693
Willis, 1704
ECKMAN
Garnett (Davis), 1206
Kenneth, 1206
ECKSPELLEN
Charles, 1730
daughter, 1730
Esther (Wieser), 1730
EDDIE
Carrie, 157
EDDINGER
Barbara, 1303
Blanch Clara (Wiser), 1303
Brenda Ann, 1303
Carolyn Jane, 1304
Cecile Luella, 1303
Charles Andrew, 1303
Charles Robert, 1304
Cynthia Lee, 1303
David Allen, 1303
Dena Marie, 1303
John Delbert, 1303
Leslie Allen, 1303
Lilian Mae, 1303
Malvern Allen, 1303
Margaret Ann (Beisel), 1303
Mary Margaret, 1303
Pearl Genevieve (Plant), 1303
Richard Allen, 1303
Ruth Lucille, 1304
Ruth Margaret (Ferguson), 1303
EDDS
Agnes (Stahl), 601
Jacob, 601
EDDY
Vivian Lucille, 1305
EDGAR
Agnes (Strachan), 338
Agnes Leroy, 338
Anna, 338
Anna Jean (Randall), 446
Caroline Strachan, 338
Daniel, 338
Daniel M, 338
Emily, 338
Eulala Anne, 446
Frederica, 338
Julia, 338
Julia (Lorillard), 338
Julia Lorillard, 338
Leroy, 338
Mary, 338
Newbold Leroy, 338
Thomas I, 446
Thomas Randall, 446
William, 338
EDGERLY
Susan Joan, 209
EDGERTON
Alice, 1231
EDISON
Hazel Grace (Weiser), 801

EIKELBERNER
(continued)
Rebecca (Weiser), 261
Rebecca Catharina
  Weiser, 261
Rebecca Elizabeth, 270
Rebecca Weiser, 276
Russell, 276
Ruth Jane, 270
Thelma, 276
Uriah Henry, 271
Uriah Mengel, 261
Uriah Mingle Mengel,
  270
William Morton, 271
Zacharias, 261, 277

EIKELBURNER
Abbie (Myers), 274
Amy Clara, 272
Ercil (Neff), 272
Faye (Slagle), 274
Fred Sutton, 274
Glenn Homer, 274
Goldie Ella, 273
Hazel Catherine, 272
Ike Kee, 273
Irene Hazel, 274
Jeffrey Ike, 273
Jessie (Light), 274
Joseph Edward, 273
Joseph Edwin, 272
Josephine, 274
June (Mitchell), 272
Kay Shirley, 272
Lora (Taulman), 273
Lucille Margaret, 273
Mary Joan, 274
Pamela Jean, 272
Rose (Brunz), 274
Verna (Light), 274
William August, 272
William Hubert, 274

EINLOTH
Carolyn Ruth, 744
Cecilia Joan, 744
Christine Anne (Bails),
  744
Christopher Gerard,
  744
Denise Marie
  (Vincevich), 744
Gerard Francis, 744
Karen Louise (Kruse),
  744
Martha Jean (Ross),
  744
Martin David, 744
Mary Colette, 744
Matthew Paul, 744
Timothy Ryan, 744

EINSTEIN
Anna Patton (Fox),
  1510
Edgar Van Sant, 1510
Mildred Martha (Kulp),
  1510
Richard Fox, 1510

EISELE
Ada Elizabeth, 1151

EISEMAN
Anita, 62

EISENBERG
Emma, 1048

EISENHARD
Edward, 1760
Jane, 1641
Mariann (Wieser),
  1760

EISENHARDT
Caroline, 1757

EISENHART
Anna D (Mitchell),
  1428
Catharine R (Schmidt),
  1428
Charles Augustus,
  1428
Elsa M (Bausch), 1428
Emma C (Pfabler),
  1428
Harry W, 1428
Hazel (Laity), 1428
Jacob C, 1428
Lillian (Cleary), 1428
Lucy A (Forry), 1428
Luther Pfabler, 1428
M Herbert, 1428
Margaret Jean (Leader),
  1422
Ruse (Butt), 1428
S Forry, 1422
William S, 1428
William Schmucker,
  1428

EISENHAUER
Margaret, 1732
Sarah, 1423

EISENHAUR
Evelyn, 1382

EISENHUTH
Sharon Kaye, 1307

EISENMENGER
Maria Margreth, 1412

EISLING
Susan, 147

EISTER
Adam, 750
Becky Jo, 754
Calvin E, 753
Clara, 744
David Henry, 753
David W, 754
Dora Elizabeth (Unger),
  754
Dorothy Mae, 751
Elizabeth, 742
Elizabeth (Broscious),
  740
Ellen E, 753
Emma Elnora, 755
Eric, 753
Eva Adaline, 744
Flora I (Epler), 753
Franklin H, 754
Gwendolyn (Oyster),
  1032
Irene, 753
Isabella Irene, 750
Jack, 1032
Jacob H, 740
Jeanne (--), 753
John Albert, 753
John O, 754
John Samuel Albert,
  750
John T, 754
Katherine, 753
Kenneth Albert, 753
Lavera (Berger), 754
Lloyd E, 754
Louisa, 743, 750
Lucas Corbett, 754
Lynn (--), 753
Margaret, 740
Margaret Elizabeth,
  754
Martha (Schaffer), 754

Martha J, 754
Mary Alice, 743
Mary Ann (Rothermal),
  754
Miriam Louise, 754
Rebecca C (Price), 750
Roselda (Krigbaum),
  750
Ruth Marie (Bird), 753
Sarah Catharine, 743
Sherry (Digan), 754
Shirley Ellen, 754
Vera Lorraine, 755
William, 753
William Webster, 754

EITNER
Alberta, 491

EKELUND
Clifford Thoren, 1458
Georgia Katharine,
  1458
Katharine Georgia
  (Weiser), 1458
Mary Sue, 1458
Sarah Ann, 1458

EKLEBERRY
-- (--), 940-941
Allen, 940
Charles, 941
Donald, 940
Edward Allen, 941
James, 940
Jennie (Hilborn), 940
Lee, 940
Margaret (--), 940
Martha (Koller), 940
Patty, 941
Peggy Lee, 941
Robert, 940
Steven, 941
Susan Kay, 941

EL BOUKHARI
Hamid, 425
Jan Carolyn (Weiser),
  425
Mouna, 425
Sanaa, 425

ELBRADOR
Theda, 52

ELDER
--, 1307
Anna, 1547
Charles, 1454
Laura Michelle, 483
Lucinda (Graham) Van
  Valzah, 1454
Margaret, 1291
Michael Joseph, 483
Patricia Louise
  (Simpson), 1307
Sharon Joyce (Blausey),
  483
Theresa Dawn, 483
Thomas Joseph, 483

ELDERKIN
Alice Louise, 262
Arthur James, 262
Effie Myrtle (Phipps),
  262
George T, 262
Harry, 262

ELDREDGE
-- (--), 1519
Alice Gail, 1520
Franklin Eugene, 1519
Helen Marguerite,
  1519
Lewellyn Orrin, 1519
Lulu Gertrude

(Matthias), 1519
Mary Elizabeth, 1519

ELDRIDGE
Dorothy, 1692
girl, 1692

ELESON
Cindy Lynnae
  (Smelser), 412
Katyana Marie, 412
Tevis James, 412
Thomas Lee, 412

ELLENBERGER
Annie A, 784
Helen Ambrose, 1034

ELLETT
Dawn Michel, 569
Frances Leigh, 1649
Harold Wayne, 568
James Douglas, 569
Jennifer Lynn, 569
Jolene Michel, 569
Katherine Jeanette, 568
Linda (Henery), 569
Mary Jeanine, 569
Phyliss Ann (Herring),
  568

ELLIFRITZ
Patricia L, 630

ELLIOT
Andrew, 562
Courtney Alyson, 1275
Dallas Alan, 562
Elizabeth, 1741
Eric Charles, 1275
Floyd, 562
J Bruces, 601
Laura (Herr), 562
Linsey, 562
Martha Louise (Banter),
  562
Nancy Sue, 562
Patricia Ann
  (McGarry), 1275
Sarah Malinda (Stahl),
  601

ELLIOTT
Adelaide, 330
Albert, 363
Albert Wesley, 362
Bretta (Shay), 363
Charley, 363
Dorothy, 363
Earl, 291
Earnest Glenn, 291
Edith, 291
Elizabeth Jane, 1346
Ethel Glenn, 291
Eva E (Atherton), 363
Ezra, 291
Frances, 295
Fred, 363
Glenna E (Smith), 1496
Harold, 363
Harriet (Ege), 291
Henrietta (Graham),
  1453
Henry, 74
James Elton, 145
James Lynn, 145
Jaydene, 601
Jennie May (Ulrich),
  74
John W, 1453
Kathleen, 554
Linda Lou, 223
Marcia Lee, 145
Mary Ellen (Powell),
  362
Pearl, 362

Sharon, 473
Virgia Mae (Evans),
  145
Walter O, 1496

ELLIS
Alma, 1825
Amanda, 1087
Christine (Knepp),
  1719
Christopher John, 798
Donna, 591
Dorothy (Wall), 126
Dorothy Ann (Naiden),
  1563
Dorothy Phyllis (Buck),
  798
Elvis Davis, 1810
Jack, 126
James, 1874-1875
John Edward, 1357
Judith Ann
  (Deffinbaugh), 591
Kay, 1440
Larry Nacif, 798
Lidia (Siegried), 39
Lola Ann, 1300
Louise Esther (Weiser),
  126
Lu Ann, 126
Maidee Virginia
  (Glavis) McMillan,
  1357
Mary (Weiser), 1874
Mary (Wiser), 1875
Melissa, 591
Mildred Lois (Wiser),
  1810
Rachel (Weiser), 1874
Rachel (Wiser), 1875
Regina, 591
Robert, 1874-1875
Sarah Elizabeth, 1563
Stanley, 1719
Steven Carroll, 798
Sue Elizabeth
  (McCreery), 1563
Susan Christine, 126
Teri Lyn, 798
Theodore, 39
Thomas John, 126
William Donohue,
  1563
William G, 798
William James, 591
William James Jr, 591
William Jr, 798
William McCreery,
  1563
William Naiden, 1563

ELLMAKER
Leonard, 1365
Mary Anna, 1365

ELLSWORTH
Jacqualyn Lee, 405
Sharon Meridith
  (Hayden), 630
Steven, 630

ELMER
Amy Jo, 478
Charles Louis, 478
Joyce Darlene (Miller),
  478
Sherry Lynn, 478

ELMORE
Ruth Elizabeth, 841

ELSESSER
Fayne, 1416

ELSEY
Eula (Wiser), 1816

ETSCHBERGER
(continued)
Ezra, 1519
Franklin, 1519
George Philip, 1522
Jacob Milton, 1521
John Jacob, 1522
John Peter, 1518
Levi, 1519
Margaret (Matthias), 1521
Marin, 1518
Melissa, 1519
Priscilla, 1519
Sarah (Conrad), 1519
William, 1519
William Jonathan, 1521
ETZLER
Tammy Lynn (Eckhart), 493
Terry Dean, 493
EUBANK
Curtis Dana, 374
Janelle Christine, 374
Jason Randall, 374
Merri Nelle (Seaman), 374
EUMAN
Cleyta Coletta (Courtright), 1121
James, 1121
EURELE
Suzanne Elaine, 404
EUSTES
Nancy Orne, 1070
EUSTON
Barbara Graham, 1510
Charles Delmar, 1510
Joan Hynicka (Fox), 1510
EUTZY
Betty, 1529
EVANGELISTA
Virginia Edna, 751
EVANS
Alfred F, 332
Alice Ann (Roth), 145
Alice Jane (Crisswel), 145
Alison Marie (Roscoe), 146
Allen Jerome, 332
Alta (Walton), 146
Alverta G (Salada), 693
Angela Jean, 332
Arthur, 1678
Arthur William, 937
Avis (Wickens), 332
Barbara Ann (McFate), 1104
Barbara Lee, 146
Belva Sarah (Thompson), 145
Brian Joseph, 937
Bridget Marie, 937
Brooke Amber, 140
Carlene Denise, 140
Carol, 1501
Carolyn Marie, 140
Catharine, 1501
Catharine Virginia (Wertz), 1501
Catherine Marie, 140
Catherine Mary, 139
Cathy Sue, 146
Charlene Elizabeth (Leibold), 382
Charles, 863
Charles Clark Jr, 1501

Charles Jr, 863
Cheryl Anne, 140
Chester, 1754
Christena (Breidenbach), 140
Christina Lynn (Seigworth), 1279
Christine Lynn, 145
Clara Belle (Wiser) Tobine, 1754
Cynthia Lynn, 140
Daisy, 502
David Blaine, 693
David G, 693
David Karl, 145
David Leslie, 146
David Weiser, 146
Dawn Marie, 146
Dawn Rene, 139
Deborah Rose (Zinser), 139
Deborah Sue, 1039
Debra Sue, 146
Dennis Todd, 145
Diana Leigh, 146
Diana Marie (Griffiths), 140
Dolores (Pitchford), 139
Donald Dwight, 146
Donna Jean (DeMarco), 145
Donna Louise (Weiser), 192
Doris (Wiggert), 139
Dorothy, 146
Edward Ethbert, 140
Edward Jr, 146
Edward Millard, 146
Eileen (Bowersock), 139
Ellen Jones, 98
Elmina (Fisher), 863
Florence (Metzler), 137
Francis Wayne, 146
Frank Earnest, 137
Frank Earnest Jr, 139
Gerald William, 145
Gertrude (Wiser), 1678
Glenn, 1279
Grace Lucy, 141
Hazel (Waltz), 146
Hazel May (Eastlake), 145
Heather Ann, 139
Helen (Edwards), 139
Helen Oakley, 332
Holly Lynn, 140
James Leonard, 382
James Winslow, 382
Janet Lee, 145
Jeffery, 139
Jennifer, 1501
Jerilee, 211
Jill (--), 1501
John, 1501
John Thomas, 68
John Walker, 332
John William, 140
Jon Eric, 192
Judith Kay, 146
Julia, 1501
Justin James, 382
Katherine Marie, 145
Katie Lee, 1501
Keith Dwight, 139
Kim Lyle, 140
Kristine Marie, 139

Larry, 1104
Linda (Seghetti), 937
Linda Marie (Hulderman), 139
Linda Mary (Meida), 140
Lindsay Mary Meida, 140
Loreen Lynne, 146
Lovina Mattie, 141
Lucy Margaretta (Walker), 332
Mable Catherine, 1549
Marcia Lynn (Goldner), 145
Margaret L (Conklin), 146
Marie (Page), 146
Marie (Thompson), 693
Marilyn Celeste (Hetrick), 139
Mark Harold, 139
Martha Eva, 138
Mary (Kelley), 937
Mary Evelyn Weiser (Moyer), 1342
Mary Jane, 120
Mary Virginia (Mesarchik), 140
Mary Weiser, 1340
Mattie Anna (Weiser), 137
Maude T (Whittredge), 140
Maureen Blee (Madden), 382
Michelle Marie, 139
Mildred Christine, 137
Monica Lee, 145
Nancy, 1209
Nancy Lee (Richter), 68
Naomi T, 251
Nicholas John, 332
Nicolette Maria, 139
Patricia (Steitler), 1501
Patricia (Trembett), 332
Rachel, 304
Randall Lee, 145
Randy Douglas, 140
Richard E, 136
Richard Edward, 140
Richard Karl, 145
Richard Wayne, 146
Robert Clark, 1501
Robert Dudly, 1342
Robert Eugene, 139
Robert Lewis, 146
Robert Michael, 139
Roberta (Nancy), 1501
Ruby Mae, 603
Ruth, 785
Ruth Emilene Hall, 933
Sandra Celeste, 139
Sandra Lee, 68
Sharon Lynn, 146
son, 68
Steven Arthur, 382
Terrence David, 146
Thelma June (Baber), 146
Thomas, 68
Valerie Nicole, 140
Virgia Mae, 145
Wilber Harold, 139
William, 1501
William E, 1501

William Harvey, 137
William Karl, 145
Wilma Ruth, 140
EVEN
Julie Ann, 1793
EVERETT
Esther Elizabeth, 739
EVERHART
Ella, 1425
EVERITT
Florence Olive, 1199
EVERLING
David Marshall, 192
Eric Elizabeth, 192
Roberta Sharlene (Rowand), 192
Steven Marshall, 192
EVERMAN
Lena, 547
Nell, 629
EVERS
Annette Kay (Veits), 1147
Brian Lee, 1147
Bruce Albert, 1147
Charles Albert, 1147
Georgeann A (Garritano), 1147
Judith Adele, 1147
Margaret Leota (Lamb), 1147
EVERSOLE
Charles William, 524
Daisy (Fisher), 626
Evelyn, 626
George, 626
Hiram, 626
Leo, 626
Mary Marjorie (Clampitt), 524
Minor, 626
Richard Arlen, 524
Willard, 626
Woodrow, 524
EVERT
Jane Isabelle, 794
John C, 793
Mary Catharine, 793
Sarah Ann (Weiser), 793
EVERTS
Gladys Irene, 206
EVICK
Sarah, 596
EVINGER
Elmer L, 854
Rena Mae (Nebinger), 854
EWEN
Bonnydelle (Willey), 58
Maurice Maynard, 58
Nancy Louise, 58
William Cliffton, 58
EWER
Charles Cary, 1356
Maidee Schutter, 1356
Mary Ellen (Schutter), 1356
Pauline Ryder, 1356
EWERS
John, 1221
Karen, 1222
Margarette (Grant), 1221
Patricia, 1221
EWING
-- (--), 1226
Alicia Esmundo

(Gonzales), 419
Allison, 808
Anna Grace, 420
Anna Mary (Zuber), 1227
Annie Elizabeth, 1227
Arnold, 1226
Arthur, 449
Bertha Adell (Weiser), 449
Beverly Jean, 692
Brent, 662
Carol, 101
Catherine Gail (Park), 419
Catherine Louise, 804
Clyde Ellis, 1226
Clyde Jr, 1226
Dale, 1226
Dell, 1439
Della, 429
Diane, 1226
Ellen Irene, 1313
Erie Elizabeth (Smith), 1227
Eva Estelle (Weiser), 416
Franklin Eugene, 1227
Gene Marie, 1227
George Thomas, 1227
Grayce Louelle, 1227
James Conrad, 419
James F, 419
Jennie Violet, 1227
Joan Louise (Robinson), 804
John Frederick, 419
John Frederick Jr, 419
Kathleen C, 419
Kenneth Charles, 419
Laura (Seal), 808
Loretta Jane (Zarnowski), 662
Lulu Caroline, 1226
Mabel, 1226
Margaret, 1226
Martha Kennerly (McVeigh), 419
Melanie Christen, 419
Michael Kennerly, 419
Michelle Leigh, 419
Oceana Grace (Kahle), 1226
Pamela, 808
Patricia Joan, 804
Paul Dwight, 419
Rhonda (Williams), 419
Robert, 808
Rodney, 808
Russell, 1226
Sandra Louise (Kuebler), 808
Sena (Thompson), 1226
Sharon Louise, 419
Stanley, 1226
Stephen Dwight, 419
Susan Kathryn, 419
Thomas Allen, 1226
Thomas Neal, 804
Warren, 1226
William Calvin, 1226
EYER
Betty Alene, 680
Sarah, 936
EYLAR
Esther, 998

FASOLD (continued)
Carrie E, 728
Catharine (Weiser), 805-806
Catharine B (Schriver), 806
Catharine Louise, 805, 809
Charles Kroh, 794
Charles L, 777
Charles Leonard, 794
Charlotte Kathryn, 812
Chesty Ann (Shutlz), 811
Christian K, 730
Christopher, 1532
Clara Minnette (Shuman), 811
Clara Vera, 806
Craig, 1042
Darlene Kay, 1042
David, 1043
Dawn Amber, 1042
Debra (Croak), 1042
Diane Elizabeth, 1042
Dolan Weiser, 794
Donald Evert, 793
Donald Robert, 1042
Doris, 1041
Dorothy Hanetta (Steese), 1042
E L, 777
Elizabeth (Greager), 794
Elizabeth Ann, 805, 811
Elwood, 1041
Emma (Stakes), 806
Emma Fasold (Kuebler), 730, 809
Emma Irene (Karbley), 730, 809
Emma Jane, 811
Emma Jean, 805
Ethel Mary (Burget), 793
Evert Lupfer, 793
Fay (Slear), 1042
Fli, 728
Florence App, 794
Forrest Elwood, 1043
Forrest Elwood Jr, 1043
Frank Rolland, 807
George McClellan, 812
Hannah, 1036
Hannah Weiser, 794
Hazel Amber (Wands), 1042
Henry, 805-806, 1883
Howard Marshall, 794
Ida Jane, 793
Irene Lulu, 794
Ivan, 777
Ivan Elwood, 807
Jack Elwood, 1042
James Paul, 1043
Janelle, 1042
Jason Lee, 1042
Jeffrey Lee, 1042
Jerry Marshall, 794
Joan (Shaffer), 1042
Joan (Swope), 1042
John, 806, 1043
John Calvin, 793
Justin Lynn, 1042
Katherine (Kroh), 794
Lena May, 794
Linda Louise, 793

Lisa Hane, 1042
Lottie (Dietz), 1041
Lottie Eva, 806
Lulu (App), 794
Lydia (Hepner), 728
Maranda F (Kimble), 806
Margaret (Albert), 793
Maria (Respelier), 793
Mary (Snyder), 1041
Mary Catharine (Evert), 793
Michelle (Rogers), 1042
Mildred, 806
Milton, 730
Minnie Arlene, 730
Miriam Rebecca, 811
Nettie Catherine, 806
Olive (Karns), 1043
Paul Snyder, 1043
Peter B, 358, 777
Peter Born, 805, 811
Philip Melanchthon, 805, 807, 811
Raymond, 1041
Richard Robert, 793
Robert Albert, 793
Robert Evert, 793
Robin, 1043
Rosa (Martz), 730
Samuel, 730, 793
Sara Claudine, 806
Sara Louise (Propst), 807
Sarah Ann, 805, 807
Solomon W, 805-806
Stella (Penny), 793
Terra Renee, 1042
Terry Ray, 1042
Thelma Sarah, 1042
Theron George, 1042
Theron Reuben, 1042
Timothy Robert, 1042
Valentine, 806
Warren Edward, 806
Willard R, 1042
William A, 730, 809
William W, 730, 777, 809
FATE
Albert Allen, 615
Cindy (Hosler), 615
Connie Diane, 615
Larry Alan, 615
Monica Sue, 616
Virginia Beverly (Long), 615
FATZINGER
Adam, 456
Hannah (Weiser), 430
Lavina (Weiser), 456
Nicholas, 430
FAUCETTE
Rebecca Carol, 1660
FAUL
Linda Marie (Wiser), 1803
Terrel Jay, 1803
FAULTERS
Theola, 136
FAUSNAUGHT
Cathy, 367
Curtis, 366
Jeff, 366
Susan K (Bauder), 366
FAUSOLD
Agnes (Kurp), 728
Arville Lerroy, 728

Charles Elmer, 728
Clarence Guy, 728
Elizabeth Emma, 728
Emma (Raker), 728
Gabrilla, 852
Helen, 728
Mable Anna (Jones), 728
Margaret (Penn), 728
William Earl, 728
FAUST
-- (--), 999
Albert B, 88
Alta, 999
Amy Patricia (Ruggles), 1512
Andy J, 999
Catherine Richter (Schoch), 66
Charles, 999
Dawn Leslie, 1512
Doug, 937
Drusilla Elizabeth, 751
Eli, 999
Elizabeth, 999
Elmer, 999
Eugean Louise (Hynicka), 1512
Evelyn, 999
Evelyn Elaine, 693
Frank, 999
Gerald, 1000
Gertie, 999
Helen, 999
Helen Dorothy (Salada), 693
Henry Arthur, 693
Herbert, 999
Howard, 999
Howard M, 148
J Frank, 66
John, 999
Kyle Allen, 937
Larraine, 1000
Lawrence, 999
Leslie L, 1512
Leslie Leroy, 1512
Marjorie, 999
Mary, 999, 1620
Minnie, 1000, 1145
Myrtle, 999
Nellie, 999
Raymond, 999
Robert Walter, 693
Rosa S, 1762
Sarah (Kehl), 999
Sherry (Phillips), 1512
Tyler Patrick, 1512
Vickie Jo (Smith), 937
Walter Joseph, 693
William, 999
Winnie, 999
FAUTH
Annie J, 1461
FAVILLE
Charles, 1549
Douglas, 1549
Gary, 1549
Thelma Corine (Ramsay), 1549
FAVRO
--, 1720
Kathryn, 1720
Mark, 1720
Michael Andrew, 1720
Michelle, 1720
Sheila Dee, 1720
FAWCET
Maude Ermina (Kahl),

1194
William Jonas, 1194
FAYFIELD
Gretchen Von Hoff (Weiser), 1462
Marsha Weiser, 1463
Robert Hoole, 1462
Robert Weiser, 1463
FEARS
Deborah E, 895
John, 895
Marian W (Eppley), 895
FEATHER
Jacob, 1365, 1402
Margaret (Weiser), 1365
Maria (--), 1402
Maria Margaretha (Weiser), 1402
Peter, 1402
Samuel, 1365
FEBRICK
Christina (Pickert), 1572
Edward, 1572
FECK
Anna Eva, 15, 25
FEDDER
Jacob, 1402
Maria (--), 1402
Maria Margaretha (Weiser), 1402
Peter, 1402
FEDIAN
Geneva, 621
Samuel, 621
FEE
David Hamilton, 83
Edward Hamilton, 83
Eleanor Ruth (Gasser), 83
Helen Anne (Nagel), 83
FEEHRER
Agnes (Coldren), 1047
Janette, 1047
Jean, 1047
Joan, 1047
Medora Susanna, 1047
Merlo, 1047
FEELEY
Kathleen, 310
FEESE
Mary Jane, 731
FEG
-- (--), 357
Agnes, 22
Anna Catharine, 21
Anna Catharine (Schutz), 22
Anna Christina (Becker), 22
Anna Elisabetha, 22
Anna Eva, 19-22, 279, 357, 1267, 1361, 1365, 1403
Anna Margaretha, 21-22
Anna Margaretha (Becker), 22
Anna Margaretha (Koch), 21-22
Anna Maria, 21
Anna Maria (Risch), 19, 21, 23
Catharine (Fischer), 1472
Christina, 21

Christina (Karr), 21
Elisabetha, 21
Eva Elisabetha, 21
Eva Magdalena, 21
Jacob, 21
Janige Johanna (Hussen), 21
Johann Leonhardt, 21
Johann Nicholas, 22
Johann Peter, 23
Johannes, 21-23, 1472
John Peter, 20-23
Leonhardt, 22
Magdalena, 21
Margaretha (Weiser), 22
Maria Catharina, 21-22
Nicholas, 21-22
Nicolaus, 22
Niklas, 357
Peter, 19, 21-22
Sophia, 21
FEGELY
Hattie E, 1638
FEGLE
Louise, 737
FEGLEY
Adam, 784
Alan Daniel, 1025
Ann Louise, 1025
Annie A (Ellenberger), 784
Barbara, 785
Beatrice, 785
Bell K, 786
Bessie, 1168
Calvin Markly, 1025
Catharine (Keefer), 784
Charles, 1025
Clifford, 784
Constance Eileen (Renn), 1025
Darla, 784
David A, 784
Donald Keith, 1025
Elizabeth, 785
Elizabeth C, 785
Ellen J, 1638
Eva Victoria (Kieffer), 1643
Florence (Ruhl), 784
Frank H, 1643
George, 784
George W, 784
Helen, 1111
Helen (Wagner), 784
Ida (Defrain), 784
Jacqueline, 784
Jean, 784
Laura Jane, 784
Luther M, 784
Mary, 784
Mary (Heim), 784
Nancy (Hetrick), 1025
Pearl (Osman), 1025
Peggy, 784
Peter Irvin, 784
Rebecca Catherine, 1522
Richard Keith, 1025
Robert, 785
Sharon, 784
Wendy Lee, 1025
William, 784, 1522
FEHL
Cheri Ann, 858
Harry Keith, 858
Harry LaForce, 858
Harry LaForce Jr, 858

FETROW (continued)
Grant William, 876
Horace Birdsell, 126
John Jacob, 876
Lucetta Eppley, 876
Miriam Elizabeth, 159
Samertha (Shettel), 876
FETT
Eli, 468
Myrtle Ruth (Binkley), 468
FETTER
-- (--), 777
Ada G (Weiser), 1614
David A, 785
Douglas Vastine, 785
Edna M (Seiler), 785
Elizabeth, 785
Elizabeth C (Fegley), 785
Grace (Ryan), 785
Harriet (Tompkins), 786
Howard Douglas, 785
Howard S, 785
Howard Sedgwick, 785
Ingrid, 106
Lauretta I, 1614
Linda Ruth, 785
Margaret (Bahner), 786
Mary Elizabeth (Braggins), 785
Maude Mae, 1614
Nancy, 785
Nancy Ellen, 785
Noreene (Bowers), 786
Paul E, 786
Phyllis, 785
Robert C, 786
Robert C Jr, 786
Russell W, 786
Ruth (Evans), 785
Sallie Ann, 786
Susan Catharine, 785
Susan June, 785
Travis, 1614
William, 777, 785
William R, 1614
FETTERHOFF
Thomas, 658
FETTEROLF
Deloris, 1085
Elinor (Stover), 1085
Gerald Samuel, 1085
Isabella, 1085
Leon Paul, 1085
Paul, 1085
Ruth (Yearick), 1085
Victoria, 1085
FICHTHORN
Elwood, 901
Emily L, 339
Grace, 901
Ivie, 901
Mary Elizabeth(Womelsdorf), 901
Sebastian, 901
FICHTNER
Donald, 370
Lynn Allen, 370
Patricia Lee, 369
Ralph, 369
Vera Jean (Cleveland), 369
FICKES
Margaret, 1586
FIDDLER
Rena Deluth, 1298

FIDLER
Adam Claude, 297
Alfred Smith, 297
Arthur Penn, 297
Brooke, 846
Elias, 296
Elias Shulze, 297
Eliza Matilda (Shulze), 296
Fannie S (Smith), 296
Frederick Augustus, 297
Frederick Ralph, 297
Henry Shulze, 296
Herbert Smith, 297
Howard V, 297
Julia Catherine, 296
Julia Eliza, 297
Kathryn (Anspach), 846
Lizzie H (Valentine), 297
Mary Frances, 296
FIEDLER
Betty (--), 1003-1004
Catherine (Weber), 1003
Darwin, 1003
daughter, 1003
Edwin Kahl, 1003
Esther, 1004
Harrison, 1003
Janet, 1003
Leroy, 1003
Lydia Mabal Eve (Kahl), 1003
Mabel, 1004
Margaret, 1003
Mary, 1004
Melvin, 1004
Nevin, 1004
Rhea Almeda, 1003
Vida, 1004
FIELD
Maria, 1508
FIELDS
--, 504, 1377
Carla Jean (Wolff), 504
Douglas, 1802
Gay Michelle, 1071
Glenora, 547
Jennifer, 1377
Mary (Wiser), 1802
Rosina, 1840
Ryan, 1377
Terri (Donahue), 1377
FIEST
David L, 287
Erika Wagner, 287
Gregory Wagner, 287
Greta Whiteman (Wagner), 287
FIGGINS
Alphonso Bernard, 558
Dora Ann, 558
Lois Blanch (Fess), 558
Phillip Fess, 558
FIKE
Donald, 817
Dorothy Jean (Womeldorf), 817
FILBERT
Jennifer Joyce, 937
Karen Ann (Smith), 936
Phoebe, 834
Ronald, 936

FILEWICH
--, 1861
Beatrice M (Wiser), 1861
FILGER
Vera M, 1488
FILION
Natalie Evelyn, 1056
FILIUS
Jessica, 1538
Joel, 1538
Lauren, 1538
Pamela (Muggiio), 1538
FILLIPI
Shirley, 490
FILONCZAK
Belinda Mae, 633
Deborah Anne, 633
Myrtle Lou (Smith), 633
Norbert, 633
FIMBRES
--, 375
Erleta (Steward), 375
Patrick Donald, 375
Paul Michael, 375
Paula Ann, 375
Peggy Juanita, 375
Perry V, 375
Peter David, 375
FINBINER
Phyllis, 1190
FINCH
Cleo Helen (Smith), 634
Dean K, 1189
Florence B, 1345
Kenneth, 634
Mary Elizabeth, 1576
Wilma Margaret (Rice), 1189
FINCHER
Daniel Lee, 1813
Tammy Sue (Wiser), 1813
FINCK
Billy Ray, 998
Helen Mae (Kahl), 998
Penny Jo, 998
FINCKH
Christiane Karoline (Heller), 1606
Georg Jakob, 1606
Philippine Elisabeth Friederike (Weisser), 1606
FINDLER
Alice Bruce (Harden), 282
Edward Price, 282
Patrick McCormack, 283
Peter Muhlenberg, 283
Robert Bruce, 282
William Edward, 282
FINDLING
Barbara Jeanne (Lau), 249
Paul Edward, 249
Paul Edward Jr, 250
FINE
David A, 1447
Nancy Jane (Spyker), 1447
FINK
Charles Edward, 890
Darlene, 588
Elizabeth Reese, 890

Emma (Johnson), 890
Frederick C, 890
Katherine Bergner, 890
Mary Elizabeth (Eppley), 890
Mary Hutter, 890
Phyllis Catharine, 1175
William Conrad, 890
FINKBONE
Alice Marie, 686
Betty Mae, 686
Dorothy Mae, 689
Jessie Marie (Conrath), 686
John Adam, 686
Kathy Marie, 686
Lena Sarah (Kocher), 686
Lois Geraldine, 686
Paula Lynn (Grubrick), 686
William Frederick, 686
William Frederick Jr, 686
FINKELSTEIN
Nan, 989
FINKS
Catherine C, 355
FINLEY
--, 1540
Clara Dock, 1540
Lillian (Dock), 1540
FINN
Betty Irene, 1494
FINNERTY
Kevin Conyers, 1691
Ryan Congers, 1691
Sara Brinanne, 1691
Susan Elaine (Kephart) Arnold, 1691
FINNEY
Bryan, 1720
Jeff, 1720
Kara (Bauman), 1720
FIRMAN
Thirzah Lenthena, 977
FIRST
Edward Curry, 794-795
Jane Isabelle (Conrad), 794
Mary Patricia, 795
Theodore Conrad, 795
FISCHER
Adam David, 107
Anna Elizabeth, 1472
Carolyn Denise, 538
Catharine, 1472
Catharine (Zimmermann), 1472
Cheryl (Stock), 92
Cheryl Kaye, 538
Christian, 1472
Cord, 92
Don, 107
Eliza Ruth, 884
Jacob, 1472
Janet Virginia, 909
Johannes, 1472
Maria (Breitenbach), 1472
Mary N C, 771
Penny Darlene, 539
Richard Eugene, 538
Sandra Lee (Eppley), 884
Sharon Puiu, 884
Sue Ann (Borror), 107
Theodore Daniel, 884

Theresa Elaine, 539
Timothy, 107
Wilma Jean (Herring), 538
FISEH
Lorraine Mary Elizabeth, 387
FISH
Belva Elizabeth (Stingly), 271
Elizabeth Ruth, 271
Guy Alonzo, 271
Marian Grace, 271
Molly Maxine (Wiser), 1815
Pamela, 1219
Wesley Merle, 1815
FISHBURN
Vonda Charlene, 745
FISHEL
Nancy Jane (Mader), 908
Vernon O, 908
FISHER
Adam, 625, 628, 1403
Albert, 1455
Albert W, 1455
Alice Marie (Charles), 520
Almanary, 510
Alton, 1758
Amelia Catharine (Weiser), 1455
Amelia Susan, 1455
Andrew, 634
Angela Carol, 139
Anna (Mounce), 628
Anna Elizabeth, 634
Anna May (Wieser), 1758
Annie, 1086
Arthur J, 1758
Avery Revere, 520
baby girl, 635
Barbara, 462, 595
Barnard, 628
Benjamin, 510
Bennet Thomas, 275
Bertha (--), 863
Bertha M, 625
Bertha May, 625
Bessie, 626
Betty, 1526
Betty (Herold), 1526
Bruce, 864
Bryan, 864
Cardiff Edwin, 753
Carl Joseph, 635
Carol Ann, 1128
Carolina (Shively), 625
Carolyn (Little), 626
Carrie A (Hamsher), 1643
Catharine, 462, 1455, 1644
Catharine Gertie, 1758
Catherine, 462, 509, 521, 597, 626-627
Catherine Lucille, 1312
Charles, 519, 864, 1455
Charles Ansell, 520
Charles E, 1455
Charles J, 634
Charles S, 1643
Charles William, 521
Chesselden, 62
Christian, 462, 509
Clara Wilma, 636

FORMAN (continued)
Lesley Bliss (Schwab), 311
Peter B, 311
FORNEY
Eli, 1427
Elizabeth (Nes), 1427
Harry, 676
Pauline Elizabeth (Lenker), 676
FORNSHELL
Archie, 560
Beatrice, 560
Chloe, 560
Clarence, 560
Daisy (Herring), 560
Everett, 560
Frieda Mae, 560
Helen, 560
Kenneth, 560
Marjorie, 560
Pauline, 560
Perna (McCally), 560
FORREST
Beatrice Pauline (Schell), 1318
Carol Ann (Fleischman), 1319, 1325
Charles Adam, 1319, 1325
Cheri Dawn (Leyes), 1319, 1325
David Ellis, 1319, 1325
Donald Eric, 1319, 1325
Douglas Daniel, 1319, 1325
Douglas Eugene, 1319, 1325
Elizabeth Amanda, 1319, 1325
Jean Marcella, 1318
Lauri (Cost), 1319
Laurie (Cost), 1325
Linda Marie (Griffo), 1319, 1325
Lois Elaine, 1318
Maude Elvira, 1321
Richard Ellis, 1319, 1325
Robert Ellis, 1318
FORRESTER
Tammy, 1673
FORRY
Lucy A, 1428
FORSHEY
Vina Blanche, 1531
FORSLUND
Esther, 149
FORST
Ruth Juanita, 572
FORSYTHE
Bert, 1225
Clifford, 1225
Edna, 1225
Ellsworth, 1225
Ethel (Jones), 1225
Eva (Thompson), 1225
Fannie Elizabeth, 1225
Frank, 1224
George, 1225
Howard, 1225
Kate, 1225
Leone, 1225
Lillian, 1225
Lucina (Kahle), 1224
Milton K, 1225

Myrtle G, 1225
Viola Lou, 1224
Wesley, 1225
FORTENBAUGH
Anna D, 882
FORTH
Magdalena, 1584
FORTNA
Ethel Sarah, 903
FORTSON
Susan, 1213
FORTUNE
--, 1507
Sarah Virginia (Rahm), 1507
FOSBINER
John Patrick, 578
Lani Jo (Byrd), 578
FOSCATO
Barbara Ann, 1170
FOSS
Signe Marie, 1462
FOSSELMAN
Brenda Lee, 1373
Helen (McCarthy), 1373
Randall J Jr, 1373
Randall Josiah, 1373
Sara Josephine (Randall), 1373
Wharton, 1373
FOSSINGER
Adam, 456
Adam Frederick, 459
Angeline, 457
Anna Sophia, 430
Barbara, 459
Bounie Weil, 461
Christie, 442
Cornelius, 456
Cuma Mae, 459
Emanuel, 442
Emeline, 457
Floy Mae (Hodges), 461
Hannah (Weiser), 430
Harriet Ellen, 442
Harvey, 442
James Berton, 461
Janett Marie, 461
Jennie (Young), 442
Julia Ann (Webb), 459
Karon Margene, 461
Lavina (Weiser), 456
Lovina Weiser, 1883
Lusina, 459
Mae (Roach), 442
Marian Lake, 442
Marion Lake, 441
Marjorie Cora (Stroudt), 461
Murrill Vaneel, 461
Myrtle, 442
Nicholas, 430
Raymond, 442
Sarah (Ginder), 442
Sharon Merlin, 461
Vancel Sidney, 461
Wilma Gail, 461
FOSTER
--, 1710
Albert III, 690
Albert Jr, 690
Alfred, 1686
Allen, 393
Berton S, 1686
Bonnie Jean, 1501
Charles Frederick, 392
Clarence, 393

Dennis, 393
Dennis Charles, 392
Diane Marie, 494
Donald, 1211
Donnie, 393
Dorothy, 392
Edna (Wisor), 1710
Elsie Ernestine (Poling), 392
Elva (Kephart), 1686
Frederick Ernest, 392
Geneva Wineford (Meeker), 392
George, 1686
Inez Blanche (Mattox), 392
Kate (Seiler), 1398
Kenneth, 528
Larry, 393
Leslie, 1519
Linwood, 1625
Lois Lee (Brammer), 392
Lori Jean, 393
Lydia Annetta (Weiser), 1625
Lynn Michelle (Martin), 1211
Maria Helen (Wickham), 528
Mary (Grimsley), 1686
Mary Ann, 642
Mary Florence (Swatsworth), 1686
Mary Jean, 393
Maynard, 1710
Melba Grace, 432
Melvin, 392
Michael P, 1398
Miriam, 1710
Morgan, 690
Nancy Jane (Smeal), 1686
Princess (Loveland), 393
Robert, 393
Stella May, 392
Stephen, 393
Susan Jean (Matter), 690
Thelma (Wisor), 1710
Wendolyn Kaye, 425
FOTE
Florence, 1107
FOTH
Christine Ruth, 1485
Eileen Marie, 1485
Gretchen Sue, 1485
Kay Jolene, 1484
Kimberly Ann, 1485
Lyle Leon, 1484
Myrnie Ruby (Leonard), 1484
Ruth Elma (Meier), 1484
Walter John, 1484
FOUGHT
Alicia Louise, 479
Gladys (Karr), 472
James Kenneth, 472
Kenneth, 472
Mary Kay, 472
Norma Jean (Minich), 472
FOULER
--, 1592
Ester (Barnett), 1592
FOULK
daughter, 192

Fiester F, 192
Helen Elizabeth (Nichols), 192
Olive Lorena (Weiser), 192
Robert E, 192
FOULKE
Charlotte Ann (Kline), 1525
James C, 1525
FOUNTAIN
Ann Elizabeth, 159
Grace Lillie, 1840
FOUST
Belle Muriel, 48
Carl, 49, 1567
Carrie (Hoffert), 1567
Carroll, 49
Charles, 1094
Cinda, 49
Emory, 552
Ernest Jr, 49
Ernest Stanley, 49
Garth Eugene, 49
Gennieve, 49
Gennieve (Sowers), 49
Hildred Louise (Stinson), 552
Joseph, 135
Kathleen Faye (Beanard), 750
Kathryn (Highland), 49
Lester Roy Jr, 750
Linda, 49
Margarite (White), 49
Marlyn Darlene, 49
Martha Ellen (Willey), 48
Myrna Sue, 552
Nancy, 147-148
Nancy (Bierly), 1094
Pauline Amelia (Oradat), 534
Priscilla (Weiser), 135
Robert, 534
Timothy Scott, 1094
William Cline, 48
Yvonne R, 1567
FOVEL
Hazel, 205
FOWKES
Donna Faye, 1394
FOWLER
Mildred, 1013
Paul, 1291
Sarah Alice (Weiser), 1291
FOX
Adelaide (Hynicka), 1510
Albert, 578
Anna, 576
Anna Patton, 1510
Anthony Lee, 536
Betty, 861
Cami Linn, 1279
Caroline Elizabeth (Hynicka), 1510
Charles, 838
Christian Amos, 1279
Christie Lynn, 537
Cindy Lou (Doverspike), 1279
Cinthia Lynn, 1279
Clara, 577
Cleo, 1051
Dale, 1052
David Carl, 1510
Dorothy, 364

E E, 1051
Earl, 1051
Edna Catherine (Herring), 536
Elizabeth, 1510
Elizabeth Ann, 142
Elizabeth Catherine, 1320, 1338
Ella (Wiser), 1862
Ella E (Wiser), 1862
Emma, 578
Eric Chris, 1279
Erin Leah, 1279
Evelyn, 1051
Fannie (Erhard), 1051
Floyd, 1051
Frances, 1051
Fred, 578
Grace Ethel, 841
Joan Hynicka, 1510
John, 1862
Julie Marie, 537
Karen Suzanne, 1279
Kelly Jo, 536
Leah (Herring), 576
Leona, 838
Lillie, 578
Lizzie, 1099
Lydia Ann, 1311
Marie (Burnw), 1510
Marilyn Louella (Seigworth), 1279
Mary Catherine, 576
Mary Elizabeth, 1240
May, 1510
Michael A, 1742
Miriam B, 1809
Natalie Ann, 1279
Noel Leon, 536
Nona Freelove, 536
Nora Amanda (Anspach), 838
Nyle Orin, 536
Oris, 536
Penalope Kay Lennon (Clouse), 536
Richard, 1510
Richard V, 1510
Roy, 1051
Ruth, 1051
Sandra Ann, 1279
Sandra Elaine (Buis), 536
Sarah Loretta, 577
Staci Lynn, 536
Suzanne L (DeHaven), 1742
Teresa (Beck), 536
Tiffany Rose, 536
William, 576
FOXWORTHY
Cora Frances (Smith), 431
Frances, 431
Glenn, 431
Homer, 431
Patty (Beck), 431
FOY
Barbara Ellen (Herring), 534
Larry Allen, 534
FOYE
Maude, 787
FRACALOSSI
Mary Jane (Beadle), 725
Norman, 725
FRAGA
Edward Lino, 372

FREED (continued)
Marion F, 872
Mary, 872
Mary (Howard), 872
Michael Scott, 872
Morgan H, 872
Nancy (McAfee), 872
Paul, 872
Paul Jr, 872
Phyllis (Fetter), 785
Ralph P, 872
Rhoda (Gress), 872
Sandra, 872
Spencer S, 872
Tyrell R, 872
William S, 872
William S Jr, 872
FREEGARD
Judith Laurel (Seaman), 374
Richard Mark, 374
FREEHAFER
Amy Clara (Eikelburner), 272
Dawn Renee, 272
Eric, 272
Jane S, 295
Leif, 272
Rhett, 272
FREEL
Ruth Agnes, 1467
FREELAND
Allison Bird, 331
Barbara Joan (Staub), 331
Dora Belle Cline, 1154
Effie May, 842
Samuel Lyles, 331
FREELING
Catherine, 1406
FREEMAN
--, 1843
Alvina, 1702
Derek, 1719
Kathy (Bauman), 1719
Katie, 1719
Marlin, 1719
Mary Tesianna (Loveless), 1843
Sally Ann, 1749
FREESE
Marianna Elizabeth, 848
FREEZE
Elizabeth W, 1822
Samantha Louise, 745
FREIMUTH
Lois Margaret, 1289
FREJAE
Derrick, 637
Sheila Dawn (Johnson), 637
FRELKE
Claude Charles, 1304
Patricia (Coukart) Butler, 1304
FRENCH
Cassidy Alexandra, 1157
John Philip Jr, 1157
Kellie Dianne (Cordier), 1157
Rylee Rebekah, 1157
FRESCHEL
Candice, 629
FRETHEIM
Myrtle Geneva, 179
FRETINA
John, 1255

John B, 1255
Myrna Lee (Chancey), 1255
Myrna Renee, 1255
FRETZ
Harriet Ann, 1627
FREW
Brian Rodney, 1282
Tina Marie (Seigworth), 1282
FREY
-- (--), 777
Antionette Kay, 412
Audrey, 789
Barbara J (Knoll), 787
Bettie (Moon), 470
C Lysle, 787
C Lysle Jr, 787
Carl, 256
Charles, 788
Charles A, 1754
Christiana (Kramer), 787
Cristin A, 788
Dana, 470
Dawn Marie, 789
Deborah M (Beard), 788
Dorothy Jean, 749
Dorothy Mabel (Brehm), 256
Douglas L, 788
Elizabeth, 787
Emma E (Wisser), 1754
Florence Haller, 1475
Frank, 787
Frederick E, 788, 1884
Frederick E Sr, 777
Frederick Eugene, 788
George Washington, 749
George Washington Jr, 749
Georgiana (Vandling), 787
Georgiana Keefer, 787
Geraldine, 789
Gordon K, 788
James E, 787
Joyce (Green), 788
Joyce (Hoover), 788
Kalaeu, 788
Kathryn B (Loetscher), 787
Kelly (Heinley), 789
Kristan L, 788
Lauren E, 788
Lillian (Sickles), 470
Lottie Irene (Ross), 749
Lyle D, 789
Lyle D Jr, 789
Lysle, 777
Manforn, 788
Mary Elizabeth, 1834
Mary Louisa, 1732
May C, 1642
Michael, 788
Michael Aiken, 470
Myrtle Eleanor (McGowin), 469
Nathan, 788
Phillip M, 789
Phyllis Victoria, 788
Regina (Roland), 788
Royal Desmond, 470
Ryan F, 788
Sharon (Noreen), 749

Shawn, 788
Shirley Ann, 470
Soren Offerson, 470
Stacy Jane, 470
Todd M, 789
William John, 469
Wilma Alida, 469
FREYTAG
Christoph Andreas, 318
Cornelia Anette, 318
Hedwig (Kulenkampff), 318
Michael Burghard, 318
FRIANT
Amanda Rachel (Krigbaum), 116
James F, 116
FRICK
Bruce G, 1033
Bruce G Jr, 1033
Dennis Joseph, 691
Florence Edna (Rhoads), 1033
Jean Catherine, 1033
Jenniebell (Stumpff), 1033
Judith L (Merrill), 1033
Justin Matthew, 691
Kristine, 582
Lorna Mae (Wade), 691
Martha, 1034
Mary Edna, 1033
Mary Margaret, 1421
Suzanne (Grugan), 1033
Terrance Craig, 1033
Thomas Rhoads, 1033
Thomas Rhoads Jr, 1033
W K, 279
FRICKE
Sandra Kay, 1799
FRICKER
--, 1462
Anna Maria, 1362
Anna Maria (Kerrstahler), 1362
Anthony, 1361-1362
Barbara (Siegfried), 1362
Beulah Helen (Weiser) Kampschroer, 1462
Catharine, 1361, 1363
Catherine Elizabeth, 1362
Elizabeth (Gravel), 1362
Ellen Rebecca, 1362
George, 1362
Henrick, 1362
Henriette, 1362
Henry George, 1361-1362
John, 1361-1363
John Franklin, 1362
John Frederick, 1362-1363
Magdalen, 1361
Margaret, 1361-1362
Margaret (Weiser) Heintzelmann, 1361
Maria, 1362
Maria Eva (Becker) Zweger, 1361
Maria Margaretha, 1362

Mary, 1361
Mary Catharine, 1361-1362
Mary Eva, 1361
Mary Jane, 1362
Peter, 1361-1362
Stephen, 1361-1363
Thomas, 1361-1363
William, 1361-1362
FRIDY
Iris Carolyn, 1014
FRIEDRICH
Alyssa Erin, 231
Cheryl, 1190
Elke, 1599
Joshua Patrick, 231
Marlis (Wagenmann) Pingel, 1599
Mary Beth (Miller), 231
Michael, 231
Wolfgang, 1599
FRIEL
Charles, 1058
Genevieve (Miller), 1058
FRIEND
Audrey Fay, 617
FRIESCH
Maria, 1599
FRITCHE
Dora Grace, 99
John, 99
Mary Ellen (Deppen), 99
FRITCHIE
Bertha, 102
Cora Ann, 101
Lucy, 104
FRITSCH
Alfred, 1742
Elda W, 1643, 1742
Franklin, 1742
Jennie, 1742
Jonas, 1742
Katie Christina Alice, 1742
Martha W, 1742
Sarah, 1742
Sarah Ann (Wieser), 1742
FRITZ
Addis, 263
Alice, 1732
Benjamin, 1732
Carol Elaine, 1333
Catherine Ulrich (Hower), 77
Charles, 782
Charles William, 783
Christina Louise, 265
Connie (Wright), 1333
Elaine Rae (Dellar), 1333
Ella A, 1758
Emma Blanche, 782
Florence May (Goodling), 714
Ida (Haschel), 263
Irene, 777
Irene Jemima, 783
Jemima (Weiser), 782
John Leo, 714
Joseph Charles, 1333
Joseph Charles II, 1333
Joseph Charles III, 1333
Kimberly Sue, 1333
Martin Luther, 783

Mary Ann (Wieser), 1732
Mary Jane, 782
Matilda, 514
Sarah Alice, 782
Steven Ray, 1333
Thelma Pauline (Daughters), 1333
Warren, 77
William, 263
FRITZEN
Frica, 342
FRIZ
Anthony, 810
Kathryn Ann (Hotvedt), 810
William, 810
FRODGE
Didi, 1179
Pamela, 1179
Pamela (Kepler), 1179
Troy R, 1179
FROEHLICH
Aleen K (--), 1214
Aleen Wilma Kahle Mowen, 1215
FROELICH
Aleen Wilma (Kahle), 1216
Frederick William, 1216
Jack L, 1418-1419
Martha Helen (Moltz), 1418
FROMAN
Barbara Jeanne, 213
FROMM
Augusta, 1880
FROMMELT
Brian, 968
David Alan, 968
Deanne Marie, 968
Dorothy Rae (White), 967
Mary Kay, 968
Merlin, 967
Michael Ray, 968
FRONK
Donald Barry, 698
Donald Emmet, 698
Jean Ann, 699
Jean Merium (Suloff), 698
FROST
-- (--), 993
Adam, 993
Barbara Jean, 434, 460
Beverly Alene, 460
Billie Mae, 1233
Caroline, 1787
Carrie Michelle, 435, 460
Charlotte Marie, 435, 460
Christopher, 993
Craig, 993
Craig Allen, 435, 460
Cuma Mae (Fossinger), 459
Diana, 1328
Donald Lewis, 993
Donna (Crockmen), 459
Douglas Day, 993
Ed, 441
Elizabeth Sylvia (Goble), 1233
Ella Mae (Ely), 435, 460

FURMAN (continued)
Patricia (Frank), 757
Paul John, 755
Reid Epler, 756
Sarah Elnora, 756
Sharon Dawn, 757
Shawn Wesley, 755
Susan (Lenker), 757
Suzanne (Brown), 756
Tammy Jane, 755
William Webster, 757
William Webster Jr,
757
FURNAS
Catherine Tyleman,
1339
FURNISH
Cathy Sue (Herring),
566
Christopher Michael,
566
Dick, 566
Melissa Renee, 566
FURR
Catharine (Wiser),
1786
Henry, 1786
John, 1786
FURST
Elizabeth (Sager), 978
Fred, 978
George Burner, 978
FUSS
Marilyn Ann, 1202
FUSSELMAN
Ruth B, 1741
FUTEY
Bonnie, 1366
Bonnie Jeanne
(Brunell), 1369
John Steven, 1369
FYE
Angela Dee, 1354
Ann Elizabeth(Norton),
1354
Charles Leverne, 1354
Lora Louise, 1354
Shirley Mason, 1304
Tamalyu Kay, 1265
FYSH
Genevieve Mae, 1691
GABLER
Ilse Johanna Hildegard,
321
Judie Ann, 227
GABY
Alison Opal Jean, 1581
Bonita Faye (Dillard),
1581
David Paul, 1581
George Edward, 1581
Lauren Elizabeth, 1581
Lydia Faye, 1581
Margaret, 1581
Margaret Elizabeth,
1581
Martha Ann (Sweazy),
1581
GADDIS
Blanche Cecil (Spyker),
1447
Clyde Albert, 1447
Frank Arthur, 1447
Helen A, 1504
John, 1447
Lois Ann, 1447
Mary Alice, 1447
Ruth Alma, 1447
Thelma, 1447

GAERTNER
Joyce Ann, 349
Oscar Max Otto, 349
Richard Otto, 349
Susan, 1459
Wilhelmine (McKnight),
349
GAFFIN
Donna Lee (Kirschke),
117
Megan Ann, 117
William Ward, 117
GAGE
Nell, 750
GAGEL
Alice S, 1859
GAHMAN
Anne Marie (Miller),
231
Brandon Brian, 231
Brian Richard, 231
Kevin Jack, 231
GAINES
Genene, 1806
GAISER
Emma, 1338
GALATRO
Elizabeth Ann (Wieser),
1738
Jefferson Charles, 1738
GALBEATH
Kathryn, 681
GALBREATH
Mary, 1217
GALE
Denise, 266
Patty (Brown), 266
Wayne, 266
GALEHER
Patricia, 1035
GALEONE
Linda Diane (Wilde),
932
Riccardo, 932
Steven, 932
GALER
Cleris M, 684
GALFORD
Joan Elizabeth
(Schmid), 1490
GALL
Catharina, 6
GALLAGHER
--, 821
Betty Lou, 444
Elizabeth (Kreible),
821
Emma, 281
Linda Ann, 1557
Lisa Ann, 728
Mary Ann (Stone),
1683
Mary Emily (Ryan),
728
Patrick, 1683
Robert, 728
GALLAHER
Betty Jo (Weiser), 1142
Carrie, 1722
Devin, 1142
Kylee, 1142
May A, 1720
Ronald, 1142
GALLAND
Mary, 585
GALLANT
Jeanmarie, 419
GALLATIN
Emily (Morris), 337

Jean B, 335
Rolaz Horace, 337
GALLEGOS
Amanda Elizabeth
(Storlie), 1318
Jesse Jr, 1318
GALLOPS
Deborah, 747
GALLUP
James, 486
Mary Elizabeth, 1827
Valerie Yvonne (Kern),
486
GALPIN
Elizabeth
(Montgomery), 311
James Lyman, 311
Katharine Baldwin, 311
Mary Baldwin, 311
Priscilla Bliss, 311
Ruth Bliss (Schwab),
311
Samuel Kellogg, 311
Stephen Kellogg, 311
Stephen Kellogg Jr,
311
Susan English, 312
GAMBER
Carrie Lynn (Smith),
229
George, 229
Joseph Thomas, 229
Nancy C, 216
Nancy Elizabeth
(Clausen), 229
Thomas Allen, 229
Trisha Nicole, 229
GAMBILL
Bertha Lee, 435
Esquire, 434
Helen Irene, 434
Marjorie Doris, 434,
460
Nellie Ocelene (Smith),
434
GAMBLE
Ada (Wiser) Smith,
1777
Harry Siddoway, 1777
GANAS
Daniel John, 969
Karen Elizabeth
(Morford), 969
GANGAWARE
Dale Raymond, 132
Donald, 132
Edith (Snyder), 132
Edward E H, 132
Evelyn Irene, 132
William John, 132
GANGLE
Adam Matthias, 407
Andrew George, 407
Katrina Annette (Guest),
407
GANN
Dorris Jean (Forbus),
527
Larry Dean, 527
Wallace A, 527
GANOE
Cheri Ann, 1273
Marcia Rayleen, 1273
Noreen Ruth
(Seigworth), 1273
Raymond Albert, 1273
Steven Ray, 1273
GANORING
Carl Albert, 863

Ruth Virginia (Wertz),
863
Steven Wayne, 863
GANT
Dixie Sarah, 1151
GANTHER
Helen, 391
GANTZ
Amy, 663
GARBER
--, 1635
Andora, 348
Barbara, 1324
Mary E (Weiser), 1635
Robert L, 1636
GARCIA
Catherine, 1386
Daniel Orlando, 123
Gloria Jean (Bradbury),
123
Guadalupe, 469
Joseph Edward, 123
Shonta Marie, 475
GARD
Brady Eugene, 572
Cynthia Sue (Lee), 572
Janet Sue, 571
Michael, 572
GARDEN
Babe, 269
Cherie, 269
Pricila (Straw), 269
GARDNER
--, 1671
-- (--), 719
Aaron Lee, 1211
Ada C, 534
Almeda Rose,
1211 1212
Amanda Leigh, 166
Angel (Tomasovsky),
438
Anita Marie, 1211
Ann Marie, 438
Anthony Stuart, 166
Beckey Lee (Weiser),
191
Bernard Charles, 165
Beverly, 722
Carol (Faile), 437
Carol (Gordon), 437
Charie (NcNair), 437
Charles, 1498
Charles Weilliam, 165
Chelsea, 438
Clarence George, 1069
Collene, 437
Connie Louise Paine
(Lynch), 166
Daniel Paul, 438
Danny, 437
David, 1069
David Edward, 166
David Thomas, 1211
Debra Ann, 166
Diane Catherine
(Worzniak), 166
Dixie Lee (Cutter),
1211
Emily, 1069
Estelle G (Poitras), 166
Eveline Noelle, 166
Flora (Hepner), 722
Grace Keyser
(MacIntire), 1069
Heather, 1069
Hilda M (Wiser), 1671
Hope, 1671
Irene (--), 1211

Jack W, 1498
James Lee, 1211
Jamie Ann, 1211
Jan Rachele, 437
Jane (West), 1498
Janell (Wiser), 1769
Jeanene (Knight), 1069
Jeffrey Lynn, 166
Jennie May, 1649
Jennifer, 1069
Jeremy Charles, 166
Jessica, 437
John Charles, 166
Jonathan, 1069
Josephine (Santore),
1498
Judy Elaine, 166
Julie Ellen, 166
Kalista Lee, 1211
Karen Jean, 438
Katie Mae, 166
Kennedy Burns, 437
Kenneth Patrick, 191
Laurlyn Amanda, 166
Leland, 1211
Linnie, 1562
Lori (Offringa), 1069
Mary Elizabeth, 1498
Matthew, 1069
Michael Anthony, 166
Michelle Cash (Wise),
437
Mitchell, 437
Mitchell II, 437
Morgan, 438
Nichele Elaine, 166
Patricia Ann, 1498
Patrick, 438
Patrick Jerome, 438
Paul, 1069, 1671
Randall Scott, 437
Rebecca (Rhodes),
1069
Rebecca Ann
(Yingling), 165
Reginald Jay, 1069
Rose Ann Almeda
(Martin), 1211
Sandra Joyce (Pappas),
166
Sarah (Sisbarro), 1069
Scott, 1069
Sean, 1069
Stella Romaine
(Weiser), 165
Stephanie Dawn, 1211
Tammy Ann, 166
Teresa (Haas), 438
Timothy Mark, 438
twin girls, 438
Vanessa, 1069
Veva Leota (Beck),
437
Victoria (Phillips),
1069
Virginia, 1069
Warren Lewis, 1069
Warren Lewis II, 1069
Wayne L, 1769
William, 719, 722
William James, 1069
Wilson Keyser, 1069
GAREY
Kenneth, 383
Mary L (Leibold), 383
Mattie Elmeda, 1041
Sandra K, 383
GARGAC
Mary Margaret, 497

GIBBONEY (continued)
Marguerite Kees
(Keen) (continued)
(Keen), 1390
Phyllis Elaine, 1390
Richard A, 1390
Richard II, 1390
Roberta (Henderson), 1390
GIBBONS
Anna Marie (Manon), 235
Brenda Kay, 276
Cheryl (--), 275
Dale Michael, 235
Gale Patrick, 235
Harold Joseph, 235
Jean Marie, 235
John Robert, 275
Joyce Ellen (Douglass), 275
Karen Sue, 275
Linda Marie, 276
Lois, 1672
Michael Joseph, 235
Reva Ellen (Roach), 235
Robert L, 275
Vonnie (Oldham), 235
GIBBS
--, 999
Charlotte Mae, 1836
Ethel, 169
Helen (Faust), 999
Katharine, 56
GIBBSON
Rebecca, 538
GIBERSON
Gary, 1385
Susan Gay (Harter), 1385
GIBLIN
Bethany Jane, 1550
Edward Gerald, 1550
Evelyn Grace, 1550
Jane Evelyn (Franck), 1550
GIBSON
--, 1183
Alan Willard, 388
Angeline, 1795
Anna B, 1184
Avery, 1183
Byrd, 1183
Charles A, 1183
Hazel Vila (Duck), 1089
Janie Elisa, 1562
Jeanne Marie, 1089
John, 1562
Laina E (--), 1183
Lena Elsie (Tuller), 388
Leslie Corrington, 218
Maggie, 1183
Martha B, 1184
Martha Belle (Kearns), 1183
Mary, 1794
Mary E, 1183
Mary Madeleine (Naiden), 1562
Orville E, 1183
Pamela Ann, 1089
Patricia Ann, 1807
Paules J, 1089
Ruby, 1184
Sally Jane, 388
Samuel, 1667

Sarah Esther, 210
Sarah Pearl, 1183
Sean Paul, 1562
Shelby, 1184
Susannah (Cecil), 1667
Thelma, 1433
Vera (--), 1184
Wilmina (--), 1183
Wilmont, 1184
GIERSDORF
Ida, 1740
GIFFIN
Aaron Thomas, 1442
Cindy (Vickers), 1442
Joel Samuel, 1442
Laura Jane, 1119
Marilyn Joanne (Mickey), 1442
Paula Ann, 1442
Robert Harold, 1442
Roger Leland, 1442
Thomas Mickey, 1442
GIFFORD
Florence Beatrice, 1215
Henrietta Caroline, 189
James Stuart, 371
Linda Pauline, 371
Martha Jane, 1215
Minerva Elinore (Weiser), 189
Nancy Ellen, 371
Orrin Philip Jr, 1215
Randy, 551
Sylvanus, 189
Terri Lynn (Riggs), 551
Virginia Pauline (Griffis), 371
Wilkie Beatricke (Kahle), 1215
GIGER
Elizabeth Ann (Gill), 209
Lawrence Eugene, 209
Paige Elane, 209
Taylor Ann, 209
GILASPIE
Linda Marie, 962
GILBERT
Adrianne, 634
Anna Elizabeth, 744
Anthony, 634
Arthur, 1079
Billie Lou, 1770
Carlotta Cornelia (Smith), 1119
Carol Margaret, 1119
Charles, 1079
Charles Walter, 1317
Daniel, 634
David Guy, 1119
David M III, 851
David McConaughy III, 890
Dorothy, 1079
Earl, 1079
Elaine Elizabeth (Klinger), 744
Elizabeth Reese (Fink), 890
Elsie, 989
Emily, 293
Gladys, 1079
Grace Bergstresser (Buck), 890
James L, 744
Janet, 914
Joel Gregory, 744

Kisha Jean, 448
Laurie Lynn, 1776
Linda Louise (Miller), 634
Marilyn Joyce (Hetzel), 1317
Mary Lucretia (Waite), 1079
Michael, 1426
Miriam Sue, 1119
Nada Jo, 1119
Pamela Jo, 1317
Sue Ann, 1317
Vincent James, 744
Virginia (Hamilton), 890
Virginia Elveretta, 893
William Kent, 890
GILBERTSON
Lyle, 60
Ruth (Schlund), 60
GILCHRIST
Charlotte (Shoemaker), 1470
Edgar, 1470
Helen, 1470
Marguerite, 1470
Miriam, 1470
Pauline, 1470
William H, 1470
GILES
Agnes, 1105
GILFILLAN
Margaret S, 1523
Mary, 1522
GILL
Adam Curtis, 209
Barbara Jo (Blagus), 636
Carol, 183
Cecil Stanley, 1688
Deborah, 472
Elizabeth Ann, 209
Hannah Rose, 70
Harriet Elane (Dwyer), 209
Jacob Allan, 209
James, 209
Jeffery Thomas, 636
Jessica Ann, 209
Lee James, 209
Mary (Youngstrom), 209
Olive Grace Manetta (Garver), 1688
Pamelia L, 857
Richard Ellis, 209
Robert Curtis, 209
Sally Beth (Tiptin), 209
Susan Joan (Edgerly), 209
GILLESPIE
Anna Spangler (Weiser), 1466
Bill, 1662
Carrie (Wysor), 1662
Charles Weiser, 1466
Clyde Gale, 1432
Clyde Raymond, 1432
Clyde Robert Sr, 1431
Cornelia Anderson, 84
Doris, 1432
Elizabeth Armstrong, 1466
Floella, 624
Franklin, 1466
Gerald Clyde, 1432
Gertrude L, 1431
Jean, 1662

Karen Tuana, 1432
Kathryn Ann, 1432
Lynda Sue (Bannion), 1432
Paul, 1662
Reva (Moore), 1431
Trenton James, 1432
Tuana (Corbet), 1432
GILLET
Elizabeth, 89
GILLETT
Craig Allen, 806
Donna Dee (Weiser), 806
Edwin, 806
Kenneth Douglas, 806
Sandra Dee, 806
GILLETTE
Virginia, 428
GILLIAM
Margaret Hannah, 889
GILLIAN
Leah, 1548
GILLILAND
Amos L, 1831
Debora Kay (Weiser), 1846
Filetta (Wiser), 1831
Joyce Ann, 367
Louis Frank, 1846
GILLISPIE
Barbara Jean, 489
GILLMOR
Dale Albert, 499
Rita Jean (Schade), 499
GILLMORE
James Clarkson, 1358
Mary Gorman (Hills), 1358
Mary Gorman Burns, 1358
Stuart H, 1358
GILMAN
Adolph, 87
Clark, 1012
Cordelia (Wisor) Flegal, 1720
Dewey E, 1685
Loy, 1720
Margaret (Brown), 1012
Ruby F (Wright), 1685
GILMER
-- (--), 1393
Albert W, 1393, 1396
Larue Hess (Schaeffer), 1396
Leslie, 828
Mary (Kienzle), 1396
Sarah Susan, 1396
Susan Sarah, 1396
William Schaeffer, 1396
GILMORE
--, 1863
Anne Elgar, 1359
Barbara Faith (Stahl), 733
Elgar Sherman (Jones), 1359
Gloria F (Weiser), 1863
Robert Campbell, 1359
Robert Lewis, 733
GILPEN
Julie Ann, 456
Patricia Ann, 456
GILPIN
Arden Jean, 422

Clifford Rodney, 422
Darcy Beth, 422
Doris Carol (Weiser), 422
Joanne Lois (Grey), 1359
Josiah Jones, 1359
Margaret Elgar, 1359
Margaret Sherman (Jones), 1359
Pearl M (Weiser), 1845
Steven Brooke, 1359
Thomas, 1845
William Edward, 1359
William Howard, 1359
GILSON
Emily T, 301
GINDER
Arthur Roger, 434
Charles Ervin, 434
Claude Ervin, 434
Edna, 431
George Walter, 59
George Walter Jr, 59
Mary Maxine (Holcomb), 59
Ora Margarett (Smith), 434
Pamela Louise, 434
Sandra Jean, 434
Sarah, 442
Virginia Mae (Wheeler), 434
GINGELE
Edith, 1609
GINGHER
Mary, 1375
GINGRICH
Christian, 78
Evalyn, 1095
Harriet, 78
Maria (Herr), 78
GINNEVER
Diedre Sue, 494
Larry, 494
Michael Eric, 494
Nancy Lou (Nowak), 494
Nicole, 494
GINOLFI
Arthur Daniel Jr, 86
Caroline Elizabeth, 86
Daniel Jr, 86
Sara Anne, 86
Susan Harrison (Miller), 86
GIONS
John, 134
Marjorie Geneva (Young), 134
GIPE
Dollie, 803
Martha Irene (Courtright), 1120
Reuben, 1120
GIRT
Joseph Clark, 1214
Pearl Hannah (McCoy), 1214
GIRTON
Harriet, 729
GIRTS
Blanche, 1291
GISH
George, 578
Jean Evelyn (Byrd), 578
GISHWILLER
May, 1105

GISNER
Frederick, 867
Frederick Jr, 867
Marriettia, 867
Mary (Still), 867
Sandra, 867
William, 867
GITHEN
Betty Jean, 1389
GIVENS
Anna (Hottenstein), 65
Charles A, 65
Elizabeth, 1424
Percival, 65
GIVLER
Alma Joyce, 257
Anneliese Nicole, 224
Barbara Glennys
(Burkey), 225
Bradley Scott, 224
Duane Lee, 224
Gary Bruce, 224
Helen Louise (Tabor),
224
Helen Marie (Coleman),
224
LeRoy E, 224
Norman LeRoy, 224
Patricia Ann, 224
Richard Alan, 225
Shannon, 225
Sharon Kay, 225
Troy Duane, 224
Vida Maye (Zuck), 224
GLADMAN
Ala Maybell (Weiser),
1187
Ernest Francis, 1187
Sandra Lee, 1187
GLANCY
Gloria Gene, 144
GLANDON
Bertha, 1689
Dale, 1689
Hazel, 1689
Irene, 1689
James, 1251
Joe, 1689
Louella (Kephart),
1689
Nicholas, 1251
Robbin (Roberts), 1251
Velma, 1689
William, 1689
Wilma, 1689
GLANZ
Sandra, 631
GLASE
Louisa A, 81
GLASGOW
Aleta, 1382
GLASS
Beth Ann, 548
Cari, 547
Jamie Renee, 547
Jonathan, 547
Larry Jo, 547
Phoebe Ann (Herring),
547
Tessa, 52
Warren Jay, 547
Wilma, 983
GLASSCOCK
Arthur Lewis, 443
Jennie Augusta (Reid),
443
GLATFELTER
-- (--), 906
Amanda Jillian, 909

Bridget Ann (Tobias),
909
Carol Ann, 909
David Patrick, 909
Ed, 906
Edward A, 906, 908
Edward Fischer, 909
Edward William, 909
Elizabeth (Leader)
Stiles, 1422
Jan, 906
Janet Virginia (Fischer),
909
Janice Ruth, 909
Jean Patricia (Peckjian),
909
John William, 909
Jonathan Edward, 909
Laura Beth, 909
Mark Daniel, 909
Nancy Ruth, 909
Ruth May (Mader),
908
Susan Joy, 909
William, 1422
GLAUBER
Caroline Coates
(Herrick), 307
Robert, 307
GLAUNER
Gertrud (Weisser),
1608
Rolf, 1608
GLAVIS
Brandon, 1357
Cheryl, 1357
Doris (Ashworth),
1357
Edward, 1356
Edward Sumner, 1356
Edward Sumner III,
1356
Edward Sumner Jr,
1356
Frances Mary (Mason),
1356
Frank Johnson, 1357
Jennifer, 1357
Judith (Otto), 1356
Maidee Virginia, 1357
Margaret, 1357
Pauline E, 1356
Pauline Ewer, 1356
Pauline Ryder (Ewer),
1356
Susan, 1357
Wendy, 1357
GLAZEBROOK
Nancy Amanda, 1788
GLAZIER
Grace Hilda (Lerew),
913
Jack, 913
GLEASON
Kenneth Ray, 609
Marlene, 609
Patty Jean, 609
Robert Lester, 609
GLEESON
Gail, 163
GLENDY
Nancy Mary, 1648
Robert Andrew, 1648
GLENN
--, 1257
Edythe, 600
Emily Helen, 1545
Gerard Ernest, 580
Howard, 1257

Linda Faye, 1212
Martha Elizabeth
(Quinlan), 1545
May (McDowell), 1257
Pearl (McDowell),
1257
Ruth June (Bowsher),
580
Thomas, 1545
Tracey Sue, 399
GLICK
Coral Agnes Ruth,
1148
Jonathan Monroe, 1148
Magdalene, 1149
Mary Alice (Alspaugh),
1148
GLIDDEN
James Arthur, 569
Patricia Lou (Smith),
569
GLINES
Sarah Marie, 1732
GLONINGER
John, 1593
GLOSSER
Bob, 1234
Elmerdeen (Kahle),
1234
James, 1709
LaVaughn (Bodle),
1709
GLOSSUP
James Dwain, 1806
Nellie Delois (Wiser),
1806
GLOVE
--, 61
GLOVER
--, 61
Alice Asenath, 1777
Bill, 665
Catherine Ann (Lynn),
1142
Christian, 502
Donald, 1142
infant, 502
Jeffrey Thomas, 1142
Kristin Lynn, 1142
Martha A (Rhoads), 61
Nettie E (Overmyer),
502
Sylvia Myrtle
(Roadenbaugh), 665
Thelma, 666
William, 502
GLUCKERT
Diane Louise, 1421
Elizabeth Anne, 1413
Elizabeth Anne (Lewis),
1420
Francis Albert, 1420
Jeanne Catharine, 1420
John Carlton, 1421
Marianne Beech, 1421
Mary Margaret (Frick),
1421
Mialisa Lewis, 1421
Suzanne Louise, 1420
GLYNN
Charlotte, 218
GNEPPER
Anna Louise (Miller),
495
Connie Sue, 495
Donald Earl, 495
Helen Blanche, 495
Howard John, 493
Ida Grace Henrietta,

493
Jeanette Louise, 495
John Harry Alvin, 493
Kathy Jo, 495
Kay Ann, 493
Lorie Lee, 495
Lucy Grace, 494
Matthew John, 494
Maxine Heath
(Heffner), 493
Melanie Rae, 494
Patricia Ann, 495
Phyllis Jeanette (Pike),
495
Priscilla Louise
(Patynko), 493
Ray Howard, 493
Willard Alvin, 495
GOBEL
Ruth Elizabeth, 582
GOBLE
Bernice Eleanor
(Mahle), 1265
Betty Kay, 1233
Charles Albert, 1231
Elizabeth Sylvia, 1233
Floyd Charles, 1233
Fred Sheldon, 1265
Hattie (Curran), 1233
Hazel (Shobert), 1233
Jessica Kathleen, 1265
Joan, 1233
Joe Kahle, 1233
Muriel Elaine, 1233
Muriel Mae, 1231
Nellie Violet, 1233
Tamalyu Kay (Fye),
1265
Thomas Albert, 1265
Winifred Arda (Kahle),
1231
Winifred Priscilla,
1232
GODAL
John, 1711
Nancy E (Wisor)
Wisor, 1711
GODDARD
Louise, 1236
GODDELL
Amanda Rea, 1432
Carmen Marie, 1432
Nancy (--), 1432
Philip Ransom II, 1432
GODFREY
Halcyon (McClurg),
524
Karen, 908
Margaret, 1373
Ralph, 524
Theresa Ann, 1283
GODMAN
Evelyn Beatrice
(Knecht), 442
Richard Alan, 442
Richard M, 442
GODSHALK
Vinie S, 897
GODSHALL
Nicholas, 25
GODWIN
Essie May, 526
Tamara Ann, 201
GOEBEL
Daniel Robert, 1156
Elisabeth Irmgard
Marianne (Willich),
321
Ellen Jeanne, 1156

Joyce (Keller), 506
Julie (Pitrowski), 1156
Karen Lee, 1155
Karl Friedrich Leopold,
321
Lynn, 506
Peter David, 1156
Susan Claire, 1155
Taylor Morgan, 1156
Zachary Ryan, 1156
GOEGEL
Claralee (Brown), 1155
Elmer Robert, 1155
Robert Gary, 1155
GOERHING
Irving, 1741
Shirley (Weiser), 1741
GOERING
Janeen Liana (Seaman),
374
Michael, 374
GOERKE
Elise, 1600
GOETZ
--, 370
Elaine, 1390
Eve Ann, 1390
Phyllis Elaine
(Gibboney), 1390
Richard, 1390
Ruth Ellen, 1390
GOEWERT
Arden Jean (Gilpin),
422
Elizabeth Caroline, 422
George, 422
John Christopher, 422
Katherine Gretchen,
422
GOFF
-- (--), 215
Dyann Cecile (Carey),
227
Fred H, 215
Fred Harvey, 227
Hazel Lorena
(Burkholder), 227
Helen Mary, 227
Hugh Marvin, 227
John Robert, 227
Norma Jeanne (Sesker),
227
Truman Burkholder,
227
GOHEEN
Debra Kaye (Heeter),
1306
Deena Kaye, 1306
Garrett Edward, 1306
Larry Edward, 1306
Marta Jenna, 1306
GOHL
Barbara Ann, 1531
Betty Virginia, 1531
Earl Forrest, 1531
Earl Forrest II, 1531
Emma (--), 1518, 1522
Emma (Weiser), 1883
Emma margaret
(Weiser), 1531
Emma Vaneta, 1531
Frederick Weiser, 1531
Frederick Weiser Jr,
1531
George Agustus, 1531
George Agustus Jr,
1531
Harold Dewain, 1531
Mary Elizabeth (Baker),

HABERSAAT
Anna Lou, 505
Charles, 505
Don, 505
Gertrude M (Cochran), 505
Hal, 505
Joyce, 505
HACH
Charles Thomas, 1285
Elizabeth Jane (Stover), 1285
James Thomas, 1285
Matthew James, 1285
Susan Jane, 1285
HACHEY
Joyce, 1239
HACKBARTH
Martha Johanna, 1305
HACKENBERG
Arla, 1391
Lucinda, 80
Lucy (Bassler), 80
Samuel, 80
HACKENBURG
Jacqueline (Fegley), 784
Laura, 1049
Verdon, 784
Wendy, 784
HACKETT
Eva Marie (Simmons), 141
Maggie, 370
Michael, 141
Sarah Marie, 142
HACKLE
Elizabeth (Eppley), 881
Elizabeth Aletha (Eppley), 883
Harr, 881
Harry, 883
HACKMAN
Cleora Geraldine, 1055
Elva Mae (Fissel), 256
Esther L, 1056
Gladys Viola, 1055
Harold, 1054
Leon Theodore Paul, 256
Lula Mae, 1054
Mary Elizabeth, 1056
Miriam, 1056
Paul Raymond, 1055
Pearl (Royer), 1054
Rose Elizabeth (Erhard), 1053
Ruth Catherine, 1053
Verna (Reish), 1055
Walter Erhard, 1054
William Henry, 1056
William W, 1053
HADAWAY
Bobby Gene, 1656
Charles Edward, 1656
Edith Ann (Wysor), 1656
Robert Wysor, 1656
HADDEN
Kimberly Beth (Watson), 204
Thomas William, 204
HADDIX
Sherry Diane, 830
HADDON
Caleb, 1055
David Anthony, 1055
Diane Victoria, 1054
Harry Harter III, 1054

Henry Harter Jr, 1054
Julia Ann, 1055
Kathy (Fitzgerald), 1055
Mara Faith, 1055
Mary Beth, 1054
Mary Elizabeth (Duck), 1054
Sharon (Sachs), 1054
HADLEY
Gladys, 518
HAEGELE
Emma, 126
HAENDLE
Gertrud, 1607
HAERDTNER
Anna Christiane, 1597
HAEUSSER
Anna Maria, 1598
HAFER
Benjamin W, 1620
Daniel, 1620
David, 1620
Elizabeth (Reider), 1620
Esther (--), 1620
Esther B (Moyer), 1620
George Francis, 1620
Henry, 1620
Isaac W, 1620
John, 1620
Maria Anna, 1620
Mary (Faust), 1620
Mary Ann O (Nein), 1620
Rebecca (Hinnershitz), 1620
Samuel, 1620
Sarah, 1620
Sarah (--), 1620
Solomon, 1620
HAFF
Daniel, 1408 1409
Experience, 1407-1408
Experience (Blachly), 1408 1409
Freelove (Blachly), 1408
Hannah, 1408
Harriet, 1409
Isaac, 1409
James, 1408-1409
Polly, 1408
Sarah (--), 1409
Sarah (Scudder), 1409
HAFFLEY
Ruth, 617
HAFFNER
Florence P, 67
HAFLEY
Brenda Lee (Wiser) Whitehouse, 1790
Steven, 1790
HAGAN
Lottie Belle, 1222
HAGARTY
Finn Edwin, 1499
Katyhrine Louise (Snider), 1499
Simon Paul, 1499
William, 1499
HAGEMAN
Amy Lynne, 1658
Carolyn (Wysor), 1658
Eric, 1658
Fred, 1658
Frederick Todd, 1658
Henry, 245

Julie, 1658
Marjorie McCord (Wolff), 245
Shelly (Teddy), 1658
HAGENBUCH
Kathryn M, 1627
Mamie A, 1761
HAGER
Albrecht, 317
Bernhard, 317
Carol (Kephart), 1690
Elena, 317
Ernst, 317
Gottfried, 317
Larry, 1690
Mechthild, 317
Waltraud (Esenwein), 317
HAGERTY
Alla Mae, 1223
HAGGARD
Flora Estelle, 1445
HAGGARDY
Emmalee, 433
HAGLAND
Becky Jean, 424
David, 424
Justin David, 424
Marsha Jean (Faidley), 424
HAGOPIAN
Elizabeth Ann, 586
HAHN
--, 837
Alta, 1578
Alvin Edward, 486
Anne Merrill (Schwab), 310
Annie, 837
Barbara Ann (Wise), 486
Catherine, 837
Catherine Anspach (Womelsdorf), 837
Curtis James, 486
Dennis Edward, 486
Doris May (Kern), 486
Elizabeth, 837
Emilie, 78
Frank Willard, 1578
Fred, 1578
Hattie L, 1259
Jacob Calvin, 486
James Russell, 486
Jennie, 1578
Jennifer Lynn (Curtis), 486
Lawrence, 310
Maxine Marie, 612
Michael Edward, 486
Minnie, 1578
Nellie, 837
Phillip, 1578
Timothy William, 486
Vernon, 1578
HAI
Chung Tai, 1172
HAIDEN
Anna Catharine (Weisser), 1595
Johann Jacob, 1595
HAIFLICH
Edith (Wiser), 1836
Jesse, 1836
HAIGHT
Susan, 171
HAIGLER
Denise Kay (Van Horn), 1321

Evan Michael, 1321
Harry Thomas, 1321
Neil, 1321
HAILS
Elizabeth Ann, 1749
HAIN
Aaron Michael, 1400
Alan Paul Jr, 1400
Catharine, 905
Elizabeth, 905, 1509
Krista Miller, 1393
Krista Suzanne (Miller), 1400
Stephen Alan, 1400
HAINCKH
Aberlin, 9
Bartel Bartholomaus, 9
Gregorius, 9
Margarethe, 8
Zeiher Cyriakus, 9
HAINES
-- (--), 157
Alene Bernice (Donne), 831
Alice (Wisor), 1707
Alma (Gramley), 1079
Bertha Virginia Laverty, 856
Charles, 1079
Charles M, 1079
Claude, 1079
David E, 831
Donna Sue, 831
Elizabeth, 1079
Elizabeth (Murphy), 1078
Emma J, 1078
Emma J (Berkert), 1078
Fletcher, 1542
George, 1079
George B, 1078
Harry, 1078
Harry Jr, 1079
Isaiah, 157, 173
Jeremiah, 1078
Julia Marie (Mulroy), 173
Karen Anne, 173
Kenneth Gramley, 1079
Kristin Marie, 173
Lydia (Ocker), 1078
Margaret (Strode), 173
Mary (Smith), 1078
Matilda, 931
Myrtle, 807
Nancy Jan, 831
Nancy Strode, 173
Olley (Weiser), 1542
Rebecca, 1453
Susanna (Brungart), 1078
William, 1707
William Burkert, 1078
HAINS
Adam, 1613
Claudia V, 1619
Mary (Rothermel) Rausch, 1613
HAIT
Ruther Boyce, 393
HAKALINEN
Edna, 1835
HALBISEN
--, 478
Karen (Miller), 478
HALDORSON
Ruth Jensine, 406

HALE
Guy, 876
Helen Constance, 1535
Marian Louise, 876
Pauline Salome (Shettel), 876
HALEY
A L, 1820
Beulah May (Werth), 480
Daniel, 480
David, 480
Josie Francis (Wiser), 1820
Karen, 480
Lawrence T, 480
Mary, 480
Susan, 480
HALL
--, 1002, 1553
Anna, 1018
Anna Justina (Brehm), 917
Anna Mae, 933
Anna Maria (Weiser), 932
Arleene, 50
Barbara, 91
Barbara Ellen (Brouches), 596
Barbara Jean, 586
Barney, 1815
Benjamin, 1041
Benson E, 917
Benson Ludlic, 917
Beryl E, 1713
Brisco, 994
Carole (Stock), 92
Carole Winkler (Heinse), 176
Christopher Allen, 1814
Christopher George, 754
Clara (Weiser), 1188
Clara Eunice, 1189
Dalton, 1807
Damon Dale, 1815
Deborah Ann, 546
Debra Ann (Hittle), 541
Deidee Seabring, 790
Diana Lorene, 541
Donald Carter, 790
Donald Carter Jr, 790
Doris (Walizer), 1002
Doris Elizabeth (Coonfare), 49
Elizabeth Mae Crownover (Hayse), 933
Elizabeth Patricia, 1339
Emma (Adams), 1189
Erin Lynn, 1123
Erleta (Steward), 375
Estella, 364
Eva Maude, 932
Everett Joseph, 175
Frances Adeline, 1189
Frances Jennie (Kahl), 994
Francis Marie (Herring), 541
Frank, 1188
Fred, 933
Freeman, 596
Freild Offord, 1189
George, 754, 932
George Weiser, 1189

HALL (continued)
Georgia, 867
Gwendolyn Alice, 1189
Helen Agatha, 1189
Herold Bryan, 520
Howard, 994
Howard E, 49
Ida Sue (Wiser), 1815
Irene (McGuigan), 1553
Isis Voss, 1189
J W, 994
JaNelle Roberta, 175
Jason Wayne, 541
Jessica Ann, 541
Jo Beth Kristine, 176
Joan Sandra (Seabring), 790
Joseph Daniel, 754
Joyce Marie, 592
Julianna (Millhouse), 934
Kayla, 754
Kelly, 541
Kristen Lynn, 1123
Lena, 267
Lillian A (Van Ormer), 934
Linda Carter, 790
Linda Gayle (Wiser), 1814
Lyda Murray (Womelsdorf), 829
Lynn (Courtright), 1123
Mabel (Benton), 175
Mable (Donmoyer), 1041
Mardean E, 92
Margaret (Wiser) Thompson Thomas, 1807
Margaret Alward, 333
Margaret Elizabeth (Eister), 754
Marguerite R, 934
Marion Elisha, 1189
Martha G (Wiser), 1802
Marvin W, 972
Mary (Simpson), 754
Mary Beth (Huse), 541
Mary Catharine, 338
Mary Elizabeth, 1189
Matthew, 1123
Matthew John, 175
McKenzie Katherine, 176
Megan Melinda, 176
Mellissa Tara, 754
Merril Dean, 546
Mitchell Vos, 175
Nancy Emelia, 122
Nelsena Jean (Vos), 175
Nettie, 619
Nicholas, 541
Norma Beth (Sours), 972
Oakie (Cressey), 1189
Olive (Pfhie), 546
Orville, 994
Orville Jr, 994
Pauline, 994
Peggy Jo, 972
Phylis Louise, 934
Phyllis Ann, 546
Phyllis Maxine (Herring), 546

Rachel Drusilla, 1189
Randolph, 829
Richard, 375
Roberta Leta (Woolridge), 175
Robyn Lynn, 747
Rodney Wayne, 541
Roger Clayton, 176
Roger Patrick, 176
Ronald, 451
Ronald John, 175
Ruth Vivian, 1189
Sandra Kay, 972
Sandra Lee, 49
Sara Beth, 972
Scott Stewart, 754
Shawn David, 754
Shirley Jean (Clevenger), 451
Sonja Glee, 175
Stephanie (Logue), 754
Sue Ellen, 972
Susan Lyn, 92
Thelma (Wrench), 1189
Thomas, 1123
Tim, 1802
Torie, 1002
Tracie Lee, 175
Trevor Sean, 451
Velma Genevieve (Fisher), 520
Wayne R, 541
William, 546, 932, 1002
William S, 934
HALLEBERG
Charlene, 1804
HALLER
Catharine, 1428
Dorothy Matz, 902
Elizabeth, 1851
Henry W, 902
Katherine (Womelsdorf), 902
Marie Helman, 902
Ralph W, 902
Urania D (Matz), 902
HALLINGSHEAD
Donna Jean, 476
HALLIWELL
Mary Catherine, 519
HALLMAN
Anita Louise, 1514
Benjamin, 1682
Cordie (Kephart), 1682
Edith (Kephart), 1682
George Lewis, 1255
Joan Jane (Mapes), 1255
Lewis Wilbur, 1255
William, 1682
HALLMEYER
Beth Ann, 92
HALLOWELL
Bruce, 947
Bruce Jr, 947
Janice Clair (Althouse), 947
HALNERS
Eulaine, 1563
HALSTEAD
Kaitlyn, 885
Patricia, 885
HAM
Donald Morrison, 1506
Florence Long (Morrison), 1506
Kimball, 1506

Richard K, 1506
Robert, 1506
HAMADA
Michiko, 313
HAMAKER
Beverly Lynn (Lemke), 497
Bradley Jacob, 497
Douglas William, 497
Lauren Ann, 497
HAMBLEN
Cathy Jo (Wiser), 1780
Michael William, 1780
HAMBY
Elanzo Carlton, 46
Lucille Mary (Willey), 46
HAMEL
Lonie, 1483
HAMER
Hattie, 1440
HAMILTON
Beverly Fay, 973
Brian, 537
Cindy (Beadle), 992
Edna, 1713
Effie Mabel (Harshe), 596
Elaine, 1292
Helen, 1228
James Samuel, 1223
Jessie, 596
Kathleen Sue, 1223
Kelly Ann (Herring), 537
Lillian Elnorah (Weiser), 1145
Linda (--), 992
Mary Elizabeth (McKinley), 1223
Rosalie, 1827
Ruth (Anderson), 992
Virginia, 158, 890
Vonda Joy, 400
William Emmett, 992
William Gordon, 1145
William Thomas, 992
HAMLETT
Reba Lynn, 1807
HAMMEL
Amanda A, 1756
Jane Marie (Thornsen), 275
Jeffrey, 275
HAMMELMAN
Letha Marie, 236
HAMMER
A R, 1795
Allan Drew, 1380
Allen Drew, 1092
Alvin, 1380
Evelyn Elizabeth (Weiser), 1380
Karen Melanie (Bierly), 1092, 1380
Kelly Lynn, 1380
Kimberly Lee, 1380
Kristy Louise, 1380
Phyllis Evelyn, 1380
Sarah, 1454
Sarah Ann (Wiser), 1795
HAMMEREL
Mary Katherine, 306
HAMMERSLY
Cheryl Leigh, 656
HAMMES
Charlotte A (Weiser), 1612

Linus, 1612
HAMMON
Catherine Ann, 622
HAMMOND
--, 504
Ala (Wiser), 1185
Alvina Sarah, 968
Angela Mae (Robinson), 1211
Bernice, 1690
Bertha Lenora, 970
Brian, 225
Catherine (Wantland), 971
Charles Leonard, 710
Charles Leonard Jr, 710
Charles Luther, 1185
Charles Wesley, 968
Christina Kay (Effinger), 486
Clara Iona, 969
Dallas Eugene, 1186
Daniel Lee, 486
David Weldon, 1185
Dea Katherine, 1190
Debra Lee, 1185
Deforest David, 968
Delores Jean (Albright), 710
Dian (Busdieker), 504
Doris (Brenner), 1186
Edith, 968
Eliza Rosetta, 968
Eva Livera, 962
Eveah Luthera, 962
Evean Ronald, 1185
Frank Melvin, 971
Gwendolyn Louise (Hardway), 1185
Harmon Porter, 962
Haven Wiser, 1185
Helen, 1691
Henretta Elizabeth (Ingles), 971
Henrietta Jean (Weldon), 1185
Jefry Alan, 1185
Jill Ellen, 1186
John, 1211
Linda Jean, 710
Lora Ann, 1185
Madison Breanne, 486
Mary Jane, 710
Nellie Lewella, 968
Nettie Loretta, 968
Randy, 225
Richard, 225
Robert Dallas, 1186
Roy William, 1186
Sarah Catherine (Bower), 962
Sharon Ann, 710
Sharon Kay (Givler), 225
Susan Elizabeth, 1185
Waldraut (Grueneberg), 1186
HAMMONDS
Chase Michael, 383
Heidi Michelle (Simpson), 383
Mary, 624
Roger Lee, 383
HAMNER
Elizabeth Mary (Pickard) Brimfield, 1573
Michal, 1573

HAMOR
Kenneth, 733
Minnie Gertrude (Malick), 733
Walter, 733
HAMPTON
Amelia (Kephart), 1682
Bertha, 1682
Dorothy Jane, 1054
Linda Sue (Duncan), 590
Pearl Biggs, 1779
Samuel S, 590
Stacy, 1682
HAMSHER
Alton P, 1643
Andora Elizabeth (Weiser), 1642
Anna Fritch, 1742
Brett, 1742
Carrie A, 1643
Cassandra (Miller), 1742
Christopher John, 1742
daughter, 1742
Douglas, 1742
Elda W (Fritsch), 1643, 1742
Elizabeth, 1742
Georgine (Lucas), 1742
Jacob E, 1742
Joseph Ezra, 1643, 1742
Joseph Fritch, 1742
Kathryn Marie, 1642
Lydia L, 1643
Mildred (Reppert), 1742
Myrtle Esther, 1643
Neil, 1742
Paul Fritch, 1742
Peter Charles, 1642
Ronald, 1742
Sallie S, 1643
Sarah E, 1742
HANAWALT
Bertha Buretta, 382
HANCE
Allen D, 155
Esther (Weiser), 155
Ethel, 240
HANCOCK
Alton Ray, 618
Heidi Lynn, 618
Linda Jane (Klingler), 618
Margaret Elizabeth (Harter), 1387
Matthew Lane, 618
William Lowell, 1387
HAND
Abigail Locke (Womelsdorf), 834
Elizabeth, 835
Francis L, 834
Frank C, 834
Harry C, 834
John David, 702
Mary H, 835
Mary L (Dunlap), 702
Robert E, 702
Ruth Marie, 702
son, 702
Susan Carol, 920
HANDLEY
Eileen, 963
HANDSCHIN
Harry, 1211
Ruth M (Martin), 1211

HARNING
Minnie M, 508
HAROLD
Bede, 1835
Sarah, 1526
HARP
Elizabeth Clara, 1476
Mary Ann, 720
HARPER
Martha E, 67
HARPHAM
Betty Louise (Banter),
564
Gilbert, 564
HARPS
Carrie (Stephens), 1014
Mabel Gertrude, 1014
William, 1014
HARPSTER
Lois, 1395
HARREL
Adam Benjamin, 452
Marjorie Ann
(Clevenger), 452
Timothy Allen, 452
HARRELL
--, 1821
Barbara Ann (Wiser),
1821
Jason Michael, 1434
Kimela Kay (Moore),
1434
Lana, 635
Michael, 1434
Misty Dawn, 1434
HARRINGER
Elizabeth (Weiser),
1269
Henry, 1269
Jacob, 1269
Jennie M, 1269
John, 1269
Mary, 1269
Michael, 1269
Sarah (Myers), 1269
HARRINGTON
Alexander, 1270
Daniel, 1270
J Earl, 1270
James L, 1270
James Mc C B, 1270
Margie, 428
Myrtle L, 681
Phillip, 1270
Washington, 1270
HARRIS
Albert Persing, 708
Ammon, 708
Ann (Wysor), 1650
Anna Gladys, 1661
Annabelle Marie
(Fulkroad), 668, 708
Annetta Maude
(Harshe), 596
Belinda Sue, 544
Bobbi Jean, 217
Bradley Charles, 217
Carol Diane, 708
Carrie Edna
(Koppenheffer), 708
Carrie Irene, 668, 708
Catherine J (Johnson),
1500
Charles Isom, 546
Christopher Davey,
120
Cindy Sue (Mick), 217
David, 905
David Richard, 419

David Wayne, 217
Ed, 596
Elaine, 668, 708
Elizabeth Spencer, 297
Evelyn Justine, 566
Franklin, 668, 708
Franklin Jr, 668, 708
Gale, 1176
Helen Marion, 32
Ian Marshall, 528
J Grafius, 297
James A, 1780
James Frederick, 419
James Frederick II, 419
James Richard, 419
James Walter, 528
Jamie Lee, 217
Jane Frances (Walter),
217
Jasper Clinton, 217
Jasper Clinton Jr, 217
Jeanmarie (Gallant),
419
Jessie Evlin (Wiser),
1780
Joel, 1650
John Sterling III, 120
Judith Flora (Herring),
544
Judy (Snider), 546
Jun (Kirpatrick), 1176
Karen Elizabeth, 668,
708
Kathleen Anne
(Josephson), 120
Lala Renee, 544
Larry Gene, 546
Lavonna (Wiser), 1872
Leslie Ray, 1872
Mamie, 458
Maria Helen
(Wickham), 528
Marian Jean (Holman),
217
Mary Elizabeth
(Smeltz), 708
Mary Jane (Novinger),
708
Mary Margaret
(Wagoner), 546
Matthew, 1650
Max, 1650
Mildred Pauline, 713
Ned, 1500
Nellie Jewel, 134
Nevin Eugene, 708
Phebe Ann Nutter
(Shulze), 297
Richard Dean, 217
Richard Lee, 708
Riley Dexter, 544
Robert Eugene, 708
Ronnie Lee, 546
Ruth Ann Taylor, 451
Ruth Arlene (Miller),
708
Sallie Grafius, 297
Sandy (Miller), 217
Sandy Kay, 544
Scott Andrew, 217
Sharon Louise (Ewing),
419
Susan Lynn (Round),
217
Teresa Ann, 544
Valerie Shane, 120
Venda Patricia
(Northway), 120
William, 668, 708

William John, 708
William Spencer, 297
HARRISON
Arthur H, 1520
Catherine Crain, 1520
Charles Edwin, 881,
883
Edythe Eppley (Scott),
883
Gertrude (Eppley), 881
Gertrude Hadden
(Eppley), 883
James Mark, 54
John Richard Stovall,
54
Julia Etchberger
(Matthias), 1520
Laura Leigh (Stovall),
54
Leigh Frances Virginia,
54
Linda Susan, 55
Louisa Hoxall, 1517
Mabel Eva, 881, 883
Rebecca Margaret, 881,
883
Victoria Stephanie
Rieck, 1486
William H, 881, 883
HARRISS
Nancy, 1179
HARROLD
Janet, 561
Louise, 490
Mary Bernice, 529
Sheila Mary, 1486
HARRSCH
Joshua, 12
HARRUFF
Terri, 385
HARRY
Cora (Frazier), 1090
Donald, 1090
Irvin, 1090
Sally Darlene, 747
HARSH
Betsy Ann (Dafler),
1324
Christopher, 1325
John, 1324
Katherine, 1324
Thelma Lenore
(Williams), 598
Theodore, 598
HARSHBARGER
Carolann (Shugarts),
1717
Darwin, 1717
Terri Rae, 1717
HARSHE
Annetta Maude, 596
Clara L, 596
Cora (Ferguson), 596
Effie Mabel, 596
Elvira Sarepta, 596
George, 596
Hazel (Waldron), 596
James Franklin, 596
James Robert, 596
John Andrew, 596
Margaret, 596
Margaret (Brouches),
596
Rebecca Jane, 596
Rose (O'Brien), 596
HART
Adeline (Hedberg), 516
Beatrice Clarabelle,
515

Belinda, 324
Carol Jean, 515
Catharine (Weiser),
1111
Cathy, 516
Charles F, 515
Debbie, 515
Dores (Mohr), 516
Douglas F, 515
Elizabeth, 1111
Frances Ann, 516
Francis Minor, 515
Grace I, 955
Helen Winnifred, 515
Irvin M, 515
Irvin Minor, 515
Ivy May (Ramsey),
515
Jane (Nelson), 515
John, 1111
Kathryn, 580
Lillian E (Burkes), 515
Lillian Gail, 516
Margaret, 1116
Mary Elizabeth
(Sperry), 303
Nancy Ann, 1834
Ray Kenneth, 515
Rosemary Lynn, 516
Ruth L (Gonser), 515
Vanessa Ray, 436
Victor R, 515
Walter Doyle, 515
William H, 303
William H Jr, 516
William Henry, 516
HARTER
Bertha, 1373, 1387
Carol Marie, 1386
Cindey Jane, 1385
David, 1385
Donald Allen, 1385
Emma Leonora (Myer),
1385
Frank Gurn, 1385
Harriet Teresta
(Weiser), 1385
Harry, 1385
Helen (Kressman),
1385
Kathleen Mary, 1385
Leora Katherine, 1386
Lonnie, 1093
Margaret Elizabeth,
1387
Mary, 1389
Mary Kellogg (Monty),
1385
Mary Lou, 1386
Noel, 1385
Ralph Weiser, 1385
Robert, 1373, 1884
Robert Elery, 1385
Robert Preston, 1385
Roger, 1385
Sharon, 616
Susan Gay, 1385
Terri, 1385
Virgene (Ecker), 1385
HARTFORD
Maria, 1765
HARTLE
Larry Wayne Jr, 925
Susan Ann (Johnson),
925
Zachary Lee, 925
HARTLEY
Fleta Dell, 147
George, 147

Sarah Ann (Weiser),
147
HARTLINE
Mary Ann, 736
HARTMAN
--, 1568
Allan, 443
Andrew D, 1514
Ann Ellen (Reid), 443
Anna I (Reedy), 837
Anna Maria (Leader),
1422
Beatrice E (Wenrich),
838
Betty, 1005
Carrie A, 837
Carrie A (Hartman),
837
Catherine May, 837
Charles Jacob, 1227
Charles William, 837
Chester, 903
Dorothy E (Hynicka),
1514
Edna I (Anspach), 837
Elizabeth, 119-122,
131
Elsie May (Stiely),
1343
Ephraim, 1343
Fred, 443
Gertrude, 1583
Ina R, 504
Jane (Smith), 1227
Katherine Lee, 1227
Katie (Kalbach), 903
Louisa L (Wisser),
1754
Margaret Lillian, 837
Margarete, 1607
Marian L, 117
Phoebe, 509
Ralph F, 837
Ralph Wilmer, 838
Ray Elwood, 837
Ray Kenneth, 837
Ruth Alvina, 1732
Sally (Weiser), 1568
Sarah Ann, 1754
Shirley Arlene, 837
Tillie Warner, 1144
twins, 837
Viola, 1344
W L, 119
William, 1754
William H, 1422
HARTMANN
Carl J, 1227
Charlotte, 1607
Helene Karoline, 1600
Jennie Violet (Ewing),
1227
HARTMEIER
Kathlyn Jill, 1334
Lorraine Winifred
(Daughters), 1334
Walter Frederick Jr,
1334
HARTPENCE
Rebecca Ann, 662
HARTSGROVE
Leanne Kay, 1740
HARTSON
Doris May, 781
HARTWAY
Andrew John, 969
Brian James, 969
Duane Joseph, 969
Francine Ruth, 969

HARTWAY (continued)
Janet Carolyn (Small), 969
Joseph Henry, 969
Lawrence Henry Jr, 969
Lynda Marie, 969
Lynette Gaye Gentham (Fraley), 969
Yvonne Marie (Ireland), 969
HARTWELL
June Marie, 1384
HARTWIG
Anna (--), 134
Charles, 134
HARTZEL
--, 273
Anna, 1425
Jantina (Blade), 273
HARTZELL
--, 1425
Allen R, 1633
Catharine May (Weiser), 1633
Edith Lillian Newhard, 887
Elsie Janet, 1633
Grace Louise (Morrison), 1227
John Robert, 1227
Ralph, 1633
Richard Wayne, 1227
Robert Wayne, 1227
Sadie (Weiser), 1425
Vivian Margaret, 685
HARTZNER
Deborah L, 793
HARVEY
Alda Marie (Bolles), 1199
Alice Josephine (Wiser), 1834
Amanda Marie, 537
Beryl Grace (Smith), 628
Betty, 1206
Brian Adam, 629
Candice (Freschel), 629
Clement Elwood, 629
David Jay, 629
Deidra Gail, 629
Diana (Purdon), 629
Douglas Gordan, 631
HARVEY
Elizabeth, 1430
HARVEY
Florence Belle (Wiser), 1834
George A, 1834
Hazel Eudene, 629
Henry W, 1199
Iris Ruth, 632
Janice Wandalee, 628
Jay Allan, 629
Justin Michael, 629
Karen Kay, 631
Kelly Jo (Fox), 536
Kenneth, 750
Kent Allen, 631
Kristine Marie, 629
Leslie Jo, 629
Linda Jean, 99
Mark Allan, 629
Mary Kay (Kaiser), 629
Matthew Michael, 629
Muriel Avis, 631

Nancy Ann, 631
Nancy Ann (Eckenrode), 750
Nathaniel Ronald, 629
Nell (Everman), 629
Othal Swineford, 628
Patricia La Moile, 630
Penny Ann, 750
Quinn O, 1834
Robert Allen, 536
Ryan Allen, 629
Sandra E (Preszler), 629
Sue (Crookshank), 629
Sue (Gordon), 631
Teresa (Knabay), 631
Verlene Marciel, 631
Vivian (Hanna), 631
Ward William, 631
Zale Addison, 631
HARVISON
Byron George, 1386
Charles A, 1386
Corinne (Rachelle), 1387
Daniel Charles, 1387
Jerome Charles, 1387
Karen (Albers), 1387
Kristen Diane, 1387
Leesa Maurine, 1387
Leora Katherine (Harter), 1386
Linda (Lee), 1386
Marcile (Herding), 1387
Marilyn Jeanette, 1386
Shirley (Clark), 1387
Stephanie Lee, 1386
Steven Charles, 1386
Susan Katherine, 1387
Wilma (Duncan), 1386
HARWELL
Gary Winston, 1817
Kathy, 1806
Pamela Kay (Wiser), 1817
HASBROOK
Katharine Rosa, 281
HASCAP
Judith Carroll (Simmons), 800
Ray Stephen, 800
HASCHEL
Alice, 263
Amanda (Reinholt), 263
Beverly Rozella (Mahler), 265
Christeen, 269
Clayton Earl, 265
Cledith, 269
Daniel, 263, 269
Dean Robert, 265
Dessie, 268
Dorothy (Berkshire), 269
Eacil Florence, 264
Edith, 265
Eugene Earl, 265
Flo, 263
Frederick Donald, 265
Frederick L, 262
Frederick Oscar Jr, 264
Goldia, 263
Gregory David, 265
Gwen Cherie, 265
Ida, 263
Ida (Reinholt), 268

Jennifer Marlene, 265
John, 269
Karen Kaye (Lange), 265
Kathryn C (Crist), 265
Lonny Eugene, 265
Luella Mae, 265
Mabel, 263
Maria (Eikelberner), 262
Mary, 269
Mary (Clemens), 269
Nellie, 264
Nettie Dell (Heland), 264
Olive (Overmyer), 263
Rick, 269
Serry, 269
Sylvia, 263
Viola, 268
Viola Belle (Hickman), 265
Wendy Catherine (Lewis), 265
William, 268
HASKINS
Jeannette, 1752
HASLAM
Emma Jones, 1767
HASLINGER
Alice Kathleen, 482
Gary Rupert, 482
Ginelle, 481
Janice Elaine (Flechtner), 482
Joanne Marie (Marquis), 482
Judith Ann, 481
Kevin, 482
Kristine, 482
Leah, 482
Michael Theodore, 482
Rupert Theodore, 481
Susan Lynn, 482
HASLOP
Beatrice Madaline (Wert), 1075
Robert D, 1075
HASSEN
Derek, 755
Ruth Edith (Severn), 755
HASSINGER
Anna, 1395
Audrey (Frey), 789
Beau Jeffrey, 687
Beth Ann (Altland), 687
Carol, 638
Carol Ella (Mattern), 687
Dale Jacob, 687
Dorothy Helen (Radel), 687
Elias Robert, 688
Eric James, 1088
Helen Marie, 688
Jacob Michael, 687
James, 1088
Jeffrey Dale, 687
Joseph, 789
Joseph E Jr, 789
Judith Carol, 687
Kali Ellen, 688
Katie Beth, 687
Kim Agnes (Kaufman), 688
Lisa Jean, 1088
Louisa, 639

Mary Colleen (Johnson), 688
Robert Eugene, 688
Sandra Faye, 688
Shirley Dorothy, 688
Sonja Roxanna (Brungart), 1088
Thomas, 638
Thomas Lamar, 688
HASSLER
Catherine, 880
Charles, 880
Charlotte Catherine (Eppley), 880
Hilda, 1638
HASTEDT
Eleanor Ann, 429
Elizabeth Ames, 429
Howard Eugene, 429
Jane Louise (Snyder), 429
Joann, 429
John Paul, 429
Josephine (Coleman), 428
Juliann (Klingsmith), 429
Kathleen Louise, 429
Kendrick Snyder, 429
Paul Randall, 428
Phyllis Jean, 429
Priscilla, 429
Randall Coleman, 429
Robert Coleman, 429
HASTINGS
--, 1540
Bert, 1578
Lillian (Dock) Finley, 1540
Ola, 1578
HATCHER
--, 919
Charlie, 500
Constance, 500
Cyrene (Wiser), 1301
Dawn Sue, 500
Douglas, 1301
Ed, 1706
Jean (Wisor), 1706
Phyllis, 1679
Phyllis Jean, 1706
Rose Marie (Weiser), 919
Tanya May, 500
HATCHETT
Mary Nadine, 1800
HATFIELD
Annie, 839
Colleen Kelly, 500
Dennis, 500
Faye, 612
Fred, 174
Fred R, 174
Margaret Louise, 174
Mary Kathryn (Heileman), 500
Tommy, 174
Virginia Louise (Arbegast), 174
HATHAWAY
Margery Estelle, 1338
HATTER
Rosemarie, 1599
HATTERMAN
David Ernest, 1379
Harry, 1379
Leah Debra (Chavalier), 1379

HAUCK
Hannah E, 935
Maria Anna (Hafer), 1620
Peter, 1620
HAUDENSCHILDE
Eric, 449
Natalie Gayle (Keysor), 449
HAUG
Lori Ann, 543
HAUGEN
Linda Christine, 411
HAUGH
Amy Elizabeth, 1056
Clarence Gene, 1055
Elizabeth Ann, 1382
Glenda Ruth, 1382
Glenn Richard, 1382
Jennifer Lea, 1056
Mary Jane, 1382
Mitchell Breon, 1056
Patricia Ann (Breon), 1055
Ruth Ann (Weiser), 1382
Suzanne Marie, 1382
HAUGHAWOUT
Mary Emogene, 396
HAUGHEY
--, 1839
Meredith L (Wiser), 1839
HAUGHN
JaLinda Eloise (Seever), 1141
James, 1141
Jeffrey Ralph, 1141
Kyle Matthew, 1141
HAUGHT
Albert, 1478
Dennis, 1479
Donald Albert, 1478
Ellen Lee (Kennedy), 1479
Hazel Ruth (Cummins), 1478
Heidi Lou, 1479
Julie (Nickelson), 1478
Kathleen, 1478
Matthew Adam, 1478
Michael Brandon, 1478
Nikki Sue, 1478
Patsy Merlyn (Knox), 1478
Richard Charles, 1478
Sheri, 1478
Shirley (Yanke), 1478
Terry Wayne, 1478
Walter Richard, 1478
Yvonne (Pester), 1479
HAUK
Edna E (Cooper), 1036
J B, 1036
Joseph, 1036
Robert, 1036
HAUL
Earl, 555
Virgil V, 555
Winifred M (Johnson), 555
Zellia, 555
HAUN
Francis Clair, 1307
Jennie Evelyn (Simpson), 1307
Sarah, 1099
HAUPERT
Eva Lavonne, 1563

HAUPT
Albert W, 1541
Carrie (--), 1518, 1540
Carrie Ellen (Gonser), 1541
Charlotte Louise, 738
Gale Ann, 286
Grace E (Long), 1541
Marie, 1400
Phyllis (Fetter), 785
Raymond, 785
Richard L, 1541
Russell G, 1541
HAUS
Alice Ada, 157
Anna Mary, 157
HAUSEN
George, 604
George Ernest Jr, 604
Linda Louise, 604
Rosemary (Stober), 604
HAUSER
Carol Lee (Lindner), 1113
Henry, 951
Jonathan, 951
Laura, 951
Leonard, 1113
Mary Jane (Brammer), 951
Melissa, 951
Stephanie Lynn, 1113
HAUSMAN
Virginia (Barnheiser), 504
Willis, 504
HAUSSOCK
Kitty, 1171
HAVENS
--, 472
Ruth Ann (Beckley), 472
HAVER
Emily Bernice, 441
HAVICE
Laura Almira (Bergstresser), 79
Leone Almarie, 80
Marcus Hill, 79
Mary Marguerite, 79
HAWK
Caroline (Womelsdorf), 827
Charles Henry, 509
David, 827
Doris, 1616
Dorothy May (Cozard), 149
Earl Eugene, 149
George Fred, 509
Gertrude, 639
Ida Belle (Womelsdorf), 827
Julia Ann, 91
Lewis, 509
Lewis Sherman, 509
Mary, 509
Nancy, 1046
Phoebe (Hartman), 509
Samuel, 827
HAWKES
Carma (Wiser), 1771·
Joseph Milton, 1771
HAWKEYE
Susan, 636
HAWKINS
Andrew J, 577
Doris Elaine, 577

Eblean (Rhodes), 577
Emma Lucretia, 577
Frederick Jr, 577
Frederick Maurice, 577
Hazel (Stayner), 577
Hildred Marie, 577
Ira Clarence, 577
John, 1582
Lori Ann, 382
Mona, 199
Ollie Ernestine, 577
Rachel (Pickard), 1582
Sarah Loretta (Fox), 577
Walter Auga, 577
HAWLEY
Mary Jane, 1668
Maude Emily, 880
HAWS
Ethel Marie, 62
HAXTON
Eileen Margean (Sours), 971
John, 971
HAY
Deborah Ann, 925
HAYD
Mary, 471
HAYDEN
Cindy (Vorlese), 630
Deborah Elizabeth (Van Valkenburgh), 270
Debra Diane, 631
Elicia Lynn, 630
Ellen Rachelle, 630
Harlan J, 270
Harold, 630
Jamie Sue, 630
John Peter, 1555
Kathleen Anne (Kenedy), 1555
Lori Ann, 631
Melissa Nicole, 630
Michael Christopher, 630
Michael Eugene, 630
Patricia L (Ellifritz), 630
Patricia La Moile (Harvey), 630
Russell Harold, 630
Sharon Meridith, 630
Sheila Marie, 630
Sherry (Hutchinson), 630
Sue (Bister), 630
Teresa Jean, 630
HAYDOCK
Jennifer Lynn, 1656
Mildred Sue (Wysor), 1656
Robert Allen, 1656
HAYES
Arthur, 1109
Carol, 86
Caroline (Graham), 1453
Charles, 1109
Chris, 550
Creed, 1868
Debra Jean (Bell), 550
Elizabeth, 559, 627
Elizabeth Blanch, 1217
Frank, 1109
Ginger Lee, 1808
Hubert, 1109
Joan Clara, 958
John, 627

Kathryn Minnette, 121
Lillian, 1109
Lorilla, 1053
Lucy, 627
Lydia (Kiplinger), 1109
Mamie, 1109
Matthew, 627
Michael Edward, 243
Minnie L (Wiser), 1868
Mona, 968
Orpha Lenora, 1316
Pamela, 1739
Robert G, 1453
Sarah (Fisher), 627
son, 627
Stephanie Jean, 550
Venda Lucille (Northway), 121
William Erie, 121
HAYLEY
Emma, 1817
HAYNES
Christopher John, 455
Dexter Craig, 455
Helen Amelia, 107
Johnny Earl, 40
Johnny M, 40
Kathy Eileen (Rheinscheld), 455
Linda Ruth, 1818
Margaret Loene, 1134
Randica Lynn, 198
Sarah Elizabeth (Farmer), 40
Tracy Marie (Groves), 455
Virginia Elizabeth, 40
Walter Richard, 455
William James, 40
HAYS
Josiah, 1665
Martha J (Wiser), 1665
HAYSE
Elizabeth Mae Crownover, 933
HAYSLIP
Candy Sue, 454
HAYTER
Almeda E, 1655
HAZEL
Emma Caroline (Wagner), 1401
Frances Helen, 1401
George H, 1401
Thelma Susanne, 1401
HAZELETT
Elias [Peter?], 813
Elva, 814
Leroy, 814
Margaret (Womelsdorf), 813
Paula Kay, 1286
HAZELTON
Albert, 1696
Viola Edith (Turner), 1696
HAZLETT
Heather Anne (Johnson), 380
Ian Lewis Johnson, 380
Jacob Royal Johnson, 380
Steven Brent, 380
HAZLEWOOD
Jack, 69
Jack Stuart, 69
Nancy Lee (Martin), 69
Tiffany Christine, 69

HEAD
Carole J (Wingo), 924
Danette Machelle, 613
David A, 924
Douglas A, 924
Glen Leo, 613
Glenda (Baker), 613
John Daniel, 613
Karen M, 924
Lucretia, 1830
HEAFFER
Anna (Weiser), 1620
George, 1620
HEANEY
Brenda Marie, 657
HEAPS
Emily (Weiser), 1469
John, 1469
HEARN
Amber Nicole, 539
Charles Gregory, 539
Justine Niles, 539
Tracy Wynn (Herring), 539
HEARVALL
Merris Steven, 1301
Sharlene Ann (Barb), 1301
HEASLEY
Brian Merve, 1280
Cameron Wayne, 1279
Deanna Lynn, 1280
Deborah Kathleen (Raber), 1279
Fredrick Wayne, 1279
Jason Wayne, 1279
Jennifer Lee, 1280
Jessican Kathleen, 1280
Laura Lynn (Dolby), 1280
Linda Lee (Seigworth), 1279
HEAST
--, 1000
Rose (Lillibridge), 1000
HEATH
--, 729
Anna Olive Klinger (Long), 729
Benjamin J, 123
daughter, 729
Jean Emelia (Jensen), 123
Mary Jane, 1764
son, 729
HEATHE
Nancy Jay, 1453
HEAVICAN
Joseph M, 1387
Matthew Joseph, 1387
Melinda Sue, 1387
Mitchell Zachary, 1387
Susan Katherine (Harvison), 1387
HEAVLIN
Arlene Mae, 453
HEBEL
James Mulhollan Jr, 925
James William, 926
Jeanette Louise, 926
Jonathan Scott, 926
Katherine Michele (Carter), 926
Wanda W, 918
Wanda Weiser, 1884
Wanda Wilma (Weiser), 925

HEBER
Nancy F, 1640
HEBERLIG
Esther, 889
HECK
June Eleanor, 697
Pamela Sue (Conley), 569
Patricia Marie, 569
Steven, 569
HECKATHORN
Patricia, 1335
HECKERT
A Franklin, 705
Alfreda Naomi (Buffington), 763
Alvine Daniel, 764
Anna Mae, 763
Arlo David, 764
Beulah Pauline (Latsha), 764
Beverly Ann, 764
Brian Christopher, 762
Bruce John, 762
Bruce Michael, 762
Cassandra, 1413
Catherine Ann, 762
Catherine May, 735
Catherine Patricia, 763
Catherine Rebecca, 764
Charles Matthew, 763
Christina Marie, 762
Christina Maritza, 764
Clara Belle (Plessinger), 763
Claudia (Del Secco), 763
Dale Daniel, 764
Daniel Alex, 763
Daniel Nevin, 762
Diane Manette, 764
Donald Lamar, 763
Doris Patterson (Watts), 705
Druann Maria, 763
Elaine Mary, 705
Emelia (Bermudez), 762
Frances Eva (Tressler), 764
George Timothy, 762
George Witmer, 762
Gerald Paul, 763
Gladys Ileen, 763
Helen, 705
infant, 764
James Quintin, 764
John Donald, 705
John Donald Jr, 705
John F, 705
Joseph Daniel, 763
Karen Eileen, 705
Katherine (Kessler), 705
Kenneth Leo, 763
Leah Charlotte (Witmer), 705
Leonard John, 764
Lois Jean, 764
Marian Josephine, 763
Marietta Barbara, 764
Mark Allen, 764
Mark Daniel, 763
Mary Edna (Witmer), 762
Mary Ellen, 763
Matthew John, 762
Melinda Catherine, 762
Nathaniel Alan, 763

HECKERT (continued)
Nolan James, 764
Paul Andrew, 763
Paul Charles, 763
Paul Kester, 763
Philina (Townley), 705
Quintin, 764
Ralph Edgar, 763
Robert Mark, 705
Ross Allen, 705
Roy Albert, 764
Sally Jane, 763
Sara Mae L (Raezer), 763
Valerie (Kaiser), 762
Virginia (Peacock), 705
Virginia Ann, 762
Virginia Mary, 763
HECKMAN
Cleora I, 1728
Daisy May (Wisser), 1728
Thorma M, 1728
Walter L, 1728
HEDBERG
Adeline, 516
HEDDINGS
Amanda Lynn, 747
Brandi Lee, 747
Christopher Daniel, 748
Deborah (Gallops), 747
Elizabeth (Wilkins), 747
Janet May (Klinger), 747
John Edward, 747
Kristina Marie, 747
Randall Lee, 747
Richard Larry, 748
Robert Lewis, 747
Robert Lewis Jr, 747
Robyn Lynn (Hall), 747
Roger Louis, 748
Ronald Leon, 748
Russel Lloyd, 747
Russel Lloyd Jr, 747
Tammy Dawn, 748
HEDGES
Darla Jean, 398
HEDKE
Donna (Kahle), 1243
Edward, 1243
HEDLIND
Irene Louise, 1259
HEDRICK
Isabelle Chase, 786
Kate (Rockey), 1129
Rufus, 1129
HEDRICKS
Thelma Mae, 856
HEDSTROM
Alice, 189
HEETER
Alysha Kaye, 1307
Amanda Kaye, 1307
Amber Kelly, 1307
Anna Kaye (Wiser), 1306
Azia Lenore (Kahle), 1230
Debra Kaye, 1306
Kimberley Raye, 1307
Merle Edwin, 1307
Richard Dean, 1306
Sharon Kaye (Eisenhuth), 1307
Shelley Jean, 1306

Walter K, 1230
HEFFELFINGER
Annie (Wisser), 1762
Charles, 1762
Clara, 1762
Stella Wilhelmina, 1354
HEFFLEFINGER
Chase, 230
Hayden, 230
Lisa Ann, 230
Logan, 230
Lori Jean, 230
Margaret Alice (Burkholder), 230
Margaret Lynn, 230
Mark William, 230
Randee (Parr), 230
Smilee, 230
William Crofford, 230
HEFFNER
Ada L, 1168
Daniel, 60
David, 60
Dolores, 1751
Ephraim, 60
Florence (Christian), 1534
James, 1534
Mary (Weiser), 60
Maxine Heath, 493
Sarah Ann, 60
Wallace G, 1534
HEFLINGER
Lisa Lynn, 486
HEFNER
Craig Eugene, 536
Glen Eugene, 536
Harry, 519
Nora Elizabeth (Fisher), 519
Selma Jean (Alexander), 536
Sonya Marie, 536
Willie Oneta, 44
HEFT
Lizzie, 1230
HEGELE
Edna Rose, 1392
HEGGINS
Paul, 55
Tina Maier (Wright), 55
HEGIE
--, 1670
Susanna (Weiser), 1670
HEGSTEDT
Maryon, 1236
HEICHEL
Emma, 873
Jack, 944
Ruth Ann (Keller), 944
HEIDE
Jeanne Mary, 1368
HEIDEL
Albert Weiser, 1625
Charles Edward, 1625
Charles Sumner, 1625
Ewart Leslie, 1625
Hattie Clara (Weiser), 1625
HEIDEMAN
Carrie Louise (Weiser), 207
Delores (Oleuinski), 207
Delores Ann, 207
Gloria Jean, 207
Melville Miller, 207

Ruby Eileen, 207
HEIDER
Gloria Jean (Bradbury), 123
Robert William, 123
HEIDLE
Laura Mae, 1057
HEIDMAN
Anna Susanna (Weiser), 378
Annie Louisa, 378
Caltha Olive, 379
Carl Graves, 379
Charlotte Celest (Roth), 378
Christopher Carl, 380
Denice Carol, 380
Elizabeth Haskell (Stoner), 378
Frank Henry, 378
George Henry, 378
Heather Nicole, 378
Henry Stello, 378
Howard Henry, 378
Jack L, 375
Jack Lane, 378
Jack Lane Jr, 378
Jerry Lee, 378
Jerry Lee Jr, 378
Joanne Joy (Flohr), 378
Joannes Edith, 379
Karen (Cutler), 380
Laura Belle (Howard), 378
Lena Gertrude, 380
Malissa Margaret, 380
Manetta Jeunie, 381
Margaret (Ledbetter), 378
Marjorie (Hanson), 379
Marvin Frank, 380
Mary Elizabeth, 381
Mary Emma, 380
Nancy (Kulpa), 380
Ollie Durella (Flemming), 378
Rita Francis (Bower), 378
Sandra (Nalie), 378
Sandra (Smart), 378
Stephanie Paige (Ford), 378
Tommy Joe, 378
HEIGES
Lucille Weiser, 1465
Marie Eichelberger (Weiser), 1465
Marie Irene, 1465
William Smith, 1465
HEIL
Charles, 401
Penny Jojane, 401
Phyllis Nadine (Moore), 401
HEILEMAN
August Carl, 502
Barbara Ann, 500
Barbara Jean (Gillispie), 489
Bereta (Riley), 489
Betty Jane, 499
Betty Joyce, 492
Boots Edward, 489
Charles Frederick, 488
Clara Augusta, 493
Constance, 500
Daniel David, 490
Donald L, 499

Doris Imogene (Leiter), 499
Edward John Henry, 490
Ellen (King), 498
Emma Catharine, 498
Ethel L, 490
Floyd J, 499
Frederick Hobsen, 492
Gary, 499
Grace (Tuckerman), 498
Grace I (Avery), 492
Harland E, 499
Hattie Lucinda, 500
Helen Louise (Nowak), 489
Henrietta (Schiller), 489
Henrietta Louisa, 482
Henry Albert, 482
James August, 489
Jan (Knight), 490
Janet Sue, 500
Joan, 499
John Benjamin, 488
John William, 499
Joyce, 499
Joyce Pauline, 490
Lake Erie, 489
Lois (--), 489
Lucinda, 500
Mable Irene, 489
Mary Ann, 490
Mary Kathryn, 500
Myrtle E, 498
Ola Dell (Henry), 500
Orland E, 500
Raymond George Dewey, 488
Reva (Courtright), 490
Richard Earl, 499
Robert Alden, 492
Robert H, 499
Samuel Jack, 489
Sharlotte (Richmond), 490
Sharon, 499
Shirley (Fillipi), 490
Shirley Jean, 499
Simon Otto, 488
stillborn female, 490
Susan (Welsh), 488
Texford Joe, 490
Viola (Courtright), 490
Virginia (Robinson), 490
Virginia Lorraine (Scott), 492
William Alexander, 498
William Sherman, 489
Winifred May, 499
HEILEMANN
Carl August, 482
Mary Elizabeth, 482
HEILER
Adolg, 1608
Silke (Weisser), 1608
HEILMAN
Melissa Ann, 483
HEIM
Catharine, 363, 375, 429-430, 443, 446, 456
Craig Grant, 684
Ernest Calvin, 684
Frances Helena (Brosious), 684

Helen, 997
John, 360
Karen Elizabeth, 1163
Maria Catharine, 360
Mary, 784
Mary Catharine, 361
Rodny Ernest, 684
HEIMADINGER
Annie, 1100
HEIMBERGER
Peggy Sue, 1140
HEIMS
Ida R, 1635
HEINBAUGH
Claudia (Boris), 1536
Erik, 1536
Harold, 1536
Harold Herbert, 1536
Heather, 1536
Kathryn, 1536
Kathryn Madaline (Muggio), 1536
Patricia (Manning), 1536
HEINEY
Lowell, 547
Michael Dean, 547
Ruth Ilene (Herring), 547
Vickie Lynn, 547
HEINLEN
Anna Marie, 943
Arthur G, 943
Carol Ann (Davidson), 943
Carol Rose, 943
Cheryl Ann, 943
Daniel David, 943
Daniel G, 943
Donald, 943
Elsie (Starner), 943
Ida, 942
John, 943
Lena Tell (Neatherly), 943
Mary Ann (Schaefer), 943
Paul, 943
Rose Ann (Sales), 943
HEINLEY
Kelly, 789
HEINRICH
--, 1
Jill Christine, 769
HEINRICKS
Elsie, 1392
HEINSE
Carole Winkler, 176
HEINTZELMAN
Harvey, 1540
Mary Cordelia (Weiser), 1540
HEINTZELMANN
Henrich Israel, 1361
John Diedrich Matthias, 1361
Margaret (Weiser), 1361
HEINZ
Bernice, 1203
Johanna Louise, 1736
HEIRMER
Clarence A, 201
Frances Roberta (McColloch), 201
HEISE
Geneva, 621
LeRoy, 621

HERRING (continued)
Nina Lucille (Karst), 543
Noah R, 535
Nora Edith, 570
Norine Delight, 572
Norma Jean, 534-535
Norma Jeann, 568
Norval Monroe, 572
Opal M (Tudor), 535
Pamela Louise (Yeager), 575
Patricia Ann (Butler), 566
Paul, 534
Paul D, 575
Paul David, 547
Paul Gerald, 575
Paul J, 546
Paul Richard, 538
Paula Dell (Secrest), 541
Paula Joan, 547
Peggy Sue, 539
Penny Denise (Smith), 547
Penrose, 1730
Perry Solomon, 545
Perry Thomas, 556
Perry Wesley, 547
Perry Wesley Jr, 547
Phoebe Ann, 547
Phyliss Ann, 534, 568
Phyllis Maxine, 546
Rachael (Morgan), 565
Ralph J, 565
Randall Everett, 567
Randy Lee, 537
Raymond Lee, 544
Rebecca, 535
Rebecca (Bricker), 565
Rebecca (Gibbson), 538
Rebecca Jo, 547
Regina Sue, 572
Rena (Morgan), 556
Renee Kae, 568
Reva Eileen, 594
Rheuben, 559-560, 627
Rhonda, 542
Rhonda Jo, 539
Rhonda Kay, 575
Richard Jerome, 538
Richard K, 535
Richard Leo, 547
Richard Leroy, 535
Rickie Lee, 566
Rita Tae (Hughes), 544
Robbie Lee, 543
Robert Eugene, 535, 541, 567, 574
Robert Ronald, 534
Roberta Joan (Neely), 541
Ronald Edwin, 567
Ronald Lee, 539
Rosa (Ralston), 536
Roy Emmons, 546
Russell, 575
Ruth (Bish), 534
Ruth Ilene, 547
Ruth Juanita (Forst), 572
Ruth Melcina (Kerlin), 566
Sabrina Marie, 544
Samantha Leeann, 547
Samuel, 594
Sarah, 549, 628

Sarah (Craig), 595
Sarah (Fisher), 627
Sarah Elizabeth, 529
Sarah J (Doyle), 549
Sarah Jane (Rodgers), 567
Sarah Loretta, 561
Sarah May, 555
Scott Aaron, 539
Scott Allen, 542
Seth Lee, 566
Shane Ladd, 539
Sharon Elaine (Nall), 566
Sharon Marie (Quinn), 538
Sharri Ann, 575
Sharron Sue, 544
Shawn Jeffery, 575
Shawna Michelle, 567
Sherry Lynn (Baker), 543
Shirley (Montgomery), 547
Shirley (Young), 566
Shirley Jean, 546
Simeon, 578
Stella (Sagers), 575
Stephanie Jo, 567
Stephen Lee, 547
Steven, 547
stillborn, 535
Susan, 628
Susan (Turner), 567
Susan Elizabeth, 535
Susan Kay, 567
Tammy Rae, 539
Terry Allen, 544
Theodore Eugene, 547
Theodore R, 595
Theodore Wilson, 546
Theola (Miller), 538
Thomas L, 561
Tony Rae, 544
Tonya (Gaunter), 542
Tracy Ann, 542
Tracy Wynn, 539
Treva Ann, 572
Trisha (Loftis), 567
Tyler Eugene, 541
Valeria Ann, 534
Verna Vember, 565
Veronica Sue, 537
Vickie Marie (Pratt), 538
Vickie Sue (Williams), 575
Violet Lucille, 543
Virginia, 534
Virginia Alice, 575
Vivian Oletha, 595
Wanda Kay David (Dyer), 538
Wanda Sue, 566
Wayne Boyd, 572
Wilbur Ellis, 535
William Earl, 543
William Ellis, 536
William Ellis Jr, 543
William F, 549
William L, 559
William Leonard, 543
Wilma Jean, 538
Wilsie Everett, 568
Wreath M, 555
HERRINGTON
Charles Raymond, 809
Kathleen Marie, 809
Laura Belle, 1445

Margaret Estelle (Kuebler), 809
HERROLD
Betty June, 704
Cora, 1457
Donald Brown, 707
Janice Ellen (Zerbe), 707
HERRON
Carol (McConnell), 64
Francis Joseph, 1546
Frank J, 1546
Jane Marie, 1547
Margaret, 158
Marguerite (Brown), 1546
Mary Lynn, 368
Paul W, 64
HERSBERGER
Carol Ann, 1511
HERSCH
Elizabeth, 1760
HERSHBERGER
Alyce Ann (Reed), 1511
Cindy Lee, 1511
Gloria Jean, 1511
Howard Eugene, 1511
Susan Joy, 1512
HERSHEY
Calvin J, 933
Carole Emilene, 933
Jeffrey Clark, 933
Judy (Clark), 933
Marilyn Jean, 933
Phyllis Irene, 608
Ronald Calvin, 933
Ronald Christopher, 933
Ruth Emilene Hall (Evans), 933
Sean Mark, 933
Shane Matthew, 933
HERSHFIELD
Mildred, 1190
HERSHISER
Mary Ann, 1879
HERSTEIN
Arthur Hayes, 882
Gideon Tong-IL, 882
Joshua Soon Shin, 882
Wendy Louise (Wise), 882
HERTZEL
Kate F, 845
HERTZOG
Terrie, 1780
HERVEY
Carol (Hayes), 86
Catherine Faith, 86
Cornelia Gillespie (Miller), 86
Geoffrey Townsen, 86
James Christopher, 86
Martha Vickery, 86
Mary (Apostolakos), 86
Mary Ann (Richmond), 86
Rosalind Wren (Thompson), 86
Sarah Elizabeth, 86
Theodore Ernst, 86
Theodore Ernst Jr, 86
HERZER
Kenneth Brian, 1297
Shelley Ann (Brosch), 1297

HESLOP
Sharon, 1777
HESNER
Eliza Jane (Spyker), 1451
William, 1451
HESS
Alan Joseph, 1678
Alexander, 1684
Alyssa Marie, 897
Andrew Ewelace, 1684
Anna Mary, 1395
Barbara (Palmer), 1678
Billy James, 897
Blanche (Felty), 1394
Carol Jean, 1450
Catherine, 1711
Catherine (Baney), 1394
Catherine Gene, 897
Charlene (Tiehl), 1393
Charles Ira, 1394
Dale Richard, 1750
Darwin Leroy, 1750
David, 1394
David Joseph, 1678
Dawn Heather (Moody), 1072
Dayton Richard, 1684
Donald Alan, 1678
Edgar E, 1394
Edna Marie, 1394
Elizabeth Jane, 1394
Emaline (Wagner), 1393
Emeline Wagner, 1394
Ernest Wagner, 1394
Ernest William, 1394
Fern (Bennett), 1395
Florence Love, 832
Francis Boyington, 1684
George Auster, 1684
Harriet Lucille (Wiser) Grimm, 1678
Harry Joseph, 1678
Heidi Lynn, 1498
Henrietta, 348
Henry, 1366
Ida A (Whitney), 1684
Joan Caroline, 1395
John E, 1394
John Michael, 1394
John Wagner, 1396
Josephine Florence, 1684
Julia Ann, 1373
Kathy Jo, 1394
Lenora Louisa (Binkley), 466
Leroy Elmer, 1750
Lucille Elinore, 1750
Lucy (--), 1684
Luella May (Wisser) Seidel, 1750
Margaret (McWilliams), 1393
Mark Allen, 1394
Mary Ann, 1394
Mary K (Thompson), 1394
Michael, 1393
Michael Aaron, 1394
Minnie (Portzline), 1393
Nancy Jane (Kephart), 1684
Naomi Ruth (Ross), 203

Newton Edgar, 1393
Newton Ernest, 1393
Nina Winona, 1395
Oscar, 466
Patricia (Mark), 1394
Phyllis, 1394
Rebecca (Weiser), 1366
Robert Calvin, 1395
Robert Eugene, 1072
Samuel McWilliams, 1393
Samuel Moser, 1396
Samuel Tiehl, 1393
Sarah, 1393
Sarah Catherine (McKinney), 1394
Sarah Weiser, 1396
Stella (Kepler), 1394
Virginia, 1395
Virginia Ann, 1394
Virginia Ann (Alex), 1678
Wilella, 466
Wilford, 1394
William, 203
HESSE
Blanche Estella (Bickel), 772
C F O, 759
Charles Felder Van Metre, 772
HESTER
Franklin, 647
Pamela Kay (Hendricks), 647
HETER
Brandi Kathryn, 474
Kathryn Virginia (Dorobek), 474
Kevin Paul, 474
Mandi Lee, 474
HETLAND
Judith Ann, 1063
HETRICH
Jacob, 1269
Mary (Harringer), 1269
HETRICK
Anna Catherine (Henrich), 16
George, 934
Guy W, 1229
Madge Evelyn (Kahle), 1229
Marily Kay, 1229
Marilyn Celeste, 139
Nancy, 1025
Peter, 16
Phylis Louise (Hall), 934
HETWORTH
Ashley Lauren, 438
Karen Jean (Gardner), 438
Robert, 438
HETZEL
Alfred Charles, 1317
Lola Jean, 1317
Marilyn Joyce, 1317
Mary Lenora (Sharritts), 1317
Phyllis Ann, 1317
HETZER
Bertha Pearl, 106
HEUSER
Alleen Deborah, 1063
Brian Michael, 1063
Curtis Noll, 1063

HILL (continued)
Thomas, 1479
Thomas Kent, 960
Timothy, 192
Valerie E Clymer, 280
Vanessa, 1006
Zelma Faye, 959
HILLARD
Harry Robert, 147
Inez, 108
Jerry Dee, 528
Julie Marlena
  (Wickham), 528
Lillian (Stevens), 147
Stephanie, 147
HILLBUSH
Anna Marsena, 767
Anna May (Witmer),
  767
Beatrice (Pordham),
  767
Celia (Bagocius), 767
Christine Anna, 767
Edward Joseph, 767
Howard Edwin, 767
Joseph Robert, 767
Kathryn Anne, 767
Robert, 767
HILLHOUSE
Benjamin Jerome, 306
Josephine Kenyon
  (Herrick), 306
HILLIARD
Billie Jo, 1307
Jennifer Leigh, 1307
Joseph Leroy, 1306
Kyle Richard, 1307
Lulu May, 368
Shelley Jean (Heeter),
  1306
HILLMAN
David Ray, 432
Edwin Ray, 432
Floyd Walker, 432
Helen Frances, 432
Laura Mildred (Smith),
  432
Mary Waldene (Scott),
  432
Melba Grace (Foster),
  432
Nancy Grace, 432
Paul Edwin, 432
Ruby Mildred, 432
Ruth Mary, 432
Warren Edwin, 432
HILLS
Arthur Gorman, 1358
Charles Warren, 1358
Elizabeth Warren, 1358
Grace Muhlenberg,
  1358
Joseph Dixon, 1358
Mary Edna (Gorman),
  1358
Mary Gorman, 1358
Mary Joe (Dixon),
  1358
Ralph G, 1358
Ralph Gorman, 1358
Ralph Warren, 1358
Sarah Elizabeth
  (Mcconnell), 1358
HILLYER
Evelyn Elizabeth, 540
HILMAN
Charles, 1443
Eleanor Jane (Spyker),
  1443

HILMER
Judith Ann, 173
HILNER
Diane Mae (Slattery),
  1171
Ron, 1171
HILSINGER
Carrie L, 1780
HILT
Hazel Matilda, 1661
HILTON
Calvin, 665
Calvin Forrest, 665
Charles Willard, 665
Vickey Arlene
  (Roadenbaugh), 665
HILTWINE
Mary, 895
HILTY
Phyllis Gaye, 852
HIMES
Donald Scott, 1230
Joan Eloise (Kahle),
  1230
Michael Scott, 1230
HIMMELBERGER
Adam E, 846
Diana, 1568
Ella M (Weiser), 1567
Hannah Amelia
  (Anspach), 846
Magdalena, 1566
Marion Virginia, 846
William Henry, 1567
HIMROD
Chris Edward, 1254
Glenn Allen, 1254
June Ann, 1254
Kenneth, 1254
Margaret Jane (Kerr),
  1254
HIMSTREET
Lora, 1580
HINDAL
Claude, 962
Mildred (Smith), 962
HINDELANG
Cynthia Ann
  (Patterson), 399
Jordan Danielle, 400
Taylor Elizabeth, 400
Tom, 399
HINDERER
Lori Maree (Troutman),
  1493
Richard Dean, 1493
HINDLEY
Barbara Jean
  (Tellefson), 457
Guy Stephen, 458
Jean Elizabeth, 458
John Parsons, 457
Thomas Rollin, 458
HINDMAN
Lilly Jane, 1239
HINDS
Adelaide (--), 183
Alexis Anne (Barrios),
  1161
Camelita J, 1160
Carl Edward, 1161
Carmelita J, 1884
Carmelita June
  (Senander), 1161
E Gladys (Madole),
  1161
Frank Leslie, 1161
Frank Leslie Jr, 1161
Jessica, 1162

John, 183
Julia Rose, 1161
Katheryn, 1718
Keith Michel, 1162
Kevin Lake, 1161
Kyle William, 1162
Lue Ann (Allen), 1162
Margaret Alice, 1162
Margaret Louise
  (Lassiter), 183
Marie Estell (Porreea),
  1162
Mary Lou, 1162
Mitchell Thomas, 1162
Robert Leonard, 1162
Robert Leonard Jr,
  1162
Robert Steve, 1162
Ruth Amelia (Weiser),
  1161
Ryan Alexander, 1161
Sandi Ann, 1162
Stacy Lynda (Story),
  1161
Thomas Edward, 1161
Vickie (McFarland),
  1162
HINER
Margaret Elizabeth,
  678
HINES
Anne Elizabeth, 831
David Early, 831
Deborah Joan
  (Otterbeck), 966
Deborah June, 1239
Dessie (Haschel), 268
Doris Fay (Wiser),
  1819
Janet McCrae, 204
John, 268
John H, 831
John Henry, 831
Kay Jolene (Foth),
  1484
Kelie Lynn, 966
Manie (Maier), 55
Mark, 966
Mary Louise, 1274
Nancy Jan (Haines),
  831
Terrance Scott, 1484
Terry Michael, 1819
Thomas C, 55
HINKE
William J, 88
HINKLE
June, 164-165
Rebecca, 1613
HINNERSHITZ
Irene, 96
Rebecca, 1620
HINNESY
Fred, 1243
Orpha (Irwin), 1243
HINSHAW
Anthony Jay, 614
Bonnie Jean (Baker),
  614
Jack, 614
HINSON
Jennifer Diane, 1387
Kristen Diane
  (Harvison), 1387
Michael Dean, 1387
HINTON
Darin Lloyd, 1778
Kim Cheree (Wiser),
  1778

Rebecca Elaine, 129
HIOSINGTON
Effie, 975
HIPPENSTEEL
Lovemma Burnice, 522
HIPPERT
Mary Catherine, 1309
HIPPLE
Annabel Lee (Eppley),
  888
Deanna Kay, 888
Earl Eugene, 888
Eleanor Elizabeth
  (Cash), 888
Gertrude Mae (Keel),
  888
Mary Lisabeth, 888
Ralph, 888
Richard Blaine, 888
Robert Allen, 888
Robert Eugene, 888
Roy Blaine, 888
Roy Gene, 888
Sara Louise (Metz),
  888
HIPPS
--, 1699
Helen (Shimmel), 1699
HIRES
Crystal Darlene, 1451
HIRNEISEN
Clifford, 285
Sarah Gardiner
  (Muhlenberg), 285
HIRSCH
Brigitte (Weisser),
  1608
Evan, 1602
Maud, 289
Sally Helen (Martin),
  1602
Stephan, 1608
HIRT
-- (--), 777
Douglas, 473
Helen Viola (Rabuck),
  778
Jean Carole, 778
Jeanne Elizabeth (Wolf),
  473
Oscar, 777-778
Patti Lynn, 778
Robert George, 778
Rose (Densavage), 778
William Richard, 778
HISCOX
Kathleen Eleanor, 1739
HISEL
Minnie Louella, 443
HISKEY
David Brian, 1289
Elizabeth Anne, 1289
Frances Yvonne
  (Vandeuren), 1289
Karen Elaine, 1289
Lois Margaret
  (Freimuth), 1289
Ralph Edward, 1289
Robert Andrew, 1289
Sarah Katherine, 1289
Susan Elizabeth, 1289
HITCHINGS
Retta A, 1702
HITE
--, 661
Betty Pauline (Herring),
  568
Carolyn Renae, 568
Cheryl Lynn, 568

Constance Ann, 568
Crystal Mae (DeBaillje),
  568
Janice Louise (Isch),
  568
John, 568
Kavin Wain, 568
Michael Eugene, 568
Minnie V
  (Roadenbaugh), 661
Monica Renee, 568
Patrick Alan, 568
Ryan Wayne, 568
HITSMAN
Vera, 1011
HITT
Eelynne Maurine
  (Wiser), 1185
Harris, 1185
HITTLE
Debra Ann, 541
HIVNER
Albert, 864
Lizzie (Smaling), 864
Martha (Greenwalt),
  864
Wayne, 864
HIXON
Betty May, 1332
HIXSON
Claude, 972
Mabel (Nelson), 972
Wilbur, 972
Zola, 972
HOAG
Dawn Lee, 202
George S, 41
Myrtle Willey
  (Appleby), 41
Sarah, 1619
HOAGLAND
Bradley S, 789
Bradley S Jr, 789
Brittan, 789
Brittany L, 789
Cynthia, 789
Georgiana, 789
Geraldine (Frey), 789
Harold, 789
Jayme D, 789
Laticia Q, 789
Lisa (Snyder), 789
Rene (Hovenstine), 789
Zachary S, 789
HOASTER
Carol Ann, 876
HOBBS
Barbara Jean
  (Whitaker), 1439
Charley Timmy, 1347
Jannifer Rae, 1347
Jonathan Allen, 1347
Julie Marie, 1347
Rex, 1439
Sharon Ann (Florek),
  1347
HOBER
Karen Ann, 1141
HOCH
Abraham, 1626
Betty Elnora (Klinger),
  745
Connie Lynn, 745
David, 1612
Elizabeth (Schwoyer),
  1612
Esther, 1613, 1626
Gary Lewis, 745
Hannah (DeTurk),

HOCH (continued)
Hannah (DeTurk)
(continued)
1637
Howard, 550
Jacob, 1612
John Daniel, 745
Josiah, 1637
Katie M, 1865
Kent T, 550
Patty (Dillon), 550
Sarah, 1625
Sibilla (Weiser), 1612
Susanna, 1626
Susanna (Schneider), 1626
Susanna (Weiser), 1626
HOCHENBERRY
Matilda, 1682
HOCHHALTER
Deanna Joyce, 414
HOCKENBROCH
ArDella Fern, 715
Dennis Ryan, 715
Ethel (Engle), 715
Gladys LeEmma, 715
Glenn Eric, 715
Howard Reuben, 715
Joyce, 82
Joyce Mae, 715
Laura Hester
(Goodling), 715
Randy Lee, 715
HOCKER
Alice J (Morgan), 588
Alvina, 585
Amanda, 580
Anna, 588
Anna Margrette
(McSpadden), 588
Annis Dale, 587
Barbara Sue, 586
Bertha Maye (Davis), 585
Betty Marie (Dodd), 590
Billy Dwane, 592
Billy Lee, 592
Birdie Irene, 591
Bobbie Gene, 585
Bonnie (Peterson), 589
Burnie Lee, 585
Candace Lynn, 584
Catherine (Herring), 578
Catherine Denise, 587
Charles Lewis, 588
Cheryl Reanee, 588
Clarence Monroe, 582
Cleo Mexia, 580
Cleo O, 591
Clifford J, 593
Daniel Leroy, 590
Danna Sue, 590
Darlene (Fink), 588
David Bradley, 588
David Donald, 588
Debra Lynn, 589
Dee Phillip, 589
Delorid (Sims), 590
Derance L, 593
Destiny Lynn, 588
Donna Ann (Stansbury), 587
Donna Gale, 593
Donna Jean (Lewis), 592
Dorothy Marie
(Wilson), 593

Earl Foster, 583
Earnest Lloyd, 589
Edward W, 280
Effie Zella (Mullen), 579
Elizabeth Ann, 589
Elizabeth C (Parrett), 593
Elizabeth May, 587
Eloise (Vargas), 588
Elsie Leela (Thomas), 585
Elsie May (Lowe), 588
Erma May, 580
Everett Leroy, 583
Fairy Nellie, 590
Faye Pauline, 584
George, 588
George Lewis, 588
Georgia Juanita
(Atkinson), 583
Grace E, 593
Hazel Lucille, 582
Irene, 585
James Lee, 590
James Lee Jr, 590
James Monroe, 585
James Monroe Jr, 585
Janet Lynn, 585
Janie Marie, 590
Jerry Glen, 593
Joanne Marie, 583
John Emanuel, 582
John Ervin, 585
John Wesley, 592
John Wesley Jr, 592
Joseph Daniel, 587
Judith Ann, 593
Julius Dwane, 592
June Alice, 589
Karelyn Kay, 592
Karl Kent, 593
Kathryn Sue, 584
Kenneth Eugene, 588
Kenneth Leroy, 583
Kenneth P, 593
Kevin Neal, 589
Kitnia Dawn, 588
Laverna Mae, 592
LaVerta A, 588
Lewis, 578
Linda Faye (Hunt), 592
Lora Lee, 586
Louise M (Kirtley), 583
Maggie Leona, 587
Marilyn Annetta, 592
Mary (Galland), 585
Mary (Lawton), 587
Mary Jane, 584
Mary Lavon
(Cappleman), 592
Mary Margaret, 578
Maxine Imogene, 589
Molly Sue, 593
Naoma Zola (Dobbs), 585
Norman Eugene, 588
Olina Jean, 589
Pamela Mary, 587
Pamela Sue (Mankin), 588
Patricia Ann (Pierce), 583
Patricia Eileen, 590
Patricia Lee, 584
Paul Cleveland, 588
Paul Isaac, 585
Paule Ann (Morris),

585
Pearl Darlene, 589
Penola (Bridge), 593
Percie J
(Webb-Hunsucker), 593
Phillip, 588
Ramona Luciela
(Snow), 592
Randall Scott, 589
Raymond Paul, 587
Raymond Pearl, 587
Richard Lee, 590
Rickey Wayne, 589
Robert Allen, 593
Robert Allen Jr, 593
Robert V, 588
Robert Vernon, 589
Robert Vernon Jr, 589
Robin Ray, 589
Rose, 588
Rose Ann, 583
Rose Ann (Barber), 583
Rose Marie (Guy), 585
Rosemary, 589
Rosemary (Hocker), 589
Roy Gene, 585
Ruth Ellen, 593
Ruth Mirriam, 586
Sandra Faye, 587
Sarah Elizabeth
(Bricker), 582
Stella Faye, 586
Stephen Louis, 588
Steven Paul, 585
Susan, 593
Tela Irene, 580
Thelma Lafon, 586
Vada Nadine, 589
Velma Avonne, 583
Velna Rose, 585
Verna Ann (Wood), 588
Virgil Eugene, 586
Virgil Lewis, 588
Wanda Maye, 585
Waunita Mae (Weeden), 588
Wetoka N, 593
William Albert, 585
William Lewis, 579
Yvonna Kathleen, 593
Zelma Lavone, 585
HODGE
--, 1424
Barbara Sue (Hocker), 586
James Riley, 1822
Mary J (Weiser), 1424
Nancy Virginia, 1822
Royce Galen, 586
HODGES
Doris Gertrude, 1488
Elton Jr, 142
Floy Mae, 461
Isaac Allen, 1829
Melinda (Wiser), 1829
Patricia Marilyn
(Hughes), 142
HOEFER
Emma Elizabeth, 1567
HOEFFER
Sophia, 1100
HOEFFLE
Jane A (Deppen), 111
William, 111

HOEHN
Ann Louise (Yoder), 830
Benjamin Randall, 830
Michael, 830
HOEL
Belinda, 1724
HOERATH
Valetta Elenora, 198
HOEY
Kathleen Alice (Kohl), 757
Matthew Christopher, 757
William, 757
HOFFA
Mary Ann, 91
HOFFBAUER
Jae, 739
HOFFER
Mary A, 1504
Naomi, 251
HOFFERT
Carrie, 1566
Catherine (Weiser), 1309
Daniel Peter, 1309
Franklin Jacob, 1309
Grace Lucilla, 1309
Kate (Weiser), 1567
Lulu (Howell), 1309
Mary Catherine
(Hippert) Burns, 1309
William, 1567
William Peter, 1309
HOFFHINES
Nelle, 1142
HOFFMAN
--, 999
-- (--), 719
-- (Emrick), 773
Ada Kathryn (Hepner), 722
Adrienne Nicole, 503
Alice Mae (Babione), 503
Allen Dean, 751
Alvin S, 1729
Amy Elizabeth, 751
Andrea, 503
Andrea Marie, 503
Andrew John, 340
Ann Muhlenberg, 340
Anna Jeanette, 770
Arleta Fern (Kiger), 1154
Arthur James, 340
Arthur James III, 1282
Arthur R, 773
Barbara, 503
Barbara (Metzler), 770
Beryl Jean, 751
Bessie (Smith), 503
Betty (Burgard), 1176
Betty (St Clair), 1175
Betty Hodge, 1176
Bobby Albert, 776
Bradley Allen, 751
Canei Vail (Carlson), 722
Carol Ann, 752
Caroline Louisa
(Paulton), 770
Caroline S (Lind), 340
Carrie, 769
Carrie Selina, 340
Catherine Rebecca
(Heckert), 764
Charles Millard, 340

Cheryl (Higley), 503
Christopher James, 1283
Clair Wilbur, 764
Clara A (Reed), 773
Clayton, 503
Cynthia Marie, 1175
Darlene Ann, 764
David William, 722-723
Delia (Berrios), 503
Derek James, 722
Diana Marie, 751
Diane (Baker), 1175
Donald, 895
Donald Eric, 752
Donald Scott, 722-723
Donna Ann, 895
Doris Mae (Eppley), 893
Drusilla Elizabeth
(Faust), 751
Edward Benjamin, 340
Effiginia Craig, 340
Elizabeth Megin, 1176
Elizabeth Shaner, 1174
Ella, 769
Elmer C McC, 773
Elura, 769
Emma (Raker), 769
Emma Jane (Fasold), 811
Emma Jean (Fasold), 805
Emma Lydia, 1077
Erma, 722
Ermal Maxine, 208
Ernest Benjamin, 340
Eva Elizabeth, 773
Eva Elizabeth (Weiser), 759
Fannie W (Clouse), 1349
Frances IV, 75
Francis Max, 340
Frank Ellis, 340
Frederick Augustus, 340
Frederick Max, 340
George, 759
George S, 1729
George William, 340
Geralding (Klimek), 722
Glenn, 503
Gloria Renee (Miller), 776
H W, 719
Harold William, 722
Hazel, 889
Hazel Emma, 675
Heather Vail, 722
Helen, 770
Helen Marie (Malick), 1174
Henry, 1349
Henry Maxwell, 340
Henry William, 769
Ida Caroline, 340
Ida Clara (Bailey), 1729
infant son, 340
Irma, 1087
J H, 1349
Jacob, 759
Jason Lee, 1282
Jeanne Carol, 724
Jeffrey Allen, 751
Jerry Lee, 503

HOFFMAN (continued)
John, 773, 1695
John Andrew, 340
John Dennis, 724
John George, 340
John Weiser, 770
Karen (Mutchler), 503
Kate, 769
Katelyn Elizabeth, 503
Kathleen Ann
  (McKinney), 1282
Keith Junior, 503
Kenneth Donald, 751
Kenneth John, 751
Kent Alan, 503
Kristin Leigh, 722-723
Kurt LaMar, 503
LaMar Edward, 503
Lance William,
  722-723
Leslie, 1615
Linda, 1176
Linda Jean (Mills), 722
Lois Ann (Eppley), 895
Louise Watson, 340
Lydia (Willier), 768
Mabel Irene, 340
Marc Christopher, 503
Marciana, 204
Margaret, 1182
Margaret (Bethell),
  1175
Margaret Elizabeth,
  1176
Mark David, 751
Mary, 340, 759
Mary (Faust), 999
Mary Catharine, 764
Mary Catherine, 1176
Mary Helen (Ulrich),
  75
Maxine, 503
Nancy (Turner), 1695
Nolan Rodger, 1176
Oscar Frederick, 340
Patricia (--), 503
Paul Phillips, 75
Paul William, 1176
Pearl Katherine, 241
Peggy Sue, 764
Ralph, 759
Ralph Raker, 770
Ray Claud, 893
Rebecca (Kuntzman),
  759
Rebecca Ann, 397
Richard J, 503
Robert Andrew, 1176
Robert William,
  722-723, 1884
Robin Elaine, 1280
Rodger David, 1175
Rodger Hodge, 1175
Rose Selina, 340
Rusha A (Teed), 340
Ruth, 769
Ruth I (Mull), 1615
Sally Ann, 724
Sandra (Berg), 1175
Sandra Diana, 651
Sandy (--), 503
Sarah (Weiss), 1349
Sarah Ann, 770
Sarah E, 768
Sarah L, 1349
Shannon St Clair, 1175
Shirley Lorraine, 752
Stephanie Ann, 1616
Susan, 1176

Susan Ann (Musser),
  340
Terri Lynn, 751
Terry Lee, 751
Thomas, 811
Thomas Paul, 752
Tina Ellen, 776
Tracey (Bowersox),
  751
Vernetta Mae (Sulouff),
  751
Virginia Edna
  (Evangelista), 751
Warren David, 1175
William, 768
William Jacob, 769
William Karl, 1155
William Luther, 1174
William M, 1160, 1884
William Malick,
  1175-1176
William Slocum, 75
William St Clair, 1175
HOFFMANN
Luise Emilie, 1607
HOFFMEIER
-- (--), 1471
Angeline, 1471
Angie, 1472
Anna Gertrude, 1471
Arthur, 1472
Catherine, 1471
Charles, 1471
Charles Frederick,
  1470
Cora, 1471
Edgar, 1471
Emelius, 1471
Emily Leman, 1471
Emmie, 1470
Frank Newcomer, 1471
Helen Weiser, 1471
Henry Asen, 1471
Henry W, 1471
Hester (Levan), 1471
Homer, 1472
John, 1471
Josephine Margaret,
  1472
Levan, 1472
Luch (Defibaugh),
  1471
Margaret (Weiser),
  1470
Mary, 1470
Mary Catherine, 1471
Nellie, 1471
Nellie I (Cordell), 1471
Thomas Franklin, 1471
HOFMA
Carol E, 1282
HOFMAN
Andrew, 758
Margareta, 758-759
HOFMANN
Elizabeth Ann
  (Arbegast), 174
Eric James, 1433
Ernie, 174
James, 174
Janice, 174
Joan, 174
Karen Lee, 1433
Lee, 174
Linda Karen, 1433
Paul, 174
Raymond J, 1433
Sandra Lee (Wetherell),
  1433

HOFMEIER
Josephine Margaret,
  1470
HOFSTETTER
Alfred F, 1270
Harold, 1270
Nettie May (Coder),
  1270
HOGAN
Adelaide, 1515
Mary Hunicka, 1515
Rebecca (Hynicka),
  1515
Richard Jr, 1515
HOGARTH
Errett, 841
Flora, 841
James, 841
Sallie Ann (Anspach),
  841
Verna, 842
Warren, 842
HOGBEN
Carrie Lee (Watson),
  204
Janet McCrae (Hines),
  204
Kathleen (McNulty),
  205
Roy, 204
Russell Roy, 205
Susan Louise, 205
William, 204
HOGELAND
Cynthia, 528
Phyllis, 836
HOGGE
Dorothy Ann Smith,
  608
HOGUE
Catherine Anne, 168
Deborah (Patenela),
  168
Douglas Todd, 168
James Burden, 168
James Burden III, 168
Jean Ann (Heisey), 168
Joseph Edward, 168
Kaitlyn Noelle, 168
Kristen Nichole, 168
Margie Ann Witt
  (Snyder), 168
Marian Elizabeth
  (Weiser), 168
Mary Elizabeth, 168
Stacy Lynn, 168
Susan Elizabeth, 168
Tammy (Rodkey), 168
Tara Alina (McKinstry),
  168
Thomas Mark, 168
Trevor Michael, 168
HOHENSEE
Ruth L, 178
HOHL
Matilda R, 1758
HOISINGTON
Claire Sue, 1200
HOKE
Alice Cora, 774
Amber, 652
Barrett Randel, 547
Beulah Marie, 761
Car Dewane, 547
Carolyn Elizabeth
  (Herring), 547
Catharine (Spitler), 914
Catharine C, 1459
Catherine, 759

Claud, 264
Dawn Lois, 165
Eric Michael, 165
Herman A, 165
Jennifer Robecca
  (Klinger), 652
John Richard, 856
Kim Eric, 165
Linda Kay (Shettel),
  856
Lois Carol, 165
Margaret Marie, 689
Marie Elizabeth
  (Weiser), 165
Marion, 264
Nellie, 264
Nellie (Haschel), 264
Ralph, 264
Randall Herman, 165
Romaine, 873
Solomon, 914
Steve, 652
HOLBROOK
Marcia A (Weiser),
  1863
Walter R, 1863
HOLCOMB
Blakeslee Raymond, 58
Dempa Sue (Knecht),
  442
Eileen (Carr), 58
Eva (Staser), 58
Gary, 442
Helen Alice (Blakeslee),
  58
Helen Rae, 58
Jerrine, 58
Joanne Partridge
  (Williams), 58
Leland Mercer, 59
Linda Marie, 58
Marjorie, 58
Mary Maxine, 59
Maurice Staser, 58
Miriam Gladys, 59
Oscar Raymond, 58
Richard Staser, 58
Sarah, 58
Silas Raymond, 58
Uva Davis, 58
Virginia (Spratt), 58
HOLCOMBE
Elizabeth Schuyler
  (Cammann), 336
Jessica Schuyler, 336
Shepherd Monson, 336
HOLDCRAFT
Danny, 943
Dorothy, 942
Dorothy (Collins), 943
Earl, 943
Emma Jane, 943
Gary, 943
Josephine (Vent), 943
Leah (Starner), 942
Leonard, 943
Mary (Starner), 943
Pearl, 942-943
Pearl Jr, 943
Peggy, 943
Robert, 943
Stanton Lee, 943
HOLDEN
Carl Frederick III,
  1035
Carl Frederick Jr, 1034
Helen Elizabeth
  (Dissinger), 1034
Laura Ann (Kratz), 974

Michael, 974
Patricia, 1035
HOLDER
Ann Barton, 1503
infant, 1503
Jean Anne (Jones),
  1503
Jean J, 1476
Michael Robert, 1503
Nancy Elizabeth
  (Johnson), 1503
Robert William, 1503
Suzanne, 1503
William Stanton, 1503
HOLDERFIELD
Dennis Lee, 947
Henry, 947
Lisa, 947
Mary Jane (Althouse),
  947
HOLDREN
Albert L, 464
Doris (Dosh), 464
HOLFORD
Linda Jane (Moore),
  141
Ralph, 141
HOLINGER
Paige, 397
HOLKESVIK
Lori, 179
HOLL
Debbie (Hoy), 1321
Delores Elizabeth (Van
  Horn), 1321
Kim Richard, 1321
Paul Richard, 1321
Scott, 1321
Sean, 1321
Susan Dianne, 1321
HOLLAND
--, 1373
Albert, 1671
Anne Wysor (Smith),
  284
Dylan Stewart, 1475
Frank S II, 1475
Lissa Kathleen (Segina),
  1475
Martha Ellen, 1671
Norman C, 284
Sara Josephine
  (Randall), 1373
HOLLAWAY
Rheta, 714
HOLLCRAFT
Margaret Mary, 922
HOLLENBACH
Cora (Miller), 1743
Emily Margaret L
  (Weiser), 1619
Henry B, 1743
Irene Mildred (Bucher),
  761
John Adam, 761
Leon Roy, 761
Robert, 1863
Samuel, 1619
Virginia (Weiser),
  1863
HOLLENSHEAD
Mary Salin, 325
HOLLERAN
Joseph Michael, 1283
Joshua Patrick, 1284
Patrick Michael, 1283
Tammy Denise (Reitz),
  1283
Tricia Ann, 1283

HOPPER (continued)
Lola (Parker), 1051
Ruth, 1829
Susan, 731
HOPPES
Delores Marie, 131
Mary J, 1639
HOPPING
Beulah Loyetta
(Pontius), 696
Walter Klots, 696
HOPPLE
Mary, 1372
HORAK
Allen C, 583
Jane A Lee (Smith),
583
Krista Kay, 583
HORCHLER
Kathy Annette, 692
HOREL
Susan Lydia, 1629
HORLEY
LaMar Victor, 673
Marian Jean (Chubb),
673
Susan Lynn, 673
Terry LaMar, 673
Tommie Charles, 673
HORLOCKER
Lisa, 125
HORN
Andrew Sheldon, 139
Angela Carol (Fisher),
139
David Riley, 139
Devin Arden, 139
Douglas Arden, 138
Eva Marie (Park), 138
Gretchen, 136
Gretchen Lynn
(Rodgers), 138
Mary Ann, 91
Paula Louise, 471
Rachel Lynn, 138
Steven Dalton, 139
Traci lee, 1499
Valerie Anne, 139
Warren Dalton, 138
HORNBARGER
Catherine, 1653
HORNBAUGH
Alberta Belle (Weiser),
1289
Donna, 1289
John, 1289
Karl Burton, 1289
Karla, 1289
M Rosalie (Bednarik),
1289
HORNBERGER
Anna (--), 16
Clarence Ira, 765
Grace, 1177
Hans Jacob, 16
Jean H, 765
Sarah Renee
(Koppenheffer), 765
HORNBURG
Arthur John, 817
Lela Malinda
(Womelsdorf), 817
HORNER
Goldie, 546
Nancy, 309
HORNICKLE
Elva, 70
HORNING
Dorothy, 700

HORSEY
Carol Ruth, 1216
James Frederick III,
1216
James Frederick Jr,
1216
Katherine Dale, 1216
Myra May (Kahle),
1216
HORTON
Donald, 1225
Dorothy, 1225
Florence P (Haffner),
67
George, 1225
James Blair, 67
James Blair Jr, 67
James C, 67
Laura Emma Richter
(Schoch), 67
Laura Lynn, 144
Lillian (Forsythe),
1225
Patti A, 67
Thomas, 67
HORVATH
Aune Theresa, 876
Beverly Jean (Knipp),
485
Cheryl Lynn, 485
Donald Michael, 485
Gladys Ann (Albright),
876
Keith Allan, 1319
Kimberly Rae
(Roelling), 876
Nancy Marlene
(Eberly), 1319
Richard Allan, 1319
Ronald Joseph, 876
Sherry Marie, 924
Timothy Joseph, 876
HOSKINS
--, 1146
Lynn, 1493
Maude (Bunn), 1146
HOSKINSON
Carrie, 1143
HOSL
Hildegard, 320
HOSLER
Cindy, 615
HOSSER
Sandra Kay, 471
HOSSLER
Benjamin Ray, 764
Mildred, 1821
Verna Marcella
(Koppenheffer), 764
HOSTERMAN
Charles S, 1441
Elisabetha, 1452
John, 1099
Margaret (Brungart),
1099
Sarah Jane (Spyker),
1441
Velma E, 1078
HOSTETLER
Carolyn Mary
(Grissom), 98
Jacob Alexander, 98
John Eby, 98
HOSTETTER
Emma Strite, 183
HOTCHKISS
Georgie, 1105
HOTTENSTEIN
Andrew, 63

Anita (Eiseman), 62
Anna, 65
Annabel (Krum), 63
Annie L, 63
Clara, 63
Clara (Motzer), 62
Craig, 63
Ethel Marie (Haws), 62
Frank, 65
Frank Haws, 62
Frank Peter, 62
George Percival, 62
George Philip, 62
Georgianna, 63
Harriet, 62
Harriet (Richter), 62
Heidi, 63
Jane Rosalie, 63
John, 63
Kathy, 63
Louisa, 65
Marc, 63
Marjorie, 63
Martha R, 63
Mary (Rohland), 62
Michael, 63
Miriam (Stroh), 63
Patricia, 63
Percival, 62
Peter Richter, 62
Ruth (Schaeffer), 63
Sally, 63
Tara, 63
Tonya, 63
Walter, 63
HOTVEDT
Barbara Elizabeth
(Sala), 810
Kathryn Ann, 810
Kermit Orville, 810
Lynne Sala, 810
Susan Margaret, 810
HOUCH
Bessie Mildred, 878
HOUCK
Louisa Marsean, 1800
Rowena, 1469
HOUCKESBELL
Harry Mead, 856
Susan Kay (Mattern),
856
HOUGH
Mabel Ruth (Kaley),
862
William J, 862
HOUGHAWOUT
Edward, 449
Martha Ellen (Weiser),
449
HOUGHER
Robert Andrew, 120
Robert Gabriel, 121
Valerie Shane (Harris),
120
HOUGHTON
Belle (Barlow), 1184
Charles, 1576
Leeta May (George),
1576
Mary, 1014
Mary (Snook), 1014
Richard, 1014
Richard T, 1184
HOULTON
Grace, 182
HOUSE
Anna, 720
John B, 1653
LaVonne, 922

Mary Elizabeth
(Reyburn), 1653
HOUSEKEEPER
Hannah, 904
HOUSELY
Carole Jane, 1489
HOUSER
Daniel Fye, 1397
Earl, 1171
James Daniel, 1397
Myrtle Steckman
(Wise), 1171
Paul Wagner, 1397
Sabrina Sarah
(Wagner), 1397
Sarah (Lenker), 1397
HOUSEWORTH
Catherine, 1524
HOUSTON
Murray, 1147
HOUTZ
Bernice Mae, 699
Billy, 854
Charlotte (Yohe), 854
Debra Ann (Hendricks),
648
Gayle, 854
George Marshall Jr,
1170
Jacqueline Kay, 1170
Joseph, 648
Juliette Georgette, 1170
Marilee Kay (Long),
1170
Mary Agnes, 1170
Michele Mary, 1170
Suzette Lee, 1170
William, 854
HOVENSTINE
Rene, 789
HOVER
Jackie, 490
HOVEY
Dorothy (Whitaker),
1439
Lisa Marie, 35
Russell, 1439
HOVIS
Mary (Leader), 1422
Raymond S, 1422
HOVIZI
Brandi Christine, 488
Brian Robert, 488
Lori J (Slasvick), 488
Robert, 488
Sharon Ann (Jaworski),
488
HOWALD
Frederick J, 155
Harriet Ann (Weiser),
155
Maud E, 155
Nettie Irene, 155
Rosetta, 114
William A, 155
HOWARD
--, 1504, 1661
Ann, 48
Anna Mae (Bowers),
686
Bertha May (Fisher),
625
Beryl Harrison, 1313
Beverly Ann, 687
Bonnie Kay (Potter),
687
Charles R, 1659
Clifford Hanna, 1331
Connie Sue, 1313

Donna Jo, 1659
Doris (Teazel), 546
Edward, 449
Elizabeth (Rahm), 1504
Elsie Marie (Herring),
546
Erma C, 1416
Ethan, 1659
Gerald William, 1331
Harold, 1037
Hazel (Malick), 1037
Hazel Lavone
(Gebhart), 1331
Helen Louise, 852
Helen Neva, 546
Jack Donald, 1659
James Warren, 687
Jean (Shane), 546
Jill, 1659
Joan (Wysor), 1659
Jody Lavelle, 687
Joyce, 1804
Laura Belle, 378
Linda Rene, 546
Martha Ellen (Weiser),
449
Martha Jane, 1659
Mary, 872
Mary Lynn, 1659
Michael Alan, 1313
Mindy La Dawn, 687
Patricia, 368
Patricia Ann, 1313
Phyllis Ann (Urschel),
1313
Renae K, 1443
Robert Eugene, 546
Rosalie Margerite, 686
Rose (Honaker), 1661
Ruth, 1105
Sandra Kay, 400
Thomas Lee, 1313
Vickie Ruth, 1659
Vicky Lynn, 1313
Warren Edward, 686
William Glen, 546
William Phin, 546
William V, 625
HOWARTH
Grace Elizabeth, 836
HOWE
Brenda, 533
Catherine Elizabeth
(Walls), 1658
Charles Thomas, 1659
Chester, 1100
Clarence, 1100
Clayton, 1099
Cyrus, 1099
Earl, 1684
Gen, 87
Irene, 1100
Isabella, 1100
Julia, 1099
Liam Walls, 1658
Lizzie (Fox), 1099
Louise (Mart), 1100
Mabel (Kephart), 1684
Maggie (Kehl), 1099
Robert, 1658
HOWELL
Beverly Diane, 469
Brittany Morgan, 748
Edith Ann, 1791
Florence Viola, 696
Justin Dale, 748
Lulu, 1309
Margaret Ruth, 1189
Olivia B, 1204

HULEATT
Chad, 1630
Debra Talitha, 1630
Helen, 1630
Jay Warren, 1630
Martin Sheppherd, 1630
Veery Maureen, 1630
HULINGS
Aleine, 1234
HULL
Alfred, 1702
Austin, 466
Charles, 725
Chrisstina, 466
David Charles, 725
JoAnn Carol, 1837
Johnny Joe, 1335
Joseph, 1703
Kenneth Michael, 876
Kenneth Stephen, 876
Madaline (Beadle), 725
Mary, 259
Mary Ann (Wiser), 1702
Nancy Lee (Shade), 1335
Rae Louise (Shettel), 876
Robert, 1305
Robert Eugene, 1335
Sarah (Parks) Louder, 1703
Sharon Louise, 725
Tillie (Wiser), 1305
HULLEN
Margaret Luinda, 1433
HULLIHAN
Kerry Jean, 408
HULMES
Clara, 1839
HULS
Gladys, 797
HULSE
Bonita Dorte, 186
James, 1321
Lois Anne, 455
Susan Dianne (Holl) Yermaatt, 1321
HULTMAN
Phyllis Elaine (Gibboney), 1390
William, 1390
HUMBERT
Ree, 1879
HUMBLE
George Anthony, 1825
Ruth Bernice (Wiser), 1825
HUMERICK
Dorothy, 1008
Edith (Kehl), 1008
Frank, 1008
Marie, 1008
Robert, 1008
HUMES
Dianna Sue, 368
Edward Eugene, 368
Kathryn Lynn, 368
Thomas Edward, 368
Verna Jo (Bauder), 368
HUMMEL
--, 826
Abraham, 1697
Aldred Clark, 1695
Anna J, 1697
Betty Jean, 652
Brandon Lee, 749
Carol Ann (Ross), 749

Carrie Viola (Turner), 1695
Catharine (Shimmel), 1697
Catherine, 1697
Charlotte (Smeal), 1697
Christina, 1476
Craig, 717
Dorothy Ann, 653
Eliza Jane, 907
Emma Amelia, 1035
Ethel (Shimmel), 1770
Ethel Marie (Herman), 652
Ethel Verda, 1695
Faye Evelyn (Arbogast), 717
George W, 1697
Hannah (Lowe), 1697
Harry Jr, 749
Henry, 1697
Jacob, 1714
Jane (Walker), 1697
John F, 1697
John William, 652
Lloyd, 1770
Loma Celissa (Womelsdorf), 826
Lydia, 1697
Margaret Elizabeth, 1770
Marie, 652
Martha S, 1712
Mary A (Baker), 1697
Mary Ann, 1697
Matilda, 1697
Michael Thomas, 1134
Michelle Annett, 749
Monte, 717
Priscilla (Emeigh), 1697
Robin Loene (Rager), 1134
Sarah A (Wisor), 1714
Sterryl, 717
Zana, 1770
HUMMELL
Bernita (Nance), 1124
Bertha Olive (Heister), 1153
Betty Jane, 1154
Bonnie Lou, 1154
Byron Courtright, 1123
Charles Foster, 1153
Connie Sue, 1154
Deborah Kay, 1154
Doyle Edward, 1154
Effie Elizabeth (Courtright), 1123
Eura Maude (Courtright), 1123
Flora Maxine, 1154
Gene Maywood, 1124
Gene Michael, 1124
Gregory Lane, 1124
James A, 1697
John Clinton, 1123
Juanita Bernadine, 1153
Kent Edward, 1154
Lois Jane, 1124
Marguertie Fern, 1124
Marilyn Louise, 1123
Marilyn Louise (Hummell), 1123
Mildred (Leist), 1154
Norma Jean (Binns), 1154

Peggy Lee, 1154
Reba Jeannine (Lane), 1124
Richard Lee, 1124
Robbin Lynn, 1124
Willis Heister, 1154
HUMMER
Viola S, 255
HUMMERLY
Dora, 1684
HUMPHREY
Charlene Mae (Cholewinski), 481
James Tobert, 909
Joseph Harold, 481
Mary Catherine (Krigbaum), 118
Nancy Ruth (Glatfelter), 909
Stephen William, 118
Trudy Darlene, 201
HUMPHREY-KRIGBAUM
Emily Ann, 119
Tyler Jon, 118
HUMPHRIES
Harry E, 37
Harry Warriner, 37
Kim Ashton, 37
Mary Lou Gleasman White, 1277
Michael E, 37
Peggy Evelyn (Ashton), 37
HUMRICH
Anna Catharina, 1591
HUND
Daniela, 1599
Dietmar, 1599
Erwin, 1599
Ewald, 1599
Irma Maria Martha Therese (Wagenmann), 1599
Monica, 1599
Rosemarie (Hatter), 1599
Walter Erwin Adolf, 1599
HUNDLEY
Patricia, 171
HUNGATE
Halden, 392
Larry Dale, 392
Marjorie Bernadine (Lugger), 392
Oscar Robert, 392
HUNSAKER
Audra Laverne, 422
HUNSBERGER
Brandon Eugene, 816
Juanita LaRee, 816
Karen Juanita (Beary), 816
Larry Dewayne, 816
Linda Susan, 1426
HUNSICKER
Maria S, 1757
HUNT
Ada A, 1849
Bebe Eileen, 109
Bessie, 1712
Charles Luther, 877
Clayton, 993
Elisa, 1782
Elizabeth, 1558
Hazel (Allinson), 993
Joseph Arthur, 73
Julia Blair, 325
Katherine, 1770

Linda, 73
Linda Faye, 592
Lydia Grace (Barnhill), 877
Mary Anne (Wood), 73
Mary Janet (Weyhrauch), 73
Max, 993
Phillip, 206
Rena Belle (Kahle), 1258
Richard, 993
Ruth, 564
Sandy, 993
Sarah, 73
Sherri, 993
Susan Annette, 452
Victoria Lynn (Williams), 206
W Preston, 1258
Wells E Jr, 73
William, 877
HUNTER
Alexandra McAlpin, 309
David, 308
Ethel Sydney (Gruver), 1225
Gov, 21
Janet, 1019
Kate Spang, 341
Kathleen Francis, 1174
Madeline Virginia Ogden (Mix), 308
Margaret, 1560
Nicholas Schwab, 308
Robert, 13
Susannah (Wiser), 1785
Timothy Mix, 309
William, 1225, 1785
HUNTSBERGER
Elaine Sue, 1489
HUNTZINGER
daughter, 833
George W, 833
Leah (Womelsdorf), 833
son, 833
HUNZICKER
Frederick Louis, 1677
Josephine (Wiggins) Reed, 1677
HUNZINGER
Albert, 734
Albert L Jr, 734
Connie Jean (Roush), 734
Lee Alan, 734
HUPP
Kimberly, 1375
Lyn, 1324
HUPRICK
Faye Elizabeth (Bohn), 1070
Kathryn Orne, 1071
Nancy Orne (Eustes), 1070
Paul Richard, 1070
Paul Wesner, 1070
HURDLE
Andy Sue, 799
Cathy Lou, 799
Claudia Lee, 799
John Franklin, 799
John Franklin Jr, 799
Lee (Martin), 799
Rosa Louise (Barbe), 799

Sheldon F, 799
HURLBURT
Joanne, 1781
Mary, 266
HURLBUT
Mathilda, 182
HURLEY
Ruth, 1703
HURMES
--, 473
Starlene, 473
HURSEN
Erin Lee, 228
HURSH
Barbara, 1081
Carroll Eugene, 1081
Frances, 1081
Myrtle Leonore (Seyler), 1081
Rose Wilson, 1059
HURST
Colleen, 1768
Joan Catherine Marsh, 69
HURT
Ashley, 1099
Freddie, 1099
Galen (Frank), 1099
Marian (Wheeler), 1553
Nicholas, 1099
Walter, 1553
HUSAR
Marquita Marie, 909
HUSE
Mary Beth, 541
HUSLER
Edna, 1226
HUSO
Mary Anne, 988
HUSSEN
Janige Johanna, 21
HUSTON
Amy Elizabeth, 1735
Darry A, 1735
Frank O, 466
Mary Ann (Binkley), 466
Meghan Ann, 1736
Sarah Alice, 1440
Sarah Katherine, 1736
Sheryl Lynne (Wieser), 1735
HUTCHENSON
Alexa R (Clifton), 664
Andrea K, 664
Janet Louise, 664
Joseph C, 663
Judith K, 664
Kevin M, 664
Larry D, 664
Larry J, 664
Michele (--), 664
Norma Louise (Balding), 663
HUTCHEON
Dane Michael, 56
Laura Ester (Wright), 56
Manie Elizabeth, 56
Michael Shawn, 56
HUTCHESON
Norma, 638
HUTCHINGS
Linda, 129
HUTCHINS
Ruby, 799
HUTCHINSON
Betty Anne, 1631

IVERS
Thelma, 1277
IVEY
Laura Page (Williams), 308
Ronald James, 308
IVY
Margaret, 1811
IZOR
Alexis S, 1330
Bessie Luella (Rabold), 1329
Catherine Louise, 1329
John Wesley, 1329
Kim Eugene, 1330
Loren Edison, 1330
Martha Jane (Korn), 1330
Peggy (Sugino), 1330
Ralph Emerson, 1330
IZZO
Madeline Teresa (Croy), 848
Nicholas John, 848
JABLONSKI
Lisa Marie (Graeff), 96
Stanley, 96
JABRE
George B, 922
Jarrod Alan, 922
Patricia Ellen (Weiser) Bixler), 922
JACK
Julia Rose, 1261
Ralph, 1235
Winnie (Pearsole), 1235
JACKSON
--, 1655
Alan L, 1014
Alva, 430
Anne Elizabeth, 1212
Beulah Mae, 1660
Blanche Myrtle, 213
Bryant Matthew, 1250
Catharine, 1655
Catharine (Wysor), 1655
Charles, 1655
Claude D, 1014
Don Stephen, 1135
Edwin, 1083
Eliza C (Wysor), 1657
Elzie Eugene, 580
Emily Helen, 1212
Emma J, 521
Gary, 554, 612
Iris Carolyn (Fridy), 1014
J Morris, 771
James M, 1657
Janie (Johnson), 554
Jean Boyer (Witherspoon), 1135
Kelly Ann (Kahle), 1250
Kevin, 1250
Leah Joy, 486
Louise, 1190
M W, 297
Mabel Gertrude (Harps), 1014
Margaret E, 1655
Mary, 297
Mary Jane, 1655
Mary Jane (Shulze), 297
Nancy Kaye (Green), 1212

Pamela Lou (Long), 612
Pattie Lou (Randall), 580
Paul Bonner, 1212
Paul Edward, 1212
Phyllis Jean, 219
Rosaline (Wolfe), 1083
Russell G, 1083
Ruth (Knecht), 430
Ruth Eleanor (Moyer), 771
Saundra Kay, 399
Sherri Dawn, 580
Stacey Denise, 580
Sue Anne, 1014
Susan Marlene, 1870
Teresa, 1808
William H, 1657
Willis C, 1014
JACOB
Frederic C, 390
Gladys O (Slack), 390
Harry E, 390
Mary Ellen, 390
Wendell P, 390
JACOBS
Alexander Marion, 1824
Alfred Ray, 731
Anita May, 608
Anna S, 1823
Barbara, 210
Barbara (Johnson), 732
Barbara Jane (Butler), 213
Beverly, 731
Brenda Kay (Sharp), 963
Calvin Alton, 732
Christ, 731
Christine Ellen (Knapp), 629
Christopher, 629
Clara Anna, 732
Clarence Calvin, 732
Cora Estella, 732
Dalphon, 732
Dalphon Una, 731
Daphne, 732
David, 732
Debbie, 379
Dorothea, 732
Dorothy (Barrett), 731
Edmund, 213
Edmund Franklin, 213
Eleanor Mae (Pfeiffer), 732
Eleanor Mae (Woomert), 732
Gaye (McFarland), 213
James Patrick, 608
Jane, 732
Jane Elizabeth, 213
Janet, 732
Janet May, 732
Janice Margie (Kirkpatrick), 1692
Janice May (Turner), 608
Josie Lee (Wiser), 1824
Kathleen, 732
Kathryn Elizabeth, 229
LeRoy, 229
Lorraine (Newberry), 732
Lulu May (Tharp), 731
Marion Elizabeth

(Burkholder), 229
Mark William, 608
Martha J (Wiser), 1812
Mary Ann, 241
Mary Jane (Feese), 731
Michael, 732
Parley M, 1812
Patricia, 732
Randy, 1869
Raymond, 731
Richard, 963, 1692
Richard Sharon, 608
Richard Stanley, 608
Robert Jr, 732
Robert Lamar, 732
Ronald, 731
Sandra, 731
Sean Michael, 629
Sharon, 732
Stephen, 732
Susan Ann, 629
Tammy Jo (Wiser), 1869
Thomas Edmund, 213
Timothy, 213
William, 213
Williard Elwood, 732
Williard Elwood Jr, 732
JACOBSEN
Judi Marie, 215
Verna Mae, 232
JACOBSON
Albin Edgar, 1077
April Lorraine, 1580
Barbara Sue (Wiest), 647
Brian Edward, 647
Carl, 647
Cynthia Ann (Pickard), 1580
Geraldine (Brungart), 1077
Lula, 1052
Michael, 1580
Patricia Ann, 1077
JACOBWITH
Louise, 1283
JACOBY
--, 864
Arlene (Spahr), 864
Ernest C, 1576
Ernest H, 1576
Jeanneane H, 1576
Jill, 1576
Joy (Hughes), 1576
Kip, 1576
Lucerne A, 1576
Lucy Anne (Schempp), 1576
Stephen A, 1576
Susan (Brandes), 1576
JACQUEL
Esther Elizabeth (Wiser), 1834
John Baptist III, 1834
JADWIN
Denise Lyn (Dafler) Nem, 1324
Donald II, 1324
Donald III, 1324
JAERCK
Sophia Salzberger, 1193
JAFFRAY
Eliza Catherine (Smith), 327
Emily Meier, 327
Lydia, 327

Robert, 327
Robert Jr, 327
JAFOLLA
D Richard, 1635
Ruth Albert (Leidy), 1634
JAGO
Jennifer Lynn Iachini, 645
JAHNSON
Chris Darin, 584
Kathryn Sue (Hocker), 584
JAKEWAY
Elizabeth Ruth (Busch), 306
Mark, 306
JAKUM
Barbara Jean (Crites), 860
Wayne A, 860
JAMES
Bartholomew Dewey, 755
Diana Sue, 481
Doyt Alan, 105
Garl, 522
Hattie, 1812
Herman, 522
Janice Louise, 105
Kathleen Y, 1692
Lois, 54
Lorena Margaret (Titus), 104
Martha Abigail, 289
Mary Elizabeth (Furman), 755
Mercy Irene, 755
Monica Lois, 1751
Nora Alice (Riggs), 522
R F, 289
Ralph, 104
Ralph Kent, 105
Randall Kay, 104
Richard, 522
Ronald, 522
Sarah Louise (Ege), 289
JAMESON
Amelia (--), 1184
Anna (--), 1184
Catherine, 1468
Charles A, 1184
Clarence S, 1184
David Merrill, 1184
Earl B, 1184
Eliza (--), 60
Elizabeth (Weiser), 1184
F E L (--), 1184
Fred, 1184
George E, 1184
Gladys E, 1184
Glenn V, 1184
Hames, 60
James E, 1184
Jessie, 1184
Joseph, 1184
Juanita Joyce, 1837
Lulu, 1184
Margaret, 1184
Mary E (--), 1184
Robert, 1184
William, 1184
JAMIESON
Nancy Anne (Beams), 1119

Robert Eugene, 1119
JAMISON
Hannah, 1047
JAMTOR
Wendy Nelson, 1276
JANDREW
Lyma, 1092
JANES
Candie Lynn, 1814
JANOWICZ
--, 1554
Carol Ann, 1554
Edward Eugene, 1554
Elizabeth Marie (Culhane), 1554
Jamaica Elizabeth, 1554
Jane Marian, 1554
Lee-wun Judith (Hong), 1554
Linell Marie, 1554
Mark Peter, 1554
Patrick Joseph Kenedy, 1554
Susan Jo (Edson), 1554
Thomas Eugene, 1554
JANSEN
Carol Elaine, 1281
JANSIK
Norman, 1228
Peggy Louise (Lutz), 1228
JANSON
Doris Elizabeth, 916
Helen May (Brehm), 916
Joel William, 916
Joyce Mary (Grim), 916
Margaret Louise (Gemmill), 916
Sandra Louise, 916
William A II, 915
William Albert, 916
William Albert II, 916
William Albert III, 916
JANTZ
Fiennes Harper, 664
Geraldine May (Roadenbaugh), 664
Geri Sue, 664
Tommy Fiennes, 664
JARDINE
Nancy M, 72
JARECKE
Judy Elaine, 1490
JARRELL
-- (Wiser), 1823
Billy, 1823
JARVIE
Ingrie Elizabeth, 917
JARVIS
Lemuel, 1409
Rebecca (Weiser), 1409
Sarah, 1408
JAVORINA
Zora, 1191
JAWORSKI
Blake, 487
Corrine (Polter), 487
Janelle, 487
Jared Austin, 487
Jennifer Darlene (Speigel), 487
Julian Boyd, 487
Julius, 487
Justin Warren, 487
Laurie, 487

JOHNSON (continued)
Esther Elizabeth
(Mader) Flemming
(continued)
(Mader) Flemming,,
910
Fannie N (Naff), 1652
Fanny Dorothy
(Cummins), 1476
Finley, 1677
Flora Mae
(Koppenhaver), 680
Florence G, 1500
Forrest, 1416
Frank Evan, 1356
Fred O, 37
Freeda (Leech), 554
Galen, 1416
Gary Lynn, 662
Gary Wayne, 1477
Gaylord Milton, 391
Gaylord Milton II, 391
George, 1676
George Frederick Betts,
1218
Georgia, 1218
Gloria, 1673
H, 1236
Harold Brady, 269
Harriet Rose, 269
Harry D, 910
Heather Anne, 380
Heather June, 925
Helen Josephine, 391
Helen M, 147
Herbert Donald, 553
Hope Ann, 391
Howard, 1031, 1432
Ida, 1677
Inez, 53
Irene Eleanor (Ocken),
1691
Isaac, 1488
Isaac Jr, 1496
Isabelle L (Kahle),
1218
Jack, 554
James, 553
James A, 149
James Arthur, 149
James Roland, 1790
Janie, 554
Jay, 1304
Jean (Good), 553
Jeannie, 57
Jeffery Neal, 554
Jeffrey David, 497
Jennifer, 1491
Jennifer Ann, 425
Jeremy, 637
Jerimiah Andrew, 637
Jessie Fern (Brown),
440
Joanna Elise, 391
John, 1495
John Brock, 637
John Earl, 391
John F, 149
John Henry, 637
John R, 532
Joni Brook, 637
Joseph, 1491
Joseph Ii, 1491
Joshua David, 859
Joshua Michael, 391
Joyce (Witmer), 1031
Joyce Yvonne (Hill),
637
Judith DeAnn, 800

Judith Fae, 691
Judy, 355
Julie Ann (Plotts), 391
Karen Kay (Foreman),
1487
Karla Marie, 1140
Kathleen (Elliott), 554
Keith Ronald, 1140
Kenneth Elwood, 925
Kevin L, 1779
Kristine, 425
Krystal (Wiser), 1779
Kyna Lynn, 1140
Lee (Brayton), 554
Leslie Ann, 458
Letitia Lynn (Wiser),
1802
Lillian, 852
Linda, 637
Linda Jane, 488
Linda Kay, 554
Linda Michelle, 637
Linda Sue, 440
Linda Sue (Kelley),
925
Lloyd Francis, 1476
Lois Alberta, 460
Lois Ellen (Dale), 529
Lois Jean, 1491
Luana (Peters), 269
Luke, 782
Lyla (Kahle), 1236
Lynn Errin (Grimm),
1304
Malcolm Andrew, 380
Margaret (Rahm), 1504
Margery Alane
(McKinnie), 186
Marian Sue
(Zarnowski), 662
Marie Lynn (Roberts),
180
Marion, 1262
Marissa Elaine, 925
Mark Anthony, 1477
Mark Duane, 216
Mark Edward, 458,
925
Martha, 1503
Martha E, 555, 1838
Martha Juanite
(Akerman), 517
Mary, 554, 1667, 1677
Mary (Johnson), 554
Mary (Shriver), 1677
Mary (Widman), 1677
Mary (Young), 1677
Mary Colleen, 688
Mary Elizabeth
(Waller), 216
Mary Ellen (Schutter)
Ewer, 1356
Mary Emma
(Heidman), 380
Mary Jane (Fritz), 782
Mary Kelly (Nixon),
380
Mary Lou, 149
Mary Rebecca
(McKibben), 1053
Mary Rebecca (Wiser),
1830
Melissa, 1676
Merle, 680
Michael, 1031
Michael Allen, 391
Michel Allen, 554
Mildred, 978
Mildred (Knoske), 37

Muriel Lucile, 1773
Nancy, 1677
Nancy Elizabeth, 1503
Nancy Lee (Wilson),
1491
Nancy Mae
(Henderson), 391
Neil Lewis, 380
Neil Malcolm, 380
Nellie C (Olds), 269
Nina C, 31
Norma, 1160
Norma Lorraine
(Rook), 1173
Norman Eugene, 554
Pat, 910, 1054
Patricia Ann (Weiser),
925
Patricia Lou (Wesco),
532
Paul, 529
Pete, 1694
Pleasant Ann, 1488
Prosper Miller, 1830
R Johnston Wayne,
1140
Rachel (Earnest), 1488
Rachel E, 1501
Rachel Earnest, 1502
Raychel Bonita, 186
Raymond, 680
Raymond E, 458
Rebecca, 477, 1780
Richard G, 1222
Ricky, 425
Robert Edwin, 1250
Robert James, 1331
Robert Michael, 1250
Robert Milton, 1173
Ron Duane, 1487
Rona Jean (Wiser),
1790
Ronald, 186
Ronald Lee, 925
Ronald Louis, 1140
Ronda Sue (Dorrell),
425
Roscoe Willard, 555
Roscoe Willard Jr, 555
Roxey, 1068
Roy, 1709
Ruth, 1851
Ruthann K (Lood), 149
Ryan David, 1487
Sara (Anderson), 1416
Scott, 553
Scott Allen, 458
Scott Lawrence, 637
Serena (Wysor), 1662
Sheila (--), 637
Sheila Dawn, 637
Sherrie Lee, 149
Simon, 1677
Skye Marie, 1140
Stacy, 532
Steven, 532
Steven Eric, 180
Sue Ann, 554
Susan Alice, 269
Susan Ann, 925
Susan Anspach
(Womelsdorf), 835
Susan Brady, 1443
Susan Elizabeth, 1398
Susan Jeanine, 1767
Susan Reese, 415
Theodore, 1503
Theresa Kay
(Richardson), 380

Thomas, 1031
Thomas Max, 269
Vela (Dishman), 553
Vickie (Arnold), 391
Virgil Cope, 390
Walter, 554
Wanda Lorraine
(Mason), 458
Wayne E, 517
Wayne V, 517
William, 555, 1676
Winifred M, 555
Wolcott Howe, 1218
Wreath M, 555
JOHNSTON
--, 1509
Anna Maria (Rahm),
1509
Anna Violet (Weiser),
1570
Brandon Scott, 1303
Carla Lucille, 1236
Cheryl Ann, 1140
Daisy Susanna, 1280
Dena Marie (Eddinger),
1303
Francis, 852
Jason Arthur, 473
Jean Maryann, 1570
Jo Anne (Wolf), 472
Kelsey Nicole, 1304
Kevin Scott, 1303
Margaret Pryor
(McVey), 852
Michael Pryor, 852
Nellie, 863
Norbert Arthur, 472
Paul, 852
Rebecca Catharine, 852
Rebecca Charlotte
(Moffitt), 852
Richard Moffitt, 852
Sarah Jane, 1509
Susan Moffitt, 852
Tiffany Brianne, 1304
William C, 1570
JOHNSTONE
Ann Jane, 973
Bonnie Jean, 1057
JOLIAT
Carter Louis, 1347
Jared Adam, 1347
Laura Marya (Florek),
1347
Philip Kent, 1347
Timothy Francis, 1347
JONAS
Alice Virginia
(Daughters), 1334
Barbara L (Branham),
1334
Gail Elaine, 1334
Gary Philip, 1334
John Philip, 1334
Kellie Elaine, 1334
JONES
--, 1109, 1592
-- (--), 1358, 1883
Adam Mark, 211
Alice Jewel, 1819
Anna, 1109
Anna Elizabeth
(Savelle), 1240
Anna J (Weiser), 1467
Anna Katharine, 281
Anna Muhlenberg
(Hiester), 281
Barbara Ann, 246
Barbara M, 1506

Betty Lou (Vernia),
1448
Beverly, 562
Beverly Ann, 1385
Blanche Marie (Weiser),
1131
Bonetha Mae, 582
Bonita May, 415
Bonnie Lee (Kifer),
1240
Carl Jackson, 1490
Carl Jackson II, 1490
Catharine Elizabeth
(Hiester), 301
Catharine Marie
(Arbogast), 246
Cathy Jean, 1817
Charles, 730
Christopher Ladd,
1240
Christopher Michael
Eugene, 1482
Cora Kraft, 1415
Dale, 518, 1482
Dan Evan, 211
Daniel Mark, 211
Darrel Wayne, 622
Dawn Elizabeth, 1240
Deborah (VanCleef),
1214
Deborah Jane, 350
Delores Dean, 34
Deloris, 267
Dennis Lynn, 1274
Dewane, 1690
Donamarie, 1555
Dorothy May, 49
Douglas Todd, 1240
Douglas Todd Jr, 1240
Edith Jonea (Mitchell),
1467
Elgar Sherman, 1359
Elizabeth (Rahm), 1506
Elizabeth Ann (Weiser),
211
Elizabeth Vaughn, 336
Elmer, 1131
Emma (Gallagher), 281
Emma Jeane, 1313
Ethel, 1225
Eulalia Lorraine, 580
Felix, 294
Floyd, 1562
Foley, 294
Frances Faye, 39
Francis, 530
Fred E, 34
Fredia, 1109
Gary, 1214
George, 1240
Grace (Cain), 1690
Harold Byrne, 1491
Harold Pete, 1490
Hattie, 1037
Henry, 1506
Henry Z Jr, 357, 1589
Howard, 1690
Ida, 1506
Ira Stanton, 1502
J W, ix, 1358, 1883
Jacqueline Susan, 1164
James Thomas, 203
Jane, 957
Jane Louise (Gearhart),
1490
Janet, 619
Janet Young (Henson),
1467
Jason Todd, 1274

KAHLE (continued)
Paulette (Grolemund)
(continued)
1263
Pauline, 1234
Pauline (Semprevira),
1252
Pearl (Lerch), 1236
Pearl (Starr), 1205
Peggy, 1242
Peggy Joan, 1262
Penny Lee (Claycomb),
1200
Perry J, 1197,
1233-1234
Phalla Blossom, 1229
Philip Ainsworth, 1218
Philip Ainsworth Jr,
1218
Philip Alan, 1254
Philip Eugene, 1201
Philip Harlan, 1201
Philip Lee, 1201
Phoebe Ann, 1220
Phyllis, 1241
Phyllis Do (Barr), 1253
Priscilla Jane, 1220
Rachael Elizabeth,
1201
Randolph Stuart, 1219
Ray, 1241
Raymond, 1243
Raymond David, 1216
Raymond David II,
1217
Raymond Frederick,
1216
Raymond Strickland,
1217
Rena, 1237
Rena Belle, 1258
Richard, 1241, 1263
Richard Allan, 1220
Richard Benton, 1215
Richard Benton Jr.
1216
Richard Daryl, 1262
Richard Jean, 1243
Richard Minnich, 1205
Richard Noble, 1236
Richard William, 1236
Rick Stephan, 1205
Robert Dean, 1243
Robert LeRoy, 1261
Robert LeRoy Jr, 1262
Robert Leslie, 1254
Robert Matthew, 1205
Robert Vinton, 1219
Robert Wayne, 1195
Roger Neal, 1216
Rona Lynn, 1202
Ronald Eugene, 1236
Ronald Lee, 1202
Rosanna B (--), 1258
Rosanna F, 1213
Rose Marie (Zacherl),
1256
Rosella, 1257
Rosella (Reed), 1247
Ross Wayne, 1257
Roween Minerva, 1218
Roy Edward, 1258
Ruby, 1242
Ruby Edna (Van
Tassell), 1242
Ruby Philistia, 1258
Russell Leroy, 1243
Ruth, 1234, 1236
Ruth Anne, 1256

Ruth Emma (Minnich),
1204
Ruth Jessica (Rogovoy),
1219
Ruth Marie, 1231
Samantha Jo, 1263
Sara Adelaide (Irwin),
1253
Sara Adeline, 1254
Sara Elizabeth, 1205
Sarah Agnes
(Dearolph), 1247
Sarah Alice, 1241
Sarah Alice (Payne),
1198
Sarah Ann (Carter),
1198
Sarah Carter, 1198
Sarah Catherine, 1246,
1265
Sarah E, 1225
Sarah Edna, 1198
Sarah Elizabeth, 1205,
1213, 1216
Sarah Jane, 1246
Sarah Lynn, 1201
Sarah Marie, 1253
Sarah Quintilla, 1259
Scott Christopher, 1203
Sheila Justine, 1236
Shelley Jean (Heeter)
Hilliard, 1306
Sheree Lynn, 1262
Sheri Kathleen, 1195
Sherman Dallas, 1243
Sherry (Russel), 1253
Shirly (Timblin), 1236
Stacey Lee, 1263
Stanley Jay, 1205
Stanley W, 1258
Stephen Earl, 1200
Steven Christopher,
1220
Sue Ann, 1200
Suellen Leslie, 1254
Susan (Rank), 1194
Susan (VanVolkeburg),
1250
Susan Adelaide, 1254
Susan Jane, 1205
Sydney Georgeanne,
1195
Sylvanus Bascom, 1220
Teresa Marie Catherine
(Schoenig), 1195
Thomas Frederick,
1201
Thomas Jacob, 1200
Thomas Jay, 1201
Thomas Muhlenberg,
1246, 1265
Thomas Neade, 1258
Timothy Michael, 1205
Travis Taylor, 1201
Twila Belle, 1237
Velma Elverda, 1263
Vera Louise (Pruett),
1201
Verna, 1257
Vicki Jean, 1236
Vickie Irene, 1262
Vinnie, 1238
Violet Jane, 1225
Virginia Ann, 1254
W Wade, 1234
Walter Wadell, 1253
Warren, 1217
Warren Francis, 1216
Warren Greer, 1216

Washington Klemer,
1230
Washington Whistler,
1197, 1221
Wayne, 1231, 1247
Wayne Allen, 1256
Wendell Malcolm,
1230
Wesley, 1241, 1247
Wesley Melvin, 1246
Wilbur Perry, 1235
Wilder Mark, 1244,
1259
Wilkie Beatricke, 1215
William, 1241
William Andrew, 1217
William Eugene, 1201
William Franklin, 1205
William Perry, 1220
William Roy, 1213
Wilma (Stone), 1258
Winifred (Geer), 1231
Winifred Arda, 1231
KAHLER
Alberta, 660
Lisa Marie, 1113
KAHMAN
Andrew D, 616
Andrew Jeffery, 617
Joan Leslie, 616
John Michael, 616
Joseph Scott, 617
Leah Annee, 616
Ledra Jane, 617
Marie (Baker), 616
Paula Kay, 616
Rebecca Marie, 616
Suzanne Nadine, 617
KAHRS
Barbara Elizabeth
(Williams), 1738
Brandon Norstrom,
1738
Brian, 1738
Brian Andrew, 1738
KAISER
Annie, 464
Gail Ann, 1205
Leota, 368
Mary Kay, 629
Valerie, 762
KAKE
Fern (Wetzel), 471
John, 471
KALBACH
Adeline (--), 903
Amelia Lucretia
(Bentz), 903
Daniel, 904
Emma, 903
Ethel Sarah (Fortna),
903
Franklin E, 903
Hannah (Housekeeper),
904
Helen M, 903
Hettie (Paffenberger),
903
James Morris, 904
John, 903
John Franklin, 903
John Howard, 904
John Peter, 903
Katie, 903
Louisa (--), 903
Mary E, 903
Mary Elizabeth, 903
Mary Elizabeth
(Womelsdorf), 903

Matthias Michael, 903
Michael, 903
Peter Womelsdorf, 904
Robert, 903
Sarah Catharine, 903
Susan Matilda, 903
Susanna, 904
Vallira Rebecca, 903
William, 903
William Albert, 903
KALCICH
Bettie, 1018
KALE
Grace Sarah, 1214
KALER
Ruth Marie, 700
KALESINSKAS
Carl, 1070
Cheryl (Webster), 1070
Frank Paul, 1070
Kipen, 1070
Leslie (Schurman),
1070
Mark Francis, 1070
Susan Anna (MacIntire),
1070
KALEY
Agnes Geraldine, 862
Betty (Fox), 861
Betty Lou, 861
Birdella (Shettel), 861
Elsie (Kling), 862
Florence, 862
Frederick, 861
Janice Elaine, 862
Judith May, 862
Jyl Freda, 861
Mabel (Rodgers), 861
Mabel Ruth, 862
Mildred L (Peters),
861
Miriam Doris, 862
Phyllis (Brown), 861
Richard, 861
Robert, 861
Rudolph, 861
Susan Dianne, 861
William, 862
William B, 862
KALLIO
Dorothy Rose (Stanley),
666
Eugene William, 666
KAMENOS
Helen Marie, 1072
KAMIN
Jodi Lynn (Seigworth),
1278
Lewis Gary, 1278
KAMMERER
Helen, 252
KAMPE
Andrew Christopher,
962
Daniel Roy, 962
Gary Roy, 962
Kay Lynn (Fahlbeck),
962
Kyle Adrin, 962
Lydia Kay, 962
KAMPEN
Getrude Ermentrout
(McCulloch), 291
Henry William, 291
KAMPES
Edward Charles, 868
John Edward, 867
Nancy Lee (Eck), 867

KAMPS
Gloria, 174
KAMPSCHROER
Beulah Helen (Weiser),
1462
Christine, 1462
Edwin J, 1462
Jack Weiser, 1462
Jacqueline, 1462
James, 1462
Joanne, 1462
Robert, 1462
KANEAFTER
Clara Lillian (Wiser),
1825
Ernest Rupert, 1825
KANG
Mak Ye, 1719
KANODE
--, 505
Velma C (Stine), 505
KANTZER
Anna Elizabeth, 944
KAPP
Mary, 1534
Sarah, 1504
KAPPENSTEIN
Deborah Lynn, 286
KARALIS
Adrian Marie, 1369
Danielle (Lefeu), 1369
Joan Esta (Chase),
1369
John Michael, 1369
John Nathaniel, 1369
Julie Anne, 1369
Kristy Lee, 1369
Mitchell, 1369
Nicholas Peter, 1369
Paulina (Fulster), 1369
Robert Mitchell, 1369
KARBLEY
Emma Irene, 730, 809
KARCHER
Anna, 1081
Barbara, 961
Barbara (Hursh), 1081
Leo, 1081
Mary Jane, 1081
Richard, 1081
Thomas, 1081
KARGE
Jennifer Renee
(Rebuck), 703
John Thomas II, 703
KARNES
George H, 823
Sara Jane
(Womelsdorf), 823
KARNS
Olive, 1043
KARPIAK
Dolores, 1022
KARPINSKY
Gregory Benedict,
1317
Jennifer Jo (Emmons),
1317
KARR
Adeline, 468
Albert Elsworth, 480
Albert Ronald, 480
Alexander James, 481
Amoretta, 468
Andrew Steven, 477
Ann Elizabeth (Haaser),
481
Anna Elizabeth (Cress),
472

KEELING (continued)
Terry, 1433
Tommy, 1433
KEEN
Anna Mary (Weiser), 1388
Barbara (Coble), 1388
Bertha (Throssell), 1388
Christopher, 1388
David A, 1389
David Calvin, 1389
Donna Christine, 1389
Dorothy Margaret, 1389
Edna Rose, 1389
Elizabeth, 1388
Eugene, 1390
Gina Collette (Wolfe), 1113
Helen Harriet, 1389
James Calvin, 1388(2)
Jane (Burns), 1388
Jeffrey, 1388
John, 1388
Kayla Berlin, 1113
Lawrence Donald, 719
Lois (Baker), 1388
Margaret Mae (Witmer), 719
Marguerite Kees, 1390
Mary (Harter), 1389
Mary Rose (Irwin), 1388
Matthew, 1388
Patricia (White), 1389
Paul Fay, 1389
Ralph John, 1389
Steven Michael, 1113
William Andrew, 1388
William Donald, 719
William Weiser, 1388
KEENE
Carolyn, 1660
KEENER
Bruce Allen, 448
Deanne Marie (Sweeting), 448
Henry S, 1566
Mary Ann, 1867
Paul Russell, 448
Rebecca Maria Elizabeth (Weiser), 1566
Ruth Ann, 448
KEERAN
Amanda Marie, 195
Debbie (Wallace), 194
Peter, 194
KEES
Mary Elizabeth, 556
KEESE
Madge Kathleen (Wysor), 1658
William Riley, 1658
KEETH
--, 865
Dorothy (Spahr), 865
KEGEL
Caroline (Kephart), 1684
William, 1684
KEGER
Charles Henry, 1155
Elvie Melvina (Alspach), 1155
June Ellen, 1152
Marvin Russell, 1158

KEHL
-- (--), 1011, 1101-1102
Abbie (Mowery), 1012
Ada, 1102
Adam, 1000
Adam N, 979
Adam Noah, 980
Agnes, 1101
Alice, 979
Alma (Popp), 1100
Amelia, 1102
Andrew, 1109
Andrew Jasper, 1011
Anna, 939
Anna (Keller), 1011
Anna (Koertner), 1102
Anna Catharine, 896
Anna Catharine (Weiser), 905, 961, 1013, 1099, 1105
Anna Louise, 1103
Anna Maria, 896, 1193
Anna Melissa, 982
Anne Marie, 1192
Annie K (Ley), 1011
Arabella (Beck), 982
Arthur, 1099
Barbara, 1105
Benjamin Franklin, 995
Bertha, 1011
Bessie, 1008
Beverly, 1102
Calvin, 1008
Calvin Newton, 1008
Carrie, 980
Catharine, 961, 1013, 1196
Catharine (Weiser), 896, 1047
Catherine, 961, 1099
Catherine (Bailey), 1099
Catherine (Rowe), 1103
Catherine (Spatz), 1193
Charles, 1011, 1101
Charles H, 1012, 1107
Charles L, 1011
Charles Nathan, 1008
Clara, 995, 1011
Clara (Kehl), 1011
Clara Ida, 983
Clayton, 1102
Clayton Jr, 1102
Constance, 1102
Daniel, 1103
Darrell, 1008
daughter, 979
David Alfred, 1008
David B, 1008
David J, 1011
David Louis, 1008
DeVere, 1011
Donald J, 1011
Donna, 1195
Dorothy, 979
Earl J, 1100
Edith, 1008
Edna A, 1100
Elizabeth, 896, 1103, 1193
Elizabeth (Fehr), 1099
Elizabeth (Hyskell), 1196-1197
Elizabeth (Moyer), 978
Elizabeth (Simmon), 995
Elizabeth Katherine,

987
Ella, 1013
Ellen (Beck), 1100
Ellen (Sheneberger), 995
Elsie (Diehl), 979
Emma, 1100
Emma (Coleman), 1099
Esther Margaret (Tyson), 979
Eva, 979
Eva (Lyon), 1011
Eva Elizabeth, 1192
Eve, 1196
Evelyn, 1102
Foster Raymond, 979
Frances Rebecca, 995
Frank, 1012
Frederick Peter, 1196-1197
George, 1012, 1100, 1192
Gerald Charles, 1011
Gertrude (Reninger), 980
Glenn, 979
Grace (Becke), 1099
Hannah (Weiser), 896, 1192
Hazel A, 1101
Henry, 1012, 1192
Henry Apple, 980
Henry H, 1100
Howard, 1101
Irene, 995, 1011
Iva, 1101
Jacob, 1099
Jacob W, 1246
Jacob Weiser, 1196, 1244-1245
Jasper, 1100, 1105
Jennie, 1012
Jeremiah, 1100
Jessie, 1101
Joel Jacob, 980
Johannes, 961
John, 1102
John Peter, 961
John Aaron, 995
John C, 1099
John George, 896, 1192
John Jacob, 896, 960, 978, 1013, 1047, 1099, 1105, 1192-1193
John Michael, 896, 982
John Peter, 896, 1099, 1192, 1196
John Vincent, 983
Jonathan, 1193
Joseph Gramley, 1011
June (Sheldon), 979
Justina, 896, 905, 914, 939
Kate (Nail), 1011
Katie, 1011
Kenneth, 1101
Ladelina (Loux), 1008
Laura Mae, 1103
Leah, 994, 1012
Leonard, 896, 994
Lester A, 1100
Ley Miller, 1011
Lilly May (Walder), 995
Lou (Lower), 1101
Louise (Strohecker),

1103
Lucille, 979
Lydia (Ferrell), 1109
Lydia Elizabeth, 980
Maggie, 1099
Maggie G, 1011
Margaret, 1008, 1107
Margaret A, 1012
Margaret Ann, 961, 1105
Margaret Hannah (Gramley), 1008
Marguerite, 1011
Maria, 1196
Maria Catharine, 1192
Marian, 1008
Marmia Catharina, 1193
Martha Amelia, 980
Mary, 1007, 1012
Mary (Kiplinger), 1011, 1107
Mary (Moore), 1008
Mary Alice (Stover), 1100, 1105
Mary Ann (Bierly), 961
Mary Elizabeth, 896
Mary Jane, 995, 1100
Mary Margaret, 979
Maude, 1103
Maxie (Musselman), 994
Mayme Ellen, 1103
Maynard, 1008
Michael, 896, 961, 987, 1192
Miles, 1101
Miles Jr, 1101
Nathaniel Jefferson, 987
Nora, 1012
Norman N, 979
Norris, 979
Olive A, 1011
Oran, 994
Orpha, 999
Peter, 1100
Pricilla (Tyson), 1000
Rebecca, 983
Robert, 1008
Rosetta Christiana, 988
Rufus H, 1101
Ruth, 1008, 1101
Ruth (Burch), 979
Sallie, 1099
Salome, 961, 1047, 1078, 1090
Salome (Weiser), 896
Salome Elizabeth, 978
Salome/ Sarah (Weiser), 1196
Samuel, 1103
Sarah, 999, 1192
Sarah (Garrett), 983
Sarah (Haun), 1099
Sarah (Herring), 1100
Sarah (Moyer), 1000
Sarah Ann (Miller), 980
Sarah Jane (Hyskell), 1244
Sarah Malizza, 1000
Sophia, 980
Sophia (Dougherty), 1008
Sophia (Hoeffer), 1100
Sophia Salzberger (Jaerck), 1193

Stella (Moore), 1008
Stella Bertha, 983
Stewart Roosevelt, 979
Susan, 1103
Susan (Ketner), 987
Tama (Miller), 979
Thomas, 1107
Thomas Clair, 979
Thomas Jefferson, 995, 1011
Tillie (Zeller), 979
Vera, 1008
Vera (Hitsman), 1011
William, 1011, 1102
William Aaron, 1099
William Henry, 1011
William Scott, 979
Zwingli Albert, 1000
KEHLER
Carl Irvin, 659
Carl Robert, 659
Gladys Elizabeth (Klinger), 659
Janice Corinne, 659
KEHRER
Catherine (Cosgrove), 947
Fredrick K, 947
Harry, 947
Lynda, 947
Martha Jane, 947
Susan, 947
Virginia (Ryland), 947
KEHRES
Jacob, 1043
KEIBLER
Kristine, 231
KEIFFER
Jorosa Hetty Ann (Weiser), 1643
Marian, 674
Peter W, 1643
KEIHL
Kristin, 900
KEIL
George Daniel, 915
Ione Jeanette (Kluiss), 915
KEIM
Abigail (Weiser), 1623
Benjamin, 1623
Clara Catharine, 1623
Isaac Weiser, 1623
Mary Ellen K (Marquette), 1623
KEIPER
Helen May, 733
KEIRMAN
Freeman, 1242
KEIRN
Philip, 1236
Ruth (English), 1236
KEIRNAN
Charlotte Miller, 86
Elizabeth Anderson, 85
Elizabeth Dessez (Miller), 85
John Semmes, 85
Kevin Harrison, 85
Kevin Wright, 85
Sally Dessez, 85
KEISER
Benjamin Jo, 1088
Cathy Jo (Leitzel), 1088
Elizabeth Jane, 716
Elva M, 504
George William, 716
Helen Martha (Snyder),

KEISER (continued)
Helen Martha (Snyder)
(continued)
716
John, 904
Justin Max, 1088
Leon Paul, 716
Mildred Shirk
(Lawver), 716
Richard Leo, 716
Richard Leon, 716
Robert Lee, 716
Ryan Benjamin, 1088
Susan Lynne, 716
William Paul, 716
KEISTER
--, 187
Ida M, 1492
Leslie Jo, 1071
Marian (Nell), 187
Sharon Gay, 930
KEITER
Elmer David, 764
Katie Alice, 661
Verna Marcella
(Koppenheffer), 764
KEITH
--, 1559
Emma (Weiser), 1559
Ruth, 1711
Vonia Rhea, 332
KEITHAN
Florence Irene, 1525
Patricia J, 1118
KELCHNER
Kathleen May, 249
KELKER
Edith Victoria, 851
KELL
Ann Elizabeth (Kahl),
1195
Duane, 1195
KELLEHER
Amy Rose, 1284
KELLER
--, 786
Albert, 944
Ann, 506
Anna, 576, 1011
Annie S (Weiser), 1614
Betty Lou, 944
Beverly Jean, 945
Bonnie (Blevins), 263
Charity (Van Slyke),
1584
Chester, 1525
Chester Jr, 1525
Christine Alison, 1160
Corey Lynn, 1160
Daniel Lee, 1159
Daniel M, 1614
Donald, 1525
Douglas, 786
Edna Mae (Derrick),
907
Elaine (--), 263
Gregory Victor, 263
John, 1584
John Henry, 907
John Patrick, 1739
Joyce, 506
Karen Lea (Wright)
Taylor, 1739
Kathi, 152
Kenneth, 944-945
Kim, 944
Loy Eugene, 605
Lucinda, 1423
Lucy Webb (Stine),

506
Margaret, 1387
Margaret (Allen), 944
Maria (Weiser), 1881
Maureen Alice, 1211
Mellie Bennettie Snider,
1139
Ned G, 1525
Neva Eleanor
(Cosgrove), 944
Patricia Mary (Scanlan),
786
Peter, 1881
Polly Ann, 1453
Prentice V, 263
Robert, 263
Robert Paul, 263
Roselyn Lee (Rhodes),
605
Roy, 263
Roy Martin, 263
Ruby (Burch), 263
Ruth, 394
Ruth Ann, 944
Ruth Ann (Kiger),
1159
Ruth Irma (Kline),
1525
Sarah, 1693
Sharon, 263
Sylvia (Haschel), 263
William E, 944
William H, 506
Wilma Jane, 944
KELLEY
--, 1340, 1579
Alva F, 798
Bessie Maude (Alton),
798
Bonnie, 624
Clifford, 1340
Cynthia Dianne, 1119
Doug, 1212
Esther Marie (Davis),
1212
Ethel (Pickard), 1579
Gloria Sue (Smith),
1119
John M, 1623
Linda Sue, 925
Louisa C (Schenke),
1623
Mary, 937
Minnie (Wagner), 1340
Nannette, 1119
Robert Thomas Jr,
1119
Ronald Shane, 1212
Sean Wesley, 1212
Shadd Manford, 1212
Sharlee Pauline, 1212
Trina (Thompson),
1212
Valerie Eileen, 128
KELLNER
Bettina (Kulenkampff),
318
Erhard Helmut Walter,
318
Kai Fabian, 319
Lars Tobias, 319
Nils Benjamin, 319
Tim Felix, 319
KELLOCK
Maggie, 1681
KELLOGG
Alvin J, 293
Chauncey Orville, 750
Dorothey Mae, 293

Lee Ann, 550
Louisa (Eister), 750
Pearl Sadie (Ege), 293
KELLY
Ada G, 1856
Amy Lynne (Hageman),
1658
Bill, 1692
Brian L, 1658
Brittany Ann, 1064
Carroll Porter, 352
David Louis, 352
Dawson William, 1803
Douglas A, 249
Jean Regina, 856
Jeannie (Masten), 352
Jestie Alexis, 127
Joseph Fitzgerald, 1064
Joye Ann, 972
Karen Virginia (Lau),
249
Katherine, 1585
Leroy, 1182
Mary Louise
(Goodrich), 352
Maxine (Colgan)
Jensen, 1692
Michelle Marie
(Maxson), 127
Paul Eugene, 972
Rebecca Louise (Noll),
1064
Robin Lynne (Wiser),
1803
Ruth, 1818
Ruth Lynn, 352
Scott, 352
Shannon Noll, 1064
Thomas Patrick, 127
Urban M, 972
Vera Gail (Sours), 972
Vera Sally (Nelson),
1182
KELOSKY
Carrie Elizabeth, 1296
Chance Edward, 1296
Christopher David,
1296
Emily Belle (Wiser),
1296
Michael Edward, 1296
Travis Michael, 1296
Zachary Andrew, 1296
KELSCH
Nichole (Whalley), 662
V Peter, 662
KELSER
Julie, 505
Russell, 505
Rustae K, 505
Todd R, 505
Vernell L (Cochran),
505
KELSEY
Delpha Lucille (Wiser),
1870
Edward, 1870
Mary, 464
KELSO
Lois Irene (Hill), 960
Robert Shaw, 960
KELTNER
Clyde Stephen, 39
Karen Anne, 38
Kathryn Jeanne, 38
Patricia Anne (Sonner),
38
Robert Edward, 38

KELVER
Mildred, 1000
KEM
Annetta, 536
KEMMER
Cheryl Lynn, 581
Eric Skyler, 581
Kathy Ellen, 581
Keith Norman, 581
Margie Ellen (Strayer),
581
Scott Norman, 581
KEMMERER
Clinton, 1636
Lillie W (Polster),
1636
KEMP
Amelia, 1730
Anna H, 787
Benjamin, 1730
Edward Ashley, 1004
Elizabeth Ann (Wieser),
1730
Eugenia Lavina, 689
Geraldine Lucille, 735
Helen (App), 1028
Kathleen Elizabeth,
1004
Marjorie Elissa (Smith),
1004
Russell, 1028
Sarah E, 1730
KEMPER
Anna Elizabeth
(Muhlenberg), 284
Brooke Elizabeth, 284
Ian William, 284
Jackson, 284
Jackson Jr, 284
John Peter, 284
Pamela (Hoyerman),
284
Peter Jackson, 284
Timothy Wood, 284
Wiliam, 284
KEMPTON
Mary Alice, 1038
KENADY
Clinton James, 665
Jennifer Jo
(Roadenbaugh), 665
Robert, 665
KENDALL
Amanda Marie Armes,
538
Carolyn Denise
(Fischer), 538
Keelli Renae, 538
Kenny, 538
Kregg Byran, 538
Kristie Lynn, 538
KENDIG
Becky (Peters), 1489
Edward Strock, 1489
Eugene, 1489
Jane Alice (Belcher),
1489
Katy, 1489
Mary E, 1614
Mary Frances (Strock),
1489
Robert Dean, 1489
KENDRICK
John, 184
John Jr, 184
Leigh, 184
Marcia Wirtz (Brown),
184

KENEDY
Angela (Downs), 1557
Anna Mercedes (Reid),
1554
Anne Loretta, 1555
Arthur Patrick, 1554
Arthur Reid, 1555
Arthur Reid Jr, 1555
Barbara Ann (Sameth),
1557
Brian Patrick, 1557
Brian Patrick Jr, 1557
Carmela Therese, 1558
Christopher Brian,
1556
Clara, 1558
Daniel Joseph, 1556
David Bradley, 1556
David Gerard, 1556
David Patrick, 1556
Elizabeth, 1558
Elizabeth Teresa
(Weiser), 1553
Eugene Thomas, 1556
Eugene Timon, 1556
Gabrielle Barzaghi,
1557
Gabrielle Marie
(Barzaghi), 1557
Gael Elizabeth, 1556
Isabel Mercedes, 1558
Jamie Alizabeth, 1556
Jed Foster, 1556
Jennifer Ann, 1557
Joan (McAvoy), 1556
Joan Marie (Accettella),
1556
John, 1553
John Justin, 1557
John Leopold, 1557
Julie Ann, 1556
Katherine Elizabeth,
1556
Kathleen Anne, 1555
Kelly Ann, 1556
Kristen Elizabeth, 1556
Linda Ann (Gallagher),
1557
Linda Anne
(Splittberger), 1555
Loretto, 1554
Lorraine Swan
(Walker), 1557
Louis, 1557
Louis Arthur, 1557
Marie Agnes, 1558
Mark William, 1556
Mary, 1554
Mary Alice (McGuirk),
1555
Mary Ann (Gornick),
1556
Megan Mariah, 1555
Olga Josephine (Silva),
1556
Patricia (Greenridge),
1557
Patricia Ann, 1557
Patricia Joan, 1557
Patrick John, 1553
Paul John, 1558
Rita Filomena (Cuzzi),
1558
Rosemary Gabrielle,
1557
Rosemary Susan, 1557
Shannon Ruth, 1557
Shaun Michael, 1557
Sheila Marie, 1556

KENEDY (continued)
Sheilah Ann (Wilson), 1555
Susan Alene, 1555
Thomas Boyd, 1558
William Wilson, 1555
KENEMORE
Donald, 591
Donita Ann, 591
Sandra Aline (Titus), 591
KENFIELD
Rose, 602
KENNEDY
Archibald, 887
Barbara (McKnight), 349
Belva, 887
Charles J, 1462
Christopher, 312
David Gregg, 295
David Scott, 295
Diana Bliss (Schwab), 312
Edgar Sloan, 295
Edna, 887
Ellen Lee, 1479
Florence Ruth (Kershner), 133
Frances Peck (Shulze), 295
Frances Scott, 295
Gail Ann (Baumann), 1735
George Washington, 189
Harry, 1735
Henrietta Caroline (Gifford), 189
Jeffrey Burle, 1814
Joseph Alexander, 133
Joseph Elliott, 295
Landis, 887
Mabel Eleanor, 190
Madge Amelia (Weiser) Wilson, 1462
Marc, 312
Margaret Jane, 295
Orpha (Eppley), 887
Raymond, 887
Thomas, 349
Tiffany Marie (Wiser), 1814
William, 887
KENNEL
Florence Viola, 1315
KENNIS
Cathy, 1302
KENT
Brenda, 444
Eurilla Emeline, 1768
Margaret, 59
Michael Shane, 570
Na Dene, 1772
Paul, 570
Retha Mae (Huffman), 570
Ruby Chloe, 397
Stacy Louise, 570
Susan Christine (Shirck), 996
Terry, 996
KENYON
Alice M, 242
Ruth Talcott, 306
KEOGEL
Florence Martha, 957
Patricia, 955
Pearl Emma, 956

KEPFORD
Joseph Leroy, 892
Zula Elizabeth (Eppley), 892
KEPHART
-- (--), 1686
A J, 1682
Ada (Barger), 1693
Addie Lorissa, 1689
Addie Lorissa (Kephart), 1689
Adie, 1687
Alana, 1692
Albert, 1690
Albert J, 1688
Alfred, 1685
Alma Mae, 1689
Alonzo Willard, 1690
Amanda Elizabeth (Dimmitt), 1696
Amelia, 1682
Andrew, 1685
Andrew E, 1686
Ann Margareet, 1695
Anna Mae (McKee), 1687
Annie, 1681
Audrey, 1689
Barbara, 1685
Barbara (Shanteau), 1691
Benjamin, 1682
Benny, 1681
Bernice (Hammond), 1690
Bertha (Hampton), 1682
Bertha Emma, 1691
Bess (--), 1687
Betty Rosalie, 1686
Burton C, 1689
Carol, 1690
Caroline, 1684, 1688
Catherine, 1681
Catherine E, 1681
Charlene, 1690
Charles, 1688
Charlott, 1682
Charlotte, 1685
Charlotte (Kephart), 1685
Christina, 1682
Cindy Ann, 1687
Clarence, 1690
Clark, 1682
Cleveland, 1682
Cora, 1687
Cora (Ogden), 1682
Cordelia, 1689, 1693
Cordie, 1682
Daniel Columbus, 1685
David J, 1688
Deborah (Medershett/ Hendershot), 1685
Delilah Jane (Rowe), 1696
Della, 1687
Delmar Charles, 1692
Delores, 1692
Doris Lorraine, 1690
Dorothy (Eldridge), 1692
Dorothy Mae, 1690
Dorothy Marie (Johnson), 1692
Douglas James, 1688
Edith, 1682
Edith (Antes), 1682
Edward, 1687

Elizabeth, 1682
Elizabeth (Koehler), 1684
Elizabeth (Lane), 1688
Elizabeth (Young), 1687
Ellan (Stormer), 1687
Ellen Frances (Ritchey), 1685
Elmer Thomas, 1690
Elmira, 1681
Elva, 1686
Elveretta (Maines), 1685
Elwood Clair, 1686
Emaline, 1688
Emma, 1687
Emma Catherine, 1696
Ernest, 1687
Evron N, 1689
Florence Katherine, 1696
Floyd William, 1688
Foster Alexander, 1688
Frances (Lorenzen), 1690
Francis, 1691
Frank, 1687
Franklin Scott, 1693
Franklin Shedrick, 1693
Fred, 1688
Genevieve Mae (Fysh), 1691
George, 1680
George Foster, 1690
George H, 1688
George Washington, 1696
Gilbert, 1688-1689
girl, 1692
Gladys (Nelson), 1692
Gladys (Schroeder), 1691
Grace B, 1688
Guy Franklin, 1692
Harold, 1686
Harold Eugene, 1690
Helen (Hammond), 1691
Helen Lucille, 1692
Henry Hunter, 1696
Henry Speaker, 1696
Hiram, 1685
Ida Ann (Rightmier), 1690
infant, 1689
Isaac, 1684
Jacob, 1682, 1685
Jean, 1689
Jennie (Ochiltree), 1687
Jennifer, 1686
Jerold Wayne, 1687
John, 1682, 1687
John C, 1685
John E, 1688
Jonathan Clair, 1686
Joseph Albert, 1696
Joshua, 1684
Joy, 1689
Joyce (Steward), 1690
Karin Lexine, 1693
Kathleen (Lampert), 1692
Kathleen Y (James), 1692
Kay (Daly), 1691
Kenneth, 1689

Lavina, 1688
Lavina (Kephart), 1688
Lavine, 1685
Leola Arlene, 1691
Leona (Lane), 1689
Leonard Eugene, 1686
Lodie May, 1682
Louella, 1682, 1689
Lucille Viola, 1690
Lucy Jane (Adams), 1686
Lulu (Stucker), 1687
Lyda May, 1682
Mabel, 1684
Mable, 1687
Margaret (Graham), 1685
Margaret (Knyper), 1685
Margaret E, 1681, 1704
Mari (Lugar), 1691
Marjorie, 1691
Martha, 1681
Martha Selina (Granville), 1686
Mary, 1682, 1703
Mary A, 1707
Mary Alta, 1690
Mary Ann, 1685, 1696
Mary Ann (Logan), 1684
Matilda (Hochenberry), 1682
Matilda Elizabeth (Turner), 1696
Maude (Clouse), 1696
May Belle, 1688
Millard Filmore, 1689
Mina (Ogden), 1682
Minnie, 1688
Minnie E, 1688
Monica (Scott), 1689
Myrtle, 1682, 1688
Nancy Jane, 1684
Nancy Jane (Smeal), 1680
Nancy May, 1696
Neil Franklin, 1692
Nellie C, 1687
Nesta (Shimmel), 1770
Nettie (Good), 1682
Oliver David, 1690
Paul, 1682
Pearl C, 1687
Peggy Anne (Blout), 1686
Percy O, 1689
Pernina, 1688, 1693
Phebe, 1685
Phoebe (Myers), 1685
Preston, 1688
Rachael (Alexander), 1685
Rachel, 1684
Rachel Ellen, 1681
Rachel Susan, 1696
Ralph, 1691
Ray Charles, 1691
Raymond, 1687
Rella Maxine, 1686
Richard Barton, 1690
Richard Earl, 1691
Rosalie, 1692
Rose Jane, 1688
Rosetta, 1687
Rozella, 1689
Ruth (Erickson), 1687
Samuel, 1685

Samuel Snyder, 1694
Sarah (Knox) Bradley, 1687
Sarah Ann, 1685
Sarah Ann (Kephart), 1685
Sarah Elizabeth (Breon), 1690
Sharon Lee, 1692
Shirley, 1690
Shirley (Shannon), 1690
Shirley LaRue, 1686
Sidna, 1693
Stacey Leigh, 1693
Stella Louise (Morris), 1688
Stella M (Long), 1688
Steven, 1691
Susan Elaine, 1691
Susan Harriett, 1689
Susanna (Phillips), 1694
Susannah, 1693
Tamer, 1684
Tami, 1691
Vella (Meints), 1689
Victor Melvin, 1687
Vida May, 1692
Viola Amy, 1692
Viola Catherine, 1681, 1696
Violet, 1693
Violet Lucille, 1688
Wallace, 1770
William, 1687
William David, 1696
William L, 1685
Winfield, 1682
Woodrow Franklin, 1692
Zoe (Mueller), 1690
KEPHART/ GEPHART
Andrew, 1681
Andrew L, 1681
Catharine (Weiser), 1681
John Asbury, 1681
Martha Jane (Haney), 1681
Mary J, 1681
Rachel Ellen (Kephart), 1681
KEPLER
Carl Theodore, 1179
Ellen Virignia (Musselman), 1179
Pamela, 1179
Penelope, 1179
Stella, 1394
KEPLINGER
Dewayne E, 523
Herbert, 523
Jane Ann, 523
Karen (Slusher), 523
Thelma Jun (Riggs), 523
Tonya, 523
KEPNER
Alice Ada (Smith), 158
William, 158
William James, 158
KEPPLE
Henry, 1361
KERBEL
Beulah Elizabeth (Rafferty), 500
Ellen Eileen, 501
Lola Jane (Sanders),

KERBEL (continued)
Lola Jane (Sanders) (continued) 500
Lynn L, 500
Orville C, 500
Sandra Sandor, 500
Stacey Lee, 501
Stanley Eugene, 500
KERCHER
Angela Sophia (Olseski), 261
Carl Frederick, 260
Earnest Richard, 260
Elizabeth Ann, 261
Esther E, 1754
Margaret W, 253
Margaret Williams (Mengel), 260
Richard James, 260
Robert Franklin, 261
KERCHEVAL
Beverly Eunice (Pearson) Leonhardt, 1483
John, 1483
KERCHNER
Elizabeth J, 1542
KEREVEN
John J, 236
John Phillip, 236
Joyce Arlene (Dietz), 236
KERFOOT
Arthur, 1709
Norma (Bodle), 1709
KERGALL
Guy Emmanuel, 282
Herve Arthur, 282
Laurent Theodore, 282
Mary Bruce (Harden), 282
KERLIN
Ruth Melcina, 566
KERN
Alma F, 1351
Amiel John, 498
Bessie Arvilda, 498
Bryan Lee, 486
Byron Lowell, 485
Connie Lou (Schmerbeck), 486
Darlene Ann, 487
Deanne, 486
Deborah Louise (Smith), 486
Donald Lee, 486
Donna Lee, 487
Dora Thomas, 1580
Doris May, 486
Dorothy Leona, 487
Earl August, 488
Emily Louise, 487
Emma Catharine (Heileman), 498
Emma Hattie (Ehlers), 485
Florence Irene, 488
Gary Lee, 486
Gertrude May (Beuhler), 485
Gloria (Carnicom), 485
Harold Lowell, 485
Hazel Mae, 498
Henrietta Louisa (Heileman), 482
Howard Leroy, 485
Joseph Michael, 486
Joyce (Camden), 486

Kay Lyn, 486
Leah Joy (Jackson), 486
Leston Lewis, 488
Lisa Lynn (Heflinger), 486
Lloyd Elroy, 485
Marilyn Yvonne (Blausey), 486
Pearl (Sands), 1634
Peggy Sue, 486
Robert S, 1634
Theodore Louis, 482
Tom Lowell, 486
Valerie Yvonne, 486
KERNS
Minnie Maxine, 1136
Sophie, 791
Steven Brent, 201
Teresa Diane (Allison), 201
Timothy James, 201
KERNY
Harold Winfred, 1834
Wynona Clarissa (Wiser), 1834
KERPER
--, 1621
Margaret L (Lykens), 1621
KERR
--, 1254
Audrey Eleanore, 559
Betty Lee, 1130
Charles J, 721
Charles Simons, 559
Clarence, 721
Clarence Gordon, 721
Cloy Cletus, 559
Connie (Szczesny), 721
Dellace Dorman, 559
Doris Jean, 559
Elizabeth Hannah, 1516
Garnet (MacDonald), 559
George Leroy, 559
Gerald Leroy, 559
Gloria Evelyn, 559
Harry Tripelette Jr, 1130
Hazel, 34
Hazel Blanche (Cook), 1254
Joyce (Kirby), 559
Lalah Marie, 559
Laurel Leroy, 559
Margaret, 163
Margaret Jane, 1254
Marie (Binkley), 559
Martha Cummins, 1517
Mary, 1261
Minta Catherine, 559
Minta Maybelle (Fess), 559
Norma Madylene, 559
Olive Pauline (Alspach), 1130
Robin, 1872
Thelma Marie (Longfellow), 721
Wendell Eugene, 559
KERRSTAHLER
Anna Maria, 1362
KERRY
Sarah, 1296
KERSCHNER
Donna Jean, 1749
Gregory Allen, 1382

Kara Elizabeth, 1382
Ted Allen, 1382
KERSEY
James, 1210
Nancy Ann (Bigler), 1210
KERSHNER
-- (--), 238
Alida May (Hanford), 133
Anna Margaret, 133
Annie (Wharton), 133
Aubrey Hanford, 133
Carolyn A (Weishaar), 133
Catherine Elizabeth, 133
Charles, 238, 250
Clara (Herb), 736
Eileen Belinda (Bryan), 133
Elizabeth Ann (Haugh), 1382
Ellgertia, 131
Ethel, 132
Florence Ruth, 133
George, 736
Glenn Aubrey, 133
Ida Katherine (Borrell), 250
Jacob, 131
Joan, 736
Karin Elizabeth, 133
Katharine Ann, 134
Linnie Elizabeth, 132
Naomi, 569
Priscilla (Weiser), 131
Richard, 736
Richard Wharton, 133
Richard Wharton Jr, 133
Ronald Eugene, 250
Ruth Weishaar, 133
Scott David, 133
Selina, 132
Thelma Evelyn (Denn), 133
Thomas Franklin, 133
Thomas Franklin III, 133
Thomas Franklin Jr, 133
William John, 132
KERSJES
Kelly, xi, 940
Michael James, 953
Tierney Elizabeth, 953
KERSTETER
Ammon, 1395
Cathy J, 1395
Harold, 1395
Lois (Harpster), 1395
Michael A, 1395
Sarah Margaret (Bottorf), 1395
Steven H, 1395
Winona Ellen, 1395
KERSTETTER
-- (--), 719
Alice (Henninger), 1541
Ashley Nicole, 650
Brian Eugene, 1006
Carol Maureen (Johnson), 650
Catharine May (Gonser), 1540
Charles, 719, 1541
Charles Edward, 726

Chris Eugene, 650
daughter, 650
David Franklin, 1006
Denise Renee, 1006
Donna, 748
Doris, 1532
Edith M, 1541
Elanore (Newberry), 1540
Eliza (Henninger), 1540
Ellis K, 1532
Ethel Jane, 726
George B, 1540
Glenn, 765
Glenn Jr, 765
Jean H (Hornberger), 765
John Charles, 726
Joyce Irene (Wertz), 1006
Kyle Evan, 650
Leon V, 1540
Leroy, 1532
Liona Grace (Bland), 726
Lorinda Lou, 1055
Louise, 1540
Madeline Janette (Kahl), 1006
Margarette, 1541
Marlin William, 1006
Melissa Ann (Williard), 650
Nathaniel, 1532
Pearl (Reitz), 1532
Robert Lewis, 1055
Robin Lynn, 1055
Rosemary (Gephart), 1055
Russell Eugene, 650
Ruth Ann, 1006
Shirley Eleanore (Welker), 650
KERSTTER
Emma, 1540
KESNEY
Sadie M, 846
KESSLER
Elizabeth Ann, 1418
Eric Paul, 1418
Galen, 616
Jack, 784
Janet Nadine (Ackers), 616
Katherine, 705
Kristy Lee (Snyder), 1418
Lavina, 507
Margaret, 88
Mary (Fegley), 784
Stephen Michael, 1418
Steven Paul, 616
KESTER
Catherine (Trinkle) Burress Clark, 1654
Paul, 1654
KESTLEU
Debra, 269
James, 269
Lee, 269
Lester, 269
Mary (Haschel), 269
KETCHAM
Hubbard, 1408
Jemima (Blachly), 1408
KETCHUM
Ada Grieve, 1488

KETNAS
Angie, 481
KETNER
David Lee, 1746
Grace marie (Wisser), 1746
Irvin Luther, 1746
Julianne Lynne, 1746
Linda Lou, 1746
Susan, 987
KETRING
Bradley Stephen, 568
Brent Alan, 568
Carolyn Kay (Herring), 568
Dawn Renee, 568
Stephen, 568
KETTLELAKE
Cheryl, 1496
Larry Edward, 1496
Miriam Ruth (Smith), 1496
KEVLER
David Peter, 219
Lynne Elizabeth (Stouffer), 219
KEY
Elizabeth Ann, 1752
KEYES
Emma Frances, 386
Louise, 1300
KEYSER
--, 672
David, 347, 672
Eleanor (Messner), 672
Emma, 895
Herbert Slemmer, 347
Lila Geneva (Roughton), 623
Margaretta Slemmer (Richards), 347
Melyne Sherie, 1113
Rollin, 623
Ronald, 672
KEYSOCK
Anthony, 658
Melba Blanche (Klinger), 658
KEYSOR
Dean, 448
Michael David, 449
Natalie Gayle, 449
Patricia Deanne, 448
Susan Patricia (Sloan), 448
KEYWORTH
Bella Weiser (Carl), 1468
William A, 1468
KHALE
Roween Minerva, 1218
KIBLER
Daniel Paul, 386
David Isaac, 386
Elizabeth Joy, 386
Joseph Patrick, 386
Joyce Eileen (Leibold), 386
Patrick Allen, 386
Rebecca Delores, 386
Ruth Eileen, 386
KICK
Alvin, 765
Sevilla (Witmer), 765
KIDDER
Lucy W, 334
KIDDOO
Dorothy Helen (Weiser), 126

KING (continued)
Gary, 564
Gladys Harriet, 1339
Grace (Donne), 830
Harriet Emily (Shulze), 296
Helen M, 142
Henry, 516
Ida (Weiser), 1292
Ines Genevieve, 36
Inez Genevieve, 36
Ira, 1292
Iva (Zerbe), 1292
James Wilson, 510
Joel Weiser, 169
John, 1654
John Connel, 296
Joshua David, 172
Joyce Irene (Weiser), 169
Joyce Rosalie, 1478
Judith Ann (Burkholder), 228
Karelyn Kay (Hocker), 592
Karen B (Blair), 169
La Vere, 1770
Leland E, 169
Leonard, 1292
Leora (Wiser), 1770
Linda (Banter), 565
Linda Leigh (Gossard), 598
Lora, 565
Lorane Kay, 604
Mabel, 1292
Madge Stewart, 296
Margaret, 1654
Martha Louise (Braumiller), 426
Mary, 1508
Mary Elizabeth Anne, 1477
Maurice Harriet, 296
Milo, 1292
Monique Kay (McAlarney), 1368
Omar Benjamin, 1812
Ora (Wiser), 1812
Patricia Jill (White), 516
Paul Anthony, 426
Phyliss, 552
Phyllis Nadine (Moore), 401
Raymond Wayne, 1478
Richard C, 517
Robert Edward, 401
Ruby, 1292
Ruth, 1292
Samuel Alsysius, 830
Sara Eleanor, 1294
Sue, 564, 1808
Thirza M, 1424
Wayne Elmer, 1477
Wendell, 565
Wesley, 1292
William, 1292
William Wiley, 35
KINGERY
Betty Jean (Tuller), 389
Clarence, 103
Clarence Richard, 103
Loretta Yvonne, 103
Margie Maxine (Shoap), 103
Merrilee Kay, 389
Sharon Maxine, 103
William Alan, 389

William Ernest, 389
KINGMAN
Clyde, 948
Clyde Jr, 949
Delores, 948
Doris (Laubrick), 948
Sheila, 949
Shelly, 949
Sherry, 949
Sheryl, 949
Shirley, 949
KINGSBOROUGH
Lucinda, 1879
KINGSLEY
Anna, 1779
Rose, 1296
KINGSTON
-- (Womelsdorf), 834
George O, 834
KINLEY
Charles, 988
Chester, 988
Clayton, 988
Elizabeth Katherine, 987
Gertrude, 988
Gladys, 988
Harrison A, 987
Helen, 988
Howard, 988
James, 988
John, 988
Olive Grace, 988
Oliver, 987
Raymond, 988
Robert, 988
Ruth, 988
KINNEY
Alexander, 1581
Alice, 979
Bonnie J (Weiser), 1846
Claire, 979
Daniel James Gaby, 1581
Darryl, 1581
Dorothy, 979
Eugene, 979
Glenn, 979
Jay Richard, 1846
Lucille, 979
Margaret Alwisha, 1732
Margaret Elizabeth (Gaby), 1581
Margaret J, 385
Mariel Christine, 1581
Mary Margaret (Kehl), 979
Norman, 979
Norris, 979
Paula Katherine, 1581
Ray, 979
KINNY
James, 654
Martha Louise (Heller), 654
KINSEY
Alyce Ann (Reed) Hershberger, 1511
Barbara Ann (Trauger), 1075
Darlene Ann, 1075
Myron, 1075
Robert Cornell, 1511
Sean Michael, 1075
KINTER
Doris Elaine, 1353
Ed, 1353

Esther Violet (Arnold), 1353
KINTNER
Karyl Yvonne, 52
KINTZ
--, 9
Jack E, 170
Jeffrey Allen, 170
Martha Lou (Weiser), 170
Patsy Ann, 170
Steve Eugene, 170
Ted Michael, 170
KINZER
Elizabeth Louise, 1418
KIPLINGER
-- (--), 1105
Agnes (Giles), 1105
Albert, 1106
Barbara, 1109
Carl, 1105
Catherine, 1109, 1654
Charles, 1105
Cora Ida, 1105
Donald, 1105
Edith, 1106
Edward, 1105
Emmie (McGullah), 1105
Fannie, 1106, 1109
Florence (Oliver), 1106
Franklin Ervin, 1106
George Edward, 1105
Georgie (Hotchkiss), 1105
Gladys, 1106
Hannah Rebecca (McDonnel), 1105
Henry, 1105
Howard, 1106
Irving, 1105
Jacob, 1105
John, 1106
Lloyd, 1105
Lucy Jane, 1106
Lula, 1105
Lydia, 1109
Mable (Stahl), 1105
Margaret, 1107
Margaret Ann (Kehl), 1105
Mary, 1011, 1106-1107
May (Gishwiller), 1105
Michael Kehl, 1105
Mildred C, 1105
Oliver, 1106
Ruth (Howard), 1105
Sally, 1106
Thomas, 1105
Ward, 1105
KIPP
David, 1714
George, 1714
Harry Burton, 1714
Joyce (Rexford), 1714
Sam, 1714
Sandy, 1714
Sue (--), 1714
Tyler, 1714
KIRBES
Sharon, 601
KIRBY
Ave Lucille (Robinson), 804
Barbara Ann (Stevenson), 804
Carl Raymond, 804
Elmo Arlene, 804

Eva (Knepp), 1719
Jerry Guy, 804
Joyce, 559
Julia Ann, 804
Kelly, 804
Kerrie, 804
Lev, 1719
Mildred Jolene, 804
Nelle Rosa, 1049
Viola Alleyne (Plassman), 804
KIRCHHOFER
Donald Ray, 108
Edward Louis, 108
Kay Ellen, 108
Mary Jean, 108
Velma Jean (Seeley), 108
Walter E, 108
KIRCHNER
Barbara, 1596
Maria Magdalena, 1595
KIRK
Allen, 633
Anita Claire, 105
Beth Ann (Stephens), 1448
Brenda Marlene, 105
Cheryl Lynn, 633
Chris, 1448
Clayborn Dale, 105
Dorothy R (Titus), 105
Gertrude C, 1618
Jeffery Allan, 633
Kathryn Luanne, 633
Margaret Ann (Smith), 633
Marjorie Dale, 105
Michael Wayne, 633
Susan Marie, 105
KIRKANDAHL
Leona, 102
KIRKENDAL
Martha, 823
KIRKLAND
Leland, 1487
Mack Alan, 44
Mary Elizabeth (Mason), 44
Russell Lee, 1487
Ruth (Pinkston), 1487
Thelma Darlene (Earnest), 1487
KIRKPARTICK
Helen Lucille (Kephart), 1692
William Hartford, 1692
KIRKPATRICK
Carrie (Womelsdorf), 834
Elisa, 1177
James L, 834
Janice Margie, 1692
Jeanne Eileen, 1692
John E, 834
Jun, 1176
Mary, 1176
Robert, 1177
Shearley (DeVore), 1177
Sybil Ann, 98
KIRKWOOD
Eliza, 252
KIROUAC
Armand H, 1228
Madge Lucille (Smith), 1228

KIRPATRICK
Florence (Weiser), 1176
June, 1176
Walton, 1176
KIRSCHKE
Donna Lee, 117
Dorothy (LaNoue), 117
Helen Chloe (Krigbaum), 117
Joan (Carpenter), 117
Lutz Theodore, 117
O T, 116
Oscar Theodore, 117
Paul Evan, 117
Paul Fuller, 117
Robert Harold, 117
KIRSHNER
Louise, 366
KIRSTEN
Diana Louise, 1465
KIRTLEY
Christopher Allen, 440
Dawn Denice, 440
Kent William, 440
Linda Sue (Johnson), 440
Louise M, 583
Stacie Renee, 440
KISER
--, 472
Barbara Sue, 1076
Donald Owen, 1076
Joan, 1076
Joann (Caskey), 472
Mildred (Brungart), 1076
Nancy, 1076
Owen Ernest, 1076
KISH
Donna Marie, 1114
KISKER
Elisabeth, 326
KISLING
Fay Etta, 1397
KISSABERTH
Minnie M, 1881
KISSICK
Donna, 797
KISSINGER
Agnes Irene (Koppenhaver), 673
Audrey Jean, 1044
DeWitt Talmadge, 1675
Edith Mildred, 1675
Elizabeth, 1675
Florence, 1675
Gurney, 1044
Henry Smith, 1675
Henry Weiser, 1675
Jacob Emanuel, 673
Nora, 1675
Raymond Emanuel, 673
Sarah Almeda (Harman), 673
Sarah Jane (Weiser), 1675
Vera Snyder (Moyer), 1044
Willis, 1675
KISSNER
Dina (Pickert), 1575
William, 1575
KISTLER
Emma Louisa, 1746
Gertrude L, 929

KISTNER
Albert John, 868
Annabell Louise (Still), 868
Darline Alice, 868
James Albert, 868
Rosina, 1724
KITCHEN
--, 1028
Delmas, 1397
Dorothy Lurene (Lenker), 675
Eugene Harry, 675
Franklin Lester, 675
Harry Wilson, 675
Hazel Catharine, 675
Judy Combs, 1159
Marjorie Elizabeth, 680
Mary Mae, 681
Mildred Sarah (Wagner), 1397
Orpha Madlene (Reed), 762
Rachel Alice (Crossley), 680
Raymond Albert, 762
Robert Eugene, 762
Sylvester Iram, 680
KITSMILLER
Barry E, 871
Bonnie (Wentz), 871
Esther (Yinger), 871
Ethel Bloser (Ernst), 890
Joyce E, 871
Keith A, 871
Robert Emmett, 890
Scotty E, 871
Vance W, 871
KITTINGER
Dorothea (Van Slyke), 1584
Sam, 1584
KITZMILLER
Maria Catharine, 896
Mary Ida, 1474
KLAAS
Eva, 1571
KLAHR
James, 1616
June Irene (Weiser), 1616
Maureen (McKay), 1616
Miltred F, 1616
Pamela, 1616
Sherri, 1616
KLAISS
Abner Weiser, 918
Albert Cooper, 918
Anna Elizabeth, 916, 916
Anna Laura (Atticks), 917
Anna Ruth (Bowers), 917
Caroline Weiser, 918
Carrie Hickok (Cooper), 918
Elsie (Bowlby), 917
Emma Jane, 916
Frederick Charles, 915
Frederick Wayne, 917
George Oliver, 917
Ione Jeanette, 915
John Abner, 915
Leila H (MacMallen), 918
Margaret Blanche, 915

Margaret Jane (Weiser), 915
Margaret Viola, 918
Mary Ellen (Grimes), 917
Mary Kathleen, 917
Mathilda M, 915
Mathilda Margaret, 918
Matilda, 1884
Ruth Emma (Young), 917
Sara Thelma, 915
Sarah Ellen, 918
Sema Aletta (Snyder), 915
Wilbur Atticks, 917
William Frederick, 915
KLAUS
Lillian Bernese, 667
KLAWITTER
Dianne, 1418
KLEBER
Bernhart, 1679
Elizabeth, 1679
Maria Elizabeth (--), 1679
KLECKNER
John, 1086
John Jr, 1086
Kathleen Winifred, 1086
Raymond, 1103
Ruth N, 1103
Vesta Viola (Brungart), 1086
KLEEMAN
Ulrich, 323
KLEES
David, 734
Jack, 734
Mary Elizabeth (Stahl), 734
Stephen Jay, 734
KLEHN
Aaron Christopher, 967
Douglas John, 967
Rachel St Andrea, 967
Rebecca Jan (Otterbeck), 967
KLEIN
--, 1
Alice M (Wisser), 1754
Anna Catharine, 1589
Anna Margaretha, 1589
Eva, 1589
Frederick, 16
Glenn Stephen, 884-885
Gretchen Lynn, 884-885
Jacob, 1589
Johann Adam, 1589
Johann Frederick, 1589
Johann Friedrich, 1589
Louise Lorraine (Caliman), 884-885
Mable, 1353
Maria, 1589
Matilda Wagner, 254
Rebecca, 1589
Rebecca (Weiser), 16, 1589
Richard Walter, 884-885
Robyn Suzanne, 884-885
William F, 1754
KLEINFELTER
-- (--), 1350

Cosmus, 1350, 1353
Edith I, 1353
Erma (Grimes), 1353
George H, 1353
Gertrude (Arnold), 1353
Harry, 1353
Hilda, 1353
Lillie (Miller), 1353
Mable (Klein), 1353
Martha (Bean), 1353
May E, 1353
Miles, 1353
Raymond A, 1353
Sterling, 1353
KLEINSCHMID
Anna Maria, 279
KLEMAN
Elizabeth, 1019
KLENCKER
John, 1103
Maude (Kehl), 1103
KLENER
Marie, 914
KLIMEK
Frances Ann, 1205
Geralding, 722
KLINE
-- (--), 961
-- (Weigle), 868
Andrew, 868
Annie (Yinger), 868
Annie Catherine (Weiser), 1525
Annie Sue, 1525
Ashley Rae, 1074
Beverly Jane, 1401
Brittany Dawn, 1074
Carol, 264
Caroline (Weiser), 1541
Charlotte Ann, 1525
child, 228
Clare, 920
Daralys (Leland), 263
Deborah Ann, 228
Desiree Jean Scholl, 1087
Donald Frederick, 1074
Dorothy R, 1748
Eleanore, 868
Elizabeth, 375-376
Elma Jane, 868
Elsie Mae (Long), 857
Florence Irene (Keithan), 1525
Francis Odea, 1525
Freda, 1030
George E, 961, 1018
Georgia (Hutton), 868
Gladys, 868
Grant, 868
Grant Jr, 868
Harry M, 857
Heidi Jane, 1074
Helen B (Yost), 1018
Henry, 1541
Ida Nadine, 1525
Isaac Dewitt, 1525
James H, 1020
Jaqueline Pamela, 644
Jeffrey C, 644
John, 868
Lois Kay, 1525
Mary Elizabeth, 1525
Maude, 868
Mayme F Wylie, 1642
Michael, 375

Michael William, 1074
Nancy Gail (Sneeringer), 227
Pamela Janine (Bixler), 644
Paul, 264
Paul Cyrus, 1525
Phyllis K (Renn), 1020
Rachel, 159, 1730
Raymond, 263
Richard Eugene, 227
Richard Paul, 1525
Roger Earl, 228
Ronald Eugene, 227
Rose Marie, 1020
Ruth Irma, 1525
Stephanie Mae, 645
Susan Rae (Wert), 1074
Susanna (--), 375
Terry Lee, 857
Thelma Susanne (Hazel), 1401
Timothy, 264
Virginia Irene, 150
William H, 1401
KLINEBRIEL
Betty Jane (Hummell), 1154
David Leonard, 1154
Lawrence, 1154
Ronald Doyle, 1154
KLINEFELTER
Florentine, 1413
KLING
Elsie, 862
Rebecca Ann (Beuchle), 1537
Robert, 1537
KLINGBERG
Elizabeth A (Wysor), 1648
Frank Joseph, 1648
KLINGEL
Lloyd, 611
Melody Sharlen, 611
Shirley Ann (Brown), 611
KLINGENSMITH
Albert Willis, 1302
Arthur Earl, 1302
Betty (--), 1302
Clair Albert, 1302
Clara Jane (Wiser), 1302
Cora Blanch, 1302
Dale, 1302
Doris (--), 1302
Elizabeth Jane, 1296
Ethel (--), 1303
Faye, 1302
Harry Hall, 1303
Hazel Fern, 1303
James, 1303
Judith, 1302
Mae Elizabeth (McDowell), 1302
Martha Elizabeth (Calhoun), 1302
Myrtle Mae, 1302
Preston Glenn, 1302
Robert, 1302
Ruth, 1302
Thomas Irvin, 1302
William, 1302
Willis Wiser, 1302
KLINGER
Ada, 657
Agatha (Heusten), 358

Agnes Grace, 661
Alberta (Kahler), 660
Alexander, 358
Amber Rae, 747
Ammon, 729
Amy Susan, 747
Anna Elizabeth (Gottman), 358
Anna Eve (--), 358, 777
Anna Maria (Snyder), 358
Anna Olive, 729
Barbara (Wysser), 6
Bessie, 1533
Bessie Elizabeth (Bush), 658
Betty Elnora, 745
Bonita, 660
Brenda Lou (Wiest), 652
Carrie E (Fasold), 728
Catharine, 245
Catharine (Steinbruck), 358
Charles Frazier, 744
Chester Leroy, 660
Christina, 358
Christina (--), 358
Clarence M, 657
Constance Mae, 659
Daniel Eston, 658
Daniel Lewis, 659
Daniel M, 652
David, 660
Debra Louise, 659
Della Louise, 661
Dennis Lee, 659
Donald Clarence, 713
Dorothy, 729
Dorothy (Manges), 745
Dorothy Marie, 661
Edith Gereon (Reed), 659
Eilene May, 661
Elaine Elizabeth, 744
Eleanor, 729
Elizabeth, 358, 360, 461-462, 637, 758, 777
Elizabeth (Brosius), 358
Ellen Mable (Groff), 661
Emmaline (Arbogast), 652
Esther (Miller), 657
Eve Elizabeth ( ), 358
Evelyn, 729
Fay Frances, 659
Florence J, 729
Forrest Edward, 661
Fred, 746
Galen Herbert, 655
Galen Oscar, 660
Gary Galen, 660
Gene Reed, 659
Georg, 358
George, 358
George Allen, 655
Gertie Mae, 657
Gertrude Isabelle, 676
Gladys Elizabeth, 659
Grace, 661
Grace (Klinger), 661
Gurney Israel, 655
Harlan Elwood, 661
Harriet Gertrude, 728
Harry, 658

KLINGER (continued)
Homer C, 729
Homer Marlin, 658
Howard A, 659
Ida Loretta, 660
Irene May (Harner), 660
Irvin, 638
Irwin Ray, 658
Jacob, 6
Jacqueline Janice, 659
James Daniel, 659
Jane Ann, 696
Janet May, 747
Jason Lynn, 652
Jay Kris, 747
Jennifer Robecca, 652
Johan Georg, 358
Johannes, 358
John Frazier, 744
John Harold, 659
John Junior, 747
John Philip, 358, 360
Joseph Harlan, 661
Josephine Eva, 746
Joyce Marie, 659
Joyce Marie (Klinger), 659
June Elizabeth, 745
Karen, 730
Karl F, 659
Katie Alice (Keiter), 661
Katie Almeda, 660
Katie Almeda (Klinger), 660
LaJuana Cheryl, 747
Leona G, 729
Lester Leroy, 660
Lillian, 1534
Linda Rose, 745
Lisa, 657
Lloyd, 729
Lois, 730
Mabel (Boyer), 729
Mabel Agnes, 655
Mable May (Boyer), 657
Magdalena (Haag), 358
Marion (Dagle), 729
Marlin, 729
Martha E (Martin), 744
Mary (Beatty), 729
Mary (Long), 729
Mary Ann, 744
Mary Anne, 659
Mary Lee, 661
Mary Louisa, 652
Melba Blanche, 658
Melba Catharine, 660
Melinda Jan, 747
Moses, 655
Nancy Ruth, 696
Nelson, 659
Oscar Preston, 661
Oscar W, 729
Pamela Inez (Bond), 747
Pauline Elizabeth (Fulkroad), 713
Peggy, 659
Peter, 358
Peter L, 728
Philip, 777
Regina (Wanger), 658
Rhea Arlene, 655
Richard Gabriel, 745
Richard Gabriel III, 745

Richard Gabriel Jr, 745
Robert Keith, 659
Robin Samantha, 747
Rodney Ray, 652
Rosa Ellen, 655
Russell, 729
Ruth Devona, 716
Ruth Elizabeth (Poticher), 696
Sallie Agnes (Rabuck), 655
Sally Darlene (Harry), 747
Sara Nicole, 747
Sarah Elizabeth (Ross), 744
Sarah Jane, 677
Sharon Ann (McNally), 745
Shirley Louise, 746
Shirley Louise (Klinger), 746
Sidney Ann (Messersmith), 655
Stephanie Lynn, 657
Steven, 660
Theresa Ann, 661
Thomas Matthew, 696
Violet Betty, 660
W Stanley, 730
Wanda Jane, 690
Yvonne Louise, 659
KLINGLE
Verna, 369
KLINGLER
Angela Marie, 607
Audrey Amelia (Maki), 618
Barbara (Parker), 607
Barbara Hetrick (Orders), 618
Bertha (Rhodes), 606
Betty (Yearick), 1372
Betty Jane, 618
Betty Jean, 1286
Bonnie Lou, 619
Brenda (Brown), 607
Carolyn Lamoyn, 619
Chester, 607
Clem, 616
David Allen, 1286
David Lee, 619
Dennis James, 618
Diamond (Shrider), 618
Dianne, 607
Donald Alan, 618
Donald Paul, 605
Douglas Warren, 607
Earl Clement, 619
Edison, 617
Edith (Arnold), 617
Elsie (Driver), 618
Elza Adam, 617
Emma (Long), 616
Ethel (Doersoam), 606
Eugene Bucher, 617
Evelyn Faye, 608
Francine Jeanette, 617
Gina Marie, 618
Gloria Eileen Ann, 607
Goldie Isabelle, 619
Gregory Lee, 618
Harold, 606
Harry Raymond, 617
Hazel N (Stober), 617
Ilo May, 608
Jack, 1372
James Dale, 605

Janet (Jones), 619
Jaqualine Lee, 605
Jeanne (Dodge), 618
Jeffery Eugene, 605
Jennifer Gaye, 1286
Jill Ann, 618
Joan Elizabeth (Rhodes), 605
John, 1372
Josephine (Rhodes), 607
Joyce (--), 617
Julia Helene, 605
Kay Ruth (Weiser), 1286
Keith Warren, 617
Kenneth Leroy, 619
Kevin Daniel, 617
Kimberly, 607
Larry Arnold Lee, 607
Lee Anne, 619
Lee Geneva, 616
Leonard, 618
Lester Clayton, 618
Linda Jane, 618
Lora Jane, 618
Marcella (Ward), 607
Marianne, 1286
Marilyn, 618
Mary Rosanna (Seigworth), 1285
Mason, 606
Matthew, 619
Max Elza, 618
Michelle Lynn, 618
Newton, 607
Norma, 606
Norma Jean, 1286
Patricia, 607
Ralph Leonard, 1285
Richard Harrison, 1286
Robert Leroy, 618
Robert Louis, 618
Robert Meredith, 1286
Rodney Allen, 607
Ronald, 607
Ronald Lee, 618
Roy Earl, 618
Ruth (Ahrens), 617
Ruth Lucille, 617
Ruth Pauling (DeVault), 607
Scot Irving, 618
Scott, 1372
Steven Ray, 619
Valerie J (Smith), 617
Victor Gale, 607
Virgil, 606
Wendy Sue, 619
Wilbert Edgar, 619
KLINGSMITH
Juliann, 429
KLINTZ
Eliza Baldwin (Schwab), 310
Jerry, 310
KLOCK
Asia Richard, 441
Donna Marie (Brown), 440
Gary Richard, 440
Jean, 774
Ruth Irene, 690
Sable Alexandria, 441
KLOEPFER
--, 8
-- (Kintz), 9
-- (Pfizenmaier), 9
-- (Wild), 8

Georg, 8
Hans, 9
Jacob, 9
Ulrich, 8
KLONSKY
Darcy Beth (Gilpin), 422
Ronald Stuart, 422
Steven Isaac Myers, 423
KLÖPFER
N, 6
KLOPP
Anna, 845
Brian, 938
Brian Keith, 938
Carol (McConnell), 64
Esther Matilda (Anspach), 842
Jerry, 64
Tammy Lou (Weiser), 938
William, 842
KLOTZ
Christina Norman, 324
KLOUSER
Charles Richard, 767
Dennis Lee, 767
Herman, 767
Kermit Woodrow, 767
Lori Ann, 656
Marie Elizabeth (Weist), 767
KLUMP
Charles James, 1316
Hazel Irene, 1316
Lulu Viola (Rabold), 1316
Russell Albert, 1316
Ruth Elizabeth (Paxton), 1316
KLUMSTRA
Harriet H, 950
KLUNDER
James, 972
Joye Ann (Kelly), 972
KLUPFEL
Clementine Sophie, 324
Eliza Henrietta Emily (Schrader), 324
Karl, 324
KLÜPFEL
Alfred Karl, 325
Bettina, 324
Christina Norman, 324
Franziska Henriette, 316
Jane Meredith, 325
Margaret Henrietta, 325
Mary Salin (Hollenshead), 325
Roland Werner, 324
KLUTZ
Michelle, 1298
KMETZ
Andrew, 674
Miriam Maybelle (Lenker), 674
KNAB
Linda Mae, 1601
KNABAY
Teresa, 631
KNABB
--, 1621
Esther L (Lykens), 1621
KNABE
Etta Sophia, 879

Mary A (Eppley), 879
Valentine R, 879
KNABERSHUE
Helen, 1879
KNAPP
Anita Louise, 630
Beatrice Elenor Marie (Heller), 654
Carol Sue, 630
Christine Ellen, 629
Gene Orlando, 629
Gene Orlando Jr, 630
Hazel Eudene (Harvey), 629
James, 654
Michele, 654
Nancy (Sawaki), 629
Orlando, 629
Scott Allen, 630
Vio, 1481
Violet Jeanene, 972
KNARR
Dawn Marie (Frey), 789
Perry, 789
Perry C Jr, 789
KNAUSS
Angelina Theresa, 1844
Johannes, 1411
Maria C R, 16
Maria Catharine (Roeder), 1411
KNEBEL
Elizabeth Ann, 1219
KNECHT
Ainslee Lenore, 431
Alice Irene, 439
Anna Lucille, 441
Anna Sophia (Fossinger), 430
Arlene Frances, 431
Bertha Salena, 440
Charley, 459
Clarence Cleveland, 441
Clarence Wilbert, 442
Dempa Sue, 442
Donna Gertrude, 442
Elvira Jennie (Sell), 435
Emily Bernice (Haver), 441
Ethel Lenora, 431
Evelyn Beatrice, 442
Frances Lee, 431
Frank Emanuel, 435
Frederick, 430
Geraldina Ida (Stafford), 430
Geraldine Elaine, 430
Hanna Ella, 441
Harold, 430
Henry Frederick, 430
Homer Wilson, 431
James Wilbert, 442
Janet Lee, 431
John Wesley, 442
Lary Van, 442
Leo, 431
Lillian B, 431
Linda Celeste, 431
Lois Beverly, 430
Loraine Izetta (Adams), 442
Louella (Stadelbauer), 435
Lula Alice (Powell), 430

KNECHT (continued)
Lusina (Fossinger), 459
Lydia Olive, 431
Mae L, 430
Margaret Jane, 431
Marlea Celeste (Pond), 431
Maurine A (Shaney), 438
Mildred B, 431
Minnie Olive, 440
Olan Emanuel, 435
Orena Faye, 436
Patricia Ann, 439
Ray Augustus, 438
Ronald, 435
Ruth, 430
Shirley May, 439
Veva Leola, 436
Viva (Hyer), 431
William Augustus, 442
Zola Elvira, 439
KNEIPLE
Amanda Geneva, 1059
Amy Augusta (Erhard), 1059
Dorothy Louise, 1059
Frances Ellen, 1059
George Erhard, 1059
William Emmet, 1059
William Emmet Jr, 1059
KNEPP
Anna (Shugarts), 1719
Benjamin, 1706
Beverly (Dickenson), 1719
Christine, 1719
Clyde, 1718
Curley Brinton, 1719
Dorothy (Wisor), 1708
Eva, 1719
Eva Marie, 1719
Fay, 1719
Frederick, 1708
Grace (Wisor), 1706
Harvey, 1719
Iola May, 1699
Janice Lynn, 1719
Jay, 1719
Joyce (Bloom), 1719
Kathleen (Carlos), 1719
Kenneth, 1706
Linda Antonio, 1719
Mak Ye (Kang), 1719
Mary (Robinson), 1719
Maureen (O'Donnell), 1719
May Belle (Wisor), 1706
Michele Catherine, 1719
Patricia, 1719
Patricia Dennis, 1719
Phyllis, 1719
R Russel, 1719
Robert Clyde, 1719
Ronald, 1719
KNEPPER
--, 1106
Albert, 1106
Beryl, 1106
Evelyn, 1107
Fannie (Bolinger), 1106
Frances, 1107
Gerald, 1106

Grace, 1106
Harvey, 1107
Jean, 1106
Kean, 1107
Maro, 1107
Othel, 1107
Paul, 1106
KNERR
Don Malick, 1524
Don Malick Jr, 1525
Fern (Koehler), 1524
Joan Yvonne, 1524
Lauren Kay, 1525
Lillian Kathryn (Malick), 1524
Nevin W, 1524
Sarah Tevilia, 1754
Steven Winfield, 1525
KNEZEVICH
Sally Jo, 1293
KNIGHT
Barbara Graham (Euston) Amy, 1510
Barbara Kay, 1276
Carol, 392
Charles William, 1510
Christopher John, 352
Irene (Alexander), 392
Jan, 490
Jeanene, 1069
Kenton, 392
Laura Ellen (Goodrich), 352
Richard Charles, 1510
Richard Charles Jr, 1510
Tawn Elizabeth, 1510
Virginia, 392
KNILEY
Mary Augusta, 639
KNIPP
Beverly Jean, 485
Debbie Jane (Lazenby), 485
Dolores Ann, 485
Eunice Irene (Schott), 485
Gary Hubert, 485
Hubert Lewis, 485
Janet Lee, 485
Laura Marie, 485
Lois Ann (Rewoldt), 485
Tyler Lewis, 485
KNIPPLE
Cindy Lynn, 872
Larry, 872
Mary (Freed), 872
KNISELY
Florence Romaine (Eppley), 894
L Donald, 894
Lloyd, 894
Nancy Romaine, 894
Ray L, 894
Sara Jane, 894
KNISPEL
Christi, 1260
Eric, 1260
Kelly, 1260
Marie Louise (McClintic), 1260
Mathew, 1260
Norman, 1260
KNISS
Algie, 1530
KNITTLE
W A, 12

KNOBEL
Alan, 1480
Kimberly Anne, 1480
Phyllis Jean (Cummins), 1480
Richard Alan, 1480
KNODT
Florence E, 95
KNOERLE
Anne Monica, 1115
KNOLL
Barbara J, 787
KNOPF
-- (--), 253
Esther, 1615
Katherine Clara (Felt), 258
Wendell, 253
Wendell Frank, 258
KNOPP
David Charles, 1018
Sarah Elizabeth (Yost), 1018
Timothy Renn, 1018
Walter, 1018
Walter George, 1018
KNORR
Charles, 733
Cornelius J, 643
Eunice Mae, 733
Gerald Leroy, 949
Jennie May (Malick), 733
John Paul, 733
Lester Leroy Jr, 949
Mary Agnes (Arbogast), 643
Mildred Abigail, 738
Virginia (Laubrick), 949
KNOSKE
Edith Clara (Willey), 37
Mildred, 37
Oscar G, 37
Vernon, 37
Virginia Inez, 37
KNOTHE
Barbara Ann (Jones), 246
Paul L, 246
KNOTTER
Elizabeth, 102
KNOTTS
Janet Louise, 401
KNOUFF
Grace, 779
KNOWIS
Mattie, 1809
KNOWLTON
Hugh Gilbert, 312
John Stanley, 312
Priscilla Bliss, 312
Ruth Christine, 312
Susan English (Galpin), 312
KNOX
Allen, 562
Anita, 1419
Estella, 252
Jane Ellen (Yoder), 198
Jody (Falk), 562
Levi Michael, 198
Michael Shane, 198
Michelle Ann (Arnett), 198
Patsy Merlyn, 1478
Sarah, 1687

Taylor Michelle, 198
KNUDSON
Mary Kay, 1195
KNUPPENBERG
Alice, 1695
Lucinda, 1696
KNUTH
Kim Lynette (Cunningham), 1632
Michael Lee, 1632
KNYPER
Margaret, 1685
KOBEL
Barbara, 812
Catharine (--), 30
John, 30
KOBER
Katie M, 1513
KOCH
Allison Leigh (Poore), 1343
Allison P, 1340
Anna L, 1617
Anna Margaretha, 21-22
Emma, 1599
Florence Elizabeth, 714
Florence May (Goodling), 714
George Thomas, 714
George Thomas Jr, 714
Hanns Diboldt Theobold, 22
Harold Eugene, 714
Lucia (--), 22
Maria Barbara (Schneider/Feg), 22
Maria Sophie, 1599
Rheta (Hollaway), 714
Wilhelm, 22
William Edward, 714
William George Jr, 1343
KOCHEL
Helen E (Lykens), 1621
Thelma S, 1636
Thomas, 1621
KOCHENOUR
Berniece (Reighter), 622
Catherine Ann (Hammon), 622
Elmer Ellsworth, 622
Imogene, 622
James, 622
Jun Rae, 622
Lila Kathryne (Edwards), 622
Mildred Geraldine, 622
Newton Howard, 622
KOCHER
Alvin Earl, 691
Audrey Louise, 760
Ben Leon, 690
Carla Marie, 692
Carol Ann, 692
Carolyn Marie (Wiest), 692
Carrie Agnes (Shoop), 685
Chad Anthony, 692
Charles, 1615
Christopher William, 690
Daniel, 1615
Daniel La Fean, 760
Daniel Milton, 1615
Diane Elizabeth, 760

Donald Lamar, 689
Dorothy Mae (Finkbone), 689
Earl Woodrow, 690
Edward Mitchell, 1851
Eldred Lamar, 760
Ellen Carrie, 686
Elsie, 1756
Esther (Knopf), 1615
Ethel (Morgan), 1615
Ethel Elizabeth (Rowe), 760
Eugene Victor, 1615
Frederick Ervin, 685
Frederick William, 690
Galen Frederick, 689
Grace (Moyer), 1615
Grovene Shoop, 691
Harold Hobson, 686
Helen Cardella, 686
Ina Naomi, 1615
Jacqueline Nicole, 690
Jennie Marie, 1615
Joan Marcella, 691
Joyce Marlene, 690
Karen Louise (Troutman), 691
Kathryn Aletha, 1615
Kendra Kristine, 692
Kenneth Kermit, 692
Lawrence Hobson, 685
Lena Sarah, 686
Leon Emanuel, 689
Linda Ann (Reese, 690
Linda Elisabeth, 760
Linda Marie (Smith), 690
Lisa Kay, 691
Mae Alvena, 686
Margaret Marie (Hoke), 689
Marie Eleanor (Reisch), 692
Mary Evelyn, 689
Matthew Benjamin, 690
May (Zerbe), 1615
Mildred Renee, 689
Nancy Ann (Wiser), 1851
Nancy Lynn, 691
Nathan Alvin, 691
Orion Cornelius, 689
Rebecca Lyn, 690
Richard Eugene, 692
Rita Agnes, 692
Ruth Irene (Klock), 690
Sadie Alvena (Brown), 685
Samuel Julius, 1615
Shirley Ann, 691
Tami Sue, 691
Violet (Weiser) Kramer, 1615
Wanda Jane (Klinger), 690
William Christopher, 690
William Franklin, 1615
KOCHERTHAL
Joshua Harrsch, 12, 20
KOCHIE
Brian Christopher, 1477
Chanda Larisse, 1477
Patricia Ann (Mullin), 1477
Thomas Andrew, 1477

LAMB (continued)
Harold Oscar, 1150
Helen Ruth, 1151
Hugh, 1151
Irma Mildred (Bell), 1151
James David, 1151
Joan Ellen, 1147
John Marc, 1147
Larry, 798
Linda Carroll, 798
Louise Cecilia (Grady), 1147
Margaret Leota, 1147
Maria, 1582
Mary Kathryn, 1150
Michelle Kathleen, 1147
Murray (Houston), 1147
Neil Woodrow, 1147
Neil Woodrow Jr, 1147
Patricia Ann (Farley), 1147
Pauline Loretta, 1151
Phoebe Madaline (Buck), 798
Robert Hugh, 1151
Ronnie Lee, 798
Roy, 1147
Tracy Lynn, 1147
William, 1696
William Asher, 1151
LAMBERT
--, 1661
Anne Reid (Belford), 1555
Carol (Kahle), 1243
Cindy, 936
Debra (Wysor), 1661
Douglas, 1243
Emily Anne, 1555
John Gallagher, 1555
Mary, 1555
Nora Kenedy, 1555
Peggy Jane, 1660
Terrence Paul, 1555
LAMBERTI
Anna Catharine (--) Weisser, 1605
Johann Gurtav, 1605
LAMBRECHT
Gisela, 327
LAMBRIGHT
Ada, 225
Garth, 940
Jody Ann, 940
Ruth May (Wilkinson), 940
LAMEY
Brian Scott, 1097
Chad Eric, 1097
Charles Dale, 1082
Edna Ruth (Fenstermaker), 1082
Harold W, 1082
Jarrad Van, 1097
Jerry Pershing, 1097
Joan Elaine (Frank), 1097
Lydia, 982
Maggie, 982
Tena, 1076
Teresa (Youngblood), 1097
Virginia Ann, 1082
Vivian Jane, 1061
LAMM
Berton Joy, 461

Charles Walter, 461
Gail Lynette, 461
Milton Charles, 461
Norlyn Carl, 461
Wilma Gail (Fossinger), 461
LAMMERS
Dave, 569
Mary Jeanine (Ellett), 569
LAMONTAGNE
Georgine Ernestine, 1558
LAMOTTE
Ilse, 322
LAMP
Montie Lynn, 398
LAMPARTER
John M, 1843
Sarah Catharine (Weiser), 1843
LAMPERT
Kathleen, 1692
LAMPLIGHTER
Lane Jagi, 753
LANAGLEY
Jody Kay, 552
LANCE
Frank, 506
Hazel (Stine), 506
Zeldon, 506
LAND
Alan James, 1256
Christopher Leon, 997
Diana Susan, 1256
Donald, 1256
Emma Leona (Kahle), 1256
Everett Wilson, 1256
Joanna (Wiser), 1798
Jocelyn, 997
Milton Lanehart, 1798
Patricia Ann (Shirck), 997
Robin Elaine, 150
Ronald Lee, 1256
LANDAUER
Arvilla, 822
LANDEFELD
Martha, 1619
LANDENBERGER
Folma Marianne Albertine (de Haan), 321
George, 321
LANDES
Barbara Jean (Frost), 434, 460
Carl Eugene, 434, 460
Cynthia Ann, 435, 460
Donna Jean, 435, 460
Janet Sue, 435, 460
LANDFAIR
Carolee, 612
LANDGREN
Dorothy Helen (Bretz), 640
Elaine, 640
Karen, 640
Robert Wunch, 640
LANDIS
--, 1543
Arthur Spencer, 1544
Aubrey Rae, 908
Bertha May, 1544
Bonnie, 846
Charles Alfred, 1544
Edward Horace, 1544
Emma Merinda (Good),

1544
Emma Penelope, 327
Herbert Davis, 1544
James Miller, 1544
Jere, 908
Josephine E, 75
Karli Jo, 908
Laura, 1628
Lori Ann (Sipes), 908
Louise Grace, 151
Nora, 874
Osbourn, 1544
Reed, 1543
Ruth, 698
Sarah Ann, 1423
Susanne, 1543
Winifred (Reed), 1543
LANDON
Mamie, 989
LANE
Angela Kay, 587
Bobby Joe, 587
Carole, 1290
Corina, 186
Debra Lynn (Wiser), 1790
Elizabeth, 1688
Frank Malcom, 587
Garland, 1790
Gertrude E, 1812
Gloria Jeane, 587
Kara Elizabeth (Smith), 206
Kerri Jo, 587
Larry Dean, 588
Leona, 1689
Maggie Leona (Hocker), 587
Margaret Bessie (Roberts), 587
Reba Jeannine, 1124
Steven Dale, 588
Terri Lynn, 588
Troy, 206
LANG
--, 1, 1299
Anthony, 854
Betty E (Buckholz), 1299
Carolyn Jean (Wolf), 1311
Fred, 1038
Grayce Arlene, 1254
Gregory Alan, 1311
Ida Laura, 1038
Ida Laura (March), 1038
James Henry, 1311
Jean Marie, 476
Joseph, 1299
Ruth (Yohe), 854
LANGE
Barbara Lee, 1169
Carol Sue, 580
Dawn Marie, 580
Edward Frederick, 580
James Edward, 581
James Michael, 580
John Frederick, 580
Karen Kaye, 265
Ruth June (Bowsher), 580
Susan (Stankula), 580
Wayne Joseph, 580
LANGENBERG
Joan Olene, 148
Louise Olene, 148
LANGER
Joseph, 1688

Pernina, 1688
LANGERMAN
Beverly June (Wyatt), 495
Carl August, 495
Clara Augusta (Heileman), 493
Cornell Lewis, 497
Edward Henry, 496
Ernest Wilfred William E, 497
Ethel Marie (Nofziger), 495
Florence (Tyler), 497
Geneva Matilda, 497
Grace I (Kay), 495
Grace M (--), 496
John Henry, 493
Juanita Marie, 496
Mary Elizabeth Fought, 496
Mary Lee (Vestel), 495
Mary Margaret (Gargac), 497
Mildred Lucille, 497
Theresa Cecelia (Szucs), 497
LANGHAUSER
Amy Katharine, 1454
Andrew Marr, 1454
Derek Peter, 1454
Dreer Purvin, 1454
Shirley Ann (Buckwalter), 1454
LANGHEAD
Charles, 1272
Emma (Coder), 1272
LANGLE
Gertrude A, 612
LANGLETZ
Elsie Rathfon, 856
LANGLEY
Fred, 595
Louetta (Herring), 595
LANGSETH
Wayne, 149
Zenda Kay (Spurgeon), 149
LANINA
Lisa Gay (Wiser), 1814
Michael, 1814
LANIUS
Ann, 1463
LANKFORD
Katherine Dale (Horsey), 1216
Roger, 1216
LANN
Patricia Jane (Maier), 55
Walter Henley Jr, 55
LANNI
Lisa, 1600
LANNING
Catherine Anna, 1840
LANOUE
Dorothy, 117
LANSBERRY
--, 1708
Alice, 1702
Blanche (Wisor), 1702
Blanche R, 1710
Clare, 1702
David E, 1702
Earl, 1702
Eleanor (Williams), 1708
Raymond, 1702

LANSBERY
Pearl, 1711
LANTELINE
Susan Ann, 1307
LANTZ
Barbara (--) Witman, 1566
Charlotte (Weiser), 1879
Elijah, 1566
Elizabeth, 38
James E, 1879
LANZ
Carol A, 1627
LAPLANTE
Andrea Lewista (Weiser), 406
Eric Mathew, 406
LAPORE
Anthony J, 221
Anthony S, 221
Dorothy Anne (Kieffer), 221
LAPP
Alfred, 1107
Annie (Schwoob), 1107
Charles, 1107
Ethel (Shippy), 1107
Florence (Fote), 1107
Irene, 1107
John, 1107
Lura, 1108
Mabel, 1107
Margaret (Kiplinger), 1107
Meda, 1108
Norman, 1107
Raymond, 1108
Thomas, 1108
Tillie (Shelhase), 1108
Vernon, 1107
Wilbur, 1108
LARABEE
Lucina Minerva, 1833
LARK
Catharine W, 696
George Robert, 931
Hannah Margaret (Weiser), 931
John E, 931
John Weiser, 931
Robert Charles, 931
LARKEY
Marjorie Estelle, 236
LARKIN
Deedra Kay (Brown), 200
Leigh Catherine, 355
Nancy Louise (Lehman), 355
Redempta Burr, 1547
Shelby Ann, 355
Steven B, 355
William Clay, 200
LARKINS
Florence Eakin (Strock), 1492
infant, 1492
Nancy Ellen (Vititoe), 1492
Nancy Richelle, 1492
Reginald Hylton, 1492
Richard Hylton, 1492
Sarah Elizabeth, 1492
Victoria Ann, 1492
LARROW
--, 1103
LARRY
Vicki Ann, 689

LONG (continued)
Cyrus, 611
David, 602
David Edward, 1170
David Frank, 615
David L, 158
David Lee, 613
David Leroy, 603
Deana Kay, 570
Debbie (Schubert), 613
Debra Frances (Deller), 1170
Derek Wayne, 615
Diana Elizabeth, 464
Diana Lee, 603
Diane (Phillip), 573
Dianne Raye, 1332
Donald Eugene, 255
Donald Keith, 574
Donald P, 709
Donna (Shrider), 620
Donna Jean, 615
Donna M (Weitzle), 255
Donnie Mae (Stauffer), 709
Doris J (Shutt), 857
Dorothy, 604
Dorothy Berdena (Herring), 573
Dorothy Louise, 615
Ed, 1524
Edward Leroy, 653
Effie Jane, 1867
Eileen, 613
Elizabeth Dee, 1170
Elsie Mae, 857
Emma, 616
Eraa Jean (Keck), 615
Ernest R, 856
Esther Ellen (Patton), 653
Eunice, 619
Evelyn II, 614
Faye (Hatfield), 612
Fern (McCarty), 619
Fern Irene, 349
Fred, 619
Gail Virginia (Shomper), 653
Garry Max, 573
Gary Kent, 604
Gary Kurtis, 614
Gene Eldon, 614
George W H, 1641
George Washington, 1641
Gerald Duane, 615
Gertrude (Zimmerman), 619
Gladys, 603
Gladys (Chambers), 615
Grace E, 1541
Harold, 612, 614
Harriet, 619
Harry, 604
Hazel (Helming), 613
Hazel R (Albaugh), 613
Helen E (Koppenheffer), 708
Henry, 613
Henry Lloyd, 255
Hilda Drusilla, 1333
Ida Leah (Wise), 1169
Ilah Jeanette, 615
Irene Catherine (Guisewhite), 1083

Irvin Eugene, 653
Iva, 611
Jack Merrill, 1170
James Douglas, 1333
James Lamar, 653
James Leroy, 615
Jan Renae (Mitchell), 541
Jane Kay, 1333
Janette Marie, 654
Jaqueline, 519
Jay, 257
Jean Ann, 604
Jean Arlene (Shutt), 653
Jeffery Lee, 574
Jeffrey William, 1170
Jerry Lee, 574
Jerry Paul, 1170
Jesse, 709
Joetta, 1280
John, 1696
John Ernest, 857
John Fount, 1868
John M, 1060
John Thomas, 603
John Timothy, 654
John Wesley, 1083
John Wilmer, 653
Joshua Dale, 574
Joshua Lee, 1170
Joyce Lynn (Mahoney), 615
Judith Ann (Rawa), 1170
Julia (Mastuson), 602
Julia Marin Lindemuth, 1297
Kathleen Sue, 604
Kathryn, 603
Kathy Annette (Edwards), 574
Kathy Lynn (Leeper), 649
Kelly A, 614
Kent Patrick, 614
Kermit Dennis, 1332
Kermit Elden, 1332
Kevin Douglas, 1085
Kevin Michael, 614
Kimberly Ann, 614
Larry Lamar, 653
Larry Lamar Jr, 649
Laura (Carr), 613
Laura Elizabeth, 541
Leotta (Yearick), 1085
Lester, 612
Lewis, 603
Linda Kay (Linton), 573
Linda Lea, 570
Lisa M, 255
Lois, 604
Lori Ann (Crosby), 1170-1171
Lori K, 573
Lottie Pearl (Gebhart), 1332
Luann Marie, 653
Lucille Dorothy (Erhard), 1050
Mabel M, 769
Mae Emma (Shettel), 856
Margaret Jane (Hoy), 602
Margaret Lavonne, 614
Margaret Pauline, 603
Margorie Jane (Pasco),

1332
Margrette Amelia, 1641
Marie Elizabeth (Mockabee), 1332
Marilee Kay, 1170
Marion (Winkelblech), 1060
Martha Ann, 1579
Martha Kansas, 1869
Martin J, 614
Mary, 602, 729
Mary (Smith), 603
Mary A (Weiser), 1641
Mary Alice (Lones), 611
Mary Ann (Kephart), 1696
Mary C, 857
Mary Catherine (Lutz), 1170
Mary Elizabeth, 1090
Mary Emma, 372
Mary Lu Cena, 800
Matthew Gilbert, 1170
Maude Priscilla, 604
Megan Elizabeth, 574
Melissa Ann (Fisher), 602
Melvin Earl, 604
Melvin Jr, 604
Merrill F Jr, iv, 1010, 1160
Merrill Franklin, 1169
Merrill Franklin Jr, 1170
Merry (Eck), 604
Michael A, 613
Michael Dene, 574
Michael Elden, 1332
Mildred, 468, 619
Mildred Louise, 1332
Mildred May (Herman), 653
Millie Ann, 605
Minnie Gertrude (Malick), 733
Minnie May (Smith), 158
Nancy Ellen (Boring), 603
Nancy Jean (Furlow), 257
Naomi, 619
Nellie, 605
Nettie (Hall), 619
Nora (Kehl), 1012
Norman, 603
Olive Mae, 614
Otto M, 613
Pamela Dawn (Royer), 1170
Pamela Kay, 603
Pamela Lou, 612
Pamela Lucille, 603
Pamelia L (Gill), 857
Pammie Michele, 857
Patrice Kay, 613
Patricia (Culberton), 613
Patricia Ann, 574
Patty, 612
Pearl (Lewis), 612
Peggy, 612
Philip, 613
Rachel Louise, 1169
Randy, 709
Randy Scott, 654
Raymond, 620

Rebecca Ann, 41
Reuben Ray, 800
Rex, 709
Richard Allen, 604
Richard Dale, 573
Richard Franklin, 1170
Richard Linn, 857
Richard Samuel, 857
Ricky Dean, 574
Robert Dale, 574
Robert Reed, 614
Robert Tomson, 573
Roger Allan, 1333
Roland, 709
Romaine E, 709
Ronald Dale, 255
Ronald Eugene, 1332
Ronald Gene, 1332
Ruby Mae (Evans), 603
Russel J, 613
Russel J Jr, 613
Ruth, 612
Sallie Ann (Wiser), 1868
Sammy Dene, 574
Scott Eugene, 604
Selma (Amstutz), 612
Seth Daniel, 257
Shelby Lynn, 603
Shirley (Witmer), 653
Shirley Jean (Hering), 573
Shirley Jean (Herring), 546
son, 653
Stella M, 1688
Stephanie Ann, 573
Steven Lewis, 603
Sue Ann, 654
Sue Elaine, 613
Susan (Weiser), 1524
Terry Lee, 653
Theodore Gerald, 615
Thomas, 1535
Tillie (Ballinger), 603
Timothy Bruce, 1170
Timothy Paul, 613
Tobias, 602
Todd Lamar, 654
Tracy Lynn, 615
twin of Naomi, 619
Valleria, 1641
Velma Ann (Sparks), 574
Vera Claudine (Simmons), 800
Virgil, 615
Virginia (Arnold), 614
Virginia Beverly, 615
Walter Martin, 613
Wanda Jun, 615
Whitney K, 614
William, 733
William Elmer, 619
William G, 708
Wilmer John, 653
Zachary Wayne, 649

LONGABAUGH
John Rutherford Jr, 187
Marian Annabelle (Snyder), 187
Pamela, 187
Susan Jane, 187

LONGACRE
Anna K, 81

LONGANBACH
Betty Arlene, 502

LONGBERRY
Burel, 450
Edna Mary (Rowland), 450

LONGCOY
Rebecca Ann, 456

LONGENBERGER
Cynthia Kay, 1325

LONGENECKER
Beth Anne, 1343
Douglas Allan, 1343
Helen Antoinette (Boulanger), 1343
Julia Suzanne Myersburg (Ritter), 1343
Lee Carl, 1343
Margaret Florence (Stiely), 1342
Marilyn Ann, 1342
Patricia Aline, 1342
Samuel Manning, 1342

LONGER
Anthony Earl, 703
Odessa, 703

LONGFELLOW
Charles A, 721
Dan, 721
Donna (Corle), 721
Elaine (Smith), 721
Frank S, 721
James L, 721
Jo Anne, 721
Mary (Hepner), 721
Oren Homer, 721
Pearl E (Hepner), 721
Ralph H, 721
Thelma Marie, 721

LONGLEY
Fannie Adelaide, 126-127

LONGSHORE
Eliza (Spyker), 1452
John, 1452

LONGSON
Joann S, 1767

LONGSWORTH
Arabella (Lemon), 525
F L, 525

LOOD
Edward Kimmel Sr, 150
Melody Renne (Simmons), 150
Ruthann K, 149

LOOK
Alice Louisa (Ege), 292
Anna, 987
Bishop Smith, 292
Grace, 292
Henry, 292

LOOKER
Jed E, 922
Julia Elizabeth, 922
Julia Elizabeth (Weiser), 922
Linda M (Harkins), 922
Mervin Edward, 922
Susanne (Derr), 922

LOOMIS
Eddie W, 902
Francis Jr, 969
James, 902
Louise, 902
Lynne Janel (Morford), 969
Mary (Homan), 902

LUKE (continued)
Michael Elwin, 142
Pamela Joyce (Hughes), 142
Randy Evans, 142
Russell Elwin, 142
LUKENS
Linda Jeanette, 93
LUMADUE
Gertrude (Parks), 1704
James, 1704
Lenora (Wisor), 1708
Merrill, 1708
LUMADUR
Josephine, 1683
LUMPKIN
Margaretta Beck (Womelsdorf), 829
Margaretta L, 829
Murray B, 829
William, 829
William J, 829
LUNCEFORD
Edith, 1868
LUND
Alice Josephine, 1735
Elsie Marinda (Wieser), 1735
Hazel Irene, 1735
Jessie Bernice, 1735
Margaret Elna, 1735
Peter Henning, 1735
LUNDBERG
Arlene Louise (Caylor), 1323
James Lawrence, 1323
John David, 1323
Judy, 176
LUNDGREN
Gayle, 1262
Lynn (Nicholson), 1262
Robert Donald, 1262
LUNDQUIST
Gilbert Carl, 1292
Marion Josephine (Weiser), 1292
LUNSFORD
Christina Marie, 500
Michelle Lee (Roschie), 500
Tony Eugene, 500
LURTON
Margaret M, 1219
LUSE
Bessie May, 935
LUSH
Helen Margaret, 836
LUSK
--, 1823
A W, 1196
Ella, 1102
Jane (Kahl), 1196
Mary Emeline (Wiser), 1823
LUST
Mabel Louise Wurm, 848
LUSTER
Nancy Jane (Stahl), 733
Orvis, 733
LUTHER
Elmer R, 108
Helen Joahan, 1414
Ola Beatrice (Seeley), 108
Wilhelmina Lee (Selier), 1116

William Walton Jr, 1116
LUTTRELL
Edward Rex, 1262
Katie Ann, 1262
Sheree Lynn (Kahle), 1262
LUTZ
--, 1
-- (--), 97
Alva Henry, 99
Audrey June (Franklin), 99
Betty Jean, 1228
Brenda Anita, 282
Christopher Michael, 99
Dale R, 97
Dale Robert, 99
Earl R, 1601
Ethel Marie (Rusk), 1228
Fred, 1228
Harold Francis, 1228
Helen (Hamilton), 1228
Laura Kathryn, 99
Linda Jean (Harvey), 99
Marie (Weisser), 1601
Mary Catherine, 1170
Mary Jane, 1332
Peggy Louise, 1228
Robert Estal, 99
Vera Virginia (Whipple), 99
William Alva, 99
Winifred, 869
Winnie May (Walker), 99
LUZIER
Jennifer Lynn, 686
LYBARGER
Barbara E, 1880
LYDON
Charles Franklin, 1521
Henry Gilbert, 1521
Keith Christopher, 1521
Melisaa Sue, 1521
Robert Morton, 1521
Susan Diane (Allison), 1521
LYERLY
Linda, 324
LYKENS
Abigail R (Weiser), 1621
Arthur S, 1621
Bertha M, 1621
Esther L, 1621
Florence (Degler), 1621
Florence C, 1621
Francis (Schnable), 1621
Harold L, 1622
Helen E, 1621
J Vernon, 1621
Margaret L, 1621
Mary Clementine, 1621
Ruth Viola R, 1621
Samuel W, 1621
Samuel Z, 1621
LYLE
Esther Jane, 1828
LYNCH
--, 1831
Alletta Remsen, 337
Ann, 1474

Arley J (Weiser), 1294
Clara Metheany, 1215
Connie Louise Paine, 166
Dorothy, 349
Frances Katherine (Saxton), 1474
Ida Dorothy (Zane) Duckstead, 1474
Jane, 590
Kenderton Smith, 1474
Kenderton Smith II, 1474
Kenderton Smith III, 1474
Kimberly Ann, 1474
Michal Lauren, 1474
Stephanie Lynn (Krafchak), 1474
Sydney, 1294
LYNE
Helen Lynne, 836
LYNN
Amy Lyn (Clevenger), 451
Barbara Sue, 1142
Bryan, 451
Catherine Ann, 1142
Cody Wayne, 451
Deborah Ann, 1121
Doris (Weiser), 1142
Frank Warren, 1121
George M, 1142
Grace Elizabeth (Courtright), 1121
Jonathon Thomas, 1143
Kathy (Sims), 1142
Michael Clayton, 1142
Sandra Kay, 1121
Thomas Michael, 1142
LYON
Eva, 1011
M Pierce, 1649
LYONS
Anna Mae (Crossley), 680
Arthur H, 771
Betty Alene (Eyer), 680
Douglas John, 680
Elizabeth, 772
Elva, 468
Florence Corinne (Moyer), 771
Harold Joseph, 680
Harriet B, 1030
James Elwin, 645
James Elwin Jr, 645
Jane Lynn (Zessis), 1252
John Milton, 771
John Milton Jr, 772
Joseph Emory, 680
Linda Dawn, 680
Martha, 697
Mary Florence, 772
Mary N C (Fischer), 771
Patty Jane (Copenhaver), 701
Richard John, 680
Robert George, 772
Roy Wayne, 701
Sherry Ann (Bixler), 645
Tanya, 636
Virginia, 362
Wayne Harry, 701
William Girard, 1252

LYTER
Dorothy Ann, 716
Hilda Lavine, 862
Violet Delight, 927
LYTLE
Abraham, 1025
Charles Richard, 928
Elda, 743
Elizabeth (Snyder), 1014
Elizabeth A (Garman), 1025
Elizabeth F, 1025
Elmer Ellsworth, 731
Faye (Smith), 1025
Flossie, 731
Frances E, 1025
Franklin Pierce, 1025
George B, 1025
Gilbert Ambrose, 1025
Isaac, 731
John C, 1014
Larry Elwood, 1025
Leon Dennis, 1025
Luther, 1025
Martha, 1014, 1016
Martin Luther, 1025
Mildred Eleanor (Shepler), 928
Minnie T, 1025
Sarah A, 1025
Sarah Ellen (Renn), 1025
Sarah Malinda (Hepner), 731
Sula (Newman), 1025
Susan (Hopper), 731
Willard Kenneth, 1025
MABEE
Laura, 1260
Linda, 1260
Robert, 1260
Susan Pearl (McClintic), 1260
MABERSON
David John, 629
Joenita Ann (Eberly), 629
John, 629
Kimberly Kay, 629
MACCHESNEY
Carlton, 1340
Mable Alberta (Rabold), 1340
MACDONALD
Garnet, 559
MACE
Allen Woodworth, 644
Alverta Romaine, 645
Bernice Leona (Wiest), 650
Beverly Ann (Robinson), 646
Bonia marie (Muggio), 1536
Brian Christopher, 650
Bruce Lamar, 651
Carol Ann, 646
Carol Ann (Bartoo), 651
Carolyn, 651
Cora Elizabeth (Nice), 646
Cynthia, 1536
David, 1536
David Earl, 646
Della Jennie (Wiest), 644
Dennis Richard, 650

Earl Raymond, 646
Elizabeth Fietta, 646
Eugene Harry, 641
Guy Larry, 651
Heidi Marie, 646
Holly Michelle, 646
Irvin Earl, 646
James Benjamin, 650
Joey Raymond, 646
Kathryn Eleanore, 644
Kimberly Ann (Wyche), 646
Lynn Alan, 646
Mearl Freeman, 646
Mervin Mearl, 646
Michael Earl, 646
Michelle Yvonne (Richards), 645
Nicole Renee, 646
Patricia Ann (Koppenhaver), 650
Paula Jean, 651
Pauline Ida (Clark), 645
Randy Alan, 645
Roni Lyn (Sigel), 646
Russel Allen, 645
Ryan Andrew, 646
Sandra Elaine (Cooper), 641
Sheila Mae (Wiest), 646
Sherry Ann, 650
Suzanne Eileen, 651
Tammy Ann, 642, 646
Terry Lynn, 645
Timothy Scott, 646
Tonya Marie, 651
William, 1536
MACEDA
Alexander Joseph, 1278
John Joseph, 1278
Lori Lee (Seigworth), 1278
MACELREE
Lawrence, 303
Mary Louise (Stokes), 303
MACEVITT
Amanda Michaelene, 1556
Anne Loretta, 1555
Christopher Hatch, 1556
James Michael III, 1555
MACGILL
Darlene Cecile, 642
Dorothy Joyce (McConnell), 642
Elva Darlene (Buffington), 642
Joseph Michael Begani, 642
Leonard, 642
Rebecca Louise, 642
MACHUSAK
Catharine May (Epler), 743
Michael, 743
MACIAS
Amy Marie, 589
Elizabeth Ann (Hocker), 589
Mary Ann, 589
Victor Frank, 589
MACINTIRE
Aleen, 1070

MACINTIRE
(continued)
Bruce, 1070
Frances Alverta, 1070
Frank Edgar, 1069
Frank Edgar III, 1070
Frank Edgar IV, 1070
Grace Keyser, 1069
Greg, 1070
Jennifer, 1070
Judith Aleen (Brull), 1070
Mary Louise, 1070
Miranda Ruth (Bohn), 1069
Sarah Miranda, 1069
Scott, 1070
Susan Anna, 1070
Wilson Filmore, 1070
MACINTOSH
Bessie May, 1179
MACINTYRE
Louise, 252
MACISAAC
Cheryl Lorraine, 394
Dawn Eleanor, 394
Eleanor Lorraine (Meeker), 393
Martin, 393
Roger Clyde, 394
Wayne Martin, 394
MACK
Anna (Weisser), 1609
Annette Marie, 1264
Annie, 930
David, 1264
Jesse, 1264
Karl-Friedrich, 1609
Marlee, 1264
Michaelyn (Smith), 1264
MACKAY
Agnes, 324
James, 1014
Marie (Wilson), 1014
MACKER
Emma, 1043
MACKEY
Lillie, 1845
Mae, 565
Thelma, 1367
MACKLIN
Harold Raymond, 1141
Kate, 467
Sharma Joan, 1141
Zella Mae (Schaffner), 1141
MACLEAN
Geneva Lydia, 790
MACMALLEN
Leila H, 918
MACMONAGEL
Marie, 420
MACNAB
John, 1633
Sara Mae (Smith), 1633
MACOM
Heather Lynette, 569
Howard Eugene, 569
Jill Ann, 569
Patricia Lou (Smith), 569
MACPHERSON
Nancy Lee, 774
MACY
Anne Fitzgerald (McKinney), 173
Charles Thomas, 173

Daniel Wayne, 173
Judith Ann (Hilmer), 173
Mark Douglas, 173
Nancy Strode (Haines), 173
MADDEN
Bernard J, 820
Bruce George, 779
Elizabeth (Cancila), 779
George James, 779
Lydia Olive (Knecht), 431
Maureen Blee, 382
Minerva Jane (Norman), 820
Reed Douglas, 779
Stephen James, 779
Thomas Francis, 431
MADEIRA
Emma R, 1559
MADER
-- (--), 911
Abraham, 905
Albert Victor, 908
Amos, 906-907
Anna, 907
Anna Catharine (Weiser), 906
Anna Mae (Snyder), 908
Beulah (--), 914
Brenda K (--), 908
Catharine, 905-907, 914
Catharine (--), 905
Catharine (Hain), 905
Catharine Jane, 906
Charles Leroy, 908
Christiana (--), 905
Clara, 912
Clarence Monroe, 908
Cora, 912
Daniel, 906
Daniel E, 907
Daniel Tobias, 907
David, 905, 907
Eddie, 913
Elenor, 906
Eliza Jane (Hummel), 907
Elizabeth, 905-907, 911
Elizabeth (Hain), 905
Elizabeth (Zarker), 907
Elsie, 906
Elsie Naomi, 910
Emeline, 906
Emiline, 907
Emmett, 914
Esther, 905
Esther Elizabeth, 910
Florence (Thompson), 911
Grace (Sloat), 908
Harriet, 907, 914
Henry, 911
Isaac, 905
Jacob, 905
Jane, 906
Jestina, 906-907
John Christiana, 914
John Earl, 908
John Jr, 905
Leah, 906
Litty Margaret, 906
Lydia, 913
Mabel V (Kuntz), 908

Maria Elizabeth, 906
Maria Lucinda, 906-907
Mary Ann, 914
May, 905
Meda O, 1084
Minnie Ellen, 907
Moses, 906
Moses Weiser, 906
Nancy Jane, 908
Paul Richard, 911
Rae Suzanne, 908
Rebecca Louise, 908
Robert, 907
Robert Paul, 908
Ruth May, 908
Sarah, 906
Sarah (--), 905
Sarah Ann, 906
Susan, 907
Susannah, 906
Veronica (Warner), 907
William, 907
William George, 908
William Raymond, 908
MADER/ MEADER
Christiana (--), 905
Daniel, 905
John, 905
MADERA
Mary, 114-115
MADGE
Helen, 1345
MADOLE
E Gladys, 1161
MAE
Edna, 518
Freda, 525
MAECHLING
Andrea Leigh, 1139
MAENTEL
Jacob, 1459
MAGEE
Edward, 1258
Evelyn (Showers), 1258
J Sample, 287
James Sean, 287
Meghan Wagner, 287
Molly Wagner, 287
Suzanne Dawson (Wagner), 287
MAGES
Christy Noel, 543
MAGGI
Joshua Andrew, 373
Ken, 373
Mary Elizabeth (Lombardi), 373
Rebecca Lynn, 373
MAGNESS
Sara Pearl (Showers), 1258
Willis, 1258
MAGNO
Christine Lou Ann (Taylor), 1239
Jinno, 1239
Jinno Antonia, 1239
Joseph Cristiano, 1239
MAGRAW
Kathy Ann (Shollenberger), 131
Richard, 131
MAGRINI
Patricia Jean, 1277
MAGUIRE
Constance Marie, 1530

Donald Matthew, 803
Frank Raum, 1508
Frank Z, 1508
Julie Jo (Fair), 803
Matthew Edward, 803
Maude (Raum), 1508
MAHAFFEY
Vida Tereasa, 1696
MAHAN
Amanda Beth, 1421
Anna Melinda, 1421
Betty Frances, 1315
Clarence, 1314
Clarence Everett, 1315
Clrence Everett, 1315
Diane Louise (Gluckert), 1421
Drucilla Pauline, 1314
Elsie Hazel (Crouch), 1315
Ethel Viola, 1314
Florence Viola (Croy), 848
Florence Viola (Kennel) Weikert, 1315
Gary Lee, 1421
James Edgar, 1314
Jennie Frances (Rabold), 1314
John Luther, 1314
John Luther Jr, 1314
Joyce Ann, 1314
Karen Sue, 1421
Minnie Elizabeth (Weidle) Baker, 1314
Ray, 848
Robert Donald, 1314
Roger Lee, 1314
Sean Patrick, 1421
Wilbur Gene, 1314
MAHER
Gloria Deneen, 1212
MAHLE
Bernice Eleanor, 1265
Evelyn Naomi, 817
Harrison Lewis, 1265
Neoskelita Pearl (Kahle), 1265
MAHLER
Beverly Rozella, 265
Evelyn Lillian, 444
MAHON
Lilette, 214
MAHONEY
Anna, 639
Carolyn Ruth, 574
Ethan Joel, 538
George T, 1751
Joyce Lynn, 615
Linda Sue (Frangowlakis) Krueger, 1751
Marcia Lynn (Miller), 538
Rolland, 538
Seth Raul, 538
MAIDEN
Vintonne A, 1562
MAIER
--, 1
Alma Sue (Craft), 53
Beverly Anne, 53
Brenda, 1020
Camille (Reed), 53
Clara, 56
Eliza Eugenia, 56
Eugene Jerome, 53
Evangeline Frances, 57
Frank Beeks, 53

Frank Beeks III, 53
Frank Beeks Jr, 53
Gertrude, 54
Grace Andres, xi, 33, 56
Grace Hildagarde Beazell (Andres), 55
Harriet Cornelia, 57
Henry Willey, 53, 55
Inez, 53
Inez (Johnson), 53
Janie Margueritte, 54
Jean (Lawrence), 53
Manie, 55
Marguerete Eliza (Willey), 53
Maria Elizabeth, 54
Marie (Beeks), 53
Melissa Catherine, 54
Miriam Camille, 53
Patricia Jane, 55
Peter August, 53-54, 56
Susan Tynes, 53
Virginia Lee, 56
Virginia Lyle (Vandeventer), 53
Willey, 54
Willey Johnson, 53
William Craft, 53
MAIER/ZEIHER
Barbara, 6
MAILEN
Caroline (Watson), 205
Tyson Harvey, 205
MAIN
-- (--), vi, 33, 361, 363, 375, 429
Carl, vi, 33, 361, 363, 375, 429
Charlene, 473
Florence Eugenia (Willey), 37
Jessie Florence, 114-115
Jonas J, 37
MAINES
Charles, 474
Charles Edward, 474
Elveretta, 1685
Geneva (Wisor), 1710
Jacquelyn Marie, 474
Megan Lee, 474
Stephanie Lynne, 474
Sylvia Ann (Dorobek), 474
Wayne, 1710
MAINHART
Mary Edith, 1115
MAINS
Louis, 555
Sarah May (Young), 555
MAIR
Gunther, 320
Julia, 320
Lore (von Wasielewski), 320
Waltraud, 320
MAIRS
Melba Jean, 616
MAITZEN
Denise, 1545
MAIZE
Donna Irene, 365
MAJOR
Diana Louise (Kirsten), 1465
Marie Irene (Heiges),

MARTIN (continued)
Justin Re, 1210
Karen Oakley (Staub), 331
Katharine Louise (Weisser), 1602
Katharine Weisser, xi
Kathleen Mae (Lau), 250
Kathleen Noel, 1602
Keith Scott, 1039
Kellie Ann, 1207
Kenneth, 754
Kenneth James, 1209
Kenneth Sylvester, 1208
Kent Gordon, 1207
Kimberly, 1210
Kimberly (--), 1209
Kimberly Joy, 1200
Larry Dean, 1210
Laura (Pollet), 151
Laura J, 1884
Laura Jane (Schwartz), 248
Laura S, 238
Lee, 799
Lela, 458
Lela Pearl, 1206
Leroy Newton, 1210
Lillian (Rabold), 1315
Linda Lee, 1209
Lisa, 1496
Lisa (Switzer), 1207
Lorene, 1377
Lori Ellen, 1209
Lori Kay, 1232
Lorraine Ann, 1210
Lynn, 1806
Lynn Michelle, 1211
Malcenia Jane, 1159
Manford Adrian, 1207
Manuel Walter, 1210
Marcella (Aslin), 1207
Marcy, 1209
Margaret (Meyer), 1208
Margaret E, 1233
Margaret Julia, 1293
Marilyn (Butterfield), 1209
Marjorie (Nielson), 69
Marsha Jean (McFarland), 586
Martha Ann, 150
Martha E, 744
Martha Elizabeth, 1658
Mary (Calhoun), 1206
Mary Louise (Donaldson), 1207
Mary Weiser, 1466
Matthew, 107
Mattie O (Shaffer), 1209
Maureen Alice (Keller), 1211
Mildred Ann (Brodland), 1210
Mildred Cecil (Green), 1207
Mildred I, 711
Mildred Joan, 535
Molly, 1207
Mona Moss, 1696
Muriel, 515
Myrtle (Wiser), 1816
Nancy (Evans), 1209
Nancy Lee, 69
Nellie Sarah Catherine

(Steward), 372
Nettie (Seamans), 113
Noel Allen, 1207
Noel Daniel, 1207
Noel Paul, 1207
Olice N, 1816
Opal Arola, 1206
Palma Marcella, 1138
Pamela May, 1211
Paul Adrian, 1207
Pauline (Shultz), 1208
Peter Kim, 69
Phyllis Anne (Sellards), 69
Phyllis Maxine (Harbison), 1231
Rachael, 1207
Rachael Leigh, 1210
Randy Floyd, 1231
Raymond Dean, 1210
Rebecca, 1207
Rebecca Jane (Farley), 1039
Richard George, 1210
Robert James, 1207
Robert Wesley, 1206
Robert Wesley III, 1208
Robert Wesley Jr, 1208
Roberta (Shultz), 1207
Rosalie (--), 1210
Rosco A, 113
Rose Ann (Newman), 1210
Rose Ann Almeda, 1211
Roy, 1206
Ruby (Schoonover), 1210
Ruth (Cunningham), 1210
Ruth M, 1211
Sadie Grace, 1210
Sally Helen, 1602
Samuel, 238, 248
Samuel James Jr, 249
Sandra Ann, 249
Sarah, 1208
Sarah Catharine Eyster (Weiser), 1466
Scott Matthew, 1210
Sean, 1209
Shela May, 585
Shirley (--), 151
Shirley Margaret (Warner), 1602
Stacey Jane, 1207
Stanley, 250
Stella Mae (Wiser), 1838
Steven Wayne, 1209
Stuart, 1207
Susan (Linderman), 1040
Susan Lynn (Rosinbum), 1210
Susan Pauline, 1211
Suzanne Christine, 69
Sylvester Newton, 1206
Tanner Lee, 1209
Templeton Willis, 69
Templeton Willis Jr, 69
Terry, 1210
Terry Lee, 1208
Theresa Rosann, 586
Thomas Haney, 1209
Timothy Dale, 151
Violet Keith, 1209

Virginia Almeda, 1208
Willard Franklin, 150
Willard Herbert, 151
William, 113
William Alder, 1040
William Franklin, 151
William H, 151
Zelma Lavone (Hocker), 585
Zelpha, 1586
MARTINCIC
Donna Louise, 770
MARTINDALE
Donna Marie (Lombardi), 372
Dorothy Grace, 373
Leah Michelle, 373
Loy Craig, 373
Timothy Craig, 373
MARTINE
Eric Arthur, 1115
Freda Ann (Foltz), 1114
James Edgar, 337
Julia Edgar (Rodman), 337
Kayla Marie, 1115
Michael Joseph, 1114
MARTINEZ
Andrea Elizabeth, 489
Angela Marie, 489
Christopher Keith, 489
Isidore Hinojosa III, 489
Lori Beth, 489
Lusindo, 882
Roberto Andres, 882
Robin Kristi (Wise), 882
Simona, 1379
Terry Lynn (Brauer), 489
MARTINS
Karl W, 866
Pearl E (Wilson), 866
Sylvia P, 866
William, 866
MARTRATT
Arthur, 513
Arthur Jr, 513
Connie (McCormick), 513
Cornelius, 513
Edwin, 513
Myra E (Akerman), 513
Ruth (Ross), 513
Vonnie, 513
MARTYNA
Jamie Marie, 1293
Kristy Leigh, 1293
Mary Martha (Weiser), 1293
Ronald, 1293
MARTZ
Bertha M (Bohner), 706
Clarence E, 706
Eben, 784
Gail, 1065
Laura Jane (Fegley), 784
Mary Henrietta (Phillips), 706
Patricia Jane (Murphy), 706
Paula Jo, 625
Rosa, 730
Russell Eugene, 706

Stella Tryphena, 702
Sterline Palmer, 706
Sterling, 638
Valeria Maxine, 706
Valerie, 1884
MARUNICK
Carly Erin, 488
John Thomas, 488
Kurt Carson, 488
Kyle Paul, 488
Wilma Jean (Jaworski), 488
MASCARELLO
Lee, 822
Martha Jean (Worrel), 822
MASCIOLA
Anthony Joseph, 1304
David Leroy Linn, 1304
Denise Marie, 1304
Mary Lou (Rupert), 1304
MASEMOU
Betty Lou, 858
MASH
Nellie, 880
Shirley Ann, 225
MASON
--, 1553
-- (--), 1883
Andrew Hugh, 44
Angie, 565
Annes, 1316
Bessie Elsie, 520
Bill, 602
Bradley Martin, 458
Charles Hugh, 44
Clarence Virgil, 457
daughter, 457
Dick, 565
Douglas Gene, 457
Emeline (Fossinger), 457
Eva, 1345
Everett P, 122
Faye M, 458
Frances, 1884
Frances Anita (Cochran), 44
Frances Lea (Murry), 457
Frances Mary, 1356
Francis Aarn, 458
Francis C, 458
Francis Douglas, 458
Francis Vernon, 458
Gerald LeRoy, 457
Gerda (McClintic), 1260
Grace Myrtle (Stingly), 271
Ida Mae, 457
James A, 457
John F, 459
John Robert, 457
Lela (Martin), 458
Leonard M, 1260
Lilas (Wolverton), 458
Linda, 603
Linda Cheryl (Basler), 458
Linda Kay (McCarroll), 44
Louise Emaline, 457
Mamie (Harris), 458
Mary Beatrice (Stahl), 602
Mary Elizabeth, 44

Mary Emeline, 459
Molly Ann, 458
Nancy Jean (Care), 457
Nancy Jo (Weiser), 122
Nettie Grace, 459
Ollie Bele, 457
Richard, 1883
Richard Eugene, 457
Richard Eugene Jr, 457
Richard Taswell, 457
Robert Paul, 122
Shirley, 540
son, 457
Stella (McGuigan), 1553
Timothy Farrin, 458
Trudy Mar, 122
Vernon Carrin, 458
Wanda (Banter), 565
Wanda Lorraine, 458
William Walker, 271
MASSARI
Judy, 1538
MASSEY
-- (--), 62
Elizabeth Ann, 65
Etoile, 183
Henry V Jr, 62
Henry Vogdes Jr, 65
Louise Cummings (Renn), 65
MASSLER
Debra Ann (Hendricks), 648
Karl Richard, 648
Richard, 648
Riki Lea, 648
MAST
Catharine Ann, 1566
MASTEN
Jeannie, 352
MASTERMAN
Carrie Emogene (Weiser), 402
Hale Clare, 402
MASTERS
Cathy Diane, 385
MASTERSON
Mary, 1038
MASTRIC
Patricia Ann, 900
MASTUSON
Julia, 602
MATALONAS
Alphonse Joseph, 659
Diane Louise, 659
Fay Frances (Klinger), 659
Gerald Klinger, 659
MATEER
Carolyn Whitaker (Snyder), 187
Elizabeth, 187
Joseph, 187
MATHE
Derek Scott, 93
Hannah Nicole, 93
Lindsey Rae, 93
Riki Ann (Grosch), 93
Scott, 93
MATHEIS
Delia, 1867
MATHENY
Anna Mildred (Black), 1124
Frank, 203
Ivan Maywood, 1123
Madlyn Louise (Ross), 203

MATHENY (continued)
Mark Hummell, 1123
Phyllis, 1448
Richard Newton, 1123
Thomas Richard, 1123
MATHEWS
Barbara (Kephart), 1685
Caroline Smith, 329
Catharine Frederica, 328
Catharine Frederica (White), 328
Clarence, 329
Clemence Florence, 329
Frederic Chapman, 328
Frederica Catharine, 329
Jacqueline Sue, 1449
John S, 328
Kate (Chapman), 328
Louise (Jerrems), 328
Louise Jerrems Muhlenberg, 328
Margaretta Muhlenberg, 329
Richard, 1685
Robert Waite, 328
MATHIAS
Audrey Elene, 1148
Bertha Alice, 1147
Claire, 734
Clark, 1130
Evelyn Marie, 1147
Holly, 1130
James, 1130
Lillian E, 1850
Marcine, 1130
Margaret Elizabeth (Alspaugh), 1147
Marshall, 1130
Melba Harryette (Wiser), 1851
Mildred (Alspach), 1130
Robert Bruce, 1851
Roy Silas, 1147
Sadie Marie (Semler), 1147
Silas S, 1147
MATLOCK
Lawrence, 817
Myrtie Almira (Womeldorf), 817
MATRANGA
Sonja Nichole, 35
MATREY
Christopher Brown, 1007
Paul, 1007
Terry (Kahl), 1007
MATSON
Cora M (Curley), 110
Darlene Joy, 189
Donna Jean, 189
Harry, 1235
Lois Dorothy (Snyder), 189
Minnie A (Shawkey), 1235
Paul B, 110
Victor, 189
MATTER
Bettie Jane (Noll), 1064
Catharine (Koppenheffer), 710
Dean R, 1084
Earl, 1064

Faye, 678
Helen May (Brungart), 1084
Ida Selena, 710
Jacqueline Lynn, 690
Jacqueline Lynn (Matter), 690
Jenna Lee, 690
Joyce Marlene (Kocher), 690
Natalie Lynne, 690
Randy Ray, 690
Ray R, 690
Robin Rachel, 690
Romaine Irene, 690
Sally Elizabeth, 691
Sandra Ann, 690
Sarah C, 685
Susan Jean, 690
William, 710
MATTERN
Carol Ella, 687
Edward Allen, 856
Edward Gerard, 856
Evan Andrew, 856
Janet Louise (Irwin), 856
Kathleen Ann (Marshall), 856
Nancy Lee, 856
Pamela, 1252
Patricia Ann (Shettel), 856
Rosalind, 832
Susan Kay, 856
MATTHEW
Sky Lyn, 1772
MATTHEWS
Bess R, 1493
Carlene Denise, 383
Carol Alice, 1500
David Barry, 689
David Paul, 689
Effie C (Moore), 1436
Elmira W (Weiss), 1350
Elwood C, 449
Francis Brooke, 816
Fred H, 1350
George, 829
George Wheeler, 829
Jacob P, 1350
Julia, 829
Lisa Ann, 819
Marcia Frances, 1223
Marilyn Kae (Radel), 689
Michael Steven, 689
Myrta Manetta (Weiser), 449
Ruth, 829
Ruth Stewart (Womelsdorf), 829
Sara Jane, 429
Tom, 1436
Wanda Lynette (Beary), 816
MATTHIAS
Adah Viola, 1521
Benjamin Franklin, 1519
Emma E, 1520
Fred, 1520
Julia Etchberger, 1520
Karen Nancy, 1191
Kathryn M, 1520
Lulu Gertrude, 1519
Margaret, 1521
Melissa (Etschberger),

1519
Wilda Grace, 1521
MATTHIES
Bonnie Lael (Bettilyon), 781
Kenneth Neil, 781
Robyn Michelle, 781
MATTINGLY
--, 1791
Betty Ann (Wiser), 1791
Dale Ellis, 586
Dick, 1012
Hope, 1012
Mary (Kehl), 1012
Pamela, 1790
Yvonne Maye (Thomas), 586
MATTIS
Esther Miriam, 642
Nina Marie, 1337
MATTOX
Inez Blanche, 392
MATUNAS
Jaclyn Renea (Johns), 129
Jason Robert, 129
Robert C, 129
MATZ
David Mohn, 902
Dorothy Ann Smith (Hogge), 608
Evelyn Faye (Klingler), 608
George, 902
George Frederick, 902
Helen (Mohn), 902
Helen Kathryn, 902
Jane Shirley, 902
John, 608
Louise Marie, 239
Margaret Ann, 902
Rhonda Lynnette, 608
Susan Jane, 655
Thomas Arnold, 608
Urania D, 902
MAUCH
Judy Lynn, 497
MAUCK
Mary, 1367
Sarah Lydia, 1391
MAUDE
Julie Ann (Earnest), 1480
Kevin, 1480
Shala Marie, 1480
MAUDSLEY
Margaret, 944
MAUER
Donald Jerome, 1316
Jerome, 1316
Lulu Viola (Rabold) Klump, 1316
Mary Nell (Hyman), 1317
MAUGHMER
Ernest, 470
Mark, 470
Noel, 470
Shirley Ann (Frey), 470
MAUK
Lovel Constance (Bowsher), 581
Ruth, 520
William E, 581
MAURER
Carl Mecker, 354
Cindy, 679

David, 679
Eva, 813
Joanna Claire (Bennetch), 354
John, 679
Mae Faith (Lenker), 679
Teresa, 679
MAUS
Earl E, 673
Ella Louise, 1352
Eve, 23
Jennie Majetta (Koppenhaver), 673
MAUST
Christophre Allen, 711
Gary Eugene, 711
Judy Lee (Hommel), 711
Steven Robert, 711
MAXEY
Audrey Mae, 234
David Randall, 234
Davis Theotie, 1752
Dorothy May (Linkenhoker), 1752
Dreama Beth, 1752
Elizabeth Ann (Key), 1752
Garret Allen, 1752
James Davis, 1752
JoAnn Lois, 234
Judith Ann, 1449
Karen Virginia, 1752
Lois Margaret (Manon), 234
Loren Ogden, 1752
Ronald William, 234
William Ralph, 234
MAXFIELD
Kelton, 1439
Sophia (Whitaker), 1439
MAXSON
Carol Bernice, 127
Dale Melvin, 127
Eldeena Bernice (Willoughby), 127
Helen Rita (Morin), 127
Marc Mitchell, 127
Michael Melvin, 127
Michelle Marie, 127
Ray Melvin, 127
MAXWELL
--, 1578
Anthony Walter, 1337
Bessie Viola, 1336
Carrie May (Highfield), 1338
Carry Luella, 1335
Charles Aquilla, 1334
Charles Woodrow, 1337
Charlotte L, 51
Clare Jean (Bartlett), 1338
Clarence Thurman, 1338
Daisy May, 1335
Daniel Eugene, 1337
David Charles, 1337
Debra Leigh, 1338
Doris mable, 1336
Douglas Bartlett, 1338
Earl Victor, 1338
Ernest Victor, 1338
Estele Lee, 1338
Esther Ruby, 1337

Florence Marie, 1338
Glena Viola (Smith), 1338
Harold Glen, 1338
Harry Wilson, 1336
Helen (McKee), 1337
Ileen (Banter), 564
Larry Lee, 1338
Lisa, 564
Lisa Marie, 1639
Lucille Jean, 1337
Lwell Edison, 1337
Margery Allen, 1338
Margery Estelle (Hathaway), 1338
Mark Alsworth, 1337
Mary M, 222
Michael Lowell, 1337
Minnie (Hahn), 1578
Nina Marie (Mattis), 1337
Norma Elizabeth (Buchanan), 1337
Phyllis Irene, 1337
Ramon Lee, 1337
Robert Byron, 1337
Robert Dillion, 470
Ruth Naomi (Patten), 1336
Sallie (Rabold), 1334
Thomas Wilson, 1337
Treva G (Miller), 1337
Violet Elizabeth (Baker), 1337
Vivian Madge (Fenner), 1338
William, 564
MAY
Colt William, 496
Cynthia Elizabeth (Shockley), 496
Elizabeth, 521
Jean Vaughan, 1098
Joseph Lynn, 119
Joseph Lynn II, 119
Loretta, 369
Lucy Jane (Krigbaum), 119
Shannon Leigh, 119
Timothy, 496
MAYBEE
John, 1586
Matilda (Pickard), 1586
MAYER
--, 1579
Carolyn, 945
Doris Janis (Cosgrove), 945
Hans, 9
J K, 945
Jane, 1728
Monica Yvonne, 882
Myrtle (Pickard), 1579
Raymond Earl, 945
MAYER/ZEIHER
Barbara, 7-8
Hans, 8
Margarethe (Hainckh), 8
MAYES
Jane Ann (Cole), 572
Jennifer Sue, 572
Nancy Jean, 933
Robert Allen, 572
MAYFIELD
Alice Naomi, 1187
MAYLAN
Elizabeth, 302

MAYNARD
Brenda Jo, 574
Helen Kathleen
(Eppley), 880
James Edward, 880
James Edward Jr, 880
Nancy Ann, 539
MAYNOR
Dorothy, 1066
MAZE
Anna (Earnest), 1487
Jacob, 1487
Sara, 1242
MAZIAR
Anna Lee (Tomlinson),
1431
Lucia Diane, 1431
Mark Gregory, 1431
Martha Inez, 1431
Stepan, 1431
MAZZA
Cindy, 1200
MCADAMS
Shawn David, 925
Susan Ann (Johnson),
925
MCAFEE
Howard, 1530
MCAFEE
Jennie, 188
MCAFEE
Margaret Helen
(Weiser), 1530
MCAFEE
Mary Jeanne, 219
Nancy, 872
MCALARNEY
Annetta Lou, 1368
Helen Pearl (Brickley),
1368
Monique Kay, 1368
Walter, 1368
MCARTHUR
Allen, 111
Leila L (Akins), 111
MCATEE
Constance Marie
(Maguire), 1530
Donald Robert, 1530
Joan, 535
Mary Priscilla (Weiser)
Zerbe, 1530
Patricia, 1531
Suzanne Marie, 1530
William, 1530
MCAVOY
Joan, 1556
MCBEAN
Angus, 69
Dorothea Francis
(Raymond), 69
MCBEE
Rebecca, 1665
Sarah C, 1664
MCBRIDE
Andrew, 609
Catherine (Cotterall),
1541
Doris (Kindle), 609
Dwight Warren, 609
Eileen J, 135
Frank, 1259
James Dean, 609
Janice (Weiser), 212
Jean, 1259
Jeffery Lynn, 609
Joseph, 1541
Lorena, 190
Michael, 212

Randall Lee, 609
Vera Myrtle (Mong),
1259
Walter, 212
MCBROOM
Ida, 1868
MCBRY
Mitchell, 466
Willella Zulah
(Binkley), 466
MCBURNEY
Lois Irene, 373
MCCABE
Edward, 1267
Enia Mae, 1438
Eva Elizabeth (Weiser),
1267
Maureen B, 832
MCCAIG
Anna Gladys, 727
Arthur Jacob, 727
Bernice Krupp
(McKune), 727
Francis, 727
Francis (--), 727
Ida (Mangle), 727
Marion Emma
(Hepner), 727
William Blaine, 727
William Blaine Jr, 727
MCCAIN
Boyd Ellsworth, 1126
Bruce David, 1126
Dorothy Elnora, 1126
Dorothy Rose (Stanley),
666
Ellsworth, 1126
Harone Marvin, 666
Helen Courtright
(Roller), 1126
James Robert, 1127
Joann (Flynn), 1126
John Stephen, 1127
Laura Theresa, 371
Norma (Scarbarry),
1126
Pamela Sue, 1126
Paul Edward, 1126
Paula Maureen, 1126
MCCALL
Brian Kenneth, 1449
Ella Irene, 1306
Emma, 1234
Jame Ann (Shidler),
1449
MCCALLISTER
John, 1585
Juanita, 1781
Mary, 1585
MCCALLUM
Catherine Love, 1624
MCCALLY
Perna, 560
MCCAMMON
Audry Lynn, 1187
Barbara Jean
(Carpenter), 1187
David Wayne, 1187
Douglas Eugene, 1187
Roy Lester, 1187
MCCANDLESS
G C, 1294
Helen (Weiser), 1294
Judy, 1214
MCCANDLISH
-- (Rick), 1561
Lindsay, 1561
MCCANN
Anthony, 1213

David Allen, 1213
Dorothy Marie (Kahle),
1213
Gary Edward, 1213
Gayle Marie, 1213
Jennifer Leigh, 1213
Joy Marie, 1213
Linda Gayle (Black),
1213
Marcus Kahle, 1213
Margaret Ann, 1280
Renata (Dudley), 1213
Susan (Fortson), 1213
William Joseph Jr,
1213
MCCARLY
Docia Dorothy (Wiser),
1810
Virgil A, 1810
MCCARROLL
Linda Kay, 44
MCCARTHY
Barbara Lee, 1399
Helen, 1373
Mary Frances (Willey),
39
Patricia, 39
Patrick, 39
Thomas Craig, 39
MCCARTNEY
--, 1671
Florence (Wiser), 1671
Fred, 1671
MCCARTY
Fern, 619
Harriet (Richter), 68
Harry, 68
MCCAULEY
Albert, 259
Bertha Margaret, 258
Christopher Michael,
1250
Ella Mary, 258
Ellen Louise (Brehm),
258
George Robert, 259
Kathryn Ann (Kahle),
1250
Kenneth Robert, 1250
Larry Lee, 1250
Louis, 259
Mark Edward, 1250
Melissa Susan (Adams),
258
Samuel Patterson, 259
Sully Reeves, 325
William Albert, 258
William Benjamin, 258
MCCLAIN
Edward, 576
Grace (Wilson), 576
Judy, 563
MCCLANHAN
Evelyn, 465
MCCLEAN
Sarah Maginley, 350
MCCLELLAND
George W, 1244
Lulu Maude (Kahle),
1244
Mark, 1244
MCCLENAHEN
Jeanne Scott, 739
MCCLENDON
Vicki Ann, 311
MCCLENNAHAN
Margaret, 1076
MCCLINTIC
Carol Lynn, 1260

Caroly Lynn, 1260
Gerda, 1260
Gerda Irene, 1260
Harold Kahle, 1259
Irene Louise (Hedlind),
1259
Maria Pearl (Kahl),
1259
Marie Louise, 1260
Michelle, 1260
Susan Pearl, 1260
William Kahle, 1260
William Lynn, 1259
MCCLINTOCK
--, 1592
Fay, 1047
Mathilda (Barnett),
1592
Traci Sue, 143
MCCLOUD
Agnes (Factor), 364
Donald F, 364
Dorothy (Fox), 364
Ethel, 364
Manetta, 364
Mary Manetta, 364
Priscilla, 364
Sarah Catharine
(Bauder), 364
William B, 364
William L, 364
MCCLOY
Jean Louise, 483
MCCLUNE
Cassandra (Weiser),
1417
Eliza Ann, 1417
Florinda Susan, 1417
Thomas, 1417
Weiser Criley, 1421
MCCLUNEY
Mark, 1297
Meagan Lynn, 1297
Tracey Lynne (Brosch),
1297
MCCLURE
Bill, 1447
Catharine, 1496
Helen Kathryn
(Snyder), 187
John Wallace, 187
Marian Carol, 187
Mary Alice (Gaddis),
1447
MCCLURG
Benjamin F, 523
Eva Dean, 524
Fern (Seber), 524
Haleyon, 524
Lessel W, 524
Lola Mae, 523
Luetta (Riggs), 523
Rachel Jane (Shafer),
524
MCCOLLOCH
Charles Asa, 201
Edna Blanch (Ross),
201
Frances Roberta, 201
Henry Ross, 201
MCCONELL
Mary Catharine
(Weiser), 1355
Robert, 1355
MCCONNAUGHEY
Thelma, 1027
MCCONNEL
--, 1270

MCCONNELL
--, 1356
Barbara Anne, 1360
Carol, 64
Catharine Weiser, 1404
Catherine (Weiser),
1360
Catherine Amelia, 1355,
1360
Cecilia, 1360
Dorothy Joyce, 642
Elizabeth (Schaeffer),
1356
Ellen, 1358
Esther, 1355, 1360
Esther Margaret, 1356
Evan, 88, 1355-1356
Frederick Augustus,
1355-1356
James, 1355, 1360
John Schaeffer, 1356
Kathy, 64
Louisa, 1355-1356
Maria, 1355-1356
Mary Catherine
(Weiser), 1356
Mary Susan, 1358
Mildred (Wilhelm), 64
Morris, 1355-1356
Oliver Robert Reily,
1356, 1360
Peter Muhlenberg
Weiser, 1355, 1360
Rebecca, 1355 1356
Rebecca (Noecker),
1360
Robert, 64, 1356, 1360
Sarah (Christ), 1356
Sarah (Miller), 1360
Sarah Elizabeth, 1358
MCCOOL
Mary Elizabeth, 1006
MCCORD
Amanda Ella, 245
Gertrude, 670
MCCORMICK
--, 549
Cody, 1040
Connie, 513
Daniel Martin, 1065
Ethel E (Lee), 549
Francis D, 1188
Goldie Lucretia
(Stover), 1065
infant son, 549
John F, 1065
John Franklin, 1065
John Lee, 1040
Kirk William, 1065
Kristee Lee, 1040
Laurie Jo (Wismer),
1040
Lisa Kay (Branson),
1065
Marilyn Kay (Sehiltz),
1065
Marjorie Lynn, 1065
Mildred Elizabeth, 810
Nancy Sidney (Duncan),
1188
Patricia Ann (Aechard),
1065
Patricia Jane, 352
Russell William, 1065
Susan, 859
Susanne (Frechette),
1065
Trevor Ryan, 1065
Wanda, 1781

MCGOWIN (continued)
Edward R, 470
Grace (Roy), 470
Harold H, 471
Henry H, 470
James Henry, 468
Myrtle Eleanor, 469
other daughters, 471
MCGRADY
Ann, 371
Anna (Dresbach), 1430
William, 1430
MCGREGOR
Bobbie Jo, 652
Bud, 1232
Carolyn Sue (Wiser)
Dotson, 1819
Margaret Lucille, 1251
Nolen, 1819
Rickey Allen, 1232
Ruth Cleone (Ripple),
1232
Vickey Ellen, 1232
MCGREW
Edith Alma, 1331
MCGUGART
Mary J, 1616
MCGUIGAN
Charles, 1553
Howard, 1553
Irene, 1553
Lillian, 1553
Loretta (Wheeler),
1553
Stella, 1553
Walbert, 1553
MCGUIRE
Betty Louise, 862
Elvina (Flegal), 1681
John, 1667
Nancy, 210
Rebecca (Cecil), 1667
W B, 1681
MCGUIRK
Mary Alice, 1555
MCGULLAH
Emmie, 1105
MCGURK
Katherine Louise, 1547
MCHENRY
--, 1655
Gussie (Wysor), 1655
John Oliver, 681
Lorraine (Barber),
1237
Marjorie Grace
(Crossley), 681
Richard, 1237
MCILVAINE
Julia, 301
MCILWAIN
Eva Mae (Riggs), 551
Madonna Lynn, 526,
551
Nancy Marie, 551
Richard, 551
MCINTIRE
Etna Eudora, 550
Shirley Morita, 1249
MCINTOSH
Lisa, 1322
Rachel (Tanner), 1406
MCINTYRE
Benjamin Franklin,
1685
Dale Donald, 811
Gale Ellen, 811
Lillian May (Wright),
1685

Lynn Elspeth, 811
Mark Ellis, 811
Ruth (Dismore), 811
MCKAY
Allen, 1298
Anna Clara (Wiser),
1298
Bessie, 1299
Maureen, 1616
Rosanna A (Wiser),
1839
Uriah, 1839
MCKEAGUE
Elizabeth Dodson,
1116
MCKEAN
Barbara, 993
Hazel Eleanor,
1134-1135
MCKEE
Alton, 1703
Anna Mae, 1687
David Ned, 954
Frances, 1798
Helen, 1337
Jennie H, 600
Josephine (Battles), 954
Millie (Parks), 1703
Nedd, 954
MCKELVEY
Ann (Richards), 46
Bernard John Michael,
46
J M, 1681
Joanne (Flegal), 1681
Michael Eugene, 46
Shirley Louise (Willey),
46
MCKENNA
James Michael, 1094
Patricia (McGovern),
1094
Thomas, 1094
MCKENZIE
Carolyn, 799
Etta (Reed), 467
Lee, 467
Linda A, 951
Nancy Carolyn, 799
Sarah, 333
MCKERNAN
Fern, 679
MCKEVITT
Cora Lilia (Fisher),
625
Earnest, 625
MCKIBBEN
Augusta Rosamond,
1218
Bonna Kay, 1053
Catherine, 1052
Clara M (Bicket), 1053
David Allison, 1053
Ethel (Waite), 1053
Frank, 960
Frank Jr, 960
Harmon Huton, 1053
Irma (Bear), 960
Isabella, 1053
Joseph Allison, 1053
Kathryn (Cohick), 1053
Kenneth George
Huston, 1053
Kenneth LeRoy, 1053
Lorilla (Hayes), 1053
Lucetta, 1053
Lucetta (Allison), 1053
Maetta J, 1053
Mary R Bridges (Wolf),

1053
Mary Rebecca, 1053
Mary Viola, 1053
Patricia Ann, 1053
Rebecca (Erhard), 1052
Romayne Ruth, 1053
Ruth, 1053
Sandra Lee, 1053
William, 1052
William Brady, 1053
MCKIM
Dana Lyn, 1230
Kenneth Michael, 1230
Nola Keith (Wheeler),
1230
Theodore, 1230
Victoria Keith, 1230
MCKINDREE
Arden, 1238
Blanch (Kahle), 1238
Delbert, 1238
Lee, 1238
Teddy, 1238
MCKINLEY
Amanda Joy, 486
Amber Mae, 486
Clarence A, 1494
Deanne (Kern), 486
Delbert Charles, 1223
Donna Larue, 1223
Gary Lee, 1494
Janet E (Shields), 1223
Kenneth Arthur, 1223
Kenneth Robert, 1223
Kyle, 1536
Leta Mae (Troutman),
1494
Mary Elizabeth, 1223
Mary Jean, 1494
Melisa Marie, 1494
Milo M, 1494
Ramona Bonita, 1223
Raymano Clark, 1494
Rick, 486
Ryan, 1536
Terry Lee, 1494
Vesta Larue (Wolfe),
1223
Victoria Ann, 1223
MCKINNA
Dean, 1437
Ester (Stinson), 1437
Fred J, 1437
Frederick, 1437
MCKINNEY
Anne Fitzgerald, 173
Emilie, 1444
Harold E, 1282
Juanita Alma
(Seigworth), 1282
Kathleen Ann, 1282
Louise Emaline
(Mason), 457
Marsha Lynne, 1283
Merle James, 457
Monte Roy, 457
Ronald Ray, 457
Sandra Diane, 1282
Sarah Catherine, 1394
MCKINNIE
Bonita Dorte (Hulse),
186
Harold A, 182
Harold Austin, 186
Kathleen
(Montgomery), 186
Kathleen Amanda, 186
Lynne Arlene, 186
Marcia Ann, 186

Margery Alane, 186
Mary or Marcia
Elizabeth (Snyder), 185
Roderic Alan, 186
MCKINSTRY
Tara Alina, 168
MCKISSICK
Mary Louise, 1104
MCKNIGHT
Andora Elizabeth
(Richards), 348
Anna Laura Shockley
(Richardson), 349
Arthur, 349
Barbara, 349
Bonnie Curtis, 350
Carrie Gertrude
(Harbach), 349
David B, 348
Deborah Anne, 350
Deborah Jane (Jones),
350
Dora Richards, 349
Dorothy (Lynch), 349
Eleanore, 350
Elizabeth, 349
Fannie E (Bowen), 349
Florence Adelaide, 349
Gertrude B (Biscoe),
349
Grace, 348
Grace Lydia, 349
James, 348
Joanne, 350
John, 348-349
John Shockley, 350
John William Richards,
349
Kerrie Anne, 1142
Kevin, 1142
Laura (Montayne), 350
Mary Anne, 339
Pamela Weiser, 350
Paul, 349
Robert, 349, 1142
Robert Brayton, 350
Robert Brayton Jr, 350
Susan Marie (Weiser),
1142
Wilhelmine, 349
William Richards, 350
MCKOON
Helen Jean (Donne),
831
Joseph W, 831
MCKUBBER
--, 1195
Josephine (Kahl), 1195
MCKUNE
Bernice Krupp, 727
MCLAIN
Doris, 920
Hazel Ruth (Cummins)
Haught, 1478
John Thomas, 856
LaVerta A (Hocker),
588
Minnie, 1052
Patricia Ann (Shettel),
856
Reggie, 1478
Virginia Smith, 919
William, 588
MCLAINE
Joyce, 353
MCLANAHAM
Isabella Craig, 301
MCLAUGHLIN
--, 1578

Anne Louise, 453
Coral (Smith), 634
Dale E, 37
Deborah Lynn (Weiser),
453
Frank L, 453
Jennie (Hahn), 1578
Jennie Eva, 779
Joseph, 1193
Leona Priscilla, 1297
Lisa Dawn Kendell
(Caylor), 1324
Madison Margaret,
1324
Mary (Beaty), 1193
Paul, 634
Sally Sue (Ashton), 37
Seth, 1324
Thomas Edmund, 453
MCLAUGHLYN
--, 907
Anna (Mader), 907
Robert, 907
MCLAUGHRY
David Edward, 314
Katharine (Schwab),
314
Stephen William, 314
William Edward, 314
MCLAWHON
Bessie Adelaide, 1113
MCLEAN
Albert R, 1685
Carrie M (Cooper),
1026
Hazel (Charmenia/
Charmain), 1685
James T, 1026
MCLENEGAN
Anna Susan, 339
Archibald Reigart, 339
Augusta, 339
Carrie Harrison
(Cutler), 339
Charles, 339
Charles Edward, 339
Clara (Rogers), 339
Cutler Sturgis, 339
David Wallace, 339
Edith Marion, 339
Edward, 338
Elizabeth (Holmes),
339
Elizabeth Hiester, 339
Emily L (Fichthorn),
339
Frederick Augustus,
339
Henrietta Augusta
(Musser), 338
Henry, 339
Henry Hall, 339
Henry Richardson, 339
James Lorraine, 339
James Lorraine Jr, 339
John, 339
John Archibald, 339
Julia (Richardson), 339
Mary Anne (McKnight),
339
Mary L (Dunn), 338
Robert Wallace, 339
Samuel Bowman, 339
Sarah F (Reigart), 339
Selina Withers, 339
William, 339
Zephaniah, 338
MCLEOD
Kim, 1802

MEEKER (continued)
Ruth (Keller), 394
Ruth Cathern (Grove), 1384
Ruth Lincoln, 395
Ruther Boyce (Hait), 393
Sarah E (Weiser), 392
Sherry, 394
Vergene, 1384
Viola (Parr), 394
MEEKS
Danny Joe, 454
DeRonald Denver, 453
Nancy Jo (Weiser), 453
Nellie (Haschel), 264
Robert, 264
MEERBACH
Doris Elizabeth (Janson), 916
John Cahin, 916
John Dahin II, 916
MEESE
Noreen Kay, 573
MEFFERD
Connie Jean, 698
Eleanor Anna (Suloff), 698
Martha Ann, 698
Robert Harold, 698
MEGONNEL
Mary Helen, 928
MEHLIN
Anna Catharina, 1595
Georg, 1595
MEIACT
Lanvency, 210
MEIDA
Linda Mary, 140
MEIER
--, 1
Amelia Henrietta, 306
Caspar, 305-306
Catharine Eliza (Kunze), 305-306
Charles Henry, 328
Eliza Catharine, 328
Elizabeth Lucie, 328
Emily Maria, 327
Erik Morgan, 459
Frances, 232
Gerald Alfred, 459
Harriet, 1837
Henry, 635
John Diedrich, 328
Mabel Viola (Fisher), 635
Margaretta Henrietta, 306
Marilyn Audie, 635
Mary Kunigunde, 328
Patricia Ann (Brown), 459
Ruth Elma, 1484
MEINHARDT
Charles Anne, 1215
Charles E, 1215
Martha Jane (Gifford), 1215
Susan, 1215
MEINTS
Vella, 1689
MEIRSMITH
Emily Stuart, 327
MEISENHELDER
Glen, 159
Kathy Marie, 159
Sally Lou (Smith), 159

MEISNER
Dorothea, 325
MEITZLER
Carol Lynn, 1751
Dolores (Heffner), 1751
Eleanor June, 1751
Gary Richard, 1751
George Edgar, 1751
Herma Frances (Wisser), 1750
Jack Richard, 1751
Joanne Marie, 1751
Kim Lee, 1751
Randy Brian, 1751
MELANDER
Rochelle Yolanda, 886
MELANDER-EPPLEY
Samuel Moffitt, 886
MELCHOIR
Blanche E (Snyder), 793
George Emil, 793
Suzanne Annette, 793
MELCOME
Margaret, 1831
MELFI
Cynthia, 501
MELHUSE
Kathleen M, 1499
MELICK
Donna M (Smith), 583
Lucinda Kay, 583
Merle D, 583
Michael Duane, 583
Trisha Lynn, 583
MELLICK
Andrew D Jr, 777
MELLINGER
Adelia (Wiser), 1677
Christian, 1677
MELLOR
Heather Lynn (Newman), 647
James, 647
Jennifer Lynn, 647
Kelly Lynn, 647
Kenneth Jay, 647
Kenneth Jay II, 647
Lisa Marie (Emerich), 647
Patricia Marie (Yalloway), 647
Sherry Ann, 647
Shirley Romaine (Zimmerman), 647
Stanley James, 647
Tracey Lynn, 647
William Joseph, 647
William Joseph Jr, 647
MELLOTT
Bonnie Jean (Wiser), 1672
Michelle Lynn, 1672
Rita Anne, 636
Tamara Jean, 1672
Timothy, 1672
MELN
Beverlyn Jean Johnson (Eckert), 1432
Mark, 1432
Paula Lee, 1432
Sam, 1432
MELO
Frances Apeler (Stiles), 287
John Edward, 287
MELTON
Barry Leroy, 1204

Caroline Omega (Wiser), 1814
Charles Richard, 1814
Doreen (--), 1204
Doris Imogene (Berry), 1204
Gregory, 1204
Michelle, 1204
Ralph, 1204
Randy, 1204
Renee, 1204
MELVILLE
-- (--), 1160
Barbara Thelma (Ritter), 1173
Frederick, 1160
Frederick Rudolph, 1173
Jodi Lee, 1174
Kathleen Francis (Hunter), 1174
Lamonte Frederick, 1174
Lois Arlene (Wanamaker), 1174
Mickie Lynn, 1174
Teri Rae, 1174
MELVIN
Carol June, 185
Elizabeth, 154
MEMMOTT
Eliza Marie (Wasden), 210
James Ammon, 210
MENCH
Arline, 741
MENDEZ
Desiree, 1249
MENEGOT
Helen, 778
MENGEL
-- (--), 88
Annie Elizabeth (Martin), 260
Benjamin, 253-254, 259-260
Catharine (--), 253
Charles Weiser, 254, 260
Edmund Weiser, 260
George, 253
George W, 254, 260
Henry Bassler, 260
Henry Weiser, 254, 260
Louisa Sarah, 254, 260
Margaret Price (Williams), 260
Margaret Williams, 260
Rebecca, 253, 259
Sarah (Weiser), 253-254, 259-260
Sarah Jane, 260
Sophia, 253-254
MENGER
Jeraldine, 1345
MENGES
Clyde D, 915
Lorrain Jeanette, 915
Margaret Blanche (Klaiss), 915
Margaret Lousie, 915
MENGLE
Catharine A, 83
MENSCH
Alice (Winkelblech), 1061
Ann Marie (Noland),

1564
Emanuel, 1061-1062
Jerry, 1564
Joel, 1564
Lodi (Winkelblech), 1062
Lynn, 1061
Mary, 1062
MENSCHING
Stacy Elaine, 1157
MENTZ
Anthony John, 1229
David Anthony, 1229
Nancy Marie, 1229
Virginia Marie (Craig), 1229
MENTZER
Alexis Nicole, 777
Anita Nichole, 777
Becci Sue (Schadle), 776
Edward George, 776
MENZIES
Diann, 1503
James Robert II, 1474
Michal Lauren (Lynch), 1474
MERAZ
Angela Marie, 372
Laura Ellen (Lombardi), 372
Ramona Briana, 372
Ron Juan, 372
MERCER
Barry Plin, 997
Lori Diane, 1139
Martha Mareen, 997
Mary Lynn (Shirck), 997
Rebecca Jane, 997
Sara Beth, 997
Vera, 1491
MERCKEL
Anna Margaretha, 1363
Francisca, 1363
Jacob, 1362
Lydia, 1363
Mary Catharine (Fricker), 1362
MERE
Charles Anthony, 1303
Lilian Mae (Eddinger), 1303
MEREDITH
Bernice Ellen (Moore), 48
Don, 48
Doris, 48
Harriet (Willey), 48
Lena (Nichols), 48
Monica, 970
Shannon, 48
Stephen Moore, 48
Von Le Van, 48
MERFERT
Charlotte Amelia (Weiser), 427
Esther Amelia, 427
Theodore Edward, 427
MERIWETHER
Norma Jane, 41
MERKEL
Betty Virginia, 1756
Carrie Esther, 1749
Clara Catharine (Keim), 1623
Earl Thomas, 1756
Edna R (Schollenberger), 1756

Eldon Floyd, 1756
Ellwood Solon, 1756
Floyd Milton, 1756
Helen Beulah, 1756
Kate E, 1614
Mary Ann Kate (Wisser), 1756
Nathaniel S, 1623
Norman Oliver, 1756
MERKLIN
Barbara (Weisser), 6
Markus, 6
MERLO
Kristen Victoria, 1388
Larry, 1388
Lee Ann (Lloyd), 1388
MERRELL
Sandra Kay, 1776
MERRELS
Ann (Pickert), 1574
Gilbert, 1574
MERRIAM
--, 471
Mercedes, 471
Musa (Lotge), 471
MERRILL
Clifford Lamer, 1157
Judith L, 1033
Kerry Lynn (Cordier), 1157
Kylene Marie, 1157
MERRIMAN
Debra Lynn, 1479
Dianne Lee, 1479
Dorothy Jean (Earnest), 1479
Douglas Dale, 1479
Heather Marie, 859
Margaret (Adams), 1479
Vernon, 1479
MERRITT
--, 1578
Amy Lynn (Shaner), 400
Berton, 1698
Emily (Dickson) Wisor, 1698
Harry, 1188
Ida (Golliday), 1188
Ida B, 559
Katherine, 303
Mary Jane (Pickard), 1578
Robert Paul, 400
MERRY
Beth, 1389
MERRYFIELD
Linda Lee, 1520
MERRYMAN
George, 445
Janet Kay, 1632
Lindsay, 445
Mary Jane (Jenkins), 445
MERSHON
Bamcy, 1733
MERTES
Aileen Ann, 1559
MERTZ
Bernard Harold, 594
Carol Louise, 594
Cindy Marie, 594
Craig, 785
Elizabeth (Fetter), 785
Estella Pauline (Cremean), 594
Gary, 785
Hannah, 1612

MERTZ (continued)
Hettie L (Kieffer), 1643
James, 1525
James Warren, 594
Joan (Neidig), 1525
June (Yohe), 854
Marilyn Anne, 594
Marlin, 785
Mildred Marian (Crowe), 594
Richard, 785
Russell, 854
Russell Jr, 854
Shirley Jean, 854
William H, 1643
MERWIN
Ann, 1683
MERZ
Gertrude, 620
MESARCHIK
Mary Virginia, 140
MESEKE
Gertrude, 220
MESNARD
Donna June, 475
MESSAMER
Fern H (Zuck), 223
Joseph Morris, 223
Randall Dean, 224
Ronald Dean, 223
Shirley Louise (Boyd), 224
Teresa Ann, 224
MESSEMER
-- (--), 215
Joe, 215
MESSER
Nicholas, 398
Steve, 398
Susan Irene (Stephenson), 398
MESSERSMITH
Dawn Loraine, 670
Dayne Donald, 669
Deborah Louise, 670
Dianna Lynn, 670
Donna Lee, 669
Emma Christine (Snyder), 643
Emma E (Koppenheffer), 642
Esther Miriam (Mattis), 642
Gladys Faye, 643
Grace R (Books), 643
Jean Elizabeth, 643
Jennie Caroline, 642
John A, 642
Mabel, 642
Percy Emmanuel, 642
Ruth Evelyn (Fulkroad), 669
Sidney Ann, 655
William Miles, 643
MESSICK
Carl Ray, 1797
Jessie Ruth, 1796
Lorene Lavergne (Wiser), 1797
Tabitha Jane, 1796
MESSINGER
Eleanore (Bender), 221
Gladys Faye (Messersmith), 643
Karl H, 221
Philip Mackhenmar, 643
Phyllis Ann, 643

MESSNER
Charles J, 1068
Darline, 672
Deborah, 672
Edward, 845
Elaine, 1514
Eleanor, 672
Florence H (Weiser), 1628
Florence May (Fulkroad), 668
Harold, 672
Hilbert, 672
Jean, 672
Lawrence, 672
Lloyd, 672
Mary Elizabeth (Patterson), 1068
Mildred Katharine, 694
Morris Gillespie, 668
Ruth, 672
Sadie, 718
Sadie Mae (Koppenhaver), 672
Sarah Marie (Anspach), 845
Stella Sarah, 1865
Virginia (--), 672
William A, 1628
MEST
Helen Eileen, 1634
Mary F, 1640
METCALFE
Anna Margaret, 218
METICK
Minerva, 154
METTLER
Dorothy Lucile, 100
Ruth Killian, 1045
METTS
Evelyn, 1166
METZ
Carrie Amelia, 672
Clara Emeline, 642
Franklin, 1369
Kay Lenora (Brunell), 1369
Kay Lenora (Chase), 1369
Sara Louise, 888
METZER
June, 1368
METZGER
--, 1
Alexander Bryant, 1554
Bertha Margaret, 718
Betty Jane (Smith), 718
Betty Lou, 718
Bonnie Lee, 718
Catharina, 6
Clara W (Woomer), 718
Colleen, 136
Daniel J, 1730
Dorothy, 785
Edwin Boyd, 719
Edwin Stanley, 718
Elizabeth Ashley, 1554
Elva Edith (Prescott), 718
Ethel (Moser), 719
Forrest Grennawalt, 718
Gail I, 719
Gail Rebecca, 718
Grace, 718
Jan Bruce, 1554
Jane Marian (Janowicz)

Van Sky, 1554
Jennie Agnes (Witmer), 718
LaRue R, 718
LaRue R Jr, 719
Mollie (Yawn), 718
Sarah E (Kemp), 1730
Susan J, 719
William Henry, 718
William M, 719
METZINGER
Bonnie Mae (Wetzel), 471
Danny Paul, 471
Elizabeth, 471
Faye Louise, 471
George, 479
Ilda, 479
Joseph, 471
Kathleen E, 479
Mary (Hayd), 471
Paula Louise (Horn), 471
Sandra Kay (Hosser), 471
Steven Luke, 471
Steven Luke Jr, 471
Tamara Ann (Mosser), 471
METZLER
Barbara, 770
Florence, 137
Gladys, 1834
MEUHLER
Pauline Elizabeth (Rice), 1189
William, 1189
MEWHORTER
Carol Kay, 583
Janet Lynn, 583
Joe Earl, 583
Ray Earl, 583
Reda Jo (Arington), 583
Velma Avonne (Hocker), 583
MEYER
Alfred, 1445
Anna Barbara, 280
Catherine Irene (Bierly), 1093
David, 557
Dorothy, 1377
Joel, 165
Josephine, 739
Lydia Maybelle (Fess), 557
Magdalena Margaret (Spyker), 1445
Margaret, 1208
Mary Elizabeth, 1445
Myralyn Katharine, 557
Patricia M (Weiser), 165
Pauline Fay, 472
Philip, 1093
Philip Duane, 1093
Solomon, 1445
MEYERS
Annie, 1109
Blanche L, 554
Carolyn Lee, 110
Charles, 1109
Connie Jean, 110
Diane (Banter), 562
Edith, 1448
Eli, 1109
Emma, 1081

Emma F, 1468
Gertrude, 1401
Hugh, 110
Joni Lynn, 1249
Joshua Allan, 991
Kelley Kristine (Flack), 952
Kevin, 562
Larry, 562
Lee, 110
Linda Joan, 110
Linda Sue (Fergien), 971
Lynn, 901
Mack, 110
Marjorie, 110
Mark, 562
Mary (Ferrell), 1109
Mary Alice (Stover), 1100, 1105
Monica Lou, 1490
Muriel Elaine (Wand), 991
Opal (Cox), 110
Otto, 110
Paul, 110
Philip Christopher, 952
Ruby (Cox), 110
Ruella L (Trueblood), 110
Sandra Kay, 110
Shanna, 562
Tim, 952
Timothy Allan, 991
William D, 1105
William J, 971
MEYETTE
Charles Phillip, 1475
Julie Ann (Segina), 1475
MEYRICK
Jean M, 1634
MICHAEL
Anna Verdilla (Koppenhaver), 682
Benjamin Franklin, 682
Benjamin Franklin Jr, 682
Grace Pauline, 682
Hattie Louisa, 682
Henery Duane, 526
James, 364
James Curtis, 526
James J, 364
Jonathan E, 364
Kevin D, 364
Lyman C, 526
Mary Manetta (McCloud), 364
Mildred Esther (Wickham), 526
Patrick W, 364
Thomas F, 364
MICHAELIS
Evelin Claudia, 321
MICHAELS
Mildred, 1712
Theresa May, 188
MICHAUS
Elizabeth, 1181
MICHEL
Jacquelyn Emma (Noll), 1063
MICHELS
Elma B (Ramsey), 517
Helen L, 517
Pete, 517
MICHELSON
Richard, 1697

Viola May (Turner), 1697
MICHOL
Jessica Caitlyn, 1274
Kristopher Robert, 1273
Nicole Leigh (Cooper), 1273
MICK
Cindy Sue, 217
MICKEY
Delores Marie, 928
Douglass Edward, 928
Eleanor Grace (Spyker), 1442
Joseph Earl, 928
Linda Louise, 1442
Marilyn Joanne, 1442
Mervin Earl Jr, 928
Robert Lee, 928
Roland Sylvester, 1442
Winifred Marie (Lineburg), 928
MICKLE
Birdina, 1729
MICKS
Julia, 953
MIDDAUGH
James W, 1531
Kim Doreen, 1531
Nancy Rae (Cobaugh), 1531
MIDDENDORF
Bobbye, 1499
Ester, 1354
MIDDLETON
Florence, 1698
John, 333
Susan Tucker (McRory), 333
MIDDLEWORTH
Patty Jean, 1007
Raymond, 1007
Ruth Aileen (Kahl), 1007
MIERZEJEWSKI
Nancy Jane (Shollenberger), 1614
Theodore, 1614
MIFFLIN
Bettie Jane (Wohlgemuth), 1064
Jeffrey D, 1064
Jordon Denton, 1064
Magen, 1064
MIKOLAJCZYK
Amy, 465
MIKSELL
Christina (Hepner), 720
James, 720
MILANO
Mary, 1520
MILBOURN
Eunice, 1496
MILBURN
Vedah, 1868
MILES
Donna Jo (Moore), 1435
Jeremy Wayne, 1435
Jodi Carman, 1435
John Reese, 827
Marlene Ann, 727
Raymond C, 1435
Ruby Myrtle, 827
Samuel Reed, 827
Sara Jane (Womelsdorf), 827

MILES (continued)
Whrena, 921
MILHOLLAND
Theresa Jill, 542
MILHOUSE
Mulianna, 934
MILKEY
Anna (Binkley), 464
Leonard A, 464
MILLAR
Emerett, 1771
MILLARD
Ann Lindsay, 353
Carol Cooper, 353
Catherine (Cooper), 352
Donald Alan III, 353
Donald Alan Jr, 352
George Milby, 698
Lisa Ann, 698
Mark William, 698
Sharon Ruth (Frye), 698
MILLER
--, 8, 390, 549, 1057, 1366, 1509, 1535, 1578
Abigail Elizabeth, 623
Ada L, 1629
Ada Lavina, 1288
Addison C, 1112
Adeline Catherine (Erhard), 1057
Alanna, 623
Albert B, 1743
Alexander, 623, 1428
Alice Jane, 511
Alice June (Furman), 757
Alice Louise (Herring), 537
Alma, 999
Alma Louise (Pickle), 1312
Althea, 252
Alverta Mae (Lenker), 676
Alwilda Esther (Renn), 1025
Amanda E (Reed), 1542
Andy Paul, 840
Ann Marie (Pontius), 694
Anna, 284, 729
Anna (Paul), 777
Anna Dora (Weiser), 1345
Anna Louise, 495
Anna Mae, 1406
Anna Mae (Smeltz), 676
Anna Margaret, 16
Anna Virginia (Geise), 1058
Anne, 1636
Anne Marie, 231
Anne Robertson, 86
Annie Maria, 244
Annie Wilma, 1743
Anson, 1688
Anthony, 1088
Arlie, 601
Barbara Ann, 1743
Barbara Lois (Warner), 692
Barry, 1089
Benjamin Charles, 1554

Benjamin Richard, 1400
Bernice Irene (Smith), 634
Bertha, 1391
Bertha Ellen, 916, 916
Bertha Helena, 86
Bertha Irene, 160-161
Betty Jean (Stahl), 601
Betty Louise, 1049
Betty Pearl (Lenker), 679
Betty Virginia (Schaffer), 765
Blanche (Kahle), 1220
Boneita Ann Corrine (Long), 709
Brenda, 589, 1131
Brenda Joyce, 623
Brenda Lee, 683, 765
Brian Lee, 746
Carl Erdman, 257
Carl F, 995
Carl Frank, 1207
Carl James, 676
Carl Rudolph Demme, 84
Carla Renee, 527
Carol (--), 478
Carol Lynn, 1141
Carolina, 89
Caroline, 39
Caroline Boyer, 86
Carolyn Sue, 622
Carrie, 853
Carrie Milinda (Rowe), 666
Cassandra, 1742
Catharine (Haller), 1428
Catherine, 1519
Catherine Elizabeth, 821
Catherine May (Weiser), 1635
Cathie Mae, 777
Charles, 89, 451
Charles Aaron, 1089
Charles Cornelius, 673
Charles Lloyd, 1554
Charlotte, 1538
Charlotte (Womelsdorf), 813
Chester W, 1543
Christian, 623
Christina, 757
Christine, 200
Christopher George, 936
Christopher Wayne, 248
Claire Elaine (Patton), 1300
Clara, 271
Clara B (Bender), 221
Clara Edna (Wolfe), 577
Clara Zelma, 545
Clark Albert, 692
Claude, 634
Cloyd Jonathan, 765
Cody Haynes, 1091
Connie Marie, 634
Cora, 1743
Cornelia Anderson (Gillespie), 84
Cornelia Gillespie, 86
Corrine L, 229
Cosby Ellen, 1657

Curtis Michael, 1400
Cynthia, 1698, 1710
Cyrus Henry Jr, 679
Dale, 1750
Dana Marie (Spears), 1207
Daniel, 19, 87, 91, 750, 813, 1360
Daniel Adam, 1745
Danielle Marie, 452
Danielle Nicole, 1141
Darla Sue, 765
David, 649
David Edgar, 185
David John, 424
David Percival, 185
David Richard, 765
Dawn, 1749
Dawn (Miller), 1749
Dawn Louise, 676
Dean C, 478
Dean Jr, 478
Deana Rozann, 765
Debbie Ann, 676
Debbie Jane, 765
Deborah Lee, 1301
Debra Christine, 840
Delores, 679
Delores Jean (White), 683
Deloris, 620
Denise A, 1113
Denise Ann, 634
Dennis, 830
Dennis Allen, 1746
Dennis Eugene, 765
Derek, 752
Diane, 214
Diane Marie, 356
Doit Alpha, 579
Doit Charles, 579
Donald, 1089
Donald E, 1536
Donna Jean (Kerschner), 1749
Donna Joan (Price), 1749
Donna Lee (Schaffner), 1141
Dorcas, 853
Dorothy, 1370, 1391
Dorothy (Schlund), 60
Dorothy Irene, 765
Dorris Jean (Forbus), 527
Drew P, 229
Durese Rene, 579
E H, 1049
Edgar, 60
Edith, 293
Edith Elizabeth, 873
Edna May, 1340
Edward, 89, 473
Elbert R, 221
Elinor Mae, 1049
Eliza (--), 849
Elizabeth, 837, 1681
Elizabeth (Gillet), 89
Elizabeth (Wheeler), 1553
Elizabeth Ann (Hails), 1749
Elizabeth Anne (Robb), 1399
Elizabeth Crilly (Snyder), 185
Elizabeth Dessez, 85
Elizabeth Gobin (Hynicka), 1510

Elizabeth R (Loebrick), 89
Ellen (Erhard), 1058
Ellen Selena (Lenker), 679
Elmer, 577
Elmer J, 1391
Elmira Rebecca Wolff (Derr), 243
Elsie Coleen, 40
Elvesta, 1743
Emaline (Kephart), 1688
Emanuel, 1519
Emma, 1636, 1638
Emma (Nebinger), 853
Emma (Weiser), 85
Emma A, 849
Emma A (Miller), 849
Emma B, 216
Emma Ebel, 86
Emma Faye, 1190
Emma H (Weiser), 1636
Emma Helena (Weiser), 84
Emma Jane (Burkholder), 230
Erma (Bozeman), 679
Ester M (Dressler), 1535
Esther, 657, 913
Esther (McConnell), 1360
Ethel, 1370
Ethel Anderson, 1845
Euphemia (--), 85
Eva Elizabeth (Snyder), 1112
Evelyn Irene, 884
Evelyn Ruth (Callender), 668
Faith Ann (Wisser), 1745
Fay Lillian (Moyer), 773
Fern (McKernan), 679
Flavius M, 579
Floyd Allen, 676
Frances Rebecca (Kehl), 995
Frank, 838, 1012
Fred Noble, 622
Frederick Franklin, 765
Frederick Gail, 623
Frederick Michael, 231
Freeman Cyrus, 679
Gary Dean, 1141
Gary Floyd, 677
Geneva, 621
Genevieve, 1058
George, 89, 936, 1370
George Frederick, 84-85
George Frederick Jr, 85
Gerald Bernard, 679
Gerald Lee, 692
Geraldine Margaret (Koppenhaver), 673
Glen Carl, 257
Glen Erdman, 257
Glenn Taylor, 257
Gloria Renee, 776
Grant L, 1510
Gregory Semmes, 86
Hannah (Logan), 1684

Hannah Elizabeth, 775
Hannah Jennie (Weiser), 774-775
Harlene B, 579
Harley Bernard, 579
Harold, 1025
Harold Leroy, 777
Harrison Dessez, 86
Harrison Edward, 666
Harry, 849, 1158
Harry Abraham, 775
Harry Bowman, 773
Harvey G, 1743
Harvey H, 1058
Hazel (Pickard), 1578
Heidi, 1324
Helen Elizabeth, 185
Helen Joan, 256
Helene, 874
Henry, 1542
Herbert, 1533
Hetty Catharine (Snyder), 1366
Hope Pearle (Royer), 1091
Howard, 1077, 1636
Irene Alice (Anspach), 840
Isaac Walter, 679
Ivan Heinly, 243
Jack L, 1536
Jaclyn Renea (Johns), 129
Jacob, 30, 39, 89, 849, 1120, 1519
James, 1106
James Levern, 634
James Richard, 231
Jan, 545
Jan Lamar, 545
Jane, 846
Janet Marie, 676
Janice Irene, 1312
Janna Mae, 840
Jason Michael, 231
Jason Richard, 248
Jaye Ellen DeGooyer, 424
Jaye Patricia, 1300
Jayne, 478
Jeanne, 1085
Jeb Kenneth, 1091
Jennie (Kehl), 1012
Jessica Lynn, 1400
Jessica Suzann, 451
Jestina, 759
Jestine Elnora, 775
Jill Marie, 840
Joan (Heileman), 499
Joan Marie (Yoder), 830
Joanne (Adams), 231
Jodia Onita (Brungart), 1089
Joelene Ann, 1300
John, 478, 527, 853, 1361, 1876
John Harry Abraham, 777
John Pearson III, 230
John Pearson IV, 230
John Sebastian, 765
Johnie Carl, 527
Jophes, 621
Joseph Alvin, 1300
Joseph S, 1424
Josephine Eva (Klinger), 746
Joshua Robb, 1400

MILLIKEN (continued)
Lorena Belle (Seaton), 1683
Louise (Vogeli), 1684
Luella May, 1684
Margaret Ellen, 1683
Mary Jane, 1683
Merwin Monroe, 1683
Rebecca H, 1683
Rosa (Becker), 1684
Samuel, 1683
Samuel David, 1684
Sarah E, 1683
William Henry, 1684
MILLINDER
Katherine (Wisor), 1713
Oliver, 1713
MILLS
--, 1671
Barbara Hiester, 282
Barbara Sue (Wesco), 532
Caroline Moyer (Hiester), 281
Caryn Helen, 282
David, 532
Dennis, 532
Effie, 993
Harold Eldon, 1686
Jack Howard, 281
James, 532
Karen Allinson (Frost), 993
Lillian Edith, 838
Linda Jean, 722
Mary Camilla, 333
Myrtle, 1221
Rebecca Alwilda, 828
Sherry, 532
Shirley LaRue (Kephart), 1686
Stanton, 1818
Tammy (Wiser), 1818
Theresa (Youngblood), 281
MILLS-MAHER
Sandra Marie, 99
MILLSAP
Gertrude, 100
MILLSAPS
Florence, 446
MILNER
Carol, 524
MILTON
Cindy Jean, 1398
Henry, 401
Jackie Ann (Snyder), 366
Jeff, 366
Mary Katherine, 366
Phyllis Nadine (Moore), 401
Thomas Franklin, 366
MINCHAUS
--, 1110
Elizabeth, 1111, 1160
MINCHAUSIN
Elizabeth, 1110
MINCHOFF
Evelyn R, 1617
MINCK
Donna Lee (Underkoffler) Sheesley, 1538
Erik B, 1538
Robert, 1538
MINER
--, 1106

Belle F, 508
Edith A, 1832
Ellis, 1704
Mabel (Rudy), 1106
Violet (Parks), 1704
MINERVA
Vesta, 1004
MINICH
Norma Jean, 472
MINICHAN
Della Marie (Burd), 162
Harry, 162
MINICK
Betty June, 826
Dorothy Ann (Lyter), 716
George Ritter, 716
James Albert, 716
James Richard, 716
Patricia Louise, 716
Ruth Catharine (Lawver), 716
MINKLE
Ann, 554
MINNICH
Esther, 1516
Henrietta, 853
Mable, 522
Ruth Emma, 1204
Susanna, 1476
MINNICK
Benjamin, 1547
Corine Mary, 1547
Florence Mae, 1549
Harold E, 828
Ida Belle (Womelsdorf), 828
Joseph E, 828
Karen Elizabeth, 1274
LaRue R, 828
Laura Teresa, 1549
Martha Caroline (Ryder), 1547
Mary Malinda, 828
Ruby A, 828
MINNIG
Sallie, 981
MINOLIVICH
Kate, 473
MINOR
Edith, 189
Jason Burdett, 1287
Karen Diane (Seigworth), 1287
Michele Lee, 1287
Ray Louis, 1287
MINSHALL
Emerson, 395
Jane Ellen, 395
Judy, 395
Michael, 395
Phyllis (Meeker), 395
MINSKER
-- (Rosen), 1417
-- (Trumbore), 1417
-- (Warner), 1417
Anna, 1417
Eliza Ann (McClune), 1417
Harry, 1417
Isabella, 1417
John, 1417
Robert, 1417
Theodore, 1417
Thomas, 1417
MINTER
Luella C, 511

MINTURN
Robert E, 444
Virginia Lee (Tuggle), 444
MIRISE
Barbara Ann (Bauder), 368
David Elwood, 368
Michael David, 368
Sandra Lee, 368
MIRRIAM
--, 554
Thetis Irene (Riggs), 554
MISENHEIMER
Byrd, 1752
MISER
Grace Lydia, 748
MISHAK
Ed, 64
Wendy (Wilhelm), 64
MISKELL
Ruby Belle, 1126
MISKONIC
Alice Angelin (Shettel), 856
David Brunis, 856
David Michael, 856
Pamela Jean, 856
MITCHEFF
Cora (Moore), 492
Daniel, 492
Deborah Ann, 492
George, 492
Gladys (Rivera), 492
Michael Allen, 492
Michael Gregory, 492
Phillip, 492
Sandra Grace, 492
Steven, 492
MITCHELFREE
Alia, 987
MITCHELL
Alfaretta, 1702
Amanda Rose, 1557
Amber Renee, 540
Anna D, 1428
Ardelle Adalene, 95
Arthur James, 1187
Barbara Dian (Bullard), 1187
Barbara Sue (Stevens), 541
Becky Louise (Karr), 478
Bert Lee, 1847
Betty (Snyder), 540
Chelsea Ruthann, 802
Christina Ray, 541
Commodore P, 362
Cynthia Sue (Douglass), 69
Danna (Vance), 69
Darrell, 362
David Malin, 69
David Malin Jr, 70
David Patrick, 1557
Deborah Lee, 540
Doris (Wilson), 540
Edith Joneu, 1467
Edna Christina (Herring), 539
Edna Sarah (Smith), 95
Edward Eugene, 540
Edward Eugene III, 540
Edward Eugene Jr, 540
Ernest, 1698
Eula, 50

Evelyn Belle, 1764
Evelyn Elizabeth (Hillyer), 540
Frank Pierre Jr, 69
George Russell, 539
Georgia Darlene (Martib), 541
Gregory Arthur, 1188
Heather, 69
Helen Ilene, 540
Helene Eugenia (Raymond), 69
Holly, 449
Ida May, 1168
Ida Myrtle, 41
Ilene (Martin), 540
Irene Beatrice (Rusk), 1228
James T, 28
Jan Renae, 541
Janet Muriel (Flynn), 540
Jeffery Russell, 541
Jeffrey Thomas, 1188
Jessica Lynn, 479
Joan Catherine Marsh (Hurst), 69
John E, 1228
Joyce Elaine, 540
Judy (Lee), 540
Julia Doris (Pine), 69
June, 272
Justin Patrick, 1557
Kali Jane, 540
Keil Thomas, 802
Kelly Ellen (Baxter), 801
Kimberly, 540
Kimberly Sue, 69
Lauren Alexandra, 1557
Lester Elsworth, 540
Lester Loren, 362
Lisa Kay, 540
Lorna Lee, 362
Lydia Ellen, 540
Marcus Homen, 1557
Margaret, 1213
Marjorie Lou, 541
Melisaa Anne, 1557
Mildred Marie (Roller), 1127
Minnie, 60
Myrtle Grace (Pennington), 362
Nancy Joan, 1188
Opal Irene (Weiser), 1847
Pamela Sue, 540
Pat (Shields), 540
Paul Irvin, 95
Peter, 69
Raymond Kenneth, 541
Rhonda Lee, 540
Rosemary Susan (Kenedy), 1557
Russell William, 540
Sheryl (Nelson), 540
Shirley (Mason), 540
Teddy Rae, 540
Terry, 478
Thomas Jude, 801
Thomas Scott, 1127
Timothy Darl, 540
Tina Marie, 540
Tracey, 540
Wendy Michell, 540
Zola (Rothrock) Wisor Graffins, 1698

MITCHELLTREE
Jane, 1591
MITMAN
Helen, 1331
MITTS
Eva May (Turner), 1696
Robert, 1696
MIX
Alice Requa (Schwab), 308
daughter, 1001
Emily Schwab, 309
Madeline Virginia Ogden, 308
Marion (Schreckangast), 1001
son, 1001
Theodore, 308
William, 1001
MIZNER
--, 1109
Irene (Schwoob), 1109
MLOCHOWSKI
Linda, 1250
MLYNAREK
Ann Rich (Krigbaum), 118
Thomas Frank, 118
Thomas Rich, 118
Ursula Ann, 118
MOATS
Catherine Louise (Izor), 1329
Leonard Garland, 1329
Myrna Rae, 1329
MOBLEY
Flossie, 620
MOCK
Bertha Irene (Boyer), 895
Clarence, 895
Helen Lenetta, 394
John Ellsworth, 394
John Lee, 1872
LaFawn (Wiser), 1872
Leonard, 394
Mary Arpinee (Meeker), 394
Norma Jean (Carrico), 394
MOCKABEE
Marie Elizabeth, 1332
MODER
Christian James, 43
Sarabeth (Enoch), 43
MOE
Dorothy, 1737
MOEBS
Susan Jane, 488
MOELICH
Peter, 777
MOELLER
Louisa Maria, 1506
Marjorie Selma, 1283
MOEN
Elizabeth Ann, 405
Ellen Meredith, 404
Kristin Rae, 404
Luis Fernando De la torre, 404
Newton Alfred, 404
Patricia Rae (Weiser), 404
Stephanie Jo, 405
MOERSHELL
Katherine, 1551
MOFFAT
Kimberly, 936

MOFFITT
Benjamin Stewert, 852
Caroline, 852
Charles Avery Homes, 852
Charles Raymond, 852
Charlotte, 852
Charlotte (Eppley), 851
Dorothy, 853
Edith Victoria (Kelker), 851
Gabrilla (Fausold), 852
George R, 852
George Reily, 852
George Washington, 851
Helen, 853
Henry Kelker, 851
Jacob Eppley, 851
John Jordon, 851-852
John Wesley, 851
Laura Edith, 852
Lillian (Johnson), 852
Luther Reily, 851
Maria Haldeman (Chamberlain), 852
Mary Edith (Ashby), 852
Myrtle (Stoops), 852
Rebecca Catharine (Witman), 851
Rebecca Catherine (Witman), 1517
Rebecca Charlotte, 852
Robert H, 1517
Robert Hopkins, 851-852
Robert Hopkins III, 852
Samuel Lewis, 851
Susan (Warren), 852
Thomas Edwin, 853
Thomas Robinson, 852
MOHAP
Linda Mae (Wisser), 1745
Ronald John, 1745
MOHLER
Mary Alice, 228
MOHN
Edna, 902
Emma (Womelsdorf), 902
Helen, 902
John Henry, 1131
John Randolph, 1131
Kerry, xiv
Luella, 902
Paul, 902
Pierce, 902
Suzanne Louise, 1131
Thomas Michael, 1131
Virginia Louise (Jones), 1131
MOHR
Carolyn Sue (Miller), 622
David Allen, 623
Deborah (Noneman), 623
Dores, 516
Jacob Banning, 623
Jeffery Daniel, 623
Joenita Ann (Eberly), 629
John Frederick, 622
John Glover, 622
John Michael, 622
Julie Ann, 623

Karen (Weiss), 622
Maegan Lorraine, 622
Michael James, 623
Paul, 629
Richard Louis, 623
MOIST
Amanda Jean, 198
Billie Jo, 1046
Douglas Michael, 198
Gordon Paul, 198
Michaela Sue (Yoder), 198
MOLD
Maria, 1865
MOLL
Friederike (Weisser), 1596
Helen M, 1743
Jacob Friedrich, 1596
MOLLENKOLF
Grace Mefferd, 624
MOLNAR
Elaine Louise (Lockhart), 1098
Scott, 1098
MOLTZ
Anita (Knox), 1419
Anthony Kyle, 1418
Catharine Ghere, 1420
Cindy Petrondi (Pratt), 1419
Donna Rae (Brownewell), 1418
Elizabeth Louise (Kinzer), 1418
Florinda Susan (McClune), 1417
Frank Kenneth, 1418
George Thomas, 1417
George Wagner, 1418
Gouverneur Warren, 1419
John Minsker, 1418
John Minsker Jr, 1418
Katherine, 1419
Khristine, 1419
Marianne, 1419
Martha Helen, 1418
Mary Ellen, 1419
Mary Gertrude (Boldridge), 1419
Michael William, 1418
Nancy Louise, 1418
Patricia Jean, 1418
Sarah (--), 1418
Susan Florinda, 1419
Susan Marcella (Wagner), 1417
Suzanne (Hopkins), 1418
Theodore, 1417
Theodore Hiney, 1419
Timothy John, 1418
Tobin Warren, 1418
Travis Daniel, 1418
MOMBERT
Adolf Wilhelm, 344
Anne Theodora, 344
Eleanor, 345
Emma (Sanger), 344
Emma Elizabeth, 344
Emma Elizabeth (Muhlenberg), 344
Francis James, 345
Frederick Augustus, 344
Gustavus Henry, 345
Henrietta Augusta, 344
Isidor Muhlenberg, 344

Jacob Isidor, 344
Joanna Muhlenberg, 344
Lily, 345
William Sanger, 344
MOMBLE
Peter, 1764
Sarah Armina (Wiser), 1764
MONAGUE
Eda Jean (Wisor), 1709, 1713
Rex, 1709, 1713
MONAHAN
Frances Mary, 1232
MONAHON
Marsha, 1142
MONCAVAGO
Melissa, 783
MONDOR
Elizabeth McKibben (Kahle), 1218
Martin Charles, 1218
MONDORF
Thelma Louise, 799
MONEYSMITH
Bertha (Kurz), 386
David Ervin, 387
David Mark, 387
Dora Anna (Leibold), 386
Eleanor (Hansen), 386
Emma Frances (Keyes), 386
Eva May, 387
Harry William, 386
James Frederick, 387
Lorraine Mary Elizabeth (Fiseh), 387
Mark David, 387
Martha Elizabeth, 387
Mary E (Yoke), 386
Paul William, 386
Peter William, 386
Ruth Elizabeth Geneva, 387
William Ervin, 386
MONG
Harvey R, 1259
Helen H (--), 1259
M, 1383
Mary Blanche (Kahle), 1259
Scott Kahle, 1259
Vera Myrtle, 1259
MONGILLO
Michelle Charlene, 1814
MONKERN
Arnold James, 1214
James, 1214
Jaqueline Sue, 1214
Judy (McCandless), 1214
Kimberly Ann, 1214
Lisa Marie, 1214
Nellie Pearl (Shottenberg), 1214
MONNTZ
--, 842
Florence May (Schoener), 842
MONOLIVICH
Katie, 473
MONREAN
Pauline Ruth, 1285
MONROE
Elna, 737
Janet, 399

MONSCHIEN
Catharine, 709
MONSELL
Miriam Jeanette, 918
MONTAGUE
Arlene E, 840
Donald W, 841
Joseph, 841
Mamie Cora (Anspach), 840
Ruth E, 840
William H, 840
Wilma, 840
MONTAYNE
Laura, 350
MONTEITH
Steven William, 1155
Terry Jean (Williamson), 1155
MONTELIUS
Alfred, 1444
Anna (Stadler), 1444
Catharine, 1444
Catharine Ann (Gast), 1444
Charles Harry, 1444
Charles Henry, 1444
Dorothy Helen, 1444
Emilie (McKinney), 1444
George, 1444
Harry, 1444
Helen (Stadler), 1444
John, 1444
Joseph K, 1444
Margaret G, 1444
Mary Rebecca, 1444
Ruth, 1444
MONTGOMERY
Amber, 113
Charlotte (Rocky), 1548
Dennis Michael, 1401
Dorothy Wagner (Runkle), 1401
Elaine (Armknecht) Soto, 1733
Elizabeth, 311
Gloria Florence (Ramsay), 1548
Ida Marie (Deradis), 1401
John Martin, 1401
Karen Lynn, 1401
Kathleen, 186
Lucinda Helen (Wiser), 1789
Morton L, 357
Ramsay, 1548
Randal Lee, 1548
Richard, 1733
Richard Martin, 1401
Ronald Michael, 1548
Ronnie, 1548
Shirley, 547
Susan (Wilkinson), 1401
Thomas John, 1401
William, 1789
MONTY
Mary Kellogg, 1385
MOODY
--, 1110
Dawn Heather, 1072
Donna Jean (Bohn), 1072
Gerald Frances Jr, 1072
Gretchen Elzine (Gass),

807
Hannah Margaret, 807
Kelly Susanne, 1072
Martha Ann, 1629
Mary Catherine, 1138
Michelle Ann, 1072
Polly Faye, 1815
Walter Thomas, 807
MOOMAW
Cecil, 1652
MOOMEY
Allen, 1689
Jean (Kephart), 1689
MOON
Bettie, 470
MOONEY
Alice, 1704
MOONEYHAM
Carol, 1804
MOOR
--, 1863
Charles, 1863
Mary (Weiser), 1863
MOORE
--, 1672, 1720
Abbie, 1437
Ada, 1439
Alberta (Eitner), 491
Alma, 491
Alonzo, 1438
Alta, 1432
Alva Rilla, 1810
Angela Marie, 1434
Anna Eliza, 1753
Anna Leah, 1435
Annie (Owens), 1436
Annie (Tucker), 1436
Anthony, 491
Arthur, 1437
Arthur J, 1437
Barbara, 490
Barbara Anne, 1434
Bernice, 1436
Bernice Ellen, 48
Bertha D, 1436
Bessie J (Showers), 1258
Betty M, 490
Bonnie Elizabeth, 1289
Brenda, 1716
Brent Edward, 401
C G, 1435
Camela Fay, 1434
Catharine (Dresbach), 1430
Cecil, 1437
Chad, 473
Charles, 492
Charles E, 1436
Charles Jr, 492
Charles Robert, 490
Cheryl Lynn (Nelson), 1691
Chester Arthur, 1437
Clarence, 1438
Clyde Austin, 1434
Compton, 1436
Cora, 492
Cora Bell, 1436
Daniel William, 1717
Danne Layne, 1044
David Charles, 141
Dee, 190
Devin, 1717
Donna Jo, 1435
Donna Sue (Hardin), 533
Earl, 491
Earl Jr, 491

MOORE (continued)
Earle, 1436
Edna, 1067
Edward, 492
Effie C, 1436
Elijah, 1430
Eliza Jane, 1435
Elizabeth, 777
Elizabeth (Peterson), 803
Ella, 1438
Erma C (Howard), 1416
Ernest O, 1416
Estella, 1438
Ethel E (Weiser), 1416
Ethel L (Heileman), 490
Eugene, 1716
Forest Lylian (Davis), 1435
Francis, 1436
Frank, 293
Gabriel D, 1440
Gary, 1434
George Frank, 1436
George Marley, 1430
George W, 1436
Georgia Lee (Shugarts), 1716
Gerta (--), 1435
Gertie (Myers), 1430
Gertie (Smith), 1436
Glenda Joy h, 1435
Glenn Edwin, 1435
Goldie, 1435
Guy Earl, 1433
Haddie (Davis), 1434
Harold, 490
Hattie, 1438
Hayden L, 803
Hayden Wilfred, 803
Hazel, 1437
Hazel Marie, 1233
Henry, 490
Henry D, 1438
Henry K, 490
Hephzibah, 1438
Howard, 492
Howard D, 1436
Ilsa (Blank), 1434
Imogene Marie (Schalbert), 1434
Iva (Baughtery), 1434
Iva Aldine, 1223
Izelia (Watson), 1436
Jacinda, 1691
Jacob D, 1436
Jacob Eliot, 803
Jacqueline, 491
James, 1592
James Austin, 1433-1434
James Lynn, 551
Jamie, 1717
Janet, 491
Janet Louise (Knotts), 401
Jeffrey Augustine, 1277
Jeffrey Scott, 1345
Jennie Green, 370
Jennifer Lynn, 1691
Jere, 185
Jerry, 1044
Jerry (Wilson), 490
Jo Ann, 1433
John A, 1431
John Earl, 1807

John H, 1258
John S, 1430
Julia, 1277
June, 1440
Justin Lee, 1434
Karen, 491
Kathleen, 1044
Katie, 1438
Keith, 1044
Kendra Sue, 803
Kenton Philip, 803
Kerry David, 1044
Kevin, 1717
Kevin Wayne, 1277
Kimberly Renee, 401
Kimela Kay, 1434
Lafayette W, 1438
Lauretta Mae, 704
Leah Reed (Dorris), 1430
Lester D, 1440
Linda (Bogan), 492
Linda Jane, 141
Linus, 1592
Lois (Moyer), 1044
Lori Ann, 1277
Lori Maurene, 152
Lorraine, 490
Lorri (Bessett), 401
Lottie C, 1440
Lottie E, 1436
Louan (Tanner), 1345
Louise (Harrold), 490
Louise Ann, 490
Lulu May, 1430
Malissa, 1367
Mamie (Sullivan), 1436
Mamie Earline (Wiser), 1807
Marcia, 1437
Marey Ellen, 1437
Margaret Luinda (Hullen), 1433
Margaret Patricia (Seigworth), 1277
Marguerita, 1433
Martin, 1479
Martin Madison, 293
Marvin Eugene, 1807
Mary, 1008
Mary (Wiser), 1672
Mary Alice, 1430
Mary Amanda (Weiser), 803
Mary Ann, 803
Mary Ann (Barnett), 1592
Mary Belle (Bullard), 1188
Mary Ellen, 1438
Mary Ellen (Weiser), 1345
Mary H, 1436
Mary Hutter (Fink), 890
Mary Jane, 1843
Mary Louisa, 293
Maud M, 1436
Maude, 1246
Mildred, 1435
Minnie, 158
Miriam Isobel (Spyker), 1442
Muriel June (Roberts), 803
Myrtle E (Heileman), 498
Nancy (Cox), 1438
Nathan John, 400

Nathan Roy, 401
Nathaniel Aaron, 803
Opal, 1437
Orella, 1438
Osceola Amelia, 293
Pamela, 490
Pat (Donato), 491
Patricia Jean (Magrini), 1277
Patricia Rae (Earnest), 1479
Patty, 1717
Paul, 492
Paul Thomas, 1277
Peggy, 1433
Pete, 966
Peter Lee, 1691
Phyllis Nadine, 401
Phyllis Nan, 1188
Ray, 1437
Ray Arlie, 1434
Rebecca, 491
Rene, 1435
Reva, 1431
Ricey G, 1873
Robert, 1345
Robert L, 1435
Robert Lee, 1188
Robin Diane, 1277
Ronald, 141
Ronine, 1345
Ronnie, 533
Roy Johny Lucus, 1434
Ruby (Henderson), 1435
Ruby Mae, 400
Rubye Ellen (Wiser), 1807
Ruth Ann, 492
Sadie (--), 1437
Sandra, 1345
Sandra Lou (Riggs), 551
Sarah, 1522
Sarah Alice (Huston), 1440
Sarah Emma (Weir), 1438
Sarah Michelle, 1479
Sharifa Daniele, 551
Sharon, 490
Sheila Dee (Favro), 1720
Shelley Lynn Hatfield (Stryker), 401
Shirlee Louise, 1435
Shirley Maxine, 1416
Sophia C, 1439
Sophia J, 1438
Stella, 1008
Steven, 491
Sybil, 1434
Tami Elizabeth, 1347
Tamme Lou, 1044
Thelma (Gibson), 1433
Thomas, 490
Thomas Dale, 1277
Timothy, 491
Vera Florence (Weiser), 400
Vera Joanne, 400
Vinton L, 1442
Vivian Wanda (Spencer), 141
Wallace, 1345
Walter, 498, 1438
Warren H, 1435
Wilbur W, 1416
Wilhelmina Maria

(Schulze), 293
William, 1438
William Barnett, 1592
William Brooke, 890
William G, 490
William Jr, 490
MOOREHOUSE
Elizabeth Louise, 808
Gertrude Arlene (Kuebler), 808
Stanley, 808
MORAN
Helen, 1272
Helen Agusta, 1845
Patricia Ann, 474
MOREHART
Geneva Ann (Alspaugh), 1150
Lisa Ann, 1150
Paul Nixon, 1150
Teri Ann, 1150
MOREHEAD
Catharine Elizabeth (Weiser), 137
John, 137
Kathryn Marie, 519
MORELAND
Ann Amandy, 1193
Catherine (Kahl), 1193
David, 1193
Elizabeth, 1193
Ella (Steinmetz), 1193
George Washington, 1193
John, 1193
Jonathan Carlton, 1193
Sarah Almira (Bagley), 1193
William, 1193
MORESEY
--, 985
Cora, 985
Ellen (Radabaugh), 985
John, 985
MORETENSON
Gilbert Henry, 220
Henry, 220
Mildred Elizabeth (Burch), 220
MORETTI
Evelyn, 150
MOREY
Clytie, 428
MORFORD
Brian Steven, 969
Donald Eugene, 968
Donald Frank, 968
Gail Patricia, 969
Heidi Ann, 969
Karen Elizabeth, 969
Lora Lee, 969
Lynne Janel, 969
Mona (Hayes), 968
Patricia (Nielson), 969
Ronald Eugene, 969
Scott, 969
Shelly Renne, 969
Sheri Lyn, 969
Vera M, 1884
Vera May (Stone), 968
Vickie Lee, 968
MORGAN
Alice J, 588
Anthony, 1692
Beverly Ann, 1776
Brad Lee, 1632
Brian Dean, 1632
Carol, 610
Catherine (Thomas),

1632
Deborah (Kahle), 1243
Denise Ann, 583
Dennis Ray, 583
Donna Jean, 543
Ethel, 576, 1615
Francis, 1292
Gary, 825
Gina Dinete, 583
Jacob, 357
James, 1243
Joanne Marie (Hocker), 583
Judith Ann (Downing), 1632
Kathlyn Jill (Hartmeier), 1334
Kellie, 1693
Kerri Ann, 825
Kevin Donald, 1780
Laura Christine, 1163
Linda L (Womelsdorf), 825
Lisa (Brooke), 1632
Lori Jane (Reser), 1632
Lori Jo, 583
Lousie, 1060
Mabel, 446
Margaret Carolyn, 78
Marilyn Baldwin (Weiser), 1632
Marlene Louise (Wiser), 1780
Mary, 1048
Mary Helen, 542
Melissa Lynn, 825
Nellie Ethel, 1375
Norman (Eighmy), 1693
Rachael, 565
Rebeca, 214
Rena, 556
Richard Joseph, 1632
Robert Dale, 1632
Robert Daryl, 1632
Ronald A, 1334
Ronald Lewis, 1334
Rosalie (Kephart), 1692
Timothy Ken, 583
Todd Landon, 1334
MORIARIT
--, 1014
Chloe (Stephens), 1014
MORIARITY
Barbara Sue (Jorden), 572
Carolyn Sue (Earhart), 573
Daniel Lee, 573
Donna Lynne, 573
Harlan K, 573
Howard A, 573
Jamie Dawn, 573
Jeffery Leon, 573
Kathlee Nichole, 573
Kenneth Wayne, 573
Kenneth Wayne Jr, 573
Lester Allen, 572
Mable Marie (Herring), 572
Margaret Joan, 572
Mary Rebecca, 573
Michael A, 573
Nanda Lou, 573
Nikki Lynn, 573
Noreen Kay (Meese), 573
Ora Alan, 572

MUHLENBERG
(continued)
Elizabeth (Schaum), 343
Elizabeth (Young), 285
Elizabeth C, 288
Ellen, 345
Ellen Maria, 345
Emanuel Samuel, 280
Emily, 342
Emma Elizabeth, 341, 343-344
Emma J (Fell), 299
Ernest A, 284
Eva Elizabeth, 238
Eve Elizabeth, 280, 289
Frances Edith, 287
Francis, 345
Francis Benjamin, 287
Francis Jr, 345
Francis Peter, 288
Francis Swaine, 289
Frederica Harriet, 286
Frederick, 304, 1403
Frederick A C, 360
Frederick Augustus, 284-287, 299-300, 344
Frederick Augustus Conrad, 280, 299
Frederick Augustus Hall, 343
Frederick Hunter, 342, 1561
Frica (Fritzen), 342
George Sheaff, 304
Georgina (Kurtz), 341
Gotthilf Henry Ernestus, 280, 338
Henrietta Augusta, 284, 342
Henrietta Augusta (Muhlenberg), 284, 342
Henry Augustus, 280, 343-344
Henry Augustus Philip, 341
Henry Ernest, 342
Henry Ernestus, 299, 343
Henry Francis, 286
Henry Jr, 1267
Henry Melchior, 14, 87, 279-280, 287, 289, 299, 304, 345, 357-358, 1361, 1365, 1403, 1587
Henry Myers, 280
Henry William, 299
Hester, 281
Hiester Henry, 284, 341-342
J Peter, 280
Jacobus Augustus, 343
Jerome David, 343
John Albert, 343
John Cameron, 299
John Charles, 280
John Christopher, 286
John D S, 280, 1884
John David Stoddard, 286
John Enoch Samuel, 280
John Peter David, 304
John Peter Gabriel, 280, 285

John William, 286
Kate Spang (Hunter), 341
Katharine Hunter, 342
Kimberly Ann (Gramlich), 286
Margaret (Orr), 287
Margaret (Spritzel), 342
Margaret Catherine, 303
Margaret Elizabeth, 344
Margaret G (Van Reed), 288
Margaretta Henrietta, 280, 304-305
Margitta Klara (Leupold), 286
Maria Salome, 345-346
Marie Wilhelmina (Thun), 342
Martha Snider, 285
Mary, 288, 342
Mary (Denny), 289
Mary (Rick), 342, 1561
Mary Ann, 300
Mary Anne, 289
Mary B, 288
Mary Catharine, 338, 344-346
Mary Catharine (Hall), 338
Mary Catharine (Sheaff), 299
Mary Catherine, 280, 301
Mary Elizabeth, 299
Mary Elizabeth (Hiester), 341
Mary Elizabeth Hiester, 341
Nicholas, 342
Nicholas Hunter, 341
Nicholous Melchior, 279
Oliver Evans, 304
Peter, 280, 283
Peter Henry, 287
Philip Dunham, 343
Phillippa Elizabeth, 343
Rachel (Evans), 304
Rebecca (Hiester), 341
Rebecca Amelia, 341
Rosa Amelia, 345
Rosa Catharine, 343
Rosa Katharine, 341-342
Sarah, 289
Sarah (Coleman), 283
Sarah Gardiner, 285
Susanna Elizabeth, 341
Virginia, 303
Virginia Dunham, 342
William, 345
William Augustus, 299
William Clement, 299
William Frederick, 284, 342
William Hiester, 285
MUIR
Anne, 1183
Barbara, 1183
Barbara Jean, 214
Beverly, 210
Beverly Myrtle (Player), 214

Blanch, 1182
Carol Jean, 214
Elmira, 1183
Eva, 1183
Frederick D, 214
Frederick D III, 215
Garrett James, 826
Guy Gerald, 1182
Helen (--), 1183
Joan Adele (Womeldorf), 826
Lewis, 1183
Marian, 1182
Randy William, 826
Robert Edward, 215
Rose, 1182
Susan Ruth (Nelson), 1182
MUIRHEAD
George Washington, 1650
Nancy Carter (Wysor), 1650
MULIALI
Leah R, 1884
MULIOLI
John Adams, 74
Leah Julianne (Rudnicki), 74
MULL
Charles H, 1615
Dwight, 937
Earl E, 1615
Earnest, 1017
Evelyn Louise (Winter), 1017
Flora B, 795
Florence Mae (Truscott), 1615
George, 1615
Lillian, 1017
Mamie O (Weiser), 1615
Newton, 1615
Robert, 1017
Robert Jr, 1017
Ruth I, 1615
Vickie Jo (Smith) Faust, 937
MULLALLY
Katherine Keller, 738
MULLEN
Bernard James, 1453
Bernard Parker, 1453
C Richard, 1498
Carolynn Jane (West), 1498
Catharine Mary, 159
Effie Zella, 579
Elizabeth Anne, 1453
Helen Winifred (Marr), 1453
Kathi Lynn, 1453
Lelia (Wisor), 1706
Marr Parker, 1453
Nancy Jay (Heathe), 1453
Rebecca (Haines), 1453
Richard Marr, 1453
William George, 1706
William Gregory, 1453
MULLER
Anna Margaretha, 1587
Clayton, 470
David A, 1845
Eleanor Alice (Orr), 1296
Frederick, 1296
Justine Annatasia

(Stasiak), 470
Nicole, 470
Norma Jean (Weiser), 1845
MULLIKEN
Mary Alice, 293
MULLIN
Dorothy Ilene (Cummins), 1476
Francis, 1476
Julia Ellen, 1476
Kelly (Bauman), 1719
Maureen Elizabeth, 1477
Miranda, 1719
Mitchell, 1719
Patricia Ann, 1477
Scott, 1719
MULLINS
Calfin Lester, 1804
Christine Loiuse, 1174
Shauna Renee, 1156
MULLIVEX
David, 794
Linda, 794
Phyllis Jean (Roos), 794
Thomas, 794
MULRANEY
James Edward, 1175
Judith Rue (Bathurst), 1175
Megan Rose, 1175
Michele Diane (Cole), 1175
Patricia Rose (McGee), 1175
Thomas Gilbert, 1175
Thomas Gilbert Jr, 1175
MULROY
Julia Marie, 173
MULVIHILL
Tersa, 1547
MUMEA
Adam, 625
Bertha M (Fisher), 625
Charles, 625
Eve, 625
George, 625
Gram, 625
Jess, 627
Lawrence, 625
Lucinda (Fisher), 627
Walter, 625
MUMMA
Emanuel, 1270
Martha (Fenton), 1031
Martha J (Coder), 1270
Samuel, 1031
MUMMERT
Betty L, 870
MUNCH
Mary Anne (Smith), 1633
William Henry, 1633
MUNDELL
Jane Esther (Martin), 249
Marc Brian, 249
Marci Jo, 249
Ronald Paul, 249
MUNDY
Dema Alice, 1189
Harold Jay, 1189
John Wesley, 1189
Lois (Laudermilk), 1189
Luella (Taylor), 1189

Susie Edith (Weiser), 1189
MUNFORD
Mary Safford, 283
MUNGER
--, 473
Marcella (Daughtery), 473
MUNGIA
Anna Marie, 544
MUNRO
Alfred Baird, 1004
Anna Elizabeth (Muhlenberg), 284
Brenda Jean, 1004
Lisa Dawne (Carlson), 1004
Scott Alfred, 1004
Walter, 284
Wanda Jean (Smith), 1004
MUNSEY
Lucille, 1656
MUNSON
Phoebe, 1543
MUNSTERMAN
John Andrew, 1483
Patricia Kaye (Leonhardt), 1483
MUNTZ
Jack, 1013
Mae (Robinson), 1013
Robert, 1013
MUNYON
Jeannette, 1736
MURDOCK
Audrey Madaline (Fess), 558
Edward, 558
MURFIN
Lynn Suzanne, 383
MURILLO
Frank Marcos, 1810
Virginia Jane (Wiser), 1810
MURPHEY
Sarah (Ogle), 1592
William, 1592
MURPHY
--, 1358
Ala Maybell (Weiser), 1187
Archie, 465
Bruce, 556
Clara (Schutter), 1358
Clarence J, 562
David, 1182
Donald E, 129
Donna (Johnson), 556
Edith (Myers), 877
Elizabeth, 1078
Elizana, 531
Eugene Leland, 1187
Eulice, 1447
Evelyn (Weiser), 129
Hannah Jeanette, 821
Jacob, 555
James, 1372
Kenneth William, 1182
Laura M (Herring), 555
Lillian Arrel (Banter), 562
Linda Michelle (Johnson), 637
Margaret, 1182
Margaret (Winkleman), 1372
Mark, 637

NALL
Sharon Elaine, 566
NANCE
Bernita, 1124
NANCY
Roberta, 1501
NAPIER
Amanda Arlene, 1494
Donna Arlene (Zook), 1494
Inez, 1431
John A, 1494
Shadrack, 1494
NAPIERE
Diana Lee, 1345
Esther Lee (Patterson), 1345
Jeraldine (Menger), 1345
Mary Esther (Weiser), 1345
Stanley Leon, 1345
Timothy William, 1345
William Herbert, 1345
NAREHOOD
Vickie, 748
NASE
Helen Marie, 728
NASH
Darrell, 215
Frank William, 995
Helen, 995
Ivan Harry, 995
Jeanne (Wall), 995
Mamie Dorinda (Kahl), 995
Mary, 1862
Pearl Marie (Weiser), 215
NASHOLD
Bess Elaine, 841
NATTER
Marie Barbara, 1605
NAUGLE
--, 1348-1349
Charles, 1348
Janet Darlene, 471
Naomi (Weiser), 1348
Thomas, 1348
NAULTY
Florine (Shaffer), 1037
James, 1037
NAUSS
Allen Howard, 168
Allen James, 168
Jonathan Michael, 168
Susan Elizabeth (Hogue), 168
NAVE
Shirley, 1448
NAVY
Charles A, 1300
Chelsea Joel, 1300
Joelene Ann (Barb), 1300
Vincente Antonio, 1300
NAY
Anna Mae (Wiser), 1190
Edgar Grant, 1190
NAYLOR
Agnes Sarah, 696
NCNAIR
Charie, 437
NEACE
Charles, 1183
Eva Ruby (Nelson), 1183
Winnifred, 1183

NEAGLE
Anna Theresa, 1749
NEAGLEY
Ann Elizabeth, 894
NEAL
Gail, 1770
Gretchen Christa (Rodziewicz), 449
Martha Ann (Ashcraft), 1195
Martha Kahle, 1192
Ronald, 449
William G, 1195
NEALE
Laura, 882
NEALLY
Muriel (McElwain), 1547
Robert, 1547
Shawn, 1548
NEAN
Ara W, 111
Winnie Maud (Akins), 111
NEARY
Linda, 82
NEATHERLY
Lena Tell, 943
NEBINGER
Alice (Shettel), 853
Alma Leora (Commerer), 854
Bertie, 854
Chapman, 854
Chapman William Jr, 854
Charles, 853
Emma, 853
Gene Melvin, 854
John Rankin, 854
Lulu (Ashenfelter), 854
Rena Mae, 854
Villa (Wolf), 854
NEDERLE
Martha, 90
NEEB
Bartley Alan, 483
Brian David, 483
Carolyn Jane (Ansted), 483
Kenneth Earl, 483
Laurene Lynette (Stucky), 483
Marylene Mae, 483
Sandra Ann, 483
Sheila Kaye, 483
Stanley Clayton, 483
NEELEY
Rhonda Lynn (Smith), 571
Roy, 571
NEELY
Bernice, 1321
Roberta Joan, 541
NEEPER
Margie Ann, 606
NEER
Janet, 1022
NEESE
Helen Edna, 1068
Sarah Catharine, 1366
NEFF
-- (--), 994
Aaron Creed, 1200
Ann Rebecca, 195
Beatrice Alice, 870
Bessie (Riland), 1114
Christopher, 195
Doris J, 1114

Ercil, 272
Francis H, 1114
George, 1114
Henry, 994
Horace B, 1114
Jennie E (Snyder), 1114
John H, 1114
Larry, xiv
Larry Melvin, iv, 1010
Laura Dee (Kahle), 1200
Leah (Kehl), 994
Lois Jeannette, 1092
Mable, 994
Marjorie Louise, 1071
Michael, 195
P J, 1200
Rebecca (Wallace), 195
Sarah May (Bohn), 1071
Susan, 994
Virginia May, 1071
William, 994
William Hoy, 1071
Zachary Todd, 1200
NEFOS
Lois Ann (Donne), 830
Thomas George, 830
NEGHERTON
Kathryn, 1017
NEIDER
Helen M, 1637
NEIDIG
Abraham, 813, 904
Albert, 740
Arline (Mench), 741
Beldon, 1525
Charles E, 741
Claud L, 741
David, 1525
Diana, 741
Domer, 741
Edna (Wolf), 741
Gordon Emerson, 740
Hannah Boyer, 742
Hannah M (Boyer), 740
Harold Leon, 741
Harold Leon Jr, 741
Henry Morris, 740
Ida Nadine (Kline), 1525
James, 741
James Raynor, 741
Jason, 741
Joan, 1525
Joy Christine (Ditty), 741
Lois Janette, 741
Margaret (Eister), 740
Mary C, 740
Mary Elizabeth, 743
Mertie Selow, 741
Ronald, 741
Ronald Henry, 741
Sarah Catharine (Eister), 743
Stephen Wilmer, 743
Truman Vernon, 743
Valerie, 741
Viola (Haas), 743
NEIDIGH
Ruth, 1534
NEIGHBERT
--, 1828
Hannah Ann (Wiser), 1828

NEIL
Belle Martha, 1258
Mary Jane (Milliken), 1683
Samuel, 1683
NEILD
Betty Packard, 790
NEILES
Brittany Jane, 290
Cyril C, 290
Cyril Joseph, 290
Diana Delane Campbell (Lind), 291
Dorothy Ann, 290
Jane Maurine (Christensen), 290
Lindsay Jo, 290
Marise Annette (Ege), 290
Shauna Marie, 290
William Ward, 291
NEILL
Betty, 35
NEILLY
Peggy Joan (Kahle), 1262
Thomas Maxwell, 1262
NEILSON
Bobbie Sue, 1262
Eloise, 502
James W, 1625
Lillian Annie (Weiser), 1625
Marilyn Eleanor, 1490
Nancy Ellen (Gifford), 371
Neil, 371
NEIMAN
Cassandra W, 1417
David William, 861
Delton Wilber, 655
Elizabeth (Weiser), 1417
Eugene Delton, 655
Floyd Joseph, 655
Jacob, 1417
Janet Lorene, 655
Jonathan David, 861
Joseph, 1417
Justina Marie, 861
Marlyn Sue (Raby), 861
Melba Mae, 655
Myrtle Marie (Herman), 655
Paula Marie (Cvek), 861
Sandra Ann, 655
William E, 861
NEIN
Mary Ann O, 1620
NEISCHWENDER
Annie E, 251
NEISWENDER
Diana Elaine (Wiest), 643
James Edward, 643
Timothy Paul, 643
NEITZ
Ellen Arlene, 683
Hilda (Shaffer), 1037
William, 1037
NEITZER
David Matthew, 956
Emily Anne, 956
Katherine Ashley, 956
Martha Jane (Denis), 956
Patrick Michael, 956

NEKOLA
Mary, 1487
NELL
Helen (Crilly), 187
Helen C, 182
Marian, 187
William H, 187
NELLANS
Alvina Agina, 1877
Emma, 1877
NELLIS
Debra, 1791
NELSON
Alan, 1798, 1835
Andrea Marie, 1581
Andrew, 972
Andrew Donald, 290
Ann Jane (Johnstone), 973
Barbara, 428
Barry Craig, 1581
Benjamin P, 38
Betty A (Erney), 870
Betty Ruth (Shugarts), 1717
Bonnie Rita, 1717
Bryan, 974
Cameron Jay, 290
Charles David, 852
Cheryl Lynn, 1691
Clinton E, 870
Colette (Tardiff), 290
Colleen (Sidle), 1678
Connie Lynn, 31
Craig Cameron, 290
Cynthia Gay, 1581
Cynthia Lynn, 974
Deborah Lou (Wiser), 1835
Della Margaret (Wiser), 1873
Don Wilton, 1873
Dorothy Ann (Naiden), 1563
Douglas Arthur, 973
Edward David, 1182
Edward Earl, 1717
Eleanor May, 973
Eliza Jane, 1181
Ellen Shirley, 1457
Erick Paul, 1563
Eugene Alfred, 1691
Eva Ruby, 1183
Evaland (Blanchard), 973
Geneanne LaRayne (Floyd), 974
Geoffrey, 1581
Gilmer, 185
Gladys, 1692
Glenn, 1563
Gregory, 1581
Grover Cleveland, 1183
Harvey Lane, 1183
Heather, 491
Helen Louise (Howard), 852
Hiram Walter, 1181
Ida May, 1181
J N, 851
James Newton, 852
Jamie, 324
Jane, 515
Janine Rae, 1691
Jeanette, 543
Jere Moore (Brown), 185
Jessie Garfield, 1183

NELSON (continued)
Kathryn Augusta (Rutherford), 38
Kevin Barry, 516
Kristine Louise, 1182
Kristine Marie, 974
Laura Edith (Moffitt), 852
Leola Arlene (Kephart), 1691
Leola K, 1885
Lois, 1733
Louise, 45
Louise Virginia, 852
Mabel, 972
Mable (--), 1183
Margaret (Bowman), 1182
Margaret (Hoffman), 1182
Marian Lucille (Barbe), 799
Marvin Leroy, 973
Mary Bell, 1181
Mary Darlene (Bonine), 290
Mary Jane (Sprague), 973
Mary Louise, 852
Mella Mae (Bower), 972
Mello Sue, 544
Melody Sue, 201
Melvin, 973
Miriam Gertrude (Wiser), 1678
Noreen Rennie, 1182
Odie Dell, 1181
Olga (Olives), 973
Opal, 799
Osa Ellen (Angell), 1182
Patricia G (Sweazy), 1581
Patty Jean, 1717
Phyllis Ann, 272
Phyllis Gaye (Hilty), 852
Raleigh P, 1182
Ray Walter, 1678
Richard Samuel, 852
Robert, 1181
Robert Edward, 1182
Robert James, 852
Ronald, 974
Ronald Allen, 974
Rose, 717
Russell Paul, 1581
Samuel McCartney, 852
Sarah Adena, 1181
Seraphine (Kearns), 1181
Shannon N, 125
Sherryl A (Weiser), 125
Sheryl, 540
Shirley Jean, 1171
Stella, 972
Stephen Michael, 974
Susan Ruth, 1182
Sylvia Lynn, 973
Tanya (Wiser), 1798
Theresa, 1183
Timothy, 491
Travis Jay, 290
Trina Margaret, 1182
Vera Sally, 1182
Verda, 1182

Verle, 974
Vern, 974
Vernon, 21
Virginia, 525
Virginia Shook, 185
Wava Joan, 1717
Wayne K, 125
Wendy K, 125
Wilbur S, 1183
Woodrow Wilson, 973
Zelpha May, 1766
NEM
Charles, 1324
Denise Lyn (Dafler), 1324
NEMEIAK
Jane, 963
NEMETH
Julie, 1600
NEMS
Velma, 101
NENDENHALL
Donna Carol, 1451
NEPPER
Damion, 176
Nicci Ann (Woolridge), 176
NEPTUNE
Harold W, 1263
Velma Elverda (Kahle), 1263
NERINO
Barbara Jean, 1112
Michael, 1112
Ralph, 1112
Ralph Anthony, 1112
Sarah Marguerite, 1112
NERMAN
Elizabeth (Moreland), 1193
Mahlon, 1193
NES
Arabella, 1427
Caroline (King), 1427
Charles M, 1427
E Gulick, 1427
Elizabeth, 1427
Elizabeth (Weiser), 1427
Frederick, 1427
Henrietta, 1427
Henry, 1427
Margaret, 1427
NESTLE
Leila Fern, 953
NESTOR
David Francis, 133
Ida (Townsend), 133
Paul, 133
NETHERY
Karen L, 118
NETTLES
Kathy, 1200
NEUBAUM
Frederick William Jr, 669
Gary, 669
June Lorraine (Pittinger), 669
Terry William, 669
NEUBERGES
Damian, 1374
Judith Ann (Weiser), 1374
NEUENSCHWANDER
baby boy, 517
baby girl, 517
Daryl G, 517
Delbert J, 517

Edwin D, 517
Gary K, 517
La Dene (Akerman), 517
NEUFER
Florence (Cooper), 1026
Harriet, 1027
Joan R, 1026
John E, 1026
Lula (Plank), 1026
Luther Earl, 1026
Mary, 1026
Samuel S, 1026
NEUMAN
Alma, 215
NEVERS
Bruce Allen, 1563
Emelia Elizabeth (Naiden), 1563
Jennifer Ida, 1563
Vanessa, 1563
NEWALL
Elinore Lee, 1545
NEWBERGER
Helen, 473
NEWBERRY
Barbara, 718
Cindy (Wysor), 1660
Elanore, 1540
Grace (Metzger), 718
Irma Virginia, 1586
James, 718
Joshua, 1660
Kundis, 1660
Lorraine, 732
Mary H, 666
Mattie Belle (Shindler), 1586
Randy, 1660
Vernon Clay, 1586
NEWBOLD
Emily, 303
NEWCOMB
Bernard, 1486
Dorys Etta, 1486
Lon, 1486
Murel Joy (Earnest), 1486
Twyla Jean, 1486
NEWCOMER
Barbara, 1125
Fannie, 1421
Frances Elizabeth (Phelps), 1125
Joanne, 1125
John Howard, 1125
NEWELL
Barbara Ann, 1124
Daniel Douglas, 1563
Greg, 1562-1563
Lance, 1563
Misty Dawn, 1563
Norma Frances (Naiden), 1562
Sarah Josephine, 1192
Sarah Maude (Naiden) Bast, 1563
NEWHOUSE
Terri, 636
NEWLAND
Cynthia, 463
NEWMAN
--, 80
Ada Lee (Wise), 1168
Annie, 1525
Anthony John, 1301
Arden Charles, 1168
Arden Neil, 1168

Barbara Ann, 1302
Bernadette Theresa, 1552
Catherine, 1524
Catherine Patricia, 1549
Cindy (Salvamosce), 1302
Clinton Joseph, 1549
Doris, 1524
Doris Elizabeth, 1551
Doris Lee, 860
Dwight, 975
Earl, 1524
Elizabeth (Weiser), 1524
Eva (Leech), 1524
Heather Lynn, 647
Ivan, 1524
Janellen, 1124
Jerome, 975
Jocelyn (Burke), 1549
John, 1524
John Mark, 1302
John Richard, 1301
June Marie, 1550
Larry, 1524
Laura Teresa (Minnick), 1549
Lila May, 1524
Lisa Mae, 1168
Lori Lee, 1168
Lucy (Bassler), 80
Mable Catherine (Evans), 1549
Mamie, 1031
Marla Ann (Wiser), 1301
Martha Evelyn, 1549, 1552
Mary Pierre, 1549
Maryalma Cecilia, 1549
Michael Gerald, 1302
Mildred (Tripp), 975
Rita May, 1550
Robert, 1524
Rose Ann, 1210
Scott Allen, 1168
Sula, 1025
Thomas, 1524
William Basil, 1549
William Clifford, 1544, 1549
William Clifford Jr, 1552
NEWPORT
Albert B, 350
Dorothea, 351
Dorothea Richards (Davison), 350
John Albert, 351
Joseph, 351
Paul Clifford, 351
NEWSOME
Betty, 936
NEWSWANGER
John E, 255
Vera Arlene (Brehm), 255
NEWTON
Amber Nicole, 42
Beatrice, 1237
Cheryl Ann, 487
Diane Esther, 868
Dolly Adeline (Still), 868
Donna Lee (Kern), 487
Dwight Rex, 42

Dwight Rex Jr, 42
Eugene Russell, 868
Flora Beatrice (Willey), 41
Hiram, 1236
Jennifer Nicole, 487
Jessica Caitlin, 41
Kathy Ann, 684
Kenneth Wesley, 487
Laura Christine, 41
Lon Willey, 41
Louvenia Myrtle, 41
Lyla (Kahle), 1236
Minnie, 771
Norma Jane (Meriwether), 41
Patricia Ann (Huff), 684
Paula Sue (Wallace), 42
Phillip Charles, 41
Raymond Edward, 868
Raymond Russell, 868
Rebecca Ann (Long), 41
Robert Lee, 684
Robert Lee Jr, 684
Sarah Kay, 41
Stanley Charles Jefferson, 41
Stanley David, 41
Suzanne, 42
Vera Rose (Belford), 41
Victor George, 41
Wilda (Cantrell), 42
NEY
Angela Diane (Stiely), 658
Jordan Michael, 658
Kate, 1519
Michael, 658
NG
Jean, 860
NGO
James Allen, 644
NICCUM
Iris, 104
NICE
Addie Juliet (Derr), 244
Benjamin, 244
Benjamin D, 238
Benjamin Derr, 244
Cora Elizabeth, 646
Edna Matilda (Seidel), 244
Laura Edna (Smithers), 244
Mary, 247
Ruthanna May, 660
Vera (Bartholomew), 244
NICHILO
Mary Pearl, 1534
NICHOLAS
Joan Faye Sannon, 424
NICHOLLS
--, 1711
Lois (Wisor), 1711
Mary Ann, 849
NICHOLS
Debra Marie (Austin), 153
Elizabeth, 153
Elsie, 971
Erma May (Hocker), 580
Eulalia Lorraine

NICHOLS (continued)
Eulalia Lorraine
(Jones) (continued)
(Jones), 580
Helen Elizabeth, 192
Joanne Evelyn, 1503
Judith (Greenwald),
580
Kathryn (Hart), 580
Lena, 48
Lucina, 1817
Rebecca (Holms), 580
Robert Ray, 580
Sarah, 1763
Shirley May, 580
Steven Ray, 580
Thomas R, 153
William Ralph, 580
William Royce, 580
NICHOLSON
Clara Lucina, 1194
John Hartman, 1262
Larry, 1439
Lynn, 1262
Michael Charles, 1262
Paul, 1439
Peggy Joan (Kahle),
1262
Velma (Whitaker),
1439
NICK
Diane Susan, 130
NICKAS
Christa, 747
Louis R, 747
Melinda Jan (Klinger),
747
Michael Art, 747
NICKEL
Edith Agnes, 674
NICKELL
Blanche Aline, 989
NICKELS
Patricia, 31
NICKELSON
Julie, 1478
NICKLES
Donald Allen, 144
Donald Zachary Allen,
144
Joshua Allen, 144
Josie Lynn (Hughes),
144
NICOLLS
Ann Hall, 282
Ann Hall (Muhlenberg),
344
Anne Hall, 344
Frederic William, 344
Frederick S Jr, 1883
Frederick W Sr, 1883
Frederick William, 344
George Taylor, 344
Gustavus Anthony,
343-344
Minnie Ransey
(Taylor), 344
Rosa Catharine
(Muhlenberg), 343
Sterne Taylor, 344
NICOLS
Helen, 1367
NIDA
Jimmy Lee, 455
Jody Lee (Green), 455
NIEBLING
Charles, 464
Mary Viola (Binkley),
464

NIEFERT
John B, 1761
Sarah (Altenderfer),
1761
NIELSEN
Amy Kaylene, 177
Ashley Beth, 177
Diana Lee (Woodridge),
177
Dorothy Marie
(Mosier), 381
Ernest, 381
Ernest Ray, 381
infant daughter, 381
May Elizabeth, 1778
Robb Howard, 177
Wayne, 177
NIELSON
Anna (Budd), 302
Betty Norine (Jensen),
123
Edward E, 123
Edward Rulon, 123
Elizabeth Inez, 123
J R Ward, 123
Joe Floyd, 123
John, 302
Karen Sue (Miller),
123
Marjorie, 69
Maxine (--), 123
Melissa Max, 123
Patricia, 969
Ward Edward, 123
Wiston Max, 123
NIEMEYER
Helene, 316
NIEMI
Arthur M, 1352
Gwen N (Clymer),
1352
Jeffrey Eric, 1352
Natalie Gwen, 1352
NIEMOND
Margaret, 1523
NIESET
Margaret Loyola, 477
NILAND
--, 1030
Agnes L (Cooper),
1030
NIMON
Frances M, 1159
NIPPERT
Harriet Ann, 57
NISLEY
Andrew Richard, 1140
Charles Ernest, 1139
Cheryl Legene, 1140
Donna Jean, 1139
Lorna Lou (Calvin),
1140
Mary Ruth (Schaffner),
1139
Matthew Scott, 1140
Richard Ernest, 1140
Zella Lou, 1140
NISSEN
Daniel P, 1564
Kim Louise (Noland),
1564
NIX
Brittany Ann, 1174
Charles Andrew,
1173-1174
Sophia Lorraine (Carn),
1173
NIXON
Dustin Charles

Brandon, 1631
Lee Edward, 584
Louise, 1631
Mary Kelly, 380
Richard Lee, 584
Richard Lee Jr, 584
Sharron Louise (Blair),
584
NOAH
Dollie Louise Ellen,
152
NOBLE
Coral, 1236
Mary, 829
NOBLES
Joanne Charrlin, 918
NOCAR
Deborah, 1550
NOECKER
Rebecca, 1360
NOEL
Charles, 926
Lydia Ann (Weiser),
926
NOFZIGER
Ambria Lynn, 632
Cheryl Lynn (Grieser),
632
Douglas, 632
Ethel Marie, 495
NOGGAL
Dorothy, 676
NOGGLE
Lillie Bell, 1142
NOHL
Daniel Eugene, 803
Kendra Sue (Moore),
803
Melissa Renae, 803
Philip Alan, 803
NOLAN
Francis Matthew, 247
Francis Matthew Jr,
247
J Bennett, 15
Kathleen Elizabeth, 247
Kathryn, 1469
Katie Rau (Fasig), 247
Mary (Nice), 247
NOLAND
Allen Kay, 1564
Ann Marie, 1564
Barry Allen, 1564
Carrie Winifred
(Naiden), 1563
Christopher Dean,
1564
Clifford C, 1563
Cyndi (Geist), 1564
Dean Carroll, 1564
Earl Lorraine, 1564
Frances Ellen
(Lonergan), 1564
Georgia Jean, 1563
Gerda Irmgard Erica
(Schultz), 1564
Johanna Wilaminia
(Vandenberg), 1564
Kim Louise, 1564
Mary Ann (Kaumanns),
1564
Mary Kay, 1564
Michael Allen, 1564
Roberta Gayle (Ringer),
1564
Sharon Kay, 1564
NOLL
Anna Grace, 705
Bailey, 1066

Bettie Jane, 1064
Charlene Marie, 1064
Charles Edwin, 1063,
1066
Charles Irvin, 1064
Clarence Emanuel,
1065
David Scott, 1065
Dorothy (Maynor),
1066
Dorothy Jean, 1065
Edna Victoria (Krape),
1063
Emma Jane (Sholl),
1063
Eva Belle (Williamson),
1063
Gail (Martz), 1065
Harry Hix, 1063
Isabella (Weiser), 1626
Jacquelyn Emma, 1063
James Clarence, 1065
Jane Marjorie (Kunkle),
1064
Jeffrey M, 1065
John H, 1626
Kenneth Leroy, 1066
Lawrence J, 1626
Matthew P, 1066
Mildred (Blythstone),
1065
Minnie Kate (Sholl),
1065
Minnie V, 1626
Nomi Eilien, 1066
Paul Leroy, 1065
Rebecca Louise, 1064
Rod, 425
Ronda Sue (Dorrell),
425
Ross, 1066
Sarah, 1626
Simon, 1626
Sylvia, 1066
Sylvia (Cooley), 1066
William Jacob, 1063
Wynn, 1066
NOLTENIUS
Agnes (MacKay), 324
Eberhard Ludwig, 324
Elisabeth Mathilde, 318
Johannes, 318
Johannes Eberhard Jr,
318
Margarethe Sophie,
318
Sophie Henriette
(Schwab), 318
Walter Hermann
Heinrich, 318
NOLTENUIS
Clementine Sophie
(Klupfel), 324
Eberhard, 324
Margaret Henrietta,
324
NOLTING
Alpheretta, 826
NONEMAN
Deborah, 623
NORBECK
Martha Jane, 910
NORDSTROM
Jane Louise, 222
NOREEN
Sharon, 749
NOREIGA
Mary Victoria, 1220

NOREMBERG
Shirley Ann, 799
NORFLEET
Barbara Jean, 1261
NORHRUP
George, 1683
Sarah E (Milliken),
1683
NORMAN
Etha May (Prewett),
445
Henry Ransome, 820
Ida Mae, 1462
Joan, 820
Minerva Esther
(Boyles), 820
Minerva Jane, 820
Richard A, 445
Ronald, 820
NORQUIST
Jodi Lea, 802
NORRIS
--, 1442
Betty Jane (Spyker),
1442
Charles, 1688
Cora Verlindia (Tuller),
388
Donna Sue
(Roadenbaugh), 665
Edith Marie, 388
Gary Lee, 665
Grace B (Kephart),
1688
Hazel, 388
Jeffrey Lynn, 1442
Jody, 205
Joe Orley, 205
Joseph Augusta, 205
Joy, 205
Kimberlee Dawn, 665
Mary Ellen (Watson),
205
Nancy Ann, 205
Ralph, 388
William, 388
NORSTROM
--, 1737
Adrian, 1737
Evelyn (Williams),
1737
NORTH
Angelina R (Richter),
68
Calvin B, 68
Isabella J (Parker), 68
Roscoe Calvin, 68
NORTHRIDGE
George A, 1401
Mary Susanna
(Wagner), 1401
Nancy Sue, 1401
NORTHRUP
Cealon, 431
Ethel Lenora (Knecht),
431
Lillian B (Knecht), 431
Raymond, 431
NORTHWAY
Frank Earl, 120
Grace (Pettit), 120
Lorenzo Marshall, 120
Mary Jane (Evans),
120
Minette Priscilla
(Crawford), 120
Venda Lucille, 121
Venda Patricia, 120

ORRIS (continued)
Walter Steven, 869
Wendy Louise (Stuck), 756
ORSINI
Kenneth, 175
Nancy Joan (Arbegast), 175
ORT
Hannah, 1475
ORTEZ
Barbara Jeanette, 436
ORTH
Adam, 1517
Adam Henry, 1517
Anna Shipley, 1517
Bertha E (Ross), 1517
Caroline, 1517
Catharine Elizabeth, 1516
Christian Henry, 1516
Edward Lawrence, 1517
Elizabeth (Cox), 1517
Elizabeth Bridgeman (Dixon), 1517
Henry, 1517
Henry L, 1517
James Wilson, 1517
Martha Cummins (Kerr), 1517
Mary W, 1517
Rebecca, 1516
Rebecca (Rahm), 1516
Rebecca Reily, 1517
Roberta Elizabeth, 1517
William, 1517
ORZECHOWSKI
Darlene (Keefer), 808
Elizabeth Anne, 808
Jennifer Sarah, 808
Joseph John, 808
ORZECK
Betty June, 733
OSANTOWSKI
Florentine Felecia, 1481
OSBORN
Alice Ada (Smith), 158
Carrie B (Linder), 154
Cynthia Gay (Nelson), 1581
Deborah Sue (Snider), 199
Diane Elizabeth, 1040
Francis, 1480
Franklin, 159
Franklin A, 158
Gretchen Louise, 1040
Joel E, 154
John William, 1039-1040
Josephine Schlesinger, 159
Patricia Ann (Linderman), 1039
Thomas, 1581
William Warren, 199
OSBORNE
--, 920
Brenda Kay (Weiser) Blair, 920
Clarence Walter, 365
Debra Lynn, 610
Edna Gaynell (Frangowlakis), 1752
Eunice M (Farney), 365

George Gordon, 365
George William, 365
Janice E, 365
Jeanine Grace, 101
Jerry, 610
John, 1399
Josephine (Walker), 101
Lester Darnell, 1752
Margaret Anne Wagner (Riglin), 1399
Ollie Gaynell, 1752
Rynne Megan, 1399
Scott Darnell, 1752
Susan (Brown), 610
Susan Elizabeth (Bauder), 365
William, 101
OSDOBA
Carolyn Mae, 405
Daniel Michael, 404
Gretchen Margaret, 404
Katie Elizabeth, 404
Kristin Rae (Moen), 404
Rachel Anne, 404
OSGOOD
Chase Ebenezer, 1764
Eliza J (Wiser), 1764
OSMAN
Donna G, 356
Joyce Mae (Hockenbroch), 715
Marlin E, 715
Mary, 1452
Pearl, 1025
OSS
Delphine, 515
OSSMAN
Ethel Mariam (Witmer), 702
Rue Weaver, 702
OSTER
Donald Eugene, 820
Kathryn Shirley (Sprinkle), 820
Steven, 820
OSTERHAUT
Elizabeth (Pickert), 1574
William, 1574
OSTERLE
Martinus, 1406
OSTERMILLER
Elizabeth Jane, 1825
OSTLE
Alexander Kyle, 422
Allan Andrew, 422
Bernard, 421
Lorene Ruth, 422
Matthew James, 422
Ruth Jean (Lowe), 421
OSTRANDER
--, 1584
Margaret (Van Slyke), 1584
OSVATH
Kornelia Maria, 381
OSWALD
Barbara, 1160
Catherine, 147
Dorothy Louise, 147
Eliza Ellen Nora (Schwoyer), 1637
Harry, 147
Nina (Weiser), 147
Peter Samuel, 1637

OSWALT
Shirley, 527
OTEY
Anita Rowene (Stephens), 1448
Cindy Mae, 1448
Jrissa Marie, 1448
Philip, 1448
OTT
Albert B, 75
Amy Lynn (Brungart), 1088
Christopher Dean, 1088
Frederick H, 75
Gayle, 75
Hildagard W (Funk), 1633
Margaretha, 6
Martha Elmire (Ulrich), 75
Pamela Sue, 481
Sandra Lee, 448
William, 75
William E. 1633
OTTAWAY
Catherine Ann, 70
OTTEMILLER
Edia C (Rockey), 1460
William H, 1460
OTTENHOUSEN
--, 976
Nettie (Rubendell), 976
OTTERBECK
Ann (--), 967
Bernice Marie (Rosenberger), 967
Brian, 967
Burdette, 967
Carol (Warner), 966
Carol Lee, 963
David Floyd, 967
Deborah Joan, 966
Donald Burdette, 967
Donald Edward, 963
Donald May, 963
Dorothy (Dole), 963
Eldon Gordon Mac, 967
Ella Mae (Steel), 966
Ellen Corinne (Skogman), 967
Gary May, 963
Gregory Lee, 967
Guy Steven, 966
Herman, 965
Herman Burdette, 967
Hermine (Waring), 967
Holly Lyn, 966
Jane (Nemeiak), 963
Jennifer Ellen, 967
Joan Marie, 963
Jonathan William, 967
Katherine L, 963
Kenneth R, 963
Kristen Marie, 967
LaVera B, 962
Lila M (Alderson), 963
Linda (Post), 966
Louis C, 962
Marilyn Melody Kay, 966
Marilyn Melody Kay (Otterbeck), 966
Marlana Vera, 967
Maxine, 966
Mildred, 965
Nancy (Gassman), 966
Nancy Ann, 967

Nettie L (Steel), 962
Pearl (Steel), 965
Peter Eugene, 966
Rebecca Jan, 967
Sandra, 967
Tizzy Dee, 966
Treasure Lee, 967
Troy Steve, 966
Wilbur Allen, 966
Wilbur Myrle, 966
William Fred, 966
William Jon, 967
William Lyle, 967
OTTERBEIN
Grace Amanda, 1615
OTTO
Craig Allan, 259
Dean Lowell, 259
Edward Eyster, 259
Elizabeth, 345
Gladys Elinor (Keeley), 259
Judith, 1356
Mary Louise, 1374
OUSLEY
Alyce Ann (Womelsdorf), 823
James Willard, 823
Lawrence Samuel, 823
Reuben James, 823
OUTCAULT
Clark, 1179
Lysbeth Ann, 1179
Lysbeth Anne (Musselman), 1179
Susan Mary, 1179
Timothy, 1179
OVERLY
Betty J (Hynicka), 1515
John, 1515
OVERMAN
Gerald, 989
Susann Jane (Rehbock), 989
OVERMEIER
Mary E, 628
OVERMEYER
Betty, 263
Flo (Haschel), 263
Fred, 263
Mabel (Haschel), 263
Perry, 263
OVERMYER
Alfred, 502
Anna Katherine, 502
Daisy (Evans), 502
Estelle, 502
George Washington, 502
Harry, 503
Howard, 479
Ilda, 479
Jeremiah, 503
Laura H, 503
Mabel E, 503
Nettie E, 502
Olive, 263
Rueben B, 502
OVERPACK
Fredric Richard, 927
Mary Frances (Raver), 927
OVERPECK
Alice Mariah (Riggs), 523
Evelynne Maurine (Wiser), 1185
Harold, 1185

Ida S, 523
John, 523
Mary, 523
Russell, 523
OVERSTREET
Elsie (Wysor), 1662
Guy, 1662
OVIEDO
Bernard, 589
Carmen Julia, 589
Jo Ann (Duncan), 589
Petra Jeanne, 589
OWEN
Archibald Alexander, 1452
Brian Craig, 418
Bruce Douglas, 418
Carter Brown, 1452
Clayton Douglas, 418
Daniel Mark, 418
Donna (Weiser), 417
Donna Mae (Weiser), 418
Douglas R, 1453
Elizabeth Fairchild (Spyker), 1452
Emily Jean, 418
Genevieve, 1507
Gina Lynn (Allender), 418
Glenda Allen (Brown), 1452
Henry Eyer Spyker, 1453
Henry Spyker, 1453
Jacob Paul, 418
Karen Sue (Wilson), 418
Kendra Lynn (Staples), 418
Kimberly Jean (Reynolds), 418
Kory Allan, 418
Laura Lynn, 418
Lyndsy Jo, 418
Mary Virginia, 1802
Molly Carrington, 1453
Morgan Lesley, 418
Paul Ronald, 418
Peggy Rae, 168
Polly Ann (Keller), 1453
Rhonda Marie, 418
Ronald Kimes, 418
Sarah Jayne, 418
Susan Spyker, 1453
Timothy Keller, 1453
OWENS
Annie, 1436
Christopher, 666
Ethan Wade, 882
Judith Marie (Wise), 882
Katie Jo, 1660
Kelly Michelle, 666
Marilou (Parent), 666
Michael Wade, 882
Mildred B (Knecht), 431
Pauline M, 590
Stanley, 431
Thomas E, 666
Toni Jean, 666
OXENREIDER
Florence Elizabeth (Koch), 714
Forrest, 714
Stephen Paul, 714

PICKERT (continued)
Conrad, 1571, 1574
Daniel, 1574-1575
Dina, 1575
Dorothy (Bishop), 1575
Eche, 1575
Edith, 1577
Elias, 1575
Elinda (Richardson), 1583
Elizabeth, 1574-1575
Elizabeth (--), 1574
Elizabeth (Felter), 1574
Ephraim, 1575
Eva (Klaas), 1571
Fannie (Makepeace), 1577
Frederick, 1575
George, 1582
George N, 1572
Gertrude, 1575
Guilbert, 1577
Henry, 1572
Isaac, 1572
Jacob, 1572, 1574
Jacobus, 1571
James, 1574
James H, 1583
Jane, 1575
Jemima (Briggs), 1575
Jennie A, 1575
Johannes, 1571-1572, 1583
John, 1575
John Heinrick, 1572
John Jr, 1571
Jonas, 1582
Joseph, 1574-1575
Josephine (Sherwood), 1577
Leah, 1571, 1583
Lelander, 1575
Louis, 1577
Louise (De Garmo), 1575
Lucina, 1575
Magdalena, 1574
Magdalena (Countryman), 1572
Margaret, 1574
Margaret (Stenzel), 1572
Margaret Marie (Garlock), 1583
Maria, 1574
Maria Catherine (--), 1574
Maria Elizabeth (--), 1571
Maria Margaret, 1572
Marilla T (--), 1583
Mary, 1575, 1582
Mary (--), 1583
Merian, 1582
Morgan, 1577
Moses, 1575
Nancy (--), 1575
Nicholas, 1572
Nicolaus, 16
Peter, 1575
Rachel, 1571
Rebecca, 1575
Roxy (Conant), 1582
Sally (--), 1575
Samantha (Franklin), 1575
Samuel, 1575
Wilhelm, 1572
William, 1571,

1574-1575, 1583
PICKERT/ BIKKERT
Anna Margrita, 1583
PICKERTT
Conrad, 1582
John Jr, 1582
Margaret, 1582
Mary B (Van Alstine), 1582
PICKETT
--, 270
Mary (Warner), 270
PICKLE
Alma Louise, 1312
Creig Marvin, 1312
Delbert John, 1312
Edgar Joseph, 1312
Glenna Jeanette (Chester), 1312
Helen Irene (Urschel), 1312
Janet Maxine, 1312
Marvin Joseph, 1312
Michael John, 1312
Nellie Frances (Scarborough), 1312
Pamela Ann, 1312
Robert Edgar, 1312
Steven Douglas, 1312
Virginia Ann, 1312
PIERCE
Ann Louise (Cook), 1148
Annebelle, 619
Armenica Janette, 1684
Barbara Leonare (Brooder), 445
Brian Neil, 445
Carol Ann (Glatfelter), 909
Carol Ann (Johnson), 440
Charles Lenlie, 1130
Clark, 1148
David Monroe, 440
Don Edward, 440
Don Everette, 440
Donald, 619
Edna Lee (Alspach), 1130
Elizabeth Ann, 909
Eric Stuart, 1317
George, 1393
Heather Lynn, 909
Jeffre Lynne, 1135
Job, 1684
Kathy Jean, 1064
Leonore (Prewett), 443, 445
Luella May (Milliken), 1684
Mary Dayton (Graff), 445
Michael S, 1317
Naomi (Long), 619
Oscar, 1684
Patricia Ann, 583
Patricia Jean, 445
Richard Brayton, 445
Richard Carl, 909
Sarah (Mallory), 1393
Sharon Virginia, 909
Stephanie Leonore, 445
Stephanie Sue, 1317
Stephen Clark, 445
Stephen Clark III, 445
Stephen Clark Jr, 445
Sue Ann (Gilbert), 1317

Susan Lynn, 440
Una Fay (Brokaw), 445
Wilbur Ray, 445
Wilbur Ray Jr, 445
William F, 619
Zada Louise (Taylor), 445
PIERPIONT
Catherine Marie (Evans), 140
Thomas Franklin, 140
PIERSON
Alta May (Wiser), 1839
Arthur C, 1839
Arthur Chester, 1839
Michael, 1064
Penny Ellen (Wohlgemuth), 1064
Roselle Virginia (Wiser), 1839
PIESECKI
Cathy, 739
PIETROWICZ
Esther madine (Weiser) Shollenberger, 1614
Walter, 1614
PIKE
Lucy Amelia, 1780
Phyllis Jeanette, 495
PILKINGTON
Josie, 1795
PILSBURY
Carol Ann (Chevalier), 1378
Christopher, 1378
Sarah Beth, 1378
PINCHIOS
Sarah Elizabeth (Smeal), 1679
William, 1679
PINE
Elizabeth Hannah (Rhoads), 61
Harley Hooker, 61
Julia Doris, 69
Lottie, 61
PINGEL
Marlis (Wagenmann), 1599
Rolf, 1599
PINKERTON
Brian Donald, 573
Karen Kay (Rittenhouse), 573
Kendra Kathlene, 573
Kristy Kaylene, 573
PINKSTON
Cecile, 1801
Elizabeth, 1483
Ruth, 1487
PINTO
Corinne, 1484
PIPER
Bertha Margaret, 1441
Caroline, 1440
Catharine Elizabeth (Orth) Whitehill, 1516
David, 627
Eileen, 1205
Elizabeth, 1443
Kendall, 369
Lydia, 578
M Salome, 1440
Patsy, 1805
Sarah (Fisher), 627
Vera Jean (Cleveland), 369
William, 1516

PIPPIN
Claude Musselman, 1180
Maude Estelle (Musselman), 1180
Robert Percy, 1180
Samuel H, 1180
PISARSKY
Gloria Ann, 476
PITCHFORD
Dolores, 139
PITROWSKI
Julie, 1156
PITTENGER
Erin Kay, 523
Jill Ellen, 523
Lynn, 523
Martha H (Brown), 523
Rebecca Ann (Clampitt), 523
Shawn, 523
PITTIGLIO
Albert, 1112
Lindo, 1112
Myrtle May (Snyder), 1112
Theodore, 1112
PITTINGER
June Lorraine, 669
PITTMAN
Florence M, 234
PIZER
Linda Kay, 817
Patricia Louise, 816
PLACE
Betty May, 110
Mary (Sankey), 110
Mina Elanore, 110
Ray Allison, 110
Ray Allison Jr, 110
Roy, 110
Sadie (Oleson), 110
Samuel, 110
Truman Samuel, 110
PLANCH
Mary E, 1671
PLANK
Lula, 1026
PLANT
Grace, 577
Pearl Genevieve, 1303
PLAPPERR
Hieka, 820
PLASSMAN
Viola Alleyne, 804
PLASTER
Delores June (Wiser), 1870
James Clyde, 1870
PLASTERER
Alma Joyce (Givler), 257
Helen Evans (Erdman), 257
Pamela Sue (Brock), 258
Parke, iv, 253, 1010
Parke Erdman, 257
Sally Lou, 257
William Givler, 258
William Singer, 257
PLATFOOT
Ernst, 1750
Sandra Faye (Schroeder), 1750
PLATT
Fanny, 304
Gwendolyn (Lee), 215

Joseph Jr, 215
Mayvon (Wiser) Brown Fallows, 1778
Ronald Ralph, 1778
PLATTENBURG
Ruth Ann, 133
Ruth Weishaar (Kershner), 133
William S Jr, 133
PLAYER
Alma (Neuman), 215
Barbara Jeanne (Froman), 213
Beverly Myrtle, 214
Blanche Myrtle (Jackson), 213
Bryan, 214
David Glen, 214
David Michael, 214
Diane (Miller), 214
Dorothea Bernice (Call), 213
Gary, 215
Glen, 210
Glen Shirl, 213
Jack Weiser, 215
Lilette (Mahon), 214
Madelyn, 214
Marc, 215
Marissa, 214
Mary Pauline, 214
Michael Glen, 214
Morgan, 214
Myrtle Eliza (Weiser), 213
Patricia Barbara, 214
Pauline (Amerson), 213
Rebeca (Morgan), 214
Rebecca, 215
Sharon, 214
Shirley, 213
PLESCIA
Gina Maria, 1157
PLESSINGER
Clara Belle, 763
PLETZ
Mary Frances, 922
PLIENINGER
Alfred Julius, 317
Elisabeth Marie, 315, 317
Emilie Sophie Elizabeth (Schwab), 317
Hanna Clementine, 315, 318
Helmut Gustav, 317
Theodora Henrietta, 317
PLOTTS
Julie Ann, 391
PLOURDE
Natalie, 1182
PLOWMAN
Barbara (Wiser), 1774
Rex Gibson, 1774
PLOZNER
Elizabeth Shaner (Hoffman), 1174
Tobias, 1174
PLUMB
John, 595
Laura Ruth (Frantz), 595
PLUMMER
Angelina Renee, 568
Craig Lee, 568
Jeffery T, 571

PRITCHEL
Alice (Haschel), 263
Louis, 263
Mary Maude, 263
PRIVET
Emma, 1828
PROBST
Catharine (Weiser), 1465
Cecilia E, 1465
Emilius, 1465
Franklin, 1465
John Augustus, 1465
Mattie B, 1855
Penny Ann (Harvey), 750
Russell Kenneth, 750
Steven, 750
PROCIOUS
George W, 1244
Nettie Maple (Kahle), 1244
PROCTOR
Hazel (Moore), 1437
J D, 1437
Joseph D, 1828
Joyce Ann, 1457
Maxine, 1437
Ray, 1437
Roena V (Wiser), 1828
PROFFITT
Cary G, 622
Ellen Kay (Edwards), 622
PROFIO
Patricia, 768
PRONSCHKE
Dorthea, 468
PROPHETER
Dorothy Evelyn, 1252
PROPST
Dora May, 757
Sara Louise, 807
PROTZELLER
-- (--), 157
Andrea (--), 171
Bessie Mabel, 170
Betty Marion, 171
Bruce, 171
Carole Ann, 172
Christine I (Caldwell), 172
Dora E, v, 157
Dora Evelyn, 170
Edward Louis, 171
Genevieve (Schutt), 171
Harry W, 157
Harry Weiser, 170-171
Hattie Minerva, 171
Helen Marguerite, 173
Helen Sarah, 171
Jane Katherine, 171
Kevin Joseph, 171
Lana (Hardman), 171
Louis, 170
Marilyn (Hollrook), 171
Mark Daniel, 171
Mary (Anderson), 171
Mary Francis (Tayler), 171
Michael, 171
Midlred (McPeek), 171
Minnie S, 170
Patricia (Hundley), 171
Patricia (McRae), 171
Raymond J, 157
Raymond Joseph, 172

Ruth (Peterson), 171
Ruth Margaret, 172
Sarah Adaline (Weiser), 170
Shirley (Enebrad), 171
Stephen, 171
Susan (Haight), 171
Susan Mary, 171
Terence Mark, 171
Teresa Ruth, 171
Thelma Mae, 172
Thomas Robert, 171
Timothy, 171
Verda (Foieman), 171
PROUD
Paul C, 841
Pauline P (Anspach), 841
PROUGH
Andrea, 1717
Tracy, 1715
PROWELL
Jeanette Irene, 870
PROWNELL
Mary Ann, 184
PRUETT
John, 1667
Margaret, 1667
Vera Louise, 1201
PRYOR
Jo Ellen (Cole), 571
Mark, 571
Steven Mitchel, 571
PUCEL
Victoria, 1194
PUCHATY
Edward F, 770
Joan Hoffman (Risser), 770
PUENT
Marian Charlotte, 1798
PUGH
Alice Eugenia, 1652
Edmar John, 258
Fern, 563
Francis, 1201
James, 150
John Howard, 258
Katherine Ann, 258
Maida Elizabeth (Sherwood), 258
Martha Ann (Martin), 150
Perry, 602
Sarah Annabell (Stahl), 602
PUGMIRE
Sharon, 1767
PUGSLEY
Blanche, 954
PULLEY
Julia K, 571
PULPHRY
--, 1106
Edith (Kiplinger), 1106
PUMP
Henry, 508
Idella (Carnicom), 508
PUMPHREY
Audrey Jean, 446
Audrey Miriam (Randall), 446
John Randall, 446
Kathlene (Sullivan), 446
Knowles, 205
Kristin, 446
Lisa (van Haam), 446
Mary Ellen (Watson),

205
Robert Earl, 446
Robert Earl III, 446
Shelley Lynn, 446
PUNNETT
Emily Meier, 328
Hermann Meier, 328
James, 328
Katharine Elizabeth Kunze, 328
Louisa, 328
Mary Kunigunde (Meier), 328
Walter, 328
PUNTY
Christine Marie (Wieser), 1738
Christopher Michael, 1738
Michael Stephan, 1738
Scott David, 1738
Zachary Stephan, 1738
PURCELL
Marie, 1384
PURDON
Diana, 629
PURDY
Abigail Ann, 897
Douglas, 1651
Ginnie (Wysor), 1651
Keith Douglas, 897
Margaret Susan (Seasholtz), 897
PURLES
Claude Edwin, 1777
Rhea Kathleen (Wiser), 1777
PURSIFUL
Amy, 561
Ann, 561
Demarus (Banter), 561
Don, 561
Jeffery, 561
Judy, 1751
Lillie (--), 1751
Lori, 561
Malcolm, 1751
Pearl Hannah (Weiser), 1751
Verna Pearl, 1751
Vernon, 1751
PUSEY
Eugene, 401
Peggy Jo, 401
Penny Jojane (Heil), 401
Yvette, 881
PUSH
Debra, 1480
PUTMAN
Carl Eugene, 1354
Carol Jean, 1354
Mary Elizabeth (Krick), 1354
Mary K, 1350
PUTNAM
--, 1592
Allan R, 768
Jane (Weiser) Wills, 1592
Judith Hope, 768
Marian Sarah (Witmer), 768
Robert Witmer, 768
Victoria May, 768
PUYANS
Catalina, 287
PYLE
Beck Ann, 936

Bruce Leon, 717
Carole Ann (Protzeller), 172
Carole Protzeller, 157
Chrisan, 172
Christine (Cornetta), 1179
Daniel Leroy, 717
Eliza A, 833
George W, 173
George William, 172
Gretchen, 173
Jeanne Laurie, 1179
Jeffrey Musselman, 1179
Jennifer Jane, 1179
Jennifer Lea, 173
Larry Ray, 717
Laura Beth, 173
Leon Roscoe, 717
Linda Sue (Oyster), 173
Naomi Ellen (Lawver), 717
Robert Delevett, 1179
Rose (Nelson), 717
Ruth Louise (Mowbray), 1179
Thomas William, 717
PYLES
Maria A, 1430
PYNCH
Caryn Helen (Mills), 282
Lawrence, 282
PYNE
Dorothy Jo, 725
QEIGLER
Cassandra (Weiser), 1472
Emanuel K, 1472
QUANDT
Emogene (Musser), 1102
Ray C, 1102
Raymond C Jr, 1102
QUAST
Shirley Mae, 437
QUATE
Edna Louise, 99
QUAY
Alice Elizabeth (Loder), 1063
Cheryl (Kindle), 609
Daryl, 609
George, 1063
Mary Ann, 1740
QUENTON
Lillian, 1838
QUERRY
Aubrey Loraine, 933
Ina Louise (Whitsel), 933
Kathy Loraine, 933
Kimberly Ann, 933
QUICK
Keith, 530
Martha Maxine (Alexander), 530
QUIDLEY
Eunice Patricia, 1330
QUIGLEY
Bessie, 880
QUILLIN
Brette Lyndell, 528
Christian Lyndell, 528
Delia Lea (Creacy), 528
J D, 528

Jennifer Denise, 528
Karen (Muckey), 528
Matthew Eric, 528
Opal Arline (Wickham), 528
Phillip Nolan, 528
Rebecca Delayne, 528
Richard Eric, 528
Sabrina Joann (Smith), 528
QUIMBLY
Deloris Jane, 1076
QUIMBY
Caroline (Weiser), 1850
Hosea, 1850
Mary (Weiser), 1850
QUINLAN
Albert Edward, 1546
Anna, 1546
Edna Marie, 1546
James, 1545
James Jr, 1545
Joseph, 1546
Joseph Augustine, 1547
Katherine Louise (McGurk), 1547
Laura Theresa, 1546
Lavinia (Ryder), 1545
Lewis Edward, 1546
Margaret Loretta (Dorman), 1546
Martha Elizabeth, 1545
Redempta Burr (Larkin), 1547
Sarah Louisa, 1546
Tersa (Mulvihill), 1547
Thomas Albert, 1545
Victor Raymond, 1547
QUINN
Abigail, 1667
Cecelia Ann (Farmer), 965
Dennis, 965
Dianne, 965
Francis, 965
Linda, 356
Sharon Marie, 538
QUINTAR
Doris (Wagner), 316
Horst, 316
Ulrike, 316
Ute, 316
QUINTARD
E L, 121
Sara Antoinette (Weiser), 121
QUINTERS
Harry, 1099
Julia (Howe), 1099
Marion, 1099
Robert, 1099
RAAB
Betty Rosalie (Kephart), 1686
William Arthur, 1686
RAABE
Adam Alexander, 185
Anne Margaret, 185
Carol June (Melvin), 185
David Paul, 185
David Rudolph, 185
Erik David, 185
Margaret Louise (Miller), 185
Margaret M, 182
Russel Benno, 185
Russel Benno Jr, 185

REINAKER
Aimee Kay, 748
Joshua Steven, 748
Linda K (Ross), 748
Steven, 748
REINBOLD
Susan Elizabeth, 802
REINBOLT
Rita Marie, 474
REINBOTH
Brett Allen, 1485
Bruce, 1485
Christine Ruth (Foth), 1485
Katie Marie, 1485
Shannon Kay, 1485
REINECKER
Carol Ann, 249
REINEKE
Margaret Ann, 350
REINER
Betty Lorraine (Wiest), 648
Deanna Louise, 648
Delight Lorraine, 648
Erika Lynn, 648
Justina Leigh, 648
Kristine Carol (George), 648
Robert Charles, 648
Ronald Charles, 648
REINERT
Christina C (Weiser), 1864
Paul K, 1864
REINHARD
Jonathan, 1761
Patricia, 775
Rebecca (Wieser), 1761
REINHART
Dixie L, 1159
Elizabeth (Andrews), 939
infant, 1727
John, 939
Lenius, 1727
Sarah Elizabeth (Wieser), 1726
REINHOLD
Harriet M, 1728
REINHOLT
Alfred R, 267
Amanda, 263
Betty, 267
Edith (Haschel), 265
Geneveive, 268
Hulda, 266
Ida, 268
Kenneth, 268
Lavon, 268
Lola, 600
Luetta, 267
Madonna, 268
Marge (Fisher), 268
Nellie, 266
Rosie (Hickman), 267
Sam, 268
Sandy (Towelson), 267
Scott, 267
Sidney, 268
Terry Jean, 267
Tony, 268
Tressa, 265
William, 265, 267
REINKING
Judy Ann (Cline), 552
Michael, 552

REINOEHL
Brian Todd, 657
Christine Lee (Daniel), 657
Cody Daniel, 657
REINSEL
Ida Mae (Womelsdorf), 827
Stanley J, 827
REISCH
Marie Eleanor, 692
Mildred, 874
REISH
Adeline May (Barnhill), 877
Alice (Hennet), 1084
Anona (Yearick), 1084
Beatrice (Smith), 1085
Brenda, 1084
Brian, 1084
Bruce, 1084
Craig, 1085
Donald, 1084
Doris (Doll), 1084
Dorothy Marie, 878
Dwayne, 1084
Gary, 1085
Gene, 1085
Glenn, 1084
Glenn Jr, 1084
Harry L Grazier, 878
Hazel Viola, 1084
Joan, 1085
Laurence, 1084
Leonard Samuel, 1084
Marian Adeline, 878
Olive (Dennis), 1084
Orien, 1084
Roy, 877
Sharon, 1084
Talitha, 1084
Verna, 1055
William Durant, 878
REISINGER
Hazel Lou, 48
Sarah, 1425
REISS
Ellen Lucille, 1121
REITER
--, 1877
Lillian, 941
Nellie (Wiser), 1877
REITZ
Ann, 730
Anna Rebecca, 1533
Annie, 1532
Bessie, 1532
Betty May, 1533
Beverly Ann, 746
Catherine, 1532
Catherine Jane (Weiser), 1532
Charles A, 1532
Clair Arthur, 1533
Clara (Farnsworth), 1532
Clara A (--), 1533
Daniel N, 1533
David C, 1533
Dawn Marie, 745
Deborah Anne, 739
Donald Nelson, 745
Donna Gae (Seigworth), 1283
Doris, 1532
Ellis Gordon, 1533
Emerson Alvin, 745
Eric, 1533
Goldie Arlene, 1533

Howard Dale, 1283
Jennifer Kathleen, 745
Jerry, 1533
Jonathan Edward, 1533
Judy, 1533
June Elizabeth (Klinger), 745
June Pauline, 684
Karen Ann, 740
Katie Jane, 1533
Kenneth, 1532
Larry Wayne, 739
Laura Weiser, 1533
Madaline, 1532
Martha (Raker), 1533
Maude (Delp), 1533
Melissa Nicole, 745
Nancy, 1533
Pearl, 1532
Peter M, 1532
Polly Ada, 746
Robert, 1532
Rodger Alvin, 745
Ronald, 1533
Sarah Jane (--), 1533
Sarah Lynn (Broscious), 739
Susan Diane (Corcoran), 745
Suzanne Lynn, 739
Tammy Denise, 1283
Urias P, 1532
Victoria Lynn, 436
REKATE
Mary Vivian, 441
REM
Peter, 26
REMALY
Susan E, 228
REMBOLD
Jean, 1253
REMINGTON
Joseph, 1582
Polly (Pickard), 1582
REMLEY
Gerald, 729
Thelma (Gearhart), 729
REMLINGER
Velma, 1181
REMPEL
Jeanne, 1547
REMPHREY
Cathy, 712
REMS
John Raymond, 1158
Mildred Jane (Kiger), 1158
REMSEL
--, 1015
Ira (Snyder), 1015
REMY
Alexandria, 384
Earl Lawrence, 384
Elizabeth, 384
Emmanuel Victory, 384
Erik Lawrence, 384
Mary Jane (Leibold), 384
RENAND
Elizabeth, 374
RENARD
Eugene, 889
Josephine, 889
Marjorie, 889
Mary Elmira (Ernst), 889
Rudolph, 889
William, 889

RENAUD
Sharon J, 375
RENBARGER
Donald Eugene, 533
Mary Levina (Arnold), 533
Mertin, 533
Oris, 533
Sandra Lou, 533
RENCHOCK
Julia, 1615
RENINGER
Gertrude, 980
RENKENBERGER
Eric, 956
Jane Lee, 956
Janet Lynne (Koegel), 956
Kyle, 956
RENN
-- (--), 961
Abraham, 1016
Adaline, 1016
Albert, 1016
Albert Wilson, 65
Alda (Unger), 1023
Alfred Willett, 1016
Alice (Ferster), 1024
Allen, 1022
Alma S, 1022
Alwilda Esther, 1025
Anna M, 1016
Beatrice M, 682
Bertha B, 1016
Beulah G, 1022
Blaine Markly, 1025
Calvin B, 961
Calvin Blair, 1024
Carl, 1022
Carol Ann, 1024
Catherine Jane (Willett), 1016
Charlotte (Snyder), 1017
Cheryl, 1024
Claude A, 1016
Clinton Smith, 1021
Constance Eileen, 1025
Daniel Blair, 1024
Daniel Jefferson, 1023
David Blair, 1022
Debbie, 1024
Dorothy (Stetler), 1024
Douglas Samuel, 1025
Elizabeth A, 1023
Elizabeth Katherine (Cummings), 65
Emerson Monroe, 1021
Emma L, 1016
Esther L, 1019
Evelyn Roselia, 1017
Florence, 1022
Foster Unger, 1023
George Baldwin, 65
George Keefer, 1019
Gertrude Elen, 1019
Harry M, 1016
Hattie, 1026
Helen (Dailey), 1024
Helen Joann, 1025
Ida (Lott), 1021
Ida (Riegle), 1019
Jean, 1022
John, 1022
Katie E (Tharp), 1024
Kay, 1045
Lonna, 1024
Louise Cummings, 65
Lulu Jane, 1016

Mabel (Chesney), 1022
Mae (Meckowiak), 1019
Maggie M (--), 1016
Margaret, 1020
Mark Blair, 1024
Martha (Lytle), 1016
Martha Ann, 1022
Mary Elizabeth, 1020
Mary Jane, 1023
Mary Lee, 1023
Maude E, 1016
Olive Margaret (Mutchler), 1024
Paul, 1024
Paul Richter, 65
Phyllis K, 1020
Rachel, 1016
Ralph Jacob, 1023
Ralph Jacob Jr, 1023
Robert Phillip, 65
Rose Marke, 1020
Samuel Lewis, 1024
Sarah Ellen, 1025
Sarah S (--), 1016
Simon Snyder, 1016
Stella, 1016
Susan Joyce, 1025
Teresa Diane, 1025
Teresa Susanne, 1025
Thaddeus R, 1016
Theo Irene, 1024
Thomas Jefferson, 1017
Thomas Jefferson Jr, 1017
Truman J, 1024
Viola Mae, 1022, 1024
Viola Mae (Yeager), 1017
Walter C, 1016
RENNER
Caroline A, 447
Dorothy Jeanne (Baird), 1520
Kristine Nina (Johns), 129
Melissa Erin, 129
Michelle Renea, 129
Robert James, 1520
Stephanie Gail, 129
William, 129
RENNICK
Helen, 1092
Lillian B, 1092
RENNINGER
--, 1002
Boyd, 697
Boyd Martin, 697
Brandi Ann, 1307
Charles Raymond, 1307
Dawn Alden, 697
Elizabeth, 1029
Geneva (Pence), 697
George William, 697
George William Jr, 697
Julie Richelle, 1307
Katharine M (Koppenhaver), 697
Kenneth Raymond, 1307
Kimberley Raye (Heeter), 1307
Marsha Larue, 697
Martha (Lyons), 697
Richard Leon, 697
Torie (Hall), 1002

RENNO
Aileen Lorraine, 700
Barry Lynn, 700
Betty Arleen (Leister), 700
George Alan, 700
George Copenhaver, 700
George Samuel, 700
Gregory Scott, 700
Keith Baxter, 700
Minnie Ellen (Koppenhaver), 700
Roger Douglas, 700
Steven Leister, 700
Viola Jane, 700
RENO
--, 1839
Rogene (Wiser), 1839
RENTSCHLER
Kim Robin, 1342
Kristie Lynn, 1342
Patricia Aline (Longenecker), 1342
Regina Barbara, 321
Robert Steven, 1342
REPAS
Constance, 1586
Gus, 1586
Irma Newberry, 1571
Irma Virginia (Newberry), 1586
Maria, 1586
REPASS
--, 1662
Laura Clark (Wysor), 1662
REPPERT
Mildred, 1742
RERRICK
Charles, 1050
Mary B (Erhard), 1050
RESER
Lori Jane, 1632
RESH
Anna, 95
RESPELIER
Maria, 793
RESSLER
Amy E, 793
Anna May, 919
Benjamin A, 793
Deborah L (Hartzner), 793
Earlene E (Bowers), 253
Jason E, 793
John Charles, 793
LeRoy W, 253
Lois (Crum), 793
Michelle N, 793
Robert W, 253
Susan, 1456
Suzanne Annette (Melchoir), 793
Thomas A III, 793
Thomas A Jr, 793
RETALLICK
Kathrine A (Pontius), 694
William J, 694
RETTER
Eva Christine, 1598
RETTKE
Muriel, 1601
RETZLAFF
Sherry Leigh, 182
RETZLER
Eleanor Rogers, 1498

Harold, 1498
Joanna (Rogers), 1498
Mary Joann, 1498
Nancy Louise, 1498
REUCHLIN
Christiane Luise (Weisser), 1606
Johan Christoph, 1606
REUTER
Eileen M, 1741
REVARD
Betty Jane (Klingler), 618
Cheryl Lee, 618
Denise Lynn, 618
Kenneth, 618
Ronie Lou, 618
REWOLDT
Lois Ann, 485
REX
Albert D, 298
Alina, 298
Bert Alan, 243
Bertram R Jr, 243
Betty Jean (Bond), 243
Bonnie Lou, 243
Carolyn Lamoyn (Klingler), 619
Emily S, 298
Frank, 298
G Albert, 298
George Abraham, 298
George Marion, 297
Isabelle Virginia, 298
Jack, 619
Leonore Leila (Gibbens), 298
Lucetta Salome (Shulze), 297
Lulu S, 298
Margaretta M, 298
Mark Alan, 619
Paula, 612
Rachel Isabelle (Felthousen), 297
Roger Jay, 619
Samuel Schaeffer, 297
Samuel Shulze, 298
Scott Monroe, 619
Shelia Kaye, 619
Susan Jane, 243
Trudy Ann, 243
REXFORD
Barbara, 1715
Dorothy, 1714
George Burton, 1715
Harry, 1714
Heidi, 1715
Jeffrey, 1715
Joyce, 1714
Tammy, 1715
Tillie (--), 1715
Wava Annabell (Shugarts), 1714
REXROTH
Albert, 865
Annie (Shettel), 865
REXTRAW
Ashlee Elizabeth, 1219
Jason, 1219
Linnaea (Sallendar), 1219
REYBURN
Catharine (Wysor), 1653
James, 1653
James M, 1653
Mary Elizabeth, 1653

REYNER
Margaret (Weiser), 1294
Samuel, 1294
REYNOLDS
--, 832
-- (Wiser), 1823
Adam Tyler, 551
Allie Christine, 42
Amber Lynn, 1276
Amy Leigh (Stoner), 42
Ann, 52
Bertha Lee (Gambill), 435
Bill, 1276
Bobby, 1797
Brian Russell, 42
Brooke Suzanne, 42
Carol Joella, 52
Carol Lee, 435
Connie, 1284
Cora Verlindia, 387
Diane, 1569
E G, 1824
Frances B (Womelsdorf), 832
Heather, 1276
Holly, 275
Howard, 52, 435
Jacqueline (Jobin), 615
John Robert, 47
Judy, 825
Justin, 1276
Kathleen (Koegel), 958
Kimberly Jean, 418
La Ruth (Wiser), 1797
Levina (Wiser), 1824
Lola Irene, 460
Mamie Magdalene, 1822
Marilyn Sue (Morris), 47
Mark Wayne, 551
Mary, 1798
Melissa Lea (Geisel), 1276
Michael J, 1162
Naomi, 1825
Pauline Louise, 698
Sara Ann, 1796, 1800
Sara Jeanne (Conley), 52
Terri Lynn (Riggs), 551
Thomas, 958
Thomas W, 551
Tom, 615
Victoria Leigh (Duniven), 1162
Wayne, 1823
Zachary Brian, 42
REYOME
Doris Marie (Karr), 472
Ivan, 472
Janet Lou, 472
REZNICEK
Donald Michael, 469
Virginia Ann, 469
RHEINSCHELD
Alton Lance, 456
Andrew Joseph, 456
Brian Wayne, 456
Carl Wayne, 456
Courtney Eileen, 456
Darryl W, 456
Douglas Henry, 456
Floyd Daniel, 455

James Daniel, 455
Jeremy Alan, 455
Jessie Elaine, 455
Joshua Foster, 455
Judith Elaine (Jenkins), 455
Julie Ann (Gilpen), 456
Kathy Eileen, 455
Linda Marie, 456
Michael Trigg, 456
Naomi Eileen (Trigg), 455
Patricia Ann (Gilpen), 456
Rachel Lynne (Brill), 455
Rebecca Ann (Longcoy), 456
Roger Alan, 455
Stephanie Lynn, 456
Tyler Matthew, 456
William Daniel, 456
RHEN
Edna, 775
RHINE
Harry Jacob, 838
Jacob, 838
Jacob D, 838
Kate L (Anspach), 838
Rosa Jane, 838
William, 838
RHINEBOLT
Mary Ann, 627
Minnie, 941
RHINEHART
Josephine, 527
RHINES
Susan Lynn, 1280
RHIVER
Elizabeth, 879
RHOAD
Daniel, 29
Francis, 29
Hannah, 29
Hannah (--), 29
RHOADES
Abby, 809
Curtis Daniel, 1331
Dorothy (Kramer), 1164
Elizabeth, 300
Elizabeth Louise (Moorehouse), 808
Grace Catherine (Weaver), 1331
Heather, 809
Hillary, 809
Mabel Luella, 1673
Mildred Gertrude (Eppley), 892
Nancy, 1164
Phoebe Mae, 714
Richard, 808-809
Robert, 1164
Thomas Winfield, 892
Victoria, 809
RHOADS, 61
Alma Catherine, 1034
Ann (Kaufmann), 901
Anna, 1066
Arthur, 785
Arthur Robert, 785
Bertha Emmadell, 447
Bertha Irene, 1034
Carolyn, 901
Catharine, 61
Charles S, 61
Dorothy (Metzger), 785

Elizabeth (Fegley), 785
Elizabeth Hannah, 61
Elwood, 901
Eugene Lorraine, 1277
Florence C (Lykens), 1621
Florence Edna, 1033
Frances (Egbert), 61
Francis, 61
George F, 901
Grace (Fichthorn), 901
Hannah Phillipina (Weiser), 61
Harriet Lucretia (Weiser), 447
Horatio, 447
Jack, 901
James, 61
James W, 61
Julia Ann, 1728
Louisa, 61
Lucy I, 61
Margaret Estelle, 447
Margaret Patricia (Seigworth) Moore, 1277
Martha A, 61
Martha Elizabeth, 1034
Marvin Kenneth, 785
Mary Aquilla Ann (Weiser), 446
Mary Catharine (Cooper), 1033
Mary Cooper, 1034
McKendree J, 446
Mildred (Borrell), 901
Minnie, 61
Miriam Mabel, 446
Pat, 1269
Peter, 29, 61
Richard Allen, 785
Sara Elma, 447
Sarah, 363
Thomas William, 1034
Vernon L, 1621
Viola, 901
Walter McKendree, 447
Walton Francis, 1033
Walton Francis Jr, 1034
RHODERICK
Ann, 1038
George, 1038
Grace, 1038
Harold, 1038
Ida (Coovert), 1038
RHODES
--, 1839
Alice (Myers), 607
Andes Forrest (Crow), 796
Bertha, 606
Bonnie Louise, 797
Charles, 607
Chester, 743
Clara Isabelle (Long), 605
Donald Eugene, 797
Eblean, 577
Edna Mable, 606
Elmer, 608
Elmer Darrel, 608
Elmer Douglas, 608
Elmer Steven, 608
Gladys (Huls), 797
Guy Edward, 797
Helen Muriel (DeVault), 605

RICKARD (continued)
June Carol, 239
Mary Anne (Klinger), 659
Russel H, 659
RICKER
Joetta, 566
RICKERT
Celeste Ann, 933
Kyle Elizabeth, 933
Parker Thomas, 933
Robert Earl, 933
Terry T, 932
Vanessa Raye (Parker), 932
RICKEY
--, 1106
Daisy Wynell (Stephens), 591
Dewitt Earl, 590
Fairy Nellie (Hocker), 590
Frank Lee, 432
Karen Wynell, 591
Madona May, 591
Marjorie Lucille, 590
Mildred Irene (Smith), 432
Nancy Louise, 432
Shirley Ann, 432
Stephen Earl, 591
William Earl, 591
William Glen, 591
RICKLES
Helen Pauline (Stahl), 602
Richard, 602
RICKMAN
Lillian, 375
RIDDICK
Meredith Anne (Cooper), 352
Ralph, 352
RIDDLE
Addie, 1819
Cynthia Louise (Wiser), 1838
John R, 1838
RIDENOUR
Beulah, 1068
Janet Lee (Wiser), 1815
Steven Edward, 1815
RIDER
Grace Pauline, 1171
Howard Earl, 393
Michael Howard, 393
Nancy Earlene (Dorsey), 393
Timothy Scott, 393
RIDGE
Frances Loraine (Weiser), 1143
Samuel, 1143
RIDGEWAY
Eugene Howard Jr, 1373
Geraldine Lynn, 1373
Hepzebah, 1854
John E, 1373
John E Jr, 1373
Josephine Marie (Bay), 1373
RIDGWAY
Byran Paul, 553
Eric Justin, 553
Linda Ann (White), 553
Ronn, 553

RIDOLFI
Carol Ann, 920
Joseph Lawrence, 920
Marian Amy (Weiser), 919
Ralph, 919-920
Richard Paul, 920
RIEBER
--, 8-9
RIEDEL
Gernot, 445
Nicole Suzanne, 445
Patricia Jean (Pierce), 445
RIEDESEL
Susan Alice, 1733
RIEGEL
Alma Rosalie (Hower), 77
Barray Lee, 1744
Crystal Ann, 78
Jody Elaine, 78
Justin Matthew, 1744
Stephanie Luann (Wisser), 1744
Truman Aucker, 77
RIEGGEL
--, 136
Mrytle (Wilcox), 136
RIEGLE
Carolee (Landfair), 612
David Ralph, 612
Diana Trudy, 612
Dianne (Laury), 612
Ernest, 612
Evelyn (Point), 612
Francine Lou (Diller), 612
Gertrude A (Langle), 612
Ida, 1019
Jenis Eileen (Point), 612
Jon Philip, 612
Judy Ann, 613
Kevin Eugene, 613
Michelle Marie, 613
Monty E, 612
Nancy Evelyn, 612
Paul Donovan, 612
Paula (Rex), 612
Philip, 612
Ralph Kenneth, 612
Robert Dean, 612
Rodney Paul, 612
Ronald Dean, 613
Ruth (Long), 612
Terry Allen, 612
Tommy Joe, 612
Victoria Lynne, 613
RIEKER
Johanna Elizabeth, 1423
RIEKKOFF
Heather Ann, 182
RIENBOLT
Darrell Ivan, 1187
Harry Ivan, 1187
Jimmy Lynn, 1187
Mary Pearl (Weiser), 1187
RIETH
Lydia, 83
RIFE
Donald Eugene, 1148
Donald Eugene Jr, 1148
Gregory Dennis, 615
Jack, 615

Josephine Margaret (Straits), 1148
Judy Ann (Jobin), 615
Nancy, 1148
Paul Holmes, 1148
Ruth Lavina (Alspaugh), 1148
RIFFLE
Betty Jean, 478
RIGGAN
Anna Blythe, 792
Catharine Anne (Snyder), 792
Jasper Simmons III, 792
RIGGS
Aaron, 741
Alice Mariah, 523
Annabelle, 1235
Ashley, 741
Austie A, 554
Avis (Brown), 551
Barbara, 522
Berlie Opal, 553
Bernice, 521
Beverly, 462
Beverly Jean (Thornburg), 551
Blanche, 553
Brian Michael, 551
Cecil Wads, 553
Charles E, 530
Charles Jerome, 553
Cherly Lynn, 530
Clara N, 553
Clement V, 550
Clyde Wilford, 550
Denton J, 524
Diana (Neidig), 741
Dora May, 551
Dorothy, 554
Dustin Robert, 551
Effie (Pearsole), 1235
Elsie Ann, 554
Emma J (Jackson), 521
Emmalou, 522
Etna Eudora (McIntire), 550
Eva (Allen), 553
Eva Mae, 551
Firman, 554
Francis (Wheeler), 554
Fred, 553
girl, 524
Glenn L, 521
Glenn Leroy Jr, 522
Guy R, 553
Homer, 522
Howard Wayne, 551
infant, 524
James E, 521
Janet, 522
Jannetta Jane, 522
Jenetta (Lemon), 521
Joan (Griffin), 521
John J, 521
Jonas, 521
Joy Michelle, 530
Julia Roda Bell (Alexander), 550
Kathy, 530
Kathy Gale, 551
Kole Kistrell, 1262
Kristopher Michael, 551
Lovemma Burnice (Hippensteel), 522
Lucille Georgia, 523
Luetta, 523

Lulu M (Prather), 524
Mable (Minnich), 522
Margaret Annabelle, 550
Mary Alta (White), 522
Mary Lucille (Mann), 530
Maryetta, 522
Melba Nile, 554
Melinda (Batten), 522
Minnie L (Sipe), 553
Nora (Cloud), 521
Nora Alice, 522
Nova May, 554
Nova P (Boxell), 550
Olive B, 553
Paul Sheldon, 522
Pearl M, 554
Phyliss, 554
Rachel Lynn, 551
Ronald, 741
Roy Allen, 522
Roy E, 521
Ruth May, 522
Samuel M, 549
Sandra Lou, 551
Sarah (Herring), 549
Sarah Renee, 522
Terri Lynn, 551
Thelma Jun, 523
Thetis Irene, 554
Tona Lea (Mannix), 522
Wallace Wayne, 554
Walter, 1235
RIGHTMIER
Audrey (Robertson), 1690
Helen (Crickton), 1690
Ida Ann, 1690
Jessa Cleveland, 1690
Marilyn, 1690
Mary Alta (Kephart), 1690
Ray Allen, 1690
Virgil Alonzo, 1690
William, 1690
RIGLIN
George Michael, 1399
Margaret Anne Wagner, 1399
Michael Edward, 1399
Susan Faye (Wagner), 1399
RIGNEY
Louise, 1799
RIKE
Beverly Jean (Gebhart), 1331
Don Eugene, 1331
Helen Annabelle (Shuck), 611
John Hugh, 611
Judy (Berry), 611
Patricia Ann, 611
Richard Alan, 611
RIKEARD
Annie C, 1416
RILAND
Bessie, 1114
Emma Jane, 782
Martha, 1027
RILEY
Bereta, 489
Charles Eugene, 1191
Cladys Ella (Hildebrandt), 1191
Clara Belle (Wiser), 1190

Dianna Jeannene Ferris, 1494
Erin Lynn, 1191
J Whitcomb, 136
Karen Ann, 1021
Karen Nancy (Matthias), 1191
Kathlenn Ann, 1021
Kristine Ann, 1021
Linda Mae (Worhacz), 1021
Linda Marie (Gibbons), 276
Margaret, 1501
Mark Andrew, 1021
Martha Baird, 1191
Mary V (Kutz), 1191
Miles Owen, 1191
Patsy Ann Anderson, 79
Paula, 1369
Robert Ronald, 1191
Scott, 276
Sharon Lynne, 1191
Susanne Irene, 276
Thomas Martin, 1021
Thomas Myles III, 1191
Thomas Seiburn Jr, 1190
Timothy Patrick, 1191
William Myles, 1191
Wynne Jill, 1191
Zora (Javorina), 1191
RIMASSA
Harry, 1289
Jeannine Marie (Vandeuren), 1289
RIMER
--, 625
Gerald, 626
Harold, 625
Joseph, 626
Leona, 625
Mary Allie (Fisher), 625
Pleasant Etta (Fisher), 626
RIMMEY
Andrew Patrick, 1094
Jane, 366
Jason Daniel, 1094
Jennifer Diane, 1094
Kevin, 1094
Tracey (McGovern), 1094
RINDNER
Benjamin Jacob, 632
Joseph, 631
Rachael Shana, 632
Susan Theo (Bloir), 631
RINE
Christian, 293
Louisa (Schulze), 293
RINEHART
Donald Lee, 779
Elizabeth, 939
Fairy, 549
Janet, 611
Keith Allen, 779
Ruth Elizabeth (Bettilyon), 779
Susan Lee, 779
RINER
Dorothy Pearl, 1797
Madge, 1797
RINGER
Manie, 894

ROGSTAD (continued)
Kent Sivern, 171
Peter, 171
ROHELIER
Leona Erma, 1809
ROHLAND
Mary, 62
ROHR
Edith Eloise (Wilson), 1128
Lois Janet, 1128
Robert Hempy, 1128
ROHRBACH
June, 1222
Sara, 1044
ROHRBAUGH
Audrey Jean (Kissinger), 1044
Deborah Ann, 1044
Howard, 1044
Robin Elaine, 1044
ROHRER
Emma, 932
Gerald C, 757
Kathleen Alice (Kohl), 757
Kayleen Marie, 757
ROHSBACH
Cheryl (Wiechart), 136
Ethan, 136
Thomas, 136
ROJOHN
D Scott, 310
Derek Schwab, 310
Eliza Baldwin (Schwab), 310
Katrina Schwab, 310
ROLAND
Julia F, 281
Regina, 788
ROLFS
Ahlert, 322
Alfke (Rullhusen), 322
Anna Elisabeth
   Gabriele Kathe
   Marianne, 322
Christian Helmut
   Heinrich, 322
Ekkehard, 322
Elke (Leuert), 322
Gabriele Luise (Beck), 322
Hans Christian
   Wolfgang, 322
Hans-Otto Rolf Walter, 322
Johannes Martin, 322
Julie Friederike, 322
Marianne Julie
   Elisabeth (Willich), 322
Matthias Jakob, 322
Raimund, 322
Rolf Albert Eckert, 322
ROLLAND
Alex, 362
Bernice Vivian (Powell), 362
ROLLER
Edward Beaty, 1125
Georgia Jeretha (Grove), 1127
Helen Courtright, 1126
May Alice, 1127
Mildred Marie, 1127
Minnie Elnora (Courtright), 1126
Ruth Olive (Courtright), 1125

Thomas, 1126
Wayne Leroy, 1127
ROLLEY
Jane, 1268
ROLLINS
Melinda Lee (Herring), 535
Stephen Eugene, 535
ROLLMAN
Rebecca, 1568
ROMAN
Alex Anthony, 1136
Anthony Jr, 1136
Erik Kristofer, 1136
Kristine Kay (Weiser), 1136
ROMANCHEK
Nancy Jo, 1293
ROMANELLA
--, 1530
Mary Eleanor (Weiser), 1530
ROMANO
Joseph Anthony, 1386
Joseph Anthony Jr, 1386
Katherine Gina Marie, 1386
Mary Lou (Harter), 1386
ROMBERGER
Alice Faye (Mozingo), 645
Ann Eliza (Koppenheffer), 671
Carol (Leitzel), 661
Charles Allen, 671
Faye Dianne (Wolfe), 645
Frances Margaurite, 671
Harry A, 671
Jason Richard
   Governatori, 645
Jennie Mae (Radel), 671
Joseph William, 759
Kathryn Eleanore (Mace), 644
Kathryn Elizabeth (Witmer), 759
Kay Louise (Engle), 759
Kelly, 661
Kerri Ann, 645
Kristy, 661
Kristy Michelle, 645
Laurie Alice, 645
Linda Marie Liberty (Governatori), 645
Michael Roger, 645
Richard Lee, 645
Robert John, 759
Rodney Roy, 759
Roger Lamar, 644
Stuart, 661
Wayne Ellis, 759
ROMERO
Rhonda, 374
ROMIG
Garry Max Jr, 1088
George A N, 1635
Nichole Erin (Brungard), 1088
Olivia W (Weiser), 1635
Sallie, 1635
ROOK
Barbara Thelma

(Ritter), 1173
Norma Lorraine, 1173
Norma Louise, 1173
Robert Edward, 1173
ROOME
Elizabeth Warren (Hills), 1358
Rodney Hills, 1358
William Journey III, 1358
William Journey IV, 1358
ROONEY
Colin Edward, 1088
Colin Edward Jr, 1088
Frances Madeline (Wilkins), 1419
Jean Francis, 649
Julie Marie (Brungart), 1088
Timothy Hayes, 1419
ROOS
Charles Howard, 794
David Allen, 794
Lena May (Fasold), 794
Norman, 794
Phyllis Jean, 794
ROOSEVELT
Teddy, 47
ROOT
Katie, 1722
Katie A, 1705
ROPER
John T, 1823
Nancy A (Wiser), 1823
RORHBACH
Mary Elizabeth, 1033
RORICK
Kirk Wyman, 465
Margaret Jean, 465
ROSALIE
Grace, 1861
ROSCHIE
Barbara Ann (Heileman), 500
Dennis Charles, 500
Michelle Lee, 500
ROSCOE
Alison Marie, 146
ROSE
Alison Lindsay, 205
Carolyn Ruth, 1778
Delaney John, 205
Jeraldine, 1569
John, 1582
John G, 205
Kimberly Ann (Wilson), 1491
Marilyn, 141
Michael Wilson, 1491
Phoebe (Pickard), 1582
Scott Wilson, 1491
Stephen, 1491
Susan Louise (Hogben), 205
ROSEBOON
Catharine, 1723
ROSELLE
Deborah Jane (Muhlenberg), 342
Ernest Muhlenberg, 342
Robert Carson, 342
ROSEN
--, 1417
ROSENBERG
Joann, 1576

ROSENBERGER
--, 1674
Bernice Marie, 967
Bobbi Jo (Kriner), 1673
Bradley Eric, 1674
Bryan Curtis, 1674
Doreen (Baillor), 1674
Gloria (Johnson) Coy, 1673
Helen Louise (Wiser), 1673
Larry Donald, 1673
Larry Donald III, 1673
Larry Donald Jr, 1673
Pamela Sue (Ocker), 1674
Rebecca Marie, 1673
Rickey Lynn, 1673
Rickey Lynn II, 1674
Taylor Bradley, 1674
ROSENBERRY
Julie Ann, 1166
Marjorie (Weiser), 1166
Michael Paul, 1166
Paul, 1166
ROSENKRANZ
Harriet L, 978
ROSENOLT
Lillian, 1047
ROSENWIE
Laurie, 1205
ROSIEK
Renee, 1416
ROSINBUM
Susan Lynn, 1210
ROSKAM
Jan, 957
Janice Louise (Thomas), 957
ROSS
-- (Rearick), 1387
Albert T, 262
Albert T Jr, 262
Barbara, 282
Beatrice Naomi, 782
Bertha E, 1517
Bertha E (Wiser), 1793
Betty Ilene, 942
Beverly (Reed), 748
Bobby, 1494
Carol Ann, 749
Charles, 1387
Charles Edward, 744
Charlyn Carol, 202
Christopher, 1430
Clarissa Rena, 203
Cleveland H, 203
Cody Thomas, 755
Cynthia Sue, 749
David James, 750
David Michael, 470
Deborah (Trumm), 749
Debra Michelle, 750
Delmar Emanuel, 750
Delores Gail, 202
Donald Edward, 744
Dorothy Mildred (Martin), 750
Edna Blanch, 201
Elizabeth, 234
Elmer, 1793
Elmer Orlando, 749
Emma Blanche (Weiser), 782
Ethel (Mustard), 202
Ethel M, 262
Eva Adaline (Eister),

744
Faye Edith, 1209
Florance May, 198
Florence Pearl (Demoss), 262
Frances (Razook), 202
George Clarence, 202
George Clarence Jr, 202
Goldie Cecelia, 772
Grace Lydia (Miser), 748
Grace Nesbit (Brooks), 744
Helen E, 262
Henry Walter, 749
Ida May, 749
James Benton, 198
James Edward, 750
Janet L, 748
Jenieve (Salander), 202
John Thomas, 42
John Wellington, 749
Joseph Lorenzo, 202
Kathleen Margaret (Sherrill), 470
Kathy Marie, 942
Kenneth Leroy, 748
Leah Nicolle, 755
Linda K, 748
Linda Margaret (Palma), 750
Linda Sue, 750
Lottie Irene, 749
Madlyn Louise, 203
Mar Jean (McKinley), 1494
Margaret (Dorn), 203
Martha Jean, 744
Mary Alice, 749
Mary Eliza (Weiser), 198
Mary Elizabeth, 202
Mary Ellen, 203
Mary Gladys, 748
Mary Louise, 484
Mary Magdalena (Dresbach), 1430
Mary Sophia (Toot), 1476
Melvin, 942
Mervin T, 782
Myrtle Ann, 201
Myrtle Elnora, 750
Nancy Lou, 749
Naomi Ruth, 203
Nelda (Starner), 942
Nell (Gage), 750
Peggy Ann, 942
Rhea Blanche, 782
Robert Francis, 748
Roy Alexander, 748
Ruth, 513
Sara Dianna, 1281
Sarah Elizabeth, 744
Shirley (Deivert), 748
Stephanie Marie, 750
Stuart, 1281
Tammy Jane (Furman), 755
Terry Gale, 470
Timothy E, 1781
Todd Leroy, 749
Tom E, 755
Vicki Lee (Wiser), 1781
Virginia Louise (Farmer), 42
Walter K, 262

RUSSELL (continued)
James Ronald, 1071
Jesse, 957
Jesse Dakota, 957
Karen, 1251
Kathryn, 234
Mark Weiser, 161
May, 533
Melissa Catherine (Maier), 54
Nathan, 487
Norma Jean, 553
Rand Howard, 161
Randall, 486
Sally Jane (Roberts), 1251
Shirley Anne (Bohn), 1071
Valerie Yvonne (Kern), 486
William, 1014
Zachary, 1251
RUST
Beverly S, 154
Eileen J, 1640
RUTE
Bessie, 982
Margaret, 1076
RUTEDGE
--, 628
Susan (Herring), 628
RUTH
Dolora Anne, 1550
Ellen Louise, 1559
Harry Joseph, 1550
Henry J, 1550
June Marie (Newman), 1550
William Newman, 1550
RUTHERFORD
Georgia Dawn, 595
Hannah, 1654
John, 595
Kathryn Augusta, 38
Ken, 1133
Kim, 1133
Linda Lou (Weber), 1133
Louise, 351
Martha Louise, 38
Olive Irene (Frantz), 595
Stacy, 1133
Verena Gertrude (Willey), 38
Walter G, 38
RUTT
Donald S, 1514
Margaret Catherine (Hynicka) Gerwer, 1514
RUTTER
Ann Marie, 846
Berlie Opal (Riggs), 553
James C, 553
RYAN
Agnes Matilda, 76
Anna M, 74
Bertha, 912
Cameron J, 912
Cameron J Jr, 913
Carolyn, 912
Clifford, 605
Dick, 38
Donald, 173
Eleanor Rogers (Retzler), 1498

Florence M (West), 912
Gail Sandra, 727
Gary Lee, 1187
Glenn, 38
Grace, 785
Harriet Jeanne (Sonner), 38
Judith, 912
June, 1005
Karene Dada, 728
Kimberly, 1759
Martin, 1498
Mary Emily, 728
Michael Raymond, 128
Nancy Strode, 1885
Nancy Strode (Haines), 173
Patricia, 912
Patrick, 605
Patrick Jr, 605
Pattie Jeanne, 38
Richard, 727-728
Rose Marie, 912
Sandra (Stober), 605
Sandra Lee (Gladman), 1187
Sarah Gladys (Hepner), 727
Sue Ann, 472
Walter, 38
Wendy Lou (Boehringer), 128
RYDER
Alexander B, 1547
Anie, 1547
Anna (Elder), 1547
Dottie, 1547
Edward, 1547
Ellen Frances, 1552
George, 1545, 1547, 1553
Grace, 1547
Helen, 1547
Helen (Lawrence), 1547
Henry, 1553
Jenny, 1547
Lavinia, 1545
Margurete (Zahn), 1553
Martha, 1553
Martha (Weiser), 1545
Martha Caroline, 1547
May, 1547
Sara (McDevitt), 1547
Thiel, 1547
Thomas, 1547
RYLAND
Virginia, 947
RYLANDER
Bernice Elizabeth (Coder), 1271
Harry, 1271
Robert, 1271
RYNARD
Diane, 885
SAALFRANK
Douglas, 553
Julie Ann, 553
Kathy, 553
Kenneth, 553
Norma Jean (Russell), 553
SABARINE
Ruth, 825
SABUDA
Eugene, 825
Jason Paul, 825

Joseph Roman, 825
Susan (Womelsdorf), 825
SACCO
D Joseph, 808
Sara Alice (Keefer), 808
Sherri (Klahr), 1616
Tony, 1616
SACHS
Sharon, 1054
SACKMAN
Helen Josephine (Garns), 227
S Kenneth, 227
SACKS
Elizabeth (Wisser), 1876
Mary Patricia, 724
William, 1876
SADDLER
George William, 1800
Linda Carolyn (Wiser), 1800
Regina Delores (Genesis), 1800
SADLER
Gaye Lynn, 563
Lelia Mabel (Phipps), 262
Pamela Ann, 858
Raymond, 262
Ruth Evelyn, 262
SAFERSTEIN
Brenda Jane (Womelsdorf), 822
Melvin Allen, 822
SAFKA
Wendy Jane, 1551
SAGE
Edwin Rodney, 1182
Kristine Louise (Nelson), 1182
Loraine (Bowers), 253
Peter, 1182
Robert Charles, 1182
Thomas, 253
SAGER
Alfred, 978
Anna Catherine, 978
Carl, 978
Cora Mabel, 979
Dora, 979
Elizabeth, 978
John R, 978
Mayme (Swavely), 978
Rena, 978
Ruth Elizabeth, 979
Salome Elizabeth (Kehl), 978
Susie (Deibler), 978
William, 979
William Harry, 978
SAGERS
Stella, 575
SAHR
Darlene Mae, 497
Lawrence August Carl, 497
Mildred Lucille (Langerman), 497
Shirley Ann, 497
SAILER
Anna Idabel, 1355
SAILOR
Brianne Canielle, 623
Court, 623
Julie Ann (Mohr), 623

SAIOMIVEBER
Mary, 1446
SAKIHARA
Miyoko, 123
SALA
Barbara Elizabeth, 810
Margaret Catharine (Anderson), 810
Roland Otto, 810
SALADA
Alice Mae, 693
Alverta G, 693
Arlene Florence, 655
Artie Foster, 693
Aurelia Lillian, 693
Carrie E, 694
Charles Henry, 694
Clement Earl, 693
Dora Elmina (Clouser), 693
Edwin Elias, 693
Eleanor Mary (Scheib), 656
Ethel (Lord), 693
Gladys Aurelia, 693
Harry Oscar, 693
Helen Dorothy, 693
Howard Edward, 693
Isaac, 693
Isaac Walter, 694
Jennie V, 694
Joseph Allen, 655
Katherine Salera (Stutzman), 693
Mabel Agnes (Klinger), 655
Mary Jane, 693
Mary Louise (Shoop), 693
Rite Iola, 693
Sadie J, 694
Sarah Elizabeth, 694
SALAKUS
Mary, 1616
SALAMI
Joseph, 1470
Virginia Jane (Rehberg), 1470
SALANDER
Jenieve, 202
SALEM
Nona, 862
SALEME
Gloria June, 1370
Louise, 1370
Sylvia Marcella (Winkleman), 1370
SALES
Rose Ann, 943
SALINAS
Pepha, 1835
SALISBURY
Joyce Ann, 138
SALISDAY
Julia, 1679
SALLACH
Joe, 1741
Lottie (Wieser), 1741
son, 1741
SALLADA
Cheryl Leigh (Hammersly), 656
Cody Ryan, 656
Devin Allen, 656
Doris Jo Ann (Bixler), 656
Eva Elizabeth (Lower), 656
Fayne Lamar, 656

Fayne Lamar Jr, 656
Gary Joseph, 656
Gary Joseph Jr, 656
Jamie Lee, 656
Jeffrey Allen, 656
Kathy (Barnwell), 656
Kayla Jean, 657
LeRoy Irwin, 656
Lori Ann (Klouser), 656
Renee JoAnna, 656
Robert Allen, 656
Robert Lamar, 656
Ronald Eugene, 656
Shirley Mae (Schoffler), 656
Sommer Lorraine, 656
son, 656
Stephanie, 656
Susan Kay (Edwards), 656
SALLADE
--, 903
John, 253
Margaret, 903
Mary E (Kalbach), 903
Susanna (--), 253
SALLEE
Fannie (Kiplinger), 1106
Florence, 1106
George, 1106
Joseph, 1106
SALLENDAR
Craig, 1219
Eric Andrew, 1219
Linda Susan (Davis), 1219
Linnaea, 1219
SALOUM
Matilda Louise (Katterhenry), 1249
Samuel, 1249
SALOVAARA
--, 1499
Beth (Stewart), 1499
Bobbye (Middendorf), 1499
Carol Alice (Matthews), 1500
Erik Jorma, 1500
Jonn Alexis, 1499
Jorma, 1499
Kaarina, 1499
Katharine Pratt, 1499
Kristian Robert, 1500
Lauri Mikael, 1499
Mary Katharine (Pratt), 1499
SALSBERG
Florence Agnes (Bower), 977
Marjory Elizabeth, 977
Reppa Leon, 977
Robert Leon, 977
SALTER
Ann Allen (Brown), 184
Taylor, 184
William Lester, 184
William Lester Jr, 184
SALTZER
Eliza (Thomas), 736
Henry G, 736
SALTZGERBER
Catharine (Weiser), 1412
John, 1412

SCANLAN (continued)
Thomas Richard Jr
(continued)
786
SCARBARRY
Norma, 1126
SCARBOROUGH
Nellie Frances, 1312
SCARBROUGH
John Frederick III,
1809
Martha Faye (Wiser),
1809
SCARPA
Letha Roselda (Sulouff),
752
Michael C, 752
SCHAAB
David, 843
Francis, 843
Frank, 843
Joan, 843
Lois Alice (Anspach),
843
Lois Anne, 843
SCHAAD
Darla, 519
SCHAAF
Grace Jeanette (Dosh),
464
Harry E, 464
SCHAAFF
Barbara Anne (Baird),
1520
Elizabeth Ann
(Sammons), 1520
Harold James, 1520
Harold James Jr, 1520
Harold Powell, 1520
Robert Paul, 1520
Susan Marie, 1520
SCHABEL
Erma Mae, 465
SCHADE
Cassandra Ann, 499
David Alan, 499
Elizabeth Ann, 499
Helen Anna
(Koppenhaver), 672
John Jacob, 672
Kathleen Marie, 499
Mary Ann, 499
Rita Jean, 499
Vickie Lynn (Garn),
499
Wilfred Aloysius, 499
Winifred May, 499
SCHADLE
Becci Sue, 776
Diane Lee Allen
(Doherty), 776
James Charles, 776
Lorraine Esther
(Koppenhaver), 776
Lynn Charles, 776
Marie Elana (Perpinka),
776
Steven James, 776
Steven Reid, 776
SCHAEFER
Catharine, 299
Friederike Karoline,
1596
Mary Ann, 943
SCHAEFFER
Bertha Mae, 1628
Dawn, 354
Elizabeth, 1356
Esther Gladys (Weiser),

1532
Harvey Pierce, 1396
Iverna, 1532
John A, 1532
John David, 1532
Larue Hess, 1396
Michelle Renee, 1249
Ruth, 63
Sarah Weiser (Hess),
1396
Wanda Jean, 858
SCHAFFER
Betty Virginia, 765
Elisabetha (Feg), 21
Martha, 754
Martha Elaine, 776
Michael, 1518
Peggie Lucille (Hower),
77
Peter, 21
Robert James, 77
SCHAFFNER
Aaron Jason, 1139
Adam Lyle, 1139
Almeda Emma
(Weiser), 1132, 1138
Andrea Leigh
(Maechling), 1139
Bruce Patrick, 1139
Bruce Patrick II, 1139
Calvin Leroy, 1139
Doloras Merlin
(Beaverson), 632
Donald L, 1131
Donald Leroy, 1141
Donna Lee, 1141
Doris Marie, 1140
Ethen Anton, 1139
Gayle Lynn, 633
Herber, 632
Jean (Flay), 1139
JoDell Jean, 1139
John, 1138
John Albert, 1139
John Michael, 1139
Karen Ann (Hober),
1141
Kim Rene, 633
Larey Dean, 1139
Leslei Herbert, 632
Linda (Reed), 1139
Lori Diane (Mercer),
1139
Luray Schirtinger,
1139
Marie Ellen (Walp),
1141
Mary Agnes (Arbogast),
643
Mary Ruth, 1139
Matthew Kerel, 1139
Mellie Bennettie Snider
(Keller), 1139
Nancee Lee, 1139
Nancy Jean (Yeager),
1139
Pauline Edith (Stalter),
1139
Philip Leroy, 1141
Roberta Irene
(Rostofer), 1139
Robin Kay, 633
Rose Ann, 632
Russell John, 1140
Ruth Ellen, 1141
Ruth Viola (Lilly),
1140
Sallie Emma J, 652
Samuel Stanley, 1139

Samuel Stanley Jr,
1139
Scott Stanley, 1139
Shawn Michael, 1139
Sheree Sue, 1139
Timoth Scott, 1141
William Isaac Lincoln,
643
Zella Mae, 1141
SCHALBERT
Imogene Marie, 1434
SCHAMBERS
Greg, 530
Penny (Alexander),
530
SCHANAFELT
Catherine Harriet, 1666
SCHANG
Hope Ann (Johnson),
391
Jessica Kathryn, 391
Tracey, 391
SCHANTZ
Frank Marshall, 635
Lois Beth (Reiling),
635
SCHAPPEL
Evelyn Jane, 838
SCHAPPELL
Clara, 1615
SCHARADIN
Carolyn Helen (Moyer),
355
Heidi Ann, 355
Nelson Swoyer, 355
Nelson Swoyer III, 355
Sara Helen, 355
SCHASSBERGER
Emma (Weisser), 1597
Karl, 1597
SCHAUER
Adam, 914
Catharine Elizabeth
(Dundore), 914
Maria, 914
Susan Ann, 411
SCHAUM
Elizabeth, 343
Rebecca (Weiser), 94
Thomas L, 94
SCHEARER
Sadie E, 1639
SCHEER
Alicia Marie, 540
Donald, 540
Elizabeth Ann, 540
Kevin Paul, 540
Rhonda Lee (Mitchell),
540
SCHEFFLER
Blanche E (Snyder),
793
Robert, 793
SCHEIB
Eleanor Mary, 656
SCHEIFLEY
Janet, 1728
SCHELL
Alvin A, 506
Anna Marie (Stine),
506
Barbara Ann, 1320
Beatrice Pauline, 1318
Bessie Olive (Getter),
1319
Bessie Viola (Maxwell),
1336
Betty Elizabeth (Braun),
1336

Betty Jo, 1336
Carol Maxwell, 1336
Christine (Becker),
1319
Clarence, 506
Daisy Alverta
(Belleman), 1320
David, 506
David John Schell,
1336
Donald Edwin, 1336
Douglas Eugene, 1336
Edna (Christian), 1336
Elmer Clarence, 1319
Emerson Dewitt, 1336
Esther (McNay), 1336
Florence Estella
(Getter), 1318
George Alfred, 1336
Gerald, 506
Harry Wilson, 1318
Henrietta Hilda (Busse),
1336
Herbert Elwood, 1320
James, 506
Jerry Lynn, 1336
Joellen, 1336
John Oliver, 859
Kenneth, 506
Lawrence G, 1336
Louvell Maxine
(Nutter), 1320
Mable Irene, 1319
Marguerite Lucille,
1320
Mary Adeline, 1336
Mary Etta (Routzahn),
1320
Mary Louise, 1320
Mary Rebecca (Rabold),
1318
Michael James, 1320
Mildred A (Swope),
1320
Molly Beth, 1336
Patrick Herbert, 1320
Paul Luther, 1320
Richard, 506
Richard Warren, 1320
Ronald, 506
Samuel, 1318
Shirley Ann, 506
Thomas Herbert, 1320
Thomas Warren, 1320
Vernie Herbert, 1320
Vinnie Rebecca
(Wenner), 1320
Viola Evelyn (Shettel),
859
Walter Emerson, 1319
SCHELLHAMMER
Anna Weiser (Croll),
1466
William Heinly, 1466
SCHELLING
--, 479
Patricia Ann (Karr),
479
SCHEMPFF
George C, 1885
SCHEMPP
Beatrice A, 1577
Beatrice Cencei, 1576
Beatrice Cencei
(George), 1576
Bethany (Fellman),
1577
Charlotte Ann, 1576
Elizabeth A (Isabell),

1577
George Christian II,
1576
George Christian III,
1576-1577
Isabel G (Poyer), 1577
Jeffrey Adam, 1577
Jennifer, 1577
John Adams, 1577
John Adams Jr, 1577
Kathryn Irene
(Marinso), 1576
Leslie A, 1577
Lucy Anne, 1576
Mary Elizabeth (Finch),
1576
Mary J, 1577
Nancy L, 1577
Natalie Elizabeth, 1577
Sarah, 1577
Susan M, 1577
William A, 1577
SCHENCK
Benjamin Forest, 1318
Cristine Stewart
(Martin), 1318
Frances N, 335
Joshua Paul, 1318
Larry Nelson, 1312
Leslie Obadiah, 1311
Lois Elaine (Forrest),
1318
Mable Vida (Rabold),
1311
Richard Elwood, 1318
Robert, 1318
Sue Anne, 1318
Teresa Anne
(Pederson), 1318
Wanda Lee, 1311
SCHENK
Catharine, 1614
Eleanor, 1397
Esther Leona (Wisor),
1710
Leon, 1710
SCHENKE
Anna, 1623
August, 1623
Charlotte Wilhelmina,
1623
John Albert, 1623
Louisa C, 1623
Maria (Weiser), 1623
William A, 1623
SCHENKEL
Jo Ann, 473
SCHERZER
Alex Louis, 997
Bradley Glenn, 996
Janice Jean (Shirck),
996
Maxwell Martin, 997
SCHICK
Berta (Weisser), 1596
Brian Curtis, 618
Ernst, 1596
Kenneth, 618
Leslie Wayne, 618
Marilyn (Klingler), 618
Michelle, 618
Patricia, 955
Phillip Arthur, 956
Randall Leroy, 618
Renee Lyndene, 618
Susan Marie, 955
Wesley Leroy, 955
SCHIEFER
Bonnie Lou, 742

SCHIEFER (continued)
Charles, 742
Charles LeRoy, 742
Ella Mae (Delbaugh),
742
Susan Kay, 742
SCHIERMEISTER
Hollie Hilda, 412
SCHIFFLER
Lona M, 920
SCHIFFNER
Elizabeth (Weiser),
1417
George, 1417
Henry, 1417
SCHILL
--, 815
Dawn, 815
Richard, 815
Shirley Diane
(Anthony), 815
SCHILLER
Henrietta, 489
SCHILLING
Christ F, 1624
Hildegard, 1599
Jennifer Nicole, 1174
Mickie Lynn (Melville),
1174
Rosa Ellen (Weiser),
1624
William Harold, 1174
SCHILLINGS
Heidie Doreen, 579
Hollie Sue, 579
Karen Louise (Arther),
579
Peter, 579
SCHILLOCKS
Erna, 316
SCHILTZ
Jennifer Lee (Jones),
1240
Michael David, 1240
SCHIMD
Nancy Nadean, 179
SCHIMMING
Mary Jane, 496
SCHINDLER
A Jackson, 511
Helna Edelburg, 1777
Phebe (Zartman), 511
SCHIRMACKER
Adolph, 1106
Mary (Kiplinger), 1106
SCHLAGHECK
Cara Ann, 404
Gary John, 403
Jacob Ward, 404
Lori Ann (Wilson),
403
SCHLECHTER
Caroline Augus, 1560
SCHLEGEL
Albert Paul, 699
Barbara Ann, 699
Carl Edward, 699
Danny, 699
Doris Irene, 707
Esther Catharine, 699
Fern Ida (Zartman),
707
Jane M, 707
Jennie (Cummings),
699
John Edward, 699
John Jacob, 699
John Milton, 699
Josephine Hardesty,

676
Karen Sue, 699
Karl E, 707
Kenneth Eugene, 707
Larry, 699
Maggie Jane (Swailes),
699
Mark Freeman, 707
Mary A (Bohner), 707
Pearl Laura
(Koppenhaver), 699
Ralphetta Jean
(Weiand), 699
Steven, 699
Tressie Arlene, 699
SCHLEH
Clyde Robert, 1372
Jeannette Fay
(Winkleman), 1372
SCHLEIG
Dada Pearl, 727
SCHLENBAKER
Betty Alice, 602
David Lester, 602
Dorothy Mae, 602
Glenn Eugene, 602
Larry Joe, 603
Lloyd George, 602
Marcella Jane, 603
Mary (Long), 602
Rose Marie, 602
S N, 602
SCHLENKER
Bartolette Owen, 1727
Curtis F, 1756
Curtis Ronald, 1757
Daisy May Jane
(Wisser), 1727
Edith Susannah, 1727
Evelyn (Wisser), 1756
Lester Harlan, 1727
SCHLESINGER
Alice Ada (Smith), 158
Emanuel, 158
Josephine, 159
SCHLICKAU
Mary Lou, 204
SCHLIEVERT
Lenore Ann, 496
SCHLINDLER
Sarah C, 511
SCHLIPP
Johann Georg, 1596
Johanna Christine
(Weisser), 1596
SCHLOTTER
Eugenia Helen, 507
SCHLOTTMAN
Lori Anne, 1746
SCHLUND
Dorothy, 60
Eloise (Staser), 60
J Benjamin, 60
Ruth, 60
SCHMECK
Emma L, 1635
Lavinia, 1543
SCHMEHL
Alice, 364
Catharine, 122
Marjorie, 368
SCHMERBECK
Connie Lou, 486
SCHMICK
Carrie Wilhemina
(Bucher), 761
Diana Lee, 761
Donna Marie, 761
James E, 761

Michael James, 761
Vickie Ann, 761
SCHMID
--, 1
Geraldine (Barton),
1495
Joan Elizabeth, 1490
Jody Marie, 1495
Kevin Michael, 1495
Robert Edward, 1495
Stacy Renee, 1495
SCHMIDLIN
Andrew John, 465
John, 465
Trina Ann (Bourdo),
465
SCHMIDT
Beverly Darlene (Reed),
135
Bruce Herman, 667
Carolyn Sue, 1320
Catharine R, 1428
Diana, 424
Diana Rae (Weiser),
1846
Geneva Ruth (Wiser),
1871
Gregory Charles, 667
Herbert Arthur, 1320
Jack, 1846
Katharine Bliss (Pool),
312
Lois, 616
Lois Suzanne (Rowe),
667
Louis H, 1871
Louis H III, 312
Mary Baldwin, 312
Mary Louise (Schell),
1320
Peter, 341
Peter Lawrence, 312
Richard H, 135
Susanna Elizabeth
(Muhlenberg), 341
Wendelyn Jean, 667
SCHMIDT/ SMITH
George, 1696
Silvia (Turner), 1696
SCHMINK
Mary Ellen, 1833
SCHMITT
Jean, 584
Paul, 1601
Sarah A, 1414
Susan Mary (Weisser),
1601
SCHMITZ
Charles, 479
Debbie, 397
Philip Andrew Michael,
128
Shirley Ann (Karr),
479
Wendy Lou
(Boehringer), 128
SCHMOYER
Erma C, 697
SCHMUCKER
Elhanan Zook, 341
Hiester Muhlenberg,
341
Jacob Zook, 341
Katharine, 338
Katharine M, 299
Katharine Muhlenberg,
341
Rebecca Amelia
(Muhlenberg), 341

SCHMULOWITZ
Harold P, 43
John Collin, 43
Kim Elizabeth
(Chappell), 43
Lily Julia, 43
SCHNABEL
Ruth, 1677
SCHNABLE
Francis, 1621
SCHNADER
Catherine (Earnest),
1504
Jonathan, 1504
Levi, 901
Sarah (Womelsdorf),
901
SCHNAIDT
Lawrence, 1260
Marie Louise
(McClintic), 1260
SCHNAITMANN
Adriane, 316
SCHNAVELY
Evelyn, 742
SCHNECK
Beth Ann (Hallmeyer),
92
Carole (Stock), 92
Courtney Elizabeth, 92
Jeryl D, 92
Linda Sue, 92
Michall Dale, 92
SCHNEIDER
, 8
Bertha E, 698
Betty Margarete
(Wetzel), 471
Catharina, 1596
Cinda Louise, 1338
Constance Marie, 1338
Dean John, 1305
Emilie Friederika,
1600
Janet Darlene (Naugle),
471
Jenny Lynn, 418
Johannes, 22
John A, 418
Jonna Joy, 418
Joy Lynn (Weiser),
418
Marilyn, 524
Nancy Jean, 471
Nicholas, 22
Paul, 471
Peggy Lou (Graham),
1338
Robert L, 471
Robert Mcinnis, 1498
Sarah Catherine (West),
1498
Susan Beth (Wiser),
1305
Susanna, 1626
Thomas Maxwell, 1338
William Fredrick, 1338
William Henry, 1338
SCHNEIDER/FEG
Anna Clara (Kruger),
22
Barbara (--), 22
Johann Otto, 22
Johannes, 22
Margaretha, 22
Maria Barbara, 22
Nicholas, 22
SCHNELL
John Robert, 1286

Laura S, 1827
Marianne (Klingler),
1286
SCHNETZLER
Clarence Earl, 635
Marilyn Audie (Meier),
635
SCHNURE
Amanda (Spyker),
1452
George, 1452
SCHOCH
Andrew Fine Derr, 66
Brewster Ames, 66
Brewster Cameron, 67
Catherine Richter, 66
Christine Zoeller, 67
Clara G, 1436
Daniel E, 1435
Dorothy Richter, 67
Eliza Jane (Moore),
1435
Elsie Mae (Strousland),
66
Frank, 1435
Georg L, 1436
Henry D, 1436
Ira Christian, 66
Laura Edith (Richter),
66
Laura Emma Richter,
67
Marilyn (Miller), 66
Mary Catherine, 1435
Pauline, 62
Pauline Richter, 66
Russell William, 67
Sarah Catharina, 1458
Sarah Ellen, 1435
Sophia M, 1436
Stephen Andrews, 67
William F, 1436
SCHOCK
Jeanette A, 1456
SCHOEN
Adalina Augusta, 403
SCHOENECK
Anna Catharina (--), 17
Fritz, 17
SCHOENECKER
Catherine Ann
(Zarnowski), 662
Eric Craig, 662
Kristin Lou, 662
Paul Michael, 662
SCHOENER
Emma Cordelia, 830
Florence May, 842
Herbert, 838
Horace Theodore, 842
James Calvin, 842
Kathy, 838
Katie Rebecca
(Anspach), 842
Lillian, 838
Louis A, 838
Morris, 838
Theodore, 838
Virdie Maria (Anspach),
838
SCHOENFELD
C W, 1724
Elizabeth (Wieser),
1724
Frederick, 1724
Ida, 1725
Rosa, 1725
SCHOENIG
Teresa Marie Catherine,

SCHOENIG (continued)
Teresa Marie Catherine
(continued)
1195
SCHOENLY
Catharine Ann B, 1627
SCHOETTLE
Mabel, 768
SCHOFF
Kimberly, 860
SCHOFFLER
Shirley Mae, 656
SCHOFFNER
Cecelia Beth, 1140
Donna Jean (Nisley),
1139
Frederick Kyle, 1140
Homer Herbert, 1139
Megan Nicole, 1140
Mitchell Patrick, 1139
Peggy Sue
(Heimberger), 1140
SCHOJTELVIG
Marit Eli, 780
SCHOLA
Bertha Lenora
(Hammond), 970
Herbert E, 970
SCHOLL
Catharina Dorothea
(Weiser), 1427
Jacob D, 1427
Shirley Fae, 677
SCHOLLENBERGER
Edna R, 1756
Mabel C, 1628
SCHOLP
Arthur, 601
Sarah Malinda (Stahl),
601
SCHOOL
Janet Marie (Miller),
676
Ralph, 676
SCHOOLER
Andrew Allen, 385
Buck, 1870
Margaret J (Kinney),
385
Nancy Lee (Allen), 384
Ronald, 385
Sarah Alexis, 385
Sherry Joann (Wiser),
1870
SCHOONOVER
Ruby, 1210
SCHOPF
Eugen, 12, 19
SCHORR
Amy Ellen (Bretz), 640
Blaine G, 640
Doris Mae (Fulkroad),
668
Lee Burns, 668
Ronald Lee, 668
Susan May, 668
Terry Lee, 668
SCHORY
Eleanor Muriel, 1520
James, 1520
Kathryn M (Matthias),
1520
Lester, 1520
Wilda, 1520
SCHOTT
Alverta Eunice (Coe),
482
Eunice Irene, 485
Hilda Mary, 483

Lorenz Carl, 485
Mildred Louise, 485
Viola Mae, 482
Walter W, 485
William Valentine, 482
SCHRACK
Alice Catherine
(Milliken), 1683
Anna Maria, 1568
David, 1683
David John, 1005
Sandra Kaye (Erb),
1005
SCHRADE
Amy Lynn, 1559
Cheryl Ann (Egan),
1559
Kelly Ann, 1559
Kyle Egan, 1559
Steven Mead, 1559
SCHRADER
Amalie Auguste
Elisabeth, 323
Amalie Elisabeth
Clementine (von Post),
323
Anna Sophie Elisabeth,
324
Clementine Luise, 326
Dorothea (Meisner),
325
Eleanore, 326
Elisabeth (Kisker), 326
Eliza Amalie (Pauli),
326
Eliza Henrietta Emily,
324
Elke, 327
Ella (Wallust), 327
Emil Karl, 326
Emily Maria, 326
Emma Pauline (Erhard),
1053
Ethel C, 1053
Friedhelm, 327
Friedrich Paul, 327
Gerhard Wilhelm Otto,
326
Gisela (Lambrecht),
327
Gustav Bernhard, 326
Hannah Henrietta
(Tiedemann), 326
Heide, 327
Heinrich Otto Hermann,
323
Heinrich Rudolph, 327
Helen, 234
Helene August (Delius),
325
Helene Elisabeth, 326
Helmuth Otto Theodor,
325
Hermann Wilhelm
Georg, 323
Hertha Flora Emily
Addy, 326
Howard John, 799
Inge, 326
J Frank, 1053
Janice Louise (Alton),
799
Kathe, 327
Käthe Henrietta Flora
(Delius), 326
Konrad Wilhelm, 325
Lorraine Mable, 643
Margret (Weddigen),
326

Otto August, 327
Otto Christoph, 326
Paul Wolfgang, 327
Rudolf Franz August,
325
Ute, 326
Wilhelm Hermann, 326
Wilhelmina
(Schumann), 327
SCHRAUDER
Annabel Lee (Eppley),
888
Harry Alfred, 888
SCHRECKANGAST
-- (Kahl), 1001
Arlene, 1001
daughter, 1001
Delilah Jane, 1001
Emery Jr, 1001
Emory, 1001
Gary, 1001
Lucille, 1001
Marion, 1001
Rebe, 1001
SCHRECKENGAST
Pearl, 980
SCHREFFLER
Carolyn, 672
Darwin, 672
Ruby Eleanor, 651
Ruth (Messner), 672
Ruth Delores, 658
Shirley, 672
SCHREIBER
Alfred D, 1762
Clarence, 1031
Daniel I, 1762
Emma (Lauer), 1031
Ida E (Wisser), 1762
SCHREINER
Katharina, 1866
SCHRENK
Nicole, 742
SCHRIDER
Martha Eldora (Fisher),
510
Oscar, 510
Verna, 510
SCHRIEBER
Kathleen Marie
(Koppenhaver), 674
Kim Rae, 674
Ray, 674
SCHRIFT
Mary Margaret, 1199
SCHRIMSHER
Denna, 477
SCHRIVER
Catharine B, 806
Marion E, 724
SCHROEDER
Anna, 1723
Anna Violet (Adam),
1750
Carl Stanley, 1750
Chris Mitchell, 1750
Delores (Huff), 104
Denton Jacob, 1750
Edward, 104
Florence Evelyn
(Wisser), 1750
Frances Lucille, 104
Gladys, 1691
Karen Beth, 1750
Kirk Daryl, 1750
Lois Joyce, 130
Mary, 1624
Miles Leroy, 1750
Miriam Ruth, 1750

Monte Carl, 1750
Randall Wisser, 1750
Sandra Faye, 1750
Shirley Maxine, 104
Todd Denton, 1750
Warren Miles, 1750
SCHROM
Gene, 810
Jeffery, 810
Lynne Sala (Hotvedt),
810
SCHUBERT
Debbie, 613
SCHUCK
James Lyle, 611
SCHUECK
Sarah, 1613
SCHUH
Amelia Charlotte
(Koerner), 51
Arleene (Hall), 50
Bell, 33, 1454
Carolyn Arleene, 50
Emily Bell, 52
Geraldine Jane, 50
Harold, 52
Harold Frederick, 52
Helen Ada, 51
Henry F, 33
Henry Frederick, 51
Herman Loy, 50
James Frederick, 52
Josephine Margaret
Virginia, 52
Lewis Herman, 50
Marjorie (Weir), 52
Mary (Loy), 50
Mary Katharine, 52
Mary Ruth, 51
Minnie Bell, 52
Nellie G (Greene), 50
Robert Hall, 50
Virginia Louise, 51
Wendell Lewis, 50
SCHULLER
Barbara Joan (Day),
524
Carman Rene, 524
Ron, 524
Ronald Lee Jr, 524
SCHULTZ
--, 1084
Adam Johnson, 1502
Alice Van Leer
(Bennetch), 356
Alison M, 1502
Andrew H, 1502
Andrew J, 1502
Barbara (--), 356
Bernice Gene Parrott,
385
Carol A (Wearath),
1502
Damon D, 1350
Diane Marie (Miller),
356
Donna G (Osman), 356
Earl, 1228
Elizabeth Earnest
Johnson (Wertz), 1502
Erica, 1502
Ervin Ivain, 356
Evelyn Mildred
(Brungart), 1084
Gerda Irmgard Erica,
1564
Harry C, 981
Hattie Esther, 260
Helen (Bierly), 981

Helen R, 807
Henrietta Rose, 233
J Ryan, 356
James, 1502
James H, 1502
Jason R, 1502
Jeffrey Dean, 356
Joanna A, 1634
John Ervin, 356
Judy, 1211
Katherine Lynn, 356
Kenneth John, 356
Kym Ann, 356
Lesley, 1502
Linda (Quinn), 356
Louise, 931
Madeline (Shellehamer),
356
Margaret, 1502
Mary Ann Elizabeth
(Arnold) Warren, 1350
Melinda (Kolb), 1502
Melissa, 1502
Nanch K (Stevens),
1502
Paul George, 356
Peter Muhlenberg, 356
Robert F, 1502
Robert G Jr, 1502
Robert Gardner, 1502
Robin (--), 1502
Rose Marie, 1530
Sharon Elaine, 692
Trista (Derby), 356
SCHULZ
Debra Dawn (Saville),
409
Emily Dawn, 410
Gerhart Otto, 409
Laura Katharine, 410
SCHULZE
Alice (Seachrist), 293
Anna Maria Margaretta,
289
August Emanuel, 293
Augusta E, 293
Charles, 293
Christopher Emanuel,
289
Edith (Miller), 293
Elizabeth, 294
Emanuel, 238
Emily (Gilbert), 293
Eva Elizabeth
(Muhlenberg), 238
Eve Elizabeth
(Muhlenberg), 289
Francis Swaine, 293
Frederick Augustus
Samuel, 293
Hans, 1607
Henry Christopher
Emanuel, 293
Hiester E, 294
John Andrew, 293
John Andrew Melchior,
293
John Frank, 293
Julia Ann, 294
Louisa, 293
Margarete (Weiser),
1607
Mary Alice, 293
Mary Alice (Mulliken),
293
Mary Elizabeth (Miller),
293
Mary Rosina (Hiester),
293

SEIP (continued)
Cynthia Johan (Donne)
(continued)
831
Emelie R, 831
Lizzie J, 1761
Lowell R, 831
Mary J (Wisser), 1761
Ramona R, 831
Robert G, 831
Tilghman, 1761
William, 1761
SEIPLE
Christie, 1045
SEISS
Helen, 298
SEITZ
Alice Marie, 875
Blaine, 875
Brigitte Hilde, 320
Gladys (Shettel), 875
Jacob Raymond, 875
Mary Louise, 1548
Melanie, 916
SEIVERTSON
Dina Ellen, 405
SELD
-- (Weisser), 6
Michael, 6
SELL
--, 1724
Albert L, 962
Bernice, 1611, 1723
Elvira Jennie, 435
Eveah Luthera
(Hammond), 962
Harriet, 1724
Kimberly Sue, 1254
Nancy Ann (Loveless),
1254
Ronald D, 1254
SELLARDS
Phyllis Anne, 69
SELLERS
--, 886
Christy, 1104
Edna, 882
Kathleen (Koegel), 958
Maria Elizabeth
(Eppley), 886
Michael, 958
Patrick Andrew, 958
Roena Geneva, 1311
Sarah Melissa, 1447
SELLMAN
Ann Adele (Henry),
418
James Kirk, 419
Stephen Michael Miller,
418
SELTZER
Catharine Priscilla,
1539
Daniel, 1539
Edward J, 1539
Edward Weiser, 1539
Emily (Spohn), 833
Frances M, 1539
George F, 833
Hannah Maria
(Williams), 1539
Helen (Peterson), 1539
Herbert Eugene, 1539
Hubert Lee, 1539
Jacob, 904
John Pool, 1539
Jonathan, 1539
Laura Marie, 1161
Maria, 1539

Maria (Weiser), 1539
Matilda Loretta (Hezel),
1539
Raymond, 1539
Sarah Dickinson
(Laughlin), 1539
Sarah M, 1539
William, 1539
William Henry, 1539
William Henry Jr,
1539
SEMAN
Annetta Kay
(Wildermuth), 1127
Mary, 1564
Robert, 1127
SEMIC
Deborah Rose
(Weikert) Cassel, 923
Nicole Juliene, 923
Steven Milan, 923
SEMLER
Caroline Virginia, 237
Sadie Marie, 1147
SEMPREVIVA
Pauline, 1252
SENANDER
Carmelita June, 1161
SENGER
Cressandra Alison, 399
John Stephen, 398
Karen Sue (Anderson),
398
Stephanie Michelle,
399
SENGLER/ SINGLE
Agnes, 1860
SENIOR
Hazel, 675
SENTRE
--, 962
Margaret Lucille
(Smith), 962
SERAFINO
Frances Ann, 694
Suzanne Marie, 694
SERAFINP
Anthony Domonick,
694
Betty Lois (Pontius),
694
SERLES
Henry, 387
Lena Ellen (Tuller),
387
SERLEY
Ines Genevieve (King),
36
Roy J, 36
SERVICE
Adeline, 507
SERVOSS
Gerald, 955
Linda Lee, 955
Marjorie (Battles),
954-955
SESKER
Norma Jeanne, 227
SETTLE
James, 48
Judy Ann (Ims), 48
SETTLES
Martha M, 1732
SEVERINSON
Harold Clifford, 213
Myrtle Eliza (Weiser),
213
SEVERN
Daniel Frank, 755

Esther Jane, 755
Frank M, 755
Grace (Creighton), 755
Jane LaRue (Furman),
755
Philip John, 755
Ruth Edith, 755
SEXTON
Andrew James, 1142
Barbara Sue (Lynn),
1142
Lucy Mae, 572
Mary (Shoemaker),
1471
Robert CArrol, 1142
Ronald, 1142
William H, 1471
SEYBERT
Jean Louise, 1305
SEYLER
Brandon Vernon, 1745
Denise Lynn, 1745
Emma (Yoder), 1081
Esther (Reigel), 1081
Gretta Renee (Wisser),
1745
Jennifer Kay, 1745
Jordan Zachary, 1745
Justin Matthew, 1745
Leon John, 1745
Miriam Henrietta, 1081
Myrtle Leonore, 1081
Paul H, 1081
Samuel Wilson, 1081
SEYMOUR
Linda, 463
SHABER
John, 29
Samuel, 29
Sophia (Weiser), 29
SHACKELFORD
Aaron George, 324
Belinda (Hart), 324
Bettina (Klüpfel), 324
David Talman, 324
Deborah
(Higginbotham), 324
George Edwin, 324
George Wiley, 324
Jamie (Nelson), 324
John Ruffin, 324
Jordan Erich, 324
Joseph Talman, 324
Leilani, 324
Linda (Lyerly), 324
Peter Rowland, 324
Rachel, 324
Roland Ruffin, 324
Sally Kate, 324
Todd Christian, 324
Virginia Kate, 324
SHACKELS
Allen, 1868
Ann Elizabeth (Wiser),
1868
SHADE
Carol Jean, 1335
Charles Evan, 1335
Charles William, 1335
Corey Steven, 690
Craig Steven, 690
Daisy May (Maxwell),
1335
David Allen, 1335
Dennis Lee, 1416
Edgar Leland, 1416
Herbert Emerson, 1335
Jeffrey Paul, 1335
Judith Ellen, 1335

Lillian Lovell (Hill),
1335
Luther William, 1335
Mabel M, 1644
Maxine (Weiser), 1416
Michael Lewis, 1335
Nancy Lee, 1335
Neal Martin, 1335
Patricia (Heckathorn),
1335
Richard Nelson, 1335
Russell Nelson, 1335
Sandra Ann (Matter),
690
Sara Ann, 690
Susan Ann, 1335
Willie Gertrude
(Tillison), 1335
Zella May (Tillison),
1335
SHADLE
Susan, 1005
SHAEFER
Thelma Louise, 1780
SHAEFFER
E Clay, 1523
Edward G, 1523
Melinda (Weiser),
1523
Rebecca, 1625
SHAFER
--, 421
Craig Allen, 537
Judith Delaine, 535
Kyle Evan, 537
Mary Jane, 512
Nancy Kay (Herring),
537
Rachel Jane, 524
Susan Jean (Lowe),
421
Terry, 537
SHAFFER
-- (--), 156
A Nello, 896
Aaron Matthew, 483
Alice R, 1847
Allyson Lee, 887
Alvena Rebecca (Long),
653
Amber Nicole, 484
Andrew William, 485
Benjamin Franklin, 483
Besse Irene, 1277
Betty Ann, 484
Betty Jane (Taylor),
483
Brock James, 483
Candace Anne, 1095
Catharine, 680
Clayton, 1037
Cora Orilla, 1493
David Kim, 483
Dawn Ann, 484
Deborah Lynn, 887
Earl, 1101
Edna (Bitner), 1037
Elizabeth, 215,
236-237
Elizabeth (West), 913
Elizabeth Reiss, 156
Ella (Cummings), 1037
Ellen, 787
Florine, 1037
Gene, 1005
Geraldine Jane
(Lenker), 680
Grace, 1101
Harriet (Malick), 1037

Harry, 1101
Helen (English), 1236
Herbert B, 1037
Hilda, 1037
Hilda Mary (Schott),
483
Jacob, 27
Jean Louise (McCloy),
483
Jessie (Kehl), 1101
Joan, 1042
Joanne, 913
John, 27, 913
John Jacob, 896
Kate, 717
Kate (Hoffman), 769
Kelly Lynn, 484
Kerri Marie, 484
Laurie Sue (Dumbroff),
484
Lester, 1101
Lori Jane, 680
Lucy Ann, 1066
Lydia Pearl, 1096
Malinda B, 1844
Margaret, 1101
Margaret Jane (Smith),
1005
Marilyn Benfer
(Eppley), 887
Marilyn Mundy, 634
Mary, 1037
Mary Louise, 484
Mary Louise (Ross),
484
Mattie O, 1209
Nello, 156
Newton Edward, 653
Osborne, 1101
Patricia (Genzman),
484
Paul, 1236
Paul James, 483
Ralph, 1101
Rebecca Lynn, 484
Robert, 887
Robert William, 484
Roy James, 483
Sarah Elizabeth, 764
Scott H, 1037
Sharon, 913
Stanley R, 680
Thomas Matthew, 484
Timothy Mark, 484
Verna, 1037
Wash, 769
William Ray, 484
Zachary Isaac, 484
SHAFFOR
Kari Anne, 402
Keith Frederick, 402
Kelsy Brooke, 402
Lindsay Renée
(Weiser), 402
Shana Nichole (Weiser),
402
SHAFTO
Sonia, 1692
SHAHABIAN
Susan Jean, 185
SHAHL
Ronald Lee, 674
SHAKELFORD
Larence, 450
Loriene June, 450
Marsha Y, 450
Paulette, 450
Winifred Ruth
(Rowland), 450

SHIPP (continued)
  Patricia Ann (White), 950
SHIPPEN
  --, 1015
  Donald, 1015
  Ella (Wilson), 1015
  Joan, 1015
SHIPPY
  Ethel, 1107
  Sadie, 1103
SHIRCHK
  James Mark, 997
  Patricia Kay (Garrison), 997
SHIRCK
  Daniel Brian, 996
  David (John), 996
  Doris (Topp), 997
  Frances (Martin), 996
  Hattie Ellen (Kahl), 995
  Janice Jean, 996
  Jared Brammer, 996
  Jean Laverne, 997
  Jeffrey Michael, 996
  Jennifer Michelle, 996
  John Kahl, 996
  Jonathan Christopher, 996
  Judy Ellen (Blitz), 996
  Karen Louise, 996
  Kari, 997
  Laurence Calvin, 997
  Linda (Anderson), 996
  Lyman Edgar, 995
  Marisa Jo, 996
  Mary Lynn, 997
  Nancy Anne, 996
  Norma Christine (Smith), 995
  Patricia Ann, 997
  Robert E, 1885
  Robert Edgar, 995
  Robert Karl, 996
  Robert S, 961
  Sarita Jean (Brammer), 996
  Susan Christine, 996
  Thomas Martin, 996
SHIRER
  Chad, 386
  Michele Renee (McElfresh), 386
SHIREY
  Amy J (Laughlin), 1305
  Brent Robert, 1305
  Kelsey Blaire, 1305
SHIRK
  Barry, 845
  Elizabeth, 716
  Kimberly, 845
  Mary, 1525
  Patricia A (Anspach), 845
SHIRLEY
  Carolyn Sue (Wiser), 1790
  Mary K, 1375
  Richard Wayne, 1790
  Susan Ann, 1326
SHISSLER
  Betty, 808
SHIVELEY
  Lester Lee, 541
  Marjorie Lou (Mitchell), 541
  Teresa Ann, 541

SHIVELHOOD
  David, 903
  Edward, 903
  Edwina, 903
  Elizabeth, 903
  Emma (Kalbach), 903
  Nancy, 903
  Sandra, 903
SHIVELY
  --, 1592
  Carolina, 625
  Estella Irene, 377, 403
  Sarah (Barnett), 1592
SHIVERY
  Elaine (Yearick), 1086
  Richard, 1086
  Tina Jean, 1086
SHOAP
  Bertha (Fritchie), 102
  Jesse, 102
  Jesse Jr, 103
  Margie Maxine, 103
  Shirley (Taylor), 103
SHOBERT
  Hazel, 1233
SHOCK
  Osa, 620
  Robert, 620
  Stacy Lynn, 859
SHOCKLEY
  Cynthia Elizabeth, 496
  Jonathan Allen, 496
  Larry Allen, 496
  Mary Elizabeth Fought (Langerman), 496
  Robin, 1656
SHOEMAKER
  A D, 1662
  Amanda Jo, 1370
  Amye Victoria (Sides), 1471
  Andrew, 813
  Barbara (Trapp), 273
  Charlotte, 1470
  Deborah (Stiffler), 1370
  Dorothy Faith (Essick), 1631
  Elias D, 1470
  Emmie, 1471
  Emmie (Hoffmeier), 1470
  Ethel L, 651
  Flora Iola (Womelsdorf), 813
  Harry, 813
  Jerry, 273
  John Nevin, 1471
  Kathryn, 1471
  Maggie (Wysor), 1662
  Mary, 1471
  Matilda (Smeal), 1680
  Moses, 1193
  Paul, 813
  Rhett, 1370
  Sarah Ann (Beaty), 1193
  Thomas, 813
  Travis James, 1370
  Wilbur Warren, 1631
  William, 1680
  William Best, 813
SHOENAMANN
  Karen, 502
SHOENER
  Andrew G, 782
  Emma Blanche (Fritz), 782
  Jean Irene, 783

  Mary Irene, 782
SHOFFER
  Lewis, 1235
  Zula (Shawkey), 1235
SHOLL
  Alice (Brungart), 1063
  Anna (Rhoads), 1066
  Anna Mazy, 1064
  daughter, 1066
  Elinora, 1066
  Elizabeth Clara, 1064
  Emma Jane, 1063
  Jacob R, 1063
  John Thomas, 1064
  John William, 1066
  Minnie Kate, 1065
  Verna Sally, 1065
  William Jacob, 1066
SHOLLENBERGER
  Anna, 845
  Edna Meryl (Gwilliam), 131
  Esther Madine (Weiser), 1614
  Ethel Marion (Gwilliam), 131-132
  Geraldine, 131
  John Robert, 131
  Kathy Ann, 131
  Nancy Jane, 1614
  Phyllis (Bailey), 1614
  Robert Leon, 131-132
  Ruppert, 1614
  Russell E, 1614
  Walter Scott, 131
SHOLLEY
  Kristen Leanne, 745
  Margaret Ann (Badman), 745
  Milton, 745
  Milton Matthew, 745
SHOMO
  --, 1707
  Carrie, 243
  Hellen Susannah (Wolff), 243
  Joseph N, 243
  Letitia, 1341
SHOMPER
  Gail Virginia, 653
SHONK
  Dierdre Lynne (Smith), 1322
  Kevin David, 1322
SHOOK
  Helene, 1058
SHOOMAKER
  Catherine (Herold), 1526
  Dell, 1526
SHOOP
  Anna Maria, 694
  Ara Priscilla, 685
  Bertha Mae, 1535
  Carrie Agnes, 685
  Carrie E (Tressler), 685
  Charles M, 696
  Dewaine Edwin, 685
  Edwin D, 685
  Elias, 684
  Elizabeth Catharine, 696
  Emanuel, 685
  Esther S, 692
  Frances, 1670
  Grovene Shoop (Kocher), 691
  Guy E, 685

  Hannah (--), 696
  Harry, 696
  Hilda Irene, 704
  Ida Louise, 685
  Isaac Newton, 694
  John E, 696
  Leon Edgar, 691
  Marie Mae (Snyder), 685
  Mary Louise, 693
  Paul Ray, 685
  Sarah Ann (Koppenheffer), 684
  Sarah C (Matter), 685
  Sarah Verdilla, 696
SHOPE
  Lucinda Mae, 1073
  Pearl, 1048
SHOPPELL
  Ellen Lavinia (Weiser), 1540
  Samuel, 1540
SHORT
  --, 1698
  James Brian, 1814
  Marcine (Rothrock), 1698
  Michael, 217
  Sandra Sue (Dooley), 217
  Tessa Lynn (Wiser), 1814
SHORTNESS
  Margaret V, 800
SHOTSBERGER
  Beatrice, 983
  Clarence, 983
  Flo Arabella, 983
  Mary Elizabeth, 983
  Stella Bertha (Kehl), 983
  Vincent, 983
SHOTTENBERG
  Dorothy G, 1214
  Gertrude (McCoy), 1214
  Nellie Pearl, 1214
  William, 1214
SHOUP
  Caroline, 1193
  Virginia Lucille, 1305
SHOVER
  Linda Lou (Troutman), 1494
  May (Venderchen), 835
  Oscar Marvin, 835
  Robert Earl, 1494
  Sophia, 29
  Thomas Hand, 835
SHOVESTALL
  Anne, 1706
  Lottie, 1706
  Sarah, 1702
SHOWER
  John, 29
  Sophia, 29
SHOWERS
  Alice Arabella (Kahle), 1257
  Amber Jo, 938
  Anna (Shawley), 1257
  Bessie J, 1258
  Bonny, 1023
  Connie, 255
  Elsie, 1062
  Elva, 1257
  Evelyn, 1258
  Evlyn (Carson), 1258

  Francis Albert, 1257
  Gerald Bird, 1257
  Margaret, 1257
  Mary Irene, 1257
  Miles, 1023
  Robert, 938
  Samuel Albert, 1258
  Sara Pearl, 1258
  Sonny, 1023
  Susan Carol, 1344
  Virginia (Snyder), 1023
  Wendy Lou (Weiser), 938
SHRADER
  Elaine (Welbourne), 1497
  Elizabeth (Rogers), 1497
  Eugenie Marie, 447
  Frances, 1497
  Gerald, 1497
  Joanna, 1497
  Lee Theodore, 1497
  Ryan West, 1497
  Sarah Elissa, 1497
SHRAWDER
  Charles Brothers, 761
  Margaret Eleanor (Bucher), 761
SHRECKENGAST
  Anna Rose (Waite), 1080
  Charles Huston, 1080
  Clyde M, 1080
  Elsie (Stover), 1080
  Huston, 1080
  Mary (Kehl), 1007
  Michael, 1007
  Paulina, 1007
  William H, 1080
SHREFFLER
  Wilma Jean, 1580
SHREINER
  Paul Myers, 255
  Ruth Hilda (Brehm), 255
SHREVE
  Amanda (Wiser), 1787
  Winkfield, 1787
SHRIDER
  Cliff, 520
  Clyde Benjamin, 520
  Diamond, 618
  Donna, 620
  Elizabeth Jane, 467
  Gale, 619
  Lois Bell (Fisher), 520
  Marie Carrie (Fisher), 520
  Mildred (Long), 619
SHRINER
  Clarence E, 1152
  Emily Lucille (Kiger), 1152
SHRIVER
  David Arlo, 410
  David Shelmerdine, 836
  Devon Marcus, 410
  Ethel, 813
  Ethel Evans (Llewellyn), 836
  Ethel Llewellyn, 828
  Justin Paul, 410
  Kelly Irene (Saville), 410
  Mary, 1677
  Patricia, 836

SKINNER (continued)
Judy Ann (Cline), 552
Michael, 544
Michael James, 546
Myks Jean, 544
Riley Dean, 544
Susan Elaine, 546
Teresa Ann (Harris), 544
William, 552
SKOGMAN
Ellen Corinne, 967
SKUSE
Craig Landis, 932
Sherri Anne (Wilde), 932
SKWERCZNSKI
Rita, 971
SLACK
Bertha Edith, 389
Charles Maynard, 390
Charles S, 389
Geraldine, 1792
Gladys O, 390
Ida Minerva (Tuller), 389
Margaret, 390
Millie B (Chambers), 390
Solomon, 390
Violet, 1291
Wilma, 390
SLAFF
Laura Louise (Yeck), 884-885
Louis Paul, 884-885
SLAGLE
Calie E, 1276
Carol Ann (Lewis) Best, 1291
Faye, 274
Garlan Delite (Eberly), 629
Jon, 629
Mikki Renee, 629
Terry, 1291
SLASVICK
Lori J, 488
SLATER
--, 1109
Addie (Daws), 1109
Almira (Wiser), 1840
Andrew, 1840
Bonnie Sue (Herring), 544
Charlotte Ann, 533
Della Nadene (Arnold), 533
Ella F, 627
Esther E (Kahle), 1257
Fannie, 1110
Farren, 533
Frederick A, 544
James, 1109
John, 627
Kathy Jo (Gnepper), 495
Louisa (Fisher), 627
Phyliss Ann, 533
Scott, 495
Skyler, 1110
Wayne, 1257
William Augustus, 627
SLATES
Betty, 780
SLATTERY
Catherine Louise, 1171
Daniel Anthony, 1171
Diane Mae, 1171

Eugene Anthony, 1171
Grace Pauline (Rider), 1171
Louise Catherine, 1171
Michelle Renee, 1171
Nellie May (Ritter), 1171
Paul E, 1160
Paul Eugene, 1171
Paul Eugene Jr, 1171
Robin (Bright), 1171
Shirley Jean (Nelson), 1171
Stephanie Renee, 1171
Steven Anthony, 1171
Terry Renee, 1171
SLAUGENHOP
Amanda (Womelsdorf), 827
Reed, 827
SLAVENS
Anna Bell, 1872
SLAVIN
Amy Lynn, 536
Charles Phillip, 536
Kristine Elizabeth, 536
Lucinda (Wearly), 536
Megan Ann, 536
SLEAR
Anna Mae, 718
Fay, 1042
SLEET
Brian, 1086
David, 1086
Donald E, 1086
Gregory, 1086
Joanne Marie (Royer), 1086
SLEMMER
Emma I, 277
SLENTZ
Belva (Binkley), 578
Betty Marie, 578
Margie, 578
Martha, 578
Oren, 578
SLICK
--, 1015
Lucy (Snyder), 1015
SLIKE
George, 1015
Ollie (Snyder), 1015
SLINEY
Carol Ann (Scott), 883
David Hammond, 883
David Scott, 883
Sean Scott, 883
Stephen Paul, 883
SLINK
Jacob, 60
Mary (--), 60
SLIPETZ
Jane Marie (Thornsen), 275
Paul, 275
SLOAN
--, 1533
Abbie (Moore), 1437
Arthur, 448
Betty (Christian), 1533
Carrie Lynn (Ackerman), 520
Charlotte, 1437
David Lee, 520
Elgin, 1437
Mande, 1437
Marie, 1437
Mary Caroline, 1509

Ruth Elizabeth (Simmons), 448
Sandra Kay, 54
Susan Patricia, 448
Vic, 1437
SLOANE
Shepard V, 44
Virginia Ellen (Cochran), 44
SLOAT
Grace, 908
SLOATMAN
--, 931
Hannah C (Weiser), 931
SLOBODA
Anna, 695
SLOCUM
Mary Elizabeth, 1833
SLOGEL
Byrd Oscar, 1687
Nellie C (Kephart), 1687
SLOON
Nettie Elizabeth, 1383
SLOOP
John Harold, 1800
Wanda Evelyn (Wiser), 1800
SLOPEY
Lagarda E, 695
SLOTHOUR
Arimetta, 1050
Doloria, 1050
Rolla, 1050
Vernie (Erhard), 1050
SLOUGH
Rachel, 1027
SLUSHER
Karen, 523
SLUTTER
Dawn E (Linderman), 1040
Lester, 1040
Sandra Jo, 1040
Scott, 1040
Steven David, 1040
SMALEY
Christopher Lee, 537
Julie Marie (Fox), 537
SMALING
Bessie, 864
Cora, 864
Ellen (Bashore), 864
Franklin, 863
George, 864
Lizzie, 864
Pearl, 864
Sallie, 863
Valeria (Shettel), 863
SMALL
Francis Randolph, 969
Janet Carolyn, 969
Maxine, 961
Maxine Sarah (Smith), 969
SMALLWOOD
Bertha, 1350
SMART
Kathleen, 447
Louis E, 447
Margaret Estelle (Rhoads), 447
Sandra, 378
SMARTT
Charles Thomas, 1821
Jewel Mae (Wiser), 1821

SMATHERS
Sarah E, 1272
SMEAL
--, 1699
Alda (Courtney), 1680
Alice (Peters), 1680
Ann (McTavish), 1681
Arthur, 1708
Barbara (McGaughey) Lines, 1720
Benjamin, 1680
Bessie (Wisor), 1707
Catherine (Hummel), 1697
Charlotte, 1697
Clayton C, 1720
Cora, 1681
Daniel, 1680
David, 1697
Dustin L, 1720
Elizabeth, 1680
Elizabeth (Barger), 1680
Elizabeth (Conaway), 1680
Elizabeth (Logan), 1680
Ellen (Flegal), 1680
Elmira (Shimel), 1680
Eva Lilly, 1681
George, 1680, 1720
George W, 1680
Grant, 1680
Harry, 1681
Henry, 1680
Henry Barnet, 1680
Henry M, 1681
Hezekiah, 1680
infant, 1680
Irene (Williams), 1708
Isaac, 1697
Isiah, 1680
Jacob, 1680
Jennie, 1680
JoAnna (Conaway), 1680
John, 1680
Josiah, 1680
Lila, 1680
Lydia (Hummel), 1697
Maria, 1679
Mary (Stives), 1680
Mary A, 1680
Mary Melinda, 1680
Mathew, 1680
Matilda, 1680
Matilda (Kramer), 1680
Nancy Jane, 1680, 1686
Nellie, 1680
Pearl (Ritchie), 1712
Rock S, 1720
Rosy, 1681
Russell J, 1720
Sam, 1712
Samuel, 1680
Sandra K, 1720
Sarah Ann, 1680
Sarah Elizabeth, 1679
Sarah J (Cowder), 1681
Sherman, 1712
Susan (Wisor), 1712
Thomas, 1712
Tillie, 1770
Tillie Oster (Henry), 1680
Vernon, 1707

SMEAL/ SCHMEHL
Abraham, 1679
Benjamin S, 1679
Elizabeth (Bailey), 1679
Elizabeth (Weiser), 1679
Ellen (Bradley), 1679
George, 1679
Julia (Salisday), 1679
Samuel Alfred, 1679
SMECK
Cecelia Beth (Schoffner), 1140
Robert D, 1140
SMELSER
Alissa Ann, 411
Antionette Kay (Frey), 412
Brady William, 412
Bret Alfred, 412
Bryon John Paul Adams, 412
Carla Beth, 412
Cindy Lynnae, 412
Darrell W, 570
Heather Christine, 412
Jonathan Tobias, 411
Leanna Sue (Smith), 570
Rebecca Grace, 412
Sharon Ann (Weiser), 411
Susan Ann (Schauer), 411
Todd William, 411
William Alfred, 411
SMELTER
Henry M, 248
Mary Esther (Loy), 248
SMELTZ
Anna Mae, 676
Janine Marie, 703
June Marie, 676
Lisa Marie (Witmer), 703
Mary Elizabeth, 708
Richard Dixon, 703
Robert Allan, 703
SMELTZER
Alton B, 1097
Ben, 1414
Bertha, 1414
Cassandra Ellen (Weiser), 1414
Charles, 1414
daughter, 817
Diane, 816
Dorothy, 816
Elizabeth Covert (Frank), 1097
Elizabeth Jean, 1098
Ellen, 1414
Enoch, 1415
Harold G, 816
Harry, 1414
Henry, 1414
Iva Nathalene, 816
James, 1414
Joe, 1414
John, 816
Margie A (Womelsdorf), 816
Mary (Sample), 1415
Mary Ann (Troup), 816
Minnie, 1414
Oliver, 1414

SMELTZER (continued)
Sallie, 1414
Sterling, 1415
Terry Lee, 816
Tina Marie, 816
Vincent Edward, 817
SMETHURST
Ashlee Dawn, 1261
Bryan, 1261
Bryan Douglas, 1261
Rebecca Sue (Abbott), 1261
Wendell Jace, 1261
SMICK
Angelina (Weiser), 1160
Austin Weiser, 1160
Eliza W, 1160
John E, 1160
Mary (--), 1160
Oscar, 1160
Stewart, 1160
SMILEY
Amy Beth, 1204
Mark Thomas, 1204
Priscilla Lynn (Berry), 1204
Sara Cathleen, 1204
Tom, 1204
SMITH
--, 214, 430, 1561, 1850
-- (Long), 1016
-- (Willett), 1016
Aaron Eldon, 571
Ada (Wiser), 1777
Ady Elizabeth, 1172
Agnes Olivia (Wiser), 1666
Albert, 327
Albert Franklin, 1004
Aletha Mae, 433
Alexander James, 1322
Alexander Ramsey, 1322
Alice, 781
Alice Ada, 158
Alice Louraine, 433
Allen Ray, 432
Alma Julia (Weiser), 936
Almeda May (Kahl), 1004
Alvan Jay, 433
Alvira, 1084
Alyssa, 1717
Amanda Jane (Wiser), 1766
Amos, 597
Andaline (Johnson), 1495
Andrea (Prough), 1717
Andrew, 1392
Andrew Eric, 1322
Anila (Wilder), 936
Anna (Resh), 95
Anna E, 1148
Anna Elizabeth, 121
Anna Kate Malara (Wisser), 1726
Anne Wysor, 284
Annes (Mason), 1316
Annie (Wiser), 1872
Archie Ford, 1321
Arna Marie, 583
Arnetti Arbella (Herring), 594
Arthur, 1713
Arthur Lynn, 1276

Avis Barilla (Wiser), 1798
Barbara, 867
Beatrice, 1085
Beck Ann (Pyle), 936
Benjamin Harrie, 452
Benjamin Wayne, 910
Bernice Irene, 634
Bert, 1694
Bertha (Miller), 1391
Bertha Elizabeth (Bricker), 576
Bertha Elizabeth (Lilly), 1118
Beryl Grace, 628
Besse Albertina (Shultz), 1118
Bessie, 503
Bessie June, 1015
Beth, 662
Bethany Jane, 1204
Bethany Marie, 452
Betty (Newsome), 936
Betty Jane, 718
Betty Jean, 937
Betty Joyce (Heileman), 492
Betty Lou (Masemou), 858
Beverly Jane Shock (Unkart), 859
Billy D, 199
Blair Shultz, 1119
Blanche Luetta (Herring), 569
Bonetha Mae (Jones), 582
Brandon Lex, 210
Brenda (--), 633
Brewster Holmes, 1458
Brian Anthony, 1329
Brittany, 1716
Buford I, 1701
Byron Douglas, 1119
Caitlin Joan Opal, 1322
Candise Emma, 937
Carl Cornelius, 1118-1119
Carl Donald Edwards, 621
Carla (Kriebel), 817
Carlotta Cornelia, 1119
Carol Grace, 447
Carol Jean, 634
Carol Virginia (Burnett), 603
Carole Jane, 1220
Caroline Jane, 1218
Carolyn, 504
Carrie E (Weiser) Shepp, 1424
Carrie Lynn, 229
Cassie, 662
Catharine Ann, 341
Catharine Augusta (Muhlenberg), 284
Catherine, 1445
Catherine A (Muhlenberg), 1649
Catherine Maria (Croy), 848
Catherine Rosella (Rabold), 1321
Cathy Sue (Baker), 583
Chad Michael, 644
Charles Edward, 158
Charles Harvey, 205
Charles Warren, 1636
Charles Weiser, 158

Cheryl Lee (Wiser), 1770
Cheryl Lynn, 1201
Chris (--), 1716
Christopher Charles, 1559
Christopher James, 203
Cindy, 614, 1716
Cindy (Lambert), 936
Clara (Stine), 503
Clara Iona (Hammond), 969
Clarence Clifford, 969
Clarence W, 95
Clarene, 390
Clay Allen, 569
Cleo A, 1839
Cleo Helen, 634
Connie D, 1160
Connie Jean, 1024
Conrad Weiser, 1172
Cora Frances, 431
Coral, 634
Corrine Lael, 781
Cynthia Christine, 1500
Cyrus B, 95
Dale, 576
Dale Lester, 569
Daniel, 962, 1681
Daniel John, 633
Danny, 390
Darrell E, 504
daughter, 435
David Clifford, 1458
David Eldon, 571
David Eugene, 859
David Gerald, 1717
David Lee, 1329
David Lloyd, 1744
David Newman, 544
David Rahm, 1505
David Rahm Jr, 1505
Debbie Jean, 433
Deborah, 1001
Deborah (Gill), 472
Deborah Ann, 1276
Deborah Lenar, 165
Deborah Louise, 486
Deborah Lynn (Toy), 1249
Debra, 221
Debra Ann, 472
Debra Larie, 1172
Debra Lynn, 1717
DeGrasse, 1218
DeGrasse Fox, 1218
Deloras Jean (Tague), 433
Delores Gail (Ross), 202
Dennis Ebert, 1309
Dennis Lynn, 1744
Diana Louse, 792
Diane Kay, 1118
Dierdre Lynne, 1322
Donald, 1547
Donald A, 1311
Donald Archie, 1322
Donald Eugene, 910
Donald Galen, 680
Donald L, 504, 839
Donald Lee, 1744
Donald Robert, 1231
Donald Wesley, 1744
Donald William, 1322
Donn J, 826
Donna (Sheely), 504
Donna I, 1278

Donna M, 583
Doris Delight (Cole), 571
Dorothy, 1390
Dorothy Jennie, 1635
Dorothy K, 162
Douglas, 1249
Douglas Alan, 1322
Douglas Edward, 206
Dwight Scott, 1329
Earl, 504
Edith L, 504
Edna, 1495
Edna (Donahue), 431
Edna (Ginder), 431
Edna Marie, 432
Edna Sarah, 95
Edna Wisser, 1726
Edward James, 1177
Edward Leroy, 648
Edward Luther, 1505
Eileen Grace, 1309
Elaine, 721, 1392
Elaine Marie (Lawless), 1744
Eleanor Scott, 1505
Elisabeth Ashley, 1450
Eliza Catherine, 327
Elizabeth, 170
Elizabeth (Snyder), 1016
Elizabeth (Weiland), 1392
Elizabeth Ann, 405, 1119
Elizabeth Ann (Weiser), 165
Elizabeth Learned, 1505
Elizabeth Otto (Richards), 347
Ellen, 1388
Ellen (Staley), 597
Elmer Edward, 1635
Eloise M, 202
Elsie Emma (Kahle), 1231
Elsie Lee, 433
Elva M (Keiser), 504
Emeline, 1392
Emily Katherine, 848
Emily Maria (Meier), 327
Emma Jane, 158
Emmalee (Haggardy), 433
Erie Elizabeth, 1227
Ernest Eugene, 492
Ernestine, 432
Essie, 1751
Esta, 1392
Estella H E (Weiser), 1635
Ethel Alberta, 1015
Ethel Althea, 594
Ethel Amanda (Wright) Flick, 1685
Ethel Cecelia (Gorr), 1744
Eunice (Milbourn), 1496
Eunice Miriam (Weiser), 1177
Eva, 95
Eva (Wisor) Weaver, 1703
Eva Adeline, 1016
Evalyn Marie, 433
Eveah Luthera

(Hammond), 962
Evelyn (Weide), 1322
Fannie S, 296
Faye, 1025, 1058
Faye Eileen (Zimmerman), 648
Fern Viola (Binner), 1744
Flora H, 464
Florence Annie, 1726
Florence Irene, 1015
Forest E, 190
Forest Edward, 206
Forest Emerson, 205
Frances Elizabeth, 1089
Frances Leigh (Ellett), 1649
Francine White, 1275
Francis L, 390
Francis Marion, 95
Frank, 1102
Frank Emanuel, 431
Frank Leroy, 680
Fred, 662
Fred G, 1726
Frederick Walker, 431
Gary, 432
Gary A, 961
Gary Albert, 1005
Gary Avon, 569
Gary Dale, 1716
Geneta Nelsine, 576
George, 1680
George Edgar, 876
George Edward, 858
George Fred, 1726
George L, 936
George Robert, 936
George Robert Jr, 937
Georgia Katharine (Ekelund), 1458
Gertie, 1436
Giselle (Bourgoin), 937
Glena Viola, 1338
Glenn D, 670
Glenna E, 1496
Gloria Sue, 1119
Grace, 1392
Grace (Auman), 1392
Grace Louise, 433
Gregory George, 1458
Hallie (Anderson), 431
Hannah Rebecca (Weiser), 1638
Harold, 495
Harold Lee, 603
Harold Lloyd, 1744
Harper R, 1717
Harriet Elizabeth, 978
Harriet Elizabeth (Crossley), 680
Harry, 1392, 1638
Harry B, 202
Harvey, 1496
Harvey Irvin, 1638
Hattie Bertha, 1635
Hazel Lucille (Hocker), 582
Hazel Marie (Tuller), 390
Heber Chase, 1766
Helen (Clark), 432
Helen Blanche (Gnepper), 495
Helen Harriet (Keen), 1389
Helen L R, 1638
Helen Marjorie, 1672

SMITH (continued)
Henry Muhlenberg, 341
Henry P, 1666
Herbert, 1685
Herbert A, 166
Herbert Roy, 433
Hilda M, 1591
Hiram W, 1495
Holly Lynn, 1249
Homer E, 435
Ida Edna (Fisher), 628
Ida Louise (Cummins), 205
Ina (Bow), 205
Ina R (Hartman), 504
Ira Milbourne, 1496
Irene, 1391
Irene (Flegal), 1681
Irene (Hinnershitz), 96
Irene (Lollar), 432
Irene (Wisor), 1701
Irene Beatrice (Rusk), 1228
Isaac H, 1015
Isaac Johnson, 1496
Isaac Johnson Jr, 1496
Ivan Roy, 433
Ivan W, 504
Jack Daniel, 1119
Jack David, 1118
Jacob C, 503
Jacob John, 1744
Jacqueline (Moyer), 1044
James, 1703
James A, 158
James Arthur, 569, 639
James Brian, 633
James Clay, 1391
James Edward Rahm, 1505
James Elmer, 158
James Harry, 1391
James Stewart, 165
James Wilson, 158-159
Jane, 1227
Jane (Donalson), 1495
Jane A Lee, 583
Jane Maria, 859
Jane Stuart, 1649
Janet, 1615
Janet (--), 202
Janet (Grundy), 504
Janet Louise (Hutchenson), 664
Janet Mae, 225
Jarred Graham, 199
Jean Karen (Egan), 1559
Jeanette Evelyn (Weiser), 1636
Jeanne (Saussman), 1392
Jeffrey Alan, 848
Jennie (Sullivan), 1102
Jennifer Leigh (Taylor), 1656
Jennifer Lynn, 197
Jesse Daniel, 211
Jessie, 561
Jill Louise (Dunlevy), 284
Jim, 664
Jimmy, 390
Jo Anne (Wolf), 472
Joan Sandra (Speedie), 1322
Jody M, 1716

Joel, 971
John, 1012, 1486, 1553
John Allen, 1744
John Allen Jr, 1744
John Carson, 435
John Charles, 936
John Charles Jr, 936
John Curtis, 817
John Donnell, 284
John Elwin, 633
John Harold, 1024
John Michael, 817
John Milhime, 1632-1633
John Milton, 158
John Wesley, 628
Jon Alan, 570
Joseph Michael, 633
Joseph Wysor, 1649
Josephine, 1118
Josie Marie (Patch), 1329
Joy Celyn Kay, 432
Juanita, 1325
Judith Ann, 495
Judith Lynn, 923
Judy, 748
Judy (--), 633
Judy A (Weiser), 1375
Judy Kay (Waring), 971
Julia Ann, 432
Julia K (Pulley), 571
Julie (--), 197
Julie Marie (Miller), 1329
Julie Rae, 1004
Justin Michael, 644
Justin Stuart, 452
Kaitlyn Marie, 1559
Kama Jean, 936
Kara Elizabeth, 206
Karen, 197, 1379
Karen Ann, 936
Karen Ann (Riley), 1021
Karen Kay, 1744
Karen Marie, 989
Karla (Wagner), 937
Karol Kay, 1779
Katherine (St Marie), 1322
Kathleen Emma, 937
Kathryn Elizabeth, 1329
Kathryn Margaret, 1228
Kathy (Summerlot), 569
Katy Sue, 1717
Kayci Lynn, 150
Kayleen Ann, 211
Keith Cameron, 1322
Kellee Jene (Wiser), 1769
Kenneth, 1392
Kilene Rochelle, 937
Kimberly Louise, 876
Lala Renee (Harris), 544
Lana Jean, 1119
Larry, 1238
Larry Edwin, 150
Larue Reardon, 1004
Laura, 95, 1496
Laura A, 1662
Laura Jane (Giffin), 1119
Laura Jean (Clevenger),

452
Laura Mildred, 432
LaVerne V, 504
Leanna Sue, 570
Lear Eugene, 937
Leland James, 583
Leland James Jr, 583
Lelia Anna, 632
Leo Frank, 1004
Leon Russell, 633
Leonard E, 432
LeRoy, 503
Leroy, 591, 1001
Lesa Leann (Graham), 199
Letty, 1408
Lewis, 1016
Lewis Andrew, 202-203
Lewis Wayne, 431
Lex Doyle, 210
Lida Marie, 936
Lillian Alice (Wisser), 1744
Lillie Mercedes (Weiser), 205
Linda (Zarnowski), 662
Linda Ann, 206
Linda Carol, 158
Linda Kathleen, 936
Linda M (Nagle), 670
Linda Marie, 690
Linda Marrol, 1309
Lindsay Ann, 165
Lisa (McIntosh), 1322
Lisa Ann, 569
Lois, 576
Lois Clare, 634
Lois Marion, 1071
Loree Lynn, 203
Lori Michele, 936
Lorraine Bernice (Roberts), 1172
Louise, 1392
Louise Grace, 229
Lucile Gladys, 433
Lucille (Schreckangast), 1001
Lucinda Mae, 633
Lucy Camille, 211
Luella, 1496
Luella May (Witters), 1309
Lulu M, 1015
Luther, 503
Lydia (Weiser), 1553
Lyman A, 431
Lyndi Kay, 203
Lynn, 571
Lynn (Coddington), 284
Lynne Elizabeth, 776
Madge Lucille, 1228
Madona May (Rickey), 591
Magdalena Ella, 95
Maggie (--), 1390
Malinda, 203
Marcia Ann, 1322
Marcia Eloise (Strader), 1329
Marcia Lynn, 1264
Margaret, 270
Margaret (--), 1390
Margaret (Herron), 158
Margaret (Taylor), 633
Margaret (Weiser), 1850

Margaret Ann, 633
Margaret Ann Hannah (Earnest), 1486
Margaret Donnell, 1649
Margaret Elizabeth, 1070
Margaret Ellen, 434
Margaret Florence, 435
Margaret Jane, 1005
Margaret Jane (Knecht), 431
Margaret Lucille, 962
Margaret Pauline (Long), 603
Margaretta Henrietta, 341
Margie Velma, 970
Maria, 662
Marian Louise (Hale), 876
Marianne Beech (Gluckert), 1421
Marilyn (Kahle), 1264
Marion (Hemminger), 158
Marjorie, 432, 911
Marjorie Elissa, 1004
Marjorie Nan, 1118
Mark, 1656
Mark Alan, 1744
Mark Daniel, 1119
Mark Joseph, 544
Marlin, 1177
Marlin Ross, 1264
Marlin Thomas, 1264
Martha Jean, 434
Marvin G, 431
Mary, 504, 603, 1078
Mary (--), 1390
Mary (Birkircher), 430
Mary (Brown), 158
Mary (Burton), 435
Mary (Stevens), 1177
Mary Amelia (Texter), 95
Mary Anne, 1633
Mary Elizabeth, 1228
Mary Elizabeth (Kahle), 1228
Mary Elizabeth (Walling), 1118
Mary Elizabeth (Weiser), 158
Mary Elizabeth (Wysor), 1649
Mary Ellen (Lowey), 431
Mary Francis, 547
Mary Gardner, 1649
Mary Judith (Wolbert), 859
Mary Kay, 441
Mary Lou, 1781
Mary Stuart (White), 327
Matson Meier, 327
Max, 1118
Maxine Sarah, 969
McKinzie Ann, 143
Melanie Leigh, 1264
Melinda, 1264
Melissa, 1001
Melissa (Smith), 1001
Melvin Albert, 435
Melvin Eugene, 142
Melvin Leroy, 603
Melvin W, 432
Merle G, 1375

Merlin Jacob Dale, 1716
Mervin Henry, 633
Michael A, 1021
Michael Charles, 158
Michael Daniel, 1172
Michael David, 859, 1177
Michael Robert, 493
Michael Shaw, 1458
Michaelyn, 1264
Mickie Jo (Constable), 569
Mildred, 962
Mildred (Crawfold), 159
Mildred Irene, 432
Mildred Louis (Rahm), 1505
Mildred Louise (Koppenhaver), 639
Mildred Maxine, 569
Mima Arlene, 1656
Minerva, 1392
Minnie (Moore), 158
Minnie Leone, 1818
Minnie May, 158
Miriam Lorene (Bierly), 1004
Miriam Ruth, 1496
Mona Lee, 1871
Monique Ann, 1275
Muriel (McElwain) Neally, 1547
Muril Elizabeth, 463
Myrtle Ann (Ross), 201
Myrtle Elizabeth (Wilson), 1119
Myrtle Lou, 633
Nadine, 1118
Nancy Lee, 1392
Naomi (Kershner), 569
Naomi Ruth (Dunlap) DeJesus, 1450
Naomi Ruth (Ross), 203
Nathan, 150
Neal Ramsey, 1322
Neil, 1118
Nellie (Smeal), 1680
Nellie Ocelene, 434
Nichele Elaine (Gardner), 166
Nila Rebecca, 583
Norma Christine, 995
Norman Samuel, 1231
Norman White, 327
Olive Neoma, 435
Ora D, 513
Ora Margarett, 434
Orville, 576
Orvis A, 594
Pamela Jo (Griffin), 1005
Pamela Sue, 536
Pamela Susan (Younkin), 1172
Pat, 1238
Patricia Ann, 859, 1309
Patricia Barbara (Player), 214
Patricia Lou, 569
Patricia Marie, 633
Patrick, 1390
Patrick James, 971
Patti (--), 493
Paul, 1392

SPRATT
Virginia, 58
SPREECE
Dura Elizabeth, 76
SPRINGER
-- (--), 78
Allis Rosanna (Kahle), 1259
Arlene Ann (Wimmer), 79
Benjamin, 565, 1259
Benjamin Lucas, 80
Charles Harold, 79
Charles Havice, 79
David, 78-79, 522
Diane (Souder), 522
Frederick Muir, 80
George, 565
Harold F, 1885
Harold Franklin, 80
Howard David, 79
Janice Jean, 80
Jarod Souder, 522
Jennifer Lynn, 80
Joan (Banter), 565
Joel David, 522
John Marvin, 247
Julia Ann, 523
Lee David, 80
Louise Marie (Teichert), 80
Margaret Leone, 79
Margaret Louise (Stands), 79
Mary Marguerite (Havice), 79
Mary Rau (Fasig), 247
Melissa Ann (Miller), 80
Nancy Ann, 79
Norma Jane (Emery), 80
Olive, 1247
Patsy Ann Anderson (Riley), 79
Paul Frederick, 80
Susan, 565
SPRINKLE
Amy Jo, 819
Angela (McGanghey), 820
April Dawn, 819
Ashley Ann, 820
Betty Jean, 820
Brian Christophr, 820
Brooke Lee, 819
Clyde Vernon, 820
Delores Violet, 819
Denise (Parker), 819
Donald Lee, 819
Donald Ream, 819
Donna Lynn, 819
Dwight, 820
Gabe Austin, 820
Ganet Earlene (Aten), 820
Gerald Wayne, 820
Grace E (Darst), 819
Heath Roscoe, 820
Hieka (Plapperr), 820
James Allen, 819
James Robert, 819
Jane Ellen, 819
Janet Lynn (Martin), 819
Kathryn Shirley, 820
Kelvin Duane, 819
Lee Roscoe, 819
Mary Ellen, 820

Mercy Leigh, 820
Molly Elizabeth, 819
Rita (Lashbrook), 820
Ronald Eugene, 819
Rose Marie (Croxton), 819
Ruth Elizabeth (Boyles), 819
Sandra Kay (Irwin), 820
Shawna Christine, 819
Sherry Lynn, 819
Tate Ross, 820
Teal Duane, 819
Terri Sue (Runkle), 820
Timothy Brandon, 820
Timothy Lynn, 820
Tina (Willcoxen), 819
Todd Lee, 820
Troy DeWayne, 820
Twylet E, 819
William Oscar, 819
SPRITZEL
Margaret, 342
SPUDIC
Rose Lucille, 1287
SPURGEON
Alice Rozelle, 149
Archie Lee, 149
Bessie Violet, 149
Carol, 149
Clarence William, 150
David Albert, 148
David William, 148
Dollie Gladys, 149
Doris, 148
Dorothy May, 149
Elmore, 149
Esther (Forslund), 149
Ethel (Hansen), 149
Ethel Marie (Cunningham), 148
Georgia (Marquarte), 149
Gilbert Martin, 148
Glenda Lou, 149
Hardy Martin, 148
Helen Marie, 225
Janet Lee, 149
Joan Olene (Langenberg), 148
June Ann, 148
Katharine Mae (Hannigan), 148
Kathryn Ann, 149
Leander Bieglow, 148
Leone (Rice), 149
Lily Violet, 148
Louise Olene (Langenberg), 148
Luanna, 549
Mabel (Collier), 148
Mabel June, 148
Martha Elizabeth, 150
Monroe Nathan, 148
Nathan Leander, 148
Olive, 149
Priscilla Almedia (Weiser), 148
Rodney Keith, 149
Ruth (Okisson), 148
Sadie Maude (Cook), 148
Sharon (Sprague), 149
Shelia, 149
Zenda Kay, 149
SPYCKER
Henry, 1412

Mary (Weiser), 1412
SPYKER
Abigail L, 1446
Addie, 1447
Agnes Selin (Davis), 1452
Agnes Selin Davis, 1452
Albert, 1448
Alfred W, 1440
Alice (Rousculp), 1446
Allen, 1446
Amanda, 1452
Anna, 1429
Anna (Rothermel), 1443
Anna Maria (Weiser), 1429
Arlene (Wertman), 1442
Baker Fairchild, 1452
Berth L, 1442
Bertha Margaret (Piper), 1441
Betty Jane, 1442
Blanche Cecil, 1447
Caroline (Piper), 1440
Catharina, 1430
Catharine, 1429, 1452
Catherine (Smith), 1445
Charles, 1445-1446, 1448
Charles Abraham, 1441
Charles Norman, 1442
Charles Richard, 1443
Chester Alton, 1441
Dale, 1447
Daniel, 1440, 1446
David A, 1447
David E, 1446
Dawn N, 1447
Dorothy (Aska), 1446
Edith (Meyers), 1448
Edna Belva, 1448
Effie, 1446
Eleanor, 1447
Eleanor Grace, 1442
Eleanor Jane, 1443
Elisabetha (Hosterman), 1452
Elisabetha (Todd), 1445
Eliza, 1452
Eliza Jane, 1451
Elizabeth, 1446, 1451-1452
Elizabeth (Kramer), 1445
Elizabeth (Piper), 1443
Elizabeth Fairchild, 1452
Ella B (Stouffer), 1443
Ellen Elizabeth, 1449
Emma (Peters), 1445
Eulice (Murphy), 1447
Eva Elizabetha, 1454
Flora Estelle (Haggard), 1445
Florence, 1447
Francis Clarence, 1449
Francis N, 1443
Franklin, 1452
Franklin Davis, 1452
Fred Bowers, 1441
George, 1444, 1447
George Allen, 1447
George Newton, 1443

George Sylvester, 1452
George W, 1440
Gertrude, 1447
Gregory Alden, 1446
Harold Leslie, 1441
Harry A, 1443
Harry Asbury, 1445
Harry W, 1440
Hattie (Hamer), 1440
Hazel Elsie, 1448
Helen, 1440
Helen (Vortkamp), 1446
Helen Jean, 1447
Henry, 1445-1446, 1452
Henry S Eyer, 1452
Ida (Chilcoat), 1442
Irene, 1445
Irma, 1447
Jack A, 1446
Jacob, 1446
James K Davis, 1452
Jeffrey Kye, 1443
Jennie Marie, 1450
Joel, 1446
Joel B, 1447
Johann Henrich, 1445
John Alfred, 1441
John Daniel, 1443
John Henry, 1429
John Parvin, 1443
John Peter, 1429
Jonathan, 1445-1446, 1452
Jonathan L, 1446
Jonathan Schnure, 1452
Julia Ann, 1447
Ladema (Cutler), 1445
Laura Belle (Herrington), 1445
Lawrence, 1446
Lawrence K, 1446
Leah (Shank), 1444
Ledy Ann, 1453
Levi, 1447, 1452
Lewis, 1446
Lidia, 1430
Luther, 1447
Lydia (Poorman), 1443
M Salome (Piper), 1440
Mabel Edith (Aggar), 1441
Madeline (Yarnell), 1443
Mae, 1440
Magdalena (Rausch), 1440
Magdalena Margaret, 1445
Margaret (Lousch), 1445
Margaret A, 1443
Margaret Winifred, 1443
Margene (Whitney), 1447
Margery E S (Cornelius), 1452
Maria, 1443
Maria Agnes, 1452
Maria Margaretha, 1453
Martha Caroline, 1441
Martin, 1445
Mary, 1444-1447, 1451
Mary (Donelson), 1441

Mary (Osman), 1452
Mary (Saiomiveber), 1446
Mary Alice, 1441
Mary Ann, 1449
Mary Ann (Petit), 1447
Mary Belle (Driscoll), 1446
Mary Catharine, 1452
Mary Elizabeth, 1443
Mary Jane, 1443
Mary Jane (Lenpel), 1442
Mary Louise, 1442
Mary Magdalene, 1430
Mary Miller (Fairchild), 1452
Meghan R, 1446
Melanie Caye, 1446
Miriam Isobel, 1442
Mitchell Alden, 1445
Myla Catherine, 1073
Myra Catherine, 1441
Nancy Jane, 1447
Nellie Catherine, 1449
Nettie, 1447
Peter, 1429, 1446
Phyllis Lorraine (Shull), 1443
Rachel, 1452
Ralph, 1441
Rebeca (Pavin), 1443
Renae K (Howard), 1443
Richard D, 1446
Richard Piper, 1443
Robert Newton, 1443
Roland Vern, 1448
Rosanna, 1443
Rosetta, 1440, 1444, 1451
Ruth Lousie, 1441
Samuel, 1440, 1445-1446
Samuel Ira, 1441
Sarah, 1446-1447
Sarah (Weaver), 1445
Sarah Anna (Butler), 1447
Sarah Jane, 1441
Sarah Margaret, 1441
Sarah Matilda, 1443
Sarah Melissa (Sellers), 1447
Sophia (Driesbach), 1429
Stephanie Joan, 1445
Stephen L, 1446
Susan, 1446
Susan (Wise), 1440
Susan B, 1446
Susanna, 1443
Susanne Carylon, 1443
Theodore, 1446
Thomas Corbett, 1445
Vera, 1448
Walter Albert, 1442
Warren, 1448, 1451
William, 1443, 1451-1452
William Donnelson, 1441
William Norman, 1442
William Peter, 1440
William Piper, 1442
SQUIRE
Barbara Lou, 893
Michael Earl, 893
Oscar Earl, 893

STEWARD (continued)
Tana (Hill), 373
Una (Younkin), 375
Wayne, 1885
Wayne Stanley, 372
William Eugene, 370, 372
Winifred Hortense, 373
STEWART
-- (--), 363
Ada Mae, 1348
Alexander Murrary, 301
Amy Helen, 1344
Anne Page (Carter), 301
Archibald, 1827
Beth, 1499
Catharine Elizabeth (Sheaff), 301
Christopher James, 997
Clementine, 1518
Dale Clark, 997
David Kenneth, 1333
Debra Jean (Wiser), 1814
Debra Kay, 997
Doris Louise, 1195
Edwin H, 363
Elaine Louise (Farrell), 1344
Elizabeth (Etschberger), 1518
Elizabeth Jo, 1344
Ellen Jeanne (Goebel), 1156
Emma Maxine (Warnica), 997
Eugenia, 301
Florence (Happenstead), 997
George Massy, 1344
Gwendolyn Ruth (Weiser), 1632
Harry Vincent, 647
Helen (Heim), 997
Helen Jane (Wiser), 1827
Hilda Drusilla (Long), 1333
Inez (Maier), 53
Jacob, 1518
James Eugene, 997
James Harvey, 997
James Luin, 997
Jan Ellen, 41
Jean Anne, 207
Jean Marilyn (Parkinson), 1482
John, 1518
Julia, 1158, 1674
Julia (McIlvaine), 301
Kathleen Ann, 1333
Kay Louise (Homuth), 1344
Kenneth Leroy, 1333
Lemuel, 1518
Leroy Neal, 997
Lydia, 1825
Margaret, 830
Mark Farrell, 1344
Martha Halstead, 962
Martha Jane, 1344
Mary Mercer Carter, 302
Matthew A, 1156
Melissa Ann (Baker), 1632
Michele, 309

Muhlenberg Hiester, 302
Murray, 301
Orville M, 363
Patricia Ann, 997
Robert Leonard, 1632
Rosa Lee Draper, 451
Ruth (Kahl), 997
Ruth Viola (Weiser), 1348
Sandra Lee, 1632
Sara Nancy, 1348
Shirley Romaine (Zimmerman), 647
Stephanie Layne, 1344
Steven Foster, 1632
Suzanne Libeth, 1344
Thelma Ruth, 1330
Tina Marie, 752
Tracey Glen, 1814
Wayne S, 363
William, 1348
William Charles, 53
William John Sheaff, 301
STICHTER
daughter, 833
Henry P, 833
Maria (Womelsdorf), 833
STICKLE
Delores Anne, 367
STIDHAM
Cathy Sue (Coomler), 555
David Ray, 555
STIEFEL
Edith, 611
STIELY
Angela Diane, 658
Charles, 1341
Clair Lamar, 658
daughter, 658
Doris L, 703
Elsie May, 1343
Emma Helen (Souders), 1340-1341
Eric Christopher, 658
Gertie Mae (Klinger), 657
Helen Mary, 1343
Joann (Zimmerman), 658
John Kirby, 657
John Roger, 658
Margaret Florence, 1342
Peggy (Stroub), 658
Peggy Wertz (Stutzman), 658
STIERS
Charles, 1350
Ida (Arnold), 1350
STIFFLER
Amie Jeanne, 1370
Deborah, 1370
Donald Ashley, 1370
Donald Eugene, 1370
Dora Lynn, 1154
Edward, 1369-1370
George Jr, 1154
Jeanne (--), 1370
Jeanne Renetta (Casner), 1369
Jennie Marie, 1370
Mitzie (Stiver), 1370
STILBOLT
Christa Dawn (Weber), 1420

Dana Karl, 1420
Oliva Ann, 1420
Weber Hans, 1420
STILES
-- (--), 280
Alisha Ann, 287
Anita Delores (Franciscus), 287
Dawn Jeanette (Johnson), 391
Elizabeth (Leader), 1422
Frances Apeler, 287
Frances Edith (Muhlenberg), 287
Ian Michael, 391
Jacob, 1422
Jan Alrich, 288
Jenny Alrich, 288
Jill Alrich, 288
Morrison N, 280, 287
Nicholas Andrew, 391
Patricia (Geist), 287
Paul Allan, 391
Peter Morrison, 287
Richard Carson, 288
Virginia (Alrich), 288
STILL
Annabell Louise, 868
Barbara (Smith), 867
Cora (Yinger), 866
Dolly Adeline, 868
Douglas Michael, 867
Edna Louise (Szech), 867
Edna Sophia, 867
Edward Jacob, 867
Edward Michael, 867
Jacob I, 866
James Robert, 867
June (Yohe), 854
Mary, 867
Michael Matthew, 867
Pearl, 867
Richard Grant, 854
Richard Grant Jr, 854
Zorado English, 866
STILLINGS
Charles F, 1230
Charles Robert, 1230
Dorothy Jane, 1230
Margaret Jane (Lucas), 1230
STIMPSON
Louis Ted, 1771
Machel (Wiser), 1771
STINE
Alice Sophia (Cochran), 504
Anna Marie, 506
Carl R Jr, 505
Carl Russell Sr, 504
Carrie A, 509
Catharine, 1427
Clara, 503
Clarence R, 505
Dorothy, 505
Ella (Batts), 1721
Eurdine M (Kreillich), 504
Evelyn (Bowersox), 505
Faye, 505
George, 1721
Grace B, 464
Hazel, 506
Katlin, 1035
Lola R, 504
Lucy Webb, 506

Lydia Matilda (Bowman), 503
Maralyn (Keefe), 505
Nellie Juanita (McCoy), 505
Raymond David, 505
Reuben, 503, 506
Robert, 504
Sarah Matilda, 505
Thomas S, 505
Urban R, 505
Velma C, 505
William Sherman, 504
STINGHEN
Donato Joseph, 693
Joel Salada, 694
Joseph Donato, 693
Mary Candice, 693
Rite Iola (Salada), 693
STINGLY
Belva Elizabeth, 271
Grace Myrtle, 271
Mary Ann (Eikelberner), 271
Peter Jacob, 271
STINHOUR
Gail, 610
STINSON
Bruce King, 551
Bruce Wayne, 530
Charles Alexander, 1437
Charles Rodger, 551
Cherly Lynn (Riggs), 530
Dora May (Riggs), 551
Doris Anna, 552
Dorothy (--), 551
Dorrance Neil, 551
Edna (King), 551
Elizabeth, 1662
Ester, 1437
Esther Lucille, 552
Forrest Edmund, 551
Gary Lee, 551
Harold, 1437
Harold James, 552
Henery F, 551
Hildred Louise, 552
James Warren, 1437
Katie (--), 551
Lillian C, 1437
Mabel Clara, 1657
Margetta (--), 551
Mark Allen, 552
Mary Ann, 1437
Mary Ellen (Moore), 1437
Michelle, 552
Phyliss (King), 552
Rene R, 1437
Robert, 1437
Sean, 551
Sophia (Arnold), 1437
Stephen, 552
Susie, 1437
Vera (Fultz), 1437
Virginia, 552
Vivian (Guldice), 551
Warren Edwin, 1437
STIREWALT
Margaret Jane, 104
STITZER
Ammon B, 1620
Ammon W, 1620
Catherine R (Weiser), 1620
Lillie M (Bloch), 1620
Loretta, 1093

Sarah (Leitzell), 1542
William, 1542
STIVER
Mitzie, 1370
STIVERS
David Arthur, 1056
Elizabeth Rey (Daugherty), 1056
Joseph A, 1056
STIVES
Mary, 1680
STOBAUGH
Adam, 1654
Margaret (Trinkle), 1654
STOBER
Barbara (Wagaman), 605
Ben, 604
Beverly (Timbs), 605
Carl, 604
Cecilia (Farley), 605
Dwight, 604
Elza, 604
Grace, 605
Hazel N, 617
Kathaleen (Duta), 604
Leroy, 605
Marlene, 604
Maude Priscilla (Long), 604
Michelle, 604
Mina, 608
Ned, 605
Ona (Jones), 604
Richard, 605
Rodney, 605
Rosemary, 604
Sandra, 605
Tracy, 605
STOCK
Albert, 93
Barbara, 92
Carole, 92
Cheryl, 92
Donna, 92
Donna (Krum), 92
Dorunda (Grimes), 91
Dorunda M (Grimes), 92
Ray, 92
Raymond, 92
Ronald Jay, 92
STOCKBERGER
Jemima, 510
STOCKBURGER
Mathilde, 1600
STOCKDALE
Gertrude, 367
STOCKING
Helen Augusta, 1453
STOCKLEY
Sydia E, 110
STOCKMAN
Daniel, 623
Deborah Lea (DeLong), 623
Lynne Annette (Wiser), 1869
Thomas, 1869
STOCKMAR
E Richard, 350
Linda Ann, 350
Margaret Ann (Richards), 350
STOCKTON
Betty (--), 351
David Reeves, 351
Ester (Kurtz), 351

TENNIS (continued)
James P, 517
Janis G, 517
Marcella M, 516
Perry D, 516
Rodney R, 517
Sherril Ann, 516
W A, 516
TENNY
April Lee (Kahle), 1202
William Lee, 1202
TENUS
Michael, 938
Missy Lou (Weiser), 938
son, 938
TEPPER
Helen (Cooper), 1031
Walter, 1031
TERHUNE
John B, 506
Rosella, 506
TERLECKY
Caroline Ann, 197
Karen (Smith), 197
Katharine Marie, 197
Myron, 197
TERMIN
Hellen, 871
TERNANE
Minnie, 291
TERPEN
Bernadette (Weiser), 212
Harold, 212
TERRES
Jennifer Ann (Rodgers), 139
John, 139
Nathan Allan, 139
Stephanie Ann, 139
TERRILL
--, 1833
Donna Jean, 1521
Marie Antoinette (Wiser), 1833
TERRINI
Leslie Ann Neil, 436
TERRY
Anna (Wiser), 1802
Dennis, 1802
Lois Jean, 454
TERWILLIGER
Mary Ann, 1220
TESKE
Carol Joy (Kuhns), 1742
David Gregory, 1742
Esther Mae, 755
Patrick Charles, 1742
Raymond, 1742
TESNER
Janis (Weiser) Teets, 1569
Paul, 1569
TETER
Alice Winifred, 713
Clara Isadore (Womelsdorf), 832
Daniel K, 832
daughter, 832
Erma Irene, 677
son, 832
TETRICK
Harold, 1233
Joan (Goble), 1233
Kelly Kay, 1233
Terry, 1233

TEWS
Charles Andrew, 543
Edith Margaret, 543
Heather Lisa, 543
Kelby Lawrence, 543
Landon Dennis, 543
Leonard Lawrence, 543
Matthew Martin, 543
Violet Lucille (Herring), 543
Windy Ann (Jungwirth), 543
TEXTER
Mary Amelia, 95
THACKER
Rebecca Jane, 1821
THAIN
Aliene, 1770
THALMAN
Beverly, 1775
THARP
Calvin George, 732
Clara Maude (Pickering), 732
Emaline (Hepner), 731
Hazel Tyler (Taby), 732
Henry, 731
Katie E, 1024
Lulu May, 731
Mae Lulu, 732
Walter Calvin, 732
THATCHER
Alma Jane, 577
Catherine Louise, 577
Ernestine Marie (Wolfe), 577
Louis, 577
Richard Eugene, 577
Smilie Clifford, 577
Stanley Eldon, 577
THAYER
Alex Willem, 746
Amy Roelina, 746
Asa Johannes, 746
Henry, 1543
Marc Willem, 746
Mary (Reed), 1543
Millie, 1543
Polly Ada (Reitz), 746
THEIS
Elizabeth Vernon, 1123
THIBAULT
Robert, 636
Susan Lynn (Bernbrock), 636
THIEL
Alma, 1725
Caroline (Wieser), 1725
Christina Lee, 631
Edwin Jacob Oscar, 1725
Elisa, 1725
Elizabeth (Williams), 1725
Evelyn, 1725
Howard, 1725
Ida, 1725
Irene, 1725
Irwin, 1725
Leroy, 631
Lori Ann (Hayden), 631
Margerite (Seabloom), 1725
Meta, 1725
Norma, 1725

Olga, 1725
Oscar, 1725
Oscar E, 1725
Tonia Renee, 631
Trinity Nathan, 631
Walter E, 1725
THIELE
Deborah Sue, 1333
Lorraine, 1600
THIELEN
Andrew Carl, 1737
Bernadine Louise, 1736
Daniel, 1737
Debbie (--), 1737
Diana, 1737
Donald Thomas, 1737
Donald Thomas Jr, 1737
Dorothy (Moe), 1737
Jennifer Michele, 1737
Joseph Edgar, 1737
Karen (Crumbley), 1737
Kathy (McCoy), 1737
Leslie Ann (Shaw), 1737
Mark William, 1737
Mary Jo, 1737
Nicholas Andrew, 1737
Raymond John, 1736
Raymond John III, 1737
Raymond John Jr, 1737
THIERET
Dianne Elyse, 454
THIMMES
Pamela Marlene Poland, 1159
THIRINGER
Charlotte Ann (Thompson), 36
Henry M, 36
Inez Genevieve (King), 36
Jon Kimberly, 36
Judy Nadine (Connooley), 36
Maika Anne, 36
Megumi Rhae, 36
Sandra Sumi (Funkhouser), 36
Sheridan Andrew, 36
Sherri Lynn, 36
Shirley Eileen, 36
THIRINGER/SANDERS
Jon Paxton, 36
Kylee Marie, 36
THOMAS
--, 736, 1406, 1807
-- (--), 1716
Alice, 31
Aline, 251
Alyson Dicole, 203
Amanda Fay, 205
April Gail, 586
Arthur, 1084
Billy Robert, 586
Brad Allen, 957
Butler, 1439
Carlene Denise (Matthews), 383
Catherine, 1632
Charles Monroe, 736
Christina, 719
Cynthia Evelyn (Wiser), 1809
Daniel Warren, 383
Danny, 1716
Denise, 1716

Dennis, 1716
Edna Grace, 736
Effie Cora, 271
Elias, 638, 736
Eliza, 736
Eliza J, 289
Ellsworth Weinmann, 957
Elsie Leela, 585
Emily, 1615
Emma Jean (Leibold), 382
Esther (Bauder), 364
Eva Candas, 558
Evelyn (Walkey), 1084
Florence Martha (Keogel), 957
George, 1238
Georgina, 1716
Grace Estella (Kahl), 1195
Gregory, 55
Gregory Allen, 957
Guy, 364
Harriet (Weiser), 426
Jane (Jones), 957
Janice Louise, 957
Jeff, 55
Jeffery Allen, 205
Jennie, 525, 600
Jennie (--), 736
John Adam, 736
John E, 736
John J, 736
John Robert, 586
Joseph Allen, 383
Joseph Franklin, 736
Joyce Marie (Shugarts), 1716
Judith Ann, 1814
Karen Marcia, 47
Karen Sue, 1439
Kate E (--), 736
Kathrine Louise (Speeks), 586
Kimberly Jane, 55
Lafayette, 1809
Lora Lee (Hocker), 586
Lucas, 1716
Lynn Suzanne (Murfin), 383
Mamie (--), 736
Margaret (Wiser) Thompson, 1807
Margaret Ann, 546
Marion, 426
Mark Edward, 200
Martha (Tanner), 1406
Mary Elizabeth, 648, 650
Marybell, 957
Merrill Jane (Wright), 55
Mona Pauline, 1489
Nancy Joann, 957
Nancy Lee, 1097
Nellie (Whitaker), 1439
Nettie Lauretta, 426
Patricia A, 382
Patricia Sue (Sturm), 202
Penney, 1716
Philip Mark, 1439
Phyllis Jeanne, 1331
Rachelle Joday, 200
Rebecca Jane, 34
Richard Allen, 957
Robert Wilson, 1195

Ronald Warren, 383
S Duane, 1716
Sally Jean, 383
Samuel, 638, 736
Sandra, 1491
Sandra Gale, 586
Sarah, 736
Sarah (Rowe), 736
Susan Elaine (Erdley), 200
Teri Anne (Tayrien), 205
Toni, 1716
Vinnie (Kahle), 1238
Warren, 382
William Eric, 202
Yvonne Maye, 586
THOME
Grace Agnes (Coonfare), 48
Paul, 48
THOMPSON
--, 1406
Alan McKinney, 1632
Alva Augustus, 1834
Andrew Howell, 1204
Anna Mae, 144
Anna Mae (Wiser), 1190
Barry Lee, 73
Belva Sarah, 145
Bonnie Kay, 1204
Brenda R, 1285
Carolyn Jean, 1815
Catherine Elizabeth, 1244
Catherine Pauline (Ulrich), 71
Charles LaVern, 1190
Charlotte Ann, 36
Cherish Amber, 1275
Christine Marie, 1200
Claudine, 403
Cynthia Renee (Strock), 1489
Daryl Ernest, 179
Dawn Marie (Wolfgong), 1275
Dean Edward, 179
Debbie Jean, 603
Dolores (Dressler), 1534
Donald Franklin, 603
Dorothy Mae (Schlenbaker), 602
Edward Duane III, 1275
Edwin John, 1505
Edwin Lewis, 1878
Edwin R, 1505
Elizabeth Jo (Stoner), 42
Ellen B, 1233
Emma Matilda (Wiser), 1878
Ernest B, 179
Eva, 1225
Florence, 911
George Lamb, 1221
Gerald Raymond, 1190
Grace May (Phebus), 1221
Hannah (--), 1406
Harold, 944
Helen (Rahm), 1505
Helen Chloe (Duffie), 796
Helen Elizabeth, 1505
Helen Lou (Starner),

THOMPSON
(continued)
Helen Lou (Starner)
(continued)
944
Homer, 1204
James Houston, 1823
James Ray, 588
James William, 1802
Jane (Inkster), 1505
Janice Elaine (Duffie),
797
Jeanette, 67
Jeffrey Alan, 179
Jeffrey Lee, 1190
Joan Eileen, 1273
John, 71, 1534, 1654,
1698
John P, 1534
Johnny Lee, 588
Judy Jean, 588
Julie (Sorenson), 179
Karen, 1206
Keith, 602
Kenneth Robert, 1489
Laura Elizabeth, 791
LaVerta A (Hocker),
588
Lillian M, 71
Lois Mae (Woolridge),
179
Lori (Holkesvik), 179
Maggie E, 1663
Manora Kathleen, 624
Margaret (Walute),
1190
Margaret (Wiser), 1807
Maribe (Tanner), 1406
Marie, 693
Mark Frederick, 1505
Marsha Kay, 603
Mary Anne (Wood), 73
Mary K, 1394
Meghan Rebecca, 1204
Melissa Sue, 179
Michael Leon, 797
Mickey Jeff, 179
Minnie (Dickson),
1698
Miranda Carole, 1489
Mona Belle, 402
Nelda Idalene (Wiser),
1834
Nicholas Wayne, 179
Norman Rahm, 1505
Olivia B (Howell),
1204
Patrick Oneil, 42
Paulette (Wiser), 1823
Peter Rahm, 1505
Peter Rutledge, 1505
Phillip George, 588
Phoebe C, 1661
Rebecca E, 74
Rebecca Marlene, 1534
Rick Wayne, 603
Robert Steven, 1204
Rosalind Wren, 86
Rose, 1102
Sandra Lee (Stewart),
1632
Sarah Alice (Berry),
1204
Sarah Ann, 1505
Sarah Henrietta, 1387
Sena, 1226
Spencer, 1489
Stephen Anthony, 944
Sue (Adrian), 179

Susannah (Anderson),
1654
Suzanne Lynnette
(Gossman), 179
Sylva Katherine
(Wiser), 1802
Sylvia Jean, 1814
Teresa, 439
Trina, 1212
Wanda, 1774
Wanda Kay, 179
William, 87
William J, 796
William Louis, 179
Woodrow Robert Jr,
1807
THOMSON
Julie Lynn
(Womeldorf), 826
Kayla Chantel, 826
Lindsay Nicole, 826
Mary Randell, 330
Robert W, 826
THORN
Michael John, 1399
Nancy Jane (Dull),
1399
THORNBERRY
Cloa S (Wiser), 1779
Thomas, 1779
THORNBRUGH
Alma Frances (Wiser),
1867
Jess, 1867
THORNBURG
April, 950
Beverly Jean, 551
Joan Darlene (Weiser),
950
Leslie Dawn, 950
Mike, 950
Robin Dodie, 950
THORNE
Alice Irene (Knecht),
439
LaVerne (Byrne), 722
Lester, 439
Robert, 722
THORNETT
Amy, 565
Don, 564
Eric, 565
Joyce (Banter), 564
Julie, 565
THORNGATE
Bradley Dale, 1480
David Allen, 1480
George, 1480
Rodney Ray, 1480
Scott Allison, 1480
Virginia Lee
(Cummins), 1480
THORNLEY
Marian, 1779
THORNSEN
Amy Lynn, 274
Ann Elizabeth, 275
Bernard Leroy, 274
Diana (Palm), 274
Holly (Reynolds), 275
Jane Marie, 275
Jeffrey Douglass, 274
Leah Kirsten, 275
Martha John, 275
Mary, 261
Mary Irene (Douglass),
274
Patrick Joseph, 275
Rebecca Christine, 275

Rebecca Lynn, 275
Thomas Cassidy, 274
THORNTON
Clara Louise, 725
THORSON
Derek, 290
Dorothy Ann (Neiles),
290
Ted, 290
THORSTAD
Amy Lynn, 180
Bradley Michael, 180
Gary Gene, 180
Michelle Ann, 180
Randee Jean, 180
Sandra Kay
(Woolridge), 180
THORTON
Austin, 1440
Helen (Spyker), 1440
THRIFT
Alice Mariah (Riggs),
523
James, 523
THROCKMORTON
James Bruce, 415
Mary Ruth (Wagner),
415
Nicholas Reed, 415
Ralph, 415
THRONEBERRY
Bertha (Wiser), 1801
Clara, 1820
S H, 1801
THROSSELL
Bertha, 1388
THROWER
Carol Lynne, 168
THUMANN
Barbara Christine,
1559
THUMM
Karen, 1019
THUN
Marie Wilhelmina, 342
THURSBY
Colleen Kay, 122
THURSTON
Edward, 1852
Lola Irene (Wiser),
1852
Nettie C, 1781
Patricia Biddulph, 309
Ruth, 464
TIBBS
Debra Sue, 644
TIBERINO
Denna Marie, 727
Gail Sandra (Ryan),
727
John, 727
John Richard, 727
TICE
John, 1518
Marin (Etschberger),
1518
TICHY
Michael, 123
Trisha Ann (McGinty),
123
TIEDEMANN
Hannah Henrietta, 326
TIEHL
Charlene, 1393
TIERNY
Edna May, 1463
TIERS
Elizabeth (Budd), 302
Theobald, 302

TILGHMAN
Erin Marie, 1378
George Christopher,
1378
George Washington,
1378
Laura Elizabeth, 1378
Linda Lee (Kuhn),
1378
TILLER
Nina, 175
TILLISON
Willie Gertrude, 1335
Zella May, 1335
TILLMAN
André Pillott, 1213
André Pillott III, 1213
Charlsie, 1213
Gayle Marie (Mccann),
1213
Sarah Wellons, 1213
TILLOTSON
Mary Margaret, 1224
TILSON
Lottie, 507
TIMBLIN
Shirly, 1236
TIMBS
Beverly, 605
TIMENS
--, 984
Amanda (Radabaugh),
984
Charles, 984
Elinora, 984
James, 985
Jonathan, 985
Margaret, 985
Robert, 985
William, 984
TIMMONS
Carol Jean (Herring),
535
Christina Dawn, 541
Dawn Louise (Martin),
1038
Heather Renee, 494
James E, 541
Janet Lucille (Nowak),
494
Jennifer Renea, 129
Joshua Scott, 541
Kenneth, 535
Lisa Diane, 1038
Martha, 148
Michael Paul, 129
Michelle Kay, 494
Michelle Lynn, 1038
Patricia Ann (Johns),
129
Paul, 129
Robert, 1038
Ronald, 494
Teresa Ann (Shiveley),
541
TIMMS
Caryol, 1778
Cassandra Marie, 822
Danielle Alyce, 822
Renee Lynnet
(Womelsdorf), 822
Robert Eugene, 822
Robert Ryan, 822
TINE
Katharine (Campbell),
170
William, 170
TINER
Donald, 973

Eleanor May (Nelson),
973
Pamela Ruth, 974
Randolph Wayne, 974
Ronald, 973
Wayne G, 973
TINGLER
Charles Edwin, 461
Clem, 461
Dorothy Ann, 461
Franz Edwin, 461
Georgia Lorrain, 461
Hattie Grace
(Gossinger), 461
Marlene Charlott
(Johannsen), 461
Virginia (Jenkins), 461
TINKEY
--, 1000
Ruth (Lillibridge),
1000
TINKLE
Mary, 1654
TINKLER
Agnes, 1193
TINNEY
Margaret, 628
TIPPERY
--, 1440
Rosetta (Spyker), 1440
TIPPIN
Barbara Maloney
(Kunkle), 129
Douglas Blaine, 129
Garold Lee, 129
Garrett Brooke, 129
Goldia La Veta (Bloyd),
128
Kay Ellen, 129
LaVonne Arlene, 129
Linda (Hutchings), 129
Perle Fremont, 128
Wanda Deloris, 128
TIPTIN
Sally Beth, 209
TISCHHAUSER
Denise Marie
(Masciola), 1304
Paul Anthony, 1304
Paul Homer, 1304
Taran Nicole, 1305
TISING
Saundra Sue, 1867
TITENSOR
Lowell Christian, 1777
Marjorie (Wiser), 1777
TITSLER
Janet Lewis, 1249
TITTLE
Donna Kay, 919
George W Jr, 919
Kenneth Lee, 919
Mary Jane (Weiser),
919
Pamela Ann, 919
TITUS
-- (--), 97
Alice Lou (Cork), 105
Billy, 591
Charles Wayne, 105
Clara Edna (Deppen),
104
David Douglas, 105
Deane Deppen, 105
Diane, 105
Dorothy R, 105
Gale Edwin, 105
Hubert W, 105
Jerrald Lynn, 105

TITUS (continued)
Juanita Wade (Redman),
105
K P, 97
Kester Riley, 104
Kester Riley Jr, 105
Lois V (Bowman), 105
Lorena Margaret, 104
Madona May (Rickey),
591
Melvin Lee, 105
Miriam Letha, 105
Robert W, 105
Sandra Aline, 591
Sharon Middleton
(Easton), 105
TOBELMAN
Carol Lynn, 756
Charles, 756
Linda (Furman), 756
Lisa, 756
TOBEY
Carol Jean (Muir), 214
Caton Elizabeth, 214
Gary, 214
Julia Mae, 214
Laura Jean, 214
TOBIAS
Bridget Ann, 909
Elizabeth Ann
(Kercher), 261
Florence Anita
(Cooper), 1035
George, 787
George Allan, 261
Georgiana Keefer
(Frey), 787
Jennie Elvira, 1836
June Anita, 1036
Lois Jean, 1036
Richard Boyd, 1035
Terry, 787
William Boyd, 1035
TOBIN
Judy Kay, 611
TOBINE
Clara Belle (Wiser),
1754
Norman B, 1754
TOCCA
Marlene, 267
TODD
Charles Edwin, 52
Eileen, 1444
Elisabetha, 1445
Harold Calvin, 52
Harold Lewis, 52
J Harold, 52
Jeanette Louise
(Gnepper), 495
Karyl Yvonne (Kintner),
52
Mary Katharine
(Schuh), 52
Matthew Lloyd, 495
Michiko (Yamada), 52
Robert Louis, 52
Robert Wayne, 495
Willie Jo (Ferguson),
52
TOLAND
Darlene Grace, 740
TOLEN
Doris Mae, 1481
TOLLE
Susan E, 83
TOLLEFSON
Kay Lynn (Bishop),
154

Ron, 154
TOLLINGER
Sara Margaret (Ulrich),
75
William Preston, 75
TOMARKO
Beverly (Gardner), 722
John, 722
TOMASKE
James, 490
Pamela (Moore), 490
TOMASOVSKY
Angel, 438
TOMBOUGH
Marie Elnor, 801
TOME
--, 1415
Burdette C (Weiser),
1292
Charles, 1415
Delma, 1292
Elmira Jane (Weiser),
1415
Harry, 1415
Janie, 1415
TOMKO
Rodger Andrew, 1512
Susan Joy
(Hershberger) Lester,
1512
TOMLINSON
Anna Lee, 1431
Brenda Jo, 441
Cartha Elaine, 441
Diane Ethel, 1431
Inez (Napier), 1431
John Winfred, 441
June Evelyn, 1430
L E, 1429
Lee Glenn, 1430
Lloyd Everett, 1431
Lulu May (Moore),
1430
Marilyn June, 1431
Reva Arline (Brown),
441
TOMOR
Craig, 483
Theresa Dawn, 483
TOMPKINS
Albert G, 953
Charles, 1206
Harriet, 786
Laura Addeline, 153
Lela Pearl (Martin),
1206
Mary A (Battles), 953
TOMPSON
Donald, 435
Margaret Florence
(Smith), 435
TONER
--, 1799
Lois Rae, 701
Shirley Ann (Wiser),
1799
TONKEL
Chad, 550
Pamela Anne (Bell),
550
TOOMEY
Cheryl, 888
Debra Lee, 189
Earl, 189
Gay, 888
Gertrude Louise
(Eppley), 888
Helen Marie (Snyder),
189

Kenneth, 888
Sherrie Dee, 189
Terrie Lynn, 189
TOONE
Kathleen, 210
TOOPS
Rita Jean, 395
TOOT
Mary Sophia, 1476
TOPP
Doris, 997
TOPTEIN
Charles, 1271
Elsie Lela (Coder),
1270
John Robert, 1271
Wilbur Milton, 1271
TORPY
Esty (Wetters), 1107
Lelia, 1107
Milon, 1107
William, 1107
TORRANCE
--, 1651
Fannie Naff (Wysor),
1651
TORRES
Bertha, 398
Norma Jean (Yost)
Crothers, 1328
Walter, 1328
TOSCHNER
Barbara Ann (Trauger),
1075
G, 1075
Gerald Lee, 1075
Joanne Marie Kinsey,
1075
TOTTEN
Miriam (Wickes), 1407
TOTZKE
Peggy Jean, 181
TOUSSAINT
Brian William, 1087
Karen Ruth (Brungard),
1087
Norbert F Jr, 1087
TOVISSI
Craig Joseph, 1199
Susan Louise (Baird),
1199
Tristan, 1199
TOWELSON
Sandy, 267
TOWNE
Kathy, 552
TOWNER
Rebecca, 485
TOWNLEY
Philina, 705
TOWNSEND
Anna Margaret
(Kershner), 133
Deborah (Wiser), 1785
Hazel, 1804
Henry, 1785
Ida, 133
Joel, 554
Johnnie Lee, 1805
Joseph S, 133
Kay Elenor, 780
Linda Kay (Johnson),
554
Martha Elizabeth, 1807
Mary Eveline, 84
Roy T, 133
Sherman J, 133
TOWNSENDE
Florence, 271

TOWNSHEND
Dianne Marie (Hill),
1098
Jesse Allan, 1098
Steven Rolph, 1098
TOY
Aliene Rosella (Kahle),
1249
Benjamin Wayne, 1249
Clayton Harold, 1250
Cody Adam, 1249
Deborah Lynn, 1249
Dennis Wayne, 1249
Doneci (Dickey), 1249
Dylan Jacob, 1249
Guy Edgar, 1249
Guy Edgar III, 1249
Guy Edgar Jr, 1249
Harold McIntire, 1249
Janet Lewis (Titsler),
1249
Joni Lynn (Meyers),
1249
Martha Jean, 1249
Michelle Renee
(Schaeffer), 1249
Nicole Louise, 1249
Pamela Joy (Troutman),
1249
Sean M, 1249
Shirley Morita
(McIntire), 1249
TOYER
Catharine C (Albright),
1080
Gershon, 1080
TOYN
Janice (Wiser), 1773
Kevin W, 1773
TRACY
Brian David, 1558
Nancy Marie
(Schwartz), 1558
Sue, 1448
TRAGER
Frances Edna (Eppley),
892
James Edward, 892
TRAIL
Alene (Wiser), 1804
Ardith E, 1804
Bazil, 1847
Caminza Jane (Wiser),
1823
Charles Calvin, 1823
Marvin, 1809
Nellie Alice (Weiser),
1847
Ozell (Wiser), 1809
Ruggie, 1803
TRAINER
Theresa, 266
TRAMMEL
Kathleen, 1798
TRAMMELL
Bessie Juanita (Young),
134
Debra Marlene (Wiser),
1781
Jeffrey, 1781
Lee, 134
TRAPHAGEN
LaVerne, 1519
Mary Elizabeth
(Eldredge), 1519
TRAPP
April Lynn, 274
Barbara, 273
Cathy, 274

Debbie Kay, 274
George, 273
Goldie Ella
(Eikelburner), 273
Janet, 273
John Herschel, 274
Larry, 273-274
Lori Ann, 274
Mary Joan
(Eikelburner), 274
Nathan Edward, 274
Peggy, 273
Susan (Miller), 274
TRAUCHT
George Edward, 1565
Katrina Jeanne, 1565
Timothy Edward, 1565
Willa Jeanne (Coburn),
1565
TRAUGER
Barbara Ann, 1075
Connie Lee (Stover),
1075
Harry, 1075
Harry Martin, 1075
Howard Albert, 1075
Jeime Lee, 1075
Jennifer Lynn, 1075
Joy Lynn (Confer),
1075
Margaret Lucille
(Wert), 1075
Robb Martin, 1075
Roxanna (Garica),
1075
Scott Allen, 1075
Shirley Ann (Ambrose),
1075
Todd Michael, 1075
William Victor, 1075
Zachary Sebastian,
1075
TRAUTMAN
Ellen, 837
TRAVERNIER
Bruce Alan, 1074
Cary Andrew, 1074
Cynthia Alice (Bradley),
1074
Gerald Earl, 1074
Kimberly Ann, 1074
Mary (Reed), 1074
Patricia Ann (Wert),
1074
TRAVIS
Anne Marie, 1740
Bertha Jean, 1739
Brandon Michael, 1739
Brittany Jean, 1739
Earle Leroy, 1739
Erica Marie, 1740
Gregory Alan, 1740
James Thompson, 1220
Jordan Jedediah, 1740
Kathleen Eleanor
(Hiscox), 1739
Leanne Kay
(Hartsgrove), 1740
Michael Earle, 1739
Priscilla Jane (Kahle),
1220
Rachael Kimberlee,
1740
Ronald Eugene, 1740
Sarah April, 1740
Teresa Lynn, 1740
TRAYNOR
Ann Veronica, 470

VARGO (continued)
Nancy (Bolig), 77
Pamela Jean, 77
VARNER
Daniel A, 749
Jerry D, 749
Michelle Annett (Hummel), 749
Sophia (Wiser), 1722
William, 1722
VASCO
Nicole Marie, 1399
VASQUEZ
Marian V, 1570
VAUGHAN
Rachel Elizabeth (Wiser), 1830
William E, 1830
VAUGHN
--, 1805
Anna V (Wiser), 1876
David, 177
David Michael, 177
Felix Johnson, 717
Harry, 1876
Judy (Wiser), 1805
Kandra Gay, 717
Karen Elsie (Weiser), 1381
Krystal Lynn, 717
Lindsay Renee, 1381
Melodie Kay, 177
Ralph, 1381
Ralph Eric, 1381
Suzanne Elizabeth (Lohafer), 176
Thelma Mae (Lawver), 717
VAUGHT
Harold David, 1752
Karen Virginia (Maxey), 1752
Mary Alice, 1792
VEASEY
Alice, 1764
VEECK
--, 22
Johannes, 22
VEH
Matilda, 466
VEIKAT
Helena Rae, 74
VEITS
Annette Kay, 1147
VELA
Jeanne, 313
VELASCO
Alexander, 581
Anthony Robert, 581
Marion Elizabeth, 581
VELEY
Betty (Neill), 35
Cherri, 35
Deborah, 35
Emma, 34
Harold, 35
Hugh, 35
James, 34
Raymond, 35
Rena (Sheets), 34
Ruth, 35
Walter, 34
Winifred M (Warren), 34
VELLINES
Diana Marie (Hoffman), 751
Steven Eric, 751
Tammy Lynn, 751

Trisha Marie, 751
VENDERCHEN
Elizabeth (Hand), 835
Frances, 835
May, 835
Samuel C, 835
VENN
Jeanne Elizabeth, 738
VENOIT
--, 1754
Dianne (Wiser), 1754
VENT
Josephine, 943
VEQUIST
Janice Marie, 1180
VERDIS
Shannon Lee, 948
VERGNON
Frederick Peter, 38
Mary Etta (Siegfried), 38
Mary Margaret, 38
VERHOFF
Judy, 136
VERNIA
Betty Lou, 1448
Dorthy, 1448
Edna Belva (Spyker), 1448
Francis, 1448
Mary, 1448
William Henry, 1448
VESTEL
Mary Lee, 495
VETOR
Mary Cheryl, 567
VIALL
Charlotte Melina, 1629
VIBBART
Olive, 1805
VIC
Jeffrey Diane, 918
VICCARO
Sandra, 1536
VICKERS
Cindy, 1442
Daphne Ann, 1039
Diane Lee (Martin), 1039
Jimmy Cole, 1039
Jimmy Cole Jr, 1039
VICKERY
Martha Jean (Smith), 434
Robert James, 434
Susan Lorraine, 434
VIELE
Frederick Frasier, 1781
Linda Ann (Wiser), 1781
VIERS
Catharine Elizabeth (Johnson), 391
Larry Bruce, 391
Teann Louise, 378
VIGAR
Lois A, 367
VIGLIOTTI
Beth Ann, 775
Diane Louise (Wasson), 775
Laura Marie, 775
Mark A, 775
Rachel Lynn, 775
Sarah Louise, 775
VILLA
Jeanine Marie (Brady), 1740
Jennifer, 64

Marguerite Marie, 336
Rene, 1740
Robert, 64
Susy (Steckbeck), 64
VINCENT
Polly, 1430
VINCEVICH
Denise Marie, 744
VINE
Anne, 1357
VITARELLI
John Michael, 1300
Marcia Kaye (Patton), 1300
VITELLO
Barbara, 276
Louis, 276
Patricia, 276
Thelma (Eikelberner), 276
VITITOE
Nancy Ellen, 1492
VITKO
Ashley Rebecca, 1511
Carol Ann (Hersberger), 1511
Joseph John III, 1511
Joseph John Jr, 1511
Lori Ann, 1511
VLEGELAR
Margareta, 1405
VOELKER
L H, 61
Lottie (Pine), 61
VOGAN
Louise C, 1633
VOGEL
Abbie Gail (Weiser), 1467
Carin, 941
Jack, 1467
VOGELI
Louise, 1684
VOLK
Bert, 610
Bessie (Shumaker), 610
Felixitus, 1353
Lori Lynn, 413
Valma, 610
VOLKERT
Donna Kay (Leibold), 383
James E, 383
Jeffrey LaVon, 384
Melissa Kay, 384
VOLLENE
Debbie, 1176
Ellen, 1176
JoAnn, 1176
Joe, 1176
June (Kirpatrick), 1176
VOLLMAR
Catherine C, 1511
VOLLOM
Tuck, 178
VOLOVICH
Vicki, 1714
VON BEHREN
Barret, 107
Linda (Buckner), 107
Mona Bernice (Starwalt), 107
Oliver Lewis, 107
Wesley Louis, 107
VON BROCKHAGEN
Kathryn (Shoemaker), 1471
William H, 1471

VON DASSEL
Maria Harriet Susanne Charlotte Metta, 319
VON DER TRENCK
Adelheid Friederike Irene (von Wasieleski), 320
Ricarda, 320
Stephan, 320
VON DUEHREN
John Bernhard, 25, 357
VON GEVEKOT
Caroline Clementine Henrietta (Gossling), 323
Elisabeth Johanna Lulu Daisy, 323
Hans Freiherr, 323
Raban Bernd Max Eduard, 323
VON HOLST
Adriane (Schnaitmann), 316
Anna Lore (Classen), 316
Dieter, 316
Karl Eberhard, 316
Walter, 316
VON KELLER
Heinrich Adalbert, 1606
Sophie Wilhelmine (Weisser), 1606
VON KNOLES
Cherri, 1011
VON NEIDA
Philip, 1459
VON PHUL
Diana (Thielen), 1737
Patricia Diana, 1737
Tracy Thielen, 1737
William, 1737
VON POST
Amalie Elisabeth Clementine, 323
Eliza Catherine, 306
Emily Maria, 327
Henrietta Margaretta, 316
Hermann Caspar, 306
Jane Scott (Whitlock), 306
Laurentius Henry, 306
Margaretta Henrietta (Meier), 306
VON SELZAM
Leonore Martha Cornelia, 319
VON WASIELESKI
Adelheid Friederike Irene, 320
Erwin Karl Thaddäus, 320
Hildegard (Hösl), 320
Jutta, 320
Reinhard Wilhelm Ludolf, 320
Sieglinde Gepa Lucy, 320
VON WASIELEWSKI
Brigitte Margarette Johanna (Gowin), 319
Dieter Vincenz Theodor, 319
Heinrich, 319
Irene Hedwig Elisabeth, 319
Lore, 320
Lucy Anne Clara

(Kulenkampff), 319
Maria Harriet Susanne Charlotte Metta (von Dassel), 319
Wilhelm Arthur Waldemar, 319
Wilhelm Traugott Theodor, 319
VON WEISSER
--, 1607
Charlotte (Hartmann), 1607
Johann Friedrich Christoph, 1606
Karl Friedrich, 1607
Luise Emilie (Hoffmann), 1607
Paul Albert, 1607
Regine Christine (Bernhard), 1606
Wilhelmine (Waechter), 1607
VONADA
Adam, 1008
Beatrice Madaline (Wert), 1075
Carrie Edith (Gentzel), 1008
Deanne Jean, 1076
Debra Susan, 1076
Deloris Jane (Quimbly), 1076
Douglas Sparr, 1076
Genevieve, 1008
Mary, 1060
Philip A, 1075
Sharlyn Mae, 1382
VOORHEES
Isaac, 15
Minnie Van, 15
VORHEES
John D, 596, 599
Lovena Ellen, 596, 599
Mary Catherine (Brouches), 596, 599
VORIS
Charles William, 1458
Clarence A, 1458
Clarence G, 1457
Mary Gray (Bruner), 1457
VORLESE
Cindy, 630
VORQUE
Cindy Ray (Armknecht), 1733
Don, 1733
VORTKAMP
Helen, 1446
VOS
Nelsena Jean, 175
VOSLER
Joan Marie, 404
VOSS
Carole, 275
VOTAW
Jessie, 59
VOUGHT
Emma, 381
VOYLES
Daniel Patrick, 636
Joseph Stephen, 636
Marcia Anne (Blagus), 636
Patrick Daniel, 636
VROMAN
Adam, 13
WABLER
Cheryl Joleen (Barse),

WEARATH
Carol A, 1502
WEARLY
Alison Marie, 536
Evelyn Francis
(Herring), 536
Lucinda, 536
Michelle Lee, 536
Paul, 536
Sam, 536
Wendy Jo (Nusbaum),
536
WEARY
Fay Catherine, 862
WEATHERBIE
David Lee, 130
Evelyn Michelle, 130
Evelyn Virginia (Tact),
130
Kenneth Lee, 130
WEATHERFIELD
Dewayne, 562
Lorada Ilene (Banter),
562
WEATHERFORD
Polly, 1788
WEATHERHOLTZ
Melissa, 1720
WEATHERILL
Albert, 681
Ann Marie, 681
Betty M (Andreas),
681
Dale, 681
David, 681
Edgar Herbert, 682
Edward Franklin, 681
Harriet Aletta, 681
Jay Edward, 681
Jill Elizabeth, 682
Julia Ann (Willis), 681
Mary Ellen, 682
Myrtle L (Harrington),
681
Paul Franklin, 681
Paul Lee, 681
Sadie Elizabeth
(Koppenhaver), 681
Susann, 681
WEAVER
-- (Thomas), 736
Albert, 1015
Anna Elizabeth
(Gebhart), 1330
Anne, 739
Ardrenna M
(Winkelblech), 1061
Bernadeni Margaret
(Jernee), 1331
Bernice Lucile, 1330
Beverly Jean (Ewing),
692
Bonnie, 1092
Brant Marvin, 1778
C Heagy, 877
Carolyn Ruth (Rose),
1778
Carrie Vella
(Koppenheffer), 709
Caryol (Timms), 1778
Charles Roy, 877
Clara Myrtle, 877
Daisey, 641
David, 578
David Mark, 692
Dawn (Davis), 692
Dennis, 1060
Dorothy, 578
Dorothy Louise, 877

Earl, 1703
Earl Raymond, 877
Edith Hazel, 877
Edna (Gramley), 1060
Edwin Johnson, 1330
Elizabeth, 1850
Elizabeth (Spitler), 914
Ellen M (Weiser),
1845
Elsie May (Wamsley),
1331
Elva Elizabeth, 679
Emma Idella (Gebhart),
1330
Eugene Forrest, 1062
Eva (Wisor), 1703
Faye Athalene, 709
Florence Irene (Smith),
1015
Florence Mae, 877
Frances Riehl, 244
Gary R, 1537
George, 1845
Gerald Franklin, 1062
Giannie Elaine, 692
Ginger Ramona, 1311
Glen Hoffman, 1311
Grace Catherine, 1331
Grace Mildred, 877
Gregory William, 1062
Hannah Rebecca, 709
Harry Allen, 1061
Heidi Allyn, 539
Helen (Mitman), 1331
Helen Barbara, 877
Homer T, 672
infant, 672
Ira Franklin, 1330
Ira Franklin Jr, 1331
J Roy, 351
Jacob, 914
James E, 1062
James Green, 1778
James J, 1367
James Russell, 1366
Joan May (Wiser),
1778
Jodi A, 1537
Joette D (Baker), 1537
John Allen, 1061
John M, 1061
John Oliver, 674
John William, 1062
Joseph, 1366
Joyce Maureen, 1062
Joyce Maureen
(Weaver), 1062
Judith Ann, 692
Kathryn Madeline,
1366
Kevin Scott, 1311
Laura, 1083
Linda, 1060, 1367
Linnie, 1083
Lois, 1378
Lori Jean (Hefflefinger),
230
Lori Marie, 1052
Margaret Viola, 1331
Marie Elaine, 653
Mark Alfred, 692
Marla Joy (Wolf), 1311
Marlin R, 1061
Marsha Ann, 1367
Marvin, 1052
Marvin Eugene, 1061
Marvin Junior, 1062
Mary Elizabeth, 877
Mary Ellen (Gheen),

1366
Mary Lou, 578
Mary Louise, 1062
Mary Roberta, 750
Minnie Mae
(Winkleman), 1366
Nancy Lee, 674
Nathan David, 692
Neal Wayne, 692
Nellie (Myers), 877
Nicholas Benjamin,
539
Paul Milton, 877
Pauline Margaret, 692
Phyllis Jeanne
(Thomas), 1331
Ralph Donald, 877
Ray, 1537
Reuben, 914
Rhonda Jo (Herring),
539
Rita Agnes (Kocher),
692
Robert Eugene, 674
Robert M, 1062
Robin Sue, 1311
Roger Lee, 1331
Ronald, 1367
Rose A, 1370
Rosemary, 1366
Ruth (Stockton), 351
Ruth Ann, 877
Ruth Arlene (Bowes),
1052
Ruth Olive (Styers),
1061
Ryan Auram, 539
Sadie Mae
(Koppenhaver), 672
Salome, 875
Samuel, 914
Samuel A, 827
Samuel Lester, 877
Sandra Snyder (Yager),
1778
Sarah, 1445
Scott Wendell, 692
Sharon Elaine (Schultz),
692
Shelia, 436
Shirley (Binkley), 578
son, 672
Steven D, 1537
Steven Lynn, 539
Thelma Hazel
(Koppenhaver), 674
Travis, 230
Twila (Womelsdorf),
827
Vivian Jane (Lamey),
1061
Walter, 230
Walter Robert, 230
Warren, 736
Wayne Conrad, 1331
Wayne Conrad Jr,
1331
Wendy S, 1537
William, 1060
William Henry, 709
Yvonne Marie, 1062
Zachary, 230
WEBB
Aline Ruth (Bettilyon),
781
Gary Eugene, 913
Grace (Gearhart), 729
Janelle, 46
Julia Ann, 459

Kathleen Susan, 781
Kenneth Thomas, 781
Kevin Lee, 913
Mark Charles, 913
Minnie Abigail, 362
Murial, 772
Pauline Frances (Haas),
913
Peggy Ann, 913
Percy Albert, 913
Richard Curtis, 913
Stanley, 729
Virginia Lee, 913
WEBB-HUNSUCKER
Percie J, 593
WEBBER
Alice, 210
Craig, 810
Mark, 810
Martin, 810
Renee, 502
Shirley Anla
(Bartholomew), 810
Terry, 810
WEBER
Ada, 1095
Alfred Jacob, 879
Barbara Jane, 452
Carolina Julia, 931
Catharine (Weiser),
1268
Catherine, 1003
Christa Dawn, 1420
Corson B, 1636
Daniel, 1268
David Paul, 1288
Donna Mae (Gephart),
1055
Edward, 1055
Eileen Elnora (Rager),
1133
Erma Fay (Wisor),
1703
Helen Dorothy (Oppelt),
879
Ira, 1703
Janet Suzette, 1288
Jessica, 126
Jill Marie, 1288
Judith Ann (Seigworth),
1288
Julia Catharine, 1420
Julia Therese, 126
Kevin Edward, 1055
Linda, 145
Linda Lou, 1133
Lottie, 1092
Mark Barton, 1420
Martha Elizabeth, 892
Michael, 126
Michele Dawn, 1055
Richard Alfred, 879
Sallie W (Polster),
1636
Sharon Sue, 1133
Suzanne Louise
(Gluckert), 1420
Tracy Ann, 1288
William Woodrow,
1133
WEBSTER
Cheryl, 1070
Debbie Marie (Leeper),
649
Jennifer Grace, 649
Jessica Faith, 649
Leonard Arthur, 649
WEDDIGEN
Margret, 326

WEDEMEYER
Charles Jefferson, 128
Wanda Deloris (Tippin),
128
WEDGE
Lucy, 948
WEEDEN
Waunita Mae, 588
WEEKES
--, 1409
Arthur Delano III, 311
Elizabeth (Scudder),
1409
Margaret Baldwin
(Schwab), 311
WEEKS
Betty Lou (Kaley), 861
Catherine (Peck), 1668
Patricia Lynnette, 861
Robert H, 1668
William J, 861
William Louis, 861
WEERMANN
Regine Dorothea
(Weisser), 1605
T J N, 1605
WEGELE
Marlene Lydia, 44
WEHR
Darlene, 125
Nevin, 1078
Pauline Susan
(Brungart), 1078
WEHRKAMP
Bernadine, 1318
WEIAND
Ralphetta Jean, 699
WEICHERT
Elaine Lynn (Bean),
371
Jeff, 371
WEICHMANN
John H, 1166
Mary (Weiser), 1166
WEIDE
Evelyn, 1322
WEIDENBACH
Barbara, 6
WEIDERMAN
Larry, 1519
Mary Elizabeth
(Eldredge), 1519
WEIDLE
Minnie Elizabeth, 1314
WEIDMAN
Dean Francis, 1747
Effie Mae, 1845
Erica Lynn, 1747
Scott Christopher, 1747
Sharon Marie (Wisser),
1747
WEIDNER
--, 1757
Beulah M (Wisser),
1757
Catharine, 1611
George Adam, 1611
WEIERICK
Dianne E, 1391
Ernest, 1391
Marjorie E (Miller),
1391
Rebecca A, 1391
Robert B, 1391
WEIGERT
Rebecca Ann, 416
WEIGLE
--, 868
Maria Johanna, 1464

WEISER (continued)
Dorothy Jean, 1381
Dorothy Lenore, 1631
Dorothy Mary, 449
Dorothy Wyoma, 124
Dorsey Eugene, 1186
Doug, xiv
Douglas Arthur, 1846
Douglas Conrad, 32
Douglas Dietrich, 806
Douglas James, iv, 169, 1010
Douglas Paul, 412
Drew Robert, 924
Drusilla Florence (Courtright), 1123, 1144
Dwayne Scott, 920
E H, 30
Earl C, 1846
Earl E, 1865
Earl Herbert, 1634
Earl Julius, 1615
Earl Lengel, 1568
Earl Randall, 1530
Earl Victor, 425
Earl W, 32
Earl William, 1568
Earnest Franklin Jr, 415
Edgar David, 1639
Edgar Sherman, 923
Edith, 155, 1625
Edith (Johnson), 1289
Edith A (Adams), 1614
Edith I, 1622
Edith L B, 1166
Edith Mae (Ashbrooke), 1144
Edmund Hartman, 125
Edmund LeRoy, 453
Edna (Burton), 949
Edna (Rhen), 775
Edna C, 1624
Edna C (Brillinger), 1426
Edna Hazel, 450
Edna Luella (Sanders), 209
Edna Mae, 1751
Edna May (Tierny), 1463
Edna S (--), 1865
Edward, xi, 1348, 1423-1424, 1844
Edward A H, 1614
Edward Benneville, 95
Edward Copeland, 1553
Edward Douglas, 1618
Edward E, 1423
Edward George, 1616
Edward H, 1009
Edward J, 1616
Edward James, 1177
Edward L, 1373
Edward Leroy, 1376
Edward S, 1614
Edwin, 1391
Edwin Christopher, 1429
Edwin Fahnestock, 1468
Edwin Hoag, 1620
Edwin Hugh, 31
Edwin Joseph, 1845
Edwin Morris, 1383
Edwin Reinke, 1428
Edwin Servatus, 86

Edythe J (Wynn), 1177
Effie Mae (Weidman), 1845
Elaine, 1144
Elaine (Hamilton), 1292
Eleanor, 1849
Eleanor (Coleman), 1848-1849
Eleanor Louise, 939
Eleanora (--), 1366
Eleanore, 1545
Elemina R (--), 1865
Elen (--), 1268
Elgin Oscar, 126
Eli Elery, 148
Elijah, 1642
Elinor, 1524
Eliora-Rae Matisse, 925
Elisabeth, 1593, 1875
Elisabeth (Leibacher), 1786
Elisabetha (Lobach), 1611
Eliza, 156, 182, 1675, 1879
Eliza (--), 1624
Eliza A, 1425
Eliza Anna, 1461
Eliza E, 114-115
Eliza Marie (Wasden), 210
Elizaberth (Anspach), 1522
Elizabeth, 30, 33, 81, 360-361, 778, 784, 812, 931, 939, 955, 1116, 1184, 1189, 1191, 1269, 1349, 1374, 1387, 1411-1413, 1417, 1427, 1458, 1472, 1524, 1542, 1544-1545, 1559, 1561, 1567, 1669, 1674-1676, 1679, 1711, 1864
Elizabeth (--), 16, 190, 1191, 1411-1412, 1544, 1591, 1679, 1786
Elizabeth (Aiken), 30
Elizabeth (Beck), 1647
Elizabeth (Bieber), 1643
Elizabeth (Bucher), 1455
Elizabeth (Copeland), 1544
Elizabeth (Crosby), 1423
Elizabeth (Custer), 236
Elizabeth (Deibler), 758-759, 774
Elizabeth (Ely), 1675
Elizabeth (Emery), 1634
Elizabeth (Givens), 1424
Elizabeth (Hartman), 119-122, 131
Elizabeth (Heister), 1567
Elizabeth (Hevener), 1633
Elizabeth (Kline), 375-376
Elizabeth (Klinger),

358, 360, 461-462, 637, 758, 777
Elizabeth (Michaus), 1181
Elizabeth (Minchaus), 1111, 1160
Elizabeth (Minchausin), 1110
Elizabeth (Musselman), 1164
Elizabeth (Rinehart), 939
Elizabeth (Shaffer), 215, 236-237
Elizabeth (Snavely), 1373-1374, 1387
Elizabeth (Snyder), 80
Elizabeth (Turner), 1587
Elizabeth (Willoughby), 1186
Elizabeth (Winn), 1181
Elizabeth A (Cassidy), 1863
Elizabeth A (Truby), 148
Elizabeth Ann, 165, 211, 415, 421
Elizabeth Ann (Smith), 405
Elizabeth Anna (Oberholtzer), 1625
Elizabeth Anne, 1348, 1844
Elizabeth Anne (Nunn), 1347
Elizabeth E A (Hanning), 1644
Elizabeth Eve (Holman), 1523
Elizabeth Jane, 1181
Elizabeth Jane (Elliott), 1346
Elizabeth Kathryn (Sheely), 160-161
Elizabeth L (Loren), 1375
Elizabeth Larue, 1562
Elizabeth Louise, 210
Elizabeth Maria, 121
Elizabeth Mary, 1456
Elizabeth Regina, 1541
Elizabeth Reiss (Shaffer), 156
Elizabeth S, x, 1189
Elizabeth S (Bohrman), 1617
Elizabeth Teresa, 1553
Elizabeth Victoria, 1638
Elizbeth (Preiss), 1412
Ella, 155
Ella (Everhart), 1425
Ella (Pemberton), 1375
Ella (Sheaffer), 1464
Ella C (Cannon), 1531
Ella Frances (Cellar), 449
Ella J (--), 1617
Ella M, 1567
Ella M (Winters), 1345
Ella Margaret, 163
Ella Stella, 1864
Ella Virginia (Powell), 1568
Ellen, 91, 190, 1268, 1413, 1633, 1676, 1842
Ellen (Smith), 1388

Ellen C H, 1644
Ellen G (--), 1618
Ellen J (Fegley), 1638
Ellen Lanius, 1465
Ellen Lavinia, 1540
Ellen M, 1845
Ellen Sarah Ann, 1640
Ellen Shirley (Nelson), 1457
Elmer, 1566
Elmer John, 929
Elmer Merle, 922
Elmer Merle Jr, 922
Elmer Sherman, 918, 1883
Elmer Theodore, 403
Elmina (Sweigert), 163
Elmira, 1636
Elmira (Brown), 1468
Elmira A, 1164
Elmira Jane, 1415
Elnora, 1568
Elsie (--), 237
Elsie Blanche (Saville), 411
Elsie Mary, 1634
Elsie Mary (Hansen), 212
Elvera (Hyberg), 1289
Elvina, 1350
Elwood, 1618
Elwood Curtis, 124
Elwood Ray, 919
Elwyn Roy, 1624
Elysbeth Ann, 1379
Emanuel, 1268, 1542
Emanuel C, 1424
Emanuel John, 1424
Emelina Jane, 795-796
Emelius Ilgenfritz, 1462
Emerson E Jr, 1374
Emerson Edgar, 1374
Emerson Frederick, 1375
Emilia, 1429
Emilie, 210
Emilius James, 1462
Emily, 205, 1468-1469, 1567
Emily (Thomas), 1615
Emily Margaret L, 1619
Emma, 85, 1463, 1526, 1559, 1638, 1883
Emma (--), 1559
Emma (Gramley), 935
Emma (Haegele), 126
Emma Blanche, 782
Emma C (Wicker), 1377
Emma C E, 1424
Emma Caroline, 1145, 1540
Emma Catharine, 1642
Emma Catherine, 1460
Emma Christine, 922
Emma E, 1847
Emma Elizabeth (Hoefer), 1567
Emma Elizabeth S, 1628
Emma Estelle, 1570
Emma F (Meyers), 1468
Emma H, 1636
Emma Helena, 84
Emma J, 1879
Emma Jane, 1186

Emma Jane (Riland), 782
Emma L (Schmeck), 1635
Emma M, 1633
Emma Margaret, 1531
Emma Rebecca, 120, 134, 137, 147
Emma Rebecca (Cox), 120, 134
Emma Rebecca Kromess (Cox), 119
Emma S (Banks), 1568
Emma Selecta, 1187
Emmaline, 1413
Emmett E, 1879
Enos Halleck, 1462
Erastus Hay, 1466
Erhard Frederick, 16
Eric Betz, 424
Eric Turner, 921
Erich W, 4
Erik, 1161
Erik Jon, 406
Erin Johnine, 1138
Erin Kathleen, 408
Ermal Maxine (Hoffman), 208
Ernest Franklin, 415
Ernest J, 1624
Errick B, 421
Ervin Miner, 1145
Ervin W, 1424
Estella H E, 1635
Estella Irene (Shively), 377, 403
Estella May, 1424
Esther, 154-155, 1366, 1561, 1566, 1612-1613, 1624, 1644
Esther (Bieber), 1637, 1642
Esther (Levan), 1544
Esther (Malick), 1540
Esther (Ward), 33
Esther (Werlein), 155
Esther D, 1620
Esther Gladys, 1532
Esther H, 1617
Esther Hoch (Pott), 1637
Esther L (Butz), 1642
Esther M (Steckle), 803
Esther Madine, 1614
Esther Ophelia, 131
Ethel, 1166, 1291, 1852
Ethel (Gibbs), 169
Ethel (Weiser), 1291
Ethel Anderson (Miller), 1845
Ethel E, 1416
Ethel Irene (Trump), 165
Ethel Irene (Wineland), 1569
Ethel M (--), 1842
Eugene, 1626
Eugene A, 165
Eugene Francis, 1464, 1883
Eugene N, 155
Eugene Robert, 1375
Eunice Miriam, 1177
Eva, 26, 360-361, 637-638, 719, 736, 1421

WEISER (continued)
John Elmer Paul, 1568
John Ernest, 1416
John Evan, 155
John F, 1624
John Franklin, 126, 1269
John Franklin Curtis, 1288
John Frederick, ix, 16, 28, 30, 33, 60, 444, 449, 1591, 1679
John G, 1635
John George, 1425
John Gillespie, 931
John H, 189, 920
John Henry, 1413, 1424
John Herbert, 920
John Holman, 1523
John Hutton, 1457
John J, 94
John Jacob, 156, 758, 1267, 1269, 1463, 1518
John Jacob Shaffer, 156-157
John Jr, 1679
John K, 1879
John Kuhy, 1272
John L, 931
John M, 444
John Melchior, 1267
John Melvin, 1566
John Monroe, 160-161
John Owen, 1845
John P, 932
John Palmer, 935
John Peter, 905, 939
John Philip, 89, 360, 408, 777-778, 1267
John Robert, 1463
John Roush, 1143
John S, 157, 189
John Silas, 918
John Solomon, 157, 169
John T, 1625, 1635
John W, 137
John Wallace, 915
John Walton, 923
John Walton III, 923
John Walton Jr, 923
John Wesley, 454
John Wesley Jr, 454
John Wesly, 1625
John William, 1879
John Ziegler, 1427
Johnathan Lewis, 1523
Johnnie, 1188
Johnny L, 949
Jon Eric, 32
Jonathan, 30, 1417, 1522, 1539, 1542, 1626, 1711
Jonathan David, 403
Jonathan G, 1637
Jonathan H, 1525
Jonathan S, 1627
JoNell Lynn, 413
Jorosa Hetty Ann, 1643
Joseph, 1294, 1842
Joseph A, 1293
Joseph Augustus, 447
Joseph Bud, 950
Joseph Edgar, 953
Joseph H, 949
Joseph Henry, 1414
Joseph J, 190

Joseph V, 1843
Josephine (Jetters), 1345
Josephine Correanna, 1414
Josephine Mary, 1468
Joshua, 915, 929, 934
Joshua Aaron, 1570
Joshua Andrew, 930
Joshua Joseph, 1379
Joshua Lee, 1846
Joshua T, 453
Josiah, 1523, 1879
Josiah S, 1624
Josie Anna (--), 1166
Joy Lynn, 418
Joyce, 1377
Joyce Ann (Proctor), 1457
Joyce Bernice, 425
Joyce Bobby (Adamson), 1846
Joyce Irene, 169
Joyce Lenore (Reese), 926
Judi Marie (Jacobsen), 215
Judith, 1753
Judith (Levan), 1365-1366
Judith (Redinger), 1366
Judith A (Dobson), 923
Judith Ann, 1374
Judith B, 1641
Judith Lynn (Smith), 923
Judith Marie, 1166
Judy, 1616
Judy (Begler), 1846
Judy (Karrer), 1844
Judy A, 1375
Judy D, 33
Judy Kay, 208
Julia, 157, 173
Julia (Micks), 953
Julia (Renchock), 1615
Julia Ann (Hess), 1373
Julia Elizabeth, 922
Julia Elizabeth (Walton), 922
Julia Faith, 926
Juliana, 1881
Juliana (Reiff), 1613
Juliana D, 1637
Julie Ann, 1634
Julius Theodore, 1614
June (Hinkle), 164-165
June Irene, 1616
June Marie, 403
Justina (Kehl), 896, 905, 914, 939
Justina (Rothermal), 774
Kaitelin Christine, 408
Kaitlyn Elizabeth, 424
Karen (Smith), 1379
Karen Elsie, 1381
Karen Kay (Swenson), 405
Karen Lee, 453
Karen Louise (Sanford), 402
Karen Michelle (Allnutt), 1379
Karl Conrad, 403
Karla Rae, 407
Kate, 1567, 1863
Kate (--), 1863
Kate B (Heist), 1622

Kate E, 1618
Kate E (Merkel), 1614
Katharine Elizabeth (Konda), 165
Katharine Fahn, 1466
Katharine Georgia, 1458
Katherine Amelia, 1382
Katherine Ann, 1143
Katherine Elizabeth, 1530
Katherine Joann (Murray), 424
Katherine Louise, 1382
Katherine M (Tshudy), 1864
Kathie Sue, 125
Kathleen (Toone), 210
Kathleen Anne Johnson (McNabb), 1143
Kathleen Mae, 1845
Kathleen Ruth, 211
Kathryn (Ernst), 1166
Kathryn Alice, 924
Kathryn Elizabeth, 1144
Kathryn Frederika (Wilkie), 416
Kathryn Lynn (Stanley), 417
Kathryn Margaret, 930
Kathryn Mary, 1167
Kathryn Pauline, 1289
Kathy (Ward), 1569
Katie, 1345
Katie Ann (Buck), 918
Katie D (Rothermel), 1638
Katie Estella (Cousey), 1569
Katie M (Hoch), 1865
Katie May, 926
Katie S (--), 1621
Katie W, 1634
Katlyn, 1622
Kay Ruth, 1286
Kayla Ann, 1616
Keith, 208
Keith A, 1846
Keith Conrad, 925
Keith R, 1617
Kelsey Rae, 408
Kenneth Dale, 405
Kenneth Eugene, 938, 1161
Kenneth F, 1616
Kenneth Miles, 190
Kenneth Noah, 190
Kenneth Thomas, 215
Kenneth Wasden, 215
Kerry Dale, 1846
Kerry Jean (Hullihan), 408
Kerry Michael, 413
Kevin, 208, 1138
Kevin Codner, 1138
Kevin D, 1846
Kevin Lee, 403
Kevin Paul, 417
Keziah A (DeLong), 1614
Kile Kerns, 1138
Kimberly, 1161
Kimberly Charlotte, 414
Kristen Elizabeth, 923
Kristine Kay, 1136
Kristy Lynn, 926

Kurt Robert, 412
Lamar Barry, 920
Lamona (Shawver), 422
Lance, 33
Landi Mae, 169
Landon Paul, 414
Lanvency (Meiact), 210
Larry Eugene, 453
Larry Lee, 122, 1375
Laura, 1424
Laura (Landis), 1628
Laura Elizabeth, 32, 364, 375
Laura Gertrude, 935
Laura Jean, 1144
Laura Jeanne, 923
Laura Marie, 421
Laura Marie (Seltzer), 1161
Laura May, 936, 1612
Laura Theresa, 1847
Laurel, 924
Laurence Arthur, 1530
Laurie Jean, 1457
Laurie Sue (Gordon), 406
LaVern A, 1616
Lavina, 154, 361, 456, 1117, 1146
Lavina Jane, 1542
Lavinia, 1543
Lavinia Elizabeth, 97
LaVonne (House), 922
Lawrence, 1426, 1849
Lawrence Clayton, 930
Lawrence Clayton Jr, 930
Lawrence Keith, 1291
Lawrence Keith III, 1292
Lawrence Keith Jr, 1292
Lawrence Y, 1615
Le Roy, 1187
Le Roy Edward, 213
Lea D, 1636
Leah, 1641
Leah (Leveknight), 1424
Leah Jane (Myers), 1423
Leander, 1637
Lee, 1618
Lela (Hughes), 1846
Lena H, 1622
Lenora May (Brewster), 1456
Leo F, 1842
Leolla Annette (Phillips), 1177
Leon, 1622
Leon Charles, 1639
Leon F, 1627
Leon H, 1622
Leona Mary (Boyer), 1636
Leonard E, 1616
Leonard Edward, 209
Leota, 1751
Leroy W, 1635
Leslie Rae, 425
Leslie Richard, 413
Leslie Sue, 192
Lester, 190
Lester George, 1133
Lettie Florence, 115
Levan, 1561

Levi, 939, 948, 1117, 1413, 1542, 1643, 1863
Levi S, 1619
Lewis, 1268, 1413, 1618, 1881
Lewis D, 1629
Lewis G, 1635
Lewis James, 60
Lewis P, 1849
Lezli Kae, 215
Lidia, 1192
Lila (Rudy), 935
Lila Lee, 215
Lillian, 1348, 1625
Lillian Annie, 1625
Lillian Carolyn, 1639
Lillian Elnorah, 1145
Lillian H (Sautter), 31
Lillian Sylinda, 795, 803
Lillie (Mackey), 1845
Lillie Bell (Noggle), 1142
Lillie Belle Flora, 1423
Lillie Dale (Baird), 114
Lillie L (Blecher), 1864
Lillie May, 1348
Lillie Mercedes, 205
Linda (Christopher), 1569
Linda Jean, 1844
Linda June (Brooks), 417
Linda Lou, 1177
Linda Louise, 212
Linda Sue, 402
Linda Susan (Hunsberger), 1426
Lindsay Renée, 402
Lisa (Antognoli), 1456
Lisa (Horlocker), 125
Lisa Ardell, 414
Lisa Christine (Avitt), 424
Lisa Jean, 1846
Lisa Kay (Moyer), 930
Lisa Lee (Bunting), 930
Lisa Lou, 938
Lisa Marie, 924
Lisa May (Holzer), 412
Lizzie, 190, 1542, 1863
Lizzie Catharine, 1568
Lizzie Mae, 1612
Lloyd Jr, 1741
Loanda Octavia, 1844
Lois Adelaide, 1624
Lois Jean (Terry), 454
Lois Lavaline McDougle (White), 191
Loisa Bell, 1269
Lola Irene (Anderson), 1456
Lona M (Schiffler), 920
Lora Jean, 454
Lorena (McBride), 190
Lorene (Martin), 1377
Lorene Elizabeth, 420
Loretta M (Brintzenhoff), 1638
Lori (Duggan), 1622
Lori Ann (Weiser), 921
Lori Lynn (Volk), 413
Lortainna F Berry

WEISER (continued)
Mary Carroll, 1467
Mary Catharine, 89, 361, 363, 779, 1267, 1355
Mary Catharine (Heim), 361
Mary Catherine, 795, 1356, 1414
Mary Catherine (--), 189
Mary Catherine (Moody), 1138
Mary Catherine (Sherman), 1881
Mary Claire, 1375
Mary Cordelia, 1540
Mary E, 774, 1425, 1624, 1626, 1635
Mary E (O'Reilly), 1863
Mary E (Tyler), 1429
Mary Edith, 126
Mary Edna, 1627
Mary Eleanor, 1530
Mary Eliza, 198
Mary Elizabeth, 60, 157-158, 206, 210, 237, 376, 381, 445
Mary Elizabeth (--), 27
Mary Elizabeth (Allen), 1624
Mary Elizabeth (Clouser), 1863
Mary Elizabeth (Hopkins), 1852
Mary Elizabeth (Wenger), 88-89, 96, 253, 261
Mary Ellen, 1345, 1426, 1628
Mary Ellen (--), 1622
Mary Ellen (Lower), 1176
Mary Ellen (Meckling), 1268
Mary Ellen (Shappstrom), 1143
Mary Emogene (Haughawout), 396
Mary Esther, 1345
Mary Esther (Woodruff), 1881
Mary Evella, 1639
Mary Evella (Kutz), 1639
Mary Fanny, 114
Mary Frances, 1177
Mary Frances (Pletz), 922
Mary G, 1636
Mary Gilfillan, 1523
Mary Hattie Eliza, 1425
Mary Helen, 1138
Mary Henricks, 1631
Mary Irene, 1424
Mary J, 1424, 1639
Mary J (Hoppes), 1639
Mary J (McGugart), 1616
Mary Jane, 30, 423, 919, 1193, 1270, 1676
Mary Jane (Culp), 1849
Mary Jane (Homrighous), 1145
Mary Jane (Moore),

1843
Mary Jane (Upp), 1465
Mary Jenny, 1294
Mary Julia, 1464
Mary K (Shirley), 1375
Mary Kathryn, 922, 1346
Mary L, 31
Mary L (Yaissle), 1614
Mary Laura, 1522
Mary Lou (Witt), 938
Mary Louisa, 1426, 1466
Mary Louise (Otto), 1374
Mary Louise (Sieber), 1426
Mary M, 94, 1117, 1132, 1141, 1146
Mary Magdalena, 1463
Mary Margaret, 1866
Mary Martha, 454, 1269, 1293
Mary Matilda, 1619
Mary May, 1565
Mary Mildred, 397
Mary Parrish (Bruce), 415
Mary Pearl, 1187
Mary Pearl (Anderson), 1186
Mary Priscilla, 1530
Mary R (DeWald), 95
Mary Ruth, 192
Mary S, 1628
Mary S (--), 1424
Mary Terese (Popowski), 415
Mary W, 1634
Mathilda (Miller), 33
Matilda, 1116, 1129, 1350, 1614
Matilda (Haines), 931
Matilda (Henritze), 1619
Matilda Ellen, 1425
Matilda Jane (Ziegler), 1427
Matilda R (Hohl), 1758
Matthew Bennett, 1347
Matthew Ray, 424
Matthew Stanley Quay, 1469
Matthew Todd, 938
Matthew William, 416, 1138, 1844
Mattie Anna, 137
Mattie Lucille, 1166
Maud Ann, 1462
Maude (--), 1880
Maude B (Yoder), 1622
Maude Emma, 161
Maude Florence, 1619
Maude H, 1622
Maude Mae (Fetter), 1614
Maude Martha (Walker), 213
Maurine (Graces), 1377
Maxine, 32, 1416
May, 1864
May Evelyne (Botha), 169
May M, 1865
Maybelle E, 1346
Mayberry, 1863
Meda, 1622

Meda H, 1622
Melinda, 1523
Melissa Nicole, 453
Melvin, 1741
Melvin Albert, 1424
Melvin Ralph, 929
Melvina, 1675
Mercedes (Schwinn), 192
Mes Maria D, 1626
Michael, 120, 1786
Michael Alan, 1456
Michael Arthur, 412
Michael David, 167-168
Michael Edgar, 923
Michael Karl, 421
Michael Louis, 1379
Michael Lynn, 1426
Michael Paul, 122
Michael Ray, 424
Michelle (Daugherty), 413
Michelle Angela (Watts), 924
Michelle Darlene (Beach), 406
Michelle Marie, 453
Michol Ilene, 211
Mignon (--), 1469
Milburn Arthur, 1289
Mildred (Treadway), 1166
Mildred Irene, 408
Mildred J (Wingard), 1379
Mildred June, 1189
Millard Fillmore, 1468
Milton Samuel, 1568
Milton U, 1885
Milton Udell, xiii
Milvina J (Clemens), 1427
Minerva, 376, 392, 1391
Minerva Ann (Dughman), 190
Minerva Elinore, 189
Minna May, 1424
Minnie (Faust), 1145
Minnie (Reichert), 1614
Minnie (Yenser), 1639
Minnie Catherine, 1533
Minnie E, 934
Minnie Edna, 1639, 1642
Minnie Elizabeth, 935
Minnie M, 1864
Minnie M (Blummer), 1468
Minnie M (Kissaberth), 1881
Minnie Maxine (Kerns), 1136
Minnie May, 1167
Minnie Metilda, 1532
Minnie S, 1628
Miriam, 1622
Miriam (Morningstar), 1468
Miriam (Palm), 1865
Miriam (Sturdevant), 1875
Miriam Frances, 1532
Miriam G, 1634
Miriam Olga (Geiss), 1177
Miriam Zipporah, 1427

Missy Lou, 938
Mollie, 1849
Molly, 89
Molly (Huber), 89
Mona Belle (Thompson), 402
Mona Louise, 422, 1346
Morgan, 120
Moses, 1614
Mulianna (Milhouse), 934
Myles Kent, 421
Myran A, 1269
Myrta Manetta, 449
Myrth Janelle, 407
Myrtle, 1192
Myrtle Eliza, 213
Nadine Joy (Perviance), 417
Nancy C (Offord), 1188
Nancy (Foust), 147-148
Nancy (McGuire), 210
Nancy (Park), 1346
Nancy (Tunison), 1844
Nancy Andrea Susan Thelander (Shropshire), 414
Nancy Catherine, 191
Nancy Dale (Fluegel), 402
Nancy Emelia (Hall), 122
Nancy Ione (Shega), 408
Nancy Jane (Swank), 1131
Nancy Jay, 32
Nancy Jo, 122, 453
Nancy Jo (Romanchek), 1293
Nancy Lida, 1143
Nancy Nadean, 411
Nannie B, 1166
Naomi, 1348
Nathalie (Ohlson), 1161
Nathan Brent, 938
Nathan Kent, 412
Neil Leonard, 923
Nelle (Hoffhines), 1142
Nelle Florence (Black), 1144
Nellie (Drake), 114
Nellie (St John), 1348
Nellie Alice, 1847
Nellie Blanche (Dishong), 1566
Nellie D, 1566
Nellie Ethel (Morgan), 1375
Nellie Kathryn, 935
Nellie Mae, 1618
Nelson, 1865
Nelson A, 1866
Nettie (--), 1426
Nettie Virginia (Koehler), 160-161
Nettie Virginia (Smyser), 1464
Nicholas, 122, 1875
Nicholas Vernon, 1347
Nickolas David, 1375
Nicole Hope, 1143
Nina, 147, 190
Nina C (Johnson), 31
Nina Nadine (Myers), 397

Nina Pearl (Clemison), 126
Noah, 363-364
Noelle, 1456
Nona (Trozel), 443
Nona Marie, 444
Nora (Coons), 949
Nora Ophelia, 123
Norla Louse, 213
Norma Jean, 1845
Norma May, 213
Olive (Starry), 167
Olive Alma, 1462
Olive Felonise, 1131
Olive Jane, 445
Olive Lorena, 192
Olive M (Rogers), 1462
Olive Weeks (Shultz), 1131
Oliver, 1883
Oliver C, 1459
Oliver David, 1414
Oliver Thomas, 1469
Oliver W, 1638
Olivia Evateny, 1614
Olivia W, 1635
Olley, 1542
Onduyln (Eckersell), 210
Opal Fae, 1845
Opal Irene, 1847
Ora (--), 1751
Ora E (Tyler), 209
Orson Frederick, 215
Orville Berneal, 1143
Orville M, 1166
Orville Samuel, 450
Oscar, 1426
Oscar Oswald, 1166
Otto H, 1881
Palma Marcella (Martin), 1138
Pamela J, 1376
Patrecia Isabel (Runyan), 403
Patricia (Burt), 1138
Patricia (Epting), 1569
Patricia Ann, 424, 925
Patricia Ellen, 922
Patricia M, 165
Patricia Rae, 404
Patterson Sterrett, 1466
Patty Ann, 1345
Paul, 84, 1568, 1622
Paul A, 1849
Paul Alexander, 163
Paul Allen, 415
Paul Alvin, 1639
Paul Andrew, 921
Paul Conrad, 1634
Paul Frederik, 406
Paul G, 136
Paul George, 147
Paul H, 95
Paul Jeremiah H, 1622
Paul Kenneth, 414, 1885
Paul Konrad, 1570
Paul Michael, 1569
Paul Richard, 1143
Paul Rolland Eckersell, 210
Paul Stanley, 416
Paul Thomas, 31
Paul W, 1568
Paul William, 416, 1883
Paul Willis, 126

WEISER (continued)
Paul Wineland, 1569
Paula Lorel, 169
Paula Michelle, 1570
Paulette J, iii-iv, xi,
  xiii, 236, 375,
  1009-1010, 1885
Paulette Jean, 414
Pauline, 361
Pauline (Killian), 937
Pauline (Starner), 169
Pauline (Young), 420
Pauline Ann, 423
Pauline J (Hanna),
  1138
Pauline S, 1885
Pauline Theresa
  (Grubic), 923
Pearl, 1622
Pearl (Hood), 1345
Pearl Hannah, 1751
Pearl I (Cortner), 129
Pearl M, 1845
Pearl Mae, 1845
Pearl Marie, 215
Pearl Marie
  (Wipperman), 416-417
Pearl Priscilla, 130
Peggy Jane, 932
Peggy Rae (Owen),
  168
Penny (Sowers), 168
Perry D, 114
Perry W, 1845
Peter, xi, 20, 26-27,
  29-30, 61, 86-87,
  357-358, 361,
  375-376, 782, 905,
  1110-1111, 1116,
  1160, 1181, 1191,
  1267, 1269, 1308,
  1355, 1365, 1522,
  1611, 1883
Peter Anthony, 1142
Peter Emanuel, 1355
Peter Oswald, 1160,
  1165-1166
Philip, 20, 25-26, 86,
  88, 97, 136-137, 147,
  357, 360, 758, 777,
  784, 791, 793, 795,
  806, 1268-1269, 1849
Philip Alden, 1144
Philip Arthur, 407
Philip Conrad, 137,
  1177
Philip Eugene, 402
Philip Konrad Richard,
  1753
Philip Lee, 408
Philip R, 125
Philip Richard, 126
Philippus, 1593
Phillip Conrad, 1569
Phoebe Anna (Ripley),
  210
Phoebe Elizabeth, 127
Phoebe Jane, 1844
Phyllis (Parker), 1161
Phyllis Amanda
  (Hueter), 1464
Phyllis L (Carlson),
  1292
Preston Thomas, 923
Priscilla, 97, 120, 131,
  135
Priscilla (Howell),
  1388
Priscilla Almedia, 148

Priscilla Estelle, 414
Priscilla Morris
  (Patton), 1161
Prudence, 1407
Quay Taylor, 1469
R Arminta (Shay), 929
Rachael Elizabeth
  (Gundrun), 926
Rachel, 1619, 1874
Rachel (--), 1591
Rachel (Kline), 159
Rachel B, 1640
Rachel Laura, 1847
Rachel Ruth, 406
Rachel Vera, 1348
Rae Eleda (Sanderson),
  405
Ralph, 1675
Ralph E, 1846
Ralph Jacob, 1636
Ralph Russell, 1864
Ralph Wilbur, 920
Ralph Wilbur Jr, 920
Randall E, 934
Randall Edward, 938
Ray J, 1849
Rayman Stanley, 1142
Raymond, 94, 1638
Raymond Alfred, 1638
Raymond Everett, 1345
Raymond Milburn,
  1292
Raymond Paul, 1292
Raymond Russell, 95
Raymond Vernon,
  1347
Raymond W C, 1644
Reba M (Craley), 1416
Rebecca, 16, 89, 94,
  156, 215-216, 218,
  220-221, 227, 231,
  236-237, 261, 363,
  370, 1366, 1407,
  1409, 1540, 1587,
  1589, 1593
Rebecca (Hinkle), 1613
Rebecca (Krotzer),
  1533
Rebecca (Rollman),
  1568
Rebecca (Shaeffer),
  1625
Rebecca (Smith), 1456
Rebecca (Udall), 16,
  1407
Rebecca Ann, 1177,
  1426
Rebecca Ann (Weigert),
  416
Rebecca Ellen, 1268
Rebecca Lynn, 210,
  1847
Rebecca Maria
  Elizabeth, 1566
Rebecca Sue, 1844
Recie Hazel, 1133
Ree (Humbert), 1879
Regina M, 1864
Renée Denise, 402
Reuben, xiii, 94, 156,
  1414, 1540
Reuben B, ix
Reuben Benjamin,
  1561
Reuben Bossart, 1565
Reuben M, 783
Reuben Roger, 926
Reuben Semler, 237
Rex Richard, 1138

Rex William, 208
Rhonda Lee, 454
Richard, 1642
Richard C, 1131, 1885
Richard Carl, 1375
Richard Charles, 919
Richard Conrad, 1138
Richard D, 1377
Richard E, 1846
Richard Elgin, 126
Richard George, 1161
Richard Jesse, 126
Richard Kaye, 1632
Richard Lenn, 1569
Richard Lynn, 1632
Richard M, 1377, 1429
Richard Matthew, 923
Richard Paul, 1374
Richard R, 1131
Richard Robert, 1144
Richard Sherman, 923
Richard Thomas, 921
Richard Wagner, 1632
Robert, 1616
Robert A, 1638, 1864
Robert Allen, 122
Robert Allen Jr, 122
Robert B, 30
Robert Brian, 1569
Robert Bruce, 32
Robert C, 1131
Robert Charles, 920,
  1142, 1289
Robert Charles Jr, 920
Robert Elwood, 1177
Robert Eugene, 1346
Robert F, 1863
Robert Haller, 1429
Robert Hoffhines, 1142
Robert Joe, 1616
Robert Kent, 412
Robert L, 189, 1864
Robert Lee, 932
Robert Luther, 411
Robert Milton, 1348
Robert Neil, 953
Robert Thomas, 1144
Robert Vernon, 1347
Robert Victor, 1161
Roberta J (Yost), 1466
Roberta Louise, 405
Robin Cathleen, 1375
Robin Keturah, 211
Robin L (Packer), 122
Roger Albert, 1462
Rolla James, 444
Rolland George, 210
Rolland Joseph, 210
Rolland S, 210
Ronald, 1615
Ronald E, 1373
Ronald Emerson, 1375
Ronald Lee, 1846
Ronald Scott, 444
Ronel Stephanie Ferrier,
  169
Ronnie Ray, 1376
Rosa (--), 189
Rosa A (Jones), 126
Rosa Ellen, 1624
Rosa M, 1842
Rosa Mitchel Martinez
  (DelBosco), 931
Rosabel Virginia, 115
Rosamund, 1843
Rosanna, 94
Roscoe M, 1881
Roscoe W, 1192
Rose Ann, 1294

Rose Ann (Moser),
  1637
Rose C, 934
Rose Marie, 451, 919,
  1884
Rose Marie (Barber),
  921
Rosetta (Howald), 114
Rosina, 1613, 1881
Roy, 1618
Roy C, 1618
Roy W, 1346
Ruby Chloe (Kent),
  397
Ruby May, 208
Russel Frederick, 408
Russell Eugene, 930,
  1161
Russell Lee, 406
Russell Shively, 405
Ruth (--), 1624
Ruth Amelia, 1161
Ruth Ann, 1382
Ruth Ann (Ramsdell),
  1457
Ruth Bertha, 421
Ruth E (Henne), 1615
Ruth Elizabeth, 1523,
  1844
Ruth Ellen, 1566
Ruth Jensine
  (Haldorson), 406
Ruth Jill, 425
Ruth M, 1849
Ruth Madeline, 1632
Ruth Marie, 163
Ruth Pauline, 1456
Ruth Viola, 1348
Ryan Thomas, 413
S Elmira, 1844
Sabina (--), 1593
Sadie, 1425, 1622
Sadie E (Schearer),
  1639
Saint Paul, 165
Salinda B (Cook), 1845
Salle, 1676
Sallie, 1186
Sallie Alice (Geiger),
  1633
Sallie F (Logan), 1429
Sallie H (Haring), 1628
Sallie R, 1623
Sally, 1529, 1568
Sally A, 209
Sally Ann, 1613
Sally Jo (Knezevich),
  1293
Salome, 358, 360, 812,
  896, 1308, 1539,
  1676
Salome/ Sally/ Sarah,
  1669
Salome/ Sarah, 1196
Samantha, 1192
Samantha Lorraine,
  191
Sammy, 357, 1365
Samuel, x-xi, 20, 89,
  155-156, 160-161,
  190, 357, 1111,
  1116-1117,
  1131-1132, 1181,
  1185, 1191, 1269,
  1365-1366,
  1373-1374, 1387,
  1403, 1412-1413,
  1459, 1463, 1611,
  1669, 1675, 1864,

  1879, 1883
Samuel A, 1670
Samuel Adam, 1566
Samuel D, 1624
Samuel David, 122
Samuel Elmer, 1145
Samuel Franklin, 97,
  119-122, 131, 134
Samuel Gardner, 1460
Samuel H, 157, 930,
  1192
Samuel Harrison, 1423
Samuel Hartman, 120,
  122
Samuel Henry, 157,
  159, 1883
Samuel J, 1374
Samuel James, 1269
Samuel John, 1566
Samuel L, 148
Samuel Lincoln, 1462
Samuel Patrick, 122
Samuel R, 1424-1425
Samuel S, 1628
Samuel Sylvester, 1531
Samuel Von Hoff,
  1463
Samuel W, 1166, 1181
Samuel Young, 1160,
  1165
Sancta Regina, 84
Sandra (Grimm), 1161
Sandra Charlotte, 405
Sandra D, 165
Sandra Faith, 169
Sandra June, 1374
Sandra Kay, 950, 953
Sandra Lee (Asbury),
  1566
Sandra Louise (Lerch),
  921
Sandra Pamela Patricia,
  1293
Sara Ann, 423
Sara Annette, 1637
Sara Antoinette, 121
Sara Elizabeth (--),
  1429
Sarah, 89, 97, 109-110,
  114, 253-254,
  259-260, 360, 363,
  370, 812, 931, 1111,
  1116, 1129, 1268,
  1270, 1310, 1373,
  1387, 1393, 1413,
  1417, 1425, 1467,
  1592, 1614, 1626,
  1643, 1676, 1697,
  1865
Sarah (--), 16, 1425,
  1561, 1587
Sarah (Allen), 1409
Sarah (Bossart), 1561
Sarah (Burns), 168
Sarah (Eisenhauer),
  1423
Sarah (Grass), 1843
Sarah (Harold), 1526
Sarah (Hoag), 1619
Sarah (Hoch), 1625
Sarah (Kraber), 1463
Sarah (Markle), 155
Sarah (Miller), 30
Sarah (Moore), 1522
Sarah (Reisinger), 1425
Sarah (Rhoads), 363
Sarah (Schueck), 1613
Sarah (Spitler),
  914-915

WILSON (continued)
Mona Cerise
(Simmons)
(continued)
(Simmons), 800
Morris, 1015
Myrtice, 1733
Myrtle Elizabeth, 1119
Nancy, 599
Nancy Lee, 1491
Nelson, 867
Norman, 663
Norris A, 867
Paul, 1015
Paul R, 866
Pearl E, 866
Peggy, 563
Randall, 1790
Ray, 1015
Richard, 131
Robert, 507, 1692
Robert Andrew, 1491
Robert F, 866
Rose, 576
Rufus William, 403
Ruth Anne (Bigelow), 576
Ruth Elizabeth, 726
Sally Jo (Strings), 686
Samantha Jean (Allen), 421
Sandra (Thomas), 1491
Sandy (Hook), 867
Sarah Ann, 867
Shara, 1491
Sharon Lee (Kephart), 1692
Sharon Lyn, 1491
Shellah Ann, 1555
Steven Wayne, 404
Stewart William, 404
Susan Diane, 1491
Suzanne Elaine (Eurele), 404
Theodore A, 866
Thomas, 867, 1015
Tina Ellen (Hoffman), 776
Tressa (Songer), 1014
Vada Belle (Abbott), 1128
Vera (Mercer), 1491
Von, 824
Wade, 1015
Weiser White, 1462
William, 599
Wilma Gertrude (Banter), 563
Zorado English (Still), 866
WILSONCROFT
Alma (Shugarts), 1718
Lulu, 1718
Naomi Bell, 1718
Thomas, 1718
WILT
Amanda Jean, 631
Harriet (Mader), 914
Hiram, 914
Joshua Alexander, 631
Nancy Ann (Harvey), 631
Paul, 631
WILTGEN
Diane Carolyn, 635
WILTON
Julie Lynn, 1240
WILTSE
Hiram, 1583

Lucy (Cook), 1583
WIMMER
Arlene Ann, 79
WIMMERGARM
Jenny, 424
WINANS
Donald Clausen, 1120
Helen Courtright (Shultz), 1120
Helen Louise (Robson), 1120
Jo Lynn Elizabeth, 1120
John Preston, 1120
John Robert, 1120
Lynn Clark, 1120
William Robert, 1120
WINCHESTER
Dora L (Weiser), 154
John, 154
WINDECKER
Ann, 1574
Catherine, 1575
WINDGROVE
Lynn L, 500
WINDSOR
Dorothy Ellen (Shepler), 928
Mitchell Jay, 458
Molly Ann (Masno), 458
Monti James, 458
Sheryl, 458
Todd Morgan, 458
William Hamilton Jr, 928
WINELAND
Ethel Irene, 1569
WINES
--, 1106
Mertie (Rudy), 1106
WING
Kay Louise, 1771
WINGARD
Charles Clifford, 1351
Charles L, 1351
Ida E (Weir), 1351
Mildred J, 1379
WINGATE
Elvira Sarepta (Harshe), 596
George, 596
WINGER
David Thomas, 1262
Kay Wildamarie (Kahle), 1262
Kristin Kay, 1262
Matthew David, 1262
WINGERT
Ascencion Michael, 647
Catherine Patricia (Heckert), 763
child, 832
Elsie, 832
John, 832
Kenneth, 647
Leighann Grace, 647
Lorena Kay (Wiest), 647
Melissa Kay, 647
Rebecca Alwilda (Womelsdorf), 832
William Nolan, 763
William Stanley, 763
WINGFIELD
Lional Dillard, 583
Rose Ann (Hocker), 583

WINGO
Douglas Perry, 183
Ethe Ray (Snyder), 183
Ethel Snyder, 182
WINK
Annie Wilma (Miller), 1743
John, 1743
WINKELBAUGH
Maria Margaret, 914
WINKELBLECH
Alice, 1061
Allen S, 1060
Ardrenna M, 1061
Bertha, 1062
Cindy, 1062
Eleanor (Wheaton), 1062
Elsie (Showers), 1062
Harold, 1062
Lodi, 1062
Lois, 1062
Mahlon, 1062
Mahlon Jr, 1062
Marion, 1060
Mary, 1062
Mary (Auman), 1060
Merle, 1062
WINKER
Peter Robert, 1686
Violet Edna (Wallingford), 1686
WINKLEMAN
Alice (Vangorder), 1368
Amanda L (Wise), 1366
Anna Louise, 1372
Arthur Percival, 1372
Audrey June, 1372
Barbara Kay, 1371
Benjamin, 1367
Benjamin J, 1367
Benjamin Schneck, 1366
Bernice, 1367
Betty, 1367
Bonny, 1367
Boyd James, 1367
Boyd James Jr, 1367
Carol, 1367
Carrie Belle (Letterman), 1367
Clair Franklin, 1367
Clevella (Wadsworth), 1367
Connie, 1372
Derbin Iona, 1367, 1370
Donald Bertram, 1367
Doris (Snyder), 1372
Dorothy (Wadsworth), 1367
Ellwood Bellmont, 1372
Esta Minerva, 1368
Esther (Weiser), 1366
Ethel Elena, 1370
Forest Kermit, 1367
Garry Lee, 1371
Genevieve, 1367-1368
Geraldine (Young), 1367
Gertrude, 1372
Gertrude (McGonigal), 1371
Gertrude Albertina (Ertley), 1372
Greggy, 1367

Guy Herbert, 1371
Guy Tressler, 1371
Harry Leroy, 1367
Hattie Agnes (Ferree), 1371
Helen (Brooks), 1372
Helen (Nicols), 1367
Henry, 1366
Herbert Ollan, 1371
Horace Wise, 1367
Irvin Holloway, 1370
James Buchanan, 1366
Jeannette Fay, 1372
John, 1367
John Henry, 1367
June (Lehman), 1372
Kenneth Guy, 1371
Larry, 1368
Larry Lyn, 1371
Leonard Guy, 1367
Leslie Marie, 1371
Loy, 1372
Lulu Bell, 1370
Mabel (--), 1367
Malissa (Moore), 1367
Margaret, 1372
Margaret (--), 1367
Margaret (McGill), 1367
Margaretha, 1366
Mary (Hopple), 1372
Mary (Mauck), 1367
Mary Ann, 1366
Mary Bello, 1373
Mary Cathrine, 1371
Merrill, 1366
Minnie Mae, 1366
Minnie Mayburn, 1371
Mirian, 1368
Mittie Ora, 1371
Naomi Grace, 1370
Paul Matthew, 1370
Pearl, 1367
Richard, 1368
Richard Herbert, 1372
Richard Jay, 1368
Robert Allan, 1371
Robert Gaylord, 1372
Rose A (Weaver), 1370
Roy Mauck, 1367
Samuel Weiser, 1366
Sarah Catharine (Neese), 1366
Sharon, 1368
Shirley Ann, 1371
Sylvia Marcella, 1370
Tessie Marie (Confer), 1371
Thelma (Mackey), 1367
Urah Boyd, 1371
Verna Margaret Waite (Tressler), 1371
Veva Pearl, 1368
Vickey, 1368
Violet Mayburn, 1370
William, 1367
WINKLER
Diane, 1736
WINN
Elizabeth, 1181
WINNER
Connie Lou, 1214
WINSLOW
--, 1625
Grace, 960
James Patrick, 1229
Madge Evelyn (Kahle), 1229

Mary (Weiser), 1625
WINSTEAD
Elizabeth Weiser, 1465
Lucille, 1459
Lucille Weiser (Heiges), 1465
Victor Lee, 1465
WINTER
Evelyn Louise, 1017
Hugo, 1017
Lillian Mae (Yost), 1017
Ruth, 1017
WINTERGILL
--, 1704
Erma (Parks), 1704
WINTERS
Cecile Inez, 1185
Ella M, 1345
Ella May, 1280
George, 620
Gertrude Eva, 330
James Earl, 402
James Earl Jr, 402
Linda Sue (Weiser), 402
Margaret Pearl (Sanderson), 620
Michael Lee, 402
WINWARD
Sarah Janet, 780
WIPP
Angelica Barbara Lucy, 319
Artur Konrad Wilhelm Traugott, 319
Benno Maximilian Martin Josef, 319
Dieter Max Eberhard Benno, 319
Elisabeth (Dorn), 319
Irene Hedwig Elisabeth (von Wasielewski), 319
Konrad Alf Theodor, 319
Leonore Martha Cornelia (von Selzam), 319
Markus Stephan Tobias, 319
Monika Barbara (Stuber), 319
Reinhold Erwin Otto Heinrich, 319
Sebastian Erasmus, 319
WIPPERMAN
Pearl Marie, 416 417
WIRE
Harry, 1562
Mary Gertrude (Lackey), 1562
WIRICK
Bruce, 631
Judith Rosalind (Jordan), 631
Sarah Ruth, 631
WIRT
Beulah R, 1540
Earl, 1540
Emma Caroline (Weiser), 1540
Emma Jane, 1540
Ethel, 1540
Jennie, 1540
John, 1540
WIS
Nancy (Wolstencroft), 1707
William, 1707

WISE
Ada L (Heffner), 1168
Ada Lee, 1168
Amanda L, 1366
Angelina
  (Koppenhaver), 682
Barbara Ann, 486
Bessie (Fegley), 1168
Bevelry June, 1342
Carroll William, 798
Charles, 1168
Charles Janton, 1168
Cora Laura (Weiser),
  1619
Edward Charles, 1168
Edward David, 1168
Elizabeth, 1455
George Feiser, 1167
Gwendolyn (Peterson),
  882
Harry Wilson, 682
Homer Franklin, 682
Ida Leah, 1169
Ida May (Mitchell),
  1168
Isador, 1619
Jacob, 15
John Christopher, 882
John H, 881
Jonathan Lawrence,
  882
Judith Marie, 882
Kelsey Lynn, 473
Laura (Neale), 882
Laura Elizabeth, 118
Lauren Nastassja, 882
Lida, 882
Margaret Ann, 118
Maria, 1080
Mary Alice (Weiser),
  1167
Mary Lorena
  (Brungart), 1083
Mary Pauline (Buck),
  798
Mervin Lamb, 881
Michelle Cash, 437
Monica Yvonne
  (Mayer), 882
Myrtle Steckman, 1171
Nancy Elizabeth
  (Krigbaum), 118
Natalie Gwendolyn,
  882
Nicole Lynette, 882
Rachel Leah, 1169
Reva Elnora (Tucker),
  682
Richard Alan, 118
Robert Arthur, 882
Robert Lawrence, 882
Robert Vincent, 1168
Robin Kristi, 882
Roscoe Harry, 682
Russell Tyler, 473
Sara Lily, 1168
Sara Louise (Eppley),
  881
Susan, 1440
Susan Leigh, 882
Vilas, 1083
Vinna, 32
Wendy Louise, 882
William, 798
William Harry, 682
William Jacob, 1167
William Vincent, 1168
Yvette (Pusey), 881

WISEGARVER
Lauren, 650
WISEMAN
Aurolyn Fern, 126
WISER
--, 1629, 1823
-- (--), 1786, 1857
-- (Lonan), 1811
-- (Lynch), 1831
-- (Shomo), 1707
-- (Stone), 1791
[See also Kreydenwys],
A Bernice, 1754
A Georgianna, 1754
Aaron Brown, 1839
Aaron Frost, 1774
Aaron Jeffrey, 1773
Aaron Talley, 1797
Aaron Todd, 1780
Abbie, 1859
Abigail, 1765, 1809
Abigail Marie, 1805
Abraham J, 1830
Abraham S, 1827
Abraham St John, 1828
Abram, 1708
Ada, 1777
Ada G (Kelly), 1856
Ada J, 1844
Ada O, 1830
Ada R, 1877
Adalade G, 1873
Adam, 1655
Addie (Riddle), 1819
Addie Belle, 1839
Addie Clay, 1792
Adelaide, 1877
Adelia, 1677
Adeline (Eager), 1851
Adeline E, 1848
Adeline Ruth
  (Lamadue), 1701
Adie (Ferrell), 1798
Adolphus, 1664
Adrian jack, 1630
Agnes, 1838, 1855
Agnes (--), 1780
Agnes Gertie (Curlee),
  1807
Agnes Olivia, 1666
Ala, 1185
Alan, 1629, 1803
Alatha, 1817
Albert, 1304, 1671,
  1831, 1857
Albert Eugene, 1877
Albert H, 1853
Albert Henry, 1782
Albert Hughes, 1837
Albert Hughes Jr, 1837
Albert Jacob, 1296
Albert N, 1847
Alberta, 1862
Alda, 1877
Alene, 1804
Alexander, 1722,
  1855-1856
Alfers C, 1859
Alfred, 1878
Alfred Roswell, 1630
Algie (Cook), 1801
Alice (Furber), 1836
Alice (Veasey), 1764
Alice Analee (Carlin),
  1773
Alice Asenath (Glover),
  1777
Alice Faye, 1807
Alice Faye (Williams),

1871
Alice Francis, 1819
Alice Jewel (Jones),
  1819
Alice Josephine, 1834
Alice Josephine (Gold),
  1799
Alice Lynn (Couch),
  1801
Alice May, 1782
Alice S (Gagel), 1859
Aliene (Thain), 1770
Aline E, 1794
Alison, 1769
Alithea, 1763
Alla Arminda, 1779
Allen Lynn, 1820
Allie, 1872
Allison, 1768
Allison Clarie, 1873
Alma, 1816
Alma (Ellis), 1825
Alma E (--), 1848
Alma Frances, 1867
Alma Jean (Wright),
  1789
Alma Ruth, 1822
Alma Sharp (Packer),
  1773
Almeda, 1851
Almira, 1840
Alonzo, 1782, 1840
Alonzo Hollister, 1832
Alta (Van Orden),
  1778
Alta B, 1701
Alta May, 1839
Alva Ellis, 1678
Alva Eunice, 1811
Alva Gerald, 1832
Alva Rilla (Moore),
  1810
Alvah B, 1840
Alvin William, 1795
Alvina (Freeman),
  1702
Alvina Agina (Nellans),
  1877
Amalia, 1875
Amanda, 1765, 1787,
  1789, 1848, 1877
Amanda (--), 1779
Amanda A, 1838
Amanda E, 1793
Amanda Elvina
  (Douglas), 1876
Amanda Jane, 1766
Amanda Lane, 1818
Amanda S, 1833
Amelia (--), 1843
Amelia (Joyce), 1838
America, 1858
Amy, 1862
Amy (Parsons), 1812
Amy Jo (Allen), 1793
Amy M, 1791
Amy Michelle
  (Westfall), 1768
Amy R, 1862
Andrea Marie, 1815
Andrea Michelle, 1801
Andrew Chase, 1801
Andrew Leroy, 1303
Andrew Scott, 1766,
  1814
Andrew Vincent, 1839
Andrew William, 1775
Angeline, 1710
Angeline (Gibson),

1795
Angie, 1819
Anita, 1776
Ann, 1785, 1804
Ann (--), 1767, 1867
Ann Elizabeth, 1868
Ann M, 1678
Ann Marie, 1305
Anna, 1802, 1831,
  1857
Anna (Kingsley), 1779
Anna Bell (Slavens),
  1872
Anna Clara, 1298
Anna E, 1816, 1873
Anna Kaye, 1306
Anna Leora, 1836
Anna Lou, 1820
Anna Louisa, 1630
Anna Mae, 1190, 1835
Anna Marie, 1801
Anna Mary (Bennett),
  1833
Anna Mary Elizabeth
  Amelia (Shufeldt),
  1781
Anna May, 1860-1861
Anna Ophelia (Wells),
  1808
Anna S, 1829
Anna S (Jacobs), 1823
Anna V, 1876
Anne Susan (Bailey),
  1807
Annette, 1771
Annie, 1788, 1872
Annie Bell (Broadrick),
  1822
Annie E (--), 1722
Annie K (--), 1857
Annie M, 1856
Annie M (--), 1856
Annie M (Bush), 1811
Annie May, 1860
Anthony, 1855-1856
Anthony J, 1855
Anthony William, 1774
Anyolina (Olivas),
  1776
Aplona, 1861
Aplona Regina, 1860
Aplonia, 1860
Archie, 1801
Archie W, 1788
Arie Ida (Simpkins),
  1812
Arielle Jane, 1814
Arletta Jerene
  (Blackburn), 1869
Arlie Jean, 1820
Arnold B, 1792
Arra Dell (Dyer), 1828
Arthur Dana, 1629
Arthur Darrell, 1630
Arthur G, 1838
Artimus A, 1830
Asa, 1831
Asa Gallup, 1833
Aseneth Arvilla, 1830
Asenith P, 1827
Ashley Ann, 1631
Ashley Louise Tahoe,
  1631
Ashley Marie, 1776
Ashley Nicole, 1798
Ashley Yvonne, 1768
Athalie Marie, 1814
Audley Marie, 1295
Audrey Ella (--), 1839

Augusta Jewell, 1834
Augustus, 1856
Auley Zathoe, 1301
Austin Calvin, 1799
Austin Lance, 1768
Austin Thomas, 1631
Authurie, 1855
Avis Barilla, 1798
Barbara, 1670-1671,
  1774, 1797, 1804,
  1856, 1861
Barbara (--), 1835
Barbara (Byroads),
  1781
Barbara (Larsen), 1776
Barbara (Stone), 1798
Barbara Ann, 1813,
  1821
Barbara Ann (Green),
  1792
Barbara Ann (Taylor),
  1766
Barbara Charlene
  (Creekmore), 1869
Barbara Clara
  (Morsback), 1812
Barbara Dean (Farris),
  1823
Barbara Gayle (Robins),
  1820
Barbara Jean (Johnson),
  1672
Barbara Jo, 1808
Barbara Joyce, 1792
Barbara Laree, 1297
Barbarra (Carr), 1767
Barney, 1871
Barney (Hall), 1815
Barry Neal, 1808
Barth, 1841
Bartholomew, 1841
Barton, 1709
Beatrice Faye (Harmer),
  1769
Beatrice Faye (Trost),
  1815
Beatrice M, 1861
Beauton C, 1816
Becky (--), 1870
Becky (Cutler), 1767
Becky Ann (Brown),
  1773
Bede (Harold), 1835
Bella E, 1861
Belle E, 1860
Ben, 1665
Benjamin, 29, 1763
Benjamin F, 1788
Benjamin Franklin,
  1830
Benjamin Jerald, 1768
Benjamin L, 1878
Benjamin Steven, 1870
Benjamin Walter, 1867
Bernard F, 1832
Bernice Mae, 1822
Bernice Marie, 1835
Bertha, 1701, 1788,
  1801
Bertha (Benedict), 1780
Bertha (Easley), 1831
Bertha A, 1788
Bertha Ann (Grimes),
  1798
Bertha E, 1793
Bertha L, 1672
Berthal C, 1799
Bertie Lee, 1804
Bessie, 1663, 1811

WISER (continued)
Eva May, 1837
Evangeline F, 1858
Eve (Helm), 1666
Evelyn, 1824, 1858
Evelyn (Hansen), 1766
Evelyn Belle (Mitchell), 1764
Evelyn Leavitt (Carter), 1775
Evelyn May, 1666
Evelynne Maurine, 1185
Everal A, 1296
Everett, 1664
Ezra, 1766
Fae (Reeves), 1767
Fannie J, 1782
Fanny (--), 1675
Fanny A, 1722
Fanny M, 1853
Farrell Dean, 1772
Faye, 1779, 1804, 1829
Faye (Henry), 1781
Faye (Walden), 1792
Faye Carol, 1789
Fern (Hansen), 1770
Fidelia, 1833
Filetta, 1831
Finley Clarence, 1877
Flora, 1827, 1859
Flora (--), 1664
Flora V (--), 1676
Florence, 1671, 1851
Florence Belle, 1782, 1834
Florence E, 1877
Florence Lillian, 1803, 1806
Florence Lillian (Wiser), 1803, 1806
Florence Wilder (Edwards), 1851
Flossie (Garner), 1817
Floy, 1827
Floyd, 1857
Floyd K George, 1295
Floyd Paul, 1869
Floyd Robert, 1781
Forest, 1798
Forest Young, 1798
Frances, 1862
Frances (McKee), 1798
Frances (Shoop), 1670
Frances Ann (Alexander), 1873
Frances E, 1856
Frances Elizabeth, 1821
Frances Lois, 1799
Frances Pearl (Wheatley), 1666
Frances Willie, 1810
Francis, 1857
Francis Caroline (Enloe), 1867
Francis E, 1812
Francis G (Blanton), 1821
Francis J (Talley), 1820
Francis Lee, 1807
Francis Marion, 1799
Frank, 1796, 1816, 1841, 1853, 1857
Frank B, 1857
Frank Clayton, 1831
Frank L, 1780

Frank Lenville, 1298
Frank W, 1839
Franklin, 1788
Franklin Delano, 1815
Fred C, 1822
Fred C Jr, 1822
Freddie Ray, 1821
Frederick, 1839, 1856
Frederick R, 1701
Frederick T, 1858
Fredona, 1825
Fronie (--), 1872
Frudie B, 1859
Gail (Neal), 1770
Gail (Roghbaugh), 1835
Gail Edward, 1869
Gail Marie, 1781
Garnet Idalene, 1834
Garnetta B, 1801
Garrett Michael, 1869
Gary, 1822
Gary Gribble, 1801
Gary Gribble Jr, 1801
Gary Kent, 1867
Gary LeMar, 1773
Gary Lynn, 1814
Gary Myron, 1769
Gaye Lynne (Gubler), 1769
Gayla, 1768
Gayle, 1663, 1774
Gayle (Breen), 1774
Gayle Elaine, 1673
Genene (Gaines), 1806
Geneva, 1796
Geneva LaVerne, 1873
Geneva Pearl (Robinson), 1813
Geneva Ruth, 1871
Genevieve, 1775
George, 1666, 1676, 1701, 1830, 1841, 1854, 1856, 1867
George A, 1848
George Adam, 1655
George C, 1860-1861
George Clay, 1791
George H, 1764, 1848
George Harmon, 1777
George Haslam, 1767
George Henry, 1853
George J, 1702
George R, 1853
George W, 1676, 1701, 1811, 1837
George Washington, 1872
George Watson, 1805-1806
Georgia A (--), 1857
Georgia M, 1853
Gerald, 1670, 1794, 1860
Gerald Allen, 1301
Gerald Clyde, 1301
Gerald E, 1802
Gerald Ethan, 1780
Gerald Lamoin, 1777
Geraldine, 1806
Geraldine (Lassiter), 1808
Geraldine (Slack), 1792
Geraldine E (Penn), 1301
Gerda, 1797
Gerrald A, 1861
Gerry Lynn, 1792
Gertha, 1797

Gertie (--), 1832
Gertrude, 1678, 1782, 1868
Gertrude E (Lane), 1812
Gilbert, 1860
Gilbert E, 1873
Ginger Lee (Hayes), 1808
Girtie Lee, 1810
Gladys, 1295, 1670, 1852, 1859
Gladys (Metzler), 1834
Gladys Rebecca (Warren), 1806
Glen, 1803
Glen Williams, 1851
Glenn, 1828
Glenn Alvin, 1835
Glenn Alvin Jr, 1835
Glenn Van Orden, 1771
Glenna Marie, 1814
Glinda Elaine (Roberts), 1818
Gloria (Gonzales), 1871
Gloria Jean, 1305
Golden Bowden, 1822
Gordon Edward, 1803
Gordon H, 1860-1861
Gordon Vernon, 1835
Grace, 1793, 1809
Grace (Rosalie), 1861
Grace Anna (Dorner), 1630
Grace Cleone, 1838
Grace Irene (Clark), 1678
Grace Lee (Russell), 1789
Grace Lillie (Fountain), 1840
Gracie, 1792
Grant Budge, 1767
Grant Earl, 1815
Grayson John, 1781
Gregory Charles, 1793
Gregory Joe, 1806
Gregory Wendrich, 1768
Gretta (Rawlings), 1767
Greyson, 1819
Grover, 1796
Grover Cleveland, 1812
Gussie Ellora (Boss), 1813
Guy Brown, 1678
Gwen, 1776, 1851
Gwendolyn Jean, 1297
H Clark, 1296
Hal, 1769
Hal Milton, 1803
Hallie (Stanch), 1872
Hannah, 29
Hannah (--), 1847
Hannah Ann, 1828
Hannah Catherine, 1805
Hannah Harrison (Larzeler), 1878
Hannah Leigh, 1800
Hardin, 1793
Harley Duane, 1190
Harmon, 1827, 1830, 1833, 1847
Harmon Levi, 1834

Harmon Walter, 1828
Harold, 1822, 1848
Harold Everett, 1781
Harold John, 1779
Harold K, 1838
Harold Victor, 1834
Harriet, 1854
Harriet (Meier), 1837
Harriet Lucille, 1678
Harriet M (Bedell), 1764
Harrison Bartley, 1862
Harry, 1862
Harry Bartley, 1862
Harry L, 1856
Harry Lee, 1799
Harry Malvern, 1851
Harry S, 1836, 1855
Harry Vanlear, 1296
Harvey, 1671, 1769, 1811, 1816, 1833
Harvey A, 1816
Harvey D, 1824
Hattie, 1788, 1812
Hattie (Chapin), 1816
Hattie (James), 1812
Hazel, 1804, 1828
Hazel (Townsend), 1804
Hazel D (Carroll), 1822
Hazel Irene, 1825
Hazel Mai, 1808
Hazel P, 1794
Heather, 1806, 1819, 1836
Hector, 1787
Helen, 1630, 1671, 1768, 1822
Helen (Dyer), 1789
Helen Alice, 1296
Helen Cadwell (Leonard), 1835
Helen E, 178
Helen Ione (Brown), 1820
Helen Jane, 1827
Helen Lorene, 1870
Helen Louise, 1673
Helen M, 1872
Helen Marie, 1868
Helen Marjorie (Smith), 1672
Helna Edelburg (Schindler), 1777
Henrietta E, 1676
Henry, 1663, 1665, 1781, 1786, 1827-1828, 1830-1831, 1858, 1866-1867
Henry Boston, 1807
Henry Carl, 1850
Henry Clay, 1666, 1859
Henry D, 1825
Henry David, 1851
Henry Eli, 1834
Henry Hunton, 1874
Henry J, 1841
Henry James, 1862
Henry Lynn, 1815
Henry Lynn Jr, 1815
Henry O, 1868
Henry S, 1854
Henry Solomon, 1308
Henry T, 1857
Henry Thomas, 1867
Henry Thomas II, 1867

Hepzebah (Ridgeway), 1854
Hepzibah M, 1855
Herbert, 1829
Herbert Grayson, 1780
Herbert Willard, 1867
Herman, 1827
Herman Alfred, 1821
Herman Kenneth, 1754
Hettie Ann Alice (Jernigan), 1810
Hilda Jean, 1797
Hilda Louise (Russell), 1873
Hilda M, 1671
Hiram, 1827-1828, 1847-1848, 1857, 1876
Hiram H, 1853
Hiram Lewis, 1832
Holly, 1803
Hope Denise, 1806
Horace, 1769, 1809
Horace C, 1859
Horace Clare, 1777
Horace Jr, 1809
Horace Lee, 1818
Houston, 1799
Howard A, 1823
Howard Shelton, 1790
Howard Verne, 1776
Hubert Joplin, 1665
Hubert Opal, 1664
Huey, 1804
Huey Wayne, 1804
Hugh G, 1832
Hyrum Leon, 1770
Ida, 1847, 1858
Ida (McBroom), 1868
Ida A, 1830
Ida Davis (Brown), 1666
Ida Hilda, 1788
Ida Sue, 1815
Ila mae, 1806
Iline, 1674
Inez (McCoy), 1871
Inez Louise (Wilson), 1851
infant, 1812, 1816, 1829, 1838
Ira, 1832, 1854
Ira Lawrence, 1830
Irene Amazon, 1796
Irene Elizabeth, 1819
Irene L, 1851
Irvin, 1301, 1857
Irvin Clyde, 1301
Irvin Milton, 1873
Irwin Don, 1767
Isaac, 1798, 1811
Isaac B, 1830
Isaac Daniel, 1798
Isaac J, 1854
Isaac William, 1830
Isabell M, 1877
Isabelle Marie (Alleman), 1877
Isaiah, 1810
Isaiah T, 1812
Isom S, 1868
Israel, 1722
Iva M, 1811
J B, 1794
J Frank, 1848
J R (Wilson), 1816
J T, 1822
Jacinta, 1769
Jack Burt, 1781

WISER (continued)
Russell Clay, 1791
Russell Cleveland, 1805
Ruth, 1773, 1829, 1834, 1872
Ruth (--), 1663
Ruth (Chamberlin), 1785, 1824
Ruth (Cheney), 1795
Ruth (Hopper), 1829
Ruth (Johnson), 1851
Ruth (Kelly), 1818
Ruth (Womble), 1797
Ruth Almira (Calhoun), 1297
Ruth Bernice, 1825
Ruth Elaine (Richards), 1772
Ruth Marie, 1869
Ruth Marie (Ayers), 1781
Ruth Marie (Goodhart), 1673
Ruth Nora, 1766
Ruth Patricia (Yaeger), 1814
Ryan H, 1837
Ryan Seth, 1772
Ryan Steven, 1307
S Arthur Austin, 1829
S Melissa (Drugs), 1701
Sadie C (--), 1301
Sadie Larcenia (Amos), 1868
Safrona Mamey (Enloe), 1871
Salina (--), 1721
Sallie Ann, 1868
Sallie Frances (Taylor), 1811
Sally (Turner), 1763
Samantha, 1818
Sammie (Ferrell), 1805
Samuel, 1675, 1765, 1854, 1857
Samuel B, 1671
Samuel E, 1833, 1838
Samuel Findley, 1677
Samuel Frost, 1771
Samuel Glenn, 1771
Samuel Henry, 1782
Samuel Isaiah, 1814
Samuel Leroy, 1834
Samuel Otis, 1678
Samuel S, 1779
Sandra, 1797, 1870
Sandra Kay, 1792
Sandra Kay (Fricke), 1799
Sandra Kay (Jones), 1813
Sandra Kay (Merrell), 1776
Sandra Lavay (Darby), 1306
Sandra Lee (Philipps), 1307
Sandy, 1674, 1807
Sara Ann, 1800
Sara Ann (Reynolds), 1796
Sara Eleanor (King), 1294
Sara Gunnell (Poppleton), 1777
Sarah, 1703, 1707, 1823, 1825, 1831,

1854
Sarah (--), 1763
Sarah (Beers), 1711
Sarah (Graham), 1840
Sarah (Hill), 1839
Sarah (Kerry), 1296
Sarah (Nichols), 1763
Sarah (Orn), 1763
Sarah (Stevens), 1764
Sarah A, 1788
Sarah Alice, 1789
Sarah Ann, 1766, 1795, 1833
Sarah Ann (Silsbee), 1766
Sarah Armina, 1764
Sarah Beth, 1867
Sarah C (--), 1788
Sarah C (McBee), 1664
Sarah Cornelia, 1854
Sarah E, 1787
Sarah E (Blodgett), 1764
Sarah E (Woodring), 1860-1861
Sarah Ellen, 1867
Sarah F, 1824
Sarah Houck, 1800
Sarah J, 1765
Sarah J (--), 1788, 1832
Sarah J (Jones), 1670
Sarah Jane, 1663, 1798
Sarah L, 1810
Sarah L (Norton), 1829
Sarah Margaret (Simpson), 1798
Sarah Rutha (Leslie), 1872
Sarah S (--), 1831
Sarah T, 1764
Sarrah E, 1854
Saundra Sue (Tising), 1867
Scott Edward, 1870
Scott Wiliam, 1629
Senna Marie (Parker), 1768
Shane Scott, 1766
Sharon, 1768, 1772
Sharon (Heslop), 1777
Sharon (Pugmire), 1767
Sharon June (Edwards), 1809
Sharon Lee (Lewis), 1870
Shasta Dawn, 1815
Shauna, 1771
Shauna Lee, 1778
Shawn Douglas, 1777
Shawna Ann, 1766
Sheila, 1820
Sheila Anna, 1672
Sheila Annette (Woodward), 1819
Shelby, 1804
Sheldon Lewis, 1774
Shelly, 1776
Shelly Ann, 1799
Sherman Layne, 1818
Sherri (Von Knoles), 1814
Sherry Joann, 1870
Sherwin Andrew, 1774
Sheryl Lynn, 1867
Sheryl Mae, 1793
Shirley, 1771
Shirley Ann, 1799,

1807
Shirley Jean (Parson), 1673
Sibbel, 1816
Simon, 1678
Sissie, 1872
Sky Lyn (Matthew), 1772
Solomon, 1676, 1764, 1832
son, 1664, 1793, 1807, 1819, 1839
Sonia (--), 1818
Sonya Ann, 1868
Sophia, 1722
Sophia (--), 1854, 1858, 1862
Sophia (Rowles), 1713
Sophia Josephine, 1798, 1803
Sophia Josephine (Wiser), 1798, 1803
Sophrona, 1787
Sophronia (Peyton), 1789
Stacey Ann, 1808
Stacy B, 1851
Stacy Lynn, 1815
Stanley, 1818, 1829
Stanley Benjamin, 1805
Stanley Bruce, 1805
Stanley Joe, 1818
Stella J (Lloyd), 1829
Stella Mae, 1838
Stephanie Andrea, 1819
Stephanie Ann, 1781
Stephen, 1629
Stephen D, 1853
Stephen Douglas, 1877
Stephen Leon, 1870
Stephen Maclain, 1815
Steven Bruce, 1776
Steven Cliff, 1771
Steven Grant, 1767, 1815
Steven H, 1768
Steven J, 1777
Steven Joseph, 1872
Steven R, 1861
Stewart Paul, 1790
Sue, 1674
Sue (King), 1808
Susan, 1855, 1876
Susan (--), 1663
Susan (Richards), 1768
Susan A (--), 1788
Susan Beth, 1305
Susan Jeanine (Johnson), 1767
Susan Lydia (Horel), 1629
Susan M, 1787
Susan Marlene (Jackson), 1870
Susan Rae, 1772
Susanna, 1721, 1824
Susannah, 1785
Susie S (--), 1860
Syble Eulalia (Smith), 1813
Sydney Marie, 1780
Sylmar Thompson, 1775
Sylva Katherine, 1802
Sylvania, 1831
Sylvanus, 1787
Sylvester, 1830
Sylvia, 1795

Sylvia Jean (Thompson), 1814
Tabitha Jane (Messick), 1796
Tabitha Lynn, 1815
Tad William, 1631
Talon Scott, 1771
Tammy, 1766, 1794, 1817-1818
Tammy Jo, 1869
Tammy Lee, 1190
Tammy Renee, 1790
Tammy Sue, 1813
Tanya, 1798
Tawnee K, 1769
Ted Keith, 1801
Teena Kay (Sterner), 1672
Temperance M, 1765
Tennessee E, 1823
Tensie West, 1869
Teresa, 1766, 1804
Teresa (Jackson), 1808
Teresa Ann (Fullmer), 1777
Teressa (Williams), 1871
Teri Jo, 1190
Terrell, 1664
Terrie (Hertzog), 1780
Terry Lynn, 1673
Terry Wayne, 1791
Tessa Lynn, 1814
Thayne Bradley, 1771
Thelma, 1671, 1803
Thelma Louise (Shaefer), 1780
Thelma Rebecca, 1822
Theodore, 1765, 1782
Theodore James, 1800
Theodore L, 1782
Theodore Ray, 1673
Theodore Sylvester, 1673
Theresa, 1819
Theresa (Murphy), 1786
Theron Telford, 1770
Thomas, 1708, 1828, 1856, 1866-1867
Thomas A, 1795
Thomas Alfred, 1818
Thomas Allen, 1820
Thomas Baxter, 1823
Thomas Carson, 1301
Thomas Coleman, 1792
Thomas Dale, 1781
Thomas Daniel, 1821
Thomas Edgar, 1795
Thomas Edward, 1808
Thomas Floyd, 1295
Thomas Franklin, 1825
Thomas H, 1828
Thomas J, 1811
Thomas Jefferson, 1764
Thomas Lynn, 1770
Thomas M, 1855, 1877
Thomas Richard, 1874
Thurman C, 1860-1861
Thurman Chester, 1807
Thurman Jr, 1860
Tiffany Marie, 1814
Tilla M (--), 1848
Tillie, 1305
Tillie (--), 1839
Tillie May (Morse), 1301

Tim, 1809
Timothy Grant, 1768
Timothy James, 1781
Timothy L, 1770
Timothy Todd, 1631
Todd Andrew, 1307
Tommy, 1820-1821
Toni Jean, 1780
Tonya Maureen, 1835
Tracy, 1669, 1792
Tracy lee, 1673
Traverse L, 1832
Travis, 1767
Trevor Lee, 1813
Trevor William, 1630
Tricia, 1836
Trina, 1775
Trisha Dee, 1781
Tyson Horatio, 1769
Urban, 1832
Uriah, 1787
Valentine, 1877
Valeria, 1805
Valerie, 1818
Van Haslam, 1768
Van Rawlings, 1767
Vedah (Milburn), 1868
Velma, 1828-1829
Velma Alice (Looney), 1816
Venus, 1773
Vera, 1809
Verda (--), 1838
Verda V, 1295
Verl Haslam, 1768
Verlon Elmer, 1800
Vern Leroy, 1851
Verna, 1803
Verna E, 1825
Verna Gertrude (Van Orden), 1771
Verna Ruth, 1840
Vernon, 1664
Vernon Victor, 1834
Verrie, 1862
Vicki Lee, 1781
Victor, 1795, 1858
Victor Lyle, 1829
Victoria, 1793, 1835
Victoria Joan, 1777
Viola, 1858
Viola Maria, 1871
Violet (Parker), 1823
Violet A, 1832
Virgie, 1665, 1805
Virgie Eugene, 1797
Virgil, 1872
Virgil Arvin, 1872
Virgil Watson, 1805
Virginia, 1809
Virginia A, 1873
Virginia Agnes, 1858
Virginia Jane, 1810
Virginia Louise (Smith), 1807
Virginia Lucille (Shoup), 1305
Vivian Gayle (Pope), 1801
Vivian Lucille (Eddy), 1305
Vola, 1665
W C, 1824
Wade Clifton, 1799
Wallace Winston, 1769
Walter A, 1858
Walter Bernard, 1878
Walter C, 1859
Walter E, 1787

WISER (continued)
Walter Harmon, 1829
Walter Newman, 1811
Walter Winthrope, 1796
Wanda (--), 1798
Wanda (Barton), 1780
Wanda (McCormick), 1781
Wanda (Thompson), 1774
Wanda Evelyn, 1800
Wanda Grace, 1820
Wanda Lee, 1871
Wanda Marie, 1871
Wanda Sue (Manes), 1813
Ward, 1672
Warren G H, 1793
Warren G Harding, 1793
Warren Herbert, 1780
Wattie Mae (Marris), 1801
Wavie (Peck), 1789
Waylon S, 1790
Wayne, 1672
Wayne Telford, 1774
Wealtha, 1812
Weasley, 1671
Wendelene, 1772
Wendell Haslam, 1767
Wendell Mark, 1772
Wendy Lynn, 1820
Wesley Aaron, 1673
Wesley Dana, 1630
Whitney, 1775, 1818
Wickey, 1858
Wilbur Dean, 1797
Wilbur Lee, 1791
Wilbur Lee Arie, 1820
Wilder, 1860
Wilders Susan, 1860-1861
Wildres F, 1860
Wilhelmina (Snyder), 1878
Willard E, 1802
William, 1308, 1630, 1663-1664, 1678, 1793, 1817, 1821, 1823, 1829, 1833, 1835, 1841, 1854-1855, 1860
William Alfred, 1821
William Bradley, 1789
William Bryan, 1812
William C, 1663, 1666
William Cecil, 1672
William D, 1817
William Dewey, 1799
William Don, 1767
William Dwain, 1871
William E, 1860
William Emmett, 1873
William F, 1671, 1788
William Franklin, 1671
William G, 1665
William Glenn, 1828
William H, 1782, 1794, 1811, 1823, 1837-1838, 1854
William H Jr, 1838
William Harold, 1817
William Harrison, 1809
William Harry, 1810
William Harvey, 1767
William Henricks,

1629
William Henry, 1779, 1835
William Homer, 1305
William Howard, 1792
William J, 1874, 1877
William James, 1812-1813, 1860-1861
William Lawrence, 1811
William Lee, 1767
William Lynn, 1813
William Lynn Jr, 1813
William M, 1789, 1877
William Mark, 1772
William Merle, 1306
William Oscar, 1869
William R, 1857
William Randall, 1793
William Robert, 1818
William Russel, 1297
William Seidgel, 1789
William T, 1790
William Terry, 1307
William Theodore, 1672
William Thomas, 1789-1790
William Wesley, 1868
Williams James, 1860
Willie, 1665, 1811, 1816
Willie Jonah, 1796
Willie Josephine, 1803
Willie May (Brown), 1666
Willis H Sr, 1670
Willis Jr, 1670
Willoughby, 1831
Wilma, 1190, 1828
Wilma Dean, 1821
Wilson, 1308
Wilton Raymond, 1190
Windell, 1802
Winfred L, 1801
Winifred, 1677
Winnie (Perry), 1824
Winston, 1803, 1851
Wiulliam, 1860
Woodrow Wilson, 1797
Woxie, 1811
Wynona (Miller), 1816
Wynona Clarissa, 1834
Yvette Marie, 1837
Yvonne Helen (Wendrich), 1767
Zacharias, 1858
Zachary William, 1768
Zachery, 1870
Zelma, 1812
Zelma (Smith), 1769
Zelpha May (Nelson), 1766
Zona (--), 1666
Zona (Blair), 1778
Zona Fay, 1871
Zona Lee (West), 1869
Zora, 1862
WISLEY
Alice (--), 111
J R, 111
John Charles, 111
Margaret E (Akins), 111
Ruby (Orndorff), 111
WISMER
David Richard, 1040

Dory Richard, 1040
Laurie Jo, 1040
Linda Jo (Linderman), 1040
Marianne (Carr), 1040
WISOR
Abraham, 1704
Abraham B, 1708
Abraham W, 1707
Adda, 1721
Adoree J (--), 1701
Agnes, 1720
Albert Louis, 1707
Alfaretta (Mitchell), 1702
Alfred, 1706
Alice, 1707
Alice Jeanine, 1708
Allen L, 1707
Allen M, 1702
Angeline, 1721
Ann Jane, 1705
Anna, 1709
Anna (Goss), 1712
Anne (Mease), 1707
Anne (Shovestall), 1706
Arnold, 1706, 1712
Arthur, 1712
Barbara, 1712
Bernice, 1706
Bernice L (--), 1702
Bertha, 1702, 1709
Beryl, 1707
Beryl E (Hall), 1713
Bessie, 1701, 1707, 1709
Bessie (Dunlap), 1705
Bessie (Hunt), 1712
Bessie (Rowles), 1705
Bessie (Wisor), 1707
Betty L, 1712
Blanche, 1702, 1712
Blanche R (Lansberry), 1710
Brooks, 1711
Burton, 1704
Carl W, 1710
Catherine, 1720
Catherine (--), 1701
Charles, 1707
Charles A, 1706
Charles Lewis, 1703
Chester, 1709, 1713, 1721
Chloe, 1707
Clair, 1706
Clara C (Leppert), 1706
Clare W, 1706
Clarence, 1705
Clarence J, 1712
Clarence Roy, 1705
Clifford, 1703, 1720
Clive E, 1701
Cloyd, 1707
Clyde, 1712
Cora Jane, 1706
Cordelia, 1720
David, 1709, 1712
David Jr, 1711
David R, 1711
Della, 1713
Dom, 1714
Donald, 1710
Dorcas (--), 1709
Dorcas (Rauch), 1714
Dorothy, 1708
Dorothy (Lowder),

1712
Dorse, 1706
Earl, 1704, 1710
Earl E, 1707
Eda Jean, 1709, 1713
Edith, 1703, 1709
Edna, 1706, 1710-1711, 1713
Edna (Graham), 1706
Edna (Hamilton), 1713
Edward, 1705
Edward L, 1710
Effie, 1713
Eleanor, 1707
Elizabeth, 1706, 1711
Elizabeth (Wisor), 1711
Ella, 1703, 1714
Elnora, 1710
Elva, 1705
Emily (Dickson), 1698
Emma, 1706
Emma J, 1702
Enlo, 1703
Erie Belle, 1703
Erma Fay, 1703
Ernest, 1705
Esther, 1713
Esther A (Green), 1707
Esther Leona, 1710
Ethel, 1706, 1709
Ethel M, 1712
Eva, 1703
Evelyn, 1712
Flora, 1704, 1707
Flora A, 1707
Floyd, 1710
Foster H, 1706
Francis, 1708
Franklin, 1713
Frederick B, 1720
Frony Jane, 1710
Gail, 1713
Geneva, 1710
George, 1702, 1705
George E, 1703
Gerald, 1707, 1713
Gerald Duane, 1713
Gertrude, 1709, 1712
Gertrude (Hendricks), 1705
Gertrude (Wisor), 1709, 1712
Gertrude J, 1706-1707
Gertrude J (Wisor), 1706-1707
Gladys, 1702
Gladys (Aughenbaugh), 1703
Goldie (Pennington), 1713
Gordon, 1704, 1714
Grace, 1705-1706, 1709
Grace (Yaeger), 1709
Guy R, 1702
Hannah, 1710, 1721
Harold, 1706, 1711
Harry, 1703, 1705
Harry Irvin, 1708
Harvey, 1714
Hazel B (--), 1706
Helen (Wilson), 1703
Henry, 1714
Henry C, 1707
Herman J, 1706
Hestor, 1705
Homer L, 1701
Howard, 1712

Hye Ray, 1713
Ida, 1714
Inez (Caldwell), 1703
infant, 1706
Irene, 1701, 1710
Iva Mae (Irvin), 1703
James, 1708-1709
James Arthur, 1703
James Ashley, 1709
Jean, 1706
Jeanette, 1709
Jesse, 1681, 1704
Jesse Henry, 1706
John, 1702, 1721
John E, 1710
John Henry, 1712
Jonathan, 1714
Joseph A, 1706
Josephine, 1709
Josephine (Wisor), 1709
Katherine, 1713
Katie, 1712
Katie A (Root), 1705
Kenneth, 1705, 1713
Laura Belle, 1721
Lavina (Litz), 1705
Lelia, 1706
Lena, 1710-1711
Lenora, 1708
Lenora (Parks), 1706
Leonard, 1707
Lester W, 1705
Lester, 1705
Lettie Mae, 1721
Lewis W, 1705
Lindsey, 1698
Lloyd, 1705
Lloyd Alfred, 1701
Lois, 1705, 1711
Lottie (Shovestall), 1706
Lucretian, 1710
Lucy (Palmer), 1710
Lula (Greene), 1706
M Margaret (Fleming), 1710
Mabel L (Robinson), 1708
Mable, 1713
Madeline (Aveni), 1707
Maggie, 1705
Margaret, 1713
Margaret E (Kephart), 1681, 1704
Marshall, 1711
Martha E (Woodel), 1702
Martha S (Hummel), 1712
Mary A (Kephart), 1707
Mary Ann (Odell), 1714
Mary E, 1708
Mary E (Druggs), 1706
Mary J (Coudriet), 1705
Mary Lettie, 1709
Mary Martha, 1709
Maude, 1702, 1709
Maude (Wisor), 1709
Maude M, 1713
Maude M (Wisor), 1713
Maurice, 1708
May A (Gallaher), 1720

WOLF (continued)
Larry Lee, 1336
Maria Catharina, 1598
Marla Joy, 1311
Mary Adeline (Schell), 1336
Mary R Bridges, 1053
Minnie, 875
Moses, 1613
Nona (Salem), 862
Patricia, 471
Pearl Olive (Wertz), 862
Peggy, 471
Regina, 464
Richard Russell, 1311
Russell Elmer, 1311
Sarah, 361
Sarah Ellen (Saville), 409
Shannon Labaun, 409
Sheldon Paul, 409
Sheridan Dale, 409
Terry, 471
Verlin, 471
Villa, 854
Virginia Lynne (Raymond), 70
WOLFE
--, 1223
Albert Edward, 980
Alberta Mae, 1147
Alma Leah Ellen, 576
Alverta Sara, 1343
Anna (Keller), 576
Anna Elizabeth (Snyder), 980
Annie Matilda, 981
Arzuba, 577
Arzuba (Blodgett), 576
Berniece Irene, 577
Beulah Elizabeth (Brungart), 980, 1083
Burt, 576
Carol, 1083
Catherine, 1086
Charles Albert, 1223
Clara Edna, 577
Delbert Kaye, 1223
Donald, 980, 1083
Doreen, 1083
Dorothy Louise, 1223
Edward Lewis, 849
Ellen, 577
Elmer, 980
Elsie Elizabeth (Croy), 849
Elva, 911
Elwood, 980
Emma Ruth (Witmer), 760
Ernestine Marie, 577
Esther, 116
Ethel (Morgan), 576
Faye Dianne, 645
Frederick, 576
George, 576
George Harold, 1223
Gina Collette, 1113
Grace (Plant), 577
James Woodrow, 981
Jennie Idella, 981
Judith Diana, 760
Kathryn Louise (Grace), 1223
Kenneth, 980
Laura Ellen, 981
Laura Verna (Truby), 1223

Lee Luther, 1083
Leotta, 1083
Leroy, 980
Linda Lee, 1223
Loretta, 980
Lorraine (Yeager), 1113
Louise (Whaley), 577
Luther Lee, 980
Marily Kay, 1223
Marion, 980, 1083
Martha (Shearer), 980
Mary C, 1099
Mary Catherine (Fox), 576
Mary Elizabeth, 981
Mary Ellen (Daniels), 1223
Mayme, 1095
Meta May, 981
Mildred (Dowdy), 1083
Nora, 981
Pearl (Schreckengast), 980
Richard, 1083
Robert, 981, 1083
Robert Leroy, 577
Rosalie, 980
Rosaline, 1083
Roscoe Leonard, 576
Ruth, 577
Samuel, 1113
Smiley Clement, 577
Smilie Clement, 576
Thomas Franklin, 760
Thomas Samuel, 760
Verna (Bressler), 980
Vesta Larue, 1223
Violet, 981
Virginia, 980, 1083
Wesley David, 980
Winifred, 1066
Woodrow, 980
WOLFER
Sue, 1483
WOLFF
Ada May, 245
Adelaide Louise, 239, 243
Amanda Ella (McCord), 245
Amy Sevilla, 239
Annie Maria (Miller), 244
Arthur Otto, 733
Arthur Otto Jr, 733
Carla Jean, 504
Charles William, 238-239
Clara May, 239
Daniel, 238
Daniel H, 240
Daniel Theodore, 238, 241
Elizabeth (Blitz), 244
Elizabeth (Cline), 240
Elmira Rebecca, 239, 243
Emma Louise, 239
Ethel (Hance), 240
Eunice Mae (Knorr), 733
Franklin Abraham, 238, 240
Hellen Susannah, 239, 243
Jennie Marie (Kocher) Boyer, 1615

Josette, 504
Joyce Jean, 733
Katie Helen, 239
Kenneth, 505
Laura Caroline, 244
Lola R (Stine), 504
Louis Daniel, 244
Louis R, 504
Louise Marie (Matz), 239
Luther, 1615
Mahlon Fasig, 238-239
Mahlon H, 240
Mahlon Matz, 239
Marjorie McCord, 245
Mary Artie (Doty), 240
Minnie Elmira, 239
Neil, 505
Oliver Jacob, 239, 244
Oliver Miller, 245
Philip, 505
Richard, 505
Rufus Daniel, 238-239
Ruth Madora, 240
Sevilla Elizabeth, 238, 240-241
Sevilla Elizabeth (Fasig), 238
Tom, 505
Vicky, 504
Virginia, 239, 245
Walter Arthur, 239, 244
Walter D, 240
William, 239
WOLFGANG
Edith Pearl, 568
Eleanor, 828
WOLFGONG
Allen Harold, 1274
Allen Harold Jr, 1274
Amber Rena, 1274
Barbara (Sharp), 1274
Christine (Rankin), 1275
Christopher Ryan, 1275
Cyrus Dean, 1275
Cyrus Emberson, 1274
Dawn lea (Barickman), 1274
Dawn Marie, 1275
Deanna Sue, 1274
Donald Wayne, 1275
Edna Maxine (Seigworth), 1274
Edward John, 1274
Edward Wayne, 1275
Francine White (Smith), 1275
Heather Marie (Stahlman), 1274
James Edward, 1274
James Edward Jr, 1274
Jeanette Dawn (Benton), 1275
Jessica Rozanna, 1274
Joyce Darlene, 1274
Justin Scott, 1274
Karen Elizabeth (Minnick), 1274
Larry Frank, 1275
Letha Mae, 1274
Letha Mae (Wolfgong), 1274
Lindsey Benet, 1275
Mary Ann (Skiba), 1275
Mary Louise (Hines),

1274
Matthew Thomas, 1275
Michael Scott, 1274
Shawna Robert, 1274
Sheryl (Bean), 1275
Susan Marie, 1274
Tammy Darlene, 1275
Thomas Lee, 1275
Timothy Ronald, 1275
Wesley William, 1275
WOLFORD
Debra Lynn (Walls), 1658
Lauren, 1658
Michael, 1658
Nancy, 1229
Terry, 1658
WOLLAM
Ellen, 365
WOLMELSDORF
Freda Cleo, 821
WOLPERT
Natalie G, 68
WOLSTENCRAFT
Nancy, 1712
WOLSTENCROFT
Alma (Shuga), 1707
George, 1707
James, 1707
Joel, 1707
John, 1707
Mamie (Holt), 1707
Nancy, 1707
Rella (Louder), 1707
Sarah (Wiser), 1707
Thomas, 1707
WOLTZ
Betty Jo, 1138
WOLVERTON
Dorothy, 1033
Julia Ann, 1041
Lilas, 458
WOMACK
Nancy Jean Jerdon, 1551
WOMBLE
Ruth, 1797
WOMELDORF
Butchie, 817
Catharine LaRee (Grant), 817
Charlotte Mae, 817
Christina Lynn, 817
Craig Douglas, 828
Donald Wallace, 827
Dorothy Jean, 817
Evelyn Naomi (Mahle), 817
Frank Edward, 827
James Alvie, 817
James Arthur, 826
Jandy Elizabeth, 817
Joan Adele, 826
Joyce Jean (Bassett), 817
Judith LaVann (Downing), 826
Judy Ann (Chestnut), 817
Julie Lynn, 826
Kassandra, 827
Leslie (Gilmer), 828
Linda Kay (Pizer), 817
Lisa (Broxson), 827
Lonnie Carl, 817
Marc Alan, 827
Myrtie Almira, 817
Pamela Lynn (Baushke), 817

Patricia, 828
Pearl M (Sherry), 827
Richard E, 817
Sandra (Kauffman), 827
Shirley Susanne, 826
Wesley Leroy, 817
WOMELSDORF
--, 823, 834
Abigail Locke, 834
Agnes Celesa, 896
Albert, 830
Albert C, 830
Alexander Livingston, 821
Alford, 821
Alice L, 823
Almira, 850
Alpheretta (Nolting), 826
Alyce Ann, 823
Amanda, 827
Amy (--), 829
Andrew Curtis, 828
Ann (--), 815
Ann (Irwin), 821
Anna Eva (Weiser), 812-813, 850, 896
Annie H (Brown), 834
Aquilla Jerome, 829
Arthur Lewis, 826
Arvilla (Landauer), 822
Benson, 817
Bertha Belle (Conner), 826
Bess (Carnathan), 824
Bessie Brancis, 826
Betty, 824
Betty June (Minick), 826
Blanche, 835
Brenda Jane, 822
Carol Ann, 825
Caroline, 827, 847
Carrie, 834
Catharine, 828, 904
Catherine (Jegley), 896
Catherine Anspach, 837
Catherine Elizabeth (Kreible), 821
Catherine Elizabeth (Miller), 821
Catherine Moni, 825
Cathryn Jane (Colwell), 825
Charles Clark, 837
Charles Edwin, 824-825
Charlotte, 813
Cheryl A, 825
Cheryl Jane, 826
Chester Henry, 828
child, 826, 828
Christine, 824
Clara Isadore, 832
Clyde, 823
Cynthia Marie, 825
Dale Russell, 826
Daniel, 88, 637, 812-813, 821, 828, 834, 847, 850, 896
Darl D, 827
David Jerald, 826
Deborah Lee, 825
Dennis Jerald, 826
Dolly, 823
Donna Marie, 825
Dorothy, 824

WYSOR (continued)
Mary (continued)
1661, 1667
Mary Anderson, 1649
Mary Belle (Ernest), 1651
Mary D, 1651
Mary E (--), 1651
Mary Elizabeth, 1649
Mary Elizabeth (Shipp), 1650
Mary Emma, 1661
Mary H (Steele), 1655
Mary Inez, 1656
Mary Jane (Lee), 1662
Mary Josephine, 1657
Mary Lynn (Van Dyke), 1660
Mary Martha Price (Templeton), 1651
Mary Shipp, 1650
Mary Ware, 1650
Maude Ellen (Call), 1658
Melissa A (Taylor), 1655
Michael Jordan, 1649
Michael Lamar, 1649
Mildred Sue, 1656
Mima Arlene (Smith), 1656
Mittie Lawrence, 1652
Mollie (Calvert), 1655
Morehead Jordan, 1650
Myrtle Alice, 1657
Myrtle M, 1662
Nancy B, 1652
Nancy Carter, 1650
Nannie Lucile, 1650
Narcie B (Brown), 1662
Nell (Davis), 1662
Nellie Audrey (Gaussoin), 1661
Nettie M, 1652
Nikki Ann, 1661
Norma Joan (Reedy), 1657
Patty Jean, 1660
Paul S, 1661
Peggy Jane, 1660
Phyllis (--), 1660
Polly (Miller), 1653
Ralph, 1657
Raymond Ware, 1650
Regina Gwen (Lawson), 1659
Robert B, 1647
Robert Burns, 1659
Robert Chet, 1660
Robert Edward, 1652
Robert Edward Jr, 1652
Robert G, 1647, 1650
Robert Meshack, 1657
Robert Wesley, 1659
Rose Anna E, 1661
Rufus Johnston, 1651
Ruth, 1651
Sally (Price), 1655
Samuel Thomas, 1661
Sandra Lyn, 1657
Sara Elizabeth Mae, 1660
Sarah, 1653
Sarah (Richardson), 1653
Sarah Katherine, 1659
Sean, 1650

Serena, 1662
Serena Cordelia, 1661
Shirley, 1648
son, 1655
Stanley, 1651
Stella (Sneed), 1655
Stephanie Page, 1662
Susan (Wohlford), 1650
Sylvester A, 1662
Tracy Jo, 1660
Vernon Clyde, 1660
Virginia, 1653
Virginia Ida (Richardson), 1660
Walter Kelly, 1656
Wilkie Collins, 1648
William, 1653
William Clarence, 1655
William Henry, 1649
William Henry III, 1650
William Henry Jr, 1650
William J, 1651
William L, 1661
William Washington, 1651
William Whitten, 1657
William Wirt, 1648
Willie Edna (Boynton), 1649
WYSS
Suzanne, 270
WYSSER
--, 9
-- (--), 9
-- (List), 9
Barbara, 6
Samuel, 9
Simon, 3-4, 6
YAEGER
Grace, 1709
Ruth Patricia, 1814
YAGER
Sandra Snyder, 1778
YAISSLE
Mary L, 1614
YAKIMICKI
Delores (Leland), 264
Donald Leland, 264
Gary Stephen, 264
J L, 264
James Scott, 264
John Robert, 264
Michael Douglas, 264
YALE
Grace Alice (Kahle), 1203
Henry, 1203
Richard Kahle, 1204
YALLOWAY
Patricia Marie, 647
YAMADA
Michiko, 52
YANARELLA
Donna, 1103
YANKE
Shirley, 1478
YANOVIAK
John Joseph Jr, 923
Rita Laraine, 923
Susan Dianne (Weiser) Case, 923
Tara Lynn, 923
YANT
Janet Merlene (Derringer), 606
Jerry Dale, 606

Pamela Elane, 606
Richard Dale, 606
YANTIS
Emory, 392
James Perry, 392
Maude (Meeker), 392
Myrtle, 392
YANTZ
Edward, 941
Wilma (Lay), 941
YARED
Karen, 1416
YARGER
Charles, 979
Charles Jr, 979
Dora (Sager), 979
Fae E, 711
YARGES
Estella, 1436
Estilene, 1436
Sophia M (Schoch), 1436
William, 1436
YARNELL
Madeline, 1443
Ruth, 1068
YATES
Charles C, 1357
Eva A, 1792
Margaret (Glavis), 1357
Maude, 558
YAWN
Mollie, 718
YEAGER
Alvin Luther, 1113
Amy Helen (Stewart), 1344
Angela Kay, 1113
Anna, 1114
Bessie Adelaide (McLawhon), 1113
Catherine Joyce, 690
Charles B, 710
Cindy L, 501
Cora M, 710
Curtis Allen, 731
Darron Reed, 1344
Dixie Lee (Parker), 1113
Edith, 1098
Edward R, 710
Elizabeth (Koppenheffer), 710
Helen Elizabeth (Shipe), 730
Jacob, 710
James Oliver, 690
John Franklin, 1113
John Michael, 1113
Joseph F, 710
Laura R, 710
Lillian F, 710
Lisa Marie (Kahler), 1113
Lorraine, 1113
Lydia Irene, 690
Madelon June, 1113
Michael Joseph, 1113
Nancy Jean, 1139
Pamela Louise, 575
Romaine Irene (Matter), 690
Sarah, 721
Shirley Arlette, 1113
Stanley, 730
Valerie, 1113
Valerie Ann, 1113
Viola Mae, 1017

Violet Kathryn (Miller), 1113
William A, 710
Zandra Merrilee, 570
YEARGAN
Juanice, 524
YEARICK
Allen, 1372
Anna Louise (Winkleman), 1372
Anona, 1084
Betty, 1372
Elaine, 1086
Homer, 1372
Iris (Ripka), 1085
Keith Douglas, 1085
Leotta, 1085
Lida B, 1067
Luzetta, 1085
Marlin Richard, 1085
Mary Ellen, 1372
Mary Ellen (Gruver), 1372
Mary Kathleen, 1086
Mary Mabel (Brungart), 1084
May Elizabeth, 1086
Nelson, 1085
Pat, 1372
Philip Samuel, 1086
Ruth, 1085
Sally Ann, 1372
Samuel C, 1084
Vesta, 1085
Victoria (Fetterolf), 1085
Wilbur, 1085
YEAROUT
Hannah, 1668
YEATER
Bonnie Jean, 715
Douglas Leroy, 715
Ethel Diane (Goodling), 714
Lois Lynn, 715
Mary Ellen, 715
William Franklin, 714
William Franklin Jr, 715
YEATMAN
Irene, 1507
YECK
Eunice Louise (Caliman), 884-885
Laura Louise, 884-885
Ronald Leslie, 884-885
Todd David, 884-885
YENSER
Emma Martha, 621
Minnie, 1639
Tina, 1749
YERGES
Ione Naomi, 680
Jacqueline, 1616
YERMAATT
Paul, 1321
Susan Dianne (Holl), 1321
YERTZY
Jacob, 1473
Mary Julia Ida (Breidenbaugh), 1473
YETTER
Sandara Darlene, 374
YINGER
Annie, 868
Arthur Leroy, 870
Barry Richard, 870
Beatrice Alice (Neff),

870
Betty (Anderson), 871
Betty L (Mummert), 870
Brenda M, 871
Carolyn L, 870
Charles C, 870
Charles K, 871
Charles S, 870
Christine, 870
Colleen M (Oppelt), 871
Cora, 866
Cora Alberta (Ulrich), 75
Craig E, 871
David A, 871
David James, 870
Diane, 871
Donald L, 870
Donna, 870
Dorothy I, 871
Elvia (Anderson), 870
Esther, 871
Ethel Goldie, 869
Florence, 876
Frank E, 871
Frank Smaling, 869
Frank Smaling Jr, 870
Glenn R, 871
Hazel Irene, 870
Helen A, 871
Hellen (Termin), 871
Irene (--), 870
Jeanette Irene (Prowell), 870
John, 866
Kathleen Elaine, 870
Kenneth Eugene, 870
Lloyd, 75
Margaret (--), 870
Marian Virginia (Dyne), 75
Mark D, 871
Michael C, 871
Murlo Linwood, 75
Nancy Virginia, 76
Pearl Elizabeth, 869
Raymond Dale, 870
Rebecca Katherine (Miller), 869
Richard E, 870
Robert Allen, 75
Ronald Dean, 870
Ruthetta, 869
Shirley, 871
Susan Darlene, 870
Suzanne K, 871
Terry L, 870
Wayne L, 871
Wayne L Jr, 871
Zorado E (Shettel), 866
YINGLING
Rebecca Ann, 165
YINGST
Adam, 1592
Catharine Ghere (Moltz), 1420
Elaine S, 871
Homer Carlton, 1420
John H, 871
Lawrence L, 871
Martha (Ogle), 1592
Shirley (Yinger), 871
Susannah (Collier), 1592
YOCKEY
Dolly, 210

YOCUM
--, 1441
Elizabeth (Graffius), 1441
Emily Lucille, 725
Frank, 1671
Hannah E, 1628
Martha Ellen, 1671

YODER
Adaline Patti, 198
Alpha, 198
Amanda (Brungart), 1080
Ann Louise, 830
Asheley Lynn, 831
Brian, 194
Catharine, 1081
Charles William, 831
Christopher Ward, 198
Clarence S, 1622
Darrell Lawrence, 198
Darrell Lynn, 198
David, 1080
Edith May, 201
Emma, 1081
Florance May (Ross), 198
Howard J, 830
James Menno, 198
James William, 198
Jane Ellen, 198
Joan Marie, 830
Justice Darian, 199
Kathy Lee (Werley), 831
Larry Eugene, 199
Lizzie, 1080
Luella Krick, 256
Marcella Rose (Muth), 198
Marie Patricia, 831
Marie W, 1622
Marion W, 1622
Marvin W, 1622
Mary L (Wittman), 1622
Mary Saloma, 199
Maude B, 1622
Maude H (Weiser), 1622
Michael, 194
Michaela Sue, 198
Paige Irene, 199
Phyllis Irene (Williams), 198
Randica Lynn (Haynes), 198
Rebecca Alwilda (Donne), 830
Sharon (Wallace), 194
Terri Lynn (Levan), 198
Thelma Jean (Ward), 198
Thomas Paul, 831
Timothy James, 198
Timothy Ward, 198
Valetta Elenora (Hoerath), 198

YOHE
Albert, 854
Barbara Jean, 854
Bellamer (Konn), 855
Bertie (Nebinger), 854
Charles, 855
Charlotte, 854
Donald, 855
Donald Ray, 854
Eleanor Beatrice, 854

Elsie (Whalen), 854
Gertrude (Taggart), 854
Glenn, 854
Ira, 854
James Donald, 855
Janet, 854
June, 854
Kenneth, 854
Larry Allen, 854
Marie (Griffith), 855
Mark Allen, 855
Mary (Gutshall), 854
Ruth, 854
Trudy Marie, 855

YOKE
--, 1039
Carol (Umplebee), 1039
Mary E, 386

YOKUM
Anna K, 1377

YONCHAK
Erin Allison, 367
Melinda Lee (Bauder), 367
Thomas Aquinas Jr, 367

YONGE
Mary E, 291

YONKER
Charles Dean, 585
Michele Yvette, 585
Pamela Marie, 585
Robert Murray, 585
Robert Murray Jr, 585
Velna Rose (Hocker), 585

YONTO
Anthony, 1845
Helen Edna (Weiser), 1845

YONTSEY
Lucille, 443

YONTZ
Barry Scott, 1492
Dorothy (Ohler), 1492
Jeffrey Dee, 1492
Steven Jay, 1492
Thomas, 1492

YOPP
Emma Donnelly, 1180

YORDY
Ethel, 1023
Grace B, 721
John, 731
Sarah Malinda (Hepner), 731

YORK
Blanche Aline (Nickell), 989
James Munro, 989
Naomi Hannah (Citzler), 989
Virginia Louise, 989
Wayne, 989

YORKE
Dorothy McLenegen, 339
Frederick Estabrooke, 339
Hazel, 932
Selina Withers (McLenegan), 339

YORKS
Jandy Elizabeth (Womeldorf), 817
W Steven, 817

YORTY
John William, 643
Nicole Wiest, 643
Reta Mae (Wiest), 643

YOSKO
Bernard James, 1758
Hannah C (Wieser), 1758
John, 1758

YOST
Albert G, 1018
Allen Richard, 1328
Anna (Hall), 1018
Barbara (Robinson), 1328
Barbara Ann, 701
Bettie (Kalcich), 1018
Betty Jo (Wallace), 194
Candy (Truesdale), 1328
Catherine Marie, 1017
Charles E, 1017
Charles Henry, 1018
Charles Henry Jr, 1018
Christopher, 194
Clara Louise, 1328
Clarra Louise, 1328
Debora Ann, 1018
Diana (Frost), 1328
Diane Marie, 684
Donna Jean, 1018
Doris Elaine, 1328
Dura Lily (Rockey), 76
Earl Edward, 1017
Earl Edward Jr, 1017
Elaine Susanne, 1018
Evelyn Roselia (Renn), 1017
Frances Elizabeth, 1018
Frances Winifred, 1328
George Daniel, 1018
George Daniel Jr, 1018
George Richard, 1328
Harold Eugene, 1328
Harriet S, 1018
Harry, 934
Helen B, 1018
Irene (Troutman), 1017
Jane (--), 1017
Jane Lois, 1018
Jean L (Bower), 1018
Jean Louise, 1019
Jeanette Ann, 1017
Joan Louis, 1018
John Calvin, 1018
Judith Lorraine, 1018
Karen Ancha (Bok), 1328
Kathryn (Negherton), 1017
Kelly Jo, 194
Lester S, 76
Lillian Evelyn, 1018
Lillian Mae, 1017
Mary Catherine, 1018
Mary Euphemia, 1648
Mildred (Stalkoski), 1018
Nelson J, 683
Norma Jean, 1328
Patricia Ann, 1017
Rita Elizabeth, 1018
Robert, 194
Robert Lee, 1017
Roberta J, 1466
Ronald C, 1018
Rose C (Weiser), 934
Ruth (Arter), 1018

Sarah Elizabeth, 1018
Thelma Lucile (Rabold), 1328
Thomas Hugo, 1018
Toletha Mae (Huff), 683
Vincent Peter, 1018
William, 934

YOTHERS
Joseph, 1722
Mary (Wiser), 1722

YOUNG
Albert, 1030
Alexander Stuart, 186
Alexander Stuart III, 186
Alexander Stuart IV, 186
Alice, 556
Alice Louisa (Ege), 292
Barbara Jo (Wiser), 1808
Barbara June, 891
Bessie Juanita, 134
Birt, 1677
Brenda (Talbert), 134
Brett Edward, 908
Carrie Maletha, 1808
Cathleen Marie (McGee), 1739
Charline, 97
Charline Ellen (Starwalt), 107
Corina (Lane), 186
Dana Louise (Morrow), 354
Deborah Diane, 134
Donna Lynn (Martin), 1602
Doyle Walter III, 1040
Eddie Wayne, 1808
Edward, 104
Edward B, 134
Edward Charles, 134
Elizabeth, 285, 1687
Eloise Elizabeth (Tschanen), 90
Emma Rebecca (Weiser), 134
Erin Lee, 354
George, 1176
George R, 1030
Gerald Edward, 134
Geraldine, 1367
Glen Harry, 891
Halsey, 90
Harriet, 1507
Harry Clarence, 891
Henry, 1722
Ida (Johnson), 1677
Ida S (Overpeck), 523
Ina M (Williams), 134
Jaime Louise, 354
James, 1739
James Arthur, 891
James Lee, 667
Jamie Renee, 908
Jane (Warner), 134
Janette Vivian, 407
Jean, 1159
Jean Cromer, 186
Jennie, 442
Joe, 555
John Clark, 354
Joseph, 821
Josephine, 707
Judith Ann, 104
June Rose (Eppley),

891
Larry Grant, 107
Linda Lou (Burch), 667
Lisa Marie, 134
Mabel (Ford), 134
Mack Leonard, 1808
Margaret A (Cooper), 1030
Marjorie (Wiser), 1722
Marjorie Geneva, 134
Mary, 1677
Mary (Kirkpatrick), 1176
Mary Jane, 1030
Mary Jane (Kreible), 821
Melvin E, 134
Michael Anthony, 134
Michael Dean, 134
Mina Geneva, 134
Natalie Kathryn, 1602
Nelle Marion (Snyder), 186
Nellie Jewel (Harris), 134
Pamela Jo (Sipes), 908
Patricia Simcox, 1005
Paul, 523
Pauline, 420
Pearl Mae (Weiser), 1845
Polly, 1786
R G, 292
Ray, 1030
Rebecca, 907
Richard A, 1845
Robert, 1602
Robert C, 1176
Robert D, 1030
Robert S, 134
Robert Samuel, 134
Roberta Ilene, 134
Ruth Emma, 917
Sandra Jo (Slutter), 1040
Sarah May, 555
Sarah May (Herring), 555
Sherrill Wayne, 134
Shirley, 566
Susan M, 1841
Thelma (Huff), 104
Thomas Allen, 891
Thomas Edward, 104
Tiffany Lynn, 134
Timothy, 908
Ulysses Grant, 107
Valarie Lynn, 134
William C, 1030
William S, 1177

YOUNGBLOOD
Teresa, 1097
Theresa, 281

YOUNGSTROM
Mary, 209

YOUNKER
Elizabeth Ann (Anspach), 847
Jill, 847
John, 847

YOUNKIN
Pamela Susan, 1172
Una, 375

YOUNT
Mary, 1476

YOUSE
Amelia, 1612
Esther (Weiser), 1612

ZIEGLER (continued)
Annie J (Fauth)
  Shenberger, 1461
Audrey Patricia, 708
C, 1645
C Walter, 1461
David, 1461, 1644
David W, 1461
Dorothy M (Doll),
  1461
Edgar D, 1461
Edgar David, 1461
Edwin, 1645
Eleanora, 1644
Elijah, 1645
Elinora (Sholl), 1066
Elizabeth, 1461
George, 623
Gertrude, 1080
Hannah (--), 1645
Harrison, 1645
Helen Irene (Roughton),
  623
Henrietta (--), 1645
Howard, 1066
Isabelle M, 787
James, 1645
John Peter, 1644
Julianna, 1645
Lucy H, 1461
Margaret (Zerbe), 707
Margerite, 623
Matilda Jane, 1427
R William, 1461
Reba, 844
Russell H, 707
Samuel Weiser, 1461
Seth Russell, 708
Stephen Paul, 708
Susanna, 1645
Susanna (Weiser), 1644
Weiser, 1461, 1645
William, 1645
ZIELINKI
Stella Florence, 1116
ZIENTA
Debra Lynne, 476
ZIERDEN
Doris (Kahle), 1243
Robert, 1243
ZIERTEN
Jenny, 522
ZIGLER
David Timothy, 1328
Rebekah Leah, 1328
Rhonda Ann (Crothers),
  1328
Timothy David, 1328
ZIGNE
Mollie, 1061
ZIM
Evelyn P, 1061
ZIMMERLY
Andrea Sue, 143
Brian Lee, 143
Kent Eugene, 143
Mark Douglas, 143
Rhonda Sue (Hughes),
  143
ZIMMERMAN
-- (--), 157, 719
Alene Fasold, 730
Alice, 737
Alice Irene (Wiest),
  647
Amos K, 1036
Amy Beth, 650
Ann Marie, 730, 742
Anna Margaret

(Weiser), 164
Anna Weiser, v
Blanche Alvenia
  (Snyder), 762
Burke, 1039
Carolyn (Dolbin), 853
Cathryn (Wilhelm), 64
Charlotte Marie, 647
Christie, 1036
Clyde Arthur, 742
Cobus, 1052
Curt, 1007
Diana Lynn, 399
Dwayne Joseph, 1007
Eddie, 64
Edward Adams, 742
Edward Adams II, 742
Elinor (Keefer), 730
Emily, 1583
Evelyn (Schnavely),
  742
Faye Eileen, 648
George, 1681
Gertrude, 619
Grace Aletha (Kahle),
  1243
H C, 157
Harriet, 961
Harriet May, 1036
Henry Clarence, 164
J C, 719
Jack E, 671
Joann, 658
John, 853
John C, 730
John Carl, 762
John Milton, 730
Joseph, 1243
Judy, 1243
Karen Lee, 743
Katie Odera (Adams),
  742
Linda Louise, 730
Lisa Ann, 650
Lisa Diane (Timmons),
  1038
Marjorie J, 671
Martha (Kephart), 1681
Martha Catherine, 1036
Mary Catherine
  (Cooper), 1036
Minnie Arlene (Fasold),
  730
Nancy, 850
Patty Jean
  (Middleworth), 1007
Peter, 64
Rachel Louise, 164
Ralph Leroy, 647
Rebecca Ann (Kreider),
  649
Richard, 64, 1243
Richard Edwin, 762
Robert Calvin, 730
Ruth, 730
Ruth Margeret (Nagle),
  671
Sadie R (Erhard), 1052
Shirley Romaine, 647
Stella C, 1036
Susan, 259
William, 649
William B, 671
Zachary Burke, 1039
ZIMMERMANN
Catharine, 1472
ZIMSEN
Rosemary Helen, 1164

ZINK
Cheryl Kay (Strader),
  1329
Darren, 491
Helen Evans (Erdman),
  257
Joan Wallis, 737
Judy, 491
Robert Witmyer, 257
Timothy Alan, 1329
Travis Daniel, 1329
Zachary Zane, 1329
ZINN
Olive, 245
ZINSER
Deborah Rose, 139
ZIPFEL
Alice, 1241
ZIRKEL
Chad Detrick, 1087
Charles Robert, 1087
Donna Mae (Royer),
  1086
Paul Eric, 1086
Paul Robert, 1086
ZITO
Angela, 1738
ZLASNEY
Karen Regine
  (Rafferty), 502
Laurie Ann, 502
Robert, 502
ZOLINSKY
Linda Maureen, 1441
ZOLLER
Erika (Weisser), 1607
Hartmut, 1607
ZOLLINGER
Catharine Charlotte,
  890
Eric Abram, 1778
Shauna Lee (Wiser),
  1778
ZOOK
Beulah Anna, 1672
Charles Curtis, 828
Dean, 1439
Donna Arlene, 1494
George, 1494
Harold, 1439
Judy, 1439
Laurie Sue, 828
Leta Mae (Troutman)
  McKinley, 1494
Letitia Eve, 828
Lisa Ann, 828
Mary (Whitaker), 1439
Patricia (Womeldorf),
  828
Virginia Maire, 1494
ZUBER
Anna Mary, 1227
ZUCK
Ada (Lambright), 225
David Lloyd, 225
David Luther, 225
David Luther Jr, 225
Dorothy Pearl, 225
Fern H, 223
Helen Elaine, 225
Helen Marie
  (Spurgeon), 225
Janice Collene, 478
Jesse H, 223
Lana Marie, 225
Rose Irene, 225
Sarah Rebecca
  (Burkholder), 223
Susan Marie, 224

Vida Maye, 224
ZUGEL
Margaretha, 17
ZUMBAUGH
Nellie (Haschel), 264
Peter, 264
ZUMBRO
Anna Lou (Wiser),
  1820
Ewell, 1820
ZUMLAUF
Marcell, 1271
ZUMMACH
Debbie Marie, 855
James Philip, 855
Jo Ann Shirley
  (Shettel), 855
Mark James, 855
Therisa Lucille, 855
ZUNKEL
Cora Evadne, 413
ZWAYER
Edith Ardell, 1126
ZWEGER
John, 1361
Maria Eva (Becker),
  1361
ZWIELY
George, 509
Myrtle, 509
ZWINCKH
Anna (Murr), 1605
ZWIRN
Berta, 1597
ZWOYER
Lulu M, 1640
Luther Daniel, 1643
Myrtle Esther
  (Hamsher), 1643
ZYSKI
Derek Ronald, 494
Diane Marie (Foster),
  494
Harvey Ronald, 494
Joanne Faye (Nowak),
  494
Marissa Jo, 494
Mark Ronald, 494
Scott Allen, 494
ZYVOLOSKI
Laurel, 166
ZYVOLOSKI/GARDNER
Danielle Monique, 166
Mesha Shawn, 166